THE INSTITUTE OF TAXATION

The Institute was founded in 1930 and its 7,500 members include most leading tax experts. Members receive 'Taxation Practitioner' monthly and copies of tax legislation with explanations and examples. Residential conferences, one-day courses and branch technical and social activities are held for members and registered students.

Associateship (ATII) is by examination in the UK; there are concessions for members of other professional bodies. Fellowship (FTII) is by thesis which can be submitted by associates and by certain other persons suitably qualified.

For further information please apply to:

RONALD J ISON LLB FTII SOLICITOR
SECRETARY
THE INSTITUTE OF TAXATION
12 UPPER BELGRAVE STREET
LONDON SW1X 8BB
TELEPHONE 01-235 9381

BUTTERWORTHS YELLOW TAX HANDBOOK

Twenty-eighth Edition

Setting out the
amended text of the Taxes Acts
relating to income tax,
corporation tax and
capital gains tax
as operative for

1989–90

EDITED BY
MOIZ SADIKALI, Barrister
of the Middle Temple

LONDON
BUTTERWORTHS
1989

United Kingdom	Butterworth & Co (Publishers) Ltd 88 Kingsway, LONDON WC2B 6AB 4 Hill Street, EDINBURGH EH2 3JZ
Australia	Butterworths Pty Ltd, SYDNEY, MELBOURNE, BRISBANE, ADELAIDE, PERTH, CANBERRA and HOBART
Canada	Butterworths Canada Ltd, TORONTO and VANCOUVER
Ireland	Butterworth (Ireland) Ltd, DUBLIN
Malaysia	Malayan Law Journal Sdn Bhd, KUALA LUMPUR
New Zealand	Butterworths of New Zealand Ltd, WELLINGTON and AUCKLAND
Singapore	Butterworth & Co (Asia) Pte Ltd, SINGAPORE
USA	Butterworth Legal Publishers, ST PAUL, Minnesota, SEATTLE, Washington, BOSTON, Massachusetts, AUSTIN, Texas and D & S Publishers, CLEARWATER, Florida

First Edition	September 1962	Seventeenth Edition	September 1978
Second Edition	September 1963	Eighteenth Edition	September 1979
Third Edition	September 1964	Nineteenth Edition	September 1980
Fourth Edition	November 1965	Twentieth Edition	September 1981
Fifth Edition	October 1966	Twenty-first Edition	August 1982
Sixth Edition	September 1967	Twenty-second Edition	June 1983
Seventh Edition	October 1968	Supplement to the	
Eighth Edition	October 1969	Twenty-second Edition	August 1983
Ninth Edition	September 1970	Twenty-third Edition	August 1984
Tenth Edition	October 1971	Twenty-fourth Edition	August 1985
Eleventh Edition	October 1972	Twenty-fifth Edition	August 1986
Twelfth Edition	October 1973	Finance Act 1987 Handbook	May 1987
Thirteenth Edition	October 1974	Twenty-sixth Edition	August 1987
Fourteenth Edition	October 1975	Twenty-seventh Edition	August 1988
Fifteenth Edition	November 1976	Twenty-eighth Edition	August 1989
Sixteenth Edition	November 1977		

©
Butterworth & Co. (Publishers) Ltd.
1989

All rights reserved. No part of this publication may be reproduced in any material form (including photocopying or storing it in any medium by electronic means and whether or not transiently or incidentally to some other use of this publication) without the written permission of the copyright owner except in accordance with the provisions of the Copyright, Designs and Patents Act 1988 or under the terms of a licence issued by the Copyright Licensing Agency Ltd, 33–34 Alfred Place, London, England WC1E 7DP. Applications for the copyright owner's written permission to reproduce any part of this publication should be addressed to the publisher.

Warning: The doing of an unauthorised act in relation to a copyright work may result in both a civil claim for damages and criminal prosecution.

ISBN 0 406 51007 5
ISSN 0141–3856

PUBLISHERS' NOTE

This edition of the Yellow Book, like its predecessors, provides the plain text of the Taxes Acts (see page iv) relating to income tax, corporation tax and capital gains tax. It also contains an extensive and comprehensive index.

The text of the legislation on inheritance tax, national insurance contributions, stamp duties and value added tax is provided in identical form in a companion volume, *Butterworths Orange Tax Handbook* (referred to in this work as the "Orange Book").

The legislation as amended for the year 1989–90 is set out in this edition as known on the date on which the Finance Act 1989 was passed.

When dealing with tax of an earlier year, the Yellow Book for that year should be used. Some of the provisions in the previous editions are affected by subsequent retrospective legislation. A list of the retrospective amending provisions in the Finance Act 1989 is provided on pages vi–vii. Provisions in that Act making amendments with effect from the Budget Day (14 March 1989), although strictly retrospective, are not listed, but the annotations under the amended provisions include the effective date.

(1) An amending or repealing provision is normally omitted, but effect is given to it in the provisions amended or repealed. The operative date is shown where this is not the beginning of the year of assessment or financial year in which the Finance Act is passed. The complete text of the latest Finance Act (including, although strictly not within the spirit of this work, the provisions which come into force next year or later) is printed in so far as it is relevant to this work. This edition includes the text of the Finance Act 1989.

(2) Where an earlier provision is modified, but the modification cannot be effected by verbal amendment, the modifying provision is printed in full where actually enacted, and is noted under the earlier provision, thus enabling it to be traced.

(3) New provisions not directly connected with any earlier provision are printed as part of the Act concerned.

(4) Prospective provisions taking effect after the year 1989–90 are not within the scope of this edition of the book and therefore are not incorporated at the appropriate places. However, they are retained in the Act which enacted them and they can be traced by referring to the list of prospective legislation on pages viii–x. Prospective provisions taking effect on a day to be appointed are, however, incorporated at the appropriate places because that day, when appointed, may fall within the current year. Any old words removed from the text as a result of incorporating such prospective provisions are retained in the annotations pertaining to the text. Moreover, the list of prospective legislation on pages viii–x also includes such prospective provisions.

Sections or Schedules which are excluded by the above rules are generally omitted from the text. If, however, for some reason they need to be included in the text, they are printed in *italics*, and the reason for their inclusion is shown in the annotations. Where subsections or smaller passages are omitted this is indicated in the annotations. The provisions of any Act which are relevant to the taxes covered by the Orange Book are identified in the Arrangement of Sections relating to that Act with the words "see Orange Book" although some provisions so identified may not necessarily appear in the Orange Book in conformity with the Publishers' Note in that book.

Statutory instruments are not printed in this book, nor are they mentioned in the annotations under the provisions to which they relate. However, the Capital Gains Tax Regulations 1967 are printed following the Taxes Management Act 1970, s. 57, so that appeals provisions for all three taxes are included.

For ease of reference, the section and Schedule numbers are conspicuously marked at the top of each page. All sections and Schedules, other than amending provisions, are indexed.

Pagination

Some pages may be numbered with an alphabetical suffix; some with a jump number. This is done to save considerable cost which would arise if the book were re-paginated consecutively.

The publishers invite suggestions for improving this Handbook in future editions.

August 1989　　　　　　　　　　　　BUTTERWORTH & CO. (PUBLISHERS) LTD.

Abbreviations

The following abbreviations are used in this book—

ACT	Advance Corporation Tax
CAA 1968	Capital Allowances Act 1968
CGTA 1979	Capital Gains Tax Act 1979
CTTA 1984	Capital Transfer Tax Act 1984
DLT	Development land tax
DLTA 1976	Development Land Tax Act 1976
FA	Finance Act
F(No. 2)A	Finance (No. 2) Act
FSA	Friendly Societies Act
IHTA 1984	Inheritance Tax Act 1984
NHA 1980	National Heritage Act 1980
OTA	Oil Taxation Act
PCTA 1968	Provisional Collection of Taxes Act 1968
S.I.	Statutory Instrument
SSA	Social Security Act
TA	Income and Corporation Taxes Act
TMA 1970	Taxes Management Act 1970
TSBA	Trustee Savings Banks Act

Meaning of "The Taxes Acts"

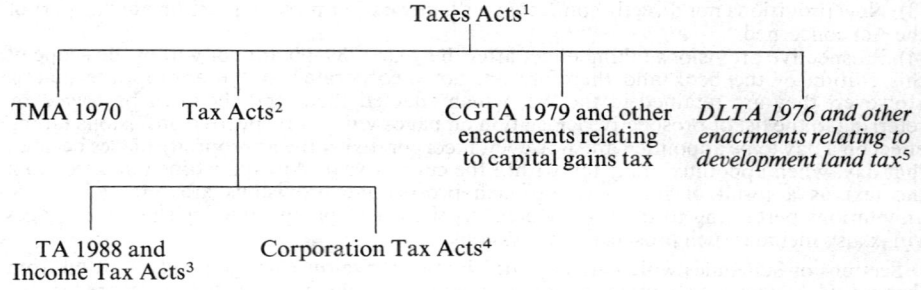

[1] Defined in TMA 1970, s. 118 (1).
[2] Defined in TA 1988, s. 831 (2).
[3] Defined in TA 1988, s. 831 (1) (*b*).
[4] Defined in TA 1988, s. 831 (1) (*a*).
[5] Repealed with effect generally from 19 March 1985 by FA 1985, s. 93, Sch. 25, Pt. I and Sch. 27, Pt. X.

CONTENTS

PUBLISHERS' NOTE

ABBREVIATIONS AND MEANING OF "THE TAXES ACTS"

RETROSPECTIVE LEGISLATION NOTES

PROSPECTIVE LEGISLATION NOTES

HOW TO TRACE LEGISLATION

- Provisional Collection of Taxes Act 1968
- Capital Allowances Act 1968
- Finance Act 1968
- Finance Act 1969
- Taxes Management Act 1970
- Income and Corporation Taxes Act 1970
- Finance Act 1970
- Finance Act 1971
- Finance Act 1972
- Finance Act 1973
- Finance Act 1974
- Finance Act 1975
- Finance (No 2) Act 1975
- Development Land Tax Act 1976
- Finance Act 1976
- Finance Act 1978
- Capital Gains Tax Act 1979
- Finance (No 2) Act 1979
- Finance Act 1980
- Finance Act 1981
- British Telecommunications Act 1981
- Finance Act 1982
- Finance Act 1983
- Finance (No 2) Act 1983
- Oil Taxation Act 1983
- Telecommunications Act 1984
- Finance Act 1984
- Films Act 1985
- Finance Act 1985
- Trustee Savings Banks Act 1985
- Transport Act 1985
- Airports Act 1986
- Finance Act 1986
- Gas Act 1986
- Building Societies Act 1986
- Finance (No 2) Act 1987
- Income and Corporation Taxes Act 1988 (including Destination Table)
- British Steel Act 1988
- Finance Act 1988
- Water Act 1989
- Finance Act 1989

INDEX

RETROSPECTIVE LEGISLATION NOTES
(continued on page vii)

Subscribers are advised to retain Handbooks for earlier years to use when dealing with tax for the corresponding years. Each Handbook shows the legislation operative for that year so far as it was known at the time of the passing of the Finance Act of that year. In view of the practice of passing legislation with retrospective effect, it is necessary when dealing with past years to consider whether the provisions have been affected or amended by subsequent legislation.

The following is a list of the retrospective provisions in FA 1989. A list of the legislation affected by these retrospective provisions appears on page vii, *post*.

The "Effective Date" column merely indicates in a general way the retrospective date. Reference must be made to the provisions mentioned under the first column to ascertain under what conditions those dates operate.

FA 1989	*Income tax, corporation tax and capital gains tax*	*Effective Date*
s 66 and Sch 17 Pt IV	Priority share allocations for employees	11 October 1988
126(1)	Non-resident carrying on profession or vocation in the UK	1988–89
128(1)	Non-residents: post-cessation disposals	1988–89
156	Interest on overdue tax	30 July 1982
180(6), (7)	Repayment interest: period of accrual	Deemed always to have had effect
Sch 6, paras 7, 8(4), 18(5), (6) and Sch 17, Pt IV	Retirement benefits schemes	1988–89
Sch 11, para 10(8)	Computation of underwriters' income tax	1987–88
Sch 15, para 2	Postponed CGT: pre-1 April 1982 events	Deemed always to have had effect
para 4	Re-basing to 1982: no gain/no loss disposals	Deemed always to have had effect
para 5	Re-basing to 1982: elections	Deemed always to have had effect

LEGISLATION AFFECTED BY RETROSPECTIVE LEGISLATION
(see page vi)

TMA 1970
  s 55(2), (6), (9)
    56(9)
    86(3), (4)

CGTA 1979
  s 12(1A)
    (2A)

FA 1985
  s 68(7A)

FA 1989
  s 156(2), (4)
    (3), (4)
    (1), (4)

  s 128(1)
    126(1)

  Sch 15 para 4(1)

TA 1988
  s 595(2), (3)

    596(3)(*a*)

    826(1)

FA 1988
  s 68(1), (1A), (2), (2A), (2B)
  Sch 8 para 1(3)
         13(5)
    9 para 3(1)

FA 1989
  Sch 11 para 10(7)

FA 1989
  Sch 6 paras 7, 18(5) and Sch 17 Pt IV
  Sch 6 paras 8(4), 18(6) and Sch 17 Pt IV
  s 180(6), (7)

  s 66 and Sch 17 Pt IV

  Sch 15, para 4(2)
            5
            2

  Sch 11 para 10(8)

PROSPECTIVE LEGISLATION NOTES
(continued on pages ix–x)

The provisions of any legislation contained in or relevant to this book which amend, modify or need to be cross-referenced and which do not take effect during the current year are listed below and will be separately noted and cross-referenced under the appropriate provisions in the Handbook for the year in which they take effect. Provisions taking effect on dates to be appointed have been incorporated at the appropriate places in this work, and are also included in the following list.

The effective date column merely indicates in a general way the prospective date. Reference must be made to the provisions mentioned under the first column to ascertain under what conditions those dates operate.

Prospective Amendments

Amended provisions	Amended by	Effective from
CAA 1968, s 7	Water Act 1989, Sch 25 para 36	1 September 1989
CAA 1968, s 68(1)–(3)	FA 1989, Sch 17 Pt VI	6 April 1993
CAA 1968, s 87(4)	ibid	6 April 1993
TMA 1970, s 37A	FA 1988, Sch 3 para 30 and FA 1989, s 149(4)(*a*)(i)	1990–91
TMA 1970, s 61	FA 1989, s 152 and Sch 17, Pt VIII	appointed day
TMA 1970, s 86(6)	FA 1989, s 158(1)(*a*) and Sch 17 Pt VIII	appointed day
TMA 1970, s 87(4), (5)	Ibid	appointed day
TMA 1970, s 98	FA 1989, ss 54(1)(*a*), 57(2)	1990–91
TMA 1970, s 98A(2)	FA 1989, s 165(2)	appointed day
F(No2)A 1975, s 47(1)	FA 1989, s 158(2)(*a*) and Sch 17, Pt VIII	appointed day
CGTA 1979, Sch 2	FA 1989, Sch 17, Pt X	appointed day
FA 1986, Sch 15 paras 1–3, 11	FA 1989, Sch 17 Pt VI	6 April 1993
TA 1988, s 257B(2)	FA 1989, ss 54(1)(*a*), 57(4)	1990–91
TA 1988, s 257D(8)	Ibid	1990–91
TA 1988, s 265(3)	Ibid	1990–91
TA 1988, s 278	FA 1988, s 31 and Sch 14, Pt IV	1990–91
TA 1988, s 685(3), (4)–(4C)	FA 1989, s 108	1990–91
TA 1988, s 824(1)(*a*), (*b*), (5)	FA 1989, s 158(2) and Sch 17, Pt VIII	appointed day
TA 1988, s 825(2)	Ibid	appointed day
TA 1988, Sch 9, para 24(2)(*a*)	FA 1989, s 62(1), (2), (4)	appointed day
FA 1988, s 38(5)	FA 1988, Sch 3, para 33	1990–91
FA 1988, s 99	FA 1988, s 99(5)	1990–91
FA 1989, s 165(2)	FA 1989, Sch 17, Pt VIII	appointed day

Married Couples

Note.—Amendments noted below are all effective from the year 1990–91.

Amended provisions	Amended by
TMA 1970	
s 8(3B)	FA 1988, Sch 14 Pt VIII
11A(3)	ibid
13(1)(*c*)	ibid
29(8)	ibid
37A (inserted)	Sch 3 para 30
93(1)	ibid
95(1)(*a*)	ibid

Married Couples (*contd*)

Amended provisions	Amended by
CGTA 1979	
s 4(2)	FA 1988, s 104(1), (2) & Sch 14 Pt VIII
5(6)	Sch 14 Pt VIII
45	s 104(1), (2) & Sch 14 Pt VIII
Sch 1 paras 2, 3	*ibid*
TA 1988	
s 256	FA 1988, Sch 14 Pt VIII
257	s 33
257A–257F (inserted)	s 33
259(1), (2), (4)	Sch 3 para 5
261	para 6
262	para 7(1), (3)
265	para 8
266(9), (11)(*a*)	para 9
273	para 10
279	s 32 & Sch 14 Pt VIII
280–281	Sch 14 Pt VIII
282	Sch 3 para 11
282A–282B (inserted)	s 34
283–288	Sch 14 Pt VIII
304(1)–(4), (5), (6)	Sch 3 para 12(1) & Sch 14 Pt VIII
325	Sch 14 Pt VIII
347B(3), (6)	Sch 3 para 13 & Sch 14 Pt VIII
356B	Sch 3 para 14
361(4)(*d*), (5)–(7)	Sch 3 para 15 & Sch 14 Pt VIII
382(1), (2)	Sch 14 Pt VIII
420(2)(*a*)(i)	Sch 3 para 16 & Sch 14 Pt VIII
467(2)	Sch 3 para 17
525(5)	Sch 14 Pt VIII
527(3)	*ibid*
535(5)	*ibid*
574(2)(*b*), (*c*)	*ibid*
590(2)(*a*), (3)(*b*)	para 18
623(1), (2), (6)(*c*), (7)(*a*), (8)	*ibid*
628(1)	Sch 3 para 19
644(7)	Sch 14 Pt VIII
646(2)(*d*), (5)(*a*), (7)	*ibid*
683(1)(*a*), (6)(*a*), (*b*), (9)	Sch 3 para 20
703(7), (8)	Sch 14 Pt VIII
833(4)	Sch 3 para 21 & Sch 14 Pt VIII
835(5)	Sch 3 para 22
Sch 14 para 1(2), (3)	Sch 14 Pt VIII
Sch 29	*ibid*
FA 1988	
s 38(5)	FA 1988, Sch 3 para 33
40(3)	Sch 14 Pt VIII
Sch 10, para 5(1), (3)–(5)	*ibid*

Married Couples *contd*)

TMA 1970, s 8	(particulars to be included in a husband's return where his income is taxable partly in 1989–90 and partly in 1990–91; see FA 1988, Sch 3 para 26).
s 93(2)	(modification of s 93(2) in its application in the year 1990–91 and subsequently; see FA 1988, Sch 3 paras 27, 28).
s 95(2)	(modification of s 95(2) in its application in the year 1990–91 and subsequently; see FA 1988, Sch 3 paras 27, 28).
CGTA 1979, s 13	(claim by husband under s 13 in respect of chargeable gains accruing to wife before 6 April 1990; see FA 1988, s 104(3)).
TA 1988, s 279	(time limits for assessments for fraud etc from the year 1990–91; see FA 1988, Sch 3 para 29).
s 279(1)	(transitional provisions in relation to the effect of the operation of s 279(1) for a year earlier than 1990–91 in the case of a wife; see FA 1988, Sch 3 para 25).

Taxes Management Provisions

Note.—The following is a list of provisions amended or modified by F(No 2)A 1987, ss 82–95, Sch 6, TA 1988, s 451(2), (3) and Sch 29, para 10. Most of these provisions are to be brought into force on appointed days, the earliest being 31 March 1992; see F(No 2)A 1987, s 95.

Amended provisions	*Amended or modified by*
TMA 1970, s 11(1), (2), (4)–(6), (8)	F(No 2)A 1987, s 82(1)–(6) and TA 1988, s 451(2)(*a*) and Sch 29 para 10(2)
TMA 1970, s 30(2A), (3A), (4), (4A)	F(No 2)A 1987, s 88 and TA 1988, Sch 29, para 10(3)
TMA 1970, s 69	F(No 2)A 1987, s 86(1)
TMA 1970, s 70(2), (5)	F(No 2)A 1987, s 84(4), 86(3)(*a*)
TMA 1970, s 85(2)	F(No 2)A 1987, Sch 6, para 7
TMA 1970, s 86(2)(*d*), (4), Table	F(No 2)A 1987, s 86(2)
TMA 1970, s 87A	F(No 2)A 1987, s 85 and TA 1988, s 451(2)(*b*) and Sch 29, para 10(4)
TMA 1970, s 88(2), (5)	F(No 2)A 1987, s 86(4)
TMA 1970, s 89	TA 1988, Sch 29, para 10(5)
TMA 1970, s 91(1A), (1B), (2), (2A)	F(No 2)A 1987, s 86(5), (6) and TA 1988, Sch 29, para 10(6)
TMA 1970, s 92	F(No 2)A 1987, s 86(3)(*a*)
TMA 1970, s 109(2), (3), (3A)	F(No 2)A 1987, s 91 and TA 1988, Sch 29, para 10(8)
TA 1970, s 267(3C)	F(No 2)A 1987, Sch 6, para 2
TA 1970, s 278(3), (3A), (5)–(6)	F(No 2)A 1987, Sch 6, para 4
FA 1973, Sch 15, para 4	F(No 2)A 1987, s 86(3)(*b*)
CGTA 1979, s 87(4), (4A)	F(No 2)A 1987, Sch 6, para 5
TA 1988, s 10(1)	TA 1988, s 451(2)(*c*)

Commercial Woodlands

See FA 1988, Sch 14, Pt V for provisions relating to commercial woodlands which are repealed with effect from the year 1993–94.

PROSPECTIVE CROSS-REFERENCES

TMA 1970, s 29(3)(*c*) 30 88	(application of these sections from 1990–91 in relation to tax relief claimed without due entitlement to it in respect of medical insurance premiums; see FA 1989, ss 54(1)(*a*), 57(3)).
TMA 1970, s 94(6)	(ascertainment of the date of payment of corporation tax where there is penalty liability under this section arising from surrender of company tax refund within group; see FA 1989, s 102(6)).
TMA 1970, s 95	(application of this section from 1990–91 in relation to incorrect return or account in respect of medical insurance premiums; see FA 1989, ss 54(1)(*a*), 57(3)).

HOW TO TRACE LEGISLATION

If the section or Schedule is known, it can be found immediately because the Acts are printed in chronological order. It should be noted that:—

(1) Amendments and repeals effected by later legislation are incorporated in the enactment amended or repealed; there is therefore no need to refer to the text of the later legislation. The annotations indicate the authority for the amendment or repeal.

(2) Where a provision is modified, a cross-reference is appended thereto, indicating where the modification is set out in full.

If only the relevant Act is known, see the Arrangement of Sections at the beginning of that Act.

Where the location of the provision is not known it may be traced through the Index.

HOW TO TRACE LEGISLATION

If the section or Schedule is known, it can be found immediately, because the Acts are printed in chronological order. It is found by noting that—

(1) Amendments and repeals effected by later legislation are incorporated in the text; consequent amendments appear: therefore no need to refer to the later enactment thereunder. The annotations indicate, inter alia, the fact, meaning, effect or extent.

(2) When a provision is obscure, a cross-reference is appended to give, for example, where the third head of its section is cited.

It only the relevant Act is known, see the arrangement of Sections at the beginning of that Act.

Where the location of the provision is not known, it may be traced through the Index.

PROVISIONAL COLLECTION OF TAXES ACT 1968

(1968 Chapter 2)

ARRANGEMENT OF SECTIONS

Section
1. Temporary statutory effect of House of Commons resolutions affecting income tax, purchase tax or customs or excise duties.
2. Payments and deductions made on account, and before renewal, of any temporary tax within s. 1.
5. House of Commons resolution giving provisional effect to motions affecting taxation.
6. Short title, repeals and saving as respects Northern Ireland.

An Act to consolidate the Provisional Collection of Taxes Act 1913 and certain other enactments relating to the provisional collection of taxes or matters connected therewith. [1st February 1968]

1. Temporary statutory effect of House of Commons resolutions affecting income tax, ...

(1) This section applies only to income tax, ...

[(1A) The reference in subsection (1) above to income tax includes a reference to any amount payable as representing income tax—

(a) under section [476 of the Income and Corporation Taxes Act 1988][3] (dividends and interest payable by building societies); or
(b) under section [479 of that Act][3] (interest paid on deposits with banks etc.).][2]

(2) Subject to that, and to the provisions of subsections (4) to (8) below, where the House of Commons passes a resolution which—

(a) provides for the renewal for a further period of any tax in force or imposed during the previous financial year (whether at the same or a different rate, and whether with or without modifications) or for the variation or abolition of any existing tax, and
(b) contains a declaration that it is expedient in the public interest that the resolution should have statutory effect under the provisions of this Act,

the resolution shall, for the period specified in the next following subsection, have statutory effect as if contained in an Act of Parliament and, where the resolution provides for the renewal of a tax, all enactments which were in force with reference to that tax as last imposed by Act of Parliament shall during that period have full force and effect with respect to the tax as renewed by the resolution.
   In this section references to the renewal of a tax include references to its reimposition, and references to the abolition of a tax include references to its repeal.

(3) The said period is—

(a) in the case of a resolution passed in March or April in any year, one expiring with 5th August in the same calendar year;
(b) in the case of any other resolution, one expiring at the end of four months after the date on which it is expressed to take effect or, if no such date is expressed, after the date on which it is passed.

(4) A resolution shall cease to have statutory effect under this section unless within the next twenty-five days on which the House of Commons sits after the day on which the resolution is passed—

(a) a Bill renewing, varying or, as the case may be, abolishing the tax is read a second time by the House, or
(b) a Bill is amended by the House [in Committee or on Report, or by any Standing Committee of the House][1] so as to include provision for the renewal, variation or, as the case may be, abolition of the tax.

(5) A resolution shall also cease to have statutory effect under this section if—

(a) the provisions giving effect to it are rejected during the passage of the Bill containing them through the House, or
(b) an Act comes into operation renewing, varying or, as the case may be, abolishing the tax, or
(c) Parliament is dissolved or prorogued.

(6) Where, in the case of a resolution providing for the renewal or variation of a tax, the resolution ceases to have statutory effect by virtue of subsection (4) or (5) above, or the period specified in subsection (3) above terminates, before an Act comes into operation renewing or varying the tax, any money paid in pursuance of the resolution shall be repaid or made good, and any deduction made in pursuance of the resolution shall be deemed to be an unauthorised deduction.

(7) Where any tax as renewed or varied by a resolution is modified by the Act renewing or varying the tax, any money paid in pursuance of the resolution which would not have been payable under the new conditions affecting the tax shall be repaid or made good, and any deduction made in pursuance of the resolution shall, so far as it would not have been authorised under the new conditions affecting the tax, be deemed to be an unauthorised deduction.

(8) When during any session a resolution has had statutory effect under this section, statutory effect shall not be again given under this section in the same session to the same resolution or to a resolution having the same effect.

Note.—Words omitted from the heading and sub-s. (1) are not relevant for the purposes of this work.
Amendments.—[1] Words in sub-s. (4) (b) added by FA 1968, s. 60.
[2] Sub-s. (1A) inserted by FA 1985, s. 97.
[3] Words in sub-s. (1A) (a), (b) substituted by TA 1988, Sch. 29, para. 32 Table.

2. Payments and deductions made on account, and before renewal, of any temporary tax within s. 1

(1) Any payment or deduction made on account of a temporary tax to which section 1 above applies and within one month after the date of its expiry shall, if the payment or deduction would have been a legal payment or deduction if the tax had not expired, be deemed to be a legal payment or deduction, subject to the condition that—

(a) if a resolution for the renewal or reimposition of the tax is not passed by the House of Commons within that month, or such a resolution is passed within that month but ceases to have statutory effect under the said section 1, any money so paid or deducted shall be repaid or made good, and
(b) if the tax is ultimately renewed or reimposed at a different rate, or with modifications, any amount paid or deducted which could not properly have been paid or deducted under the new conditions affecting the tax shall be repaid or made good.

(2) In this section "temporary tax" means a tax which has been imposed, or renewed or reimposed, for a limited period not exceeding eighteen months, and was in force or imposed during the previous financial year.

Cross references.—See TA 1988, s. 822 (over-deductions from interest on loan capital etc made before passing of annual Act).

5. House of Commons resolution giving provisional effect to motions affecting taxation

(1) This section shall apply if the House of Commons resolves that provisional statutory effect shall be given to one or more motions to be moved by the Chancellor of the Exchequer, or some other Minister, and which, if agreed to by the House, would be resolutions—

(*a*) to which statutory effect could be given under section 1 of this Act, or

(*b*) ...

(*c*) in accordance with which assessments to corporation tax could be made by virtue of [section 8 (5) of the Income and Corporation Taxes Act 1988][1].

(2) Subject to subsection (3) below, on the passing of the resolution under subsection (1) above, sections 1 to 3 of this Act, [sections 8 (5) and 822 of the 1988 Act (over-deductions from preference dividends before passing of annual Act)][1] shall apply as if each motion to which the resolution applies had then been agreed to by a resolution of the House.

(3) Subsection (2) above shall cease to apply to a motion if that motion, or a motion containing the same proposals with modifications, is not agreed to by a resolution of the House (in this section referred to as "a confirmatory resolution") within the next ten days on which the House sits after the resolution under subsection (1) above is passed, and, if it ceases to apply, all such adjustments, whether by way of discharge or repayment of tax, or discharge of security, or otherwise, shall be made as may be necessary to restore the position to what it would have been if subsection (2) above had never applied to that motion, and to make good any deductions which have become unauthorised deductions.

(4) The enactments specified in subsection (2) above shall have effect as if—

(*a*) any confirmatory resolution passed within the said period of ten sitting days had been passed when the resolution under subsection (1) above was passed, and

(*b*) everything done in pursuance of the said subsection (2) by reference to the motion to which the confirmatory resolution relates had been done by reference to the confirmatory resolution.

but any necessary adjustments shall be made, whether by way of discharge or repayment of tax, or modification of the terms of any security, or further assessment, or otherwise, where the proposals in the confirmatory resolution are not the same as those in the original motion to which that resolution relates.

Note.—Sub-s. (1) (*b*) is not relevant to this work.
Amendments.—[1] Words in sub-ss. (1) (*c*) and (2) substituted by TA 1988, Sch. 29, para. 32 Table.

6. Short title, repeals and saving as respects Northern Ireland

(1) This Act may be cited as the Provisional Collection of Taxes Act 1968.

(2) ...

(3) ...[1]

Note.—Sub-s. (2) repeals enactments specified in Sch. Effect has been given to these repeals where applicable in the relevant provisions of the earlier enactments.
Amendments.—[1] Sub-s. (3) repealed by Northern Ireland Constitution Act 1973, s. 41 (1) (*a*) and Sch. 6, Pt. 1, with effect from 18 July 1973.

CAPITAL ALLOWANCES ACT 1968
(1968 Chapter 3)

ARRANGEMENT OF SECTIONS

PART I
THE MAIN RELIEFS FOR CAPITAL EXPENDITURE

CHAPTER I
INDUSTRIAL BUILDINGS AND STRUCTURES, ETC.

Section
1. Initial allowances.
2. Writing-down allowances.
3. Balancing allowances and balancing charges.
4. Writing off of expenditure and meaning of "residue of expenditure".
5. Buildings and structures bought unused.
5A. Buildings and structures bought after use.
6. Manner of making allowances and charges.
7. Definition of "industrial building or structure".
8. Expenditure on repair of buildings.
9. Expenditure on sites for machinery and plant.
10. Sports pavilions.
11. Meanings of "the relevant interest".
12. Temporary disuse of industrial buildings or structures.
13. Requisitioned land, holding over of leased land, and other special cases.
14. Exclusion of double allowances.
15. Mining structures, etc.: balancing allowances carried back to earlier chargeable periods.
16. Transitory provision: meaning of "appointed day".
17. Interpretation of Chapter I.

CHAPTER II
MACHINERY AND PLANT

18. Initial allowances.

Writing-down allowances

19. Writing-down allowances.
20. Normal method of calculation
21. Alternative method.
22. Change from normal to alternative method.
23. Special method for use in connection with mines, oil wells, etc.
24. Adjustments of writing-down allowances in special circumstances.
25. Writing-down allowances for part of a year of assessment.
26. Determination and review of percentages.
27. Limit on writing-down allowances.
28. Part-time use otherwise than for trade purposes.
29. Effect on writing-down allowances of subsidies towards wear and tear.
30. Effect on writing-down allowances of previous user which has not attracted a writing-down allowance.

Ships and motor cars

Section
31. New ships.
32. Motor cars.

Balancing allowances, balancing charges, etc.

33. Balancing allowances and balancing charges.
34. Notional sales in certain cases.
35. Notional sale: effect on other party to transaction.
36. Demolition costs.
37. Part-time use otherwise than for trade purposes.
38. Subsidies towards wear and tear.
39. Effect on balancing allowances and balancing charges of previous user which has not attracted allowances.
40. Option in case of replacement of machinery or plant.

Supplemental

41. Meaning of "expenditure unallowed".
42. Allowances to lessors of machinery and plant.
43. Allowances to lessees of machinery and plant.
44. Partnership using property of a partner.
45. Building alterations connected with installation of machinery or plant.
46. Manner of making allowances and charges.
47. Application to professions, etc., and profits arising from occupation of land.
48. Successions to trades.
49. Transitory provisions: meaning of "appointed day" and "writing-down allowance".
50. Exclusion of double allowances.

CHAPTER III

MINES, OIL WELLS, ETC.

The main allowances

51. Qualifying expenditure: general provisions.
52. Machinery and plant used for exploration.
53. Overseas mineral rights.
54. Acquisition of land outside the United Kingdom.
55. Demolition costs.
56. Initial allowances.
57. Writing-down allowances.
58. Sale of source or part of source as going concern.
59. Expenditure incurred by persons not engaged in the trade of mining, etc.

Other allowances

60. Writing-down allowances for mineral depletion in the United Kingdom.
61. Contributions by mining concerns to public services, etc., outside the United Kingdom.
62. Expenditure by mining concerns on abortive exploration.

Supplemental

63. Regulations.
64. Expenditure prior to commencement of trade.
65. Interpretation of Chapter III.
66. Manner of making allowances and charges.

CHAPTER IV
DREDGING

Section
67. Capital allowances for expenditure on dredging.

CHAPTER V
AGRICULTURAL LAND AND BUILDINGS

68. *Allowances for capital expenditure on construction of buildings and other works.* (Spent)
69. Interpretation of preceding section.

CHAPTER VI
MISCELLANEOUS AND GENERAL

Income tax

70. Income tax allowances and charges in taxing a trade, etc.
71. Other income tax allowances.
72. Meaning of "basis period".

Corporation tax

73. Corporation tax allowances and charges in taxing a trade.
74. Other corporation tax allowances.

General

75. Writing-down allowances under sections 61, 67 and 68.
76. Companies not resident in United Kingdom.
77. Apportionment of consideration, and exchanges and surrenders of leasehold interests.
78. Special provisions as to certain sales.
79. Successions to trades, etc.
80. *Nationalisation schemes.* (repealed)
81. Procedure on apportionments, etc.
82. Interpretation of certain references to expenditure, etc.
83. Investment grants: exclusion of initial allowances.
84. Subsidies, etc.
85. Allowances in respect of contributions to capital expenditure.
86. Meaning of "sale, insurance, salvage or compensation moneys".
87. Other provisions as to interpretation of Part I.
88. Application of Part I to Scotland.
89. Transitory provisions: mills, factories and exceptional depreciation allowances.

PART II
SCIENTIFIC RESEARCH

90. Allowances for expenditure on scientific research not of a capital nature, and on payments to research associations, universities, etc.
91. Allowances for capital expenditure on scientific research.
92. Termination of user of assets provided for scientific research.
93. Prevention of double allowances.
94. Interpretation of Part II.
95. Supplemental.

PART III
GENERAL

96. Commencement and repeals.
97. Continuity.
98. Construction of existing Acts and documents.

Section
99. Construction of future enactments.
100. Short title and construction.

SCHEDULES:

Schedule 1—Initial allowances: transitory.
Schedule 2—Motor cars.
Schedule 3—Machinery and plant: hire-purchase, etc.
Schedule 4—Machinery and plant: existing writing-down percentages.
Schedule 5—Minerals: special provisions for certain expenditure.
Schedule 6—Minerals: expenditure incurred before appointed day.
Schedule 7—Operation of Parts I and II in relation to certain sales.
Schedule 8—*Assets transferred under nationalisation schemes: transitory provisions.* (repealed)
Schedule 9—Allowances for contributions towards expenditure.
Schedule 10—*Scientific research: transitory provisions.*
Schedule 11—*Repeals.*
Schedule 12—*Consequential amendments.*

An Act to consolidate Parts X and XI of the Income Tax Act 1952 with related provisions in that Act and subsequent Acts, but without the provisions of the said Part X relating to patents or to agricultural estate management expenditure which is not capital expenditure. [1st February 1968]

Cross references.—See CGTA 1979, s. 31 (2) (capital gains tax exemption for disposal consideration chargeable to income tax etc.);
TA 1988, Sch. 29, para. 1 (application of this Act in relation to income from trade etc. carried on abroad).

PART I

THE MAIN RELIEFS FOR CAPITAL EXPENDITURE

Construction.—FA 1984, Sch. 12, para. 1 to be construed as if it were contained in this Part of this Act with certain exceptions relating to the application of ss. 1 (6) and 5 (1) (*b*); see FA 1984, Sch. 12, para. 1 (3).
FA 1985, s. 66 (1) to be construed as if it were contained in this Part of this Act with certain exceptions relating to the application of ss. 1 (6) and 5 (1) (*b*); see FA 1985, s. 66 (2).
FA 1986, s. 56 (1), (2) and Sch. 15 to be construed as if they were included in this Part of this Act; see FA 1986, s. 56 (3).
The Tax Acts to have effect as if TA 1988, ss. 520–533 were contained in this Part of this Act; see TA 1988, s. 532 (1).
FA 1989, Sch. 13 to be construed as one with this Part; see FA 1989, s. 121 (2).
Cross references.—See FA 1982, Sch. 12, paras. 4 (5) (*a*), 14 (FA 1982, Sch. 12 (capital allowances for dwelling-houses let on assured tenancies) to be included in this part of this Act);
FA 1985, s. 56 (1) (*a*), (6) (for the purposes of this Part of this Act, FA 1985, s. 56 (2)–(5), (6) (*a*) to have effect to determine when capital expenditure is to be taken to be incurred with respect to any chargeable period or basis period ending after 17 December 1984),
s. 56 (8) (new rules as regards the determination of the date when capital expenditure is to be taken to be incurred with respect to any chargeable period or its basis period ending after 17 December 1984, subject to the provision that if under any provision of this Act the date would fall to be later than that determined under the new rules, the later date is to be treated as the date of the expenditure);
FA 1986, Sch. 15, para. 9 (2) (new code of allowances for capital expenditure incurred after 31 March 1986 on agricultural land and buildings: where this Act applies for the purposes of the new code, a transfer of a relevant interest (as defined in Sch. 15, para. 3) otherwise than by way of sale to be treated as a sale other than at open market value);
TA 1988, s. 532 (5) (in this Part of this Act as applied to know-how, references to property and its purchase or sale to include references to know-how and its acquisition or disposal, and s. 78, with Sch. 7 to this Act (special provisions as to controlled sales), to be omitted).

CHAPTER I

INDUSTRIAL BUILDINGS AND STRUCTURES, ETC.

Construction.—FA 1972, s. 69, to be construed as if contained in this Chapter; see FA 1972, s. 69 (6).
The Tax Acts to have effect as if FA 1978, s. 37 were contained in this Chapter where the time when the lease takes effect is on or after 15 February 1978; see FA 1978, s. 37 (7), (8).
The Tax Acts to have effect as if FA 1978, s. 38 and Sch. 6 were contained in this Chapter in relation to expenditure incurred on a qualifying hotel after 11 April 1978; see FA 1978, s. 38 (7), (8).
The Tax Acts to have effect as if FA 1980, s. 74 and Sch. 13 were contained in this Chapter in relation to expenditure on certain buildings in an enterprise zone; see FA 1980, s. 74 (7).
The Tax Acts to have effect as if FA 1980, s. 75 were contained in this Chapter in relation to expenditure after 26 March 1980 and before 27 March 1983 on small workshops; see FA 1980, s. 75 (7).
The Tax Acts to have effect as if FA 1982, s. 73 were contained in this Chapter in relation to expenditure after 26 March 1983 and before 27 March 1985 on very small workshops; see FA 1982, s. 73 (4).
The Tax Acts to have effect as if FA 1983, s. 31 were contained in this Chapter in relation to expenditure on buildings converted into very small workshops; see FA 1983, s. 31 (6).
FA 1984, Sch. 12, para. 5 to be construed as if it were contained in this Chapter with certain exceptions relating to the application of ss. 1 (6) and 5 (1) (*b*); see FA 1984, Sch. 12, para. 5 (6).
Cross references.—FA 1971, Sch. 8, para. 16 (2) (any reference in this Chapter to Part I, Chapter II, of this Act shall, in relation to capital expenditure on the provision of machinery or plant incurred on or after 27 October 1970, include a reference to FA 1971, Pt. III, Ch. I (ss. 40–50));
FA 1978, s. 37 (effect of this Chapter in relation to long leases where the time when the lease takes effect is on or after 15 February 1978),
s. 38 and Sch. 6, paras. 4, 8 (application of this Chapter to hotels in relation to expenditure incurred after 11 April 1978);
FA 1980, s. 74 and Sch. 13 (allowances for certain buildings in an enterprise zone),
s. 75 and Sch. 13 (allowances for expenditure after 26 March 1980 and before 27 March 1983 on small workshops);
FA 1981, s. 76 (1), (5) (transfer after 10 March 1981 of industrial building or structure otherwise than by way of sale to be treated as a sale for a price other than its market value);
FA 1982, s. 73 (1) (application of this Chapter as modified by FA 1980, Sch. 13, paras. 1–3 in relation to capital expenditure incurred after 26 March 1983 and before 27 March 1985 on the construction of a very small industrial building);
FA 1984, Sch. 12, paras. 5, 8, 9 (the provisions of this Chapter to apply in accordance with FA 1984, Sch. 12, paras. 5, 8, 9 to capital expenditure incurred under a contract entered into after 13 March 1984 and before 1 April 1986 stipulating full performance of the contract after 31 March 1985 or not stipulating a date for full performance);
TA 1988, s. 495 (effect of regional development grant paid in respect of expenditure incurred in connection with oil exploration, extraction, etc.);
FA 1989, Sch. 13, para. 28 (1), (4) (*a*) (exclusion of double allowances: where an allowance is made under this Chapter, no allowance to be made under other legislation).

1. Initial allowances

(1) Subject to the provisions of this Act, where a person incurs capital expenditure on the construction of a building or structure which is to be an industrial building or structure occupied for the purposes of a trade carried on either by that person or by such a lessee as is mentioned in subsection (3) of this section, there shall be made to the person who incurred the expenditure, for the chargeable period mentioned in subsection (4) below, an allowance (in this Chapter referred to as "an initial allowance").

[(1A) The reference in subsection (1) above to the occupation of a building or structure for the purposes of a trade carried on by the person who incurred the capital expenditure on that building or structure shall include a reference to the use of that building or structure for the purposes of a trade carried on by a licensee of that person or of a lessee of that person.]³

(2) An initial allowance shall be of an amount equal to [. . .]⁴ of the capital expenditure mentioned in subsection (1) above:

Provided that this subsection shall have effect subject to the provisions of Schedule 1 to this Act.

(3) The lessees mentioned in subsection (1) above are lessees occupying the building or structure on the construction of which the expenditure was incurred under a lease to which the relevant interest, as defined in section 11 of this Act, is reversionary.

(4) The chargeable period mentioned in subsection (1) above shall, in the case of a person incurring expenditure, be the chargeable period related to the incurring of that expenditure:

. . .¹⁻²

(5) Notwithstanding anything in this section, no initial allowance shall be made in respect of any expenditure if, when the building or structure comes to be used, it is not an industrial building or structure, and where an initial allowance has been granted in respect of any expenditure otherwise than in accordance with the provisions of this section, all such assessments shall be made as are necessary to secure that effect is given to those provisions.

(6) Any expenditure incurred for the purposes of a trade by a person about to carry it on shall be treated for the purposes of the preceding provisions of this section as if it had been incurred by that person on the first day on which he does carry it on.

Note.—The initial allowance under this section is abolished in respect of expenditure incurred after 31 March 1986: see FA 1984, Sch. 12, para. 1 (1).
Cross references.—See FA 1978, s. 38 (1), (8) and Sch. 6, para. 1 and FA 1985, s. 66 (in relation to expenditure incurred on a qualifying hotel after 11 April 1978, the initial allowance referred to in sub-s. (2) of this section is one-fifth of the capital expenditure incurred, subject to its abolition for expenditure after 31 March 1986),
s. 38 (4) (*a*), (8) (application of sub-s. (3) of this section in relation to expenditure incurred after 11 April 1978 on a qualifying hotel),
s. 38 (8) (expenditure on a qualifying hotel not to be treated for the purposes of that subsection as having been incurred after the date on which it was in fact incurred by reason only of sub-s. (6) of this section);
FA 1980, s. 74 and Sch. 13, para. 1 (initial allowance for industrial and commercial buildings or structures and qualifying hotels in an enterprise zone),
ss. 74 (5), 75 (5) (sub-s. (6) restricted in its application to industrial and commercial buildings or structures and qualifying hotels in an enterprise zone and certain expenditure on small workshops),
s. 75 and Sch. 13, para. 1 (initial allowance for expenditure after 26 March 1980 and before 27 March 1983 on small workshops);
FA 1981, s. 73 (2) (disclaimer or reduction of the initial allowance entitlement under sub-s. (2) above);
FA 1983, s. 30 (2) (new limit in CAA 1968, s. 7 (4) for non-industrial expenditure; sub-s. (6) above restricted in its application for the purposes of the new limit).
Amendments.—¹⁻² The proviso to sub-s. (4) repealed by FA 1980, s. 76 and Sch. 20, Pt. IX with effect generally from 27 March 1980; see s. 76 (2).
³ Sub-s. (1A) inserted by FA 1982, s. 74 (1), (4) in relation to licences granted after 9 March 1982.
⁴ The fraction under sub-s. (2) is "three-quarters" for expenditure under certain contracts entered into before 14 March 1984, "three-quarters" also for expenditure on certain projects in development areas where a written offer of financial assistance, or the Northern Ireland equivalent, was made between 1 April 1980 and 13 March 1984 (both dates inclusive), "one half" for expenditure incurred after 13 March 1984 and before 1 April 1985 and "one quarter" for expenditure incurred after 31 March 1985 and before 1 April 1986; see by FA 1984, Sch. 12, paras. 1, 4. The initial allowance is abolished in respect of expenditure incurred after 31 March 1986, see FA 1984, Sch. 12, para. 1 (1). For the spreading of capital expenditure incurred under certain contracts entered into after 13 March 1984, see FA 1984, Sch. 12, paras. 5, 8, 9.

2. Writing-down allowances

(1) Subject to the provisions of this Act, where—

(a) any person is, at the end of a chargeable period or its basis period, entitled to an interest in a building or structure, and
(b) at the end of the said chargeable period or its basis period, the building or structure is an industrial building or structure, and
(c) that interest is the relevant interest in relation to the capital expenditure incurred on the construction of that building or structure,

an allowance (in this Chapter referred to as "a writing-down allowance") shall be made to him for the said chargeable period.

(2) The writing-down allowance shall be equal to one-twentyfifth (or, where the expenditure was incurred before 6th November 1962, one-fiftieth) of the expenditure mentioned in subsection (1) (c) above, except that for a chargeable period of less than a year the said fraction of one-twentyfifth or one-fiftieth shall be proportionately reduced.

(3) Where the interest in a building or structure which is the relevant interest in relation to any expenditure is sold [and the sale is an event to which section 3 (1) of this Act applies][1], then (subject to any further adjustment under this subsection on a later sale) the writing-down allowance for any chargeable period, if that chargeable period or its basis period ends after the time of the sale, shall be the residue (as defined in section 4 (1) of this Act) of that expenditure immediately after the sale, reduced in the proportion (if it is less than one) which the length of the chargeable period bears to the part unexpired at the date of the sale of the period of twenty-five years (or, where the expenditure was incurred before 6th November 1962, fifty years) beginning with the time when the building or structure was first used.

(4) Notwithstanding anything in the preceding provisions of this section, in no case shall the amount of a writing-down allowance made to a person for any chargeable period in respect of any expenditure exceed what, apart from the writing off falling to be made by reason of the making of that allowance, would be the residue of that expenditure at the end of that chargeable period or its basis period.

Cross references.—See FA 1978, s. 38 (1), (8) and Sch. 6, para. 2 (application of sub-s. (3) of this section, with effect from 11 April 1978, to any sale (whether or not the building is then a qualifying hotel) which is an event to which s. 3 (1) of this Act applies);
FA 1980, s. 74 and Sch. 13, para. 3 (writing-down allowance for certain buildings in an enterprise zone),
s. 75 and Sch. 13, para. 3 (writing-down allowance for expenditure after 26 March 1980 and before 27 March 1983 on small workshops),
Sch. 13, para. 4 (effect for sub-ss. (1) (b) and (3) of this section of change of use of certain buildings in an enterprise zone).
Amendments.—[1] Words in sub-s. (3) substituted by FA 1981, s. 74 (2), (6) where the sale referred to in the sub-s. occurs after 17 December 1980.

3. Balancing allowances and balancing charges

(1) Where any capital expenditure has been incurred on the construction of a building or structure, and any of the following events occurs while the building or structure is an industrial building or structure [or after it has ceased to be one][1], that is to say—

(a) the relevant interest in the building or structure is sold, or
(b) that interest, being an interest depending on the duration of a foreign concession, comes to an end on the coming to an end of that concession, or
(c) that interest, being a leasehold interest, comes to an end otherwise than on the person entitled thereto acquiring the interest which is reversionary thereon, or
(d) the building or structure is demolished or destroyed, or, without being demolished or destroyed, ceases altogether to be used,

an allowance or charge (in this Chapter referred to as "a balancing allowance" or "a balancing charge") shall, in the circumstances mentioned in this section, be made to, or, as the case may be, on, the person entitled to the relevant interest immediately before that event occurs, for the chargeable period related to that event:

Provided that no balancing allowance or balancing charge shall be made by reason of any event occurring more than twenty-five years (or, where the expenditure was incurred before 6th November 1962, fifty years) after the building or structure was first used [and where two or more events occur during a period when the building or structure is not an industrial building or structure no balancing allowance or balancing charge shall be made on the occurrence of any of those events except the first][1].

(2) Where there are no sale, insurance, salvage or compensation moneys, or where the residue of the expenditure immediately before the event exceeds those moneys, a balancing allowance shall be made, and the amount thereof shall be the amount of the said residue or, as the case may be, of the excess thereof over the said moneys.

(3) If the sale, insurance, salvage or compensation moneys exceed the residue, if any, of the expenditure immediately before the event, a balancing charge shall be made, and the amount on which it is made shall be an amount equal to the excess or, where the residue is nil, to the said moneys.

[(4) If for any part of the relevant period the building or structure was neither an industrial building or structure nor used for scientific research, subsections (4A) to (5) below shall have effect instead of subsections (2) and (3) above.][2]

[(4A) Subject to subsection (4C) below, where the sale, insurance, salvage or compensation moneys are not less than the capital expenditure, a balancing charge shall be made and the amount on which it is made shall be an amount equal to the allowances given.][2]

[(4B) Subject to subsection (4C) below, where there are no sale, insurance, salvage or compensation moneys or where those moneys are less than the capital expenditure, then—

(*a*) if the adjusted net cost of the building or structure exceeds the allowances given, a balancing allowance shall be made and the amount thereof shall be an amount equal to the excess;
(*b*) if the adjusted net cost of the building or structure is less than the allowances given, a balancing charge shall be made and the amount on which it is made shall be an amount equal to the shortfall.][2]

[(4C) No balancing charge or allowance shall be made under subsection (4A) or (4B) above on the occasion of a sale if by virtue of paragraph 4 of Schedule 7 to this Act the building or structure is treated as having been sold for a sum equal to the residue of the expenditure on its construction immediately before the sale.][2]

[(5) In subsections (4) to (4B) above and in this subsection—

"the relevant period" means the period beginning at the time when the building or structure was first used for any purpose and ending with the event giving rise to the balancing allowance or balancing charge except that where there has been a sale of the building or structure after that time and before that event the relevant period shall begin on the day following that sale or, if there has been more than one such sale, the last such sale;

"the capital expenditure" means—

(*a*) where paragraph (*b*) of this definition does not apply, the capital expenditure incurred (or by virtue of section 5 of this Act deemed to have been incurred) on the construction of the building or structure;
(*b*) where the person to or on whom the balancing allowance or balancing charge falls to be made is not the person who incurred (or is deemed to have incurred) that expenditure, the residue of that expenditure at the beginning of the relevant period,

together (in either case) with any amount to be added to the residue of that expenditure by virtue of section 4 (11) of this Act;

"the allowances given" means the allowances referred to in subsection (6) of this section;

"the adjusted net cost" means—

(*a*) where there are no sale, insurance, salvage or compensation moneys, the capital expenditure;
(*b*) where those moneys are less than that expenditure, the amount by which they are less,

reduced (in either case) in the proportion that the part, or the aggregate of the parts, of the relevant period for which the building or structure was an industrial building or structure or used for scientific research bears to the whole of that period;

"scientific research" has the same meaning as in Part II of this Act.][2]

(6) Notwithstanding anything in the preceding provisions of this section, in no case shall the amount on which a balancing charge is made on a person in respect of any expenditure on the construction of a building or structure exceed the amount of the initial allowance, if any, made to him in respect of that expenditure together with the amount of any writing-down allowances or scientific research allowances in respect of that expenditure, and any

relevant mills, factories or exceptional depreciation allowances in respect of that building or structure, made to him for chargeable periods which end on or before the date of the event giving rise to the charge or of which the basis periods end on or before that date.

Cross references.—See FA 1972, s. 69 (restriction of balancing allowances on sale of industrial buildings and structures);
FA 1978, s. 37 (6) (b) (provisions whereby FA 1978, s. 37 (capital allowances for long leases) does not apply by reason of this section),
s. 38 (1), (8) and Sch. 6, paras. 3, 4 and 5 (application of sub-ss. (1) and (4) proviso of this section in relation to expenditure incurred on a qualifying hotel after 11 April 1978);
FA 1980, Sch. 13, para. 4 (effect for sub-s. (1) and proviso to sub-s. (4) of this section of change of use of certain buildings in an enterprise zone);
FA 1988, Sch. 3, para. 23 (circumstances in which an industrial buildings allowance made under this section to a husband to be treated as made to his wife).
Amendments.—[1] Words in sub-s. (1) inserted by FA 1981, s. 74 (3), (6) where any event referred to in sub-s. (1) (a)–(d) occurs after 17 December 1980.
[2] Sub-ss. (4), (4A), (4B), (4C), (5) substituted for sub-ss. (4), (5) by FA 1981, s. 75 (2), (5) where any event referred to in sub-s. (1) (a)–(d) occurs after 17 December 1980.

4. Writing off of expenditure and meaning of "residue of expenditure"

(1) Any expenditure incurred on the construction of any building or structure shall be treated for the purposes of this Chapter as written off to the extent and as at the times hereafter specified in this section, and references in this Chapter to the residue of any such expenditure shall be construed accordingly.

(2) Where an initial allowance is made in respect of the expenditure, the amount of that allowance shall be treated as written off as at the time when the building or structure is first used.

(3) Where, by reason of the building or structure being at any time an industrial building or structure, a writing-down allowance is made for any chargeable period in respect of the expenditure, the amount of that allowance shall be treated as written off as at the said time:

Provided that, where at the said time an event occurs which gives rise or may give rise to a balancing allowance or balancing charge, the amount directed to be treated as written off by this subsection as at the said time shall be taken into account in computing the residue of that expenditure immediately before that event for the purpose of determining whether any and if so what balancing allowance or balancing charge is to be made.

(4) Where a scientific research allowance is made for any chargeable period in respect of the expenditure, the amount of that allowance shall be treated as written off—

(a) in the case of an allowance under section 91 of this Act or paragraph 1 of Schedule 10 to this Act, as at the end of the chargeable period or, if it is a year of assessment, as at the end of the basis period (as defined in subsection (3) of the said section 91) for that year of assessment, and

(b) in the case of an allowance under section 92 of this Act or paragraph 2 of Schedule 10 to this Act, as at the time when the asset ceases to be used by the person in question for scientific research connected with the trade:

Provided that where, at the time as at which an amount falls to be treated as written off under this subsection, an event occurs which gives rise or may give rise to a balancing allowance or balancing charge, the amount directed to be treated as written off by this subsection as at that time shall be taken into account in computing the residue of the expenditure immediately before that event for the purpose of determining whether any and if so what balancing allowance or balancing charge is to be made.

(5) If, for any period or periods between the time when the building or structure was first used for any purpose and the time at which the residue of the expenditure falls to be ascertained, the building or structure has not been in use as an industrial building or structure, then, subject to the provisions of subsection (7) below, there shall in ascertaining that residue be treated as having been previously written off in respect of the said period or periods amounts equal to writing-down allowances made for chargeable periods of a total length equal thereto at such rate or rates as would have been appropriate having regard to any sale on which section 2 (3) of this Act operated.

(6) For the purposes of subsection (5) above a building or structure shall not be treated—

(a) by virtue of section 7 (1) (c) of this Act as having been an industrial building or structure before the year 1952–53,

(b) by virtue of section 7 (1) (i) or section 7 (6) of this Act as having been an industrial building or structure before the year 1953–54.

(7) Where any relevant mills, factories or exceptional depreciation allowances have been made in respect of the building or structure for any year of assessment before that in which the appointed day fell, and either—

(*a*) no amount falls to be treated as written off under subsection (5) above as at any date before the beginning of the year of assessment in which the appointed day fell, or
(*b*) the total amounts falling to be treated as written off thereunder as at dates before the beginning of the year of assessment in which the appointed day fell are less than the total relevant mills, factories or exceptional depreciation allowances for years of assessment before that year,

an amount equal to the total relevant mills, factories or exceptional depreciation allowances or, as the case may be, to that total amount less the total amounts falling to be treated as written off as aforesaid, shall be treated as written off as at the end of the year of assessment immediately preceding that in which the appointed day fell.

(8) Where any exceptional depreciation allowance was made in respect of a building or structure for the year of assessment in which the appointed day fell, an amount equal to that allowance shall be treated as written off as at the end of the immediately preceding year of assessment.

(9) Where, on the occasion of a sale, a balancing allowance is made in respect of the expenditure, there shall be treated as written off as at the time of the sale the amount by which the residue of the expenditure before the sale exceeds the net proceeds of the sale.

(10) Where, on the occasion of a sale, a balancing charge is made in respect of the expenditure, the residue of the expenditure shall be deemed for the purposes of this Chapter to be increased as at the time of the sale by the amount on which the charge is made.

[(10A) Where, on the occasion of a sale, a balancing charge is made under section 3 (4B) (*b*) of this Act in respect of the expenditure and, apart from this subsection, the residue of the expenditure immediately after the sale would by virtue of subsection (10) above be deemed to be greater than the net proceeds of the sale, the residue immediately after the sale shall be deemed for the purposes of this Chapter to be equal to the net proceeds.][1]

(11) Where a building or structure is demolished, and the demolition gives rise, or might give rise, to a balancing allowance or charge under this Chapter to or on the person incurring the cost of demolition, the net cost to him of the demolition (that is to say the excess, if any, of the cost of the demolition over any moneys received for the remains of the property) shall be added for the purposes of this Chapter to the residue, immediately before the demolition, of the expenditure incurred on the construction of the property; and if this subsection applies to the net cost to a person of the demolition of any property, the cost or net cost shall not be treated, for the purposes of this Part or Part II of this Act, as expenditure incurred in respect of any other property by which that property is replaced.

(12) Where the Crown is at any time entitled to the relevant interest in a building or structure, the preceding provisions of this section shall have effect as if all such writing-down allowances, balancing allowances, mills, factories or exceptional depreciation allowances and balancing charges had been made as could have been made if—

(*a*) a person other than the Crown and other than a company had been entitled to the relevant interest, and
(*b*) all things which, while the Crown is entitled to the relevant interest, have been done in relation to the building or structure by or to the Crown or by or to any person using the building or structure under the authority of the Crown, had been done by or to that other person, for the purposes of and in the course of a trade carried on by him, and
(*c*) any sale or other disposition by or on behalf of the Crown of the relevant interest in the building or structure had been made in connection with the termination of that trade, and
(*d*) the basis periods of that other person in respect of that trade had, in the case of each year of assessment, ended immediately before the beginning of the year of assessment.

[(13) In subsection (12) above references to the Crown shall include references to any person who is not within the charge to tax in the United Kingdom.][2]

Cross references.—See FA 1980, Sch. 13, para. 4 (effect for sub-ss. (3) and (5) of this section of change of use of certain buildings in an enterprise zone);
FA 1986, s. 56 (3) (application of sub-s. (11) above in relation to FA 1986, Sch. 15 (agricultural land and buildings)).
Amendments.—[1] Sub-s. (10A) inserted by FA 1981, s. 75 (3), (5) where the balancing allowance or charge arises from an event occurring after 17 December 1980.
[2] Sub-s. (13) added by FA 1988, s. 90 in relation to sales occurring after the passing of FA 1988. FA 1988 was passed on 29 July 1988.

5. Buildings and structures bought unused

(1) Where expenditure is incurred on the construction of a building or structure and, before that building or structure is used, the relevant interest therein is sold—

(a) the expenditure actually incurred on the construction thereof shall be left out of account for the purposes of the preceding provisions of this Chapter, but

(b) the person who buys that interest shall be deemed for those purposes to have incurred, on the date when the purchase price becomes payable, expenditure on the construction thereof equal to the said expenditure or to the net price paid by him for the said interest, whichever is the less:

Provided that, where the relevant interest in the building or structure is sold more than once before the building or structure is used, the provisions of paragraph (b) of this subsection shall have effect only in relation to the last of those sales.

(2) Where the expenditure incurred on the construction of a building or structure was incurred by a person carrying on a trade which consists, as to the whole or any part thereof, in the construction of buildings or structures with a view to their sale, and, before the building or structure is used, he sells the relevant interest therein in the course of that trade, or, as the case may be, of that part of that trade, paragraph (b) of subsection (1) of this section shall have effect subject to the following modifications—

(a) if that sale is the only sale of the relevant interest before the building or structure is used, the said paragraph (b) shall have effect as if the words "the said expenditure or to" and the words "whichever is the less" were omitted, and

(b) in any other case, the said paragraph (b) shall have effect as if the reference to the expenditure actually incurred on the construction of the building or structure were a reference to the price paid on the said sale.

Cross references.—See FA 1978, s. 38 (8) (expenditure incurred on a qualifying hotel after 11 April 1978 not to be treated for the purposes of that subsection as having been incurred after the date on which it was in fact incurred by reason only of sub-s. (1) of this section);
FA 1980, ss. 74 (5), 75 (5) (sub-s. (1) of this section restricted in its application to expenditure on certain buildings in an enterprise zone and certain expenditure on small workshops);
FA 1983, s. 30 (2) (increased limit in CAA 1968, s. 7 (4) for non-industrial expenditure; sub-s. (1) above to apply for the purposes of the new limit).

[5A. Buildings and structures bought after use

(1) This section applies where—

(a) expenditure is incurred on the construction of a building or structure by a person carrying on a trade which consists, in whole or part, in the construction of buildings or structures with a view to their sale, and

(b) after the building or structure has been used, he sells the relevant interest in it in the course of that trade or, as the case may be, of that part of that trade.

(2) Where this section applies, this Chapter shall have effect in relation to the person who buys the interest as if—

(a) the original expenditure had been capital expenditure,

(b) all appropriate writing-down allowances had been made to the person incurring it, and

(c) all appropriate balancing allowances or charges had been made on the occasion of the sale.][1]

Amendments.—This section inserted by FA 1989, Sch. 13, para. 1 where the purchase price on a sale becomes payable after 26 July 1989.

6. Manner of making allowances and charges

(1) Except in the cases mentioned in the following provisions of this section, any allowance or charge made to or on a person under the preceding provisions of this Chapter shall be made to or on him in taxing his trade.

(2) An initial allowance shall be made to a person by way of discharge or repayment of tax if his interest in the building or structure is subject to any lease when the expenditure is incurred or becomes subject to any lease before the building or structure is first used for any purpose.

(3) A writing-down allowance shall be made to a person for a chargeable period by way of discharge or repayment of tax if his interest is subject to any lease at the end of that chargeable period or its basis period.

(4) A balancing allowance shall be made to a person by way of discharge or repayment of tax if his interest is subject to any lease immediately before the event giving rise to the allowance.

(5) Any allowance which, under the preceding provisions of this section, is to be made by way of discharge or repayment of tax shall be available primarily against the following income, that is to say—

(a) income taxed under [Schedule A][1] in respect of any premises which at any time in the chargeable period consist of or include an industrial building or structure, or
(b) income which is the subject of a balancing charge under this Chapter.

(6) Effect shall be given to a balancing charge to be made on a person where his interest is subject to any lease immediately before the event giving rise to the charge—

(a) if it is a charge to income tax, by making the charge under Case VI of Schedule D,
(b) if it is a charge to corporation tax, by treating the amount on which the charge is to be made as income of the description in subsection (5) (a) above.

[(7) Where a balancing allowance or balancing charge falls to be made in the case of a building or structure which has ceased to be an industrial building or structure and the circumstances are such as are mentioned in paragraph (a) and (b) of subsection (2) of section 12 of this Act, the allowance or charge shall be made as provided in that subsection.][2]

Cross references.—See FA 1982, s. 74 (2) (where an industrial building or structure is used by a licensee, this section to apply as if the building or structure were subject to a lease).
Amendments.—[1] Words in sub-s. (5) (a) substituted by TA 1970, Sch. 15, para. 5 (1), (2).
[2] Sub-s. (7) inserted by FA 1981, s. 74 (4), (6) where a sale or an event occurs after 17 December 1980.

7. Definition of "industrial building or structure"

(1) Subject to the provisions of this section, in this Chapter "industrial building or structure" means a building or structure in use—

(a) for the purposes of a trade carried on in a mill, factory or other similar premises, or
(b) for the purposes of a transport, dock, inland navigation, water, [sewerage][5], electricity or hydraulic power undertaking, or
(c) subject to subsection (7) below, for the purposes of a tunnel undertaking, or
(d) subject to subsection (8) below, for the purposes of a bridge undertaking, or
(e) for the purposes of a trade which consists in the manufacture of goods or materials or the subjection of goods or materials to any process, or
(f) for the purposes of a trade which consists in the storage—

(i) of goods or materials which are to be used in the manufacture of other goods or materials, or
(ii) of goods or materials which are to be subjected, in the course of a trade, to any process, or
(iii) of goods or materials which, having been manufactured or produced or subjected, in the course of a trade, to any process, have not yet been delivered to any purchaser, or
(iv) of goods or materials on their arrival by sea or air into any part of the United Kingdom, or

(g) for the purposes of a trade which consists in the working of any mine, oil well or other source of mineral deposits, or of a foreign plantation, or
(h) for the purposes of a trade consisting in all or any of the following activities, that is to say, ploughing or cultivating land (other than land in the occupation of the person carrying on the trade) or doing any other agricultural operation on such land, or threshing the crops of another person, or
(i) for the purposes of a trade which consists in the catching or taking of fish or shellfish,

and, in particular, the said expression includes any building or structure provided by the person carrying on such a trade or undertaking for the welfare of workers employed in that trade or undertaking and in use for that purpose.

(2) The provisions of subsection (1) of this section shall apply in relation to a part of a trade or undertaking as they apply in relation to a trade or undertaking:

Provided that where part only of a trade or undertaking complies with conditions set out in the said provisions, a building or structure shall not, by virtue of this subsection, be an industrial building or structure unless it is in use for the purposes of that part of that trade or undertaking.

[(2A) The reference in paragraph (e) of subsection (1) above to the subjection of goods or materials to any process shall include a reference to the maintaining or repairing of any goods or materials but, notwithstanding subsection (2) above, paragraph (e) shall not apply to the maintenance or repair by any person of goods or materials employed by that person in any trade or undertaking unless that trade or undertaking itself falls within any of the paragraphs of that subsection (including paragraph (e)).][2]

(3) Notwithstanding anything in [the preceding provisions][3] of this section, but subject to the provisions of subsection (4) of this section, "industrial building or structure" does not include any building or structure in use as, or as part of, a dwelling-house, retail shop, showroom, hotel or office or for any purpose ancillary to the purposes of a dwelling-house, retail shop, showroom, hotel or office:

Provided that this subsection shall not apply to, or to part of, a building or structure which was constructed for occupation by, or for the welfare of, persons employed at, or in connection with the working of, a mine, oil well or other source of mineral deposits, or for occupation by, or for the welfare of, persons employed on, or in connection with the growing and harvesting of the crops on, a foreign plantation, if the building or structure is likely to have little or no value to the person carrying on the trade when the mine, oil well or other source or the plantation is not longer worked, or will cease to belong to such person on the coming to an end of a foreign concession under which the mine, oil well or other source, or the plantation, is worked.

[(3A) Where a building or structure is used by more than one licensee of the same person that building or structure shall not be an industrial building or structure unless each of the licensees uses the building or that part of it to which his licence relates for the purposes of a trade which falls within subsection (1) above.][1]

[(3B) A road on an industrial estate shall be treated as used for the purposes of a trade which falls within subsection (1) above if the buildings and structures on the estate are used wholly or mainly for such purposes.][7]

(4) Where part of the whole of a building or structure is, and part thereof is not, an industrial building or structure, and the capital expenditure which has been incurred on the construction of the second mentioned part is not more than [one quarter][4] of the total capital expenditure which has been incurred on the construction of the whole building or structure, the whole building or structure and every part thereof shall be treated as an industrial building or structure.

(5) in this section—

"retail shop" includes any premises of a similar character where retail trade or business (including repair work) is carried on;

"dock" includes any harbour, wharf, pier or jetty or other works in or at which vessels can ship or unship merchandise or passengers, not being a pier or jetty primarily used for recreation, and "dock undertaking" shall be construed accordingly;

"water undertaking" means an undertaking for the supply of water for public consumption;

["sewerage undertaking" means an undertaking for the provision of sewerage services within the meaning of the Water Act 1989;][6]

"electricity undertaking" means an undertaking for the generation, transformation, conversion, transmission or distribution of electrical energy;

"hydraulic power undertaking" means an undertaking for the supply of hydraulic power;

"undertaking" does not include an undertaking not carried on by way of trade;

"foreign plantation" means, subject to subsection (6) below, any land outside the United Kingdom used for the growing and harvesting of crops;

"crops" includes any form of vegetable produce and "harvesting" includes the collection thereof, however effected.

(6) In this section the expression "foreign plantation" shall (without prejudice to the generality of the definition in subsection (5) above) be extended so as to include any land outside the United Kingdom used for husbandry or forestry, and the reference in subsection (3) above to the growing and harvesting of crops shall be correspondingly extended.

(7) Subsection (1) (c) above shall not affect any allowance or charge which would have been made under this Part of this Act if this Act had been enacted without that paragraph and if section 25 of the Finance Act 1952 (which is the corresponding provision repealed by this Act) had not been passed, and where by virtue of the said paragraph (c) a balancing charge is made on a person in respect of any expenditure, the amount on which it is made shall not exceed the amount of the allowances made to him in respect of that expenditure by virtue of the said paragraph (c) (and the said section 25).

(8) Subsection (1) (d) above shall have effect only in relation to expenditure which is to be treated for the purposes of this Chapter as incurred after the end of the year 1956–57.

(9) For the purposes of this Chapter references to use as an industrial building or structure do not apply, in the case of a building or structure outside the United Kingdom, to use for the purposes of a trade at a time when the profits or gains of the trade are not assessable in accordance with the rules applicable to Case I of Schedule D.

Cross references.—See FA 1978 s. 38 (1), (8) and Sch. 6, para. 9 (only sub-ss. (4) and (9) of this section to be construed as applying in relation to expenditure on a qualifying hotel incurred after 11 April 1978);
FA 1980, Sch. 13, para. 5 (only sub-s. (4) of this section applies to commercial buildings and qualifying hotels in an enterprise zone).
Amendments.—[1] Sub-s. (3A) inserted by FA 1982, s. 74 (3), (4) in relation to licences granted after 9 March 1982.
[2] Sub-s. (2A) inserted by FA 1982, s. 75 (1), (3), and deemed to have come into force on 10 March 1982.
[3] Words in sub-s. (3) substituted by FA 1982, s. 75 (2).
[4] Words in sub-s. (4) substituted by FA 1983, s. 30 in relation to expenditure incurred after 15 March 1983.
[5] Word in sub-s. (1) (b) inserted by the Water Act 1989, Sch. 25, para. 36 with effect from 1 September 1989 or transfer date if later.
[6] Definition of "sewerage undertaking" in sub-s. (5) inserted by *ibid*.
[7] Sub-s. (3B) inserted by FA 1989, Sch. 13, para. 2 in relation to any chargeable period or its basis period ending after 26 July 1989.

8. Expenditure on repair of buildings

This Chapter shall have effect in relation to capital expenditure incurred by a person on repairs to any part of a building or structure as if it were capital expenditure incurred by him in the construction for the first time of that part of the building or structure, and for the purposes of this section any expenditure incurred for the purposes of a trade on repairs to a building or structure shall be deemed to be capital expenditure if it is not expenditure which would be allowed to be deducted in computing, for the purposes of tax, the profits or gains of the trade.

9. Expenditure on sites for machinery and plant

Where capital expenditure is or has been incurred on preparing, cutting, tunnelling or levelling land for the purposes of preparing the land as a site for the installation of machinery or plant, and apart from this section no allowance could be made in respect of that expenditure under this Chapter, or under Chapter II of this Part of this Act, then as regards that expenditure—

(a) the machinery or plant shall be treated for the purposes of this Chapter as a building or structure (whether or not it would be so treated apart from this section), and
(b) . . .[1]

Amendments.—[1] Paragraph (b) which is superseded by some provisions in FA 1989, Sch. 13, para. 28 (1)–(4) repealed by FA 1989, Sch. 13, para. 28 (5) (a), (6) and Sch. 17, Pt. VI in relation to any chargeable period or its basis period ending after 26 July 1989. It read—
"(b) section 14 (1) of this Act shall apply with the omission of the reference to Chapter II of this Part of this Act."

10. Sports pavilions

Where a building or structure which is not an industrial building or structure as defined in section 7 above is occupied by the person carrying on a trade and used as a sports pavilion for the welfare of all or any of the workers employed in that trade, this Chapter shall apply in relation to that building or structure as if it were an industrial building or structure.

11. Meaning of "the relevant interest"

(1) Subject to the provisions of this section, in this Chapter, "the relevant interest" means, in relation to any expenditure incurred on the construction of a building or structure, the interest in that building or structure to which the person who incurred the expenditure was entitled when he incurred it.

(2) Where, when he incurs expenditure on the construction of a building or structure, a person is entitled to two or more interests in the building or structure, and one of those

interests is an interest which is reversionary on all the others, that interest shall be the relevant interest for the purposes of this Chapter.

(3) An interest shall not cease to be the relevant interest for the purposes of this Chapter by reason of the creation of any lease or other interest to which that interest is subject, and where the relevant interest is a leasehold interest and is extinguished by reason of the surrender thereof or on the person entitled thereto acquiring the interest which is reversionary thereon, the interest into which that leasehold interest merges shall thereupon become the relevant interest.

(4) Where the relevant interest is a leasehold interest which came to an end before the appointed day, and subsection (3) of this section does not apply, the interest which is immediately reversionary thereon shall be deemed, for the purposes of the provisions of this Chapter in so far as they relate to writing-down allowances, balancing allowances and balancing charges, to have thereupon become the relevant interest.

Cross references.—See FA 1978, s. 37 (5), (8) (sub-s. (3) of this section to have effect subject to FA 1978, s. 37 (1) (c) (grant of lease affecting continuance of relevant interest) where the lease takes effect on or after 15 February 1978).

12. Temporary disuse of industrial buildings or structures

(1) For the purposes of this Chapter, a building or structure shall not be deemed to cease altogether to be used by reason that it falls temporarily out of use, and where, immediately before any period of temporary disuse, a building or structure is an industrial building or structure, it shall be deemed to continue to be an industrial building or structure during the period of temporary disuse.

(2) Where by reason of the provisions of subsection (1) of this section a building or structure is deemed to continue to be an industrial building or structure while temporarily out of use, then if—

(a) upon the last occasion upon which the building or structure was in use as an industrial building or structure, it was in use for the purposes of a trade which has since been permanently discontinued, or
(b) upon the last occasion upon which the building or structure was in use as an industrial building or structure, the relevant interest therein was subject to a lease which has since come to an end,

any writing-down allowance or balancing allowance falling to be made to any person in respect of the building or structure during any period for which the temporary disuse continues after the discontinuance of the trade or the coming to an end of the lease shall be made by way of discharge or repayment of tax, and shall be available primarily against income of the descriptions in paragraphs (a) and (b) of section 6 (5) of this Act, and effect shall be given to any balancing charge falling to be made on any person in respect of the building or structure during the period—

(i) if it is a charge to income tax, by making the charge under Case VI of Schedule D,
(ii) if it is a charge to corporation tax, by treating the amount on which the charge is to be made as income of the description in paragraph (a) of section 6 (5) of this Act.

(3) [The reference in this section to the permanent discontinuance of a trade does not include a reference to the happening of any event which, by virtue of section [113 or 337 (1)][2] of the principal Act (changes in persons carrying on a trade, and special rules for corporation tax), is to be treated as equivalent to the discontinuance of the trade][1].

(4) Subsection (1) above shall not apply by reason of a building or structure falling temporarily out of use before the appointed day, and shall not apply to a period of temporary disuse beginning before the appointed day.

Cross references.—See FA 1978, s. 38 (1), (8) and Sch. 6, para. 6 (effect of sub-s. (2) (a), (b) of this section in relation to a building which has ceased to be a qualifying hotel, with effect from 11 April 1978);
Sch. 6, para 7 (application of sub-s. (1) of this section to a qualifying hotel temporarily out of use, with effect from 11 April 1978);
FA 1980, Sch. 13, para. 4 (effect for sub-ss. (1) and (2) of this section of change of use of certain buildings in an enterprise zone).
Amendments.—[1] Sub-s. (3) substituted by TA 1970, Sch. 15, para. 5 (1), (3).
[2] Numbers in sub-s. (3) substituted by TA 1988, Sch. 29, para. 32 Table.

13. Requisitioned land, holding over of leased land, and other special cases

(1) The provisions of this Chapter shall have effect in relation to any period of requisition of any land as if the Crown had been in possession of that land for that period by virtue of a lease, and any reference in this Chapter to the surrender of a lease or the extinguishment thereof on the person entitled thereto acquiring the interest which is reversionary thereon, or to the merger of a leasehold interest, shall be construed accordingly, and any sum paid to the Crown in respect of any building or structure constructed on any land during any period of requisition of that land, being a sum paid, whether by virtue of any enactment or otherwise, by the person who, subject to the rights of the Crown, is entitled to possession of the land, shall be deemed for the purposes of this Chapter to be a sum paid in consideration of the surrender of that lease:

Provided that where a person carrying on a trade is authorised by the Crown to occupy the land or any part thereof for the whole or any part of the period of requisition, the provisions of this Chapter shall have effect as if the Crown had granted a sub-lease to that person of that land or, as the case may be, that part thereof, for the period of requisition or, as the case may be, for that part of the period for which the said person occupies the land, and the preceding provisions of this subsection shall have effect in relation to that sub-lease as they have effect in relation to the lease therein mentioned, subject, however, to the modification that for the reference to any sum paid to the Crown there shall be substituted a reference to any sum paid to the said person.

In this subsection, "period of requisition" means a period in respect of which compensation is, or, but for any agreement to the contrary, would be, payable under section 2 (1) (*a*) of the Compensation (Defence) Act 1939 by reference to the rent which might reasonably be expected to be payable under a lease granted immediately before the beginning of that period.

(2) Where, with the consent of the lessor, a lessee of any building or structure remains in possession thereof after the termination of the lease without a new lease being granted to him, that lease shall be deemed for the purposes of this Chapter to continue so long as he remains in possession as aforesaid.

(3) Where, on the termination of a lease, a new lease is granted to the lessee in pursuance of an option available to him under the terms of the first lease, the provisions of this Chapter shall have effect as if the second lease were a continuation of the first lease.

(4) Where, on the termination of a lease, the lessor pays any sum to the lessee in respect of a building or structure comprised in the lease, the provisions of this Chapter shall have effect as if the lease had come to an end by reason of the surrender thereof in consideration of the payment.

(5) Where, on the termination of a lease, another lease is granted to a different lessee and, in connection with the transaction, that lessee pays a sum to the person who was the lessee under the first lease, the provisions of this Chapter shall have effect as if both leases were the same lease and there had been an assignment thereof by the lessee under the first lease to the lessee under the second lease in consideration of the payment.

Cross references.—See FA 1978, s. 37 (4), (8) (any question whether a lease is a long lease to be determined without regard to sub-s. (3) of this section).

14. Exclusion of double allowances, etc.

(1) No allowance shall be made under or by virtue of any of the provisions of this Chapter in respect of, or of premises including, or of expenditure on, a building or structure if, for the same or any other chargeable period, an allowance is or can be made under any of the provisions of Chapter II, Chapter III or Chapter V of this Part of this Act [or Schedule 13 to the Finance Act 1986][1] in respect of, or of expenditure on, that building or structure.

(2) Without prejudice to the provisions of subsection (1) of this section, any reference in this Chapter to the incurring of expenditure on the construction of a building or structure does not include expenditure on the provision of machinery or plant or on any asset which has been treated for any chargeable period as machinery or plant.

Cross references.—See FA 1986, s. 56 (1), (2), (6) (reference to "Chapter V" in sub-s. (1) above to include a reference to FA 1986, Sch. 15 (allowances for capital expenditure other than under existing contracts incurred after 31 March 1986 on agricultural land and buildings)).
Amendments.—[1] Words in sub-s. (1) inserted by FA 1986, Sch. 13, para. 25 (1).

This section which is superseded by some provisions in FA 1989, Sch. 13, para. 28 (1)–(4) repealed by FA 1989, Sch. 13, para. 28 (5) (*a*), (6) and Sch. 17, Pt. VI in relation to any chargeable period or its basis period ending after 26 July 1989.

15. Mining structures, etc.: balancing allowances carried back to earlier chargeable periods

(1) If, in the case of a trade which consists of or includes the working of a mine, oil well or other source of mineral deposits—

(*a*) a balancing allowance falls to be made under this Chapter for the last chargeable period during which the trade is carried on, and
(*b*) the event giving rise to the allowance is the mine, oil well or other source ceasing to be worked or the coming to an end of a foreign concession, and
(*c*) the allowance is in respect of expenditure on a building or structure which was constructed for occupation by, or for the welfare of, persons employed at, or in connection with the working of, the mine, oil well or other source, and
(*d*) full effect cannot be given to the allowance because of an insufficiency of profits or gains for the said chargeable period,

the person entitled to the allowance may claim that the balance of the allowance shall be given for the last preceding chargeable period, and so on for other preceding chargeable periods, so, however, that allowances shall not be given by virtue of this subsection for periods together amounting to more than five years (inclusive of any period for which an allowance might be made but cannot be given effect for want of profits or gains) otherwise than by giving a proportionately reduced allowance for a chargeable period of which part is required to make up the five years.

(2) Allowances may be made by virtue of this section to a company for the income tax year 1964–65 or 1965–66, notwithstanding that allowances are also made for accounting periods of the company falling wholly or partly within those years and, in reckoning the period for which allowances are to be made, the periods for which allowances are so made shall be added together, notwithstanding that the same time is (according to the calendar) counted twice.

(3) In the case of a company no allowance shall be given by virtue of this section so as to create or augment a loss in any accounting period; and, where on a company ceasing to carry on a trade a claim is made both under this section and under [section 394][4] of the principal Act][1] (relief for terminal loss) the allowance for which the claim is made under this section shall be disregarded for the purposes of the claim under the said [section [394][4]][1], but effect shall be given to the claim under the said [section [394][4]][1] in priority to the claim under this section.

[(4) Section 42 of the Taxes Management Act 1970 shall apply to any claim under this section . . .[3]][2].

Amendments.—[1] Words in sub-s. (3) substituted by TA 1970, Sch. 15, para. 11. Table, Pt. II.
[2] Sub-s. (4) added by TA 1970, Sch. 15, para. 5 (1), (4).
[3] Words in sub-s. (4) repealed by FA 1970, Sch. 8, Pt. VII.
[4] Numbers in sub-s. (3) substituted by TA 1988, Sch. 29, para. 32 Table.

16. Transitory provision: meaning of "appointed day"

(1) Subject to the provisions of this section, "the appointed day" in this Chapter means 6th April 1946.

(2) Where by virtue of section 7 (2) of the Income Tax Act 1945 (which was re-enacted in Part I of Schedule 11 to the Income Tax Act 1952) an allowance fell to be made under section 15 of the Finance Act 1937 (allowances for depreciation of mills, factories and other similar premises) for the year 1946–47 or any subsequent year of assessment in the case of any trade, the provisions of this Chapter, other than this section, shall have effect in relation to the premises in question as if the appointed day were postponed until the first day of the first year of assessment for which no allowance fell to be made under the said section 15 in the case of that or any other trade.

(3) Subsection (4) below has effect as respects expenditure—

(*a*) incurred on a building or structure if used before 6th April 1956, not being premises in relation to which the appointed day is postponed to the said 6th April or a later day by subsection (2) above, and

(b) consisting in part of expenditure incurred on preparing, cutting, tunnelling or levelling any land.

The reference above to expenditure incurred on preparing, cutting, tunnelling or levelling any land does not include expenditure on work done on the land to be covered by a building or structure for the purposes of preparing the land to receive the foundations of the building or structure, being work which may be expected to be valueless when the building or structure is demolished and not being work which consists of cutting or tunnelling.

(4) The provision of this Part of this Act relating to allowances and charges under this Chapter, other than initial allowances, shall apply to the said part of the expenditure separately from the remainder, and to the remainder separately from that part, as if each had been incurred on a different building or structure from the other, and the necessary apportionments shall be made accordingly of any sale, insurance, salvage or compensation moneys or other relevant sums: and in relation to that part of the expenditure, but not in relation to the remainder, the appointed day for the purposes of any reference thereto in this Chapter shall be 6th April 1956.

(5) As regards expenditure to which this Chapter is applied by section 9 of this Act the appointed day, for the purpose of any reference thereto in this Chapter, shall be 6th April 1956.

17. Interpretation of Chapter I

(1) References in this Chapter to expenditure incurred on the construction of a building or structure do not include any expenditure incurred on the acquisition of, or of rights in or over, any land.

(2) A person who has incurred expenditure on the construction of a building or structure shall be deemed, for the purposes of any provision of this Chapter referring to his interest therein at the time when the expenditure was incurred, to have had the same interest therein as he would have had if the construction thereof had been completed at that time.

(3) Without prejudice to any of the other provisions of this Part of this Act relating to the apportionment of sale, insurance, salvage or compensation moneys, the sum paid on the sale of the relevant interest in a building or structure, or any other sale, insurance, salvage or compensation moneys payable in respect of any building or structure, shall, for the purposes of this Chapter, be deemed to be reduced by an amount equal to so much thereof as, on a just apportionment, is attributable to assets representing expenditure other than expenditure in respect of which an allowance can be made under this Chapter.

CHAPTER II

MACHINERY AND PLANT

Construction.—The Tax Acts to have effect as if TA 1988, s. 32 were contained in this Chapter; see TA 1988, s. 32 (8).
Cross references.—See FA 1971, s. 40 (1) (no allowances or charges shall be made under this Chapter in respect of capital expenditure on the provision of machinery or plant incurred on or after 27 October 1970); but see reference to FA 1976, s. 39, below;
FA 1972, s. 68 (1) (a) (restriction of capital allowances in respect of machinery and plant); but see reference to FA 1976, s. 39, below.
FA 1976, s. 39 (in the case of eligible expenditure allowances or charges to be made under 1970 system instead of this Chapter for accounting periods or basis periods ending after 5 April 1976);
TA 1988, s. 32 (capital allowances for machinery and plant used in estate management or in the management of the business of an investment company or life insurance company),
s. 198 (2) (emoluments not falling within Schedule E, Case I or II treated as not belonging to the office or employment),
s. 359 (interest on loans to purchase machinery or plant used in an office or employment),
s. 577 (1) (c) (use of asset for providing business entertainment to be treated for capital allowances purposes as use otherwise than for the purposes of a trade);
Sch. 30, para. 7 (transitional provisions with respect to claims for group relief in respect of any amount which is attributable to writing-down allowances under this Chapter in respect of expenditure incurred under a contract entered into by the surrendering company before 6 March 1973).

18. Initial allowances

(1) Subject to the provisions of this Act, where—

(a) a person carrying on a trade incurs capital expenditure on the provision of machinery or plant for the purposes of the trade, and

(b) in consequence of his incurring the expenditure the machinery or plant belongs to him at some time during the chargeable period related to the incurring of the expenditure,

there shall be made to him, for the chargeable period related to the incurring of the expenditure, an allowance (in this Chapter referred to as "an initial allowance").

(2) The initial allowance shall be of an amount equal to three-tenths of the expenditure within subsection (1) above:

Provided that this subsection shall have effect subject to the provisions of Schedule 1 to this Act.

(3) No initial allowance shall be made in respect of any expenditure incurred after 6th April 1965 on the provision of road vehicles unless they are of a type not commonly used as private vehicles and unsuitable to be so used or are provided wholly or mainly for hire to, or for the carriage of, members of the public in the ordinary course of a trade, so however that the preceding provisions of this subsection—

(a) shall not affect initial allowances in respect of any expenditure in so far as it consists (and is stated in the claim for the allowance to consist) of sums payable under a contract entered into on a date (to be specified in the claim) not later than 6 April 1965, and

(b) shall not apply, as respects expenditure incurred on the provision of vehicles after 16th January 1966, to vehicles of a construction primarily suited for the conveyance of goods or burden of any description.

and, where an initial allowance is not excluded by this subsection, subsections (1) and (2) above shall have effect as respects road vehicles subject to Schedule 2 to this Act.

(4) Any expenditure incurred for the purposes of a trade by a person about to carry it on shall be treated for the purposes of subsection (1) of this section (and accordingly, subject to the proviso below, also for the purposes of subsection (3) above) as if it had been incurred by that person on the first day on which he does carry it on:

Provided that expenditure shall not be treated for the purposes of paragraph (b) of subsection (3) above as having been incurred after 16th January 1966 by reason only of the provisions of this subsection.

(5) An initial allowance may be made to a person in respect of any machinery or plant in taxing a trade carried on by him notwithstanding that it appears that, during the period during which the machinery or plant will be used for the purposes of the trade, it will also be used for other purposes, but the allowance in any such case shall be so much only of the allowance that would be made if the machinery or plant were to be used only for the purposes of the trade as may be just and reasonable having regard to all the relevant

circumstances of the case and, in particular, to the extent to which it appears that the machinery or plant is likely to be used for the said other purposes during that period.

(6) No initial allowance shall be made to a person in respect of any machinery or plant in taxing a trade if it appears that, during the period during which the machinery or plant will be used by him for the purposes of the trade, sums which are in respect of, or take account of, the wear and tear to that machinery or plant occasioned by its use for those purposes and do not fall to be taken into account as his income or in computing the profits or gains of any trade carried on by him are, or are to be, payable to him directly or indirectly by the Crown, or by any government or public or local authority, whether in the United Kingdom or elsewhere, or by any person other than the person carrying on the trade:

Provided that where the sums referred to in this subsection are in respect of, or take account of, part only of the wear and tear therein referred to—

(*a*) the preceding provisions of this subsection shall not apply, but
(*b*) the amount of the allowance shall be reduced to such extent as may be just and reasonable having regard to all the relevant circumstances of the case.

(7) Where a person incurs capital expenditure on the provision of machinery or plant under a contract providing that he shall or may become the owner of the machinery or plant on the performance of the contract, then—

(*a*) subject to the following paragraph, the machinery or plant shall for the purposes of subsection (1) (*b*) above be treated as belonging to him at any time when he is entitled to the benefit of that contract, so far as it relates to the machinery or plant, but
(*b*) if he ceases to be so entitled without becoming the owner of the machinery or plant, the provisions of Schedule 3 to this Act shall have effect in relation to the machinery or plant.

Writing-down allowances

19. Writing-down allowances

(1) Subject to the provisions of this Act, where the person carrying on a trade in any chargeable period has incurred capital expenditure on the provision of machinery or plant for the purposes of the trade, an allowance (in this Chapter referred to as "a writing-down allowance") shall be made to him for that chargeable period on account of the wear and tear of any of the machinery or plant which belongs to him and is in use for the purposes of the trade at the end of that chargeable period or its basis period.

(2) The following provisions of this Chapter shall apply for the purposes of corporation tax notwithstanding that any provision in section 20, 21 or 26 of this Act, or in Schedule 4 to this Act, is expressed to apply in relation to a year of assessment, and for those purposes the amount of any writing-down allowance shall be determined by applying the law in force for the year of assessment in which the accounting period ends, and references in the said provisions to "the year of assessment in question" shall be construed accordingly.

(3) Where under the provisions of this Chapter a writing-down allowance falls to be determined by reference to a fraction or percentage, specified numerically, of any expenditure or other sum, or by reference to a percentage determined or deemed to be determined for a year of assessment, then for a chargeable period of less than a year the fraction or percentage shall be proportionately reduced; and similarly with the amounts by reference to which writing-down allowances for certain vehicles are limited by section 32 (1), and paragraph 6 of Schedule 2 to, this Act.

(4) In sections 20 to 24 below, and Schedule 4 to this Act, the expression "new machinery or plant" means machinery or plant being unused and not secondhand, and for the purposes of this Chapter machinery or plant which has at any time fallen within the description "new machinery or plant capital expenditure on the provision of which was incurred after 5th November 1962" shall continue to be treated as within that description notwithstanding any sale of it or other change of circumstances.

20. Normal method of calculation

(1) Subject to the provisions of this Chapter, the writing-down allowance in respect of any machinery or plant for any chargeable period shall be [25 per cent.][1] of the amount by which the capital expenditure of the person to whom the allowance is to be made in providing the machinery or plant exceeds the total amount of any initial allowance, writing-down

allowances, relevant exceptional depreciation allowances and scientific research allowances made to him in respect of that machinery or plant for previous chargeable periods.

(2)–(5) ...[2]

(6) It shall not be necessary for the Board to redetermine a percentage under this or the next following section yearly, and any such determination for any year of assessment shall apply also to subsequent years except so far as it is superseded by any subsequent determination.
Schedule 4 to this Act shall have effect as respects the application to years of assessment to which this Act applies of determinations applying to the year 1967–68.

(7) In this section "the anticipated normal working life" means, in relation to machinery or plant of any class, the period which might be expected, when machinery or plant of that class is first put into use, to be going to elapse before it is finally put out of use as being unfit for further use, it being assumed that it is going to be used in the normal manner and to the normal extent and is going to be so used throughout that period.

Amendments.—[1] Words in sub-s. (1) substituted by FA 1976, s. 39 (2) for accounting periods and basis periods ending after 5 April 1976.
[2] Sub-ss. (2) to (5) repealed by FA 1976, Sch. 15, Pt. III for accounting periods and basis periods ending after 5 April 1976.

21. Alternative method

(1) Subject to the provisions of this Chapter, the writing-down allowance in respect of any machinery or plant for any chargeable period—

(a) may, if the person to whom the allowance is to be made so elects when he makes his claim for the allowance, be computed by reference to the amount of his capital expenditure in providing the machinery or plant, and
(b) shall in that event be the percentage of that amount specified in subsection (2) below.

(2) The said percentage is such percentage as may be determined by the Board in relation to machinery or plant of the class in question for the year of assessment in question by reference to the anticipated normal working life of machinery or plant of that class.

(3) So far as the class in question consists of new machinery or plant capital expenditure on the provision of which was incurred after 5th November 1962, the said percentage shall be—

(a) where the said life is 18 years or more, $6\frac{1}{4}$ per cent.,
(b) where the life is less than 18 but not less than 14 years, $8\frac{1}{3}$ per cent.,
(c) where the life is less than 14 years, $11\frac{1}{4}$ per cent.

(4) So far as the class in question consists of other machinery or plant, the said percentage shall be five-fourths of the percentage (in this Chapter referred to as "the basic percentage") determined in accordance with this subsection.
The basic percentage is such percentage as may be determined by the Board as being in their opinion equal to nine-tenths of the fraction of which the numerator is one and the denominator is the number of years in the said life.

(5) If it is shown to the satisfaction of the Board that a percentage which, under section 282 (3) of the Income Tax Act 1952 (percentages in use in 1948–49), was deemed to be a percentage determined by them in relation to machinery or plant of any class under the said section 282 (2) for the year 1949-50 (whether or not also applying to later years) bears to the fraction (with numerator one) specified in sub-section (4) above (computed by reference to an anticipated normal working life estimated as if during the year 1948–49) a higher proportion than nine-tenths, sub-section (4) above shall have effect in relation to machinery or plant of that class as if for the reference therein to nine-tenths there were substituted a reference to the said higher proportion.

(6) Machinery or plant may be treated for the purposes of this section as being of a different class from other machinery or plant where the one is new when it is acquired and the other is not new when it is acquired, or, in the case of machinery or plant which is not new when it is acquired, where different periods have elapsed between the date when the machinery or plant was made or first put into use and the date of the acquisition thereof.

(7) An election under this section shall not be effective for any chargeable period in relation to any machinery or plant unless the Board are satisfied that the person making the election is keeping, and will keep and make available for inspection, all such records as are necessary to secure that the Board, inspectors and other officers concerned can ensure that the total

writing-down allowances made to him for all chargeable periods in respect of that machinery or plant do not exceed the limit imposed by section 27 (1) of this Act, due regard being had to any initial allowance, relevant exceptional depreciation allowances and scientific research allowances made to him in respect thereof.

(8) In this section "the anticipated normal working life" has the meaning assigned to it by subsection (7) of the last preceding section, except that, in relation to a class consisting of machinery or plant which is not new when it is acquired, the reference in the said subsection (7) to the first putting into use of the machinery or plant shall be construed as a reference to the first putting into use thereof after the acquisition thereof.

22. Change from normal to alternative method

(1) Where an election under section 21 above has effect with respect to any machinery or plant, and the writing-down allowance in respect of the same machinery or plant made to the same person for any previous chargeable period has been calculated in accordance with section 20 of this Act, the writing-down allowance for that machinery or plant for the chargeable period with respect to which the election has effect shall be computed in accordance with the following provisions, that is to say—

(*a*) instead of being computed by reference to the amount of the person's expenditure in providing the machinery or plant, it shall be computed by reference to the amount by which that amount exceeds any initial allowance, writing-down allowances, relevant exceptional depreciation allowances and scientific research allowances made to that person in respect of that machinery or plant for the chargeable periods up to and including the said previous chargeable period or, if the writing-down allowance was calculated in accordance with the said section 20 in the case of more than one previous chargeable period, up to and including the last of those previous chargeable periods, and
(*b*) it shall be computed as if for the percentage which would otherwise apply there were substituted such other percentage as the Board may determine.

In the case of expenditure to which section 21 (4) above applies, the references in paragraph (*b*) above to a percentage are references to the basic percentage.

(2) The references in subsection (1) above to allowances calculated in accordance with section 20 of this Act shall be deemed to include references to allowances for the year 1948–49 or any previous year of assessment calculated by the application of, or of five-fourths of, a percentage intended for application, or for application when multiplied by five-fourths, to a sum which, except in the case of the first year, is less than the cost of the machinery or plant.

(3) Any reference in this section to section 20 of this Act shall be deemed to include a reference to that section as modified by the following sections of this Chapter.

23. Special method for use in connection with mines, oil wells, etc.

(1) Subject to the provisions of this Chapter, the writing-down allowance for any chargeable period in respect of any machinery or plant used for the purposes of a trade which consists of or includes the working of a mine, oil well or other source of mineral deposits of a wasting nature, being machinery or plant used in connection with the working of the source, shall, if the person to whom the allowance is to be made so elects when he makes his claim for the allowance—

(*a*) be computed by reference to the amount specified in section 20 (1) or section 21 (1) of this Act, but
(*b*) be the percentage of that amount specified in subsection (2) of this section.

(2) The said percentage is such percentage as the Board may determine having regard to the date when the source is likely to cease to be worked and the probable value of the machinery or plant at that date to the person carrying on the trade.

(3) The references to section 20 of this Act contained in subsections (1) and (3) of the last preceding section shall be deemed to include references to this section where the election thereunder is that the allowance shall be computed by reference to the amount specified in section 20 (1) of this Act.

(4) The references to section 21 of this Act contained in subsection (1) of the last preceding section shall be deemed to include references to this section where the election thereunder is

that the allowance shall be computed by reference to the amount specified in section 21 (1) of this Act.

24. Adjustments of writing-down allowances in special circumstances

(1) If the Board are satisfied that the manner in which or the extent to which any machinery or plant is used in any chargeable period is such that the wear and tear thereof is greater or less than that which might be expected to be caused by the use thereof in the normal manner and to the normal extent they may give a direction under this section.

(2) If, in relation to any new machinery or plant capital expenditure on the provision of which was incurred after 5th November 1962, a direction falls to be made under this section for any chargeable period, the anticipated normal working life of the machinery or plant shall be ascertained as though it were used throughout its working life in the manner in which and to the extent to which it is used in the chargeable period in question, and the writing-down allowance in respect of the machinery or plant for that chargeable period shall be calculated as, . . .[1] by virtue of section 21 (3), of this Act, it would be if the relevant percentage for machinery or plant of that class fell to be redetermined for the relevant year of assessment and its anticipated normal working life were as so ascertained.

(3) Subject to subsection (2) above, if, in relation to any machinery or plant, a direction falls to be made under this section for any chargeable period, the writing-down allowance in respect of that machinery or plant for that chargeable period shall be ascertained as if, for the basic percentage specified in . . .[1] section 21 (4) of this Act, or the percentage specified in section 23 (2) of this Act, as the case may be, there were substituted such other percentage as the Board may determine.

(4) References in this section to the anticipated normal working life of the machinery or plant shall be construed in accordance with . . .[1] section 21 (8) of this Act.

(5) Nothing in subsection (2) of this section shall affect the operation of section 23 of this Act.

Amendments.—[1] Words in sub-ss. (2), (3) and (4) repealed by FA 1976, Sch. 15, Pt. III for accounting periods and basis periods ending after 5 April 1976.

25. Writing-down allowances for part of a year of assessment

If a writing-down allowance falls to be made for income tax purposes to any person in respect of any machinery or plant in taxing any trade which is carried on by him for part only of the year of assessment the said allowance, as computed in accordance with the preceding provisions of this Chapter (and in accordance with the provisions, where relevant, of section 31 of this Act, or of section 32 of this Act with Schedule 2) shall be proportionately reduced.

26. Determination and review of percentages

(1) If, within such time and in such manner as may be prescribed by regulations made by the Board under this section, an application is made to the Board by or on behalf of—

    (a) a considerable number of the persons engaged in any class of trade, or
    (b) a considerable number of the persons who use machinery or plant of any class for the purposes of any trade carried on by them, or
    (c) any particular person concerned,

for the increase, as respects any year of assessment, of any percentage determined or deemed to be determined by the Board for any of the purposes of this Chapter in connection with any class of machinery or plant used in the class of trade in question, in connection with the class of machinery or plant in question, or in connection with any machinery or plant, or class of machinery or plant, used by the applicant, as the case may be, the Board shall consider the application and may, if they think fit, determine or redetermine the percentage in question.

(2) Where an application has been made under subsection (1) of this section, and the Board do not determine or redetermine the percentage in question or the applicant or applicants are dissatisfied with the Board's determination or redetermination thereof, the Board, if required so to do by the applicant or applicants, shall refer the application to [the tribunal, who][2] shall consider the application:

    Provided that where the application is made under paragraph (c) of the said subsection (1), the [tribunal]² may, if they think fit, require the applicant to satisfy them, as respects the machinery or plant to which the application relates, that in all the circumstances it is reasonable that an application should be made otherwise than under paragraph (*a*) or paragraph (*b*) of that subsection and, in that event, the [tribunal]² shall consider the application only in so far as it relates to machinery or plant as respects which they are so satisfied.

(3) On the consideration of an application under subsection (1) of this section, either as respects all or as respects some only of the machinery or plant to which it relates, the [tribunal]² may, if they think fit, direct that, as respects the year of assessment to which the application relates, such percentage as the [tribunal]² may determine to be appropriate shall be substituted, either wholly or in such cases or classes of cases as the [tribunal]² may direct, for the percentage determined or deemed to be determined by the Board, and the liability of all persons concerned to tax shall be determined accordingly and all such assessments, adjustments of assessments and repayments of tax shall be made as may be necessary to give effect to the direction.

The preceding sections of this Chapter shall, in relation to the exercise by the [tribunal]² of their powers under this subsection, have effect as if the references to the Board included references to the [tribunal]².

(4) The Board may make regulations with respect to the time within which and the manner in which applications under this section are to be made and the procedure to be followed in dealing with any such application.

The power conferred by this subsection to make regulations shall be exercisable by statutory instrument, and any statutory instrument made in the exercise of that power shall be subject to annulment in pursuance of a resolution of either House of Parliament.

(5) No appeal shall lie to the General or Special Commissioners in respect of any matter which may be made or might have been made the subject of an application under this section.

(6) In the case of a percentage increased by five-fourths under . . .¹ section 21 (4) of this Act, references in this section to a percentage are references to the basic percentage.

[(7) In this section "tribunal" means the tribunal established under section [706]⁴ of the principal Act.]³

This subsection shall come into force for all purposes on 6th April 1968 to the exclusion of the provisions thereby re-enacted.

Cross references.—See FA 1989, s. 182 (3) (*c*) (criminal liability of a tribunal appointed under sub-s. (7) above for disclosing information).
Amendments.—¹ Words in sub-s. (6) repealed by FA 1976, Sch. 15, Pt. III for accounting periods and basis periods ending after 5 April 1976.
² Words in sub-ss. (2), (3) substituted by FA 1982, Sch. 21, paras. 2, 3 as a consequence of the dissolution of the Board of Referees by FA 1982, s. 156 (1).
³ Sub-s. (7) substituted by FA 1982, Sch. 21, para. 4 as a consequence of the dissolution of the Board of Referees by FA 1982, s. 156 (1).
⁴ Number in sub-s. (7) substituted by TA 1988, Sch. 29, para. 32 Table.

27. Limit on writing-down allowances

(1) No writing-down allowance shall be made in respect of any machinery or plant for any chargeable period if the allowance, when added to any initial allowance, relevant exceptional depreciation allowances or scientific research allowances given in respect of the machinery or plant to the person by whom the trade is carried on, and to any writing-down allowances for previous chargeable periods given in respect of the machinery or plant to that person, will make the aggregate amount of the allowances exceed the actual cost to that person of the machinery or plant, including in that actual cost any expenditure in the nature of capital expenditure on the machinery or plant by way of renewal, improvement or reinstatement.

(2) In the case of machinery or plant provided on or after the appointed day, the writing-down allowance for any chargeable period shall not exceed what, apart from any writing-down allowance falling to be made for that chargeable period, would be the amount of the capital expenditure on the provision of the machinery or plant still unallowed as at the beginning of the chargeable period.

28. Part-time use otherwise than for trade purposes

(1) A writing-down allowance may be made in respect of any machinery or plant in taxing a trade for any chargeable period notwithstanding that the machinery or plant is also used in that chargeable period for purposes other than those of the trade, but where, in the

chargeable period or its basis period, machinery or plant is used for purposes other than those of the trade, the writing-down allowance to be made in respect thereof shall be so much only of the allowance that otherwise would be made as may be just and reasonable having regard to all the relevant circumstances of the case and, in particular, to the extent of the use for the said other purposes during the said chargeable period or its basis period.

(2) Where an initial allowance has been made to a person in respect of any machinery or plant but the amount thereof has been reduced under section 18 (5) of this Act on the ground that the machinery or plant will be used for purposes other than those of the trade, any writing-down allowance falling to be made in respect of that machinery or plant to that person shall be calculated as if the reduction had not been made.

29. Effect on writing-down allowances of subsidies towards wear and tear

(1) No writing-down allowance shall be made to a person in respect of any machinery or plant in taxing a trade for any chargeable period if any sums which are in respect of, or take account of, the wear and tear to that machinery or plant occasioned by its use during that chargeable period or its basis period for the purposes of the trade and do not fall to be taken into account as his income or in computing the profits or gains of any trade carried on by him are, or are to be, payable to him directly or indirectly by the Crown, or by any government or public or local authority, whether in the United Kingdom or elsewhere, or by any person other than the person carrying on the trade:

Provided that where the sums referred to in this subsection are in respect of or take account of, part only of the wear and tear therein referred to—

(a) the preceding provisions of this subsection shall not apply, but
(b) the amount of the allowance shall be reduced to such extent as may be just and reasonable having regard to all the relevant circumstances of the case.

(2) Where an initial allowance has been made to a person in respect of any machinery or plant, but the amount thereof has been reduced under the proviso to section 18 (6) of this Act on the ground that sums which are in respect of, or take account of, part only of the wear and tear of that machinery or plant are or are to be payable to him as therein mentioned, any writing-down allowance falling to be made to him in respect of that machinery or plant shall be calculated as if the reduction had not been made.

30. Effect on writing-down allowances of previous user which has not attracted a writing-down allowance

(1) In determining whether any, and if so what, writing-down allowance falls to be made to a person for any chargeable period in respect of any machinery or plant which has been used by him before that chargeable period, there shall be deemed to have been made to him for every previous chargeable period (including chargeable periods during which the machinery or plant was not used for the purposes of the trade, and chargeable periods during which the trade was not carried on by him) such writing-down allowance or greater writing-down allowance, if any, as would have fallen to be made to him if all the conditions specified in subsection (2) of this section had been fulfilled in relation to every such previous chargeable period.

(2) The said conditions are as follows, that is to say—

(a) that the trade had been carried on by the person in question ever since the date on which he acquired the machinery or plant and had been so carried on by him in such circumstances that the profits or gains thereof were liable to assessment to tax, and
(b) that the machinery or plant had been used by him for the purposes of the trade ever since that date; and
(c) that a proper claim had been duly made by him for a writing-down allowance in respect of the machinery or plant for every relevant chargeable period, and
(d) that no question arose in connection with any chargeable period as to the machinery or plant having been wholly or partly used by him otherwise than for the purposes of the trade, or as to there being payable to him, directly or indirectly, any sums in respect of, or taking account of, the wear and tear of the machinery or plant.

In the case of a company paragraph (a) above shall not alter the periods which are to be taken as chargeable periods, but if during any time after the year 1965–66, and after the company acquired the machinery or plant, the company has not been within the charge to corporation tax, any year of assessment or part of a year of assessment falling within that time shall be taken as a chargeable period as if it had been an accounting period of the company.

(3) Notwithstanding anything in subsection (1) of this section, the chargeable periods for which a writing-down allowance is to be deemed thereunder to have been made shall not include chargeable periods during which machinery or plant was used only for the purposes of activities carried on by the person in question before the commencement by him of the working of a mine, oil well or other source of mineral deposits of a wasting nature, being activities consisting of—

(*a*) searching for or discovering and testing deposits or winning access thereto, or
(*b*) the construction of any works which are likely to be of little or no value when the source is no longer worked or, where the source is worked under a foreign concession, which are likely to become valueless when the concession comes to an end to the person working the source immediately before the concession comes to an end.

Ships and motor cars

31. New ships

(1) In the case of writing-down allowances in respect of capital expenditure incurred after 5th April 1965 on the provision of a new ship section 20 (1) of this Act shall apply as if, instead of requiring such an allowance for a chargeable period to be a percentage, ...[1] of the amount referred to in that subsection, it required the allowance to be so much of that amount as is specified by the person to whom the allowance is to be made in making his claim for the allowance; and accordingly the other subsections of section 20, and sections 21 and 24 of this Act, shall not apply in relation to such allowances.

(2) For the purposes of this section "new" means unused and not second-hand, but a ship shall not be treated as second-hand in relation to a claimant for an allowance in respect of it by reason of the property in the ship or any part thereof having previously passed to a person other than the claimant, if the ship has not been taken over from the builder by any such person.

Amendments.—[1] Words in sub-s. (1) repealed by FA 1976, Sch. 15, Pt. III for accounting periods and basis periods ending after 5 April 1976.

32. Motor cars

(1) Subject to the provisions of this section and of section 19 (3) of this Act, the amount of a writing-down allowance in respect of the expenditure incurred on the provision of a vehicle to which this section applies shall not exceed £500.

(2) Where the amount of a writing-down allowance, if calculated in accordance with section 20 of this Act, would be reduced by subsection (1) above, the allowance shall, notwithstanding anything in section 21 or 24 of this Act, be so calculated.

(3) Schedule 2 to this Act shall have effect as respects the application of the Income Tax Acts and the Corporation Tax Acts to vehicles to which this section applies.

(4) Subject to the provisions of this section, the vehicles to which this section applies are mechanically propelled road vehicles constructed or adapted for the carriage of passengers, other than vehicles of a type not commonly used as a private vehicle and unsuitable to be so used.

(5) This section does not apply where a vehicle is provided, or as the case may be hired, wholly or mainly for the purpose of hire to, or the carriage of, members of the public in the ordinary course of trade.

(6) This section does not apply in relation to a vehicle provided by a person who is a manufacturer of such vehicles as are mentioned in subsection (4) above, or of parts or accessories for such vehicles, if he shows that it was provided solely for the purpose of testing the vehicle or parts or accessories for such vehicles:

Provided that if during the period of five years beginning with the time when the vehicle was provided he puts it, to any substantial extent, to a use which does not serve that purpose and that purpose only, this subsection shall be deemed not to have had effect in relation to the vehicle.

(7) Subsections (1) and (2) of this section shall not apply to a writing-down allowance in

respect of expenditure incurred before 17th April 1961, or to expenditure incurred under a contract entered into before that date where either—

(a) the expenditure was incurred within twelve months after that date, or
(b) the contract is one of hire-purchase or for purchase by instalments.

Balancing allowances, balancing charges, etc.

33. Balancing allowances and balancing charges

(1) Subject to the provisions of this section, where any of the following events occurs in the case of any machinery or plant belonging to a person carrying on a trade and provided or used for the purposes of the trade, that is to say, either—

(a) any event occurring after the setting up and before the permanent discontinuance of the trade whereby the machinery or plant ceases to belong to the person carrying on the trade (whether on a sale of the machinery or plant or in any other circumstances of any description), or

(b) any event occurring after the setting up and before the permanent discontinuance of the trade whereby the machinery or plant (while continuing to belong to the person carrying on the trade) permanently ceases to be used for the purposes of a trade carried on by him, or

(c) the permanent discontinuance of the trade, the machinery or plant not having previously ceased to belong to the person carrying on the trade,

an allowance or charge (in this Chapter referred to as "a balancing allowance" or "a balancing charge") shall, in the circumstances mentioned in this section, be made to, or as the case may be, on, that person for the chargeable period related to that event:

Provided that where as respects any machinery or plant an event falling within any of paragraphs (a), (b) or (c) above is followed by another event falling within any of those paragraphs, the later event shall not be treated as an event giving rise, or which may give rise, to a balancing allowance or balancing charge in respect of that machinery or plant.

(2) Where a discontinuance within subsection (1) (c) above occurs which gives rise, or might give rise, to a balancing allowance or balancing charge under this Chapter in respect of machinery or plant, and at or about the time of the discontinuance there occurs in relation to the machinery or plant any event such as is mentioned in paragraph (a), (b), (c) or (d) of section 86 (1) of this Act, then for the purposes of this section the amount of any net proceeds, compensation, receipts or insurance moneys mentioned in the said paragraphs (a), (b), (c) and (d) of the said section 86 (1) which arise on the last-mentioned event shall be deemed to be an amount of sale, insurance, salvage or compensation moneys arising on the permanent discontinuance of the trade:

Provided that this subsection shall not apply where the event within the said section 86 (1) is a sale at less than the open-market price other than a sale to which section 78 of this Act applies; and for the purposes of this proviso—

(a) "open-market price", in relation to any machinery or plant, means the price which the machinery or plant would have fetched if sold in the open market at the time of the event in question,

(b) a sale at less than the open-market price does not include a sale in such circumstances that there is a charge to tax under Schedule E by virtue of the provisions of Chapter II of [Part V of the principal Act][1].

(3) Where there are no sale, insurance, salvage or compensation moneys, or where the amount of the capital expenditure of the person in question on the provision of the machinery or plant still unallowed as at the time of the event exceeds those moneys, a balancing allowance shall be made, and the amount thereof shall be the amount of the expenditure still unallowed as aforesaid, or, as the case may be, of the excess thereof over the said moneys.

(4) If the sale, insurance, salvage or compensation moneys exceed the amount, if any, of the said expenditure still unallowed as at the time of the event, a balancing charge shall be made, and the amount on which it is made shall be an amount equal to the excess or, where the said amount still unallowed is nil, to the said moneys.

(5) Notwithstanding anything in subsection (4) of this section, in no case shall the amount on which a balancing charge is made on a person exceed the aggregate of the following amounts, that is to say—

(*a*) the amount of the initial allowance, if any, made to him in respect of the expenditure in question, and
(*b*) the amount of any writing-down allowance made to him in respect of the machinery or plant in question, and
(*c*) the amount of any relevant exceptional depreciation allowance made to him in respect of the machinery or plant, and
(*d*) the amount of any scientific research allowances made to him in respect of the expenditure, and
(*e*) the amount of any balancing allowance previously made to him in respect of the expenditure.

(6) The proviso to subsection (1) above does not apply to any event as being later than an event which occurred before 9th July 1952 (the date of commencement of the Finance Act 1952).

(7) Where the loss of a ship is due to a war risk connected with any war in which His Majesty was engaged on 15th June 1945, then, notwithstanding that the loss occurs after the conclusion of, or of hostilities in, that war, no balancing charge shall be made by reason of the loss in respect of expenditure on the ship.

In this subsection, "war risk" means any risk falling within the definition of "war risks" contained in the form of policy set out in the First Schedule to an agreement for reinsurance of British ships made by the Minister of War Transport on 16th September 1943, a copy of which was laid before each House of Parliament on 4th November 1943, in pursuance of section 1 (2) of the War Risks Insurance Act 1939.

Amendments.—[1] Words in sub-s. (2), proviso (*b*) substituted by TA 1988, Sch. 29, para. 32 Table.

34. Notional sales in certain cases

(1) Subject to the provisions of this and the next following section, subsection (2) below shall have effect where an event occurs which gives rise or might give rise to a balancing allowance or balancing charge in respect of machinery or plant, and either—

(*a*) the event is the permanent discontinuance of the trade and immediately after the time of the discontinuance the machinery or plant continues to belong to the person by whom the trade was carried on immediately before the said time and the case is not one falling within subsection (2) of the last preceding section, or
(*b*) the event is the permanent discontinuance of the trade and at the time of the discontinuance the machinery or plant is either sold at less than the open-market price, the sale not being one to which section 78 of this Act applies, or the machinery or plant is given away, or
(*c*) the event is the sale of the machinery or plant at less than the open-market price, not being a sale to which the said section 78 applies, or is the gift of the machinery or plant, or
(*d*) the event is that, after the setting up and before the permanent discontinuance of the trade, the machinery or plant permanently ceases to be used for the purposes of a trade carried on by the person by whom the first-mentioned trade is being carried on, and so ceases either by reason of that person's transferring the machinery or plant to other use or, on a transfer of the trade which is not treated as involving the discontinuance thereof, by reason of the retention of the machinery or plant by the transferor.

(2) For the purpose of determining whether a balancing allowance or balancing charge falls to be made and, if so, the amount of the allowance or, as the case may be, the amount on which the charge is to be made, the event shall be treated as if it had given rise to sale, insurance, salvage or compensation moneys of an amount equal to the open-market price of the machinery or plant.

(3) Subsection (2) above shall not apply by reason of a gift of machinery or plant if the machinery or plant is given away in such circumstances that there is a charge to tax under Schedule E by virtue of the provisions of [Chapter II of Part V of the principal Act][1].

(4) In this and the next following section "open-market price", in relation to any machinery or plant, means the price which the machinery or plant would have fetched if sold in the open market at the time of the event in question, and for the purposes of this section a sale at less than the open-market price does not include a sale in such circumstances that there is a charge to tax under Schedule E by virtue of the provisions of Chapter II of [Part V of the principal Act][2].

Amendments.—[1] Words in sub-s. (3) substituted by TA 1988, Sch. 29, para. 32 Table.

[2] Words in sub-s. (4) substituted by *ibid*.

35. Notional sale: effect on other party to transaction

(1) Subject to the provisions of this section, where subsection (2) of the last preceding section has effect by reason of the gift or sale of machinery or plant to any person, and that person receives or purchases it with a view to using it for the purposes of a trade carried on by him, then in determining whether any, and if so what, writing-down allowances, balancing allowances or balancing charges are to be made in connection with that trade the like consequences shall ensue as if the recipient or purchaser had purchased the machinery or plant at the open-market price.

(2) Where in a case falling within subsection (1) above the recipient or purchaser and the donor or seller by notice in writing to the inspector jointly so elect, the following provisions shall have effect.

(3) Subsection (2) of the last preceding section and subsection (1) above shall have effect as if for the references to the open-market price there were substituted references to that price or the amount of the expenditure on the provision of the machinery or plant still unallowed immediately before the gift or sale, whichever is the lower.

(4) Notwithstanding anything in the preceding provisions of this Chapter, such balancing charge, if any, shall be made on the recipient or purchaser on any event occurring after the date of the gift or sale as would have fallen to be made on the donor or seller if the donor or seller had continued to own the machinery or plant and had done all such things and been allowed all such allowances in connection therewith as were done by or allowed to the recipient or purchaser.

Cross references.—See CGTA 1979, s. 34 (3) (*b*) (restriction of capital losses by reference to capital and renewals allowances).

36. Demolition costs

(1) Where machinery or plant is demolished, and the demolition either gives rise, or might give rise, to a balancing allowance or charge to or on the person incurring the cost of demolition, or (by virtue of section 33 (2) of this Act) affects or might affect such an allowance or charge on the permanent discontinuance of a trade, the net cost to him of the demolition shall be added for the purposes of this Chapter to the amount of the capital expenditure incurred on the provision of that machinery or plant still unallowed as at the time of the demolition or of the discontinuance, as the case may be.

(2) The cost or net cost to a person of the demolition of any property shall not, if subsection (1) above applies to it, be treated, for the purposes of this Part or Part II of this Act, as expenditure incurred in respect of any other property by which that property is replaced.

(3) In this section any reference to the net cost of the demolition of any property is a reference to the excess, if any, of the cost of the demolition over any moneys received for the remains of the property.

37. Part-time use otherwise than for trade purposes

Where any machinery or plant which has been used by a person for the purposes of a trade carried on by him has also been used by him for other purposes, then, in determining whether a balancing allowance or balancing charge falls to be made to or on him in taxing the trade and in determining the amount of the allowance or, as the case may be, the amount on which the charge is to be made, regard shall be had to all the relevant circumstances of the case and, in particular, to the extent of the use for the said other purposes, and there shall be made to or on him an allowance of such an amount, or, as the case may be, a charge on such an amount, as may be just and reasonable.

38. Subsidies towards wear and tear

No balancing allowance or balancing charge shall be made to or on any person in respect of any machinery or plant in taxing a trade if any sums which are in respect of, or take account of, the wear and tear to that machinery or plant occasioned by its use for the purposes of the trade, and do not fall to be taken into account as his income or in computing the profits or gains of any trade carried on by him, were paid, or are to be payable, to him directly or indirectly by the Crown, or by any government or public or local authority, whether in the United Kingdom or elsewhere, or by any person other than the person carrying on the trade:

Provided that where the sums referred to in this section are in respect of, or take account of, part only of the wear and tear therein referred to—

(a) the preceding provisions of this section shall not apply, but
(b) in determining whether it is an allowance or a charge which is to be made and the amount of the allowance or, as the case may be, the amount on which the charge is to be made, regard shall be had to all the relevant circumstances of the case and there shall be made an allowance of such an amount or, as the case may be, a charge on such an amount, as may be just and reasonable.

39. Effect on balancing allowances and balancing charges of previous user which has not attracted allowances

(1) Subject to the provisions of this section, the provisions of section 30 of this Act shall apply for the purposes of determining whether any, and if so what, balancing allowance or balancing charge falls to be made to or on a person as they apply for the purpose of determining whether any, and if so what, writing-down allowance falls to be made to a person.

(2) The only chargeable periods for which a writing-down allowance is to be deemed for the purposes of this section to have been made shall be chargeable periods during which the machinery or plant was not used by the person in question for the purposes of the trade and chargeable periods during which the trade was not carried on by him, or was not carried on by him in such circumstances that the profits or gains thereof were liable to assessment to tax.

(3) Nothing in this section shall affect the provisions of section 33 (5) of this Act.

40. Option in case of replacement of machinery or plant

(1) Where machinery or plant in the case of which any of the events mentioned in section 33 (1) of this Act has occurred is replaced by the owner thereof and a balancing charge falls to be made on him by reason of that event, or, but for the provisions of this subsection, would have fallen to be made on him by reason thereof, then, if by notice in writing to the inspector he so elects, the following provisions shall have effect, that is to say—

[(a) if the amount on which the charge would have been made is greater than the capital expenditure on the provision of the new machinery or plant, the charge shall be made on an amount equal to the difference, and
(b) for the purposes of Chapter I of Part III of the Finance Act 1971, except the bringing into account of any disposal value, the capital expenditure on the provision of the new machinery or plant shall be treated as reduced by the amount on which the charge would have been made, or, if paragraph (a) above applies, shall be disregarded.

(2) No election shall be made under this section if in relation to the new machinery or plant it appears that the provisions of paragraph 5, 6 or 10 of Schedule 8 to the said Act of 1971 will apply.][1]

Cross references.—See CGTA 1979, s. 34 (6) (restriction of capital losses by reference to capital and renewals allowances).
Amendments.—[1] Words in sub-ss. (1), (2) substituted by FA 1971, Sch. 8, para. 17 where capital expenditure on the provision of new machinery or plant is within FA 1971, Pt. III, Ch. I, i.e. incurred on or after 27 October 1970.

Supplemental

41. Meaning of "expenditure unallowed"

References in this Chapter to the amount still unallowed of any expenditure as at any time shall be construed as references to the amount of that expenditure less—

(a) the initial allowance, if any, made in respect thereof to the person who incurred it, and
(b) any writing-down allowances made to him in respect of the machinery or plant on the provision of which the expenditure was incurred, being allowances made for any

chargeable period such that the chargeable period or its basis period ended before the time in question, and

(c) any relevant exceptional depreciation allowance made to him in respect of that machinery or plant, and

(d) any scientific research allowance made to him in respect of that machinery or plant, and

(e) any balancing allowance made to him in respect of the expenditure.

42. Allowances to lessors of machinery and plant

(1) Where machinery or plant is let upon such terms that the burden of the wear and tear thereof falls directly upon the lessor, there shall be made to him, for each chargeable period, an allowance on account of the wear and tear of so much of the machinery or plant as is in use at the end of the chargeable period:

Provided that if the letting continues for part only of the chargeable period, the allowance, as computed in accordance with the preceding provisions of this Chapter, shall be proportionately reduced.

(2) The provisions of this Chapter shall apply in relation to any such lessor of machinery or plant as is mentioned in subsection (1) of this section as if the machinery or plant were, during the period of the letting, in use for the purposes of a trade carried on by him, and as if any reference to writing-down allowances included a reference to any allowance made under this section.

43. Allowances to lessees of machinery and plant

(1) Where machinery or plant is let to the person by whom the trade is being carried on, on the terms of his being bound to maintain the same and deliver it over in good condition at the end of the lease, the machinery or plant shall be deemed to belong to that person for the purposes of section 19 of this Act and that person shall be deemed for those purposes to have incurred, at the time of the letting, capital expenditure equal to so much of the capital expenditure on the provision of the machinery or plant as may appear to the inspector to be just and reasonable:

Provided that this subsection shall not apply to any machinery or plant unless the inspector is satisfied, having regard to all the relevant circumstances of the case, that the burden of the wear and tear of the machinery or plant will in fact fall directly upon that person.

On an appeal to the General Commissioners or Special Commissioners, the Commissioners shall have jurisdiction to review any relevant decision taken by the inspector under this subsection.

(2) Section 31 of this Act shall not apply to allowances falling to be made to a person in respect of expenditure on the provision of a ship treated as incurred by him by virtue of subsection (1) above unless the contract of letting provides that he shall or may become the owner of the ship on the performance of the contract; and where the contract so provides, but without becoming the owner of the ship he ceases to be entitled (otherwise than on his death) to the benefit of the contract so far as it relates to the ship, section 31 of this Act shall be deemed not to have applied to allowances falling to be made to him in respect of the ship.

(3) Where section 31 of this Act is to be deemed not to have applied to allowances for any period, there shall be made all such assessments and adjustments of assessments as may be necessary.

44. Partnership using property of a partner

(1) In taxing a trade carried on in partnership the same allowances, deductions and charges shall be allowed or made under this Chapter in respect of machinery or plant used for the purposes of that trade and belonging to one or more of the partners but not being partnership property as would fall to be allowed or made if the machinery or plant had at all material times belonged to all the partners and been partnership property and everything done by or to any of the partners in relation thereto had been done by or to all the partners.

(2) Notwithstanding anything in section 33 of this Act, a sale or gift of machinery or plant used for the purposes of a trade carried on in partnership, being a sale or gift by one or more of the partners to one or more of the partners, shall not be treated as an event giving rise to a balancing allowance or balancing charge if the machinery or plant continues to be used after the sale or gift for the purposes of that trade.

(3) References in this section to use for the purposes of a trade do not include references to use in pursuance of a letting by the partner or partners in question to the partnership or to use in consideration of the making to the partner or partners in question of any payment which may be deducted in computing the profits or gains of the trade.

Cross references.—See FA 1971, Sch. 8, para. 15 (1) (this section to have effect as if the reference in sub-s. (1) to "this Chapter" (i.e. Pt. I, Ch. II of this Act) included a reference to FA 1971, Pt. III, Ch. I (ss. 40–50), and as if the references in sub-s. (2) to "s. 33 of this Act" and "an event giving rise to a balancing allowance or balancing charge" included references respectively to FA 1971, s. 44 (5), and an event requiring any disposal value to be brought into account);
TA 1988, s. 367 (1) (interest on loans to purchase machinery or plant used by a partnership).

45. Building alterations connected with installation of machinery or plant

Where a person carrying on a trade incurs capital expenditure on alterations to an existing building incidental to the installation of machinery or plant for the purposes of the trade, the provisions of this Chapter shall have effect as if the said expenditure were expenditure on the provision of that machinery or plant and as if the works representing that expenditure formed part of that machinery or plant.

Cross references.—See FA 1971, Sch. 8, para. 15 (2) (the reference in this section to "this Chapter" (i.e. Pt. I, Ch. II of this Act) to include a reference to FA 1971, Pt. III, Ch. I (ss. 40–50)).

46. Manner of making allowances and charges

(1) Any allowance or charge made to or on any person under the preceding provisions of this Chapter shall, unless it is made under or by virtue of section 40 (2) of this Act, or under or by virtue of section 42 of this Act, be made to or on that person in taxing his trade.

(2) Any allowance made under or by virtue of section 42 of this Act shall be made by way of discharge or repayment of tax and shall be available primarily against income from the letting of machinery or plant.

(3) Effect shall be given to any charge made under or by virtue of section 42 of this Act—

(*a*) if a charge to income tax, by making the charge under Case VI of Schedule D,
(*b*) if a charge to corporation tax, by treating the amount on which the charge is to be made as income from the letting of machinery or plant.

47. Application to professions, etc., and profits arising from occupation of land

(1) Subject to the provisions of this and the next following section, the provisions of this Chapter shall, with any necessary adaptations, apply in relation to—

(*a*) professions, employments, vocations and offices, and
(*b*) the occupation of woodlands, where the profits or gains thereof are assessable under Schedule D,

as they apply in relation to trades.

(2) Where the profits or gains arising to any person from the occupation of lands (including woodlands) have, for any chargeable period, been determined by reference to assessable value, the amount still unallowed, as at any time after the end of that chargeable period, of any expenditure incurred by that person on the provision of machinery or plant in connection with those lands shall be determined, and section 27 (1) of this Act shall apply, as if there had fallen to be made to him for that chargeable period the like writing-down allowances as would have fallen to be made if, for that chargeable period, the profits or gains arising from the occupation of the lands had been determined otherwise than by reference to assessable value.

(3) The operation of the provisions of subsection (2) of this section in relation to balancing allowances and balancing charges shall not be affected by anything in section 39 of this Act, but where an allowance is deemed to have been made for any chargeable period by virtue of the said subsection (2) an allowance shall not also be deemed to have been made for the same chargeable period by virtue of the said section 39.

(4) . . .[1], the provisions of this Chapter as applied by this section have effect subject to [section [198 (2)][3] of the principal Act][2] (offices and employments with duties abroad).

Note.—See **Prospective Legislation Notes** (Commercial Woodlands).
Amendments.—[1] Words in sub-s. (4) repealed by TA 1970, Sch. 16.
[2] Words in sub-s. (4) substituted by TA 1970, Sch. 15, para. 11, Table, Pt. II.
[3] Words in sub-s. (4) substituted by TA 1988, Sch. 29, para. 32 Table.

48. Successions to trades

Note.—There are two versions of this section. The following version applies to capital expenditure on machinery or plant incurred on or after 27 October 1970 by virtue of FA 1971, Sch. 8, para. 15 (3). See *Butterworths Yellow Tax Handbook 1981–82, 20th edition*, for the other version which applies to expenditure before 27 October 1970.

(1) Where a person succeeds to any trade which until that time was carried on by another person and, by virtue of section [113 or 337 (1)][1] of the principal Act (changes in persons carrying on a trade, and special rules for corporation tax), the trade is to be treated as discontinued, any property which, immediately before the succession takes place, was in use for the purposes of the discontinued trade and, without being sold is, immediately after the succession takes place, in use for the purposes of the new trade shall, for the purposes of Chapter I of Part III of the Finance Act 1971, be treated as if it had been sold to the successor when the succession takes place, and as if the net proceeds of the sale had been the price which that property would have fetched if sold in the open market:

Provided that no first-year allowance shall be made by virtue of the provisions of this subsection.

(2) Where a person succeeds to a trade as a beneficiary under the will or on the intestacy of a deceased person who carried on that trade, the following provisions of this subsection shall, if the beneficiary by notice in writing to the inspector so elects, have effect in relation to any machinery or plant which passes to him together with the trade, being machinery or plant previously owned by the deceased person and used by him for the purposes thereof, that is to say—

(*a*) the reference in subsection (1) above to the price which the machinery or plant would have fetched if sold in the open market shall, in relation to the succession and any previous succession occurring on or after the death of the deceased, be deemed to be a reference to that price or, if it is less than that price, any excess of qualifying expenditure over disposal value which would have been taken into account under section 44 of the Finance Act 1971 for making an allowance for the chargeable period related to the permanent discontinuance of the deceased person's trade if the machinery or plant had had no disposal value.

(3) This subsection has effect as respects any allowance under Chapter I of Part III of the Finance Act 1971, other than a balancing allowance.

Where, after the setting up and before the permanent discontinuance of a trade which at any time is carried on in partnership, anything is done for the purposes thereof, any such allowance which, if the trade had at all times been carried on by one and the same person, would have fallen to be made to him shall be made to the person or persons from time to time carrying on that trade, and the amount of any such allowance shall be computed as if that person or those persons had at all times been carrying on the trade, and as if everything done to or by his or their predecessors in the carrying on thereof had been done to or by him or them.

(4) Where, after the setting up and on or before the permanent discontinuance of a trade which at any time is carried on in partnership, any event occurs which gives rise or may give rise to a balancing allowance or balancing charge under Chapter I of Part III of the Finance Act 1971 in respect of machinery or plant, any balancing allowance or balancing charge which if the trade had at all times been carried on by one and the same person, would have fallen to be made to or on him in respect of that machinery or plant by reason of that event shall be made to or on the person or persons carrying on the trade at the time of that event, and the amount of any such allowance or charge shall be computed as if that person or those persons had at all times been carrying on the trade and as if everything done to or by his or their predecessors in the carrying on thereof had been done to or by him or them.

(5) Notwithstanding section 47 (1) of the Finance Act 1971 this section shall not apply to any employment or office.

Cross references.—See FA 1971, Sch. 8, para. 13 (3A) (sub-s. (1) of this section not to apply in any case where an election is made under FA 1971, Sch. 8, para. 13);
CGTA 1979, s. 34 (3) (*b*) (restriction of capital losses by references to capital and renewals allowances).

Amendments.—[1] Numbers in sub-s. (1) substituted by TA 1988, Sch. 29, para. 32 Table.

49. Transitory provisions: meaning of "appointed day" and "writing-down allowance"

(1) In this Chapter "the appointed day" means 6th April 1946.

(2) Without prejudice to the generality of the transitional provisions in Part III of this Act, any reference to this Chapter to a writing-down allowance shall include a reference to any deduction under Rule 6 of the Rules applicable to Cases I and II of Schedule D contained in Schedule 1 to the Income Tax Act 1918.

(3) The references to a writing-down allowance in sections 21 (7), 27, 33 (5), 40 (2), 41 and 47 (2) of this Act (but not in any other provision of this Chapter) include references to any additional deduction under section 18 of the Finance Act 1932, or under that section as amended by section 22 of the Finance Act 1938.

50. Exclusion of double allowances

(1) Where an allowance under Chapter III of this Part of this Act is made by virtue of section 52 of this Act in respect of any expenditure, then for the purposes of this Chapter the amount of that expenditure (whether it is the whole or part only of the capital expenditure on the machinery or plant in question) shall be taken to be equal only to the amount of any residue of that expenditure immediately after the making of the allowance or last allowance in respect thereof under the said Chapter III, and the cost of the machinery or plant shall be treated as correspondingly reduced.

The reference in this subsection to the amount of any residue of expenditure shall be construed as if this subsection were contained in the said Chapter III.

(2) . . .[1]

Cross references.—See FA 1971, Sch. 8, para. 2 (2) (this section to have effect as if references therein to Chapter II (of this Part of this Act) included references to FA 1971, Pt. III, Ch. I (ss. 40–50));
FA 1980, s. 64 (10) (this section as applied by FA 1971, Sch. 8, para. 2 (2) to be disregarded for the purposes of FA 1980, s. 64 (2) (*a*)).
Amendments.—[1] Sub-s. (2) which is superseded by some provisions in FA 1989, Sch. 13, para. 28 (1)–(4) repealed by FA 1989, Sch. 13, para. 28 (5) (*a*), (6) and Sch. 17, Pt. VI in relation to any chargeable period or its basis period ending after 26 July 1989. It read—

"(2) No allowance shall be made under this Chapter in respect of, or of the expenditure on, any machinery or plant if, for the same or any other chargeable period, an allowance is or can be made in respect of that expenditure under the provisions of section 68 of this Act."

CHAPTER III
MINES, OIL WELLS, ETC.

Cross references.—See FA 1971, Sch. 8, para. 16 (2) (any reference in this Chapter to Part I, Chapter II, of this Act shall, in relation to capital expenditure on the provision of machinery or plant incurred on or after 27 October 1970, include a reference to FA 1971, Pt. III, Ch. I (ss. 40–50));
FA 1986, s. 55 and Sch. 13, Pts. I–IV (new code of allowances for new expenditure (i.e. subject to FA 1986, Sch. 14, expenditure incurred after 31 March 1986) on mineral extraction);
s. 55 (1), (2), (8), Sch. 14 and Sch. 23, Pt. VI (this Chapter ceases to have effect for new expenditure (i.e. subject to FA 1986, Sch. 14, expenditure incurred after 31 March 1986) except for certain expenditure incurred before 1 April 1987);
s. 55 (3), (4) (for the purposes of the old code of allowances under this Chapter, certain assumptions to apply in respect of accounting periods and basis periods);
Sch. 13, para. 2 (1) (Chapter VI *post* to apply for the purposes of FA 1986, Sch. 13 as if that Schedule were included in this Chapter).

The main allowances

51. Qualifying expenditure: general provisions

(1) "Qualifying expenditure" in the provisions of this Chapter shall be construed in accordance with this and the three next following sections.

(2) "Qualifying expenditure" means, subject to subsections (3) and (4) below, capital expenditure incurred by any person in connection with the working of a mine, oil well or other source of mineral deposits of a wasting nature—

(a) on searching for or on discovering and testing deposits, or winning access thereto, or
(b) on the construction of any works which are likely to be of little or no value when the source is no longer worked or, where the source is worked under a foreign concession, which are likely to become valueless when the concession comes to an end to the person working the source immediately before the concession comes to an end.

(3) Subject to the following provisions of this Chapter, qualifying expenditure does not include—

(a) any expenditure on the acquisition of the site of the source, or of the site of any such works as aforesaid, or of rights in or over any such site, or
(b) any expenditure on the acquisition of, or of rights in or over, the deposits, or
(c) any expenditure on works constructed wholly or mainly for subjecting the raw product of the source to any process, except a process designed for preparing the raw product for use as such, or
(d) any expenditure on buildings or structures provided for occupation by or for the welfare of workers, or
(e) any expenditure on a building where the whole of the building was constructed for use as an office, or
(f) any expenditure on so much of a building or structure as was constructed for use as an office, unless the capital expenditure on the construction of the part of the building or structure constructed for use as an office was not more than one-tenth of the capital expenditure incurred on the construction of the whole of the building or structure.

(4) Subject to the next following section, qualifying expenditure does not include any expenditure on machinery or plant, or on any asset which has been treated for any chargeable period as machinery or plant.

52. Machinery and plant used for exploration

(1) Notwithstanding section 51 (4) above expenditure within section 51 (2) (a) above shall, subject to the other provisions of this Chapter, include expenditure on machinery or plant:

Provided that this Part of this Act shall have effect subject to Schedule 5 to this Act.

(2) Notwithstanding anything in subsection (1) above, where in any chargeable period a machinery or plant allowance is or has been made in respect of any expenditure, that expenditure shall not by virtue of subsection (1) above be treated in relation to that or any subsequent chargeable period as qualifying expenditure.

In this subsection "machinery or plant allowance" means an initial allowance under Chapter II of this Part of this Act, or a writing-down allowance within the meaning of the said Chapter II.

53. Overseas mineral rights

(1) Subject to this section, capital expenditure incurred by any person in connection with the working of a mine, oil well or other source of mineral deposits of a wasting nature outside the United Kingdom, being expenditure on the acquisition of, or of rights in or over, the deposits, shall, notwithstanding anything in section 51 of this Act, be qualifying expenditure:

Provided that this Part of this Act shall have effect subject to Schedule 5 to this Act.

(2) References in this section to expenditure on the acquisition of deposits or rights shall not in any event include—

(a) expenditure which, apart from this and the next following section, is qualifying expenditure as defined in section 51 (1) of this Act, or
(b) expenditure on machinery or plant, or on any asset which has been treated for any chargeable period as machinery or plant, or
(c) expenditure on any building or structure.

(3) References in this section to capital expenditure include references to any payments of minimum royalties or dead rents, or any other similar payments, being payments of royalties or rents or other payments which cannot be taken into account as deductions in computing profits or gains for tax purposes by reason of the fact that no trade, or no relevant trade, was being carried on at the relevant time by the person making the payments.

(4) In no case shall the amount on which a balancing charge is made upon a person be increased by virtue of the provisions of this section by more than the total amount by which writing-down allowances made to that person are increased by virtue thereof.

54. Acquisition of land outside the United Kingdom

(1) Subject to this section, capital expenditure incurred by any person in connection with the working of a mine, oil well or other source of mineral deposits of a wasting nature under a foreign concession, being expenditure on the acquisition of land outside the United Kingdom which is to be used in connection with the working of the source and is likely to become valueless when the concession comes to an end to the person working the source immediately before the concession comes to an end, shall, notwithstanding anything in section 51 of this Act, be qualifying expenditure:

Provided that this Part of this Act shall have effect subject to Schedule 5 to this Act.

(2) This section shall not apply—

(a) to expenditure which, apart from this section, is qualifying expenditure, or
(b) to expenditure on machinery or plant, or on any asset which has been treated for any chargeable period as machinery or plant, or
(c) to expenditure on the acquisition of a building or structure for use in connection with the working of a source of mineral deposits, in so far as the expenditure is attributable to the building or structure and not to its site, if—

(i) the building or structure when so used in an industrial building or structure within the meaning of Chapter I or this Part of this Act, and
(ii) the interest acquired is the relevant interest, within the meaning of that Chapter, in relation to the capital expenditure incurred on the construction of that building or structure.

(3) In no case shall the amount on which a balancing charge is made upon a person be increased by virtue of the provisions of this section by more than the total amount by which writing-down allowances made to that person are increased by virtue thereof.

55. Demolition costs

(1) The net cost to a person of the demolition of an asset representing qualifying expenditure incurred by him shall be added for the purposes of this Chapter to the residue, immediately before the demolition, of the expenditure represented by the asset.

(2) The cost or net cost to a person of the demolition of any property shall not, if subsection (1) above applies to it, be treated, for the purposes of this Part of Part II or this Act, as expenditure incurred in respect of any other property by which that property is replaced.

(3) Any reference in this section to the net cost of the demolition of any property is a reference to the excess, if any, of the cost of the demolition over any moneys received for the remains of the property.

56. Initial allowances

(1) Where a person carrying on a trade which consists of or includes the working of a mine, oil well or other source of mineral deposits of a wasting nature incurs for the purposes of the trade any qualifying expenditure on the construction of works likely to have little or no value to him when the source is no longer worked, there shall be made to him, for the chargeable period related to the incurring of the expenditure, an allowance (in this Chapter referred to as "an initial allowance").

(2) The initial allowance shall be of an amount equal to two-fifths of the expenditure within subsection (1) above:

Provided that this subsection shall have effect subject to the provisions of Schedule 1 to this Act.

Cross references.—See FA 1971, s. 52 (1) (increased rate of allowance under sub-s. (2) of this section in relation to expenditure within sub-s. (1) thereof which is incurred on or after 27 October 1970 on the construction of works situated in development areas and in Northern Ireland),
s. 52 (2) (right to disclaim the allowance or specify a reduced amount thereof);
FA 1986, s. 55 (1) and Sch. 14, para. 2 (1) (*c*) (election to apply this section to certain expenditure incurred in the year ending 31 March 1987);
TA 1988, Sch. 30, para. 7 (transitional provisions in respect of claims for group relief in respect of any amount attributable to initial allowances under this section in respect of expenditure incurred under a contract entered into by the surrendering company before 6 March 1973 in respect of works in a development area or in Northern Ireland).

57. Writing-down allowances

(1) Subject to the provisions of this section, where a person carrying on a trade which consists of or includes the working of any mine, oil well or other source of mineral deposits of a wasting nature has, at any time before the end of a chargeable period or its basis period, incurred for the purposes of that trade qualifying expenditure, an allowance (in this Chapter referred to as a "writing-down allowance") shall be made to him for that chargeable period in respect of the whole of the qualifying expenditure which he has incurred for the purposes of the trade and in connection with that source at any time before the end of the said chargeable period or its basis period.

(2) The amount of the said allowance shall be the amount which results from applying to the residue of the expenditure the fraction $\frac{A}{A+B}$ where—

"A" is the output from the source in question in the chargeable period in question or its basis period, and
"B" is the total potential future output of the source, estimated as at the end of the said chargeable period or its basis period,

or the alternative fraction specified in subsection (3) below, whichever is the greater.

(3) The said alternative fraction is one-twentieth, so, however, that for a chargeable period of less than a year that alternative fraction shall be proportionately reduced.

(4) Where the source ceases to be worked or, in the case of a source worked under a foreign concession, the concession comes to an end, the person carrying on the trade may elect that the writing-down allowances, if any, for any chargeable period beginning within the six years which end with the date of that event shall be computed as if the reference in subsection (2) of this section to the total potential future output of the source estimated as at the end of the chargeable period or its basis period were a reference to the actual output of the source between the end of the chargeable period or its basis period and the happening of the said event, and the said allowances shall be computed accordingly, and notwithstanding anything in the Income Tax Acts or the Corporation Tax Acts limiting the time for the making of assessments or the allowance of claims for repayment, all such repayments and assessments shall be made as are necessary to enable effect to be given to this subsection.

(5) Subsection (1) above shall not apply to expenditure incurred before the appointed day, but where, on the appointed day, a person was carrying on a trade which consisted of or included the working of a mine, oil well or other source of mineral deposits of a wasting nature, the preceding provisions of this section shall have effect as if he had on that day incurred for the purposes of the trade and in connection with the source qualifying expenditure of the amount specified in Schedule 6 to this Act.:

Provided that if he considers that that amount is inadquate having regard to the dates on which qualifying expenditure was actually incurred in connection with the source before the appointed day, he may apply to the inspector for relief, and the inspector may authorise such increase in that amount as may be appropriate.

On an appeal to the General Commissioners or Special Commissioners, the Commissioners shall have jurisdiction to review any relevant decision taken by the inspector under this subsection.

(6) References in this section to the residue of any expenditure, in relation to the writing-down allowance to be made for any chargeable period, are references to the amount thereof which remains after deducting therefrom—

(a) any initial allowances made in respect of that expenditure or any part thereof for that or any previous chargeable period, and
(b) any writing-down allowances made in respect of that expenditure or any part thereof for any previous chargeable period, and
(c) where the expenditure consists of or includes expenditure on a building, any relevant exceptional depreciation allowances made in respect of the building for the year 1946–47, and
(d) subject to the provisions of the next following section, if, before the end of the chargeable period for which the allowance is to be made, or its basis period, any asset representing the expenditure is sold or demolished or destroyed, the sale, insurance, salvage or compensation moneys.

58. Sale of source or part of source as going concern

(1) The provisions of this section shall have effect where—

(a) a person who is carrying on a trade which consists of or includes the working of a mine, oil well or other source of mineral deposits of a wasting nature sells assets representing qualifying expenditure, and
(b) the buyer of those assets buys them for the purposes of a trade carried on or to be carried on by him, being a trade which consists of or includes the working of the whole or any part of the source in connection with which the assets were provided.

(2) If the net proceeds of the sale are less than the residue of the expenditure on the assets immediately before the sale, an allowance (in this Chapter referred to as "a balancing allowance") shall be made to the seller, for the chargeable period related to the sale, equal to the difference.

(3) If the net proceeds of the sale exceed the residue of the expenditure on the assets immediately before the sale, a charge (in this Chapter referred to as "a balancing charge") shall be made on the seller, for the chargeable period related to the sale, on the amount of the excess.

(4) If the source in connection with which the expenditure was incurred has been worked before the appointed day, subsections (2) and (3) of this section shall have effect subject to the modification that the amount of the balancing allowance or the amount on which the balancing charge is made shall be reduced by applying thereto the fraction $\frac{A}{B}$ where—

"A" is the total output from the source in the period which begins with the appointed day and ends with the time of that sale, and
"B" is the total output from the source up to the time of the sale:

Provided that if the person to whom a balancing allowance is to be made in respect of any expenditure considers that the amount by which the allowance is to be reduced under this subsection is excessive having regard to the dates on which the expenditure was actually incurred, he may apply to the inspector for relief, and the inspector may authorise such smaller reduction as may be appropriate.

On an appeal to the General Commissioners or Special Commissioners, the Commissioners shall have jurisdiction to review any relevant decision taken by the inspector under this subsection.

(5) In no case shall the amount on which a balancing charge is made upon a person in respect of any assets exceed the differences between—

(a) the qualifying expenditure which he incurred upon the assets, and
(b) the residue of that expenditure immediately before the sale.

(6) Whether a balancing allowance or balancing charge is made upon the seller or not, the deduction to be made in the case of the seller in respect of the assets under subsection (6) (d) of the last preceding section shall, instead of being the sale, insurance, salvage or compensation moneys, be the residue of the expenditure attributable to the assets immediately before the sale.

(7) The buyer shall, for the purposes of the provisions of this Chapter relating to writing-down allowances, balancing allowances and balancing charges, be deemed to have incurred on the assets

at the time of the sale qualifying expenditure equal to whichever is the less of the following amounts, that is to say—

(a) so much of the price as is attributable to the assets, and
(b) the residue of the expenditure on the assets immediately after the sale:

Provided that this subsection shall not apply in relation to a sale before the appointed day.

59. Expenditure incurred by persons not engaged in the trade of mining, etc.

Where a person incurs qualifying expenditure on searching for, discovering and testing the mineral deposits of any mine, oil well or other source of a wasting nature and winning access to those deposits, and, without having carried on any trade which consists of or includes the working of that source, he sells any assets representing that expenditure, then, if the person who acquires the assets carries on such a trade as aforesaid in connection with the source, that person shall, for the purposes of this Chapter, be deemed to have incurred for the purposes of the trade and in connection with the source qualifying expenditure equal to the amount of the qualifying expenditure which is represented by the assets of the price paid by him for the assets, whichever is the smaller.

Other allowances

60. Writing-down allowances for mineral depletion in the United Kingdom

(1) Subject to the provisions of this section, where, for the purposes of a trade carried on or about to be carried on by him, a person incurs capital expenditure on the acquisition of a mineral asset the acquisition of which entitles him to work a mine, oil well or other source of mineral deposits of a wasting nature in the United Kingdom, and the trade consists of or includes the working of that source, he shall be entitled for the chargeable period related to the incurring of the expenditure and subsequent chargeable periods to a writing-down allowance in respect of the expenditure.

(2) Subject as aforesaid, the writing-down allowance for a chargeable period shall be equal to the fraction mentioned below of the royalty value of the output in that chargeable period or its basis period from the source to which the expenditure relates, that is to say—

(a) where the first working of the source after the expenditure was incurred was less than ten years before the end of that chargeable period or its basis period, one-half,
(b) where that first working was less than twenty but not less than ten years before the end of the chargeable period or its basis period, one-quarter,
(c) in any other case, one-tenth.

(3) A writing-down allowance under this section in respect of any expenditure shall not be made to a person for a chargeable period unless the amount of the expenditure exceeds the aggregate of any allowances under this section made to him for previous chargeable periods in respect of the expenditure together with any capital sums accruing to him in or before the said chargeable period or its basis period by virtue of his acquisition of the mineral asset in question, and where made shall not be greater than the amount of the excess; and for this purpose there shall be deemed to have been made for years preceding the year 1963–64 such annual allowances as would have fallen to be made if section 37 of the Finance Act 1963 (which is re-enacted in this section) had always had effect.

(4) Where in any chargeable period or its basis period a person ceases to work the source to which capital expenditure incurred by him relates and, apart from this and the last preceding subsection, a writing-down allowance under this section would fall to be made to him for that chargeable period in respect of the expenditure, the allowance shall not be made, and—

(a) if the aggregate of any allowances under this section made to him for previous chargeable periods in respect of the expenditure exceeds so much of the expenditure as represents the cost of acquiring the output got by him from the source (other than output got before 4th April 1963), a balancing charge on an amount equal to the excess shall be made on him for that chargeable period, or
(b) if that aggregate is less than so much of the expenditure as represents the cost of acquiring that output, a balancing allowance equal to the difference shall be made to him for that chargeable period.

(5) So much of the capital expenditure incurred by a person on the acquisition of a mineral asset as remains after deducting—

(a) the market value of the asset at the time the source to which the expenditure relates ceases to be worked by him, and
(b) any capital sums accruing to him before that time by virtue of his acquisition of the asset,

shall be taken for the purposes of subsection (4) above to represent to cost of acquiring the output got by him from the source; and where part of the output was got by him before 4th April 1963, the cost of acquiring the part got on or after that date shall be taken for those purposes to be an amount which bears to the amount so remaining the same proportion as the royalty value of the output from the source on or after that date bears to the royalty value of the whole output got by virtue of the expenditure.

In this subsection "market value", in relation to an asset, means the price which it might reasonably be expected to fetch on a sale in the open market (whether for use by the purchaser for mining purposes or other purposes) if, before the sale, the owner of the asset had carried out such works (if any) for restoring or otherwise making good the land surface at the site of the source as, having regard to the obligations imposed on him and other relevant circumstances, he might reasonably be expected to carry out whether or not he sold the asset, but reduced by so much of that price as is attributable to matters not representing any part of the capital expenditure in question.

(6) Where a balancing adjustment is made in respect of a person under subsection (4) of this section, or would fall to be so made if the relevant amounts were not equal, and after ceasing to work the source he carries out any works for restoring or otherwise making good the land surface at the site of the source, the cost of those works shall not be taken into account in computing for the purposes of tax under Case I of Schedule D the profits or gains of his trade unless it was assumed, in computing the market value of the asset for the purposes of the said subsection (4), that those works would be carried out.

(7) Where any allowance under this section falls to be made to a person for the chargeable period related to his ceasing to work the source to which the expenditure relates, or for a previous chargeable period, and in a later chargeable period or its basis period he again begins to work the source, then—

(a) in computing, in accordance with subsection (2) of this section, the amount of a writing-down allowance for the later chargeable period or any subsequent chargeable period, the period between cessation and recommencement of working shall be disregarded, and
(b) in computing, for the purposes of subsection (3) or (4) of this section, the aggregate of allowances for previous chargeable periods, those allowances shall be treated as reduced by the amount on which any balancing charge under paragraph (a) of the said subsection (4) has been made in respect of the expenditure.

(8) Where a person (in this subsection referred to as "the transferee") acquires a mineral asset from another person (in this subsection referred to as "the transferor"), and the transferee is a body of persons over whom the transferor has control, or the transferor is a body of persons over whom the transferee has control, or both the transferee and the transferor are bodies of persons and some other person has control over both of them, the capital expenditure incurred by the transferee on the acquisition of the asset shall be taken for the purposes of this section (including this subsection) not to exceed the capital expenditure incurred by the transferor on the acquisition by him or, where the asset consists of an interest of right granted by the transferor, so much of the capital expenditure so incurred by the transferor as, on a just apportionment, is referable to that interest or right; and the expenditure incurred by the transferee shall where necessary be treated as reduced accordingly.

(9) Where in any chargeable period or its basis period a person, having previously incurred capital expenditure on the acquisition of a mineral asset the acquisition of which entitled him to work a source, incurs for the purposes of trade capital expenditure on the acquisition of another mineral asset the acquisition of which entitles him to work the same source, this section shall apply as respects that chargeable periods and subsequent chargeable periods as if the assets were one mineral asset capital expenditure on the acquisition of which was incurred by him when he incurred the first mentioned expenditure and was of an amount equal to the aggregate of that expenditure and the further expenditure:

Provided that where the first-mentioned expenditure was incurred before 4th April 1963 and the further expenditure on or after that date—

(a) no greater allowances shall for the purpose of subsection (3) of this section be deemed by reason of this subsection to have been made before that date, and
(b) the cost of acquiring output got before that date, as computed under subsection (5) of this section, shall not by reason of this subsection be treated as increased.

If the asset to which the further expenditure relates extends to mineral deposits or land not included in the asset to which the first-mentioned expenditure relates, so much of it as so extends shall be treated for the purposes of this section as a separate mineral asset, and the further expenditure shall be apportioned between the assets as may be just.

(10) References in this section to expenditure on the acquisition of an asset do not include—

(a) qualifying expenditure as defined in section 51 (1) of this Act, or
(b) expenditure on machinery or plant, or any asset which has been treated for any chargeable period as machinery or plant, or
(c) expenditure on any building or structure,

and where expenditure was incurred on the acquisition of an asset in respect of which, for chargeable periods previous to a chargeable period for which he first becomes entitled in respect of the expenditure to an allowance under this section, the person incurring the expenditure has been allowed any deductions under [section [87]]² of the principal Act]¹, the expenditure shall be treated for the purposes of this section as reduced by so much of those deductions as, if he had been entitled to an allowance under this section for earlier chargeable periods, would have been excluded by [subsection [(7)]² of the said section [87]²]¹.

(11) In this section—

"basis period" means, for any year of assessment, the period on the profits or gains of which income tax for that year falls to be finally computed under Case I of Schedule D in respect of the trade in question or, where, by virtue of any provision of [section [60]² of the principal Act]¹, the profits or gains of any other period are to be taken to be the profits or gains of the said period, that other period ;
"mineral asset" means any mineral deposits or land comprising mineral deposits, or any interest in or right over such deposits or land ;
"output", in relation to a source, means mineral deposits lifted or extracted from the source ;
"royalty value", in relation to any output from a source, means the amount of the royalties that would be payable on that output if the person working the source were a lessee under a lease, for a term expiring immediately after that output was produced, granted to him at the date when the expenditure in question was incurred and providing for the payment of such royalties on output from the source as might reasonably have been expected to be provided for by such a lease, but reduced by the amount of any royalties actually payable in respect of that output.

(12) This subsection shall have effect for determining for the purposes of this section the amount of any capital sum accruing to a person by virtue of his acquisition of a mineral asset.

Where the property in question is sold at a price other than that which it would have fetched if sold in the open market, the like consequences shall ensue for the said purposes as would have ensued if the property had been sold for the price which it would have fetched if sold in the open market.

Cross references.—See FA 1986, Sch. 13, para. 17 (expenditure on acquisition of land: restriction of qualifying expenditure where there is entitlement to an allowance under this section).
Amendments.—¹ Words in sub-ss. (10) and (11) substituted by TA 1970, Sch. 15, para. 11, Table, Pt. II.
² Numbers in sub-ss. (10), (11) substituted by TA 1988, Sch. 29, para. 32 Table.

61. Contributions by mining concerns to public services, etc., outside the United Kingdom

(1) Subject to the provisions of this section, where a person, for the purposes of a trade carried on by him which consists of or includes the working of a mine, oil well or other source of mineral deposits of a wasting nature outside the United Kingdom, incurs expenditure by contributing a capital sum to the cost of—

(a) buildings to be occupied by persons employed at or in connection with the working of that source, or
(b) works for the supply of water, gas or electricity wholly or mainly to buildings occupied or to be occupied by persons so employed, or
(c) works to be used in providing other services or facilities wholly or mainly for the welfare of persons so employed or their dependants,

and the buildings or works are likely to be of little or no value when the source is no longer worked, then writing-down allowances shall be made to him in respect of that expenditure during a writing-down period of ten years beginning with the chargeable period related to the incurring of the expenditure.

(2) This section shall not apply—

(a) to expenditure resulting in the acquisition of an asset by the person incurring the expenditure, or
(b) to expenditure in respect of which an allowance may be made under any other provision of the Income Tax Acts or the Corporation Tax Acts (or might be so made if this section, and section 22 of the Finance Act 1952, which is re-enacted in this section, had not been passed).

(3) If a person who has incurred expenditure to which this section applies in connection with any source of mineral deposits sells his interest in that source to a person who buys it for the purpose of a trade carried on or to be carried on by him, being a trade which consists of or includes the working of that source, then—

(a) no allowance in respect of that expenditure shall be made to the first-mentioned person for any chargeable period after the chargeable period related to the sale, and the allowance (if any) to be made to him for the chargeable period related to the sale shall be the fraction of the full allowance which the part of the chargeable period related to the sale falling before the sale is of the whole of the said chargeable period related to the sale, and
(b) for the part of the writing-down period remaining at the beginning of the last chargeable period for which an allowance is made to the first-mentioned person, allowances shall be made to the second-mentioned person as if he had incurred the expenditure for the purposes of the said trade, but so that the allowance for a chargeable period not wholly comprised in that part of the writing-down period shall be proportionately reduced.

(4) If a person who has incurred expenditure to which this section applies in connection with any source of mineral deposits sells his interest in part of that source to a person who buys it for the purpose of a trade carried on or to be carried on by him, being a trade which consists of or includes the working of that part of the source, then the last preceding subsection shall apply to so much of the expenditure as is referable to that part of the source as it would apply to the whole of the expenditure on a sale extending to the whole of the source, and any allowance in respect of the expenditure shall be apportioned accordingly.

Cross references.—See FA 1986, Sch. 13, para. 7 (3) (b) (new code of allowances with effect from 1 April 1986 for contributions falling under this section).

62. Expenditure by mining concerns on abortive exploration

(1) Subject to the provisions of this section, where the person carrying on a trade which consists of or includes the working of any mine, oil well or other source of mineral deposits of a wasting nature incurs expenditure in connection with that trade on searching for, or on discovering and testing, the mineral deposits of any source or winning access thereto, but gives up the search, exploration or inquiry upon which the expenditure is incurred without having carried on any trade which consists of or includes the working of the source in question, then in computing for the purposes of tax the profits or gains or losses of the trade in connection with which the expenditure is incurred there shall be allowed a deduction of an amount equal to the amount of that expenditure as if it were expenses incurred for the purpose of the trade at the time when he gives up the search, exploration or inquiry.

(2) This section shall not apply—

(a) to expenditure incurred in the course of a trade which consists of or includes the searching for, discovering and testing of mineral deposits and winning access thereto, if it is expenditure which is, apart from this section, allowed to be deducted in computing, for the purposes of tax, the profits or gains of that trade, or
(b) to any other expenditure incurred by a person in connection with a source, unless it would have been qualifying expenditure as defined in section 51 (1) of this Act if he had begun working the source in the course of a trade at the time when he gives up the search, exploration or inquiry,

and the same expenditure shall not be taken into account for the purposes of this section in relation to more than one trade.

(3) The preceding provisions of this section shall not affect the right to any deduction or allowance under any other provision of the Income Tax Acts or the Corporation Tax Acts, but—

(a) a person shall not be entitled to a deduction or allowance in respect of the same expenditure both under this section and under some other provision of those Acts, and
(b) section 59 of this Act shall not apply to expenditure in respect of which a deduction has been allowed under this section.

Supplemental

63. Regulations

(1) The board may make regulations for carrying this Chapter into effect, and those regulations may in particular—

(a) lay down rules for determining the extent of the mineral deposits which are to be taken,

for all or any of the purposes of this Chapter, as constituting a source and the amount of the output from a source in any year or over any period, and in estimating total potential future output for any of those purposes,

(b) lay down rules for determining the residue of the expenditure attributable to an asset immediately before, or immediately after, the sale thereof,

(c) in relation to cases in which, by virtue of the provisions of this Chapter, a person is deemed to have incurred expenditure on the appointed day, lay down rules for determining what assets are to be treated as representing that expenditure and how much of that expenditure is to be treated as incurred in any particular asset,

(d) lay down rules for determining, for the purposes of any application under this Chapter, whether and by how much—

(i) the amount of the expenditure which, under this Chapter, a person is to be treated as having incurred on the appointed day is inadequate, or

(ii) the amount by which any allowance is to be reduced under this Chapter is excessive.

(2) The power conferred by this section to make regulations shall be exercisable by statutory instrument and all regulations under this section shall be subject to annulment in pursuance of a resolution of the Commons House of Parliament.

(3) References in subsection (1) above to this Chapter do not include references to section 60 of this Act.

64. Expenditure prior to commencement of trade

Any expenditure incurred for the purposes of a trade by a person about to carry it on shall be treated for the purposes of the provisions of this Chapter, other than section 60, as if it had been incurred by that person on the first day on which he does carry it on.

65. Interpretation of Chapter III

(1) In this Chapter "the appointed day" means—

(a) in relation to expenditure which is qualifying expenditure by virtue of section 52 or section 54 of this Act, 6th April 1952,

(b) in relation to expenditure to which section 53 (1) of this Act applies, 6th April 1949,

(c) in relation to any other qualifying expenditure as defined at the beginning of this Chapter, 6th April 1946.

(2) Any reference in this Chapter to assets representing any expenditure includes, in relation to expenditure on searching for, discovering and testing deposits, any results obtained from any search, exploration or inquiry upon which the expenditure was incurred.

66. Manner of making allowances and charges

All allowances and charges falling to be made under this Chapter to or on any person shall be made to or on him in taxing his trade.

CHAPTER IV
DREDGING

Construction.—FA 1985, s. 61 to be construed as if contained in Part I of this Act; see FA 1985, s. 61 (2).
Cross references.—See FA 1971, Sch. 8, para. 16 (2) (any reference in this Chapter to Part I, Chapter II, of this Act shall, in relation to capital expenditure on the provision of machinery or plant incurred on or after 27 October 1970, include a reference to FA 1971, Pt. III, Ch. I ss. 40–50));
FA 1989, Sch. 13, para. 28 (1), (4) (b) (exclusion of double allowances: where an allowance is made under this Chapter, no allowance to be made under other legislation).

67. Capital allowances for expenditure on dredging

(1) Subject to the provisions of this section, where a person for the purposes of any qualifying trade carried on by him incurs capital expenditure on dredging, and either the trade consists of the maintenance or improvement of the navigation of a harbour, estuary or waterway or the dredging is for the benefit of vessels coming to, leaving or using any dock or other premises occupied by him for the purposes of the trade, then—

(a) an initial allowance shall be made for the first relevant chargeable period to the person incurring the expenditure, and, subject to Schedule 1 to this Act, the amount of the initial allowance shall be three-twentieths of the expenditure, and
(b) writing-down allowances shall be made up in respect of that expenditure to the person for the time being carrying on the trade during a writing-down period of twenty-five years (or, where the expenditure was incurred before 6th November 1962, fifty years) beginning with the first relevant chargeable period, but where a writing-down allowance falls to be made for a year of assessment to such a person, and he is within the charge to income tax in respect of the trade for part only of that year, that part shall be treated as a separate chargeable period for the purposes of computing allowances under this section.

(2) If the trade is permanently discontinued in any chargeable period, then for that chargeable period there shall be made to the person last carrying on the trade, in addition to any other allowance made to him, and allowance equal to the amount of the expenditure less the allowances made in respect of it under the preceding subsection for that and previous chargeable periods.

The reference in this subsection to allowances made for previous chargeable periods (which, by virtue of Part III of this Act, may include allowances under section 17 of the Finance Act 1956, which is re-enacted in this section) shall be construed, except as regards initial allowances, as if the said section 17 had always had effect (instead of having effect only for chargeable periods after the year 1955–56).

(3) [For the purposes of this section, a trade shall not be treated by virtue of section [113 or 337 (1)]² of the principal Act (changes in persons carrying on a trade, and special rules for corporation tax) as permanently discontinued]¹; but, subject to [section [343 (2)]² of the principal Act]¹ (company reconstructions, etc), where a trade is sold, it shall be treated for those purposes as having been permanently discontinued at the time of the sale, unless the sale is such a sale as is specified in section 78 of this Act.

(4) Any allowance under this section shall be made in taxing the trade.

(5) Where expenditure is incurred partly for the purposes of a qualifying trade and partly for other purposes, subsection (1) of this section shall apply to so much only of that expenditure as on a just apportionment ought fairly to be treated as incurred for the purposes of that trade.

(6) In this section "qualifying trade" means any trade or undertaking which, or a part of which, complies with any of the following conditions, that is to say—

(a) the condition that it consists of the maintenance or improvement of the navigation of a harbour, estuary or waterway, or
(b) any condition set out in the provisions of section 7(1) of this Act,

but where part only of a trade or undertaking complies with those conditions, subsection (5) of this section shall apply as if the part which does and the part which does not comply were separate trades.

(7) Where a person incurs capital expenditure for the purposes of a trade or part of a trade not yet carried on by him but with a view to carrying it on, or incurs capital expenditure in connection with a dock or other premises not yet occupied by him for the purposes of a qualifying trade but with a view to so occupying the dock or premises, the preceding

provisions of this section shall apply as if he had been carrying on the trade or part of the trade or occupying the dock or premises for the purposes of the qualifying trade, as the case may be, at the time when the expenditure was incurred.

(8) For the purposes of this section, the first relevant chargeable period, in relation to expenditure incurred by any person, is the chargeable period related to the following event or occasion, that is—

(a) the incurring of the expenditure, or

(b) in the case of expenditure for which allowances are to be made by virtue of subsection (7) of this section, the occasion when he first both carries on the trade or part of the trade for the purpose of which the expenditure was incurred, and occupies for the purposes of that trade or part of the trade the dock or other premises in connection with which it was incurred.

(9) Where a person contributes a capital sum to expenditure on dredging incurred by another person, he shall be treated as incurring capital expenditure on that dredging, and capital expenditure incurred by any person shall not be treated as incurred for the purposes of any trade carried on or to be carried on by him in so far as it has been or is to be met directly or indirectly by the Crown or by any government or public or local authority, whether in the United Kingdom or elsewhere, or by capital sums contributed by any other person for purposes other than those of that trade.

(10) In this section "dredging" does not include things done otherwise than in the interests of navigation, but (subject to that) includes the removal of anything forming part of or projecting from the bed of the sea or of any inland water, by whatever means it is removed and whether or not at the time of removal it is wholly or partly above water; and this section shall apply to the widening of an inland waterway in the interests of navigation as it applies to dredging.

(11) . . .[3]

Cross references.—See FA 1985, s. 61 (no initial allowance to be made under this section in respect of capital expenditure incurred after 31 March 1986, subject to certain transitional provisions).
Amendments.—[1] Words in sub-s. (3) substituted by TA 1970, Sch 15, para 5 (1), (6) and para. 11, Table, Pt. II, respectively.
[2] Numbers in sub-s. (3) substituted by TA 1988, Sch. 29, para. 32 Table.
[3] Sub-s. (11) which is superseded by some provisions in FA 1989, Sch. 13, para. 28 (1)–(4) repealed by FA 1989, Sch 13, para. 28 (5) (a), (6) and Sch. 17, Pt. VI in relation to any chargeable period or its basis period ending after 26 July 1989. It read—

"(11) No allowance shall be made by virtue of this section in respect of any expenditure if for the same or any other chargeable period an allowance is or can be made in respect of it under any of the provisions of Chapter I or II of this Part of this Act."

CHAPTER V

AGRICULTURAL LAND AND BUILDINGS

Cross references.—See FA 1982, Sch. 12, para. 11 (capital allowances for expenditure incurred after 9 March 1982 and before 1 April 1987 on buildings and dwelling-houses let on assured tenancies not available under Sch. 12 if available under any provisions of this Chapter);
FA 1989, Sch. 13, para. 28 (1), (4) (c) (exclusion of double allowances: where an allowance is made under this Chapter, no allowance to be made under other legislation).

68. Allowances for capital expenditure on construction of buildings and other works

(1) Subject to the provisions of this section, where the owner or tenant of any agricultural or forestry land incurs any capital expenditure on the construction of farmhouses, farm or forestry buildings, cottages, fences or other works, [there shall be made to him—

(a) For the chargeable period related to the incurring of that expenditure, an initial allowance of an amount equal to one-fifth of that expenditure; and

(b) during a writing-down period of eight years beginning with that period, writing-down allowances of an aggregate amount equal to four-fifths of that expenditure.][1]

(2) Any allowance under this section shall be made by way of discharge or repayment of tax and shall be available primarily against agricultural income and forestry income.

(3) No expenditure shall be taken into account for the purposes of this section unless it is incurred for the purposes of husbandry or forestry on the agricultural or forestry land in question, and—

(a) where the expenditure is on a farmhouse, one-third only of the expenditure shall be taken into account, or, if the accommodation and amenities of the farmhouse are out of due relation to the nature and extent of the farm, such proportion thereof not grater than one-third as may be just,

(b) where expenditure is incurred on any asset other than a farmhouse, being an asset which is to serve partly the purposes of husbandry or forestry and partly other purposes, such apportionment of the expenditure shall be made for the purposes of this subsection as may be just.

[(3A) A person in making a claim by virtue of this section as it applies for income tax purposes in respect of the chargeable period mentioned in paragraph (a) of subsection (1) above may require the initial allowance to be reduced to a specified amount, and a company may by notice in writing given to the inspector not later than two years after the end of that period disclaim the initial allowance or require it to be so reduced; and

(a) where the initial allowance is not claimed or, in the case of a company, is disclaimed, the period and amount mentioned in paragraph (b) of that subsection shall be ten years and the whole amount of the expenditure; and

(b) where the initial allowance is reduced, that period and amount shall be a fraction of the period of ten years and of the whole amount of the expenditure equal to the fraction of the whole amount of the expenditure that remains after deducting the part covered by the initial allowance].[2]

(4) Where a person would, if he continued to be the owner or, as the case may be, the tenant of any land, be entitled under this section to [a writing-down allowance][3] *in respect of any expenditure, and the whole of his interest in the land in question, or in any part of the land in question, is transferred, whether by operation of law or otherwise, to some other person, then, for the part of the writing-down period falling after the date of the transfer, the person to whom the interest is transferred shall, to the exclusion of the person from whom it is tranferred, be entitled to the allowances (any allowance to either of them for a chargeable period falling partly before and partly within that part of the writing-down period being reduced accordingly):*

Provided that, where the interest transferred is in part only of the land, this subsection shall apply to so much of the allowance as is properly referable to that part of the land as if it were a separate allowance.

(5) For the purposes of the last preceding subsection, where an interest in land is a tenancy and that tenancy comes to an end, that interest shall be deemed to have been transferred—

(a) if an incoming tenant makes any payment to the outgoing tenant in respect of assets representing the expenditure in question, to the incoming tenant, and

(b) in any other case, to the owner of the interest in immediate reversion on the tenancy.

(6) For the purposes of this section as it applies for income tax purposes, the basis period for a

year of assessment is the year ending with 31st March next preceding that year of asessment, or with such other date as may be agreed by the owner or tenant in question and the inspector, and section 72 of this Act shall not apply for the purposes of this section.

Note.—See **Prospective Legislation Notes.**
Cross references.—See FA 1986, s. 56 (1), (2) (with respect to capital expenditure incurred after 31 March 1986, other than expenditure under existing contracts as defined, FA 1986, Sch. 15 to have effect in place of this section); FA 1989, s. 120 (1) (*a*) (forestry land: abolition of agricultural buildings allowances).
Amendments.—[1] Words in sub-s. (1) substituted by FA 1978, s. 39 (1), (5), in relation to expenditure incurred after 11 April 1978.
[2] Sub-s. (3A) inserted by FA 1978, s. 39 (2), (5), in relation to expenditure incurred after 11 April 1978.
[3] Words in sub-s. (4) substituted by FA 1978, s. 39 (3), (5), in relation to expenditure incurred after 11 April 1978.
This section repealed by FA 1986, Sch. 23, Pt. VI with respect to capital expenditure incurred after 31 March 1986, other than expenditure under existing contracts as defined in FA 1986, s 56 (2).

69. Interpretation of preceding section

In section 68 above [and Schedule 15 to the Finance Act 1986][2]—

"agricultural land" means land, houses or other buildings in the United Kingdom occupied wholly or mainly for the purpose of husbandry [(as defined below)][3];

"agricultural income" means income chargeable under [Schedule A][1] in respect of agricultural land, and income chargeable under Schedule D in respect of farming or market gardening in the United Kingdom;

"forestry land" means woodlands in the United Kingdom in respect of which an election is in force for assessment and charge to tax under Schedule D by virtue of [paragraph 5 of Schedule 6 to the Finance Act 1988][5], and any houses or other buildings in the United Kingdom which are occupied together with, and wholly or mainly for the purposes of, such woodlands;

"forestry income" means income chargeable under [Schedule A][1] in respect of forestry land, and income chargeable under Schedule D in respect of the occupation of woodlands in the United Kingdom;

["husbandry" includes any method of intensive rearing of livestock or fish on a commercial basis for the production of food for human consumption.][4]

Note.— See **Prospective Legislation Notes** (Commercial Woodlands).
Amendments.—[1] Words in definitions of "agricultural income" and "forestry income" substituted by TA 1970, Sch. 15, para. 5 (1), (7).
[2] Words inserted by FA 1986, s. 56 (4) (*a*).
[3] Words at the end of the definition of "agricultural land" inserted by FA 1986, s. 56 (4) (*b*).
[4] Words added by FA 1986, s. 56 (4) (*c*).
[5] Words in the definition of "forestry land" substituted for the words "section 54 of the principal Act" (i.e. TA 1988, s. 54) by virtue of FA 1988, Sch. 6, para. 6 (1), (9). The definition as amended applies from 15 March 1988.

CHAPTER VI

MISCELLANEOUS AND GENERAL

Cross references.—See FA 1986, s. 56 (3) (application of this Chapter in relation to FA 1986, Sch. 15 (agricultural land and buildings)),
Sch. 13, para. 2 (1) (this Chapter to apply for the purposes of that Schedule (new code of allowances for capital expenditure on mineral extraction with effect from 1 April 1986) as if that Schedule were included in Chapter III of this Part of this Act).

Income tax

70. Income tax allowances and charges in taxing a trade, etc.

(1) This and the next following section have effect as respects allowances and charges which fall to be made under the provisions of this Part of this Act as they apply for the purposes of income tax.

(2) Allowances which fall to be made to a person in taxing his trade shall be made as a deduction in charging the profits or gains of the trade to income tax.

(3) Any claim by a person for an allowance falling to be made to him in taxing his trade shall be made in his returns of income for income tax purposes, . . .[5]. [Section 42 of the Taxes Management Act 1970 shall not apply to any such claim][1].

(4) Where full effect cannot be given in any year to any allowance falling to be made in taxing a trade owing to there being no profits or gains of the trade chargeable for that year, or owing to the profits or gains chargeable being less than the allowance, the allowance or part of the allowance to which effect has not been given, as the case may be, [shall be carried forward and, so far as may be, made as a deduction in charging the profits or gains of the trade in subsequent years of assessment.][4]

[(4A) Where the allowances in respect of which deductions can be made under this section for any year include allowances carried forward under subsection (4) above from a previous year the allowances shall, subject to paragraph 5 of Schedule 9 to the Finance Act 1981, be deducted in the following order—

(a) allowances other than those carried forward under subsection (4) above from an earlier year;
(b) allowances carried forward as aforesaid from years of assessment not earlier than the year for which the basis period ended on or included 14th November 1980;
(c) allowances carried forward as aforesaid from years of assessment earlier than those referred to in paragraph (b) above.][4]

(5) . . .[2], subsection (4) above has effect subject to [section [383][6] of the principal Act][3] (right to set capital allowances against general income).

(6) Any charge falling to be made on a person for any year of assessment in taxing his trade shall be made by means of an assessment to income tax on the profits or gains of that trade for that year of assessment in addition to any other assessment falling to be made thereon for that year.

(7) This section shall apply in relation to professions, employments, vocations and offices, and the occupation of woodlands the profits or gains whereof are assessable under Schedule D, as it applies in relation to trades, and nothing in this section applies to any deduction allowable under any provision of this Part of this Act in computing the profits or gains of a trade.

Note.—See **Prospective Legislation Notes** (Commercial Woodlands).
Cross references.—See FA 1971, s. 48 (4) (this section to have effect, as respects capital expenditure on the provision of machinery or plant incurred on or after 27 October 1970, as if references therein to Part I of this Act included references to FA 1971, Pt. III, Ch. I (ss. 40–50));

FA 1982, s. 79 (written agreement between taxpayer and inspector as regards allowances under this section to be treated as equivalent to an assessment).
Amendments.—[1] Words at the end of sub-s. (3) added by TA 1970, Sch. 15, para. 5 (1), (8).
[2] Words in sub-s. (5) repealed by TA 1970, Sch. 16.
[3] Words in sub-s. (5) substituted by TA 1970, Sch. 15, para. 11, Table, Pt. II.
[4] Sub-s. (4A) inserted and words in sub-s. (4) substituted by FA 1981, s. 77 with effect from the year of assessment for which the basis period ended on or after 14 November 1980.
[5] Words "and, in the case of an allowance under section 60 of this Act, the claim shall be in such form and accompanied by such plans and other particulars as the Board may direct" in sub-s. (3) repealed by FA 1986, Sch. 23, Pt. VI in relation to new expenditure (i.e. subject to FA 1986, Sch. 14, expenditure incurred after 31 March 1986).
[6] Number in sub-s. (5) substituted by TA 1988, Sch. 29, para. 32 Table.

71. Other income tax allowances

(1) Where an allowance falls to be made to a person for any year of assessment which is to be given by way of discharge or repayment of tax, and is to be available primarily against a specified class of income—

(*a*) the amount of the allowance shall be deducted from or set off against income of his of that class for that year of assessment, and
(*b*) if the amount to be allowed is greater than the amount of his income of that class for that year of assessment, the balance shall be deducted from or set off against his income of that class for the next year of assessment, and so on for subsequent years of assessment, and tax shall be discharged or repaid accordingly:

Provided that where the amount of the allowance is greater than the amount of the person's income of that class for the first-mentioned year of assessment, he may elect that the excess shall be deducted from or set off against his other income for that year of assessment, and it shall be deducted from or set off against that income and tax discharged or repaid accordingly, and only the excess, if any, of the amount of the allowance over all his income for that year of assessment shall be deducted from or set off against his income of the specified class for succeeding years.

An election under this proviso as respects an allowance for any year of assessment shall be made by giving notice in writing to the inspector not later than two years after the end of that year of assessment.

(2) An election under the proviso to subsection (1) above may be made for any year of assessment with respect to an allowance for the last preceding year of assessment, so far as not previously allowed, as if the allowance were or formed part of the allowance for the year for which the election is made; and in applying that subsection as extended by this provision to any allowances, relief shall be deemed to be given in respect of an allowance carried forward from an earlier year before it is given in respect of an allowance arising in a later year.

(3) Relief under this section shall be given on a claim [(that is to say, a claim to which section 42 of the Taxes Management Act 1970 applies)][1].

Cross references.—See FA 1971, s. 48 (4) (this section to have effect, as respects capital expenditure on the provision of machinery or plant incurred on or after 27 October 1970, as if references therein to Part I of this Act included references to FA 1971, Pt. III, Ch. I (ss. 40–50));
Oil Taxation Act 1975, s. 13 (3), (6) (capital allowances not to be made under this section for oil extraction activities for chargeable periods beginning after 11 July 1974);
FA 1976, s. 41 (6) (for expenditure incurred after 15 December 1975 or 6 April 1976 (see s. 41 (7)), restriction of set-off of capital allowances against general income to apply to relief under the proviso to sub-s. (1) of this section);
FA 1982, s. 79 (written agreement between taxpayer and inspector as regards allowances under this section to be treated as equivalent to an assessment);
Sch. 12, para. 14 (application of this section for the purposes of capital allowances on expenditure incurred after 9 March 1982 and before 1 April 1987 for dwelling-houses let on assured tenancies);
FA 1985, s. 48 and Sch. 12, para. 2 (3) (*c*) (restriction of relief under this section for chargeable periods beginning after 19 March 1985 or, subject to certain conditions, for chargeable periods beginning on or before that date and ending after it in the case of a trade carried on by limited partners who are individuals);
TA 1988, s. 279 (7) (for the purposes of this section, TA 1988, s. 279 (1) (*b*) to have effect as if the words "being a part beginning with 6th April" were omitted).
Amendments.—[1] Words in sub-s. (3) substituted by TA 1970, Sch. 15, para. 5 (1), (9).

72. Meaning of "basis period"

(1) Except as otherwise expressly provided, in this Part of this Act as it applies for income tax purposes "basis period" has the meaning assigned to it by the following provisions of this section.

(2) In the case of a person to or on whom an allowance or charge falls to be made in taxing his trade, his basis period for any year of assessment is the period on the profits or gains of which income tax for that year falls to be finally computed under Case I of Schedule D in respect of the trade in question or, where, by virtue of any provision of [section [60]² of the principal Act]¹, the profits or gains of any other period are to be taken to be the profits or gains of the said period, that other period:

Provided that, in the case of any trade—

(a) where two basis periods overlap, the period common to both shall be deemed for the purpose of this subsection to fall in the first basis period only,
(b) where there is an interval between the end of the basis period for one year of assessment and the basis period for the next year of assessment, then, unless the second-mentioned year of assessment is the year of the permanent discontinuance of the trade, the interval shall be deemed to be part of the second basis period, and
(c) where there is an interval between the end of the basis period for the year of assessment preceding that in which the trade is permanently discontinued and the basis period for the year in which it is permanently discontinued, the interval shall be deemed to form part of the first basis period.

(3) Where an allowance falls to be made under Chapter II of this Part of this Act to a person carrying on a profession or vocation, subsection (2) of this section shall apply as if the references to a trade included references to a profession or vocation and as if the reference to Case I of Schedule D included a reference to Case II of Schedule D.

(4) In the case of any other person to or on whom an allowance or charge falls to be made under this Part of this Act, his basis period for any year of assessment is the year of assessment itself.

(5) Any reference in this section to the overlapping of two periods shall be construed as including a reference to the coincidence of two periods or to the inclusion of one period in another, and references to the period common to both of two periods shall be construed accordingly.

Cross references.—See FA 1971, s. 50 (2) (for income tax purposes "basis period" to be construed according to sub-ss. (2)–(5) of this section, and allowances and charges to be made according to FA 1971, Pt. III, Ch. I (ss. 40–50) in relation to capital expenditure on machinery or plant incurred on or after 27 October 1970);
FA 1982, Sch. 12, para. 14 (application of this section for the purposes of capital allowances on expenditure incurred after 9 March 1982 and before 1 April 1987 for dwelling-houses let on assured tenancies).
Amendments.—¹ Words in sub-s. (2) substituted by TA 1970, Sch. 15, para. 11, Table, Pt. II.
² Number in sub-s. (2) substituted by TA 1988, Sch. 29, para. 32 Table.

Corporation tax

73. Corporation tax allowances and charges in taxing a trade

(1) In computing for the purposes of corporation tax a company's profits for any accounting period there shall be made all such deductions and additions as are required to give effect to the provisions of this Part of this Act which relate to allowances and charges in respect of capital expenditure; and subsection (2) of this section and the next following section have effect as respects allowances and charges which fall to be made under the provisions of this Part of this Act as they apply for the purposes of corporation tax.

(2) Allowances and charges which fall to be made for any accounting period in taxing a trade under the provisions of this Part of this Act as they apply for the purposes of corporation tax shall be given effect by treating the amount of any allowance as a trading expense of the trade in that period, and by treating the amount on which any such charge is to be made as a trading receipt of the trade in that period.

Cross references.—FA 1971, s. 48 (4) (this section to have effect, as repects capital expenditure on the provision of machinery or plant incurred on or after 27 October 1970, as if references therein to Part I of this Act included references to FA 1971, Pt. III, Ch. I (ss. 40–50));
FA 1982, Sch. 12, para. 14 (application of this section for the purposes of capital allowances on expenditure incurred after 9 March 1982 and before 1 April 1987 for dwelling-houses let on assured tenancies).

74. Other corporation tax allowances

(1) Where an allowance falls to be made to a company for any accounting period which is to be given by discharge or repayment of tax, and is to be available primarily against a specified class of income, it shall, as far as may be, be given effect by deducting the amount of the allowance from any income of the period, being income of the specified class.

(2) Where such an allowance which is to be made for any accounting period cannot be given full effect under subsection (1) above in that period by reason of a want or deficiency of income of the relevant class, then (so long as the company remains within the charge to tax) the amount unallowed shall be carried forward to the succeeding accounting period, except in so far as effect is given to it under subsection (3) below; and the amount so carried forward shall be treated for the purposes of subsection (1) of this section, and of any further application of this subsection, as the amount of a corresponding allowance for that period.

(3) Where such an allowance which is to be made for any accounting period (otherwise than by being carried forward from an earlier accounting period) cannot be given full effect under subsection (1) above in that period by reason of a want or deficiency of income of the relevant class, the company [may, on making a claim (to which section 42 of the Taxes Management Act 1970 applies), require][1] that effect shall be given to the allowance against the profits (of whatever description) of that accounting period and, if the company was then within the charge to tax, of preceding accounting periods ending within the time specified in subsection (4) below; and, subject to that subsection and to any relief for earlier allowances or for losses, the profits of any of those accounting periods shall then be treated as reduced by the amount unallowed under subsection (1) above, or by so much of that amount as cannot be given effect under this subsection against profits of a later accounting period.

(4) The time referred to in subsection (3) above is a time equal in length to the accounting period for which the allowance falls to be made; but the amount or aggregate amount of the reduction which may be made under that subsection in the profits of an accounting period falling partly before that time shall not, with the amount of any reduction falling to be made therein under any corresponding provision of [the Corporation Tax Acts][1] relating to losses, exceed a part of those profits proportionate to the part of the period falling within that time.

(5) A claim under subsection (3) above shall be made within two years from the end of the accounting period first mentioned in that subsection.

(6) . . .[2]

Cross references.—See FA 1971, s. 48 (4) (this section to have effect, as repects capital expenditure on the provision of machinery or plant incurred on or after 27 October 1970, as if references therein to Part I of this Act included references to FA 1971, Pt. III, Ch. I. (ss. 40–50));
FA 1982, Sch. 12, para. 14 (application of this section for the purposes of capital allowances on expenditure incurred after 9 March 1982 and before 1 April 1987 for dwelling-houses let on assured tenancies);

TA 1988, s. 118 (restriction of relief under this section in the case of a trade carried on by limited partners which are companies);
s. 242 (2) (*d*), (4), (8) (*c*) (set-off of losses, etc., against surplus of franked investment income in relation to sub-ss. (3) and (4) of this section);
s. 400 (2) (write-off of government investment after 9 March 1981: any allowance under sub-s. (2) of this section to be reduced by the amount written-off);
s. 400 (4) (any allowance under sub-s. (3) of this section not to be reduced by the amount written-off);
s. 492 (capital allowances not to be made under this section for oil extraction activities for chargeable periods beginning after 11 July 1974).
Amendments.—[1] Words in sub-ss. (3) and (4) substituted by TA 1970, Sch. 15, para. 5 (1), (10), (11).
[2] Sub-s. (6) repealed by FA 1986, Sch. 23, Pt. VI with respect to expenditure incurred after 31 March 1986 other than expenditure under existing contracts as defined in FA 1986, s. 56 (2).

General
75. Writing-down allowances under sections 61, 67 and 68

(1) This section has effect where it is provided under section . . .[1] 67 or 68 of this Act that writing-down allowances shall be made in respect of any expenditure during a writing-down period of a specified length.

(2) There shall for any chargeable period wholly or partly comprised in the writing-down period be made an allowance equal to the appropriate fraction of the expenditure; and, subject to any provision to the contrary, the appropriate fraction is such fraction of the writing-down period as falls within the chargeable period:

Provided that the aggregate amount of the allowances made whether to the same or to different persons, together with the amount of any initial allowance, shall not exceed the amount of the expenditure.

(3) Where under paragraph 27 (2) of Schedule 14 to the Finance Act 1965 allowances were made for accounting periods of a company falling wholly or partly within the year 1964–65 or 1965–66 in addition to allowances (for income tax purposes) made for either of those years, then in reckoning the period for which allowances are to be made, the periods for which allowances were so made shall be added together, notwithstanding that the same time is (according to the calendar) counted twice.

Cross references.—See FA 1986, s. 56 (6) (the reference to "section 68" in this section to include a reference to FA 1986, Sch. 15 (allowances for capital expenditure on agricultural land and buildings incurred after 31 March 1986 other than expenditure under existing contracts as defined in FA 1986, s. 56 (2));
Sch. 15, para. 4 (6) (adjustment for shortfall in allowances under sub-s. (2) above for agricultural land and buildings);
TA 1988, s. 530 (8) (application of sub-s. (2) of this section to writing-down allowances for know-how).
Amendments.—[1] Word "61," in sub-s. (1) repealed by FA 1986, Sch. 23, Pt. VI.

76. Companies not resident in United Kingdom

Where a company not resident in the United Kingdom is within the charge to corporation tax in respect of one source of income and to income tax in respect of another source, then, in applying the provisions of this Part of this Act, allowances related to any source of income shall be given effect against income chargeable to the same tax as is chargeable on income from that source.

Cross references.—See FA 1982, Sch. 12, para. 14 (application of this section for the purposes of capital allowances on expenditure incurred after 9 March 1982 and before 1 April 1987 for dwelling-houses let on assured tenancies).

77. Apportionment of consideration, and exchanges and surrenders of leasehold interests

(1) Any reference in this Part of this Act to the sale of any property includes a reference to the sale of that property together with any other property and, where property is sold together with other property, so much of the net proceeds of the sale of the whole property as, on a just apportionment, is properly attributable to the first-mentioned property shall, for the purposes of this Part of this Act, be deemed to be the net proceeds of the sale of the first-mentioned property, and references to expenditure incurred on the provision or the purchase of property shall be construed accordingly.

For the purposes of this subsection, all the property which is sold in pursuance of one bargain shall be deemed to be sold together, notwithstanding that separate prices are or purport to be agreed for separate items of that property or that there are or purport to be separate sales of separate items of that property.

(2) The provisions of subsection (1) of this section shall, with the necessary adaptations, apply in relation to other sale, insurance, salvage or compensation moneys as they apply in relation to the net proceeds of sales.

(3) This Part of this Act shall have effect as if any reference therein (including any reference in the preceding provisions of this section) to the sale of any property included a reference to the exchange of any property and, in the case of a leasehold interest, also included a reference to the surrender thereof for valuable consideration, and any provisions of this Part of this Act referring to sales shall have effect accordingly with the necessary adaptations and, in particular, with the adaptations that references to the net proceeds of sale and to the price shall be taken to include references to the consideration for the exchange or surrender and references to capital sums included in the price shall be taken to include references to so much of the consideration as would have been a capital sum if it had taken the form of a money payment.

(4) The reference in subsection (1) above to expenditure incurred on the provision or the purchase of property shall—

(a) in relation to section 53 of this Act, be deemed to include a reference to expenditure on the acquisition of, or of rights in or over, mineral deposits,
(b) in relation to section 54 of this Act, be deemed to include a reference to expenditure on the acquisition of land,
(c) in relation to section 60 of this Act, be deemed to include a reference to expenditure on the acquisition of a mineral asset.

Cross references.—See FA 1971, Sch. 8, para. 15 (4) (references in this section to Part I of this Act to include, in relation to capital expenditure on the provision of machinery or plant incurred on or after 27 October 1970, references to FA 1971, Pt. III, Ch. I (ss. 40–50));
FA 1982, Sch. 12, para. 14 (application of sub-ss. (1)–(3) of this section for the purposes of capital allowances on expenditure incurred after 9 March 1982 and before 1 April 1987 for dwelling-houses let on assured tenancies);
FA 1986, Sch. 13, para. 2 (2) (references to specific provisions of this Act in sub-s. (4) above to include a reference to FA 1986, Sch. 13, Pts. II–IV (mineral extraction: new code of reliefs)).

78. Special provisions as to certain sales

(1) The provisions of Schedule 7 to this Act shall have effect in relation to sales of any property where either—

(a) the buyer is a body of persons over whom the seller has control, or the seller is a body of persons over whom the buyer has control, or both the seller and the buyer are bodies of persons and some other person has control over both of them [or the buyer and the seller are connected with each other within the meaning of section [839][3] of the principal Act][1], or
(b) it appears with respect to the sale, or with respect to transactions of which the sale is one, that the sole or main benefit which, apart from the provisions of the said Schedule, might have been expected to accrue to the parties or any of them was the obtaining of an allowance or deduction [, the obtaining of a greater allowance or deduction or the avoidance or reduction of a charge][1] under this Part or Part II of this Act.

(2) References in this section to a body of persons include references to a partnership.

(3) *This section and the said Schedule shall not apply in relation to section 60 of this Act.*[2]

Cross references.—See FA 1982, Sch. 12, para. 14 (application of this section for the purposes of capital allowances on expenditure incurred after 9 March 1982 and before 1 April 1987 for dwelling-houses let on assured tenancies);
Sch. 12, para. 5 (a) (reference in sub-s. (1) (b) of this section to "this Part" to include a reference to FA 1982, Sch. 12 (see preceding cross reference));
TA 1988, s. 532 (this section, with Sch. 7 to this Act, not applicable to dealings in know-how).
Amendments.—[1] Words in sub-s. (1) (a), (b) inserted by FA 1981, s. 76 (3), (5) where the sale occurs after 10 March 1981.
[2] Sub-s. (3) repealed by FA 1986, Sch. 23, Pt. VI, subject to the provisions of FA 1986, Sch. 14.
[3] Number in sub-s. (1) (a) substituted by TA 1988, Sch. 29, para. 32 Table.

79. Succession to trades, etc.

(1) Where a person succeeds to any trade, profession or vocation which until that time was carried on by another person and, by virtue [of section [113 or 337 (1)][3] of the principal Act (changes in persons carrying on a trade, and special rules for corporation tax)],[1] the trade, profession or vocation is to be treated as discontinued, any property which, immediately before the succession takes place, was in use for the purposes of the discontinued trade, profession or vocation and, without being sold, is immediately after the succession takes place, in use for the purposes of the new trade, profession or vocation, shall, for the purposes of this Part of this Act, be treated as if it had been sold to the successor when the succession takes place, and as if the net proceeds of the sale had been the price which that property would have fetched if sold in the open market:

Provided that no initial allowance shall be made by virtue of the provisions of this subsection.

(2) Where, after the setting up and before the permanent discontinuance of a trade, profession or vocation which at any time is carried on in partnership, anything is done for the purposes thereof, any allowance or charge which, if the trade, profession or vocation had at all times been carried on by one and the same person, would have fallen to be made to or on him under any of the provisions of this Part of this Act shall be made to or on the person or persons from time to time carrying on that trade, profession or vocation, and the amount of any such allowance or charge shall be computed as if that person or those persons had at all times been carrying on the trade, profession or vocation and as if everything done to or by his or their predecessors in the carrying on thereof had been done to or by him or them.

(3) This section shall, with the necessary adaptations, apply in relation to the occupation of woodlands the profits or gains of which are assessable under Schedule D as it applies in relation to a trade.

(4) Subsection (1) above shall not apply as respects a succession before the appointed day, and in that subsection the reference to [section [113][3] of the principal Act][1] includes a reference to section 145 of the Income Tax Act 1952.

In this subsection "the appointed day" means 6th April 1946, but subject to section 16 (2) . . .[2] of this Act.

(5) This section shall not apply to allowances and charges under Chapter II of this Part of this Act.

Note.—See **Prospective Legislation Notes** (Commercial Woodlands).
Amendments.—[1] Words in sub-ss. (1) and (4) substituted by TA 1970, Sch. 15, para. 5 (1), (12) and para. 11, Table, Pt. II, respectively.
[2] Words "and section 65 (1)" in sub-s. (4) above repealed by FA 1986, Sch. 23, Pt. VI, subject to the provisions of FA 1986, Sch. 14.
[3] Numbers in sub-ss. (1), (4) substituted by TA 1988, Sch. 29, para. 32 Table.

80. Nationalisation schemes

Amendments.—This section repealed by FA 1989, Sch. 17, Pt. VI.

81. Procedure on apportionments, etc.

(1) Where, under or by virtue of any provisions of this Part of this Act, any sum falls to be apportioned and, at the time of the apportionment, it appears that it is material as respects the liability to tax (for whatever period) of two or more persons, any question which arises as to the manner in which the sum is to be apportioned shall be determined, for the purposes of the tax of all those persons—

(a) in a case where the same body of General Commissioners have jurisdiction with respect to all those persons, by those Commissioners, unless all those persons agree that it shall be determined by the Special Commissioners,

(*b*) in a case where different bodies of Commissioners have jurisdiction with respect to those persons, by such of those bodies as the Board may direct, unless all those persons agree that it shall be determined by the Special Commissioners, and
(*c*) in any other case, by the Special Commissioners,

and any such Commissioners shall determine the question in like manner as if it were an appeal . . .[1]:

Provided that all the said persons shall be entitled to appear and be heard by the Commissioners who are to make the determination or to make representations to them in writing.

(2) This section applies in relation to any determination, under section 48 or section 79 of, or Schedule 7 to, this Act, of the price which property would have fetched if sold in the open market as it applies in relation to apportionments.

(3) This section shall come into force for all purposes on 6th April 1968, to the exclusion of section 329 of the Income Tax Act 1952 (which is re-enacted in this section).

Cross references.—See TMA 1970, s. 58 (3) (*b*) and FA 1988, s. 134 (4) (with effect from an appointed day, proceedings under this section to be in Northern Ireland if the place given by certain rules in relation to the parties to the proceedings is in Northern Ireland);
FA 1971, Sch. 8, para. 15 (4) (FA 1971, Pt. III, Ch. I (ss. 40–50) to be treated as included in the provisions referred to in sub-s. (2) of this section);
FA 1982, Sch. 12, para. 14 (application of this section for the purposes of capital allowances on expenditure incurred after 9 March 1982 and before 1 April 1987 for dwelling-houses let on assured tenancies).
Amendments.—[1] Words in sub-s. (1) repealed by TA 1970, Sch. 16.

82. Interpretation of certain references to expenditure, etc.

(1) References in this Part of this Act to capital expenditure and capital sums—

(*a*) in relation to the person incurring the expenditure or paying the sums, do not include any expenditure or sum which is allowed to be deducted in computing, for the purposes of tax, the profits or gains of a trade, profession, office, employment or vocation carried on or held by him, and
(*b*) in relation to the person receiving the amounts expended or the sums in question, do not include references to any amounts or sums which fall to be taken into account as receipts in computing the profits or gains of any trade, profession, office, employment or vocation carried on or held by him,

and do not include, in relation to any such person as aforesaid, any expenditure or sum in the case of which a deduction of tax falls or may fall to be made under [section [348 or 349 (1)][4] of the principal Act][1] (. . .[2] annual payments).

(2) . . .[2], Chapter II of this Part of this Act has effect subject to [section [577 (1) (*c*)][4] of the principal Act][1] (under which the use of an asset for providing business entertainment is not to be treated as use for the purposes of a trade).

(3) . . .[3]

Cross references.—See FA 1971, s. 50 (3) (sub-s. (1) of this section to apply for the purposes of FA 1971, Pt. III, Ch. I (ss. 40–50) as it applies for the purposes of Part I of this Act);
FA 1982, Sch. 12, para. 14 (application of sub-ss. (1), (3) of this section for the purposes of capital allowances on expenditure incurred after 9 March 1982 and before 1 April 1987 for dwelling-houses let on assured tenancies).
Amendments.—[1] Words in sub-ss. (1) and (2) substituted by TA 1970, Sch. 15, para. 11, Table, Pt. II; see also, as to sub-s. (1), TA 1970, s. 387 (3).
[2] Words in sub-ss. (1) and (2) repealed by TA 1970, Sch. 16.
[3] Sub-s. (3) repealed by FA 1985, s. 56 (6) (*a*) and Sch. 27, Pt. VI with respect to any chargeable period or its basis period ending after 17 December 1984.
[4] Numbers in sub-ss. (1), (2) substituted by TA 1988, Sch. 29, para. 32 Table.

83. Investment grants: exclusion of initial allowances

(1) No initial allowance under section 1, section 18 . . .[6] of this Act shall be made in respect of so much of any expenditure as is taken into account for the purposes of any investment grant made towards that expenditure, or be made by virtue of section 85 of this Act in respect of a proportionate part of any contribution towards that expenditure.

(2) If any such grant is made after the making of any such allowance, that allowance shall to that extent be withdrawn; and where the amount of any investment grant towards any expenditure is repaid in whole or in part by the grantee to the grantor, then to the extent to which it has been so repaid it shall be deemed never to have been made.

(3) All such assessments or adjustments of assessments to income tax or corporation tax shall be made as may be necessary in consequence of the last preceding subsection and, notwithstanding anything in any other provision, the time within which such an assessment or adjustment may be made shall not expire before the expiration of three years from the end of the chargeable period in which the investment grant, or, as the case may be, the repayment referred to in that subsection, was made.

(4) In this section "investment grant" means a grant towards capital expenditure incurred by a person carrying on a business, being—

(a) a grant made under the Industrial Development Act 1966 or the Agriculture Act 1967 or in pursuance of a scheme under an enactment amended by either of those Acts, or
(b) a grant made under an enactment of the Parliament of Northern Ireland or out of moneys provided by that Parliament which appears to the Treasury to be made towards expenditure and for a purpose corresponding respectively to expenditure towards which and a purpose for which a grant such as is mentioned in paragraph (a) above may be made, [or
(c) a grant made under section 32, 34 (1) or 56 (1), or a payment made under section 56 (2), of the Transport Act 1968,][1] [or][3]
[(d) a grant made under section [12 of the London Regional Transport Act 1984][5]][3] [or
(e) a grant made under section 29 of the Agriculture Act 1970][4]

and being . . .[2] a grant declared by the Treasury by order made by statutory instrument to be relevant for the purposes of the withholding or withdrawal of investment and initial allowances.

(5) So much of subsection (4) above as authorises the Treasury to make orders shall come into force for all purposes on 6th April 1968 to the exclusion of so much of section 35 (3) of the Finance Act 1966 as authorises the Treasury to make orders, and accordingly—

(a) any order made by the Treasury before that date under the said section 35 (3) shall be treated from that date as if it were an order under subsection (4) above, and
(b) the reference in the said section 35 (3) (as it applies in relation to chargeable periods ending before 6th April 1968) to an order made by the Treasury under that subsection shall include a reference to an order made by the Treasury under subsection (4) above.

Note.—Sub-s. (4) (c), in its application to Scotland only, should read as follows, with effect from 16 May 1975:
"(c) a grant made under section 32, 34 (1) or (2) or 56 (1), or a payment made under section 56 (2), of the Transport Act 1968, or"
See the Local Government (Scotland) Act 1973, s. 214 (2) and Sch. 27, Pt. II, para. 173.
Amendments.—[1] Sub-s. (4) (c) and the word "or" preceding it inserted by the Transport Act 1968, s. 161 (3), with effect from 18 November 1968; see the Transport Act 1968 (Commencement No. 1) Order 1968, Sch. 1, S. I. 1968 No. 1822.
[2] Words in sub-s. (4) repealed by the Transport Act 1968, with effect from 18 November 1968; see the Transport Act 1968 (Commencement No. 1) Order 1968, Sch. 1, S. I. 1968 No. 1822.
[3] Sub-s. (4) (d) and the word "or" preceding it inserted by the Transport (London) Act 1969, s. 3 (2).
[4] Sub-s. (4) (e) and the word "or" preceding it inserted by the Agriculture Act 1970, s. 30 (5).
[5] Words in sub-s. (4) (d) substituted by virtue of the London Regional Transport Act 1984, Sch. 6, para. 4 with effect from 29 June 1984 by virtue of the London Regional Transport (Appointed Day) Order 1984, S. I. 1984 No. 877.
[6] Words "or section 56" in sub-s. (1) above repealed by FA 1986, Sch. 23, Pt. VI, subject to the provisions of FA 1986, Sch. 14.

84. Subsidies, etc.

(1) Expenditure shall not be regarded for any of the purposes of this Part of this Act as having been incurred by any person in so far as it has been or is to be met directly or indirectly by the Crown or by any government or public or local authority, whether in the United Kingdom or elsewhere, or by any person other than the first-mentioned person [unless it is so met by a grant made [under the provisions of Part II of the Industrial Development Act 1982 or Part I][2] of the Industry Act 1972 or such grant made under an enactment of the Parliament of Northern Ireland as may be declared by the Treasury by order made by statutory instrument to correspond to a grant made under [those provisions]][2].
   A statutory instrument made under this section shall be subject to annulment in pursuance of a resolution of the Commons House of Parliament.][1]

(2) In considering, for the purposes of this section, how far any expenditure has been or is to be met directly or indirectly by the Crown or by any authority or person other than the person incurring the expenditure, there shall be left out of account—

(a) any insurance moneys or other compensation moneys payable in respect of any asset which has been demolished, destroyed or put out of use, and
(b) any expenditure met or to be met by any person other than the Crown or a government or public or local authority, being expenditure in respect of which, apart from the provisions of this paragraph, no allowance could be made under the provisions of the next following section [and not being expenditure which is allowed to be deducted in computing the profits or gains of a trade, profession or vocation carried on by that person].[3]

[(2A) In determining for the purposes of subsection (2) (b) above whether an allowance could be made under the provisions of section 85 below, it shall be assumed that the person by whom expenditure has been or is to be met is within the charge to tax, whether or not that is in fact the case.][4]

(3) This section shall not apply—

(a) in considering whether any, and if so what, writing-down allowance or balancing charge is to be made to or on a person under Chapter II in respect of any machinery or plant provided before the appointed day (as defined in Chapter II),
(b) in considering what deduction may be made under section 40 (2) of this Act in respect of expenditure on the replacement of machinery or plant provided before that day,
(c) for the purposes of Chapter IV.

Cross references.—See FA 1971, Sch. 8, para. 15 (5) (in sub-s. (1) of this section, the reference to Part I of this Act shall include a reference to FA 1971, Pt. III, Ch. I (ss. 40–50)): see also FA 1971, Sch. 8, para. 10 (3) (b);
FA 1982, s. 137 (2) (a), (7) (regional development grant paid in respect of expenditure incurred after 9 March 1982 in connection with oil exploration, extraction, etc.);
Sch. 12, para. 14 (application of this section for the purposes of capital allowances on expenditure incurred after 9 March 1982 and before 1 April 1987 for dwelling-houses let on assured tenancies);
TA 1988, s. 400 (write-off of government investment after 9 March 1981 not to be treated for the purposes of this section as an expenditure met by the Crown).
Amendments.—[1] Words at the end of sub-s. (1) added by FA 1972, s. 67 (3).
[2] Words in sub-s. (1) substituted by the Industrial Development Act 1982, Sch. 2, Pt. II, para. 4 (1) with effect from 28 January 1983.
[3] Words in sub-s. (2) (b) added by FA 1989, Sch. 13, para. 3 in relation to expenditure incurred after 26 July 1989 except in so far as a contribution to the expenditure was made before 26 July 1989.
[4] Sub-s. (2A) inserted by *ibid*.

85. Allowances in respect of contributions to capital expenditure

(1) Where a person, for the purposes of a trade carried on or to be carried on by him or by a tenant of land in which he has an interest, contributes a capital sum to expenditure on the provision of an asset, being expenditure which, apart from the provisions of the last preceding section, would have been regarded as wholly incurred by another person and in respect of which, apart from the last preceding section—

(a) an allowance would have been made under Chapter I, or
(b) an initial allowance or a writing-down allowance would have been made under Chapter II, or
(c) an allowance would have been made under any provision of Chapter III, . . .[3], or
(d) an allowance would have been made under Chapter V,

then, subject to the provisions of Schedule 9 to this Act and to the following provisions of this section, such initial and writing-down allowances, if any, shall be made to the contributor as would have been made to him if his contribution had been expenditure on the provisison, for the purposes of that trade, of a similar asset.

[(1A) Subsection (1) above shall not apply where the person making the contribution and the person receiving it are connected persons within the meaning of section [839][4] of the principal Act.][2]

(2) For the purpose of initial allowances given by virtue of subsection (1) above, section 18 (1) (b) of this Act, shall, subject to the provisions of Schedule 3 to this Act, apply as if the relevant asset belonged to the person making the contribution at any time when the machinery or plant belongs, or is treated under section 18 (7) of this Act as belonging, to the person for the time being carrying on the trade for the purposes of which the machinery or plant is provided.

[(2A) In relation to any contribution made after 5th April 1970 to expenditure incurred after that date by the Crown, or by any public or local authority in the United Kingdom, subsection (1) above shall have effect as if the words from "and in respect" to the end of paragraph (d) were omitted].[1]

(3) Where a sewerage authority in the United Kingdom incurs expenditure on the provision of an asset to be used in the treatment of trade effluents, then, in relation to any contribution of a capital sum made to that expenditure, this section shall apply as if such allowances fell to be made to the sewerage authority in respect of the expenditure as, apart from the last preceding section, would fall to be made if the asset were to be so used for the purposes of a trade carried on by the sewerage authority.

In this subsection—

"sewerage authority" means a public body having power under any enactment relating to the public health to construct and maintain sewers,
"trade effluents" means liquid or other matter discharged into public sewers from premises occupied for the purposes of a trade,

and this subsection shall apply only where [subsection (2A) above does not apply but][1] the contribution was made, and the expenditure in question was incurred, after 31st May 1963.

[(3A) References in this section, and in Schedule 9 to this Act, to a trade shall be construed as including references to a profession or vocation.][6]

(4) In subsection (1) of this section, and in Schedule 9 to this Act, "trade" includes the occupation of woodlands in the United Kingdom in respect of which the assessment and charge to tax falls to be made under Schedule D by virtue of [paragraph 5 of Schedule 6 to the Finance Act 1988][5].

(5) This section shall not apply to any contribution made before the appointed day.

In this subsection "the appointed day" means 6th April 1946, but subject to section 16 (2) and section 65 (1) of this Act.

Note.—See **Prospective Legislation Notes** (Commercial Woodlands).
Cross references.—See FA 1971, Sch 8, para. 15 (6) (sub-s. (1) of this section, with modification, applies to expenditure to which FA 1971, Pt. III, Ch. I (ss. 40–50) applies); see also FA 1971, Sch. 8, para. 11;
FA 1985, s. 59 (8) (allowances under this section not to be affected by allowances for machinery and plant which are fixtures);
FA 1986, s. 56 (6) (b) (any reference to Chapter V of this Part of this Act in this section to include a reference to FA 1986, Sch. 15 (allowances for capital expenditure on agricultural land and buildings incurred after 31 March 1986 other than expenditure under existing contracts as defined in s. 56 (2));
FA 1989, Sch. 13, para. 5 (the provisions in FA 1989, Sch. 13, para. 5 to apply where by virtue of this section allowances are made in respect of contributions made after 26 July 1989).
Amendments.—[1] Sub-s. (2A), and words in sub-s. (3), inserted by FA 1970, Sch. 4, para. 7.
[2] Sub-s. (1A) inserted by FA 1976, s. 42 in relation to contributions made after 8 July 1976.
[3] Words "other than section 60" in sub-s. (1) (c) above repealed by FA 1986, Sch. 23, Pt. VI, subject to the provisions of FA 1986, Sch. 14.
[4] Number in sub-s. (1A) substituted by TA 1988, Sch. 29, para. 32 Table.
[5] Words in sub-s. (4) substituted for the words "section 54 of the principal Act" (i.e. TA 1988, s. 54) by virtue of FA 1988, Sch. 6, para. 6 (1), (9). The subsection as amended applies from 15 March 1988.
[6] Sub-s. (3A) inserted by FA 1989, Sch. 13, para. 4 in relation to contributions made after 26 July 1989.

---

86. Meaning of "sale, insurance, salvage or compensation moneys"

(1) Subject to subsection (2) below, in this Part of this Act, except where the context otherwise requires, "sale, insurance, salvage or compensation moneys" means, in relation to an event which gives rise or might give rise to a balancing allowance or a balancing charge to or on any person, or is material in determining whether any, and if so what, writing-down allowance is to be made to a person under Chapter III of this Part of this Act—

(a) where the event is a sale of any property, the net proceeds to that person of the sale;
(b) where the event is the coming to an end of an interest in property on or by reason of the coming to an end of a foreign concession, any compensation payable to that person in respect of that property;
(c) where the event is the demolition or destruction of any property, the net amount received by him for the remains of the property, together with any insurance moneys received by him in respect of the demolition or destruction and any other compensation of any description received by him in respect thereof, in so far as that compensation consists of capital sums;
(d) as respects machinery or plant, where the event is the permanent loss thereof otherwise than in consequence of its demolition or destruction, any insurance moneys received by him in respect of the loss and any other compensation of any description received by him in respect thereof, in so far as that compensation consists of capital sums;
(e) where the event is that a building or structure ceases altogether to be used, any

compensation of any description received by him in respect of that event, in so far as that compensation consists of capital sums.

(2) So far as this section has effect for purposes other than those of Chapter II of this Part of this Act, subsection (1) above shall have effect as if—

(*a*) paragraph (*d*) were omitted, and
(*b*) paragraph (*e*) applied where machinery or plant is put out of use as it applies where a building or structure ceases altogether to be used.

Cross references.—See FA 1982, Sch. 12, para. 14 (application of this section for the purposes of capital allowances on expenditure incurred after 9 March 1982 and before 1 April 1987 for dwelling-houses let on assured tenancies).

87. Other provisions as to interpretation of Part I

(1) In this Part of this Act, except where the context otherwise requires—

"the Board" means the Commissioners of Inland Revenue;
"chargeable period" means an accounting period of a company or a year of assessment; and

(*a*) a reference to a "chargeable period or its basis period" is a reference to the chargeable period if it is an accounting period and to the basis period for it if it is a year of assessment,
(*b*) a reference to a "chargeable period related to" the incurring of expenditure, or a sale or other event, is a reference to the chargeable period in which, or to that in the basis period for which, the expenditure is incurred or the sale or other event takes place, and means the latter if, but only if, the chargeable period is a year of assessment; ...[1];

"control", in relation to a body corporate, means the power of a person to secure, by means of the holding of shares or the possession of voting power in or in relation to that or any other body corporate, or by virtue of any powers conferred by the articles of association or other document regulating that or any other body corporate, that the affairs of the first-mentioned body corporate are conducted in accordance with the wishes of that person, and, in relation to a partnership, means the right to a share of more than one-half of the assets, or of more than one-half of the income, of the partnership;
"foreign concession" means a right or privilege granted by the government of, or any municipality or other authority in, any territory outside the United Kingdom;
"income" includes any amount on which a charge to tax is authorised to be made under any of the provisions of this Part of this Act;
"lease" includes an agreement for a lease where the term to be covered by the lease has begun, and any tenancy, but does not include a mortgage, and "lessee", "lessor" and "leasehold interest" shall be construed accordingly;
"mineral deposits" includes any natural deposits capable of being lifted or extracted from the earth [and, for this purpose, geothermal energy, whether in the form of aquifers, hot dry rocks or otherwise, shall be treated as a natural deposit][2];
"scientific research allowance" means an allowance made under Part II of this Act, other than an allowance under section 90;
"tax", where neither corporation tax nor income tax is specified, means either of those taxes;
"writing-down allowance", where the reference is partly to years of assessment before the year 1966–67, includes an annual allowance in the sense which in the context that phrase had immediately before the commencement of the Finance Act 1965,

and for the purposes of this Part of this Act a source of income is "within the charge to" corporation tax or income tax if that tax is chargeable on the income arising from it, or would be so chargeable if there were any such income, and references to a person, or to income, being within the charge to tax shall be similarly construed.

(2) In this Part of this Act a reference to allowances or charges being made in taxing a trade is a reference to their being made in computing the trading income for corporation tax or in charging the profits or gains of the trade to income tax.

(3) Any reference in this Part of this Act to an allowance made or deduction allowed includes a reference to an allowance or deduction which would be made or allowed but for an insufficiency of profits or gains, or other income, against which to make it:

Provided that this subsection shall not apply to the references in section 40 (2) of this Act to writing-down allowances, exceptional depreciation allowances and scientific research allowances.

(4) Any reference in this Part of this Act to any building, structure, machinery, plant, works, asset, farmhouse, farm or forestry building, cottage or fence shall be construed as including a reference to a part of any building, structure, machinery, plant, works, asset, farmhouse, farm or forestry building, cottage or fence:

Provided that where the reference is expressed to be to the whole of a building or structure, this subsection shall not apply.

(5) The provisions of Chapter II of this Part of this Act, and the provisions of this Chapter so far as it applies for the purposes of the said Chapter II, shall apply in relation to a share in machinery or plant as they apply in relation to a part of machinery or plant, and for the purposes of the said provisions a share in machinery or plant shall be deemed to be used for the purposes of a trade, profession or vocation so long as, and only so long as, the machinery or plant is used for the purposes thereof.

This subsection shall, with any necessary adaptations, apply in relation to the occupation of woodlands where the profits or gains thereof are assessable under Schedule D as they apply in relation to trades.

(6) Any reference in this Part of this Act to the time of any sale shall be construed as a reference to the time of completion or the time when possession is given, whichever is the earlier.

(7) Any reference in this Part of this Act to the setting up or permanent discontinuance of a trade includes, except where the contrary is expressly provided, a reference to the occurring of any event which, under any of the provisions of the Income Tax Acts or the Corporation Tax Acts, is to be treated as equivalent to the setting up or permanent discontinuance of a trade:

Provided that the reference above to the Corporation Tax Acts shall not include a reference to paragraph 7 of Schedule 16 to the Finance Act 1965 (overseas trade corporations).

(8) In the application of this Part of this Act in relation to assets which have been used for the purposes of a trade carried on by a company which, at any time when the assets were so used, was for the purposes of Part IV of the Finance Act 1957 an Overseas Trade Corporation, there shall be deducted from expenditure to which this Part of this Act applies all such amounts as would have been deducted if, throughout the period when the company was an Overseas Trade Corporation, the said Part IV had not had effect and allowances and balancing charges had been made accordingly:

Provided that, where there was an interval between the end of the last basis period related to a year of assessment falling before the date when the company ceased to be an Overseas Trade Corporation and that date, the interval shall be deemed for the purposes of this subsection to have been part of that basis period.

(9) In connection with the transition for companies from income tax to corporation tax effected by the Finance Act 1965 the provisions of this Act and any other provisions of the Income Tax Acts relevant thereto shall have effect with such modifications as are necessary to preserve the continuity of the system of allowances and charges under this Part of this Act, and so that in particular references to a previous chargeable period or to a subsequent chargeable period, or to a time before, or a time after, a chargeable period, shall have effect in relation to a company as if the year 1965-66 or any earlier year of assessment preceded that company's first accounting period for corporation tax.

This subsection shall not be taken to require any time to be counted twice in reckoning duration.

Note.—See **Prospective Legislation Notes** (Prospective Amendments and Commercial Woodlands).
Cross references.—See FA 1982, Sch. 12, para. 14 (application of sub-ss. (1), (3), (6) of this section for the purposes of capital allowances on expenditure incurred after 9 March 1982 and before 1 April 1987 for dwelling-houses let on assured tenancies);
FA 1986, Sch 13, para. 2 (4) (extension of the application of sub-s. (4) above to a share in an asset used for the purposes of a trade).
TA 1988, s. 768 (6), (7) (change in ownership of company: disallowance of trading losses as respects sub-s. (3));
Amendments.—[1] Words in sub-s. (1) repealed by TA 1970, Sch. 16.
[2] Words in the definition of "mineral deposits" in sub-s. (1) added by FA 1986, Sch. 13, para. 2 (3).

88. Application of Part I to Scotland

In the application of this Part of this Act to Scotland, "leasehold interest" means the interest of a tenant in property subject to a lease; and any reference to an interest which is reversionary on a leasehold interest or on a lease shall be construed as a reference to the interest of the landlord in the property subject to the leasehold interest of lease.

89. Transitory provisions: mills, factories and exceptional depreciation allowances

(1) In this Part of this Act, "exceptional depreciation allowance" means an allowance made under section 19 of the Finance Act 1941 and "mills, factories or exceptional depreciation allowances" means any allowance made under section 15 of the Finance Act 1937 or any exceptional depreciation allowances.

(2) Any reference in this Part of this Act to the relevant exceptional depreciation allowances shall be construed, in relation to any building, machinery or plant, as a reference to an exceptional depreciation allowance in respect of that building, machinery or plant, or to so much of any exceptional depreciation allowance granted in respect of any building, machinery or plant of which it forms part as is properly attributable to it.

(3) Any reference in this Part of this Act to the relevant mills, factories or exceptional depreciation allowances shall be construed, in relation to any building or structure, as a reference to any allowances granted under section 15 of the Finance Act 1937 in respect of it or premises of which it forms part, and any relevant exceptional depreciation allowances:

Provided that where an allowance under the said section 15 was in respect of premises which include several buildings or structures, the whole amount of the allowance under the said section 15 shall be apportioned between all the buildings or structures, and only that part of the allowance which is apportioned to the building or structure in question shall be taken into account.

(4) Any reference in this Part of this Act to the allowance made under said section 15 for any year of assessment shall be construed as a reference to an amount which, under the said section 15, was to be allowed as a deduction in computing profits or gains for that year of assessment.

PART II
SCIENTIFIC RESEARCH

Cross references.—See FA 1971, s. 44 (6) (*b*) (i) (capital allowances under this Part of this Act for expenditure on the acquisition of machinery or plant);
Sch. 8, para. 16 (2) (any reference in this Part to Part I, Chapter II, of this Act shall include a reference to FA 1971, Pt. III, Ch. I (ss. 40–50));
FA 1985, s. 56 (1) (*a*), (7) (for the purposes of this Part of this Act, FA 1985, s. 56 (2)–(5) to have effect to determine when capital expenditure is to be taken to be incurred with respect to any chargeable period ending after 31 March 1985);
s. 56 (8) (new rules as regards the determination of the date when capital expenditure is to be taken to be incurred with respect to any chargeable period or its basis period ending after 17 December 1984, subject to the provision that if under any provision of this Act the date would fall to be later than that determined under the new rules, the later date is to be treated as the date of the expenditure);
TA 1988, s. 495 (effect of regional development grant paid in respect of expenditure incurred in connection with oil exploration, extraction, etc.);
FA 1989, Sch. 13, para. 28 (1), (4) (*d*) (exclusion of double allowances: where an allowance is made under this Part of this Act, no allowance to be made under other legislation).

90. Allowances for expenditure on scientific research not of a capital nature, and on payments to research associations, universities, etc.

Notwithstanding anything in [section [74]² of the principal Act]¹ (general rules as to deductions not allowable in computing the profits or gains of a trade), where a person carrying on a trade—

(*a*) incurs expenditure not of a capital nature on scientific research related to that trade and directly undertaken by him or on his behalf, or

(*b*) pays any sum to any scientific research association for the time being approved for the purposes of this section by the Secretary of State or the Minister of Technology, being an association which has as its object the undertaking of scientific research related to the class of trade to which the trade he is carrying on belongs, or

(*c*) pays any sum to be used for such scientific research as is mentioned in paragraph (*b*) above to any such university, college research institute or other similar institution as is for the time being approved for the purposes of this section by the Secretary of State or the Minister of Technology,

the expenditure incurred or sum paid, as the case may be, may be deducted as an expense in computing the profits or gains of the trade for the purposes of tax.

Amendments.—¹ Words substituted by TA 1970, Sch. 15, para. 11, Table, Pt. II.
² Number substituted by TA 1988, Sch. 29, para. 32 Table.

91. Allowances for capital expenditure on scientific research

(1) Subject to the provisions of this and the next following section, where a person—

(*a*) while carrying on a trade, incurs expenditure of a capital nature on scientific research related to that trade and directly undertaken by him or on his behalf, or

(*b*) incurs expenditure of a capital nature on scientific research directly undertaken by him or on his behalf, and thereafter sets up and commences a trade connected with that research,

a deduction equal to the whole of the expenditure shall be allowed in taxing the trade for the relevant chargeable period as defined in the following provisions of this section.

[(1A) No allowance shall be made under subsection (1) above in respect of expenditure on the acquisition of, or of rights in or over, any land except in so far as, on a just apportionment, that expenditure is referable to the acquisition of, or of rights in or over, or of machinery or plant which forms part of, a building or other structure already constructed on that land.]²

[(1B) For the purposes of this section, expenditure on the provision of a dwelling is not scientific research expenditure; but where part of a building is used for scientific research and part consists of a dwelling and the capital expenditure which it is just to apportion to the construction or acquisition of the dwelling is not more than one quarter of the capital expenditure which is referable to the construction or acquisition of the whole building, the whole of the building shall be treated for the purposes of this Part of this Act as used for scientific research.]²

[(1C) Subject to subsections (1A) and (1B) above, where a person incurs capital expenditure which is partly within subsection (1) above and partly not, such apportionment of the expenditure shall be made for the purposes of this Part of this Act as may be just.][4]

(2) For corporation tax purposes the relevant chargeable period shall be the accounting period in which the expenditure was incurred or, if it was incurred before the setting up and commencement of the trade, the accounting period beginning with that setting up and commencement.

(3) For income tax purposes the relevant chargeable period shall be—

(a) in the case of expenditure incurred before the end of the year of assessment in which the trade was set up and commenced, that year of assessment,
(b) in the case of expenditure incurred after the end of that year of assessment but not later than twelve months from the setting up and commencement of the trade, the year of assessment next following that in which the trade was set up and commenced,
(c) in the case of expenditure incurred after twelve months from the setting up and commencement of the trade and during the basis year for any year of assessment, but subject to subsection (4) below, that year of assessment,
(d) in the case of expenditure incurred during the year of assessment in which the trade is permanently discontinued, that year of assessment.

In paragraph (c) above "basis year" means, in relation to a year of assessment, the period the profits or gains of which are, under [section [60][3] of the principal Act][1], to be taken to be the profits or gains of the year preceding that year of assessment.

(4) For the purposes of the said paragraph (c)—

(a) where two basis years overlap, any expenditure incurred in the period common to both shall be deemed to have been incurred in the first basis year only,
(b) where there is an interval between the end of the basis year for one year of assessment and the beginning of the basis year for the next year of assessment, any expenditure incurred during the interval shall be deemed to have been incurred in the second basis year, and
(c) any expenditure which is incurred before the end of, but after the end of the basis year for, the last complete year of assessment before the permanent discontinuance of the trade shall be deemed to have been incurred in that basis year,

and, in paragraph (a) of this subsection, the reference to the overlapping of two basis years includes a reference to the coincidence of two basis years, or to the inclusion of one basis year in another, and the reference to the period common to both of two basis years shall be construed accordingly.

(5) This section shall not apply to expenditure incurred before 6th November 1962, but deductions in respect of such expenditure shall be allowed instead in accordance with the transitory provisions contained in Schedule 10 to this Act.

Note.—Sch. 10 referred to in sub-s. (5) above is not reproduced in this edition. It is printed in the 1985–86 edition of this book.
Cross references.—See TA 1988, Sch. 30, para. 7 (1) (c) (transitional provisions with respect to claims for group relief in respect of any amount attributable to allowances under this section in respect of expenditure incurred under a contract entered into by the surrendering company before 6 March 1973);
FA 1988, s. 63 (1), (2) (b), (6) (a) (disposal of oil licences relating to undeveloped areas; treatment of oil drilling expenditure, whenever incurred, for the purpose of allowances under this section and for chargeable gains).
Amendments.—[1] Words in sub-s. (3) substituted by TA 1970, Sch. 15, para. 11, Table, Pt. II.
[2] Sub-ss. (1A), (1B) inserted by FA 1985, s. 63 (1), (7) with respect to capital expenditure incurred after 31 March 1985 unless that expenditure is incurred before 1st April 1987, and consists of the payment of sums under a contract entered into on or before 19th March 1985 by the person incurring the expenditure.
[3] Number in sub-s. (3) substituted by TA 1988, Sch. 29, para. 32 Table.
[4] Sub-s. (1C) inserted by FA 1989, Sch. 13, para. 7 in relation to expenditure incurred after 26 July 1989.

92. Termination of user of assets provided for scientific research

(1) Subject to subsection (6) below, the two next following subsections shall have effect where an asset representing [allowable][1] scientific research expenditure of a capital nature incurred by the person carrying on a trade ceases to [belong to him; and the occasion of that asset ceasing to belong to him is in the following provisions of this section referred to as "the relevant event".][2]

(2) If [the relevant event][2] occurs in or after the chargeable period for which an allowance in respect of the expenditure is made under the last preceding section, then, subject to subsection (5) below—

(a) the sum by which the aggregate of the [disposal value of the asset][2] and the amount of the allowance exceeds the amount of the expenditure, or

(b) the amount of the allowance if it is less than that sum,

shall be treated as a trading receipt of the trade accruing at the time of [the relevant event][2] or, if [the relevant event][2] occurs on or after the date on which the trade is permanently discontinued, accruing immediately before the discontinuance.

(3) If [the relevant event][2] occurs before the chargeable period for which an allowance in respect of the expenditure would fall to be so made, that allowance shall not be made, but, subject to subsection (5) below, if the [disposal value of the asset is][2] less than the expenditure a deduction equal to the difference shall be allowed in taxing the trade for the chargeable period in which [the relevant event][2] occurs.

[(3A) For the purposes of this section the disposal value of an asset depends upon the nature of the relevant event, and—

(a) if that event is the actual sale of the asset at a price not lower than that which it would have fetched if sold in the open market, equals the proceeds of that sale;

(b) if that event is the deemed sale of the asset under subsection (4) below, equals the deemed proceeds of sale under that subsection; and

(c) in any other event, equals the price which the asset would have fetched if sold in the open market.][3]

(4) Where an asset is destroyed, it shall for the purposes of this section be treated as if it had been sold immediately before its destruction, and any insurance moneys or other compensation of any description received by the person carrying on the trade in respect of the destruction, and any moneys received by him for the remains of the asset, shall be treated as if they were proceeds of that sale; and, where this subsection has effect on the demolition of an asset—

(a) the cost of the demolition to the person carrying on the trade shall, for the purposes of subsections (2) and (3) above, be added to the expenditure represented by the asset, and

(b) if the case falls within the first of those subsections but, by reason of that addition, the aggregate there referred to is less than the amount of the expenditure represented by the asset, then, [unless, prior to its demolition, the asset had begun to be used for purposes other than][2] scientific research related to the trade, and subject to subsection (5) below, a deduction equal to the difference shall be allowed in taxing the trade for the chargeable period in which the asset is treated as having been sold or, if it is treated as having been sold on or after the date on which the trade is permanently discontinued, for the last chargeable period in which the trade was carried on before the discontinuance.

(5) No amount shall be . . .[4] charged by virtue of this section in respect of any [relevant event if that event][2] gives rise to a . . .[5] balancing charge under Chapter I or Chapter II of Part I of this Act.

(6) This section shall not apply as respects assets representing expenditure incurred before 6th November 1962, but the transitory provisions contained in Schedule 10 to this Act shall have effect instead.

Cross references.—See FA 1988, s. 63 (1), (2) (c), (6) (b) (disposal of oil licences relating to undeveloped areas; no deduction allowed under sub-s. (3) above for certain oil drilling expenditure);

FA 1989, Sch. 13, para. 8 (this section as amended by FA 1985, s. 63 to have effect where the termination of user occurs after 31 March 1989 as well as where it occurs before 1 April 1989 in the cases provided for by FA 1985, s. 63 (7).

Amendments.—[1] Word in sub-s. (1) inserted by FA 1985, s. 63 (2), (7) with respect to capital expenditure incurred after 31 March 1985 unless that expenditure is incurred before 1st April 1987, and consists of the payment of sums under a contract entered into on or before 19th March 1985 by the person incurring the expenditure. But see FA 1989, Sch. 13, para. 8 which extends the period of application of this section as amended by FA 1985, s. 63.

[2] Words in sub-ss. (1), (2), (3), (4) (b), (5) substituted by FA 1985, s. 63 (2), (3), (5)–(7) with respect to capital expenditure incurred after 31 March 1985 unless that expenditure is incurred before 1st April 1987, and consists of the payment of sums under a contract entered into on or before 19th March 1985 by the person incurring the expenditure. But see FA 1989, Sch. 13, para. 8 which extends the period of application of this section as amended by FA 1985, s. 63.

[3] Sub-s. (3A) inserted by FA 1985, s. 63 (4), (7) with respect to capital expenditure incurred after 31 March 1985 unless that expenditure is incurred before 1st April 1987, and consists of the payment of sums under a contract entered into on or before 19th March 1985 by the person incurring the expenditure. But see FA 1989, Sch. 13, para. 8 which extends the period of application of this section as amended by FA 1985, s. 63.

This section as originally enacted read—

"(1) Subject to subsection (6) below, the two next following subsections shall have effect where an asset representing scientific research expenditure of a capital nature incurred by the person carrying on a trade ceases to be used by that person for scientific research related to that trade and is then or thereafter sold by him.

(2) If the sale occurs in or after the chargeable period for which an allowance in respect of the expenditure is made under the last preceding section, then, subject to subsection (5) below—

(a) the sum by which the aggregate of the proceeds of sale and the amount of the allowance exceeds the amount of the expenditure, or

(b) the amount of the allowance if it is less than that sum,

shall be treated as a trading receipt of the trade accruing at the time of the sale or, if the sale occurs on or after the date on which the trade is permanently discontinued, accruing immediately before the discontinuance.
(3) If the sale occurs before the chargeable period for which an allowance in respect of the expenditure would fall to be so made, that allowance shall not be made, but, subject to subsection (5) below, if the proceeds of sale are less than the expenditure a deduction equal to the difference shall be allowed in taxing the trade for the chargeable period in which the sale occurs.
(4) Where an asset is destroyed, it shall for the purposes of this section be treated as if it had been sold immediately before its destruction, and any insurance moneys or other compensation of any description received by the person carrying on the trade in respect of the destruction, and any moneys received by him for the remains of the asset, shall be treated as if they were proceeds of that sale; and, where this subsection has effect on the demolition of an asset—
    (*a*) the cost of the demolition to the person carrying on the trade shall, for the purposes of subsections (2) and (3) above, be added to the expenditure represented by the asset, and
    (*b*) if the case falls within the first of those subsections but, by reason of that addition, the aggregate there referred to is less than the amount of the expenditure represented by the asset, then, unless the asset was used for other purposes after it ceased to be used for scientific research related to the trade, and subject to subsection (5) below, a deduction equal to the difference shall be allowed in taxing the trade for the chargeable period in which the asset is treated as having been sold or, if it is treated as having been sold on or after the date on which the trade is permanently discontinued, for the last chargeable period in which the trade was carried on before the discontinuance.
(5) No amount shall be allowed or charged by virtue of this section in respect of any sale if the sale gives rise to a balancing allowance or balancing charge under Chapter I or Chapter II of Part I of this Act.
(6) This section shall not apply as respects assets representing expenditure incurred before 6th November 1962, but the transitory provisions contained in Schedule 10 to this Act shall have effect instead."
[4] Words "allowed or" in sub-s. (5) repealed by FA 1989, Sch. 13, para. 28 (5), (6) and Sch. 17, Pt. VI in relation to any chargeable period or its basis period ending after 26 July 1989.
[5] Words "balancing allowance or" in sub-s. (5) repealed by *ibid.*

93. Prevention of double allowances

(1)–(2) . . .[1]

(3) The cost to a person of the demolition of any property shall not, if section 92 (4) (*a*) above or paragraph 2 (4) of Schedule 10 to this Act applies to it, be treated for the purposes of this Act as expenditure incurred in respect of any other property by which that property is replaced.

Amendments.—[1] Sub-ss. (1), (2) which are superseded by some provisions in FA 1989, Sch. 13, para. 28 (1)–(4) repealed by FA 1989, Sch. 13, para. 28 (5) (*a*) and Sch. 17, Pt. VI in relation to any chargeable period or its basis period ending after 26 July 1989. They read—

"(1) No initial allowances under Chapter I or Chapter II of Part I of this Act shall be made in respect of expenditure on the provision of an asset if that expenditure is expenditure in respect of which a deduction may be allowed under section 91 above or the corresponding provisions of Schedule 10 to this Act and no allowance under Schedule 13 to the Finance Act 1986 shall be made in respect of any expenditure if it is expenditure in respect of which such a deduction may be allowed.
(2) Where a deduction is allowed for any chargeable period under section 91 or 92 above, or the corresponding provisions of Schedule 10 to this Act, in respect of expenditure represented wholly or partly by any assets, there shall not be made or allowed—
    (*a*) any writing-down allowance under Chapter I of Part I of this Act, or
    (*b*) except under this Part of this Act, any allowance or deduction in respect of wear and tear, obsolescence or depreciation of those assets,
for any chargeable period during any part of which they are used by the person carrying on a trade for scientific research related to that trade."

94. Interpretation of Part II

(1) In this Part of this Act—

    "scientific research" means any activities in the fields of natural or applied science for the extension of knowledge;
    "scientific research expenditure" means expenditure incurred on scientific research;
    references to expenditure incurred on scientific research do not include any expenditure incurred in the acquisition of rights in, or arising out of, scientific research, but, subject to that, include all expenditure incurred for the prosecution of, or the provision of facilities for the prosecution of, scientific research;
references to scientific research related to a trade or a class of trades include—

    (*a*) any scientific research which may lead to or facilitate an extension of that trade or, as the case may be, of trades of that class;
    (*b*) any scientific research of a medical nature which has a special relation to the welfare of workers employed in that trade or, as the case may be, trades of that class;

    "asset" includes part of an asset.

(2) In this Part of this Act, unless the context otherwise requires—

"the Board" means the Commissioners of Inland Revenue;
"chargeable period" means an accounting period of a company or a year of assessment; ...[1]
"tax", where neither corporation tax nor income tax is specified, means either of those taxes;
"writing-down allowance", where the reference is partly to years of assessment before the year 1966–67, includes an annual allowance in the sense which in the context that phrase had immediately before the commencement of the Finance Act 1965.

(3) In this Part of this Act a reference to allowances being made in taxing a trade is a reference to their being made in computing the trading income for corporation tax or in charging the profits or gains of the trade to income tax.

(4) References in this Part of this Act to the setting up and commencement of a trade and to the permanent discontinuance of a trade include references to the occurring of any event which, under any of the provisions of the Income Tax Acts or the Corporation Tax Acts, is to be treated as equivalent to the setting up and commencement of a trade or, as the case may be, to the permanent discontinuance thereof:

Provided that the reference above to the Corporation Tax Acts shall not include a reference to paragraph 7 of Schedule 16 to the Finance Act 1965 (overseas trade corporations).

[(4A) Any reference in this Part of this Act to the time when an asset ceases to belong to a person shall, in the case of a sale, be construed as a reference to the time of completion or the time when possession is given, whichever is the earlier.][3]

(5) ...[2]

Amendments.—[1] Words in sub-s. (2) repealed by TA 1970, Sch. 16.
[2] Sub-s. (5) repealed by FA 1985, Sch. 27, Pt. VI with respect to capital expenditure incurred after 31 March 1985 unless that expenditure is incurred before 1 April 1987 and consists of the payment of sums made under a contract entered into before 20 March 1985 by the person incurring the expenditure.
[3] Sub-s. (4A) inserted by FA 1989, Sch. 13, para. 9 with effect in any case where sale is effected or contract for sale is entered into after 26 July 1989.

95. Supplemental

(1) Deductions allowable in taxing a trade under the provisions of this Part of this Act as they apply for the purposes of income tax shall be given effect in accordance with subsections (2) and (4) of section 70 of this Act, and deductions so allowable under those provisions as they apply for the purposes of corporation tax shall be given effect in accordance with section 73 of this Act.

(2) Section 77 of this Act shall have effect in relation to section 92 above and the corresponding provisions of Schedule 10 to this Act as if that section and those provisions were contained in Part I of this Act.

(3) Sections 91 and 92 above, and the corresponding provision of Schedule 10 to this Act, shall have effect subject to the provisions of section 78 of, and Schedule 7 to, this Act.

(4) In section 80 of this Act references to sections 70, 73 and 78 of this Act, and to Schedule 7 to this Act, are references to those provisions as extended by this section, and this Part of this Act has effect subject to Schedule 8 to this Act.

(5) Subsections (8) and (9) of section 87 of this Act shall apply for the purposes of this Part of this Act as they apply for the purposes of Part I of this Act, but as if, in the proviso to the said subsection (8), references to a basis period were references to a basis year.

(6) For the purposes of this Part of this Act, expenditure shall not be regarded as incurred by a person in so far as it is, or is to be, met directly or indirectly by the Crown or by any government or public or local authority, whether in the United Kingdom or elsewhere, or by any person other than the first-mentioned person [unless it is so met by a grant made [under the provisions of Part II of the Industrial Development Act 1982 or Part I][2] of the Industry Act 1972 or such grant made under an enactment of the Parliament of Northern Ireland as may be declared by the Treasury by order made by statutory instrument to correspond to a grant made under [those provisions][2].

A statutory instrument made under this section shall be subject to annulment in pursuance of a resolution of the Commons House of Parliament.][1]

(7) The same expenditure shall not be taken into account for any of the purposes of this Part of this Act in relation to more than one trade.

(8) If any question arises under this Part of this Act as to whether, and if so to what extent, any activities constitute or constituted, or any asset is or was being used for, scientific research, the Board shall refer the question for decision to the Secretary of State or the Minister of Technology, as may be appropriate in relation to the activities in question, and his decision shall be final.

Cross references.—See FA 1982, s. 137 (2) (*b*), (7) (regional development grant paid in respect of expenditure incurred after 9 March 1982 in connection with oil exploration, extraction, etc.).
Amendments.—[1] Words at the end of sub-s. (6) added by FA 1972, s. 67 (3).
[2] Words in sub-s. (6) substituted by the Industrial Development Act 1982, Sch. 2, Pt. II, para. 4 (1) with effect from 28 January 1983.

PART III
GENERAL

Cross references.—See FA 1971, Sch. 8, para. 16 (2) (any reference in this Part to Part I, Chapter II, of this Act shall include a reference to FA 1971, Pt. III, Ch. I (ss. 40–50)).

96. Commencement and repeals

(1) Except as otherwise provided by Part I of this Act, Parts I and II of this Act shall come into force and have effect as respects allowances and charges falling to be made for chargeable periods ending after 5th April 1968.

(2) The provisions of this Act applied by subsection (1) above include those under which effect may be given to allowances falling to be made for a chargeable period by setting any part of them against the profits of gains of some other chargeable period, and subsection (1) above shall apply to allowances falling to be made for the chargeable periods there mentioned notwithstanding that, under any such provision of this Act, or under any other provision of the Income Tax Acts or the Corporation Tax Acts, effect is to be given to those allowances by setting any part of them off against the profits or gains of a chargeable period ending before 6th April 1968.

(3) The enactments mentioned in Schedule 11 to this Act shall be repealed to the extent specified in the third column of that Schedule, and the provisions of this Act brought into force by subsection (1) above shall have effect to the exclusion of the corresponding provisions so repealed, and those repeals shall take effect accordingly.

(4) The said repeals shall not affect any enactment so far as it authorises effect to be given to an allowance falling to be made for a chargeable period ending before 6th April 1968 by setting any part of it against profits or gains of a chargeable period ending after 5th April 1968, and subsection (1) above shall not be read as referring to any such allowance.

97. Continuity

(1) The continuity of the operation of the Income Tax Acts and the Corporation Tax Acts shall not be affected by the substitution of this Act for the repealed enactments.

(2) Any reference, whether express or implied, in this Act to, or to things done or falling to be done under or for the purposes of, any provision of this Act shall, if and so far as the nature of the reference permits, be construed as including, in relation to the times, years or periods, circumstances or purposes in relation to which the corresponding provision in the repealed enactments has or had effect, a reference to, or as the case may be to things done or falling to be done under or for the purposes of, that corresponding provision.

(3) The repeals made by this Part of this Act shall not affect any instrument made or other thing done under the repealed enactments and, so far as any such instrument or other thing could have affected the allowances, deductions and charges as respects which this Act has effect if this Act had not passed, this Act shall have effect as if the instrument or other thing had been made or done under the corresponding provisions of this Act.

(4) Subsection (3) above applies in particular to any election, to any appointment, to any claim for an allowance, and to any proceedings on any such claim.

(5) Without prejudice to the said subsection (3), the repeals made by this Part of this Act in Schedule 2 to the Science and Technology Act 1965 shall not affect that Schedule so far as it provides for approvals given under section 335 (*b*) or (*c*) of the Income Tax Act 1952 before its coming into force as respects that section to be treated as given by the Secretary of State or the Minister of Technology.

(6) In this and the next following section "the repealed enactments" means the enactments repealed by Schedule 11 to this Act, and such of the enactments repealed by the Income Tax Act 1952 as correspond to the provisions of that Act so repealed.

98. Construction of existing Acts and documents

(1) Any reference, whether express or implied, in any enactment, instrument or document passed or made before or in the same Session as this Act to, or to things done or falling to be done under or for the purposes of, any of the repealed enactments shall, if and so far as the

nature of the reference permits, be construed as including, in relation to the times, years or periods, circumstances or purposes in relation to which the corresponding provision of this Act has effect, a reference to, or as the case may be to things done or deemed to be done or falling to be done under or for the purposes of, that corresponding provision.

(2) ...[1]

(3) The provisions of this Part of this Act are without prejudice to the provisions of the Interpretation Act 1889 as respects the effect of repeals.

Amendments.—[1] Sub-s. (2) repealed by TA 1970, Sch. 16.

99. Construction of future enactments

(1) Except as otherwise expressly provided or where the context otherwise requires, section 97 of this Act shall apply for the purpose of construing any provision contained in an Act passed after this Act, or in an instrument made after the passing of this Act under any Act, past or future [(including any amendment made by any such provision in any enactment or instrument passed or made before the passing of this Act)][1], which refers to a provision of this Act, as it applies for the purposes of construing this Act.

(2) This subsection has effect in applying for corporation tax any Act passed after this Act.

For the purposes of corporation tax, the right to an allowance or liability to a charge under this Act for an accounting period, and the rate or amount of any such allowance or charge, shall be determined by applying the law in force for the year of assessment in which the accounting period ends.

Amendments.—[1] Words in sub-s. (1) inserted by TA 1970, Sch. 15, para. 12 (2).

100. Short title and construction

(1) This Act may be cited as the Capital Allowances Act 1968.

(2) Except in so far as this Act otherwise provides, its provisions shall apply equally for purposes of income tax and for purposes of corporation tax; and [section [9(5)]][3] of the principal Act][1] (which relates to the construction of income tax provisions applying both to income tax and corporation tax) shall apply to this Act as it applies to any such provisions of the Income Tax Acts.

(3) This Act, so far as it relates to income tax, shall be construed as one with the Income Tax Acts and, so far as it relates to corporation tax, shall be construed as one with the Corporation Tax Acts.

(4) Any reference in this Act to any other enactment shall, except so far as the context otherwise requires, be construed as a reference to that enactment as amended or applied by or under any other enactment including this Act.

[(5) In this Act "the principal Act" means the Income and Corporation Taxes Act [1988][3].][2]

Amendments.—[1] Words in sub-s. (2) substituted by TA 1970, Sch. 15, para. 11, Table, Pt. II.
[2] Sub-s. (5) added by TA 1970, Sch. 15, para. 5 (1), (13).
[3] Section number in sub-s. (2) and year in sub-s. (5) substituted by TA 1988, Sch. 29, para. 32 Table.

SCHEDULES

SCHEDULE 1

Sections 1 (2), 18 (2), 56 (2) and 67 (1)

INITIAL ALLOWANCES: TRANSITORY

1.—(1) This paragraph has effect as regards the relationship between initial allowances and investment allowances (that is the investment allowances under the provisions repealed by section 35 of the Finance Act 1966 except as regards expenditure incurred before 17th January 1966 and certain expenditure under contracts before that date).

(2) If any such investment allowance falls to be made in respect of any expenditure, this Act shall apply to that expenditure with the following modifications—

(*a*) in section 1 (2), for the words "three-twentieths" there shall be substituted the words "one-twentieth",
(*b*) in section 18 (2), for the words "three-tenths" there shall be substituted the words "one-tenth",
(*c*) in section 56 (2), for the words "two-fifths" there shall be substituted the words "one-fifth",
(*d*) in section 67 (1) (*a*), for the words "three-twentieths" there shall be substituted the words "one-twentieth".

(3) Where an investment allowance in respect of any expenditure is withheld or withdrawn under paragraph 1 of Schedule 2 to the Finance Act 1954 then—

(*a*) if it is withheld or withdrawn by reason of a sale or transfer such initial allowance (if any) as might have been made in addition to the investment allowance if it had not been withheld or withdrawn shall be made, or
(*b*) if it is withheld or withdrawn otherwise than by reason of a sale or transfer such initial allowance (if any) as might have been made in respect of the said expenditure but for sub-paragraph (2) above shall be made.

(4) In the case of an initial allowance under section 67 (1) (*a*) of this Act, sub-paragraph (3) above shall not apply, but if an investment allowance in respect of any expenditure is withheld or withdrawn otherwise than by reason of a sale of the trade deemed for the purposes of the said section 67 to constitute the permanent discontinuance thereof such initial allowance as might have been made in respect of the said expenditure but for sub-paragraph (2) above shall be made.

(5) Subject to sub-paragraphs (3) and (4) above, where an investment allowance falls to be made in addition to an initial allowance, no greater initial allowance shall be made by reason that the investment allowance is for any reason not made.

Machinery and plant

2.—(1) Where an investment allowance is made or falls to be made in respect of expenditure on machinery or plant, and the machinery or plant is sold by the person incurring the expenditure or an associate of his, then if either—

(*a*) the buyer is an associate of the person incurring the expenditure, or
(*b*) it appears with respect to the sale either—
   (i) that it is one in contemplation of which the expenditure was incurred, or
   (ii) that the sole or main benefit which, apart from this paragraph, might have been expected to accrue to the parties or any of them would have been or have derived from the allowances (whether investment allowances or initial allowances) obtained or to be obtained in respect of the machinery or plant sold or any machinery or plant by which it is or is to be replaced;

the amount of the initial allowance (if any) to which the buyer is entitled shall be reduced by two-thirds, unless the investment allowance is withheld or withdrawn under paragraph 1 of

Schedule 2 to the Finance Act 1954 or the initial allowance is reduced in accordance with the provisions of Schedule 7 to this Act.

(2) For the purposes of this paragraph machinery or plant shall be deemed to be sold, or as the case may be bought, by an associate of the person incurring the expenditure—

> (*a*) if it is sold, or as the case may be bought, by a body of persons which is at the time of the sale under the control of the person incurring the expenditure, or
> (*b*) if the expenditure was incurred by a body of persons which either is at the time of the sale or was when the expenditure was incurred under control of the seller, or as the case may be the buyer, or
> (*c*) if the expenditure was incurred by one body of persons and the machinery or plant is sold, or as the case may be bought, by another, and the seller, or as the case may be the buyer, is at the time of the sale under the control of the same person as the body incurring the expenditure either is at that time or was when the expenditure was incurred,

or if it is sold by a person to whom the machinery or plant was transferred by the person incurring the expenditure or an associate of his and it appears that the transfer was made in contemplation of the sale.

In this sub-paragraph "body of persons" includes a partnership.

Ships

3.—(1) Where an investment allowance falls to be made in respect of any expenditure incurred on the provision of a ship, no initial allowance shall be made in respect of that expenditure, and paragraph 1 above shall not apply.

(2) Where an investment allowance in respect of any expenditure incurred on the provision of a ship is withheld or withdrawn under paragraph 1 of Schedule 2 to the Finance Act 1954 otherwise than by reason of a sale or transfer, such initial allowance (if any) as might have been made in respect of that expenditure but for sub-paragraph (1) above shall be made.

(3) In the case of expenditure incurred on the provision of a ship paragraph 2 (1) above shall apply as if for the words following sub-paragraphs (*a*) and (*b*) in the said paragraph 2 (1) there were substituted the words—

> "the buyer shall not be entitled to an initial allowance, unless the investment allowance is withheld or withdrawn under paragraph 1 of Schedule 2 to the Finance Act 1954".

(4) Subject to sub-paragraph (2) above, where an investment allowance falls to be made in respect of expenditure incurred on the provision of a ship, no initial allowance shall be made in respect of that expenditure notwithstanding that the investment allowance is for any reason not made.

Supplemental

4.—(1) All such assessments and adjustments of assessments shall be made as may be necessary for or in consequence of the substitution for an investment allowance of an initial allowance under the preceding provisions of this Schedule, and may be so made at any time.

(2) In the case of the death of a person who, if he had not died, would, under the preceding provisions of this Schedule, have become chargeable to income tax for any year, the tax which would have been so chargeable shall be assessed and charged upon his excutors or administrators and shall be a debt due from and payable out of his estate.

Expenditure incurred before 8th April 1959

5.—(1) This paragraph has effect as respects expenditure incurred before 8th April 1959 (that is to say expenditure incurred before the coming into force of the rates of allowance prescribed by section 21 of the Finance Act 1959 and in respect of which an initial allowance would only fall to be made under this Act where section 1 (4) proviso applies of where, under section 1 (6), section 18 (4) or section 64, expenditure incurred before 8th April 1959 is to be treated as having been incurred at a later time).

(2) In the case of such expenditure the rate of any initial allowance under this Act shall be such as would have applied if this Act had not passed, and neither the rates substituted by paragraph 1 (2) above nor the rates for which they are substituted shall apply.

SCHEDULE 2

Sections 18 (3), 19 (3) and 32 (3)

MOTOR CARS

Cross references.—See FA 1971, s. 40 (1) (no allowances or charges shall made under Pt. I, Chapter II (ss. 18–50) of this Act in respect of capital expenditure on the provision of machinery or plant incurred on or after 27 October 1970).

Preliminary

1.—(1) Except as otherwise provided in paragraphs 9 and 10 below, the descriptions of vehicles to which this Schedule applies are those to which section 32 of this Act applies.

(2) Paragraphs 2 to 7 of this Schedule have effect as respects initial allowances, writing-down allowances and balancing allowances in respect of expenditure incurred on the provision of a vehicle to which this Schedule applies, not being—

(*a*) expenditure incurred before 17th April 1961, nor
(*b*) expenditure incurred under a contract entered into before that day where either the expenditure was incurred within twelve months after that day or the contract was one of hire-purchase or for purchase by instalments,

and references in paragraphs 8 and 9 of this Schedule to expenditure incurred on the provision or hiring of a vehicle do not include references to expenditure within paragraph (*a*) or paragraph (*b*) above.

Initial allowances: transitory provisions

2. Where an initial allowance is not precluded by section 18 (3) of this Act, the amount to be allowed by way of initial allowance for any one vehicle shall not exceed £600 (whether the allowance falls to be made by reference to lump sum expenditure or by reference to the amounts of instalments), and the references in paragraph 3 (2) of Schedule 7 to this Act to the appropriate fraction of the limit of recharge on the seller shall have effect accordingly as references to the limit of recharge reduced by £600.

Writing-down allowances: previous user which has not attracted allowances

3.—(1) Section 30 of this Act shall have effect as if at the end of subsection (1) thereof there were added "and in any case where the machinery or plant was not in fact used for the purposes of the trade in the first of those previous chargeable periods (whether or not the trade was then being carried on) there shall be deemed to have been made to him for that chargeable period the maximum allowances permitted by subsections (1) and (2) of section 32 of this Act".

(2) The reference in sub-paragraph (1) above to the maximum allowances permitted by subsections (1) and (2) of section 32 of this Act includes (where the initial allowance would not have been precluded by section 18 (3) of this Act) a reference to the maximum allowances permitted by paragraph 2 above.

Restriction of balancing allowances

4. Where apart from this paragraph a balancing allowance would fall to be made in respect of any vehicle, and the event giving rise to the allowance takes place within a chargeable period or its basis period, being a chargeable period as respects which subsections (1) and (2) of section 32 of this Act, or paragraph 3 above, would operate to reduce the amount of any writing-down allowance falling to be made in respect of the vehicle, or would so operate but for any provision of the Income Tax Acts or the Corporation Tax Acts (other than this paragraph) reducing writing-down allowances—

(*a*) if the person to whom the balancing allowance would fall to be made proves that as respects the period during which the vehicle has been used for the purposes of his trade the amount (if any) falling to be made to him by way of writing-down allowances in respect of the vehicle is less than an amount at a rate of £500 a year, the amount of the balancing allowance shall not exceed the amount of the difference, increased, if any amount which could have been allowed by way of initial allowance was not claimed, by that amount;

(b) in any other case no balancing allowance shall be made unless any amount which could have been allowed by way of initial allowance was not claimed, and if so the balancing allowance shall not exceed that amount.

Reduction of allowances for part-time use, etc.

5. It is hereby declared that the provisions of the Income Tax Acts and the Corporation Tax Acts (other than this paragraph) which in special circumstances reduce initial or writing-down allowances, and balancing allowances, apply to allowances after modification by subsections (1) and (2) of section 32 of this Act and the preceding provisions of this Schedule; and, in particular, where, in a case falling within section 37 or the proviso to section 38 of this Act, it is just and reasonable that paragraph 4 above should apply with the substitution for the references to £500 of a reference to a smaller amount, that paragraph shall so apply, without prejudice to the determination in accordance with the said section 37 or the said proviso whether any balancing allowance falls to be made, or would fall to be made apart from paragraph 4 above.

Subsidies and contributions to expenditure

6. Where under section 84 of this Act any part of the expenditure incurred on the provision of a vehicle is to be treated as not having been incurred by a person, or under section 85 of this Act a person's contribution to such expenditure is to be treated as expenditure on the provision of a similar vehicle, subsections (1) and (2) of section 32 of this Act and the preceding provisions of this Schedule shall have the like effect as if for the references to £500 (read with section 19 (3) of this Act) and to £600 there were substituted references to sums which bear the same proportion thereto as the amount of expenditure which is to be treated as having been incurred by the person providing the vehicle, or as the case may be the amount of the contribution, bears to the whole expenditure incurred on the provision of the vehicle.

Option in case of replacement of machinery or plant

7. Section 40 (1) of this Act shall not have effect where the vehicle is the new plant referred to in that subsection, and this provision shall apply in relation to balancing charges as well as in relation to initial and writing-down allowances.

Limit on renewals allowances

8.—(1) In determining what amount (if any) is allowable—

(a) to be deducted in computing profits or gains chargeable to tax under [Schedule A or][1] Schedule D, or

(b) to be deducted from emoluments chargeable to tax under Schedule E, or

(c) to be taken account for the purposes of any allowances falling to be made by virtue of [section 32 (1) of the principal Act or section 306 (1) of the Income and Corporation Taxes Act 1970][2],

in respect of capital expenditure, being expenditure exceeding £2,000 incurred on the provision of a vehicle, the excess over £2,000 shall be disregarded for all purposes; but if on the replacement of the vehicle any amount becomes allowable as aforesaid in respect of capital expenditure on any other vehicle, any deduction falling to be made, in determining the last-mentioned amount, for the value or proceeds of sale of the replaced vehicle or otherwise in respect thereof shall be reduced in the proportion which £2,000 bears to the cost of the replaced vehicle.

(2) Where a vehicle to which this Schedule applies is replaced by another such vehicle, and sub-paragraph (1) above has effect, the capital expenditure on the provision of the replacement vehicle shall be taken for the purposes of Chapter II of Part I of this Act (including this Schedule) to be the amount of the deduction (if any) falling to be made, in determining what amount is allowable as mentioned in sub-paragraph (1) above, by reason of the cost of the replacement vehicle exceeding the cost of the replaced vehicle.

(3) In sub-paragraph (1) above "capital expenditure" shall be construed without regard to section 82 (1) of this Act.

Amendments.—[1] Words in sub-para. (1) (*a*) inserted by TA 1970, Sch. 15, para. 5 (1), (14).
[2] Words in sub-para. (1) (*c*) substituted by TA 1988, Sch. 29, para. 32 Table.

Limit on deductions, etc. for hiring cars

9.—(1) Where apart from this paragraph the amount of any expenditure on the hiring (otherwise than by way of hire-purchase) of a vehicle to which this paragraph applies would be allowed to be deducted or taken into account as mentioned in paragraph 8 (1) above, and the retail price of the vehicle at the time when it was made exceeded £2,000, the said amount shall be reduced in the proportion which £2,000, together with one half of the excess, bears to the said price.

(2) Where a person, having on or after 4th April 1963 hired (otherwise than by way of hire-purchase) a vehicle to which this paragraph applies, subsequently becomes the owner thereof, and the retail price of the vehicle at the time it was made exceeded £2,000, then for the purposes of the Income Tax Acts and the Corporation Tax Acts (and in particular section 32 of this Act and this Schedule)—

(*a*) so much of the aggregate of the payments for the hire of the vehicle and of any payment for the acquisition thereof as does not exceed the retail price of the vehicle at the time it was made shall be treated as capital expenditure incurred on the provision of the vehicle, and as having been incurred when the hiring began, and
(*b*) the payments to be treated as expenditure on the hiring of the vehicle shall be rateably reduced so as to amount the aggregate to the balance.

(3) The descriptions of vehicles to which this paragraph applies are those to which section 32 of this Act applies, and those to which it would apply but for subsection (6) of that section.

Apportionment of hire-purchase payments

10.—(1) Where the person providing a vehicle takes it under a hire-purchase contract, and the retail price at the time of the contract exceeds £2,000, then in apportioning the payments under the contract between capital expenditure incurred on the provision of the vehicle and other expenditure so much of those payments shall be treated as such capital expenditure as is equal to the price which would be chargeable, at the time the contract is entered into, to the person providing the vehicle if he were acquiring it on a sale outright.

(2) This paragraph applies to all mechanically propelled road vehicles constructed or adapted for the carriage of passengers, other than vehicles of a type not commonly used as a private vehicle and unsuitable to be so used.

Supplemental

11.—(1) There shall be made all such assessments and adjustments of assessments as may be necessary for the purpose of giving effect to section 32 (6) of this Act, and to paragraph 9 (2) above, and any such assessments may be made at any time.

(2) In the case of the death of a person who, if he had not died, would, under the said provisions, have become chargeable to tax for any year, the tax which would have been so chargeable shall be assessed and charged upon his executors or administrators and shall be a debt due from and payable out of his estate.

(3) Any claim for an allowance by virtue of paragraph 9 (2) above may be made in connection with the making or adjusting of assessments under this paragraph, and whether so made or not may notwithstanding anything in section 70 of this Act be made at any time not later than two years after the claimant became the owner of the vehicle.

SCHEDULE 3

Sections 18 (7) and 85 (2)

MACHINERY AND PLANT: HIRE-PURCHASE, ETC.

Cross references.—See FA 1971, s. 40 (1) (no allowances or charges shall be made under Pt. I, Chapter II (ss. 18–50) of this Act in respect of capital expenditure on the provision of machinery or plant incurred on or after 27 October 1970).

1.—(1) Where a person, having incurred capital expenditure on the provision of machinery or plant under a contract providing that he shall or may become the owner of the machinery or plant on the performance of the contract—

(*a*) without becoming the owner of it ceases to be entitled to the benefit of the contract, so far as it relates to the machinery or plant, and
(*b*) receives or is entitled to any capital sum by way of consideration, compensation damages or insurance moneys in respect of his rights under the contract or of the machinery or plant,

then (subject to paragraph 2 of this Schedule) that expenditure shall be left out of account for the purposes of Chapter II of Part I of this Act.

(2) Where—

(*a*) a person who has incurred capital expenditure as aforesaid dies or otherwise ceases to be entitled to the benefit of the contract, so far as it relates to the machinery or plant, without either becoming the owner of the machinery or plant or receiving or being entitled to any such capital sum as aforesaid, and
(*b*) another person, having become entitled to the benefit of that expenditure—

(i) ceases to be entitled to it without becoming the owner of the machinery or plant, and
(ii) receives or is entitled to any capital sum by way of consideration, compensation, damages or insurance moneys in respect of that benefit or of the machinery or plant,

the preceding sub-paragraph shall apply as if the person incurring the expenditure had received such a capital sum as is mentioned in paragraph (*b*) of that sub-paragraph.

2. Paragraph 1 above shall not affect any allowance given by virtue of section 85 of this Act in respect of a person's contribution to another person's expenditure; but an initial allowance shall not be given by virtue of that section in respect of a person's contribution or, if previously given, shall be withdrawn where, without the machinery or plant belonging to the person making the contribution or to the person for the time being carrying on the trade for the purposes of which it is provided, the relevant asset ceases to be treated under section 85 (2) of this Act as belonging to the person making the contribution, and he receives any capital sum by way of consideration, compensation, damages or insurance moneys in respect of his contribution or of the machinery or plant.

3.—(1) Where a person has incurred capital expenditure on the provision of machinery or plant for the purposes of his trade (without the machinery or plant belonging to him), and he or the person for the time being entitled to the benefit of that expenditure enters into any arrangement which, with or without any associated transactions, has the effect (or would if tax were chargeable in respect of any profits or gains of the trade have the effect) both—

(*a*) that, under paragraph 1 of this Schedule, that expenditure falls to be left out of account for the purposes of the said Chapter II, and
(*b*) that another person ("the successor") incurs capital expenditure on the provision of machinery or plant for the purposes of his trade in securing for himself the benefit of that expenditure incurred by the first-mentioned person,

then that expenditure incurred by the successor, in so far as it exceeds that expenditure incurred by the first-mentioned person, shall also be left out of account for the purposes of the said Chapter II, if in addition—

(i) of the successor and the person last previously entitled to the benefit aforesaid, either is a body of persons over whom the other has control or both are bodies of persons and some other person has control over both, or
(ii) it appears with respect to the arrangement, or with respect to transactions of which

the arrangement is one, that the sole or main benefit which, apart from the provisions of this paragraph, might have been expected to accrue to the parties or any of them was the obtaining of an allowance under the said Chapter II.

(2) In this paragaraph "body of persons" includes a partnership.

4.—(1) There shall be made all such assessments and adjustments of assessments as may be necessary for or in consequence of the withdrawal of any allowance given in respect of expenditure falling to be left out of account under this Schedule, or as may otherwise be necessary for the purpose of giving effect to this Schedule, and any such assessments or adjustments of assessments may be made at any time.

(2) In the case of the death of a person who, if he had not died, would, under the provisions of this Schedule, have become chargeable to tax for any year, the tax which would have been so chargeable shall be assessed and charged upon his executors or administrators and shall be a debt due from and payable out of his estate.

SCHEDULE 4

Section 20 (6)

MACHINERY AND PLANT: EXISTING WRITING-DOWN PERCENTAGES

Cross references.—See FA 1971, s. 40 (1) (no allowances or charges shall be made under Pt. I, Chapter II (ss. 18–50) of this Act in respect of capital expenditure on the provisions of machinery or plant incurred on or after 27 October 1970).

Application of existing determinations to 1968–69 and later years

1.—(1) The provisions of this paragraph are without prejudice to section 20 (6) of this Act as read with Part III of this Act, and shall have effect, as respects machinery or plant to which paragraphs 2 and 3 below apply, subject to the provisions of those paragraphs.

(2) Except so far as it is superseded by any subsequent determination under . . .[1] section 21 (3) of this Act, any determination under section 35 (3) of the Finance Act 1963 (. . .[1] as applied by subsection (6) of the same section) made for or applied to the year 1967–68 shall apply also to subsequent years as if made under . . .[1] section 21 (3) of this Act . . .[1]

(3) Except so far as it is superseded by any subsequent determination under . . .[1] section 21 (4) of this Act, any determination made or deemed to be made under . . .[1] section 282 of the Income Tax Act 1952, being a determination made for or applied to the year 1967–68, shall apply also to subsequent years as if it were the determination of a basic percentage under . . .[1] the said section 21 (4) . . .[1].

(4) . . .[2]

Amendments.—[1] Words in sub-paras. (2) and (3) repealed by FA 1976, Sch. 15, Pt. III for accounting periods and basis periods ending after 5 April 1976.
[2] Sub-para. (4) repealed by FA 1976, Sch. 15, Pt. III for accounting periods and basis periods ending after 5 April 1976.

New machinery and plant provided after 5th November 1962

2.—(1) This and the next following paragraph apply to new machinery or plant capital expenditure on the provision of which was incurred after 5th November 1962 (within the meaning of that expression as defined in section 19(4) of this Act) [and, for accounting periods ending on or after 27th October 1970 and years of assessment from the year 1971–72 onwards, also to any machinery or plant not within the meaning of that expression.][1]

(2) . . .[2]

(3) Where a writing-down allowance under section 21 of this Act in respect of machinery or plant to which this paragraph applies falls to be computed by reference to a percentage established before the year 1963–64, the amount of the allowance resulting under sub-paragraph (4) below from the application of that percentage—

(a) where it is less than $6\frac{1}{4}$ per cent. of the relevant capital amount, shall be increased so as to equal $6\frac{1}{4}$ per cent. of that amount,
(b) where it is between $6\frac{1}{4}$ and $8\frac{1}{2}$ per cent. of the relevant capital amount, shall be increased so as to equal $8\frac{1}{2}$ per cent. of that amount,
(c) where it is less than $11\frac{1}{4}$ but not less than $8\frac{1}{2}$ per cent. of the relevant capital amount, shall be increased so as to equal $11\frac{1}{4}$ per cent. of that amount.

(4) Paragraph 1 (3) above shall apply to a determination carried forward from a year before 1963–64 in respect of a class of machinery or plant notwithstanding that it includes machinery or plant to which this paragraph applies and in that case the basic percentage established by the determination and the provisions of . . .[3], section 21 (4) of this Act increasing it by one-quarter shall have effect as respects the said machinery or plant for the purposes of—

(a) deciding whether or not a writing-down allowance falls to be increased under sub-paragraph . . .[3] (3) above, (*b*) arriving at the amount of a writing-down allowance which does not fall to be so increased, and

(*c*) the calculation referred to in sub-paragraph (5) below.

(5) Where paragraph 1 (3) above applies in accordance with sub-paragraph (4) of this paragraph to a determination carried forward from a year before 1963–64—

(*a*) the said paragraph 1 (3) shall have effect, as respects machinery or plant to which this paragraph applies, as if for the reference to any subsequent determination under section 20 (4) or section 21 (4) of this Act there were substituted a reference to any subsequent determination under . . .[3] section 21 (3) of this Act, and

(*b*) in deciding whether or not, as respects such machinery or plant as aforesaid, a redetermination of the percentage established by the first-mentioned determination is necessary, the amount of the basic percentage as falling to be adjusted, that is to say, as increased by one-quarter under the last preceding sub-paragraph and further increased, where so required, under sub-paragraph . . .[3] (3) above, shall be treated as if it were a percentage determined in accordance with the said . . .[3] section 21 (3), . . .[3],

so, however, that where the basic percentage, as increased by one-quarter, is greater than the percentage mentioned in . . .[3], sub-paragraph (3) (*c*), above, paragraph (*b*) of this sub-paragraph shall apply as if that greater percentage were instead so mentioned.

Amendments.—[1] Words in sub-para. (1) were inserted by FA 1971, s. 53.
[2] Sub-para. (2) repealed by FA 1976, Sch. 15, Pt. III for accounting periods and basis periods ending after 5 April 1976.
[3] Words in sub-paras. (4) and (5) repealed by FA 1976, Sch. 15, Pt. III for accounting periods and basis periods ending after 5 April 1976.

3.—(1) References in paragraph 2 above to a percentage established before the year 1963–64 shall be construed as references to a percentage established by a determination which before the commencement of this Act was made or deemed to be made under . . .[1], section 282 (2), of the Income Tax Act 1952 for a year before the year 1963–64.

(2) Where in the case of machinery or plant of any class, annual allowances for the year 1962–63 or any earlier year of assessment falling to be computed in accordance with the said section . . .[1] 282 were computed by reference to a percentage which, though not determined or deemed to have been determined by the Board under that section, was commonly treated as if it had been so determined, that percentage shall, notwithstanding that a percentage has, after the commencement of the Finance Act 1963, been so determined for the year, be regarded for the purposes of this Schedule as the percentage so determined in respect of machinery or plant of that class for the year 1962–63 or that earlier year, as the case may be.

(3) In paragraph 2 of this Schedule "relevant capital amount" means the amount specified in . . .[1], section 21 (1) of this Act as the amount by reference to which a writing-down allowance is to be computed.

Amendments.—[1] Words in sub-paras. (1), (2) and (3) repealed by FA 1976, Sch. 15, Pt. III for accounting periods and basis periods ending after 5 April 1976.

SCHEDULE 5

Sections 52, 53 and 54

MINERALS: SPECIAL PROVISIONS FOR CERTAIN EXPENDITURE

Cross references.—See FA 1986, s. 55 (new code of allowances for certain capital expenditure on mineral extraction incurred after 31 March 1986 subject to transitional provisions in FA 1986, Sch. 14 for expenditure incurred before 1 April 1987),
s. 55 (3), (4) (for the purposes of the old code of allowances, certain assumptions to apply in respect of accounting periods and basis periods).
Amendments.—This Schedule repealed by FA 1986, Sch. 23, Pt. VI in respect of expenditure incurred after 31 March 1986 subject to the provisions of FA 1986, Sch. 14.

Exploration machinery and plant

1.—*(1) Where machinery or plant used by any person in searching for, or discovering and testing, the mineral deposits of any source, or winning access thereto, either—*

(a) is not sold, demolished or destroyed before the source is worked in the course of a trade, or
(b) before being sold, demolished or destroyed as aforesaid, or before being used as aforesaid, is used by him for some other purpose,

then of the capital expenditure incurred by him on the machinery or plant so much only shall be treated for the purposes of Chapter III of Part I of this Act as incurred in connection with that source as in the opinion of the inspector (or, on appeal, of the Commissioners having jurisdiction in the matter) does not exceed the amount of the diminution in the value of the machinery or plant attributable to its use in searching for, discovering and testing and winning access to the deposits of that source, and the remainder shall not be treated as qualifying expenditure by reason of the use of the machinery or plant in connection with that source.

(2) In the case of machinery or plant used in searching for, or discovering and testing, or winning access to, the deposits of more than one source the aggregate amount of the expenditure treated under this paragraph as incurred by any person in connection with those sources shall not exceed the total amount of the expenditure incurred by him on the machinery or plant.

2.—*(1) Where a person carrying on a trade which consists of or includes the working of any mine, oil well or other source of mineral deposits of a wasting nature has incurred qualifying expenditure on machinery or plant for the purposes of that trade, then for the purposes of Chapter III of Part I of this Act any sale, insurance, salvage or compensation moneys in respect of the machinery or plant shall—*

(a) if by virtue of the preceding paragraph the qualifying expenditure is not the whole of the capital expenditure incurred by him on the machinery or plant, by disregarded except in so far as they exceed the difference between the said capital expenditure and the qualifying expenditure on the machinery or plant,
(b) subject to paragraph (a) of this sub-paragraph, if the qualifying expenditure on the machinery or plant was incurred in connection with more than one source, be apportioned between the sources in such manner as appears to the inspector (or, on appeal, to the Commissioners having jurisdiction in the matter) to be appropriate.

(2) The deductions to be made under section 57 (6) of this Act in respect of any machinery or plant shall not, in the case of any source, exceed the amount of the qualifying expenditure on the machinery or plant incurred in connection with that source.

(3) In Schedule 7 to this Act references to machinery or plant shall not apply in the case of machinery or plant which for the seller of the machinery or plant is an asset representing qualifying expenditure.

Overseas mineral rights and land

3.—*(1) Where—*

(a) a person incurs expenditure to which section 53 (1) of this Act applies on acquiring any deposits or rights, and
(b) those deposits or rights had previously been acquired by some other person, being, or being

a body corporate or partnership under the control of, a person resident in the United Kingdom, and

(c) the case is not one to which section 58 (7) of this Act applies,

then subject to paragraph 5 below, the said expenditure of the first-mentioned person shall be left out of account for the purposes of Chapters III of Part I of this Act so far as it exceeds the capital expenditure incurred by the said other person in acquiring the deposits or rights.

(2) In the case specified in this sub-paragraph, sub-paragraph (1) above and paragraph 5 below shall have effect subject to the following provisions—

(a) if there has been more than one acquisition to which sub-paragraph (1) (b) above applies, regard shall be had only to that one of the other persons mentioned in the said sub-paragraph (1) (b) who first acquired the deposits or rights.

(b) where any such other person as is mentioned in the said sub-paragraph (1) (b) carried on a trade which consisted of or included the buying or selling of, or of rights in or over, mineral deposits, references to capital expenditure shall, in relation to him, be deemed to include expenditure which would have been capital expenditure if his trade had been the working of the deposits or rights in question and had not included such buying and selling as aforesaid,

(c) in computing the expenditure of any such other person, liabilities undertaken by him which, in connection with the disposal by him of the deposits or rights in question, have been taken over by some other person may, notwithstanding anything in section 82 (3) of this Act, be taken into account.

4.—(1) Where—

(a) a person incurs or has incurred in connection with any source of mineral deposits any such expenditure as is mentioned in section 54 (1) of this Act, and

(b) the land acquired by him had previously been acquired by some other person, being, or being a body corporate or partnership under the control of, a person resident in the United Kingdom, and had been so acquired either for use in connection with the working of that source or for the purpose of a trade consisting of or including the buying and selling of land containing mineral deposits, and

(c) the case is not one to which sections 58 (7) of this Act applies,

then subject to paragraph 5 below, that expenditure shall not be treated by virtue of the said section 54 as qualifying expenditure so far as it exceeds the capital expenditure incurred by the said other person in acquiring the land.

(2) In the cases specified in this sub-paragraph, sub-paragraph (1) above and paragraph 5 below shall have effect subject to the following provisions—

(a) if there has been more than one acquisition to which sub-paragraph (1) (b) above applies, regard shall be had only to the first of those acquisitions,

(b) where the person making the acquisition to which the said sub-paragraph (1) (b) applies (or, if there has been more than one such acquisition the one to which regard is to be had) carried on a trade consisting of or including the buying and selling of land containing mineral deposits, references to capital expenditure shall, in relation to him, be taken to include expenditure which would have been capital expenditure if his trade had been the working of the source in question and had not included such buying and selling as aforesaid,

(c) in computing the expenditure of the person making the said acquisition, liabilities undertaken by him which, in connection with the disposal by him of the land in question, have been taken over by some other person may, notwithstanding anything in section 82 (3) of this Act, be taken into account.

5.—(1) Where the source or part of the source in question in paragraph 3 or the source in question in paragraph 4 above has been worked between the dates of the two acquisitions, the capital expenditure of the other person mentioned in paragraph 3 (1) (b) or paragraph 4 (1) (b), as the case may be, incurred in acquiring the deposits or rights, or, as the case may be, the land, shall be treated for the purposes of paragraphs 3 (1) and 4 (1) above as reduced as follows.

(2) In a case where the expenditure is incurred on or after the appointed day it shall be reduced by

applying the fraction $\dfrac{A}{A+B}$ where—

"A" is the total potential future output from the source or part, estimated as at the later of those dates, and

"B" is the actual output from the source or part between those dates.

(3) In a case where the expenditure was incurred before the appointed day it shall be reduced by

applying the fraction $\dfrac{A+C}{B+C}$ where—

"A" is the actual total output from the source or part from the later of those dates to the appointed day;

"B" is the actual total output from the source or part from the earlier of those dates up to the appointed day, and

"C" is the total potential future output from the source or part, estimated as at the appointed day.

SCHEDULE 6

Section 57 (5)

MINERALS: EXPENDITURE INCURRED BEFORE APPOINTED DAY

Appointed day.—For definition, see s. 65, *ante*.
Cross references.—See FA 1986, s. 55 (new code of allowances for certain capital expenditure on mineral extraction incurred after 31 March 1986 subject to transitional provisions in FA 1986, Sch. 14 for expenditure incurred before 1 April 1987),
s. 55 (3), (4) (for the purposes of the old code of allowances, certain assumptions to apply in respect of accounting periods and basis periods).
Amendments.—This Schedule repealed by FA 1986, Sch. 23, Pt. VI in respect of expenditure incurred after 31 March 1986 subject to the provisions of FA 1986, Sch. 14.

PART I

PRELIMINARY

1. The amount of expenditure which a person who, on the appointed day, was carrying on a trade which consisted of or included the working of a mine, oil well or other source of mineral deposits of a wasting nature is to be treated for certain purposes of Chapter III of Part I of this Act as having incurred on that day shall, except in the cases dealt with in Part III of this Schedule, be the amount specified in Part II thereof.

2. In the following provisions of this Schedule, the said expenditure is referred to as "the appointed day expenditure" and the said person is referred to as "the trader".

PART II

PROVISIONS APPLICABLE WHERE PART III OF THIS SCHEDULE DOES NOT APPLY

3. Except in cases to which Part III of this Schedule applies, the amount of the appointed day expenditure shall be ascertained by—

(a) ascertaining the total qualifying expenditure which was incurred by the trader before the appointed day for the purposes of the trade and in connection with the source, and
(b) subtracting therefrom the amounts specified in paragraph 4 of this Schedule, and
(c) applying the fraction specified in paragraph 5 of this Schedule to the result.

4. The said amounts are—

(a) where any asset representing any part of the expenditure incurred by the trader as aforesaid before the appointed day has, before the appointed day, been sold by him, the amount of the expenditure so incurred which is attributable to that asset, and
(b) where the assets representing the expenditure so incurred, not being assets sold by the trader before the appointed day, consist of or include buildings or structures, any relevant mills, factories or exceptional depreciation allowances made in respect of the buildings or structures for any year of assessment before that in which the appointed day fell.

5. The said fraction is $\dfrac{A}{A+B}$ where—

"A" is the total potential future from the source, estimated as at the appointed day, and
"B" is the total output from the source before the appointed day.

6.—*(1)* In relation to expenditure which is qualifying expenditure by virtue of section 52 or section 54 of this Act—

(a) references in this Part of this Schedule to qualifying expenditure shall be taken as referring only to expenditure which is qualifying expenditure by virtue of those sections, and
(b) in applying paragraph 5 above, there shall be left out of account under head B, in the case of expenditure on machinery or plant, any output from the source before the machinery or plant was used in connection with the source and, in the case of expenditure on land, any output from the source before the trader acquired the land.

(2) In relation to expenditure to which section 53 (1) of this Act applies—

*(a) references in this Part of this Schedule to qualifying expenditure shall be taken as referring only to expenditure which is qualifying expenditure by virtue of the said section 53, and
(b) in applying paragraph 5 above, there shall be left out of account under head B any output before the trader acquired the source.*

PART III
ASSETS PURCHASED FROM A PREDECESSOR

7.—*(1) Where, at or about the time when the trader began to work the source, he acquired from a predecessor in the working of the source assets representing qualifying expenditure, incurred by that or any other predecessor in the working of the source, the amount of the appointed day expenditure shall be whichever of the amounts respectively specified in the two next following paragraphs is the smaller.*

(2) In this paragraph and the following provisions of this Part of this Schedule, "predecessor in the working of the source" means a person who has, before the appointed day, carried on a trade which consisted of or included the working of the source but has, before that day, ceased to work it.

(3) In the following provisions of this Part of this Schedule, the assets mentioned in sub-paragraph (1) of this paragraph are referred to as "the acquired assets".

8.—*(1) The first of the amounts mentioned in the last preceding paragraph is the amount which results from—*

*(a) ascertaining the total qualifying expenditure which was incurred either on the acquired assets by any predecessor in the working of the source for the purposes of his trade and in connection with that source or by the trader for the purposes of his trade and in connection with the source, and
(b) subtracting therefrom the sums specified in sub-paragraph (2) of this paragraph, and
(c) applying to the result the fraction specified in sub-paragraph (3) of this paragraph.*

(2) The said sums are—

*(a) where any of the acquired assets has, before the appointed day, been sold by the trader, so much of the said expenditure incurred by any predecessor in the working of the source as is attributable to that asset,
(b) where any asset representing any part of the expenditure incurred by the trader as aforesaid before the appointed day has, before the appointed day, been sold by him, the amount of that expenditure which is attributable to that asset, and
(c) where any of the acquired assets or any asset representing any such expenditure as aforesaid of the trader consists of buildings or structures (not being buildings or structures sold by the trader before the appointed day (any relevant mills, factories or exceptional depreciation allowances made in respect of the buildings or structures for any year of assessment before that in which the appointed day fell.*

(3) The said fraction is $\frac{A}{A+B}$ where—

*"A" is the total potential future output from the source, estimated as at the appointed day, and
"B" is the total output from the source before the appointed day.*

9.—*(1) The second of the said amounts is the amount which results from—*

*(a) adding the price paid by the trader for the acquired assets to all the qualifying expenditure which he incurred for the purposes of the trade and in connection with the source between the time when he acquired those assets and the appointed day, and
(b) subtracting from the total the sums specified in sub-paragraph (2) of this paragraph, and
(c) applying to the result the fraction specified in sub-paragraph (3) of this paragraph.*

(2) The said sums are—

*(a) where any asset representing the expenditure mentioned in sub-paragraph (1) (a) above has, before the appointed day, been sold by the trader, the amount of that expenditure which is attributable to that asset, and
(b) where any of the acquired assets has, before the appointed day, been sold by the trader, the price paid by the trader for the asset, and
(c) where the assets representing that expenditure, not being assets sold by the trader before*

the appointed day, consist of or include buildings or structures, any relevant mills, factories or exceptional depreciation allowances made to him in respect of the buildings or structures for any year of assessment before the year in which the appointed day fell.

(3) The said fraction is $\dfrac{A}{A+B}$ where—

"A" is the total potential future output from the source, estimated as at the appointed day, and "B" is the total output from the source between the date of the acquisition of the acquired assets and the appointed day.

10. This Part of this Schedule shall not apply in relation to—

(a) expenditure which is qualifying expenditure by virtue of section 52 or section 54 of this Act, or

(b) expenditure to which section 53 *(1)* of this Act applies.

SCHEDULE 7

Sections 78, 81 (2), 95 (3) and Schedules 1, 2, 5 and 12

OPERATION OF PARTS I AND II IN RELATION TO CERTAIN SALES

Cross references.—See FA 1981, s. 76 (2) (application of this Schedule to a transfer after 10 March 1981 of an industrial building or structure otherwise than by way of sale);
FA 1982, Sch. 12, para. 14 (application of this Schedule for the purposes of capital allowances on expenditure incurred after 9 March 1982 and before 1 April 1987 for dwelling-houses let on assured tenancies),
Sch. 12, para. 4 (5) (*a*) (references in this Schedule to CAA 1968, Part I to include a reference to FA 1982, Sch. 12, (see preceding cross reference)).
FA 1985, s. 64 (2) (*h*) (notwithstanding TA 1988, s. 532, this Schedule not to apply in relation to writing-down allowances for expenditure on purchase of patent rights incurred after 31 March 1986);
FA 1986, Sch. 15, para. 9 (modification of this Schedule in its application to the new code of capital allowances under FA 1986, s. 56 in relation to agricultural land and buildings);
TA 1988, s. 532 (s. 78 of this Act, with this Schedule, not applicable to dealings in know-how).

General

1.—(1) This Schedule has effect in relation to the sales specified in section 78 of this Act, that is to say, sales of any property where either—

(*a*) the buyer is a body of persons over whom the seller has control, or the seller is a body of persons over whom the buyer has control, or both the seller and the buyer are bodies of persons and some other person has control over both of them [or the buyer and the seller are connected with each other within the meaning of section [839][2] of the principal Act][1], or

(*b*) it appears with respect to the sale, or with respect to transactions of which the sale is one, that the sole or main benefit which, apart from the provisions of this Schedule, might have been expected to accrue to the parties or any of them was the obtaining of an allowance or deduction [, the obtaining of a greater allowance or deduction or the avoidance or reduction of a charge][1] under Part I or Part II of this Act.

References in this sub-paragraph to a body of persons include references to a partnership.

(2) Subject to paragraph 4 (3) below, this Schedule shall have effect in relation to a sale notwithstanding that it is not fully applicable by reason of the non-residence of a party to the sale or otherwise:

Provided that this sub-paragraph and the said paragraph 4 (3) shall not apply in the case of a sale made before 6th April 1954 where the property was sold at a price other than that which it would have fetched if sold in the open market.

Cross references.—See FA 1981, s. 76 (2) (transfer after 10 March 1981 of an industrial building or structure otherwise than by way of sale to be treated for the application of this Schedule as a sale under sub-para. (1) (*a*));
FA 1982, Sch. 12, para. 4 (6) (application of sub-para. (1) (*a*) above to a transfer otherwise than by sale of a dwelling-house constructed after 9 March 1982 and before 1 April 1987 and let on assured tenancy);
FA 1986, Sch. 15, para. 9 (3) (this Schedule to have effect in relation to capital expenditure incurred after 31 March 1986 on agricultural land and buildings as if a transfer of a relevant interest as defined in Sch. 15, para. 3 were a sale falling within sub-para. (1) (*a*) above.
Amendments.—[1] Words in sub-para. (1) (*a*), (*b*) inserted by FA 1981, s. 76 (3), (5) where the sale occurs after 10 March 1981.
[2] Number in sub-para. (1) (*a*) substituted by TA 1988, Sch. 29, para. 32 Table.

2. Where the property is sold at a price other than that which it would have fetched if sold in the open market, then, subject to the following provisions of this Schedule, the like consequences shall ensue for the purposes of the said Parts I and II, in their application to the tax of all persons concerned, as would have ensued if the property had been sold for the price which it would have fetched if sold in the open market.

Cross references.—See FA 1986, Sch. 13, para. 23 (2) (notwithstanding anything in this paragraph, para. 23 to apply to capital expenditure incurred after 31 March 1986 on the acquisition of mineral assets within a group unless the acquisition is a sale in respect of which an election is made under para. 4 of this Schedule).

Machinery or plant

3.—(1) Subject to the provisions of this paragraph, where the sale is a sale of machinery or plant—

(a) no initial allowance shall be made to the buyer, and
(b) subject to the provisions of paragraph 4 of this Schedule, if the price which the property would have fetched if sold in the open market is greater than the limit of recharge on the seller, paragraph 2 of this Schedule shall have effect as if for each of the references to the price which the property would have fetched if sold in the open market there were substituted a reference to the said limit of recharge:

Provided that this sub-paragraph shall not apply in relation to a sale of machinery or plant which has never been used if the business or part of the business of the seller was the manufacture or supply of machinery or plant of that class and the sale was effected in the ordinary course of the seller's business.

(2) Where, in the case of any sale of machinery or plant—

(a) the sale is one to which sub-paragraph (1) (a) of paragraph 1 of this Schedule applies and sub-paragraph (1) (b) of the said paragraph 1 does not apply, and
(b) an initial allowance fell to be made to the seller of the machinery or plant in respect of the capital expenditure which he incurred on the provision thereof, and
(c) a balancing charge is made on the seller by reason of the sale, and
(d) the price which the machinery or plant would have fetched if sold in the open market at the time of the sale exceeds the appropriate fraction of the limit of recharge on the seller,

sub-paragraph (1) (a) of this paragraph shall not apply, but the initial allowance to the buyer shall not exceed whichever of the three following amounts is the least, that is to say—

(i) the excess of the said price over the appropriate fraction of the said limit of recharge,
(ii) the initial allowance which fell to be made to the seller as aforesaid, and
(iii) the amount on which a balancing charge is made on the seller as aforesaid.

(3) In sub-paragraph (2) above the appropriate fraction is—

(a) seven-tenths where the rate of the seller's initial allowance was three-tenths by virtue of section 18 of this Act or section 15 of the Finance Act 1958 (expenditure incurred on or after 15th April 1958),
(b) subject to the provisions of paragraph 1 of Schedule 1 to this Act, nine-tenths where the rate of the seller's initial allowance was one-tenth by virtue of paragraph 1 or paragraph 2 of the said Schedule 1 or section 21 of the Finance Act 1959 (expenditure incurred after 7th April 1959 on assets qualifying for investment allowance),
(c) four-fifths where the rate of the seller's initial allowance was one-fifth by virtue of section 16 of the Finance Act 1953 (expenditure incurred on or after 15th April 1953),
(d) three-fifths where the rate of the seller's initial allowance was two-fifths by virtue of the proviso to section 279 (5) of the income Tax Act 1952 or the proviso to section 20 (1) of the Finance Act 1951 (expenditure on ship under contract entered into at 10th April 1951) or section 20 of the Finance Act 1949 (expenditure incurred on or after 6th April 1949 and before 6th April 1952),
(e) four-fifths where the expenditure referred to in sub-paragraph (2) (b) above was incurred before 6th April 1949.

(4) In this paragraph, "the limit of recharge" means, in relation to a person who sells machinery or plant—

(a) if he provided that machinery or plant for himself before the appointed day, the actual cost to him of the machinery or plant, including in that actual cost any expenditure in the nature of capital expenditure on machinery or plant by way of renewal, improvement or reinstatement,
(b) if he provided the machinery or plant for himself on or after the appointed day, the expenditure incurred by him on the provision thereof.

In this sub-paragraph "the appointed day" means 6th April 1946.

Sales without change of control

4.—(1) Subject to sub-paragraph (3) below, where the sale is one to which sub-paragraph (1) (a) of paragraph 1 of this Schedule applies and sub-paragraph (1) (b) of that paragraph does not apply, and the parties to the sale [so elect by notice in writing given to the inspector not later than two years after the sale][5], the following provisions shall have effect—

(a) paragraph 2 of this Schedule shall have effect as if for each of the references to the price which the property would have fetched if sold in the open market there were substituted a reference to that price or to the sum hereinafter mentioned, whichever is the lower, and

(b) paragraph 3 (1) (b) above shall not apply, and

(c) notwithstanding anything in the preceding provisions of this Schedule, such balancing charge, if any, shall be made on the buyer on any event occurring after the date of the sale as would have fallen to be made on the seller if the seller had continued to own the property and had done all such things and been allowed all such allowances or deductions in connection therewith as were done by or allowed to the buyer.

(2) The sum referred to in sub-paragraph (1) (a) of this paragraph is—

(a) in the case of an industrial building or structure the residue of the expenditure on the construction of that building or structure immediately before the sale, computed in accordance with the provisions of section 4 of this Act,

(b) in the case of machinery or plant, the amount of the expenditure on the provision thereof still unallowed immediately before the sale, computed in accordance with the provisions of section 41 of this Act,

(c) *in the case of assets representing qualifying expenditure as defined in section 51 (1) of this Act, the residue of the expenditure attributable to those assets immediately before the sale, computed in accordance with the provisions of Chapter III of Part I of this Act,*[1]

[(d) in the case of assets representing qualifying expenditure, within the meaning of Schedule 13 to the Finance Act 1986, the excess of that expenditure attributable to those assets over the aggregate of—

(i) any allowances made under that Schedule to the seller in respect of that expenditure before the sale; and

(ii) any disposal receipts which the seller has been required to bring into account by reference to that expenditure by reason of any event occurring before the sale.][2]

(3) An election may not be made under this paragraph if—

(a) any of the parties to the sale is not resident in the United Kingdom at the time of sale, and

(b) the circumstances are not at that time such that an allowance or charge under Part I or Part II of this Act falls or might fall to be made to or on that party in consequence of the sale

[nor may such an election be made if the buyer is a dual resident investing company, within the meaning of section [404 of the principal Act][4].][3]

[(4) All such assessments and adjustments of assessments shall be made as may be necessary to give effect to this paragraph.][6]

Cross references.—See CGTA 1979, s. 34 (3) (a) (restriction of capital losses by reference to capital and renewals allowances);
FA 1982, Sch. 12, para. 4 (5) (b), (c) (modification of sub-paras. (2) (a), (3) (a), (b) of this paragraph in their application for the purposes of capital allowances on expenditure incurred after 9 March 1982 and before 1 April 1987 for dwelling-houses let on assured tenancies),
Sch. 12, para. 5 (4) (no balancing charge or allowance to be made on the sale of a dwelling-house subject to the modified provisions of this paragraph (see preceding cross reference) where the dwelling-house was not a qualifying dwelling-house for the whole of the relevant period);
FA 1986, s. 56 (1), (2) and Sch. 15, para. 9 (omission of this paragraph and references to its provisions in this Schedule in relation to any sale which is material for the purposes of capital allowances for expenditure on agricultural land and buildings incurred after 31 March 1986 other than expenditure under existing contracts);
TA 1988, s. 532 (3) (computation of sum referred to in sub-para. (1) (a)).
Amendments.—[1] Sub-para. (2) (c) repealed by FA 1986, Sch. 23, Pt. VI, subject to the provisions of FA 1986, Sch. 14.
[2] Sub-para. (2) (d) added by FA 1986, Sch. 13, para. 25 (3).
[3] Words in sub-para. (3) added by F (No. 2) A 1987, s. 64 (1).
[4] Words in sub-para. (3) substituted by TA 1988, Sch. 29, para. 32 Table.
[5] Words in sub-para. (1) substituted by FA 1988, s. 91 in relation to sales occurring after the passing of FA 1988. FA 1988 was passed on 29 July 1988.
[6] Sub-para. (4) inserted by *ibid.*

SCHEDULE 9
Section 85 (1)

ALLOWANCES FOR CONTRIBUTIONS TOWARDS EXPENDITURE

1. Subject to the provisions of this Schedule, the amount of the allowances and the manner in which they are to be made shall be determined on the following basis—

(a) the asset shall be deemed to continue at all material times to be in use for the purposes of the trade,
(b) where the asset is machinery or plant and, when the contribution was made, the trade was carried on or to be carried on by a tenant of land in which the contributor has an interest, the contributor shall be deemed to have let the machinery or plant to the said tenant on such terms that the burden of the wear and tear thereof falls directly on the contributor.

2. Where, when the contribution was made, the trade for the purposes of which it was made was carried on or to be carried on by the contributor, the following provisions shall have effect on any transfer of the trade or any part of the trade—

(a) where the transfer is of the whole trade, writing-down allowances for chargeable periods ending after the date of transfer shall be made to the transferee, and shall not be made to the transferor,
(b) where the transfer is of part only of the trade, the provisions of sub-paragraph (a) of this paragraph shall have effect with respect to so much of the allowance as is properly referable to the part of the trade transferred.

3.—(1) Where, when the contribution was made, the trade was carried on or to be carried on by a tenant of land in which the contributor had an interest, a writing-down allowance shall be made to a person for a chargeable period if at the end of that period he is entitled to the contributor's interest in the land, and section 11 of this Act shall, with the necessary modifications, apply in relation to a contribution made for the purposes of a trade carried on or to be carried on by a tenant of land as it applies in relation to expenditure incurred on the construction of a building or structure.

(2) Section 2 (3) of this Act shall not apply in relation to writing-down allowances to be made in respect of contributions.

Cross references.—See FA 1989, Sch. 13 para. 6 (in relation to contributions made after 26 July 1989, this paragraph to apply with certain modifications in relation to allowances under FA 1986, Sch. 15).

4. Paragraphs 2 and 3 of this Schedule shall not apply where the trade is husbandry in the United Kingdom or the occupation of woodlands in the United Kingdom, and in lieu thereof the provisions of section 68 (4), (5) of this Act shall apply with any necessary modifications.

Note.—See **Prospective Legislation Notes** (Commercial Woodlands).
Cross references.—See FA 1989, Sch. 13 para. 6 (in relation to contributions made after 26 July 1989, this paragraph not to apply in relation to allowances under FA 1986, Sch. 15).

FINANCE ACT 1968
(1968 Chapter 44)

55. Exchange Control

(3) In this section—

"certificate of deposit" means a document relating to money, in any currency, which has been despoited with the issuer or some other person, being a document which recognises an obligation to pay a stated amount to bearer or to order, with or without interest, and being a document by the delivery of which, with or without endorsement, the right to receive that stated amount, with or without interest, is transferable,

---

Note.—This provision is printed because a certificate of deposit mentioned in other provisions is defined by reference to this provision.

FINANCE ACT 1969

(1969 Chapter 32)

ARRANGEMENT OF SECTIONS

Note.—Provisions of this Act relevant to the taxes covered in this Handbook and not reproduced are either spent or repealed by TA 1988, Sch. 31 and other legislation.

PART II
INCOME TAX AND CORPORATION TAX

Children

Section
16. Reduction in age of majority for tax purposes.

PART VI
MISCELLANEOUS

58. Disclosure of information for statistical purposes by Board of Inland Revenue.
61. Citation, interpretation, construction, extent and repeals.

An Act to grant certain duties, to alter other duties, and to amend the law relating to the National Debt and the Public Revenue, and to make further provision in connection with Finance.

[25th July 1969]

PART II
INCOME TAX AND CORPORATION TAX

Children

16. Reduction in age of majority for tax purposes

(1) Subject to the following provisions of this section, section 1 of the Family Law Reform Act 1969 and section 1 of the Age of Majority (Scotland) Act 1969 (which reduce the age of majority to eighteen except for the purposes of the statutory provisions referred to in Schedule 2 thereof) shall apply for the purposes of any statutory provision, as defined in those sections, relating to income tax (including surtax), capital gains tax, corporation tax or estate duty; and accordingly paragraph 3 of Schedule 2 to each of those acts shall cease to have effect.

(2) ...[2]

(3)–(5) ...[1]

Amendments.—[1] Sub-ss. (3)–(5) repealed by TA 1970, Sch. 16.
[2] Sub-s. (2) repealed by Northern Ireland Constitution Act 1973, s. 41 (1) (*a*) and Sch. 6, Pt. I, with effect from 18th July 1973.

PART VI
MISCELLANEOUS

58. Disclosure of information for statistical purposes by Board of Inland Revenue

(1) For the purpose of any statistical survey conducted or to be conducted by the Department of Employment and Productivity or by the Business Statistics Office of the Board of Trade, the Board of Inland Revenue may disclose to an authorised officer of that Department or Office—

(a) the names and addresses of persons (in this section referred to as "employers") required under [section 203 of the Income and Corporation Taxes Act 1988][1] (pay as you earn) to make deductions of tax from payments of, or on account of, emoluments to which that section applies; and
(b) information concerning the number of persons (in this section referred to as "employees") in receipt of emoluments paid by an employer.

(2) For the purpose of any statistical survey relating to earnings conducted or to be conducted by the Department of Employment and Productivity, the Board of Inland Revenue may disclose to an authorised officer of that Department the name and address of the employer of any person who is one of a number of employees selected (as a statistical sample) for the purpose of that survey.

(3) Subsections (1) and (2) above shall have effect notwithstanding any obligation as to secrecy imposed on the Board or any officer of the Board under the Income Tax Management Act 1964 or otherwise.

(4) Subject to subsection (5) below, no information obtained by virtue of this section by an officer of the Department of Employment and Productivity or of the Business Statistics Office of the Board of Trade may be disclosed except—

(a) to [an][2] officer of that Department or Office for the purpose of the statistical survey concerned, or
(b) to another department (including a department of the Government of Northern Ireland) for the purpose of a statistical survey conducted or to be conducted by that department, [or][3]
[(c) to an authorised officer of any body specified in the first column of the following Table for the purposes of functions of that body under any enactment specified in relation to it in the second column of the Table.

TABLE

Body	Enactment
A local education authority in England and Wales.	Section 8 of the Employment and Training Act 1973.
An education authority in Scotland.	Section 126 of the Education (Scotland) Act 1980.
The Northern Ireland Training Authority.	The Industrial Training (Northern Ireland) Order 1984.
A local planning authority within the meaning of the Town and Country Planning Act 1971 and any board which exercises for any area the functions of such an authority.	Part II of the Town and Countrry Planning Act 1971.
A planning authority as defined in section 172 (3) of the Local Government (Scotland) Act 1973.	Part II of the Town and Country Planning (Scotland) Act 1972.
The Welsh Development Agency.	The Welsh Development Agency Act 1975.
The Scottish Development Agency.	The Scottish Development Agency Act 1975.
The Development Board for Rural Wales.	The Development of Rural Wales Act 1976.
The Highlands and Islands Development Board.	The Highlands and Islands Development (Scotland) Acts 1965 and 1968.

Body	Enactment
A development corporation within the meaning of the New Towns Act 1981.	Section 4 of the New Towns Act 1981.
A development corporation within the meaning of the New Towns (Scotland) Act 1968.	Section 3 of the New Towns (Scotland) Act 1968.
A new town commission within the meaning of the New Towns Act (Northern Ireland) 1965.	Section 7 of the New Towns Act (Northern Ireland) 1965.][3]

(5) Subsection (4) above does not apply to the disclosure of any such information as is mentioned in subsection (1) or subsection (2) above—

(a) in the form of a summary so framed as not to enable particulars relating to an employer or employee to be ascertained from it, or

(b) in the case of such information as is mentioned in subsection (1) above, with the consent of the employer concerned and, in the case of such information as is mentioned in subsection (2) above, with the consent of the employee concerned.

(6) If any person who has obtained any information by virtue of any provision of this section discloses that information otherwise than in accordance with paragraph (a) [paragraph (b) or paragraph (c) of subsection (4) above][4] or subsection (5) above, he shall be liable on summary conviction to a fine not exceeding . . . or on conviction on indictment to imprisonment for a term not exceeding two years or to fine or to both.

(7) References in this section to the Department of Employment and Productivity or the Business Statistics Office of the Board of Trade include references to any department of the Government of Northern Ireland carrying out similar functions.

Note.—By virtue of the Magistrates' Courts Act 1980, s. 32 (2), (9) and the Criminal Penalties etc (Increase) Order 1984, S.I. 1984 No. 447, Sch. 1, the amount of fine in sub-s. (6) is £2,000 for offences committed after 1 May 1984 or such other sum as may be substituted by the Secretary of State under s. 143 (1), (2) (b) of that Act.
Cross references.—See the Employment and Training Act 1973, s. 4 (6) (reference in this section to an officer of the Department of Employment to include a reference to an officer of the Manpower Services Commission).
Amendments.—[1] Words in sub-s. (1) (a) substituted by TA 1988, Sch. 29, para. 32 Table.
[2] Word in sub-s. (4) (a) substituted by the Employment and Training Act 1973, s. 4 (6), with effect from 1 January 1974; see the Employment and Training Act 1973 (Commencement No. 1) Order 1973, S.I. 1973 No. 2063.
[3] Sub-s. (4) (c) and the word "or" preceding it added by F (No. 2) A 1987, s. 69 (1), (2).
[4] Words in sub-s. (6) substituted by F (No. 2) A 1987, s. 69 (1), (3).

61. Citation, interpretation, construction, extent and repeals

(1) This Act may be cited as the Finance Act 1969.

(2) In this Act, except where the context otherwise requires, "the Board" means the Commissioners of Inland Revenue.

(3) In this Act—

(a), (b) . . .
(c) . . .[1];
(d) . . .
(e) . . .[2].

(4) Any reference in this Act to any other enactment shall, except so far as the context otherwise requires, be construed as a reference to that enactment as amended or applied by or under any other enactment, including this Act.

(5) Except as otherwise expressly provided, such of the provisions of this Act as relate to matters in respect of which the Parliament of Northern Ireland has power to make laws shall not extend to Northern Ireland.

(6) . . .

Note.—Sub-s. (3) (a), (b), (d) are outside the scope of this work.
Sub-s. (6) repeals enactments specified in Sch. 21. Effect has been given to these repeals, where applicable, in the relevant provisions of the earlier enactments.
Amendments.—[1] Sub-s. (3) (c) repealed by TA 1970, Sch. 16.
[2] Sub-s. (3) (e) repealed by CGTA 1979, s. 158 and Sch. 8.

TAXES MANAGEMENT ACT 1970

(1970 Chapter 9)

ARRANGEMENT OF SECTIONS

PART I
ADMINISTRATION

Section
1. Taxes under care and management of the Board.
2. General Commissioners.
3. Clerk to General Commissioners.
4. Special Commissioners.
4A. Deputy Special Commissioners.
5. General and Special Commissioners.
6. Declarations on taking office.

PART II
RETURNS OF INCOME AND GAINS

Income tax

7. Notice of liability to income tax.
8. Return of income.
9. Partnership return.

Corporation tax

10. Notice of liability to corporation tax.
11. Return of profits.

Capital gains

11A. Notice of liability to capital gains tax.
12. Information about chargeable gains.

PART III
OTHER RETURNS AND INFORMATION

13. Persons in receipt of taxable income belonging to others.
14. Return of lodgers and inmates.
15. Return of employees emoluments, etc.
16. Fees, commissions, etc.
16A. Agency workers.
17. Interest paid or credited by banks etc. without deduction of income tax.
18. Interest paid without deduction of income tax.
18A. Other payments and licences etc.
19. Information for purposes of Schedule A.

Production of accounts, books and other information

20. Power to call for documents of taxpayer and others.

Section
20A. Power to call for papers of tax accountant.
20B. Restrictions on powers under ss. 20 and 20A.
20BB. Falsification etc. of documents.
20C. Entry with warrant to obtain documents.
20CC. Procedure where documents etc. are removed.
20D. Interpretation of ss. 20 to 20C.
21. Stock jobbers' transactions.

"Surtax"

22. Additional particulars for "surtax".
23. Power to obtain copies of registers of securities.
24. Power to obtain information as to income from securities.

Chargeable gains

25. Issuing houses, stockbrokers, auctioneers, etc.
26. Nominee shareholders.
27. Settled property.
28. Non-resident companies and trusts.

PART IV
ASSESSMENT AND CLAIMS

29. Assessing procedure.
30. Recovery of overpayment of tax, etc.
31. Right of appeal.

Relief for excessive assessments

32. Double assessment.
33. Error or mistake.

Time limits

34. Ordinary time limit of six years.
35. Emoluments received after year for which they are assessable.
36. Fraudulent or negligent conduct.
37. Neglect: income tax and capital gains tax.
37A. Effect of assessment where allowances transferred.
38. Modification of s. 37 in relation to partnerships.
39. Neglect: corporation tax.
40. Assessment on personal representatives.
41. Leave of General or Special Commissioners required for certain assessments.

Claims

42. Procedure for making claims.
43. Time limit for making claims.
43A. Further assessments: claims etc.
43B. Limits on application of section 43A.

PART V
APPEALS AND OTHER PROCEEDINGS

Jurisdiction

44. General Commissioners.
45. Quorum of Special Commissioners.
46. General and Special Commissioners.
47. Special jurisdiction relating to tax on chargeable gains.
47A. *Special jurisdiction relating to development land tax.*
47B. Special jurisdiction relating to Business Expansion Scheme.

Proceedings before Commissioners

Section
48. Application to appeals and other proceedings.
49. Proceedings brought out of time.
50. Procedure.
51. Power of Commissioners to obtain information from appellant.
52. Evidence.
53. Summary award of penalties.
54. Settling of appeals by agreement.
55. Recovery of tax not postponed.
56. Statement of case for opinion of the High Court.
56A. Statement of case: Special Commissioners to Court of Appeal.

Chargeable gains

57. Regulations about appeals.

Capital Gains Tax Regulations

Development land tax

57A. *Regulations about appeals.* (Repealed).

Procedural rules

57B. Commissioners: procedural rules.

Northern Ireland

58. Proceedings in tax cases in Northern Ireland.
59. Election for county court in Northern Ireland.

PART VI

COLLECTION AND RECOVERY

60. Issue of demand notes and receipts.

Distraint and poinding

61. Distraint by collectors.
62. Priority of claim for tax.
63. Recovery of tax in Scotland.
63A. Sheriff officer's fees and outlays.
64. Priority of claim for tax in Scotland.

Court proceedings

65. Magistrates' courts.
66. County courts.
67. Inferior courts in Scotland.
68. High Court, etc.

Supplemental

69. Interest on tax.
70. Evidence.

PART VII
PERSONS CHARGEABLE IN A REPRESENTATIVE CAPACITY, ETC.

Income tax

Section
71. Bodies of persons.
72. Trustees, guardians, etc. of incapacitated persons.
73. Further provision as to infants.
74. Personal representatives.
75. Receivers appointed by a court.
76. Protection for certain trustees, agents and receivers.

Capital gains tax

77. Application of Part VII to capital gains tax.

PART VIII
CHARGES ON NON-RESIDENTS

Income tax

78. Method of charging non-residents.
79. Profits from branch or agency.
80. Charge on percentage of turnover.
81. Taxation on basis of merchanting profit.
82. Savings.
83. Responsibilities and indemnification of persons in whose name a non-resident person is chargeable.

Capital gains tax

84. Gains from branch or agency.

Corporation tax

85. Application of Part VIII to corporation tax.

PART IX
INTEREST ON OVERDUE TAX

86. Interest on overdue tax.
87. Interest on overdue advance corporation tax and income tax on company payments.
87A. Interest on overdue corporation tax etc.
88. Interest on tax recovered to make good loss due to taxpayer's fault.
88A. Determinations under section 88.
89. The prescribed rate of interest.
90. Disallowance of relief for interest on tax.
91. Effect on interest of reliefs.
92. Remission in certain cases of interest on tax in arrear by reason of exchange restrictions.

PART X
PENALTIES, ETC.

93. Failure to make return for income tax or capital gains tax.
94. Failure to make return for corporation tax.
95. Incorrect return or accounts for income tax or capital gains tax.
96. Incorrect return or accounts for corporation tax.
97. Incorrect return or accounts: supplemental.
97A. Two or more tax-geared penalties in respect of same tax.
98. Special returns, etc.
98A. Special penalties in the case of certain returns
99. Assisting in preparation of incorrect return etc.
100. Determination of penalties by officer of Board.

Section
100A. Provisions supplementary to section 100.
100B. Appeals against penalty determinations.
100C. Penalty proceedings before Commissioners.
100D. Penalty proceedings before court.
101. Evidence of profits for purposes of preceding provisions of Part X.
102. Mitigation of penalties.
103. Time limits for penalties.
104. Saving for criminal proceedings.
105. Evidence in cases of fraudulent conduct.
106. Refusal to allow a deduction of income tax, and avoidance of agreements for payment without deduction.

Scotland

107. Criminal liability for false statements made to obtain allowances.

PART XI

MISCELLANEOUS AND SUPPLEMENTAL

Companies

108. Responsibility of company officers.
109. Corporation tax on close company in connection with loans to participators etc.

Valuation

110. Valuation of land: power of entry.
111. Valuation of assets: power to inspect.

Documents

112. Loss, destruction or damage to assessments, returns, etc.
113. Form of returns and other documents.
114. Want of form or errors not to invalidate assessments, etc.
115. Delivery and service of documents.
116. *Receipts, etc. exempt from stamp duty.*

Northern Ireland

117. Action of ejection in Northern Ireland.

Interpretation

118. Interpretation.

PART XII

GENERAL

119. Commencement and construction.
120. Short title.

SCHEDULES:

Schedule 1—Forms of declarations.
Schedule 2—Jurisdiction in appeals on claims.
Schedule 3—Rules for assigning proceedings to Commissioners.
Schedule 4—*Savings and transitory provisions.*

An Act to consolidate certain of the enactments relating to income tax, capital gains tax and corporation tax, including certain enactments relating also to other taxes. [12th March 1970]

Construction.—FA 1988, s. 127 to be construed as if it were contained in this Act; see FA 1988, s. 127 (6).

PART I
ADMINISTRATION

1. Taxes under care and management of the Board

(1) Income tax, corporation tax and capital gains tax shall be under the care and management of the Commissioners of Inland Revenue (in this Act referred to as "the Board"), and the definition of "inland revenue" in section 39 of the Inland Revenue Regulation Act 1890 shall have effect accordingly.

(2) The Board shall appoint inspectors and collectors of taxes who shall act under the direction of the Board.

(3) Any legal proceedings or administration act relating to any tax begun by one inspector or collector may be continued by another inspector or, as the case may be, another collector; and any inspector or collector may act for any division or other area.

2. General Commissioners

(1) For the purpose of exercising such powers relating to appeals and other matters as are conferred on them by the Taxes Acts there shall be "Commissioners for the general purposes of the income tax" (in the Taxes Acts referred to as "General Commissioners") who shall act for the same separate areas in Great Britain as heretofore [or for the separate areas in Northern Ireland defined by an order made by the Lord Chancellor][4] (in the Taxes Acts referred to as "divisions").

(2) General Commissioners for divisions in England and Wales [or Northern Ireland][5] shall be appointed by, and shall hold office during the pleasure of, the Lord Chancellor.

(3) General Commissioners for divisions in Scotland shall be appointed by, and shall hold office during the pleasure of, [the Secretary of State][2] . . .[3]

(4) In Scotland a sheriff shall be ex officio a General Commissioner for any division wholly or partly within his sheriffdom, and a salaried sheriff-substitute shall be ex officio a General Commissioner for any division wholly or partly within his district.

(5) General Commissioners shall be entitled to receive out of moneys provided by Parliament payments by way of travelling allowance or subsistence allowance of such amounts and in such circumstances as may be determined by [the Minister for the Civil Service].[1]

(6) The Lord Chancellor or, in Scotland, the Secretary of State may by order create a new division or abolish an existing division or alter in any other respect the divisions or their boundaries; and any such order may contain such consequential and transitional provisions as the Lord Chancellor or the Secretary of State, as the case may be, thinks fit and may be revoked or varied by a subsequent order under this subsection.

. . .[6]

(7) A General Commissioner shall not continue in office after he attains the age of seventy-five years.

(8) The validity of any proceedings of General Commissioners shall not be affected by a defect in the appointment of any of them, or by a failure to observe the requirements of the last preceding subsection.

Cross references.—See FA 1972, s. 130 (compensation for loss of office, etc., by clerks to General Commissioners which is attributable to any order affecting a division made (whether before or after the passing of FA 1972) under sub-s. (6) of this section);
FA 1973, s. 41 (the alteration of local government areas due to take effect on 1 April 1974 (16 May 1975 in Scotland) is not to affect divisions, although orders may be made to take the changes into account).
Amendments.—[1] Words in sub-s. (5) substituted by the Minister for the Civil Service Order 1971, S.I. 1971 No. 2099, Art. 4 (2).
[2] Words in sub-s. (3) substituted by FA 1975, s. 57 (1) (*a*), with effect from 16 May 1975.

[3] Words in sub-s. (3) repealed by FA 1975, s. 57 (1) (*b*) and Sch. 13, Pt. II, with effect from 16 May 1975.
[4] Words in sub-s. (1) inserted by FA 1988, s. 134 (1), (4) with effect from 3 April 1989 by virtue of FA 1988 (Commencment) Order 1989, S.I. 1989 No. 473, subject to special provisions for proceedings instituted before 3 April 1989.
[5] Words in sub-s. (2) inserted by *ibid*.
[6] Words in sub-s. (6) repealed by FA 1988, Sch. 14 Pt. IX with effect from 3 April 1989 by virtue of FA 1988 (Commencment) Order 1989, S.I. 1989 No. 473.

3. Clerk to General Commissioners

(1) The General Commissioners for every division shall appoint a clerk and, if they think it necessary, an assistant clerk, and persons appointed under this subsection shall hold office during the pleasure of the Commissioners and act under their direction.

(2) A clerk shall be paid such remuneration in respect of his services as the Board may with the consent of the Minister for the Civil Service determine.

(3) The Board may, in such cases as they may in their discretion determine, pay to or in respect of any full-time clerk such pension [allowance][1] or gratuity, or make such provision for the payment of pension [allowance][1] or gratuity to or in respect of any full-time clerk, as they may with the consent of the Minister for the Civil Service determine.

In this subsection "full-time clerk" means a clerk as regards whom the Board are satisfied that he is required to devote substantially the whole of his time to the duties of his office.

(4) Without prejudice to the power of any General Commissioners to dismiss their clerk or assistant clerk, the Lord Chancellor or, in Scotland, the Secretary of State may, after consulting the General Commissioners for any division, dismiss their clerk or assistant clerk.

(5) A clerk or assistant clerk shall not continue in office after he has attained the age of seventy years unless the General Commissioners for whom he acts think it desirable in the public interest and extend his term of office; and the term shall not be extended beyond the age of seventy-five years.

Amendments.—[1] Word inserted in both places in sub-s. (3) by the Superannuation Act 1972, s. 29 and Sch 6, para. 77, with effect from 25 March 1972: the Superannuation Act 1972 (Commencement No. 1) Order 1972, S.I. 1972 No. 325, reg. 2.

[4. Special Commissioners

(1) The Lord Chancellor shall, after consultation with the Lord Advocate, appoint such persons as he thinks fit as "Commissioners for the special purposes of the Income Tax Acts" (in the Taxes Acts referred to as "Special Commissioners") and shall designate one of the Special Commissioners as the Presiding Special Commissioner.

(2) No person shall be appointed under subsection (1) above unless he is a barrister, advocate or solicitor of not less than ten years' standing.

(3) If the Presiding Special Commissioner is temporarily absent or unable to act or there is a vacancy in his office, the Lord Chancellor may designate another Special Commissioner to act as deputy Presiding Special Commissioner and the Commissioner so designated shall, when so acting, have all the functions of the Presiding Special Commissioner.

(4) The Lord Chancellor may, if he thinks fit, and after consultation with the Lord Advocate, remove a Special Commissioner from office on the grounds of incapacity or misbehaviour.

(5) By virtue of their appointment the Special Commissioners shall have authority to execute such powers, and to perform such duties, as are assigned to them by any enactment.

(6) Such sums shall be allowed to Special Commissioners in respect of salary and incidental expenses and such pensions (including allowances and gratuities) shall be paid to, or in respect of, them as the Lord Chancellor may, with the approval of the Treasury, determine.

(7) Officers and staff may be appointed under section 27 of the Courts Act 1971 (court staff) for carrying out the administrative work of the Special Commissioners.][1]

Amendments.—[1] This section substituted by FA 1984, Sch. 22, para. 1 and came into force on 1 January 1985 by virtue of FA 1984 (Commencement No. 2) Order 1984, S.I. 1984 No. 1836.

[4A. Deputy Special Commissioners

(1) If it appears to the Lord Chancellor expedient to do so in order to facilitate the performance of any functions of the Special Commissioners, he may, after consultation with the Lord Advocate, appoint a person to be a deputy Special Commissioner during such period or on such occasions as the Lord Chancellor thinks fit.

(2) A person shall not be qualified for appointment as a deputy Special Commissioner unless he is qualified for appointment as a Special Commissioner.

(3) A deputy Special Commissioner while acting under this section shall have all the jurisdiction and functions of a Special Commissioner and any reference to a Special Commissioner in the following provisions of this Act or in any other enactment or any instrument made under any enactment (whenever passed or made) shall include a reference to a deputy Special Commissioner.

(4) The duty under section 6 (1) below shall only apply to a deputy Special Commissioner on his first appointment to that office.

(5) Notwithstanding the expiry of any period for which a person is appointed under this section, he may continue to act under the appointment for the purpose of continuing to deal with any matter with which he was concerned during that period.

(6) The Lord Chancellor may pay to any person appointed under this section such remuneration and allowances as he may, with the approval of the Treasury, determine.][1]

Amendments.—[1] This section inserted by FA 1984, s. 127 and Sch. 22, para 1 and came into force on 1 January 1985 by virtue of FA 1984 (Commencement No. 2) Order 1984, S.I. 1984 No. 1836.

5. General and Special Commissioners

(1) No General Commissioner or Special Commissioner shall act as such in relation to any matter in which he has a personal interest, or is interested on behalf of another person, except with the express consent of the parties to the proceedings.

(2) . . .[1]

Amendments.—[1] Sub-s. (2) repealed by the Criminal Justice Act 1972, Sch. 6, Pt. I, with effect from 30 March 1974; see the Criminal Justice Act 1972 (Commencement No. 3) Order 1973, S.I. 1973 No. 1472.

6. Declarations on taking office

(1) Every person who is appointed to be—

(a) a General Commissioner or a Special Commissioner, or
(b) . . .[1]
(c) a member of the tribunal established under section [706][2] of the principal Act (cancellation of tax advantages),

shall make a declaration in the form set out in Part I of Schedule 1 to this Act before another person holding the same office, or before a General Commissioner.

(2) Every person who is appointed to be a clerk or assistant clerk to the General Commissioners for any division, or who assists any such clerk, shall make a declaration in the form set out in Part I of Schedule 1 to this Act.

A clerk or assistant clerk shall make the declaration before a General Commissioner for the division, and a person who assists any such clerk shall make the declaration before such a General Commissioner or the clerk.

(3) Every person who is appointed to be a member of the Board shall make a declaration in the form set out in Part II of Schedule 1 to this Act before another member of the Board.

(4) Every person who is appointed an inspector or collector, or who is appointed by the Board to serve in any other capacity, shall make a declaration in the form set out in Part III of Schedule 1 to this Act before such person as the Board may direct.

(5) A declaration under this section shall be made as soon as may be after first appointment to the office in question.

Amendments.—[1] Sub-s. (1) (b) repealed by FA 1982, Sch. 22, Pt. X.
[2] Number substituted by TA 1988, Sch. 29, para. 32 Table.

PART II
RETURNS OF INCOME AND GAINS

Cross references.—See TA 1988, ss. 253, 350 (4)–(7) (power of Board to make regulations modifying or replacing TA 1988, s. 234(5)–(9) and Schs. 13, 16).

Income tax

[7. Notice of liability to income tax

(1) Every person who is chargeable to income tax for any year of assessment and has neither—

 (*a*) delivered a return of his profits or gains or his total income for that year, nor
 (*b*) received a notice under section 8 of this Act requiring such a return,

shall, subject to subsections (2) to (5) below, within twelve months from the end of that year, give notice to the inspector that he is so chargeable, specifying each separate source of income.

(2) A source of income is excluded for the purposes of subsection (1) above in relation to any year of assessment if—

 (*a*) all payments of, or on account of, income from it during that year, and
 (*b*) all income from it for that year which does not consist of payments,

have or has been taken into account in the making of deductions or repayments of tax under section 203 of the principal Act.

(3) A source of income is excluded for the purposes of subsection (1) above in relation to any person and any year of assessment if all income from it for that year has been assessed or has been taken into account—

 (*a*) in determining that person's liability to tax, or
 (*b*) in the making of deductions or repayments of tax under section 203 of the principal Act.

(4) A source of income is excluded for the purposes of subsection (1) above in relation to any person and any year of assessment if all income from it for that year is—

 (*a*) income from which income tax has been deducted;
 (*b*) income from or on which income tax is treated as having been deducted or paid (not being income consisting of a payment to which section 559 of the principal Act applies); or
 (*c*) income chargeable under Schedule F,

and that person is not for that year liable to tax at a rate other than basic rate.

(5) A person shall not be required to give notice under subsection (1) above in respect of a year of assessment if and to the extent that his total income for that year consists of income from sources—

 (*a*) which are excluded under subsections (2) to (4) above, or
 (*b*) in respect of income from which he could not become liable to tax under assessments made more than twelve months after the end of that year.

(6) If any person, for any year of assessment, fails to comply with subsection (1) above as respects any source of income, he shall be liable to a penalty not exceeding the amount of the tax for which he is liable, in respect of income from that source for that year, under assessments made more than twelve months after the end of that year.

(7) In the case of a partner, the reference in subsection (6) above to the tax for which he is liable in respect of income from any source does not include a reference to tax assessable in the name of the partnership on so much of the income from that source as falls to be included in the total income of any other person.][1]

Amendments.—[1] This section substituted by FA 1988, s. 120.

8. Return of income

(1) Any person may be required by a notice given to him by an inspector or other officer of the Board to deliver to the officer within the time limited by the notice a return of his income, computed in accordance with the Income Tax Acts and specifying each separate source of income and the amount from each source.

(2) Any person may be required by a notice given to him by an inspector or other officer of the Board to deliver to the officer within the time limited by the notice a return of income which is not his income, but in respect of which he is chargeable in any capacity specified the notice, computed in accordance with the Income Tax Acts and specifying each separate source of income and the amount from each source.

(3) A notice under this section may require a return of income for a specified year of assessment, or a return which is, so far as relates to certain sources of income, a return of income for one year of assessment, and so far as relates to the remaining sources of income, a return of income for the preceding year of assessment.

[(3A) A notice given to trustees under this section may require a return of the income arising to them to include particulars of the manner in which the income has been applied, including particulars as to the exercise of any discretion and of the persons in whose favour it has been exercised.

In this subsection "trustees" and "income" have the same meaning as in section 686 of the principal Act.][5]

[(3B) A notice given to a person under this section may require him to include in the return of his income particulars of premiums paid by him or his wife living with him under policies of life insurance or contracts for deferred annuities and of deductions made from the premiums payable.][5]

(4) So far as a notice under this section relates to income chargeable under Case I or Case II of Schedule D, or any other income which may be computed by reference to the profits or gains of a period which is not a year of assessment, the notice may require a return of profits or gains (computed in accordance with the Income Tax Acts) for a period for which accounts are made up or a period by reference to which income is to be computed.

(5), (6) . . .[1]

(7) Every return under this section shall include a declaration by the person making the return to the effect that the return is to the best of his knowledge correct and complete.

(8) In this section references to returns of income computed in accordance with the Income Tax Acts are references to returns which include, as well as all particulars relating to income from which tax has not been deducted, all particulars relating to income from which tax has been deducted before receipt, and relating to charges on income, . . .[2]; and in this subsection the expression "charges on income" means amounts which fall to be deducted in computing total income . . .[2], or which would fall to be so deducted if the person to whose income the return relates were an individual [or would fall to be so deducted but for section [683 or 684][6] of the principal Act][3].

[(9) Where a person's income of which particulars are required to be included in a return under this section comprises a distribution chargeable under Schedule F there shall be separately stated in the return the amount or value of the distribution and the amount of any tax credit under section [231 of the principal Act][6] to which that person is entitled in respect of that distribution.][4]

Note.—See **Prospective Legislation Notes** (Married Couples).
Cross references.—See FA 1974, s. 24 (return of income of a person treated as employee to include emoluments, whether or not tax is chargeable on them),
CGTA 1979, s. 5 (5) (circumstances in which a statement by an individual will be sufficient compliance with any notice under this section),
s. 45 (3) (return under this section as regards capital gains accruing to a married woman);
FA 1988, Sch. 3, para. 26 (particulars to be included in a husband's return where his income is taxable partly in 1989–90 and partly in 1990–91 when new provisions regarding taxation of married couples come into effect).
Amendments.—[1] Sub-ss. (5) and (6) were repealed by FA 1971, ss. 37, 38 (1), Sch. 6, paras. 81, 82 (*a*), and Sch. 14, Pt. II, with effect from the year 1973–74.
[2] Words in sub-s. (8) were repealed, in both places, by FA 1971, ss. 37, 38 (1), Sch. 6, paras. 81, 82 (*b*) and Sch. 14, Pt. II, with effect from the year 1973–74.
[3] Words at end of sub-s. (8) were added by FA 1971, s. 37 (1) and Sch. 6, paras. 81, 82 (*b*), with effect from the year 1973–74.
[4] Sub-s. (9) was added by FA 1972, s. 111 and Sch. 24, para. 4, with effect from 6 April 1973.
[5] Sub-ss. (3A), (3B) inserted by TA 1988, Sch. 29, para. 4.
[6] Words in sub-ss. (8), (9) substituted by TA 1988, Sch. 29, para. 32 Table.

9. Partnership return

(1) Where a trade or profession is carried on by two or more persons jointly, the precedent partner, that is to say, the partner who, being resident in the United Kingdom—

(*a*) is first named in the agreement of partnership, or
(*b*) if there is no agreement, is named singly, or with precedence to the other partners in the usual name of the firm, or
(*c*) is the precedent acting partner, if the person named with precedence is not an acting partner.

shall make and deliver a return under section 8 above of the profits or gains of the trade or profession, on behalf of himself and the other partners, and declare in the return the names and residences of the other partners.

(2) Where no partner is resident in the United Kingdom, the return shall be made and delivered by the agent, manager or factor of the firm resident in the United Kingdom.

(3) . . .[1] an inspector may, if he thinks fit, require from every partner a like return, and the like information and evidence, as he is entitled to require from the precedent partner.

(4) This section shall apply to income chargeable to income tax in accordance with section [114][3] of the principal Act (partnerships involving companies), matters relevant only to corporation tax being omitted from the return, and the obligation to make and deliver the return being that of the individual partner or partners.

(5) . . .[2]

Amendments.—[1] Words in sub-s. (3) repealed by FA 1970, Sch. 8, Pt. VII.
[2] Sub-s. (5) was repealed by FA 1971, Sch. 14, Pt. IV.
[3] Number in sub-s. (4) substituted by TA 1988, Sch. 29, para. 32 Table.

Corporation tax

[10. Notice of liability to corporation tax

(1) Every company which is chargeable to corporation tax for any accounting period and has neither—

(*a*) made a return of its profits for that period, nor
(*b*) received a notice under section 11 of this Act requiring such a return,

shall, within twelve months from the end of that period, give notice to the inspector that it is so chargeable.

(2) If any company, for any accounting period ending on or before the appointed day, fails to comply with subsection (1) above, it shall be liable to a penalty not exceeding the amount of the corporation tax for which it is liable, in respect of its profits for that period, under assessments made more than twelve months after the end of that period.

(3) If any company, for any accounting period ending after the appointed day, fails to comply with subsection (1) above, it shall be liable to a penalty not exceeding the amount by which so much of the corporation tax chargeable on its profits for that period as remains unpaid twelve months after the end of that period exceeds any income tax borne by deduction from payments included in those profits.

(4) In determining—

(*a*) for the purposes of subsection (2) above, for how much corporation tax a company is liable, in respect of its profits for an accounting period, under assessments made more than twelve months after the end of that period; or
(*b*) for the purposes of subsection (3) above, how much of the corporation tax chargeable on the profits of a company for an accounting period remained unpaid at the time of any failure to comply with subsection (1) above,

no account shall be taken of the discharge of any liability for that tax which, pursuant to a claim under subsection (3) of section 239 of the principal Act, is attributable to an amount of surplus advance corporation tax, as defined in that subsection.

(5) In this section "the appointed day" means the day appointed for the purposes of section 8(3) of the principal Act.][1]

Amendments.—[1] This section substituted by FA 1988, s 121 with respect to notices required to be given in respect of accounting periods ending after 31 March 1989.

11. Return of profits

(1) A company may be required by a notice served on the company by an inspector or other officer of the Board to deliver to the officer within the time limited by the notice a return of the profits of the company computed in accordance with the Corporation Tax Acts—

(a) specifying the income taken into account in computing those profits, with the amount from each source,
(b) giving particulars of all disposals giving rise to chargeable gains or allowable losses under the provisions of [the Capital Gains Tax Act 1979][2] and the Corporation Tax Acts and particulars of those chargeable gains or allowable losses, and
(c) giving particulars of all charges on income to be deducted against those profits for the purpose of assessment to corporation tax.

(2) A notice under this section may require a return of profits arising in any period during which the company was within the charge to corporation tax.

(3) Every return under this section shall include a declaration to the effect that the return is correct and complete.

(4) A return under this section which includes profits which are payments on which the company has borne income tax by deduction shall specify the amount of income tax so borne.

(5) A notice under this section may require the inclusion in the return of particulars of management expenses, capital allowances and balancing charges which have been taken into account in arriving at the profits included in the return.

[(6) A notice under this section may require the inclusion in the return of particulars of advance corporation tax paid by the company (and not repaid) and of any surplus advance corporation tax carried forward under section [239 (4) of the principal Act][3].][1]

Note.—See **Prospective Legislation Notes** (Taxes Management Provisions).
Cross references.—See TA 1988, s. 239 (5) (a return made by a company under this section containing particulars of advance corporation tax or surplus advance corporation tax which falls to be dealt with under sub-ss. (1) and (4) of that section to be treated as a claim).
Amendments.—[1] Sub-s. (6) added by FA 1972, s. 111 and Sch. 24, para. 5, with effect from 6 April 1973.
[2] Words in sub-s. (1) (b) substituted by CGTA 1979, s. 157 (2)–(4) and Sch. 7, para. 8 Table, Pt. I.1, with effect from 22 March 1979.
[3] Words in sub-s. (6) substituted by TA 1988, Sch. 29, para. 32 Table.

Capital gains

[11A. Notice of liability to capital gains tax

(1) Every person who is chargeable to capital gains tax for any year of assessment and has neither—

(a) delivered a return of his chargeable gains for that year, nor
(b) received a notice under section 8 of this Act requiring such a return,

shall, within twelve months from the end of that year, give notice to the inspector that he is so chargeable; but a person all of whose chargeable gains for a year of assessment have been assessed shall not be required to give notice under this subsection in respect of that year.

(2) If any person, for any year of assessment, fails to comply with subsection (1) above, he shall be liable to a penalty not exceeding the amount of the tax for which he is liable, in respect of his chargeable gains for that year, under assessments made more than twelve months after the end of that year.

(3) In this section references to a person's chargeable gains for a year of assessment include, if section 45 (1) of the Capital Gains Tax Act 1979 applies in relation to him and his wife in that year, her chargeable gains for that year.][1]

Note.—See **Prospective Legislation Notes** (Married Couples).
Amendments.—[1] This section inserted by FA 1988, s. 122 (1).

12. Information about chargeable gains

[(1) Section 8 of this Act shall apply in relation to capital gains tax as it applies in relation to income tax, and subject to any necessary modifications.][1]

(2) A notice under section 8 or section 11 of this Act may require particulars of any assets

acquired by the person on whom the notice was served (or if the notice relates to income or chargeable gains of some other person, of any assets acquired by that other person) in the period specified in the notice (being a period beginning not earlier than 6th April 1965) but excluding—

[(*a*) any assets exempted by the following provisions of the Capital Gains Tax Act 1979, namely—

(i) section 19 (4) (rights to winnings from pool betting, lotteries or games with prizes),
(ii) section 71 (government non-marketable securities),
(iii) section 130, 131 or 133 (passenger vehicles, decorations for valour or gallant conduct and foreign currency for personal expenditure)][1]

(*b*) unless the amount or value of the consideration for its acquisition exceeded [£6,000][5], any asset which is tangible movable property and is not within the exceptions in [section 128 (6)][2] of the said Act (terminal markets and currency), or
(*c*) any assets acquired as trading stock.

(3) The particulars required under this section may include particulars of the person from whom the asset was acquired, and of the consideration for the acquisition.

(4) A return of income of a partnership under section 9 of this Act shall include—

(*a*) with respect to any disposal of partnership property during a period to which any part of the return relates, the like particulars as if the partnership were liable to tax on any chargeable gain accruing on the disposal, and
(*b*) with respect to any acquisition of partnership property, the particulars required under subsection (2) above.

(5) In this section "trading stock" has the meaning given by section [100 (2)][3] of the principal Act.

Amendments.—[1] Sub-s. (2) (*a*) substituted by CGTA 1979, s. 157 (2)–(4) and Sch. 7, para. 1 (2), with effect from 22 March 1979.
[2] Words in sub-s. (2) (*b*) substituted by CGTA 1979, s. 157 (2)–(4) and Sch. 7, para. 9 Table, with effect from 22 March 1979.
[3] Number in sub-s. (5) substituted by TA 1988, Sch. 29, para. 32 Table.
[4] Sub-s. (1) substituted by FA 1988, s. 122 (2).
[5] Amount in sub-s. (2) (*b*) substituted by FA 1989, s. 123 (1) (*b*), (2) in relation to assets acquired after 5 April 1989.

PART III

Cross references.—See TA 1988, ss. 253, 350 (4)–(7) (power of Board to make regulations modifying or replacing TA 1988, s. 234 (5)–(9) and Schs. 13, 16.

OTHER RETURNS AND INFORMATION

13. Persons in receipt of taxable income belonging to others

(1) Every person who, in whatever capacity, is in receipt of any money or value, or of any profits or gains from any of the sources mentioned in the Income Tax Acts, of or belonging to another person who is chargeable to income tax in respect thereof, or who would be so chargeable if he were resident in the United Kingdom and not an incapacitated person, shall, whenever required to do so by a notice given to him by an inspector, prepare and deliver, within the time mentioned in the notice, a return . . .[1], signed by him, containing—

(a) a statement of all such money, value, profits or gains, and
(b) the name and address of every person to whom the same belong, and
(c) a declaration whether every such person is of full age, or is a married woman, or is resident in the United Kingdom or is an incapacitated person.

(2) If any person described above is acting jointly with any other person, he shall, in like manner, deliver a return of the names and addresses of all persons joined with him at the time of delivery of the return mentioned in subsection (1) above.

[(3) A notice under this section shall not require information as to any money, value, profits or gains received in a year of assessment ending more than three years before the date of the giving of the notice.][2]

Note.—See **Prospective Legislation Notes** (Married Couples).
Amendments.—[1] Words in sub-s. (1) repealed by FA 1970, Sch. 8, Pt. VII.
[2] Sub-s. (3) added by FA 1988, s. 123 (1), (5) with respect to notices given after the passing of FA 1988. FA 1988 was passed on 29 July 1988.

14. Return of lodgers and inmates

Every person, when required to do so by a notice served on him by an inspector, shall, within the time limited by the notice, prepare and deliver to the inspector a return, in writing, containing to the best of his belief—

(a) the name of every lodger or inmate resident in his dwelling-house, and
(b) the name and ordinary place of residence of any such lodger or inmate who has any ordinary place of residence elsewhere at which he can be assessed and who desires to be assessed at such ordinary place of residence.

[15. Return of employees emoluments, etc.

(1) Every employer, when required to do so by notice from an inspector, shall, within the time limited by the notice, prepare and deliver to the inspector a return relating to persons who are or have been employed by him, containing the information required under the following provisions of this section.

(2) An employer shall not be required to include in his return information relating to a year of assessment beginning more than six years before the year of assessment in which the notice is given.

(3) A notice under subsection (1)—

(a) shall specify the employees for whom a return is to be made and may, in particular, specify individuals (by name or otherwise) or all employees of an employer or all his employees who are in [employment to which Chapter II of Part V of the principal Act applies][3]; and
(b) shall specify the years of assessment of other periods with respect to which the information is to be provided.

(4) A notice under subsection (1) may require the return to state the name and place of residence of an employee to whom it relates.

(5) A notice under subsection (1) may require the return to contain, in respect of an

employee to whom it relates, particulars of the payments made to him in respect of his employment including—

(*a*) payments to him in respect of expenses (including sums put at his disposal and paid away by him).
(*b*) payments made on his behalf and not repaid, and
(*c*) payments to him for services rendered in connection with a trade or business, whether the services were rendered in the course of his employment or not.

(6) Where, for the purposes of his return, an employer apportions expenses incurred partly in or in connection with a particular matter and partly in or in connection with other matters—

(*a*) the return shall contain a statement that the sum included in the return is the result of such an apportionment; and
(*b*) if required to do so by notice from the inspector, he shall prepare and deliver to the inspector within the time limited by the notice, a return containing full particulars as to the amount apportioned and the manner in which, and the grounds on which, the apportionment has been made.

(7) A notice under subsection (1) may require the return—

(*a*) to state in respect of an employee to whom it relates whether any benefits are or have been provided for him (or for any other person) by reason of his employment, such as may give rise to charges to tax under [sections 141, 142, 143, 145 or 154 to 165 of the principal Act][2] (miscellaneous benefits in cash or in kind); and
(*b*) if such benefits are or have been provided, to contain such particulars of those benefits as may be specified in the notice.

(8) Where such benefits are provided the notice may, without prejudice to subsection (7) (*b*), require the return to contain the following particulars—

(*a*) where the benefits are or have been provided by the employer, particulars of the cost of providing them; and
(*b*) where the benefits are or have been provided otherwise than by the employer himself, the name and business address of any person who has (either by arrangement with the employer, or to his knowledge) provided them.

(9) Where it appears to an inspector that a person has, in any year of assessment, been concerned in providing benefits to or in respect of employees of another, the inspector may at any time up to 6 years after the end of that year of assessment by notice require him to deliver to the inspector, within the time limited by the notice, such particulars of those benefits as may be specified in the notice (so far as known to him) and to include with those particulars the names and addresses (so far as known to him) of the employees concerned.

(10) Where the employer is a body of persons, the secretary of the body or other officer (by whatever name called) performing the duties of secretary shall be treated as the employer for the purposes of this section.
Provided that, where the employer is a body corporate, that body corporate, as well as the secretary or other officer, shall be liable to a penalty for failure to comply with this section.

(11) In this section—

(*a*) "employee" means an office holder or employee whose emoluments fall to be assessed under Schedule E, and related expressions are to be construed accordingly; . . . [4]
(*b*) . . .[4]][1]

Cross references.—See FA 1974, s. 24 (application of this section where employer not resident but duties performed for benefit of person resident or trading in U.K.);
FA 1976, Sch. 9, para. 6 (validation of anything done before 29 July 1976 in reliance on the old s. 15);
Amendments.—[1] This section substituted by FA 1976, Sch. 9, para. 1.
[2] Words in sub-ss. (7) (*a*), (11) (*b*) substituted by TA 1988, Sch. 29, para. 32 Table.
[3] Words in sub-s. (3) (*a*) substituted by FA 1989, s. 53 (2) (*g*).
[4] Sub-s. (11) (*b*) and the word "and" preceding it repealed by FA 1989, Sch. 17, Pt. IV.

16. Fees, commissions, etc.

(1) Every person carrying on a trade or business shall, if required to do so by notice from an inspector, make and deliver to the inspector a return of all payments of any kind specified in the notice made during a period so specified, being—

(*a*) payments made in the course of the trade or business, or of such part of the trade or business as may be specified in the notice, for services rendered by persons not employed in the trade or business, or

(b) payments for services rendered in connection with the formation, acquisition, development or disposal of the trade or business, or any part of it, by persons not employed in the trade or business, or

(c) periodical or lump sum payments made in respect of any copyright [, public lending right, right in a registered design or design right][1].

(2) Every body of persons carrying on any activity which does not constitute a trade or business shall, if required to do so by notice from an inspector, make and deliver to the inspector a return of all payments of a kind specified in the notice made during a period so specified, being—

(a) payments made in the course of carrying on the activity, or such part of the activity as may be specified in the notice, for services rendered by persons not employed by the said body of persons, or

(b) periodical or lump sum payments made in respect of any copyright [, public lending right, right in a registered design or design right][1].

(3) A return required under either of the preceding subsections shall, if the trade or business or other activity is carried on by an unincorporated body of persons (other than a company), be made and delivered by the person who is or performs the duties of secretary of the body, and the notice shall be framed accordingly.

(4) A return under the preceding provisions of this section shall give the name of the person to whom each payment was made, the amount of the payment and such other particulars (including particulars as to the services or rights in respect of which the payment was made, the period over which any services were rendered and any business name and any business or home address of the person to whom payment was made) as may be specified in the notice.

(5) No person shall be required under the preceding provisions of this section to include in a return—

(a) particulars of any payment from which income tax is deductible, or

(b) particulars of payments made to any one person where the total of the payments to that person which would otherwise fall to be included in the return does not exceed £15, or

(c) particulars of any payment made in a year of assessment ending more than three years before the service of the notice requiring him to make the return.

(6) . . .[3]

(7) In this section—

(a) references to payments for services include references to payments in the nature of commission of any kind and references to payments in respect of expenses incurred in connection with the rendering of services, and

(b) references to the making of payments include references to the giving of any valuable consideration,

and the requirement imposed by subsection (4) above to state the amount of a payment shall, in relation to any consideration given otherwise than in the form of money, be construed as a requirement to give particulars of the consideration.

[(8) In subsection (2) above references to a body of persons include references to any department of the Crown, any public or local authority and any other public body.][2]

Amendments.—[1] Words in sub-ss. (1) (c), (2) (b) substituted for the words "or public lending right" by the Copyright, Designs and Patents Act 1988, Sch. 7, para. 13 with effect from 1 August 1989 by virtue of the Copyright, Designs and Patents Act 1988 (Commencement No. 1) Order 1989, S.I. 1989 No. 816.
[2] Sub-s. (8) added by FA 1988, s. 124.
[3] Sub-s. (6) repealed by FA 1989, s. 164 (6), (7) (a) and Sch. 17, Pt. VIII in relation to any failure to comply with a notice served after 26 July 1989. Sub-s. (6) read—

"(6) A person who fails to deliver, within the time limited in any notice served on him under this section, a true and correct return which he is required by the notice to deliver shall be liable to a penalty not exceeding £50 and, after judgment has been given for that penalty, to a further penalty of the like amount for every day during which the failure continues."

16A. Agency workers

(1) Where—

(a) any services which an individual renders or is under an obligation to render under a contract are treated under section 134(1) of the principal Act as the duties of an office or employment held by him; or

(b) any remuneration receivable under or in consequence of arrangements to which subsection (6) of that section applies is treated under that subsection as emoluments of an office or employment held by an individual,

section 15 above shall apply as if that individual were employed—

(i) in a case within paragraph (*a*) above, by the persons or each of the persons from whom he receives any remuneration under or in consequence of the contract; and
(ii) in a case within paragraph (*b*) above, by the other party to the arrangements,

and section 16 above shall not apply to any payments made to that individual under or in consequence of that contract or those arrangements.

(2) In subsection (1) above "remuneration", in relation to an individual, does not include anything in respect of which he would not have been chargeable to tax under Schedule E if it had been receivable in connection with an office or employment held by him but, subject to that, includes every form of payment and all perquisites, benefits and profits whatsoever.][1]

Amendments.—[1] This section inserted by TA 1988, Sch. 29, para. 6.

17. Interest paid or credited by banks etc. without deduction of income tax

(1) Every person carrying on a trade or business who, in the ordinary course of the operations thereof, receives or retains money in such circumstances that interest becomes payable thereon which is paid or credited without deduction of income tax, and, in particular, every person carrying on the trade or business of banking, shall, if required to do so by notice from an inspector, make and deliver to the inspector, within the time specified in the notice, a return of all interest paid or credited by him as aforesaid during a year [of assessment][1] specified in the notice in the course of his trade or business or any such part of his trade or business as may be so specified, giving the names and addresses of the persons to whom the interest was paid or credited and stating, in each case, the amount of the interest:

Provided that—

(*a*) no interest paid or credited to any person shall be required to be included in any such return if the total amount of the interest paid or credited to that person which would otherwise have fallen to be included in the return does not exceed £15, and
(*b*) the year specified in a notice under this subsection shall not be a year ending more than three years before the date of the service of the notice.

(2) Without prejudice to the generality of so much of subsection (1) above as enables different notices to be served thereunder in relation to different parts of a trade or business, separate notices may be served under that subsection as respects the transactions carried on at any branch or branches respectively specified in the notices, and any such separate notice shall, if served on the manager or other person in charge of the branch or branches in question, be deemed to have been duly served on the person carrying on the trade or business; and where such a separate notice is so served as respects the transactions carried on at any branch or branches, any notice subsequently served under the said subsection (1) on the person carrying on the trade or business shall not be deemed to extend to any transaction to which the said separate notice extends.

(3) This section shall, with any necessary adaptations, apply in relation to the National Savings Bank as if it were a trade or business carried on by the Director of Savings.

(4) This section shall apply only to money received or retained in the United Kingdom, and if a person to whom any interest is paid or credited in respect of any money received or retained in the United Kingdom by notice in writing served on the person paying or crediting the interest—

(*a*) declares that the person who was beneficially entitled to that interest when it was paid or credited was not then ordinarily resident in the United Kingdom, and
(*b*) requests that the interest shall not be included in any return under this section,

the person paying or crediting the interest shall not be required to include that interest in any such return.

Amendments.—[1] Words in sub-s. (1) inserted by FA 1988, s. 123 (2), (5) with respect to notices given after the passing of FA 1988. FA 1988 was passed on 29 July 1988.

18. Interest paid without deduction of income tax

(1) Any person by whom any interest is paid in the year 1969–70 or any subsequent year of assessment without deduction of income tax . . .[1] shall, on being so required by a notice given to him by an inspector, furnish to the inspector, within the time limited by the notice—

    (a) the name and address of the person to whom the interest has been paid or on whose behalf the interest has been received, and
    (b) the amount of the interest so paid or received,

and any person who receives any such interest on behalf of another person shall on being so required furnish to the inspector the name and address of the person on whose behalf the interest has been received, and its amount.

(2) The persons to whom [subsection (1) above][2] applies include any officer in any public office or in any department of the Crown.

(3) [Subsection (1) above][2] shall not impose any obligation on a bank carrying on a bona fide business in the United Kingdom in respect of any interest paid by the bank in the ordinary course of that business.

[(3A) A notice under this section shall not require information with respect to interest paid in a year of assessment ending more than three years before the date of the giving of the notice.][4]

[(4) . . .[3]

Amendments.—[1] Words in sub-s. (1) which were inserted by TA 1988, Sch. 29, para. 7 repealed by FA 1988, Sch. 14, Pt. IV.
[2] Words in sub-ss. (2), (3) substituted by TA 1988, Sch. 29, para. 7.
[3] Sub-s. (4) which was inserted by TA 1988, Sch. 29, para. 7 repealed by FA 1988, Sch. 14, Pt. IV.
[4] Sub-s. (3A) added by FA 1988, s. 123 (3), (5) with respect to notices given after the passing of FA 1988. FA 1988 was passed on 29 July 1988.

[18A. Other payments and licences etc.

(1) Any person by whom any payment out of public funds is made by way of grant or subsidy shall, on being so required by a notice given to him by an inspector, furnish to the inspector, within the time limited by the notice—

    (a) the name and address of the person to whom the payment has been made or on whose behalf the payment has been received, and
    (b) the amount of the payment so made or received,

and any person who receives any such payment on behalf of another person shall on being so required furnish to the inspector the name and address of the person on whose behalf the payment has been received, and its amount.

(2) Any person by whom licences or approvals are issued or a register is maintained shall, on being so required by a notice given to him by an inspector, furnish to the inspector, within the time limited by the notice—

    (a) the name and address of any person who is or has been the holder of a licence or approval issued by the first-mentioned person, or to whom an entry in that register relates or related; and
    (b) particulars of the licence or entry.

(3) the persons to whom this section applies include any department of the Crown, any public or local authority and any other public body.

(4) A notice is not to be given under this section unless (in the inspector's reasonable opinion) the information required is or may be relevant to any tax liability to which a person is or may be subject, or the amount of any such liability.

(5) A notice under this section shall not require information with respect to a payment which was made, or to a licence, approval or entry which ceased to subsist—

    (a) before 6th April 1988; or
    (b) in a year of assessment ending more than three years before the date of the giving of the notice.

(6) For the purposes of this section a payment is a payment out of public funds if it is

provided directly or indirectly by the Crown, by any Government, public or local authority whether in the United Kingdom or elsewhere or by any Community institution.][1]

Amendments.—[1] This section inserted by FA 1988, s. 125.

19. Information for purposes of Schedule A

(1) For the purpose of obtaining particulars of profits or gains chargeable to tax under Schedule A (or, for chargeable periods ending before 6th April 1970, under Case VIII of Schedule D), the inspector may by notice in writing require—

(*a*) any lessee, occupier or former lessee or occupier of land (including any person having, or having had, the use of land) to give such information as may be prescribed by the Board as to the terms applying to the lease, occupation or use of the land, and where any of those terms are established by any written instrument, to produce the instrument to the inspector,

(*b*) any lessee or former lessee of land to give such information as may be so prescribed as to any consideration given for the grant or assignment to him of the tenancy,

(*c*) any person who as agent manages land or is in receipt of rent or other payments arising from land to furnish the inspector with such particulars relating to payments arising therefrom as may be specified in the notice.

(2) Subsection (1) above shall apply in relation to sums chargeable to tax under Case VI of Schedule D by virtue of any provision of sections [34 to 36][1] of the principal Act as it applies to profits or gains chargeable to tax under Schedule A or Case VIII of Schedule D.

(3) In this section—

(*a*) "lease" includes an agreement for a lease, and any tenancy, but does not include a mortgage or heritable security, and "lessee" shall be construed accordingly but shall include the successor in title of a lessee,

(*b*) in relation to Scotland "assignment" means an assignation.

[(4) A notice under this section shall not require information with respect to—

(*a*) the terms applying to the lease, occupation or use of the land, or
(*b*) consideration given, or
(*c*) payments arising,

in a year of assessment ending more than three years before the date of the giving of the notice.][2]

Amendments.—[1] Numbers in sub-s. (2) substituted by TA 1988, Sch. 29, para. 32 Table.
[2] Sub-s. (4) added by FA 1988, s. 123 (4), (5) with respect to notices given after the passing of FA 1988. FA 1988 was passed on 29 July 1988.

Production of accounts, books and other information

[20. Power to call for documents of taxpayer and others

(1) Subject to this section, an inspector may by notice in writing require [a person—

(*a*) to deliver to him such documents as are in the person's possession or power and as (in the inspector's reasonable opinion) contain, or may contain, information relevant to—

(i) any tax liability to which the person is or may be subject, or
(ii) the amount of any such liability, or

(*b*) to furnish to him such particulars as the inspector may reasonably require as being relevant to, or to the amount of, any such liability.]

(2) Subject to this section, the Board may by notice in writing require [a person—

(*a*) to deliver to a named officer of the Board such documents as are in the person's possession or power and as (in the Board's reasonable opinion) contain, or may contain, information relevant to—

(i) any tax liability to which the person is or may be subject, or
(ii) the amount of any such liability, or

(*b*) to furnish to a named officer of the Board such particulars as the Board may reasonably require as being relevant to, or to the amount of, any such liability.][6]

(3) Subject to this section, an inspector may, for the purpose of enquiring into the tax liability of any person ("the taxpayer"), by notice in writing require any [other person][7] to deliver to the inspector or, if the person to whom the notice is given so elects, to make available for inspection by a named officer of the Board, such documents as are in his possession or power and as (in the inspector's reasonable opinion) contain, or may contain, information relevant to any tax liability to which the taxpayer is or may be, or may have been, subject, or to the amount of any such liability [; and the persons who may be required to deliver or make available a document under this subsection include the Director of Savings.][8]

(4) The persons so subject are—

    (a) the taxpayer's spouse, and any son or daughter of his;
    (b) in so far as the inspector's enquiries relate to liability of the taxpayer in respect of income, profits or gains that were, or may have been, derived from—

        (i) any business (past or present) carried on by the taxpayer or his spouse, or
        (ii) any business (past or present) with whose management either of them was concerned at a material time,

any person who is carrying on a business, or was doing so at a material time, [any company, whether carrying on a business or not, and the Director of Savings][2]][9].

(5) For the purposes of subsection (4) above, every director of a company is to be taken as being concerned with the management of any business carried on by the company; and a material time is any time which (in the inspector's reasonable opinion) is, or may have been, material in the ascertainment of any past or present tax liability of the taxpayer.[9]

(6) The persons who may be treated as "the taxpayer" [for the purposes of this section][10] include a company which has ceased to exist and an individual who has died; . . .[11]

(7) Notices under [subsection (1) or (3) above][3] are not to be given by an inspector unless he is authorised by the Board for its purposes; and—

    (a) a notice is not to be given by him except with the consent of a General or Special Commissioner; and
    (b) the Commissioner is to give his consent only on being satisfied that in all the circumstances the inspector is justified in proceeding under this section.

[(8) Subject to subsection (8A) below, a notice under subsection (3) above shall name the taxpayer with whose liability the inspector (or, where section 20B(3) below applies, the Board) is concerned.][12]

[(8A) If, on an application made by an inspector and authorised by order of the Board, a Special Commissioner gives his consent, the inspector may give such a notice as is mentioned in subsection (3) above but without naming the taxpayer to whom the notice relates; but such a consent shall not be given unless the Special Commissioner is satisfied—

    (a) that the notice relates to a taxpayer whose identity is not known to the inspector or to a class of taxpayers whose individual identities are not so known;
    (b) that there are reasonable grounds for believing that the taxpayer or any of the class of taxpayers to whom the notice relates may have failed or may fail to comply with any provision of the Taxes Acts;
    (c) that any such failure is likely to have led or to lead to serious prejudice to the proper assessment or collection of tax; and
    (d) that the information which is likely to be contained in the documents to which the notice relates is not readily available from another source.][4]

[(8B) A person to whom there is given a notice under subsection (8A) above may, by notice in writing given to the inspector within thirty days after the date of the notice under that subsection, object to that notice on the ground that it would be onerous for him to comply with it; and if the matter is not resolved by agreement, it shall be referred to the Special Commissioners, who may confirm, vary or cancel that notice.][4]

[(8C) In this section references to documents do not include—

    (a) personal records (as defined in section 12 of the Police and Criminal Evidence Act 1984), or
    (b) journalistic material (as defined in section 13 of that Act),

and references to particulars do not include particulars contained in such personal records or journalistic material.][13]

[(8D) Subject to subsection (8C) above, references in this section to documents and particulars are to those specified or described in the notice in question; and—

(a) the notice shall require documents to be delivered (or delivered or made available), or particulars to be furnished, within such time (which, except in the case of a notice under subsection (2) above, shall not be less than thirty days after the date of the notice) as may be specified in the notice; and

(b) the person to whom they are delivered, made available or furnished may take copies of them or of extracts from them.][13]

(9) To the extent specified in section 20 B below, the above provisions are subject to the restrictions of that section.][1]

Amendments.—[1] This section and ss. 20A to 20D, *post,* substituted for s. 20 by FA 1976, Sch. 6.
[2] Words in sub-s. (4) (b) substituted by FA 1988, s. 126 (1), (6) with respect to notices given after the passing of FA 1988. FA 1988 was passed on 29 July 1988.
[3] Words in sub-s. (7) substituted by FA 1988, s. 126 (2), (6) with respect to notices given after the passing of FA 1988. FA 1988 was passed on 29 July 1988.
[4] Sub-ss. (8A), (8B) inserted by FA 1988, s. 126 (3), (6) with respect to notices given after the passing of FA 1988. FA 1988 was passed on 29 July 1988.
[5] Words in sub-s. (1) substituted by FA 1989, s. 142 with respect to notices given after 26 July 1989. The original words are—

"a person to deliver to him such documents as are in the person's possession or power and as (in the inspector's reasonable opinion) contain, or may contain, information relevant to any tax liability to which the person is or may be subject, or to the amount of any such liability."

[6] Words in sub-s. (2) substituted by *ibid.* The original words are—

"a person to deliver, to a named officer of theirs, such documents as are in the person's possession or power and as (in the Board's reasonable opinion) contain, or may contain, information relevant to any tax liability to which he is or may be subject, or to the amount of any such liability."

[7] Words in sub-s. (3) substituted by *ibid.* The original words are "of the persons who in relation to the taxpayer are subject to this subsection".
[8] Words in sub-s. (3) added by *ibid.*
[9] Sub-ss (4), (5) repealed by *ibid* and Sch. 17, Pt. VIII with respect to notices given after 26 July 1989.
[10] Words in sub-s. (6) substituted by FA 1989, s. 142. The original words are "under subsections (3) and (4)".
[11] Words "and in relation to such an individual the references in subsection (4) to the spouse are then instead to the widow or widower (the circumstance that she or he may have re-married being immaterial for the purposes of those subsections)." in sub-s. (6) repealed by *ibid* and Sch. 17, Pt. VIII with respect to notices given after 26 July 1989.
[12] Sub-s. (8) substituted by *ibid.* The original sub-s. (8) reads—

"(8) The references in subsections (1), (2) and (3) above to documents are to those specified or described in the notice in question; and—

(a) the notice shall require them to be delivered or (as the case may be) made available within such time as may be there specified; and
(b) the person to whom they are delivered or made available may take copies of, or extracts from them;

and a notice under subsection (3) shall name the taxpayer with whose liability the inspector (or, as the case may be, the Board) is concerned."

[13] Sub-ss. (8C), (8D) inserted by *ibid.*

[20A. Power to call for papers of tax accountant

(1) Where after the passing of the Finance Act 1976 a person—

(a) is convicted of an offence in relation to tax (whenever committed) by or before any court in the United Kingdom; or
(b) has [a penalty imposed on][3] him (whether before or after the passing of that Act) under section 99 of this Act,

and he has stood in relation to others as tax accountant, an inspector authorised by the Board for the purpose of this section may by notice in writing require the person to deliver to him such documents as are in his possession or power and as (in the inspector's reasonable opinion) contain information relevant to any tax liability to which any client of his is or has been, or may be or have been, subject, or to the amount of any such liability.

[(1A) The reference to documents in subsection (1) above does not include—

(a) personal records (as defined in section 12 of the Police and Criminal Evidence Act 1984), or
(b) journalistic material (as defined in section 13 of that Act).][2]

[(1B) Subject to subsection (1A) above, the reference to documents in subsection (1) above is to those specified or described in the notice in question; and—

(a) the notice shall require documents to be delivered within such time (which shall not be less than thirty days after the date of the notice) as may be specified in the notice; and
(b) the inspector may take copies of them or of extracts from them.][2]

(2) Subsection (1) above does not have effect in relation to a person convicted or penalised as there mentioned for so long as an appeal is pending against the conviction or [penalty][3]; and—

(a) for this purpose an appeal is to be treated as pending (where one is competent but has not been brought) until the expiration of the time for bringing it or, in the case of a conviction in Scotland, until the expiration of 28 days from the date of conviction; and
(b) references here to appeal include further appeal but, in relation to the [imposition][3] of a penalty, do not include appeal against the amount of the penalty.

(3) A notice is not to be given to any person under this section unless with the consent of the appropriate judicial authority; and that authority is to give his consent only on being satisfied that in all the circumstances the inspector is justified in so proceeding.

(4) The power to give a notice under this section, by reference to a person's conviction or the [imposition on][3] him of a penalty, ceases at the expiration of the period of 12 months beginning with the date on which it was first exercisable in his case by virtue of that conviction or [penalty][3].

(5) To the extent specified in section 20B below, the above provisions are subject to the restrictions of that section.]¹

Note.—FA 1976 was passed on 29 July 1976.
Amendments.—¹ This section, s. 20, *ante*, and ss. 20B to 20D, *post*, substituted for s. 20 by FA 1976, Sch. 6.
² Sub-ss. (1A), (1B) substituted for the last sentence of sub-s. (1) by FA 1989, s. 143 with respect to notices given after 26 July 1989. The last sentence of sub-s. (1) read—
"For this purpose section 20 (8) above applies, substituting "the client" for "the taxpayer"."
³ Words in sub-ss. (1), (2), (4) substituted by FA 1989, s. 168(1), (2).

[20B. Restrictions on powers under ss. 20 and 20A

(1) Before a notice is given to a person by an inspector under [section 20 (1), (3) or (8A)]² or under section 20A, the person must have been given a reasonable opportunity to deliver (or, in the case of section 20 (3), to deliver or make available) the documents in question [, or to furnish the particulars in question]⁵; and the inspector must not apply for consent under [section 20 (7) or (8A)]³ or, as the case may be, section 20A (3), until the person has been given that opportunity.

[(1A) Subject to subsection (1B) below, where a notice is given to any person under section 20 (3) the inspector shall give a copy of the notice to the taxpayer to whom it relates.]⁶

(1B) If, on an application by the inspector, a General or Special Commissioner so directs, a copy of a notice under section 20 (3) need not be given to the taxpayer to whom it relates; but such a direction shall not be given unless the Commissioner is satisfied that the inspector has reasonable grounds for suspecting the taxpayer of fraud.]⁶

(2) A notice under section 20 (1) does not oblige a person to deliver documents [or furnish particulars]⁵ relating to the conduct of any pending appeal by him; a notice under section 20 (3) [or (8A)]⁴ does not oblige a person to deliver or make available documents relating to the conduct of a pending appeal by the taxpayer; and a notice under section 20A does not oblige a person to deliver documents relating to the conduct of a pending appeal by the client.

"Appeal" means appeal relating to tax.

(3) An inspector cannot under section 20 (1) or (3) or under section 20A (1), give notice to a barrister, advocate or solicitor, but the notice must in any such case be given (if at all) by the Board; and accordingly in relation to a barrister, advocate or solicitor for references in section 20 (3) and (4) and section 20A to the inspector there are substituted references to the Board.

(4) To comply with a notice under section 20 (1) or section 20A (1), and as an alternative to delivering documents to comply with a notice under section 20 (3) [or (8A)]⁴, copies of documents may be delivered instead of the originals; but—

(a) the copies must be photographic or otherwise by way of facsimile; and
(b) if so required by the inspector (or, as the case may be, the Board) in the case of any documents specified in the requirement, the original must be made available for inspection by a named officer of the Board (failure to comply with this requirement counting as failure to comply with the notice).

(5) A notice under section 20 (3), [does not oblige a person]⁷ to deliver or make available any document the whole of which originates more than 6 years before the date of the notice.

(6) But subsection (5) does not apply where the notice is so expressed as to exclude the restrictions of that subsection; and it can only be so expressed where—

(a) the notice being given by an inspector with consent under section 20 (7), the Commissioner giving consent has also given approval to the exclusion;

(b) the notice being given by the Board, they have applied to a General or Special Commissioner for, and obtained, that approval.

For this purpose the Commissioner gives approval only if satisfied, on the inspector's or the Board's application, that there is reasonable ground for believing that tax has, or may have been, lost to the Crown owing to the fraud of the taxpayer.

(7) A notice under section 20 (3) in relation to a taxpayer who has died cannot be given . . .[8] if more than 6 years have elapsed since the death.

(8) A notice under section 20 (3) [or (8A)][4] or section 20A (1) does not oblige a barrister, advocate or a solicitor to deliver or make available, without his client's consent, any document with respect to which a claim to professional privilege could be maintained.

[(9) Subject to subsections (11) and (12) below, a notice under section 20 (3) or (8A)—

(a) does not oblige a person who has been appointed as an auditor for the purposes of any enactment to deliver or make available documents which are his property and were created by him or on his behalf for or in connection with the performance of his functions under that enactment, and
(b) does not oblige a tax adviser to deliver or make available documents which are his property and consist of relevant communications.][9]

[(10) In subsection (9) above "relevant communications" means communications between the tax adviser and—

(a) a person in relation to whose tax affairs he has been appointed, or
(b) any other tax adviser of such a person,

the purpose of which is the giving or obtaining of advice about any of those tax affairs; and in subsection (9) above and this subsection "tax adviser" means a person appointed to give advice about the tax affairs of another person (whether appointed directly by that other person or by another tax adviser of his).][9]

[(11) Subject to subsection (13) below, subsection (9) above shall not have effect in relation to any document which contains information explaining any information, return, accounts or other document which the person to whom the notice is given has, as tax accountant, assisted any client of his in preparing for, or delivering to, the inspector or the Board.][9]

[(12) Subject to subsection (13) below, in the case of a notice under section 20 (8A) subsection (9) above shall not have effect in relation to any document which contains information giving the identity or address of any taxpayer to whom the notice relates or of any person who has acted on behalf of any such person.][9]

[(13) Subsection (9) above is not disapplied by subsection (11) or (12) above in the case of any document if—

(a) the information within subsection (11) or (12) is contained in some other document, and
(b) either—

(i) that other document, or a copy of it, has been delivered to the inspector or the Board, or
(ii) that other document has been inspected by an officer of the Board.][9]

[(14) Where subsection (9) above is disapplied by subsection (11) or (12) above in the case of a document, the person to whom the notice is given either shall deliver the document to the inspector or make it available for inspection by an officer of the Board or shall—

(a) deliver to the inspector (or, where subsection (3) above applies, the Board) a copy (which is photographic or otherwise by way of facsimile) of any parts of the document which contain the information within subsection (11) or (12), and
(b) if so required by the inspector (or, as the case may be, the Board), make available for inspection by a named officer of the Board such parts of the document as contain that information;

and failure to comply with any requirement under paragraph (b) above shall constitute a failure to comply with the notice.][9][1]

Amendments.—[1] This section, ss. 20 and 20A, *ante*, and s. 20C and 20D, *post*, substituted for s. 20 by FA 1976, Sch. 6.
[2] Words in sub-s. (1) substituted by FA 1988, s. 126 (4), (6) with respect to notices given after the passing of FA 1988. FA 1988 was passed on 29 July 1988.
[3] Words in sub-s. (1) substituted by *ibid*.
[4] Words in sub-ss. (2), (4), (8), (9) inserted by *ibid*.
[5] Words in sub-ss. (1), (2) inserted by FA 1989, s. 144 with respect to notices given after 26 July 1989.
[6] Sub-ss. (1A), (1B) inserted by *ibid*.
[7] Words in sub-s. (5) substituted for the words "if given to a person who is carrying on a business or was doing so at

any time material to the subject matter of the inspector's (or the Board's) enquiries, or if given to a company (whether carrying on a business or not), does not oblige the person or company" by *ibid*.
[8] Words "to a person by virtue of her or his being the taxpayer's widow, widower, son or daughter" in sub-s. (7) repealed by *ibid* and Sch. 17, Pt. VIII with respect to notices given after 26 July 1989.
[9] Sub-ss. (9)–(14) substituted for sub-s. (9) by *ibid*. The old sub-s. (9) as amended by FA 1988, s. 126 (4), (6) read—

"(9) A notice under section 20 (3) or (8A) does not, in the case of a person who (in the course of a business carried on by him) has stood in relation to another as tax accountant, oblige that person to deliver or make available documents which are his (the accountant's) property and originate as working papers of that relationship."

[20BB. Falsification etc. of documents

(1) Subject to subsections (2) to (4) below, a person shall be guilty of an offence if he intentionally falsifies, conceals, destroys or otherwise disposes of, or causes or permits the falsification, concealment, destruction or disposal of, a document which—

(*a*) he has been required by a notice under section 20 or 20A above, or
(*b*) he has been given an opportunity in accordance with section 20B(1) above,

to deliver, or to deliver or make available for inspection.

(2) A person does not commit an offence under subsection (1) above if he acts—

(*a*) with the written permission of a General or Special Commissioner, the inspector or an officer of the Board,
(*b*) after the document has been delivered or, in a case within section 20(3) or (8A) above, inspected, or
(*c*) after a copy has been delivered in accordance with section 20B(4) or (14) above and the original has been inspected.

(3) A person does not commit an offence under subsection (1) (*a*) above if he acts after the end of the period of two years beginning with the date on which the notice is given, unless before the end of that period the inspector or an officer of the Board has notified the person in writing that the notice has not been complied with to his satisfaction.

(4) A person does not commit an offence under subsection (1) (*b*) above if he acts—

(*a*) after the end of the period of six months beginning with the date on which an opportunity to deliver the document was given, or
(*b*) after an application for consent to a notice being given in relation to the document has been refused.

(5) A person guilty of an offence under subsection (1) above shall be liable—

(*a*) on summary conviction, to a fine not exceeding the statutory maximum;
(*b*) on conviction on indictment, to imprisonment for a term not exceeding two years or to a fine or to both.][1]

Amendments.—[1] This section inserted by FA 1989, s. 145 and applies to any falsification, concealment, destruction or disposal of a document occurring after 26 July 1989.

[20C. Entry with warrant to obtain documents

(1) If the appropriate judicial authority is satisfied on information on oath given by an officer of the Board that—

(*a*) there is reasonable ground for suspecting that an offence involving [serious fraud][2] in connection with, or in relation to, tax [is being, has been or is about to be][3] committed and that evidence of it is to be found on premises specified in the information; and
(*b*) in applying under this section, the officer acts with the approval of the Board given in relation to the particular case,

the authority may issue a warrant in writing authorising an officer of the Board to enter the premises, if necessary by force, at any time within 14 days from the time of issue of the warrant, and search them.

[(1A) Without prejudice to the generality of the concept of serious fraud—

(*a*) any offence which involves fraud is for the purposes of this section an offence involving serious fraud if its commission had led, or is intended or likely to lead, either to substantial financial gain to any person or to serious prejudice to the proper assessment or collection of tax; and
(*b*) an offence which, if considered alone, would not be regarded as involving serious fraud may nevertheless be so regarded if there is reasonable ground for suspecting that it

forms part of a course of conduct which is, or but for its detection would be, likely to result in serious prejudice to the proper assessment or collection of tax.][4]

[(1B) The powers conferred by a warrant under this section shall not be exercisable—

(a) by more than such number of officers of the Board as may be specified in the warrant;
(b) outside such times of day as may be so specified;
(c) if the warrant so provides, otherwise than in the presence of a constable in uniform.][4]

(2) Section 4A of the Inland Revenue Regulation Act 1890 (Board's functions to be exercisable by an officer acting under their authority) does not apply to the giving of Board approval under this section.

[(3) An officer who enters the premises under the authority of a warrant under this section may—

(a) take with him such other persons as appear to him to be necessary;
(b) seize and remove any things whatsoever found there which he has reasonable cause to believe may be required as evidence for the purposes of proceedings in respect of such an offence as is mentioned in subsection (1) above; and
(c) search or cause to be searched any person found on the premises whom he has reasonable cause to believe to be in possession of any such things;

but no person shall be searched except by a person of the same sex.][5]

[(4) Nothing in subsection (3) above authorises the seizure and removal of documents in the possession of a barrister, advocate or solicitor with respect to which a claim to professional privilege could be maintained.][5]

[(5) An officer of the Board seeking to exercise the powers conferred by a warrant under this section or, if there is more than one such officer, that one of them who is in charge of the search—

(a) if the occupier of the premises concerned is present at the time the search is to begin, shall supply a copy of the warrant endorsed with his name to the occupier;
(b) if at that time the occupier is not present but a person who appears to the officer to be in charge of the premises is present, shall supply such a copy to that person; and
(c) if neither paragraph (a) nor paragraph (b) above applies, shall leave such a copy in a prominent place on the premises.][5]

[(6) Where entry to premises has been made with a warrant under this section, and the officer making the entry has seized any things under the authority of the warrant, he shall endorse on or attach to the warrant a list of the things seized.][5]

[(7) Subsections (10) to (12) of section 16 of the Police and Criminal Evidence Act 1984 (return, retention and inspection of warrants) apply to a warrant under this section (together with any list endorsed on or attached to it under subsection (6) above) as they apply to a warrant issued to a constable under any enactment.][5]

[(8) Subsection (7) above extends to England and Wales only.][5]][1]

Amendments.—[1] This section, ss. 20, 20A and 20B, *ante*, and s. 20D, *post*, substituted for s. 20 by FA 1976, Sch. 6.
[2] Words in sub-s. (1) (a) substituted for the words "any form of fraud" by FA 1989, s. 146 with respect to warrants issued after 26 July 1989.
[3] Words in sub-s. (1) (a) substituted for the words "has been" by *ibid*.
[4] Sub-ss. (1A), (1B) inserted by *ibid*.
[5] Sub-ss. (3)–(8) substituted by for sub-ss. (3)–(5) by *ibid*. The old sub-ss. (3)–(5) read—

"(3) On entering the premises with a warrant under this section, the officer may seize and remove any things whatsoever found there which he has reasonable cause to believe may be required as evidence for the purposes of proceedings in respect of such an offence as is mentioned in subsection (1) above.

But this does not authorise the seizure and removal of documents in the possession of a barrister, advocate or solicitor with respect to which a claim to professional privilege could be maintained.

(4) Where entry to premises has been made with a warrant under this section, and the officer making the entry has seized any things under the authority of the warrant, he shall, if so requested by a person showing himself either—

(a) to be the occupier of the premises; or
(b) to have had the possession or custody of those things immediately before the seizure,

provide that person with a list of them.

(5) Where documents are seized which relate to any business, and it is shown that access to them is required for the continued conduct of the business, the officer who has seized them shall afford reasonable access to the documents to the person carrying on the business."

[20CC. Procedure where documents etc. are removed

(1) An officer of the Board who removes anything in the exercise of the power conferred by section 20C above shall, if so requested by a person showing himself—

 (*a*) to be the occupier of premises from which it was removed, or
 (*b*) to have had custody or control of it immediately before the removal,

provide that person with a record of what he removed.

(2) The officer of the Board shall provide the record within a reasonable time from the making of the request for it.

(3) Where anything which has been removed by an officer of the Board as mentioned in subsection (1) above is of such a nature that a photograph or copy of it would be sufficient—

 (*a*) for use as evidence at a trial for an offence, or
 (*b*) for forensic examination or for investigation in connection with an offence,

it shall not be retained longer than is necessary to establish that fact and to obtain the photograph or copy.

(4) Subject to subsection (8) below, if a request for permission to be granted access to anything which—

 (*a*) has been removed by an officer of the Board, and
 (*b*) is retained by the Board for the purpose of investigating an offence,

is made to the officer in overall charge of the investigation by a person who had custody or control of the thing immediately before it was so removed or by someone acting on behalf of any such person, the officer shall allow the person who made the request access to it under the supervision of an officer of the Board.

(5) Subject to subsection (8) below, if a request for a photograph or copy of any such thing is made to the officer in overall charge of the investigation by a person who had custody or control of the thing immediately before it was so removed, or by someone acting on behalf of any such person, the officer shall—

 (*a*) allow the person who made the request access to it under the supervision of an officer of the Board for the purpose of photographing it or copying it, or
 (*b*) photograph or copy it, or cause it to be photographed or copied.

(6) Where anything is photographed or copied under subsection (5) (*b*) above the photograph or copy shall be supplied to the person who made the request.

(7) The photograph or copy shall be supplied within a reasonable time from the making of the request.

(8) There is no duty under this section to grant access to, or to supply a photograph or copy of, anything if the officer in overall charge of the investigation for the purposes of which it was removed has reasonable grounds for believing that to do so would prejudice—

 (*a*) that investigation;
 (*b*) the investigation of an offence other than the offence for the purposes of the investigation of which the thing was removed; or
 (*c*) any criminal proceedings which may be brought as a result of—
  (i) the investigation of which he is in charge, or
  (ii) any such investigation as is mentioned in paragraph (*b*) above.

(9) Any reference in this section to the officer in overall charge of the investigation is a reference to the person whose name and address are endorsed on the warrant concerned as being the officer so in charge.][1]

Amendments.—[1] This section inserted by FA 1989, s. 147 with respect to warrants issued after 26 July 1989.

[20D. Interpretation of ss. 20 to 20C

(1) For the purposes of section 20A and 20C above, "the appropriate judicial authority" is—

 (*a*) in England and Wales, a Circuit judge;
 (*b*) in Scotland, a sheriff; and
 (*c*) in Northern Ireland, a county court judge.

(2) For the purposes of sections 20 and 20A, a person stands in relation to another as tax accountant at any time when he assists the other in the preparation [or delivery of any information, return, accounts or other document which he knows will be, or is or are likely to be, used][2] for any purpose of tax; and his clients are all those to whom he stands or has stood in that relationship.

[(3) Without prejudice to section 127 of the Finance Act 1988, in sections 20 to 20CC above "document" has, subject to sections 20 (8C) and 20A (1A), the same meaning as it has—

(*a*) in relation to England and Wales, in Part I of the Civil Evidence Act 1968,
(*b*) in relation to Scotland, in Part III of the Law Reform (Miscellaneous Provisions) (Scotland) Act 1968, and
(*c*) in relation to Northern Ireland, in Part I of the Civil Evidence Act (Northern Ireland) 1971.][3]][1]

Amendments.—[1] This section and ss. 20 to 20C, *ante,* substituted for s. 20 by FA 1976, Sch. 6.
[2] Words in sub-s. (2) substituted for the words "of returns or accounts to be made or delivered by the other" by FA 1989, s. 148 (2).
[3] Sub-s. (3) substituted by FA 1989, s. 148 (3), (4), subject to transitional meaning of "business" in ss. 20 and 20C above. The old sub-s. (3) read—

"(3) In sections 20 and 20C above "business" includes trade, profession and vocation; and in those sections and in section 20B "documents" includes books, accounts and other documents or records whatsoever."

21. Stock jobbers' transactions

(1) The Board may exercise the powers conferred by this section as respects, and in connection with, any business which is, or has been, carried on by a [market maker][2] ...[1] whose liability to tax in respect of the business is determined on the footing that any excess of his payments in respect of interest on securities over his receipts in respect thereof, being payments made or receipts accrued in pursuance of a contract for the sale or purchase of the securities, is to be treated for all the purposes of the Income Tax Acts or the Corporation Tax Acts as an annual payment made by him.

(2) With a view to obtaining information about transactions in the course of a business within subsection (1) above, the Board may serve on the [market maker][2] ...[1] by whom the business is or has been carried on a notice requiring him to make available within a time specified in the notice, for inspection by an inspector or other officer of the Board, all such books, accounts and other documents in his possession or power as may be specified or described in the notice, being books, accounts or other documents which in the opinion of the Board contain or may contain information directly or indirectly relating to any such transactions.

(3) The Board may serve on any broker a notice requiring him to make available within a time specified in the notice, for inspection by an inspector or other officer of the Board, all such books, accounts or other documents in his possession or power as may be specified or described in the notice, being books, accounts or other documents which in the opinion of the Board contain or may contain information relating directly or indirectly to transactions in the course of a business within subsection (1) above.

(4) The Board may by notice in writing require—

(*a*) a person, other than a broker, who has directly or indirectly received from a [market maker][2] ...[1] any payment made by the [market maker][2] ...[1] in the course of a business within subsection (1) above, being a payment treated by the [market maker][2] ...[1] as made in respect of interest on securities, to state within a time specified in the notice whether the amount received is in whole or in part received on behalf of, or for payment on to, any other person and, if so, to furnish the name and address of that other person, or
(*b*) a person who has directly or indirectly paid to a [market maker][2] ...[1] any sum constituting a receipt by him in the course of a business within subsection (1) above, being a receipt treated by the [market maker][2] ...[1] as accruing in respect of interest on securities, to state within a time specified in the notice whether the amount paid is in whole or in part received from, or paid on account of, any other person and, if so, to furnish the name and address of that other person.

(5) If, for the purpose of obtaining (from any persons whether brokers or [market makers][3] or not) information directly or indirectly relating to any transactions in the course of a business within subsection (1) above, any person in whose name any securities are registered is so required by notice in writing by the Board, he shall state whether or not he is the

beneficial owner of those securities, and, if not the beneficial owner of those securities or any of them, shall furnish the name and address of the person or persons on whose behalf the securities are registered in his name.

(6) The Board may not exercise their powers under the preceding provisions of this section for the purpose of obtaining information relating to transactions in any year of assessment ending more than six years before the service of the notice.

(7) In this section—

> ["broker", in relation to securities, means a member of The Stock Exchange who carries on his business in the United Kingdom and is not a market maker in securities of the kind concerned;][4]
>
> ["market maker", in relation to securities, means a person who—
> (a) holds himself out at all normal times in compliance with the rules of The Stock Exchange as willing to buy and sell securities of the kind concerned at a price specified by him, and
> (b) is recognised as doing so by the Council of The Stock Exchange.][5]
>
> "securities" includes shares and stock, and references to interest include references to dividends.

Cross references.—See FA 1986, Sch. 18, para. 7(4), (5) (Board's powers to extend the scope of the definitions of "broker" and "market maker" in sub-s. (7) with effect from an appointed day),
Sch. 18, para. 9 (1) (b), (c), (3) (Board's powers to amend this section with effect from an appointed day).
Amendments.—[1] Words in sub-ss. (1), (2) and (4) repealed by FA 1973, Sch. 21, para. 5 (a), and Sch. 22, Pt. IV.
[2] Words "market maker" in sub-ss. (1), (2), (4) substituted for the word "jobber" by FA 1986, Sch. 18, para. 7 (1), (3) in relation to transactions effected on or after 27 October 1986 (i.e. the day on which the Stock Exchange rule prohibiting a person from carrying on business as both a broker and a jobber is abolished).
[3] Words "market makers" in sub-s. (5) substituted for the word "jobbers" by *ibid*.
[4] The definition of "broker" in sub-s. (7) substituted by FA 1986, Sch. 18, para. 7 (2), (3) in relation to transactions effected on or after 27 October 1986 (i.e. the day on which the Stock Exchange rule prohibiting a person from carrying on business as both a broker and a jobber is abolished).
[5] The definition "market maker" in sub-s. (7) substituted for the definition of "jobber" by *ibid*.

"Surtax"

22. Additional particulars for "surtax"

The Board may, . . .[1], by notice in writing require any individual to furnish to them within such time as they may prescribe, not being less than twenty-eight days, such particulars as to the several sources of his income and the amount arising from each source, and as to the nature and the amount of any deductions claimed to be allowed therefrom, as they consider necessary.

Amendments.—[1] Words repealed by FA 1971, ss. 37, 38 (1), Sch. 6, paras. 81, 83 and Sch. 14, Pt. II, with effect from the year 1973–74.

23. Power to obtain copies of registers of securities

(1) The Board may cause to be served upon any body corporate a notice requiring them to deliver to the Board within a specified time, being not less than twenty-one days, a copy, certified by a duly authorised officer of such body, of the whole of, or any specified class of entries in, any register containing the names of the holders of any securities issued by them.

(2) On delivery of the copy in accordance with the notice payment shall be made therefor at the rate of five shillings in respect of each one hundred entries.

(3) In this section, "security" includes shares, stock, debentures and debenture stock, and "entry" means, in relation to any register, so much thereof as relates to the securities held by any one person.

24. Power to obtain information as to income from securities

(1) The Board may by notice in writing require—

> (a) any person, being a registered or inscribed holder of any United Kingdom securities, who, in any year of assessment, has received on behalf of any other person any income arising from any such securities, or
> (b) any person by or through whom, in any year of assessment, any income in respect of United Kingdom securities has been paid in any case where—

(i) the registered or inscribed holder of the securities is not the person to whom the income was paid or,
(ii) the securities are bearer securities,

to furnish them, within such time as may be specified in the notice (not being less than twenty-eight days) with particulars of the amounts so received or, as the case may be, paid in that year (other than amounts received or paid in that year on behalf of or to any one person which did not exceed in the aggregate the sum of £15), the securities to which those amounts respectively relate, and the names and addresses of the persons on whose behalf or to whom those amounts were respectively received or paid.

(2) The Board may similarly require any person who acts or has acted, directly or indirectly, as an intermediary or as one of a series of intermediaries between any such person as is specified in subsection (1) (*a*) or (*b*) above and the person or persons beneficially entitled to the income in question to furnish such information as the Board may require for the purpose of enabling them to ascertain the names and addresses of the person or persons beneficially entitled to the income and the respective amounts to which those persons were beneficially entitled.

(3) Nothing in this section shall impose on any bank the obligation to disclose any particulars relating to income from securities in cases where the person beneficially entitled to the income is not resident in the United Kingdom.

(4) In this section—

"securities" includes shares, stocks, bonds, debentures and debenture stock, and
"United Kingdom securities" means any securities issued by or on behalf of Her Majesty's Government in the United Kingdom or the Government of Northern Ireland and any securities of a body corporate incorporated in any part of the United Kingdom.

Chargeable gains

25. Issuing houses, stockbrokers, auctioneers, etc.

(1) For the purpose of obtaining particulars of chargeable gains an inspector may by notice in writing require a return under any of the provisions of this section.

(2) An issuing house or other person carrying on a business of effecting public issues of shares or securities in any company, or placings of shares or securities in any company, either on behalf of the company, or on behalf of holders of blocks of shares or securities which have not previously been the subject of a public issue or placing, may be required to make a return of all such public issues or placings effected by that person in the course of the business in the period specified in the notice requiring the return, giving particulars of the persons to or with whom the shares or securities are issued, allotted or placed, and the number or amount of the shares or securities so obtained by them respectively.

(3) A person not carrying on such a business may be required to make a return as regards any such public issue or placing effected by that person and specified in the notice, giving particulars of the persons to or with whom the shares or securities are issued, allotted, or placed and the number or amount of the shares or securities so obtained by them respectively.

(4) A member of a stock exchange in the United Kingdom, other than a [market maker][3], may be required to make a return giving particulars of any transactions effected by him in the course of his business in the period specified in the notice requiring the return and giving particulars of—

(*a*) the parties to the transactions,
(*b*) the number or amount of the shares or securities dealt with in the respective transactions, and
(*c*) the amount or value of the consideration.

(5) A person (other than a member of a stock exchange in the United Kingdom) who acts as an agent or broker in the United Kingdom in transactions in shares or securities may be required to make a return giving particulars of any such transactions effected by him after 5th April 1968 and in the period specified in the notice, and giving particulars of—

(*a*) the parties to the transactions,
(*b*) the number or amount of the shares or securities dealt with in the respective transactions, and
(*c*) the amount or value of the consideration.

(6) The committee or other person or body of persons responsible for managing a clearing house for any terminal market in commodities may be required to make a return giving particulars of any transactions effected through the clearing house in the period specified in the notice requiring the return and giving particulars of—

(a) the parties to the transactions,
(b) the amounts dealt with in those transactions respectively, and
(c) the amount or value of the consideration.

(7) An auctioneer, and any person carrying on a trade of dealing in any description of tangible movable property, or of acting as an agent or intermediary in dealings in any description of tangible movable property, may be required to make a return giving particulars of any transactions effected by or through him in which any asset which is tangible movable property is disposed of for a consideration the amount or value of which, in the hands of the recipient, exceeds [£6,000][5].

(8) No person shall be required under this section to include in a return particulars of any transaction effected more than three years before the service of the notice requiring him to make the return.

(9) In this section "company" and "shares" shall be construed in accordance with [sections 64, 93 and 155 (1) of the Capital Gains Tax Act 1979][1-2].

[(10) In this section "market maker", in relation to shares or securities, means a person who—

(a) holds himself out at all normal times in compliance with the rules of The Stock Exchange as willing to buy and sell shares or securities of the kind concerned at a price specified by him, and
(b) is recognised as doing so by the Council of The Stock Exchange.][4]

Cross references.—See FA 1986, Sch. 18, para. 8 (4), (5) (Board's powers to extend the scope of sub-ss. (4), (5), (10) above with effect from an appointed day).
Amendments.—[1-2] Words in sub-s. (9) substituted by CGTA 1979, s. 157 (2)–(4) and Sch. 7, para. 9 Table, with effect from 22 March 1979.
[3] Words "market maker" in sub-s. (4) substituted for the word "jobber" by FA 1986, Sch. 18, para. 8 (1), (3) in relation to transactions on or after 27 October 1986 (i.e. the day on which the Stock Exchange rule prohibiting a person from carrying on business as both a broker and a jobber is abolished).
[4] Sub-s. (10) inserted by FA 1986, Sch. 18, para. 8 (2), (3).
[5] Amount in sub-s. (7) substituted by FA 1989, s. 123 (1) (c), (2) in relation to disposals after 5 April 1989.

26. Nominee shareholders

(1) If, for the purpose of obtaining particulars of chargeable gains, any person in whose name any shares of a company are registered is so required by notice in writing by the Board or an inspector, he shall state whether or not he is the beneficial owner of those shares and, if not the beneficial owner of those shares or any of them, shall furnish the name and address of the person or persons on whose behalf the shares are registered in his name.

(2) In this section references to shares include references to securities and loan capital.

27. Settled property

(1) The Board may by notice in writing require any person, being a party to a settlement, to furnish them within such time as they may direct (not being less than twenty-eight days) with such particulars as they think necessary for the purposes of [the Capital Gains Tax Act 1979][1].

(2) In this section "settlement" has the meaning given by section [681 (4)][2] of the principal Act.

Amendments.—[1] Words in sub-s. (1) substituted by CGTA 1979, s. 157 (2)–(4) and Sch. 7, para. 8 Table, Pt. II. 2, with effect from 22 March 1979.
[2] Number in sub-s. (2) substituted by TA 1988, Sch. 29, para. 32 Table.

28. Non-resident companies and trusts

(1) A person holding shares or securities in a company which is not resident or ordinarily resident in the United Kingdom, or who is interested in settled property under a settlement the trustees of which are not resident or ordinarily resident in the United Kingdom, may be required by a notice by the Board to give such particulars as the Board may consider are

required to determine whether the company or trust falls within [section 15][1] (non-resident companies) or [section 17][1] (non-resident trusts) of the [Capital Gains Tax Act 1979][1], and whether any chargeable gains have accrued to that company, or to the trustees of that settlement, in respect of which the person to whom the notice is given is liable to capital gains tax under the said [section 15][1] or the said [section 17][1].

(2) In this section "settled property" has the meaning given by [section 51 of the Capital Gains Tax Act 1979][2], and "company" and "shares" shall be construed in accordance with [sections 64, 93 and 155 (1) of that Act][2].

Amendments.—[1] Words in sub-s. (1) substituted by CGTA 1979, s. 157 (2)–(4) and Sch. 7, Para. 1 (3), with effect from 22 March 1979.
[2] Words in sub-s. (2) substituted by CGTA 1979, s. 157 (2)–(4) and Sch. 7, para. 9 Table, with effect from 22 March 1979.

PART IV
ASSESSMENT AND CLAIMS

Cross references.—See TA 1988, ss. 253, 350 (4)–(7) (power of Board to make regulations modifying or replacing TA 1988, s. 234 (5)–(9) and Schs. 13, 16).

29. Assessing procedure

(1) Except as otherwise provided, all assessments to tax shall be made by an inspector, and—

(a) if the inspector is satisfied that any return under the Taxes Acts affords correct and complete information concerning profits in respect of which tax is chargeable, he shall make an assessment accordingly,

(b) if it appears to the inspector that there are any profits in respect of which tax is chargeable and which have not been included in a return under Part II of this Act, or if the inspector is dissatisfied with any return under Part II of this Act, he may make an assessment to tax to the best of his judgment.

[(c) where income tax is charged for a year of assessment in respect of income arising in that year, the inspector may make an assessment during that year to the best of his judgment, by reference to actual income or estimated income (whether from any particular source or generally) or partly by reference to one and partly by reference to the other.][5]

[(1A) Where an assessment is made by virtue of subsection (1) (c) above, any necessary adjustments shall be made after the end of the year (whether by way of assessment, repayment of tax or otherwise) to secure that tax is charged in respect of income actually arising in the year.][5]

(2) ...[6]

(3) If an inspector or the Board discover—

(a) that any profits which ought to have been assessed to tax have not been assessed, or
(b) that an assessment to tax is or has become insufficient, or
(c) that any relief which has been given is or has become excessive,

the inspector or, as the case may be, the Board may make an assessment in the amount, or the further amount, which ought in his or their opinion to be charged.

(4) All income tax ...[1-2] which is charged for any year on any person under subsection (3) (c) above may, notwithstanding that it was chargeable under more than one Schedule, be included in one assessment and an appeal against an assessment under subsection (3) (c) above shall be to the Commissioners to whom an appeal would lie on a claim for the relief in connection with which the assessment is made.

(5) Notice of any assessment to tax shall be served on the person assessed and shall state [the date on which it is issued and][3] the time within which any appeal against the assessment may be made.

(6) After the notice of assessment has been served on the person assessed, the assessment shall not be altered except in accordance with the express provisions of the Taxes Acts.

(7) Assessments to income tax ...[1-2] which are under any provision in the Income Tax Acts to be made by the Board shall be made in accordance with this section, and as if in subsection (1) (a) and (b) above the references to the inspector were references to the Board.

(8) In this section "profits"—

(a) in relation to income tax, means income,
(b) in relation to capital gains tax, means chargeable gains,
(c) in relation to corporation tax, means profits as computed for the purposes of that tax,

and "return under Part II of this Act" includes a return under that Part as extended by section [284 (4)][4] of the principal Act (returns of income of husband and wife).

Note.—See **Prospective Legislation Notes** (Married Couples) and **Prospective Cross References**.
Cross references.—See TA 1988, Sch. 14, para. 7 (3) (a) (application of sub-s. (3) (c) of this section in respect of repayment claims for tax deducted at source from life assurance premiums).
Amendments.—[1-2] Words in sub-ss. (4) and (7) repealed by FA 1971, ss. 37, 38 (1), Sch. 6, paras. 81, 84 (b), (c) and Sch. 14, Pt. II, with effect from the year 1973–74.

[3] Words in sub-s. (5) inserted by F (No. 2) A 1975, s. 44 (5), (7) in relation to tax charged by assessment notice issued after 31 July 1975.
[4] Words in sub-ss. (2), (8) substituted by TA 1988, Sch. 29, para. 32 Table.
[5] Sub-ss. (1) (c), (1A) inserted by FA 1988, s. 119.
[6] Sub-s. (2) repealed by FA 1989, Sch. 17, Pt. V.

[30. Recovery of overpayment of tax, etc.

(1) Where an amount of tax has been repaid to any person which ought not to have been repaid to him, that amount of tax may be assessed and recovered as if it were unpaid tax.

(2) In any case where—

(*a*) a repayment of tax has been increased in accordance with section [824 or 825 of the principal Act or section 47][2] of the Finance (No. 2) Act 1975 (supplements added to repayments of tax, etc.); and
(*b*) the whole or any part of that repayment has been paid to any person but ought not to have been paid to him; and
(*c*) that repayment ought not to have been increased either at all or to any extent;

then the amount of the repayment assessed under subsection (1) above may include an amount equal to the amount by which the repayment ought not to have been increased.

(3) In any case where—

(*a*) a payment, other than a repayment of tax to which subsection (2) above applies, is increased in accordance with section [824 or 825 of the principal Act or section 47][2] of the Finance (No. 2) Act 1975; and
(*b*) that payment ought not to have been increased either at all or to any extent;

then an amount equal to the amount by which the payment ought not to have been increased may be assessed and recovered as if it were unpaid income tax or corporation tax.

(4) An assessment to income tax or corporation tax under this section shall be made under Case VI of Schedule D.

(5) An assessment under this section shall not be out of time under section 34 of this Act if it is made before the end of the chargeable period following that in which the amount so assessed was repaid or paid as the case may be.

(6) Subsection (5) above is without prejudice to [section 36][3] of this Act.

(7) In this section any reference to an amount repaid or paid includes a reference to an amount allowed by way of set-off.][1]

Note.—See **Prospective Legislation Notes** (Taxes Management Provisions) and **Prospective Cross References**.
Cross references.—See TA 1988, s. 813 (3), (6) (application of this section for the purpose of recovering from certain non-resident companies a fine for the violation of the provisions withdrawing the right of tax credits),
Sch. 14, para. 7 (3) (*b*) (application of this section in respect of repayment claims for tax deducted at source from life assurance premiums).
Amendments.—[1] This section substituted by FA 1982, s. 149 (1).
[2] Words in sub-ss. (2) (*a*), (3) (*a*) substituted by TA 1988, Sch. 29, para. 32 Table.
[3] Words in sub-s. (6) substituted for the words "sections 36, 37 and 39" by FA 1989, s. 149 (3) (*a*).

31. Right of appeal

(1) An appeal may be brought against an assessment to tax by a notice of appeal in writing given within thirty days after the date of the notice of assessment.

(2) The notice of appeal shall be given to the inspector or other officer of the Board by whom the notice of assessment was given.

[(3) The appeal shall be to the Special Commissioners if the assessment is made—

(*a*) by the Board; or
(*b*) under section 350, . . .[3] 445, 740, 743 (1) or 747 (4) (*a*) of the principal Act; or
(*c*) under section 38 of the Finance Act 1973 or section 830 of the principal Act and is not an assessment to tax under Schedule E;

or if the appeal involves any question as to the application of Part XV or XVI of the principal Act.][2]

(4) Subject to subsection (3) above the appeal shall be to the General Commissioners, except that the appellant may elect (in accordance with section 46 (1) of this Act) to bring the appeal before the Special Commissioners instead of the General Commissioners.

(5) The notice of appeal against any assessment shall specify the grounds of appeal, but on the hearing of the appeal the Commissioners may allow the appellant to put forward any ground not specified in the notice, and take it into consideration if satisfied that the omission was not wilful or unreasonable.

[(5A) An election under subsection (4) above shall be disregarded if—

(*a*) the appellant and the inspector or other officer of the Board agree in writing, at any time before the determination of the appeal, that it is to be disregarded; or
(*b*) the General Commissioners have given a direction under subsection (5C) below and have not revoked it.][1]

[(5B) At any time before the determination of an appeal in respect of which an election has been made under subsection (4) above, the inspector or other officer of the Board after giving notice to the appellant may refer the election to the General Commissioners.][1]

[(5C) On any such reference the Commissioners shall, unless they are satisfied that the appellant has arguments to present or evidence to adduce on the merits of the appeal, direct that the election be disregarded.][1]

[(5D) If, at any time after the giving of a direction under subsection (5C) above (but before the determination of the appeal) the General Commissioners are satisfied that the appellant has arguments to present or evidence to adduce on the merits of the appeal, they shall revoke the direction.][1]

[(5E) Any decision to give a direction under subsection (5C) above or revoke such a direction under subsection (5D) above shall be final.][1]

(6) This section has effect subject to any express provision in the Taxes Acts, including in particular any provision under which an appeal lies to the Special Commissioners to the exclusion of the General Commissioners, any provision transferring jurisdiction to some other tribunal, and any provision making one kind of assessment conclusive in an appeal against another kind of assessment.

Cross references.—See F (No. 2) A 1975, s. 67 (1) (in sub-s. (1) of this section, the reference to the date of the notice of assessment is a reference to the date on which the notice was issued);
TA 1988, Sch. 19A, para. 5 (2) (application of sub-ss. (5A)–(5E) of this section in respect of certain appeals by underwriting agents),
Sch. 19A, para. 8 (2) (*a*) (modification of the reference in this section to the date of the notice of assessment in a case where a determination by an Inspector of Taxes of Lloyd's underwriting syndicate's profit or loss is varied or modified);
FA 1988, s. 134 (4), (8), (9) (application of sub-ss. (5A)–(5E) of this section, with effect from 3 April 1989 by virtue of FA 1988 (Commencement) Order 1989, S.I. 1989 No. 473, where parties have elected against transfer of a tax appeal in Northern Ireland from Special Commissioners to General Commissioners).
Amendments.—[1] Sub-ss. (5A)–(5E) inserted by FA 1984, Sch. 22, para. 3 (1) and came into force on 1 January 1985 by virtue of FA 1984 (Commencement No. 2) Order 1984, S.I. 1984 No. 1836.
[2] Sub-s. (3) substituted by TA 1988, Sch. 29, para. 32 Table.
[3] Number in sub-s. (3) (*b*) repealed by FA 1989, Sch. 17, Pt. V.

Relief for excessive assessments

32. Double assessment

(1) If on a claim made to the Board it appears to their satisfaction that a person has been assessed to tax more than once for the same cause and for the same chargeable period, they shall direct the whole, or such part of any assessment as appears to be an overcharge, to be vacated, and thereupon the same shall be vacated accordingly.

(2) An appeal on a claim under this section shall lie to any of the bodies of Commissioners having jurisdiction to hear an appeal against the assessment, or the later of the assessments, to which the claim relates.

33. Error or mistake

(1) If any person who has paid tax charged under an assessment alleges that the assessment was excessive by reason of some error or mistake in a return, he may by notice in writing at any time not later than six years after the end of the year of assessment (or, if the assessment is to corporation tax, the end of the accounting period) in which the assessment was made, make a claim to the Board for relief.

(2) On receiving the claim the Board shall inquire into the matter and shall, subject to the provisions of this section, give by way of repayment such relief . . .[1] in respect of the error or mistake as is reasonable and just:

Provided that no relief shall be given under this section in respect of an error or mistake as to the basis on which the liability of the claimant ought to have been computed where the return was in fact made on the basis or in accordance with the practice generally prevailing at the time when the return was made.

(3) In determining the claim the Board shall have regard to all the relevant circumstances of the case, and in particular shall consider whether the granting of relief would result in the exclusion from charge to tax of any part of the profits of the claimant, and for this purpose the Board may take into consideration the liability of the claimant and assessments made on him in respect of chargeable periods other than that to which the claim relates.

(4) If any appeal is brought from the decision of the Board on the claim the Special Commissioners shall hear and determine the appeal in accordance with the principles to be followed by the Board in determining claims under this section; and neither the appellant nor the Board shall be entitled to require a case to be stated under section 56 of this Act otherwise than on a point of law arising in connection with the computation of profits.

(5) In this section "profits"—

(*a*) in relation to income tax, means income,
(*b*) in relation to capital gains tax, means chargeable gains,
(*c*) in relation to corporation tax, means profits as computed for the purposes of that tax.

Amendments.—[1] Words in sub-s. (2) repealed by FA 1971, ss. 37 (2), 38 and Sch. 14, Pt. II, with effect from the year 1973–74.

Time limits

Note.—See **Prospective Legislation Notes** (Taxes Management Provisions).

34. Ordinary time limit of six years

(1) Subject to the following provisions of this Act, and to any other provisions of the Taxes Acts allowing a longer period in any particular class of case, an assessment to tax may be made at any time not later than six years after the end of the chargeable period to which the assessment relates.

(2) An objection to the making of any assessment on the ground that the time limit for making it has expired shall only be made on an appeal against the assessment.

35. Emoluments received after year for which they are assessable

(1) Where income to which this section applies is received in a year of assessment subsequent to that for which it is assessable, assessments to income tax as respects that income may be made at any time within six years after the year of assessment in which it was received.

(2) The income to which this section applies is any income which is chargeable to tax under Schedule E, but which is not taken into account in an assessment to income tax for the year of assessment in which it is received; and for the purposes of this section—

(*a*)...[1]
(*b*) any payment chargeable to tax by virtue of section [148][2] of the principal Act (payments on retirement or loss of office or employment) shall notwithstanding anything in subsection (4) of that section (notional date of payment) be treated as having been received at the time it was actually received.

Amendments.—[1] Sub-s. (2) (*a*) repealed by FA 1976, Sch. 9, para. 10 and Sch. 15, Pt. III, in relation to income assessable for 1977–78 and subsequent years.
[2] Number in sub-s. (2) (*b*) substituted by TA 1988, Sch. 29, para. 32 Table.

[36. Fraudulent or negligent conduct

(1) An assessment on any person (in this section referred to as "the person in default") for the purpose of making good to the Crown a loss of tax attributable to his fraudulent or negligent conduct or the fraudulent or negligent conduct of a person acting on his behalf may be made at any time not later than twenty years after the end of the chargeable period to which the assessment relates.

(2) Where the person in default is an individual who carried on a trade or profession in partnership with another individual, or with other persons at least one of whom is an

individual, at any time in the year for which the assessment is made, an assessment in respect of the profits or gains of the trade or profession for the purpose mentioned in subsection (1) above may be made not only on the person in default but also on his partner or, as the case may be, on any of his partners who is an individual.

(3) If the person on whom the assessment is made so requires, in determining the amount of the tax to be charged for any chargeable period in any assessment made for the purpose mentioned in subsection (1) above, effect shall be given to any relief or allowance to which he would have been entitled for that chargeable period on a claim or application made within the time allowed by the Taxes Acts.][1]

Cross references.—See TA 1988, Sch. 13, para. 10 (1) (application of this section to assessments and due date of advance corporation tax),
Sch. 16, para. 10 (1) (application of this section to assessments and due date of income tax on company payments which are not distributions),
Sch. 19A, para. 9 (liability of each member of Lloyd's underwriting syndicate for fraud etc. committed by syndicate's agent).
Amendments.—[1] This section substituted by FA 1989 s. 149 (1), (7), but does not affect the making of assessments for years of assessment before 1983–84 or for accounting periods ending before 1 April 1983. Previously this section read—

"**36. Fraud or wilful default**
Subject to section 41 below, where any form of fraud or wilful default has been committed by or on behalf of any person in connection with or in relation to tax, assessments on that person to tax may, for the purpose of making good to the Crown any loss of tax attributable to the fraud or wilful default, be made at any time."

37. Neglect: income tax and capital gains tax

(1) Where, for the purpose of making good to the Crown a loss of tax wholly or partly attributable to the fraud, wilful default or neglect of any person, an assessment for any year (in this section referred to as "the normal year") has been made on him not later than six years after the end of that year, assessments to tax for earlier years may, to the extent provided by the following provisions of this section, be made on him notwithstanding that, but for this section, they would be out of time.

(2) No assessment under this section shall be made on any person except for the purpose of making good to the Crown a loss of tax attributable to his neglect.

(3) An assessment under this section for any year ending not earlier than six years before the end of the normal year may, subject to section 41 below, be made at any time not later than the end of the year of assessment following that in which the tax covered by the assessment mentioned in subsection (1) of this section is finally determined.

(4) An assessment under this section for any year ending earlier than six years before the end of the normal year may only be made with the leave of the General or Special Commissioners, given under the following provisions of this section.

(5) Where an assessment for any year (in this section referred to as "the earlier year") has been made on any person more than six years after the end of that year—

(a) under this section; or
(b) (in the circumstances mentioned in subsection (6) below) under section 36 above,

and it appears to the General or Special Commissioners, on an application made to them not later than the end of the year of assessment following that in which the tax covered by the assessment for the earlier year is finally determined, that there are reasonable grounds for believing that tax for a year ending not earlier than six years before the end of the earlier year was or may have been lost to the Crown owing to the neglect of that person, they may give leave for the making on him of an assessment under this section for that year.

(6) The circumstances referred to in subsection (5) (b) above are that the assessment for the earlier year was one of a number of assessments made on that person for the purpose mentioned in subsection (1) above and that of the years for which those assessments were made—

(a) the latest, apart from the normal year, ended not more than six years before the end of the normal year,
(b) the next, if any, ended not more than six years before the end of the said latest year,

and so on for any earlier years.

(7) An application for leave under this section may be made by the inspector or the Board, and on any such application the person to be assessed shall be entitled to appear and be heard.

(8) In determining the amount of the tax to be charged for any year in any assessment made under this section effect shall be given, if the person to be assessed so requires, to any relief or

allowance to which he would have been entitled for that year on a claim or application made within the time allowed by the Taxes Acts.

(9) In this section and section 38 below "tax" does not include corporation tax, and this section shall apply separately to income tax and to capital gains tax, so that the making of an assessment to one of those taxes shall not affect the time allowed for the making of an assessment to the other tax.

Cross references.—See FA 1988, Sch. 3, para. 29 (husband's liability to the Crown for loss of tax due to wife's neglect before 1990–91 when new system of taxing married couples comes into force).
Amendments.—This section repealed by FA 1989, s. 149 (2), (7) and Sch. 17, Pt. VIII without affecting the making of assessments for years of assessment before 1983–84 or for accounting periods ending before 1 April 1983.

38. Modification of s. 37 in relation to partnerships

(1) The following provisions of this section shall have effect where such an assessment to tax as is mentioned in section 37 (1) above was made on any person who at any time carried on a trade, profession or vocation in partnership with any other person (whether the assessment was made in respect of the profits or gains thereof or not).

(2) In this section—

"*the business*" *means the trade, profession or vocation mentioned in subsection (1) of this section,*
"*the normal year*" *has the same meaning as in section 37 above,*
" *the person in default*" *means the person mentioned in section 37 (1) above.*

(3) Subject to subsection (5) of this section, an assessment in respect of the profits or gains of the business may be made under section 37 above not only on the person in default but on any person who carried on the business at any time in the year for which the assessment is made and either—

(a) then carried it on in partnership with the person in default or with a person who at any time in the normal year carried it on in partnership with the person in default; or
(b) at any time in the normal year carried on the business in partnership with the person in default;

and may be made for the purpose of making good to the Crown a loss of tax attributable to the neglect of any person who carried on the business at any time in the year for which the assessment is made.

(4) For the purpose of determining whether leave may be given for the making of such an assessment on two or more persons who carried on the business in partnership subsections (5) and (6) of section 37 above shall have effect as if the neglect referred to therein were the neglect of any of those persons and as if the assessments referred to therein were assessments made on any one of those persons.

(5) Where such an assessment is made on two or more persons who carried on the business in partnership and those persons include any person (in this subsection referred to as "the exempted partner") who was not charged in any such assessment as is mentioned in subsection (1) of this section, the tax charged in the assessment—

(a) shall not include tax on so much of the profits or gains as would fall to be included in the exempted partner's total income; and
(b) shall not be recoverable from the exempted partner;

and where a person who was not charged as aforesaid carried on the business otherwise than in partnership no such assessment shall be made on him.

Amendments.—This section repealed by FA 1989, s. 149 (2), (7) and Sch. 17, Pt. VIII without affecting the making of assessments for years of assessment before 1983–84 or for accounting periods ending before 1 April 1983.

39. Neglect: corporation tax

(1) Where, for the purpose of making good to the Crown a loss of tax wholly or partly attributable to the fraud, wilful default or neglect of any person, an assessment to corporation tax

for any accounting period (in this section referred to as "the normal accounting period") has been made on him not later than six years after the end of that accounting period, assessments to corporation tax, income tax and the profits tax for earlier accounting periods, years of assessment and chargeable accounting periods may, to the extent provided by the following provisions of this section, be made on him notwithstanding that, but for this section, they would be out of time.

(2) No assessment under this section shall be made on any person except for the purpose of making good to the Crown a loss of tax attributable to his neglect.

(3) An assessment under this section for any accounting period, year of assessment or chargeable accounting period ending not earlier than six years before the end of the normal accounting period may, subject to section 41 below, be made at any time not later than one year after the time when the tax covered by the assessment mentioned in subsection (1) above is finally determined.

(4) An assessment under this section for any accounting period, year of assessment or chargeable accounting period ending earlier than six years before the end of the normal accounting period may only be made with the leave of the General or Special Commissioners, given under the following provisions of this section.

(5) Where an assessment for any accounting period, year of assessment or chargeable accounting period (in this section referred to as "the earlier period") has been made on any person more than six years after the end of that period—

(a) under this section, or
(b) (in the circumstances mentioned in sub-section (6) below) under section 36 above,

and it appears to the General or Special Commissioners, on an application made to them not later than one year after the tax covered by the assessment for the earlier period is finally determined, that there are reasonable grounds for believing that tax for an accounting period, year of assessment or chargeable accounting period ending not earlier than six years before the end of the earlier period was or may have been lost to the Crown owing to the neglect of that person, they may give leave for the making on him of an assessment under this section for that accounting period, year of assessment or chargeable accounting period.

(6) The circumstances referred to in subsection (5) (b) above are that the assessment for the earlier period was one of a number of assessments made on that person for the purpose mentioned in subsection (1) above and that of the accounting periods, years of assessment and chargeable accounting periods for which those assessments were made—

(a) the latest, apart from the normal accounting period, ended not more than six years before the end of the normal accounting period,
(b) the next, if any, ended not more than six years before the end of the said latest accounting period, year of assessment or chargeable accounting period,

and so on for any earlier accounting periods, years of assessment or chargeable accounting periods.

(7) An application for leave under subsection (5) above may be made by the inspector or the Board, and on any such application the person to be assessed shall be entitled to appear and be heard.

(8) In determining the amount of the tax to be charged for any accounting period, year of assessment or chargeable accounting period in any assessment made under this section effect shall be given, if the person to be assessed so requires, to any relief or allowance to which he would have been entitled for that accounting period, year of assessment or chargeable accounting period on a claim or application made within the time allowed by the Taxes Acts or the enactments relating to the profits tax, as the case may be.

(9) For the purposes of this section the year 1965–66 and any earlier year of assessment, and any chargeable accounting period, is to be regarded as earlier than any corporation tax accounting period.

(10) For the purpose of making assessments to income tax for the year 1965–66 and earlier years of assessment, section 38 above shall apply in relation to this section as it applies in relation to section 37 above, but as if references in the said section 38 to the normal year were references to the normal accounting period, and with any other necessary modifications.

Amendments.—This section repealed by FA 1989, s. 149 (2), (7) and Sch. 17, Pt. VIII without affecting the making of assessments for years of assessment before 1983–84 or for accounting periods ending before 1 April 1983.

40. Assessment on personal representatives

(1) For the purpose of the charge of tax on the executors or administrators of a deceased person in respect of the income, or chargeable gains, which arose or accrued to him before his death, the time allowed by section 34, 35 or 36 above shall in no case extend beyond the end of the third year next following the year of assessment in which the deceased died.

(2) ...[1], for the purpose of making good to the Crown any loss of tax attributable to the [fraudulent or negligent conduct][2] of a person who has died, an assessment on his personal representatives to tax for any year of assessment ending not earlier than six years before his death may be made at any time before the end of the third year next following the year of assessment in which he died.

(3) In this section "tax" means income tax or capital gains tax.

Cross references.—See TA 1988, Sch. 19A, para. 9 (for the purposes of this section, any fraud etc. committed by Lloyd's underwriting syndicates's agent to be attributed to each member of the syndicate).
Amendments.—[1] Words "Subject to section 41 below" in sub-s (2) repealed by FA 1989, Sch. 17, Pt. VIII.
[2] Words in sub-s. (2) substituted for the words "fraud, wilful default or neglect" by FA 1989, s. 149 (4) (a) (ii), (7).

41. Leave of General or Special Commissioners required for certain assessments

(1) An assessment to tax made by virtue of—

  (a) section 36 of this Act, or
  (b) so far as they relate to an assessment for a period ending not earlier than six years before the end of the normal year or normal accounting period, section 37, 38 or 39 of this Act, or
  (c) section 40 (2) of this Act,

may only be made with the leave of a General or Special Commissioner given on being satisfied by an inspector or other officer of the Board that there are reasonable grounds for believing that tax has or may have been lost to the Crown owing to the fraud or wilful default or neglect of any person.

(2) The General or Special Commissioner giving leave to make such an assessment shall take no part in the proceedings, and shall not be present, when any appeal against the assessment is heard or determined.

Amendments.—This section repealed by FA 1989, s. 149 (2), (7) and Sch. 17, Pt. VIII without affecting the making of assessments for years of assessment before 1983–84 or for accounting periods ending before 1 April 1983.

Claims

42. Procedure for making claims

(1) Where any provision of the Taxes Acts provides for relief to be given, or any other thing to be done, on the making of a claim, this section shall, unless otherwise provided, have effect in relation to the claim.

(2) Subject to any provision in the Taxes Acts for a claim to be made to the Board, every claim shall be made to an inspector.

(3) An appeal may be brought against the decision of the inspector or the Board on a claim by giving written notice to the inspector or the Board as the case may be within thirty days of receipt of written notice of that decision:

Provided that the time for appealing against the Board's decision—

  (a) under section [278][1] of the principal Act (personal reliefs for non-residents), or
  (b) on a question of residence, ordinary residence or domicile, or
  (c) in the case of a claim under [subsection (5) of section 614][1] of the principal Act (pension funds for service abroad) on the question whether a fund is one to which [section 615 (3) of that Act][1] applies,

shall be three months from receipt of notice of their decision.

(4) Schedule 2 to this Act shall have effect as respects the Commissioners to whom an appeal lies under this section.

(5) A claim shall be in such form as the Board may determine and the form of claim—

(a) shall provide for a declaration to the effect that all the particulars given in the form are correctly stated to the best of the knowledge and belief of the person making the claim, and
(b) may require—
  (i) a return of profits to be made in support of the claim, and
  (ii) any such particulars of assets acquired as may be required in a return by virtue of subsections (2) and (3) of section 12 of this Act,

and, in the case of a claim made by or on behalf of a person who is not resident, or who claims to be not resident or not ordinarily resident or not domiciled, in the United Kingdom, the inspector or the Board may require a statement or declaration in support of the claim to be made by affidavit.

(6) A claim may be made on behalf of an incapacitated person by his trustee, guardian, tutor or curator; and a person who under Part VIII of this Act has been charged with tax on the profits of another person may make any such claim for relief by discharge or repayment of that tax.

(7) The inspector or the Board may give effect to any claim by discharge of tax or, on proof to the satisfaction of the inspector or the Board that any tax has been paid by the claimant by deduction or otherwise, by repayment of tax.

(8) Where a claim has been made and the claimant subsequently discovers that an error or mistake has been made in the claim, the claimant may make a supplementary claim within the time allowed for making the original claim.

(9) On an appeal on a claim, the Commissioners may vary the decision appealed against whether or not the variation is to the advantage of the appellant.

(10) Where it is necessary, in order to give effect to a claim, or as a result of allowing a claim, to make any adjustment by way of an assessment on any person, the assessment shall not be out of time if it is made within one year of the final determination of the claim.

For the purposes of this subsection, a claim shall not be deemed to be finally determined until the amount recoverable under the claim can no longer be varied, whether by any Commissioners on appeal or by the order of any court.

(11) In this section "profits"—
  (a) in relation to income tax, means income,
  (b) in relation to capital gains tax, means chargeable gains,
  (c) in relation to corporation tax, means profits as computed for the purposes of that tax.

Cross references.—See CGTA 1979, s. 45 (3) (return under sub-s. (5) of this section as regards capital gains accruing to a married woman).
Amendments.—[1] Words in sub-s. (3) (a), (c) substituted by TA 1988, Sch. 29, para. 32 Table.

43. Time limit for making claims

(1) Subject to any provision of the Taxes Acts prescribing a longer or shorter period, no claim for relief under the Taxes Acts shall be allowed unless it is made within six years from the end of the chargeable period to which it relates.

(2) A claim (including a supplementary claim) which could not have been allowed but for the making of an assessment to income tax or capital gains tax after the year of assessment to which the claim relates may be made at any time before the end of the year of assessment following that in which the assessment was made.

Cross references.—See TA 1988, Sch. 26, para. 1 (6) (application of this section to claims for group relief or relief for trading losses by UK controlled foreign companies).

[43A. Further assessments: claims etc.

(1) This section applies where—
  (a) by virtue of section 29 (3) of this Act an assessment is made on any person for a chargeable period, and
  (b) the assessment is not made for the purpose of making good to the Crown any loss of tax attributable to his fraudulent or negligent conduct or the fraudulent or negligent conduct of a person acting on his behalf.

(2) Without prejudice to section 43 (2) above but subject to section 43B below, where this section applies—

(*a*) any relevant claim, election, application or notice which could have been made or given within the time allowed by the Taxes Acts may be made or given at any time within one year from the end of the chargeable period in which the assessment is made, and
(*b*) any relevant claim, election, application or notice previously made or given may at any such time be revoked or varied—

(i) in the same manner as it was made or given, and
(ii) by or with the consent of the same person or persons who made, gave or consented to it (or, in the case of any such person who has died, by or with the consent of his personal representatives),

except where by virtue of any enactment it is irrevocable.

(3) For the purposes of this section and section 43B below, a claim, election, application or notice is relevant in relation to an assessment for a chargeable period if—

(a) it relates to that chargeable period or is made or given by reference to an event occurring in that chargeable period, and
(*b*) it or, as the case may be, its revocation or variation has or could have the effect of reducing any of the liabilities mentioned in subsection (4) below.

(4) The liabilities referred to in subsection (3) above are—

(*a*) the increased liability to tax resulting from the assessment,
(*b*) any other liability to tax of the person concerned for—

(i) the chargeable period to which the assessment relates, or
(ii) any chargeable period which follows that chargeable period and ends not later than one year after the end of the chargeable period in which the assessment is made.

(5) Where a claim, election, application or notice is made, given, revoked or varied by virtue of subsection (2) above, all such adjustments shall be made, whether by way of discharge or repayment of tax or the making of assessments or otherwise, as are required to take account of the effect of the taking of that action on any person's liability to tax for any chargeable period.

(6) The provisions of this Act relating to appeals against decisions on claims shall apply with any necessary modifications to a decision on the revocation or variation of a claim by virtue of subsection (2) above.][1]

Amendments.—[1] This section inserted by FA 1989, s. 150 in relation to assessment notices issued after 26 July 1989.

[43B. Limits on application of section 43A

(1) If the effect of the exercise by any person of a power conferred by section 43A (2) above—

(*a*) to make or give a claim, election, application or notice, or
(*b*) to revoke or vary a claim, election, application or notice previously made or given,

would be to alter the liability to tax of another person, that power may not be exercised except with the consent in writing of that other person or, where he has died, his personal representatives.

(2) Where—

(*a*) a power conferred by subsection (2) of section 43A above is exercised in consequence of an assessment made on a person, and
(*b*) the exercise of the power increases the liability to tax of another person,

that section shall not apply by reason of any assessment made because of that increased liability.

(3) In any case where—

(*a*) one or more relevant claims, elections, applications or notices are made, given, revoked or varied by virtue of the application of section 43A above in the case of an assessment, and
(*b*) the total of the reductions in liability to tax which, apart from this subsection, would result from the action mentioned in paragraph (*a*) above would exceed the additional liability to tax resulting from the assessment,

the excess shall not be available to reduce any liability to tax.

(4) Where subsection (3) above has the effect of limiting either the reduction in a person's liability to tax for more than one period or the reduction in the liability to tax of more than one person, the limited amount shall be apportioned between the periods or persons concerned—

    (*a*) except where paragraph (*b*) below applies, in such manner as may be specified by the inspector by notice in writing to the person or persons concerned, or
    (*b*) where the person concerned gives (or the persons concerned jointly give) notice in writing to the inspector within the relevant period, in such manner as may be specified in the notice given by the person or persons concerned.

(5) For the purposes of paragraph (*b*) of subsection (4) above the relevant period is the period of 30 days beginning with the day on which notice under paragraph (*a*) of that subsection is given to the person concerned or, where more than one person is concerned, the latest date on which such notice is given to any of them.][1]

Amendments.—[1] This section inserted by FA 1989, s. 150 in relation to assessment notices issued after 26 July 1989.

PART V
APPEALS AND OTHER PROCEEDINGS

Cross references.—See TA 1988, ss. 253, 350 (4)–(7) (power of Board to make regulations modifying or replacing TA 1988, s. 234 (5)–(9) and Schs. 13, 16).

Jurisdiction

44. General Commissioners

(1) Proceedings before the General Commissioners under the Taxes Acts shall, subject to the provisions of this section, be brought before the General Commissioners for the division in which the place given by the rules in Schedule 3 to this Act is situated.

[(1A) Subject to subsections (1B) and (2) below, the Board may direct that, notwithstanding the said rules, proceedings before the General Commissioners under the Taxes Acts of any description specified in the direction shall be brought before the General Commissioners for the division so specified in relation to proceedings of that description.][2]

[(1B) A direction under subsection (1A) above shall have effect subject to the provisions referred to in the last paragraph of Schedule 3 to this Act and shall not apply to any proceedings if—

(*a*) the inspector has not served on the other party a notice stating the effect of the direction in relation to those proceedings;
(*b*) that party has served on the inspector, within thirty days of the service of the inspector's notice, a notice objecting to the direction so applying; or
(*c*) in the case of an appeal, that party has elected under rule 3 or 5 of the said rules for the place where he ordinarily resides.][2]

[(2) Where—

(*a*) the parties to any proceedings under the Taxes Acts which are to be heard by any General Commissioners have agreed, whether before or after the institution of the proceedings, that the proceedings shall be brought before the General Commissioners for a division specified in the agreement; and
(*b*) in the case of an agreement made before the time of the institution of the proceedings, neither party has determined that agreement by a notice served on the other party before that time,

the proceedings shall be brought before the General Commissioners for the division so specified, notwithstanding the said rules and any direction under subsection (1A) above.][3]

(3) In any case in which proceedings under the Taxes Acts may be brought at the election of any person before the Special Commissioners instead of before the General Commissioners, the Commissioners before whom the proceedings are to be brought or have been brought may, if they think fit, on an application made by the parties, arrange with the other Commissioners concerned for the transfer of the proceedings to those other Commissioners; and the proceedings may be so transferred notwithstanding that the election has been exercised, or that the time for exercising the election has expired without its being exercised.

[(3A) Where in any case (including one in which proceedings may be brought as mentioned in subsection (3) above)—

(*a*) an appeal has been brought before the General Commissioners; and
(*b*) those Commissioners consider that, because of the complexity of the appeal or the length of time likely to be required for hearing it, the appeal should be brought before the Special Commissioners;

the General Commissioners may, with the agreement of the Special Commissioners, and having considered any representations made to them by the parties, arrange for the transfer of the proceedings to the Special Commissioners.][1]

(4) No determination of any General Commissioners under the Taxes Acts shall be questioned, whether by a case stated under section 56 of this Act or otherwise, on the ground that this section did not authorise those General Commissioners to make the determination, except by a party by whom or on whose behalf an objection to the jurisdiction was made to

those General Commissioners before or in the course of the proceedings leading to the determination.

(5) Anything to be done by the General Commissioners may, save as otherwise expressly provided by the Taxes Acts, be done by any two or more General Commissioners.

Cross references.—See FA 1988, s. 134 (4), (7), (9) (application of this section, with effect from 3 April 1989 by virtue of FA 1988 (Commencement) Order 1989, S.I. 1989 No. 473, in relation to proceedings in Northern Ireland transferred from the Special Commissioners to the General Commissioners).
Amendments.—[1] Sub-s. (3A) inserted by FA 1984, Sch. 22, para. 5 and came into force on 1 January 1985 by virtue of FA 1984 (Commencement No. 2) Order 1984, S.I. 1984 No. 1836.
[2] Sub-ss. (1A), (1B) inserted by FA 1988, s. 133 (1), (3) and have effect in relation to proceedings instituted after 31 December 1988.
[3] Sub-s (2) substituted by FA 1988, s. 133 (2), (3) and has effect in relation to proceedings instituted after the passing of FA 1988. FA 1988 was passed on 29 July 1988.

45. Quorum of Special Commissioners

(1) Anything to be done under any Act (including, except where otherwise expressly provided, any Act passed after this Act) by, to or before the Special Commissioners [shall, except in any case where the Presiding Special Commissioner directs otherwise,][1] be done by, to or before a single Special Commissioner, . . .[2]; and this section applies not only for the purposes of the Taxes Act but also for the purposes of any other affairs under the care and management of the Board.

(2) . . .[2]

(3) Proceedings brought [, in accordance with a direction of the Presiding Special Commissioner][3] before two or more Special Commissioners may be continued and determined by any one or more of them if the parties to the proceedings have given their consent, and if the continuing Special Commissioner or Commissioners, after such consultation as is practicable with any Special Commissioner retiring from the proceedings, is or are satisfied that to do so will avoid undue delay in the hearing of those or any other proceedings.

(4)–(6) . . .[2]

Amendments.—[1] Words in sub-s. (1) substituted by FA 1984, Sch. 22, para. 2 (2) with effect from 1 January 1985 by virtue of FA 1984 (Commencement No. 2) Order 1984, S.I. 1984 No. 1836.
[2] Sub-ss. (2), (4)–(6) repealed in sub-s. (1) repealed by FA 1984, Sch. 22, para. 2 (2), (4) and Sch. 23, Pt. XIII with effect from 1 January 1985 by virtue of S.I. 1984 No. 1836.
[3] Words in sub-s. (3) inserted by FA 1984, Sch. 22, para. 2 (3) with effect from 1 January 1985 by virtue of S.I. 1984 No. 1836.

46. General and Special Commissioners

(1) A right to elect to bring an appeal or other proceedings under the Taxes Acts before the Special Commissioners instead of before the General Commissioners shall be exercised by notice combined (in the case of an appeal) with the notice of appeal, or by a separate notice in writing to the inspector or other officer of the Board within the time limited for bringing the proceedings, and if no such notice of election is given the appeal or other proceedings shall be brought before the General Commissioners.

(2) Save as otherwise provided in the Taxes Acts, the determination of the General Commissioners or the Special Commissioners in any proceedings under the Taxes Acts shall be final and conclusive.

47. Special jurisdiction relating to tax on chargeable gains

(1) If and so far as the question in dispute on any appeal against an assessment to tax (whether capital gains tax or corporation tax) on chargeable gains, or against a decision on a claim under [the Capital Gains Tax Act 1979][3] is a question of the value of any land, or of a lease of land then—

(a) if the land is in England or Wales the question shall be determined on a reference to the Lands Tribunal, and
(b) if the land is in Northern Ireland the question shall be determined on a reference to the Lands Tribunal for Northern Ireland.

(2) In relation to land and leases of land in Scotland for any reference to the Lands Tribunal

in subsection (1) above there shall be substituted a reference to the Lands Tribunal for Scotland:
. . .¹

(3) If and so far as any appeal mentioned in subsection (1) above involves the question of the value of any shares or securities in a company resident in the United Kingdom, other than shares or securities dealt in on a stock exchange in the United Kingdom, that question shall be determined [by the Special Commissioners]², and those Commissioners shall hear and determine the question in the same way as an appeal.

(4) . . .⁴

Amendments.—¹ Proviso to sub-s. (2) repealed by FA 1974, Sch 14, Pt. VII.
² Words in sub-s. (3) substituted by FA 1975, s. 54 (1), with effect from 13 March 1975.
³ Words in sub-s. (1) substituted by CGTA 1979, s. 157 (2)–(4) and Sch. 7, para. 8 Table, Pt. I. 1, with effect from 22 March 1979.
⁴ Sub-s. (4) repealed by CGTA 1979, Sch. 8.

[47B. Special jurisdiction relating to Business Expansion Scheme

If and so far as the question in dispute on any appeal against the refusal of relief under [Chapter III of Part VII of the principal Act]² (relief for investment in corporate trades), or against an assessment withdrawing any such relief, is a question of the value of an interest in land (within the meaning of [section 294 (5) of that Act]²), it shall be determined—

(a) if the land is in England and Wales, on a reference to the Lands Tribunal;
(b) if the land is in Scotland, on a reference to the Lands Tribunal for Scotland; and
(c) if the land is in Northern Ireland, on a reference to the Lands Tribunal for Northern Ireland.]¹

Amendments.—¹ This section inserted by FA 1986, Sch. 9, para. 1 (2) and 22 in relation to shares issued after 18 March 1986.
² Words substituted by TA 1988, Sch. 29, para. 32 Table.

Proceedings before Commissioners

48. Application to appeals and other proceedings

(1) In the following provisions of this Part of this Act, unless the context otherwise requires—

"appeal" means any appeal to the General Commissioners or to the Special Commissioners under the Taxes Acts,
"the Commissioners" means the General Commissioners or the Special Commissioners as the case may be.

(2) The following provisions of this Part of this Act shall apply in relation to—

(a) appeals other than appeals against assessments, and
(b) proceedings which under the Taxes Acts are to be heard and determined in the same way as an appeal,

subject [to any necessary modifications, including (except in the case of applications under section 55 below) the omission of section 56 (9) below].¹

Amendments.—¹ Words in sub-s. (2) substituted by F (No. 2) A 1975, s. 45 (4) in relation to tax charged by assessment notice issued after 31 July 1975; see F (No. 2) A 1975, s. 44 (7).

49. Proceedings brought out of time

(1) An appeal may be brought out of time if on an application for the purpose an inspector or the Board is satisfied that there was a reasonable excuse for not bringing the appeal within the time limited, and that the application was made thereafter without unreasonable delay, and gives consent in writing; and the inspector or the Board, if not satisfied, shall refer the application for determination by the Commissioners.

(2) If there is a right to elect to bring the appeal before the Special Commissioners instead of before the General Commissioners, the Commissioners to whom an application under this section is to be referred shall be the General Commissioners unless the election has been exercised before the application is so referred.

50. Procedure

(1) The Commissioners shall cause notice of the day for hearing appeals to be given to every appellant, and shall meet together for the hearing of appeals from time to time, with or without adjournment until all appeals have been determined.

(2) Notice of appeal meetings to be held by the Commissioners shall also be given to the inspector by the clerk to the Commissioners, except that in proceedings to which the Board, or an officer of the Board other than an inspector, are parties, the notice shall be given to the Board or to that officer.

(3) Any officer of the Board may attend every appeal, and shall be entitled—

(*a*) to be present during all the time of the hearing and at the determination of the appeal, and
(*b*) to give reasons in support of the assessment or other decision against which the appeal is made.

(4) If it is shown to the satisfaction of the Commissioners that owing to absence, sickness or other reasonable cause any person has been prevented from attending at the hearing of an appeal on the day fixed for that purpose, they may postpone the hearing of his appeal for such reasonable time as they think necessary, or may admit the appeal to be made by any agent, clerk or servant on his behalf.

(5) Upon any appeal the Commissioners shall permit any barrister or solicitor to plead before them on behalf of any party to the appeal, either orally or in writing, and shall hear any accountant, that is to say, any person who has been admitted a member of an incorporated society of accountants:

. . .[2]

(6) If, on an appeal, it appears to the majority of the Commissioners present at the hearing, by examination of the appellant on oath or affirmation, or by other lawful evidence, that the appellant is overcharged by any assessment, the assessment shall be reduced accordingly, but otherwise every such assessment shall stand good.

(7) If on any appeal it appears to the Commissioners that the person assessed ought to be charged in an amount exceeding the amount contained in the assessment, the assessment shall be increased accordingly.

[(8) Where, on an appeal against an assessment which—

(*a*) assesses an amount which is chargeable to tax, and
(*b*) charges tax on the amount assessed,

it appears to the Commissioners as mentioned in subsection (6) or (7) above, they may, unless the circumstances of the case otherwise require, reduce or, as the case may be, increase only the amount assessed; and where any appeal is so determined the tax charged by the assessment shall be taken to have been reduced or increased accordingly.][1]

Note.—See **Prospective Legislation Notes** (Taxes Management Provisions and Commercial Woodlands).
Amendments.—[1] Sub-s. (8) added by F (No. 2) A 1975, s. 67 (2), and this section, as amended, to have effect and be deemed always to have had effect except that the addition of sub-s. (8) does not affect the judgment of any court given in proceedings commenced before 29 April 1975; see F (No. 2) A 1975, s. 67 (3).
[2] The proviso in sub-s. (5) repealed by FA 1988, Sch. 14, Pt. V.

51. Power of Commissioners to obtain information from appellant

(1) The Commissioners may at any time before the determination of an appeal give notice to the appellant or other party to the proceedings (not being an inspector or the Board) requiring him within the time specified in the notice—

(*a*) to deliver to them such particulars as they may require for the purpose of determining the appeal, and
(*b*) to make available for inspection by them, or by any officer of the Board, all such books, accounts or other documents in his possession or power as may be specified or described in the notice, being books, accounts or other documents which, in the opinion of the Commissioners issuing the notice, contain or may contain information relating to the subject matter of the proceedings.

(2) Any officer of the Board may, at all reasonable times, inspect and take copies of, or extracts from, any particulars delivered under subsection (1) (*a*) above; and the Commissioners or any officer of the Board may take copies of, or extracts from, any books,

accounts, or other documents made available for their or his inspection under subsection (1) (*b*) above.

52. Evidence

(1) Any party to an appeal shall be entitled to adduce any lawful evidence.

(2) The Commissioners may summon any person (other than the appellant) to appear before them and give evidence, and a witness before the Commissioners may be examined on oath:

Provided that any agent or servant of the appellant, and any other person confidentially employed in the affairs of the appellant, may refuse to be sworn or to answer any question to which he objects.

(3) A person who after being duly summoned—

(*a*) neglects or refuses to appear before the Commissioners at the time and place appointed for that purpose, or
(*b*) appears, but refuses to be sworn, or
(*c*) refuses to answer any lawful question concerning the matters under consideration,

shall incur a penalty not exceeding £50:

Provided that the penalty imposed in respect of any offence under paragraph (*b*) or paragraph (*c*) of this subsection shall not apply to any such person as is within the proviso to subsection (2) above.

53. Summary award of penalties

(1) Any penalty incurred by any person for a failure to comply with a notice under section 51 above, or incurred by any person under section 52 above, may be [determined][2] summarily by the Commissioners notwithstanding that no proceedings [under section 100C of this Act][2] have been commenced, and accordingly [section 98 of this Act shall have effect, in relation to a penalty so [determined][2], as if subsection (3) were omitted . . .[3]][1].

(2) An appeal shall lie to the High Court or, in Scotland, the Court of Session as the Court of Exchequer in Scotland, from the [determination][2] of any penalty under this section, and on any such appeal the court may either confirm or reverse the [determination][2] of the Commissioners or reduce or increase the sum [determined][2].

(3) Any penalty [determined][2] by virtue of this section shall for all purposes be treated as if it were tax charged in an assessment and due and payable.

Amendments.—[1] Words in sub-s. (1) substituted by FA 1972, s. 129 in relation to a penalty awarded on or after 27 July 1972.
[2] Words in sub-ss. (1), (2), (3) substituted by FA 1989, s. 168 (1), (3).
[3] Words in sub-s. (1) repealed by FA 1989, Sch. 17, Pt. VIII.

54. Settling of appeals by agreement

(1) Subject to the provisions of this section, where a person gives notice of appeal and, before the appeal is determined by the Commissioners, the inspector or other proper officer of the Crown and the appellant come to an agreement, whether in writing or otherwise, that the assessment or decision under appeal should be treated as upheld without variation, or as varied in a particular manner or as discharged or cancelled, the like consequences shall ensue for all purposes as would have ensued if, at the time when the agreement was come to, the Commissioners had determined the appeal and had upheld the assessment or decision without variation, had varied it in that manner or had discharged or cancelled it, as the case may be.

(2) Subsection (1) of this section shall not apply where, within thirty days from the date when the agreement was come to, the appellant gives notice in writing to the inspector or other proper officer of the Crown that he desires to repudiate or resile from the agreement.

(3) Where an agreement is not in writing—

(*a*) the preceding provisions of this section shall not apply unless the fact that an agreement was come to, and the terms agreed, are confirmed by notice in writing given by the inspector or other proper officer of the Crown to the appellant or by the appellant to the inspector or other proper officer; and
(*b*) the references in the said preceding provisions to the time when the agreement was

come to shall be construed as references to the time of the giving of the said notice of confirmation.

(4) Where—

(*a*) a person who has given a notice of appeal notifies the inspector or other proper officer of the Crown, whether orally or in writing, that he desires not to proceed with the appeal; and
(*b*) thirty days have elapsed since the giving of the notification without the inspector or other proper officer giving to the appellant notice in writing indicating that he is unwilling that the appeal should be treated as withdrawn,

the preceding provisions of this section shall have effect as if, at the date of the appellant's notification, the appellant and the inspector or other proper officer had come to an agreement, orally or in writing, as the case may be, that the assessment or decision under appeal should be upheld without variation.

(5) The references in this section to an agreement being come to with an appellant and the giving of notice or notification to or by an appellant include references to an agreement being come to with, and the giving of notice or notification to or by, a person acting on behalf of the appellant in relation to the appeal.

Cross references.—See FA 1982, Sch. 21, para. 4 (1) (this section to apply to the tribunal established under TA 1988, s. 706).

[55. Recovery of tax not postponed

(1) This section applies to an appeal to the Commissioners against—

(*a*) an assessment to income tax under Schedule A, Schedule C or Schedule D,
(*b*) an assessment charging income tax at a rate other than the basic rate on income from which income tax has been deducted (otherwise than under section [203][8] of the principal Act) or from or on which income tax is treated as having been deducted or paid or income chargeable under Schedule F,
(*c*) an assessment to income tax made under [Schedule 16 to the principal Act][8] (income tax on company payments) other than an assessment charging tax the time for the payment of which is given by paragraph 4 (1) or 9 of that Schedule,
(*d*) an assessment to capital gains tax,
(*e*) an assessment to corporation tax other than an assessment made under [Schedule 13 to the principal Act][8] (advance corporation tax) charging tax the time for the payment of which is given by paragraph 3 (1) or 9 of that Schedule.
(*f*) ...[4]
[(*g*) a notice under subsection (1) or subsection (3) of section 753 of the principal Act where, before the appeal is determined, the appellant is assessed to tax under section 747 (4) (*a*) of that Act by reference to an amount of chargeable profits specified in that notice.][6]

(2) [Except as otherwise provided by the following provisions of this section][2], the tax charged by the assessment shall be due and payable as if [there had been no appeal][9].

(3) If the appellant has grounds for believing that he is overcharged to tax by the assessment, he may, by notice in writing given to the inspector within thirty days after the date of the issue of the notice of assessment, apply to the Commissioners for a determination of the amount of tax the payment of which should be postponed pending the determination of the appeal.

A notice of application under this subsection shall state the amount in which the appellant believes that he is overcharged to tax and his grounds for that belief.

[(3A) An application under subsection (3) above may be made more than thirty days after the date of the issue of the notice of assessment if there is a change in the circumstances of the case as a result of which the appellant has grounds for believing that he is over-charged to tax by the assessment.][3]

(4) If, after any determination of the amount of tax the payment of which should be so postponed, there is a change in the circumstances of the case as a result of which either party has grounds for believing that the amount so determined has become excessive or, as the case may be, insufficient, he may, by notice in writing given to the other party at any time before the determination of the appeal, apply to the Commissioners for a further determination of that amount.

A notice of application under this subsection shall state the amount in which the applicant believes that the amount previously determined has become excessive or, as the case may be, insufficient and his grounds for that belief.

(5) An application under subsection (3) or (4) above shall be heard and determined in the same way as the appeal; and where any such application is heard and determined by any Commissioners, that shall not preclude them from hearing and determining the appeal or any application or further application under subsection (4) above.

(6) The amount of tax the payment of which shall be postponed pending the determination of the appeal shall be the amount (if any) in which it appears to the Commissioners, having regard to the representations made and any lawful evidence adduced, that there are reasonable grounds for believing that the appellant is overcharged to tax; and—

[(a) in the case of a determination made on an application under subsection (3) above, other than an application made by virtue of subsection (3A) above, the date on which any tax the payment of which is not so postponed is due and payable shall be determined as if the tax were charged by an assessment notice of which was issued on the date of that determination and against which there had been no appeal; and][10]

[(b) in the case of a determination made on an application under subsection (4) above—

(i) the date on which any tax the payment of which ceases to be so postponed is due and payable shall be determined as if the tax were charged by an assessment notice of which was issued on the date of that determination and against which there had been no appeal; and

(ii) any tax overpaid shall be repaid.][10]

[(6A) Where an appeal is brought against an assessment to tax under section 747 (4) (a) of the principal Act as well as against a notice under section 753 (1) or (3) of that Act—

(a) an application under subsection (3) above may relate to matters arising on both appeals and, in determining the amount of tax the payment of which should be postponed, the Commissioners shall consider the matters so arising together; and

(b) if the Commissioners have determined the amount of tax the payment of which should be postponed solely in relation to one of the appeals, the bringing of the other appeal shall be taken to be a change of circumstances falling within subsection (4) above; and

(c) any reference in this section to the determination of the appeal shall be construed as a reference to the determination of the two appeals, but the determination of one before the other shall be taken to be a change of circumstances falling within subsection (4) above.][7]

(7) If the appellant and the inspector come to an agreement, whether in writing or otherwise, as to the amount of tax the payment of which should be postponed pending the determination of the appeal, the like consequences shall ensue as would have ensued if the Commissioners had made a determination to that effect under subsection (6) above on the date when the agreement was come to, but without prejudice to the making of a further agreement or of a further determination under that subsection.

(8) Where an agreement is not in writing—

(a) subsection (7) above shall not apply unless the fact that an agreement was come to, and the terms agreed, are confirmed by notice in writing given by the inspector to the appellant or by the appellant to the inspector, and

(b) the reference in that subsection to the time when the agreement was come to shall be construed as a reference to the time of the giving of the notice of confirmation.

[(9) On the determination of the appeal—

(a) the date on which any tax payable in accordance with that determination is due and payable shall, so far as it is tax the payment of which had been postponed, or which would not have been charged by the assessment if there had been no appeal, be determined as if the tax were charged by an assessment—

(i) notice of which was issued on the date on which the inspector issues to the appellant a notice of the total amount payable in accordance with the determination, and

(ii) against which there had been no appeal; and

(b) any tax overpaid shall be repaid.][10]

(10) In this section "inspector" means the inspector or other officer of the Board by whom the notice of assessment was issued; and references in this section to an agreement being come to with an appellant and the giving of notice to or by an appellant include references to an agreement being come to with, and the giving of notice to or by, a person acting on behalf of the appellant in relation to the appeal.

(11) . . .[5] the transfer of proceedings under this Act from one body of Commissioners to

another body of Commissioners shall not affect the validity of a determination under subsection (6) above.][1]

Cross references.—See TA 1988, s. 10 (5) (application under sub-ss. (3), (4) above may be combined with an application under TA 1988, s. 10 (3), (4) for repayment of excess corporation tax becoming due owing to a change in a company's circumstances), an assessment for recovering from taxpayer excess relief under TA 1988, s. 266 (life assurance premiums) to be treated as if it were among those specified in sub-s. (1) of this section),
s. 306 (8) (application for postponement of tax under sub-s. (3) or (4) by an individual subscribing for shares in a qualifying company),
s. 375 (4) (MIRAS; application of this section to assessments for recovery of tax deducted by a borrower after ceasing to be entitled to it);
Sch. 19A, para. 6 (modification of this section in its application to appeals by Lloyd's underwriters against determination by inspector of tax liability),
Sch. 19A, para. 8 (2) (*a*) (modification of the reference in this section to the date of the notice of assessment in a case where an inspector's determination of Lloyd's underwriting profit or loss is varied or modified),
Sch. 27, para. 19 (3) (application of sub-ss. (3A) onwards of this section to an application for postponement of tax on non-qualifying offshore fund pending its certification as a distributing fund).
Amendments.—[1] This section was substituted by F (No. 2) A 1975, s. 45 (1) in relation to tax charged by assessment notices issued after 31 July 1975.
[2] Words in sub-s. (2) substituted by FA 1982, s. 68 (1), (4) in relation to assessment notices issued after 30 July 1982.
[3] Sub-s. (3A) inserted by FA 1982, s. 68 (2)–(4) in relation to assessment notices issued after 30 July 1982.
[4] Sub-s. (1) (*f*) relates to development land tax and is not relevant to this work.
[5] Words in sub-s. (11) repealed by FA 1984, Sch. 23, Pt. XIII with effect from 1 January 1985 by virtue of FA 1984 (Commencement No. 2) Order 1984, S.I. 1984 No. 1836.
[6] Sub-s. (1) (*g*) substituted by TA 1988, Sch. 29, para. 8.
[7] Sub-s. (6A) inserted by *ibid*.
[8] Words in sub-s. (1) (*b*), (*c*), (*e*) substituted by TA 1988, Sch. 29, para. 32 Table.
[9] Words in sub-s. (2) substituted by FA 1989, s. 156 (2), (4) in respect of tax charged by assessment notices issued after 30 July 1982.
[10] Sub-ss. (6) (*a*), (6) (*b*), (9) substituted by *ibid*.

56. Statement of case for opinion of the High Court

(1) Immediately after the determination of an appeal by the Commissioners, the appellant or the inspector or other officer of the Board, if dissatisfied with the determination as being erroneous in point of law, may declare his dissatisfaction to the Commissioners who heard the appeal.

(2) The appellant or the inspector or other officer of the Board, as the case may be, having declared his dissatisfaction, may, within thirty days after the determination, by notice in writing addressed to the clerk to the Commissioners, require the Commissioners to state and sign a case for the opinion of the High Court thereon.

(3) The party requiring the case shall pay to the clerk to the Commissioners a fee of [£25][2] for and in respect of the same, before he is entitled to have the case stated.

(4) The case shall set forth the facts and the determination of the Commissioners, and the party requiring it shall transmit the case, when stated and signed, to the High Court, within thirty days after receiving the same.

(5) At or before the time when he transmits the case to the High Court, the party requiring it shall send notice in writing of the fact that the case has been stated on his application, together with a copy of the case, to the other party.

(6) The High Court shall hear and determine any question or questions of law arising on the case, and shall reverse, affirm or amend the determination in respect of which the case has been stated, or shall remit the matter to the Commissioners with the opinion of the Court thereon, or may make such other order in relation to the matter as to the Court may seem fit.

(7) The High Court may cause the case to be sent back for amendment, and thereupon the case shall be amended accordingly, and judgment shall be delivered after it has been amended.

(8) An appeal shall lie from the decision of the High Court to the Court of Appeal and thence to the House of Lords:

Provided that—

(*a*) no appeal shall lie to the House of Lords from the Court of Appeal unless leave has been given under and in accordance with section 1 of the Administration of Justice (Appeals) Act 1934, and
(*b*) this subsection has effect subject to Part II of the Administration of Justice Act 1969 (appeal from High Court to House of Lords).

(9) Where the appeal is against an assessment, then notwithstanding that a case has been required to be stated or is pending before the High Court, tax shall be paid in accordance with the determination of the Commissioners who have been required to state the case:

Provided that, if the [amount charged by][3] the assessment is altered by the order or judgement of the High Court, then—

(a) if too much tax has been paid the amount overpaid shall be refunded with such interest, if any, as the High Court may allow; or
[(b) if too little tax has been charged, the amount undercharged shall be due and payable at the expiration of a period of thirty days beginning with the date on which the inspector issues to the other party a notice of the total amount payable in accordance with the order or judgment of that Court.]][1]

(10) All matters within the jurisdiction of the High Court under this section shall be assigned in Scotland to the Court of Session sitting as the Court of Exchequer, and an appeal shall lie from the decision under this section of the Court of Session, as the Court of Exchequer in Scotland, to the House of Lords.

(11) This section has effect in Northern Ireland subject to section 58 below.

Note.—The Revenue Appeals Order 1987, S.I. 1987 No. 1422 made under s. 56A of this Act with effect from 1 October 1987 provides that a case stated by the Special Commissioners under this section for the opinion of the High Court shall be referred direct to the Court of Appeal if—

(a) the parties consent to such referral;
(b) the Special Commissioners have endorsed the case with a certificate that their determination involves a point of law relating wholly or mainly to the construction of an enactment or of a statutory instrument which has been fully argued before them and fully considered by them; and
(c) the leave of a single judge of the Court of Appeal has been obtained pursuant to section 54 (6) of the Supreme Court Act 1981

and applies this section to a referral to the Court of Appeal subject to—

(a) for references to the High Court (other than that in sub-section (2)) there were references to the Court of Appeal;
(b) the following words appeared at the end of subsection (2)—

"and, if the other party consents, may, before the case is stated and signed, request the Commissioners to endorse the case with a certificate that their determination involves a point of law relating wholly or mainly to the construction of an enactment or of a statutory instrument which has been fully argued before them and fully considered by them";

(c) for subsection (4) there were substituted—

"(4) The case shall set forth the facts and the determination of the Commissioners, and when stated and signed the party requiring it shall—

(a) where the case has not been endorsed with a certificate pursuant to subsection (2) above, transmit it to the High Court within 30 days after receiving the same; or
(b) where the case has been so endorsed, either:

(i) transmit it to the High Court within that period; or
(ii) apply to the Court of Appeal for leave for the case to be referred direct to that Court, and the party shall, if such leave is refused, transmit the case to the High Court within 30 days after the refusal.";

(d) In subsection (8)—

(i) for the words "from the decision of the High Court to the Court of Appeal and thence to the House of Lords" there were substituted the words "from the decision of the Court of Appeal to the House of Lords", and
(ii) paragraph (b) of the proviso were omitted.

Amendments.—[1] In sub-s. (9), para. (b) of the proviso substituted by F (No. 2) A 1975, s. 45 (3) in relation to tax charged by assessment notice issued after 31 July 1975.
[2] Amount in sub-s. (3) substituted by FA 1984, Sch. 22, para. 6 with effect from 1 January 1985 by virtue of FA 1984 (Commencement No. 2) Order 1984, S.I. 1984 No. 1836.
[3] Words in sub-s. (9) proviso substituted by FA 1989, s. 156 (3).

[56A. Statement of case: Special Commissioners to Court of Appeal

(1) The Lord Chancellor may by order provide that—

(a) in such classes of appeal in England and Wales as may be prescribed by the order; and
(b) subject to the consent of the parties and to such other conditions as may be so prescribed;

a case stated by the Special Commissioners under section 56 above, for the opinion of the High Court, shall be referred to the Court of Appeal.

(2) An order under this section—

(a) may provide that section 56 above shall have effect, in relation to any appeal to which the order applies, with such modifications as may be specified in the order; and
(b) shall be made by statutory instrument subject to annulment in pursuance of a resolution of either House of Parliament.][1]

Note.—The Revenue Appeals Order 1987, S.I. 1987 No. 1422 has been made under this section for the effect of which see s. 56 above.
Amendments.—[1] This section inserted by FA 1984, Sch. 22, para. 7 with effect from 1 January 1985 by virtue of FA (Commencement No. 2) Order 1984, S.I. 1984 No. 1836.

Chargeable gains

57. Regulations about appeals

(1) The Board may make regulations—

(*a*) as respects the conduct of appeals against assessments and decisions on claims under [the Capital Gains Tax Act 1979][2],
(*b*) entitling persons, in addition to those who would be so entitled apart from the regulations, to appear on such appeals,
(*c*) regulating the time within which such appeals or claims may be brought or made,
(*d*) where the market value of an asset on a particular date, or an apportionment or any other matter, may affect the liability to capital gains tax of two or more persons, enabling any such person to have the matter determined by the tribunal having jurisdiction to determine that matter if arising on an appeal against an assessment, and prescribing a procedure by which the matter is not determined differently on different occasions,
(*e*) authorising an inspector or other officer of the Board, notwithstanding the obligation as to secrecy imposed by virtue of this or any other Act, to disclose to a person entitled to appear on such an appeal the market value of an asset as determined by an assessment or decision on a claim, or to disclose to a person whose liability to tax may be affected by the determination of the market value of an asset on a particular date, or an apportionment or any other matter, any decision on the matter made by an inspector or other officer of the Board.

(2) . . .[1]

(3) Regulations under this section may contain such supplemental and incidental provisions as appear to the Board to be expedient including in particular—

(*a*) provisions as to the choice of the Commissioners, whether a body of General Commissioners or the Special Commissioners, to hear the appeal where, in addition to the appellant against an assessment, or the claimant in the case of an appeal against the decision on a claim, and in addition to the inspector or other officer of the Board, some other person is entitled to be a party to the appeal, and
(*b*) provisions corresponding to section 81 of the Capital Allowances Act 1968 (procedure on apportionments where more than one body of General Commissioners has jurisdiction), and
(*c*) provisions authorising the giving of conditional decisions where, under section 47 of this Act, . . .[3], questions on an appeal against an assessment or a decision on a claim may go partly to one tribunal and partly to another.

(4) Regulations under this section—

(*a*) shall be made by statutory instrument subject to annulment in pursuance of a resolution of the House of Commons, and
(*b*) shall have effect notwithstanding anything in this Act.

Amendments.—[1] Sub-s. (2) repealed by FA 1971, Sch. 14, Pt. III.
[2] Words in sub-s. (1) (*a*) substituted by CGTA 1979, s. 157 (2)–(4) and Sch. 7, para. 8 Table, Pt. I. 1, with effect from 22 March 1979.
[3] Words in sub-s. (3) (*c*) repealed by CGTA 1979, Sch. 8.

CAPITAL GAINS TAX REGULATIONS

Note.—Statutory instruments are outside the scope of this publication (see p. iii). These regulations are included only because all the provisions in relation to income tax and corporation tax appeals are covered by statutory provisions and are therefore included in this Handbook; it would be anomalous to exclude provisions in relation to capital gains tax appeals. Furthermore, because of its portability, this Handbook is invaluable when attending appeal meetings, where questions as to procedure covered by these regulations are likely to arise.

S.I. 1967 No. 149

The Capital Gains Tax Regulations 1967

Made on 9 February 1967 by the Commissioners of Inland Revenue under FA 1965,

Sch. 10, para. 2, now TMA 1970; s. 57; see TA 1970, s. 539 (1), (3), (5).

Citation and commencement

1. These Regulations may be cited as the Capital Gains Tax Regulations 1967, and shall come into operation on 16th February 1967.

Interpretation

2.—(1) In the Regulations, unless the context otherwise requires—

"appeal" means an appeal against an assessment to capital gains tax or against a decision on a claim relating to capital gains tax;

"The Board" means the Commissioners of Inland Revenue;

"Commissioners" means (subject to Regulation 17) General Commissioners or Special Commissioners;

"third party" means a third or subsequent party joined under Regulation 8;

references to the Income Tax Management Act 1964 are references to that Act as applied in relation to capital gains tax by paragraph 1 of Schedule 10 to the Finance Act 1965;

references to Part III of the Finance Act 1965 include Schedules 6 to 10 to that Act and any other enactment to be construed as one with the said Part III;

subject to Regulation 15, other expressions have the same meaning as in Part III of the Finance Act 1965.

(2) The Interpretation Act 1889 shall apply to these Regulations as it applies to an Act of Parliament.

Note.—FA 1965, Pt. III has been consolidated in CGTA 1979.

Notices of appeals against assessments

3. . . .[1]

Amendments.—[1] Repealed by FA 1969, Sch. 21, Pt. VIII.

Choice of appeal Commissioners

4. . . .[1]

Amendments.—[1] Repealed by FA 1969, Sch. 21, Pt. VIII.

Assignment of appeals to General Commissioners

5. . . .[1]

Amendments.—[1] Repealed by FA 1969, Sch. 21, Pt. VIII.

Representations in writing

6. The Commissioners hearing an appeal or a question in an appeal shall consider any representations in writing made to them by any party entitled to be present who is not present or represented at the hearing, other than the inspector and—

(*a*) the appellant, if the hearing is before Commissioners ascertained under the rules in Schedule 3 to the Income Tax Management Act 1964, or by an election made by him; or

(*b*) a third party, if the hearing is before Commissioners to whom the appeal has been transferred on his application under Regulation 8 (6).

Capital Gains Tax Regulations 1967, *continued*

Representation of the inspector

7. Any officer of the Board may represent the inspector on or in connection with the hearing of an appeal or of any question in an appeal.

Joinder of third parties in appeals

8.—(1) Where the market value of an asset on a particular date or the apportionment of any amount or value is a material question in an appeal any person whose liability to capital gains tax for any period may be affected by that market value or by the manner in which that amount or value is apportioned may apply under this Regulation to be joined as a party in the appeal.

(2) An application under this Regulation to be joined as a party in an appeal shall be made in writing to the inspector stating—

    (*a*) the name and address of the applicant;
    (*b*) the question which may affect his liability to capital gains tax;
    (*c*) how his liability may be affected; and
    (*d*) his contention with regard to that question.

(3) The inspector shall send a copy of the application to the appellant and to any other party to the appeal.

(4) If the application is received by the inspector not later than thirty days before the date fixed for the hearing of the appeal (or of the question), or if when he receives the application no date has been fixed, he shall, if he is satisfied that it is proper to join the applicant as a party in the appeal, join him as a third party and give notice of the joinder to the appellant and any other party to the appeal.

(5) If the application is received by the inspector later than thirty days before the date fixed for the hearing of the appeal (or of the question) but before it has been determined, or if he is not satisfied that it is proper to join the applicant as a party in the appeal, he shall refer the application to the Commissioners before whom the appeal is brought, and those Commissioners may in their discretion allow or refuse the application.

(6) The Commissioners before whom the appeal is brought may on the application of a third party transfer the appeal to the General Commissioners for the division in which the applicant ordinarily resides at the date of the application, or to the Special Commissioners:

    Provided that an appeal shall not be so transferred unless the Commissioners to whom the application is made are satisfied that the balance of convenience to the parties is in favour of the transfer.

(7) At the hearing and on the determination of the appeal or of any question in the appeal a third party shall, so far as relates to the question in which he is interested, have the same rights as an appellant, including any right to require the statement of a case for the opinion of any Court.

(8) On the hearing of the appeal or of any question in the appeal a third party shall not (unless the appellant consents) be entitled to be present except during such part of the hearing as relates to a question in which he is interested, and the Commissioners shall if necessary hear any such question separately from the rest of the appeal.

(9) A person entitled under section 26 (5) of the Finance Act 1965 (proceedings consequent on death) to be a party to an appeal shall, if he wishes to be made a party, apply to be joined under this Regulation.

Applications for determination of market value

9.—(1) Where the market value of an asset on a particular date or the apportionment of any amount or value may affect the liability to capital gains tax for any period (and whether for the same or different periods) of two or more persons and is not (and has not been) a material question in an appeal already brought by any of them, any of those persons may apply to the Commissioners to determine that market value or the manner in which that amount or value should be apportioned.

(2) An application under this Regulation shall be made by notice in writing sent to the inspector stating the question for determination and (to the best of the applicant's

Capital Gains Tax Regulations 1967, *continued*

knowledge) the names and addresses of the other persons whose liability to capital gains tax may be affected by the question.

(3) In relation to proceedings under this Regulation references in Schedule 3 to the Income Tax Management Act 1964 (rules for assigning proceedings to Commissioners) to the place where the appellant ordinarily resided in the year of assessment to which the proceedings relate shall, in cases where the application does not relate to any ascertained year of assessment, be construed as references to the place where the applicant ordinarily resides at the time of making the application.

(4) The inspector shall be a party to proceedings under this Regulation.

(5) An election to bring proceedings under this Regulation before the Special Commissioners instead of before the General Commissioners (or, if the proceedings are in Northern Ireland, before a county court instead of before the Special Commissioners) shall, if not made in the notice of application, be made by notice in writing to the inspector within thirty days thereafter.

(6) Subject to paragraphs (1) to (5) above, these Regulations, Part III of the Finance Act 1965, and any enactment directly or indirectly applied by the said Part III shall, so far as they are applicable and with any necessary modifications, apply in relation to proceedings under this Regulation as they apply in relation to an appeal against an assessment to capital gains tax.

References of questions of value to other tribunals

10.—(1) A question in an appeal which is required to be determined in accordance with section 44 (6), (7) and (8) of the Finance Act 1965 (questions of the value of land or unquoted shares or securities) may be referred to the appropriate tribunal by the Commissioners before whom the appeal is brought or, if the hearing of the appeal has not begun, by the inspector.

(2) ...[1]

(3) Where any question in an appeal has been referred to another tribunal in accordance with section 44 (6), (7) or (8) of the Finance Act 1965 the Commissioners before whom the appeal is brought may determine the remaining questions in the appeal and may at the request of any party (whether or not he declared his dissatisfaction immediately after that determination) state a case thereon under section 64 of the Income Tax Act 1952 without awaiting the determination of the question referred to the other tribunal.

Amendments.—[1] Para. (2) repealed by FA 1969, Sch. 21, Pt. VIII.

Conclusive effect of a determination on appeal

11.—(1) Where the market value of an asset on a particular date or the apportionment of any amount or value (being a market value or apportionment affecting or which may affect the liability to capital gains tax of two or more persons) is finally determined on an appeal that determination shall, subject to Regulation 14, be in all proceedings relating to capital gains tax conclusive between the Board or any officer of the Board and the following persons—

(*a*) parties to the appeal; and
(*b*) any person who was entitled to apply to be joined as a third party in the appeal, and had notice, in reasonable time for making such application, of the appeal and of the question in the appeal entitling him so to apply, not being a person who did so apply without undue delay and whose application was not allowed.

(2) For the purposes of these Regulations—

(*a*) the determination of an appeal or a question in an appeal shall be treated as final when the determination can no longer be varied by the tribunal making it or by the order of any court;
(*b*) the market value of an asset on a particular date or the apportionment of any amount or value shall be deemed to have been finally determined on an appeal notwithstanding that there was no dispute concerning that market value or apportionment if the market value or apportionment was a material question in the appeal and the appeal has been finally determined.

Capital Gains Tax Regulations 1967, *continued*

(3) The Commissioners shall, if required by any party to an appeal, record in their decision the market value of an asset on a particular date or the apportionment of an amount or value if that market value or apportionment was a material question in the appeal.

(4) The final determination on an appeal of the market value of an asset on a particular date or of the apportionment of any amount or value may be proved in any proceedings relating to capital gains tax by a certificate stating the material particulars signed by the inspector or by the clerk or registrar of the Commissioners or other tribunal who determined the appeal or determined the question in accordance with section 44 (6), (7) or (8) of the Finance Act 1965 or in accordance with Regulation 10 (3); and a document purporting to be such a certificate may be received in evidence in any such proceedings without further proof.

Agreements in writing of market value or apportionment

12.—(1) An agreement or notification which apart from this Regulation would have effect under section 510 of the Income Tax Act 1952 (settlement of appeals by agreement or withdrawal) as if an appeal had been determined by Commissioners shall not have that effect in relation to any appeal in which a third party has been joined unless, at the time when such agreement is made or notification is given, the question in which the third party is interested has been finally determined on the appeal or disposed of by an agreement made in accordance with paragraph (2) below.

(2) Where the market value of an asset on a particular date or the apportionment of any amount or value may affect the liability to capital gains tax of two or more persons and is a material question in an appeal, then if the market value or apportionment is agreed in writing between the inspector or any other officer of the Board and all the parties to the appeal whose liability may be affected by it the agreement shall in all proceedings relating to the capital gains tax be conclusive between the Board or any officer of the Board and the following persons—

(*a*) parties to the agreement; and
(*b*) any person who was entitled, in respect of the question in the appeal to which the agreement relates, to apply to be joined as a third party in the appeal, and had notice of the appeal and of the question in the appeal not less than thirty days before the agreement was made, not being a person who did so apply before the agreement was made.

(3) A document purporting to be an agreement made in accordance with paragraph (2) above and produced from proper custody may be received in evidence in any proceedings relating to capital gains tax without further proof as such an agreement made by the persons by whom it purports to be signed.

Persons affected by a determination or agreement in writing

13.—(1) A determination or agreement which is by virtue of these Regulations conclusive against or in favour of any person shall to the same extent be conclusive against or in favour of his personal representatives and his trustee or assignee in bankruptcy or under a deed of arrangement.

(2) A determination or agreement relating to any settled property which is by virtue of these Regulations conclusive against or in favour of the trustees of the settlement shall to the same extent be conclusive against or in favour of any person becoming absolutely entitled to that property as against the trustees.

(3) A determination or agreement relating to an asset comprised in the estate of a deceased person, or in a testamentary disposition made by him, which is by virtue of these Regulations conclusive against or in favour of his personal representatives shall to the same extent be conclusive against or in favour of any person acquiring the asset as legatee.

(4) Where paragraph 20 of Schedule 7 to the Finance Act 1965 (disposals between husband and wife) or section 31 (4) of that Act (disposals of certain works of art, etc.) applies in respect of the disposal of an asset, a determination or agreement relating to the asset which is by virtue of these Regulations conclusive against or in favour of the person making the disposal shall to the same extent be conclusive against or in favour of the person acquiring the asset.

Capital Gains Tax Regulations 1967, *continued*

Fraud or wilful default

14. A determination or agreement shall not by virtue of these Regulations be conclusive in favour of any person if it is shown that any form of fraud or wilful default committed by or on behalf of that person procured or contributed to procure the determination or agreement.

Interpretation of certain expressions

15. For the purposes of these Regulations—

(*a*) The market value of an asset or the apportionment of any amount or value is a material question in an appeal notwithstanding that there is no dispute thereon between the appellant and the inspector if the adoption of a different market value or of a different apportionment might produce a different determination on the appeal.

(*b*) A person shall not be treated as being at any date a person whose liability to capital gains tax may be affected by the market value of an asset or by the apportionment of any amount or value paid, payable or ascertained in connection with an asset unless—

(i) on or before that date, but since 6th April 1965, there has been (or is deemed to have been) a disposal or acquisition of the asset by him, or by personal representatives from whom he may acquire the asset as legatee, or by a company or trustees whose chargeable gains may to any extent be treated as having accrued to him under section 41 or 42 of the Finance Act 1965 (non-resident companies and trusts); and

(ii) he is at that date, or was during the year of assessment in which any such disposal or acquisition was made, resident or ordinarily resident in the United Kingdom or carrying on a trade in the United Kingdom:

Provided that section 10 (3) of the Finance Act 1956 (determination of questions of ordinary residence) shall not apply to a question arising under this paragraph.

(*c*) Personal representatives or trustees who are for the purposes of Part III of the Finance Act 1965 treated as a single and continuing body of persons shall be treated as a single person distinct from the persons who may from time to time be the personal representatives or trustees, and if the same persons are personal representatives or trustees in respect of more than one estate or settlement they shall be treated as a separate person in respect of each estate or settlement.

Notification of third parties

16. Where it appears to the inspector that a person is entitled to apply to be joined as a third party in an appeal the inspector may, and at that person's request shall, notify him of the appeal and disclose to him (so far as relevant to his interest in that appeal) the market value of any asset or the apportionment of any amount or value used in making the assessment or decision from which the appeal is brought.

Proceedings in Northern Ireland

17. Section 14 (1) of the Income Tax Management Act 1964 (meaning of "General Commissioners" in relation to proceedings in Northern Ireland) shall apply to these Regulations as it applies to Part III of the Finance Act 1965.

Service by post

18. Any notice or other document to be given, served, sent or delivered under these Regulations may be served by post.

Procedural rules

[57B. Commissioners: procedural rules

(1) The Lord Chancellor may, with the consent of the Lord Advocate, make rules—

(*a*) as to the procedure of the Special Commissioners and the procedure in connection with the bringing of matters before them;

(b) as to the time within which matters may be brought before the Special Commissioners; and

(c) providing for appeals which have been heard by the Special Commissioners in the absence of the appellant to be reheard, in such circumstances and subject to such conditions, as the rules may prescribe.

(2) Rules under this section may make such consequential provision (including the amendment of any enactment or instrument made under any enactment) as the Lord Chancellor considers necessary.

(3) Rules under this section shall be made by statutory instrument subject to annulment in pursuance of a resolution of either House of Parliament.][1]

Amendments.—[1] This section inserted by FA 1984, Sch. 22, para. 4 with effect from 1 January 1985 by virtue of FA 1984 (Commencement No. 2) Order 1984, S.I. 1984 No. 1836.

Northern Ireland

58. Proceedings in tax cases in Northern Ireland

(1) ...[2]

(2) A case concerning tax which is stated by the ...[2] Commissioners under section 56 of this Act in proceedings in Northern Ireland shall be a case for the opinion of the Court of Appeal in Northern Ireland, and the Taxes Acts shall have effect as if that section applied in relation to such proceedings—

(a) with the substitution for references to the High Court of references to the Court of Appeal in Northern Ireland, and
(b) with the omission of subsections (4), (5) and (8) of that section,

and the procedure relating to the transmission of the case to, and the hearing and determination of the case by, the Court of Appeal in Northern Ireland shall be that for the time being in force in Northern Ireland as respects cases stated by a county court in exercise of its general jurisdiction, and an appeal shall lie from the Court of Appeal to the House of Lords in accordance with [section 42 of the Judicature (Northern Ireland) Act 1978][1].

[(2A) Where in proceedings in Northern Ireland an application is made for a case to be stated by the Commissioners under section 56 of this Act the case must be settled and sent to the applicant as soon after the application as is reasonably practicable.][3]

[(3) For the purposes of this section—

(a) "proceedings in Northern Ireland" means proceedings as respects which the place given by the rules in Schedule 3 to this Act is in Northern Ireland;
(b) proceedings under section 102, 113 (5), 260 (3), 281 (4), 343 (10) or 783 (9) of the principal Act (or the corresponding enactments repealed by that Act), section 11 of or paragraph 22 of Schedule 7 to the Income and Corporation Taxes Act 1970 or section 81 of the Capital Allowances Act 1968 (proceedings to which more than one taxpayer is a party) shall be proceedings in Northern Ireland if the place given by the rules in Schedule 3 to this Act in relation to each of the parties concerned in the proceedings is in Northern Ireland,

and sections 21 and 22 of the Interpretation Act (Northern Ireland) 1954 shall apply as if references in those provisions to any enactment included a reference to this section.][4]

(4) ...[2]

Cross references.—See FA 1988, s. 134 (4), (6), (9) (application of sub-s. (3) of this section, with effect from 3 April 1989 by virtue of FA 1988 (Commencement) Order 1989, S.I. 1989 No. 473, where pending proceedings are transferred from Special Commissioners to General Commissioners, subject to any provision made under s. 134 (9)).
Amendments.—[1] Words in sub-s. (2) substituted by the Judicature (Northern Ireland) Act 1978, s. 122 (1) and Sch. 5, Pt. II, with effect from 21 August 1978 by virtue of the Judicature (Northern Ireland) Act 1978 (Commencement No. 1) Order 1978, S.I. 1978 No. 1101.
[2] Sub-ss. (1), (4) and the word "special" in sub-s. (2) repealed by FA 1988, s. 134 (2), (4) and Sch. 14, Pt. IX with effect from 3 April 1989 by virtue of FA 1988 (Commencement) Order 1989, S.I. 1989 No. 473, subject to any provision made under s. 134 (9).
[3] Sub-s. (2A) inserted by FA 1988, ss. 134 (4), 135 (1) with effect from 3 April 1989 by virtue of FA 1988 (Commencement) Order 1989, S.I. 1989 No. 473.
[4] Sub-s. (3) substituted by FA 1988, ss. 134 (4), (5), 135 (2) with effect from 3 April 1989 by virtue of FA 1988 (Commencement) Order 1989, S.I. 1989 No. 473.

59. Election for county court in Northern Ireland

Amendments.—This section repealed by FA 1988, s. 134 (2), (4) and Sch. 14, Pt. IX with effect from 3 April 1989 by virtue of FA 1988 (Commencement) Order 1989, S.I. 1989 No. 473.

PART VI
COLLECTION AND RECOVERY

Cross references.—See TA 1988, ss. 253, 350 (4)–(7) (power of Board to make regulations, modifying or replacing TA 1988, s. 234 (5)–(9) and Schs. 13, 16).

60. Issue of demand notes and receipts

(1) Every collector shall, when the tax becomes due and payable, make demand of the respective sums given to him in charge to collect, from the persons charged therewith, or at the places of their last abode, or on the premises in respect of which the tax is charged, as the case may require.

(2) On payment of the tax, the collector shall if so requested give a receipt.

Distraint and poinding

61. Distraint by collectors

(1) If a person neglects or refuses to pay the sum charged, upon demand made by the collector, [the collector may distrain upon the goods and chattels of the person charged (in this section referred to as "the person in default")][1].

(2) For the purpose of levying any such distress, [a justice of the peace, on being satisfied by information on oath that there is reasonable ground for believing that a person is neglecting or refusing to pay a sum charged, may issue a warrant in writing authorising a collector to][2] break open, in the daytime, any house or premises, calling to his assistance any constable.
Every such constable shall, when so required, aid and assist the collector in the execution of the warrant and in levying the distress in the house or premises.

(3) A levy or warrant to break open shall be executed by, or under the direction of, and in the presence of, the collector.

(4) A distress levied by the collector shall be kept for five days, at the costs and charges of the person [in default][3].

(5) If the person [in default][4] does not pay the sum due, together with the costs and charges ...[5], the distress shall be appraised by [one or more independent persons appointed by the collector][6], and shall be sold by public auction by the collector for payment of the sum due and all costs and charges.
...[7] any overplus coming by the distress, after the deduction of the costs and charges and of the sum due, shall be restored to the owner of the goods distrained.

[(6) The Treasury may by regulations make provision with respect to—

(a) the fees chargeable on or in connection with the levying of distress, and
(b) the costs and charges recoverable where distress has been levied;

and any such regulations shall be made by statutory instrument which shall be subject to annulment in pursuance of a resolution of the House of Commons.][8]

Amendments.—[1] Words in sub-s. (1) substituted by FA 1989, s. 152 with effect from an appointed day. The original words read—
"the collector shall, for non-payment thereof, distrain upon the lands, tenements and premises in respect of which the tax is charged, or distrain the person charged by his goods and chattels, and all such other goods and chattels as the collector is hereby authorised to distrain."
[2] Words in sub-s. (2) substituted by *ibid*. The original words read—
"a collector may, after obtaining a warrant for the purpose signed by the General Commissioners"
[3] Words in sub-s. (4) substituted by *ibid*. The original words read—
"neglecting or refusing to pay"
[4] Words in sub-s. (5) substituted for the word "aforesaid" by *ibid*.
[5] Words in sub-s. (5) repealed by *ibid* and Sch. 17, Pt. VIII. They read—
"within the said five days"
[6] Words in sub-s. (5) substituted by *ibid*. The original words read—
"two or more inhabitants of the parish in which the distress is taken, or by other sufficient persons"
[7] Words in sub-s. (5) repealed by *ibid*. and Sch. 17, Pt. VIII. They read—
"The costs and charges of taking, keeping and selling the distress shall be retained by the collector, and"
[8] Sub-s. (6) added by *ibid*.

62. Priority of claim for tax

(1) [If at any time at which any goods or chattels belonging to any person (in this section referred to as "the person in default") are][1] liable to be taken by virtue of any execution or other process, warrant, or authority whatever, or by virtue of any assignment, on any account or pretence whatever, except at the suit of the landlord for rent, [the person in default is·in arrears in respect of any such sums as are referred to in subsection (1A) below, the goods or chattels may not be so taken unless on demand made by the collector"][2] the person at whose suit the execution or seizure is made, or to whom the assignment was made, pays or causes to be paid to the collector, before the sale or removal of the goods or chattels, all [such sums as have fallen due at or before the date of seizure][3]:

Provided that, where tax is claimed for more than one year, the person at whose instance the seizure has been made may, on paying to the collector the tax which is due for one whole year, proceed in his seizure in like manner as if no tax had been claimed.

[(1A) The sums referred to in subsection (1) above are—

(*a*) sums due from the person in default on account of deductions of income tax from emoluments paid during the period of twelve months next before the date of seizure, being deductions which the person in default was liable to make under section 203 of the principal Act (pay as you earn) less the amount of the repayments of income tax which he was liable to make during that period; and
(*b*) sums due from the person in default in respect of deductions required to be made by him for that period under section 559 of the principal Act (sub-contractors in the construction industry).][4]

(2) [If the sums referred to in subsection (1) above are not paid within ten days of the date of the demand referred to in that subsection, the collector may][5] distrain the goods and chattels notwithstanding the seizure or assignment, and [may proceed][6] to the sale thereof, as prescribed by this Act, for the purpose of obtaining payment of the whole of [those sums][7], and the reasonable costs and charges attending such distress and sale, and every collector so doing shall be indemnified by virtue of this Act.

Amendments.—[1] Words in sub-s. (1) substituted by FA 1989, s. 153. The original words read—
"No goods or chattels whatever, belonging to any person at the time any tax becomes in arrear, shall be"
[2] Words in sub-s. (1) substituted for the word "unless" by *ibid*.
[3] Words in sub-s. (1) substituted by *ibid*. The original words read—
"arrears of tax which are due at the time of seizure, or which are payable for the year in which the seizure is made".
[4] Sub-s. (1A) inserted by *ibid*.
[5] Words in sub-s. (2) substituted by *ibid*. The original words read—
"In case of neglect or refusal to pay the tax so claimed or the tax for one whole year, as the case may be, the collector shall".
[6] Words in sub-s. (2) substituted for the words "shall proceed" by *ibid*.
[7] Words in sub-s. (2) substituted by *ibid*. The original words read—
"the tax charged and claimed".

[63. Recovery of tax in Scotland

(1) Subject to subsection (3) below, in Scotland, where any tax is due and has not been paid, the sheriff, on an application by the collector accompanied by a certificate by the collector—

(*a*) stating that none of the persons specified in the application has paid the tax due by him;
(*b*) stating that the collector has demanded payment under section 60 of this Act from each such person of the amount due by him;
(*c*) stating that 14 days have elapsed since the date of such demand without payment of the said amount; and
(*d*) specifying the amount due and unpaid by each such person,

shall grant a summary warrant in a form prescribed by Act of Sederunt authorising the recovery, by any of the diligences mentioned in subsection (2) below, of the amount remaining due and unpaid.

(2) The diligences referred to in subsection (1) above are—

(*a*) a poinding and sale in accordance with Schedule 5 to the Debtors (Scotland) Act 1987;
(*b*) an earnings arrestment;
(*c*) an arrestment and action of furthcoming or sale.

(3) Paragraph (c) of subsection (1) above shall not apply to an application under that subsection [insofar as it relates to sums due in respect of—]²

[(a) deductions of income tax which any person specified in the application was liable to make under section 203 of the principal Act (pay as you earn); or]²
[(b) deductions required to be made under section 559 of the principal Act (sub-contractors in the construction industry) by any person specified in the application.]²]¹

[(4) In this section references to amounts of tax due and references to sums due in respect of deductions include references to amounts which are deemed to be—

(a) amounts of tax which the person is liable to pay by virtue of the Income Tax (Employments) Regulations 1973; or
(b) amounts which the person is liable to pay by virtue of the Income Tax (Sub-Contractors in the Construction Industry) Regulations 1975.]³

Amendments.—¹ This section and s. 63A below substituted for s. 63 by the Debtors (Scotland) Act 1987, Sch. 4, para. 2 with effect from 30 November 1988 by virtue of the Debtors (Scotland) Act 1987 (Commencement No. 2) Order 1988, S.I. 1988 No. 1818.
² Sub-s. (3) (a), (b) and the preceding words substituted by FA 1989, s. 154. The original words as amended by TA 1988, Sch. 29, para. 32 read—
"which relates to tax deducted from the emoluments of an office or employment by virtue of regulations under section 203 of the principal Act".
³ Sub-s. (4) added by *ibid.*

[**63A. Sheriff officer's fees and outlays**

(1) Subject to subsection (2) below and without prejudice to paragraphs 25 to 34 of Schedule 5 to the Debtors (Scotland) Act 1987 (expenses of poinding and sale), the sheriff officer's fees, together with the outlays necessarily incurred by him, in connection with the execution of a summary warrant shall be chargeable against the debtor.

(2) No fee shall be chargeable by the sheriff officer against the debtor for collecting, and accounting to the collector for, sums paid to him by the debtor in respect of the amount owing.]¹

Amendments.—¹This section and s. 63 above substituted for s. 63 by the Debtors (Scotland) Act 1987, Sch. 4, para. 2 with effect from 30 November 1988 by virtue of the Debtors (Scotland) Act 1987 (Commencement No. 2) Order 1988, S.I. 1988 No. 1818.

64. Priority of claim for tax in Scotland

(1) [If at any time at which any moveable goods and effects belonging to any person (in this section referred to as "the person in default") are]¹ liable to be taken by virtue of any poinding, sequestration for rent, or diligence whatever, or by any assignation, [the person in default is in arrears in respect of any such sums as are referred to in subsection (1A) below, the goods and effects may not be so taken unless on demand made by the collector]², the person proceeding to take the said goods and effects pays [such sums as have fallen due at or before the date of poinding or, as the case may be, other diligence or assignation.]³

[(1A) The sums referred to in subsection (1) above are—

(a) sums due from the person in default on account of deductions of income tax from emoluments paid during the period of twelve months next before the date of poinding, being deductions which the person in default was liable to make under section 203 of the principal Act (pay as you earn) less the amount of the repayments of income tax which he was liable to make during that period; and
(b) sums due from the person in default in respect of deductions required to be made by him for that period under section 559 of the principal Act (sub-contractors in the construction industry).]⁴

(2) [If the sums referred to in subsection (1) above are not paid within ten days of the date of the demand referred to in that subsection, the sums shall]⁵, notwithstanding any [proceedings]⁶ for the purpose of taking the said moveable goods and effects, be recoverable by poinding and selling the said moveable goods and effects under warrant obtained in conformity with the provisions contained in section 63 above.

Amendments.—¹ Words in sub-s. (1) substituted by FA 1989, s. 155. The original words read—
"No moveable goods and effects belonging to any person in Scotland, at the time any tax became in arrear or was payable, shall be".
² Words in sub-s. (1) substituted for the word "unless" by *ibid.*

[3] Words in sub-s. (1) substituted by *ibid*. The original words read—

"the tax so in arrears or payable:

Provided that where the tax is claimed for more than one year the person proceeding to take the said goods and effects may on paying the tax for one whole year proceed as he might have done if no tax had been so claimed."

[4] Sub-s. (1A) inserted by *ibid*.
[5] Words in sub-s. (2) substituted by *ibid*. The original words read—

"If the said person neglects or refuses to pay the tax so in arrear or payable, or the tax for one whole year, as the case may be, the tax claimed shall,".

[6] Words in sub-s. (2) substituted by *ibid*. The original words read—

"proceeding at his instance".

Court proceedings

65. Magistrates' courts

(1) Where—

(*a*) the amount of any tax for the time being due and payable under any assessment is less than [£250][1], or
(*b*) the tax under any assessment is payable by instalments and the sum for the time being due and payable in respect of any of those instalments is less than [£250][1],

the tax shall, without prejudice to any other remedy, be recoverable summarily as a civil debt by proceedings commenced in the name of a collector.

(2) All or any of the sums due in respect of tax from any one person and payable to any one collector (being sums which are by law recoverable summarily) may, whether or not they are due under one assessment, be included in the same complaint, summons, order, warrant or other document required by law to be laid before justices or to be issued by justices, and every such document as aforesaid shall, as respects each such sum, be construed as a separate document and its invalidity as respects any one such sum shall not affect its validity as respects any other such sum.

(3) Proceedings under this section for the recovery of any tax charged under Schedule E may be brought in England and Wales at any time within one year from the time when the matter complained of arose.

(4) It is hereby declared that in subsection (1) above the expression "recoverable summarily as a civil debt" in respect of proceedings in Northern Ireland means recoverable [in proceedings under Article 62 of the Magistrates' Courts (Northern Ireland) Order 1981][1].

[(5) The Treasury may by order made by statutory instrument increase the sums specified in subsection (1) above; and any such statutory instrument shall be subject to annulment in pursuance of a resolution of the Commons House of Parliament.][2]

Amendments.—[1] Amounts in sub-s. (1) and words in sub-s. (4) substituted by FA 1984, s. 57 (1) (*a*), (*b*).
[2] Sub-s. (5) added by FA 1984, s 57 (1) (*c*).

66. County courts

(1) Where the amount of tax for the time being due and payable under any assessment does not exceed the [county court limit][3], the tax may, without prejudice to any other remedy, be sued for and recovered from the person charged therewith as a debt due to the Crown by proceedings in a county court commenced in the name of a collector.

[(2) An officer of the Board who is authorised by the Board to do so may address the court in any proceedings under this section in a county court in England and Wales.][2]

[(2A) In subsection (1) of this section "the county court limit" means the amount which for the time being is the county court limit for the purposes of section 16 of the County Courts Act 1984.][4]

(3) In the application of subsection (1) of this section to Northern Ireland, for the reference to [the county court limit there shall be substituted a reference to the limit specified in][5] [Article 10 (1) of the County Courts (Northern Ireland) Order 1980][1], and in this section as it applies in Northern Ireland the expression "county court" shall mean a county court held for a division under [that Order][1].

(4) Sections 21 and 42 (2) of the Interpretation Act (Northern Ireland) 1954 shall apply as if any reference in those provisions to any enactment included a reference to this section, and Part III of the County Courts [(Northern Ireland) Order 1980][1] (general civil jurisdiction) shall apply for the purposes of this section in Northern Ireland.

Amendments.—[1] Words in sub-ss. (3), (4) substituted by the County Courts (Northern Ireland) Order 1980, S. I. 1980 No. 397, Sch. 1, Pt. II.
[2] Sub-s. (2) substituted by FA 1984, s 57 (2).
[3] Words in sub-s (1) substituted by the County Courts Act 1984, Sch. 2, para. 36 (*a*) with effect from 1 August 1984.
[4] Sub-s. (2A) inserted by the County Courts Act 1984, Sch. 2, para 36 (*b*).
[5] Words in sub-s. (3) substituted by the County Courts Act 1984, Sch. 2, para. 36 (*c*).

67. Inferior courts in Scotland

(1) In Scotland, where the amount of tax for the time being due and payable under any assessment [does not exceed the sum for the time being specified in section 35 (1) (*a*) of the Sheriff Courts (Scotland) Act 1971][1] the tax may, without prejudice to any other remedy, be sued for and recovered from the person charged therewith as a debt due to the Crown by proceedings commenced in the name of a collector in the sheriff court . . .[2].

(2) Section 65 and 66 above shall not apply in Scotland.

Amendments.—[1] Words in sub-s. (1) substituted by FA 1976, s. 58, with effect from 1 September 1976.
[2] Words in sub-s. (1) repealed by FA 1976, s. 58 and Sch. 15, Pt. III, with effect from 1 September 1976.

68. High Court, etc.

(1) Any tax may be sued for and recovered from the person charged therewith in the High Court as a debt due to the Crown, or by any other means whereby any debt of record or otherwise due to the Crown can, or may at any time, be sued for and recovered, as well as by the other means specially provided by this Act for levying the tax.

(2) All matters within the jurisdiction of the High Court under this section shall be assigned in Scotland to the Court of Session sitting as the Court of Exchequer.

Supplemental

69. Interest on tax

Interest charged under Part IX of this Act shall be treated for the purposes—

(*a*) of sections 61, 63 and 65 to 68 above, and
(*b*) of section 35 (2) (*g*) (i) of the Crown Proceedings Act 1947 (rules of court to impose restrictions on set-off and counterclaim where the proceedings or set-off or counterclaim relate to taxes) and of any rules of court (including county court rules) for England and Wales or Northern Ireland, which impose such a restriction, and
(*c*) of section 35 (2) (*b*) of the said Act of 1947 as set out in section 50 of that Act (which imposes corresponding restrictions in Scotland).

as if it were tax charged and due and payable under the assessment to which it relates.

Note.—See **Prospective Legislation Notes** (Taxes Management Provisions).
Cross references.—See TA 1988, Sch. 19A, para. 11 (1) (extension of this section to interest payable on tax paid in advance of the due payment date by Lloyd's underwriters);
FA 1989, s. 157 (5), (6) (modification of this section where a claim is made after 13 March 1989 to carry back surplus ACT to reduce mainstream corporation tax except corporation tax for any accounting period ending after the day appointed under F(No. 2)A 1987, s.85).

70. Evidence

(1) Where tax is in arrear, a certificate of the inspector or any other officer of the Board that tax has been charged and is due, together with a certificate of the collector that payment of the tax has not been made to him, or, to the best of his knowledge and belief, to any other collector, or to any person acting on his behalf or on behalf of another collector, shall be sufficient evidence that the sum mentioned in the certificate is unpaid and is due to the Crown; and any document purporting to be such a certificate as is mentioned in this subsection shall be deemed to be such a certificate until the contrary is proved.

(2) A certificate of a collector that interest is payable under section 86 or 87 of this Act and that payment of the interest has not been made to him, or, to the best of his knowledge and belief, to any other collector, or to any person acting on his behalf or on behalf of another collector, shall be sufficient evidence that the sum mentioned in the certificate is unpaid and is due to the Crown, and any document purporting to be such a certificate as is mentioned in this subsection shall be deemed to be such a certificate unless the contrary is proved.

[(3) A certificate of the inspector or any other officer of the Board that it has been determined that tax carries interest under section 88 of this Act, together with a certificate of the collector that payment of the interest has not been made to him, or, to the best of his knowledge and belief, to any other collector, or to any person acting on his behalf or on behalf of another collector, shall be sufficient evidence—

(*a*) that interest is chargeable on the tax from the date when for the purposes of section 88 of this Act the tax ought to have been paid, and

(*b*) that the sum mentioned in the certificate is unpaid and is due to the Crown;

and any document purporting to be such a certificate as is mentioned in this subsection shall be deemed to be such a certificate unless the contrary is proved.][1]

(4) A written statement as to the wages, salaries, fees, and other emoluments paid for any period to the person against whom proceedings are brought under section 65, 66 or 67 of this Act, purporting to be signed by his employer for that period or by any responsible person in the employment of the employer, shall in such proceedings be prima facie evidence that the wages, salaries, fees and other emoluments therein stated to have been paid to the person charged have in fact been so paid.

Note.—See **Prospective Legislation Notes** (Taxes Management Provisions).
Cross references.—See TA 1988, Sch. 19A, para. 11 (2) (reference to section 86 in sub-s. (2) of this section to include a reference to TA 1988, Sch. 19A, para. 3 (4)).
Amendments.—[1] Sub-s. (3) substituted by FA 1989, s. 160 (3). The original sub-s. (3) read—

"(3) A certificate by the General or Special Commissioners that the tax or a specified part of the tax charged by an assessment specified in the certificate carries interest under section 88 of this Act from a date so specified shall be sufficient evidence of that fact in proceedings for the recovery of that interest.

A certificate under this subsection shall not be given except on the application of the inspector or the Board, and on any such application the person charged by the assessment (or, if he has died, his personal representatives) shall be entitled to appear and be heard."

PART VII
PERSONS CHARGEABLE IN A REPRESENTATIVE CAPACITY, ETC.

Income tax

71. Bodies of persons

(1) Subject to [sections 6 to 12 and Parts VIII and XI]¹ of the principal Act (charge of corporation tax on companies), every body of persons shall be chargeable to income tax in like manner as any person is chargeable under the Income Tax Acts.

(2) Subject to section 108 of this Act, the chamberlain or other officer acting as treasurer, auditor or receiver for the time being of any body of persons chargeable to income tax shall be answerable for doing all such acts as are required to be done under the Income Tax Acts for the purpose of the assessment of the body and for payment of the tax.

(3) Every such officer as aforesaid may from time to time retain, out of any money coming into his hands on behalf of the body, so much thereof as is sufficient to pay the income tax charged upon the body, and shall be indemnified for all such payments made in pursuance of the Income Tax Acts.

Amendments.—¹ Words in sub-s. (1) substituted by TA 1988, Sch. 29, para. 32 Table.

72. Trustees, guardians, etc. of incapacitated persons

(1) The trustee, guardian, tutor, curator or committee of any incapacitated person having the direction, control or management of the property or concern of any such person, whether such person resides in the United Kingdom or not, shall be assessable and chargeable to income tax in like manner and to the like amount as that person would be assessed and charged if he were not an incapacitated person.

(2) The person who is chargeable in respect of an incapacitated person shall be answerable for all matters required to be done under the Income Tax Acts for the purpose of assessment and payment of income tax.

(3) Any person who has been charged under the Income Tax Acts in respect of any incapacitated person as aforesaid may retain, out of money coming into his hands on behalf of any such person, so much thereof from time to time as is sufficient to pay the tax charged, and shall be indemnified for all such payments made in pursuance of the Income Tax Acts.

73. Further provision as to infants

If a person chargeable to income tax is an infant, then his parent, guardian or tutor—

(*a*) shall be liable for the tax in default of payment by the infant, and
(*b*) on neglect or refusal of payment, may be proceeded against in like manner as any other defaulter, and
(*c*) if he makes such payment, shall be allowed all sums so paid in his accounts.

74. Personal representatives

(1) If a person chargeable to income tax dies, the executor or administrator of the person deceased shall be liable for the tax chargeable on such deceased person, and may deduct any payments made under this section out of the assets and effects of the person deceased.

(2) On neglect or refusal of payment, any person liable under this section may be proceeded against in like manner as any other defaulter.

75. Receivers appointed by a court

(1) A receiver appointed by any court in the United Kingdom which has the direction and control of any property in respect of which income tax is charged in accordance with the provisions of the Income Tax Acts shall be assessable and chargeable with the tax in like manner and to the like amount as would be assessed and charged if the property were not under the direction and control of the court.

(2) Every such receiver shall be answerable for doing all matters and things required to be done under the Income Tax Acts for the purpose of assessment and payment of income tax.

76. Protection for certain trustees, agents and receivers

(1) A trustee who has authorised the receipt of profits arising from trust property by, or by the agent of, the person entitled thereto shall not, if—

    (*a*) that person or agent actually received the profits under that authority, and
    (*b*) the trustee makes a return, as required by section 13 of this Act, of the name, address and profits of that person,

be required to do any other act for the purpose of the assessment of that person to income tax.

(2) An agent or receiver of any person resident in the United Kingdom, other than an incapacitated person, shall not, if he makes a return, as required by section 13 of this Act, of the name, address and profits of that person, be required to do any other act for the purpose of the assessment of that person to income tax.

Capital gains tax

77. Application of Part VII to capital gains tax

(1) This Part of this Act (except section 76 above) shall apply in relation to capital gains tax as it applies in relation to income tax. . .[1], and subject to any necessary modifications.

(2) This Part of this Act as applied by this section shall not affect the question of who is the person to whom chargeable gains accrue, or who is chargeable to capital gains tax, so far as that question is relevant for the purposes of any exemption, or of any provision determining the rate at which capital gains tax is chargeable.

Amendments.—[1] Words in sub-s. (1) repealed by FA 1971, ss. 37 (2), 38 (1) and Sch. 14, Pt. II, with effect from the year 1973–74.

PART VIII
CHARGES ON NON-RESIDENTS

Income tax

78. Method of charging non-residents

(1) Subject to [subsection (2) below and][1] section [43][3] of the principal Act (Schedule A etc.) a person not resident in the United Kingdom, whether a British subject or not, shall be assessable and chargeable to income tax in the name of any such trustee, guardian, tutor, curator or committee as is mentioned in section 72 of this Act, or of any branch or agent, whether the branch or agent has the receipt of the profits or gains or not, in like manner and to the like amount as such non-resident person would be assessed and charged if he were resident in the United Kingdom and in the actual receipt of such profits or gains.

[(2) Subject to the following provisions of this section, a person who is not resident in the United Kingdom shall not, by virtue of this section, be chargeable in the name of an agent in respect of profits or gains arising from investment transactions carried out by the agent if—

(*a*) the agent is carrying on a business of providing investment management services to a number of clients of whom the non-resident person is one; and
(*b*) the investment transactions concerned were carried out in the ordinary course of the business referred to in paragraph (*a*) above; and
(*c*) the remuneration which the agent receives for the provision of investment management services to the non-resident person is at a rate which is not less than that which is customary for that class of business; and
(*d*) in the case of profits or gains which are chargeable to tax as the profits or income of the non-resident person from carrying on a trade in the United Kingdom through a branch or agency, the agent carrying out the investment transaction is also the agency through which the trade is carried on;

and in the case of an agent who provides investment management services as part only of a business, paragraphs (*a*) to (*d*) above shall apply as if that part were a separate business.][2]

[(3) In subsection (2) above "investment transactions" means—

(*a*) transactions in shares, stock or securities of any other description, excluding commodity or financial futures,
(*b*) transactions on a recognised futures exchange, within the meaning of the Capital Gains Tax Act 1979, and
(*c*) the placing of money at interest,

and for the purposes of that subsection an agent carries out such a transaction on behalf of his client whether he undertakes the transaction himself or by giving instructions to another person.][2]

[(4) Subsection (2) above does not apply to profits or gains which constitute income of an offshore fund, within the meaning of Chapter [V of Part XVII of the principal Act][3].][2]

[(5) Subsection (2) above does not apply if the non-resident person and the agent are connected with each other, within the terms of section [839][3] of the principal Act.][2]

Amendments.—[1] Words in sub-s. (1) inserted by FA 1985, s. 50 (1), (2).
[2] Sub-ss. (2)–(5) inserted by FA 1985, s. 50 (1), (3) with effect from 6 April 1985 or, in the case of a company, for accounting periods ending after 31 March 1985.
[3] Words in sub-ss. (1), (4), (5) substituted by TA 1988, Sch. 29, para. 32 Table.

79. Profits from branch or agency

A non-resident person shall be assessable and chargeable to income tax in respect of any profits or gains arising, whether directly or indirectly, through or from any branch or agency, and shall be so assessable and chargeable in the name of the branch or agent.

80. Charge on percentage of turnover

(1) Where it appears to the inspector or, on appeal, to the General or Special Commissioners, that the true amount of the profits or gains of any non-resident person chargeable with

income tax in the name of a resident person cannot in any case be readily ascertained, the inspector or Commissioners may, if he or they think fit, assess and charge the non-resident person on a percentage of the turnover of the business done by the non-resident person through or with the resident person in whose name he is chargeable as aforesaid, and the inspector may by notice require the resident person to deliver a return of the business so done by the non-resident person through or with the resident person.

(2) The amount of percentage under subsection (1) of this section shall in each case be determined, having regard to the nature of the business, by the inspector or Commissioners.

(3) If either the resident person or the non-resident person is dissatisfied with the percentage as confirmed or determined by the General or Special Commissioners on appeal, he may within four months of the determination, require the Commissioners to refer the question of the percentage to a referee or board of referees to be appointed for the purpose by the Treasury and the decision of the referee or board shall be final and conclusive.

Cross references.—See FA 1989, s. 182 (3) (c) (criminal liability of a referee or board of referees appointed under sub-s. (3) above for disclosing information).

81. Taxation on basis of merchanting profit

Where a non-resident person is chargeable to income tax in the name of any branch or agent in respect of any profits or gains arising from the sale of goods or produce manufactured or produced out of the United Kingdom by the non-resident person, the person in whose name the non-resident person is so chargeable may, by notice included in a return of income delivered within six years from the end of the year of assessment for which he is chargeable, elect to be assessed in respect of those profits or gains on the basis of the profits which might reasonably be expected to have been earned by a merchant or, where the goods are retailed by or on behalf of the manufacturer or producer, by a retailer of the goods sold, who had bought from the manufacturer or producer direct.

82. Savings

(1) Nothing in this Part of this Act shall render a non-resident person chargeable in the name of a broker or in the name of an agent not being an authorised person carrying on the regular agency of the non-resident person, in respect of profits or gains arising from sales or transactions carried out through such a broker or agent:

Provided that where sales or transactions are carried out on behalf of a non-resident person through a broker in the ordinary course of his business as such and the broker—

(*a*) is a person carrying on bona fide the business of a broker in the United Kingdom, and
(*b*) receives in respect of the business of the non-resident person which is transacted through him remuneration at a rate not less than that customary in the class of business in question,

then, notwithstanding that the broker is a person who acts regularly for the non-resident person as such broker, the non-resident person shall not be chargeable in the name of that broker in respect of profits or gains arising from those sales or transactions.

In this subsection, "broker" includes a general commission agent.

(2) The fact that a non-resident person executes sales or carries out transactions with other non-residents which would make him chargeable in pursuance of this Part of this Act in the name of a resident person shall not of itself make him chargeable in respect of profits arising from those sales or transactions.

Cross references.—See CGTA 1979, s. 12 (3) (capital gains tax exemption for a non-resident person trading in the UK through a person within the exemptions in this section).

83. Responsibilities and indemnification of persons in whose name a non-resident person is chargeable

(1) A person in whose name a non-resident person is chargeable shall be answerable for all matters required to be done under the Income Tax Acts for the purpose of assessment and payment of income tax.

(2) A person who has been charged under the Income Tax Acts in respect of any non-resident person as aforesaid may retain, out of money coming into his hands on behalf of any such person, so much thereof from time to time as is sufficient to pay the tax charged, and shall be indemnified for all such payments made in pursuance of the Income Tax Acts.

Capital gains tax

84. Gains from branch or agency

(1) A non-resident person shall be assessable and chargeable to capital gains tax in respect of any chargeable gains arising, whether directly or indirectly, through or from any branch or agency, and shall be so assessable and chargeable in the name of the branch or agent.

(2) The person in whose name the non-resident person is chargeable shall be answerable for all matters required to be done under the enactments relating to capital gains tax for the purpose of assessment and payment of that tax.

(3) A person who has been charged under this section in respect of any non-resident person may retain, out of money coming into his hands on behalf of any such person, so much thereof from time to time as is sufficient to pay the tax charged, and shall be indemnified for all such payments made in pursuance of the enactments relating to capital gains tax.

Corporation tax

85. Application of Part VIII to corporation tax

The provisions of this Part of this Act relating to income tax, so far as they are applicable to tax chargeable on a company, shall apply with any necessary adaptations in relation to corporation tax chargeable on companies not resident in the United Kingdom.

Note.—See **Prospective Legislation Notes** (Taxes Management Provisions).

PART IX
INTEREST ON OVERDUE TAX

Cross references.—See FA 1984, Sch. 14, para. 6 (4) (this Part not to apply, subject to certain time limits, where capital gains tax due from beneficiaries on gains of non-resident trustees is postponed).

[86. Interest on overdue tax

(1) Any tax charged by an assessment to which this section applies shall carry interest at the [rate applicable under section 178 of the Finance Act 1989][10] from the reckonable date until payment.

(2) This section applies to—

(*a*) an assessment to income tax under Schedule A, Schedule C, Schedule D or Schedule E,
(*b*) an assessment charging income tax at a rate other than the basic rate on income from which income tax has been deducted (otherwise than under section [203][6] of the principal Act) or from or on which income tax is treated as having been deducted or paid or income chargeable under Schedule F,
(*c*) an assessment to capital gains tax,
(*d*) an assessment to corporation tax other than an assessment made under Schedule [13 to the principal Act][6] (advance corporation tax).

[(3) For the purposes of this section—

(*a*) the reckonable date in relation to any tax charged by an assessment to income tax under Schedule E, and
(*b*) subject to subsection (3A) below, the reckonable date in relation to tax charged by any other assessment to which this section applies,

is the date on which the tax becomes due and payable.][7]

[(3A) Where an appeal has been made against an assessment and any of the tax charged by the assessment is due and payable on a date later than the date given by the Table in subsection (4) below, the reckonable date in relation to the tax so due and payable is the later of—

(*a*) the date given by that Table, and
(*b*) the date on which the tax would have been due and payable if there had been no appeal against the assessment (assuming in a case where the tax would not have been charged by the assessment if there had been no appeal that it was so charged).][7]

[(4) The Table referred to in subsection (3A) above is as follows—][8]

TABLE

Description of tax	Date applicable
1. Tax charged by an assessment to income tax under Schedule A or an assessment to income tax under Schedule D other than an assessment made under Part III of Schedule [3][6] to the principal Act (machinery for assessment, charge and payment of income tax under Schedule C and, in certain cases, Schedule D).	1. The 1st July following the end of the year of assessment.
2. Tax charged by an assessment to income tax under Schedule C or an assessment to income tax under Schedule D made under Part III of Schedule [3][6] to the principal Act.	2. The last day of the six months following the end of the thirty days mentioned in paragraph 9 of the said Schedule [3][6].
3. Tax charged by an assessment charging income tax as mentioned in subsection (2) (*b*) above.	3. [The 1st June following the 1st December mentioned in section [5 (4)][6] of the principal Act][2].

Description of tax	Date applicable
4. Tax charged by an assessment to capital gains tax.	4. [The 1st June following the 1st December mentioned in section 7 of the Capital Gains Tax Act 1979][2].
5. Tax charged by an assessment to corporation tax other than an assessment made under Schedule [13 to the principal Act][6].	5. The last day of the six months following— (a) in a case where section [10 (1)][6] of the principal Act applies, the end of the nine months there mentioned; (b) in a case where section 244 (1) of that Act applies, the end of the interval there mentioned from the end of the accounting period to which the assessment relates; or[5] (c) in a case where section [478][6] of that Act applies, the last day on which the tax could have been paid within the time limit imposed by subsection (2) (a) of that section.

(5) Tax charged by an assessment to which this section applies shall carry interest from the reckonable date even if that date is a non-business day within the meaning of section 92 of the Bills of Exchange Act 1882.

(6) Where the amount of interest payable under this section on the tax charged by any assessment does not exceed [£30][3–4], that interest may, if the Board think fit, be remitted.][9]][1]

Note.—See **Prospective Legislation Notes** (Taxes Management Provisions).
Cross references.—See CGTA 1979, s. 8 (2) (interest on capital gains tax payable by instalments);
TA 1988, s. 307 (6) (meaning of "reckonable date" for the purposes of the withdrawal of tax relief on investment in new corporate trades),
s. 375 (4) (MIRAS: application of certain provisions of this section to tax recoverable from a borrower after ceasing to be entitled to it),
s. 478 (6) (modification of para. 5 (a) of the Table in sub-s. (4) in its application to building societies),
Sch. 14, para. 6 (2) (an assessment for recovering from taxpayer excess relief in respect of life assurance premiums to be treated as if it were among those specified in sub-s. (2) of this section, and as if the sum charged by such assessment were tax specified in para. 3 of the Table in sub-s. (4) of this section),
Sch. 30, para. 1 (7) (modification of para. 5 (a) of the Table in sub-s. (4) in its application to certain old companies for their accounting periods beginning after 16 March 1987);
FA 1989, s. 157 (1), (6) (reckonable date from which interest is chargeable on additional corporation tax following the surrender of ACT to another company),
s. 157 (2) (c) (i), (3), (4), (6) (calculation of interest payable under this section where surplus ACT of a later period is utilised to meet corporation tax liability of an earlier period).
Amendments.—[1] This section was substituted by F (No. 2) A 1975, s. 46 (1) in relation to tax charged by assessment notice issued after 31 July 1975.
[2] Paras. 3 and 4 in the second column of the Table in sub-s. (4) substituted by FA 1980, s. 61 (3).
[3–4] Amount in sub-s. (6) substituted by FA 1980, s. 62 (1), (2) (a), (3), where interest accrues on tax assessed after 1 August 1980.
[5] Para. 5 (b) of the Table in sub-s. (4) repealed by FA 1987, Sch. 16, Pt. V with respect to accounting periods beginning after 16 March 1987.
[6] Words in sub-ss. (2) (b), (d), (4) substituted by TA 1988, Sch. 29, para. 32 Table.
[7] Sub-ss. (3), (3A) substituted for sub-s. (3) by FA 1989, s. 156 (1).
[8] Words in sub-s. (4) substituted by *ibid*.
[9] Sub-s. (6) repealed by FA 1989, s. 158 (1) (a) and Sch. 17, Pt. VIII with effect from an appointed day.
[10] Words in sub-s. (1) substituted for the words "prescribed rate" by FA 1989, s. 179 (1) (b) (i).

[87. Interest on overdue advance corporation tax and income tax on company payments

(1) Any tax assessable in accordance with Schedule [13][4] or [16 to the principal Act][4] shall carry interest at the [rate applicable under section 178 of the Finance Act 1989][6] from the date when the tax becomes due and payable until payment.

(2) Where—

(a) advance corporation tax paid in respect of distributions made in any return period is repaid under paragraph 4 of the said Schedule [13][4] in consequence of the receipt of franked investment income in a later period; or

(b) income tax paid in respect of payments made in any return period is repaid or discharged under paragraph 5 of the said Schedule [16][4] in consequence of the receipt in a later return period of a payment on which income tax is borne by deduction,

the repayment or discharge shall not affect interest under this section on the tax so repaid or discharged for such time as is specified in subsection (3) below but, subject to that, this section shall apply as if any such tax which is repaid or discharged had never become payable.

(3) The time for which interest is not affected is—

(*a*) any time before the expiration of fourteen days from the end of the later return period, unless the return for that period is made earlier in those fourteen days; and

(*b*) if that return is made earlier in those fourteen days, any time ending before the date on which the return is made.

(4) Interest shall not be payable under this section on the tax charged by any assessment unless the total amount of the interest exceeds [£30][3, 5].

(5) Subsection (4) above shall have effect as if all advance corporation tax due from a company in accordance with paragraph 3 (1) of the said Schedule [13][4] *for any return period, whether or not it is actually assessed, were included in a single assessment, and similarly in the case of all income tax due from a company in accordance with paragraph 4 (1) of the said Schedule [16]*[4] *for any return period.*[5]

(6) In this section "return period" means a period for which a return is required to be made under the said Schedule [13][4] or [16][4].

(7) It is hereby declared that this section applies to advance corporation tax and income tax which, in accordance with either of those Schedules, is paid without the making of any assessment (but is paid after it is due), and that where the tax is charged by an assessment (whether or not any part of it has been paid when the assessment is made) this section applies as respects interest running before as well as after the making of the assessment].[1]

[(8) Tax assessable as mentioned in subsection (1) above shall carry interest from the date when it becomes due and payable even if that date is a non-business day within the meaning of section 92 of the Bills of Exchange Act 1882.][2]

Amendments.—[1] This section was substituted by FA 1972, s. 111 and Sch. 24, para 10, with effect from 6 April 1973.
[2] Sub-s. (8) added by F (No. 2) A 1975, s. 46 (3) (*b*) in relation to tax charged by assessment notice issued after 31 July 1975; see F (No. 2) A 1975, s. 44 (7).
[3] Amount in sub-s. (4) substituted by FA 1980, s. 62 (1), (2) (*b*), (3), where interest accrues on tax assessed after 1 August 1980.
[4] Numbers and words in sub-ss. (1), (2) (*a*), (*b*), (5), (6) substituted by TA 1988, Sch. 29, para. 32 Table.
[5] Sub-ss. (4), (5) repealed by FA 1989, s. 158 (1) (*b*) and Sch. 17, Pt. VIII with effect from an appointed day.
[6] Words in sub-s. (1) substituted for the words "prescribed rate" by FA 1989, s. 179 (1) (*b*) (i).

88. Interest on tax recovered to make good loss due to taxpayer's fault

(1) Where an assessment has been made for the purpose of making good to the Crown a loss of tax wholly or partly attributable to—

[(*a*) a failure to give a notice, make a return or produce or furnish a document or other information required by or under the Taxes Acts, or][6]

[(*b*) an error in any information, return, accounts or other document delivered to an inspector or other officer of the Board,][6]

the tax charged by the assessment, or as the case may be such part thereof as corresponds to the part so attributable, [shall, if an inspector or the Board so determine, carry][8] interest at the [rate applicable under section 178 of the Finance Act 1989][10] from the date on which the tax ought to have been paid until payment.

(2) This section shall not apply in relation to tax under [Schedule 13 or 16 to the principal Act][5].

[(3) Where it is finally determined that any tax carries interest under this section, the tax shall carry no interest under section 86 or 86A above (and, accordingly, any interest under either of those sections which has been paid before the final determination shall be set off against the amount of the interest under this section); and for the purposes of this subsection a determination that tax carries interest is not final until it can no longer be varied, whether by any Commissioners on appeal or by the order of any court.][9]

(4) The Board may at their discretion mitigate (whether before or after judgment) any interest due under this section and may stay or compound any proceedings for the recovery thereof.

(5) For the purposes of this section the date when tax ought to have been paid shall be taken to be—

(*a*) in the case of income tax, 1st January in the year of assessment for which the tax is charged, but subject to paragraphs (*b*) and (*c*) below,

(*b*) in the case of one-half of any income tax specified in section [5 (2)][5] of the principal Act, the following 1st July,

[(*c*) in the case of any income tax specified in section [5 (4)][5] of the principal Act, the following [1st December][3]][1], (*d*) in the case of capital gains tax, [1st December]³ in the year of assessment next following the year for which the tax is charged,

(*e*) in the case of corporation tax, the date nine months from the end of the accounting period for which the tax is charged . . .⁴

[(6) Tax charged by an assessment mentioned in subsection (1) above shall carry interest from the date when it ought to have been paid even if that date was a non-business day within the meaning of section 92 of the Bills of Exchange Act 1882.]²

[(7) In paragraph (*a*) of subsection (1) above the reference to a failure to do something includes, in relation to anything required to be done at a particular time or within a particular period, a reference to a failure to do it at that time or within that period; and, accordingly, section 118 (2) of this Act shall not apply for the purposes of that paragraph.]⁷

Note.—See **Prospective Legislation Notes** (Taxes Management Provisions) and **Prospective Cross References**.
Cross references.—See TA 1988, Sch. 14, para. 7 (3) (*c*) (application of this section in respect of overdeduction of tax at source from life insurance premiums),
Sch. 30, para. 1 (transitional provisions with regard to the application of sub-s. (5) (*e*)—see the appropriate **Amendment** note below);
Amendments.—¹ Sub-s. (5) (*c*) substituted by FA 1971, ss. 37 (1), 38 (1) and Sch. 6, para. 87, with effect from the year 1973–74.
² Sub-s. (6) added by F (No. 2) A 1975, s. 46 (4), s. 44 (7) in relation to tax charged by assessment notice issued after 31 July 1975.
³ Date in sub-s. (5) (*c*), (*d*) substituted by FA 1980, s. 61 (4).
⁴ Words in sub-s. (5) (*e*) repealed by TA 1988, Sch. 31, subject to the transitional provisions in TA 1988, Sch. 30, para. 1. For the purpose of the transitional provisions, sub-s. (5) (*e*) as amended by TA 1988, Sch. 30, para. 1 (8) reads—

"(*e*) in the case of corporation tax, the date nine months from the end of the accounting period for which the tax is charged or, [in the case of an accounting period in respect of which section 10 (1) of the principal Act applies as modified by sub-paragraph 1 (3) or (4) of Schedule 30 to that Act, at the end of the period which, under that sub-paragraph, is substituted for the period of nine months] mentioned in that subsection (without the alternative of one month from the making of the assessment)."

⁵ Words and numbers in sub-ss. (2), (5) (*b*), (*c*) substituted by TA 1988, Sch. 29, para. 32 Table.
⁶ Sub-s. (1) (*a*), (*b*) substituted for the words "the fraud, wilful default or neglect of any person" by FA 1989, s. 159 in relation to failures to give notice, etc. and errors in any information, etc. after 26 July 1989.
⁷ Sub-s. (7) added by *ibid*.
⁸ Words in sub-s. (1) substituted by the words "shall carry" by FA 1989, s. 160 (1).
⁹ Sub-s. (3) substituted by FA 1989, s. 161. The original sub-s. (3) read—

"(3) Tax carrying interest under this section shall not carry interest under section 86 above."

¹⁰ Words in sub-s. (1) substituted for the words "prescribed rate" by FA 1989, s. 179 (1) (*b*) (i).

[88A. Determinations under section 88

(1) Notice of a determination under section 88 above shall be served on the person liable to pay the interest to which it relates and shall specify—

(*a*) the date on which it is issued,
(*b*) the amount of the tax which carries interest and the assessment by which that tax was charged,
(*c*) the date when for the purposes of section 88 above that tax ought to have been paid, and
(*d*) the time within which an appeal against the determination may be made.

(2) After the notice of a determination under section 88 above has been served the determination shall not be altered except in accordance with this section.

(3) A determination under section 88 above may be made at any time—

(*a*) within six years after the end of the chargeable period for which the tax carrying the interest is charged (or, in the case of development land tax, of the financial year in which the liability for that tax arose), or
(*b*) within three years after the date of the final determination of the amount of that tax.

(4) An appeal may be brought against a determination under section 88 above and, subject to the following provisions of this section, the provisions of this Act relating to appeals shall have effect in relation to an appeal against such a determination as they have effect in relation to an appeal against an assessment to tax.

(5) On an appeal against a determination under section 88 above section 50 (6) to (8) of this Act shall not apply but the Commissioners may—

(*a*) if it appears to them that the tax carries no interest under that section, set the determination aside,
(*b*) if the determination appears to them to be correct, confirm the determination, or
(*c*) if the determination appears to them to be incorrect as to the amount of tax or the date on which the tax ought to have been paid, revise the determination accordingly.]¹

Amendments.—[1] This section inserted by FA 1989, s. 160 (2).

89. The prescribed rate of interest

[(1) For the purposes of any provision of this Part of this Act and of section 87 of the Finance (No. 2) Act 1987 "the prescribed rate" means such rate as may for the time being be prescribed for the purposes of the provision in question by order made by the Treasury.][1]

(2) [The power to make an order under this section shall be exercisable by][2] *statutory instrument subject to annulment in pursuance of a resolution of the Commons House of Parliament, [and any such order may be framed either so as to prescribe a single rate]*[2] *for the purposes of all the provisions of this Part of this Act, or so as to prescribe different rates for different purposes.*

(3) [Any rate of interest prescribed by order under this section][2] *shall apply to interest for periods beginning on or after the date when the order is expressed to come into force, whether or not interest runs from before that date.*

Note.—For the purposes of sections 86, 87 and 88 of this Act, the rate of interest fixed by the Income Tax (Interest on Unpaid Tax and Repayment Supplement) Orders is—
  8·25 per cent. from 6 December 1987: S.I. 1987 No. 1988.
  7·75 per cent. from 6 May 1988: S.I. 1988 No. 756.
  9·75 per cent. from 6 August 1988: SI 1988 No. 1278.
  10·75 per cent. from 6 October 1988: SI 1988 No. 1621.
  11·5 per cent. from 6 January 1989: SI 1988 No. 2185.
  12·25 per cent. from 6 July 1989: S.I. 1989 No. 1000.
F(No. 2)A 1987, s. 87 is repealed by TA 1988, Sch. 31 and superseded by TA 1988, s. 826 which will come into force on an appointed day as provided for in s. 826 (9).
Amendments.—[1] Sub-s. (1) substituted by F(No. 2)A 1987, s. 89 (1).
[2] Words in sub-ss. (2), (3) substituted by F(No. 2)A 1987, s. 89 (2), (3).
This section repealed by FA 1989, Sch. 17, Pt. XI with effect as mentioned in FA 1989, s. 178 (7).

90. Disallowance of relief for interest on tax

Interest payable under this Part of this Act shall be paid without any deduction of income tax and shall not be allowed as a deduction in computing any income, profits or losses for any tax purposes.

Cross references.—See TA 1988, Sch. 19A, para. 3 (4) (*b*) (application of this section in relation to interest on outstanding tax payable by underwriters).

91. Effect on interest of reliefs

(1) Where any amount of interest is payable under section 86 or section 88 of this Act in relation to an assessment, and relief from tax charged by the assessment is given to any person by a discharge of any of that tax, such adjustment shall be made of the said amount, and such repayment shall be made of any amounts previously paid under those provisions in relation to the assessment, as are necessary to secure that the total sum, if any, paid or payable under those provisions in relation to the assessment, is the same as it would have been if the tax discharged had never been charged.

(2) Where relief from tax paid for any chargeable period is given to any person by repayment, he shall be entitled to require that the amount repaid shall be treated for the purposes of this section, so far as it will go, as if it were a discharge of the tax charged on him (whether alone or together with other persons) by or by virtue of any assessment for or relating to the same chargeable period, so, however, that it shall not be applied to any assessment made after the relief was given and that it shall not be applied to more than one assessment so as to reduce, without extinguishing, the amount of tax charged thereby.

(3) Notwithstanding anything in the preceding provisions of this section, no relief, whether given by way of discharge or repayment, shall be treated for the purposes of this section as—

  (*a*) . . .[1]
  (*b*) affecting tax charged by any assessment to income tax made under Schedule A or Schedule D if either—
    (i) . . .[1]

(ii) it arises in connection with income taxable otherwise than under Schedule A or Schedule D, or

(iii) it relates to a source income from which is taxable otherwise than under Schedule A or Schedule D, [or

(c) affecting tax charged at a rate other than the basic rate on income from which tax has been deducted (otherwise than under section [203][3] of the principal Act) or is treated as having been deducted, unless it is a relief from the tax so charged.][2]

(4) For the purposes of this section a relief from corporation tax or capital gains tax shall not be treated as affecting tax charged by any assessment unless the assessment is to the same tax.

Note.—See **Prospective Legislation Notes** (Taxes Management Provisions).
Cross references.—See TA 1988, s. 306 (9) (income tax relief to individuals investing in new corporate trades under Business Expansion Scheme: this section restricted in its application to that relief).
Amendments.—[1] Sub-s. (3) (a), (b) (i) repealed by FA 1971, ss. 37, 38 (1), and Sch. 6, para. 88 (a) and Sch. 14, Pt. II, with effect from 1973–74.
[2] Sub-s. (3) (c) added by FA 1971, ss. 37 (1), 38 (1) and Sch. 6, para. 88 (b), with effect from 1973–74.
[3] Number in sub-s. (3) substituted by TA 1988, Sch. 29, para. 32 Table.

92. Remission in certain cases of interest on tax in arrear by reason of exchange restrictions

(1) The provisions of this section shall have effect where the Board are satisfied as respects any tax carrying interest under section 86 of this Act—

(a) that the tax is in respect of income or chargeable gains arising in a country outside the United Kingdom, and
(b) that, as the result of action of the government of that country, it is impossible for the income or gains to be remitted to the United Kingdom, and
(c) that having regard to the matters aforesaid and to all the other circumstances of the case it is reasonable that the tax should for the time being remain uncollected,

and the Board allow the tax to remain uncollected accordingly.

(2) Interest on the said tax shall, subject to subsection (3) below, cease to run under the said section 86 as from the date on which the Board were first in possession of the information necessary to enable them to be satisfied as aforesaid and, if the said date is not later than three months from the time when the tax became due and payable, the interest thereon under the said section 86 in respect of the period before the said date shall be remitted.

(3) Where, under subsection (2) above, interest has ceased to run on any tax and thereafter demand is made by the collector or other proper officer for payment of all or any of that tax, interest under the said section 86 shall again begin to run from the date of the demand in respect of the amount demanded.

Provided that where all or any part of the amount demanded is paid not later than three months from the date of the demand, the interest under the said section 86 on the amount so paid running from the date of the demand shall be remitted.

Note.—See **Prospective Legislation Notes** (Taxes Management Provisions).
Cross references.—See TA 1988, Sch. 19A, para. 11 (2) (references to s. 86 in this section to include references to TA 1988, Sch. 19A, para. 3 (4)).

PART X
PENALTIES, ETC.

93. Failure to make return for income tax or capital gains tax

(1) If any person has been required by a notice served under or for the purposes of section 8 or 9 of this Act (or either of those sections as extended by section 12 of this Act or section [284 (4)][2] of the principal Act (husband and wife)) to deliver any return, and he fails to comply with the notice he shall be liable, subject to the provisions of this section—

    [(a) to a penalty not exceeding £300, and][3]
    [(b) if the failure continues after a penalty is imposed under paragraph (a) above, to a further penalty or penalties not exceeding £60 for each day on which the failure continues after the day on which the penalty under paragraph (a) above was imposed (but excluding any day for which a penalty under this paragraph has already been imposed).][3]

[(2) If a failure by a person to comply with a notice such as is referred to in subsection (1) above continues after the end of the year of assessment following that during which it was served then, without prejudice to any penalty under subsection (1) above, he shall be liable to a penalty of an amount not exceeding so much of the tax with which he is charged (whether for one or for more than one year of assessment) in assessments—

    (a) based wholly or partly on any income or chargeable gains that ought to have been included in the return required by the notice, and
    (b) made after the end of the year next following the year of assessment in which the notice was served,

as is attributable to the income or chargeable gains that ought to have been so included.][3]

(3) Where in any year of assessment any amount was deducted from the said person's emoluments under section [203][2] of the principal Act (pay as you earn), and that amount exceeds the total amount (if any) charged in any assessments under Schedule E made on him for that year before the end of the year of assessment next following that in which the said notice was served, the amount of the excess shall be treated, for the purposes of subsection (2) of this section, as reducing the amount of the tax charged in assessments under Schedule E made on him for the first-mentioned year after the end of the said following year.

(4) [In relation to a return required for the purposes of section 9 of this Act the reference in subsection (2) above to tax][1] does not include any tax not chargeable in the partnership name; and in relation to a person's failure to deliver any other return it does not include tax assessed in the name of a partnership on so much of the profits or gains assessed as falls to be included in the total income of any other person.

[(5) No penalty shall be imposed under subsection (1) above in respect of a failure at any time after the failure has been remedied.][3]

(6) Where a person is liable to more than one penalty of an amount determined under subsection (2) above, any assessment taken into account for the purposes of one of those penalties shall be left out of account for the purposes of the other or others.

[(7) If the person on whom a notice is served proves that there was no income or chargeable gain to be included in the return, the penalty under this section shall not exceed £100.][3]

(8) References in this section to the amount of tax with which a person is charged for any year of assessment and to assessments made on him include, in the case of a person who has died, references to any amount with which his personal representatives are charged for that year and to assessments made on them.

Note.—See **Prospective Legislation Notes** (Married Couples).
Amendments.—[1] Words at the beginning of sub-s. (4) substituted by FA 1971, ss. 37 (1), 38 (1) and Sch. 6, para. 89, with effect from the year 1973–74.
[2] Numbers in sub-ss. (1), (3) substituted by TA 1988, Sch. 29, para. 32 Table.
[3] Sub-ss. (1) (a), (b), (2), (5), (7) substituted by FA 1989, s. 162 in relation to a failure to comply with a notice served after 5 April 1989.

---

94. Failure to make return for corporation tax

(1) If any company has been required by a notice served under section 11 of this Act (or under that section as extended by section 12 of this Act) to deliver a return and the company fails to comply with the notice the company shall be liable, subject to subsection (3) of this section—

(a) to a penalty not exceeding, except in the case mentioned in subsection (2) of this section £50, and
(b) if the failure continues after it has been declared by the court or Commissioners before whom proceedings for the penalty have been commenced, to a further penalty not exceeding £10 for each day on which the failure so continues.

(2) If the failure continues after the end of the period of two years beginning with the date on which the notice was served, the penalty under subsection (1) (a) above shall be an amount not exceeding the aggregate of £50 and the total amount of the tax with which the said company is charged (whether for one or more accounting periods) in assessments to corporation tax—

(a) based wholly or partly on any profits that ought to have been included in the return required by the notice, and
(b) made after the end of the said period of two years,

and in arriving at the amount of corporation tax with which the company is so charged no account shall be taken of any income tax which under section [7 (2) or 11 (3)][1] of the principal Act (income tax borne by deduction from receipts) may be set off against corporation tax.

(3) Except in the case mentioned in subsection (2) above, the company shall not be liable to any penalty incurred under this section for failure to comply with a notice, if the failure is remedied before proceedings for the recovery of the penalty are commenced.

(4) If in proceedings under this section it is proved that there were no profits to be included in the return, the penalty under this section shall not exceed £5.

Note.—See **Prospective Legislation Notes** (Taxes Management Provisions) and **Prospective Cross References**.
Amendments.—[1] Numbers in sub-s. (2) substituted by TA 1988, Sch. 29, para. 32 Table.

95. Incorrect return or accounts for income tax or capital gains tax

(1) Where a person fraudulently or negligently—

(a) delivers any incorrect return of a kind mentioned in section 8 or 9 of this Act (or either of those sections as extended by section 12 of this Act or section [284 (4)][2] of the principal Act (husband and wife)), or
(b) makes any incorrect return, statement or declaration in connection with any claim for any allowance, deduction or relief in respect of income tax or capital gains tax, or
(c) submits to an inspector or the Board or any Commissioners any incorrect accounts in connection with the ascertainment of his liability to income tax or capital gains tax,

he shall be liable to a penalty not exceeding [the amount of the difference specified in subsection (2) below.][3]

(2) The difference is that between—

(a) the amount of income tax and capital gains tax payable for the relevant years of assessment by the said person (including any amount of income tax deducted at source and not repayable), and
(b) the amount which would have been the amount so payable if the return, statement, declaration or accounts as made or submitted by him had been correct.

(3) The relevant years of assessment for the purposes of this section are, in relation to anything delivered, made or submitted in any year of assessment, that, the next following, and any preceding year of assessment; and the references in subsection (2) to the amount of income tax payable [do not, in relation to anything done in connection with a partnership],[1] include any income tax not chargeable in the partnership name.

Note.—See **Prospective Legislation Notes** (Married Couples) and **Prospective Cross References**.
Cross references.—See TA 1988, Sch. 14, para. 7 (3) (d) (application of this section in respect of tax deducted at source from life insurance premiums).
Amendments.—[1] Words in sub-s. (3) substituted by FA 1971, ss. 37 (1), 38 (1) and Sch. 6, para. 90, with effect from the year 1973–74.
[2] Numbers in sub-s. (1) (a) substituted by TA 1988, Sch. 29, para. 32 Table.
[3] Words in sub-s. (1) substituted by FA 1989, s. 163 (1) (a), (2) in relation to returns, etc. submitted after 26 July 1989. The original words read—

"the aggregate of—
(i) £50, and
(ii) the amount, or, in the case of fraud, twice the amount of the difference specified in subsection (2) below."

96. Incorrect return or accounts for corporation tax

(1) Where a company fraudulently or negligently—

  (*a*) delivers any incorrect return under section 11 of this Act (or under that section as extended by section 12 of this Act), or
  (*b*) makes any incorrect return, statement or declaration in connection with any claim for any allowance, deduction or relief in respect of corporation tax, or
  (*c*) submits to an inspector or any Commissioners any incorrect accounts in connection with the ascertainment of the company's liability to corporation tax,

the company shall be liable to a penalty not exceeding [the amount of the difference specified in subsection (2) below.][1]

(2) The difference is that between—

  (*a*) the amount of corporation tax payable by the said company for the accounting period or accounting periods comprising the period to which the return, statement, declaration or accounts relate, and
  (*b*) the amount which would have been the amount so payable if the return, statement, declaration or accounts had been correct.

Amendments.—[1] Words in sub-s. (1) substituted by FA 1989, s. 163 (1) (*b*), (2) in relation to returns, etc. submitted after 26 July 1989. The original words read—
  "the aggregate of—
    (i) £50, and
    (ii) the amount, or, in the case of fraud, twice the amount of the difference specified in subsection (2) below."

97. Incorrect return or accounts: supplemental

(1) Where any such return, statement, declaration or accounts as are mentioned in sections 95 and 96 above were made or submitted by any person neither fraudulently nor negligently and it comes to his notice (or, if he has died, to the notice of his personal representatives) that they were incorrect, then, unless the error is remedied without unreasonable delay, the return, statement, declaration or accounts shall be treated for the purposes of those sections as having been negligently made or submitted by him.

(2) For the purpose of sections 95 and 96 above, any accounts submitted on behalf of any person shall be deemed to have been submitted by him unless he proves that they were submitted without his consent or connivance.

[97A. Two or more tax-geared penalties in respect of same tax

Where two or more penalties—

  (*a*) are incurred by any person and fall to be determined by reference to any income tax or capital gains tax with which he is chargeable for a year of assessment; or
  (*b*) are incurred by any company and fall to be determined by reference to any corporation tax with which it is chargeable for an accounting period,

each penalty after the first shall be so reduced that the aggregate amount of the penalties, so far as determined by reference to any particular part of the tax, does not exceed whichever is or, but for this section, would be the greater or greatest of them, so far as so determined.][1]

Amendments.—[1] This section inserted by FA 1988, s. 129; paragraph (*a*) comes into effect from 1988–89 and paragraph (*b*) comes into effect for accounting periods ending after 31 March 1989.

98. Special returns, etc.

(1) [Subject to section 98A below, where][5] any person—

  (*a*) has been required, by a notice served under or for the purposes of any of the provisions specified in the first column of the Table below, to deliver any return or other document, to furnish any particulars, to produce any document, or to make anything available for inspection, and he fails to comply with the notice, or
  (*b*) fails to furnish any information, give any certificate or produce any document or record in accordance with any of the provisions specified in the second column of the Table below,

he shall be liable, subject to [subsections (3) and (4) below—

  (i) to a penalty not exceeding £300, and

(ii) if the failure continues after a penalty is imposed under paragraph (i) above, to a further penalty or penalties not exceeding £60 for each day on which the failure continues after the day on which the penalty under paragraph (i) above was imposed (but excluding any day for which a penalty under this paragraph has already been imposed).][6]

(2) [Subject to section 98A below, where][5] a person fraudulently or negligently furnishes, gives, produces or makes any incorrect information, certificate, document, record or declaration of a kind mentioned in any of the provisions specified in either column of the Table below, he shall be liable to a penalty not exceeding [£3,000][7].

[(3) No penalty shall be imposed under subsection (1) above in respect of a failure within paragraph (*a*) of that subsection at any time after the failure has been remedied.][8]

[(4) No penalty shall be imposed under paragraph (ii) of subsection (1) above in respect of a failure within paragraph (*b*) of that subsection at any time after the failure has been remedied.][8]

[TABLE]

1	2
Part III of this Act...[9] Section 51 of this Act. In the principal Act— [section 38 (5);][10] [section 42;][11] section 181 (1); regulations under section 202; section 217; section 226 (3) and (4); section 234 (7) (*b*), (8) and (9); section 250 (6) and (7); section 272 (7); section 310 (4) and (5); regulations under section 333; regulations under section 476 (1); ...[12] section 482 (3); regulations under section 482 (11); section 483; regulations under section 555 (7); section 561 (8); section 588 (7); regulations under section 602; section 605 (1), (2), (3) (*b*) and (4); regulations under section 612 (3); regulations under section 639; section 652; section 669; section 680; section 700 (4); section 708; section 728; section 729 (11); section 730 (8); section 737 (8); section 745 (1); section 755; section 768 (9); section 772 (1) and (3); section 774 (5); section 778; section 815; Schedule 3, paragraph 13 (1); Schedule 5, paragraph 10; Schedule 9, paragraphs 6 and 25; Schedule 15, paragraph 14 (5); ...[16]; Schedule 22, paragraph 4. Section 32 of the Finance Act 1973. Paragraph 2 of Schedule 15 to the Finance Act 1973. Regulations under section 149D of the Capital Gains Tax Act 1979.	In the principal Act— ...[10] section 41 (2); ...[11] section 124 (3); section 136 (6); ...[2]; section 148 (7); section 180 (1); regulations under section 202; regulations under section 203; section 216; section 226 (1) and (2); section 234 (5), (6) and (7) (*a*); section 250 (1) to (5); section 310 (1), (2) and (3); section 313 (5); regulations under section 333; section 350 (1); section 375 (5); regulations under section 476 (1); [section 482 (2);][13] regulations under section 482 (11); section 552; regulations under section 555 (7); regulations under section 566 (1) or (2); section 577 (4); section 588 (6); regulations under section 602; section 605 (3) (*a*); regulations under section 612 (3); regulations under section 639; section 772 (6); Schedule 3, paragraph 6; Schedule 13; regulations under paragraph 7 of Schedule 14; Schedule 15, paragraph 14 (4); Schedule 16; Schedule 22, paragraph 2. Regulations under section 149D of the Capital Gains Tax Act 1979. Section 67 (2) of, and paragraph 4 (1) of Schedule 12 to, the Finance Act 1980. Regulations 16 and 17 of the Income Tax (Interest Relief) Regulations 1982. Paragraph 15 (3) of Schedule 14 to the Finance Act 1984. Paragraph 10 of Schedule 16 to the Finance Act 1986. [Section 85 (1) and (2) of the Finance Act 1988.][3]

1	2
Paragraph 6 (9) of Schedule 1 to the Capital Gains Tax Act 1979.	
Section 67 (4) of, and paragraph 4 (3) of Schedule 12 to, the Finance Act 1980.	
Section 84 of the Finance Act 1981.	
Paragraph 15 (1) of Schedule 14 to the Finance Act 1984.	
Paragraph 6 (1) of Schedule 22 to the Finance Act 1985.	
[Paragraph 7 (1) of Schedule 10 to the Finance Act 1988.][4]	
[Section 73 of the Finance Act 1989.][14]	
[Paragraphs 2 to 4 of Schedule 12 to the Finance Act 1989.][15]	

The references in this Table to regulations under section 602 have effect only for the purpose of giving effect to any provision mentioned in paragraphs (*a*) and (*b*) of subsection (2) of that section.][1]

Note.—See **Prospective Legislation Notes**.
Amendments.—[1] The Table substituted by TA 1988, Sch. 29, para. 9.
[2] Words in column 2 repealed by FA 1988, Sch. 14, Pt. VI.
[3] Words in column 2 added by FA 1988, s. 85 (3).
[4] Words in column 1 added by FA 1988, Sch. 10, para. 7 (2).
[5] Words in sub-ss. (1), (2) substituted for the word "Where" by FA 1989, s. 164.
[6] Words in sub-s. (1) substituted by *ibid.* in relation to any failure to comply with a notice or to furnish information, give a certificate or produce a document or record beginning after 26 July 1989, and the furnishing, giving, producing or making of any incorrect information, certificate, document, record or declaration after 26 July 1989.
The original words read—
"subsection (3) below—
   (i) to a penalty not exceeding £50, and
   (ii) if the failure continues after it has been declared by the court or Commissioners before whom proceedings for the penalty have been commenced, to a further penalty not exceeding £10 for each day on which the failure so continues."
[7] Amount in sub-s. (2) substituted for the words "£250, or, in the case of fraud, £500" by *ibid.*
[8] Sub-ss. (3), (4) substituted for sub-s. (3) by *ibid.* The original sub-s. (3) read—
"(3) A person shall not be liable to any penalty incurred under this section for a failure to comply with any notice, if the failure is remedied before proceedings for the recovery of the penalty are commenced."
[9] Words ", except sections 16 and 24 (2)" in column 1 repealed by *ibid.* and Sch. 17, Pt. VIII.
[10] Entry transferred from column 2 to column 1 by *ibid.*
[11] Entry transferred from column 2 to column 1 by *ibid.*
[12] Entry "section 481 (5) (*k*)" in column 1 repealed by *ibid.* and Sch. 17, Pt. VIII.
[13] Words in column 2 inserted by *ibid.*
[14] Words in column 1 added by FA 1989, s. 73 (9).
[15] Words in column 1 added by FA 1989, Sch. 12, para. 5.
[16] Words "Schedule 19, paragraph 17" in column 1 repealed by FA 1989, Sch. 17, Pt. V with effect from 27 July 1989.

[98A. Special penalties in the case of certain returns

(1) Regulations under section 203 (2) (PAYE) or 566 (1) (sub-contractors) of the principal Act may provide that this section shall apply in relation to any specified provision of the regulations.

(2) Where this section applies in relation to a provision of regulations, any person who fails to make a return in accordance with the provision shall be liable—

(*a*) to a penalty or penalties of the relevant monthly amount for each month (or part of a month) during which the failure continues, but excluding any month after the twelfth or for which a penalty under this paragraph has already been imposed, and
(*b*) if the failure continues beyond twelve months, without prejudice to any penalty under paragraph (*a*) above, to a penalty not exceeding so much of the amount payable by him in accordance with the regulations for the year of assessment to which the return relates as remained unpaid at the end of 19th April after the end of that year.

(3) For the purposes of subsection (2) (*a*) above, the relevant monthly amount in the case of a failure to make a return—

(a) where the number of persons in respect of whom particulars should be included in the return is fifty or less, is £100, and
(b) where that number is greater than fifty, is £100 for each fifty such persons and an additional £100 where that number is not a multiple of fifty.

(4) Where this section applies in relation to a provision of regulations, any person who fraudulently or negligently makes an incorrect return of a kind mentioned in the provision shall be liable to a penalty not exceeding the difference between—

(a) the amount payable by him in accordance with the regulations for the year of assessment to which the return relates, and
(b) the amount which would have been so payable if the return had been correct.][1]

Amendments.—[1] This section inserted by FA 1989, s. 165. In relation to a failure to make a return beginning before such day as the Treasury may by order made by statutory instrument appoint, sub-s. (2) shall have effect with the substitution of the following paragraph for paragraph (a)—
  "(a) to—
    (i) a penalty not exceeding twelve times the relevant monthly amount, and
    (ii) if the failure continues after a penalty is imposed under sub-paragraph (i) above, a further penalty or penalties of the relevant monthly amount for each month (or part of a month) during which the failure continues, but excluding any month after the twelfth or for which a penalty under this sub-paragraph has already been imposed,"

[99. Assisting in preparation of incorrect return etc.

Any person who assists in or induces the preparation or delivery of any information, return, accounts or other document which—

(a) he knows will be, or is or are likely to be, used for any purpose of tax, and
(b) he knows to be incorrect,

shall be liable to a penalty not exceeding £3,000.][1]

Amendments.—[1] This section substituted by FA 1989, s. 166 in relation to assistance and inducements occurring after 26 July 1989. The original section read—
  "**99. Assisting in making incorrect return, etc.**
  Any person who assists in or induces the making or delivery for any purposes of tax of any return or accounts which he knows to be incorrect shall be liable to a penalty not exceeding £500."

[100. Determination of penalties by officer of Board

(1) Subject to subsection (2) below and except where proceedings for a penalty have been instituted under section 100D below or a penalty has been imposed by the Commissioners under section 53 of this Act, an officer of the Board authorised by the Board for the purposes of this section may make a determination imposing a penalty under any provision of the Taxes Acts and setting it at such amount as, in his opinion, is correct or appropriate.

(2) Subsection (1) above does not apply where the penalty is a penalty under—

(a) section 93 (1) above as it has effect before the amendments made by section 162 of the Finance Act 1989 or section 93 (1) (a) above as it has effect after those amendments,
(b) section 94 (1) above as it has effect before the substitution made by section 83 of the Finance (No. 2) Act 1987,
(c) section 98 (1) above as it has effect before the amendments made by section 164 of the Finance Act 1989 or section 98 (1) (i) above as it has effect after those amendments, or
(d) paragraph (a) (i) of section 98A (2) above as it has effect by virtue of section 165 (2) of the Finance Act 1989.

(3) Notice of a determination of a penalty under this section shall be served on the person liable to the penalty and shall state the date on which it is issued and the time within which an appeal against the determination may be made.

(4) After the notice of a determination under this section has been served the determination shall not be altered except in accordance with this section or on appeal.

(5) If it is discovered by an officer of the Board authorised by the Board for the purposes of this section that the amount of a penalty determined under this section is or has become insufficient the officer may make a determination in a further amount so that the penalty is set at the amount which, in his opinion, is correct or appropriate.

(6) In any case where—

(a) a determination under this section is of a penalty under section 94 (6) above, and
(b) after the determination has been made it is discovered by an officer of the Board

authorised by the Board for the purposes of this section that the amount which was taken into account as the relevant amount of tax is or has become excessive,

the determination shall be revised so that the penalty is set at the amount which is correct; and, where more than the correct amount has already been paid, the appropriate amount shall be repaid.][1]

Amendments.—[1] This section and ss. 100A to 100D below substituted for s. 100 by FA 1989, s. 167. See *post* after s. 100D for the old s. 100.

[100A. Provisions supplementary to section 100

(1) Where a person who has incurred a penalty has died, a determination under section 100 above which could have been made in relation to him may be made in relation to his personal representatives, and any penalty imposed on personal representatives by virtue of this subsection shall be a debt due from and payable out of his estate.

(2) A penalty determined under section 100 above shall be due and payable at the end of the period of thirty days beginning with the date of the issue of the notice of determination.

(3) A penalty determined under section 100 above shall for all purposes be treated as if it were tax charged in an assessment and due and payable.][1]

Amendments.—[1] This section and ss. 100, 100B to 100D substituted for s. 100 by FA 1989, s. 167. See *post* after s. 100D for the old s. 100.

[100B. Appeals against penalty determinations

(1) An appeal may be brought against the determination of a penalty under section 100 above and, subject to the following provisions of this section, the provisions of this Act relating to appeals shall have effect in relation to an appeal against such a determination as they have effect in relation to an appeal against an assessment to tax.

(2) On an appeal against the determination of a penalty under section 100 above section 50 (6) to (8) of this Act shall not apply but—

(*a*) in the case of a penalty which is required to be of a particular amount, the Commissioners may—

(i) if it appears to them that no penalty has been incurred, set the determination aside,
(ii) if the amount determined appears to them to be correct, confirm the determination, or
(iii) if the amount determined appears to them to be incorrect, increase or reduce it to the correct amount,

(*b*) in the case of any other penalty, the Commissioners may—

(i) if it appears to them that no penalty has been incurred, set the determination aside,
(ii) if the amount determined appears to them to be appropriate, confirm the determination,
(iii) if the amount determined appears to them to be excessive, reduce it to such other amount (including nil) as they consider appropriate, or
(iv) if the amount determined appears to them to be insufficient, increase it to such amount not exceeding the permitted maximum as they consider appropriate.

(3) Without prejudice to section 56 of this Act, an appeal from a decision of the Commissioners against the amount of a penalty which has been determined under section 100 above or this section shall lie, at the instance of the person liable to the penalty, to the High Court or, in Scotland, to the Court of Session as the Court of Exchequer in Scotland; and on that appeal the court shall have the like jurisdiction as is conferred on the Commissioners by virtue of this section.][1]

Amendments.—[1] This section and ss. 100, 100A, 100C, 100D substituted for s. 100 by FA 1989, s. 167. See *post* after s. 100D for the old s. 100.

[100C. Penalty proceedings before Commissioners

(1) An officer of the Board authorised by the Board for the purposes of this section may commence proceedings before the General or Special Commissioners for any penalty to which subsection (1) of section 100 above does not apply by virtue of subsection (2) of that section.

(2) Proceedings under this section shall be by way of information in writing, made to the Commissioners, and upon summons issued by them to the defendant (or defender) to appear before them at a time and place stated in the summons; and they shall hear and decide each case in a summary way.

(3) Any penalty determined by the Commissioners in proceedings under this section shall for all purposes be treated as if it were tax charged in an assessment and due and payable.

(4) An appeal against the determination of a penalty in proceedings under this section shall lie to the High Court or, in Scotland, the Court of Session as the Court of Exchequer in Scotland—

(*a*) by any party on a question of law, and
(*b*) by the defendant (or, in Scotland, the defender) against the amount of the penalty.

(5) On any such appeal the court may—

(*a*) if it appears that no penalty has been incurred, set the determination aside,
(*b*) if the amount determined appears to be appropriate, confirm the determination,
(*c*) if the amount determined appears to be excessive, reduce it to such other amount (including nil) as the court considers appropriate, or
(*d*) if the amount determined appears to be insufficient, increase it to such amount not exceeding the permitted maximum as the court considers appropriate.][1]

Amendments.—[1] This section and ss. 100, 100A, 100B, 100D substituted for s. 100 by FA 1989, s. 167. See *post* after s. 100D for the old s. 100.

[100D. Penalty proceedings before court

(1) Where in the opinion of the Board the liability of any person for a penalty arises by reason of the fraud of that or any other person, proceedings for the penalty may be instituted before the High Court or, in Scotland, the Court of Session as the Court of Exchequer in Scotland.

(2) Proceedings under this section which are not instituted (in England, Wales or Northern Ireland) under the Crown Proceedings Act 1947 by and in the name of the Board as an authorised department for the purposes of that Act shall be instituted—

(*a*) in England and Wales, in the name of the Attorney General,
(*b*) in Scotland, in the name of the Lord Advocate, and
(*c*) in Northern Ireland, in the name of the Attorney General for Northern Ireland.

(3) Any proceedings under this section instituted in England and Wales shall be deemed to be civil proceedings by the Crown within the meaning of Part II of the Crown Proceedings Act 1947 and any such proceedings instituted in Northern Ireland shall be deemed to be civil proceedings within the meaning of that Part of that Act as for the time being in force in Northern Ireland.

(4) If in proceedings under this section the court does not find that fraud is proved but consider that the person concerned is nevertheless liable to a penalty, the court may determine a penalty notwithstanding that, but for the opinion of the Board as to fraud, the penalty would not have been a matter for the court.][1]

Amendments.—[1] This section and ss.100, 100A to 100C substituted for s. 100 by FA 1989, s. 167. See below for the old s. 100.

100. Procedure for recovery of penalties

(1) Except as otherwise provided in this section, no proceedings shall be commenced against any person for the recovery of any penalty under the Taxes Acts except by order of the Board.

(2) Any such proceedings which are not instituted (in England, Wales or Northern Ireland) under the Crown Proceedings Act 1947 by and in the name of the Board as an authorised department for the purposes of that Act shall be instituted in the name of an officer, or—

(a) in England and Wales, in the name of the Attorney General,
(b) in Scotland, in the name of the Lord Advocate, and
(c) in Northern Ireland, in the name of the Attorney General for Northern Ireland.

(3) Any such proceedings may, except as otherwise provided in the Taxes Acts, be commenced either before the General or Special Commissioners, or

(a) in England, Wales or Northern Ireland, in the High Court,
(b) in Scotland, in the Court of Session as the Court of Exchequer in Scotland,

and any proceedings commenced as mentioned in paragraph (a) of this subsection shall be deemed to be civil proceedings by the Crown within the meaning of Part II of the Crown Proceedings Act 1947 or, as the case may be, that Part as for the time being in force in Northern Ireland.

(4) The inspector may, without an order of the Board, commence before the General Commissioners . . .¹ proceedings for a penalty incurred by any person under section 93 (1) or section 98 (1) of this Act for a failure to deliver, furnish or produce anything to the inspector; but in any proceedings so commenced the Commissioners shall not in any case award, in respect of the penalty under paragraph (a) of the said section 93 (1) a sum exceeding £50.

(5) Where the person who has incurred any penalty has died, any proceedings under this section which have been or could have been commenced against him may be continued or commenced against his personal representatives, and any penalty awarded in proceedings so continued or commenced shall be a debt due from and payable out of his estate; but nothing in this subsection shall extend the time for commencing proceedings against personal representatives.

(6) Where any proceedings under this section are brought before any Commissioners, an appeal shall lie to the High Court or, in Scotland, the Court of Session as the Court of Exchequer in Scotland, from their decision—

  (a) by any party, on a question of law, and
  (b) by the defendant (or, in Scotland, the defender) against the amount of any penalty awarded,

and on any appeal under paragraph (b) above the court may either confirm the decision or reduce or increase the sum awarded.

(7) Proceedings under this section before any Commissioners shall be by way of information in writing, made to them, and upon summons issued by them to the defendant (or defender) to appear before them at a time and place stated in the summons, and they shall hear and determine each case in a summary way; and any penalty awarded by them in such proceedings shall for all purposes be treated as if it were tax charged in an assessment and due and payable.

(8) The Commissioners or the court before whom any proceedings for a penalty of a fixed amount are brought under this section may, if they think fit, give judgment for a less amount.

(9) The Governor of Northern Ireland may, if he thinks fit, appoint some other person to act instead of the Attorney General for Northern Ireland in relation to any matters to which this section relates, and in that case the reference in this section to the Attorney General for Northern Ireland shall be construed as a reference to the person so appointed.

Note.—This section substituted for by ss. 100 to 100D; see above.
Amendments—¹ Words in sub-s. (4) repealed by FA 1988, Sch. 14, Pt. IX with effect from 3 April 1989 by virtue of FA 1988 (Commencement) Order 1989, S.I. 1989 No. 473, subject to any provision made under FA 1988, s. 134 (9).

101. Evidence of profits for purposes of preceding provisions of Part X

For the purposes of the preceding provisions of this Part of this Act, any assessment which can no longer be varied by any Commissioners on appeal or by order of any court shall be sufficient evidence that the income or chargeable gains in respect of which tax is charged in the assessment arose or were received as stated therein.

102. Mitigation of penalties

The Board may in their discretion mitigate any penalty, or stay or compound any proceedings for [a penalty]¹, and may also, after judgment, further mitigate or entirely remit the penalty.

Amendments.—¹ Words substituted by FA 1989, s. 168 (4).

[103. Time limits for penalties

(1) Subject to subsection (2) below, where the amount of a penalty is to be ascertained by reference to tax payable by a person for any period, the penalty may be determined by an officer of the Board, or proceedings for the penalty may be commenced before the Commissioners or a court—

  (a) at any time within six years after the date on which the penalty was incurred, or
  (b) at any later time within three years after the final determination of the amount of tax by reference to which the amount of the penalty is to be ascertained.

(2) Where the tax was payable by a person who has died, and the determination would be made in relation to his personal representatives, subsection (1) (b) above does not apply if the tax was charged in an assessment made later than six years after the end of the chargeable period for which it was charged.

(3) A penalty under section 99 of this Act may be determined by an officer of the Board, or proceedings for such a penalty may be commenced before a court, at any time within twenty years after the date on which the penalty was incurred.

(4) A penalty to which neither subsection (1) nor subsection (3) above applies may be so determined, or proceedings for such a penalty may be commenced before the Commissioners or a court, at any time within six years after the date on which the penalty was incurred or began to be incurred.][1]

Amendments.—[1] This section substituted by FA 1989, s. 169, but it does not affect the application of TMA 1970, s. 103(4) to proceedings under TMA 1970, s.100 as originally enacted.
This section as originally enacted read—

"**103. Time limit for recovery of penalties**

(1) Proceedings for the recovery of any penalty incurred under the Taxes Acts in connection with or in relation to tax may be commenced at any time within six years next after the date on which it was incurred, or at any later time allowed under the following provisions of this section.

(2) Proceedings for the recovery of any penalty from any person in connection with or in relation to any tax covered by any assessment may, where any form of fraud or wilful default has been committed by him or on his behalf in connection with or in relation to that tax, be commenced at any time within three years from the final determination of the amount of tax covered by the assessment:

Provided that this subsection shall not extend the time for the bringing of any proceedings against the personal representatives of any person by whom or on whose behalf any form of fraud or wilful default has been committed.

(3) Where the amount of any penalty to which a person is liable under the Taxes Acts is determined by reference to tax charged in an assessment for any chargeable period which is made not later than six years after the end of that chargeable period, proceedings for the recovery of the penalty may be commenced within three years from the final determination of the amount of that tax.

(4) In any proceedings for the recovery of a penalty which could not have been commenced but for subsection (3) above, any tax charged in an assessment made under section 37, 39 or 40 (2) of this Act shall be left out of account in determining the amount of the penalty."

104. Savings for criminal proceedings

The provisions of the Taxes Acts shall not, save so far as is otherwise provided, affect any criminal proceedings for any misdemeanour.

105. Evidence in cases of [fraudulent conduct]

(1) Statements made or documents produced by or on behalf of a person shall not be inadmissible in any such proceedings as are mentioned in subsection (2) below by reason only that it has been drawn to his attention that—

[(*a*) pecuniary settlements may be accepted instead of a penalty being determined, or proceedings being instituted, in relation to any tax,][2]
(*b*) though no undertaking can be given as to whether or not the Board will accept such a settlement in the case of any particular person, it is the practice of the Board to be influenced by the fact that a person has made a full confession of any [fraudulent conduct][1] to which he has been a party and has given full facilities for investigation,

and that he was or may have been induced thereby to make the statements or produce the documents.

(2) The proceedings mentioned in subsection (1) above are—

(*a*) any criminal proceedings against the person in question for any form of [fraudulent conduct][1] in connection with or in relation to tax, and
(*b*) any proceedings against him for the recovery of any [tax due from him, and][2]
[(*c*) any proceedings for a penalty or on appeal against the determination of a penalty.][3]

Amendments.—[1] Words in sub-s. (1) (*b*), (2) (*a*) substituted for the words "fraud or default" and "fraud or wilful default" respectively by FA 1989, s. 149 (5).
[2] Sub-s. (1) (*a*) and words in sub-s. (2) (*b*) substituted by FA 1989, s. 168 (5).
[3] Sub-s. (2) (*c*) inserted by *ibid.*

106. Refusal to allow a deduction of income tax, and avoidance of agreements for payment without deduction

(1) A person who refuses to allow a deduction of income tax authorised by the Taxes Acts to be made out of any payment shall incur a penalty of £50.

(2) Every agreement for payment of interest, rent or other annual payment in full without allowing any such deduction shall be void.

Scotland

107. Criminal liability for false statements made to obtain allowances

(1) This section applies only in Scotland.

(2) If any person, for the purpose of obtaining any allowance, reduction, rebate or repayment in respect of tax, either for himself or for any other person, or, in any return made with reference to tax, knowingly makes any false statement or false representation, he shall be liable, on summary conviction, to imprisonment for a term not exceeding six months.

(3) Notwithstanding anything in the Summary Jurisdiction (Scotland) Act 1954, proceedings for an offence under this section may be commenced at any time within three years from the time when the offence was committed.

(4) The expression "return" in this section shall be construed without regard to the definition in section 118 (1) of this Act.

PART XI

MISCELLANEOUS AND SUPPLEMENTAL

Companies

108. Responsibility of company officers

(1) Everything to be done by a company under the Taxes Acts shall be done by the company acting through the proper officer of the company, and service on a company of any document under or in pursuance of the Taxes Acts may be effected by serving it on the proper officer.

This subsection is without prejudice to Part VIII of this Act (charges on non-residents) as it applies to corporation tax.

(2) Corporation tax or other tax chargeable under the Corporation Tax Acts on a company which is not a body corporate, or which is a body corporate not incorporated under the [Companies Act 1985][1] or any other enactment forming part of the law of the United Kingdom, or by Charter, may, at any time after the tax becomes due, and without prejudice to any other method of recovery, be recovered from the proper officer of the company, and that officer may retain out of any money coming into his hands on behalf of the company sufficient sums to pay that tax, and, so far as he is not so reimbursed, shall be entitled to be indemnified by the company in respect of the liability so imposed on him.

(3) For the purposes of this section—

(*a*) the proper officer of a company which is a body corporate shall be the secretary or person acting as secretary of the company, except that if a liquidator has been appointed for the company the liquidator shall be the proper officer,
(*b*) the proper officer of a company which is not a body corporate or for which there is no proper officer within paragraph (*a*) above, shall be the treasurer or the person acting as treasurer, of the company.

Amendments.—[1] Words in sub-s. (2) substituted by the Companies Consolidation (Consequential Provisions) Act 1985, Sch. 2 with effect from 1 July 1985.

[109. Corporation tax on close company in connection with loans to participators etc.

(1) The provisions of [sections 419 and 420][4] of the principal Act (charge of tax in connection with loans by close companies to participators etc.) directing that tax be assessed and recoverable as if it were an amount of corporation tax shall be taken as applying, subject to the provisions of the Taxes Act, and to any necessary modifications, all enactments applying generally to corporation tax, including those relating to the assessing, collecting and receiving of corporation tax, those conferring or regulating a right of appeal and those concerning administration, penalties, interest on unpaid tax and priority of tax in cases of insolvency under the law of any part of the United Kingdom.

(2) Section 86 of this Act shall apply in relation to tax under the said [sections 419 and 420][4] as if [the date given by the Table in subsection (4) of the said section 86 were the last day of the three months following the end of the financial year in which the loan or advance was made].[2]

(3) For the purposes of section 88 of this Act as applied by subsection (1) above, the date when tax charged under the said [sections 419 and 420][4] ought to have been paid shall be taken to be the first day of the [financial year][3] following that in which the loan or advance was made.

(4) Section 91 of this Act shall not apply in consequence of any discharge or repayment of tax under section [419 (4)] of the principal Act.

(5) For the purposes of the said section 91, a relief from tax under the said [sections 419 and 420][4] shall not be treated as affecting tax charged by any assessment unless the assessment is to tax under that section.][1]

Note.—See **Prospective Legislation Notes** (Taxes Management Provisions).
Amendments.—[1] This section was substituted by FA 1972, s. 111 and Sch. 24, para. 13, with effect from 6 April 1973.
[2] Words in sub-s. (2) substituted by F (No. 2) A 1975, s. 46 (5) (*b*) in relation to tax charged by assessment notice issued after 31 July 1975.
[3] Words in sub-s. (3) substituted by F (No. 2) A 1975, s. 46 (5) (*c*) in relation to tax charged by assessment notice issued after 31 July 1975.
[4] Words in sub-ss. (1)–(5) substituted by TA 1988, Sch. 29, para. 32 Table.

Valuation

110. Valuation of land: power of entry

Any person authorised in that behalf by the Board may, on producing if so required evidence of his authority, at any reasonable time enter on and inspect, with a view to establishing its annual value, any land the annual value of which falls to be determined for purposes of income tax or corporation tax.

111. Valuation of assets; power to inspect

(1) If for the purposes of [the Capital Gains Tax Act 1979][1] the Board authorise an inspector or other officer of the Board to inspect any property for the purpose of ascertaining its market value the person having the custody or possession of that property shall permit the inspector or other officer so authorised to inspect it at such reasonable times as the Board may consider necessary.

(2) If any person wilfully delays or obstructs an inspector or other officer of the Board acting in pursuance of this section he shall be liable on summary conviction to a fine not exceeding £5.

Amendments.—[1] Words in sub-s. (1) substituted by CGTA 1979, s. 157 (2)–(4) and Sch. 7, para. 8 Table, Pt. I. 1, with effect from 22 March 1979.

Documents

112. Loss, destruction or damage to assessments, returns, etc.

(1) Where any assessment to tax, or any duplicate of assessment to tax, or any return or other document relating to tax, has been lost or destroyed, or been so defaced or damaged as to be illegible or otherwise useless, the Commissioners, inspectors, collectors and other officers having powers in relation to tax may, notwithstanding anything in any enactment to the contrary, do all such acts and things as they might have done, and all acts and things done under or in pursuance of this section shall be as valid and effectual for all purposes as they would have been, if the assessment or duplicate of assessment had not been made, or the return or other document had not been made or furnished or required to be made or furnished:

Provided that, where any person who is charged with tax in consequence or by virtue of any act or thing done under or in pursuance of this section proves to the satisfaction of the Commissioners having jurisdiction in the case that he has already paid any tax for the same chargeable period in respect of the subject matter and on the account in respect of and on which he is so charged, relief shall be given to the extent to which the liability of that person has been discharged by the payment so made either by abatement from the charge or by repayment, as the case may require.

(2) In this section, "the Commissioners" means, as the case may require, either the Board or the General or Special Commissioners concerned.

[(3) The references in subsection (1) above to assessments to tax include references to determinations of penalties; and in its application to such determinations the proviso to that subsection shall have effect with the appropriate modifications.][1]

Amendments.—[1] Sub-s. (3) added by FA 1989, s. 168 (6).

113. Form of returns and other documents

(1) Any returns under the Taxes Acts shall be in such form as the Board prescribe, and in prescribing income tax forms under this subsection the Board shall have regard to the desirability of securing, so far as may be possible, that no person shall be required to make more than one return annually of the sources of his income and the amounts derived therefrom.

[(1A) Any notice or direction requiring any return to be made under the Taxes Acts to an inspector or other officer of the Board may be issued or given in the name of that officer, or as the case may be in the name of the Board, by any officer of the Board, and so as to require the return to be made to the first-mentioned officer]¹.

[(1B) Where the Board or an inspector or other officer of the Board have in accordance with section 29 of this Act, or any other provision of the Taxes Acts, decided to make an assessment to tax, and have taken all other decisions needed for arriving at the amount of the assessment, they may entrust to some other officer of the Board responsibility for completing the assessing procedure, whether by means involving the use of a computer or otherwise, including responsibility for serving notice of the assessment on the person liable for tax]¹.

[(1C) Where an officer of the Board has decided that an amount of tax carries interest under section 88 of this Act and has taken the decisions needed for arriving at the date when for the purposes of that section that tax ought to have been paid, he may entrust to any other officer of the Board responsibility for completing the determination procedure, whether by means involving the use of a computer or otherwise, including responsibility for serving notice of the determination on the person liable to the interest.]²

[(1D) Where an officer of the Board has decided to impose a penalty under section 100 of this Act and has taken all other decisions needed for arriving at the amount of the penalty, he may entrust to any other officer of the Board responsibility for completing the determination procedure, whether by means involving the use of a computer or otherwise, including responsibility for serving notice of the determination on the person liable to the penalty.]³

(2) Any return or assessment or other document relating to chargeable gains or tax on capital gains may be combined with one relating to income or income tax.

(3) Every assessment, [determination of a penalty]⁴ duplicate, warrant, notice of assessment [, of determination]⁴ or of demand, or other document required to be used in assessing, charging, collecting and levying tax [or determining a penalty]⁴ shall be in accordance with the forms prescribed from time to time in that behalf by the Board, and a document in the form prescribed and supplied or approved by them shall be valid and effectual.

Amendments.—¹ Sub-ss. (1A) and (1B) inserted by FA 1970, Sch. 4, para. 10.
² Sub-s. (1C) inserted by FA 1989, s. 160 (4).
³ Sub-s. (1D) inserted by FA 1989, s. 168 (7) (*a*).
⁴ Words in sub-s. (3) inserted by FA 1989, s. 168 (7) (*b*).

114. Want of form or errors not to invalidate assessments, etc.

(1) An assessment [or determination]¹, warrant or other proceeding which purports to be made in pursuance of any provision of the Taxes Acts shall not be quashed, or deemed to be void or voidable, for want of form, or be affected by reason of a mistake, defect or omission therein, if the same is in substance and effect in conformity with or according to the intent and meaning of the Taxes Acts, and if the person or property charged or intended to be charged or affected thereby is designated therein according to common intent and understanding.

(2) An assessment [or determination]¹ shall not be impeached or affected—

(*a*) by reason of a mistake therein as to—

(i) the name or surname of a person liable, or
(ii) the description of any profits or property, or
(iii) the amount of the tax charged, or

(*b*) by reason of any variance between the notice and the assessment [or determination]¹.

Amendments.—¹ Words in sub-ss. (1), (2) inserted by FA 1989, s. 160 (5).

115. Delivery and service of documents

(1) A notice or form which is to be served under the Taxes Acts on a person may be either delivered to him or left at his usual or last known place of residence.

(2) Any notice or other document to be given, sent, served or delivered under the Taxes Acts may be served by post, and, if to be given, sent, served or delivered to or on any person

by the Board, by any officer of the Board, or by or on behalf of any body of Commissioners, may be so served addressed to that person—

(*a*) at his usual or last known place of residence, or his place of business or employment, or
(*b*) in the case of a company, at any other prescribed place and, in the case of a liquidator of a company, at his address for the purposes of the liquidation or any other prescribed place.

(3) In subsection (2) above "prescribed" means prescribed by regulations made by the Board, and the power of making regulations for the purposes of that subsection shall be exercisable by statutory instrument subject to annulment in pursuance of a resolution of the House of Commons.

(4) Notices to be given or delivered to, or served on, the General Commissioners shall be valid and effectual if given or delivered to or served on their clerk.

116. Receipts, etc. exempt from stamp duty[1]

Amendments.—[1] Repealed by FA 1970, Sch. 8, Pt. V, with effect from 1 February 1971.

Northern Ireland

117. Action of ejectment in Northern Ireland

Unless other provision is made in that behalf by any enactment, an action of ejectment in Northern Ireland for non-payment of rent shall not be defeated on the ground that the person liable to pay the rent is entitled under the Income Tax Acts to a deduction which would reduce the amount due by him below a year's rent.

Interpretation

118. Interpretation

(1) In this Act, unless the context otherwise requires—

"Act" includes an Act of the Parliament of Northern Ireland and "enactment" shall be construed accordingly,
"the Board" means the Commissioners of Inland Revenue,
"body of persons" means any body politic, corporate or collegiate, and any company, fraternity, fellowship and society of persons, whether corporate or not corporate,
"branch or agency" means any factorship, agency, receivership, branch or management, and "branch or agent" shall be construed accordingly,
"chargeable gain" has the same meaning as in [the Capital Gains Tax Act 1979][4],
"chargeable period" means a year of assessment or a company's accounting period,
"collector" means any collector of taxes,
"company" has the meaning given by section [832 (1)][6] of the principal Act (with section [468][6] of that Act),
"incapacitated person" means any infant, person of unsound mind, lunatic, idiot or insane person,
"inspector" means any inspector of taxes,
. . .[9]
"the principal Act" means the Income and Corporation Taxes Act [1988][6],
"return" includes any statement or declaration under the Taxes Acts,
"tax", where neither income tax nor capital gains tax nor corporation tax [nor development land tax][2] is specified, means any of those taxes [except that in sections 20, 20A, 20B, 20C and 20D it does not include development land tax][3],
"the Taxes Acts" means this Act and—
  (*a*) the Tax Acts . . .[7],
  (*b*) [the Capital Gains Tax Act 1979][4] and all other enactments relating to capital gains tax, [and
  (*c*) the Development Land Tax Act 1976 and any other enactment relating to development land tax][2],
"trade" includes every trade, manufacture, adventure or concern in the nature of trade.

(2) For the purposes of this Act, a person shall be deemed not to have failed to do anything required to be done within a limited time if he did it within such further time, if any, as the

Board or the Commissioners or officer concerned may have allowed; and where a person had a reasonable excuse for not doing anything required to be done he shall be deemed [not to have failed to do it unless the excuse ceased and, after the excuse ceased, he shall be deemed][5] not to have failed to do it if he did it without unreasonable delay after the excuse had ceased : . . .[1]

(3) For the purposes of [section 36][8] and Part X of this Act, an assessment made in the partnership name and the tax charged in such an assessment shall, according to the law in Scotland as well as according to the law elsewhere in the United Kingdom, be deemed to be respectively an assessment made on the partners and tax charged on and payable by them.

(4) For the purposes of this Act, the amount of tax covered by any assessment shall not be deemed to be finally determined until that assessment can no longer be varied, whether by any Commissioners on appeal or by the order of any court.

Cross references.—See the Interpretation Act 1978, ss. 5, 24 (4), 26 and Sch. 1 (meaning of "The Tax Acts").
Amendments.—[1] In sub-s. (2), the proviso repealed by FA 1970, Sch. 8, Pt. VII.
[2] Words in the definition of "tax" and para. (c) in the definition of "the Taxes Acts" in sub-s. (1) added by the Development Land Tax Act 1976, Sch. 8, para. 32 (c), (d).
[3] Words in the definition of "tax" in sub-s. (1) inserted by FA 1976, s. 57 (2).
[4] Words in sub-s. (1), in the definitions of "chargeable gain" and "the Taxes Acts" substituted by CGTA 1979, s. 157 (2)–(4) and Sch. 7, para. 8 Table, Pt. I. 1, with effect from 22 March 1979.
[5] Words in sub-s. (2) inserted by F (No. 2) A 1987, s. 94.
[6] Numbers in sub-s. (1) substituted by TA 1988, Sch. 29, para. 32 Table.
[7] Words in sub-s. (1) repealed by TA 1988, Sch. 31.
[8] Words in sub-s. (3) substituted for the words "sections 37 to 39" by FA 1989, s. 149 (3) (b).
[9] The definition of "neglect" repealed by FA 1989, Sch. 17, Pt. VIII.

PART XII
GENERAL

119. Commencement and construction

This Act shall come into force for all purposes on 6th April 1970 to the exclusion of the corresponding enactments repealed by the principal Act.

(2) This Act, and the repeals made by the principal Act, have effect subject to Schedule 4 to this Act.

(3) This Act, so far as it relates to income tax or corporation tax, shall be construed as one with the principal Act.

(4) This Act, so far as it relates to chargeable gains, shall be construed as one with [the Capital Gains Tax Act 1979][1].

Amendments.—[1] Words in sub-s. (4) substituted by CGTA 1979, s. 157 (2)–(4) and Sch. 7, para. 8 Table, Pt. I. 1, with effect from 22 March 1979.

120. Short title

This Act may be cited as the Taxes Management Act 1970.

SCHEDULES

SCHEDULE 1
Section 6

FORMS OF DECLARATIONS

PART I
GENERAL AND SPECIAL COMMISSIONERS AND OTHERS

"I, A.B., do solemnly declare that I will impartially and to the best of my ability execute [the duties of my office][1]; and that I will not disclose any information received by me in the execution of [those duties][1] except for the purposes of [those duties][1] or for the purposes of any prosecution for an offence relating to [inland revenue][1], or in such other cases as may be required by law."

Amendments.—[1] Words substituted by FA 1975, s. 57 (2), with effect from 13 March 1975.

PART II
COMMISSIONERS OF INLAND REVENUE

"I, A.B., do solemnly declare that I will not disclose any information received by me in the execution of my duties except for the purposes of those duties or for the purposes of any prosecution for an offence relating to inland revenue, or in such other cases as may be required by law."

PART III
INSPECTORS, COLLECTORS AND OTHER OFFICERS

"I, A.B., do solemnly declare that I will not disclose any information received by me in the execution of the duties which may from time to time be assigned to me by the Board of Inland Revenue except for the purposes of my duties, or to the Board of Inland Revenue or in accordance with their instructions, or for the purposes of any prosecution for an offence relating to inland revenue, or in such other cases as may be required by law."

SCHEDULE 2

Section 42

JURISDICTION IN APPEALS ON CLAIMS

Appeal from Inspector

1.—(1) Except as otherwise provided by the following provisions of this Schedule, or any other provision of the Taxes Acts, an appeal against the decision of an inspector on a claim shall lie to the General Commissioners, but the appellant may elect to bring the appeal before the Special Commissioners instead of the General Commissioners.

[(1A) An election under sub-paragraph (1) above shall be disregarded if—

(*a*) the appellant and the inspector or other officer of the Board agree in writing, at any time before the determination of the appeal, that it is to be disregarded; or

(*b*) the General Commissioners have given a direction under sub-paragraph (1C) below and have not revoked it.][1]

[(1B) At any time before the determination of an appeal in respect of which an election has been made under sub-paragraph (1) above, the inspector or other officer of the Board after giving notice to the appellant may refer the election to the General Commissioners.][1]

[(1C) On any such reference the Commissioners shall, unless they are satisfied that the appellant has arguments to present or evidence to adduce on the merits of the appeal, direct that the election be disregarded.][1]

[(1D) If, at any time after the giving of a direction under sub-paragraph (1C) above (but before the determination of the appeal) the General Commissioners are satisfied that the appellant has arguments to present or evidence to adduce on the merits of the appeal, they shall revoke the direction.][1]

[(1E) Any decision to give a direction under sub-paragraph (1C) or revoke such a direction under sub-paragraph (1D) above shall be final.][1]

(2) If an appeal to either body of Commissioners is pending against an assessment on the appellant which relates to the same source of income as that to which the claim relates, the appeal on the claim shall lie to that body of Commissioners.

Amendments.—[1] Sub-paras. (1A)–(1E) inserted by FA 1984, Sch. 22, para. 3 (2) with effect from 1 January 1985 by virtue of FA 1984 (Commencement No. 2) Order 1984, S.I. 1984 No. 1836.

2.—(1) An appeal from a decision of an inspector on a claim under any provision in column 1 of the Table below shall be to the General Commissioners, and paragraph 1 of this Schedule shall not apply.

(2) An appeal from a decision of an inspector on a claim under any provision in column 2 of the said Table shall be to the Special Commissioners, and paragraph 1 of this Schedule shall not apply.

TABLE

1 *Appeal exclusively to* *General Commissioners*	2 *Appeal exclusively to* *Special Commissioners*
In the principal Act—	In the principal Act—
Chapter [I of Part VII][1]	section [121 (1), (2)][1]
section [351 (5)][1]	*section 310*
Schedule [2][1]	. . .[2]
	section [441 (3)][1]
	section [459][1]
	section [460][1]
	section [467][1]
	section [484][1]
	section [527][1]
	section [534][1]
	section [536][1]
	section [538][1]
	Chapter I of Part XVIII

Note.—The reference to "section 310" in column 2 appears to be obsolete because the reference is to TA 1970, s. 310, whereas the principal Act now is TA 1988 and TA 1970, s. 310 is now repealed by TA 1988, Sch. 31.
Amendments.—[1] Numbers in columns 1 and 2 substituted by TA 1988, Sch. 29, para. 32 Table.
[2] Words in column 2 repealed by TA 1988, Sch. 31.

Appeal from Board

3. Except as otherwise provided by any provision of the Taxes Acts, an appeal against the decision of the Board on a claim shall lie to the Special Commissioners.

SCHEDULE 3

Section 44

RULES FOR ASSIGNING PROCEEDINGS TO COMMISSIONERS

Description of proceedings   *Place given by these rules*

Income tax and capital gains tax

Description of proceedings	Place given by these rules
1. An appeal against an assessment under Case I of Case II of Schedule D. 2. Any other proceedings relating to a trade, profession or vocation the profits of which are assessable under Case I or Case II of Schedule D, or would be so assessable if there were any.	The place where the trade, profession or vocation is carried on, or in which the head office or principal place of business is situated.
3. An appeal against an assessment under Schedule E and any appeal in exercise of a right conferred by regulations under Section [203][8] of the principal Act (pay as you earn).	Subject to the right of election for place of residence, the place of employment or such other place as may be assigned instead by regulations under section [203][8] of the principal Act.
4. ...[9] any proceedings concerning the annual value of land.	The place where the property is situated.
[5. An appeal against an assessment under Schedule A or under Schedule D, other than Cases I and II. An appeal against an assessment charging income tax at a rate other than the basic rate on income from which income tax has been deducted (otherwise than under section [203][8] of the principal Act) or from or on which income tax is treated as having been deducted or paid or income chargeable under Schedule F. An appeal against an assessment to capital gains tax. [An appeal against a determination under section 88 of this Act.][10] Proceedings for a penalty under [section 100C or an appeal under section 100B against the determination of a penalty][11] of this Act.	If the appellant or other party to the proceedings (not being an inspector or the Board) is carrying on a trade, profession or vocation, then, subject (in the case of an appeal) to the right of election for place of residence, the place in which the trade, profession or vocation is carried on, or in which the head office or principal place of business is situated. If the appellant or other party is employed and does not carry on a trade, profession or vocation, then, subject (in the case of an appeal) to the right of election for place of residence, the place of employment. In any other case, the place where the appellant or other party ordinarily resides.][3]
[5A.] ...	
[5B. An appeal against the decision of an inspector under section [159 of the principal Act][8].	The place where the employees concerned (or most of them) are employed.][7]
6. Any proceedings under the Income Tax Acts not covered by the preceding rules. Any proceedings relating to capital gains tax not covered by rule 5.	The place where the appellant or other party to the proceedings (not being an inspector or the Board) ordinarily [resides].[4] ...[6]

Corporation tax, etc.

7. Proceedings which relate to corporation tax. Proceedings which relate to income tax, but which a company resident in the United Kingdom and within the charge to corporation tax is a party.	The place where the company or other body concerned carries on its trade or business, or in which its head office or principal place of business is situated, or where it resides.
8. Proceedings relating to tax assessable under [sections 419 and 420][8] ...[1-2] of the principal Act ...[1-2]	The place where the company concerned carries on its trade or business, or in which its head office or principal place of business is situated, or where it resides.

Rules 3 and 5 have effect subject to rule 4 above.

Rules 7 and 8 have effect to the exclusion of any other rules.

Where under rules 3 and 5 above a right of election for the place of residence is provided in column 2 above, the appellant may, by notice in writing to the inspector or the Board (given not later than the notice of appeal), elect for the place where he ordinarily [resides].[4]

[If the place given by any of the rules in this Schedule is outside the United Kingdom, the Board may give directions, which may be either general or addressed to a particular occasion, to meet the case.][5]

The rules in this Schedule have effect subject to sections [102, 113 (5), 263 (5) and (6), 343 (10) and 783 (9) of the principal Act, to paragraph 22 of Schedule 7 to the Income and Corporation Taxes Act 1970][8], to paragraph 22 of Schedule 7 to the principal Act and to section 81 of the Capital Allowances Act 1968 (all of which relate to proceedings to which more than one taxpayer may be a party) and to any other express provisions in the Taxes Acts.

Note.—See **Prospective Legislation Notes** (Commercial Woodlands).
Cross references.—See FA 1988, s. 134(7) (transfer of appeals from Special to General Commissioners for Northern Ireland; time limit for notice of election under rule 3 or 5 above).
Amendments.—[1-2] Words in column 1 of rule 8 repealed by FA 1972, s. 111, Sch. 24, para. 14, and Sch. 28, Pt. VI, with effect from 6 April 1973.
[3] Rule 5 substituted by F (No. 2) A 1975, s. 66 (2).
[4] The word "resides" substituted in both places by F (No. 2) A 1975, s. 66 (3).
[5] Paragraph inserted by F (No. 2) A 1975, s. 66 (4).
[6] Second paragraph in rule 6, column 2, repealed by F (No. 2) A 1975, Sch. 14, Pt. IV.
[7] Rule 5B inserted by FA 1976, Sch. 9, paras. 7, 11, with effect from the year 1977-78.
[8] Words in rules 3, 5, 5B, 8 and the last paragraph substituted by TA 1988, Sch. 29, para. 32 Table.
[9] Words in rule 4 repealed by FA 1988, Sch. 14, Pt. V with effect from 6 April 1988.
[10] Words in column 1 of rule 5 inserted by FA 1989, s. 160 (6).
[11] Words in column 1 of rule 5 substituted by FA 1989, s. 168 (8).

SCHEDULE 4

Section 119

SAVINGS AND TRANSITORY PROVISIONS

Note.—See *Butterworths Tax Handbook*, 1975–76, 14th Edition, for the text of this Schedule.

INCOME AND CORPORATION TAXES ACT 1970

(1970 Chapter 10)

ARRANGEMENT OF PARTS

Part		Sections
I.	*Charge of income tax, and general provisions relating only to income tax*	*1–51*
II.	*Annual payments and interest*	*52– 66*
III.	*Schedule A, and associated charges under Schedule D*	*67– 90*
IV.	*Schedule B*	*91– 92*
V.	*Schedule C, and general provisions about Government securities*	*93–107*
VI.	*Schedule D*	*108–167*
VII.	*Loss relief*	*168–180*
VIII.	*Schedule E*	*181–207*
IX.	*Pension schemes, life annuities etc.*	*208–231*
X.	*Schedule F and company distributions*	*232–237*
XI.	Company taxation	238
		239–242
		243–244
		245–266
		267–276
		277
		278–281
		282–303
XII.	Special classes of companies and businesses	*304–305*
		306
		307–341A
		342–342B
		343–359
XIII.	Special exemptions	*360–377*
XIV.	Miscellaneous special provisions	*378–425*
XV.	Estates of deceased persons in course of administration	*426–433*
XVI.	Settlements	*434–459*
XVII.	Tax avoidance	*460–496*
XVIII.	Double taxation relief	*497–518*
XIX.	Supplemental	*519–535*
XX.	General	536–540

Note.—The Parts printed in italics are repealed by TA 1988, Sch. 31.

ARRANGEMENT OF SECTIONS

Note.—Sections 243 and 244 are among the provisions of this Act repealed by TA 1988, Sch. 31. However, they are reproduced in this Handbook for the purpose of the transitional provisions in TA 1988, Sch. 30. Provisions of this Act not reproduced are either spent or repealed by TA 1988, Sch. 31 and other legislation.

PART XI

COMPANY TAXATION

CHAPTER I

MAIN PROVISIONS

General system of taxation

Section
238. Charge to corporation tax.

Corporation tax

243. General scheme of corporation tax.
244. Time for payment of corporation tax: companies trading before financial year 1965.

CHAPTER II

COMPANIES' CAPITAL GAINS

General provisions

267. Company reconstruction or amalgamation: transfer of assets.
268. *Postponement of charge on transfer of assets to non-resident company.*
268A. Postponement of charge on transfer of assets to non-resident company.
269. Interest charged to capital.

Gilt-edged securities: restrictions on exemptions

270. Charge to tax on certain disposals of United Kingdom securities.
271. *Charge to tax on certain disposals of Guaranteed Stock issued at a discount.*

Groups of companies

272. Groups of companies: definitions.
273. Transfers within a group.
274. Transfers within a group: trading stock.
275. Disposal or acquisition outside a group.
276. Replacement of business assets by members of a group.
278. Company ceasing to be member of a group.
278A. Exemption from charge under s. 278 in the case of certain mergers.
279. Shares in subsidiary member of a group.

Losses attributable to depreciatory transactions

280. Transactions in a group.
281. Dividend stripping.

PART XII

SPECIAL CLASSES OF COMPANIES AND BUSINESSES

CHAPTER I

INVESTMENT AND INSURANCE COMPANIES: EXPENSES OF MANAGEMENT AND CAPITAL ALLOWANCES

Section
306. Capital allowances for machinery and plant.

CHAPTER IV

SAVINGS BANKS, INDUSTRIAL AND PROVIDENT SOCIETIES, BUILDING SOCIETIES AND MUTUAL BUSINESS

342. Disposals of land between the Housing Corporation and housing societies.
342A. Disposals by Housing Corporation and certain housing associations.
342B. Disposals by Northern Ireland housing associations.

PART XX

GENERAL

536. Commencement.
537. Savings, transitory provisions and consequential amendments.
538. Repeals.
539. Continuity and construction of references to old and new law.
540. Short title and construction.

SCHEDULES:

Schedule 14—Savings and transitory provisions.

An Act to consolidate certain of the enactments relating to income tax and corporation tax, including certain enactments relating also to other taxes. [12th March 1970]

Cross references.—See the Interpretation Act 1978, ss. 5, 24, (4), 26 and Sch. 1 (meaning of "The Tax Acts").

PART XI
COMPANY TAXATION

Cross references.—See the Interpretation Act 1978, ss. 5, 24 (4), 26 and Sch. 1 (meaning of "The Corporation Tax Acts" and "The Income Tax Acts");
CGTA 1979, s. 1 (2) (company's chargeable gains to be taxed according to the provisions of this Part, and CGTA 1979 to have effect subject thereto).

CHAPTER I
MAIN PROVISIONS

General system of taxation

238. Charge to corporation tax

(1)–(3) . . .[1]

(4) In this Part of this Act, except in so far as the context otherwise requires—

(*a*) "profits" means income and chargeable gains, and
(*b*) "trade includes "vocation", and includes also an office or employment or the occupation of woodlands in any context in which the expression is applied to that in the Income Tax Acts.

Amendments.—[1] Sub-ss. (1)–(3) repealed by TA 1988, Sch. 31.

Corporation tax

243. General scheme of corporation tax

(1)–(3) . . .

(4) *Except as provided by section 244 below and section 344 of this Act (special provisions for building societies), corporation tax assessed for an accounting period shall be paid within nine months from the end of that period or, if it is later, within [thirty days from the date of the issue of the notice of assessment].*[1]

(5)–(7) . . .

Cross references.—See TA 1988, Sch. 30, para. 1 (new provisions in respect of date of payment of corporation tax; modification of sub-s. (4) above for accounting periods of certain old companies beginning after 16 March 1987).
Amendments.—[1] Words in sub-s. (4) substituted by F (No. 2) A 1975, s. 44 (2), (7), in relation to tax charged by assessments notice of which is issued after 31 July 1975.
This section is repealed by TA 1988, Sch. 31. Sub-s. (4) is retained for the benefit of TA 1988, Sch. 30, para. 1.

244. Time for payment of corporation tax: companies trading before financial year 1965

(1) Where, in respect of a trade chargeable under Case I or II of Schedule D, a company was within the charge to income tax from a time before the financial year 1965, then (so long as the company continues to be within the charge to corporation tax in respect of that trade) section 243 (4) above shall not apply to the company, but corporation tax assessed on the company (or on some person in its place) for any accounting period, whether or not in respect of the trade, shall be paid within the like interval from the end of the accounting period as there was between the end of the basis period of the trade for the year 1965–66 and 1st January 1966 or, if it is later, within [thirty days from the date of the issue of the notice of assessment]:[1]

Provided that this subsection shall not apply unless the said interval is longer than nine months.

(2) Where subsection (1) above applies to a company having distinct trades which had different

basis periods for the year 1965–66, that one of the basis periods which ended earliest shall be taken.

(3) References in this section to the basis period for the year 1965–66 are, in relation to any source of income, references to the period on the income of which the income tax (if any) chargeable for that year fell to be finally computed in respect of the source or, where by virtue of any provision of the Income Tax Acts the income of any period was to be taken to be the income of the said period, that other period.

Cross references.—See TA 1988, Sch. 30, para. 1 (transitional provisions in respect of date of payment of corporation tax).
Amendments.—[1] Words in sub-s. (1) substituted by F (No. 2) A 1975, s. 44 (2), (7), in relation to tax charged by assessments notice of which is issued after 31 July 1975.
This section repealed by TA 1988, Sch. 31. It is reproduced here for the benefit of TA 1988, Sch. 30, para. 1.

CHAPTER II
COMPANIES' CAPITAL GAINS

General provisions

267. Company reconstruction or amalgamation: transfer of assets

(1) Subject to the provisions of this section, where—

(*a*) any scheme of reconstruction or amalgamation involves the transfer of the whole or part of a company's business to another company, and
(*b*) the transfer takes effect after 5th April 1970, and
(*c*) at the time of the transfer both the companies are resident in the United Kingdom, and
(*d*) the first-mentioned company receives no part of the consideration for the transfer (otherwise than by the other company taking over the whole or part of the liabilities of the business),

then so far as relates to corporation tax on chargeable gains the two companies shall be treated as if any assets included in the transfer were acquired by the one company from the other company for a consideration of such amount as would secure that on the disposal by way of transfer neither a gain nor a loss would accrue to the company making the disposal, and for the purposes of [Schedule 5 to the Capital Gains Tax Act 1979][2] (assets held on 6th April 1965) the acquiring company shall be treated as if the respective acquisitions of the assets by the other company had been the acquiring company's acquisition of them.

(2) This section does not apply in relation to an asset which, until the transfer, formed part of trading stock of a trade carried on by the company making the disposal, or in relation to an asset which is acquired as trading stock for the purposes of a trade carried on by the company acquiring the asset.

(3) This section does not apply in the case of a transfer of the whole or part of a company's business to a unit trust scheme to which [section 96 . . .][3] of the Capital Gains Tax Act 1979][2] (unit trusts for exempt unit holders) applies [or which is an authorised unit trust within the meaning of [section 468 of the Taxes Act 1988][5] or to an investment trust within the meaning of [section 842 of that Act][5]][4].

[(3A) This section does not apply unless the reconstruction or amalgamation is effected for bona fide commercial reasons and does not form part of a scheme or arrangements of which the main purpose, or one of the main purposes, is avoidance of liability to corporation tax, capital gains tax or income tax; but the foregoing provisions of this subsection shall not affect the operation of this section in any case where, before the transfer, the Board have, on the application of the acquiring company, notified the company that the Board are satisfied that the reconstruction or amalgamation will be effected for bona fide commercial reasons and will not form part of any such scheme or arrangements as aforesaid.

[Subsections (2) to (5) of section 88 of the Capital Gains Tax Act 1979][2] shall have effect in relation to this subsection as they have effect in relation to [subsection (1)][2] of that section.][1]

[(3B) Where, if the company making the disposal had not been wound up, tax could have been assessed on it by virtue of subsection (3A) above, that tax may be assessed and charged (in the name of the company making the disposal) on the company to which the disposal is made.][1]

[(3C) If any tax assessed on a company (the chargeable company) by virtue of subsection (3A) or (3B) above is not paid within six months from the date when it is payable, any other person who—

(*a*) holds all or any part of the assets in respect of which the tax is charged; and
(*b*) either is the company to which the disposal was made or has acquired the assets without there having been any subsequent disposal not falling within this section or section 273 below,

may, within two years from the time when the tax became payable, be assessed and charged (in the name of the chargeable company) to all or, as the case may be, a corresponding part of the unpaid tax; and a person paying any amount of tax under this section shall be entitled to recover a sum of that amount from the chargeable company.][1]

(4) In this section—

"scheme of reconstruction or amalgamation" means a scheme for the reconstruction of any company or companies or the amalgamation of any two or more companies,
"trading stock" has the meaning given by section [100 (2) of the Taxes Act 1988]⁵.

Note.—See **Prospective Legislation Notes** (Taxes Management Provisions).
Cross references.—See CGTA 1979, s. 98 (1) (transfer of assets to a unit trust scheme which becomes tax exempt after the transfer);
FA 1983, Sch. 6, para. 9 (disposal of securities under this section; treatment of indexation allowance where the transferee company has elected for pooling under the new pooling provisions for securities disposed of after 31 March 1982);
FA 1984, Sch. 13, para. 10 (2) (*bb*) (disposals of qualifying corporate bonds);
FA 1985, s. 68 (7) (modification of indexation allowance with respect to disposals of assets after 31 March or 5 April 1985);
FA 1988, Sch. 8, para. 1 (capital gains: re-basing to 1982 of assets held on 31 March 1982).
Amendments.—¹ Sub-ss. (3A), (3B) and (3C) inserted by FA 1977, s. 41, with effect from 19 April 1977.
² Words in sub-ss. (1), (3) and (3A) substituted by CGTA 1979, s. 157 (2)–(4) and Sch. 7, para. 9 Table, with effect from 22 March 1979.
³ Words in sub-s. (3) repealed by FA 1980, s. 81 (2) and Sch. 20, Pt. X.
⁴ Words in sub-s. (3) inserted by FA 1980, s. 81 (2).
⁵ Words in sub-ss. (3), (4) substituted by TA 1988, Sch. 29, para. 32 Table.

268. Postponement of charge on transfer of assets to non-resident company

Note.—This section replaced by s. 268A below by FA 1977, s. 42 with effect from 29 March 1977.

[268A. Postponement of charge on transfer of assets to non-resident company

(1) This section applies where a company resident in the United Kingdom carries on a trade outside the United Kingdom through a branch or agency and—

(*a*) that trade, or part of it, together with the whole assets of the company used for the purposes of the trade or part (or together with the whole of those assets other than cash) is transferred to a company not resident in the United Kingdom;
(*b*) the trade or part is so transferred wholly or partly in exchange for securities consisting of shares, or of shares and loan stock, issued by the transferee company to the transferor company;
(*c*) the shares so issued, either alone or taken together with any other shares in the transferee company already held by the transferor company, amount in all to not less than one quarter of the ordinary share capital of the transferee company; and
(*d*) either no allowable losses accrue to the transferor company on the transfer or the aggregate of the chargeable gains so accruing exceeds the aggregate of the allowable losses so accruing.

(2) In any case to which this section applies the transferor company may claim that [the Capital Gains Tax Act 1979]² shall have effect in accordance with the following provisions.

(3) Any allowable losses accruing to the transferor company on the transfer shall be set off against the chargeable gains so accruing and the transfer shall be treated as giving rise to a single chargeable gain equal to the aggregate of those gains after deducting the aggregate of those losses and—

(*a*) if the securities are the whole consideration for the transfer, the whole of that gain shall be treated as not accruing to the transferor company on the transfer but an equivalent amount ("the deferred gain") shall be brought into account in accordance with subsections (4) and (5) below;
(*b*) if the securities are not the whole of that consideration—

(i) paragraph (*a*) above shall apply to the appropriate proportion of that gain; and
(ii) the remainder shall be treated as accruing to the transferor company on the transfer.

In paragraph (*b*) (i) above "the appropriate proportion" means the proportion that the market value of the securities at the time of the transfer bears to the market value of the whole of the consideration at that time.

(4) If at any time after the transfer the transferor company disposes of the whole or part of the securities held by it immediately before that time, the consideration received by it on the disposal shall be treated as increased by the whole or the appropriate proportion of the deferred gain so far as not already taken into account under this subsection or subsection (5) below.

In this subsection "the appropriate proportion" means the proportion that the market value of the part of the securities disposed of bears to the market value of the securities held immediately before the disposal.

(5) If at any time within six years after the transfer the transferee company disposes of the whole or part of the relevant assets held by it immediately before that time there shall be deemed to accrue to the transferor company as a chargeable gain on that occasion the whole or the appropriate proportion of the deferred gain so far as not already taken into account under this subsection or subsection (4) above.

In this subsection "relevant assets" means assets the chargeable gains on which were taken into account in arriving at the deferred gain and "the appropriate proportion" means the proportion which the chargeable gain so taken into account in respect of the part of the relevant assets disposed of bears to the aggregate of the chargeable gains so taken into account in respect of the relevant assets held immediately before the time of the disposal.

(6) There shall be disregarded—

(*a*) for the purposes of subsection (4) above any disposal to which section 273 of this Act applies; and
(*b*) for the purposes of subsection (5) above any disposal to which that section would apply apart from section 272 (1) (*a*) or (2) of this Act;

and where a person acquires securities or an asset on a disposal disregarded for the purposes of subsection (4) or (5) above (and without there having been a previous disposal not so disregarded) a disposal of the securities or asset by that person shall be treated as a disposal by the transferor or, as the case may be, transferee company.

(7) This section applies where the transfer mentioned in subsection (1) (*a*) above is on or after 29th March 1977.

(8) If in the case of any such transfer as was mentioned in subsection (1) of section 268 of this Act there were on the said 29th March chargeable gains which by virtue of subsection (2) of that section were treated as not yet having accrued to the transferor company, subsections (4) and (5) above shall (without any claim in that behalf) apply to the aggregate of those gains as if references to the deferred gain were references to that aggregate and as if references to the transfer and the securities were references to the transfer and the shares, or shares and loan stock, mentioned in subsection (1) of that section.][1]

Note.—Sub-s. (8) of this section refers to s. 268 (1), (2), which read as follows—
(1) This section applies where a company resident in the United Kingdom which is carrying on a trade outside the United Kingdom through a branch or agency transfers the trade carried on through that branch or agency, together with the whole assets of the business used for the purposes of that trade, or together with the whole of those assets other than cash, to a company not resident in the United Kingdom, and the business is so transferred wholly or partly in exchange for shares or for shares and loan stock issued by the transferee company to the transferor company, and the shares so issued, either alone or taken together with any other shares in the transferee company already held by the transferor company, amounted in all to not less than one quarter of the ordinary share capital of the transferee company.
(2) For the purposes of Part III of the Finance Act 1965, the transferor company shall be treated as if a fraction of any chargeable gain accruing to it on its disposal of any asset so transferred to the transferee company did not accrue to the transferor company until—
(*a*) the transferee company disposes or partly disposes of that asset, or ceases to use it, or is wound up or dissolved, or
(*b*) the transferor company disposes of all or any of the shares or loan stock issued in exchange by the transferee company, or
(*c*) the expiration of a period of ten years beginning with the transfer, or
(*d*) the passing of a resolution or the making of an order, or any other act, for the winding up of the transferor company (unless that company is not in fact wound up or dissolved),
whichever event comes first.
Cross references.—See FA 1988, Sch. 9, para. 3 (reduction of a deferred charge to tax where the charge is wholly or partly attributable to an increase in the value of an asset before 31 March 1982);
FA 1989, Sch. 15, para. 1 (1), (2) (*a*) (sub-s. (4) of this section not to apply in consequence of an event occurring after 5 April 1988 if its application is directly attributable to the disposal of an asset before 1 April 1982).
Amendments.—[1] This section (i.e. 268A) substituted for s. 268 by FA 1977, s. 42, with effect from 29 March 1977.
[2] Words in sub-s. (2) substituted by CGTA 1979, s. 157 (2)–(4) and Sch. 7, para. 8 Table, Pt. I. 2, with effect from 22 March 1979.

269. Interest charged to capital

(1) Where—

(*a*) a company incurs expenditure on the construction of any building, structure or works, being expenditure allowable as a deduction under [section 32 of the Capital Gains Tax Act 1979][2] in computing a gain accruing to the company on the disposal of the building, structure or work, or of any asset comprising it, and
(*b*) that expenditure was defrayed out of borrowed money, . . .[3]

(c) ...³

[the sums so allowable under the said section 32 shall, subject to subsection (1A) below, include the amount of any interest on that borrowed money which is referable to a period or part of a period ending on or before the disposal.]⁴

[(1A) Subsection (1) above has effect subject to section 33 of the said Act of 1979 and does not apply to interest which is a charge on income.]⁴

(2) ...¹

Cross references.—See CGTA 1979, s. 32 (3) (capital gains tax relief for interest charged to capital).
Amendments.—¹ Sub-s. (2) repealed by FA 1971, Sch. 14, Pt. III.
² Words in sub-s. (1) substituted by CGTA 1979, s. 157 (2)–(4) and Sch. 7, para. 9 Table, with effect from 22 March 1979.
³ Words in sub-s. (1) repealed by FA 1981, s. 38 (3), (4) and Sch. 19, Pt. VI in relation to interest paid in accounting period ending after 31 March 1981.
⁴ Words in sub-s. (1) substituted and sub-s. (1A) inserted by FA 1981, s. 38 (3), (4) in relation to interest paid in accounting period ending after 31 March 1981.

Gilt-edged securities: restrictions on exemptions

270. Charge to tax on certain disposals of United Kingdom securities

(1), (2) ...¹

(3) ...⁶

(4) In any case where—

(a) at 3.30 p.m. on 15th April 1969 (in the following provisions of this section referred to as "the relevant time") or at any time thereafter (whether before or after the commencement of this Act) any specified securities were held by a company in such circumstances that any gain or loss on their disposal would, apart from [section 67 of the Capital Gains Tax Act 1979]³ ...², have been taken into account in determining the company's liability to corporation tax on chargeable gains, and
(b) those securities are subsequently appropriated by the company in such circumstances that if they were disposed of after the appropriation, any profit accruing on their disposal would be brought into account in computing the company's income for corporation tax,

then for the purposes of corporation tax any loss incurred by the company on the disposal of those securities shall not exceed the loss which would have been incurred on that disposal if the amount or value of the consideration for the acquisition of the securities had been equal to their market value at the time of the appropriation.

(5) In any case where—

(a) at the relevant time or at any time thereafter (whether before or after the commencement of this Act) any specified securities were held by a company in such circumstances that any profit accruing on their disposal would be brought into account in computing the company's income for corporation tax, and
(b) those securities are subsequently appropriated by the company in such circumstances that any gain accruing on their disposal would, by virtue of [section 67 of the Capital Gains Tax Act 1979]³, be exempt from corporation tax on chargeable gains,

then for the purposes of corporation tax the company shall be treated as if, immediately before the appropriation, it had sold and repurchased the specified securities at their market value at the time of the appropriation.

[(6) In this section "specified securities" means securities which are gilt-edged securities as defined by Schedule 2 to the Capital Gains Tax Act 1979]⁴ [or qualifying corporate bonds, within the meaning of section 64 of the Finance Act 1984]⁵.

Cross references.—See TA 1988, s. 484 (2) (certain savings banks' loss not subject to the restriction provided for in sub-s. (4) of this section).
Amendments.—¹ Sub-ss. (1), (2) repealed by FA 1971, Sch. 14, Pt. IV. See now FA 1971, Sch. 10, para. 4.
² Words in sub-s. (4) (a) repealed by FA 1977, Sch. 9, Pt. VI.
³ Words in sub-ss. (4) (a) and (5) (b) substituted by CGTA 1979, s. 157 (2)–(4) and Sch. 7, para. 9 Table, with effect from 22 March 1979.
⁴ Sub-s. (6) substituted by CGTA 1979, s. 157 (2)–(4) and Sch. 7, para. 2 (3), with effect from 22 March 1979.
⁵ Words in sub-s. (6) added by FA 1985, s. 67 (2) (a) with respect to disposals occurring after 1 July 1986.
⁶ Sub-s. (3) repealed by FA 1985, Sch. 27, Pt. VII with respect to disposals after 1 July 1986.

271. Charge to tax on certain disposals of Guaranteed Stock issued at a discount

(1)–(3) . . .[1]

(4) . . .[2]

Amendments.—[1] Sub-ss. (1)–(3) repealed by FA 1971, Sch. 14, Pt. IV. See now FA 1971, Sch. 10, para. 4.
[2] Sub-s. (4) repealed by FA 1977, Sch. 9, Pt. VI.

Groups of companies

272. Groups of companies: definitions

(1) For the purposes of this and the following sections of this Chapter—

(*a*) references to a company, subject to section 280 (7) below, apply only to a company, as that expression is limited by subsection (2) below, which is resident in the United Kingdom;
[(*b*) subsections (1A) to (1D) below apply to determine whether companies form a group and, where they do, which is the principal company of the group;][6]
(*c*) . . .[6];
(*d*) in applying the definition of "75 per cent. subsidiary" in section [838 of the Taxes Act 1988][5] any share capital of a registered industrial and provident society shall be treated as ordinary share capital; and
(*e*) "group" and "subsidiary" shall be construed with any necessary modifications where applied to a company incorporated under the law of a country outside the United Kingdom.

[(1A) Subject to subsections (1B) to (1D) below—

(*a*) a company (referred to below in this Chapter as the "principal company of the group") and all its 75 per cent. subsidiaries form a group and, if any of those subsidiaries have 75 per cent. subsidiaries, the group includes them and their 75 per cent. subsidiaries, and so on, but
(*b*) a group does not include any company (other than the principal company of the group) that is not an effective 51 per cent. subsidiary of the principal company of the group.][7]

[(1B) A company cannot be the principal company of a group if it is itself a 75 per cent. subsidiary of another company.][7]

[(1C) Where a company ("the subsidiary") is a 75 per cent. subsidiary of another company but those companies are prevented from being members of the same group by subsection (1A) (*b*) above, the subsidiary may, where the requirements of subsection (1A) above are satisfied, itself be the principal company of another group notwithstanding subsection (1B) above unless this subsection enables a further company to be the principal company of a group of which the subsidiary would be a member.][7]

[(1D) A company cannot be a member of more than one group; but where, apart from this subsection, a company would be a member of two or more groups (the principal company of each group being referred to below as the "head of a group"), it is a member only of that group, if any, of which it would be a member under one of the following tests (applying earlier tests in preference to later tests)—

(*a*) it is a member of the group it would be a member of if, in applying subsection (1A) (*b*) above, there were left out of account any amount to which a head of a group is or would be beneficially entitled of any profits available for distribution to equity holders of a head of another group or of any assets of a head of another group available for distribution to its equity holders on a winding-up,
(*b*) it is a member of the group the head of which is beneficially entitled to a percentage of profits available for distribution to equity holders of the company that is greater than the percentage of those profits to which any other head of a group is so entitled,
(*c*) it is a member of the group the head of which would be beneficially entitled to a percentage of any assets of the company available for distribution to its equity holders on a winding-up that is greater than the percentage of those assets to which any other head of a group would be so entitled,
(*d*) it is a member of the group the head of which owns directly or indirectly a percentage of the company's ordinary share capital that is greater than the percentage of that capital owned directly or indirectly by any other head of a group (interpreting this paragraph as if it were included in section 838 (1) (*a*) of the Taxes Act 1988).][7]

[(1E) For the purposes referred to in subsection (1) above, a company ("the subsidiary") is an effective 51 per cent. subsidiary of another company ("the parent") at any time if and only if—

(a) the parent is beneficially entitled to more than 50 per cent. of any profits available for distribution to equity holders of the subsidiary; and
(b) the parent would be beneficially entitled to more than 50 per cent. of any assets of the subsidiary available for distribution to its equity holders on a winding-up.][7]

(1F) Schedule 18 to the Taxes Act 1988 (group relief: equity holders and profits or assets available for distribution) shall apply for the purposes of subsections (1D) and (1E) above as if the references to subsection (7), or subsections (7) to (9), of section 413 of that Act were references to subsections (1D) and (1E) above and as if, in paragraph 1 (4), the words from "but" to the end and paragraph 7 (1) (b) were omitted.][7]

(2) For the purposes referred to in subsection (1) above references to a company apply only to—

(a) a company within the meaning of the [Companies Act 1985][3] or the corresponding enactment in Northern Ireland, and
(b) a company which is constituted under any other Act or a Royal Charter or letters patent or (although resident in the United Kingdom) is formed under the law of a country or territory outside the United Kingdom, and
(c) a registered industrial and provident society within the meaning of section [486 of the Taxes Act 1988][5] [; and][1]
[(d) a trustee savings bank as defined in section 54 (1) of the Trustee Savings Banks Act 1981][1], [and][4]
[(e) a building society within the meaning of the Building Societies Act 1986.][4]

(3) For the purposes referred to in subsection (1) above a group remains the same group so long as the same company remains the principal company of the group, and if at any time the principal company of a group becomes a [member of another group, the first group and the other group shall be regarded as the same][8], and the question whether or not a company has ceased to be a member of a group shall be determined accordingly.

(4) For the purposes referred to in subsection (1) above the passing of a resolution or the making of an order, or any other act, for the winding-up of [a member of a group of companies][8] shall not be regarded as the occasion of [that or any other company ceasing to be a member of the group][8].

(5) The following sections of this Chapter, except in so far as they relate to recovery of tax, shall also have effect in relation to bodies from time to time established by or under any enactment for the carrying on of any industry or part of an industry, or of any undertaking, under national ownership or control as if they were companies within the meaning of those sections, and as if any such bodies charged with related functions (and in particular the Boards and Holding Company established under the Transport Act 1962 and the new authorities within the meaning of the Transport Act 1968 established under that Act of 1968) and subsidiaries of any of them formed a group, and as if also any two or more such bodies charged at different times with the same or related functions were members of a group:

Provided that this subsection shall have effect subject to any enactment by virtue of which property, rights, liabilities or activities of one such body fall to be treated for corporation tax as those of another, including in particular any such enactment in Chapter [VI of Part XII of the Taxes Act 1988][5].

(6) The following sections of this Chapter, except in so far as they relate to recovery of tax, shall also have effect in relation to ...[2] the Executive for a designated area within the meaning of section 9 (1) of the Transport Act 1968 as if [that Executive][2] were a company within the meaning of these sections.

Cross references.—See FA 1973, s. 38 (5) (ss. 273 to 275 and 278 to 279 of this Act to apply to companies disposing of exploration or exploitation rights as if sub-ss. (1) (a) and (2) of this section were omitted);
CGTA 1979, s. 16 (4) (b) (application of this section for taxation of capital gains of non-resident group of companies),
s. 26 (7) (a) (provisions to counter avoidance of capital gains tax by value-shifting disposals),
s. 26C (10) (application of sub-ss. (1)–(4) of this section for the purposes of CGTA 1979, ss. 26, 26A, 26B (value shifting)),
s. 70 (7) (provisions to counter avoidance of capital gains tax by re-acquisition of gilts after their sale at a loss),
s. 136 (10) (c) (capital gains tax relief for irrecoverable loans to traders),
Sch. 5, para. 5 (5) (quoted securities held on 6.4.65; election for pooling);
FA 1984, s. 44 (1), (4) (for the purposes of this section, a trustee savings bank is deemed to be a body corporate with effect from 21 November 1982);

FA 1988, Sch. 8, para. 14 (3) (application of this section where market value election is made by a member of a group of companies making a disposal after 5 April 1988 of assets held on 31 March 1982).
Amendments.—[1] Sub-s. (2) (*d*) and the word "and" preceding it added by FA 1984, s. 44 (2), (4) with effect from 21 November 1982.
[2] Words in sub-s. (6) repealed and substituted by the London Regional Transport Act 1984, Sch. 6, para. 7 and Sch. 7 with effect from 29 June 1984 by virtue of the London Regional Transport (Appointed Day) Order 1984, S.I. 1984 No. 877.
[3] Words in sub-s. (2) substituted by the Companies Consolidation (Consequential Provisions) Act 1985, Sch. 2 with effect from 1 July 1985.
[4] Sub-s. (2) (*e*) and the word "and" preceding it added by F (No. 2) A 1987, s. 79.
[5] Words in sub-ss. (1) (*d*), (2) (*c*), (5) substituted by TA 1988, Sch. 29, para. 32 Table.
[6] Sub-s. (1) (*b*) substituted for sub-s. (1) (*b*), (*c*) by FA 1989, s. 138 (1). Previous sub-s. (1) (*b*), (*c*) read as follows and are reproduced for the benefit of FA 1989, s. 138 (12)—

"(*b*) a principal company and all its 75 per cent. subsidiaries form a group, and where a principal company is a member of a group as being itself a 75 per cent. subsidiary that group shall comprise all its 75 per cent. subsidiaries;

(*c*) "principal company" means a company of which another company is a 75 per cent. subsidiary."

[7] Sub-ss. (1A)–(1F) inserted by FA 1989, s. 138 (2) with effect from 14 March 1989, but subject to the provisions in FA 1989, s. 138 (7)–(12).
[8] Words in sub-ss. (3), (4) substituted by FA 1989, s. 138 (3), (4). The original sub-ss. (3), (4) read as follows and are reproduced for the benefit of FA 1989, s. 138 (12)—

"(3) For the purposes referred to in subsection (1) above a group remains the same group so long as the same company remains the principal company of the group, and if at any time the principal company of a group becomes a 75 per cent. subsidiary of another company the group of which it was the principal company before that time shall be regarded as the same as the group of which that other company, or one of which it is a 75 per cent. subsidiary, is the principal company, and the question whether or not a company has ceased to be a member of a group shall be determined accordingly.

(4) For the purposes referred to in subsection (1) above the passing of a resolution or the making of an order, or any other act, for the winding-up of a company shall not be regarded as the occasion of that company, or of any 75 per cent. subsidiary of that company, ceasing to be a member of a group of companies."

273. Transfers within a group

(1) Notwithstanding any provision in [the Capital Gains Tax Act 1979][1] fixing the amount of the consideration deemed to be received on a disposal or given on an acquisition, where a member of a group of companies disposes of an asset to another member of the group, both members shall, except as provided by subsections (2) and (3) below, be treated, so far as relates to corporation tax on chargeable gains, as if the asset acquired by the member to whom the disposal is made were acquired for a consideration of such amount as would secure that on the other's disposal neither a gain nor a loss would accrue to that other; but where it is assumed for any purpose that a member of a group of companies has sold or acquired an asset, it shall be assumed also that it was not a sale to or acquisition from another member of the group.

(2) Subsection (1) above shall not apply where the disposal is—

(*a*) a disposal of a debt due from a member of a group of companies effected by satisfying the debt or part of it; or

(*b*) a disposal of redeemable shares in a company on the occasion of their redemption; [or][3]

[(*c*) a disposal by or to an investment trust within the meaning of [section 842 of the Taxes Act 1988][5];][3] [or][4]

[(*d*) a disposal to a dual resident investing company, within the meaning of section [404 of the Taxes Act 1988][5]][4]

and the reference in that subsection to a member of a group of companies disposing of an asset shall not apply to anything which under [section 72 of the Capital Gains Tax Act 1979][2] is to be treated as a disposal of an interest in shares in a company in consideration for a capital distribution (as defined in [that section][2] from that company, whether or not involving a reduction of capital.

[(2A) Subsection (1) above shall not apply to a transaction treated by virtue of sections 78 and 85 of the Capital Gains Tax Act 1979 as not involving a disposal by the company first mentioned in that subsection.][6]

(3) For the purposes of subsection (1) above, so far as the consideration for the disposal consists of money or money's worth by way of compensation for any kind of damage or injury to assets, or for the destruction or dissipation of assets or for anything which depreciates or might depreciate an asset, the disposal shall be treated as being to the person who, whether as an insurer or otherwise, ultimately bears the burden of furnishing that consideration.

Cross references.—See FA 1973, s. 38 (5) (application of this section to companies disposing of exploration or exploitation rights);
CGTA 1979, s. 16 (2) (chargeable gains accruing to non-resident group of companies),
s. 26 (1A) (a), (6) (c), (7) (b) (anti-avoidance of capital gains tax; value-shifting disposals),
s. 26A (6) (a), (7) (a) (value shifting: reductions attributable to distributions within a group),
s. 26B (1) (value shifting: disposals within a group followed by a disposal of shares),
s. 35 (5) (c) (computation of capital gains: apportionment of deductible expenditure on a part disposal),
s. 75 (4) (anti-avoidance of capital gains tax; transfer of assets at undervalue),
s. 87 (4) (b) (chargeable person failing to pay capital gains tax; liability of other persons to pay it),
s. 107 (1) (b) (small part disposals),
s. 126C (4) (capital gains tax relief under CGTA 1979, s. 126 in respect of a disposal of an asset to a company controlled by the trustees of a settlement not resident in UK before the disposal),
Sch. 5, para. 4 (3) (b) (quoted securities held on 6.4.65; election for pooling);
FA 1983, Sch. 6, para. 9 (disposal of securities under this section; treatment of indexation allowance where the transferee company has elected for pooling under the new pooling provisions for securities disposed of after 31 March 1982);
FA 1984, s. 44 (1), (4) (for the purposes of this section, a trustee savings bank is deemed to be a body corporate with effect from 21 November 1982),
Sch. 13, para. 10 (2) (c) (treatment of deemed gain or loss in relation to transactions within this section involving qualifying corporate bonds);
FA 1985, s. 68 (7) (modification of indexation allowance with respect to disposals of assets after 31 March or 5 April 1985),
s. 71 (6), (7) (modification of no gain/no loss provisions of this section where after 19 March 1985 assets are disposed of by way of gift or otherwise by a member of a group to a person connected with another member of the group);
TA 1988, s. 245B (1) (c) (restriction on set-off of ACT where asset transferred after change in ownership of company);
FA 1988, Sch. 8, paras. 1, 2 (capital gains: re-basing to 1982 of assets held on 31 March 1982);
Sch. 11, para. 5 (capital gains indexation: groups and associated companies).
Amendments.—[1] Words in sub-s. (1) substituted by CGTA 1979, s. 157 (2)–(4) and Sch. 7, para. 8 Table, Pt. I. 2, with effect from 22 March 1979.
[2] Words in sub-s. (2) substituted by CGTA 1979, s. 157 (2)–(4) and Sch. 7, para. 9 Table, with effect from 22 March 1979.
[3] Sub-s. (2) (c) and the word "or" preceding it inserted by FA 1980, s. 81 (4).
[4] Sub-s. (2) (d) and the word "or" preceding it inserted by F (No. 2) A 1987, s. 64 (3).
[5] Words in sub-s. (2) (c), (d) substituted by TA 1988, Sch. 29, para. 32 Table.
[6] Sub-s. (2A) inserted by FA 1988, s. 115 and apply to transactions after 14 March 1988.

274. Transfers within a group: trading stock

(1) Where a member of a group of companies acquires an asset as trading stock from another member of the group, and the asset did not form part of the trading stock of any trade carried on by the other member, the member acquiring it shall be treated for purposes of [section 122 of the Capital Gains Tax Act 1979][1] as having acquired the asset otherwise than as trading stock and immediately appropriated it for the purposes of the trade as trading stock.

(2) Where a member of a group of companies disposes of an asset to another member of the group, and the asset formed part of the trading stock of a trade carried on by the member disposing of it but is acquired by the other member otherwise than as trading stock of a trade carried on by it, the member disposing of the asset shall be treated for purposes of [section 122 of the Capital Gains Tax Act 1979][1] as having immediately before the disposal appropriated the asset for some purpose other than the purpose of use as trading stock.

Cross references.—See FA 1973, s. 38 (5) (application of this section to companies disposing of exploration or exploitation rights);
CGTA 1979, s. 16 (2) (chargeable gains accruing to non-resident group of companies);
FA 1984, s. 44 (1), (4) (for the purposes of this section, a trustee savings bank is deemed to be a body corporate with effect from 21 November 1982).
Amendments.—[1] Words in sub-ss. (3) and (2) substituted by CGTA 1979, s. 157 (2)–(4) and Sch. 7, para. 9 Table, with effect from 22 March 1979.

275. Disposal or acquisition outside a group

(1) Where a company which is or has been a member of a group of companies disposes of an asset which it acquired from another member of the group at a time when both were members of the group, [section 34 of the Capital Gains Tax Act 1979][1] (restriction of losses by reference to capital allowances) shall apply in relation to any capital allowances made to the other member (so far as not taken into account in relation to a disposal of the asset by that other member), and so on as respects previous transfers of the asset between members of the group (but this shall not be taken as affecting the consideration for which an asset is deemed under section 273 (1) above to be acquired).

(2) [Schedule 5 to the Capital Gains Tax Act 1979][1] (assets acquired before 6th April 1965) shall apply in relation to a disposal of an asset by a company which is or has been a member of a group of companies, and which acquired the asset from another member of the group at a time when both were members of the group, as if all members of the group for the time

being were the same person, and as if the acquisition or provision of the asset by the group, so taken as a single person, had been the acquisition or provision of it by the member disposing of it.

[(3) Subsection (2) above does not apply where the asset was acquired on a disposal within section 273 (2) (c) above.][2]

Cross references.—See FA 1973, s. 38 (5) (application of this section to companies disposing of exploration or exploitation rights);
CGTA 1979, s. 16 (2) (chargeable gains accruing to non-resident group of companies);
FA 1984, s. 44 (1), (4) (for the purposes of this section, a trustee savings bank is deemed to be a body corporate with effect from 21 November 1982).
Amendments.—[1] Words in sub-ss. (1) and (2) substituted by CGTA 1979, s. 157 (2)–(4) and Sch. 7, para. 9 Table, with effect from 22 March 1979.
[2] Sub-s. (3) inserted by FA 1980, s. 81 (5).

276. Replacement of business assets by members of a group

(1) [Subject to subsection (1A) below][2] for the purposes of [section 115 to 121 of the Capital Gains Tax Act 1979][1] (replacement of business assets) all the trades carried on by members of a group of companies shall be treated as a single trade (unless it is a case of one member of the group acquiring, or acquiring the interest in, the new assets from another or disposing of, or of the interest in, the old assets to another).

[(1A) Subsection (1) above does not apply where so much of the consideration for the disposal of the old assets as is applied in acquiring the new assets or the interest in them is so applied by a member of the group which is a dual resident investing company; and in this subsection—

(a) "the old assets" and "the new assets" have the same meaning as in section 115 of the Capital Gains Tax Act 1979; and

(b) "dual resident investing company" has the same meaning as in section [404 of the Taxes Act 1988][4].][3]

(2) [Section 117 (2) of the Capital Gains Tax Act 1979][1] (special rules for depreciating assets) shall apply where the company making the claim is a member of a group of companies as if all members of the group for the time being were the same person (and, in accordance with subsection (1) above, as if all trades carried on by members were the same trade) and so that the gain shall accrue to the member of the group holding the asset concerned on the occurrence of the event mentioned in the said section 117 (2)][1].

Cross references.—See CGTA 1979, s. 16 (2) (application of sub-s. (1) of this section to non-resident groups of companies);
FA 1984, s. 44 (1), (4) (for the purposes of this section, a trustee savings bank is deemed to be a body corporate with effect from 21 November 1982),
s. 80 (4) (modification of this section in its application to rollover relief for business assets used in connection with oil fields),
Amendments.—[1] Words in sub-ss. (1) and (2) substituted by CGTA 1979, s. 157 (2)–(4) and Sch. 7, para. 9 Table, with effect from 22 March 1979.
[2] Words in sub-s. (1) inserted by F (No. 2) A 1987, s. 64 (4).
[3] Sub-s. (1A) inserted by *ibid*.
[4] Words in sub-s. (1A) (b) substituted by TA 1988, Sch. 29, para. 32 Table.

278. Company ceasing to be member of a group

(1) If a company (in this section called the chargeable company) ceases to be a member of a group of companies, this section shall have effect as respects any asset which the chargeable company acquired from another company which was at the time of acquisition a member of that group of companies, but only if the time of acquisition fell—

(a) on or after 6th April 1965, and

(b) within the period of six years ending with the time when the company ceases to be a member of the group;

and references in this section to a company ceasing to be a member of a group of companies do not apply to cases where a company ceases to be a member of a group by being wound up or dissolved or in consequence of another member of the group being wound up or dissolved.

(2) Where two or more associated companies cease to be members of the group at the same time, subsection (1) above shall not have effect as respects an acquisition by one from another of those associated companies.

(3) If, when the chargeable company ceases to be a member of the group, the chargeable

company, or an associated company also leaving the group, owns, otherwise than as trading stock—

(a) the asset, or
(b) property to which a chargeable gain has been carried forward from the asset on a replacement of business assets,

the chargeable company shall be treated for all the purposes of [the Capital Gains Tax Act 1979][1] as if immediately after its acquisition of the asset it had sold, and immediately reacquired, the asset at market value at that time.

(3A) . . .

[(3B) Where, apart from subsection (3C) below, a company ceasing to be a member of a group by reason only of the fact that the principal company of the group becomes a member of another group would be treated by virtue of subsection (3) above as selling an asset at any time, subsections (3C) to (3E) below shall apply.][3]

[(3C) The company in question shall not be treated as selling the asset at that time; but if—

(a) within six years of that time the company in question ceases at any time ("the relevant time") to satisfy the following conditions, and
(b) at the relevant time, the company in question, or a company in the same group as that company, owns otherwise than as trading stock the asset or property to which a chargeable gain has been carried forward from the asset on a replacement of business assets,

the company in question shall be treated for all the purposes of the Capital Gains Tax Act 1979 as if, immediately after its acquisition of the asset, it had sold and immediately reacquired the asset at the value that, at the time of acquisition, was its market value.][3]

[(3D) Those conditions are—

(a) that the company is a 75 per cent. subsidiary of one or more members of the other group referred to in subsection (3B) above, and
(b) that the company is an effective 51 per cent. subsidiary of one or more of those members.][3]

[(3E) . . .][4]

[(3F) Where—

(a) by virtue of this section a company is treated as having sold an asset at any time, and
(b) if at that time the company had in fact sold the asset at market value at that time, then, by virtue of section 26 of that Act, any allowable loss or chargeable gain accruing on the disposal would have been calculated as if the consideration for the disposal were increased by an amount,

subsections (3) and (3C) above shall have effect as if the market value at that time had been that amount greater.][3]

(4) For the purposes of this section—

(a) two or more companies are associated companies if, by themselves, they would form a group of companies,
(b) a chargeable gain is carried forward from an asset to other property on a replacement of business assets if, by one or more claims under [sections 115 to 121 of the Capital Gains Tax Act 1979][2], the chargeable gain accruing on a disposal of the asset is reduced, and as a result an amount falls to be deducted from the expenditure allowable in computing a gain accruing on the disposal of the other property,
(c) an asset acquired by the chargeable company shall be treated as the same as an asset owned at a later time by that company or an associated company if the value of the second asset is derived in whole or in part from the first asset, and in particular where the second asset is a freehold, and the first asset was a leasehold and the lessee has acquired the reversion.

(5) If any of the corporation tax assessed on a company in consequence of this section is not paid within six months from the date when it becomes payable then—

(a) a company which on the said date, or immediately after the chargeable company ceased to be a member of the group, was the principal company of the group, and
(b) a company which owned the asset on the said date, or when the chargeable company ceased to be a member of the group,

may at any time within two years from the time when the tax became payable, be assessed and charged (in the name of the chargeable company) to all or any part of that tax; and a company paying any amount of tax under this subsection shall be entitled to recover a sum of that amount from the chargeable company.

(6) Notwithstanding any limitation on the time for making assessments, an assessment to corporation tax chargeable in consequence of this section may be made at any time within six years from the time when the chargeable company ceased to be a member of the group, and where under this section the chargeable company is to be treated as having disposed of, and reacquired, an asset, all such recomputations of liability in respect of other disposals, and all such adjustments of tax, whether by way of assessment or by way of discharge or repayment of tax, as may be required in consequence of the provisions of this section shall be carried out.

(7) The provision in subsection (3) above making the assumption that an asset is sold and re-acquired at market value shall, in accordance with paragraph 7 (1) of Schedule 14 to the Finance Act 1967, have effect subject to the provisions of section 33 of that Act (current use value of land in Great Britain).

(8) This section has effect, to the exclusion of the corresponding enactments repealed by this Act, where the chargeable company ceases to be a member of the group in an accounting period ending after 5th April 1970, and not only in respect of tax for such an accounting period but also in respect of tax for accounting periods ending on or before that date.

Note.—See **Prospective Legislation Notes** (Taxes Management Provisions).
Sub-s. (3A) is to be inserted with effect from an appointed day; see F(No 2)A 1987, s. 95 and Sch. 6, para. 4 (2).
Cross references.—See FA 1973, s. 38 (5) (application of this section to companies disposing of exploration or exploitation rights);
CGTA 1979, s. 16 (3) (application of this section to non-resident groups of companies),
s. 26 (1A) (*b*) (value shifting disposals),
s. 26A (7) (*b*) (value shifting: reductions attributable to distributions within a group);
FA 1980, Sch. 18, para. 10 (this section not to apply in a case where a company ceases to be a member of a group by reason only of an exempt distribution under that Schedule);
FA 1984, s. 44 (1), (4) (for the purposes of this section, a trustee savings bank is deemed to be a body corporate with effect from 21 November 1982);
Trustee Savings Banks Act 1985, Sch. 2, para. 4 (2) (this section not to apply as respects any assets transferred at any time by a trustee savings bank to a 75 per cent. subsidiary of the bank's successor),
Sch. 2, para. 4 (2) (this section to apply as if the assets acquired from a trustee savings bank by a 75 per cent. subsidiary of the successor of the bank had been acquired by the subsidiary from the successor where the subsidiary ceases to be a member of a group of companies of which the successor and the new holding company are both members);
Transport Act 1985, s. 130 (4) (this section not to apply in certain circumstances as respects assets of a company formed by a Passenger Transport Executive on its ceasing to be a 75 per cent. subsidiary of the Executive);
TA 1988, s. 214 (1) (time limit for making amendments on chargeable payments under that section);
FA 1988, Sch. 9, para. 3 (reduction of a deferred charge to tax where the charge is wholly or partly attributable to an increase in the value of an asset before 31 March 1982);
Sch. 12, para. 4 (building society's change of status to company: capital gains tax position where the society and the company are not members of the same group or cease to be so).
Amendments.—[1] Words in sub-s. (3) substituted by CGTA 1979, s. 157 (2)–(4) and Sch. 7, para. 8 Table, Pt. I.2, with effect from 22 March 1979.
[2] Words in sub-s. (4) (*b*) substituted by CGTA 1979, s. 157 (2)–(4) and Sch. 7, para. 9 Table, with effect from 22 March 1979.
[3] Sub-ss. (3B), (3C), (3D), (3F) inserted by FA 1989, s. 138 (5) with effect from 14 March 1989, but subject to the provisions of FA 1989, s. 138 (7)–(12).
[4] Sub-s. (3E) to be inserted by FA 1989, s. 138 (5), (7) is to have effect where the accounting period in which the company referred to in sub-s. (3B) above ceases to be a member of a group ends after the day appointed for the purposes of F(No. 2)A 1987, Sch. 6, para. 4.

[278A. Exemption from charge under s. 278 in the case of certain mergers

(1) Subject to the following provisions of this section, section 278 above shall not apply in a case where—

(*a*) as part of a merger, a company (in this section referred to as "company A") ceases to be a member of a group of companies (in this section referred to as "the A group"); and

(*b*) it is shown that the merger was carried out for bona fide commercial reasons and that the avoidance of liability to tax was not the main or one of the main purposes of the merger.

(2) In this section "merger" means an arrangement (which in this section includes a series of arrangements)—

(*a*) whereby one or more companies (in this section referred to as "the acquiring company" or, as the case may be, "the acquiring companies") none of which is a member of the A group acquires or acquire, otherwise than with a view to their disposal, one or more interests in the whole or part of the business which, before the arrangement took effect, was carried on by company A; and

(*b*) whereby one or more members of the A group acquires or acquire, otherwise than with a view to their disposal, one or more interests in the whole or part of the business or each of the businesses which, before the arrangement took effect, was carried on either by the acquiring company or acquiring companies or by a company at least 90 per cent. of the ordinary share capital of which was then beneficially owned by two or more of the acquiring companies; and

(c) in respect of which the conditions in subsection (4) below are fulfilled.

(3) For the purposes of subsection (2) above, a member of a group of companies shall be treated as carrying on as one business the activities of that group.

(4) The conditions referred to in subsection (2) (c) above are—

(a) that not less than 25 per cent. by value of each of the interests acquired as mentioned in paragraphs (a) and (b) of subsection (2) above consists of a holding of ordinary share capital, and the remainder of the interest, or as the case may be of each of the interests, acquired as mentioned in the said paragraph (b) consists of a holding of share capital (of any description) or debentures or both; and
(b) that the value or, as the case may be, the aggregate value of the interest or interests acquired as mentioned in subsection (2) (a) above is substantially the same as the value or, as the case may be, the aggregate value of the interest or interests acquired as mentioned in subsection (2) (b) above; and
(c) that the consideration for the acquisition of the interest or interests acquired by the acquiring company or acquiring companies as mentioned in subsection (2) (a) above, disregarding any part of that consideration which is small by comparison with the total, either consists of, or is applied in the acquisition of, or consists partly of and as to the balance is applied in the acquisition of, the interest or interests acquired by members of the A group as mentioned in subsection (2) (b) above;

and for the purposes of this subsection the value of an interest shall be determined as at the date of its acquisition.

(5) Notwithstanding the provisions of section 272 (1) (a) above, references in this section to a company include references to a company resident outside the United Kingdom][1].

Note.—See **Prospective Legislation Notes** (Taxes Management Provisions).
Cross references.—See FA 1973, s. 38 (5) (application of this section to companies disposing of exploration or exploration rights);
FA 1984, s. 44 (1), (4) (for the purposes of this section, a trustee savings bank is deemed to be a body corporate with effect from 21 November 1982).
Amendments.—[1] This section was inserted by FA 1970, s. 27.

279. Shares in subsidiary member of a group

(1) This section has effect if a company (in this section called "the subsidiary") ceases to be a member of a group of companies, and on an earlier occasion shares in the subsidiary were disposed of by another company (in this section called "the chargeable company") which was then a member of that group in the course of an amalgamation or reconstruction in the group, but only if that earlier occasion fell—

(a) on or after 6th April 1965 [but before 20th April 1977][1], and
(b) within the period of six years ending with the date on which the subsidiary ceases to be a member of the group;

and references in this section to a company ceasing to be a member of a group of companies do not apply to cases where a company ceases to be a member of a group by being wound up or dissolved or in consequence of another member of the group being wound up or dissolved.

(2) The chargeable company shall be treated, for all the purposes of [the Capital Gains Tax Act 1979][2], as if immediately before the earlier occasion it had sold, and immediately reacquired, the said shares at market value at that time.

(3) If, before the subsidiary ceases to be a member of the group, the chargeable company has ceased to exist, or a resolution has been passed, or an order made, for the winding up of the company, or any other act has been done for the like purpose, any corporation tax to which, if the chargeable company had continued in existence, it would have been chargeable in consequence of this section may be assessed and charged (in the name of the chargeable company) on the company which is, at the time when the subsidiary ceases to be a member of the group, the principal company of the group.

(4) If any of the corporation tax assessed on a company in consequence of this section, or in pursuance of subsection (3) above, is not paid within six months from the date when it becomes payable, then—

(*a*) a company which is on the said date, or was on the earlier occasion, the principal company of the group, and

(*b*) any company taking an interest in the subsidiary as part of the amalgamation or reconstruction in the group,

may at any time within two years from the time when the tax became payable, be assessed and charged (in the name of the chargeable company) to all or any part of that tax; and a company paying any amount of tax under this subsection shall be entitled to recover a sum of that amount from the chargeable company, or as the case may be from the company assessed under subsection (3) above.

(5) Notwithstanding any limitation on the time for making assessments, an assessment to corporation tax chargeable in consequence of this section may be made at any time within six years from the time when the subsidiary ceased to be a member of the group and, in relation to any disposal of the property after the earlier occasion, there shall be made all such adjustments of tax, whether by way of assessment or by way of discharge or repayment of tax, as may be required in consequence of the provisions of this section.

(6) For the purposes of this section there is a disposal of shares in the course of an amalgamation or reconstruction in a group of companies if [section 85 or section 86 of the Capital Gains Tax Act 1979][3] (company amalgamations) applies to shares in a company so as to equate them with shares in or debentures of another company, and the companies are members of the same group, or become members of the same group as a result of the amalgamation or reconstruction.

(7) Where by virtue of [section 86 of the Capital Gains Tax Act 1979][3] shares are to be treated as cancelled and replaced by a new issue, references in this section to a disposal of shares include references to the occasion of their being so treated.

(8) This section has effect, to the exclusion of the corresponding enactments repealed by this Act, where the subsidiary ceases to be a member of the group in an accounting period of the chargeable company (or, as the case may be, of the company assessable under subsection (3) above) ending after 5th April 1970, and not only in respect of tax for such an accounting period but also in respect of tax for accounting periods ending on or before that date.

Cross references.—See FA 1973, s. 38 (5) (application of this section to companies disposing of exploration or exploitation rights);
CGTA 1979, s. 16 (3) (application of this section to non-resident groups of companies);
FA 1980, Sch. 18, para. 10 (this section not to apply in a case where a company ceases to be a member of a group by reason only of an exempt distribution under that Schedule);
FA 1984, s. 44 (1), (4) (for the purposes of this section, a trustee savings bank is deemed to be a body corporate with effect from 21 November 1982);
TA 1988, s. 214 (1) (time limit for making amendments on chargeable payments under that section).
Amendments.—[1] Words in sub-s. (1) (*a*) inserted by CGTA 1979, s. 157 (2)–(4) and Sch. 7, para. 2 (4), with effect from 22 March 1979.
[2] Words in sub-s. (2) substituted by CGTA 1979, s. 157 (2)–(4) and Sch. 7, para. 8 Table, Pt. I.2, with effect from 22 March 1979.
[3] Words in sub-ss. (6) and (7) substituted by CGTA 1979, s. 157 (2)–(4) and Sch. 7, para. 9 Table, with effect from 22 March 1979.

Losses attributable to depreciatory transactions

280. Transactions in a group

(1) This section has effect as respects a disposal of shares in, or securities of, a company (in this section referred to as an "ultimate disposal") if the value of the shares or securities has been materially reduced by a depreciatory transaction effected on or after 6th April 1965; and for this purpose "depreciatory transaction" means—

(*a*) any disposal of assets at other than market value by one member of a group of companies to another, or

(*b*) . . .[4] any other transaction satisfying the conditions of subsection (2) below:

Provided that a transaction shall not be treated as a depreciatory transaction to the extent that it consists of a payment which is required to be or has been brought into account, for the purposes of corporation tax on chargeable gains, in computing a chargeable gain or allowable loss accruing to the person making the ultimate disposal

(2) The conditions referred to in subsection (1) (*b*) above are—

(*a*) that the company, the shares in which, or securities of which, are the subject of the ultimate disposal, or any 75 per cent, subsidiary of that company, was a party to the transaction, and

(b) that the parties to the transaction were or included two or more companies which at the time of the transactions were members of the same group of companies.

(3) Without prejudice to the generality of subsection (1) above, the cancellation of any shares in or securities of one member of a group of companies under [section 135 of the Companies Act 1985][3] shall, to the extent that immediately before the cancellation those shares or securities were the property of another member of the group, be taken to be a transaction fulfilling the conditions in subsection (2) above.

(4) If the person making the ultimate disposal is, or has at any time been, a member of the group of companies referred to in subsection (1) or (2) above, any allowable loss accruing on the disposal shall be reduced to such extent as appears to the inspector, or on appeal the Commissioners concerned, to be just and reasonable having regard to the depreciatory transaction:

Provided that if the person making the ultimate disposal is not a member of the said group when he disposes of the shares or securities, no reduction of the loss shall be made by reference to a depreciatory transaction which took place when that person was not a member of the said group.

(5) The inspector or the Commissioners shall make the decision under subsection (4) above on the footing that the allowable loss ought not to reflect any diminution in the value of the company's assets which was attributable to a depreciatory transaction . . .[1], but allowance may be made for any other transaction on or after 6th April 1965 which has enhanced the value of the company's assets and depreciated the value of the assets of any other member of the group.

(6) If, under subsection (4) above, a reduction is made in an allowable loss, any chargeable gain accruing on a disposal of the shares or securities of any other company which was a party to the depreciatory transaction by reference to which the reduction was made, being a disposal not later than six years after the depreciatory transaction, shall be reduced to such extent as appears to the inspector, or on appeal to the Commissioners concerned, to be just and reasonable having regard to the effect of the depreciatory transaction on the value of those shares or securities at the time of their disposal:

Provided that the total amount of any one or more reductions in chargeable gains made by reference to a depreciatory transaction shall not exceed the amount of the reductions in allowable losses made by reference to that depreciatory transaction.

All such adjustments, whether by way of discharge or repayment of tax, or otherwise, as are required to give effect to the provisions of this subsection may be made at any time.

(7) For the purposes of this section—

"securities" includes any loan stock or similar security whether secured or unsecured,
references to the disposal of assets include references to any method by which one company which is a member of a group appropriates the goodwill of another member of the group,
a "group of companies" may consist of companies some or all of which are not resident in the United Kingdom.

(8) References in this section to the disposal of shares or securities include references to the occasion of the making of a claim under [section 22 (2) of the Capital Gains Tax Act 1979][2] that the value of shares or securities had become negligible, and references to a person making a disposal shall be construed accordingly.

Cross references.—See FA 1984, s. 44 (1), (4) (for the purposes of this section, a trustee savings bank is deemed to be a body corporate with effect from 21 November 1982);
FA 1988, Sch. 8, para. 6 (modification of sub-ss. (1), (5) of this section by substitution of "31st March 1982" for "6th April 1965" in relation to disposals after 5 April 1988 of assets held on 31 March 1982).
Amendments.—[1] Words in sub-s. (5) repealed by FA 1974, s. 29 and Sch. 14, Part VI, in relation to any disposal made (within the meaning of this section) after 26 March 1974.
[2] Words in sub-s. (8) substituted by CGTA 1979, s. 157 (2)–(4) and Sch. 7, para. 9 Table, with effect from 22 March 1979.
[3] Words in sub-s. (3) substituted by the Companies Consolidation (Consequential Provisions) Act 1985, Sch. 2 with effect from 1 July 1985.
[4] Words in sub-s. (1) (b) repealed by FA 1988, Sch. 14, Pt. VII in relation to disposals made after 5 April 1988.

281. Dividend stripping

(1) The provisions of this section apply where one company (in this section referred to as "the first company") has a holding in another company (in this section referred to as "the second company") and the following conditions are fulfilled—

(*a*) that the holding amounts to, or is an ingredient in a holding amounting to, 10 per cent. of all holdings of the same class in the second company,
(*b*) that the first company is not a dealing company in relation to the holding,
(*c*) that a distribution is or has been made after 29th April 1969 to the first company in respect of the holding, and
(*d*) that the effect of the distribution is that the value of the holding is or has been materially reduced.

(2) Where this section applies in relation to a holding section 280 above shall apply in relation to any disposal of any shares or securities comprised in the holding, whether the disposal is by the first company or by any other company to which the holding is transferred by a transfer to which section 273 above applies, as if the distribution were a depreciatory transaction and, if the companies concerned are not members of a group of companies, as if they were:

Provided that the distribution shall not be treated as a depreciatory transaction to the extent that it consists of a payment which is required to be or has been brought into account, for the purposes of corporation tax on chargeable gains, in computing a chargeable gain or allowable loss accruing to the person making the ultimate disposal.

(3) This section shall be construed as one with section 280 above.

(4) For the purposes of this section a company is "a dealing company" in relation to a holding if a profit on the sale of the holding would be taken into account in computing the company's trading profits.

(5) References in this section to a holding in a company refer to a holding of shares or securities by virtue of which the holder may receive distributions made by the company, but so that—

(*a*) a company's holdings of different classes in another company shall be treated as separate holdings, and
(*b*) holdings of securities which differ in the entitlements or obligations they confer or impose shall be regarded as holdings of different classes.

(6) For the purposes of subsection (1) above—

(*a*) all a company's holdings of the same class in another company are to be treated as ingredients constituting a single holding, and
(*b*) a company's holding of a particular class shall be treated as an ingredient in a holding amounting to 10 per cent. of all holdings of that class if the aggregate of that holding and other holdings of that class held by connected persons amounts to 10 per cent. of all holdings of that class,

and section [839 of the Taxes Act 1988][1] (definition of connected persons) shall have effect in relation to paragraph (*b*) above as if, in subsection (7) of that section, after the words "or exercise control of" in each place where they occur there were inserted the words "or to acquire a holding in".

Cross references.—See FA 1984, s. 44 (1), (4) (for the purposes of this section, a trustee savings bank is deemed to be a body corporate with effect from 21 November 1982).
Amendments.—[1] Words in sub-s. (6) substituted by TA 1988, Sch. 29, para. 32 Table.

PART XII
SPECIAL CLASSES OF COMPANIES AND BUSINESSES

CHAPTER I
INVESTMENT AND INSURANCE COMPANIES: EXPENSES OF MANAGEMENT AND CAPITAL ALLOWANCES

Cross references.—See TA 1988, s. 592 (4)–(6) (occupational pension schemes).

306. Capital allowances for machinery and plant

(1) Subject to the provisions of this section, Chapter II of Part I of the Capital Allowances Act 1968, and such other provisions of the Corporation Tax Acts as relate to allowances or charges under that Chapter, shall apply with any necessary adaptations in relation to machinery or plant provided for use or used for the purposes of the management of the business—

(*a*) of an investment company (as defined in section [130 of the Taxes Act 1988][1]), or

(*b*) of a company carrying on the business of life assurance,

as they apply in relation to machinery or plant provided for use or used for the purposes of a trade; and, except as provided by subsection (2) below, in relation to any allowances and balancing charges which fall to be made by virtue of this section the Corporation Tax Acts shall apply as if they were to be made in taxing a trade.

(2) As respects allowances or charges falling to be made by virtue of this section in relation to any business—

(*a*) allowances for any accounting period shall, as far as may be, be given effect by deducting the amount of the allowance from any income for the period of the business, and in so far as effect cannot be so given section [75 (4) of the Taxes Act 1988][1] shall apply; and

(*b*) effect shall be given to any charge by treating the amount on which the charge is to be made as income of the business;

and section 46 of the Capital Allowances Act 1968 (manner of making allowances and charges under Chapter II) shall not apply.

(3) No allowance, other than an investment allowance, and no balancing charge shall be made by virtue of this section for any accounting period in respect of expenditure incurred by any person on machinery or plant, except in pursuance of an election made by him for that accounting period; but an election for any chargeable period shall have effect as an election for that and all subsequent chargeable periods.

(4) An election under subsection (3) above shall be made by notice in writing to the inspector either for all machinery or plant provided for use or used for the purposes of the management of the relevant business, or for any class of machinery or plant so provided or used; but an election for machinery or plant of any class shall not be made for any accounting period after an assessment in respect of the business for that or a subsequent accounting period has been finally determined without such an election.

(5) Corresponding allowances or charges in the case of the same machinery or plant shall not be made under Chapter II of Part I of the Capital Allowances Act 1968 (whether for the same chargeable period or for different chargeable periods) both under subsection (2) above and in some other way; and, on any assessment to tax, expenditure to which an election under this section applies shall not be taken into account otherwise than under the said Chapter II (and except as provided by section [75 (4) of the Taxes Act 1988][1]).

(6) In this section references to the purposes of the management of a business are to be taken as referring to those purposes expenditure on which would, apart from this section, be treated as expenses of management within the meaning of section [75 of the Taxes Act 1988][1].

(7) The Tax Acts shall have effect as if this section were contained in Chapter II of Part I of the Capital Allowances Act 1968.

Cross references.—See FA 1971, s. 47 (2) (this section to have effect as if the references therein to CAA 1968, Pt. I, Ch. II, included references to FA 1971, Pt. III, Ch. I (ss. 40–50), and as if the reference in sub-s. (2) thereof to CAA 1968, s. 46, included a reference to FA 1971, s. 48);

TA 1988, s. 75 (4) (management expenses of an investment company to be given effect under TA 1988, s. 75 in so far as effect cannot be given under sub-s. (2) above),

s. 487 (4) (credit unions not to be regarded as investment companies for the purposes of this section).

CHAPTER IV

SAVINGS BANKS, INDUSTRIAL AND PROVIDENT SOCIETIES, BUILDING SOCEITIES AND MUTUAL BUSINESS

342. Disposals of land between the Housing Corporation [or Housing for Wales][3] and housing societies

Where—

(a) in accordance with a scheme approved under section 5 of the Housing Act 1964 [or paragraph 5 of Schedule 7 to the Housing Associations Act 1985][1] the Housing Corporation [or Housing for Wales][3] acquires from a [housing association][2] the [association's][2] interest in all the land held by the [association][2] for carrying out its objects, or

(b) after the Housing Corporation [or Housing for Wales][3] has so acquired from a [housing association][2] all the land so held by it the Corporation disposes to a single [housing association][2] of the whole of that land (except any part previously disposed of or agreed to be disposed of otherwise than to a [housing association][2]), together with all related assets,

then both parties to the disposal of the land to or, as the case may be, by the Housing Corporation [or Housing for Wales][3] shall be treated for the purposes of corporation tax in respect of chargeable gains as if the land and any related assets disposed of therewith (and each part of that land and those assets) were acquired from the party making the disposal for a consideration of such an amount as would secure that on the disposal neither a gain nor a loss accrued to that party.

In this section, "[housing association][2]" has the same meaning as in [the Housing Associations Act 1985][2], and "related assets" means, in relation to an acquisition of land by the Housing Corporation [or Housing for Wales][3], assets required by the Corporation in accordance with the same scheme as that land, and in relation to a disposal of land by the Housing Corporation [or Housing for Wales][3], assets held by the Corporation for the purposes of the same scheme as that land.

Cross references.—See FA 1985, s. 68 (7), (7A) (b) (modification of indexation allowance with respect to disposals of assets after 31 March or 5 April 1985);
FA 1988, Sch. 8, para. 1 (capital gains: re-basing to 1982 of assets held on 31 March 1982).
Amendments.—[1] Words in para. (a) inserted by the Housing (Consequential Provisions) Act 1985, Sch. 2, para. 18 (4).
[2] Words substituted by *ibid*.
[3] Words inserted by the Housing Act 1988, ss. 140 (1), 141 (2) and Sch. 17, para. 93 with effect from 1 December 1988 by virtue of the Housing Act 1988 (Commencement No. 1) Order 1988, S.I. 1988 No. 2056. It seems the same words ought to be inserted after the words "the Corporation" wherever they occur in this section, but there is no such amending provision in the Housing Act 1988.

[342A. Disposals by Housing Corporation [or Housing for Wales][3] and certain housing associations

(1) In any case where—

(a) The Housing Corporation [or Housing for Wales][3] dispose of any land to a registered housing association, or

(b) a registered housing association disposes of any land to another registered housing association, or

(c) in pursuance of a direction of the Housing Corporation [or Housing for Wales][3] given under [Part I of the Housing Associations Act 1985][2] requiring it to do so, a registered housing association disposes of any of its property, other than land, to another registered housing association, or

(d) a registered housing association or an unregistered self-build society disposes of any land to the Housing Corporation [or Housing for Wales][3],

both parties to the disposal shall be treated for the purposes of corporation tax in respect of chargeable gains or, as the case may require, capital gains tax as if the land or property disposed of were acquired from the Housing Corporation [or Housing for Wales][3], registered housing association or unregistered self-build society making the disposal for a consideration of such an amount as would secure that on the disposal neither a gain nor a loss accrued to the Corporation or, as the case may be, that association or society.

(2) In this section "registered housing association" and "unregistered self-build society" have the same meanings as in [the Housing Associations Act 1985]²].¹

Cross references.—See FA 1985, s. 68 (7), (7A) (b) (modification of indexation allowance with respect to disposals of assets after 31 March or 5 April 1985);
FA 1988, Sch. 8, para. 1 (capital gains: re-basing to 1982 of assets held on 31 March 1982).
Amendments.—¹ This section was inserted by the Housing Act 1974, s. 11. It came into operation on 18 September 1974 by virtue of the Housing Act 1974 (Commencement No. 2) Order 1974, S.I. 1974 No. 1562.
² Words in sub-ss. (1), (2) substituted by the Housing (Consequential Provisions) Act 1985, Sch. 2, para. 18 (5).
³ Words inserted by the Housing Act 1988, ss. 140 (1), 141 (2) and Sch. 17, para. 93 with effect from 1 December 1988 by virtue of the Housing Act 1988 (Commencement No. 1) Order 1988, S.I. 1988 No. 2056. It seems the same words ought to be inserted after the words "the Corporation" wherever they occur in this section, but there is no such amending provision in the Housing Act 1988.

[342B. Disposals by Northern Ireland housing associations

(1) In any case where—

(a) a registered Northern Ireland housing association disposes of any land to another such association, or
(b) in pursuance of a direction of the Department of the Environment for Northern Ireland given under Chapter II of Part VII of the Housing (Northern Ireland) Order 1981 requiring it to do so, a registered Northern Ireland housing association disposes of any of its property, other than land, to another such housing association,

both parties to the disposal shall be treated for the purposes of corporation tax in respect of chargeable gains as if the land or property disposed of were acquired from the association making the disposal for a consideration of such an amount as would secure that on the disposal neither a gain nor a loss accrued to that association.

(2) In subsection (1) above "registered Northern Ireland housing association" means a registered housing association within the meaning of Part VII of the Order referred to in paragraph (b) of that subsection.]¹

Cross references.—See FA 1985, s. 68 (7), (7A) (b) (modification of indexation allowance with respect to disposals of assets after 31 March or 5 April 1985);
FA 1988, Sch. 8, para. 1 (capital gains: re-basing to 1982 of assets held on 31 March 1982).
Amendments.—¹ This section inserted by FA 1984, s. 56 (3).

PART XX
GENERAL

536. Commencement

(1) Except as otherwise provided by the following provisions of this section, this Act shall come into force in relation to tax for the year 1970–71 and subsequent years of assessment, and for companies' accounting periods ending after 5th April 1970.

(2) Except as otherwise provided by the following provisions of this section, such of the provisions of this Act as relate to capital gains tax (including the provisions of Part XVIII of this Act as applied to capital gains tax by section 39 of the Finance Act 1965) shall come into force in relation to that tax for the year 1970–71 and subsequent years of assessment.

(3) The following provisions of this Act, that is—

(*a*) so much of any provision of this Act as authorises the making, variation or revocation of any Order in Council or regulation or other instrument,
(*b*) so much of any provision of this Act as relates to the making of a return, the furnishing of a certificate or the giving of any other information, including any such provision which imposes a duty on the Board or an officer of the Board as well as any such provision which imposes a duty on any other person,
(*c*) so much of any provision of this Act as imposes any penalty.
(*d*) except where the tax concerned is all tax for years of assessment before the year 1970–71 or accounting periods ending before 6th April 1970, so much of any other provision of this Act as confers any power or imposes any duty the exercise or performance of which operates or may operate in relation to tax for more than one chargeable period,

shall come into force for all purposes on 6th April 1970 to the exclusion of the corresponding enactments repealed by this Act.

(4) This section has effect except as otherwise provided by any other provision of this Act.

537. Savings, transitory provisions and consequential amendments

(1) Schedule 14 to this Act which contains savings and transitory provisions, shall have effect, and the repeals made by section 538 below have effect subject to that Schedule.

(2) For the avoidance of doubt it is hereby declared that this Act and the Taxes Management Act 1970 have effect subject to those provisions of the Tax Acts and the enactments relating to chargeable gains which are not repealed by this Act, and, with a view to preserving the existing effect of such enactments and instruments as are mentioned in Schedule 15 to this Act, they shall be amended in accordance with that Schedule.

(3) The provisions of the said Schedule 15, and the other provisions of this Part of this Act, are without prejudice to the provisions of the Interpretation Act 1889 as respects the effect of repeals; and section 38 (1) of the Interpretation Act 1889 shall have effect as if the Taxes Management Act 1970 formed part of this Act.

(4) This section and the said Schedules 14 and 15 shall come into force on the passing of this Act.

538. Repeals

(1) The enactments mentioned in Schedule 16 to this Act are hereby repealed to the extent specified in the third column of that Schedule.

(2) Subject to the following provisions of this section, the said repeals shall come into force in accordance with subsections (1) and (2) of section 536 above.

(3) Subsection (2) above has effect subject to section 119 (1) of the Taxes Management Act 1970, to section 536 (3) above and to any other provision of this Act by which any provision is brought into force to the exclusion of the corresponding enactments repealed by this Act.

(4) No provision mentioned in subsection (3) above shall be taken as bringing a repeal into force except to the extent that the repealed enactment is being superseded, and in particular where part of the effect of any repealed enactment is reproduced in this Act, or is not reproduced, nothing in section 119 (1) of the Taxes Management Act 1970 shall be taken as

bringing the repeal into force except so far as the enactment is reproduced in the Taxes Management Act 1970.

(5) In this section "enactments" includes any statutory instrument mentioned in Schedule 16 to this Act, and references in this Act and the Taxes Management Act 1970 to the enactments repealed by this Act shall be construed accordingly.

539. Continuity and construction of references to old and new law

(1) The continuity of the operation of the Tax Acts and of the law relating to chargeable gains shall not be affected by the substitution of this Act and of the Taxes Management Act 1970 (in this section referred to as "the new Acts") for the repealed enactments.

(2) Any reference, whether express or implied, in any enactment, instrument or document (including the new Acts and any enactment amended by Schedule 15 to this Act) to, or to things done or falling to be done under or for the purposes of, any provision of the new Acts shall, if and so far as the nature of the reference permits, be construed as including, in relation to the times, years or periods, circumstances or purposes in relation to which the corresponding provision in the repealed enactments has or had effect, a reference to, or as the case may be to things done or falling to be done under or for the purposes of, that corresponding provision.

(3) Any reference, whether express or implied, in any enactment, instrument or document (including the repealed enactments and enactments, instruments and documents passed or made after the passing of this Act) to, or to things done or falling to be done under or for the purposes of, any of the repealed enactments shall, if and so far as the nature of the reference permits, be construed as including, in relation to the times, years or periods, circumstances or purposes in relation to which the corresponding provision of the new Acts has effect, a reference to, or as the case may be to things done or deemed to be done or falling to be done under or for the purposes of, that corresponding provision.

(4) Any reference to Case VIII of Schedule D, whether a specific reference or one imported by more general words, in any enactment, instrument or document shall, in relation to the chargeable periods to which section 536 (1) above applies, be construed as a reference to Schedule A, and for the purposes of subsection (2) above Schedule A in this Act shall be treated as corresponding to Case VIII of Schedule D in the repealed enactments, and any provision of the new Acts referring to Schedule A shall be construed accordingly.

(5) The repeals made by this Act shall not affect any instrument made or other thing done under the repealed enactments and, if it was made or done under an enactment reproduced in the new Acts, the new Acts shall have effect as if it had also been made or done under the corresponding provision in the new Acts.

(6) In this section "the repealed enactments" means the enactments repealed by this Act, and such of the enactments repealed by the Income Tax Act 1952 or the Capital Allowances Act 1968 as correspond to the provisions of those Acts of 1952 and 1968 so repealed.

540. Short title and construction

(1) This Act may be cited as the Income and Corporation Taxes Act 1970.

(2) This Act, so far as it relates to capital gains tax, shall be construed as one with [the Capital Gains Tax Act 1979][1] [and any reference in this Act to the Taxes Act 1988 is a reference to the Income and Corporation Taxes Act 1988][2].

(3) Any reference in this Act to any other enactment shall, except so far as the context otherwise requires, be construed as a reference to that enactment as amended or applied by or under any other enactment, including this Act.

Amendments.—[1] Words in sub-s. (2) substituted by CGTA 1979, s. 157 (2)–(4) and Sch. 7, para. 8 Table, Pt. I. 2, with effect from 22 March 1979.
[2] Words in sub-s. (2) added by TA 1988, Sch. 29, para. 32 Table.

FINANCE ACT 1970

(1970 Chapter 24)

ARRANGEMENT OF SECTIONS

Note.—Provisions of this Act relevant to the taxes covered by this Handbook and not reproduced are either spent or repealed by TA 1988, Sch. 31 and other legislation.

PART II
INCOME TAX AND CORPORATION TAX

CHAPTER I
GENERAL

Section
15. Increase in initial allowance for industrial buildings.

PART III
MISCELLANEOUS

Mineral royalties

29. Taxation of mineral royalties.

Stamp duties

Sections 32–33. (see Orange Book)

Other provisions

Section
36. Citation, interpretation, construction, extent and repeals.

SCHEDULES:

Schedule 6—Taxation of capital element in mineral royalties.
Schedule 7—*Stamp duties.* (see Orange Book)

An Act to grant certain duties, to alter other duties, and to amend the law relating to the National Debt and the Public Revenue, and to make further provision in connection with Finance.
[29th May 1970]

PART II
INCOME TAX AND CORPORATION TAX

CHAPTER I
GENERAL

15. Increase in initial allowances for industrial buildings

(1) In relation to capital expenditure incurred [in a case falling within subsection (2) below on or after 6th April 1970, and in any other case][1] at any time within the period beginning on 6th April 1970 and ending on 5th April 1972, on the construction of a building or structure in such circumstances that a person becomes entitled to an initial allowance within the meaning of section 1 of the Capital Allowances Act 1968, for the words "three-twentieths" in subsection (2) of that section (the rate of allowance) there shall be substituted—

(a) in a case falling within subsection (2) below, the words "two-fifths"; and
(b) in any other case, the words "three-tenths".

(2) The higher rate of initial allowance specified in subsection (1) (a) above applies if the building or structure concerned is situated in an area which is a development area or an intermediate area—

(a) on the date on which the capital expenditure is incurred; or
(b) if the contract under which the capital expenditure is incurred was entered into on or after 6th April 1970, on the date on which that contract was entered into;

or if the building or structure concerned is situated in Northern Ireland.

(3) [For the purposes of subsection (2) above "development area" and "intermediate area" have the same meaning as in the Local Employment Act 1972.][2]

(4) Expenditure shall not be treated for the purposes of this section as having been incurred after the date on which it was in fact incurred by reason only of section 1 (6) of the Capital Allowances Act 1968 (expenditure incurred before trade began) or section 5 (1) of that Act (purchase of unused buildings and structures).

Cross references.—See FA 1972, s. 67 (2) (sub-s. (1) (b) of this section not to apply to expenditure incurred after 21 March 1972).
Amendments.—[1] Words in sub-s. (1) inserted by FA 1971, s. 51.
[2] Sub-s. (3) substituted by the Local Employment Act 1972, s. 23 (2) and Sch. 3 with effect from 10 March 1972.

PART III
MISCELLANEOUS

Mineral royalties

29. Taxation of mineral royalties

(1)–(4) . . .[1]

(5) The provisions of Part II of Schedule 6 to this Act shall have effect in relation to capital losses which accrue during the currency of a mineral lease or agreement.

(6) In this section and in Schedule 6 to this Act, references to mineral royalties refer only to royalties receivable on or after 6th April 1970, and the expression "mineral royalties" means so much of any rents, tolls, royalties and other periodical payments in the nature of rent payable under a mineral lease or agreement as relates to the winning and working of minerals; [and any other payment or part of a payment which is to be treated as mineral royalties by virtue of regulations made under section 122(5) of the Income and Corporation Taxes Act 1988][1].

(7) In this section and in Schedule 6 to this Act—

"minerals" means all minerals and substances in or under land which are ordinarily worked for removal by underground or surface working, but excluding water, peat, topsoil and vegetation; and
"mineral lease or agreement" means—

(*a*) a lease, profit a prendre, licence or other agreement conferring a right to win and work minerals in the United Kingdom;
(*b*) a contract for the sale, or a conveyance, of minerals in or under land in the United Kingdom; and
(*c*) a grant of a right under section 1 of the Mines (Working Facilities and Support) Act 1966, other than an ancillary right within the meaning of that Act.

(8) . . .[2]

(9) In the application of this section to Northern Ireland—

(*a*) paragraphs (*a*) to (*c*) of subsection (3) above shall not apply but the relevant fraction referred to in subsection (1) (*b*) above shall be one half;
(*b*) references to mineral royalties include references—

(i) to periodical payments of compensation under section 29 or section 35 of the Mineral Development Act (Northern Ireland) 1969 or under section 4 of the Petroleum (Production) Act (Northern Ireland) 1964; and
(ii) to periodical payments made as mentioned in section 37 of the said Act of 1969 or under section 55 (4) (*b*) of that Act or under section 11 of the said Act of 1964 (payments in respect of minerals to persons entitled to a share of royalties under section 13 (3) of the Irish Land Act 1903); and

(*c*) in the application of this section to any such payments as are referred to in paragraph (*b*) above, subsection (5) above shall be omitted, and references in any other provision of this section to the mineral lease or agreement under which mineral royalties are payable shall be construed as references to the enactment under which the payments are made.

Amendments.—[1] Words in sub-s. (6) substituted by TA 1988, Sch. 29, para. 32 Table.
[2] Sub-ss. (1)–(4), (8) repealed (so far as unrepealed by previous enactments) by TA 1988, Sch. 31.

Other provisions

36. Citation, interpretation, construction, extent and repeals

(1) This Act may be cited as the Finance Act 1970.

(2) In this Act—

(*a*) except where the context otherwise requires, "the Board" means the Commissioners of Inland Revenue,
(*b*) "the Taxes Act" means the Income and Corporation Taxes Act 1970,
(*c*) "the Management Act" means the Taxes Management Act 1970.

(3) ...

(4) Part II of this Act, so far as it relates to income tax, shall be construed as one with the Income Tax Acts and, so far as it relates to corporation tax, shall be construed as one with the Corporation Tax Acts.

(5) ...

(6) Any reference in this Act to any other enactment shall, except so far as the context otherwise requires, be construed as a reference to that enactment as amended or applied by or under any other enactment, including this Act.

(7) Except as otherwise expressly provided such of the provisions of this Act as relate to matters in respect of which the Parliament of Northern Ireland has power to make laws shall not extend to Northern Ireland.

(8) ...

Notes.—Sub-ss. (3), (5) are outside the scope of this work.
Sub-s. (8) repeals enactments specified in Sch. 8. Effect has been given to these repeals, where applicable, in the relevant provisions of the earlier enactments.

SCHEDULES

SCHEDULE 6

Section 29

TAXATION OF CAPITAL ELEMENT IN MINERAL ROYALTIES

PART I

CALCULATION OF CAPITAL ELEMENT

1, 2 ...[1]

Amendments.—[1] Repealed by FA 1971, Sch. 14, Pt. III

PART II

TERMINAL LOSS RELIEF

3.—(1) The provisions of this Part of this Schedule apply in a case where, at the time of the occurrence of a relevant event in relation to a mineral lease or agreement, the person who immediately before that event occurred was entitled to receive mineral royalties under the lease or agreement (in this Part of this Schedule referred to as "the taxpayer") has an interest in the land to which the mineral lease or agreement relates (in this Part of this Schedule referred to, in relation to the lease or agreement, as "the relevant interest").

(2) For the purposes of this Part of this Schedule a relevant event occurs in relation to a mineral lease or agreement—

(*a*) on the expiry or termination of the mineral lease or agreement;
(*b*) if the relevant interest is disposed of, or is treated as having been disposed of by virtue of any provision of [the Capital Gains Tax Act 1979][1].

Amendments.—[1] Words in sub-para. (2) (*b*) substituted by CGTA 1979, s. 157 (2)–(4) and Sch. 7, para. 8 Table, Pt. II. 4, with effect from 22 March 1979.

4.—(1) Subject to sub-paragraph (2) below, on the expiry or termination of a mineral lease or agreement the taxpayer shall, if he makes a claim in that behalf, be treated for purposes of capital gains tax, or as the case may be corporation tax on chargeable gains, as if he had disposed of and immediately re-acquired the relevant interest for a consideration equal to its market value ...[1].

(2) A claim may not be made under this paragraph—

(*a*) if the expiry or termination of the mineral lease or agreement is also a relevant event falling within paragraph 3 (2) (*b*) above; nor
(*b*) unless, on the notional disposal referred to in sub-paragraph (1) above, an allowable loss would accrue to the taxpayer.

(3) In the following provisions of this Part of this Schedule "the terminal loss", in relation to a relevant event in respect of which a claim is made under this paragraph, means the allowable loss which accrues to the taxpayer by virtue of the notional disposal occurring on that relevant event by virtue of sub-paragraph (1) above.

Amendments.—[1] Words in para. 4 (1) repealed by FA 1971, Sch. 14, Pt. III.

5.—(1) On making a claim under paragraph 4 above, the taxpayer shall specify whether he requires the terminal loss to be dealt with in accordance with this paragraph or with paragraph 7 below.

(2) Where the taxpayer requires the loss to be dealt with in accordance with this paragraph

it shall be treated as an allowable loss accruing to him in the year of assessment or accounting period in which the mineral lease or agreement expires.

6.—(1) If on the occurrence of a relevant event falling within paragraph 3 (2) (*b*) above, an allowable loss accrues to the taxpayer on the disposal or notional disposal which constitutes that relevant event, the taxpayer may make a claim under this paragraph requiring the loss to be dealt with in accordance with paragraph 7 below and not in any other way.

(2) In the following provisions of this part of this Schedule "the terminal loss" in relation to a relevant event in respect of which a claim is made under this paragraph means the allowable loss which accrues to the taxpayer as mentioned in sub-paragraph (1) above.

7.—(1) Where, as a result of a claim under paragraph 4 or paragraph 6 above, the terminal loss is to be dealt with in accordance with this paragraph, then, subject to sub-paragraph (2) below, it shall be deducted from or set off against the amount on which the taxpayer was chargeable to capital gains tax, or as the case may be corporation tax, for years of assessment or accounting periods preceding the year of assessment or accounting period in which occurred the relevant event giving rise to the terminal loss and falling wholly or partly within the period of fifteen years ending with the date of that event.

(2) The amount of the terminal loss which, by virtue of sub-paragraph (1) above, is to be deducted from or set off against the amount on which the taxpayer was chargeable to capital gains tax, or as the case may be corporation tax, for any year of assessment or accounting period shall not exceed the amount of the gain which in that year or period was treated, by virtue of subsection (1) (*b*) of section [122 of the Income and Corporation Taxes Act 1988][1], as accruing to the taxpayer in respect of mineral royalties under the mineral lease or agreement in question; and subject to this limit any relief given to the taxpayer by virtue of sub-paragraph (1) above shall be given as far as possible for a later rather than an earlier year of assessment or accounting period.

(3) If in any case where relief has been given to the taxpayer in accordance with sub-paragraphs (1) and (2) above there remains an unexpended balance of the terminal loss which cannot be applied in accordance with those sub-paragraphs, there shall be treated as accruing to the taxpayer in the year of assessment or accounting period in which the relevant event occurs an allowable loss equal to that unexpended balance.

Amendments.—[1] Words in sub-para. (2) substituted by TA 1988, Sch. 29, para. 32 Table.

8.—(1) No claim under paragraph 4 or paragraph 6 above shall be allowed unless it is made within six years from the date of the relevant event by virtue of which the taxpayer is entitled to make the claim.

(2) All such repayments of tax shall be made as may be necessary to give effect to any such claim.

9. This Part of this Schedule shall be construed as one with [the Capital Gains Tax Act 1979][1].

Amendments.—[1] Words substituted by CGTA 1979, s. 157 (2)–(4) and Sch. 7, para. 8 Table, Pt. I. 3, with effect from 22 March 1979.

FINANCE ACT 1971

(1971 Chapter 68)

ARRANGEMENT OF SECTIONS

Note.—Provisions of this Act relevant to the taxes covered in this Handbook and not reproduced are either spent or repealed by TA 1988, Sch. 31 and other legislation.

PART II

INCOME TAX AND CORPORATION TAX

CHAPTER I

GENERAL

Section
21. Occupational pension schemes.

PART III

INCOME TAX AND CORPORATION TAX: CAPITAL ALLOWANCES

CHAPTER I

NEW SYSTEM OF ALLOWANCES AND CHARGES IN RESPECT OF TRADE (ETC.) MACHINERY AND PLANT

Introductory

40. Application of new system.

First-year allowances, writing-down allowances and balancing adjustments

41. First-year allowances—general rules.
42. First-year allowances—rates.
43. First-year allowances—exclusion of certain road vehicles.
44. Writing-down allowances and balancing adjustments

Application to machinery and plant on hire-purchase etc. or lease, and to activities other than trades

45. Machinery and plant on hire-purchase etc.
46. Machinery and plant on lease.
47. Application to activities other than trades.

Supplementary

48. Manner of making allowances and charges.
49. Minor rules, and consequential amendments.
50. Interpretation etc.

226

Section

CHAPTER II

OTHER PROVISIONS

51. Initial allowances for industrial buildings—continuance of increased rate for development and intermediate areas and Northern Ireland.
52. Initial allowances for mining etc. works—increased rate for development areas and Northern Ireland, and right of disclaimer.

PART V

MISCELLANEOUS

69. Citation, interpretation, construction, extent and repeals.

SCHEDULES:

Schedule 3—Occupational pension schemes.
     Part II—Taxation of Refunds of Contributions and Certain Other Payments.

An Act to grant certain duties, to alter other duties, and to amend the law relating to the National Debt and the Public Revenue, and to make further provision in connection with Finance.

[5th August 1971]

PART II
INCOME TAX AND CORPORATION TAX

CHAPTER I
GENERAL

21. Occupational pension schemes

(1)–(5) . . .[2]

[(6) Part II of Schedule 3 to this Act shall have effect.][1]

Amendments.—[1] Sub-s. (6) substituted by TA 1988, Sch. 29, para. 32 Table.
[2] Sub-ss. (1)–(5) repealed by TA 1988, Sch. 31.

PART III

INCOME TAX AND CORPORATION TAX: CAPITAL ALLOWANCES

Cross references.—See Trustee Savings Banks Act 1985, Sch. 2, para. 1 (1) (for the purposes of this Part, the transfer of a trustee savings bank's business to a company not to be treated as discontinuation of an existing trade and setting up of a new trade).

CHAPTER I

NEW SYSTEM OF ALLOWANCES AND CHARGES IN RESPECT OF TRADE (ETC.) MACHINERY AND PLANT

Construction.—FA 1972, s. 68, to be construed as if contained in this Chapter; see FA 1972, s. 68 (1), (10).
FA 1974, s. 17, to be construed as if contained in this Chapter; see FA 1974, s. 17 (2).
FA 1975, s. 14, to be construed as if contained in this Chapter; see FA 1975, s. 14 (4).
FA 1975, s. 15, to be construed as if contained in this Chapter; see FA 1975, s. 15 (3).
F (No. 2) A 1975, s. 49, to be construed as if contained in this Chapter; see F (No. 2) A 1975, s. 49 (3).
FA 1976, s. 39, to be construed as if contained in this Chapter; see FA 1976, s. 39 (7).
The Tax Acts to have effect as if FA 1978, s. 40 were contained in this Chapter; see FA 1978, s. 40 (6).
The Tax Acts to have effect as if FA 1980, ss. 60–66 and Sch. 12 (capital allowances on machinery and plant for leasing) were contained in this Chapter, subject to certain exceptions; see FA 1980, s. 67 (1).
FA 1982, s. 72, to be construed as if comprised in this Chapter; see FA 1982, s. 72 (10).
FA 1984, s. 59 (2)–(7) to be construed as if contained in this Chapter; see FA 1984, s 59 (8).
FA 1984, Sch. 12, paras. 2 and 6 to be construed as if contained in this Chapter with exception in relation to the application of s. 50 (4) below; see FA 1984, Sch. 12, paras. 2 (4), 6 (7).
FA 1985, s. 59 and Sch. 17 to be construed as if contained in this chapter with exception in relation to the application of s. 50 (4) below; see FA 1985, s. 59 (7).
The Tax Acts to have effect as if TA 1988, s. 32 were contained in this Chapter; see TA 1988, s. 32 (8).
TA 1988, Sch. 24, para. 10 to be construed as one with this Chapter; see TA 1988, Sch. 24, para. 10 (2).
FA 1989, s. 119 to be construed as if contained in this Chapter; see FA 1989, s. 119 (3).
Cross references.—FA 1974, s. 17 (1) (expenditure on fire safety treated as if it were capital expenditure on machinery or plant for the purposes of trade);
FA 1975, s. 14 (1) (expenditure incurred after 12 November 1974 on thermal insulation of industrial buildings or structures treated as if it were capital expenditure on machinery or plant for the purposes of trade);
s. 15 (expenditure incurred on or after relevant date (as defined) on fire safety treated as if it were capital expenditure on machinery or plant for the purposes of trade);
F (No. 2) A 1975, s. 49 (1), (3) (expenditure on safety at sports grounds incurred after 31 July 1975 treated as if it were capital expenditure on machinery or plant for the purposes of trade);
CGTA 1979, s. 34 (4) (*a*), (7) (restriction of capital losses by reference to capital and renewals allowances);
FA 1980, ss. 64–72 and Sch. 12 (capital allowances on machinery and plant for leasing),
s. 71 (quarantine premises);
FA 1982, s. 72 (1) (*b*) (capital expenditure on production and acquisition of films, tapes or discs to be regarded, subject to certain exceptions, as revenue expenditure);
s. 78 (2) (acquisition of machinery or plant for use in connection with an oil field; disregard of certain expenditure for the purposes of capital allowances under this Chapter),
Sch. 12, paras. 6, 8, 9 (spreading of capital expenditure incurred under certain contracts entered into after 13 March 1984),
FA 1985, s. 56 (1) (*b*), (6), (8) (new rules as regards the determination of the date when capital expenditure is to be taken to be incurred with respect to any chargeable period or its basis period ending after 17 December 1984, subject to the provision that if under any provision of this Chapter the date would fall to be later than that determined under the new rules, the later date is to be treated as the date of the expenditure),
s. 59 (1), (2) (FA 1985, Sch. 17 to apply to determine entitlement to an allowance under this Chapter in respect of expenditure incurred after 11 July 1984 (subject to exception for expenditure in relation to contracts or leases entered into on or before that date) for machinery and plant which are fixtures);
FA 1986, s. 55 (5), (6), (8) (where a person incurs new expenditure (i.e. subject to FA 1986, Sch. 14, expenditure incurred after 31 March 1986) on machinery or plant for mineral exploration before commencing trade of mineral extraction, that expenditure is, subject to certain conditions, treated as expenditure incurred for the purposes of his trade).
s. 57 (2) (expenditure on the provision of machinery or plant for leasing deemed under this Chapter to have been incurred after 31 March 1986 to fall under the new code in FA 1986 instead of under this Chapter);
TA 1988, s. 32 (capital allowances for machinery and plant used in estate management or in the management of the business of an investment company or life assurance company),
s. 198 (2) (emoluments not falling within Schedule E, Case I or II treated as not belonging to the office or employment),
s. 198 (4) (allowances under this Chapter cannot be claimed by Members of Parliament in respect of expenditure for temporary accommodation),
s. 359 (3) (*a*) (interest on loans to purchase machinery or plant used in an office or employment),
s. 384 (6) (restrictions on right of set-off to capital allowances made to an individual under this Chapter in respect of expenditure incurred on the provision of machinery or plant for leasing),
s. 393 (4) (loss other than terminal loss incurred by a company in an accounting period for which first-year allowances fall to be made under this Chapter),
s. 495 (effect of regional development grant paid in respect of expenditure incurred in connection with oil exploration, extraction, etc.),
s. 503 (treatment of the commercial letting of furnished holiday accommodation for the purposes of this Chapter),
s. 577 (1) (*c*) (use of asset for providing business entertainment to be treated for capital allowances purposes as use otherwise than for the purposes of a trade),

Sch. 24, para. 10 (1) (relief for capital expenditure on machinery and plant incurred before the introduction of tax liability of UK controlled foreign companies);
FA 1989, s. 117 (application of this Chapter in respect of expenditure for personal physical security),
s. 119 (application of this Chapter in respect of expenditure on improving safety of stands at sports grounds).

Introductory

40. Application of new system

(1) Subject to subsections (2) and (3) below, this Chapter applies to capital expenditure on the provision of machinery or plant incurred on or after 27th October 1970; and, in the case of expenditure to which this Chapter applies, no allowances or charges shall be made under Chapter II of Part I of the Capital Allowances Act 1968.

(2) This Chapter shall not apply to capital expenditure incurred by any person on the provision of second-hand machinery or plant if capital expenditure on providing the machinery or plant was incurred by another person before the said 27th October and—

(*a*) he and that other person are connected with each other within the terms of section [839][1] of the Taxes Act, or
(*b*) it appears with respect to the transaction under which the first-mentioned expenditure is incurred, or with respect to the transactions of which it is one, that the sole or main benefit which, but for this subsection, might have been expected to accrue to the parties or any of them was the obtaining of an allowance under this Chapter.

(3) Where any capital expenditure is incurred before the said 27th October on the provision of machinery or plant under a contract which provides that a person shall or may become the owner of the machinery or plant on the performance of the contract, this Chapter shall not apply to any capital expenditure incurred under the contract in respect of that machinery or plant unless it is first brought into use by that person on or after that date.

Cross references.—See FA 1976, s. 39 (the system of capital allowances introduced by this Act to include certain expenditure otherwise excluded from that system by this section);
FA 1980, ss. 64–72 and Sch. 12 (capital allowances on machinery and plant for leasing).
Amendments.—[1] Number in sub-s. (2) (*a*) substituted by TA 1988, Sch. 29, para. 32 Table.

First-year allowances, writing-down allowances and balancing adjustments

41. First-year allowances—general rules

(1) Subject to the provisions of this Chapter, where—

(*a*) a person carrying on a trade incurs capital expenditure on the provision of machinery or plant [wholly and exclusively][1] for the purposes of the trade, and
(*b*) in consequence of his incurring the expenditure, the machinery or plant belongs to him at some time during the chargeable period related to the incurring of the expenditure,

there shall be made to him for that period an allowance (in this Chapter referred to as "a first-year allowance") which shall be of an amount determined in accordance with section 42 below:

Provided that no first-year allowance shall be made in respect of any expenditure if the chargeable period related to the incurring of the expenditure is also the chargeable period related to the permanent discontinuance of the trade.

(2) . . .[2]

(3) Where one or more first-year allowances fall to be made for any chargeable period in connection with a trade carried on by a company, the company may, by notice in writing given to the inspector not later than two years after the end of that period, either disclaim the allowance or allowances or require that the amount, or aggregate amount, thereof be reduced to an amount specified in that behalf in the notice; and a claim for one or more first-year allowances to be made for any chargeable period in connection with a trade carried on by a person other than a company may contain a similar requirement as to the amount or aggregate amount thereof:

Provided that this subsection shall not apply to allowances in respect of expenditure on the provision of new ships.

(4) All such assessments and adjustments of assessments shall be made as may be necessary to give effect to subsection (2) or (3) above.

Cross references.—See FA 1978, s. 40 (3) (disclaimer or claims under sub-s. (3) of this section in respect of relief available under that section);
FA 1984, s. 58 (1) (*b*) (progressive withdrawal of first-year allowances under this section),
s. 59 (4) (*c*) (capital expenditure incurred after 13 March 1984; effect of a disclaimer under sub-s. (3) above for the purposes of s. 44 of this Act),
s. 59 (6) (*c*) (capital expenditure incurred after 13 March 1984; effect of a reduction of allowances under sub-s. (3) above for the purposes of s. 44 of this Act),
s. 78 (2) (*b*) (acquisition of machinery or plant to which sub-s. (2) above applies for use in oil fields; first-year allowances under this section to be based on the expenditure incurred by the person disposing it);
FA 1985, s. 58 (3), FA 1989, Sch. 13, para. 15 (2) (no disclaimer or claim under sub-s. (3) above may be made after 26 July 1989 in respect of ships which are not new);
TA 1988, s. 393 (4) (loss other than terminal loss incurred by a company in an accounting period for which first-year allowances fall to be made).
Amendments.—[1] Words in sub-s. (1) (*a*) inserted by FA 1985, s. 55 (1) with respect to capital expenditure incurred after 31 March 1985.
[2] Sub-s. (2) repealed by FA 1985, s. 55 (2) (*a*) and Sch. 27, Pt. VI with respect to any chargeable period or its basis period ending after 31 March 1985.

42. First-year allowances—rates

(1) ...[1], *a first-year allowance shall be of an amount equal to [...]*[3] *of the expenditure in respect of which it is made.*

(2)–(6) ...[2]

Amendments.—[1] Words in sub-s. (1) repealed by FA 1972, Sch. 28, Pt. XII, in relation to expenditure incurred after 21 March 1972.
[2] Sub-ss. (2)–(6) repealed by FA 1972, s. 67 (2) (*a*) and Sch. 28, Pt. XII, in relation to expenditure incurred after 21 March 1972.
[3] The first-year allowance is abolished in respect of capital expenditure incurred after 31 March 1986; see FA 1984, Sch. 12, para. 2 (1).
The fraction in sub-s. (1) is "one half" with respect to expenditure incurred after 31 March 1985 and before 1 April 1986. It is "three-quarters" for expenditure incurred after 13 March 1984 and before 1 April 1985, and for expenditure before 14 March 1984 the allowance equals the whole of the expenditure. The allowance also equals the whole of the expenditure where it is incurred under certain contracts entered into before 14 March 1984 and where it is incurred on certain projects in development areas where a written offer of financial assistance, on the Northern Ireland equivalent, was made between 1 April 1980 and 13 March 1984 (both dates inclusive); see FA 1984, Sch. 12, paras. 2, 4.
For the spreading of expenditure incurred under certain contracts entered into after 13 March 1984, see FA 1984, Sch. 12, paras. 6, 8, 9.

43. First-year allowances—exclusion of certain road vehicles

[(1)] First-year allowances shall not be made in respect of capital expenditure on the provision of mechanically-propelled road vehicles, except—

(*a*) vehicles of a construction primarily suited for the conveyance of goods or burden of any description,
(*b*) vehicles of a type not commonly used as private vehicles and unsuitable to be so used, and
(*c*) [subject to subsection (2) below,][1] vehicles provided wholly or mainly for hire to, or for the carriage of, members of the public in the ordinary course of a trade.

[(2) Subsection (1) (*c*) above applies to a vehicle only if—

(*a*) the following conditions are satisfied—

(i) the number of consecutive days for which it is on hire to, or used for the carriage of, the same person will normally be less than thirty; and
(ii) the total number of days for which it is on hire to, or used for the carriage of, the same person in any period of twelve months will normally be less than ninety; or

(*b*) it is provided for hire to a person who will himself use it wholly or mainly for hire to, or the carriage of, members of the public in the ordinary course of a trade and in a manner complying with the conditions specified in paragraph (*a*) above.][1]

[(3) For the purposes of subsection (2) above persons who are connected with each other within the meaning of section [839][3] of the Taxes Act shall be treated as the same person; and that subsection does not affect vehicles provided wholly or mainly for the use of persons in receipt of—

(*a*) a mobility allowance under the Social Security Act 1975 or the Social Security (Northern Ireland) Act 1975][1]
[(*b*) a mobility supplement under a scheme made under the Personal Injuries (Emergency Provisions) Act 1939; or

(c) a mobility supplement under an Order in Council made under section 12 of the Social Security (Miscellaneous Provisions) Act 1977; or
(d) any payment appearing to the Treasury to be of a similar kind and specified by them by order made by statutory instrument.

An order made under paragraph (d) above may provide that it has effect in relation to expenditure incurred on or after 21st November 1983 (expenditure being taken to be incurred for this purpose on the date when the sums in question become payable).][2]

Note.—This section as originally enacted did not have subsections. The original provisions became sub-s. (1) by F (No. 2) A 1979, s. 14 (2).
Cross references.—See F (No. 2) A 1979, s. 14 (7), (8) (this section as amended by F (No. 2) A 1979, s. 14 to apply to expenditure incurred after 12 June 1979, with transitional provisions expiring on 12 June 1980 for expenditure after 12 June 1979 on contracts entered into on or before 12 June 1979);
FA 1985, s. 57 (10) and Sch. 15, para 2. (election to treat as short-life assets cannot be made in respect of vehicles precluded from first-year allowance under this section).
Amendments.—[1] Words in sub-s. (1) (c) inserted and sub-ss. (2), (3) inserted by F (No. 2) A 1979, s. 14 (2), (3), (7), (8), where the contract for the purchase of a vehicle was entered into after 12 June 1979.
[2] Sub-s. (3) (b)–(d) and the words following para. (d) added by virtue of FA 1984, s. 61 in relation to supplements, etc. becoming payable after 20 November 1983.
[3] Number in sub-s. (3) substituted by TA 1988, Sch. 29, para. 32 Table.

44. Writing-down allowances and balancing adjustments

(1) Subject to the provisions of this Chapter, where—

(a) a person carrying on a trade has incurred capital expenditure on the provision of machinery or plant [wholly and exclusively][4] for the purposes of the trade, and
(b) in consequence of his incurring the expenditure, the machinery or plant belongs, or has belonged, to him, . . .[5]
(c) . . .[5]

allowances and charges shall be made to and on him in accordance with the following provisions of this section.

(2) For any chargeable period for which a person within subsection (1) above has qualifying expenditure as defined in subsection (4) below which exceeds any disposal value to be brought into account by him in accordance with subsection (5) below, there shall be made to him—

(a) unless the period is the chargeable period related to the permanent discontinuance of the trade, an allowance (in this Chapter referred to as "a writing-down allowance") of an amount equal to—
  (i) 25 per cent. of the excess, or
  (ii) a proportionately reduced percentage of the excess if the period is part only of a year, or if the period is a year of assessment but the trade has been carried on for part only thereof;
(b) if the period is the chargeable period related to the permanent discontinuance of the trade, an allowance (in this Chapter referred to as "a balancing allowance") equal to the whole of the excess:

Provided that a claim for a writing-down allowance to be made for any chargeable period in connection with a trade carried on by a person other than a company may require that the amount of the allowance be reduced to an amount specified in that behalf in the claim.

[(2A) For any chargeable period ending after 13th March 1984 for which a company has qualifying expenditure, the company may, by notice in writing given to the inspector not later than two years after the end of that period, either disclaim a writing-down allowance or require that the allowance be reduced to an amount specified in that behalf in the notice [and all such assessments and adjustments of assessments shall be made as may be necessary to give effect to this subsection][6].][3]

(3) For any chargeable period for which a person's qualifying expenditure is less than the disposal value which he is to bring into account, there shall be made on him a charge (in this Chapter referred to as "a balancing charge"), and the amount on which the charge is made shall be an amount equal to the difference.

(4) For the purposes of subsections (2) [(2A)][3] and (3) above, a person's qualifying expenditure for a chargeable period is the aggregate of the following amounts—

(a) the balance remaining after deducting any first-year allowances made in respect thereof of any capital expenditure incurred by him on the provision for the purposes of

the trade of machinery or plant [being expenditure incurred in the chargeable period in question or its basis period or at any previous time, and]⁷ not being—
  (i) expenditure which, or any part of which, has formed part of his qualifying expenditure for any previous chargeable period, or
  (ii) expenditure in respect of which a first-year allowance is or could (assuming a claim therefor in the case of a person other than a company, and disregarding any notice of disclaimer in the case of a company) be made for the chargeable period in question; and
(b) if for the chargeable period immediately preceding the chargeable period in question there was an excess of qualifying expenditure over disposal value, the balance of that excess after deducting any writing-down allowance made by reference thereto.

(5) For the purposes of subsections (2) and (3) above, the disposal value to be brought into account by a person for any chargeable period is the disposal value (calculated in accordance with subsection (6) below) of all machinery or plant—

[(a) on the provision of which for the purposes of the trade he has incurred capital expenditure; and
(b) which belongs to him at some time in the chargeable period or its basis period; and
(c) in respect of which, in the chargeable period or its basis period, one of the following events occurs, namely—
  (i) the machinery or plant ceases to belong to him;
  (ii) he loses possession of the machinery or plant in circumstances where it is reasonable to assume that the loss is permanent [or, in the case of machinery or plant which was in use for mineral exploration and access, he abandons the machinery or plant at the site where it was in use for that purpose]⁹;
  (iii) the machinery or plant ceases to exist as such (as a result of destruction, dismantling or otherwise);
  (iv) the machinery or plant begins to be used wholly or partly for purposes which are other than those of the trade;
  (v) the trade is permanently discontinued (or is treated by virtue of any provision of the Tax Acts as permanently discontinued);
and that is the first such event to occur.]⁸

Provided that this subsection shall not require a person to bring into account the disposal value of any machinery or plant which he disposes of by way of gift in such circumstances that there is a charge to tax under [Schedule E]¹¹.

(6) The disposal value of any machinery or plant depends upon the event by reason of which it falls to be taken into account, and—

(a) unless paragraph (b) below applies, if that event is the sale of the machinery or plant, equals the net proceeds to the person in question of the sale, together with any insurance moneys received by him in respect of the machinery or plant by reason of any event affecting the price obtainable on the sale, and, so far as it consists of capital sums, any other compensation of any description so received,
(b) if that event is the sale of the machinery or plant at a price lower than that which it would have fetched if sold in the open market, and otherwise than in circumstances such that—
  (i) the buyer's expenditure on the acquisition of the machinery or plant can be taken into account in making allowances to him under this Chapter or Part II of the Capital Allowances Act 1968 (scientific research allowances) [and the buyer is not a dual resident investing company, within the meaning of section [404 of the Taxes Act]¹¹, which is connected with the seller within the terms of section [839 of that Act]¹¹]¹⁰, or
  (ii) there is a charge to tax under [Schedule E]¹¹,
equals the price which the machinery or plant would have fetched if sold in the open market,
(c) if the event is the demolition or destruction of the machinery or plant, equals the net amount received by the person in question for the remains of the machinery or plant, together with any insurance moneys received by him in respect of the demolition or destruction and, so far as it consists of capital sums, any other compensation of any description so received,
(d) if that event is the permanent loss of the machinery or plant otherwise than in consequence of its demolition or destruction, equals any insurance moneys received by him in respect of the loss and, so far as it consists of capital sums, any other compensation of any description so received,
(e) if that event is the permanent discontinuance of the trade before the occurrence of an

event within paragraph (a), (b), (c) or (d) above, is the same as the disposal value specified for the last-mentioned event, and

(f) in the case of any other event, equals the price which the machinery or plant would have fetched if sold in the open market at the time of the event:

Provided that the disposal value of any machinery or plant shall in no case exceed the capital expenditure incurred by the person in question on the provision of the machinery or plant for the purposes of the trade.

[(7) Where the person mentioned in the proviso to subsection (6) above has acquired the machinery or plant as a result of a transaction which was, or a series of transactions each of which was, between connected persons within the meaning of section [839][11] of the Taxes Act, that proviso shall have effect as if it referred to the capital expenditure on the provision of the machinery or plant incurred by whichever party to that transaction, or to any of those transactions, incurred the greatest such expenditure.][1-2]

Cross references.—See TA 1970, s. 306 (4B) (close investment-holding companies: restriction on allowances);
FA 1976, s. 39 (inclusion in sub-s. (4) (a) for first accounting period or basic period ending after 5 April 1976 of unallowed eligible expenditure, and references in this section to capital expenditure to include eligible expenditure);
FA 1980, s. 64 (2) (a) (expenditure which is qualifying expenditure under this section is also qualifying expenditure for the purposes of allowances on expenditure for certain leased assets),
s. 65 (1), (6) (application of this section where first-year allowances precluded under FA 1980, s. 64),
s. 66 (1) (b) (application of this section in a case of recovery of excess first-year allowance on leased machinery or plant not used for a qualifying purpose),
s. 66 (7) (b) (application of this section with FA 1980, s. 65 in respect of new ships used otherwise than for qualifying purposes under FA 1980, s. 64),
s. 68 (3), (5) (b) (application of this section in certain circumstances where machinery or plant leased to joint lessees),
s. 69 and Sch. 12, para. 9 (additional assets in respect of which this section has effect for the purposes of FA 1980, s. 65);
FA 1982, s. 70 (2) (modification of sub-s. (2) of this section in respect of capital allowances for assets leased outside the United Kingdom),
Sch. 11, para. 2 (separate application of this section to expenditure for assets leased outside the United Kingdom and to other expenditure),
Sch. 11, paras. 3 (1) (c), 6 (4) (extension of this section for the purposes of FA 1982, s. 70 (capital allowances for assets leased outside the United Kingdom));
FA 1984, s. 59 (4)–(6) (capital expenditure incurred after 13 March 1984; treatment of that expenditure for the purposes of this section in the event of a disclaimer of writing-down allowances),
s. 78 (2) (a) (acquisition after 12 March 1984 of machinery or plant for use in oil fields; restriction on capital allowances);
FA 1985, s. 57 (effect on and modification of this section where an election is made for certain machinery and plant to be treated as short-life assets),
s. 59 (2) and Sch. 17, paras. 1 (4) (b), 4 (c), 7 (1) (capital allowances in respect of expenditure incurred after 11 July 1984 subject to exception for expenditure in relation to contracts or leases entered into on or before that date) for machinery and plant which are fixtures),
s. 59 (2) and Sch. 17, para. 9 (disposal value of fixtures in certain cases where capital expenditure on them is incurred after 11 July 1984 subject to exception for expenditure in relation to contracts or leases entered into on or before that date);
FA 1986, s. 56 (1), (2), (5) (no allowance under this section to be made in respect of capital expenditure on agricultural land and buildings for which an allowance is made under the new code in FA 1986 for expenditure incurred after 31 March 1986 other than expenditure under existing contracts),
s. 57 (7) (notwithstanding the new code of allowances for expenditure on assets for leasing, this section to continue to apply separately to expenditure on cars falling within FA 1980, s. 69, that is cars not qualifying for first year allowances and not exceeding certain value),
Sch. 13, para. 10 (3) (application of sub-ss. (6), (7) above for determining the disposal value of certain assets used in relation to mineral extraction),
Sch. 16, para. 8 (treatment for the purposes of this section of new capital expenditure incurred on the provision of machinery or plant for leasing outside the United Kingdom; new expenditure means expenditure incurred after 31 March 1986 with certain exceptions—see FA 1986, s. 57 (1)–(3)).
Sch. 16, para 8 (7) (treatment of any allowance in respect of a ship leased outside the United Kingdom which has been postponed under Sch. 8, para. 8A of this Act),
Sch. 16, para. 9 (4) (b) (apportionment of any disposal value brought into account under this section in respect of machinery or plant leased to two or more persons jointly and in respect of which new capital expenditure is incurred);
FA 1989, s. 117 (1) (d) (capital allowances for expenditure in relation to personal physical security),
Sch. 13, para. 5 (2) (certain assumptions to apply for the purposes of this section where allowances are made in respect of a contribution made after 26 July 1989 by virtue of CAA 1968, s. 85),
Sch. 13, para. 28 (1) (b) (certain capital expenditure not to be taken into account in determining qualifying expenditure for the purpose of any allowance or charge under this section).
Amendments.—[1-2] Sub-s. (7) inserted by FA 1976, s. 40 (1), (3) and applies as respects disposals after 15 April 1976.
[3] Sub-s. (2A) and "(2A)" in sub-s. (4) inserted by FA 1984, s. 59 (1).
[4] Words in sub-s. (1) (a) inserted by FA 1985, s. 55 (1) with respect to capital expenditure incurred after 31 March 1985.
[5] Sub-s (1) (c) and the word "and" preceding it repealed by FA 1985, s. 55 (2) (b) and Sch. 27, Pt. VI with respect to any chargeable period or its basis period ending after 31 March 1985.
[6] Words in sub-s. (2A) added by FA 1985, Sch. 14, para. 3 (1) with respect to any chargeable period or its basis period ending after 31 March 1985.
[7] Words in sub-s. (4) substituted by FA 1985, Sch. 14, para. 3 (2) with respect to any chargeable period or its basis period ending after 31 March 1985.
[8] Words in sub-s. (5) substituted by FA 1985, Sch. 14, para. 3 (3) with respect to any chargeable period or its basis period ending after 31 March 1985.
[9] Words in sub-s. (5) (c) (ii) added by FA 1986, s. 55 (7) (c) and have effect according to the provisions of FA 1986, s. 55 (5), (6).
[10] Words in sub-s. (6) (b) (i) inserted by F (No. 2) A 1987, s. 64 (5).

[11] Words in sub-ss. (5), (6), (7) substituted by TA 1988, Sch. 29, para. 32 Table.

Application to machinery and plant on hire-purchase etc. or lease, and to activities other than trades

45. Machinery and plant on hire-purchase etc.

(1) Where a person carrying on a trade incurs capital expenditure on the provision of machinery or plant for the purposes thereof under a contract providing that he shall or may become the owner of the machinery or plant on the performance of the contract—

(*a*) the machinery or plant shall be treated for the purposes of this Chapter as belonging to him [(and not to any other person)][1] at any time when he is entitled to the benefit of the contract so far as it relates to that machinery or plant, and
(*b*) all capital expenditure in respect of that machinery or plant to be incurred by him under the contract after the time when the machinery or plant is brought into use for the purposes of the trade shall be treated for the purposes of this Chapter as having been incurred by him at that time.

(2) Where a person to whom any machinery or plant is treated as belonging by virtue of subsection (1) (*a*) above ceases to be entitled to the benefit of the contract in question so far as it relates to that machinery or plant without in fact becoming the owner of the machinery or plant—

(*a*) the machinery or plant shall be treated for the purposes of this Chapter as ceasing to belong to him at the time when he ceases to be so entitled, and
(*b*) if he ceases to be so entitled after the machinery or plant has been brought into use for the purposes of the trade, the disposal value of the machinery or plant—
  (i) shall not exceed the total capital expenditure which he would have incurred in respect of the machinery or plant if he had wholly performed the contract, but
  (ii) subject to that limitation, shall be taken as an amount equal to any capital sums which he receives, or is entitled to receive, by way of consideration, compensation, damages or insurance moneys in respect of his rights under the contract, or in respect of the machinery or plant, together with so much of the said capital expenditure as he has not in fact incurred.

Cross references.—See FA 1984, Sch. 12, para. 6 (3) (exclusion of the provisions in respect of the spreading of capital expenditure on machinery and plant under certain contracts entered into after 13 March 1984).
Amendments.—[1] Words in sub-s. (1) (*a*) inserted by FA 1989, Sch. 13, para. 10 in relation to capital expenditure incurred under contracts entered into after 26 July 1989.

46. Machinery and plant on lease

(1) Where machinery or plant is first let by any person otherwise than in the course of a trade, then, whether or not it is used for the purposes of a trade carried on by the lessee—

(*a*) the capital expenditure incurred by the lessor in providing the machinery or plant shall be treated for the purposes of this Chapter as having been incurred in providing it for the purposes of a trade begun to be carried on by him, separately from any other trade which he may carry on, at the commencement of the letting, and
[(*b*) at the time when the lessor permanently ceases to let the machinery or plant otherwise than in the course of a trade, the machinery or plant shall be treated for the purposes of this Chapter as being used wholly for purposes other than those of the trade referred to in paragraph (*a*) above:][1]

Provided that this subsection shall not apply to machinery or plant let for use in a dwelling house.

[(1A) Where subsection (1) above applies, the question whether the provision of the machinery or plant is to be treated as being wholly and exclusively or only partly for the purposes of the trade referred to in paragraph (*a*) of that subsection shall be determined according to whether the machinery or plant was in fact provided wholly and exclusively for the purpose of letting otherwise than in the course of a trade or only partly for that purpose.][2]

(2) Where—

[(*a*)][3] a lessee incurs capital expenditure on the provision for the purposes of a trade carried on by him of machinery or plant which he is required to provide under the terms of the lease [and

(b) the machinery or plant is not so installed or otherwise fixed in or to a building or any other description of land as to become, in law, part of that building or other land,

then, if the machinery or plant would not otherwise belong to him][3], the machinery or plant shall be treated for the purposes of this Chapter as belonging to him for so long as it continues to be used for the purposes of the trade; but, as from the determination of the lease, section 44 (5) above shall have effect as if the capital expenditure on providing the machinery or plant had been incurred by the lessor and not by the lessee.

[(2A) In this section "lease" includes an agreement for a lease where the term to be covered by the lease has begun, and any tenancy, but does not include a mortgage, and "lessee" and other cognate expressions shall be construed accordingly.][4]

Cross references.—See FA 1982, s. 70 (2) (*e*) (capital allowances in respect of machinery and plant leased outside the United Kingdom);
FA 1985, Sch. 15, para. 3 (election to treat as short-life assets cannot be made in respect of machinery or plant to which this section applies);
TA 1988, s. 116 (4) (*b*) (partnerships involving companies: effect of arrangements for transferring relief).
Amendments.—[1] Sub-s. (1) (*b*) substituted by FA 1985, Sch. 14, para. 4 with respect to any chargeable period or its basis period ending after 31 March 1985.
[2] Sub-s. (1A) inserted by FA 1985, Sch. 14, para. 1 with respect to capital expenditure incurred after 31 March 1985.
[3] Words in sub-s. (2) inserted by FA 1985, s. 59 (5), (6) in relation to any lease entered into after 11 July 1984, unless it was entered into pursuant to an agreement made on or before that date.
[4] Sub-s. (2A) inserted by FA 1989, Sch. 13, para. 11.

47. Application to activities other than trades

(1) Except as otherwise provided, the provisions of this Chapter shall, with any necessary adaptations, apply in relation to—

(*a*) professions, employments, vocations and offices, and
(*b*) the occupation of woodlands, where the profits or gains thereof are assessable under Schedule D.

as they apply in relation to trades:

Provided that—
(i) in their application to an office or employment, the said provisions shall apply only to machinery or plant which is necessarily provided for use in the performance of the duties thereof, and
[(ii) the provisions of this Chapter as applied by this subsection shall have effect subject to section 198 (2) of the Taxes Act (offices and employments with duties abroad).][1]

(2) [Section 306 of the Income and Corporation Taxes Act 1970 (capital allowances for machinery and plant used by investment or life assurance companies) shall][2] have effect as if the references therein to Chapter II of Part I of the Capital Allowances Act 1968 included a reference to this Chapter, and as if the reference in subsection (2) thereof to section 46 of the said Act of 1968 included a reference to section 48 below.

Note.—See **Prospective Legislation Notes** (Commercial Woodlands).
Amendments.—[1] Sub-s. (1) proviso (ii) substituted by TA 1988, Sch. 29, para. 32 Table.
[2] Words in sub-s. (2) substituted by TA 1988, Sch. 29, para. 32 Table.

Supplementary

48. Manner of making allowances and charges

(1) Subject to subsection (2) below, any allowance or charge made to or on any person under this Chapter shall be made to or on that person in taxing his trade.

(2) Any allowance made by virtue of section 46 (1) above shall be made by way of discharge or repayment of tax, and, subject to subsection (3) below, shall be available primarily against income from the letting of machinery or plant; and effect shall be given to any charge made by virtue of the said section 46 (1)—

(*a*) if a charge to income tax, by making the charge under Case VI of Schedule D,
(*b*) if a charge to corporation tax, by treating the amount on which the charge is to be made as income from the letting of machinery or plant.

(3) Where an allowance falling to be made for any chargeable period by virtue of section 46 (1) above is in respect of expenditure on the provision of machinery or plant which for the whole or any part of that period or its basis period is not used for the purposes

of a trade carried on by the lessee, that allowance or, as the case may require, a proportionate part thereof shall be available primarily against income from the letting of that machinery or plant only.

(4) The following provisions of the Capital Allowances Act 1968 with respect to the manner of making allowances and charges, that is to say, sections 70 and 71 (allowances and charges under Part I of that Act as it applies for the purposes of income tax) and sections 73 and 74 (corresponding provisions for corporation tax) shall have effect as if the references therein to the said Part I included references to this Chapter:

Provided that [the proviso to subsection (1) of the said section 71 shall not apply to an allowance made by virtue of section 46 (1) above and][1], where an allowance falling to be made for any chargeable period by virtue of section 46 (1) above is in respect of expenditure on the provision of machinery or plant which for the whole or any part of that period or its basis period is not used for the purposes of a trade carried on by the lessee, [subsection (3) of the said section 74][2] shall not apply to that allowance or, as the case may require, to a proportionate part thereof.

[(4A) Section 403 (3) of the Taxes Act (group relief) shall not apply to an allowance if or to the extent that, by virtue of the proviso to subsection (4) above, subsection (3) of the said section 74 does not apply to it.][3]

Cross references.—See FA 1975, s. 14 (3) (allowance under s. 46 (1) of this Act for thermal insulation of industrial buildings or structures available primarily against Schedule A income or income subject of a balancing charge, notwithstanding sub-s. (2) of this section).
FA 1980, s. 64 (11) (so much of the proviso to sub-s. (4) of this section as relates to CAA 1968, s. 74 (3) not to apply to any allowance under FA 1980, s. 64).
Amendments.—[1] Words in the proviso to sub-s. (4) inserted by FA 1980, s. 70 (3) (a), (6), without prejudice to FA 1976, s. 41.
[2] Words in the proviso to sub-s. (4) substituted by FA 1980, s. 70 (3) (b), (6), without prejudice to FA 1976, s. 41.
[3] Sub-s. (4A) inserted by FA 1989, Sch. 13, para. 12 and applies where the accounting period of the surrendering company ends after 26 July 1989.

49. Minor rules, and consequential amendments

The provisions of Schedule 8 to this Act shall have effect, being provisions supplementing the foregoing provisions of this Chapter, and provisions making consequential amendments in certain enactments.

50. Interpretation etc.

(1) In this Chapter—

"capital expenditure" means capital expenditure to which this Chapter applies in accordance with section 40 above;
"chargeable period" means an accounting period of a company or a year of assessment; and
  (a) a reference to a "chargeable period or its basis period" is a reference to the chargeable period if it is an accounting period and to the basis period for it if it is a year of assessment,
  (b) a reference to a "chargeable period related to" the incurring of expenditure, or a sale or other event, is a reference to the chargeable period in which, or to that in the basis period for which, the expenditure is incurred or the sale or other event takes place, and means the latter if, but only if, the chargeable period is a year of assessment;

"income" includes any amount on which a charge to tax is authorised to be made under this Chapter;
["mineral exploration and access" and "trade of mineral extraction" have the same meaning as in Schedule 13 to the Finance Act 1986;][2]
"new" means unused and not second-hand;
"tax", where neither income tax nor corporation tax is specified, means either of those taxes.

(2) In this Chapter as it applies for income tax purposes "basis period" shall be construed in accordance with subsections (2) to (5) of section 72 of the Capital Allowances Act 1968, with references in those provisions to Part I of that Act or Chapter II of that Part read for the purpose as references to this Chapter.

(3) Section 82 (1) of the Capital Allowances Act 1968 (construction of references to capital expenditure and capital sums) shall apply for the purposes of this Chapter as it applies for the purposes of Part I of that Act.

(4) ...¹ for the purposes of this Chapter, any expenditure incurred for the purposes of a trade by a person about to carry it on shall be treated as if it had been incurred by him on the first day on which he does carry it on.

(5) Any reference in this Chapter to an allowance made includes a reference to an allowance which would be made but for an insufficiency of profits or gains, or other income, against which to make it.

(6) Any reference in this Chapter to any machinery, plant, building, structure or works shall be construed as including a reference to a part of any machinery, plant, building, structure or works.

(7) The provisions of this Chapter, and the provisions applying for the purposes of this Chapter, shall apply in relation to a share in machinery or plant as they apply in relation to a part of machinery or plant; and, for the purposes of the said provisions, a share in machinery or plant shall be deemed to be used for the purposes of a trade so long as, and only so long as, the machinery or plant is used for the purposes thereof.

[(7A) For the purposes of this Chapter, where a person is carrying on a trade of mineral extraction, expenditure incurred by him in connection with that trade on the provision of machinery or plant for mineral exploration and access shall be taken to be incurred on the provision of the machinery or plant wholly and exclusively for the purposes of that trade.]³

(8) ...⁴

Cross references.—See FA 1972, s. 67 (4) (expenditure shall not be treated for the purposes of FA 1972, s. 67, as having been incurred after the date on which it was in fact incurred by reason only of so much of sub-s. (4) of this section as relates to expenditure incurred before trade began);
FA 1980, s. 73 (1) (expenditure not to be treated for the purposes of FA 1980, s. 72 as having been incurred after the date it was in fact incurred by virtue of sub-s. (4) of this section);
FA 1982, s. 72 (10) (sub-s. (4) above to apply in relation to FA 1982, s. 72 (expenditure on production and acquisition of films, etc.) as though it were comprised in Pt. III, Ch. I of this Act).
Amendments.—¹ Words in sub-s. (4) repealed by FA 1985, s. 56 (6) (*b*) and Sch. 27, Pt. VI with respect to any chargeable period or its basis period ending after 17 December 1984.
² Definition of "mineral exploration and access" in sub-s. (1) inserted by FA 1986, s. 55 (7) and has effect according to FA 1986, s. 55 (6).
³ Sub-s. (7A) inserted by *ibid.*
⁴ Sub-s. (8) repealed by TA 1988, Sch. 31.

CHAPTER II
OTHER PROVISIONS

51. Initial allowances for industrial buildings—continuance of increased rate for development and intermediate areas and Northern Ireland

The rate of initial allowance under section 1 of the Capital Allowances Act 1968 (industrial buildings and structures) provided for by section 15 (1) of the Finance Act 1970 in a case falling within subsection (2) of that section (that is to say, a rate of two-fifths in the case of buildings and structures in development areas, intermediate areas and Northern Ireland) shall apply in relation to expenditure incurred after 5th April 1972 as well as in relation to expenditure incurred during the period beginning on 6th April 1970 and ending on the said 5th April; . . .

Note.—Words omitted amend FA 1970, s. 15 (1).

52. Initial allowances for mining etc. works—increased rate for development areas and Northern Ireland, and right of disclaimer

(1) In relation to expenditure within section 56 (1) of the Capital Allowances Act 1968 (works in connection with mines, oil wells and other sources of mineral deposits of a wasting nature) which is incurred on or after 27th October 1970 on the construction of works situated—

(a) in an area which is a development area [(that is to say, an area specified as such by an order made, or having effect as if made, under section 1 of the Industrial Development Act 1982 or, in relation to a time before the commencement of that Act, a development area within the meaning of the Local Employment Act 1972)][1] on the date on which the expenditure is incurred or, if the expenditure is incurred under a contract entered into on or after the said 27th October, on the date on which the contract was entered into, or

(b) in Northern Ireland,

section 56 (2) of that Act (which provides for an initial allowance of an amount equal to two-fifths of any expenditure within the said section 56 (1)) shall have effect with the substitution for the words "two-fifths" of the words "the whole".

Expenditure shall not be treated for the purposes of this subsection as having been incurred after the date on which it was in fact incurred by reason only of section 64 of the said Act of 1968 (expenditure incurred before trade began).

(2) A company to whom an initial allowance under the said section 56 (1) falls to be made for any chargeable period in respect of expenditure incurred on or after 27th October 1970 may, by notice in writing given to the inspector not later than two years after the end of that period, either disclaim the allowance or require that the amount thereof be reduced to an amount specified in the notice; and a person other than a company claiming an initial allowance under the said section 56 (1) in respect of expenditure so incurred may require the amount thereof to be reduced to an amount specified in the claim.

Cross references.—See TA 1988, Sch. 30, para. 7 (1) (*b*) (application of TA 1988, Sch. 30, para.7 in respect of claims for group relief for expenditure falling within sub-s. (1) of this section incurred under a contract entered into by the surrendering company before 6 March 1973).
Amendments.—[1] Words in sub-s. (1) substituted by the Industrial Development Act 1982, Sch. 2, Pt. II, para. 6 with effect from 28 January 1983.
This section repealed by FA 1986, s. 55 (2) and Sch. 23, Pt. VI in relation to expenditure incurred after 31 March 1986, but subject to FA 1986, Sch. 14.

PART V
MISCELLANEOUS

69. Citation, interpretation, construction, extent and repeals

(1) This Act may be cited as the Finance Act 1971.

(2) In this Act "the Taxes Act" means the Income and Corporation Taxes Act [1988][2].

(3) In this Act—

...

Parts II and III, so far as they relate to income tax, shall be construed as one with the Income Tax Acts and, so far as they relate to corporation tax, shall be construed as one with the Corporation Tax Acts.

...[1]

(4) Except so far as the context otherwise requires, any reference in this Act to any enactment shall be construed as a reference to that enactment as amended, and as including a reference to that enactment as applied, by or under any other enactment, including this Act.

(5) Except as otherwise expressly provided, such of the provisions of this Act as relate to matters in respect of which the Parliament of Northern Ireland has power to make laws do not extend to Northern Ireland.

(6) If the Parliament of Northern Ireland passes provisions amending or replacing any enactment of that Parliament referred to in this Act the reference shall be construed as a reference to the enactment as so amended or, as the case may be, as a reference to those provisions.

(7) ...

Notes.—Words in sub-s. (3) are outside the scope of this work.
Sub-s. (7) repeals enactments specified in Sch. 14. Effect has been given to these repeals, where applicable, in the relevant provisions of the earlier enactments.
Amendments.—[1] Words in sub-s. (3) repealed by CGTA 1979, s. 158 and Sch. 8.
[2] Year in sub-s. (2) substituted by TA 1988, Sch. 29, para. 32 Table.

SCHEDULES

SCHEDULE 3

Section 21

OCCUPATIONAL PENSION SCHEMES

PART II

TAXATION OF REFUNDS OF CONTRIBUTIONS
AND CERTAIN OTHER PAYMENTS

Schemes approved under old law
Taxation of refunds of contributions and commutation payments

8.—(1) This paragraph has effect as respects any payment chargeable to tax for the year 1971–72 or any later year of assessment under Regulation 7, 8 or 13 of the Regulations dated November 10th 1921 made by the Board under section 32 of the Finance Act 1921 (which corresponds to section 208 of [the Income and Corporation Taxes Act 1970]¹).

(2) Where tax is chargeable under the said Regulation 7 (or Regulation 13 with that Regulation) then—

(*a*) if the scheme relates to a trade, profession or vocation carried on by the employer, the payment shall be treated for the purposes of the Tax Acts as a receipt of that trade, profession or vocation receivable when the payment falls due or on the last day on which the trade, profession or vocation is carried on by the employer, whichever is the earlier;
(*b*) if the scheme does not relate to such a trade, profession or vocation, the employer shall be charged to tax on the amount of the payment under Case VI of Schedule D.

(3) Where tax is chargeable under the said Regulation 8 (or Regulation 13 with that Regulation), [section 598 (2) to (4) of the Taxes Act]¹ shall apply as they apply to tax chargeable under that paragraph.

(4) If at any time the scheme becomes an approved scheme (that is to say approved for the purposes of Chapter II of Part II of the Finance Act [1970 or Chapter I of Part XIV of the Taxes Act]¹) no tax shall be chargeable under the said Regulations on any payment made under the scheme after that time.

(5) The provisions of this paragraph shall have effect in substitution for the provisions of the said Regulations as to the rate of tax and the manner of charging tax, and the said Regulations 7, 8 and 13 shall not cease to be in force by reason of the provisions of this Act repealing the said section 208 of [the Income and Corporation Taxes Act 1970]¹, or of the provisions of this Act under which in certain cases the said section 208 ceases to apply to a scheme before the date of that repeal.

Cross references.—See TA 1988, s. 599A(9) (tax charge on repayment of surplus funds to members of AVC schemes).
Amendments.—¹ Words in sub-paras. (1), (3), (4), (5) substituted by TA 1988, Sch. 29, para. 32 Table.

SCHEDULE 8
Section 49

CAPITAL ALLOWANCES

Investment grants etc.: exclusion of first-year allowances

1.—(1) No first-year allowance shall be made in respect of so much of any expenditure as is taken into account for the purposes of—

(*a*) any grant towards that expenditure made under the Industrial Development Act 1966, or

(*b*) any grant towards that expenditure made under the Industrial Investment (General Assistance) Act (Northern Ireland) 1966 by virtue of the Industrial Investment Grant (Addition of Eligible Assets) Order (Northern Ireland) 1967, or

(*c*) any grant towards that expenditure made under the last-mentioned Act and exceeding [20 per cent.][1] of that expenditure, or

(*d*) any grant towards that expenditure made under any agreement under the Industries Development Act (Northern Ireland) 1966 made before 1st August 1971 other than one made after 16th February 1971 and providing that no grant payable thereunder in respect of expenditure on machinery or plant is to exceed 40 per cent. of the expenditure:

Provided that the Treasury may from time to time, by order made by statutory instrument, vary as respects expenditure incurred after the passing of this Act, or any description of such expenditure specified in the order, the percentages specified in paragraphs (*c*) and (*d*) above or either of them.

(2) If any such grant is made after the making of any such allowance, that allowance shall to that extent be withdrawn; and where the amount of any such grant is repaid in whole or in part by the grantee to the grantor, then, to the extent to which it has been so repaid, it shall be deemed never to have been made.

(3) All such assessments and adjustments shall be made as may be necessary to give effect to sub-paragraph (2) above; and, notwithstanding anything in any other provision, the time within which such an assessment or adjustment may be made shall not expire before the expiry of three years from the end of the chargeable period in which the grant or, as the case may be, repayment is made.

(4) The paragraph does not apply to expenditure on the provision of ships.

Amendments.—[1] An increase in the rate from 20 per cent. to 30 per cent. applies to expenditure incurred on or after 27 July 1972. This increase does not apply to specified expenditure which is related to contracts made before 8 December 1970: for such expenditure there is a reduction in the rate from 20 per cent. to 19 per cent. which applies to expenditure incurred after 30 January 1973: The Capital Allowances (Northern Ireland Grants) Order 1973, S.I. 1973 No. 113.

Effect of other capital allowances

2.—(*1*) *Expenditure in respect of which a deduction may be allowed under section 91 of the Capital Allowances Act 1968 (which gives a deduction of 100 per cent. in the case of capital expenditure on scientific research) shall be disregarded for all the purposes of Chapter I of Part III of this Act; and where a deduction in respect of any expenditure has been allowed under the said section 91 in taxing a trade carried on by any person, paragraph 7 of this Schedule shall not apply on that person's bringing into use for the purposes of the trade of any machinery or plant representing that expenditure.*

(2) Section 50 of the said Act of 1968 (effect on allowances under Chapter II of Part I of that Act of allowances in respect of machinery or plant used for exploration or in respect of agricultural or forestry works) shall have effect as if references therein to the said Chapter II included references to Chapter I of Part III of this Act.

Cross references.—See FA 1980, s. 64 (10) (sub-para. (1) to be disregarded for the purposes of sub-s. (2) (*a*) of that section).

Amendments.—This paragraph superseded by FA 1989, Sch. 13, para. 28 (1)–(4) and repealed by FA 1989, Sch. 13, para. 28 (5) (*b*) and Sch. 17, Pt. VI in relation to any chargeable period or its basis period ending after 26 July 1989.

Effect of sales between connected persons, sale and lease-back etc.

3.—(1) Where a person incurs capital expenditure on the provision by purchase of machinery or plant . . .[1], and—

(a) he and the seller are connected with each other within the terms of section [839][4] of the Taxes Act, or
(b) the machinery or plant continues to be used for the purposes of a trade carried on by the seller, or
(c) it appears with respect to the sale, or with respect to transactions of which the sale is one, that the sole or main benefit which, but for this sub-paragraph, might have been expected to accrue to the parties or any of them was the obtaining of an allowance under Chapter I of Part III of this Act,

a first-year allowance shall not be made in respect of the expenditure, or if made shall be withdrawn, and there shall be disregarded for the purposes of section 44 of this Act so much (if any) of the expenditure as exceeds the disposal value to be brought into account under that section by reason of the sale.

(2) Where a person enters into a contract under which, on the performance thereof, he will or may become the owner of machinery or plant [belonging to another person][2], and—

(a) he and that person are connected with each other within the terms of section [839][4] of the Taxes Act, or
(b) the machinery or plant continues to be used for the purposes of a trade carried on by that person, or
(c) it appears with respect to the transaction, or with respect to the transactions of which it is one, that the sole or main benefit which, but for this sub-paragraph, might have been expected to accrue to the parties or any of them was the obtaining of an allowance under Chapter I of Part III of this Act,

a first-year allowance shall not be made in respect of any expenditure incurred by him under the contract so far as relating to that machinery or plant, or if made shall be withdrawn, and there shall be disregarded for the purposes of section 44 of this Act so much (if any) of the expenditure as exceeds the disposal value to be brought into account under that section by reason of the contract so far as so relating.

(3) Where a person, being entitled to the benefit of a contract under which, on the performance thereof, he will or may become the owner of any machinery or plant . . .[3], assigns the benefit of the contract so far as it relates to that machinery or plant to another person, and—

(a) he and the assignee are connected with each other within the terms of section [839][4] of the Taxes Act, or
(b) the machinery or plant continues to be used for the purposes of a trade carried on by him, or
(c) it appears with respect to the assignment, or with respect to transactions of which the assignment is one, that the sole or main benefit which, but for this sub-paragraph, might have been expected to accrue to the parties or any of them was the obtaining of an allowance under Chapter I of Part III of this Act,

a first-year allowance shall not be made in respect of any expenditure incurred by the assignee under the contract so far as so relating, or by way of consideration for the assignment, or if so made shall be withdrawn, and there shall be disregarded for the purposes of section 44 of this Act so much (if any) of the assignee's expenditure as exceeds the disposal value to be brought into account under section 45 of this Act by reason of the assignment.

(4) All such assessments and adjustments of assessments shall be made as may be necessary to give effect to the preceding provisions of this paragraph.

Cross references.—See FA 1984, s. 78 (4) (application of this section in relation to transfers after 12 March 1984 of interests in oil fields between connected persons);
FA 1985, s. 57 (7) (b) (disposal to a connected person of machinery or plant which is treated as a short-life asset; disapplication of this paragraph to that disposal).
Amendments.—[1] Words in sub-para. (1) repealed by FA 1972, s. 68 (3) (a), (9), and Sch. 28, Pt. XII. in relation to cases where the incurring of the capital expenditure occurs on or after 14 June 1972; see also FA 1972, s. 68 (3)–(7).
[2] Words in sub-para. (2) substituted by FA 1972, s. 68 (3) (b), (9), in relation to cases where the making of the contract occurs on or after 14 June 1972; see also FA 1972, s. 68 (3), (6), (7).
[3] Words in sub-para. (3) repealed by FA 1972, s. 68 (3) (c), (9), and Sch. 28, Pt. XII, in relation to cases where the assignment of the benefit of the contract occurs on or after 14 June 1972; see also FA 1972, s. 68 (3), (6).
[4] Number in sub-paras. (1) (a), (2) (a), (3)(a) substituted by TA 1988, Sch. 29, para. 32 Table.

Further effects of disposal etc. before bringing into use

4.—(1) Subject to sub-paragraph (2) below, [where—]²

[(*a*) a first year allowance is made in respect of capital expenditure on the provision of machinery or plant, and
(*b*) in the chargeable period related to the incurring of that expenditure, the disposal value of that machinery or plant falls to be brought into account in accordance with subsection (5) of section 44 of this Act,

that expenditure shall not, by virtue of sub-paragraph (ii) of paragraph (*a*) of subsection (4) of that section be excluded from the capital expenditure referred to in that paragraph.]²

(2) Where the event [by reason of which disposal value falls to be brought into account as mentioned in]³ sub-paragraph (1) above is the assignment of the benefit of a contract—

[section 44 of this Act, as modified by that sub-paragraph, shall have effect as if any reference in subsection (4) (*a*) of that section to capital expenditure incurred were a reference to]⁴ the total capital expenditure which the person in question would have incurred in respect of the machinery or plant if he had wholly performed the contract, . . .¹

(*b*) . . .¹

(3) All such assessments and adjustments of assessments shall be made as may be necessary to give effect to the preceding provisions of this paragraph.

Amendments.—¹ Sub-para. (2) (*b*), together with the word preceding it, repealed by FA 1972, s. 68 (8), (9), and Sch. 28, Pt. XII, with effect from 14 June 1972.
² Words in sub-para. (1) substituted by FA 1985, Sch. 14, para. 5 (1) with respect to any chargeable period or its basis period ending after 31 March 1985.
³ Words in sub-para. (2) substituted by FA 1985, Sch. 14, para. 5 (2) with respect to any chargeable period or its basis period ending after 31 March 1985.
⁴ Words in sub-para. (2) substituted by *ibid*.

Effect of use partly for trade etc. purposes and
partly for other purposes

5.—(1) A first-year allowance may be made to a person in respect of any machinery or plant notwithstanding that it appears [that the provision of the machinery or plant is partly for purposes other than those of a trade carried on by him]¹; but the allowance in such case shall be so much only of the allowance that would fall to be made if the [provision of the machinery or plant were wholly and exclusively]² for the purposes of the trade as may be just and reasonable having regard to all the relevant circumstances of the case and, in particular, to the extent to which it appears that the machinery or plant is likely to be used for the said other purposes . . .³.

[(2) Where a person carrying on a trade incurs capital expenditure on the provision of machinery or plant partly for the purposes of that trade (in sub-paragraphs (4) to (6) below referred to as "the actual trade") and partly for other purposes, it shall be assumed for the purposes of section 44 of this Act that he incurred the expenditure on the provision of the machinery or plant wholly and exclusively for the purposes of a trade (in sub-paragraphs (4) to (6) below referred to as "the notional trade") carried on by him separately from the actual trade and any other trade carried on by him.]⁴

[(3) If, for any chargeable period, a person who has incurred expenditure on the provision of machinery or plant for the purposes of a trade (in sub-paragraphs (4) to (6) below referred to as "the actual trade") is required to bring the disposal value of the machinery or plant into account by reason of it beginning in that chargeable period or its basis period to be used partly, but not wholly, for purposes other than those of the actual trade, it shall be assumed for the purposes of section 44 of this Act that, immediately after the beginning of that chargeable period or its basis period, he incurs capital expenditure equal to that disposal value on the provision of the machinery or plant wholly and exclusively for the purposes of a trade (in sub-paragraphs (4) to (6) below referred to as "the notional trade") carried on by him separately from the actual trade and any other trade carried on by him.]⁴

[(4) Without prejudice to sub-paragraphs (i) to (iii) of paragraph (*c*) of subsection (5) of section 44 of this Act, it shall be assumed for the purposes of that section that the notional trade is permanently discontinued on the machinery or plant beginning to be used wholly for purposes other than those of the actual trade.]⁴

[(5) The allowance or charge under section 44 of this Act which, on the above assumptions, and having regard to sub-paragraph (6) below, would fall to be made for any chargeable period in the case of the notional trade—

(*a*) shall be reduced to such extent as may be just and reasonable having regard to all the relevant circumstances of the case and, in particular, to the extent to which the machinery or plant was used in that chargeable period or its basis period otherwise than for the purposes of the actual trade; and
(*b*) shall, as so reduced, be made for that chargeable period in the case of the actual trade.]⁴

[(6) If an allowance under section 44 of this Act falling to be made by virtue of this paragraph for any chargeable period in the case of the actual trade is not claimed or is disclaimed under subsection (2A) of that section, or is reduced in amount in accordance with a requirement under the proviso of subsection (2) of that section or under subsection (2A) of that section then, in determining the allowance or charge under that section which would fall to be made for any subsequent chargeable period in the case of the notional trade, any allowance falling to be made in the case of that trade for the first-mentioned chargeable period shall be treated as not claimed or as disclaimed or, as the case may require, as proportionately reduced.]⁴

Cross references.—See CGTA 1979, s. 34 (7) (restriction of capital losses by reference to capital and renewals allowances);
FA 1985, Sch. 15, para. 4 (election to treat as short-life assets cannot be made in respect of machinery or plant to which sub-para. (2) above applies).
Amendments.—¹ Words in sub-para. (1) substituted by FA 1985, Sch. 14, para. 2 (*a*) with respect to capital expenditure incurred after 31 March 1985.
² Words in sub-para. (1) substituted by FA 1985, Sch. 14, para. 2 (*b*) with respect to capital expenditure incurred after 31 March 1985.
³ Words in sub-para. (1) repealed by FA 1985, Sch. 14, para. 2 (*c*) and Sch. 27, Pt. VI with respect to capital expenditure incurred after 31 March 1985.
⁴ Sub-paras. (2)–(6) substituted for sub-paras. (2)–(5) by FA 1985, Sch. 14, para. 6 with respect to any chargeable period or its basis period ending after 31 March 1985.

Effect of subsidies towards wear and tear

6.—(1) If it appears that, during the period during which any machinery or plant will be used by a person for the purposes of his trade, sums which—

(*a*) are in respect of, or take account of, the wear and tear to the machinery or plant occasioned by its use for those purposes, and
(*b*) do not fall to be taken into account as income of that person, or in computing the profits or gains of any trade carried on by him,

are, or are to be, payable to that person directly or indirectly by the Crown, or by any government or public or local authority (whether in the United Kingdom or elsewhere), or by any other person, then, unless those sums are in respect of, or take account of, part only of the said wear and tear, any expenditure incurred by the first-mentioned person in providing the machinery or plant shall be wholly disregarded for the purposes of Chapter I of Part III of this Act.

(2) Where sub-paragraph (1) above would apply to a person's expenditure on the provision of machinery or plant but for the fact that the sums there referred to are in respect of, or take account of, part only of the wear and tear to the machinery or plant, a first-year allowance may be made in respect of the expenditure, but the amount thereof shall be reduced to such extent as may be just and reasonable having regard to all the relevant circumstances of the case.

(3) Where sums within sub-paragraph (1) above are paid as mentioned in that sub-paragraph to a person carrying on a trade, but are in respect of, or take account of, part only of the wear and tear to the machinery or plant in respect of which they are paid, the following provisions of this paragraph shall have effect with respect to the allowances and charges to be made in the case of the trade (hereafter called the "actual trade") under section 44 of this Act.

(4) [If an allowance has been made under section 44 of this Act for a chargeable period prior to that in which or, as the case may be, in the basis period of which the first sum is so paid in respect of the machinery or plant]¹, it shall be treated for the purposes of the said section 44 as having [begun to be used wholly for purposes other than those]¹ of the actual trade immediately after the beginning of the said chargeable or basis period.

(5) Whether or not sub-paragraph (4) above applies, it shall be assumed for the purposes of the said section 44—

(a) that (with paragraph 7 of this Schedule applying where appropriate) immediately after the beginning of the said chargeable or basis period [capital expenditure was incurred on providing the machinery or plant wholly and exclusively][1] for the purposes of a trade (hereafter called "the notional trade") carried on by the person carrying on the actual trade separately from that and any other trade carried on by him,

(b) that from then until [the notional trade is treated by virtue of paragraph (c) below as permanently discontinued][1] no sums within sub-paragraph (1) above [are][1] paid in respect thereof to the persons carrying on that trade,

(c) that [without prejudice to sub-paragraphs (i) to (iii) of paragraph (c) of subsection (5) of that section][2] the notional trade is permanently discontinued on the machinery or plant [beginning to be used wholly or partly for the purposes other than those of the actual trade][1]

(d) . . .[3]

and the allowance or charge under that section which, on the above assumptions and having regard to sub-paragraph (6) below, would fall to be made for any chargeable period in the case of the notional trade—

(i) shall be reduced to such extent as may be just and reasonable having regard to all the relevant circumstances of the case, and

(ii) shall, as so reduced, be made for that chargeable period in the case of the actual trade.

(6) If an allowance under the said section 44 falling by virtue of this paragraph to be made for any chargeable period in the case of the actual trade is not claimed [or is disclaimed under subsection (2A) of that section][2], or is reduced in amount in accordance with a requirement under the proviso to subsection (2) of that section [or under subsection (2A) of that section][2], then, in determining the allowance or charge under that section which would fall to be made for any subsequent chargeable period in the case of the notional trade, any allowance falling to be made in the case of that trade for the first-mentioned chargeable period shall be treated as not [claimed or as disclaimed or, as the case may require, as proportionately reduced][1].

Cross references.—See CGTA 1979, s. 34 (7) (restriction of capital losses by reference to capital and renewals allowances);
FA 1982, s. 70 (2) (b) (modification of s. 44 of this Act in its application in accordance with this paragraph to expenditure for assets leased outside the United Kingdom);
FA 1985, Sch. 15, para. 5 (election to treat as short-life assets cannot be made in respect of machinery or plant to which this paragraph applies).
Amendments.—[1] Words in sub-paras. (4), (5), (6) substituted by FA 1985, Sch. 14, para. 7 in respect of any chargeable period or its basis period ending after 31 March 1985.
[2] Words in sub-para. (5) (c), (6) inserted by FA 1985, Sch. 14, para. 7 in respect of any chargeable period or its basis period ending after 31 March 1985.
[3] Sub-para. (5) (d) repealed by FA 1985, Sch. 14, para. 7 (2) (d) and Sch. 27, Pt. VI in respect of any chargeable period or its basis period ending after 31 March 1985.

Effect of use after user not attracting capital allowances, or after receipt by way of gift

7.—(1) . . .[4], where a person—

(a) brings into use for the purposes of a trade carried on by him machinery or plant which belongs to him in consequence of his having incurred capital expenditure on its provision, [for purposes which were][1] such that that expenditure has not been taken into account in computing any allowance falling to be made in the case of the trade under Chapter I of Part III of this Act, or

(b) brings into use for the purposes of a trade carried on by him machinery or plant which belongs to him in consequence of a disposition by way of gift . . .[5]

the said section 44 shall have effect as if that person had incurred capital expenditure on the provision of the machinery or plant for the purposes of the trade in the chargeable period related to its bringing into use for those purposes, the amount of that expenditure being taken as the price which the machinery or plant would have fetched if sold in the open market on the date when it was so brought into use, and the machinery or plant being treated as belonging to that person in consequence of his having incurred that expenditure.

[(1A) Where sub-paragraph (1) above applies, the question whether the provision of the machinery or plant is to be taken to be wholly and exclusively or only partly for the purposes of the trade shall be determined according to whether the use referred to in paragraph (a) or, as the case may be, paragraph (*b*) of that sub-paragraph is wholly and exclusively or only partly for those purposes.]²

[(1B) Where a person is treated as having incurred capital expenditure on the provision of machinery or plant by virtue of sub-paragraph (1) (*b*) above, he shall for the purposes of paragraph 3 above be treated as having done so by way of purchase from the donor.]⁶

(2) Sub-paragraph (1) above shall not apply where a person brings into use for the purposes of a trade carried on by him machinery or plant which belongs to him in consequence of his having incurred capital expenditure on its provision and which he has previously used only for the purposes of activities carried on by him before commencing to work a mine, oil well, or other source of mineral deposits of a wasting nature, being activities consisting of—

(a) searching for or discovering and testing deposits or winning access thereto, or
(b) the construction of any works which are likely to be of little or no value when the source is no longer worked, or, where the source is worked under a foreign concession, which are likely to become valueless when the concession comes to an end to the person working the source immediately before the concession comes to an end;

but, in any such case, the actual expenditure incurred by that person on the provision of the machinery or plant shall be treated for the purposes of the said section 44 as having been incurred by him on its provision for the purposes of the trade in the chargeable period related to its bringing into use for those purposes.

In this sub-paragraph—

"foreign concession" means a right or privilege granted by the government of, or any municipality or other authority in, any territory outside the United Kingdom, and
*"mineral deposits" includes any natural deposits capable of being lifted or extracted from the earth.*³

Cross references.—See FA 1985, Sch. 15, para. 6 (election to treat as short-life assets cannot be made in respect of machinery or plant to which this paragraph applies);
TA 1988, Sch. 24, para. 10 (1) (application of this paragraph in relation to capital expenditure on machinery and plant incurred by a UK controlled foreign company before the year in which tax liability was imposed).
Amendments.—¹ Words in sub-para. (1) (*a*) substituted by FA 1985, Sch. 14, para. 8 (1) with respect to any chargeable period or its basis period ending after 31 March 1985.
² Sub-para. (1A) inserted by FA 1985, Sch. 14, para 8 (2) with respect to any chargeable period or its basis period ending after 31 March 1985.
³ Sub-para. (2) repealed by FA 1989, Sch. 17, Pt. VI. It was repealed also by FA 1986, s. 55 (7) (*d*) in relation to capital expenditure incurred after 31 March 1986, but subject to FA 1986, s. 55 (6).
⁴ Words "Subject to sub-paragraph (2) below" in sub-para. (1) repealed by FA 1989, Sch. 13, para. 13 (1), (2), (4) and Sch. 17, Pt. VI where machinery or plant is brought into use after 26 July 1989.
⁵ Words in sub-para. (1) (*b*) repealed by *ibid*. They read—
"by reason of which the donor was required by virtue of section 44 (5) of this Act to bring into account for the purposes there mentioned a disposal value equal to the price which the machinery or plant would have fetched if sold in the open market at the time of the gift,".
⁶ Sub-para. (1B) inserted FA 1989, Sch. 13, para. 13 (3), (4) and applies where machinery or plant is brought into use after 26 July 1989.

*Special rules for . . .*⁶ *ships*

8.—(1) Where for any chargeable period a first-year allowance falls to be made to a person carrying on a trade in respect of expenditure incurred by him on the provision of a . . .⁶ ship, that person may, by notice in writing given to the inspector not later than two years after the end of the period,

[(*a*) require the postponement of the whole allowance or, in the case of a company, disclaim it, or
(*b*) require that the amount of the allowance be reduced to an amount specified in the notice, or
(*c*) require the postponement of so much of the allowance as is so specified,

and a notice which contains a requirement under paragraph (*b*) above may also contain a requirement under paragraph (*c*) above with respect to the reduced amount of the allowance.]¹⁻²

(2) Where a notice has been given under sub-paragraph (1) above [requiring the postponement of the whole or part]³ of any first-year allowance—

(*a*) the allowance shall, as the case may require, be withheld or withdrawn, or partially withheld or withdrawn, and
(*b*) [so much of the expenditure as is equal to the whole allowance]⁴ shall be disregarded

for all the purposes of section 44 of this Act except the purposes of subsections (5) and (6) of that section, and

(c) the person giving the notice may claim the amount withheld or withdrawn as a first-year allowance for any subsequent chargeable period in which he carries on the trade, or may claim first-year allowances not exceeding that amount in the aggregate for any two or more such periods.

(3) All such assessments and adjustments of assessments shall be made as may be necessary to give effect to the provisions of this paragraph.

(4) An allowance which is postponed by virtue of this paragraph shall not by reason only of the postponement fall within the references to allowances or amounts carried forward from an earlier year or period in sections [383 (5) (*d*), 388 (7) and 403 (3)][8] of the Taxes Act (loss relief and group relief).

(5) . . .[7]

[(6) In any case where a notice under sub-paragraph (1) above contains requirements under both paragraphs (*b*) and (*c*) of that sub-paragraph, any reference in sub-paragraphs (2) to (5) above to the first-year allowance is a reference to the reduced amount of that allowance as specified in the notice.][5]

Cross references.—See FA 1980, s. 66 (7) (*a*) (restriction of allowances under sub-para. (2) (*c*) in respect of new ships used otherwise than for qualifying purposes under FA 1980, s. 64);
FA 1984, s. 59 (4) (*c*), (6) (*c*) (capital expenditure incurred after 13 March 1984; effect of a disclaimer or a reduction under sub-paras. (1) (*a*) or (1) (*b*) above for the purposes of s. 44 of this Act).
Amendments.—[1-2] Words in sub-para. (1), including the words following para. (*c*), substituted by FA 1984, s. 59 (2) with respect to expenditure incurred after 13 March 1984.
[3] Words in sub-para. (2) substituted by FA 1984, s. 59 (3) with respect to expenditure incurred after 13 March 1984.
[4] Words in sub-para. (2) (*b*) substituted by FA 1984, s. 58 (3).
[5] Sub-s. (6) added by FA 1984, s. 59 (3) (*b*) with respect to expenditure incurred after 13 March 1984.
[6] Word in the heading and in sub-para (1) repealed by FA 1985, s. 58 (1) (*a*) and Sch. 27, Pt. VI with respect to capital expenditure incurred after 31 March 1985.
[7] Sub-para. (5) repealed by FA 1985, s. 58 (1) (*b*) and Sch. 27, Pt. VI with respect to capital expenditure incurred after 31 March 1985.
[8] Numbers in sub-para. (4) substituted by TA 1988, Sch. 29, para. 32 Table.

[**8A.**—(1) This paragraph and paragraphs 8B and 8C below apply in any case where,—

(*a*) after the relevant date, a person (in this paragraph referred to as "the shipowner") carrying on a trade incurs expenditure on the provision of a ship for the purposes of that trade (in this paragraph referred to as his "actual trade");
(*b*) [the ship is not provided for leasing or letting on charter otherwise than by way of lease, or is so provided but it appears that the ship will be used in the requisite period (within the meaning of section 64 of the Finance Act 1980) for a qualifying purposes (within the meaning of that section) and will not at any time in that period be used for any other purpose, and the expenditure does not fall][4] within subsection (1) of section 70 of the Finance Act 1982 (which provides for only a 10 per cent. writing-down allowance for assets leased outside the United Kingdom); and
(*c*) the actual trade is not a separate trade which the shipowner is treated as carrying on by virtue of section 46(1) of this Act (machinery or plant let otherwise than in the course of a trade).

(2) In sub-paragraph (1) (*a*) above "the relevant date" means, in the case of expenditure on the provision of a new ship, 13th March 1984 and, in the case of expenditure on the provision of a ship which is not new, 31st March 1985; and for this purpose a ship which is not new is nevertheless to be regarded as a new ship if, at any time after 13th March 1984, it fell to be treated as a new ship for the purposes of paragraph 8 above (by virtue of sub-paragraph (5) of that paragraph).

(3) Subject to paragraphs 8B and 8C below, it shall be assumed for the purposes of section 44 of this Act and the following provisions of this paragraph—

(*a*) that the shipowner incurred the expenditure on the provision of the ship wholly and exclusively for the purposes of a trade (in this paragraph referred to as a "single ship trade") carried on by him separately from his actual trade and from any other trade which he may in fact carry on or is assumed for any purpose to carry on; and
(*b*) that, without prejudice to sub-paragraphs (i) to (iii) of paragraph (*c*) of subsection (5) of the said section 44, the single ship trade is permanently discontinued when the ship begins to be used wholly or partly for purposes other than those of the actual trade or, if it is earlier, at a time within the requisite period, within the meaning of section 64 of the Finance Act 1980, when the ship begins to be used otherwise than for a qualifying purpose within the meaning of that section;

and subject to the following provisions of this paragraph, any allowance or charge which, on those assumptions, would fall to be made for any chargeable period in the case of the single ship trade shall be made for that period in the case of the actual trade.

(4) The shipowner may, by notice in writing given to the inspector not later than two years after the end of a chargeable period for which he has qualifying expenditure in respect of his single ship trade, require the postponement of the whole of the writing-down allowance to be made to him for that period or of so much of it as is specified in the notice.

(5) Where notice has been given under sub-paragraph (4) above in respect of a chargeable period,—

> (*a*) the writing-down allowance which would otherwise have been made to the shipowner for that period in respect of his single ship trade shall not be made or, as the case may be, shall be made only to the extent that the notice does not require it to be postponed; and
> (*b*) the amount of any writing-down allowance falling to be made to the shipowner for any subsequent chargeable period of his single ship trade shall be determined as if the writing-down allowance referred to in paragraph (*a*) above had been made (or, as the case may be, had been made in full) for the chargeable period concerned; and
> (*c*) on a claim made by the shipowner, the whole or part of the amount of that allowance or, as the case may be, of so much of it as was not made to him shall be treated as a writing-down allowance to be made to him for any subsequent chargeable period in which his actual trade is carried on (whether or not his single ship trade is treated as carried on in that period),

and, where a claim under paragraph (*c*) above relates to only part of the amount postponed, a further claim or claims may be made under that paragraph in relation to the balance or any part thereof until the aggregate of the amounts claimed equals the amount postponed.

(6) A claim under sub-paragraph (5) (*c*) above shall not affect any right of the shipowner to (or the determination of the amount of) any writing-down allowance to which, apart from the claim, he is entitled for the chargeable period to which the claim relates.

(7) For any chargeable period of the single ship trade for which the amount of a writing-down allowance is reduced by virtue of a requirement—

> (*a*) in a claim made by virtue of the proviso to subsection (2) of section 44 of this Act, or
> (*b*) in a notice under subsection (2A) of that section,

any reference in sub-paragraphs (4) to (6) above to the writing-down allowance is a reference to the reduced amount of the allowance, as specified in the claim or notice concerned.

(8) For any chargeable period of the single ship trade for which the disposal value of the ship falls to be brought into account in accordance with section 44 of this Act, no balancing allowance or balancing charge shall be made to or on the shipowner in respect of that trade but, in such a case,—

> (*a*) if, apart from this sub-paragraph, a balancing allowance would have fallen to be made to the shipowner, an amount equal to that allowance shall for the purposes of section 44 of this Act be added to the shipowner's qualifying expenditure for that period in respect of his actual trade; and
> (*b*) if, apart from this sub-paragraph, a balancing charge would have fallen to be made on the shipowner, an amount equal to that on which the charge would have been made shall be brought into account for that chargeable period as an item of disposal value referable to machinery or plant which, in respect of that chargeable period, falls within subsection (5) of section 44 of this Act.

(9) In any case where sub-paragraph (8) above applies by reason of the ship beginning to be used otherwise than for a qualifying purpose, within the meaning of section 64 of the Finance Act 1980,—

> *(a) any reference in that sub-paragraph to section 44 of his Act shall be construed as a reference to that section as it has effect in accordance with section 65 of that Act; and*
> *(b) any reference therein to the shipowner's actual trade shall be construed as a reference to the separate trade referred to in subsection (2) of that section.*[2]

(10) All such assessments and adjustments of assessments shall be made as may be necessary to give effect to the provisions of this paragraph and paragraphs 8B and 8C below.

(11) An allowance which is postponed by virtue of this paragraph shall not by reason of the postponement fall within the references to allowances or amounts carried forward from an earlier year or period in section [383 (5) (*d*), 388 (7) and 403 (3)][3] of the Taxes Act (loss relief and group relief).][1]

Cross references.—See FA 1986, Sch. 16, para. 8 (7) (new capital expenditure (i.e. expenditure incurred after 31 March 1986 with certain exceptions mentioned in FA 1986, s. 57 (2), (3)) incurred for the provision of a ship used in the requisite period for lease outside the United Kingdom; no allowance can be claimed under sub-para. (5) (*c*) above).
Amendments.—[1] This paragraph inserted by FA 1985, Sch. 16.
[2] Sub-para. (9) repealed by FA 1986, s. 57 (5) in relation to capital expenditure incurred after 31 March 1986 on the provision of machinery or plant for leasing, but subject to FA 1986, s. 57 (1)–(4).
[3] Numbers in sub-para. (11) substituted by TA 1988, Sch. 29, para. 32 Table.
[4] Words in sub-para. (1) (*b*) substituted by FA 1989, Sch. 13, para. 14 in relation to expenditure incurred after 26 July 1989. The original words read—
"the expenditure is not such that section 64 of the Finance Act 1980 (which applies to leased assets used for certain purposes) precludes (or but for the provisions of paragraph 2 of Schedule 12 to the Finance Act 1984 would preclude) the making of a first-year allowance in respect of it and is not expenditure falling".

[**8B.**—(1) If the ship ceases to belong to the shipowner without having in fact been brought into use for the purposes of his actual trade, then,—

(*a*) on that event, the single ship trade shall be treated as permanently discontinued, but paragraph 4 above shall not apply;
(*b*) any writing-down allowances which, by virtue of paragraph 8A above, have previously been made to the shipowner or have been postponed by him shall be withdrawn; and
(*c*) without prejudice to the operation of paragraph 8A (8) above, an amount equal to any writing-down allowances withdrawn by virtue of paragraph (*b*) above shall be added to the shipowner's qualifying expenditure in respect of his actual trade for the chargeable period related to that event.

(2) In this paragraph "the shipowner", "actual trade" and "single ship trade" have the same meaning as in paragraph 8A above.][1]

Amendments.—[1] This paragraph inserted by FA 1985, Sch. 16.

[**8C.**—(1) The shipowner may, by notice in writing given to the inspector not later than two years after the end of a chargeable period of a single ship trade, not being the chargeable period relating to the permanent discontinuance of that trade, require that, with effect from the beginning of that chargeable period, paragraph 8A above shall not or, as the case may be, shall no longer apply.

(2) Where a notice under sub-paragraph (1) above is given before any writing-down allowance has been made to the shipowner in respect of the expenditure referred to in sub-paragraph (1) of paragraph 8A above, the provisions of that paragraph shall be deemed never to have applied with respect to that expenditure.

(3) If a notice under sub-paragraph (1) above is given after any writing-down allowance has been so made, then, for the purposes of section 44 of this Act and paragraph 8A above,—

(*a*) the single ship trade shall be treated as permanently discontinued in the chargeable period to which the notice relates or, as the case may be, in its basis period but no balancing allowance or charge shall be made to or on the shipowner by reason thereof; and
(*b*) the amount which, apart from this paragraph, would be the shipowner's qualifying expenditure for that chargeable period in respect of the single ship trade shall be added to his qualifying expenditure for that period in respect of his actual trade.

(4) The shipowner may, by notice in writing given to the inspector not later than two years after the end of a chargeable period of a single ship trade, require that an amount of expenditure specified in the notice, being less than the amount which, apart from this sub-paragraph, would be his qualifying expenditure for that period in respect of the single ship trade, shall be attributed to his actual trade.

(5) If a notice is given under sub-paragraph (4) above, then, for the purposes of section 44 of this Act and paragraph 8A above,—

(*a*) the shipowner's qualifying expenditure for that period in respect of the single ship trade shall be reduced by deducting therefrom the amount specified in the notice; and
(*b*) the amount specified in the notice shall be added to his qualifying expenditure for that period in respect of his actual trade.

(6) In this paragraph "the shipowner", "actual trade" and "single ship trade" have the same meaning as in paragraph 8A above.][1]

Amendments.—[1] This paragraph inserted by FA 1985, Sch. 16.

Special rules for motor cars

9. In paragraphs 10 to 12 below "motor car" means any mechanically-propelled road vehicle other than one within paragraph (*a*), (*b*) or (*c*) of [section 43 (1) of this Act][1].

Amendments—[1] Words substituted by F (No. 2) A 1979, s. 14 (4).

10.—(1) The following provisions of this paragraph shall have effect where capital expenditure exceeding [£8,000][1] is incurred, or is treated under any provision of this Schedule as incurred, on the provision of a motor car for the purposes of a trade.

(2) It shall be assumed for the purposes of section 44 of this Act—

(*a*) that . . .[2] the person carrying on the trade (hereafter called "the actual trade") [incurred the expenditure on the provision of the motor car wholly and exclusively][3] for the purposes of a trade carried on by him separately from the actual trade and any other trade he may carry on,
(*b*) . . .[2] and
(*c*) that [without prejudice to sub-paragraphs (i) to (iii) of paragraph (*c*) of subsection (5) of that section][4] the separate trade is permanently discontinued when the motor car [begins to be used wholly or partly for purposes other than those of the actual trade];[3]

and, subject to sub-paragraphs (3) to (5) below, the allowance or charge under that section which, on these assumptions, would fall to be made for any chargeable period in the case of the separate trade shall be made for that period in the case of the actual trade.

(3) If on the assumptions in sub-paragraph (2) above a writing-down allowance would fall to be made for any chargeable period in the case of the separate trade, the amount thereof shall be treated as not exceeding—

(*a*) except in a case falling within paragraph (*b*) below, [£2,000][1] or, if the period is part only of a year, a proportionate part of [£2,000][1],
(*b*) if (by virtue of section 84 of the Capital Allowances Act 1968 as applied by this Schedule) the person carrying on the trade is regarded as having incurred a part only of the expenditure actually incurred on the provision of the motor car, a proportionate part of [£2,000][1] or, if the period is part only of a year, that proportionate part proportionately reduced.

(4) [Where the disposal value of the motor car falls to be taken into account by reason of an event falling within section 44 (5) (*c*) (i) of this Act and that event is such a sale or the performance of such a contract as is referred to in paragraph 3 of this Schedule][5]—

(*a*) the disposal value to be brought into account under section 44 of this Act in the case of the separate trade shall be an amount equal to the price which the motor car would have fetched on a sale at the same time in the open market or, if less, the capital expenditure incurred, or treated as incurred, on the provision of the motor car by the person disposing of it, and
(*b*) the person acquiring the motor car shall be treated for the purposes of Chapter I of Part III of this Act as having incurred on its provision capital expenditure equal to that disposal value.

(5) If either of the following events occurs in relation to the motor car—

(*a*) it is used partly for the purposes of the actual trade and partly for other purposes, or
(*b*) while it is in use for the purposes of the actual trade, there is paid to the person carrying on the trade any sum which is in respect of, or takes account of, part of the wear and tear to it occasioned by that use,

neither paragraph 5 nor paragraph 6 of this Schedule shall apply, but for the chargeable period related to the event and any subsequent period, instead of there being made in the case of the actual trade the allowance or charge which under the preceding provisions of this paragraph would fall to be made for that period in the case of the separate trade, there shall be made so much of that allowance or charge as, in accordance with the said paragraph 5 or 6, would be just and reasonable if it were one falling to be made for that period in the case of the notional trade referred to in that paragraph.

Cross references.—See FA 1980, s. 69 (1) (*c*) (exclusion of writing-down allowance in respect of expenditure incurred on the provision of expensive cars for leasing);
FA 1982, s. 70 (2) (*c*) (modification of s. 44 of this Act in its application in accordance with this paragraph to expenditure for assets leased outside the United Kingdom);
FA 1985, Sch. 15, para. 7 (election to treat as short-life assets cannot be made in respect of motor cars falling within this paragraph).

Amendments.—[1] Amounts in sub-paras. (1) and (3) substituted by F (No. 2) A 1979, s. 14 (5), (7), (8), where the contract for the purchase of motor car was entered into after 12 June 1979.
[2] Words in sub-para. (2) (a), (c) repealed by FA 1985, Sch. 14, para. 9 (1) (a), (b) and Sch. 27, Pt. VI with respect to any chargeable period or its basis period ending after 31 March 1985.
[3] Words in sub-paras. (2) (a), (c) substituted by FA 1985, Sch. 14, para. 9 (1) (a), (c) with respect to any chargeable period or its basis period ending after 31 March 1985.
[4] Words in sub-para. (2) (c) inserted by FA 1985, Sch. 14, para. 9 (1) (c) with respect to any chargeable period or its basis period ending after 31 March 1985.
[5] Words in sub-para. (4) substituted by FA 1985, Sch. 14, para. 9 (2) with respect to any chargeable period on its basis period ending after 31 March 1985.

11. Where capital expenditure exceeding [£8,000][1] is incurred on the provision of a motor car and, by virtue of section 85 of the Capital Allowances Act 1968 as applied by this Schedule, writing-down allowances may be made to a person as if a contribution made by him to the expenditure had been expenditure on the provision of the motor car for the purposes of a trade, the amount of the allowance to be made for any chargeable period—

(a) shall be determined as if the contribution had been expenditure on the provision of the motor car for the purposes of a trade carried on by that person separately from any other trade carried on by him, and

(b) shall not exceed an amount bearing to [£2,000][1] the same proportion as that borne by the contribution to the capital expenditure actually incurred on the provision of the motor car or, if the chargeable period is part only of a year, that amount proportionately reduced.

Cross references.—See FA 1982, s. 70 (2) (d) (modification of s. 44 of this Act in its application in accordance with this paragraph to expenditure for assets leased outside the United Kingdom).
Amendments.—[1] Amounts substituted by F (No. 2) A 1979, s. 14 (5), (7), (8), where the contract for the purchase of motor car was entered into after 12 June 1979.

12. Where, apart from this paragraph, the amount of any expenditure on the hiring of a motor car the retail price of which when new exceeds [£8,000][1] would be allowed to be deducted in computing for the purposes of tax the profits or gains of any trade, the said amount shall be reduced in the proportion which [£8,000][1] together with one half of the excess, bears to the said retail price.

Amendments.—[1] Amounts substituted by F (No. 2) A 1979, s. 14 (5), (7), (8), where the contract for the purchase of motor car was entered into after 12 June 1979.

[12A. The Treasury may by order increase or further increase the sums of money specified in paragraphs 10, 11 and 12 above; and any such order shall be made by statutory instrument subject to annulment in pursuance of a resolution of the House of Commons.][1]

Amendments.—[1] This paragraph inserted by F (No. 2) A 1979, s. 14 (6).

Effect of successions to trades between connected persons

[13.—(1) Where at any time a person ("the successor") succeeds to a trade which was until that time carried on by another person ("the predecessor") and—

(a) the two persons are connected with each other;
(b) each of them is within the charge to tax in the United Kingdom on the profits of the trade; and
(c) the successor is not a dual resident investing company within the meaning of section 404 of the Taxes Act,

those persons may, by notice in writing given to the inspector not later than two years after that time, elect that the provisions of this paragraph shall have effect.

(2) In the event of such an election—

(a) for the purpose of making allowances and charges under Chapter I of Part III of this Act, any machinery or plant which—

(i) immediately before the time when the succession took place, belonged to the predecessor and was in use for the purposes of the trade; and
(ii) immediately after that time, belonged to the successor and was in use for those purposes,

shall (notwithstanding any actual sale or transfer) be treated as sold by the predecessor to the successor at a price which does not give rise to a balancing allowance or a balancing charge; and (*b*) allowances and charges shall be made under that Chapter to or on the successor as if everything done to or by the predecessor had been done to or by the successor.

(3) The predecessor and the successor are connected with each other for the purposes of this paragraph if—

(*a*) they are connected with each other within the meaning of section 839 of the Taxes Act;
(*b*) one of them is a partnership and the other has the right to a share in that partnership;
(*c*) one of them is a body corporate and the other has control over that body;
(*d*) both of them are partnerships and some other person has the right to a share in both of them; or
(*e*) both of them are bodies corporate, or one of them is a partnership and the other is a body corporate, and (in either case) some other person has control over both of them.

[(3A) Section 48 (1) of the Capital Allowances Act 1968 and section 65 (5) of the Finance Act 1980 shall not apply in any case where an election is made under this paragraph.]²

(4) All such assessments and adjustments of assessments shall be made as may be necessary to give effect to this paragraph.

(5) In this paragraph "control" shall be construed in accordance with section 840 of the Taxes Act; and any reference to the right to a share in a partnership is a reference to the right to a share of the assets or income of that partnership.]¹

Amendments.—¹ This paragraph substituted by FA 1988, s. 92 in relation to successions occurring after the passing of FA 1988. FA 1988 was passed on 29 July 1988.
² Sub-para. (3A) inserted by FA 1989, Sch. 13, para. 16 in relation to successions occurring after 26 July 1989.

Treatment of demolition costs

14.—(1) Where any machinery or plant which is in use for the purposes of a trade is demolished, then—

(*a*) if the person carrying on the trade replaces the machinery or plant by other machinery or plant, the net cost to him of the demolition shall be treated for the purposes of Chapter I of Part III of this Act as expenditure incurred by him on the provision of that other machinery or plant, and
(*b*) if the person carrying on the trade does not replace the machinery or plant, his qualifying expenditure for the chargeable period related to the demolition shall be treated for the purposes of section 44 of this Act as increased by the net cost to him of the demolition.

(2) In this paragraph any references to the net cost of the demolition of any machinery or plant is a reference to the excess, if any, of the cost of the demolition over any moneys received for the remains of the machinery or plant.

Application of certain provisions of Capital Allowances Act 1968

15.—(1) Section 44 of the Capital Allowances Act 1968 (partnership using property of a partner) shall have effect as if the reference in subsection (1) to Chapter II of Part I of that Act included a reference to Chapter I of Part III of this Act, and as if the references in subsection (2) to section 33 of that Act and an event giving rise to a balancing allowance or balancing charge included references respectively to section 44 (5) of this Act and an event requiring any disposal value to be brought into account.

(2) In section 45 of the said Act of 1968 (building alterations connected with installation of machinery or plant), the reference to the said Chapter II shall include a reference to the said Chapter I.

(3) Section 48 of the said Act of 1968 (successions to trades) shall, with the omission of the proviso to subsection (4) and subsection (6), have effect as if references therein to initial allowances, the said Chapter II, and section 47 (1) of that Act included references respectively to first-year allowances, the said Chapter I and section 47 (1) of this Act; but, in its application by virtue of this sub-paragraph, the section shall be modified by substituting—

[(*a*) in subsection (1), for the words "in use", in each place where they occur, the words "either in use or provided and available for use"; and

(b) in subsection (2), for the word "used" the words "either used or provided and available for use"; and

(c)][2] for all the words in subsection (2) from "be deemed to be a reference" to the end of that subsection, the words "be deemed to be a reference to that price or, if it is less than that price, any excess of qualifying expenditure over disposal value which would have been taken into account under section 44 of the Finance Act 1971 for making an allowance for the chargeable period related to the permanent discontinuance of the deceased person's trade if the machinery or plant had had no disposal value."

(4) In section 77 of the said Act of 1968 (apportionments etc.) references to Part I of that Act shall include references to the said Chapter I; and the said Chapter I shall be treated as included in the provisions referred to in section 81 (2) of that Act (procedure on apportionments etc.).

(5) In section 84 (1) of the said Act of 1968 (subsidies etc.), the reference to Part I of that Act shall include a reference to the said Chapter I.

(6) Section 85 (1) of the said Act (allowances in respect of contributions to capital expenditure) shall have effect as if the references therein to initial allowances and writing-down allowances included references respectively to first-year allowances and writing-down allowances under the said Chapter I, but, in its application by virtue of this sub-paragraph, modified by substituting the words "of that asset" for the words "of a similar asset"; and, for the purpose of any allowance under the said Chapter I given by virtue of the said section 85 (1) in respect of any asset, that asset shall be treated as belonging to the person making the contribution in respect of which the allowance is given at any time when it belongs, or is treated under the said Chapter I [or Schedule 17 to the Finance Act 1985][1] as belonging, to the recipient of the contribution.

Amendments.—[1] Words in sub-para. (6) inserted by FA 1985, s. 59 (8) in relation to expenditure incurred after 11 July 1984; see FA 1985, s. 59 (2).
[2] Words in sub-para. (3) substituted by FA 1985, Sch. 14, para. 10 with respect to any chargeable period or its basis period ending after 31 March 1985.

Amendments of other enactments

16.—(1)[1]

(2) Any reference in the Capital Allowances Act 1968 to Chapter II of Part I of that Act shall, unless it is in the said Chaper II or in Chapter VI of the said Part I, include a reference to Chapter I of Part III of this Act.

(3)–(9) . . .[3]

(10) . . .[2]

Amendments.—[1] Sub-para. (1) repealed by CGTA 1979, s. 158 and Sch. 8.
[2] Sub-para. (10) repealed by the Civil Aviation Act 1982, Sch. 16.
[3] Sub-paras. (3)–(9) repealed by TA 1988, Sch. 31.

Transitional provision as to roll-over relief

17. Where section 40 of the Capital Allowances Act 1968 applies on a person's replacement of any machinery or plant by other machinery or plant on the provision of which his expenditure is capital expenditure to which Chapter I of Part III of this Act applies, it shall so apply with the substitution of the following for all the words from the beginning of paragraph (a) of subsection (1) to the end of the section—

. . .

. . .

Notes.—Words omitted amend CAA 1968, s. 40.
Chapter I of Part III of this Act applies to capital expenditure incurred on or after 27 October 1970.

FINANCE ACT 1972

(1972 Chapter 41)

ARRANGEMENT OF SECTIONS

Note.—Provisions of this Act relevant to the taxes covered by this Handbook and not reproduced are either spent or repealed by TA 1988, Sch. 31 and other legislation.

PART IV

INCOME TAX AND CORPORATION TAX

Section
67. Capital allowances.
68. Restriction of capital allowances in respect of machinery and plant.
69. Restriction of balancing allowances on sale of industrial buildings and structures.

PART V

TAXATION OF COMPANIES AND COMPANY DISTRIBUTIONS

Supplementary

111. Consequential amendments.

PART VII

MISCELLANEOUS

127. Disclosure of information between revenue departments.
130. Compensation for loss of office etc. by clerks to General Commissioners.
131. Post-war credits.
134. Citation, interpretation, construction, extent and repeals.

An Act to grant certain duties, to alter other duties, and to amend the law relating to the National Debt and the Public Revenue, and to make further provision in connection with Finance.
[27th July 1972]

PART IV
INCOME TAX AND CORPORATION TAX

67. Capital allowances

(1) . . .

(2) In relation to expenditure incurred after 21st March 1972—

(a)–(d) . . .

and accordingly subsection (1) (b) of section 15 of the Finance Act 1970 shall not apply to expenditure so incurred.

(4) Expenditure shall not be treated for the purposes of this section as having been incurred after the date on which it was in fact incurred by reason only of section 1 (6) of the Capital Allowances Act 1968 (expenditure incurred before trade began) or section 5 (1) of that Act (purchase of unused buildings) or so much of section 50 (4) of the Finance Act 1971 as relates to expenditure incurred before trade began.

Notes.—Sub-s. (1) amends FA 1971, s. 42 in relation to expenditure incurred after 19 July 1971 and before 22 March 1972.
Sub-s. (2) (a)–(d) amend CAA 1968, s. 1 (2), TA 1970, s. 177 (3A), FA 1971, s. 42 and Sch. 8, para. 8.
Sub-s. (3) amends CAA 1968, ss. 84 (1), 95 (6).

68. Restriction of capital allowances in respect of machinery and plant

(1) Chapter I of Part III of the Finance Act 1971 shall not apply to capital expenditure on the provision of second-hand machinery or plant incurred by any person on or after 14th June 1972 if—

(a) the machinery or plant belonged to him at any time before 27th October 1970 or fell to be treated as belonging to him at any such time for the purposes of any provision of Chapter II of Part I of the Capital Allowances Act 1968; or

(b) capital expenditure on providing the machinery or plant was incurred by another person before the said 27th October and the machinery or plant continues after the date of the transaction under which the first-mentioned expenditure is incurred to be used for the purposes of a trade carried on by that other person.

(2) . . .[1]

(3) Paragraph 3 of Schedule 8 to the said Act of 1971 shall be amended as follows—

(a)–(c) . . .

and paragraph (b) of each of those sub-paragraphs shall have effect as if the reference to the machinery or plant continuing to be used for the purposes of a trade carried on by the person there mentioned included a reference to its being used after the date of the sale, the making of the contract or the assignment of the benefit of the contract (as the case may be) for the purposes of a trade carried on by that person or another person who is connected with him (other than the buyer, the person entering into the contract or the assignee) without having been used since that date for the purposes of any other trade except that of leasing machinery or plant.

(4) In a case in which no disposal value falls to be brought into account as mentioned in sub-paragraph (1) of the said paragraph 3, that sub-paragraph shall have effect as if for the reference to the disposal value to be so brought into account there were substituted a reference to an amount equal to whichever of the following is the smallest—

(a) the open market value of the machinery or plant;
[(b) where capital expenditure was incurred by the seller on the provision of the machinery or plant, the amount of that expediture;][3]
[(c) where capital expenditure was incurred by any person connected with the seller on the provision of the machinery or plant, the amount of the expenditure incurred by that person.][3]

(5) The said sub-paragraph (1) shall not by virtue of paragraph (*a*) or (*b*) thereof deny a first-year allowance if the machinery or plant has not before the sale been used for the purposes of a trade by the seller or any person connected with him but for the purposes of that allowance there shall be disregarded so much (if any) of the expenditure as exceeds whichever is the smallest of the amounts mentioned in subsection (4) (*a*), (*b*) and (*c*) above.

(6) Subsections (4) and (5) above shall apply in relation to sub-paragraphs (2) and (3) of the said paragraph 3 as they apply in relation to sub-paragraph (1) of that paragraph but taking references—

(*a*) to the sale as references to the making of the contract and to the assignment of the benefit of the contract respectively;
(*b*) to the seller as references to the person to whom the machinery or plant belongs and to the assignor respectively.

(7) Neither sub-paragraph (1) nor sub-paragraph (2) of the said paragraph 3 shall apply in relation to a sale or contract if the machinery or plant has never been used before the sale or the making of the contract and the business or part of the business of the seller or owner was the manufacture or supply of machinery or plant of that class and the sale was effected or the contract was made in the ordinary course of that business.

(8) . . .

(9) Subsections (3) to (7) above apply in relation to cases where the incurring of the capital expenditure, the making of the contract or the assignment of the benefit of the contract mentioned in the said paragraph 3 (1), (2) or (3) occurs on or after 14th June 1972, and subsection (8) above has effect from that date.

(10) This section shall be construed as if contained in Chapter I of Part III of the said Act of 1971; and in this section "open market value" in relation to any machinery or plant means an amount equal to the price which the machinery or plant would have fetched if sold in the open market and references to persons connected with each other shall be construed in accordance with section [839][2] of the Taxes Act.

Notes.—Sub-s. (3) (*a*)–(*c*) amend FA 1971, Sch. 8, para. 3.
Sub-s. (8) amends FA 1971, Sch. 8, para. 4.
Cross references.—See FA 1976, s. 39 (the system of capital allowances introduced by FA 1971 to include certain expenditure otherwise excluded from that system by sub-s. (1) of this section).
Amendments.—[1] Sub-s. (2) repealed by FA 1976, s. 40 (2), (3) and Sch. 15, Pt. III as respect disposals after 15 April 1976.
[2] Number in sub-s. (10) substituted by TA 1988, Sch. 29, para. 32 Table.
[3] Sub-s. (4) (*b*), (*c*) substituted by FA 1989, Sch. 13, para. 17.

69. Restriction of balancing allowances on sale of industrial buildings and structures

(1) This section has effect where—

(*a*) the relevant interest in a building or structure is sold subject to a subordinate interest; and
(*b*) a balancing allowance would, apart from this section, fall to be made to the person who is entitled to the relevant interest immediately before the sale ("the relevant person") under section 3 of the Capital Allowances Act 1968 by virtue of the sale; and
(*c*) either—

(i) the relevant person, the person to whom the relevant interest is sold and the grantee of the subordinate interest, or any two of them, are connected with each other within the terms of section [839][1] of the Taxes Act, or
(ii) it appears with respect to the sale or to the grant of the subordinate interest, or with respect to transactions including the sale or grant, that the sole or main benefit which, but for this section, might have been expected to accrue to the parties or any of them was the obtaining of an allowance under Chapter I of Part I of the said Act of 1968.

(2) For the purposes of section 3 of the said Act of 1968 the net proceeds to the relevant person of the sale—

(*a*) shall be taken to be increased by an amount equal to any premium receivable by him for the grant of the subordinate interest; and
(*b*) where no rent, or no commercial rent, is payable in respect of the subordinate interest, shall be taken to be what those proceeds would have been if a commercial rent had been payable and the relevant interest had been sold in the open market (increased by any amount to be added under paragraph (*a*) of this subsection);

but the net proceeds of sale shall not by virtue of this subsection be taken to be greater than such amount as will secure that no balancing allowance falls to be made.

(3) Where subsection (2) above operates, in relation to a sale, to deny or reduce a balancing allowance in respect of any expenditure the residue of that expenditure immediately after the sale shall be calculated for the purposes of Chapter I of Part I of the said Act of 1968 as if that balancing allowance had been made or, as the case may be, had not been reduced.

(4) In this section—

"subordinate interest" means any interest in or right over the building or structure in question (whether granted by the relevant person or by somebody else);
"premium" includes any capital consideration except so much if any sum as corresponds to any amount of rent or profits falling to be computed by reference to that sum under section [34][1] of the Taxes Act (premium treated as rent or Schedule D profits);
"capital consideration" means consideration which consists of a capital sum or would be a capital sum if it had taken the form of a money payment;
"rent" includes any consideration which is not capital consideration;
"commercial rent" means such rent as may reasonably be expected to have been required in respect of the subordinate interest in question (having regard to any premium payable for the grant of the interest) if the transaction had been at arm's length.

(5) Where the terms on which a subordinate interest is granted are varied before the sale of the relevant interest any capital consideration for the variation shall be treated for the purposes of this section as a premium for the grant of the interest, and the question whether any and, if so, what rent is payable in respect of the interest shall be determined by reference to the terms as in force immediately before the sale.

(6) This section shall be construed as if contained in Chapter I of Part I of the said Act of 1968 and applies where the relevant interest is sold on or after 14th June 1972.

Amendments.—[1] Numbers in sub-s. (1) (*c*) (i), (4) substituted by TA 1988, Sch. 29, para. 32 Table.

PART V

TAXATION OF COMPANIES AND COMPANY DISTRIBUTIONS

111. Consequential amendments

(1) ...

(2) ...[1]

(3) This section has effect from 6th April 1973 and does not affect the operation of any enactment in relation to any previous time; and no amendment in the said Schedule 24 adapting an enactment so as to make it apply or refer to a provision of this Act instead of a provision repealed thereby shall be construed as affecting the operation of that enactment in relation to the repealed provision so far as concerns matters occurring before the repeal or otherwise unaffected by it.

Note.—Sub-s. (1) amends the enactments specified in Sch. 24.
Amendments.—[1] Sub-s. (2) repealed by TA 1988, Sch. 31.

PART VII

MISCELLANEOUS

127. Disclosure of information between revenue departments

(1) No obligation as to secrecy or other restriction upon the disclosure of information imposed by statute or otherwise shall prevent either—

(*a*) the Commissioners of Inland Revenue or an authorised officer of those Commissioners; or
(*b*) the Commissioners of Customs and Excise or an authorised officer of those Commissioners;

from disclosing information to the other Commissioners or an authorised officer of the other Commissioners for the purpose of assisting them in the performance of their duties.

(2) Information obtained in pursuance of this section shall not be disclosed except—

(*a*) to the Commissioners or an authorised officer of the Commissioners on whose behalf it was obtained; or
(*b*) for the purpose of any proceedings connected with a matter in relation to which those Commissioners perform duties.

130. Compensation for loss of office etc. by clerks to General Commissioners

(1) The Commissioners of Inland Revenue may, with the concurrence of the Minister for the Civil Service, by regulations provide for the payment out of money provided by Parliament of compensation to or in respect of any clerk to the General Commissioners for any division who suffers or has suffered loss of office or loss or diminution of emoluments which is attributable to any order affecting that division made (whether before or after the passing of this Act) under section 2 (6) of the Taxes Management Act 1970 (alteration and abolition of divisions).

(2) Regulations under this section may—

(*a*) include provision as to the manner in which and the person to whom any claim for compensation under the regulations is to be made, and for the determination of all questions arising under the regulations;
(*b*) make different provision for different classes of persons and for different circumstances, and make, or authorise the Commissioners of Inland Revenue to make, exceptions and conditions;
(*c*) be framed so as to have effect from a date earlier than the making of the regulations,

but so that regulations having effect from a date earlier than their making shall not place any individual in a worse position than he would have been in if the regulations had been so framed as to have effect only from the date of their making.

(3) Regulations under this section shall be made by statutory instrument subject to annulment in pursuance of a resolution of either House of Parliament.

131. Post-war credits

(1) On the repayment of any post-war credit, or payment to a building society of any amount outstanding under section 3 of the Income Tax (Repayment of Post-War Credits) Act 1959, the sum payable, inclusive of the interest, may be taken by the Commissioners of Inland Revenue as amounting to 138 per cent. of the credit as notified under section 7 of the Finance Act 1941 or of the amount so outstanding, as the case may be.

(2) An application for such a repayment made before the applicant is qualified may, if he later becomes qualified, be treated as made on the date when he does so.

(3) No such repayment shall be made unless application therefor is made before such time (not earlier than the beginning of the year 1974) as the Treasury may by order direct.

Any order under this subsection shall be made by statutory instrument, which shall be laid before Parliament after being made, and may be varied by a subsequent order so as to extend the time for applications for repayment.

[(3A) An order under subsection (3) above may make different provision for different cases or classes of case and may provide that no amount shall be ascertained, recorded or notified under section 7 of the Finance Act 1941 after any such time as may be specified in the order.]¹

(4) In this section "post-war credit" has the same meaning as in the Income Tax (Repayment of Post-War Credits) Act 1959.

(5) This section shall be deemed to have had effect from the beginning of April 1972.

Amendments.—¹ Sub-s. (3A) inserted by FA 1976, s. 59.

134. Citation, interpretation, construction, extent and repeals

(1) This Act may be cited as the Finance Act 1972.

(2) In this Act "the Taxes Act" means the Income and Corporation Taxes Act [1988]².

(3) In this Act—

(a) . . .
(b) Parts IV and V, so far as they relate to income tax, shall be construed as one with the Income Tax Acts and, so far as they relate to corporation tax, shall be construed as one with the Corporation Tax Acts;
(c) . . .¹
(d) . . .

(4) Except so far as the context otherwise requires, any reference in this Act to any enactment shall be construed as a reference to that enactment as amended, and as including a reference to that enactment as applied, by or under any other enactment, including this Act.

(5) Except as otherwise expressly provided, such of the provisions of this Act as relate to matters in respect of which the Parliament of Northern Ireland has power to make laws do not extend to Northern Ireland.

(6) If the Parliament of Northern Ireland passes provisions amending or replacing any enactment of that Parliament referred to in this Act the reference shall be construed as a reference to the enactment as so amended or, as the case may be, as a reference to those provisions.

(7) . . .

Notes.—Sub-s. (3), paras. (a), (d) are outside the scope of this work.
Sub-s. (7) repeals enactments specified in Sch. 28. Effect has been given to these repeals, where applicable, in the relevant provisions of the earlier enactments.
Amendments.—¹ Sub-s. (3) (c) repealed by CGTA 1979, s. 158 and Sch. 8.
² Year in sub-s. (2) substituted by TA 1988, Sch. 29, para. 32 Table.

FINANCE ACT 1973

(1973 Chapter 51)

ARRANGEMENT OF SECTIONS

Note.—Provisions of this Act relevant to the taxes covered in this Handbook and not reproduced are either spent or repealed by TA 1988, Sch. 31 and other legislation.

PART III

INCOME TAX, CORPORATION TAX AND CAPITAL GAINS TAX

Section
32. Information as to arrangements for transferring relief, etc.
38. Territorial extension of charge to income tax, capital gains tax and corporation tax.

PART VI

MISCELLANEOUS AND GENERAL

59. Citation, interpretation, construction, extent and repeals.

SCHEDULES:

Schedule 15—Territorial extension of charge to tax—supplementary provisions.

An Act to grant certain duties, to alter other duties, and to amend the law relating to the National Debt and the Public Revenue, and to make further provision in connection with Finance.
[25th July 1973]

PART III
INCOME TAX, CORPORATION TAX AND CAPITAL GAINS TAX

32. Information as to arrangements for transferring relief, etc.

(1) If a company—

(*a*) makes a claim for group relief, or
(*b*) being a party to a leasing contract, as defined in section [395 of the Taxes Act 1988]², claims relief as mentioned in subsection (1) (*b*) of that section, or
(*c*) being a member of a partnership, either claims any relief which, if subsection (2) of section [116 of that Act]² applied in relation to it, it would not be entitled to claim, or makes a return which is treated as a claim by virtue of section [239 (5) of that Act]², or
(*d*) makes a claim under section [240 of that Act]² (surrender of advance corporation tax),

and the inspector has reason to believe that any relevant arrangements may exist, or may have existed at any time material to the claim, then at any time after the claim (or return) is made he may serve notice in writing on the company requiring it to furnish him, within such time being not less than thirty days from the giving of the notice as he may direct, with—

(i) a declaration in writing stating whether or not any such arrangements exist or existed at any material time, or
(ii) such information as he may reasonably require for the purpose of satisfying himself whether or not any such arrangements exist or existed at any material time, or
(iii) both such a declaration and such information.

(2) In this section "relevant arrangements", in relation to a claim (including a return which is treated as a claim) falling within any of paragraphs (*a*) to (*d*) of subsection (1) above, means such arrangements as are referred to in that enactment which is specified in the corresponding paragraph below, that is to say,—

[(*a*) section 410 (1) or (2) of or paragraph 5 (3) of Schedule 18 to the Taxes Act 1988;
(*b*) section 395 (1) (*c*) of that Act;
(*c*) section 116 (1) of that Act;
(*d*) paragraph 5 (3) of Schedule 18 to or section 240 (11) of that Act.]³

(3) In a case falling within paragraph (*a*) of subsection (1) above, a notice under that subsection may be served on the surrendering company, within the meaning of section [402 of the Taxes Act 1988]², instead of or as well as on the company claiming relief.

(4) In a case falling within paragraph (*c*) of subsection (1) above, a notice under that subsection may be served on the partners instead of or as well as on the company alone, and accordingly may require them, instead of or as well as the company, to furnish the declaration, information or declaration and information concerned.

(5) ...¹

(6) In this section, ...¹ "arrangements" means arrangements of any kind, whether in writing or not.

Amendments.—¹ Sub-s. (5) and words in sub-s. (6) repealed by TA 1988, Sch. 31.
² Words in sub-ss. (1) (*b*), (*c*), (*d*), (3) substituted by TA 1988, Sch. 29, para. 32 Table.
³ Sub-s. (2) (*a*)–(*d*) substituted by TA 1988, Sch. 29, para. 32 Table.

38. Territorial extension of charge to income tax, capital gains tax and corporation tax

(1) The territorial sea of the United Kingdom shall for all purposes of ...⁵, capital gains tax ...⁵ (including the following provisions of this section) be deemed to be part of the United Kingdom.

(2) In this section and in Schedule 15 to this Act—

(a) "exploration or exploitation activities" means activities carried on in connection with the exploration or exploitation of so much of the seabed and subsoil and their natural resources as is situated in the United Kingdom or a designated area; and

(b) "exploration or exploitation rights" means rights to assets to be produced by exploration or exploitation activities or to interests in or to the benefit of such assets; and

(c) references to the disposal of exploration or exploitation rights include references to the disposal of shares deriving their value or the greater part of their value directly or indirectly from such rights, other than shares quoted on a recognised stock exchange (within the meaning of the Corporation Tax Acts); and

(d) "shares" includes stock and any security as defined in section [254 (1) of the Taxes Act 1988][7]; and

(e) "designated area" means an area designated by Order in Council under section 1 (7) of the Continental Shelf Act 1964.

(3) [Any gains accruing on the disposal of exploration or exploitation rights][7] shall be treated for the purposes of [the Capital Gains Tax Act 1979][1] as gains accruing on the disposal of assets situated in the United Kingdom.

[(3A) Gains accruing on the disposal of—

(a) exploration or exploitation assets which are situated in a designated area, or

(b) unquoted shares deriving their value or the greater part of their value directly or indirectly from exploration or exploitation assets situated in the United Kingdom or a designated area or from such assets and exploration or exploitation rights taken together,

shall be treated for the purposes of the Capital Gains Tax Act 1979 as gains accruing on the disposal of assets situated in the United Kingdom.][2]

[(3B) For the purposes of this section, an asset disposed of is an exploration or exploitation asset if either—

(a) it is not a mobile asset and it is being or has at some time . . .[8] been used in connection with exploration or exploitation activities carried on in the United Kingdom or a designated area; or

(b) it is a mobile asset which [has at some time][9] been used in connection with exploration or exploitation activities so carried on and is dedicated to an oil field in which the person making the disposal, or a person connected with him within the meaning of section [839 of the Taxes Act 1988][7], is or has been a participator;

and expressions used in paragraphs (a) and (b) above have the same meaning as if those paragraphs were included in Part I of the Oil Taxation Act 1975.][2]

[(3C) In paragraph (b) of subsection (3A) above "unquoted shares" means shares other than those which are quoted on a recognised stock exchange (within the meaning of the Corporation Tax Acts); and references in subsections (4) and (5) below to exploration or exploitation assets include references to unquoted shares falling within that paragraph.][2]

[(4) Gains accruing to a person not resident in the United Kingdom on the disposal of exploration or exploitation rights or of exploration or exploitation assets shall, for the purposes of capital gains tax or corporation tax on chargeable gains, be treated as gains accruing on the disposal of assets used for the purposes of a trade carried on by that person in the United Kingdom through a branch or agency.

This subsection shall have effect in relation to gains accruing on disposals before 13th March 1984 with the omission of the words "exploration or exploitation assets".][4]

(5) In relation to exploration or exploitation rights [or exploration or exploitation assets][3] disposed of by a company resident in a territory outside the United Kingdom to a company resident in the same territory or in the United Kingdom, sections 273 to 275 and 278 to 279 of [the Taxes Act 1970][7] (transfer within group and company ceasing to be member of group) shall apply as if in section 272 of that Act (definition of "group" etc.) subsections (1) (a) and (2) were omitted.

(6) . . .[6]

(7) This section shall have effect for the purposes of income tax and capital gains tax for the year 1973–74 and subsequent years of assessment and for the purposes of corporation tax for the financial year 1973 and subsequent years.

(8) Schedule 15 to this Act shall have effect for supplementing this section.

Cross references.—See CGTA 1979, s. 2 (2) (territorial sea of the UK as part of the UK for capital gains tax purposes); FA 1982, s. 70 (1) (*b*) (capital allowances for machinery or plant leased outside the UK and used for earning profits not falling within sub-s. (4) above).
Amendments.—[1] Words in sub-s. (3) substituted by CGTA 1979, s. 157 (2)–(4) and Sch. 7, para. 8 Table, Pt. I. 5, with effect from 22 March 1979.
[2] Sub-ss. (3A)–(3C) inserted by FA 1984, s. 81 (2), (5) in relation to disposals after 12 March 1984.
[3] Words in sub-ss. (4), (5) inserted by FA 1984, s. 81 (3)–(5) in relation to disposals after 12 March 1984.
[4] Sub-s. (4) substituted by TA 1988, Sch. 29, para. 12.
[5] Words in sub-s. (1) repealed by TA 1988, Sch. 31.
[6] Sub-s. (6) repealed by *ibid*.
[7] Words in sub-ss. (2) (*d*), (3), (3B), (5) substituted by TA 1988, Sch. 29, para. 32 Table.
[8] Words in sub-s. (3B) (*a*) repealed by FA 1989, s. 130 (1) (*a*) and Sch. 17, Pt. VII where assets are disposed of after 13 March 1989.
[9] Words in sub-s. (3B) (*b*) substituted by FA 1989, s. 130 (1) (*b*) where assets are disposed of after 13 March 1989.

41. General Commissioners' divisions

The boundaries of any division specified by an order made or having effect as if made under section 2 (6) of the Taxes Management Act 1970 and in operation immediately before—

(*a*) 1st April 1974, if the division is in England or Wales; and
(*b*) 16th May 1975, if the division is in Scotland;

shall remain the same on and after that day as if there were then no change of local government areas (but without prejudice to the making of new orders under that section).

PART VI
MISCELLANEOUS AND GENERAL

59. Citation, interpretation, construction, extent and repeals

(1) This Act may be cited as the Finance Act 1973.

[(2) In this Act—

(a) "the Taxes Act 1970" means the Income and Corporation Taxes Act 1970; and
(b) "the Taxes Act 1988" means the Income and Corporation Taxes Act 1988.][2]

(3) In this Act—

(a) ...
(b) ...
(c) Part III, so far as it relates to income tax, shall be construed as one with the Income Tax Acts, so far as it relates to corporation tax, shall be construed as one with the Corporation Tax Acts and, so far as it relates to capital gains tax, shall be construed as one with [the Capital Gains Tax Act 1979][1];
(d) ...
(e) ...

(4) Except so far as the context otherwise requires, any reference in this Act to any enactment shall be construed as a reference to that enactment as amended, and as including a reference to that enactment as applied, by or under any other enactment, including this Act.

(5) Except as otherwise expressly provided, such of the provisions of this Act to relate to matters in respect of which the Parliament of Northern Ireland has power to make laws do not extend to Northern Ireland.

(6) If the Parliament of Northern Ireland passes provisions amending or replacing any enactment of that Parliament referred to in this Act the reference shall be construed as a reference to the enactment as so amended or, as the case may be, as a reference to those provisions.

(7) The enactments mentioned in Schedule 22 to this Act (which include certain enactments which had ceased to have effect before the commencement of this Act) are hereby repealed to the extent specified in the third column of that Schedule, but subject to any provision at the end of any Part of that Schedule.

Note.—Sub-s. (3), paras. (a), (b), (d) and (e) are outside the scope of this work.
Amendments.—[1] Words in sub-s. (3) (c) substituted by CGTA 1979, s. 157 (2)–(4) and Sch. 7, para. 8 Table, Pt. I. 5, with effect from 22 March 1979.
[2] Sub-s. (2) substituted by TA 1988, Sch. 29, para. 32 Table.

SCHEDULES

SCHEDULE 15
Section 38

TERRITORIAL EXTENSION OF CHARGE TO TAX—SUPPLEMENTARY PROVISIONS

Information

2. The holder of any licence granted under the Petroleum (Production) Act 1934 shall, if required to do so by a notice served on him by an inspector, give to the inspector within the time limited by the notice (which shall not be less than thirty days) such particulars as may be required by the notice of—

(*a*) transactions in connection with activities authorised by the licence as a result of which any person is or might be liable to tax by virtue of section 38 of [this Act or section 830 of the Taxes Act 1988][2]; and

(*b*) [emoluments or other payments paid or payable in respect of duties or services][1] performed in an area in which those activities may be carried on under the licence and the persons to whom they were paid or are payable;

and shall take reasonable steps to obtain the information necessary to enable him to comply with the notice.

Amendments.—[1] Words in sub-para. (*b*) substituted by FA 1978, s. 29 (3), (4).
[2] Words in para. (*a*) substituted by TA 1988, Sch. 29, para. 32 Table.

Collection

4.—(1) Subject to the following provisions of this Schedule, where any tax is assessed by virtue of section 38 of [this Act or section 830 of the Taxes Act 1988][2] on a person not resident in the United Kingdom in respect of—

(*a*) profits or gains from activities authorised, or carried on in connection with activities authorised, by a licence granted under the Petroleum (Production) Act 1934, or

(*b*) profits or gains from, or chargeable gains accruing on the disposal of, exploration or exploitation rights connected with activities so authorised or carried on,

then, if the tax remains unpaid later than thirty days after it has become due and payable, the Board may serve a notice on the holder of the licence stating particulars of the assessment, the amount remaining unpaid and the date when it became payable, and requiring the holder of the licence to pay that amount, together with any interest due thereon under section 86 of the Taxes Management Act 1970, within thirty days of the service of the notice.

(2) Any amount which a person is required to pay by a notice under this paragraph may be recovered from him as if it were tax due and duly demanded from him; and he may recover any such amount paid by him from the person on whom the assessment was made.

[(3) A payment in pursuance of a notice under this paragraph shall not be allowed as a deduction in computing any income, profits or losses for any tax purposes.][1]

Note.—See **Prospective Legislation Notes** (Taxes Management Provisions).
Cross references.—See FA 1988, s. 130 (7) (*e*) (securing payment from a migrating company of outstanding amount under this paragraph).
Amendments.—[1] Sub-para. (3) inserted by FA 1984, s. 124 (1).
[2] Words in sub-para. (1) substituted by TA 1988, Sch. 29, para. 32 Table.

[**4A.**—(1) Subject to the following provisions of this Schedule, the power of the Board under paragraph 4 above to serve a notice in respect of tax remaining unpaid as there mentioned shall also apply where—

(a) tax is assessed on any person not resident in the United Kingdom as mentioned in paragraph 4 (1) (a) or (b) but more than one licence under the Petroleum (Production) Act 1934 is the basis for the assessment; or

(b) tax assessed on any such person includes, but is not limited to, tax assessed on him as so mentioned (whether by reference to one or to more than one such licence);

but in any such case the amount the holder of any licence in question may be required to pay by a notice under that paragraph shall be the amount of the tax remaining unpaid under the assessment which is attributable to the profits or gains in respect of which that licence was the basis for the assessment, together with a corresponding proportion of any interest due as mentioned in paragraph 4 (1).

(2) For the purposes of sub-paragraph (1) above the amount of the tax remaining unpaid under the assessment which is attributable to the profits or gains in respect of which any licence in question was the basis for the assessment is such part of the total amount of that tax as bears to that total amount the same proportion as the proportion borne by the amount of the profits or gains in respect of which that licence was the basis for the assessment to the total amount of the profits or gains in respect of which the assessment was made.][1]

Amendments.—[1] This paragraph inserted by FA 1984, s. 124 (2), (8) and applies in any case where a period of thirty days relevant for the purposes of the service of a notice under para. 4 above in relation to any tax expires after 11 March 1984.

5. Paragraph 4 above does not apply to any assessment to tax under Schedule E.

6. Paragraph 4 above does not apply [in relation to the holder of any licence][1] if the profits or gains arose or the chargeable gains accrued to the person on whom the assessment is made in consequence of a contract made by the holder of the licence before 23rd March 1973, unless he is a person connected with the holder within the meaning of section [839 of the Taxes Act 1988][2] or the contract was substantially varied on or after that date.

Amendments.—[1] Words inserted by FA 1984, s. 124 (3), (8) and apply in any case where a period of thirty days relevant for the purposes of the service of a notice under paragraph 4 above in relation to any tax expires after 11 March 1984.
[2] Words substituted by TA 1988, Sch. 29, para. 32 Table.

7. Where, on an application made by a person who will or might become liable to tax which, if remaining unpaid, could be recovered under paragraph 4 above from the holder of a licence, the Board are satisfied that the applicant will comply with any obligations imposed on him by the Taxes Acts, they may issue a certificate to the holder of the licence exempting him from the provisions of that paragraph with respect to any tax payable by the applicant; and where such a certificate is issued that paragraph shall not apply to any such tax which becomes due while the certificate is in force [or, if the certificate is cancelled under paragraph 8 below, to any such tax which becomes due after the cancellation of the certificate in respect of profits or gains arising while the certificate is in force (referred to below in this Schedule as pre-cancellation profits or gains)].[1]

Amendments.—[1] Words added by FA 1984, s. 124 (4).

[7A.—(1) Paragraph 7 above is subject to the following provisions of this paragraph in any case where—

(a) after the cancellation of a certificate issued to the holder of a licence under that paragraph tax is assessed as mentioned in paragraph 4 (1) (a) or (b) above on the person who applied for the certificate; and

(b) the relevant profits or gains include (but are not limited to) pre-cancellation profits or gains.

(2) In this paragraph "the relevant profits or gains" means—

(a) in a case where the amount of the tax remaining unpaid under the assessment which, but for paragraph 7 above, the holder of the licence could be required to pay by a notice under paragraph 4 above (referred to below in this paragraph as the amount otherwise applicable in his case) is the whole of the amount remaining unpaid, all the profits or gains in respect of which the assessment was made; or

(b) in a case where the amount otherwise applicable in his case falls under paragraph 4A above to be determined by reference to profits or gains in respect of which the licence was the basis for the assessment, the profits or gains in question.

(3) In any case to which this paragraph applies, the amount the holder of the licence may be required to pay by a notice under paragraph 4 shall be the amount otherwise applicable in his case reduced by the amount of the tax remaining unpaid under the assessment which

is attributable to the pre-cancellation profits or gains, together with a corresponding proportion of any interest due as mentioned in paragraph 4 (1).

(4) For the purposes of sub-paragraph (3) above the amount of the tax remaining unpaid under the assessment which is attributable to the pre-cancellation profits or gains is such part of the amount otherwise applicable in the case of the holder of the licence as bears to the whole of the amount otherwise so applicable the same proportion as the proportion borne by the amount of the pre-cancellation profits or gains to the total amount of the relevant profits or gains.][1]

Amendments.—[1] This paragraph inserted by FA 1984, s. 124 (5).

8. The Board may, by notice in writing to the holder of a certificate issued under paragraph 7 above, cancel the certificate from such date, not earlier than thirty days after the service of the notice, as may be specified in the notice.

[**8A.**—(1) For the purposes of paragraphs 4A and 7A above and this paragraph, profits or gains in respect of which an assessment is made as mentioned in paragraph 4 (1) (*a*) or (*b*) above are profits or gains in respect of which any licence in question was the basis for the assessment if those profits or gains fall within paragraph 4 (1) (*a*) or (*b*) by reference to that licence.

(2) In determining—

(*a*) for the purposes of paragraph 4A (2) or 7A (4) above, the amount of the profits or gains in respect of which any licence was the basis for an assessment; or
(*b*) for the purposes of paragraph 7A (4) above, the amount of any pre-cancellation profits or gains;

the Board shall compute that amount as if for the purposes of making a separate assessment in respect of those profits or gains on the person on whom the assessment was made, making all such allocations and apportionments of receipts, expenses, allowances and deductions taken into account or made for the purposes of the actual assessment as appear to the Board to be just and reasonable in the circumstances.

(3) A notice under paragraph 4 above as it applies by virtue of paragraph 4A or 7A above shall give particulars of the manner in which the amount required to be paid was determined.

(4) References in paragraphs 4A, 7 and 7A above and in this paragraph to profits or gains include chargeable gains.][1]

Amendments.—[1] This paragraph inserted by FA 1984, s. 124 (6).

9. In this Schedule "The Taxes Acts" has the same meaning as in the Taxes Management Act 1970.

FINANCE ACT 1974

(1974 Chapter 30)

ARRANGEMENT OF SECTIONS

Note.—Provisions of this Act relevant to the taxes covered by this Handbook and not reproduced are either spent or repealed by TA 1988, Sch. 31 and other legislation.

PART II
INCOME TAX, CORPORATION TAX AND CAPITAL GAINS TAX (GENERAL)

Section
17. Expenditure on fire safety.
24. Returns of persons treated as employees.

PART III
CAPITAL GAINS FROM LAND

CHAPTER I
DEVELOPMENT GAINS FROM LAND

44. Supplementary.

PART IV
MISCELLANEOUS AND GENERAL

52. Definition of "local authority" for certain tax purposes.
57. Citation, interpretation, construction and repeals.

SCHEDULES:
Schedule 3—Provisions supplementary to section 38.

An Act to grant certain duties, to alter other duties, and to amend the law relating to the National Debt and the Public Revenue, and to make further provision in connection with Finance.

[31st July 1974]

PART II

INCOME TAX, CORPORATION TAX AND CAPITAL GAINS TAX (GENERAL)

17. Expenditure on fire safety

(1) If a person carrying on a trade has on or after 1st June 1972 incurred expenditure in taking steps specified in a notice served on him by the fire authority under section 5 (4) of the Fire Precautions Act 1971, and—

(*a*) the notice was issued on an application for a fire certificate in respect of premises used by him for the purposes of the trade; and

(*b*) an allowance or deduction in respect of the expenditure could not, apart from this section, be made in taxing the trade or computing the profits or gains arising from it;

Chapter I of Part III of the Finance Act 1971 shall apply as if the expenditure were capital expenditure incurred on the provision of machinery or plant for the purposes of the trade, and as if the machinery or plant had, in consequence of his incurring the expenditure, belonged to him . . .[1]; and as if the disposal value of the machinery or plant were nil.

(2) This section shall be construed as if contained in Chapter I of Part III of the Finance Act 1971.

Cross references.—See FA 1975, s. 15 (capital allowance for expenditure on fire safety); FA 1978, s. 38 (1), (8) and Sch. 6, para. 8 (in relation to expenditure on a qualifying hotel incurred after 11 April 1978, references in CAA 1968, Pt. I, Ch. I to expenditure on the construction of a building or structure not to include references to expenditure incurred under this section).
Amendments.—[1] Words in sub-s. (1) repealed by FA 1985, Sch. 14, para. 11 and Sch. 27, Pt. VI with respect to any chargeable period or its basis period ending after 31 March 1985.

24. Returns of persons treated as employees

Where a person performs in the United Kingdom for a continuous period of not less than thirty days duties of an office or employment and—

(*a*) the office or employment is under or with a person resident outside and not resident in the United Kingdom; but

(*b*) the duties are performed for the benefit of a person resident or carrying on a trade, profession or vocation in the United Kingdom;

section 15 of the Taxes Management Act 1970 (return of employees) [shall apply as if the person for whose benefit the duties were performed were the employer, but only so as to require him to make a return of the name and place of residence of the person performing the duties;][1] and any notice given to him under section 8 of the Taxes Management Act 1970 may require a return of his income to include particulars of any emoluments paid to him, whether or not tax is chargeable on them.

Amendments.—[1] Words substituted by FA 1976, Sch. 9, para. 5.

PART III
CAPITAL GAINS FROM LAND

CHAPTER I
DEVELOPMENT GAINS FROM LAND

44. Supplementary

(1) For the purposes of this Chapter—

. . .

"interest in land" means any estate or interest in land, any right in or over land or affecting the use or disposition of land, and any right to obtain such an estate, interest or right from another which is conditional on that other's ability to grant the estate, interest or right in question, except that it does not include the interest of a creditor (other than a creditor in respect of a rentcharge) whose debt is secured by way of a mortgage, an agreement for a mortgage or a charge of any kind over land, or, in Scotland, the interest of a creditor in a charge or security of any kind over land;

"land" includes buildings;

. . .

(5) This Chapter shall be deemed to have come into force on 18th December 1973.

Note.—The provisions omitted from this section are not relevant for the purpose of CGTA 1979, Sch. 5, Pt. II.
Cross references.—See CGTA 1979, Sch. 5, para. 9 (5) (*a*) (market valuation of land held at 6 April 1965 sold at a price reflecting development value).
Amendments.—This section repealed by FA 1985, Sch. 27, Pt. X, but the provisions reproduced above are relevant for the purpose of, *inter alia*, CGTA 1979, Sch. 5, Pt. II; see also provision No. 1 at the end of FA 1985, Sch. 27, Pt. X.

PART IV

MISCELLANEOUS AND GENERAL

52. Definition of "local authority" for certain tax purposes

(1) The definition of "local authority" set out below (which reproduces the effect of that in section 353 of the Taxes Act with modifications necessary to take account of the reorganisation of local government in all parts of the United Kingdom) shall have effect for the purposes of the Income Tax Acts, the Corporation Tax Acts and the enactments relating to capital gains tax; . . .

(2) "Local authority" means—

(*a*) any authority having power to make or determine a rate;
(*b*) any authority having power to issue a precept, requisition or other demand for the payment of money to be raised out of a rate;

and in this subsection "rate" means a rate the proceeds of which are applicable for public local purposes and which is leviable by reference to the value of land or other property.

(3) This section shall come into operation or, as the case may be, be deemed to have come into operation—

(*a*) in its application to England and Wales, on 1st April 1974;
(*b*) in its application to Scotland, on 16th May 1975; and
(*c*) in its application to Northern Ireland, on 1st October 1973.

Note.—Words omitted from sub.-s. (1) are outside the scope of this work.

57. Citation, interpretation, construction and repeals

(1) This Act may be cited as the Finance Act 1974.

(2) In this Act "the Taxes Act" means the Income and Corporation Taxes Act 1970.

(3) In this Act—

(*a*) . . .
(*b*) Part II, so far as it relates to income tax, shall be construed as one with the Income Tax Acts, so far as it relates to corporation tax, shall be construed as one with the Corporation Tax Acts . . .[2];
(*c*) . . .[3]
(*d*) . . .

(4) Except so far as the context otherwise requires, any reference in this Act to any enactment shall be construed as a reference to that enactment as amended, and as including a reference to that enactment as applied, by or under any other enactment, including this Act.

(5) If the Northern Ireland Assembly passes provisions amending or replacing any enactment of the Parliament of Northern Ireland, or any Order in Council made under section 1 (3) of the Northern Ireland (Temporary Provisions) Act 1972, referred to in this Act, the reference shall be construed as a reference to the enactment or order as so amended or, as the case may be, as a reference to those provisions.

(6) The enactments mentioned in Schedule 14 to this Act (which include certain enactments which had ceased to have effect before the commencement of this Act) are hereby repealed to the extent specified in the third column of that Schedule, but subject to any provisions at the end of any Part of that Schedule.

Note.—Sub-s. (3), paras. (*a*) and (*d*) are outside the scope of this work.
Amendments.—[1] Words in sub-s. (3) (*c*) substituted by CGTA 1979, s. 157 (2)–(4) and Sch. 7, para. 8 Table, Pt. I.6, with effect from 22 March 1979.
[2] Words in sub-s. (3) (*b*) repealed by CGTA 1979, s. 158 and Sch. 8.
[3] Sub-s. (3) (*c*) repealed by FA 1985, Sch. 27, Pt. X.

SCHEDULES

SCHEDULE 3
PROVISIONS SUPPLEMENTARY TO SECTION 38

Note.—Section 38 and this Schedule repealed by FA 1985, Sch. 27, Pt. X, but the provisions reproduced below are relevant for the purpose, *inter alia*, of CGTA 1979, Sch. 5, Pt. II; see also provision No. 1 at the end of FA 1985, Sch. 27, Pt. X.

PART I
DEFINITION OF CURRENT USE VALUE, MATERIAL DEVELOPMENT, ETC.

Cross references.—See CGTA 1979, Sch. 5, para. 9 (5) (c) (capital gains tax consequences on disposal of land at a price in excess of the current use value, calculated in accordance with this Part of this Schedule).

Definition of current use value

1.—(1) For the purposes of the principal section and this Schedule the current use value of an interest in land shall be ascertained in accordance with this Part of this Schedule; and in this Part of this Schedule the time as at which current use value is to be ascertained is referred to as "the relevant time".

(2) Subject to the following provisions of this Part of this Schedule, the current use value of an interest in land at the relevant time is the market value of that interest at that time calculated on the assumption that it was at that time, and would continue to be, unlawful to carry out any material development of the land other than any material development thereof which, being authorised by planning permission in force at that time, was begun before that time.

(3) In this paragraph "planning permission" has the same meaning as in the Town and Country Planning Act 1971, or, in Scotland, the Town and Country Planning (Scotland) Act 1972, or, in Northern Ireland, the Planning (Northern Ireland) Order 1972; and in determining for the purposes of this paragraph what material development of any land was authorised by planning permission at a time when there was in force in respect of the land planning permission granted on an outline application (that is to say, an application for planning permission subject to subsequent approval on any matters), any such development of the land which at that time—

(a) was authorised by that permission without any requirement as to subsequent approval; or
(b) not being so authorised, had been approved in the manner applicable to that planning permission

but no other material development, shall for those purposes be taken to have been authorised by that permission at that time.

Cross references.—See CGTA 1979, Sch. 5, para. 9 (5) (c) (modification of this paragraph for capital gains tax purposes).

Current use value—part disposals

2.—(1) Subject to sub-paragraphs (5) to (7) below, this paragraph shall apply as regards the current use value of an interest in land which has been disposed of by way of a part disposal of an asset (in this paragraph referred to as "the relevant asset") consisting of an interest in land.

(2) The current use value at the relevant time of the interest disposed of shall be the relevant fraction of the current use value of the relevant asset at that time, calculated on the same assumptions as to the lawfulness or otherwise of any material development as fall to be made under this Schedule in calculating the current use value at that time of the interest disposed of.

(3) For the purposes of the preceding sub-paragraph "the relevant fraction" means that fraction of the sums mentioned in the following sub-paragraph which under [subsection (2) of section 35 of the Capital Gains Tax Act 1979][1] is, or would but for [subsection (4) of that section][1] be,

allowable as a deduction in computing under [Chapter II of Part II of that Act]¹ the amount of the gain accruing on the part disposal.

(4) The sums referred to in the preceding sub-paragraph are the sums which, if the entire relevant asset had been disposed of at the time of the part disposal, would be allowable by virtue of [section 32 (1) (a) and (b) of the Capital Gains Tax Act 1979]¹ as a deduction in computing under [Chapter II of Part II of that Act]¹ the gain accruing on that disposal of the relevant asset.

(5) Sub-paragraphs (2) to (4) above shall not apply—

  (a) in the case of a disposal of an interest in land by way of a part disposal if, on making the disposal, the person doing so no longer has any interest in the land which is subject to that interest; or
  (b) in a case to which the following provisions of this paragraph apply.

(6) In computing under this Chapter any gain accruing to a person on a part disposal of a lease which is a wasting asset by way of the grant of a sub-lease for a premium, the current use value of the lease at the time of its acquisition by the person making the disposal shall be the relevant fraction of what its current use value at that time would be apart from sub-paragraphs (2) to (4) above.

(7) For the purposes of the preceding sub-paragraph "the relevant fraction" means that fraction of the expenditure attributable to the lease under [section 32 (1) (a) and (b) of the Capital Gains Tax Act 1979]¹ which under paragraph 4 of [Schedule 3]¹ to that Act (sub-leases out of short leases) falls to be apportioned to what is disposed of.

Amendments.—¹ Words in sub-paras. (3), (4), (7) substituted by CGTA 1979, s. 157 (2)–(4) and Sch. 7, para. 9 Table, with effect from 22 March 1979.

3. *In computing under this Chapter any gain accruing to a person on a part disposal of an interest in land resulting under [subsection (1) of section 20 of the Capital Gains Tax Act 1979]¹ from the receipt as mentioned in paragraph (a), (c) or (d) of that subsection of a capital sum, the current use value at the relevant time of the interest out of which the part disposal was made shall be taken to be what it would have been at that time if the circumstances which caused the capital sum to be received had not arisen.*

Amendments.—¹ Words substituted by CGTA 1979, s. 157 (2)–(4) and Sch. 7, para. 9 Table, with effect from 22 March 1979.

Current use value—leases and reversions

4.—*(1) The current use value of an interest in land which is either—*

  (a) a freehold interest which is subject to a lease or an agreement for a lease; or
  (b) an interest under a lease or agreement for a lease,

shall be ascertained without regard to any premium required under the lease or agreement for a lease or any sublease, or otherwise under the terms subject to which the lease or sublease was or is to be granted, but with regard to all other rights under the lease or prospective lease (and, for the current use value of an interest under a lease subject to a sublease, under the sublease).

(2) If under the preceding sub-paragraph an interest under a lease or agreement for a lease would have a negative value, the current use value of the interest shall be nil.

(3) If a lease is granted out of any interest in land after 17th December 1973, then, in computing under this Chapter any gain accruing on any disposal of the reversion on the lease made while the lease subsists, the current use value of the reversion at any time after the grant of the lease shall not exceed what would have been at that time the current use value of the interest in the land of the person then owning the reversion if that interest had not been subject to the lease.

(4) In the application of this paragraph to Scotland, "freehold" means the estate or interest of the proprietor of the dominium utile or, in the case of property other than feudal property, of the owner, and "reversion" means the interest of the landlord in property subject to a lease.

5.—*(1) In computing under this Chapter any gain accruing to a person on a disposal of a lease which is a wasting asset, the current use value of the lease at the time of its acquisition by the person making the disposal shall be the relevant fraction of what its current use value at that time would be apart from this paragraph.*

(2) For the purposes of the preceding sub-paragraph "the relevant fraction" means the fraction of which the numerator is equal to so much of the expenditure attributable to the lease under [section 32 (1) (a) and (b) of the Capital Gains Tax Act 1979]¹ as is not under paragraph 1 of

[Schedule 3][1] *to that Act excluded therefrom for the purposes of the computation under [Chapter II of Part II of that Act]*[1] *of the gain accruing on the disposal, and the denominator is equal to the whole of the expenditure which would be so attributable to the lease for those purposes apart from the said paragraph 1.*

Amendments.—[1] Words in sub-para. (2) substituted by CGTA 1979, s. 157 (2)–(4) and Sch. 7, para. 9 Table, with effect from 22 March 1979.

Definition of material development

6. *In this Schedule, subject to the following paragraph, "material development", in relation to any land, means the making of any change in the state, nature or use of the land.*

Cross references.—See CGTA 1979, Sch. 5, para. 9 (5) (*b*) (land reflecting development value; valuation at 6 April 1965 for capital gains tax purposes).

7.—*(1) The doing of any of the following things in the case of any land shall not be taken for the purposes of this Schedule to involve material development of the land, that is to say—*

(a) the carrying out of works for the maintenance, improvement, enlargement or other alteration of any building, so long as the cubic content of the original building is not exceeded by more than one-tenth;

(b) the carrying out of works for the rebuilding, as often as occasion may require, of any building which was in existence at the relevant time, or of any building which was in existence in the period of ten years immediately preceding the day on which that time falls but was destroyed or demolished before the relevant time, so long as (in either case) the cubic content of the original building is not exceeded by more than one-tenth;

(c) the use of any land for the purposes of agriculture or forestry, the use for any of those purposes of any building occupied together with land so used, and the carrying out on any land so used of any building or other operations required for the purposes of that use;

(d) the carrying out of operations on land for, or the use of land for, the display of an advertisement, announcement or direction of any kind;

(e) the carrying out of operations for, or the use of the land for, car parking, provided that such use shall not exceed three years;

(f) in the case of a building or other land which at the relevant time was used for a purpose falling within any class specified in paragraph 8 below or which, being unoccupied at that time, was last used for any such purpose, the use of that building or land for any other purpose falling within the same class;

(g) in the case of a building or other land which at the relevant time was in the occupation of a person by whom it was used as to part only for a particular purpose, the use for that purpose of any additional part of the building or land not exceeding one-tenth of the cubic content of the part of the building used for that purpose at the relevant time or, as the case may be, one-tenth of the area of the land so used at that time;

(h) in the case of land which at the relevant time was being temporarily used for a purpose other than the purpose for which it was normally used, the resumption of the use of the land for the last-mentioned purpose;

(i) in the case of land which was unoccupied at the relevant time, the use of the land for the purpose for which it was last used before that time.

(2) In determining for the purposes of sub-paragraph (1) (a) or (b) above whether or not the cubic content of the original building has been exceeded by more than one-tenth, the cubic content of the building after the carrying out of the works in question shall be treated as reduced by the amout (if any) by which so much of that cubic content as is attributable to one or more of the matters mentioned in the following sub-paragraph exceeds so much of the cubic content of the original building as was attributable to one or more of the matters so mentioned.

(3) The matters referred to in the preceding sub-paragraph are the following, that is to say—

(a) means of escape in case of fire;
(b) car-parking or garage space;
(c) accommodation for plant providing heating, air-conditioning or similar facilities.

8. *The classes of purposes mentioned in paragraph 7 (1) (f) above are the following—*

Class A—Use as a dwelling-house or for the purpose of any activities which are wholly or mainly carried on otherwise than for profit, except use for a purpose falling within Class B, C or E.

Class B—Use as an office or retail shop.

Class C—Use as a hotel, boarding house or guest-house, or as premises licensed for the sale of intoxicating liquors for consumption on the premises.

Class D—Use for the purpose of any activities wholly or mainly carried on for profit, except—

(a) use as a dwelling-house or for the purposes of agriculture or forestry; and
(b) use for a purpose falling within Class B, C or E.

Class E—Use for any of the following purposes, namely—

(a) the carrying on of any process for or incidental to any of the following purposes, namely—

(i) the making of any article or of part of any article, or the production of any substance;
(ii) the altering, repairing, ornamenting, finishing, cleaning, washing, packing or canning, or adapting for sale, or breaking up or demolishing of any article; or
(iii) without prejudice to (i) or (ii) above, the getting, dressing or treatment of minerals,

being a process carried on in the course of a trade or business other than agriculture or forestry, but excluding any process carried on at a dwelling-house or retail shop;
(b) storage purposes (whether or not involving use as a warehouse or repository) other than storage purposes ancillary to a purpose falling within Class B or C.

Date when material development is begun

9.—(1) For the purposes of this Schedule material development shall be taken to be begun on the earliest date on which any specified operation comprised in the material development is begun.

(2) In this paragraph "specified operation" means any of the following, that is to say—

(a) any work of construction in the course of the erection of a building;
(b) the digging of a trench which is to contain the foundations or part of the foundations, of a building;
(c) the laying of any underground main or pipe to the foundations, or part of the foundations, of a building or to any such trench as is mentioned in (b) above;
(d) any operation in the course of laying out or constructing a road or part of a road;
(e) any change in the use of any land.

Cross references.—See CGTA 1979, Sch. 5, para. 9 (5) (d) (land reflecting development value; valuation at 6 April 1965 for capital gains tax purposes).

Interpretation

10.—(1) In this Part of this Schedule, unless the context otherwise requires—

"agriculture" includes horticulture, fruit growing, seed growing, dairy farming, the keeping and breeding of livestock (including any creature kept for the production of food, wool, skins or fur, or for the purpose of its use in the farming of land), the use of land as grazing land, meadow land, osier land, market gardens and nursery grounds, and the use of land for woodlands where that use is ancillary to the farming of land for other agricultural purposes, and "agricultural" shall be construed accordingly; "article" means an article of any description;
"building" includes part of a building and references to a building may include references to land occupied therewith and used for the same purposes;
"forestry" includes afforestation;
"minerals" includes all minerals and substances in or under land of a kind ordinarily worked for removal by underground or surface working;
"retail shop" includes any premises of a similar character where retail trade or business (including repair work) is carried on;
"substance" means any natural or artificial substance or material, whether in solid or liquid form or in the form of a gas or vapour.

(2) Any reference in this part of this Schedule to the cubic content of a building is a reference to that content as ascertained by external measurement.

(3) For the purposes of paragraph 7 (1) (a) and (b) of this Schedule where two or more buildings are included in a single development the whole of that development may be regarded as a single building, and where two or more buildings result from the redevelopment of a single building the new buildings may together be regarded as a single building.

For the purposes of this sub-paragraph two or more buildings shall not be treated as included in a single development unless they are or were comprised in the same curtilage.

PART II

OTHER PROVISIONS SUPPLEMENTARY TO SECTION 38

Computation of development gain in respect of disposal of interest in land after material development has been carried out

11.—(1) This paragraph shall apply in relation to a disposal of an interest in land to which the principal section applies if material development of the land has been carried out after 17th December 1973 [and][1] since the person making the disposal acquired the interest [but before the appointed day, within the meaning of the Development Land Tax Act 1976][1].

(2) Subsection (3) of the principal section shall apply in relation to the disposal as if paragraph (b) were omitted, and as if for the words "whichever is the least" there were substituted the words "whichever is the smaller".

(3) For the purpose of computing the amount given by subsection (3) (c) of the principal section, the amount by which the current use value of the interest in land at the time of the disposal exceeds the current use value of the interest at the time of its acquisition by the person making the disposal or, if the interest was acquired by him before 6th April 1965, its current use value at that date shall be taken to be equal to the sum of the amounts mentioned in the following sub-paragraph (or, if both those amounts are nil, to be nil).

(4) The amounts referred to in the preceding sub-paragraph are the following, that is to say—

(a) the amount (if any) by which the current use value of the interest immediately before the date on which the material development mentioned in sub-paragraph (1) above was begun exceeds the current use value of the interest at the time of its acquisition by the person making the disposal or on 6th April 1965, as the case may be; and
(b) the amount (if any) by which the current use value of the interest at the time of the disposal exceeds the aggregate of the amounts mentioned in the following sub-paragraph.

(5) The amounts referred to in sub-paragraph (4) (b) above are the following, that is to say—

(a) the current use value of the interest immediately after the date on which the material development mentioned in sub-paragraph (1) above was begun, calculated on the assumption that it was lawful for that development to be carried out; and
(b) the amount of any expenditure attributable to that development which is allowable under [section 32 (1) (b) of the Capital Gains Tax Act 1979][2] as a deduction from the consideration for the disposal in computing the chargeable gain accruing thereon.

(6) Where material development of the land in question has been carried out on two or more different occasions after 17th December 1973 [and][1] since the person making the disposal acquired the interest [but before the appointed day, within the meaning of the Development Land Tax Act 1976][1], then for the purposes of this paragraph—

(a) there shall be calculated for the first of those occasions the amount mentioned in sub-paragraph (4) (a) above (the reference there to the material development mentioned in sub-paragraph (1) above being for this purpose read as a reference to the material development carried out on that occasion);
(b) there shall be calculated for each of those occasions other than the first the amount (if any) by which the current use value of the interest immediately before the date on which the material development carried out on that occasion was begun exceeds the aggregate of the amounts mentioned in sub-paragraph (5) above (the references there to the material development mentioned in sub-paragraph (1) above being for this purpose read as references to the material development carried out on the occasion preceding the one for which the calculation is being made); and
(c) there shall be calculated the amount (if any) by which the current use value of the interest at the time of the disposal exceeds the aggregate of the amounts mentioned in sub-paragraph (5) above (the references there to the material development mentioned in sub-paragraph (1) above being for this purpose read as references to the material development carried out on the last of those occasions);

and sub-paragraph (3) above shall apply as if for the words from "the sum of the amounts mentioned in the following sub-paragraph" to the end of the paragraph there were substituted the words "the sum of the amounts calculated under sub-paragraph (6) (a) to (c) below (or, if those amounts are each nil, to be nil)".

Note.—The appointed day, within the meaning of DLTA 1976, is 1 August 1976: the Development Land Tax (Appointed Day) Order 1976, S.I. 1976 No. 1148.

Amendments.—[1] Words in sub-paras. (1) and (6) added and inserted by DLTA 1976, s. 35 (3).
[2] Words in sub-para. (5) (*b*) substituted by CGTA 1979, s. 157 (2)–(4) and Sch. 7, para. 9 Table, with effect from 22 March 1979.

Computation of development gain in respect of disposal of interest in land reflecting expenditure on enhancement

12.—*(1)* This paragraph shall apply in relation to a disposal of an interest in land to which the principal section applies if any expenditure which is or, but for paragraph 1 of [Schedule 3 to the Capital Gains Tax Act 1979][2], would be allowable under [section 32 (1) (b) of that Act][2] as a deduction from the consideration for the disposal in computing the chargeable gain accruing thereon has been incurred since the person making the disposal acquired the interest, not being expenditure attributable to material development of the land carried out as mentioned in paragraph 11 (1) of this Schedule (that is, carried out after 17th December 1973 [and][1] since the person making the disposal acquired the interest [but before the appointed day, within the meaning of the Development Land Tax Act 1976][1]).

(2) For the purpose of computing the amount given by subsection (3) (c) of the principal section the current use value of the interest in land at the time of its acquisition by the person making the disposal or, if the interest was acquired by him before 6th April 1965, its current use value at that date shall be taken to be equal to the sum of the amounts mentioned in the following sub-paragraph.

(3) The amounts referred to in the preceding sub-paragraph are the following, that is to say—

(a) the current use value of the interest at the time of its acquisition by the person making the disposal or on 6th April 1965, as the case may be; and
(b) so much of the expenditure mentioned in sub-paragraph (1) above as is reflected in the current use value of the interest at the time of the disposal.

(4) Where material development of the land has been carried out (whether on only one occasion or on two or more different occasions) after 17th December 1973 [and][1] since the person making the disposal acquired the interest, [but before the appointed day, within the meaning of the Development Land Tax Act 1976][1] sub-paragraphs (2) and (3) above shall not apply, and paragraph 11 of this Schedule shall have effect subject to the following provisions of this paragraph.

(5) Where any expenditure mentioned in sub-paragraph (1) above was incurred before the date on which the material development of the land carried out after 17th December 1973 on the first or only occasion was begun, then in calculating under paragraph 11 (4) (a) or 11 (6) (a) of this Schedule the amount mentioned in the said paragraph 11 (4) (a), the current use value of the interest at the time of its acquisition by the person making the disposal or on 6th April 1965, as the case may be, shall be increased by so much of the expenditure so incurred as is reflected in the current use value of the interest immediately before the date on which the material development carried out on that occasion was begun.

(6) Where any expenditure so mentioned was incurred on or after the date on which the material development of the land so carried out on the last or only occasion was begun, then in calculating under paragraph 11 (5) (b) or 11 (6) (c) of this Schedule the expenditure attributable to that material development which is allowable as mentioned in the said paragraph 11 (5) (b) there shall be included in that expenditure so much of the expenditure so incurred as is reflected in the current use value of the interest at the time of the disposal.

(7) Where any expenditure so mentioned was incurred on or after the date on which the material development ("the preceding development") so carried out on any but the last of two or more occasions was begun but before the date on which the material development ("the following development") carried out on the next of those occasions was begun, then, in calculating under paragraph 11 (6) (b) of this Schedule the expenditure attributable to the preceding development which is allowable as mentioned in paragraph 11 (5) (b) of this Schedule, there shall be included in that expenditure so much of the expenditure so incurred as is reflected in the current use value of the interest immediately before the date on which the following development was begun.

Note.—The appointed day, within the meaning of DLTA 1976, is 1 August 1976: the Development Land Tax (Appointed Day) Order 1976, S.I. 1976 No. 1148.
Amendments.—[1] Words in sub-paras. (1) and (4) added and inserted by DLTA 1976, s. 35 (3).
[2] Words in sub-para. (1) substituted by CGTA 1979, s. 157 (2)–(4) and Sch. 7, para. 9 Table, with effect from 22 March 1979.

Provisions supplementary to paragraphs 11 and 12

13.—*(1) Where paragraph 11 of this Schedule would, apart from this paragraph, apply in relation to a disposal of an interest in land because of any material development of the land carried out after 17th December 1973 [and]¹ since the person making the disposal acquired the interest [but before the appointed day, within the meaning of the Development Land Tax Act 1976]¹, the said paragraph 11 shall not so apply if the amount by which the current use value of the interest immediately after the date on which that material development was begun, calculated on the assumption that it was lawful for that development to be carried out, exceeds the current use value of the interest immediately before that date—*

(a) is not greater than one-tenth of the current use value of the interest immediately before that date; and
(b) does not exceed £2,500.

(2) Where material development of the land in question has been carried out on two or more different occasions after 17th December 1973 [and]¹ since the person making the disposal acquired the interest [but before the appointed day, within the meaning of the Development Land Tax Act 1976]¹, then for the purposes of this paragraph there shall be calculated for each of those occasions the amount by which the current use value of the interest immediately after the date on which the material development carried out on that occasion was begun, calculated on the assumption that it was lawful for that development to be carried out, exceeds the current use value of the interest immediately before that date, and the preceding sub-paragraph shall not apply in relation to the disposal if the aggregate of the amounts so calculated exceeds £2,500.

(3) Where by virtue of the preceding provisions of this paragraph, paragraph 11 of this Schedule does not apply in relation to a disposal of an interest in land even though material development of the land has been carried out as aforesaid, the material development in question shall be disregarded for the purposes of paragraph 12 of this Schedule.

Note.—The appointed day, within the meaning of DLTA 1976, is 1 August 1976: the Development Land Tax (Appointed Day) Order 1976, S.I. 1976 No. 1148.
Amendments.—¹ Words in sub-paras. (1) and (2) inserted by DLTA 1976, s. 35 (3).

14. *(1) Subject to the following sub-paragraph, material development shall for the purposes of paragraphs 11 to 13 of this Schedule not be treated as carried out after a particular date if it was begun on or before that date.*

(2) If, in the case of any land—

(a) material development thereof was begun on or before 17th December 1973 but was not completed on or before that date; and
(b) the development was on that date to any extent not authorised by planning permission then in force,

then, for the purposes of paragraphs 11 to 13 of this Schedule, so much of the development carried out after that date as was not so authorised on that date shall be treated as begun on the earliest date after 17th December 1973 on which any specified operation comprised therein is begun, and shall accordingly be treated as material development of the land carried out after 17th December 1973.

(3) Sub-paragraph (3) of paragraph 1 of this Schedule shall apply for the purposes of this paragraph as it applies for the purposes of paragraph 1; and in this paragraph "specified operation" has the same meaning as in paragraph 9 of this Schedule.

Cross references.—See CGTA 1979, Sch. 5, para. 9 (5) (*e*) (land reflecting development value; valuation at 6 April 1965 for capital gains tax purposes).

FINANCE ACT 1975

(1975 Chapter 7)

ARRANGEMENT OF SECTIONS

Note.—Provisions of this Act relevant to the taxes covered by this Handbook and not reproduced are either spent or repealed by TA 1988, Sch. 31 and other legislation.

PART II

INCOME TAX AND CORPORATION TAX

Section
13. Initial allowances for industrial buildings and structures, etc.
14. Expenditure on thermal insulation.
15. Expenditure on fire safety.

PART III

CAPITAL TRANSFER TAX

19. *Capital transfer tax.* (see Orange Book)
49. *Abolition of estate duty and transitional provisions.* (see Orange Book)

PART IV

MISCELLANEOUS AND GENERAL

59. Citation, interpretation, construction and repeals.

SCHEDULES:

Schedule 4—*Administration and collection of capital transfer tax.* (see Orange Book)

An Act to grant certain duties, to alter other duties, and to amend the law relating to the National Debt and the Public Revenue, and to make further provision in connection with Finance

[13th March 1975]

PART II
INCOME TAX AND CORPORATION TAX

13. Initial allowances for industrial buildings and structures, etc.

(1) ...

(2) Expenditure shall not be treated for the purposes of this section as having been incurred after the date on which it was in fact incurred by reason only of section 1 (6) of the Capital Allowances Act 1968 (expenditure incurred before trade began) or section 5 (1) of that Act (purchase of unused buildings or structures).

Note.—Sub-s. (1) amends CAA 1968, s. 1 (2).

14. Expenditure on thermal insulation

(1) If a person carrying on a trade has after 12th November 1974 incurred expenditure in adding any insulation against loss of heat to any industrial building or structure occupied by him for the purposes of that trade, Chapter I of Part III of the Finance Act 1971 shall apply as if the expenditure were capital expenditure incurred on the provision of machinery or plant for the purposes of the trade, and as if the machinery or plant had, in consequence of his incurring the expenditure, belonged to him ...[1], and as if the disposal value of the machinery or plant were nil.

(2) If a person has after 12 November 1974 incurred expenditure in adding any insulation against loss of heat to any industrial building or structure let by him otherwise than in the course of a trade, Chapter I of Part III of the Finance Act 1971 shall apply as if the expenditure were capital expenditure incurred in providing machinery or plant first let by that person, otherwise than in the course of a trade, at the time when the expenditure was incurred, and as if the property comprised in the lease of the building or structure had as from that time included the machinery or plant, and as if the disposal value of the machinery or plant were nil.

(3) Any allowance made by virtue of section 46 (1) of the Finance Act 1971 in a case where it applies by virtue of subsection (2) above shall (notwithstanding section 48 (2) of that Act) be available primarily against the following income, that is to say—

(a) income taxed under Schedule A in respect of any premises which at any time in the chargeable period for which the allowance falls to be made consist of or include an industrial building or structure; or

(b) income which is the subject of a balancing charge under Chapter I (industrial buildings and structures, etc.) of Part I of the Capital Allowances Act 1968.

(4) This section shall be construed as if contained in Chapter I of Part III of the Finance Act 1971; and in this section "industrial building or structure" has the meaning given by section 7 of the Capital Allowances Act 1968.

Amendments.—[1] Words in sub-s. (1) repealed by FA 1985, Sch. 14, para. 12 and Sch. 27, Pt. VI with respect to any chargeable period or its basis period ending after 31 March 1985.

15. Expenditure on fire safety

(1) If a person carrying on a trade has on or after the relevant date incurred expenditure in taking, in respect of any premises used by him for the purposes of the trade—

(a) steps specified, in a letter or other document sent or given to him by or on behalf of the fire authority on an application for a fire certificate under the Fire Precautions Act 1971 in respect of those premises, as steps that would have to be taken in order to satisfy the authority as mentioned in subsection (4) of section 5 of that Act, being steps that might have been, but were not, specified in a notice under that subsection; or

(b) steps which, in consequence of the making of an order under section 10 of that Act prohibiting or restricting the use of the premises, had to be taken to enable the premises to be used without contravention of the order,

then, if an allowance or deduction in respect of the expenditure could not, apart from this section, be made in taxing the trade or computing the profits or gains arising from it, Chapter I of Part III of the Finance Act 1971 shall apply as regards the expenditure as it would apply by virtue of section 17 of the Finance Act 1974 if the expenditure fell within the said section 17.

(2) For the purposes of this section the relevant date, in relation to expenditure incurred in taking steps falling within subsection (1) (a) above, is 1st June 1972 and, in relation to expenditure incurred in taking steps falling within subsection (1) (b) above, is 20th March 1972.

(3) This section shall be construed as if contained in Chapter I of Part III of the Finance Act 1971.

Cross references.—See FA 1978, s. 38 (1), (8) and Sch. 6, para. 8 (in relation to expenditure on a qualifying hotel incurred after 11 April 1978, references in CAA 1968 Pt. I, Ch. 1 to expenditure on the construction of a building or structure not to include references to espenditure incurred under this section).

PART IV

MISCELLANEOUS AND GENERAL

59. Citation, interpretation construction and repeals

(1) This Act may be cited as the Finance Act 1975.

(2) In this Act "the Taxes Act" means the Income and Corporation Taxes Act 1970.

(3) In this Act—

(a) ...
(b) Part II, so far as it relates to income tax, shall be construed as one with the Income Tax Acts and, so far as it relates to corporation tax, shall be construed as one with the Corporation Tax Acts.

(4) Except so far as the context otherwise requires, any references in this Act to any enactment shall be construed as a reference to that enactment as amended, and as including a reference to that enactment as applied, by or under any other enactment, including this Act.

(5) The enactments mentioned in Schedule 13 to this Act are hereby repealed to the extent specified in the third column of that Schedule, but subject to any provision at the end of any Part of that Schedule.

Note.—Sub-s. (3) (a) is outside the scope of this work.

FINANCE (NO. 2) ACT 1975

(1975 Chapter 45)

ARRANGEMENT OF SECTIONS

Note.—Provisions of this Act relevant to the taxes covered by this Handbook and not reproduced are either spent or repealed by TA 1988, Sch. 31 and other legislation.

PART III

INCOME TAX, CORPORATION TAX AND CAPITAL GAINS TAX

CHAPTER I

GENERAL

Section
47. Repayment supplement in respect of delayed repayments of certain taxes to persons other than companies.
49. Expenditure on safety at sports grounds.
58. Disposal of shares and securities within prescribed period of acquisition.
67. Appeals.

PART IV

MISCELLANEOUS AND GENERAL

72. *Extension of Finance Act 1973, s. 50 to stamp duties in Northern Ireland.* (see Orange Book)
75. Citation, interpretation, construction and repeals.

An Act to grant certain duties, to alter other duties, and to amend the law relating to the National Debt and the Public Revenue, and to make further provision in connection with Finance. [1st August 1975]

PART III
INCOME TAX, CORPORATION
TAX AND CAPITAL GAINS TAX

CHAPTER I
GENERAL

47. Repayment supplement in respect of delayed repayments of certain taxes to persons other than companies

(1) Subject to the provisions of this section, where—

(a) in the case of . . .[1] capital gains tax paid by or on behalf of an individual for a year of assessment for which he was resident in the United Kingdom, a repayment thereof *of not less than £25*[3] is (after the passing of this Act) made by the Board or an inspector after the end of the twelve months following that year of assessment; . . .[1]

(b) . . .[2]

the repayment shall be increased under this section by an amount (in this section referred to as a "repayment supplement") equal to interest on the amount repaid at the [rate applicable under section 178 of the Finance Act 1989][4] for the period (if any) between the relevant time and the end of the tax month in which the order for the repayment is issued.

(2) In relation to so much (if any) of the last-mentioned period as preceded 6th April 1974, subsection (1) above shall have effect as if the rate of interest there specified were 6 per cent. per annum (instead of the rate there specified or any other rate in force . . .[1]*).*[5]

(3) . . .[2]

(4) For the purposes of subsection (1) above—

(a) if the repayment is of tax that was paid after the end of the twelve months following the year of assessment for which it was payable, the relevant time is the end of the year of assessment in which that tax was paid;

(b) . . .[2]

(c) in any other case, the relevant time is the end of the twelve months mentioned in that subsection;

and . . .[1] where a repayment to which subsection (1) above applies is of tax paid in two or more years of assessment, the repayment shall as far as possible be treated for the purposes of this subsection as a repayment of tax paid in a later rather than an earlier year among those years.

(5)–(7) . . .[2]

(8) A repayment supplement shall not be payable under this section in respect of a repayment or payment made in consequence of an order or judgment of a court having power to allow interest on the repayment or payment, . . .[1].

(9)–(10) . . .[2]

(11) The preceding provisions of this section shall apply in relation to a partnership, or a United Kingdom trust (as defined in section [231 (5) of the Income and Corporation Taxes Act 1988][4], or, in the case of a United Kingdom estate, the personal representatives of a deceased person as such (within the meaning of section [701 (4) of that Act][4]) as they apply in relation to an individual.

(12) In this section—

"tax month" means the period beginning with the 6th day of any calendar month and ending with the 5th day of the following calendar month;

"United Kingdom estate" has the meaning given by section [701 (9) of the Income and Corporation Taxes Act 1988][4].

Notes.—For the purposes of sub-s. (1) above, the rate of interest prescribed by the Income Tax (Interest on Unpaid Tax and Repayment Supplement) Orders is—
    8·25 per cent. from 6 December 1987: S.I. 1987 No. 1988.
    7·75 per cent. from 6 May 1988: S.I. 1988 No. 756.
    9·75 per cent. from 6 August 1988: S.I. 1988 No. 1278.
    10·75 per cent. from 6 October 1988: S.I. 1988 No. 1621.
    11·50 per cent. from 6 January 1989: S.I. 1988 No. 2185.
    12·25 per cent. from 6 July 1989: S.I. 1989 No. 1000.
See **Prospective Legislation Notes.**
Cross references.—See TMA 1970, s. 30 (2) (*a*) (recovery of overpayment of tax and any increase of it under this section);
TA 1988, s. 824 (8) (repayment supplement paid under this section is not income of the payee for any tax purposes);
Amendments.—[1] Words in sub-ss. (1) (*a*), (2), (4), (8) repealed by FA 1988, Sch. 14, Pt. IV.
[2] Sub-ss. (1) (*b*), (3), (4) (*b*), (5)–(7), (9), (10) repealed by *ibid.*
[3] Words "of not less than £25" in sub-s. (1) (*a*) repealed by FA 1989, s. 158 (2) (*a*), (5) and Sch. 17, Pt. VIII in relation to repayments of tax made on or after a day to be appointed.
[4] Words in sub-s. (1) substituted for the words "rate of . . . per cent. per annum" by FA 1989, s. 179 (1) (*a*) (vi), (4) for periods beginning on or after a day to be appointed and for interest running from before that day as well as from or from after that day.
[5] Sub-s. (2) repealed by FA 1989, Sch. 17, Pt. X.

49. Expenditure on safety at sports grounds

(1) If a person carrying on a trade has on or after the relevant date incurred expenditure in taking, in respect of any [sports ground][2] used by him for the purposes of the trade—

    (*a*) steps necessary for compliance with the terms and conditions of a safety certificate issued for the [sports ground][2]; or
    (*b*) steps specified in a letter or other document sent or given to him by or on behalf of the local authority for the area in which the [sports ground][2] is situated as steps the taking of which would be taken into account by them in deciding what terms and conditions to include in a safety certificate to be issued for the [sports ground][2] or lead to the amendment or replacement of a safety certificate issued or to be issued for it,

then, if an allowance or deduction in respect of the expenditure could not, apart from this section, be made in taxing the trade or computing the profits or gains arising from it, Chapter I of Part III of the Finance Act 1971 shall apply as if the expenditure were capital expenditure incurred on the provision of machinery or plant for the purposes of the trade, and as if the machinery or plant had, in consequence of his incurring the expenditure, belonged to him . . .[1] and as if the disposal value of the machinery or plant were nil.

(2) In this section "[sports ground][2]", "safety certificate" and "local authority" have the same meaning as in the Safety of Sports Grounds Act 1975, and "the relevant date", in relation to any [sports ground][2], means the date on which a designation order under section 1 of that Act comes into operation in respect of that [sports ground][2].

(3) This section shall be construed as if contained in Chapter I of Part III of the Finance Act 1971 and shall be deemed to have come into force on the passing of the Safety of Sports Grounds Act 1975.

Cross references.—See FA 1978, s. 40 (availability of capital allowances for sports grounds in the absence of a designation order and safety certificate).
Amendments.—[1] Words in sub-s. (1) repealed by FA 1985, Sch. 14, para. 13 and Sch. 27, Pt. VI with respect to any chargeable period or its basis period ending after 31 March 1985.
[2] Words in sub-ss. (1), (2) substituted by FA 1988, s. 93 with effect from 1 January 1988.

58. Disposal of shares and securities within prescribed period of acquisition

(1) For the purposes of corporation tax on chargeable gains, shares disposed of by a company shall be identified in accordance with the following provisions where—

    (*a*) the number of shares of that kind held by the company at any time during the prescribed period before the disposal amounted to not less than 2 per cent. of the number of issued shares of that kind; and
    (*b*) shares of that kind have been or are acquired by the company within the prescribed period before or after the disposal.

(2) Where a company is a member of a group, shares held or acquired by another member of the group shall be treated for the purposes of paragraphs (*a*) and (*b*) of subsection (1) above as held or acquired by that company and for the purposes of paragraph (*b*) any shares acquired by that company from another company which was a member of the group throughout the prescribed period before and after the disposal shall be disregarded.

(3) References in subsection (1) above to a company's disposing, holding and acquiring shares are references to its doing so in the same capacity; and references in that subsection to the holding or acquisition of shares do not include references to the holding or acquisition of shares as trading stock.

(4) The shares disposed of shall be identified—

(a) with shares acquired as mentioned in subsection (1) (b) above (in this section referred to as "available shares") rather than other shares; and

(b) with available shares acquired by the company making the disposal rather than other available shares.

(5) The shares disposed of shall be identified with available shares acquired before the disposal rather than available shares acquired after the disposal and—

(a) in the case of available shares acquired before the disposal, with those acquired later rather than those acquired earlier;

(b) in the case of available shares acquired after the disposal, with those acquired earlier rather than those acquired later.

(6) Where available shares could be identified—

(a) with shares disposed of either by the company that acquired them or by another company; or

(b) with shares disposed of either at an earlier date or at a later date,

they shall in each case be identified with the former rather than the latter; and the identification of any available shares with shares disposed of by a company on any occasion shall preclude their identification with shares comprised in a later disposal by that company or in a disposal by another company.

(7) Where a company disposes of shares which have been identified with shares disposed of by another company, the shares disposed of by the first-mentioned company shall be identified with the shares that would, apart from this section, have been comprised in the disposal by the other company or, if those shares have themselves been identified with shares disposed of by a third company, with the shares that would, apart from this section, have been comprised in the disposal by the third company and so on.

(8) Where shares disposed of by one company are identified with shares acquired by another, the sums allowable to the company making the disposal under [section 32 of the Capital Gains Tax Act 1979][1] shall be—

(a) the sums allowable under [subsection (1) (c) of that section][1] (incidental cost of disposal); and

(b) the sums that would have been allowable under [subsection (1) (a) and (b) of that section][1] (acquisition cost etc.) to the company that acquired the shares if they had been disposed of by that company.

(9) This section shall have effect subject to [section 66 (1) of the Capital Gains Tax Act 1979][1] (identification of shares acquired and disposed of on same day); and [subsection (2) of the said section 66][1] (identification of shares not identified [under subsection (1)[1]]) shall have effect subject to this section.

(10) In this section—

"group" has the meaning given in section 272 of the Taxes Act;

"the prescribed period" means—

(a) in the case of a disposal through a stock exchange or Automated Real-Time Investments Exchange Limited, one month;

(b) in the case of a disposal otherwise than as aforesaid, six months;

"trading stock", in relation to a company carrying on life assurance business as defined in section [431 of the Income and Corporation Taxes Act 1988][3], does not include investments held in connection with that business except in so far as they are referable to general annuity business or pension business as defined in that section.

(11) Shares shall not be treated for the purpose of this section as being of the same kind unless they are treated as being of the same class by the practice of a recognised stock exchange or would be so treated if dealt with on such a stock exchange.

(12) This section applies to securities as defined in [section 82 of the Capital Gains Tax Act 1979][1] . . .[2] as it applies to shares.

(13) This section applies where the acquisition and disposal mentioned in subsection (1) above is after 14th April 1975.

Cross-references.—See FA 1982, ss. 86 (6), 88 (1) (*a*) (application of this section to new rules (in consequence of indexation allowance) for the identification of securities held on or acquired on or after 6 April 1982);
FA 1985, Sch. 19, para. 17 (1) (*b*) (modification of indexation allowance with respect to securities (other than those in existence on 1 or 6 April 1982) held on or acquired after 1 April 1985 by companies or after 6 April 1985 by persons other than companies).
Amendments.—[1] Words in sub-ss. (8), (9), (12) substituted by CGTA 1979, s. 157 (2)–(4) and Sch. 7, para. 9 Table, with effect from 22 March 1979.
[2] Words in sub-s. (12) repealed by FA 1985, Sch. 27, Pt. VII with respect to disposals after 1 July 1986.
[3] Words in sub-s. (10) substituted by TA 1988, Sch. 29, para. 32 Table.

67. Appeals

(1) For the removal of doubt it is hereby declared that in section 31 (1) of the Taxes Management Act 1970 (right of appeal) the reference to the date of the notice of assessment is a reference to the date on which the notice was issued.

(2), (3) . . .

Notes.—Sub-ss. (2) and (3) amend TMA 1970, s. 50.

PART IV
MISCELLANEOUS AND GENERAL

75. Citation, interpretation, construction and repeals

(1) This Act may be cited as the Finance (No. 2) Act 1975.

(2) In this Act "the Taxes Act" means the Income and Corporation Taxes Act 1970: ....

(3) In this Act—

(*a*), (*b*) ...

(*c*) Part III, so far as it relates to income tax, shall be construed as one with the Income Tax Acts, so far as it relates to corporation tax shall be construed as one with the Corporation Tax Acts...[1]

(4) Except so far as the context otherwise requires, any reference in this Act to any enactment shall be construed as a reference to that enactment as amended, and as including a reference to that enactment as applied, by or under any other enactment, including this Act.

(5) The enactments mentioned in Schedule 14 to this Act (Part IV of which includes certain enactments which had ceased to have effect before the commencement of this Act) are hereby repealed to the extent specified in the third column of that Schedule, but subject to any provision at the end of any Part of that Schedule.

Note.—Words omitted from sub-ss. (2), (3) are outside the scope of this work.
Amendments.—[1] Words in sub-s. (3) (*c*) repealed by CGTA 1979, s. 158 and Sch. 8.

DEVELOPMENT LAND TAX ACT 1976

(1976 Chapter 24)

34. Interaction of development land tax with other taxes

(1) The provisions of Schedule 6 to this Act shall have effect where development land tax falls to be charged on the realisation of development value which is also brought into account, in whole or in part, for the purposes of—

(a) tax on chargeable gains;
(b) tax on profits or gains of a trade;
(c) ...
(d) ...
(e) section 80 or section 82 of the Income and Corporation Taxes Act 1970 (certain capital sums to be taxable as rent); or
(f) Chapter I of Part III of the Finance Act 1974 (development gains from land).

(2) Without prejudice to subsection *(1)* above, payments of development land tax shall not be available as a deduction in computing the amount of the profits or gains of a trade or the amount of a chargeable gain.

(3) In Schedule 6 to this Act—

(a) a "CGT disposal" means a disposal, for the purposes of tax on chargeable gains, of an asset consisting of an interest in land;
(b) a "DLT disposal" means a disposal (within the meaning of this Act) of an interest in land, other than a disposal for which no consideration is given;
(c) a "trading disposal" means a disposal of an interest in land where the proceeds of the disposal or the market value of the interest disposed of fell or falls to be included in the computation of the profits or gains of a trade carried on by any person; and
(d) ...

(4) If, by virtue of any provision of this Act, liability for development land tax on any realised development value which accrues on a deemed disposal is deferred until a subsequent disposal or other event, then, without prejudice to the operation of section 12 *(8)* of this Act, for the purposes of Schedule 6 to this Act and, in particular, for the purpose of determining whether any chargeable realised development value accrues on that deemed disposal and, if so, the amount of that chargeable realised development value, the liability shall be assumed not to have been deferred.

(5) ...

(6) ...

(7) For the purposes of Schedule 6 to this Act, a person (in this subsection referred to as "A") who makes a disposal of an interest in land (in this subsection referred to as "the relevant interest") claims for DLT purposes through another person (in this subsection referred to as "B") if—

(a) no consideration was given for A's acquisition of the relevant interest, and
(b) B has made a disposal of an interest in land for which no consideration was given, and
(c) in the application of subsection *(2)* of section 10 above for the purpose of determining the relevant base value of the relevant interest on the disposal in question, the disposal referred to in paragraph (b) above is the previous disposal,

and in any case where, by virtue of the preceding provisions of this subsection, B himself claimed for DLT purposes through another person in relation to the making of the disposal referred to in paragraph (b) above, A also claims for DLT purposes through that other person.

Notes.—Sub-ss. (1) (*c*), (*d*), (3) (*d*), (5) and (6) are not relevant for the purposes of this work.

Amendments.—DLTA 1976 repealed by FA 1985, Sch. 27, Pt. X, but the repeal does not have effect in relation to a disposal, as defined in FA 1985, s. 93 (1), which takes place before 19 March 1985. FA 1985, s. 93 (1) reads—

"**93.**—(1) Development land tax shall not be charged in respect of any disposal taking place on or after 19th March 1985; and for this purpose 'disposal' includes a deemed disposal within the meaning of the Development Land Tax Act 1976 (in this section referred to as 'the 1976 Act') and any other event which, but for the repeals effected by Part X of Schedule 27 to this Act, would constitute a disposal of an interest in land for the purposes of that Act."

SCHEDULE 6
Section 34

INTERACTION OF DEVELOPMENT LAND TAX WITH OTHER TAXES

Cross references.—See CGTA 1979, s. 114 (*a*) (CGTA 1979 to have effect subject to this Act and in particular this Schedule);
FA 1985, Sch. 25, para. 2 (waiver of deferred DLT liability on a deemed DLT disposal before 19 March 1985 to have the corresponding effect of cancelling any relief in respect of other taxes under Part I of this Schedule).
Amendments.—DLTA 1976 repealed by FA 1985, Sch. 27, Pt. X, but the repeal does not have effect in relation to a disposal, as defined in FA 1985, s. 93 (1), which takes place before 19 March 1985. FA 1985, s. 93 (1) reads—
"**93.**—(1) Development land tax shall not be charged in respect of any disposal taking place on or after 19th March 1985; and for this purpose 'disposal' includes a deemed disposal within the meaning of the Development Land Tax Act 1976 (in this section referred to as 'the 1976 Act') and any other event which, but for the repeals effected by Part X of Schedule 27 to this Act, would constitute a disposal of an interest in land for the purposes of that Act."

PART I
DLT DISPOSAL PRECEDES OR IS CONTEMPORANEOUS WITH CGT DISPOSAL OR TRADING DISPOSAL

Reduction of chargeable gain on contemporaneous disposal

1.—*(1) If chargeable realised development value accrues to any person on a DLT disposal and that disposal is also a CGT disposal then, subject to the provisions of this Part of this Schedule, a sum equal to the amount of that chargeable realised development value shall be available as a deduction in accordance with sub-paragraph (2) below.*

(2) If a chargeable gain accrues (or would but for this Part of this Schedule accrue) on the CGT disposal referred to in sub-paragraph (1) above, then, for the purposes of capital gains tax or, as the case may require, corporation tax on chargeable gains, the sum available as a deduction by virtue of that sub-paragraph shall be deducted from the amount which, apart from this Part of this Schedule, would be the amount of the chargeable gain.

(3) Where chargeable realised development value accrues to any person on a DLT disposal and, by virtue of Part II of this Schedule, the amount of development land tax chargeable in respect of that value is reduced by an amount which is the credit for other tax paid, within the meaning of that Part, then, for the purposes of this Part of this Schedule, the amount of chargeable realised development value which accrues on that DLT disposal shall be taken to be reduced by an amount equal, subject to sub-paragraph (4) below, to the amount of the notional reduction in liability, within the meaning of that Part, relevant to the calculation of that credit.

(4) Where sub-paragraph (1) of paragraph 14 below applies to the DLT disposal referred to in sub-paragraph (3) above and the case is one to which sub-paragraph (2) of that paragraph applies, the reference in sub-paragraph (3) above to the amount of the notional reduction in liability relevant to the calculation of the credit for other tax paid shall be construed as follows—

(a) except where paragraph 15 below applies, the reference shall be construed as a reference to the aggregate of the amounts of the notional reductions in liability determined in relation to each of the relevant CGT disposals, as defined in paragraph 14 (2) below; and
(b) where paragraph 15 below applies, the reference shall be construed as a reference to the relevant proportion of the amount which was the notional reduction in liability for the purpose of determining, in accordance with sub-paragraph (2) of that paragraph, the amount of the gross credit referred to in sub-paragraph (1) of that paragraph;

and, for the purposes of paragraph (b) above, the relevant proportion is the proportion which the credit for other tax paid appropriate to the DLT disposal referred to in sub-paragraph (3) above bears to the total of the gross credit referred to in paragraph (b) above.

(5) The deduction from the amount of a chargeable gain which is provided for by sub-paragraph (2) above shall be applied to the amount of that gain—

(a) before making any reduction under [section 124 or 125 of the Capital Gains Tax Act 1979][1] *(transfer of business on retirement) or under any other enactment providing for relief by reference to the aggregate of a loss and a gain or of two or more gains or losses, and*
(b) before making any adjustment . . .[2] *under the proviso to section 208 (2) of the Income and*

Corporation Taxes Act 1970 (partially approved superannuation funds: part of gain not to be chargeable gain) or under section 21 (7) of the Finance Act 1970 (investments held partially for purposes of certain retirement benefit schemes: part of gain not to be chargeable gain), and (c) before making any reduction under section 93 of the Finance Act 1972 (reduction in amount of chargeable gains to be included in company's total profits),

but after taking account of any other provision affecting the determination of the amount of any chargeable gain.

(6) Subject to the following provisions of this Part of this Schedule, in any case where, apart from this sub-paragraph, the sum available as a deduction as mentioned in sub-paragraph (1) above would be greater than the amount from which, by virtue of sub-paragraph (2) above, it falls to be deducted, that sum shall be treated for the purposes of those sub-paragraphs as equal to that amount.

Amendments.—[1] Words in sub-para. (5) (*a*) substituted by CGTA 1979, s. 157 (2)–(4) and Sch. 7, para. 9 Table, with effect from 22 March 1979.
[2] Words in sub-para. (5) (*b*) repealed by FA 1980, Sch. 20, Pt. X.

Reduction where DLT disposal precedes CGT disposal

2.—*(1) Subject to sub-paragraph (2) below, if chargeable realised development value accrues to any person on a DLT disposal which is a deemed disposal and, accordingly, does not constitute a CGT disposal of the interest in question and that deemed disposal is followed by a CGT disposal (in this paragraph referred to as "the subsequent disposal") of that interest or any part of it, then,—*

(a) if the subsequent disposal is not also a DLT disposal, it shall be treated as such for the purposes of paragraph 1 above; and
(b) whether or not paragraph (a) above applies, the chargeable realised development value which accrued on the earlier deemed DLT disposal shall be treated for the purposes of paragraph 1 above as accruing on the subsequent DLT disposal (in addition to any chargeable realised development value which in fact accrues or is otherwise treated as accruing on that disposal).

(2) Sub-paragraph (1) above does not apply if, in the period between the earlier deemed DLT disposal and the subsequent disposal, the interest which is the subject matter of the subsequent disposal was acquired in circumstances falling within [section 49 (1) of the Capital Gains Tax Act 1979][1] *(for capital gains tax purposes, personal representatives acquire deceased's assets at market value but without there being a CGT disposal).*

Amendments.—[1] Words in sub-para. (2) substituted by CGTA 1979, s. 157 (2)–(4) and Sch. 7, para. 9 Table, with effect from 22 March 1979.

Part disposals

3.—*(1) The provisions of this paragraph apply if, in a case where paragraph 1 (1) above applies,—*

(a) chargeable realised development value accrues to any person on a DLT disposal which is a part disposal consisting of the grant of a lease; or
(b) if paragraph 2 above also applies, the subsequent disposal referred to in that paragraph is a part disposal;

and in the following provisions of this paragraph the part disposal referred to in paragraph (a) or, as the case may be, paragraph (b) above is referred to as "the principal disposal" (and references to the principal DLT disposal and the principal CGT disposal shall be construed accordingly) and the interest of which the principal disposal is a part disposal is referred to as "the relevant interest".

(2) If, in a case where this paragraph applies, the principal disposal consists of the grant of a lease and, apart from this sub-paragraph, paragraph 2 of [Schedule 3 to the Capital Gains Tax Act 1979][1] *(premiums for leases) would not apply to the principal disposal by reason only that no premium is required as mentioned in sub-paragraph (1) of that paragraph, it shall be assumed for the purposes of the application of this Part of this Schedule that the payment of a premium of £1 was required under the lease and, accordingly, that the principal disposal is such a CGT disposal as is referred to in the said paragraph 2.*

(3) Where this paragraph applies in a case falling within sub-paragraph (1) (b) above, then, for

the purposes of the following provisions of this paragraph, the consideration for the principal DLT disposal shall be taken to be the aggregate of—

(a) the consideration for the earlier deemed DLT disposal referred to in paragraph 2 above; and
(b) the amount which would be the amount of expenditure on improvements for the purposes of a DLT disposal of the relevant interest, assuming that DLT disposal to occur contemporaneously with the principal disposal.

(4) If, in a case where this paragraph applies, the consideration for the principal DLT disposal (in this paragraph referred to as "CD") exceeds the consideration for the principal CGT disposal, as determined for the purposes of tax on chargeable gains, paragraph 1 (1) above shall have effect as if the reference therein to a sum equal to the amount of the chargeable realised development value which accrues on the DLT disposal were a reference to a sum equal to that fraction of that value of which the numerator is the consideration for the CGT disposal, as so determined, and the denominator, subject to sub-paragraph (5) below, is CD.

(5) If, in a case where paragraph 1 (1) above has effect in accordance with sub-paragraph (4) above,—

(a) the relevant interest is itself a lease, and
(b) the principal disposal is the grant of a sub-lease,

the denominator in the fraction referred to in that sub-paragraph shall be $CD - (HR \times F)$ where—

"HR" is the amount which, for the purposes of Part III of Schedule 2 to this Act, is the value at the time of the principal disposal of the rights of the landlord under the relevant interest; and
"F" is the fraction which, under sub-paragraph (1) of paragraph 10 of that Schedule is applied (or would but for paragraph 11 of that Schedule be applied) to the matters specified in paragraphs (a) to (d) of that sub-paragraph for the purpose of determining the amount of chargeable realised development value which accrues on the principal DLT disposal.

(6) Subject to sub-paragraph (9) below,—

(a) where paragraph 1 (1) above has had effect in accordance with sub-paragraph (4) above in relation to the principal disposal, and
(b) there is a subsequent disposal (in this paragraph referred to as "the later disposal") of the balance of the relevant interest which is either a CGT disposal alone or both a DLT disposal and a CGT disposal,

then, if the later disposal is not also a DLT disposal, it shall be treated as such for the purposes of this paragraph and paragraph 1 above and (in every case) there shall be treated, for the purposes of paragraph 1 above, as accruing on the later disposal, in addition to any chargeable realised development value which in fact accrues on that disposal, such part of the chargeable realised development value which accrued on the principal disposal as is represented by the difference between the fraction of that value appropriate to the later disposal and the fraction of that value appropriate to the last preceding disposal of the relevant interest (whether that is the principal disposal or a subsequent disposal of the balance of the relevant interest).

(7) For the purposes of this paragraph a disposal of the balance of the relevant interest means—

(a) a disposal of the interest which was the retained interest in relation to the principal disposal, or
(b) a disposal which would fall within paragraph (a) above if, in the period beginning immediately after the principal disposal and ending immediately after the disposal in question, no disposal had occurred which falls within either paragraph (a) above or this paragraph.

(8) For the purposes of this paragraph, in relation to the chargeable realised development value which accrued on the principal disposal, the fraction appropriate to that disposal is the fraction applied under sub-paragraph (4) above, and the fraction appropriate of any subsequent disposal of the balance of the relevant interest is the fraction of which the denominator is the amount which is the denominator in the fraction appropriate to the principal disposal and the numerator is CA, where "CA" is the aggregate of the following, as determined for the purposes of tax on chargeable gains, namely,—

(a) the consideration for the principal disposal;
(b) the consideration for the subsequent disposal; and
(c) the consideration for any disposal of the balance of the relevant interest which occurred between the principal disposal and the subsequent disposal.

(9) On the occasion of the first disposal of the balance of the relevant interest where the fraction which, in accordance with sub-paragraph (8) above, is appropriate to the disposal is or exceeds unity, sub-paragraph (6) above shall have effect in relation to the disposal as if for the words "as is represented by the difference between the fraction of that value appropriate to the later disposal and" there were substituted the words "as remains after deducting therefrom"; and thereafter the preceding provisions of this paragraph shall no longer apply in relation to any part of the chargeable realised development value which accrued on the principal disposal.

(10) In determining for the purposes of this paragraph the consideration for a CGT disposal, no account shall be taken of the exclusion of any amount from any consideration by virtue of [paragraph 5 (1) or (3) of Schedule 3 to the Capital Gains Tax Act 1979][1] *(where, by reference to any premium, income tax becomes chargeable under section 80 or section 82 of the Income and Corporation Taxes Act 1970 on any amount, that amount is to be excluded from the consideration brought into account for the purpose of computing any chargeable gain).*

Amendments.—[1] Words in sub-paras. (2), (10) substituted by CGTA 1979, s. 157 (2)–(4) and Sch. 7, para. 9 Table, with effect from 22 March 1979.

Modifications where part of premium, etc. taxable as income

4.—*(1) If, in a case where paragraph 1 (1) above applies on the disposal of an interest in land,—*

(a) the CGT disposal is such that, by virtue of any provision of paragraph 5 of [Schedule 3 to the Capital Gains Tax Act 1979][1] *an amount (in this paragraph referred to as "the income element") falls to be excluded either from the consideration brought into account in making a computation under [Chapter II of Part II of]*[1] *that Act or from any gain accruing on the disposal, and*
(b) by virtue of section 80 or section 82 of the Income and Corporation Taxes Act 1970, the income element falls to be taxable as rent or is chargeable to tax under Case VI of Schedule D,

paragraph 1 (2) above shall have effect in accordance with sub-paragraph (2) below.

(2) Where sub-paragraph (1) above applies, paragraph 1 (2) above shall have effect as if—

(a) the reference to the amount of the chargeable gain were a reference to the aggregate of the income element and the amount of the chargeable gain; and
(b) the reference to capital gains tax included a reference to income tax; and
(c) in the phrase "corporation tax on chargeable gains" the words "on chargeable gains" were omitted.

(3) If, in a case where sub-paragraph (1) above applies, the sum available as a deduction as mentioned in paragraph 1 (1) above is less than the aggregate referred to in sub-paragraph (2) (a) above, the deduction provided for by paragraph 1 (2) above shall be made in the first instance from the amount which, apart from this Part of this Schedule, would be the income element, so that only if the sum so available exceeds that amount will the balance of that sum fall to be deducted from the amount which, apart from this Part of this Schedule, would be the amount of the chargeable gain.

(4) In determining in any case—

(a) the amount excluded from any consideration or chargeable gain by virtue of any provision of paragraph 5 of [Schedule 3 to the Capital Gains Tax Act 1979][1]*, or*
(b) the amount of any deduction under section 83 or section 134 of the Income and Corporation Taxes Act 1970 (deduction for other tax purposes where tax has become chargeable under any provision of sections 80 to 82 of that Act),

no account shall be taken of any deduction made by virtue of any provision of this Schedule on account of any chargeable realised development value.

(5)–(9) . . .[2]

Cross references.—See F (No. 2) A 1979, s. 24 (5) (*a*) (cessation of Schedule D Case VI charge to tax after the year 1978–79).
Amendments.—[1] Words in sub-paras. (1) (*a*), (4) (*a*) substituted by CGTA 1979, s. 157 (2)–(4) and Sch. 7, para. 9 Table, with effect from 22 March 1979.
[2] Sub-paras. (5)–(9) repealed by F (No. 2) A 1979, Sch. 5, Pt. IV, in relation to years of assessment after 1978–79.

Modifications where roll-over relief applies on CGT disposal

5.—*(1)* If, in a case where paragraph 1 *(1)* above applies on the disposal of an interest in land,—

(a) *[sections 115 to 121 of the Capital Gains Tax Act 1979]*[1] *(replacement of business assets) [apply]*[1] *in relation to the CGT disposal in such circumstances that the interest disposed of constitutes or is included among the old assets, and*
(b) *the chargeable realised development value referred to in that paragraph is greater than the chargeable gain, if any, which, apart from this Schedule, would accrue on the disposal,*

paragraph 1 *(6)* above shall not apply and, subject to sub-paragraph *(2)* below, the amount by which that chargeable realised development value exceeds that chargeable gain *(in this paragraph referred to as "the unapplied balance of chargeable development value")* shall be carried forward from the disposal and applied in accordance with the provisions of this paragraph.

(2) If, in a case falling within sub-paragraph *(1)* above, the chargeable realised development value referred to in paragraph 1 *(1)* above exceeds what would be the amount of the chargeable gain accruing on the disposal in question if *[sections 115 to 121 of the Capital Gains Tax Act 1979]*[1] *did not apply, the chargeable realised development value shall be treated for the purposes of sub-paragraph *(1)* above and the following provisions of this paragraph as equal to that amount.

(3) Subject to sub-paragraph *(4)* below, the unapplied balance of chargeable development value shall be set off against the amount of any chargeable gain which *(apart from this paragraph)* would accrue on a subsequent CGT disposal of the new assets and, if the unapplied balance is greater than the amount of any such chargeable gain, the remainder shall again be carried forward to set off against subsequent chargeable gains accruing on the disposal of further replacement assets, and so on until the whole of the balance is exhausted.

(4) If, in a case falling within sub-paragraph *(1)* above, *[sections 115 and 116 of the Capital Gains Tax Act 1979 have effect subject to the provisions of section 117 of that Act]*[1] *(depreciating assets)* in such circumstances that the whole or any part of the chargeable gain referred to in *[subsection (2) of the said section 117 accrues in accordance with that subsection]*[1],—

(a) the unapplied balance of chargeable development value shall be set off against the amount of any chargeable gain which accrues as mentioned in *[subsection (2) of the said section 117]*[1] and
(b) if the unapplied balance is greater than the amount of any such chargeable gain and part of the postponed gain is carried forward to asset No. 3 under *[subsection (3) of the said section 117]*[1], the remainder of the unapplied balance shall be dealt with under sub-paragraph *(3)* above.

(5) In any case where, by virtue of sub-paragraph *(3)* or sub-paragraph *(4)* above, the unapplied balance of chargeable development value or any part of it falls to be set off against the amount of a chargeable gain, a sum equal to that unapplied balance or part thereof shall be deducted from the amount which, apart from this paragraph, would be the amount of the chargeable gain and, if the unapplied balance or part thereof exceeds that amount, the chargeable gain shall be extinguished.

(6) In this paragraph "the old assets" and "the new assets" have the same meaning as in *[sections 115 to 121 of the Capital Gains Tax Act 1979]*[1] and "asset No. 3" has the same meaning as in *[section 117 of that Act]*[1].

Amendments.—[1] Words in sub-paras. (1) (*a*), (2), (4), (6) substituted by CGTA 1979, s. 157 (2)–(4) and Sch. 7, para. 6, with effect from 22 March 1979.

Reduction of profits or gains on contemporaneous disposal

6.—*(1)* If chargeable realised development value accrues to any person on a DLT disposal and that disposal is also a trading disposal, then, subject to the following provisions of this paragraph, a sum equal to the amount of that chargeable realised development value shall be allowable as a deduction in accordance with sub-paragraph *(2)* below in computing the profits or gains of the trade in question.

(2) For the purpose of determining the year of assessment or accounting period in which account is to be taken of the deduction referred to in sub-paragraph *(1)* above, that deduction shall be treated as if it were a trading expense incurred on the date on which occurred the trading disposal referred to in that sub-paragraph.

(3)–(9) . . .[1]

Cross references.—See F (No. 2) A 1979, s. 24 (5) (*a*) (cessation of Schedule D Case VI charge to tax after the year 1978–79).
Amendments.—¹ Sub-paras. (3)–(9) repealed by F (No. 2) A 1979, Sch. 5, Pt. IV, in relation to years of assessment after 1978–79.

Reduction where DLT disposal precedes trading disposal

7. *If chargeable realised development value accrues to any person on a DLT disposal which is a deemed disposal and, accordingly, does not constitute a trading disposal of the interest in question and that deemed DLT disposal is followed by a trading disposal (in this paragraph referred to as "the subsequent disposal") of that interest or any part of it, then,—*

(a) if the subsequent disposal is not also a DLT disposal, it shall be treated as such for the purposes of paragraph 6 above; and
(b) whether or not paragraph (a) above applies, the chargeable realised development value which accrued on the earlier deemed DLT disposal shall be treated for the purposes of paragraph 6 above as accruing on the subsequent DLT disposal (in addition to any chargeable realised development value which in fact accrues or is otherwise treated as accruing on that disposal).

Part disposals

8.—*(1) The provisions of this paragraph apply if, in a case where paragraph 6 (1) applies,—*

(a) chargeable realised development value accrues to any person on a DLT disposal which is a part disposal consisting of the grant of a lease; or
(b) if paragraph 7 above also applies, the subsequent DLT disposal referred to in that paragraph is a part disposal,

and in the following provisions of this paragraph the part disposal referred to in paragraph (a) or, as the case may be, paragraph (b) above is referred to as "the principal disposal" (and references to the principal DLT disposal and the principal trading disposal shall be construed accordingly) and the interest of which the principal DLT disposal is a part disposal is referred to as "the relevant interest".

(2) If in a case where this paragraph applies, the principal disposal consists of the grant of a lease and, apart from this sub-paragraph, the principal disposal would not be a trading disposal by reason only that no part of the consideration would fall to be included in the computation of the profits or gains of the trade in question, then, for the purposes of this paragraph and paragraphs 6 and 7 above, the disposal shall be treated as a trading disposal and the sum of £1 shall be taken to be the consideration for the disposal which falls to be included in the computation of those profits or gains.

(3) Where this paragraph applies in a case falling within sub-paragraph (1) (b) above, then, for the purposes of the following provisions of this paragraph, the consideration for the principal DLT disposal shall be taken to be the aggregate of—

(a) the consideration for the earlier deemed disposal referred to in paragraph 7 above; and
(b) the amount which would be the amount of expenditure on improvements for the purposes of a DLT disposal of the relevant interest, assuming that DLT disposal to occur contemporaneously with the principal disposal.

(4) If, in a case where this paragraph applies, the consideration for the principal DLT disposal (in this paragraph referred to as "CD") exceeds the consideration for the principal trading disposal (in this paragraph referred to as "CT") as brought into account in computing the profits or gains of the trade in question, paragraph 6 (1) above shall have effect as if the reference therein to a sum equal to the amount of the chargeable realised development value which accrues on the DLT disposal were a reference to a sum equal to that fraction of that value of which the numerator is CT and the denominator, subject to sub-paragraph (5) below, is CD.

(5) Sub-paragraphs (5) to (9) of paragraph 3 above shall have effect in relation to the preceding provisions of this paragraph as if, in those sub-paragraphs,—

(a) any reference to paragraph 1 or paragraph 1 (1) above were a reference to paragraph 6 or paragraph 6 (1) above;
(b) any expression to which a meaning is assigned by the preceding provisions of this paragraph had that meaning;

(c) any reference to sub-paragraph (4) of paragraph 3 above were a reference to sub-paragraph (4) of this paragraph; and
(d) any reference to a CGT disposal were a reference to a trading disposal;

and as if, in sub-paragraph (8) of paragraph 3 above, for the words "as determined for the purposes of tax on chargeable gains" there were substituted the words "as brought into account in computing the profits or gains of the trade in question."

FINANCE ACT 1976

(1976 Chapter 40)

ARRANGEMENT OF SECTIONS

Note.—Provisions of this Act relevant to the taxes covered by this Handbook and not reproduced are either spent or repealed by TA 1988, Sch. 31 and other legislation.

PART III
INCOME TAX, CORPORATION TAX AND CAPITAL GAINS TAX

CHAPTER I
GENERAL

Section
39. Capital allowances: writing-down allowances.
41. Capital allowances: restriction of set-off against general income.
54. Capital gains: compulsory acquisition of aircraft and shipbuilding shares.

CHAPTER II
BENEFITS DERIVED BY COMPANY DIRECTORS AND OTHERS FROM THEIR EMPLOYMENT

72. Interpretation of this Chapter; supplementary.

PART V
MISCELLANEOUS AND SUPPLEMENTARY

127. *Stamp duty: stock exchange transfers.* (see Orange Book)
128. *Stamp duty: chargeable transactions in respect of capital companies.* (see Orange Book)
131. Inter-American Development Bank.
132. Citation, interpretation, construction and repeals.

SCHEDULES:

Schedule 9—Amendments of Tax Acts consequent on Part III, Chapter II.
    Part I—Replacement of section 15 of the Taxes Management Act 1970.
    Part II—Other amendments.

An Act to grant certain duties, to alter other duties, and to amend the law relating to the National Debt and the Public Revenue, and to make further provision in connection with Finance.
[29th July 1976]

PART III
INCOME TAX, CORPORATION TAX AND CAPITAL GAINS TAX

CHAPTER I
GENERAL

39. Capital allowances: writing-down allowances

(1) Notwithstanding section 40 of the Finance Act 1971 and section 68 (1) of the Finance Act 1972 (which exclude from the system of capital allowances introduced in 1971 expenditure incurred before 27th October 1970 and certain expenditure incurred later), the expenditure to which subsection (4) (*a*) of section 44 of the said Act of 1971 applies in the case of a person's first new chargeable period shall include the amount still unallowed, at the beginning of that period or its basis period, of any eligible expenditure incurred by him on the provision for the purposes of his trade of machinery or plant which then—

(*a*) belongs to him; and
(*b*) is or has been used for those purposes; and
(*c*) has not permanently ceased to be so used;

and elsewhere in the said section 44 references to capital expenditure shall include references to such eligible expenditure as aforesaid.

(2) In the case of such eligible expenditure as is mentioned in subsection (1) above no allowances or charges shall be made under Chapter II of Part I of the Capital Allowances Act 1968 for any new chargeable period; and in the case of other expenditure section 20 (1) of that Act (normal method of calculating writing-down allowances) shall have effect for any such period with the substitution of the words "a percentage" of the words "25 per cent".

(3) In this section "eligible expenditure" means, subject to subsection (4) below, expenditure in respect of which an allowance or allowances have been (or, if claimed, could have been) made under the said Chapter II; and in subsection (1) above the reference to the amount of any such expenditure still unallowed shall be construed in accordance with section 41 in that Chapter.

(4) The following is not eligible expenditure—

(*a*) expenditure on the provision of a new ship within the meaning of section 31 of the said Act of 1968;
(*b*) expenditure in respect of which an allowance or allowances have been (or, if claimed, could have been) made by virtue of or in accordance with the following provisions of the said Act of 1968—

(i) section 18 (5) or 28 (assets used partly for trade and partly for other purposes);
(ii) section 18 (6) or 29 (subsidies for wear and tear);
(iii) section 32 (cars); or
(iv) section 42 or 43 (lessors or lessees);

(*c*) expenditure in respect of which an allowance or allowances have been made in accordance with section 21 of the said Act of 1968 (alternative method of calculating writing-down allowances);
(*d*) expenditure incurred by a person under a contract which provides that he shall or may become the owner of the machinery or plant on the performance of the contract and which has not been performed before the beginning of his first new chargeable period or its basis period;
(*e*) expenditure to which the person by whom it was incurred elects that subsection (1) above shall not apply.

(5) Any election under subsection (4) (*e*) above shall be made by notice in writing to the inspector given within two years from the end of the first new chargeable period of the person concerned.

(6) In this section "new chargeable period" means—

(*a*) where the chargeable period is a company's accounting period, an accounting period ending after 5th April 1976;
(*b*) where the chargeable period is a year of assessment, a year of assessment the basis period for which ends after that date.

(7) This section shall be construed as if contained in Chapter I of Part III of the said Act of 1971.

41. Capital allowances: restriction of set-off against general income

(1) Relief shall not be given to an individual under [sections 380 and 381 of the Income and Corporation Taxes Act 1988][1] (set-off against general income) by reference to a first-year allowance made to him in respect of expenditure incurred on the provision of machinery or plant for leasing in the course of a trade if—

(*a*) at the time when the expenditure was incurred the trade was carried on by him in partnership with a company (with or without other partners); or
(*b*) a scheme had been effected or arrangements have been made (whether before or after that time) with a view to the trade being carried on by him as aforesaid.

(2) Relief shall not be given to an individual under the said [sections 380 and 381][1] by reference to a first-year allowance if—

(*a*) the allowance is made in connection with—

(i) a trade which at the time when the expenditure was incurred was carried on by him in partnership or which has subsequently been carried on by him in partnership or transferred to a person who was connected with him within the meaning of section [839 of the Income and Corporation Taxes Act 1988][1]; or
(ii) an asset which after that time has been transferred by him to a person who was connected with him as aforesaid or, at a price lower than that which it would have fetched if sold in the open market, to any other person; and

(*b*) a scheme has been effected or arrangements have been made (whether before or after that time) such that the sole or main benefit that might be expected to accrue to the individual from the transaction under which the expenditure was incurred was the obtaining of a reduction in tax liability by means of such relief as aforesaid.

(3) Where relief has been given in a case to which subsection (1) or (2) above applies it shall be withdrawn by the making of an assessment under Case VI of Schedule D.

(4) For the purposes of subsection (1) above letting a ship on charter shall be regarded as leasing it if, apart from this provision, it would not be so regarded.

(5) In this section "first-year allowance" means a first-year allowance under Chapter I of Part III of the Finance Act 1971, "trade" includes any activity in connection with which a first-year allowance can be given and any expression defined in section 50 of the said Act of 1971 has the meaning given in that section.

(6) This section applies to relief under the proviso to section 71 (1) of the Capital Allowances Act 1968 as it applies to relief under the said [sections 380 and 381][1].

(7) Subsections (1) and (2) above apply where the expenditure in respect of which the allowance is made to the individual in question was incurred by him after the commencement date and otherwise than under a contract entered into by him on or before that date; and "the commencement date" is, in relation to subsection (1), 15th December 1975 and, in relation to subsection (2), 6th April 1976.

Amendments.—[1] Words in sub-ss. (1), (2), (6) substituted by TA 1988, Sch. 29, para. 32 Table.

54. Capital gains: compulsory acquisition of aircraft and shipbuilding shares

(1) This section has effect where, in pursuance of any enactment to which this subsection applies, gilt-edged securities are exchanged for shares in a company and, immediately before the exchange, those shares are owned by another company—

(*a*) which is a member of the same group of companies as the first-mentioned company; or

(*b*) which is a member of a consortium by which the first-named company is owned.

(2) Subsection (1) above applies to any enactment providing for the compulsory acquisition of shares in companies engaged in manufacturing aircraft or guided weapons or in shipbuilding or allied industries.

(3) In any case in which this section has effect the company owning the shares immediately before the exchange may by notice in writing given to the inspector within four years after the exchange, elect—

(*a*) that [section 84 (3) of the Capital Gains Tax Act 1979]² shall not apply to the exchange; and

(*b*) that [sections 115 to 121 of the Capital Gains Tax Act 1979]² (replacement of business assets) shall have effect in relation to the disposal on the occasion of the exchange as if the shares were assets falling within the classes listed in [section 118 of that Act]² and had, throughout the period of ownership been used and used only for the purposes of a trade carried on by that company.

(4) For the purposes of this section—

(*a*) two companies shall be deemed to be members of a group of companies if one is the 75 per cent. subsidiary of the other or both are 75 per cent. subsidiaries of a third company;

(*b*) a company is owned by a consortium if all of the ordinary share capital of that company is directly and beneficially owned between them by five or fewer companies, and those companies are called the members of the consortium.

[(5) Subsection (6) of section 84 of the Capital Gains Tax Act 1979 (gilt-edged securities not issued until after the date when shares are compulsorily acquired) shall apply in relation to this section as it applies in relation to that section, and in this section—

"gilt-edged securities" has the meaning given by Schedule 2 to that Act;
"shares" includes securities within the meaning of section 82 of that Act.]¹

Cross references.—See CGTA 1979, s. 84 (8) (gilt-edged securities issued in exchange for securities as a result of nationalisation).
Amendments.—¹ Sub-s. (5) substituted by CGTA 1979, s. 157 (2)–(4) and Sch. 7, para. 7, with effect from 22 March 1979.
² Words in sub-s. (3) (*a*), (*b*) substituted by CGTA 1979, s. 157 (2)–(4) and Sch. 7, para. 9 Table, with effect from 22 March 1979.

CHAPTER II
BENEFITS DERIVED BY COMPANY DIRECTORS AND OTHERS FROM THEIR EMPLOYMENT

72. Interpretation of this Chapter; supplementary

(1)–(12) ...[1]

(13) The enactments specified in Schedule 9 to this Act shall be amended as there specified (which are amendments consequential on the replacement by this Chapter of Chapter II or Part VIII of the Taxes Act and other provisions); Part I of that Schedule substitutes a new section for section 15 of the Taxes Management Act 1970, and contains consequential amendments; Part II contains other amendments.

Amendments.—[1] Sub-ss. (1)–(12) repealed by TA 1988, Sch. 31.

PART V
MISCELLANEOUS AND SUPPLEMENTARY

131. Inter-American Development Bank

(1) The following provisions of this section shall have effect on the United Kingdom's becoming a member of the Inter-American Development Bank ("the Bank").

(2) [A security issued by the Inter-American Development Bank][1] shall be taken for the purposes of capital transfer tax and capital gains tax to be situated outside the United Kingdom.

(3) ...

Note.—Sub-s. (3) is outside the scope of this work.
Cross references.—See FA 1986, s. 100 (1), (2) (the reference in sub-s. (2) above to CTT to be construed as a reference to inheritance tax where the liability arises on or after 25 July 1986).
Amendments.—[1] Words in sub-s. (2) substituted by TA 1988, Sch. 29, para. 32 Table.

132. Citation, interpretations, construction and repeals

(1) This Act may be cited as the Finance Act 1976.

(2) In this Act "the Taxes Act" means the Income and Corporation Taxes Act 1970.

(3) In this Act—

(*a*) ...
(*b*) ...
(*c*) Part III, so far as it relates to income tax, shall be construed as one with the Income Tax Acts, so far as it relates to corporation tax shall be construed as one with the Corporation Tax Acts and, so far as it relates to capital gains tax, shall be construed as one with [the Capital Gains Tax Act 1979][1];
(*d*) ...

(4) Except so far as the context otherwise requires, any reference in this Act to any enactment shall be construed as a reference to that enactment as amended, and as including a reference to that enactment as applied, by or under any other enactment, including this Act.

(5) The enactments mentioned in Schedule 15 to this Act (which include spent enactments) are hereby repealed to the extent specified in the third column of that Schedule, but subject to any provision at the end of any Part of that Schedule.

Note.—In sub-s. (3), paras. (*a*), (*b*) and (*d*) are outside the scope of this work.
Amendments.—[1] Words in sub-s. (3) (*c*) substituted by CGTA 1979, s. 157 (2)–(4) and Sch. 7, para. 8 Table, Pt. I. 9, with effect from 22 March 1979.

SCHEDULES

SCHEDULE 9
Section 72

AMENDMENTS OF TAX ACTS CONSEQUENT ON PART III, CHAPTER II

PART I
REPLACEMENT OF SECTION 15 OF THE TAXES MANAGEMENT ACT 1970 (c. 9)

Taxes Management Act 1970 (c. 9)

Savings

6. Nothing in this Part of this Act shall prejudice the validity of anything done before the passing of this Act for the purposes of section 15 of the Taxes Management Act 1970 or section 200 of the Taxes Act, including any notice given, return made or proceedings taken, and anything so done shall be complied with and proceeded with, and proceedings for failure to comply with those sections may be instituted or continued, as if this Part of this Act had not been passed.

FINANCE ACT 1978

(1978 Chapter 42)

ARRANGEMENT OF SECTIONS

Note.—Provisions of this Act relevant to the taxes covered by this Handbook and not reproduced are either spent or repealed by TA 1988, Sch. 31 and other legislation.

PART III
INCOME TAX, CORPORATION TAX AND CAPITAL GAINS TAX
CHAPTER I
GENERAL

Section
37. Capital allowances: long leases.
38. Capital allowances: hotels.
40. Capital allowances: sports grounds.

PART V
MISCELLANEOUS AND SUPPLEMENTARY

77. Disclosure of information to tax authorities in other member States.
80. Short title, interpretation, construction and repeals.

SCHEDULES:
 Schedule 6—Capital allowances: hotels.

An Act to grant certain duties, to alter other duties, and to amend the law relating to the National Debt and the Public Revenue, and to make further provision in connection with Finance. [31st July 1978]

PART III

INCOME TAX, CORPORATION TAX AND CAPITAL GAINS TAX

CHAPTER I

GENERAL

37. Capital allowances: long leases

(1) Subject to the provisions of this section, where expenditure has been incurred on the construction of a building or structure and a long lease of that building or structure is granted out of an interest therein which is, within the meaning of Chapter I of Part I of the Capital Allowances Act 1968, the relevant interest in relation to that expenditure, that Chapter shall, if the lessor and lessee so elect, have effect as if—

(*a*) the grant of the lease were a sale of the relevant interest by the lessor to the lessee at the time when the lease takes effect;
(*b*) any capital sum paid by the lessee in consideration for the grant of the lease were the purchase price on the sale; and
(*c*) the interest out of which the lease is granted had at that time ceased to be, and the interest granted by the lease had at that time become, the relevant interest in relation to that expenditure.

(2) Any election under this section shall have effect in relation to all the expenditure in relation to which the interest out of which the lease is granted is the relevant interest and which relates to the building or structure or (if more than one) the buildings or structures which are the subject of the lease.

(3) Any election under this section shall be by notice in writing to the inspector given within two years after the date on which the lease takes effect; and all such adjustments shall be made, whether by discharge or repayment of tax or by further assessments, as may be required for giving effect to the election.

(4) In this section "long lease" means a lease the duration of which (ascertained according to [subsections (1) to (4) and (6) of section 38 of the Income and Corporation Taxes Act 1988][1]) exceeds fifty years; and any question whether a lease is a long lease shall be determined without regard to section 13 (3) of the said Act of 1968 (options for renewal).

(5) Section 11 (3) of the said Act of 1968 (under which the creation of a lease does not affect the continuance of a relevant interest) shall have effect subject to subsection (1) (*c*) above.

(6) This section does not apply where—

(*a*) the lessor and lessee are connected with each other within the terms of section [839 of the Income and Corporation Taxes Act 1988][1]; or
(*b*) it appears that the sole or main benefit which may be expected to accrue to the lessor from the grant of the lease and the making of an election is the obtaining of a balancing allowance under section 3 of the said Act of 1968;

but paragraph (*a*) above shall not prevent the application of this section where the lessor is a body discharging statutory functions and the lessee a company of which it has control.

(7) The Tax Acts shall have effect as if this section were contained in Chapter I of Part I of the said Act of 1968.

(8) This section applies where the time when the lease takes effect is on or after 15th February 1978.

Amendments.—[1] Words in sub-ss. (4), (6) (*a*) substituted by TA 1988, Sch. 29, para. 32 Table.

38. Capital allowances: hotels

(1) Chapter I of Part I of the Capital Allowances Act 1968 shall apply in relation to a qualifying hotel as if it were an industrial building or structure; but the provisions of that Chapter shall have effect in relation to any such hotel with the modifications specified in Schedule 6 to this Act.

(2) A qualifying hotel is a hotel the accommodation in which is in a building or buildings of a permanent nature and which complies with the following requirements—

> (a) that it is open for at least four months in the season; and
> (b) that during the time when it is open in the season—
>
>> (i) it has at least ten letting bedrooms;
>> (ii) the sleeping accommodation offered at the hotel consists wholly or mainly of letting bedrooms; and
>> (iii) the services provided for guests normally include the provision of breakfast and an evening meal, the making of beds and the cleaning of rooms.

(3) In subsection (2) above "the season" means April, May, June, July, August, September and October; and for the purposes of that subsection a letting bedroom is a private bedroom available for letting to the public generally and not normally in the same occupation for more than one month.

(4) Subject to subsection (5) below, any question whether a hotel complies with the requirements in subsection (2) (a) and (b) above at any time in a person's chargeable period or its basis period shall be determined—

> (a) if the hotel has been in use for the purposes of the trade carried on by that person or by such a lessee as is mentioned in section 1 (3) of the said Act of 1968 throughout the twelve months ending with the last day of that chargeable period or its basis period, by reference to those twelve months;
> (b) if the hotel was first used as aforesaid on a date after the beginning of those twelve months, by reference to the twelve months beginning with that date;

but a hotel shall not by virtue of this subsection be treated as complying with those requirements at any time in a chargeable period or its basis period after it has ceased altogether to be used.

(5) Where, during the twelve months mentioned in paragraph (a) of subsection (4) above, a hotel had fewer than ten letting-bedrooms until a date which was too late for it to qualify by reference to those twelve months, it may instead qualify under paragraph (b) of that subsection by reference to the twelve months beginning with that date as if it had then first been used.

(6) For the purposes of this section—

> (a) there shall be treated as included in a qualifying hotel any building (whether or not on the same site as any other part of the hotel) which is provided by the person carrying on the hotel for the welfare of workers employed in the hotel and is in use for that purpose; and
> (b) where a qualifying hotel is carried on by an individual, whether alone or in partnership, there shall be treated as excluded from the hotel any accommodation which, during the time when the hotel is open in the season, is normally used as a dwelling by that person or by any member of his family or household.

(7) The Tax Acts shall have effect as if this section and Schedule 6 to this Act were contained in Chapter I of Part I of the said Act of 1968.

(8) This section applies in relation to expenditure incurred after 11th April 1978; and expenditure shall not be treated for the purposes of this subsection as having been incurred after the date on which it was in fact incurred by reason only of section 1 (6) or 5 (1) of the said Act of 1968.

Cross references.—See FA 1980, s. 74 (3) (sub-s. (1) of this section not to apply to hotels in enterprise zones); FA 1981, ss. 74 (5), 75 (4), 76 (4) (for the purposes of this section, CAA 1968, Pt. I, Ch. I to apply as amended by FA 1981, ss. 74, 75, 76);
FA 1985, s. 66 (1) (no initial allowance to be made under this section in respect of expenditure incurred after 31 March 1986, subject to certain savings).

40. Capital allowances: sports grounds

(1) If a person carrying on a trade has since the passing of the Safety of Sports Grounds Act 1975 incurred expenditure in respect of a [sports ground][1] used for the purposes of the trade, then, if—

    (*a*) at the time when the expenditure was incurred the [sports ground][1] was of the description specified in subsection (1) of section 1 of that Act but no designation order under that section had come into operation in respect of the [sports ground][1]; and

    (*b*) the expenditure was incurred in taking steps which the local authority for the area in which the [sports ground][1] is situated certify would have fallen within subsection (1) (*a*) or (*b*) of section 49 of the Finance (No. 2) Act 1975 (relief for safety expenditure at a designated [sports ground][1]) if such an order had then been in operation and a safety certificate had then been issued or applied for,

subsection (1) of the said section 49 shall have effect in relation to the expenditure as it has effect in relation to the expenditure mentioned in that subsection.

(2) All such adjustments shall be made by discharge or repayment of tax as may be required for giving effect to the relief available under this section for expenditure incurred before the passing of this Act.

(3) Any disclaimer or claim under section 41 (3) of the Finance Act 1971 in respect of the relief available under this section for expenditure incurred before the passing of this Act, and any claim for relief (or additional relief) under any other provision of the Tax Acts which is made in consequence of the relief available under this section for such expenditure, shall not be out of time if made within twelve months after the passing of this Act.

(4) Any provision of regulations made under section 6 (1) (*b*) of the Safety of Sports Grounds Act 1975 (power of local authorities to charge fees) shall, with the necessary modifications, apply to the issue of a certificate for the purposes of this section as it applies to the issue of a safety certificate.

(5) In this section "[sports ground][1]", "safety certificate" and "local authority" have the same meaning as in the said Act of 1975.

(6) The Tax Acts shall have effect as if this section were contained in Chapter I of Part III of the Finance Act 1971.

Amendments.—[1] Words in sub-ss. (1), (5) substituted by FA 1988, s. 93 with effect from 1 January 1988.

PART V
MISCELLANEOUS AND SUPPLEMENTARY

77. Disclosure of information to tax authorities in other member States

(1) No obligation as to secrecy imposed by statute or otherwise shall preclude the Commissioners of Inland Revenue or an authorised officer of those Commissioners from disclosing to the competent authorities of another member State any information required to be so disclosed by virtue of the Directive of the Council of the European Communities dated 19th December 1977 No. 77/799/EEC.

(2) Neither the Commissioners nor an authorised officer shall disclose any information in pursuance of the said Directive unless satisfied that the competent authorities of the other State are bound by, or have undertaken to observe, rules of confidentiality with respect to the information which are not less strict than those applying to it in the United Kingdom.

(3) Nothing in this section shall permit the Commissioners of Inland Revenue or an authorised officer of those Commissioners to authorise the use of information disclosed by virtue of the said Directive other than for the purposes of taxation or to facilitate legal proceedings for failure to observe the tax laws of the receiving State.

80. Short title, interpretation, construction and repeals

(1) This Act may be cited as the Finance Act 1978.

(2) In this Act "the Taxes Act" means the Income and Corporation Taxes Act 1970.

(3) In this Act—

(a) ...
(b) ...
(c) Part III, so far as it relates to income tax, shall be construed as one with the Income Tax Acts, so far as it relates to corporation tax shall be construed as one with the Corporation Tax Acts...[1]
(d) ...

(4) Except so far as the context otherwise requires, any reference in this Act to any enactment shall be construed as a reference to that enactment as amended, and as including a reference to that enactment as applied, by or under any other enactment, including this Act.

(5) The enactments mentioned in Schedule 13 to this Act (which include spent enactments) are hereby repealed to the extent specified in the third column of that Schedule, but subject to any provision at the end of any Part of that Schedule.

Note.—In sub-s. (3), paras. (a), (b) and (d) are outside the scope of this work.
Amendments.—Words in sub-s. (3) (c) repealed by CGTA 1979, s. 158 and Sch. 8.

SCHEDULES

SCHEDULE 6
Section 38

CAPITAL ALLOWANCES: HOTELS

Initial allowances

1. *In section 1 (2) of the Capital Allowances Act 1968 for the reference to . . . of the capital expenditure there shall be substituted a reference to one-fifth of that expenditure.*

Note.—For the omitted fraction, see the annotation under CAA 1968, s. 1.
Cross references.—See FA 1980, s. 74 and Sch. 13, para. 1 (initial allowance for qualifying hotels in enterprise zones); FA 1984, s. 58 (4) (*a*) (20 per cent. initial allowance for hotels); FA 1985, s. 66 (1) (abolition of initial allowance under this paragraph in respect of expenditure incurred after 31 March 1986, subject to certain savings).

Balancing allowances and balancing charges

4. Where, after a building has ceased to be a qualifying hotel otherwise than on the occurrence of an event to which subsection (1) of the said section 3 applies, a period of two years elapses in which it is not a qualifying hotel and without the occurrence of any such event, that section and the other provisions of Chapter I of Part I of the said Act of 1968 shall have effect as if—

(*a*) the relevant interest in the building had been sold at the end of that period; and
(*b*) the net proceeds of the sale were equal to the price which that interest would then have fetched if sold in the open market.

Temporary disuse

7. Paragraph 4 above has effect subject to section 12 (1) of the said Act of 1968; but a building shall not by virtue of that section be deemed to continue to be a qualifying hotel for more than two years after the end of the chargeable period or its basis period in which it falls temporarily out of use.

Eligible expenditure

8. *References in Chapter I of Part I of the said Act of 1968 to expenditure on the construction of a building or structure shall not include references to expenditure incurred in taking any such steps as are mentioned in section 17 of the Finance Act 1974 or section 15 of the Finance Act 1975 (expenditure on fire safety).*

Amendments.—This paragraph superseded by FA 1989, Sch. 13, para. 28 (1)–(4) and repealed by FA 1989, Sch. 13, para. 28 (5) (*c*), (6) and Sch. 17, Pt. VI in relation to any chargeable period or its basis period ending after 26 July 1989.

Definitions

9. None of the provisions of section 7 of the said Act of 1968 except subsections (4) and (9) shall be construed as applying to a qualifying hotel.

CAPITAL GAINS TAX ACT 1979

(1979 Chapter 14)

ARRANGEMENT OF PARTS

Part		Sections	Schedule
I.	General	1–18	1
II.	Gains and Losses	19–43	5
III.	Persons and Trusts	44–63	—
IV.	Shares and Securities	64–100	2
V.	Land	101–114	3
VI.	Property: Further Provisions	115–139	4
VII.	Other Provisions	140–149	—
VIII.	Supplemental	150–155	—
IX.	General	156–160	6–8

CAPITAL GAINS TAX ACT 1979

(1979 Chapter 14)

ARRANGEMENT OF SECTIONS

PART I
GENERAL

Capital gains tax and corporation tax

Section
1. Taxation of capital gains.

Capital gains tax

2. Persons chargeable.
3. *Rate of tax.* (repealed)
4. Gains chargeable to tax.
5. Exemption for first £5,000 of gains.
6. *Small gifts.* (repealed)
7. Time for payment of tax.
7A. Payment by instalments of tax on gifts.
8. *Postponement of payment of tax.* (repealed)
9. *Postponement of payment of tax: further provisions.* (repealed)

The foreign element

10. Double taxation relief.
11. Allowance for foreign tax.
12. Non-resident with United Kingdom branch or agency.
13. Foreign assets: delayed remittances.
14. Foreign assets of person with foreign domicile.
15. Non-resident company.
16. Non-resident group of companies.
17. *Non-resident trust.* (spent)
18. Residence etc. and location of assets.

PART II
GAINS AND LOSSES

CHAPTER I
DISPOSALS

19. Disposal of assets.
20. Capital sums derived from assets.
21. Capital sums: compensation and insurance money.
22. Assets lost or destroyed, or whose value becomes negligible.
23. Mortgages and charges.
24. Hire-purchase.
25. Value shifting.
26. Value shifting: further provisions.
26A. Value shifting: distributions within a group followed by a disposal of shares.
26B. Value shifting: disposals within a group followed by a disposal of shares.
26C. Value shifting: supplementary.
26D. Value shifting: transactions treated as a reorganisation of share capital.
27. Time of disposal and acquisition where asset disposed of under contract.

CHAPTER II
COMPUTATION

Section
28. Chargeable gains.
29. Losses.
29A. Disposals and acquisitions treated as made at market value.

Computation of gains

30. Introductory.
31. Consideration chargeable to tax on income.
32. Expenditure: general.
32A. Expenditure: amounts to be included as consideration.
33. Exclusion of expenditure by reference to tax on income.
33A. Transfer of certain securities.
34. Restriction of losses by reference to capital allowances and renewals allowances.
35. Part disposals.
36. Assets derived from other assets.
37. Wasting assets.
38. Wasting assets: straightline restriction of allowable expenditure.
39. Wasting assets qualifying for capital allowances.
40. Consideration due after time of disposal.
41. Contingent liabilities.
42. Expenditure reimbursed out of public money.
43. Supplemental.

PART III
PERSONS AND TRUSTS

Married persons

44. Husband and wife.
45. Tax on married woman's gains.

Trustees, nominees and personal representatives

46. Nominees and bare trustees.
47. Expenses in administration of estates and trusts.
48. Liability for tax.

Death

49. Death: general provisions.
50. Death: application of law in Scotland.

Settlements

51. Meaning of "settled property".
52. Trustees of settlements.
53. Gifts in settlement.
54. Person becoming absolutely entitled to settled property.
55. Termination of life interest etc.
56. Death of life tenant: exclusion of chargeable gain.
56A. Effect on sections 55 and 56 of relief under Finance Act 1980, section 79.
57. Death of annuitant.
58. Disposal of interests in settled property.

Other cases

59. Gifts: recovery from donee.
60. Partnerships.
61. Insolvents' assets.

Section
62. Transactions between connected persons.
63. Connected persons: interpretation.

PART IV
SHARES AND SECURITIES

CHAPTER I
GENERAL

64. Interpretation.

Rules of identification

65. Pooling.
66. Disposal on or before day of acquisition.

Gilt-edged securities

67. Exemptions for gilt-edged securities and qualifying corporate bonds etc.
68. *Identification (general).* (repealed)
69. *Identification: disposal to husband or wife and third person.* (repealed)
70. *Re-acquisition after sale at a loss.* (repealed)

Savings certificates, etc.

71. Exemption for government non-marketable securities.

Capital distribution in respect of shares, etc.

72. Distribution which is not a new holding within Chapter II.
73. Disposal of right to acquire shares.

Close companies

74. Disposal of shares: relief in respect of income tax consequent on shortfall in distributions.
75. Shares in close company transferring assets at an undervalue.

Share option schemes

76. Consideration for acquisition of shares under share option schemes.

CHAPTER II
REORGANISATION OF SHARE CAPITAL, CONVERSION OF SECURITIES, ETC.

Reorganisation or reduction of share capital

77. Application of sections 78 to 81.
78. Equation of original shares and new holding.
79. Consideration given or received by holder.
80. Part disposal of new holding.
81. Composite new holdings.

Conversion of securities

82. Equation of converted securities and new holding.
83. Premiums on conversion of securities.
84. Compensation stock.

Company reconstructions and amalgamations

Section
85. Exchange of securities for those in another company.
86. Reconstruction or amalgamation involving issue of securities.
87. Restriction on application of sections 85 and 86.
88. Procedure for clearance in advance.

Stock dividends

89. Stock dividends: consideration for new holding.
90. Capital gains on certain stock dividends.

Quoted options

91. Application of Chapter II to quoted options.

CHAPTER III

UNIT TRUSTS ETC.

Preliminary

92. Interpretation.
93. Application of Act to unit trusts.

General

94. *Reduction of tax liability on disposal of units or shares.* (repealed)

Unit trusts

95. *Valuation of assets and rights.* (repealed)
96. Unit trusts for exempt unit holders.
97. *Unit trusts for pension schemes.* (repealed)
98. Transfer of company's assets to unit trust which later comes within section 96 or 97.

Court investment funds etc.

99. Funds in court.
100. *Reduced rate of tax.* (repealed)

PART V

LAND

Private residences

101. Relief on disposal of private residence.
102. Amount of relief.
103. Amount of relief: further provisions.
104. Private residence occupied under terms of settlement.
105. Private residence occupied by dependent relative.

Leases

106. Leases of land and other assets.

Part disposals

107. Small part disposals.
108. Part disposal to authority with compulsory powers.
109. Part disposal: consideration exceeding allowable expenditure.

Compulsory acquisition

Section
110. Compensation paid on compulsory acquisition.
111. Time of disposal and acquisition.
111A. Rollover relief on compulsory acquisition.
111B. Provisions supplementary to section 111A.

Agricultural land and woodlands

112. Grants for giving up agricultural land.
113. Woodlands.

Development land tax etc.

114. Interaction with development land tax and other taxation. (repealed)

PART VI
PROPERTY: FURTHER PROVISIONS

Replacement of business assets

115. Roll-over relief.
116. Assets only partly replaced.
117. New assets which are depreciating assets.
118. Relevant classes of assets.
119. Assets of Class 1.
120. Trade carried on by family company: business assets dealt with by individual.
121. Activities other than trades, and interpretation.

Stock in trade

122. Appropriations to and from stock.

Transfer of business to a company

123. Roll-over relief on transfer of business.
123A. Harbour authorities.

Transfer of business on retirement

124. Relief on transfer.
125. Transfer by way of capital distribution from family company.

Gifts of business assets

126. Relief for gifts of business assets.
126A. Section 126 relief: gifts to non-residents.
126B. Section 126 relief: gifts to foreign-controlled companies.
126C. Section 126 relief: emigration of controlling trustees.

Movable property

127. Wasting assets.
128. Chattel exemption.
129. Leases of property other than land.
130. Passenger vehicles.
131. Decorations for valour or gallant conduct.

Other property

132. Commodities and other assets without earmark.
132A. Deep discount securities.
133. Foreign currency for personal expenditure.

Section
134. Debts.
135. Debts: foreign currency bank accounts.
136. Relief in respect of loans to traders.
137. Options and forfeited deposits.
138. Options: application of rules as to wasting assets.
139. Quoted options treated as part of new holdings.

PART VII

OTHER PROVISIONS

Insurance

140. Policies of insurance.
141. Disallowance of insurance premiums as expenses.
142. Underwriters.
142A. Disposal of assets in premiums trust fund etc.
143. Life assurance and deferred annuities.

Superannuation funds, annuities and annual payments

144. Superannuation funds, annuities and annual payments.

Profit sharing and share option schemes

144A. Approved profit sharing and share option schemes.

Other exemptions and reliefs

145. Charities.
146. Gifts to charities etc.
146A. Gifts to housing associations.
147. Works of art etc.
147A. Gifts on which inheritance tax is chargeable etc.
147B. Section 147A relief: gifts to non-residents.
148. *Maintenance funds for historic buildings.* (repealed)
149. Employee trusts.
149A. Building societies and life policies.
149B. Miscellaneous exemptions.
149C. Business expansion schemes.
149D. Personal equity plans.

PART VIII

SUPPLEMENTAL

Valuation

150. Valuation: general.
151. *Assets disposed of in a series of transactions.* (repealed)
152. Unquoted shares and securities.
153. Value determined for capital transfer tax.

Other provisions

154. Income tax decisions.
155. Interpretation.

PART IX

GENERAL

156. Commencement.
157. Savings, transitory provisions and consequential amendments.
158. Repeals.
159. Continuity and construction of references to old and new law.
160. Short title.

SCHEDULES:
Schedule 1—Exemption for first £5,900 of gains.
Schedule 2—Gilt-edged securities.
Schedule 3—Leases.
Schedule 4—Relief for gifts of business assets.
Schedule 5—Assets held on 6th April 1965.
Schedule 6—Transitory.
Schedule 7—*Consequential amendments*. (amending)
Schedule 8—*Repeals*. (amending)

An Act to consolidate Part III of the Finance Act 1965 with related provisions in that Act and subsequent Acts. [22 March 1979]

Construction.—TMA 1970, so far as it relates to chargeable gains, to be construed as one with this Act; see TMA 1970, s. 119 (4).
TA 1970, so far as it relates to capital gains tax, to be construed as one with this Act; see TA 1970, s. 540 (2).
FA 1970, Sch. 6, Pt. II, to be construed as one with this Act; see FA 1970, Sch. 6, para. 9.
FA 1980, Pt. III, in so far as it relates to capital gains tax, to be construed as one with this Act; see FA 1980, s. 122 (3) (*a*).
Sch. 18, so far as it relates to capital gains tax, to be construed as one with this Act; see FA 1980, Sch. 18, para. 23 (5).
FA 1981, Pt. IV, in so far as it relates to capital gains tax, to be construed as one with this Act; see FA 1981, s. 139 (3);
FA 1982, Pt. III, in so far as it relates to capital gains tax, to be construed as one with this Act; see FA 1982, s. 157 (3).
FA 1983, Pt. II, in so far as it relates to capital gains tax, to be construed as one with this Act; see FA 1983, s. 48 (3).
F(No. 2)A 1983, Pt. I, in so far as it relates to capital gains tax, to be construed as one with this Act; see F(No. 2)A 1983, s. 16 (2).
FA 1984, Pt. II, in so far as it relates to capital gains tax, to be construed as one with this Act; see FA 1984, s. 128 (3).
FA 1985, Pt. II, in so far as it relates to capital gains tax, to be construed as one with this Act; see FA 1985, s. 98 (3).
FA 1986, Pt. II, in so far as it relates to capital gains tax, to be construed as one with this Act; see FA 1986, s. 114 (3).
FA 1987, Pt. II, in so far as it relates to capital gains tax, to be construed as one with this Act; see FA 1987, s. 72(3).
F (No. 2) A 1987, Pt. I, in so far as it relates to capital gains tax, to be construed as one with this Act; see F (No. 2) A 1987, s. 104 (3).
FA 1988, Pt. III, in so far as it relates to capital gains tax, to be construed as one with this Act; see FA 1988, s. 147 (3).
Cross references.—See TMA 1970, s. 11 (1) (*b*) (return of profits required to be made by a company),
s. 27 (1) (settlor, trustee or beneficiary of settled property may be required to give necessary particulars for capital gains tax purposes),
s. 47 (1) (appeal against capital gains tax assessment on land to be referred to Lands Tribunal),
s. 57 (1) (*a*) (regulations about appeals on capital gains tax),
s. 111 (1) (inspector of taxes to be permitted to inspect property for ascertainment of market value for capital gains tax purposes);
TA 1970, s. 268A (2) (postponement of capital gains tax on transfer of assets to non-resident company),
s. 273 (1) (capital gains tax relief on transfer of assets within group of companies),
s. 278 (3) (charge to capital gains tax when a company ceases to be a member of a group),
s. 279 (2) (charge to capital gains tax when a subsidiary company leaves a group on company reorganisation),
FA 1970, Sch. 6, para. 3 (2) (*b*) (terminal loss relief in relation to mineral royalties);
FA 1973, s. 38 (3) (territorial extension of charge to capital gains tax),
s. 38 (3A) (extension of this Act to disposals by non-residents etc. of assets used in connection with exploration and exploitation activities);
TA 1988, s. 122 (1), (2) (taxation of mineral royalties),
s. 345 (4) (computation of companies' capital gains),
s. 442 (3) (insurance companies' overseas business; treatment of profit or loss for the purposes of capital gains tax).

PART I
GENERAL

Capital gains tax and corporation tax

1. Taxation of capital gains

(1) Tax shall be charged in accordance with this Act in respect of capital gains, that is to say chargeable gains computed in accordance with this Act and accruing to a person on the disposal of assets.

(2) In the circumstances prescribed by the provisions of Part XI of the [Taxes Act 1970 and Part VIII of the Taxes Act 1988][1] (taxation of companies and certain other bodies and associations) the tax shall be chargeable in accordance with those provisions, and all the provisions of this Act have effect subject to those provisions.

(3) Subject to the said provisions, capital gains tax shall be charged for all years of assessment in accordance with the following provisions of this Act.

Amendments.—[1] Words in sub-s. (2) substituted by TA 1988, Sch. 29, para. 32 Table.

Capital gains tax

2. Persons chargeable

(1) Subject to any exceptions provided by this Act, a person shall be chargeable to capital gains tax in respect of chargeable gains accruing to him in a year of assessment during any part of which he is resident in the United Kingdom, or during which he is ordinarily resident in the United Kingdom.

(2) This section is without prejudice to the provisions of section 12 below (non-resident with UK branch or agency), and of section 38 of the Finance Act 1973 (territorial sea of the United Kingdom).

Cross references.—See TA 1988, s. 761 (2) (extension of this section to offshore income gains).

3. Rate of tax

. . .

Amendments.—This section repealed by FA 1988, Sch. 14, Pt. VII in relation to disposals made after 5 April 1988. See now FA 1988, s. 98.

4. Gains chargeable to tax

(1) Capital gains tax shall be charged on the total amount of chargeable gains accruing to the person chargeable in the year of assessment, after deducting—

(*a*) any allowable losses accruing to that person in that year of assessment, and
(*b*) so far as they have not been allowed as a deduction from chargeable gains accruing in any previous year of assessment, any allowable losses accruing to that person in any previous year of assessment (not earlier than the year 1965–66)

(2) In the case of a woman who in a year of assessment is a married woman living with her husband any allowable loss which, under subsection (1) above, would be deductible from the chargeable gains accruing in that year of assessment to the one but for an insufficiency of chargeable gains shall, for the purposes of that subsection, be deductible from chargeable gains accruing in that year of assessment to the other:

Provided that this subsection shall not apply in relation to losses accruing in a year of assessment to either if, before 6th July in the year next following that year of assessment, an application is made by the man or the wife to the inspector in such form and manner as the Board may prescribe.

Note.—See **Prospective Legislation Notes** (Married Couples).

5. Exemption for first [£5,000][5] of gains[1]

[(1) An individual shall not be chargeable to capital gains tax in respect of so much of his taxable amount for any year of assessment as does not exceed [the exempt amount for the year][3].[2]

[(1A) Subject to subsection (1B) below, the exempt amount for any year of assessment shall be [£5,000][5].][4]

[(1B) If the retail prices index for the month of December preceding the year 1983–84 or any subsequent year of assessment is higher than it was for the previous December, then, unless Parliament otherwise determines, subsection (1A) above shall have effect for that year as if for the amount specified in that subsection as it applied for the previous year (whether by virtue of this subsection or otherwise) there were substituted an amount arrived at by increasing the amount of the previous year by the same percentage as the percentage increase in the retail prices index and, if the result is not a multiple of £100, rounding it up to the nearest amount which is such a multiple.][4]

[(1C) The Treasury shall, before the year 1983–84 and each subsequent year, make an order specifying the amount which by virtue of this section is the exempt amount for that year; and any such order shall be made by statutory instrument.][4]

(4) For the purposes of this section an individual's taxable amount for a year of assessment is the amount on which he is chargeable under section 4 (1) above for that year but—

(*a*) Where the amount of chargeable gains less allowable losses accruing to an individual in any year of assessment does not exceed [the exempt amount for the year][3], no deduction from that amount shall be made for that year in respect of allowable losses carried forward from a previous year or carried back from a subsequent year in which the individual dies, and

(*b*) where the amount of chargeable gains less allowable losses accruing to an individual in any year of assessment exceeds [the exempt amount for the year][3], the deduction from that amount for that year in respect of allowable losses carried forward from a previous year or carried back from a subsequent year in which the individual dies shall not be greater than the excess.

(5) Where in a year of assessment—

(a) the amount of chargeable gains accruing to an individual does not exceed [the exempt amount for the year]³, and
(b) the aggregate amount or value of the consideration for all the disposals of assets made by him (other than disposals gains accruing on which are not chargeable gains) does not exceed [an amount equal to twice the exempt amount for the year]³,

a statement to the effect of paragraphs (a) and (b) above shall, unless the inspector otherwise requires, be sufficient compliance with any notice under section 8 of the Taxes Management Act 1970 requiring the individual to make a return of the chargeable gains accruing to him in that year.

(6) Schedule 1 to this Act shall have effect as respects the application of this section to husbands and wives, personal representatives and trustees.

Note.—See **Prospective Legislation Notes** (Married Couples).
Cross references.—See FA 1989, s. 122 (sub-s. (1B) above not to apply for the year 1989–90).
Amendments.—¹ The heading substituted by FA 1980, s. 77 (2).
² Sub-s. (1) substituted for sub-ss. (1)–(3) by FA 1980, s. 77 (2).
³ Words in sub-ss. (1), (4) (a), (b), (5) (a), (b) substituted by FA 1982, s. 80 (1).
⁴ Sub-ss. (1A), (1B), (1C) inserted by FA 1982, s. 80 (2).
⁵ Amount in the heading and in sub-s. (1A) substituted by virtue of FA 1989, s. 122.

6. Small gifts

Amendments.—Repealed by FA 1984, s. 63 (1) (a) and Sch. 23, Pt. VIII.

7. Time for payment of tax

Capital gains tax assessed on any person in respect of gains accruing in any year shall be payable by that person [on or before 1st December following the end of that year]¹, or at the expiration of a period of thirty days beginning with the date of the issue of the notice of assessment, whichever is the later.

Amendments.—¹ Words substituted by FA 1980, s. 61 (2).

[7A. Payment by instalments of tax on gifts

(1) Subsection (2) below applies where—

(a) the whole or any part of any assets to which this section applies is disposed of by way of gift or is deemed to be disposed of under section 54(1) or 55(1) below, and
(b) the disposal is one—

(i) to which neither section 126 (3) nor section 147A (3) below applies (or would apply if a claim were duly made), or
(ii) to which either of those sections does apply but on which the held-over gain (within the meaning of the section applying) is less than the chargeable gain which would have accrued on that disposal apart from that section.

(2) Where this subsection applies, the capital gains tax chargeable on a gain accruing on the disposal may, if the person paying it by notice in writing to the inspector so elects, be paid by ten equal yearly instalments.

(3) The assets to which this section applies are—

(a) land or an estate or interest in land,
(b) any shares or securities of a company which, immediately before the disposal, gave control of the company to the person by whom the disposal was made or deemed to be made, and
(c) any shares or securities of a company not falling under paragraph (b) above and not quoted on a recognised stock exchange nor dealt in on the Unlisted Securities Market.

(4) Where tax is payable by instalments by virtue of this section, the first instalment shall be due on the day on which the tax would be payable apart from this section.

(5) Subject to the following provisions of this section—
 (a) tax payable by instalments by virtue of this section shall carry interest in accordance with Part IX (except section 88) of the Taxes Management Act 1970, and
 (b) the interest on the unpaid portion of the tax shall be added to each instalment and paid accordingly.

(6) Tax payable by instalments by virtue of this section which is for the time being unpaid, with interest to the date of payment, may be paid at any time.

(7) Tax which apart from this subsection would be payable by instalments by virtue of this section and which is for the time being unpaid, with interest to the date of payment, shall become due and payable immediately if—
 (a) the disposal was by way of gift to a person connected with the donor or was deemed to be made under section 54 (1) or 55 (1) below, and
 (b) the assets are disposed of for valuable consideration under a subsequent disposal (whether or not the subsequent disposal is made by the person who acquired them under the first disposal).][1]

Amendments.—[1] This section inserted by FA 1989, s. 124 (2), (3) and Sch. 14, para. 5 in relation to disposals after 13 March 1989 with certain exceptions; see FA 1989, s. 124 (3).

8. Postponement of payment of tax

Amendments.—Repealed by FA 1984, s. 63 (1) (b) and Sch. 23, Pt. VIII.

9. Postponement of payment of tax: further provisions

Amendments.—Repealed by FA 1984, s. 63 (1) (b) and Sch. 23, Pt. VIII.

The foreign element

10. Double taxation relief

(1) For the purpose of giving relief from double taxation in relation to capital gains tax and tax on chargeable gains charged under the law of any country outside the United Kingdom, in Chapters I and II of Part XVIII of the Taxes Act [1988][1], as they apply for the purposes of income tax, for references to income there shall be substituted references to capital gains and for references to income tax there shall be substituted references to capital gains tax meaning, as the context may require, tax charged under the law of the United Kingdom or tax charged under the law of a country outside the United Kingdom.

(2) Any arrangements set out in an order made under section 347 of the Income Tax Act 1952 before 5th August 1965 (the date of the passing of the Finance Act 1965) shall so far as they provide (in whatever terms) for relief from tax chargeable in the United Kingdom on capital gains have effect in relation to capital gains tax.

(3) So far as by virtue of this section capital gains tax charged under the law of a country outside the United Kingdom may be brought into account under the said Chapters I and II as applied by this section, that tax, whether relief is given by virtue of this section in respect of it or not, shall not be taken into account for the purposes of those Chapters as they apply apart from this section.

(4) Section [816][2] of the Taxes Act (disclosure of information for purposes of double taxation) shall apply in relation to capital gains tax as it applies in relation to income tax.

Amendments.—[1] "1988" in sub-s. (1) inserted by virtue of TA 1988, Sch. 29, para. 15 (a).
[2] Number in sub-s. (4) substituted by TA 1988, Sch. 29, para. 32 Table.

11. Allowance for foreign tax

Subject to section 10 above, the tax chargeable under the law of any country outside the United Kingdom on the disposal of an asset which is borne by the person making the disposal shall be allowable as a deduction in the computation under Chapter II of Part II of this Act.

12. Non-resident with United Kingdom branch or agency

(1) Subject to any exceptions provided by this Act a person shall be chargeable to capital gains tax in respect of chargeable gains accruing to him in a year of assessment in which he is not resident and not ordinarily resident in the United Kingdom but is carrying on a trade in the United Kingdom through a branch or agency, and shall be so chargeable on chargeable gains accruing on the disposal—

(a) of assets situated in the United Kingdom and used in or for the purposes of the trade at or before the time when the capital gain accrued, or
(b) of assets situated in the United Kingdom and used or held for the purposes of the branch or agency at or before that time, or assets acquired for use by or for the purposes of the branch or agency.

[(1A) Subsection (1) above does not apply unless the disposal is made at a time when the person is carrying on the trade in the United Kingdom through a branch or agency.][2]

(2) This section shall not apply to a person who, by virtue of Part XVIII of the Taxes Act [1988][1] (double taxation agreements), is exempt from income tax chargeable for the year of assessment in respect of the profits or gains of the branch or agency.

[(2A) This section shall apply as if references to a trade included references to a profession or vocation.][3]

(3) In this Act, unless the contest otherwise requires, "branch or agency" means any factorship, agency, receivership, branch or management, but does not include any person within the exemptions in section 82 of the Taxes Management Act 1970 (general agents and brokers).

Cross references.—See TA 1988, s. 761 (2)–(4) (extension with modification of this section to offshore income gains);
FA 1989, s. 126 (5), (6) (non-residents carrying on profession or vocation in the UK through a branch or agency),
s. 127 (6) (a) (anti-avoidance provisions to counter avoidance of tax under this section by non-residents removing the chargeable assets outside the UK or by ceasing to trade in the UK after 13 March 1989),
s. 129 (6) (a) (anti-avoidance provisions in relation to roll-over relief to counter avoidance of tax under this section by non-residents where disposal of old assets or acquisition of new assets takes place after 13 March 1989),
s. 131 (6) (a) (CGT charge under this section where certain events occur after 13 March 1989 in relation to exploration or exploitation of oil assets by non-residents having a branch or agency in the UK).
Amendments.—[1] "1988" in sub-s. (2) inserted by virtue of TA 1988, Sch. 29, para. 15 (a).
[2] Sub-s. (1A) inserted by FA 1989, s. 128 (2) from the year 1989–90 onwards. For the year 1988–89, sub-s. (1A) reads as follows, see FA 1989, s. 128 (1)—

"(1A) In the case of a disposal made on or after 14th March 1989, subsection (1) above only applies—

(a) if it is made at a time when the person is carrying on the trade in the United Kingdom through a branch or agency, or
(b) if he ceased to carry on the trade in the United Kingdom through a branch or agency before 14th March 1989."

[3] Sub-s. (2A) inserted by FA 1989, s. 126 (2) from the year 1989–90 onwards. For the year 1988–89, sub-s. (2A) reads as follows, see FA 1989, s. 126 (1)—

"(2A) In the case of a disposal made on or after 14th March 1989, this section shall apply as if references to a trade included references to a profession or vocation, but not so as to make a person chargeable to capital gains tax by virtue of a profession or vocation which he ceased to carry on in the United Kingdom through a branch or agency before 14th March 1989."

13. Foreign assets: delayed remittances

(1) Subsection (2) below applies where—

(a) chargeable gains accrue from the disposal of assets situated outside the United Kingdom, and
(b) the person charged or chargeable makes a claim and shows that the conditions set out in subsection (3) below are, so far as applicable, satisfied as respects those gains ("the qualifying gains").

(2) For the purposes of capital gains tax—

(a) the amount of the qualifying gains shall be deducted from the amounts on which the claimant is assessed to capital gains tax for the year in which the qualifying gains accrued to the claimant, but
(b) the amount so deducted shall be assessed to capital gains tax on the claimant (or his personal representatives) as if it were an amount of chargeable gains accruing in the year of assessment in which the conditions set out in subsection (3) below cease to be satisfied.

(3) The said conditions are—

(*a*) that the claimant was unable to transfer the qualifying gains to the United Kingdom, and

(*b*) that that inability was due to the laws of the territory where the income arose, or to the executive action of its government, or to the impossibility of obtaining foreign currency in that territory, and

(*c*) that the inability was not due to any want of reasonable endeavours on the part of the claimant.

(4) Where under an agreement entered into under arrangements made by the Secretary of State in pursuance of section 1 of the Overseas Investment and Export Guarantees Act 1972 or section 11 of the Export Guarantees and Overseas Investment Act 1978 any payment is made by the Exports Credits Guarantee Department in respect of any gains which cannot be transferred to the United Kingdom, then, to the extent of the payment, the gains shall be treated as gains with respect to which the conditions mentioned in subsection (3) above are not satisfied (and accordingly cannot cease to be satisfied).

(5) No claim under this section shall be made in respect of any chargeable gain more than six years after the end of the year of assessment in which that gain accrues.

(6) The personal representatives of a deceased person may make any claim which he might have made under this section if he had not died.

Note.—See **Prospective Legislation Notes** (Married Couples).
Cross-references.—See FA 1988, s. 104 (3) (claim by husband under this section in respect of chargeable gains accruing to wife before 6 April 1990).

14. Foreign assets of person with foreign domicile

(1) In the case of individuals resident or ordinarily resident but not domiciled in the United Kingdom, capital gains tax shall not be charged in respect of gains accruing to them from the disposal of assets situated outside the United Kingdom (that is chargeable gains accruing in the year 1965–66 or a later year of assessment) except that the tax shall be charged on the amounts (if any) received in the United Kingdom in respect of those chargeable gains, any such amounts being treated as gains accruing when they are received in the United Kingdom.

(2) For the purposes of this section there shall be treated as received in the United Kingdom in respect of any gain all amounts paid, used or enjoyed in or in any manner or form transmitted or brought to the United Kingdom, and subsections [(6) to (9) of section 65][2] of the Taxes Act [1988][1] (under which income applied outside the United Kingdom in payment of debts is, in certain cases, treated as received in the United Kingdom) shall apply as they would apply for the purposes of subsection [(5) of the section][2] if the gain were income arising from possessions out of the United Kingdom.

Cross references.—See TA 1988, s. 761 (5) (extension of this section to offshore income gains).
Amendments.—[1] "1988" in sub-s. (2) inserted by virtue of TA 1988, Sch. 29, para. 15 (*a*).
[2] Words in sub-s. (2) substituted by TA 1988, Sch. 29, para. 32 Table.

15. Non-resident company

(1) This section applies as respects chargeable gains accruing to a company—

(*a*) which is not resident in the United Kingdom, and

(*b*) which would be a close company if it were resident in the United Kingdom.

(2) Subject to this section, every person who at the time when the chargeable gain accrues to the company is resident or ordinarily resident in the United Kingdom, who, if an individual, is domiciled in the United Kingdom, and who holds shares in the company, shall be treated for the purposes of this Act as if a part of the chargeable gain had accrued to him.

(3) That part shall be equal to the proportion of the assets of the company to which that person would be entitled on a liquidation of the company at the time when the chargeable gain accrues to the company

(4) If the part of a chargeable gain attributable to a person under subsection (2) above is less than one-twentieth, the said subsection (2) shall not apply to that person.

(5) This section shall not apply in relation to—

(*a*) any amount in respect of the chargeable gain which is distributed, whether by way of dividend or distribution of capital or on the dissolution of the company, to persons holding shares in the company, or creditors of the company, within two years from the time when the chargeable gain accrued to the company, or

(*b*) a chargeable gain accruing on the disposal of assets, being tangible property, whether movable or immovable, or a lease of such property, where the property was used, and used only, for the purposes of a trade carried on by the company wholly outside the United Kingdom, or

(c) a chargeable gain accruing on the disposal of currency or of a debt within section 135 (1) below (foreign currency bank accounts), where the currency or debt is or represents money in use for the purposes of a trade carried on by the company wholly outside the United Kingdom, or

(d) to a chargeable gain in respect of which the company is chargeable to tax by virtue of section [11 (2) (b)][2] of the Taxes Act [1988][1] (gains corresponding to those charged under section 12 above).

(6) Subsection (5) (a) above shall not prevent the making of an assessment in pursuance of this section but if, by virtue of that paragraph, this section is excluded all such adjustments, whether by way of repayment or discharge of tax or otherwise, shall be made as will give effect to the provisions of that paragraph.

(7) The amount of capital gains tax paid by a person in pursuance of subsection (2) above (so far as not reimbursed by the company) shall be allowable as a deduction in the computation under this Act of a gain accruing on the disposal by him of the shares by reference to which the tax was paid.

(8) So far as it would go to reduce or extinguish chargeable gains accruing by virtue of this section to a person in a year of assessment this section shall apply in relation to a loss accruing to the company on the disposal of an asset in that year of assessment as it would apply if a gain instead of a loss had accrued to the company on the disposal, but shall only so apply in relation to that person; and subject to the preceding provisions of this subsection this section shall not apply in relation to a loss accruing to the company.

(9) If the person owning any of the shares in the company at the time when the chargeable gain accrues to the company is itself a company which is not resident in the United Kingdom but which would be a close company if it were resident in the United Kingdom, an amount equal to the amount apportioned under subsection (3) above out of the chargeable gain to the shares so owned shall be apportioned among the issued shares of the second-mentioned company, and the holders of those shares shall be treated in accordance with subsection (2) above, and so on through any number of companies.

(10) If any tax payable by any person by virtue of subsection (2) above is paid by the company to which the chargeable gain accrues, or in a case under subsection (9) above is paid by any such other company, the amount so paid shall not for the purposes of income tax, capital gains tax or corporation tax be regarded as a payment to the person by whom the tax was originally payable.

Cross references.—See TMA 1970, s. 28 (1) (non-resident companies and trusts);
FA 1981, s. 85 (sub-s. (2) above to apply to shareholders who are non-resident trustees as regards gains accruing after 9 March 1981);
TA 1988, s. 762 (1) (extension with modification of this section to offshore income gains).
Amendments.—[1] "1988" in sub-s. (5) (d) inserted by virtue of TA 1988, Sch. 29, para. 15 (a).
[2] Number in sub-s. (5) substituted by TA 1988, Sch. 29, para. 32 Table.

16. Non-resident group of companies

(1) This section has effect for the purposes of section 15 above.

(2) Sections 273 to 275 and 276 (1) of the Taxes Act [1970][1] shall apply in relation to non-resident companies which are members of a non-resident group of companies, as they apply in relation to companies resident in the United Kingdom which are members of a group of companies.

(3) Sections 278 and 279 of the Taxes Act [1970][1] shall apply for the said purposes as if for any reference therein to a group of companies there were substituted a reference to a non-resident group of companies, and as if references to companies were references to companies not resident in the United Kingdom.

(4) For the purposes of this section—

(a) a "non-resident group" of companies—

(i) in the case of a group, none of the members of which are resident in the United Kingdom, means that group, and
(ii) in the case of a group, two or more members of which are not resident in the United Kingdom means the members which are not resident in the United Kingdom;

(*b*) "group" shall be construed in accordance with subsections (1) (without paragraph (*a*)), (3) and (4) of section 272 of the Taxes Act [1970][1].

Amendments.—[1] "1970" in sub-ss. (2), (3), (4) (*b*) inserted by virtue of TA 1988, Sch. 29, para. 15 (*b*).

17. Non-resident trust

(1) This section applies as respects chargeable gains accruing to the trustees of a settlement if the trustees are not resident and not ordinarily resident in the United Kingdom, and if the settlor, or one of the settlors, is domiciled and either resident or ordinarily resident in the United Kingdom, or was domiciled and either resident or ordinarily resident in the United Kingdom when he made his settlement.

(2) Any beneficiary under the settlement who is domiciled and either resident or ordinarily resident in the United Kingdom during any year of assessment shall be treated for the purposes of this Act as if an apportioned part of the amount, if any, on which the trustees would have been chargeable to capital gains tax under section 4 (1) above, if domiciled and either resident or ordinarily resident in the United Kingdom in that year of assessment, had been chargeable gains accruing to the beneficiary in that year of assessment; and for the purposes of this section any such amount shall be apportioned in such manner as is just and reasonable between persons having interests in the settled property, whether the interest be a life interest or an interest in reversion, and so that the chargeable gain is apportioned, as near as may be, according to the respective values of those interests, disregarding in the case of a defeasible interest the possibility of defeasance.

(3) For the purposes of this section—

(a) if in any of the three years ending with that in which the chargeable gain accrues a person has received a payment or payments out of the income of the settled property made in exercise of a discretion he shall be regarded, in relation to that chargeable gain, as having an interest in the settled property of a value equal to that of an annuity of a yearly amount equal to one-third of the total of the payments so received by him in the said three years, and

(b) if a person receives at any time after the chargeable gain accrues [but before 6th April 1984][1] a capital payment made out of the settled property in exercise of a discretion, being a payment which represents the chargeable gain in whole or part then, except so far as any part of the gain has been attributed under this section to some other person who is domiciled and resident or ordinarily resident in the United Kingdom, that person shall, if domiciled and resident or ordinarily resident in the United Kingdom, be treated as if the chargeable gain, or as the case may be the part of the chargeable gain represented by the capital payment, had accrued to him at the time when he received the capital payment.

(4) In the case of a settlement made before 6th April 1965—

(a) subsection (2) above shall not apply to a beneficiary whose interest is solely in the income of the settled property, and who cannot, by means of the exercise of any power of appointment or power of revocation or otherwise, obtain for himself, whether with or without the consent of any other person, any part of the capital represented by the settled property, and

(b) payment of capital gains tax chargeable on a gain apportioned to a beneficiary in respect of an interest in reversion in any part of the capital represented by the settled property may be postponed until that person becomes absolutely entitled to that part of the settled property, or disposes of the whole or any part of his interest, unless he can, by any means described in paragraph (a) above, obtain for himself any of it at any earlier time,

and for the purposes of this subsection, property added to a settlement after the settlement is made shall be regarded as property under a separate settlement made at the time when the property is so added.

(5) In any case in which the amount of any capital gains tax payable by a beneficiary under a settlement in accordance with the provisions of this section is paid by the trustees of the settlement that amount shall not for the purposes of taxation be regarded as a payment to the beneficiary.

(6) This section shall not apply in relation to a loss accruing to the trustees of the settlement.

(7) In this section "settlement" and "settlor" have the meanings given by section 454 (3) of the Taxes Act and "settled property" shall be construed accordingly.

Cross references.—See FA 1981, s. 80 (8) (this section not to apply as respects chargeable gains accruing to the trustees of a settlement after 5 April 1981);
FA 1984, s. 70 (1) and Sch. 14, para. 2 (3) (*a*) (postponement of tax due at 29 March 1983 from beneficiaries on gains of non-resident trustees provided no postponement has been made under sub-s. (4) (*b*) above).

Amendments.—This section repealed by FA 1981, Sch. 19, Pt. VIII. It is reproduced here because it may be relevant for the purposes of e.g. FA 1984, s. 70 and Sch. 14.
[1] Words in sub-s. (3) (*b*) inserted by FA 1984, s. 70 (2).

18. Residence etc. and location of assets

(1) In this Act "resident" and "ordinarily resident" have the same meanings as in the Income Tax Acts.

(2) Section 207 of the Taxes Act [1988][2] (disputes as to domicile or ordinary residence) shall apply in relation to capital gains tax as it applies for the purposes mentioned in that section.

(3) Subject to section 12 (1) above, an individual who is in the United Kingdom for some temporary purpose only and not with any view or intent to establish his residence in the United Kingdom shall be charged to capital gains tax on chargeable gains accruing in any year of assessment if and only if the period (or the sum of the periods) for which he is resident in the United Kingdom in that year of assessment exceeds six months.

(4) For the purposes of this Act—

(*a*) the situation of rights or interests (otherwise than by way of security) in or over immovable property is that of the immovable property,
(*b*) subject to the following provisions of this subsection, the situation of rights or interests (otherwise than by way of security) in or over tangible movable property is that of the tangible movable property,
(*c*) subject to the following provisions of this subsection, a debt, secured or unsecured, is situated in the United Kingdom if and only if the creditor is resident in the United Kingdom,
(*d*) shares or securities issued by any municipal or governmental authority, or by any body created by such an authority, are situated in the country of that authority,
(*e*) subject to paragraph (*d*) above, registered shares or securities are situated where they are registered and, if registered in more than one register, where the principal register is situated,
(*f*) a ship or aircraft is situated in the United Kingdom if and only if the owner is then resident in the United Kingdom, and an interest or right in or over a ship or aircraft is situated in the United Kingdom if and only if the person entitled to the interest or right is resident in the United Kingdom,
(*g*) the situation of good-will as a trade, business or professional asset is at the place where the trade, business or profession is carried on,
[(*ha*) patents, trade-marks, service marks and registered designs are situated where they are registered, and if registered in more than one register, where each register is situated, and rights or licences to use a patent, trade-mark, service mark or registered design are situated in the United Kingdom if they or any right derived from them are exercisable in the United Kingdom,][4]
[(*hb*) copyright, design right and franchises, and rights or licences to use any copyright work or design in which design rights subsists, are situated in the United Kingdom if they or any right derived from them are exercisable in the United Kingdom,][4]
(*i*) a judgment debt is situated where the judgment is recorded.
[(*j*) a debt which—

(i) is owed by a bank, and
(ii) is not in sterling, and
(iii) is represented by a sum standing to the credit of an account in the bank of an individual who is not domiciled in the United Kingdom,

is situated in the United Kingdom if and only if that individual is resident in the United Kingdom and the branch or other place of business of the bank at which the account is maintained is itself situated in the United Kingdom.][1]

[(5) A period during which a member of a visiting force to whom section 323 (1) of the Taxes Act 1988 applies is in the United Kingdom by reason solely of his being a member of that force shall not be treated for the purposes of capital gains tax either as a period of residence in the United Kingdom or as creating a change in his residence or domicile.][3]

This subsection shall be construed as one with subsection (2) of section 323 and subsections (4) to (8) of that section shall apply accordingly.

[(6) An Agent-General who is resident in the United Kingdom shall be entitled to the same immunity from capital gains tax as that to which the head of a mission so resident is entitled under the Diplomatic Privileges Act 1964.][3]

[(7) Any person having or exercising any employment to which section 320 (2) of the Taxes Act 1988 applies (not being a person employed in any trade, business or other undertaking carried on for the purposes of profit) shall be entitled to the same immunity from capital gains tax as that to which a member of the staff of a mission is entitled under the Diplomatic Privileges Act 1964.][3]

[(8) Subsections (6) and (7) above shall be construed as one with section 320 of the Taxes Act 1988].[3]

Amendments.—[1] Sub-s. (4) (*j*) added by FA 1984, s. 69 with effect from 6 April 1983.
[2] "1988" in sub-s. (2) inserted by virtue of TA 1988, Sch. 29, para. 15 (*a*).
[3] Sub-ss. (5)–(8) inserted by TA 1988, Sch. 29, para. 16.
[4] Sub-s. (4) (*ha*), (*hb*) substituted for sub-s. (4) (*h*) by the Copyright, Designs and Patents Act 1988, Sch. 7, para. 26 with effect from 1 August 1989 by virtue of the Copyright, Designs and Patents Act 1988 (Commencement No. 1) Order 1989, S.I. 1989 No. 816. The original para. (*h*) read—

"(*h*) patents, trade-marks and designs are situated where they are registered, and if registered in more than one register, where each register is situated, and copyright, franchises, rights and licences to use any copyright material, patent, trade-mark or design are situated in the United Kingdom if they, or any rights derived from them, are exercisable in the United Kingdom,"

PART II
GAINS AND LOSSES

CHAPTER I
DISPOSALS

19. Disposal of assets

(1) All forms of property shall be assets for the purposes of this Act, whether situated in the United Kingdom or not, including—

(a) options, debts and incorporeal property generally, and
(b) any currency other than sterling, and
(c) any form of property created by the person disposing of it, or otherwise coming to be owned without being acquired.

(2) For the purposes of this Act—

(a) references to a disposal of an asset include, except where the context otherwise requires, references to a part disposal of an asset, and
(b) there is a part disposal of an asset where an interest or right in or over the asset is created by the disposal, as well as where it subsists before the disposal, and generally, there is a part disposal of an asset where, on a person making a disposal, any description of property derived from the asset remains undisposed of.

(3) Subject to the provisions of this Act, a person's acquisition of an asset and the disposal of it to him shall for the purposes of this Act be deemed to be for a consideration equal to the market value of the asset—

(a) where he acquires the asset otherwise than by way of a bargain made at arm's length and in particular where he acquires it by way of gift or by way of distribution from a company in respect of shares in the company, or
(b) where he acquires the asset wholly or partly for a consideration that cannot be valued, or in connection with his own or another's loss of office or employment or diminution of emoluments, or otherwise in consideration for or recognition of his or another's services or past services in any office or employment or of any other service rendered or to be rendered by him or another.[1]

(4) It is hereby declared that winnings from betting, including pool betting, or lotteries or games with prizes are not chargeable gains, and no chargeable gain or allowable loss shall accrue on the disposal of rights to winnings obtained by participating in any pool betting or lottery or game with prizes.

(5) It is hereby declared that sums obtained by way of compensation or damages for any wrong or injury suffered by an individual in his person or in his profession or vocation are not chargeable gains.

Cross references.—See TMA 1970, s. 12 (2) (information about chargeable gains).
Amendments.—[1] Sub-s. (3) repealed by FA 1981, s. 90 (3), (4) and Sch. 19, Pt. VIII in relation to acquisitions and disposals after 9 March 1981. It may, however, apply in the current year for the purposes of the acquisition value of a property acquired on or before 9 March 1981 and disposed of after that date.

20. Capital sums derived from assets

(1) Subject to sections 21 and 23 (1) below, and to any other exceptions in this Act, there is for the purposes of this Act a disposal of assets by their owner where any capital sum is derived from assets notwithstanding that no asset is acquired by the person paying the capital sum, and this subsection applies in particular to—

(a) capital sums received by way of compensation for any kind of damage or injury to assets or for the loss, destruction or dissipation of assets or for any depreciation or risk of depreciation of an asset,
(b) capital sums received under a policy of insurance of the risk of any kind of damage or injury to, or the loss or depreciation of, assets,
(c) capital sums received in return for forfeiture or surrender of rights, or for refraining from exercising rights, and
(d) capital sums received as consideration for use or exploitation of assets.

(2) In the case of a disposal within paragraph (*a*), (*b*), (*c*) or (*d*) of subsection (1) above the time of the disposal shall be the time when the capital sum is received as described in that subsection.

(3) In this section "capital sum" means any money or money's worth which is not excluded from the consideration taken into account in the computation under Chapter II below.

21. Capital sums: compensation and insurance money

(1) If the recipient so claims, receipt of a capital sum within paragraph (*a*), (*b*), (*c*) or (*d*) of section 20 (1) above derived from an asset which is not lost or destroyed shall not be treated for the purposes of this Act as a disposal of the asset if—

(*a*) the capital sum is wholly applied in restoring the asset, or
(*b*) (subject to subsection (2) below), the capital sum is applied in restoring the asset except for a part of the capital sum which is not reasonably required for the purpose and which is small as compared with the whole capital sum, or
(*c*) (subject to subsection (2) below), the amount of the capital sum is small, as compared with the value of the asset,

but, if the receipt is not treated as a disposal, all sums which would, if the receipt had been so treated, have been brought into account as consideration for that disposal in the computation under Chapter II below of a gain accruing on the disposal shall be deducted from any expenditure allowable under Chapter II below as a deduction in computing a gain on the subsequent disposal of the asset.

(2) If the allowable expenditure is less than the consideration for the disposal constituted by the receipt of the capital sum (or is nil)—

(*a*) paragraphs (*b*) and (*c*) of subsection (1) above shall not apply, and
(*b*) if the recipient so elects (and there is any allowable expenditure)—

(i) the amount of the consideration for the disposal shall be reduced by the amount of the allowable expenditure, and
(ii) none of that expenditure shall be allowable as a deduction in computing a gain accruing on the occasion of the disposal or any subsequent occasion.

In this subsection "allowable expenditure" means expenditure which, immediately before the disposal, was attributable to the asset under paragraphs (*a*) and (*b*) of section 32 (1) below.

(3) If, in a case not falling within subsection (1) (*b*) above, a part of a capital sum within paragraph (*a*) or paragraph (*b*) of section 20 (1) above derived from an asset which is not lost or destroyed is applied in restoring the asset, then if the recipient so claims, that part of the capital sum shall not be treated as consideration for the disposal deemed to be effected on receipt of the capital sum but shall be deducted from any expenditure allowable under Chapter II below as a deduction in computing a gain on the subsequent disposal of the asset.

(4) If an asset is lost or destroyed and a capital sum received by way of compensation for the loss or destruction, or under a policy of insurance of the risk of the loss or destruction, is within one year of receipt, or such longer period as the inspector may allow, applied in acquiring an asset in replacement of the asset lost or destroyed the owner shall if he so claims be treated for the purposes of this Act—

(*a*) as if the consideration for the disposal of the old asset were (if otherwise of a greater amount) of such amount as would secure that on the disposal neither a gain nor a loss accrues to him, and
(*b*) as if the amount of the consideration for the acquisition of the new asset were reduced by the excess of the amount of the capital sum received by way of compensation or under the policy of insurance, together with any residual or scrap value, over the amount of the consideration which he is treated as receiving under paragraph (*a*) above.

(5) A claim shall not be made under subsection (4) above if part only of the capital sum is applied in acquiring the new asset but if all of that capital sum except for a part which is less than the amount of the gain (whether all chargeable gain or not) accruing on the disposal of the old asset is so applied, then the owner shall if he so claims be treated for the purposes of this Act—

(*a*) as if the amount of the gain so accruing were reduced to the amount of the said part (and, if not all chargeable gain, with a proportionate reduction in the amount of the chargeable gain), and

(b) as if the amount of the consideration for the acquisition of the new asset were reduced by the amount by which the gain is reduced under paragraph (a) of this subsection.

(6) Subsections (4) and (5) above have effect subject to paragraph 18 of Schedule 5 to this Act (application to gain which in consequence of that Schedule is not all chargeable gain).

(7) This section shall not apply in relation to a wasting asset.

Cross references.—See FA 1988, Sch. 9, paras. 1, 2 (reduction of a deferred charge to tax where the charge is wholly or partly attributable to an increase in the value of an asset before 31 March 1982);
FA 1989, Sch. 15, para. 3 (expenditure disallowed under sub-s. (2) of this section to be deducted from the new 1982 base cost where the disallowance relates to past disposals made after 31 March 1982 but before 6 April 1988).

22. Assets lost or destroyed, or whose value becomes negligible

(1) Subject to the provisions of this Act and, in particular to section 137 below (options), the occasion of the entire loss, destruction, dissipation or extinction of an asset shall, for the purposes of this Act, constitute a disposal of the asset whether or not any capital sum by way of compensation or otherwise is received in respect of the destruction, dissipation or extinction of the asset.

(2) If, on a claim by the owner of an asset, the inspector is satisfied that the value of an asset has become negligible, he may allow the claim and thereupon this Act shall have effect as if the claimant had sold, and immediately re-acquired, the asset for a consideration of an amount equal to the value specified in the claim.

(3) For the purposes of subsections (1) and (2) above, a building and any permanent or semi-permanent structure in the nature of a building, may be regarded as an asset separate from the land on which it is situated, but where either of those subsections applies in accordance with this subsection, the person deemed to make the disposal of the building or structure shall be treated as if he had also sold, and immediately re-acquired, the site of the building or structure (including in the site any land occupied for purposes ancillary to the use of the building or structure) for a consideration equal to its market value at that time.

Cross references.—See TA 1970, s. 280 (1), (8) (a claim under sub-s. (2) above is a disposal for purposes of TA 1970, s. 280, i.e. losses attributable to depreciatory transactions);
TA 1988, s. 575 (1) (c) (tax relief for losses on certain shares of an unquoted trading company).

23. Mortgages and charges

(1) The conveyance or transfer by way of security of an asset or of an interest or right in or over it, or transfer of a subsisting interest or right by way of security in or over an asset (including a retransfer on redemption of the security), shall not be treated for the purposes of this Act as involving any acquisition or disposal of the asset.

(2) Where a person entitled to an asset by way of security or to the benefit of a charge or incumbrance on an asset deals with the asset for the purpose of enforcing or giving effect to the security, charge or incumbrance his dealings with it shall be treated for the purposes of this Act as if they were done through him as a nominee by the person entitled to it subject to the security, charge or incumbrance; and this subsection shall apply to the dealings of any person appointed to enforce or give effect to the security, charge or incumbrance as receiver and manager or judicial factor as it applies to the dealings of the person entitled as aforesaid.

(3) An asset shall be treated as having been acquired free of any interest or right by way of security subsisting at the time of any acquisition of it, and as being disposed of free of any such interest or right subsisting at the time of the disposal; and where an asset is acquired subject to any such interest or right the full amount of the liability thereby assumed by the person acquiring the asset shall form part of the consideration for the acquisition and disposal in addition to any other consideration.

24. Hire-purchase

A hire-purchase or other transaction under which the use and enjoyment of an asset is obtained by a person for a period at the end of which the property in the asset will or may pass to that person shall be treated for the purposes of this Act, both in relation to that person and in relation to the person from whom he obtains the use and enjoyment of the asset, as if it amounted to an entire disposal of the asset to that person at the beginning of the period for which he obtains the use and enjoyment of the asset, but subject to such adjustments of tax, whether by way of repayment or discharge of tax or otherwise, as may be required where the period for which that person has the use and enjoyment of the asset terminates without the property in the asset passing to him.

25. Value shifting

(1) Without prejudice to the generality of the provisions of this Act as to the transactions which are disposals of assets, any transaction which under the following subsections is to be treated as a disposal of an asset shall be so treated (with a corresponding acquisition of an interest in the asset) notwithstanding that there is no consideration and so far as, on the assumption that the parties to the transaction were at arm's length, the party making the disposal could have obtained consideration, or additional consideration, for the disposal the transaction shall be treated as not being at arm's length and the consideration so obtainable, or the additional consideration so obtainable added to the consideration actually passing, shall be treated as the market value of what is acquired.

(2) If a person having control of a company exercises his control so that value passes out of shares in the company owned by him or a person with whom he is connected, or out of rights over the company exercisable by him or by a person with whom he is connected, and passes into other shares in or rights over the company, that shall be a disposal of the shares or rights out of which the value passes by the person by whom they were owned or exercisable.

(3) A loss on the disposal of an asset shall not be an allowable loss to the extent to which it is attributable to value having passed out of other assets, being shares in or rights over a company which by virtue of the passing of value are treated as disposed of under subsection (2) above.

(4) If, after a transaction which results in the owner of land or of any other description of property becoming the lessee of the property there is any adjustment of the rights and liabilities under the lease, whether or not involving the grant of a new lease, which is as a whole favourable to the lessor, that shall be a disposal by the lessee of an interest in the property.

(5) If an asset is subject to any description of right or restriction the extinction or abrogation, in whole or in part, of the right or restriction by the person entitled to enforce it shall be a disposal by him of the right or restriction.

26. Value shifting: further provisions

(1) This section has effect as respects the disposal of an asset if a scheme has been effected or arrangements have been made (whether before or after the disposal) whereby—

    (*a*) the value of the asset [or a relevant asset][2] has been materially reduced, and
    (*b*) a tax-free benefit has been or will be conferred—

        (i) on the person making the disposal or a person with whom he is connected, or
        (ii) subject to subsection (3) below, on any other person.

[(1A) For the purposes of this section, where the asset disposed of by a company ("the disposing company") consists of shares in, or securities of, another company, another asset is a relevant asset if, at the time of the disposal, it is owned by a company associated with the disposing company; but no account shall be taken of any reduction in the value of a relevant asset except in a case where—

    (*a*) during the period beginning with the reduction in value and ending immediately before the disposal by the disposing company, there is no disposal of the asset to any person, other than a disposal falling within section 273 (1) of the Taxes Act 1970 (transfers within a group: no gain/no loss),
    (*b*) no disposal of the asset is treated as having occurred during that period by virtue of section 278 of the Taxes Act 1970 (company ceasing to be member of group), and
    (*c*) if the reduction had not taken place but any consideration given for the relevant asset and any other material circumstances (including any consideration given before the disposal for the asset disposed of) were unchanged, the value of the asset disposed of would, at the time of the disposal, have been materially greater;

and in this subsection "securities" has the same meaning as in section 82 below.][3]

(2) For the purposes of subsection (1) (*b*) above a benefit is conferred on a person if he becomes entitled to any money or money's worth or the value of any asset in which he has an interest is increased or he is wholly or partly relieved from any liability to which he is subject; and a benefit is tax-free unless it is required, on the occasion on which it is conferred on the person in question, to be brought into account in computing his income, profits or gains for the purposes of income tax, capital gains tax or corporation tax.

(3) This section shall not apply by virtue of subsection (1) (*b*) (ii) above if it is shown that avoidance of tax was not the main purpose or one of the main purposes of the scheme or arrangements in question.

(4) Where this section has effect in relation to any disposal, any allowable loss or chargeable gain accruing on the disposal shall be calculated as if the consideration for the disposal were increased by such amount as appears to the inspector, or on appeal the Commissioners concerned, to be just and reasonable having regard to the scheme or arrangements and the tax-free benefit in question.

(5) Where—
   (*a*) by virtue of subsection (4) above the consideration for the disposal of an asset has been treated as increased, and
   (*b*) the benefit taken into account under subsection (1) (*b*) above was an increase in the value of another asset,

any allowable loss or chargeable gain accruing on the first disposal of the other asset after the increase in its value shall be calculated as if the consideration for that disposal were reduced by such amount as appears to the inspector, or on appeal the Commissioners concerned, to be just and reasonable having regard to the scheme or arrangements in question and the increase made in relation to the disposal mentioned in paragraph (*a*) above.

(6) References in this section to a disposal do not include references to any disposal falling within—
   (*a*) section 44 (1) below (disposals between husband and wife), or
   (*b*) section 49 (4) below (disposals by personal representatives to legatees), or
   (*c*) section 273 (1) of the Taxes Act [1970][1] (disposals within a group of companies).

[(7) References in this section, in relation to any disposal, to a reduction in the value of an asset, where the asset consists of shares owned by a company in another company, shall be interpreted in accordance with sections 26A to 26C below and, in those sections, the disposal, the asset and those companies are referred to respectively as "the section 26 disposal", "the principal asset", "the first company" and "the second company".][4]

(8) In relation to a case in which the disposal of an asset precedes its acquisition the [references in subsections (1) (*a*) and (1A)][4] above to a reduction shall be read as including a reference to an increase.

Cross references.—See TA 1970, s. 278 (3F) (*b*) (deemed disposal of certain assets held by company leaving group); Trustee Savings Banks Act 1985, Sch. 2, para. 4 (3) (no provision made by that Act to be treated for the purposes of this section as a scheme or arrangement); TA 1988, s. 576 (2) (modification of sub-ss. (1) (*b*), (4) of this section where tax relief is claimed for losses on unquoted shares in trading companies).
Amendments.—[1] "1970" in sub-ss. (6) (*c*), (7) (*a*) inserted by virtue of TA 1988, Sch. 29, para 15 (*b*).
[2] Words in sub-s. (1) (*a*) inserted by FA 1989, s. 135 (1), (4) in respect of disposals after 13 March 1989.
[3] Sub-s. (1A) inserted by *ibid*.
[4] Sub-s. (7) and words in sub-s. (8) substituted by FA 1989, s. 135 (2)–(4) in respect of disposals after 13 March 1989.

[26A. Value shifting: distributions within a group followed by a disposal of shares

(1) The references in section 26 above to a reduction in the value of an asset, in the case mentioned in subsection (7) of that section, do not include a reduction attributable to the payment of a dividend by the second company at a time when it and the first company are associated, except to the extent (if any) that the dividend is attributable to chargeable profits of the second company and, in such a case, the tax-free benefit shall be ascertained without regard to any part of the dividend that is not attributable to such profits.

(2) Subsections (3) to (11) below apply for the interpretation of subsection (1) above.

(3) Chargeable profits shall be ascertained as follows—
   (*a*) the distributable profits of any company are chargeable profits of that company to the extent that they are profits arising on a transaction caught by this section, and
   (*b*) where any company makes a distribution attributable wholly or partly to chargeable profits (including any profits that are chargeable profits by virtue of this paragraph) to another company, the distributable profits of the other company, so far as they represent that distribution or so much of it as was attributable to chargeable profits, are chargeable profits of the other company,

and for this purpose any loss or other amount to be set against the profits of a company in determining the distributable profits shall be set first against profits other than the profits so arising or, as the case may be, representing so much of the distribution as was attributable to chargeable profits.

(4) The distributable profits of a company are such profits computed on a commercial basis as, after allowing for any provision properly made for tax, the company is empowered, assuming sufficient funds, to distribute to persons entitled to participate in the profits of the company.

(5) Profits of a company ("company A") are profits arising on a transaction caught by this section where each of the following three conditions is satisfied.

(6) The first condition is that the transaction is—

(*a*) a disposal of an asset by company A to another company in circumstances such that company A and the other company are treated as mentioned in section 273 (1) of the Taxes Act 1970 (transfers within a group: no gain/no loss), or

(*b*) an exchange, or a transaction treated for the purposes of section 85 (2) and (3) below as an exchange, of shares in or debentures of a company held by company A for shares in or debentures of another company, being a company associated with company A immediately after the transaction, and is treated by virtue of section 85 (3) below as a reorganisation of share capital, or

(*c*) a revaluation of an asset in the accounting records of company A.

In the following conditions the "asset with enhanced value" means (subject to section 26C below), in the paragraph (*a*) case, the asset acquired by the person to whom the disposal is made, in the paragraph (*b*) case, the shares in or debentures of the other company and, in the paragraph (*c*) case, the revalued asset.

(7) The second condition is that—

(*a*) during the period beginning with the transaction referred to in subsection (6) above and ending immediately before the section 26 disposal, there is no disposal of the asset with enhanced value to any person, other than a disposal falling within section 273 (1) of the Taxes Act 1970, and

(*b*) no disposal of the asset with enhanced value is treated as having occurred during that period by virtue of section 278 of the Taxes Act 1970 (company ceasing to be member of group).

(8) The third condition is that, immediately after the section 26 disposal, the asset with enhanced value is owned by a person other than the company making that disposal or a company associated with it.

(9) The conditions in subsections (6) to (8) above are not satisfied if—

(*a*) at the time of the transaction referred to in subsection (6) above, company A carries on a trade and a profit on a disposal of the asset with enhanced value would form part of the trading profits, or

(*b*) by reason of the nature of the asset with enhanced value, a disposal of it could give rise neither to a chargeable gain nor to an allowable loss, or

(*c*) immediately before the section 26 disposal, the company owning the asset with enhanced value carries on a trade and a profit on a disposal of the asset would form part of the trading profits.

(10) The amount of chargeable profits of a company to be attributed to any distribution made by the company at any time in respect of any class of shares, securities or rights shall be ascertained by—

(*a*) determining the total of distributable profits, and the total of chargeable profits, that remains after allowing for earlier distributions made in respect of that or any other class of shares, securities or rights, and for distributions made at or to be made after that time in respect of other classes of shares, securities or rights, and

(*b*) attributing first to that distribution distributable profits other than chargeable profits.

(11) The amount of chargeable profits of a company to be attributed to any part of a distribution made at any time to which a person is entitled by virtue of any part of his holding of any class of shares, securities or rights, shall be such proportion of the chargeable profits as are attributable under subsection (10) above to the distributions made at that time in respect of that class as corresponds to that part of his holding.][1]

Amendments.—[1] This section inserted by FA 1989, s. 136 in respect of disposals after 13 March 1989, but subject to the provisions in FA 1989, s. 136(2).

[26B. Value shifting: disposals within a group followed by a disposal of shares

(1) The references in section 26 above to a reduction in the value of an asset, in the case mentioned in subsection (7) of that section, do not include a reduction attributable to the

disposal of any asset ("the underlying asset") by the second company at a time when it and the first company are associated, being a disposal falling within section 273 (1) of the Taxes Act 1970 (transfers within group: no gain/no loss), except in a case within subsection (2) below.

(2) A case is within this subsection if the amount or value of the actual consideration for the disposal of the underlying asset—

(*a*) is less than the market value of the underlying asset, and
(*b*) is less than the cost of the underlying asset,

unless the disposal is effected for bona fide commercial reasons and does not form part of a scheme or arrangements of which the main purpose, or one of the main purposes, is avoidance of liability to corporation tax.

(3) For the purposes of subsection (2) above, the cost of an asset owned by a company is the aggregate of—

(*a*) any capital expenditure incurred by the company in acquiring or providing the asset, and
(*b*) any other capital expenditure incurred by the company in respect of the asset while owned by that company.

(4) For the purposes of this section, where the disposal of the underlying asset is a part disposal, the reference in subsection (2)(*a*) above to the market value of the underlying asset is to the market value of the asset acquired by the person to whom the disposal is made and the amounts to be attributed to the underlying asset under paragraphs (*a*) and (*b*) of subsection (3) above shall be reduced to the appropriate proportion of those amounts, that is—

(*a*) the proportion of capital expenditure in respect of the underlying asset properly attributed in the accounting records of the company to the asset acquired by the person to whom the disposal is made, or
(*b*) where paragraph (*a*) above does not apply, such proportion as appears to the inspector, or on appeal the Commissioners concerned, to be just and reasonable.

(5) Where by virtue of a distribution in the course of dissolving or winding up the second company the first company is treated as disposing of an interest in the principal asset, the exception mentioned in subsection (1) above does not apply.][1]

Amendments.—[1] This section inserted by FA 1989, s. 136 in respect of disposals after 13 March 1989, but subject to the provisions in FA 1989, s. 136 (2).

[26C. Value shifting: supplementary

(1) For the purposes of sections 26 (1A) and 26A (7) to (9) above, subsections (2) to (6) below apply for the purpose of determining in the case of any asset ("the original asset") whether it is subsequently disposed of or treated as disposed of or owned or any other condition is satisfied in respect of it.

(2) References in sections 26 (1A) (*a*) and (*b*) and 26A (7) to a disposal are to a disposal other than a part disposal.

(3) References to an asset are to the original asset or, where at a later time one or more assets are treated by virtue of subsections (5) or (6) below as the same as the original asset—

(*a*) if no disposal falling within paragraph (*a*) or (*b*) of section 26 (1A) or, as the case may be, of 26A (7) has occurred, those references are to the asset so treated or, as the case may be, all the assets so treated, and
(*b*) in any other case, those references are to an asset or, as the case may be, all the assets representing that part of the value of the original asset that remains after allowing for earlier disposals falling within the paragraphs concerned,

references in this subsection to a disposal including a disposal which would fall within the paragraphs concerned but for subsection (2) above.

(4) Where by virtue of subsection (3) above those references are to two or more assets—

(*a*) those assets shall be treated as if they were a single asset,
(*b*) any disposal of any one of them is to be treated as a part disposal, and
(*c*) the reference in section 26 (1A) to the asset owned at the time of the disposal by a company associated with the disposing company and the reference in section 26A (8) to the asset with enhanced value is to all or any of those assets.

(5) Where there is a part disposal of an asset, that asset and the asset acquired by the person to whom the disposal is made are to be treated as the same.

(6) Where the value of an asset is derived from any other asset in the ownership of the same or an associated company, in a case where assets have been merged or divided or have changed their nature or rights or interests in or over assets have been created or extinguished, the first asset is to be treated as the same as the second.

(7) For the purposes of section 26 (1A) above, where account is to be taken under that subsection of a reduction in the value of a relevant asset and at the time of the disposal by the disposing company referred to in that subsection—

(a) references to the relevant assets are by virtue of this section references to two or more assets treated as a single asset, and
(b) one or more but not all of those assets are owned by a company associated with the disposing company,

the amount of the reduction in the value of the relevant asset to be taken into account by virtue of that subsection shall be reduced to such amount as appears to the inspector, or on appeal to the Commissioners concerned, to be just and reasonable.

(8) For the purposes of section 26A above, where—

(a) a dividend paid by the second company is attributable to chargeable profits of that company, and
(b) the condition in subsection (7), (8) or (9) (c) of that section is satisfied by reference to an asset, or assets treated as a single asset, treated by virtue of subsection (3) (b) above as the same as the asset with enhanced value,

the amount of the reduction in value of the principal asset shall be reduced to such amount as appears to the inspector, or on appeal to the Commissioners concerned, to be just and reasonable.

(9) For the purposes of sections 26 to 26B above and this section, companies are associated if they are members of the same group.

(10) Section 272 (1) to (4) of the Taxes Act 1970 (groups of companies: definitions) applies for the purposes of sections 26 to 26B above and this section as it applies for the purposes of that section.][1]

Amendments.—[1] This section inserted by FA 1989, s. 136 in respect of disposals after 13 March 1989, but subject to the provisions in FA 1989, s. 136(2).

[26D. Value shifting: transactions treated as a reorganisation of share capital

(1) Where—

(a) but for sections 78 and 85 (3) below, section 26 above would have effect as respects the disposal by a company ("the disposing company") of an asset consisting of shares in or debentures of another company ("the original holding") in exchange for shares in or debentures of a further company which, immediately after the disposal, is not a member of the same group as the disposing company, and
(b) if section 26 above had effect as respects that disposal, any allowable loss or chargeable gain accruing on the disposal would be calculated as if the consideration for the disposal were increased by an amount,

the disposing company shall be treated for the purposes of section 79 (2) below as receiving, on the reorganisation of share capital that is treated as occurring by virtue of section 85 (3) below, that amount for the disposal of the original holding.

(2) For the purposes of subsection (1) above it shall be assumed that section 86 below has effect generally for the purposes of this Act, and in that subsection "group" has the same meaning as in sections 26 to 26C above.][1]

Amendments.—[1] This section inserted by FA 1989, s. 137 where the reduction in value, by reason of which the amount referred to in sub-s. (1) (b) above falls to be calculated, occurs after 13 March 1989.

27. Time of disposal and acquisition where asset disposed of under contract

(1) Where an asset is disposed of and acquired under a contract the time at which the disposal and acquisition is made is the time the contract is made (and not, if different, the time at which the asset is conveyed or transferred).

This subsection has effect subject to section 20 (2) above, and subsection (2) below.

(2) If the contract is conditional (and in particular if it is conditional on the exercise of an option) the time at which the disposal and acquisition is made is the time when the condition is satisfied.

CHAPTER II
COMPUTATION

Cross references.—See TA 1988, s. 763 (3) (deduction of offshore income gains from the disposal value in computing the gains under this Chapter),
Sch. 26, para. 3 (2) (computation under this Chapter of gains on disposal of shares in UK controlled foreign company).

28. Chargeable gains

(1) The amount of the gains accruing on the disposal of assets shall be computed in accordance with this Chapter, and subject to the other provisions of this Act [and sections 86 and 87 of the Finance Act 1982]¹.

(2) Every gain shall, except as otherwise expressly provided, be a chargeable gain.

(3) Schedule 5 to this Act (which restricts the amount of chargeable gains accruing on the disposal of assets owned on 6th April 1965) shall have effect.

Amendments.—¹ Words in sub-s. (1) added by FA 1982, s. 86 (4).

29. Losses

(1) Except as otherwise expressly provided, the amount of a loss accruing on a disposal of an asset shall be computed in the same way as the amount of a gain accruing on a disposal is computed.

(2) Except as otherwise expressly provided, all the provisions of this Act which distinguish gains which are chargeable gains from those which are not, or which make part of a gain a chargeable gain, and part not, shall apply also to distinguish losses which are allowable losses from those which are not, and to make part of a loss an allowable loss, and part not; and references in this Act to an allowable loss shall be construed accordingly.

(3) A loss accruing to a person in a year of assessment during no part of which he is resident or ordinarily resident in the United Kingdom shall not be an allowable loss for the purposes of this Act unless, under section 12 above (non-resident with U.K. branch or agency), he would be chargeable to capital gains tax in respect of a chargeable gain if there had been a gain instead of a loss on that occasion.

(4) In accordance with section 14 (1) above (foreign assets of person with foreign domicile), losses accruing on the disposal of assets situated outside the United Kingdom to an individual resident or ordinarily resident but not domiciled in the United Kingdom shall not be allowable losses.

(5) Except as provided by section 49 below (death), an allowable loss accruing in a year of assessment shall not be allowable as a deduction from chargeable gains accruing in any earlier year of assessment, and relief shall not be given under this Act more than once in respect of any loss or part of a loss, and shall not be given under this Act if and so far as relief has been or may be given in respect of it under the Income Tax Acts.

Cross references.—See FA 1981, s. 83 (6) (capital losses of non-resident settlements to be set off against capital gains accruing after 5 April 1981, notwithstanding sub-s. (3) above);
TA 1988, Sch. 28, para. 3 (5) (computation of offshore income gains; determination of losses not to be in like manner as determination of gains).

[29A. Disposals and acquisitions treated as made at market value

(1) Subject to the provisions of this Act, a person's acquisition or disposal of an asset shall for the purposes of this Act be deemed to be for a consideration equal to the market value of the asset—

(*a*) where he acquires or, as the case may be, disposes of the asset otherwise than by way of a bargain made at arm's length, and in particular where he acquires or disposes of it by way of gift or on a transfer into settlement by a settlor or by way of distribution from a company in respect of shares in the company, or
(*b*) where he acquires or, as the case may be, disposes of the asset wholly or partly for a consideration that cannot be valued, or in connection with his own or another's loss of

office or employment or diminution of emoluments, or otherwise in consideration for or recognition of his or another's services or past services in any office or employment or of any other service rendered or to be rendered by him or another.

(2) . . .[2], subsection (1) above shall not apply to the acquisition of an asset if—

(*a*) there is no corresponding disposal of it, . . .[2], and
(*b*) there is no consideration in money or money's worth or the consideration is of an amount or value lower than the market value of the asset.

[(3) In any case where—

(*a*) apart from this subsection, subsection (1) above would apply to the acquisition of an asset, and
(*b*) the condition in subsection (2) (*b*) above is fulfilled with respect to the acquisition, and
(*c*) the corresponding disposal is made on or after 6th April 1983 and before 6th April 1985, and
(*d*) the corresponding disposal is made by an excluded person who is within the charge to capital gains tax or corporation tax in respect of any chargeable gain accruing to him on the disposal,

then, if the person acquiring the asset and the excluded person so elect by notice in writing given to the Board within the period of two years beginning at the end of the chargeable period in which the corresponding disposal is made, subsection (1) above shall not apply to the acquisition or the corresponding disposal.][3]

[(4) There shall be made all such adjustments of capital gains tax or corporation tax (in respect of chargeable gains), whether by way of assessment or by way of discharge or repayment of tax, as may be required in consequence of the making of an election under subsection (3) above.][3]

(5) In this section "excluded person" means—

(*a*) a person who is neither resident nor ordinarily resident in the United Kingdom; or
(*b*) a person who is wholly exempt from tax in respect of chargeable gains, or would be so exempt on making a claim for exemption; or
(*c*) a charity; or
(*d*) a registered friendly society; or
(*e*) a person making the disposal for the purposes of—

(i) a fund to which section 218 or 226 (6) of the Taxes Act [1970][4] or section 36 of the Finance Act 1980 applies, or
(ii) an exempt approved scheme or statutory scheme as defined in Chapter II of Part II of the Finance Act 1970.][1]

Cross references.—See TA 1988, s. 185 (3) (*b*) (capital gains tax charge on disposal of shares acquired under a share option scheme; the market value rule in sub-s. (1) above not to apply in calculating acquisition cost or disposal value);
FA 1988, s. 68 (4) (sub-s. (1) of this section not to apply to any acquisition in relation to which FA 1988, s. 68 (1) (priority share acquisition by a director or an employee) applies).
Amendments.—[1] This section inserted by FA 1981, s. 90 (1), (4) in relation to acquisitions and disposals after 9 March 1981.
[2] Words in sub-s. (2) repealed by FA 1984, s. 66 (1), (4) and Sch. 23, Pt. VIII in relation to acquisitions and disposals after 5 April 1983.
[3] Sub-ss. (3), (4) substituted by FA 1984, s. 66 (2), (4) in relation to acquisitions and disposals after 5 April 1983.
[4] "1970" in sub-s. (5) (*e*) (i) inserted by virtue of TA 1988, Sch. 29, para. 15 (*b*).

Computation of gains

30. Introductory

The following provisions of this Chapter, and Schedule 5 to this Act, shall have effect for computing for the purposes of this Act the amount of a gain accruing on the disposal of an asset.

31. Consideration chargeable to tax on income

(1) There shall be excluded from the consideration for a disposal of assets taken into account in the computation under this Chapter of the gain accruing on that disposal any money or money's worth charged to income tax as income of, or taken into account as a receipt in computing income or profits or gains or losses of, the person making the disposal for the purposes of the Income Tax Acts.

(2) Subsection (1) above shall not be taken as excluding from the consideration so taken into account any money or money's worth which is taken into account in the making of a balancing charge under the Capital Allowances Act 1968 (including the provisions of [the Taxes Act 1970 or the Taxes Act 1988 which under either of those Acts][3] are to be treated as contained in the said Act of 1968) [or which is brought into account as the disposal value of machinery or plant under section 44 of the Finance Act 1971][1].

(3) This section shall not preclude the taking into account in a computation under this Chapter, as consideration for the disposal of an asset, of the capitalised value of a rentcharge (as in a case where a rentcharge is exchanged for some other asset) or of the capitalised value of a ground annual or feu duty, or of a right of any other description to income or to payments in the nature of income over a period, or to a series of payments in the nature of income.

[(4) The reference in subsection (1) above to computing income or profits or gains or losses shall not be taken as applying to a computation of a company's income for the purposes of subsection (2) of section 76 of the Taxes Act 1988.][2]

Cross references.—See FA 1986, s. 56 (7) (*c*) (reference in sub-s. (2) above to CAA 1968 to include a reference to FA 1986, Sch. 15 (new code of allowances and charges from 1 April 1986 in respect of capital expenditure on agricultural land and buildings)),
Sch. 13, para. 2 (5) (*c*) (reference in sub-s. (2) above to CAA 1968 to include a reference to FA 1986, Sch. 13, Part III (new code of allowances and charges from 1 April 1986 in respect of capital expenditure on mineral extraction));
TA 1988, s. 450 (6) (disposal of assets in premiums trust fund of underwriters),
s. 763 (2) (modification of this section where a disposal constitutes a disposal for capital gains tax purposes and also gives rise to an offshore income gain),
s. 777 (12) (sales of income from personal activities and transactions in land),
Sch. 28, para. 3 (4) (sub-s. (1) above not to apply in the case of an insurance company's profits from general annuity business and attributable to disposals of offshore funds);
FA 1988, s. 63 (5) (application of this section on disposal of oil drilling licence).
Amendments.—[1] Words in sub-s. (2) inserted by FA 1980, s. 83, in relation to disposals after 25 March 1980.
[2] Sub-s. (4) inserted by TA 1988, Sch. 29, para. 17.
[3] Words in sub-s. (2) substituted by TA 1988, Sch. 29, para. 32 Table.

32. Expenditure: general

(1) Except as otherwise expressly provided, the sums allowable as a deduction from the consideration in the computation under this Chapter of the gain accruing to a person on the disposal of an asset shall be restricted to—

(*a*) the amount or value of the consideration, in money or money's worth, given by him or on his behalf wholly and exclusively for the acquisition of the asset, together with the incidental costs to him of the acquisition or, if the asset was not acquired by him, any expenditure wholly and exclusively incurred by him in providing the asset,
(*b*) the amount of any expenditure wholly and exclusively incurred on the asset by him or on his behalf for the purpose of enhancing the value of the asset, being expenditure reflected in the state or nature of the asset at the time of the disposal, and any expenditure wholly and exclusively incurred by him in establishing, preserving or defending his title to, or to a right over, the asset,
(*c*) the incidental costs to him of making the disposal.

(2) For the purposes of this section and for the purposes of all other provisions of this Act the incidental costs to the person making the disposal of the acquisition of the asset or of its disposal shall consist of expenditure wholly and exclusively incurred by him for the purposes of the acquisition or, as the case may be, the disposal, being fees, commission or remuneration paid for the professional services of any surveyor or valuer, or auctioneer, or accountant, or agent or legal adviser and costs of transfer or conveyance (including stamp duty) together—

(*a*) in the case of the acquisition of an asset, with costs of advertising to find a seller, and
(*b*) in the case of a disposal, with costs of advertising to find a buyer and costs reasonably incurred in making any valuation or apportionment required for the purposes of the computation under this Chapter, including in particular expenses reasonably incurred in ascertaining market value where required by this Act.

(3) Except as provided by section 269 of the Taxes Act [1970][2] (companies: interest charged to capital), no payment of interest shall be allowable under this section.

(4) Any provision in this Act introducing the assumption that assets are sold and

immediately re-acquired shall not imply that any expenditure is incurred as incidental to the sale or re-acquisition.

[(5)–(6) . . .[1]

Cross references.—See TA 1970, s. 269 (1) (*a*), (1A) (interest charged to capital by a company);
F (No. 2) A 1975, s. 58 (8) ("bed and breakfast" and "double banking" transactions by companies);
FA 1982, ss. 86, 87 and Sch. 13, para. 10 (3) (indexation allowance on certain expenditure falling under this section);
TA 1988, s. 185 (7) (computation of chargeable gains accruing on shares in a share option scheme);
FA 1988, s. 84 (application of sub-s. (1) (*a*) of this section on the first disposal of shares acquired under unapproved employee share schemes).
Amendments.—[1] Sub-ss. (5), (6) repealed by FA 1984, s. 66 (3) and Sch. 23, Pt. VIII where the disposal by the person who is neither resident nor ordinarily resident in the UK is made after 5 April 1985.
[2] "1970" in sub-s. (3) inserted by virtue of TA 1988, Sch. 29, para. 15 (*b*).

[32A. Expenditure: amounts to be included as consideration

(1) Section 32 (1) (*a*) above applies as if the relevant amount as defined in the following provisions of this section in the cases there specified had formed part of the consideration given by the person making the disposal for his acquisition of the assets in question.

(2) Where an amount is chargeable to tax by virtue of section 162 (5) of the Taxes Act 1988 in respect of shares or an interest in shares, then—

(*a*) on a disposal of the shares or interest, where that is the event giving rise to the charge; or
(*b*) in any case, on the first disposal of the shares or interest after the event,

the relevant amount is a sum equal to the amount so chargeable.
(3) If a gain chargeable to tax under section 135 (1) or (6) of the Taxes Act 1988 is realised by the exercise of a right to acquire shares, the relevant amount is a sum equal to the amount of the gain so chargeable to tax.

(4) Where an amount is chargeable to tax under section 138 of the Taxes Act 1988 on a person acquiring any shares or interest in shares, then on the first disposal (whether by him or another person) of the shares after his acquisition, the relevant amount is an amount equal to the amount so chargeable.

(5) Where an amount was chargeable to tax under secton 185 (6) of the Taxes Act 1988 in respect of shares acquired in exercise of any such right as is mentioned in section 185 (1) of that Act, the relevant sum in relation to those shares is an amount equal to the amount so chargeable.

(6) Subsections (2), (3), (4) and (5) above shall be construed as one with sections 162, 135, 138 and 185 of the Taxes Act 1988 respectively.][1]

Cross references.—See TA 1988, s. 139 (3) (application of sub-s. (4) of this section with necessary modifications where a person connected with a director or employee acquires shares in a company),
s. 139 (14) (*a*) (acquisition of units in an authorised unit trust by a director or an employee).
Amendments.—[1] This section inserted by TA 1988, Sch. 29, para. 18.

33. Exclusion of expenditure by reference to tax on income

(1) There shall be excluded from the sums allowable under section 32 above as a deduction in the computation under this Chapter any expenditure allowable as a deduction in computing the profits or gains or losses of a trade, profession or vocation for the purposes of income tax or allowable as a deduction in computing any other income or profits or gains or losses for the purposes of the Income Tax Acts and any expenditure which, although not so allowable as a deduction in computing any losses, would be so allowable but for an insufficiency of income or profits or gains; and this subsection applies irrespective of whether effect is or would be given to the deduction in computing the amount of tax chargeable or by discharge or repayment of tax or in any other way.

(2) Without prejudice to the provisions of subsection (1) above there shall be excluded from the sums allowable under section 32 above as a deduction in the computation under this Chapter any expenditure which, if the assets, or all the assets to which the computation relates, were, and had at all times been, held or used as part of the fixed capital of a trade the profits or gains of which were (irrespective of whether the person making the disposal is a company or not) chargeable to income tax would be allowable as a deduction in computing the profits or gains or losses of the trade for the purposes of income tax.

[(3) No account shall be taken of any relief under Chapter II of Part IV of the Finance Act

1981 or under Schedule 5 to the Finance Act 1983, in so far as it is not withdrawn and relates to shares issued before 19th March 1986, in determining whether any sums are excluded by virtue of subsection (1) or (2) above from the sums allowable as a deduction in the computation of gains or losses for the purposes of this Act.][1]

Cross references.—See TA 1988, s. 450 (6) (disposal of assets in premiums trust fund of underwriters), s. 777 (12) (sales of income from personal activities and transactions in land).
Amendments.—[1] Sub-s. (3) inserted by TA 1988, Sch. 29, para. 19.

[33A. Transfer of certain securities

(1) Where there is a transfer of securities within the meaning of section 710 of the Taxes Act 1988 (accrued income scheme)—

(*a*) if section 713 (2) (*a*) or (3) (*a*) of that Act applies, section 31 above shall be disregarded in computing for capital gains tax purposes the gain accruing on the disposal concerned;
(*b*) if section 713 (2) (*b*) or (3) (*b*) of that Act applies, section 33 above shall be disregarded in computing for capital gains tax purposes the gain accruing to the transferee if he disposes of the securities;

but subsections (2) and (3) below shall apply.

(2) where the securities are transferred with accrued interest (within the meaning of section 711 of that Act)—

(*a*) if section 713 (2) (*a*) of that Act applies, an amount equal to the accrued amount (determined under that section) shall be excluded from the consideration mentioned in subsection (8) below;
(*b*) if section 713 (2) (*b*) of that Act applies, an amount equal to that amount shall be excluded from the sums mentioned in subsection (9) below.

(3) Where the securities are transferred without accrued interest (within the meaning of section 711 of that Act)—

(*a*) if section 713 (3) (*a*) of that Act applies, an amount equal to the rebate amount (determined under that section) shall be added to the consideration mentioned in subsection (8) below;
(*b*) if section 713 (3) (*b*) of that Act applies, an amount equal to that amount shall be added to the sums mentioned in subsection (9) below.

(4) Where section 716 of that Act applies—

(*a*) if subsection (2) or (3) of that section applies, section 31 above shall be disregarded in computing for capital gains tax purposes the gain accruing on the disposal concerned, but the relevant amount shall be excluded from the consideration mentioned in subsection (8) below; and
(*b*) if subsection (4) of that section applies and the securities were transferred as mentioned in subsection (1) of that section after 18th March 1986, section 33 above shall be disregarded in computing for capital gains tax purposes the gain accruing on the disposal concerned, but the relevant amount shall be excluded from the sums mentioned in subsection (9) below.

(5) In subsection (4) above "the relevant amount" means an amount equal to—

(*a*) if paragraphs (*b*) and (*c*) below do not apply, the amount of the unrealised interest in question;
(*b*) if section 719 of the Taxes Act 1988 applies—

(i) in a case falling within subsection (4)(*a*) above, amount A (within the meaning of section 719);
(ii) in a case falling within subsection (4) (*b*) above, amount C (within the meaning of section 719);

(*c*) if the unrealised interest is subject to the provisions of regulations under section 476(1) of that Act and would not on being paid (to whatever person) be a gross payment within the meaning of those regulations, the grossed up equivalent of the unrealised interest (calculated in accordance with section 726 of that Act).

Paragraphs (*a*), (*b*) and (*c*) above shall be construed as one with sections 716, 719 and 726 respectively.

(6) In relation to any securities which by virtue of subsection (7) below are treated for the purposes of this sub-paragraph as having been transferred, subsections (2) and (3) above

shall have effect as if for "applies" (in each place where it occurs) there were substituted "would apply if the disposal were a transfer".

(7) Where there is a disposal of securities for capital gains tax purposes which is not a transfer for the purposes of section 710 of the Taxes Act 1988 but, if it were such a transfer, one or more of the following paragraphs would apply, namely, paragraphs (*a*) and (*b*) of section 713 (2) and paragraphs (*a*) and (*b*) of section 713 (3) of that Act, the securities shall be treated—

(*a*) for the purposes of subsection (6) above, as transferred on the day of the disposal, and
(*b*) for the purposes of subsections (2) and (3) above, as transferred with accrued interest if, had the disposal been a transfer for the purposes of section 710, it would have been a transfer with accrued interest and as transferred without accrued interest if, had the disposal been such a transfer, it would have been a transfer without accrued interest.

(8) The consideration is the consideration for the disposal of the securities transferred which is taken into account in the computation for capital gains tax purposes of the gain accruing on the disposal.

(9) The sums are the sums allowable to the transferee as a deduction from the consideration in the computation for capital gains tax purposes of the gain accruing to him if he disposes of the securities.

(10) Where on a conversion or exchange of securities a person is treated as entitled to a sum under subsection (2) (*a*) of section 713 of the Taxes Act 1988 an amount equal to the accrued amount (determined under that section) shall, for capital gains tax purposes, be treated as follows—

(*a*) to the extent that it does not exceed the amount of any consideration which the person receives (or is deemed to receive) or becomes entitled to receive on the conversion or exchange (other than his new holding), it shall be treated as reducing that consideration; and
(*b*) to the extent that it does exceed that amount, it shall be treated as consideration which the person gives on the conversion or exchange;

and where on a conversion or exchange of securities a person is treated as entitled to relief under subsection (3) (*a*) of that section an amount equal to the rebate amount (determined under that section) shall, for capital gains tax purposes, be treated as consideration which the person receives on the conversion or exchange.

(11) In subsection (10) above "conversion" means conversion within the meaning of section 82 below and "exchange" means an exchange which by virtue of Chapter II of Part IV of this Act does not involve a disposal.][1]

Cross references.—See TA 1988, s. 726 (5) (grossing up of a building society's interest for the purposes of sub-s. (5) (*c*) of this section).
Amendments.—[1] This section inserted by TA 1988, Sch. 29, para 20.

34. Restriction of losses by reference to capital allowances and renewals allowances

(1) Section 33 above shall not require the exclusion from the sums allowable as a deduction in the computation under this Chapter of any expenditure as being expenditure in respect of which a capital allowance or renewals allowance is made, but the amount of any losses accruing on the disposal of an asset shall be restricted by reference to capital allowances and renewals allowances as follows.

(2) In the computation under this Chapter of the amount of a loss accruing to the person making the disposal, there shall be excluded from the sums allowable as a deduction any expenditure to the extent to which any capital allowance or renewals allowance has been or may be made in respect of it.

(3) If the person making the disposal acquired the asset—

(*a*) by a transfer by way of sale in relation to which an election under paragraph 4 of Schedule 7 to the Capital Allowances Act 1968 was made, or
(*b*) by a transfer to which section 35 (2) to (4) or section 48 (2) of that Act applies,

(being enactments under which a transfer is treated for the purposes of capital allowances as being made at written down value), the preceding provisions of this section shall apply as if any capital allowance made to the transferor in respect of the asset had (except so far as any loss to the transferor was restricted under those provisions) been made to the person making the disposal (that is the transferee); and where the transferor acquired the asset by such a transfer, capital allowances which by virtue of this subsection can be taken into account in relation to the transferor shall also be taken into account in relation to the transferee (that is the person making the disposal), and so on for any series of transfers before the disposal.

(4) In this section "capital allowance" means—

(a) any allowance under the Capital Allowances Act 1968 (including the provisions of [the Taxes Act 1970 or the Taxes Act 1988 which under either of those Acts][2] are to be treated as contained in the said Act of 1968) or under Chapter I of Part III of the Finance Act 1971, other than an allowance under [section 33 (1) of the Taxes Act 1988][4] (relief for cost of maintenance of agricultural land),

[(aa) an allowance under Schedule 12 to the Finance Act 1982][1],

(b) any relief given under section [30][2] of the Taxes Act [1988][3] (expenditure on sea walls), and

(c) any deduction in computing profits or gains allowable under section [91][2] of the Taxes Act [1988][3] (cemeteries).

(5) In this section "renewals allowance" means a deduction allowable in computing the profits or gains of a trade, profession or vocation for the purpose of income tax by reference to the cost of acquiring an asset for the purposes of the trade, profession or vocation in replacement of another asset, and for the purposes of this Chapter a renewals allowance shall be regarded as a deduction allowable in respect of the expenditure incurred on the asset which is being replaced.

(6) The amount of capital allowances to be taken into account under this section in relation to a disposal include any allowances falling to be made by reference to the event which is the disposal, and there shall be deducted from the amount of the allowances the amount of any balancing charge to which effect has been or is to be given by reference to the event which is the disposal, or any earlier event, and of any balancing charge to which effect might have been so given but for the making of an election under section 40 of the Capital Allowances Act 1968 (option in case of replacement of machinery or plant).

(7) Where the disposal is of machinery or plant in relation to expenditure on which allowances or charges have been made under Chapter I of Part III of the Finance Act 1971, and neither paragraph 5 (assets used partly for trade purposes and partly for other purposes) nor paragraph 6 (wear and tear subsidies) of Schedule 8 to that Act applies, the capital allowances to be taken into account under this section are to be regarded as equal to the difference between the capital expenditure incurred, or treated as incurred, under that Chapter on the provision of the machinery or plant by the person making the disposal and the disposal value required to be brought into account in respect of the machinery or plant.

Cross references.—See FA 1985, s. 68 (5A) (application of this section in relation to any capital or renewals allowances made in respect of expenditure incurred before 31 March 1982);
FA 1986, s. 56 (7) (reference in sub-s. (4) above to CAA 1968 to include a reference to FA 1986, Sch. 15 (new code of allowances and charges from 1 April 1986 in respect of capital expenditure on agricultural land and buildings)),
Sch. 13, para. 2 (5) (d) (reference in sub-s. (4) above to CAA 1968 to include a reference to FA 1986, Sch. 13, Part III (new code of allowances and charges from 1 April 1986 in respect of capital expenditure on mineral extraction));
FA 1988, s. 62 (4) (disposal of oil licences relating to undeveloped areas; application of this section in relation to capital allowance made for an accounting period ending after 31 March 1982 in respect of expenditure actually incurred in providing the licence),
s. 63 (5) (application of this section on disposal of oil licence),
Sch. 8, para. 3 (re-basing to 1982: disposal after 5 April 1988 of assets held on 31 March 1982; application of this section in relation to any capital or renewals allowances made in respect of expenditure incurred before 31 March 1982).
Amendments.—[1] Sub-s. (4) (aa) inserted by F (No. 2) A 1983, s. 6 (3) and deemed always to have had effect except that it does not affect the computation under CGTA 1979, Pt. II, Ch. II of any loss on a disposal before 1 April 1983.
[2] Words in sub-s. (4) (a)–(c) substituted by TA 1988, Sch. 29, para. 32 Table.
[3] "1988" in sub-s. (4) (b), (c) inserted by virtue of TA 1988, Sch. 29, para. 15.
[4] Words in sub-s. (4) (a) substituted by FA 1988, Sch. 13, para. 16.

35. Part disposals

(1) Where a person disposes of an interest or right in or over an asset, and generally wherever on the disposal of an asset any description of property derived from that asset remains undisposed of, the sums which under paragraphs (a) and (b) of section 32 (1) above are attributable to the asset shall, both for the purposes of the computation under this Chapter of the gain accruing on the disposal and for the purpose of applying this Chapter in relation to the property which remains undisposed of, be apportioned.

(2) The apportionment shall be made by reference—

(*a*) to the amount or value of the consideration for the disposal on the one hand (call that amount or value A), and
(*b*) to the market value of the property which remains undisposed of on the other hand (call that market value B),

and accordingly the fraction of the said sums allowable as a deduction in computing under this Chapter the amount of the gain accruing on the disposal shall be $\dfrac{A}{A+B}$, and the remainder shall be attributed to the property which remains undisposed of.

(3) Any apportionment to be made in pursuance of this section shall be made before operating the provisions of section 34 above and if, after a part disposal, there is a subsequent disposal of an asset the capital allowances or renewals allowances to be taken into account in pursuance of that section in relation to the subsequent disposal shall, subject to subsection (4) below, be those referable to the sums which under paragraphs (*a*) and (*b*) of section 32 (1) above are attributable to the asset whether before or after the part disposal, but those allowances shall be reduced by the amount (if any) by which the loss on the earlier disposal was restricted under the provisions of section 34 above.

(4) This section shall not be taken as requiring the apportionment of any expenditure which, on the facts, is wholly attributable to what is disposed of, or wholly attributable to what remains undisposed of.

(5) It is hereby declared that this section, and all other provisions for apportioning on a part disposal expenditure which is deductible in computing a gain, are to be operated before the operation of, and without regard to—

(*a*) section 44 (1) below (disposals between husband and wife),
(*b*) sections 115 to 121 below (replacement of business assets), but without prejudice to the provisions of subsection (8) of the said section 115,
(*c*) section 273 (1) of the Taxes Act [1970][1] (transfers within a group of companies), or
(*d*) any other enactment making an adjustment to secure that neither a gain nor a loss occurs on a disposal.

Cross references.—See FA 1982, Sch. 13, para. 1 (indexation allowance on part disposals; the apportionment under this section to be effected before calculating the indexation allowance);
TA 1988, s. 763 (4) (disposal constituting part disposal for capital gains tax purposes and also giving rise to an offshore income gain; the offshore income gain not to be deducted from the disposal consideration for the purposes of the apportionment fraction in sub-s. (2) above);
FA 1988, s. 62 (5), (6) (disposals of oil licences relating to undeveloped areas: modification of this section),
s. 63 (7) (allowance of certain drilling chargeable expenditure in determining chargeable gains),
Sch. 8, para. 4 (re-basing to 1982: part disposals of assets held on 31 March 1982).
Amendments.—"1970" in sub-s. (5) (*c*) inserted by virtue of TA 1988, Sch. 29, para. 15 (*b*).

36. Assets derived from other assets

If and so far as, in a case where assets have been merged or divided or have changed their nature or rights or interests in or over assets have been created or extinguished, the value of an asset is derived from any other asset in the same ownership, an appropriate proportion of the sums allowable as a deduction in a computation under this Chapter in respect of the other asset under paragraphs (*a*) and (*b*) of section 32 (1) above shall, both for the purpose of the computation of a gain accruing on the disposal of the first-mentioned asset and, if the other asset remains in existence, on a disposal of that other asset, be attributed to the first-mentioned asset.

Cross references.—See FA 1985, s. 68 (6) (modification of indexation allowance in respect of assets derived after 31 March 1982 from assets held on that date);
FA 1988, Sch. 8, para. 5 (re-basing to 1982: disposal of assets derived from other assets held on 31 March 1982).

37. Wasting assets

(1) In this Chapter "wasting asset" means an asset with a predictable life not exceeding fifty years but so that—

(*a*) freehold land shall not be a wasting asset whatever its nature, and whatever the nature of the buildings or works on it,
(*b*) "life", in relation to any tangible movable property, means useful life, having regard to the purpose for which the tangible assets were acquired or provided by the person making the disposal,
(*c*) plant and machinery shall in every case be regarded as having a predictable life of less

than fifty years, and in estimating that life it shall be assumed that its life will end when it is finally put out of use as being unfit for further use, and that it is going to be used in the normal manner and to the normal extent and is going to be so used throughout its life as so estimated,

(*d*) a life interest in settled property shall not be a wasting asset until the predictable expectation of life of the life tenant is fifty years or less, and the predictable life of life interests in settled property and of annuities shall be ascertained from actuarial tables approved by the Board.

(2) In this Chapter "the residual or scrap value", in relation to a wasting asset, means the predictable value, if any which the wasting asset will have at the end of its predictable life as estimated in accordance with this section.

(3) The question what is the predictable life of an asset, and the question what is its predictable residual or scrap value at the end of that life, if any, shall, so far as those questions are not immediately answered by the nature of the asset, be taken, in relation to any disposal of the asset, as they were known or ascertainable at the time when the asset was acquired or provided by the person making the disposal.

38. Wasting assets: straightline restriction of allowable expenditure

(1) In the computation under this Chapter of the gain accruing on the disposal of a wasting asset it shall be assumed—

(*a*) that any expenditure attributable to the asset under section 32 (1) (*a*) above after deducting the residual or scrap value, if any, of the asset, is written off at a uniform rate from its full amount at the time when the asset is acquired or provided to nothing at the end of its life, and

(*b*) that any expenditure attributable to the asset under section 32 (1) (*b*) above is written off from the full amount of that expenditure at the time when that expenditure is first reflected in the state or nature of the asset to nothing at the end of its life,

so that an equal daily amount is written off day by day.

(2) Thus, calling the predictable life of a wasting asset at the time when it was acquired or provided by the person making the disposal L, the period from that time to the time of disposal T(1), and, in relation to any expenditure attributable to the asset under section 32 (1) (*b*) above, the period from the time when that expenditure is first reflected in the state or nature of the asset to the said time of disposal T(2), there shall be excluded from the computation under this Chapter—

(*a*) out of the expenditure attributable to the asset under section 32 (1) (*a*) above a fraction $\dfrac{T(1)}{L}$ of an amount equal to the amount of that expenditure minus the residual or scrap value, if any, of the asset, and

(*b*) out of the expenditure attributable to the asset under section 32 (1) (*b*) above a fraction $\dfrac{T(2)}{L-(T(1)-T(2))}$ of the amount of the expenditure.

(3) If any expenditure attributable to the asset under section 32 (1) (*b*) above creates or increases a residual or scrap value of the asset, the provisions of subsection (1) (*a*) above shall be applied so as to take that into account.

39. Wasting assets qualifying for capital allowances

(1) Section 38 above shall not apply in relation to a disposal of an asset—

(*a*) which, from the beginning of the period of ownership of the person making the disposal to the time when the disposal is made, is used and used solely for the purposes of a trade, profession or vocation and in respect of which that person has claimed or could have claimed any capital allowance in respect of any expenditure attributable to the asset under paragraph (*a*) or paragraph (*b*) of section 32 (1) above, or

(*b*) on which the person making the disposal has incurred any expenditure which has otherwise qualified in full for any capital allowance.

(2) In the case of the disposal of an asset which, in the period of ownership of the person making the disposal, has been used partly for the purposes of a trade, profession or vocation and partly for other purposes, or has been used for the purposes of a trade, profession or vocation for part of that period, or which has otherwise qualified in part only for capital allowances—

(a) the consideration for the disposal, and any expenditure attributable to the asset by paragraph (a) or paragraph (b) of section 32 (1) above shall be apportioned by reference to the extent to which that expenditure qualified for capital allowances, and
(b) the computation under this Chapter shall be made separately in relation to the apportioned parts of the expenditure and consideration, and
(c) section 38 above shall not apply for the purposes of the computation in relation to the part of the consideration apportioned to use for the purposes of the trade, profession or vocation, or to the expenditure qualifying for capital allowances, and
(d) if an apportionment of the consideration for the disposal has been made for the purposes of making any capital allowance to the person making the disposal or for the purpose of making any balancing charge on him, that apportionment shall be employed for the purposes of this section, and
(e) subject to paragraph (d) above, the consideration for the disposal shall be apportioned for the purposes of this section in the same proportions as the expenditure attributable to the asset is apportioned under paragraph (a) above.

Cross references.—FA 1985, s. 68 (5A) (application of this section in relation to any allowance made in respect of expenditure incurred before 31 March 1982);
FA 1988, Sch. 8, para. 3 (re-basing to 1982: disposal after 5 April 1988 of assets held on 31 March 1982; application of this section in relation to any allowance made in respect of expenditure incurred before 31 March 1982).

40. Consideration due after time of disposal

(1) If the consideration, or part of the consideration, taken into account in the computation under this Chapter is payable by instalments over a period beginning not earlier than the time when the disposal is made, being a period exceeding eighteen months, then, if the person making the disposal satisfies the Board that he would otherwise suffer undue hardship, the tax on a chargeable gain accruing on the disposal may, at his option, be paid by such instalments as the Board may allow over a period not exceeding eight years and ending not later than the time at which the last of the first-mentioned instalments is payable.

(2) In the computation under this Chapter consideration for the disposal shall be brought into account without any discount for postponement of the right to receive any part of it and, in the first instance, without regard to a risk of any part of the consideration being irrecoverable or to the right to receive any part of the consideration being contingent; and if any part of the consideration so brought into account is subsequently shown to the satisfaction of the inspector to be irrecoverable, such adjustment, whether by way of discharge or repayment of tax or otherwise, shall be made as is required in consequence.

41. Contingent liabilities

(1) In the first instance no allowance shall be made in the computation under this Chapter—

(a) in the case of a disposal by way of assigning a lease of land or other property, for any liability remaining with, or assumed by, the person making the disposal by way of assigning the lease which is contingent on a default in respect of liabilities thereby or subsequently assumed by the assignee under the terms and conditions of the lease,
(b) for any contingent liability of the person making the disposal in respect of any covenant for quiet enjoyment or other obligation assumed as vendor of land, or of any estate or interest in land, or as a lessor,
(c) for any contingent liability in respect of a warranty or representation made on a disposal by way of sale or lease of any property other than land.

(2) If it is subsequently shown to the satisfaction of the inspector that any such contingent liability has become enforceable, and is being or has been enforced, such adjustment, whether by way of discharge or repayment of tax or otherwise, shall be made as is required in consequence.

42. Expenditure reimbursed out of public money

There shall be excluded from the computation under this Chapter any expenditure which has been or is to be met directly or indirectly by the Crown or by any Government, public or local authority whether in the United Kingdom or elsewhere.

Cross references.—See TA 1988, s. 400 (6) (writing-off of government investment in a company not to be treated as expenditure met by the Crown).

43. Supplemental

(1) No deduction shall be allowable in a computation under this Chapter more than once from any sum or from more than one sum.

(2) References in this Chapter to sums taken into account as receipts or as expenditure in computing profits or gains or losses for the purposes of income tax shall include references to sums which would be so taken into account but for the fact that any profits or gains of a trade, profession, employment or vocation are not chargeable to income tax or that losses are not allowable for those purposes.

(3) In this Chapter references to income or profits charged or chargeable to tax include references to income or profits taxed or as the case may be taxable by deduction at source.

(4) For the purposes of any computation under this Chapter any necessary apportionments shall be made of any consideration or of any expenditure and the method of apportionment adopted shall, subject to the express provisions of this Chapter, be such method as appears to the inspector or on appeal the Commissioners concerned to be just and reasonable.

(5) In this Chapter "capital allowance" and "renewals allowance" have the meanings given by subsections (4) and (5) of section 34 above.

PART III
PERSONS AND TRUSTS

Married persons

44. Husband and wife

(1) If, in any year of assessment, and in the case of a woman who in that year of assessment is a married woman living with her husband, the man disposes of an asset to the wife, or the wife disposes of an asset to the man, both shall be treated as if the asset was acquired from the one making the disposal for a consideration of such amount as would secure that on the disposal neither a gain nor a loss would accrue to the one making the disposal.

(2) This section shall not apply—

(a) if until the disposal the asset formed part of trading stock of a trade carried on by the one making the disposal, or if the asset is acquired as trading stock for the purposes of a trade carried on by the one acquiring the asset, or

(b) if the disposal is by way of donatio mortis causa,

but this section shall have effect notwithstanding the provisions of section 62 (transactions between connected persons) or section 122 (appropriations to and from stock in trade) below, or of any other provisions of this Act fixing the amount of the consideration deemed to be given on a disposal or acquisition.

Cross references.—See FA 1984, Sch. 13, para. 10 (2) (a) (disposals of qualifying corporate bonds between husband and wife);
FA 1985, s. 68 (7) (modification of indexation allowance with respect to disposals of assets after 5 April 1988);
FA 1988, Sch. 8, paras. 1, 2 (capital gains; re-basing of indexation to 1982 for assets held on 31 March 1982).

45. Tax on married woman's gains

(1) Subject to this section, the amount of capital gains tax on chargeable gains accruing to a married woman in—

(a) a year of assessment, or
(b) any part of a year of assessment, being a part beginning with 6th April,

during which she is a married woman living with her husband shall be assessed and charged on the husband and not otherwise but this subsection shall not affect the amount of capital gains tax chargeable on a man apart from this subsection nor result in the additional amount of capital gains tax charged on a man by virtue of this subsection being different from the amount which would otherwise have remained chargeable on the married woman.

(2) Subsection (1) above shall not apply in relation to a husband and wife in any year of assessment if, before 6th July in the year next following that year of assessment, an application is made by either the husband or wife, and such an application duly made shall have effect not only as respects the year of assessment for which it is made but also for any subsequent year of assessment:

Provided that the applicant may give, for any subsequent year of assessment, a notice to withdraw that application and where such a notice is given the application shall not have effect with respect to the year for which the notice is given or any subsequent year.

A notice of withdrawal under this proviso shall not be valid unless it is given within the period for making, for the year for which the notice is given, an application similar to that to which the notice relates.

(3) Returns under section 8 or 42 (5) of the Taxes Management Act 1970 as respects chargeable gains accruing to a married woman may be required either from her or, if her husband is liable under subsection (1) above, from him.

(4) Section [285][2] (collection from wife of tax assessed on husband attributable to her income) and section [286][2] (right of husband to disclaim liability for tax on deceased wife's income) of the Taxes Act [1988][1] shall apply with any necessary modifications in relation to capital gains tax as they apply in relation to income tax.

(5) An application or notice of withdrawal under this section shall be in such form and made in such manner as may be prescribed by the Board.

Note.—See **Prospective Legislation Notes** (Married Couples).
Cross references.—See FA 1984, Sch. 14, para. 1 (3) (postponement of tax due at 29 March 1983 from the husband under sub-s. (1) above on gains of non-resident trustees);
FA 1988, s. 99 (2), (3), (5) (special provisions for the years 1988–89 and 1989–90 in respect of capital gains tax on married woman's gains).
Amendments.—[1] "1988" in sub-s. (4) inserted by virtue of TA 1988, Sch. 29, para. 15 (*a*).
[2] Numbers in sub-s. (4) substituted by TA 1988, Sch. 29, para. 32 Table.

Trustees, nominees and personal representatives

46. Nominees and bare trustees

(1) In relation to assets held by a person as nominee for another person, or as trustee for another person absolutely entitled as against the trustee, or for any person who would be so entitled but for being an infant or other person under disability (or for two or more persons who are or would be jointly so entitled), this Act shall apply as if the property were vested in, and the acts of the nominee or trustee in relation to the assets were the acts of, the person or persons for whom he is the nominee or trustee (acquisitions from or disposals to him by that person or persons being disregarded accordingly).

(2) It is hereby declared that references in this Act to any asset held by a person as trustee for another person absolutely entitled as against the trustee are references to a case where that other person has the exclusive right, subject only to satisfying any outstanding charge, lien or other right of the trustees to resort to the asset for payment of duty, taxes, costs or other outgoings, to direct how that asset shall be dealt with.

47. Expenses in administration of estates and trusts

(1) In the case of a gain accruing to a person on the disposal of, or of a right or interest in or over, an asset to which he became absolutely entitled as legatee or as against the trustees of settled property—

(*a*) any expenditure within section 32 (2) above incurred by him in relation to the transfer of the asset to him by the personal representatives or trustees, and
(*b*) any such expenditure incurred in relation to the transfer of the asset by the personal representatives or trustees,

shall be allowable as a deduction in the computation under Chapter II of Part II above of the gain accruing to that person on the disposal.

(2) In this Act, unless the context otherwise requires, "legatee" includes any person taking under a testamentary disposition or on an intestacy or partial intestacy, whether he takes beneficially or as trustee, and a person taking under a donatio mortis causa shall be treated (except for the purposes of section 49 below (death)) as a legatee and his acquisition as made at the time of the donor's death.

(3) For the purposes of the definition of "legatee" above, and of any reference in this Act to a person acquiring an asset "as legatee", property taken under a testamentary disposition or on an intestacy or partial intestacy includes any asset appropriated by the personal representatives in or towards satisfaction of a pecuniary legacy or any other interest or share in the property devolving under the disposition or intestacy.

48. Liability for tax

(1) Capital gains tax chargeable in respect of chargeable gains accruing to the trustees of a settlement or capital gains tax due from the personal representatives of a deceased person may be assessed and charged on and in the name of any one or more of those trustees or personal representatives, but where an assessment is made in pursuance of this subsection otherwise than on all the trustees or all the personal representatives the persons assessed shall not include a person who is not resident or ordinarily resident in the United Kingdom.

(2) Subject to section 46 above, chargeable gains accruing to the trustees of a settlement or to the personal representatives of a deceased person, and capital gains tax chargeable on or in the name of such trustees or personal representatives, shall not be regarded for the purposes of this Act as accruing to, or chargeable on, any other person, nor shall any trustee or personal representative be regarded for the purposes of this Act as an individual.

Death

49. Death: general provisions

(1) For the purposes of this Act the assets of which a deceased person was competent to dispose—

(*a*) shall be deemed to be acquired on his death by the personal representatives or other person on whom they devolve for a consideration equal to their market value at the date of the death, but
(*b*) shall not be deemed to be disposed of by him on his death (whether or not they were the subject of a testamentary disposition).

(2) Allowable losses sustained by an individual in the year of assessment in which he dies may, so far as they cannot be deducted from chargeable gains accruing in that year, be deducted from chargeable gains accruing to the deceased in the three years of assessment preceding the year of assessment in which the death occurs, taking chargeable gains accruing in a later year before those accruing in an earlier year.

(3) In relation to property forming part of the estate of a deceased person the personal representatives shall for the purposes of this Act be treated as being a single and continuing body of persons (distinct from the persons who may from time to time be the personal representatives), and that body shall be treated as having the deceased's residence, ordinary residence, and domicile at the date of death.

(4) On a person acquiring any asset as legatee (as defined in section 47 above)—

(*a*) no chargeable gain shall accrue to the personal representatives, and
(*b*) the legatee shall be treated as if the personal representatives' acquisition of the asset had been his acquisition of it.

(5) Notwithstanding [section 29A (1)][1] above (gifts) no chargeable gain shall accrue to any person on his making a disposal by way of donatio mortis causa.

(6) Subject to subsections (7) and (8) below, where within the period of two years after a person's death any of the dispositions (whether effected by will, under the law relating to intestacy or otherwise) of the property of which he was competent to dispose are varied, or the benefit conferred by any of those dispositions is disclaimed, by an instrument in writing made by the persons or any of the persons who benefit or would benefit under the dispositions—

(*a*) the variation or disclaimer shall not constitute a disposal for the purposes of this Act, and
(*b*) this section shall apply as if the variation had been effected by the deceased or, as the case may be, the disclaimed benefit had never been conferred.

(7) Subsection (6) above does not apply to a variation unless the person or persons making the instrument so elect by written notice given to the Board within six months after the date of the instrument or such longer time as the Board may allow.

(8) Subsection (6) above does not apply to a variation or disclaimer made for any consideration in money or money's worth other than consideration consisting of the making of a variation or disclaimer in respect of another of the dispositions.

(9) Subsection (6) above applies whether or not the administration of the estate is complete or the property has been distributed in accordance with the original dispositions.

(10) In this section references to assets of which a deceased person was competent to dispose are references to assets of the deceased which (otherwise than in right of a power of appointment or of the testamentary power conferred by statute to dispose of entailed interests) he could, if of full age and capacity, have disposed of by his will, assuming that all the assets were situated in England and, if he was not domiciled in the United Kingdom, that he was domiciled in England, and include references to his severable share in any assets to which, immediately before his death, he was beneficially entitled as a joint tenant.

Cross references.—See FA 1984, Sch. 13, para. 10 (2) (*b*) (disposals of qualifying corporate bonds by personal representatives to legatees).
TA 1988, s. 757 (3) (material interest in non-qualifying offshore fund which a deceased person was competent to dispose of; the interest to be deemed to have been disposed of immediately before death notwithstanding sub-s. (1) (*b*) above),
s. 757 (4) (application of this section for the purposes of TA 1988, Pt. XVII, Ch. V (disposals of material interests in non-qualifying offshore funds),
Sch. 4, para. 7 (2) (deep discount securities which a deceased person was competent to dispose of; the securities to be deemed to have been disposed of immediately before death notwithstanding sub-s. (1) (*b*) above),

Amendments.—[1] Words in sub-s. (5) substituted by FA 1981, s. 90 (3) (*a*).

50. Death: application of law in Scotland

(1) The provisions of this Act, so far as relating to the consequences of the death of an heir of entail in possession of any property in Scotland subject to an entail, whether sui juris or not, or of a proper liferenter of any property, shall have effect subject to the provisions of this section.

(2) For the purposes of this Act, on the death of any such heir or liferenter the heir of entail next entitled to the entailed property under the entail or, as the case may be, the person (if any) who, on the death of the liferenter, becomes entitled to possession of the property as fiar shall be deemed to have acquired all the assets forming part of the property at the date of the deceased's death for a consideration equal to their market value at that date.

Settlements

51. Meaning of "settled property"

In this Act, unless the context otherwise requires, "settled property" means any property held in trust other than property to which section 46 above (nominees and bare trustees) applies.

This definition has effect subject to section 61 (4) (insolvents' assets) and 93 (unit trusts) below.

52. Trustees of settlements

(1) In relation to settled property, the trustees of the settlement shall for the purposes of this Act be treated as being a single and continuing body of persons (distinct from the persons who may from time to time be the trustees), and that body shall be treated as being resident and ordinarily resident in the United Kingdom unless the general administration of the trusts is ordinarily carried on outside the United Kingdom and the trustees or a majority of them for the time being are not resident or not ordinarily resident in the United Kingdom.

(2) Notwithstanding subsection (1) above, a person carrying on a business which consists of or includes the management of trusts, and acting as trustee of a trust in the course of that business, shall be treated in relation to that trust as not resident in the United Kingdom if the whole of the settled property consists of or derives from property provided by a person not at the time (or, in the case of a trust arising under a testamentary disposition or on an intestacy or partial intestacy, at his death) domiciled, resident or ordinarily resident in the United Kingdom, and if in such a case the trustees or a majority of them are or are treated in relation to that trust as not resident in the United Kingdom, the general administration of the trust shall be treated as ordinarily carried on outside the United Kingdom.

(3) For the purposes of this section, and of sections 54 (1) and 55 (1) below, where part of the property comprised in a settlement is vested in one trustee or set of trustees and part in another (and in particular where settled land within the meaning of the Settled Land Act 1925 is vested in the tenant for life and investments representing capital money are vested in the trustees of the settlement), they shall be treated as together constituting and, in so far as they act separately, as acting on behalf of a single body of trustees.

(4) If tax assessed on the trustees, or any one trustee, of a settlement in respect of a chargeable gain accruing to the trustees is not paid within six months from the date when it becomes payable by the trustees or trustee, and before or after the expiration of that period of six months the asset in respect of which the chargeable gain accrued, or any part of the proceeds of sale of that asset, is transferred by the trustees to a person who as against the trustees is absolutely entitled to it, that person may at any time within two years from the time when the tax became payable be assessed and charged (in the name of the trustees) to an amount of capital gains tax not exceeding tax chargeable on an amount equal to the amount of the chargeable gain and, where part only of the asset or of the proceeds was transferred, not exceeding a proportionate part of that amount.

Cross references.—See FA 1986, s. 58 (3) (hold over relief on a gift into a settlement not available where the gift is made after 17 March 1986 into a foreign settlement the trustees of which are treated under this section as resident and ordinarily resident in the UK).

53. Gifts in settlement

A [transfer into]¹ settlement, whether revocable or irrevocable, is a disposal of the entire property thereby becoming settled property notwithstanding that the [transferor]¹ has some interest as a beneficiary under the settlement and notwithstanding that he is a trustee, or the sole trustee, of the settlement.

Amendments.—¹ Words substituted by FA 1981, s. 86 with effect from 10 March 1981.

54. Person becoming absolutely entitled to settled property

(1) On the occasion when a person becomes absolutely entitled to any settled property as against the trustee all the assets forming part of the settled property to which he becomes so entitled shall be deemed to have been disposed of by the trustee, and immediately reacquired by him in his capacity as a trustee within section 46 (1) above, for a consideration equal to their market value.

(2) On the occasion when a person becomes absolutely entitled to any settled property as against the trustee, any allowable loss which has accrued to the trustee in respect of property which is, or is represented by, the property to which that person so becomes entitled (including any allowable loss carried forward to the year of assessment in which that occasion falls), being a loss which cannot be deducted from chargeable gains accruing to the trustee in that year, but before that occasion, shall be treated as if it were an allowable loss accruing at that time to the person becoming so entitled, instead of to the trustee.

[(3) References in this section to the case where a person becomes absolutely entitled to settled property as against the trustee shall be taken to include references to the case where a person would become so entitled but for being an infant or other person under disability.]¹

Cross references.—See FA 1988, Sch. 12, para. 5 (4) (c) (building society changing into a company; transfer of shares to trustees as settled property; this section not to apply where a member becomes absolutely entitled to such shares as against the trustees).
Amendments.—¹ Sub-s. (3) added by FA 1981, s. 87 (1), (3) with effect from 10 March 1981.

55. Termination of life interest etc.

(1) [On the termination, on the death of the person entitled to it, of a life interest in possession in all or any part of settled property—

   (a) the whole or a corresponding part of each of the assets forming part of the settled property and not ceasing at that time to be settled property shall be deemed for the purposes of this Act at that time to be disposed of and immediately re-acquired by the trustee for a consideration equal to the whole or a corresponding part of the market value of the asset; but
   (b) no chargeable gain shall accrue on that disposal.]¹

For the purposes of this subsection a life interest which is a right to part of the income of settled property shall be treated as a life interest in a corresponding part of the settled property.

(2) . . .²

(3) Subsection (1) above shall apply where the person entitled to a life interest in possession in all or any part of settled property dies (although the interest does not then terminate) as it applies on the termination of such a life interest.

(4) In this section "life interest" in relation to a settlement—

   (a) includes a right under the settlement to the income of, or the use or occupation of, settled property for the life of a person other than the person entitled to the right, or for lives,
   (b) does not include any right which is contingent on the exercise of the discretion of the trustee or the discretion of some other person, and
   (c) subject to subsection (5) below, does not include an annuity, notwithstanding that the annuity is payable out of or charged on settled property or the income of settled property.

(5) In this section the expression "life interest" shall include entitlement to an annuity created by the settlement if—

   (a) some or all of the settled property is appropriated by the trustees as a fund out of which the annuity is payable, and

(b) there is no right of recourse to settled property not so appropriated, or to the income of settled property not so appropriated,

and, without prejudice to subsection (6) below, the settled property so appropriated shall, while the annuity is payable, and on the occasion of the death of the annuitant, be treated for the purposes of this section as being settled property under a separate settlement.

(6) If there is a life interest in a part of the settled property and, where that is a life interest in income, there is no right of recourse to, or to the income of, the remainder of the settled property, the part of the settled property in which the life interest subsists shall while it subsists be treated for the purposes of this section as being settled property under a separate settlement.

Amendments.—[1] Words in sub-s. (1) substituted by FA 1982, s. 84 (1).
[2] Sub-s. (2) repealed by FA 1982, s. 84 (1) and Sch. 22, Pt. VI.

56. Death of life tenant: exclusion of chargeable gain

(1) Where, by virtue of section 54 (1) above, the assets forming part of any settled property are deemed to be disposed of and re-acquired by the trustee on the occasion when a person becomes [(or would but for a disability become)][1] absolutely entitled thereto as against the trustee, then, if that occasion is the termination of a life interest (within the meaning of section 55 above) by the death of the person entitled to that interest—

(a) no chargeable gain shall accrue on the disposal, and
(b) if on the death the property reverts to the disponer the disposal and re-acquisition under that subsection shall be deemed to be for such consideration as to secure that neither a gain nor a loss accrues to the trustee, and shall, if the trustee had first acquired the property at a date earlier than 6th April 1965, be deemed to be at that earlier date.

[(1A) Where the life interest referred to in subsection (1) above is an interest in part only of the settled property to which section 54 applies, subsection (1) (a) above shall not apply but any chargeable gain accruing on the disposal shall be reduced by a proportion corresponding to that represented by the part.][2]

[(1B) The last sentence of subsection (1) of section 55 above, and subsection (6) of that section, shall apply for the purposes of subsection (1A) above as they apply for the purposes of section 55 (1).][2]

(2) ...[3]

Cross references.—See FA 1985, s. 68 (7A) (a) (disposal after 5 April 1988 of assets held on 31 March 1982; computation of indexation allowance for the purposes of this section);
FA 1988, Sch. 8, para. 1 (3) (disposal after 5 April 1988 of assets held on 31 March 1982; application of indexation allowance re-based to 1982 in relation to unindexed gains and losses).
Amendments.—[1] Words in sub-s. (1) inserted by FA 1981, s. 87 (2), (3) with effect from 10 March 1981.
[2] Sub-ss. (1A), (1B) inserted by FA 1982, s. 84 (2).
[3] Sub-s. (2) repealed by FA 1982, s. 84 (2) and Sch. 22, Pt. VI.

[56A. Effect on sections 55 and 56 of relief under Finance Act 1980, section 79

(1) This section applies where—

(a) a claim for relief was made under section [126 or 147A below][2] in respect of the disposal of an asset to a trustee, and
(b) the trustee is deemed to have disposed of the asset, or part of it, by virtue of section 54 (1) or 55 (1) (a) above.

(2) Sections 56 (1) (a) and 55 (1) (b) shall not apply to the disposal of the asset or part by the trustee, but any chargeable gain accruing to the trustee on the disposal shall be restricted to the amount of the held-over gain (or a corresponding part of it) on the disposal of the asset to him.

(3) Subsection (2) above shall not have effect in a case within section 56 (1A) above; but in such a case the reduction provided for by section 56 (1A) above shall be diminished by an amount equal to the proportion there mentioned of the held-over gain.

(4) In this section "held-over gain" has the same meaning as in section [126 or, as the case may be, 147A below][2].][1]

Amendments.—[1] This section inserted by FA 1982, s. 84 (3).
[2] Words in sub-ss. (1) (a), (4) substituted by FA 1989, Sch. 14, para. 6 (1).

57. Death of annuitant

Sections 54 (1) and 55 (1) above shall apply, where an annuity which is not a life interest is terminated by the death of the annuitant, as they apply on the termination of a life interest by the death of the person entitled thereto.

In this section "life interest" has the same meaning as in section 55 above.

58. Disposal of interests in settled property

(1) No chargeable gain shall accrue on the disposal of an interest created by or arising under a settlement (including, in particular, an annuity or life interest, and the reversion to an annuity or life interest) by the person for whose benefit the interest was created by the terms of the settlement or by any other person except one who acquired, or derives his title from one who acquired, the interest for a consideration in money or money's worth, other than consideration consisting of another interest under the settlement.

(2) Subject to subsection (1) above, where a person who has acquired an interest in settled property (including in particular the reversion to an annuity or life interest) becomes, as the holder of that interest, absolutely entitled as against the trustee to any settled property, he shall be treated as disposing of the interest in consideration of obtaining that settled property (but without prejudice to any gain accruing to the trustee on the disposal of that property deemed to be effected by him under section 54 (1) above).

Cross references.—See FA 1981, s. 88 (1), (2) (exclusion of sub-s. (1) above as regards non-resident settlements and deemed accrual of chargeable gains where settlement subsequently becomes non-resident);
FA 1984, Sch. 14, para. 11 (2) (postponement of tax due at 29 March 1983 from a beneficiary on gains of non-resident trustees; postponed tax becoming payable when beneficiary makes a disposal of his interest in the non-resident trust in circumstances such that by virtue of sub-s. (1) above no chargeable gain could accrue on the disposal);
FA 1988, Sch. 12, para. 5 (4) (*d*) (building society changing into a company; sub-s. (1) above not to apply in relation to a disposal by a member of shares to which he became absolutely entitled as against the trustees to whom the shares were transferred as settled property).

Other cases

59. Gifts: recovery from donee

(1) If in any year of assessment a chargeable gain accrues to any person on the disposal of an asset by way of gift and any amount of capital gains tax assessed on that person for that year of assessment is not paid within twelve months from the date when the tax becomes payable the donee may, by an assessment made not later than two years from the date when the tax became payable, be assessed and charged (in the name of the donor) to capital gains tax on an amount not exceeding the amount of the chargeable gain so accruing, and not exceeding the grossed up amount of that capital gains tax unpaid at the time when he is so assessed, grossing up at the marginal rate of tax, that is to say taking capital gains tax on a chargeable gain at the amount which would not have been chargeable but for that chargeable gain.

(2) A person paying any amount of tax in pursuance of this section shall be entitled to recover a sum of that amount from the donor.

(3) References in this section to a donor include, in the case of an individual who has died, references to his personal representatives.

(4) In this section references to a gift include references to any transaction otherwise than by way of a bargain made at arm's length so far as money or money's worth passes under the transaction without full consideration in money or money's worth, and "donor" and "donee" shall be construed accordingly; and this section shall apply in relation to a gift made by two or more donors with the necessary modifications and subject to any necessary apportionments.

60. Partnerships

Where two or more persons carry on a trade or business in partnership—

(*a*) tax in respect of chargeable gains accruing to them on the disposal of any partnership assets shall, in Scotland as well as elsewhere in the United Kingdom, be assessed and charged on them separately, and
(*b*) any partnership dealings shall be treated as dealings by the partners and not by the firm as such, and
(*c*) section [112 (1), (2)][2] of the Taxes Act [1988][1] (residence of partnerships) shall apply

in relation to tax chargeable in pursuance of this Act as it applies in relation to income tax.

Amendments.—[1] "1988" in para. (c) inserted by virtue of TA 1988, Sch. 29, para. 15 (a).
[2] Number in para. (c) substituted by TA 1988, Sch. 29, para. 32 Table.

61. Insolvents' assets

(1) In relation to assets held by a person as trustee or assignee in bankruptcy or under a deed of arrangement this Act shall apply as if the assets were vested in, and the acts of the trustee or assignee in relation to the assets were the acts of, the bankrupt or debtor (acquisitions from or disposals to him by the bankrupt or debtor being disregarded accordingly), and tax in respect of any chargeable gains which accrue to any such trustee or assignee shall be assessable on and recoverable from him.

(2) Assets held by a trustee or assignee in bankruptcy or under a deed of arrangement at the death of the bankrupt or debtor shall for the purposes of this Act be regarded as held by a personal representative of the deceased and—

(a) subsection (1) above shall not apply after the death, and
(b) section 49 (1) above (under which assets passing on a death are deemed to be acquired by the persons on whom they devolve) shall apply as if any assets held by a trustee or assignee in bankruptcy or under a deed of arrangement at the death of the bankrupt or debtor were assets of which the deceased was competent to dispose and which then devolved on the trustee or assignee as if he were a personal representative.

(3) Assets vesting in a trustee in bankruptcy after the death of the bankrupt or debtor shall for the purposes of this Act be regarded as held by a personal representative of the deceased, and subsection (1) above shall not apply.

(4) The definition of "settled property" in section 51 above shall not include any property as being property held by a trustee or assignee in bankruptcy or under a deed of arrangement.

(5) In this section "deed of arrangement" means a deed of arrangement to which the Deeds of Arrangement Act 1914 or any corresponding enactment forming part of the law of Scotland or Northern Ireland applies.

62. Transactions between connected persons

(1) This section shall apply where a person acquires an asset and the person making the disposal is connected with him.

(2) Without prejudice to the generality of section [29A (1)][1] above the person acquiring the asset and the person making the disposal shall be treated as parties to a transaction otherwise than by way of a bargain made at arm's length.

(3) If on the disposal a loss accrues to the person making the disposal, it shall not be deductible except from a chargeable gain accruing to him on some other disposal of an asset to the person acquiring the asset mentioned in subsection (1) above, being a disposal made at a time when they are connected persons:

Provided that this subsection shall not apply to a disposal by way of gift in settlement if the gift and the income from it is wholly or primarily applicable for educational, cultural or recreational purposes, and the persons benefiting from the application for those purposes are confined to members of an association of persons for whose benefit the gift was made, not being persons all or most of whom are connected persons.

(4) Where the asset mentioned in subsection (1) above is an option to enter into a sale or other transaction given by the person making the disposal a loss accruing to the person acquiring the asset shall not be an allowable loss unless it accrues on a disposal of the option at arm's length to a person who is not connected with him.

(5) In a case where the asset mentioned in subsection (1) above is subject to any right or restriction enforceable by the person making the disposal, or by a person connected with him, then [where the amount of the consideration for the acquisition is][1], in accordance with subsection (2) above, deemed to be equal to the market value of the asset) that market value shall be—

(a) what its market value would be if not subject to the right or restriction, minus—
(b) the market value of the right or restriction or the amount by which its extinction would enhance the value of the asset to its owner, whichever is the less:

Provided that if the right or restriction is of such a nature that its enforcement would or might effectively destroy or substantially impair the value of the asset without bringing any countervailing advantage either to the person making the disposal or a person connected with him or is an option or other right to acquire the asset or, in the case or incorporeal property, is a right to extinguish the asset in the hands of the person giving the consideration by forfeiture or merger or otherwise, that market value of the asset shall be determined, and the amount of the gain accruing on the disposal shall be computed, as if the right or restriction did not exist.

(6) Subsection (5) above shall not apply to a right of forfeiture or other right exercisable on breach of a convenant contained in a lease of land or other property, and shall not apply to any right or restriction under a mortgage or other charge.

Cross references.—See FA 1984, s. 79 (7) (*b*), (8) (treatment of losses on disposals after 12 March 1984 between connected persons of oil rights or assets used in connection with oil fields).
Amendments.—[1] Words in sub-ss. (2), (5) substituted by FA 1981, s. 90 (3) (*a*), (*b*).

63. Connected persons: interpretation

(1) Any question whether a person is connected with another shall for the purposes of this Act be determined in accordance with the following subsections of this section (any provision that one person is connected with another being taken to mean that they are connected with one another).

(2) A person is connected with an individual if that person is the individual's husband or wife, or is a relative, or the husband or wife of a relative, of the individual or of the individual's husband or wife.

(3) A person, in his capacity as trustee of a settlement, is connected with any individual who in relation to the settlement is a settlor, with any person who is connected with such an individual and with a body corporate which, under section [681][2] of the Taxes Act [1988][1], is deemed to be connected with that settlement ("settlement" and "settlor" having for the purposes of this subsection the meanings assigned to them by subsection [(4)][2] of the said section [681][2]).

(4) Except in relation to acquisitions or disposals of partnership assets pursuant to bona fide commercial arrangements, a person is connected with any person with whom he is in partnership, and with the husband or wife or a relative of any individual with whom he is in partnership.

(5) A company is connected with another company—

(*a*) if the same person has control of both, or a person has control of one and persons connected with him, or he and persons connected with him, have control of the other, or
(*b*) if a group of two or more persons has control of each company, and the groups either consist of the same persons or could be regarded as consisting of the same persons by treating (in one or more cases) a member of either group as replaced by a person with whom he is connected.

(6) A company is connected with another person, if that person has control of it or if that person and persons connected with him together have control of it.

(7) Any two or more persons acting together to secure or exercise control of a company shall be treated in relation to that company as connected with one another and with any person acting on the directions of any of them to secure or exercise control of the company.

(8) In this section "relative" means brother, sister, ancestor or lineal descendant.

Amendments.—[1] "1988" in sub-s. (3) inserted by virtue of TA 1988, Sch. 29, para. 15 (*a*).
[2] Numbers in sub-s. (3) substituted by TA 1988, Sch. 29, para. 32 Table.

PART IV
SHARES AND SECURITIES

CHAPTER I
GENERAL

64. Interpretation

(1) In this Act, unless the context otherwise requires—
"gilt-edged securities" has the meaning given by Schedule 2 to this Act,
["qualifying corporate bonds" has the meaning given by section 64 of the Finance Act 1984][1],
"shares" includes stock,
"class", in relation to shares or securities, means a class of shares or securities of any one company.

(2) For the purposes of this Act shares or debentures comprised in any letter of allotment or similar instrument shall be treated as issued unless the right to the shares or debentures thereby conferred remains provisional until accepted, and there has been no acceptance.

Cross references.—See TMA 1970, s. 25 (9) (powers of inspector of taxes to obtain particulars of chargeable gains of issuing houses, stockbrokers, auctioneers, etc.).
Amendments.—[1] Words in sub-s. (1) inserted by FA 1984, Sch. 13, para. 1.

Rules of identification

Note.—The provisions of sections 65 and 66 do not apply to securities held on, or acquired on or after, 6 April 1982 or, in the case of a company, 1 April 1982. Instead FA 1982, ss. 88, 89 apply; see FA 1982, s. 88 (1); see also FA 1983, Sch. 6 (new pooling rules with effect from 6 April 1982).

65. Pooling

(1) This section has effect subject to—

(*a*) section 66 below, and

(*b*) paragraphs 3 and 13 (2) of Schedule 5 to this Act, . . .[1]

(2) Any number of securities of the same class held by one person in one capacity shall for the purposes of this Act be regarded as indistinguishable parts of a single asset (in this section referred to as a holding) growing or diminishing on the occasions on which additional securities of the class in question are acquired, or some of the securities of the class in question are disposed of.

(3) Without prejudice to the generality of subsection (2) above, a disposal of securities in a holding, other than the disposal outright of the entire holding, is a disposal of part of an asset and the provisions of this Act relating to the computation of a gain accruing on a disposal of part of an asset shall apply accordingly.

(4) Shares, or securities of a company, shall not be treated for the purposes of this section as being of the same class unless they are so treated by the practice of a recognised stock exchange in the United Kingdom or elsewhere or would be so treated if dealt with on such a stock exchange, but shall be treated in accordance with this section notwithstanding that they are identified in some other way by the disposal or by the transfer or delivery giving effect to it.

(5) This section shall apply separately in relation to any securities held by a person to whom they were issued as an employee of the company or of any other person on terms which restrict his rights to dispose of them, so long as those terms are in force, and, while applying separately to any such securities, shall have effect as if the owner held them in a capacity other than that in which he holds any other securities of the same class.

(6) Nothing in this section shall be taken as affecting the manner in which the market value of any asset is to be ascertained.

(7) In this section "securities" means—

(a) shares, or securities of a company, and
(b) ...[1] any other assets where they are of a nature to be dealt in without identifying the particular assets disposed of or acquired.

Note.—The provisions of this section and section 66 below do not apply to securities held on, or acquired on or after 6 April 1982 or, in the case of a company, 1 April 1982. Instead FA 1982, ss. 88, 89 apply; see FA 1982, s. 88 (1); see also FA 1983, Sch. 6 (new pooling rules with effect from 6 April 1982).
Cross references.—See FA 1982, Sch. 13, Pt. II (discontinuation of pooling rules under this section for securities subject to indexation allowance; provisions for existing share pools);
FA 1983, Sch. 6, para. 1 (2) (b) (new pooling rules with effect from 6 April 1982);
FA 1985, Sch. 19, para. 17 (1) (disposal of securities after 5 April 1985 or 31 March 1985 in the case of companies; new pooling provisions replacing the provisions of this section).
Amendments.—[1] Words in sub-ss. (1) (b), (7) (b) repealed by FA 1985, Sch. 27, Pt. VII with respect to disposals after 1 July 1986.

66. Disposal on or before day of acquisition

Note.—The provisions of this section and section 65 above do not apply to securities held on, or acquired on or after 6 April 1982 or, in the case of a company, 1 April 1982. Instead FA 1982, ss. 88, 89 apply; see FA 1982, s. 88 (1); see also FA 1983, Sch. 6 (new pooling rules with effect from 6 April 1982).

(1) The following provisions shall apply where securities of the same kind are acquired or disposed of by the same person on the same day and in the same capacity—

(a) all the securities so acquired shall be treated as acquired by a single transaction and all the securities so disposed of shall be treated as disposed of by a single transaction, and
(b) all the securities so acquired shall, so far as their quantity does not exceed that of the securities so disposed of, be identified with those securities.

(2) Where the quantity of the securities so disposed of exceeds the quantity of the securities so acquired, then so far as the excess—

(a) is not required by paragraph 2 (2), 3 (3) or 13 (3) of Schedule 5 to this Act to be identified with securities held on or acquired before 6th April 1965, and
(b) cannot be treated under section 65 above as diminishing a holding,

it shall be treated as diminishing a quantity subsequently acquired, and a quantity so acquired at an earlier date, rather than one so acquired at a later date.

(3) Shares shall not be treated for the purposes of this section as being of the same kind unless they are treated as being of the same class by the practice of a recognised stock exchange in the United Kingdom or elsewhere or would be so treated if dealt with on such a stock exchange.

(4) In this section "securities" includes shares and any assets dealt with without identifying the particular assets disposed of or acquired, ...[1]

Cross references.—See FA 1985, Sch. 19, para. 17 (extension and modification of this section in respect of securities not forming part of a pre-April 1982 holding),
Sch. 19, para. 18 (disposal and acquisition after 5 April 1985 or 31 March 1985 in the case of companies of securities of the same class made within a period of ten days),
Sch. 19 para. 19 (1) (extension of this section in relation to identification of securities not included in a pre-April 1982 holding not in a post-April 1982 holding).
Amendments.—[1] Words in sub-s. (4) repealed by FA 1985, Sch. 27, Pt. VII with respect to disposals after 1 July 1986.

Gilt-edged securities

[67. Exemptions for gilt-edged securities and qualifying corporate bonds etc.

(1) A gain which accrues on the disposal by any person of—

(a) gilt-edged securities or qualifying corporate bonds, or
(b) any option or contract to acquire or dipsose of gilt-edged securities or qualifying corporate bonds,

shall not be a chargeable gain.

(2) In subsection (1) above the reference to the disposal of a contract to acquire or dispose of gilt-edged securities or qualifying corporate bonds is a reference to the disposal of the outstanding obligations under such a contract.

(3) Without prejudice to section 72 (3) of the Finance Act 1985 (closing out of certain

futures contracts dealt in on a recognised futures exchange), where a person who has entered into any such contract as is referred to in subsection (1) (*b*) above closes out that contract by entering into another contract with obligations which are reciprocal to those of the first-mentioned contract, that transaction shall for the purposes of this section constitute the disposal of an asset, namely, his outstanding obligations under the first-mentioned contract.]¹

Cross references.—See FA 1984, s. 64 (7) and Sch. 13, para. 10 (1) (*c*) (reorganisations etc. involving transactions whereby qualifying corporate bonds are exchanged for other securities);
TA 1988, s. 439 (8) (restricted government securities).
Amendments.—¹ This section substituted by FA 1986, s. 59 with respect to disposals occurring after 1 July 1986.

68. Identification (general)

Amendments.—This section repealed by FA 1985, Sch. 27, Pt. VII with respect to disposals after 1 July 1986.

69. Identification: disposal to husband or wife and third person

Amendments.—This section repealed by FA 1985, Sch. 27, Pt. VII with respect to disposals after 1 July 1986.

70. Re-acquisition after sale at a loss

Amendments.—This section repealed by FA 1985, Sch. 27, Pt. VII with respect to disposals after 1 July 1986.

Savings certificates, etc.

71. Exemption for government non-marketable securities

(1) Savings certificates and non-marketable securities issued under the National Loans Act 1968 or the National Loans Act 1939, or any corresponding enactment forming part of the law of Northern Ireland, shall not be chargeable assets, and accordingly no chargeable gain shall accrue on their disposal.

(2) In this section—

(*a*) "savings certificates" means savings certificates issued under section 12 of the National Loans Act 1968, or section 7 of the National Debt Act 1958, or section 59 of the Finance Act 1920, and any war savings certificates as defined in section 9 (3) of the National Debt Act 1972, together with any savings certificates issued under any enactment forming part of the law of Northern Ireland and corresponding to the said enactments, and

(*b*) "non-marketable securities" means securities which are not transferable, or which are transferable only with the consent of some Minister of the Crown, or the consent of a department of the Government of Northern Ireland, or only with the consent of the National Debt Commissioners.

Cross references.—See TMA 1970, s. 12 (2) (information about chargeable gains).

Capital distribution in respect of shares, etc.

72. Distribution which is not a new holding within Chapter II

(1) Where a person receives or becomes entitled to receive in respect of shares in a company any capital distribution from the company (other than a new holding as defined in section 77 below) he shall be treated as if he had in consideration of that capital distribution disposed of an interest in the shares.

(2) If the inspector is satisfied that the amount distributed is small, as compared with the value of the shares in respect of which it is distributed, and so directs—

(*a*) the occasion of the capital distribution shall not be treated for the purposes of this Act as a disposal of the asset, and

(*b*) the amount distributed shall be deducted from any expenditure allowable under this Act as a deduction in computing a gain or loss on the disposal of the shares by the person receiving or becoming entitled to receive the distribution of capital.

(3) A person who is dissatisfied with the refusal of the inspector to give a direction under this section may appeal to the Commissioners having jurisdiction on an appeal against an assessment to tax in respect of a gain accruing on the disposal.

(4) Where the allowable expenditure is less than the amount distributed (or is nil)—

(a) subsections (2) and (3) above shall not apply, and
(b) if the recipient so elects (and there is any allowable expenditure)—

(i) the amount distributed shall be reduced by the amount of the allowable expenditure, and
(ii) none of that expenditure shall be allowable as a deduction in computing a gain accruing on the occasion of the capital distribution, or on any subsequent occasion.

In this subsection "allowable expenditure" means the expenditure which immediately before the occasion of the capital distribution was attributable to the shares under paragraphs (a) and (b) of section 32 (1) above.

(5) In this section—

(a) the "amount distributed" means the amount or value of the capital distribution,
(b) "capital distribution" means any distribution from a company, including a distribution in the course of dissolving or winding up the company, in money or money's worth except a distribution which in the hands of the recipient constitutes income for the purposes of income tax.

Cross references.—See FA 1980, Sch. 18, para. 9 (a) (exempt distribution under para. 2 (1) (a) of that Schedule not to be a capital distribution for the purposes of this section);
FA 1985, s. 69 (2) (c) (capital gains tax relief in respect of a disposal within this section made after 5 April 1985 by an individual who is retired from family business or at the time of disposal is 60 or suffering from ill-health),
Sch. 20, paras. 11 (1) (a), 12 (5) (a) (computation of capital gains qualifying for relief in respect of disposals falling within this section and FA 1985, ss. 69, 70 (CGT relief on retirement));
FA 1989, Sch. 15, para. 3 (expenditure disallowed under sub-s. (4) of this section to be deducted from the new 1982 base cost where the disallowance relates to part disposals made after 31 March 1982 but before 6 April 1988).

73. Disposal of right to acquire shares

(1) Where a person receives or becomes entitled to receive in respect of any shares in a company a provisional allotment of shares in or debentures of the company and he disposes of his rights section 72 above shall apply as if the amount of the consideration for the disposal were a capital distribution received by him from the company in respect of the first-mentioned shares, and as if that person had, instead of disposing of the rights, disposed of an interest in those shares.

(2) If under Schedule 5 to this Act it is to be assumed that, at a time after the creation of the rights and before their disposal, the said person sold and immediately re-acquired the shares in respect of which the rights were created, the same assumption shall be made as respects the rights.

(3) This section shall apply in relation to rights obtained in respect of debentures of a company as it applies in relation to rights obtained in respect of shares in a company.

Close companies

74. Disposal of shares: relief in respect of income tax consequent on shortfall in distributions

(1) If in pursuance of [section 426 of the Taxes Act 1988][1] (consequences for income tax of apportionment of income etc. of close company) a person is assessed to income tax, then, in the computation under Chapter II of Part II of this Act of the gain accruing on a disposal by him of any shares forming part of his interest in the company to which the relevant apportionment relates, the amount of the income tax paid by him, so far as attributable to those shares, shall be allowable as a deduction.

(2) Subsection (1) above shall not apply in relation to tax charged in respect of undistributed income which has, before the disposal, been subsequently distributed and is then exempt from tax by virtue of [section 427 (4) of the Taxes Act 1988][1] or in relation to tax treated as having been paid by virtue of [section 426 (b) of that Act].[1]

(3) For the purposes of this section the income assessed to tax shall be the highest part of the individual's income for the year of assessment in question, but so that if the highest part of the said income is taken into account under this section in relation to an assessment to

tax the next highest part shall be taken into account in relation to any other relevant assessment, and so on.

(4) For the purpose of identifying shares forming part of an interest in a company with shares subsequently disposed of which are of the same class, shares bought at an earlier time shall be deemed to have been disposed of before shares bought at a later time.

(5) The provisions of this section shall be construed as if this section [were included in sections 426 to 428 of the Taxes Act 1988].[1]

Amendments.—[1] Words in sub-ss. (1), (2), (5) substituted by TA 1988, Sch. 29, para. 32 Table.

75. Shares in close company transferring assets at an undervalue

(1) If after 6th April 1965 a company which is a close company transfers an asset to any person otherwise than by way of a bargain made at arm's length and for a consideration of an amount or value less than the market value of the asset an amount equal to the difference shall be apportioned among the issued shares of the company, and the holders of those shares shall be treated in accordance with the following provisions of this section.

(2) For the purposes of the computation under Chapter II of Part II of this Act of a gain accruing on the disposal of any of those shares by the person owning them on the date of transfer an amount equal to the amount so apportioned to that share shall be excluded from the expenditure allowable as a deduction under section 32 (1) (a) above from the consideration for the disposal.

(3) If the person owning any of the said shares at the date of transfer is itself a close company an amount equal to the amount apportioned to the shares so owned under subsection (1) above to that close company shall be apportioned among the issued shares of that close company, and the holders of those shares shall be treated in accordance with subsection (2) above, and so on through any number of close companies.

(4) This section shall not apply where the transfer of the asset is a disposal to which section 273 (1) of the Taxes Act [1970][1] (transfers within a group of companies) applies.

Cross references.—See FA 1988, Sch. 8, para. 7 (application of indexation allowance re-based to 1982 in relation to unindexed capital gains and losses accruing on disposals after 5 April 1988 of assets held on 31 March 1982; this section to apply with the date in sub-s. (1) as 31 March 1982 instead of 6 April 1965).
Amendments.—[1] "1970" in sub-s. (4) inserted by virtue of TA 1988, Sch. 29, para. 15 (b).

Share option schemes

76. Consideration for acquisition of shares under share option schemes

Section 19 (3) above (assets deemed acquired and disposed of at market value) shall not apply in calculating the consideration for the acquisition of shares in pursuance of a share option scheme as defined in Schedule 12 to the Finance Act 1972.

Note.—S. 19 (3) is repealed by FA 1981, s. 90 (3), (4) and Sch. 19, Pt. VIII and is superseded by s. 29A (1), *ante* in relation to acquisitions and disposals after 9 March 1981.

CHAPTER II

REORGANISATION OF SHARE CAPITAL, CONVERSION OF SECURITIES, ETC.

Cross references.—See FA 1984, s. 64 (7) and Sch. 13, paras. 7, 8 (reorganisations etc. involving transactions whereby qualifying corporate bonds are exchanged for other securities).

Reorganisation or reduction of share capital

77. Application of sections 78 to 81

(1) For the purposes of this section and sections 78 to 81 below "reorganisation" means a reorganisation or reduction of a company's share capital, and in relation to the reorganisation—

(*a*) "original shares" means shares held before and concerned in the reorganisation,
(*b*) "new holding" means, in relation to any original shares, the shares in and debentures of the company which as a result of the reorganisation represent the original shares (including such, if any, of the original shares as remain).

(2) The reference in subsection (1) above to the reorganisation of a company's share capital includes—

(*a*) any case where persons are, whether for payment or not, allotted shares in or debentures of the company in respect of and in proportion to (or as nearly as may be in proportion to) their holdings of shares in the company or of any class of shares in the company, and
(*b*) any case where there are more than one class of share and the rights attached to shares of any class are altered.

(3) The reference in subsection (1) above to a reduction of share capital does not include the paying off of redeemable share capital, and where shares in a company are redeemed by the company otherwise than by the issue of shares or debentures (with or without other consideration) and otherwise than in a liquidation, the shareholder shall be treated as disposing of the shares at the time of the redemption.

Cross references.—See FA 1980, Sch. 18, para. 9 (*b*) (application of this section to exempt distributions on a demerger); TA 1988, s. 139 (13) (application of this section in the case of a person who acquires new shares after 18 March 1986 in exchange for original shares),
s. 305 (business expansion scheme: reorganisation of share capital after 18 March 1986),
s. 473 (2) (*a*) (conversion of securities held as trading stock by banks, insurance companies and dealers in securities).

78. Equation of original shares and new holding

Subject to sections 79 to 81 below, a reorganisation shall not be treated as involving any disposal of the original shares or any acquisition of the new holding or any part of it, but the original shares (taken as a single asset) and the new holding (taken as a single asset) shall be treated as the same asset acquired as the original shares were acquired.

Cross references.—See FA 1980, Sch. 18, para. 9 (*b*) (application of this section to exempt distributions on a demerger); FA 1982, Sch. 13, para. 5 (on a reorganisation or a reconstruction after 31 March 1982, the new shares will be equated with the original shares as provided for in this section, but for calculating the indexation allowance any consideration for the new shares will be treated as paid on the date on which it was actually paid);
FA 1984, s. 64 (7) and Sch.13, para. 7, 8 (reorganisations etc. involving transactions whereby qualifying corporate bonds are exchanged for other securities);
FA 1985, Sch. 20, para. 2 (discretion to exclude the application of this section where as part of a reorganisation of a company the disposal of securities attract CGT retirement relief under FA 1985, ss. 69, 70);
TA 1988, s. 139 (13) (application of this section in the case of a person who acquires new shares after 18 March 1986 in exchange for original shares),
s. 305 (business expansion scheme: reorganisation of share capital after 18 March 1986),
s. 473 (2) (*a*) (conversion of securities held as trading stock by banks, insurance companies and dealers in securities),
s. 757 (1) (disposals after 31 December 1984 of material interest in certain assets of UK resident companies or unit trust schemes which at a material time after 31 December 1984 were non-qualifying offshore funds),
Sch. 4, para. 7 (3) (reorganisations etc. involving transactions whereby deep discount securities are exchanged; notwithstanding this section, the original securities are deemed to have been disposed of by the beneficiary);
FA 1988, s. 82 (3) (*a*) (acquisition of shares after 25 October 1987 in an unapproved employee share scheme; application of this section where new holding is acquired in place of original shares);
FA 1989, s. 140 (3), (4), (5) (notwithstanding this section, exchange of rights after 13 March 1989 in collective investment schemes to constitute a disposal and acquisition).

79. Consideration given or received by holder

(1) Where, on a reorganisation, a person gives or becomes liable to give any consideration for his new holding or any part of it, that consideration shall in relation to any disposal of the new holding or any part of it be treated as having been given for the original shares, and if the new holding or part of it is disposed of with a liability attaching to it in respect of that consideration, the consideration given for the disposal shall be adjusted accordingly:

Provided that there shall not be treated as consideration given for the new holding or any part of it any surrender, cancellation or other alteration to the original shares or of the rights attached thereto, or any consideration consisting of any application, in paying up the new holding or any part of it, of assets of the company or of any dividend or other distribution declared out of those assets but not made.

[Provided also that, in the case of a reorganisation on or after 10th March 1981, any consideration given for the new holding or any part of it otherwise than by way of a bargain made at arm's length shall be disregarded to the extent that its amount or value exceeds the relevant increase in value; and for this purpose "the relevant increase in value" means the amount by which the market value of the new holding immediately after the reorganisation exceeds the market value of the original shares immediately before the reorganisation.][1]

(2) Where on a reorganisation a person receives (or is deemed to receive), or becomes entitled to receive, any consideration, other than the new holding, for the disposal of an interest in the original shares, and in particular—

(*a*) where under section 72 above he is to be treated as if he had in consideration of a capital distribution disposed of an interest in the original shares, or
(*b*) where he receives (or is deemed to receive) consideration from other shareholders in respect of a surrender of rights derived from the original shares,

he shall be treated as if the new holding resulted from his having for that consideration disposed of an interest in the original shares (but without prejudice to the original shares and the new holding being treated in accordance with section 78 above as the same asset).

(3) Where for the purpose of subsection (2) above it is necessary in computing the gain or loss accruing on the disposal of the interest in the original shares mentioned in subsection (2) above to apportion the cost of acquisition of the original shares between what is disposed of and what is retained, the apportionment shall be made in the like manner as under section 80 (1) below.

Cross references.—See FA 1980, Sch. 18, para. 9 (*b*) (application of this section to exempt distributions on a demerger); FA 1982, Sch. 13, para. 5 (on a reorganisation or a reconstruction after 31 March 1982, the date of payment of consideration for the new shares will be the date on which it was actually paid);
FA 1984, s. 64 (7) and Sch. 13, paras. 7, 8 (reorganisations etc. involving transactions whereby qualifying corporate bonds are exchanged for other securities);
TA 1988, s. 139 (13) (acquisition of new shares after 18 March 1986 in exchange for the original holding; treatment of the consideration given or received as mentioned in sub-ss. (1), (2) above),
s. 305 (business expansion scheme: reorganisation of share capital; this section not to apply in relation to reorganisation after 18 March 1986 affecting ordinary shares if certain conditions exist),
s. 473 (2) (*a*) (conversion of securities held as trading stock by banks, insurance companies and dealers in securities).
Amendments.—[1] Second proviso in sub-s. (1) added by FA 1981, s. 91 (1).

80. Part disposal of new holding

(1) Where for the purpose of computing the gain or loss accruing to a person from the acquisition and disposal of any part of the new holding it is necessary to apportion the cost of acquisition of any of the original shares between what is disposed of and what is retained, the apportionment shall be made by reference to market value at the date of the disposal (with such adjustment of the market value of any part of the new holding as may be required to offset any liability attaching thereto but forming part of the cost to be apportioned).

(2) This section has effect subject to section 81 (2) below.

Cross references.—See FA 1980, Sch. 18, para. 9 (*b*) (application of this section to exempt distributions on a demerger);
FA 1984, s. 64 (7) and Sch. 13, paras. 7, 8 (reorganisations etc. involving transactions whereby qualifying corporate bonds are exchanged for other securities);
TA 1988, s. 305 (business expansion scheme: reorganisation of share capital; this section not to apply in relation to reorganisation after 18 March 1986 affecting ordinary shares if certain conditions exist),
s. 473 (2) (*a*) (conversion of securities held as trading stock by banks, insurance companies and dealers in securities).

81. Composite new holdings

(1) This section shall apply to a new holding—

(a) if it consists of more than one class of shares in or debentures of the company and one or more of those classes is of shares or debentures which, at any time not later than the end of the period of three months beginning with the date on which the reorganisation took effect, or of such longer period as the Board may by notice in writing allow, had quoted market values on a recognised stock exchange in the United Kingdom or elsewhere, or

(b) if it consists of more than one class of rights of unit holders and one or more of those classes is of rights the prices of which were published daily by the managers of the scheme at any time not later than the end of that period of three months (or longer if so allowed).

(2) Where for the purpose of computing the gain or loss accruing to a person from the acquisition and disposal of the whole or any part of any class of shares or debentures or rights of unit holders forming part of a new holding to which this section applies it is necessary to apportion costs of acquisition between what is disposed of and what is retained, the cost of acquisition of the new holding shall first be apportioned between the entire classes of shares or debentures or rights of which it consists by reference to market value on the first day (whether that day fell before the reorganisation took effect or later) on which market values or prices were quoted or published for the shares, debentures or rights as mentioned in subsection (1) (a) or (1) (b) above (with such adjustment of the market value of any class as may be required to offset any liability attaching thereto but forming part of the cost to be apportioned).

(3) For the purposes of this section the day on which a reorganisation involving the allotment of shares or debentures or unit holders' rights takes effect is the day following the day on which the right to renounce any allotment expires.

Cross references.—See FA 1980, Sch. 18, para. 9 (b) (application of this section to exempt distributions on a demerger); FA 1984, s. 64 (7) and Sch. 13, paras. 7, 8 (reorganisations etc. involving transactions whereby qualifying corporate bonds are exchanged for other securities);
TA 1988, s. 305 (business expansion scheme: reorganisation of share capital; this section not to apply in relation to reorganisation after 18 March 1986 affecting ordinary shares if certain conditions exist),
s. 473 (2) (a) (conversion of securities held as trading stock by banks, insurance companies and dealers in securities).

Conversion of securities

82. Equation of converted securities and new holding

(1) Sections 78 to 81 above shall apply with any necessary adaptations in relation to the conversion of securities as they apply in relation to a reorganisation (that is to say a reorganisation or reduction of a company's share capital).

(2) This section has effect subject to sections 83 and 84 below.

(3) For the purposes of this section and section 83 below—

(a) "conversion of securities" includes—

(i) a conversion of securities of a company into shares in the company, and
(ii) a conversion at the option of the holder of the securities converted as an alternative to the redemption of those securities for cash, and
(iii) any exchange of securities effected in pursuance of any enactment (including an enactment passed after this Act) which provides for the compulsory acquisition of any shares or securities and the issue of securities or other securities instead,

(b) "security" includes any loan stock or similar security whether of the Government of the United Kingdom or of any other government, or of any public or local authority in the United Kingdom or elsewhere, or of any company, and whether secured or unsecured.

Cross references.—See F (No. 2) A 1975, s. 58 (12) (provisions to counter avoidance of corporation tax on capital gains on disposal, after 14 April 1975, of securities, as defined in this section, within prescribed period of acquisition);
FA 1976, s. 54 (5) (capital gains: compulsory acquisition of aircraft and shipbuilding shares);
TA 1988, s. 473 (2) (a) (conversion of securities held as trading stock by banks, insurance companies and dealers in securities),
Sch. 4, para. 2 (4) (acceleration of tax charge in respect of deep discount securities issued by a company after 18 March 1985 on a conversion to which this section applies),
Sch. 4, para. 7 (3) (reorganisations etc. involving transactions in which securities converted or exchanged include deep discount securities).

83. Premiums on conversion of securities

(1) This section applies where, on a conversion of securities, a person receives, or becomes entitled to receive, any sum of money (in this section called "the premium") which is by way of consideration (in addition to his new holding) for the disposal of the converted securities.

(2) If the inspector is satisfied that the premium is small, as compared with the value of the converted securities, and so directs—

(a) receipt of the premium shall not be treated for the purposes of this Act as a disposal of part of the converted securities, and
(b) the premium shall be deducted from any expenditure allowable under this Act as a deduction in computing a gain or loss on the disposal of the new holding by the person receiving or becoming entitled to receive the premium.

(3) A person who is dissatisfied with the refusal of the inspector to give a direction under subsection (2) above may appeal to the Commissioners having jurisdiction on an appeal against an assessment to tax in respect of a gain accruing to him on a disposal of the securities.

(4) Where the allowable expenditure is less than the premium (or is nil)—

(a) subsections (2) and (3) above shall not apply, and
(b) if the recipient so elects (and there is any allowable expenditure)—

(i) the amount of the premium shall be reduced by the amount of the allowable expenditure, and
(ii) none of that expenditure shall be allowable as a deduction in computing a gain accruing on the occasion of the conversion, or on any subsequent occasion.

(5) In subsection (4) above "allowable expenditure" means expenditure which immediately before the conversion was attributable to the converted securities under paragraphs (a) and (b) of section 32 (1) above.

Cross references.—See TA 1988, s. 473 (2) (a) (conversion of securities held as trading stock by banks, insurance companies and dealers in securities;
FA 1989, Sch. 15, para. 3 (expenditure disallowed under sub-s. (4) of this section to be deducted from the new 1982 base cost where the disallowance relates to part disposals made after 31 March 1982 but before 6 April 1988).

84. Compensation stock

(1) This section has effect where gilt-edged securities are exchanged for shares in pursuance of any enactment (including an enactment passed after this Act) which provides for the compulsory acquisition of any shares and the issue of gilt-edged securities instead.

(2) The exchange shall not constitute a conversion of securities within section 82 above and accordingly the gilt-edged securities shall not be treated as having been acquired on any date earlier than that on which they were issued or for any consideration other than the value of the shares as determined for the purposes of the exchange.

(3) The exchange shall be treated as not involving any disposal of the shares by the person from whom they were compulsorily acquired but—

(a) there shall be calculated the gain or loss that would have accrued to him if he had then disposed of the shares for a consideration equal to the value mentioned in subsection (2) above, and
(b) on a subsequent disposal of the whole or part of the gilt-edged securities by the person to whom they were issued—

(i) there shall be deemed to accrue to him (in addition to any gain or loss that actually accrues) the whole or a corresponding part of the gain or loss mentioned in paragraph (a) above, and
(ii) . . .[1] section 67 (1) above (exemption for gilt-edged securities) . . .[1] shall have effect only in relation to any gain or loss that actually accrues and not in relation to any gain or loss that is deemed to accrue as aforesaid.

(4) Where a person to whom gilt-edged securities of any kind were issued as mentioned in subsection (1) above disposes of securities of that kind, the securities of which he disposes—

[(a) shall, so far as possible, be identified with securities which were issued to him as mentioned in subsection (1) above rather than with other securities of that kind, and
(b) subject to paragraph (a) above, shall be identified with securities issued at an earlier time rather than with those issued at a later time][2].

(5) Subsection (3) (*b*) above shall not apply to any disposal falling within the provisions of—

(*a*) section 44 (1) above (disposals between husband and wife),
(*b*) section 49 (4) above (disposals by personal representatives to legatees), or
(*c*) section 273 (1) of the Taxes Act [1970][3] (disposals within a group of companies);

but a person who has acquired the securities on a disposal falling within those provisions (and without there having been a previous disposal not falling within those provisions or a devolution on death) shall be treated for the purposes of subsections (3) (*b*) and (4) above as if the securities had been issued to him.

(6) Where the gilt-edged securities to be exchanged for any shares are not issued until after the date on which the shares are compulsorily acquired but on that date a right to the securities is granted, this section shall have effect as if the exchange had taken place on that date, as if references to the issue of the securities and the person to whom they were issued were references to the grant of the right and the person to whom it was granted and references to the disposal of the securities included references to disposals of the rights.

(7) In this section "shares" includes securities within the meaning of section 82 above.

(8) This section has effect subject to section 54 of the Finance Act 1976 (compulsory acquisition from certain companies of aircraft and shipbuilding shares).

Cross references.—See FA 1976, s. 54 (5) (capital gains: compulsory acquisition of aircraft and shipbuilding shares);
TA 1988, s. 473 (2) (*a*) (conversion of securities held as trading stock by banks, insurance companies and dealers in securities);
FA 1988, Sch. 9, para. 3 (reduction of a deferred charge to tax where the charge is wholly or partly attributable to an increase in the value of an asset before 31 March 1982);
FA 1989, Sch. 15, para. 1 (this section not to apply in consequence of an event occurring after 5 April 1988 if its application is directly attributable to the disposal of an asset before 1 April 1982).
Amendments.—[1] Words in sub-s. (3) (*b*) (ii) repealed by FA 1985, Sch. 27, Pt. VII with respect to disposals after 1 July 1986.
[2] Sub-s. (4) (*a*), (*b*) substituted by FA 1985, s. 67 (2) (*b*) with respect to disposals after 1 July 1986.
[3] "1970" in sub-s. (5) (*c*) inserted by virtue of TA 1988, Sch. 29, para. 15 (*b*).

Company reconstructions and amalgamations

85. Exchange of securities for those in another company

(1) Subsection (3) below has effect where a company (company A) issues shares or debentures to a person in exchange for shares in or debentures of another company (company B) and—

(*a*) company A holds, or in consequence of the exchange will hold, more than one quarter of the ordinary share capital (as defined in section [832 (1)][2] of the Taxes Act [1988][1]) of company B, or
(*b*) company A issues the shares or debentures in exchange for shares as the result of a general offer—

(i) which is made to members of company B or any class of them (with or without exceptions for persons connected with company A), and
(ii) which is made in the first instance on a condition such that if it were satisfied company A would have control of company B.

(2) Subsection (3) below also has effect where under section 86 below persons are to be treated as exchanging shares or debentures for shares or debentures held by them in consequence of the arrangement there mentioned.

(3) Subject to the provisions of sections 87 and 88 below, sections 78 to 81 above shall apply with any necessary adaptations as if the two companies mentioned in subsection (1) above, or as the case may be in section 86 below, were the same company and the exchange were a reorganisation of its share capital.

Cross references.—See FA 1985, Sch. 20, para. 2 (2) (deemed reorganisation under sub-s. (3) above to be regarded as reorganisation for the purposes of CGT retirement relief under FA 1985, ss. 69, 70);
TA 1988, s. 473 (2) (*a*) (conversion of securities held as trading stock by banks, insurance companies and dealers in securities),
s. 757 (5), (6) (reconstructions etc. after 31 December 1984 where company A is not a non-qualifying offshore fund and company B is a non-qualifying offshore fund),
Sch. 4, para. 2 (4) (*b*) (acceleration of tax charge in respect of deep discount securities issued by a company after 18 March 1985 in exchange of old securities in circumstances in which sub-s. (3) above applies),
Sch. 4, para. 7 (3) (reconstructions etc. involving transactions whereby securities including deep discount securities are exchanged for other securities in circumstances in which sub-s. (3) above applies);

Amendments.—[1] "1988" in sub-s. (1) (*a*) inserted by virtue of TA 1988, Sch. 29, para. 15 (*a*).
[2] Number in sub-s. (1) substituted by TA 1988, Sch. 29, para. 32 Table.

86. Reconstruction or amalgamation involving issue of securities

(1) Where—

(*a*) an arrangement between a company and the persons holding shares in or debentures of the company, or any class of such shares or debentures, is entered into for the purposes of or in connection with a scheme of reconstruction or amalgamation, and

(*b*) under the arrangement another company issues shares or debentures to those persons in respect of and in proportion to (or as nearly as may be in proportion to) their holdings of shares in or debentures of the first-mentioned company, but the shares in or debentures of the first-mentioned company are either retained by those persons or cancelled,

then those persons shall be treated as exchanging the first-mentioned shares or debentures for those held by them in consequence of the arrangement (any shares or debentures retained being for this purpose regarded as if they had been cancelled and replaced by a new issue), and subsections (2) and (3) of section 85 above shall apply accordingly.

(2) In this section "scheme of reconstruction or amalgamation" means a scheme for the reconstruction of any company or companies or the amalgamation of any two or more companies, and references to shares or debentures being retained include their being retained with altered rights or in an altered form whether as the result of reduction, consolidation, division or otherwise.

(3) This section, and section 85 (2) above, shall apply in relation to a company which has no share capital as if references to shares in or debentures of a company included references to any interests in the company possessed by members of the company.

Cross references.—See TA 1988, s. 473 (2) (*a*) (conversion of securities held as trading stock by banks, insurance companies and dealers in securities),
s. 757 (5) (reconstructions etc. after 31 December 1984 involving transactions whereby interests in non-qualifying offshore funds are exchanged for assets which are not non-qualifying offshore funds),
Sch. 4, para. 2 (4) (*b*) (acceleration of tax charge in respect of deep discount securities issued by a company after 18 March 1985 and treated under sub-s. (1) as issued in exchange for old securities),
Sch. 4, para. 7 (3) (reconstructions etc. involving transactions whereby securities including deep discount securities are treated by virtue of sub-s. (1) above as exchanged for other securities in circumstances in which s. 85 (3) of this Act applies).

87. Restriction on application of sections 85 and 86

(1) Subject to subsection (2) below, and section 88 below, neither section 85 nor section 86 above shall apply to any issue by a company of shares in or debentures of that company in exchange for or in respect of shares in or debentures of another company unless the exchange, reconstruction or amalgamation in question is effected for bona fide commercial reasons and does not form part of a scheme or arrangements of which the main purpose, or one of the main purposes, is avoidance of liability to capital gains tax or corporation tax.

(2) Subsection (1) above shall not affect the operation of section 85 or 86 in any case where the person to whom the shares or debentures are issued does not hold more than 5 per cent. of, or of any class of, the shares in or debentures of the second company mentioned in subsection (1) above.

(3) For the purposes of subsection (2) above shares or debentures held by persons connected with the person there mentioned shall be treated as held by him.

(4) If any tax assessed on a person (the chargeable person) by virtue of subsection (1) above is not paid within six months from the date when it is payable, any other person who—

(*a*) holds all or any part of the shares or debentures that were issued to the chargeable person, and

(*b*) has acquired them without there having been, since their acquisition by the chargeable person, any disposal of them not falling within section 44 (1) above or section 273 of the Taxes Act [1970][1] (disposals between spouses or members of a group of companies),

may, at any time within two years from the time when the tax became payable, be assessed and charged (in the name of the chargeable person) to all or, as the case may be, a corresponding part of the unpaid tax; and a person paying any amount of tax under this subsection shall be entitled to recover a sum of that amount from the chargeable person.

(5) In this section references to shares or debentures include references to any interests or options to which this Chapter applies by virtue of section 86 (3) above (interests in a company with no share capital) or section 139 below (quoted options).

Note.—See **Prospective Legislation Notes** (Taxes Management Provisions).
Cross references.—See TA 1988, s. 473 (7) (reference in sub-s. (1) of this section to capital gains tax to be construed as a reference to income tax for determining whether conversion of certain securities would result in the original holding being equated with a new holding).
Amendments.—[1] "1970" in sub-s. (4) (b) inserted by virtue of TA 1988, Sch. 29, para. 15 (b).

88. Procedure for clearance in advance

(1) Section 87 above shall not affect the operation of section 85 or 86 above in any case where, before the issue is made, the Board have, on the application of either company mentioned in section 87 (1) above, notified the company that the Board are satisfied that the exchange, reconstruction or amalgamation will be effected for bona fide commercial reasons and will not form part of any such scheme or arrangements as are mentioned in section 87 (1) above.

(2) Any application under subsection (1) above shall be in writing and shall contain particulars of the operations that are to be effected and the Board may, within thirty days of the receipt of the application or of any further particulars previously required under this subsection, by notice require the applicant to furnish further particulars for the purpose of enabling the Board to make their decision; and if any such notice is not complied with within thirty days or such longer period as the Board may allow, the Board need not proceed further on the application.

(3) The Board shall notify their decision to the applicant within thirty days of receiving the application or, if they give a notice under subsection (2) above, within thirty days of the notice being complied with.

(4) If the Board notify the applicant that they are not satisfied as mentioned in subsection (1) above or do not notify their decision to the applicant within the time required by subsection (3) above, the applicant may within thirty days of the notification or of that time require the Board to transmit the application, together with any notice given and further particulars furnished under subsection (2) above, to the Special Commissioners; and in that event any notification by the Special Commissioners shall have effect for the purposes of subsection (1) above as if it were a notification by the Board.

(5) If any particulars furnished under this section do not fully and accurately disclose all facts and considerations material for the decision of the Board or the Special Commissioners, any resulting notification that the Board or Commissioners are satisfied as mentioned in subsection (1) above shall be void.

Cross references.—See TA 1970, s. 267 (3A) (sub-ss. (2) to (5) of this section to have effect in relation to TA 1970, s. 267 (3A)).

Stock dividends

89. Stock dividends: consideration for new holding

(1) In applying section 79 (1) above in relation to the issue of any share capital to which section [249 of the Taxes Act 1988][2] (stock dividends) applies as involving a reorganisation of the company's share capital, there shall be allowed, as consideration given for so much of the new holding as was issued as mentioned in—

(a) subsection (4), (5) or (6) of [that section],[2] . . .[3]
(b) . . .[3]

(read in each case with subsection (3) of [that section][2]) an amount equal to what is, for that much of the new holding, the appropriate amount in cash within the meaning of [section 251 (2) of the Taxes Act 1988].[2]

(2) This section shall have effect notwithstanding the [provisos][1] to section 79 (1) above.

Amendments.—[1] Word in sub-s. (2) substituted by FA 1981, s. 91 (2) (a).
[2] Words in sub-s. (1) substituted by TA 1988, Sch. 29, para. 32 Table.
[3] Sub-s. (1)(b) and the preceding word "or" repealed by FA 1989, Sch. 17, Pt. V.

90. Capital gains on certain stock dividends

(1) This section applies where a company issues any share capital to which section [249 of the Taxes Act 1988][2] applies in respect of shares in the company held by a person as trustee, and another person is at the time of the issue absolutely entitled thereto as against the trustee or would be so entitled but for being an infant or other person under disability (or two or more other persons are or would be jointly so entitled thereto).

(2) Notwithstanding paragraph (*a*) of section 77 (2) above the case shall not constitute a reorganisation of the company's share capital for the purposes of sections 77 to 79 above.

(3) Notwithstanding section [29A (1)][1] above (disposal at market value) the person who is or would be so entitled to the share capital (or each of the persons who are or would be jointly so entitled thereto) shall be treated for the purposes of section 32 (1) (*a*) above as having acquired that share capital, or his interest in it, for a consideration equal to the appropriate amount in cash within the meaning of [section 251 (2) to (4) of the Taxes Act 1988].[2]

Amendments.—[1] Words in sub-s. (3) substituted by FA 1981, s. 90 (3) (*a*).
[2] Words in sub-ss. (1), (3) substituted by TA 1988, Sch. 29, para. 32 Table.

Quoted options

91. Application of Chapter II to quoted options

The preceding provisions of this Chapter have effect subject to section 139 below (quoted option to be regarded for the purposes of this Chapter as the shares which could be acquired by exercising the option).

CHAPTER III

UNIT TRUSTS ETC.

Preliminary

92. Interpretation

[(1) Subject to subsection (2) below, in this Act—][1]

[(a) "unit trust scheme" has the same meaning as in the Financial Services Act 1986][1],
(b) "authorised unit trust" has the meaning given by section [468 (6)][4] of the Taxes Act [1988][3],
(c) "investment trust" has the meaning given by section [842][4] of the Taxes Act [1988][3],
(d) "court investment fund" means a common investment fund established under section 1 of the Administration of Justice Act 1965.

[(2) The Treasury may by regulations provide that any scheme of a description specified in the regulations shall be treated as not being a unit trust scheme for the purposes of this Act.][2]

[(3) Regulations under this section—

(a) may contain such supplementary and transitional provisions as appear to the Treasury to be necessary or expedient, and
(b) shall be made by statutory instrument, which shall be subject to annulment in pursuance of a resolution of the House of Commons.][2]

Amendments.—Sub-s. (1) (a) and the words preceding it substituted by FA 1987, s. 40 (3), (5) with effect from 11 March 1988 by virtue of FA 1987 (Commencement) (No. 1) Order 1988, S.I. 1988 No. 179.
[2] Sub-ss. (2), (3) added by FA 1987, s. 40 (4), (5) with effect from 18 February 1988 by virtue of FA 1987 (Commencement) (No. 1) Order 1988, S.I. 1988 No. 179.
[3] "1988" in sub-s. (1) (b), (c) inserted by virtue of TA 1988, Sch. 29, para. 15 (a).
[4] Numbers in sub-s. (1) (b), (c) substituted by TA 1988, Sch. 29, para. 32 Table.

93. Application of Act to unit trusts

This Act shall apply in relation to any unit trust scheme as if—

(a) the scheme were a company,
(b) the rights of the unit holders were shares in the company, and
(c) in the case of an authorised unit trust, the company were resident and ordinarily resident in the United Kingdom.

General

94. Reduction of tax liability on disposal of units or shares

Amendments.—Repealed by FA 1980, s. 81 (6), (7) and Sch. 20, Pt. X, in relation to disposals after 5 April 1980.

Unit trusts

95. Valuation of assets and rights

Amendments.—Repealed by FA 1980, Sch. 20, Pt. X, in relation to accounting periods beginning after 5 April 1980.

96. Unit trusts for exempt unit holders

If throughout a year of assessment all the issued units in a unit trust scheme are assets such that any gain accruing if they were disposed of by the unit holder would be wholly exempt from capital gains tax or corporation tax (otherwise than by reason of residence) gains accruing to the unit trust scheme in that year of assessment shall not be chargeable gains.

Cross references.—See TA 1970, s. 267 (3) (company amalgamations and reconstructions).

97. Unit trusts for pension schemes

Amendments.—Repealed by FA 1980, Sch. 20, Pt. X, in relation to disposals after 5 April 1980.

98. Transfer of company's assets to unit trust which later comes within section 96 *or 97*

(1) Where section 267 of the Taxes Act [1970][3] (roll-over for assets transferred on company reconstruction or amalgamation) has applied on the transfer of a company's business (in whole or in part) to a unit trust scheme [or a company which at the time of the transfer was not such a unit trust scheme or investment trust as is mentioned in subsection (3) of that section, then if—

(*a*) at any time after the transfer—

(i) the unit trust scheme becomes in a year of assessment one which is such as is mentioned in that subsection; or
(ii) the company becomes for an accounting period an investment trust such as is there mentioned, and

(*b*) at the beginning of that year of assessment or accounting period the unit trust scheme or company still owns any of the assets of the business transferred,

the unit trust scheme or company shall be treated][1] for all the purposes of this Act as if immediately after the transfer it had sold, and immediately re-acquired, the assets referred to in paragraph (*b*) above at their market value at that time.

(2) Notwithstanding any limitation on the time for making assessments, an assessment to corporation tax chargeable in consequence of subsection (1) above may be made at any time within six years after the end of the year of assessment [or accounting period][2] referred to in subsection (1) above, and where under this section a unit trust scheme [or company][2] is to be treated as having disposed of, and reacquired, an asset of a business, all such recomputations of liability in respect of other disposals and all such adjustments of tax, whether by way of assessment or by way of discharge or repayment of tax, as may be required in consequence of the provisions of this section shall be carried out.

Note.—The words "or 97" in the heading should (though they have not) have been deleted as a result of the amendments made by FA 1980.
Amendments.—[1] Words in sub-s. (1) substituted by FA 1980, s. 81 (3).
[2] Words in sub-s. (2) inserted by FA 1980, s. 81 (3).
[3] "1970" in sub-s. (1) inserted by virtue of TA 1988, Sch. 29, para. 15 (*b*).

Court investment funds etc.

99. Funds in court

(1) For the purposes of section 46 above (nominees and bare trustees) funds in court held by the Accountant General shall be regarded as held by him as nominee for the persons entitled to or interested in the funds, or as the case may be for their trustees.

(2) Where funds in court standing to an account are invested or, after investment, are realised the method by which the Accountant General effects the investment or the realisation of investments shall not affect the question whether there is for the purposes of this Act an acquisition, or as the case may be a disposal, of an asset representing funds in court standing to the account, and in particular there shall for those purposes be an acquisition or disposal of shares in a court investment fund notwithstanding that the investment in such shares of funds in court standing to an account, or the realisation of funds which have been so invested, is effected by setting off, in the Accountant General's accounts, investment in one account against realisation of investments in another.

(3) In this section "funds in court" means—

(*a*) money in the Supreme Court, money in county courts and statutory deposits described in [section 40 of the Administration of Justice Act 1982][1], and
(*b*) [money in the Supreme Court of Judicature of Northern Ireland][1] and money in a county court in Northern Ireland,

and investments representing such money; and references in this section to the Accountant General are references to the Accountant General of the Supreme Court of Judicature in England and, in relation to money within paragraph (*b*) above and investments representing such money, include references to the Accountant General of the Supreme Court of Judicature of Northern Ireland or any other person by whom such funds are held.

Amendments.—[1] Words in sub-s. (3) (*a*), (*b*) substituted by the Administration of Justice Act 1982, s. 46 (2) (*f*) (i) with effect from 12 March 1986 by virtue of the Administration of Justice Act 1982 (Commencement) Order 1986, S.I. 1986 No. 364.

100. Reduced rate of tax

Amendments.—Repealed by FA 1980, Sch. 20, Pt. X in relation to disposals after 5 April 1980.

PART V
LAND

Private residences

101. Relief on disposal of private residence

(1) This section applies to a gain accruing to an individual so far as attributable to the disposal of, or of an interest in—

(a) a dwelling-house or part of a dwelling-house which is, or has at any time in his period of ownership been, his only or main residence, or
(b) land which he has for his own occupation and enjoyment with that residence as its garden or grounds up to the permitted area.

(2) In this section "the permitted area" means, subject to subsections (3) and (4) below, an area (inclusive of the site of the dwelling-house) of one acre.

(3) In any particular case the permitted area shall be such area, larger than one acre, as the Commissioners concerned may determine if satisfied that, regard being had to the size and character of the dwelling-house, that larger area is required for the reasonable enjoyment of it (or of the part in question) as a residence.

(4) Where part of the land occupied with a residence is and part is not within subsection (1) above, then (up to the permitted area) that part shall be taken to be within subsection (1) above which, if the remainder were separately occupied, would be the most suitable for occupation and enjoyment with the residence.

(5) So far as it is necessary for the purposes of this section to determine which of two or more residences is an individual's main residence for any period—

(a) the individual may conclude that question by notice in writing to the inspector given within two years from the beginning of that period, or given by the end of the year 1966–67, if that is later, but subject to a right to vary that notice by a further notice in writing to the inspector as respects any period beginning not earlier than two years before the giving of the further notice,
(b) subject to paragraph (a) above, the question shall be concluded by the determination of the inspector, which may be as respects either the whole or specified parts of the period of ownership in question,

and notice of any determination of the inspector under paragraph (b) above shall be given to the individual who may appeal to the General Commissioners or the Special Commissioners against that determination within thirty days of service of the notice.

(6) In the case of a man and his wife living with him—

(a) there can only be one residence or main residence for both, so long as living together, and, where a notice under subsection (5) (a) above affects both the husband and the wife, it must be given by both, and
(b) any notice under subsection (5) (b) above which affects a residence owned by the husband and a residence owned by the wife shall be given to each and either may appeal under that subsection.

(7) In this section, and sections 102 to 105 below, "the period of ownership" where the individual has had different interests at different times shall be taken to begin from the first acquisition taken into account in arriving at the expenditure which under Chapter II of Part II of this Act is allowable as a deduction in computing under that Chapter the amount of the gain to which this section applies, and in the case of a man and his wife living with him—

(a) if the one disposes of, or of his or her interest in, the dwelling-house or part of a dwelling-house which is their only or main residence to the other, and in particular if it passes on death to the other as legatee, the other's period of ownership shall begin with the beginning of the period of ownership of the one making the disposal, and
(b) if paragraph (a) above applies, but the dwelling-house or part of a dwelling-house was not the only or main residence of both throughout the period of ownership of the one making the disposal, account shall be taken of any part of that period during which it was his only or main residence as if it was also that of the other.

(8) If at any time . . .[3] during an individual's period of ownership of a dwelling-house or part of a dwelling-house he—

(a) resides in living accommodation which is for him job-related within the meaning of [section 356 of the Taxes Act 1988],[2] and
(b) intends in due course to occupy the dwelling-house or part of a dwelling-house as his only or main residence,

this section, and sections 102 to 105 below, shall apply as if the dwelling-house or part of a dwelling-house were at that time occupied by him as a residence.

[(8A) Section 356 (3) (b) and (5) of the Taxes Act 1988 shall apply for the purposes of subsection (8) above only in relation to residence on or after 6th April 1983 in living accommodation which is job-related within the meaning of that section.][1]

(9) Apportionments of consideration shall be made wherever required by this section or sections 102 to 105 below and, in particular, where a person disposes of a dwelling-house only part of which is his only or main residence.

Cross references.—See FA 1980, s, 80 (1) (relief where dwelling-house let during period of ownership);
FA 1984, Sch. 11, para. 5 (reduction of relief under this section where a residence let as furnished holiday accommodation is disposed of and a new residence is acquired after 5 April 1982 or, in the case of a company, after 31 March 1982 and for which rollover relief has been allowed).
Amendments.—[1] Sub-s. (8A) inserted by TA 1988, Sch. 29, para. 21.
[2] Words in sub-s. (8) (a) substituted by TA 1988, Sch. 29, para. 32 Table.
[3] Words in sub-s. (8) repealed by FA 1988, Sch. 14, Pt. VII in relation to disposals made after 5 April 1988.

102. Amount of relief

(1) No part of a gain to which section 101 above applies shall be a chargeable gain if the dwelling-house or part of a dwelling-house has been the individual's only or main residence throughout the period of ownership, or throughout the period of ownership except for all or any part of the last [twenty-four months][1] of that period.

(2) Where subsection (1) above does not apply, a fraction of the gain shall not be a chargeable gain, and that fraction shall be—

(a) the length of the part or parts of the period of ownership during which the dwelling-house or the part of the dwelling-house was the individual's only or main residence, but inclusive of the last [twenty-four months][1] of the period of ownership in any event, divided by
(b) the length of the period of ownership.

(3) For the purposes of subsections (1) and (2) above—

(a) a period of absence not exceeding three years (or periods of absence which together did not exceed three years), and in addition
(b) any period of absence throughout which the individual worked in an employment or office all the duties of which were performed outside the United Kingdom, and in addition
(c) any period of absence not exceeding four years (or periods of absence which together did not exceed four years) throughout which the individual was prevented from residing in the dwelling-house or part of the dwelling-house in consequence of the situation of his place of work or in consequence of any condition imposed by his employer requiring him to reside elsewhere, being a condition reasonably imposed to secure the effective performance by the employee of his duties,

shall be treated as if in that period of absence the dwelling-house or the part of the dwelling-house was the individual's only or main residence if both before and after the period there was a time when the dwelling-house was the individual's only or main residence.

In this subsection "period of absence" means a period during which the dwelling-house or the part of the dwelling-house was not the individual's only or main residence and throughout which he had no residence or main residence eligible for relief under this section.

(4) In this section "period of ownership" does not include any period before [31st March 1982][2].

Cross references.—See FA 1980, s. 80 (1) (amount of relief where dwelling-house let during period of ownership).
Amendments.—[1] Words in sub-ss. (1), (2) (a) substituted by FA 1980, s. 80 (2).
[2] Date in sub-s. (4) substituted for "6th April 1965" by FA 1988, Sch. 8, para. 8 in relation to disposals after 5 April 1988.

103. Amount of relief: further provisions

(1) If the gain accrues from the disposal of a dwelling-house or part of a dwelling-house part of which is used exclusively for the purposes of a trade or business, or of a profession or vocation, the gain shall be apportioned and section 102 above shall apply in relation to the part of the gain apportioned to the part which is not exclusively used for those purposes.

(2) If at any time in the period of ownership there is a change in what is occupied as the individual's residence, whether on account of a reconstruction or conversion of a building or for any other reason, or there have been changes as regards the use of part of the dwelling-house for the purpose of a trade or business, or of a profession or vocation, or for any other purpose, the relief given by section 102 above may be adjusted in such manner as the Commissioners concerned may consider to be just and reasonable.

(3) Section 102 above shall not apply in relation to a gain if the acquisition of, or of the interest in, the dwelling-house or the part of a dwelling-house was made wholly or partly for the purpose of realising a gain from the disposal of it, and shall not apply in relation to a gain so far as attributable to any expenditure which was incurred after the beginning of the period of ownership and was incurred wholly or partly for the purpose of realising a gain from the disposal.

Cross references.—See TA 1988, s. 776 (9), (14) (artificial transactions in land).

104. Private residence occupied under terms of settlement

Sections 101 to 103 above shall also apply in relation to a gain accruing to a trustee on a disposal of settled property being an asset within section 101 (1) above where during the period of ownership of the trustee the dwelling-house or part of the dwelling-house mentioned in that subsection has been the only or main residence of a person entitled to occupy it under the terms of the settlement, and in those sections as so applied—

(a) references to the individual shall be taken as references to the trustee except in relation to the occupation of the dwelling-house or part of the dwelling-house, and
(b) the notice which may be given to the inspector under section 101 (5) (a) above shall be a joint notice by the trustee and the person entitled to occupy the dwelling-house or part of the dwelling-house.

Cross references.—See FA 1980, s. 80 (1) (relief where dwelling-house let during period of ownership).

105. Private residence occupied by dependent relative

(1) This section applies to a gain accruing to an individual so far as attributable to the disposal of, or of an interest in, a dwelling-house or part of a dwelling-house which is, or has at any time in his period of ownership been, the sole residence of a dependent relative of the individual, provided rent-free and without any other consideration.

(2) If the individual so claims, such relief shall be given in respect of it and its garden or grounds as would be given under sections 101 to 103 above if the dwelling-house (or part of the dwelling-house) had been the individual's only or main residence in the period of residence by the dependent relative, and shall be so given in addition to any relief available under those sections apart from this section.

(3) Not more than one dwelling-house (or part of a dwelling-house) may qualify for relief as being the residence of a dependent relative of the claimant at any one time nor, in the case of a man and his wife living with him, as being the residence of a dependent relative of the claimant or of the claimant's husband or wife at any one time.

(4) The inspector, before allowing a claim, may require the claimant to show that the giving of the relief claimed will not under subsection (3) above preclude the giving of relief to the claimant's wife or husband or that a claim to any such relief has been relinquished.

(5) In this section "dependent relative" means, in relation to an individual—

(a) any relative of his or of his wife who is incapacitated by old age or infirmity from maintaining himself, or
(b) his or his wife's mother who, whether or not incapacitated, is either widowed, or living apart from her husband, or a single woman in consequence of dissolution or annulment of marriage.

(6) If the individual mentioned in subsection (5) above is a woman the references in that subsection to the individual's wife shall be construed as references to the individual's husband.

Amendments.—This section not to apply to disposals after 5 April 1988, subject to certain savings; see FA 1988, s. 111.

Leases
106. Leases of land and other assets
Schedule 3 to this Act shall have effect as respects leases of land and of other assets.

Part disposals
107. Small part disposals
(1) This section applies to a transfer of land forming part only of a holding of land, where—

(a) the amount or value of the consideration for the transfer [does not exceed one-fifth of]² the market value of the holding as it subsisted immediately before the transfer, and
(b) the transfer is not one which, by virtue of section 44 above (transfers between husband and wife) or section 273 (1) of the Taxes Act [1970]³ (transfers within groups of companies), is treated as giving rise to neither a gain nor a loss.

(2) Subject to subsection (3) below, if the transferor so claims, the transfer shall not be treated for the purposes of this Act as a disposal, but all sums which, if it had been so treated, would have been brought into account as consideration for that disposal in the computation under Chapter II of Part II of this Act of a gain accruing on the disposal shall be deducted from any expenditure allowable under that Chapter as a deduction in computing a gain on any subsequent disposal of the holding.

(3) This section shall not apply—

(a) if the amount or value of the consideration for the transfer exceeds [£20,000]¹, or
(b) where in the year of assessment in which the transfer is made, the transferor made any other disposal of land, if the total amount or value of the consideration for all disposals of land made by the transferor in that year exceeds [£20,000]¹.

(4) No account shall be taken under subsection (3) above of any transfer of land to which section 108 below applies.

(5) In relation to a transfer which is not for full consideration in money or money's worth "the amount or value of the consideration" in this section shall mean the market value of the land transferred.

(6) For the purposes of this section the holding of land shall comprise only the land in respect of which the expenditure allowable under paragraphs (a) and (b) of section 32 (1) above would be apportioned under section 35 above if the transfer had been treated as a disposal (that is, as a part disposal of the holding).

(7) In this section references to a holding of land include references to any estate or interest in a holding of land, not being an estate or interest which is a wasting asset, and references to part of a holding shall be construed accordingly.

Amendments.—¹ Amount in sub-s. (3) (a), (b) substituted by FA 1984, s. 63 (2), (5) with respect to disposals after 5 April 1983.
² Words in sub-s. (1) (a) substituted by FA 1986, s. 60.
³ "1970" in sub-s. (1) (b) inserted by virtue of TA 1988, Sch. 29, para. 15 (b).

108. Part disposal to authority with compulsory powers

(1) This section applies to a transfer of land forming part only of a holding of land to an authority exercising or having compulsory powers where—

(a) the amount or value of the consideration for the transfer, or if the transfer is not for full consideration in money or money's worth, the market value of the land transferred, is small, as compared with the market value of the holding as it subsisted immediately before the transfer, and
(b) the transferor had not taken any steps by advertising or otherwise to dispose of any part of the holding or to make his willingness to dispose of it known to the authority or others.

(2) If the transferor so claims, the transfer shall not be treated for the purposes of this Act as a disposal, but all sums which, if it had been so treated, would have been brought into account as consideration for that disposal in the computation under Chapter II of Part II of this Act of a gain accruing on the disposal shall be deducted from any expenditure allowable under that Chapter as a deduction in computing a gain on any subsequent disposal of the holding.

(3) For the purposes of this section the holding of land shall comprise only the land in respect of which the expenditure allowable under paragraphs (*a*) and (*b*) of section 32 (1) above would be apportioned under section 35 above if the transfer had been treated as a disposal (that is, as a part disposal of the holding).

(4) In this section references to a holding of land include references to an estate or interest in a holding of land, not being an estate or interest which is a wasting asset, and references to part of a holding shall be construed accordingly.

(5) In this section "authority exercising or having compulsory powers" means, in relation to the land transferred, a person or body of persons acquiring it compulsorily or who has or have been, or could be, authorised to acquire it compulsorily for the purposes for which it is acquired, or for whom another person or body of persons has or have been, or could be, authorised so to acquire it.

109. Part disposal: consideration exceeding allowable expenditure

(1) The provisions of section 107 (2) and 108 (2) above shall have effect subject to this section.

(2) Where the allowable expenditure is less than the consideration for the part disposal (or is nil)—

(*a*) the said provisions shall not apply, and
(*b*) if the recipient so elects (and there is any allowable expenditure)—

(i) the consideration for the part disposal shall be reduced by the amount of the allowable expenditure, and,
(ii) none of that expenditure shall be allowable as a deduction in computing a gain accruing on the occasion of the part disposal or on any subsequent occasion.

In this subsection "allowable expenditure" means expenditure which, immediately before the part disposal, was attributable to the holding of land under paragraphs (*a*) and (*b*) of section 32 (1) above.

Cross references.—FA 1989, Sch. 15, para. 3 (expenditure disallowed under this section to be deducted from the new 1982 base cost where the disallowance relates to part disposals made after 31 March 1982 but before 6 April 1988).

Compulsory acquisition

110. Compensation paid on compulsory acquisition

(1) Where land or an interest in or right over land is acquired and the acquisition is, or could have been, made under compulsory powers, then in considering whether, under section 43 (4) above, the purchase price or compensation or other consideration for the acquisition should be apportioned and treated in part as a capital sum within section 20 (1) (*a*) above (disposal arising on receipt of capital sum), whether as compensation for loss of goodwill or for disturbance or otherwise, or should be apportioned in any other way, the fact that the acquisition is or could have been made compulsorily, and any statutory provision treating the purchase price or compensation or other consideration as exclusively paid in respect of the land itself, shall be disregarded.

(2) In any case where land or an interest in land is acquired as mentioned in subsection (1) above from any person and the compensation or purchase price includes an amount in respect of severance of the land comprised in the acquisition or sale from other land in which that person is entitled in the same capacity to an interest, or in respect of that other land as being injuriously affected, there shall be deemed for the purposes of this Act to be a part disposal of that other land.

111. Time of disposal and acquisition

Where an interest in land is acquired, otherwise than under a contract, by an authority possessing compulsory purchase powers the time at which the disposal and acquisition is made is the time at which the compensation for the acquisition is agreed or otherwise determined (variations on appeal being disregarded for this purpose) or, if earlier (but after 20th April 1971), the time when the authority enter on the land in pursuance of their powers.

[**111A. Rollover relief on compulsory acquisition**

(1) This section applies where—

(*a*) on or after 6th April 1982 land (in this section referred to as "the old land") is disposed of by any person (in this section referred to as "the landowner") to an authority exercising or having compulsory powers; and
(*b*) the landowner did not take any steps, by advertising or otherwise, to dispose of the old land or to make his willingness to dispose of it known to the authority or others; and
(*c*) the consideration for the disposal is applied by the landowner in acquiring other land (in this section referred to as "the new land") not being land excluded from this paragraph by section 111B below.

(2) Subject to section 111B below, in a case where the whole of the consideration for the disposal was applied as mentioned in subsection (1) (*c*) above, the landowner, on making a claim as respects the consideration so applied, shall be treated for the purposes of this Act—

(*a*) as if the consideration for the disposal of the old land were (if otherwise of a greater amount or value) of such amount as would secure that on the disposal neither a gain nor a loss accrues to him; and
(*b*) as if the amount or value of the consideration for the acquisition of the new land were reduced by the excess of the amount or value of the actual consideration for the disposal of the old land over the amount of the consideration which he is treated as receiving under paragraph (*a*) above.

(3) If part only of the consideration for the disposal of the old land was applied as mentioned in subsection (1) (*c*) above, then, subject to section 111B below, if the part of the consideration which was not so applied (in this subsection referred to as "the unexpended consideration") is less than the amount of the gain (whether all chargeable gain or not) accruing on the disposal of the old land, the landowner, on making a claim as respects the consideration which was so applied, shall be treated for the purposes of this Act—

(*a*) as if the amount of the gain so accruing were reduced to the amount of the unexpended consideration (and, if not all chargeable gain, with a proportionate reduction in the amount of the chargeable gain); and
(*b*) as if the amount or value of the consideration for the acquisition of the new land were reduced by the amount by which the gain is reduced (or, as the case may be, the amount by which the chargeable gain is proportionately reduced) under paragraph (*a*) above.

(4) Nothing in subsection (2) or subsection (3) above affects the treatment for the purposes of this Act of the authority by whom the old land was acquired or of the other party to the transaction involving the acquisition of the new land.

(5) For the purposes of this section—

(*a*) subsection (2) of section 115 below shall apply in relation to subsection (2) (*a*) and subsection (2) (*b*) above as it applies in relation to subsection (1) (*a*) and subsection (1) (*b*) of that section; and
(*b*) subsection (3) of that section shall apply as if any reference to the new assets were a reference to the new land, any reference to the old assets were a reference to the old land and any reference to that section were a reference to this.

(6) Where this section applies, any such amount as is referred to in subsection (2) of section 110 above shall be treated as forming part of the consideration for the disposal of the old land and, accordingly, so much of that subsection as provides for a deemed disposal of other land shall not apply.

(7) The provisions of this Act fixing the amount of the consideration deemed to be given for the acquisition or disposal of assets shall be applied before this section is applied.

(8) In this section—

"land" includes any interest in or right over land; and
"authority exercising or having compulsory powers" shall be construed in accordance with section 108 (5) above.][1]

Cross references.—See FA 1988, Sch. 9, paras. 1, 2 (reduction of a deferred charge to tax where the charge is wholly or partly attributable to an increase in the value of an asset before 31 March 1982).
Amendments.—[1] This section inserted by FA 1982, s. 83.

[**111B. Provisions supplementary to section 111A**

(1) Land is excluded from paragraph (*c*) of subsection (1) of section 111A above if—

(*a*) it is a dwelling-house or part of a dwelling-house (or an interest in or right over a dwelling-house), and
(*b*) by virtue of, or of any claim under, any provision of sections 101 to 105 above (private residences) the whole or any part of a gain accruing on a disposal of it by the landowner at a material time would not be a chargeable gain;

and for the purposes of this subsection "a material time" means any time during the period of six years beginning on the date of the acquisition referred to in the said paragraph (*c*).

(2) If, at any time during the period of six years referred to in subsection (1) above, land which at the beginning of that period was not excluded from section 111A (1) (*c*) above by virtue of that subsection becomes so excluded, the amount of any chargeable gain accruing on the disposal of the old land shall be redetermined without regard to any relief previously given under section 111A above by reference to the amount or value of the consideration for the acquisition of that land; and all such adjustments of capital gains tax, whether by way of assessment or otherwise, may be made at any time, notwithstanding anything in section 34 of the Taxes Management Act 1970 (time limit for assessments).

(3) Where the new land is a depreciating asset, within the meaning of section 117 below, that section has effect as if—

(*a*) any reference in subsection (1) or subsection (3) to section 115 or section 116 were a reference to subsection (2) or subsection (3) respectively of section 111A above; and
(*b*) paragraph (*b*) of subsection (2) were omitted; and
(*c*) the reference in subsection (4) to section 115 (3) were a reference to that provision as applied by section 111A (5) above.

(4) No claim may be made under section 108 above in relation to a transfer which constitutes a disposal in respect of which a claim is made under section 111A above.

(5) Expressions used in this section have the same meaning as in section 111A above.][1]

Cross references.—See FA 1988, Sch. 9, para. 3 (reduction of a deferred charge to tax where the charge is wholly or partly attributable to an increase in the value of an asset before 31 March 1982);
FA 1989, Sch. 15, para. 1 (sub-s. (3) of this section not to apply in consequence of an event occurring after 5 April 1988 if its application is directly attributable to the disposal of an asset before 1 April 1982).
Amendments.—[1] This section inserted by FA 1982, s. 83.

Agricultural land and woodlands

112. Grants for giving up agricultural land

For the purposes of capital gains tax, a sum payable to an individual by virtue of a scheme under section 27 of the Agriculture Act 1967 (grants for relinquishing occupation of uncommercial agricultural units) shall not be treated as part of the consideration obtained by him for, or otherwise as accruing to him on, the disposal of any asset.

113. Woodlands

(1) (*a*) Consideration for the disposal of trees standing or felled or cut on [woodlands managed by the occupier on a commerecial basis and with a view to the realisation of profits][1], and
(*b*) capital sums received under a policy of insurance in respect of the destruction of or damage or injury to trees by fire or other hazard on [such woodlands][1],

shall be excluded from the computation under Chapter II of Part II of this Act of the gain accruing on the disposal if the person making the disposal is [the occupier][1].

(2) Subsection (1) (*b*) above has effect notwithstanding section 20 (1) above (disposal arising on receipt of capital sum).

(3) In the computation under Chapter II of Part II above so much of the cost of woodland in the United Kingdom shall be disregarded as is attributable to trees growing on the land.

(4) In the computation under Chapter II of Part II above of the gain accruing on a disposal of woodland in the United Kingdom so much of the consideration for the disposal as is attributable to trees growing on the land shall be excluded.

(5) References in this section to trees include references to saleable underwood.

Amendments.—¹ Words in sub-s. (1) substituted by FA 1988, Sch. 6, para. 6 (5), (9).

Development land tax etc.

114. Interaction with development land tax and other taxation

The provisions of this Act have effect subject to—

(a) the Development Land Tax Act 1976, and in particular Schedule 6 to that Act,
(b) the taxation of development gains under Part III of the Finance Act 1974, which is to be terminated in accordance with the provisions of the Development Land Tax Act 1976,
(c) the extension of the taxation of chargeable gains by Chapter II of the said Part III (the first letting charge), subject to termination in accordance with the said Act of 1976.

Amendments.—This section repealed by FA 1985, Sch. 27, Pt. X but the repeal does not have effect in relation to a disposal as defined in FA 1985, s. 93 (1) which takes place before 19 March 1985. FA 1985, s. 93 (1) reads—

"**93.**—(1) Development land tax shall not be charged in respect of any disposal taking place on or after 19th March 1985; and for this purpose "disposal" includes a deemed disposal within the meaning of the Development Land Tax Act 1976 (in this section referred to as "the 1976 Act") and any other event which, but for the repeals effected by Part X of Schedule 27 to this Act, would constitute a disposal of an interest in land for the purposes of that Act."

PART VI
PROPERTY: FURTHER PROVISIONS

Replacement of business assets
115. Roll-over relief

(1) If the consideration which a person carrying on a trade obtains for the disposal of, or of his interest in, assets (in this section referred to as "the old assets") used, and used only, for the purposes of the trade throughout the period of ownership is applied by him in acquiring other assets, or an interest in other assets (in this section referred to as "the new assets") which on the acquisition are taken into use, and used only, for the purposes of the trade, and the old assets and new assets are within the classes of assets listed in section 118 below, then the person carrying on the trade shall, on making a claim as respects the consideration which has been so applied, be treated for the purposes of this Act—

(*a*) as if the consideration for the disposal of, or of the interest in, the old assets were (if otherwise of a greater amount or value) of such amount as would secure that on the disposal neither a gain nor a loss accrues to him, and

(*b*) as if the amount or value of the consideration for the acquisition of, or of the interest in, the new assets were reduced by the excess of the amount or value of the actual consideration for the disposal of, or of the interest in, the old assets over the amount of the consideration which he is treated as receiving under paragraph (*a*) above.

but neither paragraph (*a*) nor paragraph (*b*) above shall affect the treatment for the purposes of this Act of the other party to the transaction involving the old assets, or of the other party to the transaction involving the new assets.

(2) Where subsection (1) (*a*) above applies to exclude a gain which, in consequence of Schedule 5 to this Act, is not all chargeable gain, the amount of the reduction to be made under subsection (1) (*b*) above shall be the amount of the chargeable gain, and not the whole amount of the gain.

(3) This section shall only apply if the acquisition of, or of the interest in, the new assets takes place, or an unconditional contract for the acquisition is entered into, in the period beginning twelve months before and ending three years after the disposal of, or of the interest in, the old assets, or at such earlier or later time as the Board may by notice in writing allow:

Provided that, where an unconditional contract for the acquisition is so entered into, this section may be applied on a provisional basis without waiting to ascertain whether the new assets, or the interest in the new assets, is acquired in pursuance of the contract, and, when that fact is ascertained, all necessary adjustments shall be made by making assessments or by repayment or discharge of tax, and shall be so made notwithstanding any limitation on the time within which assessments may be made.

(4) This section shall not apply unless the acquisition of, or of the interest in, the new assets was made for the purpose of their use in the trade, and not wholly or partly for the purpose of realising a gain from the disposal of, or of the interest in, the new assets.

(5) If, over the period of ownership or any substantial part of the period of ownership, part of a building or structure is, and part is not, used for the purposes of a trade, this section shall apply as if the part so used, with any land occupied for purposes ancillary to the occupation and use of that part of the building or structure, were a separate asset, and subject to any necessary apportionments of consideration for an acquisition or disposal of, or of an interest in, the building or structure and other land.

(6) If the old assets were not used for the purposes of the trade throughout the period of ownership this section shall apply as if a part of the asset representing its use for the purposes of the trade having regard to the time and extent to which it was, and was not, used for those purposes, were a separate asset which had been wholly used for the purposes of the trade, and this subsection shall apply in relation to that part subject to any necessary apportionment of consideration for an acquisition or disposal of, or of the interest in, the asset.

(7) This section shall apply in relation to a person who, either successively or at the same time, carries on two or more trades as if both or all of them were a single trade.

[(7A) In this section "period of ownership" does not include any period before 31st March 1982.][1]

(8) The provisions of this Act fixing the amount of the consideration deemed to be given for the acquisition or disposal of assets shall be applied before this section is applied.

(9) Without prejudice to section 43 (4) above (general provision for apportionments), where consideration is given for the acquisition or disposal of assets some or part of which are assets in relation to which a claim under this section applies, and some or part of which are not, the consideration shall be apportioned in such manner as is just and reasonable.

Cross references.—See TA 1970, s. 278 (1), (4) (*b*) (effect of claims under this section when a company ceases to be a member of a group of companies);
FA 1976, s. 54 (3) (*b*) (compulsory acquisition of aircraft and shipbuilding shares);
FA 1984, s. 80 (application of this section, subject to certain conditions, in relation to replacement of business assets used in connection with oil fields);
F (No. 2) A 1987, s. 80 (1), (2) (roll-over relief to be assumed never to have been available for gains on oil licences except for any relief given by any Commissioners or court before 14 May 1987);
TA 1988, s. 503 (treatment of the commercial letting of furnished holiday accommodation for the purposes of this section);
FA 1988, s. 105 (3), (4), (7) (relief under this section not available in certain circumstances to companies migrating without Treasury consent),
s. 106 (3) (this section not to apply in respect of certain companies which are resident in the UK but are regarded under double taxation relief arrangements as resident outside the UK),
Sch. 9, paras. 1, 2 (reduction of a deferred charge to tax where the charge is wholly or partly attributable to an increase in the value of an asset before 31 March 1982);
FA 1989, s. 129 (1), (4) (anti-avoidance provisions in relation to roll-over relief to counter avoidance of tax by non-residents where disposal of old assets or acquisition of new assets takes place after 13 March 1989),
s. 133 (1), (2) (restriction of roll-over relief to dual resident companies where disposal of old assets or acquisition of new assets takes place after 13 March 1989).
Amendments.—[1] Sub-s. (7A) inserted by FA 1988, Sch. 8, para. 9 in relation to disposals after 5 April 1988.

116. Assets only partly replaced

(1) Section 115 (1) above shall not apply if part only of the amount or value of the consideration for the disposal of, or of the interest in, the old assets is applied as described in that subsection, but if all of the amount or value of the consideration except for a part which is less than the amount of the gain (whether all chargeable gain or not) accruing on the disposal of, or of the interest in, the old assets is so applied, then the person carrying on the trade, on making a claim as respects the consideration which has been so applied, shall be treated for the purposes of this Act—

(*a*) as if the amount of the gain so accruing were reduced to the amount of the said part (and, if not all chargeable gain, with a proportionate reduction in the amount of the chargeable gain), and
(*b*) as if the amount or value of the consideration for the acquisition of, or of the interest in, the new assets were reduced by the amount by which the gain is reduced (or as the case may be the amount by which the chargeable gain is proportionately reduced) under paragraph (*a*) of this subsection,

but neither paragraph (*a*) nor paragraph (*b*) above shall affect the treatment for the purposes of this Act of the other party to the transaction involving the old assets, or of the other party to the transaction involving the new assets.

(2) Subsections (3) to (9) of section 115 above shall apply as if this section formed part of that section.

Cross references.—See TA 1970, s. 278 (1), (4) (*b*) (effect of claims under this section when a company ceases to be a member of a group of companies);
FA 1976, s. 54 (3) (*b*) (compulsory acquisition of aircraft and shipbuilding shares);
FA 1984, s. 80 (application of this section, subject to certain conditions, in relation to replacement of business assets used in connection with oil fields);
TA 1988, s. 503 (treatment of the commercial letting of furnished holiday accommodation for the purposes of this section).

117. New assets which are depreciating assets

(1) Sections 115 and 116 above shall have effect subject to the provisions of this section in which—

(*a*) the "held over gain" means the amount by which, under those sections, and apart from the provisions of this section, any chargeable gain on one asset (called "asset No. 1") is reduced, with a corresponding reduction of the expenditure allowable in respect of another asset (called "asset No. 2").
(*b*) any reference to a gain of any amount being carried forward to any asset is a reference

to a reduction of that amount in a chargeable gain coupled with a reduction of the same amount in expenditure allowable in respect of that asset.

(2) If asset No. 2 is a depreciating asset, the held over gain shall not be carried forward, but the claimant shall be treated as if so much of the chargeable gain on asset No. 1 as is equal to the held over gain did not accrue until—

    (*a*) the claimant disposes of asset No. 2, or
    (*b*) he ceases to use asset No. 2 for the purposes of a trade carried on by him, or
    (*c*) the expiration of a period of ten years beginning with the acquisition of asset No. 2,

whichever event comes first.

(3) If, in the circumstances specified in subsection (4) below, the claimant acquires an asset (called "asset No. 3") which is not a depreciating asset, and so claims under section 115 or 116 above—

    (*a*) the gain held over from asset No. 1 shall be carried forward to asset No. 3, and
    (*b*) the claim which applies to asset No. 2 shall be treated as withdrawn (so that subsection (2) above does not apply).

(4) The circumstances are that asset No. 3 is acquired not later than the time when the chargeable gain postponed under subsection (2) above would accrue and, assuming—

    (*a*) that the consideration for asset No. 1 was applied in acquiring asset No. 3, and
    (*b*) that the time between the disposal of asset No. 1 and the acquisition of asset No. 3 was within the time limited by section 115 (3) above,

the whole amount of the postponed gain could be carried forward from asset No. 1 to asset No. 3; and the claim under subsection (3) above shall be accepted as if those assumptions were true.

(5) If part only of the postponed gain could be carried forward from asset No. 1 to asset No. 3, and the claimant so requires, that and the other part of the postponed gain shall be treated as derived from two separate assets, so that, on that claim—

    (*a*) subsection (3) above applies to the first-mentioned part, and
    (*b*) the other part remains subject to subsection (2) above.

(6) For the purposes of this section, an asset is a depreciating asset at any time if—

    (*a*) at that time it is a wasting asset, as defined in section 37 above, or
    (*b*) within the period of ten years beginning at that time it will become a wasting asset (so defined).

Cross references.— See TA 1970, s. 278 (1), (4) (*b*) (effect of claims under this section when a company ceases to be a member of a group of companies);
FA 1976, s. 54 (3) (*b*) (compulsory acquisition of aircraft and shipbuilding shares);
FA 1984 s. 80 (application of this section, subject to certain conditions, in relation to replacement of business assets used in connection with oil fields),
TA 1988, s. 503 (treatment of the commercial letting of furnished holiday accommodation for the purposes of this section);
FA 1988, Sch. 9, para. 3 (reduction of a deferred charge to tax where the charge is wholly or partly attributable to an increase in the value of an asset before 31 March 1982);
FA 1989, Sch. 15, para. 1 (sub-s. (2) of this section not to apply in consequence of an event occurring after 5 April 1988 if its application is directly attributable to the disposal of an asset before 1 April 1982).

118. Relevant classes of assets

The classes of assets for the purposes of section 115 (1) above are as follows.

Class 1. Assets within heads A and B below.

Head A

1. Any building or part of a building and any permanent or semi-permanent structure in the nature of a building, occupied (as well as used) only for the purposes of the trade.
2. Any land occupied (as well as used) only for the purposes of the trade.
Head A has effect subject to section 119 below.

Head B

Fixed plant or machinery which does not form part of a building or of a permanent or semi-permanent structure in the nature of a building.

Class 2

Ships, aircraft and hovercraft ("hovercraft" having the same meaning as in the Hovercraft Act, 1968).

[Class 2A

Satellites space stations and spacecraft (including launch vehicles).][1]

Class 3

Goodwill.

[Class 4

Milk quotas (that is, rights to sell dairy produce without being liable to pay milk levy or to deliver daily produce without being liable to pay a contribution to milk levy) and potato quotas (that is, rights to produce potatoes without being liable to pay more than the ordinary contribution to the Potato Marketing Board's fund).][2]

Cross references.—See TA 1970, s. 278 (1), (4) (*b*) (effect of claims under this section when a company ceases to be a member of a group of companies);
FA 1976, s. 54 (3) (*b*) (compulsory acquisition of aircraft and shipbuilding shares);
F (No. 2) A 1987, s. 80 (1), (2) (roll-over relief to be assumed never to have been available for gains on oil licences except for any relief given by any Commissioners or court before 14 May 1987);
TA 1988, s. 503 (treatment of the commercial letting of furnished holiday accommodation for the purposes of this section).
Amendments.—[1] Class 2A inserted by FA 1988, s. 112 and apply where disposal of old assets or acquisition of new assets takes place after 27 July 1987.
[2] Class 4 inserted by FA 1988, s. 112 and apply where disposal of old assets or acquisition of new assets takes place after 29 October 1987.

119. Assets of Class 1

(1) This section has effect as respects head A of Class 1 in section 118 above.

(2) Head A shall not apply where the trade is a trade—

(*a*) of dealing in or developing land, or
(*b*) of providing services for the occupier of land in which the person carrying on the trade has an estate or interest.

(3) Where the trade is a trade of dealing in or developing land, but a profit on the sale of any land held for the purposes of the trade would not form part of the trading profits, then, as regards that land, the trade shall be treated for the purposes of subsection (2) (*a*) of this section as if it were not a trade of dealing in or developing land.

(4) A person who is a lessor of tied premises shall be treated as if he occupied (as well as used) those tied premises only for the purposes of the relevant trade.

This subsection shall be construed in accordance with section [98 (2)][2] of the Taxes Act [1988][1] (income tax and corporation tax on tied premises).

Cross references.—See TA 1970, s. 278 (1), (4) (*b*) (effect of claims under this section when a company ceases to be a member of a group of companies);
FA 1976, s. 54 (3) (*b*) (compulsory acquisition of aircraft and shipbuilding shares);
TA 1988, s. 503 (treatment of the commercial letting of furnished holiday accommodation for the purposes of this section).
Amendments.—[1] "1988" in sub-s. (4) inserted by virtue of TA 1988, Sch. 29, para. 15 (*a*).
[2] Number in sub-s. (4) substituted by TA 1988, Sch. 29, para. 32 Table.

120. Trade carried on by family company: business assets dealt with by individual

In relation to a case where—

(*a*) the person disposing of, or of his interest in, the old assets and acquiring the new assets, or an interest in them, is an individual, and
(*b*) the trade or trades in question are carried on not by that individual but by a company which, both at the time of the disposal and at the time of the acquisition referred to in paragraph (*a*) above, is his family company, within the meaning of [Schedule 20 to the Finance Act 1985][1],

any reference in sections 115 to 119 above to the person carrying on the trade (or the two or more trades) includes a reference to that individual.

Cross references.—See TA 1970, s. 278 (1), (4) (*b*) (effect of claims under this section when a company ceases to be a member of a group of companies);
FA 1976, s. 54 (3) (*b*) (compulsory acquisition of aircraft and shipbuilding shares);
TA 1988, s. 503 (treatment of the commercial letting of furnished holiday accommodation for the purposes of this section).
Amendments.—[1] Words in para. (*b*) substituted by FA 1985, s. 70 (9) with respect to disposals and associated acquisitions made after 5 April 1985.

121. Activities other than trades, and interpretation

(1) Sections 115 to 120 above shall apply with the necessary modifications—

(*a*) in relation to the discharge of the functions of a public authority, and
(*b*) in relation to the occupation of woodlands where the woodlands are managed by the occupier on a commercial basis and with a view to the realisation of profits, and
(*c*) in relation to a profession, vocation, office or employment, and
(*d*) in relation to such of the activities of a body of persons whose activities are carried on otherwise than for profit and are wholly or mainly directed to the protection or promotion of the interests of its members in the carrying on of their trade or profession as are so directed, and
(*e*) in relation to the activities of an unincorporated association or other body chargeable to corporation tax, being a body not established for profit whose activities are wholly or mainly carried on otherwise than for profit, but in the case of assets within head A of class 1 only if they are both occupied and used by the body, and in the case of other assets only if they are used by the body,

as they apply in relation to a trade.

(2) In sections 115 to 120 above and this section the expressions "trade", "profession", "vocation", "office" and "employment" have the same meanings as in the Income Tax Acts, but not so as to apply the provisions of the Income Tax Acts as to the circumstances in which, on a change in the persons carrying on a trade, a trade is to be regarded as discontinued, or as set up and commenced.

(3) Sections 115 to 120 above, and this section, shall be construed as one.

Cross references.—See TA 1970, s. 278 (1), (4) (*b*) (effect of claims under this section when a company ceases to be a member of a group of companies);
FA 1976, s. 54 (3) (*b*) (compulsory acquisition of aircraft and shipbuilding shares).

Stock in trade

122. Appropriations to and from stock

(1) Subject to subsection (3) below, where an asset acquired by a person otherwise than as trading stock of a trade carried on by him is appropriated by him for the purposes of the trade as trading stock (whether on the commencement of the trade or otherwise) and, if he had then sold the asset for its market value, a chargeable gain or allowable loss would have accrued to him, he shall be treated as having thereby disposed of the asset by selling it for its then market value.

(2) If at any time an asset forming part of the trading stock of a person's trade is appropriated by him for any other purpose, or is retained by him on his ceasing to carry on the trade, he shall be treated as having acquired it at that time for a consideration equal to the amount brought into the accounts of the trade in respect of it for tax purposes on the appropriation or on his ceasing to carry on the trade, as the case may be.

(3) Subsection (1) above shall not apply in relation to a person's appropriation of an asset for the purposes of a trade if he is chargeable to income tax in respect of the profits of the trade under Case I of Schedule D, and elects that instead the market value of the asset at the time of the appropriation shall, in computing the profits of the trade for purposes of tax, be treated as reduced by the amount of the chargeable gain or increased by the amount of the allowable loss referred to in that subsection, and where that subsection does not apply by reason of such an election, the profits of the trade shall be computed accordingly:

Provided that if a person making an election under this subsection is at the time of the appropriation carrying on the trade in partnership with others, the election shall not have effect unless concurred in by the others.

Cross references.—See TA 1988, s. 777 (11) (transactions in land).

Transfer of business to a company

123. Roll-over relief on transfer of business

(1) This section shall apply for the purposes of this Act where a person who is not a company transfers to a company a business as a going concern, together with the whole assets of the business, or together with the whole of those assets other than cash, and the business is so transferred wholly or partly in exchange for shares issued by the company to the person transferring the business.

Any shares so received by the transferor in exchange for the business are referred to below as "the new assets".

(2) The amount determined under subsection (4) below shall be deducted from the aggregate (referred to below as "the amount of the gain on the old assets") of the chargeable gains less allowable losses.

(3) For the purpose of computing any chargeable gain accruing on the disposal of any new asset—

(*a*) the amount determined under subsection (4) below shall be apportioned between the new assets as a whole, and
(*b*) the sums allowable as a deduction under section 32 (1) (*a*) above shall be reduced by the amount apportioned to the new asset under paragraph (*a*) above;

and if the shares which comprise the new assets are not all of the same class, the apportionment between the shares under paragraph (*a*) above shall be in accordance with their market values at the time they were acquired by the transferor.

(4) The amount referred to in subsections (2) and (3) (*a*) above shall not exceed the cost of the new assets but, subject to that, the said amount shall be a fraction $\frac{A}{B}$ of the amount of the gain on the old assets where—

"A" is the cost of the new assets, and
"B" is the value of the whole of the consideration received by the transferor in exchange for the business;

and for the purposes of this subsection "the cost of the new assets" means any sums which would be allowable as a deduction under section 32 (1) (*a*) above if the new assets were disposed of as a whole in circumstances giving rise to a chargeable gain.

(5) References in this section to the business, in relation to shares or consideration received in exchange for the business, include references to such assets of the business as are referred to in subsection (1) above.

Cross references.—See TA 1988, s. 763 (5) (disposal constituting disposal for capital gains tax purposes and also giving rise to an offshore income gain; deduction of the offshore income gain in determining fraction "B" in sub-s. (4) above),
Sch. 28, para. 3 (2) (calculation of unindexed gain for the purpose of computation of offshore income gains; unindexed gain accruing on transfers to which this section applies);
FA 1988, Sch. 9, paras. 1, 2 (reduction of a deferred charge to tax where the charge is wholly or partly attributable to an increase in the value of an asset before 31 March 1982).

[123A. Harbour authorities

(1) For the purposes of this Act any asset transferred on the transfer of the trade shall be deemed to be for a consideration such that no gain or loss accrues to the transferor on its transfer; and for the purposes of Schedule 5 to this Act the transferee shall be treated as if the acquisition by the transferor of any asset so transferred had been the transferee's acquisition thereof.

(2) This section applies only where the trade transferred is transferred from any body corporate other than a limited liability company to a harbour authority by or under a certified harbour reorganisation scheme (within the meaning of section 518 of the Taxes Act 1988) which provides also for the dissolution of the transferor.][1]

Former enactment.—TA 1970, s. 352 (1), (7).
Cross references.—See FA 1985, s. 68 (7A) (*a*), (*b*) (new rules for calculation of indexation allowance in respect of assets held on 31st March 1982);
FA 1988, Sch. 8, para. 1 (3) (*a*), (*b*) (extension of indexation allowance to unindexed gains and losses in relation to assets held on 31 March 1982).
Amendments.—[1] This section inserted by TA 1988, Sch. 29, para. 22.

Transfer of business on retirement

124. Relief on transfer

(1) If an individual who has attained the age of 60 years—

(a) *disposes by way of sale or gift of the whole or part of a business, or*
(b) *disposes by way of sale or gift of shares or securities of a company,*

and throughout a period of at least one year ending with the disposal the relevant conditions have been fulfilled, relief shall be given under this section in respect of gains accruing to him on the disposal.

(2) For the purposes of subsection (1) above the relevant conditions are fulfilled at any time if at that time,—

(a) *in the case of a disposal falling within paragraph (a) of that subsection, the business in question is owned either by the individual or by a company with respect to which the following conditions are at that time fulfilled, namely—*

(i) *it is a trading company,*
(ii) *it is the individual's family company, and*
(iii) *he is a full-time working director of it;*

and
(b) *in the case of a disposal falling within paragraph (b) of that subsection, either the conditions in sub-paragraphs (i) to (iii) of paragraph (a) above are fulfilled with respect to the company in question or the individual owns the business which, at the time of the disposal, is owned by the company;*

and in relation to a particular disposal the period, up to a maximum of 10 years, which ends with the disposal and throughout which the relevant conditions are fulfilled is in this section referred to as "the qualifying period".

(3) The amount available for relief under this section shall be—

(a) *in the case of an individual who has attained the age of 65 years, the relevant percentage of [£100,000][1], and*
(b) *in the case of an individual who has not attained that age, the relevant percentage of the aggregate of [£20,000][1] for every year by which his age exceeds 60 and a corresponding part of [£20,000][1] for any odd part of a year;*

and for the purpose of this subsection "the relevant percentage" means a percentage determined according to the length of the qualifying period on a scale rising arithmetically from 10 per cent. where that period is precisely one year to 100 per cent. where it is ten years.

(4) Where subsection (1) (a) above applies the gains accruing to the individual on the disposal of chargeable business assets comprised in the disposal by way of sale or gift shall be aggregated, and only so much of that aggregate as exceeds the amount available for relief under this section shall be chargeable gains (but not so as to affect liability in respect of gains accruing on the disposal of assets other than chargeable business assets).

(5) Where subsection (1) (b) above applies—

(a) *the gains which accrue to the individual on the disposal of the shares or securities shall be aggregated, and*
(b) *of a proportion of that aggregate sum which is equal to the proportion which the part of the value of the company's chargeable assets at the time of the disposal which is attributable to the value of the company's chargeable business assets bears to the whole of that value, only so much as exceeds the amount available for relief under this section shall constitute chargeable gains (but not so as to affect liability in respect of gains representing the balance of the said aggregate sum),*

and for the purposes of paragraph (b) above every asset is a chargeable asset except one, on the disposal of which by the company at the time of the disposal of the shares or securities no chargeable gain would accrue.

(6) So far as the amount available for relief under this section is applied in giving relief to an individual as respects a disposal it shall not be applied in giving relief to that individual as respects any other disposal (and the relief shall be applied in the order in which any disposals take place).

(7) In arriving at the aggregate under subsection (4) or subsection (5) above—

(a) *the respective amounts of the gains shall be computed in accordance with the provisions of this Act (other than this section) fixing the amount of chargeable gains, and*
(b) *any allowable loss which accrues on the disposal shall be deducted,*

and the provisions of this section shall not affect the computation of the amount of any allowable loss.

(8) In this section—

"*chargeable business asset*" means an asset (including goodwill but not including shares or securities or other assets held as investments) which is, or is an interest in, an asset used for the purposes of a trade, profession, vocation, office or employment carried on by the individual, or as the case may be by the individual's family company, other than an asset on the disposal of which no chargeable gain accrues or (where the disposal is of shares or securities in the family company) on the disposal of which no chargeable gain would accrue if the family company disposed of the asset at the time of the disposal of the shares or securities,

"*family company*" means, in relation to an individual, a company the voting rights in which are—
 (a) as to not less than 25 per cent., exercisable by the individual, or
 (b) as to not less than 51 per cent., exercisable by the individual or a member of his family, and, as to not less than 5 per cent., exercisable by the individual himself,

"*family*" means, in relation to an individual, the husband or wife of the individual, and a relative of the individual or the individual's husband or wife, and "relative" means brother, sister, ancestor or lineal descendant,

"*full time working director*" means a director who is required to devote substantially the whole of his time to the service of the company in a managerial or technical capacity,

"*trade*", "*profession*", "*vocation*", "*office*" and "*employment*" have the same meanings as in the Income Tax Acts,

"*trading company*" has the meaning given by paragraph [7 of schedule 19 to the Taxes Act 1988];[2]

and in this section references to the disposal of the whole or part of a business include references to the disposal of the whole or part of the assets provided or held for the purposes of an office or employment by the person exercising that office or employment.

Cross references.—See FA 1985, Sch. 20, para. 15 (4), 16 (5) (new provisions in FA 1985, ss. 69, 70 and Sch. 20 in respect of transfer of assets on retirement or ill-health; extension of the relief under this section to the new provisions); TA 1988, s. 503 (treatment of the commercial letting of furnished holiday accommodation for the purposes of this section).
Amendments.—[1] Amounts in sub-s. (3) (a), (b) substituted by FA 1984, s. 63 (4), (5) with respect to disposals after 5 April 1983.
This section repealed by FA 1985, s. 69 (1) and Sch. 27, Pt. VII in relation to any disposal made after 5 April 1985 and in respect of which the qualifying period (as defined in FA 1985, Sch. 20, para. 4 (2)) ends after 5 April 1985.
[2] Words in sub-s. (8) substituted by TA 1988, Sch. 29, para. 32 Table.

125. Transfer by way of capital distribution from family company

(1) Subject to subsection (2) below, section 124 (1) (b) above shall apply where under section 72 above (distribution which is not a new holding) the individual is treated as disposing of interests in shares or securities of a company in consideration of a capital distribution from the company in the course of dissolving or winding up the company as it applies where he disposes of shares or securities of a company by way of sale or gift.

(2) Subsection (1) above shall not apply if the capital distribution consists wholly of chargeable business assets of the company, and if it consists partly of chargeable business assets (and partly of money or money's worth), relief shall only be given under section 124 above in respect of that proportion of the gains accruing on the disposal which the part of the capital distribution not consisting of chargeable business assets bears to the entire capital distribution.

Amendments.—This section repealed by FA 1985, s. 69 (1) and Sch. 27, Pt. VII in relation to any disposal made after 5 April 1985 and in respect of which the qualifying period (as defined in FA 1985, Sch. 20, para. 4 (2)) ends after 5 April 1985.

Gifts of business assets

126. Relief for gifts of business assets

[(1) If—
 (a) an individual (in this section referred to as "the transferor") makes a disposal

otherwise than under a bargain at arm's length of an asset within subsection (1A) below, and

(b) a claim for relief under this section is made by the transferor and the person who acquires the asset (in this section referred to as "the transferee") or, where the trustees of a settlement are the transferee, by the transferor alone,

then, subject to subsection (2) and sections 126A and 126B below, subsection (3) below shall apply in relation to the disposal.][7]

[(1A) An asset is within this subsection if—

(a) it is, or is an interest in, an asset used for the purposes of a trade, profession or vocation carried on by—

(i) the transferor, or
(ii) his family company, or
(iii) a member of a trading group of which the holding company is his family company, or

(b) it consists of shares or securities of a trading company, or of the holding company of a trading group, where—

(i) the shares or securities are neither quoted on a recognised stock exchange nor dealt in on the Unlisted Securities Market, or
(ii) the trading company or holding company is the transferor's family company.][7]

(2) Subsection (3) below does not apply in relation to a disposal if—

(a) in the case of a disposal of an asset, any gain accruing to the transferor on the disposal is (apart from this section) wholly relieved under [Schedule 20 to the Finance Act 1985][6],
(b) in the case of a disposal of shares or securities, [the appropriate proportion][2] determined under [paragraph 7 (2) or paragraph 8 (2) of Schedule 20 to the Finance Act 1985][3] of any gain accruing to the transferor on the disposal is (apart from this section) wholly relieved under [that Schedule][4], [or][8],
[(c) in the case of a disposal of qualifying corporate bonds within the meaning of section 64 of the Finance Act 1984, a gain is deemed to accrue by virtue of paragraph 10 (1) (b) of Schedule 13 to that Act, or]
[(d) subsection (3) of section 147A below applies in relation to the disposal (or would apply if a claim for relief were duly made under that section).]

(3) Where a claim for relief is made under this section in respect of a disposal—

(a) the amount of any chargeable gain which, apart from this section, would accrue to the transferor on the disposal, and
(b) the amount of the consideration for which, apart from this section, the transferee would be regarded for the purposes of capital gains tax as having acquired the asset or, as the case may be, the shares or securities,

shall each be reduced by an amount equal to the held-over gain on the disposal.

(4) Part I of Schedule 4 to this Act shall have effect for extending the relief provided for by virtue of subsections (1) to (3) above in the case of agricultural property and for applying it in relation to settled property.

(5) Subject to Part II of Schedule 4 to this Act (which provides for reductions in the held-over gain in certain cases) and subsection (6) below, the reference in subsection (3) above to the held-over gain on a disposal is a reference to the chargeable gain which would have accrued on that disposal apart from subsection (3) above and (in appropriate cases) [Schedule 20 to the Finance Act 1985][6], and in subsection (6) below that chargeable gain is referred to as the unrelieved gain on the disposal.

(6) In any case where—

(a) there is actual consideration (as opposed to the consideration equal to the market value which is deemed to be given by virtue of section [29A (1)][1] above) for a disposal in respect of which a claim for relief is made under this section, and
(b) that actual consideration exceeds the sums allowable as a deduction under section 32 above,

the held-over gain on the disposal shall be the amount by which the unrelieved gain on the disposal exceeds the excess referred to in paragraph (b) above.

(7) Subject to subsection (8) below, in this section and Schedule 4 to this Act—

(a) "family company" [, "holding company", "trading company" and "trading group" have the meanings][9] given by [paragraph 1 of Schedule 20 to the Finance Act 1985][5],

(b) ...[11],
(c) "trade", "profession" and "vocation" have the same meaning as in the Income Tax Acts.

(8) In this section and Schedule 4 to this Act and in determining whether a company is a trading company for the purposes of this section and that Schedule, the expression "trade" shall be taken to include the occupation of woodlands where the woodlands are managed by the occupier on a commercial basis and with a view to the realisation of profits.

[(9) Where a disposal in respect of which a claim is made under this section is (or proves to be) a chargeable transfer for inheritance tax purposes, there shall be allowed as a deduction in computing (for capital gains tax purposes) the chargeable gain accruing to the transferee on the disposal of the asset in question an amount equal to whichever is the lesser of—

(a) the inheritance tax attributable to the value of the asset, and
(b) the amount of the chargeable gain as computed apart from this subsection,

and, in the case of a disposal which, being a potentially exempt transfer, proves to be a chargeable transfer, all necessary adjustments shall be made, whether by the discharge or repayment of capital gains tax or otherwise.][10]

[(10) Where an amount of inheritance tax—

(a) falls to be redetermined in consequence of the transferor's death within seven years of making the chargeable transfer in question, or
(b) is otherwise varied,

after it has been taken into account under subsection (9) above, all necessary adjustments shall be made, whether by the making of an assessment to capital gains tax or by the discharge or repayment of such tax.][10]

Cross references.—See FA 1981, s. 79 (1) (a) (charge on held-over gain where transferee migrates);
FA 1986, s. 58 (1) (charge on held-over gain where transferee is or becomes a dual resident trust);
TA 1988, s. 503 (treatment of the commercial letting of furnished holiday accommodation for the purposes of this section),
Sch. 28, para. 3 (3) (claim under this section in respect of gains from a disposal of an offshore fund);
FA 1988, Sch. 9, paras. 1, 2 (reduction of a deferred charge to tax where the charge is wholly or partly attributable to an increase in the value of an asset before 31 March 1982).
Amendments.—[1] Words in sub-s. (6) (a) substituted by FA 1981, s. 90 (3) (a).
[2] Words in sub-s. (2) (b) substituted by FA 1985, s. 70 (9) (a) in relation to disposals made after 5 April 1985.
[3] Words in sub-s. (2) (b) substituted by FA 1985, s. 70 (9) (a) in relation to disposals made after 5 April 1985.
[4] Words in sub-s. (2) (b) substituted by FA 1985, s. 70 (9) (a).
[5] Words in sub-s. (7) (a) substituted by FA 1985, s. 70 (9) (b) in relation to disposals made after 5 April 1985.
[6] Words in sub-ss. (2) (a), (5) substituted by FA 1985, s. 70 (9) (d) in relation to disposals made after 5 April 1985.
[7] Sub-ss. (1), (1A) substituted for sub-s. (1) by FA 1989, s. 124 (2), (3) and Sch. 14, para. 1 in relation to disposals after 13 March 1989 with certain exceptions; see FA 1989, s. 124 (3).
[8] Sub-s. (2) (c), (d) and the word "or" at the end of sub-s. (2) (b) added by *ibid*.
[9] Words in sub-s. (7) (a) substituted by *ibid*.
[10] Sub-ss. (9), (10) added by *ibid*.
[11] Sub-s. (7) (b) repealed by *ibid*. and Sch. 17, Pt. VII in relation to disposals after 13 March 1989.

[126A. Section 126 relief: gifts to non-residents

(1) Section 126 (3) above shall not apply where the transferee is neither resident nor ordinarily resident in the United Kingdom.

(2) Section 126 (3) above shall not apply where the transferee is an individual or a company if that individual or company—

(a) though resident or ordinarily resident in the United Kingdom, is regarded for the purposes of any double taxation arrangements having effect by virtue of section 788 of the Taxes Act 1988 as resident in a territory outside the United Kingdom, and
(b) by virtue of the arrangements would not be liable in the United Kingdom to tax on a gain arising on a disposal of the asset occurring immediately after its acquisition.][1]

Amendments.—[1] This section inserted by FA 1989, s. 124 (2), (3) and Sch. 14, para. 2 in relation to disposals after 13 March 1989 with certain exceptions; see FA 1989, s. 124 (3).

[126B. Section 126 relief: gifts to foreign-controlled companies

(1) Section 126 (3) above shall not apply where the transferee is a company which is within subsection (2) below.

(2) A company is within this subsection if it is controlled by a person who, or by persons each of whom,—

(*a*) is neither resident nor ordinarily resident in the United Kingdom, and
(*b*) is connected with the person making the disposal.

(3) For the purposes of subsection (2) above, a person who (either alone or with others) controls a company by virtue of holding assets relating to that or any other company and who is resident or ordinarily resident in the United Kingdom shall be regarded as neither resident nor ordinarily resident there if—

(*a*) he is regarded for the purposes of any double taxation arrangements having effect by virtue of section 788 of the Taxes Act 1988 as resident in a territory outside the United Kingdom, and
(*b*) by virtue of the arrangements he would not be liable in the United Kingdom to tax on a gain arising on a disposal of the assets.][1]

Amendments.—[1] This section inserted by FA 1989, s. 124 (2), (3) and Sch. 14, para. 2 in relation to disposals after 13 March 1989 with certain exceptions; see FA 1989, s. 124 (3).

[126C. Section 126 relief: emigration of controlling trustees

(1) Subsection (2) below applies where—

(*a*) relief under section 126 above is given in respect of a disposal of an asset to a company which is controlled by the trustees of a settlement ("the relevant disposal"),
(*b*) at the time of the relevant disposal the person making it is connected with the trustees, and
(*c*) at a time when the company has not disposed of the asset and the trustees have not ceased to control the company, they become neither resident nor ordinarily resident in the United Kingdom.

(2) Where this subsection applies then, subject to the following provisions of this section, a chargeable gain shall be deemed to have accrued to the trustees immediately before the time mentioned in subsection (1) (*c*) above, and its amount shall be equal to the held-over gain (within the meaning of section 126 above) on the relevant disposal.

(3) For the purposes of paragraph (*c*) of subsection (1) above, the company shall be taken to have disposed of an asset before the time referred to in that paragraph only if it has made a disposal or disposals in connection with which the whole of the held-over gain on the relevant disposal was represented by reductions made in accordance with section 126 (3) (*b*) above; and where the company has made a disposal in connection with which part of that gain was so represented, the amount of chargeable gain deemed by virtue of this section to accrue to the trustees shall be correspondingly reduced.

(4) The disposals by the company that are to be taken into account under subsection (3) above shall not include any disposal to which section 273 of the Taxes Act 1970 (transfers within a group) applies; but where the company disposes of an asset by a disposal to which that section applies, the first subsequent disposal of the asset by another member of the group which is a disposal to which that section does not apply shall be taken into account under subsection (3) above as if it had been made by the company.

(5) Where an amount of tax assessed on trustees by virtue of this section is not paid within the period of twelve months beginning with the date when the tax becomes payable then, subject to subsection (6) below, the transferor may be assessed and charged (in the name of the trustees) to all or any part of that tax.

(6) No assessment shall be made under subsection (5) above more than six years after the end of the year in which the relevant disposal was made.

(7) Where the transferor pays an amount of tax in pursuance of subsection (5) above, he shall be entitled to recover a corresponding sum from the trustees.

(8) Gains on disposals made after a chargeable gain has under this section been deemed to accrue by reference to a held-over gain shall be computed without any reduction under section 126 (3) (*b*) above in respect of that held-over gain.

(9) Section 126B (3) above shall for the purposes of subsection (1) (*c*) above as it applies for the purposes of section 126B (2).][1]

Amendments.—[1] This section inserted by FA 1989, s. 124 (2), (3) and Sch. 14, para. 2 in relation to disposals after 13 March 1989 with certain exceptions; see FA 1989, s. 124 (3).

Movable property

127. Wasting assets

(1) Subject to the provisions of this section, no chargeable gain shall accrue on the disposal of, or of an interest in, an asset which is tangible movable property and which is a wasting asset.

(2) Subsection (1) above shall not apply to a disposal of, or of an interest in, an asset—

(*a*) if, from the beginning of the period of ownership of the person making the disposal to the time when the disposal is made, the asset has been used and used solely for the purposes of a trade, profession or vocation and if that person has claimed or could have claimed any capital allowance in respect of any expenditure attributable to the asset or interest under paragraph (*a*) or paragraph (*b*) of section 32(1) above (allowable expenditure), or

(*b*) if the person making the disposal has incurred any expenditure on the asset or interest which has otherwise qualified in full for any capital allowance.

(3) In the case of the disposal of, or of an interest in, an asset which, in the period of ownership of the person making the disposal, has been used partly for the purposes of a trade, profession or vocation and partly for other purposes, or has been used for the purposes of a trade, profession or vocation for part of that period, or which has otherwise qualified in part only for capital allowances—

(*a*) the consideration for the disposal, and any expenditure attributable to the asset or interest by virtue of section 32(1)(*a*) and (*b*) above, shall be apportioned by reference to the extent to which that expenditure qualified for capital allowances, and

(*b*) the computation under Chapter II of Part II above shall be made separately in relation to the apportioned parts of the expenditure and consideration, and

(*c*) subsection (1) above shall not apply to any gain accruing by reference to the computation in relation to the part of the consideration apportioned to use for the purposes of the trade, profession or vocation, or to the expenditure qualifying for capital allowances.

(4) Subsection (1) above shall not apply to a disposal of commodities of any description by a person dealing on a terminal market or dealing with or through a person ordinarily engaged in dealing on a terminal market.

(5) This section shall be construed as one with Chapter II of Part II above.

128. Chattel exemption

(1) Subject to this section a gain accruing on a disposal of an asset which is tangible movable property shall not be a chargeable gain if the amount or value of the consideration for the disposal does not exceed [£6,000][1].

(2) Where the amount or value of the consideration for the disposal of an asset which is tangible movable property exceeds [£6,000][1], there shall be excluded from any chargeable gain accruing on the disposal so much of it as exceeds five-thirds of the difference between—

(*a*) the amount or value of the consideration, and

(*b*) [£6,000][1].

(3) Subsections (1) and (2) above shall not affect the amount of an allowable loss accruing on the disposal of an asset, but for the purposes of computing under this Act the amount of a loss accruing on the disposal of tangible movable property the consideration for the disposal shall, if less than [£6,000][1], be deemed to be [£6,000][1] and the losses which are allowable losses shall be restricted accordingly.

(4) If two or more assets which have formed part of a set of articles of any description all owned at one time by one person are disposed of by that person, and—

(*a*) to the same person, or

(*b*) to persons who are acting in concert or who are connected persons,

whether on the same or different occasions, the two or more transactions shall be treated as a single transaction disposing of a single asset, but with any necessary apportionments of the reductions in chargeable gains, and in allowable losses, under subsections (2) and (3) above.

(5) If the disposal is of a right or interest in or over tangible movable property—

(*a*) in the first instance subsections (1), (2) and (3) above shall be applied in relation to the asset as a whole, taking the consideration as including the market value of what remains undisposed of, in addition to the actual consideration,

(b) where the sum of the actual consideration and that market value exceeds [£6,000][1], the part of any chargeable gain that is excluded from it under subsection (2) above shall be so much of the gain as exceeds five-thirds of the difference between that sum and [£6,000][1] multiplied by the fraction equal to the actual consideration divided by the said sum, and

(c) where that sum is less than [£6,000][1] any loss shall be restricted under subsection (3) above by deeming the consideration to be the actual consideration plus the said fraction of the difference between the said sum and [£6,000][1].

(6) This section shall not apply—

(a) in relation to a disposal of commodities of any description by a person dealing on a terminal market or dealing with or through a person ordinarily engaged in dealing on a terminal market, or

(b) in relation to a disposal of currency of any description.

Cross references.—See TMA 1970, s. 12 (2) (b) (information about chargeable gains).
Amendments.—[1] Amount "£6,000" in sub-ss. (1), (2), (3), (5) substituted by FA 1989, s. 123 (1) (a).

129. Leases of property other than land

Schedule 3 to this Act has effect, to the extent specified in paragraph 9 of that Schedule, as respects leases of property other than land.

130. Passenger vehicles

A mechanically propelled road vehicle constructed or adapted for the carriage of passengers, except for a vehicle of a type not commonly used as a private vehicle and unsuitable to be so used, shall not be a chargeable asset; and accordingly no chargeable gain or allowable loss shall accrue on its disposal.

Cross references.—See TMA 1970, s. 12 (2) (information about chargeable gains).

131. Decorations for valour or gallant conduct

A gain shall not be a chargeable gain if accruing on the disposal by any person of a decoration awarded for valour or gallant conduct which he acquired otherwise than for consideration in money or money's worth.

Cross references.—See TMA 1970, s. 12 (2) (information about chargeable gains).

Other property

132. Commodities and other assets without earmark

Sections 65 and 66 above (rules of identification), and paragraph 13 of Schedule 5 to this Act (assets held on 6th April 1965) have effect, to the extent there specified, as respects assets dealt with without identifying the particular assets disposed of or acquired.

[132A. Deep discount securities

(1) Subject to subsections (2) and (3) below, in computing for the purposes of capital gains tax, the gain accruing on the disposal by any person of any deep discount securities (within the meaning of Schedule 4 of the Taxes Act 1988—

(a) section 31 above shall not apply but the consideration for the disposal shall be treated as reduced by the amount mentioned in paragraph 4 (1) (a) of that Schedule (including any amount mentioned in paragraph 3 of that Schedule); and

(b) where that amount exceeds the consideration for the disposal, the amount of the excess shall be treated as expenditure within section 32 (1) (b) above incurred by that person on the security immediately before the disposal.

(2) Subsection (3) below applies where—

(a) there is a conversion of securities to which section 82 above applies and those securities include deep discount securities; or

(b) securities including deep discount securities are exchanged (or by virtue of section

86 (1) above are treated as exchanged) for other securities in circumstances in which section 85 (3) above applies.

(3) Where this subsection applies—

(a) subsection (1) and section 31 above shall not apply but any sum payable to the beneficial owner of the deep discount securities by way of consideration for their disposal (in addition to his new holding) shall be treated for the purpose of capital gains tax as reduced by the amount of the accrued income on which he is chargeable to income tax by virtue of paragraph 7 (3) of Schedule 4 to the Taxes Act 1988 or, in a case where paragraph 3 of that Schedule applies, on which he would be so chargeable if that paragrah did not apply; and
(b) where that amount exceeds any such sum, the excess shall be treated as expenditure within section 32 (1) (b) above incurred by him on the security immediately before the time of the conversion or exchange.

(4) Where a disposal of a deep discount security is to be treated for the purposes of capital gains tax as one on which neither a gain nor a loss accrues to the person making the disposal, the consideration for which the person acquiring the security would, apart from this subsection, be treated for those purposes as having acquired the security shall be increased by the amount mentioned in paragraph 4 (1) (a) of Schedule 4 to the Taxes Act 1988 (including any amount mentioned in paragraph 3 of that Schedule).][1]

[(5) Where by virtue of paragraph 18 (3) of Schedule 4 to the Taxes Act 1988 trustees are deemed for the purposes of that Schedule to dispose of a security at a particular time—

(a) they shall be deemed to dispose of the security at that time for the purposes of this Act, and
(b) the disposal deemed by paragraph (a) above shall be deemed to be at the market value of the security.][2]

[(6) Where by virtue of paragraph 18 (4) of Schedule 4 to the Taxes Act 1988 trustees are deemed for the purposes of that Schedule to acquire a security at a particular time—

(a) they shall be deemed to acquire the security at that time for the purposes of this Act, and
(b) the acquisition deemed by paragraph (a) above shall be deemed to be at the market value of the security.][2]

Amendments.—[1] This section inserted by TA 1988, Sch. 29, para. 23.
[2] Sub-ss (5), (6) inserted by FA 1989, s. 96 (3).

133. Foreign currency for personal expenditure

A gain shall not be a chargeable gain if accruing on the disposal by an individual of currency of any description acquired by him for the personal expenditure outside the United Kingdom of himself or his family or dependants (including expenditure on the provision or maintenance of any residence outside the United Kingdom).

Cross references.—See TMA 1970, s. 12 (2) (information about chargeable gains).

134. Debts

(1) Where a person incurs a debt to another, whether in sterling or in some other currency, no chargeable gain shall accrue to that (that is the original) creditor or his personal representative or legatee on a disposal of the debt, except in the case of the debt on a security (as defined in section 82 above).

(2) Subject to the provisions of sections 82 and 85 above (conversion of securities and company amalgamations), and subject to subsection (1) above, the satisfaction of a debt or part of it (including a debt on a security as defined in section 82 above) shall be treated as a disposal of the debt or of that part by the creditor made at the time when the debt or that part is satisfied.

(3) Where property is acquired by a creditor in satisfaction of his debt or part of it, then subject to the provisions of sections 82 and 85 above the property shall not be treated as disposed of by the debtor or acquired by the creditor for a consideration greater than its market value at the time of the creditor's acquisition of it; but if under subsection (1) above (and in a case not falling within either of the said sections 82 and 85) no chargeable gain is to accrue on a disposal of the debt by the creditor (that is the original creditor), and a

chargeable gain accrues to him on a disposal by him of the property, the amount of the chargeable gain shall (where necessary) be reduced so as not to exceed the chargeable gain which would have accrued if he had acquired the property for a consideration equal to the amount of the debt or that part of it.

(4) A loss accruing on the disposal of a debt acquired by the person making the disposal from the original creditor or his personal representative or legatee at a time when the creditor or his personal representative or legatee is a person connected with the person making the disposal, and so acquired either directly or by one or more purchases through persons all of whom are connected with the person making the disposal, shall not be an allowable loss.

(5) Where the original creditor is a trustee and the debt, when created, is settled property, subsections (1) and (4) above shall apply as if for the references to the original creditor's personal representative or legatee there were substituted references to any person becoming absolutely entitled, as against the trustee to the debt on its ceasing to settled property, and to that person's personal representative or legatee.

Cross references.—See Trustee Savings Banks Act 1985, Sch. 2, para. 4 (1) (reorganisation of trustee savings banks; transfer of debts owed to trustee savings banks etc to companies; transferee to be treated as the original creditor for the purposes of this section).

135. Debts: foreign currency bank accounts

(1) Subject to subsection (2) below, section 134 (1) above shall not apply to a debt owed by a bank which is not in sterling and which is represented by a sum standing to the credit of a person in an account in the bank.

(2) Subsection (1) above shall not apply to a sum in an individual's bank account representing currency acquired by the holder for the personal expenditure outside the United Kingdom of himself or his family or dependants (including expenditure on the provision or maintenance of any residence outside the United Kingdom).

136. Relief in respect of loans to traders

(1) In this section "a qualifying loan" means a loan in the case of which—

(a) the money lent is used by the borrower wholly for the purposes of a trade carried on by him, not being a trade which consists of or includes the lending of money, and
(b) the borrower is resident in the United Kingdom, and
(c) the borrower's debt is not a debt on a security as defined in section 82 above;

and for the purposes of paragraph (a) above money used by the borrower for setting up a trade which is subsequently carried on by him shall be treated as used for the purposes of that trade.

(2) In subsection (1) above references to a trade include references to a profession or vocation; and where money lent to a company is lent by it to another company in the same group, being a trading company, that subsection shall apply to the money lent to the first-mentioned company as if it had used it for any purpose for which it is used by the other company while a member of the group.

(3) If, on a claim by a person who has made a qualifying loan, the inspector is satisfied that—

(a) any outstanding amount of the principal of the loan has become irrecoverable, and
(b) the claimant has not assigned his right to recover that amount, and
(c) the claimant and the borrower were not each other's spouses, or companies in the same group, when the loan was made or at any subsequent time,

this Act shall have effect as if an allowable loss equal to that amount had accrued to the claimant when the claim was made.

(4) If, on a claim by a person who has guaranteed the repayment of a loan which is, or but for subsection (1) (c) above would be, a qualifying loan, the inspector is satisfied that—

(a) any outstanding amount of, or of interest in respect of, the principal of the loan has become irrecoverable from the borrower, and
(b) the claimant has made a payment under the guarantee (whether to the lender or a co-guarantor) in respect of that amount, and
(c) the claimant has not assigned any right to recover that amount which has accrued to

him (whether by operation of law or otherwise) in consequence of his having made the payment, and

(d) the lender and the borrower were not each other's spouses, or companies in the same group, when the loan was made or at any subsequent time and the claimant and the borrower were not each other's spouses, and the claimant and the lender were not companies in the same group, when the guarantee was given or at any subsequent time,

this Act shall have effect as if an allowable loss had accrued to the claimant when the payment was made; and the loss shall be equal to the payment made by him in respect of the amount mentioned in paragraph (a) above less any contribution payable to him by any co-guarantor in respect of the payment so made.

(5) Where an allowable loss has been treated under subsection (3) or (4) above as accruing to any person and the whole or any part of the outstanding amount mentioned in subsection (3) (a) or, as the case may be, subsection (4) (a) is at any time recovered by him, this Act shall have effect as if there had accrued to him at that time a chargeable gain equal to so much of the allowable loss as corresponds to the amount recovered.

(6) For the purposes of subsection (5) above, a person shall be treated as recovering an amount if he (or any other person by his direction) receives any money or money's worth in satisfaction of his right to recover that amount or in consideration of his assignment of the right to recover it; and where a person assigns such a right otherwise than by way of a bargain made at arm's length he shall be treated as receiving money or money's worth equal to the market value of the right at the time of the assignment.

(7) No amount shall be treated under this section as giving rise to an allowable loss or chargeable gain in the case of any person if it falls to be taken into account in computing his income for the purposes of income tax or corporation tax.

(8) Where an allowable loss has been treated as accruing to a person under subsection (4) above by virtue of a payment made by him at any time under a guarantee—

(a) no chargeable gain shall accrue to him otherwise than under subsection (5) above, and
(b) no allowable loss shall accrue to him under this Act,

on his disposal of any rights that have accrued to him (whether by operation of law or otherwise) in consequence of his having made any payment under the guarantee at or after that time.

(9) References in this section to an amount having become irrecoverable do not include references to cases where the amount has become irrecoverable in consequence of the terms of the loan, of any arrangements of which the loan forms part, or of any act or omission by the lender or, in a case within subsection (4) above, the guarantor.

(10) In this section

(a) "spouses" means spouses who are living together (construed in accordance with section 155 (2) below),
(b) "trading company" has the meaning given by [paragraph 1 of Schedule 20 to the Finance Act 1985][2], and
(c) "group" shall be construed in accordance with section 272 of the Taxes Act [1970][1].

(11) Subsection (3) above applies where the loan is made after 11th April 1978 and subsection (4) above applies where the guarantee is given after that date.

Cross references.—See TA 1988, s. 503 (treatment of the commercial letting of furnished holiday accommodation for the purposes of this section).
Amendments.—[1] "1970" in sub-s. (10) (c) inserted by virtue of TA 1988, Sch. 29, para. 15 (b).
[2] Words in sub-s. 10 (b) substituted by FA 1989, Sch. 12, para. 6 where the claim under this section is made after 31 March 1989.

137. Options and forfeited deposits

(1) Without prejudice to section 19 above (general provisions about the disposal of assets), the grant of an option, and in particular—

(a) the grant of an option in a case where the grantor binds himself to sell what he does not own, and because the option is abandoned, never has occasion to own, and
(b) the grant of an option in a case where the grantor binds himself to buy what, because the option is abandoned, he does not acquire,

is the disposal of an asset (namely of the option), but subject to the following provisions of this section as to treating the grant of an option as part of a larger transaction.

(2) If an option is exercised the grant of the option and the transaction entered into by the grantor in fulfilment of his obligations under the option shall be treated as a single transaction and accordingly—

(a) if the option binds the grantor to sell, the consideration for the option is part of the consideration for the sale, and

(b) if the option binds the grantor to buy, the consideration for the option shall be deducted from the cost of acquisition incurred by the grantor in buying in pursuance of his obligations under the option.

(3) The exercise of an option by the person for the time being entitled to exercise it shall not constitute the disposal of an asset by that person, but, if an option is exercised then the acquisition of the option (whether directly from the grantor or not) and the transaction entered into by the person exercising the option in exercise of his rights under the option shall be treated as a single transaction and accordingly—

(a) if the option binds the grantor to sell, the cost of acquiring the option shall be part of the cost of acquiring what is sold, and

(b) if the option binds the grantor to buy, the cost of the option shall be treated as a cost incidental to the disposal of what is bought by the grantor of the option.

(4) The abandonment of—

(a) a quoted option to subscribe for shares in a company, or

[(aa) a traded option or financial option, or][1]

(b) an option to acquire assets exercisable by a person intending to use them, if acquired, for the purpose of a trade carried on by him,

shall constitute the disposal of an asset (namely of the option); but the abandonment of any other option by the person for the time being entitled to exercise it shall not constitute the disposal of an asset by that person.

(5) In the case of an option relating to shares or securities this section shall apply subject to the provisions of section 65 above (rules for identification: pooling) and, accordingly, the option may be regarded, in relation to the grantor or in relation to the person entitled to exercise the option, as relating to part of a holding (as defined in section 65 above) of shares or securities.

(6) This section shall apply in relation to an option binding the grantor both to sell and to buy as if it were two separate options with half the consideration attributed to each.

(7) In this section references to an option include references to an option binding the grantor to grant a lease for a premium, or enter into any other transaction which is not a sale, and references to buying and selling in pursuance of an option shall be construed accordingly.

(8) This section shall apply in relation to a forfeited deposit of purchase money or other consideration money for a prospective purchase or other transaction which is abondoned as it applies in relation to the consideration for an option which binds the grantor to sell and which is not exercised.

[(9) In subsection (4) above and sections 138 and 139 below—

(a) "quoted option" means an option which, at the time of the abandonment or other disposal, is quoted on a recognised stock exchange;

(b) "traded option" means an option which, at the time of the abandonment or other disposal, is quoted on a recognised stock exchange or a recognised futures exchange; and

(c) "financial option" means an option which is not a traded option, as defined in paragraph (b) above, but which, subject to subsection (10) below,—

(i) relates to currency, shares, securities or an interest rate and is granted (otherwise than as agent) by a member of a recognised stock exchange, by an authorised person within the meaning of the Financial Services Act 1986 or by a listed institution within the meaning of section 43 of that Act; or

(ii) relates to shares or securities which are dealt in on a recognised stock exchange and is granted by a member of such an exchange, acting as agent; or

(iii) relates to currency, shares, securities or an interest rate and is granted to such an authorised person or institution as is referred to in sub-paragraph (i) above and concurrently and in association with an option falling within that sub-paragraph which is granted by that authorised person or institution to the grantor of the first-mentioned option; or

(iv) relates to shares or securities which are dealt in on a recognised stock exchange and is granted to a member of such an exchange, including such a member acting as agent;

and in this subsection "recognised stock exchange" has the meaning given by section [841][4] of the Taxes Act [1988][3].][2]

[(10) If the Treasury by order so provide, an option of a description specified in the order shall be taken to be within the definition of "financial option" in subsection (9) (c) above; and the power to make an order under this subsection shall be exercisable by statutory instrument which shall be subject to annulment in pursuance of a resolution of the House of Commons.][2]

Cross references.—See FA 1982, Sch. 13, para. 7 (4) (this section not to apply (with certain exceptions) to options subject to indexation allowance).
Amendments.—[1] Sub-s. (4) (aa) substituted by F (No. 2) A 1987, s. 81 (4), (8) with effect from 29 April 1988 by virtue of F (No. 2) A 1987 (Commencement) Order 1988, S.I. 1988 No. 744.
[2] Sub-ss. (9), (10) substituted for sub-s. (9) by F (No. 2) A 1987, s. 81 (5), (8) with effect from 29 April 1988 by virtue of F (No. 2) A 1987 (Commencement) Order 1988, S.I. 1988 No. 744.
[3] "1988" in sub-s. (9) inserted by virtue of TA 1988, Sch. 29, para. 15 (a).
[4] Number in sub-s. (9) substituted by TA 1988, Sch. 29, para. 32 Table.

138. Options: application of rules as to wasting assets

(1) Section 38 above (wasting assets: restriction of allowable expenditure) shall not apply—

(a) to a quoted option to subscribe for shares in a company, or
[(aa) to a traded option or financial option, or][2]
(b) to an option to acquire assets exercisable by a person intending to use them, if acquired, for the purpose of a trade carried on by him.

(2) In relation to the disposal by way of transfer of an option [(other than an option falling within subsection (1) (a) or (aa) above)][1] binding the grantor to sell or buy quoted shares or securities, the option shall be regarded as a wasting asset the life of which ends when the right to exercise the option ends, or when the option becomes valueless, whichever is the earlier.

Subsections (6) and (7) of section 137 above shall apply in relation to this subsection as they apply in relation to that section.

(3) The preceding provisons of this section are without prejudice to the application of sections 37 to 39 above (wasting assets) to options not within those provisions.

(4) In this section—

[(a) "financial option", "quoted option" and "traded option" have the meaning given by section 137 (9) above, and][3]
(b) "quoted shares or securities" means shares or securities which have a quoted market value on a recognised stock exchange in the United Kingdom or elsewhere.

Amendments.—[1] Words in sub-s. (2) substituted by FA 1980, s. 84 (5).
[2] Sub-s. (1) (aa) substituted by F (No. 2) A 1987, s. 81 (6), (8) with effect from 29 April 1988 by virtue of F (No. 2) A 1987 (Commencement) Order 1988, S.I. 1988 No. 744.
[3] Sub-s (4) (a) substituted by F (No. 2) A 1987, s. 81 (7), (8) with effect from 29 April 1988 by virtue of F (No. 2) A 1987 (Commencement) Order 1988, S.I. 1988 No. 744.

139. Quoted options treated as part of new holdings

(1) If a quoted option to subscribe for shares in a company is dealt in (on the stock exchange where it is quoted) within three months after the taking effect, with respect to the company granting the option, of any reorganisation, reduction, conversion or amalgamation to which Chapter II of Part IV above applies, or within such longer period as the Board may by notice in writing allow—

(a) the option shall, for the purposes of the said Chapter II (under which a holding prior to the reorganisation or reduction of capital, conversion or amalgamation is to be treated as the same as the resulting new holding) be regarded as the shares which could be acquired by exercising the option, and
(b) section 150 (3) below shall apply for determining its market value.

(2) In this section "quoted option" has the meaning given by section 137 (9) above.

PART VII
OTHER PROVISIONS

Insurance

140. Policies of insurance

(1) The rights of the insurer under any policy of insurance shall not constitute an asset on the disposal of which a gain may accrue, whether the risks insured relate to property or not; and the rights of the insured under any policy of insurance of the risk of any kind of damage to, or the loss or depreciation of, assets shall constitute an asset on the disposal of which a gain may accrue only to the extent that those rights relate to assets on the disposal of which a gain may accrue or might have accrued.

(2) Notwithstanding subsection (1) above, sums received under a policy of insurance of the risk of any kind of damage to, or the loss or depreciation of, assets are for the purposes of this Act, and in particular for the purposes of section 20 above (disposal of assets by owner where any capital sum is derived from assets), sums derived from the assets.

(3) In this section "policy of insurance" does not include a policy of assurance on human life.

141. Disallowance of insurance premiums as expenses

Without prejudice to the provisions of section 33 above (exclusion of expenditure by reference to tax on income), there shall be excluded from the sums allowable as a deduction in the computation under Part II of Chapter II above of the gain accruing to a person on the disposal of an asset any premiums or other payments made under a policy of insurance of the risk of any kind of damage or injury to, or loss or depreciation of, the asset.

142. Underwriters

(1) An underwriting member of Lloyd's or of an approved association of underwriters shall, subject to the following provisions of this section, be treated for the purposes of this Act as absolutely entitled as against the trustees to the investments of his premiums trust fund, his special reserve fund (if any) and any other trust fund required or authorised by the rules of Lloyd's or the association in question, or required by the underwriting agent through whom his business or any part of it is carried on, to be kept in connection with the business.

(2) The trustees of any premiums trust fund shall, subject to [subsections (2A) and (3)]¹ below, be assessed and charged to capital gains tax as if subsection (1) above had not been passed.

[(2A) Tax assessed by virtue of subsection (2) above for a year of assessment shall be assessed at a rate equivalent to the basic rate of income tax for the year; and if an assessment to tax at a higher rate is subsequently made on an underwriting member in respect of the same gains, an appropriate credit shall be given for the tax assessed on the trustees.]²

(3) The assessment to be made on the trustees of a fund by virtue of subsection (2) above for any year of assessment shall not take account of losses accruing in any previous year of assessment, and if for that or any other reason the tax paid on behalf of an underwriting member for any year of assessment by virtue of assessments so made exceeds the capital gains tax for which he is liable, the excess shall, on a claim by him, be repaid.

(4) For the purposes of subsections (2) and (3) above the underwriting agent may be treated as a trustee of the premiums trust fund.

Amendments.—¹ Words in sub-s. (2) substituted by FA 1988, s. 101.
² Sub-s. (2A) inserted by *ibid*.

[142A. Disposal of assets in premiums trust fund etc.

(1) Subject to subsection (4) below, for the year 1972–73 and subsequent years of assessment the chargeable gains or allowable losses accruing on the disposal of assets forming part of a premiums trust fund shall be taken to be those allocated to the corresponding underwriting year.

(2) The amount of the gains or losses so allocated at the end of any accounting period shall

be such proportion of the difference mentioned in subsection (3) below as is allocated to the underwriting year under the rules or practice of Lloyd's.

(3) That difference is the difference between the valuations at the beginning and at the end of the accounting period of the assets forming part of the fund, the value at the beginning of the period of assets acquired during the period being taken as the cost of acquisition and the value at the end of the period of assets disposed of during the period being taken as the consideration for the disposal.

(4) Subsections (1) to (3) above do not apply to the computation of chargeable gains or allowable losses on the disposal of gilt-edged securities as defined in Schedule 2 to this Act or of qualifying corporate bonds as defined in section 64 of the Finance Act 1984.

[(4A) Subsection (4B) below applies where the following state of affairs exists at the beginning of an accounting period or the end of an accounting period—

(*a*) securities have been transferred by the trustees of a premiums trust fund in pursuance of an arrangement mentioned in section 129 (1) or (2) of the Taxes Act 1988 (stock lending),
(*b*) the transfer was made to enable another person to fulfil a contract or to make a transfer,
(*c*) securities have not been transferred in return, and
(*d*) the transfer made by the trustees constitutes a disposal which by virtue of section 149B (9) below is to be disregarded as there mentioned.][2]

[(4B) The securities transferred by the trustees shall be treated for the purposes of subsection (3) above as if they formed part of the premiums trust fund at the beginning concerned or the end concerned (as the case may be).][2]

(5) The Board may, by regulations made by statutory instrument which shall be subject to annulment in pursuance of a resolution of the House of Commons, provide—

(*a*) for the assessment and collection of tax charged in accordance with this section;
(*b*) for modifying the provisions of this section in relation to syndicates continuing for more than two years after the end of an underwriting year;
(*c*) . . .[4]
(*d*) for giving credit for foreign tax.][1]

[(6) Regulations under subsection (5) above may make provision with respect to any year or years of assessment; and the year (or any of the years) may be the one in which the regulations are made or any year falling before or after that year.][3]

[(7) But the regulations may not make provision with respect to any year of assessment which precedes the next but one preceding the year of assessment in which the regulations are made.][3]

Amendments.—[1] This section inserted by TA 1988, Sch. 29, para. 24.
[2] Sub-ss. (4A), (4B) inserted by FA 1989, s. 91 (2), (3) where the transfer by the trustees is made after an appointed day.
[3] Sub-ss. (6), (7) inserted by FA 1989, s. 92 (3).
[4] Sub-s. (5) (*c*) repealed by FA 1989, s. 92 (3) and Sch. 17, Pt. VII.

143. Life assurance and deferred annuities

(1) This section has effect as respects any policy of assurance or contract for a deferred annuity on the life of any person.

(2) No chargeable gain shall accrue on the disposal of, or of an interest in, the rights under any such policy of assurance or contract except where the person making the disposal is not the original beneficial owner and acquired the rights or interest for a consideration in money or money's worth.

(3) Subject to subsection (2) above, the occasion of—

(*a*) the payment of the sum or sums assured by a policy of assurance, or
(*b*) the transfer of investments or other assets to the owner of a policy of assurance in accordance with the policy,

and the occasion of the surrender of a policy of assurance, shall be the occasion of a disposal of the rights under the policy of assurance.

(4) Subject to subsection (2) above, the occasion of the payment of the first instalment of a deferred annuity, and the occasion of the surrender of the rights under a contract for a

deferred annuity, shall be the occasion of a disposal of the rights under the contract for a deferred annuity and the amount of the consideration for the disposal of a contract for a deferred annuity shall be the market value at that time of the right to that and further instalments of the annuity.

Superannuation funds, annuities and annual payments

144. Superannuation funds, annuities and annual payments

No chargeable gain shall accrue to any person on the disposal of a right to, or to any part of—

(*a*) any allowance, annuity or capital sum payable out of any superannuation fund, or under any superannuation scheme, established solely or mainly for persons employed in a profession, trade, undertaking or employment, and their dependants,

(*b*) an annuity granted otherwise than under a contract for a deferred annuity by a company as part of its business of granting annuities on human life, whether or not including instalments of capital, or an annuity granted or deemed to be granted under the Government Annuities Act 1929, or

(*c*) annual payments which are due under a covenant made by any person and which are not secured on any property.

[*Profit sharing and share option schemes*]

144A. Approved profit sharing and share option schemes

(1) Notwithstanding anything in a profit sharing scheme approved under Schedule 9 of the Taxes Act 1988 or in paragraph 2 (2) of that Schedule or in the trust instrument relating to that scheme, for the purposes of capital gains tax a person who is a participant in relation to that scheme shall be treated as absolutely entitled to his shares as against the trustees of the scheme.

(2) For the purposes of capital gains tax—

(*a*) no deduction shall be made from the consideration for the disposal of any shares by reason only that an amount determined under section 186 or 187 of or Schedule 9 or 10 to the Taxes Act 1988 is chargeable to income tax under section 186 (3) or (4) of that Act;

(*b*) any charge to income tax by virtue of section 186 (3) of that Act shall be disregarded in determining whether a distribution is a capital distribution within the meaning of section 72 (5) (*b*) above;

(*c*) nothing in any provision of section 186 or 187 of or Schedule 9 or 10 to that Act with respect to—

(i) the order in which any of a participant's shares are to be treated as disposed of for the purposes of those provisions as they have effect in relation to profits sharing schemes, or

(ii) the shares in relation to which an event is to be treated as occurring for any such purpose,

shall affect the rules applicable to the computation of a gain accruing on a part disposal of a holding of shares or other securities which were acquired at different times; and

(*d*) a gain accruing on an appropriation of shares to which section 186 (11) applies shall not be a chargeable gain.

(3) In subsection (2) above "participant" and "the trust instrument" have the meanings given by section 187 of the Taxes Act 1988.

(4) Where a right to acquire shares in a body corporate is released in consideration of the grant of a right to acquire shares in another body corporate in accordance with a provision included in a scheme pursuant to paragraph 15 of Schedule 9 to the Taxes Act 1988, the transaction shall not be treated for the purposes of this Act as involving any disposal of the first-mentioned right but for those purposes the other right shall be treated as the same asset acquired as the first-mentioned right was acquired.

This subsection does not apply in relation to a savings-related share option scheme, within the meaning of section 187 of that Act, unless the first-mentioned right was acquired as mentioned in section 185 (1) of that Act.][1]

Amendments.—[1] This section inserted by TA 1988, Sch. 29, para. 25.

Other exemptions and reliefs

145. Charities

(1) [Subject to section 505 (3) of the Taxes act 1988 and][1] subsection (2) below a gain shall not be a chargeable gain if it accrues to a charity and is applicable and applied for charitable purposes.

(2) If property held on charitable trusts ceases to be subject to charitable trusts—

(*a*) the trustees shall be treated as if they had disposed of, and immediately re-acquired, the property for a consideration equal to its market value, any gain on the disposal being treated as not accruing to a charity, and
(*b*) if and so far as any of that property represents, directly or indirectly, the consideration for the disposal of assets by the trustees, any gain accruing on that disposal shall be treated as not having accrued to a charity,

and an assessment to capital gains tax chargeable by virtue of paragraph (*b*) above may be made at any time not more than three years after the end of the year of assessment in which the property ceases to be subject to charitable trusts.

Cross references.—See TA 1988, s. 505 (5), (6) (certain gains not relieved under this section; charity's discretion to specify).
Amendments.—[1] Words in sub-s. (1) substituted by TA 1988, Sch. 29, para. 32 Table.

146. Gifts to charities etc.

(1) Subsection (2) below shall apply where a disposal of an asset is made otherwise than under a bargain at arm's length—

(*a*) to a charity, or
(*b*) to any bodies mentioned in [Schedule 3 to the Capital Transfer Tax Act 1984][3] (gifts for national purposes, etc.).

(2) Section [29A (1)][1] above (consideration deemed to be equal to market value) and section 147 (3) below shall not apply; but if the disposal is by way of gift (including a gift in settlement) or for a consideration not exceeding the sums allowable as a deduction under section 32 above, then—

(*a*) the disposal and acquisition shall be treated for the purposes of this Act as being made for such consideration as to secure that neither a gain nor a loss accrues on the disposal, and
(*b*) where, after the disposal, the asset is disposed of by the person who acquired it under the disposal, its acquisition by the person making the earlier disposal shall be treated for the purposes of this Act as the acquisition of the person making the later disposal.

(3) Where, otherwise than on the termination of a life interest (within the meaning of section 55 above) by the death of the person entitled thereto, any assets or parts of any assets forming part of settled property are under section 54 . . .[2] above, deemed to be disposed of and re-acquired by the trustee, and—

(*a*) the person becoming entitled as mentioned in section 54 (1) above is a charity, or a body mentioned in [Schedule 3 to the Capital Transfer Tax Act 1984][3] (gifts for national purposes, etc.), . . .[2]

then, if no consideration is received by any person for or in connection with any transaction by virtue of which the charity or other body becomes so entitled . . .[2], the disposal and re-acquisition of the assets to which the charity or other body becomes so entitled . . .[2] shall, notwithstanding sections 54 . . .[2] above, be treated for the purposes of this Act as made for such consideration as to secure that neither a gain nor a loss accrues on the disposal.

Note.—For CTTA 1984 (now Inheritance Tax Act 1984), see the current edition of *Butterworths Orange Tax Handbook*.
Cross references.—See FA 1985, s. 68 (7A) (*a*) (new rules for calculation of indexation allowance in respect of assets held on 31 March 1982);
FA 1986, s. 100 (CTTA 1984 may be cited as Inheritance Tax Act 1984 after 24 July 1986);
FA 1988, Sch. 8, para. 1 (3) (extension of indexation allowance to unindexed gains and losses in relation to assets held on 31 March 1982).
Amendments.—[1] Words in sub-s. (2) substituted by FA 1981, s. 90 (3) (*a*).
[2] Words in sub-s. (3) repealed by FA 1982, Sch. 22, Pt. VI.
[3] Words in sub-ss. (1) (*b*), 3 (*a*) substituted by IHTA 1984, Sch. 8, para. 9 with effect from 1 January 1985.

[146A. Gifts to housing associations

(1) Subsection (2) below shall apply where—

(a) a disposal of an estate or interest in land in the United Kingdom is made to a registered housing association otherwise than under a bargain at arm's length, and
(b) a claim for relief under this section is made by the transferor and the association.

(2) Section 29A (1) above (consideration deemed to be equal to market value) shall not apply; but if the disposal is by way of gift or for a consideration not exceeding the sums allowable as a deduction under section 32 above, then—

(a) the disposal and acquisition shall be treated for the purposes of this Act as being made for such consideration as to secure that neither a gain nor a loss accrues on the disposal, and
(b) where, after the disposal, the estate or interest is disposed of by the association, its acquisition by the person making the earlier disposal shall be treated for the purposes of this Act as the acquisition of the association.

(3) In this section "registered housing association" means a registered housing association within the meaning of the Housing Associations Act 1985 or Part VII of the Housing (Northern Ireland) Order 1981.][1]

Cross references.—See FA 1985, s. 68 (7A) (a) (new rules for calculation of indexation allowance in respect of assets held on 31 March 1982).
Amendments.—[1] This section inserted by FA 1989, s. 125 for disposals made after 13 March 1989.

147. Works of art etc.

(1) A gain accruing on the disposal of an asset by way of gift shall not be a chargeable gain if the asset is property falling within [subsection (2) of section 26 of the Capital Transfer Tax Act 1984][2] (gifts for public benefit) and the Treasury give a direction in relation to it under [subsection (1) of that section][3].

(2) A gain shall not be a chargeable gain if it accrues on the disposal of an asset with respect to which a capital transfer tax undertaking or an undertaking under the following provisions of this section has been given and—

(a) the disposal is by way of sale by private treaty to a body mentioned in [Schedule 3 to the Capital Transfer Tax Act 1984][4] (museums, etc), or is to such a body otherwise than by sale, or
(b) the disposal is to the Board in pursuance of [section 230 of the Capital Transfer Tax Act 1984][5] or in accordance with directions given by the Treasury under section 50 or 51 of the Finance Act 1946 (acceptance of property in satisfaction of tax).

(3) Subsection (4) below shall have effect in respect of the disposal of any asset which is property which has been or could be designated under [section 31 of the Capital Transfer Tax Act 1984][6], being—

(a) a disposal by way of gift, including a gift in settlement, or
(b) a disposal of settled property by the trustee on an occasion when, under section 54 (1) ...[1] above, the trustee is deemed to dispose of and immediately re-acquire settled property (other than any disposal on which by virtue of section 56 above no chargeable gain or allowable loss accrues to the trustee),

if the requisite undertaking described in [the said section 31][7] (maintenance, preservation and access) is given by such person as the Treasury think appropriate in the circumstances of the case.

(4) The person making a disposal to which subsection (3) above applies and the person acquiring the asset on the disposal shall be treated for all the purposes of this Act as if the asset was acquired from the one making the disposal for a consideration of such an amount as would secure that on the disposal neither a gain nor a loss would accrue to the one making the disposal.

(5) If—

(a) there is a sale of the asset and capital transfer tax is chargeable under [section 32 of the Capital Transfer Tax Act 1984][8] (or would be chargeable if a capital transfer undertaking as well as an undertaking under this section had been given), or
(b) the Treasury are satisfied that at any time during the period for which any such undertaking was given it has not been observed in a material respect,

the person selling that asset or, as the case may be, the owner of the asset shall be treated for the purposes of this Act as having sold the asset for a consideration equal to its market value, and, in the case of a failure to comply with the undertaking, having immediately re-acquired it for a consideration equal to its market value.

(6) The period for which an undertaking under this section is given shall be until the person beneficially entitled to the asset dies or it is disposed of, whether by sale or gift or otherwise; and if the asset subject to the undertaking is disposed of—

(*a*) otherwise than on sale, and
(*b*) without a further undertaking being given under this section,

subsection (5) above shall apply as if the asset had been sold to an individual.

References in this subsection to a disposal shall be construed without regard to any provision of this Act under which an asset is deemed to be disposed of.

(7) Where under subsection (5) above a person is treated as having sold for a consideration equal to its market value any asset within [section 31 (1) (*c*), (*d*) or (*e*) of the Capital Transfer Tax Act 1984][9], he shall also be treated as having sold and immediately re-acquired for a consideration equal to its market value any asset associated with it; but the Treasury may direct that the preceding provisions of this subsection shall not have effect in any case in which it appears to them that the entity consisting of the asset and any assets associated with it has not been materially affected.

For the purposes of this subsection two or more assets are associated with each other if one of them is a building falling within [the said section 31 (1) (*c*)][10] and the other or others such land or objects as, in relation to that building, fall within [the said section 31 (1) (*d*) or (*e*)][11].

(8) If in pursuance of subsection (5) above a person is treated as having on any occasion sold an asset and capital transfer tax becomes chargeable on the same occasion, then, in determining the value of the asset for the purposes of that tax, an allowance shall be made for the capital gains tax chargeable on any chargeable gain accruing on that occasion.

(9) In this section "capital transfer tax undertaking" means an undertaking under [Chapter II of Part II or section 78 of, or Schedule 5 to, the Capital Transfer Tax Act 1984][12].

Note.—For CTTA 1984 (now Inheritance Tax Act 1984), see the current edition of *Butterworths Orange Tax Handbook*.
Cross references.—See FA 1985, s. 68 (7A) (*a*) (new rules for calculation of indexation allowance in respect of assets held on 31 March 1982),
s. 95 (1) (*b*) (transfer of Treasury functions under this section to the Commissioners of Inland Revenue);
FA 1986, s. 100 (CTT renamed as inheritance tax and CTTA 1984 may be cited as Inheritance Tax Act 1984 after 24 July 1986);
FA 1988, Sch. 8, para. 1 (3) (extension of indexation allowance to unindexed gains and losses in relation to assets held on 31 March 1982).
Amendments.—[1] Words in sub-s. (3) repealed by FA 1982, Sch. 22, Pt. VI.
[2] Words in sub-s. (1) substituted by IHTA 1984, Sch. 8, para. 10 with effect from 1 January 1985.
[3] Words in sub-s. (1) substituted by *ibid*.
[4] Words in sub-s. (2) (*a*) substituted by *ibid*.
[5] Words in sub-s. (2) (*b*) substituted by *ibid*.
[6] Words in sub-s. (3) substituted by *ibid*.
[7] Words in sub-s. (3) substituted by *ibid*.
[8] Words in sub-s. (5) substituted by *ibid*.
[9] Words in sub-s. (7) substituted by *ibid*.
[10] Words in sub-s. (7) substituted by *ibid*.
[11] Words in sub-s. (7) substituted by *ibid*.
[12] Words in sub-s. (9) substituted by *ibid*.

[147A. Gifts on which inheritance tax is chargeable etc.

(1) If—

(*a*) an individual or the trustees of a settlement (in this section referred to as "the transferor") make a disposal within subsection (2) below of an asset,
(*b*) the asset is acquired by an individual or the trustees of a settlement (in this section referred to as "the transferee"), and
(*c*) a claim for relief under this section is made by the transferor and the transferee or, where the trustees of a settlement are the transferee, by the transferor alone,

then, subject to subsection (6) and section 147B below, subsection (3) below shall apply in relation to the disposal.

(2) A disposal is within this subsection it it is made otherwise than under a bargain at arm's length and—

(*a*) is a chargeable transfer within the meaning of the Inheritance Tax Act 1984 (or would be but for section 19 of that Act) and is not a potentially exempt transfer (within the meaning of that Act),

(b) is an exempt transfer by virtue of—

(i) section 24 of that Act (transfers to political parties),
(ii) section 26 of that Act (transfers for public benefit),
(iii) section 27 of that Act (transfers to maintenance funds for historic buildings etc.), or
(iv) section 30 of that Act (transfers of designated property),

(c) is a disposition to which section 57A of that Act applies and by which the property disposed of becomes held on trusts of the kind referred to in subsection (1) (b) of that section (maintenance funds for historic buildings etc.),

(d) by virtue of subsection (4) of section 71 of that Act (accumulation and maintenance trusts) does not constitute an occasion on which inheritance tax is chargeable under that section,

(e) by virtue of section 78 (1) of that Act (transfers of works of art etc.) does not constitute an occasion on which tax is chargeable under Chapter III of Part III of that Act, or

(f) is a disposal of an asset comprised in a settlement where, as a result of the asset or part of it becoming comprised in another settlement, there is no charge, or a reduced charge, to inheritance tax by virtue of paragraph 9, 16 or 17 of Schedule 4 to that Act (transfers to maintenance funds for historic buildings etc.).

(3) Where this subsection applies in relation to a disposal—

(a) the amount of any chargeable gain which, apart from this section, would accrue to the transferor on the disposal, and

(b) the amount of the consideration for which, apart from this section, the transferee would be regarded for the purposes of capital gains tax as having acquired the asset in question,

shall each be reduced by an amount equal to the held-over gain on the disposal.

(4) Subject to subsection (5) below, the reference in subsection (3) above to the held-over gain on a disposal is a reference to the chargeable gain which would have accrued on that disposal apart from this section.

(5) In any case where—

(a) there is actual consideration (as opposed to the consideration equal to the market value which is deemed to be given by virtue of any provision of this Act) for a disposal in respect of which a claim for relief is made under this section, and

(b) that actual consideration exceeds the sums allowable as a deduction under section 32 above,

the held-over gain on the disposal shall be reduced by the excess referred to in paragraph (b) above or, if part of the gain on the disposal is relieved under Schedule 20 to the Finance Act 1985 (retirement relief), by so much, if any, of that excess as exceeds the part so relieved.

(6) Subsection (3) above does not apply in relation to a disposal of assets within section 67 (1) above on which a gain is deemed to accrue by virtue of paragraph 10 (1) (b) of Schedule 13 to the Finance Act 1984.

(7) In the case of a disposal within subsection (2) (a) above there shall be allowed as a deduction in computing the chargeable gain accruing to the transferee on the disposal of the asset in question an amount equal to whichever is the lesser of—

(a) the inheritance tax attributable to the value of the asset, and
(b) the amount of the chargeable gain as computed apart from this subsection.

(8) Where an amount of inheritance tax is varied after it has been taken into account under subsection (7) above, all necessary adjustments shall be made, whether by the making of an assessment to capital gains tax or by the discharge or repayment of such tax.

(9) Where subsection (3) above applies in relation to a disposal which is deemed to occur by virtue of section 54 (1) or 55 (1) above, subsection (5) above shall not apply.

(10) Where a disposal is partly within subsection (2) above, or is a disposal within paragraph (e) of that subsection on which there is a reduced charge such as is mentioned in that paragraph, the preceding provisions of this section shall have effect in relation to an appropriate part of the disposal.][1]

Note.—For the Inheritance Tax Act 1984, see the current edition of *Butterworths Orange Tax Handbook*.
Cross references.—See FA 1981, s. 79 (1) (a) (charge on held-over gain where transferee migrates);
FA 1986, s. 58 (1) (charge on held-over gain where transferee is or becomes a dual resident trust);
TA 1988, Sch. 28, para. 3 (3) (claim under this section in respect of gains from a disposal of an offshore fund).

Amendments.—[1] This section inserted by FA 1989, s. 124 (2), (3) and Sch. 14, para. 4 in relation to disposals after 13 March 1989 subject to certain exceptions; see FA 1989, s. 124 (3).

[147B. Section 147A relief: gifts to non-residents

(1) Section 147A (3) above shall not apply where the transferee is neither resident nor ordinarily resident in the United Kingdom.

(2) Section 147A (3) above shall not apply where the transferee is an individual who—

(*a*) though resident or ordinarily resident in the United Kingdom, is regarded for the purposes of any double taxation arrangements having effect by virtue of section 788 of the Taxes Act 1988 as resident in a territory outside the United Kingdom, and
(*b*) by virtue of the arrangements would not be liable in the United Kingdom to tax on a gain arising on a disposal of the asset occurring immediately after its acquisition.][1]

Note.—For the Inheritance Tax Act 1984, see the current edition of *Butterworths Orange Tax Handbook*.
Amendments.—[1] This section inserted by FA 1989, s. 124 (2), (3) and Sch. 14, para. 4 in relation to disposals after 13 March 1989 subject to certain exceptions; see FA 1989, s. 124 (3).

148. Maintenance funds for historic buildings

Amendments.—In consequence of the operation of FA 1980, s. 79 (general relief for gifts), this section repealed by FA 1984, s. 68 and Sch. 23, Pt. VIII.

149. Employee trusts

(1) Where—

(*a*) a close company disposes of an asset to trustees in circumstances such that the disposal is a disposition which by virtue of [section 13 of the Capital Transfer Tax Act 1984][2] (employee trusts) is not a transfer of value for the purposes of capital transfer tax, or
(*b*) an individual disposes of an asset to trustees in circumstances such that the disposal is an exempt transfer by virtue of [section 28 of the Capital Transfer Tax Act 1984][3] (employee trusts: capital transfer tax),

this Act shall have effect in relation to the disposal in accordance with subsections (2) and (3) below.

(2) Section [29A (1)][1] above (consideration deemed to be equal to market value) shall not apply to the disposal; and if the disposal is by way of gift or is for a consideration not exceeding the sums allowable as a deduction under section 32 above—

(*a*) the disposal, and the acquisition by the trustees, shall be treated for the purposes of this Act as being made for such consideration as to secure that neither a gain nor a loss accrues on the disposal, and
(*b*) where the trustees dispose of the asset, its acquisition by the company or individual shall be treated as its acquisition by the trustees.

(3) Where the disposal is by a close company, section 75 (1) above (assets disposed of for less than market value) shall apply to the disposal as if for the reference to market value there were substituted a reference to market value or the sums allowable as a deduction under section 32 above, whichever is the less.

(4) Subject to subsection (5) below, this Act shall also have effect in accordance with subsection (2) above in relation to any disposal made by a company other than a close company if—

(*a*) the disposal is made to trustees otherwise than under a bargain made at arm's length, and
(*b*) the property disposed of is to be held by them on trusts of the description specified in [section 86 (1) of the Capital Transfer Tax Act 1984 (that is to say, those in relation to which the said section 13 of that Act has effect)][4] and the persons for whose benefit the trusts permit the property to be applied include all or most of either—

(i) the persons employed by or holding office with the company, or
(ii) the persons employed by or holding office with the company or any one or more subsidiaries of the company.

(5) Subsection (4) above does not apply if the trusts permit any of the property to be applied

at any time (whether during any such period as is referred to in [the said section 86 (1)]⁵ later) for the benefit of—

(a) a person who is a participator in the company ("the donor company"), or
(b) any other person who is a participator in any other company that has made a disposal of property to be held on the same trusts as the property disposed of by the donor company, being a disposal in relation to which this Act has had effect in accordance with subsection (2) above, or
(c) any other person who has been a participator in the donor company or any such company as is mentioned in paragraph (b) above at any time after, or during the ten years before, the disposal made by that company, or
(d) any person who is connected with a person within paragraph (a), (b) or (c) above.

(6) The participators in a company who are referred to in subsection (5) above do not include any participator who—

(a) is not beneficially entitled to, or to rights entitling him to acquire, 5 per cent. or more of, or of any class of the shares comprised in, its issued share capital, and
(b) on a winding-up of the company would not be entitled to 5 per cent. or more of its assets;

and in determining whether the trusts permit property to be applied as mentioned in that subsection, no account shall be taken—

(i) of any power to make a payment which is the income of any person for any of the purposes of income tax, or would be the income for any of those purposes of a person not resident in the United Kingdom if he were so resident, or
(ii) if the trusts are those of a profit sharing scheme approved under the Finance Act 1978, of any power to appropriate shares in pursuance of the scheme.

(7) In subsection (4) above "subsidiary" has the same meaning as in the [Companies Act 1985]⁶ and in subsections (5) and (6) above "participator" has the meaning given in section [417 (1)]⁸ of the Taxes Act [1988]⁷, except that it does not include a loan creditor.

(8) In this section "close company" includes a company which, if resident in the United Kingdom, would be a close company as defined in section 155 (1) below.

Note.—For CTTA 1984 (now Inheritance Tax Act 1984), see the current edition of *Butterworths Orange Tax Handbook*.
Cross references.—See FA 1986, s. 100 (CTT renamed as inheritance tax and CTTA 1984 may be cited as Inheritance Tax Act 1984 after 24 July 1986).
Amendments.—¹ Words in sub-s. (2) substituted by FA 1981, s. 90 (3) (a).
² Words in sub-s. (1) (a) substituted by IHTA 1984, Sch. 8, para. 11 with effect from 1 January 1985.
³ Words in sub-s. (1) (b) substituted by *ibid*.
⁴ Words in sub-s. (4) (b) substituted by *ibid*.
⁵ Words in sub-s. (5) substituted by *ibid*.
⁶ Words in sub-s. (7) substituted by the Companies Consolidation (Consequential Provisions) Act 1985, Sch. 2 with effect from 1 July 1985.
⁷ "1988" in sub-s. (7) inserted by virtue of TA 1988, Sch. 29, para. 15 (a).
⁸ Number in sub-s. (7) substituted by TA 1988, Sch. 29, para. 32 Table.

[149A. Building societies and life policies

(1) If in the course of or as part of an amalgamation of two or more building societies or a transfer of engagements from one building society to another, there is a disposal of an asset by one society to another, both shall be treated for the purposes of corporation tax on chargeable gains as if the asset were acquired from the one making the disposal for a consideration of such amount as would secure that on the disposal neither a gain nor a loss would accrue to the one making the disposal.

In this subsection "building society" means a building society within the meaning of the Building Societies Act 1986.

(2) Where any investments or other assets are or have been, in accordance with a policy issued in the course of life assurance business carried on by an insurance company, transferred to the policy holder on or after 6th April 1967, the policy holder's acquistion of the assets and the disposal of them to him shall be deemed to be, for the purposes of this Act, for a consideration equal to the market value of the assets.

In this subsection "life assurance business" and "insurance company" have the same meaning as in Chapter I of Part XII of the Taxes Act 1988.]¹

Former enactments.—Sub-s. (1): TA 1970, s. 343 (5), (8).
Sub-s. (2): TA 1970, s. 321.
Cross references.—See FA 1985, s. 68 (7), (7A) (*b*) (modification of indexation allowance with respect to disposals of assets after 31 March or 5 April 1985);
FA 1988, Sch. 8, para. 1 (capital gains: re-basing to 1982 of assets held on 31 March 1982).
Amendments.—¹ This section inserted by TA 1988, Sch. 29, para. 26.

[**149B. Miscellaneous exemptions**

(1) The following gains shall not be chargeable gains—

(*a*) gains accruing on the disposal of stock—

(i) transferred to accounts in the books of the Bank of England in the name of the Treasury or the National Debt Commissioners in pursuance of any Act of Parliament; or
(ii) belonging to the Crown, in whatever name it may stand in the books of the Bank of England;

(*b*) any gain accruing to a person from his acquisition and disposal of assets held by him as part of a fund mentioned in section 613 (4) of the Taxes Act 1988 (Parliamentary pension funds) or of which income is exempt from income tax under section 614 (1) of that Act (social security supplementary schemes);
(*c*) any gain accruing to a person from his acquisition and disposal of assets held by him as part of a fund mentioned in section [614 (2)]² or paragraph (*b*), (*c*), (*d*), (*f*) or (*g*) of section 615 (2) of the Taxes Act 1988 (India etc. pension funds) or as part of a fund to which subsection (3) of that section applies (pension funds for overseas employees);
(*d*) any gain accruing to a person from his acquisition and disposal of assets held by him as part of any fund maintained for the purpose mentioned in subsection (5) (*b*) of section 620 or subsection (5) of section 621 of the Taxes Act 1988 under a scheme for the time being approved under that subsection;
(*e*) any gain accruing on the disposal by the trustees of any settled property held on trusts in accordance with directions which are valid and effective under section 9 of the Superannuation and Trust Funds (Validation) Act 1927 (trust funds for the reduction of the National debt);
(*f*) any gain accruing to a consular officer or employee, within the meaning of section 322 of the Taxes Act 1988, of any foreign state to which that section applies on the disposal of assets which at the time of the disposal were situated outside the United Kingdom;
(*g*) any gain accruing to a person from his disposal of investments if, or to such extent as the Board are satisfied that, those investments were held by him or on his behalf for the purposes of a scheme which at the time of the disposal is an exempt approved scheme;
(*h*) any gain accruing to a person on his disposal of investments held by him for the purposes of an approved personal pension scheme;
(*j*) any gain accruing to a unit holder on his disposal of units in an authorised unit trust which is also an approved personal pension scheme or is one to which section 592 (10) of the Taxes Act 1988 applies.

In this subsection "exempt approved scheme" and "approved personal pension scheme" have the same meanings as in Part XIV of the Taxes Act 1988.

(2) Where a claim is made in that behalf, a gain which accrues to a person on the disposal of investments shall not be a chargeable gain for the purposes of capital gains tax if, or to such extent as the Board are satisfied that, those investments were held by him or on his behalf for the purposes of a fund to which section 608 of the Taxes Act 1988 applies.

A claim under this subsection shall not be allowed unless the Board are satisfied that the terms on which benefits are payable from the fund have not been altered since 5th April 1980.

(3) A local authority, and a local authority association, within the meaning of section 519 of the Taxes Act 1988, shall be exempt from capital gains tax.

(4) Any terminal bonus, or interest or other sum, payable under a certified contractual savings scheme—

(*a*) in respect of money raised under section 12 of the National Loans Act 1968; or
(*b*) in respect of shares in a building society,

shall be disregarded for all purposes of the enactments relating to capital gains tax.

This subsection shall be construed as one with section 326 of the Taxes Act 1988.

(5) A signatory to the Operating Agreement made pursuant to the Convention on the International Maritime Satellite Organisation which came into force on 16th July 1979, other than a signatory designated for the purposes of the Agreement by the United Kingdom in accordance with the Convention, shall be exempt from capital gains tax in respect of any payment received by that signatory from the Organisation in accordance with the Agreement.

(6) The following shall, on a claim made in that behalf to the Board, be exempt from tax in respect of all chargeable gains—

(*a*) the Trustees of the British Museum and the Trustees of the British Museum (Natural History); and
(*b*) an Association within the meaning of section 508 of the Taxes Act 1988 (scientific research organisations).

(7) The Historic Buildings and Monuments Commission for England, the Trustees of the National Heritage Memorial Fund, the United Kingdom Atomic Energy Authority and the National Radiological Protection Board shall be exempt from tax in respect of chargeable gains; and for the purposes of this subsection gains accruing from investments or deposits held for the purposes of any pension scheme provided and maintained by the United Kingdom Atomic Energy Authority shall be treated as if those gains and investments and deposits belonged to the Authority.

(8) There shall be exempt from tax any chargeable gains accruing to the issue department of the Reserve Bank of India constituted under an Act of the Indian legislature called the Reserve Bank of India Act 1934, or to the issue department of the State Bank of Pakistan constituted under certain orders made under section 9 of the Indian Indpendence Act 1947.

(9) Any disposal and acquisition made in pursuance of an arrangement mentioned in subsection (1) or (2) of section 129 of the Taxes Act 1988 (stock lending) shall, subject to regulations under subsection (4) of that section, be disregarded for the purposes of capital gains tax.][1]

Cross references.—See TA 1988, s. 438 (8) (nothing in this section to be construed as affording relief in respect of any sums to be brought into account under TA 1988, s. 438 (pension business: exemption from tax)),
Sch. 22, para. 7 (3) (*d*) (curtailment under certain circumstances of tax exemption under sub-s. (1) (*g*) above);
FA 1988, Sch. 12, para. 7 (*b*) (building societies change of status; continuation of tax exemption under sub-s. (4) above where contractual savings schemes are in operation before change of status).
Amendments.—[1] This section inserted by TA 1988, Sch. 29, para. 26.
[2] Number in sub-s. (1) (*c*) substituted by FA 1988, Sch. 13, para. 17.

[149C. Business expansion schemes

(1) In this section "relief" means relief under Chapter III of Part VII of the Taxes Act 1988, Schedule 5 to the Finance Act 1983 ("the 1983 Act") or Chapter II of Part IV of the Finance Act 1981 ("the 1981 Act") and "eligible shares" has the meaning given by section 289 (4) of the Taxes Act 1988.

(2) A gain or loss which accrues to an individual on the disposal of any shares issued after 18th March 1986 in respect of which relief has been given and not withdrawn shall not be a chargeable gain or allowable loss for the purposes of capital gains tax.

(3) The sums allowable as deductions from the consideration in the computation for the purposes of capital gains tax of the gain or loss accruing to an individual on the disposal of shares issued before 19th March 1986 in respect of which any relief has been given and not withdrawn shall be determined without regard to that relief, except that where those sums exceed the consideration they shall be reduced by an amount equal to—

(*a*) the amount of that relief; or
(*b*) the excess,

whichever is the less, but the foregoing provisions of this subsection shall not apply to a disposal falling within section 44 (1) above.

(4) Sections 88 and 89 of the Finance Act 1982 (identification of securities disposed of) shall not apply to shares in respect of which any relief has been given and not withdrawn; and any question—

(*a*) as to which of any such shares issued to a person at different times a disposal relates; or
(*b*) whether a disposal relates to such shares or to other shares;

shall for the purposes of capital gains tax be determined as for the purposes of section 299 of the Taxes Act 1988, or section 57 of the Finance Act 1981 if the relief has only been given under that Act.

(5) Where an individual holds shares which form part of the ordinary share capital of a company and the relief has been given (and not withdrawn) in respect of some but not others, then, if there is within the meaning of section 77 above a reorganisation affecting those shares, section 78 shall apply separately to the shares in respect of which the relief has been given (and not withdrawn) and to the other shares (so that shares of each kind are treated as a separate holding of original shares and identified with a separate new holding).

(6) Where section 44 above has applied to any eligible shares disposed of by an individual to his or her spouse ("the transferee"), subsection (2) above shall apply in relation to the subsequent disposal of the shares by the transferee to a third party.

(7) Where section 85 or 86 above would, but for this subsection, apply in relation to eligible shares in respect of which an individual has been given relief, that section shall apply only if the relief is withdrawn.

(8) Sections 78 to 81 above shall not apply in relation to any shares in respect of which relief (other than relief under the 1981 Act) has been given and which form part of a company's ordinary share capital if—

(*a*) there is, by virtue of any such allotment for payment as is mentioned in section 77(2)(*a*) above, a reorganisation occurring after 18th March 1986 affecting those shares; and
(*b*) immediately following the reorganisation, the relief has not been withdrawn in respect of those shares or relief has been given in respect of the allotted shares and not withdrawn.

(9) Where relief is reduced by virtue of subsection (2) of section 305 of the Taxes Act 1988—

(*a*) the sums allowable as deductions from the consideration in the computation, for the purposes of capital gains tax, of the gain or loss accruing to an individual on the disposal, after 18th March 1986, of any of the allotted shares or debentures shall be taken to include the amount of the reduction apportioned between the allotted shares or (as the case may be) debentures in such a way as appears to the inspector, or on appeal to the Commissioners concerned, to be just and reasonable; and
(*b*) the sums so allowable on the disposal (in circumstances in which subsections (2) to (7) above do not apply) of any of the shares referred to in section 305 (2) (*a*) shall be taken to be reduced by the amount mentioned in paragraph (*a*) above, similarly apportioned between those shares.

(10) These shall be made all such adjustments of capital gains tax, whether by way of assessment or by way of discharge or repayment of tax, as may be required in consequence of the relief being given or withdrawn.][1]

Amendments.—[1] This section inserted by TA 1988, Sch. 29, para. 26.

[149D. Personal equity plans

(1) The Treasury may make regulations providing that an individual who invests under a plan shall be entitled to relief from capital gains tax in respect of the investments.

(2) Subsections (2) to (5) of section 333 of the Taxes Act 1988 (personal equity plans) shall apply in relation to regulations under subsection (1) above as they apply in relation to regulations under subsection (1) of that section but with the substitution for any reference to income tax of a reference to capital gains tax.

[(2A) Regulations under this section may include provision securing that losses are disregarded for the purposes of capital gains tax where they accrue on the disposal of investments on or after 18th January 1988.][2]

(3) Regulations under this section shall be made by stautory instrument which shall be subject to annulment in pursuance of a resolution of the House of Commons.][1]

Amendments.—[1] This section inserted by TA 1988, Sch. 29, para. 26.
[2] Sub-s. (2A) inserted by FA 1988, s. 116.

PART VIII
SUPPLEMENTAL

Valuation

150. Valuation: general

(1) In this Act "market value" in relation to any assets means the price which those assets might reasonably be expected to fetch on a sale in the open market.

(2) In estimating the market value of any assets no reduction shall be made in the estimate on account of the estimate being made on the assumption that the whole of the assets is to be placed on the market at one and the same time.

(3) The market value of shares or securities listed in The Stock Exchange Daily Official List shall, except where in consequence of special circumstances prices quoted in that List are by themselves not a proper measure of market value, be as follows—

(a) the lower of the two prices shown in the quotations for the shares or securities in The Stock Exchange Daily Official List on the relevant date plus one-quarter of the difference between those two figures, or
(b) halfway between the highest and lowest prices at which bargains, other than bargains done at special prices, were recorded in the shares or securities for the relevant date,

choosing the amount under paragraph (a) if less than that under paragraph (b), or if no such bargains were recorded for the relevant date, and choosing the amount under paragraph (b) if less than that under paragraph (a):

Provided that—

(i) this subsection shall not apply to shares or securities for which The Stock Exchange provides a more active market elsewhere than on the London trading floor, and
(ii) if the London trading floor is closed on the relevant date the market value shall be ascertained by reference to the latest previous date or earliest subsequent date on which it is open, whichever affords the lower market value.

(4) In this Act "market value" in relation to any rights of unit holders in any unit trust scheme the buying and selling prices of which are published regularly by the managers of the scheme shall mean an amount equal to the buying price (that is the lower price) so published on the relevant date, or if none were published on that date, on the latest date before.

(5) In relation to an asset of a kind the sale of which is subject to restrictions imposed under the Exchange Control Act 1947 such that part of what is paid by the purchaser is not retainable by the seller the market value, as arrived at under subsection (1), subsection (3) or subsection (4) above, shall be subject to such adjustment as is appropriate having regard to the difference between the amount payable by a purchaser and the amount receivable by a seller.[1]

(6) The provisions of this section, with sections 151 to 153 below, have effect subject to Part I of Schedule 6 to this Act (market value at a time before the commencement of this Act).

Cross references.—See TA 1988, s. 251 (5) (sub-s. (3) of this section to apply for the purposes of taxation of stock dividends).
Amendments.—[1] Sub-s. (5) repealed by FA 1987, s. 68 (3) and Sch. 16, Pt. XI except in relation to the determination of the market value of any assets before 13 December 1979.

151. Assets disposed of in a series of transactions

If a person is given, or acquires from one or more persons with whom he is connected, by way of two or more gifts or other transactions, assets of which the aggregate market value, when considered separately in relation to the separate gifts or other transactions, is less than their aggregate market value when considered together, then for the purposes of this Act their market value, where relevant, shall be taken to be the larger market value, to be apportioned rateably to the respective disposals.

Cross references.—See FA 1985, s. 71 (5) (for the purposes of this section any gift or other transaction occurring after 19 March 1985 to be disregarded),
s. 71 (8) (application of the new code for assets disposed of in a series of transactions in respect of certain transactions to which this section would otherwise have applied).
Amendments.—This section repealed by FA 1985, Sch. 27, Pt. VII with respect to gifts or other transactions occurring after 19 March 1985.

152. Unquoted shares and securities

(1) The provisions of subsection (3) below shall have effect in any case where, in relation to an asset to which this section applies, there falls to be determined by virtue of section 150 (1) above the price which the asset might reasonably be expected to fetch on a sale in the open market.

(2) The assets to which this section applies are shares and securities which are not quoted on a recognised stock exchange, within the meaning of section [841][2] of the Taxes Act [1988][1], at the time as at which their market value for the purposes of tax on chargeable gains falls to be determined.

(3) For the purposes of a determination falling within subsection (1) above, it shall be assumed that, in the open market which is postulated for the purposes of that determination, there is available to any prospective purchaser of the asset in question all the information which a prudent prospective purchaser of the asset might reasonably require if he were proposing to purchase it from a willing vendor by private treaty and at arm's length.

Cross references.—See TA 1988, s. 251 (6) (application of this section to determine market value of securities, not quoted on stock exchange, issued in lieu of cash dividends).
Amendments.—[1] "1988" in sub-s. (2) inserted by virtue of TA 1988, Sch. 15, para. 15 (*a*).
[2] Number in sub-s. (2) substituted by TA 1988, Sch. 29, para. 32 Table.

153. Value determined for capital transfer tax

Where on the death of any person capital transfer tax is chargeable on the value of his estate immediately before his death and the value of an asset forming part of that estate has been ascertained (whether in any proceedings or otherwise) for the purposes of that tax, the value so ascertained shall be taken for the purposes of this Act to be the market value of that asset at the date of the death.

Cross references.—See CTTA 1984 (now cited as Inheritance Tax Act 1984), s. 187 (determination of the market value of "specific investment" for the purposes of capital gains tax under this section);
FA 1986, s. 100 (CTT renamed as inheritance tax and CTTA 1984 may be cited as Inheritance Tax Act 1984 after 24 July 1986).

Other provisions

154. Income tax decisions

Any assessment to income tax or decision on a claim under the Income Tax Acts, and any decision on an appeal under the Income Tax Acts against such an assessment or decision, shall be conclusive so far as under Chapter II of Part II of this Act, or any other provisions of this Act, liability to tax depends on the provisions of the Income Tax Acts.

155. Interpretation

(1) In this Act, unless the context otherwise requires—

"allowable loss" has the meaning given by section 29 above,
"the Board" means the Commissioners of Inland Revenue,
"chargeable gain" has the meaning given by section 28 (2) above,
"chargeable period" means a year of assessment or an accounting period of a company for purposes of corporation tax,
"close company" has the meaning given by sections [414 and 415][4] of the Taxes Act [1988][3],
"company" includes any body corporate or unincorporated association but does not include a partnership, and shall be construed in accordance with section 93 above (application of Act to unit trusts),
"control" shall be construed in accordance with section [416][4] of the Taxes Act [1988][3],
"inspector" means any inspector of taxes,
"land" includes messuages, tenements, and hereditaments, houses and buildings of any tenure,
"married woman living with her husband": see subsection (2) below,
"part disposal" has the meaning given by section 19 (2) above,
"personal representatives" has the meaning given by section [701 (4)][4] of the Taxes Act [1988][3],
"quoted" on a stock exchange, or recognised stock exchange, in the United Kingdom: see subsection (3) below,

["recognised stock exchange" has the meaning given by section 841 of the Taxes Act 1988.][7]
["the Taxes Act 1970" and "the Taxes Act 1988" mean the Income and Corporation Taxes Act 1970 and Income and Corporation Taxes Act 1988 respectively,][4]
"trade" has the same meaning as in the Income Tax Acts,
"trading stock" has the meaning given by section [100 (2)][4] of the Taxes Act [1988][3],
"wasting asset" has the meaning given by section 37 above and paragraph 1 of Schedule 3 to this Act,
"year of assessment" means, in relation to capital gains tax, a year beginning on 6th April and ending on 5th April in the following calendar year, and "1979–80" and so on indicate years of assessment as in the Income Tax Acts.

(1A) In this Act "retail prices index" shall have the same meaning as in the Income Tax Acts and, accordingly, any reference in this Act to the retail prices index shall be construed in accordance with section 833 (2) of the Taxes Act 1988.][2]

(2) References in this Act to a married woman living with her husband shall be construed in accordance with section [282][6] of the Taxes Act [1988][3].

(3) References in this Act to quotation on a stock exchange in the United Kingdom or a recognised stock exchange in the United Kingdom shall be construed as references to listing in the Official List of The Stock Exchange.

[(3A) In this Act "recognised futures exchange" means the London International Financial Futures Exchange and any other futures exchange which is for the time being designated for the purposes of this Act by order made by the Board.][1]

[(3B) An order made by the Board under subsection (3A) above.

(a) may designate a futures exchange by name or by reference to any class or description of futures exchanges, including in the case of futures exchanges in a country outside the United Kingdom, a class or description framed by reference to any authority or approval given in that country; and
(b) may contain such transitional and other supplemental provisions as appear to the Board to be necessary or expedient.][1]

(4) The Table below indexes other general definitions in this Act.

Expression defined	Reference
"Absolutely entitled as against the trustee"	S. 46 (2).
"Authorised unit trust"	S. 92.
"Branch or agency"	S. 12 (3).
"Class", in relation to shares or securities	S. 64 (1).
"Connected", in references to persons being connected with one another.	S. 63.
"Court investment fund"	S. 92.
"Gilt-edged securities"	Schedule 2.
"Investment trust"	S. 92.
"Issued", in relation to shares or debentures	S. 64 (2).
"Lease" and cognate expressions	Paragraph 10 (1) of Schedule 3.
"Legatee"	S. 47 (2) (3).
"Market value"	Ss. 150 to 153; Part I of Schedule 6.
"Resident" and "ordinarily resident"	S. 18 (1).
"Settled property"	S. 51.
"Shares"	S. 64 (1).
"Unit trust scheme"	S. 92.

(5) ...[5]

Amendments.—[1] Sub-ss. (3A), (3B) inserted by FA 1985, s. 72 (6).
[2] Sub-s. (1A) inserted by TA 1988, Sch. 29, para. 27.
[3] "1988" in sub-ss. (1), (2) inserted by virtue of TA 1988, Sch.29, para. 15 (a).
[4] Words in sub-s (1) substituted by TA 1988, Sch. 29, para. 32 Table.
[5] Sub-s. (5) repealed by TA 1988, Sch. 31.
[6] Number in sub-s. (2) substituted by FA 1988, Sch. 13, para. 18.
[7] Definition of "recognised stock exchange" in sub-s (1) inserted by FA 1989, Sch. 14, para. 6 (2).

PART IX
GENERAL

156. Commencement

(1) Except as otherwise provided by this Part of this Act, this Act shall come into force in relation to tax for the year 1979–80 and subsequent years of assessment, and tax for other chargeable periods beginning after 5th April 1979.

(2) The following provisions of this Act, that is—

(*a*) so much of any provision of this Act as authorises the making of any order or other instrument,
(*b*) except where the tax concerned is all tax for chargeable periods to which this Act does not apply, so much of any provision of this Act as confers any power or imposes any duty the exercise or performance of which operates or may operate in relation to tax for more than one chargeable period,

shall come into force for all purposes on 6th April 1979 to the exclusion of the corresponding enactments repealed by this Act.

157. Savings, transitory provisions and consequential amendments

(1) Schedule 6 to this Act, which contains transitory provisions and savings, shall have effect, and the repeals made by section 158 (1) below have effect subject to that Schedule.

[1A) No letters patent granted or to be granted by the Crown to any person, city, borough or town corporate of any liberty, privilege, or exemption from subsidies, tolls, taxes, assessments or aids, and no statute which grants any salary, annuity or pension to any person free of any taxes, deductions or assessments, shall be construed or taken to exempt any person, city, borough or town corporate, or any inhabitant of the same, from tax chargeable in pursuance of this Act.][2]

(2) For the avoidance of doubt it is hereby declared that this Act has effect subject to those provisions of the Taxes Act [1988][1] and other enactments relating to chargeable gains which are not repealed by this Act; and with a view to preserving the existing effect of such enactments as are mentioned in Schedule 7 to this Act, they shall be amended in accordance with that Schedule.

(3) The provisions of the said Schedule 7, and the other provisions of this Part of this Act, are without prejudice to the provisions of the Interpretation Act 1978 as respects the effect of repeals.

(4) This section and the said Schedules 6 and 7 shall come into force on the passing of this Act.

Amendments.—[1] "1988" in sub-s (2) inserted by virtue of TA 1988, Sch. 29, para. 15 (*a*).
[2] Sub-s. (1A) inserted by TA 1988, Sch. 29, para. 28.

158. Repeals

(1) The enactments and instruments mentioned in Schedule 8 to this Act are hereby repealed to the extent specified in the third column of that Schedule.

(2) The said repeals shall come into force in accordance with section 156 above.

159. Continuity and construction of references to old and new law

(1) The continuity of the operation of the law relating to chargeable gains shall not be affected by the substitution of this Act for the repealed enactments.

(2) Any reference, whether express or implied, in any enactment, instrument or document (including this Act and any enactment amended by Schedule 7 to this Act) to, or to things done or falling to be done under or for the purposes of, any provision of this Act shall, if and so far as the nature of the reference permits, be construed as including, in relation to the times, years or periods, circumstances or purposes in relation to which the corresponding provision in the repealed enactments has or had effect, a reference to, or as the case may be

to things done or falling to be done under or for the purposes of, that corresponding provision.

(3) Any reference, whether express or implied, in any enactment, instrument or document (including the repealed enactments and enactments, instruments and documents passed or made after the passing of this Act) to, or to things done or falling to be done under or for the purposes of, any of the repealed enactments shall, if and so far as the nature of the reference permits, be construed as including, in relation to the times, years or periods, circumstances or purposes in relation to which the corresponding provision of this Act has effect, a reference to, or as the case may be to things done or falling to be done under or for the purposes of, that corresponding provision.

(4) In this section "the repealed enactments" means the enactments repealed by this Act.

160. Short title

This Act may be cited as the Capital Gains Tax Act 1979.

SCHEDULES

SCHEDULE 1

Section 5

[APPLICATION OF EXEMPT AMOUNT IN PARTICULAR CASES][1]

Amendments.—[1] The heading substituted by FA 1982, s. 80 (3) (*a*).

Preliminary

1. In this Schedule references to any subsections not otherwise identified are references to subsections of section 5 of this Act.

Husband and wife

2.—(1) For any year of assessment during which a married woman is living with her husband [subsections (1) and (4)][1] shall apply to them as if [the exempt amount for the year][2] were divided between them—

(*a*) in proportion to their respective taxable amounts for that year (disregarding for this purpose paragraphs (*a*) and (*b*) of subsection (4)), or
(*b*) where the aggregate of those amounts does not exceed [the exempt amount for the year][2] and allowable losses accruing to either of them in a previous year are carried forward from that year, in such other proportion as they may agree.

(2) Sub-paragraph (1) above shall also apply for any year of assessment during a part of which (being a part beginning with 6th April) a married woman is living with her husband but—

(*a*) her taxable amount for that year shall not include chargeable gains or allowable losses accruing to her in the remainder of the year, and
(*b*) [subsections (1) and (4)][1] shall apply to her (without the modification in sub-paragraph (1) above) for the remainder of the year as if it were a separate year of assessment.

Note.—See **Prospective Legislation Notes** (Married Couples).
Amendments.—[1] Words in sub-paras. (1) and (2) (*b*) substituted by FA 1980, s. 77 (4) (*b*).
[2] Words in sub-para. (1) substituted by FA 1982, s. 80 (3) (*b*).

3.—(1) For any year of assessment during which or during a part of which (being a part beginning with 6th April) the individual is a married man whose wife is living with him and in relation to whom section 45 (1) of this Act applies subsection (5) shall apply as if—

(*a*) the chargeable gains accruing to him in the year included those accruing to her in the year or the part of the year, and
(*b*) all the disposals of assets made by her in the year or the part of the year were made by him.

(2) Subsection (5) shall not apply for any year of assessment during which or during a part of which (being a part beginning with 6th April)—

(*a*) the individual is a married man whose wife is living with him but in relation to whom the said section 45 (1) does not apply, or
(*b*) the individual is a married woman living with her husband.

Note.—See **Prospective Legislation Notes** (Married Couples).

Personal representatives

4. For the year of assessment in which an individual dies and for the two next following years of assessment, [subsections (1), (4) and (5)][1] shall apply to his personal representatives as they apply to an individual.

Amendments.—[1] Words substituted by FA 1980, s. 77 (4) (*c*).

Trustees

5.—(1) For any year of assessment during the whole or part of which settled property is held on trusts which secure that, during the lifetime of a mentally disabled person or a person in receipt of attendance allowance,

[(*a*) not less than half of the property which is applied is applied for the benefit of that person, and
(*b*) that person is entitled to not less than half of the income arising from the property, or no such income may be applied for the benefit of any other person.]²

[subsections (1), (4) and (5)]¹ shall apply to the trustees of the settlement as they apply to an individual.

[(1A) The trusts on which settled property is held shall not be treated as falling outside sub-paragraph (1) above by reason only of the powers conferred on the trustees by section 32 of the Trustee Act 1925 or section 33 of the Trustee Act (Northern Ireland) 1958 (powers of advancement); and the reference in that sub-paragraph to the lifetime of a person shall, where the income from the settled property is held for his benefit on trusts of the kind described in section 33 of the Trustee Act 1925 (protective trusts), be construed as a reference to the period during which the income is held on trust for him.]³

[(1B) In relation to a settlement which is one of two or more qualifying settlements comprised in a group, this paragraph shall have effect as if for the references in section 5 of this Act to [the exempt amount for the year]⁵ there were substituted references to [one tenth of that exempt amount]⁵ or, if it is more, to such amount as results from dividing [the exempt amount for the year]⁵ by the number of settlements in the group.]³

[(1C) For the purposes of sub-paragraph (1B) above—

(*a*) a qualifying settlement is any settlement (other than an excluded settlement) which is made on or after 10th March 1981 and to the trustees of which this paragraph applies for the year of assessment; and
(*b*) all qualifying settlements in relation to which the same person is the settlor constitute a group.]³

[(1D) If, in consequence of two or more persons being settlors in relation to it, a settlement is comprised in two or more groups comprising different numbers of settlements, sub-paragraph (1B) above shall apply to it as if the number by which the amount of [the exempt amount for the year]⁵ is to be divided were the number of settlements in the largest group.]³

(2) In this paragraph "mentally disabled person" means a person who by reason of mental disorder within the meaning of [the Mental Health Act 1983]⁶ is incapable of administering his property or managing his affairs and "attendance allowance" means an allowance under section 35 of the Social Security Act 1975 or the Social Security (Northern Ireland) Act 1975 [; and "settlor" and "excluded settlement" have the same meanings as in paragraph 6 below]⁴.

[(3) An inspector may by notice in writing require any person, being a party to a settlement, to furnish him within such time as he may direct (not being less than twenty-eight days) with such particulars as he thinks necessary for the purposes of this paragraph.]³

Cross references.—See TA 1988, s. 715 (8) (exemption from tax in relation to trusts falling under sub-para. (1) above in respect of deemed income on disposal of certain securities).
Amendments.—¹ Words in sub-para. (1) substituted by FA 1980, s. 77 (4) (*c*).
² Words in sub-para. (1) substituted by FA 1981, s. 89 (2).
³ Sub-paras. (1A), (1B), (1C), (1D), (3) inserted by FA 1981, s. 89 (3), (5).
⁴ Words in sub-para. (2) added by FA 1981, s. 89 (4).
⁵ Words in sub-paras. (1B), (1D) substituted by FA 1982, s. 80 (3) (*b*), (*c*).
⁶ Words in sub-para. (2) substituted by the Mental Health Act 1983, Sch. 4, para. 49.

6.—(1) For any year of assessment during the whole or part of which any property is settled property, not being a year of assessment for which paragraph 5(1) above applies, [subsections (1), (4) and (5)]¹ shall apply to the trustees of a settlement as they apply to an individual but with the following modifications.

[(2) In subsections (1) and (4) for "[the exempt amount for the year]³" there shall be substituted "[one half of the exempt amount for the year]³"]².

[(3) Subsection (5) shall apply only to the trustees of a settlement made before 7 June 1978 and, in relation to such trustees, shall have effect with the substitution for "[the exempt amount for the year]³" and ["twice the exempt amount for the year" of "one half of the exempt amount for the year" and " the exempt amount for the year" respectively.]³]².

[(4) In relation to a settlement which is one of two or more qualifying settlements comprised in a group, sub-paragraph (2) above shall have effect as if for the reference to [one half of the exempt amount for the year]³ there were substituted a reference to [one tenth of that exempt amount]³ or, if it is more, to such amount as results from dividing [one half of the exempt amount for the year]³ by the number of settlements in the group.]²

[(5) For the purposes of sub-paragraph (4) above—

(*a*) a qualifying settlement is any settlement (other than an excluded settlement) which is made after 6th June 1978 and to the trustees of which this paragraph applies for the year of assessment; and
(*b*) all qualifying settlements in relation to which the same person is the settlor constitute a group.]²

[(6) If, in consequence of two or more persons being settlors in relation to it, a settlement is comprised in two or more groups comprising different numbers of settlements, sub-paragraph (4) above shall apply to it as if the number by which the amount of [one half of the exempt amount for the year]³ is to be divided were the number of settlements in the largest group.]²

[(7) In this paragraph "settlor" has the meaning given by section 681 (4) of the Taxes Act [1988]⁴ and includes, in the case of a settlement arising under a will or intestacy, the testator or intestate and "excluded settlement" means—

(*a*) any settlement the trustees of which are not for the whole or any part of the year of assessment treated under section 52 (1) of this Act as resident and ordinarily resident in the United Kingdom; and
(*b*) any settlement the property comprised in which—

(i) is held for charitable purposes only and cannot become applicable for other purposes; or
(ii) is held for the purposes of any such scheme or fund as is mentioned in sub-paragraph (8) below (retirement benefits and compensation funds).]²

[(8) The schemes and funds referred to in sub-paragraph (7) (*b*) (ii) above are funds to which section 615 (3) of the Taxes Act 1988 applies, schemes and funds approved under section 620 or 621 of that Act, sponsored superannuation schemes as defined in section 624 of that Act and exempt approved schemes and statutory schemes as defined in Chapter I of Part XIV of that Act.]⁶

[(9) An inspector may by notice in writing require any person, being a party to a settlement, to furnish him within such time as he may direct (not being less than twenty-eight days) with such particulars as he thinks necessary for the purposes of this paragraph.]²

Amendments.—¹ Words in sub-para. (1) substituted by FA 1980, s. 78 (2).
² Sub-paras. (2)–(7), (9) substituted by FA 1980, s. 78 (3).
³ Words in sub-paras. (2)–(4), (6) substituted by FA 1982, s. 80 (3).
⁴ "1988" in sub-para. 7 inserted by virtue of TA 1988, Sch. 29, para. 15 (*a*).
⁵ Number in sub-para (7) substituted by TA 1988, Sch. 29, para. 32 Table.
⁶ Sub-para. (8) substituted by TA 1988, Sch. 29, para. 32 Table.

SCHEDULE 2

Section 64 (1)

Gilt-Edged Securities

Cross references.—See TA 1970, s. 270 (6) (taxation of capital gains on certain disposals of UK securities); FA 1976, s. 54 (5) (capital gains: compulsory acquisition of aircraft and shipbuilding shares).

Part I

1. For the purposes of this Act "gilt-edged securities" means the securities specified in Part II of this Schedule, and such of the following securities, denominated in sterling and issued after 15th April 1969, as may be specified by order made by the Treasury by statutory instrument, namely—

(a) stocks and bonds issued under section 12 of the National Loans Act 1968, and
(b) stock and bonds guaranteed by the Treasury and issued under the Electricity (Scotland) Acts 1943 to 1954, the Electricity Acts 1947 and 1957 . . . [1]

Amendments.—[1] Words in sub-para. (b) repealed by the Gas Act 1986, Sch. 9, Pt. II with effect from 24 August 1986 by virtue of S.I. 1986 No. 1318.

2. The Treasury shall cause particulars of any order made under paragraph 1 above to be published in the London and Edinburgh Gazettes as soon as may be after the order is made.

3. Section 14 (b) of the Interpretation Act 1978 (implied power to amend orders made by statutory instrument) shall not apply to the power of making orders under paragraph 1 above.

Part II

Existing Gilt-Edged Securities

Stocks and bonds charged on the National Loans Fund

$11\frac{1}{2}\%$ Treasury Stock 1979
3% Treasury Stock 1979
$10\frac{1}{2}\%$ Treasury Stock 1979
9% Treasury Convertible Stock 1980
4% British Overseas Airways Stock 1974–80
$9\frac{1}{2}\%$ Treasury Stock 1980
$3\frac{1}{2}\%$ Treasury Stock 1977–80
$5\frac{1}{4}\%$ Funding Stock 1978–80
13% Exchequer Stock 1980
$11\frac{1}{2}\%$ Treasury Stock 1981
$3\frac{1}{2}\%$ Treasury Stock 1979–81
$9\frac{3}{4}\%$ Treasury Stock 1981
$8\frac{1}{4}\%$ Exchequer Stock 1981
$9\frac{1}{2}\%$ Exchequer Stock 1981
3% Exchequer Stock 1981
Variable Rate Treasury Stock 1981
$12\frac{3}{4}\%$ Exchequer Stock 1981
$8\frac{1}{2}\%$ Treasury Loan 1980–82
3% Treasury Stock 1982
14% Treasury Stock 1982
$2\frac{1}{2}\%$ British Overseas Airways Stock 1977–82
Variable Rate Treasury Stock 1982
$8\frac{1}{4}\%$ Treasury Stock 1982
$9\frac{1}{4}\%$ Exchequer Stock 1982
$8\frac{3}{4}\%$ Exchequer Stock 1983
3% British Overseas Airways Stock 1980–83
3% Exchequer Stock 1983

12 %	Treasury Loan 1983
[12 %	Treasury Loan 1983 "A"][1]
9$\frac{1}{4}$%	Treasury Stock 1983
10 %	Exchequer Stock 1983
[Variable	Rate Treasury Stock 1983][1]
[13$\frac{1}{2}$%	Exchequer Stock 1983][3]
[3 %	Exchequer Stock 1983 "A"][5]
5$\frac{1}{2}$%	Funding Stock 1982–84
[12 %	Treasury Stock 1984][2]
[3 %	Exchequer Stock 1984][2]
[11$\frac{1}{4}$%	Exchequer Stock 1984][2]
[14 %	Exchequer Stock 1984][3]
12$\frac{1}{4}$%	Exchequer Stock 1985
[12$\frac{1}{4}$%	Exchequer Stock 1985 "A"][16]
[12$\frac{1}{2}$%	Exchequer Stock 1985 "A"][5]
[15 %	Treasury Stock 1985][3]
[3 %	Treasury Stock 1985][4]
[3 %	Treasury Stock 1985 "A"][6]
[12 %	Exchequer Convertible Stock 1985][6]
[11$\frac{1}{2}$%	Treasury Stock 1985][7]
[8$\frac{3}{4}$%	Treasury Convertible Stock 1985][9]
8$\frac{1}{2}$%	Treasury Stock 1984–86
[11$\frac{3}{4}$%	Exchequer Stock 1986][5]
[14 %	Exchequer Stock 1986][7]
[3 %	Treasury Stock 1986][7]
[12 %	Treasury Stock 1986][7]
[12$\frac{1}{4}$%	Treasury Convertible Stock 1986][9]
[10$\frac{1}{2}$%	Exchequer Convertible Stock 1986][10]
[10 %	Treasury Convertible Stock 1986][10]
[2$\frac{1}{2}$%	Exchequer Stock 1986][11]
6$\frac{1}{2}$%	Funding Loan 1985–87
[13$\frac{1}{4}$%	Exchequer Stock 1987][1]
[13$\frac{1}{4}$%	Exchequer Stock 1987 "A"][8]
[12 %	Treasury Stock 1987][5]
[12 %	Treasury Stock 1987 "A"][9]
[3 %	Treasury Stock 1987][8]
[10$\frac{1}{2}$%	Exchequer Stock 1987][9]
[10$\frac{1}{2}$%	Exchequer Stock 1987 "A"][10]
[2$\frac{1}{2}$%	Exchequer Stock 1987][10]
[10$\frac{1}{4}$%	Treasury Convertible Stock 1987][10]
[10 %	Treasury Stock 1987][10]
3 %	British Transport Stock 1978–88
[3 %	British Transport Stock 1978–88][11]
7$\frac{3}{4}$%	Treasury Loan 1985–88
[2 %	Index-linked Treasury Stock 1988][8]
[10$\frac{1}{2}$%	Exchequer Stock 1988][9]
[9$\frac{1}{2}$%	Treasury Stock 1988][9]
[9$\frac{1}{2}$%	Treasury Stock 1988 "A"][10]
[9$\frac{3}{4}$%	Treasury Convertible Stock 1988][10]
5 %	Treasury Stock 1986–89
[11$\frac{1}{2}$%	Treasury Stock 1989][2]
[11$\frac{1}{2}$%	Treasury Stock 1989 "A"][6]
[10$\frac{1}{2}$%	Treasury Stock 1989][10]
[3 %	Treasury Stock 1989][12]
[10 %	Exchequer Stock 1989][10]
[10%	Exchequer Stock 1989 "A"][11]
[9$\frac{1}{2}$%	Treasury Convertible Stock 1989][11]
[11%	Exchequer Stock 1989][11]
[10$\frac{1}{4}$%	Exchequer Convertible Stock 1989][12]
8$\frac{1}{4}$%	Treasury Loan 1987–90
13 %	Treasury Stock 1990
[2%	Index-linked Treasury Stock 1990][11]
[10%	Treasury Convertible Stock 1990][11]
[12$\frac{1}{2}$%	Exchequer Stock 1990][7]
[11%	Exchequer Stock 1990][12]
[3 %	Treasury Stock 1990][12]

[$2\frac{1}{2}\%$	Exchequer Stock 1990][13]
[11 %	Exchequer Loan 1990][13]
[8 %	Treasury Convertible Stock 1990][14]
$5\frac{3}{4}\%$	Funding Loan 1987–91
[8 %	Treasury Loan 1991][14]
[8 %	Treasury Stock 1991][16]
$11\frac{3}{4}\%$	Treasury Stock 1991
[$11\frac{3}{4}\%$	Treasury Stock 1991 "A"][5]
[11 %	Exchequer Stock 1991][1]
[3 %	Treasury Stock 1991][13]
[10 %	Treasury Convertible Stock 1991][13]
$12\frac{3}{4}\%$	Treasury Loan 1992
[8 %	Treasury Loan 1992][14]
10 %	Treasury Stock 1992
[3 %	Treasury Stock 1992][14]
$12\frac{1}{4}\%$	Exchequer Stock 1992
[$13\frac{1}{2}\%$	Exchequer Stock 1992][4]
[$10\frac{1}{2}\%$	Treasury Convertible Stock 1992][11]
[2 %	Index-linked Treasury Stock 1992][14]
$12\frac{1}{2}\%$	Treasury Loan 1993
6 %	Funding Loan 1993
$13\frac{3}{4}\%$	Treasury Loan 1993
[10 %	Treasury Loan 1993][13]
[$8\frac{1}{4}\%$	Treasury Stock 1993][16]
$14\frac{1}{2}\%$	Treasury Loan 1994
$12\frac{1}{2}\%$	Exchequer Stock 1994
9 %	Treasury Loan 1994
[10 %	Treasury Loan 1994][14]
[$13\frac{1}{2}\%$	Exchequer Stock 1994][4]
[$8\frac{1}{2}\%$	Treasury Stock 1994][16]
[$8\frac{1}{2}\%$	Treasury Stock 1994 "A"][16]
[2 %	Index-linked Treasury Stock 1994][16]
12 %	Treasury Stock 1995
$10\frac{1}{4}\%$	Exchequer Stock 1995
$12\frac{3}{4}\%$	Treasury Loan 1995
9 %	Treasury Loan 1992–96
$15\frac{1}{4}\%$	Treasury Loan 1996
$13\frac{1}{4}\%$	Exchequer Loan 1996
[14 %	Treasury Stock 1996][4]
[2 %	Index-linked Treasury Stock 1996][8]
[10 %	Conversion Stock 1996][13]
$13\frac{1}{4}\%$	Treasury Loan 1997
$10\frac{1}{2}\%$	Exchequer Stock 1997
$8\frac{3}{4}\%$	Treasury Loan 1997
[$8\frac{3}{4}\%$	Treasury Loan 1997 "B"][14]
[$8\frac{3}{4}\%$	Treasury Loan 1997 "C"][16]
[15 %	Exchequer Stock 1997][7]
$6\frac{3}{4}\%$	Treasury Loan 1995–98
$15\frac{1}{2}\%$	Treasury Loan 1998
12 %	Exchequer Stock 1998
[12 %	Exchequer Stock 1998 "A"][5]
[$9\frac{3}{4}\%$	Exchequer Stock 1998][11]
[$9\frac{3}{4}\%$	Exchequer Stock 1998 "A"][14]
$9\frac{1}{2}\%$	Treasury Loan 1999
$10\frac{1}{2}\%$	Treasury Stock 1999
[$12\frac{1}{4}\%$	Exchequer Stock 1999][1]
[$12\frac{1}{4}\%$	Exchequer Stock 1999 "A"][2]
[$12\frac{1}{4}\%$	Exchequer Stock 1999 "B"][6]
[$2\frac{1}{2}\%$	Index-linked Treasury Convertible Stock 1999][10]
[$10\frac{1}{4}\%$	Conversion Stock 1999][11]
[9 %	Conversion Stock 2000][4]
[9 %	Conversion Stock 2000 "A"][14]
[13 %	Treasury Stock 2000][5]
[$8\frac{1}{2}\%$	Treasury Loan 2000][14]
[14 %	Treasury Stock 1998–2001][3]
[$2\frac{1}{2}\%$	Index-linked Treasury Stock 2001][9]

[9¾%	Conversion Stock 2001][11]
[10 %	Treasury Stock 2001][12]
[9½%	Conversion Loan 2001][13]
12 %	Exchequer Stock 1999–2002
[12 %	Exchequer Stock 1999–2002 "A"][2]
[9½%	Conversion Stock 2002][11]
[10%	Conversion Stock 2002][11]
[9 %	Exchequer Stock 2002][14]
[9¾%	Treasury Stock 2002][12]
[13¾%	Treasury Stock 2000–2003][1]
[13¾%	Treasury Stock 2000–2003 "A"][3]
[2½%	Index-linked Treasury Stock 2003][9]
[9¾%	Conversion Loan 2003][14]
[10 %	Treasury Stock 2003][13]
3½%	Funding Stock 1999–2004
[11½%	Treasury Stock 2001—2004][2]
[9½%	Conversion Stock 2004][11]
[10 %	Treasury Stock 2004][12]
12½%	Treasury Stock 2003–2005
[12½%	Treasury Stock 2003–2005 "A"][3]
[10½%	Exchequer Stock 2005][12]
[9½%	Conversion Stock 2005][13]
[9½%	Conversion Stock 2005 "A"][14]
8 %	Treasury Loan 2002–2006
[8 %	Treasury Loan 2002–2006 "A"][14]
[2 %	Index-linked Treasury Stock 2006][8]
[9¾%	Conversion Stock 2006][13]
[11¾%	Treasury Stock 2003–2007][2]
[11¾%	Treasury Stock 2003–2007 "A"][6]
[8½%	Treasury Loan 2007][13]
[13½%	Treasury Stock 2004–2008][4]
[9 %	Treasury Loan 2008][14]
[9 %	Treasury Loan 2008 "A"][14]
[2½%	Index-linked Treasury Stock 2009][9]
[8 %	Treasury Stock 2009][13]
[2½%	Index-linked Treasury Stock 2011][8]
[9 %	Conversion Loan 2011][13]
5½%	Treasury Stock 2008–2012
[2½%	Index-linked Treasury Stock 2013][12]
7¾%	Treasury Loan 2012–2015
2½%	Treasury Stock 1986–2016
[2½%	Index-linked Treasury Stock 2016][10]
[2½%	Index-linked Treasury Stock 2016 "A"][13]
12 %	Exchequer Stock 2013–2017
[2½%	Index-linked Treasury Stock 2020][10]
[2½%	Index-linked Treasury Stock 2024][14]
2½%	Annuities 1905 or after
2¾%	Annuities 1905 or after
2½%	Consolidated Stock 1923 or after
4 %	Consolidated Loan 1957 or after
3½%	Conversion Loan 1961 or after
2½%	Treasury Stock 1975 or after
3 %	Treasury Stock 1966 or after
3½%	War Loan 1952 or after

Securities issued by the Treasury under Part II of the Tithe Act 1936

3 % Redemption Stock 1986–96[15]

Securities issued by certain public corporations and guaranteed by the Treasury

4¼% North of Scotland Electricity Stock 1974–79
4¼% British Electricity Stock 1974–79
3½% British Electricity Stock 1976–79

3½%   North of Scotland Electricity Stock 1977–80
3 %   British European Airways Stock 1980–83
3 %   North of Scotland Electricity Stock 1989–92
3 %   British Gas Stock 1990–95

Amendments.—Securities in square brackets are added as specified by the Capital Gains Tax (Gilt-edged Securities) Orders—
S.I. 1979 Nos. [1] 1231; [2] 1676; S.I. 1980 Nos. [3] 507, [4] 922, [5] 1910; S.I. 1981 Nos. [6] 615, [7] 1879; S.I. 1982 Nos. [8] 413, [9] 1774; S.I. 1983 Nos. [10] 1774; S.I. 1984 No. [11] 1966; S.I. 1986 No. [12] 12; S.I. 1987 No. [13] 259; S.I. 1988 No. [14] 360; S.I. 1989 No. [16] 944.
[15] Entry relating to securities issued under Part II of the Tithe Act 1936 repealed by FA 1989, Sch. 17, Pt. XIV with effect from an appointed day.

SCHEDULE 3

Section 106

Leases

Leases of land as wasting assets: curved line restriction of allowable expenditure

1.—(1) A lease of land shall not be a wasting asset until the time when its duration does not exceed fifty years.

(2) If at the beginning of the period of ownership of a lease of land it is subject to a sub-lease not at a rackrent and the value of the lease at the end of the duration of the sub-lease, estimated as at the beginning of the period of ownership, exceeds the expenditure allowable under section 32 (1) (*a*) of this Act in computing the gain accruing on a disposal of the lease, the lease shall not be a wasting asset until the end of the duration of the sub-lease.

(3) In the case of a wasting asset which is a lease of land the rate at which expenditure is assumed to be written off shall, instead of being a uniform rate as provided by section 38 of this Act, be a rate fixed in accordance with the Table below.

(4) Accordingly, for the purposes of the computation under Chapter II of Part II of this Act of the gain accruing on a disposal of a lease, and given that—

(*a*) the percentage derived from the Table for the duration of the lease at the beginning of the period of ownership is $P(1)$.
(*b*) the percentage so derived for the duration of the lease at the time when any item of expenditure attributable to the lease under section 32 (1) (*b*) of this Act is first reflected in the nature of the lease is $P(2)$, and
(*c*) the percentage so derived for the duration of the lease at the time of the disposal is $P(3)$.

then—

(i) there shall be excluded from the expenditure attributable to the lease under section 32 (1) (*a*) of this Act a fraction equal to $\dfrac{P(1)-P(3)}{P(1)}$ and

(ii) there shall be excluded from any item of expenditure attributable to the lease under section 32 (1) (*b*) of this Act a fraction equal to $\dfrac{P(2)-P(3)}{P(2)}$

(5) This paragraph applies notwithstanding that the period of ownership of the lease is a period exceeding fifty years and, accordingly, no expenditure shall be written off under this paragraph in respect of any period earlier than the time when the lease becomes a wasting asset.

(6) Section 39 of this Act (wasting assets qualifying for capital allowances) shall apply in relation to this paragraph as it applies in relation to section 38.

TABLE

Years	Percentage	Years	Percentage
50 (or more)	100	25	81·100
49	99·657	24	79·622
48	99·289	23	78·055
47	98·902	22	76·399
46	98·490	21	74·635
45	98·059	20	72·770
44	97·595	19	70·791
43	97·107	18	68·697
42	96·593	17	66·470
41	96·041	16	64·116
40	95·457	15	61·617
39	94·842	14	58·971
38	94·189	13	56·167
37	93·497	12	53·191
36	92·761	11	50·038
35	91·981	10	46·695
34	91·156	9	43·154
33	90·280	8	39·399
32	89·354	7	35·414
31	88·371	6	31·195
30	87·330	5	26·722
29	86·226	4	21·983
28	85·053	3	16·959
27	83·816	2	11·629
26	82·496	1	5·983
		0	0

If the duration of the lease is not an exact number of years the percentage to be derived from the Table above shall be the percentage for the whole number of years plus one twelfth of the difference between that and the percentage for the next higher number of years for each odd month counting an odd 14 days or more as one month.

Premiums for leases

2.—(1) Subject to this Schedule where the payment of a premium is required under a lease of land, or otherwise under the terms subject to which a lease of land is granted, there is a part disposal of the freehold or other asset out of which the lease is granted.

(2) In applying section 35 of this Act to such a part disposal, the property which remains undisposed of includes a right to any rent or other payments, other than a premium, payable under the lease, and that right shall be valued as at the time of the part disposal.

3.—(1) This paragraph applies in relation to a lease of land.

(2) Where, under the terms subject to which a lease is granted, a sum becomes payable by the tenant in lieu of the whole or part of the rent for any period, or as consideration for the surrender of the lease, the lease shall be deemed for the purposes of this Schedule to have required the payment of a premium to the landlord (in addition to any other premium) of the amount of that sum for the period in relation to which the sum is payable.

(3) Where, as consideration for the variation or waiver of any of the terms of a lease, a sum becomes payable by the tenant otherwise than by way of rent, the lease shall be deemed for the purposes of this Schedule to have required the payment of a premium to the landlord (in addition to any other premium) of the amount of that sum for the period from the time when the variation or waiver takes effect to the time when it ceases to have effect.

(4) If under sub-paragraph (2) or (3) above a premium is deemed to have been received by the landlord, otherwise than as consideration for the surrender of the lease, then subject to sub-paragraph (5) below, both the landlord and the tenant shall be treated as if that premium were, or were part of, the consideration for the grant of the lease due at the time when the lease was granted, and the gain accruing to the landlord on the disposal by way of grant of the lease shall be recomputed and any necessary adjustments of tax, whether by way of assessment for the year in which the premium is deemed to have been received, or by way of discharge or repayment of tax, made accordingly.

(5) If under sub-paragraph (2) or (3) above a premium is deemed to have been received by

the landlord, otherwise than as consideration for the surrender of the lease, and the landlord is a tenant under a lease the duration of which does not exceed fifty years this Schedule shall apply as if an amount equal to the amount of that premium deemed to have been received had been given by way of consideration for the grant of the part of the sub-lease covered by the period in respect of which the premium is deemed to have been paid as if that consideration were expenditure incurred by the sub-lessee and attributable to that part of the sub-lease under section 32 (1) (*b*) of this Act.

(6) Where under sub-paragraph (2) above a premium is deemed to have been received as consideration for the surrender of a lease the surrender of the lease shall not be the occasion of any recomputation of the gain accruing on the receipt of any other premium, and the premium which is consideration for the surrender of the lease shall be regarded as consideration for a separate transaction consisting of the disposal by the landlord of his interest in the lease.

(7) Sub-paragraph (3) above shall apply in relation to a transaction not at arm's length, and in particular in relation to a transaction entered into gratuitously, as if such sum had become payable by the tenant otherwise than by way of rent as might have been required of him if the transaction had been at arm's length.

Sub-leases out of short leases

4.—(1) In the computation under Chapter II of Part II of this Act of the gain accruing on the part disposal of a lease which is a wasting asset by way of the grant of a sub-lease for a premium the expenditure attributable to the lease under paragraphs (*a*) and (*b*) of section 32 (1) of this Act shall be apportioned in accordance with this paragraph, and section 35 of this Act shall not apply.

(2) Out of each item of the expenditure attributable to the lease under paragraphs (*a*) and (*b*) of section 32 (1) of this Act there shall be apportioned to what is disposed of—

(*a*) if the amount of the premium is not less than what would be obtainable by way of premium for the said sub-lease if the rent payable under that sub-lease were the same as the rent payable under the lease, the fraction which, under paragraph 1 (3) of this Schedule, is to be written off over the period which is the duration of the sub-lease, and
(*b*) if the amount of the premium is less than the said amount so obtainable, the said fraction multiplied by a fraction equal to the amount of the said premium divided by the said amount so obtainable.

(3) If the sub-lease is a sub-lease of part only of the land comprised in the lease this paragraph shall apply only in relation to a proportion of the expenditure attributable to the lease under paragraphs (*a*) and (*b*) of section 32 (1) of this Act which is the same as the proportion which the value of the land comprised in the sub-lease bears to the value of that and the other land comprised in the lease; and the remainder of that expenditure shall be apportioned to what remains undisposed of.

Exclusion of premiums taxed under Schedule A etc.

5.—(1) Where by reference to any premium income tax has become chargeable under section [34][2] of the Taxes Act [1988][1] on any amount, that amount out of the premium shall be excluded from the consideration brought into account in the computation under Chapter II of Part II of this Act of a gain accruing on the disposal for which the premium is consideration except where the consideration is taken into account in the denominator of the fraction by reference to which an apportionment is made under section 35 of this Act (part disposals).

(2) Where by reference to any premium in respect of a sub-lease granted out of a lease the duration of which (that is of the lease) does not, at the time of granting the lease, exceed fifty years, income tax has become chargeable under section [34][2] of the Taxes Act [1988][1] on any amount that amount shall be deducted from any gain accruing on the disposal for which the premium is consideration as computed in accordance with the provisions of this Act apart from this sub-paragraph, but not so as to convert the gain into a loss, or to increase any loss.

(3) Where income tax has become chargeable under section [36][2] of the Taxes Act [1988][1] (sale of land with right of re-conveyance) on any amount a sum of that amount shall be excluded from the consideration brought into account in the computation under Chapter II of Part II of this Act of a gain accruing on the disposal of the estate or interest in respect of which income tax becomes so chargeable, except where the consideration is taken into

account in the denominator of the fraction by reference to which an apportionment is made under section 35 of this Act:

Provided that if what is disposed of is the remainder of a lease or a sub-lease out of a lease the duration of which does not exceed fifty years the preceding provisions of this sub-paragraph shall not apply but the said amount shall be deducted from any gain accruing on the disposal as computed in accordance with the provisions of this Act apart from this sub-paragraph, but not so as to convert the gain into a loss, or to increase any loss.

(4) References in sub-paragraph (1) and (2) above to a premium include references to a premium deemed to have been received under subsection [(4) or (5)][2] of section [34][2] of the Taxes Act [1988][1] (which correspond to paragraph 3 (2) and (3) of this Schedule).

(5) Section 31 of this Act (exclusion of consideration chargeable to tax on income) shall not be taken as authorising the exclusion of any amount from the consideration for a disposal of assets taken into account in the computation under Chapter II of Part II of this Act by reference to any amount chargeable to tax under [section 348 or 349][2] of the Taxes Act [1988][1].

Amendments.—[1] "1988' in sub-paras. (1)–(5) inserted by virtue of TA 1988, Sch. 29, para. 15 (a).
[2] Words in sub-paras. (1)–(5) substituted by TA 1988, Sch. 29, para. 32 Table.

6.—(1) If under section [37 (4)][2] of the Taxes Act [1988][1] (allowance where, by the grant of a sub-lease, a lessee has converted a capital amount into a right to income) a person is to be treated as paying additional rent in consequence of having granted a sub-lease, the amount of any loss accruing to him on the disposal by way of the grant of the sub-lease shall be reduced by the total amount of rent which he is thereby treated as paying over the term of the sub-lease (and without regard to whether relief is thereby effectively given over the term of the sub-lease), but not so as to convert the loss into a gain, or to increase any gain.

(2) Nothing in section 31 of this Act shall be taken as applying in relation to any amount on which tax is paid under section [35][2] of the Taxes Act [1988][1] (charge on assignment of lease granted at undervalue).

(3) If any adjustment is made under section [36 (2) (b)][2] of the Taxes Act [1988][1] on a claim under that paragraph, any necessary adjustment shall be made to give effect to the consequences of the claim on the operation of this paragraph or paragraph 5 above.

Amendments.—[1] "1988' in sub-paras. (1)–(3) inserted by virtue of TA 1988, Sch. 29, para. 15 (a).
[2] Numbers in sub-paras. (1)–(3) substituted by TA 1988, Sch. 29, para. 32 Table.

7. If under section [34 (2) and (3)][2] of the Taxes Act [1988][1] income tax is chargeable on any amount, as being a premium the payment of which is deemed to be required by the lease, the person so chargeable shall be treated for the purposes of the computation of any gain accruing to him as having incurred at the time the lease was granted expenditure of that amount (in addition to any other expenditure) attributable to the asset under section 32 (1) (b) of this Act.

Amendments.—[1] "1988" inserted by virtue of TA 1988, Sch. 29, para. 15 (a).
[2] Number substituted by TA 1988, Sch. 29, para. 32 Table.

Duration of leases

8.—(1) In ascertaining for the purposes of this Act the duration of a lease of land the following provisions shall have effect.

(2) Where the terms of the lease include provision for the determination of the lease by notice given by the landlord, the lease shall not be treated as granted for a term longer than one ending at the earliest date on which it could be determined by notice given by the landlord.

(3) Where any of the terms of the lease (whether relating to forfeiture or to any other matter) or any other circumstances render it unlikely that the lease will continue beyond a date falling before the expiration of the term of the lease, the lease shall not be treated as having been granted for a term longer than one ending on that date.

(4) Sub-paragraph (3) applies in particular where the lease provides for the rent to go up after a given date, or for the tenant's obligations to become in any other respect more onerous after a given date, but includes provision for the determination of the lease on that date, by notice given by the tenant, and those provisions render it unlikely that the lease will continue beyond that date.

(5) Where the terms of the lease include provision for the extension of the lease beyond a given date by notice given by the tenant this paragraph shall apply as if the term of the lease extended for as long as it could be extended by the tenant, but subject to any right of the landlord by notice to determine the lease.

(6) It is hereby declared that the question what is the duration of a lease is to be decided, in relation to the grant or any disposal of the lease, by reference to the facts which were known or ascertainable at the time when the lease was acquired or created.

Leases of property other than land

9.—(1) Paragraphs 2, 3, 4 and 8 of this Schedule shall apply in relation to leases of property other than land as they apply to leases of land, but subject to any necessary modifications.

(2) Where by reference to any capital sum within the meaning of section [785][2] of the Taxes Act [1988][1] (leases of assets other than land) any person has been charged to income tax on any amount, that amount out of the capital sum shall be deducted from any gain accruing on the disposal for which that capital sum is consideration, as computed in accordance with the provisions of this Act apart from this sub-paragraph, but not so as to convert the gain into a loss, or increase any loss.

(3) In the case of a lease of a wasting asset which is movable property the lease shall be assumed to terminate not later than the end of the life of the wasting asset.

Amendments.—[1] "1988" in sub-para. (2) inserted by virtue of TA 1988, Sch. 29, para. 15 (*a*).
[2] Number in sub-para. (2) substituted by TA 1988, Sch. 29, para. 32 Table.

Interpretation

10.—(1) In this Act, unless the context otherwise requires "lease"—

(*a*) in relation to land, includes an underlease, sublease or any tenancy or licence, and any agreement for a lease, underlease, sublease or tenancy or licence and, in the case of land outside the United Kingdom, any interest corresponding to a lease as so defined,

(*b*) in relation to any description of property other than land, means any kind of agreement or arrangement under which payments are made for the use of, or otherwise in respect of, property,

and "lessor", "lessee" and "rent" shall be construed accordingly.

(2) In this Schedule "premium" includes any like sum, whether payable to the intermediate or a superior landlord, and for the purposes of this Schedule any sum (other than rent) paid on or in connection with the granting of a tenancy shall be presumed to have been paid by way of premium except in so far as the other sufficient consideration for the payment is shown to have been given.

(3) In the application of this Schedule to Scotland "premium" includes in particular a grassum payable to any landlord or intermediate landlord on the creation of a sublease.

SCHEDULE 4
Section 126

RELIEF FOR GIFTS OF BUSINESS ASSETS

PART I
AGRICULTURAL PROPERTY AND SETTLED PROPERTY

Agricultural property

1.—(1) This paragraph applies where—

(*a*) there is a disposal of an asset which is, or is an interest in, agricultural property within the meaning of [Chapter II of Part V of the Capital Transfer Tax Act 1984][3] (capital transfer tax relief for agricultural property), and

(*b*) apart from this paragraph, the disposal would not fall within [section 126 (1)][4] of this Act by reason only that the agricultural property is not used for the purposes of a trade carried on as mentioned in [section 126 (1A) (*a*)][4].

(2) Where this paragraph applies, section 126 (1) of this Act shall apply in relation to the disposal if the circumstances are such that a reduction . . .[5] in respect of the asset—

(*a*) is made under [Chapter II of Part V of the Capital Transfer Tax Act 1984][3] in relation to a chargeable transfer taking place on the occasion of the disposal, or

(*b*) would be so made if there were a chargeable transfer on that occasion . . .[1-2]. [, or][6]

[(*c*) would be so made but for section 124A of that Act (assuming, where there is no chargeable transfer on that occasion, that there were).][6]

Note.—For CTTA 1984 (now cited as Inheritance Tax Act 1984), see the current edition of *Butterworths Orange Tax Handbook*.
Cross references.—See FA 1986, s. 100 (CTTA 1984 may be cited as Inheritance Tax Act 1984 after 24 July 1986).
Amendments.—[1-2] Words in sub-para. (2) (*b*) repealed by FA 1981, Sch. 19, Pt. VIII.
[3] Words in sub-paras. (1) (*a*), (2) (*a*) substituted by IHTA 1984, Sch. 8, para. 12 with effect from 1 January 1985.
[4] Words in sub-para. (1) (*b*) substituted by FA 1989, Sch. 14, para. 3 (2).
[5] Words in sub-para. (2) repealed by FA 1989, Sch. 14, para. 3 (2) (*b*) and Sch. 17, Pt. VII with effect in relation to disposals after 13 March 1989, subject to certain exceptions; see FA 1989, Sch. 17, Pt. VII, Note 7.
[6] Sub-para. (2) (*c*) and the preceding word "or" added by FA 1989, Sch. 14, para. 3 (2) (*b*) in relation to disposals after 13 March 1989, subject to certain exceptions; see FA 1989, s. 124(3).

Settled property

[2.—(1) If—

(*a*) the trustees of a settlement make a disposal otherwise than under a bargain at arm's length of an asset within sub-paragraph (2) below, and

(*b*) a claim for relief under section 126 of this Act is made by the trustees and the person who acquires the asset (in this Schedule referred to as "the transferee") or, where the trustees of a settlement are also the transferee, by the trustees making the disposal alone,

then, subject to subsection (2) of section 126 and to sections 126A and 126B, subsection (3) of section 126 shall apply in relation to the disposal.

(2) An asset is within this sub-paragraph if—

(*a*) it is, or is an interest in, as asset used for the purposes of a trade, profession or vocation carried on by—

(i) the trustees making the disposal, or
(ii) a beneficiary who had an interest in possession in the settled property immediately before the disposal, or

(*b*) it consists of shares or securities of a trading company, or of the holding company of a trading group, where—

(i) the shares or securities are neither quoted on a recognised stock exchange nor dealt in on the Unlisted Securities Market, or

(ii) not less than 25 per cent. of the voting rights exercisable by shareholders of the company in general meeting are exercisable by the trustees at the time of the disposal.

(3) Where section 126 (3) applies by virtue of this paragraph, references to the trustees shall be substituted for the references in sections 126 (3) (a) and 126C to the transferor; and where it applies in relation to a disposal which is deemed to occur by virtue of section 54 (1) or 55 (1) of this Act, section 126 (6) shall not apply.][1]

Amendments.—[1] This paragraph substituted by FA 1989, s. 124 (2), (3) and Sch. 14, para. 3 (3) in relation to disposals made after 13 March 1989 subject to certain exceptions; see FA 1989, s. 124 (3).

3.—(1) This paragraph applies where—

(a) there is, . . .[4], a disposal of an asset which is, or is an interest in, agricultural property within the meaning of [Chapter II of Part V of the Capital Transfer Tax Act 1984][3], and

(b) apart from this paragraph, the disposal would not fall within paragraph [2 (1) (a)][5] above by reason only that the agricultural property is not used for the purposes of a trade as mentioned in [paragraph 2 (2) (a) above][5].

(2) Where this paragraph applies, paragraph 2 (1) above shall apply in relation to the disposal if the circumstances are such that a reduction . . .[6] in respect of the asset—

(a) is made under [Chapter II of Part V of the Capital Transfer Tax Act 1984][3] in relation to a chargeable transfer taking place on the occasion of the disposal, or

(b) would be so made if there were a chargeable transfer on that occasion . . .[1–2]. [, or][7]

[(c) would be so made but for section 124A of that Act (assuming, where there is no chargeable transfer on that occasion, that there were).][7]

Note.—For CTTA 1984 (now cited as Inheritance Tax Act 1984), see the current edition of *Butterworths Orange Tax Handbook*.
Cross references.—See FA 1986, s. 100 (CTTA 1984 may be cited as Inheritance Tax Act 1984 after 24 July 1986).
Amendments.—[1–2] Words in sub-para. (2) (b) repealed by FA 1981, Sch. 19, Pt. VIII.
[3] Words in sub-paras. (1) (a), (2) (a) substituted by IHTA 1984, Sch. 8, para. 12 with effect from 1 January 1985.
[4] Words in sub-para. (1) (a) repealed by FA 1989, Sch. 14, para. 3 (4) (a) and Sch. 17, Pt. VII subject to certain exceptions; see FA 1989, s. 124 (3) and Sch. 17, Pt. VII, Note 7.
[5] Words in sub-para. (1) (a), (b) substituted by FA 1989, Sch. 14, para. 3 (4) (a) (ii), (iii).
[6] Words in sub-para. (2) repealed by FA 1989, Sch. 14, para. 3 (4) (a) (i) and Sch. 17, Pt. VII with effect in relation to disposals after 13 March 1989, subject to certain exceptions; see FA 1989, Sch. 17, Pt. VII, Note 7.
[7] Sub-para. (2) (c) and the preceding word "or" added by FA 1989, Sch. 14, para. 3 (4) (b) in relation to disposals after 13 March 1989, subject to certain exceptions; see FA 1989, s. 124 (3).

PART II

REDUCTIONS IN HELD-OVER GAIN

Application and interpretation

4.—(1) The provisions of this Part of this Schedule apply in cases where a claim for relief is made under section 126 of this Act.

(2) In this Part of this Schedule—

(a) "the principal provision" means [section 126 (1A)][1], of this Act, or, as the case may require, [sub-paragraph (2)][1] of paragraph 2 above,

(b) "shares" includes securities,

[(c) "the transferor" has the same meaning as in section 126 of this Act except that, in a case where paragraph 2 above applies, it refers to the trustees mentioned in that paragraph,]

(d) "unrelieved gain", in relation to a disposal, has the same meaning as in section 126 (6) of this Act.

[(3) In this Part of this Schedule—

(a) any reference to a disposal of an asset is a reference to a disposal which falls within subsection (1) of section 126 of this Act by virtue of subsection (1A) (a) of that section or, as the case may be, falls within sub-paragraph (1) of paragraph 2 above by virtue of sub-paragraph (2) (a) of that paragraph, and

(b) any reference to a disposal of shares is a reference to a disposal which falls within subsection (1) of section 126 of this Act by virtue of subsection (1A) (b) of that section or, as the case may be, falls within sub-paragraph (1) of paragraph 2 above by virtue of sub-paragraph (2) (b) of that paragraph.][2]

(4) In relation to a disposal of an asset or of shares, any reference in the following provisions of this Part of this Schedule to the held-over gain is a reference to the held-over gain on that disposal as determined under subsection (5) or, [where it applies]¹, subsection (6) of section 126 of this Act . . .³.

Amendments.—¹ Words in sub-para. (2) (*a*), (4) substituted by FA 1989, Sch. 14, para. 3 (5) (*a*).
² Sub-paras. (2) (*c*), (3) substituted by FA 1989, s. 124 (2), (3) and Sch. 14, para. 3 (5) (*b*), (*c*) in relation to disposals after 13 March 1989 subject to certain exceptions; see FA 1989, s. 124 (3).
³ Words in sub-para. (4) repealed by FA 1989, Sch. 14, para. 3 (5) (*d*) and Sch. 17, Pt. VII subject to certain exceptions; see FA 1989, Sch. 17, Pt. VII, Note 7.

Reductions peculiar to disposals of assets

5.—(1) If, in the case of a disposal of an asset, the asset was not used for the purposes of the trade, profession or vocation referred to in paragraph (*a*) of the principal provision throughout the period of its ownership by the transferor, the amount of the held-over gain shall be reduced by multiplying it by the fraction of which the denominator is the number of days in that period of ownership and the numerator is the number of days in that period during which the asset was so used.

[(2) This paragraph shall not apply where the circumstances are such that a reduction in respect of the asset—

(*a*) is made under Chapter II of Part V of the Inheritance Tax Act 1984 in relation to a chargeable transfer taking place on the occasion of the disposal, or
(*b*) would be so made if there were a chargeable transfer on that occasion, or
(*c*) would be so made but for section 124A of that Act (assuming, where there is no chargeable transfer on that occasion, that there were).]¹

Note.—For the Inheritance Tax Act 1984, see the current edition of *Butterworths Orange Tax Handbook*.
Amendments.—¹ Sub-para. (2) added by FA 1989, Sch. 14, para. 3 (6) in relation to disposals after 13 March 1989, subject to certain exceptions; see FA 1989, s. 124 (3).

6.—(1) If, in the case of a disposal of an asset, the asset is a building or structure and, over the period of its ownership by the transferor or any substantial part of that period, part of the building or structure was, and part was not, used for the purposes of the trade, profession or vocation referred to in paragraph (*a*) of the principal provision, there shall be determined the fraction of the unrelieved gain on the disposal which it is just and reasonable to apportion to the part of the asset which was so used, and the amount of the held-over gain (as reduced, if appropriate, under paragraph 5 above) shall be reduced by multiplying it by that fraction.

[(2) This paragraph shall not apply where the circumstances are such that a reduction in respect of the asset—

(*a*) is made under Chapter II of Part V of the Inheritance Tax Act 1984 in relation to a chargeable transfer taking place on the occasion of the disposal, or
(*b*) would be so made if there were a chargeable transfer on that occasion, or
(*c*) would be so made but for section 124A of that Act (assuming, where there is no chargeable transfer on that occasion, that there were).]¹

Note.—For the Inheritance Tax Act 1984, see the current edition of *Butterworths Orange Tax Handbook*.
Amendments.—¹ Sub-para. (2) added by FA 1989, Sch. 14, para. 3 (6) in relation to disposals after 13 March 1989, subject to certain exceptions; see FA 1989, s. 124 (3).

Reduction peculiar to disposal of shares

[**7.**—(1) If in the case of a disposal of shares assets which are not business assets are included in the chargeable assets of the company whose shares are disposed of, or, where that company is the holding company of a trading group, in the group's chargeable assets, and either—

(*a*) at any time within the period of twelve months before the disposal not less than 25 per cent. of the voting rights exercisable by shareholders of the company in general meeting are exercisable by the transferor, or
(*b*) the transferor is an individual and, at any time within that period, the company is his family company,

the amount of the held-over gain shall be reduced by multiplying it by the fraction defined in sub-paragraph (2) below.

(2) The fraction referred to in sub-paragraph (1) above is that of which—

(*a*) the denominator is the market value on the date of the disposal of all the chargeable assets of the company, or as the case may be of the group, and
(*b*) the numerator is the market value on that date of those chargeable assets of the company or of the group which are business assets.

(3) For the purposes of this paragraph—

(*a*) an asset is a business asset in relation to a company or a group if it is or is an interest in an asset used for the purposes of a trade, profession or vocation carried on by the company, or as the case may be by a member of the group; and
(*b*) an asset is a chargeable asset in relation to a company or a group at any time if, on a disposal at that time, a gain accruing to the company, or as the case may be to a member of the group would be a chargeable gain.

(4) Where the shares disposed of are shares of the holding company of a trading group, then for the purposes of this paragraph—

(*a*) the holding by one member of the group of the ordinary share capital of another member shall not count as a chargeable asset, and
(*b*) if the whole of the ordinary share capital of 51 per cent. subsidiary of the holding company is not owned directly or indirectly by that company, the value of the chargeable assets of the subsidiary shall be taken to be reduced by multiplying it by the fraction of which the denominator is the whole of the ordinary share capital of the subsidiary and the numerator is the amount of that share capital owned directly or indirectly by the holding company.

(5) Expressions used in sub-paragraph (4) above have the same meanings as in section 838 of the Taxes Act 1988.][1]

Amendments.—[1] This paragraph substituted by FA 1989, Sch. 14, para. 3 (7) in relation to disposals after 13 March 1989, subject to certain exceptions; see FA 1989, s. 124 (3).

Reduction where gain partly relieved by retirement relief

8.—(1) If, in the case of a disposal of an asset—

(*a*) the disposal is of a chargeable business asset and is comprised in a disposal of the whole or part of a business in respect of gains accruing on which the transferor is entitled to relief under [Schedule 20 to the Finance Act 1985][1] (transfer of business on retirement), and
(*b*) apart from this paragraph, the held-over gain on the disposal (as reduced, where appropriate, under the preceding provisions of this Part of this Schedule) would exceed the amount of the chargeable gain which, apart from section 126 of this Act, would accrue on the disposal.

the amount of that held-over gain shall be reduced by the amount of the excess.

(2) In sub-paragraph (1) above "chargeable business asset" has the same meaning as in [Schedule 20 to the Finance Act 1985][1].

(3) If, in the case of a disposal of shares,—

(*a*) the disposal is or forms part of a disposal of shares in respect of the gains accruing on which the transferor is entitled to relief under [Schedule 20 to the Finance Act 1985][1], and
(*b*) apart from this paragraph, the held-over gain on the disposal (as reduced, where appropriate, under paragraph 7 above) would exceed an amount equal to the relevant proportion of the chargeable gain which, apart from section 126 of this Act, would accrue on the disposal.

the amount of that held-over gain shall be reduced by the amount of the excess.

(4) In sub-paragraph (3) above "the relevant proportion", in relation to a disposal falling within paragraph (*a*) of that sub-paragraph, means [the appropriate proportion determined under Schedule 20 to the Finance Act 1985][2] in relation to the aggregate sum of the gains which accrue on that disposal.

Amendments.—[1] Words in sub-paras. (1) (*a*), (2), (3) (*a*) substituted by FA 1985, s. 70 (9) (*c*), (*d*).
[2] Words in sub-para. (4) substituted by FA 1985, s. 70 (9) (*c*).

SCHEDULE 5

Section 28 (3)

ASSETS HELD ON 6TH APRIL 1965

Cross references.—See FA 1982, s. 148 (1) (transfer of assets of the Hops Marketing Board to specified transferees; effect of this Schedule on the transfer of assets held by the Board on 6 April 1965);
Trustee Savings Banks Act 1985, Sch. 2, para. 2 (2) (application of this Schedule in relation to certain transfers of assets in the course of the reorganisation of trustee savings banks).

PART I

QUOTED SECURITIES

Deemed acquisition at 6th April 1965 value

1.—(1) This paragraph applies—

(*a*) to shares and securities which on 6th April 1965 have quoted market values on a recognised stock exchange in the United Kingdom or elsewhere, or which have had such quoted market values at any time in the period of six years ending on 6th April 1965, and
(*b*) to rights of unit holders in any unit trust scheme the prices of which are published regularly by the managers of the scheme.

(2) For the purposes of this Act it shall be assumed, wherever relevant, that any assets to which this paragraph applies were sold by the owner, and immediately re-acquired by him, at their market value on 6th April 1965.

(3) This paragraph shall not apply in relation to a disposal of shares or securities of a company by a person to whom those shares or securities were issued as an employee either of the company or of some other person on terms which restrict his rights to dispose of them.

Restriction of gain or loss by reference to actual cost

2.—(1) Subject to the rights of election conferred by paragraphs 4 to 7 below, paragraph 1 (2) above shall not apply in relation to a disposal of assets—

(*a*) if on the assumption in paragraph 1 (2) a gain would accrue on that disposal to the person making the disposal and either a smaller gain or a loss would so accrue (computed in accordance with Chapter II of Part II) if paragraph 1 (2) did not apply, or
(*b*) if on the assumption in paragraph 1 (2) a loss would so accrue and either a smaller loss or a gain would accrue if paragraph 1 (2) did not apply,

and accordingly the amount of the gain or loss accruing on the disposal shall be computed without regard to the preceding provisions of this Schedule except that in a case where this sub-paragraph would otherwise substitute a loss for a gain or a gain for a loss it shall be assumed, in relation to the disposal, that the relevant assets were sold by the owner, and immediately re-acquired by him, for a consideration such that, on the disposal, neither a gain nor a loss accrued to the person making the disposal.

(2) For the purpose of—

(*a*) identifying shares or securities held on 6th April 1965 with shares or securities previously acquired, and
(*b*) identifying the shares or securities held on that date with shares or securities subsequently disposed of, and distinguishing them from shares or securities acquired subsequently,

so far as that identification is needed for the purposes of sub-paragraph (1) above, and so far as the shares or securities are of the same class, shares or securities acquired at a [later time][1] shall be deemed to be disposed of before shares or securities acquired at an [earlier time][1].

(3) Sub-paragraph (2) above has effect subject to section 66 of this Act (disposal on or before day of acquisition).

Cross references.—See FA 1985, Sch. 19, para. 6 (3) (*b*) (election to pool quoted securities held before 1 April 1985 or 6 April 1985 with the securities held on 1 April 1982 or 6 April 1982; exclusion of para. 2 above where such election is made).
Amendments.—[1] Words in sub-para. (2) substituted by FA 1982, Sch. 13, para. 11.

Exclusion of pooling

3.—(1) Subject to the rights of election conferred by paragraphs 4 to 7 below, section 65 of this Act (pooling of shares and other assets) shall not apply to quoted securities held on 6th April 1965.

(2) Where—

(*a*) a disposal was made out of quoted securities before 20th March 1968 (that is to say before the date on which the provisions re-enacted in sub-paragraph (1) above took effect), and
(*b*) by virtue of paragraph 2 of Schedule 7 to the Finance Act 1965 (re-enacted as section 65 of this Act) some of the quoted securities out of which the disposal was made were acquired before 6th April 1965, and some later

then in computing the gain accruing on any disposal of quoted securities the question of what remained undisposed of on the earlier disposal shall be decided on the footing that sub-paragraph (1) above had effect as respects that earlier disposal.

(3) The rules of identification in paragraph 2 (2) above shall apply for the purposes of this paragraph as they apply for the purposes of the said paragraph 2.

Election for pooling

4.—(1) If a person so elects, quoted securities covered by the election shall be excluded from paragraphs 2 and 3 above (so that neither paragraph 1 (2) above nor section 65 of this Act is excluded by those paragraphs as respects those securities).

(2) An election made by any person under this paragraph shall be as respects all disposals made by him at any time, including disposals made before the election but after 19th March 1968—

(*a*) of quoted securities of kinds other than fixed-interest securities and preference shares, or
(*b*) of fixed-interest securities and preference shares,

and references to the quoted securities covered by an election shall be construed accordingly.

Any person may make both of the elections.

(3) An election under this paragraph shall not cover quoted securities which the holder acquired on a disposal after 19th March 1968 in relation to which either of the following enactments (which secure that neither a gain nor a loss accrues on the disposal) applies, that is—

(*a*) section 44 of this Act (disposals between husband and wife),
(*b*) section 273 (1) of the Taxes Act [1970][1] (disposals within a group of companies),

but this paragraph shall apply to the quoted securities so held if the person making the original disposal (that is to say the wife or husband of the holder, or the other member of the group of companies) makes an election covering quoted securities of the kind in question.

For the purpose of identifying quoted securities disposed of by the holder with quoted securities acquired by him on a disposal in relation to which either of the said enactments applies, so far as they are of the same class, quoted securities acquired at an earlier time shall be deemed to be disposed of before quoted securities acquired at a later time.

(4) For the avoidance of doubt it is hereby declared—

(*a*) that where a person makes an election under this paragraph as respects quoted securities which he holds in one capacity, that election does not cover quoted securities which he holds in another capacity, and
(*b*) that an election under this paragraph is irrevocable.

(5) An election under this paragraph shall be made by notice in writing to the inspector not later than the expiration of two years from the end of the year of assessment or accounting

period of a company in which the first relevant disposal is made, or such further time as the Board may allow.

(6) Subject to paragraph 5 below, in this paragraph the "first relevant disposal", in relation to each of the elections referred to in sub-paragraph (2) of this paragraph, means the first disposal after 19th March 1968 by the person making the election of quoted securities of the kind covered by that election.

(7) All such adjustments shall be made, whether by way of discharge or repayment of tax, or the making of assessments or otherwise, as are required to give effect to an election under this paragraph.

Cross references.—See FA 1985, Sch. 19, para. 6 (4) (this paragraph except sub-para. (1) to apply in relation to an election for the pooling of securities held on 1 April or 6 April 1985 with the securities held on 1 April or 6 April 1982.
Amendments.—[1] "1970" in sub-para. (3) (*b*) inserted by virtue of TA 1988, Sch. 29, para. 15 (*b*).

Election by principal company of group

5.—(1) In the case of companies which at the relevant time are members of a group of companies—

(*a*) an election under paragraph 4 above by the company which at that time is the principal company of the group shall have effect also as an election by any other company which at that time is a member of the group, and
(*b*) no election under that paragraph may be made by any other company which at that time is a member of the group.

(2) In this paragraph "the relevant time", in relation to a group of companies, and in relation to each of the elections referred to in paragraph 4 (2) above, is the first occasion after 19th March 1968 when any company which is then a member of a group disposes of quoted securities of a kind covered by that election, and for the purposes of paragraph 4 (5) above that occasion is, in relation to the group, "the first relevant disposal".

(3) This paragraph shall not apply in relation to quoted securities of either kind referred to in paragraph 4 (2) above which are owned by a company which, in some period after 19th March 1968 and before the relevant time, was not a member of the group if in that period it had made an election under paragraph 4 above in relation to securities of that kind (or was treated by virtue of this paragraph, in relation to another group, as having done so), or had made a disposal of quoted securities of that kind and did not make an election within the time limited by paragraph 4 (5) above.

(4) This paragraph shall apply notwithstanding that a company ceases to be a member of the group at any time after the relevant time.

(5) In this paragraph "company" and "group" shall be construed in accordance with subsections (1) and (2) of section 272 of the Taxes Act [1970][1].

Cross references.—See FA 1985, Sch. 19, para. 6 (4) (this paragraph to apply in relation to an election for the pooling of securities held on 1 April or 6 April 1985 with the securities held on 1 April or 6 April 1982).
Amendments.—[1] "1970" in sub-para. (5) inserted by virtue of TA 1988, Sch. 29, para. 15 (*b*).

*Pooling at value on 6th April 1965 :
exchange of securities etc.*

6.—(1) Where a person who has made only one of the elections under paragraph 4 above disposes of quoted securities which, in accordance with Chapter II of Part IV of this Act, are to be regarded as being or forming part of a new holding, the election shall apply according to the nature of the quoted securities disposed of, notwithstanding that under the said Chapter the new holding is to be regarded as the same asset as the original holding and that the election would apply differently to the original holding.

(2) Where the election does not cover the disposal out of the new holding, but does cover quoted securities of the kind comprised in the original holding, then in computing the gain accruing on the disposal out of the new holding (in accordance with paragraph 3 above) the question of what remained undisposed of on any disposal out of the original holding shall be decided on the footing that paragraph 3 above applied to that earlier disposal.

(3) In the case converse to that in sub-paragraph (2) above (that is to say where the election covers the disposal out of the new holding, but does not cover quoted securities of the kind

comprised in the original holding) the question of how much of the new holding derives from quoted securities held on 6th April 1965, and how much derives from other quoted securities, shall be decided as it is decided for the purposes of paragraph 3 above.

Cross references.—See FA 1985, Sch. 19, para. 6 (4) (this paragraph to apply in relation to an election for the pooling of securities held on 1 April or 6 April 1985 with the securities held on 1 April or 6 April 1982).

Underwriters

7. No election under paragraph 4 above shall cover quoted securities comprised in any underwriter's premiums trust fund, or premiums trust fund deposits, or personal reserves, being securities comprised in funds to which section 142 of this Act applies.

Cross references.—See FA 1985, Sch. 19, para. 6 (4) (this paragraph to apply in relation to an election for the pooling of securities held on 1 April or 6 April 1985 with the securities held on 1 April or 6 April 1982).

Interpretation of paragraphs 3 to 7

8.—(1) In paragraphs 3 to 7 above—

"quoted securities" means assets to which paragraph 1 above applies,
"fixed interest security" means any security as defined by section 82 of this Act,
"preference share" means any share the holder whereof has a right to a dividend at a fixed rate, but has no other right to share in the profits of the company.

(2) If and so far as the question whether at any particular time a share was a preference share depends on the rate of dividends payable on or before 5th April 1973, the reference in the definition of "preference share" in sub-paragraph (1) above to a dividend at a fixed rate includes a dividend at a rate fluctuating in accordance with the standard rate of income tax.

Cross references.—See FA 1985, Sch. 19, para. 6 (4) (this paragraph to apply in relation to an election for the pooling of securities held on 1 April or 6 April 1985 with the securities held on 1 April or 6 April 1982).

PART II

LAND REFLECTING DEVELOPMENT VALUE

Valuation at 6th April 1965

9.—(1) This paragraph shall apply in relation to a disposal of an asset which is an interest in land situated in the United Kingdom—

(*a*) if, but for this paragraph, the expenditure allowable as a deduction in computing under Chapter II of Part II of this Act the gain accruing on the disposal would include any expenditure incurred before 6th April 1965, and
(*b*) if the consideration for the asset acquired on the disposal exceeds the current use value of the asset at the time of the disposal, or if any material development of the land has been carried out after 17th December 1973 since the person making the disposal acquired the asset.

(2) For the purposes of this Act, including Chapter II of Part II, it shall be assumed in relation to the disposal and, if it is a part disposal, in relation to any subsequent disposal of the asset which is an interest in land situated in the United Kingdom that that asset was sold by the person making the disposal, and immediately re-acquired by him, at its market value on 6th April 1965.

(3) Sub-paragraph (2) above shall apply also in relation to any prior part disposal of the asset and, if tax has been charged, or relief allowed, by reference to that part disposal on a different footing, all such adjustments shall be made, whether by way of assessment or discharge or repayment of tax, as are required to give effect to the provisions of this sub-paragraph.

(4) Sub-paragraph (2) above shall not apply in relation to a disposal of assets—

(*a*) if on the assumption in that sub-paragraph a gain would accrue on that disposal to the person making the disposal and either a smaller gain or a loss would so accrue (computed in accordance with the provisions of Chapter II of Part II of this Act) if the said sub-paragraph (2) did not apply, or

(b) if on the assumption in the said sub-paragraph (2) a loss would so accrue and either a smaller loss or a gain would accrue if the said sub-paragraph (2) did not apply.

and accordingly the amount of the gain or loss accruing on the disposal shall be computed without regard to the provisions of this Schedule except that in a case where this sub-paragraph would otherwise substitute a loss for a gain or a gain for a loss it shall be assumed, in relation to the disposal, that the relevant assets were sold by the owner, and immediately re-acquired by him, for a consideration such that, on the disposal, neither a gain not a loss accrued to the person making the disposal.

(5) For the purposes of this paragraph—

(a) "interest in land" has the meaning given by section 44 (1) of the Finance Act 1974,
(b) "material development" has the meaning given by paragraph 6 of Schedule 3 to the Finance Act 1974,
(c) the current use value of an interest in land shall be computed in accordance with Part I of the said Schedule 3, but so that, in relation to any material development which was begun before 18th December 1973, sub-paragraph (2) of paragraph 1 of that Schedule (definition of current use value) shall have effect as if the words from "other than" to the end of the sub-paragraph (which allow for the completion of duly authorised material development already begun) were omitted,
(d) paragraph 9 of the said Schedule 3 (date when material development is begun) shall apply as it applies for the purposes of that Schedule, and
(e) paragraph 14 of the said Schedule 3 (meaning of the material development "carried out after" a particular date) shall apply as it applies for the purposes of paragraphs 11 to 13 of that Schedule.

Allowance for betterment levy

10. Paragraph 9 (1) above has effect subject to paragraph 21 (2) of Schedule 6 to this Act (valuation at 6th April 1965 on a claim under that paragraph).

PART III
OTHER ASSETS

Apportionment by reference to straightline growth of gain or loss over period of ownership

11.—(1) This paragraph applies subject to Parts I and II of this Schedule.

(2) On the disposal of assets by a person whose period of ownership began before 6th April 1965 only so much of any gain accruing on the disposal as is under this paragraph to be apportioned to the period beginning with 6th April 1965 shall be a chargeable gain.

(3) Subject to the following provisions of this Schedule, the gain shall be assumed to have grown at a uniform rate from nothing at the beginning of the period of ownership to its full amount at the time of the disposal so that, calling the part of that period before 6th April 1965, P, and the time beginning with 6th April 1965 and ending with the time of the disposal T, the fraction of the gain which is a chargeable gain is, $\dfrac{T}{P+T}$

(4) If any of the expenditure which is allowable as a deduction in the computation under Chapter II of Part II of this Act of the gain is within section 32 (1) (b) of this Act—

(a) the gain shall be attributed to the expenditure, if any, allowable under paragraph (a) of the said section 32 (1) as one item of expenditure, and to the respective items of expenditure under the said section 32 (1) (b) in proportion to the respective amounts of those items of expenditure,
(b) sub-paragraph (3) of this paragraph shall apply to the part of the gain attributed to the expenditure under the said section 32 (1) (a),
(c) each part of the gain attributed to the items of expenditure under the said section 32 (1) (b) shall be assumed to have grown at a uniform rate from nothing at the time when the relevant item of expenditure was first reflected in the value of the asset to the full amount of that part of the gain at the time of the disposal,

so that, calling the respective proportions of the gain E(0), E(1), E(2) and so on (so that they add up to unity) and calling the respective periods from the times when the items under the said section 32 (1) (b) were reflected in the value of the asset to 5th April 1965 P(1), P(2) and so on, and employing also the abbreviations in sub-paragraph (3) above, the fraction of the gain which is a chargeable gain is

$$E(0)\frac{T}{P+T} + E(1)\frac{T}{P(1)+T} + E(2)\frac{T}{P(2)+T} \text{ and so on}$$

(5) In a case within sub-paragraph (4) above where there is no initial expenditure (that is no expenditure under section 32 (1) (*a*) of this Act) or that initial expenditure is, compared with any item of expenditure under section 32 (1) (*b*), disproportionately small having regard to the value of the asset immediately before the subsequent item of expenditure was incurred, the part of the gain which is not attributable to the enhancement of the value of the asset due to any item of expenditure under the said section 32 (1) (*b*) shall be deemed to be attributable to expenditure incurred at the beginning of the period of ownership and allowable under section 32 (1) (*a*), and the part or parts of the gain attributable to expenditure under section 32 (1) (*b*) shall be reduced accordingly.

(6) The beginning of the period over which a gain, or a part of a gain is, under sub-paragraphs (3) and (4) above, to be treated as growing shall not be earlier than 6th April 1945, and this sub-paragraph shall have effect notwithstanding any provision in this Schedule or elsewhere in this Act.

(7) If in pursuance of section 35 of this Act (part disposals) an asset's market value at a date before 6th April 1965 is to be ascertained sub-paragraphs (3) to (5) above shall have effect as if that asset had been on that date sold by the owner, and immediately re-acquired by him, at that market value.

(8) If in pursuance of section 35 of this Act an asset's market value at a date on or after 6th April 1965 is to be ascertained sub-paragraphs (3) to (5) above shall have effect as if—

(*a*) the asset on that date had been sold by the owner, and immediately re-acquired by him, at that market value, and
(*b*) accordingly, the computation of any gain on a subsequent disposal of that asset shall be computed—
(i) by apportioning in accordance with this paragraph the gain or loss over a period ending on the said date (the date of the part disposal), and
(ii) by bringing into account the entire gain or loss over the period from the date of the part disposal to the date of subsequent disposal.

(9) For the purposes of this paragraph the period of ownership of an asset shall, where under section 36 of this Act (assets derived from other assets) account is to be taken of expenditure in respect of an asset from which the asset disposed of was derived, or where it would so apply if there were any relevant expenditure in respect of that other asset, include the period of ownership of that other asset.

(10) If under this paragraph part only of a gain is a chargeable gain, the fraction in 102 (2) of this Act (private residences: amount of relief) shall be applied to that part instead of to the whole of the gain.

Cross references.—See FA 1988, Sch. 8, para. 10 (re-basing of indexation allowance to 1982 in respect of part of the unindexed gains and losses from disposals of assets held before 6 April 1965).

Election for valuation at 6th April 1965

12.—(1) If the person making a disposal so elects paragraph 11 of this Schedule shall not apply in relation to that disposal and it shall be assumed, both for the purposes of computing under Chapter II of Part II of this Act the gain accruing to that person on the disposal, and for all other purposes both in relation to that person and other persons, that the assets disposed of, and any assets of which account is to be taken in relation to the disposal under section 36 of this Act, being assets which were in the ownership of the said person on 6th April 1965, were on that date sold, and immediately re-acquired, by him at their market value on the said 6th April 1965.

(2) Sub-paragraph (1) above shall not apply in relation to a disposal of assets if on the assumption in that sub-paragraph a loss would accrue on that disposal to the person making the disposal and either a smaller loss or a gain would accrue if the said sub-paragraph (1) did not apply, but in a case where this sub-paragraph would otherwise substitute a gain for a loss it shall be assumed, in relation to the disposal, that the relevant assets were sold by the owner, and immediately re-acquired by him, for a consideration such that, on the disposal, neither a gain nor a loss accrued to the person making the disposal.

The displacement of sub-paragraph (1) above by this sub-paragraph shall not be taken as bringing paragraph 11 above into operation.

(3) An election under this paragraph shall be made by notice in writing to the inspector given within two years from the end of the year of assessment or accounting period of a company in which the disposal is made or such further time as the Board may by notice in writing allow.

(4) For the avoidance of doubt it is hereby declared that an election under this paragraph is irrevocable.

(5) An election may not be made under this paragraph as respects, or in relation to, an asset the market value of which at a date on or after 6th April 1965, and before the date of the disposal to which the election relates, is to be ascertained in pursuance of section 35 of this Act (part disposals).

Unquoted shares, commodities, etc.

13.—(1) This paragraph has effect as respects shares held by any person on 6th April 1965 other than shares which are to be treated under this Act as if disposed of and immediately re-acquired by him on that date.

(2) Section 65 of this Act (pooling of shares and other assets) shall not apply in relation to the shares while that person continues to hold them and, in particular, shall not apply in relation to a disposal of the shares by him.

(3) For the purpose of—

(*a*) identifying the shares so held on 6th April 1965 with shares previously acquired, and
(*b*) identifying the shares so held on that date with shares subsequently disposed of, and distinguishing them from shares acquired subsequently,

so far as the shares are of the same class shares bought at a [later time][1] shall be deemed to have been disposed of before shares bought at an [earlier time][1].

(4) Sub-paragraph (3) above has effect subject to section 66 of this Act (disposal on or before day of acquisition).

(5) Shares shall not be treated for the purposes of this paragraph as being of the same class unless if dealt with on a recognised stock exchange in the United Kingdom or elsewhere they would be so treated, but shall be treated in accordance with this paragraph notwithstanding that they are identified in a different way by a disposal or by the transfer or delivery giving effect to it.

(6) This paragraph, without sub-paragraph (5), shall apply in relation to any assets, other than shares, which are of a nature to be dealt with without identifying the particular assets disposed of or acquired.

Amendments.—[1] Words in sub-para. (3) substituted by FA 1982, Sch. 13, para. 11.

Reorganisation of share capital, conversion of securities, etc.

14.—(1) For the purposes of this Act, including Chapter II of Part II, it shall be assumed that any shares or securities held by a person on 6th April 1965 (identified in accordance with paragraph 13 above) which, in accordance with Chapter II of Part IV of this Act, are to be regarded as being or forming part of a new holding were sold and immediately re-acquired by him on 6th April 1965 at their market value on that date.

(2) If at any time after 5th April 1965, a person comes to have, in accordance with the said Chapter II of Part IV, a new holding sub-paragraphs (3) to (5) of paragraph 11 above shall have effect as if—

(*a*) the new holding had at that time been sold by the owner, and immediately re-acquired by him, at its market value at that time, and
(*b*) accordingly, the amount of any gain on a disposal of the new holding or any part of it shall be computed—
  (i) by apportioning in accordance with paragraph 11 above the gain or loss over a period ending at the said time, and
  (ii) by bringing into account the entire gain or loss over the period from that time to the date of the disposal.

(3) This paragraph shall not apply in relation to a reorganisation of a company's share capital if the new holding differs only from the original shares in being a different number, whether greater or less, of shares of the same class as the original shares.

PART IV
MISCELLANEOUS

Capital allowances

15. If under any provision in this Schedule it is to be assumed that any asset was on 6th April 1965 sold by the owner, and immediately re-acquired by him, sections 34 and 39 of this Act (restriction of losses by reference to capital allowances, and wasting assets qualifying for capital allowances) shall apply in relation to any capital allowance or renewals allowance made in respect of the expenditure actually incurred by the owner in providing the asset, and so made for the year 1965–66 or for any subsequent year of assessment, as if it were made in respect of the expenditure which, on the said assumption, was incurred by him in re-acquiring the asset on 7th April 1965.

Assets transferred to close companies

16.—(1) This paragraph has effect where—

(*a*) at any time, including a time before 7th April 1965, any of the persons having control of a close company, or any person who is connected with a person having control of a close company, has transferred assets to the company, and
(*b*) paragraph 11 above applies in relation to a disposal by one of the persons having control of the company of shares or securities in the company, or in relation to a disposal by a person having, up to the time of disposal, a substantial holding of shares or securities in the company, being in either case a disposal after the transfer of the assets.

(2) So far as the gain accruing to the said person on the disposal of the shares is attributable to a profit on the assets so transferred, the period over which the gain is to be treated under paragraph 11 above as growing at a uniform rate shall begin with the time when the assets were transferred to the company, and accordingly a part of a gain attributable to a profit on assets transferred on or after 6th April 1965 shall all be a chargeable gain.

(3) This paragraph shall not apply where a loss, and not a gain, accrues on the disposal.

Husbands and wives

17. Where section 44 of this Act is applied in relation to a disposal of an asset by a man to his wife, or by a man's wife to him, then in relation to a subsequent disposal of the asset (not within section 44) the one making the disposal shall be treated for the purposes of this Schedule as if the other's acquisition or provision of the asset had been his or her acquisition or provision of it.

Compensation and insurance money

18. Where section 21 (4) (*a*) of this Act applies to exclude a gain which, in consequence of this Schedule, is not all chargeable gain, the amount of the reduction to be made under section 21 (4) (*b*) (corresponding reduction in allowable expenditure in respect of new asset) shall be the amount of the chargeable gain and not the whole amount of the gain; and in section 21 (5) (*b*) of this Act (corresponding reduction in allowable expenditure in respect of the new asset where part only of the consideration in respect of the old asset has been applied as such expenditure) for the reference to the amount by which the gain is reduced under section 21 (5) (*a*) there shall be substituted a reference to the amount by which the chargeable gain is proportionately reduced under the said section 21 (5) (*a*).

SCHEDULE 6

Section 157 (1)

TRANSITORY

PART I

VALUATION

Preliminary

1. This Part of this Schedule has effect in cases where the market value of an asset or any part of it at a time before the commencement of this Act is material to the computation of a gain under this Act, and in those cases—

(*a*) section 150 of this Act (which is the same as paragraph 2 below with the amendments in paragraph 4) shall not apply,
(*b*) section 152 of this Act shall only apply to the extent specified in paragraphs 5 to 8 below,

(but sections 151 and 153 of this Act shall apply in those cases as in later cases).

Original rules

2.—(1) "Market value" in relation to any assets means the price which those assets might reasonably be expected to fetch on a sale in the open market.

(2) In estimating the market value of any assets no reduction shall be made in the estimate on account of the estimate being made on the assumption that the whole of the assets is to be placed on the market at one and the same time:

Provided that where capital gains tax is chargeable, or an allowable loss accrues, in consequence of a death before 31st March 1971 and the market value of any property on the date of death taken into account for the purposes of that tax or loss has been depreciated by reason of the death the estimate of the market value shall take that depreciation into account.

(3) The market value of shares or securities quoted on the London Stock Exchange shall, except where in consequence of special circumstances prices so quoted are by themselves not a proper measure of market value, be as follows—

(*a*) the lower of the two prices shown in the quotations for the shares or securities in the Stock Exchange Official Daily List on the relevant date plus one-quarter of the difference between those two figures, or
(*b*) halfway between the highest and lowest prices at which bargains, other than bargains done at special prices, were recorded in the shares or securities for the relevant date,

choosing the amount under paragraph (*a*) if less than that under paragraph (*b*), or if no such bargains were recorded for the relevant date, and choosing the amount under paragraph (*b*) if less than that under paragraph (*a*):

Provided that—

(i) this sub-paragraph shall not apply to shares or securities for which some other stock exchange in the United Kingdom affords a more active market, and
(ii) if the London Stock Exchange is closed on the relevant date the market value shall be ascertained by reference to the latest previous date or earliest subsequent date on which it is open, whichever affords the lower market value.

(4) "Market value" in relation to any rights of unit holders in any unit trust scheme the buying and selling prices of which are published regularly by the managers of the scheme shall mean an amount equal to the buying price (that is the lower price) so published on the relevant date, or if none were published on that date, on the latest date before.

(5) In relation to an asset of a kind the sale of which is subject to restrictions imposed under the Exchange Control Act 1947 such that part of what is paid by the purchaser is not retainable by the seller the market value, as arrived at under sub-paragraph (1), (3) or (4)

above, shall be subject to such adjustment as is appropriate having regard to the difference between the amount payable by a purchaser and the amount receivable by a seller.

(6) This paragraph has effect subject to the following provisions of this Part of this Schedule.

Value of quoted securities on 6th April 1965

3.—(1) For the purpose of ascertaining the market value of any shares or securities in accordance with paragraph 1 (2) of Schedule 5 to this Act, paragraph 2 above shall have effect subject to the provisions of this paragraph.

(2) Sub-paragraph (3) (*a*) of that paragraph shall have effect as if for the words, "one-quarter" there were substituted the words "one-half", and as between the amount under paragraph (*a*) and the amount under paragraph (*b*) of that sub-paragraph the higher, and not the lower, amount shall be chosen.

(3) Sub-paragraph (4) of that paragraph shall have effect as if for the reference to an amount equal to the buying price there were substituted a reference to an amount halfway between the buying and selling prices.

(4) Where the market value of any shares or securities not within the said sub-paragraph (3) falls to be ascertained by reference to a pair of prices quoted on a stock exchange, an adjustment shall be made so as to increase the market value by an amount corresponding to that by which any market value is increased under sub-paragraph (2) above.

References to Stock Exchange on or after 25th March 1973

4. Except in relation to anything done before 25th March 1973, paragraph 2 (3) above shall have effect subject to the following amendments—

(*a*) for the words "quoted on the London Stock Exchange" there shall be substituted the words "listed in The Stock Exchange Daily Official List" and for the words "so quoted" the words "quoted in that List";
(*b*) for the words "the Stock Exchange Official Daily List" there shall be substituted the words "The Stock Exchange Daily Official List";
(*c*) for the words "some other stock exchange in the United Kingdom affords a more active market" there shall be substituted the words "The Stock Exchange provides a more active market elsewhere than on the London trading floor"; and
(*d*) for the words "if the London Stock Exchange is closed" there shall be substituted the words "if the London trading floor is closed".

Unquoted shares and securities: application of section 152 to acquisitions before commencement of this Act

5. Paragraphs 6 to 8 below shall have effect with respect to the application of section 152 of this Act, and in those paragraphs "asset" means an asset to which that section applies.

6. Subject to paragraphs 7 and 8 below, if the market value of an asset or any part of it at the time of its acquisition is material to the computation of any chargeable gain under this Act then, notwithstanding that the acquisition may have occurred before 6th July 1973 (the date on which the provision re-enacted in section 152 of this Act first came into operation as respects disposals) or that the market value of the asset at the time of its acquisition may have been fixed for the purposes of a contemporaneous disposal, section 152 of this Act shall apply for the purposes of the determination of the market value of the asset or, as the case may be, that part of it at the time of its acquisition.

Unquoted shares or securities: acquisition on death

7.—(1) This paragraph applies if, in a case where the market value of an asset at the time of its acquisition is material as mentioned in paragraph 6 above,—

(*a*) the acquisition took place on the occasion of a death occurring after 30th March 1971 and before 6th July 1973, and
(*b*) by virtue of paragraph 9 below, the principal value of the asset for the purposes of estate duty on that death would, apart from this paragraph, be taken to be the market value of the asset at the date of the death for the purposes of this Act.

(2) If the principal value referred to in sub-paragraph (1) (*b*) above falls to be determined as

mentioned in section 55 of the Finance Act 1940 or section 15 of the Finance (No. 2) Act (Northern Ireland) 1946 (certain controlling shareholdings to be valued on an assets basis), nothing in section 152 of this Act shall affect the operation of paragraph 9 below for the purpose of determining the market value of the asset at the date of the death.

(3) If sub-paragraph (2) above does not apply, paragraph 9 below shall not apply as mentioned in sub-paragraph (1)(b) above and the market value of the asset on its acquisition at the date of the death shall be determined in accordance with paragraphs 2, 4 and 6 above.

Unquoted shares or securities: prior part disposal

8.—(1) In any case where—

(a) before 6th July 1973 there has been a part disposal of an asset to which section 152 of this Act applies (in this paragraph referred to as "the earlier disposal"), and

(b) by virtue of any enactment, the acquisition of the asset or any part of it was deemed to be for a consideration equal to its market value, and

(c) on or after 6th July 1973 there is a disposal (including a part disposal) of the property which remained undisposed of immediately before that date (in this paragraph referred to as "the later disposal").

sub-paragraph (2) below shall apply in computing any chargeable gain accruing on the later disposal.

(2) Where this sub-paragraph applies, the apportionment made by virtue of paragraph 7 of Schedule 6 to the Finance Act 1965 (corresponding to section 35 of this Act) on the occasion of the earlier disposal shall be recalculated on the basis that section 152 (3) of this Act was in force at the time, and applied for the purposes of, the determination of—

(a) the market value referred to in sub-paragraph (1)(b) above, and

(b) the market value of the property which remained undisposed of after the earlier disposal, and

(c) if the consideration for the earlier disposal was, by virtue of any enactment, deemed to be equal to the market value of the property disposed of, that market value.

Value determined for estate duty

9.—(1) Where estate duty (including estate duty leviable under the law of Northern Ireland) is chargeable in respect of any property passing on a death after 30th March 1971 and the principal value of an asset forming part of that property has been ascertained (whether in any proceedings or otherwise) for the purposes of that duty, the principal value so ascertained shall, subject to paragraph 7 (3) above, be taken for the purposes of this Act to be the market value of that asset at the date of the death.

(2) Where the principal value has been reduced under section 35 of the Finance Act 1968 or section 1 of the Finance Act (Northern Ireland) 1968 (tapering relief for gifts inter vivos etc.), the reference in sub-paragraph (1) above to the principal value as ascertained for the purposes of estate duty is a reference to that value as so ascertained before the reduction.

PART II

Assets Acquired Before Commencement

Events before commencement

10.—(1) The substitution of this Act for the corresponding enactments repealed by this Act shall not alter the effect of any provision enacted before this Act (whether or not there is a corresponding provision in this Act) so far as it determines whether and to what extent events in, or expenditure incurred in, or other amounts referable to, a period earlier than the chargeable periods to which this Act applies may be taken into account for any tax purposes in a chargeable period to which this Act applies.

(2) Without prejudice to sub-paragraph (1) above, the repeals made by this Act shall not affect—

(a) the enactments specified in Part V of Schedule 14 to the Finance Act 1971 (charge on death) so far as their operation before repeal falls to be taken into account in chargeable periods to which this Act applies,

(b) the application of the enactment repealed by this Act to events before 6th April 1965 in accordance with paragraph 31 of Schedule 6 to the Finance Act 1965.

(3) This paragraph has no application to the law relating to the determination of the market value of assets (which is stated for all relevant times and occasions in Part I of this Schedule, with Part VIII of this Act).

PART III
Other Transitory Provisions

Value-shifting

11. Section 26 of this Act applies only where the reduction in value mentioned in subsection (1) of that section (or, in a case within subsection (8) of that section, the reduction or increase in value) is after 29th March 1977.

Assets acquired on disposal chargeable under Case VII of Schedule D

12.—(1) In this paragraph references to a disposal chargeable under Case VII are references to cases where the acquisition and disposal was in circumstances that the gain accruing on it was chargeable under Case VII of Schedule D, or where it would have been so chargeable if there were a gain so accruing.

(2) The amount or value of the consideration for the acquisition of an asset by the person acquiring it on a disposal chargeable under Case VII shall not under any provision of this Act be deemed to be an amount greater than the amount taken into account as consideration on that disposal for the purposes of Case VII.

(3) Any apportionment of consideration or expenditure falling to be made in relation to a disposal chargeable under Case VII in accordance with section 164 (4) of the Taxes Act [1970][1], and in particular in a case where section 164 (6) of that Act (enhancement of value of land by acquisition of adjoining land) applied, shall be followed for the purposes of this Act both in relation to a disposal of the assets acquired on the disposal chargeable under Case VII and, where the disposal chargeable under Case VII was a part disposal, in relation to a disposal of what remains undisposed of.

(4) Sub-paragraph (3) above has effect notwithstanding section 43 (4) of this Act (general provisions for apportionment).

Amendments.—[1] "1970" in sub-para. (3) inserted by virtue of TA 1988, Sch. 29, para. 15 (b).

Unrelieved Case VII losses

13. Where no relief from income tax (for a year earlier than 1971–72) has been given in respect of a loss or part of a loss allowable under Case VII of Schedule D the loss or part shall, notwithstanding that the loss accrued before that year, be an allowable loss for the purposes of capital gains tax, but subject to any restrictions imposed by section 62 of this Act (transactions between connected persons).

Dispositions before 27th March 1974 which attract capital transfer tax

14. Paragraphs 15 and 16 below have effect in respect of dispositions before 27th March 1974 where the disponer dies before 27th March 1981.

Gifts subject to capital transfer tax on death

15.—(1) Where the value of any asset comprised in a gift inter vivos is by virtue of section 22 (5) of the Finance Act 1975 included in the value of the estate of any person for the purposes of capital transfer tax, and at the time of that person's death the asset—

(a) is owned by the donee, or
(b) is property settled by the gift or property which for the purposes of section 38 of the Finance Act 1957 would by virtue of subsection (9) thereof be treated as property settled by the gift,

then, subject to sub-paragraph (2) below, the asset shall for the purposes of this Act be deemed to be disposed of and immediately re-acquired at that time by the donee or trustee for a consideration equal to the value so included; but no chargeable gain shall accrue on the disposal.

(2) Where the value so included is reduced by virtue of section 35 of the Finance Act 1968, the appropriate portion only of the asset shall be deemed to be so disposed of and re-acquired; and for this purpose the appropriate portion is the reduced value so included divided by the value before the reduction.

Life interest terminated on death on which capital transfer tax is chargeable

16. Where a life interest within the meaning of section 55 of this Act in settled property is terminated by the death of a person on whose death capital transfer tax is chargeable under section 22 of the Finance Act 1975 and, under subsection (5) of that section, a value falls to be included in respect of the settled property, then—

(*a*) if that value is the principal value of the property, section 56 of this Act shall apply as if that person had been entitled to the life interest at his death, and

(*b*) if that value is a value reduced by any percentage under paragraph 3 of Part II of Schedule 17 to the Finance Act 1969, any chargeable gain or allowable loss accruing on the disposal deemed to be made under section 54 (1) or 55 (1) of this Act shall be reduced by the complementary percentage, that is to say the percentage found by subtracting the first-mentioned percentage from one hundred per cent.

Devaluation of sterling: securities acquired with borrowed foreign currency

17.—(1) This paragraph applies where, in pursuance of permission granted under the Exchange Control Act 1947, currency other than sterling was borrowed before 19th November 1967 for the purpose of investing in foreign securities (and had not been repaid before that date), and it was a condition of the permission—

(*a*) that repayment of the borrowed currency should be made from the proceeds of the sale in foreign currency of the foreign securities so acquired or out of investment currency, and

(*b*) that the foreign securities so acquired should be kept in separate accounts to distinguish them from others in the same ownership,

and securities held in such a separate account on 19th November 1967 are in this paragraph referred to as "designated securities".

(2) In computing the gain accruing to the borrower on the disposal of any designated securities or on the disposal of any currency or amount standing in a bank account on 19th November 1967 and representing the loan the sums allowable as a deduction under section 32 (1) (*a*) of this Act shall be increased by multiplying by seven sixths:

Provided that the total amount of the increases so made in computing all gains (and losses) which are referable to any one loan (made before 19th November 1967) shall not exceed one sixth of the sterling parity of that loan at the time it was made.

(3) Section 65 of this Act (rules for identification: pooling) shall apply separately in relation to any designated securities held in a particular account until such time as a disposal takes place on the occurrence of which the proviso to sub-paragraph (2) above operates to limit the increases which would otherwise be made under that sub-paragraph in allowable deductions.

(4) In this paragraph and paragraph 18 below "foreign securities" means securities expressed in a currency other than sterling, or shares having a nominal value expressed in a currency other than sterling, or the dividends on which are payable in a currency other than sterling.

Devaluation of sterling: foreign insurance funds

18.—(1) The sums allowable as a deduction under section 32 (1) (*a*) of this Act in computing any gains to which this paragraph applies shall be increased by multiplying by seven-sixths.

(2) This paragraph applies to gains accruing—

(a) to any underwriting member of Lloyd's or to any other approved association of underwriters, or

(b) to any company engaged in the business of marine protection and indemnity insurance on a mutual basis,

on the disposal by that person after 18th November 1967 of any foreign securities which on that date formed part of a trust fund—

(i) established by that person in any country or territory outside the United Kingdom, and
(ii) representing premiums received in the course of that person's business, and
(iii) wholly or mainly used for the purpose of meeting liabilities arising in that country or territory in respect of that business.

Gilt-edged securities past redemption date

19.—(1) So far as material for the purposes of this or any other Act, the definition of "gilt-edged securities" in Schedule 2 to this Act shall include any securities which were specified securities for the purposes of section 41 of the Finance Act 1969, and the redemption date of which fell before 1st January 1979.

*Reorganisation of share capital,
conversion of securities, etc.*

20.—(1) Chapter II of Part IV of this Act has effect subject to the provisions of this paragraph.

(2) The substitution of the said Chapter II for the enactments repealed by this Act shall not alter the law applicable to any reorganisation or reduction of share capital, conversion of securities or company amalgamation taking place before the commencement of this Act.

(3) Sub-paragraph (2) above applies in particular to the law determining whether or not any assets arising on an event mentioned in that sub-paragraph are to be treated as the same asset as the original holding of shares, securities or other assets.

(4) Notwithstanding the preceding provisions of this paragraph, section 84 of this Act (compensation stock) shall apply where the compulsory acquisition took place after 6th April 1976, but before the commencement of this Act, as well as where it took place after the commencement of this Act.

Land : allowance for betterment levy

21.—(1) Where betterment levy charged in the case of any land in respect of an act or event falling within Case B or Case C or, if it was the renewal, extension or variation of a tenancy, Case F—

(a) has been paid, and
(b) has not been allowed as a deduction in computing the profits or gains or losses of a trade for the purposes of Case I of Schedule D;

then, if the person by whom the levy was paid disposes of the land or any part of it and so claims, the following provisions of this paragraph shall have effect for the purposes of applying Chapter II of Part II of, and Schedule 5 to, this Act to the disposal.

(2) Paragraph 9 of Schedule 5 to this Act (sales of land reflecting development value) shall apply where the condition stated in sub-paragraph (1) (a) thereof is satisfied, notwithstanding that the condition stated in sub-paragraph (1) (b) thereof is not satisfied.

(3) Subject to the following provisions of this paragraph, there shall be ascertained the excess, if any, of—

(a) the net development value ascertained for the purposes of the levy, over
(b) the increment specified in sub-paragraph (6) below;

and the amount of the excess shall be treated as an amount allowable under section 32 (1) (b) of this Act.

(4) Where the act or event in respect of which the levy was charged was a part disposal of the land, the said section 32 shall apply as if the part disposal had not taken place and sub-paragraph (5) below shall apply in lieu of sub-paragraph (3) above.

(5) The amount or value of the consideration for the disposal shall be treated as increased

by the amount of any premium or like sum paid in respect of the part disposal, and there shall be ascertained the excess, if any, of—

(a) the aggregate specified in sub-paragraph (7) below, over
(b) the increment specified in sub-paragraph (6) below;

and the amount of the excess shall be treated as an amount allowable under section 32 (1) (b) of this Act.

(6) The increment referred to in sub-paragraphs (3) (b) and (5) (b) above is the excess, if any, of—

(a) the amount or value of the consideration brought into account under section 32 (1) (a) of this Act, over
(b) the base value ascertained for the purposes of the levy.

(7) The aggregate referred to in sub-paragraph (5) (a) above is the aggregate of—

(a) the net development value ascertained for the purposes of the levy, and
(b) the amount of any premium or like sum paid in respect of the part disposal, in so far as charged to tax under Schedule A (or, as the case may be, Case VIII of Schedule D), and
(c) the chargeable gain accruing on the part disposal.

(8) Where betterment levy in respect of more than one act or event has been charged and paid as mentioned in sub-paragraph (1) above sub-paragraphs (2) to (7) above shall apply without modifications in relation to the betterment levy in respect of the first of them; but in relation to the other or others sub-paragraph (3) or, as the case may be, (5) above shall have effect as if the amounts to be treated thereunder as allowable under section 32 (1) (b) of this Act were the net development value specified in sub-paragraph (3) (a) or, as the case may be, the aggregate referred to in sub-paragraph (5) (a) of this paragraph.

(9) Where the disposal is of part only of the land sub-paragraphs (2) to (8) above shall have effect subject to the appropriate apportionments.

(10) References in this paragraph to a premium include any sum payable as mentioned in subsection (3) or (4) of section 80 of the Taxes Act [1970][1] (sums payable in lieu of rent or as consideration for the surrender of lease or for variation or waiver of term) and, in relation to Scotland, a grassum.

Amendments.—[1] "1970" in sub-para. (10) inserted by virtue of TA 1988, Sch. 29, para. 15 (b).

Replacement of business assets

22.—(1) Sections 115 to 121 of this Act (which are substituted for section 33 of the Finance Act 1965 as amended by subsequent enactments) have effect subject to the provisions of this paragraph.

(2) The substitution of those sections for the enactments repealed by this Act shall not alter the effect of those repealed enactments so far as they apply where the acquisition of, or of the interest in, the new assets (but not the disposal of, or of the interest in, the old assets) was before the commencement of this Act.

(3) Where the said section 33 of the Finance Act 1965 applied on the acquisition, before 23rd July 1970, of, or of an interest in, any new assets and the adjustment required to be made under subsection (1) (a) or subsection (2) (a) of that section was, by virtue of paragraph 9 (5) of Schedule 14 to the Finance Act 1967 (allowance for development value), required to be computed as mentioned therein, any adjustment required to be made under section 115 (1) (b), or 116 (1) (b), of this Act shall also be so computed, notwithstanding the repeals made by the Finance Act 1971 (restoring development value).

Transfer of business to a company

23. Section 123 of this Act shall have effect as if after subsection (4) there were inserted as subsection (4A)—

"(4A) If any development gains within the meaning of Part III of the Finance Act 1974 accrue to the transferor in respect of his disposal of the assets included in the business, then for the purposes of subsection (4) above B (that is, the value of the whole of the consideration received by the transferor in exchange for the business) shall be taken to be what it would be if the value of the consideration other than shares so received by him were less by an amount equal to those gains".

Works of art etc.

24. The repeals made by this Act do not affect the continued operation of sections 31 and 32 of the Finance Act 1965, in the form in which they were before 13th March 1975, in relation to estate duty in respect of deaths occurring before that date.

Disposal before acquisition

25. The substitution of this Act for the corresponding enactments repealed by this Act shall not alter the effect of any provision enacted before this Act (whether or not there is a corresponding provision in this Act) so far as it relates to an asset which—

(a) was disposed of before being acquired, and
(b) was disposed of before the commencement of this Act.

Estate duty

26. Nothing in the repeals made by this Act shall affect any enactment as it applies to the determination of any principal value for the purposes of estate duty.

Income and corporation tax: premiums on leases

27. The repeal by this Act of section 116 (3) of the Finance Act 1972 shall not affect its application by paragraph 3 of Schedule 13 to that Act.

Validity of subordinate legislation

28. So far as this re-enacts any provision contained in a statutory instrument made in exercise of powers conferred by any Act, it shall be without prejudice to the validity of that provision, and any question as to its validity shall be determined as if the re-enacted provision were contained in a statutory instrument made under those powers.

Savings for Part II of this Schedule

29. The provisions of this Part of this Schedule are without prejudice to the generality of Part II of this Schedule.

FINANCE (NO. 2) ACT 1979
(1979 Chapter 47)

ARRANGEMENT OF SECTIONS

Note.—Provisions of this Act relevant to the taxes covered by this Handbook and not reproduced are either spent or repealed by TA 1988, Sch. 31 and other legislation.

PART II
INCOME TAX, CORPORATION TAX AND CAPITAL GAINS TAX
Section
14. Capital allowances: motor vehicles.
17. Compensation for delay in national savings payments.

PART IV
MISCELLANEOUS AND SUPPLEMENTARY
25. Short title, interpretation, construction and repeals.

An Act to grant certain duties, to alter other duties, and to amend the law relating to the National Debt and the Public Revenue, and to make further provision in connection with Finance.
[26th July 1979]

PART II

INCOME TAX, CORPORATION TAX AND CAPITAL GAINS TAX

14. Capital allowances: motor vehicles

(1)–(3) . . .

(4)–(5) . . .

(6) . . .

(7) Subject to subsection (8) below, this section applies in relation to expenditure incurred after 12th June 1979, and for the purposes of this subsection expenditure is incurred on the date when the sums in question become payable.

(8) This section does not affect the operation of the said section 43 in relation to any expenditure on the provision of a vehicle if the expenditure consists of the payment of sums payable under a contract entered into on or before the said 12th June and the vehicle is brought into use not later than 12th June 1980.

Note.—Sub-ss. (1)–(3) amend FA 1971, s. 43.
Sub-ss. (4), (5) amend FA 1971, Sch. 8, paras. 9–12.
Sub-s. (6) inserts FA 1971, Sch. 8, para. 12A.
s. 43 referred to in sub-s (8) is FA 1971, s. 43.

17. Compensation for delay in national savings payments

(1) There shall be disregarded for all purposes of . . .[1] capital gains tax any sums paid by the Department for National Savings as compensation for delay in making any such payments or repayments as are mentioned in subsection (2) below, being delay attributable to industrial action by staff of the Department between 22nd February 1979 and 4th May 1979.

(2) The payments and repayments referred to above are—

(*a*) payments of dividends or interest on stocks and securities registered on the National Savings Stock Register;
(*b*) repayments of national savings certificates;
(*c*) repayments of contributions, and payments of bonuses or interest, under certified contractual saving schemes as defined by section 415 (2) of the Taxes Act;
(*d*) payments of premium savings bond prizes and repayments of premium savings bonds;
(*e*) repayments of money deposited in the National Savings Bank.

(3) This section does not affect the tax treatment of interest to which a person is entitled under any express provision in that behalf contained in the terms of issue of any such stock, securities or certificates as are mentioned in paragraph (*a*) or (*b*) of subsection (2) above, in the conditions applying to a contract made under any such scheme as is mentioned in paragraph (*c*) of that subsection or in the National Savings Bank Act 1971.

Amendments.—[1] Words in sub-s. (1) repealed by TA 1988, Sch. 31.

PART IV
MISCELLANEOUS AND SUPPLEMENTARY

25. Short title, interpretation, construction and repeals

(1) This Act may be cited as the Finance (No. 2) Act 1979.

(2) In this Act "the Taxes Act" means the Income and Corporation Taxes Act 1970.

(3) Part II of this Act so far as it relates to income tax shall be construed as one with the Income Tax Acts and so far as it relates to corporation tax shall be construed as one with the Corporation Tax Acts.

(5) The enactments mentioned in Schedule 5 to this Act are hereby repealed to the extent specified in the third column of that Schedule, but subject to any provision at the end of any Part of that Schedule.

Note.—Sub-s. (4) is not relevant to this work.

FINANCE ACT 1980

(1980 Chapter 48)

ARRANGEMENT OF SECTIONS

Note.—Provisions of this Act relevant to the taxes covered by this Handbook and not reproduced are either spent or repealed by TA 1988, Sch. 31 and other legislation.

PART II
VALUE ADDED TAX

Section
17. *Mutual recovery and disclosure of information between member States* (see Orange Book)

PART III
INCOME TAX, CORPORATION TAX AND CAPITAL GAINS TAX

CHAPTER II
CAPITAL ALLOWANCES

Machinery and plant

Section
64. Exclusion of first-year allowances for certain leased assets.
65. Writing-down allowances etc. in case of leased assets.
66. Recovery of excess relief.
67. Information.
68. Joint lessees.
69. Writing-down allowances etc. for cars.
72. Commencement and transitional provisions.
73. Interpretation.

Industrial and commercial buildings

74. Enterprise zones.
75. Small workshops.
76. Tenancies.

CHAPTER III
CAPITAL GAINS

80. Exemption for private residences.
81. Exemption for authorised unit trusts etc.

PART V
STAMP DUTY

Sections 95–103 (see Orange Book)

451

PART VIII
MISCELLANEOUS AND SUPPLEMENTARY

Section
117. Demergers.
118. National Heritage Memorial Fund.
122. Short title, interpretation, construction and repeals.

SCHEDULES:
- Schedule 12—Transitional restriction of first-year allowances.
- Schedule 13—Industrial and commercial buildings.
- Schedule 18—Demergers.
  - Part I—Relief from advance corporation tax and income tax.
  - Part II—Relief from tax in respect of capital gains.
  - Part IV—*Relief from stamp duty*. (see also Orange Book)
  - Part V—Prevention of tax avoidance.
  - Part VI—Administration.
  - Part VII—Interpretation.

An Act to grant certain duties, to alter other duties, and to amend the law relating to the National Debt and the Public Revenue, and to make further provision in connection with Finance.
[1st August 1980]

PART III
INCOME TAX, CORPORATION TAX AND CAPITAL GAINS TAX
CHAPTER II
CAPITAL ALLOWANCES

Cross references.—See FA 1982, s. 70 (9) (*a*) (application of certain provisions of this Chapter to capital allowances for expenditure incurred for assets leased outside the United Kingdom);
FA 1986, s. 57 (4), (7) (the separate pooling provisions contained in ss. 64–68 below not to apply to "new expenditure" (i.e. expenditure incurred after 31 March 1986, subject to qualifications in s. 57 (2), (3)) on the provision of leased assets except cars qualifying for allowances under s. 69 of this Act and assets leased outside the United Kingdom and qualifying for allowances under FA 1982, s. 70).

Machinery and plant

64. Exclusion of first-year allowances for certain leased assets

(1) No first-year allowance shall be made in respect of expenditure on the provision of machinery or plant for leasing, whether in the course of a trade or otherwise, unless it appears that the machinery or plant will be used for a qualifying purpose in the requisite period and will not at any time in that period be used for any other purpose.[1,3]

(2) Machinery or plant is used for a qualifying purpose at any time when—

(*a*)[7] it is leased to a lessee who uses it for the purposes of a trade, otherwise than for leasing, and the circumstances are such that . . .[6] if he had bought the machinery or plant at that time and had incurred capital expenditure in doing so [that expenditure would have fallen to be included, in whole or in part, in his qualifying expenditure for any chargeable period for the purposes of subsections (2), (2A) and (3) of section 44 of the Finance Act 1971 (writing-down allowances)][8]; or

(*b*) the person who incurred the expenditure uses it for short-term leasing; or

(*c*) it is leased to a lessee who uses it for short-term leasing and either is resident in the United Kingdom or so uses it in the course of a trade carried on by him there; or

(*d*) the person who incurred the expenditure uses it for the purposes of a trade otherwise than for leasing.

(3) In subsection (2) (*b*) and (*c*) above "short-term leasing" means leasing the machinery or plant in such a manner—

(*a*) that—

(i) the number of consecutive days for which it is leased to the same person will normally be less than thirty; and
(ii) the total number of days for which it is leased to the same person in any period of twelve months will normally be less than ninety; or

(*b*) that—

(i) the number of consecutive days for which it is leased to the same person will not normally exceed three hundred and sixty-five; and
(ii) [subject to subsection (3A) below][1] the aggregate of the periods for which it is leased in the requisite period to lessees not falling within subsection (2) (*a*) above will not exceed two years.

[(3A) In a case where the requisite period exceeds four years the reference in subsection (3) (*b*) (ii) above to that period shall be construed as a reference to any period of four consecutive years which falls within the requisite period.][2]

(4) For the purposes of subsection (3) above persons who are connected with each other shall be treated as the same person and where any machinery or plant is leased as one of a number of items which form part of a pool of items of the same or a similar description and are not separately identifiable all the items in the pool may be treated as used for short-term

leasing within the meaning of that subsection if substantially the whole of the items in the pool are so used.

(5) Without prejudice to subsection (2) above [but subject to subsection (6A) below][3], a ship is also used for a qualifying purpose at any time when it is let on charter in the course of a trade which consists of or includes operating ships if—

(a) the person carrying on the trade is resident in the United Kingdom or carries on the trade there; and
(b) that person is responsible as principal (or appoints another person to be responsible in his stead) for navigating and managing the ship throughout the period of the charter and for defraying all expenses in connection with the ship throughout that period or substantially all such expenses other than those directly incidental to a particular voyage or to the employment of the ship during that period.

(6) Subsection (5) above shall with the necessary modifications apply also in relation to aircraft.

[(6A) Subsection (5) above does not apply if the main object, or one of the main objects, of the letting of the ship or aircraft on charter, or of a series of transactions of which the letting on charter was one, or of any of the transactions in such a series was to obtain a [writing-down allowance of an amount determined without regard to section 70 (2) of the Finance Act 1982][9] in respect of expenditure incurred on the provision of the ship or aircraft, whether by the person referred to in subsection (5) (a) above or some other person.][4]

(7) Without prejudice to subsection (2) above, a transport container is also used for a qualifying purpose at any time when it is leased in the course of a trade which is carried on by a person who is resident in the United Kingdom or who carries on the trade there if—

(a) the trade consists of or includes the operation of ships or aircraft and the container is at other times used by that person in connection with the operation of ships or aircraft; or
(b) the container is leased under a succession of leases to different persons who, or most of whom, are not connected with each other.

(8) [Subject to subsection (8A) below][10] the requisite period is the period of [ten][11] years beginning with the date on which the machinery or plant is first brought into use by the person who incurred the expenditure, except that where the machinery or plant ceases at any time before the end of those [ten][11] years to belong to that person the requisite period shall end at that time.

[(8A) If the circumstances are such that machinery or plant is used for a qualifying purpose, subsection (8) above shall have effect as if each reference therein to ten years were a reference to four years.][12]

(9) For the purposes of subsection (8) above machinery or plant shall be treated as continuing to belong to the person who incurred the expenditure so long as it belongs to—

(a) a person who is connected with him; or
(b) a person who acquired it from him as a result of one or more disposals on the occasion of which, or each of which, the trade carried on by the person making the disposal was treated as continuing by virtue of section [113 (2) or 114 (1) of the Taxes Act 1988];[17]

and for any part of the requisite period for which the machinery or plant belongs to a person falling within paragraph (a) or (b) above that person shall be treated for the purposes of subsections (2) (b) and (d) above as the person who incurred the expenditure.

(10) For the purposes of subsection (2) (a) above there shall be disregarded paragraph 2 (1) of Schedule 8 to the Finance Act 1971 and section 50 of the Capital Allowances Act 1968 as applied by paragraph 2 (2) of that Schedule (which precludes the making of a first year allowance where certain other allowances are available).[13]

(11) [Where expenditure is incurred][14] on the provision of machinery or plant [which][15] is fixed to a building or land of which the person who incurs the expenditure is the lessor and the circumstances are such that a transfer of his interest in the building or land would operate to transfer his interest in the machinery or [plant, so][16] much of the proviso to section 48 (4) of the said Act of 1971 as relates to section 74 (3) of the said Act of 1968 (restriction of relief for leased asset not used for trade) shall not apply to any allowance in respect of such expenditure.

(12) Nothing in this section affects expenditure on the provision of vehicles if they are provided wholly or mainly for the use of persons in receipt of—

(*a*) mobility allowance under the Social Security Act 1975 or the Social Security (Northern Ireland) Act 1975.
[(*b*) a mobility supplement under a scheme made under the Personal Injuries (Emergency Provisions) Act 1939; or
(*c*) a mobility supplement under an Order in Council made under section 12 of the Social Security (Miscellaneous Provisions) Act 1977; or
(*d*) any payment appearing to the Treasury to be of a similar kind and specified by them by order made by statutory instrument.

An order made under paragraph (*d*) above may provide that it has effect in relation to expenditure incurred on or after 21st November 1983 (expenditure being taken to be incurred for this purpose on the date when the sums in question become payable.]⁵

Note.—This section and ss. 65–68 below have a limited application generally after 31 March 1986 by virtue of FA 1986, s. 57 and all cross references to and amendments by FA 1986, s. 57 and Sch. 16 are to be read accordingly.
Cross references.—See FA 1982, s. 70 (capital allowances for expenditure incurred for assets leased outside the United Kingdom),
s. 71 (3) (this section as amended by FA 1982, s. 71 to apply in relation to expenditure incurred after 9 March 1982, with certain exceptions);
FA 1985, s. 57 (10) and Sch. 15, para. 8 (election to treat as short-life assets certain machinery or plant and vehicles provided for leasing);
FA 1986, s. 57 (3) (new code of allowances in respect of "new expenditure" (i.e. expenditure incurred after 31 March 1986, subject to qualifications in s. 57 (2), (3)) on the provision of machinery or plant for leasing not to apply to expediture incurred after that date by an associate or successor in acquiring the machinery or plant for which expenditure was incurred on or before that date),
s. 57 (4), (7) (the separate pooling provisions contained in ss. 64–68 of this Chapter not to apply to "new expenditure" (i.e. expenditure incurred after 31 March 1986, subject to qualifications in s. 57 (2), (3)) on the provision of leased assets except cars qualifying for allowances under s. 69 of this Act and assets leased outside the United Kingdom and qualifying for allowances under FA 1982, s. 70).
Amendments.—¹ Words in sub-s. (3) (*b*) (ii) inserted by FA 1982, s. 70 (7), (10).
² Sub-s. (3A) added by FA 1982, s. 70 (7), (10).
³ Words in sub-s. (5) inserted by FA 1982, s. 71 (1), (3).
⁴ Sub-s. (6A) inserted by FA 1982, s. 71 (2), (3).
⁵ Sub-s. (12) (*b*)–(*d*) and the words following para. (*d*) inserted by FA 1984, s. 61 in relation to expenditure incurred after 20 November 1983 and expenditure is incurred on the date when the sums in question become payable.
⁶ Words "a first-year allowance could have been made to the lessee" in sub-s. (2) (*a*) repealed by FA 1986, s. 57 (4) and Sch. 16, para. 1 in relation to "new expenditure" (i.e. expenditure incurred after 31 March 1986, subject to qualifications in s. 57 (2), (3)) on the provision of machinery or plant for leasing.
⁷ Sub-s. (2) (*a*) as it applies to expenditure which is not "new expenditure" as defined in FA 1986, s. 57 (2), (3), reads—

"(*a*) it is leased to a lessee who uses it for the purposes of a trade, otherwise than for leasing, and the circumstances are such that a first-year allowance could have been made to the lessee [(disregarding for this purpose paragraph 2 of Schedule 12 to the Finance Act 1984)] if he had bought the machinery or plant at that time and had incurred capital expenditure in doing so; or"

The words "(disregarding for this purpose paragraph 2 of Schedule 12 to the Finance Act 1984)" inserted by FA 1986, s. 57 (9) for expenditure which is not "new expenditure", but the notional purchase by the lessee referred to in the said sub-s. (2) (*a*) would at any time mean the incurring of new expenditure.
⁸ Words in sub-s. (2) (*a*) inserted by FA 1986, s. 57 (4) and Sch. 16, para. 1 in relation to "new expenditure" (i.e. expenditure incurred after 31 March 1986, subject to qualifications in s. 57 (2), (3)) on the provision of machinery or plant for leasing.
⁹ Words in sub-s. (6A) substituted for the words "first-year allowance" by *ibid*.
¹⁰ Words in sub-s. (8) inserted by *ibid*.
¹¹ In sub-s. (8) "ten" substituted for "four" by *ibid*.
¹² Sub-s. (8A) inserted by *ibid*.
¹³ Sub-ss (1), (10) repealed by *ibid*.
¹⁴ Words in sub-s. (11) substituted for the words "This section does not preclude the making of a first-year allowance in respect of expenditure" by *ibid*.
¹⁵ Word in sub-s. (11) substituted for the words "if it" by *ibid*.
¹⁶ Words in sub-s. (11) substituted for the words "plant; and so" by *ibid*.
¹⁷ Words in sub-s. (9) (*b*) substituted by TA 1988, Sch. 29, para. 32 Table.

---

65. Writing-down allowances etc. in case of leased assets

(1) [Where section 70 of the Finance Act 1982 applies to expenditure on the provision of machinery or plant for leasing]⁷ in the course of a trade, the following provisions shall have effect with respect to the allowances and charges to be made in the case of the trade ("the actual trade") under section 44 of the Finance Act 1971 (writing-down allowances and balancing adjustments).

(2) It shall be assumed for the purposes of the said section 44—

(*a*) that, . . .¹, the person carrying on the trade [incurred the expenditure on the provision of the machinery or plant wholly and exclusively]² for the purposes of a trade carried on by him separately from the actual trade and any other trade carried on by him;
(*b*) . . .¹; and
(*c*) that [without prejudice to sub-paragraphs (i) to (iii) of paragraph (*c*) of subsection (5)

of that section]³ the separate trade is permanently discontinued when the machinery or plant [begins to be used wholly or partly for purposes other than those of the actual trade]²

and the allowance or charge under that section which, on those assumptions and having regard to subsections (3) and (4) below, would fall to be made for any chargeable period in the case of the separate trade shall be made for that period in the case of the actual trade.

(3) If an allowance under the said section 44 falling by virtue of this section to be made for any chargeable period in the case of the actual trade is not claimed [or is disclaimed under subsection (2A) of that section]⁵, or is reduced in amount in accordance with a requirement under the proviso to subsection (2) of that section [or under subsection (2A) of that section]⁵, then, in determining the allowance or charge under that section which would fall to be made for any subsequent chargeable period in the case of the separate trade, any allowance falling to be made in the case of that trade for the first-mentioned chargeable period shall be treated as not [claimed or as disclaimed or, as the case may require, as proportionately reduced]⁴.

(4) Where in the case of any person the said section 44 applies in accordance with this section to different items of machinery or plant it shall apply as if the separate trade for which each item is treated as used were the same trade, and accordingly that trade shall not by virtue of subsection (2) (c) above be treated as permanently discontinued until all those items [begin to be used wholly or partly for purposes other than those of the actual trade]⁶.

(5) Where the said section 44 has effect in accordance with this section in respect of expenditure incurred by a person providing machinery or plant for the purposes of a trade, then, if the machinery or plant is disposed of by him to a person who is connected with him and the disposal is not on an occasion on which the trade is treated as continuing by virtue of section [113 (2), 114 (1) or 343 (2) of the Taxes Act 1988]¹⁰ or paragraph 13 of Schedule 8 to the said Act of 1971—

(a) the disposal value to be brought into account under the said section 44 in the case of the separate trade shall be of an amount equal to the price which the machinery or plant would have fetched on a sale at the same time in the open market or, if less, the capital expenditure incurred or treated as incurred on the provision of the machinery or plant by the person disposing of it; and

(b) the person acquiring it shall be treated for the purposes of Chapter I of Part III of the said Act of 1971 as having incurred on its provision expenditure equal to that disposal value.

(6) . . .⁸ this section does not apply to machinery or plant in relation to which the said section 44 applies in accordance with paragraph 5, 6 or 10 of [Schedule 8 to the Finance Act 1971]⁹.

Note.—This section, s. 64 above and ss. 66–68 below have a limited application generally after 31 March 1986 by virtue of FA 1986, s. 57 and all cross references to and amendments by FA 1986, s. 57 and Sch. 16 are to be read accordingly.

Cross references.—See FA 1971, Sch. 8, para. 13 (3A) (sub-s. (5) of this section not to apply where an election is made under FA 1971, Sch. 8, para. 13 (effect of successions to trades between connected persons));
FA 1982, s. 70 (capital allowances for expenditure incurred for assets leased outside the United Kingdom);
FA 1986, s. 57 (4), (7) (the separate pooling provisions contained in ss. 64–68 of this Chapter not to apply to "new expenditure" (i.e. expenditure incurred after 31 March 1986, subject to qualifications in s. 57 (2), (3)) on the provision of leased assets except cars qualifying for allowances under s. 69 of this Act and assets leased outside the United Kingdom and qualifying for allowances under FA 1982, s. 70).

Amendments.—¹ Words in sub-s. (2) (a), (b) repealed by FA 1985, Sch. 14, para. 14 (1) (a) and Sch. 27, Pt. VI with respect to any chargeable period or its basis period ending after 31 March 1985.
² Words in sub-ss. (2) (a), (c) substituted by FA 1985, Sch. 14, para. 14 (1) (a), (c), (2) (c), (3) with respect to any chargeable period or its basis period ending after 31 March 1985.
³ Words in sub-ss. (2) (c) inserted by FA 1985, Sch. 14, para. 14 (1) (c) (2) (a), (b) with respect to any chargeable period or its basis period ending after 31 March 1985.
⁴ Words in sub-s. (3) substituted by FA 1985, Sch. 14, para. 14 (2) with respect to any chargeable period or its basis period ending after 31 March 1985.
⁵ Words in sub-s. (3) inserted by *ibid.*
⁶ Words in sub-s. (4) substituted by FA 1985, Sch. 14, para. 14 (3) with respect to any chargeable period or its basis period ending after 31 March 1985.
⁷ Words in sub-s. (1) substituted for the words "Where section 64 above precludes the making of a first-year allowance in respect of expenditure incurred by a person on the provision of machinery or plant for leasing" by FA 1986, s. 57 (4) and Sch. 16, para. 2 in relation to "new expenditure" (i.e. expenditure incurred after 31 March 1986, subject to qualifications in s. 57 (2), (3)) on the provision of machinery or plant for leasing).
⁸ Words "This section applies also where section 64 above would have precluded the making of a first-year allowance in respect of any expenditure if the making of such an allowance in respect of the expenditure were not already precluded by paragraph 3 of Schedule 8 to the said Act of 1971; but" in sub-s. (6) repealed by *ibid.*
⁹ Words in sub-s. (6) substituted for the words "that Schedule" by *ibid.*
¹⁰ Words in sub-s. (5) substituted by TA 1988, Sch. 29, para. 32 Table.

66. Recovery of excess relief

(1) Where a first-year allowance has been made in respect of expenditure incurred in providing machinery or plant and the machinery or plant is at any time in the requisite period used otherwise than for a qualifying purpose—

(a) an amount equal to the excess relief shall, in relation to the person to whom the machinery or plant then belongs, be treated as if it were a balancing charge to be made on him for the chargeable period in which, or in the basis period for which, the machinery or plant is first so used; and

(b) section 44 of the Finance Act 1971 (as it has effect in accordance with section 65 above) shall apply as if that amount were qualifying expenditure of that person for the next chargeable period and, for the purpose of bringing any disposal value into account, as if the machinery or plant had always been used for the purposes of the separate trade.

(2) The excess relief is the excess, if any, of—

(a) the first-year allowance made in respect of the expenditure and any writing-down allowance or allowances made in respect of it for the chargeable period related to the incurring of the expenditure and any subsequent chargeable period up to and including that mentioned in subsection *(1) (a)* above, over

(b) the maximum writing-down allowance or allowances that could have been made in respect of it for those chargeable periods if the first-year allowance had not and could not have been made.

(3) Where as a result of a requirement under section 41 *(3)* of the said Act of 1971 (reduction of first-year allowances) an aggregate amount of first-year allowances in respect of different items of machinery or plant is reduced there shall be treated for the purposes of subsection *(2)* above as having been made in respect of each item a reduction proportionate to the capital expenditure on the provision of that item.

(4) For the purposes of subsection *(2)* above the writing-down allowance or allowances that were made or would have been made in respect of any item of machinery or plant shall be determined as if that item were the only item of machinery or plant in relation to which the said section 44 had effect.

(5) Where the person to whom any machinery or plant belongs at a time when it is first used otherwise than for a qualifying purpose has acquired it as a result of a transaction which was, or a series of transactions each of which was, between connected persons and a first-year allowance in respect of expenditure on the provision of the machinery or plant has been made to any of those persons—

(a) subsection *(2)* above shall have effect as if it referred to that first-year allowance and to the expenditure in respect of which it was made;

(b) for the purposes of that subsection any consideration paid or received on a disposal of the machinery or plant between connected persons shall be disregarded; and

(c) if a balancing allowance or balancing charge is made in respect of the machinery or plant there shall be made such adjustments of the total relief falling to be taken into account under paragraph *(a)* of that subsection as are just and reasonable in the circumstances;

but this subsection does not apply where section [113*(2)*, 114 *(1)* or 343 *(2)* of the Taxes Act 1988]¹ or paragraph 13 *(a)* and *(b)* of Schedule 8 to the said Act of 1971 (succession to trades) applied on the occasion of the transaction or transactions in question.

(6) Where the person to whom any machinery or plant belongs at such a time as is mentioned in subsection *(5)* above acquired it as there mentioned and—

(a) a first-year allowance in respect of expenditure on the provision of the machinery or plant could have been made to any of the connected persons but was not claimed or was disclaimed; and

(b) a balancing allowance is made to any of those persons in respect of that expenditure,

this section shall with the necessary modifications apply as it applies where a first-year allowance has been made.

(7) If at any time in the requisite period a new ship is used otherwise than for a qualifying purpose, then, without prejudice to the other provisions of this section—

(a) no allowance shall be made in respect of it under sub-paragraph *(2) (c)* of paragraph 8 of Schedule 8 to the said Act of 1971 for the chargeable period in which it is first so used or for any subsequent chargeable period; and

(b) section 44 of that Act (as it has effect in accordance with section 65 above) shall apply as if the amount of any allowance in respect of the ship which has been postponed under that

paragraph and not made were qualifying expenditure for the next chargeable period after that in which the ship is first so used.

Note.—This section, ss. 64–65 above and ss. 67–68 below have a limited application generally after 31 March 1986 by virtue of FA 1986, s. 57 and its repeal by FA 1986, Sch. 16, para. 3 is to be considered accordingly.
Cross references.—See FA 1982, s. 70 (capital allowances for expenditure incurred for assets leased outside the United Kingdom),
Sch. 11, para. 3 (application of this section with modifications to FA 1982, s. 70 (1) (capital allowances for assets leased outside the United Kingdom));
FA 1985, s. 58 (3) (*b*) (application of sub-s. (7) of this section with modifications in relation to first-year allowances to ships which are not new).
Amendments.—This section repealed by FA 1986, s. 57 (4) and Sch. 16, para. 3 in relation to "new expenditure" (i.e. expenditure incurred after 31 March 1986, subject to qualifications in s. 57 (2), (3)) on the provision of machinery or plant for leasing.
[1] Words in sub-s. (5) substituted by TA 1988, Sch. 29, para. 32 Table.

67. Information

(1) A claim by a person other than a company for a first-year allowance in respect of expenditure to which section 64 above applies, and a return by a company of profits in the computation of which a deduction is made on account of such an allowance, shall be accompanied by a certificate—

(a) stating that the machinery or plant in question will be used for a qualifying purpose in the requisite period, will not be used for any other purpose in that period and has not been used for any other purpose in any part of that period which has already elapsed; and
(b) containing a description of the machinery or plant in question or, if the claim or deduction relates to more than one item of machinery or plant and those items are of different kinds, a description of the different kinds and the amount claimed or deducted in respect of each of them.

(2) Where a person other than a company has claimed a first-year allowance in respect of any expenditure, or a deduction on account of such an allowance has been made in computing profits in respect of which a return has been made by a company, and the machinery or plant in question is at any time in the requisite period used otherwise than for a qualifying purpose, the person to whom it then belongs shall give written notice of that fact to the inspector, specifying the use to which the machinery or plant has been put; and, subject to (3) below, any such notice shall—

(a) be given within three months after the end of the chargeable period or its basis period in which the machinery or plant is first used as aforesaid; and
(b) relate to all the items of machinery or plant (if more than one) in respect of which that person is required to give notice under this subsection in respect of that period.

(3) If at the end of the three months mentioned in paragraph (a) of subsection (2) above the person concerned does not know and cannot reasonably be expected to know that any item of machinery or plant in respect of which he is required to give a notice under that subsection has been used otherwise than for a qualifying purpose he shall in respect of that item give the notice within thirty days of his coming to know that it has been so used.

(4) Where a first-year allowance has been made in respect of any expenditure, the inspector may by notice in writing require—

(a) any person to whom the machinery or plant belongs or has belonged, or who is or has been in possession of it under a lease, during the requisite period; and
(b) the personal representatives of any such person,

to furnish him, within such period (not being less than thirty days) as may be specified in the notice, with such information as he may require and the person to whom the notice is addressed has or can reasonably obtain about the leasing of the machinery or plant or the use to which it is being or has been put.

Note.—This section, ss. 64–66 above and s. 68 below have a limited application generally after 31 March 1986 by virtue of FA 1986, s. 57 and its repeal by FA 1986, Sch. 16, para. 3 is to be considered accordingly.
Cross references.—See FA 1982, s. 70 (capital allowances for expenditure incurred for assets leased outside the United Kingdom),
Sch. 11, para. 5 (application of this section with modifications to FA 1982, s. 70 (3) (capital allowances for assets leased outside the United Kingdom)).
Amendments.—This section repealed by FA 1986, s. 57 (4) and Sch. 16, para. 3 in relation to "new expenditure" (i.e. expenditure incurred after 31 March 1986, subject to qualifications in s. 57 (2), (3)) on the provision of machinery or plant for leasing.

68. Joint lessees

(1) The foregoing provisions of this Chapter shall have effect in accordance with this section where machinery or plant is leased to two or more persons jointly [and—]¹

[(a) at least one of the joint lessees is a person falling within paragraphs (a) and (b) of subsection (1) of section 70 of the Finance Act 1982; and
(b) the leasing is not permitted leasing as defined in paragraph 7 of Schedule 16 to the Finance Act 1986.]¹

(2) [If]² at any time when the machinery or plant is leased as aforesaid . . .³ the lessees use the machinery or plant for the purposes of a trade or trades, otherwise than for leasing, [the expenditure on the provision of the machinery or plant shall be treated as not falling within subsection (1) of the said section 70]⁴ if and to the extent to which it appears that the profits or gains of the trade or trades arising throughout the requisite period (or the period of the lease, if shorter) will be chargeable to income tax or corporation tax.

(3) Where by virtue of subsection (2) above . . .⁵ part only of the expenditure on the provision of any machinery or plant [is treated as not falling within subsection (1) of section 70 of the Finance Act 1982]¹, then, whether or not the machinery or plant continues to be leased as aforesaid, section 44 of the Finance Act 1971 (writing-down allowances and balancing adjustments) [the said section 70 and section 65 above]⁶ shall have effect as if—

(a) that part were expenditure on the provision of a separate item of machinery or plant; and
(b) the remainder were expenditure [(falling within subsection (1) of the said section 70)]¹ on the provision of another item of machinery or plant [used otherwise than for a qualifying purpose]¹;

and there shall be made all such apportionments as are necessary in consequence of this subsection.

(4) Where by virtue of subsection (2) above a first-year allowance has been made in respect of the whole or part of the expenditure on the provision of any machinery or plant and at any time in the requisite period while it is leased as aforesaid no lessee uses it for the purpose of a trade or trades the profits or gains of which are chargeable to income tax or corporation tax, section 66 above shall have effect as if the machinery or plant or, as the case may be, the separate item referred to in subsection (3) (a) above had at that time been used otherwise than for a qualifying purpose.

(5) Where by virtue of subsection (2) above a first-year allowance has been made in respect of the whole or part of the expenditure on the provision of any machinery or plant and at the end of the requisite period the machinery or plant is leased as aforesaid but subsection (4) above has not had effect, then, if it appears that the extent to which the machinery or plant has been used for the purposes of such trade or trades as aforesaid is less than that by reference to which the amount of the first-year allowance was determined—

(a) section 66 above shall have effect as if a part of the expenditure corresponding to the reduction in the extent of such use were expenditure on the provision of a separate item of machinery or plant used otherwise than for a qualifying purpose on the last day of that period; and
(b) any disposal value subsequently brought into account in respect of the machinery or plant under section 44 of the said Act of 1971 shall, instead of being apportioned in accordance with subsection (3) above, be apportioned by reference to the extent of such use as determined at the end of that period.

(6) Where the claim or deduction referred to in subsection (1) of section 67 above relates to a first-year allowance which by virtue of subsection (2) above is in respect of part only of any expenditure, the certificate required by the said subsection (1) shall include a statement of the extent to which the profits or gains referred to in subsection (2) above will be chargeable to tax as there mentioned.

(7) In subsection (2) of section 67 above the reference to machinery or plant being used otherwise than for a qualifying purpose shall include a reference to machinery or plant being treated as so used by virtue of subsection (4) above.

(8) Where a first-year allowance has been made in respect of expenditure on the provision of machinery or plant otherwise than by virtue of subsection (2) above and the machinery or plant is subsequently leased in the requisite period to two or more persons jointly, subsections (4), (5) and (7) above shall apply as if the first-year allowance had been made by virtue of subsection (2) above and had been so made in respect of the whole of the expenditure.

Note.—This section and ss. 64–67 above have a limited application generally after 31 March 1986 by virtue of FA 1986, s. 57 and all cross references to and amendments by FA 1986, s. 57 and Sch. 16 are to be read accordingly.
Cross references.—See FA 1982, Sch. 11, para. 6 (application of this section with modifications to FA 1982, s. 70 (capital allowances for assets leased outside the United Kingdom));
FA 1985, s. 57 (10) and Sch. 15, para. 9 (election to treat as short-life assets cannot be made in respect of machinery or plant precluded from first-year allowance under this section);
FA 1986, s. 57 (4), (7) (the separate pooling provisions contained in ss. 64–68 of this Chapter not to apply to "new expenditure" (i.e. expenditure incurred after 31 March 1986, subject to qualifications in s. 57 (2), (3) on the provision of leased assets except cars qualifying for allowances under s. 69 of this Act and assets leased outside the United Kingdom and qualifying for allowances under FA 1982, s. 70),
Sch. 16, para. 9 (provisions supplementing this section),
Sch. 16, para. 10 (5) (certain information to be given to the inspector in writing by the lessor within certain time limit where machinery or plant is leased as mentioned in sub-s. (1) above).
Amendments.—[1] Sub-s. (1) (*a*), (*b*) and words in sub-s. (3) and (3) (*b*) inserted by FA 1986, s. 57 (1), (4) and Sch. 16, para. 4 in relation to "new expenditure" (i.e. expenditure incurred after 31 March 1986, subject to qualifications in s. 57 (2), (3)) on the provision of machinery or plant for leasing.
[2] Word in sub-s. (2) substituted for the words "Subsection (2) (*a*) of section 64 above shall not apply" by *ibid*.
[3] Words "but if" in sub-s. (2) repealed by *ibid*.
[4] Words in sub-s. (2) substituted for the words "it shall be regarded as used for a qualifying purpose" by *ibid*.
[5] Words "a first-year allowance may be made in respect of" in sub-s. (3) repealed by *ibid*.
[6] Words in sub-s. (3) substituted for the words "and sections 65 and 66 above" by *ibid*.

69. Writing-down allowances etc. for cars

The machinery or plant in relation to which section 44 of the Finance Act 1971 (writing-down allowances and balancing adjustments) has effect in accordance with section 65 above shall include [any mechanically propelled vehicle other than—

(*a*) a vehicle of a construction primarily suited for the conveyance of goods or burden of any description;

(*b*) a vehicle of a type not commonly used as a private vehicle and unsuitable to be so used;

(*c*) a vehicle to which paragraph 10 of Schedule 8 to the Finance Act 1971 applies (expensive motor cars); and

(*d*) subject to subsection (2) below, a vehicle provided wholly or mainly for hire to, or for the carriage of, members of the public in the ordinary course of a trade.][1]

[(2) Subsection (1) (*d*) above applies to a vehicle only if—

(*a*) the following conditions are satisfied—

(i) the number of consecutive days for which it is on hire to, or used for the carriage of, the same person will normally be less than 30; and

(ii) the total number of days for which it is on hire to, or used for the carriage of, the same person in any period of 12 months will normally be less than 90; or

(*b*) it is provided for hire to a person who will himself use it wholly or mainly for hire to, or the carriage of, members of the public in the ordinary course of a trade and in a manner complying with the conditions in paragraph (*a*) above.][1]

[(3) For the purposes of subsection (2) above, persons who are connected with each other shall be treated as the same person; and that subsection does not affect vehicles provided wholly or mainly as mentioned in section 64 (12) above.][1]

Cross references.—See FA 1986, s. 57 (7) (exclusion of the new code for expenditure on leased assets (that is, expenditure incurred after 31 March 1986, subject to qualifications in s. 57 (2), (3)) with respect to vehicles falling within this section).
Amendments.—[1] This section amended by FA 1986, s. 57 (8) and Sch. 16, para. 11 with respect to "new expenditure" (i.e. expenditure incurred after 31 March 1986, subject to qualifications in s. 57 (2), (3)) on leased assets and in consequence of the withdrawal of first-year allowances by FA 1984, s. 58 and Sch. 12. This section as originally enacted read—

"The machinery or plant in relation to which section 44 of the Finance Act 1971 (writing-down allowances and balancing adjustments) has effect in accordance with section 65 above shall include any vehicle in respect of which the making of a first-year allowance is precluded by section 43 of that Act other than a vehicle to which paragraph 10 of Schedule 8 to that Act applies."

72. Commencement and transitional provisions

(1) Subject to subsection (5) below, sections 64 to 69 above apply to expenditure incurred on or after 1st June 1980 except that those sections do not affect expenditure incurred by a person on the provision of machinery or plant if the expenditure consists of the payment of sums payable under a contract entered into by him before 27th March 1980 and the machinery or plant is brought into use not later than 27th March 1982.

(2) Those sections apply also to expenditure incurred by a person before 1st June 1980 if the expenditure—

(*a*) is on the provision of machinery or plant which does not belong to him before that date; and
(*b*) consists of the payment of sums payable under a contract entered into by him on or after 27th March 1980 with a connected person.

(3) Section 70 above applies to expenditure incurred on or after 27th March 1980 except that that section does not affect expenditure incurred by a person on the provision of machinery or plant if the expenditure consists of the payment of sums payable under a contract entered into by him before that date and the machinery or plant is brought into use not later than 27th March 1982.

(4) Part I of Schedule 12 to this Act shall have effect for restricting first-year allowances in respect of certain expenditure incurred on or after 24th October 1979 and before 1st June 1980 but that Part does not affect expenditure incurred by a person on the provision of machinery or plant if the expenditure consists of the payment of sums payable under a contract entered into by him before the said 24th October and the machinery or plant is brought into use not later than 24th October 1981.

(5) Part II of Schedule 12 to this Act shall have effect for excluding from section 64 above certain expenditure incurred before 1st June 1986 and for restricting first-year allowances in respect of that expenditure.

73. Interpretation

(1) The Tax Acts shall have effect as if the foregoing provisions of this Chapter and the provisions of Schedule 12 to this Act were contained in Chapter I of Part III of the Finance Act 1971 except that expenditure shall not be treated for the purposes of section 72 above as having been incurred after the date on which it was in fact incurred by reason only of so much of section 50(4) of that Act as relates to expenditure incurred before a trade begins.

(2) References in those provisions to a lease include references to a sub-lease and references to a lessor or lessee shall be construed accordingly.

(3) For the purposes of those provisions letting a ship on charter or any other asset on hire shall be regarded as leasing it if, apart from this subsection, it would not be so regarded.

(4) In those provisions "qualifying purpose" and "requisite period" have the meanings given in section 64 above.

(5) Without prejudice to section 47 of the said Act of 1971 (application to activities other than trades) references in those provisions to the use of machinery or plant for the purposes of a trade include references to its use for any purpose in connection with which a [writing-down][2] allowance can be given by virtue of that section.

(6) Section [839 of the Taxes Act 1988][1] (connected persons) applies for the purposes of those provisions.

Cross references.—See FA 1982, s. 70 (9) (application of this section with modifications to FA 1982, s. 70 and Sch. 11 (capital allowances for assets leased outside the United Kingdom)).
Amendments.—[1] Words in sub-s. (6) substituted by TA 1988, Sch. 29, para. 32 Table.
[2] Words in sub-s. (5) substituted by FA 1989, Sch. 13, para. 18.

Industrial and commercial buildings

74. Enterprise zones

(1) Chapter I of Part I of the Capital Allowances Act 1968 (industrial buildings allowances)—

(*a*) shall apply with the modifications specified in Schedule 13 to this Act in relation to capital expenditure on the construction of an industrial building or structure; and
(*b*) shall, as so modified, apply also in relation to capital expenditure on the construction of a qualifying hotel or of a commercial building or structure as if it were an industrial building or structure,

in any case where the expenditure is incurred, or is incurred under a contract entered into, at a time when the site of the industrial building or structure, the qualifying hotel or the commercial building or structure is in an enterprise zone, being a time not more than ten years after the site was first included in the zone.

(2) In this section "enterprise zone" means an area designated as such by an order made by the Secretary of State under powers in that behalf conferred by any Act passed in the same Session as this Act or, in Northern Ireland, by an order made by the Department of the Environment for Northern Ireland under powers in that behalf conferred by an Order in Council under the Northern Ireland Act 1974.

(3) In this section "qualifying hotel" has the same meaning as for the purposes of section 38 of the Finance Act 1978; and Chapter I of Part I of the said Act of 1968 shall not by virtue of that section apply to expenditure to which that Chapter applies by virtue of this section.

(4) In this section "commercial building or structure" means a building or structure, other than an industrial building or structure or a qualifying hotel, which is used for the purposes of a trade, profession or vocation or, whether or not for such a purpose, as an office or offices but does not include any building or structure in use as, or as part of, a dwelling-house.

(5) For the purposes of subsection (1) above expenditure shall not by reason only of section 1 (6) or 5 (1) of the said Act of 1968 be treated as having been incurred after the date on which it was in fact incurred.

(6) . . .[1] section 64 above shall not apply to expenditure incurred at any time on the provision of machinery or plant which is to be an integral part of a building or structure if this section would apply to expenditure incurred at that time on the construction of that building or structure.

(7) The Tax Acts shall have effect as if this section and Schedule 13 to this Act were contained in Chapter I of Part I of the said Act of 1968.

Cross references.—See FA 1981, ss. 74 (5), 75 (4), 76 (4) (for the purposes of this section, CAA 1968, Pt. I, Ch. I to apply as amended by FA 1981, ss. 74–76).
Amendments.—[1] Words in sub-s. (6) superseded by FA 1989, Sch. 13, para. 28 (1)–(4) and repealed by FA 1989, Sch. 13. para. 28 (5) (*d*), (6) and Sch. 17, Pt. VI in relation to any chargeable period or its basis period ending after 26 July 1989. The repealed words read—
"Section 14 of the Finance Act 1975 (expenditure on thermal insulation) shall not apply to expenditure to which this section applies; and".

75. Small workshops

(1) Chapter I of Part I of the Capital Allowances Act 1968 (industrial buildings allowances) shall apply with the modifications specified in paragraphs 1 to 3 of Schedule 13 to this Act in relation to capital expenditure on the construction of an industrial building to which this section applies if the expenditure is incurred after 26th March 1980 and before 27th March 1983.

(2) This section applies to an industrial building if the gross internal floor space of the whole building will not exceed 2,500 square feet.

(3) Where the industrial building is part of a larger building the reference in subsection (2) above to the gross internal floor space of the whole of the building shall be construed as a reference to the gross internal floor space of the whole of that part and this section shall not apply unless that part is permanently separated from the remainder of the building, is intended for occupation separately from the remainder of the building and is suitable for being so occupied.

(4) The reference in subsection (1) above to capital expenditure on the construction of a building includes a reference to capital expenditure on the construction of any ancillary works.

(5) For the purposes of subsection (1) above expenditure shall not by reason only of section 1 (6) or 5 (1) of the said Act of 1968 be treated as having been incurred after the date on which it was in fact incurred.

(6) . . .[1] section 64 above shall not apply to expenditure incurred at any time on the provision of machinery or plant which is to be an integral part of a building if this section would apply to expenditure incurred at that time on the construction of the building.

(7) The Tax Acts shall have effect as if this section were contained in Chapter I of Part I of the said Act of 1968.

Cross references.—See FA 1982, s. 73 (3) (application of sub-ss. (3)–(6) of this section to very small workshops, i.e. gross internal floor space not exceeding 1,250 square feet).

Amendments.—[1] Words in sub-s. (6) superseded by FA 1989, Sch. 13, para. 28 (1)–(4) and repealed by FA 1989, Sch. 13. para. 28 (5) (*d*), (6) and Sch. 17, Pt. VI in relation to any chargeable period or its basis period ending after 26 July 1989. The repealed words read—

"Section 14 of the Finance Act 1975 (expenditure on thermal insulation) shall not apply to expenditure to which this section applies; and".

76. Tenancies

(1) The proviso to section 1 (4) of the Capital Allowances Act 1968 (which defers the making of an initial allowance where the building or structure is first used by a tenant) shall cease to have effect.

(2) This section applies in relation to—

(*a*) expenditure incurred on or after 27th March 1980; and
(*b*) expenditure which was incurred before that date but by reason of the said proviso has not before that date become eligible for an initial allowance;

but expenditure to which this section applies by virtue of paragraph (*b*) above shall be treated for the purposes of the said section 1 (4) as if it had been incurred on that date.

CHAPTER III
CAPITAL GAINS

80. Exemption for private residences

(1) Where a gain to which section 101 of the Capital Gains Tax Act 1979 (disposals of private residences) applies accrues to any individual and the dwelling-house in question or any part of it is or has at any time in his period of ownership been wholly or partly let by him as residential accommodation the part of the gain, if any, which, apart from this section, would be a chargeable gain by reason of the letting, shall be such a gain only to the extent, if any, to which it exceeds whichever is the lesser of—

    (*a*) the part of the gain which is not a chargeable gain by virtue of the provisions of section 102 of that Act or that section as applied by section 104 of that Act; and
    (*b*) [£20,000][1].

(2) . . .

(3) This section has effect in relation to disposals after 5th April 1980.

Note.—Sub-s. (2) amends CGTA 1979, s. 102 (1), (2) (*a*).
Amendments.—[1] Amount in sub-s. (1) (*b*) substituted by FA 1984, s. 63 (3), (5) with respect to disposals after 5 April 1983.

81. Exemption for authorised unit trusts etc

(1) Gains accruing to an authorised unit trust, an investment trust or a court investment fund shall not be chargeable gains.

(2) . . .

(3) . . .

(4) . . .

(5) . . .

(6) . . .

(7) Subsections (1), (4) and (5) above have effect in relation to disposals after 31st March 1980, subsections (2) and (3) above have effect where the transfer referred to in section 267 (3) is after that date and subsection (6) above has effect in relation to disposals after 5th April 1980.

Notes.—Sub-s. (2) amends TA 1970, s. 267 (3).
Sub-s. (3) amends CGTA 1979, s. 98 (1), (2).
Sub-s. (4) amends TA 1970, s. 273 (2).
Sub-s. (5) amends TA 1970, s. 275 (2).
Sub-s. (6) repeals CGTA 1979, s. 94.

PART VIII
MISCELLANEOUS AND SUPPLEMENTARY

117. Demergers

Schedule 18 to this Act shall have effect for facilitating certain transactions whereby trading activities carried on by a single company or group are divided so as to be carried on by two or more companies not belonging to the same group or by two or more independent groups.

118. National Heritage Memorial Fund

(1) ...[2]

(2) ...[2]

[(3) The trustees of the National Heritage Memorial Fund shall be treated for the purposes of section 49 (2) of the Finance Act 1974 and section 99 above as a body of persons established for charitable purposes only.][1]

(4)–(5) ...

(6) This section shall be deemed to have come into force on 1 April 1980.

Note.—Sub-ss. (4)–(5) and words omitted from sub-s. (3) are not relevant to this work.
Amendments.—[1] Sub-s. (3) substituted by TA 1988, Sch. 29, para. 32 Table.
[2] Sub-ss. (1), (2) repealed by TA 1988, Sch. 31.

122. Short title, interpretation, construction and repeals

(1) This Act may be cited as the Finance Act 1980.

(2) In this Act "the Taxes Act" means the Income and Corporation Taxes Act [1970 and "the Taxes Act 1988" means the Income and Corporation Taxes Act 1988].[1]

(3) In this Act—

(*a*) Part III, so far as it relates to income tax, shall be construed as one with the Income Tax Acts, so far as it relates to corporation tax, shall be construed as one with the Corporation Tax Acts and, so far as it relates to capital gains tax, shall be construed as one with the Capital Gains Tax Act 1979; and

(*b*) ...

(4) The enactments mentioned in Schedule 20 to this Act (which include spent enactments) are hereby repealed to the extent specified in the third column of that Schedule, but subject to any provision at the end of any Part of that Schedule.

Note.—Sub-s. (3) (*b*) is not relevant to this work
Amendments.—[1] Words in sub-s. (2) substituted by TA 1988, Sch. 29, para. 32 Table.

SCHEDULES

SCHEDULE 12
Section 72

TRANSITIONAL RESTRICTION OF FIRST-YEAR ALLOWANCES

PART I
EXPENDITURE INCURRED AFTER 23RD OCTOBER 1979 AND BEFORE 1ST JUNE 1980

PART II
EXPENDITURE INCURRED AFTER 31ST MAY 1980 AND BEFORE 1ST JUNE 1986

7.—(1) Section 64 of this Act does not preclude the making of a first-year allowance in respect of expenditure on the provision of a television set if the expenditure is incurred and the set is delivered to the person incurring the expenditure before the end of the transitional period.

(2) In this Part of this Schedule "the transitional period" means—

(a) in relation to expenditure on the provision of a television set other than [a teletext receiver or][1] a viewdata receiver, the period of four years beginning with 1st June 1980;
(aa) . . .[4];
(b) in relation to expenditure on the provision of [a teletext receiver or][5] a viewdata receiver, the period of six years beginning with that date.

(3) In this Part of this Schedule "a viewdata receiver" means a television set [which is not a teletext receiver but which is][1] constructed for displaying information received by means of a telephone land-line connection in response to a request for specified information communicated by those means to a computer data bank; . . .[2]

[(4) In this Part of this Schedule "a teletext receiver" means a television set—

(a) which is constructed for receiving teletext transmissions, that is to say, transmissions intended for general reception and consisting of a succession of visual displays (with or without accompanying sound) each capable of being selected and held for separate viewing or other use; and
(b) which is not also constructed for displaying information received as mentioned in sub-paragraph (3) above.][3]

[(5) In relation to expenditure incurred after 9th March 1982—

(a) this Part of this Schedule, other than sub-paragraph (6) below, shall have effect as if any reference to a television set included a reference to a teletext adaptor or a viewdata adaptor; and
(b) sub-paragraph (2) above shall have effect as if any reference to a teletext receiver included a reference to a teletext adaptor and as if any reference to a viewdata receiver included a reference to a viewdata adaptor.][3]

[(6) In this Part of this Schedule—

(a) "teletext adaptor" means a device external to a television set which, after it is connected to that television set, allows the set to display transmissions in the same manner as a teletext receiver; and
(b) "viewdata adaptor" means a device external to a television set which, afer it is connected to that television set, allows the set to display information received in the same manner as a viewdata receiver.][3]

Cross references.—See FA 1986, s. 57 (2) (c) (new code of allowances in respect of "new expenditure" (i.e. expenditure incurred after 31 March 1986, subject to qualifications in s. 57 (2), (3)) on leased assets not to apply to expenditure falling within this paragraph).
Amendments.—[1] Words in sub-paras. (2) (a), (3) inserted by FA 1982, s. 77 (1)–(3).

[2] Words in sub-para. (3) repealed by FA 1982, s. 77 (1), (3) and Sch. 22, Pt. IV.
[3] Sub-paras. (4), (5), (6) inserted by FA 1982, s. 77 (1), (4).
[4] Sub-para. (2) (*aa*) repealed by FA 1983, s. 33 (*a*) and Sch. 10, Pt. II.
[5] Words in sub-para. (2) (*b*) inserted by FA 1983, s. 33 (*b*).

8. Where section 64 of this Act would, apart from paragraph 7 above, have precluded the making of a first-year allowance in respect of any expenditure, the first-year allowance in respect of that expenditure shall—

(*a*) if the person who incurs the expenditure has the set delivered to him in the penultimate year of the transitional period, be of an amount equal to 75 per cent. of the expenditure;
(*b*) if that person has the set delivered to him in the last year of that period, be of an amount equal to 50 per cent. of the expenditure.

Cross references.—See FA 1985, Sch. 15, para. 10 (election to treat as short-life assets cannot be made in respect of television sets to which this paragraph applies).

9. The machinery or plant in relation to which section 44 of the Finance Act 1971 (writing-down allowances and balancing adjustments) has effect in accordance with section 65 of this Act shall include any television set in respect of which the amount of a first-year allowance is determined in accordance with paragraph 8 above.

10. Where section 66 of this Act has effect in relation to expenditure incurred on the provision of a television set which the person who incurs the expenditure has delivered to him in the last two years of the transitional period subsection (2) (*b*) of that section shall have effect as if the allowances there mentioned were the maximum first-year allowance and the writing-down allowance or allowances that could have been made in respect of the expenditure if the amount of the first-year allowance had been determined in accordance with paragraph 8 above.

11. Section 67 of this Act applies where the claim or deduction referred to in subsection (1) of that section relates to a first-year allowance in respect of a television set which the person who incurs the expenditure has delivered to him in the last two years of the transitional period and the amount of which falls to be determined otherwise than in accordance with paragraph 8 above.

SCHEDULE 13

Sections 74 and 75

INDUSTRIAL AND COMMERCIAL BUILDINGS

PART I

ENTERPRISE ZONES AND SMALL WORKSHOPS

Initial allowances

1. In section 1 (2) of the Capital Allowances Act 1968 for the reference to . . . of the capital expenditure there shall be substituted a reference to the whole of that expenditure.

Note.—For the omitted fraction, see the annotation under CAA 1968, s. 1.
Cross references.—See FA 1982, s. 73 (1) (this paragraph to apply in relation to very small workshops of gross internal floor area of 1,250 square feet or less);
FA 1984, s. 58 (4) (100 per cent. allowance under this paragraph not affected by a reduction of allowances for other expenditure).

2. A person making a claim by virtue of the said section 1 (2) (modified by paragraph 1 above) as it applies for income tax purposes may require the initial allowance to be reduced to a specified amount; and a company may by notice in writing given to the inspector not later than two years after the end of the chargeable period for which the allowance falls to be made disclaim the initial allowance or require it to be reduced to a specified amount.

Cross references.—See FA 1982, s. 73 (1) (this paragraph to apply in relation to very small workshops of gross internal floor area of 1,250 square feet or less).

Writing-down allowances

3. In section 2 (2) of the said Act of 1968 for the references to one twenty-fifth of the expenditure there shall be substituted references to one quarter of the expenditure.

Cross references.—See FA 1982, s. 73 (1) (this paragraph to apply in relation to very small workshops of gross internal floor area of 1,250 square feet or less).

PART II

ENTERPRISE ZONES

Use as a qualifying building or structure

4. For the purposes of sections 2 (1) (*b*) . . .[1] and 3 (1), . . .[1] of sections 4 (3) and (5) and of section 12 (1) and (2) of the said Act of 1968 a building or structure of any description (including a qualifying hotel) in relation to which Chapter I of Part I of that Act has effect in accordance with section 74 of this Act shall be regarded as continuing to be, or to be used as, a building or structure of that description notwithstanding that it has become a building or structure of another such description.

Amendments.—[1] Words repealed by FA 1981, Sch. 19, Pt. VI with effect from 18 December 1980.

Definitions

5. None of the provisions of section 7 of the said Act of 1968 except subsection (4) shall be construed as applying by virtue of section 74 of this Act to a qualifying hotel or a commercial building or structure.

SCHEDULE 18

Section 117

DEMERGERS

PART II

Relief From Tax in Respect of Capital Gains

9. Where a company makes an exempt distribution which falls within [section 213 (3) (*a*) of the Taxes Act 1988]—[1]

(*a*) the distribution shall not be a capital distribution for the purposes of section 72 of the Capital Gains Tax Act 1979 (disposal on receipt of capital distribution); and
(*b*) sections 77 to 81 of that Act shall, with the necessary modifications, apply as if that company and the subsidiary whose shares are transferred were the same company and the distribution were a reorganisation of its share capital.

Amendments.—[1] Words in this para. substituted by TA 1988, Sch. 29, para. 32 Table.

10. Subject to paragraph 15 below, neither section 278 nor section 279 of the Taxes Act (charge of tax where company ceases to be a member of a group) shall apply in a case where a company ceases to be a member of a group by reason only of an exempt distribution.

PART IV

Relief From Stamp Duty

12. . . .

Note.—See *Butterworths Orange Tax Handbook* for the provisions of this paragraph.

PART V

Prevention of Tax Avoidance

Re-instatement of charge in respect of capital gains

15. Paragraph 10 above does not apply if within five years after the making of the exempt distribution there is chargeable payment; and the time for making an assessment under section 278 or 279 of the Taxes Act by virtue of this paragraph shall not expire before the end of three years after the making of the chargeable payment.

PART VII

Interpretation

23.—(1) In this Schedule—

"chargeable payment" has the meaning given in [section 214 (2) of the Taxes Act 1988];[1]
. . .[2]
. . .[2]
"exempt distribution" means a distribution which is exempt by virtue of [section 213 (2) of that Act];[1]
"group" . . .[2] means a company which has one or more 75 per cent. subsidiaries together with that or those subsidiaries . . .[2]
. . .[2]
"shares" includes stock;
. . .[2]

(2) . . .[2]

(3) In determining for the purposes of this Schedule whether one company is a 75 per cent. subsidiary of another, the other company shall be treated as not being the owner of—

(*a*) any share capital which it owns directly in a body corporate if a profit on a sale of the shares would be treated as a trading receipt of its trade; or

(*b*) any share capital which it owns indirectly and which is owned directly by a body corporate for which a profit on the sale of the shares would be a trading receipt.

(4) ...[2]

(5) This Schedule, so far as it relates to income tax, shall be construed as one with the Income Tax Acts, so far as it relates to corporation tax, shall be construed as one with the Corporation Tax Acts, and, so far as it relates to capital gains tax, shall be construed as one with the Capital Gains Tax Act 1979.

Amendments.—[1] Words in sub-s. (1) substituted by TA 1988, Sch. 29, para. 32 Table.
[2] Sub-paras. (2), (4) and words in sub-para. (1) repealed by TA 1988, Sch. 31.

FINANCE ACT 1981

(1981 Chapter 35)

ARRANGEMENT OF SECTIONS

Note.—Provisions of this Act relevant to the taxes covered by this Handbook and not reproduced are either spent or repealed by TA 1988, Sch. 31 and other legislation.

PART IV

INCOME TAX, CORPORATION TAX AND CAPITAL GAINS TAX

CHAPTER IV

CAPITAL ALLOWANCES

Section
73. Industrial buildings etc.: increase of initial allowances.
74. Industrial buildings etc.: sales after cessation of use for qualifying purpose.
75. Industrial buildings etc.: balancing adjustments in cases of use for non-qualifying purpose.
76. Transfers other than sales and transactions between connected persons.

CHAPTER V

CAPITAL GAINS

79. Emigration of donee.
80. Gains of non-resident settlements.
81. Migrant settlements.
82. Transfers between settlements.
83. Provisions supplementary to sections 80 to 82.
84. Power to obtain information for purposes of sections 80 to 82.
85. Non-resident trustees and non-resident companies.
88. Disposal of interests in non-resident settlements.

PART VI

STAMP DUTY

Sections 107–110 (see Orange Book)

PART VIII

SUPPLEMENTARY PETROLEUM DUTY

127. Deduction of duty in computing income for corporation tax

PART X

MISCELLANEOUS AND SUPPLEMENTARY

135. Chevening Estate.
139. Short title, interpretation, construction and repeals.

An Act to grant certain duties, to alter other duties, and to amend the law relating to the National Debt and the Public Revenue, and to make further provision in connection with Finance.
[27th July 1981]

PART IV
INCOME TAX, CORPORATION TAX AND CAPITAL GAINS TAX
CHAPTER IV
CAPITAL ALLOWANCES

73. Industrial buildings etc.: increase of initial allowances

(2) A person other than a company may, in making a claim to an initial allowance at the rate applying by virtue of this section, require the initial allowance to be reduced to a specified amount; and a company may, by notice in writing given to the inspector not later than two years after the end of the chargeable period for which an initial allowance at that rate falls to be made, disclaim the allowance or require it to be reduced to a specified amount.

(3) This section has effect in relation to expenditure incurred after 10th March 1981 and to expenditure which by virtue of section 5 (1) of the said Act of 1968 (purchase of unused buildings or structures) is deemed to have been incurred after that date; but expenditure shall not be treated for the purposes of this section as having been incurred after the date on which it was in fact incurred by reason only of section 1 (6) of that Act (expenditure incurred before trade begins).

Notes.—Sub-s. (1) amends CAA 1968, s. 1 (2), FA 1978, Sch. 6, para. 1 and FA 1980, Sch. 13, para. 1.

74. Industrial buildings etc.: sales after cessation of use for qualifying purpose

(5) In section 38 of the Finance Act 1978 (application of the said Chapter I to qualifying hotels) and in section 74 of the Finance Act 1980 (application of that Chapter to commercial buildings and qualifying hotels in enterprise zones) references to that Chapter shall be construed as references to that Chapter as amended by this section.

(6) This section has effect where the sale referred to in section 2 (3) of the said Act of 1968 or, as the case may be, the event referred to in paragraph (*a*), (*b*), (*c*) or (*d*) of section 3 (1) of that Act occurs after 17th December 1980 but not where the sale is pursuant to a contract of sale made on or before that date or the event is a sale pursuant to such a contract.

Notes.—Sub-ss. (1)–(4) amend CAA 1968, ss. 2 (3), 3 (1) and inserts CAA 1968, s. 6 (7).

75. Industrial buildings etc.: balancing adjustments in cases of use for non-qualifying purpose

(4) In section 38 of the Finance Act 1978 (application of the said Chapter I to qualifying hotels) and in section 74 of the Finance Act 1980 (application of that Chapter to commercial buildings and qualifying hotels in enterprise zones) references to that Chapter shall be construed as references to that Chapter as amended by this section.

(5) This section has effect where the event referred to in paragraph (*a*), (*b*), (*c*) or (*d*) of section 3 (1) of the said Act of 1968 occurs after 17th December 1980 but not where that event is a sale pursuant to a contract of sale made on or before that date.

Notes.—Sub-ss. (1)–(3) substitute CAA 1968, ss. 3 (4)–(5) and inserts CAA 1968, s. 4 (10A).

76. Transfers other than sales and transactions between connected persons

(1) For the purposes of Chapter I of Part I of the Capital Allowances Act 1968 (industrial buildings and structures etc.) and the other provisions of that Act which are relevant to that Chapter any transfer of the relevant interest in a building or structure otherwise than by way of sale shall be treated as a sale of the interest for a price other than that which it would have fetched if sold on the open market.

(2) If Schedule 7 to the said Act of 1968 (special provisions as to certain sales) would not apart from this subsection have effect in relation to a transfer treated as a sale by virtue of subsection (1) above, that Schedule shall have effect in relation to it as if it were a sale falling within paragraph 1 (1) (*a*) of that Schedule.

(4) In section 38 of the Finance Act 1978 (application of the said Chapter I to qualifying hotels) and in section 74 of the Finance Act 1980 (application of that Chapter to commercial buildings and qualifying hotels in enterprise zones) references to that Chapter shall be construed as references to that Chapter as amended by this section.

(5) This section has effect where the transfer or sale occurs after 10th March 1981 but not when the transfer or sale is pursuant to a contract for the carrying out of the transaction or sale made on or before that date.

Notes.—Sub-s. (3) amends CAA 1968, s. 78 (1) and Sch. 7, para. 1 (1).

CHAPTER V
CAPITAL GAINS

79. Emigration of donee

(1) If—

[(a) relief is given under section 126 of the Capital Gains Tax Act 1979 in respect of a disposal to an individual or the trustees of a settlement or under section 147A of that Act in respect of any disposal ("the relevant disposal");][1]
(b) at a time when he has not disposed of the asset in question, the transferee becomes neither resident nor ordinarily resident in the United Kingdom,

then, subject to the following provisions of this section, a chargeable gain shall be deemed to have accrued to the transferee immediately before that time, and its amount shall be equal to the held-over gain (within the meaning of [section 126 or 147A][2] on the relevant disposal.

(2) For the purposes of subsection (1) above the transferee shall be taken to have disposed of an asset before the time there referred to only if he has made a disposal or disposals in connection with which the whole of the held-over gain on the relevant disposal was represented by reductions made in accordance with [section 126 (3) (b) or 147A (3) (b) of the Capital Gains Tax Act 1979][2]; and where he has made a disposal in connection with which part of that gain was so represented, the amount of the chargeable gain deemed by virtue of this section to accrue to him shall be correspondingly reduced.

(3) The disposals by the transferee that are to be taken into account under subsection (2) above shall not include any disposal to which section 44 of the Capital Gains Tax Act 1979 (disposals between spouses) applies; but where any such disposal is made by the transferee, disposals by his spouse shall be taken into account under subsection (2) above as if they had been made by him.

(4) Where the relevant disposal was made to an individual subsection (1) above shall not apply by reason of his becoming neither resident nor ordinarily resident more than six years after the end of the year of assessment in which the relevant disposal was made.

(5) Subsection (1) above shall not apply where the relevant disposal was made to an individual and—

(a) the reason for his becoming neither resident nor ordinarily resident in the United Kingdom is that he works in an employment or office all the duties of which are performed outside the United Kingdom, and
(b) he again becomes resident or ordinarily resident in the United Kingdom within the period of three years from the time when he ceases to be so, without having meanwhile disposed of the asset in question;

and accordingly no assessment shall be made by virtue of subsection (1) above before the end of the said period of three years in any case where the condition in paragraph (a) above is, and the condition in paragraph (b) above may be satisfied.

(6) For the purposes of subsection (5) above a person shall be taken to have disposed of an asset if he has made a disposal in connection with which the whole or part of the held-over gain on the relevant disposal would, had he been resident in the United Kingdom, have been represented by a reduction made in accordance with [section 126 (3) (b) or 147A (3) (b) of the Capital Gains Tax Act 1979][2]; and subsection (3) above shall have effect for the purposes of this subsection as it has effect for the purposes of subsection (2) above.

(7) Where an amount of tax assessed on a transferee by virtue of subsection (1) above is not paid within the period of twelve months beginning with the date when the tax becomes payable then, subject to subsection (8) below, the transferor may be assessed and charged (in the name of the transferee) to all or any part of that tax.

(8) No assessment shall be made under subsection (7) above more than six years after the end of the year of assessment in which the relevant disposal was made.

(9) Where the transferor pays an amount of tax in pursuance of subsection (7) above, he shall be entitled to recover a corresponding sum from the transferee.

(10) Gains on disposals made after a chargeable gain has under this section been deemed to accrue by reference to a held-over gain shall be computed without any reduction under

[section 126 (3) (*b*) or 147A (3) (*b*) of the Capital Gains Tax Act 1979][2] in respect of that held-over gain.

Cross references.—See FA 1986, s. 58 (5) (claw-back under this section of relief obtained under FA 1980, s. 79 (general relief for gifts) in respect of gifts into dual resident trusts);
FA 1988, Sch. 9, para. 3 (reduction of a deferred charge to tax where the charge is wholly or partly attributable to an increase in the value of an asset before 31 March 1982).
Amendments.—[1] Sub-s. (1) (*a*) substituted by FA 1989, s. 124 (2), (3) and Sch. 14, para. 6 (3) in relation to disposals made after 13 March 1989 subject to certain exceptions; see FA 1989, s. 124 (3).
[2] Words in sub-ss. (1), (2), (6), (10) substituted by *ibid.*

80. Gains of non-resident settlements

(1) This section applies to a settlement for any year of assessment (beginning on or after 6th April 1981) during which the trustees are at no time resident or ordinarily resident in the United Kingdom if the settlor or one of the settlors is at any time during that year, or was when he made his settlement, domiciled and either resident or ordinarily resident in the United Kingdom.

(2) There shall be computed in respect of every year of assessment for which this section applies the amount on which the trustees would have been chargeable to tax under section 4 (1) of the Capital Gains Tax Act 1979 if they had been resident or ordinarily resident in the United Kingdom in the year; and that amount, together with the corresponding amount in respect of any earlier such year so far as not already treated under subsection (3) or section 81 (2) below as chargeable gains accruing to beneficiaries under the settlement, is in this section and sections 81 and 82 below referred to as the trust gains for the year.

(3) Subject to the following provisions of this section, the trust gains for a year of assessment shall be treated as chargeable gains accruing in that year to beneficiaries of the settlement who receive capital payments from the trustees in that year or have received such payments in any earlier year.

(4) The attribution of chargeable gains to beneficiaries under subsection (3) above shall be made in proportion to, but shall not exceed, the amounts of the capital payments received by them.

(5) A capital payment shall be left out of account for the purposes of subsections (3) and (4) above to the extent that chargeable gains have by reason of the payment been treated as accruing to the recipient in an earlier year.

(6) A beneficiary shall not be charged to tax on chargeable gains treated by virtue of subsection (3) above as accruing to him in any year unless he is domiciled in the United Kingdom at some time in that year.

(7) For the purposes of this section a settlement arising under a will or intestacy shall be treated as made by the testator or intestate at the time of his death.

(8) Section 17 of the Capital Gains Tax Act 1979 shall not apply as respects chargeable gains accruing to the trustees of a settlement after 5th April 1981; and the references in subsections (3) and (4) above to capital payments received by beneficiaries do not include references to any payment received before 10th March 1981, or any payment received on or after that date [and before 6th April 1984][1] so far as it represents a chargeable gain which accrued to the trustees before 6th April 1981.

Cross references.—See FA 1984, Sch. 14, paras. 7–12 (postponement of CGT due at 29 March 1983 from beneficiaries on gains of non-resident trustees; effect of capital payments received by beneficiaries subsequent to postponement);
TA 1988, s. 762 (2)–(4) (extension of this section, with modifications, to offshore income gains accruing to persons resident or domiciled abroad).
Amendments.—[1] Words in sub-s. (8) inserted by FA 1984, s. 70 (3).

81. Migrant settlements

(1) Where a period of one or more years of assessment for which section 80 above applies to a settlement (in this section referred to as a "non-resident period") succeeds a period of one or more years of assessment in each of which the trustees were at some time resident or ordinarily resident in the United Kingdom (in this section referred to as a "resident period"), a capital payment received by a beneficiary in the resident period shall be disregarded for the purposes of section 80 if it was not made in anticipation of a disposal made by the trustees in the non-resident period.

(2) Where—

(a) a non-resident period is succeeded by a resident period, and
(b) the trust gains for the last year of the non-resident period are not (or not wholly) treated as chargeable gains accruing in that year to beneficiaries,

then, subject to subsection (3) below, those trust gains (or the outstanding part of them) shall be treated as chargeable gains accruing in the first year of the resident period to beneficiaries of the settlement who receive capital payments from the trustees in that year; and so on for the second and subsequent years until the amount treated as accruing to beneficiaries is equal to the amount of the trust gains for the last year of the non-resident period.

(3) Subsections (4) and (6) of section 80 above shall apply in relation to subsection (2) above as they apply in relation to subsection (3) of that section.

Cross references.—See TA 1988, s. 762 (2) (extension of this section, with modifications, to offshore income gains accruing to persons resident or domiciled abroad).

82. Transfers between settlements

(1) If in a year of assessment for which section 80 or 81 (2) above applies to a settlement ("the transferor settlement") the trustees transfer all or part of the settled property to the trustees of another settlement ("the transferee settlement") then, subject to the following provisions—

(a) if section 80 applies to the transferee settlement for the year, its trust gains for the year shall be treated as increased by an amount equal to the outstanding trust gains for the year of the transferor settlement or, where part only of the settled property is transferred, to a proportionate part of those trust gains;
(b) if section 81 (2) applies to the transferee settlement for the year (otherwise than by virtue of paragraph (c) below), the trust gains referred to in section 81 (2) shall be treated as increased by the amount mentioned in paragraph (a) above;
(c) if (apart from this paragraph) neither section 80 nor section 81 (2) above applies to the transferee settlement for the year, section 81 (2) shall apply to it as if the year were the first year of a resident period succeeding a non-resident period and the trust gains referred to in section 81 (2) were equal to the amount mentioned in paragraph (a) above.

(2) Subject to subsection (3) below the reference in subsection (1) (a) above to the outstanding trust gains for the year of the transferor settlement is a reference to the amount of its trust gains for the year so far as they are not treated under section 80 (3) above as chargeable gains accruing to beneficiaries in that year.

(3) Where section 81 (2) above applies to the transferor settlement for the year, the reference in subsection (1) (a) above to the outstanding trust gains of the settlement is a reference to the trust gains referred to in section 81 (2) so far as not treated as chargeable gains accruing to beneficiaries in that or an earlier year.

(4) This section shall not apply to a transfer so far as it is made for consideration in money or money's worth.

Cross references.—See TA 1988, s. 762 (extension of this section, with modifications, to offshore income gains accruing to persons resident or domiciled abroad).

83. Provisions supplementary to sections 80 to 82

(1) In sections 80 to 82 above "capital payment" means any payment which is not chargeable to income tax on the beneficiary or, in the case of a beneficiary who is neither resident nor ordinarily resident in the United Kingdom, any payment received otherwise than as income.

(2) In subsection (1) above references to a payment include references to the transfer of an asset and the conferring of any other benefit, and to any occasion on which settled property becomes property to which section 46 of the Capital Gains Tax Act 1979 applies.

(3) The fact that the whole or part of a benefit is by virtue of section 45 (2) (b) above treated as the recipient's income for a year of assessment after that in which it is received—

(a) shall not prevent the benefit or that part of it being treated for the purposes of sections 80 to 82 above as a capital payment in relation to any year of assessment earlier than that in which it is treated as his income; but
(b) shall preclude its being treated for those purposes as a capital payment in relation to that or any later year of assessment.

(4) For the purposes of sections 80 to 82 above the amount of a capital payment made by

way of loan, and of any other capital payment which is not an outright payment of money, shall be taken to be equal to the value of the benefit conferred by it.

(5) For the purposes of sections 80 to 82 above a capital payment shall be regarded as received by a beneficiary from the trustees of a settlement if—

(a) he receives it from them directly or indirectly, or
(b) it is directly or indirectly applied by them in payment of any debt of his or otherwise paid or applied for his benefit, or
(c) it is received by a third person at the beneficiary's direction.

(6) Section 29 (3) of the Capital Gains Tax Act 1979 (losses accruing to non-residents not to be allowable losses) shall not prevent losses accruing to trustees in a year of assessment for which section 80 above or section 17 of that Act applied to the settlement from being allowed as a deduction from chargeable gains accruing in any later year beginning after 5th April 1981 (so far as they have not previously been set against gains for the purposes of a computation under either of those sections or otherwise).

[(7) In sections 80 to 82 above and in the preceding provisions of this section—

"settlement" and "settlor" have the meaning given by section [681 (4)][2] of the Taxes Act and "settlor" includes, in the case of a settlement arising under a will or intestacy, the testator or intestate; and
"settled property" shall be construed accordingly.][1]

Cross references.—See FA 1984, Sch. 14, para. 1 (2) (application of this section in relation to the postponement of a beneficiary's CGT liability on the gains of non-resident settlement);
TA 1988, s. 762 (extension of this section, with modifications, to offshore income gains accruing to persons resident or domiciled abroad).
Amendments.—[1] Sub-s. (7) added by FA 1984, s. 71.
[2] Number in sub-s. (7) substituted by TA 1988, Sch. 29, para. 32 Table.

84. Power to obtain information for purposes of sections 80 to 82

(1) The Board may by notice in writing require any person to furnish them within such time as they may direct, not being less than twenty-eight days, with such particulars as they think necessary for the purposes of sections 80 to 82 above.

(2) Subsections (2) to [(5) of section 745][1] of the Taxes Act shall have effect in relation to subsection (1) above as they have effect in relation to section [745 (1)][1], but in their application by virtue of this subsection—

(a) references to Chapter III of Part XVII of the Taxes Act shall be construed as references to sections 80 to 82 above; and
(b) the expressions "settlement" and "settlor" have the same meanings as in those sections.

Cross references.—See TA 1988, s. 762 (extension of this section, with modifications, to offshore income gains accruing to persons resident or domiciled abroad).
Amendments.—[1] Words in sub-s. (2) substituted by TA 1988, Sch. 29, para. 32 Table.

85. Non-resident trustees and non-resident companies

(1) The persons treated by section 15 of the Capital Gains Tax Act 1979 as if a part of a chargeable gain accruing to a company had accrued to them shall include trustees owning shares in the company if when the gain accrues to the company the trustees are neither resident nor ordinarily resident in the United Kingdom.

(2) This section applies to gains accruing to a company on or after 10th March 1981.

88. Disposal of interests in non-resident settlements

(1) Subsection (1) of section 58 of the Capital Gains Tax Act 1979 shall not apply to the disposal of an interest in settled property, other than one treated under subsection (2) of that section as made in consideration of obtaining the settled property, if at the time of the disposal the trustees are neither resident nor ordinarily resident in the United Kingdom.

(2) If—

(a) a gain accrues to a person ("the transferor") on the disposal by him of an interest in settled property but, by reason of section 58 (1) of the Capital Gains Tax Act 1979, it is not a chargeable gain, and (*b*) at any time after the disposal the trustees of the settlement become neither resident nor ordinarily resident in the United Kingdom,

then, subject to subsection (3) below, a chargeable gain shall be deemed to have accrued to the trustees immediately before that time, and its amount shall be equal to that of the gain which accrued to the transferor.

(3) Subsection (2) above shall not apply if, before the end of the year in which they become neither resident nor ordinarily resident, the trustees have disposed of all the assets which, when the transferor disposed of his interest, constituted the settled property in which the interest subsisted; and where under that subsection a chargeable gain is deemed to accrue to the trustees at any time its amount shall not exceed the market value at that time of such of those assets as have not been disposed of by the trustees before the end of that year.

(4) For the purposes of subsection (3) above the trustees shall be regarded as not having disposed of an asset if and to the extent that they retain part of it, an interest in or right over it, or property derived from it.

(5) Where an amount of tax assessed on trustees by virtue of this section is not paid within the period of twelve months beginning with the date when the tax becomes payable, the transferor may be assessed and charged (in the name of the trustees) to all or any part of that tax; but no assessment may be made under this subsection after the end of the period of six years beginning with the date when the transferor disposed of his interest.

(6) Where the transferor pays an amount of tax in pursuance of subsection (5) above, he shall be entitled to recover a corresponding sum from the trustees.

(7) This section applies to disposals on or after 10th March 1981.

PART VIII
SUPPLEMENTARY PETROLEUM DUTY

127. Deduction of duty in computing income for corporation tax

(1) Where a participator in an oil field has paid any duty with which he was chargeable for a chargeable period, then, in computing for corporation tax the amount of his income arising in the relevant accounting period from oil extraction activities or oil rights, there shall be deducted an amount equal to that duty; and there shall be made all such adjustments of assessments to corporation tax as are required in order to give effect to this subsection.

(2) For the purposes of subsection (1) above the relevant accounting period, in relation to any duty paid by a company is—

(a) the accounting period of the company in or at the end of which the chargeable period for which the duty was charged ends; or
(b) if that chargeable period ends after the accounting period of the company in or at the end of which the trade giving rise to the income referred to in subsection (1) above is permanently discontinued, that accounting period.

(3) Subject to subsection (4) below, if some or all of the duty in respect of which a deduction has been made under subsection (1) above is subsequently repaid, that deduction shall be reduced or extinguished accordingly; and any additional assessment to corporation tax required in order to give effect to this subsection may be made at any time not later than six years after the end of the accounting period in which the duty was repaid.

(4) Subsection (3) above does not apply to any repayment of duty under section 125 above but any amount of duty repaid to a person under that section shall be treated as his income for the purpose of corporation tax.

(5) Where, because of a deduction made under subsection (1) above in computing for corporation tax the amount of a company's income of any kind, the amount of advance corporation tax which can be set against the company's liability to corporation tax for an accounting period is less than the amount of advance corporation tax which could have been set against that liability if the deduction had not been made, then, if a claim in that behalf is made by the company not later than two years after the end of that accounting period, an amount of advance corporation tax equal to the difference shall be repaid to the company.

(6) In this section "oil extraction activities" and "oil rights" have the meaning given in section 19 (1) of the principal Act.

Note.—The principal Act referred to in sub-s (6) above is the Oil Taxation Act 1975.
Cross references.—See TA 1988, s. 498 (8) (*b*) (oil company's right to set off surrendered ACT against corporation tax liability of previous accounting periods; ACT for distributions actually made after 16 March 1987 to be left out of account for determining ACT under sub-s. (5) above).
Amendments.—This section repealed by FA 1982, Sch. 22, Pt. IX in relation to chargeable periods ending after 31 December 1982.

PART X
MISCELLANEOUS AND SUPPLEMENTARY

135. Chevening Estate

(1) The enactments relating to capital gains tax, ... shall not apply in respect of property held on the trusts of the trust instrument set out in the Schedule to the Chevening Estate Act 1959.

(2) This section shall be deemed always to have had effect.

Note.—Words omitted from sub-s. (1) are not relevant to this work.

139. Short title, interpretation, construction and repeals

(1) This Act may be cited as the Finance Act 1981.

(2) In this Act "the Taxes Act" means the Income and Corporation Taxes Act [1988][1].

(3) Part IV of this Act, so far as it relates to income tax, shall be construed as one with the Income Tax Acts, so far as it relates to corporation tax, shall be construed as one with the Corporation Tax Acts and, so far as it relates to capital gains tax, shall be construed as one with the Capital Gains Tax Act 1979.

(4) ...

(5) ...

(6) The enactments mentioned in Schedule 19 to this Act are hereby repealed to the extent specified in the third column of that Schedule, but subject to any provision at the end of any Part of that Schedule.

Note.—Sub-ss. (4), (5) are not relevant to this work.
Amendments.—[1] Year in sub-s. (2) substituted by TA 1988, Sch. 29, para. 32 Table.

BRITISH TELECOMMUNICATIONS ACT 1981

(1981 Chapter 38)

82. Tax provisions

(1) For the purposes of the Capital Gains Tax Act 1979 any asset transferred by this Act from the Post Office to the Corporation, or from the Corporation to the Post Office, shall be deemed to be for a consideration such that no gain or loss accrues to the transferor on its transfer; and Schedule 5 to that Act shall have effect in relation to any asset so transferred as if the acquisition or provision of it by the transferor, or the acquisition or provision of it by the Crown which is treated as the acquisition or provision of it by the transferor, had been the acquisition or provision of it by the transferee.

(2) For the purposes of the Corporation Tax Acts—

(a) the part of the Post Office's trade transferred by this Act to the Corporation ("the transferred trade") and the part thereof retained by the Post Office ("the retained trade") shall be treated as having been, at all times since the commencement of the Post Office's trade, separate trades carried on by the Corporation and the Post Office respectively; and

(b) the trade carried on by each of those bodies after the appointed day shall be treated as the same trade as that which, by virtue of paragraph (a), it is treated as having carried on before that day.

(3) The aggregate of the amounts for which the Corporation and the Post Office are entitled to relief under section 177 (1) of the Income and Corporation Taxes Act 1970, as for losses sustained by them before the appointed day in carrying on the transferred trade and the retained trade, shall not exceed the amount which, if subsection (2) had not been enacted and the Post Office had continued to carry on both trades, would have been available to it for carrying forward against trading income from the trades in succeeding accounting periods.

(4) Where, in the discharge of any liability which is transferred to the Corporation by this Act, the Corporation makes payments to the trustees of a retirement benefits scheme with a view to the provision of relevant benefits for persons who are employees of the Post Office, the Tax Acts shall have effect in relation to those payments—

(a) as if those persons were employees of the Corporation; and

(b) where the scheme is an exempt approved scheme, as if paragraph (a) of the proviso to section 21 (3) of the Finance Act 1970 were omitted;

and in this subsection expressions which are also used in Chapter II of Part II of the said Act of 1970 have the same meanings as in that Chapter.

(5)–(6) . . .

(7) Subsections (2) and (3) shall have effect in relation to accounting periods of the Corporation and of the Post Office ending on or after the appointed day.

Notes.—Sub-ss. (5), (6) are not relevant to this work.

FINANCE ACT 1982

(1982 Chapter 39)

ARRANGEMENT OF SECTIONS

Note.—Provisions of this Act relevant to the taxes covered by this Handbook and not reproduced are either spent or repealed by TA 1988, Sch. 31 and other legislation.

PART III
INCOME TAX, CORPORATION TAX AND CAPITAL GAINS TAX
CHAPTER II
CAPITAL ALLOWANCES

Section
70. Allowances for assets leased outside the United Kingdom.
71. Restriction on first-year allowances in respect of ships and aircraft let on charter.
72. Expenditure on production and acquisition of films etc.
73. Industrial buildings allowance: very small workshops.
74. Industrial buildings allowance: licensees.
76. Allowances for dwelling houses let on assured tenancies.
79. Capital allowances and stock relief.

CHAPTER III
CAPITAL GAINS

86. Indexation allowance on certain disposals.
87. Calculation of indexation allowance.
88. Identification of securities etc. disposed of: general rules.

PART V
STAMP DUTY

Sections 128–131 (see Orange Book)

PART VI
OIL TAXATION
CHAPTER I
GENERAL

Section
137. Expenditure met by regional development grants to be disregarded for certain purposes.

PART VII
MISCELLANEOUS AND SUPPLEMENTARY

145. Certificates of tax deposit: extension of interest period.
148. Transfer of assets of Hops Marketing Board.

Section
156. Dissolution of Board of Referees.
157. Short title, interpretation, construction and repeals.

SCHEDULES

Schedule 11—Allowances for assets leased outside the United Kingdom.
Schedule 12—Capital allowances for dwelling-houses let on assured tenancies.
Schedule 13—The indexation allowance.
Schedule 21—Dissolution of Board of Referees: consequential provisions.

PART III
INCOME TAX, CORPORATION TAX AND CAPITAL GAINS TAX
CHAPTER II
CAPITAL ALLOWANCES
70. Allowances for assets leased outside the United Kingdom

(1) The provisions of this section have effect with respect to expenditure on the provision of machinery or plant for leasing where the machinery or plant is at any time in the requisite period used for the purpose of being leased to a person who—

(a) is not resident in the United Kingdom, and
(b) does not use the machinery or plant for the purposes of a trade carried on there or for earning profits or gains chargeable to tax by virtue of section [830 (4) of the Taxes Act 1988][13],

and where the leasing is [neither short-term leasing nor the leasing of a ship, aircraft or transport container which is used for a qualifying purpose by virtue of subsections (5) to (7) of section 64 of the Finance Act 1980][1].

(2) In its application to expenditure falling within subsection (1) above, section 44 of the Finance Act 1971 (writing-down allowances and balancing adjustments) as it has effect—

(a) in accordance with section 65 of the Finance Act 1980 [(as amended by Part I of Schedule 16 to the Finance Act 1986)][2], or
(b) in accordance with paragraph 6 of Schedule 8 to the Finance Act 1971 (effect of subsidies towards wear and tear of assets), or
(c) in accordance with paragraph 10 of that Schedule (cars costing more than £8,000), or
(d) with respect to any motor car to which paragraph 11 of that Schedule applies (contributions towards expenditure on cars costing more than £8,000), or
(e) with respect to machinery or plant to which section 46 of the Finance Act 1971 applies (assets leased otherwise than in the course of a trade),

shall have effect, subject to subsection (4) below, as if the reference in subsection (2) of section 44 to 25 per cent were a reference to 10 per cent.

(3) In any case where—

(a) machinery or plant is used for the purpose of being leased to such a person as is referred to in paragraphs (a) and (b) of subsection (1) above, and
(b) the circumstances are such that the machinery or plant is used otherwise than for a qualifying purpose, within the meaning of section 64 of the Finance Act 1980 (exclusion of first-year allowances for certain leased assets),

any question whether that use falls within the requisite period, as defined in subsection (8) of that section, shall be determined as if, for each reference in that subsection to four years, there were substituted a reference to ten years; and any reference to the requisite period in sections 66 and 67 of that Act shall be construed accordingly.[3]

(4) No . . .[4], balancing allowances or writing-down allowances shall be available in respect of expenditure falling within subsection (1) above if the circumstances are [such that the machinery or plant in question is used otherwise than for a qualifying purpose, within the meaning of section 64 of the Finance Act 1980][5] and—

(a) there is a period of more than one year between the dates on which any two consecutive payments become due under the lease; or
(b) any payments other than periodical payments are due under the lease or under any agreement which might reasonably be construed as being collateral to the lease; or
(c) disregarding variations made under the terms of the lease which are attributable to—

(i) changes in the rate of corporation tax or income tax, or
(ii) changes in the rate of capital allowances, or
(iii) changes in any rate or interest where the changes are linked to changes in the rate of interest applicable to inter-bank loans, or

(iv) changes in the premiums charged for insurance of any description by a person who is not connected with the lessor or the lessee,

any of the payments due under the lease or under any such agreement as is referred to in sub-paragraph (b) above, expressed as monthly amounts over the period for which that payment is due, is not the same as any other such payment expressed in the same way; or

(d) either the lease is expressed to be for a period which exceeds thirteen years or there is, in the lease or a separate agreement, provision for extending or renewing the lease or for the grant of a new lease so that, by virtue of that provision, the machinery or plant could be leased for a period which exceeds thirteen years; or

(e) at any time the lessor or a person connected with him will, or may in certain circumstances, become entitled to receive from the lessee or any other person a payment, other than a payment of insurance moneys, which is of an amount determined before the expiry of the lease and which is referable to a value of the machinery or plant at or after that expiry (whether or not the payment relates to a disposal of the machinery or plant).

(5) Where ...[6], a balancing allowance or a writing-down allowance has been made in respect of expenditure incurred in providing machinery or plant and, at any time in the requisite period, an event occurs such that, by virtue of subsection (4) above, there is no right to that allowance, an amount equal to any such allowance which has previously been given (less any excess reliefs previously recovered by the operation of [paragraph 8 of Schedule 16 to the Finance Act 1986][7]) shall, in relation to the person to whom the machinery or plant belongs immediately before the occurrence of that event, be treated as if it were a balancing charge to be made on him for the chargeable period in which, or in the basis period for which, the machinery or plant is used at the time that event occurs.

[(6) For the purposes of subsection (5) above, the allowances that have been made in respect of expenditure on any item of machinery or plant shall be determined as if that item were the only item of machinery or plant in respect of which section 44 of the Finance Act 1971 had effect.][8]

(7) In subsection (1) above "short-term leasing" has the same meaning as in subsection (2) (b) of section 64 of the Finance Act 1980 [(as amended by Part I of Schedule 16 to the Finance Act 1986)][9], ...

(8) The provisions of Schedule 11 to this Act shall have effect for supplementing the preceding provisions of this section.

(9) In subsections (1) and (5) above "the requisite period" has the same meaning [as it has in section 64 of the Finance Act 1980 (as amended by Part I of Schedule 16 to the Finance Act 1986)][10]; and section 73 of that Act (interpretation), with the exception of subsection (4) thereof, has effect in relation to the preceding provisions of this section ...[11]—

(a) as if those provisions were comprised in the foregoing provisions of Chapter II of Part III of that Act; and

(b) as if the reference in subsection (1) of that section to section 72 of that Act included a reference to subsection (10) below.

[(c) as if the reference in subsection (5) of that section to a first-year allowance were a reference to a writing-down allowance][12].

(10) Subject to subsection (11) below, this section applies to expenditure incurred on or after 10th March 1982 unless—

(a) the expenditure consists of the payment of sums payable under a contract entered into before that date by the person incurring the expenditure; or

(b) the expenditure consists of the payment of sums payable under a contract entered into not later than 31st March 1984 and the conditions in subsection (12) below are fulfilled;

and, in either case, the machinery or plant concerned is brought into use not later than 31st March 1985.

(11) In its application to subsections (4) to (6) above, subsection (10) above has effect as if for the references to 10th March 1982 there were substituted references to 23rd June 1982.

(12) The conditions referred to in paragraph (b) of subsection (10) above are—

(a) that the expenditure referred to in that paragraph is incurred in fulfilment of arrangements (not necessarily amounting to contractual obligations) under which the person incurring the expenditure (in this subsection referred to as "the lessor") would lease the machinery or plant in question to another person (in this subsection referred to as "the lessee"); and

(b) that those arrangements were in existence on 10th March 1982 and are evidenced by writing dating from a time before that date; and

(c) that, in reliance upon the arrangements and before 10th March 1982, the lessee had entered into a contract with a third party (in this subsection referred to as "the supplier") to incur expenditure on the provision of the machinery or plant in question; and

(d) that, pursuant to the arrangements,—

(i) the obligations of the lessee under the contract referred to in paragraph (c) above are, before 31st March 1984, either taken over by the lessor or discharged on the lessor entering into a new contract with the supplier; or

(ii) the lessee purchases the machinery or plant in question and transfers it to the lessor before 8th July 1982; and

(e) that, on or before 31st March 1984, the lessor enters into a contract to lease the machinery or plant to the lessee; and

(f) that, disregarding any use before 8th July 1982, the machinery or plant in question is not brought into use by the lessee before it is leased to him by the lessor; and

(g) that the lessor and the lessee are not connected persons and neither of them is connected with the supplier;

and section [839 of the Taxes Act 1988][13] (connected persons) applies for the purposes of this section.

Notes.—Words omitted from sub-s. (7) amend FA 1980, s. 64 (3) and add s. 64 (3A).
Cross references.—See FA 1980, s. 68 (1), (3) (machinery or plant leased to two or more lessees jointly at least one of whom falls within sub-s. (1) (a), (b) above).
FA 1985, Sch. 15, para. 11 (election to treat as short-life assets cannot be made in respect of machinery and plant with a 10 per cent. writing-down allowance under this section);
FA 1986, s. 57 (7) (a) (application of this section as amended by FA 1986, Sch. 16, para. 5 with respect to expenditure on the provision of cars for leasing as mentioned in sub-s (1) above).
Amendments.—[1] Words in sub-s. (1) substituted for the words "not short-term leasing" by FA 1986, s. 57 (4) (b), (7) (a) and Sch. 16, para. 5 in respect of "new expenditure" (i.e. expenditure incurred after 31 March 1986, subject to qualifications in s. 57 (2), (3)).
[2] Words in sub-s. (2) (a) substituted for the words "(assets leased in the course of a trade)" by ibid.
[3] Sub-s. (3) repealed by ibid.
[4] Words "first-year allowances" in sub-s. (4) repealed by ibid.
[5] Words in sub-s. (4) substituted for the words "as mentioned in subsection (3) (b) above" by ibid.
[6] Words "a first-year allowance" in sub-s. (5) repealed by ibid.
[7] Words in sub-s. (5) substituted for the words "section 66 of the Finance Act 1980" by ibid.
[8] Sub-s. (6) substituted by ibid. As originally enacted it read—
(6) Subsections (3) and (4) of section 66 of the Finance Act 1980 apply in relation to the allowances mentioned in subsection (5) above as they apply in relation to the allowances mentioned in subsection (2) of that section.
[9] Words in sub-s. (7) inserted by ibid.
[10] Words in sub-s. (9) substituted for the words "as, in a case where subsection (3) above applies, it has in sections 64 to 68 of the Finance Act 1980" by ibid.
[11] Words "and the provisions of Schedule 11 to this Act" in sub-s. (9) repealed by ibid.
[12] Sub-s. (9) (c) added by ibid.
[13] Words in sub-ss. (1), (12) substituted by TA 1988, Sch. 29, para. 32 Table.

71. Restriction on first-year allowances in respect of ships and aircraft let on charter

(3) This section applies in relation to expenditure incurred on or after 10th March 1982 unless—

(a) the expenditure consists of the payment of sums payable under a contract entered into before that date by the person incurring the expenditure; and

(b) the ship or aircraft concerned is brought into use not later than 31st March 1984.

Notes.—Sub-ss. (1), (2) amend FA 1980, s. 64 (5) and insert s. 64 (6A).

72. Expenditure on production and acquisition of films etc

(1) Expenditure which—

(a) is incurred on or after 10th March 1982 on the production or acquisition of a film, tape or disc, and

(b) would, apart from this subsection, constitute capital expenditure on the provision of machinery or plant for the purposes of Chapter I of Part III of the Finance Act 1971 (first-year and other allowances in respect of machinery and plant),

shall be regarded for the purposes of the Tax Acts as expenditure of a revenue nature unless it is expenditure falling within subsection (7) below.

(2) In this section—

(a) any reference to a film is . . .[8] a reference to an original master negative of the film and its soundtrack (if any);
(b) any reference to a tape is a reference to an original master film tape or original master audio tape; and
(c) any reference to a disc is a reference to an original master film disc or original master audio disc;

and any reference to the acquisition of a film, tape or disc includes a reference to the acquisition of any description of rights in a film, tape or disc.

(3) Subject to the following provisions of this section, in computing the profits or gains accruing to any person from a trade or business which consists of or includes the exploitation of a film, tape or disc, expenditure which—

(a) is incurred on or after 10th March 1982 on the production or acquisition of a film, tape or disc, and
(b) is expenditure of a revenue nature (whether by virtue of subsection (1) above or otherwise),

shall be allocated to relevant periods in accordance with [subsections (4) to (4B)][3] below; and in this subsection and [subsections (4) to (4B)][3] below "relevant period" means a period for which the accounts of the trade or business concerned are made up or, if those accounts are not made up for any period, a period the profits or gains of which are taken into account in assessing the income of the trade or business for any chargeable period.

(4) [Subject to subsection (4A) below][4] the amount of expenditure falling within subsection (3) above which falls to be allocated to any relevant period shall be such as is just and reasonable, having regard to—

(a) the amount of that expenditure which remains unallocated at the beginning of that period;
(b) the proportion which the estimated value of the film, tape or disc which is realised in that period (whether by way of income or otherwise) bears to the aggregate of the value so realised and the estimated remaining value of the film, tape or disc at the end of that period; and
(c) the need to bring the whole of the expenditure falling within subsection (3) above into account over the time during which the value of the film, tape or disc is expected to be realised.

[(4A) In addition to any expenditure which is allocated to a relevant period in accordance with subsection (4) above, if a claim is made in that behalf not later than two years after the end of that period, there shall also be allocated to that period so much of the unallocated expenditure as is specified in the claim and does not exceed the difference between—

(a) the amount allocated to that period in accordance with subsection (4) above; and
(b) the value of the film, tape or disc which is realised in that period (whether by way of income or otherwise).][5]

[(4B) As respects any relevant period, 'the unallocated expenditure' referred to in subsection (4A) above is that expenditure falling within subsection (3) above—

(a) which does not fall to be allocated to that period in accordance with subsection (4) above; and
(b) which has not been allocated to any earlier relevant period in accordance with subsection (4) or subsection (4A) above.][5]

(5) Subsections (3) [to (4B)][3] above do not apply to the profits or gains of a trade in which the film, tape or disc concerned constitutes trading stock, as defined in section [100 (2) of the Taxes Act 1988][9].

(6) In a case where any expenditure on the production or acquisition of a film, tape or disc is expenditure to which subsection (1) above applies, sums received from the disposal of that film, tape or disc shall be regarded for the purposes of the Tax Acts as receipts of a revenue nature (if they would not be so regarded apart from this subsection); and the reference in this subsection to sums received from the disposal of any film, tape or disc shall be construed as including—

(a) sums received from the disposal of any interest or right in or over the film, tape or disc, including an interest or right created by the disposal; and
(b) insurance or compensation moneys and other moneys of a like nature which are derived from the film, tape or disc.

(7) The preceding provisions of this section do not apply to expenditure which is incurred

by any person on or before 31st March 1984 if it consists of the payment of sums payable under a contract entered into by him before 10th March 1982 [nor to expenditure which is incurred by any person . . .⁶ if it is incurred]¹⁻²—

(a) by a person who carries on a trade or business which consists of or includes the exploitation of films, tapes or discs; and

(b) on the production or acquisition of a film, tape or disc which is certified by the Secretary of State [under Schedule 1 to the Films Act 1985 as a qualifying film, tape or disc for the purposes of this section]⁷ and the value of which is expected to be realisable over a period of not less than two years.

(8) . . .⁸

(9) In this section "expenditure of a revenue nature" means expenditure which, if it were incurred in the course of a trade the profits or gains of which are chargeable to tax under Case I of Schedule D, would be taken into account for the purpose of computing the profits, gains or losses of the trade; and "receipts of a revenue nature" means receipts which, if they were receipts of such a trade, would be taken into account for that purpose.

[(10) Section 50 (4) of the Finance Act 1971 (construction of references to the date on which expenditure is incurred for the purposes of Chapter I of Part III of that Act) applies in relation to the preceding provisions of this section as though they were comprised in that Chapter.]¹.

Cross references.—See the Films Act 1985, ss. 7 (5), 8 (2) (c) (application of sub-s. (7) above to films etc. certified under sub-s. (7) (b) as originally enacted),
ss. 7 (6), 8 (2) (c) (exclusion by written notice of the modifications of this section made by the Films Act 1985, s. 6 where the contract for the production or acquisition of a master negative etc has been entered into before 23 July 1985),
Sch. 1 (application of that Schedule from 23 July 1985 for the purposes of this section).
Amendments.—¹⁻² Words in sub-s. (7) substituted and sub-s. (10) added by FA 1983, s. 32.
³ Words in sub-ss. (3), (5) substituted by FA 1984, s. 62 (1), (2), (4).
⁴ Words in sub-ss. (4), (8) inserted by FA 1984, s. 62 (1), (2), (6).
⁵ Sub-ss. (4A), (4B) inserted by FA 1984, s. 62 (1), (3).
⁶ Words in sub-s. (7) repealed by FA 1984, s. 62 (5) and Sch. 27, Pt. V.
⁷ Words in sub-s. (7) (b) substituted by the Films Act 1985, ss. 6 (2), 8 (2) (a) with effect from 23 July 1985.
⁸ Sub-s. (8) and words in sub-s. (2) (a) repealed by the Films Act 1985, ss. 6 (2) (b), 8 (2) (a), (b) and Sch. 2 with effect from 23 July 1985.
⁹ Words in sub-s. (5) substituted by TA 1988, Sch. 29, para. 32 Table.

73. Industrial buildings allowance: very small workshops

(1) Chapter I of Part I of the Capital Allowances Act 1968 (industrial buildings allowances) shall apply with the modifications specified in paragraphs 1 to 3 of Schedule 13 to the Finance Act 1980 in relation to capital expenditure on the construction of an industrial building to which this section applies if the expenditure is incurred after 26th March 1983 and before 27th March 1985.

(2) This section applies to an industrial building if the gross internal floor space of the whole building will not exceed 1,250 square feet.

(3) Subsections (3) to (6) of section 75 of the Finance Act 1980 (small workshops allowance) shall apply for the purposes of this section as they apply for the purposes of that section and accordingly—

(a) in subsection (3) the reference to subsection (2) of that section shall be construed as including a reference to subsection (2) of this section; and

(b) in subsections (4) and (5) the references to subsection (1) of that section shall be construed as including a reference to subsection (1) of this section.

(4) The Tax Acts shall have effect as if this section were contained in Chapter I of Part I of the said Act of 1968.

Cross references.—See FA 1983, s. 31 (application of this section in relation to capital expenditure incurred in converting large buildings into small workshops satisfying sub-s. (2) above).

74. Industrial buildings allowance: licensees

(2) Section 6 of that Act (method of making allowances and charges) shall apply where the building or structure in question is used by a licensee of the person entitled to the relevant interest as if that interest were subject to a lease.

(4) Subsections (1) and (3) above shall apply in relation to licences granted on or after 10th March 1982.

Notes.—Sub-ss. (1), (3) insert CAA 1968, s. 1 (1A) and s. 7 (3A).

76. Allowances for dwelling-houses let on assured tenancies

(1) The provisions of Schedule 12 to this Act shall have effect to provide for reliefs in respect of expenditure incurred on the construction of buildings consisting of or including dwelling-houses let on assured and certain other tenancies.

(2) Schedule 12 to this Act has effect only where the expenditure concerned is incurred on or after 10th March 1982 and before 1st April [1992][1] or is deemed to have been so incurred by virtue of paragraph 8 of that Schedule.

Amendments.—[1] Year in sub-s. (2) substituted by F (No. 2) A 1987, s. 72 (1).

79. Capital allowances and stock relief

(1) This section applies in any case where a person is entitled to an allowance or relief for a year of assessment and—

(*a*) he and the inspector have come to an agreement, in writing, as to the extent to which the allowance or relief is to be given effect in that year (whether by deduction from profits or gains or by discharge or repayment of tax, or both); and

(*b*) no assessment giving effect to the allowance or relief is made for that year.

(2) In a case to which this section applies the allowance or relief shall be taken to have been given effect in the year of assessment in question, as if an assessment had been made, to the extent set out in the agreement mentioned in subsection (1) above.

(3) In this section—

"allowance" means an allowance to which section 70 or 71 of the Capital Allowances Act 1968 applies (income tax allowances in taxing a trade); and

"relief" means a relief to which Part II of Schedule 9 to the Finance Act 1981 applies (income tax: stock relief).

(4) This section has effect in relation to agreements made on or after 6th April 1982.

CHAPTER III

CAPITAL GAINS

86. Indexation allowance on certain disposals

(1) This section applies to any disposal of an asset—

(a) which occurs on or after 6th April 1982, or, if the disposal is by a company, on or after 1st April 1982; *and*
(b) ...[1]
(c) ...[1]

(2) In relation to a disposal to which this section applies—

[(a) "the unindexed gain or loss" means the amount of the gain or loss on the disposal computed in accordance with Chapter II of Part II of the Capital Gains Tax Act 1979 and, if there is neither a gain nor a loss on the disposal as so computed, the unindexed gain or loss shall be nil][2]; and
(b) "relevant allowable expenditure" means, subject to subsection (3) below, any sum which, in the computation of the [unindexed gain or loss][3], was taken into account by virtue of paragraph (a) or paragraph (b) of subsection (1) of section 32 of that Act.

(3) In determining what sum (if any) was taken into account as mentioned in subsection (2) (b) above, account shall be taken of any provision of any enactment which, for the purpose of the computation under the said Chapter II, increases, excludes or reduces the whole or any part of any item of expenditure falling within the said section 32 or provides for it to be written-down.

(4) The following provisions of this Chapter have effect to provide for an allowance (in those provisions referred to as "the indexation allowance") which, on a disposal to which this section applies, is to be [set against the unindexed gain or, as the case may be, added to the unindexed loss so as to give the gain or loss for the purposes of the Capital Gains Tax Act 1979 as follows,—

(a) if there is an unindexed gain, the indexation allowance shall be deducted from the gain and, if the allowance exceeds the unindexed gain, the excess shall constitute a loss;
(b) if there is an unindexed loss, the indexation allowance shall be added to it so as to increase the loss; and
(c) if the unindexed gain or loss is nil, there shall be a loss equal to the indexation allowance][4]; ...

(5) ...[1]

(6) The provisions of Schedule 13 to this Act have effect for supplementing this section and the following provisions of this Chapter and the preceding provisions of this section have effect subject to the provisions of that Schedule.

Notes.—Words omitted from sub-s. (4) amend CGTA 1979, s. 28 (1).
Cross references.—See FA 1983, Sch. 6, para. 3 (3), (6) (new rules for pooling of securities of the same class; in its application to a holding (as defined in para. 3 (3)), sub-s. (1) above to have effect as if the condition in para. (b) of that subsection were always fulfilled),
Sch. 6, para. 5 (1) (new provisions for calculating indexation allowance on a disposal to which this section applies and in respect of which an election has been made for pooling),
Sch. 6, para. 7 (4) (c) (disposal of shares out of pooled holding resulting in a reduction in expenditure of unindexed pool; proportionate reduction in the expenditure of indexed pool);
FA 1985, Sch. 19, paras. 22, 23 (this section to apply with necessary modifications to premium trust funds of underwriters);
FA 1988, s. 113 (in relation to disposals after 3 July 1987, this section not to apply in the case of building society shares or registered industrial and provident society shares).
Amendments.—[1] Sub-ss. (1) (b), (c), (5) repealed by FA 1985, Sch. 19, para. 1 (1), (4) and Sch. 27, Pt. VII with respect to disposals of assets after 5 April 1985 or 31 March 1985 (in the case of disposals by companies) except that with respect to disposals of certain securities the repeal has effect from 28 February 1986 or 2 July 1986; see FA 1985, s. 68 (1), (2) and Sch. 27, Pt. VII, para. 4.
[2] Sub-s. (2) (a) substituted by FA 1985, Sch. 19, para. 1 with respect to disposals of assets after 5 April 1985 or 31 March 1985 (in the case of disposals by companies) or in the case of certain securities with respect to their disposals after 27 February 1986; see FA 1985, s. 68 (1), (2).
[3] Words in sub-s. (2) (b) substituted by *ibid.*
[4] Words in sub-s. (4) substituted by *ibid.*

87. Calculation of indexation allowance

(1) The provisions of this section have effect for the purpose of computing the indexation allowance on a disposal to which section 86 above applies.

(2) The indexation allowance is the aggregate of the indexed rise in each item of relevant allowable expenditure; and, in relation to any such item of expenditure, the indexed rise is a sum produced by multiplying the amount of that item by a figure expressed as a decimal and determined, subject to subsections (3) and (4) below, by the formula $(RD-RI) \div RI$ where—

> RD is the retail prices index for the month in which the disposal occurs; and
> RI is the retail prices index for March 1982 or the month . . .[1] in which the expenditure was incurred, whichever is the later.

(3) If, in relation to any item of expenditure,—

> [(*a*) the expenditure is attributable to the acquisition of relevant securities, within the meaning of section 88 below, which are disposed of within the period of ten days beginning on the day on which the expenditure was incurred, or][2]
> (*b*) RD, as defined in subsection (2) above, is equal to or less than RI, as so defined,

the indexed rise in that item is nil.

(4) If, in relation to any item of expenditure, the figure determined in accordance with the formula in subsection (2) above would, apart from this subsection, be a figure having more than three decimal places, it shall be rounded to the nearest third decimal place.

(5) For the purposes of this section—

> (*a*) relevant allowable expenditure falling within paragraph (*a*) of subsection (1) of section 32 of the Capital Gains Tax Act 1979 shall be assumed to have been incurred at the time when the asset in question was acquired or provided; and
> (*b*) relevant allowable expenditure falling within paragraph (*b*) of that subsection shall be assumed to have been incurred at the time when that expenditure became due and payable.

Cross references.—See FA 1983, Sch. 6, para. 5 (1) (new provisions in place of the provisions of this section for calculating indexation allowance on a disposal to which s. 86 of this Act applies and in respect of which an election has been made for pooling),
Sch. 6, para. 6 (6) (sub-s. (5) above (with FA 1982, Sch. 13) to apply for the purpose of computing indexation allowance in relation to pooled securities);
FA 1985, s. 68 (3) and Sch. 19, para. 7 (3) (relevant allowable expenditure attributable to securities in a 1982 holding, as defined in para. 6 (1) of that Schedule, to be deemed to be expenditure falling within sub-s. (5) (*a*) above),
s. 68 (3) and Sch. 19, para. 11 (1) (new provisions to apply in place of this section for computing indexation allowance in relation to disposals of new holdings of securities as defined in s. 68 (7) and Sch. 19, para. 9 (3).
s. 68 (3), (9) and Sch. 19, para 13 (2) (determination of the indexed pool of expenditure in relation to new holdings of securities),
s. 68 (3), (9) and Sch. 19, para. 18 (4) (securities acquired and disposed of within ten days; treatment of such securities for the purposes of sub-s. (3) above),
Sch. 19, paras. 22, 23 (this section to apply with necessary modifications to premium trust funds of underwriters);
FA 1988, s. 113 (in relation to disposals after 3 July 1987, this section not to apply in the case of building society shares or registered industrial and provident society shares).
Amendments.—[1] Words in the definition of "RI" in sub-s. (2) repealed by FA 1985, Sch. 19, para. 2 (1) and Sch. 27, Pt. VII with respect to disposals of assets after 5 April 1985 or 31 March 1985 (in the case of disposals by companies) except that with respect to disposals of certain securities the repeal has effect from 28 February 1986 or 2 July 1986; see FA 1985, s. 68 (1), (2) and Sch. 27, Pt. VII, para. 4.
[2] Sub-s. (3) (*a*) substituted by FA 1985, Sch. 19, para. 2 (2) with respect to disposals of assets after 5 April 1985 or 31 March 1985 (in the case of disposals by companies) or in the case of certain securities with respect to their disposals after 27 February 1986; see FA 1985, s. 68 (1), (2).

88. Identification of securities etc. disposed of: general rules

(1) With respect to [relevant securities][2] held on, or acquired on or after, 6th April 1982 or, in the case of a company, 1st April 1982 the provisions of this section (other than subsection (8)) . . .[1] have effect in place of sections 65 and 66 of the Capital Gains Tax Act 1979 (pooling and other rules for identification of securities); and, in taking account of those provisions,—

> (*a*) this section, . . .[1] and Part II of Schedule 13 shall have effect subject to section 58 of the Finance (No. 2) Act 1975 (disposal of shares and securities within prescribed period of acquisition); *and*
> (*b*) . . .[1]

(2) Where a person disposes of [relevant securities][2], the securities disposed of shall be identified in accordance with the rules contained in this section with the securities of the

same class acquired by him which could be comprised in that disposal, and shall be so identified notwithstanding that they are otherwise identified by the disposal or by a transfer or delivery giving effect to it (but so that where a person disposes of securities in one capacity, they shall not be identified with securities which he holds or can dispose of only in some other capacity).

(3) [Relevant securities]² disposed of on an earlier date shall be identified before securities disposed of on a later date, and the identification of the securities first disposed of shall accordingly determine the securities which could be comprised in the later disposal.

(4) [Relevant securities]² disposed of for transfer or delivery on a particular date or in a particular period—

(a) shall not be identified with securities acquired for transfer or delivery on a later date or in a later period; and
(b) shall be identified with securities acquired for transfer or delivery on or before that date or in or before that period, but on or after the date of the disposal, rather than with securities not so acquired.

(5) The [relevant securities]² disposed of shall be identified—

(a) with securities acquired within the twelve months preceding the disposal rather than with securities not so acquired, and with securities so acquired on an earlier date rather than with securities so acquired on a later date; and
(b) subject to paragraph (a) above, with securities acquired on a later date rather than with securities acquired on an earlier date; and
(c) with securities acquired at different times on any one day in as nearly as may be equal proportions.

[(5A) ...]¹

(6) The rules contained in the preceding subsections shall have priority according to the order in which they are so contained.

(7) Notwithstanding anything in subsections (3) to (5) above, where, under arrangements designed to postpone the transfer or delivery of [relevant securities]² disposed of, a person by a single bargain acquires securities for transfer or delivery on a particular date or in a particular period and disposes of them for transfer or delivery on a later date or in a later period, then—

(a) the securities disposed of by that bargain shall be identified with the securities thereby acquired; and
(b) securities previously disposed of which, but for the operation of paragraph (a) above in relation to acquisitions for transfer or delivery on the earlier date or in the earlier period, would have been identified with the securities acquired by that bargain—

(i) shall, subject to subsection (3) above, be identified with any available securities acquired for such transfer or delivery (that is to say, any securities so acquired other than securities to which paragraph (a) above applies and other than securities with which securities disposed of for such transfer or delivery would be identified apart from this subsection); and
(ii) in so far as they cannot be so identified shall be treated as disposed of for transfer or delivery on the later date, or in the later period, mentioned above.

(8) The provisions of Part II of Schedule 13 to this Act have effect with respect to [relevant securities]² acquired before 6th April 1982 or, in the case of a company, before 1st April 1982.

(9) In this section and Schedule 13 to this Act ["relevant securities" means—

(a) securities, within the meaning of [section 710 of the Taxes Act 1988]⁴;
(b) deep discount securities, within the meaning of [Schedule 4 to that Act]⁴; and
(c) securities which are, or have at any time been, material interests in a non-qualifying offshore fund, within the meaning of Chapter [V of Part XVII of the Taxes Act 1988]⁴]³;

and shares or securities of a company shall not be treated for the purposes of this section and that Schedule as being of the same class unless they are so treated by the practice of The Stock Exchange or would be so treated if dealt with on The Stock Exchange.

Cross references.—See CGTA 1979, s. 149C (4) (this section not to apply to shares in respect of which business expansion scheme relief has been given and not withdrawn);
FA 1983, Sch. 6, para. 1 (2) (new provisions for pooling of securities defined in sub-s. (9) above),
Sch. 6, para. 4 (1) (limited application of this section in respect of pooled securities).

FA 1985, Sch. 19, paras. 22, 23 (this section to apply with necessary modifications to premium trust funds of underwriters);
TA 1988, Sch. 4, para. 12 (extension of this section for the identification of deep discount securities disposed of);
FA 1989, Sch. 11, para. 19 (extension of the identification rules in this section to deep gain securities).

Amendments.—[1] Sub-s. (1) (*b*), words in sub-s. (1), sub-s. (5A) (which was inserted by FA 1983, s. 34 (2)) repealed by FA 1985, Sch. 19, para. 3 (2) and Sch. 27, Pt. VII with respect to disposals after 5 April 1985 or 31 March 1985 (in the case of disposals by companies) except that with respect to disposals of certain securities it applies with respect to disposals after 27 February 1986 or 1 July 1986; see FA 1985, s. 68 (1), (2) and Sch. 27, Pt. VII, para. 4.

[2] Words in sub-ss. (1)–(5), (7), (8) substituted by FA 1985, Sch. 19, para. 3 (1) with respect to disposals after 5 April 1985 or 31 March 1985 (in the case of disposals by companies) except that with respect to disposals of certain securities it applies with respect to disposals after 27 February 1986 or 1 July 1986; see FA 1985, s. 68 (1), (2) and Sch. 27, Pt. VII, para. 4.

[3] Words in sub-s. (9) substituted by FA 1985, Sch. 19, para. 3 (3) with respect to disposals after 5 April 1985 or 31 March 1985 (in the case of disposals by companies) except that with respect to disposals of certain securities it applies with respect to disposals after 27 February 1986 or 1 July 1986; see FA 1985, s. 68 (1), (2) and Sch. 27, Pt. VII, para. 4.

[4] Words in sub-s. (9) (*a*), (*b*), (*c*) substituted by TA 1988, Sch. 29, para. 32 Table.

PART VI
OIL TAXATION
CHAPTER I
GENERAL

137. Expenditure met by regional development grants to be disregarded for certain purposes

(2) Subject to subsection (3) below, in any case where, by virtue of the said paragraph 8 as amended by subsection (1) above, expenditure which has been or is to be met by a regional development grant is not to be regarded for any of the purposes of Part I of the principal Act as having been incurred by any person, that particular grant shall be regarded as not falling within the reference to a regional development grant in—

   (a) section 84 (1) of the Capital Allowances Act 1968 (treatment of subsidised expenditure for the purposes of the main reliefs for capital expenditure); or
   (b) section 95(6) of that Act (treatment of subsidised expenditure for the purposes of allowances relevant to scientific research).

(3) If, in a case falling within subsection (2) above, only a proportion of the expenditure which has been or is to be met by a regional development grant is expenditure which, if it were not so met, would be allowable under section 3 or section 4 of the principal Act, only a corresponding proportion of the grant shall be regarded as not falling within the reference to regional development grant in the provisions referred to in subsection (2) above.

(4)–(5) . . .[2]

(6) In this section "regional development grant" means a grant made [under the provisions of Part II of the Industrial Development Act 1982 or Part I][1] of the Industry Act 1972 or such grant made under an enactment of the Parliament of Northern Ireland or Measure of the Northern Ireland Assembly as has been or may be declared by the Treasury under section 84 or section 95 of the Capital Allowances Act 1968 to correspond to a grant made under [those provisions][1].

(7) This section applies in any case where—

   (a) the expenditure to which the regional development grant relates is incurred after 9th March 1982; and
   (b) the regional development grant concerned is paid after that date.

Notes.—The principal Act referred to in this section is the Oil Taxation Act 1975.
Sub-s. (1) amends the Oil Taxation Act 1975, Sch. 3, para. 8 (1).
Cross references.—See TA 1988, s. 495 (3) (certain expenditure met by regional development grants not to be disregarded notwithstanding the provisions of this section).
Amendments.—[1] Words in sub-s. (6) substituted by the Industrial Development Act 1982, Sch. 2, Pt. II, para. 18 with effect from 28 January 1983.
[2] Sub-ss. (4), (5) repealed by TA 1988, Sch. 31.

PART VII
MISCELLANEOUS AND SUPPLEMENTARY

145. Certificates of tax deposit: extension of interest period

For the purposes of certificates of tax deposit issued by the Treasury under section 12 of the National Loans Act 1968 on terms published before 31st July 1980, the date which is the due date in relation to—

(a) income tax charged at a rate other than the basic rate, and
(b) capital gains tax,

is by virtue of this section postponed, with respect to the year 1980–81 and any subsequent year of assessment, from the date specified in the prospectuses concerned to 1st December following the end of the year of assessment for which the tax is payable.

148. Transfer of assets of Hops Marketing Board

(1) For the purposes of the Capital Gains Tax Act 1979, the transfer by virtue of the Hops Marketing Act 1982 of any asset from the Hops Marketing Board to any person or persons specified as mentioned in section 2 (1) of that Act (in this section referred to as "the transferee") shall be deemd to be for a consideration such that no gain or loss accrues to the Board; and Schedule 5 to the Capital Gains Tax Act 1979 shall have effect in relation to any asset so transferred as if the acquisition or provision of it by the Board had been the acquisition or provision of it by the transferee.

(2) Any transfer by virtue of the Hops Marketing Act 1982 of any interest in land from the Hops Marketing Board to the transferee shall be deemed to be a disposal to which subsection (1) of section 20 of the Development Land Tax Act 1976 (groups of companies) applies.

Cross references.—See FA 1985, s. 68 (7) (modification of indexation allowance with respect to disposals of assets after 1 April 1985),
s. 68 (7A) (c) (re-basing of indexation allowance to 1982 in relation to disposals after 5 April 1988);
FA 1988, Sch. 8, para. 1 (3) (c) (re-basing of indexation allowance to 1982 in relation to unindexed gains and losses on disposals after 5 April 1988 of assets held on 31 March 1982).

156. Dissolution of Board of Referees

(1) The Board of Referees mentioned in section 26 of the Capital Allowances Act 1968 is hereby dissolved and the functions of the Board transferred to the tribunal established under section 463 of the Taxes Act.

(2) Schedule 21 to this Act shall have effect for the purpose of making provision consequential on this section.

157. Short title, interpretation, construction and repeals

(1) This Act may be cited as the Finance Act 1982.

[(2) In this Act—

(a) "the Taxes Act 1970" means the Income and Corporation Taxes Act 1970; and
(b) "the Taxes Act 1988" means the Income and Corporation Taxes Act 1988][1].

(3) Part III of this Act, so far as it relates to income tax, shall be construed as one with the Income Tax Acts, so far as it relates to corporation tax, shall be construed as one with the Corporation Tax Acts and, so far as it relates to capital gains tax shall be construed as one with the Capital Gains Tax Act 1979.

(4) ...

(5) ...

(6) The enactments and Orders mentioned in Schedule 22 to this Act (which include spent enactments) are hereby repealed to the extent specified in the third column of that Schedule, but subject to any provision at the end of any part of that Schedule.

(7) The provisions of Part XI of Schedule 22 to this Act, except in so far as they relate to the Wellington Museum Act 1947 and the Finance (No. 2) Act 1975, shall have effect in substitution for the provisions of Section B of Part VI of Schedule 20 to the Finance Act

1980 and, accordingly, that Section shall be deemed not to have taken effect at the beginning of the year 1982–83.

Note.—Sub-ss. (4), (5) are not relevant to this work.
Amendments.—[1] Sub-s. (2) substituted by TA 1988, Sch. 29, para. 32 Table.

SCHEDULE 11

Section 70

ALLOWANCES FOR ASSETS LEASED OUTSIDE THE UNITED KINGDOM

Interpretation

1. In this Schedule "the principal section" means section 70 of this Act.

Separate pooling of writing-down allowances

2. In any case where section 44 of the Finance Act 1971 has effect as mentioned in paragraphs (*a*) to (*e*) of subsection (2) of the principal section, section 44 shall apply separately with respect to expenditure falling within subsection (1) of the principal section and with respect to other expenditure.

Recovery of excess relief

3.—(1) In relation to expenditure falling within subsection (1) of the principal section, section 66 of the Finance Act 1980 shall apply subject to the following modifications:—

(*a*) any reference in that section to machinery or plant (or a new ship) being used otherwise than for a qualifying purpose shall be construed as a reference to its being used as mentioned in paragraphs (*a*) and (*b*) of subsection (3) of the principal section; and

(*b*) any reference in section 66 to a first-year allowance shall be construed as including a reference to a writing-down allowance of an amount determined without regard to subsection (2) of the principal section; and

(*c*) the reference in subsection (1) (*b*) of section 66 to section 44 of the Finance Act 1971, as it has effect in accordance with section 65 of the Finance Act 1980, shall be construed as including a reference to section 44 as it has effect as mentioned in paragraphs (*b*) to (*e*) of subsection (2) of the principal section; and

(*d*) in determining the amount of any excess relief under section 66 in a case where that section had previously applied, account shall be taken of the relief already recovered.

(2) If subsection (7) of section 66 of the Finance Act 1980 has already applied in relation to expenditure on a new ship before subsection (1) of the principal section applied to that expenditure, then, on the subsequent application of the said subsection (7) by virtue of sub-paragraph (1) (*a*) above, paragraph (*b*) of that subsection shall not again apply.

Cross references.—See FA 1985, s. 58 (3) (*b*) (application of this paragraph with modifications in relation to the extension of first-year allowances to ships which are not new).
Amendments.—This paragraph repealed by FA 1986, s. 57 (2), (4) (*b*), (7) (*a*) and Sch. 16, para. 6 in respect of "new expenditure" (i.e. expenditure incurred after 31 March 1986, subject to qualifications in s. 57 (2), (3)).

4.—(1) Subject to sub-paragraph (3) below, the provisions of sub-paragraph (2) below apply where—

(*a*) by virtue of subsection (5) of the principal section any amount falls to be treated as if it were a balancing charge, and

(*b*) the person on whom the balancing charge is, by virtue of that subsection, to be made acquired the machinery or plant in question as a result of a transaction which was, or a series of transactions each of which was, between connected persons, and

(*c*) a first-year allowance, a balancing allowance, or a writing-down allowance in respect of expenditure on the provision of that machinery or plant has been made to any of those persons.

(2) Where this sub-paragraph applies—

(*a*) subsection (5) of the principal section shall have effect as if it referred to the allowances specified in sub-paragraph (1) (*c*) above; and

(*b*) for the purposes of that subsection any consideration paid or received on a disposal of the machinery or plant between connected persons shall be disregarded; and

(*c*) if a balancing allowance or balancing charge is made in respect of the machinery or plant, there shall be made such adjustments of the relief falling to be taken into account by virtue of paragraph (*a*) above as are just and reasonable in the circumstances.

(3) Sub-paragraph (2) above does not apply where section [113 (2), 114 (1) or [343 (2)]² of the Taxes Act 1988]¹ or sub-paragraph (*a*) or sub-paragraph (*b*) of paragraph 13 of Schedule 8 to the Finance Act 1971 (succession to trades) applied on the occasion of the transaction or transactions referred to in sub-paragraph (1) (*b*).

(4) Section [839 of the Taxes Act 1988]¹ (connected persons) applies for the purposes of this paragraph.

Amendments.—¹ Words in sub-paras. (3), (4) substituted by TA 1988, Sch. 29, para. 32 Table.
² Number substituted by FA 1989, Sch. 13, para. 19.

Information

5.—*(1) The obligation to give notice by virtue of subsection (2) or subsection (3) of section 67 of the Finance Act 1980 where machinery or plant becomes used otherwise than for a qualifying purpose shall arise a second time where machinery or plant which has been used otherwise than for a qualifying purpose but not as mentioned in paragraphs (a) and (b) of subsection (3) of the principal section subsequently becomes used as mentioned in those paragraphs.*

(2) In the case of any expenditure in respect of which a first-year allowance has not been made but a writing-down allowance of an amount determined without regard to subsection (2) of the principal section has been or may be made, then—

(a) any reference in subsections (2), (3) and (4) of section 67 of the Finance Act 1980 to a first-year allowance shall be construed as a reference to a writing-down allowance of an amount so determined; and
(b) any reference in those subsections to the use of machinery or plant otherwise than for a qualifying purpose shall be construed as a reference to the use of machinery or plant as mentioned in paragraphs (a) and (b) of subsection (3) of the principal section.

Amendments.—This paragraph repealed by FA 1986, s. 57 (4) (*b*), (7) (*a*) and Sch. 16, para. 6 in respect of "new expenditure" (i.e. expenditure incurred after 31 March 1986, subject to qualifications in s. 57 (2), (3)).

Joint lessees

6.—*(1) The provisions of this paragraph have effect where machinery or plant is leased to two or more persons jointly and at least one of the joint lessees is a person falling within paragraphs (a) and (b) of subsection (1) of the principal section (in this paragraph referred to as a "non-resident lessee").*

(2) Where this paragraph applies, any reference in section 68 of the Finance Act 1980 to the requisite period shall be construed in accordance with subsection (3) of the principal section, whether or not there is also a joint lessee who is not a non-resident lessee.

(3) If the circumstances are such that no first-year allowance has been or may be made in respect of any part of the expenditure on the provision of the machinery or plant in question, the principal section shall apply in relation to that expenditure as if all the joint lessees were non-resident lessees.

(4) Where, by virtue of subsection (3), subsection (4) or subsection (5) of section 68 of the Finance Act 1980 (cases of joint lessees where first-year allowances may be or have been made) section 44 of the Finance Act 1971 has effect (directly or through the operation of section 66 of the Finance Act 1980) in relation to the whole or any part of the expenditure on the machinery or plant in question, it shall have effect, in accordance with subsection (2) of the principal section, as if that expenditure were expenditure falling within subsection (1) of that section.

Amendments.—This paragraph repealed by FA 1986, s. 57 (4) (*b*), (7) (*a*) and Sch. 16, para. 6 in respect of "new expenditure" (i.e. expenditure incurred after 31 March 1986, subject to qualifications in s. 57 (2), (3)).

SCHEDULE 12

Section 76

CAPITAL ALLOWANCES FOR DWELLING-HOUSES LET ON ASSURED TENANCIES

Construction.—FA 1984, Sch. 12, paras. 3 (1), (2), 7 to be construed as if contained in this Schedule; see FA 1984, Sch. 12, paras. 3 (3), 7 (6) with certain exception as regards the application of para. 8 (1) (*b*).
Cross references.—See FA 1984, Sch. 12, paras. 7, 8, 9 (spreading of capital expenditure incurred under certain contracts entered into after 13 March 1984);
FA 1985, s. 56 (1) (*d*), (6), (8) (new rules to determine when capital expenditure is to be taken to be incurred for the purposes of this Schedule with respect to any chargeable period or its basis period ending after 17 December 1984);
F (No. 2) A 1987, s. 72 (2), (3) (extension of time for claiming initial allowance under this Schedule);
FA 1988, s. 95 (transitional provisions to extend the application of this Schedule after the coming into effect of the Housing Act 1988, Pt. I which will result in this Schedule ceasing to have effect);
FA 1989, Sch. 13, para. 28 (1), (4) (*e*), (6) (exclusion of double allowances; where an allowance is made under this Schedule, no allowance to be made under any other legislation in relation to any chargeable period or its basis period ending after 26 July 1989.

Initial allowances

1.—*(1) Subject to the provisions of this Schedule, where an approved body incurs capital expenditure on the construction of a building which is to be or to include a qualifying dwelling-house, then, for the chargeable period related to the incurring of that expenditure an allowance (in this Schedule referred to as an "initial allowance") shall be made to that body in respect of each qualifying dwelling-house to be comprised in the building.*

(2) An initial allowance in respect of a qualifying dwelling-house shall be of an amount equal to [. . .]¹ of the capital expenditure appropriate to that dwelling-house.

(3) No initial allowance shall be made in respect of any expenditure if, when the dwelling-house to which it relates comes to be used, it is not a qualifying dwelling-house; and where an initial allowance has been granted in respect of any expenditure otherwise than in accordance with the provisions of this paragraph, all such assessments shall be made as are necessary to secure that effect is given to those provisions.

(4) For the purposes of this Schedule, the capital expenditure appropriate to a dwelling-house shall be determined as follows:—

(a) if the building concerned consists of a single qualifying dwelling-house, then, subject to the relevant limit, the whole of the capital expenditure referred to in sub-paragraph (1) above is appropriate to that dwelling-house; and
(b) in the case of a dwelling-house which forms part of a building, the capital expenditure appropriate to it is, subject to the relevant limit, the aggregate of—

(i) that proportion of the capital expenditure referred to in sub-paragraph (1) above which is properly attributable to the construction of that dwelling-house; and
(ii) where there are common parts of the building, such proportion of the capital expenditure on those common parts as it is just and reasonable to attribute to the dwelling-house and as does not exceed one-tenth of that proportion of the capital expenditure referred to in paragraph (i) above;

and in this Schedule "the relevant limit" means £60,000, if the dwelling-house is in Greater London, and £40,000 if it is elsewhere.

(5) In sub-paragraph (4) above "common parts", in relation to a building, means common parts of the building which—

(a) are not intended to be in separate occupation (whether for domestic, commercial or other purposes); and
(b) are intended to be of benefit to some or all of the qualifying dwelling-houses included in the building.

and the capital expenditure on any such parts of the building is so much of the expenditure referred to in sub-paragraph (1) above as it is just and reasonable to attribute to those parts.

Note.—This paragraph ceases to apply in respect of expenditure incurred after 31 March 1986; see FA 1984, Sch. 12, para. 3 (1).
Amendments.—[1] The fraction in sub-para. (2) is "one quarter" with respect to capital expenditure incurred after 31 March 1985 and before 1 April 1986. The fraction is "one half" for expenditure after 13 March 1984 and before 1 April 1985; see FA 1984, Sch. 12, paras. 1 (1), 3 (1) (*a*).

The fraction is "three-quarters" for expenditure under certain contracts entered into before 14 March 1984; see FA 1984, Sch. 12, para. 3 (2).
It is "three-quarters" also for expenditure on certain projects in development areas (and in Northern Ireland) where a written offer of financial assistance was made between 1 April 1980 and 13 March 1984 (both dates inclusive), see FA 1984, Sch. 12, para. 4.
The initial allowance is abolished in respect of expenditure incurred after 31 March 1986; see FA 1984, Sch. 12, para. 3 (1).
For the spreading of capital expenditure incurred under certain contracts entered into after 13 March 1984, see FA 1984, Sch. 12, paras. 7, 8, 9.

Writing-down allowances

2.—(1) Subject to the provisions of this Schedule, where—

(*a*) an approved body or a body which has been an approved body is, at the end of a chargeable period or its basis period, entitled to an interest in a building, and

(*b*) at the end of that chargeable period or its basis period, the building is or includes a qualifying dwelling-house or two or more qualifying dwelling-houses, and

(*c*) that interest is the relevant interest in relation to the capital expenditure incurred on the construction on that building,

an allowance (in this Schedule referred to as "a writing-down allowance") shall be made to that body for that chargeable period in respect of the dwelling-house or, as the case may be, each dwelling-house falling within paragraph (*b*) above.

(2) The writing-down allowance in respect of a dwelling-house shall be equal to one twenty-fifth of the capital expenditure which is appropriate to that dwelling-house, except that for a chargeable period of less than a year that fraction shall be proportionately reduced.

(3) If, in the case of a building which is or includes a qualifying dwelling-house—

(*a*) the interest which is the relevant interest in relation to any expenditure is sold, and

(*b*) the sale is an event to which paragraph 4 (1) below applies,

then (subject to any further adjustment under this sub-paragraph on a later sale) the writing-down allowance in respect of that dwelling-house for any chargeable period, if that chargeable period or its basis period ends after the time of the sale, shall be the residue, as defined in paragraph 7 (1) below, of that expenditure immediately after the sale, reduced in the proportion (if it is less than one) which the length of the chargeable period bears to the part unexpired at the date of the sale of the period of 25 years beginning with the time when the building was first used.

(4) Notwithstanding anything in the preceding provisions of this paragraph, in no case shall the amount of a writing-down allowance made to a body for any chargeable period in respect of any expenditure exceed what, apart from the writing-off falling to be made by reason of the making of that allowance, would be the residue of that expenditure at the end of that chargeable period of its basis period.

Qualifying dwelling-house

3.—(1) In this Schedule "qualifying dwelling-house" means, subject to the following provisions of this paragraph, a dwelling-house let on a tenancy which is for the time being an assured tenancy, within the meaning of section 56 of the Housing Act 1980.

(2) Without prejudice to section 57 of the Housing Act 1980 (by virtue of which certain tenancies continue to be treated as assured tenancies notwithstanding that the landlord has ceased to be an approved body by reason of a variation in the description of bodies for the time being approved) a dwelling-house which has been a qualifying dwelling-house by virtue of sub-paragraph (1) above shall be regarded as a qualifying dwelling-house at any time when—

(*a*) it is for the time being subject to regulated tenancy or a housing association tenancy; and

(*b*) the landlord under that tenancy either is an approved body or was an approved body but has ceased to be such for any reason.

(3) Notwithstanding that a dwelling-house is let as mentioned in sub-paragraph (1) or sub-paragraph (2) above, it is not a qualifying dwelling-house for the purposes of this Schedule—

(*a*) unless the landlord [is a company and either][1] is for the time being entitled to the relevant interest in the dwelling-house or is the person who incurred the capital expenditure on the construction of the building in which the dwelling-house is comprised; or

(b) if the landlord is a housing association which is approved for the purposes of section [488 of the Taxes Act 1988][3] (co-operative housing associations) or is a self-build society, within the meaning of [the Housing Associations Act 1985][2]; or

(c) if the landlord and the tenant are connected persons; or

(d) if the tenant is a director of a company which is or is connected with the landlord; or

(e) if the landlord is a close company and the tenant is, for the purposes of [Part XI of the Taxes Act 1988][3], a participator in that company or an associate of such a participator; or

(f) if the tenancy is entered into as part of an arrangement between the landlords (or owners) of different dwelling houses under which one landlord takes a person as a tenant in circumstances where, if that person was the tenant of a dwelling-house let by the other landlord, that dwelling-house would not be a qualifying dwelling-house by virtue of any of paragraphs (c) to (e) above;

and section [839 of the Taxes Act 1988][3] (connected persons) applies for the purposes of this sub-paragraph.

(4) In this paragraph "regulated tenancy" and "housing association tenancy" have the same meaning as in the Rent Act 1977.

Cross references.—See F (No. 2) A 1983, s. 6 (6) (effective date in respect of **Amendment** [1]; see below).
Amendments.—[1] Words in sub-para. (3) (a) inserted by F (No. 2) A 1983, s. 6 (5) in relation to expenditure incurred after 4 May 1983; but see s. 6 (6) for further provisions as to the effective date.
[2] Words in sub-para. (3) (b) substituted by Housing (Consequential Provisions) Act 1985, Sch. 2, para. 54 (1), (3) with effect from 1 April 1986.
[3] Words in sub-para. 3 (3) substituted by TA 1988, Sch. 29, para. 32 Table.

Balancing allowances and balancing charges

4.—(1) Where any capital expenditure has been incurred on the construction of such a building as is referred to in paragraph 1 (1) above and any of the following events occur while a dwelling-house comprised in that building is a qualifying dwelling-house, that is to say—

(a) the relevant interest in the dwelling-house is sold, or

(b) that interest, being a leasehold interest, comes to an end otherwise than on the person entitled to it acquiring the interest which is reversionary on it, or

(c) the dwelling-house is demolished or destroyed or, without being demolished or destroyed, ceases altogether to be used,

then, subject to sub-paragraph (2) below, for the chargeable period related to that event an allowance or charge (in this Schedule referred to as a "balancing allowance" or a "balancing charge") shall, in the circumstances mentioned below, be made to or, as the case may be, on the person entitled to the relevant interest immediately before that event occurs.

(2) No balancing allowance or balancing charge shall be made by reason of any event occurring more than twenty-five years after the dwelling-house was first used.

(3) Subject to paragraph 5 below, where there are no sale, insurance, salvage or compensation moneys, or where the residue of the expenditure immediately before the event exceeds those moneys, a balancing allowance shall be made and the amount of it shall be the amount of that residue or, as the case may be, of the excess of that residue over those moneys.

(4) Subject to paragraph 5 below, if the sale, insurance, salvage or compensation moneys exceed the residue, if any, of the expenditure immediately before the event, a balancing charge shall be made, and the amount on which it is made shall be an equal amount to the excess or, where the residue is nil, to those moneys.

(5) The provisions of section 78 of and Schedule 7 to the Capital Allowances Act 1968 (special provisions as to certain sales) apply for the purposes of this Schedule as they apply in relation to the sale of an industrial building and as if—

(a) any reference in those provisions to Part I of that Act included a reference to this Schedule; and

(b) for the words in sub-paragraph (2) (a) of paragraph 4 of that Schedule following "the case of" there were substituted the words "a qualifying dwelling-house, the residue of the expenditure immediately before the sale, computed in accordance with paragraph 7 of Schedule 12 to the Finance Act 1982"; and

(c) for paragraphs (a) and (b) of sub-paragraph (3) of paragraph 4 of that Schedule [and the word "if" preceding them there were substituted the words "unless both][1] the seller and the buyer [at the time of the sale are or at any earlier time were][2] approved bodies, as defined in section 56 (4) of the Housing Act 1980".

(6) For the purposes of this Schedule, any transfer of the relevant interest in a dwelling-house, otherwise than by way of sale, shall be treated as a sale of that interest for a price other than that which it would have fetched if sold on the open market; and if Schedule 7 to the Capital Allowances Act 1968 would not, apart from this sub-paragraph have effect in relation to a transfer treated as a sale by virtue of this sub-paragraph, that Schedule shall have effect in relation to it as if it were a sale falling within paragraph 1 (1) (a) of that Schedule.

(7) Notwithstanding anything in the preceding provisions of this paragraph (or in paragraph 5 below), in no case shall the amount on which a balancing charge is made on any person in respect of any expenditure on the construction of a dwelling-house comprised in a building exceed the amount of the initial allowance, if any, made to him in respect of the expenditure appropriate to that dwelling-house together with the amount of any writing-down allowances made to him in respect of that expenditure for chargeable periods which end on or before the date of the event giving rise to the charge or of which the basis periods ends on or before that date.

Amendments.—[1] Words in sub-para. (5) (c) substituted by F (No. 2) A 1983, s. 6 (1), (2) and deemed always to have had effect except that the validity of an election made before 1 April 1983 under CAA 1968, Sch. 7, para. 4 is not affected.
[2] Words in sub-para. (5) (c) substituted by FA 1989, Sch. 13, para. 20 where the time of the sale is after 14 January 1989.

5.—(1) If, in a case where paragraph 4 (1) above applies, a dwelling-house which had been a qualifying dwelling-house was not, for any part of the relevant period, such a dwelling-house, the provisions of this paragraph shall have effect instead of sub-paragraphs (3) and (4) of paragraph 4 above.

(2) Subject to sub-paragraph (4) below, where the sale, insurance, salvage or compensation moneys are not less than the capital expenditure appropriate to the dwelling-house, a balancing charge shall be made and the amount on which it is made shall be an amount equal to the allowances given.

(3) Subject to sub-paragraph (4) below, where there are no sale, insurance, salvage or compensation moneys or where those moneys are less than the capital expenditure appropriate to the dwelling-house, then—

(a) if the adjusted net cost of the dwelling-house exceeds the allowances given, a balancing allowance shall be made and the amount thereof shall be an amount equal to the excess;
(b) if the adjusted net cost of the dwelling-house is less than the allowances given, a balancing charge shall be made and the amount on which it is made shall be an amount equal to the shortfall.

(4) No balancing charge or allowance shall be made under this paragraph on the occasion of a sale if, by virtue of paragraph 4 of Schedule 7 to the Capital Allowances Act 1968, as applied by paragraph 4 (5) above, the dwelling-house is treated as having been sold for a sum equal to the residue of the expenditure before sale.

(5) In this paragraph—

"the relevant period" means the period beginning at the time when the dwelling-house was first used for any purpose and ending with the event giving rise to the balancing allowance or balancing charge, except that where there has been a sale of the dwelling-house after that time and before that event the relevant period shall begin on the day following that sale or, if there has been more than one such sale, the last such sale;
"the capital expenditure" means—

(a) where paragraph (b) of this definition does not apply, the capital expenditure incurred (or by virtue of paragraph 8 below deemed to have been incurred) on the construction of the dwelling-house;
(b) where the person to or on whom the balancing allowance or balancing charge falls to be made is not the person who incurred (or is deemed to have incurred) that expenditure the residue of that expenditure at the beginning of the relevant period,

together (in either case) with any amount to be added to the residue of that expenditure by virtue of paragraph 7 (9) below;

"the allowances given" means the allowance referred to in paragraph 4 (7) above;
"the adjusted net cost" means—

(*a*) where there are no sale, insurance, salvage or compensation moneys, the capital expenditure appropriate to the dwelling-house; and
(*b*) where those moneys are less than that expenditure, the amount by which they are less,

reduced (in either case) in the proportion that the part or the aggregate of the parts, of the relevant period for which the building is a qualifying dwelling-house bears to the whole of that period.

6.—(1) If a dwelling-house ceases to be a qualifying dwelling-house otherwise than by reason of a sale or transfer of the relevant interest in it, that relevant interest shall be treated for the purposes of this Schedule as having been sold, at the time the dwelling-house ceases to be a qualifying dwelling-house, for the price which it would have fetched if sold in the open market.

(2) For the purposes of this Schedule, a dwelling-house shall not be regarded as ceasing altogether to be used by reason that it falls temporarily out of use, and where, immediately before any period of temporary disuse, it is a qualifying dwelling-house, it shall be regarded as continuing to be a qualifying dwelling-house during the period of temporary disuse.

Writing off of expenditure and meaning of "residue of expenditure"

7.—(1) Any expenditure appropriate to a qualifying dwelling-house shall be treated for the purposes of this Schedule as written off to the extent and as at the times specified below, the references in this Schedule to the residue of any such expenditure shall be construed accordingly.

(2) Where an initial allowance is made in respect of a qualifying dwelling-house, the amount of that allowance shall be treated as written off as at the time when the qualifying dwelling-house is first used.

(3) Where, by reason of the whole or part of a building being at any time a qualifying dwelling-house, a writing-down allowance is made for any chargeable period in respect of the expenditure, the amount of that allowance shall, subject to sub-paragraph (4) below, be treated as written off as at that time.

(4) Where, at a time which is material for the purposes of sub-paragraph (3) above, an event occurs which gives rise or may give rise to a balancing allowance or balancing charge, the amount directed to be treated as written off by that sub-paragraph as at that time shall be taken into account in computing the residue of that expenditure immediately before that event for the purpose of determining whether any and if so what balancing allowance or balancing charge is to be made.

(5) If, for any period or periods between the time when the whole or part of a building was first used for any purpose and the time at which the residue of the expenditure falls to be ascertained, the building or part, as the case may be, has not been a qualifying dwelling-house, there shall in ascertaining that residue be treated as having been previously written off in respect of the said period or periods amounts equal to writing-down allowances made for chargeable periods of a total length equal thereto at such rate or rates as would have been appropriate having regard to any sale on which paragraph 2 (3) above operated.

(6) Where, on the occasion of a sale, a balancing allowance is made in respect of the expenditure, there shall be treated as written off as at the time of the sale the amount by which the residue of the expenditure before the sale exceeds the net proceeds of the sale.

(7) Where, on the occasion of a sale, a balancing charge is made in respect of the expenditure, the residue of the expenditure shall be deemed for the purposes of this Schedule to be increased as at the time of the sale by the amount on which the charge is made.

(8) Where, on the occasion of a sale, a balancing charge is made under paragraph 5 (3) (*b*) above in respect of the expenditure and, apart from this sub-paragraph, the residue of the expenditure immediately after the sale would by virtue of sub-paragraph (7) above be deemed to be greater than the net proceeds of the sale, the residue immediately after the sale shall be deemed for the purposes of this Schedule to be equal to the net proceeds.

(9) Where a dwelling-house is demolished, and the demolition gives rise, or might give rise, to a balancing allowance or charge under this Schedule to or on the person incurring the cost of demolition, the net cost to him of the demolition (that is to say the excess, if any, of the cost of the demolition over any moneys received for the remains of the property) shall be

added for the purposes of this Schedule to the residue, immediately before the demolition, of the expenditure appropriate to the dwelling-house; and if this sub-paragraph applies to the net cost to a person of the demolition of any property, the cost or net cost shall not be treated, for the purpose of this Schedule, as expenditure incurred in respect of any other property by which that property is replaced.

Buildings bought unused

8.—(1) Subject to sub-paragraph (2) below, where expenditure is incurred on the construction of such a building as is referred to in paragraph 1 (1) above and the relevant interest in that building is sold before any of the dwelling-houses comprised in it are used,—

(*a*) the expenditure actually incurred on the construction of the building shall be left out of account for the purposes of the preceding provisions of this Schedule; but

(*b*) the person who buys that interest shall be deemed for those purposes to have incurred, on the date when the purchase price becomes payable, expenditure on the construction of the building equal to the expenditure actually incurred or to the net price paid by him for that interest, whichever is the less.

(2) Where the relevant interest in such a building as is referred to in paragraph 1 (1) above is sold more than once before any of the dwelling-houses comprised in it is used, the provisions of sub-paragraph (1) (*b*) above shall have effect only in relation to the last of those sales.

(3) Where the expenditure incurred on the construction of such a building as is referred to in paragraph 1 (1) above was incurred by a person carrying on a trade which consists, as to the whole or any part thereof, in the construction of buildings with a view to their sale, and, before any of the dwelling-houses comprised in it is used, he sells the relevant interest in the building in the course of that trade, or, as the case may be, of that part of that trade, paragraph (*b*) of sub-paragraph (1) above shall have effect subject to the following modifications—

(*a*) if that sale is the only sale of the relevant interest before any of the dwelling-house comprised in the building is used that paragraph shall have effect as if the words "the expenditure actually incurred or to" and the words "whichever is the less" were omitted, and

(*b*) in any other case, that paragraph shall have effect as if the reference to the expenditure actually incurred on the construction of the building were a reference to the price paid on that sale.

Manner of making allowances and charges

9.—(1) Any allowance under this Schedule shall be made to a person by way of discharge or repayment of tax and shall be available primarily against the following income, that is to say—

(*a*) income taxed under Schedule A in respect of any premises which at any time in the chargeable period consist of a qualifying dwelling-house; or

(*b*) income which is subject of a balancing charge under this Schedule.

(2) Effect shall be given to a balancing charge to be made on a person—

(*a*) if it is a charge to income tax, by making the charge under Case VI of Schedule D,

(*b*) if it is a charge to corporation tax, by treating the amount on which the charge is to be made as income of the description in sub-paragraph (1) (*a*) above.

Expenditure on repair of buildings

10. This Schedule shall have effect in relation to capital expenditure incurred by a person on repairs to any part of a building as if it were capital expenditure incurred by him in the construction for the first time of that part of the building.

Exclusion of double allowances

11. *No allowance shall be made under this Schedule in respect of any expenditure on a building or in respect of a dwelling-house if for the same or any other chargeable period an allowance is or can be made under any provisions of Chapter V of Part I of the Capital Allowances Act 1968 (agricultural land or buildings) in respect of that expenditure or that dwelling-house.*

Cross references.—See FA 1986, s. 56 (6) (c) (reference in this paragraph to CAA 1968, Pt. I, Ch. V to include a reference to FA 1986, Sch. 15 (new code of allowances and charges from 1 April 1986 in respect of capital expenditure on agricultural land and buildings)).
Amendments.—This paragraph superseded by FA 1989, Sch. 13, para. 28 (1)–(4) and repealed by FA 1989, Sch. 13, para. 28 (5) (e) and Sch. 17, Pt. VI in relation to any chargeable period or its basis period ending after 26 July 1989.

Holding over by lessee etc.

12.—(1) Where the relevant interest in relation to the capital expenditure incurred on the construction of a building is an interest under a lease, this Schedule shall have effect subject to the following provisions of this paragraph, and in those provisions—

(*a*) except in sub-paragraph (5), any reference to a lessor or lessee is a reference to the lessor or lessee under that lease; and
(*b*) in sub-paragraph (5) the reference to the first lease is a reference to that lease.

(2) Where, with the consent of the lessor, a lessee of any building remains in possession thereof after the termination of the lease without a new lease being granted to him, that lease shall be deemed for the purposes of this Schedule to continue so long as he remains in possession as aforesaid.

(3) Where, on the termination of a lease, a new lease is granted to the lessee in pursuance of an option available to him under the terms of the first lease, the provisions of this Schedule shall have effect as if the second lease were a continuation of the first lease.

(4) Where, on the termination of a lease, the lessor pays any sum to the lessee in respect of a building comprised in the lease, the provisions of this Schedule shall have effect as if the lease had come to an end by reason of the surrender thereof in consideration of the payment.

(5) Where, on the termination of a lease, another lease is granted to a different lessee and, in connection with the transaction, that lessee pays a sum to the person who was the lessee under the first lease, the provisions of this Schedule shall have effect as if both leases were the same lease and there had been an assignment thereof by the lessee under the first lease to the lessee under the second lease in consideration of the payment.

Meaning of "the relevant interest"

13.—(1) Subject to the provisions of this paragraph, in this Schedule "the relevant interest" means,—

(*a*) in relation to any expenditure incurred on the construction of a building, the interest in that building to which the person who incurred the expenditure was entitled when he incurred it; and
(*b*) in relation to a dwelling-house comprised in such a building as is referred to in paragraph 1 (1) above, that interest, to the extent that it subsists in the dwelling-house, which is the relevant interest in relation to the capital expenditure incurred on the construction of that building.

(2) Where, when it incurs expenditure on the construction of a building, a body is entitled to two or more interests in the building and one of those interests is an interest which is reversionary on all the others, that interest shall be the relevant interest for the purposes of this Schedule.

(3) An interest shall not cease to be the relevant interest for the purposes of this Schedule by reason of the creation of any lease or other interest to which that interest is subject, and where the relevant interest is a leasehold interest and is extinguished by reason of the surrender thereof or on the body entitled thereto acquiring the interest which is reversionary on it, the interest into which that leasehold interest merges shall thereupon become the relevant interest.

Application of provisions of Capital Allowances Act 1968

14. The following provisions of the Capital Allowances Act 1968, namely—

section 71 to 74 (income tax and corporation tax allowances and charges),
section 76 (companies not resident in the United Kingdom),
subsections (1) to (3) of section 77 (apportionment of consideration etc.),
section 81 (procedure on apportionments),
subsections (1) . . .[1] of section 82 (interpretation of certain references to expenditure etc.),

section 84 (subsidies),
section 86 (meaning of "sale, insurance, salvage or compensation moneys"), and
subsections (1), (3) and (6) of section 87 (interpretation of Part I),

shall apply for the purposes of this Schedule as they apply for the purposes of Part I of that Act and, accordingly, any reference in those provisions to Part I of that Act shall include a reference to this Schedule.

Amendments.—[1] Words repealed by FA 1985, Sch. 27, Pt. VI.

Interpretation

15.—(1) In this Schedule—

"approved body" has the meaning given by section 56 (4) of the Housing Act 1980;
"building", except where the context otherwise requires, includes part of a building;
"dwelling-house" except where the context otherwise requires, has the same meaning as in the Rent Act 1977;
"expenditure appropriate to a dwelling-house" has the meaning given by paragraph 1 (4) above; and
"qualifying dwelling-house" has the meaning given by paragraph 3 above.

(2) References in this Schedule to expenditure incurred on the construction of a building do not include any expenditure incurred on the acquisition of, or of rights in or over any land.

(3) A person who has incurred expenditure on the construction of a building shall be deemed, for the purposes of any provision of this Schedule referring to his interest therein at the time when the expenditure was incurred, to have had the same interest therein as if the construction thereof had been completed at that time.

(4) Without prejudice to any of the other provisions of this Schedule relating to the apportionment of sale, insurance, salvage or compensation moneys, the sum paid on the sale of the relevant interest in a building or structure, or any other sale, insurance, salvage or compensation moneys payable in respect of any building or structure, shall, for the purposes of this Schedule, be deemed to be reduced by an amount equal to so much thereof, as, on a just apportionment, is attributable to assets representing expenditure other than expenditure in respect of which an allowance can be made under this Schedule.

SCHEDULE 13

Sections 86 and 88

THE INDEXATION ALLOWANCE

Cross references.—See FA 1983, Sch. 6, para. 6 (6) (certain provisions of this Schedule to apply for the purpose of calculating indexation allowance in relation to pooled securities);
FA 1985, Sch. 19, paras. 22, 23 (this Schedule to apply with modifications to underwriters' premiums trust funds).

PART I

GENERAL

Part disposals

1. For the purpose of determining the indexation allowance (if any) on the occasion of a part disposal of an asset, the apportionment under section 35 of the Capital Gains Tax Act 1979 of the sums which make up the relevant allowable expenditure shall be effected before the application of section 87 of this Act and, accordingly, in relation to a part disposal—

> (*a*) references in section 87 to an item of expenditure shall be construed as references to that part of that item which is so apportioned for the purposes of the computation under Chapter II of Part II of that Act of the [unindexed gain or loss][1] on the part disposal; and
> (*b*) no indexation allowance shall be determined by reference to the part of each item of relevant allowable expenditure which is apportioned to the property which remains undisposed of.

Cross references.—See FA 1988, s. 113 (for disposals after 3 July 1987 this paragraph not to apply in the case of building society shares and registered industrial and provident society shares).
Amendments.—[1] Words in para. (*a*) substituted by FA 1985, Sch. 19, para. 5 (1).

Disposals on a no-gain/no-loss basis

2.—(1) This paragraph applies to a disposal of an asset which falls within subsection (1) (*a*) of section 86 of this Act if, by virtue of any enactment other than . . .[1] any provision of this Schedule, the disposal is treated as one on which neither a gain nor a loss accrues to the person making the disposal.

(2) In relation to a disposal to which this paragraph applies—

> "the transferor" means the person making the disposal of the asset concerned; and
> "the transferee" means the person acquiring the asset on the disposal.

(3) On a disposal to which this paragraph applies . . .[1], the amount of the consideration shall be calculated for the purposes of the Capital Gains Tax Act 1979 on the assumptions that—

> (*a*) the disposal is one to which that section applies; and
> (*b*) on the disposal [an unindexed gain][2] accrues to the transferor which is equal to the indexation allowance on the disposal;

and, accordingly, the disposal shall be one on which, after taking account of the indexation allowance, neither a gain nor a loss accrues.

(4) Except as provided by paragraph 3 below, for the purposes of the application of sections 86 and 87 of this Act there shall be disregarded so much of any enactment as provides that, on the subsequent disposal by the transferee of the asset acquired by him on a disposal to which this paragraph applies, the transferor's acquisition of the asset is to be treated as the transferee's acquisition of it.

Cross references.—See FA 1983, Sch. 6, para. 9 (3), (4) (transfers on a no gain/no loss basis on a company reconstruction and within a group of companies);
TA 1988, Sch. 28, para. 3 (1) (calculation of the unindexed gain for the purposes of the computation of income gains on disposals of non-qualifying offshore funds);
FA 1988, s. 113 (for disposals after 3 July 1987 this paragraph not to apply in the case of building society shares and registered industrial and provident society shares).
Amendments.—[1] Words in sub-paras. (1), (3) repealed by FA 1985, Sch. 19, para. 5 (2) and Sch. 27, Pt. VII.
[2] Words in sub-para. (3) (*b*) substituted by FA 1985, Sch. 19, para. 5 (2) (*b*).

Receipts etc. which are not treated as disposals but affect relevant allowable expenditure

4.—(1) This paragraph applies where, in determining the relevant allowable expenditure in relation to a disposal to which section 86 of this Act applies, account is required to be taken, as mentioned in subsection (3) of that section, of any provision of any enactment which, by reference to a relevant event . . .[1], reduces the whole or any part of an item of expenditure as mentioned in that subsection.

(2) For the purpose of determining, in a case where this paragraph applies, the indexation allowance (if any) to which the person making the disposal is entitled, no account shall in the first instance be taken of the provision referred to in sub-paragraph (1) above in calculating the indexed rise in the item of expenditure to which that provision applies but, from that indexed rise as so calculated, there shall be deducted a sum equal to the indexed rise (determined as for the purposes of the actual disposal) in a notional item of expenditure which—

(*a*) is equal to the amount of the reduction effected by the provision concerned; and
(*b*) was incurred on the date of the relevant event referred to in sub-paragraph (1) above.

(3) In this paragraph "relevant event" means any event which does not fall to be treated as a disposal for the purposes of the Capital Gains Tax Act 1979.

Cross references.—See FA 1983, Sch. 6, para. 6 (4) (new provisions for calculating indexation allowance in relation to pooled securities the expenditure in respect of which falls to be reduced on the occurrence of an event under this paragraph);
FA 1988, s. 113 (for disposals after 3 July 1987 this paragraph not to apply in the case of building society shares and registered industrial and provident society shares).
Amendments.—[1] Words in sub-para. (1) repealed by FA 1985, Sch. 19, para. 5 (4) and Sch. 27, Pt. VII with respect to disposals after 5 April 1985 or, in the case of companies, after 31 March 1985 except that in the case of disposals of certain securities the repeal has effect from 28 February 1986 or 2 July 1986; see FA 1985, s. 68 (1), (2) and Sch. 27, Pt. VII, para. 4.

Reorganisations, reconstructions etc.

5.—(1) This paragraph applies where,—

(*a*) by virtue of section 78 of the Capital Gains Tax Act 1979, on a reorganisation the original shares (taken as a single asset) and the new holding (taken as a single asset) fall to be treated as the same asset acquired as the original shares were acquired; and
(*b*) on the reorganisation, a person gives or becomes liable to give any consideration for his new holding or any part of it.

(2) Where this paragraph applies, so much of the consideration referred to in sub-paragraph (1) (*b*) above as, on a disposal to which section 86 of this Act applies of the new holding, will, by virtue of section 79 (1) of the Capital Gains Tax Act 1979, be treated as having been given for the original shares, shall be treated for the purposes of section 87 of this Act as an item of relevant allowable expenditure incurred not at the time the original shares were acquired but at the time the person concerned gave or became liable to give the consideration (and, accordingly, subsection (5) of section 87 of this Act shall not apply in relation to that item of expenditure).

(3) In the preceding provisions of this paragraph the expressions "reorganisation", "the original shares" and "the new holding" have the meanings assigned by section 77 of the Capital Gains Tax Act 1979 except that in a case where, by virtue of any other provision of Chapter II of Part IV of that Act (which extends to conversion of securities, company reconstructions and amalgamations etc.) sections 78 and 79 of that Act apply in circumstances other than a reorganisation (within the meaning of section 77 of that Act), those expressions shall be construed in like manner as they fall to be construed in sections 78 and 79 as so applied.

Cross references.—See FA 1988, s. 113 (for disposals after 3 July 1987 this paragraph not to apply in the case of building society shares and registered industrial and provident society shares).

Calls on shares etc.

6.—(1) Sub-paragraph (2) below applies where,—

(*a*) on disposal to which section 86 of this Act applies, the relevant allowable expenditure is or includes the amount or value of the consideration given for the issue of shares or securities in, or debentures of, a company; and

(b) the whole or some part of that consideration was given after the expiry of the [period of twelve months beginning on the date of the issue of the shares, securities or debentures][1].

(2) For the purpose of computing the indexation allowance (if any) on the disposal referred to in sub-paragraph (1) (a) above,—

(a) so much of the consideration as was given after the expiry of the [period referred to in sub-paragraph (1) (b) above][1] shall be regarded as an item of expenditure separate from any consideration given during that period; and
(b) subsection (5) of section 87 of this Act shall not apply to that separate item of expenditure which, accordingly, shall be regarded as incurred at the time the consideration in question was actually given.

Cross references.—See FA 1988, s.113 (for disposals after 3 July 1987 this paragraph not to apply in the case of building society shares and registered industrial and provident society shares).
Amendments.—[1] Words in sub-paras. (1) (b), (2) (a) substituted by FA 1985, Sch. 19, para. 5 (5) (a) with respect to disposals after 5 April 1985 or, in the case of companies, after 31 March 1985 except that in the case of disposals of certain securities the substituted words have effect from 28 February 1986; see FA 1985, s. 68 (1), (2).

Options

7.—(1) This paragraph applies where, on a disposal to which section 86 of this Act applies, the relevant allowable expenditure includes both—

(a) the cost of acquiring an option binding the grantor to sell (in this paragraph referred to as "the option consideration"); and
(b) the cost of acquiring what was sold as a result of the exercise of the option (in this paragraph referred to as "the sale consideration").

(2) . . .[1]

(3) For the purpose of computing the indexation allowance (if any) on the disposal referred to in sub-paragraph (1) above,—

(a) the option consideration and the sale consideration shall be regarded as separate items of expenditure; and
(b) subsection (5) of section 87 of this Act shall apply to neither of those items and, accordingly, they shall be regarded as incurred when the option was acquired and when the sale took place, respectively.

(4) The preceding provisions of this paragraph have effect notwithstanding section 137 of the Capital Gains Tax Act 1979 (under which the grant of an option and the transaction entered into by the grantor in fulfilment of his obligations under the option are to be treated as a single transaction); but expressions used in this paragraph have the same meaning as in that section and subsection (6) of that section (division of consideration for option both to sell and to buy) applies for the purpose of determining the cost of acquiring an option binding the grantor to sell.

Cross references.—See FA 1983, Sch. 6, para. 7 (2) (b) (computation of indexation allowance in respect of pooled securities; application of sub-para. (3) above);
FA 1988, s. 113 (for disposals after 3 July 1987 this paragraph not to apply in the case of building society shares and registered industrial and provident society shares).
Amendments.—[1] Sub-para. (2) repealed by FA 1985, Sch. 19, para. 5 (6) and Sch. 27, Pt. VII with respect to disposals after 5 April 1985 or, in the case of companies, 31 March 1985 except that with respect to disposals of certain securities the repeal has effect from 28 February 1986 or 2 July 1986; see FA 1985, s. 68 (1), (2) and Sch. 27, Pt. VII, para. 4.

PART II
EXISTING SHARE POOLS

Cross references.—See FA 1983, Sch. 6, para. 3 (5) (*b*) (disposals of securities after 31 March 1982; new provisions for pooling; where this Part of this Schedule applies, the pooled holding comes into existence on 1 April 1982);
FA 1985, s. 68 (3) and Sch. 19, Pt. II (new rules of pooling with respect to holdings of securities to which this Part applies);

8.—(1) The provisions of this Part of this Schedule have effect in relation to a number of securities of the same class which, immediately before the operative date, are held by one person in one capacity and, by virtue of section 65 of the Capital Gains Tax Act 1979 are to be regarded for the purposes of that Act as indistinguishable parts of a single asset (in that section and in this Part of this Schedule referred to as a holding).

(2) Subject to paragraph 9 below, on and after the operative date,—

(*a*) the holding shall continue to be regarded as a single asset for the purposes of the Capital Gains Tax Act 1979 (but one which cannot grow by the acquisition of additional securities of the same class); and

(*b*) the holding shall be treated for the purposes of section 86 of this Act as having been acquired twelve months before the operative date; and

(*c*) every sum which, on a disposal of the holding occurring after the operative date, would be an item of relevant allowable expenditure shall be regarded for the purposes of section 87 of this Act as having been incurred at such a time that the month which determines RI, in the formula in subsection (2) of that section, is March 1982.

(3) Nothing in sub-paragraph (2) above affects the operation of section 78 of the Capital Gains Tax Act 1979 (equation of original shares and new holding on a reorganisation etc.) in relation to the holding, but without prejudice to paragraph 5 above.

(4) In this Part of this Schedule "the operative date" means—

(*a*) where the holding is held by a company, 1st April 1982; and

(*b*) in any other case, 6th April 1982.

Cross references.—See FA 1983, Sch. 6, para. 3 (5) (*b*) (disposals of securities after 31 March 1982; new provisions for pooling; the pooled holding comes into existence on 1 April 1982 where it includes the holding referred to in this paragraph),
Sch. 6, para. 4 (2) (qualifying securities continuing in existence after 31 March 1982 by virtue of this paragraph to be treated as qualifying securities for the purposes of pooling);
FA 1985, Sch. 19, para. 6 (1) (identification of securities held immediately before 1 or 6 April 1985 with share pools in existence on 1 or 6 April 1982);
FA 1988, s. 113 (for disposals after 3 July 1987, sub-para. (2) (*c*) above not to apply in the case of building society shares and registered industrial and provident society shares).

9.—(1) For the purposes of this paragraph there shall be ascertained—

(*a*) the amount which would be the relevant allowable expenditure on a disposal of the whole of the holding on the day in 1982 which immediately precedes the operative date; and

(*b*) the amount which would have been the relevant allowable expenditure on a disposal of the whole of the holding (as then constituted) on the same day in 1981;

and in this paragraph these amounts are referred to as the 1982 amount and the 1981 amount respectively.

(2) If the 1982 amount exceeds the 1981 amount, paragraph 8 (2) above shall not apply to the holding and the following provisions of this paragraph shall have effect in relation to it.

(3) Where sub-paragraph (2) above applies, the identification rules set out in sub-paragraph (4) below shall be assumed to have applied in relation to every acquisition or disposal of securities which occurred after the day referred to in sub-paragraph (1) (*b*) above and before the operative date and which, apart from this paragraph, would have increased or reduced the size of the holding; and accordingly—

(*a*) only such of the securities (if any) which constituted the holding on that day as are not identified, by virtue of those rules, with securities disposed of before the operative date shall be regarded as constituting the holding on the operative date; and

(*b*) all securities acquired after that day and before the operative date, so far as they are not so identified with securities disposed of before the operative date, shall be regarded as separate assets.

(4) The identification rules referred to in sub-paragraph (3) above are—

(*a*) that securities disposed of on an earlier date shall be identified before securities disposed of on a later date, and the identification of the securities first disposed of shall accordingly determine the securities which could be comprised in the later disposal; and
(*b*) that securities disposed of shall be identified with securities acquired on a later date rather than with securities acquired on an earlier date; and
(*c*) that securities disposed of shall be identified with securities acquired at different times on any one day in as nearly as may be equal proportions;

and these rules shall have priority according to the order in which they are set out above.

(5) In this paragraph and paragraph 10 below—

(*a*) "the reduced holding" means the securities referred to in sub-paragraph (3) (*a*) above; and
(*b*) "relevant allowable expenditure" has, in relation to a disposal taking place at any time, the meaning assigned to it by subsection (2) (*b*) of section 86 of this Act in relation to a disposal to which that section applies.

(6) Sub-paragraph (2) of paragraph 8 above shall apply in relation to the reduced holding but, so far as paragraph (*c*) of that sub-paragraph is concerned, subject to paragraph 10 (1) below.

Cross references.—See FA 1983, Sch. 6, para. 3 (5) (*b*) (disposals of securities after 31 March 1982; new provisions for pooling; the pooled holding comes into existence on 1 April 1982 where it includes the reduced holding referred to in this paragraph),
Sch. 6, para. 4 (2) (qualifying securities continuing in existence after 31 March 1982 by virtue of this paragraph to be treated as qualifying securities for the purposes of pooling);
FA 1985, Sch. 19, para. 6 (2) (pooling of a reduced holding of securities existing immediately before 1 or 6 April 1985 with securities not disposed of before that date and constituting separate assets under sub-para. (3) (*b*) above).

10.—(1) For the purpose of computing the indexation allowance (if any) on a disposal of—

(*a*) the reduced holding, or
(*b*) any other securities which, by virtue of sub-paragraph (3) (*b*) of paragraph 9 above, constitute one or more separate assets,

the 1982 amount, as defined in that paragraph, shall be apportioned between the reduced holding and that asset or those assets in proportion to the number of securities comprised in each of them on the operative date.

(2) In relation to a disposal on or after the operative date, the amount apportioned to the reduced holding or to any asset by virtue of sub-paragraph (1) above shall be regarded for all purposes of capital gains tax as the relevant allowable expenditure attributable to the securities comprised in the reduced holding or, as the case may be, in the asset in question.

(3) For the purposes of section 87 (5) of this Act any relevant allowable expenditure which is attributable to any securities by virtue of sub-paragraph (2) above shall be deemed to be expenditure falling within paragraph (*a*) of subsection (1) of section 32 of the Capital Gains Tax Act 1979.

Cross references.—See FA 1985, Sch. 19, para. 7 (2) (*a*) (relevant allowable expenditure attributable to the 1982 holding of securities where such holding comprises a reduced holding existing immediately before 1 or 6 April 1985 and securities not disposed of before that date and constituting separate assets by virtue of para. 9 (3) (*b*) of this Schedule);
FA 1988, s. 113 (for disposals after 3 July 1987, sub-para. (3) above not to apply in the case of building society shares and registered industrial and provident society shares).

SCHEDULE 21
Section 156

DISSOLUTION OF BOARD OF REFEREES: CONSEQUENTIAL PROVISIONS

Capital Allowances

2. The Income Tax (Applications for Increase of Wear and Tear Percentages) Regulations 1950 shall have effect as if for references to the Board of Referees there were substituted references to the tribunal.

The tribunal

3.—(1) . . .[2]

(2) In this Schedule "tribunal" means the tribunal established under section [706 of the Taxes Act 1988][1].

Amendments.—[1] Words in sub-para. (2) substituted by TA 1988, Sch. 29, para. 32 Table.
[2] Sub-para. (1) repealed by TA 1988, Sch. 31.

Savings and transitionals

4.—(1) Section 54 of the Taxes Management Act 1970 (settling of appeals by agreement) shall apply to the tribunal in relation to the exercise of functions transferred by section 156 of this Act as it applied, by virtue of paragraph 8 of Schedule 4 to that Act, to the Board of Referees.

(2) Section 156 of this Act shall not affect the validity of anything done by or in relation to the Board of Referees before the commencement of that section; and anything which at that date is in process of being done by or in relation to the Board may be continued by or in relation to the tribunal.

FINANCE ACT 1983

(1983 Chapter 28)

ARRANGEMENT OF SECTIONS

Note.—Provisions of this Act relevant to the taxes covered by this Handbook and not reproduced are either spent or repealed by TA 1988, Sch. 31 and other legislation.

PART II
INCOME TAX, CORPORATION TAX AND CAPITAL GAINS TAX

CHAPTER II
CAPITAL ALLOWANCES

Section
30. Industrial building or structure.
31. Buildings converted into very small workshops.

CHAPTER III
CAPITAL GAINS

34. Election for pooling: indexation.

PART IV
MISCELLANEOUS AND SUPPLEMENTARY

Miscellaneous

48. Short title, interpretation, construction and repeals.
    SCHEDULE:
    Schedule 6—Capital gains: election for pooling.

An Act to grant certain duties, to alter other duties, and to amend the law relating to the National Debt and the Public Revenue, and to make further provision in connection with Finance.
[13th May 1983]

PART II

INCOME TAX, CORPORATION TAX AND CAPITAL GAINS TAX

CHAPTER II
CAPITAL ALLOWANCES

30. Industrial building or structure

(1) . . .

(2) Subsection (1) above has effect in relation to expenditure incurred after 15th March 1983 and to expenditure which, by virtue of section 5 (1) of the Capital Allowances Act 1968 (purchase of unused buildings or structures), is deemed to have been incurred after that date; but expenditure shall not be treated for the purposes of this section as having been incurred after the date on which it was in fact incurred by reason only of section 1 (6) of that Act (expenditure incurred before trade begins).

Note.—Sub-s. (1) amends CAA 1968, s. 7 (4).

31. Buildings converted into very small workshops

(1) Where the conditions mentioned in subsection (2) below are satisfied in relation to an industrial building, section 73 of the Finance Act 1982 (industrial buildings allowance: very small workshops) shall apply in relation to capital expenditure on the construction of that building notwithstanding that the gross internal floor space of the whole building will exceed 1,250 square feet.

(2) The conditions referred to in subsection (1) above are that—

(*a*) the industrial building has been constructed by means of the conversion of a building (the "existing building") into two or more industrial buildings;
(*b*) each of those industrial buildings is—

(i) permanently separated from the remainder of the existing building;
(ii) intended for occupation separately from the remainder of the existing building; and
(iii) suitable for being so occupied; and

(*c*) the average gross internal floor space does not exceed 1,250 square feet.

(3) For the purposes of subsection (2) (*c*) above, the average gross internal floor space shall be calculated—

(*a*) as at the date at which the following condition is first satisfied, namely that all the buildings which have been constructed by means of the conversion have come into use; or
(*b*) if that condition is not satisfied before 27th March 1986, as at that date;

and shall be taken to be the average of the gross internal floor space of all those parts of the existing building which are industrial buildings at that date.

(4) This section does not apply where the existing building, or any part of it, remained unused throughout the period before the conversion.

(5) Where—

(*a*) in anticipation of the conditions mentioned in subsection (2) above being complied with in relation to an industrial building, section 73 of the Act of 1982 has been taken to apply in relation to capital expenditure on the construction of that building; and
(*b*) those conditions have not been complied with in relation to that industrial building;

all such assessments shall be made as are necessary to secure that the Capital Allowances

Act 1968 shall have effect in relation to that expenditure as if it had never been expenditure to which section 73 applies.

(6) The Tax Acts shall have effect as if this section were contained in Chapter I of Part I of the Act of 1968.

CHAPTER III
CAPITAL GAINS

34. Election for pooling: indexation

(1) The provisions of Schedule 6 to this Act shall have effect for the purposes of, and in connection with,—

(*a*) enabling a company to elect that, with respect to disposals after 31st March 1982, each of its holdings of certain securities of the same class which are held by it solely and beneficially and which have been so held for the length of time referred to in that Schedule shall be regarded for the purposes of the Capital Gains Tax Act 1979 as constituting a single asset; and

(*b*) computing the indexation allowance applicable on a disposal of such a single asset.

(2) ...

Note.—Sub-s. (2) inserts FA 1982, s. 88 (5A); repealed by FA 1985, Sch. 27, Pt. VII.

PART IV
MISCELLANEOUS AND SUPPLEMENTARY

48. Short title, interpretation, construction and repeals

(1) This Act may be cited as the Finance Act 1983.

(2) In this Act "the Taxes Act" means the Income and Corporation Taxes Act 1970.

(3) Part II of this Act, so far as it relates to income tax, shall be construed as one with the Income Tax Acts, so far as it relates to corporation tax, shall be construed as one with the Corporation Tax Acts and, so far as it relates to capital gains tax, shall be construed as one with the Capital Gains Tax Act 1979.

(5) The enactments specified in Schedule 10 to this Act are hereby repealed to the extent specified in the third column of that Schedule, but subject to any provision at the end of any Part of that Schedule.

Note.—Sub-s. (4) is not relevant to this work.

SCHEDULE 6
Section 34

CAPITAL GAINS: ELECTION FOR POOLING

Cross references.—See FA 1985, s. 68 (3) (*d*) (application of FA 1985, Sch. 19, Pt. V (modification of indexation allowance) to have effect with respect to securities in respect of which elections have been or could be made under this Schedule);
TA 1988, Sch. 28, para. 8 (4), (5) (computation of offshore income gains; disposals involving an equalisation element made by a company which has made an election under this Schedule).

Interpretation

1.—(1) In this Schedule—

(*a*) "the principal Act" means the Capital Gains Tax Act 1979;
(*b*) "the 1982 Act" means the Finance Act 1982;
(*c*) "the qualifying period" has the meaning assigned to it by section 86 (1) (*b*) of the 1982 Act; and
(*d*) "relevant allowable expenditure" has the meaning assigned to it by subsections (2) (*b*) and (3) of section 86 of the 1982 Act.

(2) For the purposes of this Schedule, "qualifying securities" are securities, as defined in section 88 (9) of the 1982 Act, which are neither—

(*a*) gilt-edged securities, as defined in Schedule 2 to the principal Act; [nor][2]
[(*aa*) qualifying corporate bonds, as defined in section 64 of the Finance Act 1984; nor][2]
[(*ab*) deep discount securities (within the meaning of Schedule 4 to the Income and Corporation Taxes Act 1988); nor][3]
(*b*) securities which on 6th April 1965 were held by the company making the election concerned and which, disregarding the effect of sections 88 and 89 of the 1982 Act, would for the time being be excluded from the effect of section 65 of the principal Act by virtue of subsection (1) (*b*) of that section; [nor][1]
[(*c*) securities which are, or have at any time after the expiry of the period which, in relation to a disposal of them, would be the qualifying period, been material interests in a non-qualifying offshore fund, whithin the meaning of Chapter [V of Part XVII of the Income and Corporation Taxes Act 1988][4].][1]

Amendments.—[1] Sub-para. (2) (*c*) and the word "nor" preceding it added by FA 1984, s. 67 (1), (2) and to be deemed always to have had effect.
[2] Sub-para. (2) (*aa*) added by FA 1984, Sch. 13, para. 6.
[3] Sub-para. (2) (*ab*) substituted by TA 1988, Sch. 29, para. 32 Table.
[4] Words in sub-para. (2) (*c*) substituted by TA 1988, Sch. 29, para. 32 Table.

Election for pooling

2.—(1) An election under this Schedule shall be made by notice in writing to the inspector not later than the expiry of two years from the end of the accounting period in which the first relevant disposal is made or such further time as the Board may allow.

(2) For the avoidance of doubt it is hereby declared—

(*a*) that where a company makes an election under this Schedule with respect to qualifying securities which it holds solely and beneficially, that election does not apply to qualifying securities which it holds in another capacity; and
(*b*) that an election under this Schedule is irrevocable [except in accordance with Part V of Schedule 19 to the Finance Act 1985][1].

(3) In this paragraph the "first relevant disposal", in relation to an election, means the first disposal after 31st March 1982 by the company making the election of qualifying securities which are held by it solely and beneficially.

Amendments.—[1] Words in sub-para. (2) (*b*) added by FA 1985, Sch. 19, para. 20 (2).

Effect of election

3.—(1) The provisions of this paragraph have effect where an election is made under this Schedule.

(2) The election shall have effect with respect to all disposals after 31st March 1982 of qualifying securities held solely and beneficially by the company making the election.

(3) For the purposes of the principal Act, qualifying securities—

(*a*) which are of the same class, and
(*b*) which have been held by the company making the election for such a length of time that, on a disposal of them, the disposal would not be regarded as occurring within the qualifying period,

shall be regarded as indistinguishable parts of a single asset (in this paragraph referred to as a holding) diminishing or growing on the occasions on which some of the securities of the class in question are disposed of or additional securities of the class in question which have been previously acquired become held as mentioned in paragraph (*b*) above.

(4) Without prejudice to the generality of sub-paragraph (3) above, a disposal of securities in a holding, other than the disposal outright of the entire holding, is a disposal of part of an asset and the provisions of the principal Act relating to the computation of a gain accruing on a disposal of part of an asset shall apply accordingly.

(5) In accordance with the preceding provisions of this paragraph, where an election is made under this Schedule, the holding shall come (or, as the case may be, shall be treated as having come) into being—

(*a*) on the first anniversary of the first acquisition of qualifying securities of a particular description; or
(*b*) if Part II of Schedule 13 to the 1982 Act applies so that "the holding" for the purposes of this paragraph consists of or includes what is "the holding" or "the reduced holding" referred to in paragraph 8 or paragraph 9 of that Schedule, [immediately before 1st April 1982][1].

(6) In its application to a holding, subsection (1) of section 86 of the 1982 Act (conditions for the existence of the indexation allowance) shall have effect as if the condition in paragraph (*b*) (the qualifying period) were always fulfilled.

(7) Shares or securities of a company shall not be treated for the purposes of this Schedule as being of the same class unless they are so treated by the practice of The Stock Exchange or would be so treated if dealt with on The Stock Exchange.

Amendments.—[1] Words in sub-para. (5) (*b*) substituted by FA 1984, s. 67 (1), (3) and are deemed always to have had effect.

The 1982 identification rules

4.—(1) The provisions of sections 88 and 89 of, and Part II of Schedule 13 to, the 1982 Act shall have effect for determining whether qualifying securities have been held as mentioned in paragraph (*b*) of sub-paragraph (3) of paragraph 3 above but, subject to that, those provisions shall not apply to securities forming part of the single asset referred to in that sub-paragraph.

(2) Any reference in sub-paragraph (1) above to qualifying securities includes a reference to a single asset consisting of qualifying securities which continued in existence on and after 1st April 1982 by virtue of paragraph 8 or paragraph 9 (3) (*a*) of Schedule 13 to the 1982 Act.

The indexation allowance

5.—(1) Where an election has been made under this Schedule, the following provisions of this Schedule have effect in place of the provisions of section 87 of the 1982 Act for the purpose of computing the indexation allowance on a disposal to which section 86 of that Act applies of the single asset (in the following provisions of this Schedule referred to as "the holding") which by virtue of paragraph 3 (3) above results from the election.

(2) On any disposal of the holding falling within sub-paragraph (1) above, other than a disposal of the whole of it,—

(*a*) the unindexed and indexed pools of expenditure shall each be apportioned between the part disposed of and the remainder in the same proportions as, under the principal Act, the relevant allowable expenditure is apportioned; and

(b) the indexation allowance is the amount by which the portion of the indexed pool which is attributed to the part disposed of exceeds the portion of the unindexed pool which is attributed to that part.

(3) On a disposal falling within sub-paragraph (1) above of the whole of the holding, the indexation allowance is the amount by which the indexed pool of expenditure at the time of the disposal exceeds the unindexed pool of expenditure at that time.

6.—(1) Subject to sub-paragraph (2) below, in relation to the holding, the unindexed pool of expenditure is at any time the amount which would be the aggregate of the relevant allowable expenditure in relation to a disposal of the whole of the holding occurring at that time.

(2) Where any item of the relevant allowable expenditure referred to in sub-paragraph (1) above was incurred after the time at which the securities to which it relates were acquired, it shall not be taken into account for the purpose of determining the unindexed pool of expenditure at any time before the expiry of the period of twelve months beginning on the date on which it was incurred; but at the expiry of that period the unindexed pool of expenditure shall be increased, subject to sub-paragraph (3) below, by the addition of a sum equal to it.

(3) If, before the expiry of the period of twelve months referred to in sub-paragraph (2) above, there is a disposal of any of the securities to which the item of relevant expenditure referred to in that sub-paragraph relates, only the portion of that expenditure which is attributable to the securities which are not so disposed of shall be added to the unindexed pool of expenditure by virtue of sub-paragraph (2) above.

(4) If, by virtue of any enactment, any item of the relevant allowable expenditure referred to in sub-paragraph (1) above falls to be reduced by reference to a relevant event, within the meaning of paragraph 4 of Schedule 13 to the 1982 Act, occurring after the time at which the securities to which it relates were acquired, that reduction shall not be taken into account for the purpose of determining the unindexed pool of expenditure until the expiry of the period of twelve months beginning on the date of the relevant event in question.

(5) If, before the expiry of the period of twelve months referred to in sub-paragraph (4) above, there is a disposal of any of the securities to which the item of relevant expenditure referred to in that sub-paragraph relates, the amount by which the unindexed pool of expenditure falls to be reduced at the expiry of that period shall itself be reduced so that only that portion of the reduction which is attributable to the securities which are not so disposed of shall then be made in the unindexed pool of expenditure.

(6) Subsection (5) of section 87 of the 1982 Act (date on which expenditure was incurred) and any provision of Schedule 13 to that Act which, in particular circumstances, displaces that subsection shall apply for the purposes of sub-paragraph (2) above as they apply for the purpose of computing the indexation allowance in accordance with that section.

7.—(1) The provisions of this paragraph have effect, subject to paragraphs 9 and 10 below, for determining, in relation to the holding, the indexed pool of expenditure at any time.

(2) The indexed pool of expenditure shall come into being at the time that the holding comes into being and shall at that time consist of the aggregate of—

(a) the unindexed pool of expenditure at that time; and
(b) any indexation allowance which, by virtue of paragraph 7 (3) of Schedule 13 to the 1982 Act (options), would have applied to a disposal of the whole of the holding at that time.

(3) Any reference in the following provisions of this Schedule to an operative event is a reference to any event (whether a disposal, the expiry of a period of twelve months from an acquisition or otherwise) which has the effect of reducing or increasing the unindexed pool of expenditure attributable to the holding.

(4) Whenever an operative event occurs,—

(a) there shall be added to the indexed pool of expenditure the indexed rise, as calculated under paragraph 8 below, in the value of that pool since the last operative event or, if there has been no previous operative event, since the pool came into being; and
(b) if the operative event results in an increase in the unindexed pool of expenditure then,

in addition to any increase under paragraph (*a*) above, the same increase shall be made to the indexed pool of expenditure;

(*c*) if the operative event is a disposal resulting in a reduction in the unindexed pool of expenditure, then, whether or not it is a disposal to which section 86 of the 1982 Act applies, the indexed pool of expenditure shall be reduced in the same proportion as the unindexed pool is reduced; and

(*d*) if the operative event results in a reduction in the unindexed pool of expenditure but is not a disposal, the same reduction shall be made to the indexed pool of expenditure.

(5) Where the operative event is a disposal to which section 86 of the 1982 Act applies,—

(*a*) any addition under paragraph (*a*) of sub-paragraph (4) above shall be made before the calculation of the indexation allowance under paragraph 5 above; and

(*b*) the reduction under paragraph (*c*) of that sub-paragraph shall be made after that calculation.

8.—(1) At the time of any operative event, the indexed rise in the indexed pool of expenditure is a sum produced by multiplying the value of that pool immediately before the event by a figure expressed as a decimal and determined, subject to sub-paragraphs (2) and (3) below, by the formula—

$$\frac{RE - RL}{RL}$$

where—

RE is the retail prices index for the month in which the operative event occurs; and
RL is the retail prices index for the month in which occurred the immediately preceding operative event or, if there has been no such event, in which the indexed pool of expenditure came into being.

(2) If RE, as defined in sub-paragraph (1) above, is equal to or less than RL, as so defined, the indexed rise is nil.

(3) If the figure determined in accordance with the formula in sub-paragraph (1) above would, apart from this sub-paragraph, be a figure having more than three decimal places, it shall be rounded to the nearest third decimal place.

Transfers on a no gain/no loss basis

9.—(1) This paragraph applies in any case where—

(*a*) a company (in this paragraph referred to as "the first company") disposes of securities to another company (in this paragraph referred to as "the second company") which has made an election under this Schedule, and

(*b*) the disposal is one to which section 267 or section 273 of the Taxes Act applies (transfers on a company reconstruction etc. and within a group of companies to be on a no gain/no loss basis), and

(*c*) the disposal by the first company takes place outside the qualifying period.

[(2) The disposal referred to in sub-paragraph (1) above shall be regarded for the purposes of this Schedule as an operative event][1]

[(3) Notwithstanding anything in paragraph 2 of Schedule 13 to the 1982 Act, the amount which, on the disposal referred to in sub-paragraph (1) above, is to be regarded as the consideration given by the second company for the acquisition of the securities (and, accordingly, the amount which is to be added to that company's unindexed pool of expenditure on the disposal) shall not include the indexation allowance on that disposal.][1]

[(4) Nothing in sub-paragraph (3) above affects the amount which, by virtue of paragraph 2 (3) of Schedule 13 to the 1982 Act, is to be treated as the consideration received by the first company on the disposal referred to in sub-paragraph (1) above, and it shall be that amount (rather than the smaller amount referred to in sub-paragraph (3) above) which, on that disposal, shall be added to the second company's indexed pool of expenditure.][1]

[(5) Paragraph 3 of Schedule 13 to the 1982 Act shall not apply on any subsequent disposal of the holding in which the securities referred to in sub-paragraph (1) above are comprised.][1]

Amendments.—[1] Sub-paras. (2)–(5) substituted for sub-paras. (2), (3) by FA 1984, s. 67 (1), (4) and are deemed always to have had effect.

Consideration for options

10.—(1) If, in a case where sub-paragraph (4) (*b*) of paragraph 7 above applies, the increase in the unindexed pool of expenditure is, in whole or in part, attributable to the cost of acquiring an option binding the grantor to sell (in this paragraph referred to as "the option consideration"), then, in addition to any increase under paragraph (*a*) or paragraph (*b*) of sub-paragraph (4) of paragraph 7 above, the indexed pool of expenditure shall be increased by an amount equal to the indexed rise in the option consideration, as determined under sub-paragraph (2) below.

(2) The indexed rise in the option consideration is a sum produced by multiplying the consideration by a figure expressed as a decimal and determined, subject to sub-paragraphs (3) and (4) below, by the formula—

$$\frac{RO - RA}{RA}$$

where—

RO is the retail prices index for the month in which falls the first anniversary of the date on which the option is exercised; and

RA is the retail prices index for the month in which falls the first anniversary of the date on which the option was acquired or, if it is later, March 1982.

(3) If RO, as defined in sub-paragraph (2) above, is equal to or less than RA, as so defined, the indexed rise is nil.

(4) If the figure determined in accordance with the formula in sub-paragraph (2) above would, apart from this sub-paragraph, be a figure having more than three decimal places, it shall be rounded to the nearest third decimal place.

Supplementary

11. All such adjustments shall be made, whether by way of discharge or repayment of tax, or the making of assessments or otherwise, as are required to give effect to an election under this Schedule.

FINANCE (No. 2) ACT 1983

(1983 Chapter 49)

ARRANGEMENT OF SECTIONS

Note.—Provisions of this Act relevant to the taxes covered by this Handbook and not reproduced are either spent or repealed by TA 1988, Sch. 31 and other legislation.

PART I
INCOME TAX, CORPORATION TAX AND CAPITAL GAINS TAX

Section
6. Allowances for dwelling-houses let on assured tenancies.
7. Relief for local constituency associations of political parties on reorganisation of constituencies.

PART III
MISCELLANEOUS AND SUPPLEMENTARY

15. *Relief from stamp duty for local constituency associations of political parties on reorganisation of constituencies.* (see Orange Book)
16. Short title, construction and repeals.

An Act to grant certain duties, to alter other duties, and to amend the law relating to the National Debt and the Public Revenue, and to make further provision in connection with Finance.
[26th July 1983]

PART I
INCOME TAX, CORPORATION TAX AND CAPITAL GAINS TAX

6. Allowances for dwelling-houses let on assured tenancies

(1) . . .

(2) The amendment made by subsection (1) above shall be deemed always to have had effect, except that it shall not affect the validity of any election under paragraph 4 of Schedule 7 to the Capital Allowances Act 1968 which was made before 1st April 1983 in reliance on the provisions of paragraph 4 (5) (*c*) of Schedule 12 to the Finance Act 1982, as originally enacted.

(3) . . .

(4) The amendment made by section (3) above shall be deemed always to have had effect, except that it shall not affect the computation under Chapter II of Part II of the Capital Gains Tax Act 1979 of the amount of any loss accruing on a disposal before 1st April 1983.

(5) . . .

(6) The amendment made by subsection (5) above shall have effect in relation to—

(*a*) expenditure incurred on or after 5th May 1983 otherwise than pursuant to a contract entered into before that date by the person incurring the expenditure, and
(*b*) expenditure which, by virtue of paragraph 8 of Schedule 12 to the Finance Act 1982, is deemed to be incurred on or after that date,

and also in any case where a person other than a company becomes entitled to the relevant interest, within the meaning of that Schedule, on or after that date.

Notes.—Sub-s. (1) amends FA 1982, Sch. 12, para. 4 (5) (*c*).
Sub-s. (3) inserts CGTA 1979, s. 34 (4) (*aa*).
Sub-s. (5) amends FA 1982, Sch. 12, para. 3 (3) (*a*).

7. Relief for local constituency associations of political parties on reorganisation of constituencies

(1) In this section "relevant date" means the date of coming into operation of an Order in Council under section 3 of the House of Commons (Redistribution of Seats) Act 1949 (orders specifying new parliamentary constitutences) and, in relation to any relevant date,—

(*a*) "former parliamentary constituency" means an area which, for the purposes of parliamentary elections, was a constituency immediately before that date but is no longer such a constituency after that date; and
(*b*) "new parliamentary constituency" means an area which, for the purposes of parliamentary elections, is a constituency immediately after that date but was not such a constituency before that date.

(2) In this section "local constituency association" means an unincorporated association (whether described as an association, a branch or otherwise) whose primary purpose is to further the aims of a political party in an area of a parliamentary constituency or two or more parliamentary constituencies and, in relation to any relevant date,—

(*a*) "existing association" means a local constituency association whose area was the same, or substantially the same, as the area of a former parliamentary constituency or two or more such constituencies; and
(*b*) "new association" means a local constituency association whose area is the same, or substantially the same, as the area of a new parliamentary constituency or two or more such constituencies.

(3) For the purposes of this section, a new association is a successor to an exisitng association if any part of the existing association's area is comprised in the new association's area.

(4) In any case where, before, on or after a relevant date,—

(a) an existing association disposes of land to a new association which is a successor to the existing association, or

(b) an existing association disposes of land to a body (whether corporate or unincorporated) which is an organ of the political party concerned and, as soon as practicable thereafter, that body disposes of the land to a new association which is a successor to the existing association,

the parties to the disposal or, where paragraph (b) above applies, to each of the disposals, shall be treated for the purposes of corporation tax in respect of chargeable gains or, as the case may require, capital gains tax as if the land disposed of were acquired from the existing association or the body making the disposal for a consideration of such an amount as would secure that on the disposal neither a gain nor a loss accrued to that association or body.

(5) In a case falling within subsection (4) above, the new association shall be treated for the purposes of Schedule 5 to the Capital Gains Tax Act 1979 (assets held on 6th April 1965) as if the acquisition by the existing association of the land disposed of as mentioned in that subsection had been the new association's acquisition of it; . . .

(6) In any case where—

(a) before, on or after a relevant date, an existing association disposes of any land which was used and occupied by it for the purposes of its functions, and

(b) the existing association transfers the whole or part of the proceeds of the disposal to a new association which is a successor to the existing association,

then, subject to subsection (7) below, the Capital Gains Tax Act 1979 (and, in particular the provisions of section 115 to 121 providing for roll-over relief on the replacement of business assets) shall have effect as if, since the time it was acquired by the existing association, the land disposed of had been the property of the new association and, accordingly, as if the disposal of it had been by the new association.

(7) If, in a case falling within subsection (6) above, only part of the proceeds of the disposal is transferred to the new association, that subsection shall apply—

(a) as if there existed in the land disposed of as mentioned in paragraph (a) of that subsection a separate asset in the form of a corresponding undivided share in that land, and subject to any necessary apportionments of consideration for an acquisition or disposal of, or of an interest in, that land; and

(b) as if the references in that subsection (other than paragraph (a) thereof) to the land disposed of and the disposal of it were references respectively to the corresponding undivided share referred to in paragraph (a) above and the disposal of that share;

and for this purpose a corresponding undivided share in the land disposed of is a share which bears to the whole of that land the same proportion as the part of the proceeds transferred bears to the whole of those proceeds.

(8) In this section "political party" means a political party which qualifies for exemption under [section 24 of the Capital Transfer Tax Act 1984][1] (gifts to political parties).

(9) This section applies in any case where the relevant date falls after 1st January 1983 and the disposal referred to in subsection (4) or subsection (6) above is on or after 6th April 1983.

Notes.—Words omitted from sub-s. (5) insert FA 1982, Sch. 13, para. 3 (3) (d).
Cross references.—See FA 1985, s. 68 (7) (modification of indexation allowance with respect to disposal of assets after 1 April or 6 April 1985),
s. 68 (7A) (d) (re-basing of indexation allowance to 1982 in relation to disposals after 5 April 1988);
FA 1986, s. 100 (CTTA 1984 renamed as Inheritance Tax Act 1984 from 25 July 1986);
FA 1988, Sch. 8, para. 1 (3) (d) (re-basing of indexation allowance to 1982 in relation to unindexed gains and losses on disposals after 5 April 1988 of assets held on 31 March 1982).
Amendments.—[1] Words in sub-s. (8) substituted by IHTA 1984, Sch. 8, para. 23 with effect from 1 January 1985.

PART III
MISCELLANEOUS AND SUPPLEMENTARY

16. Short title, construction and repeals

(1) This Act may be cited as the Finance (No. 2) Act 1983.

(2) Part I of this Act, so far as it relates to income tax, shall be construed as one which the Income Tax Acts, so far as it relates to Income Tax Acts, so far as it relates to corporation tax, shall be construed as one with the Corporation Tax Acts and, so far as it relates to capital gains tax, shall be construed as one with the Capital Gains Tax Act 1979.

(4) The enactments specified in Schedule 2 to this Act are hereby repealed to the extent specified in the third column of that Schedule, but subject to any provision at the end of any part of that Schedule.

Note.—Sub-s. (3) is not relevant.

OIL TAXATION ACT 1983

(1983 Chapter 56)

An Act to vary the reliefs available for certain expenditure incurred in connection with assets used or to be used in connection with oil fields; to bring into charge to petroleum revenue tax certain sums received or receivable in respect of such assets and of certain other assets situated in the United Kingdom, the territorial sea thereof or a designated area, within the meaning of the Continental Shelf Act 1964; to amend Part II of the Oil Taxation Act 1975 in relation to sums so received or receivable; and for connected purposes.

[1st December 1983]

12. Charge of receipts attributable to U.K. use of foreign field asset

(1) The provisions of Schedule 4 to this Act have effect for the purpose of bringing into charge to tax the amount or value of certain consideration (whether in the nature of income or capital) which is received or receivable after 30th June 1982 by a participator in a foreign field—

(*a*) in respect of the United Kingdom use of a field asset; or

(*b*) in respect of the provision, in connection with the United Kingdom use of a field asset, of services or other business facilities of whatever kind; or

(*c*) in respect of the disposal of a field asset or an interest in such an asset where either the asset has already been in United Kingdom use or it is reasonable to expect that, after the disposal, the asset will be in United Kingdom use.

(2) In this section and Schedule 4 to this Act—

(*a*) "foreign field" means subject to subsection (3) below, an area which is not under the jurisdiction of the government of the United Kingdom but which, by an order made by statutory instrument by the Secretary of State for the purposes of this Act, is specified as a foreign field; and

(*b*) in relation to a foreign field, "participator" means a person who is, or has rights, interests or obligations of, a licensee in respect of the foreign field under the law of a country outside the United Kingdom.

(3) For the purposes of this section and Schedule 4 to the Act, in the case of an oil field which, by virtue of section 107 of the Finance Act 1980 (transmedian fields) is deemed to include the sector mentioned in subsection (1) (*a*) (ii) of that section—

(*a*) that sector shall be treated as a foreign field; and

(*b*) the remainder of that field shall be treated as a separate oil field.

(4) In this section and Schedule 4 to this Act—

(*a*) "field asset", in relation to a foreign field, means an asset which—

(i) is not a mobile asset, and

(ii) is situated in the United Kingdom, the territorial sea thereof or a designated area, and

(iii) subject to subsection (6) below, is, has been or is expected to be used in a way which, on the assumptions in subsection (5) below, would be use in connection with the foreign field; and

(*b*) "United Kingdom use", in relation to a field asset, means the use of the asset in connection with the exploration or exploitation of so much of the seabed and subsoil and their natural resources as is situated in the territorial sea of the United Kingdom or a designated area.

(5) The assumptions referred to in subsection (4) (*a*) above are—

(*a*) that every foreign field is situated in a designated area and is an oil field within the meaning of Part I of the principal Act; and

(*b*) that references in Part I of the principal Act to oil are references to any substance that would be oil if the enactments mentioned in section 1 (1) thereof extended to the foreign field.

(6) For the purposes of this section and Schedule 4 to this Act an asset which falls within sub-paragraphs (i) and (ii) of paragraph (*a*) of subsection (4) above but does not fall within sub-paragraph (iii) of that paragraph is nevertheless a field asset if—

(*a*) its use gives rise or is expected to give rise to consideration which, assuming the asset to be a field asset, would fall within subsection (1) above; and
(*b*) its useful life continues, or is expected to continue, for more than six months after the time at which the consideration referred to in paragraph (*a*) above is first received or receivable; and
(*c*) it is, or is expected to be, used in association with another asset which is a field asset.

(7) For the purposes of subsection (6) (*c*) above, an asset shall not be regarded as used in association with a field asset unless it is so used in a way which constitutes use in connection with an oil field or would constitute such use but for section 10 (2) of the principal Act (exempt gas).

15. Short title, interpretation, construction and repeals

(1) This Act may be cited as the Oil Taxation Act 1983.

(2) In this Act "the principal Act" means the Oil Taxation Act 1975.

(3) In this Act—
"chargeable field" shall be construed in accordance with section 8 (5) above;
"disposal receipts" shall be construed in accordance with section 7 (2) above;
"qualifying asset" shall be construed in accordance with [section 8][1] above; and
"tariff receipts" shall be construed, subject to Schedule 5 to this Act, in accordance with section 6 (2) above.

(4) Section [839][2] of the Taxes Act (connected persons) applies for the purposes of this Act.

Note.—Sub-ss. (5), (6) are not relevant to this work.
Amendments.—[1] Words in sub-s. (3) substituted by FA 1985, s. 92 (3).
[2] Number in sub-s. (4) substituted by TA 1988, Sch. 29, para. 32 Table.

SCHEDULES

SCHEDULE 2

SUPPLEMENTAL PROVISIONS AS TO RECEIPTS FROM QUALIFYING ASSETS

Use by connected or associated person: avoidance devices

11.—(1) This paragraph applies in any case where—

(*a*) any consideration in respect of the use of an asset is received or receivable by a person (in this paragraph referred to as "the recipient") in relation to whom the asset is not a qualifying asset; and
(*b*) the asset is at any time used in connection with an oil field by a person (in this paragraph referred to as "the user") who is connected or associated with the recipient and who is a participator in that or any other oil field; and
(*c*) the consideration is so received or receivable under or in consequence of a scheme or arrangements the main purpose or one of the main purposes of which is the avoidance of petroleum revenue tax or corporation tax.

(2) Subject to sub-paragraphs (5) and (6) below, the user shall be treated for the purposes of this Act and Part I [of the principal Act and section 500 of the Taxes Act][1] as if—

(*a*) any consideration arising from the use of the asset and received or receivable at any time by the recipient or a person connected or associated with him, other than consideration received or receivable from the user himself, had been received or receivable at that time by the user; and
(*b*) such proportion of any expenditure incurred by the recipient at any time in connection with the asset as it is just and reasonable to apportion to the use which gives rise to the consideration had been incurred at that time by the user for the purpose for which it was in fact incurred by the recipient.

(3) For the purposes of this paragraph, a participator in an oil field is associated with another person if the participator, by acting together with a person who is, or two or more persons each of whom is, a participator in that oil field or in any other relevant field, would be able to secure or exercise control of that other person, and for this purpose—

(*a*) "control" shall be construed in accordance with section [416][1] of the Taxes Act; and
(*b*) "relevant field" means an oil field in connection with which the asset referred to in sub-paragraph (1) (*a*) above has been, is, or is expected to be, used.

(4) For the purposes of sub-paragraph (3) above—

(*a*) a foreign field, within the meaning of section 12 of this Act, shall be treated as an oil field, and
(*b*) an asset is used in connection with a relevant field which is a foreign field if it is used in a way which, on the assumptions set out in subsection (5) of that section, would be use in connection with the foreign field,

and, in relation to a relevant field which is a foreign field, the reference in sub-paragraph (3) above to a participator shall be construed in accordance with section 12 (2) (*b*) of this Act.

(5) If, in relation to the recipient, there is more than one person who is the user, any consideration or expenditure falling within paragraph (*a*) or paragraph (*b*) of sub-paragraph (2) above shall be apportioned between those persons in such manner as is just and reasonable.

(6) Sub-paragraph (2) (*b*) above does not apply if the asset is a mobile asset which is not dedicated to an oil field.

Amendments.—[1] Words in sub-paras. (2), (3) (*a*) substituted by TA 1988, Sch. 29, para. 32 Table.

Purchase at place of extraction

12.—(1) Subject to sub-paragraphs (4) and (5) below, in any case where—

a participator in an oil field or any person connected with him purchases any oil, otherwise than in pursuance of such an agreement as is mentioned in paragraph 6A of Schedule 3 to the principal Act (transactions between participators), and takes delivery of that oil at the place of extraction, and

(b) any of that oil is transported, initially treated or initially stored (or subjected to any two or more of those operations) by means of any asset which is a qualifying asset in relation to that field, and

(c) when the oil is disposed of or relevantly appropriated by the participator or the person connected with him, the selling price of the oil exceeds the price paid for it on the purchase referred to in paragraph (a) above,

the participator shall be treated for the purposes of this Act and Part I [of the principal Act and section 500 of the Taxes Act][1] as having received an amount equal to that excess as tariff receipts which arise in the chargeable period in which the selling price falls to be determined and are attributable to the use of the asset for carrying out the operation or operations referred to in paragraph (b) above.

(2) In this paragraph "selling price", in relation to any oil, means the aggregate of the amounts determined in relation to that oil in accordance with paragraphs (a) to (c) of subsection (5) of section 2 of the principal Act; and for the purpose of the application of those paragraphs and of determining whether any oil falling within sub-paragraph (1) above is relevantly appropriated,—

(a) a person who is connected with the participator and who purchases oil as mentioned in sub-paragraph (1) (a) above shall be deemed to be a participator; and

(b) oil falling within sub-paragraph (1) above shall be treated, for the purposes of section 2 (5) of the principal Act and the definition of "relevantly appropriated" in section 12 of that Act as if it were oil won from the field referred to in paragraph (a) of that sub-paragraph.

(3) A person who takes delivery of oil—

(a) before it has been transported to the place at which it is first landed in the United Kingdom, or

(b) which is not in fact landed in the United Kingdom,

shall be treated for the purposes of sub-paragraph (1) (a) above as having taken delivery of the oil at the place of extraction.

(4) Sub-paragraph (1) above does not apply to oil if, at a time before the participator's selling price for that oil falls to be determined as mentioned in sub-paragraph (2) above, the oil is either—

(a) stored in the field referred to in paragraphs (a) and (b) of sub-paragraph (1) above; or

(b) used for the purpose of assisting the extraction of oil from that field.

(5) Sub-paragraph (1) above does not apply to oil if, by virtue of section 2 (5) (b) of the principal Act (oil disposed of crude, otherwise than in sales at arm's length), the market value of the oil is taken into account in calculating the gross profit and loss (if any) accruing to a participator from an oil field in any chargeable period.

Amendments.—[1] Words in sub-para. (1) substituted by TA 1988, Sch. 29, para. 32 Table.

SCHEDULE 4

Section 12

RECEIPTS ATTRIBUTABLE TO UNITED KINGDOM USE OF FOREIGN FIELD ASSETS

Interpretation

1. In this Schedule—

(a) "the principal section" means section 12 of this Act;

Income and corporation taxes

16.—(1) Section 11 of this Act shall have effect as if—

(a) any reference therein to an oil field included a reference to a foreign field; and
(b) any reference therein to a participator were to be construed, in relation to a foreign field, in accordance with subsection (2) (b) of the principal section; and
(c) any reference therein to a tariff receipt included a reference to a chargeable receipt consisting of consideration received or receivable as mentioned in paragraph (a) or paragraph (b) of subsection (1) of the principal section.

(2) Paragraphs (a) and (b) of sub-paragraph (1) above apply in relation to paragraph 11 (3) of Schedule 2 to this Act in so far as that paragraph has effect for the purposes of section 11 of this Act by virtue of subsection (4) thereof.

TELECOMMUNICATIONS ACT 1984

(1984 Chapter 12)

72. Tax provisions

(1) Subject to subsection (2) below and paragraph 39 of Schedule 5 to this Act, the successor company shall be treated for all purposes of corporation tax ... as if it were the same person as British Telecommunications.

(2) The successor company shall not by virtue of subsection (1) above be regarded as a body falling within section 272 (5) of the Income and Corporation Taxes Act 1970 (bodies established for carrying on industries or undertakings under national ownership or control) ...

(3) Where, in the discharge of any liability which is vested in the successor company by this Act, the successor company makes payments to a retirement benefits scheme with a view to the provision of relevant benefits for persons who are employees of the Post Office, the Tax Acts shall have effect in relation to those payments—

    (a) as if those persons were employees of the successor company; and
    (b) where the scheme is an exempt approved scheme, as if [section 592 (5) of the Income and Corporation Taxes Act 1988][1] were omitted;

and in this subsection expressions which are also used in Chapter [I of Part XIV of that Act][1] have the same meanings as in that Chapter.

(4) The vesting in the successor company by virtue of section 60 above of liability for any loan made to British Telecommunications shall not affect any direction in respect of the loan which has been given by the Treasury under section [581][1] of the Income and Corporation Taxes Act [1988][1] (income tax exemption for interest on foreign currency securities).

(5) ...

Notes.—Sub-s. (5) and words omitted from sub-ss. (1), (2) are not relevant to this work.
Amendments.—[1] Words in sub-ss. (3), (4) substituted by TA 1988, Sch. 29, para. 32 Table.

SCHEDULE 5

39. (1)–(6) ...

(7) British Telecommunications shall be exempt from income tax and corporation tax in respect of—

    (a) income accruing to it in right of the transferred debentures; and
    (b) chargeable gains accruing to it on the disposal of those debentures;

and in so far as the exemption conferred by this sub-paragraph calls for repayment of tax, effect shall be given thereto by means of a claim.

(8) Nothing in section 72 (1) of this Act shall be taken—

    (a) as requiring any payments made or expenses incurred by British Telecommunications under this paragraph to be regarded for corporation tax purposes as made or incurred by the successor company; or
    (b) as requiring any payments made by the successor company to British Telecommunications in pursuance of the transferred debentures to be disregarded for those purposes.

(9) Section 82 (4) of the 1981 Act (tax provisions) shall have effect during the transitional period as if any reference to persons who are employees of the Post Office included a reference to persons who are employees of the successor company.

(10) ...

Notes.—The 1981 Act referred to in sub-para. (9) is the British Telecommunications Act 1981.

FINANCE ACT 1984

(1984 Chapter 43)

ARRANGEMENT OF SECTIONS

Note.—Provisions of this Act relevant to the taxes covered by this Handbook and not reproduced are either spent or repealed by TA 1988, Sch. 31 and other legislation.

PART I

CUSTOMS AND EXCISE, VALUE ADDED TAX AND CAR TAX

CHAPTER I

CUSTOMS AND EXCISE

Section
8. *Free zones* (see Orange Book)
9. *Entry of goods on importation* (see Orange Book)

CHAPTER II

VALUE ADDED TAX

Sections 10–13 (see Orange Book)

CHAPTER III

MISCELLANEOUS

Sections 14–16 (see Orange Book : VAT)

PART II

INCOME TAX, CORPORATION TAX AND CAPITAL GAINS TAX ETC.

CHAPTER I

GENERAL

Section
44. Trustee savings banks.
50. Furnished holiday lettings.

CHAPTER II

CAPITAL ALLOWANCES

58. Withdrawal of initial and first year allowances.
59. Disclaimer of writing-down and first-year allowances.
60. Transfer under Oil and Gas (Enterprise) Act 1982.

533

CHAPTER III
CAPITAL GAINS

64. Exemption for qualifying corporate bonds.
68. Maintenance funds for historic buildings.
70. Postponement of tax due from beneficiaries on gains of non-resident trustees.

CHAPTER IV
INSURANCE

Section
73. Insurance business of registered friendly societies.

CHAPTER V
OIL AND GAS INDUSTRY

78. Transfer of interests in oil fields: capital allowances.
79. Gains on certain disposals.
80. Replacement of business assets used in connection with oil fields.

PART IV
STAMP DUTY

Sections 109–112 (see Orange Book)

PART VI
MISCELLANEOUS AND SUPPLEMENTARY

Miscellaneous

Section
126. Tax exemptions in relation to designated international organisations.
128. Short title, interpretation, construction and repeals.

SCHEDULES:
    Schedule 4—*Free zones.* (see Orange Book: VAT)
    Schedule 5—*Entry on importation: amendment of Customs and Excise Management Act 1979.* (see Orange Book)
    Schedule 6—*Modifications of Schedule 5 to Value Added Tax Act 1983.* (see Orange Book)
    Schedule 11—Furnished holiday lettings.
    Schedule 12—Initial allowances and first-year allowances.
    Schedule 13—Qualifying corporate bonds.
    Schedule 14—Beneficiary's liability for tax on gains of non-resident trustees.
    Schedule 23—Repeals.
        Part III   *Value Added Tax.* (see Orange Book)
        Part IV   *Customs and Excise: Miscellaneous.* (see Orange Book)
        Part X   *Stamp Duty.* (see Orange Book)

An Act to grant certain duties, to alter other duties, and to amend the law relating to the National Debt and the Public Revenue, and to make further provision in connection with Finance.
[26th July 1984]

PART II
INCOME TAX, CORPORATION TAX AND CAPITAL GAINS TAX ETC.

CHAPTER I
GENERAL

44. Trustee savings banks

(1) For the purposes of sections ...[1] 272 to 281 (groups of companies) of the Taxes Act, a trustee savings bank as defined in section 54 (1) of the Trustee Savings Banks Act 1981 shall be deemed to be a body corporate.

(2) ...

(3) ...[1]

(4) Subsection (2) above, and subsection (1) above so far as it applies to sections 272 to 281, shall be deemed to have come into force on 21st November 1982.

Note.—Sub-s. (2) amends TA 1970, s. 272(2).
Amendment.—[1] Words in sub-s. (1) and sub-s. (3) repealed by TA 1988, Sch. 31.

50. Furnished holiday lettings

(1) Schedule 11 to this Act shall have effect with respect to the treatment for the purposes of [capital gains tax or corporation tax on chargeable gains][1] of the commercial letting of furnished holiday accommodation in the United Kingdom.

(2) For the purposes of this section a letting—

(*a*) is a commercial letting if it is on a commercial basis and with a view to the realisation of profits; and
(*b*) is of furnished accommodation if the tenant is entitled to the use of furniture.

(3) Accommodation shall not be treated as holiday accommodation for the purposes of this section unless—

(*a*) it is available for commercial letting to the public generally as holiday accommodation for periods which amount, in the aggregate, to not less than 140 days;
(*b*) the periods for which it is so let amount, in the aggregate, to at least 70 days; and
(*c*) for a period comprising at least seven months (which need not be continuous but includes any months in which it is let as mentioned in paragraph (*b*) above) it is not normally in the same occupation for a continuous period exceeding 31 days.

(4) Any question whether accommodation let by any person other than a company is, at any time in a year of assessment, holiday accommodation shall be determined—

(*a*) if the accommodation was not let by him as furnished accommodation in the preceding year of assessment but is so let in the following year of assessment, by reference to the 12 months beginning with the date on which he first so let it in the year of assessment;
(*b*) if the accommodation was let by him as furnished accommodation in the preceding year of assessment but is not so let in the following year of assessment, by reference to the 12 months ending with the date on which he ceased so to let it in the year of assessment; and
(*c*) in any other case, by reference to the year of assessment.

(5) Any question whether accommodation let by a company is at any time in an accounting period holiday accommodation shall be determined—

(*a*) if the accommodation was not let by it as furnished accommodation in the period of 12 months immediately preceding the accounting period but is so let in the period of 12 months immediately following the accounting period, by reference to the 12 months beginning with the date in the accounting period on which it first so let it;
(*b*) if the accommodation was let by it as furnished accommodation in the period of

12 months immediately preceding the accounting period but is not so let by it in the period of 12 months immediately following the accounting period, by reference to the 12 months ending with the date in the accounting period on which it ceased so to let it; and

(c) in any other case, by reference to the period of 12 months ending with the last day of the accounting period.

(6) Where, in any year of assessment or accounting period, a person lets furnished accommodation which is treated as holiday accommodation for the purposes of this section in that year or period ("the qualifying accommodation"), he may make a claim under this subsection, within two years after that year or period, for averaging treatment to apply for that year or period to that and any other accommodation specified in the claim which was let by him as furnished accommodation during that year or period and would fall to be treated as holiday accommodation in that year or period if paragraph (b) of subsection (3) were satisfied in relation to it.

(7) Where a claim is made under subsection (6) above in respect of any year of assessment or accounting period, any such other accommodation shall be treated as being holiday accommodation in that year or period if the number of days for which the qualifying accommodation and any other such accommodation was let by the claimant as mentioned in paragraph (a) of subsection (3) above during the year or period amounts on average to at least 70.

(8) Qualifying accommodation may not be specified in more than one claim in respect of any one year of assessment or accounting period.

(9) For the purposes of this section a person lets accommodation if he permits another person to occupy it, whether or not in pursuance of a lease; and "letting" and "tenant" shall be construed accordingly.

(10) This section has effect—

(a) ...[2]

(b) for the purposes of capital gains tax and corporation tax on chargeable gains—

(i) in so far as it applies in relation to sections 115 to 120 of the Capital Gains Tax Act 1979, where the acquisition of, or of the interest in, the new assets takes place on or after 6th April 1982, and

(ii) otherwise, in relation to disposals made on or after that date; and

(c) ...[2]

Amendments.—[1] Words in sub-s. (1) substituted by TA 1988, Sch. 29, para. 32 Table.
[2] Sub-s. (10)(a), (c) repealed by TA 1988, Sch. 31.

CHAPTER II

CAPITAL ALLOWANCES

58. Withdrawal of initial and first-year allowances

(1) Each of the following allowances in respect of capital expenditure, namely,—

(*a*) initial allowances under section 1 of the Capital Allowances Act 1968 (industrial buildings and structures),
(*b*) first-year allowances under section 41 of the Finance Act 1971 (machinery and plant), and
(*c*) initial allowances under Schedule 12 to the Finance Act 1982 (dwelling-houses let on assured tenancies),

shall be progressively withdrawn in accordance with Part I of Schedule 12 to this Act.

(2) Part II of Schedule 12 to this Act shall have effect—

(*a*) to provide transitional relief in respect of certain capital expenditure incurred in connection with projects in development areas and Northern Ireland; and
(*b*) with respect to the treatment of certain capital expenditure incurred in the financial years 1984 and 1985 under contracts entered into after 13th March 1984 and on or before 31st March 1986.

(3) . . .

(4) Nothing in subsection (1) (*a*) above or in paragraph 1 of Schedule 12 to this Act affects the continuing operation of—

(*a*) paragraph 1 of Schedule 6 to the Finance Act 1978 (20 per cent. initial allowance for capital expenditure in respect of hotels); or
(*b*) paragraph 1 of Schedule 13 to the Finance Act 1980 (100 per cent. initial allowance for capital expenditure in respect of industrial buildings etc. in enterprise zones and for capital expenditure incurred before 27th March 1985 in respect of small workshops);

and paragraph 5 of Schedule 12 to this Act does not apply to expenditure in respect of which the rate of initial allowance is determined by the provision referred to in paragraph (*b*) above.

Note.—Sub-s. (3) amends FA 1971, Sch. 8, para. 8(2) (*b*).

59. Disclaimer of writing-down and first-year allowances

(1) . . .

(2)–(3) . . .

(4) In any case where—

(*a*) after 13th March 1984, a company carrying on a trade incurs capital expenditure on the provision of machinery or plant for the purposes of the trade, and
(*b*) apart from any disclaimer of the allowance a first-year allowance would fall to be made for any chargeable period in respect of that expenditure, and
(*c*) the company disclaims the allowance by notice under section 41(3) of the Finance Act 1971 or (in the case of new ships) under paragraph 8 (1) (*a*) of Schedule 8 to that Act,

then, for the purposes of section 44 of that Act, that expenditure shall not, by virtue of sub-paragraph (ii) of paragraph (*a*) of subsection (4) of that section, be excluded from the capital expenditure referred to in that paragraph.

(5) In any case where—

(*a*) after 13th March 1984, a person carrying on a trade, but not being a company, incurs capital expenditure on the provision of machinery or plant for the purposes of the trade, and
(*b*) if a claim were made in that behalf, a first-year allowance would fall to be made in respect of that expenditure for the chargeable period related to the incurring of it, and
(*c*) no claim is so made but, by notice in writing given to the inspector not later than two

years after the end of that chargeable period, the person concerned elects that this subsection shall apply,

then, for the purposes of section 44 of the Finance Act 1971, that expenditure shall not, by virtue of sub-paragraph (ii) of paragraph (a) of subsection (4) of that section, be excluded from the capital expenditure referred to in that paragraph.

(6) In any case where—

(a) after 13th March 1984, a person (whether a company or not) carrying on a trade has incurred capital expenditure on the provision of machinery or plant for the purposes of the trade, and

(b) a first-year allowance falls to be made to that person in respect of that expenditure (and, in the case of a person other than a company, a claim is made for that allowance), and

(c) for the chargeable period related to the incurring of that expenditure, the amount of that first-year allowance or, as the case may be, the aggregate amount of that and other first-year allowances which fall to be made to that person is required to be reduced by virtue of section 41 (3) of the Finance Act 1971 or (in the case of new ships) paragraph 8 (1) (b) of Schedule 8 to that Act,

then, for the purposes of section 44 of that Act, an amount equal to the relevant portion of so much of the expenditure giving rise to the first-year allowance or allowances referred to in paragraph (c) above as was incurred after 13th March 1984 shall be treated as expenditure in respect of which no first-year allowance is or could be made for the chargeable period in question.

(7) In subsection (6) above "the relevant portion" of expenditure giving rise to a first-year allowance or allowances and incurred after 13th March 1984 is that which bears to the whole of that expenditure the same proportion as the amount of the reduction mentioned in paragraph (c) of that subsection bears to what the amount of the allowance or allowances would have been apart from that reduction.

(8) Subsections (2) to (7) above shall be construed as if they were contained in Chapter I of Part III of the Finance Act 1971.

Notes.—Sub-s. (1) amends FA 1971, s. 44.
Sub-ss. (2), (3) amend FA 1971, Sch. 8, para. 8.
Cross references.—See FA 1985, s. 58 (3) (c) (sub-ss. (4) (c), (6) (c) of this section to apply with modifications in relation to first-year allowances to ships which are not new).

60. Transfers under Oil and Gas (Enterprise) Act 1982

(1) This section shall have effect in relation to any transfer of assets made pursuant to a direction under section 11 of the Oil and Gas (Enterprise) Act 1982 by the British Gas Corporation or any relevant subsidiary, within the meaning of that section, other than a transfer of assets made on any transfer of a trade to which section [343 of the Taxes Act 1988][1] applies.

(2) The transfer shall not give rise to any allowance or charge provided for by Chapter I of Part III of the Finance Act 1971 (capital allowances and charges in respect of machinery and plant) or the Capital Allowances Act 1968.

(3) Paragraph 3 of Schedule 8 to the 1971 Act and section 78 of, and Schedule 7 to, the 1968 Act (special rules for sales between connected persons) shall not apply in relation to the transfer.

(4) In respect of any chargeable period beginning after the transfer there shall be made in accordance with the provisions mentioned in subsection (2) above all such further allowances and charges in respect of the assets transferred by the transfer as would have fallen to be made if—

(a) everything done to or by the transferor in relation to the assets (other than the transfer) had been done to or by the transferee;

(b) the trade carried on by the transferee, in relation to which the assets are first used by it after the transfer, were the same trade as the trade in relation to which the transferor used the assets at the time of the transfer; and (*c*) that trade had been carried on by the transferee since the transferor began to carry it on.

(5) This section has effect in relation to transfers whenever made.

Amendments.—[1] Words in sub-s. (1) substituted by TA 1988, Sch. 29, para. 32 Table.

CHAPTER III

CAPITAL GAINS

64. Exemption for qualifying corporate bonds

(1) Part I of Schedule 13 to this Act shall have effect for the purpose of—

(*a*) providing, in relation to qualifying corporate bonds, an exemption from capital gains tax and corporation tax on chargeable gains similar to that provided in relation to gilt-edged securities by Part IV of the Capital Gains Tax Act 1979; and
(*b*) making corresponding amendments of other enactments.

(2) For the purposes of this section, a "corporate bond" is a security, as defined in section 82 (3) (*b*) of the Capital Gains Tax Act 1979,—

(*a*) ...[1]
(*b*) the debt on which represents and has at all times represented a normal commercial loan, as defined in paragraph 1 (5) of Schedule 12 to the Finance Act 1973; and
(*c*) which is expressed in sterling and in respect of which no provision is made for conversion into, or redemption in, a currency other than sterling.

(3) For the purposes of subsection (2) (*c*) above,—

(*a*) a security shall not be regarded as expressed in sterling if the amount of sterling falls to be determined by reference to the value at any time of any other currency or asset; and
(*b*) a provision for redemption in a currency other than sterling but at the rate of exchange prevailing at redemption shall be disregarded.

[(3A) For the purposes of this section "corporate bond" also includes a security—

(*a*) which is not included in the definition in subsection (2) above, and
(*b*) which is a deep gain security for the purposes of Schedule 11 to the Finance Act 1989.][2]

[(3B) For the purposes of this section "corporate bond" also includes a security—

(*a*) which is not included in the definition in subsection (2) above, and
(*b*) which, by virtue of paragraph 21 (2) of Schedule 11 to the Finance Act 1989, falls to be treated as a deep gain security as there mentioned.][2]

[(3C) For the purposes of this section "corporate bond" also includes a security—

(*a*) which is not included in the definition in subsection (2) above, and
(*b*) which, by virtue of paragraph 22 (2) of Schedule 11 to the Finance Act 1989, falls to be treated as a deep gain security as there mentioned.][2]

(4) Subject to subsection (6) below, for the purposes of this section and Schedule 13 to this Act, a corporate bond—

(*a*) is a "qualifying" corporate bond if it is issued after 13th March 1984; and
(*b*) becomes a "qualifying" corporate bond if, having been issued on or before that date, it is acquired by any person after that date and that acquisition is not as a result of a disposal which is excluded for the purposes of this subsection.

(5) Where a person disposes of a corporate bond which was issued on or before 13th March 1984 and, before the disposal, the bond had not become a qualifying corporate bond, the disposal is excluded for the purposes of subsection (4) above if, by virtue of any enactment,—

(*a*) the disposal is treated for the purposes of the Capital Gains Tax Act 1979 as one on which neither a gain nor a loss accrues to the person making the disposal; or
(*b*) the consideration for the disposal is treated for the purposes of that Act as reduced by an amount equal to the held-over gain on that disposal, as defined for the purposes of section 126 [or 147A of that Act][4].

[(5A) Subject to subsection (6) below, for the purposes of this section and Schedule 13 to this Act a corporate bond which falls within subsection (3A) above is a qualifying corporate bond, whatever the date of its issue; and subsections (4) and (5) above shall not apply in the case of such a bond.][2]

[(5B) Subject to subsection (6) below, for the purposes of this section and Schedule 13 to this Act a corporate bond which falls within subsection (3B) above is a qualifying corporate bond as regards a disposal made after the time mentioned in paragraph 21 (1) (c) of Schedule 11 to the Finance Act 1989, whatever the date of its issue; and subsections (4) and (5) above shall not apply in the case of such a bond.]²

[(5C) Subject to subsection (6) below, for the purposes of this section and Schedule 13 to this Act a corporate bond which falls within subsection (3C) above is a qualifying corporate bond as regards a disposal made after the time the agreement mentioned in paragraph 22 (1) (b) of Schedule 11 to the Finance Act 1989 is made, whatever the date of its issue; and subsections (4) and (5) above shall not apply in the case of such a bond.]²

(6) A security which is issued by a member of a group of companies to another member of the same group is not a qualifying corporate bond for the purposes of this section or Schedule 13 to this Act [except in relation to a disposal by a person who (at the time of the disposal) is not a member of the same group as the company which issued the security]³; and references in this subsection to a group of companies or to a member of a group shall be construed in accordance with section 272 of the Taxes Act.

(7) Part II of Schedule 13 to this Act shall have effect in any case where a transaction occurs of such a description that, apart from the provisions of that Schedule,—

(a) sections 78 to 81 of the Capital Gains Tax Act 1979 would apply by virtue of any provision of Chapter II of Part IV of that Act; and
(b) either the original shares would consist of or include a qualifying corporate bond and the new holding would not, or the original shares would not and the new holding would consist of or include such a bond;

and in paragraph (b) above "the original shares" and "the new holding" have the same meaning as they have for the purposes of the said sections 78 to 81.

(8) For the purposes of this section, in any case where—

(a) a security is comprised in a letter of allotment or similar instrument, and
(b) the right to the security thereby conferred remains provisional until accepted,

the security shall not be treated as issued until there has been acceptance.

Amendments.—[1] Sub-s. (2) (a) repealed by FA 1989, s. 139 (1), (2) and Sch. 17, Pt. VII in relation to disposals after 13 March 1989 and in relation to such disposals the repeal is deemed always to have had effect.
[2] Sub-ss. (3A), (3B), (3C), (5A), (5B), (5C) inserted by FA 1989, s. 139 (1), (3), (4) in relation to disposals after 13 March 1989 and in relation to such disposals the new subsections are deemed always to have had effect.
[3] Words in sub-s. (6) inserted by FA 1989, s. 139 (1), (5) in relation to disposals after 13 March 1989 and in relation to such disposals are deemed always to have had effect.
[4] Words in sub-s. (5) (b) substituted by FA 1989, Sch. 14, para. 6 (4).

68. Maintenance funds for historic buildings

In consequence of the operation of section 79 of the Finance Act 1980 (general relief for gifts) section 148 of the Capital Gains Tax Act 1979 (specific relief in the case of certain disposals relating to maintenance funds for historic buildings) shall cease to have effect with respect to disposals made on or after 6th April 1984.

70. Postponement of tax due from beneficiaries on gains of non-resident trustees

(1) The provisions of Schedule 14 to this Act have effect in any case where,—

(a) before 6th April 1981, a chargeable gain accrued to the trustees of a settlement in such circumstances that section 17 of the Capital Gains Tax Act 1979 (non-resident trust) applies as respects that chargeable gain; and
(b) by virtue of that section a beneficiary under the settlement is treated for the purposes of that Act as if, in the year 1983–84 or any earlier year of assessment, an amount determined by reference to the chargeable gain which accrued to the trustees or, as the case may be, the whole or part of that gain had been a chargeable gain accruing to the beneficiary; and
(c) at 29th March 1983 some or all of the capital gains tax payable in respect of the chargeable gain accruing to the beneficiary had not been paid.

(2) In subsection (3) (b) of the said section 17 (which relates to capital payments which are made in the exercise of a discretion, which are received at any time and which represent a chargeable gain to which that section applies) after the words "after the chargeable gain accrues" there shall be inserted the words "but before 6th April 1984".

(3) In consequence of the amendment made by subsection (2) above, in section 80 of the Finance Act 1981 (new provisions as to gains of non-resident settlements) in subsection (8) (which, among other things, excludes from the scope of that section payments received on or after 10th March 1981 so far as they represent chargeable gains accruing to the trustees before 6th April 1981) after the words "received on or after that date" there shall be inserted the words "and before 6th April 1984".

(4) In this section and Schedule 14 to this Act "settlement", "settlor" and "settled property" have the same meaning as in section 17 of the Capital Gains Tax Act 1979.

CHAPTER IV

INSURANCE

73. Insurance business of registered friendly societies

(1) ...²

(2) ...²

(3) ...²

(4) In consequence of the preceding provisions of this section and subsection (5) below, in section 1 of the Friendly Societies Act (Northern Ireland) 1970 and section 7 of the Friendly Societies Act 1974 (societies which may be registered),—

    (*a*) paragraph (*a*) of subsection (3), and
    (*b*) subsection (3A),

shall not have effect with respect to benefits secured by contracts made after 13th March 1984.

(5) ...²

(6) ...²

(7) If, after 13th March 1984, the committee of a registered society or branch whose rules make provision for it to carry on life or endowment business resolve to accept, in respect of any contract falling within subsection (8) below, premiums of amounts arrived at by deducting 15 per cent. from the premiums provided for by the rules of the society or branch (that is to say by deducting the same amount as, apart from section 72 above, would have been deductible by way of relief under section 19 of the Taxes Act),—

    (*a*) the resolution shall be deemed to be permitted by the principal Act and the rules of the society or branch; and
    (*b*) nothing in the principal Act shall require the registration of the resolution; and
    (*c*) together with the annual return of the society or branch for the year of account ending 31st December 1984, the society or branch shall send a copy of the resolution to the registrar.

(8) Subsection (7) above applies to any contract entered into by a registered society or branch—

    (*a*) which is for the assurance under life or endowment business of any gross sum; and
    (*b*) which is entered into pursuant to a proposal received by the society or branch on or before 13th March 1984; and
    (*c*) which is one which the society might lawfully have entered into on that date; and
    (*d*) which is entered into after 13th March 1984 and before 1st May 1984.

(9) In subsection (7) above "the principal Act" means, according to the enactment under which the society or branch is registered,—

    (*a*) the Friendly Societies Act (Northern Ireland) 1970; or
    (*b*) the Friendly Societies Act 1974;

and subsections (7) and (8) above shall be construed as one with the principal Act.

Amendments.—[1] Words in sub-s. (5) repealed by FA 1985, Sch. 27, Pt. V with respect to business of friendly societies and branches thereof carried on after 18 March 1985.
[2] Sub-ss. (1)–(3), (5), (6) repealed by TA 1988, Sch. 31.

CHAPTER V

OIL AND GAS INDUSTRY

78. Transfers of interests in oil fields: capital allowances

(1) This section applies where,—

(a) there is, for the purposes of Schedule 17 to the Finance Act 1980, a transfer by a participator in an oil field of the whole or part of his interest in the field; and
(b) in pursuance of that transfer, the old participator disposes of, and the new participator acquires, machinery or plant used, or expected to be used, in connection with the field, or a share in such machinery or plant.

(2) In the application of Chapter I of Part III of the Finance Act 1971 (capital allowances) to expenditure incurred by the new participator in the acquisition referred to in subsection (1) (b) above, there shall be disregarded so much (if any) of that expenditure as exceeds—

(a) the disposal value to be brought into account by the old participator under section 44 of that Act (balancing adjustments etc.) by reason of the disposal; or
(b) if subsection (2) of section 41 of that Act applies in relation to the old participator (machinery or plant disposed of before being brought into use), the amount of the expenditure in respect of which, but for that subsection, a first-year allowance would have been made (and not withdrawn).

(3) In this section—

(a) "machinery or plant" has the same meaning as in Chapter I of Part III of the Finance Act 1971 (capital allowances);
(b) subsection (7) of section 50 of that Act applies to any reference to a share in machinery or plant; and
(c) "the old participator" and "the new participator" have the same meaning as in Schedule 17 to the Finance Act 1980;

and, subject thereto, expressions used in subsection (1) above have the same meaning as in Part I of the Oil Taxation Act 1975 and expressions used in subsection (2) above have the same meaning as in Chapter I of Part III of the Finance Act 1971.

(4) Nothing in this section affects the operation of paragraph 3 of Schedule 8 to the Finance Act 1971 (which restricts allowable expenditure on sales between connected persons etc.).

(5) This section applies where the acquisition referred to in subsection (1) (b) above occurs on or after 13th March 1984.

79. Gains on certain disposals

(1) This section applies where, on or after 13th March 1984 and in pursuance of a transfer by a participator in an oil field of the whole or part of his interest in the field, there is—

(a) a disposal of an interest in oil to be won from the oil field; or
(b) a disposal of an asset used in connection with the field;

and section 12 of the Oil Taxation Act 1975 (interpretation of Part I of that Act) applies for the interpretation of this subsection and the reference to the transfer by a participator in an oil field of the whole or part of his interest in the field shall be construed in accordance with paragraph 1 of Schedule 17 to the Finance Act 1980.

(2) In this section "disposal" has the same meaning as in the Capital Gains Tax Act 1979 and "material disposal" means—

(a) a disposal falling within paragraph (a) or paragraph (b) of subsection (1) above; or
(b) the sale of an asset referred to in subsection (3) of section 278 of the Taxes Act (company ceasing to be a member of a group: notional sale and repurchase of asset acquired from another member) where the asset was acquired by the chargeable company (within the meaning of that section) on a disposal falling within one of those paragraphs.

(3) For any chargeable period (within the meaning of the Taxes Act) in which a chargeable gain or allowable loss accrues to any person (in the following provisions of this section

referred to as "the chargeable person") on a material disposal (whether taking place in that period or not), subject to subsection (7) below there shall be aggregated—

(a) the chargeable gains accruing to him in that period on such disposals, and
(b) the allowable losses accruing to him in that period on such disposals,

and the lesser of the two aggregates shall be deducted from the other to give an aggregate gain or, as the case may be, an aggregate loss for that chargeable period.

(4) For the purposes of capital gains tax and corporation tax in respect of capital gains,—

(a) the several chargeable gains and allowable losses falling within paragraphs (a) and (b) of subsection (3) above shall be left out of account; and
(b) the aggregate gain or aggregate loss referred to in that subsection shall be treated as a single chargeable gain or allowable loss accruing to the chargeable person in the chargeable period concerned on the notional disposal of an asset; and
(c) if in any chargeable period there is an aggregate loss, then, except as provided by subsection (6) below, it shall not be allowable as a deduction against any chargeable gain arising in that or any later period, other than an aggregate gain treated as accruing in a later period by virtue of paragraph (b) above (so that the aggregate gain of that later period shall be reduced or extinguished accordingly); and
(d) if in any chargeable period there is an aggregate gain, no loss shall be deducted from it except in accordance with paragraph (c) above; and
(e) without prejudice to any indexation allowance which was taken into account in determining an aggregate gain or aggregate loss under subsection (3) above, no further indexation allowance shall be allowed on a notional disposal referred to in paragraph (b) above.

(5) Where, in accordance with subsection (3) above, the chargeable person has an aggregate gain, that ...[1] and his ring fence income (if any) for the chargeable period concerned together constitute, for the purposes of this section, his ring fence profits for that period ...[4]

(6) In any case where—

(a) by virtue of subsection (4) (b) above, an aggregate loss is treated as accruing to the chargeable person in any chargeable period, and
(b) before the expiry of the period of two years beginning at the end of the chargeable period concerned, the chargeable person makes a claim under this subsection,

the whole, or such portion as is specified in the claim, of the aggregate loss shall be treated for the purposes of capital gains tax or corporation tax, as the case may be, as an allowable loss arising in that chargeable period otherwise than on a material disposal.

(7) In any case where a loss accrues to the chargeable person on a material disposal made to a person who is connected with him (within the meaning of section 63 of the Capital Gains Tax Act 1979)—

(a) the loss shall be excluded from those referred to in paragraph (b) of subsection (3) above and, accordingly, shall not be aggregated under that subsection; and
(b) except as provided by subsection (8) below, section 62 of that Act shall apply in relation to the loss as if, in subsection (3) of that section (losses on disposals to a connected person to be set only against gains on disposals made to the same person at a time when he is a connected person), any reference to a disposal were a reference to a disposal which is a material disposal; and
(c) to the extent that the loss is set against a chargeable gain by virtue of paragraph (b) above, the gain shall be excluded from those referred to in paragraph (a) of subsection (3) above and, accordingly, shall not be aggregated under that subsection.

(8) In any case where—

(a) the losses accruing to the chargeable person in any chargeable period on material disposals to a connected person exceed the gains accruing to him in that chargeable period on material disposals made to that person at a time when they are connected persons, and
(b) before the expiry of the period of two years beginning at the end of the chargeable period concerned, the chargeable person makes a claim under this subsection,

the whole, or such part as is specified in the claim, of the excess referred to in paragraph (a) above shall be treated for the purposes of section 62 of the Capital Gains Tax Act 1979 as if it were a loss accruing on a disposal in that chargeable period, being a disposal which is not a material disposal and which is made by the chargeable person to the connected person referred to in paragraph (*a*) above.

(9) Where a claim is made under subsection (6) or subsection (8) above, all such adjustments shall be made, whether by way of discharge or repayment of tax (including capital gains tax) or otherwise, as may be required in consequence of the operation of that subsection.

(10) In subsection (5) above "ring fence income" means income arising from oil extraction activities or oil rights, within the meaning of [Chapter V of Part XII of the Taxes Act 1988].[3]

Amendments.—[1] Words in sub-s. (5) repealed by F (No. 2) A 1987, s. 76 (3) and Sch. 9, Pt. II with respect to accounting periods beginning after 16 March 1987.
[2] Words in sub-s. (5) substituted by F (No. 2) A 1987, s. 76 (1), (3) with respect to accounting periods beginning after 16 March 1987.
[3] Words in sub-s. (10) substituted by TA 1988, Sch. 29, para. 32 Table.
[4] Words in sub-s. (5) repealed by TA 1988, Sch. 31.

80. Replacement of business assets used in connection with oil fields

(1) If the consideration which a person obtains on a material disposal is applied, in whole or in part, as mentioned in subsection (1) of section 115 or section 116 of the Capital Gains Tax Act 1979 (replacement of business assets), that section shall not apply unless the new assets are taken into use, and used only, for the purposes of the ring fence trade.

(2) Subsection (1) above has effect notwithstanding subsection (7) of the said section 115 (which treats two or more trades as a single trade for certain purposes).

(3) Where the said section 115 or the said section 116 applies in relation to any of the consideration on a material disposal, the asset which constitutes the new assets for the purposes of that section shall be conclusively presumed to be a depreciating asset, and section 117 of the Capital Gains Tax Act 1979 (special rules for depreciating assets) shall have effect accordingly, except that—

(*a*) the reference in subsection (2) (*b*) of that section to a trade carried on by the claimant shall be construed as a reference solely to his ring fence trade; and
(*b*) subsections (3) to (6) of that section shall be omitted.

(4) In any case where sections 115 to 117 of the Capital Gains Tax Act 1979 have effect in accordance with the preceding provisions of this section, the operation of section 276 of the Taxes Act (replacement of business assets by members of a group) shall be modified as follows:—

(*a*) only those members of a group which actually carry on a ring fence trade shall be treated for the purposes of those sections as carrying on a single trade which is a ring fence trade; and
(*b*) only those activities which, in relation to each individual member of the group, constitute its ring fence trade shall be treated as forming part of that single trade.

(5) In this section—

(*a*) "material disposal" has the meaning assigned to it by section 79 above; and
(*b*) "ring fence trade" means a trade consisting of either or both of the activities mentioned in paragraphs (*a*) and (*b*) of subsection (1) of section [492 of the Taxes Act 1988][1].

Amendments.—[1] Words in sub-s. (5) (*b*) substituted by FA 1988, Sch. 13, para. 22.

PART VI
MISCELLANEOUS AND SUPPLEMENTARY

Miscellaneous

126. Tax exemptions in relation to designated international organisations

(1) Where—

(*a*) the United Kingdom or any of the Communities is a member of an international organisation; and
(*b*) the agreement under which it became a member provides for exemption from tax, in relation to the organisation, of the kind for which provision is made by this section;

the Treasury may, by order made by statutory instrument, designate that organisation for the purposes of this section.

(2) Where an organisation has been so designated, the provisions mentioned in subsection (3) below shall, with the exception of any which may be excluded by the designation order, apply in relation to that organisation.

(3) The provisions are—

(*a*) . . .[2]
(*b*) any security issued by the organisation shall be taken, for the purposes of . . . capital gains tax, to be situated outside the United Kingdom; and
(*c*) . . .

[(4) The Treasury may, by order made by statutory instrument, designate any of the Communities or the European Investment Bank for the purposes of this section, and references in subsections (2) and (3) above to an organisation designated for the purposes of this section include references to a body so designated by virtue of this subsection.][1]

[(5)] . . .

Note.—Words omitted from sub-s. (3) are not relevant to this work.
Sub-s. (5) inserted by FA 1985, s. 96 (1) is not relevant to this work.
Amendments.—[1] Sub-s. (4) inserted by FA 1985, s. 96 (1).
[2] Sub-s. (3)(*a*) repealed by TA 1988, Sch. 31.

128. Short title, interpretation, construction and repeals

(1) This Act may be cited as the Finance Act 1984.

(2) In this Act "the Taxes Act" means the Income and Corporation Taxes Act [1970; and "the Taxes Act 1988" means the Income and Corporation Taxes Act 1988].[1]

(3) Part II of this Act, so far as it relates to income tax, shall be construed as one with the Income Tax Acts, so far as it relates to corporation tax, shall be construed as one with the Corporation Tax Acts and, so far as it relates to capital gains tax, shall be construed as one with the Capital Gains Tax Act 1979.

(4) . . .

(5) . . .

(6) The enactments specified in Schedule 23 to this Act are hereby repealed to the extent specified in the third column of that Schedule, but subject to any provision at the end of any Part of that Schedule.

Note.—Sub-ss. (4), (5) are not relevant to this work.
Amendment.—[1] Words in sub-s. (2) substituted by TA 1988, Sch. 29, para. 32 Table.

SCHEDULES

SCHEDULE 11
Section 50 (1)

FURNISHED HOLIDAY LETTINGS

Treatment of lettings as a trade for certain purposes

1.—(1) Subject to the provisions of this Schedule, for the purposes of the provisions mentioned in sub-paragraph (2) below—

(a) the commercial letting of furnished holiday accommodation in respect of which the profits or gains are chargeable under Case VI of Schedule D shall be treated as a trade; and

(b) all such lettings made by a particular person or partnership or body of persons shall be treated as one trade.

(2) The provisions mentioned in sub-paragraph (1) above are—

(a) ...[3]
(b) ...[3]
(c) ...[3]
(d) ...[3]
(e) ...[3]
(f) sections 115 to 120 of the Capital Gains Tax Act 1979 (roll-over relief for replacement of business assets);
(g) [Schedule 20 to the Finance Act 1985][1] (transfer of business on retirement);
(h) section 126 of [the Capital Gains Tax Act 1979][1] (relief for gifts of business assets);
(i) section 136 of that Act (relief in respect of loans to traders); and
(j) ...[3]
[(k) subsection (2) (c) of section 35 of the Finance (No. 2) Act 1987 (personal pension schemes).][2]

Amendments.—[1] Words in sub-para. (2) (g), (h) substituted by FA 1985, s. 70 (10).
[2] Sub-para. (2) (k) added by F (No. 2) A 1987, Sch. 2, para. 6.
[3] Sub-para. (2)(a)–(e), (j) repealed by TA 1988, Sch. 31.

Capital gains tax

4.—(1) Subject to sub-paragraph (2) below, for the purposes of the provisions mentioned in sub-paragraph (2) (f) to (i) of paragraph 1 above as they apply by virtue of that paragraph, where in any year of assessment a person makes a commercial letting of furnished holiday accommodation—

(a) the accommodation shall be taken to be used in that year only for the purposes of the trade of making such lettings; and
(b) that trade shall be taken to be carried on throughout that year.

(2) Sub-paragraph (1) above does not apply to any period in a year of assessment during which the accommodation is neither let commercially nor available to be so let unless it is prevented from being so let or available by any works of construction or repair.

5. Where—

(a) a gain to which section 101 of the Capital Gains Tax Act 1979 (relief on disposal of private residence) applies accrues to any individual on the disposal of an asset; and
(b) by virtue of paragraph 1 above the amount or value of the consideration for the acquisition of the asset is treated as reduced under section 115 or 116 of that Act,

the gain to which section 101 applies shall be reduced by the amount of the reduction mentioned in paragraph (b) above.

Power to make apportionments

6. Where there is a letting of accommodation only part of which is holiday accommodation such apportionments shall be made for the purposes of this Schedule as appear to the inspector, or on appeal the Commissioners, to be just and reasonable.

Adjustments of tax charged

7. Where a person has been charged to . . .[1] capital gains tax otherwise than in accordance with the provisions of this Schedule, such assessment, reduction or discharge of an assessment or, where a claim for repayment is made, such repayment, shall be made as may be necessary to give effect to those provisions.

Amendments.—[1] Words in this para. repealed by TA 1988, Sch. 31.

SCHEDULE 12
Section 58

INITIAL ALLOWANCES AND FIRST-YEAR ALLOWANCES

PART I
WITHDRAWAL OF ALLOWANCES

Initial allowances for industrial buildings and structures

1.—(1) In section 1 (2) of the Capital Allowances Act 1968 (rate of initial allowances for capital expenditure on the construction of industrial buildings or structures) for the words "three-quarters" there shall be substituted,—

(a) with respect to capital expenditure incurred after 13th March 1984 and before 1st April 1985, the words "one half"; and
(b) with respect to capital expenditure incurred on or after 1st April 1985 and before 1st April 1986, the words "one quarter";

and no initial allowance shall be made in respect of expenditure incurred on or after 1st April 1986.

(2) Nothing in sub-paragraph (1) above applies to capital expenditure which—

(a) is incurred after 13th March 1984 and before 1st April 1987; and
(b) consists of the payment of sums under a contract entered into on or before 13th March 1984 by the person incurring the expenditure.

(3) Sub-paragraphs (1) and (2) above shall be construed as if they were contained in Part I of the Capital Allowances Act 1968 except that—

(a) expenditure shall not be treated for the purposes of those sub-paragraphs as having been incurred after the date on which it was in fact incurred by reason only of section 1 (6) of that Act (expenditure incurred before a trade begins); and
(b) expenditure falling within subsection (1) (b) of section 5 of that act (purchase price of building or structure bought unused) shall be treated for the purposes of those sub-paragraphs as having been incurred at the latest time when any expenditure falling within subsection (1) (a) of that section (expenditure on the construction of the building or structure) was incurred.

First-year allowances for machinery and plant

2.—(1) In section 42 (1) of the Finance Act 1971 (rate of first-year allowance for capital expenditure incurred on provision of machinery or plant) for the words "the whole" there shall be substituted,—

(a) with respect to capital expenditure incurred after 13th March 1984 and before 1st April 1985, the words "three-quarters"; and
(b) with respect to capital expenditure incurred on or after 1st April 1985 and before 1st April 1986, the words "one half";

and no first-year allowance shall be made in respect of expenditure incurred on or after 1st April 1986.

(2) Nothing in sub-paragraph (1) above applies to capital expenditure which—

(a) is incurred after 13th March 1984 and before 1st April 1987; and
(b) consists of the payment of sums under a contract entered into on or before 13th March 1984 by the person incurring the expenditure or by a person whose contractual obligations that person has assumed with a view to entering into leasing arrangements.

(3) For the purposes of sub-paragraph (2) (b) above, a person incurring expenditure on the provision of machinery or plant (in this sub-paragraph referred to as "the lessor") shall be taken to have assumed, with a view to entering into leasing arrangements, the contractual obligations of a person who entered into a contract for the provision of that machinery or plant (in this sub-paragraph referred to as "the lessee") if, and only if,—

(a) arrangements exist under which the lessor will lease the machinery or plant to the lessee, and
(b) the obligations of the lessee under the contract either have been taken over by the lessor or have been discharged on the lessor's entering into a new contract for the provision of the machinery or plant concerned;

and, where there is such a new contract as is referred to in paragraph (b) above, sums paid under that contract shall be treated for the purposes of sub-paragraph (2) (b) above and Part II of this Schedule as paid under the contract referred to in that sub-paragraph.

(4) Sub-paragraphs (1) to (3) above shall be construed as if they were contained in Chapter I of Part III of the Finance Act 1971, except that expenditure shall not be treated for the purposes of those sub-paragraphs as having been incurred after the date on which it was in fact incurred by reason only of so much of section 50 (4) of that Act as relates to expenditure incurred before a trade begins.

Cross references.—See FA 1980, s. 64 (2) (a) (this paragraph to be disregarded for the purposes of FA 1980, s. 64 (exclusion of first-year allowances for certain leased assets); see annotations under FA 1980, s. 64).
FA 1985, Sch. 15, para. 12 (election to treat as short-life assets cannot be made in respect of machinery or plant falling within sub-para. (2) above);
FA 1986, s. 57 (2) (a) (new code of allowances for "new expenditure" (i.e. expenditure incurred after 31 March 1986, subject to qualifications in s. 57 (2), (3)) on leased assets not to apply to expenditure falling within sub-para. (2) above).

Initial allowances in respect of dwelling-houses let on assured tenancies

3.—(1) In paragraph 1 (2) of Schedule 12 to the Finance Act 1982 (rate of initial allowance in respect of qualifying dwelling-house on the construction of which capital expenditure is incurred) for the words "three-quarters" there shall be substituted,—

(a) with respect to capital expenditure incurred after 13th March 1984 and before 1st April 1985, the words "one half"; and
(b) with respect to capital expenditure incurred on or after 1st April 1985 and before 1st April 1986, the words "one quarter";

and no initial allowance shall be made in respect of expenditure incurred on or after 1st April 1986.

(2) Nothing in sub-paragraph (1) above applies to capital expenditure which—

(a) is incurred after 13th March 1984 and before 1st April 1987; and
(b) consists of the payment of sums under a contract entered into on or before 13th March 1984 by the person incurring the expenditure.

(3) Sub-paragraphs (1) and (2) above shall be construed as if they were contained in Schedule 12 to the Finance Act 1982 except that expenditure falling within sub-paragraph (1) (b) of paragraph 8 of that Schedule (purchase price of building bought unused) shall be treated for the purposes of those sub-paragraphs as having been incurred at the latest time when any expenditure falling within sub-paragraph (1) (a) of that paragraph (expenditure on the construction of the building) was incurred.

PART II
SUPPLEMENTARY

Transitional relief for regional projects

4.—(1) The provisions of Part I of this Schedule do not apply to so much of any expenditure as is certified by the Secretary of State for the purposes of this paragraph to be expenditure which, in his opinion, qualifies for a regional development grant or a grant under Part IV of the relevant Order and consists of the payment of sums on a project—

(a) either in an area which on 13th March 1984 was a development area, within the meaning of the Industrial Development Act 1982, or in Northern Ireland; and
(b) in respect of which a written offer of financial assistance under section 7 or section 8 of that Act was made on behalf of the Secretary of State, in the period beginning on 1st April 1980 and ending on 13th March 1984 or in respect of which a written offer of financial assistance was made in that period by the Highlands and Islands Development Board.

(2) The provisions of Part I of this Schedule do not apply to so much of any expenditure as is certified by the Department of Economic Development in Northern Ireland for the purposes of this paragraph to be expenditure which, in the opinion of that Department, qualifies for a grant under Part IV of the relevant Order and consists of the payment of sums on a project—

(a) in Northern Ireland; and
(b) in respect of which a written offer of financial assistance under Article 7 or Article 8 of the relevant Order was made on behalf of a Department of the Government of Northern Ireland, in the period beginning on 1st April 1980 and ending on 13th March 1984 or in respect of which a written offer of financial assistance was made in that period by the Local Enterprise Development Unit.

(3) In this paragraph—

"regional development grant" means a grant under Part II of the Industrial Development Act 1982;
"the relevant Order" means the Industrial Development (Northern Ireland) Order 1982;

and any reference to a particular provision of that Act or Order includes a reference to the corresponding provision of any Act or Order which was in force before and repealed by the said Act or Order of 1982.

Cross references.—See FA 1985, Sch. 15, para. 12 (election to treat as short-life assets cannot be made in respect of machinery or plant to which this paragraph applies);
FA 1986, s. 57 (2) (b) (new code of allowances for "new expenditure" (i.e. expenditure incurred after 31 March 1986, subject to qualifications in s. 57 (2), (3)) on leased assets not to apply to expenditure falling within this paragraph).

Spreading of expenditure under certain contracts

5.—(1) Where in circumstances falling within paragraph 8 below a person incurs such capital expenditure as is referred to in section 1 of the Capital Allowances Act 1968 under a contract—

(a) which is entered into after 13th March 1984 and on or before 31st March 1986, and
(b) which either specifies no date on or by which the contractual obligations must be fully performed or specifies such a date which is after 31st March 1985,

Chapter I of Part I of that Act shall have effect in relation to the capital expenditure so incurred subject to the following provisions of this paragraph.

(2) In this Part of this Schedule, in relation to a contract falling within sub-paragraph (1) above,—

"the contract date" means the date on which the contract is entered into;
"the contract price" means the total capital expenditure on the construction of the building or structure concerned which the person referred to in sub-paragraph (1) above is to incur pursuant to the contract;
"the completion date" means the date specified as mentioned in sub-paragraph (1) (b) above or, if no date is so specified, 31st March 1987; and
"the maximum allowable expenditure" shall be construed in accordance with paragraph 9 below.

(3) In respect of capital expenditure incurred in either of the financial years 1984 and 1985 under a contract falling within sub-paragraph (1) above, the initial allowance under section 1 of the Capital Allowances Act 1968 shall not exceed the fraction appropriate under paragraph 1 above of the maximum allowable expenditure for that year.

(4) So much (if any) of the capital expenditure incurred in the financial year 1984 under a contract falling within sub-paragraph (1) above as exceeds the maximum allowable expenditure for that year shall be deemed for all purposes of Chapter I of Part I of the Capital Allowances Act 1968 to be incurred on 1st April 1985.

(5) So much (if any) of the aggregate of—

(a) the capital expenditure incurred in the financial year 1985 under a contract falling within sub-paragraph (1) above, and
(b) any excess relating to that contract which, by virtue of sub-paragraph (4) above, is deemed to be incurred in that financial year,

as exceeds the maximum allowable expenditure for that financial year shall be deemed for all purposes of Chapter I of Part I of the Capital Allowances Act 1968 to be incurred on 1st April 1986.

(6) This paragraph shall be construed as if it were contained in Chapter I of Part I of the Capital Allowances Act 1968 except that—

(*a*) expenditure shall not be treated for the purposes of this paragraph as having been incurred after the date on which it was in fact incurred by reason only of section 1 (6) of that Act; and
(*b*) expenditure falling within subsection (1) (*b*) of section 5 of that Act shall be treated for the purposes of this paragraph as having been incurred at the latest time when any expenditure falling within subsection (1) (*a*) of that section was incurred.

6.—(1) Where in circumstances falling within paragraph 8 below a person carrying on a trade incurs capital expenditure on the provision of machinery or plant for the purposes of that trade under a contract—

(*a*) which is entered into after 13th March 1984 and on or before 31st March 1986, and
(*b*) which provides that he shall or may become the owner of the machinery or plant on or before the performance of the contract, and
(*c*) which either specifies no date on or by which the contractual obligations must be fully performed or specifies such a date which is after 31st March 1985,

Chapter I of Part III of the Finance Act 1971 shall have effect in relation to the capital expenditure so incurred subject to the following provisions of this paragraph.

(2) In this Part of this Schedule, in relation to a contract falling within sub-paragraph (1) above,—

"the contract date" means the date on which the contract is entered into;
"the contract price" means the total capital expenditure on the provision of the machinery or plant which the person referred to in sub-paragraph (1) above is to incur pursuant to the contract;
"the completion date" means the date specified as mentioned in sub-paragraph (1) (*c*) above or, if no date is so specified, 31st March 1987; and
"the maximum allowable expenditure" shall be construed in accordance with paragraph 9 below.

(3) The provisions of this paragraph do not apply in relation to capital expenditure to which section 45 (1) (*b*) of the Finance Act 1971 (machinery and plant on hire-purchase etc.) applies.

(4) In respect of capital expenditure incurred in either of the financial years 1984 and 1985 under a contract falling within sub-paragraph (1) above, the first-year allowance under section 42 (1) of the Finance Act 1971 shall not exceed the fraction appropriate under paragraph 2 above of the maximum allowable expenditure for that year.

(5) So much (if any) of the capital expenditure incurred in the financial year 1984 under a contract falling within sub-paragraph (1) above as exceeds the maximum allowable expenditure for that year shall be deemed for all purposes of Chapter I of Part III of the Finance Act 1971 to be incurred on 1st April 1985.

(6) So much (if any) of the aggregate of—

(*a*) the capital expenditure incurred in the financial year 1985 under a contract falling within sub-paragraph (1) above; and
(*b*) any excess relating to that contract which, by virtue of sub-paragraph (5) above, is deemed to be incurred in that financial year,

as exceeds the maximum allowable expenditure for that financial year shall be deemed for all purposes of Chapter I of Part III of the Finance Act 1971 to be incurred on 1st April 1986.

(7) This paragraph shall be construed as if it were contained in Chapter I of Part III of the Finance Act 1971 except that expenditure shall not be treated for the purposes of this paragraph as having been incurred after the date on which it was in fact incurred by reason only of so much of section 50 (4) of that Act as relates to expenditure incurred before a trade began.

Cross references.—See FA 1986, s. 57 (2) (new code of allowances for "new expenditure" (i.e. expenditure incurred after 31 March 1986, subject to qualifications in s. 57 (2), (3)) on leased assets to apply for the purposes of this paragraph).

7.—(1) Where in circumstances falling within paragraph 8 below an approved body incurs such capital expenditure as is referred to in paragraph 1 (1) of Schedule 12 to the Finance Act 1982 under a contract—

(a) which is entered into after 13th March 1984 and on or before 31st March 1986, and
(b) which either specifies no date on or by which the contractual obligations must be fully performed or specifies such a date which is after 31st March 1985,

that Schedule shall have effect in relation to the capital expenditure so incurred subject to the following provisions of this paragraph.

(2) In this Part of this Schedule, in relation to a contract falling within sub-paragraph (1) above,—

"the contract date" means the date on which the contract was entered into;
"the contract price" means the total capital expenditure on the construction of the building concerned which the approved body referred to in sub-paragraph (1) above is to incur pursuant to the contract;
"the completion date" means the date specified as mentioned in sub-paragraph (1) (b) above or, if no date is so specified, 31st March 1987; and
"the maximum allowable expenditure" shall be construed in accordance with paragraph 9 below.

(3) In respect of capital expenditure incurred in either of the financial years 1984 and 1985 under a contract falling within sub-paragraph (1) above, the initial allowance under paragraph 1 of Schedule 12 to the Finance Act 1982 shall not exceed the fraction appropriate under paragraph 3 above of the maximum allowable expenditure for that year.

(4) So much (if any) of the capital expenditure incurred in the financial year 1984 under a contract falling within sub-paragraph (1) above as exceeds the maximum allowable expenditure for that year shall be deemed for all purposes of Schedule 12 to the Finance Act 1982 to be incurred on 1st April 1985.

(5) So much (if any) of the aggregate of—

(a) the capital expenditure incurred in the financial year 1985 under a contract falling within sub-paragraph (1) above, and
(b) any excess relating to that contract which, by virtue of sub-paragraph (4) above, is deemed to be incurred in that financial year,

as exceeds the maximum allowable expenditure for that financial year shall be deemed for all purposes of Schedule 12 to the Finance Act 1982 to be incurred on 1st April 1986.

(6) This paragraph shall be construed as if it were contained in Schedule 12 to the Finance Act 1982 except that expenditure falling within sub-paragraph (1) (b) of paragraph 8 of that Schedule shall be treated for the purposes of this paragraph as having been incurred at the latest time when any expenditure falling within sub-paragraph (1) (a) of that paragraph was incurred.

8.—(1) The circumstances referred to in sub-paragraph (1) of each of paragraphs 5 to 7 above is that the sole or main benefit which (apart from this Part of this Schedule) might have been expected to be gained by incurring the expenditure at the time at which it was incurred was either—

(a) the securing of an initial allowance or first-year allowance in respect of the expenditure, rather than a writing-down allowance; or
(b) the securing of a higher rate of initial or first-year allowance in respect of the expenditure.

(2) In sub-paragraph (1) above—

"initial allowance" means an initial allowance under section 1 of the Capital Allowances Act 1968 or Schedule 12 to the Finance Act 1982; and
"first-year allowance" means a first-year allowance under section 41 of the Finance Act 1971.

9.—(1) References in paragraphs 5 to 7 above to the maximum allowable expenditure for each of the financial years 1984 and 1985 shall be construed in accordance with this paragraph.

(2) For each contract falling within sub-paragraph (1) of any of paragraphs 5 to 7 above, the maximum allowable expenditure shall be that fraction of the contract price of which—

(a) the numerator,—

(i) for the financial year 1984, is the number of complete months in the period beginning on the contract date and ending on 31st March 1985; and

(ii) for the financial year 1985, is 12 or, if it is less, the number of complete months in the period beginning on the contract date and ending on 31st March 1986; and

(*b*) the denominator is the number of complete months in the period beginning on the contract date and ending on the completion date or, if it is earlier, 31st March 1987.

10.—(1) Where, by virtue of paragraph 5 (4), paragraph 6 (5) or paragraph 7 (4) above, a portion of any expenditure which is incurred by any person in the financial year 1984 is deemed to be incurred on 1st April 1985, so much of that expenditure as is not deemed to be incurred on that date shall be apportioned to the chargeable periods or their basis periods which begin or end in the financial year 1984 on a time basis according to the respective lengths of those periods which fall within that financial year.

(2) Where, by virtue of paragraph 5 (5), paragraph 6 (6) or paragraph 7 (5) above, a portion of the aggregate of any capital expenditure incurred and deemed to be incurred by any person in the financial year 1985 is deemed to be incurred on 1st April 1986, so much of that aggregate expenditure as is not deemed to be incurred on that date shall be apportioned to the chargeable periods or their basis periods which begin or end in the financial year 1985 on the like time basis as is specified in sub-paragraph (1) above.

SCHEDULE 13

Section 64

QUALIFYING CORPORATE BONDS

PART I

Note.—Part I amends TA 1970, s. 270, FA 1973, Sch. 16, para. 7, CGTA 1979, ss. 64, 67, 70 and FA 1983, Sch. 6, para. 1.

PART II

REORGANISATIONS, CONVERSIONS, RECONSTRUCTIONS ETC.

7.—(1) In this Part of this Schedule "relevant transaction" means a reorganisation, conversion of securities or other transaction such as is mentioned in subsection (7) of section 64 of this Act.

(2) Where the qualifying corporate bond referred to in paragraph (*b*) of that subsection would constitute the original shares for the purposes of sections 78 to 81 of the principal Act, it is in this Part of this Schedule referred to as "the old asset" and the shares or securities which would constitute the new holding for those purposes are referred to as "the new asset".

(3) Where the qualifying corporate bond referred to in section 64 (7) (*b*) of this Act would constitute the new holding for the purposes of sections 78 to 81 of the principal Act, it is in this Part of this Schedule referred to as "the new asset" and the shares or securities which would constitute the original shares for those purposes are referred to as "the old asset".

(4) In this Part of this Schedule "the principal Act" means the Capital Gains Tax Act 1979.

8.—(1) So far as the relevant transaction relates to the old asset and the new asset, sections 78 to 81 of the principal Act shall not apply in relation to it.

(2) In accordance with sub-paragraph (1) above, the new asset shall not be treated as having been acquired on any date other than the date of the relevant transaction or, subject to sub-paragraphs (3) and (4) below, for any consideration other than the market value of the old asset as determined immediately before that transaction.

(3) If, on the relevant transaction, the person concerned receives, or becomes entitled to receive, any sum of money which, in addition to the new asset, is by way of consideration for the old assets, that sum shall be deducted from the consideration referred to in sub-paragraph (2) above.

(4) If, on the relevant transaction, the person concerned gives any sum of money which, in addition to the old asset, is by way of consideration for the new asset, that sum shall be added to the consideration referred to in sub-paragraph (2) above.

9. In any case where—

(*a*) the old asset consists of a qualifying corporate bond, *and*
(*b*) . . .[1],

then, so far as it relates to the old asset and the new asset, the relevant transaction shall be treated for the purposes of that Act as a disposal of the old asset and an acquisition of the new asset.

Amendments.—[1] Sub-para. (*b*) repealed by FA 1985, Sch. 27, Pt. VII with respect to disposals after 1 July 1986.

10.—(1) Except in a case falling within paragraph 9 above, so far as it relates to the old asset and the new asset, the relevant transaction shall be treated for the purposes of the principal Act as not involving any disposal of the old asset but—

(*a*) there shall be calculated the chargeable gain or allowable loss that would have accrued if, at the time of the relevant transaction, the old asset had been disposed of for a consideration equal to its market value immediately before that transaction; and
(*b*) subject to paragraph 11 below, the whole or a corresponding part of the chargeable gain or allowable loss mentioned in paragraph (*a*) above shall be deemed to accrue on a

subsequent disposal of the whole or part of the new asset (in addition to any gain or loss that actually accrues on that disposal); and

(c) [on that subsequent disposal section 67 of the principal Act][1] shall have effect only in relation to any gain or loss that actually accrues and not in relation to any gain or loss which is deemed to accrue by virtue of paragraph (b) above.

(2) Paragraphs (b) and (c) of sub-paragraph (1) above shall not apply to any disposal falling within the provisions of—

(a) section 44 (1) of the principal Act (disposals between husband and wife); or
(b) section 49 (4) of that Act (disposals by personal representatives to legatees); or
[(bb) section 267 of the Taxes Act (company reconstructions and amalgamations); or][2]
(c) section 273 (1) of the Taxes Act (disposals within a group of companies);

but a person who has acquired the new asset on a disposal falling within those provisions (and without there having been a previous disposal [not][3] falling within those provisions or a devolution on death) shall be treated for the purposes of paragraphs (b) and (c) of sub-paragraph (1) above as if the new asset had been acquired by him at the same time and for the same consideration as, having regard to paragraph 8 above, it was acquired by the person making the disposal.

Cross references.—See CGTA 1979, s. 126 (2) (c) (relief for gifts of business assets), s. 147A (6) (gifts on which inheritance tax is chargeable);
FA 1988, Sch. 9, para. 3 (reduction of a charge to tax where the charge is wholly or partly attributable to an increase in the value of an asset before 31 March 1982).
Amendments.—[1] Words in sub-para. (1) (c) substituted by FA 1985, s. 67 (2) (c) with respect to disposals occurring after 1 July 1986.
[2] Sub-para. (2) (bb) inserted by FA 1989, s. 139 (1), (6) (a) in relation to any disposal after 13 March 1989 and in relation to such disposal is deemed always to have had effect.
[3] Word in sub-para. (2) inserted by FA 1989, s. 139 (1), (6) (b) in relation to any disposal after 13 March 1989 and in relation to such disposal is deemed always to have had effect.

11.—(1) In any case where—

(a) on the calculation under paragraph 10 (1) (a) above, a chargeable gain would have accrued, and
(b) the consideration for the old asset includes such a sum of money as is referred to in paragraph 8 (3) above,

then, subject to sub-paragraph (2) below, the proportion of that chargeable gain which that sum of money bears to the market value of the old asset immediately before the relevant transaction shall be deemed to accrue at the time of that transaction.

(2) If the inspector is satisfied that the sum of money referred to in sub-paragraph (1) (b) above is small, as compared with the market value of the old asset immediately before the relevant transaction, and so directs, sub-paragraph (1) above shall not apply.

(3) In a case where sub-paragraph (1) above applies, the chargeable gain which, apart from this paragraph, would by virtue of paragraph 10 (1) (b) above be deemed to accrue on a subsequent disposal of the whole or part of the new asset shall be reduced or, as the case may be, extinguished by deducting therefrom the amount of the chargeable gain which, by virtue of sub-paragraph (1) above, is deemed to accrue at the time of the relevant transaction.

SCHEDULE 14

Section 70

BENEFICIARY'S LIABILITY FOR TAX ON GAINS OF NON-RESIDENT TRUSTEES

Interpretation

1.—(1) In this Schedule—

"attributed gain", in relation to the beneficiary, means the chargeable gain which, as mentioned in paragraph (*b*) of subsection (1) of the principal section, is treated as accruing to him;
"the beneficiary" means the beneficiary referred to in that paragraph and paragraph (*c*) of that subsection;
"claim" means a claim under paragraph 2 (1) below;
"close relative", in relation to any person, means his spouse or a child or remoter descendant of his;
"ineligible gain" shall be construed in accordance with paragraph 2 (3) below;
"offshore income gain" has the same meaning as in Chapter [V of Part XVII of the Taxes Act 1988];[1]
"the principal Act" means the Capital Gains Tax Act 1979;
"the principal section" means section 70 of this Act;
"related settlement" shall be construed in accordance with paragraph 5 (6) below;
"relevant benefit" shall be construed in accordance with paragraph 5 below; and
"the relevant year of assessment", in relation to an attributed gain, means the year of assessment in which the gain is treated as accruing to the beneficiary.

(2) Subject to subsection (4) of the principal section, section 83 of the Finance Act 1981 (meaning of "capital payment" etc.) applies for the purposes of this Schedule as it applies for the purposes of sections 80 to 82 of that Act.

(3) In any case where the beneficiary is a married woman, any reference in the following provisions of this Schedule to the payment of capital gains tax by the beneficiary shall be construed as including a reference to the payment by her husband of capital gains tax which, under subsection (1) of section 45 of the principal Act, is assessed and charged on him.

Amendments.—[1] Words in sub-para. (1) substituted by TA 1988, Sch. 29, para. 32 Table.

Claims for postponement of tax

2.—(1) Subject to sub-paragraph (3) below, in a case falling within the principal section, the provisions of this Schedule have effect to determine whether, on a claim made to the Board, payment of any of the capital gains tax referable to an attributed gain may be postponed and, if so, to what extent and for how long.

(2) A claim must be made before 1st July 1985 or, if it is later, the expiry of the period of thirty days beginning with the date of the issue of a notice of assessment requiring the payment of an amount of capital gains tax assessed, in whole or in part, by reason of an attributed gain to which the claim relates.

(3) The provisions of this Schedule do not have effect to allow postponement of the payment of the capital gains tax referable to an attributed gain if the capital gains tax chargeable on the gain—

(*a*) has previously been postponed under section 17 (4) (*b*) of the principal Act (pre-6th April 1965 settlements); or

(*b*) subject to sub-paragraph (4) below, carries interest, by virtue of section 88 (1) of the Taxes Management Act 1970 (interest on tax recovered to make good tax lost due to fraud, wilful default or neglect), from the date on which the tax ought to have been paid until payment;

and an attributed gain falling within paragraph (*a*) or paragraph (*b*) above is in this Schedule referred to as an ineligible gain.

(4) Sub-paragraph (3) (*b*) above does not apply where the tax carries interest by reason only of the neglect of any person and that neglect is remedied before 1st July 1985.

(5) In relation to a claim, any reference in this Schedule to an attributed gain to which the claim relates is a reference to such a gain—

(*a*) which is specified in the claim, and
(*b*) which is not an ineligible gain, and
(*c*) in respect of which the claim is not out of time by virtue of sub-paragraph (2) above,

and any reference to the settlement to which the claim relates is a reference to the settlement under which the beneficiary is a beneficiary and to the trustees of which accrued the chargeable gain which gives rise to the attributed gain or gains to which the claim relates.

(6) In a case where a claim relates to attributed gains accruing to the beneficiary by virtue of more than one settlement, the provisions of this Schedule shall have effect as if there were separate claims, each relating to the attributed gain or gains accruing by virtue of a single settlement.

(7) Without prejudice to the application of sub-paragraph (2) above in a case where the personal representatives of the beneficiary receive a notice of assessment requiring the payment by them of an amount of capital gains tax assessed, in whole or in part, by reason of an attributed gain, if—

(*a*) before his death the beneficiary or, where paragraph 1 (3) above applies, the beneficiary's husband received a notice of assessment requiring the payment by him of such an amount of capital gains tax, and
(*b*) at the time of his death the period within which he might make a claim in respect of any of the tax assessed by that notice had not expired,

a claim by his personal representatives relating to that tax may be made at any time before the expiry of the period of six months beginning on the date of the death of the beneficiary or, as the case may be, her husband (or, if it is later, before 1st July 1985).

(8) In relation to any claim by the personal representatives of the beneficiary, references in this Schedule to the postponement of the payment of any tax shall be construed as references to the discharge of that tax and, accordingly, paragraphs 11 and 12 below do not apply where a claim is made by the personal representatives.

Tax referable to attributed gains

3.—(1) Any reference in this Schedule to the tax referable to an attributed gain is a reference to the amount determined by multiplying the total capital gains tax on chargeable gains accruing to the beneficiary in the relevant year of assessment by a fraction—

(*a*) of which the numerator is the amount of the attributed gain; and
(*b*) the denominator is the total of the chargeable gains accruing to the beneficiary in the relevant year of assessment.

Initial calculations relevant to tax which may be postponed

4.—(1) Where a claim is made, the determination referred to in paragraph 2 (1) above shall, in the first instance, be made (in accordance with paragraph 6 below) by reference to—

(*a*) the amount defined in sub-paragraph (4) below as the unpaid tax;
(*b*) the amount defined in sub-paragraph (5) below as the tax already paid; and
(*c*) the aggregate value of any relevant benefits which, by virtue of paragraph 5 below, fall to be taken into account in relation to the claim.

(2) Subject to sub-paragraph (3) below, in this paragraph and paragraph 5 below "the base year" means the year of assessment which precedes the relevant year of assessment in relation to the attributed gain or, as the case may be, the earliest of the attributed gains to which the claim relates.

(3) Where the relevant year of assessment referred to in sub-paragraph (2) above is the year 1965–66, the base year is also that year of assessment.

(4) In relation to a claim "the unpaid tax" means the amount of tax—

(*a*) which is referable to the attributed gain (or attributed gains) to which the claim relates; and
(*b*) which remains unpaid at the date of the claim.

(5) In relation to a claim, "the tax already paid" means the amount of tax—

(a) which has been paid at the date of the claim, excluding any tax which was so paid, or is or was otherwise borne, by the trustees of the settlement to which the claim relates; and

(b) which is referable to any attributed gains—

(i) which have accrued to the beneficiary by virtue of the settlement to which the claim relates; and
(ii) for which the relevant year of assessment is, or is later than, the base year; and
(iii) which are not ineligible gains.

Relevant benefits

5.—(1) The provisions of this paragraph have effect to determine what are the relevant benefits to be taken into account (as mentioned in paragraph 4 (1) (c) above) in relation to a claim; and in the following provisions of this paragraph "the calculation period" means the period beginning at the beginning of the base year and ending on 9th March 1981.

(2) Subject to sub-paragraph (3) below, if, under or by reference to the settlement to which the claim relates or a related settlement, the beneficiary received a capital payment from the trustees of the settlement—

(a) at any time in the calculation period, or
(b) after the end of that period but before 6th April 1984, in so far as that payment represented a chargeable gain which, before 6th April 1981, accrued to the trustees of the settlement to which the claim relates,

the amount of that capital payment is a relevant benefit.

(3) In any case where, apart from this sub-paragraph, sub-paragraph (2) above would bring into account, as a relevant benefit in relation to a claim, a capital payment received under or by reference to a related settlement, and either—

(a) on a claim relating to the related settlement, the payment falls to be taken into account under this paragraph as a relevant benefit, or
(b) it appears to the Board to be likely that the payment will fall to be so taken into account on a claim relating to the related settlement,

the payment shall not be taken into account as a relevant benefit in relation to the claim referred to in sub-paragraph (2) above except to the extent that it constitutes a surplus benefit by virtue of paragraph 6 (5) below.

(4) If, at any time in the period beginning at the beginning of the base year and ending at the beginning of the year of assessment in which the claim is made, the beneficiary disposed of his interest in the settlement to which the claim relates in circumstances such that, by virtue of section 58 (1) of the principal Act, no chargeable gain could accrue on the disposal, then the amount or value of the consideration for the disposal is a relevant benefit.

(5) Where the disposal referred to in sub-paragraph (4) above was made before 6th April 1984, the reference in that sub-paragraph to the consideration for the disposal shall be construed as a reference only to such consideration (if any) as was actually given for the disposal.

(6) For the purposes of this Schedule, a settlement is a related settlement in relation to the settlement to which a claim relates if, by the exercise in the base year or later (whether before or after the making of the claim) of a power conferred by one of the settlements, or by the combination of such an exercise and any other transactions, property of any description forming part of the settled property of one of the settlements is at any time appointed to the other settlement or otherwise dealt with so as to increase the value of the settled property of the other settlement.

The basic rules as to postponement

6.—(1) Unless on a claim the aggregate of—

(a) the unpaid tax (as defined in paragraph 4 (4) above), and
(b) the tax already paid (as defined in paragraph 4 (5) above),

exceeds 30 per cent. of the aggregate of the relevant benefits referred to in paragraph 4 (1) (c) above, there is no postponement of the payment of any of the capital gains tax referable to the attributed gains to which the claim relates.

(2) Subject to the following provisions of this Schedule, the amount of capital gains tax

payment of which is, on a claim, postponed by virtue of this Schedule is whichever is the smaller of—

(a) the unpaid tax; and
(b) the amount of the excess referred to in sub-paragraph (1) above;

and, where the amount in paragraph (b) above is the smaller, payment of tax assessed for a later year shall be postponed in priority to payment of tax assessed for an earlier year.

(3) Without prejudice to paragraph 2 (8) above, if at any time after a claim is made the beneficiary dies, any tax the payment of which would, by virtue of this Schedule, still be postponed at the date of his death shall be discharged on that date.

(4) Notwithstanding anything in Part IX of the Taxes Management Act 1970 (interest on overdue tax), where payment of an amount of capital gains tax is postponed by virtue of this Schedule none of that tax shall carry interest (or be taken to have carried interest) for any period before the time when the tax becomes payable in accordance with paragraph 11 below.

(5) In any case where, by virtue of sub-paragraph (1) above, there is on a claim no postponement of the payment of capital gains tax, there shall be determined—

(a) whether there would still be no postponement if there were left out of account all relevant benefits (if any) referable to capital payments received under or by reference to a related settlement, and
(b) if so, what is the excess of all the other relevant benefits over $3\frac{1}{3}$ times the aggregate of the tax referred to in paragraphs (a) and (b) of sub-paragraph (1) above,

and so much of those other relevant benefits as are referable to capital payments falling within sub-paragraph (2) of paragraph 5 above and equal (or do not exceed) that excess shall be regarded as a surplus benefit for the purposes of sub-paragraph (3) of that paragraph.

Effect of subsequent capital payments received by the beneficiary

7.—(1) The provisions of this paragraph apply if—

(a) on a claim there would, in accordance with paragraph 6 (2) above, be an amount of capital gains tax payment of which is postponed by virtue of this Schedule; but
(b) before the beginning of the year of assessment in which the claim is made, the beneficiary has received from the trustees of the settlement to which the claim relates or a related settlement a capital payment which is not a relevant benefit and has not been brought into account under subsections (3) and (4) of section 80 of the Finance Act 1981 (new provisions as to gain of non-resident settlements) in determining whether chargeable gains or offshore income gains should be attributed to the beneficiary by reference to any trust gains for any previous year of assessment.

(2) If the amount of capital gains tax referred to in paragraph (a) of sub-paragraph (1) above exceeds 30 per cent. of the aggregate of the amount of the capital payments which fall within paragraph (b) of that sub-paragraph, then, subject to paragraph 9 below, the amount of capital gains tax payment of which is postponed by virtue of this Schedule is an amount equal to that excess.

(3) If the amount of capital gains tax referred to in paragraph (a) of sub-paragraph (1) above is less than or equal to 30 per cent. of the aggregate of the amount of the capital payments which fall within paragraph (b) of that sub-paragraph, then there is no postponement of the payment of any of that capital gains tax.

(4) In any case where—

(a) the amount of capital gains tax referred to in sub-paragraph (1) (a) above equals or exceeds 30 per cent. of the aggregate of those capital payments falling within sub-paragraph (1) (b) above which the beneficiary has received from the trustees of the settlement to which the claim relates, and
(b) apart from this paragraph, those capital payments would fall to be brought into account under subsections (3) and (4) of section 80 of the Finance Act 1981 (new provisions as to gains of non-resident settlements) in determining whether chargeable gains or offshore income gains should be attributed to the beneficiary by reference to any trust gains for the year of assessment in which the claim is made,

then, as respects that year of assessment and any subsequent year, those capital payments shall be left out of account for the purposes of the said subsections (3) and (4).

(5) In any case where—

(a) the condition in sub-paragraph (4) (a) above is not fulfilled, but
(b) the condition in sub-paragraph (4) (b) above is fulfilled,

then, as respects the year of assessment in which the claim is made and any subsequent year, so much of the capital payments referred to in sub-paragraph (4) above as is equal to $3\frac{1}{3}$ times the amount of capital gains tax referred to in sub-paragraph (1) (a) above shall be left out of account for the purposes of subsections (3) and (4) of section 80 of the Finance Act 1981.

(6) Where, by virtue of sub-paragraph (4) or sub-paragraph (5) above, the whole or any part of a capital payment falls to be left out of account as mentioned in that sub-paragraph—

(a) the payment shall to the same extent be left out of account for the purposes of the application on any other occasion of any provision of paragraphs 7 to 12 of this Schedule; and
(b) section [740 of the Taxes Act 1988][1] (transfer of assets abroad: liability of non-transferors) shall have effect in relation to a benefit received by the beneficiary which, in whole or in part, consists of that payment as if, in the year of assessment in which the claim is made, chargeable gains equal to so much of that payment as falls to be so left out of account were, by reason of that payment, treated under section 80 of that act as accruing to the beneficiary.

(7) Where any capital payments falling within sub-paragraph (1) (b) above which the beneficiary has received from the trustees of the settlement to which the claim relates are not such as are referred to in sub-paragraph (4) (b) above, sub-paragraph (6) (a) above shall apply to each of those payments in like manner as if it had been such a payment as is referred to in sub-paragraph (4) (b) above and the amount of it to be left out of account had been determined accordingly under sub-paragraph (4) or sub-paragraph (5) above.

Amendments.—[1] Words in sub-para. (6)(b) substituted by TA 1988, Sch. 29, para. 32 Table.

8.—(1) The provisions of this paragraph apply if, in a case where paragraph 7 above applies, the amount of capital gains tax referred to in sub-paragraph (1) (a) of that paragraph exceeds 30 per cent. of the aggregate of those capital payments falling within sub-paragraph (1) (b) of that paragraph which the beneficiary has received from the trustees of that settlement to which the claim relates.

(2) In the following provisions of this paragraph—

(a) the capital payments falling within sub-paragraph (1) (b) of paragraph 7 above which the beneficiary has received otherwise than from the trustees of the settlement to which the claim relates are referred to as "related payments"; and
(b) any of those related payments which, apart from this paragraph, would fall to be brought into account as mentioned in sub-paragraph (4) (b) of paragraph 7 above is referred to as a "related section 80 payment".

(3) If sub-paragraph (2) of paragraph 7 above applies, then—

(a) as respects the year of assessment in which the claim is made and any subsequent year, any related section 80 payment shall be left out of account for the purposes of sub-paragraphs (3) and (4) of section 80 of the Finance Act 1981; and
(b) all the related payments shall be left out of account for the purposes of the application on any other occasion of any provision of paragraphs 7 to 12 of this Schedule.

(4) If sub-paragraph (3) of paragraph 7 above applies, then—

(a) as respects the year of assessment in which the claim is made and any subsequent year, so much of any related section 80 payment as is equal to $3\frac{1}{3}$ times the amount of capital gains tax released by that payment shall be left out of account for the purposes of subsections (3) and (4) of section 80 of the Finance Act 1981; and
(b) so much of each of the related payments as is equal to $3\frac{1}{3}$ times the amount of capital gains tax released by the payment shall be left out of account for the purposes mentioned in sub-paragraph (3) (b) above.

(5) For the purposes of sub-paragraph (4) above, the amount of capital gains tax released by a related payment shall be determined by the formula—

$$(A - B) \times \frac{C}{D}$$

where—

"A" is the capital gains tax referred to in sub-paragraph (1) (*a*) of paragraph 7 above;
"B" is an amount equal to 30 per cent. of the aggregate of those capital payments falling within sub-paragraph (1) (*b*) of that paragraph which the beneficiary has received from the trustees of trhe settlement to which the claim relates;
"C" is the related payment in question; and
"D" is the aggregate of all the related payments.

(6) Where, by virtue of sub-paragraph (3) (*a*) or sub-paragraph (4) (*a*) above, the whole or any part of a related section 80 payment falls to be left out of account as mentioned in that sub-paragraph, section [740 of the Taxes Act 1988][1] shall have effect in relation to the benefit received by the beneficiary which, in whole or in part, consists of that payment as if, in the year of assessment in which the claim is made, chargeable gains equal to so much of that payment as falls to be so left out of account were, by reason of that payment, treated under section 80 of that Act as accruing to the beneficiary.

Amendments.—[1] Words in sub-para. (6) substituted by TA 1988, Sch. 29, para. 32 Table.

Effect of related benefits derived from payments received by close relatives of the beneficiary

9.—(1) The provisions of this paragraph apply if,—

(*a*) on a claim, payment of an amount of capital gains tax determined in accordance with paragraph 6 (2) or paragraph 7 (2) above would, apart from this paragraph, be postponed by virtue of this Schedule; and
(*b*) as a result of a capital payment received by a close relative of the beneficiary, there is, in accordance with paragraph 10 below, a related benefit which falls to be taken into account in relation to the claim.

(2) If the amount of capital gains tax referred to in sub-paragraph (1) (*a*) above exceeds 30 per cent. of the aggregate of the related benefits which fall to be taken into account in relation to the claim, then the amount of capital gains tax payment of which is postponed by virtue of this Schedule is an amount equal to that excess.

(3) If the amount of capital gains tax referred to in sub-paragraph (1) (*a*) above is less than or equal to 30 per cent. of the aggregate of the related benefits which fall to be taken into account in relation to the claim, then there is no postponement of the payment of any of that capital gains tax.

Related benefits

10.—(1) The provisions of this paragraph have effect to determine what are, in relation to a claim, the related benefits which are to be taken into account under paragraph 9 above.

(2) If, on or after 6th April 1984 and before the beginning of the year of assessment in which the claim is made, a close relative of the beneficiary has received from the trustees of the settlement to which the claim relates or a related settlement a capital payment which has not been brought into account under subsections (3) and (4) of section 80 of the Finance Act 1981 in determining whether chargeable gains or offshore income gains should be attributed to the close relative by reference to any trust gains for any previous year of assessment, then, subject to sub-paragraphs (3) and (4) below, that capital payment is a related benefit which falls to be taken into account in relation to the claim.

(3) A capital payment falling within sub-paragraph (2) above is not a related benefit which falls to be taken into account as mentioned in that sub-paragraph to the extent that it has already been taken into account on any previous operation of sub-paragraph (4) or sub-paragraph (5) of paragraph 7 above on the occasion of a claim in respect of which the close relative himself or a close relative of his or a person whose close relative he is was the beneficiary.

(4) A capital payment falling within sub-paragraph (2) above is not a related benefit which falls to be taken into account as mentioned in that sub-paragraph if the Board so direct on the grounds that it appears likely that the payment will fall to be taken into account, either as giving rise to a relevant benefit or under paragraph 7 above, in relation to such a claim as is referred to in sub-paragraph (3) above.

(5) Sub-paragraphs (3) to (6) of paragraph 8 above shall have effect for the purposes of this paragraph—

(a) as if any reference to a provision of paragraph 7 above were a reference to the corresponding provision of paragraph 9 above; and
(b) as if any reference to a related payment were a reference to a related benefit which falls to be taken into account as mentioned in sub-paragraph (2) above; and
(c) as if any reference to a related section 80 payment were a reference to a related benefit which falls to be taken into account as mentioned in sub-paragraph (2) above and which, apart from this paragraph, would fall to be taken into account under sub-paragraphs (3) and (4) of section 80 of the Finance Act 1981 in determining whether chargeable gains or offshore income gains should be attributed to the close relative concerned by reference to any trust gains for the year of assessment in which is made the claim referred to in sub-paragraph (2) above; and
(d) as if "B" in the formula in sub-paragraph (5) were nil; and
(e) as if any reference in sub-paragraph (6) to the beneficiary were a reference to the close relative concerned.

Time when postponed tax becomes payable

11.—(1) The provisions of this paragraph apply where, as a result of a claim, payment of an amount of capital gains tax, determined in accordance with paragraphs 6 to 9 above, is postponed by virtue of this Schedule; and, subject to sub-paragraph (6) below, any reference in the following provisions of this paragraph to postponed tax is a reference to tax the payment of which is so postponed.

(2) Postponed tax shall become payable in accordance with sub-paragraph (5) below if, at any time in the year of assessment in which the claim is made or any later year, the beneficiary disposes of his interest in the settlement to which the claim relates in circumstances such that, by virtue of section 58 (1) of the principal Act, no chargeable gain could accrue on the disposal; and in sub-paragraph (5) below "the relevant consideration" means the amount or value of the consideration for such a disposal.

(3) Subject to paragraph 12 below, postponed tax shall become payable in accordance with sub-paragraph (5) below if in the year of assessment in which the claim is made or any later year, the beneficiary or a close relative of his receives a capital payment from the trustees of the settlement to which the claim relates or a related settlement.

(4) In the following provisions of this paragraph and paragraph 12 below, any reference to a material year of assessment is a reference to one in which the beneficiary disposes of his interest as mentioned in sub-paragraph (2) above or in which sub-paragraph (3) above applies.

(5) For any material year of assessment, so much of the postponed tax as does not exceed 30 per cent. of the aggregate of—

(a) the relevant consideration in respect of any disposal in that year, and
(b) subject to paragraph 12 below, the capital payments received in that year as mentioned in sub-paragraph (3) above,

shall become payable as if it were capital gains tax assessed in respect of gains accruing in that year.

(6) If, for any material year of assessment, the amount of the postponed tax exceeds 30 per cent. of the aggregate referred to in sub-paragraph (5) above, only the excess shall continue after the end of that year to be postponed tax for the purposes of this paragraph, but without prejudice to the subsequent operation of this paragraph in relation to a later year of assessment which is a material year.

(7) Where part, but not the whole, of any postponed tax becomes payable in accordance with sub-paragraph (5) above, tax assessed for an earlier year shall be regarded as becoming so payable before tax assessed for a later year.

Balance of capital payments

12.—(1) If any capital payments received in any year of assessment as mentioned in paragraph 11 (3) above fall to be brought into account for that year for the purposes of subsections (3) and (4) of section 80 of the Finance Act 1981, those capital payments shall be disregarded for the purposes of sub-paragraph (5) or, as the case may be, sub-paragraph (6) of paragraph 11 above except to the extent that the aggregate of those payments exceeds the chargeable gains and offshore income gains which in that year are treated under the said section 80 as accruing to the beneficiary or, as the case may be, the close relative; and any such excess is in the following provisions of this paragraph referred to as the balance of section 80 payments for that year.

(2) Subject to the following provisions of this paragraph, as respects any year of assessment subsequent to a material year of assessment for which there is a balance of section 80 payments there shall be left out of account for the purposes of subsections (3) and (4) of section 80 of the Finance Act 1981 so much of the capital payments as made up that balance.

(3) If paragraph 11 (6) above did not apply for any material year of assessment for which there is a balance of section 80 payments then, as respects years of assessment subsequent to that year, sub-paragraph (2) above shall apply only to so much of the capital payments mentioned therein as is equal to $3\frac{1}{3}$ times the amount of postponed tax released by that balance.

(4) For any material year of assessment, the amount of postponed tax released by a balance of section 80 payments for that year shall be determined by that formula:—

$$(E-F) \times \frac{G}{H}$$

where

"E" is the postponed tax, within the meaning of paragraph 11 above;
"F" is an amount equal to 30 per cent. of any consideration for that year which falls within sub-paragraph (5) (*a*) of that paragraph;
"G" is the balance of the section 80 payments for that year; and
"H" is the aggregate of the capital payments (including that balance) taken into account under sub-paragraph (5) (*b*) of that paragraph for that year.

(5) If, in a case where sub-paragraph (2) above applies in accordance with sub-paragraph (3) above, there were, for the material year of assessment concerned,—

(*a*) a balance of section 80 payments derived from payments received by the beneficiary, and
(*b*) another such balance derived from payments received by a close relative of his,

sub-paragraph (2) above shall apply (in accordance with sub-paragraph (3) above) to the capital payments which made up the balance derived from payments received by the beneficiary in priority to capital payments which made up the other balance.

(6) Subject to sub-paragraph (5) above, where there is more than one capital payment to which sub-paragraph (2) above applies, the proportion of each of them which is left out of account as mentioned in that sub-paragraph shall be the same.

(7) Where, by virtue of the preceding provisions of this paragraph, the whole or any part of a capital payment falls to be left out of account as mentioned in sub-paragraph (2) above, section [740 of the Taxes Act 1988][1] shall have effect in relation to a benefit which is received by the beneficiary or, as the case may be, a close relative of his and which, in whole or in part, consists of that payment as if, in the material year of assessment concerned, chargeable gains equal to so much of that payment as falls to be so left out of account were, by reason of that payment, treated under section 80 of that Act as accruing to the beneficiary or, as the case may be, the close relative.

Amendments.—[1] Words in sub-para. (7) substituted by TA 1988, Sch. 29, para. 32 Table.

13.—(1) Where, by virtue of sub-paragraph (2) of paragraph 12 above, the whole or any part of a capital payment falls to be left out of account as mentioned in that sub-paragraph, it shall to the same extent be left out of account for the purposes of the application on any other occasion of any provision of paragraphs 7 to 12 of this Schedule.

(2) Where sub-paragraph (6) of paragraph 11 above applies for any material year of assessment, any capital payments which—

(*a*) fall to be taken into account under sub-paragraph (5) (*b*) of that paragraph for that year, and
(*b*) are not such as to fall within paragraph 12 (1) above,

shall be left out of account for the purposes referred to in sub-paragraph (1) above.

(3) Where sub-paragraph (6) of paragraph 11 above does not apply for any material year of assessment, so much of any capital payment falling within paragraphs (*a*) and (*b*) of sub-paragraph (2) above as is equal to $3\frac{1}{3}$ times the amount of postponed tax released by that payment shall be left out of account for the purposes referred to in sub-paragraph (1) above.

(4) The amount of postponed tax released by a capital payment shall be determined for the purposes of sub-paragraph (3) above by the formula in paragraph 12 (4) above, except that, in applying that formula for those purposes, "G" shall be the amount of the capital payment in question.

(5) In this paragraph, "material year of assessment" shall be construed in accordance with paragraph 11 (4) above.

Second and later claims

14.—(1) This paragraph applies where—

(*a*) as a result of a claim (in this paragraph referred to as "the earlier claim"), payment of an amount of capital gains tax (in this paragraph referred to as "the original tax"), determined in accordance with paragraph 6 or paragraph 7 above, is or was postponed by virtue of this Schedule; and
(*b*) after the making of the earlier claim, another claim (in this paragraph referred to as "the later claim") is made in relation to an attributed gain to which the earlier claim did not relate; and
(*c*) the settlement to which the earlier and the later claims relate is the same.

(2) If the year of assessment which is the relevant year of assessment in relation to any attributed gain to which the later claim relates is earlier than the earliest year of assessment which is the relevant year of assessment in relation to any attributed gain to which the earlier claim related, then,—

(*a*) the earlier claim and the postponement resulting from it shall be set aside; and
(*b*) the provisions of this Schedule shall have effect as if (notwithstanding paragraph 2 (2) above) the attributed gains to which the later claim relates included the attributed gains to which the earlier claim related.

(3) Where sub-paragraph (2) above does not apply and, at the time the later claim is made, payment of any of the original tax remains postponed by virtue of this Schedule, then, subject to sub-paragraph (4) below,—

(*a*) paragraphs 4 to 10 above shall not apply in relation to the later claim; and
(*b*) payment of the tax referable to the attributed gain or gains to which the later claim relates shall be postponed by virtue of this Schedule; and
(*c*) paragraphs 11 and 12 above shall apply as if the payment of that tax had been postponed as a result of the earlier claim and, accordingly, that tax shall be added to the original tax.

(4) If, in a case where sub-paragraph (3) above applies, the relevant year of assessment in relation to an attributed gain (in this sub-paragraph referred to as "the later gain") to which the later claim relates is the same as the relevant year of assessment in relation to an attributed gain to which the earlier claim related,—

(*a*) paragraph 3 above shall not apply in relation to the later gain; and
(*b*) in relation to the later gain, the references in sub-paragraph (3) above to the tax referable to the gain shall be construed as references to the capital gains tax assessed by reason of the gain.

(5) Where sub-paragraph (2) above does not apply and, at the time the later claim is made, there is no longer any postponement of the payment of any of the original tax, then, in the application of the provisions of this Schedule in relation to the later claim, paragraph 4 (2) above shall not apply and "the base year" for the purposes of paragraphs 4 and 5 above shall be that year of assessment which was the base year in relation to the earlier claim.

Information

15.—(1) The Board may by notice in writing require any person to furnish them, within such time as they may direct, not being less than twenty-eight days, with such particulars as they think necessary for the purposes of section 70 of this Act and this Schedule.

(2) Subsections (2) to [(6) of section 745 of the Taxes Act 1988][1] shall have effect in relation to sub-paragraph (1) above as they have effect in relation to subsection (1) of that section; but, in the application of those subsections by virtue of this sub-paragraph, references to Chapter III of Part XVII of the Taxes Act shall be construed as references to section 70 of this Act and this Schedule.

(3) In any case where—

(a) a claim has been made, and
(b) as a result of the claim, payment of an amount of capital gains tax was postponed by virtue of this Schedule, and
(c) at a time when any of that tax remains unpaid, there is a disposal to which paragraph 11 (2) above applies or the beneficiary or a close relative of his receives such a capital payment as is referred to in paragraph 11 (3) above,

then, not later than three months after the end of the year of assessment in which the disposal occurs or the payment is received, the beneficiary shall inform the Board of the disposal or receipt, as the case may be.

Amendments.—[1] Words in sub-para. (2) substituted by TA 1988, Sch. 29, para. 32 Table.

FILMS ACT 1985

(1985 Chapter 21)

6. Certification of master negatives, tapes and discs for purposes of section 72 of Finance Act 1982

(1) Schedule 1 to this Act shall have effect with respect to the certification by the Secretary of State of a master negative, tape or disc of a film as a qualifying film, tape or disc for the purposes of section 72 of the Finance Act 1982 (expenditure on production and acquisition of films etc.).

(2) . . .

Note.—Sub-s. (2) amends FA 1982, s. 72 (7) and repeals FA 1982, s. 72 (8).

7. Repeals, etc

(1) The enactments mentioned in Schedule 2 to this Act are repealed to the extent specified in the third column of that Schedule.

(2)–(4) . . .

(5) In subsection (7) (*b*) of section 72 of the Finance Act 1982, as amended by section 6 of this Act, the reference to a film, tape or disc which is certified by the Secretary of State under Schedule 1 to this Act as a qualifying film, tape or disc for the purposes of section 72 shall include a reference to a film, tape or disc which was certified by the Secretary of State as aforesaid in pursuance of subsection (7) (*b*) as originally enacted.

(6) Where—

(*a*) a contract for the production or acquisition of a master negative, master tape or master disc of a film has been entered into before the commencement of section 6 of this Act; and
(*b*) any person, having incurred expenditure in pursuance of the contract (before or after that commencement) on the production or acquisition of the negative, tape or disc, makes an application under paragraph 2 of Schedule 1 to this Act with respect to it,

that person may by notice in writing require that the question whether the negative, tape or disc ought to be certified as a qualifying film, tape or disc for the purposes of section 72 of the Finance Act 1982 shall be determined by the Secretary of State in accordance with the law in force immediately before the commencement of section 6 in like manner as if his application had been a request for certification made under section 72 (8).

Any expression used in this subsection has the same meaning as it has in paragraph 2 (1) of Schedule 1 to this Act.

(7) The Secretary of State may by order made by statutory instrument provide for such further transitional and saving provisions to have effect in connection with the coming into operation of any provision of this Act as appear to him to be necessary or expedient.

Note.—Sub-ss. (2)–(4) are not relevant to this work.

8. Short title, commencement and extent

(1) This Act may be cited as the Films Act 1985.

(2) The following provisions of this Act shall come into force at the end of the period of two months beginning with the day on which it is passed, namely—

(a) section 6 and Schedule 1;
(b) section 7 (1) and Schedule 2 so far as relating to the Finance Act 1982 and the Finance Act 1984;
(c) section 7 (5) and (6).

(3) The following provisions of this Act extend to Northern Ireland, namely—

(a) ...
(b) section 6 and Schedule 1;
(c) section 7 and Schedule 2;
(d) this section.

Note.—Sub-s. (3) (a) is not relevant to this work.
This Act was passed on 23 May 1985.

SCHEDULE 1

Sections 3, 5 and 6

CERTIFICATION FOR PURPOSES OF SECTION 72 OF FINANCE ACT 1982 IN CASE OF BRITISH FILMS

Preliminary

1.—(1) In this Schedule—

"Commonwealth country" means the United Kingdom, any country for the time being specified in Schedule 3 to the British Nationality Act 1981 (countries whose citizens are Commonwealth citizens), and any territory for whose international relations Her Majesty's Government in the United Kingdom is responsible;

"film" includes any record, however made, of a sequence of visual images, which is a record capable of being used as a means of showing that sequence as a moving picture;

"maker", in relation to a film, means the person by whom the arrangements necessary for the making of the film are undertaken;

"master disc", in relation to a film, means the original master film disc or the original master audio disc of the film;

"master negative", in relation to a film, means the original master negative of the film and its soundtrack (if any);

"master tape", in relation to a film, means the original master film tape or the original master audio tape of the film;

"sound recording" means a sound recording which is either an original recording or a re-recording;

"studio" (except in paragraph 5 (1) (*b*)) means a building or group of buildings constructed or adapted for the purpose of making films therein and includes any land occupied with such a building or group of buildings.

(2) For the purposes of this Schedule a studio shall be deemed to be used for making a film if any part of that film, or of any other film used in making it, consists of photographs taken or sound recordings made in that studio.

(3) Subject to sub-paragraph (4), each part of a series of films shall be treated as a separate film for the purposes of this Schedule.

(4) Where—

(*a*) any series of films consists of a number of parts (not exceeding sixteen) whose combined playing time does not exceed eight hours; and
(*b*) those parts, when shown consecutively in the sequence intended, constitute in the opinion of the Secretary of State a self-contained work,

the Secretary of State may, if he thinks fit, direct that those parts, taken together, are to be treated as constituting a single film for the purposes of this Schedule.

(5) Any reference in this Schedule to a master negative, tape or disc certified under paragraph 3 (1) or to a certificate issued under that provisions includes a reference to a master negative, tape or disc certified in pursuance of section 72 (7) (*b*) of the Finance Act 1982 as originally enacted or to a certificate issued in pursuance of that provision.

Applications for certification of master negatives, tapes and discs

2.—(1) An application for the certification by the Secretary of State of a master negative, master tape or master disc of a film as a qualifying film, qualifying tape or qualifying disc for the purposes of section 72 of the Finance Act 1982 may be made by any person who has incurred expenditure on the production or acquisition of that negative, tape, or disc.

(2) In sub-paragraph (1) the reference to the acquisition of a master negative, tape or disc includes a reference to the acquisition of any description of rights in it.

(3) On an application under this paragraph for the certification of a master negative, tape or disc the applicant shall—

(a) produce to the Secretary of State such books and other documents relating to it; and
(b) furnish to the Secretary of State such other information with respect to it,

as the Secretary of State may require for the purpose of determining the application.

(4) Any information furnished for the purposes of sub-paragraph (3) shall, if the Secretary of State so directs, be accompanied by a statutory declaration as to the truth of the information made by the person furnishing it.

Certification by Secretary of State of master negatives, tapes and discs

3.—(1) If the Secretary of State is satisfied that a master negative, tape or disc with respect to which an application is made under paragraph 2 is a master negative, tape or disc of a film which, in his opinion, is a British film for the purposes of this Schedule, he shall certify that negative, tape or disc as a qualifying film, qualifying tape or qualifying disc for the purposes of section 72 of the Finance Act 1982.

(2) If the Secretary of State is for any reason not satisfied as mentioned in sub-paragraph (1) he shall refuse the application.

(3) If it appears to the Secretary of State that any negative, tape or disc certified by him under sub-paragraph (1) ought for any reason not to have been so certified he shall revoke its certification.

(4) Where an application is made under paragraph 2 in relation to a negative, tape or disc of a film which has already been certified by the Secretary of State under sub-paragraph (1) on a prior application, the Secretary of State may issue the applicant with a duplicate or copy of the certificate issued on that prior application.

British films for purposes of the Schedule

4.—(1) Subject to paragraph 5, a film is a British film for the purposes of this Schedule if all the requirements specified in sub-paragraph (2) are satisfied with respect to it.

(2) Those requirements are—

(a) that the maker of the film was, throughout the time during which the film was being made, either—

(i) a person ordinarily resident in a member State, or
(ii) a company registered in a member State, being a company the central management and control of whose business was throughout the said time exercised in a member State;

(b) that the studio (if any) used in making the film was in a Commonwealth country or the Republic of Ireland; and
(c) that not less than the requisite amount of labour costs (as determined under paragraph 7) represents payments paid or payable in respect of the labour or services of Commonwealth citizens or citizens of any member State or persons ordinarily resident in a Commonwealth country or a member State.

(3) For the purpose of determining whether the requirements specified in sub-paragraph (2) are satisfied with respect to any film, any other film used for making photographs depicted as part of any scene in the first-mentioned film shall be treated as part of that film.

(4) Subject to paragraph 5 (4), if on an application under paragraph 2 in relation to a negative, tape or disc of any film the applicant requests the Secretary of State to do so, the Secretary of State shall, for the purpose of determining whether the film is a British film for the purposes of this Schedule, treat the film as if such portions of it as may be designated by the applicant did not form part of it; but the playing time of the portions so designated must not exceed $7\frac{1}{2}$ per cent. of the total playing time of the film.

(5) Her Majesty may by Order in Council provide for films which are made in accordance with the terms of any agreement between Her Majesty's Government in the United Kingdom and any other government or any international organisation or authority, and which would not, apart from such an Order, be British films for the purposes of this Schedule, to be treated as British films for those purposes.

Excluded films

5.—(1) A film is not a British film for the purposes of this Schedule by virtue of paragraph 4 (1)—

(*a*) if parts of the film are derived, as regards the photographs comprised in it, from—

(i) any film of which the master negative, tape or disc has already been certified under paragraph 3 (1), or
(ii) any film the maker of which was not the maker of the first-mentioned film,

and the playing time of those parts exceeds 10 per cent. of the total playing time of the film; or
(*b*) if the playing time of so much of the film as consists of photographs taken or sound recordings made in any studio outside the United Kingdom exceeds 7½ per cent. of the total playing time of the film; or
(*c*) (subject to sub-paragraph (3)) if the playing time of so much of the film as consists of photographs taken or sound recordings made outside the United Kingdom exceeds 20 per cent. of the total playing time of the film.

(2) In sub-paragraph (1) (*b*) "studio"—

(*a*) in relation to photographs, means any building or group of buildings constructed or adapted wholly or mainly for the purpose of taking photographs therein;
(*b*) in relation to sound recordings, means any building or group of buildings constructed or adapted wholly or mainly for the purpose of making sound recordings therein.

(3) Sub-paragraph (1) (*c*) shall not apply to a film if—

(*a*) the preparation for the making of the film was so far as practicable carried out in the United Kingdom; and
(*b*) the normal laboratory processing work incidental to the making of the film was carried out in the United Kingdom; and
(*c*) at least 50 per cent. (in terms of value) of the technical equipment used in the making of the film was provided from sources in the United Kingdom.

(4) In determining the playing time of a film for the purposes of sub-paragraph (1) (*c*) any portions of the film designated in accordance with paragraph 4 (4) shall nevertheless be treated as forming part of the film.

Ascertainment of labour costs and playing time

6.—(1) For the purposes of this Schedule the labour costs of a film shall be taken to be, subject to paragraph 8, the total amount of the payments paid or payable in respect of the labour or services of persons directly engaged in the making of the film, in so far as those payments are attributable to the making of that film, but shall not be taken to include payments in respect of copyright unless it is copyright in a work created for the purpose of its use in the film.

(2) For the purposes of sub-paragraph (1)—

(*a*) the author of the scenario of the film shall be deemed to be a person directly engaged in the making of the film;
(*b*) a person shall not be taken to be directly engaged in the making of a film by reason only—

(i) that he is financially interested in the making of the film or is engaged in a clerical capacity as a servant of an undertaking concerned with the making of the film; or
(ii) that he supplies goods used in the making of the film or is in the employment of a person who supplies such goods;

(*c*) payments paid or payable to a person who is engaged in an administrative capacity as an officer or servant of an undertaking concerned with the making of a film shall not be taken to be attributable to the making of the film except in so far as they are payments in respect of services directly concerned with the making of that film.

(3) Subject to paragraph 5 (4), in determining the playing time of a film for the purposes of this Schedule any portions of the film designated in accordance with paragraph 4 (4) shall be treated as not forming part of the film.

Determination of requisite amount of labour costs

7.—(1) For the purposes of paragraph 4 (2) (*c*) the requisite amount of the labour costs of a film shall be taken to be (subject to sub-paragraph (3) of this paragraph) whichever is the lesser of the two amounts specified in sub-paragraph (2) of this paragraph.

(2) The amounts referred to in sub-paragraph (1) are—

(*a*) the amount arrived at by applying the fraction three-quarters to the total labour costs of the film, after deducting from those costs, if the applicant on an application under paragraph 2 so desires, the amount of any payment which, as part of those costs, has been paid or is payable in respect of the labour or services of any one person who was not, while engaged in the making of the film—

(i) a Commonwealth citizen or a citizen of a member State, nor
(ii) a person ordinarily resident in a Commonwealth country or a member State; and

(*b*) the amount arrived at by applying the fraction four-fifths to the total labour costs of the film, after deducting from those costs the amount of any payments which, as part of those costs, have been paid or are payable in respect of the labour or services of any two persons neither of whom was, while engaged in the making of the film, such a citizen or person as is referred to in paragraph (*a*) (i) or (ii), and at least one of whom was so engaged in the capacity of an actor or actress and in no other capacity.

(3) If on an application under paragraph 2 in relation to a negative, tape or disc of a film with respect to which the requirement specified in paragraph 4 (2) (*c*) is not fulfilled the Secretary of State is satisfied that the maker of the film took all reasonable steps to fulfil that requirement, and that its non-fulfilment was due to exceptional circumstances beyond his control, the Secretary of State, if he thinks fit, may direct that sub-paragraph (2) of this paragraph shall have effect in relation to that film as if for "three-quarters" and "four-fifths" there were substituted "seven-tenths" and "three-quarters" respectively.

Power of Secretary of State to direct alteration of labour costs

8. Where it is material, in connection with an application under paragraph 2 in relation to a negative, tape or disc of a film, to ascertain the labour costs of the film or the proportion of those costs which represents payments in respect of the labour or services of persons of any particular class, then—

(*a*) if it appears to the Secretary of State that any sum which, as part of those costs, is paid or payable in respect of the labour or services of any particular person is so great as not to be a bona fide payment by way of remuneration for the said labour or services, the Secretary of State may direct that that sum, or part of that sum, shall be disregarded in ascertaining the said labour costs or the said proportion thereof, as the case may be; and
(*b*) if it appears to the Secretary of State that no sum or a sum so small as not bona fide to represent all the remuneration therefor is paid or payable as part of those costs in respect of the labour or services of any particular person, the Secretary of State may direct that such sum, or (as the case may be) such greater sum, as may be specified in the direction shall be treated as so paid or payable.

Determination of disputes

9.—(1) Any person who is aggrieved by any decision of the Secretary of State to refuse an application under paragraph 2 or to revoke any certification under paragraph 3 (1) may, subject to rules of court, apply to the High Court, and the decision of that Court shall be final.

(2) In relation to any person whose principal place of business is in Scotland, sub-paragraph (1) shall have effect as if for any reference to the High Court there were substituted a reference to the Court of Session.

Regulations and orders

10.—(1) The Secretary of State may make regulations—

(*a*) prescribing the form of applications under paragraph 2;
(*b*) prescribing the particulars and evidence necessary for satisfying the Secretary of State that a film is a British film for the purposes of this Schedule;
(*c*) providing that any statutory declaration which is required by paragraph 2 (4) to be

made by any person shall be deemed to be properly made if it is made on his behalf by any such person as may be specified in the regulations.

(2) The Secretary of State with the approval of the Treasury may by order make such modifications of any of the provisions of paragraphs 1 and 4 to 8 as he considers appropriate; and any such order may contain such incidental, supplemental and transitional provisions as he considers appropriate in connection with the order.

(3) In sub-paragraph (2) "modifications" includes additions, omissions and alterations.

(4) Any regulations or order under this paragraph shall be made by statutory instrument.

(5) Any regulations under this paragraph shall be laid before Parliament after being made; but no order shall be made under this paragraph unless it has been laid before Parliament and approved by a resolution of each House.

FINANCE ACT 1985

(1985 Chapter 54)

ARRANGEMENT OF SECTIONS

Note.—Provisions of this Act relevant to the taxes covered by this Handbook and not reproduced are either spent or repealed by TA 1988, Sch. 31 and other legislation.

PART I

CUSTOMS AND EXCISE AND VALUE ADDED TAX

CHAPTER I
CUSTOMS AND EXCISE

Section
10. *Computer records etc.* (see Orange Book)

CHAPTER II
VALUE ADDED TAX

Sections 11–33 (see Orange Book)

PART II

INCOME TAX, CORPORATION TAX AND CAPITAL GAINS TAX

CHAPTER II
CAPITAL ALLOWANCES

Section
56. Time when capital expenditure is incurred.
57. Election for certain machinery or plant to be treated as short-life assets.
58. Allowances for ships.
59. Entitlement to allowances for machinery and plant which are fixtures.
61. Dredging.
63. Allowances for capital expenditure on scientific research.
66. Hotels.

CHAPTER III
CAPITAL GAINS

68. Modification of indexation allowance.
69. Relief for disposals by individuals on retirement from family business.
70. Relief for other disposals associated with retirement.
71. Assets disposed of in a series of transactions.
72. Commodity and financial futures and traded options.

PART III

STAMP DUTY

Sections 78–89 (see Orange Book)

PART V

MISCELLANEOUS AND SUPPLEMENTARY

Section
93. Abolition of development land tax and tax on development gains.
94. *Capital transfer tax: conditional exemption.* (see Orange Book)
95. The national heritage: transfer of Treasury functions to Board.
98. Short title, interpretation, construction and repeals.

SCHEDULES:

Schedule 6—*Section 39 of the principal Act, as amended, excluding subsection (8).* (see Orange Book)
Schedule 7—*Amendments of Schedule 7 to the principal Act.* (see Orange Book)
Schedule 8—*Value added tax tribunals.* (see Orange Book)
Schedule 15—Machinery and plant excluded from treatment as short-life assets.
Schedule 17—Capital allowances for fixtures.
Schedule 19—Indexation.
Schedule 20—Retirement relief etc.
Schedule 21—Assets disposed of in a series of linked transactions.
Schedule 24—*Stamp duty: headings omitted.* (see Orange Book)
Schedule 25—Abolition of development land tax and tax on development gains.
Schedule 26—*Capital transfer tax: conditional exemption.* (see Orange Book)
Schedule 27—Repeals.
    Part IV   *Value Added Tax.* (see Orange Book)
    Part IX   *Stamp Duty.* (see Orange Book)

An Act to grant certain duties, to alter other duties, and to amend the law relating to the National Debt and the Public Revenue, and to make further provision in connection with Finance.
[25th July 1985]

PART II

INCOME TAX, CORPORATION TAX AND CAPITAL GAINS TAX

CHAPTER II

CAPITAL ALLOWANCES

56. Time when capital expenditure is incurred

(1) The provisions of this section have effect to determine when capital expenditure is to be taken to be incurred for the purposes of—

(*a*) Parts I and II of the Capital Allowances Act 1968;
(*b*) Chapter I of Part III of the Finance Act 1971 (machinery and plant);
(*c*) any [enactment (including any contained in the Taxes Act)][3] which falls to be construed (or is expressed to have effect) as if it were contained in any of those enactments; and
(*d*) Schedule 12 to the Finance Act 1982 (dwelling-houses let on assured tenancies); [and][1]
(*e*) Section 57 of the Finance Act 1986;][1] [and][2]
(*f*) Schedule 13 to the Finance Act 1986;][2] [and][4]
[(*g*) sections 117 and 118 of the Finance Act 1989.][4]

(2) Subject to subsections (3) to (5) below, an amount of capital expenditure is to be taken to be incurred on the date on which the obligation to pay that amount becomes unconditional (whether or not there is a later date on or before which the whole or any part of that amount is required to be paid).

(3) If, under or by virtue of any agreement,—

(*a*) as a result of the issue of a certificate or some other event, an obligation to pay an amount of capital expenditure on the provision of an asset becomes unconditional, and
(*b*) at a time before that obligation becomes unconditional, the asset becomes the property of or is otherwise under the contract attributed to the person having that obligation,

then, in a case where the obligation referred to in paragraph (*a*) above becomes unconditional within the period of one month beginning at the end of a chargeable period or its basis period but the time referred to in paragraph (*b*) above falls at or before the end of that chargeable period or its basis period, subsection (2) above shall apply as if the obligation became unconditional immediately before the expiry of that period.

(4) Where, under or by virtue of any agreement, the whole or any part of an amount of capital expenditure is required to be paid on (or not later than) a date which is more than four months after the date on which the obligation to pay that amount becomes unconditional, so much of that expenditure as is required to be so paid shall be taken to be incurred on the date on or before which it is required to be so paid.

(5) In any case where—

(*a*) under or by virtue of any agreement, an obligation to pay an amount of capital expenditure becomes unconditional on a date earlier than that which accords with normal commercial usage, and
(*b*) the sole or main benefit which (apart from this subsection) might have been expected to be obtained from the obligation becoming unconditional on that earlier date is that, by virtue of subsection (2) above, the expenditure would be taken to be incurred in a chargeable period or its basis period which is earlier than would otherwise have been the case,

then, in relation to that amount of expenditure, subsection (2) above shall have effect as if, for the words from "on which" onwards there were substituted "on or before which it is required to be paid"; and, accordingly, subsection (4) above shall be disregarded.

(6) Subject to subsection (7) below, the preceding provisions of this section have effect with respect to any chargeable period or its basis period ending on or after 18th December 1984

and, accordingly, the following provisions shall not have effect with respect to any such period, namely,—

(a) section 82 (3) of the Capital Allowances Act 1968; and
(b) in subsection (4) of section 50 of the Finance Act 1971, the words from the beginning to "payable; and".

(7) In relation to Part II of the Capital Allowances Act 1968 (scientific research), the preceding provisions of this section have effect with respect to any chargeable period (within the meaning of that Part) ending on or after 1st April 1985.

(8) In so far as (apart from subsections (2) to (6) above) any provision of the Capital Allowances Act 1968, [sections 520 to 533]³ of the Taxes Act (patents and know-how) [the Finance Act 1971, Schedule 12 to the Finance Act 1982 or Schedules 13 and 15 to the Finance Act 1986]⁵ would have the effect that any expenditure would for any purpose fall to be treated as incurred on a date which is later than that which would result from the application of those subsections, nothing in this section shall affect the continuing operation of that provision.

Amendments.—¹ Sub-s. (1) (e) and the word "and" preceding it added by FA 1986, s. 57 (10).
² Sub-s. (1) (f) and the word "and" preceding it added by FA 1986, Sch. 13, para. 28.
³ Words in sub-ss. (1) (c), (8) substituted by TA 1988, Sch. 29, para. 32 Table.
⁴ Sub-s. (1) (g) and the preceding word "and" added by FA 1989, Sch. 13, para. 29.
⁵ Words in sub-s. (8) substituted by FA 1989, Sch. 13, para. 30 in relation to any chargeable period or its basis period ending after 26 July 1989.

57. Election for certain machinery or plant to be treated as short-life assets

(1) The provisions of this section apply where—

(a) a person carrying on a trade (in this section referred to as "the trader") incurs capital expenditure on or after 1st April 1986 on the provision of machinery or plant wholly and exclusively for the purposes of the trade; and
(b) the machinery or plant is not of a description specified in Schedule 15 to this Act; and
(c) the trader makes an election under this section requiring the machinery or plant to be treated as a short-life asset;

and any machinery or plant to which an election under this section applies is in the following provisions of this section referred to as a "short-life asset".

(2) An election under this section—

(a) shall be made in writing to the inspector;
(b) shall specify the short-life asset, the capital expenditure concerned and the date on which it was incurred;
(c) may not be made more than two years after the end of the chargeable period or its basis period in which the capital expenditure was incurred; and
(d) shall be irrevocable;

and if different parts of the capital expenditure are incurred at different times, only that part of the expenditure which is first incurred shall be taken into account for the purposes of paragraph (c) above.

(3) Where an election is made under this section, it shall be assumed for the purposes of section 44 of the Finance Act 1971 (in the following provisions of this section referred to as "section 44")—

(a) that the trader incurred the expenditure on the provision of the short-life asset wholly and exclusively for the purposes of a trade (in the following provisions of this section referred to as "the notional trade") carried on by him separately from the trade referred to in subsection (1) above (in those provisions referred to as his "actual trade") and from any other trade which he in fact carries on or is assumed for any other purpose to carry on; and
(b) that, without prejudice to sub-paragraphs (i) to (iii) of paragraph (c) of subsection (5) of section 44, the notional trade is permanently discontinued when the short-life asset begins to be used wholly or partly for purposes other than those of the actual trade.

(4) Any allowance or charge which, on the assumptions in subsection (3) above, would fall to be made for any chargeable period in the case of the notional trade shall be made for that period in the case of the actual trade; and all such assessments and adjustments of assessments shall be made as may be necessary to give effect to an election under this section.

(5) If the disposal value of a short-life asset does not fall to be brought into account in accordance with section 44 for any of the chargeable periods ending on or before the fourth anniversary of the end of the chargeable period related to the incurring of the capital expenditure concerned or, as the case may be, the first part of that expenditure, then,—

(a) in the first chargeable period ending after that fourth anniversary or, as the case may be, in its basis period, the notional trade shall be treated as permanently discontinued but no balancing allowance or charge shall be made to or on the trader by reason thereof; and
(b) the amount which, apart from this subsection, would be the trader's qualifying expenditure for the chargeable period referred to in paragraph (a) above in respect of the notional trade shall be added to his qualifying expenditure for that period in respect of his actual trade.

(6) If, at a time before the notional trade would otherwise be permanently discontinued for the purposes of section 44, [a short-life asset provided for leasing]³ begins to be used otherwise than for a qualifying purpose, within the meaning of section 64 of the Finance Act 1980 (leased assets used for certain purposes) and the occasion of its beginning to be so used falls within the requisite period, within the meaning of that section, then at that time—

(a) the notional trade shall be treated as permanently discontinued but no balancing allowance or charge shall be made to or on the trader by reason thereof, and
(b) the amount which, apart from this subsection, would be the trader's qualifying expenditure [in respect of the notional trade]⁴ for the chargeable period in which, or in the basis period for which, the asset began to be so used shall for the purposes of section 44 . . .¹ [be, or be added to, the trader's qualifying expenditure for that chargeable period.]⁵

(7) Subject to subsection (8) below, if, at a time before the notional trade is permanently discontinued for the purposes of section 44, the trader disposes of a short-life asset to a person with whom he is connected within the terms of section [839]² of the Taxes Act,—

(a) the disposal shall be treated for the purposes of section 44 (in its application both to the trader and to the connected person) as a sale of the short-life asset at a price equal to the amount of the trader's qualifying expenditure in respect of the notional trade for the chargeable period related to the disposal;
(b) nothing in paragraph 3 of Schedule 8 to the Finance Act 1971 (sales between connected persons etc.) shall apply in relation to the disposal;
(c) immediately after his acquisition of the short-life asset, the connected person shall be taken to have made an election under this section (so that, in his hands, the machinery or plant concerned is also a short-life asset for the purposes of this section); and
(d) in relation to the connected person, subsection (5) above shall have effect as if any reference to the fourth anniversary of the end of the chargeable period related to the incurring of the capital expenditure concerned were a reference to the date which was (or which, by virtue of the previous operation of this paragraph, had effect as) that fourth anniversary in relation to the trader.

(8) Paragraphs (a) and (b) of subsection (7) above do not apply in relation to a disposal unless, by notice in writing given to the inspector not more than two years after the end of the chargeable period or its basis period in which the disposal occurred, the trader and the connected person so elect.

(9) In the application of subsection (6) of section 44 (disposal value) where a short-life asset is disposed of at a price lower than that which it would have fetched if sold in the open market, paragraph (b) (i) (which excludes open market value where the buyer is entitled to allowances) shall not apply unless an election is made under subsection (8) above.

(10) Any reference in Schedule 15 to this Act to expenditure in respect of which the making of a first-year allowance is precluded by any enactment shall be construed without regard to paragraph 2 of Schedule 12 to the Finance Act 1984 (which terminates first-year allowances in respect of expenditure incurred on the provision of machinery or plant on or after 1st April 1986).

Cross references.—See FA 1986, s. 55 (5), (8) (where a person incurs new expenditure (i.e. subject to FA 1986, Sch. 14, expenditure incurred after 31 March 1986) on machinery or plant for mineral exploration before commencing trade of mineral extraction, that expenditure is, subject to certain conditions, treated as expenditure incurred for the purposes of his trade).
Amendments.—¹ Words "(as it has effect in accordance with section 65 of the Finance Act 1980)" in sub-s. (6) (b) repealed by FA 1986, s. 57 (6) in respect of "new expenditure" (i.e. expenditure incurred after 31 March 1986, subject to qualifications in s. 57 (2), (3)) on any machinery or plant except a vehicle falling within FA 1980, s. 69; see FA 1986, s. 57 (7) (b).
² Number in sub-s. (7) substituted by TA 1988, Sch. 29, para. 32 Table.
³ Words in sub-s. (6) substituted for the words "the short-life asset" by FA 1989, Sch. 13, para. 21 (1) (a), (3) in relation to any chargeable period or its basis period ending after 26 July 1989.

[4] Words in sub-s. (6) (*b*) inserted by FA 1989, Sch. 13, para. 21 (1) (*b*) (i), (3) in relation to any chargeable period or its basis period ending after 26 July 1989; but subject to FA 1989, Sch. 13, para. 21 (2).
[5] Words in sub-s. (6) (*b*) substituted by FA 1989, Sch. 13, para. 21 (1) (*b*) (ii), (3) in relation to any chargeable period or its basis period ending after 26 July 1989; but subject to FA 1989, Sch. 13, para. 21 (2). Previously sub-s. (6) (*b*) read—

"(*b*) the amount which, apart from this subsection, would be the trader's qualifying expenditure for the chargeable period in which, or in the basis period for which, the asset began to be so used shall for the purposes of section 44 (as it has effect in accordance with section 65 of the Finance Act 1980) be added to the trader's qualifying expenditure for that chargeable period in respect of the separate trade referred to in subsection (2) of the said section 65."

And as amended by FA 1986, s. 57 (6) it read—

"(*b*) the amount which, apart from this subsection, would be the trader's qualifying expenditure for the chargeable period in which, or in the basis period for which, the asset began to be so used shall for the purposes of section 44 be added to the trader's qualifying expenditure for that chargeable period in respect of his actual trade."

58. Allowances for ships

(1) With respect to expenditure incurred on or after 1st April 1985, paragraph 8 of Schedule 8 to the Finance Act 1971 (first-year allowances for new ships) shall have effect in relation to ships which are not new as well as in relation to new ships and accordingly—

(*a*) the word "new", wherever appearing, shall be omitted; and
(*b*) sub-paragraph (5) (previous ownership disregarded in certain cases in determining whether ship is new) shall also be omitted.

(2) After the said paragraph 8 there shall be inserted the paragraphs set out in Schedule 16 to this Act, being provisions relating to writing-down allowances for ships.

[(3) In consequence of subsection (1) above—

(*a*) no disclaimer or claim under section 41 (3) of the Finance Act 1971 may be made in respect of any ship,
(*b*) section 66 (7) of the Finance Act 1980 and paragraph 3 of Schedule 11 to the Finance Act 1982 shall have effect with the omission of the word "new" in each place where it occurs, and
(*c*) section 59 (4) (*c*) and (6) (*c*) of the Finance Act 1984 shall have effect with the omission of the word "new".][1]

Amendments.—[1] Sub-s. (3) added by FA 1989, Sch. 13, para. 15. Sub-s. (3) (*a*) has effect in relation to disclaimers and claims made after 26 July 1989, sub-s. (3) (*b*) has effect in any case where the requisite period begins after that day and sub-s. (3) (*c*) comes into force on that day.

59. Entitlement to allowances for machinery and plant which are fixtures

(1) The provisions of Schedule 17 to this Act apply to determine entitlement to an allowance under Chapter I of Part III of the Finance Act 1971 in respect of expenditure on the provision of machinery or plant which is so installed or otherwise fixed in or to a building or any other description of land as to become, in law, part of that building or other land; and at any time when, by virtue of that Schedule, any machinery or plant is treated as belonging to any person, no other person shall be entitled to such an allowance in respect of it.

(2) Schedule 17 to this Act applies to expenditure incurred after 11th July 1984, unless that expenditure—

(*a*) consists of the payment of sums payable under a contract entered into on or before that date; or
(*b*) is incurred pursuant to an obligation contained in a lease or agreement for a lease entered into on or before that date.

(3) All such assessments and adjustments of assessments shall be made as may be necessary to give effect to the provisions of Schedule 17 to this Act.

(4) Where any question arises as to whether any machinery or plant has become, in law, part of a building or other land and that question is material with respect to the liability to tax (for whatever period) of two or more persons, that question shall be determined, for the purposes of the tax of all those persons, by the Special Commissioners who shall determine the question in like manner as if it were an appeal, except that, for the purposes of the determination, all those persons shall be entitled to appear and be heard by, or to make representations in writing to, the Special Commissioners.

(5) . . .

(6) The amendments made by subsection (5) above have effect in relation to any lease

entered into after 11th July 1984, unless it was entered into pursuant to an agreement made on or before that date.

(7) This section and Schedule 17 to this Act shall be construed as if they were contained in Chapter I of Part III of the Finance Act 1971, except that expenditure shall not be treated for the purposes of that Schedule as having been incurred after the date on which it was in fact incurred by reason only of so much of section 50 (4) of that Act as relates to expenditure incurred before a trade begins.

(8) Nothing in subsection (1) above affects the entitlement of any person to an allowance by virtue of section 85 of the Capital Allowances Act 1968 (allowances in respect of contributions of a capital nature)...

Notes.—Sub-s. (5) amends FA 1971, s. 46 (2).
Words omitted from sub-s. (8) amend FA 1971, Sch. 8, para. 15 (6).

61. Dredging

(1) No initial allowance shall be made under section 67 of the Capital Allowances Act 1968 (dredging) in respect of capital expenditure incurred on or after 1st April 1986 unless that expenditure—

(*a*) consists of the payment of sums under a contract entered into on or before 13th March 1984 by the person incurring the expenditure, and
(*b*) is incurred before 1st April 1987.

(2) Subsection (1) above shall be construed as if it were contained in Part I of the Capital Allowances Act 1968.

63. Allowances for capital expenditure on scientific research

(1)–(6) ...

(7) This section has effect with respect to capital expenditure incurred on or after 1st April 1985 unless that expenditure—

(*a*) is incurred before 1st April 1987, and
(*b*) consists of the payment of sums under a contract entered into on or before 19th March 1985 by the person incurring the expenditure.

Notes.—Sub-ss. (1)–(6) amend CAA 1968, ss. 91, 92.

66. Hotels

(1) No initial allowance shall be made in respect of capital expenditure incurred on or after 1st April 1986 in respect of a qualifying hotel (within the meaning of section 38 of the Finance Act 1978) unless that expenditure—

(*a*) consists of the payment of sums under a contract entered into on or before 13th March 1984 by the person incurring the expenditure, and
(*b*) is incurred before 1st April 1987.

(2) Subsection (1) above shall be construed as if it were contained in Part I of the Capital Allowances Act 1968 except that—

(*a*) expenditure shall not be treated for the purposes of that subsection as having been incurred after the date on which it was in fact incurred by reason only of section 1 (6) of that Act (expenditure incurred before a trade begins); and
(*b*) expenditure falling within subsection (1) (*b*) of section 5 of that Act (purchase price of building bought unused) shall be treated for the purposes of that subsection as having been incurred at the latest time when any expenditure falling within subsection (1) (*a*) of that section (expenditure on the construction of the building) was incurred.

CHAPTER III

CAPITAL GAINS

68. Modification of indexation allowance

(1) Subject to subsection (2) below, with respect to disposals of assets on or after 6th April 1985 or, in the case of disposals by companies, 1st April 1985, the provisions of Chapter III of Part III of the Finance Act 1982 shall have effect subject to the amendments in Part I of Schedule 19 to this Act, being amendments designed—

(a) to remove the twelve month qualifying period for the indexation allowance; and
(b) to extend the indexation allowance to cases where there is a loss on a disposal; and
(c) to make provisions supplementary to those matters.

(2) In the case of securities within the meaning of Chapter IV of this Part of this Act, the amendments in Part I of Schedule 19 to this Act—

(a) shall not have effect with respect to disposals of gilt-edged securities as defined in Schedule 2 to the Capital Gains Tax Act 1979 or qualifying corporate bonds as defined in section 64 of the Finance Act 1984; and
(b) shall have effect with respect to disposals of other securities on or after 28th February 1986.

(3) In Schedule 19 to this Act—

(a) Part II shall have effect with respect to holdings of securities to which Part II of Schedule 13 to the Finance Act 1982 applied (share pools in existence on 1st or 6th April 1982);
(b) Part III shall have effect with respect to other holdings of securities held on or acquired after the 1985 date;
(c) Part IV shall have effect with respect to the identification of securities disposed of on or after the 1985 date;
(d) Part V has effect with respect to securities in respect of which elections have been or could be made under Schedule 6 to the Finance Act 1983; and
(e) Part VI contains consequential provisions relating to assets forming part of a premiums trust fund;

and in that Schedule and paragraphs (b) and (c) above "the 1985 date" means 1st April 1985 in the case of holdings or disposals by companies and 6th April 1985 in any other case.

(4) For the purpose of computing the indexation allowance on a disposal of an asset . . .[4] where, on 31st March 1982, the asset was held by the person making the disposal, it shall be assumed that on that date the asset was sold by the person making the disposal and immediately reacquired by him at its market value on that date.

[(5) Except where an election under section 96 (5) of the Finance Act 1988 has effect, neither subsection (4) above nor section 96 (2) of the Finance Act 1988 shall apply for the purpose of computing the indexation allowance in a case where that allowance would be greater if they did not apply.][3]

[(5A) If under subsection (4) above it is to be assumed that any asset was on 31st March 1982 sold by the person making the disposal and immediately re-acquired by him, sections 34 and 39 of the Capital Gains Tax Act 1979 shall apply in relation to any capital allowance or renewals allowance made in respect of the expenditure actually incurred by him in providing the asset as if it were made in respect of expenditure which, on that assumption, was incurred by him in re-acquiring the asset on 31st March 1982.][1]

(6) Where, after 31st March 1982, an asset which was held on that date has been merged or divided or has changed its nature or rights in or over the asset have been created, then, subject to subsection (5) above, subsection (4) above shall have effect to determine for the purposes of section 36 of the Capital Gains Tax Act 1979 (assets derived from other assets) the amount of the consideration for the acquisition of the asset which was so held.

(7) Subsection (8) below applies to a disposal of an asset which is not a no gain/no loss disposal if—

(a) the person making the disposal acquired the asset after 31st March 1982; and
(b) the disposal by which he acquired the asset and any previous disposal of the asset after 31st March 1982 was a no gain/no loss disposal;

and for the purposes of this subsection a no gain/no loss disposal is one on which, by virtue of [any of the enactments specified in subsection (7A) below]², neither a gain nor a loss accrues to the person making the disposal.

[(7A) The enactments mentioned in subsection (7) above are—

(a) sections 44, 56, 123A, [146 (2) or (3), 146A (2)]⁵ 147 (4), 148 and 149A of the Capital Gains Tax Act 1979;
(b) sections 267, 273, 340 (7), 342, 342A, 342B, 343 (5) and 352 (7) of the Income and Corporation Taxes Act 1970;
(c) section 148 of the Finance Act 1982;
(d) section 7 of the Finance (No 2) Act 1983;
(e) paragraph 2 of Schedule 2 to the Trustee Savings Banks Act 1985;
[(ee) section 130 (3) of the Transport Act 1985]⁶
(f) section 486 (8) of the Taxes Act; and
(g) paragraph 4 of Schedule 12 to the Finance Act 1988.]¹

(8) Where this subsection applies to a disposal—

(a) the person making the disposal shall be treated for the purpose referred to in subsection (4) above as having held the asset on 31st March 1982; and
(b) for the purpose of determining any gain or loss on the disposal, the consideration which, apart from this subsection, that person would be treated as having given for the asset shall be taken to be reduced by deducting therefrom any indexation allowance brought into account by virtue of Part I of Schedule 13 to the Finance Act 1982 on any disposal falling within subsection (7) (b) above.

(9) In paragraphs (b) and (c) of subsection (3) above and in Parts III and IV of Schedule 19 to this Act "securities" does not include relevant securities as defined in section 88 (9) of the Finance Act 1982 (as amended by paragraph 3 (3) of Schedule 19 to this Act) but, subject to that, means—

(a) shares or securities of a company; and
(b) any other assets where they are of a nature to be dealt in without identifying the particular assets disposed of or acquired.

(10) Shares or securities of a company shall not be treated for the purposes of subsection (9) above or Part III of Schedule 19 to this Act as being of the same class unless they are so treated by the practice of the Stock Exchange or would be so treated if dealt with on the Stock Exchange.

Cross references.—See FA 1988, ss. 62 (4), (7) (b), 64 (6) (d) (claim under sub-s. (5) (b) as originally enacted (see under Amendments below) on material disposal of oil licence relating to undeveloped areas), s. 113 (for disposals after 3 July 1987, sub-ss. (4)–(8) above not to apply in the case of building society shares and registered industrial and provident society shares).
Amendments.—¹ Sub-ss. (5A), (7A) inserted by FA 1988, s. 118 (1), (2), (4) in relation to disposals after 5 April 1988.
² Words in sub-s. (7) substituted by FA 1988, s. 118 (3).
³ Sub-s. (5) substituted by FA 1988, Sch. 8, para. 11 in relation to disposals after 5 April 1988.
⁴ Words in sub-s. (4) repealed by FA 1988, Sch. 14, Pt. VII.
⁵ Numbers in sub-s. (7A) (a) substituted by FA 1989, Sch. 15, para. 4 (1) and deemed always to have had effect.
⁶ Sub-s. (7A) (ee) inserted by *ibid*.

---

69. Relief for disposals by individuals on retirement from family business

(1) Relief from capital gains tax shall be given, subject to and in accordance with Schedule 20 to this Act, in any case where a material disposal of business assets is made by an individual who, at the time of the disposal,—

(a) has attained the age of 60, or
(b) has retired on ill-health grounds below the age of 60,

and sections 124 and 125 of the Capital Gains Tax Act 1979 shall not apply to any disposal made on or after 6th April 1985 unless it is a disposal in respect of which, by virtue only of paragraph 5 (1) of Schedule 20 to this Act, relief in accordance with that Schedule cannot be given.

(2) For the purposes of this section and Schedule 20 to this Act, a disposal of business assets is—

(a) a disposal of the whole or part of a business, or
(b) a disposal of one or more assets which, at the time at which a business ceased to be carried on, were in use for the purposes of that business, or

(*c*) a disposal of shares or securities of a company (including a disposal of an interest in shares which a person is treated as making by virtue of section 72 of the Capital Gains Tax Act 1979—capital distributions),

and the question whether such a disposal is a material disposal shall be determined in accordance with the following provisions of this section.

(3) A disposal of the whole or part of a business is a material disposal if, throughout a period of at least one year ending with the date of the disposal, the relevant conditions are fulfilled and, in relation to such a disposal, those conditions are fulfilled at any time if at that time the business is owned by the individual making the disposal or—

(*a*) the business is owned by a company—

(i) which is a trading company, and
(ii) which is either that individual's family company or a member of a trading group of which the holding company is that individual's family company; and

(*b*) that individual is a full-time working director of that company or, if that company is a member of a group or commercial association of companies, of one or more companies which are members of the group or association.

(4) A disposal of assets such as is mentioned in subsection (2) (*b*) above is a material disposal if—

(*a*) throughout a period of at least one year ending with the date on which the business ceased to be carried on the relevant conditions are fulfilled and, in relation to such a disposal, those conditions are fulfilled at any time if at that time either the business was owned by the individual making the disposal or paragraphs (*a*) and (*b*) of subsection (3) above apply; and
(*b*) on or before the date on which the business ceased to be carried on, the individual making the disposal had either attained the age of 60 or retired on ill-health grounds below that age; and
(*c*) the date on which the business ceased to be carried on falls within the permitted period before the date of the disposal.

(5) A disposal of shares or securities of a company (including such a disposal of an interest in shares as is mentioned in subsection (2) (*c*) above) is a material disposal if, throughout a period of at least one year ending with the operative date, the relevant conditions are fulfilled and, in relation to such a disposal, those conditions are fulfilled at any time if at that time—

(*a*) the individual making the disposal owns the business which, at the date of the disposal, is owned by the company or, if the company is the holding company of a trading group, by any member of the group; or
(*b*) the company is the individual's family company and is either a trading company or the holding company of a trading group and the individual is a full-time working director of the company or, if the company is a member of a group or commercial association of companies, of one or more companies which are members of the group or association;

and, except where subsection (6) or subsection (7) below applies, the operative date for the purposes of this subsection is the date of the disposal.

(6) In any case where—

(*a*) within the permitted period before the date of the disposal referred to in subsection (5) above, the company concerned either ceased to be a trading company without continuing to be or becoming a member of a trading group or ceased to be a member of a trading group without continuing to be or becoming a trading company, and
(*b*) on or before the date of that cessation, the individual making the disposal attained the age of 60 or retired on ill-health grounds below that age,

then, subject to subsection (7) below, the operative date for the purposes of subsection (5) above is the date of the cessation referred to in paragraph (*a*) above; and, where this subsection applies, the reference in subsection (5) (*a*) above to the date of the disposal shall also be construed as a reference to the date of that cessation.

(7) If, throughout a period which ends on the date of the disposal referred to in subsection (5) above or, if subsection (6) above applies, on the date of the cessation referred to in paragraph (*a*) of that subsection and which begins when the individual concerned ceased to be a full-time working director of the company or, if that company is a member of a group or commercial association of companies, of one or more companies which are members of the group or association,—

(*a*) the company concerned was his family company and either a trading company or the holding company of a trading group, and

(*b*) he was a director of the company concerned or, as the case may be, of one or more members of the group or association and, in that capacity, devoted at least ten hours per week (averaged over the period) to the service of the company or companies in a technical or managerial capacity,

the operative date for the purposes of subsection (5) above is the date on which the individual ceased to be a full-time working director as mentioned above.

(8) For the purposes of this section—

(*a*) any reference to the disposal of the whole or part of a business by an individual includes a reference to the disposal by him of his interest in the assets of a partnership carrying on the business; and

(*b*) subject to paragraph (*a*) above, at any time when a business is carried on by a partnership, the business shall be treated as owned by each individual who is at that time a member of the partnership.

(9) Part I of Schedule 20 to this Act shall have effect for the interpretation of this section as well as of that Schedule.

70. Relief for other disposals associated with retirement

(1) Relief from capital gains tax shall be given, subject to and in accordance with Schedule 20 to this Act, in any case where an individual—

(*a*) who has attained the age of 60, or
(*b*) who has retired on ill-health grounds below the age of 60,

makes a relevant disposal of the whole or part of the assets provided or held for the purposes of an office or employment exercised by him; and, if he ceases to exercise that office or employment before the date of the relevant disposal, the date on which he ceased to exercise it is in subsection (2) below referred to as the "prior cessation date".

(2) For the purposes of subsection (1) above, a disposal of the whole or part of the assets provided or held as mentioned in that subsection is a relevant disposal if—

(*a*) throughout a period of at least one year ending with the date of the disposal or, where applicable, the prior cessation date, the office or employment was the full-time occupation of the individual making the disposal; and

(*b*) that office or employment is other than that of director of a company which is either the family company of the individual concerned or is a member of a trading group of which the holding company is his family company; and

(*c*) where there is a prior cessation date, the individual either had attained the age of 60 on or before that date or on that date retired on ill-health grounds below that age; and

(*d*) where there is a prior cessation date, the disposal takes place within the permitted period after the cessation date.

(3) Relief from capital gains tax shall be given, subject to and in accordance with Schedule 20 to this Act, where—

(*a*) the trustees of a settlement dispose of—

(i) shares or securities of a company, or
(ii) an asset used or previously used for the purposes of a business,

being, in either case, part of the settled property; and

(*b*) the conditions in subsection (4) or, as the case may be, subsection (5) below are fulfilled with respect to a beneficiary who, under the settlement, has an interest in possession in the whole of the settled property or, as the case may be, in a part of it which consists of or includes the shares or securities or the asset referred to in paragraph (*a*) above, but excluding, for this purpose, an interest for a fixed term; and in those subsections that beneficiary is referred to as "the qualifying beneficiary".

(4) In relation to a disposal of shares or securities of a company (including such a disposal of an interest in shares as is mentioned in section 69 (2) (*c*) above), the conditions referred to in subsection (3) (*b*) above are—

(*a*) that, throughout a period of at least one year ending not earlier than the permitted period before the disposal, the company was the qualifying beneficiary's family company and either a trading company or the holding company of a trading group; and

(*b*) that, throughout a period of at least one year ending as mentioned in paragraph (*a*) above, the qualifying beneficiary was a full-time working director of the company or, if the company is a member of a group or commercial association of companies, of one or more companies which are members of the group or association; and

(*c*) that, on the date of the disposal or within the permitted period before that date, the qualifying beneficiary ceased to be a full-time working director as mentioned in paragraph (*b*) above, having attained the age of 60 or retired on ill-health grounds below that age.

(5) In relation to a disposal of an asset, the conditions referred to in subsection (3) (*b*) above are—

(*a*) that, throughout a period of at least one year ending not earlier than the permitted period before the disposal, the asset was used for the purposes of a business carried on by the qualifying beneficiary; and

(*b*) that, on the date of the disposal or within the permitted period before that date, the qualifying beneficiary ceased to carry on the business referred to in paragraph (*a*) above; and

(*c*) that, on or before the date of the disposal or, if it was earlier, the date on which the qualifying beneficiary ceased to carry on that business, he attained the age of 60 or retired on ill-health grounds below that age.

(6) In any case where—

(*a*) by virtue of section 69 above, relief falls to be given, in accordance with Schedule 20 to this Act, in respect of a material disposal of business assets which either consists of the disposal by an individual of his interest in the assets of a partnership or is of a description falling within subsection (5) of that section, and

(*b*) the individual making that material disposal makes an associated disposal of assets, as defined in subsection (7) below,

relief from capital gains tax shall also be given, subject to and in accordance with that Schedule, in respect of the associated disposal.

(7) In relation to a material disposal of business assets, a disposal of an asset is an associated disposal if—

(*a*) it takes place as part of a withdrawal of the individual concerned from participation in the business carried on by the partnership referred to in subsection (6) (*a*) above or, as the case may be, by the company which owns the business as mentioned in subsection (5) (*a*) of section 69 above; and

(*b*) immediately before the material disposal or, if it was earlier, the cessation of the business mentioned in paragraph (*a*) above, the asset was in use for the purposes of that business; and

(*c*) during the whole or part of the period in which the asset has been in the ownership of the individual making the disposal the asset has been used—

(i) for the purposes of the business mentioned in paragraph (*a*) above (whether or not carried on by the partnership or company there referred to); or

(ii) for the purposes of another business carried on by the individual or by a partnership of which the individual concerned was a member; or

(iii) for the purposes of another business in respect of which the conditions in paragraphs (*a*) and (*b*) of subsection (3) of section 69 above were fulfilled.

(8) In subsections (6) and (7) above "material disposal of business assets" has the same meaning as in section 69 above and Part I of Schedule 20 to this Act shall have effect for the interpretation of this section as well as of that Schedule.

(9) In consequence of the provisions of this section and section 69 above, with respect to disposals on which relief falls to be given under Schedule 20 to this Act, section 126 of and Schedule 4 to the Capital Gains Tax Act 1979 (gifts of business assets) shall be amended as follows—

. . .

(10) . . .

Notes.—Words omitted from sub-s. (9) amend CGTA 1979, ss. 120, 126, Sch. 4, para. 8.
Sub-s. (10) amends FA 1980, s. 79 (3), FA 1984, Sch. 11, para. 1 (2) (*g*), (*h*).

71. Assets disposed of in a series of transactions

(1) For the purposes of the Capital Gains Tax Act 1979 (in this section referred to as "the principal Act"), in any case where,—

> (*a*) by way of two or more material transactions which are linked (in this section referred to as a series of linked transactions), one person disposes of assets to another person with whom he is connected or to two or more other persons with each of whom he is connected, and
> (*b*) the original market value of the assets disposed of by any of the transactions in the series, as determined under Schedule 21 to this Act, is less than the appropriate portion of the aggregate market value of the assets disposed of by all the transactions in the series, as so determined,

then, subject to subsection (2) below, the disposal effected by any linked transaction in the series in respect of which the condition in paragraph (*b*) above is fulfilled shall be deemed to be for a consideration equal to the appropriate portion referred to in that paragraph.

(2) Where the disposal effected by a material transaction is one to which section 44 of the principal Act applies (disposals of assets between husband and wife) nothing in subsection (1) above shall affect the amount which, for the purposes of the principal Act, is the consideration for that disposal.

(3) Subject to subsections (6) to (8) below, any reference in this section to a material transaction is a reference to a transaction by way of gift or otherwise which takes place after 19th March 1985; and for the purposes of this section two or more material transactions are linked if they occur within the period of six years ending on the date of the last of them.

(4) This section shall apply or, as the case may be, shall again apply—

> (*a*) when a second material transaction causes a series of linked transactions to come into being; and
> (*b*) whenever, on the occurrence of a further material transaction, an existing series is extended by the inclusion of that transaction (whether or not an earlier transaction ceases to form part of the series);

and all such assessments and adjustments of assessments shall be made as may be necessary to give effect to this section on each such occasion.

(5) In consequence of the preceding provisions of this section, any gift or other transaction which occurs after 19th March 1985 shall be disregarded for the purposes of section 151 of the principal Act (the previous code for assets disposed of in a series of transactions).

(6) Where a member of a group of companies disposes of an asset to another member of the group in circumstances such that, by virtue of section 273 of [the Income and Corporation Taxes act 1970],[1] both companies are treated, so far as relates to corporation tax on chargeable gains, as if the consideration for the disposal were of such an amount as would secure that neither a gain nor a loss would accrue, the transaction by which that disposal is effected is not a material transaction; and a disposal in these circumstances is in this section referred to as an "inter-group transfer".

(7) In any case where—

> (*a*) a company (in this subsection referred to as "company A") disposes of an asset by way of a material transaction, and
> (*b*) company A acquired the asset after 19th March 1985 by way of an inter-group transfer, and
> (*c*) the disposal by company A is to a person who is connected with another company (in this subsection referred to as "company B") which at some time after 19th March 1985 disposed of the asset by way of an inter-group transfer, and
> (*d*) either the disposal by way of inter-group transfer which is referred to in paragraph (*c*) above was the occasion of the acquisition referred to in paragraph (*b*) above or, between that disposal and that acquisition, there has been no disposal of the asset which was not an inter-group transfer,

then, for the purpose of determining whether subsection (1) above applies in relation to a series of linked transactions, the disposal by company A shall be treated as having been made by company B; but any increase in the consideration for that disposal resulting from the application of subsection (1) above shall have effect with respect to company A.

(8) In any case where one or more transactions occur on or before 19th March 1985 and one or more transactions occur after that date in circumstances such that—

(a) if all the transactions had occurred before that date, section 151 of the principal Act would have applied in relation to them, and

(b) if all the transactions occurred after that date, subsection (1) above would apply to them,

such of the transactions which occurred on or before that date as occurred not more than two years before the first of the transactions occurring after that date shall be treated as material transactions.

Amendments.—[1] Words in sub-s. (6) substituted by TA 1988, Sch. 29, para. 32 Table.

72. Commodity and financial futures and traded options

(1) If, apart from [section 128 of the Taxes Act],[5] gains arising to any person in the course of dealing in commodity or financial futures or in [qualifying options][1] would constitute, for the purposes of the Tax Acts, profits or gains chargeable to tax under Schedule D otherwise than as the profits of a trade, then, on and after 6th April 1985,—

(a) his outstanding obligations under any futures contract entered into in the course of that dealing and any [qualifying option][1] granted or acquired in the course of that dealing shall be regarded as assets to the disposal of which the Capital Gains Tax Act 1979 (in this section referred to as "the principal Act") applies; . . .[6]

(b) . . .[6]

(2) In subsection (1) above—

(a) "commodity or financial futures" means commodity futures or financial futures which are for the time being dealt in on a recognised futures exchange, within the meaning of the principal Act; and

[(b) "qualifying option" means a traded option or financial option as defined in section 137 (9) of that Act.][2]

[(2A) Notwithstanding the provisions of subsection (2) (a) above, where, otherwise than in the course of dealing on a recognised futures exchange, within the meaning of the principal Act,—

(a) an authorised person or listed institution enters into a commodity or financial futures contract with another person, or

(b) the outstanding obligations under a commodity or financial futures contract to which an authorised person or listed institution is a party are brought to an end by a further contract between the parties to the futures contract,

then, except in so far as any gain or loss arising to any person from that transaction arises in the course of a trade, that gain or loss shall be regarded for the purposes of subsection (1) above as arising to him in the course of dealing in commodity or financial futures.][3]

[(2B) In subsection (2A) above—

"authorised person" has the same meaning as in the Financial Services Act 1986, and "listed institution" has the same meaning as in section 43 of that Act.][3]

(3) For the purposes of the principal Act, where, in the course of dealing in commodity or financial futures, a person who has entered into a futures contract closes out that contract by entering into another futures contract with obligations which are reciprocal to those of the first-mentioned contract, that transaction shall constitute the disposal of an asset (namely, his outstanding obligations under the first-mentioned contract) and, accordingly,—

(a) any money or money's worth received by him on that transaction shall constitute consideration for the disposal; and

(b) any money or money's worth paid or given by him on that transaction shall be treated as incidental costs to him of making the disposal.

(4) In any case where,—

(a) a person who, in the course of dealing in financial futures, has entered into a futures contract does not close out that contract (as mentioned in subsection (3) above), and

(b) the nature of the futures contract is such that, at its expiry date, the person concerned is entitled to receive or liable to make a payment in full settlement of all obligations under that contract,

then, for the purposes of the principal Act, he shall be treated as having disposed of an asset (namely, his outstanding obligations under the futures contract) and the payment received or made by him shall be treated as consideration for that disposal or, as the case may be, as incidental costs to him of making the disposal.

(5) ...[4]

(6) ...

(7) ...[6]

Notes.—Sub-s. (6) inserts CGTA 1979, s. 155 (3A), (3B).
Cross references.—See CGTA 1979, s. 67 (3) (exemption for gain accruing on the diposal of options and futures contracts in gilt-edged securities and qualifying bonds).
Amendments.—[1] Words in sub-s. (1) substituted by F (No. 2) A 1987, s. 81 (1), (8) with effect from 29 April 1988 by virtue of F (No. 2) A 1987 (Commencement) Order 1988, S.I. 1988 No. 744.
[2] Sub-s. (2) (b) substituted by F (No. 2) A 1987, s. 81 (2), (8) with effect from 29 April 1988 by virtue of F (No. 2) A 1987 (Commencement) Order 1988, S.I. 1988 No. 744.
[3] Sub-ss. (2A), (2B) inserted by F (No. 2) A 1987, s. 81 (3), (8) with effect from 29 April 1988 by virtue of F (No. 2) A 1987 (Commencement) Order 1988, S.I. 1988 No. 744.
[4] Sub-s. (5) which amended CGTA 1979, s. 137 (9) repealed by F (No. 2) A 1987, Sch. 9, Pt II.
[5] Words in sub-s. (1) substituted by TA 1988, Sch. 29, para. 32 Table.
[6] Words in sub-s. (1) (a), sub-ss. (1) (b), (7) repealed by TA 1988, Sch. 31.

PART V

MISCELLANEOUS AND SUPPLEMENTARY

93. Abolition of . . . tax on development gains

(1)–(5) . . .

(6) No part of a chargeable gain which accrues to any person on the disposal of an interest in land on or after 19th March 1985 shall be a development gain by virtue of Chapter 1 of Part III of the Finance Act 1974; and for this purpose "disposal of an interest in land" means any event which, but for the repeals effected by Part X of Schedule 27 to this Act, would be (or be deemed to be) a disposal of an interest in land to which section 38 of that Act would apply.

(7) In consequence of the preceding provisions of this section and of the repeals effected by Part X of Schedule 27 to this Act, the enactments specified in Part II of Schedule 25 to this Act shall have effect subject to the amendments in that Part; but those amendments do not affect the operation of the enactments concerned in relation to—

(*a*) a disposal, as defined in subsection (1) above, taking place before 19th March 1985; or

(*b*) a disposal of an interest in land, as defined in subsection (6) above, taking place before that date.

Note.—Words omitted from the heading and sub-ss. (1)–(5) are not relevant for the purposes of this book.

95. The national heritage: transfer of Treasury functions to Board

(1) The functions of the Treasury under—

(*a*) . . .
(*b*) section 147 of the Capital Gains Tax Act 1979 (works of art etc.);
(*c*) the enactments re-enacted by those provisions;

. . . are hereby transferred to the Commissioners of Inland Revenue ("the Board").

(2) This section shall not affect the validity of anything done by or in relation to the Treasury before the passing of this Act; and anything which at that date is in the process of being done by or in relation to the Treasury may, if it relates to functions transferred by this section to the Board, be continued by or in relation to the Board.

(3) Any authorisation, designation, direction, approval, determination, or other thing given, made or done by the Treasury in connection with functions transferred by this section shall have effect as if given, made or done by the Board in so far as that is required for continuing its effect after the passing of this Act.

(4) Any enactment passed or instrument or other document made before the coming into operation of this section shall have effect, so far as may be necessary, for the purpose or in consequence of the transfer of functions effected by this section as if any reference to the Treasury were or included a reference to the Board.

Note.—Words omitted from sub-s. (1) are not relevant for the purposes of this book.

98. Short title, interpretation, construction and repeals

(1) This Act may be cited as the Finance Act 1985.

(2) In this Act "the Taxes Act" means the Income and Corporation Taxes Act [1988].[1]

(3) Part II of this Act, so far as it relates to income tax, shall be construed as one with the Income Tax Acts, so far as it relates to corporation tax, shall be construed as one with the Corporation Tax Acts and, so far as it relates to capital gains tax, shall be construed as one with the Capital Gains Tax Act 1979.

(4)–(5) . . .

(6) The enactments specified in Schedule 27 to this Act are hereby repealed to the extent specified in the third column of that Schedule, but subject to any provision at the end of any Part of that Schedule.

Note.—Sub-ss. (4), (5) are not relevant for the purposes of this book.
Amendments.—[1] Number in sub-s. (2) substituted by TA 1988, Sch. 29, para. 32 Table.

SCHEDULES

SCHEDULE 15
Section 57

MACHINERY AND PLANT EXCLUDED FROM TREATMENT AS SHORT-LIFE ASSETS

1. Ships.

2. Any vehicle which is of such a description that section 43 of the Finance Act 1971 (exclusion of certain road vehicles) precludes the making of a first-year allowance in respect of capital expenditure incurred on its provision.

3. Machinery or plant to which section 46 of that Act applies (machinery or plant let by any person otherwise than in the course of a trade).

4. Machinery or plant falling within paragraph 5 (2) of Schedule 8 to that Act (machinery or plant used partly for trade purposes and partly for other purposes).

5. Machinery or plant where the capital expenditure on its provision is expenditure to which paragraph 6 of that Schedule applies (subsidies towards wear and tear).

6. Machinery or plant falling within paragraph 7 (1) (*a*) or paragraph 7 (1) (*b*) of that Schedule (user after user not attracting capital allowances or after receipt by way of gift).

7. Motor cars falling within paragraph 10 of that Schedule.

[**8.** Machinery or plant provided for leasing, except—
   (*a*) machinery or plant which it appears will be used in the requisite period (within the meaning of section 64 of the Finance Act 1980) for a qualifying purpose (within the meaning of that section) and will not at any time in that period be used for any other purpose,
   (*b*) vehicles of the kind mentioned in subsection (12) of that section.][1]

Amendments.—[1] This paragraph substituted by FA 1989, Sch. 13, para. 22 (1), (3) in relation to expenditure incurred after 26 July 1989. Previously it read—
   "**8.** Machinery or plant which is used in such a way that section 64 of the Finance Act 1980 (leased assets) precludes the making of a first-year allowance in respect of expenditure incurred on the provision of it for leasing."

9. Machinery or plant which is leased to two or more persons jointly in such circumstances that section 68 of the Finance Act 1980 [applies][1].

Amendments.—[1] Word substituted by FA 1989, Sch. 13, para. 22 (2), (3) in relation to expenditure incurred after 26 July 1989. The original words read—
   "precludes the making of a first-year allowance in respect of the whole or part of the capital expenditure incurred on its provision."

10. Television sets in respect of which the amount of a first-year allowance falls to be determined in accordance with paragraph 8 of Schedule 12 to the Finance Act 1980.

11. Machinery or plant in respect of expenditure on which section 70 of the Finance Act 1982 (assets leased outside the United Kingdom) provides for only a 10 per cent. writing-down allowance.

12. Machinery or plant in respect of which first-year allowances continue to be available by virtue of paragraph 2 (2) of Schedule 12 to the Finance Act 1984 (contracts entered into on or before 13th March 1984) or paragraph 4 of that Schedule (expenditure qualifying for regional development grants etc.).

SCHEDULE 17

Section 59

CAPITAL ALLOWANCES FOR FIXTURES

Interpretation

1.—(1) In this Schedule—

"allowance" means an allowance under Chapter I of Part III of the Finance Act 1971;
"fixture" means any such machinery or plant as is referred to in section 59 (1) of this Act;
"interest in land" and "lease" shall be construed in accordance with sub-paragraph (2) below;
"material purposes" means the purposes of Chapter I of Part III of the Finance Act 1971; and
"relevant land", in relation to a fixture, means the building or other description of land of which the fixture becomes part.

(2) In this Schedule "interest in land" means—

(*a*) the fee simple estate in the land or an agreement to acquire that estate;
(*b*) in Scotland, the estate or interest of the proprietor of the *dominium utile* (or, in the case of property other than feudal property, of the owner) and any agreement to acquire such an estate or interest;
(*c*) any leasehold estate in, or in Scotland lease of, the land (whether in the nature of a head-lease, sub-lease or under-lease) and any agreement to acquire such an estate or, in Scotland, lease;
(*d*) an easement or servitude or any agreement to acquire an easement or servitude; and
(*e*) a licence to occupy land;

and, except in the context of leasing machinery or plant, any reference in the following provisions of this Schedule to a lease is a reference to such a leasehold estate or, in Scotland, lease as is mentioned in paragraph (*c*) above or to such an agreement as is mentioned in that paragraph (and, in relation to such an agreement, the expression "grant" shall be construed accordingly).

(3) If an interest in land is conveyed or assigned by way of security and subject to a right of redemption, then, so long as such a right subsists, the interest held by the creditor shall be treated for the purposes of this Schedule as held by the person having that right.

(4) Any reference in the following provisions of this Schedule to a person being entitled to an allowance in respect of any capital expenditure incurred on the provision of a fixture is a reference to a case where—

(*a*) that person is, for any chargeable period, entitled to a first-year allowance in respect of that expenditure, or
(*b*) that expenditure is taken into account in determining his qualifying expenditure for a chargeable period for the purposes of subsections (2) and (3) of section 44 of the Finance Act 1971 (whether or not an allowance is made to him for that period),

and any reference to a chargeable period for which a person is so entitled is a reference—

(i) to the chargeable period referred to in paragraph (*a*) above; or
(ii) to the chargeable period referred to in paragraph (*b*) above; or
(iii) to any chargeable period which is subsequent to that referred to in paragraph (*b*) above but is not later than the chargeable period in which he is required to bring the disposal value of the fixture concerned into account for the purposes mentioned in paragraph (*b*) above.

Expenditure incurred by holder of interest in land

2.—(1) Subject to sub-paragraph (2) below, in any case where—

(*a*) a person incurs capital expenditure on the provision of machinery or plant either for the purposes of a trade carried on by him or for leasing otherwise than in the course of a trade, and
(*b*) the machinery or plant becomes a fixture, and

(c) at the time the machinery or plant becomes a fixture he has an interest in the relevant land,

then, subject to paragraphs 3 and 7 below, on and after that time the fixture shall be treated for material purposes as belonging to the person concerned in consequence of his incurring the expenditure.

(2) If, in respect of the same fixture, there are two or more persons with different interests in the relevant land to whom, by virtue of sub-paragraph (1) above, the fixture would (apart from this sub-paragraph), be treated as belonging for material purposes, the only interest which shall be taken into account under that sub-paragraph is,—

(a) if one of the interests is an interest falling within paragraph 1 (2) (d) above, that interest;
(b) if paragraph (a) above does not apply but one of the interests is an interest falling within paragraph 1 (2) (e) above, that interest; and
(c) in any other case,—

(i) except in Scotland, that interest which is not in reversion (at law or in equity and whether directly or indirectly) on any other interest in the relevant land which is held by any of the persons referred to above; and
(ii) in Scotland, that of whichever of those persons has, or last had, the right of use of the relevant land.

Expenditure incurred by equipment lessor

3.—(1) In any case where—

(a) a person (in this Schedule referred to as "the equipment lessor") incurs capital expenditure on the provision of machinery or plant for leasing, and
(b) an agreement is entered into for the lease, directly or indirectly from the equipment lessor, of the machinery or plant (otherwise than as part of the relevant land) to another person (in this Schedule referred to as "the equipment lessee") for the purposes of a trade carried on by the equipment lessee or for leasing otherwise than in the course of a trade, and
(c) the machinery or plant becomes a fixture, and
(d) if the expenditure referred to in paragraph (a) above had been incurred by the equipment lessee, the fixture would, by virtue of paragraph 2 above, have been treated for material purposes as belonging to him in consequence of his incurring the expenditure, and
(e) the equipment lessor and the equipment lessee elect that this paragraph should apply,

then, subject to paragraph 7 below, on and after the time at which the expenditure is incurred the fixture shall be treated for material purposes as belonging to the equipment lessor in consequence of his incurring the expenditure.

(2) An election under this paragraph shall be made by notice in writing to the inspector given before the expiry of the period of two years beginning at the end of the chargeable period related to the incurring of the expenditure referred to in sub-paragraph (1) (a) above; but no election may be made under this paragraph if the equipment lessor and the equipment lessee are connected with each other within the terms of section [839][1] of the Taxes Act.

(3) Where an election has been made under this paragraph with respect to a fixture, nothing in paragraph 2 above shall have the effect of treating the fixture for material purposes as belonging to the equipment lessee.

(4) In the following provisions of this Schedule "equipment lease" means such an agreement as is mentioned in sub-paragraph (1) (b) above or a lease entered into pursuant to such an agreement.

Amendments.—[1] Number in sub-para. (2) substituted by TA 1988, Sch. 29, para. 32 Table.

Expenditure included in consideration for acquisition of existing interest in land

4.—(1) In any case where,—

(a) after any machinery or plant has become a fixture, a person (in this paragraph referred to as "the purchaser") acquires an interest in the relevant land, being an interest which was in existence prior to his acquisition of it, and

(b) the consideration which the purchaser gives for that interest is or includes a capital sum which, in whole or in part, falls to be treated for material purposes as expenditure on the provision of the fixture, and

(c) at the time of the purchaser's acquisition of his interest in the relevant land, either no person has previously become entitled to an allowance in respect of any capital expenditure incurred on the provision of the fixture or, if any person has become so entitled, that person has been or is required to bring the disposal value of the fixture into account under section 44 of the Finance Act 1971,

then, subject to paragraph 7 below, on and after the purchaser's acquisition of his interest in the relevant land, the fixture shall be treated for material purposes as belonging to him in consequence of his incurring expenditure as mentioned in paragraph (b) above.

(2) If, in a case where paragraph (a) of sub-paragraph (1) above applies,—

(a) the machinery or plant was, prior to the purchaser's acquisition of the interest in the relevant land, let under an equipment lease, and
(b) in connection with the acquisition of the interest in the relevant land, the purchaser pays a capital sum to discharge the obligations of the equipment lessee under the equipment lease,

sub-paragraph (1) above shall apply as if that capital sum were such a capital sum as is referred to in paragraph (b) of that sub-paragraph.

Expenditure incurred by income lessee: election to transfer right to allowances

5.—(1) In any case where—

(a) after any machinery or plant has become a fixture, a person (in this paragraph referred to as "the lessor") who has an interest in the relevant land grants a lease, and
(b) apart from paragraph 7 below, the lessor would be entitled, for the chargeable period related to the grant of the lease, to an allowance in respect of expenditure incurred on the provision of the fixture, and
(c) the consideration which the lessee gives for the lease is or includes a capital sum which, in whole or in part, falls to be treated for material purposes as expenditure on the provision of the fixture, and
(d) the lessor and the lessee make an election under this paragraph,

then, subject to paragraph 7 below, on and after the grant of the lease, the fixture shall be treated for material purposes as belonging to the lessee in consequence of his incurring expenditure as mentioned in paragraph (c) above.

(2) If in any case the lessor is not within the charge to tax, it shall be assumed that he is within that charge for the purpose of determining whether the condition in sub-paragraph (1)(b) above is fulfilled.

(3) An election under this paragraph shall be made by notice in writing to the inspector given within two years after the date on which the lease takes effect.

(4) No election may be made under this paragraph if—

(a) the lessor and the lessee are connected with each other within the terms of section [839][1] of the Taxes Act; or
(b) it appears that the sole or main benefit which may be expected to accrue to the lessor from the grant to the lease and the making of an election is the obtaining of an allowance or deduction or a greater allowance or deduction or the avoidance or reduction of a charge under Chapter I of Part III of the Finance Act 1971.

Amendments.—[1] Number in sub-para. (4)(a) substituted by TA 1988, Sch. 29, para. 32 Table.

Expenditure incurred by incoming lessee: lessor not entitled to allowances

6. In any case where—

(a) after any machinery or plant has become a fixture, a person (in this paragraph referred to as "the lessor") who has an interest in the relevant land grants a lease, but paragraph 5 (1) (b) above does not apply in this case, and
(b) the consideration which the lessee gives for the lease is or includes a capital sum

which, in whole or in part, falls to be treated for material purposes as expenditure on the provision of the fixture, and

(c) at the time of the grant of the lease, no person has previously become entitled to an allowance in respect of any capital expenditure incurred on the provision of the fixture, and

(d) the fixture has not before that time been used for the purposes of a trade by the lessor or any person connected with him within the terms of section [839][1] of the Taxes Act,

then, subject to paragraph 7 below, on and after the grant of the lease, the fixture shall be treated for material purposes as belonging to the lessee in consequence of his incurring expenditure as mentioned in paragraph (b) above.

Amendments.—[1] Number in sub-para. (6) (d) substituted by TA 1988, Sch. 29, para. 32 Table.

Cases where fixture is to be treated as ceasing to belong to particular person

7.—(1) The provisions of this paragraph and paragraph 8 below are without prejudice to any other circumstances in which the disposal value of a fixture falls to be brought into account in accordance with section 44 of the Finance Act 1971.

(2) Subject to sub-paragraph (4) below, if at any time the person to whom a fixture is treated for material purposes as belonging by virtue of any of paragraphs 2, 4, 5 and 6 above ceases (whether by reason of the transfer, surrender, or expiry of the interest or otherwise) to have the qualifying interest, the fixture shall be treated for those purposes as ceasing to belong to him at that time.

(3) In this paragraph and paragraph 9 below, "the qualifying interest" means—

(a) where paragraph 2 or paragraph 4 above applies, the interest in the relevant land referred to in that paragraph; and
(b) where paragraph 5 or paragraph 6 above applies, the lease referred to in that paragraph;

but if the qualifying interest is an agreement to acquire an interest in land and that interest in land is subsequently transferred or granted to the person referred to in sub-paragraph (2) above, the interest so transferred or granted shall be treated as the same interest as the qualifying interest.

(4) For the purposes of sub-paragraph (2) above,—

(a) if the qualifying interest ceases to exist by reason of its merger in another interest acquired by the person referred to in that sub-paragraph, that other interest shall be treated as the same interest as the qualifying interest;
(b) if the qualifying interest is a lease and, on its termination, a new lease of the relevant land (with or without other land) is granted to the lessee, the new lease shall be treated as the same interest as the qualifying interest;
(c) if the qualifying interest is a licence and, on its termination, a new licence to occupy the relevant land (with or without other land) is granted to the licensee, the new licence shall be treated as the same interest as the qualifying interest;
(d) if the qualifying interest is a lease and, with the consent of the lessor, the lessee remains in possession of the relevant land after the termination of the lease but without a new lease being granted to him, the qualifying interest shall be treated as continuing to subsist so long as the lessee remains in possession of the relevant land.

(5) At the time at which, by virtue of paragraph 5 above, the fixture concerned begins to be treated for material purposes as belonging to the lessee, it shall be treated for those purposes as ceasing to belong to the lessor (as defined in that paragraph).

(6) Where, by virtue of sub-paragraph (2) above, on the termination of a lease or licence, a fixture is treated for material purposes as ceasing to belong to the outgoing lessee or licensee, it shall, on that termination, be treated for material purposes as beginning to belong to the person who, immediately before the termination, was the lessor under the lease or, as the case may be, the licensor under the licence.

(7) If at any time a fixture is permanently severed from the relevant land (so that it ceases to be a fixture) and, immediately before that time, it was treated for material purposes as belonging to any person by virtue of any of the preceding provisions of this Schedule or sub-paragaph (2) or sub-paragraph (4) of paragraph 8 below, then, unless on its severance the fixture does in fact belong to that person, it shall be treated for those purposes as ceasing to belong to him at that time.

Special provisions as to equipment lessors

8.—(1) If, by virtue of an election under paragraph 3 above, a fixture is treated for material purposes as belonging to the equipment lessor and either,—

(a) the equipment lessor at any time assigns his rights under an equipment lease, or
(b) the financial obligations of the equipment lessee under an equipment lease are at any time discharged, on the payment of a capital sum or otherwise,

then, at that time (or, as the case may be, at the earliest of those times) the fixture shall be treated for material purposes as ceasing to belong to the equipment lessor by reason of a sale by him of the fixture.

(2) If paragraph (a) of sub-paragraph (1) above applies, then, on and after the time of the assignment referred to in that paragraph, the fixture to which the agreement in question relates shall be treated for material purposes as belonging to the assignee and the consideration given by him for the assignment shall be treated for those purposes—

(a) as the price received for the sale of the fixture by the assignor; and
(b) as expenditure incurred by the assignee on acquiring the fixture.

(3) On and after an assignment falling within paragraph (a) of sub-paragraph (1) above, that sub-paragraph shall have effect as if the machinery or plant (as a fixture) were treated for material purposes as belonging to the assignee by virtue of an election under paragraph 3 above and, accordingly, as if the assignee were the equipment lessor, as defined in that paragraph.

(4) Where a capital sum is paid as mentioned in paragraph (b) of sub-paragraph (1) above, that capital sum shall be treated for material purposes—

(a) as the price received for the sale of the fixture by the equipment lessor; and
(b) if that capital sum is paid by the equipment lessee, as expenditure incurred by him on the provision of the fixture;

and where paragraph (b) above applies, on and after the time of that payment, the fixture shall be treated for material purposes as belonging to the equipment lessee.

(5) Where the financial obligations of the equipment lessee under an equipment lease have become vested in any other person (by assignment, operation of law or otherwise) any reference in sub-paragraph (1) (b) or sub-paragraph (4) above to the equipment lessee shall be construed as a reference to the person in whom those obligations are for the time being vested when the capital sum is paid.

Disposal value of fixtures in certain cases

9.—(1) In any case where—

(a) by virtue of paragraph 7 above, a fixture is at any time treated for material purposes as ceasing to belong to any person (in this paragraph referred to as "the former owner"), and
(b) the qualifying interest continues in existence after that time (whether in the hands of the former owner or any other person) or would so continue but for its becoming merged in another interest, and
(c) the occasion of the fixture ceasing to belong to the former owner is not its permanent severance from the relevant land (whether on disposal, demolition, destruction or otherwise),

the fixture shall be treated for material purposes as sold at that time by the former owner for a price determined in accordance with sub-paragraphs (2) to (6) below.

(2) Subject to sub-paragraph (6) below, if the occasion of the fixture ceasing to belong to the former owner is the sale of the qualifying interest, the price referred to in sub-paragraph (1) above is that portion of the sale price of the qualifying interest which falls (or, if the purchaser were entitled to an allowance, would fall) to be treated for material purposes as expenditure incurred by the purchaser on the provision of the fixture.

(3) If the fixture ceases to belong to the former owner by virtue of sub-paragraph (5) of paragraph 7 above, the price referred to in sub-paragraph (1) above is so much of the capital sum referred to in sub-paragraph (1) (c) of paragraph 5 above as falls to be treated for material purposes as expenditure by the lessee on the provision of the fixture.

(4) If neither sub-paragraph (2) nor sub-paragraph (3) above applies, the price referred to in sub-paragraph (1) above is that portion of the price which, on a sale of the qualifying

interest in the open market, would fall to be treated for material purposes as expenditure by the purchaser on the provision of the fixture.

(5) The sale referred to in sub-paragraph (4) above shall be assumed to take place immediately before the event which causes the fixture to be treated for material purposes as ceasing to belong to the former owner; but that event shall be disregarded in determining the open market price on that sale.

(6) If the sale referred to in sub-paragraph (2) above is at a price lower than that which the qualifying interest would have fetched if sold in the open market, that sub-paragraph shall not apply unless the purchaser's expenditure on the acquisition of the fixture can be taken into account as mentioned in section 44 (6) (*b*) (i) of the Finance Act 1971.

(7) If the occasion of the fixture ceasing to belong to the former owner is the expiry of the qualifying interest, then, except in so far as the former owner receives any capital sum, by way of compensation or otherwise, by reference to the fixture, the disposal value of the fixture which falls to be brought into account under section 44 of the Finance Act 1971 shall be nil.

(8) In any case where—

(*a*) the disposal value of a fixture falls to be brought into account in accordance with section 44 of the Finance Act 1971 on the permanent discontinuance of the trade in circumstances where that value falls to be determined under paragraph (*e*) of subsection (6) of that section; and

(*b*) before the occurrence of the later event referred to in that paragraph, the fixture is not permanently severed from the relevant land,

that paragraph shall apply as if the reference therein to paragraph (*a*) and paragraph (*b*) of that subsection were omitted; but if the event which follows the discontinuance of the trade is the sale of the qualifying interest, the disposal value of the fixture to be brought into account under that section shall be that portion of the sale price referred to in sub-paragraph (2) above.

(9) If the disposal value of the fixture falls to be brought into account in accordance with section 44 of the Finance Act 1971 on its beginning to be used wholly or partly for purposes which are other than those of the trade, paragraph (*f*) of subsection (6) of that section shall apply as if the reference to the price which the machinery or plant would have fetched if sold on the open market were a reference to that portion of the price referred to in sub-paragraph (4) above.

(10) If, on the occasion of the fixture being treated, by virtue of paragraph 7 above, as ceasing to belong to the former owner,—

[(*a*) another person incurs expenditure on the provision of the fixture, and][1]

[(*b*) the former owner brings a disposal value into account in accordance with section 44 of the Finance Act 1971,][1]

[there shall be disregarded for material purposes so much (if any) of that expenditure as exceeds that disposal value.][1]

Amendments.—[1] Sub-para. (10) (*a*), (*b*) and the words following substituted by FA 1989, Sch. 13, para. 23 in relation to expenditure incurred after 26 July 1989. The original words read—

"another person incurs expenditure on the provision of the fixture, there shall be disregarded for material purposes so much (if any) of that expenditure as exceeds the disposal value which the former owner is required to bring into account in accordance with section 44 of the Finance Act 1971."

SCHEDULE 19

Section 68

INDEXATION

PART I

Note.—This Part amends FA 1982, ss. 86–89 and Sch. 13, paras. 1–4, 6, 7.

PART II

PRE-APRIL 1982 SHARE POOLS

6.—(1) Subject to sub-paragraphs (2) and (3) below, a holding of securities, as it exists immediately before the 1985 date, is for the purposes of this Part of this Schedule a 1982 holding if, by virtue of paragraph 8 (2) of Schedule 13 to the Finance Act 1982, it is regarded for the purposes of the Capital Gains Tax Act 1979 as a single asset.

(2) If the holding of securities referred to in sub-paragraph (1) above is "the reduced holding", within the meaning of paragraph 9 of Schedule 13 to the Finance Act 1982, then, for the purposes of this Part of this Schedule, the 1982 holding is the aggregate of—

(*a*) the reduced holding, (as it exists immediately before the 1985 date); and
(*b*) such of the separate assets (derived from the same holding as the reduced holding) which, by virtue of sub-paragraph (3) (*b*) of the said paragraph 9, constitute separate assets as have not been disposed of before that date.

(3) If a person so elects, quoted securities, as defined in paragraph 8 of Schedule 5 to the Capital Gains Tax Act 1979 (assets held on 6th April 1965) which are covered by the election—

(*a*) shall be treated as an accretion to an existing 1982 holding or, as the case may be, as constituting a new 1982 holding; and
(*b*) shall be excluded from paragraph 2 of that Schedule (restriction of gain or loss by reference to actual cost);

and the relevant allowable expenditure (as defined in relation to a disposal to which section 86 of the Finance Act 1982 applies) which is attributable to that 1982 holding shall be adjusted or determined accordingly.

(4) Paragraphs 4 to 8 of the said Schedule 5 (except paragraph 4 (1)) shall apply in relation to an election under sub-paragraph (3) above as they apply in relation to an election under paragraph 4 of that Schedule, but with the substitution for any reference to 19th March 1968 of a reference to 31st March 1985 in the case of holdings or disposals by companies and 5th April 1985 in any other case.

7.—(1) For the purposes of the Capital Gains Tax Act 1979, on and after the 1985 date, a 1982 holding shall continue to be regarded or, if it comes into being by virtue of paragraph 6 above, shall begin to be regarded as a single asset (but one which cannot grow by the acquisition of additional securities of the same class).

(2) In a case where the 1982 holding is determined by paragraph 6 (2) above, for all purposes of capital gains tax the relevant allowable expenditure attributable to the securities comprised in the 1982 holding shall be taken to be the aggregate of—

(*a*) the amount which, by virtue of sub-paragraph (2) of paragraph 10 of Schedule 13 to the Finance Act 1982, would for those purposes be regarded as the relevant allowable expenditure attributable to the reduced holding referred to in paragraph 6 (2) (*a*) above on a disposal of the whole of it immediately before the 1985 date; and
(*b*) the amount which, by virtue of that sub-paragraph, would for those purposes be regarded as the relevant allowable expenditure attributable to the separate assets referred to in paragraph 6 (2) (*b*) above on a disposal of them immediately before that date.

(3) For the purposes of section 87 (5) of the Finance Act 1982 (indexation of allowable expenditure) the relevant allowable expenditure which by virtue of sub-paragraph (2) above is attributable to the securities comprised in a 1982 holding shall be deemed to be expenditure falling within section 32 (1) (*a*) of the Capital Gains Tax Act 1979.

Cross references.—See FA 1988, s. 113 (in respect of disposals after 3 July 1987, sub-para. (3) above not to apply in the case of building society shares and registered industrial and provident society shares).

PART III

POOLING OF OTHER SECURITIES

8.—(1) In this Part of this Schedule—

(*a*) "the principal Act" means the Capital Gains Tax Act 1979;
(*b*) "the 1982 Act" means the Finance Act 1982; and
(*c*) "relevant allowable expenditure" has the meaning assigned to it by subsections (2) (*b*) and (3) of section 86 of the 1982 Act.

(2) This Part of this Schedule shall apply separately in relation to any securities held by a person to whom they were issued as an employee of the company or of any other person on terms which restrict his rights to dispose of them, so long as those terms are in force, and, while applying separately to any such securities, this Part of this Schedule shall have effect as if the owner held them in a capacity other than that in which he holds any other securities of the same class.

(3) Nothing in this Part of this Schedule shall be taken as affecting the manner in which the market value of any securities is to be ascertained.

Cross references.—See FA 1988, s. 113 (in respect of disposals after 3 July 1987, sub-para. (1) (*b*), (*c*) above not to apply in the case of building society shares and registered industrial and provident society shares).

9.—(1) Any number of securities of the same class which—

(*a*) were held by the same person in the same capacity immediately before the 1985 date and
(*b*) were acquired on or after 6th April 1982 or, in the case of a company, 1st April 1982,

shall for the purposes of the principal Act be regarded as indistinguishable parts of a single asset growing or diminishing on the occasions on which additional securities of the same class are acquired or some of the securities of that class are disposed of.

(2) Any number of securities of the same class which—

(*a*) are acquired by the same person in the same capacity on or after the 1985 date, and
(*b*) do not form part of a single asset by virtue of sub-paragraph (1) above,

shall for the purposes of the principal Act be regarded as indistinguishable parts of a single asset growing or diminishing on the occasions on which additional securities of the same class are acquired or some of the securities of that class are disposed of.

(3) A holding of securities which, by virtue of sub-paragraph (1) or sub-paragraph (2) above, is to be regarded as a single asset is in this Part of this Schedule referred to as a "new holding".

10. Without prejudice to the generality of paragraph 9 above, a disposal of securities in a new holding, other than a disposal of the whole of it, is a disposal of part of an asset and the provisions of the principal Act relating to the computation of a gain accruing on a disposal of part of an asset shall apply accordingly.

11.—(1) In relation to a disposal of a new holding, the following provisions of this Part of this Schedule have effect in place of the provisions of section 87 of the 1982 Act for the purpose of computing the indexation allowance.

(2) On any disposal of a new holding, other than a disposal of the whole of it,—

(*a*) the qualifying expenditure and the indexed pool of expenditure shall each be apportioned between the part disposed of and the remainder in the same proportions as, under the principal Act, the relevant allowable expenditure is apportioned; and
(*b*) the indexation allowance is the amount by which the portion of the indexed pool which is attributed to the part disposed of exceeds the portion of the qualifying expenditure which is attributable to that part.

(3) On a disposal of the whole of a new holding, the indexation allowance is the amount by which the indexed pool of expenditure at the time of the disposal exceeds the qualifying expenditure at that time.

Cross references.—See FA 1988, s. 113 (in respect of disposals after 3 July 1987, this paragraph not to apply in the case of building society shares and registered industrial and provident society shares).

12. In relation to a new holding, the qualifying expenditure is at any time the amount which would be the aggregate of the relevant allowable expenditure in relation to a disposal of the whole of the holding occurring at that time.

Cross references.—See FA 1988, s. 113 (in respect of disposals after 3 July 1987, this paragraph not to apply in the case of building society shares and registered industrial and provident society shares).

13.—(1) The provisions of this paragraph have effect, subject to paragraph 15 below, for determining, in relation to a new holding, the indexed pool of expenditure at any time.

(2) In the case of a new holding falling within paragraph 9 (1) above, the indexed pool of expenditure shall come into being immediately before the 1985 date and shall at that time consist of the aggregate of—

    (*a*) the qualifying expenditure at that time; and
    (*b*) any indexation allowance which, in accordance with section 87 of the 1982 Act, would have applied to a disposal at that time of all of the securities comprised in the holding, on the assumption that the amendments made by paragraphs 1 and 2 above had always had effect.

(3) In the case of any other new holding, the indexed pool of expenditure shall come into being at the time that the holding comes into being or, if it is earlier, when any of the qualifying expenditure is incurred and shall at the time it comes into being be the same as the qualifying expenditure at that time.

(4) Any reference in the following provisions of this Part of this Schedule to an operative event is a reference to any event (whether a disposal or otherwise) which has the effect of reducing or increasing the qualifying expenditure referable to the new holding.

(5) Whenever an operative event occurs,—

    (*a*) there shall be added to the indexed pool of expenditure the indexed rise, as calculated under paragraph 14 below, in the value of the pool since the last operative event or, if there has been no previous operative event, since the pool came into being; and
    (*b*) if the operative event results in an increase in the qualifying expenditure then, in addition to any increase under paragraph (*a*) above, the same increase shall be made to the indexed pool of expenditure; and
    (*c*) if the operative event is a disposal resulting in a reduction in the qualifying expenditure, the indexed pool of expenditure shall be reduced in the same proportion as the qualifying expenditure is reduced; and
    (*d*) if the operative event results in a reduction in the qualifying expenditure but is not a disposal, the same reduction shall be made to the indexed pool of expenditure.

(6) Where the operative event is a disposal—.

    (*a*) any addition under paragraph (*a*) of sub-paragraph (5) above shall be made before the calculation of the indexation allowance under paragraph 11 above; and
    (*b*) the reduction under paragraph (*c*) of that sub-paragraph shall be made after that calculation.

Cross references.—See FA 1988, s. 113 (in respect of disposals after 3 July 1987, this paragraph not to apply in the case of building society shares and registered industrial and provident society shares).

14.—(1) At the time of any operative event, the indexed rise in the indexed pool of expenditure is a sum produced by multiplying the value of the pool immediately before the event by a figure expressed as a decimal and determined, subject to sub-paragraph (2) below, by the formula—

$$\frac{RE - RL}{RL}$$

where—

    RE is the retail prices index for the month in which the operative event occurs; and
    RL is the retail prices index for the month in which occurred the immediately preceding operative event or, if there has been no such event, in which the indexed pool of expenditure came into being.

(2) If RE, as defined in sub-paragraph (1) above, is equal to or less than RL, as so defined, the indexed rise is nil.

Cross references.—See FA 1988, s. 113 (in respect of disposals after 3 July 1987, this paragraph not to apply in the case of building society shares and registered industrial and provident society shares).

Consideration for options

15.—(1) If, in a case where sub-paragraph (5)(*b*) of paragraph 13 above applies, the increase in the qualifying expenditure is, in whole or in part, attributable to the cost of acquiring an option binding the grantor to sell (in this paragraph referred to as "the option consideration"), then, in addition to any increase under paragraph (*a*) or paragraph (*b*) of sub-paragraph (5) of paragraph 13 above, the indexed pool of expenditure shall be increased by an amount equal to the indexed rise in the option consideration, as determined under sub-paragraph (2) below.

(2) The indexed rise in the option consideration is a sum produced by multiplying the consideration by a figure expressed as a decimal and determined, subject to sub-paragraph (3) below, by the formula—

$$\frac{RO - RA}{RA}$$

Where—

RO is the retail prices index for the month in which falls the date on which the option is exercised; and

RA is the retail prices index for the month in which falls the date in which the option was acquired or, if it is later, March 1982.

(3) If RO, as defined in sub-paragraph (2) above, is equal to or less than RA, as so defined, the indexed rise is nil.

Cross references.—See FA 1988, s. 113 (in respect of disposals after 3 July 1987, this paragraph not to apply in the case of building society shares and registered industrial and provident society shares).

PART IV

IDENTIFICATION OF SECURITIES ETC.

16.—(1) This Part of this Schedule applies where a person disposes of securities on or after the 1985 date, and in such a case the securities disposed of shall be identified in accordance with the provisions of this Part of this Schedule with securities of the same class acquired by him which could be comprised in that disposal.

(2) The provisions of this Part of this Schedule apply notwithstanding that securities disposed of are otherwise identified by the disposal or by a transfer or delivery giving effect to it (but so that where a person disposes of securities in one capacity, they shall not be identified with securities which he holds or can dispose of only in some other capacity).

(3) Notwithstanding anything in sub-paragraphs (1) and (2) above, the provisions of this Part of this Schedule do not apply to shares in respect of which relief under [Chapter III of Part VIII of the Taxes Act][1] (relief for investment in corporate trades) has been given and not withdrawn.

Amendments.—[1] Words in sub-para. (3) substituted by TA 1988, Sch. 29, para. 32 Table.

17.—(1) Part III of this Schedule shall have effect with respect to securities in place of section 65 of the Capital Gains Tax Act 1979 (pooling) but subject to—

(*a*) section 66 of that Act (disposals on or before day of acquisition); and
(*b*) section 58 of the Finance (No. 2) Act 1975 (disposal of certain shares and securities within prescribed period of acquisition).

(2) In relation to disposals of securities on or after the 1985 date, section 66 of the Capital Gains Tax Act 1979 shall have effect—

(*a*) as if the reference in subsection (2) (*a*) to provisions of Schedule 5 to that Act included a reference to paragraph 19 (3) below; and
(*b*) as if the reference in subsection (2) (*b*) to section 65 of that Act were a reference to Part III of this Schedule.

18.—(1) Without prejudice to section 66 of the Capital Gains Tax Act 1979 if, within a period of ten days, a number of securities are acquired and subsequently a number of securities are disposed of and, apart from this paragraph,—

(*a*) the securities acquired would increase the size of, or constitute a new holding, and
(*b*) the securities disposed of would decrease the size of, or extinguish, the same new holding,

then, subject to sub-paragraphs (2) and (3) below, the securities disposed of shall be identified with the securities acquired and none of them shall be regarded as forming part of an existing new holding or constituting a new holding.

(2) If, in a case falling within sub-paragraph (1) above, the number of securities acquired exceeds the number disposed of,—

(*a*) the excess shall be regarded as forming part of an existing new holding or, as the case may be, as constituting a new holding; and
(*b*) if the securities acquired were acquired at different times (within the ten days referred to in sub-paragraph (1) above) the securities disposed of shall be identified with securities acquired at an earlier time rather than with securities acquired at a later time.

(3) If, in a case falling within sub-paragraph (1) above, the number of securities disposed of exceeds the number acquired, the excess shall be not identified in accordance with that sub-paragraph.

(4) Securities which, by virtue of this paragraph, do not form part of or constitute a new holding shall be treated for the purposes of section 87 (3) of the Finance Act 1982 (cases where indexation allowance is nil) as relevant securities within the meaning of section 88 of that Act.

Cross references.—See FA 1988, s. 113 (in respect of disposals after 3 July 1987, this paragraph not to apply in the case of building society shares and registered industrial and provident society shares).

19.—(1) The identification rules set out in sub-paragraphs (2) and (3) below have effect subject to section 66 of the Capital Gains Tax Act 1979 but, subject to that, have priority according to the order in which they are so set out.

(2) Securities disposed of shall be identified with securities forming part of a new holding, within the meaning of Part III of this Schedule, rather than with other securities.

(3) Securities disposed of shall be identified with securities forming part of a 1982 holding, within the meaning of Part II of this Schedule, rather than with other securities and, subject to that, shall be identified with securities acquired at a later time rather than with securities acquired at an earlier time.

PART V

PARALLEL POOLING

20.—(1) Where an election has been made under Schedule 6 to the Finance Act 1983 (parallel pooling) that election may be revoked, by notice in writing to the inspector not later than 31st March 1987 or within such further time as the Board may allow.

(2) . . .

(3) All such adjustments shall be made, whether by way of discharge or repayment of tax, or the making of assessments or otherwise, as are required in consequence of a revocation under sub-paragraph (1) above.

Note.—Sub-para. (2) amends FA 1983, Sch. 6, para. 2 (2) (*b*).

21.—(1) An election under Schedule 6 to the Finance Act 1983 shall not have effect with respect to any disposal on or after 1st April 1985.

(2) The Treasury may by regulations make such provisions as are referred to in sub-paragraph (3) below in relation to qualifying securities, within the meaning of the said Schedule 6,—

    (*a*) in respect of which an election under that Schedule has been made and not revoked under paragraph 20 above; and

    (*b*) which, immediately before 1st April 1985, were regarded as indistinguishable parts of a single asset by virtue of paragraph 3 of that Schedule.

(3) The provisions referred to in sub-paragraph (2) above are such as appear to the Treasury to be appropriate to enable section 68 of this Act and the preceding provisions of this Schedule to take full effect in relation to the securities concerned.

(4) Regulations under this paragraph shall be made by statutory instrument which shall be subject to annulment in pursuance of a resolution of the Commons House of Parliament.

PART VI

UNDERWRITERS' PREMIUMS TRUST FUNDS

22. This Part of this Schedule has effect with respect to premiums trust funds, within the meaning of [section 457 of the Taxes Act][1] (underwriters), and any reference in paragraph 23 below to a fund is a reference to such a premiums trust fund.

Cross references.—See FA 1988, s. 113 (in respect of disposals after 3 July 1987, this paragraph not to apply in the case of building society shares and registered industrial and provident society shares).
Amendments.—[1] Words substituted by TA 1988, Sch. 29, para. 32 Table.

23.—(1) Subject to the following provisions of this paragraph, the enactments relating to indexation shall apply with any necessary modifications in relation to assets forming part of a fund as they apply in relation to other assets.

(2) In this paragraph "the enactments relating to indexation" means—

(*a*) sections 86 to 88 of and Schedule 13 to the Finance Act 1982; and
(*b*) section 68 of this Act and Parts I to III of this Schedule.

(3) For the purposes of the application of the enactments relating to indexation in accordance with sub-paragraph (1) above, it shall be assumed—

(*a*) that assets forming part of a fund are disposed of and immediately reacquired on the last day of each accounting period; and
(*b*) that the indexation allowance computed for that accounting period is allocated to the corresponding underwriting year in the same proportion as the gains or losses referred to in [section 142A of the Capital Gains Tax Act 1979][1].

Cross references.—See FA 1988, s. 113 (in respect of disposals after 3 July 1987, this paragraph not to apply in the case of building society shares and registered industrial and provident society shares).
Amendments.—[1] Words substituted by TA 1988, Sch. 29, para. 32 Table.

SCHEDULE 20

Sections 69 and 70

RETIREMENT RELIEF ETC.

PART I

INTERPRETATION

1.—(1) This paragraph and paragraphs 2 and 3 below have effect for the purposes of this Schedule and sections 69 and 70 of this Act.

(2) In the provisions referred to above—

"commercial association of companies" means a company together with such of its associated companies, within the meaning of section [416][1] of the Taxes Act, as carry on businesses which are of such a nature that the businesses of the company and the associated companies taken together may be reasonably considered to make up a single composite undertaking;

"family company" means, in relation to an individual, a company the voting rights in which are—

(a) as to not less than 25 per cent., exercisable by the individual, or
(b) as to more than 50 per cent., exercisable by the individual or a member of his family and, as to not less than 5 per cent., exercisable by the individual himself;

"family" means, in relation to an individual, the husband or wife of the individual and a relative of the individual or of the individual's husband or wife and, for this purpose, "relative" means brother, sister, ancester or lineal descendant;

"full-time working director", in relation to one or more companies, means a director who is required to devote substantially the whole of his time to the service of that company or, as the case may be, those companies taken together, in a managerial or technical capacity;

"group of companies" means a company which has one or more 51 per cent. subsidiaries together with those subsidiaries;

"holding company" means a company whose business (disregarding any trade carried on by it) consists wholly or mainly of the holding of shares or securities of one or more companies which are its 51 per cent. subsidiaries;

"permitted period" means a period of one year or such longer period as the Board may, in any particular case, by notice in writing allow;

"trade", "profession", "vocation", "office" and "employment" have the same meaning as in the Income Tax Acts;

"trading company" means a company whose business consists wholly or mainly of the carrying on of a trade or trades;

"trading group" means a group of companies the business of whose members, taken together, consists wholly or mainly of the carrying on of a trade or trades.

(3) For the purposes of sub-paragraph (2) above, voting rights exercisable by trustees of a settlement are to be treated as voting rights exercisable by a member of the family of an individual if—

(a) the individual or any member of his family is a beneficiary under the settlement; and
(b) no one, other than the individual or a member of his family, is for the time being entitled under the settlement to receive any capital or income of the settled property; and
(c) the terms of the settlement are such that no one other than the individual or a member of his family can become entitled to capital or income except upon the failure (for whatever reason) of the individual or a member of his family to become so entitled.

(4) Any reference in sub-paragraph (3) above to a person being or becoming entitled to any capital or income of the settled property includes a reference to a person—

(a) whose entitlement is subject to a power which could be so exercised as to require all or any of the capital or income in question to be paid to some other person; or
(b) whose entitlement depends upon his exercising a power in his own favour.

Amendments.—[1] Number in the definition of "commercial association of companies" in sub-para. (2) substituted by TA 1988, Sch. 29, para. 32 Table.

2.—(1) For the purposes of the provisions referred to in paragraph 1 (1) above, where, as part of a reorganisation, within the meaning of section 77 of the Capital Gains Tax Act 1979, there is a disposal of shares or securities of a company and, apart from this sub-paragraph, the shares disposed of and the new holding (as defined in that section) would fall to be treated, by virtue of section 78 of that Act, as the same asset, the said section 78 shall not apply if the individual concerned so elects or, in the case of a trustees' disposal, if the trustees and the individual concerned jointly so elect; and an election under this sub-paragraph shall be made by notice in writing given to the Board not more than two years after the end of the year of assessment in which the disposal occurred.

(2) In sub-paragraph (1) above, the reference to a reorganisation, within the meaning of section 77 of the Capital Gains Tax Act 1979, includes a reference to an exchange of shares or securities which is treated as such a reorganisation by virtue of section 85 (3) of that Act.

3.—(1) A person who has been concerned in the carrying on of a business shall be treated as having retired on ill-health grounds if, on production of such evidence as the Board may reasonably require, the Board are satisfied—

(*a*) that he has ceased to be engaged in and, by reason of ill-health, is incapable of engaging in work of the kind which he previously undertook in connection with that business; and
(*b*) that he is likely to remain permanently so incapable.

(2) In sub-paragraph (1) above, the reference to a person being concerned in the carrying on of a business is a reference to his being so concerned personally or as a member of a partnership carrying on the business; and the business which is relevant for the purposes of the provisions referred to in paragraph 1 (1) above is that referred to—

(*a*) in subsection (3) or subsection (4) of section 69 of this Act in relation to a material disposal of business assets;
(*b*) in subsection (5) of section 70 of this Act in relation to a trustees' disposal; and
(*c*) in subsection (7) of section 70 of this Act in relation to an associated disposal.

(3) A person who has been a full-time working director of a company or of two or more companies shall be treated as having retired on ill-health grounds if, on production of such evidence as the Board may reasonably require, the Board are satisfied—

(*a*) that he has ceased to serve and, by reason of ill-health, is incapable of serving that company or, as the case may be, those companies in a managerial or technical capacity; and
(*b*) that he is likely to remain permanently incapable of serving in such a capacity that company or those companies (as the case may be) or any other company engaged in business of a kind carried on by that company or those companies.

(4) In relation to an employee's disposal, a person who has been exercising any office or employment shall be treated as having retired on ill-health grounds if, on production of such evidence as the Board may reasonably require, the Board are satisfied—

(*a*) that he has ceased to exercise and, by reason of ill-health, is incapable of exercising that office or employment; and
(*b*) that he is likely to remain permanently so incapable.

4.—(1) In this Schedule—

(*a*) "material disposal of business assets" has the same meaning as in section 69 of this Act;
(*b*) "employee's disposal" means a disposal falling within subsection (1) of section 70 of this Act;
(*c*) "trustees' disposal" means a disposal falling within subsection (3) of section 70 of this Act and, in relation to such a disposal, "the qualifying beneficiary" has the meaning assigned to it by paragraph (*b*) of that subsection;
(*d*) "associated disposal" has the meaning assigned to it by section 70 (7) of this Act;

and "qualifying disposal" means any of the disposals referred to in paragraphs (*a*) to (*d*) above.

(2) Any reference in this Schedule to the qualifying period is a reference to the period of at least one year which,—

(*a*) in relation to a material disposal of business assets, is referred to in subsection (3), subsection (4) (*a*) or subsection (5) (as the case may require) of section 69 of this Act;
(*b*) in relation to an employee's disposal, is referred to in section 70 (2) (*a*) of this Act;

(c) in relation to a trustee's disposal, is referred to in subsection (4) or subsection (5) (as the case may require) of section 70 of this Act;

and, in relation to an associated disposal, any reference in this Schedule to the qualifying period is a reference to that period which is the qualifying period in relation to the material disposal of business assets with which the associated disposal is associated in accordance with section 70 (7) of this Act.

(3) In relation to a qualifying disposal, any reference in this Schedule to the amount available for relief is a reference to the amount determined in accordance with paragraphs 13 to 16 below.

PART II

THE OPERATION OF THE RELIEF

Disposals on which relief may be given

5.—(1) Relief in accordance with this Schedule shall not be given in respect of any disposal unless the qualifying period relating to that disposal ends on or after 6th April 1985.

(2) Except in the case of a disposal which is made by an individual who has attained the age of 60, relief in accordance with this Schedule shall be given only on the making of a claim not later than two years after end of the year of assessment in which the disposal occurred.

(3) In the case of a trustees' disposal, relief in accordance with this Schedule shall be given only on a claim made jointly by the trustees and the beneficiary concerned.

(4) Where a claim for relief in accordance with this Schedule is dependent upon an individual having retired on ill-health grounds below the age of 60, the claim shall be made to the Board.

Gains qualifying for relief

6. Subject to paragraphs 9 and 10 below, in the case of any qualifying disposal other than one of shares or securities of a company, the gains accruing to the individual or, in the case of a trustees' disposal, the trustees on the disposal of chargeable business assets comprised in the qualifying disposal shall be aggregated, and only so much of that aggregate as exceeds the amount available for relief shall be chargeable gains (but not so as to affect liability in respect of gains accruing on the disposal of assets other than chargeable business assets).

7.—(1) Subject to paragraphs 9 to 11 below, in the case of a qualifying disposal of shares or securities of a trading company which is not a holding company,—

(a) the gains which on the disposal accrue to the individual or, as the case may be, the trustees shall be aggregated, and
(b) of the appropriate proportion of the aggregated gains, only so much as exceeds the amount available for relief shall constitute chargeable gains (but not so as to affect liability in respect of gains representing the balance of the aggregated gains).

(2) For the purposes of sub-paragraph (1) (b) above, "the appropriate proportion" is that which that part of the value of the company's chargeable assets immediately before the end of the qualifying period which is attributable to the value of the company's chargeable business assets bears to the whole of that value, but, in the case of a company which has no chargeable assets, "the appropriate proportion" is the whole.

(3) For the purposes of this paragraph, every asset is a chargeable asset except one, on the disposal of which by the company immediately before the end of the qualifying period, no gain accruing to the company would be a chargeable gain.

8.—(1) Subject to paragraphs 9 to 11 below, in the case of a qualifying disposal of shares or securities of a holding company,—

(a) the gains which on the disposal accrue to the individual or, as the case may be, the trustees shall be aggregated, and
(b) of the appropriate proportion of the aggregated gains, only so much as exceeds the amount available for relief shall constitute chargeable gains (but not so as to affect liability in respect of gains representing the balance of the aggregated gains).

(2) For the purposes of sub-paragraph (1) (b) above, "the appropriate proportion" is that

which that part of the value of the trading group's chargeable assets immediately before the end of the qualifying period which is attributable to the value of the trading group's chargeable business assets bears to the whole of that value; but, in the case of a trading group which has no chargeable assets, "the appropriate proportion" is the whole.

(3) For the purpose of sub-paragraph (2) above,—

(*a*) any reference to the trading group's chargeable assets or chargeable business assets is a reference to the chargeable assets or, as the case may be, chargeable business assets of every member of the trading group; and
(*b*) subject to paragraph (*c*) below, every asset is a chargeable asset except one, on the disposal of which by the member of the group concerned immediately before the end of the qualifying period no gain accruing to that member would be a chargeable gain; and
(*c*) a holding by one member of the trading group of the ordinary share capital of another member of the group is not a chargeable asset.

(4) Where the whole of the ordinary share capital of a 51 per cent. subsidiary of the holding company is not owned directly or indirectly by that company, then, for the purposes of sub-paragraph (2) above, the value of the chargeable assets and chargeable business assets of that subsidiary shall be taken to be reduced by multiplying it by a fraction of which the denominator is the whole of the ordinary share capital of the subsidiary and the numerator is the amount of that share capital owned, directly or indirectly, by the holding company.

(5) Expressions used in sub-paragraph (4) above have the same meaning as in section [838 (1)][1] of the Taxes Act (subsidiaries).

Amendments.—[1] Number in sub-para. (5) substituted by TA 1988, Sch. 29, para. 32 Table.

9.—(1) If, in the case of a trustees' disposal, there is, in addition to the qualifying beneficiary, at least one other beneficiary who, at the end of the qualifying period, has an interest in possession in the whole of the settled property or, as the case may be, in a part of it which consists of or includes the shares, securities or asset which is the subject matter of the disposal, only the relevant proportion of the gain which accrues to the trustees on the disposal shall be brought into account under paragraph 6, paragraph 7 or paragraph 8 above (as the case may require) and the balance of the gain shall, accordingly, be a chargeable gain.

(2) For the purposes of sub-paragraph (1) above, the relevant proportion is that which, at the end of the qualifying period, the qualifying beneficiary's interest in the income of the part of the settled property comprising the shares, securities or asset in question bears to the interests in that income of all the beneficiaries (including the qualifying beneficiary) who then have interests in possession in that part.

(3) The reference in sub-paragraph (2) above to the qualifying beneficiary's interest is a reference to the interest by virtue of which he is the qualifying beneficiary and not to any other interest he may hold.

10.—(1) If, in the case of an associated disposal,—

(*a*) the asset in question was in use for the purposes of a business as mentioned in section 70 (7) (*c*) of this Act for only part of the period in which it was in the ownership of the individual making the disposal, or
(*b*) for any part of the period in which the asset in question was in use for the purposes of a business as mentioned in section 70 (7) (*c*) of this Act, the individual making the disposal was not concerned in the carrying on of that business (whether personally, as a member of a partnership or as a full-time working director of any such company as is referred to in section 69 (3) (*b*) of this Act), or
(*c*) for the whole or any part of the period in which the asset in question was in use for the purposes of a business as mentioned in section 70 (7) (*c*) of this Act, its availability for that use was dependent upon the payment of rent,

only such part of the gain which accrues on the disposal as appears to the Board to be just and reasonable shall be brought into account under paragraph 6, paragraph 7 or paragraph 8 above (as the case may require) and the balance of the gain shall, accordingly, be a chargeable gain.

(2) In determining how much of a gain it is just and reasonable to bring into account as mentioned in sub-paragraph (1) above, the Board shall have regard to the length of the period the asset was in use as mentioned in that sub-paragraph and the extent to which any

rent paid was less than the amount which would have been payable in the open market for the use of the asset.

(3) In sub-paragraphs (1) and (2) above "rent" includes any form of consideration given for the use of the asset.

11.—(1) This paragraph applies where—

(*a*) there is a material disposal of business assets or a trustees' disposal which (in either case) consists of a disposal which the individual or trustees is or are treated as making by virtue of section 72 of the Capital Gains Tax Act 1979 in consideration of a capital distribution; and

(*b*) the capital distribution consists wholly of chargeable business assets of the company or partly of such assets and partly of money or money's worth.

(2) Where the capital distribution consists wholly of chargeable business assets, no relief shall be given under this Schedule in respect of the gains accruing on the disposal.

(3) Where the capital distribution consists only partly of chargeable business assets, the gains accruing on the disposal (aggregated as mentioned in paragraph 7 (1) (*a*) or paragraph 8 (1) (*a*) above) shall be reduced for the purposes of this Schedule by multiplying them by the fraction of which—

(*a*) the numerator is the part of the capital distribution which does not consist of chargeable business assets; and

(*b*) the denominator is the entire capital distribution;

and it shall be to that reduced amount of aggregated gains that, in accordance with sub-paragraph (1) (*b*) of paragraph 7 or, as the case may be, paragraph 8 above, the appropriate proportion determined under sub-paragraph (2) of that paragraph shall be applied.

(4) Any question whether or to what extent a capital distribution consists of chargeable business assets shall be determined by reference to the status of the assets immediately before the end of the qualifying period.

12.—(1) Subject to paragraphs 9 to 11 above, in arriving at the aggregate gains under any of paragraphs 6, 7 (1) and 8 (1) above,—

(*a*) the respective amounts of the gains shall be computed in accordance with the provisions of the Capital Gains Tax Act 1979 fixing the amount of chargeable gains, and

(*b*) any allowable loss which accrues on the qualifying disposal concerned shall be deducted,

and the provisions of this Schedule shall not affect the computation of the amount of any allowable loss.

(2) Subject to the following provisions of this paragraph, in paragraphs 6 to 11 above, "chargeable business asset" means an asset (including goodwill but not including shares or securities or other assets held as investments) which is, or is an interest in, an asset used for the purposes of a trade, profession, vocation, office or employment carried on by—

(*a*) the individual concerned; or

(*b*) that individual's family company; or

(*c*) a member of a trading group of which the holding company is that individual's family company; or

(*d*) a partnership of which the individual concerned is a member.

(3) An asset is not a chargeable business asset if, on the disposal of it, no gain which might accrue would be a chargeable gain.

(4) In relation to a trustees' disposal, references in sub-paragraph (2) above to the individual shall be construed as references to the beneficiary concerned.

(5) Sub-paragraph (6) below applies if—

(*a*) a qualifying disposal falling within paragraph 7 or paragraph 8 above is a disposal which the individual or trustees concerned is or are treated as making by virtue of section 72 of the Capital Gains Tax Act 1979 in consideration of a capital distribution; and

(*b*) not later than two years after the end of the year of assessment in which the individual or the trustees received the capital distribution, the individual or trustees by notice in writing to the inspector elects or elect that that sub-paragraph should apply.

(6) If, in a case where this sub-paragraph applies in relation to a qualifying disposal, any part of the assets of the company concerned consists, as at the end of the qualifying period, of the proceeds of the sale of an asset sold not more than six months before the end of that

period, then, sub-paragraph (2) above and paragraph 7 or, as the case may be, paragraph 8 above shall have effect as if, at that time—

(a) the asset remained the property of the company and was in use for the purposes for which it was used before its sale; and
(b) the proceeds of sale of the asset did not form part of the assets of the company.

The amount available for relief: the basic rule

13.—(1) Subject to the following provisions of this Part of this Schedule, on a qualifying disposal by an individual the amount available for relief by virtue of sections 69 and 70 of this Act is [an amount equal to the aggregate of—

(a) so much of the gains qualifying for relief as do not exceed the appropriate percentage of £125,000; and
(b) one half of so much of those gains as exceed the appropriate percentage of £125,000 but do not exceed that percentage of £500,000;

and for the purposes of this sub-paragraph "the appropriate percentage" is a percentage][1] determined according to the length of the qualifying period which is appropriate to the disposal on a scale rising arithmetically from 10 per cent. where that period is precisely one year to 100 per cent. where it is ten years.

[(1A) In sub-paragraph (1) above "the gains qualifying for relief" means, in relation to any qualifying disposal, so much of the gains accruing on that disposal (aggregated under paragraph 6, 7(1)(a) or 8(1)(a) above) as would, by virtue of this Schedule, not be chargeable gains if—

(a) sub-paragraph (1) above had specified as the amount available for relief a fixed sum in excess of those aggregate gains; and
(b) paragraphs 14 to 16 below were disregarded.][2]

(2) The amount available for relief by virtue of section 70 of this Act on a trustees' disposal shall be determined, subject to sub-paragraph (3) below, in accordance with sub-paragraph (1) above on the assumption that the trustees' disposal is a qualifying disposal by the qualifying beneficiary.

(3) If, on the same day, there is both a trustees' disposal and a material disposal of business assets by the qualifying beneficiary, the amount available for relief shall be applied to the beneficiary's disposal in priority to the trustees' disposal.

Amendments.—[1] Words in sub-para. (1) substituted by FA 1988, s. 110 (1), (8) with respect to qualifying disposals after 5 April 1988.
[2] Sub-para. (1A) inserted by FA 1988, s. 110 (2), (8) with respect to qualifying disposals after 5 April 1988.

Aggregation of earlier business periods

14.—(1) If, apart from this paragraph, the qualifying period appropriate to a qualifying disposal (in this paragraph referred to as "the original qualifying period") would be less than ten years but throughout some period (in this paragraph referred to as "the earlier business period") which—

(a) ends not earlier than two years before the beginning of the original qualifying period, and
(b) falls, in whole or in part, within the period of ten years ending at the end of the original qualifying period,

the individual making the disposal or, as the case may be, the relevant beneficiary was concerned in the carrying on of another business (in this paragraph referred to as the "previous business") then, for the purpose of determining the amount available for relief on the qualifying disposal, the length of the qualifying period appropriate to that disposal shall be redetermined on the assumptions and subject to the provisions set out below.

(2) For the purposes of the redetermination referred to in subparagraph (1) above, it shall be assumed that the previous business is the same business as the business at retirement and, in the first instance, any time between the end of the earlier business period and the beginning of the qualifying period shall be disregarded (so that those two periods shall be assumed to be one continuous period).

(3) The reference in sub-paragraph (1) above to a person being concerned in the carrying

on of a business is a reference to his being so concerned personally or as a member of a partnership or, if the business was owned by a company, then as a full-time working director of that company or, as the case may be, of any member of the group or commercial association of which it is a member; and the reference in sub-paragraph (2) above to the business at retirement is a reference to that business which, in relation to the qualifying disposal, is referred to—

(a) in subsection (3), subsection (4) or subsection (5) of section 69 of this Act where the qualifying disposal is a material disposal of business assets;
(b) in subsection (5) of section 70 of this Act where that disposal is a trustees' disposal; and
(c) in subsection (7) of section 70 of this Act where that disposal is an associated disposal.

(4) Any extended qualifying period resulting from the operation of sub-paragraph (2) above shall not begin earlier than the beginning of the period of ten years referred to in sub-paragraph (1) (b) above.

(5) If the earlier business period ended before the beginning of the original qualifying period, any extended qualifying period which would otherwise result from the operation of the preceding provisions of this paragraph, shall be reduced by deducting therefrom a period equal to that between the ending of the earlier business period and the beginning of the original qualifying period.

(6) Where there is more than one business which qualifies as the previous business and, accordingly, more than one period which qualifies as the earlier business period, this paragraph shall apply first in relation to that one of those businesses in which the individual in question was last concerned and shall then again apply (as if any extended qualifying period resulting from the first application were the original qualifying period) in relation to the next of those businesses and so on.

Relief given on earlier disposal

15.—(1) In any case where—

(a) an individual makes a qualifying disposal or is the qualifying beneficiary in relation to a trustees' disposal, and
(b) relief has been (or falls to be) given under this Schedule in respect of an earlier disposal which was either a qualifying disposal made by the individual or a trustees' disposal in respect of which he was the qualifying beneficiary,

the amount which, apart from this paragraph, would be the amount available for relief on the disposal mentioned in paragraph (a) above shall not exceed the limit in sub-paragraph (3) below.

(2) [In the following provisions of this paragraph][1]—

(a) the disposal falling within sub-paragraph (1) (a) above is referred to as "the later disposal"; and
(b) the disposal falling within sub-paragraph (1) (b) above or, if there is more than one such disposal, each of them is referred to as "the earlier disposal".

(3) The limit referred to in sub-paragraph (1) above is the difference between—

(a) the amount which would be available for relief on the later disposal—

[(i) if the gains qualifying for relief on that disposal were increased by the amount of the underlying gains relieved on the earlier disposal (or the aggregate amount of the underlying gains relieved on all the earlier disposals, as the case may be); and
(ii) if the qualifying period appropriate to the later disposal][1]

(as redetermined where appropriate under paragraph 14 above) were extended by the addition of a period equal to so much (if any) of the qualifying period appropriate to the earlier disposal (or, as the case may be, to each of the earlier disposals) as does not already fall within the qualifying period appropriate to the later disposal; and

(b) the amount of relief given under this Schedule on the earlier disposal or, as the case may be, the aggregate of the relief so given on all the earlier disposals.

[(3A) Where there is only one earlier disosal, or where there are two or more such disposals but none of them took place on or after 6th April 1988, then, for the purposes of sub-paragraph (3) (a) (i) above—

(a) if the earlier disposal took place on or after 6th April 1988, the amount of the underlying gains relieved on that disposal is the aggregate of—

(i) so much of the gains qualifying for relief on that disposal as were, by virtue of paragraph 13 (1) (*a*) above, not chargeable gains; and
(ii) twice the amount of so much of those gains as were, by virtue of paragraph 13(1)(*b*) above, not chargeable gains; and

(*b*) if the earlier disposal took place before 6th April 1988, the amount of the underlying gains relieved on that disposal (or on each such disposal) is so much of the gains qualifying for relief on that disposal as were, by virtue of paragraph 13 above, not chargeable gains.]²

[(3B) Where there are two or more earlier disposals and at least one of them took place on or after 6th April 1988, then, for the purposes of sub-paragraph (3) (*a*) (i) above, the aggregate amount of the underlying gains relieved on all those disposals shall be determined as follows—

(*a*) it shall be assumed for the purposes of paragraph (*b*) below—

(i) that the amount which resulted from the calculation under sub-paragraph (3) (*a*) above on the last of those disposals ("the last disposal") was the amount of the gains qualifying for relief on that disposal which were, by virtue of this Schedule, not chargeable gains (the "gains actually relieved");
(ii) that the qualifying period appropriate to that disposal (as redetermined where appropriate under paragraph 14 above) was that period as extended in accordance with sub-paragraph (3) (*a*) (ii) above; and
(iii) that the last disposal was the only earlier disposal;

(*b*) there shall then be ascertained in accordance with paragraph 13 (1) above (but on the assumptions in paragraph (*a*) above)—

(i) how much of the gains actually relieved would, by virtue of paragraph 13 (1) (*a*) above, not have been chargeable gains; and
(ii) how much of those gains would, by virtue of paragraph 13 (1) (*b*) above, not have been chargeable gains; and

(*c*) the aggregate amount of the underlying gains relieved on all the earlier disposals is the sum of—

(i) the amount ascertained under paragraph (*b*) (i) above; and
(ii) twice the amount ascertained under paragraph (*b*) (ii) above.]²

[(3C) In this paragraph "the gains qualifying for relief" has the meaning given by paragraph 13 (1A) above.]²

(4) References in this paragraph to relief given under this Schedule include references to relief given under section 34 of the Finance Act 1965 or section 124 of the Capital Gains Tax Act 1979; and—

(*a*) in relation to relief given under either of those sections paragraph (*b*) of sub-paragraph (1) above shall have effect as if, for the words from "which was" onwards, there were substituted "made by the individual"; and
[(*b*) for the purpose of determining the limit in sub-paragraph (3) above where the earlier disposal (or any of the earlier disposals) was a disposal in respect of which relief was given under either of those sections—

(i) the underlying gains relieved on that disposal shall (subject to sub-paragraph (3B) above) be taken to be gains of an amount equal to the relief given under the section in question in respect of that disposal; and
(ii) the reference in sub-paragraph (3) (*a*) (ii) above to the qualifying period appropriate to the earlier disposal shall be construed in accordance with paragraph (*c*) below;]¹

[(*c*) for the purpose mentioned in paragraph (*b*) above, that reference shall, as respects the earlier disposal in question, be taken to be]¹ a reference,—

(i) if the disposal took place on or before 11th April 1978, to the period of ten years ending with the disposal; and
(ii) in any other case, to the qualifying period within the meaning of the section in question.

Amendments.—¹ Words in sub-paras. (2), (3) (*a*), (4) substituted by FA 1988, s. 110 (3), (4), (6), (8) with respect to qualifying disposals after 5 April 1988.
² Sub-paras. (3A), (3B), (3C) inserted by FA 1988, s. 110 (5), (8) with respect to qualifying disposals after 5 April 1988.

Aggregation of spouse's interest in the business

16.—(1) In any case where—

(*a*) an individual makes a material disposal of business assets, and
(*b*) the subject matter of that disposal (whether business, assets or shares or securities) was acquired, in whole or in part, from that individual's spouse, and
(*c*) that acquisition was either under the will or intestacy of the spouse or by way of lifetime gift and in the year of assessment in which occurred in the spouse's death or, as the case may be, the lifetime gift, the individual and his spouse were living together, and
(*d*) as a result of the acquisition the individual acquired the whole of the interest in the business, assets, shares or securities concerned which, immediately before the acquisition or, as the case may be, the spouse's death, was held by the spouse, and
(*e*) not later than two years after the end of the year of assessment in which the material disposal occurred, the individual elects that this paragraph should apply,

the period which, apart from this paragraph, would be the qualifying period appropriate to that disposal shall be extended by assuming that, in the conditions which under section 69 of this Act are the relevant conditions applicable to the disposal, any reference to the individual were a reference either to the individual or his spouse.

(2) An election under sub-paragraph (1) (*e*) above shall be made by notice in writing to the inspector.

(3) Where the acquisition referred to in sub-paragraph (1) (*c*) above was by way of lifetime gift, the amount available for relief on the material disposal concerned, having regard to the extension of the qualifying period under sub-paragraph (1) above, shall not exceed [the limit][1] specified in sub-paragraph (4) below.

(4) The [limit][1] referred to in sub-paragraph (3) above [is][1]—

(*a*) . . .[2]
(*b*) the amount which would have been available for relief on the material disposal if—

   (i) the lifetime gift had not occurred; and
   (ii) the material disposal had been made by the spouse; and
   (iii) anything done by the individual in relation to the business concerned after the lifetime gift was in fact made had been done by the spouse.

(5) . . .[2]

Amendments.—[1] Words in sub-paras. (3), (4) substituted by FA 1988, s. 110 (7), (8) with respect to qualifying disposals after 5 April 1988.
[2] Sub-paras. (4) (*a*), (5) repealed by FA 1988, s. 110 (7), (8) and Sch. 14, Pt. VII in relation to qualifying disposals after 5 April 1988.

SCHEDULE 21
Section 71

ASSETS DISPOSED OF IN A SERIES OF LINKED TRANSACTIONS

1.—(1) This Schedule has effect for determining the original market value of assets and the aggregate market value of assets as mentioned in subsection (1) (*b*) of section 71 of this Act (in this Schedule referred to as "the principal section").

(2) Expressions used in this Schedule have the same meaning as in the principal section.

2. Where there is a series of linked transactions, the original market value of the assets disposed of by each transaction in the series shall be determined as follows—

(*a*) if at the time in question the transaction is the most recent in the series, the original market value of the assets disposed of by that transaction is the market value which, apart from the principal section, would be deemed to be the consideration for that transaction for the purposes of the principal Act; and

(*b*) in the case of any other transaction in the series, the original market value of the assets disposed of by that transaction is the value which, prior to the occurrence of the most recent transaction in the series, was or would have been deemed for the purposes of the principal Act to be the consideration for the transaction concerned (whether by virtue of that Act or the previous operation of the principal section).

3.—(1) Subject to paragraph 4 below, in relation to any transaction in a series of linked transactions,—

(*a*) any reference in the principal section or this Schedule to the aggregate market value of the assets disposed of by all the transactions in the series is a reference to what would have been the market value of all those assets for the purposes of the principal Act if, considering all the assets together, they had been disposed of by one disposal occurring at the time of the transaction concerned; and

(*b*) any reference in the principal section to the appropriate portion of the aggregate market value of the assets disposed of by all the transactions in the series is a reference to that portion of the market value determined in accordance with paragraph (*a*) above which it is reasonable to apportion to those of the assets which were actually disposed of by the transaction concerned.

(2) The reference in sub-paragraph (1) (*a*) above to considering all the assets together includes a reference not only to considering them as a group or holding or collection of assets retaining their separate identities but also (if it gives a higher market value) to considering them as brought together, physically or in law, so as to constitute either a single asset or a number of assets which are distinct from those which were comprised in each of the transactions concerned.

4.—(1) If any of the assets disposed of by all the transactions in a series of linked transactions were acquired after the time of the first of those transactions, then, in the application of paragraph 3 above in relation to each of the transactions in the series,—

(*a*) no account shall be taken of any assets which were acquired after the time of that transaction unless they were acquired by way of an inter-group transfer; and

(*b*) subject to sub-paragraph (2) below, the number of assets of which account is to be taken shall be limited to the maximum number which were held by the person making the disposal at any time in the period beginning immediately before the first of the transactions in the series and ending immediately before the last.

(2) If, before the first of the transactions referred to in paragraph (*b*) of sub-paragraph (1) above, the person concerned (being a company) disposed of any assets by way of an inter-group transfer, the maximum number of assets referred to in that paragraph shall be determined as if the inter-group transfer had occurred after that first transaction.

(3) In the application of sub-paragraph (1) above in a case where the assets disposed of are securities, the assets disposed of by any of the transactions in a series of linked transactions shall be identified with assets acquired on an earlier date rather than with assets acquired on a later date.

(4) In sub-paragraph (3) above "securities" includes any assets which are of a nature to be dealt in without identifying the particular assets disposed of or acquired.

SCHEDULE 25

Section 93

ABOLITION OF DEVELOPMENT LAND TAX AND TAX ON DEVELOPMENT GAINS

PART I

PROVISIONS SUPPLEMENTARY TO ABOLITION OF DEVELOPMENT LAND TAX

1.—(1) In this Part of this Schedule "the 1976 Act" means the Development Land Tax Act 1976.

(2) Expressions used in this Part of this Schedule have the same meaning as in the 1976 Act.

2.—(1) In any case where—

(*a*) before 19th March 1985 there was a DLT disposal which was a deemed disposal, and
(*b*) by virtue of any provision of the 1976 Act, liability for development land tax on all or any of the realised development value which accrued on the DLT disposal stands deferred immediately before that date and, accordingly, is extinguished under section 93 (3) of this Act,

then, except as respects the interaction of the DLT disposal with a CGT disposal or trading disposal occurring before 19th March 1985, for the purposes of Part I of Schedule 6 to the 1976 Act (interaction of development land tax with other taxes) so much of the realised development value as is referable to the deferred tax shall be assumed not to have accrued on the DLT disposal and, accordingly, no sum shall be regarded as being available or allowable as a deduction under any provision of that Part by virtue of that amount of realised development value.

(2) If, in a case falling within paragraphs (*a*) and (*b*) of sub-paragraph (1) above, liability for only some of the tax which accrued on the DLT disposal stands deferred as mentioned in paragraph (*b*), any reference in that sub-paragraph to the amount of realised development value which is referable to the deferred tax is a reference to that proportion of the whole of the realised development value accruing on the DLT disposal which the tax the liability for which stands so deferred bears to the whole of the tax the liability for which arose on the DLT disposal.

(3) In this paragraph, "DLT disposal", "CGT disposal" and "trading disposal" have the meaning assigned by section 34 (3) of the 1976 Act.

3. Where, by virtue of paragraph 21 or paragraph 22 of Schedule 2 to the 1976 Act (general rules for determining amount of consideration),—

(*a*) consideration is brought into account without any discount for postponed payment or without regard to any risk of irrecoverability, or
(*b*) consideration is determined without taking account of any contingent liability,

no further assessment to tax shall be raised by reason of anything occurring on or after 19th March 1985, but relief by way of discharge or repayment of tax or otherwise shall continue to be available on and after that date under sub-paragraph (2) of the paragraph in question.

SCHEDULE 27
Section 98

REPEALS

PART X
DEVELOPMENT LAND TAX AND TAX ON DEVELOPMENT GAINS

Chapter	Short title	Extent of repeal
1974 c. 30.	The Finance Act 1974.	Sections 38 to 47.
		Schedules 3 and 4.

1. The repeals in the Finance Act 1974 . . .—

(*a*) do not have effect in relation to a disposal of an interest in land, as defined in section 93 (6) of this Act, which takes place before 19th March 1985; and
(*b*) do not affect the construction of paragraph 9 of Schedule 5 to the Capital Gains Tax Act 1979 (of which sub-paragraph (5) adopts for the purposes of that paragraph certain provisions of the Finance Act 1974).

2. . . .

Note.—The provisions reproduced above are relevant for the purpose of CGTA 1979, Sch. 5, Pt. II.

TRUSTEE SAVINGS BANKS ACT 1985

(1985 Chapter 58)

An Act to make provision for the purposes of or in connection with the reorganisation into companies incorporated under the Companies Acts of the institutions regulated by or existing under the Trustee Savings Banks Act 1981 and for the treatment for the purposes of the Banking Act 1979 of any Scottish savings bank established before 28th July 1863 which has not since become a trustee savings bank. [25th July 1985]

Preliminary

1. Preliminary

(1) In this Act—

  (*a*) "the existing TSB group" means the following, taken as a whole—

   (i) the existing trustee savings banks certified under the Trustee Savings Banks Act 1969 or 1981 ("the existing banks");
   (ii) the Trustee Savings Banks Central Board ("the Central Board");
   (iii) Trustee Savings Banks (Holdings) Limited ("the existing holding company"); and
   (iv) the existing subsidiaries of any of the existing banks, the Central Board or the existing holding company;

  and "existing" with reference to any of those banks or companies means existing immediately before the vesting day, in the case of a bank, with a certification under the Trustee Savings Banks Act 1969 or 1981 effective on 17th December 1984;

  (*b*) "the new TSB group" means the following, taken as a whole—

   (i) the companies formed or to be formed with objects including that of assuming and conducting, after the vesting day, the respective businesses of the existing banks and eligible to succeed them;
   (ii) the companies which, immediately before the vesting day, are subsidiaries of the existing banks, the Central Board or the existing holding company;
   (iii) the company formed or to be formed with objects including that of acting as the holding company for the companies falling within (i) and (ii) above and which, immediately before the vesting day, is a subsidiary of the Central Board ("the new holding company");

  and for the purposes of this section "formed", with reference to the objects of a company, includes the alteration of its objects (with or without an alteration of its name);

  (*c*) "successor", with reference to an existing bank, means the company formed or to be formed with objects including that of assuming and conducting its business and eligible to succeed it; and
  (*d*) "the vesting day" means the day appointed for the transfer by virtue of section 3 below of the assets and liabilities of any of the bodies comprising the existing TSB group to any of the bodies comprising the new TSB group.

(2) For a company to be "eligible to succeed" an existing bank it must have been, immediately before the vesting day, a subsidiary of the Central Board or the exisitng holding company and it must—

  (*a*) in the case of the company which is to succeed the existing bank for England and Wales, be registered (and accordingly have its registered office) in England and Wales;
  (*b*) in the case of the company which is to succeed the existing bank for Scotland, be registered (and accordingly have its registered office) in Scotland;
  (*c*) in the case of the company which is to succeed the existing bank for Northern Ireland, be registered (and accordingly have its registered office) in Northern Ireland; and
  (*d*) in the case of the company which is to succeed the existing bank for the Channel

Islands, be incorporated (and accordingly have its registered office) in any of the Channel Islands.

(3) References in this Act to a company being a subsidiary of another or being a holding company as regards another company are to be construed in accordance with the Companies Act 1985.

(4) The vesting day shall be appointed by the Treasury by order made by statutory instrument after consulting the Central Board.

(5) This Act, except section 6, has effect for the purpose of enabling the existing TSB group to be reorganised into the new TSB group and any reference in it to "the reorganisation" shall be construed accordingly.

Note.—The vesting day appointed under sub-s. (4) above is 21 July 1986 by virtue of TSBA 1985 (Appointed Day) (No. 3) Order 1986, S.I. 1986 No. 1222.

Taxation

5. Taxation

Schedule 2 to this Act shall have effect for the purpose of making provision about taxation in relation to the reorganisation.

SCHEDULE 2

Section 5

TAXATION

Capital allowances

1.—(1) For the purposes of the allowances and charges provided for by the Capital Allowances Act 1968 and by Part III of the Finance Act 1971 (capital allowances) the trade of an existing bank shall not be treated as permanently discontinued and the trade of its successor shall not be treated as a new trade set up and commenced by the successor.

(2) There shall be made to or on the successor in accordance with those Acts all such allowances and charges as would, if the bank had continued to carry on the trade, have fallen to be made to or on it, and the amount of any such allowance or charge shall be computed as if the successor had been carrying on the trade since the bank began to do so and as if everything done to or by the bank had been done to or by the successor.

(3) No transfer of assets from the bank to its successor effected by section 3 above shall be treated as giving rise to any such allowance or charge.

Chargeable gains

2.—(1) For the purposes of the Capital Gains Tax Act 1979, the transfer of any assets effected by section 3 above shall be deemed to be for a consideration such that no gain or loss accrues to the transferor.

(2) Schedule 5 to the Act of 1979 shall have effect in relation to any asset so transferred as if the acquisition or provision of it by the transferor had been the acquisition or provision of it by the transferee.

(3) ...

Note.—Sub-para. (3) adds FA 1982, Sch. 13, para. 3 (3) (*e*).

3.—(1) For the purposes of Chapter II of Part II of the Act of 1979 (computation of chargeable gains)—

(*a*) the shares in the successor to Trustee Savings Bank of the Channel Islands acquired by the new holding company on or before the vesting day shall be taken to have been so acquired for a consideration equal to the value of the assets transferred to the successor by section 3 above (as shown by the statutory accounts for the final financial year of Trustee Savings Bank of the Channel Islands) less the amount of any liabilities so transferred (as so shown); and

(*b*) the shares in the other successors to the existing banks acquired by the new holding company on or before the vesting day shall be deemed to have been acquired by the new holding company before 6th April 1945 and for no consideration or incidental cost.

(2) For the purposes of paragraph 12 of Schedule 5 to the Act of 1979 (election for valuation at 6th April 1965) the market value of the shares mentioned in sub-paragraph (1) (*b*) above, shall be determined by applying the formula—

$$£X = £Y \times \frac{A}{B}$$

Where—

X is the market value of those shares;

Y is the value of the assets of the transferor (as shown by the statutory accounts for its final financial year) less the aggregate of the amount of its liabilities (as so shown);

A is the period beginning with 6th April 1945 and ending with 5th April 1965; and

B is the period beginning with 6th April 1945 and ending with the vesting day.

4.—(1) Where the liability in respect of any debt owed to an existing bank, the existing holding company or the Central Board, is transferred by section 3 above, the transferee shall be treated as the original creditor for the purposes of section 134 of the Act of 1979 (debts).

(2) On a 75 per cent. subsidiary ("the existing subsidiary") of an existing bank becoming a 75 per cent. subsidiary of the bank's successor, section 278 of the [Income and Corporation Taxes Act 1970]¹ (company ceasing to be a member of a group) shall not have effect as respects any assets transferred (at any time) by the bank to the subsidiary; but on the subsidiary ceasing to be a member of the group of companies ("the group") of which the successor and the new holding company are both members, section 278 of the [Income and Corporation Taxes Act 1970]¹ shall apply as if the assets acquired by the subsidiary from the bank had been acquired by it from the bank's successor.

(3) No provision made by this Act shall be treated, for the purposes of section 26 of the Act of 1979 (value-shifting), as a scheme or arrangement.

(4) For the purposes of the Act of 1979, any allowable losses accruing in any accounting period to the Central Board or to an existing bank shall, so far as they have not been allowed as a deduction from chargeable gains, be treated as allowable losses which accrued in that accounting period to the new holding company or, as the case may be, successor.

Amendments.—¹ Words in sub-para. (2) substituted by TA 1988, Sch. 29, para. 32 Table.

5. For the purposes of the Act of 1979, gains arising on the disposal by the Central Board of any shares or rights to shares in the new holding company shall not be chargeable gains.

General

6.—(1) Section [100]¹ of the Taxes Act (valuation of trading stock on discontinuance of trade) shall not apply in relation to the discontinuance of the business of an existing bank.

(2) The transfer of any trading stock investment from an existing bank to its successor effected by section 3 above shall be treated, for the purposes of corporation tax, as not constituting a disposal of that investment by the bank; but on the disposal of any such investment by the successor, the gain or, as the case may be, loss accruing to the successor shall be calculated (for the purposes of corporation tax) as if the investment had been acquired by the successor for the same consideration as that for which it was acquired by the bank.

(3) . . .²

(4) Subject to any claim made by an existing bank under subsection (2) of section [393]¹ of the Taxes Act (set off of losses against total profits), its successor shall be entitled to relief under subsection (1) of that section (carry forward of losses), as for a loss sustained by the successor in carrying on the trade, for any amount for which the bank would have been entitled to claim relief if it had continued to carry on the trade.

(5)–(7). . .²

(8) Section [410 (1) to (6) of the Taxes Act]¹ (group relief: effect of arrangements for transfer of company to another group) shall not apply in relation to any transfer effected by section 3 above.

Amendments.—¹ Words in sub-paras. (1), (4), (8) substituted by TA 1988, Sch. 29, para. 32 Table.
² Sub-paras. (3), (5)–(7) repealed by TA 1988, Sch. 31.

Deduction of tax from certain loan interest

7.—(1) . . .²

(2) Section [369 of the Taxes Act]¹ (deduction of tax from certain loan interest) shall have effect, on and after the vesting day, in relation to any loans made by an existing bank, as if the bank and its successor were a single qualifying lender.

Amendments.—¹ Words in sub-para. (2) substituted by TA 1988, Sch. 29, para. 32 Table.
² Sub-para. (1) repealed by TA 1988, Sch. 31.

8. . . .

Note.—Para. 8 provides for stamp duty exemption; see *Butterworths Orange Tax Handbook*.

Interpretation

9.—(1) In this Schedule—

...²

"further successor", in relation to the successor to an existing bank, means any body to which the bank's business, or any part of that business, is transferred after having been assumed by the successor;

"the Taxes Act" means the Income and Corporation Taxes Act [1988]¹;

"trading stock investment" means any investment on the disposal of which any gain or loss accruing would be treated as a trading profit or, as the case may be, loss for the purposes of Case I of Schedule D; and

"transferee" and "transferor", in relation to any transfer of property, rights, liabilities or obligations effected by section 3 above, means respectively the person to whom and the person from whom they are so transferred.

(2) Paragraph 1 above shall be construed as one with the provisions mentioned there and the other provisions of this Schedule shall be construed, so far as they relate to corporation tax, as one with the Corporation Taxes Act and, so far as they relate to capital gains tax, as one with the Capital Gains Tax Act 1979.

Amendments.—¹ Year in the definition of "the Taxes Act" in sub-para. (1) substituted by TA 1988, Sch. 29, para. 32 Table.
² Definition of "exempt investment" repealed by TA 1988, Sch. 31.

TRANSPORT ACT 1985

(1985 Chapter 67)

130. Corporation tax and capital gains tax

(1) Section 16 (1) (*a*) of the Finance Act 1970 (which excludes precept income and grants in computing the profits of a Passenger Transport Executive chargeable to corporation tax) shall not apply with respect to any accounting period beginning on or after the passing of this Act.

(2) In computing for the purposes of the Corporation Tax Acts the profit or loss of a Passenger Transport Executive for any accounting period beginning on or after the passing of this Act, the loss of any earlier accounting period shall be computed as if section 16 (1) (*a*) of the Finance Act 1970 had not been enacted.

(3) For the purposes of the Capital Gains Tax Act 1979, the transfer under section 59 (8) or section 85 (4) of this Act of any asset from a Passenger Transport Executive to a Passenger Transport Authority shall be deemed to be for a consideration such that no gain or loss accrues to the Executive; and Schedule 5 to that Act (assets held on 6th April 1965) shall have effect in relation to any asset so transferred as if the acquisition or provision of it by the Executive had been the acquisition or provision of it by the Authority.

(4) If, under section 59 of this Act, a company is formed by a Passenger Transport Executive and the shares in or securities of that company are subsequently transferred to a Passenger Transport Authority, section 278 of the Income and Corporation Taxes Act 1970 (deemed disposals of assets for capital gains purposes where member leaves group) shall not have effect as respects any of the assets of the company on its ceasing to be a 75 per cent. subsidiary (within the meaning of the Tax Acts) of the Executive.

Note.—This section came into force on 6 January 1986 by virtue of the Transport Act 1985 (Commencement No. 1) Order 1985, S.I. 1985 No. 1887.

Cross references.—See FA 1985, s. 68 (7A) (*ee*) (re-basing of indexation allowance to 1982 in relation to disposals after 5 April 1988);
FA 1988, Sch. 8, para. 1 (3) (*ee*) (re-basing of indexation allowance to 1982 in relation to unindexed gains and losses on disposals after 5 April 1988 of assets held on 31 March 1982).

AIRPORTS ACT 1986
(1986 Chapter 31)

77. Corporation tax

(1) Subject to subsection (2), the successor company shall be treated for all purposes of corporation tax as if it were the same person as the BAA.

(2) The successor company shall not by virtue of subsection (1) be regarded as a body falling within section 272 (5) of the [Income and Corporation Taxes Act 1970][1] (bodies established for carrying on industries or undertakings under national ownership or control).

(3) Where any debentures are issued in pursuance of section 4, any annual payment secured by those debentures shall be treated for all purposes of corporation tax as if it were a charge on income of the successor company.

(4) For the avoidance of doubt it is hereby declared that—

(a) any issue of shares in pursuance of section 4 is to be regarded as a subscription for shares for the purposes of section [400 (9) of the 1988 Act][1] (write-off of government investment: restriction of tax losses); and
(b) where any debentures are issued in pursuance of section 4, the principal sums payable under the debentures are to be regarded as money lent for those purposes.

(5) Where in the case of a claim for group relief—

(a) the claimant company is the BAA or the successor company and the surrendering company is a company to whom property, rights or liabilities have been transferred by a scheme made under section 1, and
(b) the claim relates to the accounting period of the surrendering company first ending after that transfer, and
(c) the corresponding accounting period of the claimant company ends with the same date as that accounting period,

then, for the purposes of section [408 (2) of the 1988 Act][1] (corresponding accounting periods) as it applies in relation to the claim, those accounting periods shall be taken to coincide and, for the purposes of section [409 (1) of that Act][1] (companies joining or leaving group) as it so applies, the claimant company and the surrendering company shall be taken to have been members of the same group throughout each of those periods (notwithstanding anything in section [409 (2)][1] and (3) of that Act).

(6) In this section "the [1988][1] Act" means the Income and Corporation Taxes Act [1988][1], and in subsection (5) above expressions used in sections [Chapter IV of Part X] of that Act (group relief) have the same meanings as in those sections.

Amendments.— Words in sub-paras. (2), (4) (a), (5), (6) substituted by TA 1988, Sch. 29, para. 32 Table.

FINANCE ACT 1986

(1986 Chapter 41)

ARRANGEMENT OF SECTIONS

PART I
CUSTOMS AND EXCISE AND VALUE ADDED TAX

Note.—Provisions of this Act relevant to the taxes covered by this Handbook and not reproduced are either spent or repealed by TA 1988, Sch. 31 and other legislation.

CHAPTER II
VALUE ADDED TAX

Sections 9–15 (see Orange Book)

PART II
INCOME TAX, CORPORATION TAX AND CAPITAL GAINS TAX

CHAPTER I
GENERAL

Employee shareholding

Section
24. Approved profit sharing schemes: workers' co-operatives.

CHAPTER II
CAPITAL ALLOWANCES

55. New code of allowances for capital expenditure on mineral extraction.
56. Agricultural land and buildings.
57. New expenditure on leased assets etc.

CHAPTER III
CAPITAL GAINS

58. Gifts into dual resident trusts.

PART III
STAMP DUTY

Sections 64–85 (see Orange Book)

PART IV
STAMP DUTY RESERVE TAX

Sections 86–91 (see Orange Book)
Section
92. Repayment or cancellation of tax.
Sections 93–99 (see Orange Book)

PART V
INHERITANCE TAX

Section
100. Capital transfer tax to be known as inheritance tax.
Sections 101–107 (see Orange Book)

PART VII
MISCELLANEOUS AND SUPPLEMENTARY

Section
114. Short title, interpretation, construction and repeals.

SCHEDULES:

Schedule 6—*Consideration for fuel supplied for private use.* (see Orange Book)
Schedule 13—Mineral extraction: the new code of reliefs.
Schedule 14—Mineral extraction: old expenditure.
Schedule 15—Agricultural land and buildings.
Schedule 16—New expenditure on leased assets and on certain vehicles.
Schedule 18—Securities: other provisions.
Schedule 19—*Inheritance tax.* (see Orange Book)
Schedule 20—*Gifts with reservation.* (see Orange Book)
Schedule 23—Repeals.
        Part IX   *Stamp Duty.* (see Orange Book)
        Part X   *Inheritance Tax.* (see Orange Book)

An Act to grant certain duties, to alter other duties, and to amend the law relating to the National Debt and the Public Revenue, and to make further provision in connection with Finance.

[25 July 1986]

PART II

INCOME TAX, CORPORATION TAX AND CAPITAL GAINS TAX

CHAPTER I

GENERAL

Employee shareholding

24. Approved profit sharing schemes: workers' co-operatives

(4) Where, for the purpose of securing (and maintaining) approval of its profit sharing scheme in accordance with Part I of Schedule 9 to the [Taxes Act 1988][1], the rules of a society which is a workers' co-operative or which is seeking to be registered under the industrial and provident societies legislation as a workers' co-operative contain—

    (a) provision for membership of the society by the trustees of the scheme,
    (b) provision denying voting rights to those trustees, or
    (c) other provisions which appear to the registrar to be reasonably necessary for that purpose,

those provisions shall be disregarded in determining whether the society should be or continue to be registered under the industrial and provident societies legislation as a bona fide co-operative society.

(5) In subsection (4) above "the industrial and provident societies legislation" means—

    (a) the Industrial and Provident Societies Act 1965, or
    (b) the Industrial and Provident Societies Act (Northern Ireland) 1969,

and "registrar" has the same meaning as in each of those Acts and "co-operative society" has the same meaning as in section 1 of those Acts.

Notes.—Sub-s. (1) amends FA 1978, Sch. 9 by adding para. 18.
Sub-s. (2) substitutes FA 1978, Sch. 9, para. 7 (b).
Sub-s. (3) amends FA 1978, s. 54 (1) (d), (4).
Amendments.—[1] Words in sub-s. (4) substituted by TA 1988, Sch. 29, para. 32 Table.

CHAPTER II
CAPITAL ALLOWANCES

55. New code of allowances for capital expenditure on mineral extraction

(1) The provisions of Chapter III of Part I of the Capital Allowances Act 1968 (which relate to allowances for certain capital expenditure incurred in connection with mineral extraction activities and which are in this section referred to as "the old code of allowances") shall cease to have effect on 31st March 1986 except as provided by Schedule 14 to this Act.

(2) The provisions of Parts I to IV of Schedule 13 to this Act have effect to provide for relief in respect of certain new expenditure incurred by persons carrying on a trade of mineral extraction; and the provisions of Schedule 14 to this Act have effect with respect to certain expenditure incurred before 1st April 1987 by persons carrying on such a trade.

(3) Subject to paragraph 2 of Schedule 14 to this Act, for the purposes of the old code of allowances, the following provisions of this section and Schedules 13 and 14 to this Act, as respects any company which on 31st March 1986 was carrying on a trade of mineral extraction, it shall be assumed that, unless the latest accounting period of the company which begins on or before 31st March 1986 in fact ends on that date,—

    (*a*) that accounting period ends on that date; and
    (*b*) a new one begins on 1st April 1986, the new accounting period to end with the end of the true accounting period.

(4) Subject to paragraph 2 of Schedule 14 to this Act, for the purposes of the provisions referred to in subsection (3) above as they apply to a person who on 31st March 1986 was within the charge to income tax in respect of the profits or gains of a trade of mineral extraction carried on by him, it shall be assumed that, unless the latest basis period of his (determined in accordance with section 72 of the Capital Allowances Act 1968) which begins on or before 31st March 1986 in fact ends on that date,—

    (*a*) that basis period ends on that date; and
    (*b*) a new basis period begins on 1st April 1986, the new basis period to end with the end of the true basis period.

(5) In any case where—

    (*a*) new expenditure is incurred by any person on the provision of machinery or plant for the purposes of mineral exploration and access, as defined in paragraph 1 of Schedule 13 to this Act, and
    (*b*) that expenditure is so incurred before the first day on which that person begins to carry on a trade of mineral extraction, and
    (*c*) on that first day the machinery or plant belongs to him, and does not fall within paragraph 5 (1) (*d*) of Schedule 13 to this Act,

that person shall be treated for the purposes of Chapter I of Part III of the Finance Act 1971 (the normal code applicable to machinery or plant) and section 57 of the Finance Act 1985 (short-life assets) as if he had sold the machinery or plant immediately before that first day and had on that first day incurred capital expenditure on the provision of the machinery or plant wholly and exclusively for the purposes of the trade, being expenditure equal to the expenditure incurred (or, where there has been an actual previous sale and re-acquisition, last incurred) as mentioned in paragraph (*a*) above.

(6) For the purpose of the application of Chapter I of Part III of the Finance Act 1971—

    (*a*) in relation to expenditure treated by virtue of subsection (5) above as incurred on the first day on which a person begins to carry on a trade of mineral extraction, and
    (*b*) in relation to expenditure actually incurred on or after that day on the provision of machinery or plant for the purposes of mineral exploration and access,

that Chapter shall have effect subject to the amendments in subsection (7) below.

(7) . . .

(8) In this section—

    "new expenditure" means, subject to Schedule 14 to this Act, expenditure incurred on or after 1st April 1986;

"old expenditure" means expenditure which is not new expenditure; and
"trade of mineral extraction" has the meaning assigned to it by paragraph 1 of Schedule 13 to this Act.

(9) In consequence of and in connection with the provisions of this section and Parts I to IV of Schedule 13, the amendments in Part V of that Schedule shall have effect.

Note.—Sub-s. (7) amends FA 1971, ss. 44, 50 and Sch. 8, para. 7.

56. Agricultural land and buildings

(1) With respect to capital expenditure incurred on or after 1st April 1986, other than expenditure under existing contracts, the provisions of Schedule 15 to this Act shall have effect in place of section 68 of the Capital Allowances Act 1968 (allowances for capital expenditure on construction of agricultural buildings and works etc.).

(2) In subsection (1) above "expenditure under existing contracts" means expenditure which—

(a) consists of the payment of sums under a contract entered into on or before 13th March 1984 by the person incurring the expenditure; and
(b) is incurred before 1st April 1987.

(3) The preceding provisions of this section and Schedule 15 to this Act shall be construed as if they were included in Part I of the Capital Allowances Act 1968 [and section 4 (11) of and Chapter VI of Part I of the Capital Allowances Act 1968 shall apply in relation to Schedule 15 as they apply in relation to section 68 of that Act][2].

(4) ...

(5) Where an allowance is or has been made under Schedule 15 to this Act in respect of any capital expenditure, none of that expenditure shall be taken into account in determining qualifying expenditure for the purpose of any allowance or charge under section 44 of the Finance Act 1971 (machinery and plant); and where such an allowance or charge is or has been made by reference to an amount of qualifying expenditure which took account of a particular amount of capital expenditure, that capital expenditure shall be left out of account for the purposes of Schedule 15 of this Act.[3]

(6) Any reference to Chapter V of Part I of the Capital Allowances Act 1968 in—

(a) section 14 of that Act (exclusion of double allowances), and
(b) section 85 of that Act (allowances in respect of contributions to capital expenditure), and
(c) paragraph 11 of Schedule 12 to the Finance Act 1982 (capital allowances for dwelling-houses let on assured tenancies),

includes a reference to Schedule 15 to this Act; and the reference to section 68 of the said Act of 1968 in section 75 thereof (writing-down allowances during a period of specified length) includes a reference to that Schedule.

(7) In the following provisions—

(a) ...[1]
(b) ...[1]
(c) section 31 (2) of the Capital Gains Tax Act 1979, and
(d) the definition of "capital allowance" in subsection (4) of section 34 of the said Act of 1979,

any reference to the Capital Allowances Act 1968 or to Part I thereof includes a reference to Schedule 15 to this Act.

Note.—Sub-s. (4) amends CAA 1968, s. 69.
Amendments.—[1] Sub-s. (7) (a), (b) repealed by TA 1988, Sch. 31.
[2] Words in sub-s. (3) added by FA 1989, Sch.13, para. 25.
[3] Sub-s. (5) superseded by FA 1989, Sch. 13, para. 28 (1)–(4) and repealed by FA 1989, Sch. 13, para. 28 (5) (f), (6) and Sch. 17, Pt. VI in relation to any chargeable period or its basis period ending after 26 July 1989.

57. New expenditure on leased assets etc.

(1) The provisions of subsections (4) to (8) below and Schedule 16 to this Act (which relate to allowances in respect of expenditure on the provision of machinery or plant for leasing

and on the provision of certain vehicles) shall have effect with respect to new expenditure, as defined in subsections (2) and (3) below.

(2) In this section and Schedule 16 to this Act, new expenditure means expenditure incurred on or after 1st April 1986, other than—

(a) expenditure to which, by virtue of sub-paragraph (2) of paragraph 2 of Schedule 12 to the Finance Act 1984 (expenditure incurred under contracts entered into on or before 13th March 1984), sub-paragraph (1) of that paragraph (progressive withdrawal of first-year allowances) does not apply; and
(b) expenditure to which, by virtue of paragraph 4 of that Schedule (transitional relief for regional projects) Part I of that Schedule does not apply; and
(c) expenditure falling within paragraph 7 of Schedule 12 to the Finance Act 1980 (television sets, etc.); and
(d) expenditure excluded by subsection (3) below;

and any expenditure which, by virtue of paragraph 6 of Schedule 12 to the Finance Act 1984 (spreading of expenditure under certain contracts) is deemed for the purposes of Chapter I of Part III of the Finance Act 1971 to be incurred on 1st April 1986 shall also be deemed to be incurred on that date for the purposes of this section and Schedule 16 to this Act.

(3) In any case where—

(a) before 1st April 1986 a person (in this subsection referred to as "the original lessor") incurred expenditure on the provision of machinery or plant for leasing, and
(b) on or after that date the machinery or plant ceases to belong to the original lessor on being acquired by an associate or successor of his, and
(c) by virtue of subsection (9) of section 64 of the Finance Act 1980 (connected persons etc.), the machinery or plant is treated for the purposes of subsection (8) of that section (the requisite period) as continuing to belong to the original lessor so long as it belongs to his associate or successor,

expenditure incurred by his associate or successor on the acquisition of the machinery or plant is excluded from new expenditure; and in this subsection "associate or successor" means a person who, in relation to the original lessor, is of a description specified in paragraph (a) or paragraph (b) of the said subsection (9).

(4) Subject to subsection (7) below, the separate pooling provisions which are contained in sections 64 to 68 of the Finance Act 1980 and which are applicable to expenditure on machinery or plant which is not used for a qualifying purpose shall not apply to new expenditure but, for the purpose of maintaining a separate pool for expenditure falling within section 70 of the Finance Act 1982 (assets leased outside the United Kingdom) and for excluding from that section certain ships, aircraft and transport containers,—

(a) sections 64 to 68 of the Finance Act 1980 shall have effect as amended by Part I of Schedule 16 to this Act;
(b) section 70 of, and Schedule 11 to, the Finance Act 1982 shall have effect as amended by Part II of that Schedule; and
(c) Part III of that Schedule shall have effect for supplementing the enactments amended by Parts I and II of that Schedule.

(5) In consequence of the preceding provisions of this section, in paragraph 8A of Schedule 8 to the Finance Act 1971 (writing-down allowances for ships) sub-paragraph (9) shall be omitted.

(6) In consequence of the preceding provisions of this section, but subject to subsection (7) below, in subsection (6) (b) of section 57 of the Finance Act 1985 (short-life assets: transfer of expenditure on asset beginning to be used otherwise than for a qualifying purpose)—

(a) the words "(as it has effect in accordance with section 65 of the Finance Act 1980)" shall be omitted; and
(b) for the words from "the separate trade" onwards there shall be substituted "his actual trade".

(7) Notwithstanding anything in the preceding provisions of this section, section 44 of the Finance Act 1971 shall continue to apply separately with respect to expenditure on the provision of any vehicle falling within section 69 of the Finance Act 1980 (writing-down allowances for cars) and, accordingly,—

(a) except where such a vehicle is used for the purpose of being leased to such a person as is referred to in paragraphs (a) and (b) of subsection (1) of section 70 of the Finance Act 1982 and the leasing is not short-term leasing, within the meaning of that section, nothing in Parts I to III of Schedule 16 to this Act applies with respect to any such expenditure; and

(b) the amendments made by subsection (6) above do not apply where the asset in question is a vehicle falling within section 69 of the Finance Act 1980.

(8) In consequence of the withdrawal of first-year allowances by section 58 of, and Schedule 12 to, the Finance Act 1984, section 69 of the Finance Act 1980 shall be amended, with respect to new expenditure, in accordance with Part IV of Schedule 16 to this Act.

(9) In section 64 of the Finance Act 1980, as it has effect where—

(a) the expenditure on the provision of machinery or plant referred to in subsection (1) of that section is not new expenditure, but

(b) the notional purchase of the machinery or plant by the lessee which is referred to in subsection (2) (a) of that section would at any time mean the incurring of new expenditure,

after the words "could have been made to the lessee" there shall be inserted "(disregarding for this purpose paragraph 2 of Schedule 12 to the Finance Act 1984)".

(10) . . .

Note.—Sub-s. (10) amends FA 1985, s. 56 (1).

CHAPTER III

CAPITAL GAINS

58. Gifts into dual resident trusts

(1) This section applies where there is or has been a disposal of an asset to the trustees of a settlement in such circumstances that, on a claim for relief, section [126 or 147A of the Capital Gains Tax Act 1979 (relief][2] for gifts) applies, or would but for this section apply, so as to reduce the amounts of the chargeable gain and the consideration referred to in [subsection (3)][2] of that section.

(2) In this section—

(a) "a relevant disposal" means such a disposal as is referred to in subsection (1) above; ...[3]

(b) ...[3]

(3) Relief under [section 126 or 147A of the Capital Gains Tax Act 1979][2] shall not be available on a relevant disposal occurring on or after 18th March 1986 if—

(a) at the material time the trustees to whom the disposal is made fall to be treated, under section 52 of the Capital Gains Tax Act 1979, as resident and ordinarily resident in the United Kingdom, although the general administration of the trust is ordinarily carried on outside the United Kingdom; and

(b) on a notional disposal of the asset concerned occurring immediately after the material time, the trustees would be regarded for the purposes of any double taxation relief arrangements—

(i) as resident in a territory outside the United Kingdom; and

(ii) as not liable in the United Kingdom to tax on a gain arising on that disposal.

(4) In subsection (3) above—

(a) "the material time" means the time of the relevant disposal;

(b) a "notional disposal" means a disposal by the trustees of the asset which was the subject of the relevant disposal; and

(c) "double taxation relief arrangements" means arrangements having effect by virtue of section [788 or 789 of the Taxes Act 1988][1] (as extended to capital gains tax by section 10 of the Capital Gains Tax Act 1979).

(5) In any case where—

(a) relief under [section 126 or 147A of the Capital Gains Tax Act 1979][2] has been allowed on a claim relating to a relevant disposal (whether occurring before, on or after 18th March 1986), and

(b) at a time subsequent to that relevant disposal, but not earlier than 18th March 1986, the circumstances become such that paragraphs (a) and (b) of subsection (3) above would apply if that time were the material time referred to in that subsection, and

(c) section 79 of the Finance Act 1981 (which provides for the recovery of relief under [section 126 or 147A of the Capital Gains Tax Act 1979][2] in the event of the emigration of the donee) has not had effect in relation to the relevant disposal before that time and would not (apart from this subsection) have effect at that time,

section 79 of the Finance Act 1981 shall have effect as if, at that time, the trustees had become neither resident nor ordinarily resident in the United Kingdom.

Amendments.—[1] Words in sub-s. (4) (c) substituted by TA 1988, Sch. 29, para. 32 Table.
[2] Words in sub-ss. (1), (3), (5) (a), (c) substituted by FA 1989, s. 124 (2), (3) and Sch. 14, para. 6 (5) in relation to disposals after 13 March 1989, subject to certain exceptions; see FA 1989, s. 124 (3).
[3] Sub-s. (2) (b) and the preceding word "and" repealed by *ibid.* and Sch. 17, Pt. VII, subject to certain exceptions; see FA 1989, Sch. 17, Pt. VII, Note 7.

PART IV

STAMP DUTY RESERVE TAX

The principal charge

92. Repayment or cancellation of tax

(1) ...

(2) If any of the tax charged has been paid, and a claim for repayment is made within the period of six years mentioned in subsection (1) above, the tax paid shall be repaid; and where the tax paid is not less than £25 it shall be repaid with interest on it at the [rate applicable under section 178 of the Finance Act 1989][2] from [the date on which the payment was made until the order for repayment is issued][3].

(3) ...

(4) ...

[(4A) Interest paid under subsection (2) above shall not constitute income for any tax purposes.][1]

(5) ...

Note.—"tax" in the above provisions means stamp duty reserve tax.
Sub-ss. (1), (3), (4), (5) are outside the scope of this work; but see Orange Book.
Amendments.—[1] Sub-s. (4A) inserted by FA 1987, Sch. 7, para. 7 and is deemed always to have had effect.
[2] Words in sub-s. (2) substituted by FA 1989, s. 179 (1) (f).
[3] Words in sub-s. (2) substituted by FA 1989, s. 180 (5).

PART V

INHERITANCE TAX

100. Capital transfer tax to be known as inheritance tax

(1) On and after the passing of this Act, the tax charged under the Capital Transfer Tax Act 1984 (in this Part of this Act referred to as "the 1984 Act") shall be known as inheritance tax and, accordingly, on and after that passing,—

(*a*) the 1984 Act may be cited as the Inheritance Tax Act 1984; and

(*b*) subject to subsection (2) below, any reference to capital transfer tax in the 1984 Act, in any other enactment passed before or in the same Session as this Act or in any document executed, made, served or issued on or before the passing of this Act or at any time thereafter shall have effect as a reference to inheritance tax.

(2) Subsection (1) (*b*) above does not apply where the reference to capital transfer tax relates to a liability to tax arising before the passing of this Act.

(3) In the following provisions of this Part of this Act, any reference to tax except where it is a reference to a named tax is a reference to inheritance tax and, in so far as it occurs in a provision which relates to a time before the passing of this Act, includes a reference to capital transfer tax.

PART VII

MISCELLANEOUS AND SUPPLEMENTARY

114. Short title, interpretation, construction and repeals

(1) This Act may be cited as the Finance Act 1986.

(2) In this Act "the Taxes Act" means the Income and Corporation Taxes Act [1970 and "the Taxes Act 1988" means the Income and Corporation Taxes Act 1988][1].

(3) Part II of this Act, so far as it relates to income tax, shall be construed as one with the Income Tax Acts, so far as it relates to corporation tax, shall be construed as one with the Corporation Tax Acts and, so far as it relates to capital gains tax, shall be construed as one with the Capital Gains Tax Act 1979.

(4) ...

(5) ...

(6) The enactments and Orders specified in Schedule 23 to this Act are hereby repealed to the extent specified in the third column of that Schedule, but subject to any provision at the end of any Part of that Schedule.

Note.—Sub-ss. (4), (5) are not relevant to this work.
Amendments.—[1] Words in sub-s. (2) substituted by TA 1988, Sch. 29, para. 32 Table.

SCHEDULE 13

Section 55

MINERAL EXTRACTION: THE NEW CODE OF RELIEFS

Cross references.—See FA 1985, s. 56 (8) (rules to determine when capital expenditure is to be taken to be incurred for the purposes of this Schedule with respect to any chargeable period or its basis period ending after 26 July 1989);
FA 1989, Sch. 13, para. 28 (1), (4) (*f*), (6) (exclusion of double allowances in relation to any chargeable period or its basis period ending after July 1989; where an allowance is made in respect of capital expenditure under this Schedule, no allowance to be made under any other legislation).

PART I
PRELIMINARY

Defined terms

1.—(1) In this Schedule—

"development" and "development order" have the meaning assigned to them by the relevant planning enactment;

"mineral asset" means any mineral deposits or land comprising mineral deposits, or any interest in or right over such deposits or land;

"mineral exploration and access" means searching for or discovering and testing the mineral deposits of any source or winning access to any such deposits;

"planning permission" has the meaning assigned to it by the relevant planning enactment;

"pre-trading expenditure on machinery or plant" shall be construed in accordance with paragraph 5 below;

"pre-trading exploration expenditure" shall be construed in accordance with paragraph 6 below;

"qualifying expenditure" shall be construed in accordance with Parts II and IV of this Schedule;

"the relevant planning enactment" means—

(*a*) in relation to land in England and Wales, section 290 (1) of the Town and Country Planning Act 1971;
(*b*) in relation to land in Scotland, section 275 (1) of the Town and Country Planning (Scotland) Act 1972; and
(*c*) in relation to land in Northern Ireland, Article 2 (2) of the Planning (Northern Ireland) Order 1972;

"source of mineral deposits" includes a mine, an oil well and a source of geothermal energy; and

"trade of mineral extraction" means a trade which consists of or includes the working of a source of mineral deposits.

(2) Any reference in this Schedule to mineral deposits is a reference to mineral deposits of a wasting nature and, in the case of a mineral asset which consists of or includes an interest in or right over mineral deposits or land, the asset shall not be regarded as situated in the United Kingdom unless the deposits or land are or is so situated.

(3) Any reference in this Schedule to assets representing any expenditure includes, in relation to expenditure on mineral exploration and access, any results obtained from any search, exploration or inquiry upon which the expenditure was incurred.

(4) Any reference in this Schedule to a chargeable period or its basis period is a reference to a chargeable period or, as the case may be, basis period beginning (or treated by virtue of section 55 of this Act as beginning) on or after 1st April 1986.

Application of Capital Allowances Act 1968 etc.

2.—(1) Chapter VI of Part I of the Capital Allowances Act 1968 (miscellaneous and general) applies for the purposes of this Schedule as if it were included in Chapter III of that Part.

(2) In section 77 (4) of that Act, any reference to a specific provision of that Act includes a reference to Parts II to IV of this Schedule.

(3) . . .

(4) The provisions of this Schedule apply in relation to a share in an asset of any description as, by virtue of the application of section 87 (4) of that Act, they apply to a part of an asset; and, for the purposes of those provisions, a share in an asset of any description shall be deemed to be used for the purposes of a trade so long as, and only so long as, the asset is used for those purposes.

(5) In the following provisions—

(a) ...[1]
(b) ...[1]
(c) section 31 (2) of the Capital Gains Tax Act 1979, and
(d) the definition of "capital allowance" in subsection (4) of section 34 of the said Act of 1979,

any reference to the Capital Allowances Act 1968 or to Part I thereof includes a reference to Part III of this Schedule.

Note.—Sub-para. (3) amends CAA 1968, s. 87 (1).
Amendments.—[1] Sub-para. (5) (a), (b) repealed by TA 1988, Sch. 31.

Time when expenditure is incurred

3.—(1) For the purposes of this Schedule, expenditure incurred for the purposes of a trade by a person about to carry it on shall be treated as if it had been incurred by him on the first day on which he does carry it on.

(2) Without prejudice to sub-paragraph (1) above, pre-trading expenditure on machinery or plant and pre-trading exploration expenditure shall be treated for the purposes of Part III of this Schedule as incurred on the first day on which the person who incurred the expenditure carries on a trade of mineral extraction.

PART II
QUALIFYING EXPENDITURE

General provisions

4.—(1) Subject to sub-paragraphs (2) to (5) below, in relation to a person carrying on a trade of mineral extraction, the following capital expenditure is qualifying expenditure, namely,—

(a) expenditure on mineral exploration and access;
(b) expenditure on the acquisition of a mineral asset;
(c) expenditure on the construction of any works in connection with the working of a source of mineral deposits, being works which, when the source is no longer worked, are likely to be of little or no value to the person working it immediately before that time; and
(d) where a source of mineral deposits is worked under a foreign concession, expenditure on the construction of works which, when the concession comes to an end, are likely to become valueless to the person working the source immediately before that time.

(2) Where expenditure falling within sub-paragraph (1) (a) above is incurred by any person before he begins to carry on a trade of mineral extraction, it shall not be qualifying expenditure except to the extent that paragraph 5 or paragraph 6 below provides.

(3) Part IV of this Schedule shall have effect to limit in certain cases the amount of expenditure which is qualifying expenditure.

(4) Except as provided by paragraph 5 below, expenditure on the provision of machinery or plant or on any asset which has been treated for any chargeable period as machinery or plant is not qualifying expenditure.

(5) The following expenditure is not qualifying expenditure by virtue of this paragraph—

(a) any expenditure on the acquisition of the site of any such works as are referred to in sub-paragraph (1) above, or of rights in or over any such site;
(b) any expenditure on works constructed wholly or mainly for subjecting the raw product of a source to any process, except a process designed for preparing the raw product for use as such;
(c) any expenditure on buildings or structures provided for occupation by or for the welfare of workers;
(d) any expenditure on a building where the whole of the building was constructed for use as an office; and
(e) any expenditure on so much of a building or structure as was constructed for use as an office, unless the capital expenditure on the construction of the part of the building or

structure constructed for use as an office was not more than one-tenth of the capital expenditure incurred on the construction of the whole building or structure.

(6) Where a person carrying on a trade of mineral extraction incurs expenditure on seeking any planning permission necessary to enable any mineral exploration and access to be undertaken at any place or any mineral deposits to be worked and that permission is not granted, the expenditure shall be treated for the purposes of this Schedule as expenditure on mineral exploration and access; and in this sub-paragraph "seeking", in relation to planning permission, includes not only making any necessary application but also pursuing any appeal against a refusal of permission.

(7) In so far as any provision of this Schedule or of any other enactment is expressed to be about expenditure falling within sub-paragraph (1) (*a*) above or sub-paragraph (1) (*b*) above—

(*a*) expenditure on the acquisition of, or of rights in or over, the site of a source, and
(*b*) expenditure on the acquisition of, or of rights in or over, mineral deposits,

shall be treated as falling within sub-paragraph (1) (*b*) above and not within sub-paragraph (1) (*a*) above.

Cross references.—See TA 1988, s. 87 (7) (allowance in respect of expenditure on the acquisition of a mineral asset in taxing premiums in respect of land).

Pre-trading expenditure on machinery or plant which is sold etc.

5.—(1) This paragraph applies where—

(*a*) capital expenditure is incurred by any person on the provision of machinery or plant; and
(*b*) that expenditure falls within paragraph 4 (1) (*a*) above; and
(*c*) that expenditure is so incurred before he begins to carry on a trade of mineral extraction; and
(*d*) before he begins to carry on that trade, the machinery or plant is sold, demolished, destroyed or abandoned.

(2) Where this paragraph applies and there is such an excess of expenditure as is referred to in sub-paragraph (3) below, then, for the purposes of this Schedule the person concerned shall be treated as incurring qualifying expenditure equal to that excess on the first day on which he begins to carry on a trade of mineral extraction; and that qualifying expenditure is in this Schedule referred to as pre-trading expenditure on machinery or plant.

(3) Subject to sub-paragraph (4) below, the excess referred to in sub-paragraph (2) above is the amount by which the capital expenditure referred to in sub-paragraph (1) above exceeds any sale, insurance, salvage or compensation moneys resulting from the event mentioned in paragraph (*d*) of that sub-paragraph.

(4) If, in a case where this paragraph applies, the mineral exploration and access at the source in connection with which the machinery or plant was used ceased before the first day referred to in sub-paragraph (2) above, any capital expenditure which was incurred more than six years before that day shall be left out of account in determining the amount of any excess under sub-paragraph (3) above.

Pre-trading exploration expenditure

6.—(1) This paragraph applies to capital expenditure which—

(*a*) is incurred by any person on mineral exploration and access at any source, and
(*b*) is so incurred before he begins to carry on a trade of mineral extraction, and
(*c*) is not incurred on the provision of machinery or plant.

(2) Where this paragraph applies to any capital expenditure and the mineral exploration and access is continuing at the source in question at the time when the person concerned begins to carry on a trade of mineral extraction, so much of the expenditure as exceeds any relevant capital sum received by him is qualifying expenditure.

(3) Where this paragraph applies to any capital expenditure and the mineral exploration and access has ceased at the source in question before the time when the person concerned begins to carry on a trade of mineral extraction, so much of that expenditure as was incurred within the six years ending at that time and exceeds any relevant capital sum received by him shall be treated as qualifying expenditure incurred on the first day on which he begins to carry on that trade.

(4) In relation to capital expenditure to which this paragraph applies, a relevant capital sum is a capital sum—

(a) which is received by the person incurring the expenditure before he begins to carry on a trade of mineral extraction; and

(b) which is or, as the case may be, to the extent to which it is reasonably attributable to the incurring of the expenditure at the source in question.

(5) Expenditure which is qualifying expenditure by virtue of sub-paragraph (2) or sub-paragraph (3) above is in this Schedule referred to as pre-trading exploration expenditure.

Contributions by mining concerns to public services etc. outside the United Kingdom

7.—(1) Subject to sub-paragraphs (2) and (3) below, expenditure incurred by a person carrying on a trade of mineral extraction outside the United Kingdom and consisting of contributions of capital sums to the cost of—

(a) buildings to be occupied by persons employed at or in connection with the working of a source outside the United Kingdom, or

(b) works for the supply of water, gas or electricity wholly or mainly to buildings occupied or to be occupied by persons so employed, or

(c) works to be used in providing other services or facilities wholly or mainly for the welfare of persons so employed or their dependants,

is by virtue of this paragraph qualifying expenditure.

(2) Expenditure incurred by any person as mentioned in sub-paragraph (1) above is not qualifying expenditure unless—

(a) it is incurred for the purposes of his trade of mineral extraction; and

(b) when the source in question is no longer worked, the buildings or works concerned are likely to be of little or no value to the person working the source immediately before that time.

(3) Sub-paragraph (1) above does not apply—

(a) to expenditure resulting in the acquisition of an asset by the person incurring the expenditure; nor

(b) to expenditure in respect of which an allowance may be made under any provision of the Tax Acts (other than this Schedule, section 61 of the Capital Allowances Act 1968 or any enactment which was re-enacted by that section).

Restoration expenditure

8.—(1) Where a person who has ceased to carry on a trade of mineral extraction incurs expenditure on the restoration of the site of a source to the working of which that trade related and all or any of that expenditure—

(a) is incurred within the period of three years immediately following the last day on which he carried on that trade, and

(b) has not been deducted for the purposes of corporation tax or income tax in relation to that or any other trade carried on by him, and

(c) is expenditure which, if it had been incurred while that trade was being carried on, either would have been qualifying expenditure by virtue of any of the preceding provisions of this Part of this Schedule or would have been allowable as a deduction in computing the profits or gains from that trade,

so much of that expenditure as falls within paragraphs (a) to (c) above and does not exceed the net cost of the restoration of the site shall be qualifying expenditure by virtue of this paragraph and shall be treated as incurred by him on the last day on which he carried on that trade.

(2) Any reference in this paragraph to the site of a source includes a reference to land used in connection with the working of the source.

(3) In this paragraph "restoration" includes landscaping and—

(a) in relation to land in the United Kingdom, the carrying out of any works required by a condition subject to which planning permission for development consisting of the winning and working of minerals was granted; and

(b) in relation to land outside the United Kingdom, the carrying out of any works required by any equivalent condition imposed under the law of the territory in which the land is situated.

(4) For the purpose of this paragraph, the net cost to any person of the restoration of the site of a source is the excess, if any, of expenditure falling within paragraphs (*a*) to (*c*) of sub-paragraph (1) above over any receipts which—

(*a*) are attributable to the restoration (whether for spoil or other assets removed from the site or for tipping rights or otherwise); and
(*b*) are received within the period of three years immediately following the last day on which the person concerned carried on a trade of mineral extraction.

(5) As respects the person by whom is incurred any expenditure which is qualifying expenditure by virtue of this paragraph,—

(*a*) expenditure falling within paragraphs (*a*) to (*c*) of sub-paragraph (1) above (not only so much of it as constitutes qualifying expenditure) shall not be deductible in computing his income for any purpose of income tax or corporation tax; and
(*b*) to the extent that any receipts are, under sub-paragraph (4) above, taken into account to determine the net cost of the restoration of the site of a source, those receipts shall not constitute income of his for any purpose of income tax or corporation tax.

(6) All such adjustments shall be made, whether by way of discharge or repayment of tax or otherwise, as may be required in consequence of the preceding provisions of this paragraph.

PART III
ALLOWANCES AND CHARGES

Cross references.—See TA 1988, s. 87 (7) (allowance in respect of expenditure on the acquisition of a mineral asset in taxing premiums in respect of land).

Writing-down and balancing allowances

9.—(1) Allowances shall be made in accordance with this paragraph to a person who carries on a trade of mineral extraction in respect of qualifying expenditure incurred by him for the purposes of that trade.

(2) Subject to sub-paragraph (4) below, for the chargeable period related to the incurring of the expenditure, there shall be made to the person incurring it an allowance equal to the appropriate percentage of the excess (if any) of that expenditure over any disposal receipts which he is required to bring into account by reference to that expenditure for that chargeable period.

(3) Subject to sub-paragraph (4) below, for each of the chargeable periods following that related to the incurring of the expenditure, there shall be made to the person incurring it an allowance equal to the appropriate percentage of the excess (if any) of that expenditure over the aggregate of—

(*a*) the allowances made in respect of the expenditure for earlier chargeable periods by virtue of sub-paragraph (2) above and this sub-paragraph; and
(*b*) any disposal receipts which he is or was required to bring into account by reference to that expenditure for the chargeable period in question and any earlier chargeable periods.

(4) For a chargeable period for which, in accordance with paragraph 12 below, a balancing allowance falls to be made to any person in respect of any expenditure, sub-paragraph (2), or, as the case may be, sub-paragraph (3) above shall have effect with the omission of the words "the appropriate percentage of".

(5) Subject to sub-paragraph (6) below, in relation to expenditure which is qualifying expenditure falling within paragraph 4, paragraph 7 or paragraph 8 above, other than expenditure falling within paragraph 4 (1) (*b*), the appropriate percentage is 25 and, in relation to all other qualifying expenditure, the appropriate percentage is 10.

(6) If a chargeable period or its basis period is part only of a year or if the period is a year of assessment but the trade has been carried on for part only of it, the percentage appropriate under sub-paragraph (5) above shall be correspondingly reduced.

Disposal receipts

10.—(1) In any case where—

(*a*) qualifying expenditure has been incurred by any person on the provision of any assets (including the construction of any works), and
(*b*) in any chargeable period or its basis period any of those assets is disposed of or otherwise permanently ceases (whether because of the discontinuance of the trade or for any other reason) to be used by him for the purposes of a trade of mineral extraction,

he shall bring into account as a disposal receipt in respect of that expenditure for the chargeable period related to the disposal or, as the case may be, cessation the disposal value of any asset falling within paragraph (*b*) above.

(2) If, at any time after a mineral asset has been acquired by any person, it begins to be used (by him or any other person) in a way which constitutes development but is neither existing permitted development nor development for the purposes of a trade of mineral extraction carried on by him, the asset shall be treated as having permanently ceased, immediately before that time, to be used by him for the purposes of that trade; and for the purposes of this sub-paragraph, "existing permitted development" means—

    (*a*) development which, prior to the acquisition, had been or had begun to be lawfully carried out; and
    (*b*) any other development for which planning permission is granted by a development order made as a general order and in force at the time of the acquisition;

and sub-paragraph (3) of paragraph 16 below applies for the purposes of this sub-paragraph as it applies for the purposes of sub-paragraph (2) of that paragraph.

(3) Subject to paragraph 18 below, subsections (6) and (7) of section 44 of the Finance Act 1971 (disposal value of machinery or plant) shall apply to determine the disposal value of any asset falling within sub-paragraph (1) above, substituting a reference to that asset for any reference in those subsections to machinery or plant.

(4) In any case where—

    (*a*) qualifying expenditure has been incurred by any person, and
    (*b*) in any chargeable period or its basis period he receives any capital sum which, in whole or in part, it is reasonable to attribute to that expenditure, and
    (*c*) that capital sum does not fall to be brought into account as a disposal receipt by virtue of sub-paragraph (1) above,

he shall bring into account as a disposal receipt in respect of that expenditure for the chargeable period related to the receipt of that capital sum so much of it as is reasonably attributable to the expenditure.

Balancing charges: excess of allowances and disposal receipts over expenditure

11.—(1) If, for any chargeable period for which a person is required to bring into account a disposal receipt in respect of qualifying expenditure incurred by him, the aggregate of—

    (*a*) the disposal receipts in respect of that expenditure which he is required to bring into account for that period, and
    (*b*) any disposal receipts in respect of that expenditure which he was required to bring into account for earlier chargeable periods, and
    (*c*) the net amount of the allowances made to him for earlier chargeable periods under paragraph 9 above in respect of that expenditure,

exceeds the expenditure concerned, there shall be made on him a charge (in this Part of this Schedule referred to as a "balancing charge".)

(2) In relation to any qualifying expenditure, the amount on which a balancing charge is made for a chargeable period shall be whichever is the less of—

    (*a*) the amount by which the aggregate referred to in sub-paragraph (1) above exceeds the expenditure; and
    (*b*) the net amount of the allowances made as mentioned in paragraph (*c*) of that sub-paragraph.

(3) In relation to any chargeable period, the net amount of the allowances made to any person for earlier chargeable periods under paragraph 9 above in respect of expenditure incurred by him means the total of those allowances less the total of the amounts on which balancing charges have been made on him for earlier chargeable periods, being charges arising by reason of his bringing into account disposal receipts in respect of that expenditure.

Occasions of balancing allowances

12.—(1) For the chargeable period related to the permanent discontinuance of a trade of mineral extraction, any allowance to which the person carrying on that trade is entitled under paragraph 9 above in respect of qualifying expenditure incurred by him for the purposes of that trade shall be a balancing allowance.

(2) If in any chargeable period or its basis period a person carrying on a trade of mineral

extraction permanently ceases to work particular mineral deposits (and sub-paragraph (1) above does not apply in respect of that period) any allowance to which he is entitled under paragraph 9 above in respect of—

(*a*) expenditure on mineral exploration and access which relates solely to those deposits, or
(*b*) expenditure on the acquisition of a mineral asset which consists of those deposits or any part of them,

shall be a balancing allowance.

(3) Where a person carrying on a trade of mineral extraction is for the time being entitled to two or more mineral assets which at any time were comprised in a single mineral asset or were otherwise derived from a single mineral asset, sub-paragraph (2) above shall not apply until such time as he permanently ceases to work the deposits comprised in all the mineral assets concerned taken together and, for this purpose, where a mineral asset relates to, but does not actually consist of mineral deposits, the deposits to which the asset relates shall be treated as comprised in the asset.

(4) If, in a case where sub-paragraph (1) of paragraph 10 above applies, neither sub-paragraph (1) nor sub-paragraph (2) above has effect in relation to the expenditure referred to in sub-paragraph (1) (*a*) of that paragraph, then for the chargeable period related to the disposal or cessation referred to in sub-paragraph (1) (*b*) of that paragraph, any allowance in respect of that expenditure shall be a balancing allowance.

(5) In relation to pre-trading expenditure on machinery or plant and pre-trading exploration expenditure falling within paragraph 6 (3) above, any allowance under paragraph 9 above shall be a balancing allowance.

(6) If in any chargeable period or its basis period a person who has incurred qualifying expenditure on mineral exploration and access (including pre-trading exploration expenditure falling within paragraph 6 (2) above) gives up the search, exploration or inquiry to which the expenditure related and does not carry on then or subsequently a trade of mineral extraction which consists of or includes the working of any mineral deposits to which the mineral exploration and access related, any allowance to which he is entitled for that chargeable period under paragraph 9 above in respect of that expenditure shall be a balancing allowance.

(7) In any case where—

(*a*) a person has incurred expenditure consisting of contributions falling within paragraph 7 above to the cost of any buildings or works, and
(*b*) in any chargeable period or its basis period the buildings or works permanently cease to be used for the purposes of, or in connection with, a trade of mineral extraction carried on by him,

then, without prejudice to sub-paragraph (1) above, any allowance to which he is entitled for that chargeable period under paragraph 9 above in respect of that expenditure shall be a balancing allowance.

(8) If in any chargeable period or its basis period any of the following events occurs in relation to assets representing any qualifying expenditure, namely—

(*a*) the person by whom the expenditure was incurred loses possession of the assets in circumstances where it is reasonable to assume that the loss is permanent,
(*b*) the assets cease to exist as such (as a result of destruction, dismantling or otherwise),
(*c*) the assets begin to be used wholly or partly for purposes other than those of the trade of mineral extraction carried on by that person,

any allowance to which that person is entitled for that chargeable period under paragraph 9 above in respect of that expenditure shall be a balancing allowance.

Treatment of qualifying expenditure on mineral exploration and access

13. For the purposes of this Part of this Schedule, where a person is carrying on a trade of mineral extraction, qualifying expenditure incurred by him in connection with that trade (whether before or after the trade began to be carried on) on mineral exploration and access shall be taken to be incurred for the purposes of the trade.

Demolition costs

14.—(1) The net cost to a person of the demolition of an asset representing qualifying expenditure shall, for the purposes of this Part of this Schedule, be added to that qualifying expenditure in determining the amount of any balancing allowance or balancing charge for the chargeable period related to the demolition of the asset.

(2) The cost or net cost to a person of the demolition of any asset shall not, if sub-paragraph (1) applies to it, be treated for the purposes of this Schedule as expenditure incurred in respect of any other asset by which that asset is replaced.

(3) Any reference in this paragraph to the net cost of the demolition of any asset is a reference to the excess (if any) of the cost of the demolition over any moneys received for the remains of the asset.

Manner of making allowances and charges

15. All allowances and charges falling to be made under this Part of this Schedule to or on any person shall be made to or on him in taxing his trade of mineral extraction.

PART IV
LIMITATIONS ON QUALIFYING EXPENDITURE ETC.

Expenditure on the acquisition of land: restriction of qualifying expenditure

16.—(1) In so far as capital expenditure falling within paragraph 4 (1) (*b*) above consists of expenditure on the acquisition of an interest in land (whether in the United Kingdom or elsewhere) and that land includes a source of mineral deposits, so much of that expenditure as is equal to the undeveloped market value of the interest shall not constitute qualifying expenditure.

(2) In relation to the acquisition of an interest in land, the undeveloped market value means the consideration which at the time of the acquisition the interest might reasonably be expected to fetch on a sale in the open market on the assumptions—

(*a*) that there is no source of mineral deposits on or in the land; and
(*b*) that it is and will continue to be unlawful to carry out any development of the land other than—

(i) development which, at the time of the acquisition, has been or has begun to be lawfully carried out; and
(ii) any other development for which planning permission is granted by a development order which is made as a general order and is in force at that time.

(3) In the application of sub-paragraph (2) above to the acquisition of an interest in land outside the United Kingdom,—

(*a*) any question whether development has been or is being lawfully carried out shall be determined in accordance with the law of the territory in which the land is situated; and
(*b*) any question whether development is of a character for which planning permission is granted by a general development order shall be determined as if the land were situated in England or Wales.

(4) In any case where—

(*a*) the preceding provisions of this paragraph have effect to limit the amount of expenditure falling within paragraph 4 (1) (*b*) above which is qualifying expenditure, and
(*b*) the undeveloped market value of the interest in land in question includes the value of any buildings or other structures on the land, and
(*c*) at the time of the acquisition of the interest in land or at any time thereafter, those buildings or structures cease permanently to be used for any purpose,

then at the time referred to in paragraph (*c*) above, the person who incurred the expenditure referred to in paragraph (*a*) above shall be treated as having incurred qualifying expenditure falling within paragraph 4 (1) (*b*) above equal to the unrelieved value of the buildings or structures referred to in paragraph (*b*) above.

(5) In sub-paragraph (4) above "the unrelieved value" of buildings or structures falling within paragraph (*b*) thereof means the value of those buildings or structures determined as at the date of the acquisition of the interest in land (and without regard to any value properly attributable to the land on which the buildings or structures stand) less the excess of any allowances over balancing charges which the person treated by sub-paragraph (4) above as incurring expenditure has received in respect of the buildings or structures or assets therein under—

(*a*) the Capital Allowances Act 1968;
(*b*) Chapter I of Part III of the Finance Act 1971 (machinery or plant); and

(c) [Schedule 15]¹ to this Act.

(6) References in the preceding provisions of this paragraph to the time of the acquisition of an interest in land are not affected by paragraph 3 of this Schedule.

Amendments.—¹ Words in sub-para. (5) (c) substituted for the words "section 55" by FA 1989, Sch. 13, para. 24 in cases where buildings or structures cease, after 26 July 1989, permanently to be used for any purpose.

17. In any case where—

(a) a person incurs capital expenditure falling within paragraph 4 (1) (b) above on the acquisition of an asset which is or includes an interest in land, and

(b) for chargeable periods previous to the chargeable period for which he first becomes entitled in respect of the expenditure to an allowance under paragraph 9 above, the person incurring the expenditure has been allowed, in respect of that land, any deductions under section [87 of the Taxes Act 1988]¹ (deductions where premiums etc. taxable),

the expenditure shall be treated for the purposes of this Schedule as reduced by so much of those deductions as would have been excluded by subsection [(7) of that section]¹ if the person concerned had been entitled to an allowance under paragraph 9 above (or, as the case may be, section 60 of the Capital Allowances Act 1968) for the previous chargeable periods referred to in sub-paragraph (b) above.

Amendments.—¹ Words substituted by TA 1988, Sch. 29, para. 32 Table.

Restriction of disposal receipts

18.—(1) Where a disposal receipt to be brought into account in respect of any expenditure for a chargeable period would, apart from this paragraph, be the disposal value of an interest in land (determined as mentioned in paragraph 10 (3) above), only so much of that disposal value as exceeds the undeveloped market value of the interest shall constitute a disposal receipt for the purposes of Part III of this Schedule.

(2) Sub-paragraphs (2) and (3) of paragraph 16 above shall apply to determine the undeveloped market value of an interest for the purposes of this paragraph as they would apply in relation to an acquisition of that interest at the time the disposal value falls to be determined.

Assets formerly owned by traders

19.—(1) Subject to sub-paragraph (2) below, paragraph 20 below applies where a person carrying on a trade of mineral extraction (in this paragraph referred to as "the buyer") incurs capital expenditure in acquiring an asset (in this paragraph referred to as "the purchased asset") from another person in circumstances falling within sub-paragraph (3) below.

(2) This paragraph and paragraph 20 below have effect subject to paragraph 22 below, and neither this paragraph, paragraph 20 nor paragraph 22 below applies if—

(a) the purchased asset is a mineral asset situated in the United Kingdom; and

(b) the capital expenditure incurred by the buyer consists of the payment of sums under a contract entered into by him before 16th July 1985.

(3) Subject to sub-paragraph (5) below, the circumstances referred to in sub-paragraph (1) above are—

(a) that, in connection with a trade of mineral extraction carried on by him, the other person referred to in sub-paragraph (1) above incurred expenditure on the acquisition or bringing into existence of the purchased asset; or

(b) that that other person has not incurred expenditure as mentioned in paragraph (a) above but, at any time prior to the buyer's acquisition, the purchased asset was owned by a person who, in connection with a trade of mineral extraction carried on by him, had incurred such expenditure as is mentioned in paragraph (a) above;

and, in a case where the purchased asset is a mineral asset situated in the United Kingdom, the reference in paragraph (b) above to a time prior to the buyer's acquisition does not include any time earlier than 1st April 1986.

(4) In this paragraph "the previous trader" means—

(a) where the circumstances are as mentioned in paragraph (a) of sub-paragraph (3) above, the person referred to in that paragraph; and

(b) where the circumstances are as mentioned in paragraph (b) of that sub-paragraph, the last person who, prior to the buyer's acquisition, incurred such expenditure as is mentioned in paragraph (*a*) thereof;

and, subject to sub-paragraphs (5) and (6) below, any reference in paragraph 20 below to the previous trader's qualifying expenditure is a reference to so much of the expenditure incurred by him on the acquisition or bringing into existence of the purchased asset as constituted his qualifying expenditure for the purposes of this Schedule.

(5) Any reference in sub-paragraphs (3) and (4) above to the purchased asset includes a reference—

(*a*) to two or more assets which together make up the purchased asset; and
(*b*) to an asset from which or, as the case may be, to two or more assets from the combination of which the purchased asset is derived.

(6) Where the previous trader in fact incurred expenditure on the acquisition or bringing into existence of one or more assets from which the purchased asset is derived, so much of that expenditure as was qualifying expenditure of his for the purposes of this Schedule and as it is just and reasonable to attribute to the purchased asset shall be taken to be the previous trader's qualifying expenditure.

Limitation of expenditure on asset by reference to previous acquisition

20.—(1) In this paragraph "the buyer's expenditure" means the capital expenditure incurred by him as mentioned in paragraph 19 (1) above, less any amount of that expenditure which, by virtue of paragraph 16 above, does not constitute qualifying expenditure.

(2) If the previous trader did not become entitled to an allowance or liable to a balancing charge in respect of his qualifying expenditure, so much of the buyer's expenditure as does not exceed the amount of the previous trader's qualifying expenditure shall be the buyer's qualifying expenditure in respect of the acquisition of the purchased asset.

(3) If the previous trader became entitled to an allowance or liable to a balancing charge in respect of his qualifying expenditure, so much of the buyer's expenditure as does not exceed the residue of the previous trader's qualifying expenditure shall be the buyer's qualifying expenditure in respect of the acquisition of the purchased asset.

(4) In relation to the previous trader's qualifying expenditure, the residue referred to in sub-paragraph (3) above is that expenditure—

(*a*) less the total of all allowances made to him in respect of that expenditure; and
(*b*) plus the amount (if any) on which a balancing charge was made in respect of that expenditure.

(5) For the purposes of sub-paragraph (4) above, where the previous trader's qualifying expenditure is an amount attributed to the purchased asset on a just and reasonable basis in accordance with paragraph 19 (6) above, any allowances and any balancing charge made by reference to a greater amount of expenditure shall be apportioned on the like basis.

(6) In this paragraph

"allowance" means an allowance under paragraph 9 above;
"balancing charge" means a balancing charge under paragraph 11 above; and
"the buyer", "the previous trader" and "the purchased asset" have the same meaning as in paragraph 19 above.

Part of expenditure on mineral asset treated as expenditure on mineral exploration and access

21.—(1) This paragraph applies where, in a case falling within sub-paragraph (1) of paragraph 19 above,—

(*a*) the purchased asset is a mineral asset; and
(*b*) part of the value of that asset is attributable to expenditure incurred by the previous trader on mineral exploration and access.

(2) Where this paragraph applies—

(*a*) such part of the buyer's expenditure as it is just and reasonable to attribute to the part of the value referred to in sub-paragraph (1) (*b*) above (being no greater than the amount of the previous trader's expenditure on mineral exploration and access which is properly attributable to that part of the value) shall be treated for the purposes of Parts II and III of this Schedule as expenditure on mineral exploration and access and the remainder shall be treated for those purposes as expenditure on the acquisition of a mineral asset; and

(b) if, under Part II of the Capital Allowances Act 1968 (scientific research) allowances were made to the previous trader in taxing his trade, the existence of these allowances shall not affect the question whether any of his expenditure on the purchased asset was qualifying expenditure.

(3) In this paragraph "the previous trader" and "the purchased asset" have the same meaning as in paragraphs 19 and 20 above, and "the buyer's expenditure" has the same meaning as in paragraph 20 above.

Oil licences etc.

22.—(1) Where a person carrying on a trade of mineral extraction (in this paragraph referred to as "the buyer") incurs capital expenditure falling within paragraph 4 (1) (b) above in acquiring a Petroleum Act licence or any interest in such a licence, only so much of that expenditure as does not exceed the corresponding expenditure of the original licensee shall be the buyer's qualifying expenditure.

(2) In this paragraph a "Petroleum Act licence" means a licence under the Petroleum (Production) Act 1934 or the Petroleum (Production) Act (Northern Ireland) 1964 authorising the winning of oil, as defined in section 1 of the Oil Taxation Act 1975; and in relation to such a licence, "the original licensee" means the person to whom the licence was granted under the enactment in question.

(3) In relation to the acquisition of a Petroleum Act licence "the corresponding expenditure" of the original licensee is the amount of the payment made by him (whether before or after the passing of this Act) to the Secretary of State or, in Northern Ireland, to the Department of Economic Development for the purpose of obtaining the licence, and, in relation to an interest in such a licence, that corresponding expenditure is such portion of the amount of that payment as it is just and reasonable to attribute to that interest.

Transfer of mineral assets within a group

23.—(1) Subject to sub-paragraph (2) below, this paragraph applies where a company (in this paragraph referred to as "the transferee") acquires a mineral asset from another company (in this paragraph referred to as "the transferor") and either—

(a) the transferor has control of the transferee or the transferee has control of the transferor, or

(b) both the transferor and the transferee are under the control of another person.

(2) This paragraph does not apply—

(a) where the acquisition is a sale in respect of which an election is made under paragraph 4 of Schedule 7 to the Capital Allowances Act 1968; nor

(b) where the mineral asset in question is, or is an interest in, a Petroleum Act licence as defined in paragraph 22 above;

but, subject to paragraph (a) above, this paragraph applies notwithstanding anything in paragraph 2 of the said Schedule 7.

(3) Subject to sub-paragraph (4) below, so much (if any) of the capital expenditure incurred by the transferee on the acquisition of the mineral asset as exceeds the capital expenditure incurred by the transferor on the acquisition of the mineral asset by him shall be left out of account for the purposes of this Schedule (and, accordingly, if the transferee is carrying on a trade of mineral extraction, shall not be qualifying expenditure).

(4) Where the mineral asset acquired by the transferee consists of an interest or right granted by the transferor in a mineral asset acquired by him, the reference in sub-paragraph (3) above to the capital expenditure incurred by the transferor on the acquisition of the mineral asset by him shall be construed as a reference to so much of that expenditure as, on a just apportionment, is referable to the interest or right granted by the transferor.

(5) If the transferee is carrying on a trade of mineral extraction and the expenditure incurred by him on the acquisition of the mineral asset is expenditure falling within paragraph 16 above, any reference in that paragraph to the time it was acquired by the transferor or, if there is a sequence of two or more acquisitions each of which falls within sub-paragraph (1) above, the time at which the interest was acquired by the company which was the transferor under the earliest of those acquisitions.

(6) If, in a case where sub-paragraph (5) above applies, there is a sequence of two or more acquisitions each of which falls within sub-paragraph (1) above,—

(a) any expenditure which one of the companies involved in the sequence is treated as incurring under sub-paragraph (4) of paragraph 16 above shall be treated as incurred by the company which is the transferee from that company and by any subsequent transferee company in the sequence; and

(b) the reference in sub-paragraph (5) of that paragraph to the person treated by sub-paragraph (4) thereof as incurring expenditure shall be construed as including a reference to any other company which, under paragraph (a) above, is treated as incurring that expenditure.

Assets formerly owned by non-traders

24. Where a person incurs expenditure on mineral exploration and access and, without having carried on a trade of mineral extraction, he sells any assets representing that expenditure, then, if the person who acquires the assets carries on such a trade, only so much of the price paid by him for the assets as does not exceed the amount of the seller's expenditure which is represented by the assets shall be qualifying expenditure for the purposes of this Schedule.

SCHEDULE 14

Section 55

MINERAL EXTRACTION: OLD EXPENDITURE

Interpretation

1.—(1) In this Schedule—

"mineral asset" and "mineral exploration and access" have the same meaning as in Schedule 13 to this Act;

"new expenditure" and "old expenditure" have the same meaning as in the principal section;

"the new code of allowances" means subsections (5) to (7) of the principal section and Schedule 13 to this Act;

"the old code of allowances" has the same meaning as in the principal section;

"the principal section" means section 55 of this Act;

"the relevant day" means, subject to paragraph 2 below, 1st April 1986;

"trade of mineral extraction" has the same meaning as in Schedule 13 to this Act; and

"the 1968 Act" means the Capital Allowances Act 1968.

(2) In relation to any item of old expenditure "outstanding balance" means, subject to the following provisions of this paragraph,—

(*a*) in the case of old expenditure falling within section 57 of the 1968 Act, so much of that expenditure as, if the old code of allowances had continued in force, would have been the residue of that expenditure in relation to a writing-down allowance under that section to be made for the chargeable period which, or the basis period of which, begins on the relevant day;

(*b*) in the case of old expenditure falling within section 60 of the 1968 Act, the excess referred to in subsection (3) of that section by reference to which, if the old code of allowances had continued in force, a writing-down allowance under that section would fall to be made for the chargeable period referred to in paragraph (*a*) above; and

(*c*) in the case of old expenditure falling within section 61 of the 1968 Act, so much of that expenditure as exceeds any writing-down allowances under that section made in respect of that expenditure for chargeable periods which, or the basis periods of which, ended before the relevant day.

(3) In determining the residue of expenditure mentioned in paragraph (*a*) of sub-paragraph (2) above, it shall be assumed that, in the chargeable period or its basis period referred to in that paragraph, no asset representing expenditure which is qualifying expenditure for the purposes of section 57 of the 1968 Act is sold, demolished or destroyed.

(4) In determining, in relation to the chargeable period referred to in paragraph (*a*) of sub-paragraph (2) above, the excess mentioned in paragraph (*b*) of that sub-paragraph—

(*a*) no account shall be taken of any capital sum accruing in that chargeable period or its basis period to the person to whom a writing-down allowance would fall to be made as mentioned in that paragraph; and

(*b*) it shall be assumed that that person does not cease to work the source in question in that chargeable period or its basis period.

*Election to treat certain post March 1986 expenditure
as old expenditure*

2.—(1) This paragraph applies to expenditure—

(*a*) which is incurred in the year ending 31st March 1987 by a person carrying on a trade of mineral extraction; and

(*b*) which consists of the payment of sums under a contract entered into before 16th July 1985 by the person incurring the expenditure; and

(*c*) in respect of which, but for the provisions of the principal section, an initial allowance would have been made to the person concerned under section 56 of the 1968 Act.

(2) If the person incurring the expenditure so elects, expenditure to which this paragraph applies shall be treated for the purposes of the principal section and Schedule 13 to this Act as not being new expenditure and the old code of allowances shall continue to apply to it until 31st March 1987.

(3) An election under this paragraph—

(a) shall be made in writing to the inspector;
(b) may not be made more than two years after the end of the chargeable period or its basis period in which the expenditure was incurred; and
(c) shall be irrevocable;

and if different parts of the expenditure are incurred at different times, only that part of the expenditure which is first incurred on or after 1st April 1986 shall be taken into account for the purposes of paragraph (b) above.

(4) In relation to expenditure to which an election under this paragraph applies—

(a) subsections (3) and (4) of the principal section shall have effect as if for any reference to 31st March 1986 or 1st April 1986 there were substituted a reference to 31st March 1987 or 1st April 1987 respectively; and
(b) in this Schedule "the relevant day" means 1st April 1987.

Outstanding balances: general rules

3.—(1) If there is an outstanding balance in relation to any item of old expenditure, then, subject to the following provisions of this Schedule, for the purposes of the new code of allowances,—

(a) an amount of expenditure equal to that balance shall be treated as expenditure incurred on the relevant day (and, accordingly, as new expenditure); and
(b) that amount shall be taken to have been incurred for the same purposes as the item of old expenditure was incurred.

(2) If any item of old expenditure was incurred for more than one purpose, then, so far as may be necessary for the application of the new code of allowances, the outstanding balance of that expenditure shall be apportioned to those different purposes in such manner as may be just and reasonable and sub-paragraph (1) above shall apply separately in relation to the apportioned parts as if they were referable to different items of old expenditure.

Old expenditure with no outstanding balance

4.—(1) This paragraph applies to old expenditure—

(a) in respect of which allowances were made under the old code of allowances, and
(b) in respect of which there is no outstanding balance on the relevant day.

(2) Where this paragraph applies, the new code of allowances shall have effect as if—

(a) the whole of the old expenditure had been incurred on the relevant day; and
(b) under the appropriate provisions of the new code of allowances there had been made allowances equal to that expenditure;

and the provisions of the new code about disposal receipts shall have effect accordingly in relation to events happening on or after the relevant day.

Unrelieved expenditure on mineral exploration and access

5.—(1) This paragraph applies to old expenditure incurred on mineral exploration and access.

(2) If, immediately before the relevant day, no allowance had been made in respect of the expenditure under the old code of allowances, and on that day the mineral exploration and access at the source in connection with which the expenditure was incurred has not ceased, and either—

(a) the person by whom the expenditure was incurred began to carry on a trade of mineral extraction before the relevant day, or
(b) on or after the relevant day and before mineral exploration and access ceases at the source in question, the person by whom the expenditure was incurred begins to carry on a trade of mineral extraction,

then, subject to sub-paragraph (3) below, paragraph 5 or paragraph 6 of Schedule 13 to this Act or, as the case may be, subsection (5) of the principal section shall apply as if the expenditure were new expenditure and, if the expenditure was in fact incurred after the person concerned began to carry on a trade of mineral extraction, as if he had not begun to carry on that trade until the relevant day.

(3) Where sub-paragraph (2) above applies to any item of old expenditure which, apart from this sub-paragraph, would not fall to be treated as incurred on or after the relevant

day, it shall (as new expenditure) be treated for the purposes of the new code of allowances as incurred on the relevant day.

Old expenditure on acquisition of mineral asset

6.—(1) This paragraph applies to old expenditure incurred on the acquisition of a mineral asset.

(2) If, immediately before the relevant day, no allowance has been made in respect of the expenditure under the old code of allowances, the expenditure shall be treated for the purposes of the new code of allowances as having been incurred on the relevant day.

(3) Nothing in sub-paragraph (2) above shall affect the time as at which, under paragraph 16 of Schedule 13 to this Act, the undeveloped market value of an interest is to be determined.

(4) If sub-paragraph (2) above does not apply in relation to an item of old expenditure to which this paragraph applies,—

(*a*) paragraph 16 of Schedule 13 to this Act shall not apply in relation to any amount which, by virtue of paragraph 3 (1) above, is to be treated as expenditure incurred on the relevant day (and, accordingly, the whole of any such amount shall be qualifying expenditure for the purposes of the new code of allowances); and

(*b*) in determining the amount of any disposal receipt which, by virtue of paragraph 3 or paragraph 4 above, falls to be brought into account in respect of that expenditure under Part III of Schedule 13 to this Act, paragraph 18 of that Schedule shall not apply (so that no deduction shall be made by reference to the undeveloped market value of the land).

Old expenditure on construction of certain works

7.—(1) This paragraph applies to old expenditure which does not fall within paragraph 5 above but which is incurred—

(*a*) on the construction of any works in connection with the working of a source of mineral deposits, being works which, when the source is no longer worked, are likely to be of little or no value to the person working it immediately before that time; or

(*b*) where a source of mineral deposits is worked under a foreign concession, on the construction of works which, when the concession comes to an end, are likely to become valueless to the person working the source immediately before that time.

(2) If, immediately before the relevant date, no allowance has been made in respect of the expenditure under the old code of allowances, the expenditure shall be treated for the purposes of the new code of allowances as having been incurred on the relevant day.

Balancing charges: old allowances to be brought into account

8.—(1) In any case where—

(*a*) by virtue of any of the preceding provisions of this Schedule, the whole or any part of the outstanding balance of an item of old expenditure is treated for the purposes of Schedule 13 to this Act as qualifying expenditure, and

(*b*) a balancing charge falls to be made under paragraph 11 of that Schedule in respect of that expenditure,

then, in determining the amount on which that charge falls to be made, sub-paragraph (2) (*b*) of the said paragraph 11 shall have effect as if it referred not only to allowances made as mentioned in sub-paragraph (1) (*c*) of that paragraph but also, subject to sub-paragraph (2) below, to allowances made in respect of the item of old expenditure under the old code of allowances.

(2) Where the qualifying expenditure in respect of which a balancing charge falls to be made represents part only of the outstanding balance of an item of old expenditure, the reference in sub-paragraph (1) above to allowances made in respect of that item shall be construed as a reference to such part of those allowances as it is just and reasonable to apportion to that part of the balance (having regard to the apportionment of the balance under paragraph 3 (2) above).

SCHEDULE 15

Section 56

AGRICULTURAL LAND AND BUILDINGS

Cross references.—See CAA 1968, s. 69 (interpretation of certain words used in this Schedule);
FA 1985, s. 56 (8) (rules to determine when capital expenditure is to be taken to be incurred for the purposes of this Schedule with respect to any chargeable period or its basis period ending after 26 July 1989);
FA 1989, s. 120 (1) (b) (forestry land: abolition of agricultural buildings allowances for a chargeable period beginning after 19 June 1989, subject to certain exceptions; see FA 1989, s. 120 (2)–(4)),
Sch. 13, para. 6 (modification of CAA 1968, Sch. 9 (allowances for contributions) in its application to this Schedule in relation to contributions made after 26 July 1989),
Sch. 13, para. 28 (1), (4) (g), (6) (exclusion of double allowances in relation to any chargeable period or its basis period ending after 26 July 1989: where an allowance is made in respect of capital expenditure under this Schedule, no allowance to be made under any other legislation).

Writing-down allowances

1.—(1) If a person having a major interest in any agricultural or forestry land incurs any capital expenditure on the construction of farmhouses, farm or forestry buildings, cottages, fences or other works, then, during a writing-down period of twenty-five years beginning on the first day of the chargeable period related to the incurring of the expenditure, there shall be made to him, subject to the following provisions of this Schedule, writing-down allowances of an aggregate amount equal to that expenditure.

(2) In any case where—

(a) capital expenditure is incurred on the construction of any building, fence or other works, but

(b) when the building, fence or other works comes to be used it is not used for the purposes of husbandry or forestry,

the expenditure shall be left out of account for the purposes of this Schedule and, accordingly, any writing-down allowance made in respect of the expenditure under sub-paragraph (1) above shall be withdrawn and all such assessments and adjustments of assessments shall be made as may be necessary to give effect to that withdrawal.

(3) In this Schedule a "major interest" in land means—

(a) the fee simple estate in the land or an agreement to acquire that estate;

(b) in Scotland, the estate or interest of the proprietor of the *dominium utile* (or, in the case of property other than feudal property, of the owner) and any agreement to acquire such an estate or interest, and

(c) a lease.

(4) If an interest in land is conveyed or assigned by way of security and subject to a right of redemption, then, so long as such a right subsists, the interest held by the creditor shall be treated for the purposes of this Schedule as held by the person having that right.

(5) Any reference in the following provisions of this Schedule to a writing-down allowance is a reference to an allowance under sub-paragraph (1) above.

Note.—See **Prospective Legislation Notes.**
Cross references.—See FA 1988, Sch. 3, para. 24 (allowance made to a husband under sub-para. (1) above to be treated under certain circumstances to have been made to his wife).

Expenditure qualifying for allowances

2.—(1) No expenditure shall be taken into account for the purposes of this Schedule unless it is incurred for the purposes of husbandry or forestry on the agricultural or forestry land referred to in paragraph 1 above.

(2) Where capital expenditure is incurred on a farmhouse, one-third only of that expenditure shall be taken into account for the purposes of this Schedule or, if the accommodation and amenities of the farmhouse are out of due relation to the nature and extent of the farm, such proportion thereof not greater than one-third as may be just.

(3) Where capital expenditure is incurred on any asset other than a farmhouse and the asset is to serve partly the purposes of husbandry or forestry and partly other purposes, such apportionment of the expenditure shall be made for the purposes of this Schedule as may be just.

Note.—See **Prospective Legislation Notes.**

Meaning of "the relevant interest"

3.—(1) Subject to the provisions of this paragraph, in this Schedule "the relevant interest" means, in relation to any expenditure falling within paragraph 1 (1) above, the major interest in the agricultural or forestry land concerned to which the person who incurred the expenditure was entitled when he incurred it.

(2) Where, when he incurs expenditure falling within paragraph 1 (1) above, a person is entitled to two or more major interests in the agricultural or forestry land concerned, and one of those interests is an interest which is in reversion on all the others, that interest is the relevant interest for the purposes of this Schedule.

(3) A major interest shall not cease to be the relevant interest for the purposes of this Schedule by reason of the creation of any lease (or other interest) to which the interest is subject; and where the relevant interest is a lease which is extinguished—

(*a*) by reason of the surrender thereof, or
(*b*) on the person entitled thereto acquiring the interest which is the reversion on the relevant interest,

then, unless a new lease of the land concerned is granted to take effect on the extinguishment of the former lease, the interest into which that lease merges shall thereupon become the relevant interest.

(4) In the application of this paragraph to Scotland "reversion" means the interest of a landlord in property subject to a lease.

Note.—See **Prospective Legislation Notes.**

Transfers of relevant interest

4.—(1) In any case where—

(*a*) if a person (in this paragraph referred to as "the former owner") continued to be the owner of the relevant interest in any land, he would be entitled to a writing-down allowance in respect of any expenditure, and
(*b*) another person (in this paragraph referred to as "the new owner") acquires the relevant interest in the whole or part of that land (whether by transfer, by operation of law or otherwise),

the former owner shall not be entitled to an allowance under this Schedule for any chargeable period of his after that related to the acquisition and the new owner shall be entitled to allowances under this Schedule for the chargeable period of his related to the acquisition and for subsequent chargeable periods falling within the writing-down period.

(2) If, in a case falling within sub-paragraph (1) above, the date of the acquisition occurs during a chargeable period of the former owner or its basis period, he shall be entitled only to an appropriate portion of an allowance for the chargeable period related to the acquisition and, similarly, if the date of the acquisition occurs during a chargeable period of the new owner or its basis period, he shall be entitled only to an appropriate portion of an allowance for the chargeable period (of his) related to the acquisition.

(3) Where the new owner acquires the relevant interest in part only of the land concerned, sub-paragraphs (1) and (2) above shall apply to so much only of the allowance as is properly referable to that part of the land as if it were a separate allowance.

(4) Where paragraph 3 (3) above applies and the person who owns the interest into which the lease is merged is not the same as the person who owned the lease, the relevant interest shall be treated for the purposes of this Schedule as acquired by the owner of the interest into which the lease is merged.

(5) Where the relevant interest is a lease which comes to an end and paragraph 3 (3) above does not apply, then, for the purposes of this Schedule,—

(*a*) if a new lease is granted to a person who makes any payment to the outgoing lessee in respect of assets representing the expenditure in question, the new lease shall be treated as the same interest as the former lease and, accordingly, the relevant interest shall be treated as acquired by the incoming lessee; and
(*b*) if a new lease is granted to the person who was the lessee under the former lease, the new lease shall be treated as the same interest as the former lease; and
(*c*) in any other case, the former lease and the interest of the person who was the landlord under the former lease shall be treated as the same interest and, accordingly, the relevant interest shall be treated as acquired by that person.

(6) If, by virtue only of the operation of the preceding provisions of this paragraph and, where appropriate, section 75 (2) of the Capital Allowances Act 1968, the total allowances which, apart from this sub-paragraph, would fall to be made under this Schedule in respect

of any expenditure during the writing-down period appropriate to it would be less than the amount of that expenditure, then, for the chargeable period in which that writing-down period ends, the allowance in respect of that expenditure shall be increased to such amount as will secure that the total of the allowances equals the amount of that expenditure.

(7) This paragraph has effect subject to the following provisions of this Schedule.

Buildings etc. bought unused

5.—(1) This paragraph applies where expenditure falling within paragraph 1 (1) above is expenditure on the construction of a building, fence or other works and, before the building, fence or works comes to be used, the relevant interest is sold.

(2) Where this paragraph applies—

(a) the expenditure shall be left out of account for the purposes of this Schedule and, accordingly, any writing-down allowance made in respect of the expenditure shall be withdrawn and all such assessments and adjustments of assessments shall be made as may be necessary to give effect to that withdrawal;
(b) paragraph 4 above shall not apply; and
(c) the person who buys the relevant interest shall be treated for the purposes of this Schedule as having incurred, on the date when the purchase price becomes payable, expenditure falling within paragraph 1 (1) above on the construction of the building, fence or other works.

(3) The expenditure referred to in sub-paragraph (2) (c) above is whichever is the lesser of—

(a) the net price paid by the person concerned for the purchase of the relevant interest; and
(b) the expenditure referred to in sub-paragraph (1) above.

(4) Where the relevant interest is sold more than once in circumstances falling within sub-paragraph (1) above, sub-paragraphs (2) (c) and (3) above shall have effect only in relation to the last of those sales.

Balancing allowances and charges

6.—(1) If, in respect of any expenditure falling within paragraph 1 (1) above, a balancing event occurs in a chargeable period or its basis period and, apart from this paragraph, a person would be entitled to a writing-down allowance in respect of that expenditure for the chargeable period related to that event, no such allowance shall be made but an allowance or charge (in this paragraph referred to as a "balancing allowance" or a "balancing charge") shall, in the circumstances mentioned below, be made for that period to or, as the case may be, on the person entitled to the relevant interest immediately before that event occurs.

(2) In relation to any expenditure, the amount of any balancing allowance or charge shall be determined in accordance with the following provisions of this paragraph by reference to—

(a) the residue of that expenditure, that is to say, the amount of that expenditure falling to be taken into account for the purposes of this Schedule less the aggregate of any writing-down allowances made in respect of it (whether or not to the person to or on whom the allowance or charge is to be made); and
(b) subject to sub-paragraph (3) below, any sale, insurance, salvage or compensation moneys related to the event which gives rise to the balancing allowance or balancing charge.

(3) If, by virtue of sub-paragraph (2) or sub-paragraph (3) of paragraph 2 above only a portion of any expenditure falls to be taken into account for the purposes of this Schedule, any reference in the following provisions of this paragraph to sale, insurance, salvage or compensation moneys is a reference only to the like portion of those moneys.

(4) Where there are no sale, insurance, salvage or compensation moneys or where the residue of the expenditure immediately before the balancing event exceeds those moneys, a balancing allowance shall be made of an amount equal to that residue or, as the case may be, to the excess of it over those moneys.

(5) If the sale, insurance, salvage or compensation moneys exceed the residue of the expenditure immediately before the event, a balancing charge shall be made on an amount equal to that excess.

(6) Notwithstanding anything in sub-paragraph (5) above, in no case shall the amount on

which a balancing charge is made on any person exceed the amount of the writing-down allowances made to him in respect of that expenditure before the balancing event.

(7) If a balancing event relates to—

(*a*) the acquisition of the relevant interest in part only of the land in which it subsisted at the time the expenditure was incurred, or
(*b*) only part of the building, fence or other works on the construction of which the expenditure was incurred,

the preceding provisions of this paragraph shall apply to so much of the expenditure as is properly attributable to the part of the land, building, fence or other works concerned, as if it were an item of expenditure separate from the rest.

(8) This paragraph has effect subject to paragraph 9 below.

Cross references.—See FA 1988, Sch. 3, para. 24 (allowance made to a husband under para. 1 (1) of this Schedule to be treated for the purposes of sub-para. (6) above as having been made under certain circumstances to his wife).

Balancing events

7.—(1) Subject to sub-paragraph (2) below, in relation to expenditure (in this paragraph referred to as "the original expenditure") for which, apart from paragraph 6 above, a person (in this paragraph referred to as "the former owner") would be entitled to a writing-down allowance, the following events are balancing events for the purposes of this Schedule—

(*a*) the acquisition of the relevant interest by another person (in this paragraph referred to as "the new owner") as mentioned in paragraph 4 above; and
(*b*) where any building, fence or other works on the construction of which the expenditure was incurred is demolished, destroyed or otherwise ceases to exist as such.

(2) An event falling within sub-paragraph (1) above is not a balancing event for the purposes of this Schedule unless an election is made with respect to that event by notice in writing given to the inspector not more than two years after the end of the chargeable period related to the occurrence of the event.

(3) Where, during the writing-down period applicable to the original expenditure, a balancing event falling within sub-paragraph (1) (*a*) above occurs, the amount of any writing-down allowances to which the new owner is entitled for chargeable periods which, or the basis periods for which, end after the balancing event shall be determined as if—

(*a*) that part of the writing-down period applicable to the original expenditure which falls after the balancing event were itself the writing-down period in which the allowances in respect of that expenditure were to be made; and
(*b*) . . .[1] the allowances were in respect of expenditure equal to the residue of the original expenditure (determined under paragraph 6 (2) (*a*) above) immediately before the balancing event less the amount of any balancing allowance made to the former owner or, as the case may be, plus the amount on which any balancing charge was made on him by reason of the balancing event.

(4) Subject to sub-paragraph (5) below, an election under this paragraph shall be made as follows—

(*a*) where the event falls within sub-paragraph (1) (*a*) above, jointly by the former owner and the new owner; and
(*b*) where the event falls within sub-paragraph (1) (*b*) above, by the former owner.

(5) No election may be made under this paragraph if any person by whom that election should be made is not within the charge to tax in the United Kingdom; and no election may be made in relation to an acquisition falling within sub-paragraph (1) (*a*) above if it appears with respect to that acquisition, or with respect to transactions of which that acquisition is one, that the sole or main benefit which (apart from Schedule 7 to the Capital Allowances Act 1968) might have been expected to accrue to the parties or any of them was the obtaining of an allowance, or a greater allowance under this Schedule.

Amendments.—[1] Words in sub-para. (3) (*b*) repealed by FA 1989, Sch. 13, para. 26 and Sch. 17, Pt. VI.

Exclusion of land values etc.

8.—(1) Any reference in this Schedule to expenditure incurred on the construction of a building does not include any expenditure incurred on the acquisition of, or of rights in or over, any land.

(2) Without prejudice to any provision of Part I of the Capital Allowances Act 1968 relating to the apportionment of sale, insurance, salvage or compensation moneys, the sum paid on the sale of the relevant interest in a building, fence or other works or any other sale, insurance, salvage or compensation moneys payable in respect of any building, fence or other works shall, for the purposes of this Schedule, be deemed to be reduced by an amount equal to so much thereof as, on a just apportionment, is attributable to assets representing expenditure other than expenditure in respect of which an allowance can be made under this Schedule.

Special provisions as to certain sales

9.—(1) In its application in relation to any sale which is material for the purposes of this Schedule, Schedule 7 to the Capital Allowances Act 1968 (transactions between connected persons etc.) shall have effect with the omission—

(*a*) of paragraph 4 (sales without change of control); and
(*b*) of any reference to paragraph 4 or any provision thereof in any other paragraph of that Schedule.

(2) For the purposes of this Schedule and the provisions of the Capital Allowances Act 1968 which are relevant to this Schedule, any transfer of the relevant interest (in relation to any expenditure falling within paragraph 1 (1) above) otherwise than by way of sale shall be treated as a sale of the interest for a price other than that which it would have fetched if sold on the open market.

(3) If Schedule 7 to the Capital Allowances Act 1968 would not, apart from this sub-paragraph, have effect in relation to a transfer treated as a sale by virtue of sub-paragraph (2) above, that Schedule shall have effect in relation to it as if it were a sale falling within paragraph 1 (1) (*a*) of that Schedule.

Restriction of balancing allowances on sale of buildings

10.—(1) This paragraph has effect where—

(*a*) the relevant interest in a building is sold subject to a subordinate interest; and
(*b*) a balancing allowance under paragraph 6 above would, apart from this paragraph, fall to be made to the person who is entitled to the relevant interest immediately before the sale (in this paragraph referred to as "the former owner") by virtue of the sale; and
(*c*) either—

(i) the former owner, the person to whom the relevant interest is sold and the grantee of the subordinate interest, or any two of them, are connected with each other within the terms of section [839 of the Taxes Act 1988][1], or
(ii) it appears with respect to the sale or to the grant of the subordinate interest, or with respect to transactions including the sale or grant, that the sole or main benefit which, but for this paragraph, might have been expected to accrue to the parties or any of them was the obtaining of an allowance under this Schedule.

(2) For the purposes of paragraph 6 above the net proceeds to the former owner of the sale—

(*a*) shall be taken to be increased by an amount equal to any premium receivable by him for the grant of the subordinate interest; and
(*b*) where no rent, or no commercial rent, is payable in respect of the subordinate interest, shall be taken to be what those proceeds would have been if a commercial rent had been payable and the relevant interest had been sold in the open market (increased by any amount to be added under paragraph (*a*) of this sub-paragraph);

but the net proceeds of sale shall not by virtue of this sub-paragraph be taken to be greater than such amount as will secure that no balancing allowance falls to be made.

(3) Where sub-paragraph (2) above operates, in relation to a sale, to deny or reduce a balancing allowance in respect of any expenditure, paragraph 7 (3) above shall have effect as if that balancing allowance had been made or, as the case may be, had not been reduced.

(4) In this paragraph—

"subordinate interest" means any interest in or right over the building in question (whether granted by the former owner or by somebody else);
"premium" includes any capital consideration except so much of any sum as corresponds to any amount of rent or profits falling to be computed by reference to that sum under section [34 of the Taxes Act 1988][1] (premium treated as rent or Schedule D profits);

"capital consideration" means consideration which consists of a capital sum or would be a capital sum if it had taken the form of a money payment;

"rent" includes any consideration which is not capital consideration;

"commercial rent" means such rent as may reasonably be expected to have been required in respect of the subordinate interest in question (having regard to any premium payable for the grant of the interest) if the transaction had been at arm's length.

(5) Where the terms on which a subordinate interest is granted are varied before the sale of the relevant interest, any capital consideration for the variation shall be treated for the purposes of this paragraph as a premium for the grant of the interest, and the question whether any and, if so, what rent is payable in respect of the interest shall be determined by reference to the terms as in force immediately before the sale.

Amendments.—[1] Words in sub-paras. (1) (c) (i), (4) substituted by TA 1988, Sch. 29, para. 32 Table.

Manner of making allowances and charges

11.—(1) Except as provided below, any allowance or charge made to or on any person under this Schedule shall be made to or on him in taxing his trade; and any reference in the following provisions of this paragraph to an allowance or charge of any description is a reference to an allowance or charge under this Schedule.

(2) Any allowance which falls to be made to a person for a chargeable period in which he is not carrying on a trade shall be made by way of discharge or repayment of tax.

(3) Any allowance which, under this paragraph, is to be made by way of discharge or repayment of tax shall be available primarily against agricultural income and forestry income and income which is the subject of a balancing charge.

(4) Effect shall be given to a balancing charge to be made on a person for a chargeable period in which he is not carrying on a trade,—

(*a*) if it is a charge to income tax, by making the charge under Case VI of Schedule D; and

(*b*) if it is a charge to corporation tax, by treating the amount on which the charge is to be made as agricultural income or forestry income.

Note.—See **Prospective Legislation Notes.**
Cross references.—See FA 1989, s. 120 (5) (forestry land: abolition of agricultural buildings allowances).

SCHEDULE 16
Section 57

NEW EXPENDITURE ON LEASED ASSETS AND ON CERTAIN VEHICLES

PART I

Note.—This Part amends FA 1980, ss. 64–68.

PART II

Note.—This Part amends FA 1982, s. 70 and Sch. 11.

PART III

SUPPLEMENTARY PROVISIONS AS TO ASSETS LEASED OUTSIDE THE UNITED KINGDOM

Interpretation

7.—(1) In this Part of this Schedule—

(a) "the principal section" means section 70 of the Finance Act 1982;
(b) a "non-resident" means such a person as is referred to in paragraphs (a) and (b) of subsection (1) of the principal section;
(c) "normal writing-down allowance" means a writing-down allowance of an amount determined without regard to subsection (2) of the principal section;
(d) "permitted leasing" means short-term leasing or the leasing of a ship, aircraft or transport container which is used for a qualifying purpose by virtue of subsections (5) to (7) of section 64 of the Finance Act 1980; and
(e) "short-term leasing" has the meaning assigned to it by section 64 (3) of the Finance Act 1980;

and other expressions have the same meaning as in the principal section.

(2) Where new expenditure has been incurred by any person, any reference in this Part of this Schedule to the new expenditure having qualified for a normal writing-down allowance is a reference to the expenditure having fallen to be included, in whole or in part, in that person's qualifying expenditure for any chargeable period for the purposes of sub-sections (2), (2A) and (3) of section 44 of the Finance Act 1971, as that section has effect with respect to expenditure which does not fall within subsection (1) of the principal section.

Recovery of excess relief

8.—(1) Where new expenditure incurred by any person in providing machinery or plant has qualified for a normal writing-down allowance and the machinery or plant is at any time in the requisite period used for the purpose of being leased to a non-resident, otherwise than by permitted leasing,—

(a) an amount equal to the excess relief shall, in relation to the person to whom the machinery or plant then belongs, be treated as if it were a balancing charge to be made on him for the chargeable period for which, or in the basis period for which, the machinery or plant is first so used; and
(b) for the purposes of section 44 of the Finance Act 1971 (as it has effect with respect to expenditure which does not fall within subsection (1) of the principal section), an amount equal to the unused expenditure shall, in relation to that person, be treated as if it were a disposal value to be brought into account for the chargeable period referred to in paragraph (a) above; and
(c) section 44 of the Finance Act 1971 (as it has effect as mentioned in paragraphs (a) to (e) of subsection (2) of the principal section) shall apply as if a sum equal to the aggregate of the amounts in paragraphs (a) and (b) above were qualifying expenditure of that person for the next chargeable period and, for the purpose of subsequently bringing any disposal value into account, as if the machinery or plant had always been used for the purposes of the separate trade.

(2) The excess relief is the excess, if any, of—

(a) any normal writing-down allowances made in respect of the new expenditure for the chargeable period related to the incurring of the expenditure and any subsequent chargeable period up to and including that mentioned in sub-paragraph (1) (a) above, over
(b) the maximum writing-down allowance or allowances that could have been made in respect of the expenditure for those chargeable periods if no normal writing-down allowance had been or could have been made.

(3) The unused expenditure is the amount by which the new expenditure incurred in providing the machinery or plant exceeds the allowances referred to in sub-paragraph (2) (a) above.

(4) For the purposes of sub-paragraph (2) above, the normal writing-down allowances that were made in respect of new expenditure on any item of machinery or plant shall be determined as if that item were the only item of machinery or plant in relation to which the said section 44 had effect.

(5) Where the person to whom any machinery or plant belongs at a time when it is first used for the purpose of being leased to a non-resident, otherwise than by permitted leasing, has

acquired it as a result of a transaction which was, or a series of transactions each of which was, between connected persons and a normal writing-down allowance in respect of expenditure on the provision of the machinery or plant has been made to any of those persons—

(a) sub-paragraph (2) above shall have effect as if it referred to that allowance and to the expenditure in respect of which it was made;
(b) for the purposes of that sub-paragraph any consideration paid or received on a disposal of the machinery or plant between connected persons shall be disregarded; and
(c) if a balancing allowance or balancing charge is made in respect of the machinery or plant there shall be made such adjustments of the total relief falling to be taken into account under paragraph (a) of that sub-paragraph as are just and reasonable in the circumstances;

but this sub-paragraph does not apply where section [113(2), 114(1) or 343 (2) of the Taxes Act 1988][1] or sub-paragraphs (a) and (b) of paragraph 13 of Schedule 8 to the Finance Act 1971 (succession to trades), applied on the occasion of the transaction or transactions in question.

(6) Where the person to whom any machinery or plant belongs at such a time as is mentioned in sub-paragraph (5) above acquired it as there mentioned and—

(a) new expenditure incurred on the provision of the machinery or plant by any of the connected persons would have qualified for a normal writing-down allowance but such an allowance was not claimed or was disclaimed; and
(b) a balancing allowance is made to any of those persons in respect of that expenditure,

this paragraph shall with the necessary modifications apply as it applies where a normal writing-down allowance has been made.

(7) If at any time in the requisite period a ship is used for the purpose of being leased to a non-resident, otherwise than by permitted leasing, then, without prejudice to the other provisions of this paragraph,—

(a) no allowance shall be made in respect of it under sub-paragraph (5) (c) of paragraph 8A of Schedule 8 to the Finance Act 1971 for the chargeable period in which it is first so used or for any subsequent chargeable period;
(b) nothing in sub-paragraphs (8) and (9) of that paragraph shall affect the operation of sub-paragraph (1) above; and
(c) section 44 of that Act (as it has effect in accordance with section 65 of the Finance Act 1980) shall apply as if the amount of any allowance in respect of the ship which has been postponed under the said paragraph 8A and not made were qualifying expenditure for the next chargeable period after that in which the ship is first so used.

(8) Section [839 of the Taxes Act 1988][1] (connected persons) applies for the purposes of this paragraph.

Amendments.—[1] Words in sub-paras. (5), (8) substituted by TA 1988, Sch. 29, para. 32 Table.

Joint lessees

9.—(1) Without prejudice to the operation of paragraph 8 above, the provisions of this paragraph have effect where new expenditure is incurred on the provision of machinery or plant which is leased as mentioned in subsection (1) of section 68 of the Finance Act 1980, and any reference in the following provisions of this paragraph to section 68 is a reference to that section.

(2) Where, by virtue of subsection (2) of section 68, the whole or part of the new expenditure has qualified for a normal writing-down allowance and, at any time in the requisite period while it is leased as mentioned in that subsection—

(a) no lessee uses the machinery or plant for the purposes of a trade or trades the profits or gains of which are chargeable to income tax or corporation tax, and
(b) subsection (5) of the principal section does not apply at that time and has not applied at any earlier time,

paragraph 8 above and paragraph 10 (2) below shall have effect as if the separate item of machinery or plant referred to in subsection (3) (a) of section 68 had at that time begun to be used for the purpose of being leased to a non-resident, otherwise than by permitted leasing.

(3) Where the whole or part of any new expenditure has qualified for a normal writing-

down allowance and the machinery or plant is subsequently leased in the requisite period as mentioned in subsection (1) of section 68, sub-paragraph (2) above shall apply as if the whole of the expenditure had qualified for a normal writing-down allowance by virtue only of subsection (2) of that section.

(4) Where, by virtue of subsection (2) of section 68, the whole or part of the new expenditure has qualified for a normal writing-down allowance and, at the end of the requisite period, the machinery or plant in question is leased as mentioned in subsection (1) of that section but sub-paragraph (2) above has not had effect, then, if it appears that the extent to which the machinery or plant has been used for the purposes of such a trade or trades as are referred to in that sub-paragraph is less than that which was taken into account in determining the amount of the new expenditure which qualified for a normal writing-down allowance,—

   (*a*) paragraph 8 above shall have effect as if a part of the expenditure corresponding to the reduction in the extent of such use were expenditure on the provision of a separate item of machinery or plant used for the purpose of leasing to a non-resident, otherwise than by permitted leasing, on the last day of the requisite period; and
   (*b*) any disposal value subsequently brought into account in respect of the machinery or plant under section 44 of the Finance Act 1971 shall, instead of being apportioned in accordance with subsection (3) of section 68, be apportioned by reference to the extent of such use as determined at the end of that period.

Information

10.—(1) Where new expenditure is incurred on the provision of machinery or plant and, before the expenditure has qualified for a normal writing-down allowance, it is used for leasing to a non-resident and that leasing is permitted leasing, a claim by a person other than a company for a writing-down allowance which takes account of that expenditure and a return by a company of profits in the computation of which a deduction is made on account of such an allowance shall be accompanied by a certificate to that effect, setting out the description of permitted leasing.

(2) If, after any new expenditure has qualified for a normal writing-down allowance, the machinery or plant in question is at any time in the requisite period used for the purpose of being leased to a non-resident, otherwise than by permitted leasing, the person to whom it belongs at that time shall give written notice of that fact to the inspector.

(3) Subject to sub-paragraph (6) below, notice under sub-paragraph (2) above shall be given within three months after the end of the chargeable period or its basis period in which the machinery or plant is first used for leasing as mentioned in that sub-paragraph.

(4) A certificate or notice given by any person under sub-paragraph (1) or sub-paragraph (2) above by reference to any chargeable period or its basis period shall specify the non-resident to whom the machinery or plant has been leased and shall specify all the items of machinery or plant (if more than one) in respect of which the person in question is required to give a certificate or notice under this paragraph by reference to that period.

(5) Subject to sub-paragraph (6) below, where new expenditure is incurred on the provision of machinery or plant which is leased as mentioned in section 68 (1) of the Finance Act 1980, the lessor shall, within three months after the end of the chargeable period or its basis period in which the machinery or plant is first so leased, give written notice to the inspector specifying—

   (*a*) the names and addresses of the persons to whom the asset is jointly leased;
   (*b*) the portion of the new expenditure which is properly attributable to each of those persons; and
   (*c*) so far as it is within his knowledge, which of those persons is resident in the United Kingdom.

(6) If, at the end of the three months referred to in sub-paragraph (3) or sub-paragraph (5) above, the person required to give a notice under that sub-paragraph does not know and cannot reasonably be expected to know that any item of machinery or plant in respect of which he is required to give such a notice has been used or leased as mentioned in the sub-paragraph in question, he shall in respect of that item give the notice within thirty days of his coming to know that it has been so used or leased.

(7) . . .[1]

Amendments.—[1] Sub-para. (7) repealed by TA 1988, Sch. 31.

PART IV

Note.—This Part amends FA 1980, s. 69.

SCHEDULE 18

Section 63

SECURITIES: OTHER PROVISIONS

Information

7.—(1)–(3) . . .

(4) The Board may by regulations provide that section 21 (7) (as amended by sub-paragraph (2) above) shall have effect—

(*a*) as if references to The Stock Exchange in the definition of "broker" and in paragraph (*a*) of the definition of "market maker" were to any recognised investment exchange or to any of those exchanges specified in the regulations, and

(*b*) as if the reference to the Council of The Stock Exchange in paragraph (*b*) of the definition of "market maker" were to the investment exchange concerned.

(5) Regulations under sub-paragraph (4) above shall apply in relation to transactions effected on or after such day, after the day of The Stock Exchange reforms, as is specified in the regulations.

Note.—Sub-paras. (1)–(3) amend TMA 1970, s. 21.

8.—(1)–(3) . . .

(4) The Board may by regulations provide that—

(*a*) subsections (4) and (5) of section 25 and paragraph (*a*) of subsection (10) (as inserted by sub-paragraph (2) above) shall have effect as if references to The Stock Exchange were to any recognised investment exchange or to any of those exchanges specified in the regulations, and

(*b*) paragraph (*b*) of subsection (10) shall have effect as if the reference to the Council of The Stock Exchange were to the investment exchange concerned.

(5) Regulations under sub-paragraph (4) above shall apply in relation to transactions effected on or after such day, after the day of The Stock Exchange reforms, as is specified in the regulations.

Note.—Sub-paras. (1)–(3) amend TMA 1970, s. 25.

Miscellaneous

9.—(1) The Board may by regulations—

(*a*) . . .[1]

(*b*) substitute for section 21 (1) of the Taxes Management Act 1970 a provision that the Board may exercise the powers conferred by section 21 in such circumstances as are specified in the substituted provision;

(*c*) make such incidental and consequential provisions (which may include the amendment of other provisions of . . .[2] section 21) as appear to the Board to be appropriate.

(2) . . .[1]

(3) So far as they relate to section 21, the regulations shall apply in relation to transactions effected on or after such day, after the day of The Stock Exchange reforms, as is specified in the regulations.

Amendments.—[1] Sub-paras. (1) (*a*), (2) repealed by TA 1988, Sch. 31.
[2] Words in sub-para. (1) (*c*) repealed by *ibid.*

General

10.—(1) In this Schedule "the day of The Stock Exchange reforms" means the day on which the rule of The Stock Exchange that prohibits a person from carrying on business as both a broker and a jobber is abolished.

(2) In this Schedule "recognised investment exchange" means a recognised investment exchange within the meaning of the Financial Services Act 1986.

(3) Any power to make regulations under this Schedule shall be exercisable by statutory instrument subject to annulment in pursuance of a resolution of the House of Commons.

GAS ACT 1986

(1986 Chapter 44)

60. Tax provisions

(1) The successor company shall be treated—

    (*a*) for all purposes of corporation tax . . . ; and
    (*b*) . . . ;

as if it were the same person as the Corporation.

(2) The successor company shall not by virtue of subsection (1) above be regarded as a body falling within section 272(5) of the Income and Corporation Taxes Act 1970 (bodies established for carrying on industries or undertakings under national ownership or control).

(3) Where any debentures are issued in pursuance of section 51 above, any annual payment secured by those debentures shall be treated for all purposes of corporation tax as if it were a charge on income of the successor company.

(4) . . .

Note.—Sub-ss. (1) (*b*), (4) and words omitted from sub-s. (1) (*a*) are not relevant to this work.

BUILDING SOCIETIES ACT 1986
(1986 Chapter 53)

30. Tax treatment of contributions and repayments

In computing for the purposes of the Tax Acts the profits or gains arising from the trade carried on by a contributory building society—

(*a*) to the extent that it would not be deductible apart from this paragraph, any sum expended or trated under section 29 as expended by the society in paying a contribution to the Fund may be deducted as an expense; and

(*b*) any payment which is made or treated as made to the society by the Board under section 29 (3) or (7) shall be treated as a trading receipt.

62. Prohibition of tax-free payments to directors

(1) A building society shall not pay a director remuneration (whether as director or otherwise) free of income tax, or otherwise calculated by reference to or varying with the amount of his income tax, or to or with any rate of income tax.

(2) Any rule of a building society and any provision of any contract, or in any resolution of a building society, for payment to a director of remuneration falling within subsection (1) above has effect as if it provided for payment, as a gross sum subject to income tax, of the net sum for which the rule, contract or resolution actually provides.

FINANCE (NO. 2) ACT 1987

(1987 Chapter 51)

ARRANGEMENT OF SECTIONS

Note.—Provisions of this Act relevant to the taxes covered by this Handbook and not reprodced are either spent or repealed by TA 1988, Sch. 31 and other legislation.

PART I
INCOME TAX, CORPORATION TAX AND CAPITAL GAINS TAX

Miscellaneous

Section
72. Allowances for dwelling-houses let on assured tenancies.
73. Recognised investment exchanges.

CHAPTER IV
CAPITAL GAINS

Miscellaneous

78. Collective investment schemes.
80. Roll-over relief not available for gains on oil licences.

CHAPTER V
TAXES MANAGEMENT PROVISIONS

Company returns

82. Return of profits.
83. Failure to make return for corporation tax.
84. *Assessment of amounts due by way of penalty.* (repealed)

Interest, etc.

85. Interest on overdue corporation tax etc.
86. Supplementary provisions as to interest on overdue tax.
88. Recovery of overpayment of tax etc.

Miscellaneous

91. Close companies: loans to participators.
95. Interpretation of Chapter V and consequential and supplementary provisions.

PART II
INHERITANCE TAX, ETC.

Sections 96–98 (see Orange Book)

PART III
MISCELLANEOUS AND SUPPLEMENTARY

99. *Stamp duty: options etc.* (see Orange Book)
100. *Stamp duty reserve tax.* (see Orange Book)

Section
103. *Consumption in port of goods transhipped for use as stores etc.* (see Orange Book)
104. Short title, interpretation, construction and repeals.

SCHEDULES:

Schedule 6—Management provisions: supplementary and consequential provisions.
Schedule 7—*Inheritance tax: interests in possession.* (see Orange Book)
Schedule 9—Repeals.
        Part III   *Inheritance Tax.* (see Orange Book)
        Part IV   *Stamp Duty Reserve Tax.* (see Orange Book)

An Act to grant certain duties, to alter other duties, and to amend the law relating to the National Debt and the Public Revenue, and to make further provision in connection with Finance.

[23rd July 1987]

PART I

INCOME TAX, CORPORATION TAX AND CAPITAL GAINS TAX

72. Allowances for dwelling-houses let on assured tenancies

(1) . . .

(2) In any case where—

(*a*) by reason only of the enactment (by the Housing and Planning Act 1986) of section 56B of the Housing Act 1980 (extension of assured tenancies scheme to cases where works have been carried out) an approved body is entitled to an initial allowance in respect of any expenditure under Schedule 12 to the Finance Act 1982 (capital allowances for dwelling-houses let on assured tenancies); and

(*b*) effect has not been and, apart from this subsection, no longer can be given to the initial allowance referred to in paragraph (*a*) above,

then, if a claim is made in that behalf before 1st April 1988, all such adjustments shall be made as may be necessary to give effect to that initial allowance.

(3) Expressions used in subsection (2) above have the same meaning as in Schedule 12 to the Finance Act 1982.

Note.—Sub-s. (1) amends FA 1982, s. 76 (2).

73. Recognised investment exchanges

(1) The Board may by regulations make provision securing that enactments relating to income tax, corporation tax or capital gains tax and referring to The Stock Exchange have effect, for such purposes and subject to such modifications as may be prescribed by the regulations, in relation to all other recognised investment exchanges (within the meaning of the Financial Services Act 1986), or in relation to such of those exchanges as may be so prescribed.

(2) The power to make regulations under this section shall be exercisable by statutory instrument, which shall be subject to annulment in pursuance of a resolution of the House of Commons.

Miscellaneous

78. Collective investment schemes

Where arrangements within section 75 of the Financial Services Act 1986 provide for pooling of the kind mentioned in subsection (3) (a) of that section in relation to different parts of the property concerned, any question whether the arrangements constitute a single collective investment scheme shall be determined for the purposes of capital gains tax without regard to any entitlement of the participants to exchange rights in one part of the property for rights in another.[1]

Amendments.—[1] This section repealed by FA 1989, s. 140 (6) and Sch. 17, Pt. VII where the question whether any arrangements constitute a single collective investment scheme is determined in relation to disposals made after 13 March 1989.

80. Roll-over relief not available for gains on oil licences

(1) A licence under the Petroleum (Production) Act 1934 or the Petroleum (Production) Act (Northern Ireland) 1964 is not and, subject to subsection (2) below, shall be assumed never to have been an asset falling within any of the classes in section 118 of the Capital Gains Tax Act 1979 (classes of assets for the purposes of roll-over relief under section 115 of that Act).

(2) Nothing in subsection (1) above affects the determination of any Commissioners or the judgment of any court made or given before 14th May 1987.

(3) A reference in subsection (1) above to a provision of the Capital Gains Tax Act 1979 includes a reference to the corresponding enactment in Part III of the Finance Act 1965 which is re-enacted in that provision.

CHAPTER V

TAXES MANAGEMENT PROVISIONS

Company returns

82. Return of profits

(1) With respect to any notice served after the appointed day, section 11 of the Management Act (return of profits) shall be amended in accordance with this section.

(2) In subsection (1) for the words from "within the time limited by the notice" to the end there shall be substituted "not later than the final day determined under subsection (4) below a return of the profits and losses of the company containing such information and accompanied by such accounts, statements and reports as, subject to subsection (6) below, may be required in pursuance of the notice."

(3) For subsection (2) there shall be substituted the following subsection—

"(2) A notice under this section may require a return of profits and losses arising in any period specified in the notice (in this subsection referred to as "the specified period") but, if the specified period does not coincide with an accounting period of the company and the company is within the charge to corporation tax in the whole or some part of the specified period, then—

(*a*) if an accounting period of the company ends in or at the end of the specified period, the notice shall be taken to require a return for that accounting period or, if there is more than one, for each of them;
(*b*) if no accounting period of the company ends in or at the end of the specified period but there is a part of the specified period which does not fall within an accounting period of the company, the notice shall be taken to require a return for that part of the specified period; and;
(*c*) if the specified period begins in or at the beginning of an accounting period of the company and ends before the end of that period, the notice shall be of no effect and, accordingly, the company shall not be required to make any return pursuant to it."

(4) For subsections (4) to (6) there shall be substituted the following subsections—

"(4) Subject to subsection (5) below, the final day for the delivery of any return required by a notice under this section shall be whichever is the later of—

(*a*) the first anniversary of the last day of the period to which the return relates;
(*b*) the first anniversary of the last day of that period of account of the company in which falls the last day of the accounting period (if any) to which the return relates; and
(*c*) the end of the period of three months beginning on the day following that on which the notice was served.

(5) In paragraph (*b*) of subsection (4) above "period of account" has the same meaning as in the principal Act, but for the purposes of that paragraph the last day of a period of account which is longer than eighteen months shall be treated as the day on which expires the period of eighteen months beginning on the first day of the period of account.

(6) In relation to a company which—

(*a*) is resident in the United Kingdom throughout the period to which the return relates (in this subsection referred to as "the return period"); and
(*b*) is required under the Companies Act 1985 to prepare accounts for a period consisting of or including the return period,

the reference to accounts in subsection (1) above is a reference only to such accounts, containing such particulars and having annexed to them such documents, as are required under that Act to be so prepared.

(7) The statements which may be required in pursuance of a notice under this section include statements showing the amount of tax (if any) chargeable.

(8) Different information, accounts, statements and reports may be required in pursuance of a notice under this section in relation to different descriptions of company or different descriptions of profits and losses; and, in particular, information may be so required with

respect to tax recoverable by virtue of section [419][1] of the principal Act (loans to participators) as if it were corporation tax, to advance corporation tax and to corporation tax already paid.

(9) In the application of this section to a company registered in Northern Ireland, references to the Companies Act 1985 shall be construed as references to the Companies (Northern Ireland) Order 1986."

Amendments.—[1] Number in sub-s. (8) substituted by TA 1988, Sch. 29, para. 10 (2).

83. Failure to make return for corporation tax

With respect to failures to deliver returns required by notices served under section 11 of the Management Act after the appointed day, for section 94 of that Act (failure to make return for corporation tax) there shall be substituted the following section—

"94. Failure to make return for corporation tax

(1) If a company has been required by a notice served under section 11 of this Act (or under that section as extended by section 12 of this Act) to deliver a return for any period (in this section referred to as "the return period") and the company fails to make proper delivery of the return, then, subject to subsections (3) and (5) below, the company shall be liable to a penalty which,—

(*a*) if the return is delivered before the expiry of the period of three months beginning on the day following the final day for the delivery of the return, shall be £100; and
(*b*) in any other case, shall be £200.

(2) In relation to a return required by such a notice as is referred to in subsection (1) above,—

(*a*) any reference in this section (however expressed) to the delivery of the return is a reference to its delivery together with the accompanying accounts, statements and reports referred to in section 11 (1) of this Act; and
(*b*) any reference in this section to making proper delivery of the return is a reference to the delivery of the return on or before the day which (in accordance with section 11 (4) of this Act) is the final day for the delivery of the return.

(3) In a case where—

(*a*) a company is required to deliver a return for a return period, and
(*b*) the return period is a period for which, under the Companies Act 1985, the company is required to deliver accounts to the Registrar of Companies,

the company shall not be liable to a penalty under subsection (1) above by reason of a failure to make proper delivery of the return if the return is delivered on or before the day which is the last day for the delivery to the Registrar of the accounts referred to in paragraph (*b*) above.

(4) In the application of this section to a company registered in Northern Ireland, the reference in subsection (3) above to the Companies Act 1985 shall be construed as a reference to the Companies (Northern Ireland) Order 1986 and references to the Registrar of Companies shall be construed accordingly.

(5) In any case where—

(*a*) a company is within the charge to corporation tax for three consecutive accounting periods, each of which is a return period, and
(*b*) at no time between the beginning of the first of those periods and the end of the last is the company outside the charge to corporation tax, and
(*c*) the company fails to make proper delivery of the return for the third of those periods, and
(*d*) the company was liable to a penalty under this section in respect of each of the first two of those periods,

subsection (1) above shall have effect in relation to the failure referred to in paragraph (*c*) above as if for "£100" there were substituted "£500" and for "£200" there were substituted "£1,000".

(6) If a company which has been required as mentioned in subsection (1) above to deliver a return fails to deliver the return before the expiry of the period of eighteen months beginning on the day following the last day of the return period, then (without prejudice to any penalty under the preceding provisions of this section) the company shall be liable to a penalty which,—

(*a*) if the return is delivered before the expiry of the period of two years beginning on the day following that last day, shall be 10 per cent. of the tax unpaid at the end of the eighteen months referred to above; and

(*b*) in any other case, shall be 20 per cent. of the tax unpaid at the end of those eighteen months.

(7) In subsection (6) above "the tax unpaid" at any time means the amount by which the corporation tax chargeable on the profits of the company for the return period which then remains unpaid exceeds any income tax borne by deduction from payments included in those profits.

(8) In determining for the purposes of subsection (7) above how much of the corporation tax chargeable on the profits of a company for the return period remains unpaid at any time, no account shall be taken of the discharge of any liability for that tax which, pursuant to a claim under [section 239 (3) of the principal Act][1], is attributable to an amount of surplus advance corporation tax, as defined in that subsection, unless it is a surplus for an accounting period ending not later than two years after the end of the return period."

Amendments.—[1] Words in sub-s. (8) substituted by TA 1988, Sch. 29, para. 10 (7).

Interest etc.

85. Interest on overdue corporation tax etc.

With respect to accounting periods ending after the appointed day, after section 87 of the Management Act there shall be inserted the following section—

"87A. Interest on overdue corporation tax etc.

(1) Corporation tax shall carry interest at the [rate applicable under section 178 of the Finance Act 1989][2] from the date when the tax becomes due and payable (in accordance with section [10][1] of the principal Act) until payment.

(2) Subsection (1) above applies even if the date when the tax becomes due and payable (as mentioned in that subsection) is a non-business day within the meaning of section 92 of the Bills of Exchange Act 1882.

(3) In relation to corporation tax assessed by virtue of section [346 (2) or 347 (1) of the principal Act, section 267 (3C) or 278 (5) of the Income and Corporation Taxes Act 1970][1] or section 87 (4) of the Capital Gains Tax Act 1979 (which enable unpaid corporation tax assessed on a company to be assessed on other persons in certain circumstances), the reference in subsection (1) above to the date when the tax becomes due and payable is a reference to the date when it became due and payable by the company.

(4) In any case where—

(*a*) there is in any accounting period of a company (in this subsection referred to as "the later period") an amount of surplus advance corporation tax, as defined in subsection (3) of section [239 of the principal Act][1], and

(*b*) pursuant to a claim under the said subsection (3), the whole or any part of that amount is treated for the purposes of the said section [239][1] as discharging liability for an amount of corporation tax for an earlier accounting period (in this subsection referred to as "the earlier period"), and

(*c*) disregarding the effect of the said subsection (3), an amount of corporation tax for the earlier period would carry interest in accordance with this section,

then, in determining the amount of interest payable under this section on corporation tax unpaid for the earlier period, no account shall be taken of any reduction in the amount of that tax which results from the said subsection (3) except so far as concerns interest for any time after the date on which any corporation tax for the later period became due and payable (as mentioned in subsection (1) above).

(5) A sum assessed on a company by such an assessment as is referred to in [section 252 (5) of the principal Act][1] (recovery of payment of tax credit or interest on such a payment) shall carry interest at the prescribed rate from the date when the payment of tax credit or interest was made until the sum assessed is paid."

Amendments.—[1] Words in sub-ss. (1), (3)–(5) substituted by TA 1988, Sch. 29, para. 10 (4).
[2] Words in sub-s. (1) substituted by FA 1989, s. 179 (1) (*b*) (i).

86. Supplementary provisions as to interest on overdue tax

(1) At the end of section 69 of the Management Act (recovery of interest on tax) there shall be added the words "or, if it is interest on tax which is not in fact assessed, as if it were tax charged and due and payable under an assessment".

(2) In section 86 of the Management Act (interest on overdue tax), subsection (2) (*d*) and paragraph 5 of the Table (which relate to assessed corporation tax) shall be omitted.

(3) References to section 86 of the Management Act in—

(*a*) sections 70 (2) and 92 of that Act (evidence, and remission of interest in certain cases), and
(*b*) paragraph 4 of Schedule 15 to the Finance Act 1973 (territorial extension of tax),

shall include a reference to section 87A of the Management Act.

(4) In section 88 of the Management Act (interest on tax recovered to make good loss due to taxpayer's fault)—

(*a*) in subsection (2) (exclusion of certain non-assessed tax) after the words "in relation to" there shall be inserted "corporation tax or"; and
(*b*) in subsection (5), paragraph (*e*) (which relates to corporation tax) shall be omitted.

(5) In section 91 of the Management Act (effect on interest of reliefs) after subsection (1) there shall be inserted the following subsections—

"(1A) Where interest is payable under section 87A of this Act in respect of an amount of corporation tax for an accounting period, and relief from tax is given by a discharge of any of that corporation tax—

(*a*) such adjustment shall be made of the amount of interest payable under that section in respect of corporation tax for that accounting period, and
(*b*) such repayment shall be made of any amounts of interest previously paid under that section in respect of that corporation tax,

as are necessary to secure that the total sum (if any) paid or payable under that section in respect of corporation tax for that accounting period is the same as it would have been if the tax discharged had never been charged.

(1B) Subsection (1A) above has effect subject to section 87A (4) of this Act."

(6) At the beginning of subsection (2) of that section there shall be inserted the words "Subject to subsection (2A) below" and at the end of that subsection there shall be added the following subsection—

"(2A) In any case where—

(*a*) relief from corporation tax is given to any person by repayment, and
(*b*) that tax was paid for an accounting period ending after the day which is the appointed day for the purposes of section [10 of the principal Act][1],

that person shall be entitled to require that the amount repaid shall be treated for the purposes of this section, so far as it will go, as if it were a discharge of the corporation tax charged on him for that period."

Amendments.—[1] Words in para. (*b*) substituted by TA 1988, Sch. 29, para. 10 (6).

(7) This section has effect with respect to accounting periods ending after the appointed day.

88. Recovery of overpayment of tax etc.

(1) In section 30 of the Management Act (recovery of overpayment of tax etc.) after subsection (2) there shall be inserted the following subsection—

"(2A) In any case where—

(*a*) interest has been paid under section [826 of the principal Act][1] on a repayment of tax, and
(*b*) the whole or any part of that repayment has been paid to any person but ought not to have been paid to him, and
(*c*) interest ought not to have been paid on that repayment, either at all or to any extent,

then the amount of the repayment assessed under subsection (1) above may include an amount equal to the interest that ought not to have been paid."

Amendments.—[1] Words in para. (a) substituted by TA 1988, Sch. 29, para. 10 (3).

(2) After subsection (3) of that section there shall be inserted the following subsection—

"(3A) If, in a case not falling within subsection (2A) above,—

(a) interest has been paid under section [826 of the principal Act][1] on a repayment of tax, and

(b) that interest ought not to have been paid, either at all or to any extent,

then an amount equal to the interest that ought not to have been paid may be assessed and recovered as if it were unpaid corporation tax."

Amendments.—[1] Words in para. (a) substituted by TA 1988, Sch. 29, para. 10 (3).

(3) At the end of subsection (4) of that section there shall be added the words "and an assessment to recover—

(a) an amount of corporation tax repaid to a company in respect of an accounting period, or

(b) an amount of income tax repaid to a company in respect of a payment received by the company in any accounting period, or

(c) interest on any such repayment of tax,

shall be treated as an assessment to corporation tax for the accounting period referred to in paragraph (a) or (b) above, as the case may be, and the sum assessed shall carry interest at the prescribed rate for the purposes of section 87A of this Act from the date when the payment being recovered was made until payment."

(4) After subsection (4) of that section there shall be inserted the following subsection—

"(4A) Where an assessment is made under this section to recover—

(a) corporation tax repaid to a company in respect of an accounting period, or

(b) income tax repaid to a company in respect of payments received by the company in an accounting period,

and more than one repayment of that tax has been made in respect of that period, any sum recovered in respect of income tax or corporation tax repaid shall as far as possible be treated as relating to a repayment of that tax made later rather than to a repayment made earlier."

(5)–(6) . . .[1]

(7) Subsections (1) to (4) above have effect with respect to the recovery of—

(a) repayments of corporation tax paid for accounting periods ending after the appointed day,

(b) repayments of income tax on payments received by a company in any such accounting period, and

(c) interest on such repayments;

. . .[1]

Amendments.—[1] Sub-ss. (5), (6) and words in sub-s. (7) repealed by TA 1988, Sch. 31.

91. Close companies: loans to participators

(1) In section 109 of the Management Act (close companies: loans to participators) subsection (2) shall be omitted.

(2) In subsection (3) of that section for "88" there shall be substituted "87A" and for the words from "charged" onwards there shall be substituted "under the said section [419][1] became due and payable shall be that determined in accordance with subsection [(3)][1] of that section".

(3) After subsection (3) of that section there shall be inserted the following subsection—

"(3A) If there is such a repayment of the whole or any part of a loan or advance as is referred to in subsection [(4)][1] of section [419][1] of the principal Act, interest under section 87A of this Act on so much of the tax under the said section [419][1] as is referable to the amount repaid shall not be payable in respect of any period after the date on which the repayment was made."

(4) This section has effect with respect to loans or advances made (or treated as made) in any accounting period ending after the appointed day.

Amendments.—[1] Figures substituted by TA 1988, Sch. 29, para. 10 (8).

95. Interpretation of Chapter V and consequential and supplementary provisions

(1) In this Chapter "the Management Act" means the Taxes Management Act 1970.

(2) Subject to subsection (3) below, any reference in this Chapter to the appointed day is a reference to such day as the Treasury may by order made by statutory instrument appoint, and different days may be so appointed for different provisions of this Chapter.

(3) No day may be appointed by virtue of subsection (2) above which falls earlier than 31st March 1992.

(4) The provisions of Schedule 6 to this Act shall have effect, being provisions consequential on and supplementary to the provisions of this Chapter.

PART III
MISCELLANEOUS AND SUPPLEMENTARY

104. Short title, interpretation, construction and repeals

(1) This Act may be cited as the Finance (No. 2) Act 1987.

(2) In this Act "the Taxes Act" means the Income and Corporation Taxes Act 1970.

(3) Part I of this Act, so far as it relates to income tax, shall be construed as one with the Income Tax Acts, so far as it relates to corporation tax, shall be construed as one with the Corporation Tax Acts and, so far as it relates to capital gains tax, shall be construed as one with the Capital Gains Tax Act 1979.

(4) The enactments specified in Schedule 9 to this Act (which include enactments which are spent or otherwise unnecessary) are hereby repealed to the extent specified in the third column of that Schedule, but subject to any provision at the end of any Part of that Schedule.

SCHEDULE 6

Section 95

MANAGEMENT PROVISIONS: SUPPLEMENTARY AND CONSEQUENTIAL PROVISIONS

Companies' capital gains

1.—...[1]

Amendments.—[1] This paragraph repealed by TA 1988, Sch. 31.

2. With respect to chargeable gains accruing in accounting periods ending after the appointed day, in subsection (3C) of section 267 of the Taxes Act (company reconstruction or amalgamation: transfer of assets)—

(a) for the words "when it is payable" there shall be substituted "when it is due and payable or, if later, the date when the assessment is made on the company";
(b) for the words "the time when the tax became payable" there shall be substituted "the later of those dates"; and
(c) for the words from "a sum" onwards there shall be substituted "from the chargeable company a sum equal to that amount together with any interest paid by him under section 87A of the Taxes Management Act 1970 on that amount".

3.—...[1]

Amendments.—[1] This paragraph repealed by TA 1988, Sch. 31.

4.—(1) Section 278 of the Taxes Act (company ceasing to be member of a group) shall be amended as follows.

(2) In subsection (3) at the beginning of the words following paragraph (b) there shall be inserted "then, subject to subsection (3A) below", and after that subsection there shall be inserted the following subsection—

"(3A) Any chargeable gain or allowable loss which, apart from this subsection, would accrue to the chargeable company on the sale referred to in subsection (3) above shall be treated as accruing to the chargeable company as follows—

(a) for the purposes for which the assumptions in section [409 (2) of the Taxes Act 1988][1] apply, it shall be assumed to accrue in the notional or actual accounting period which ends when the company ceases to be a member of the group; and
(b) subject to paragraph (a) above, it shall be treated as accruing immediately before the company ceases to be a member of the group."

Amendments.—[1] Words in paragraph (a) substituted by TA 1988, Sch. 29, para. 32 Table.

(3) In subsection (5)—

(a) the words "of the", in the first place where they occur, shall be omitted;
(b) for the words "the date when it become payable" there shall be substituted "the date determined under subsection (5A) below";
(c) for the words "the time when the tax became payable" there shall be substituted "the said date"; and
(d) for the words "a sum" onwards there shall be substituted "from the chargeable company a sum equal to that amount together with any interest paid by the company concerned under section 87A of the Taxes Management Act 1970 on that amount".

(4) After subsection (5) there shall be inserted the following subsection—

"(5A) The date referred to in subsection (5) above is whichever is the later of—

(a) the date when the tax becomes due and payable by the company; and
(b) the date when the assessment was made on the chargeable company."

(5) In subsection (6) the words from the beginning to "group, and" shall be omitted.

(6) This paragraph has effect where the accounting period in which the chargeable company ceases to be a member of the group ends after the appointed day.

5.—(1) With respect to chargeable gains accruing in chargeable periods ending after the appointed day, section 87 of the Capital Gains Tax Act 1979 (restriction on application of sections 85 and 86 of that Act) shall be amended as follows.

(2) In subsection (4)—

(*a*) for the words "the date when it is payable" there shall be substituted "the date determined under subsection (4A) below";

(*b*) for the words "the time when the tax became payable" there shall be substituted "that date"; and

(*c*) for the words from "a sum" onwards there shall be substituted "from the chargeable person a sum equal to that amount together with any interest paid by him under section 87A of the Taxes Management Act 1970 on that amount".

(3) After subsection (4) there shall be inserted the following subsection—

"(4A) The date referred to in subsection (4) above is whichever is the later of—

(*a*) the date when the tax becomes due and payable by the chargeable person; and

(*b*) the date when the assessment was made on the chargeable person."

Relief for unremittable income

6.—...[1]

Amendments.—[1] This paragraph repealed by TA 1988, Sch. 31.

Charges on non-residents

7. With respect to tax in respect of accounting periods ending after the appointed day and interest on such tax, at the end of section 85 of the Management Act (application to corporation tax of provisions of Part VIII of that Act) there shall be added the following subsection—

"(2) Subsection (2) of section 83 above shall apply—

(*a*) to corporation tax to which a person is chargeable in respect of a non-resident company and which has become due and payable without the making of an assessment; and

(*b*) to interest to which he is chargeable on such tax under section 87A below,

as it applies (by virtue of subsection (1) above) to corporation tax which has been assessed on him in respect of such a company."

Lloyd's underwriting agents

8.—(1)...[1]

Amendments.—[1] This paragraph repealed by TA 1988, Sch. 31.

DESTINATION TABLE

This table lists the provisions of the Income and Corporation Taxes Act 1970 and subsequent Finance Acts and other Acts which are re-enacted in the Income and Corporation Taxes Act 1988. Where no corresponding provision appears under the 1988 Act in the third column, the former enactment may be spent or may have been repealed as indicated in the "Remarks" column.

For the operative date of the re-enacted provisions, please see sections 843 and 844 of the 1988 Act.

Finance Acts are referred to in this table by their years only, *e.g.* 1971 means Finance Act 1971. References to other Acts are abbreviated as shown in the abbreviation list below.

Abbreviations used in this table are—

1970 or 1970(F)	= Finance Act 1970
1971	= Finance Act 1971 and so on as respects subsequent years
1975(2)	= Finance (No. 2) Act 1975 and so on as respects subsequent years
§	= paragraph
AFA 1981	= Armed Forces Act 1981
AJA 1982	= Administration of Justice Act 1982
Am.	= Amended by
BA 1987	= Banking Act 1987
BNA	= British Nationality Act 1981
BSA 1986	= Building Societies Act 1986
CGTA 7	= Capital Gains Tax Act 1979 Sch. 7 and so on
CCCPA	= Companies Consolidation (Consequential Provisions) Act 1985 Sch. 2
CCA 1974	= Consumer Credit Act 1974
CCA 1984	= County Courts Act 1984
CUA 1979	= Credit Unions Act 1979
CJA 1975	= Criminal Jurisdiction Act 1975
DCA 1969	= Decimal Currency Act 1969
EP(C)A	= Employment Protection (Consolidation) Act 1978
FA	= Finance Act
FSA	= Friendly Societies Act
HSA 1984	= Health and Social Security Act 1984
HCPA 1985	= Housing (Consequential Provisions) Act 1985
IDA 1982	= Industrial Development Act 1982
ITA	= Inheritance Tax Act 1984
IA 1986	= Insolvency Act 1986
ICA	= Insurance Companies Act
IA 1978	= Interpretation Act 1978
J(NI)A	= Judicature (Northern Ireland) Act 1978
LGA	= Local Government Act 1972
LRTA	= London Regional Transport Act 1984
NHS 1977	= National Health Service Act 1977
NHS 1978	= National Health Service (Scotland) Act 1978
NICA	= Northern Ireland Constitution Act 1973
OTA	= Oil Taxation Act
OPA 1973	= Overseas Pensions Act 1973
para	= paragraph
PPA 1972	= Parliamentary and other Pensions Act 1972
PPA 1987	= Parliamentary and other Pensions Act 1987
PPA 1976	= Parliamentary and other Pensions and Salaries Act 1976
Pt.	= Part
Rep.	= Repealed
Sch.	= Schedule
s.	= section
SSA	= Social Security Act
SSCPA	= Social Security (Consequential Provisions) Act 1975
S.I.	= Statutory Instrument
Subst.	= Substituted by
SBA 1976	= Supplementary Benefits Act 1976
TA	= Income and Corporation Taxes Act
TA 1984	= Telecommunications Act 1984
TSB 1985	= Trustee Savings Banks Act 1985

The above abbreviations are also used as applicable in the annotations under the sections and the schedules paragraphs of the 1988 Act.

The statutory instruments are referred to in this table by their numbers only. The following list shows their full titles—

1970/1537 = Secretary of State for Trade and Industry Order 1970
1970/1681 = Secretary of State for the Environment Order 1970
1971/2099 = Minister for the Civil Service Order 1971
1977/2158 = Supplementary Benefits etc. (Consequential Provisions) (Northern Ireland) Order 1977
1979/1573 = Statutory Rules (Northern Ireland) Order 1979
1979/1574 = Industrial Assurance (Northern Ireland) Order 1979
1979/1576 = Tax, Consumer Credit and Judicature (Northern Ireland Consequential Amendments) Order 1979
1980/1171 = Income Tax (Construction Operations) Order 1980
1981/157 = Building Societies and Tax (Northern Ireland Consequential Amendments) Order 1981
1981/1670 = Transfer of Functions (Minister for the Civil Service and the Treasury) Order 1981
1982/338 = The Departments (Northern Ireland) Order 1982 (S.I. No. 338 (N.I. 6))
1983/50 = Companies (Northern Ireland) Order 1983
1985/1205 = Credit Unions (Northern Ireland) Order 1985
1985/1598 = Income Tax (Cash Equivalents of Car Benefits) Order 1985
1986/702 = Income Tax (Cash Equivalents of Car Fuel Benefits) Order 1986
1986/703 = Income Tax (Cash Equivalents of Car Benefits) Order 1986
CCCP(NI) = Companies Consolidation (Consequential Provisions) (Northern Ireland) Order 1986
1986/771 = Income Tax (Composite Rates) (Relevant Deposits) Order 1986
1986/1888 = Social Security (Northern Ireland) Order 1986
1987/434 = Income Tax (Indexation) Order 1987
1987/898 = Income Tax (Interest on Unpaid Tax and Repayment Supplement) (No. 2) Order 1987

INCOME AND CORPORATION TAXES ACT 1970
(c. 10)

TA 1970	Subject Matter	Re-enacted in TA 1988	Remarks
s. 1	The charge to income tax.	s. 1(1), (2)	
s. 2	Fractions of a pound, and yearly assessments.	s. 2	Am. 1970(F) Sch. 4 §11; partly spent.
s. 3	Certain income charged at basic rate.	s. 3	Subst. 1971 Sch. 6 §2.
s. 4	Dates for payment.	s. 5	Rep. in part 1971 Sch. 14 Pt. II; am. 1971 Sch. 6 §3; 1975(2) s. 44(1); 1972 Sch. 24 §15; 1980 s. 61(1).
s. 5	Personal reliefs: general.	s. 256	Am. 1975(2) s. 31(3); 1976 Sch. 4 §18.
s. 6	—	—	Rep. 1971 Sch. 14 Pt. II.
s. 7	—	—	Rep. 1975(2) Sch. 14 Pt. IV.
s. 8(1)	Personal relief.	s. 257(1)	Am. 1971 Sch. 6 §5; 1987/434.
s. 8(1A)		s. 257(2)	Added 1975(2) s. 31(1); am. 1977 s. 22(1); 1987/434.
s. 8(1B)		s. 257(5)	Added 1975(2) s. 31(1); am. 1987/434.
s. 8(2)		s. 257(6), (7)	Am. 1971 Sch. 6 §5; 1979(2) Sch. 2 §1; 1981 s. 27(9); 1987 s. 27(1); 1987/434; rep. in part 1981 Sch. 19 Pt. VI; 1982 Sch. 22 Pt. IV.
s. 8(3)		s. 257(8)	Am. 1970(F) s. 14(1).
s. 9	—	—	Rep. 1971 Sch. 14 Pt. II.
s. 10	—	—	Rep. 1982 Sch. 22 Pt. XI.
s. 11(1)–(3), (6)	—	—	Rep. 1982 Sch. 22 Pt. XI.
s. 11(4), (5)	Apportionment of relief.	s. 263(5), (6)	Applied by 1970 s. 16(3).
s. 12	Widow's or widower's housekeeper.	s. 258	Rep. in part 1978 Sch. 13 Pt. III; 1971 Sch. 14 Pt. II; am. 1971 s. 15(5), Sch. 6 §7; 1978 s. 19(2).
s. 13			Rep. 1979(2) Sch. 5 Pt. II.
s. 14	Relief in respect of children.	s. 259	Rep. in part 1970(F) Sch. 8 §6; am. 1976 s. 36(4); 1979(2) Sch. 1 §2; 1980 s. 24(6); 1987 Sch. 15 §2(2).
s. 14A	Apportionment of relief.	s. 260	Added 1979(2) Sch. 1 §3; am. 1980 s. 24(6).
s. 15	Claims under ss. 12–14 for year of marriage.	s. 261	
s. 15A	Widow's bereavement allowance.	s. 262	Added 1980 s. 23; am. 1980 s. 24(6); 1983 s. 15(1).
s. 16(1), (2)	Dependent relatives.	s. 263(1), (2)	Am. 1973 s. 12(2).
s. 16(2A)		s. 263(3)	Added 1979(2) Sch. 2 §2.
s. 16(3)		s. 263(4)	Am. 1973 s. 12(2).
s. 16(4)		s. 263(7)	
s. 16(5)			Spent.
s. 17	Claim for services of son or daughter.	s. 264	Am. 1971 Sch. 6 §11; 1978 s. 19(5).
s. 18(1), (2)	Relief for blind persons.	s. 265(1), (2)	Am. 1978 s. 19(6); 1981 s. 23(2), (3); 1987 s. 28; rep. in part 1981 Sch. 19 Pt. VI.
s. 18(3), (4)		—	Rep. 1978 Sch. 13 Pt. III.
s. 18(5), (6)		s. 265(3), (4)	Am. 1978 s. 19(5); 1987 Sch. 15 §2(3); rep. in part 1981 Sch. 19 Pt. VI.
s. 19(1)	Relief for certain premiums.	s. 266(1)	Am. 1976 Sch. 4 §3(1).

TA 1970	Subject Matter	Re-enacted in TA 1988	Remarks
s. 19(2)		s. 266(2)	Am. 1976 s. 36(5), Sch. 4 §3(2); ICA 1982 Sch. 5 §10.
s. 19(3)(a), (b)		s. 266(3)(a), (d)	
s. 19(3)(i), (ii)		s. 266(11)	
s. 19(4)		s. 266(3)(b), (10)	Rep. in part 1971 Sch. 14 Pt. I; am. 1971 Sch. 3 §11.
s. 19(5)		Sch. 14 §8(1), (2)	
s. 19(6)		s. 267	
s. 19(7), (8)		—	Rep. 1971 Sch. 14 Pt. II; 1976 Sch. 15 Pt. IV.
s. 20(1)	Further relief for premiums and other payments.	s. 273	Rep. in part 1972 Sch. 28 Pt. IV; 1976 Sch. 15 Pt. IV; 1987 Sch. 15 §2(4).
s. 20(2)–(5)		—	Rep. 1987 Sch. 16 Pt. VII.
s. 21(1)	Limits on relief under ss. 19 and 20.	s. 274(1)	Am. 1976 Sch. 4 §21.
s. 21(1A), (2)		—	Rep. 1976 Sch. 4 §21(3); 1975 Sch. 13 Pt. II.
s. 21(3)		s. 274(2)	Am. 1976 Sch. 4 §21; 1975 Sch. 2 §6.
s. 21(4)		s. 274(3)	Am. 1975 Sch. 2 §6; 1980 s. 29; 1987 Sch. 15 §2(5); rep. in part 1976 Sch. 15 Pt. IV.
s. 21(5)		s. 274(4)	Rep. in part 1975 Sch. 13 Pt. II.
s. 22	—	—	Rep. 1970(F) Sch. 8 Pt. IV.
s. 23	Meaning of relative.	s. 275	
s. 24	—	—	Rep. 1977 Sch. 9 Pt. IV; 1976 Sch. 15 Pt. III.
s. 25	Effect on relief of charges on income.	s. 276	Subst. 1971 s. 33(5); rep. in part 1976 Sch. 15 Pt. IV.
s. 26	Partners.	s. 277	Rep. in part 1970(F) Sch. 8 Pt. VII.
s. 27(1), (2)	Non-residents.	s. 278(1)–(3)	Am. BNA s. 51(1)(b), (2); rep. in part 1971 Sch. 14 Pt. II.
s. 27(3)–(5)		s. 278(5)–(8)	Rep. in part 1972 Sch. 28 Pt. VI.
s. 28, 29	—	—	Rep. 1971 Sch. 14 Pt. II.
s. 30	—	—	Rep. 1985 Sch. 27 Pt. VIII.
s. 31, 32	—	—	Rep. 1971 Sch. 14 Pt. II.
s. 33	—	—	Rep. 1985 Sch. 27 Pt. VIII.
s. 34(1)	Tax on consideration for certain restrictive covenants.	s. 313(1)–(3)	Am. 1971 Sch. 16 §15; rep. in part 1980 Sch. 20 Pt. V.
s. 34(2)–(5)		s. 313(4)–(6)	Rep. in part 1987 Sch. 16 Pt. VII.
s. 35	—	—	Rep. 1971 Sch. 14 Pt. II.
s. 36	Recovery from trustees of tax due from certain beneficiaries.	s. 689	Am. 1971 Sch. 6 §16; 1978 Sch. 2 §3; rep. in part 1980 Sch. 20 Pt. V; 1984 Sch. 23 Pt. VI.
s. 37(1)	Aggregation of wife's income with husband's.	s. 279(1), (2)	Am. 1976 s. 36(2), (9); 1978 s. 30(7)(e).
s. 37(2)		s. 279(3), (4)	
s. 37(3)		s. 279(5)	Subst. 1971 Sch. 6 §17.
s. 37(4)		s. 279(6)	
s. 37(5)		—	Rep. 1971 Sch. 14 Pt. II.
s. 38(1)	Options for separate assessment.	s. 283(1)	Rep. in part 1971 Sch. 14 Pt. II; 1976 Sch. 15 Pt. III; am. 1976 s. 36(3).
s. 38(2)		s. 283(2)	Subst. 1971 Sch. 6 §18; rep. in part 1984 Sch. 23 Pt VI.
s. 38(3)–(5)		s. 283(3)–(5)	Rep. in part 1971 Sch. 14 Pt. II.
s. 39(1)(a), (b)	Separate assessments and personal reliefs.	—	Rep. 1971 Sch. 14 Pt. II.

TA 1970	Subject Matter	Re-enacted in TA 1988	Remarks
s. 39(1)(c)–(e)		s. 284(1), (5)	Rep. in part 1971 Sch. 14 Pt. II; 1982 Sch. 22 Pt. XI; am. 1978 s. 19(5); 1971 Sch. 6 §19.
s. 39(1) proviso		s. 284(2)	Am. 1971 Sch. 6 §19.
s. 39(2)		s. 284(3)	Rep. in part 1971 Sch. 14 Pt. II.
s. 39(3)		s. 284(4)	
s. 39(4)		—	Rep. 1971 Sch. 14 Pt. II.
s. 40	Collection from wife of tax on her income.	s. 285	Rep. in part 1971 Sch. 14 Pt. II.
s. 41	Husband's disclaimer of tax on dead wife's income.	s. 286	Rep. in part 1971 Sch. 14 Pt. II.
s. 42	Interpretation.	s. 282	Rep. in part 1971 Sch. 14 Pt. II.
s. 43–48	—	—	Rep. 1971 Sch. 14 Pt. VII.
s. 49	Residence: temporary absence.	s. 334	Am. BNA s. 51(1)(b), (2).
s. 50(1)	Working abroad.	s. 335(1)	
s. 50(2)		s. 335(1)(b)	
s. 50(3)		s. 335(2)	
s. 51	Temporary residents in U.K.	s. 336	
s. 51A	Annual payments	s. 347A	Added 1988 s. 36(2).
s. 51B	Qualifying maintenance payments	s. 347B	Added 1988 s. 36(2).
s. 52(1)(a)	Deduction of tax: payments out of profits etc. brought into charge to income tax.	—	Rep. in part 1971 Sch. 14 Pt. II.
s. 52(1)(b)		s. 348(1)(a)	
s. 52(1)(c)		s. 348(1)(b)	Rep. 1971 Sch. 14 Pt. II.
s. 52(1)(d)		s. 348(1)(c)	
s. 52(1)(e)		s. 348(1)(d)	Added 1971 Sch. 6 §20(c).
s. 52(2)		s. 348(2)	Rep. in part 1971 Sch. 14 Pt. II.
s. 53(1)	Payments not out of profits etc. brought into charge to income tax.	s. 349(1)	Rep. in part 1971 Sch. 14 Pt. II.
s. 53(2)		s. 350(1)	Am. 1971 Sch. 6 §21.
s. 53(3)		s. 350(3)	
s. 53(4)		s. 350(4)(a)	Am. 1972 Sch. 24 §16.
s. 54(1)	Annual interest.	s. 349(2)	Am. 1971 Sch. 1 §22.
s. 54(2)		s. 349(3)(a), (b)	
s. 54(3)		s. 350(1), (3), (4)	
s. 55(1)	Certificates of deduction of tax.	s. 352(1)	Am. 1973 s. 17(4); 1986 s. 29(3).
s. 55(2)		s. 352(2)	
s. 56	Interpretation.	s. 350(2)	
s. 57–64	—	—	Rep. 1972 Sch. 28 Pt. V.
s. 64A	Employee share schemes.	s. 688	Added 1970(F) Sch. 4 §9(5); am. CCCPA.
s. 65(1), (1A)	Small maintenance payments.	s. 351(1), (2)	Subst. 1982 s. 33(2); am. Income Tax (Small Maintenance Payments) Order 1986 (S.I. No. 328).
s. 65(2)		s. 348(3), 349(3)(d), 351(3)	
s. 65(3), (4)		s. 351(4), (5)	
s. 65(5)		s. 351(6)	Am. 1982 s. 33(3).
s. 65(6)		s. 351(7)	Am. 1982 s. 33(4).
s. 65(7)		s. 351(8)	
s. 66	—	—	Rep. 1977 Sch. 9 Pt. V.
s. 67	Schedule A.	s. 15	
s. 68	Persons chargeable.	s. 21	
s. 69(1)	Assessments.	s. 22(1)	
s. 69(2)		s. 22(2), (3)	

TA 1970	Subject Matter	Re-enacted in TA 1988	Remarks
s. 70(1)	Collection from lessees and agents.	s. 23(1)–(6)	
s. 70(2)		s. 23(7), (8)	
s. 71(1)	Deductions from rents etc.	s. 25(1), 28(1), 29(1), 31(1)	
s. 71(2)	Interpretation.	s. 24(6), (7)	
s. 72(1)	Deductions from rents: general rules.	s. 25(1), (2)	
s. 72(2)		s. 25(3), (4)	
s. 72(3)		s. 25(5), (6)	
s. 72(4)–(6)		s. 25(7)–(9)	
s. 72(7)		s. 25(2)	
s. 73(1)	Deductions from rents: land managed as one estate.	s. 26(1), (2)	
s. 73(2)		s. 26(3)	
s. 73(3)		s. 26(4), (5)	Am. 1987 Sch. 15 §2(6).
s. 73(4)		s. 26(6)	
s. 74	Deductions from receipts other than rent.	s. 28	
s. 75(1)	Sporting rights.	s. 29(1), (2)	
s. 75(2), (3), (4)		s. 29(3), (4), (5)	Am. 1976 Sch. 9 §12.
s. 76	Expenditure on sea walls.	s. 30	
s. 77	Interpretation.	s. 31(2)–(7)	
s. 78(1)	Capital allowances for machinery etc.	s. 32(1), (2)	Am. 1971 s. 47(2).
s. 78(2)		s. 32(3), (4)	Am. 1971 s. 47(2).
s. 78(3)–(6)		s. 32(5)–(8)	Partly spent; am. 1971 s. 47(2).
s. 79(1)	Agricultural land.	s. 33(1), (2), (4)	
s. 79(2)		s. 33(3)	
s. 80(1)	Premiums as rent or Schedule D profits.	s. 34(1)	
s. 80(2)		s. 34(2), (3)	Am. 1987 Sch. 15 §13.
s. 80(3), (4)		s. 34(4), (5)	
s. 80(5)		s. 34(6), (7)	
s. 80(6), (7)		s. 34(8), (9)	Am. 1972 s. 81(1).
s. 81(1)	Assignment of lease granted at an undervalue.	s. 35(1), (2)	
s. 81(2)		s. 35(3)	
s. 82(1), (2)	Sale of land with right to reconveyance.	s. 36(1), (2), (5)	
s. 82(3)		s. 36(3), (4), (5)	
s. 83(1)	Deductions from premium and rents received.	s. 37(1)–(3)	Am. 1978 s. 32(2); rep. in part 1972 Sch. 28 Pt. XII.
s. 83(2)		s. 37(4)	Rep. in part 1978 Sch. 13 Pt. III.
s. 83(3)		s. 37(5), (6)	
s. 83(4)(a)		s. 37(7)(a)	
s. 83(4)(b)(i), (ii)		s. 37(7)(b)	
s. 83(4)(b)(iii)		—	Rep. 1978 Sch. 13 Pt. III.
s. 83(5)		s. 37(8)	
s. 83(6)		—	Rep. 1978 Sch. 13 Pt. III.
s. 83(7)		s. 37(9)	
s. 84(1)(a)	Rules for ascertaining duration of leases.	—	Rep. 1972 Sch. 28 Pt. XII.
s. 84(1)(b)–(d)		s. 38(1)	Am. 1972 s. 81(2).
s. 84(2)		s. 38(2), (3), (4)	Am. 1972 s. 81(2).
s. 84(3)		s. 38(6)	Am. 1972 s. 81(2).
s. 84(3A)		s. 38(5)	Added 1972 s. 81(5).
s. 84(4)		s. 38(7)	
s. 85(1)	Pre-1963 leases and special relief for individuals.	s. 39(1), (2)	
s. 85(2)		s. 39(3)	Rep. in part 1972 Sch. 28 Pt. XII.
s. 86	Receipts and outgoings on sale of land.	s. 40	
s. 87(1)	Relief for rent not paid.	s. 41(1), (2)	
s. 87(2)		s. 41(3)	
s. 88	—	—	Rep. 1971 Sch. 14 Pt. III.

TA 1970	Subject Matter	Re-enacted in TA 1988	Remarks
s. 89	Non-residents.	s. 43	
s. 90(1)	Interpretation.	s. 24(1)	Am. 1972 s. 81(3).
s. 90(2)		s. 24(2)	
s. 90(2A), (2B)		s. 24(3), (4)	Added 1972 s. 81(4).
s. 90(3)		s. 24(5)	
s. 91	Schedule B.	s. 16(1)	
s. 92(1)–(3)	Supplementary provisions.	s. 16(2)–(5)	
s. 92(4)		s. 16(6)	Added 1984 s. 51.
s. 93	Schedule C.	s. 17	Am. DCA 1969 s. 10.
s. 94	Mode of charge.	s. 44	
s. 95–97	—	—	Rep. 1981 Sch. 19 Pt VI.
s. 98	Tax reserve certificates.	s. 46(2)	
s. 99	U.K. government securities.	s. 47	
s. 100	Securities of foreign states.	s. 48(1)–(3)	
s. 101(1)	Payment of interest without deduction of tax.	s. 50(1)	
s. 101(2)		s. 50(2), (3)	
s. 101(3)–(6)		s. 50(4)–(7)	
s. 102	Northern Ireland securities.	s. 51	Am. NICA Sch. 5 §8(1); 1982/338.
s. 103	Information.	Sch. 29	Am. 1987 Sch. 15 §2(7).
s. 104	Converted government securities.	s. 52	
s. 105	War loans.	—	Rep. 1987 Sch. 16 Pt. VII.
s. 106(1), (2)	Treasury and Crown holdings etc.	s. 49	
s. 106(3)		Sch. 29	
s. 107	Interpretation.	s. 45	
s. 108	Schedule D.	s. 18(1), (4)	Rep. in part 1973 Sch. 22 Pt II; am. BNA s. 51(1), (2).
s. 109	The six Cases.	s. 18(2)–(4)	Rep. in part 1971 Sch. 14 Pt. IV.
s. 110(1), (2)	Farming etc.	s. 53(1), (2)	
s. 110(3)		s. 53(3), (4)	
s. 111	Woodlands.	s. 54	
s. 112	Mines etc.	s. 55	
s. 113	Foreign pensions.	s. 58	
s. 114	Persons chargeable.	s. 59	
s. 115(1)	Case I and II assessments on preceding year basis.	s. 60(1)	
s. 115(2)		s. 60(2)–(4)	
s. 115(3)–(6)		s. 60(5)–(8)	
s. 116(1)	Special basis on start of business.	s. 61(1), (2)	Am. 1985 s. 47.
s. 116(2)		s. 61(3)	
s. 117(1)	Special basis for two years after start.	s. 62(1)	Am. 1985 s. 47.
s. 117(2)		s. 62(2), (3)	
s. 117(3)		s. 62(6)–(8)	Am. 1987 Sch. 15 §2(8).
s. 117(4), (5)		s. 62(9), (10)	Am. 1987 Sch. 15 §2(8).
s. 118	Special basis on discontinuance.	s. 63	
s. 119	Case III assessments.	s. 64	
s. 120	Special rules for fresh income.	s. 66(1)–(4)	
s. 121(1), (2)	Special rules where source of income ceases.	s. 67(1), (2)	
s. 121(3)		s. 67(4), (5)	
s. 121(4), (5)		s. 67(7), (8)	
s. 122(1)(*a*), (*b*)	Case IV and V assessments.	s. 65(1)	
s. 122(1)(*c*)		—	Rep. 1987 Sch. 16 Pt. VII.
s. 122(2)(*a*)		s. 65(4)	Am. BNA s. 51(1), (2).
s. 122(2)(*b*), (*c*)		—	Rep. 1974 Sch. 14 Pt. VI.
s. 122(3)–(7)		s. 65(5)–(9)	
s. 123(1)–(3)	Special rules for fresh income.	s. 66(1)–(3)	
s. 123(4), (5)		s. 66(5), (6)	

TA 1970	Subject Matter	Re-enacted in TA 1988	Remarks
s. 124(1)	Special rules where source of income ceases.	s. 67(1)	
s. 124(2)		s. 67(3)	
s. 124(3)		s. 67(4), (5)	
s. 124(4)–(6)		s. 67(6)–(8)	
s. 125	Case VI assessments.	s. 69	
s. 126	Taxation where no profits.	s. 71	
s. 127	Apportionments for Cases I, II and VI.	s. 72	
s. 128	Single assessments.	s. 73	
s. 129(1)	Corporation tax.	s. 70(1)	
s. 129(2)		s. 72(1)	
s. 129(3)		s. 73	
s. 129(4), (5)		s. 70(2), (3)	
s. 130(*a*)–(*m*)	Deductions not allowable.	s. 74(*a*)–(*n*)	Am. 1987 Sch. 15 §2(9).
s. 130(*n*), (*o*)		s. 74(*p*), (*q*)	
s. 131(1)–(5)	Interest paid to non-residents.	s. 82(1)–(5)	S. 131(2)(*c*)(ii) am. 1982 s. 64(1).
s. 131(6)		—	Rep. 1982 Sch. 22 Pt. IV.
s. 131(7)		s. 82(6)	
s. 132	Patent fees etc.	s. 83	
s. 133	Payments for technical education.	s. 84	Am. 1987 Sch. 15 §2(10).
s. 134(1)	Taxable premiums etc.	s. 87(1), (9)	Rep. in part 1972 Sch. 28 Pt. XII, 1978 Sch. 13 Pt. III; am. 1978 s. 32.
s. 134(2)		s. 87(2)	Am. 1978 s. 32; rep. in part 1978 Sch. 13 Pt. III.
s. 134(3)		s. 87(3)	
s. 134(4)		s. 87(4), (5), (6)	
s. 134(5), (6)		s. 87(7), (8)	Am. 1986 Sch. 13 §26.
s. 134(7)		—	Rep. 1978 Sch. 13 Pt. III.
s. 135	Irrecoverable debts.	s. 89	
s. 136	Released debts.	s. 94	
s. 137(1)	Valuation of trading stock.	s. 100(1)	
s. 137(2), (3)		s. 102(1), (2)	
s. 137(4)		s. 100(2)	
s. 138(1)	Valuation of work in progress.	s. 101(1)	
s. 138(2)		s. 102(1)	
s. 138(3)		s. 101(2)	
s. 138(4)		s. 102(2)	
s. 138(5)		s. 101(3)	
s. 139	Treatment of farm animals etc.	s. 97	
s. 140	Tied premises.	s. 98	
s. 141(1)	Cemeteries.	s. 91(1)	
s. 141(2)		s. 91(2), (3)	
s. 141(3)–(8)		s. 91(4)–(9)	
s. 142(1)	Dealers in land.	s. 99(1), (4)	
s. 142(2)		s. 99(2)	
s. 142(3)		—	Rep. 1972 Sch. 28 Pt. XII.
s. 142(4)		s. 99(2), (3)	
s. 143	Receipts after discontinuance.	s. 103	
s. 144(1)		s. 104(1)–(3)	
s. 144(2)		s. 104(4), (5)	
s. 144(3), (4)		s. 104(6), (7)	
s. 144(5)		—	Unnecessary.
s. 145	Allowable deductions.	s. 105	
s. 146	Permanent discontinuance of business.	s. 110(2)	
s. 147	Transfer of rights to certain payments.	s. 106	Partly spent.
s. 148	Receipts as earned income.	s. 107	
s. 149	Election for carry-back.	s. 108	
s. 150	Relief for individuals over 71.	s. 109	
s. 151	Interpretation.	s. 110(1), (3)–(6)	
s. 152	Partnership assessments.	s. 111	
s. 153	Foreign partnerships.	s. 112	Am. 1987(2) s. 62.

TA 1970	Subject Matter	Re-enacted in TA 1988	Remarks
s. 154	Change in ownership of business.	s. 113	Am. 1971 s. 17.
s. 155(1)	Partnerships involving companies.	s. 114(1)	Am. 1980 s. 39(3).
s. 155(2)		s. 114(2)	Subst. 1972 s. 107(2).
s. 155(3), (4)		s. 114(3), (4)	
s. 155(5)		s. 115(1), (2), (3)	
s. 155(6)–(9)		s. 115(4)–(7), 6(4)	Am. 1971 Sch. 8 §16; 1986 s. 56(7)(*a*), Sch. 13 §2(5).
s. 156	Mining rents etc.	s. 119	
s. 157	Rent for certain wayleaves.	s. 120	Am. DCA 1969 s. 10(1).
s. 158(1)	Management expenses of mine owners.	s. 121(1), (2)	
s. 158(2)		s. 121(3)	
s. 158(3)		—	Rep. 1971 Sch. 14 Pt. III.
s. 159	Foreign dividends.	s. 123	Am. 1986 s. 48(2).
s. 160–167	—	—	Rep. 1971 Sch. 14 Pt. IV.
s. 168(1), (2)	Set off of losses against general income.	s. 380(1), (2)	
s. 168(3)		s. 382(1)	Subst. 1971 s. 16(2)(*a*).
s. 168(4)		s. 382(2)	Rep. in part 1971 Sch. 14 Pt. VII.
s. 168(5)		s. 382(3)	
s. 168(6)		s. 380(3)	
s. 168(7)		s. 382(4)	Am. 1987 Sch. 15 §2(11).
s. 168(8)		s. 380(4)	
s. 169(1)–(3)	Extension of right of set off to capital allowances.	s. 383(1)–(3)	
s. 169(4)–(7)		s. 383(5)–(8)	
s. 169(8)		s. 383(9), (10)	
s. 169(9)		s. 383(11)	
s. 169(10)		s. 383(12)	
s. 170(1)	Restrictions on right of set-off.	s. 384(1), (2)	
s. 170(2)–(4)		s. 384(3)–(5)	
s. 170(5), (6)		s. 384(9), (10)	
s. 171(1)	Carry-forward against subsequent profits.	s. 385(1), (2)	
s. 171(2)–(6)		s. 385(3)–(7)	
s. 171(7)		s. 385(8)	Partly spent.
s. 172	Carry-forward where business transferred to a company.	s. 386	
s. 173(1), (2)	Carry-forward as losses of amounts taxed under 1970 s. 53.	s. 387(1), (2)	
s. 173(3)(*aa*)		s. 387(3)(*a*)	Added 1970(F) Sch. 4 §9(6).
s. 173(3)(*a*)–(*e*)		s. 387(3)(*b*)–(*f*)	
s. 174(1)	Carry-back of terminal losses.	s. 388(1), (2)	
s. 174(2)–(6)		s. 388(3)–(7)	
s. 174(7)–(11)		s. 389(1)–(5)	Am. 1986 Sch. 13 §27.
s. 174(12)		s. 389(6), (7)	Am. 1971 Sch. 8 §16(5).
s. 174(13)		s. 389(8)	
s. 175(1)	Treatment of interest as a loss.	s. 390	
s. 175(2)(*a*)		s. 390	New para. (*a*) subst. for paras. (*a*) & (*b*) by 1972 Sch. 11 §3; am. 1974 Sch. 1 §28.
s. 175(2)(*b*)		—	Rep. 1977 Sch. 9 Pt. V.
s. 175(2)(*c*)		—	Rep. 1987 Sch. 16 Pt. VII.
s. 175(2)(*d*)		—	
s. 175(3)		—	Unnecessary.
s. 176	Case VI losses.	s. 392	
s. 177(1)–(3)	Losses other than terminal losses: corporation tax.	s. 393(1)–(3)	
s. 177(3A)		s. 393(4)	Added 1971 Sch. 8 §16; am. & rep. in part 1972 s. 67(2)(*c*); am. 1985 s. 60.

TA 1970	Subject Matter	Re-enacted in TA 1988	Remarks
s. 177(4)–(10)		s. 393(5)–(11)	
s. 178(1)	Terminal losses: corporation tax.	s. 394(1), (2)	
s. 178(2)–(5)		s. 394(3)–(6)	
s. 179	Case VI losses: corporation tax.	s. 396	
s. 180(1)–(7)	Loss relief in case of farming and market gardening.	s. 397(1)–(7)	Am. 1971 Sch. 8 §16(5); 1986 s. 56(7)(*a*), Sch. 13 §2(5).
s. 180(8)		s. 397(8), (9)	
s. 180(9)		s. 397(10)	
s. 181(1)	Schedule E.	s. 19(1), 192(1)	Am. 1974 s. 21(1); 1977 s. 31(3)(*a*); BNA Sch. 7.
s. 181(2)		s. 19(2)	
s. 182	Voluntary pensions.	s. 133	
s. 183	Taxable emoluments.	s. 131	Partly spent.
s. 184	Place of performance etc.	s. 132(1), (2), (4), (5)	Am. 1977 s. 31(3)(*b*); 1986 s. 34(7).
s. 185	—	—	Rep. 1977 Sch. 9 Pt. VI.
s. 186(1)–(3)	Gains by directors etc. from share options.	s. 135(1)–(4)	
s. 186(4), (5)		s. 135(6), (7)	
s. 186(5A), (5B)		s. 135(8), (9)	Added 1986 s. 26(1).
s. 186(6)–(8)		s. 136(1)–(4)	
s. 186(9)		s. 140(1)	
s. 186(10)		s. 140(2), (3), 136(5)	
s. 186(11)		s. 136(6)	Am. 1986 s. 26(2).
s. 186(12)(*a*)		Sch. 29	Am. CGTA 7.
s. 186(12)(*b*)		—	Rep. 1971 Sch. 14 Pt. IV.
s. 187	Payments on retirement etc.	s. 148	
s. 188(1)	Exemptions from s. 187.	s. 188(1)	Am. 1971 Sch. 6 §24; 1970(F) Sch. 5 Pt. III §12(1).
s. 188(2)(*a*)		—	Rep. 1984 s. 30(7).
s. 188(2)(*b*)		—	Rep. 1974 Sch. 14 Pt. VI.
s. 188(2)(*c*)		s. 188(3)	1974 s. 21(3) altered §(*c*) to (*b*); rep. in part 1974 Sch. 14 Pt. VI.
s. 188(3)		s. 188(4), (5)	Am. 1981 s. 31(1).
s. 188(4), (5)		s. 188(6), (7)	
s. 188(6)		s. 188(8)	Rep. in part 1981 Sch. 19 Pt. VI.
s. 189	Relief for necessary expenses.	s. 198	Am. 1971 s. 47(1)(ii); 1984 s. 28(2).
s. 190	—	—	Rep. 1972 Sch. 28 Pt. V.
s. 191	Expenses: official emoluments.	s. 199	Am. 1971/2099 Art. 4(1).
s. 192	Fees to professional bodies etc.	s. 201	
s. 193		—	Rep. 1971 Sch. 14 Pt. II.
s. 194(1), (2)	Expenses etc. of Minister of religion.	s. 332(1), (2)	Am. 1977 Sch. 8 §3(2), (3); 1987 Sch. 15 §2(12).
s. 194(3), (4)		s. 332(3), (4)	
s. 195–203		—	Rep. 1976 Sch. 15 Pt. III.
s. 204(1)	P.A.Y.E.	s. 203(1)	
s. 204(2)		s. 203(2), (3), (5)	Am. 1971 Sch. 6 §25; 1987(2) s. 92(2).
s. 204(3)		s. 203(6)–(8)	Rep. in part 1971 Sch. 14 Pt. II.
s. 204(3A)		s. 203(4)	Added 1987(2) s. 92(3).
s. 204(4)		s. 828	
s. 205(1)	Assessments unnecessary in certain cases.	s. 205(1), (2)	
s. 205(2)	Additional provision for certain assessments. s. 205(3)		
s. 206		s. 206	
s. 207	Disputes as to domicile or ordinary residence.	s. 207	
s. 208, 209	—	—	Rep. 1971 Sch. 14 Pt. I.

TA 1970	Subject Matter	Re-enacted in TA 1988	Remarks
s. 210		—	Rep. 1972 Sch. 28 Pt. IV.
s. 211(1)	Parliamentary pension funds.	s. 613(1), (2)	
s. 211(2)		s. 613(4)	Am. PPA 1972 Sch. 3; 1981 s. 50(1); PPA 1987 Sch. 3 §2(1).
s. 211(3)		Sch. 29	Rep. in part 1971 Sch. 14 Pt. IV.
s. 211(4)		s. 613(3)	
s. 211(5)		—	Rep. 1971 Sch. 14 Pt. I.
s. 212(1)	National insurance supplementary schemes.	s. 614(1)	Subst. SSCPA Sch. 2 §28.
s. 212(2)		—	Rep. 1987 Sch. 16 Pt. VII.
s. 212(3)		s. 614(6)	
s. 212(4)		Sch. 29	Rep. in part 1971 Sch. 14 Pt. IV.
s. 213(1)	Indian pensions.	s. 614(2)	Am. OPA 1973 s. 2; 1987 Sch. 15 §2(13).
s. 213(2)		Sch. 29	Rep. in part 1971 Sch. 14 Pt. IV; am. OPA 1973 s. 2.
s. 214(1)	Colonial pensions.	s. 615(1), (2)(a)–(d), (4)	Am. BNA Sch. 7; 1973 s. 53(1); rep. in part 1987 Sch. 16 Pt. VII.
s. 214(2)		s. 614(3)	Am. 1973 s. 53(1).
s. 214(3)		s. 614(6), 615(1)	
s. 214(4)		Sch. 29	Am. 1973 s. 53(1); rep. in part 1971 Sch. 14 Pt. IV.
s. 214(5)		s. 615(7), (8)(a)	
s. 214(6)		s. 615(5)	Added BNA Sch. 7; am. 1987 Sch. 15 §2(14).
s. 215(1), (2)	Overseas Service Act 1958 pensions.	s. 615(1), (2)(e)	Am. OPA 1973 s. 2.
s. 215(3)		s. 615(7), (8)(b)	
s. 216(1)	Central African Pension Fund.	s. 615(1), (2)(f)	
s. 216(2)		s. 614(3)	Am. 1987 Sch. 15 §2(13).
s. 216(3)		Sch. 29	Rep. in part 1971 Sch. 14 Pt. IV.
s. 216(4)		s. 615(2)(f), (7)	
s. 217(1)	Overseas Service Pensions Fund.	s. 615(1), (2)(g)	
s. 217(2)		s. 614(4)	Am. 1987 Sch. 15 §2(13).
s. 217(3)		Sch. 29	
s. 217(4)		s. 614(4), 615(2)(g), (7)	
s. 218(1)	Pension funds for overseas employees.	s. 614(5), (6)	Rep. in part 1971 Sch. 14 Pt. IV.
s. 218(2)		Sch. 29	
s. 218(3), (4)		s. 615(3), (6)	
s. 219(1)(a)	Social security benefits etc.	s. 617(1)	Am. SSCPA Sch. 2 §39; 1979(2) Sch. 1 §4(1), Sch. 2 §3; 1981 s. 27(1); 1982 s. 30(1); HSA 1984 Sch. 4 §2; rep. in part 1979(2) Sch. 5 Pt. II; SSA 1986 Sch. 11.
s. 219(1)(b)		—	Rep. 1977 Sch. 9 Pt. IV.
s. 219(2)		s. 617(2)	Subst. 1987 s. 29(1).
s. 219(3)		s. 617(3), (4)	Am. SSCPA Sch. 2 §39; rep. in part Social Security Pensions Act 1975 c. 60 Sch. 5.
s. 219A	Job release scheme allowances etc.	s. 150	Added 1982 s. 31(1); am. & rep. in part SSA 1986 Sch. 10 §71, Sch. 11.
s. 220–225	—	—	Rep. 1971 Sch. 14 Pt. I.
s. 226(1)	Tax exemption for qualifying premiums.	s. 619(1), 620(1)	Am. 1971 s. 20(1).
s. 226(2)		s. 620(2), (3)	Am. 1971 s. 20(3); 1976 s. 30(2); rep. in part 1980 Sch. 20 Pt. VII.

TA 1970	Subject Matter	Re-enacted in TA 1988	Remarks
s. 226(3)		s. 620(4)	Rep. in part 1983 Sch. 10 Pt. II.
s. 226(4)		s. 619(1)	
s. 226(5)		s. 620(5)	
s. 226(6)		s. 620(6), Sch. 29	Rep. in part 1971 Sch. 14 Pt. IV.
s. 226(7)		s. 620(7)	
s. 226(8)–(10)		s. 623(1)–(4), 624(3)	Am. 1972 Sch. 24 §17; 1970(F) Sch. 5 Pt. III §12(7); 1976 s. 30(2); rep. in part 1987 Sch. 16 Pt. VII.
s. 226(11)		s. 624(1), (2)	
s. 226(12), (13)		s. 620(8), (9)	Am. 1987(2) Sch. 2 §1.
s. 226A	Other approved contracts.	s. 621, Sch. 29	Added 1971 Sch. 2 §1; am. 1976 s. 30(2); rep. in part 1980 Sch. 20 Pt. VII.
s. 227(1), (1A), (1B)	Qualifying premiums.	s. 619(1)–(3)	Subst. 1971 s. 20(2); am. 1980 s. 31(1), (2).
s. 227(1BB)		s. 619(4)	Added 1980 s. 33(2).
s. 227(1C), (2), (2A), (2B), (3)		—	Rep. 1980 Sch. 20 Pt. VII.
s. 227(4)		s. 623(5)	
s. 227(5)(*a*)		s. 623(6)(*a*)	Subst. 1980 s. 33(3); rep. in part 1971 Sch. 14 Pt. II; 1980 Sch. 20 Pt. VII.
s. 227(5)(*aa*)		s. 623(6)(*b*)	Added 1980 s. 33(3).
s. 227(5)(*b*)		s. 623(6)(*c*)	Rep. in part 1987 Sch. 16 Pt. VII.
s. 227(6)		s. 623(7)	
s. 227(7)		—	Rep. 1980 Sch. 20 Pt. VII.
s. 227(8), (9)		s. 623(8), (9)	Partly spent; rep. in part 1987 Sch. 16 Pt. VII.
s. 227(10), (11)		s. 619(5), (6)	
s. 227(12)		—	Rep. 1987 Sch. 16 Pt. VII.
s. 227(13)		s. 619(7)	
s. 227A	Carry-forward of unused relief.	s. 625	Added 1980 s. 32(1).
s. 228	Increased relief in certain cases.	s. 626	Subst. 1987(2) s. 54(2).
s. 229(1), (1A), (1B)	Annuity premiums for Ministers etc.	s. 629	Rep. in part 1980 Sch. 20 Pt. VII; am. PPA 1972 s. 32; PPA 1976 s. 1(3); PPA 1987 Sch. 3 §2(2).
s. 229(2)		—	Rep. 1987 Sch. 16 Pt. VII.
s. 230(1)	Purchased life annuities.	s. 656(1)	
s. 230(2)		s. 656(3)(*a*)–(*d*)	
s. 230(2A)		s. 656(2), (3)(*e*)	Added 1970(F) Sch. 4 §8.
s. 230(3)–(5)		s. 656(4)–(6)	
s. 230(6), (7)		s. 657	Rep. in part 1976 Sch. 15 Pt. IV; am. 1978 s. 26(4); 1987(2) s. 41(3).
s. 231	Supplementary provisions.	s. 658, 828	
s. 232(1)	Schedule F.	s. 20	Subst. 1972 s. 87(2).
s. 232(2), (3)		—	Rep. 1972 Sch. 28 Pt. VI.
s. 232(4)		s. 234(1), (2)	Subst. 1972 Sch. 24 §18.
s. 233(1)	Meaning of "distribution".	s. 209(1)	Am. 1980 s. 45(2).
s. 233(2)(*a*)		s. 209(2)(*a*)	
s. 233(2)(*b*)		s. 209(2)(*b*)	Am. 1972 Sch. 22 §1.
s. 233(2)(*c*)		s. 209(2)(*c*)	Subst. 1972 Sch. 22 §2(1).
s. 233(2)(*d*)(i)		s. 209(2)(*e*)(i)	
s. 233(2)(*d*)(ii)		s. 209(2)(*e*)(ii)	Subst. 1972 Sch. 22 §3(1).
s. 233(2)(*d*)(iii)		s. 209(2)(*d*), (*e*)(iii)	Am. 1972 Sch. 22 §3(2).
s. 233(2)(*d*)(iv)(*aa*)		s. 209(2)(*e*)(iv)	
s. 233(2)(*d*)(iv)(*bb*)		s. 209(2)(*e*)(iv)	Subst. 1970(F) Sch. 4 §6(1).
s. 233(2)(*d*)(iv)(*cc*)		s. 209(2)(*e*)(v)	Subst. 1970(F) Sch. 4 §6(1).
s. 233(2)(*d*)(v)		s. 209(2)(*e*)(vi)	
s. 233(2)(*e*)		s. 209(2)(*f*)	
s. 233(3)		s. 209(4), (5)	
s. 233(4)		s. 209(7)	

TA 1970	Subject Matter	Re-enacted in TA 1988	Remarks
s. 234(1)	Bonus issue following repayment of capital.	s. 210(1)	Rep. in part 1972 Sch. 28 Pt. VI.
s. 234(2)		s. 210(2)	
s. 234(3)		s. 210(4)	Rep. in part 1972 Sch. 28 Pt. VI.
s. 235(1)	Matters to be treated or not to be treated as repayments of share capital.	s. 211(1)	Am. 1972 Sch. 22 §6(1), (3).
s. 235(2)–(5)		s. 211(3)–(7)	
s. 236	—	—	Rep. 1972 Sch. 28 Pt. VI.
s. 237(1)		s. 254(1), (5)	
s. 237(2)		s. 254(9)	
s. 237(3)		s. 254(1)	
s. 237(4)		s. 254(10)	
s. 237(5)		s. 254(1)	
s. 237(6)		s. 254(11)	
s. 237(7)		s. 254(12)	
s. 238	Charge to corporation tax.	s. 6(1)–(4)	Rep. in part 1971 Sch. 14 Pt. II. Subsection (4) not repealed.
s. 239	Certain distributions not chargeable to corporation tax.	s. 208	
s. 240(1)–(3), (6)	—	—	Rep. 1972 Sch. 28 Pt. VI.
s. 240(4), (5), (7)	Payments exempt from income tax.	s. 7(1), (2), (4)	Rep. in part 1972 Sch. 28 Pt. VI.
s. 240A	—	—	Added 1971 Sch. 4 §§1, 5; rep. 1972 Sch. 28 Pt. VI.
s. 241	Claims for repayment etc.	s. 7(5)	
s. 242	Information to be attached to dividend warrants etc.	s. 234(3), (4)	Am. 1972 Sch. 24 §19; CCCPA; CCCP(NI).
s. 243(1)–(3)	General scheme of corporation tax.	s. 8(1)–(3)	Am. 1974 s. 36; 1987(2) s. 90(1)(a).
s. 243(4)		s. 10(1)	Rep. in part 1987 Sch. 16 Pt. V; am. 1975(2) s. 44(2); 1987(2) s. 90(1)(b).
s. 243(5)–(7)		s. 8(4)–(6)	
s. 244		—	Rep. 1987 Sch. 16 Pt. V.
s. 245(1)	Tax on company in liquidation.	s. 342(1)	
s. 245(2), (3)		s. 342(2), (3)	Subst. 1974 s. 37(1).
s. 245(4)–(6)		s. 342(4)–(6)	
s. 245(7)–(9)		s. 342(7)–(9)	Subst. 1974 s. 37(1).
s. 246	Non-resident companies.	s. 11(1)–(3)	Am. CGTA 7.
s. 247	Basis of and periods for assessment.	s. 12	Am. 1972 s. 107(1); CCCPA.
s. 248(1), (2)	Allowance of charges on income and capital.	s. 338(1), (2)(a)	Am. 1981 s. 38(1); 1973 s. 54(1).
s. 248(3)		s. 338(3)	
s. 248(4)		s. 338(4)	Am. 1972 Sch. 24 §20; 1984 s. 35(4).
s. 248(5)		s. 338(5)	Am. 1981 s. 38(2).
s. 248(6)		s. 338(6)	Am. 1974 Sch. 1 §27; rep. in part 1987 Sch. 16 Pt. VI.
s. 248(7)		—	Rep. 1977 Sch. 9 Pt. V.
s. 248(8)		s. 339(6)	Am. 1972 Sch. 24 §20.
s. 248(8A)		s. 339(7)	Added 1986 s. 30(2).
s. 248(9)		s. 339(8)	Am. 1980 s. 55(3).
s. 249(1)–(4)	Interest payable to non-residents.	s. 340	Am. 1982 s. 64(1).
s. 249(5)		—	Rep. 1982 Sch. 22 Pt. IV.
s. 250	Computation of income: general.	s. 9	Rep. in part 1971 Sch. 14 Pts. II, IV.
s. 251	Computation of income: special rules.	s. 337	

TA 1970	Subject Matter	Re-enacted in TA 1988	Remarks
s. 252	Company reconstructions without change of ownership.	s. 343	Am. 1971 Sch. 8 §16; 1986 s. 42, 56(7)(*a*), Sch. 10 §1, Sch. 13 §2(5); 1987(2) s. 64(2).
s. 253(1)–(4)	Supplemental.	s. 344(1)–(4)	
s. 253(5)–(12)		s. 344(5)–(12)	Added 1986 Sch. 10 §2.
s. 254(1)	Set-off of losses etc. against franked investment income.	s. 242(1)	Section 254 subst. by 1972 Sch. 15 Pt. I.
s. 254(2)		s. 242(2)	Am. 1981 s. 37; 1984 Sch. 9 §13.
s. 254(3)		s. 242(3)	
s. 254(4)		s. 242(4)	Am. 1981 s. 37.
s. 254(5)		s. 242(5)	
s. 254(6)		s. 242(6), (7)	Am. 1981 s. 37.
s. 254(7)		s. 242(8)	Am. 1981 s. 37; 1984 Sch. 9 §13.
s. 254(8)		s. 242(9)	
s. 255	Set-off of loss brought forward etc.	s. 243	Subst. 1972 Sch. 15 Pt. I.
s. 256(1)	Group income.	s. 247(1)–(3)	Subst. 1972 Sch. 15 Pt. II.
s. 256(2)		s. 247(4)	
s. 256(3)		s. 247(5)	Am. 1973 s. 24.
s. 256(4), (4A)		s. 247(6), (7)	Subst. 1972 Sch. 15 Pt. II.
s. 256(5)		s. 247(8)	
s. 256(6)		s. 247(9)	Rep. in part 1984 s. 46(1).
s. 256(7)		s. 247(10)	
s. 257	Election for group income etc.	s. 248	
s. 258(1)	Group relief.	s. 402(1), (2)	
s. 258(2)		s. 402(3), (4)	Subst. 1981 s. 40(2).
s. 258(3), (4)		s. 402(5), (6)	
s. 258(5)		s. 413(3)	
s. 258(6), (7)		s. 413(4), (5)	
s. 258(8)		s. 413(6)	Subst. 1984 s. 46(2).
s. 259(1)–(7)	Kinds of group relief.	s. 403(1)–(8)	
s. 259(8)		s. 403(9)	Subst. 1981 s. 40(3).
s. 260(1)	Relation to other relief.	s. 407(1)	
s. 260(2)		s. 407(1)(*b*)	
s. 260(3)(*a*)		s. 407(2)(*a*)	
s. 260(3)(*b*)		s. 407(2)(*b*)	
s. 260(3)(*c*)		—	Spent.
s. 260(3)(*d*)		s. 407(2)(*a*)	
s. 260(4)		s. 407(3)	Partly spent.
s. 261	Corresponding accounting periods.	s. 408	
s. 262(1)	Companies joining groups etc.	s. 409(1)	
s. 262(2)		s. 409(2)	Rep. in part and am. 1984 s. 47(1).
s. 262(3)		s. 409(3)	
s. 262(4)		s. 409(4)	Am. 1984 s. 47(2).
s. 263	Exclusion of double allowances etc.	s. 411	Am. 1985 Sch. 9 Pt. II.
s. 264	Claims and adjustments.	s. 412	Am. 1981 s. 40(4).
s. 265(1)	Computation of chargeable gains.	s. 345(1)(*a*)	
s. 265(2)		s. 345(2)	
s. 265(3)(*a*)		s. 345(3)(*a*)	Am. CGTA 7.
s. 265(3)(*b*)		—	Rep. 1978 Sch. 13 Pt. IV.
s. 265(3)(*c*)		s. 345(3)(*b*)	
s. 265(4), (5)		s. 345(4), (5)	Am. CGTA 7; CCCPA; CCCP(NI).
s. 266	Corporation tax attributable to chargeable gains.	s. 346	Am. CGTA 7; 1987(2) Sch. 6 §1.
s. 277	Tax on one member of group recoverable from another.	s. 347(1)–(4)	Am. 1987(2) Sch. 6 §3.
s. 282(1)	Meaning of close company.	s. 414(1)	Partly spent (1970 s. 343(9) rep. 1985).
s. 282(2)		s. 414(2), (3)	Subst. 1972 Sch. 17 §1(2).

TA 1970	Subject Matter	Re-enacted in TA 1988	Remarks
s. 282(3)		s. 414(4)	
s. 282(4), (5)		s. 414(5), (6)	Subst. 1972 Sch. 17 §1(3).
s. 283(1)–(3)	Certain companies with quoted shares not to be close companies.	s. 415(1)–(3)	
s. 283(4)(*a*)		s. 415(4)(*a*)	
s. 283(4)(*b*)		—	Rep. 1971 Sch. 14 Pt. I.
s. 283(4)(*bb*)		s. 415(4)(*b*)	Added 1970(F) Sch. 5 Pt. III §12(3).
s. 283(4)(*c*)		s. 415(4)(*c*)	
s. 283(5)–(8)		s. 415(5)–(8)	
s. 284(1)(*a*), (*b*)	Payments to participators and associates.	—	Rep. 1972 Sch. 28 Pt. VI.
s. 284(1)(*c*)		s. 418(1)	
s. 284(2)		s. 418(2), (3)	Am. 1976 Sch. 9 §15; 1977 s. 35(4); 1980 s. 51(4).
s. 284(3)		s. 418(4)	Subst. 1976 Sch. 9 §16.
s. 284(4)–(7)		s. 418(5)–(8)	
s. 285(1)–(5)		—	Rep. 1980 Sch. 20 Pt. VIII.
s. 285(6)	Persons materially interested in companies.	s. 187(3)	Rep. in part 1980 Sch. 20 Pt. VIII; am. 1971 Sch. 6 §30; 1978 Sch. 9 §11(3); 1980 Sch. 10 §26(2); 1984 Sch. 10 §4(4).
s. 286(1)	Loans to participators etc.	s. 419(1)	Am. 1972 Sch. 17 §3(2).
s. 286(2)		s. 419(2), 420(1)	
s. 286(3)		s. 420(2)	Am. 1971 s. 25(5)(*c*); 1972 Sch. 17 §3(3).
s. 286(3)(*a*)		—	Rep. 1971 s. 25(5)(*a*).
s. 286(3)(*b*)		s. 420(2)(*a*)	Subst. 1971 s. 25(5)(*b*).
s. 286(3)(*c*), (*d*)		s. 420(2)(*b*), (*c*)	
s. 286(4)		s. 419(3)	Am. 1986 s. 43.
s. 286(5)		s. 419(4)	Am. 1972 Sch. 17 §3(4); 1976 s. 44(1); 1986 s. 43.
s. 286(6)		—	Rep. 1972 Sch. 28 Pt. VI.
s. 286(7)		s. 419(5)	Rep. in part 1971 Sch. 14 Pt. II; 1972 Sch. 28 Pt. VI.
s. 286(8)		s. 419(6)	
s. 286(9)		s. 419(7), 420(2)	
s. 287(1)(*a*), (*b*)	Release of debt in respect of loan under s. 286.	s. 421(1)(*a*), (*b*)	Am. 1971 Sch. 6 §32(1).
s. 287(1)(*c*)		s. 421(1)(*c*)	Am. 1971 Sch. 6 §32(1); 1978 Sch. 2 §4; rep. in part 1980 Sch. 20 Pt. V.
s. 287(1)(*d*)		s. 421(1)(*d*)	Am. 1971 Sch. 6 §32(1).
s. 287(2)		s. 421(2)	Am. & rep. in part 1971 Sch. 6 §32(2), Sch. 14 Pt. II.
s. 287(3), (4)		s. 421(3), (4)	
s. 287A	Loans by controlled companies.	s. 422	Added 1976 s. 44.
s. 288–301	—	—	Rep. 1972 Sch. 28 Pts. V & VI.
s. 302(1)	"Associated company" and "control".	s. 416(1)	Am. 1972 Sch. 24 §21; rep. in part 1972 Sch. 28 Pt. VI.
s. 302(2)–(4)		s. 416(2)–(4)	Added 1972 Sch. 17 §5.
s. 302(5), (6)		s. 416(5), (6)	
s. 303(1), (2)	"Participator" etc.	s. 417(1), (2)	
s. 303(3)		s. 417(3)	Am. 1970 Sch. 5 Pt. III §12(4); rep. in part 1971 Sch. 14 Pt. I; 1987 Sch. 16 Pt. V.
s. 303(4)		s. 417(4)	
s. 303(5)(*a*)		s. 417(5)(*a*)	
s. 303(5)(*b*)		—	Rep. 1972 Sch. 28 Pt. VI.
s. 303(5)(*c*)		s. 417(5)(*b*)	
s. 303(6)		s. 417(6)	Rep. in part 1987 Sch. 16 Pt. V.
s. 303(7)		s. 417(7), (9)	

TA 1970 — Destination Table — 696

TA 1970	Subject Matter	Re-enacted in TA 1988	Remarks
s. 303(8)		s. 417(8)	Added 1972 Sch. 17 §7.
s. 304(1)	Expenses of management: investment companies.	s. 75(1), (2)	Am. 1984 s. 54(2)(b); 1987 s. 41.
s. 304(2)–(4)		s. 75(3)–(5)	
s. 304(5)		s. 130	Am. 1980 Sch. 11 §1; Trustee Savings Bank Act 1981 c. 65 Sch. 6; TSB 1985 Sch. 2 §6.
s. 305(1)	Insurance companies.	s. 76(1)	
s. 305(2)		s. 76(2), (5), Sch. 29	Rep. in part 1972 Sch. 28 Pt. VI; am. CGTA 7.
s. 305(3)		s. 76(8)	
s. 307	Insurance business.	s. 432	
s. 308		s. 434(1), (2)	
s. 309		s. 433	
s. 310(1)–(4)		—	Rep. 1984 Sch. 23 Pt. V; 1972 Sch. 28 Pt. VI.
s. 310(5)		s. 434(3)	Subst. 1972 Sch. 18 §2(3).
s. 310(6)		s. 434(4), (5)	
s. 310(7)		s. 434(7)	Added 1984 s. 18(5).
s. 311	—	—	Rep. 1972 Sch. 28 Pt.VI.
s. 312(1)	Annuity business.	s. 436(1), (2)	Am. 1970(F) Sch. 5 Pt. III §11(3).
s. 312(2), (3)		s. 436(3)(a)–(c), (4)	Am. 1970(F) Sch. 5 Pt. III §11(6); rep. in part 1987 Sch. 16 Pt. VII.
s. 312(4)		Sch. 30	
s. 313(1)	General annuity business.	s. 437(1)	
s. 313(2)		s. 437(2)	Am. 1985 Sch. 25 §7.
s. 313(4)		s. 437(4)	Am. 1972 Sch. 18 §3.
s. 313(5), (6)		s. 437(5), (6)	
s. 314(1)	Pension annuity business.	s. 438(1)	Rep. in part 1972 Sch. 18 Pt. VI; am 1970(F) Sch. 5 Pt. III §11(3), (6).
s. 314(2)		s. 438(2)	
s. 314(3)		s. 438(3)	Rep. in part 1972 Sch. 18 Pt. VI.
s. 314(4)		s. 438(6), (7)	Am. 1970(F) Sch. 5 Pt. III §11(3); rep. in part 1972 Sch. 28 Pt. VI.
s. 314(5)		s. 436(3)(d)	
s. 315(1)–(6)	Foreign life assurance funds.	s. 441(1)–(6)	
s. 315(7), (8)		—	Rep. 1976 Sch. 15 Pt. III.
s. 315(9)		s. 441(7)	
s. 316(1)	Overseas life assurance companies.	s. 445(1)	Am. 1970(F) Sch. 5 Pt. III §11(6).
s. 316(1A)		s. 445(2)(a)	Subst. 1985 Sch. 25 §8.
s. 316(2)		s. 445(3)	Am. 1972 Sch. 18 §5.
s. 316(3)		s. 445(4)	Am. 1970(F) Sch. 5 Pt. III §11(6).
s. 316(4)–(6)		s. 445(5)–(7)	
s. 317	Management expenses.	s. 76(6)	
s. 318(1)	Overseas life assurance companies.	s. 446(1)	Am. 1970(F) Sch. 5 Pt. III §11(3); 1972 Sch. 18 §5.
s. 318(2)–(4)		s. 446(2)–(4)	
s. 319	Set off of income tax against corporation tax.	s. 447(1)–(3)	Am. 1971 Sch. 6 §39.
s. 320(1)	Double taxation agreements.	s. 449(1)	Am. 1970(F) Sch. 5 Pt. III §11(6).
s. 320(2)		s. 449(2), (3)	Am. 1970(F) Sch. 5 Pt. III §11(6); 1972 Sch. 18 §5.
s. 321(1)(b), (2)	Life policies.	s. 443	
s. 321(1)(a)		Sch. 29	
s. 321(1)(c)		—	Rep. 1971 Sch. 14 Pt. IV.
s. 322	Pre-5/8/65 life policies.	s. 444	
s. 323(1), (2)	Interpretation.	s. 431(1), (2)	Am. ICA 1973 s. 54(2); 1970(F) Sch. 5 Pt. III §11(4); ICA 1974 Sch. 1; ICA 1982 Sch. 5 §10(b); rep. in part ICA 1981 Sch. 5.

TA 1970	Subject Matter	Re-enacted in TA 1988	Remarks
s. 323(3)		s. 431(3)	Subst. 1970(F) Sch. 5 Pt. III §11(5).
s. 323(4)		s. 431(4), (6)	Rep. in part & am. 1970(F) Sch. 5 Pt. III §11(1)–(3); am. 1978 s. 26(5); 1987(2) s. 39(3), Sch. 3 §16.
s. 324	Capital redemption policies.	s. 458	
s. 325		—	Rep. 1987 Sch. 16 Pt. VII.
s. 326(1)	Exchange of certain securities.	s. 471(1), (2)	
s. 326(2), (3)		s. 471(3), (4)	
s. 327	Distribution of certain securities.	s. 472	
s. 328(1), (2)	Tax-free income.	s. 474	Am. 1970(F) Sch. 5 Pt. III §11.
s. 328(3)		s. 445(8)	
s. 329	Tax-free Treasury securities.	s. 475	
s. 330	—	—	Unnecessary.
s. 331	Unregistered friendly societies.	s. 459	
s. 332(1)	Registered friendly societies.	s. 460(1), 461(1)	
s. 332(2)		s. 460(2)(*b*), (*c*), (*d*)	Am. 1984 s. 73(1), (2); 1987 s. 30(2); 1987(2) Sch. 2 §2.
s. 332(3)		s. 460(3), (4)	Am. 1984 s. 73(1), (2); FSA 1984 s. 2; 1987 s. 30(3).
s. 332(4)–(9)		s. 460(5)–(10)	Added 1975(2) s. 52(1); am. 1980 s. 57(1); 1984 s. 73(3).
s. 332(10)		s. 460(11)	Added 1976 s. 48(1).
s. 332(11)		s. 461(4)	Added 1976 s. 48(1).
s. 332(12)(*a*)		s. 460(12)	Added 1976 s. 48(1).
s. 332(12)(*b*)		s. 461(5)	Added 1976 s. 48(1).
s. 333(1)(*a*)	Distinction between old and new societies.	s. 460(2)(*a*)	
s. 333(1)(*b*), (2)		—	Rep. 1985 Sch. 27 Pt. V.
s. 334	Tax exempt business.	s. 462(1), Sch. 15 §3, 4	Am. 1985 s. 41(6); 1979/1576; rep. in part 1985 Sch. 27 Pt. V.
s. 335(1)	Life or endowment business.	s. 463, 828	
s. 335(2)–(5)		—	Rep. 1985 Sch. 27 Pt. V.
s. 336	Pre-3/5/66 contracts.	s. 462(2)	Partly spent.
s. 337(1)	Interpretation.	—	Unnecessary.
s. 337(2)		s. 466(1)	Am. FSA 1974 Sch. 9 §23; 1985 s. 41(7)(*b*), (*c*); 1987(2) Sch. 2 §2.
s. 337(3)		s. 466(2), 832	Am. 1985 s. 41(7)(*d*); 1987(2) Sch. 2 §2.
s. 337(4)		s. 466(3), (4)	Am. 1975(2) s. 52(2); 1985 s. 41(7)(*e*); rep. in part 1985 Sch. 27 Pt. V.
s. 337(5)		s. 832, Sch. 15 §3	Am. 1979/1576; FSA 1974 Sch. 9 §23.
s. 338(1)	Trade unions.	s. 467(1)	Am. 1982 s. 36.
s. 338(2)		s. 467(2)	Rep. in part 1974 Sch. 14 Pt. VI.
s. 338(3)		s. 467(3)	Am. 1982 s. 36.
s. 339	Savings banks.	s. 484(1)	Am. 1980 Sch. 11 §5; TSB 1985 Sch. 2 §6(6); partly spent.
s. 340	Industrial and provident societies.	s. 486	Am. CUA 1979 s. 25(2); NICA Sch. 5 §8.
s. 340A(1)–(4), (7)	Credit unions.	s. 487	Added CUA 1979 s. 25(1); am. Credit Unions (Northern Ireland) Order 1985 (S.I. No. 1205).

TA 1970	Subject Matter	Re-enacted in TA 1988	Remarks
s. 340A(5), (6)		—	Spent.
s. 341	Co-operative housing associations.	s. 488	Am. 1972 Sch. 11 §6; 1981/157; HCPA 1985 Sch. 2 §18; 1979/1573 Art. 4; 1970/1681.
s. 341A	Self-build societies.	s. 489	Added Housing Act 1974 c. 44 s. 120; am. HCPA 1985 Sch. 2 §18; 1984 s. 56(1).
s. 343(1)	Building societies.	—	Spent: rep. in part 1984 s. 26(5); am. 1985 s. 40(2).
s. 343(1A), (1B)		s. 476(1), (2), 828	Added 1985 s. 40(3); am. 1986 s. 47(1).
s. 343(2)		s. 476(3), 477(3)	Rep. in part 1971 Sch. 14 Pt. II; 1985 Sch. 27 Pt. V; am. 1985 s. 40(4); 1986 s. 47(2).
s. 343(3)(a)		s. 476(5)(a)	Am. 1985 s. 40(5).
s. 343(3)(b)		s. 476(5)(b)	Am. 1971 Sch. 6 §40(c).
s. 343(3)(c)		s. 476(5)(c)	Subst. 1971 Sch. 6 §40(d); am. 1978 Sch. 2 §5(8); rep. in part 1980 Sch. 20 Pt. V.
s. 343(3)(d)		s. 476(5)(d)	Am. 1971 Sch. 6 §40(e).
s. 343(3)(i)		s. 476(6)	Subst. 1971 Sch. 6 §40(f).
s. 343(3)(ii)		s. 476(8)	Subst. 1971 Sch. 6 §40(f); rep. in part 1975(2) Sch. 14 Pt. IV.
s. 343(3)(iii), (iv)		—	Rep. 1985 Sch. 27 Pt. V.
s. 343(4)		s. 476(9)	Am. 1985 s. 40(6).
s. 343(5)		Sch. 29	Rep. in part BSA 1986 Sch. 19 Pt. I.
s. 343(6)		—	Rep. 1985 Sch. 27 Pt. V.
s. 343(7)		s. 476(11)	Am. 1985 s. 40(7); 1986 s. 47(3).
s. 343(8)		s. 832(1)	Am. BSA 1986 Sch. 18.
s. 343(8A)–(9)		—	Rep. 1985 Sch. 27 Pt. V.
s. 344(1)	Time for payment of tax.	s. 478(1)	See 1987 s. 36(2), Sch. 6 Pt. II.
s. 344(2)		s. 478(2), (3)	Am. 1975(2) s. 45(2).
s. 345	Companies trading with members etc.	s. 486(10), (11)	Rep. in part 1987 Sch. 16 Pt. VII.
s. 346	Companies carrying on mutual business etc.	s. 490	
s. 347	Distribution of assets.	s. 491	
s. 348	Agricultural marketing boards etc.	s. 509	Subst. 1971 s. 28; am. NICA Sch. 5.
s. 349(1)–(3)	Electricity Council etc.	s. 511(1)–(3)	
s. 349(4)		s. 511(6)	
s. 350(1), (2)	Gas Council etc.	—	Rep. Gas Act 1986 c. 44.
s. 350(3)		s. 511(7)	
s. 351	Atomic Energy Authority etc.	s. 512, Sch. 29	
s. 352(1)–(3)	Harbour re-organisation schemes.	s. 518(1)–(3)	
s. 352(4)		s. 518(4), (5)	Am. 1971 Sch. 8 §16(5); 1986 s. 56(7)(a), Sch. 13 §2(5).
s. 352(5), (6)		s. 518(6), (7)	Partly spent.
s. 352(7)		Sch. 29	Am. CGTA Sch. 7.
s. 352(8), (9)		s. 518(8), (9)	
s. 352(10)		—	Rep. 1987 Sch. 16 Pt. VII.
s. 352(11)		s. 518(10)	
s. 353(1)	Local authorities.	s. 519(1), (2), Sch. 29	
s. 353(2), (3)		—	Rep. 1974 Sch. 14 Pt. VI.
s. 353(4)		s. 519(3)	
s. 354	Authorised unit trusts.	s. 468(1)–(4), (6)	Subst. 1987 s. 38.
s. 354A	Other unit trusts.	s. 469	Added 1987 s. 39.
s. 355		—	Rep. 1980 Sch. 20 Pt. X.
s. 356		—	Rep. 1972 Sch. 28 Pt. VI.
s. 357		—	Rep. 1972 Sch. 28 Pt. X.

TA 1970	Subject Matter	Re-enacted in TA 1988	Remarks
s. 358	Interpretation.	s. 832(1)	Subst. 1987 s. 40(1).
s. 359	Investment trusts.	s. 842	Am. CGTA Sch. 7.
s. 360(1)	Charities.	s. 505(1)	Rep. in part 1971 Sch. 14 Pt. VI.
s. 360(2)		—	Unnecessary.
s. 360(3)		s. 506(1)	Am. CGTA 7.
s. 361	Agricultural societies.	s. 510	
s. 362(1)–(3)	Scientific research organisations.	s. 508, Sch. 29	Am. 1970/1537.
s. 362(4)		—	Rep. 1987 Sch. 16 Pt. VII.
s. 363	British Museum.	s. 507(2), Sch. 29	
s. 364	National Debt.	s. 514, Sch. 29	
s. 365(1), (2)	Wounds & disability pensions.	s. 315	
s. 365(3)		—	Rep. 1979(2) Sch. 5 Pt. II.
s. 366	Allowances, bounties & gratuities.	s. 316	Am. 1981/1670; rep. in part AFA 1981 Sch. 5 Pt. I.
s. 367(1)–(6)	Visiting forces.	s. 323, Sch. 29	Am. BNA s. 51(3)(a).
s. 367(7)		—	Unnecessary: see IA 1978 s. 14.
s. 368	Victoria Cross etc.	s. 317	Am. 1980 s. 26.
s. 369	Foreign service allowance.	s. 319	Am. 1981/1670.
s. 370	Non-resident central banks.	s. 516	
s. 371	Issue departments of certain banks.	s. 517, Sch. 29	
s. 372	Commonwealth Agents General.	s. 320, Sch. 29	Am. BNA Sch. 7.
s. 373	Consuls.	s. 321	Am. BNA s. 51(1)(b), (2).
s. 374(1)	Consular officers etc.	s. 322(1)	Am. BNA s. 51(3)(a); rep. in part 1971 Sch. 14 Pt. IV.
s. 374(2)		Sch. 29	
s. 374(3)–(7)		s. 322(2)–(6)	Am. BNA s. 51(3)(a).
s. 375	Scholarship income.	s. 331	Rep. in part 1987 Sch. 16 Pt. VII.
s. 375A(1)	Interest on damages.	s. 329(1)	Am. AJA 1982 s. 74.
s. 375A(1A)		s. 329(3)	Added 1981 s. 39.
s. 375A(1B)		s. 329(2)	Added 1971 s. 19; am. CCA 1984 Sch. 2 §37; AJA 1982 s. 74.
s. 375A(2)		s. 329(4)	Added 1971 s. 19.
s. 376	Housing grants.	s. 578	
s. 377	Certain compensation.	s. 330	Subst. 1986 s. 51.
s. 378(1), (2)	Writing down allowances in respect of patent rights.	s. 520(1)–(3), 522(1)–(6)	Am. 1985 s. 64(1), (2)(a)–(c).
s. 378(3)		s. 522(7)	
s. 379	Effect of lapses of patent rights.	s. 523	Am. 1985 s. 64(2)(c).
s. 380	Taxation of receipts from sale of patent rights.	s. 524	Rep. in part 1970(F) Sch. 8 Pt. VII; 1971 Sch. 14 Pt. II.
s. 381	Capital sums: death etc.	s. 525	Rep. in part 1971 Sch. 14 Pt. II.
s. 382	Relief for expenses.	s. 526	
s. 383	Patent income.	s. 529	
s. 384	Spreading of royalties.	s. 527	Rep. in part 1971 Sch. 14 Pt. II.
s. 385	Manner of making allowances etc.	s. 528	Am. 1985 s. 64(2)(d)–(f).
s. 386(1)	Disposal of know-how.	s. 530(1), (6), (7)	Am. 1985 s. 65(1).
s. 386(2)–(6)		s. 531(1)–(7)	Am. 1985 s. 65(3).
s. 386(7)		s. 533(7)	
s. 386(8)		s. 531(8)	
s. 386(9)		s. 530(8)	
s. 387	Application of 1968 Act.	s. 532	
s. 388	Interpretation.	s. 533(1)–(6)	Am. 1985 s. 64(2)(g); rep. in part 1987 Sch. 16 Pt. VII.
s. 389	Copyright.	s. 534	

TA 1970	Subject Matter	Re-enacted in TA 1988	Remarks
s. 390	Sale of copyright ten years after first publication.	s. 535	Rep. in part 1971 Sch. 14 Pt. II.
s. 391	Owner resident abroad.	s. 536	
s. 392	Artists' receipts.	s. 538	
s. 393(1)	Life policies etc.: general.	s. 539(1)	Am. 1971 Sch. 6 §41; 1972 Sch. 24 §23.
s. 393(2)(a)		s. 539(2)(a)	
s. 393(2)(b)		—	Rep. 1971 Sch. 14 §1.
s. 393(2)(c)		s. 539(2)(b)	Added 1971 Sch. 3 §11.
s. 393(2A)		s. 539(2)(c)	Added 1971 Sch. 2 §6.
s. 393(3)		s. 539(3)	Am. 1985 s. 41(8).
s. 393(4), (5)		s. 539(5)–(7)	
s. 394(1)	Life policies: chargeable events.	s. 540(1)	Rep. in part 1975 Sch. 13 Pt. II; am. 1975 Sch. 2 §9.
s. 394(2)		s. 540(1)(b)	
s. 394(3)		s. 540(2)	Am. 1984 s. 75.
s. 394(4)		s. 540(3)	Am. 1983 s. 18(1); 1975 Sch. 2 §10.
s. 394(5), (6)		s. 540(4), (5)	Rep. in part 1975 Sch. 13 Pt. II.
s. 395(1)	Computation of gain.	s. 541(1)	Am. 1975 Sch. 2 §11(1); rep. in part 1975 Sch. 13 Pt. II.
s. 395(2), (3)		s. 541(2), (3)	
s. 395(3A)		s. 541(4)	Added 1975 Sch. 2 §11(2).
s. 395(4)		s. 541(5)	Rep. in part 1975 Sch. 13 Pt. II.
s. 396(1)	Life annuity contracts.	s. 542(1), (2)	Rep. in part 1975 Sch. 13 Pt. II; am. 1975 Sch. 2 §§9(3), 12(1).
s. 396(2), (3)		s. 542(3), (4)	Am. 1975 Sch. 2 §12(2); 1983 s. 18(2).
s. 397(1)	Computation of gain.	s. 543(1)	Rep. in part 1975 Sch. 13 Pt. II; am. 1975 Sch. 2 §13(1).
s. 397(2), (3)		s. 543(2), (3)	Am. 1975 Sch. 2 §13(2), (3).
s. 398(1)	Capital redemption policies.	s. 545(1)	Rep. in part 1975 Sch. 13 Pt. II; am. 1975 Sch. 2 §§9(4), 14.
s. 398(2)–(4)		s. 545(2)–(4)	
s. 399(1)	Charge to tax.	s. 547(1), (2)	Rep. in part 1971 Sch. 14 Pt. II; am. 1972 Sch. 24 §24.
s. 399(2), (3)		s. 547(3), (4)	
s. 399(4)		s. 547(5)	Added 1971 Sch. 6 §42; 1978 Sch. 2 §6; rep. in part 1980 Sch. 20 Pt. V.
s. 400(1)–(3)	Relief for higher rate tax payer.	s. 550(1)–(4)	Am. 1971 Sch. 6 §43; 1978 Sch. 2 §7; rep. in part 1980 Sch. 20 Pt. V.
s. 400(4), (5)		s. 550(6), (7)	Am. 1971 Sch. 6 §43.
s. 401	Recovery of tax from trustees.	s. 551	
s. 402	Information.	s. 552(1), (2)	
s. 403, 404		—	Rep. 1987 Sch. 16 Pt. VII.
s. 405	Certain loans treated as income.	s. 554	
s. 406	Deduction of contributions to schemes for rationalizing industry.	s. 568	Am. 1970/1537.
s. 407	Repayment of contributions.	s. 569	Am. 1971 Sch. 6 §45.
s. 408	Other payments.	s. 570	Am. 1970/1537.
s. 409	Cancellation of certificates.	s. 571	Am. 1970/1537.
s. 410	Statutory redundancy schemes.	s. 572	
s. 411(1)	Business entertaining expenses.	s. 577(1)	Am. 1971 s. 50(8).
s. 411(2)–(7)		s. 577(2)–(7)	

TA 1970	Subject Matter	Re-enacted in TA 1988	Remarks
s. 411(8)		s. 577(8)	Am. 1985 s. 43.
s. 411(9)		s. 577(10)	
s. 412(1)–(6)	Statutory redundancy schemes.	s. 579	Am. EP(C)A Sch. 16 §9.
s. 412(7), (8)		s. 580	Am. EP(C)A Sch. 16 §9.
s. 413(1), (2)	Funds in court.	s. 328(1)	Am. AJA 1982 s. 46(2).
s. 413(3)		s. 328(5)	
s. 413(4), (5)		s. 328(6), (7)	Am. AJA s. 46(2).
s. 413(6)		s. 328(8)	Am. Supreme Court Act 1981 c. 54 s. 1(1); Judicature (Northern Ireland) Act 1978 c. 23 Sch. 5.
s. 414(1)(*a*)	Savings bank interest.	s. 325	Rep. in part 1971 Sch. 14 Pt. II; am. 1977 s. 29; 1980 s. 59.
s. 414(1)(*b*)		—	Rep. 1980 Sch. 20 Pt. IX.
s. 414(1)(*c*)		—	Rep. Merchant Shipping Act 1970 c. 36 Sch. 5.
s. 414(2)		—	Rep. 1971 Sch. 14 Pt. II.
s. 414(3)–(7)		—	Rep. 1980 Sch. 20 Pt. IX.
s. 415(1)–(3)	Contractual savings schemes.	s. 326, Sch. 29	
s. 415(4)		s. 476(4)	
s. 415(5)		s. 832	
s. 416(1)–(3)	Borrowings in foreign currency.	s. 581(1)–(3)	Am. 1982 s. 64(2).
s. 416(4)		s. 581(6)	Rep. 1982 Sch. 22 Pt. IV.
s. 417	Funding bonds.	s. 582	Am. 1971 Sch. 6 §47.
s. 418(1), (2)	Relief for unremittable overseas income.	s. 584(1), (2)	Am. 1987(2) Sch. 6 §6(2).
s. 418(2A), (2B)		s. 584(3), (4)	Added 1987(2) Sch. 6 §6(3).
s. 418(3)–(6)		s. 584(6)–(9)	
s. 418(7)		—	Rep. 1971 Sch. 14 Pt. IV.
s. 419	Delayed remittances.	s. 585	
s. 420	War risk premiums.	s. 586	Rep. in part 1987 Sch. 16 Pt. VII.
s. 421	War injuries.	s. 587	
s. 422–424	—	—	Rep. 1987 Sch. 16 Pt. VII.
s. 425	Payments of interest less tax.	s. 818	Am. 1971 Sch. 6 §51.
s. 426	Limited interests in residue.	s. 695	Am. 1971 Sch. 6 §52.
s. 427	Absolute interests in residue.	s. 696, 701(14)	Rep. in part 1975 Sch. 13 Pt. I; am. 1971 Sch. 6 §53; 1974 Sch. 7 §9(3).
s. 428	Supplementary provisions.	s. 697	Am. 1971 Sch. 6 §54.
s. 429	Special provisions.	s. 698, 701(14)	Am. 1971 Sch. 6 §55; 1974 Sch. 7 §9(4).
s. 430	Inheritance tax.	s. 699	Am. 1971 Sch. 6 §56; 1975 Sch. 12 §16; 1978 Sch. 2 §11; 1986 s. 100; rep. in part 1975 Sch. 13 Pt. I; 1980 Sch. 20 Pt. V; 1984 Sch. 23 Pt. VI.
s. 431	Adjustments etc.	s. 700	Rep. in part 1971 Sch. 14 Pt. II; am. 1971 Sch. 6 §57.
s. 432	Interpretation.	s. 701	Rep. in part 1971 Sch. 14 Pt. II; 1972 Sch. 24 §25; 1975 Sch. 13 Pt. I; am. 1972 Sch. 24 §25; 1975(2) s. 34(5).
s. 433	Scotland.	s. 702	Am. 1987 Sch. 15 §2(15).
s. 434(1)	Dispositions for short periods.	s. 660(1)	Am. 1980 s. 55(1).
s. 434(1A)		s. 660(2)	Added 1980 s. 55(1); subst. 1987 Sch. 15 §2(16).
s. 434(2)		s. 660(3)	Am. 1980 s. 55(1).
s. 435	Adjustments between disponor and trustees.	s. 661	Rep. in part 1971 Sch. 14 Pt. II.

TA 1970	Subject Matter	Re-enacted in TA 1988	Remarks
s. 436	Cases involving more than disponor.	s. 662	
s. 437(1)	Settlements on children: general rule.	s. 663(1)	Am. 1971 s. 16(2)(*b*).
s. 437(2), (3)		s. 663(3), (4)	Am. 1971 s. 16(2)(*d*).
s. 437(4)		—	Rep. 1971 s. 16(2)(*d*).
s. 437(5)		s. 663(5)	
s. 438(1)	Accumulation settlements.	s. 664(1)	
s. 438(2)		s. 664(2), (3)	Am. 1971 s. 16(2)(*c*); 1987 Sch. 15 §2(17).
s. 438(3)		—	Unnecessary.
s. 439(1)	Meaning of "irrevocable".	s. 665	
s. 439(2)		—	Spent.
s. 440(1)–(3)	Interest paid by trustees.	s. 666(1)–(3)	Rep. in part 1971 Sch. 14 Pt. II; am. 1971 s. 16(2).
s. 440(4)		s. 666(4), (5)	
s. 441	Adjustments between settlor and trustees.	s. 667	Rep. in part 1971 Sch. 14 Pt. II.
s. 442(1)	Cases involving more than settlor.	s. 668(1)	
s. 442(2)		s. 668(2), (3)	
s. 442(3)–(5)		s. 668(4)–(6)	
s. 443	Power to obtain information.	s. 669	Rep. in part 1971 Sch. 14 Pt. II; am. 1971 Sch. 6 §62.
s. 444(1), (2)	Interpretation.	s. 670	Rep. in part 1971 Sch. 14 Pt. VII.
s. 444(3), (4)		—	Rep. 1971 Sch. 14 Pt. IV.
s. 445(1)	Revocable settlements allowing release of obligation.	s. 671(1), (2)	
s. 445(1A)		s. 671(2)(*b*)	Added 1980 s. 55(2).
s. 445(2)		s. 671(3)	
s. 445(3)		Sch. 30	
s. 446(1)	Revocable settlements allowing reversion of property.	s. 672(1), (2)	
s. 446(2)		s. 672(3)	
s. 446(3)		Sch. 30	
s. 447(1)	Settlements where settlor retains an interest.	s. 673(1)	
s. 447(2)		s. 673(2), (3)	
s. 448(1)	Discretionary power for benefit of settlor etc.	s. 674(1), (2)	
s. 448(2), (3)		s. 674(3), (4)	
s. 448(4)		Sch. 30	
s. 449	Supplementary provisions.	s. 675	Rep. in part 1971 Sch. 14 Pt. II.
s. 450	Disallowance of certain deductions from total income.	s. 676	Rep. in part 1971 Sch. 14 Pt. II.
s. 451(1)	Capital sums paid to settlor.	s. 677(1)	Am. 1981 s. 42(2)(*a*), (*b*); 1982 s. 63(3).
s. 451(2)(*aa*)		s. 677(2)(*a*)	Added 1981 s. 42(3).
s. 451(2)(*a*)		s. 677(2)(*b*)	
s. 451(2)(*b*)		s. 677(2)(*c*)	Am. 1981 s. 42(3).
s. 451(2)(*c*)		s. 677(2)(*d*)	
s. 451(2)(*d*)		s. 677(2)(*e*)	
s. 451(2)(*dd*)		s. 677(2)(*f*)	Added 1981 s. 42(3).
s. 451(2)(*ddd*)		s. 677(2)(*g*)	Added 1981 s. 42(3).
s. 451(2)(*e*)		s. 677(2)(*h*)	Am. 1973 s. 16(7); 1981 s. 42(3)(*d*); 1971 Sch. 6 §64.
s. 451(3)		s. 677(3)	
s. 451(3A), (3B)		s. 677(4), (5)	Added 1981 s. 42(4).
s. 451(4)		—	Rep. 1981 Sch. 19 Pt. VI.
s. 451(5)		s. 677(6)	Am. 1973 s. 16(7); 1971 Sch. 6 §64.
s. 451(6)		s. 677(7)	Rep. in part 1971 Sch. 14 Pt. II; am. 1981 s. 42(5).
s. 451(7)		s. 677(8)	
s. 451(8)		s. 677(9)	Am. 1981 s. 42(6)(*a*), (*b*).

TA 1970	Subject Matter	Re-enacted in TA 1988	Remarks
s. 451(9)		s. 677(10)	Added 1981 s. 42(7).
s. 451A	Capital payments by connected bodies.	s. 678	Added 1981 s. 43(2).
s. 452	Cases involving more than one settlor.	s. 679	
s. 453	Power to obtain information.	s. 680	Rep. in part 1971 Sch. 14 Pt. II; am. 1971 Sch. 6 §65.
s. 454(1)	Interpretation.	s. 681(1), (2)	Am. 1972 Sch. 24 §26; 1981 s. 44(1); partly spent.
s. 454(1A)		s. 681(3)	Added 1981 s. 44(1).
s. 454(2)		—	Rep. 1971 Sch. 14 Pt. IV.
s. 454(3)		s. 681(4)	
s. 454(4)		s. 681(5)	Subst. 1981 s. 44(2).
s. 454(5)		—	Spent.
s. 454(6)		s. 681(6)	
s. 455	Ascertainment of undistributed income.	s. 682(1)	
s. 456		s. 682(2)–(6)	Rep. in part 1971 Sch. 14 Pt. II.
s. 457(1)	Post-6th April 1965 settlements.	s. 683(1), (2)	Am. 1971 Sch. 6 §67; 1978 Sch. 2 §12; 1980 s. 56(1); rep. in part 1980 Sch. 20 Pt. V; 1984 Sch. 23 Pt. VI.
s. 457(1A)		s. 683(3)	Added 1980 s. 56(2); am. 1985 s. 49(1); 1986 s. 32(2); rep. in part 1986 Sch. 23 Pt. V.
s. 457(1B), (1C)		s. 683(4), (5)	Added 1986 s. 32(2).
s. 457(2)–(4)		s. 683(6)–(8)	
s. 457(4A)		s. 683(9)	Added 1980 s. 34(4).
s. 457(5)		s. 683(10)	Am. 1980 s. 56(3).
s. 457(6)		s. 685(1), (2)	
s. 458(1)	Pre-7th April 1965 settlements.	s. 684(1)–(3)	Am. 1971 Sch. 6 §68; 1978 Sch. 2 §13; rep. in part 1980 Sch. 20 Pt. V; 1984 Sch. 23 Pt. VI.
s. 458(2)		s. 685(1), (2)	
s. 459	Interpretation.	s. 685(4), (5)	
s. 460(1)–(3)	Cancellation of tax advantage.	s. 703(1)–(3)	Rep. in part 1987 Sch. 16 Pt. VII.
s. 460(4), (4A), (4B)		s. 703(4)–(6)	Added 1973 Sch. 11 §1.
s. 460(5)–(9)		s. 703(7)–(12)	
s. 461	The prescribed circumstances.	s. 704	Am. 1973 s. 54, Sch. 11 §2; rep. in part 1973 Sch. 22 Pt. II.
s. 462	Appeals.	s. 705(1)–(5)	
s. 462A	Appeals.	s. 705(6)–(8)	Added 1973 Sch. 11 §3.
s. 463	The tribunal.	s. 706	Am. 1982 Sch. 21 §3(1).
s. 464	Advance clearance.	s. 707	
s. 465	Information.	s. 708	
s. 466(1)	"Tax advantage".	s. 709(1)	Am. 1973 Sch. 11 §4.
s. 466(2)		—	Rep. 1973 Sch. 22 Pt. II.
s. 467	Interpretation.	s. 709(2)–(6)	Am. 1973 Sch. 11 §5; rep. in part 1987 Sch. 16 Pt. VII.
s. 468		—	Rep. 1987 Sch. 16 Pt. VII.
s. 469(1)	Sale and repurchase of securities.	s. 729(1)	Rep. in part 1971 Sch. 14 Pt. II; am. 1971 Sch. 6 §70.
s. 469(2)–(6)		s. 729(2)–(6)	
s. 469(6A), (6B), (6C)		s. 729(7)–(9)	Added 1986 Sch. 18 §1(1).
s. 469(7)		s. 729(10)	Am. 1986 Sch. 18 §1(4).
s. 469(8)		s. 729(11)	
s. 470	Transfers of income.	s. 730	Am. 1971 Sch. 6 §71.
s. 471	Application of sections 472–474.	s. 731	Am. 1973 Sch. 11 §6; 1986 Sch. 18 §2(1).
s. 472(1)	Dealers in securities.	s. 732(1)	
s. 472(2)		s. 732(2)	Subst. 1986 Sch. 18 §3(1).

TA 1970 — Destination Table — 704

TA 1970	Subject Matter	Re-enacted in TA 1988	Remarks
s. 472(3), (4)		s. 732(3), (4)	Am. 1986 Sch. 18 §1(3).
s. 472(5)		s. 732(5)	Added 1982 s. 57.
s. 472(6)		s. 732(6)	Added 1986 Sch. 18 §3(2).
s. 473(1)	Persons entitled to exemptions.	s. 733	
s. 473(2)		—	Rep. 1986 Sch. 15 Pt. III.
s. 474(1), (2)	Persons other than dealers in securities.	s. 734(1), (2)	Am. 1978 s. 30(7); CGTA 7.
s. 474(3)		s. 734(3)	Added 1973 Sch. 11 §7.
s. 475(1)–(5)	"Appropriate amount" in respect of interest.	s. 735	Am. 1973 s. 54, Sch. 21 §7.
s. 475(6)		—	Rep. 1986 Sch. 23 Pt. VIII.
s. 476	Company dealing in securities.	s. 736	
s. 477(1)–(6)	Manufactured dividends.	s. 737(1)–(6)	Am. 1973 Sch. 11 §8; 1982 s. 59(1); 1986 Sch. 18 §5, 6(2), (3); rep. in part 1973 Sch. 22 Pt. IV.
s. 477(6A)		s. 737(7)	Added 1973 Sch. 11 §8.
s. 477(7)		s. 737(8)	
s. 478(1), (2)	Transfer of assets abroad.	s. 739(1)–(4)	Am. 1981 s. 46(3).
s. 478(2A), (2B)		s. 739(5), (6)	Added 1981 s. 46(3).
s. 478(3)		s. 741	
s. 478(4)–(6)		s. 742(1)–(3)	Am. 1981 s. 46(5).
s. 478(7), (8)		s. 742(8), (9)	Am. 1972 Sch. 24 §27; rep. in part 1971 Sch. 14 Pt. II.
s. 478(9)		s. 742(10)	Added 1981 s. 46.
s. 479	Irish residents.	s. 746	
s. 480	Supplemental.	s. 743	Am. 1971 Sch. 6 §72; 1981 s. 46(7); rep. in part 1971 Sch. 14 Pt. II.
s. 481	Information.	s. 745	Rep. in part 1971 Sch. 14 Pt. II; am. 1972 Sch. 24 §28.
s. 482(1)–(4)	Migration of companies.	s. 765	
s. 482(5)		s. 766(1), (2)	
s. 482(6)		s. 766(3)	See Criminal Law Act 1977 c. 45 s. 32(1), Criminal Procedure (Scotland) Act 1975 c. 21 s. 193A, Fines and Penalties (Northern Ireland) Order 1984 (S.I. No. 703 (N.I. 3)).
s. 482(7)		s. 767(1), (2)	
s. 482(8)–(10)		s. 767(3)–(5)	Am. CCCPA.
s. 482(11)		s. 766(4)	Rep. in part CJA 1975 Sch. 6 Pt. I.
s. 482(12)		s. 767(6)	
s. 483	Change in ownership of company.	s. 768	
s. 484	Rules for section 483.	s. 769	Partly spent.
s. 485(1)	Sales at an undervalue etc.	s. 770(1), (2)(a)	Am. 1975 s. 17(2).
s. 485(2)		s. 770(1), (2)(b)	Am. 1975 s. 17(2).
s. 485(3)		s. 770(2)(d), (3)	
s. 485(4), (5)		s. 773(1), (2)	Am. 1971 Sch. 8 §16(5).
s. 485(5A)		s. 773(3)	Added 1975 s. 17(1).
s. 485(6)		s. 773(4)	
s. 486	Dealing company and associated companies.	s. 774	
s. 487(1)–(7)	Sale of certain income.	s. 775	
s. 487(8)		—	Spent.
s. 488(1)–(13)	Artificial transactions in land.	s. 776	
s. 488(14)		—	Spent.
s. 489	Supplemental.	s. 777	Am. CGTA 7; rep. in part 1971 Sch. 14 Pt. III.
s. 490	Information.	s. 778	
s. 491	Limitation of tax reliefs.	s. 779	
s. 492(1)–(5)	Assets leased to traders etc.	s. 781(1)–(6)	
s. 492(6)		s. 785	

TA 1970	Subject Matter	Re-enacted in TA 1988	Remarks
s. 492(7)–(9)		s. 781(7)–(9)	Am. 1971 Sch. 8 §16(7).
s. 493	Special cases.	s. 782	Am. 1971 Sch. 8 §16(8).
s. 494	Supplemental.	s. 783	
s. 495	Hire-purchase agreements.	s. 784	Am. CCA 1974 Sch. 4 §29; rep. in part 1987 Sch. 16 Pt. VII.
s. 496	Credit transactions.	s. 786	Rep. in part 1971 Sch. 14 Pt. II.
s. 497(1)–(8)	Double taxation relief.	s. 788	Am. 1972 ss. 100(1), 98(2); 1976 s. 50(2); 1987 s. 70(1).
s. 497(9), (10)		s. 789	Am. 1971 Sch. 6 §74; partly spent.
s. 498(1)–(4)	Unilateral relief.	s. 790(1)–(6)	Rep. in part 1976 Sch. 15 Pt. III; 1971 Sch. 14 Pt. VII; am. 1972 s. 83, 100(1); 1971 s. 26.
s. 498(5), (6)		s. 790(11), (12)	Am. 1972 s. 100(1).
s. 499		—	Rep. 1972 Sch. 28 Pt. VI.
s. 500	Interpretation of credit code.	s. 792	Rep. in part 1971 Sch. 14 Pt. VII.
s. 501	Relief by way of credit.	s. 793	Am. 1972 s. 100(1).
s. 502	Requirements as to residence.	s. 794	Am. 1982 s. 67.
s. 503	Computation of certain income.	s. 795	Am. 1972 s. 100(1); 1987 Sch. 15 §2(18).
s. 504	Limits on credit.	s. 796	
s. 505	Limits on credit.	s. 797(1)	Am. 1972 s. 100(3)–(7).
s. 506(1)	Underlying tax.	s. 799(1)	
s. 506(1A)		s. 799(2)	Added 1976 s. 50(3).
s. 506(2), (3)		s. 799(3), (4)	
s. 507(1)	Related companies' dividends.	s. 800	Am. 1971 s. 26(4).
s. 507(2), (3)		—	Rep. 1971 Sch. 14 Pt. VII.
s. 508		s. 801	Subst. 1971 s. 26(2).
s. 509	Insurance companies.	s. 802	
s. 510	Relief against income tax.	s. 804	Am. 1971 Sch. 6 §75.
s. 511	Elections against credit.	s. 805	Am. 1972 s. 100(1).
s. 512	Time limit for claims etc.	s. 806	Am. 1972 s. 100(1).
s. 513	—	—	Rep. 1976 Sch. 15 Pt. III.
s. 514	—	—	Rep. 1987 Sch. 16 Pt. VII.
s. 515	Capital allowances.	s. 810	Am. 1971 s. 54(1); 1982 s. 78(1); rep. in part 1970(F) Sch. 8 Pt. VII.
s. 516	Deductions for foreign tax.	s. 811	Am. 1973 s. 40(1); 1987 Sch. 15 §2(19).
s. 517(1)	Regulations.	s. 791, 828	
s. 517(2)		—	Rep. 1972 Sch. 28 Pt. VI.
s. 518	Information.	s. 816	
s. 519(1), (2)	Deductions not allowed.	s. 817	
s. 519(3)		—	Rep. 1987 Sch. 16 Pt. VII.
s. 520	Income tax provisions.	s. 820	
s. 521(1), (2)		s. 821(1), (2)	Rep. in part 1972 Sch. 28 Pt. VI.
s. 521(3)(a)		—	Rep. 1972 Sch. 28 Pt. VI.
s. 521(3)(b), (c), (d)		s. 821(3)	Am. 1983 s. 27.
s. 521(4)		s. 821(4)	Added 1972 Sch. 24 §29.
s. 522		s. 822	Am. 1971 Sch. 6 §76; 1972 Sch. 24 §30; rep. in part 1972 Sch. 28 Pt. VI.
s. 523		s. 823	
s. 524		s. 829(1)–(3)	
s. 525(1)		s. 829(4)	
s. 525(2)		Sch. 29	Am. CGTA 7.
s. 526(1), (2)	Interpretation.	s. 831(1), (2)	
s. 526(3), (4)		s. 832(3), (4)	
s. 526(5)		s. 832(1)	Am. NICA Sch. 5; 1971 Sch. 8 §16(3); CGTA 7; 1972 Sch. 24 §31; 1974 Sch. 12 §10; 1979(2) Sch. 2 §4; 1987 Sch. 15 §2(20); rep. in part 1972 Sch. 28 Pt. VI.

TA 1970	Subject Matter	Re-enacted in TA 1988	Remarks
s. 526(5A)		s. 832(5)	Added 1987 Sch. 15 §2(21).
s. 526(6)		s. 832(2)	
s. 527	Interpretation.	s. 834	Am. 1980 s. 45(2).
s. 528(1), (2)		s. 835(1), (2)	Am. 1971 Sch. 6 §78.
s. 528(3)–(5)		s. 835(6)–(8)	Am. 1971 Sch. 6 §78; 1972 Sch. 11 §8, Sch. 24 §32; rep. in part 1971 Sch. 14 Pt. II.
s. 529		s. 833(3)	
s. 530		s. 833(4)–(6)	Am. 1982 s. 31(2); 1981 s. 27(10); rep. in part 1977 Sch. 9 Pt. IV.
s. 531		s. 837	
s. 532		s. 838	
s. 533		s. 839	Rep. in part 1987 Sch. 16 Pt. VII.
s. 534		s. 840	
s. 535		s. 841	Am. 1973 s. 54, Sch. 21 §9.
Sch. 1	Qualifying policies.		
para. 1(1)–(4A)		Sch. 15 §1(1)–(5)	Am. 1975 Sch. 2 §4.
para. 1(5)–(7)		Sch. 15 §1(7)–(9)	Am. 1975 Sch. 2 §4.
para. 2		Sch. 15 §2(1)–(3)	Am. 1975 Sch. 2 §4.
para. 3, 3A		Sch. 15 §3, 4, 6(1)	Subst. 1985 Sch. 10 Pt. I; 1985 s. 41(4).
para. 4		Sch. 15 §7	Am. 1976 Sch. 4 §12; rep. in part 1976 Sch. 15 Pt. IV.
para. 5		Sch. 15 §9	
para. 6, 7		Sch. 15 §12, 13	
para. 8		Sch. 15 §15	
para. 9		Sch. 15 §17(1)–(3)	Am. 1984 s. 76(3), (6).
para. 10		Sch. 15 §18	
para. 11		Sch. 15 §22(1)–(3)	Rep. in part 1978 Sch. 14 Pt. III; am. 1975 Sch. 2 §2; 1976 s. 33(2); 1978 Sch. 3 §13.
Sch. 2	Restrictions on Schedule A deductions.		
para. 1–3		Sch. 1 §1–3	
para. 4		—	Rep. 1977 Sch. 9 §5.
Sch. 3	Taxable premiums.	Sch. 2	Rep. in part 1971 Sch. 14 Pt. II; 1970(F) Sch. 8 Pt. VI.
Sch. 4	—	—	Rep. 1971 Sch. 14 Pt. III.
Sch. 5	Tax under Schedule C.		
para. 1–13		Sch. 3 §1–13	Am. 1971 Sch. 6 §80; DCA 1969 s. 10; 1975(2) s. 44(3).
para. 14		s. 45, Sch. 3 §14	
Sch. 6	Farm animals etc.		
para. 1–11		Sch. 5 §1–11	
Sch. 7	—	—	Rep. 1971 Sch. 14 Pt. IV.
Sch. 8	Schedule E: retirement benefits etc.		
para. 1		Sch. 11 §1	
para. 2		Sch. 11 §2	Rep. in part 1971 Sch. 14 Pt. II.
para. 3–5		Sch. 11 §13	Am. 1978 s. 24; 1970(F) Sch. 5 Pt. III §12(6); 1971 Sch. 3 §12(6); 1981 s. 31(7); rep. in part 1973 Sch. 22 Pt. II.
para. 6		Sch. 11 §3, 14	Rep. in part 1971 Sch. 14 Pt. VI; 1981 Sch. 19 Pt. VI.
para. 7		Sch. 11 §4, 15	Am. 1981 s. 31(3); 1982 s. 43(1).
para. 7A		Sch. 11 §5	Added 1982 s. 43(1).
para. 8, 9		Sch. 11 §16	See 1981 s. 31(7).
para. 10		Sch. 11 §6, 7	Rep. in part 1981 Sch. 19 Pt. VI; see 1981 s. 31(7); am. 1986 s. 45(2).

TA 1970	Subject Matter	Re-enacted in TA 1988	Remarks
Sch. 8 (contd)			
para. 11		Sch. 11 §7, 18	Rep. in part 1981 Sch. 19 Pt. VI; see 1981 s. 31(7).
para. 12		—	Rep. 1986 Sch. 23 Pt. V.
para. 13		Sch. 11 §19	Rep. in part 1981 Sch. 19 Pt. VI; see 1981 s. 31(7).
para. 14		Sch. 11 §8	Am. 1971 Sch. 8 §16.
para. 15		Sch. 11 §9	
para. 16		Sch. 11 §10	Am. 1974 s. 21; 1977 s. 31.
para. 17		Sch. 11 §11	
Sch. 9		—	Rep. 1972 Sch. 28 Pt. VI.
Sch. 10	Underwriters.		
para. 1		s. 452(1)	Rep. in part 1973 Sch. 22 Pt. III; 1987 Sch. 16 Pt. VII.
para. 2–4		—	Rep. 1973 Sch. 22 Pt. III.
para. 5		s. 452(2), (3)	
para. 6		s. 452(4)(a)	
para. 7(1)–(3)		s. 452(5)–(9)	Am. 1973 Sch. 16 §10; 1985 Sch. 23 §29; rep. in part 1973 Sch. 22 Pt. III; 1987 Sch. 16 Pt. VII.
para. 7(4)		—	Rep. 1971 Sch. 14 Pt. IV.
para. 8		s. 453(1)–(4)	
para. 9		s. 453(5)–(7)	
para. 10		s. 452(4)(b)	
para. 11		s. 454	Rep. in part 1973 Sch. 22 Pt. III; 1971 Sch. 14 Pt. II; am. 1973 Sch. 16 §§8, 11, 12.
para. 12		s. 455	Rep. in part 1971 Sch. 14 Pt. II.
para. 12A		s. 456(1), (2)	Added 1973 Sch. 16 §§8, 13.
para. 13		s. 456(3)	
para. 14(a)		—	Rep. 1973 Sch. 22 Pt. III.
para. 14(b)		s. 456(4)	Rep. in part 1987 Sch. 16 Pt. VII.
para. 15		—	Rep. 1971 Sch. 14 Pt. IV.
para. 16		s. 457	Partly spent; am. 1987 Sch. 15 §2(22); rep. in part 1987 Sch. 16 Pt. VII.
Sch. 11	Tax relief in connection with certain schemes.	Sch. 21	
Sch. 12			
Pt. I, II		—	Rep. 1976 Sch. 15 Pt. III.
Pt. III			
para. 1		—	Rep. 1976 Sch. 15 Pt. III.
para. 2	Double taxation relief: Republic of Ireland.	s. 68(1)–(4)	Am. 1974 Sch. 1 §§27, 29; 1976 s. 49(4); rep. in part 1984 Sch. 23 Pt. VII; partly spent.
para. 3(1), (2)		—	Rep. 1976 Sch. 15 Pt. III.
para. 3(3)		s. 192(1)	Am. 1974 s. 21(6).
para. 4, 5		—	Rep. 1976 Sch. 15 Pt. III.
para. 6		Sch. 3 §15	Am. 1987 Sch. 15 §2(23).
Sch. 13	Returns of total income.	s. 836	
Sch. 14	Transitionals.		
para. 1, 2		—	Spent.
para. 3, 4		Sch. 30	
para. 5		—	Spent.
para. 6		Sch. 30	
para. 7, 8		—	Rep. 1971 Sch. 14 Pt. IV.
para. 9		Sch. 30	
para. 10		—	Rep. 1972 Sch. 28 Pt. V.
para. 11			Not repealed.
para. 12		—	Rep. 1980 Sch. 20 Pt. VIII.
para. 13–17			Spent.
para. 18		Sch. 30	
para. 19(1)		—	Rep. 1972 Sch. 28 Pt. VI.
para. 19(2), 20–22		—	Spent.

TA 1970   *Destination Table*   708

TA 1970	Subject Matter	Re-enacted in TA 1988	Remarks
Sch. 14 (contd) para. 23		—	Rep. in part 1972 Sch. 28 Pt. VI; spent.
para. 24–27		—	Spent.
para. 28		—	Rep. 1971/2099.
para. 29		—	Rep. 1970(F) Sch. 8 Pt. VII.
Sch. 16	Repeals.	—	

FINANCE ACT 1970
(c. 24)

FA 1970	Subject Matter	Re-enacted in TA 1988	Remarks
s. 11–13	IT, CT & surtax rates.	—	Spent; rep. in part 1971 Sch. 14 Pt. II.
s. 14(1)(*a*)(i)–(iii)	Personal reliefs.	—	Rep. 1971 Sch. 14 Pt. II.
s. 14(1)(*a*)(iv)		s. 257(8)	
s. 14(1)(*b*)–(*e*)		—	Rep. 1971 Sch. 14 Pt. II, VII.
s. 14(1)(*f*)		—	Spent.
s. 14(2)		—	Spent.
s. 16(1)	Passenger transport executives.	—	Rep. Transport Act 1985 c. 67 Sch. 8.
s. 16(2), (3)		Sch. 30	
s. 16(4)		—	Unnecessary.
s. 17		—	Rep. 1972 Sch. 28 Pt. V.
s. 19(1)	Occupational pension schemes.	s. 590(1)	Subst. 1971 s. 21(2).
s. 19(2)(*a*)–(*e*)		s. 590(2)(*a*)–(*e*)	
s. 19(2)(*f*)		—	Rep. 1973 Sch. 22 Pt. II.
s. 19(2)(*g*)		s. 590(2)(*f*)	
s. 19(2A)		s. 590(3), (4)	Added 1971 s. 21(3).
s. 19(2B)		s. 590(3)	Added 1987(2) Sch. 3 §1.
s. 19(3)		s. 590(5)	Am. 1987(2) Sch. 3 §2.
s. 19(4)		s. 590(6)	Subst. 1971 Sch. 3 §12(1).
s. 19(5)		s. 590(7)	
s. 19(6)	Commencement.	—	Spent.
s. 20(1)		s. 591(1)	Am. 1987(2) Sch. 3 §3.
s. 20(2)(*a*)–(*f*)		s. 591(2)(*a*)–(*f*)	Subst. 1971 s. 21(4).
s. 20(2)(*g*), (*h*)		s. 591(2)(*g*), (*h*)	Added 1981 s. 32; subst. 1987(2) Sch. 3 §3.
s. 20(2A)		s. 591(3)	Added 1981 s. 32; am. ICA 1982.
s. 20(3)		s. 591(4)	
s. 20(4), (5)		s. 591(5), (6)	Added 1987 Sch. 15 §3.
s. 20(6)		s. 612(3), 828	
s. 21(1), (2)		s. 592(1), (2)	
s. 21(2A)		s. 592(3)	Added 1971 s. 21(5).
s. 21(3)		s. 592(4)–(6)	
s. 21(4)		s. 592(7)	Rep. in part 1987(2) Sch. 9 Pt. I.
s. 21(4A)		s. 592(8)	Subst. 1987(2) Sch. 3 §4.
s. 21(5)		s. 592(9)	
s. 21(6)		—	Rep. 1971 Sch. 14 Pt. IV.
s. 21(7)		Sch. 29	
s. 21(7A), (7B)		s. 592(10), Sch. 29	Added 1987(2) Sch. 3 §5.
s. 21(8), (9)		s. 592(11), (12)	
s. 21(10), (11)		—	Rep. 1971 Sch. 14 Pt. I.
s. 22(1), (2), (2A)	Statutory schemes.	s. 594	Am. 1972 s. 74(3); 1987(2) Sch. 3 §6.
s. 22(3)		—	Rep. 1972 Sch. 28 Pt. IV.

FA 1970	Subject Matter	Re-enacted in TA 1988	Remarks
s. 22(4)		—	Rep. 1971 Sch. 14 Pt. I.
s. 23(1)–(5)	Payments by employer etc.	s. 595	
s. 23(6)		—	Rep. 1971 Sch. 14 Pt. I.
s. 24(1)	Exceptions from s. 23.	s. 596(1)	
s. 24(2)		s. 596(2)	Subst. 1974 s. 21(7).
s. 24(3)		s. 596(3)	
s. 25	Definitions.	s. 611(1)–(4)	
s. 26(1)	Further interpretation.	s. 612(1)	Rep. in part 1971 Sch. 14 Pt. I; 1973 Sch. 22 Pt. II; am. 1971 Sch. 3 §12(4); NICA Sch. 5; 1987(2) Sch. 3 §7.
s. 26(2)		s. 612(2)	Am. 1987(2) Sch. 3 §8.
s. 26(3)		—	Unnecessary.
s. 29(1), (2)	Mineral royalties.	s. 122(1), (2)	Rep. in part 1971 Sch. 14 Pt. II, III; am. CGTA 7.
s. 29(3)(a)		s. 122(1)(b), (3)	See 1971 Sch. 9 §4.
s. 29(3)(b), (c)		—	Rep. 1971 Sch. 14 Pt. III.
s. 29(4)		s. 122(4)	Rep. in part 1971 Sch. 14 Pt. II.
s. 29(6)–(9)		s. 122(5)–(7), Sch. 29	Not wholly repealed.
Sch. 3	London transport authorities.		
para. 2–7		Sch. 30	Partly spent.
Sch. 4	Amendments.		
para. 1–5		—	Rep. 1972 Sch. 28 Pt. VI.
para. 6		s. 209(2)(e)(iv), (v)	
para. 7		—	Not repealed.
para. 8		s. 656(2), (3)(e)	
para. 9(1)–(5), (7)–(9)		—	Rep. 1972 Sch. 28 Pt. V.
para. 9(6)		s. 387(3)(a)	
para. 10		—	Not repealed.
para. 11		—	Unnecessary.
Sch. 5	Occupational pensions schemes.		
Pt. I		—	Rep. 1971 Sch. 14 Pt. I.
Pt. II para. 1		s. 597	
para. 2		s. 598, 828	Subst. 1971 Sch. 3 §7.
para. 3(1)–(5)		s. 599	Subst. 1971 Sch. 3 §7; am. 1987(2) Sch. 3 §9.
para. 3(6)			Spent.
para. 4		s. 601(5), (6)	Am. 1971 Sch. 3 §12(5).
para. 5		—	Rep. 1971 Sch. 14 Pt. I.
para. 6		s. 604	Am. 1987(2) Sch. 3 §11.
para. 6A		s. 593	Added 1987(2) Sch. 3 §12.
para. 7, 8		s. 605	Am. 1987(2) Sch. 3 §13, 14.
para. 9		s. 606	Am. 1987(2) Sch. 3 §15.
para. 10		s. 612(3)	
Pt. III para. 11, 12	Amendments.		See destinations of enactments amended.

INCOME AND CORPORATION TAXES (No. 2) ACT 1970
(c. 54)

T (No. 2) A 1970	Subject Matter	Re-enacted in TA 1988	Remarks
s. 1	IT rates.	—	Spent.
s. 2		—	Rep. 1973 Sch. 22 Pt. II.
s. 3	CT rates.	—	Spent.
s. 4		—	Unnecessary.

FINANCE ACT 1971
(c. 68)

FA 1971	Subject Matter	Re-enacted in TA 1988	Remarks
s. 13, 14	IT & CT rates.	—	Spent.
s. 15(1)	—	—	Unnecessary.
s. 15(2)–(4)	Personal reliefs.	—	Rep. 1974 Sch. 14 Pt. VI, VII.
s. 15(5)		s. 258(2)(c)	
s. 15(6)		—	Rep. 1973 Sch. 23 Pt. II.
s. 15(7)		—	Rep. 1977 Sch. 9 Pt. IV.
s. 16(1)	Settlements.	—	Unnecessary.
s. 16(2)(a)		s. 382(1)	
s. 16(2)(b)		s. 663(1)	
s. 16(2)(c)		s. 664(2)(b), 666(1)	
s. 16(2)(d)		s. 663(4)	
s. 17(1)	Partnerships.	s. 113(2)	
s. 17(2)		—	Spent.
s. 18(1)	Social security benefits.	s. 617(1)(a)	
s. 18(2)		—	Rep. 1973 Sch. 22 Pt. II.
s. 19	Damages for personal injuries.	s. 329	Am. NICA Sch. 5 §4(1); AJA 1982 s. 74; 1981 s. 39; CCA 1984 Sch. 2 §37.
s. 20(1)	Annuities.	s. 620(1)	
s. 20(2)		s. 619(2), (3)	Rep. in part 1980 Sch. 20 Pt. VII; am. 1980 s. 31(1), (2).
s. 20(3)		s. 620(3)	
s. 20(4)		—	Unnecessary.
s. 21(1)		—	Unnecessary.
s. 21(2), (3)	Occupational pensions schemes.	s. 590(1), (3)	
s. 21(4)		s. 591(2)	Am. 1981 s. 32.
s. 21(5)		s. 592(3)	
s. 21(6)		—	Not repealed.
s. 22(1)–(3)	Pensions.	s. 610	
s. 22(4)–(10)		—	Rep. SSA 1973 Sch. 28.
s. 23(1)	Taxation of wife's earnings.	s. 287(1)	
s. 23(2)–(5)		s. 288	Am. 1976 s. 36(10).
s. 24	—	—	Spent.
s. 25(1)–(4)(a)	—	—	Rep. 1972 Sch. 28 Pt. VI.
s. 25(4)(b)	—	—	Spent.
s. 25(5)	Close companies.	s. 420(2)	
s. 25(6)		s. 414(7)	
s. 25(7)		—	Unnecessary.
s. 26(1)	D.T.R.	—	Unnecessary.
s. 26(2)		s. 801	
s. 26(3)		s. 790(6)(a)	
s. 26(4)		s. 800	
s. 26(5)		—	Spent.
s. 27	—	—	Spent.
s. 28	Marketing boards.	s. 509	
s. 29–31	—	—	Rep. 1975(2) Sch. 14 Pt. IV.
s. 32(1)(a)	Basic and higher rates.	s. 1(2)(a)	
s. 32(1)(aa)		—	Added 1978 s. 14(1); rep. 1980 Sch. 20 Pt. V.
s. 32(1)(b)		s. 1(2)(b)	
s. 32(1)		s. 832(1)	Am. 1984 Sch. 7 §1.
s. 32(1A), (1B), (1C)		—	Added 1978 s. 14(2); rep. 1980 Sch. 20 Pt. V.
s. 32(1D)		s. 832(1)	Added 1978 s. 14(1); rep. in part 1980 Sch. 20 Pt. V.
s. 32(2)		—	Spent.
s. 32(3), (4)		—	Rep. 1984 Sch. 23 Pt. VI.
s. 33(1)		—	Spent.
s. 33(2), (3)	Amendments.		See destinations of enactments amended.
s. 33(4)		—	Rep. 1977 Sch. 9 Pt. IV.
s. 33(5)		s. 276	

FA 1971	Subject Matter	Re-enacted in TA 1988	Remarks
s. 34(1)–(3)	Deductions.	s. 835(3)–(5)	Am. 1975(2) s. 31(4).
s. 34(4)			Rep. 1984 Sch. 23 Pt. VI.
s. 35	Surtax.	—	Spent.
s. 36	Deduction of tax.	s. 4	Am. 1975(2) s. 44(6).
s. 39	IT rate.	—	Spent.
s. 54(1)	DTR: capital allowances.	s. 810(4)(*b*)	
s. 54(2)			Spent.
Sch. 2	Amendments.		
para. 1		s. 621, Sch. 29	Am. 1976 s. 30(2); rep. in part 1980 Sch. 20 Pt. VII.
para. 2–5			Rep. 1980 Sch. 20 Pt. VII.
para. 6		s. 539(2)(*c*)	
para. 7	Commencement.	—	Spent; rep. in part 1980 Sch. 20 Pt. VII.
Sch. 3	Occupational pension schemes.		
para. 1–3		—	Spent.
para. 4		—	Spent.
para. 5		s. 611(5)	
para. 6		—	Spent.
para. 7		s. 598, 599	
para. 8		—	Not repealed.
para. 9		s. 600	
para. 10		—	Rep. CGTA 8.
para. 11, 12			See destinations of enactments amended.
para. 13		—	Unnecessary.
Sch. 4	Separate taxation of wife's earnings.		
para. 1, 2		s. 287(2), (3)	Am. 1979(2) Sch. 2 §5; 1987 s. 27(3).
para. 3		s. 287(4)–(6)	Rep. in part 1971 Sch. 4 §8; 1979(2) Sch. 5 Pt. II; 1982 Sch. 22 Pt. XI; am. 1975(2) s. 31(5); 1987 s. 26(5).
para. 4, 5		s. 287(7)–(9)	
para. 6		—	Rep. 1971 Sch. 4 §8.
para. 7		s. 287(10)	
para. 8		—	Spent.
Sch. 5	—	—	Rep. 1975(2) Sch. 14 Pt. IV.
Sch. 6	Amendments.		
Pt. I			See destinations of enactments amended.
Pt. III			
para. 91, 92		—	Rep. CGTA 8; 1972 Sch. 28 Pt. VI.
para. 93		—	Spent.
Sch. 7	Income tax provisions.		
para. 1		—	Spent.
para. 2–4		s. 819	Am. 1978 Sch. 2 §14; rep. in part 1980 Sch. 20 Pt. V; 1984 Sch. 23 Pt. VI.
Sch. 9	Development value.		
para. 4		s. 122	

FINANCE ACT 1972
(c. 41)

FA 1972	Subject Matter	Re-enacted in TA 1988	Remarks
s. 62–64	IT, CT & surtax rates.	—	Spent.
s. 65	—	—	Rep. 1973 Sch. 23 Pt. II; 1974 Sch. 14 Pt. VI, VII.
s. 66	IT rates.	—	Spent.

FA 1972	Subject Matter	Re-enacted in TA 1988	Remarks
s. 70	Grants for the disabled.	s. 327	Am. NHS 1977 Sch. 15 §57; NHS 1978 Sch. 16 §37.
s. 71	—	—	Spent.
s. 72	Terminal grants to Members of Parliament.	s. 190	
s. 73	Compensation for early retirement etc.	s. 188(2)	
s. 74(1), (2)	—	—	Spent.
s. 74(3)	Pensions.	s. 594	
s. 75(1)	Relief for payment of interest.	s. 353(1)	Am. 1974 s. 19(1)(a); 1973 s. 54.
s. 75(1A)		s. 353(3)(a)	Added 1974 s. 19(1)(b).
s. 75(2)		s. 353(3)(b)	
s. 75(3)–(5)		—	Rep. 1974 Sch. 14 Pt. I.
s. 75(6)		s. 353(1)(b)	Subst. 1976 s. 49(5).
s. 75(7)		s. 353(1)	Am. 1974 s. 19(1)(d).
s. 75(8)		—	Unnecessary.
s. 76	Securities.	—	Rep. 1987 Sch. 16 Pt. VII.
s. 77(1)	Share options.	s. 135(2), (5)	
s. 77(2), (3)		s. 135(5)	
s. 78		—	Rep. 1974 Sch. 14 Pt. II.
s. 79(1)	Share incentive schemes.	s. 138(1)	
s. 79(1A), (1B)		s. 139(1), (2)	Added 1984 s. 41(1).
s. 79(2)(a)		—	Rep. 1974 Sch. 14 Pt. II.
s. 79(2)(b)		s. 138(2)(a)	Rep. in part 1974 Sch. 14 Pt. II.
s. 79(2)(bb)		s. 138(3)(b)	Added 1984 s. 40(1).
s. 79(2)(c)		s. 138(3)(a), (5)	Subst. 1973 Sch. 8 §4(1)(a).
s. 79(2A)		s. 138(6)	Added 1973 Sch. 8 §4(1)(b).
s. 79(2B)		s. 138(7)	Added 1984 s. 40(2).
s. 79(3)		s. 138(2)(a), (12)	Rep. in part 1974 Sch. 14 Pt. II.
s. 79(4)		s. 138(1)(a)	
s. 79(4A)		s. 139(14)	Added 1984 s. 40(3).
s. 79(5)		s. 138(8)	
s. 79(5A), (5B)		s. 138(10), (11)	Added 1986 s. 26(3).
s. 79(6)		s. 138(9)	Am. 1973 Sch. 8 §4(1)(c); 1986 s. 26(4).
s. 79(6A)		s. 139(13)	Added 1986 s. 26(5).
s. 79(7)		s. 138(1)(b)	
s. 79(8)		s. 138(2)(a)	
s. 79(9)		Sch. 29	Am. CGTA 7.
s. 79(10), (11)		s. 139(3), (4)	
s. 79(12)		—	Unnecessary.
s. 80	Sale & lease-back of land.	s. 780	
s. 81(1)	Premiums for and duration of leases.	s. 34(8)	
s. 81(2)(a), (b)		s. 38(1)	
s. 81(2)(c)		s. 38(2), (3), (4)	
s. 81(2)(d)		s. 38(6)	
s. 81(3)		s. 24(1)	
s. 81(4)		s. 24(3), (4)	
s. 81(5)		s. 38(5), Sch. 29	
s. 81(6)		Sch. 30	Partly spent.
s. 82	Appeals against certain determinations.	s. 42	
s. 83	Double taxation relief.	s. 790(6)–(10)	
s. 84(1)	Advance corporation tax.	s. 14(1)	Partly spent.
s. 84(2)		s. 14(3)	Am. 1986 s. 17(1).
s. 84(3)		s. 238(1)	
s. 84(4)		s. 14(2)	
s. 84(5)		s. 238(5)	
s. 85(1), (2)	Set-off of ACT against liability to corporation tax.	s. 239(1), (2)	Am. 1987(2) s. 74(2).
s. 85(3)		s. 239(3)	Am. 1984 ss. 52(1), 53(2); 1987(2) s. 74(2).
s. 85(4), (5)		s. 239(4), (5)	
s. 85(6)		s. 239(6)	Am. 1974 Sch. 7 §3(1); 1987(2) s. 74(2).

FA 1972	Subject Matter	Re-enacted in TA 1988	Remarks
s. 85(7)		s. 239(7)	Partly spent.
s. 86	Tax credits.	s. 231	
s. 87(1)	Schedule F.	—	Unnecessary.
s. 87(2), (3)		s. 20(1), (2)	
s. 87(4)		—	Spent.
s. 87(5), (6)		s. 233	Rep. in part 1984 Sch. 23 Pt. VI.
s. 88(1)	Franked investment income.	s. 238(1)	
s. 88(2)		—	Unnecessary.
s. 89(1)–(5)	Calculation of ACT.	s. 241	
s. 89(6)		s. 238(1)	Partly unnecessary.
s. 90(1)	Set-off of losses etc. against franked investment income.	—	Unnecessary.
s. 90(2), (3)		s. 244	Am. 1973 Sch. 13 §9.
s. 91(1), (2)	Group income.	—	Spent.
s. 91(3)		s. 248(1), (6), 828	
s. 91(4)		—	Effect preserved by IA 1978 s. 17(2)(b).
s. 92(1)	Setting of company's surplus ACT against subsidiary's liability.	s. 240(1)	Am. 1973 Sch. 13 §2.
s. 92(2)		s. 240(2)	Am. and rep. in part 1973 Sch. 13 §§3, 4.
s. 92(3)		s. 240(3)	
s. 92(3A)		s. 240(4)	Added 1973 Sch. 13 §5.
s. 92(4)		s. 240(5)	
s. 92(5)		s. 240(6)	Am. 1973 Sch. 13 §6.
s. 92(6), (7)		s. 240(7), (8)	
s. 92(7A)		s. 240(9)	Added 1982 s. 55.
s. 92(8)		s. 240(10)	Am. 1973 Sch. 13 §7.
s. 92(9)–(11)		s. 240(11), (13)	Added 1973 Sch. 13 §8.
s. 93		—	Rep. 1987(2) Sch. 9 Pt. I.
s. 94	Close companies.	—	Unnecessary.
s. 95	Small companies' relief.	s. 13	Am. 1973 Sch. 14 §2; 1983(2) s. 2(2); 1987(2) s. 74(4).
s. 96		—	Rep. 1984 Sch. 23 Pt. V.
s. 97	—	—	Unnecessary.
s. 98(1), (3), (4)	Tax credits for non-U.K. residents.	s. 232	
s. 98(2)		s. 788	
s. 99	—	—	Spent.
s. 100(1)	Double taxation relief.	Pt. XVIII	
s. 100(2)		—	Spent.
s. 100(3)–(6)		s. 797(1)–(4)	Am. 1984 s. 53; 1986 s. 49(2); rep. in part 1986 Sch. 23 Pt. V; 1987(2) s. 77(2).
s. 100(6A)		s. 797(5)	Added 1986 s. 49(3); am. 1987(2) s. 77(2).
s. 100(7), (8)		—	Spent.
s. 101	Calculation of ACT etc. on change of ownership of company.	s. 245	Am. 1987(2) s. 74(5).
s. 102	Rectification of excessive set-off of ACT or tax credit.	s. 252	Am. 1987(2) s. 88(5)–(7).
s. 103(1)–(3)	Charge of ACT at old rates.	—	Rep. 1986 Sch. 23 Pt. V.
s. 103(4), (5)		s. 246(5), (6)	Am. 1973 Sch. 14 §5; 1987(2) s. 74(5).
s. 104	Liability to account for income tax.	s. 350(4)	
s. 105	—	—	Unnecessary.
s. 106	—	—	Unnecessary.
s. 107	Amendments.		See destinations of enactments amended; rep. in part 1986 Sch. 23 Pt. V.

FA 1972 — Destination Table

FA 1972	Subject Matter	Re-enacted in TA 1988	Remarks
s. 108	Power to modify 1972 Sch. 14, 20 or 21.	s. 253, 350(4)–(7)	
s. 109	—	—	Spent.
s. 110(1)–(4)	Interpretation.	s. 238(1)–(4), 231(5)	
s. 110(5)		—	Spent.
s. 111(1)	—	—	Unnecessary.
s. 111(2)	Relationship between provisions about ACT and corporation tax.	s. 14(4)	
		—	Spent.
s. 111(3)		—	Spent.
s. 124(1)	Payments to E.C.G.D.	s. 88	Rep. in part CGTA 8.
s. 124(2)(*a*)		s. 584(5)	
s. 124(2)(*b*)		s. 441(9)	
Sch. 9	Relief for payment of interest.		Am. 1974 Sch. 1 §§1, 2; 1983 s. 17(5).
para. 1		s. 354(1)	
para. 2		s. 367(2)	
para. 3, 4		s. 354(2)	
para. 5		s. 354(1), (3)	Am. 1974 Sch. 1 §1.
para. 5A		s. 354(1), 367(1)	Added 1974 Sch. 1 §3.
para. 6		s. 354(4)	
para. 7		s. 354(7)	
para. 8		s. 355(5)	
para. 9		s. 367(1)	
para. 10–13		s. 359(1)–(4)	Am. 1974 Sch. 1 §1.
para. 14		s. 367(3)	
para. 15		s. 367(4)	Am. 1974 Sch. 1 §1.
Sch. 10	Relief for interest: supplementary provisions.		
para. 1–6		s. 368	
para. 7		s. 366(1)	Am. 1974 Sch. 1 §25(1).
para. 8, 9		s. 366(2), (3)	
para. 10, 11		—	Spent.
Sch. 11	Amendments.		Rep. in part 1974 Sch. 14 Pt. I; see destinations of enactments amended.
Sch. 12	Share option and share incentive schemes.		
Pts. I to VI		—	Rep. 1974 Sch. 14 Pt. II.
Pt. VII para. 1, 2		—	Rep. 1974 Sch. 14 Pt. II.
para. 3(1)		s. 139(5)	
para. 3(2)		s. 139(5)	Added 1984 s. 41(2).
para. 3A		s. 139(6)	Added 1984 s. 40(4).
para. 4		—	Rep. 1974 Sch. 14 Pt. II.
para. 5		Sch. 40	
para. 6		s. 139(11), 140(2)	Rep. in part 1974 Sch. 14 Pt. II; am. CGTA 7.
para. 7		s. 140(1)	Rep. in part 1974 Sch. 14 Pt. II.
para. 8		s. 139(12)	
para. 9		s. 140(2)	Rep. in part 1974 Sch. 14 Pt. II.
Sch. 13	Leases.		
para. 1–5		—	Spent.
para. 6, 7		Sch. 30 §3	
Sch. 14	Collection of ACT.	Sch. 13	
Sch. 15	Loss relief.		
Pt. I		s. 242, 243	
Pt. II		s. 247	
Sch. 16	Apportionment of income etc. of close companies.		
para. 1(1)		s. 423(1)(*a*)	Am. 1987(2) s. 61(3).
para. 1(2)		s. 424(1)(*a*), 423(7)	Am. 1974 Sch. 1 §26.
para. 1(3)		s. 424(1)(*b*)	
para. 1(4)		s. 423(3)	Am. 1987(2) s. 61(3).
para. 1(5)		s. 423(6)	
para. 2		s. 424(2)	
para. 3(1)		s. 423(1)(*b*)	Am. 1980 s. 56(4); 1987(2) s. 61(4).
para. 3(2)		s. 424(3)	

FA 1972	Subject Matter	Re-enacted in TA 1988	Remarks
Sch. 16 (contd)			
para. 3(3)		s. 423(2), 424(1)	
para. 3A(1)		s. 423(1)(c)	Para. 3A added 1974 Sch. 1 §26; am. 1987(2) s. 61(1).
para. 3A(2)		s. 424(4)	
para. 3A(3)		s. 424(6)	
para. 3A(4)		s. 423(4)	
para. 3A(5)		s. 423(2), 424(1)	
para. 3A(6)		s. 423(5)	
para. 3A(7)		s. 424(5)	
para. 4	Manner of apportionment.	s. 425	
para. 5(1)–(3)	Consequences of apportionment: income tax.	s. 426	Rep. in part 1980 Sch. 20 Pt. V.
para. 5(4)		s. 427(1)	Am. 1984 s. 32.
para. 5(5)		s. 427(2)	
para. 5(5A)		s. 427(3)	Added 1980 s. 56(5); am. 1986 s. 32(3).
para. 5(6)		s. 427(4)	Am. 1973 Sch. 9 §1(2).
para. 5(6A)		s. 427(5)	Added 1973 Sch. 9 §1(3); 1978 Sch. 2 §16(b); rep. in part 1980 Sch. 20 Pt. V; 1984 Sch. 23 Pt. VI.
para. 5(7)		s. 428(1)	Am. 1974 Sch. 1 §26; rep. in part 1973 Sch. 22 Pt. II.
para. 5(8)		s. 428(2)	
para. 6	Payment and collection of income tax.	s. 429	Am. 1976 s. 45; 1980 s. 61(4).
para. 7(1)	Consequences of apportionment: ACT.	s. 430(1)	
para. 7(2)–(5)		s. 430(3)–(6)	
para. 7(6)(a)		s. 430(7)(a)	
para. 7(6)(aa)		s. 430(7)(b)	Added 1975(2) s. 46(6).
para. 7(6)(b)		s. 430(7)(c)	
para. 7(7)		—	Rep. 1973 Sch. 22 §2.
para. 7(8), (9)		s. 430(8), (9)	
para. 8(1)	"Relevant income".	Sch. 19 §1(1)	Am. 1980 Sch. 9 §1.
para. 8(2)		Sch. 19 §1(2)	
para. 8(3)–(5)		Sch. 19 §1(3)–(5)	Added 1978 Sch. 5 §1.
para. 9(1)		Sch. 19 §2(1)	
para. 9(2)		Sch. 19 §2(2)	Subst. 1980 Sch. 9 §2.
para. 9(3)		Sch. 19 §2(3)	Am. 1978 s. 35(1).
para. 9(4)		Sch. 19 §2(4)	Am. 1978 s. 35(2).
para. 9(5), (6)		Sch. 19 §2(5), (6)	
para. 10(1)	Distributions and distributable income.	Sch. 19 §3(1), (2)	
para. 10(2)		Sch. 19 §4(1)	Am. 1980 Sch. 9 §3.
para. 10(3)		Sch. 19 §4(2)	Am. 1978 s. 35(3); 1980 s. 44(2).
para. 10(4), (4A)		Sch. 19 §5(1), (2)	Subst. and added 1980 Sch. 9 §4.
para. 10(5)		Sch. 19 §5(3)	Am. 1980 Sch. 9 §5.
para. 10(6)		Sch. 19 §5(4)	
para. 10(7)		Sch. 19 §6(1)	
para. 10(8)		Sch. 19 §6(2)	Am. 1985 Sch. 25 §9.
para. 10(9)		Sch. 19 §6(3)	Added 1980 Sch. 9 §6; am. 1987 Sch. 15 §4.
para. 10A		Sch. 19 §3(3)–(5)	Added 1973 Sch. 9 §3.
para. 11	Trading company.	Sch. 19 §7	
para. 12(1)		Sch. 19 §8(1)	Am. 1974 Sch. 9 §4; rep. in part 1987 Sch. 16 Pt. VII.
para. 12(2)		Sch. 19 §8(2)	
para. 12(2A)		Sch. 19 §8(3)	Added 1973 Sch. 9 §4.
para. 12(2B)		Sch. 19 §8(4)	Added 1982 s. 56(2).
para. 12(3)		Sch. 19 §8(5)	
para. 12A		Sch. 19 §9	Added 1978 Sch. 5 §2.
para. 13		Sch. 19 §10	Am. 1980 Sch. 9 §7.
para. 14		Sch. 19 §11	

FA 1972 — Destination Table — 716

FA 1972	Subject Matter	Re-enacted in TA 1988	Remarks
Sch. 16 (contd)			
para. 14A		—	Rep. 1985 Sch. 27 Pt. X.
para. 15–18	Procedure.	Sch. 19 §13–16	Am. 1987(2) s. 61(5).
para. 19		Sch. 19 §17	Am. 1976 s. 44(3).
para. 20		Sch. 19 §18	Am. 1987(2) s. 61(6).
Sch. 17	Close companies.		
paras. 1, 3, 5, 7	Amendments.		See destinations of enactments amended.
paras. 2, 4, 6		—	Spent.
para. 7	Commencement.	—	Spent.
Sch. 18	Insurance companies.		
para. 1		s. 76(2)–(4)	
para. 2(1)		—	Rep. 1984 Sch. 23 Pt. V.
para. 2(2)		—	Spent.
para. 2(3)		s. 434(3)	
para. 2(4)		s. 434(6)	Am. 1987(2) s. 75(1)(b).
para. 2(5)		s. 434(8)	
para. 3		s. 437(4)	
para. 4(1)		s. 438(4)	
para. 4(2)		s. 438(5), (6)	
para. 4(3)		—	Spent.
para. 4(4)		—	Spent.
para. 5		s. 436(3)(e), 445(2)(a), 449(2)	
para. 6		s. 447(4)	
Sch. 19	—		Spent.
Sch. 20	Collection of income tax on payments which are not distributions.	Sch. 16	
Sch. 21	Returns of non-qualifying distributions.	s. 234(5)–(9)	
Sch. 22	Meaning of "distribution".		
para. 1		s. 209(2)(b)	
para. 2(1)		s. 209(2)(c)	
para. 2(2)		s. 209(8)	
para. 3(1)		s. 209(2)(e)(ii)	
para. 3(2)		s. 209(2)(d)	
para. 3(3)		s. 209(3)	
para. 4(1), (2)		s. 209(6)	
para. 4(3)		s. 209(5)	
para. 5(1)		—	Spent.
para. 5(2), (3)		s. 210(3)	
para. 6		s. 211(1), (2)	
para. 7		—	Spent.
para. 8(1), (2)		s. 254(6), (7)	
para. 9		s. 254(8)	
para. 10(1)–(3)		s. 254(1)–(4)	
para. 10(4)		s. 254(1)	
para. 11		—	Unnecessary.
Sch. 23	Transitional provisions.		
paras. 1–17	—	—	Spent.
para. 18	References to gross distributions etc.	s. 255	Am. 1976 s. 46(1).
para. 19	—	—	Spent.

Finance Act 1973
(c. 51)

FA 1973	Subject Matter	Re-enacted in TA 1988	Remarks
s. 10, 11	IT & surtax rates.	—	Spent.
s. 12(1)	Personal reliefs.	—	Rep. 1974 Sch. 14 Pt. VI.
s. 12(2)		s. 263	Rep. in part 1979(2) Sch. 5 Pt. II.
s. 13	—	—	Rep. 1977 Sch. 9 Pt. VI.
s. 14	Retirement benefits.	s. 189	Am. 1987(2) Sch. 2 §3.

FA 1973	Subject Matter	Re-enacted in TA 1988	Remarks
s. 15			Spent.
s. 16(1)–(6)	Additional rate tax on certain income from discretionary trusts.	s. 686	Am. 1986 s. 47(4)(*a*).
s. 16(7)		s. 677(2)(*h*), (6)	
s. 16(8)		Sch. 29	
s. 17(1)	Payments under discretionary trusts.	s. 687(1), 348(3), 349(1)	
s. 17(2)		s. 687(2)	
s. 17(3)		s. 687(3)	Am. 1975(2) s. 34(6); 1984 s. 100(2); 1985 Sch. 23 §8(3); 1974 Sch. 7 §8.
s. 17(4)		s. 352(1)	
s. 17(5)		s. 687(4)	
s. 18	Discretionary trusts.	s. 809	
s. 19		—	Unnecessary; rep. in part 1974 Sch. 14 Pt. II.
s. 20		—	Rep. 1974 Sch. 14 Pt. II.
s. 21		—	Spent.
s. 22(1)–(5)	Distribution to exempt funds etc.	s. 235	
s. 22(6)		—	Unnecessary.
s. 23	Bonus issues: disallowance of reliefs.	s. 237	
s. 24	Group income.	s. 247(5)	
s. 25		—	Unnecessary.
s. 26(1)	Certificates of deposit.	s. 56(1)–(3)	Am. 1975(2) s. 50.
s. 26(2)		s. 398	
s. 26(3), (4)		s. 56(5), (6)	
s. 27	Discounted Treasury securities.	s. 126	
s. 28(1)	Group relief.	—	Unnecessary.
s. 28(2)–(5)		s. 413(7)–(10)	Am. 1981 s. 40(5).
s. 28(6)(*a*)		—	Rep. 1981 Sch. 19 Pt. VI.
s. 28(6)(*b*)		—	Spent.
s. 28(7)		s. 413	
s. 29	Group relief.	s. 410(1)–(6)	Am. 1981 s. 40(6); 1973 s. 32(6).
s. 30	Leasing contracts.	s. 395	
s. 31(1)–(5)	Partnerships involving companies.	s. 116	
s. 31(6)–(8)		—	Rep. 1987 Sch. 16 Pt. VII.
s. 31(9)		s. 834(1), 116(7)	
s. 32(5)	Amends TMA s. 98.	Sch. 29	
s. 32(6)		s. 116, 240(11), 395, 410, Sch. 18	
s. 33	—	—	Unnecessary.
s. 34	—	—	Unnecessary.
s. 35	Election for herd basis.	Sch. 5 §12	
s. 36(1)		s. 513(1)	
s. 36(2)		—	Spent.
s. 37	—	—	Rep. CGTA 8.
s. 38(6)	Territorial sea etc.	s. 830(5)	
s. 39	—	—	Unnecessary.
s. 40(1)	Overseas life assurance companies.	s. 811	
s. 40(2)–(6)		s. 448	
s. 40(7)		s. 431	
s. 43	Chevening House.	s. 147	Am. 1977 Sch. 8 §4.
s. 51	—	—	Rep. CGTA 8.
s. 52	Charities.	—	Spent.
s. 53(1)	Overseas pensions.	s. 614(3), 615(2)(*d*), (4), Sch. 29	
s. 53(2)		s. 615(2)(*e*)	Rep. in part 1975 Sch. 13 Pt. I.
s. 53(3)–(5)		s. 616	
s. 53(6)–(8)		—	Rep. 1975 Sch. 13 Pt. I.
s. 53(9)		s. 616	Rep. in part 1975 Sch. 13 Pt. I.
s. 54	The Stock Exchange.	Passim	

FA 1973	Subject Matter	Re-enacted in TA 1988	Remarks
Sch. 8	Share option and share incentive schemes.		
para. 1		s. 138(2)	Am. 1974 s. 20(2).
para. 2		s. 138(4)(*b*)	
para. 3		s. 138(4)(*a*)	
para. 4(1)		s. 138(3)(*a*), (5)	
para. 4(2)		—	Unnecessary.
para. 5		s. 139(7)	Rep. in part 1974 Sch. 14 Pt. II.
para. 6		s. 139(8)	
para. 7		s. 139(9)	Rep. in part 1974 Sch. 14 Pt. II; am. 1982 s. 41.
paras. 8–34		—	Rep. 1974 Sch. 14 Pt. II.
para. 35		s. 139(11), (12), 140	
para. 36		—	Unnecessary.
Sch. 9	Close companies.		
Pt. I	Amendments.		See destinations of enactments amended.
Pt. II	Transitionals.	—	Spent.
Sch. 10	Exempt funds.	s. 236	
Sch. 11	Amendments.		See destinations of enactments amended.
Sch. 12	Group relief.		
Pt. I		Sch. 18	Am. 1987 Sch. 15 §5.
Pt. II			
paras. 8, 9		—	Spent.
paras. 10, 11		Sch. 30	Partly spent.
Sch. 13, 14	Amendments.		See destinations of enactments amended.
Sch. 15	Territorial sea etc.		
paras. 1, 3		Sch. 29	
Sch. 16	Underwriters.		
para. 1		s. 457	
para. 2		s. 450(1)	
paras. 3–5		s. 450(3), (4), (6)	
paras. 6, 7		Sch. 29	
paras. 8–14	Amendments.		See destinations of enactments amended.
para. 15		—	Rep. CGTA 8.
para. 16		s. 450(2)	
para. 17(1)(*a*)		s. 451(1)(*a*), Sch. 29	
para. 17(1)(*b*)		s. 451(4)	
para. 17(1)(*c*)		s. 451(1)(*b*), Sch. 29	
para. 17(1)(*d*)		Sch. 29	
para. 17(1)(*e*)		s. 451(1)(*c*)	
para. 17(2)		s. 828	
Sch. 16A	Underwriters: assessment and collection of tax	Sch. 19A	Inserted 1988, s. 58(4)(*b*) and Sch. 5.
Sch. 21 paras. 6–9	Amendments.		See destinations of enactments amended.

FINANCE ACT 1974
(c. 30)

FA 1974	Subject Matter	Re-enacted in TA 1988	Remarks
s. 7–13	IT, CT & ACT rates.	—	Spent; rep. in part 1984 Sch. 23 Pt. V.

FA 1974	Subject Matter	Re-enacted in TA 1988	Remarks
s. 14	—	—	Spent; rep. in part 1975(2) Sch. 14 Pt. IV; 1980 Sch. 20 Pt. VI; 1977 Sch. 9 Pt. IV.
s. 15	—	—	Rep. 1984 Sch. 23 Pt. VI.
s. 16(1)	Annuities.	s. 628(1)	Rep. in part 1984 Sch. 23 Pt. VI.
s. 16(2)		s. 628(2)	
s. 16(2A)		s. 628(3)	Added 1982 s. 39(1).
s. 16(3), (4)		s. 628(4), (5)	Added 1980 s. 34(3).
s. 18	—	—	Rep. 1976 Sch. 15 Pt. III.
s. 19(1)(a)	Relief for payment of interest.	s. 353(1)	
s. 19(1)(b)		s. 353(3)(a)	
s. 19(1)(c)		—	Spent.
s. 19(1)(d)		s. 353(1)	
s. 19(2)		—	Unnecessary.
s. 19(3)–(7)		—	Spent.
s. 20(1)		—	Spent.
s. 20(2)		s. 138(4)(a)	
s. 21(1)	Amends Sch. E.	s. 19	
s. 21(2)		—	Rep. 1977 Sch. 9 Pt. VI.
s. 21(3)	Amends 1970 s. 188(2).	s. 188(3)	Partly spent.
s. 21(4)	Amends 1970 Sch. 8.	Sch. 11 §10	
s. 21(5)		—	Spent.
s. 21(6)	Amends 1970 Sch. 12.	s. 192(1)	
s. 21(7)	Amends 1970(F) s. 24(2).	s. 596(2)	
s. 21(8)		—	Unnecessary.
s. 21(9)		—	Spent.
s. 22(1)	Foreign pensions.	s. 65(2)	
s. 22(2)		—	Rep. 1986 Sch. 23 Pt. V.
s. 22(3)		s. 196	
s. 22(4), (5)		—	Spent.
s. 23(1)	Income from foreign trade etc.	s. 65(3)	
s. 23(2)(a)		s. 391(1)	
s. 23(2)(b)		Sch. 29	
s. 23(3)		—	Rep. 1984 Sch. 23 Pt. VII.
s. 23(4)		s. 391(2)	Am. 1984 s. 30.
s. 23(5)		—	Spent.
s. 23(6)(a)		Sch. 29	
s. 23(6)(b)		s. 65(3)	
s. 23(7)		—	Spent.
s. 25	—	—	Rep. 1975(2) Sch. 14 Pt. IV.
s. 26(1)	Life insurance companies.	s. 435(1)	
s. 26(2), (3)		s. 435(2), (3)	Am. CGTA 7; 1987(2) s. 75(2), (3).
s. 26(4)		s. 435(1)	
s. 26(5)		—	Unnecessary.
s. 27(1)(a)	Friendly societies.	s. 461(1)	
s. 27(1)(b)		s. 461(3)	
s. 27(2)		s. 461(2)	
s. 27(3)–(7)		s. 461(6)–(10)	Am. 1985 s. 41(10); 1987 Sch. 15 §6.
s. 27(8)		s. 466(1), (2), (5)	
s. 27(9)		—	Spent.
s. 28(1)(a)	Trade unions.	s. 467(4)(a)	
s. 28(1)(b)		s. 467(2)	
s. 28(2)		—	Spent.
s. 30(1)	Transactions in deposits without certificate or in debts.	s. 56(1), (2), (6)	CGTA 7.
s. 30(2)		s. 398, 56(5), (6)	
s. 30(3)		—	Spent.
s. 31–33	—	—	Rep. CGTA 8.
s. 34	—	—	Rep. 1978 Sch. 13 Pt. IV.
s. 35	—	—	Rep. 1980 Sch. 20 Pt. VIII.
s. 36	CT.	s. 8	
s. 37(1)	CT.	s. 342	
s. 37(2)		—	Rep. 1986 Sch. 23 Pt. V.

FA 1974

FA 1974	Subject Matter	Re-enacted in TA 1988	Remarks
Sch. 1	Relief for payment of interest.		
para. 1		s. 354(1), 359, 367(4)	
para. 2		s. 354(1)	
para. 3		s. 354(1), 367(1)	
para. 4(1)–(3)		s. 355(1)–(3)	
para. 4(4)		s. 367(1)	
para. 4A(1), (2)		s. 356(1), (2)	Para. 4A added 1977 s. 36(1).
para. 4A(3)		s. 356(3)(a)	
para. 4A(3A)		s. 356(3)(b)	Added 1984 s. 25.
para. 4A(3B)		s. 356(5)	Added 1984 s. 25.
para. 4A(4), (5)		s. 356(4)	
para. 4A(6)		s. 356(6)	
para. 4A(7)		—	Unnecessary.
para. 5(1)		s. 357(1)	Am. 1977 Sch. 8 §8(2); 1984 s. 22(1)(a), (b).
para. 5(1A)		s. 367(5)	Added 1984 s. 22(1)(c).
para. 5(2)(a)		s. 357(1)	
para. 5(2)(b), (c)		—	Spent.
para. 5(3)		s. 357(2)	Am. 1977 Sch. 8 §8(3).
para. 5(4), (5)		s. 357(3), (5)	
para. 5(6)		s. 357(6)	Added 1982 s. 25(2).
para. 6(1)		s. 354(5)	
para. 6(1A)		s. 357(4)	Added 1984 s. 22(2).
para. 6(2)		s. 354(6)	
para. 7		s. 355(4)	Am. 1977 Sch. 8 §9.
para. 8		s. 358	Subst. 1977 Sch. 8 §10.
para. 9(1)		s. 360(1)	Am. 1982 s. 49(2).
para. 9(2)		—	Spent.
para. 10(1)		s. 360(2)	Am. 1982 s. 49(3).
para. 10(1)(a)		s. 360(2)(a)	
para. 10(1)(b)		—	Rep. 1980 Sch. 20 Pt. IX.
para. 10(1)(c)		s. 360(2)(b)	Am. 1980 s. 28(1)(b).
para. 10(1)(d)		s. 360(2)(c)	Added 1980 s. 28(1)(c).
para. 10(2)		s. 360(3)	Added 1982 s. 49(3).
para. 10A(1)		s. 361(1)	Added 1981 s. 25(3).
para. 10A(2)		s. 363(5)	Added 1981 s. 25(3).
para. 10B		s. 361(2)(b)–(d)	Added 1981 s. 25(3).
para. 10C		s. 361(3)	Added 1983 s. 24(1).
para. 10D(1)		s. 361(4)	Added 1983 s. 24(1).
para. 10D(2)		s. 361(5)	Am. 1984 s. 24(2).
para. 10D(3)		s. 361(6)	Am. 1984 s. 24(3).
para. 10D(3A)		s. 361(7)	Added 1984 s. 24(4).
para. 10D(4)		s. 361(8)	
para. 11(1)		s. 362(1)	
para. 11(2)		—	Spent.
para. 12		s. 362(2)	Am. 1981 s. 25(2).
para. 13		s. 363(1)	
para. 14(1)		s. 363(2)	Am. 1981 s. 25(4); 1983 s. 24(2)(a); rep. in part 1984 Sch. 23 Pt. V.
para. 14(2)		s. 363(3)	
para. 15		s. 363(4)	Am. 1981 s. 25(4); 1983 s. 24(2)(b).
para. 16		s. 360(4)	
para. 17(1)		s. 364(1)	Am. 1975 Sch. 12 §19(2); 1986 s. 100(1).
para. 17(2)		—	Spent.
para. 18		s. 364(2)	
para. 19		—	Rep. 1975 Sch. 13 Pt. I.
para. 20		s. 364(3)	Subst. 1975 Sch. 12 §19(3).
para. 21		s. 364(4)	Am. 1975 Sch. 12 §19(4).
para. 22			Rep. 1975 Sch. 13 Pt. I.
para. 23		s. 367(2)–(4)	
para. 24		s. 365	Am. 1984 s. 22(3).
para. 25(1)		s. 366(1)	
para. 25(2)		—	Spent.

721 Finance Act 1975 **FA 1975**

FA 1974	Subject Matter	Re-enacted in TA 1988	Remarks
Sch. 1 (contd) para. 26–29	Amendments.	—	See destinations of enactments amended and notes on clauses.
Sch. 2 paras. 1, 2	Foreign emoluments.	—	Rep. 1977 Sch. 9 Pt. VI.
para. 3		s. 192(4)	Rep. & am. 1984 s. 30(9)–(12), Sch. 23 Pt. VII.
para. 4		s. 192(2)	
para. 5		s. 192(5)	
para. 6		s. 192(3)	
Sch. 12 paras. 7–12	Amendments.		See destinations of enactments amended.

FRIENDLY SOCIETIES ACT 1974
(c. 46)

FSA 1974	Subject Matter	Re-enacted in TA 1988	Remarks
s. 64	Limits on benefits.	s. 464, Sch. 15 §6(2)	Am. 1985 s. 41(1), (2); 1980 s. 57(2)(b); FSA 1984 s. 2; rep. in part FSA 1984 s. 2(5).
Sch. 9 para. 23	Amendments.	s. 466	

FINANCE ACT 1975
(c. 7)

FA 1975	Subject Matter	Re-enacted in TA 1988	Remarks
s. 5	IT rates.	—	Spent.
s. 6	Pension funds.	s. 476(7)	Am. 1987(2) s. 39(4).
s. 7	Life policies.	s. 268	Am. 1976 Sch. 4 §19(1); 1984 s. 72(5).
s. 8		s. 269, 832	Am. 1976 Sch. 4 §19(2); 1984 s. 72(5).
s. 9(1)–(4)		s. 270	Am. 1976 Sch. 4 §19(3); rep. in part 1976 Sch. 15 Pt. IV.
s. 9(5)		—	Unnecessary.
s. 10		—	Unnecessary.
s. 11		—	Rep. 1981 Sch. 19 Pt. VI.
s. 12	Borrowing in foreign currency.	s. 581(4)	Am. 1987 Sch. 15 §7.
s. 16	Trade unions.	—	Spent.
s. 17(1)	Sales at undervalue etc.	s. 773(3)	
s. 17(2)		s. 770(1)(a)	
s. 17(3)–(8)		s. 772	
s. 17(9)		Sch. 29	
Sch. 1	Life policies.	s. 272	
Sch. 2	Qualifying policies.		
para. 1		Sch. 15 §21	Am. 1987 Sch. 15 §7.
para. 1A		Sch. 15 §24	Added 1984 Sch. 15 Pt. I.
para. 2(1), (2)		Sch. 15 §22	
para. 3		Sch. 15 §19	
para. 4(1)		—	Unnecessary.
para. 4(2)		Sch. 15 §1(1)	
para. 4(3)		Sch. 15 §1(5)	
para. 4(4)		Sch. 15 §1(6)	

FA 1975	Subject Matter	Re-enacted in TA 1988	Remarks
Sch. 2 (contd)			
para. 4(5)–(8)	Amendments.		See destinations of enactments amended.
para. 5		Sch. 15 §17(4)	
para. 6		s. 274	
para. 7		Sch. 15 §8	Am. S.I. 1979/1576; 1976 Sch. 4 §19(4).
para. 8		—	Unnecessary.
para. 9(1)–(4)	Amendments.		See destinations of enactments amended.
para. 9(5)–(9)		s. 546	
paras. 10–14	Amendments.		See destinations of enactments amended.
para. 15		s. 539(4)	
para. 16(1)		s. 548(1), 271(1)	
para. 16(2)		s. 548(2)	
para. 16(3)		s. 548(3)(*a*), 271(2)(*a*)	
para. 16(4)		s. 548(4)	
para. 17		s. 547(6)	
para. 18		s. 550(5)	
para. 19		s. 549	Am. 1975(2) s. 40; 1978 Sch. 2 §18; rep. in part 1980 Sch. 20 Pt. V; 1984 Sch. 23 Pt. VI.
para. 20		s. 552(3)–(5)	
Sch. 12			
para. 16		s. 699	
para. 19		s. 364(1), (3), (4)	

OIL TAXATION ACT 1975
(c. 22)

OTA 1975	Subject Matter	Re-enacted in TA 1988	Remarks
s. 13(1)	Taxation relating to oil extraction activities etc.	s. 492(1)	
s. 13(2)		s. 492(2), (3)	Am. 1978 s. 30(7)(*d*); 1984 s. 79(5).
s. 13(2A)		s. 492(4)	Added 1982 s. 136(1).
s. 13(3)		s. 492(5), (6)	Am. 1984 s. 79(5).
s. 13(4)		s. 492(7)	
s. 13(5)		s. 492(8)	Am. 1984 s. 79(5).
s. 13(6)		—	Spent.
s. 14(1)–(4)	Valuation of oil.	s. 493(1)–(3)	Am. 1985 s. 53; 1987 Sch. 11 §6; rep. in part 1987 Sch. 16 Pt. X.
s. 14(4A)		s. 493(4)	Added 1985 s. 53(1); rep. in part 1987 Sch. 16 Pt. X.
s. 14(5)		s. 493(5)	Am. 1984 s. 79(5); 1985 s. 53(2).
s. 14(6)		s. 770(2)(*c*)	
s. 15(1)–(3)	Charges on income.	s. 494(1)–(3)	Am. 1984 s. 79(5).
s. 15(4)		—	Spent.
s. 15(5)		s. 494(4)	Added 1982 s. 136(2).
s. 16	ACT: restrictions on set-off.	s. 497	Am. 1987 s. 46; 1987(2) s. 76(2).
s. 17(1), (2)	Deduction of PTR.	s. 500(1)–(4)	Am. 1981 s. 120.
s. 17(3)		—	Rep. 1984 Sch. 23 Pt. V.
s. 17(4)		s. 502, 500(5)	
s. 18(1)	Interest on PRT.	s. 501	
s. 18(2)		s. 502	
s. 19(1)–(3)	Interpretation.	s. 502(1)–(3)	
s. 19(4)		s. 502(4)	Added 1986 s. 54(1).
s. 20(1)	Miscellany.	s. 771	

OTA 1975	Subject Matter	Re-enacted in TA 1988	Remarks
s. 20(2)		s. 772(8)	
s. 20(3)		—	Unnecessary.
Sch. 9	Extension of 1970 s. 485.	s. 771	Am. 1987 Sch. 11 §7.

FINANCE (NO. 2) ACT 1975
(c. 45)

F(No. 2)A 1975	Subject Matter	Re-enacted in TA 1988	Remarks
s. 25–29	IC, CT & ACT rates.	—	Spent.
s. 30	—	—	Rep. 1976 Sch. 15 Pt. III; 1981 Pt. VI.
s. 31	Amendments.		See destinations of enactments amended.
s. 32	—	—	Rep. 1976 Sch. 15 Pt. III.
s. 33	—	—	Spent.
s. 34(1)–(6)	Stock dividends.	s. 249(1)–(6), 687(3)(b), 701	
s. 34(7)		—	Unnecessary.
s. 34(8)		s. 251(1)	
s. 34(9)–(11)		s. 249(7)–(9)	
s. 35		—	Rep. 1976 Sch. 15 Pt. III.
s. 36(1)	Non-cash vouchers.	s. 141(1), (2)	Am. 1982 s. 44(2).
s. 36(2)		s. 141(3)	Subst. 1982 s. 44(3).
s. 36(2A)		s. 141(4)	Added 1981 s. 70(2).
s. 36(3)		s. 141(5)	
s. 36(3A)		s. 141(6)	Added 1982 s. 44(4).
s. 36(4)		s. 141(7), 144(5)	Added 1982 s. 44(5); am. CCCPA.
s. 36(5)(a)		—	Rep. 1982 Sch. 22 Pt. IV.
s. 36(5)(b)		s. 144(3)	Am. 1981 s. 70(5)(b).
s. 36(5)(c)		s. 144(4)(a)	
s. 36(5)(d)		s. 144(4)(b)	Am. 1981 s. 70(5)(b); rep. in part 1981 Sch. 19 Pt. VI.
s. 36(5A)		s. 144(1), (2)	Added 1982 s. 44(6).
s. 36(6)		—	Unnecessary.
s. 36A	Credit tokens.	s. 142	Added 1981 s. 71.
s. 36A(1)(a)		—	Rep. 1982 Sch. 22 Pt. IV.
s. 36A(1)(b)		s. 142(1)(a)	Am. 1982 s. 45(2).
s. 36A(1)(c)		s. 142(1)(b)	Rep. in part 1982 Sch. 22 Pt. IV.
s. 36A(2), (3)		s. 142(2), (3)	Am. 1982 s. 45(2).
s. 36A(4)		s. 142(4)	Subst. 1982 s. 45(3).
s. 36A(4A)		s. 142(5)	Added 1982 s. 45(3).
s. 36A(4B)		s. 142(4), 144(5)	Added 1982 s. 45(3).
s. 36A(5)		s. 144(3), (4)	
s. 36A(6), (7)		s. 144(1), (2)	
s. 37(1)–(4)	Cash vouchers.	s. 143(1)–(4)	
s. 37(5)		s. 143(5)	Am. 1976 s. 71(2).
s. 37(6)		s. 144(4), (5)	Rep. in part 1976 Sch. 15 Pt. III.
s. 37(7)		—	Unnecessary.
s. 38(1)–(6)	Agency workers.	s. 134(1)–(6)	
s. 38(7)		Sch. 29	
s. 38(8)		s. 134(7), Sch. 29	
s. 38(9), (10)		—	Unnecessary.
s. 39	—	—	Rep. 1975(2) Sch. 14 Pt. IV.
s. 40	Amendments.	s. 549	
s. 41	—	—	Rep. 1987 Sch. 16 Pt. VII.
s. 42(1)	Insurance companies.	s. 440(1)	
s. 42(2)		—	Spent.
s. 42(3)–(11)		s. 440(2)–(10)	Am. CGTA 7; 1987 Sch. 15 §8.
s. 42(12)		—	Spent.

F(No. 2)A 1975	Subject Matter	Re-enacted in TA 1988	Remarks
s. 43	Oil losses.	Sch. 30	
s. 44(1)–(3), (6)	Amendments.		See destinations of enactments amended; rep. in part 1987 Sch. 16 Pt. V.
s. 47(1)(a)	Repayment supplements.	s. 824(1)	(Not repealed); rep. in part 1987 Sch. 16 Pt. VII; am. 1987/1988.
s. 47(1)(b)		—	Rep. 1987 Sch. 16 Pt. VII.
s. 47(2)		—	Rep. 1987 Sch. 16 Pt. VII.
s. 47(3)(a)		s. 824(2)	
s. 47(3)(b)		—	Rep. 1987 Sch. 16 Pt. VII.
s. 47(4)(a), (c)		s. 824(3)	(Not repealed.)
s. 47(4)(b)		—	Rep. 1987 Sch. 16 Pt. VII.
s. 47(5)–(7)		s. 824(4)–(6)	
s. 47(8)		s. 824(7)	(Not repealed.)
s. 47(9)		s. 824(8)	
s. 47(10)		s. 828	
s. 47(11), (12)		s. 824(9), (10)	(Not repealed.)
s. 48(1), (2)	Repayment supplements.	s. 825(1), (2)	Am. 1987/1988.
s. 48(3)		—	Spent.
s. 48(4), (5)		s. 825(3), (4)	
s. 48(6)		s. 825(5), 828	
s. 48(7)–(9)		s. 825(6)–(8)	Rep. in part 1987 Sch. 16 Pt. V.
s. 50	Certificates of deposits.	s. 56	
s. 51		—	Rep. 1980 Sch. 20 Pt. IX.
s. 52(1)	Friendly societies.	s. 460(5)–(10)	
s. 52(2)		s. 466(1)	
s. 52(3)		—	Spent.
s. 52(4)		—	Unnecessary.
s. 53	Employers' associations.	s. 467(4)(b)	
s. 68		—	Spent.
s. 69(1)	Sub-contractors in the construction industry.	s. 559(1), (2)(a)	
s. 69(2)		s. 560(1)	
s. 69(3)		s. 560(2)(a)–(e)	Rep. in part HCPA 1985 Sch. 1.
s. 69(3A)		s. 560(2)(f)	Added 1980 Sch. 8 §1.
s. 69(3B), (3C)		s. 560(3), (4)	Added 1980 Sch. 8 §1.
s. 69(4), (5)		s. 559(3), (4)	Am. 1979(2) s. 15; 1987 s. 23.
s. 69(6)		s. 566(1)	
s. 69(7)		s. 559(5)	
s. 69(8)		Sch. 29	
s. 69(9)		s. 828	
s. 69(10)		s. 559(7)	
s. 70(1)–(6)		s. 561(1)–(3), (6)–(9)	Am. 1982 Sch. 8 §1, 2; 1987(2) s. 93; rep. in part 1980 Sch. 20 Pt. IX.
s. 70(7)		s. 566(2)	Am. 1982 Sch. 8 §§3, 4; 1987(2) s. 93.
s. 70(8)		s. 828	
s. 70(9)–(11)		s. 561(8)–(10)	
s. 70(12)		Sch. 29	
s. 70A		s. 561(3), (4)	Added 1982 Sch. 8 §5.
s. 71(1)		—	Unnecessary.
s. 71(2)		—	Rep. 1980 Sch. 20 Pt. IX.
s. 71(3)		s. 560(5)	Am. & rep. in part HCPA 1985 Sch. 1, 2 §28.
s. 71(4)		s. 561(4)	
s. 71(5)		s. 559(7)	Subst. 1982 Sch. 8 §6.
s. 71(6)		s. 559(6)	Rep. in part Insolvency Act 1985 c. 65 Sch. 10; Bankruptcy (Scotland) Act 1985 c. 66 Sch. 8.
s. 71(7)		—	Rep. 1980 Sch. 20 Pt. IX.
s. 71(8)		s. 567(1)	
s. 71(9), (10)		s. 567(5), (6)	
Sch. 8	Stock dividends.		
para. 1		s. 251(2)–(4)	Rep. in part CGTA 8.
para. 2(1)		s. 251(3)	

F(No. 2)A 1975	Subject Matter	Re-enacted in TA 1988	Remarks
Sch. 8 (contd)			
para. 2(2), (3)		s. 251(5), (6)	Am. CGTA 7.
para. 3(1)–(3)		Sch. 19 §12(1)–(3)	
para. 3(4)		s. 430(2)	
para. 4		Sch. 19 §12(4)	
para. 5		—	Rep. CGTA 8.
para. 6		s. 230	
para. 7(1)–(6)		s. 250	
para. 7(7)		—	Spent.
para. 8		Sch. 29	
Sch. 12	Sub-contractors in the construction industry.		
Pt. I			
para. 1		s. 562(2)	
para. 2(1)		s. 562(3)	Am. 1980 Sch. 8 §4(2); 1982 Sch. 8 §7; rep. in part 1980 Sch. 20 Pt. IX.
para. 2(2), (3)		s. 562(5), (6)	Added 1980 Sch. 8 §4(3); am. 1982 Sch. 8 §8.
para. 2(4)		s. 562(14)	Added 1980 Sch. 8 §4(3).
para. 2(5)		s. 562(7)	Added 1982 Sch. 8 §9.
para. 2A		s. 562(4)	Added 1982 Sch. 8 §10.
para. 3(1)		s. 562(8)	Am. 1982 Sch. 8 §11.
para. 3(1A)		s. 562(9)	Added 1982 Sch. 8 §12.
para. 3(2)		s. 562(10)	Am. 1982 Sch. 8 §13; 1980 Sch. 8 §7.
para. 3(3)		s. 562(11)	Subst. 1980 Sch. 8 §6(1).
para. 4		s. 562(12)	Partly spent.
para. 5		—	Rep. 1982 Sch. 22 Pt. XI.
para. 6		—	Rep. 1980 Sch. 20 Pt. IX.
para. 7		s. 562(13)	
Pt. II			
para. 1(1)		s. 563(2)	Rep. in part 1980 Sch. 20; am. 1982 Sch. 8 §14.
para. 1(2), (3)		s. 563(3), (4)	Added 1980 Sch. 8 §§4, 5.
para. 1(4)		s. 563(10)	Added 1980 Sch. 8 §5.
para. 2		s. 563(5)–(7)	Am. 1980 Sch. 8 §6, 7.
para. 3		s. 563(8)	Partly spent.
para. 4		s. 563(9)	
Pt. III			
para. 1, 2		s. 564(2)–(4)	Am. 1980 Sch. 8 §7.
para. 3		—	Rep. 1982 Sch. 22 Pt. XI.
para. 4		—	Rep. 1980 Sch. 20 Pt. IX.
para. 5		s. 564(5)	
Pt. IV			
para. 1		s. 565(2)	
para. 2(1), (2)		s. 565(3), (4)	Am. 1982 Sch. 8 §15; 1980 Sch. 8 §7.
para. 2(3)		s. 565(9)	
para. 3		s. 565(5)	Partly spent.
para. 4		—	Rep. 1982 Sch. 22 Pt. XI.
para. 5		—	Rep. 1980 Sch. 20 Pt. IX.
para. 6		s. 565(6), (7)	Am. & rep. in part CCCPA; CCCP(NI); 1987 Sch. 15 §8.
para. 7		s. 565(8)	
Sch. 13	Construction operations.		
Pt. I		s. 567(2), (4)	Am. TA 1984 Sch. 4 §62.
Pt. II		s. 567(3)	Am. 1980/1171.

FINANCE ACT 1976
(c. 40)

FA 1976	Subject Matter	Re-enacted in TA 1988	Remarks
s. 24–27	IC, CT & ACT rates.	—	Spent.

FA 1976 — Destination Table

FA 1976	Subject Matter	Re-enacted in TA 1988	Remarks
s. 28	—	—	Rep. 1977 Sch. 9 Pt. VI.
s. 29	—	—	Rep. 1977 Sch. 9 Pt. VI; 1979(2) Sch. 5 Pt. II; 1980 Sch. 20 Pt. VI; 1982 Sch. 22 Pt. XI.
s. 30(1)	—	—	Rep. 1977 Sch. 9 Pt. VI.
s. 30(2)		s. 620(2), 621(1), (3), 623(3)	
s. 30(3)	—	—	Spent.
s. 31	—	—	Rep. 1979(2) Sch. 5 Pt. VI.
s. 32	—	—	Rep. 1977 Sch. 9 Pt. IV; partly spent.
s. 33	Certification of life policies.	Sch. 15 §22(2)	Rep. in part 1987 Sch. 16 Pt. VII.
s. 34	—	—	Unnecessary.
s. 35	Loan annuity contracts by elderly.	s. 271(2)(b)	
s. 36(1)–(6)	Amendments.		See destinations of enactments amended.
s. 36(7), (8)		s. 280	Am. 1983 s. 15(2).
s. 36(9)		s. 279(7)	
s. 36(10)		s. 288(1), (3)	
s. 37	—	—	Rep. 1981 Sch. 19 Pt. VII.
s. 38(1)–(3)	Interest payments.	s. 787	
s. 38(4), (5)		—	Spent.
s. 44, 45	Amendments.		See destinations of enactments amended.
s. 46(1)	ACT.	s. 255	
s. 46(2)–(6)		—	Spent.
s. 47	Levies on insurance companies.	s. 76(7)	
s. 48	Amendments.		See destinations of enactments amended.
s. 49(1)–(3)	DTR: Ireland.	—	Spent & Order in Council saved by IA 1978.
s. 49(4)		s. 68(4)	
s. 49(5)		s. 353(1)(b)	
s. 49(6)		s. 68(5)	
s. 49(7), (8)		—	Spent.
s. 50(1)	DTR.	s. 808	
s. 50(2)		s. 788	
s. 50(3)		s. 799	
s. 60(1)–(3)	Payments in respect of expenses.	s. 153	
s. 60(4)	Commencement.	—	Unnecessary.
s. 61(1)–(3)	Benefits in kind: general charging provision.	s. 154	Am. 1977 Sch. 8 §5; 1981 s. 30(3), 72(3).
s. 61(4)	Commencement.	—	Unnecessary.
s. 62(1)	Exceptions from the general charge.	s. 155(1)	Subst. 1980 s. 48(1).
s. 62(2)		—	Rep. 1980 s. 48(1).
s. 62(3)		s. 155(2)	
s. 62(4)		s. 155(3)	Subst. 1977 Sch. 8 §6; am. HCPA Sch. 2 §31.
s. 62(5)		—	Rep. 1977 Sch. 8 §6.
s. 62(6), (7)		s. 155(4), (5)	
s. 62(8)		s. 155(6)	Subst. 1981 s. 72.
s. 62A(1)–(3)	Scholarships.	s. 165(1)–(3)	Added 1983 s. 20(1); am. 1984 s. 31(1).
s. 62A(4)		s. 165(6)	Added 1983 s. 20(1); am. 1984 s. 31(2).
s. 63(1)–(3)	Cash equivalents of benefits in kind.	s. 156(1)–(3)	
s. 63(3A)		s. 156(4)	Added 1980 s. 49(2).
s. 63(4)		s. 156(5)	Added 1980 s. 51(1)(a).
s. 63(5)(a)		s. 156(6)(a)	
s. 63(5)(b)		—	Rep. 1980 Sch. 20 Pt. IX.
s. 63(5)(c)		s. 156(6)(b)	Am. 1980 s. 49(3).
s. 63(6)		s. 156(7)	Am. 1980 s. 51(1)(b).
s. 63(7)			Rep. 1977 Sch. 9 Pt. VI.
s. 63(8)		s. 156(8)	

Finance Act 1976 — FA 1976

FA 1976	Subject Matter	Re-enacted in TA 1988	Remarks
s. 63A	Expenses connected with living accommodation.	s. 163	Added 1977 s. 34.
s. 64(1)	Cars available for private use.	s. 157(1)	
s. 64(2)		s. 157(2)	Am. 1985/1598.
s. 64(2A)		s. 157(3)	Added 1981 s. 68(3); am. 1982 s. 46(2).
s. 64(2B)		—	Spent.
s. 64(3)	Commencement.	—	Unnecessary.
s. 64(4)		s. 157(4)	Am. 1980 s. 51(2).
s. 64(5)		s. 157(5)	
s. 64A(1)	Car fuel.	s. 158(1)	Subst. 1981 s. 69(1); am. 1982 s. 46(4).
s. 64A(2)		s. 158(2)	Subst. 1981 s. 69(1); am. 1986/702.
s. 64A(3)		s. 158(3)	Subst. 1981 s. 69(1).
s. 64A(4)		s. 158(4)	Subst. 1981 s. 69(1); partly spent.
s. 64A(5), (6)		s. 158(5), (6)	Subst. 1981 s. 69(1).
s. 64A(7), (8)		—	Subst. 1981 s. 69(1); rep. 1982 Sch. 22 Pt. IV.
s. 65	Pooled cars.	s. 159	
s. 66(1)	Beneficial loan arrangements.	s. 160(1)	
s. 66(2)		s. 161(1)	Am. 1980 s. 50(1).
s. 66(3)		s. 160(2)	
s. 66(4), (5)		s. 161(4), (5)	
s. 66(6)		s. 160(3)	
s. 66(7)		s. 161(6)	
s. 66(8)–(11)		s. 160(4)–(7), 161(7)	Partly spent; am. 1982 s. 26(9)(*a*).
s. 66A	Tax paid by employer.	s. 164	Added 1983 s. 22.
s. 67(1)–(12)	Employee shareholdings.	s. 162	Am. CGTA 7.
s. 67(13)		Sch. 29	
s. 67(14)	Commencement.	—	Unnecessary.
s. 68		—	Rep. 1981 Sch. 19 Pt. VI.
s. 69	"Director's or higher paid employment".	s. 167	Subst. 1977 s. 35; am. 1978 s. 23(1); 1981 s. 71(2); 1982 s. 46(2).
s. 70	Notice of nil liability.	s. 166(1), (2)	
s. 71(1)		—	Spent.
s. 71(2)	Cash vouchers.	s. 143	
s. 72(1)–(12)	Interpretation of 1976 Pt. III Ch. II.	s. 168	Am. 1980 s. 51(3).
Sch. 4	Life policies etc.		
para. 1		—	Unnecessary.
para. 2		Sch. 15 §10	
para. 2A		Sch. 15 §11	Added 1978 Sch. 3 §4; am. 1982 s. 35(1); ICA 1982 Sch. 5 §17.
para. 3		s. 266(1), (2)	
para. 4(1)		s. 266(4)	
para. 4(2)		s. 266(8)	
para. 5		s. 266(5)	Am. 1980 s. 29(2)(*b*).
para. 5A		s. 266(9)	Added 1978 Sch. 3 §5; am. AFA 1981 Sch. 3 §1.
para. 6		—	Rep. 1978 Sch. 13 Pt. III.
para. 7		—	Spent.
para. 8–10		Sch. 14 §1	
para. 11		Sch. 14 §2, cl. 832	Am. 1979/1576; 1982 s. 35(2).
para. 12		Sch. 15 §7	
para. 13		Sch. 14 §3	Am. 1978 Sch. 3 §7(1); 1980 s. 28(2)(*c*); 1987 Sch. 15 §9.
para. 14		Sch. 14 §4	Am. 1978 Sch. 3 §8.
para. 14A		Sch. 14 §5	Partly spent; added 1978 Sch. 3 §9.
para. 15		Sch. 14 §6	
para. 16(1), (2)		Sch. 14 §7(1), (2)	Am. 1978 Sch. 3 §10.
para. 16(3)		Sch. 29	
para. 16(4)		Sch. 14 §7(3)	

FA 1976	Subject Matter	Re-enacted in TA 1988	Remarks
Sch. 4 (contd)			
para. 17		Sch. 29	
para. 18–21	Amendments.		See destinations of enactments amended.
Sch. 7	Taxation of directors etc. in respect of cars.	Sch. 6	
Pt. I		Pt. I	Subst. 1987/1897.
Pt. II para. 1		Pt. II §1	Am. 1985/1598.
Pt. II para. 2		§2	
para. 3		§3	Am. 1980 s. 48(2).
para. 4		§4	
para. 5		§5	Added 1980 s. 48(3).
Sch. 8	Taxation of benefit of loans.	Sch. 7	
para. 1(1)		§1(1), (2)	
para. 1(2)		§1(5)	
para. 2		§1(3)	
para. 3		§1(4)	
para. 4		§2	
para. 5–7		§3–5	
para. 8(1)		§6	Subst. 1982 s. 26(9)(*b*).
para. 8(2)		—	Spent.
para. 9–11		§7–9	
para. 12–14		§10–12	Added 1983(2) s. 4.
Sch. 9	Consequential amendments.		
para. 3, 4		—	Spent.
para. 8, 9		Sch. 29	
para. 12, 13	Amendments.		See destinations of enactments amended.
para. 14(1)		—	Spent.
para. 14(2)–(4)		s. 166(4)	
para. 15, 16		s. 418(3), (4)	

Finance Act 1977
(c. 36)

FA 1977	Subject Matter	Re-enacted in TA 1988	Remarks
s. 17–20	IT, CT & ACT rates.	—	Spent.
s. 21	M.I.R.	—	Rep. 1978 Sch. 13 Pt. III.
s. 22(1)	Personal reliefs.	s. 257(2)	Rep. in part 1978 Sch. 13 Pt. III; 1979(2) Sch. 5 Pt. II.
s. 22(2), (3)		—	Rep. 1980 Sch. 20 Pt. IX.
s. 23(1)	Child benefit etc.	—	Spent.
s. 23(2), (5)		—	Spent.
s. 23(3), (4)		—	Rep. 1979(2) Sch. 5 Pt. II.
s. 24	—	—	Rep. 1978 Sch. 13 Pt. III.
s. 25	—	—	Rep. 1982 Sch. 22 Pt. XI.
s. 26	—	—	Rep. 1980 Sch. 20 Pt. VI; 1978 Sch. 13 Pt. III.
s. 27	—	—	Rep. in part 1980 Sch. 20 Pt. VII; spent.
s. 28	—	—	Rep. 1978 Sch. 13 Pt. III.
s. 29	Savings bank interest.	s. 325	
s. 30	Job release scheme allowances.	s. 191	Am. Departments (No. 2) (Northern Ireland) Order 1982 (S.I. No. 846 (N.I. 11)) Art. 3.
s. 31(1)	Earnings from work done abroad.	—	Unnecessary.
s. 31(2)		s. 192(5)	Rep. in part & am. 1984 s. 30(14).
s. 31(3)(*a*)	Amends Sch. E.	s. 19	

FA 1977	Subject Matter	Re-enacted in TA 1988	Remarks
s. 31(3)(b)	Amends 1970 s. 184(3).	s. 132(4)	
s. 31(3)(c)	Amends 1980 Sch. 8 § 16.	Sch. 11 §10	
s. 31(3)(d)	—	—	Spent.
s. 31(4)	—	—	Spent.
s. 32(1)	Expenses in connection with work done abroad.	s. 193(2)	
s. 32(2)		s. 193(3)	Am. 1986 s. 34(2).
s. 32(3)–(5)		s. 193(4)–(6)	
s. 32(6)		s. 194(2)	Added. 1986 s. 34(3).
s. 32(6A)–(6D)		s. 194(3)–(6)	Added 1986 s. 34(4).
s. 32(7)		s. 194(1)	Am. 1986 s. 34(5).
s. 32(7A)–(7C)		s. 194(7)–(9)	Added 1986 s. 34(6).
s. 32(8)		s. 193(7), 194(10)	
s. 32(9)		—	Unnecessary.
s. 33(1)–(8)	Living accommodation for employees.	s. 145	
s. 33(9)		—	Unnecessary.
s. 33A	Additional charge in certain cases.	s. 146	Added 1983 s. 21(1).
s. 34(1)	Expenses connected with living accommodation.	s. 163	
s. 34(2)		—	Unnecessary.
s. 35(1)	Miscellaneous amendments.	s. 167	
s. 35(2), (3)		—	Unnecessary.
s. 35(4)		s. 418	
s. 36(1)	Interest relief.	s. 356	
s. 36(2)		—	Unnecessary.
s. 37(1), (2)	Leave travel for services.	s. 197	
s. 37(3)		—	Unnecessary.
s. 38	Maintenance funds.	s. 691	Am. 1980 s. 88(7); 1982 Sch. 10 §1; ITA Sch. 8; 1987 Sch. 15 §10.
s. 39	—	—	Spent.
s. 45(1)–(4)	Insurance companies.	s. 442	Am. CGTA 7.
s. 45(5)		—	Unnecessary.
s. 46(1)–(7)	Conversion of certain securities.	s. 473	Am. CGTA 7.
s. 46(8)		—	Unnecessary.
s. 47(1)	Police provident benefits.	s. 467(4)(c)	
s. 47(2)		—	Unnecessary.
s. 48	Annual payments.	s. 125	
Sch. 7	Foreign earnings.		
para. 1(1)		s. 193(1)	
para. 1(2)–(4)		Sch. 12 §3	
para. 1(5)		—	Spent.
para. 2, 3		—	Rep. 1984 Sch. 23 Pt. VII.
para. 4(1), (2)		Sch. 12 §2(1), (2)	
para. 4(3), (4)		—	Rep. 1984 Sch. 23 Pt. VII.
para. 4(5)		Sch. 12 §2(3)	
para. 5		—	Rep. 1984 Sch. 23 Pt. VII.
paras. 6–8		Sch. 12 §4–6	
para. 9		s. 132(3)	
para. 10		—	Rep. 1984 Sch. 23 Pt. VII.
para. 11		Sch. 12 §7	
Sch. 8	Amendments.		See destinations of enactments amended.

FINANCE ACT 1978
(c. 42)

FA 1978	Subject Matter	Re-enacted in TA 1988	Remarks
s. 13	IT rates.	—	Spent.
s. 14	—	—	Spent; rep. 1980 Sch. 20 Pt. V.

FA 1978 — Destination Table

FA 1978	Subject Matter	Re-enacted in TA 1988	Remarks
s. 15–17	CT rates.	—	Spent.
s. 18	Mortgage interest relief limit.	—	Rep. 1979(2) Sch. 5 Pt. II.
s. 19(1)	Personal reliefs.	—	Rep. 1979(2) Sch. 5 Pt. II.
s. 19(2)		s. 258(2)	
s. 19(3), (4)		—	Rep. 1979(2) Sch. 5 Pt. II.
s. 19(5)		s. 264, 265(3), 284	
s. 19(6)		s. 265	
s. 20	—	—	Rep. 1979(2) Sch. 5 Pt. II; 1980 Sch. 20 Pt. VI; 1982 Sch. 22 Pt. XI.
s. 21		—	Spent.
s. 22(1)–(4)	Tax repayments.	s. 281(1)–(4)	
s. 22(5)		—	Spent: see 1982 s. 149(2).
s. 22(6)–(9)		s. 281(5)–(8)	
s. 22(10)		—	Spent.
s. 23	Benefits in kind.	s. 167	
s. 24	—	—	Rep. 1981 Sch. 19 Pt. VI.
s. 25	—	—	Unnecessary.
s. 26(1)–(3)	Annuities.	s. 622	Am. 1987(2) Sch. 2 §4.
s. 26(4)		s. 657	
s. 26(5)		s. 431(4)(*a*)	
s. 27	—	—	Rep. 1984 s. 30(2).
s. 28(1)–(4)	Farming and market gardening.	s. 96(1)–(4)	
s. 28(5)		s. 96(5)	Rep. in part 1981 Sch. 19 Pt. VII.
s. 28(6)–(12)		s. 96(6)–(12)	Am. 1981 s. 35(4).
s. 29(1), (2)	Divers and diving supervisors.	s. 314	
s. 29(4)		—	Spent.
s. 30(1)–(6)	Loss relief.	s. 381(1)–(6)	
s. 30(7)(*a*)		s. 382, 734(1)	
s. 30(7)(*b*)		s. 391(1)	
s. 30(7)(*c*)		Sch. 29	Am. 1987 Sch. 15 §11(1).
s. 30(7)(*d*)		s. 492(2)	
s. 30(7)(*e*)		s. 279(7)	
s. 30(7)(*f*)		—	Spent.
s. 30(8)(*a*)		s. 383(4)	
s. 30(8)(*b*)		s. 383(7)(*b*)	
s. 30(8)(*c*)		s. 383(9)	
s. 30(9)		—	Spent.
s. 30(10)		s. 381(7)	
s. 30(11)		—	Spent.
s. 31	Commodity futures.	s. 399(2)–(4)	Am. 1987 Sch. 15 §11(2).
s. 32(1)	—	—	Unnecessary.
s. 32(2)(*a*)		s. 37(1)	
s. 32(2)(*b*), (*c*)		—	Spent.
s. 32(3)(*a*)		s. 87(1)(*a*)	
s. 32(3)(*b*), (*c*)		—	Spent.
s. 32(3)(*d*)		s. 87(2)	
s. 32(4)		—	Unnecessary.
s. 33, 34	—	—	Spent.
s. 35	Amendments.		See destinations of enactments amended.
s. 36	—	—	Unnecessary.
s. 41, 42	—	—	Spent.
s. 53(1)	Profit sharing schemes.	s. 186(1)	
s. 53(2)		s. 187(2)	
s. 53(3)		s. 186(2)	
s. 53(4)		Sch. 9 §30(4)	
s. 53(5)		Sch. 29	
s. 53(6)		s. 186(11), Sch. 29	
s. 53(7)		Sch. 9 §6	
s. 53(8)		Sch. 29	
s. 54(1)	Supplementary provisions.	Sch. 9 §2(2)	Am. 1986 s. 24(3)(*a*).
s. 54(1A)		Sch. 10 §1(2)	Added 1980 s. 46(2).
s. 54(2)		Sch. 10 §1(1), s. 187(2)	
s. 54(3)		Sch. 10 §1(3)	
s. 54(4), (5)		Sch. 10 §2	Am. 1980 s. 46(3); 1986 s. 24(3)(*b*).

FA 1978	Subject Matter	Re-enacted in TA 1988	Remarks
s. 54(6)		s. 187(2)	Am. 1980 s. 46(4); 1985 s. 45(2).
s. 54(7)		Sch. 10 §3	Am. 1980 s. 46(5); 1985 s. 45(3).
s. 55(1)–(5)	Disposal of scheme shares.	s. 186(4)–(8)	
s. 55(6)		s. 187(8)	
s. 55(7), (8)		s. 186(9), (10)	
s. 55(9)		s. 186(8)	
s. 56(1)	Capital receipts.	s. 186(3)	Am. 1982 s. 42(1).
s. 56(2)–(5)		Sch. 10 §4	
s. 56(6)		s. 186(12)	Added 1980 s. 46(6); subst. 1982 s. 42(2); am. 1985 s. 45(4).
s. 57	Company reconstructions etc.	Sch. 10 §5	Am. CGTA 7.
s. 58(1)	Excess shares etc.	Sch. 10 §6(1)(a), (2)	Am. 1982 s. 42(3); 1983 s. 25(1).
s. 58(2)		Sch. 10 §6(3)	Am. 1982 s. 42(3); 1983 s. 25(1).
s. 58(3)		Sch. 10 §6(1)(b), (2)	
s. 58(4)–(7)		Sch. 10 §6(4)–(7)	
s. 59(1)	PAYE deduction of tax.	Sch. 10 §7(1)	
s. 59(1A)		Sch. 10 §7(2)	Added 1980 s. 46(8).
s. 59(2)–(7)		Sch. 10 §7(3)–(8)	Am. 1987 Sch. 15 §11(3).
s. 60	Schedule D deductions.	s. 85	
s. 61(1)	Interpretation.	s. 187(2)	Am. CGTA 7; 1983 s. 25(1); 1982 s. 42(3).
s. 61(2)		s. 187(9)	
s. 61(3)		Sch. 29	
s. 61(4)		s. 187(5)	Added 1983 s. 25(2).
Sch. 2	Amendments		Partly spent; see destinations of enactments.
Sch. 3			
para. 1		—	Unnecessary.
para. 2		s. 266(4)	
para. 3–10, 13	Amendments.		See destinations of enactments amended.
para. 11, 12		s. 266(6), (7)	Am. 1981 s. 33.
Sch. 4		—	Rep. 1984 Sch. 23 Pt. VIII.
Sch. 5	Close companies.	Sch. 19 §1, 9	
Sch. 9	Profit sharing schemes.		
para. 1(1)		Sch. 9 §1(1), 2(1)	
para. 1(2)		Sch. 9 §1(3), (4)	
para. 1(3)		Sch. 9 §30(1)	
para. 1(4)		Sch. 9 §30(3)	Am. 1983 s. 25(1).
para. 1(5)		Sch. 9 §1(2)	
para. 2		Sch. 9 §36, 2(3), (4)	Am. 1983 s. 25(4), (5).
para. 3(1)		Sch. 9 §3(2)	Am. 1983 s. 25(6).
para. 3(2)		Sch. 9 §4, 30(2)	
para. 3(3)		Sch. 9 §3(3)	
para. 4		Sch. 9 §5	
para. 5		Sch. 9 §10	
para. 6		Sch. 9 §11	Am. 1980 s. 46(10).
para. 7		Sch. 9 §12	Am. 1986 s. 22(1), (4), (5), 24.
para. 8		Sch. 9 §14	Am. 1980 s. 46(11); 1986 s. 23(2), (3).
para. 9		Sch. 9 §35(1)	
para. 10		Sch. 9 §35(2)	
para. 11(1), (2), (3)(a)		Sch. 9 §8, cl. 832	
para. 11(3)(b)		s. 187(3)	
para. 11(3)(c)		—	Rep. 1987 Sch. 16 Pt. V.
para. 12		Sch. 9 §31	
para. 13		Sch. 9 §32	Am. 1980 s. 46(13).
paras. 14, 15		Sch. 9 §§33, 34	
para. 16		s. 187(2)	
para. 17		s. 187(7)	
para. 18		s. 187(10)	Added 1986 s. 24(1).

Capital Gains Tax Act 1979
(c. 14)

CGTA 1979	Subject Matter	Re-enacted in TA 1988	Remarks
s. 155(5)	Chargeable gains.	s. 833(1)	

Credit Unions Act 1979
(c. 34)

CUA 1979	Subject Matter	Re-enacted in TA 1988	Remarks
s. 25(1)	Credit unions.	s. 487	

Finance (No. 2) Act 1979
(c. 47)

F (No. 2) A 1979	Subject Matter	Re-enacted in TA 1988	Remarks
s. 5–7	IT & CT rates.	—	Spent.
s. 8	Personal reliefs.	—	Spent.
s. 9	War service pensions.	s. 318	
s. 10	—	—	Spent.
s. 11, 12	—	—	Unnecessary.
s. 13	—	—	Rep. 1981 Sch. 19 Pt. VII.
s. 15	—	—	Spent.
s. 16	DTR.	Sch. 30	
s. 17	—	—	Spent.
Schs. 1, 2	Amendments.		See destinations of enactments amended.

Finance Act 1980
(c. 48)

FA 1980	Subject Matter	Re-enacted in TA 1988	Remarks
s. 18–21	IT, CT & ACT rates.	—	Spent.
s. 22	Personal reliefs.	—	Spent.
s. 23	Widow's bereavement allowance.	s. 262	Am. 1983 s. 15(1).
s. 24(1)	Indexation.	—	Spent.
s. 24(2)(a)		s. 1(2)(b)	
s. 24(2)(b)		—	Spent.
s. 24(3)		s. 1(3)	Am. & rep. in part 1984 Sch. 7 §3(5), Sch. 23 Pt. VI.
s. 24(4)		s. 1(4)	
s. 24(5)		s. 257(9)	
s. 24(6)	Amendments.		See destinations of enactments amended.
s. 24(7)		s. 1(5), 257(10)	
s. 24(8)		s. 833(2), Sch. 29	
s. 24(9)		s. 1(6), 257(11)	
s. 25	—	—	Rep. 1982 Sch. 22 Pt. XI.

FA 1980	Subject Matter	Re-enacted in TA 1988	Remarks
s. 26	Amendments.		See destinations of enactments amended.
s. 27	Mortgage interest relief limit.	—	Spent.
s. 28, 29	Amendments.		See destinations of enactments amended.
s. 30	Life policies.	Sch. 15 §14	Am. 1984 s. 74.
s. 31	Amendments.		See destinations of enactments amended.
s. 32(1)	Adds s. 227A to ICTA 1970.	s. 625	
s. 32(2)–(4)		—	Spent.
s. 33, 34	Amendments.		See destinations of enactments amended.
s. 35	Pilots' benefit fund.	s. 607	Am. Pilotage Act 1983 (c. 21) Sch. 3 §10; Pilotage Act 1987 (c. 21) Sch. 2 §4.
s. 36(1), (2)	Old approved funds.	s. 608(1), (2)	Rep. in part 1987 Sch. 16 Pt. VII.
s. 36(3)		Sch. 29	
s. 36(4)		s. 608(3)	
s. 36(5)		s. 431(5)	
s. 36(6)		s. 608(4)	
s. 37(1)–(4)	Relief for certain losses.	s. 574	Rep. in part 1981 Sch. 19 Pt. VIII.
s. 37(5)		s. 576(4)	
s. 37(6)–(8)		s. 575	
s. 37(9)–(11)		s. 576(1)–(3)	
s. 37(12)		s. 576(5)	Am. 1981 s. 36(7); 1987(2) s. 71.
s. 37(13)			Spent.
s. 38(1)	Incidental cost of obtaining loan finance.	s. 77(1)	Am. 1984 s. 43(1)(*a*).
s. 38(2)		s. 77(2)(*a*)	Am. 1984 s. 43(1)(*b*).
s. 38(3)		s. 77(3)	Am. 1984 s. 43(1)(*c*).
s. 38(3A), (3B)		s. 77(4), (5)	Added 1984 s. 43(2).
s. 38(4), (5)		s. 77(6), (7)	
s. 38(6)		—	Unnecessary.
s. 39(1), (2), (4)	Relief for pre-trading expenditure.	s. 401	Am. 1982 s. 50.
s. 39(3)		s. 114(1)(*b*)	
s. 40		—	Rep. 1981 Sch. 19 Pt. VII.
s. 41	Redundancy payments.	s. 90	
s. 42	Grants under Industrial Development Act 1982 etc.	s. 93	Am. IDA 1982 Sch. 2 Pt. II §16; 1984 s. 55.
s. 43	—	—	Unnecessary.
s. 44, 45	Amendments.		See destinations of enactments amended.
s. 46(1)	Profit sharing schemes.	—	Unnecessary.
s. 46(2)		Sch. 10 §1(2)	
s. 46(3)		Sch. 10 §2	
s. 46(4)		s. 187(2)	
s. 46(5)		Sch. 10 §3(1)	
s. 46(6)		s. 187(12)	Subst. 1982 s. 42(2).
s. 46(7)		—	Spent.
s. 46(8)		Sch. 10 §7	
s. 46(9)		—	Spent.
s. 46(10)		Sch. 9 §11	
s. 46(11)		Sch. 9 §14	
s. 46(12)		—	Rep. 1987 Sch. 16 Pt. V.
s. 46(13)		Sch. 9 §32	
s. 46(14)		—	Spent.
s. 47(1)	Savings-related share option schemes.	s. 185(1)–(3)	See Finance Act 1980 (Savings-related Share Option Schemes) Commencement Order 1980 S.I. 1980/1546; am. 1981 s. 90(3)(*a*); 1984 s. 39(1).

FA 1980	Subject Matter	Re-enacted in TA 1988	Remarks
s. 47(2)		s. 185(4)	
s. 47(2A)		Sch. 29	Added 1987 Sch. 4 §4; am. 1987(2) s. 59(1).
s. 47(3)		—	Spent.
s. 48(1)	Cars available for private use.	s. 155(1)	
s. 48(2)		Sch. 6 §3	
s. 48(3)		Sch. 6 §5	
s. 48(4)		—	Unnecessary.
s. 49(1)	Cash equivalents.	—	Unnecessary.
s. 49(2)		s. 156(4)	
s. 49(3)		s. 156(6)	
s. 49(4)		s. 156(9)	
s. 50(1)	Beneficial loans.	s. 161(1)	
s. 50(2), (3)		s. 161(2), (3)	
s. 50(4)		—	Unnecessary.
s. 51(1)	Benefits in kind.	s. 156(5), (7)	
s. 51(2)		s. 157(4)	
s. 51(3)		s. 168(5)	
s. 51(4)		s. 418	
s. 51(5)		Sch. 29	
s. 52	Maintenance funds.	s. 694	Am. 1982 Sch. 10 §2; ITA Sch. 8 §17.
s. 53	Maintenance funds.	s. 27	Am. 1982 Sch. 10 §3; ITA Sch. 8 §18; 1987 Sch. 15 §13(1).
s. 54	Charitable gifts by traders.	s. 577(9)	
s. 55(1)	Charitable dispositions.	s. 660	Subst. 1987 Sch. 15 §2(16).
s. 55(2)		s. 671(2)	
s. 55(3)		s. 339(8)	
s. 55(4)		—	Spent.
s. 56, 57(1), (3), (4)	Amendments.		See destinations of enactments amended.
s. 59	Trustee Savings Banks.	—	Spent.
s. 60	Authorised unit trusts.	s. 468(4)	Rep. in part 1987 Sch. 16 Pt. VI.
s. 61(1)	Amendment.	s. 5(4)	
s. 63	INMARSAT.	s. 515, Sch. 29	
s. 70(1), (2)	Loss relief.	s. 384(6), (7)	
s. 109(11)	Oil.	Sch. 30	
s. 118(1)	National Heritage Memorial Fund.	s. 507(1)	
s. 118(2)		Sch. 29	
s. 119(1)–(3)	British Airways etc.	s. 513	Partly spent.
s. 119(4)		—	Rep. 1981 Sch. 19 Pt. VI.
s. 121	Penalties.	Sch. 29	
Sch. 8, 9	Amendments.		See destinations of enactments amended.
Sch. 10	Savings related share option schemes.	Sch. 9	
para. 1(1), (1A)		Sch. 9 §1(1), (3), 2	Am. 1984 s. 39(2), (3); 1987 Sch. 15 §13(2).
para. 1(2)		Sch. 9 §1(2)	
para. 1(3)		Sch. 9 §1(3), (4)	
para. 2		—	Rep. 1986 Sch. 23 Pt. V.
para. 3(1)		Sch. 9 §3(1)	
para. 3(2)		Sch. 9 §4	
para. 4		Sch. 9 §5	
para. 5(*a*)		Sch. 9 §9(1)	
para. 5(*b*)		Sch. 9 §16(1), cl. 187(2)	
para. 6, 7		Sch. 9 §17, 18	
para. 8		Sch. 9 §19	Am. 1986 s. 25(3).
para. 9		Sch. 9 §20	
para. 10		Sch. 9 §21	Am. 1986 s. 25(4).
para. 10A		Sch. 9 §15(1)–(4)	Added 1987 Sch. 4 §1; am. 1987(2) s. 59.
para. 11		Sch. 9 §22	
para. 12		Sch. 9 §23	Am. 1986 s. 25(5).
para. 13		Sch. 9 §24	Am. 1984 s. 39(5).

FA 1980	Subject Matter	Re-enacted in TA 1988	Remarks
Sch. 10 (contd)			
para. 14		Sch. 9 §25	
para. 15		Sch. 9 §10	
para. 16		Sch. 9 §11	
para. 17		Sch. 9 §12	Am. 1986 s. 22(2).
para. 18		Sch. 9 §13(1)	Am. 1982 s. 41; 1986 s. 23(4).
para. 19		Sch. 9 §14	Am. 1986 s. 23.
para. 20		Sch. 9 §26(1), (2)	Am. 1984 s. 39(6).
para. 21		Sch. 9 §26(3)	Am. 1986 s. 25(6).
para. 22		—	Rep. 1986 Sch. 23 Pt. V.
para. 23		Sch. 9 §8	
para. 24		Sch. 9 §16(2), (3)	
para. 25		Sch. 9 §6	
para. 26(1)		s. 187(2)	Am. 1982 s. 40(8).
para. 26(2)		s. 187(3)	
para. 26(3)		—	Rep. 1987 Sch. 16 Pt. V.
para. 26(4)		s. 187(6)	
para. 26(5)		s. 187(7)	Am. 1986 s. 23(5).
Sch. 11	Trustee savings banks.		
para. 1(1)		s. 130	
para. 1(2)		—	Unnecessary.
para. 2(1)		Sch. 30	
para. 2(2)		—	Spent.
para. 2(3)–(6)		s. 484	Am. TSB 1985 Sch. 2 §6(3); partly spent.
para. 3, 4		—	Spent.
para. 5		s. 484	
para. 6(1)		Sch. 30	
para. 6(2)–(4)		s. 485	
para. 7, 8		—	Spent.
Sch. 18	Demergers.		
para. 1–8		s. 213	
para. 13		s. 214(2)–(6)	
para. 14		s. 214(1)	
para. 17		s. 215(1)–(4)	
para. 18		s. 215(5)–(8)	
para. 19		s. 216(1)	
para. 20		s. 216(2)–(4)	
para. 21		s. 217(1)	
para. 22		s. 217(2)–(4)	
para. 23		s. 218(1), 213(10), 214	Not wholly repealed.

FINANCE ACT 1981
(c. 35)

FA 1981	Subject Matter	Re-enacted in TA 1988	Remarks
s. 19–22	IT, CT & ACT rates.	—	Spent.
s. 23(1)	Personal reliefs.	—	Spent.
s. 23(2)		s. 265(1)	
s. 23(3)		s. 265(2)	
s. 23(4)		—	Spent.
s. 24		—	Rep. 1982 Sch. 22 Pt. IV.
s. 25	Amendments.		See destinations of enactments amended.
s. 26		—	Spent.
s. 27		—	Rep. 1987 Sch. 16 Pt. V.
s. 28	Notification of taxable amounts.	s. 152	Am. 1987 Sch. 3 §6.

FA 1981 *Destination Table* 736

FA 1981	Subject Matter	Re-enacted in TA 1988	Remarks
s. 29	PAYE repayments.	s. 204	Am. 1987 Sch. 3 §7.
s. 30(1), (2)	Sick pay.	s. 149(1), (2)	
s. 30(3)		s. 154(2)	
s. 30(4)		s. 149(3)	
s. 30(5)		—	Unnecessary.
s. 31(1)	Payments for loss of employment etc.	s. 188(4)	
s. 31(2), (4), (7)		Sch. 11 Pt. II	
s. 31(3)		Sch. 11 §4	
s. 31(5), (6), (8)		—	Spent.
s. 32	Occupational pension schemes.	s. 591	
s. 33	Police provident benefits.	s. 266(7)	
s. 34	Savings certificates.	s. 46, 832	
s. 35	Stock relief.	s. 96(7)(c)	
s. 36(1)–(5)	Relief for losses.	s. 573(1)–(5)	
s. 36(6)		s. 573(6), 575, 576	
s. 37	Amendments.		See destinations of enactments amended.
s. 38(1), (2)	Interest charged to capital.	s. 338	
s. 39	Damages for personal injuries.	s. 329(3)	
s. 40	Amendments.		See destinations of enactments amended.
s. 41	Insurance companies.	s. 439(1)–(5)	Am. ICA 1982 Sch. 5 §25.
s. 42(1)–(7)	Amendments.		See destinations of enactments amended.
s. 42(8)		s. 677(11)	
s. 43, 44	Amendments.		See destinations of enactments amended.
s. 45(1)–(6)	Transfer of assets abroad.	s. 740	
s. 45(7)		s. 741, 742	
s. 45(8)		s. 745, Sch. 29	
s. 45(9)		s. 740	
s. 46(1), (2)	Transfer of assets abroad.	s. 744	
s. 46(3)–(7)	Amendments.		See destinations of enactments amended.
s. 46(8)		—	Rep. ITA Sch. 9.
s. 47	Assets of statutory bodies.	s. 410, 240(12)	
s. 48	Write-off of government investment.	s. 400	Am. 1987 Sch. 15 §14(1).
s. 49	National Heritage Memorial Fund.	s. 339(9)	
s. 50(1)	Northern Ireland.	s. 613(4)	
s. 50(2)		—	Spent.
s. 50(3), (4)		s. 511(4), (5)	
s. 51		—	Spent.
s. 52(1)–(6)	Relief for investment in new corporate trades: the Business Expansion Scheme.	—	Spent, but see 1983 Sch. 5 & 1986 Sch. 9 for application with amendments of ss. 52 to 67 and Sch. 11 & 12.
s. 52(7), (8)		s. 289(14), (15)	Am. 1983 Sch. 5 §2(9).
s. 52(8A)		Sch. 29	Added 1982 s. 51(1); rep. 1986 Sch. 9 §19.
s. 52(9)		—	Spent.
s. 53		—	Spent.
s. 54(1)		—	Spent.
s. 54(2)–(8)		s. 291(2)–(8)	Applied 1983 Sch. 5 §4(2).
s. 54(9)		—	Spent.
s. 55		—	Spent.
s. 56(1)		—	Spent.
s. 56(2)		s. 297(2)(a)–(c), (e)–(g)	Applied 1983 Sch. 5 §6(2).
s. 56(3)		s. 297(3)	Applied 1983 Sch. 5 §6(2).
s. 56(4)–(7)		—	Spent.
s. 56(8)–(10)		s. 298(1)–(3)	Applied 1983 Sch. 5 §5(9), 6(4).
s. 57(1)–(3)		—	Spent.
s. 57(4)		s. 299(5)	Am. 1983 Sch. 5 §7(3).
s. 58(1)		—	Spent.

FA 1981	Subject Matter	Re-enacted in TA 1988	Remarks
s. 58(2)–(4)		s. 300(2)–(4)	Am. 1983 Sch. 5 §8(2); 1986 Sch. 9 §10.
s. 58(5)		s. 301(1)	Am. 1983 Sch. 5 §8(2).
s. 58(6)–(9)		s. 301(3)–(6)	Applied 1983 Sch. 5 §8(2); 1986 Sch. 9 §10(3); 1987 Sch. 15 §14(2).
s. 59(1), (2)		—	Spent.
s. 59(3)–(8)		s. 303(2)–(7)	Am. 1983 Sch. 5 §10(2); rep. in part 1983 Sch. 10 Pt. II.
s. 60(1)		—	Spent.
s. 60(2)		s. 284(1)(a), (5), 287(7)(a), 283(2)	Am. 1983 Sch. 5 §12(2).
s. 60(3)		s. 280	Am. 1983 Sch. 5 §12(2).
s. 60(4)–(7)		s. 304(2), (3), (5), (6)	Am. 1983 Sch. 5 §12(2).
s. 61(1)–(5), (7)		—	Spent.
s. 61(6)		s. 306(8)	Applied 1983 Sch. 5 §13(8).
s. 62(1)		—	Spent.
s. 62(2)–(7)		s. 307(2)–(7), (9)	Am. 1983 Sch. 5 §14(2).
s. 63		s. 310(7)–(9)	Am. 1983 Sch. 5 §15(6).
s. 64		Sch. 29	Am. 1982 s. 52(1); partly spent.
s. 65(1)		—	Spent.
s. 65(2), (3)		s. 308(6)	Applied 1983 Sch. 5 §17(1).
s. 65(4)		—	Spent.
s. 66		—	Spent.
s. 67		s. 312	Applied 1983 Sch. 5 §20.
s. 68(1)	Cars available for private use.	—	Unnecessary.
s. 68(3)		s. 157(3)	
s. 68(6)		Sch. 6 Pt. II §5	
s. 68(7)		—	Unnecessary.
s. 68(2), (4), (5)		—	See 1982 s. 46(1).
s. 69(1)	Car fuel.	s. 158	Am. 1986/702.
s. 69(2)		—	Unnecessary.
s. 70(1)	Transport vouchers.	—	Unnecessary.
s. 70(2)		s. 141(4)	
s. 70(3), (4)		—	Spent.
s. 70(5)(a)		—	Rep. 1982 Sch. 22 Pt. IV.
s. 70(5)(b)		s. 144(4)	
s. 70(6)		—	Unnecessary.
s. 71(1)	Credit-tokens.	s. 142, 144	
s. 71(2)		Sch. 29	
s. 71(3)		—	Unnecessary.
s. 72(1)	Medical insurance etc.	s. 155(6)	
s. 72(2)		—	
s. 72(3)		Sch. 29	
s. 72(4)		—	Unnecessary.
s. 138		Sch. 29	Partly spent.
Sch. 9	Stock relief.	Sch. 30	
Sch. 10	Stock relief.	—	Spent.
Sch. 11	Relief for investment in new corporate trades.	s. 297(3)(d)	Applied 1983 Sch. 5 §6(2).
Sch. 12			
para. 1		—	Spent.
para. 2		s. 309(5)–(7)	Am. 1982 s. 52(2); 1983 Sch. 5 §18(5).
para. 3		—	Spent.
para. 4		s. 309(8)	Am. 1982 s. 52(3); 1983 Sch. 5 §18(5).
para. 4A, 5		—	Spent; am. 1982 s. 52(4).
para. 6, 7		s. 310(11)	

FA 1982   *Destination Table*   738

FINANCE ACT 1982
(c. 39)

FA 1982	Subject Matter	Re-enacted in TA 1988	Remarks
s. 20–23	IT, CT & ACT rates.	—	Spent.
s. 24	Personal reliefs.	—	Spent.
s. 25(1)	Mortgage interest relief limit.	—	Spent.
s. 25(2)		s. 357(6)	
s. 26(1)	M.I.R.A.S.	s. 369(1), 349(3)(d), 353(2), 476(10)	
s. 26(2)		s. 369(2)	
s. 26(3)		—	Unnecessary.
s. 26(4)–(6)		s. 369(3)–(5)	
s. 26(7)		s. 7(3), 11(4), 396(6)	
s. 26(8)		s. 74(*o*)	
s. 26(9)		s. 160(4), Sch. 7 §6	
s. 28(1)–(3)	Variation of loan agreements.	s. 377(1)–(3)	
s. 28(4)		s. 377(4), (5)	Am. 1984 s. 23(1), (2).
s. 28(4A)		s. 377(6)	Added 1984 s. 23(3).
s. 28(5)		s. 377(8), 832	Am. BSA 1986 Sch. 18 §15.
s. 28(6)		s. 377(9)	
s. 28(7)		s. 377(10), 379	
s. 29(1)	Supplementary regulations.	s. 378(1), (4)(*a*)	Am. 1984 s. 56(2); HCPA 1985 Sch. 2 §54(2).
s. 29(2), (3)		s. 378(2), (3)	
s. 29(4)		s. 378(4), (6)	
s. 29(5)		s. 828	
s. 30(1)	Amends 1970 s. 219.	s. 617	
s. 30(2), (3)	—	—	Spent.
s. 31	Income taxable under Schedule E.	s. 150	
s. 32		—	Rep. 1987 Sch. 16 Pt. V.
s. 33	Small maintenance payments.	s. 351	
s. 34	Qualifying policies.	Sch. 15 §20	
s. 35, 36	Amendments.		See destinations of enactments amended.
s. 37	Annuities.	s. 627	
s. 38		—	Spent.
s. 39	Annuities.	s. 628(3)	
s. 40(1)–(7)	Share options.	s. 137	Am. and rep. in part 1984 s. 39(7), (8).
s. 40(8)		s. 187(2)	
s. 41	Share options etc.: insider dealing.	s. 139(10), Sch. 9 §13	Am. 1986 s. 23(4).
s. 42(1)	Approved profit sharing schemes.	s. 186(3)	
s. 42(2)		s. 186(12)	
s. 42(3)–(5)		—	Spent.
s. 43(1)	Payments for loss of employment etc.	Sch. 11 §4, 5	
s. 43(2)		—	Unnecessary.
s. 44	Non-cash vouchers.	s. 141(1)–(3), (6), (7), 144(1), (2), (5)	
s. 45(1)	Credit tokens.	—	Unnecessary.
s. 45(2)		s. 142(1), (3)	
s. 45(3)		s. 142(4), (5)	
s. 45(4)		—	Unnecessary.
s. 46(1)	Cars and car fuel.	—	Spent.
s. 46(2)		s. 157(3), 167(2)	
s. 46(3)		—	Spent.
s. 46(4)		s. 158(1)	
s. 46(5)–(7)		—	Spent.
s. 47		—	Unnecesssary.
s. 48(1)–(4)	Contributions to local enterprise agencies.	s. 79(1)–(4)	

FA 1982	Subject Matter	Re-enacted in TA 1988	Remarks
s. 48(5)		s. 79(5)–(7)	
s. 48(6)–(9)		s. 79(8)–(11)	
s. 49–52	Amendments.		See destinations of enactments amended.
s. 53	Purchase by company of own shares: distributions.	s. 219	Am. 1986 s. 100.
s. 54	Dealer's receipts.	s. 95	
s. 55–57	Amendments.		See destinations of enactments amended.
s. 58(1)	Index-linked Treasury stock.	s. 439(6)	
s. 58(2)		—	Spent.
s. 58(3)		s. 439(6)	
s. 58(4)		s. 439(7)(a)	
s. 58(5)		s. 439(7)(b)	
s. 58(6)		s. 439(8)	
s. 58(7)		s. 431	
s. 59	Manufactured dividends.	s. 737	
s. 60(1)	Meaning of "distribution".	s. 212(1)	
s. 60(2)		s. 209(2)(d)	
s. 60(3), (4)		s. 212(2), (3)	
s. 60(5), (6)		—	Unnecessary.
s. 61	Maintenance funds.	s. 692	
s. 62(1), (2)		s. 693	
s. 62(3)		—	Unnecessary.
s. 63	Amends ICTA 1970 s. 451.	s. 677, Sch. 30	
s. 64	Amendments.		See destinations of enactments amended.
s. 65	D.T.R.	s. 798	Am. 1987(2) s. 67.
s. 66		s. 803	
s. 67		s. 794	
s. 136(1)	Oil activities.	s. 492(3)	
s. 136(2)		s. 494(4)	
s. 136(3)		Sch. 30	
s. 137(4)–(6)	Regional development grants.	s. 495(1), (2), (7)	Am. IDA 1982 Sch. 2 Pt. II §18.
s. 138		s. 495(3)–(7)	
s. 142(3), (4)		—	Rep. 1987 Sch. 16 Pt. VII.
Sch. 7	M.I.R.A.S.		
para. 1		s. 379	Partly unnecessary.
para. 2(1)		s. 370(1)	
para. 2(2)		s. 370(2)	Partly spent.
para. 2(3)		s. 370(3)	
para. 2(4)–(6)		—	Spent.
para. 2(7)		s. 370(4)	
para. 3(1)–(3)		s. 370(5)–(7)	
para. 3(4)–(6)		s. 371	
para. 4(1)(a), (b)		s. 372(1), 379	Am. BSA 1986 Sch. 18 §15.
para. 4(1)(c)		s. 372(1)	Added 1983 s. 17(1).
para. 4(2)–(4)		s. 372(2)–(4)	
para. 5(1)–(3)		s. 373(1)–(3)	Am. 1985 s. 37(2).
para. 5(3A)		s. 373(4)	Added 1983 s. 17(2).
para. 5(4)		s. 373(5)	Am. 1983 s. 17(2); 1985 s. 37(3).
para. 6(1), (2)		s. 373(6), (7)	
para. 7(1)–(3)		s. 374(1)–(3)	
para. 7(4)		s. 374(1)(d)(iii)	
para. 7(5)		s. 374(1)(d)(i)	
para. 8		s. 375(1)–(4), 74(o)	
para. 9(1)		s. 375(5)	
para. 9(2)		Sch. 29	
para. 10		s. 375(6), (7)	
para. 11		s. 375(8)	
para. 12		s. 375(9), (10)	
para. 13(1)		s. 376(1), 379	
para. 13(2), (3)		s. 376(2), (3)	
para. 14(1)		s. 376(4), 379	Am. ICA 1982 Sch. 5 §28(b); 1983 s. 17(3); TSB 1985 Sch. 2 §7(1); BSA 1986 Sch. 18 §15; BA 1987 Sch. 6 §13.

FA 1982   *Destination Table*   740

FA 1982	Subject Matter	Re-enacted in TA 1988	Remarks
Sch. 7 (contd) para. 14(2)		s. 376(5)	Am. 1983 s. 17(4); 1985 s. 37(4).
para. 15		s. 376(6)	
Sch. 8	Amendments.		See destinations of enactments amended.
Sch. 9	Distributions: purchase of own shares.		
para. 1, 2		s. 220	
para. 3(1)		s. 221(1)	
para. 3(2)–(7)		s. 221(4)–(8)	Am. CCCPA.
para. 4		s. 221(2), (3)	
para. 5(1), (2)		s. 222(1), (2)	
para. 5(3)–(10)		s. 222(5)–(12)	
para. 6(1), (2)		s. 222(3)	
para. 6(3)		s. 222(4)	
para. 6(4)		s. 222(9)	
para. 7		s. 223(1)	
para. 8		s. 223(2), (3)	
para. 9		s. 224	
para. 10(1)		s. 225(1)(*a*)	
para. 10(2)		s. 225(1)(*b*)	
para. 10(3)–(6)		s. 225(2)–(5)	
para. 11		s. 226(1), (2)	
para. 12		s. 226(3), (4)	
para. 13		Sch. 29	
para. 14		s. 227	
para. 15		s. 228	
para. 16		s. 229	
Sch. 10	Amendments.		See destinations of enactments amended.
Sch. 21 para. 3(1)	Amendments.	s. 706	

Finance Act 1983
(c. 28)

FA 1983	Subject Matter	Re-enacted in TA 1988	Remarks
s. 10–13	IT, CT & ACT rates.	—	Spent; rep. in part 1983(2) Sch. 2 Pt. I.
s. 14	Personal reliefs.	—	Spent.
s. 15(1)		s. 262	
s. 15(2)		s. 280	
s. 15(3)		—	Spent.
s. 16		—	Rep. 1983(2) Sch. 2 Pt. I.
s. 17(1)	M.I.R.A.S.	s. 372(1)	
s. 17(2)		s. 373(4), (5)	
s. 17(3)		s. 376(4)(*o*), (*p*)	
s. 17(4)		s. 828	
s. 17(5)		s. 354(1)(*c*)	
s. 17(6)		—	Spent.
s. 18(1)		s. 540(3)	
s. 18(2)		s. 542(3)	
s. 18(3)–(5)		—	Unnecessary.
s. 19	Repeals.	—	Spent.
s. 20(1)	Scholarships.	s. 165	
s. 20(2)		s. 165(4)	
s. 20(3)(*a*), (*b*)		s. 165(4)(*a*), (*b*)	
s. 20(3)(*c*)		s. 165(4)(*c*)	Subst. 1984 s. 31(3).
s. 20(3A)		s. 165(5)	Added 1984 s. 31(3).
s. 20(4)		—	Rep. 1984 Sch. 23 Pt. V.
s. 21	Additional charge for living accommodation.	s. 146	
s. 22	Director's tax paid by employer.	s. 164	
s. 23		—	Spent.

FA 1983	Subject Matter	Re-enacted in TA 1988	Remarks
s. 24, 25	Amendments.		See destinations of enactments amended.
s. 26	Business expansion scheme.	s. 289	Am. 1986 s. 40(2).
s. 27(*a*)	Public lending right.	Sch. 29	
s. 27(*b*)		s. 103(3), 537, 821(3)(*a*)	
s. 28(1), (2)	Employees seconded to charities.	s. 86(1), (2)	
s. 28(2A), (2B)		s. 86(1), (2)	Added 1984 s. 33.
s. 28(3)		—	Unnecessary.
s. 46(1)	Historic Buildings and Monuments Commission for England.	s. 507(1)	
s. 46(2)		Sch. 29	
s. 46(3)(*a*), (*b*)		s. 339(9), 577(9), 660(4)	
Sch. 4	Life policies etc.	s. 544	
Sch. 5	Business expansion scheme.		
para. 1		—	Unnecessary.
para. 2(1)		s. 289(1)(*a*)	
para. 2(2), (3)		s. 289(4), (5)	
para. 2(4)		s. 289(8)	
para. 2(4A), (4B)		s. 289(6), (7)	Added 1987 s. 42(1).
para. 2(5)		s. 289(9)	
para. 2(6)		s. 289(10)	
para. 2(7), (8)		s. 289(12), (13)	Am. 1986 Sch. 9 §2.
para. 2(9), (10)		s. 289(14), (15), Sch. 29	Applies 1981 s. 52(7); subst. 1987 s. 42(2).
para. 2A(1)		—	Unnecessary; added 1985 s. 44(2); am. 1986 Sch. 9 §3(*a*).
para. 2A(2)		s. 289(1)(*b*), (*c*)	Added 1985 s. 44(2); am. 1986 Sch. 9 §3(*b*).
para. 2A(3)		s. 289(8)(*b*)	Added 1985 s. 44(2); am. 1986 Sch. 9 §3(*c*).
para. 2A(4)		s. 289(9)	Added 1985 s. 44(2); am. 1986 Sch. 9 §3(*d*).
para. 2A(5)		s. 289(12)(*b*)	Added 1985 s. 44(2).
para. 2B		s. 289(1)(*d*), (2), (3), (8)(*c*), (9), 12(*b*), 297(9)	Added 1986 Sch. 9 §4.
para. 3		s. 290	Am. 1987 s. 42(3).
para. 4(1)		s. 291(1)	Am. 1983(2) Sch. 1 §2.
para. 4(2)		s. 291(2)–(8)	Applies 1981 s. 54(2)–(8).
para. 4(3), (4)		s. 291(9), (10)	
para. 4(5)		s. 291(1)	Added 1986 Sch. 9 §5.
para. 5(1)–(7)		s. 293(1)–(8)	Am. 1983(2) Sch. 1 §3; CCCPA; CCCP(NI); 1986 Sch. 9 §6; IA 1986 Sch. 14.
para. 5(9)		s. 298	Applies 1981 s. 56(8), (9).
para. 5(8), (10), (11)		s. 293(9)–(11)	Am. 1983(2) Sch. 1 §3; rep. 1986 Sch. 9 §6.
para. 5A		s. 294, 307(8), 828	Added 1986 Sch. 9 §7.
para. 5B		s. 295	Added 1986 Sch. 9 §7.
para. 5C		s. 296	Added 1986 Sch. 9 §7.
para. 6(1)		s. 297(1)	
para. 6(2)		s. 297(2)(*a*)–(*h*), 298(5)	Subst. 1986 Sch. 9 §8(2); am. 1984 s. 37(1); 1985 s. 44(3).
para. 6(2A)		s. 297(4)	Added 1984 s. 37(2).
para. 6(2AA)		s. 297(5)	Added 1985 s. 44(4).
para. 6(2B)		s. 297(6), 298(5)	Added 1984 s. 37(2); subst. 1986 Sch. 9 §8(3).
para. 6(2C)		s. 297(7)	Added 1986 Sch. 9 §8(3).
para. 6(3)		s. 297(8)	
para. 6(4)		ss. 297(3), 298(3)	Subst. 1986 Sch. 9 §8(4).
para. 6(5)–(10)		s. 298(1)–(5), 828	Added 1986 Sch. 9 §8(4).

FA 1983 — Destination Table — 742

FA 1983	Subject Matter	Re-enacted in TA 1988	Remarks
Sch. 5 (contd)			
para. 7(1)		s. 299(1)	
para. 7(1A)		s. 299(2)	Added 1986 Sch. 9 §9(2).
para. 7(2)		s. 299(3)	Am. 1983(2) Sch. 1 §4(2); 1986 Sch. 9 §9(3).
para. 7(2A)		s. 299(4)	Added 1983(2) Sch. 1 §4(3); am. 1986 Sch. 9 §9(4).
para. 7(3)		s. 299(5)	Applies 1981 s. 57(4); am. 1983(2) Sch. 1 §4(4).
para. 7(4)		s. 299(6)	Added 1983(2) Sch. 1 §4(5); subst. 1986 Sch. 9 §9(5).
para. 8(1)		s. 300(1)	
para. 8(2)		s. 300(2)–(4), 301	Subst. 1986 Sch. 9 §10(3); applies 1981 s. 58(2)–(9).
para. 8(3)		s. 300(5)	Am. 1983(2) Sch. 1 §5.
para. 8(4)		s. 301(2)	Added 1986 Sch. 9 §10(4).
para. 9		s. 302	Am. 1983(2) Sch. 1 §6.
para. 10(1)		s. 303(1)	Am. 1986 Sch. 9 §11(2).
para. 10(2)		s. 303(2)–(7)	Applies 1981 s. 59(3)–(8).
para. 10(3), (4)		s. 303(8), (9)	Am. 1987 Sch. 15 §15(1).
para. 10(5)		—	Am. 1983(2) Sch. 1 §7; spent.
para. 10(5A)		s. 303(10)	Added 1983(2) Sch. 1 §7; subst. 1986 Sch. 9 §11(3).
para. 10A		s. 292	Added 1986 Sch. 9 §12.
para. 11		s. 289(11)	
para. 12(1)		s. 304(1)	
para. 12(2), (3)		s. 280(2), 283(2), 284(1), (5), 287(7), 304(2)–(5)	Applies 1981 s. 60(2)–(7); am. 1987 s. 42(4).
para. 13		s. 306	Am. 1986 Sch. 9 §13.
para. 14(1), (1A)		s. 307(1)	Am. 1987 s. 42(5).
para. 14(2)		s. 307(2)–(7), (9)	Applies & amends 1981 s. 62(2)–(7); am. 1983(2) Sch. 1 §8; 1986 Sch. 9 §14.
para. 15(1), (2)		s. 310(1), (2)	
para. 15(3)–(5)		s. 310(4)–(6)	
para. 15(6)		s. 310(7)–(9)	Applies 1981 s. 63(7)–(9).
para. 15A		s. 310(3), (4)	Added 1986 Sch. 9 §15.
para. 16		Sch. 29	Am. 1986 Sch. 9 §16.
para. 16A(1)		s. 305(1)	Added 1986 Sch. 9 §17.
para. 16A(2)		Sch. 29	Added 1986 Sch. 9 §17.
para. 16A(3), (4)		s. 305(2), (3)	Added 1986 Sch. 9 §17.
para. 16A(5)		Sch. 29	Added 1986 Sch. 9 §17.
para. 17(1)–(1D)		s. 308(1)–(5)	Subst. 1986 Sch. 9 §18; am. 1987 Sch. 15 §15(2).
para. 17(2)		s. 309(1)	
para. 18(1)–(3)		s. 309(2)–(4)	
para. 18(4)		s. 310(5), (6)	
para. 18(5)		s. 309(5)–(8)	Applies 1981 Sch. 12 §§2, 4; am. 1982 s. 52(2).
para. 19		s. 311(1), (3)–(6)	
para. 19A		s. 311(2)	Added 1986 Sch. 9 §20.
para. 20		s. 312	Am. 1985 s. 44(6); CCCPA; 1986 Sch. 9 §21.
paras. 21–23		—	Spent.

Finance (No. 2) Act 1983
(c. 49)

F(No. 2)A 1983	Subject Matter	Re-enacted in TA 1988	Remarks
s. 1, 2	IT & CT rates.	—	Spent.
s. 3	Mortgage interest relief limit.	—	Spent.
s. 4	Loans.	Sch. 7 §§10, 11	
s. 5	—	—	Unnecessary.
Sch. 1	Amendments.		See destinations of enactments amended.

Oil Taxation Act 1983
(c. 56)

OTA 1983	Subject Matter	Re-enacted in TA 1988	Remarks
s. 11	Tariff receipts.	s. 496	

Finance Act 1984
(c. 43)

FA 1984	Subject Matter	Re-enacted in TA 1988	Remarks
s. 17, 18(1)–(4)	IT & CT rates.	—	Spent.
s. 18(5)		s. 434(7)	
s. 18(6)		—	Spent.
s. 19, 20	ACT & CT rates.	—	Spent.
s. 21	Personal reliefs.	—	Spent.
s. 22(1)	M.I.R.A.S.	s. 357(1), 367(5)	
s. 22(2)		s. 357(4)	
s. 22(3)		s. 365(3)	
s. 22(4), (5)		—	Spent.
s. 23	Variation of loan agreements.	s. 377(4)–(6), 379	
s. 24(1)–(4)	Relief for interest.	s. 361(4)–(7)	
s. 24(5)		—	Spent.
s. 25(1)	Job-related accommodation.	s. 356(3)(*b*), (5)	
s. 25(2)(*a*)		—	Spent.
s. 25(2)(*b*)		Sch. 29	
s. 26(1)–(4)	The composite rate.	s. 483(1)–(4)	
s. 26(5)		—	Spent.
s. 26(6), (7)		s. 483(5), 832	
s. 26(8)		Sch. 29	
s. 26(9)		s. 483(5)	
s. 27(1)	Interest paid on bank deposits etc.	s. 479(1)	
s. 27(2)		s. 349(3)(*d*)	
s. 27(3), (4)		—	Unnecessary.
s. 28(1)	M.P.s' allowances.	s. 200	
s. 28(2)(*a*)		s. 198(4)	
s. 28(2)(*b*)		Sch. 29	
s. 29	Grant to M.E.P.s.	s. 190(*b*), (*c*)	
s. 30(1)–(3)	Foreign emoluments.	—	Spent.
s. 30(4)		Sch. 29, Sch. 30	
s. 30(5)		—	Spent.
s. 30(6)		Sch. 29	
s. 30(7), (8)		—	Spent.
s. 30(9)–(12)		s. 192(4)	
s. 30(13)		s. 391	

FA 1984 — Destination Table

FA 1984	Subject Matter	Re-enacted in TA 1988	Remarks
s. 30(14)(a)		—	Spent.
s. 30(14)(b)		s. 192(5)	
s. 30(15)		—	Unnecessary.
s. 31–33	Amendments.		See destinations of enactments amended.
s. 34		—	Rep. 1985 Sch. 27 Pt. V.
s. 35(1)–(3)	Eurobonds.	s. 124(1)–(3)	
s. 35(4)		s. 338(4)(b)	
s. 35(5)–(8)		s. 124(4)–(7)	
s. 35(9)		Sch. 29	
s. 35(10)		—	Unnecessary.
s. 36(1)	Deep discount securities.	s. 57	
s. 36(2)		Sch. 4 §1(1)	
s. 36(3), (4)		Sch. 4 §1(2), (3)	
s. 36(5)		Sch. 4 §1(1)	
s. 37(1)	Business expansion scheme.	s. 297(2)(j)	
s. 37(2)		s. 297(4), 298(5)	Am. 1985 s. 44(5); 1986 Sch. 9 §3.
s. 37(3)		s. 298(6)(b)	
s. 38(1)–(3)	Share option schemes.	s. 185(1)–(3)	
s. 38(4)–(9)		s. 185(5)–(8)	Am. 1987 Sch. 4 §5.
s. 38(10)		Sch. 29	
s. 39–41	Amendments.		See destinations of enactments amended.
s. 42	Discounted bills of exchange.	s. 78	
s. 43	Loan finance.	s. 77	
s. 45	Pension funds.	s. 659	Am. 1987(2) Sch. 2 §5.
s. 46(1)	Group relief etc.	—	Spent.
s. 46(2)		s. 413(6)	
s. 46(3)–(5)		—	Spent.
s. 47(1), (2)		s. 409	
s. 47(3)		—	Spent.
s. 48, 49	—	—	Spent.
s. 50(1)	Furnished holiday lettings.	—	[Not repealed].
s. 50(2)–(9)		s. 504(2)–(9)	[Not repealed].
s. 50(10)(a)		—	Spent.
s. 50(10)(b)		—	[Not repealed].
s. 50(10)(c)		—	Spent.
s. 51	Woodlands.	s. 16	
s. 52(1)	ACT.	s. 239(3)	
s. 52(2), (3)		—	Spent.
s. 53	DTR: amendments.		See destinations of enactments amended.
s. 54	Regional development grants.	s. 92	
s. 55	Other grants.	s. 93	
s. 56, 57	Amendments.		See destinations of enactments amended.
s. 56(1)	Northern Ireland self-build societies etc.	s. 489(11), (12)	
s. 56(2)		s. 378(1)(b), (4)(a)	
s. 72(1)	Premium relief.	s. 266(3)(c)	
s. 72(2)–(4)		Sch. 14 §8(3)–(5)	
s. 72(5)		s. 268(7)(a), 269(5)(a)	
s. 72(6), (7)		Sch. 14 §8(6), (7)	
s. 72(8)		—	Spent.
s. 72(9)		Sch. 15 §16, s. 541(6), 546(5)	
s. 73(1)	Friendly societies.	s. 460(2)	
s. 73(2), (3)		s. 460(6)	
s. 73(4)		—	[Not repealed].
s. 73(5), (6)		s. 464(1)	
s. 74	Life policies.	Sch. 15 §14(1)–(7)	
s. 75, 76	Amendments.		See destinations of enactments amended.
s. 77		—	Spent.
s. 79(5), (10)	Oil taxation.	s. 492, 494, 502	
s. 82	Foreign controlled companies.	s. 747	

FA 1984	Subject Matter	Re-enacted in TA 1988	Remarks
s. 83	Limits on directions.	s. 748	
s. 84	Residence etc.	s. 749	
s. 85	Lower level of tax.	s. 750	
s. 86	Accounting periods etc.	s. 751	
s. 87	Apportionment of profits etc.	s. 752	
s. 88	Notices etc.	s. 753	
s. 89(1), (2)		s. 754(1), (2)	
s. 89(3)		Sch. 29, s. 754(3)	
s. 89(4)		s. 754(4)	
s. 89(5), (6)		Sch. 29	
s. 89(7)–(11)		s. 754(5)–(9)	
s. 90(1)–(7)	Information.	s. 755	
s. 90(8)		Sch. 29	
s. 91	Interpretation.	s. 756	
s. 92(1)–(6)	Offshore funds.	s. 757(1)–(6)	Partly spent.
s. 92(7)		s. 757(1)	Rep. in part 1987 Sch. 16 Pt. VI.
s. 92(8)		s. 757(7)	
s. 93	Equalisation arrangements.	s. 758	
s. 94	Material interests.	s. 759	Rep. in part 1987 Sch. 16 Pt. VI.
s. 95	Non-qualifying funds.	s. 760	
s. 96(1)–(7)	Charge to tax.	s. 761	Am. 1987 Sch. 15 §16(1).
s. 96(8)		—	Rep. ITA Sch. 8.
s. 97	Foreign residents etc.	s. 762	
s. 98	Deductions.	s. 763	
s. 99(1)	Insurance companies.	s. 441(8)	
s. 99(2)		s. 437(2)(a)	Rep. in part and superseded 1985 Sch. 25 §7, Sch. 27 Pt. X.
s. 99(3)		—	Rep. 1985 Sch. 27 Pt. X.
s. 99(4)		s. 431	
s. 100(1)	Trustees.	s. 764	
s. 100(2)		s. 687(3)	
s. 100(3)		s. 663(2)	
s. 126(1)–(3)(a)	International organisations.	s. 324	Only s. 126(3)(a) repealed; am. 1985 s. 96.
Sch. 7	The additional rate: amendments.		See destinations of enactments amended.
Sch. 8	Interest on bank deposits etc.		
para. 1(1)		—	Unnecessary.
para. 1(2)		s. 482(1)	
para. 2(1)		s. 481(1), (2)	Am. 1985 s. 38(2); 1987 Sch. 15 §16(2); BA 1987 Sch. 6 §16.
para. 2(2)		s. 482(10)	Subst. 1985 s. 38(2).
para. 2(3)		s. 828	
para. 3(1)–(3)		s. 481(3)–(5)	Am. 1985 s. 38(3), (4).
para. 3(4)–(9)		s. 482(2)–(7)	Am. 1985 s. 38(5), (6); Income Tax (Composite Rate) (Relevant Deposits) Order 1986 S.I. No. 771.
para. 3A		s. 481(6), 482(11), (12), 828	Added 1985 s. 38(7).
para. 4		s. 479(2)–(4)	
para. 5		s. 479(5)–(7)	
para. 6(1)		—	Spent.
para. 6(2), (3)		s. 482(8), (9)	
para. 6(4)		—	Spent.
para. 6(5)–(8)		s. 480	
para. 7		Sch. 29	
Sch. 9	Deep discount securities.		
para. 1(1)(a), (b)		Sch. 4 §4(1)	
para. 1(1)(c)		Sch. 29	
para. 1(2)–(6)		Sch. 4 §4(2)–(6)	
para. 1(7)		Sch. 4 §1(1)	Am. 1985 Sch. 11 §4.
para. 1(8)		Sch. 4 §13(1)	
para. 1(9)		Sch. 4 §4(7)	

FA 1984 — Destination Table — 746

FA 1984	Subject Matter	Re-enacted in TA 1988	Remarks
Sch. 9 (contd)			
para. 2		Sch. 4 §7(1), (2)	
para. 3(1)–(5)		Sch. 4 §5(1)–(5)	
para. 3(6), (7)		s. 77	
para. 3(8)		—	Spent.
para. 3(9), (10)		Sch. 4 §5(6), (7)	
para. 4		Sch. 4 §6	
para. 5–7		Sch. 4 §9–11	
para. 8(1), (2)(*a*)		Sch. 4 §7(3)	
para. 8(2)(*b*), (*c*)		Sch. 29	
para. 8(3)		Sch. 4 §7(4)	
para. 9		Sch. 29	
para. 10		Sch. 4 §8	
para. 11(1)		Sch. 4 §12	
para. 11(2)		Sch. 29	
para. 12		Sch. 4 §14	Subst. 1987 Sch. 15 §16(3).
para. 13		s. 242	
para. 14		—	Rep. ITA Sch. 9.
Sch. 10	Approved share option schemes.		
para. 1(1)		Sch. 9 §1(1), 2(1)	
para. 1(2)–(4)		Sch. 9 §1(2)–(4)	
para. 1(5)		s. 185(9)	
para. 2(1)		Sch. 9 §3(1)	
para. 2(2)		Sch. 9 §4	
para. 3		Sch. 9 §5	
para. 4(1)(*a*), (2)		Sch. 9 §27(1)	
para. 4(1)(*b*), (3)		Sch. 9 §8	
para. 4(4)		s. 187(3)(*c*)	Rep. in part 1987 Sch. 16 Pt. V.
para. 4A		Sch. 9 §15(1)–(4)	
para. 5		Sch. 9 §28	
para. 6		Sch. 9 §9(1)	
para. 7–11		Sch. 9 §10–14	Am. 1986 s. 22, 23.
para. 12		Sch. 9 §27(2), (3)	
para. 13		Sch. 9 §29	
para. 14		Sch. 9 §6	
para. 15		s. 187(2), (3), (6), (7), Sch. 9 §27(4)	
Sch. 11	Furnished holiday lettings.		
para. 1(1)		s. 503(1)	Not repealed; am. 1987(2) Sch. 2 §6.
para. 1(2)(*a*)–(*e*)		s. 503(1)	
para. 1(2)(*f*)–(*i*)		—	Not repealed.
para. 1(2)(*j*)		s. 503(1)	
para. 2		s. 503(2)–(4)	
para. 3		s. 503(5)	
paras. 4, 5		—	Not repealed.
para. 6		s. 503(6)	Not repealed.
para. 7		s. 503(7)	Not wholly repealed.
Sch. 15	Life policies.		
Pt. I		Sch. 15 §24	
Pt. II		Sch. 15 Pt. III	
Pt. III		s. 553	Am. 1985 s. 51.
Sch. 16	Controlled foreign companies.		
para. 1–11, 13		Sch. 24	Am. 1985 Sch. 14 §16.
para. 12		—	Spent.
Sch. 17	Exceptions from directions.	Sch. 25	Am. 1987(2) s. 65.
Sch. 18	Relief from tax.	Sch. 26	
Sch. 19	Offshore funds.	Sch. 27	Am. 1986 s. 50; 1987(2) s. 66.
Sch. 20	Offshore income gains.	Sch. 28	

FINANCE ACT 1985
(c. 54)

FA 1985	Subject Matter	Re-enacted in TA 1988	Remarks
s. 34, 35	IT & CT rates.	—	Spent.
s. 36	Personal reliefs.	—	Spent.
s. 37(1)	Relief for interest.	—	Spent.
s. 37(2)		s. 373(2)	
s. 37(3)		s. 373(5)	
s. 37(4)		s. 376(5)	
s. 38(1)	Interest on bank deposits.	—	Unnecessary.
s. 38(2)		s. 482(10)	
s. 38(3)		s. 481(4)(b)	
s. 38(4)		s. 481(5)(e), (f)	
s. 38(5)		s. 482(2)(b)	
s. 38(6)		s. 482(6)	
s. 38(7)		s. 481(6), 482(11), (12), 828	
s. 38(8), (9)		—	Spent.
s. 38(10)		Sch. 29	
s. 39	Group relief.	—	Unnecessary.
s. 40(1)	Building societies.	—	Unnecessary.
s. 40(2)		—	Spent.
s. 40(3)		s. 476(1), (2), 828	
s. 40(4)		s. 476(3)	
s. 40(5)		s. 476(5)	
s. 40(6)		s. 476(9)	
s. 40(7)		s. 476(11)	
s. 40(8), (9)		—	Spent.
s. 40(10)		Sch. 29	
s. 41(1)	Friendly societies.	s. 464, Sch. 15 §6	
s. 41(2)		—	Unnecessary.
s. 41(3)		—	Spent.
s. 41(4)		Sch. 29, Sch. 15 §3–6	
s. 41(5)		—	
s. 41(6)		s. 462	
s. 41(7)		s. 466	
s. 41(8)		s. 539(3)	
s. 41(9)		s. 547(7)	
s. 41(10)		s. 461(6)	
s. 42(1)	Class 4 contributions.	s. 617(5)	
s. 42(2)		Sch. 29	
s. 43	Business entertaining expenses.	s. 577(8)(b)	
s. 44(1)	Business expansion scheme.	—	Unnecessary.
s. 44(2)		s. 289(1), (8), (9), (12)(b)(i)	
s. 44(3)		s. 297(2)(h)	
s. 44(4)		s. 297(5)	
s. 44(5)		s. 298(5)	
s. 44(6)		s. 312(1)	
s. 44(7)		s. 289(1)(c), 298(6)(a)	
s. 45(1)	Profit sharing schemes.	—	Unnecessary.
s. 45(2)		s. 187(2)	
s. 45(3)		Sch. 10 §3(1)	
s. 45(4)		s. 186(12)	
s. 45(5)		—	Spent.
s. 46	—	—	Unnecessary.
s. 47	Partnerships.	s. 61(4), 62(1), (4), (5)	
s. 48	—	—	Unnecessary.
s. 49	—	—	Rep. 1986 Sch. 23 Pt. V.
s. 51	Offshore life assurance.	s. 553(5)	
s. 52	London Transport.	Sch. 30	
s. 53	Oil taxation.	s. 493(4), (5)	
s. 54	Companies connected with unitary states.	s. 812	
s. 60	Loss relief.	s. 393(4)	

FA 1985	Subject Matter	Re-enacted in TA 1988	Remarks
s. 64, 65	Amendments.		See destinations of enactments amended.
s. 72(1)(*b*)	Commodity futures.	s. 128, 399(5)	
s. 72(7)		s. 436(5)	
s. 73	Bondwashing.	s. 713(1)–(6)	
s. 74		s. 714	
s. 75(1)		s. 715(1)(*a*)–(*c*), (*e*)–(*j*)	
s. 75(2)		s. 715(2)	
s. 75(3), (4)		s. 715(4), (5)	
s. 75(5), (6)		s. 715(8)	
s. 76		—	Spent.
s. 77		—	Unnecessary.
Sch. 9	Group relief.		
para. 1		s. 413(2)	
para. 2		s. 405(1)–(3)	
para. 3		s. 405(4)–(6)	
para. 4		s. 403(10), (11)	
para. 5		s. 406(1)–(4)	
para. 6		s. 406(1), (5)–(8)	
para. 7(1), (2)		s. 409(5), (6)	
para. 7(3)		s. 409(8)	
para. 8(1), (2)		s. 409(7)	
para. 8(3)		s. 409(8)	
para. 9		s. 411(3)	
para. 10		s. 411(4), (5)	
para. 11		s. 411(6)	
para. 12		s. 411(7), (8)	
para. 13		s. 411(9)	
Sch. 10	Friendly societies.		
Pt. I		Sch. 15 §§3, 4	
Pt. II		s. 462(3), (4)	
Pt. III		s. 465	
Sch. 11	Deep discount securities.		
para. 1		Sch. 4 §1, 2	
para. 2(1)–(3)		Sch. 4 §3	
para. 2(4)		Sch. 4 §4(1)(*a*)	
para. 2(5)		Sch. 4 §7	
para. 2(6)		Sch. 29	
para. 2(7)		Sch. 4 §11(2)	
para. 2(8)		—	Rep. 1987 Sch. 16 Pt. VII.
para. 2(9)		Sch. 4 §1	
para. 3		Sch. 4 §13	
para. 4		Sch. 4 §1(1)(*f*)(ii)	
Sch. 12	Limited partners.		
para. 1		s. 117(2)	
para. 2(1)–(3)		s. 117(1)	
para. 2(4)		s. 117(2)	
para. 2(5)		s. 117(4)	
para. 3(1)–(3)		s. 118(1)	
para. 3(4)		s. 118(2)	
para. 4		s. 117(3)	
Sch. 13	Companies connection with unitary states.		
para. 1		s. 813	
para. 2		—	Unnecessary.
para. 3		s. 814	
para. 4		s. 815	
para. 5		s. 812(2), (5), (6)	
Sch. 14			
para. 16	Amendments.	Sch. 24 §10	
Sch. 18	Writing-down allowances.		
para. 1		s. 520(4)–(6)	
para. 2		s. 521(1)	
para. 3		s. 521(2)–(4)	
para. 4		s. 521(5)	
para. 5		s. 530(2), (3)	
para. 6		s. 530(4)	
para. 7		s. 530(5)	
para. 8		s. 533	

FA 1985	Subject Matter	Re-enacted in TA 1988	Remarks
Sch. 22		—	Spent.
Sch. 23	Bondwashing.		
para. 1		s. 710(1)–(4)	
para. 2		s. 710(5)–(10)	
para. 3		s. 711(1)–(5), (7)–(9)	
para. 4		s. 712	
para. 5		s. 710(11)	
para. 6		s. 720(1), (2)	
para. 7		s. 720(4), 711(6)	
para. 8(1), (2)		s. 720(5)	
para. 8(3)		s. 687(3)(*f*)	
para. 8(4)		s. 720(5)	Am. 1986 Sch. 17 §1(1).
para. 8(5), (6)		s. 328(2)–(4)	Added 1986 Sch. 17 §1(1).
para. 9		s. 720(6)–(8)	
para. 10(1)–(3)		s. 713(7), (8)	
para. 10(4), (5)		—	Spent.
para. 10(6)		s. 710(12)	Partly spent.
para. 10(7)		s. 713(9), 710(12)	
para. 11		s. 723	
para. 12		s. 721(1)–(4), 711(6)	Partly spent.
para. 13		s. 722, 711(6)	
para. 14		s. 710(13), 711(6)	
para. 15(1)–(4)		s. 716(1)–(4)	
para. 15(5)		s. 716(5)	Subst. 1986 Sch. 17 §2(2).
para. 15(6)		s. 720(1)	
para. 15(7)		Sch. 29	
para. 15(7A)		Sch. 29	Added 1986 Sch. 17 §3.
para. 15(8)		s. 716(6)	
para. 15A, 15B		s. 717, 718	Added 1986 Sch. 17 §3.
para. 15C		s. 719, Sch. 29	Added 1986 Sch. 17 §3.
para. 16		s. 724(1)	Partly spent.
para. 17		s. 724(2)	Partly spent.
para. 18(1), (2)		s. 724(3), (4)	
para. 18(3)		—	Spent.
para. 19(1), (2)		s. 724(3), (4)	
para. 19(3)		—	Spent.
para. 19(4), (5)		s. 724(3), (4)	
para. 19(6)		—	Spent.
para. 20(1)		s. 445(2)	
para. 20(2)–(6)		s. 724(5)–(8)	
para. 21		s. 710(14)	Rep. in part 1987 Sch. 16 Pt. VII.
para. 22		s. 720(3)	Rep. in part 1987 Sch. 16 Pt. VII.
para. 23		—	Spent.
para. 24		s. 725(1)–(3)	
para. 25		s. 725(4)–(6)	
para. 26		s. 725(7)–(9)	
para. 27		s. 721(5), (6)	Rep. in part 1987 Sch. 16 Pt. VII.
para. 28		—	Spent.
para. 29		s. 452(9)	Partly spent.
para. 30(1)		s. 715(1)(*d*)(i)	
para. 30(2)		s. 715(2)(*b*)	
para. 30(3)		—	Spent.
para. 30(4)		s. 715(1)(*d*)(ii)	
para. 30(5)		s. 715(2)(*b*)	
para. 30(6)		—	Spent.
para. 31		s. 715(3)	
para. 32(1), (2)		s. 715(1), (2)	
para. 32(3)		—	Spent.
para. 32A		s. 726(1)–(6), Sch. 29	Added 1986 Sch. 17 §4.
para. 32B		s. 726(7)	Added 1986 Sch. 17 §4.
para. 32C		s. 727	Added 1986 Sch. 17 §4.
para. 33–35		Sch. 29	
para. 36		—	Spent.
para. 37, 38		s. 807	

FA 1974	Subject Matter	Re-enacted in TA 1988	Remarks
Sch. 23 (contd)			
para. 39		s. 742(4)–(7)	
para. 40		—	Spent.
para. 41, 42		—	Rep. 1986 Sch. 23 Pt. VIII.
para. 43		s. 715(6), (7)	Am. 1986 Sch. 17 §5.
para. 44(1)–(5A)		s. 728	Am. 1986 Sch. 17 §6.
para. 44(6)		Sch. 29	
Sch. 25	Amendments.		
para. 7		s. 437(2)(*a*)	
para. 8		s. 445(2)(*a*)	
para. 9		Sch. 19 §6(2)	

FINANCE ACT 1986
(c. 41)

FA 1986	Subject Matter	Re-enacted in TA 1988	Remarks
s. 16	IT rates.	—	Spent.
s. 17(1)	ACT rate.	s. 14(3), 246(4)	
s. 17(2)–(4)		s. 246(1)–(3)	
s. 17(5)		s. 14(3)	
s. 17(6), (7)		—	Spent.
s. 18	CT rates.	—	Spent.
s. 19	PAYE.	—	Spent.
s. 20	—	—	Spent.
s. 21–23	Amendments.		See destinations of enactments amended.
s. 24(1)–(3)	Amendments.		See destinations of enactments amended.
s. 25(1)–(7)	Amendments.		See destinations of enactments amended.
s. 25(8), (9)		Sch. 9 §21(3)	
s. 26(1)	Shares acquired by directors etc.	s. 135(8)(*a*)	
s. 26(2)		s. 136(6)	
s. 26(3)		s. 138(10), (11)	
s. 26(4)		s. 138(9)	
s. 26(5)		s. 139(13)	
s. 26(6)		s. 138(10)	Partly spent.
s. 27(1)–(7)	Payroll deduction scheme.	s. 202(1)–(7)	
s. 27(8)		s. 202(11)	
s. 27(9)		—	Spent.
s. 28(1), (2)		s. 202(8)	
s. 28(3)		s. 202(9)	
s. 28(4)		s. 202(10)	
s. 28(5)		s. 202(9)	
s. 28(6)		Sch. 29	
s. 28(7)		s. 828	
s. 29(1)	Company gifts to charity.	s. 338(1), 339(2)	
s. 29(2)		s. 339(1)	
s. 29(3)		s. 339(3), 352	
s. 29(4), (5)		s. 339(4), (5)	
s. 29(6)		s. 339(9)	
s. 29(7)		—	Spent.
s. 30(1)	Charities.	s. 505(2)	
s. 30(2)		s. 505(6)	
s. 30(3)		s. 506	
s. 31(1), (2)	Charities.	s. 505(3), (4)	
s. 31(3)(*a*)		s. 506(1)	
s. 31(3)(*b*)		s. 339(8)	
s. 31(3)(*c*)		s. 505, 506	
s. 31(3)(*d*)		s. 505(5)	

FA 1986	Subject Matter	Re-enacted in TA 1988	Remarks
s. 31(4)–(6)		s. 506(4)–(6)	
s. 31(7)–(9)		s. 505(6)–(8)	
s. 31(10), (11)		—	Spent.
s. 32(1)	Payments to charities.	s. 683(3)	
s. 32(2)		s. 683(4), (5)	
s. 32(3)		s. 427(3)	
s. 34	Amendments.		See destinations of enactments amended.
s. 35	Expenses.	s. 80	
s. 36		s. 81	
s. 37		s. 195(1)–(12)	
s. 38(1)–(3)		—	Spent.
s. 38(4)		s. 195(13)	
s. 38(5)		—	Spent.
s. 39		—	Unnecessary.
s. 40	Business expansion scheme.	s. 289	
s. 41(1)–(3)	Enterprise allowance.	s. 127	
s. 41(4)		Sch. 29	
s. 41(5)		—	Spent.
s. 42	Company reconstructions.	s. 343(4)	
s. 43	Close companies.	s. 419(3), (4)	
s. 44	—	—	Unnecessary.
s. 45	Amendments.		See destinations of enactments amended.
s. 46		—	Unnecessary.
s. 47(1)	Building societies.	s. 476(1)	
s. 47(2)		s. 476(3)	
s. 47(3)		s. 476(11)	
s. 47(4)(a)		s. 686(5)	
s. 47(4)(b)		s. 476(7)	
s. 47(5), (6)		s. 477(1), (2)	
s. 47(7)		—	Spent.
s. 47(8)		s. 477(3)	
s. 47(9)		—	Spent.
s. 48(1)	Foreign dividends.	s. 48(4)	
s. 48(2)–(5)		s. 123(1)(b), (2), 832	
s. 49	D.T.R.	s. 797(4), (5)	
s. 50	Offshore funds.		See destinations of enactments amended.
s. 51	Foreign pensions etc.	s. 330	
s. 52	—	—	Spent.
s. 53	VAT penalties etc.	s. 827	
s. 54	Oil taxation.	s. 502(4)	
s. 56(7)(a)	Amendments.		See destinations of enactments amended.
s. 61	Stock lending.	s. 129, Sch. 29, s. 828	
s. 62, 63	—	—	Unnecessary.
Sch. 7 Pt. I	Private indirect charities.	s. 506(1)–(3)	
Pts. II–IV		Sch. 20	Am. BA 1987 Sch. 6 §24.
Sch. 8	Personal equity plans.	s. 333, Sch. 29, s. 828	
Sch. 9	Business expansion scheme.		See destinations of enactments amended.
Sch. 10	Amendments.		See destinations of enactments amended.
Sch. 11	Entertainers and sportsmen.		
para. 1		s. 555(1)	
para. 2(1)		s. 555(2)	
para. 2(2)		s. 555(4)	
para. 2(3)		s. 555(3)	
para. 2(4)		s. 555(4)	
para. 2(5)		s. 555(5)(a)	
para. 2(6)		s. 555(5)(b)	
para. 2(7)		s. 555(6)	
para. 3(1)		s. 555(7)	
para. 3(2)		Sch. 29	

FA 1986 — Destination Table

FA 1986	Subject Matter	Re-enacted in TA 1988	Remarks
Sch. 11 (contd)			
para. 4		s. 555(8)–(11)	
para. 5		s. 558(4)	
para. 6		s. 556(1), (4), (5)	
para. 7		s. 556(2)–(5)	
para. 8		s. 557	
para. 9		s. 558(1)–(3)	
para. 10–12		s. 558(5), (6), 828	
Sch. 12	Pension scheme surpluses.		
para. 1(1)		s. 601(1)	
para. 1(2)		s. 601(2)	
para. 1(3)		s. 601(1)	
para. 1(4)		s. 601(5)	
para. 1(5)		s. 601(3)(*a*)	
para. 1(6)		s. 601(4)	
para. 1(7)		s. 601(3)(*c*)	
para. 1(8)		s. 601(3)(*b*)	
para. 1(9)		s. 601(6)(*a*)	
para. 1(10)		s. 612(1)	
para. 1(11)		—	Unnecessary.
para. 1(12)		s. 601(3)(*d*)	
para. 1(13)		s. 601(3)(*e*)	
para. 2		s. 602, Sch. 29	
para. 3		s. 601(6), 602(1), 828	
para. 4–11		Sch. 22, s. 828	
Sch. 17	Amendments.		See destinations of enactments amended.
Sch. 18	Securities.		
para. 1(1)		s. 729(7)–(9)	
para. 1(2)		—	Unnecessary.
para. 1(3)		s. 732(3)	
para. 1(4)		s. 729(10)(*b*)	
para. 1(5)		s. 729(12)	
para. 2(1)		s. 731(9)	
para. 2(2)		—	Spent.
para. 3(1)		s. 732(2)	
para. 3(2)		s. 732(6)	
para. 3(3)		—	Spent.
para. 4		s. 738(1)	
para. 5		s. 737	
para. 6(1)		—	Unnecessary.
para. 6(2)		s. 737(3)	
para. 6(3)		s. 737(6)	
para. 6(4)		—	Spent.
para. 6(5), (6)		s. 738(2), (4)	
para. 9(1)(*a*)		s. 738(3)	
para. 9(2)		s. 738(4)	

Finance Act 1987
(c. 16)

FA 1987	Subject Matter	Re-enacted in TA 1988	Remarks
s. 20, 21, 22	IT & CT rates.	—	Spent.

Finance Act 1987 — FA 1987

FA 1987	Subject Matter	Re-enacted in TA 1988	Remarks
s. 23	Sub-contractors.	s. 559(3)	
s. 24	—	—	Spent.
s. 25	—	—	Spent.
s. 26(1), (2)	Personal reliefs.	s. 257(3)	
s. 26(3)		s. 257(4)	
s. 26(4)		s. 257(3)	
s. 26(5)(a)		s. 257(5)	
s. 26(5)(b)		s. 259(2)	
s. 26(5)(c)		s. 287(5)	
s. 26(6)		s. 280(2)(b)(i)	
s. 26(7)		s. 257(9)	
s. 26(8)		—	Spent.
s. 27(1)	Wife's earnings.	s. 257(7)(b)(iii)	
s. 27(2)		s. 287(2)(b)	
s. 27(3)		—	Spent.
s. 28	Blind persons.	s. 265	
s. 29(1)	Social security benefits.	s. 617(2)	
s. 29(2)–(4)		s. 151(1)–(4)	
s. 29(5)		s. 151(9)	
s. 29(6)		—	Unnecessary.
s. 29(7)–(9)		Sch. 30	
s. 30(1)	Friendly societies.	—	
s. 30(2)		s. 460(2)(c)(i)	
s. 30(3)		s. 460(3)	
s. 30(4)		s. 464(2)–(4)	
s. 30(5)		s. 464(5)(d)	
s. 30(6)		Sch. 15 §6(2)	
s. 30(7)		s. 464(7)	
s. 30(8)		s. 547(7)	
s. 31	Trade unions.	s. 467(1), (3)	
s. 32	Charities.	s. 202(7)	
s. 33(1), (2)	Employee share schemes.	s. 187, Sch. 9	
s. 33(3)		s. 360(4)(a)	
s. 33(4)		—	Unnecessary.
s. 34(1), (2)	Charities.	s. 86(3)	
s. 34(3)		—	Spent.
s. 35(1)–(7)	Training costs.	s. 588	
s. 35(8)		Sch. 29	
s. 36(1)	Corporation tax.	—	Spent.
s. 36(2)		s. 478(1)	
s. 36(3)(a)		Sch. 30	
s. 36(3)(b)		s. 478(4)–(7)	
s. 37(1)	Associates.	s. 417(3)(c)	
s. 37(2)		s. 360(4)(b)	
s. 37(3)		—	Spent.
s. 38(1)	Authorised unit trusts.	s. 468(1)–(4), (6)	
s. 38(2)		—	Spent.
s. 39	Other unit trusts.	s. 469, 828	
s. 40(1), (2)	Definitions.	s. 468(6), 832	Subsections (4), (5), (6) not repealed.
s. 41	Expenses of management.	s. 75(1)	
s. 42(1)	Business Expansion Scheme.	s. 289(6), (7)	
s. 42(2)		s. 289(14), (15)	
s. 42(3)		s. 290(2)	
s. 42(4)		s. 304(4)	
s. 42(5)		s. 307(1)	
s. 42(6)		—	Spent.
s. 43(1)		s. 297(4)	
s. 43(2)		s. 298(8)	
s. 44, 45	Oil: ACT.	s. 498, 499	Am. 1987(2) s. 76(4), (5).
s. 46(1)		s. 497(2)	
s. 46(2)		s. 497(3), (4)	
s. 46(3)		s. 497(6), (7)	
s. 70(1)		s. 788(2)	
s. 71		—	Unnecessary.
Sch. 3	Income support.		
para. 1(1)		s. 151(5)	
para. 1(2)		s. 151(2)	
para. 2–4		s. 151(6)–(8)	
para. 5		s. 833(5)(c)	
para. 6		s. 152(1)	
para. 7		s. 204(b)	

FA 1987   *Destination Table*   754

FA 1987	Subject Matter	Re-enacted in TA 1988	Remarks
Sch. 3 (cont)			
Sch. 4	Employee share schemes.		
para. 1, 2		Sch. 9 §15(1)–(4)	Am. & rep. in part 1987(2) s. 59(2), (3), Sch. 9 Pt. I.
para. 3		Sch. 9 §15(5)–(8)	
para. 4, 5		Sch. 29	Am. 1987(2) s. 56.
para. 6–8		Sch. 9 §37–39	
Sch. 5	Training costs.	s. 589	
Sch. 6	Corporation tax.		
para. 1–8		Sch. 30 §1	
para. 9–12		s. 478(4)–(7)	
Sch. 15	Pre-consolidation amendments.		See destinations of enactments amended.

Finance (No. 2) Act 1987
(c. 51)

F(No. 2)A 1987	Subject Matter	Re-enacted in TA 1988	Remarks
s. 1	Profit-related pay.	s. 169	
s. 2		s. 170	
s. 3		s. 171	
s. 4		s. 172	
s. 5		s. 173	
s. 6		s. 174	
s. 7		s. 175	
s. 8		s. 176	
s. 9		s. 177	
s. 10		s. 178	
s. 11		s. 179	
s. 12		s. 180	
s. 13		s. 181	
s. 14		Sch. 29	
s. 15		s. 182	
s. 16		s. 183	
s. 17		s. 184	
s. 18	Personal pension schemes.	s. 630	
s. 19		s. 631(1)–(4)	
s. 20		s. 632, 828	
s. 21		s. 633	
s. 22		s. 634	
s. 23		s. 635, 828	
s. 24		s. 636	
s. 25		s. 637(1)	
s. 26		s. 637(2)	
s. 27		s. 638(1)	
s. 28		s. 638(2), 828	
s. 29		s. 638(3)–(5)	
s. 30		s. 638(6), (7)	
s. 31		s. 639(1)	
s. 32		s. 640	
s. 33		s. 641	
s. 34		s. 642	
s. 35		s. 644	
s. 36		s. 645	
s. 37		s. 646	
s. 38		s. 643(1)	
s. 39(1)		s. 643(2)	
s. 39(2)		Sch. 29	
s. 39(3)		s. 431(4)(c), 438(8)	
s. 39(4)		s. 476(7)	
s. 40		s. 468(2), Sch. 29	
s. 41(1), (2)		s. 643(3), (4)	

F(No. 2)A 1987	Subject Matter	Re-enacted in TA 1988	Remarks
s. 41(3)		s. 657(2)(e)	
s. 42		s. 649, 828	
s. 43		s. 650	
s. 44		s. 647	
s. 45		s. 639(2)–(5), 828	
s. 46		s. 639(1)	
s. 47		s. 651	
s. 48		s. 639(6)	
s. 49		s. 639(7), (8)	
s. 50		s. 652	
s. 51(1)		s. 653	
s. 51(2)		Sch. 29	
s. 52		s. 654	
s. 53		s. 648	
s. 54(1)		s. 618	
s. 54(2)		s. 626	
s. 54(3)–(6)		s. 618	
s. 55		s. 655(1)–(3)	
s. 56		s. 655(4), (5), 828	
s. 57, 58		—	Unnecessary.
s. 59(1)	Employee share schemes.	Sch. 29	
s. 59(2), (3)		Sch. 9 §15	
s. 60	Payments between related companies.	s. 341	
s. 61(1), (2)	Close companies.	—	Unnecessary.
s. 61(3), (4)		s. 423(1), (3)	
s. 61(5), (6)		Sch. 19 §15(1), 18	
s. 62(1)	Partnerships.	s. 112(4), (5)	
s. 62(2)		—	Spent.
s. 63	Group relief.	s. 404	
s. 64(2)		s. 343(2)	
s. 65	Controlled foreign companies.	Sch. 25 §2(1)(c), 4(1)(c)	
s. 66	Offshore funds.	Sch. 27 §1(1)(c), 14	
s. 67	D.T.R.	s. 798(1), (2), (5)(b), (6)–(11)	
s. 68		s. 803(2)–(5), (11)	
s. 70	Lloyd's underwriters.	s. 450(5)	
s. 71	Loss relief.	s. 576(5)	
s. 74(1)	Companies' chargeable gains.	—	Unnecessary.
s. 74(2)		s. 239	
s. 74(3)		—	Spent.
s. 74(4)		s. 13	
s. 74(5)		s. 245(2), 246(5)	
s. 75(1)		s. 434(6)	
s. 75(2), (3)		s. 435(2), (3)	
s. 75(4)		—	Spent.
s. 76(1)	Oil.	—	Unnecessary.
s. 76(2)		s. 497(5)	
s. 76(3)		s. 497(1)	
s. 76(4)		s. 498	
s. 76(5)		s. 499(4)	
s. 77(2)		s. 797(4), (5)	
s. 77(3)–(5)		—	Spent.
s. 87	Interest on overpaid tax.	s. 826	
s. 90(1)	Payment of corporation tax.	s. 8(3), 10(1)	
s. 90(2), (3)		s. 419(1), (3)	
s. 90(4)–(7)		s. 10(2)–(5)	
s. 92	PAYE.	s. 203	
s. 93	Sub-contractors.	s. 561, 566	
Sch. 1	Profit-related pay schemes.	Sch. 8	
Sch. 2	Amendments.		See destinations of enactments amended.
Sch. 3	Occupational pension schemes.		
Pt. I	Amendments.		See destinations of enactments amended.
Pt. II	Pre-19th March 1987 schemes.	Sch. 23	

F(No.2)A 1987	Subject Matter	Re-enacted in TA 1988	Remarks
Sch. 3 (contd)			
Sch. 4	Dual resident investing companies.	Sch. 17	
Sch. 5	—	—	Spent.
Sch. 6	Management provisions.		
para. 1		s. 346	
para. 2		—	Not repealed.
para. 3		s. 347	
para. 4, 5		—	Not repealed.
para. 6		s. 584	
para. 7		—	Not repealed.
para. 8		s. 451(2), 828	

INCOME AND CORPORATION TAXES ACT 1988

(1988 Chapter 1)

ARRANGEMENT OF PARTS

PART	CHAPTER		Sections
I		The charge to tax	1–20
II		Provisions relating to the Schedule A charge and the associated Schedule D charges	21–43
III		Provisions relating to the Schedule C charge and general provisions about Government securities	44–52
IV		Provisions relating to the Schedule D charge	
	I	Supplementary charging provisions	53–59
	II	Income tax: basis of assessment etc.	60–69
	III	Corporation tax: basis of assessment etc.	70
	IV	Provisions supplementary to Chapters II and III	71–73
	V	Computational provisions	74–99
	VI	Discontinuance, and change of basis of computation	100–110
	VII	Partnerships and successions	111–118
	VIII	Miscellaneous and supplemental	119–130
V		Provisions relating to the Schedule E charge	
	I	Supplementary charging provisions of general application	131–152
	II	Supplementary charging provisions applicable to directors and higher-paid employees and office holders	153–168
	III	Profit-related pay	169–184
	IV	Other exemptions and reliefs	185–202
	V	Assessment, collection, recovery and appeals	203–207
VI		Company distributions, tax credits etc.	
	I	Taxation of company distributions	208
	II	Matters which are distributions for the purposes of the Corporation Tax Acts	209–211
	III	Matters which are not distributions for the purposes of the Corporation Tax Acts	212–230
	IV	Tax credits	231–237
	V	Advance corporation tax and franked investment income	238–246
	VI	Miscellaneous and supplemental	247–255
VII		General provisions relating to taxation of income of individuals	
	I	Personal reliefs	256–278
	II	Taxation of income of spouses	279–288
	III	Relief for investment in new corporate trades: the business expansion scheme	289–312
	IV	Special provisions	313–333
	V	Residence of individuals	334–336
VIII		Taxation of income and chargeable gains of companies	337–347
IX		Annual payments and interest	348–379
X		Loss relief and group relief	
	I	Loss relief: income tax	380–392
	II	Loss relief: corporation tax	393–396
	III	Loss relief: miscellaneous provisions	397–401
	IV	Group relief	402–413

PART	CHAPTER		Sections
XI		Close companies	
	I	Interpretative provisions	414–418
	II	Charges to tax in connection with loans	419–422
	III	Apportionment of undistributed income etc.	423–430
XII		Special classes of companies and businesses	
	I	Insurance companies, underwriters and capital redemption business	431–458
	II	Friendly societies, trade unions and employers' associations	459–467
	III	Unit trust schemes, dealers in securities etc.	468–475
	IV	Building societies, banks, savings banks, industrial and provident societies and others	476–491
	V	Petroleum extraction activities	492–502
	VI	Miscellaneous businesses and bodies	503–519
XIII		Miscellaneous special provisions	
	I	Intellectual property	520–538
	II	Life policies, life annuities and capital redemption policies	539–554
	III	Entertainers and sportsmen	555–558
	IV	Sub-contractors in the construction industry	559–567
	V	Schemes for rationalizing industry	568–572
	VI	Other provisions	573–589
XIV		Pension schemes, social security benefits, life annuities etc.	
	I	Retirement benefit schemes	590–612
	II	Other pension funds and social security benefits and contributions	613–617
	III	Retirement annuities	618–629
	IV	Personal pension schemes	630–655
	V	Purchased life annuities	656–658
	VI	Miscellaneous	659
XV		Settlements	
	I	Dispositions for short periods	660–662
	II	Settlements on children	663–670
	III	Revocable settlements etc.	671–682
	IV	Liability to higher rate and additional rate tax	683–689
	V	Maintenance funds for historic buildings	690–694
XVI		Estates of deceased persons in course of administration	695–702
XVII		Tax avoidance	
	I	Cancellation of tax advantages from certain transactions in securities	703–709
	II	Transfers of securities	710–738
	III	Transfer of assets abroad	739–746
	IV	Controlled foreign companies	747–756
	V	Offshore funds	757–764
	VI	Miscellaneous	765–787
XVIII		Double taxation relief	
	I	The principal reliefs	788–791
	II	Rules governing relief by way of credit	792–806
	III	Miscellaneous provisions	807–816
XIX		Supplemental	817–845

ARRANGEMENT OF SECTIONS

PART I

THE CHARGE TO TAX

Income Tax

Section
1. The charge to income tax.
2. Fractions of a pound, and yearly assessments.
3. Certain income charged at basic rate.
4. Construction of references in Income Tax Acts to deduction of tax.
5. Date for payment.

Corporation tax

6. The charge to corporation tax and exclusion of income tax and capital gains tax.
7. Treatment of certain payments and repayment of income tax.
8. General scheme of corporation tax.
9. Computation of income: application of income tax principles.
10. Time for payment of tax.
11. Companies not resident in United Kingdom.
12. Basis of, and periods for, assessment.

Small companies' rate

13. Small companies' relief.
13A. Close investment-holding companies.

Advance corporation tax

14. Advance corporation tax and qualifying distributions.

The six Schedules

15. Schedule A.
16. *Schedule B* (repealed).
17. Schedule C.
18. Schedule D.
19. Schedule E.
20. Schedule F.

PART II

PROVISIONS RELATING TO THE SCHEDULE A CHARGE AND THE ASSOCIATED SCHEDULE D CHARGES

General

21. Persons chargeable.
22. Assessments.
23. Collection from lessees and agents.
24. Construction of Part II.

Deductions and other allowances

25. Deductions from rent: general rules.
26. Deductions from rent: land managed as one estate.
27. Deductions from rent: maintenance funds for historic buildings.
28. Deductions from receipts other than rent.
29. Sporting rights.
30. Expenditure on making sea walls.
31. Provisions supplementary to sections 25 to 30.
32. Capital allowances for machinery and plant used in estate management.
33. Agricultural land: allowance for excess expenditure on maintenance.

Premiums, leases at undervalue etc.

34. Treatment of premiums etc. as rent or Schedule D profits.
35. Schedule D charge on assignment of lease granted at an undervalue.
36. Schedule D charge on sale of land with right to reconveyance.

Section
37. Premiums paid etc.: deductions from premiums and rent received.
38. Rules for ascertaining duration of leases.
39. Saving for pre-1963 leases, and special relief for individuals.

Supplemental: Schedules A and D

40. Tax treatment of receipts and outgoings on sale of land.
41. Relief for rent etc. not paid.
42. Appeals against determinations under sections 34 to 36.
43. Non-residents.

PART III

PROVISIONS RELATING TO THE SCHEDULE C CHARGE AND GENERAL PROVISIONS ABOUT GOVERNMENT SECURITIES

General

44. Income tax: mode of charge.
45. Interpretation of Part III.

Government securities: exemptions from tax

46. Savings certificates and tax reserve certificates.
47. United Kingdom government securities held by non-residents.
48. Securities of foreign states.
49. Stock and dividends in name of Treasury etc.

Government securities: interest payable without deduction of tax

50. United Kingdom securities: Treasury directions for payment without deduction of tax.
51. Treasury directions as respects Northern Ireland securities.
52. Taxation of interest on converted government securities and interest which becomes subject to deduction.

PART IV

PROVISIONS RELATING TO THE SCHEDULE D CHARGE

CHAPTER I
SUPPLEMENTARY CHARGING PROVISIONS

53. Farming and other commercial occupation of land (except woodlands).
54. *Woodlands managed on a commercial basis.* (repealed)
55. Mines, quarries and other concerns.
56. Transactions in deposits with and without certificates or in debts.
57. Deep discount securities.
58. Foreign pensions.
59. Persons chargeable.

CHAPTER II
INCOME TAX: BASIS OF ASSESSMENT ETC.

Cases I and II

60. Assessment on preceding year basis.
61. Special basis at commencement of trade, profession or vocation.
62. Special basis for early years following commencement.
63. Special basis on discontinuance.

Cases III, IV and V

64. Case III assessments: general.
65. Cases IV and V assessments: general.
66. Special rules for fresh income.
67. Special rules where source of income disposed of or yield ceases.
68. Special rules where property etc. situated in Republic of Ireland.

Section

Case VI

69. Assessment on current year basis unless otherwise directed.

CHAPTER III

CORPORATION TAX: BASIS OF ASSESSMENT ETC.

70. Basis of assessment etc.

CHAPTER IV

PROVISIONS SUPPLEMENTARY TO CHAPTERS II AND III

71. Computation of income tax where no profits in year of assessment.
72. Apportionments etc. for purposes of Cases I, II and VI.
73. Single assessments for purposes of Cases III, IV and V.

CHAPTER V

COMPUTATIONAL PROVISIONS

Deductions

74. General rules as to deductions not allowable.
75. Expenses of management: investment companies.
76. Expenses of management: insurance companies.
77. Incidental costs of obtaining loan finance.
78. Discounted bills of exchange.
79. Contributions to local enterprise agencies.
80. Expenses connected with foreign trades etc.
81. Travel between trades etc.
82. Interest paid to non-residents.
83. Patent fees etc. and expenses.
84. Payments for technical education.
85. Payments to trustees of approved profit sharing schemes.
86. Employees seconded to charities and educational establishments.
87. Taxable premiums etc.
88. Payments to Export Credit Guarantee Department.
89. Debts proving irrecoverable after event treated as discontinuance.
90. Additional payments to redundant employees.
91. Cemeteries.

Treatment of regional development and other grants and debts released etc.

92. Regional development grants.
93. Other grants under Industrial Development Act 1982 etc.
94. Debts deducted and subsequently released.
95. Taxation of dealer's receipts on purchase by company of own shares.

Special provisions

96. Farming and market gardening: relief for fluctuating profits.
97. Treatment of farm animals etc.
98. Tied premises.
99. Dealers in land.

CHAPTER VI

DISCONTINUANCE, AND CHANGE OF BASIS OF COMPUTATION

Valuation of trading stock etc.

100. Valuation of trading stock at discontinuance of trade.
101. Valuation of work in progress at discontinuance of profession or vocation.
102. Provisions supplementary to sections 100 and 101.

Case VI charges on receipts

103. Receipts after discontinuance: earnings basis charge and related charge affecting conventional basis.

Section
104. Conventional basis: general charge on receipts after discontinuance or change of basis.
105. Allowable deductions.
106. Application of charges where rights to payments transferred.

Reliefs

107. Treatment of receipts as earned income.
108. Election for carry-back.
109. Charge under section 104: relief for individuals born before 6th April 1917.

Supplemental

110. Interpretation etc.

CHAPTER VII
PARTNERSHIPS AND SUCCESSIONS

General

111. Partnership assessments to income tax.
112. Partnerships controlled abroad.
113. Effect, for income tax, of change in ownership of trade, profession or vocation.

Partnerships involving companies

114. Special rules for computing profits and losses.
115. Provisions supplementary to section 114.
116. Arrangements for transferring relief.

Limited partners

117. Restriction on relief: individuals.
118. Restriction on relief: companies.

CHAPTER VIII
MISCELLANEOUS AND SUPPLEMENTAL

119. Rent etc. payable in connection with mines, quarries and similar concerns.
120. Rent etc. payable in respect of electric line wayleaves.
121. Management expenses of owner of mineral rights.
122. Relief in respect of mineral royalties.
123. Foreign dividends.
124. Interest on quoted Eurobonds.
125. Annual payments for non-taxable consideration.
126. Treasury securities issued at a discount.
127. Enterprise allowance.
128. Commodity and financial futures etc.: losses and gains.
129. Stock lending.
130. Meaning of "investment company" for the purposes of Part IV.

PART V
PROVISIONS RELATING TO THE SCHEDULE E CHARGE

CHAPTER I
SUPPLEMENTARY CHARGING PROVISIONS OF GENERAL APPLICATION

Miscellaneous provisions

131. Chargeable emoluments.
132. Place of performance, and meaning of emoluments received in the U.K.
133. Voluntary pensions.
134. Workers supplied by agencies.

Shareholdings, loans etc.

135. Gains by directors and employees from share options.

Section
136. Provisions supplementary to section 135.
137. Payment of tax under section 135 by instalments.
138. Share acquisitions by directors and employees.
139. Provisions supplementary to section 138.
140. Further interpretation of sections 135 to 139.

Vouchers etc.

141. Non-cash vouchers.
142. Credit-tokens.
143. Cash vouchers taxable under P.A.Y.E.
144. Supplementary provisions.

Living accommodation

145. Living accommodation provided for employee.
146. Additional charge in respect of certain living accommodation.
147. Occupation of Chevening House.

Payments on retirement, sick pay etc.

148. Payments on retirement or removal from office or employment.
149. Sick pay.
150. Job release scheme allowances, maternity pay and statutory sick pay.
151. Income support etc.
152. Notification of amount taxable under section 151.

CHAPTER II

SUPPLEMENTARY CHARGING PROVISIONS APPLICABLE TO DIRECTORS AND HIGHER-PAID EMPLOYEES AND OFFICE HOLDERS

Expenses

153. Payments in respect of expenses.

Benefits in kind

154. General charging provision.
155. Exceptions from the general charge.
156. Cash equivalents of benefits charged under section 154.
157. Cars available for private use.
158. Car fuel.
159. Pooled cars.
160. Beneficial loan arrangements.
161. Exceptions from section 160.
162. Employee shareholdings.
163. Expenses connected with living accommodation.
164. Director's tax paid by employer.
165. Scholarships.

General supplementary provisions

166. Notice of nil liability under this Chapter.
167. Employment to which this Chapter applies.
168. Other interpretative provisions.

CHAPTER III

PROFIT-RELATED PAY

Preliminary

169. Interpretation.
170. *Taxation of profit-related pay.* (repealed)

The relief

171. Relief from tax.
172. Exceptions from tax.

Section

Registration

173. Persons who may apply for registration.
174. Excluded employments.
175. Applications for registration.
176. Registration.
177. Change of scheme employer.
177A. Death of scheme employer.
177B. Alteration of scheme's terms.
178. Cancellation of registration.

Administration

179. Recovery of tax from scheme employer.
180. Annual returns etc.
181. Other information.
182. Appeals.

Supplementary

183. Partnerships.
184. Independent accountants.

CHAPTER IV
OTHER EXEMPTIONS AND RELIEFS

Share option and profit sharing schemes

185. Approved share option schemes.
186. Approved profit sharing schemes.
187. Interpretation of sections 185 and 186 and Schedules 9 and 10.

Retirement benefits etc.

188. Exemptions from section 148.
189. Lump sum benefits on retirement.
190. Payments to Members of Parliament, Representatives to the European Parliament and others.
191. Job release scheme allowances not to be treated as income.

Foreign emoluments and earnings, pensions and certain travel facilities

192. Relief from tax for foreign emoluments.
193. Foreign earnings and travel expenses.
194. Other foreign travel expenses.
195. Travel expenses of employees not domiciled in the United Kingdom.
196. Foreign pensions.
197. Leave travel facilities for the armed forces.
197A. Car parking facilities.

Other expenses, subscriptions etc.

198. Relief for necessary expenses.
199. Expenses necessarily incurred and defrayed from official emoluments.
200. Expenses of Members of Parliament.
201. Fees and subscriptions to professional bodies, learned societies etc.
202. Donations to charity: payroll deduction scheme.

CHAPTER V
ASSESSMENT, COLLECTION, RECOVERY AND APPEALS

202A. Assessment on receipts basis.
202B. Receipts basis: meaning of receipt.
203. Pay as you earn.
203A. PAYE: meaning of payment.
204. PAYE repayments.
205. Assessments unnecessary in certain circumstances.
206. Additional provision for certain assessments.
207. Disputes as to domicile or ordinary residence.

Section

PART VI

COMPANY DISTRIBUTIONS, TAX CREDITS ETC.

CHAPTER I

TAXATION OF COMPANY DISTRIBUTIONS

208. U.K. company distributions not generally chargeable to corporation tax.

CHAPTER II

MATTERS WHICH ARE DISTRIBUTIONS FOR THE PURPOSES OF THE CORPORATION TAX ACTS

209. Meaning of "distribution".
210. Bonus issue following repayment of share capital.
211. Matters to be treated or not to be treated as repayments of share capital.

CHAPTER III

MATTERS WHICH ARE NOT DISTRIBUTIONS FOR THE PURPOSES OF THE CORPORATION TAX ACTS

Payments of interest

212. Interest etc. paid in respect of certain securities.

Demergers

213. Exempt distributions.
214. Chargeable payments connected with exempt distributions.
215. Advance clearance by Board of distributions and payments.
216. Returns.
217. Information.
218. Interpretation of sections 213 to 217.

Purchase of own shares

219. Purchase by unquoted trading company of own shares.
220. Conditions as to residence and period of ownership.
221. Reduction of vendor's interest as shareholder.
222. Conditions applicable where purchasing company is member of group.
223. Other conditions.
224. Relaxation of conditions in certain cases.
225. Advance clearance of payments by Board.
226. Returns and information.
227. Associated persons.
228. Connected persons.
229. Other interpretative provisions.

Stock dividends

230. Stock dividends: distributions.

CHAPTER IV

TAX CREDITS

231. Tax credits for certain recipients of qualifying distributions.
232. Tax credits for non-U.K. residents.
233. Taxation of certain recipients of distributions and in respect of non-qualifying distributions.
234. Information relating to distributions.
235. Distributions of exempt funds etc.
236. Provisions supplementary to section 235.
237. Disallowance of reliefs in respect of bonus issues.

Section

CHAPTER V
ADVANCE CORPORATION TAX AND FRANKED INVESTMENT INCOME

238. Interpretation of terms and collection of ACT.
239. Set-off of ACT against liability to corporation tax.
240. Set-off of company's surplus ACT against subsidiary's liability to corporation tax.
241. Calculation of ACT where company receives franked investment income.
242. Set-off of losses etc. against surplus of franked investment income.
243. Set-off of loss brought forward, or terminal loss.
244. Further provisions relating to claims under section 242 or 243.
245. Calculation etc. of ACT on change of ownership of company.
245A. Restriction on application of section 240 in certain circumstances.
245B. Restriction on set-off where asset transferred after change in ownership of company.
246. Charge of ACT at previous rate until new rate fixed, and changes of rate.

CHAPTER VI
MISCELLANEOUS AND SUPPLEMENTAL

Group income

247. Dividends etc. paid by one member of a group to another.
248. Provisions supplementary to section 247.

Stock dividends

249. Stock dividends treated as income.
250. Returns.
251. Interpretation of sections 249 and 250.

Supplemental

252. Rectification of excessive set-off etc. of ACT or tax credit.
253. Power to modify or replace section 234(5) to (9) and Schedule 13.
254. Interpretation of Part VI.
255. "Gross rate" and "gross amount" of distributions to include ACT.

PART VII
GENERAL PROVISIONS RELATING TO TAXATION OF INCOME OF INDIVIDUALS

CHAPTER I
PERSONAL RELIEFS

The reliefs

256. General.
257. Personal relief.
258. *Widower's or widow's housekeeper.* (repealed)
259. Additional relief in respect of children.
260. Apportionment of relief under section 259.
261. Claims under sections 258 and 259 for year of marriage.
262. Widows' bereavement allowance.
263. *Dependent relatives.* (repealed)
264. *Claimant depending on services of a son or daughter.* (repealed)
265. Relief for blind persons.
266. Life assurance premiums.
267. Qualifying policies.
268. Early conversion or surrender of life policies.
269. Surrender etc. of policies after four years.
270. Provisions supplementary to sections 268 and 269.
271. Deemed surrender in cases of certain loans.
272. Collection of sums payable under sections 268 and 269.
273. Payments securing widows' and children's annuities.
274. Limits on relief under section 266 and 273.

Supplemental

275. Meaning of "relative".

Section
276. Effect on relief of charges on income.
277. Partners.
278. Non-residents.

CHAPTER II

TAXATION OF INCOME OF SPOUSES

General rules

279. Aggregation of wife's income with husband's.
280. Transfer of reliefs.
281. Tax repayments to wives.
282. Construction of references to married women living with their husbands.

Separate assessments

283. Option for separate assessment.
284. Effect of separate assessment on personal reliefs.
285. Collection from wife of tax assessed on husband but attributable to her income.
286. Right of husband to disclaim liability for tax on deceased wife's income.

Separate taxation

287. Separate taxation of wife's earnings.
288. Elections under section 287.

CHAPTER III

RELIEF FOR INVESTMENT IN NEW CORPORATE TRADES: THE BUSINESS EXPANSION SCHEME

289. The relief.
290. Minimum and maximum subscriptions.
290A. Restrictions of relief where amounts raised exceed permitted maximum.
291. Individuals qualifying for relief.
292. Parallel trades.
293. Qualifying companies.
294. Companies with interests in land.
295. Valuation of interests in land for purposes of section 294(1)(*b*).
296. Section 294 disapplied where amounts raised total £50,000 or less.
297. Qualifying trades.
298. Provisions supplementary to sections 293 and 297.
299. Disposal of shares.
300. Value received from company.
301. Provisions supplementary to section 300.
302. Replacement capital.
303. Value received by persons other than claimants.
304. Husband and wife.
305. Reorganisation of share capital.
306. Claims.
307. Withdrawal of relief.
308. Application to subsidiaries.
309. Further provisions as to subsidiaries.
310. Information.
311. Nominees, bare trustees and approved investment funds.
312. Interpretation of Chapter III.

CHAPTER IV

SPECIAL PROVISIONS

313. Taxation of consideration for certain restrictive undertakings.
314. Divers and diving supervisors.
315. Wounds and disability pensions.
316. Allowances, bounties and gratuities.
317. Victoria Cross and other awards.
318. Other pensions in respect of death due to war service etc.
319. Crown servants: foreign service allowance.

Section
320. Commonwealth Agents—General and official agents etc.
321. Consuls and other official agents.
322. Consular officers and employees.
323. Visiting forces.
324. Designated international organisations.
325. Interest on deposits with National Savings Bank.
326. Interest etc. under contractual savings schemes.
327. Disabled persons' vehicle maintenance grant.
328. Funds in court.
329. Interest on damages for personal injuries.
330. Compensation for National–Socialist persecution.
331. Scholarship income.
332. Expenditure and houses of ministers of religion.
333. Personal equity plans.

CHAPTER V

RESIDENCE OF INDIVIDUALS

334. Commonwealth citizens and others temporarily abroad.
335. Residence of persons working abroad.
336. Temporary residents in the United Kingdom.

PART VIII

TAXATION OF INCOME AND CHARGEABLE GAINS OF COMPANIES

Taxation of income

337. Companies beginning or ceasing to carry on a trade.
338. Allowance of charges on income and capital.
339. Charges on income: donations to charity.
340. Charges on income: interest payable to non-residents.
341. Payments of interest etc. between related companies.
342. Tax on company in liquidation.
343. Company reconstructions without a change of ownership.
344. Company reconstructions: supplemental.

Chargeable gains

345. Computation of chargeable gains.
346. Capital distribution of chargeable gains: recovery of tax from shareholder.
347. Tax on one member of group recoverable from another member.

PART IX

ANNUAL PAYMENTS AND INTEREST

Annual payments

347A. General rule.
347B. Qualifying maintenance payments.
348. Payments out of profits or gains brought into charge to income tax: deduction of tax.
349. Payments not out of profits or gains brought into charge to income tax, and annual interest.
350. Charge to tax where payments made under section 349.
351. *Small maintenance payments* (repealed).
352. Certificates of deduction of tax.

Relief for payments of interest (excluding MIRAS)

353. General provision.
354. Loans to buy land etc.
355. Matters excluded from section 354.
356. Job-related accommodation.
356A. Limit on relief for home loans: residence basis.
356B. Residence basis: married couples.
356C. Payments to which sections 356A and 356B apply.
356D. Provisions supplementary to sections 356A to 356C.

Section
357. Limit on amount of loan eligible for relief by virtue of section 354.
358. Relief where borrower deceased.
359. Loan to buy machinery or plant.
360. Loan to buy interest in close company.
360A. Meaning of "material interest" in section 360.
361. Loan to buy interest in co-operative or employee-controlled company.
362. Loan to buy into partnership.
363. Provisions supplementary to sections 360 to 362.
364. Loan to pay inheritance tax.
365. Loan to buy life annuity.
366. Information.
367. Provisions supplementary to sections 354 to 366.
368. Exclusion of double relief etc.

Mortgage interest relief at source

369. Mortgage interest payable under deduction of tax.
370. Relevant loan interest.
371. Second loans.
372. Home improvement loans.
373. Loans in excess of the qualifying maximum, and joint borrowers.
374. Conditions for application of section 369.
375. Interest ceasing to be relevant loan interest etc.
376. Qualifying borrowers and qualifying lenders.
377. Variation of terms of repayment of certain loans.
378. Supplementary regulations.
379. Interpretation of sections 369 to 378.

PART X

LOSS RELIEF AND GROUP RELIEF

CHAPTER I

LOSS RELIEF: INCOME TAX

Trade etc. losses

380. Set-off against general income.
381. Further relief for individuals for losses in early years of trade.
382. Provisions supplementary to sections 380 and 381.
383. Extension of right of set-off to capital allowances.
384. Restrictions on right of set-off.
385. Carry-forward against subsequent profits.
386. Carry-forward where business transferred to a company.
387. Carry-forward as losses of amounts taxed under section 350.
388. Carry-back of terminal losses.
389. Supplementary provisions relating to carry-back of terminal losses.
390. Treatment of interest as a loss for purposes of carry-forward and carry-back.
391. Losses from trade etc. carried on abroad.

Case VI losses

392. Case VI losses.

CHAPTER II

LOSS RELIEF: CORPORATION TAX

Trade etc. losses

393. Losses other than terminal losses.
394. Terminal losses.
395. Leasing contracts and company reconstructions.

Case VI losses

396. Case VI losses.

Section

CHAPTER III

LOSS RELIEF: MISCELLANEOUS PROVISIONS

397. Restriction of relief in case of farming and market gardening.
398. Transactions in deposits with and without certificates or in debts.
399. Dealings in commodity futures etc.: withdrawal of loss relief.
400. Write-off of government investment.
401. Relief for pre-trading expenditure.

CHAPTER IV

GROUP RELIEF

402. Surrender of relief between members of groups and consortia.
403. Losses etc. which may be surrendered by way of group relief.
404. Limitation of group relief in relation to certain dual resident companies.
405. Claims relating to losses etc. of members of both group and consortium.
406. Claims relating to losses etc. of consortium company or group member.
407. Relationship between group relief and other relief.
408. Corresponding accounting periods.
409. Companies joining or leaving group or consortium.
410. Arrangements for transfer of company to another group or consortium.
411. Exclusion of double allowances.
412. Claims and adjustments.
413. Interpretation of Chapter IV.

PART XI

CLOSE COMPANIES

CHAPTER I

INTERPRETATIVE PROVISIONS

414. Close companies.
415. Certain quoted companies not to be close companies.
416. Meaning of "associated company" and "control".
417. Meaning of "participator", "associate", "director" and "loan creditor".

Additional matters to be treated as distributions

418. "Distribution" to include certain expenses of close companies.

CHAPTER II

CHARGES TO TAX IN CONNECTION WITH LOANS

419. Loans to participators etc.
420. Exceptions from section 419.
421. Taxation of borrower when loan under section 419 released etc.
422. Extension of section 419 to loans by companies controlled by close companies.

CHAPTER III

APPORTIONMENT OF UNDISTRIBUTED INCOME ETC.

423. Apportionment of certain income, deductions and interest.
424. Exclusions from section 423.
425. Manner of apportionment.
426. Charge to income tax where apportionment is to an individual.
427. Reduction of charge under section 426 in certain cases.
428. Increase of apportioned sum etc. by reference to ACT.
429. Payment and collection of income tax.
430. Consequences of apportionment: ACT.

Section

PART XII
SPECIAL CLASSES OF COMPANIES AND BUSINESSES

CHAPTER I
INSURANCE COMPANIES, UNDERWRITERS AND CAPITAL REDEMPTION BUSINESS

Insurance companies: general

431. Interpretative provisions relating to insurance companies.
432. Separation of different classes of business.
433. Profits reserved for policy holders and annuitants.
434. Franked investment income etc.
434A. Limitations on loss relief and group relief.
435. Taxation of gains reserved for policy holders and annuitants.
436. Annuity business and pension business: separate charge on profits.
437. General annuity business.
438. Pension business: exemption from tax.
439. Restricted government securities.
440. Identification or exchange of long term assets.
441. Foreign life assurance funds.
442. Overseas business of U.K. companies.
443. Life policies carrying rights not in money.
444. Life policies issued before 5th August 1965.

Provisions applying only to overseas life insurance companies

445. Charge to tax on investment income.
446. Annuity business.
447. Set-off of income tax and tax credits against corporation tax.
448. Qualifying distributions and tax credits.
449. Double taxation agreements.

Underwriters

450. Assessment, set-off of losses and reinsurance.
451. Regulations.
452. Special reserve funds.
453. Payments into premiums trust fund on account of losses.
454. Income tax consequences on payments into and out of special reserve fund.
455. Income tax consequences on death of underwriter.
456. Unearned income, variation of arrangements and cancellation of approval etc.
457. Interpretation of sections 450 to 456.

Capital redemption business

458. Capital redemption business.

CHAPTER II
FRIENDLY SOCIETIES, TRADE UNIONS AND EMPLOYERS' ASSOCIATIONS

Unregistered friendly societies

459. Exemption from tax.

Registered friendly societies

460. Exemption from tax in respect of life or endowment business.
461. Taxation in respect of other business.
462. Conditions for tax exempt business.
463. Life or endowment business: application of the Corporation Tax Acts.
464. Maximum benefits payable to members.
465. Old societies.
466. Interpretation of Chapter II.

Trade unions and employers' associations

467. Exemption for trade unions and employers' associations.

Section

CHAPTER III
UNIT TRUST SCHEMES, DEALERS IN SECURITIES ETC.
Unit trust schemes

468. Authorised unit trusts.
468A. Certified unit trusts.
468B. Certified unit trusts: corporation tax.
468C. Certified unit trusts: distributions.
468D. Funds of funds: distributions.
469. Other unit trusts.
470. Transitional provisions relating to unit trusts.

Dealers in securities, banks and insurance businesses

471. Exchange of securities in connection with conversion operations, nationalisation etc.
472. Distribution of securities issued in connection with nationalisation etc.
473. Conversion etc. of securities held as circulating capital.
474. Treatment of tax-free income.
475. Tax-free Treasury securities: exclusion of interest on borrowed money.

CHAPTER IV
BUILDING SOCIETIES, BANKS, SAVINGS BANKS, INDUSTRIAL AND PROVIDENT SOCIETIES AND OTHERS

476. Building societies: regulations for payment of tax.
477. Investments becoming or ceasing to be relevant building society investments.
478. Building societies: time for payment of tax.
479. Interest paid on deposits with banks etc.
480. Deposits becoming or ceasing to be composite rate deposits.
481. "Deposit-taker", "deposit" and "relevant deposit".
482. Supplementary provisions.
483. Determination of reduced rate for building societies and composite rate for banks etc.
484. Savings banks: exemption from tax.
485. Savings banks: supplemental.
486. Industrial and provident societies and co-operative associations.
487. Credit unions.
488. Co-operative housing associations.
489. Self-build societies.
490. Companies carrying on a mutual business or not carrying on a business.
491. Distribution of assets of body corporate carrying on mutual business.

CHAPTER V
PETROLEUM EXTRACTION ACTIVITIES

492. Treatment of oil extraction activities etc. for tax purposes.
493. Valuation of oil disposed of or appropriated in certain circumstances.
494. Charges on income.
495. Regional development grants.
496. Tariff receipts.
497. Restriction on setting ACT against income from oil extraction activities etc.
498. Limited right to carry back surrendered ACT.
499. Surrender of ACT where oil extraction company etc. owned by a consortium.
500. Deduction of PRT in computing income for corporation tax purposes.
501. Interest on repayment of PRT.
502. Interpretation of Chapter V.

CHAPTER VI
MISCELLANEOUS BUSINESSES AND BODIES

503. Letting of furnished holiday accommodation treated as a trade.
504. Supplementary provisions.
505. Charities: general.
506. Qualifying expenditure and non-qualifying expenditure.
507. The National Heritage Memorial Fund, the Historic Buildings and Monuments Commission for England and the British Museum.
508. Scientific research organisations.
509. Reserves of marketing boards and certain other statutory bodies.
510. Agricultural societies.

Section
511. The Electricity Council and Boards, the Northern Ireland Electricity Service and the Gas Council.
512. Atomic Energy Authority and National Radiological Protection Board.
513. British Airways Board and National Freight Corporation.
514. Funds for reducing the National Debt.
515. Signatories to Operating Agreement for INMARSAT.
516. Government securities held by non-resident central banks.
517. Issue departments of the Reserve Bank of India and the State Bank of Pakistan.
518. Harbour reorganisation schemes.
519. Local authorities.

PART XIII

MISCELLANEOUS SPECIAL PROVISIONS

CHAPTER I

INTELLECTUAL PROPERTY

Patents and know-how

520. Allowances for expenditure on purchase of patent rights: post-31st March 1986 expenditure.
521. Provisions supplementary to section 520.
522. Allowances for expenditure on purchase of patent rights: pre-1st April 1986 expenditure.
523. Lapses of patent rights, sales etc.
524. Taxation of receipts from sale of patent rights.
525. Capital sums: death, winding up or partnership change.
526. Relief for expenses.
527. Spreading of royalties over several years.
528. Manner of making allowances and charges.
529. Patent income to be earned income in certain cases.
530. Disposal of know-how.
531. Provisions supplementary to section 530.
532. Application of the 1968 Act.
533. Interpretation of sections 520 to 532.

Copyright and public lending right

534. Relief for copyright payments etc.
535. Relief where copyright sold after ten years or more.
536. Taxation of royalties where owner abroad.
537. Public lending right.
537A. Relief for payments in respect of designs.
537B. Taxation of design royalties where owner abroad.

Artists' receipts

538. Relief for painters, sculptors and other artists.

CHAPTER II

LIFE POLICIES, LIFE ANNUITIES AND CAPITAL REDEMPTION POLICIES

539. Introductory.
540. Life policies: chargeable events.
541. Life policies: computation of gain.
542. Life annuity contracts: chargeable events.
543. Life annuity contracts: computation of gain.
544. Second and subsequent assignment of life policies and contracts.
545. Capital redemption policies.
546. Calculation of certain amounts for purposes of sections 540, 542 and 545.
547. Method of charging gain to tax.
548. Deemed surrender of certain loans.
549. Certain deficiencies allowable as deductions.
550. Relief where gain charged at a higher rate.
551. Right of individual to recover tax from trustees.
552. Information: duty of insurers.

Section
553. Non-resident policies and off-shore capital redemption policies.
554. Borrowings on life policies to be treated as income in certain cases.

CHAPTER III

ENTERTAINERS AND SPORTSMEN

555. Payment of tax.
556. Activity treated as trade etc. and attribution of income.
557. Charge on profits or gains.
558. Supplementary provisions.

CHAPTER IV

SUB-CONTRACTORS IN THE CONSTRUCTION INDUSTRY

559. Deductions on account of tax etc. from payments to certain sub-contractors.
560. Persons who are sub-contractors or contractors for purposes of Chapter IV.
561. Exceptions from section 559.
562. Conditions to be satisfied by individuals.
563. Conditions to be satisfied by partners who are individuals.
564. Conditions to be satisfied by firms.
565. Conditions to be satisfied by companies.
566. General powers to make regulations under Chapter IV.
567. Meaning of "construction operations".

CHAPTER V

SCHEMES FOR RATIONALIZING INDUSTRY

568. Deductions from profits of contributions paid under certified schemes.
569. Repayment of contributions.
570. Payments under certified schemes which are not repayments of contributions.
571. Cancellation of certificates.
572. Application to statutory redundancy schemes.

CHAPTER VI

OTHER PROVISIONS

Relief for losses on unquoted shares in trading companies

573. Relief for companies.
574. Relief for individuals.
575. Exclusion of relief under section 573 or 574 in certain cases.
576. Provisions supplementary to sections 573 to 575.

Miscellaneous

577. Business entertaining expenses.
578. Housing grants.
579. Statutory redundancy payments.
580. Provisions supplementary to section 579.
581. Borrowing in foreign currency by local authorities and statutory corporations.
582. Funding bonds issued in respect of interest on certain debts.
583. Inter-American Development Bank.
584. Relief for unremittable overseas income.
585. Relief from tax on delayed remittances.
586. Disallowance of deductions for war risk premiums.
587. Disallowance of certain payments in respect of war injuries to employees.
588. Training courses for employees.
589. Qualifying courses of training etc.

PART XIV

PENSION SCHEMES, SOCIAL SECURITY BENEFITS, LIFE ANNUITIES ETC.

CHAPTER I

RETIREMENT BENEFIT SCHEMES

Approval of schemes

590. Conditions for approval of retirement benefit scheme.
590A. Section 590: supplementary provisions.
590B. Section 590: further supplementary provisions.
590C. Earnings cap.
591. Discretionary approval.

Tax reliefs

592. Exempt approved schemes.
593. Relief by way of deductions from contributions.
594. Exempt statutory schemes.

Charge to tax in certain cases

595. Charge to tax in respect of certain sums paid by employer etc.
596. Exceptions from section 595.
596A. Charge to tax: benefits under non-approved schemes.
597. Charge to tax: pensions.
598. Charge to tax: repayment of employee's contributions.
599. Charge to tax: commutation of entire pension in special circumstances.
599A. Charge to tax: payments out of surplus funds.
600. Charge to tax: unauthorised payments to or for employees.
601. Charge to tax: payments to employers.
602. Regulations relating to pension fund surpluses.
603. Reduction of surpluses.

Supplementary provisions

604. Application for approval of a scheme.
605. Information.
606. Responsibilities of administrator of scheme, and employer.
607. Pilots' benefit fund.
608. Superannuation funds approved before 6th April 1980.
609. Schemes approved before 23rd July 1987.
610. Amendments of schemes.
611. Definition of "retirement benefits scheme".
611A. Definition of relevant statutory scheme.
612. Other interpretative provisions, and regulations for purposes of this Chapter.

CHAPTER II

OTHER PENSION FUNDS AND SOCIAL SECURITY BENEFITS AND CONTRIBUTIONS

613. Parliamentary pension funds.
614. Exemptions and reliefs in respect of income from investments etc. of certain pension schemes.
615. Exemption from tax in respect of certain pensions.
616. Other overseas pensions.
617. Social security benefits and contributions.

CHAPTER III

RETIREMENT ANNUITIES

618. Termination of relief under this Chapter, and transitional provisions.
619. Exemption from tax in respect of qualifying premiums.
620. Qualifying premiums.
621. Other approved contracts.
622. Substituted retirement annuity contracts.
623. Relevant earnings.
624. Sponsored superannuation schemes and controlling directors.
625. Carry-forward of unused relief under section 619.
626. Modification of section 619 in relation to persons over 50.
627. Lloyd's underwriters.

Section
628. Partnership retirement annuities.
629. Annuity premiums of Ministers and other officers.

CHAPTER IV
PERSONAL PENSION SCHEMES
Preliminary

630. Interpretation.
631. Approval of schemes.

Restrictions on approval

632. Establishment of schemes.
633. Scope of benefits.
634. Annuity to member.
635. Lump sum to member.
636. Annuity after death of member.
637. Lump sum on death of member.
638. Other restrictions on approval.

Tax reliefs

639. Member's contributions.
640. Maximum amount of deductions.
640A. Earnings cap.
641. Carry-back of contributions.
642. Carry-forward of relief.
643. Employer's contributions and personal pension income etc.
644. Meaning of "relevant earnings".
645. Earnings from pensionable employment.
646. Meaning of "net relevant earnings".
646A. Earnings from associated employments.

Charge to tax

647. Unauthorised payments.
648. Contributions under unapproved arrangements.

Miscellaneous

649. Minimum contributions under Social Security Act 1986.
650. Withdrawal of approval.
651. Appeals.
652. Information about payments.
653. Information: penalties.
654. Remuneration of Ministers and other officers.
655. Transitional provisions.

CHAPTER V
PURCHASED LIFE ANNUITIES

656. Purchased life annuities other than retirement annuities.
657. Purchased life annuities to which section 656 applies.
658. Supplementary.

CHAPTER VI
MISCELLANEOUS

659. Financial futures and traded options.

PART XV
SETTLEMENTS

CHAPTER I
DISPOSITIONS FOR SHORT PERIODS

660. Dispositions for period which cannot exceed six years.

Section
661. Adjustments between disponor and trustees.
662. Application of Chapter I to dispositions by two or more disponors.

CHAPTER II
SETTLEMENTS ON CHILDREN

663. The general rule.
664. Accumulation settlements.
665. Meaning of "irrevocable".
666. Interest paid by trustees.
667. Adjustments between disponor and trustees.
668. Application of Chapter II to settlements by two or more settlors.
669. Power to obtain information under Chapter II.
670. Interpretation of Chapter II.

CHAPTER III
REVOCABLE SETTLEMENTS ETC.

671. Revocable settlements allowing release of obligation.
672. Revocable settlements allowing reversion of property.
673. Settlements where settlor retains an interest.
674. Settlements: discretionary power for benefit of settlor, etc.
674A. Other settlements where settlor retains interest in settled property.
675. Provisions supplementary to sections 671 to 674.
676. Disallowance of deduction from total income of certain sums paid by settlor.
677. Sums paid to settlor otherwise than as income.
678. Capital sums paid by body connected with settlement.
679. Application of Chapter III to settlements by two or more settlors.
680. Power to obtain information for purposes of Chapter III.
681. Interpretation of Chapter III.
682. Ascertainment of undistributed income.

CHAPTER IV
LIABILITY TO HIGHER RATE AND ADDITIONAL RATE TAX

Liability of settlors

683. Settlements made after 6th April 1965.
684. Settlements made before 7th April 1965 but after 9th April 1946.
685. Provisions supplementary to sections 683 and 684.

Liability of trustees

686. Liability to additional rate tax of certain income of discretionary trusts.
687. Payments under discretionary trusts.
688. Schemes for employees and directors to acquire shares.
689. Recovery from trustees of discretionary trusts of higher rate tax due from beneficiaries.

CHAPTER V
MAINTENANCE FUNDS FOR HISTORIC BUILDINGS

690. Schedule 4 directions.
691. Certain income not to be income of settlor etc.
692. Reimbursement of settlor.
693. Severance of settled property for certain purposes.
694. Trustees chargeable to income tax at 30 per cent. in certain cases.

PART XVI
ESTATES OF DECEASED PERSONS IN COURSE OF ADMINISTRATION

695. Limited interests in residue.
696. Absolute interests in residue.
697. Supplementary provisions as to absolute interests in residue.
698. Special provisions as to certain interests in residue.
699. Relief from higher rate tax for inheritance tax on accrued income.
700. Adjustments and information.

Section
701. Interpretation.
702. Application to Scotland.

PART XVII
TAX AVOIDANCE

CHAPTER I
CANCELLATION OF TAX ADVANTAGES FROM CERTAIN TRANSACTIONS IN SECURITIES

703. Cancellation of tax advantage.
704. The prescribed circumstances.
705. Appeals against Board's notices under section 703.
706. The tribunal.
707. Procedure for clearance in advance.
708. Power to obtain information.
709. Meaning of "tax advantage" and other expressions.

CHAPTER II
TRANSFERS OF SECURITIES

Transfers with or without accrued interest: introductory

710. Meaning of "securities", "transfer" etc. for purposes of sections 711 to 728.
711. Meaning of "interest", "transfers with or without accrued interest" etc.
712. Meaning of "settlement day" for purposes of sections 711 to 728.

Transfers with or without accrued interest: charge to tax and reliefs

713. Deemed sums and reliefs.
714. Treatment of deemed sums and reliefs.
715. Exceptions from sections 713 and 714.
716. Transfer of unrealised interest.
717. Variable interest rate.
718. Interest in default.
719. Unrealised interest in default.

Transfers with or without accrued interest: supplemental

720. Nominees, trustees etc.
721. Death.
722. Trading stock.
723. Foreign securities: delayed remittances.
724. Insurance companies.
725. Lloyd's underwriters.
726. Building societies.
727. Stock lending.
728. Information.

Other transfers of securities

729. Sale and repurchase of securities.
730. Transfers of income arising from securities.

Purchase and sale of securities

731. Application and interpretation of sections 732 to 734.
732. Dealers in securities.
733. Persons entitled to exemptions.
734. Persons other than dealers in securities.
735. Meaning of "appropriate amount in respect of" interest.

Miscellaneous provisions relating to securities

736. Company dealing in securities: distribution materially reducing value of holding.
737. Manufactured dividends: treatment of tax deducted.

Section

Supplemental

738. Power to amend sections 732, 735 and 737.

CHAPTER III
TRANSFER OF ASSETS ABROAD

739. Prevention of avoidance of income tax.
740. Liability of non-transferors.
741. Exemption from sections 739 and 740.
742. Interpretation of sections 739 to 741.
743. Supplemental provisions.
744. No duplication of charge.
745. Power to obtain information.
746. Persons resident in the Republic of Ireland.

CHAPTER IV
CONTROLLED FOREIGN COMPANIES

747. Imputation of chargeable profits and creditable tax of controlled foreign companies.
748. Limitations on direction-making power.
749. Residence and interest.
750. Territories with a lower level of taxation.
751. Accounting periods and creditable tax.
752. Apportionment of chargeable profits and creditable tax.
753. Notices and appeals.
754. Assessment, recovery and postponement of tax.
755. Information relating to controlled foreign companies.
756. Interpretation and construction of Chapter IV.

CHAPTER V
OFFSHORE FUNDS

Material interests in non-qualifying offshore funds

757. Disposal of material interests in non-qualifying offshore funds.
758. Offshore funds operating equalisation arrangements.
759. Material interests in offshore funds.
760. Non-qualifying offshore funds.

Charge to tax of offshore income gains

761. Charge to income tax or corporation tax of offshore income gain.
762. Offshore income gains accruing to persons resident or domiciled abroad.
763. Deduction of offshore income gain in determining capital gain.
764. Offshore income gains of trustees.

CHAPTER VI
MISCELLANEOUS

Migration etc. of company

765. Migration etc. of companies.
766. Offences under section 765.
767. Interpretation and commencement of sections 765 and 766.

Change in ownership of company

768. Change in ownership of company: disallowance of trading losses.
769. Rules for ascertaining change in ownership of company.

Transactions between associated persons

770. Sales etc. at an undervalue or overvalue.
771. Transactions by petroleum companies.
772. Information for purposes of section 770, and appeals.
773. Interpretation of sections 770 and 771.
774. Transactions between dealing company and associated company.

Section

Other provisions

775. Sale by individual of income derived from his personal activities.
776. Transactions in land: taxation of capital gains.
777. Provisions supplementary to sections 775 and 776.
778. Power to obtain information.
779. Sale and lease-back: limitation on tax reliefs.
780. Sale and lease-back: taxation of consideration received.
781. Assets leased to traders and others.
782. Leased assets: special cases.
783. Leased assets: supplemental.
784. Leased assets subject to hire-purchase agreements.
785. Meaning of "asset", "capital sum" and "lease" for purposes of sections 781 to 784.
786. Transactions associated with loans or credit.
787. Restriction of relief for payments of interest.

PART XVIII
DOUBLE TAXATION RELIEF

CHAPTER I
THE PRINCIPAL RELIEFS

788. Relief by agreement with other countries.
789. Arrangements made under old law.
790. Unilateral relief.
791. Power to make regulations for carrying out section 788.

CHAPTER II
RULES GOVERNING RELIEF BY WAY OF CREDIT

General

792. Interpretation of credit code.
793. Reduction of United Kingdom taxes by amount of credit due.
794. Requirement as to residence.
795. Computation of income subject to foreign tax.
796. Limits on credit: income tax.
797. Limits on credit: corporation tax.
798. Interest on certain overseas loans.

Tax underlying dividends

799. Computation of underlying tax.
800. Dividends paid between related companies but not covered by arrangements.
801. Dividends paid between related companies: relief for U.K. and third country taxes.
802. U.K. insurance companies trading overseas.
803. Underlying tax reflecting interest on loans.

Miscellaneous rules

804. Relief against income tax in respect of income arising in years of commencement.
805. Elections against credit.
806. Time limit for claims etc.

CHAPTER III
MISCELLANEOUS PROVISIONS

807. Sale of securities with or without accrued interest.
808. Restriction on deduction of interest or dividends from trading income.
809. Relief in respect of discretionary trusts.
810. Postponement of capital allowances to secure double taxation relief.
811. Deduction for foreign tax where no credit allowable.
812. Withdrawal of right to tax credit of certain non-resident companies connected with unitary states.
813. Recovery of tax credits incorrectly paid.
814. Arrangements to avoid section 812.

Section
815. Power to inspect documents.
816. Disclosure of information.

PART XIX

SUPPLEMENTAL

Miscellaneous

817. Deductions not to be allowed in computing profits or gains.
818. Arrangements for payments of interest less tax or of fixed net amount.
819. Old references to standard rate tax.
820. Application of Income Tax Acts from year to year.
821. Under-deductions from payments made before passing of annual Act.
822. Over-deductions from interest on loan capital etc. made before passing of annual Act.
823. Adjustment of reliefs where given at different times.
824. Repayment supplements: individuals and others.
825. Repayment supplements: companies.
826. Interest on tax overpaid.
827. VAT penalties etc.
828. Orders and regulations made by the Treasury or the Board.
829. Application of Income Tax Acts to public departments and avoidance of exempting provisions.
830. Territorial sea and designated areas.

Interpretation

831. Interpretation of this Act.
832. Interpretation of the Tax Acts.
833. Interpretation of Income Tax Acts.
834. Interpretation of the Corporation Tax Acts.
835. "Total income" in the Income Tax Acts.
836. Returns of total income.
837. "Annual value" of land.
838. Subsidiaries.
839. Connected persons.
840. Meaning of "control" in certain contexts.
841. Recognised stock exchange and recognised investment exchanges.
842. Investment trusts.

Commencement, savings, repeals etc.

843. Commencement.
844. Savings, transitional provisions, consequential amendments and repeals.
845. Short title.

SCHEDULES:

Schedule 1—Restrictions on Schedule A deductions.
Schedule 2—*Premiums etc. taxable under Schedules A and D: special relief for individuals.* (repealed)
Schedule 3—Machinery for assessment, charge and payment of income tax under Schedule C and, in certain cases, Schedule D.
 Part I Public revenue dividends etc. payable to the Bank of England or the Bank of Ireland or entrusted for payment to the Bank of England, the Bank of Ireland or the National Debt Commissioners.
 Part II Public revenue dividends payable by public offices and departments.
 Part III Other public revenue dividends, foreign dividends and proceeds of coupons.
 Part IV Interest payable out of the public revenue of the Republic of Ireland etc.
Schedule 4—Deep discount securities.
Schedule 5—Treatment of farm animals etc. for purposes of Case I of Schedule D.
Schedule 6—Taxation of directors and others in respect of cars.
 Part I Tables of flat rate cash equivalents.

      Part II Supplementary provisions.
Schedule 7—Taxation of benefit from loans obtained by reason of employment.
      Part I   Meaning of "obtained by reason of employment".
      Part II Calculation of cash equivalent of loan benefit.
      Part III Exceptions where interest eligible for relief.
Schedule 8—Profit-related pay schemes: conditions for registration.
Schedule 9—Approved share option schemes and profit sharing schemes.
      Part I   General.
      Part II Requirements generally applicable.
      Part III Requirements applicable to savings-related share option schemes.
      Part IV Requirements applicable to other share option schemes.
      Part V Requirements applicable to profit sharing schemes.
      Part VI Material interest test.
Schedule 10—Further provisions relating to profit sharing schemes.
Schedule 11—Relief as respects tax on payments on retirement or removal from office or employment.
      Part I   General provisions.
      Part II Payments in pursuance of pre-10th March 1981 obligations.
Schedule 12—Foreign earnings.
Schedule 13—Collection of advance corporation tax.
Schedule 14—Provisions ancillary to section 266.
      Part I   Modification of section 266 in certain cases.
      Part II Supplementary provisions as to relief under section 266.
Schedule 15—Qualifying policies.
      Part I   Qualifying conditions.
      Part II Certification of qualifying policies.
      Part III Policies issued by non-resident companies.
Schedule 16—Collection of income tax on company payments which are not distributions.
Schedule 17—Dual resident investing companies.
      Part I   Division of accounting periods covering 1st April 1987.
      Part II Early payments of interest etc. and charges on income.
      Part III General.
Schedule 18—Group relief: equity holders and profits or assets available for distribution.
Schedule 19—Apportionment of income of close companies.
      Part I   Determination of relevant income and distributions.
      Part II Procedure.
Schedule 19A—Underwriters: Assessment and Collection of Tax.
Schedule 20—Charities: qualifying investments and loans.
      Part I   Qualifying investments.
      Part II Qualifying loans.
      Part III Attribution of excess non-qualifying expenditure to earlier chargeable periods.
Schedule 21—Tax relief in connection with schemes for rationalizing industry and other redundancy schemes.
      Part I   Preliminary.
      Part II Relief in respect of certain payments.
      Part III Exclusion of relief in respect of contributions paid after relief has been given under Part II.
Schedule 22—Reduction of pension fund surpluses.
Schedule 23—Occupational pension schemes: schemes approved before 23rd July 1987.
Schedule 24—Assumptions for calculating chargeable profits, creditable tax and corresponding United Kingdom tax of foreign companies.
Schedule 25—Cases excluded from direction-making powers.
      Part I   Acceptable distribution policy.
      Part II Exempt activities.
      Part III The public quotation condition.
      Part IV Reductions in United Kingdom tax and diversion of profits.
Schedule 26—Reliefs against liability for tax in respect of chargeable profits.
Schedule 27—Distributing funds.
      Part I   The distribution test.

         Part II   Modifications of conditions for certification in certain cases.
         Part III   Certification procedure.
         Part IV   Supplementary.
Schedule 28—Computation of offshore income gains.
         Part I   Disposals of interests in non-qualifying funds.
         Part II   Disposals involving an equalisation element.
Schedule 29—Consequential amendments.
Schedule 30—Transitional provisions and savings.
Schedule 31—*Repeals*. (amending)

An Act to consolidate certain of the enactments relating to income tax and corporation tax, including certain enactments relating also to capital gains tax; and to repeal as obsolete section 339(1) of the Income and Corporation Taxes Act 1970 and paragraphs 3 and 4 of Schedule 11 to the Finance Act 1980. [9th February 1988]

PART I

THE CHARGE TO TAX

Income tax

1. The charge to income tax

(1) Income tax shall be charged in accordance with the provisions of the Income Tax Acts in respect of all property, profits or gains respectively described or comprised in the Schedules, A, . . .[4], C, D, E and F, set out in sections 15 to 20 or which in accordance with the Income Tax Acts are to be brought into charge to tax under any of those Schedules or otherwise.

(2) Where any Act enacts that income tax shall be charged for any year, income tax shall be charged for that year—

(*a*) in respect of any income which does not fall within paragraph (*b*) below, at such rate as Parliament may determine to be the basic rate for that year;
[(*b*) in respect of so much of an individual's total income as exceeds £[. . .][5], at such higher rate as Parliament may determine][1];

but this subsection has effect subject to any provision of the Income Tax Acts providing for income tax to be charged at a different rate in certain cases.

(3) The amount up to which an individual's income is by virtue of subsection (2) above chargeable for any year at the basic rate shall be known as the basic rate limit; . . .[3]

(4) If the retail prices index for the month of December preceding a year of assessment is higher than it was for the previous December, then, unless Parliament otherwise determines, subsection (2) above shall apply for that year as if for [the amount][2] specified in that subsection as it applied for the previous year (whether by virtue of this subsection or otherwise) there were substituted an amount arrived at by increasing the amount for the previous year by the same percentage as the percentage increase in the retail prices index and, if the result is not a multiple of £100, rounding it up to the nearest amount which is such a multiple.

(5) Subsection (4) above shall not require any change to be made in the amounts deductible or repayable under section 203 between the beginning of a year of assessment and [. . . May][6] in that year.

(6) The Treasury shall before each year of assessment make an order specifying the [amount][2] which by virtue of subsection (4) above will be treated as specified for that year in subsection (2) above.

(7) Part VII contains general provisions relating to the taxation of income of individuals.

Former enactments.—Sub-s. (1): TA 1970, s. 1.
Sub-s. (2): TA 1970, s. 1; FA 1971, s. 32(1); FA 1980, s. 24(2); FA 1987, s. 20(1).
Sub-s. (3): FA 1980, s. 24(3); FA 1984, Sch. 7, para 3(5).
Sub-ss. (4)–(6): FA 1980, s. 24(4), (7), (9).
Cross references.—See FA 1989, s. 30 (the basic rate for the year 1989–90 is 25 per cent.; the higher rate for the year 1989–90 is 40 per cent.).
Amendments.—[1] Sub-s. (2)(*b*) substituted by FA 1988, s. 24(2).
[2] Words in sub-ss. (4), (6) substituted by *ibid*.
[3] Words in sub-s. (3) repealed by FA 1988, s. 24(2)(*b*) and Sch. 14, Pt. IV.
[4] The reference to Schedule B in sub-s. (1) repealed by FA 1988, Sch. 14, Pt. V.
[5] The amount in sub-s. (2)(*b*) is £20,700 for the year 1989–90 by virtue of FA 1989, s. 30 and the Income Tax (Indexation) Order 1989, S.I. 1989 No. 467.
[6] The date in sub-s. (5) is "18th May" for the year 1989–90 by virtue of FA 1989, s. 32.

2. Fractions of a pound, and yearly assessments

(1) The due proportion of income tax shall be charged for every fractional part of one pound.

(2) Every assessment and charge to income tax shall be made for a year commencing on the 6th April and ending on the following 5th April.

Former enactment.—TA 1970, s. 2.

3. Certain income charged at basic rate

Where a person is required to be assessed and charged with income tax in respect of any property, profits or gains out of which he makes any payment in respect of—

   (a) any annuity or other annual payment (not being interest); or
   (b) any royalty or other sum in respect of the user of a patent; or
   (c) any rent, royalty or other payment which is declared by section 119 or 120 to be subject to deduction of tax under section 348 or 349 as if it were a royalty or other sum paid in respect of a patent;

he shall, in respect of so much of the property, profits or gains as is equal to the payment and may be deducted in computing his total income, be charged at the basic rate.

Former enactments.—TA 1970, s. 3; FA 1971, Sch. 6, para. 2.

4. Construction of references in Income Tax Acts to deduction of tax

(1) Any provision of the Income Tax Acts requiring, permitting or assuming the deduction of income tax from any amount (otherwise than in pursuance of section 203) or treating income tax as having been deducted from or paid on any amount, shall, subject to any provision to the contrary, be construed as referring to deduction or payment of income tax at the basic rate in force for the relevant year of assessment.

(2) For the purposes of subsection (1) above, the relevant year of assessment shall be taken to be (except where otherwise provided)—

   (a) if the amount is an amount payable wholly out of profits or gains brought into charge to tax, the year in which the amount becomes due;
   (b) in any other case, the year in which the amount is paid.

Former enactments.—FA 1971, s. 36; F (No. 2) A 1975, s. 44(6).

5. Date for payment

(1) Subject to the provisions of the Income Tax Acts and in particular to subsection (2) below and section 203, income tax contained in an assessment for any year shall be payable on or before the 1st January in that year, or at the expiration of a period of 30 days beginning with the date of the issue of the notice of assessment, whichever is the later.

(2) Subject to subsection (3) below, income tax under Schedule D charged for any year on any individual or firm in respect of the profits or gains of any trade, profession or vocation and contained in an assessment for that year shall, instead of being payable in accordance with subsection (1) above, be payable in two equal instalments, the first on or before the 1st January in that year or at the expiration of the period referred to in subsection (1) above, and the second on or before the following 1st July; and the provisions of the Income Tax Acts as to the recovery of income tax shall apply to each instalment of the tax in the same manner as they apply to the whole amount of the tax.

(3) Where the date of the issue of the notice of assessment is later than the 1st June following the end of the year of assessment, subsection (2) above shall not have effect, and the tax shall be due and payable as provided in subsection (1) above.

(4) Except as otherwise provided by the Income Tax Acts, any income tax charged at a rate other than the basic rate on—

   (a) income from which income tax has been deducted (otherwise than under section 203); or
   (b) income from or on which income tax is treated as having been deducted or paid; or
   (c) income chargeable under Schedule F;

shall be due and payable on or before 1st December following the end of the year for which it is assessed, or at the expiration of a period of 30 days beginning with the date of the issue of the notice of assessment, whichever is the later.

Former enactments.—TA 1970, s. 4; FA 1971, Sch. 6, para. 3; FA 1972, Sch. 24, para 15; F (No. 2) A 1975, s. 44(1); FA 1980, s. 61(1).

Corporation tax

6. The charge to corporation tax and exclusion of income tax and capital gains tax

(1) Corporation tax shall be charged on profits of companies, and the Corporation Tax Acts shall apply, for any financial year for which Parliament so determines, and where an Act charges corporation tax for any financial year the Corporation Tax Acts apply, without any express provision, for that year accordingly.

(2) The provisions of the Income Tax Acts relating to the charge of income tax shall not apply to income of a company (not arising to it in a fiduciary or representative capacity) if—

(*a*) the company is resident in the United Kingdom, or
(*b*) the income is, in the case of a company not so resident, within the chargeable profits of the company as defined for the purposes of corporation tax by section 11(2).

(3) A company shall not be chargeable to capital gains tax in respect of gains accruing to it so that it is chargeable in respect of them to corporation tax or would be so chargeable but for an exemption from corporation tax.

(4) In this section, sections 7 to 12, 114, 115 (but subject to subsection (7)), 242, 243, 247 and 248, Part VIII, Chapter IV of Part X and Part XI, except in so far as the context otherwise requires—

(*a*) "profits" means income and chargeable gains; and
(*b*) "trade" includes "vocation", and also includes an office or employment or the occupation of woodlands in any context in which the expression is applied to that in the Income Tax Acts.

(5) Part VIII contains general provisions relating to the taxation of profits of companies.

Former enactment.—TA 1970, s. 238.
Note.—See **Prospective Legislation Notes** (Commercial Woodlands).

7. Treatment of certain payments and repayment of income tax

(1) No payment made by a company resident in the United Kingdom shall be treated for any purpose of the Income Tax Acts as paid out of profits or gains brought into charge to income tax; nor shall any right or obligation under the Income Tax Acts to deduct income tax from any payment be affected by the fact that the recipient is a company not chargeable to income tax in respect of the payment.

(2) Subject to the provisions of the Corporation Tax Acts, where a company resident in the United Kingdom receives any payment on which it bears income tax by deduction, the income tax thereon shall be set off against any corporation tax assessable on the company by an assessment made for the accounting period in which that payment falls to be taken into account for corporation tax (or would fall to be taken into account but for any exemption from corporation tax); and accordingly in respect of that payment the company, unless wholly exempt from corporation tax, shall not be entitled to a repayment of income tax before the assessment for that accounting period is finally determined and it appears that a repayment is due.

(3) Subsection (2) above does not apply to a payment of relevant loan interest to which section 369 applies.

(4) References in this section to payments received by a company apply to any received by another person on behalf of or in trust for the company, but not to any received by the company on behalf of or in trust for another person.

(5) Effect shall be given to section 6(2), to that section as modified by subsection (2) above and by section 11(3) and, so far as exemptions from income tax conferred by the Corporation Tax Acts call for repayment of tax, to those exemptions by means of a claim.

Former enactments.—Sub-ss. (1), (2): TA 1970, s. 240(4), (5).
Sub-s. (3): FA 1982, s. 26(7).
Sub-s (4): TA 1970, s. 240(7).
Sub-s. (5): TA 1970, s. 241.

8. General scheme of corporation tax

(1) Subject to any exceptions provided for by the Corporation Tax Acts, a company shall be chargeable to corporation tax on all its profits wherever arising.

(2) A company shall be chargeable to corporation tax on profits accruing for its benefit under any trust, or arising under any partnership, in any case in which it would be so chargeable if the profits accrued to it directly; and a company shall be chargeable to corporation tax on profits arising in the winding up of the company, but shall not otherwise be chargeable to corporation tax on profits accruing to it in a fiduciary or representative capacity except as respects its own beneficial interest (if any) in those profits.

(3) Corporation tax for any financial year shall be charged on profits arising in that year; but assessments to corporation tax shall be made on a company by reference to accounting periods, and the amount chargeable (after making all proper deductions) of the profits arising in an accounting period shall, where necessary, be apportioned between the financial years in which the accounting period falls.

In relation to accounting periods ending after such day, not being earlier than 31st March 1992, as the Treasury may by order appoint for the purposes of this subsection, this subsection shall have effect with the substitution for "assessments to corporation tax shall be made on a company" of "corporation tax shall be computed and chargeable (and any assessments shall accordingly be made)".

(4) In any financial year assessments for accounting periods falling wholly or partly in that year or (subject to subsection (5) below) in the preceding year may, notwithstanding that corporation tax has not at the time been charged for the year in question, charge tax for so much of the period as falls within that year according to the rate of tax and the other rates and the fractions last fixed, but any such charge shall be subject to later adjustment, if need be, by discharge or repayment of tax or by a further assessment if for that year corporation tax is not charged by an Act of Parliament passed not later than 5th August next after the end of the year or is charged otherwise than as it has been assessed.

(5) Where the House of Commons passes a resolution for fixing the rate of corporation tax for any financial year or for altering the tax for any financial year, then any assessment to tax afterwards made by virtue of subsection (4) above may be made in accordance with the resolution; but no assessment made by virtue of that subsection later than 5th May next after the end of any financial year shall charge tax for that year, unless a resolution for charging corporation tax for that year has been so passed, nor shall any assessment be made by virtue of any such resolution later than the prescribed period from the date on which the resolution is passed.

(6) In subsection (5) above "the prescribed period" means—

(*a*) as respects a resolution passed in March or April in any year, a period beginning with the passing of the resolution and ending with 5th August in the same calendar year,
(*b*) as respects any other resolution, four months after the date on which the resolution is passed.

Former enactments.—TA 1970, s. 243(1)–(3), (5)–(7); FA 1974, s. 36; F (No. 2) A 1987, s. 90(1)(*a*).

9. Computation of income: application of income tax principles

(1) Except as otherwise provided by the Tax Acts, the amount of any income shall for purposes of corporation tax be computed in accordance with income tax principles, all questions as to the amounts which are or are not to be taken into account as income, or in computing income, or charged to tax as a person's income, or as to the time when any such amount is to be treated as arising, being determined in accordance with income tax law and practice as if accounting periods were years of assessment.

(2) For the purposes of this section "income tax law" means, in relation to any accounting period, the law applying, for the year of assessment in which the period ends, to the charge on individuals of income tax, except that it does not include such of the enactments of the

Income Tax Acts as make special provision for individuals in relation to matters referred to in subsection (1) above.

(3) Accordingly, for purposes of corporation tax, income shall be computed, and the assessment shall be made, under the like Schedules and Cases as apply for purposes of income tax, and in accordance with the provisions applicable to those Schedules and Cases, but (subject to the provisions of the Corporation Tax Acts) the amounts so computed for the several sources of income, if more than one, together with any amount to be included in respect of chargeable gains, shall be aggregated to arrive at the total profits.

(4) Without prejudice to the generality of subsection (1) above, any provision of the Income Tax Acts which confers an exemption from income tax, or which provides for a person to be charged to income tax on any amount (whether expressed to be income or not, and whether an actual amount or not), shall, except as otherwise provided, have the like effect for purposes of corporation tax.

(5) Where, by virtue of this section or otherwise, any enactment applies both to income tax and to corporation tax—

(a) it shall not be affected in its operation by the fact that they are distinct taxes but, so far as is consistent with the Corporation Tax Acts, shall apply in relation to income tax and corporation tax as if they were one tax, so that, in particular, a matter which in a case involving two individuals is relevant for both of them in relation to income tax shall in a like case involving an individual and a company be relevant for him in relation to that tax and for it in relation to corporation tax; and

(b) for that purpose references in any such enactment to a relief from or charge to income tax, or to a specified provision of the Income Tax Acts shall, in the absence of or subject to any express adaptation, be construed as being or including a reference to any corresponding relief from or charge to corporation tax, or to any corresponding provision of the Corporation Tax Acts.

(6) The provisions of the Income Tax Acts applied by this section do not include sections 1 to 5, 60 to 69, Part VII or sections 348 to 350 of this Act; and nothing in this section shall be taken to mean that income arising in any period is to be computed by reference to any other period (except in so far as this results from apportioning to different parts of a period income of the whole period).

Former enactment.—TA 1970, s. 250.

10. Time for payment of tax

(1) Except as provided by section 478—

(a) corporation tax for an accounting period ending after such day or days (not being earlier than 31st March 1992) as the Treasury may by order appoint for the purposes of this section shall be due and payable on the day following the expiry of nine months from the end of that period; and

(b) corporation tax assessed for any other accounting period shall be paid within nine months from the end of that period or, if it is later, within 30 days from the date of the issue of the notice of assessment.

(2) Notwithstanding that, by virtue of subsection (1)(a) above or section 419(1), any corporation tax (or any amount payable as if it were corporation tax) is due without the making of an assessment, no proceedings for collecting that tax (or other amount) shall be instituted—

(a) unless it has been assessed; and
(b) until the expiry of the period of 30 days beginning on the date on which the notice of assessment is issued;

and the reference in this subsection to proceedings for collecting tax or any other amount includes a reference to proceedings by way of distraint or poinding for that tax or other amount.

(3) If, with respect to any accounting period—

(a) a company has paid an amount of corporation tax without the making of an assessment; and
(b) at any time before an assessment to corporation tax for the period becomes final, the company has grounds for believing that, by reason of a change in the circumstances of the case since the tax was paid, the amount paid exceeds the company's probable liability for corporation tax,

the company may, by notice given to the inspector on or after the date which, under section 826, is the material date in relation to that tax, make a claim for the repayment to the company of the amount of that excess; and a notice under this subsection shall state the amount which the company considers should be repaid and the grounds referred to in paragraph (*b*) above.

(4) If, apart from this subsection, a claim would fall to be made under subsection (3) above at a time when the company concerned has appealed against such an assessment as is referred to in paragraph (*b*) of that subsection but that appeal has not been finally determined, that subsection shall have effect as if, for the words from "make a claim" to "excess", there were substituted "apply to the Commissioners to whom the appeal stands referred for a determination of the amount which should be repaid to the company pending a determination of the company's liability for the accounting period in question"; and such an application shall be determined in the same way as the appeal.

(5) Where on an appeal against an assessment to corporation tax a company makes an application under section 55(3) or (4) of the Management Act (postponement of tax charged but not paid etc.), that application may be combined with an application under subsections (3) and (4) above (relating to tax which was paid prior to the assessment).

Former enactments.—TA 1970, s. 243(4); F (No. 2) A 1975, s. 44(2); F (No. 2) A 1987, s. 90(1)(*b*), (4)–(7).
Note.—See **Prospective Legislation Notes** (Taxes Management Provisions).

11. Companies not resident in United Kingdom

(1) A company not resident in the United Kingdom shall not be within the charge to corporation tax unless it carries on a trade in the United Kingdom through a branch or agency but, if it does so, it shall, subject to any exceptions provided for by the Corporation Tax Acts, be chargeable to corporation tax on all its chargeable profits wherever arising.

(2) For purposes of corporation tax the chargeable profits of a company not resident in the United Kingdom but carrying on a trade there through a branch or agency shall be—

(*a*) any trading income arising directly or indirectly through or from the branch or agency, and any income from property or rights used by, or held by or for, the branch or agency (but so that this paragraph shall not include distributions received from companies resident in the United Kingdom); and
(*b*) such chargeable gains accruing on the disposal of assets situated in the United Kingdom as are by section 12 of the 1979 Act made chargeable to capital gains tax in the case of an individual not resident or ordinarily resident in the United Kingdom.

(3) Subject to section 447, where a company not resident in the United Kingdom receives any payment on which it bears income tax by deduction, and the payment forms part of, or is to be taken into account in computing, the company's income chargeable to corporation tax, the income tax thereon shall be set off against any corporation tax assessable on that income by an assessment made for the accounting period in which the payment falls to be taken into account for corporation tax; and accordingly in respect of that payment the company shall not be entitled to a repayment of income tax before the assessment for that accounting period is finally determined and it appears that a repayment is due.

(4) Subsection (3) above does not apply to a payment of relevant loan interest to which section 369 applies.

Former enactments.—Sub-ss. (1)–(3): TA 1970, s. 246; CGTA 1979, Sch. 7.
Sub-s. (4): FA 1982, s. 26(7).
Cross references.—See FA 1989, s. 127(6)(*b*) (deemed disposals of assets ceasing to be situated in the UK or of assets belonging to persons ceasing to carry on trade etc. in the UK through a branch or agency after 13 March 1989),
s. 129(6)(*b*) (withdrawal of roll-over relief in certain circumstances after 13 March 1989 in relation to non-residents trading through a branch or agency),
s. 131(6)(*b*) (deemed disposals of oil exploration or exploitation assets ceasing to be dedicated to a participator's oil field or of such assets belonging to non-residents ceasing to carry on trade in the UK through a branch or agency after 13 March 1989),
s. 134(1)(*b*) (provisions authorising the Board to take certain actions for recovering tax owed by non-resident companies for chargeable gains on disposals after 13 March 1989).

12. Basis of, and periods for, assessment

(1) Except as otherwise provided by the Corporation Tax Acts, corporation tax shall be assessed and charged for any accounting period of a company on the full amount of the profits arising in the period (whether or not received in or transmitted to the United Kingdom) without any other deduction than is authorised by those Acts.

(2) An accounting period of a company shall begin for purposes of corporation tax whenever—

(*a*) the company, not then being within the charge to corporation tax, comes within it, whether by the company becoming resident in the United Kingdom or acquiring a source of income, or otherwise; or

(*b*) an accounting period of the company ends without the company then ceasing to be within the charge to corporation tax.

(3) An accounting period of a company shall end for purposes of corporation tax on the first occurrence of any of the following—

(*a*) the expiration of 12 months from the beginning of the accounting period;
(*b*) an accounting date of the company or, if there is a period for which the company does not make up accounts, the end of that period;
(*c*) the company beginning or ceasing to trade or to be, in respect of the trade or (if more than one) of all the trades carried on by it, within the charge to corporation tax;
(*d*) the company beginning or ceasing to be resident in the United Kingdom;
(*e*) the company ceasing to be within the charge to corporation tax.

(4) For the purposes of this section a company resident in the United Kingdom, if not otherwise within the charge to corporation tax, shall be treated as coming within the charge to corporation tax at the time when it commences to carry on business.

(5) If a company carrying on more than one trade makes up accounts of any of them to different dates, and does not make up general accounts for the whole of the company's activities, subsection (3)(*b*) above shall apply with reference to the accounting date of such one of the trades as the Board may determine.

(6) If a chargeable gain or allowable loss accrues to a company at a time not otherwise within an accounting period of the company, an accounting period of the company shall then begin for the purposes of corporation tax, and the gain or loss shall accrue in that accounting period.

(7) Notwithstanding anything in subsections (1) to (6) above, where a company is wound up, an accounting period shall end and a new one begin with the commencement of the winding up, and thereafter, subject to section 342(6), an accounting period shall not end otherwise than by the expiration of 12 months from its beginning or by the completion of the winding up.

For this purpose a winding up is to be taken to commence on the passing by the company of a resolution for the winding up of the company, or on the presentation of a winding up petition if no such resolution has previously been passed and a winding up order is made on the petition, or on the doing of any other act for a like purpose in the case of a winding up otherwise than under the Insolvency Act 1986.

(8) Where it appears to the inspector that the beginning or end of any accounting period of a company is uncertain, he may make an assessment on the company for such period, not exceeding 12 months, as appears to him appropriate, and that period shall be treated for all purposes as an accounting period of the company unless either—

(*a*) the inspector on further facts coming to his knowledge sees fit to revise it; or
(*b*) on an appeal against the assessment in respect of some other matter the company shows the true accounting periods;

and if on an appeal against an assessment made by virtue of this subsection the company shows the true accounting periods, the assessment appealed against shall, as regards the period to which it relates, have effect as an assessment or assessments for the true accounting periods, and there may be made such other assessments for any such periods or any of them as might have been made at the time when the assessment appealed against was made.

Former enactments.—TA 1970, s. 247; FA 1972, s. 107(1).
Note.—See **Prospective Legislation Notes** (Taxes Management Provisions).

Small companies' rate

13. Small companies' relief

(1) Where in any accounting period the profits of [a company which—

(*a*) is resident in the United Kingdom, and
(*b*) is not a close investment-holding company (as defined in section 13A) at the end of that period,]²

do not exceed the lower relevant maximum amount, the company may claim that the corporation tax charged on its basic profits for that period shall be calculated as if the rate of corporation tax (instead of being the rate fixed for companies generally) were such lower rate (to be known as the "small companies' rate") as Parliament may from time to time determine.

(2) Where in any accounting period the profits of any such company exceed the lower relevant maximum amount but do not exceed the upper relevant maximum amount, the company may claim that the corporation tax charged on its basic profits for that period shall be reduced by a sum equal to such fraction as Parliament may from time to time determine of the following amount—

$$(M-P) \times \frac{I}{P}$$

where—

M is the upper relevant maximum amount;

P is the amount of the profits; and

I is the amount of the basic profits.

(3) The lower and upper relevant maximum amounts mentioned above shall be determined as follows—

(*a*) where the company has no associated company in the accounting period, those amounts are [£150,000][1] and [£750,000][1] respectively;

(*b*) where the company has one or more associated companies in the accounting period, the lower relevant maximum amount is [£150,000][1] divided by one plus the number of those associated companies, and the upper relevant maximum amount is [£750,000][1] divided by one plus the number of those associated companies.

(4) In applying subsection (3) above to any accounting period of a company, an associated company which has not carried on any trade or business at any time in that accounting period (or, if an associated company during part only of that accounting period, at any time in that part of that accounting period) shall be disregarded and for the purposes of this section a company is to be treated as an "associated company" of another at a given time if at that time one of the two has control of the other or both are under the control of the same person or persons.

In this subsection "control" shall be construed in accordance with section 416.

(5) In determining how many associated companies a company has got in an accounting period or whether a company has an associated company in an accounting period, an associated company shall be counted even if it was an associated company for part only of the accounting period, and two or more associated companies shall be counted even if they were associated companies for different parts of the accounting period.

(6) For an accounting period of less than 12 months the relevant maximum amounts determined in accordance with subsection (3) above shall be proportionately reduced.

(7) For the purposes of this section the profits (but not the basic profits) of a company for an accounting period shall be taken to be the amount of its profits for that period on which corporation tax falls finally to be borne, with the addition of franked investment income other than franked investment income which the company (if a member of a group) receives from companies within the group; and for this purpose distributions received by the company from another are to be treated as coming from within the company's group if, but only if, dividends so received are group income or would be group income if the companies so elected.

(8) For the purposes of this section the basic profits of a company for an accounting period shall be taken to be the amount of its profits for that period on which corporation tax falls finally to be borne.

(9) Any power which the inspector may exercise under [paragraphs 2 to 4 of Schedule 12 to the Finance Act 1989][3] may be exercised by him for the purposes of this section.

Former enactments.—FA 1972, s. 95; FA 1973, Sch. 14, para. 2; F (No. 2) A 1983, s. 2(2); F (No. 2) A 1987, s. 74(4).

Cross references.—See FA 1989, s. 35(1)(*b*) (the fraction for the purposes of sub-s. (2) of this section is one fortieth for the year 1989),

s. 88(4) (policy holder's fraction of profits to be disregarded in calculating for the purposes of this section a life assurance company's profits).

Amendments.—[1] Amounts in sub-s. (3)(*a*), (*b*) substituted for "£100,000" and "£500,000" by FA 1989, s. 35(2), (3) from the financial year 1989. Where this section has effect with different relevant maximum amounts in relation to different parts of a company's accounting period, those parts are to be treated as if they were separate accounting periods and the profits and basic profits of the company for that period are to be apportioned between those parts.

[2] Words in sub-s. (1) substituted by FA 1989, s. 105(1).

[3] Words in sub-s. (9) substituted by FA 1989, Sch. 12, para. 7.

[13A. Close investment-holding companies

(1) A close company is for the purposes of section 13(1) a "close investment-holding company" unless it complies with subsection (2) below.

(2) A company ("the relevant company") complies with this subsection in any accounting period if throughout that period it exists wholly or mainly for any one or more of the following purposes—
: (a) the purpose of carrying on a trade or trades on a commercial basis,
: (b) the purpose of making investments in land or estates or interests in land in cases where the land is, or is intended to be, let to persons other than—
:: (i) any person connected with the relevant company, or
:: (ii) any person who is the wife or husband of an individual connected with the relevant company, or is a relative, or the wife or husband of a relative, of such an individual or of the husband or wife of such an individual,
: (c) the purpose of holding shares in and securities of, or making loans to, one or more companies each of which is a qualifying company or a company which—
:: (i) is under the control of the relevant company or of a company which has control of the relevant company, and
:: (ii) itself exists wholly or mainly for the purpose of holding shares in or securities of, or making loans to, one or more qualifying companies,
: (d) the purpose of co-ordinating the administration of two or more qualifying companies,
: (e) the purpose of a trade or trades carried on on a commercial basis by one or more qualifying companies or by a company which has control of the relevant company, and
: (f) the purpose of the making, by one or more qualifying companies or by a company which has control of the relevant company, of investments as mentioned in paragraph (b) above.

(3) For the purposes of subsection (2) above, a company is a "qualifying company", in relation to the relevant company, if it—
: (a) is under the control of the relevant company or of a company which has control of the relevant company, and
: (b) exists wholly or mainly for either or both of the purposes mentioned in subsection (2)(a) or (b) above.

(4) Where a company is wound up, it shall not be treated as failing to comply with subsection (2) above in the accounting period that (by virtue of subsection (7) of section 12) begins with the time which is for the purposes of that subsection the commencement of the winding up, if it complied with subsection (2) above in the accounting period that ends with that time.

(5) In this section—
: "control" shall be construed in accordance with section 416, and
: "relative" has the meaning given by section 839(8).

(6) Section 839 shall apply for the purposes of this section.][1]

Cross references.—See FA 1989, Sch. 12, para.1 (administrative provisions relating to close companies).
Amendments.—[1] This section inserted by FA 1989, s. 105(2), (3) in relation to accounting periods beginning after 31 March 1989.

Advance corporation tax

14. Advance corporation tax and qualifying distributions

(1) Subject to section 247, where a company resident in the United Kingdom makes a qualifying distribution it shall be liable to pay an amount of corporation tax ("advance corporation tax") in accordance with subsection (3) below.

(2) In this Act "qualifying distribution" means any distribution other than—
: (a) a distribution which, in relation to the company making it, is a distribution by virtue only of section 209(2)(c); or
: (b) a distribution consisting of any share capital or security which the company making the distribution has directly or indirectly received from the company by which the share capital or security was issued and which, in relation to the latter company, is a distribution by virtue only of section 209(2)(c).

(3) Subject to section 241, for the financial year 1988 and any subsequent financial year advance corporation tax shall be payable on an amount equal to the amount or value of the distribution, and shall be so payable at a rate which shall be fixed by the fraction—

$$\frac{I}{100-I}$$

where I is the percentage at which income tax at the basic rate is charged for the year of assessment which begins on 6th April in that financial year.

(4) The provisions of this Act as to the charge, calculation and payment of corporation tax (including provisions conferring any exemption) shall not be construed as affecting the charge, calculation or payment of advance corporation tax, and the Corporation Tax Acts shall apply for the purposes of advance corporation tax whether or not they are for the time being applicable for the purposes of corporation tax other than advance corporation tax.

(5) Part VI contains further provisions relating to advance corporation tax and company distributions.

Former enactments.—Sub-s. (1): FA 1972, s. 84(1).
Sub-s. (2): FA 1972, s. 84(4).
Sub-s. (3): FA 1972, s. 84(2); FA 1986, s. 17(1), (5).
Sub-s (4): FA 1972, s. 111(2).

The six Schedules

15. Schedule A

(1) The Schedule referred to as Schedule A is as follows:—

SCHEDULE A

1. Tax under this Schedule shall be charged on the annual profits or gains arising in respect of any such rents or receipts as follows, that is to say—
    (*a*) rents under leases of land in the United Kingdom;
    (*b*) rentcharges, ground annuals and feuduties, and any other annual payments reserved in respect of, or charged on or issuing out of, such land;
    (*c*) other receipts arising to a person from or by virtue of his ownership of an estate or interest in or right over such land or any incorporeal hereditament or incorporeal heritable subject in the United Kingdom.

2. Tax under this Schedule shall be charged by reference to the rents or receipts to which a person becomes entitled in the chargeable period.

Exceptions

3. Paragraph 1 above does not apply—
    (*a*) to any yearly interest, or
    [(*aa*) to any profits or gains arising from a person's occupation of any woodlands which are managed on a commercial basis and with a view to the realisation of profits, or]¹
    (*b*) to any profits or gains charged to tax under Schedule D by virtue of section 55, or
    (*c*) to any payment so charged by virtue of section 119 or 120;
and has effect subject also to the provisions of section 98 with respect to tied premises.

4. Where rent is payable under a lease under which the tenant is entitled to the use of furniture and tax in respect of the payment for its use is chargeable under Case VI of Schedule D, tax in respect of the rent shall be charged under that Case instead of under this Schedule unless the landlord elects that this paragraph shall not apply.

(2) An election that paragraph 4 of Schedule A shall not apply shall be made by notice to the inspector given within two years after the end of the chargeable period; and where such notice is given, any adjustment of the liability to tax of the person giving it which is required in consequence thereof may be made by an assessment or by repayment or otherwise as the case may require.

(3) . . .²

(4) Part II contains further provisions relating to the charge to tax under Schedule A.

Former enactment.—Sub-s (1): TA 1970, s. 67.
Cross references.—See FA 1988, Sch. 6, para. 6(2), (9) and Sch. 14, Pt. V (amendment to TA 1970, s. 67(1), (3) effective from 6 April 1988).
Amendments.—¹ Para. 3(*aa*) in sub-s. (1) inserted by FA 1988, Sch. 6, para. 6(6), (9).
² Sub-s. (3) repealed by FA 1988, Sch. 14, Pt. V.

16. Schedule B

Former enactments.—Sub-s. (1): TA 1970, s. 91.
Sub-ss. (2)–(6): TA 1970, s. 92; FA 1984, s. 51.

Cross references.—See FA 1988, Sch. 14, Pt. V (repeal of TA 1970, Pt. IV (i.e. ss. 91, 92) with effect from 6 April 1988).
Amendments.—This section repealed by FA 1988, Sch. 14, Pt. V.

17. Schedule C

(1) The Schedule referred to as Schedule C is as follows:—

SCHEDULE C

1. Tax under this Schedule shall be charged in respect of all profits arising from public revenue dividends payable in the United Kingdom in any chargeable period.

2. Tax under this Schedule shall also be charged in respect of profits arising from public revenue dividends payable in the Republic of Ireland in any chargeable period, being dividends on securities of the United Kingdom government entered in the register of the Bank of Ireland in Dublin.

[3. Where a banker or any other person in the United Kingdom obtains payment of any overseas public revenue dividends by means of coupons received from any other person or otherwise on his behalf and either—

(*a*) the payment of those dividends was not entrusted to any person in the United Kingdom, or

(*b*) the securities in respect of which those dividends are paid are held in a recognised clearing system,

tax under this Schedule shall be charged in respect of those dividends.][1]

4. Where—

(*a*) any banker in the United Kingdom sells or otherwise realises coupons for any overseas public revenue dividends and pays over the proceeds to any person or carries them to his account, or

(*b*) any dealer in coupons in the United Kingdom purchases any such coupons otherwise than from a banker or another dealer in coupons,

tax under this Schedule shall be charged in respect of the proceeds of the sale or other realisation.

5. Notwithstanding anything in paragraphs 1 to 4 above but subject to paragraph 6 below, where any half-yearly payment in respect of any dividend entrusted to the Bank of England or the Bank of Ireland for payment and distribution or which is payable by the National Debt Commissioners or of which they have the distribution does not exceed £2.50, it shall not be charged under this Schedule, but shall be assessed and charged under Case III of Schedule D.

6. Paragraph 5 above does not apply to any payment obtained by means of a coupon in respect of a bond to bearer or stock certificate.

(2) Part III contains further provisions relating to the charge to tax under Schedule C and to government securities; and section 45 shall apply for the interpretation of Schedule C.

Former enactments.—TA 1970, s. 93; Decimal Currency Act 1969, s. 10.
Amendments.—[1] Para. 3 in sub-s. (1) substituted by FA 1988, s. 76(1), (6) with respect to payments obtained after the passing of FA 1988. FA 1988 was passed on 29 July 1988.

18. Schedule D

(1) The Schedule referred to as Schedule D is as follows:—

SCHEDULE D

Tax under this Schedule shall be charged in respect of—

(*a*) the annual profits or gains arising or accruing—

(i) to any person residing in the United Kingdom from any kind of property whatever, whether situated in the United Kingdom or elsewhere, and

(ii) to any person residing in the United Kingdom from any trade, profession or vocation, whether carried on in the United Kingdom or elsewhere, and

(iii) to any person, whether a Commonwealth citizen or not, although not resident in the United Kingdom from any property whatever in the United Kingdom or from any trade, profession or vocation exercised within the United Kingdom, and

(*b*) all interest of money, annuities and other annual profits or gains not charged under Schedule A, ...[1] C or E, and not specially exempted from tax.

(2) Tax under Schedule D shall be charged under the Cases set out in subsection (3) below, and subject to and in accordance with the provisions of the Tax Acts applicable to those Cases respectively.

(3) The Cases are—

Case I: tax in respect of any trade carried on in the United Kingdom or elsewhere;

Case II: tax in respect of any profession or vocation not contained in any other Schedule;

Case III: tax in respect of—

(*a*) any interest of money, whether yearly or otherwise, or any annuity or other annual payment, whether such payment is payable within or out of the United Kingdom, either as a charge on any property of the person paying the same by virtue of any deed or will or otherwise, or as a reservation out of it, or as a personal debt or obligation by virtue of any contract, or whether the same is received and payable half-yearly or at any shorter or more distant periods, but not including any payment chargeable under Schedule A, and

(*b*) all discounts, and

(*c*) income, except income charged under Schedule C, from securities bearing interest payable out of the public revenue;

Case IV: tax in respect of income arising from securities out of the United Kingdom except such income as is charged under Schedule C;

Case V: tax in respect of income arising from possessions out of the United Kingdom not being income consisting of emoluments of any office or employment;

Case VI: tax in respect of any annual profits or gains not falling under any other Case of Schedule D and not charged by virtue of Schedule A, . . .[1] C or E.

(4) The provisions of Schedule D and of subsection (2) above are without prejudice to any other provision of the Tax Acts directing tax to be charged under Schedule D or under one or other of the Cases set out in subsection (3) above, and tax directed to be so charged shall be charged accordingly.

(5) Part IV contains further provisions relating to the charge to tax under Schedule D.

Former enactments.—Sub-s. (1): TA 1970, s. 108(1); British Nationality Act 1981, s. 51.
Sub-ss. (2), (3): TA 1970, s. 109(1), (2).
Sub-s. (4): TA 1970, ss. 108(3), 109(3).
Cross references.—See FA 1988, Sch. 14, Pt. V (repeal of the reference to Schedule B in TA 1970, ss. 108(1)(*b*), 109(2) Case VI with effect from 6 April 1988).
Amendments.—[1] The reference to Schedule B in sub-ss. (1)(*b*), (3) Case VI repealed by FA 1988, Sch. 14, Pt. V.

19. Schedule E

(1) The Schedule referred to as Schedule E is as follows—

SCHEDULE E

1. Tax under this Schedule shall be charged in respect of any office or employment on emoluments therefrom which fall under one or more than one of the following Cases—

[Case I: any emoluments for any year of assessment in which the person holding the office or employment is resident and ordinarily resident in the United Kingdom, subject however to section 192 if the emoluments are foreign emoluments (within the meaning of that section) and to section 193(1) if in the year of assessment concerned he performs the duties of the office or employment wholly or partly outside the United Kingdom;][1]

[Case II: any emoluments, in respect of duties performed in the United Kingdom, for any year of assessment in which the person holding the office or employment is not resident (or, if resident, not ordinarily resident) in the United Kingdom, subject however to section 192 if the emoluments are foreign emoluments (within the meaning of that section);][1]

[Case III: any emoluments for any year of assessment in which the person holding the office or employment is resident in the United Kingdom (whether or not ordinarily resident there) so far as the emoluments are received in the United Kingdom;][1]

and tax shall not be chargeable in respect of emoluments of an office or employment under any other paragraph of this Schedule.

2. Tax under this Schedule shall be charged in respect of every annuity, pension or stipend payable by the Crown or out of the public revenue of the United Kingdom or of Northern Ireland, other than annuities charged under Schedule C.

3. Tax under this Schedule shall also be charged in respect of any pension which is paid otherwise than by or on behalf of a person outside the United Kingdom.

4. Where—

(*a*) any pension or annuity is payable in the United Kingdom by or through any public department, officer or agent of a government of a territory to which this paragraph applies (but otherwise than out of the public revenue of the United Kingdom or of Northern Ireland) to a person who has been employed in relevant service outside the United Kingdom in respect of that service, or

(*b*) any pension or annuity is so payable to the widow, child, relative or dependant of any such person as is mentioned above,

and the person in receipt of the pension or annuity is chargeable to tax as a person resident in the United Kingdom, the pension or annuity shall be chargeable to tax under this Schedule.

The territories to which this paragraph applies are—

(i) any country forming part of Her Majesty's dominions,
(ii) any other country for the time being mentioned in Schedule 3 to the British Nationality Act 1981, and
(iii) any territory under Her Majesty's protection;

and in this paragraph "relevant service" means the service of the Crown or service under the government of a territory to which this paragraph applies.

[4A. Where (apart from this paragraph) emoluments from an office or employment would be for a year of assessment in which a person does not hold the office or employment, the following rules shall apply for the purposes of the Cases set out in paragraph 1 above—

(*a*) if in the year concerned the office or employment has never been held, the emoluments shall be treated as emoluments for the first year of assessment in which the office or employment is held;

(*b*) if in the year concerned the office or employment is no longer held, the emoluments shall be treated as emoluments for the last year of assessment in which the office or employment was held.][2]

5. The preceding provisions of this Schedule are without prejudice to any other provision of the Tax Acts directing tax to be charged under this Schedule and tax so directed to be charged shall be charged accordingly.

(2) References in the Tax Acts to Cases I, II and III of Schedule E shall be taken as referring to the Cases under which tax is chargeable under paragraph 1 of that Schedule.

(3) Part V contains further provisions relating to the charge to tax under Schedule E.

Former enactments.—TA 1970, s. 181; FA 1974, s. 21(1); FA 1977, s. 31(3)(*a*); British Nationality Act 1981, Sch. 7.
Cross references.—See FA 1989, s. 41(1)(*a*) (income tax in respect of pension, stipend or annuity chargeable under this section to be charged in the year it accrues irrespective of when it is paid).
Amendments.—[1] Cases I, II, III substituted by FA 1989, s. 36(2), (4) from the year 1989–90. Originally Cases I, II, III read as follows and are reproduced for the benefit of FA 1989, ss. 38(1)(*b*), 39(1)(*c*)—

"Case I: where the person holding the office or employment is resident and ordinarily resident in the United Kingdom, any emoluments for the chargeable period, subject however to section 192 if the emoluments are foreign emoluments (within the meaning of that section) and to section 193(1) if in the chargeable period he performs the duties of the office or employment wholly or partly outside the United Kingdom and subject also to section 170;

Case II: where that person is not resident or, if resident, then not ordinarily resident in the United Kingdom, any emoluments for the chargeable period in respect of duties performed in the United Kingdom, subject however to section 192 if the emoluments are foreign emoluments (within the meaning of that section) and subject also to section 170;

Case III: where that person is resident in the United Kingdom (whether or not ordinarily resident there) any emoluments received in the United Kingdom in the chargeable period being emoluments either for that period or for an earlier period in which he has been resident there and any emoluments for that period received in the United Kingdom in an earlier period;".

[2] Paragraph 4A in sub-s. (1) inserted by FA 1989, s. 36(3), (5) where each of the years mentioned in sub-paras. (*a*) or (*b*) (as the case may be) is 1989–90 or a subsequent year.

20. Schedule F

(1) The Schedule referred to as Schedule F is as follows:—

SCHEDULE F

1. Subject to section 95(1)(*a*), income tax under this Schedule shall be chargeable for any year of assessment in respect of all dividends and other distributions in that year of a company resident in the United Kingdom which are not specially excluded from income tax, and for the purposes of income tax all such distributions shall be regarded as income however they fall to be dealt with in the hands of the recipient.

2. [Except as provided by section 450 (underwriters)][1] for the purposes of this Schedule and all other purposes of the Tax Acts any such distribution in respect of which a person is entitled to a tax credit shall be treated as representing income equal to the aggregate of the amount or value of that distribution and the amount of that credit, and income tax under this Schedule shall accordingly be charged on that aggregate.

(2) No distribution which is chargeable under Schedule F shall be chargeable under any other provision of the Income Tax Acts.

(3) Part VI contains further provisions relating to company distributions and tax credits.

Former enactments.—Sub-s. (1): TA 1970, s. 232(1); FA 1972, s. 87(2).
Sub-s. (2): FA 1972, s. 87(3).
Cross references.—See FA 1988, s. 61(3), (5) (amendment to FA 1972, s. 87(3) effective for the years 1986–87 and 1987–88).
Amendments.—[1] Words in para. 2 of Schedule F under sub-s. (1) inserted by FA 1988, s. 61(1)(*a*).

PART II

PROVISIONS RELATING TO THE SCHEDULE A CHARGE AND THE ASSOCIATED SCHEDULE D CHARGES

General

21. Persons chargeable

(1) Income tax under Schedule A shall be charged on and paid by the persons receiving or entitled to the profits or gains in respect of which tax under that Schedule is directed by the Income Tax Acts to be charged.

(2) Subsection (1) above does not apply for the purposes of the Corporation Tax Acts.

Former enactment.—TA 1970, s. 68.

22. Assessments

(1) The profits or gains arising to a person for any chargeable period which are assessable to tax under Schedule A may, if they arise from more than one source, be assessed in one or more assessments, and in the latter case, each assessment may relate to profits or gains from one or more sources.

(2) Subject to subsection (3) below, where an assessment to income tax under Schedule A for any year of assessment is made in that year—

(a) it shall be made on the basis that all sources of income and all amounts relevant in computing profits or gains are the same as for the last preceding year of assessment, and
(b) tax shall be leviable accordingly, but any necessary adjustments shall be made after the end of the year, whether by way of assessment, repayment of tax or otherwise, to secure that tax is charged by reference to the rents or receipts to which the person assessed becomes entitled in the year of assessment.

(3) If before the 1st January in any year a person delivers a statement in writing to the inspector—

(a) showing that since the beginning of the last preceding year of assessment he has ceased to possess one or more sources of income chargeable under Schedule A, and
(b) giving the aggregate of the rents and receipts relevant for the purposes of Schedule A to which he has become or is likely to become entitled in the current year ("the current aggregate"), and
(c) showing that the current aggregate is less than the aggregate of such rents and receipts to which he became entitled in the last preceding year ("the previous aggregate"), and that it would not have been less if he had not ceased to possess the said source or sources,

then, if the inspector is satisfied as to the correctness of the statement, an assessment made on that person in the current year shall be made on an amount which bears to the amount arrived at under subsection (2)(a) above the same proportion as the current aggregate bears to the previous aggregate, and subsection (2)(b) above shall apply accordingly.

Former enactments.—Sub-s. (1): TA 1970, s. 69(1).
Sub-ss. (2), (3): TA 1970, s. 69(2).

23. Collection from lessees and agents

(1) In any case where—

(a) any tax under Schedule A is charged in respect of profits or gains arising from any land to a person who is not the occupier of the land, and
(b) the tax is not paid by that person ("the person in default"),

the tax may be recovered in accordance with the following provisions of this section.

(2) Subject to subsection (3) below, the collector may from time to time, by notice in such

form as may be prescribed by the Board, require any lessee of the land or any part thereof whose interest is derived, directly or indirectly, from that held by the person in default, (a "derivative lessee"), to pay to him, on the date or dates specified in the notice, such sum or sums as may be required to satisfy the tax.

(3) The sum demanded from a derivative lessee to be paid during any period shall not exceed the amount of the rent or other payments arising out of the land which becomes due from him at the end of the period and payable to the person in default or to another derivative lessee.

(4) In default of payment by a derivative lessee of any amount duly demanded of him under subsection (2) above, that amount may be recovered from him in like manner as if he had been charged with tax of that amount.

(5) Where any sum on account of tax has been collected from a derivative lessee in pursuance of this section, he may deduct that sum from any subsequent payment arising and payable as mentioned in subsection (3) above, and shall be acquitted and discharged of the amount so deducted.

(6) Where under subsection (5) above, or under that subsection as applied by this subsection, a sum is deducted from an amount payable to another derivative lessee—

(a) that subsection shall apply as if the sum had been collected from him under a demand made under subsection (2) above by the collector; and
(b) where the amounts from which he is entitled, under subsection (5) above, to make deductions during the following 12 months are less than that sum, he shall be entitled to recover from the Board an amount equal to the difference, which shall be treated as reducing the tax recovered under the preceding provisions of this section.

(7) In any case where—

(a) rents or receipts from land are received by any person ("the agent") on behalf of another ("the principal"), and
(b) any tax under Schedule A charged on the principal has not been paid,

the collector may by notice, in such form as may be prescribed by the Board, require the agent to pay to the collector in or towards the satisfaction of the tax any sums from time to time received by the agent on behalf of the principal on account of rents or receipts from any land (including any sums so received which are in his hands when the notice is given) until the liability in respect of the tax has been satisfied; and the agent shall pay all such sums over to the collector accordingly, and the payment shall acquit and discharge him as against the person on whose behalf he received them.

(8) If the agent fails to comply with the requirements of a notice duly served on him, he shall be liable to a penalty not exceeding [£300][1] for each failure, and non-compliance as respects sums in his hands when the notice is given, or as respects any one payment subsequently received by him, shall be treated as a separate failure.

Former enactments.—Sub-s. (1): TA 1970, s. 70(1).
Sub-s. (2): TA 1970, s. 70(1)(a).
Sub-s. (3): TA 1970, s. 70(1)(b).
Sub-s. (4): TA 1970, s. 70(1)(c).
Sub-s. (5): TA 1970, s. 70(1)(d).
Sub-s. (6): TA 1970, s. 70(1)(e).
Sub-ss. (7), (8): TA 1970, s. 70(2).
Amendments.—[1] Amount in sub-s. (8) substituted for "£50" by FA 1989, s. 170(1), (6) in relation to things done or omitted after 26 July 1989.

24. Construction of Part II

(1) In this Part, except where the context otherwise requires—

"lease" includes an agreement for a lease, and any tenancy, but does not include a mortgage or heritable security, and "lessee", "lessor" and "letting" shall be construed accordingly;
"lessee" and "lessor" include respectively the successors in title of a lessee or a lessor;
"premises" includes any land; and
"premium" includes any like sum, whether payable to the immediate or a superior landlord or to a person connected (within the meaning of section 839) with the immediate or a superior landlord.

(2) For the purposes of this Part, any sum (other than rent) paid on or in connection with

the granting of a tenancy shall be presumed to have been paid by way of premium except in so far as other sufficient consideration for the payment is shown to have been given.

(3) Where paragraph (c) of section 38(1) applies, the premium, or an appropriate part of the premium, payable for or in connection with either lease mentioned in that paragraph may be treated as having been required under the other.

(4) References in this section to a sum shall be construed as including the value of any consideration, and references to a sum paid or payable or to the payment of a sum shall be construed accordingly.

(5) In the application of this Part to Scotland—

"assignment" means an assignation;
"intermediate landlord" means, where an occupying lessee is a sub-lessee, any person for the time being holding the interest of landlord under a sub-lease which comprises the property of which the occupying lessee is sub-lessee, but does not include the immediate landlord;
"premium" includes in particular a grassum payable to any landlord or intermediate landlord on the creation of a sub-lease; and
"reversion" means the interest of the landlord in the property subject to the lease.

(6) In Schedule A and in sections 25 to 31—

(a) references to a lease extend only to a lease conferring a right, as against the person whose interest is subject to the lease, to the possession of the premises;
(b) "rent" includes a payment by the tenant to defray the cost of work of maintenance of, or repairs to, the demised premises, not being work required by the lease to be carried out by the tenant; and
(c) "tenant's repairing lease" means a lease where the tenant is under an obligation to maintain and repair the whole or substantially the whole of the premises comprised in the lease.

(7) For the purposes of Schedule A and sections 25 to 31, a lease shall be taken to be at a full rent if the rent reserved under the lease (including an appropriate sum in respect of any premium under the lease) is sufficient, taking one year with another, to defray the cost to the lessor of fulfilling his obligations under the lease and of meeting any expenses of maintenance, repairs, insurance and management of the premises subject to the lease which fall to be borne by him.

Former enactments.—Sub-s. (1): TA 1970, s. 90(1); FA 1972, s. 81(3).
Sub-s. (2): TA 1970, s. 90(2).
Sub-ss. (3), (4): TA 1970, s. 90(2A), (2B); FA 1972, s. 81(4).
Sub-s. (5): TA 1970, s. 90(3).
Sub-ss. (6), (7): TA 1970, s. 71(2).

Deductions and other allowances

25. Deductions from rent: general rules

(1) In computing for the purposes of Schedule A the profits or gains arising to a person (the "person chargeable") in any chargeable period, the amounts of any permitted deductions shall be deducted from rent to which he becomes entitled under a lease in that period.

(2) In this section—

"permitted deductions" means any payments, except any payment of interest, made by the person chargeable in respect of any of the following matters—

(a) maintenance, repairs, insurance or management;
(b) any services provided by him otherwise than by way of maintenance or repairs, being services which he was obliged to provide but in respect of which he received no separate consideration;
(c) rates or other charges on the occupier which the person chargeable was obliged to defray;
(d) any rent, rentcharge, ground annual, feuduty or other periodical payment reserved in respect of, or charged on or issuing out of, land;

being payments which are deductible in accordance with subsections (3) to (9) below and section 26; and

"void period" means a period during which the person chargeable was not in occupation of the premises or any part thereof but was entitled to possession thereof.

(3) There may be deducted from rent to which the person chargeable becomes entitled in a chargeable period the amount of any permitted deduction which became due in that period, or at an earlier time falling within the currency of the lease, in so far as the payment—

    (*a*) was made in respect of the premises comprised in the lease, and
    (*b*) in the case of a payment for maintenance or repairs, was incurred by reason of dilapidation attributable to a period falling within the currency of the lease or, in the case of any other payment, was incurred in respect of such a period.

(4) Where the person chargeable became the landlord after the lease began, references in subsection (3) above to the currency of the lease shall not include any time before he became the landlord.

(5) In the case of a lease at a full rent, subsection (3) above shall have effect as if references to the currency of the lease included any period ("a previous qualifying period")—

    (*a*) during which the person chargeable was the landlord in relation to a previous lease of the premises, being a lease at a full rent; or
    (*b*) which was a void period beginning either with the termination of an earlier lease at a full rent of the premises or with the acquisition by the person chargeable of the interest in the premises giving him the right to possession thereof;

but a period shall not be a previous qualifying period if it preceded a period ending before the beginning of the lease which was not itself a previous qualifying period.

(6) Where during any period the conditions necessary for the period to be a previous qualifying period were fulfilled as respects part of the premises, but not the whole, the period shall be treated as a previous qualifying period as respects that part of the premises only, and subsection (5) above shall have effect accordingly, any necessary apportionment being made of rent, payments or other matters.

(7) In the case of a lease at a full rent, not being a tenant's repairing lease, there may also be deducted the amount of any payment made in respect of other premises by the person chargeable—

    (*a*) in so far as that amount could be deducted under subsections (3) and (5) above from rent to which he became entitled in the chargeable period under a lease of those other premises, being a lease at a full rent, or could be so deducted if that rent were not insufficient, or
    (*b*) if any part of the chargeable period is, in respect of those other premises, a void period beginning with the termination of a lease at a full rent, in so far as the amount could be so deducted if the lease had continued until the end of the period.

(8) Where by reason of any change of circumstances a lease ceases to be, or becomes, a tenant's repairing lease, or ceases to be, or becomes, a lease at a full rent, subsections (5) and (7) above shall apply in relation to the lease as it subsists after the change of circumstances as if it were a new lease granted when the change occurred.

(9) Where the person chargeable retains possession of a part of the premises and that part is used in common by persons respectively occupying other parts of the premises, this section shall apply as if a payment made in respect of the part used in common had been made in respect of those other parts.

Former enactments.—Sub-s. (1): TA 1970, ss. 71(1), 72(1).
Sub-s. (2): TA 1970, s. 72(1), (3), (7).
Sub-ss. (3), (4): TA 1970, s. 72(2).
Sub-ss. (5), (6): TA 1970, s. 72(3).
Sub-s. (7): TA 1970, s.72(4).
Sub-s. (8): TA 1970, s.72(5).
Sub-s. (9): TA 1970, s. 72(6).

26. Deductions from rent: land managed as one estate

(1) Where this section applies to an estate for a chargeable period, the owner shall be treated—

    (*a*) in relation to a part of the estate which for any portion of that period is not comprised in a lease under which he is the landlord, as if he were entitled under a lease of that part at a full rent (not being a tenant's repairing lease) to rent for that portion, becoming due from day to day, at a rate per annum equal to the relevant annual value, and
    (*b*) in relation to a part of the estate which for any portion of that period is comprised in a lease under which he is the landlord, not being a lease at a full rent, as if the lease were

at a full rent, and as if the rent so far as it relates to that part were at a rate per annum not less than the relevant annual value;

and section 25 shall apply accordingly.

(2) In any case where subsection (1) above applies—

(*a*) a payment relating to premises comprised in the estate shall not be deductible from rent in respect of premises not so comprised; and
(*b*) paragraph (*a*) of that subsection shall not apply to premises occupied by the owner wholly and exclusively for purposes connected with the management of the estate or for the purposes of a trade, profession or vocation.

(3) This section shall apply to an estate if, at the end of the year 1962–63, the land comprised in the estate was managed as one estate and the owner for the time being of the estate by notice to the inspector so elects; but such an election—

(*a*) must be made within 12 months after the end of the first chargeable period for which the person making it became entitled to make it or such further time as the Board may allow;
(*b*) except in the case of the first election that can be made under this subsection or the first election made under section 73(2) of the 1970 Act, shall not have effect unless an election under this section has had effect as respects the immediately preceding ownership;
(*c*) shall apply in relation to the estate throughout the ownership of the person making it.

(4) Where in any chargeable period the estate comprises premises not included in it at the end of the year 1962–63, subsection (1) above (but not subsection (2)) shall apply in relation to the chargeable period as if the premises were not included in the estate in that period.

(5) Subsection (4) above shall not have effect in relation to any premises if—

(*a*) at the end of the year 1962–63 the owner of the remainder of the estate as then subsisting was entitled under trusts arising under a settlement or on an intestacy, or in Scotland, under a disposition by way of liferent and fee, to an interest such that, on the occurrence of some future event or events, he might become the owner of the premises in question, and
(*b*) before the end of that year, the premises and the remainder of the estate, as then subsisting, were together managed as one estate.

(6) In this section—

"estate" means land in one ownership managed as one estate (but without prejudice to section 27); and
"relevant annual value", in relation to any part of an estate, means the annual value of that part ascertained in accordance with section 837.

Former enactments.—Sub-ss. (1), (2): TA 1970, s. 73(1).
Sub-s. (3): TA 1970, s.73(2).
Sub-s. (4): TA 1970, s.73(3).
Sub-s. (5): TA 1970, s. 73(3); FA 1987, Sch. 15, para. 2(6).
Sub-s. (6): TA 1970, s. 73(4).

27. Deductions from rent: maintenance funds for historic buildings

(1) Where a building or land which is qualifying property for the purposes of paragraph 3(1) of Schedule 4 to the Inheritance Tax Act 1984 (maintenance funds for historic buildings) forms part of an estate in relation to which an election has effect under section 26—

(*a*) the election shall not cease to have effect by reason only of another part of the estate becoming comprised in, and managed by the trustees of, a settlement in relation to which the Treasury give a direction under paragraph 1 of that Schedule, and
(*b*) while such a direction has effect that other part shall be treated as continuing to form part of the estate to which the election relates.

(2) In any case where—

(*a*) a person becomes the owner of any such building or land as is mentioned in subsection (1) above, and
(*b*) that building or land, in the immediately preceding ownership, formed part of an estate in relation to which an election under section 26 had effect,

any other part of that estate which continues to be or becomes comprised in a settlement of the kind mentioned in subsection (1) above shall, while such a direction as is mentioned in that subsection has effect, be treated as part of the estate in relation to which an election under section 26 may be made by him.

(3) Where by virtue of this section an election has effect in relation to an estate part of which is comprised in a settlement—

    (*a*) there may be treated as deductible from the rents arising from that part—

        (i) any payments which are made in respect of the other part of the estate by the trustees of the settlement and which would be so deductible under section 25 if that part were also comprised in the settlement; and
        (ii) any payments made in respect of the other part of the estate by its owner to the extent to which they cannot be deducted by him under that section in the chargeable period in which they become due because of an insufficiency of the rents arising in that period from that part; and

    (*b*) any relief available to the trustees under section 33 in respect of the part of the estate comprised in the settlement shall instead be available to the owner of the other part of the estate.

(4) Where by virtue of this section an election has effect in relation to an estate part of which is comprised in a settlement, the election shall not cease to have effect in relation to any of that part by reason of its ceasing to be comprised in that settlement if either—

    (*a*) it becomes comprised in another settlement in circumstances such that by virtue of paragraph 9(1) of Schedule 4 to the Inheritance Tax Act 1984 there is (or would but for paragraph 9(4) be) no charge to inheritance tax in respect of the property so ceasing; or
    (*b*) both immediately before and immediately after its so ceasing it is property in respect of which a direction has effect under paragraph 1 of that Schedule.

(5) The inclusion by virtue of this section in an estate of property comprised in a settlement shall not be construed as requiring it to be treated as the property of the person who owns the remainder of the estate or as affecting any question as to the person entitled to the income arising from that property.

Former enactments.—FA 1980, s. 53; FA 1982, Sch. 10, para. 3; IHTA 1984, Sch. 8, para. 18.
Note.—For the Inheritance Tax Act 1984, Sch. 4, para. 3(1), see *Butterworths Orange Tax Handbook*.

28. Deductions from receipts other than rent

Subject to section 122, where a person becomes entitled in a chargeable period to a sum other than rent payable under a lease, then in computing for the purposes of Schedule A the profits or gains arising to that person in that period, there shall be deducted from that sum—

    (*a*) so much of any payment made by that person as was made in respect of maintenance, repairs, insurance or management of premises to which the sum relates and constituted an expense of the transaction under which he became entitled to that sum;
    (*b*) so much of any rent, rentcharge, ground annual, feuduty or other periodical payment made by that person as was reserved in respect of, or was charged upon or issued out of, premises to which the sum relates and constituted an expense of that transaction;
    (*c*) so much of any other payment made by that person as constituted an expense of that transaction, not being an expense of a capital nature; and
    (*d*) where, in or before the chargeable period, that person entered into any like transaction, any amount which, under paragraphs (*a*) to (*c*) above, is deductible from a sum to which he is entitled under that like transaction in the period, or was deductible from a sum to which he was so entitled in a previous chargeable period but has not been deducted.

Former enactments.—Sub-s. (1): TA 1970, ss. 71(1), 74(1).Sub-s. (2): TA 1970, s. 74(2).

29. Sporting rights

(1) Subject to subsection (2) below, in any case where the person entitled to possession of any land ("the person chargeable")—

    (*a*) is in the practice of granting sporting rights over the land for payment, but
    (*b*) in any year of assessment, such rights are for any reason not granted by him,

the aggregate of any amounts paid by him which, if such rights had been granted in that year (the "relevant year"), would have been deductible under section 28 from payments receivable by him in respect of the grant shall be treated for the purposes of section 25(7) as a deduction which, by virtue of section 25(3), might have been made by him from rent to which he was entitled for that year under a lease of the land, being a lease at a full rent.

(2) If in the relevant year sporting rights over the land are exercised—

(*a*) by the person chargeable, or
(*b*) by any other person at his invitation, or
(*c*) where the person chargeable is a close company, by a person who is, within the meaning of Part XI, a director of, or a participator in, that company,

the aggregate referred to in subsection (1) above shall be treated as reduced by an amount equal to the price which might reasonably be expected to have been paid for that exercise of the rights if the person exercising them had had to give full consideration therefor.

(3) For the purposes of subsection (2) above, an exercise of sporting rights shall be disregarded if it gives rise to a charge to tax under Schedule E by virtue of section 154.

(4) Where the person chargeable is a company, section 9(1) shall not have effect so as to require references in that subsection to a year of assessment to be read as references to an accounting period, but any deduction thereby authorised shall be apportioned between the accounting periods (if more than one) comprising the year of assessment.

(5) In this section, "sporting rights" means rights of fowling, shooting or fishing, or of taking or killing game, deer or rabbits.

Former enactments.—Sub-s. (1): TA 1970, ss. 71(1), 75(1).
Sub-s. (2): TA 1970, s. 75(1).
Sub-ss. (3), (4), (5): TA 1970, s. 75(2), (3), (4); FA 1976, Sch. 9, para. 12.

30. Expenditure on making sea walls

(1) Where in any year of assessment the owner or tenant of any premises incurs any expenditure in the making of any sea wall or other embankment necessary for the preservation or protection of the premises against the encroachment or overflowing of the sea or any tidal river, he shall be treated for the purposes of sections 25, 28 and 31 as making in that year of assessment and in each of the succeeding 20 years of assessment a payment in relation to the premises preserved or protected by the embankment of an amount equal to a twenty-first part of the expenditure and incurred in respect of dilapidation attributable to the year.

(2) Where the whole of that person's interest in the premises or any part thereof is transferred (whether by operation of law or otherwise) to some other person—

(*a*) the amount of the payment which he would be so treated as making for the year of assessment in which the transfer takes place shall be treated as being made partly by the transferor and partly by the transferee, as may be just; and
(*b*) the transferee shall, to the exclusion of the transferor, be treated in any subsequent year—
  (i) where the interest transferred is in the whole of the premises, as having made the whole of the payment for that year, and
  (ii) where the interest transferred is in part only of the premises, as having made so much of the payment as is properly referable to that part of the premises.

(3) For the purposes of subsection (2) above, where an interest in any premises is a lease and that lease comes to an end, that interest shall be deemed to have been transferred—

(*a*) if an incoming lessee makes any payment to the outgoing lessee in respect of the embankment in question, to the incoming lessee, and
(*b*) in any other case, to the owner of the interest in immediate reversion on the lease and, in relation to Scotland, the expression "the owner of the interest in immediate reversion on the lease" shall be construed as a reference to the landlord.

(4) In relation to a company, section 9(1) shall not have effect so as to require references in this section to a year of assessment to be read as references to an accounting period, but any deduction authorised by this section shall be apportioned between the accounting periods (if more than one) comprising the year of assessment, other than any such period ended before the expenditure is incurred, or transfer takes place, by virtue of which the company is entitled to the deduction.

(5) This section shall not apply in relation to any expenditure in respect of which a capital allowance has been made.

Former enactment.—TA 1970, s. 76.

31. Provisions supplementary to sections 25 to 30

(1) Schedule 1, which makes provision in relation to certain expenditure incurred before the beginning of the year 1963–64, shall have effect (and the preceding provisions of this Part shall have effect subject to that Schedule).

(2) Any reference in this section to a deduction is a reference to a sum which is deductible under any of the provisions of sections 25 to 30 and Schedule 1, and any reference to a sum which can be deducted or which is deductible shall be construed accordingly.

(3) Subject to subsections (4) to (7) below, where a sum or part of a sum can be deducted for the chargeable period in which it is paid, it shall be so deducted, and, where it cannot, it shall be deducted for the earliest chargeable period for which it can be deducted.

(4) Where for any chargeable period the amount from which deductions can be made is sufficient to allow the deduction from that amount of some, but not all, of different sums or parts of sums which are deductible, the sum or parts to be deducted for that period shall in the aggregate be equal to that amount, and, subject to that requirement, shall be such as the person whose liability to tax is in question may choose.

(5) No deduction shall be made in respect of—

   (*a*) a payment made by any person to the extent that the payment has been or will be—
      (i) balanced by the receipt of insurance moneys, or
      (ii) recovered from, or in any other manner borne by, some other person, otherwise than by means of an amount on the profits or gains arising from which the first-mentioned person would be chargeable under Schedule A, or

   (*b*) a payment made by a person other than a company, if payable under deduction of income tax.

(6) An amount, or part of an amount, shall not be deducted more than once from any sum, or from more than one sum, and shall not in any case be deducted if it has otherwise been allowed as a deduction in computing the income of any person for tax purposes.

(7) Where, on account of a payment made in any chargeable period, a deduction falls to be made from any rents or receipts to which the person making the payment became entitled in a previous period, all such adjustments of liability to tax shall be made, by repayment or otherwise, as may be necessary to give effect to the deduction.

Former enactments.—Sub-s. (1): TA 1970, s. 71(1).
Sub-ss. (2), (3): TA 1970, s. 77(1); FA 1987, Sch. 15, para. 13.
Sub-ss. (4)–(7): TA 1970, s. 77(2)–(5).

32. Capital allowances for machinery and plant used in estate management

(1) Subject to the provisions of this section, Chapter II of Part I of the 1968 Act and Chapter I of Part III of the Finance Act 1971, and such other provisions of the Tax Acts as relate to allowances or charges under those Chapters, shall apply with any necessary adaptations in relation to machinery or plant provided for use or used by a person entitled to rents or receipts falling within Schedule A for the maintenance, repair or management of premises in respect of which those rents or receipts arise as they apply in relation to machinery or plant provided for use or used for the purposes of a trade.

(2) Except as provided by subsection (3) below, the Tax Acts shall apply in relation to any allowances or balancing charges which fall to be made by virtue of this section as if they were to be made in taxing a trade.

(3) Allowances and balancing charges which by virtue of this section fall to be made to or on a person for any chargeable period shall be made by—

   (*a*) adding the amount of any such allowances to the expenditure on maintenance, repair or management of the premises which is deductible under sections 25 or 28 in computing his profits or gains for the purposes of Schedule A; and

   (*b*) deducting the amount on which any such charge is to be made from that expenditure (or from the sum of that expenditure and any addition made to it under this subsection);

and sections 46 of the 1968 Act and 48 of the Finance Act 1971 (manner of making allowances or charges) shall not apply.

(4) Any charge falling to be made under this section shall, in so far as a deduction cannot be made for it under subsection (3)(*b*) above, be made under Case VI of Schedule D.

(5) No allowance or balancing charge shall be made by virtue of this section for any chargeable period in respect of expenditure incurred by any person on machinery or plant, except in pursuance of an election made by him for that period; but an election for any chargeable period shall have effect as an election for that and all subsequent chargeable periods.

(6) Any such election shall be made by notice to the inspector either for all machinery or plant provided for use or used for the maintenance, repair or management of the relevant premises or for any class of machinery or plant so provided or used; but an election for machinery or plant of any class shall not be made for any chargeable period after payments made in that or a subsequent chargeable period for the maintenance, repair or management of the relevant premises have been taken into account in an assessment or claim for repayment of tax which has been finally determined.

(7) Corresponding allowances or charges in the case of the same machinery or plant shall not be made under Chapter II of Part I of the 1968 Act or Chapter I of Part III of the Finance Act 1971 (whether for the same or different chargeable periods) both in computing profits or gains for the purposes of Schedule A and in some other way; and, on any assessment to tax, expenditure to which an election under this section applies shall not be taken into account otherwise than under those Chapters.

(8) The Tax Acts shall have effect as if this section were contained in Chapter II of Part I of the 1968 Act or Chapter I of Part III of the Finance Act 1971, as the case may require.

Former enactments.—Sub-ss. (1), (2): TA 1970, s. 78(1); FA 1971, s. 47(2).
Sub-ss. (3), (4): TA 1970, s. 78(2); FA 1971, s. 47(2).
Sub-ss. (5)–(8): TA 1970, s. 78(3)–(6); FA 1971, s. 47(2).

33. Agricultural land: allowance for excess expenditure on maintenance

(1) Where in the case of an estate which consists of or includes agricultural land—

(*a*) provision is made in sections 25 to 32 for the deduction of a sum in respect of payments in a chargeable period for maintenance, repairs, insurance or management of the estate, or in respect of allowances for machinery or plant provided for use or used on the estate, and

(*b*) owing to the insufficiency of rents and receipts to which the owner of the estate becomes entitled in that period, whether from the estate or from other property, the sum in question cannot be deducted (other amounts deductible under Schedule A being treated as deductible in priority thereto),

then, subject to subsection (2) below, the sum in question shall be treated as if it were the amount of an allowance falling to be made under the 1968 Act by way of discharge or repayment of tax, and available primarily against agricultural income as defined in section 69 of that Act.

(2) The sum in question shall not exceed the sum which would have fallen to be so treated if—

(*a*) the estate had not included such parts thereof as were used wholly for purposes other than purposes of husbandry, and

(*b*) payments or allowances in respect of parts thereof which were used partly for purposes of husbandry and partly for other purposes were reduced to an extent corresponding to the extent to which those parts were used for other purposes.

(3) In this section—

"agricultural land" means land, houses or other buildings in the United Kingdom occupied wholly or mainly for the purposes of husbandry; and

"estate" means any land (including any houses or other buildings) managed as one estate.

(4) Sections 71 and 74 of the 1968 Act shall apply as if this section were contained in Part I of that Act.

Former enactments.—Sub-ss. (1), (2): TA 1970, s. 79(1); FA 1987, Sch. 15, para. 13.
Sub-s. (3): TA 1970, s. 79(2).
Sub-s. (4): TA 1970, s. 79(1).

Premiums, leases at undervalue etc.

34. Treatment of premiums etc. as rent or Schedule D profits

(1) Where the payment of any premium is required under a lease, or otherwise under the terms subject to which a lease is granted, and the duration of the lease does not exceed 50 years, the landlord shall be treated for the purposes of the Tax Acts as becoming entitled when the lease is granted to an amount by way of rent (in addition to any actual rent) equal to—

$$P - \frac{(P \times Y)}{50}$$

where P is the premium and Y is the number of complete periods of 12 months (other than the first) comprised in the duration of the lease.

(2) Where the terms subject to which a lease is granted impose on the tenant an obligation to carry out any work on the premises, the lease shall be deemed for the purposes of this section to have required the payment of a premium to the landlord (in addition to any other premium) of an amount equal to the amount by which the value of the landlord's estate or interest immediately after the commencement of the lease exceeds what its then value would have been if those terms did not impose that obligation on the tenant.

(3) Subsection (2) above shall not apply in so far as the obligation requires the carrying out of work the payment for which would, if the landlord and not the tenant were obliged to carry it out, be deductible from the rent under sections 25 to 30.

(4) Where, under the terms subject to which a lease is granted, a sum becomes payable by the tenant in lieu of the whole or a part of the rent for any period, or as consideration for the surrender of the lease, the lease shall be deemed for the purposes of this section to have required the payment of a premium to the landlord (in addition to any other premium) of the amount of that sum; but—

(*a*) in computing tax chargeable by virtue of this subsection in respect of a sum payable in lieu of rent, the duration of the lease shall be treated as not including any period other than that in relation to which the sum is payable; and

(*b*) notwithstanding anything in subsection (1) above, rent treated as arising by virtue of this subsection shall be deemed to become due when the sum in question becomes payable by the tenant.

(5) Where, as a consideration for the variation or waiver of any of the terms of a lease, a sum becomes payable by the tenant otherwise than by way of rent, the lease shall be deemed for the purposes of this section to have required the payment of a premium to the landlord (in addition to any other premium) of the amount of that sum; but—

(*a*) in computing tax chargeable by virtue of this subsection, the duration of the lease shall be treated as not including any period which precedes the time at which the variation or waiver takes effect, or falls after the time at which it ceases to have effect; and

(*b*) notwithstanding anything in subsection (1) above, rent treated as arising by virtue of this subsection shall be deemed to become due when the contract providing for the variation or waiver is entered into.

(6) Where a payment falling within subsection (1), (4) or (5) above is due to a person other than the landlord, no charge to tax shall arise under that subsection, but any amount which would otherwise fall to be treated as rent shall be treated as profits or gains of that other person chargeable under Case VI of Schedule D.

(7) Subsection (6) above shall not apply in relation to any payment falling within subsection (5) above unless it is due to a person who is, within the meaning of section 839, connected with the landlord.

(8) Where an amount by reference to which a person is chargeable to tax by virtue of this section is payable by instalments ("the tax instalments"), the tax chargeable by reference to that amount may, if that person satisfies the Board that he would otherwise suffer undue hardship, be paid at his option by such instalments as the Board may allow over a period not exceeding eight years and ending not later than the time at which the last of the tax instalments is payable.

(9) Section 22(2) and (3) shall not apply in relation to amounts which, in computing profits or gains for the purposes of Schedule A, are relevant only by virtue of this section.

Former enactments.—Sub-ss. (1), (2): TA 1970, s. 80(1), (2).
Sub-s. (3): TA 1970, s. 80(2); FA 1987, Sch. 15, para. 13.

Sub-ss. (4), (5): TA 1970, s. 80(3), (4).
Sub-ss. (6), (7): TA 1970, s. 80(5).
Sub-ss. (8), (9): TA 1970, s. 80(6), (7); FA 1972, s. 81(1).

35. Schedule D charge on assignment of lease granted at an undervalue

(1) This section applies to any lease of a duration not exceeding 50 years where the terms subject to which it was granted are such that the grantor, having regard to values prevailing at the time it was granted and on the assumption that the negotiations for the lease were at arm's length, could have required the payment of an additional sum by way of premium, or additional premium, for the grant of the lease; and in this section any such additional sum is referred to as the "amount foregone".

(2) On any assignment of a lease to which this section applies for a consideration—

(a) where the lease has not previously been assigned, exceeding the premium, if any, for which it was granted, or
(b) where the lease has been previously assigned, exceeding the consideration for which it was last assigned,

the amount of the excess, in so far as it is not greater than the amount foregone reduced by the amount of any such excess arising on a previous assignment of the lease, shall in the same proportion as the amount foregone would, under section 34(1), have fallen to be treated as rent if it had been a premium under the lease, be treated as profits or gains of the assignor chargeable to tax under Case VI of Schedule D.

(3) If there is submitted to the inspector, by the grantor or any assignor or assignee of the lease, a statement showing whether or not a charge to tax arises or may arise under this section and, if so, the amount on which the charge arises or may arise, then, if the inspector is satisfied as to the accuracy of the statement, he shall certify the accuracy thereof.

Former enactments.—Sub-ss. (1), (2): TA 1970, s. 81(1).
Sub-s. (3): TA 1970, s. 81(2).

36. Schedule D charge on sale of land with right to reconveyance

(1) Where the terms subject to which an estate or interest in land is sold provide that it shall be, or may be required to be, reconveyed at a future date to the vendor or a person connected with him, the vendor shall be chargeable to tax under Case VI of Schedule D on any amount by which the price at which the estate or interest is sold exceeds the price at which it is to be reconveyed or, if the earliest date at which in accordance with those terms it would fall to be reconveyed is a date two years or more after the sale, on that excess reduced by one-fiftieth thereof for each complete year (other than the first) in the period between the sale and that date.

(2) Where, under the terms of the sale, the date of the reconveyance is not fixed, then—

(a) if the price on reconveyance varies with the date, the price shall be taken, for the purposes of this section, to be the lowest possible under the terms of the sale, and
(b) there shall be repaid to the vendor, on a claim made before the expiry of six years after the reconveyance takes place, any amount by which tax assessed on him by virtue of this section exceeded the amount which would have been so assessed if that date had been treated for the purposes of this section as the date fixed by the terms of the sale.

(3) Where the terms of the sale provide for the grant of a lease directly or indirectly out of the estate or interest to the vendor or a person connected with him, this section shall, subject to subsection (4) below, apply as if the grant of the lease were a reconveyance of the estate or interest at a price equal to the sum of the amount of the premium (if any) for the lease and the value at the date of the sale of the right to receive a conveyance of the reversion immediately after the lease begins to run.

(4) Subsection (3) above shall not apply in any case where the lease is granted and begins to run within one month after the sale.

(5) In this section references to a person connected with another shall be construed in accordance with section 839.

Former enactments.—Sub-ss. (1), (2): TA 1970, s. 82(1), (2).
Sub-ss. (3), (4): TA 1970, s. 82(3).
Sub-s. (5): TA 1970, s. 82(1), (3).

37. Premiums paid etc.: deductions from premiums and rent received

(1) This section applies in any case where in respect of a lease of any premises—

(*a*) tax has become chargeable under the provisions of section 34 or 35 on any amount (disregarding any reduction in that amount under subsection (2) below); or

(*b*) tax would have become so chargeable on that amount but for the operation of this subsection, or but for any exemption from tax;

and the amount of that tax is in this section referred to as "the amount chargeable on the superior interest" and any such lease is referred to as "the head lease".

(2) Where—

(*a*) a lease is granted out of, or there is a disposition of, the head lease, and

(*b*) in respect of that grant or disposition a person would, apart from this subsection, be chargeable under section 34 or 35 on any amount ("the later chargeable amount"),

then the amount on which he is so chargeable shall, subject to subsection (3) below, be the excess (if any) of the later chargeable amount over the appropriate fraction of the amount chargeable on the superior interest.

(3) Where a person would, apart from subsection (2) above, be chargeable under section 34 or 35 in respect of a lease or disposition which extends to a part only of the premises subject to the head lease, the amount on which he is so chargeable shall be the excess (if any) of the later chargeable amount over the appropriate fraction of the amount chargeable on the superior interest as, on a just apportionment, is attributable to that part of the premises.

(4) Subject to subsection (5) below, the person for the time being entitled to the head lease shall be treated for the purposes of deductions under sections 25 and 26 from rent receivable by him in respect of those or other premises as paying rent for those premises (in addition to any actual rent), becoming due from day to day, during any part of the period in respect of which the amount chargeable on the superior interest arose for which he was entitled to the head lease, and, in all, bearing to that amount the same proportion as that part of the period bears to the whole.

(5) Where subsection (2) above applies, subsection (4) above shall apply for the period in respect of which the later chargeable amount arose only if the appropriate fraction of the amount chargeable on the superior interest exceeds the later chargeable amount, and shall then apply as if the amount chargeable on the superior interest were reduced in the proportion which that excess bears to that appropriate fraction.

(6) Where subsection (3) above applies, subsections (4) and (5) above shall be applied separately to the part of the premises referred to in subsection (3) above and to the remainder of the premises, but as if for any reference to the amount chargeable on the superior interest there were substituted a reference to that amount proportionately adjusted.

(7) For the purposes of this section—

(*a*) the appropriate fraction of the amount chargeable on the superior interest is the fraction—

$$\frac{A}{B}$$

where—

A is the period in respect of which the later chargeable amount arose; and
B is the period in respect of which the amount chargeable on the superior interest arose; and

(*b*) the period in respect of which an amount arose—

(i) where it arose under section 34, shall be the period treated in computing the amount as being the duration of the lease;

(ii) where it arose under section 35, shall be the period treated in computing the amount as being the duration of the lease remaining at the date of the assignment.

(8) Where the amount chargeable on the superior interest arose under section 34(2) by reason of an obligation which included the carrying out of work in respect of which any capital allowance has fallen or will fall to be made, subsections (1) to (6) above shall apply as if the obligation had not included the carrying out of that work and that amount had been calculated accordingly.

(9) An amount or part of an amount shall not be deducted under this section more than once from any sum, or from more than one sum, and shall not in any case be so deducted if

it has been otherwise allowed as a deduction in computing the income of any person for tax purposes.

Former enactments.—Sub-ss. (1), (2), (3): TA 1970, s. 83(1); FA 1978, s. 32(2).
Sub-s. (4): TA 1970, s. 83(2).
Sub-ss. (5), (6): TA 1970, s. 83(3).
Sub-s. (7): TA 1970, s. 83(4).
Sub-s. (8): TA 1970, s. 83(5).
Sub-s. (9): TA 1970, s. 83(7).

38. Rules for ascertaining duration of leases

(1) In ascertaining the duration of a lease for the purposes of sections 34 to 36—

(*a*) in any case where—

(i) any of the terms of the lease (whether relating to forfeiture or any other matter) or any other circumstances render it unlikely that the lease will continue beyond a date falling before the expiry of the term of the lease, and
(ii) the premium was not substantially greater than it would have been, on the assumptions required by subsections (3) and (4) below, had the term been one expiring on that date,

the lease shall not be treated as having been granted for a term longer than one ending on that date;
(*b*) where the terms of the lease include provision for the extension of the lease beyond a given date by notice given by the tenant, account may be taken of any circumstances making it likely that the lease will be so extended; and
(*c*) where the tenant or a person connected with him (within the meaning of section 839) is or may become entitled to a further lease or the grant of a further lease (whenever commencing) of the same premises or of premises including the whole or part of the same premises, the term of the lease may be treated as not expiring before the term of the further lease.

(2) Subsection (1) above shall be applied by reference to the facts which were known or ascertainable at the time of the grant of the lease, or in relation to tax under section 34(5), at a time when the contract providing for the variation or waiver is entered into.

(3) It shall be assumed in applying subsection (1) above that all parties concerned, whatever their relationship, act as they would act if they were at arm's length.

(4) In any case where—

(*a*) by the lease or in connection with the granting of it benefits were conferred other than—

(i) vacant possession and beneficial occupation of the premises, or
(ii) the right to receive rent at a reasonable commercial rate in respect of the premises, or

(*b*) payments were made which would not be expected to be made by parties acting at arm's length if no other benefits had been so conferred,

it shall also be assumed, unless it is shown that the benefits were not conferred or the payments made for the purpose of securing a tax advantage in the application of this Part, that the benefits would not have been conferred nor the payments made had the lease been for a term ending on the date mentioned in subsection (1)(*a*) above.

(5) Where an inspector has reason to believe that a person has information relevant to the ascertainment of the duration of a lease in accordance with subsections (1) to (4) above, the inspector may by notice require him to give, within a time specified in the notice, such information on the matters so specified as is in his possession; but a solicitor shall not be so required to do more, in relation to anything done by him on behalf of a client, than state that he is or was so acting and give the name and address of his client.

(6) In this section in relation to Scotland, the expression "term", where referring to the duration of a lease, means period.

(7) This section has effect subject to paragraphs 2 and 3 of Schedule 30.

Former enactments.—Sub-s. (1): TA 1970, s. 84(1)(*b*)–(*d*); FA 1972, s. 81(2)(*a*), (*b*).
Sub-ss. (2), (3), (4): TA 1970, s. 84(2); FA 1972, s. 81(2)(*c*).
Sub-s. (5): TA 1970, s. 84(3A); FA 1972, s. 81(5).
Sub-s. (6): TA 1970, s. 84(3); FA 1972, s. 81(2)(*d*).
Sub-s. (7): TA 1970, s. 84(4).

39. Saving for pre-1963 leases, and special relief for individuals

(1) Subject to subsection (2) below, sections 34 to 36 shall not apply in relation to a lease granted, or an estate or interest in land sold, before the beginning of the year 1963–64 or in pursuance of a contract entered into before 4th April 1963.

(2) Section 34(5) shall apply to the variation or waiver of any terms of a lease (not being a variation or waiver made in pursuance of a contract entered into before 4th April 1963) notwithstanding that the lease was granted before the beginning of the year 1963–64.

(3) . . .[1]

Former enactments.—Sub-ss. (1), (2): TA 1970, s. 85(1).
Sub-s. (3): TA 1970, s. 85(2).
Amendments.—[1] Sub-s. (3) repealed by FA 1988, s. 75 and Sch. 14, Pt. IV.

Supplemental: Schedules A and D

40. Tax treatment of receipts and outgoings on sale of land

(1) Where—

(*a*) by virtue of a contract for the sale of an estate or interest in land there falls to be apportioned between the parties a receipt or outgoing in respect of the estate or interest which becomes due after the making of the contract but before the time to which the apportionment falls to be made, and
(*b*) a part of the receipt is therefore receivable by the vendor in trust for the purchaser or, as the case may be, a part of the outgoing is paid by the vendor as trustee for the purchaser,

the purchaser shall be treated for the purposes of tax under Schedule A as if that part had become receivable or payable on his behalf immediately after the time to which the apportionment falls to be made.

(2) Where by virtue of such a contract there falls to be apportioned between the parties a receipt or outgoing in respect of the estate or interest which became due before the making of the contract, the parties shall be treated for the purposes of tax under Schedule A as if the contract had been entered into before the receipt or outgoing became due, and subsection (1) above shall apply accordingly.

(3) Where on the sale of an estate or interest in land there is apportioned to the vendor a part of a receipt or outgoing in respect of the estate or interest which is to become receivable or be paid by the purchaser after the making of the apportionment, then for the purposes of tax under Schedule A—

(*a*) when the receipt becomes due or, as the case may be, the outgoing is paid, the amount of it shall be treated as reduced by so much thereof as was apportioned to the vendor, and
(*b*) the part apportioned to the vendor shall be treated as if it were of the same nature as the receipt or outgoing and had become receivable, or had been paid, directly by him immediately before the time to which the apportionment is made and, where it is part of an outgoing, had become due immediately before that time.

(4) Any reference in subsection (1) or (2) above to a party to a contract shall include a person to whom the rights and obligations of that party under the contract have passed by assignment or otherwise.

(5) This section shall apply as respects tax under Case VI of Schedule D in a case falling within paragraph 4 of Schedule A as it applies as respects tax under Schedule A in other cases.

Former enactment.—TA 1970, s. 86.

41. Relief for rent etc. not paid

(1) Where on a claim in that behalf a person proves—

(*a*) that he has not received an amount which he was entitled to receive in respect of any rents or receipts on the profits or gains arising from which he would be chargeable under Schedule A; and
(*b*) if the non-receipt of that amount was attributable to the default of another person by whom it was payable, that the claimant has taken any reasonable steps available to him to enforce payment; or

(c) if the claimant waived payment of that amount, that the waiver was made without consideration, and was reasonably made in order to avoid hardship;

then subject to subsection (2) below, the claimant shall be treated for tax purposes for all relevant chargeable periods as if he had not been entitled to that amount, and such adjustments shall be made, by repayment or otherwise, as the case may require.

(2) If all or any part of that amount is subsequently received, the claimant or, if he is dead, his executors or administrators shall not later than six months thereafter give notice to the inspector, and such readjustment of liability to tax (for all relevant chargeable periods) shall be made as may be necessary, and may be made at any time at which it could be made if it related only to tax for the chargeable period in which the amount, or that part of the amount, is received.

(3) Subsection (1) above shall apply in relation to sums chargeable to tax under Case VI of Schedule D by virtue of any provision of sections 34 to 36 as it applies to profits or gains chargeable to tax under Schedule A.

Former enactments.—Sub-ss. (1), (2): TA 1970, s. 87(1).
Sub-s. (3): TA 1970, s. 87(2).

42. Appeals against determinations under sections 34 to 36

(1) Where it appears to the inspector that the determination of any amount on which a person may be chargeable to tax by virtue of section 34, 35 or 36 may affect the liability to income tax, corporation tax or capital gains tax of other persons he may give notice to those persons as well as to the first-mentioned person of the determination he proposes to make and of the rights conferred on them by this section.

(2) Any person to whom such a notice is given may, within 30 days after the date on which it is given, object to the proposed determination by notice given to the inspector.

(3) Where notices have been given under subsection (1) above and no notice of objection is duly given under subsection (2) above the inspector shall make the determination as proposed in his notices and the determination shall not be called in question in any proceedings.

(4) Where a notice of objection is duly given the amount mentioned in subsection (1) above shall be determined in like manner as an appeal and shall be so determined by the Special Commissioners or such body of General Commissioners as may be agreed on by the person to be charged and all persons who have given notice of objection.

(5) All persons to whom notices have been given under subsection (1) above may take part in any proceedings under subsection (4) above and in any appeal arising out of those proceedings and shall be bound by the determination made in the proceedings or on appeal, whether or not they have taken part in the proceedings; and their successors in title shall also be so bound.

(6) A notice under subsection (1) above may, notwithstanding any obligation as to secrecy or other restriction on the disclosure of information, include a statement of the grounds on which the inspector proposes to make the determination.

(7) An inspector may by notice require any person to give within the time specified in the notice such information as appears to the inspector to be required for deciding whether to give a notice under subsection (1) above to any person.

Former enactment.—FA 1972, s. 82.

43. Non-residents

(1) Section 78 of the Management Act (taxation of non-residents in name of agent) shall not apply to tax on profits or gains chargeable to tax under Schedule A, or on any of the profits or gains chargeable under Case VI of Schedule D—

(a) in a case falling within paragraph 4 of Schedule A; or
(b) which arise under the terms of a lease, but to a person other than the landlord, or otherwise arise out of any disposition or contract such that if they arose to the person making it they would be chargeable under Schedule A,

where payment is made (whether in the United Kingdom or elsewhere) directly to a person whose usual place of abode is outside the United Kingdom, but sections 349(1) and 350 shall apply in relation to the payment as they apply to annual payments charged with tax under Case III or IV of Schedule D and not payable out of profits or gains brought into charge to income tax.

(2) Subsection (1) above shall apply in relation to sums chargeable to tax under Case VI of Schedule D by virtue of any provision of sections 34 to 36 as it applies to profits or gains chargeable to tax under Schedule A.

(3) Where by virtue of subsection (1) above the income tax chargeable for any year of assessment on a person's profits or gains chargeable to tax under Schedule A or Case VI of Schedule D or both would, apart from this subsection, be greater than the tax which would be chargeable thereon apart from section 22(2) and (3), then, on a claim in that behalf being made, relief shall be given from the excess, whether by way of repayment or otherwise.

Former enactment.—TA 1970, s. 89.

PART III

PROVISIONS RELATING TO THE SCHEDULE C CHARGE AND GENERAL PROVISIONS ABOUT GOVERNMENT SECURITIES

General

44. Income tax: mode of charge

(1) Income tax under Schedule C shall be charged by the Board, and shall be paid on behalf of the persons entitled to the profits, dividends or proceeds which are the subject of the tax—

(*a*) in the case of tax charged under paragraph 1 of that Schedule, by the persons and bodies of persons respectively entrusted with payment;
(*b*) in the case of tax charged under paragraph 2 of that Schedule, by the Bank of England;
(*c*) in the case of tax charged under paragraph 3 or 4 of that Schedule, by the banker or other person, or by the banker or dealer in coupons, as the case may be.

(2) Schedule 3 shall have effect in relation to the assessment, charge and payment of income tax under Schedule C.

Former enactment.—TA 1970, s. 94.

45. Interpretation of Part III

In this Part—

"banker" includes a person acting as a banker;
"coupons" and "coupons for any overseas public revenue dividends" include warrants for and bills of exchange purporting to be drawn or made in payment of any overseas public revenue dividends;
"dividends" means any interest, public annuities, dividends or shares of annuities;
["overseas public revenue dividends" means public revenue dividends payable out of any public revenue other than that of the United Kingdom;][1]
"public revenue", except where the context otherwise requires, includes the public revenue of any government whatsoever, and the revenue of any public authority or institution in any country outside the United Kingdom; and
"public revenue dividends" means dividends payable out of any public revenue.

Former enactment.—TA 1970, s. 107, Sch. 5, para. 14.
Amendments.—[1] Definition of "overseas public revenue dividends" substituted by FA 1988, s. 76(2), (6) with effect after the passing of FA 1988. FA 1988 was passed on 29 July 1988.

Government securities: exemptions from tax

46. Savings certificates and tax reserve certificates

(1) Subject to subsections (3) to (6) below, income arising from savings certificates shall not be liable to tax.

(2) Tax shall not be chargeable in respect of the interest on tax reserve certificates issued by the Treasury.

(3) Subsection (1) above does not apply to any savings certificates which are purchased by or on behalf of a person in excess of the amount which a person is for the time being authorised to purchase under regulations made by the Treasury or, as respects Ulster Savings Certificates, by the Department of Finance and Personnel.

(4) Subsection (1) above does not apply to Ulster Savings Certificates unless—

(*a*) the holder is resident and ordinarily resident in Northern Ireland when the certificates are repaid; or
(*b*) the certificates were purchased by him and he was so resident and ordinarily resident when they were purchased.

(5) A claim under this section in respect of Ulster Savings Certificates shall be made to the Board.

(6) In this section "savings certificates" means savings certificates issued under section 12 of the National Loans Act 1968 or section 7 of the National Debt Act 1958 or section 59 of the Finance Act 1920 and any war savings certificates as defined in section 9(3) of the National Debt Act 1972, together with any savings certificates issued under any corresponding enactment forming part of the law of Northern Ireland.

Former enactments.—Sub-s. (1): FA 1981, s. 34(1).
Sub-s. (2): TA 1970, s. 98.
Sub-ss. (3)–(6): FA 1981, s. 34(2)–(5); CGTA 1979, s. 71(2)(*a*); Departments (Northern Ireland) Order 1982, S.I. 1982 No. 338.

47. United Kingdom government securities held by non-residents

(1) The interest on securities which—

(*a*) the Treasury have power to issue for the purpose of raising any money or any loan with a condition that the interest thereon shall not be liable to income tax so long as it is shown that the securities are in the beneficial ownership of persons who are not ordinarily resident in the United Kingdom, and
(*b*) have been issued with such a condition,

shall, subject to subsection (3) below, be exempt from tax accordingly.

(2) A claim under this section shall be made to the Board.

(3) Where any income of any person is, by virtue of any provision of the Tax Acts (and, in particular, but without prejudice to the generality of the preceding words, by virtue of Chapter III of Part XVII) to be deemed to be income of any other person, that income is not exempt from tax as being derived from a security issued by the Treasury with any condition regulating the treatment of the interest thereon for tax purposes by reason of the first-mentioned person not being ordinarily resident, or being neither domiciled nor ordinarily resident, in the United Kingdom.

Former enactment.—TA 1970, s. 99.

48. Securities of foreign states

(1) Subject to subsection (3) below, no tax shall be chargeable in respect of—

(*a*) dividends payable in the United Kingdom on the securities of any state or territory outside the United Kingdom, or
(*b*) any dividends or proceeds chargeable apart from this subsection under paragraph 3 or 4 of Schedule C,

if it is proved, on a claim in that behalf made to the Board, that the person owning the securities and entitled to the dividends or proceeds is not resident in the United Kingdom.

(2) Where—

(*a*) securities are held under a trust, and
(*b*) the person who is the beneficiary in possession is the sole beneficiary in possession and can, by means either of revocation of the trust or of the exercise of any powers under the trust, call upon the trustees at any time to transfer the securities to him absolutely free from any trust,

that person shall for the purposes of subsection (1) above be deemed to be the person owning the securities.

(3) Where any income of any person is, by virtue of any provision of the Tax Acts (and in particular, but without prejudice to the generality of the preceding words, by virtue of Chapter III of Part XVII) to be deemed to be income of any other person, that income is not exempt from tax by virtue of this section by reason of the first-mentioned person not being resident in the United Kingdom.

(4) Paragraph 1 of Schedule C shall not apply, in the case of dividends payable out of any public revenue other than the public revenue of the United Kingdom, if the securities in respect of which the dividends are payable are held in a recognised clearing system.

Former enactments.—Sub-ss. (1)–(3): TA 1970, s. 100.
Sub-s. (4): FA 1986, s. 48(1).

49. Stock and dividends in name of Treasury etc

(1) No tax shall be chargeable in respect of the stock or dividends transferred to accounts in the books of the Bank of England in the name of the Treasury or the National Debt Commissioners in pursuance of any Act of Parliament, but the Bank of England shall transmit to the Board an account of the total amount thereof.

(2) No tax shall be chargeable in respect of the stock or dividends belonging to the Crown, in whatever name they may stand in the books of the Bank of England.

Former enactment.—TA 1970, s. 106(1), (2).

Government securities: interest payable without deduction of tax

50. United Kingdom securities: Treasury directions for payment without deduction of tax

(1) The Treasury may direct that any of the following securities, that is to say—

(*a*) any securities issued under the War Loan Acts 1914 to 1919 or under section 60 of the Finance Act 1916;
(*b*) any securities issued or deemed to be issued under the National Loans Act 1939 or issued under the National Loans Act 1968;
(*c*) any government stock issued under section 1 of the Bank of England Act 1946, section 1 of the Cable and Wireless Act 1946, section 65(1) of the Town and Country Planning Act 1947 or section 62(1) of the Town and Country Planning (Scotland) Act 1947; and
(*d*) any such stock as is mentioned in section 33(1) of the Coal Industry Nationalisation Act 1946 or section 26(1) of the Iron and Steel Act 1967;

shall be issued, or shall be deemed to have been issued, subject to the condition that the interest thereon shall be paid without deduction of income tax; and subject to the provisions of this section the interest shall be so paid accordingly, but shall be chargeable under Case III of Schedule D.

(2) The holder of any registered securities the interest on which is by virtue of directions given under subsection (1) above payable without deduction of tax may make an application to the Bank under this subsection requesting that income tax shall be deducted from the interest on those securities before payment thereof.

(3) Where any such application is made, income tax in respect of the interest on those securities shall, so long as they remain registered in the name of the applicant and subject to the withdrawal of the application under subsection (5) below, be deducted and charged in the same manner as if they were not securities to which subsection (1) above applied.

(4) An application under subsection (2) above shall be made in such form as the Bank with the approval of the Treasury may prescribe, and any application made less than two months before the date on which a payment of interest falls due shall only have effect as regards any payment of interest subsequent to that payment.

(5) An application made under subsection (2) above may at any time be withdrawn by notice to the Bank in such form as the Bank may with the approval of the Treasury prescribe, but an application so withdrawn shall, notwithstanding the withdrawal, continue to have effect as regards any interest payable less than two months after the date the notice is received at the Bank.

(6) Where any securities to which subsection (2) above applies are held on trust, the holders of the securities may make an application under that subsection in respect thereof without the consent of any other person, notwithstanding anything in the instrument creating the trust.

(7) In this section—

"the Bank" means the Bank of England or the Bank of Ireland as the case requires, and "registered" means entered in the register of the Bank.

Former enactments.—Sub-s. (1): TA 1970, s. 101(1).
Sub-ss. (2), (3): TA 1970, s. 101(2).
Sub-ss. (4)–(7): TA 1970, s. 101(3)–(6).

51. Treasury directions as respects Northern Ireland securities

(1) The Treasury may, on the application of the Department of Finance and Personnel, as respects any securities to which this section applies, direct that the securities specified in the

direction shall be issued, or shall be deemed to have been issued, subject to the condition that the interest thereon shall be paid without deduction of income tax; and in relation to any securities so specified and the interest thereon, section 50 shall have effect as if—

(a) the securities were securities in respect of which a direction had been given by the Treasury under subsection (1) of that section;
(b) references in that section to "the Bank" were (notwithstanding subsection (7) of that section) references to the bank in the books of which the securities are registered or inscribed; and
(c) the references in subsections (4) and (5) of that section to the Treasury were references to the Department of Finance and Personnel.

(2) The securities to which this section applies are securities issued under section 11(1)(c) of the Exchequer and Financial Provisions Act (Northern Ireland) 1950 for money borrowed by the Department of Finance and Personnel for the purposes of making issues from the Consolidated Fund of Northern Ireland.

Former enactments.—TA 1970, s. 102; Northern Ireland Constitution Act 1973, Sch. 5, para. 8(1); Departments (Northern Ireland) Order 1982, S.I. 1982 No. 338.

52. Taxation of interest on converted government securities and interest which becomes subject to deduction

(1) Where the income which any individual is required under the Income Tax Acts to include in a statement of his total income for any year includes both—

(a) interest received without deduction of income tax in respect of government securities ("the original securities") which have been exchanged for any other government securities ("substituted securities"), and
(b) interest taxed by deduction in respect of such substituted securities,

and the amount of the interest so included exceeds the full amount of the interest for a complete year on the original securities, then, if that individual so requires—

(i) the excess shall not be taken into account in ascertaining his total income for that year for the purposes of income tax, but
(ii) the excess shall nevertheless be chargeable to income tax for that year at such rate or rates, and subject to such reliefs, if any, as would be applicable if it constituted the highest part of an income equal, subject to section 833(3), to the amount of his total income exclusive of the excess.

(2) Where an application is made under section 50(2) with respect to any securities, subsection (1) above shall have effect as if—

(a) during the period in which the interest on those securities was paid without deduction of income tax, those securities were original securities, and
(b) during any later period, they were substituted securities.

Former enactment.—TA 1970, s. 104.

PART IV

PROVISIONS RELATING TO THE SCHEDULE D CHARGE

CHAPTER I

SUPPLEMENTARY CHARGING PROVISIONS

53. Farming and other commercial occupation of land (except woodlands)

(1) All farming and market gardening in the United Kingdom shall be treated as the carrying on of a trade or, as the case may be, of a part of a trade, and the profits and gains thereof shall be charged to tax under Case I of Schedule D accordingly.

(2) All the farming carried on by any particular person or partnership or body of persons shall be treated as one trade.

(3) Subject to subsection (4) below, the occupation of land in the United Kingdom for any purpose other than farming or market gardening shall, if the land is managed on a commercial basis and with a view to the realisation of profits, be treated as the carrying on of a trade or, as the case may be, of a part of a trade, and the profits or gains thereof shall be charged to tax under Case I of Schedule D accordingly.

[(4) Subsection (3) above shall not apply in relation to the occupation of land which comprises woodlands or is being prepared for use for forestry purposes.][1]

Former enactments.—Sub-ss. (1), (2): TA 1970, s. 110(1), (2).
Sub-ss. (3), (4): TA 1970, s. 110(3).
Cross references.—See FA 1988, Sch. 6, para. 6(7) (the new sub-s. (4) as substituted by FA 1988, Sch. 6, para. 6(7) not to apply in certain circumstances),
Sch. 6, para. 6(3), (9) (amendment to TA 1970, s. 110(3) effective from 6 April 1988).
Amendments.—[1] Sub-s. (4) substituted by FA 1988, Sch. 6, para. 6(7). As originally enacted it read—
"(4) Subsection (3) above shall not affect the taxation of woodlands which are managed on a commercial basis and with a view to the realisation of profits."

54. Woodlands managed on a commercial basis

Former enactment.—TA 1970, s. 111.
Cross references.—See FA 1988, Sch. 6, para. 3(1), (7) and Sch. 14, Pt. V (repeal of TA 1970, s. 111 from 15 March 1988),
Sch. 6, paras. 4(7), (9), 5(1), (5) (an election under TA 1970, s. 111 made before 15 March 1988 in respect of commercial woodlands to have effect as if the election is for assessment and charge to tax under Schedule D).
Amendments.—This section repealed by FA 1988, Sch. 6, para. 3(1), (7) and Sch. 14, Pt. V with effect from 15 March 1988.

55. Mines, quarries and other concerns

(1) Profits or gains arising out of land in the case of any concern specified in subsection (2) below shall be charged to tax under Case I of Schedule D.

(2) The concerns are—

(*a*) mines and quarries (including gravel pits, sand pits and brickfields);
(*b*) ironworks, gasworks, salt springs or works, alum mines or works (not being mines falling within the preceding paragraph) and waterworks and streams of water;
(*c*) canals, inland navigation, docks and drains or levels;
(*d*) fishings;
(*e*) rights of markets and fairs, tolls, bridges and ferries;
(*f*) railways and other ways;
(*g*) other concerns of the like nature as any of the concerns specified in paragraphs (*b*) to (*e*) above.

Former enactment.—TA 1970, s. 112.

56. Transactions in deposits with and without certificates or in debts

(1) Subsection (2) below applies to the following rights—

(a) the right to receive the amount, with or without interest, stated in a certificate of deposit;

(b) the right to receive an amount payable with interest—

(i) in a transaction in which no certificate of deposit or security is issued, and

(ii) which is payable by a bank or similar institution or a person regularly engaging in similar transactions;

and the right to receive that interest.

(2) Profits or gains arising to a person from the disposal of a right to which this subsection applies or, except so far as it is a right to receive interest, from the exercise of any such right (whether by the person to whom the certificate was issued or by some other person, or, as the case may be, by the person who acquired the right in the transaction referred to in subsection (1) above or by some person acquiring it directly or indirectly from that person), shall, if not falling to be taken into account as a trading receipt, be treated as annual profits or gains chargeable to tax under Case VI of Schedule D.

(3) Subsection (2) above does not apply in the case of the disposal or exercise of a right to receive an amount stated in a certificate of deposit or interest on such an amount—

(a) if the person disposing of the right acquired it before 7th March 1973;

(b) to any profits or gains arising to a fund or scheme in the case of which provision is made by section 592(2), 613, 614(1) to (3) or 620(6) for exempting the whole or part of its income from income tax;

(c) in so far as they are applied to charitable purposes only, to any profits or gains arising to a charity within the meaning of section 506.

(4) For the purposes of this section, profits or gains shall not be treated as falling to be taken into account as a trading receipt by reason only that they are included in the computation required by section 76(2).

(5) In this section—

"certificate of deposit" means a document relating to money, in any currency, which has been deposited with the issuer or some other person, being a document which recognises an obligation to pay a stated amount to bearer or to order, with or without interest, and being a document by the delivery of which, with or without endorsement, the right to receive that stated amount, with or without interest, is transferable; and

"security" has the same meaning as in section 82 of the 1979 Act.

Former enactments.—Sub-s. (1)(a): FA 1973, s. 26(1); sub-s. (1)(b): FA 1974, s. 30(1).
Sub-s. (2): FA 1973, s. 26(1); FA 1974, s. 30(1).
Sub-s. (3): FA 1973, s. 26(1)(a), (b); F(No. 2)A 1975, s. 50(1).
Sub-s. (4): FA 1973, s. 26(3); FA 1974, s. 30(2).
Sub-s. (5): FA 1968, s. 55(3); FA 1973, s. 26(4); FA 1974, s. 30(1), (2); CGTA 1979, Sch. 7.

57. Deep discount securities

Schedule 4 shall have effect with respect to the treatment for the purposes of income tax and corporation tax of deep discount securities (within the meaning of that Schedule).

Former enactment.—FA 1984, s. 36(1).

58. Foreign pensions

(1) A pension which—

(a) is paid by or on behalf of a person outside the United Kingdom, and

(b) is not charged under paragraph 4 of Schedule E,

shall be charged to tax under Case V of Schedule D.

(2) Where—

(a) a person has ceased to hold any office or employment, and

(b) a pension or annual payment is paid to him, or to his widow or child or to any relative or dependant of his, by the person under whom he held the office or by whom he was employed, or by the successors of that person, and

(c) that pension or annual payment is paid by or on behalf of a person outside the United Kingdom,

then, notwithstanding that the pension or payment is paid voluntarily, or is capable of being discontinued, it shall be deemed to be income for the purposes of assessment to tax and shall be assessed and charged to tax under Case V of Schedule D as income from a pension.

Former enactment.—TA 1970, s. 113.

59. Persons chargeable

(1) Subject to subsections (2) and (3) below, income tax under Schedule D shall be charged on and paid by the persons receiving or entitled to the income in respect of which the tax is directed by the Income Tax Acts to be charged.

(2) Income tax to be charged under Schedule D in respect of any of the concerns mentioned in section 55 shall be assessed and charged on the person carrying on the concern, or on the agents or other officers who have the direction or management of the concern or receive the profits thereof.

(3) Where, in accordance with that section, income tax is charged under Schedule D on the profits of markets or fairs, or on tolls, fisheries or any other annual or casual profits not distrainable, the owner or occupier or receiver of the profits thereof shall be answerable for the tax so charged, and may retain and deduct the same out of any such profits.

(4) Subsections (1) to (3) above shall not apply for the purposes of corporation tax.

Former enactment.—TA 1970, s. 114.

CHAPTER II

INCOME TAX: BASIS OF ASSESSMENT ETC.

Cases I and II

60. Assessment on preceding year basis

(1) Subject to the provisions of this section and sections 61 to 63, income tax shall be charged under Cases I and II of Schedule D on the full amount of the profits or gains of the year preceding the year of assessment.

(2) Subsection (3) or (4) below shall apply where, in the case of a trade, profession or vocation, an account has, or accounts have, been made up to a date or dates within the period of three years immediately preceding the year of assessment.

(3) If—

    (*a*) an account was made up to a date within the year preceding the year of assessment, and
    (*b*) that account was the only account made up to a date in that year, and
    (*c*) it was for a period of one year beginning either—

        (i) at the commencement of the trade, profession or vocation, or
        (ii) at the end of the period on the profits or gains of which the assessment for the last preceding year of assessment was to be computed,

the profits or gains of the year ending on that date shall be taken to be the profits or gains of the year preceding the year of assessment.

(4) If subsection (3) does not apply, the Board shall decide what period of 12 months ending on a date within the year preceding the year of assessment shall be deemed to be the year the profits or gains of which are to be taken to be the profits or gains of the year preceding the year of assessment.

(5) Where—

    (*a*) the Board have given a decision under subsection (4) above, and
    (*b*) it appears to them that, in consequence of that decision, income tax for the last preceding year of assessment in respect of the profits or gains from the same source should be computed on the profits or gains of a corresponding period,

they may give a direction to that effect, and an assessment or, on a claim therefor, repayment of tax shall be made accordingly.

(6) The decision whether or not to give a direction under subsection (5) above shall be subject to an appeal which shall lie to the General Commissioners unless the appellant elects (in accordance with section 46(1) of the Management Act) to bring it before the Special Commissioners, and the Commissioners hearing the appeal shall grant such relief, if any, as is just.

(7) An appeal under subsection (6) above shall be brought within 30 days of receipt of notice of the decision, save that, if the decision is to give a direction and an assessment is made in accordance with the direction, the appeal against the decision shall be by way of an appeal against the assessment.

(8) In the case of the death of a person who, if he had not died, would under subsections (2) to (5) above have become chargeable to income tax for any year, the tax which would have been so chargeable shall be assessed and charged on his executors or administrators, and shall be a debt due from and payable out of his estate.

Former enactments.—Sub-s. (1): TA 1970, s. 115(1).
Sub-s. (2): TA 1970, s. 115(2).
Sub-s. (3): TA 1970, s. 115(2)(*a*).
Sub-s. (4): TA 1970, s. 115(2)(*b*).
Sub-ss. (5)–(8): TA 1970, s. 115(3)–(6).

61. Special basis at commencement of trade, profession or vocation

(1) Subject to subsection (4) below, where the trade, profession or vocation has been set up and commenced within the year of assessment, the computation of the profits or gains chargeable to income tax under Case I or Case II of Schedule D shall be made either on the full amount of the profits or gains arising in the year of assessment or according to the average of such period, not being greater than one year, as the case may require and as may be directed by the inspector.

(2) On an appeal to the General or Special Commissioners, the Commissioners shall have jurisdiction to review the inspector's decision under subsection (1) above.

(3) Where the trade, profession or vocation has been set up and commenced within the year preceding the year of assessment, the computation of the profits or gains chargeable to income tax under Case I or Case II of Schedule D shall be made on the profits or gains for one year from its first being set up.

(4) Subsections (1) to (3) above shall not apply in any case where [there is a change in the persons engaged in carrying on a trade, profession or vocation in partnership and][1] section 113(1) and (2) apply but no election is made under section 113(2), but in such a case the computation of the profits or gains chargeable to income tax under Case I or II of Schedule D for the year of assessment in which the new trade, profession or vocation is treated as having been set up and commenced, and for each of the three years following that year of assessment, shall be made on the full amount of the profits or gains arising in the year of assessment in question.

Former enactments.—Sub-ss. (1)–(3): TA 1970, s. 116.
Sub-ss. (4), (5): FA 1985, s. 47(1)–(3).
Amendments.—Words in sub-s. (4) inserted by FA 1988, Sch. 13, para. 2

62. Special basis for early years following commencement

(1) In this section—

"charged" means charged to income tax in respect of the profits or gains of a trade, profession or vocation;

"the second year of assessment" and "the third year of assessment" mean respectively the year next after, and the year next but one after, the year of assessment in which the trade, profession or vocation in question was set up and commenced; and

"the fifth year of assessment" and "the sixth year of assessment" mean respectively the year next but three after, and the year next but four after, the year of assessment in which the trade, profession or vocation in question was set up and commenced.

(2) Subject to subsection (4) below, the person charged, or liable to be charged, shall be entitled, on giving notice to the inspector within seven years after the end of the second year of assessment, to require that tax shall be charged for both the second year of assessment and the third year of assessment (but not for one or other only of those years) on the amount of the profits or gains for each such year respectively.

[(2A) Where—

(a) the second year of assessment is the year 1989–90,
(b) the person charged, or liable to be charged, for that year is a married man, and
(c) the person charged, or liable to be charged, for the year 1990–91 is his wife,

subsection (2) above shall have effect as if it conferred the right to give notice on her and not on him.][1]

(3) A notice under subsection (2) above may be revoked by the person who gave it by notice given to the inspector within six years after the end of the third year of assessment and, where it is so revoked, tax shall be charged for both the second year of assessment and the third year of assessment as if the first notice had never been given.

(4) Subsections (2) and (3) above shall not apply in any case where—

(a) section 113(1) and (2) apply and the change in the persons engaged in carrying on the trade, profession or vocation in partnership occurs after 19th March 1985; but
(b) no election is made under section 113(2);

but in such a case the person charged, or liable to be charged, shall be entitled, on giving notice to the inspector within seven years after the end of the fifth year of assessment, to require that tax shall be charged for both the fifth year of assessment and the sixth year of assessment (but not for one or other only of those years) on the amount of the profits or gains for each such year respectively.

(5) A notice under subsection (4) above may be revoked by the person who gave it by notice given to the inspector within six years after the end of the sixth year of assessment and, where it is so revoked, tax shall be charged for both the fifth year of assessment and the sixth year of assessment as if the first notice had never been given.

(6) If at any time during the second or third year of assessment—

(a) a change occurs, by reason of retirement or death, in a partnership of persons engaged in the trade, profession or vocation, or the dissolution of the partnership as to one or more of the partners, or the admission of a new partner, in such circumstances that one or more of the persons who until that time were engaged in the trade, profession or vocation continue to be engaged in it; or

(b) a change occurs such that a person who until that time was engaged in the trade, profession or vocation on his own account continues to be engaged in it but as a partner in a partnership;

a notice given for the purposes of subsection (2) above must, if given after the occurrence of the change and after notice has been given as respects the change under section 113(2), comply with the requirements of subsection (7) or (8) below, as the case may require.

(7) A notice given within 12 months after the end of the second year of assessment must be signed by—

(a) each of the individuals who were engaged in the trade, profession or vocation at any time between the commencement of that year and the giving of the notice; or

(b) in the case of a deceased person, his personal representatives.

(8) A notice given after the end of the third year of assessment must be signed by—

(a) each of the individuals who were engaged in the trade, profession or vocation at any time during the second or third year of assessment; or

(b) in the case of a deceased person, his personal representatives.

(9) In the case of the death of a person who, if he had not died, would under the provisions of this section have become chargeable to income tax for any year, the tax which would have been so chargeable shall be assessed and charged on his personal representatives, and shall be a debt due from and payable out of his estate.

(10) There shall be made such assessments, reductions of assessments or, on a claim in that behalf, repayments of tax as may in any case be required in order to give effect to the preceding provisions of this section.

Former enactments.—Sub-s. (1): TA 1970, s. 117(1); FA 1985, s. 47(2), (4)(a).
Sub-ss. (2), (3): TA 1970, s. 117(2).
Sub-ss. (4), (5): TA 1970, s. 117(2); FA 1985, s. 47(2), (4)(b).
Sub-ss. (6)–(8): TA 1970, s. 117(3); FA 1987, Sch. 15, para. 2(8).
Sub-ss. (9), (10): TA 1970, s. 117(4), (5); FA 1987, Sch. 15, para. 2(8).
Amendments.—[1] Sub-s. (2A) inserted by FA 1988, Sch. 3, para. 2.

63. Special basis on discontinuance

(1) Where in any year of assessment a trade, profession or vocation is permanently discontinued, then notwithstanding anything in sections 60 to 62—

(a) the person charged or chargeable with income tax in respect thereof shall be charged for that year on the amount of the profits or gains of the period beginning on the 6th April in that year and ending on the date of the discontinuance, but subject to any deduction or set-off to which he may be entitled under section 385 in respect of any loss; and

(b) if the aggregate of the profits or gains (if any) of the years ending on the 5th April in each of the two years preceding the year of assessment in which the discontinuance occurs exceeds—

(i) the aggregate of the amounts on which [income tax][1] has been charged for each of those two years; or

(ii) the aggregate of the amounts on which [income tax][1] would have been so charged if no deduction or set-off under section 385 had been allowed;

[income tax][1] may be charged instead, for each of those two years, but subject to any such deduction or set-off, on the amount of the profits or gains of the year ending on the 5th April in that year.

(2) Where [income tax has been charged][1] otherwise than in accordance with subsection (1)

above, any such assessment to tax, reduction or discharge of an assessment to tax, or on a claim therefor, repayment of tax shall be made as may be necessary to give effect to that subsection.

(3) In the case of the death of a person who, if he had not died, would under the provisions of this section have become chargeable to income tax for any year, the tax which would have been so chargeable shall be assessed and charged on his executors or administrators, and shall be a debt due from and payable out of his estate.

(4) Subsection (1)(*b*) above shall not apply where a trade is permanently discontinued in consequence of the nationalisation of any property constituting the assets of the trade.

For the purposes of this subsection "nationalisation" means, in relation to any property, a transfer of the property for which provision is made by any Act passed after the beginning of August 1945 and embodying a scheme for the carrying on of any industry or part of an industry, or of any undertaking, under national ownership or control, being a transfer, as part of the initial putting into force of the scheme, either to the Crown or to a body corporate constituted for the purposes of the scheme or of some previous scheme for such national ownership or control.

Former enactment.—TA 1970, s. 118.
Amendments.—[1] Words in sub-ss. (1)(*b*), (2) substituted by FA 1988, Sch. 3, para. 3.

Cases III, IV and V

64. Case III assessments: general

Subject to sections 66 and 67, income tax under Case III of Schedule D shall be computed on the full amount of the income arising within the year preceding the year of assessment, and shall be paid on the actual amount of that income, without any deduction.

Former enactment.—TA 1970, s. 119.
Cross references.—See FA 1988, ss. 37–40 (maintenance payments under existing obligations), s. 38(8) (tax chargeable under Schedule D Case III in respect of certain maintenance payments to be computed on current year basis).

65. Cases IV and V assessments: general

(1) Subject to the provisions of this section and sections 66 and 67, income tax chargeable under Case IV or Case V of Schedule D shall be computed on the full amount of the income arising in the year preceding the year of assessment, whether the income has been or will be received in the United Kingdom or not, subject in the case of income not received in the United Kingdom—

(*a*) to the same deductions and allowances as if it had been so received, and
(*b*) to a deduction on account of any annuity or other annual payment (not being interest) payable out of the income to a person not resident in the United Kingdom.

(2) Subject to section 330, income tax chargeable under Case IV or V of Schedule D on income arising from any pension shall be computed on the amount of that income subject to a deduction of one-tenth of the amount of the income.

(3) Income tax chargeable under Case IV or V of Schedule D on income which is immediately derived by a person from the carrying on by him of any trade, profession or vocation either solely or in partnership shall be computed in accordance with the rules applicable to Cases I and II of Schedule D; and subsection (1)(*a*) above shall not apply.

Nothing in this subsection shall be taken to apply sections 60 to 63 or 113 in relation to income chargeable under Case V of Schedule D but computed in accordance with this subsection.

(4) Subsections (1), (2) and (3) above shall not apply to any person who, on a claim made to the Board, satisfies the Board that he is not domiciled in the United Kingdom, or that, being a Commonwealth citizen or a citizen of the Republic of Ireland, he is not ordinarily resident in the United Kingdom.

(5) Where subsection (4) above applies the tax shall, subject to sections 66 and 67, be computed—

(*a*) in the case of tax chargeable under Case IV, on the full amount, so far as the same can be computed, of the sums received in the United Kingdom in the year preceding the year of assessment, without any deduction or abatement; and
(*b*) in the case of tax chargeable under Case V, on the full amount of the actual sums

received in the United Kingdom in the year preceding the year of assessment from remittances payable in the United Kingdom, or from property imported, or from money or value arising from property not imported, or from money or value so received on credit or on account in respect of any such remittances, property, money or value brought or to be brought into the United Kingdom, without any deduction or abatement other than is allowed under the provisions of the Income Tax Acts in respect of profits or gains charged under Case I of Schedule D.

(6) For the purposes of subsection (5) above, any income arising from securities or possessions out of the United Kingdom which is applied outside the United Kingdom by a person ordinarily resident in the United Kingdom in or towards satisfaction of—
 (a) any debt for money lent to him in the United Kingdom or for interest on money so lent, or
 (b) any debt for money lent to him outside the United Kingdom and received in or brought to the United Kingdom, or
 (c) any debt incurred for satisfying in whole or in part a debt falling within paragraph (a) or (b) above,
shall be treated as received by him in the United Kingdom (and, for the purposes of subsection (5)(b) above, as so received from remittances payable in the United Kingdom).

(7) Where a person ordinarily resident in the United Kingdom receives in or brings to the United Kingdom money lent to him outside the United Kingdom, but the debt for that money is wholly or partly satisfied before he does so, subsection (6) above shall apply as if the money had been received in or brought to the United Kingdom before the debt was so satisfied, except that any sums treated by virtue of that subsection as received in the United Kingdom shall be treated as so received at the time when the money so lent is actually received in or brought to the United Kingdom.

(8) Where—
 (a) a person ("the borrower") is indebted for money lent to him, and
 (b) income is applied by him in such a way that the money or property representing it is held by the lender on behalf of or to the account of the borrower in such circumstances as to be available to the lender for the purpose of satisfying or reducing the debt by set-off or otherwise,
that income shall be treated as applied by the borrower in or towards satisfaction of the debt if, under any arrangement between the borrower and the lender, the amount for the time being of the borrower's indebtedness to the lender, or the time at which the debt is to be repaid in whole or in part, depends in any respect directly or indirectly on the amount or value so held by the lender.

(9) For the purposes of subsections (6) to (8) above—
 (a) a debt for money lent shall, to the extent to which that money is applied in or towards satisfying another debt, be deemed to be a debt incurred for satisfying that other debt, and a debt incurred for satisfying in whole or in part a debt falling within paragraph (c) of subsection (6) above shall itself be treated as falling within that paragraph; and
 (b) "lender" includes, in relation to any money lent, any person for the time being entitled to repayment.

Former enactments.—Sub-s. (1): TA 1970, s. 122(1)(a), (b).
Sub-s. (2): FA 1974, s. 22(1).
Sub-s. (3): FA 1974, s. 23(1), (6)(b).
Sub-s. (4): TA 1970, s. 122(2)(a); British Nationality Act 1981, s. 51(1)(b), (2).
Sub-ss. (5)–(9): TA 1970, s. 122(3)–(7).
Cross references.—See FA 1988, ss. 37–40 (maintenance payments under existing obligations),
s. 38(8) (tax chargeable under Schedule D Case III in respect of certain maintenance payments to be computed on current year basis),
s. 38(9) (no deduction to be made under sub-s. (1)(b) on account of certain maintenance payments);
FA 1989, Sch. 11, para. 13(3)(b) (extension of the application of sub-ss. (6)–(9) above to income from deep gain securities of a non-resident).

66. Special rules for fresh income

(1) Income tax under Case III, IV or V of Schedule D shall, in the following cases, be computed on the following amounts, and, where the tax is charged under Case III, paid on those actual amounts without any deduction—
 (a) as respects the year of assessment in which the income first arises, on the full amount of the income arising within that year;
 (b) where the income first arose on some day in the year preceding the year of assessment other than 6th April, on the amount of the income of the year of assessment; and

(*b*) on the full amount thereof on an average of such period as the case may require and as may be directed by the inspector;

so that, according to the nature of the income, the tax may be computed on the same basis as that on which it would have been computed if the income had arisen in the United Kingdom, and subject in either case to a deduction on account of any annuity or other annual payment (not being interest) payable out of the income to a person not resident in the United Kingdom; and the person chargeable and assessable shall be entitled to the same allowances, deductions and reliefs as if the income had arisen in the United Kingdom.

The jurisdiction of the General or Special Commissioners on any appeal shall include jurisdiction to review the inspector's decision under this subsection.

(4) In charging any income which is excluded from subsection (1) above by subsection (2)(*a*) above there shall be the same limitation on reliefs as under section 391(2) in the case of income computed by virtue of section 65(3) in accordance with the rules applicable to Cases I and II of Schedule D.

(5) In charging income arising from a pension under subsection (3) above, a deduction of one-tenth shall be allowed unless it is the income of a person falling within section 65(4).

Former enactments.—TA 1970, Sch. 12, Pt. III, para. 2; FA 1976, s. 49(4), (6).

Case VI

69. Assessment on current year basis unless otherwise directed

(1) Income tax under Case VI of Schedule D shall be computed either on the full amount of the profits or gains arising in the year of assessment or according to an average of such period, not being greater than one year, as the case may require and as may be directed by the inspector.

(2) On an appeal to the General or Special Commissioners, the Commissioners shall have jurisdiction to review the inspector's decision under this section.

Former enactment.—TA 1970, s. 125.

CHAPTER III

CORPORATION TAX: BASIS OF ASSESSMENT ETC.

70. Basis of assessment etc.

(1) In accordance with sections 6 to 12 and 337 to 344, for the purposes of corporation tax for any accounting period income shall be computed under Cases I to VI of Schedule D on the full amount of the profits or gains or income arising in the period (whether or not received in or transmitted to the United Kingdom), without any other deduction than is authorised by the Corporation Tax Acts.

(2) Where a company is chargeable to corporation tax in respect of a trade or vocation under Case V of Schedule D, the income from the trade or vocation shall be computed in accordance with the rules applicable to Case I of Schedule D.

(3) Cases IV and V of Schedule D shall for the purposes of corporation tax extend to companies not resident in the United Kingdom, so far as those companies are chargeable to tax on income of descriptions which, in the case of companies resident in the United Kingdom, fall within those Cases (but without prejudice to any provision of the Tax Acts specially exempting non-residents from tax on any particular description of income).

Former enactments.—Sub-s. (1): TA 1970, s. 129(1).
Sub-s. (2): TA 1970, s. 129(4).
Sub-s. (3): TA 1970, s. 129(5).

CHAPTER IV

PROVISIONS SUPPLEMENTARY TO CHAPTERS II AND III

71. Computation of income tax where no profits in year of assessment

Where it is provided by the Income Tax Acts that income tax under Schedule D in respect of profits or gains or income from any source is to be computed by reference to the amount of the profits or gains or income of some period preceding the year of assessment, tax as so computed shall be charged for that year of assessment notwithstanding that no profits or gains or income arise from that source for or within that year.

Former enactment.—TA 1970, s. 126.

72. Apportionments etc. for purposes of Cases I, II and VI

(1) Where in the case of any profits or gains chargeable under Case I, II or VI of Schedule D it is necessary in order to arrive for the purposes of income tax or corporation tax at the profits or gains or losses of any year of assessment, accounting period or other period, to divide and apportion to specific periods the profits or gains or losses for any period for which the accounts have been made up, or to aggregate any such profits, gains or losses or any apportioned parts thereof, it shall be lawful to make such a division and apportionment or aggregation.

(2) Any apportionment under this section shall be made in proportion to the number of months, or fractions of months, in the respective periods.

Former enactments.—Sub-s. (1): TA 1970, ss. 127(1), 129(2).
Sub-s. (2): TA 1970, s. 127(2), 527(4).

73. Single assessments for purposes of Cases III, IV and V

Except as otherwise provided by the Tax Acts all income in respect of which a person is chargeable to tax under Case III, IV or V of Schedule D may respectively be assessed and charged in one sum.

Former enactment.—TA 1970, ss. 128, 129(3).

CHAPTER V

COMPUTATIONAL PROVISIONS

Deductions

74. General rules as to deductions not allowable

Subject to the provisions of the Tax Acts, in computing the amount of the profits or gains to be charged under Case I or Case II of Schedule D, no sum shall be deducted in respect of—

(a) any disbursements or expenses, not being money wholly and exclusively laid out or expended for the purposes of the trade, profession or vocation;

(b) any disbursements or expenses of maintenance of the parties, their families or establishments, or any sums expended for any other domestic or private purposes distinct from the purposes of the trade, profession or vocation;

(c) the rent of the whole or any part of any dwelling-house or domestic offices, except any such part as is used for the purposes of the trade, profession or vocation, and where any such part is so used, the sum so deducted shall not, unless in any particular case it appears that having regard to all the circumstances some greater sum ought to be deducted, exceed two-thirds of the rent bona fide paid for that dwelling-house or those offices;

(d) any sum expended for repairs of premises occupied, or for the supply, repairs or alterations of any implements, utensils or articles employed, for the purposes of the trade, profession or vocation, beyond the sum actually expended for those purposes;

(e) any loss not connected with or arising out of the trade, profession or vocation;

(f) any capital withdrawn from, or any sum employed or intended to be employed as capital in, the trade, profession or vocation, but so that this paragraph shall not be treated as disallowing the deduction of any interest;

(g) any capital employed in improvements of premises occupied for the purposes of the trade, profession or vocation;

(h) any interest which might have been made if any such sums as aforesaid had been laid out at interest;

(j) any debts, except bad debts proved to be such, and doubtful debts to the extent that they are respectively estimated to be bad, and in the case of the bankruptcy or insolvency of a debtor the amount which may reasonably be expected to be received on any such debt shall be deemed to be the value thereof;

(k) any average loss beyond the actual amount of loss after adjustment;

(l) any sum recoverable under an insurance or contract of indemnity;

(m) any annuity or other annual payment (other than interest) payable out of the profits or gains;

(n) any interest paid to a person not resident in the United Kingdom if and so far as it is interest at more than a reasonable commercial rate;

(o) any relevant loan interest within the meaning of section 369, other than interest to which section 375(2) applies;

(p) any royalty or other sum paid in respect of the user of a patent;

(q) any rent, royalty or other payment which is by section 119 or 120 declared to be subject to deduction of tax under section 348 or 349 as if it were a royalty or other sum paid in respect of the user of a patent.

Former enactments.—Sub-paras. (a)–(n): TA 1970, s. 130(a)–(m); FA 1987, Sch. 15, para. 2(9).
Sub-para. (o): FA 1982, s. 26(8).
Sub-paras. (p), (q): TA 1970, s. 130(n), (o).
Cross references.—See FA 1988, s. 73(2) (notwithstanding anything in this section, any sum to which s. 313 of this Act applies (consideration for certain restrictive undertakings) to be an allowable deduction from the profits or gains of a trade etc.);
FA 1989, s. 112(2) (the limitations of this section not to apply to expenditure incurred to acquire assets or services for personal physical security).

75. Expenses of management: investment companies

(1) In computing for the purposes of corporation tax the total profits for any accounting period of an investment company resident in the United Kingdom there shall be deducted any sums disbursed as expenses of management (including commissions) for that period, except any such expenses as are deductible in computing profits apart from this section.

(2) For the purposes of subsection (1) above there shall be deducted from the amount treated as expenses of management the amount of any income derived from sources not charged to tax, other than franked investment income, group income and any regional development grant. In this subsection "regional development grant" means a payment by way of grant under Part II of the Industrial Development Act 1982.

(3) Where in any accounting period of an investment company the expenses of management deductible under subsection (1) above, together with any charges on income paid in the accounting period wholly and exclusively for purposes of the company's business, exceed the amount of the profits from which they are deductible—

(a) the excess shall be carried forward to the succeeding accounting period; and
(b) the amount so carried forward to the succeeding acounting period shall be treated for the purposes of this section, including any further application of this subsection, as if it had been disbursed as expenses of management for that accounting period.

(4) For the purposes of this section there shall be added to a company's expenses of management in any accounting period the amount of any allowances falling to be made to the company for that period by virtue of section 306 of the 1970 Act (capital allowances for machinery and plant) in so far as effect cannot be given to them under subsection (2) of that section.

(5) Where an appeal against an assessment to corporation tax or against a decision on a claim under section 242 relates exclusively to the relief to be given under subsection (1) above, the appeal shall lie to the Special Commissioners, and if and so far as the question in dispute on any such appeal which does not lie to the Special Commissioners relates to that relief, that question shall, instead of being determined on the appeal, be referred to and determined by the Special Commissioners, and the Management Act shall apply as if that reference were an appeal.

Former enactments.—Sub-ss. (1), (2): TA 1970, s. 304(1); FA 1984, s. 54(2)(b); FA 1987, s. 41.
Sub-ss. (3), (4): TA 1970, s. 304(2), (3).
Sub-s. (5): TA 1970, s. 304(4).
Cross references.—See FA 1988, s. 73(3) (any sum to which s. 313 of this Act applies (consideration for restrictive undertakings) to be treated for the purposes of this section as management expenses);
FA 1989, s. 67(2)(b) (contributions by companies mentioned in s. 76 below to employee share ownership trusts to enjoy relief given by this section),
s. 76(1), (4)(b) (the relief given by this section not to apply to certain management expenses of non-approved retirement benefits schemes),
ss. 84(1), 86 (spreading of relief over a seven year period for certain management expenses incurred in accounting periods beginning after 31 December 1989 in relation to basic life assurance business),
ss. 84(1), 87(5), (6) (in the case of certain management expenses incurred in the accounting periods beginning after 31 December 1989 in relation to basic life assurance business, this section to apply subject to the amendments made to s. 76 below by FA 1989, s. 87(1)–(3) and subject to the provisions regarding a straddling period).

76. Expenses of management: insurance companies

(1) Subject to the provisions of this section and of section 432, section 75 shall apply for computing the profits of a company carrying on life assurance business, whether mutual or proprietary, (and not charged to corporation tax in respect of it under Case I of Schedule D), whether or not the company is resident in the United Kingdom, as that section applies in relation to an investment company except that—

(a) there shall be deducted from the amount treated as the expenses of management for any accounting period the amount of any fines, fees or profits arising from reversions; and
(b) no deduction shall be made under section 75(2); [and]¹
[(c) there shall be deducted from the amount treated as the expenses of management for any accounting period any repayment or refund (in whole or in part) of a sum disbursed by the company (for that or any earlier period) as acquisition expenses; and]¹
[(d) the amount treated as expenses of management shall not include any amount in respect of expenses referable to general annuity business or pension business; and]¹
[(e) the amount of profits from which expenses of management may be deducted for any accounting period shall not exceed the net income and gains of that accounting period referable to basic life assurance business;]¹

[and for this purpose "net income and gains" means income and gains after deducting any reliefs or exemptions which fall to be applied before taking account of this section.]¹

(2) Relief in respect of management expenses shall not be given to any such company, whether under section 242 or subsection (1) above, so far as it would, if given in addition to

all other reliefs to which the company is entitled, reduce the corporation tax borne by the company on the income and gains of its life assurance business for any accounting period to less than would have been paid if the company had been charged to tax in respect of that business under Case I of Schedule D.

In this subsection the references to reliefs do not include references to any set-off under section 239.

(3) For the purposes of subsection (2) above—

(a) any tax credit to which the company is entitled in respect of a distribution received by it shall be treated as an equivalent amount of corporation tax borne or paid in respect of that distribution; and

(b) any payment in respect of that credit under section 242 shall be treated as reducing the tax so treated as borne or paid.

(4) In applying subsection (2) above to an accounting period in which a company—

(a) carries on any business in addition to life assurance business, or

(b) carries on both ordinary life assurance business and industrial life assurance business,

the tax that would have been paid if the company had been charged under Case I of Schedule D in respect of its life assurance business, or its life assurance business of either of those classes, shall be calculated as if any advance corporation tax set against the company's liability to corporation tax for that accounting period were apportioned to the corporation tax attributable to each business in proportion to the profits of that business charged to corporation tax for that accounting period.

(5) Where relief has been withheld in respect of any accounting period by virtue of subsection (2) above, the excess to be carried forward by virtue of section 75(3) shall be increased accordingly.

(6) The relief under this section available to an overseas life insurance company (within the meaning of section 431) in respect of its expenses of management shall be limited to expenses attributable to the life assurance business carried on by the company at or through its branch or agency in the United Kingdom.

(7) For the purposes of this section any sums paid by a company under a long term business levy imposed by virtue of the Policyholders Protection Act 1975 shall be treated as part of its expenses of management.

[(8) In this section—

"acquisition expenses" means expenses falling within paragraphs (a) to (c) of subsection (1) of section 86 of the Finance Act 1989;

"basic life assurance business" has the meaning assigned by section 84(1) of that Act;

and other expressions have the same meaning as in Chapter I of Part XII.][2]

Former enactments.—Sub-s. (1): TA 1970, s. 305(1).
Sub-s. (2): TA 1970, s. 305(2); FA 1972, Sch. 18, para. 1(2).
Sub-ss. (3), (4): FA 1972, Sch. 18, para. 1(1), (3).
Sub-s. (5): TA 1970, s. 305(2).
Sub-s. (6): TA 1970, s. 317.
Sub-s. (7): FA 1976, s. 47.
Sub-s. (8): TA 1970, ss. 305(3), 323(2).
Cross references.—See CGTA 1979, s. 31(4) (reference in sub-s. (1) of that section to computing income etc not to apply to computation of a company's income for the purposes of sub-s. (2) of this section);
FA 1989, ss. 84(1), 85(2)(d) (charge of certain receipts of basic life assurance business),
ss. 84(1), 86 (spreading of relief over a seven year period for certain management expenses incurred in accounting periods beginning after 31 December 1989 in relation to basic life assurance business),
ss. 84(1), 87(5), (6) (in the case of certain management expenses incurred in the accounting periods beginning before 1 January 1990 in relation to basic life assurance business this section to apply as if the amendments by FA 1989, s. 87(1)–(3) were not made, but subject to the provisions regarding a straddling period).
Amendments.—[1] Sub-s. (1)(c) and the preceding word "and", (d), (e) and the words following inserted by FA 1989, s. 87(1)–(3), (5) with respect to accounting periods beginning after 31 December 1989.
[2] Sub-s. (8) substituted by *ibid*. Originally it read—

"(8) In subsections (2) and (6) above "life assurance business" includes the business of granting annuities on human life."

77. Incidental costs of obtaining loan finance

(1) Subject to subsection (5) below, in computing the profits or gains to be charged under Case I or II of Schedule D there may be deducted the incidental costs of obtaining finance by means of a qualifying loan or the issue of qualifying loan stock or a qualifying security; and the incidental costs of obtaining finance by those means shall be treated for the purposes of section 75 as expenses of management.

(2) Subject to subsections (3) and (4) below, in this section—

(*a*) "a qualifying loan" and "qualifying loan stock" mean a loan or loan stock the interest on which is deductible—

(i) in computing for tax purposes the profits or gains of the person by whom the incidental costs in question are incurred; or
(ii) under section 338 against his total profits; and

(*b*) "qualifying security" means any deep discount security, as defined by paragraph 1 of Schedule 4, in respect of which the income elements, as defined by paragraph 4 of that Schedule, are deductible under paragraph 5(1) of that Schedule in computing the total profits of the company by which the incidental costs in question are incurred.

(3) Except as provided by subsection (4) below, a loan or loan stock which carries the right of conversion into or to the acquisition of—

(*a*) shares, or
(*b*) other securities not being a qualifying loan or qualifying loan stock,

is not a qualifying loan or qualifying loan stock if that right is exercisable before the expiry of the period of three years from the date when the loan was obtained or the stock issued.

(4) A loan or loan stock—

(*a*) which carries such a right as is referred to in subsection (3) above, and
(*b*) which by virtue of that subsection is not a qualifying loan or qualifying loan stock,

shall nevertheless be regarded as a qualifying loan or qualifying loan stock, as the case may be, if the right is not, or is not wholly, exercised before the expiry of the period of three years from the date when the loan was obtained or the stock was issued.

(5) For the purposes of the application of subsection (1) above in relation to a loan or loan stock which is a qualifying loan or qualifying loan stock by virtue of subsection (4) above—

(*a*) if the right referred to in subsection (4)(*a*) above is exercised as to part of the loan or stock within the period referred to in that subsection, only that proportion of the incidental costs of obtaining finance which corresponds to the proportion of the stock in respect of which the right is not exercised within that period shall be taken into account; and
(*b*) in so far as any of the incidental costs of obtaining finance are incurred before the expiry of the period referred to in subsection (4) above they shall be treated as incurred immediately after that period expires.

(6) In this section "the incidental costs of obtaining finance" means expenditure on fees, commissions, advertising, printing and other incidental matters (but not including stamp duty), being expenditure wholly and exclusively incurred for the purpose of obtaining the finance (whether or not it is in fact obtained), or of providing security for it or of repaying it.

(7) This section shall not be construed as affording relief—

(*a*) for any sums paid in consequence of, or for obtaining protection against, losses resulting from changes in the rate of exchange between different currencies; or
(*b*) for the cost of repaying a loan or loan stock or a qualifying security so far as attributable to its being repayable at a premium or to its having been obtained or issued at a discount.

Former enactments.—Sub-s. (1): FA 1980, s. 38(1); FA 1984, s. 43(1), Sch. 9, para. 3(6).
Sub-s. (2)(*a*): FA 1980, s. 38(2); FA 1984, s. 43(1).
Sub-s. (2)(*b*): FA 1984, Sch. 9, para. 3(7).
Sub-s. (3): FA 1980, s. 38(3); FA 1984, s. 43(1).
Sub-ss. (4), (5): FA 1980, s. 38(3A), (3B); FA 1984, s. 43(2).
Sub-ss. (6), (7): FA 1980, s. 38(4), (5); FA 1984, Sch. 9, para. 3(6).

78. Discounted bills of exchange

(1) This section applies in any case where—

(*a*) a bill of exchange drawn by a company is or was accepted by a bank and discounted by that or any other bank or by a discount house; and
(*b*) the bill becomes or became payable on or after 1st April 1983; and
(*c*) the discount suffered by the company is not (apart from this section) deductible in computing the company's profits or any description of those profits for purposes of corporation tax.

(2) Subject to subsection (3) below, in computing, in a case where this section applies, the

corporation tax chargeable for the accounting period of the company in which the bill of exchange is paid, an amount equal to the discount referred to in subsection (1)(*c*) above shall be allowed as a deduction against the total profits for the period as reduced by any relief other than group relief and, except for the purposes of an allowance under section 338(1), that amount shall be treated for the purposes of the Corporation Tax Acts as a charge on income.

(3) Subsection (2) above shall not apply if the discount is not ultimately suffered by the company and shall not apply unless—

(*a*) the company exists wholly or mainly for the purposes of carrying on a trade; or
(*b*) the bill is drawn to obtain funds which are wholly and exclusively expended for the purposes of a trade carried on by the company; or
(*c*) the company is an investment company.

(4) Where an amount falls to be allowed as mentioned in subsection (2) above, there may be deducted, in computing the profits or gains of the company to be charged under Case I of Schedule D, the incidental costs incurred on or after 1st April 1983 in securing the acceptance of the bill by the bank; and those incidental costs shall be treated for the purposes of section 75 as expenses of management.

(5) For the purposes of subsection (4) above "incidental costs" means fees, commission and any other expenditure wholly and exclusively incurred for the purpose of securing the acceptance of the bill.

(6) In this section "bank" means a bank carrying on a bona fide banking business in the United Kingdom and "discount house" means a person bona fide carrying on the business of a discount house in the United Kingdom.

Former enactment.—FA 1984, s. 42.

79. Contributions to local enterprise agencies

(1) Notwithstanding anything in section 74, but subject to the provisions of this section, where a person carrying on a trade, profession or vocation makes any contribution (whether in cash or in kind) to an approved local enterprise agency, any expenditure incurred by him in making the contribution may be deducted as an expense in computing the profits or gains of the trade, profession or vocation for the purposes of tax if it would not otherwise be so deductible.

(2) Where any such contribution is made by an investment company any expenditure allowable as a deduction under subsection (1) above shall for the purposes of section 75 be treated as expenses of management.

(3) Subsection (1) above does not apply in relation to a contribution made by any person if either he or any person connected with him receives or is entitled to receive a benefit of any kind whatsoever for or in connection with the making of that contribution, whether from the agency concerned or from any other person.

(4) In this section "approved local enterprise agency" means a body approved by the Secretary of State for the purposes of this section; but he shall not so approve a body unless he is satisfied that—

(*a*) its sole objective is the promotion or encouragement of industrial and commercial activity or enterprise in a particular area in the United Kingdom with particular reference to encouraging the formation and development of small businesses; or
(*b*) one of its principal objectives is that set out in paragraph (*a*) above and it maintains or is about to maintain a fund separate from its other funds which is or is to be applied solely in pursuance of that objective;

and where the Secretary of State approves a body by virtue of paragraph (*b*) above, the approval shall specify the fund concerned and, in relation to a body so approved, any reference in this section to a contribution is a reference to a contribution which is made wholly to or for the purposes of that fund.

(5) A body may be approved under subsection (4) above whether or not it is a body corporate or a body of trustees or any other association or organisation and whether or not it is described as a local enterprise agency.

(6) A body may not be approved under subsection (4) above unless it is precluded, by virtue of any enactment, contractual obligation, memorandum or otherwise, from making any direct or indirect payment or transfer to any of its members, or to any person charged with

the control and direction of its affairs, of any of its income or profit by way of dividend, gift, division, bonus or otherwise howsoever by way of profit.

(7) For the purposes of subsection (6) above, the payment—

(*a*) of reasonable remuneration for goods, labour or power supplied or for services rendered, or
(*b*) of reasonable interest for money lent, or
(*c*) of reasonable rent for any premises,

does not constitute a payment or transfer which is required to be so precluded.

(8) Any approval given by the Secretary of State may be made conditional upon compliance with such requirements as to accounts, provision of information and other matters as he considers appropriate; and if it appears to the Secretary of State that—

(*a*) an approved local enterprise agency is not complying with any such requirement, or
(*b*) one or other of the conditions for his approval contained in subsection (4) above or the precondition for his approval in subsection (6) above has ceased to be fulfilled with respect to an approved local enterprise agency,

he shall by notice withdraw his approval from the body concerned with effect from such date as he may specify in the notice (which may be a date earlier than the date on which the notice is given).

(9) In any case where—

(*a*) a contribution has been made to an approved local enterprise agency in respect of which relief has been given under subsection (1) above, and
(*b*) any benefit received in any chargeable period by the contributor or any person connected with him is in any way attributable to that contribution,

the contributor shall in respect of that chargeable period be charged to tax under Case I or Case II of Schedule D or, if he is not chargeable to tax under either of those Cases for that period, under Case VI of Schedule D on an amount equal to the value of that benefit.

(10) Section 839 applies for the purposes of subsections (3) and (9) above.

(11) This section applies to contributions made on or after 1st April 1982 and before 1st April 1992.

Former enactments.—Sub-ss. (1)–(4): FA 1982, s. 48(1)–(4).
Sub-ss. (5)–(7): FA 1982, s. 48(5).
Sub-ss. (8)–(11): FA 1982, s. 48(6)–(9).

80. Expenses connected with foreign trades etc.

(1) This section applies in the case of a trade, profession or vocation carried on wholly outside the United Kingdom by an individual ("the taxpayer") who does not satisfy the Board as mentioned in section 65(4); and it is immaterial in the case of a trade or profession whether the taxpayer carries it on solely or in partnership.

(2) Expenses of the taxpayer—

(*a*) in travelling from any place in the United Kingdom to any place where the trade, profession or vocation is carried on;
(*b*) in travelling to any place in the United Kingdom from any place where the trade, profession or vocation is carried on; or
(*c*) on board and lodging for the taxpayer at any place where the trade, profession or vocation is carried on;

shall, subject to subsections (3) and (4) below, be treated for the purposes of section 74(*a*) as having been wholly and exclusively expended for the purposes of the trade, profession or vocation.

(3) Subsection (2) above does not apply unless the taxpayer's absence from the United Kingdom is occasioned wholly and exclusively for the purpose of performing the functions of the trade, profession or vocation or of performing those functions and the functions of any other trade, profession or vocation (whether or not one in the case of which this section applies).

(4) Where subsection (2) above applies and more than one trade, profession or vocation in the case of which this section applies is carried on at the place in question, the expenses shall be apportioned on such basis as is reasonable between those trades, professions or vocations; and the expenses so apportioned to a particular trade, profession or vocation

shall be treated for the purposes of section 74(*a*) as having been wholly and exclusively expended for the purposes of that trade, profession or vocation.

(5) Where the taxpayer is absent from the United Kingdom for a continuous period of 60 days or more wholly and exclusively for the purpose of performing the functions of one or more trades, professions or vocations in the case of which this section applies, expenses to which subsection (6) below applies shall be treated in accordance with subsection (7) or (8) below (as the case may be).

(6) This subsection applies to the expenses of any journey by the taxpayer's spouse, or any child of his, between any place in the United Kingdom and the place of performance of any of those functions outside the United Kingdom, if the journey—

(*a*) is made in order to accompany him at the beginning of the period of absence or to visit him during that period; or
(*b*) is a return journey following a journey falling within paragraph (*a*) above;

but this subsection does not apply to more than two outward and two return journeys by the same person in any year of assessment.

(7) The expenses shall be treated for the purposes of section 74(*a*) as having been wholly and exclusively expended for the purposes of the trade, profession or vocation concerned (if there is only one).

(8) The expenses shall be apportioned on such basis as is reasonable between the trades, professions or vocations concerned (if there is more than one) and the expenses so apportioned to a particular trade, profession or vocation shall be treated for the purposes of section 74(*a*) as having been wholly and exclusively expended for the purposes of that trade, profession or vocation.

(9) In subsection (6) above "child" includes a stepchild and an illegitimate child but does not include a person who is aged 18 or over at the beginning of the outward journey.

(10) Nothing in this section shall permit the same sum to be deducted for more than one trade, profession or vocation in respect of expenses in computing profits or gains.

Former enactment.—FA 1986, s. 35.

81. Travel between trades etc.

(1) Where a taxpayer (within the meaning of section 80) travels between a place where he carries on a trade, profession or vocation in the case of which section 80 applies and a place outside the United Kingdom where he carries on another trade, profession or vocation (whether or not one in the case of which that section applies) expenses of the taxpayer on such travel shall, subject to subsections (3) to (5) below, be treated for the purposes of section 74(*a*) as having been wholly and exclusively expended for the purposes of the trade, profession or vocation mentioned in subsection (2) below.

(2) The trade, profession or vocation is—

(*a*) the one carried on at the place of the taxpayer's destination; or
(*b*) if that trade, profession or vocation is not one in the case of which section 80 applies, the one carried on at the place of his departure.

(3) This section does not apply unless the journey was made—

(*a*) after performing functions of the trade, profession or vocation carried on at the place of departure; and
(*b*) for the purpose of performing functions of the trade, profession or vocation carried on at the place of destination.

(4) This section does not apply unless the taxpayer's absence from the United Kingdom is occasioned wholly and exclusively for the purpose of performing the functions of both the trades, professions or vocations concerned or of performing those functions and the functions of any other trade, profession or vocation.

(5) Where this section applies and more than one trade, profession or vocation in the case of which section 80 applies is carried on at the place of the taxpayer's destination or (in a case falling within subsection (2)(*b*) above) at the place of his departure, the expenses shall be apportioned on such basis as is reasonable between those trades, professions or vocations; and the expenses so apportioned to a particular trade, profession or vocation shall be treated for the purposes of section 74(*a*) as having been wholly and exclusively expended for the purposes of that trade, profession or vocation.

(6) Nothing in this section shall permit the same sum to be deducted for more than one trade, profession or vocation in respect of expenses in computing profits or gains.

Former enactment.—FA 1986, s. 36.

82. Interest paid to non-residents

(1) In computing the profits or gains arising from a trade, profession or vocation, no sum shall be deducted in respect of any annual interest paid to a person not resident in the United Kingdom unless—

(a) the person making the payment has deducted income tax from the payment in accordance with section 349(2) and accounts for the tax so deducted, or
(b) the conditions set out in subsection (2) below are satisfied.

(2) The conditions referred to in subsection (1)(b) above are as follows—

(a) that the trade, profession or vocation is carried on by a person residing in the United Kingdom, and
(b) that the liability to pay the interest was incurred exclusively for the purposes of the trade, profession or vocation, and
(c) that either—

(i) the liability to pay the interest was incurred wholly or mainly for the purposes of activities of the trade, profession or vocation carried on outside the United Kingdom, or
(ii) the interest is payable in a currency other than sterling, and

(d) that, under the terms of the contract under which the interest is payable, the interest is to be paid, or may be required to be paid, outside the United Kingdom, and
(e) that the interest is in fact paid outside the United Kingdom.

(3) Where the trade, profession or vocation is carried on by a partnership, subsection (1)(b) above shall not apply to any interest which is payable to any of the partners, or is payable in respect of the share of any partner in the partnership capital.

(4) Subsection (1)(b) above shall not apply where—

(a) the trade, profession or vocation is carried on by a body of persons over whom the person entitled to the interest has control; or
(b) the person entitled to the interest is a body of persons over whom the person carrying on the trade, profession or vocation has control; or
(c) the person carrying on the trade, profession or vocation and the person entitled to the interest are both bodies of persons and some other person has control over both of them.

In this subsection, the references to a body of persons include references to a partnership, and "control" has the meaning given by section 840.

(5) If interest paid under deduction of tax in accordance with section 349(2) is deductible in computing the profits or gains of a trade, profession or vocation the amount so deductible shall be the gross amount.

(6) This section does not apply for the purposes of corporation tax.

Former enactments.—TA 1970, s. 131(1)–(5), (7); FA 1982, s. 64(1).

83. Patent fees etc. and expenses

Notwithstanding anything in section 74, in computing the profits or gains of a trade there may be deducted as expenses any fees paid or expenses incurred—

(a) in obtaining for the purposes of the trade the grant of a patent, an extension of the term of a patent, the registration of a design or trade mark, [an extension of the period for which the right in a registered design subsists][1] or the renewal of registration of a trade mark, or
(b) in connection with a rejected or abandoned application for a patent made for the purposes of the trade.

References in this section to a trade mark include references to a service mark within the meaning of the Trade Marks (Amendment) Act 1984.

Former enactments.—TA 1970, s. 132; Patents, Designs and Marks Act 1986, Sch. 2, para. 1.
Amendments.—[1] Words in para. (*a*) substituted by the Copyright, Designs and Patents Act 1988, Sch. 7, para. 36(1), (2) with effect from 1 August 1989 by virtue of the Copyright, Designs and Patents Act 1988 (Commencement No. 1) Order 1989, S.I. 1989 No. 816. The original words read—
"the extension of the period of copyright in a design"

84. Payments for technical education

(1) Notwithstanding anything in section 74, where a person carrying on a trade makes any payment to be used for the purposes of technical education related to that trade at any university or university college or at any such technical college or other similar institution as may for the time being be approved for the purposes of this section by the Secretary of State, the payment may be deducted as an expense in computing the profits or gains of the trade for the purposes of tax.

(2) For the purposes of this section, technical education shall be deemed to be related to a trade if, and only if, it is technical education of a kind specially requisite for persons employed in the class of trade to which that trade belongs.

(3) In relation to technical colleges or other institutions in Northern Ireland, this section shall have effect as if for the reference to the Secretary of State there were substituted a reference to the Department of Education for Northern Ireland.

Former enactments.—TA 1970, s. 133; FA 1987, Sch. 15, para. 2(10).

85. Payments to trustees of approved profit sharing schemes

(1) Any sum expended in making a payment to the trustees of an approved profit sharing scheme by a company which is in relation to that scheme the grantor or a participating company—

(*a*) shall be deducted in computing for the purposes of Schedule D the profits or gains of a trade carried on by that company; or
(*b*) if that company is an investment company or a company in the case of which section 75 applies by virtue of section 76, shall be treated as expenses of management,

if, and only if, one of the conditions in subsection (2) below is fulfilled.

(2) The conditions referred to in subsection (1) above are—

(*a*) that before the expiry of the relevant period the sum in question is applied by the trustees in the acquisition of shares for appropriation to individuals who are eligible to participate in the scheme by virtue of their being or having been employees or directors of the company making the payment; and
(*b*) that the sum is necessary to meet the reasonable expenses of the trustees in administering the scheme.

(3) For the purposes of subsection (2)(*a*) above "the relevant period" means the period of nine months beginning on the day following the end of the period of account in which the sum in question is charged as an expense of the company incurring the expenditure or such longer period as the Board may allow by notice given to that company.

(4) For the purposes of this section, the trustees of an approved profit sharing scheme shall be taken to apply sums paid to them in the order in which the sums are received by them.

(5) In this section—

"approved profit sharing scheme" means a profit sharing scheme approved under Schedule 9; and
"the grantor" and "participating company" have the meaning given by paragraph 1(3) and (4) of that Schedule.

Former enactment.—FA 1978, s. 60.

86. Employees seconded to charities and educational establishments

(1) If a person ("the employer") carrying on a trade, profession, vocation or business for the purposes of which he employs a person ("the employee") makes available to a charity, on a basis which is expressed and intended to be of a temporary nature, the services of the employee then, notwithstanding anything in section 74 or 75, any expenditure incurred (or disbursed) by the employer which is attributable to the employment of that employee shall continue to be deductible in the manner and to the like extent as if, during the time that his

services are so made available to the charity, they continued to be available for the purposes of the employer's trade, business, profession or vocation.

(2) In subsection (1) above—
"charity" has the same meaning as in section 506;
"deductible" means deductible as an expense in computing the profits or gains of the employer to be charged under Case I or II of Schedule D or, as the case may be, deductible as expenses of management for the purposes of section 75.

(3) With respect to expenditure attributable to the employment of a person on or after 26th November 1986 and before 1st April 1997, this section shall have effect as if the references to a charity included references to any of the following bodies, that is to say—

(*a*) in England and Wales, any local education authority and any educational institution maintained by such an authority;
(*b*) in Scotland, any education authority, any educational establishment maintained by such an authority, and any college of education or central institution within the meaning of the Education (Scotland) Act 1980;
(*c*) in Northern Ireland, any education and library board, college of education or controlled school within the meaning of the Education and Libraries (Northern Ireland) Order 1986 and any institution of further education which is under the management of an education and library board by virtue of Article 28 of that Order; and
(*d*) any other educational body which is for the time being approved for the purposes of this section by the Secretary of State or, in Northern Ireland, the Department of Education for Northern Ireland.

Former enactments.—FA 1983, s. 28; FA 1984, s. 33; FA 1987, s. 34.

87. Taxable premiums etc.

(1) This section applies where in relation to any land used in connection with a trade, profession or vocation—

(*a*) tax has become chargeable under section 34 or 35 on any amount (disregarding any reduction in that amount under section 37(2) and (3)); or
(*b*) tax would have become so chargeable on that amount but for the operation of section 37(2) and (3) or but for any exemption from tax;

and that amount is referred to below as "the amount chargeable".

(2) Subject to subsections (3) to (8) below, where—

(*a*) during any part of the relevant period the land in relation to which the amount chargeable arose is occupied by the person for the time being entitled to the lease as respects which it arose, and
(*b*) that occupation is for the purposes of a trade, profession or vocation carried on by him,

he shall be treated, in computing the profits or gains of the trade, profession or vocation chargeable to tax under Case I or II of Schedule D, as paying in respect of that land rent for the period (in addition to any actual rent), becoming due from day to day, of an amount which bears to the amount chargeable the same proportion as that part of the relevant period bears to the whole.

(3) As respects any period during which a part only of the land in relation to which the amount chargeable arose is occupied as mentioned in subsection (2) above, that subsection shall apply as if the whole were so occupied, but the amount chargeable shall be treated as reduced by so much thereof as, on a just apportionment, is attributable to the remainder of the land.

(4) Where a person, although not in occupation of the land or any part of the land, deals with his interest in the land or that part as property employed for the purposes of a trade, profession or vocation carried on by him, subsections (2) and (3) above shall apply as if the land or part were occupied by him for those purposes.

(5) Where section 37(2) and (3) has effect in relation to a lease granted out of the interest referred to in subsection (4) above, subsections (5) and (6) of that section shall apply for modifying the operation of subsections (2) and (3) above as they apply for modifying the operation of subsection (4) of that section.

(6) In computing profits or gains chargeable under Case I or II of Schedule D for any chargeable period, rent shall not by virtue of subsection (4) above be treated as paid by a

person for any period in respect of land in so far as rent treated under section 37(4) as paid by him for that period in respect of the land has in any previous chargeable period been deducted, or falls in that chargeable period to be deducted under Part II.

(7) Where, in respect of expenditure on the acquisition of his interest in the land in relation to which the amount chargeable arose, a person has become entitled to an allowance under section 60 of the 1968 Act (mineral depletion) for any chargeable period, then—

(a) if the allowance is in respect of the whole of the expenditure, no deduction shall be allowed him under this section for that or any subsequent chargeable period; or

(b) if the allowance is in respect of part only of the expenditure ("the allowable part"), a deduction allowed him under this section for that or any subsequent chargeable period shall be the fraction—

$$\frac{A-B}{A}$$

of the amount which apart from this subsection would fall to be deducted, where—

A is the whole of the expenditure, and

B is the allowable part of the expenditure;

and the reference in this subsection to an allowance under section 60 of the 1968 Act includes a reference to an allowance under Part III of Schedule 13 to the Finance Act 1986 in respect of expenditure falling within paragraph 4(1)(b) of that Schedule.

(8) Where the amount chargeable arose under section 34(2) by reason of an obligation which included the carrying out of work in respect of which any capital allowance has fallen or will fall to be made, this section shall apply as if the obligation had not included the carrying out of that work and the amount chargeable had been calculated accordingly.

(9) In this section "the relevant period" means—

(a) where the amount chargeable arose under section 34, the period treated in computing that amount as the duration of the lease;

(b) where the amount chargeable arose under section 35, the period treated in computing that amount as the duration of the lease remaining at the date of the assignment.

Former enactments.—Sub-s. (1): TA 1970, s. 134(1); FA 1978, s. 32.
Sub-ss. (2), (3): TA 1970, s. 134(2), (3); FA 1978, s. 32.
Sub-s. (4): TA 1970, s. 134(4).
Sub-s. (5): TA 1970, s. 134(4)(a).
Sub-s. (6): TA 1970, s. 134(4)(b).
Sub-ss. (7), (8): TA 1970, s. 134(5), (6); FA 1986, Sch. 13, para. 26.
Sub-s. (9): TA 1970, s. 134(1)(i), (ii).

88. Payments to Export Credit Guarantee Department

Any sums paid by a person to the Export Credits Guarantee Department under an agreement entered into under arrangements made by the Secretary of State in pursuance of section 11 of the Export Guarantees and Overseas Investment Act 1978, or with a view to entering into such an agreement, shall be included—

(a) in the sums to be deducted in computing for the purposes of Case I or Case II of Schedule D the profits or gains of any trade, profession or vocation carried on by that person; or

(b) if that person is an investment company or a company in the case of which section 75 applies by virtue of section 76, in the sums to be deducted as expenses of management in computing the company's profits for the purposes of corporation tax;

whether or not they would fall to be so included apart from this section.

Former enactment.—FA 1972, s. 124(1).

89. Debts proving irrecoverable after event treated as discontinuance

Where section 113 or 337(1) applies to treat a trade, profession or vocation as discontinued by reason of any event, then, in computing for tax purposes the profits or gains of the trade, profession or vocation in any period after the event, there may be deducted a sum equal to any amount proved during that period to be irrecoverable in respect of any debts credited in computing for tax purposes the profits or gains for any period before the event (being debts the benefit of which was assigned to the persons carrying on the trade, profession or vocation after the event) in so far as the total amount proved to be irrecoverable in respect of those debts exceeds any deduction allowed in respect of them under section 74(*j*) in a computation for any period before the event.

Former enactment.—TA 1970, s. 135.

90. Additional payments to redundant employees

(1) Where a payment is made by way of addition to a redundancy payment or to the corresponding amount of any other employer's payment and the additional payment would be—

(*a*) allowable as a deduction in computing for the purposes of Schedule D the profits or gains or losses of a trade, profession or vocation; or
(*b*) eligible for relief under section 75 or 76 as expenses of management of a business,

but for the permanent discontinuance of the trade, profession, vocation or business, the additional payment shall, subject to subsection (2) below, be so allowable or so eligible notwithstanding that discontinuance and, if made after the discontinuance, shall be treated as made on the last day on which the trade, profession, vocation or business was carried on.

(2) Subsection (1) above applies to an additional payment only so far as it does not exceed three times the amount of the redundancy payment or of the corresponding amount of the other employer's payment.

(3) In this section references to the permanent discontinuance of a trade, profession, vocation or business include references to any occasion on which it is treated as permanently discontinued by virtue of section 113(1) or 337(1).

(4) In this section references to a redundancy payment or to the corresponding amount of an employer's payment shall be construed as in sections 579 and 580.

Former enactment.—FA 1980, s. 41.

91. Cemeteries

(1) In computing the profits or gains or losses for any period of a trade which consists of or includes the carrying on of a cemetery, there shall be allowed as a deduction—

(*a*) any capital expenditure incurred by the person engaged in carrying on the trade in providing any land in the cemetery sold during that period for the purpose of interments, and
(*b*) the appropriate fraction of the residue at the end of that period of the relevant capital expenditure.

(2) Subject to subsection (3) below, the relevant capital expenditure is capital expenditure incurred for the purposes of the trade in question by the person engaged in carrying it on, being—

(*a*) expenditure on any building or structure other than a dwelling-house, being a building or structure in the cemetery likely to have little or no value when the cemetery is full; and
(*b*) expenditure incurred in providing land taken up by any such building or structure, and any other land in the cemetery not suitable or adaptable for use for interments and likely to have little or no value when the cemetery is full.

(3) Relevant capital expenditure—

(*a*) does not include expenditure incurred on buildings or structures which have been destroyed before the beginning of the first period to which subsection (1) above applies in the case of the trade in question; and
(*b*) of other expenditure incurred before that time, includes only the fraction—

$$\frac{A}{A+B}$$

where—
A is the number of grave-spaces which at that time were or could have been made available in the cemetery for sale, and
B is the number already sold.

(4) For the purposes of this section—

(a) the residue of any expenditure at the end of a period is the amount incurred before that time which remains after deducting—

(i) any amount allowed in respect of that expenditure under subsection (1)(b) above in computing the profits or gains or losses of the trade for any previous period, and
(ii) if, after the beginning of the first period to which subsection (1) above applies in the case of a trade and before the end of the period mentioned at the beginning of this subsection, any asset representing that expenditure is sold or destroyed, the net proceeds of sale or, as the case may be, any insurance money or other compensation of any description received by the person carrying on the trade in respect of the destruction and any money received by him for the remains of the asset; and

(b) the appropriate fraction of the residue of any expenditure at the end of any period is—

$$\frac{A}{A+B}$$

where—

A is the number of grave-spaces in the cemetery sold in the period, and

B is the number of grave-spaces which at the end of the period are or could be made available in the cemetery for sale.

(5) Where in any chargeable period there is a change in the persons engaged in carrying on a trade which consists of or includes the carrying on of a cemetery, any allowance to be made under this section to the persons carrying on the trade after the change shall, whether or not it is to be assumed for other purposes that the trade was discontinued and a new trade set up and commenced, be computed—

(a) as if they had at all times been engaged in carrying on the trade;
(b) as if everything done to or by any of their predecessors in carrying on the trade had been done to or by them; and
(c) without regard to the price paid on any sale on the occasion of any such change.

(6) No expenditure shall be taken into account under both paragraph (a) and paragraph (b) of subsection (1) above, whether for the same or different periods.

(7) This section shall apply in relation to a trade which consists of or includes the carrying on of a crematorium and, in connection therewith, the maintenance of memorial garden plots, as it applies in relation to a trade which consists of or includes the carrying on of a cemetery, but subject to the modifications that—

(a) references to the cemetery or land in the cemetery shall be taken as references to the land which is devoted wholly to memorial garden plots, and
(b) references to grave-spaces shall be taken as references to memorial garden plots, and
(c) references to the sale or use of land for interments shall be taken as references to its sale or use for memorial garden plots.

(8) In this section—

(a) references to the sale of land include references to the sale of a right of interment in land, and to the appropriation of part of a memorial garden in return for a dedication fee or similar payment;
(b) references to capital expenditure incurred in providing land shall be taken as references to the cost of purchase and to any capital expenditure incurred in levelling or draining it or otherwise rendering it suitable for the purposes of a cemetery or a memorial garden; and
(c) the reference in subsection (4)(a)(ii) to subsection (1) above includes a reference to section 141 of the 1970 Act and section 22 of the Finance Act 1952 (which made similar provision to that made by this section).

(9) Section 84 of the 1968 Act (which relates to expenditure which is reimbursed to a person carrying on a trade) shall apply for the purposes of this section as it applies for the purposes of Part I of that Act.

Former enactments.—Sub-s. (1): TA 1970, s. 141(1).
Sub-ss. (2), (3): TA 1970, s. 141(2).
Sub-ss. (4)–(9): TA 1970, s. 141(3)–(8).

Treatment of regional development and other grants and debts released etc.

92. Regional development grants

(1) A regional development grant which, apart from this subsection, would be taken into account as a receipt in computing the profits of a trade, profession or vocation which are chargeable under Case I or II of Schedule D, shall not be taken into account as a receipt in computing those profits.

(2) A regional development grant which is made to an investment company—

(*a*) shall not be taken into account as a receipt in computing its profits under Case VI of Schedule D; and
(*b*) shall not be deducted, by virtue of section 75(2), from the amount treated as expenses of management.

(3) In this section "regional development grant" means a payment by way of grant under Part II of the Industrial Development Act 1982.

Former enactments.—Sub-s. (1): FA 1984, s. 54(1), (4).
Sub-ss. (2), (3): FA 1984, s. 54(2), (3).

93. Other grants under Industrial Development Act 1982 etc.

(1) A payment to which this section applies which is made to a person carrying on a trade the profits of which are chargeable under Case I of Schedule D shall be taken into account as a receipt in computing those profits; and any such payment which is made to an investment company shall be taken into account as a receipt in computing its profits under Case VI of Schedule D.

(2) This section applies to any payment which would not, apart from this section, be taken into account as mentioned in subsection (1) above, being a payment by way of a grant under—

(*a*) section 7 or 8 of the Industrial Development Act 1982 or section 7 or 8 of the Industry Act 1972; or
(*b*) section 1 of the Industries Development Act (Northern Ireland) 1966 or section 4 of the Industries Development Act (Northern Ireland) 1971; or
(*c*) any of Articles 7, 9 and 30 of the Industrial Development (Northern Ireland) Order 1982;

other than a grant designated as made towards the cost of specified capital expenditure or as made by way of compensation for the loss of capital assets and other than a grant falling within subsection (3) below.

(3) A payment by way of grant which is made—

(*a*) under Article 7 of the Order referred to in subsection (2)(*c*) above, and
(*b*) in respect of a liability for corporation tax (including a liability which has already been met),

shall not be taken into account as mentioned in subsection (1) above, whether by virtue of this section or otherwise.

Former enactments.—Sub-s. (1): FA 1980, s. 42(1).
Sub-s. (2)(*a*), (*b*): FA 1980, s. 42(2); Industrial Development Act 1982, Sch. 2, para. 16.
Sub-s. (2)(*c*): FA 1980, s. 42(2); FA 1984, s. 55(1).
Sub-s. (3): FA 1980, s. 42(3); FA 1984, s. 55(2).

94. Debts deducted and subsequently released

Where, in computing for tax purposes the profits or gains of a trade, profession or vocation, a deduction has been allowed for any debt incurred for the purposes of the trade, profession or vocation, then, if the whole or any part of the debt is thereafter released, the amount released shall be treated as a receipt of the trade, profession or vocation arising in the period in which the release is effected.

Former enactment.—TA 1970, s. 136.

95. Taxation of dealer's receipts on purchase by company of own shares

(1) Where a company purchases its own shares from a dealer, the purchase price shall be taken into account in computing the profits of the dealer chargeable to tax under Case I or II of Schedule D; and accordingly—

  (a) tax shall not be chargeable under Schedule F in respect of any distribution represented by any part of the price, and
  (b) the dealer shall not be entitled in respect of the distribution to a tax credit under section 231, and
  (c) sections 208 and 234(1) shall not apply to the distribution.

(2) For the purposes of subsection (1) above a person is a dealer in relation to shares of a company if the price received on their sale by him otherwise than to the company would be taken into account in computing his profits chargeable to tax under Case I or II of Schedule D.

(3) Subject to subsection (4) below, in subsection (1) above—

  (a) the reference to the purchase of shares includes a reference to the redemption or repayment of shares and to the purchase of rights to acquire shares, and
  (b) the reference to the purchase price includes a reference to any sum payable on redemption or repayment.

(4) Subsection (1) above shall not apply in relation to—

  (a) the redemption of fixed-rate preference shares, or
  (b) the redemption, on terms settled or substantially settled before 6th April 1982, of other preference shares issued before that date,

if in either case the shares were issued to and continuously held by the person from whom they are redeemed.

(5) In this section—

"fixed-rate preference shares" means shares which—

  (a) were issued wholly for new consideration, and
  (b) do not carry any right either to conversion into shares or securities of any other description or to the acquisition of any additional shares or securities, and
  (c) do not carry any right to dividends other than dividends which—

    (i) are of a fixed amount or at a fixed rate per cent. of the nominal value of the shares, and
    (ii) together with any sum paid on redemption, represent no more than a reasonable commercial return on the consideration for which the shares were issued;

"new consideration" has the meaning given by section 254; and
"shares" includes stock.

Former enactment.—FA 1982, s. 54.

Special provisions

96. Farming and market gardening: relief for fluctuating profits

(1) Subject to the provisions of this section, a person who is or has been carrying on a trade of farming or market gardening in the United Kingdom may claim that subsection (2) or (3) below shall have effect in relation to his profits from that trade for any two consecutive years of assessment if his profits for either year do not exceed such part of his profits for the other year as is there specified.

(2) If the claimant's profits for either year do not exceed seven-tenths of his profits for the other year or are nil, his profits for each year shall be adjusted so as to be equal to one-half of his profits for the two years taken together or, as the case may be, for the year for which there are profits.

(3) If the claimant's profits for either year exceed seven-tenths but are less than three-quarters of his profits for the other year, his profits for each year shall be adjusted by adding to the profits that are lower and deducting from those that are higher an amount equal to three times the difference between them less three-quarters of those that are higher.

(4) No claim shall be made under this section—

(a) in respect of any year of assessment before a year in respect of which a claim has already been made under this section; or
(b) in respect of a year of assessment in which the trade is (or by virtue of section 113(1) is treated as) set up and commenced or permanently discontinued.

(5) Any adjustment under this section shall have effect for all the purposes of the Income Tax Acts (including any further application of this section where the second of any two years of assessment is the first of a subsequent pair) except that—

(a) subsection (2) above shall not prevent a person obtaining relief under those Acts for a loss sustained by him in any year of assessment;
(b) any adjustment under this section shall be disregarded for the purposes of section 63(1)(b); and
(c) where, after a claim has been made under this section in respect of the profits for any two years of assessment, the profits for both or either of those years are adjusted for any other reason, this section shall have effect as if the claim had not been made but without prejudice to the making of a further claim in respect of those profits as so adjusted.

(6) This section applies to the profits of a trade carried on by a person in partnership as it applies to the profits of a sole trader except that—

(a) the profits to which the claim relates shall be those chargeable in accordance with section 111; and
(b) any claim in respect of those profits shall be made jointly by all the partners who are individuals;

and where during the years of assessment to which the claim relates there is a change in the persons engaged in carrying on the trade but a notice is given under section 113(2), the claim shall be made jointly by all the persons who are individuals and have been engaged in carrying on the trade at any time during those years.

Where a person who is required by this subsection to join in the making of a claim has died, this subsection shall have effect as if it required his personal representatives to join in making the claim.

(7) In this section references to profits from a trade for a year of assessment are references to the profits or gains from that trade which are chargeable to income tax for that year before—

(a) any deduction for losses sustained in any year of assessment;
(b) any deduction or addition for capital allowances or charges (not being allowances or charges given or made by deduction or addition in the computation of profits or gains);
(c) any deduction for relief under Schedule 9 to the Finance Act 1981 (stock relief).

(8) Any claim under this section shall be made by notice given to the inspector not later than two years after the end of the second of the years of assessment to which the claim relates but any such further claim as is mentioned in subsection (5)(c) above shall not be out of time if made before the end of the year of assessment following that in which the adjustment is made.

(9) Where a person makes a claim under this section in respect of any year of assessment, any claim by him for relief for that year under any other provision of the Income Tax Acts—

(a) shall not be out of time if made before the end of the period in which the claim under this section is required to be made; and
(b) if already made, may be revoked or amended before the end of that period;

but no claim shall by virtue of this subsection be made, revoked or amended after the determination of the claim under this section.

(10) There shall be made all such alterations of assessments or repayments of tax (whether in respect of such profits as are mentioned in subsection (1) above or of other income of the person concerned) as may be required in consequence of any adjustment under this section.

(11) Nothing in this section shall be construed as applying to profits chargeable to corporation tax.

(12) This section applies where the first of the two years mentioned in subsection (1) above is the year 1987–88 or a subsequent year of assessment.

Former enactments.—FA 1978, s. 28; FA 1981, s. 35(4).

97. Treatment of farm animals etc.

Schedule 5 shall have effect with respect to the treatment, in computing profits or gains for the purposes of Case I of Schedule D, of animals and other living creatures kept for the purposes of farming or any other trade.

Former enactment.—TA 1970, s. 139.

98. Tied premises

(1) In computing for tax purposes the profits or gains or losses of a trade carried on by a lessor of tied premises—

   (a) there shall be taken into account as a trading receipt any rent payable for the premises to him, and there shall be allowed as deduction any rent paid for the premises by him, but
   (b) no deduction shall be allowed in respect of the premises either by reference to his being entitled to a rent for the premises which is less than the rent which might have been obtained (or less than their annual value or the rent payable by him for them) or in respect of the annual value of the premises.

(2) For the purposes of this section, premises shall be deemed to be tied premises in relation to any lessor of the premises, and in relation to any trade carried on by him, if, but only if, in the course of that trade, he is concerned (whether as principal or agent) in the supply of goods sold or used on the premises and accordingly deals with the premises or his interest in the premises as property employed for the purposes of that trade; and in this section "the relevant trade", in relation to any tied premises and to any lessor thereof, means any trade carried on by him in relation to which they are tied premises.

(3) Where part only of premises in respect of which rent is paid by or payable to a lessor of the premises are tied premises in relation to him, the rent paid or payable for the tied premises shall for the purposes of this section be taken to be that part of the entire rent which, on a fair and just apportionment, is attributable to them.

(4) Subject to subsection (5) below, a lessor of tied premises who is chargeable to tax for any chargeable period in respect of the profits or gains of the relevant trade shall not be liable for that period (or for the part of it during which he carries on that trade) to any tax in respect of the premises under Schedule A.

(5) Where, for any chargeable period or part of a chargeable period, a lessor of tied premises becomes entitled to any rent under a lease comprising the tied premises and other premises, but is by virtue of subsection (4) above relieved of liability to tax in respect of the tied premises under Schedule A—

   (a) his liability in respect of the rent shall be computed in the first instance as it would be apart from this section, but
   (b) his total liability (so computed) in respect of the rent shall be reduced by the part which, on a fair and just apportionment, is attributable to the tied premises for the chargeable period or part thereof for which he is so relieved of liability in respect of them.

(6) If the lessor of tied premises outside the United Kingdom is chargeable to tax for any chargeable period in respect of the profits or gains of the relevant trade, he shall not be liable for that period (or for the part of it during which he carried on that trade) to tax under Case V of Schedule D in respect of any rent for the premises.

(7) Where the person carrying on a trade is, in the case of any premises, entitled in equity to the interest of any lessor of those premises, then, in relation to that person, subsections (1) to (3) above shall apply as if he were the lessor of the premises, and as if any rent payable to or paid by the lessor were payable to or paid by him; and, in relation to the lessor of the premises, subsections (4) and (5) above (or, in the case of premises outside the United Kingdom, subsection (6) above) shall apply as they would apply to the person carrying on the trade if the lessor's interest in the premises and in any other relevant land were vested in him.

(8) In this section "lease" includes an agreement for a lease if the term to be covered by the lease has begun, and any tenancy, but does not include a mortgage or heritable security, and "lessor" shall be construed accordingly, and includes the successors in title of a lessor.

Former enactment.—TA 1970, s. 140.

99. Dealers in land

(1) In computing for tax purposes the profits or gains of a trade of dealing in land, there shall be disregarded—

(*a*) so much of the cost of woodlands in the United Kingdom purchased in the course of the trade as is attributable to trees or saleable underwood growing on the land; and

(*b*) where any amount has been disregarded under paragraph (a) above and, on a subsequent sale of the woodlands in the course of the trade, all or any of the trees or underwood to which the amount disregarded was attributable are still growing on the land, so much of the price for the land as is equal to the amount so disregarded in respect of those trees or underwood.

(2) In computing the profits or gains of a trade of dealing in land, any trading receipt falling within subsection (1), (4) or (5) of section 34 or section 35 or 36 shall be treated as reduced by the amount on which tax is chargeable by virtue of that section.

(3) Where, on a claim being made under subsection (2)(*b*) of section 36, the amount on which tax was chargeable by virtue of that section is treated as reduced, subsection (2) above shall be deemed to have applied to the amount as reduced, and any such adjustment of liability to tax shall be made (for all relevant chargeable periods) whether by means of an assessment or otherwise, as may be necessary, and may be so made at any time at which it could be made if it related only to tax for the chargeable period in which that claim is made.

(4) Subsection (1) above shall not apply where the purchase mentioned in paragraph (*a*) of that subsection was made under a contract entered into before 1st May 1963.

Former enactments.—Sub-s. (1): TA 1970, s. 142(1).
Sub-ss. (2), (3): TA 1970, s. 142(2), (4).
Sub-s. (4): TA 1970, s. 142(1).

CHAPTER VI

DISCONTINUANCE, AND CHANGE OF BASIS OF COMPUTATION

Valuation of trading stock etc.

100. Valuation of trading stock at discontinuance of trade

(1) In computing for any tax purpose the profits or gains of a trade which has been discontinued, any trading stock belonging to the trade at the discontinuance shall be valued as follows—

(*a*) if—

(i) the stock is sold or transferred for valuable consideration to a person who carries on, or intends to carry on, a trade in the United Kingdom, and
(ii) the cost of the stock may be deducted by the purchaser as an expense in computing for any tax purpose the profits or gains of that trade,

the value of the stock shall be taken to be the amount realised on the sale or the value of the consideration given for the transfer; and

(*b*) if the stock does not fall to be valued under paragraph (*a*) above, its value shall be taken to be the amount which it would have realised if it had been sold in the open market at the discontinuance of the trade.

(2) For the purposes of this section "trading stock", in relation to any trade—

(*a*) means property of any description, whether real or personal, being either—

(i) property such as is sold in the ordinary course of the trade, or would be so sold if it were mature or if its manufacture, preparation or construction were complete; or
(ii) materials such as are used in the manufacture, preparation or construction of any such property as is referred to in sub-paragraph (i) above; and

(*b*) includes also any services, article or material which would, if the trade were a profession or vocation, be treated, for the purposes of section 101, as work in progress of the profession or vocation, and references to the sale or transfer of trading stock shall be construed accordingly.

Former enactments.—Sub-s. (1): TA 1970, s. 137(1).
Sub-s. (2): TA 1970, s. 137(4).
Cross references.—See FA 1988, Sch. 12, para. 2 (valuation of a building society's financial trading stock at the time of its change into a company).

101. Valuation of work in progress at discontinuance of profession or vocation

(1) Where, in computing for any tax purpose the profits or gains of a profession or vocation which has been discontinued, a valuation is taken of the work of the profession or vocation in progress at the discontinuance, that work shall be valued as follows—

(*a*) if—

(i) the work is transferred for money or any other valuable consideration to a person who carries on, or intends to carry on, a profession or vocation in the United Kingdom, and
(ii) the cost of the work may be deducted by that person as an expense in computing for any tax purpose the profits or gains of that profession or vocation,

the value of the work shall be taken to be the amount paid or other consideration given for the transfer; and

(*b*) if the work does not fall to be valued under paragraph (*a*) above, its value shall be taken to be the amount which would have been paid for a transfer of the work on the date of the discontinuance as between parties at arm's length.

(2) Where a profession or vocation is discontinued, and the person by whom it was carried on immediately before the discontinuance so elects by notice sent to the inspector at any time within 12 months after the discontinuance—

(*a*) the amount (if any) by which the value of the work in progress at the discontinuance (as ascertained under subsection (1) above) exceeds the actual cost of the work shall not be brought into account in computing the profits or gains of the period immediately before the discontinuance; but

(b) the amount by which any sums received for the transfer of the work exceed the actual cost of the work shall be included in the sums chargeable to tax by virtue of section 103 as if it were a sum to which that section applies received after the discontinuance.

(3) References in this section to work in progress at the discontinuance of a profession or vocation shall be construed as references to—

(a) any services performed in the ordinary course of the profession or vocation, the performance of which was wholly or partly completed at the time of the discontinuance and for which it would be reasonable to expect that a charge would have been made on their completion if the profession or vocation had not been discontinued; and

(b) any article produced, and any such material as is used, in the performance of any such services,

and references in this section to the transfer of work in progress shall include references to the transfer of any benefits and rights which accrue, or might reasonably be expected to accrue, from the carrying out of the work.

Former enactments.—Sub-s. (1): TA 1970, s. 138(1).
Sub-s. (2): TA 1970, s. 138(3).
Sub-s. (3): TA 1970, s .138(5).

102. Provisions supplementary to sections 100 and 101

(1) Any question arising under section 100(1)(a) or 101(1)(a) shall be determined as follows, for the purpose of computing for any tax purpose the profits or gains of both the trades or, as the case may be, the professions or vocations concerned—

(a) in a case where the same body of General Commissioners have jurisdiction with respect to both the trades, professions or vocations concerned, the question shall be determined by those Commissioners unless all parties concerned agree that it shall be determined by the Special Commissioners;

(b) in any other case, the question shall be determined by the Special Commissioners; and

(c) the General or Special Commissioners shall determine the question in like manner as an appeal.

(2) Where, by virtue of section 113 or 337(1), a trade, profession or vocation is treated as having been permanently discontinued for the purpose of computing tax, it shall also be so treated for the purposes of sections 100 and 101; but those sections shall not apply in a case where a trade, profession or vocation carried on by a single individual is discontinued by reason of his death.

Former enactments.—Sub-s. (1): TA 1970, ss. 137(2), 138(2).
Sub-s. (2): TA 1970, ss. 137(3), 138(4).
Cross references.—See TMA 1970, s. 58(3)(b) and FA 1988 ss. 134(4), 135(2) (with effect from an appointed day, proceedings under this section to be in Northern Ireland if the place given by certain rules in relation to the parties to the proceedings is in Northern Ireland).

Case VI charges on receipts

103. Receipts after discontinuance: earnings basis charge and related charge affecting conventional basis

(1) Where any trade, profession or vocation the profits or gains of which are chargeable to tax under Case I or II of Schedule D has been permanently discontinued, tax shall be charged under Case VI of that Schedule in respect of any sums to which this section applies which are received after the discontinuance.

(2) Subject to subsection (3) below, this section applies to the following sums arising from the carrying on of the trade, profession or vocation during any period before the discontinuance (not being sums otherwise chargeable to tax)—

(a) where the profits or gains for that period were computed by reference to earnings, all such sums in so far as their value was not brought into account in computing the profits or gains for any period before the discontinuance, and

(b) where those profits or gains were computed on a conventional basis (that is to say, were computed otherwise than by reference to earnings), any sums which, if those profits or gains had been computed by reference to earnings, would not have been brought into the computation for any period before the discontinuance because the date on which they became due, or the date on which the amount due in respect thereof was ascertained, fell after the discontinuance.

(3) This section does not apply to any of the following sums—

(a) sums received by a person beneficially entitled thereto who is not resident in the United Kingdom, or by a person acting on his behalf, which represent income arising directly or indirectly from a country or territory outside the United Kingdom, or

(b) a lump sum paid to the personal representatives of the author of a literary, dramatic, musical or artistic work as consideration for the assignment by them, wholly or partially, of the copyright in the work, or

[(bb) a lump sum paid to the personal representatives of the designer of a design in which design right subsists as consideration for the assignment by them, wholly or partially, of that right,][1]

(c) sums realised by the transfer of trading stock belonging to a trade at the discontinuance of the trade, or by the transfer of the work of a profession or vocation in progress at its discontinuance.

Paragraph (b) above shall have effect in relation to public lending right as it has effect in relation to copyright.

(4) Where—

(a) in computing for tax purposes the profits or gains of a trade, profession or vocation a deduction has been allowed for any debt incurred for the purposes of the trade, profession or vocation, and

(b) the whole or any part of that debt is thereafter released, and

(c) the trade, profession or vocation has been permanently discontinued at or after the end of the period for which the deduction was allowed and before the release was effected,

subsections (1) to (3) above shall apply as if the amount released were a sum received after the discontinuance.

(5) For the purposes of this section the value of any sum received in payment of a debt shall be treated as not brought into account in the computation of the profits or gains of a trade, profession or vocation to the extent that a deduction has been allowed in respect of that sum under section 74(j).

Former enactments.—TA 1970, s. 143; FA 1983, s. 27(b).
Amendments.—[1] Sub-s. (3)(bb) inserted by the Copyright, Designs and Patents Act 1988, Sch. 7, para. 36(3) with effect from 1 August 1989 by virtue of the Copyright, Designs and Patents Act 1988 (Commencement No. 1) Order 1989, S.I. 1989 No. 816.

104. Conventional basis: general charge on receipts after discontinuance or change of basis

(1) Where any trade, profession or vocation the profits or gains of which are chargeable to tax under Case I or II of Schedule D has been permanently discontinued, and the profits or gains for any period before the discontinuance were computed on a conventional basis, tax shall be charged under Case VI of that Schedule in respect of any sums to which this subsection applies which are received on or after the discontinuance.

(2) Subject to subsection (3) below, subsection (1) above applies to all sums arising from the carrying on of the trade, profession or vocation during any period before the discontinuance, not being sums otherwise chargeable to tax, in so far as the amount or value of the sums was not brought into account in computing the profits or gains for any period before the discontinuance.

(3) In subsection (2) above the reference to sums otherwise chargeable to tax includes any sums which (disregarding this section) are chargeable to tax under section 103 or to which that section would have applied but for subsection (3)(a) and (b) of that section.

(4) Where, in the case of any trade, profession or vocation the profits or gains of which are chargeable to tax under Case I or II of Schedule D, there has been—

(a) a change from a conventional basis to the earnings basis, or

(b) a change of conventional basis which may result in receipts dropping out of computation,

tax shall be charged under Case VI of that Schedule in respect of sums to which this subsection applies which are received after the change and before the trade, profession or vocation is permanently discontinued.

(5) Subsection (4) above applies to all sums arising from the carrying on of the trade, profession or vocation during any period before the change, not being sums otherwise

chargeable to tax, in so far as the amount or value of the sums was not brought into account in computing the profits or gains for any period.

(6) It is hereby declared that where work in progress at the discontinuance of a profession or vocation, or the responsibility for its completion, is transferred, the sums to which subsection (1) above applies include any sums received by way of consideration for the transfer, and any sums received by way of realisation by the transferee, on behalf of the transferor, of the work in progress transferred.

(7) Where in the case of any profession or vocation, the profits or gains of which are chargeable to tax under Case II of Schedule D—

(a) there has been a change from a conventional basis to the earnings basis, or a change of conventional basis, and
(b) the value of the work in progress at the time of the change was debited in the accounts and allowed as a deduction in computing profits for tax purposes for a period after the change,

then, in so far as no counterbalancing credit was brought into account in computing profits for tax purposes for any period ending before or with the date of the change, tax shall be charged under subsection (4) above in respect of that amount for the year of assessment in which the change occurred as if that amount were a sum to which that subsection applies, and the change of basis were a change of the kind described in that subsection.

Former enactments.—Sub-ss. (1), (2), (3): TA 1970, s. 144(1).
Sub-ss. (4), (5): TA 1970, s. 144(2).
Sub-ss. (6), (7): TA 1970, s. 144(3), (4).

105. Allowable deductions

(1) In computing the charge to tax in respect of sums received by any person which are chargeable to tax by virtue of section 103 or 104(1) (including amounts treated as sums received by him by virtue of section 103(4)), there shall be deducted from the amount which, apart from this subsection, would be chargeable to tax—

(a) any loss, expense or debit (not being a loss, expense or debit arising directly or indirectly from the discontinuance itself) which, if the trade, profession or vocation had not been discontinued, would have been deducted in computing for tax purposes the profits or gains of the person by whom it was carried on before the discontinuance, or would have been deducted from or set off against those profits or gains as so computed, and
(b) any capital allowance to which the person who carried on the trade, profession or vocation was entitled immediately before the discontinuance and to which effect has not been given by way of relief before the discontinuance.

(2) No amount shall be deducted under subsection (1) above if that amount has been allowed under any other provision of the Tax Acts.

(3) No amount shall be deducted more than once under subsection (1) above; and—

(a) any expense or debit shall be apportioned between a sum chargeable under section 103 and a sum chargeable under section 104(1) in such manner as may be just;
(b) as between sums chargeable, whether under section 103 or 104(1), for one chargeable period and sums so charged for a subsequent chargeable period, any deduction in respect of a loss or capital allowance shall be made against sums chargeable for the earlier chargeable period;
(c) subject to paragraph (b) above, as between sums chargeable for any chargeable period under section 103 and sums so chargeable under section 104(1), any deduction in respect of a loss or capital allowance shall be made against the last-mentioned sums rather than the first-mentioned;

but, in the case of a loss which is to be allowed after the discontinuance, not so as to authorise its deduction from any sum chargeable for a chargeable period preceding that in which the loss is incurred.

(4) In computing the charge to tax in respect of sums received by any person which are chargeable to tax by virtue of section 104(4), there shall be deducted any expense or debit which is not otherwise allowable and which, but for the change in basis, would have been deducted in computing for tax purposes the profits or gains of the trade, profession or vocation, but no amount shall be deducted more than once under this subsection.

Former enactment.—TA 1970, s. 145.

106. Application of charges where rights to payments transferred

(1) Subject to subsection (2) below, in the case of a transfer for value of the right to receive any sum to which section 103, 104(1) or 104(4) applies, any tax chargeable by virtue of either of those sections shall be charged in respect of the amount or value of the consideration (or, in the case of a transfer otherwise than at arm's length, in respect of the value of the right transferred as between parties at arm's length), and references in this Chapter, except section 101(2), to sums received shall be construed accordingly.

(2) Where a trade, profession or vocation is treated as permanently discontinued by reason of a change in the persons carrying it on, and the right to receive any sum to which section 103 or 104(1) applies is or was transferred at the time of the change to the persons carrying on the trade, profession or vocation after the change, tax shall not be charged by virtue of either of those sections, but any sum received by those persons by virtue of the transfer shall be treated for all purposes as a receipt to be brought into the computation of the profits or gains of the trade, profession or vocation in the period in which it is received.

Former enactment.—TA 1970, s. 147.

Reliefs

107. Treatment of receipts as earned income

Where an individual is chargeable to tax by virtue of section 103 or 104, and the profits or gains of the trade, profession or vocation to which he was entitled before the discontinuance or, as the case may be, change of basis fell to be treated as earned income for the purposes of income tax, the sums in respect of which he is so chargeable shall also be treated as earned income for those purposes (but, in the case of sums chargeable by virtue of section 104, after any reduction in those sums under section 109).

Former enactment.—TA 1970, s. 148.

108. Election for carry-back

Where any sum is—

    (*a*) chargeable to tax by virtue of section 103 or 104, and
    (*b*) received in any year of assessment beginning not later than six years after the discontinuance or, as the case may be, change of basis by the person by whom the trade, profession or vocation was carried on before the discontinuance or change, or by his personal representatives,

that person or (in either case) his personal representatives may, by notice sent to the inspector within two years after that year of assessment, elect that the tax so chargeable shall be charged as if the sum in question were received on the date on which the discontinuance took place or, as the case may be, on the last day of the period at the end of which the change of basis took place; and, in any such case, an assessment shall (notwithstanding anything in the Tax Acts) be made accordingly, and, in connection with that assessment, no further deduction or relief shall be made or given in respect of any loss or allowance deducted in pursuance of section 105.

Former enactment.—TA 1970, s. 149.

109. Charge under section 104: relief for individuals born before 6th April 1917

(1) If an individual born before 6th April 1917, or the personal representatives of such an individual, is chargeable to tax under section 104 and—

    (*a*) the individual was engaged in carrying on a trade, profession or vocation on 18th March 1968, and
    (*b*) the profits or gains of the trade, profession or vocation were not computed by reference to earnings in the period in which that 18th March fell, or in any subsequent period ending before or with the relevant date,

the net amount with which he is so chargeable to tax shall be reduced by multiplying that net amount by the fraction given below.

(2) Where section 104(4) applies in relation to a change of basis taking place on a date before 19th March 1968, then, in relation to tax chargeable by reference to that change of basis, that earlier date shall be substituted for the date in subsection (1)(*a*) above and subsection (1)(*b*) above shall be omitted.

(3) The fraction referred to in subsection (1) above is—

(*a*) where on 5th April 1968 the individual had not attained the age of 52—

$$\frac{19}{20}$$

(*b*) where on that date he had attained the age of 52, but had not attained the age of 53—

$$\frac{18}{20}$$

and so on, reducing the fraction by—

$$\frac{1}{20}$$

for each year he had attained up to the age of 64;

(*c*) where on that date he had attained the age of 65, or any greater age—

$$\frac{5}{20}$$

(4) In this section—

"the net amount" with which a person is chargeable to tax under section 104 means the amount with which he is so chargeable after making any deduction authorised by section 105 but before giving any relief under this section; and

"relevant date"—

(*a*) in relation to tax under section 104(1), means the date of the permanent discontinuance, and

(*b*) in relation to tax under section 104(4), means the date of the change of basis.

(5) Subsections (1) to (4) above shall apply as follows as respects the net amount of any sum chargeable under section 104 which is assessed by reference to a sum accruing to a partnership—

(*a*) the part of that net amount which is apportioned to any partner (who is an individual), or the personal representative of such an individual, shall be a net amount with which that person is chargeable under that section, and

(*b*) if the part of that net amount which is so apportioned is a greater proportion of that amount than is the individual's share (that is to say, the part to be included in his total income) of the total amount of the partnership profits assessed to income tax for the three years of assessment ending with the year in which the discontinuance or change of basis took place, the amount of the reduction to be given by way of relief shall not exceed the amount of relief which would have been so given if the apportionment had been made by reference to his share of that total amount.

(6) For the purposes of this section the trade, profession or vocation carried on before a permanent discontinuance shall not be treated as the same as any carried after the discontinuance.

Former enactment.—TA 1970, s. 150.

Supplemental

110. Interpretation etc.

(1) The following provisions have effect for the purposes of sections 103 to 109.

(2) For the purposes of those sections, any reference to the permanent discontinuance of a trade, profession or vocation includes a reference to the occurring of any event which, under section 113 or 337(1), is to be treated as equivalent to the permanent discontinuance of a trade, profession or vocation.

(3) The profits or gains of a trade, profession or vocation in any period shall be treated as

computed by reference to earnings where all credits and liabilities accruing during that period as a consequence of its being carried on are brought into account in computing those profits or gains for tax purposes, and not otherwise, and "earnings basis" shall be construed accordingly.

(4) "Conventional basis" has the meaning given by section 103(2), so that profits or gains are computed on a conventional basis if computed otherwise than by reference to earnings.

(5) There is a change from a conventional basis to the earnings basis at the end of a period the profits or gains of which were computed on a conventional basis if the profits or gains of the next succeeding period are computed by reference to earnings; and, if the profits or gains of two successive periods are computed on different conventional bases, a change of conventional basis occurs at the end of the earlier period.

(6) In sections 103 and 104—
  (a) "trading stock" has the meaning given by section 100(2);
  (b) references to work in progress at the discontinuance of a profession or vocation, and to the transfer of work in progress, are to be construed in accordance with section 101(3); and
  (c) the reference to work in progress at the time of a change of basis is also to be construed in accordance with section 101(3), substituting therein for this purpose references to the change of basis for references to the discontinuance.

Former enactments.—Sub-s. (1): TA 1970, s. 151(1).
Sub-s. (2): TA 1970, s. 146.
Sub-ss. (3)–(6): TA 1970, s. 151(2)–(5).

CHAPTER VII

PARTNERSHIPS AND SUCCESSIONS

General

111. Partnership assessments to income tax

Where a trade or profession is carried on by two or more persons jointly, income tax in respect thereof shall be computed and stated jointly, and in one sum, and shall be separate and distinct from any other tax chargeable on those persons or any of them, and a joint assessment shall be made in the partnership name.

Former enactment.—TA 1970, s. 152.

112. Partnerships controlled abroad

(1) Where a trade or business is carried on by two or more persons in partnership, and the control and management of the trade or business is situated abroad, the trade or business shall be deemed to be carried on by persons resident outside the United Kingdom, and the partnership shall be deemed to reside outside the United Kingdom, notwithstanding the fact that some of the members of the partnership are resident in the United Kingdom and that some of its trading operations are conducted within the United Kingdom.

(2) Where any part of the trade or business of a partnership firm whose management and control is situated abroad consists of trading operations within the United Kingdom, the firm shall, subject to subsection (3) below, be chargeable in respect of the profits of those trading operations within the United Kingdom to the same extent as, and no further than, a person resident abroad is chargeable in respect of trading operations by him within the United Kingdom, notwithstanding the fact that one or more members of the firm are resident in the United Kingdom.

(3) For the purpose of charging any such firm as is mentioned in subsection (2) above in respect of the profits of its trading operations within the United Kingdom, an assessment may be made on the firm in respect of those profits in the name of any partner resident in the United Kingdom.

(4) In any case where—

    (*a*) a person resident in the United Kingdom (in this subsection and subsection (5) below referred to as "the resident partner") is a member of a partnership which resides or is deemed to reside outside the United Kingdom; and
    (*b*) by virtue of any arrangements falling within section 788 any of the income or capital gains of the partnership is relieved from tax in the United Kingdom,

the arrangements referred to in paragraph (*b*) above shall not affect any liability to tax in respect of the resident partner's share of any income or capital gains of the partnership.

(5) If, in a case where subsection (4) above applies, the resident partner's share of the income of the partnership consists of or includes a share in a qualifying distribution made by a company resident in the United Kingdom, then, notwithstanding anything in the arrangements, the resident partner (and not the partnership as a whole) shall be regarded as entitled to that share of the tax credit in respect of the distribution which corresponds to his share of the distribution.

(6) Section 115(5) has effect as respects the application of this section where the partners in a partnership include a company.

Former enactments.—TA 1970, s. 153; F(No. 2)A 1987, s. 62.

113. Effect, for income tax, of change in ownership of trade, profession or vocation

(1) Where there is a change in the persons engaged in carrying on any trade, profession or vocation chargeable under Case I or II of Schedule D, then, subject to the provisions of this section and of section 114(3)(*b*), the amount of the profits or gains of the trade, profession or vocation on which income tax is chargeable for any year of assessment and the persons on

whom it is chargeable, shall be determined as if the trade, profession or vocation had been permanently discontinued, and a new one set up and commenced, at the date of the change.

(2) Subject to section 114(3)(*b*), where there is such a change as is mentioned in subsection (1) above, and a person engaged in carrying on the trade, profession or vocation immediately before the change continues to be so engaged immediately after it, the persons so engaged immediately before and the persons so engaged immediately after the change may, by notice signed by them and sent to the inspector at any time within two years after the date of the change, elect that subsection (1) above shall not apply to treat the trade, profession or vocation as discontinued or a new one as set up and commenced.

(3) Where there is in any year of assessment a change in the persons engaged in carrying on a trade, profession or vocation, and subsection (1) above does not apply by reason of a notice under subsection (2) above, then—

(*a*) income tax in respect of the trade, profession or vocation for that year shall be assessed and charged separately on those so engaged before the change and on those so engaged after the change, but the amount on which tax is chargeable shall be computed as if there had been no such change in that year, and shall be apportioned as may be just; and

(*b*) if, after the change but before the end of the second year of assessment following that in which the change occurred, there is a permanent discontinuance of the trade, profession or vocation (including a change treated as such), then, on that discontinuance, section 63 shall apply, as respects any period before the first-mentioned change, to the persons charged or chargeable for that period as it would apply if no such change had taken place and they had been charged to tax accordingly for the subsequent period up to the discontinuance.

(4) There shall be made any such assessment, reduction of an assessment or, on the making of a claim therefor, repayment of income tax as may in any case be necessary for giving effect to this section.

(5) Any question which arises as to the manner in which any sum is to be apportioned under subsection (3)(*a*) above shall be determined, for the purposes of the tax of all of the persons as respects whose liability to tax the apportionment is material—

(*a*) in a case where the same body of General Commissioners have jurisdiction with respect to all those persons, by those Commissioners, unless all those persons agree that it shall be determined by the Special Commissioners;

(*b*) in a case where different bodies of Commissioners have jurisdiction with respect to those persons, by such of those bodies as the Board may direct, unless all those persons agree that it shall be determined by the Special Commissioners; and

(*c*) in any other case, by the Special Commissioners;

and any such Commissioners shall determine the question in like manner as an appeal, except that all those persons shall be entitled to appear and be heard by the Commissioners who are to make the determination, or to make representations to them in writing.

(6) In the case of the death of a person who, if he had not died, would under the provisions of this section have become chargeable to tax for any year, the tax which would have been so chargeable shall be assessed and charged upon his executors or administrators, and shall be a debt due from and payable out of his estate; and where under those provisions an election may be made by any person, it may in the case of his death be made by his executors or administrators instead of by him.

(7) For the purposes of this section, a change in the personal representatives of any person, or in the trustees of any trust, shall not be treated as a change in the persons engaged in the carrying on any trade, profession or vocation carried on by those personal representatives or trustees as such.

Former enactments.—TA 1970, s. 154; FA 1971, s. 17(1).
Cross references.—See TMA 1970, s. 58(3)(*b*) and FA 1988, ss. 134(4), 135(2) (with effect from an appointed day, proceedings under sub-s. (5) above to be in Northern Ireland if the place given by certain rules in relation to the parties to the proceedings is in Northern Ireland).

Partnerships involving companies

114. Special rules for computing profits and losses

(1) So long as a trade is carried on by persons in partnership, and any of those persons is a company, the profits and losses (including terminal losses) of the trade shall be computed for the purposes of corporation tax in like manner, and by reference to the like accounting

periods, as if the partnership were a company, and without regard to any change in the persons carrying on the trade, except that—

(*a*) references to distributions shall not apply; and
(*b*) subject to section 116(5), no deduction or addition shall be made for charges on income, or for capital allowances and charges, nor in any accounting period for losses incurred in any other period nor for any expenditure to which section 401(1) applies; and
(*c*) a change in the persons engaged in carrying on the trade shall be treated as the transfer of the trade to a different company if there continues to be a company so engaged after the change, but not a company that was so engaged before the change.

(2) A company's share in the profits or loss of any accounting period of the partnership, or in any matter excluded from the computation by subsection (1)(*b*) above, shall be determined according to the interests of the partners during that period, and corporation tax shall be chargeable as if that share derived from a trade carried on by the company alone in its corresponding accounting period or periods; and the company shall be assessed and charged to tax for its corresponding accounting period or periods accordingly.

In this subsection "corresponding accounting period or periods" means the accounting period or periods of the company comprising or together comprising the accounting period of the partnership, and any necessary apportionment shall be made between corresponding accounting periods if more than one.

(3) Where any of the persons engaged in carrying on the trade is an individual, income tax shall be chargeable in respect of his share of the profits, and he shall be entitled to relief for his share of any loss, as if all the partners had been individuals except that—

(*a*) income tax shall be chargeable, and any relief from income tax shall be given, by reference to the computations made for corporation tax, but so that the amounts so computed for an accounting period of the capital allowances and charges falling to be made in taxing the trade shall (as regards the individual's share of them) be given or made for the year or years of assessment comprising that period and, where necessary, apportioned accordingly; and
(*b*) section 113 shall not apply by reason of any change in the persons engaged in carrying on the trade unless an individual begins or ceases to be so engaged, and, where it does apply, an election under subsection (2) of that section shall be made only by the individuals so engaged, and only if an individual so engaged before the change continues to be so engaged after it; and
(*c*) sections 388 and 389 shall not apply except where section 394 applies to the partnership as a whole.

(4) Section 111 shall apply to income tax chargeable in accordance with this section, matters relevant only to corporation tax being omitted from the assessment.

Former enactments.—Sub-s. (1): TA 1970, s. 155(1); FA 1973, s. 31(5); FA 1980, s. 39(3).
Sub-s. (2): TA 1970, s. 155(2); FA 1972, s. 107(2).
Sub-ss. (3), (4): TA 1970, s. 155(3), (4).

115. Provisions supplementary to section 114

(1) Subsections (2) and (3) below have effect as respects income tax chargeable in accordance with section 114 for any year of assessment throughout all or any part of which one or more of the persons engaged in carrying on the trade is an individual.

(2) Notwithstanding any difference between the partners' interests during the basis period and their interests during the year of assessment, the amount of the individual's income from the partnership for the year of assessment, or the total of the amounts of the individuals' incomes from the partnership for that year, shall be deemed to be not less than the profits of the basis period, reduced, where any share was apportioned to a company under section 114(2), by the amount of that company's share.

(3) Where there are two or more individuals and, but for subsection (2) above, the total of the amounts of the individuals' incomes from the partnership for the year would fall short of the profits of the basis period reduced, where any share was apportioned to a company under section 114(2), by the amount of that company's share, that amount shall be apportioned—

(*a*) according to the individuals' interests during the year of assessment, disregarding any company's interest; and
(*b*) in so far as that does not determine, or fully determine, the apportionment, between the individuals in equal shares.

(4) Where a trade or business is carried on by two or more persons in partnership, and the control and management of the trade or business is situated abroad but those persons include a company resident in the United Kingdom, then as regards that company, this section and section 114 shall have effect as if the partnership were resident in the United Kingdom, and an assessment may be made on the company accordingly.

(5) Subject to subsection (4) above, where the partners in a partnership include a company, section 112 shall apply whether for corporation tax or for income tax; and this section and section 114 shall have effect accordingly.

(6) In this section and section 114—

"basis period", in relation to a year of assessment, means any accounting period or part of an accounting period which is, or forms part of, the period on the profits or gains of which income tax for the year of assessment in question falls to be computed under Schedule D in respect of the trade;

"capital allowances and charges" means any allowances or charges under any of the Capital Allowances Acts, not being allowances or charges which, for income tax, are given or made by deduction or addition in the computation of profits or gains;

and references in subsection (1) above to an individual's income from the partnership are references to that income before deduction of capital allowances or charges on income.

(7) For the purposes of this section and section 114 "profits" shall not be taken as including chargeable gains.

Former enactments.—Sub-ss. (1)–(3): TA 1970, s. 155(5).
Sub-ss. (4)–(7): TA 1970, s. 155(6)–(9); FA 1971, Sch. 8, para. 16(5); FA 1986, s. 56(7)(*a*), Sch. 13, para. 2(5)(*a*).

116. Arrangements for transferring relief

(1) The provisions of subsection (2) below shall apply in relation to a company ("the partner company") which is a member of a partnership carrying on a trade if arrangements are in existence (whether as part of the terms of the partnership or otherwise) whereby—

(*a*) in respect of the whole or any part of the value of, or of any portion of, the partner company's share in the profits or loss of any accounting period of the partnership, another member of the partnership or any person connected with another member of the partnership receives any payment or acquires or enjoys, directly or indirectly, any other benefit in money's worth; or

(*b*) in respect of the whole or any part of the cost of, or of any portion of, the partner company's share in the loss of any accounting period of the partnership, the partner company or any person connected with that company receives any payment or acquires or enjoys, directly or indirectly, any other benefit in money's worth, other than a payment in respect of group relief to the partner company by a company which is a member of the same group as the partner company for the purposes of group relief.

(2) In any case where the provisions of this subsection apply in relation to the partner company—

(*a*) the company's share in the loss of the relevant accounting period of the partnership and its share in any charges on income, within the meaning of section 338, paid by the partnership in that accounting period shall not be available for set-off for the purposes of corporation tax except against its share in the profits of the trade carried on by the partnership; and

(*b*) except in accordance with paragraph (*a*) above, no trading losses shall be available for set-off for the purposes of corporation tax against the company's share in the profits of the relevant accounting period of the partnership; and

(*c*) except in accordance with paragraphs (*a*) and (*b*) above, no amount which, apart from this subsection, would be available for relief against profits shall be available for set-off for the purposes of corporation tax against so much of the company's total profits as consists of its share in the profits of the relevant accounting period of the partnership; and

(*d*) notwithstanding anything in section 239, no advance corporation tax may be set against the company's liability to corporation tax on its share in the profits of the relevant accounting period of the partnership.

(3) In subsection (2) above "relevant accounting period of the partnership" means any accounting period of the partnership in which any such arrangements as are specified in subsection (1) above are in existence or to which any such arrangements apply.

(4) If a company is a member of a partnership and tax in respect of any profits of the partnership is chargeable under Case VI of Schedule D, this section shall apply in relation to the company's share in the profits or loss of the partnership as if—

(a) the profits or loss to which the company's share is attributable were the profits of, or the loss incurred in, a trade carried on by the partnership; and
(b) any allowance which falls to be made under section 46(1) of the Finance Act 1971 (machinery and plant on lease) were an allowance made in taxing that trade.

(5) For the purposes of this section, subsection (2) of section 114 shall have effect for determining a company's share in the profits or loss of any accounting period of a partnership as if, in subsection (1)(b) of that section, the words "or for capital allowances and charges" were omitted.

(6) In this section "arrangements" means arrangements of any kind whether in writing or not.

(7) Section 839 shall apply for the purposes of this section.

Former enactment.—FA 1973, ss. 31(1)–(5), 32(6).

Limited partners

117. Restriction on relief: individuals

(1) An amount which may be given or allowed to an individual under section 353, 380 or 381 below or section 71 of the 1968 Act—

(a) in respect of a loss sustained by him in a trade, or of interest paid by him in connection with the carrying on of a trade, in a relevant year of assessment; or
(b) as an allowance falling to be made to him for a relevant year of assessment either in taxing a trade or by way of discharge or repayment of tax to which he is entitled by reason of his participation in a trade,

may be given or allowed otherwise than against income consisting of profits or gains arising from the trade only to the extent that the amount given or allowed or (as the case may be) the aggregate amount does not exceed the relevant sum.

(2) In this section—

"limited partner" means—

(i) a person who is carrying on a trade as a limited partner in a limited partnership registered under the Limited Partnership Act 1907;
(ii) a person who is carrying on a trade as a general partner in a partnership, who is not entitled to take part in the management of the trade and who is entitled to have his liabilities, or his liabilities beyond a certain limit, for debts or obligations incurred for the purposes of the trade discharged or reimbursed by some other person; or
(iii) a person who carries on a trade jointly with others and who, under the law of any territory outside the United Kingdom, is not entitled to take part in the management of the trade and is not liable beyond a certain limit for debts or obligations incurred for the purposes of the trade;

"relevant year of assessment" means a year of assessment at any time during which the individual carried on the trade as a limited partner;
"the aggregate amount" means the aggregate of any amounts given or allowed to him at any time under section 353, 380 or 381 below or section 71 of the 1968 Act—

(a) in respect of a loss sustained by him in the trade, or of interest paid by him in connection with carrying it on, in a relevant year of assessment; or
(b) as an allowance falling to be made to him for a relevant year of assessment either in taxing the trade or by way of discharge or repayment of tax to which he is entitled by reason of his participation in the trade;

"the relevant sum" means the amount of his contribution to the trade as at the appropriate time; and
"the appropriate time" is the end of the relevant year of assessment in which the loss is sustained or the interest paid or for which the allowance falls to be made (except that where he ceased to carry on the trade during that year of assessment it is the time when he so ceased).

(3) A person's contribution to a trade at any time is the aggregate of—

(a) the amount which he has contributed to it as capital and has not, directly or indirectly, drawn out or received back (other than anything which he is or may be entitled so to draw out or receive back at any time when he carries on the trade as a limited partner or which he is or may be entitled to require another person to reimburse to him), and

(*b*) the amount of any profits or gains of the trade to which he is entitled but which he has not received in money or money's worth.

(4) To the extent that an allowance is taken into account in computing profits or gains or losses in the year of the loss by virtue of section 383(1) it shall, for the purposes of this section, be treated as falling to be made in the year of the loss (and not the year of assessment for which the year of loss is the basis year).

Former enactments.—Sub-s. (1): FA 1985, Sch. 12, para. 2(1)–(3).
Sub-s. (2): FA 1985, Sch. 12, paras. 1, 2(4).
Sub-s. (3): FA 1985, Sch. 12, para. 4.
Sub-s. (4): FA 1985, Sch. 12, para. 2(5).

118. Restriction on relief: companies

(1) An amount which may be given or allowed under section 338, 393(2) or 403(1) to (3) and (7) below or section 74 of the 1968 Act—

(*a*) in respect of a loss incurred by a company in a trade, or of charges paid by a company in connection with the carrying on of a trade, in a relevant accounting period; or

(*b*) as an allowance falling to be made to a company for a relevant accounting period either in taxing a trade or by way of discharge or repayment of tax to which it is entitled by reason of its participation in a trade,

may be given or allowed to that company ("the partner company") otherwise than against profits or gains arising from the trade, or to another company, only to the extent that the amount given or allowed or (as the case may be) the aggregate amount does not exceed the relevant sum.

(2) In this section—

"relevant accounting period" means an accounting period of the partner company at any time during which it carried on the trade as a limited partner (within the meaning of section 117(2));

"the aggregate amount" means the aggregate of any amounts given or allowed to the partner company or another company at any time under section 338, 393(2) or 403(1) to (3) and (7) below or section 74 of the 1968 Act—

(*a*) in respect of a loss incurred by the partner company in the trade, or of charges paid by it in connection with carrying it on, in any relevant accounting period; or

(*b*) as an allowance falling to be made to the partner company for any relevant accounting period either in taxing the trade or by way of discharge or repayment of tax to which it is entitled by reason of its participation in the trade;

"the relevant sum" means the amount of the partner company's contribution (within the meaning of section 117(3)) to the trade as at the appropriate time; and

"the appropriate time" is the end of the relevant accounting period in which the loss is incurred or the charges paid or for which the allowance falls to be made (except that where the partner company ceased to carry on the trade during that accounting period it is the time when it so ceased).

Former enactments.—Sub-s. (1): FA 1985, Sch. 12, para. 3(1)–(3).
Sub-s. (2): FA 1985, Sch. 12, para. 3(4).

CHAPTER VIII

MISCELLANEOUS AND SUPPLEMENTAL

119. Rent etc. payable in connection with mines, quarries and similar concerns

(1) Where rent is payable in respect of any land or easement, and either—

(*a*) the land or easement is used, occupied or enjoyed in connection with any of the concerns specified in section 55(2); or

(*b*) the lease or other agreement under which the rent is payable provides for the recoupment of the rent by way of reduction of royalties or payments of a similar nature in the event of the land or easement being so used, occupied or enjoyed,

the rent shall, subject to section 122, be charged to tax under Schedule D, and, subject to subsection (2) below, shall be subject to deduction of income tax under section 348 or 349 as if it were a royalty or other sum paid in respect of the user of a patent.

(2) Where the rent is rendered in produce of the concern, it shall, instead of being treated as provided by subsection (1) above, be charged under Case III of Schedule D, and the value of the produce so rendered shall be taken to be the amount of the profits or income arising therefrom.

(3) For the purposes of this section—

"easement" includes any right, privilege or benefit in, over or derived from land; and

"rent" includes a rent service, rentcharge, fee farm rent, feuduty or other rent, toll, duty, royalty or annual or periodical payment in the nature of rent, whether payable in money or money's worth or otherwise.

Former enactment.—TA 1970, s. 156.

120. Rent etc. payable in respect of electric line wayleaves

(1) Where rent is payable in respect of any easement enjoyed in the United Kingdom in connection with any electric, telegraphic or telephonic wire or cable (not being such an easement as is mentioned in section 119(1)), the rent shall be charged to tax under Schedule D, and, subject to subsections (2) to (5) below, shall be subject to deduction of income tax under section 348 or 349 as if it were a royalty or other sum paid in respect of the user of a patent.

(2) Any payment of rent to which subsection (1) above applies which does not exceed £2.50 per year may, if the payer so elects, be treated as not affected by so much of that subsection as provides that the rent shall be subject to deduction of income tax, and shall in that event be made without deduction of income tax accordingly.

(3) Any payment of rent to which subsection (1) above applies which is made without deduction of income tax, whether by virtue of subsection (2) above or otherwise, shall, unless income tax is assessed thereon under section 350, be chargeable to tax under Case III of Schedule D.

(4) Any payment of rent to which subsection (1) above applies which is made subject to deduction of income tax shall, if it is paid by a person carrying on a trade which consists of or includes the provision of a radio relay service and the wire or cable in question is used by that person for the purposes of that service—

(*a*) be deductible (notwithstanding anything in section 74(*q*)) in computing the amount of the profits or gains of the trade to be charged under Case I of Schedule D, and

(*b*) be deemed for the purposes of sections 348 and 349 not to be payable out of profits or gains brought into charge to income tax.

(5) In this section—

(*a*) "easement" and "rent" have the same meanings as in section 119;

(*b*) the reference to easements enjoyed in connection with any electric, telegraphic or telephonic wire or cable includes (without prejudice to the generality of that expression) references to easements enjoyed in connection with any pole or pylon supporting any such wire or cable, or with any apparatus (including any transformer) used in connection with any such wire or cable; and

(*c*) "radio relay service" means the retransmission by wire to their customers of broadcast programmes (which may or may not be television programmes) which the persons carrying on the service receive either by wire or by wireless from the British Broadcasting Corporation or from the persons outside the United Kingdom who broadcast the programmes in question.

Former enactments.—Decimal Currency Act 1969, s. 10(1); TA 1970, s. 157.

121. Management expenses of owner of mineral rights

(1) Where for any year of assessment rights to work minerals in the United Kingdom are let, the lessor shall, subject to subsection (2) below, be entitled, on making a claim for the purpose, to be repaid so much of the income tax paid by him by deduction or otherwise in respect of the rent or royalties for that year as is equal to the amount of the tax on any sums proved to have been wholly, exclusively and necessarily disbursed by him as expenses of management or supervision of those minerals in that year.

(2) No repayment of tax shall be made under subsection (1) above if, or to such extent as, the expenses in question have been otherwise allowed as a deduction in computing income for the purposes of income tax.

(3) In computing for the purposes of corporation tax the income of a company for any accounting period from the letting of rights to work minerals in the United Kingdom, there may be deducted any sums disbursed by the company wholly, exclusively and necessarily as expenses of management or supervision of those minerals in that period.

Former enactment.—TA 1970, s. 158(1), (2).

122. Relief in respect of mineral royalties

(1) Subject to the following provisions of this section, a person resident or ordinarily resident in the United Kingdom who in any year of assessment or accounting period is entitled to receive any mineral royalties under a mineral lease or agreement shall be treated—

(*a*) for the purposes of income tax, or as the case may be for the purposes of corporation tax on profits exclusive of chargeable gains, as if the total of the mineral royalties receivable by him under that lease or agreement in that year or period and any management expenses available for set-off against those royalties in that year or period were each reduced by one-half; and

(*b*) for the purposes of the 1979 Act or as the case may be for the purposes of corporation tax on chargeable gains, as if there accrued to him in that year or period a chargeable gain equal to one-half of the total of the mineral royalties receivable by him under that lease or agreement in that year or period;

and this section shall have effect notwithstanding any provision of section 119(1) making the whole of certain kinds of mineral royalties chargeable to tax under Schedule D, but without prejudice to any provision of that section providing for any such royalties to be subject to deduction of income tax under section 348 or 349.

(2) For the purposes of subsection (1)(*a*) above, "management expenses available for set-off" against royalties means—

(*a*) where section 121 applies in respect of the royalties, any sum brought into account under subsection (1) of that section in determining the amount of the repayment of income tax in respect of those royalties or, as the case may be, deductible from those royalties under subsection (2) of that section in computing the income of a company for the purposes of corporation tax; and

(*b*) if the royalties are chargeable to tax under Schedule A, any sums deductible under Part II as payments made in respect of management of the property concerned;

and if neither paragraph (*a*) nor paragraph (*b*) above applies, the reference in subsection (1)(*a*) above to management expenses available for set-off shall be disregarded.

(3) The amount of the chargeable gain treated as accruing to any person by virtue of subsection (1)(*b*) above shall, notwithstanding anything in the enactments relating to the computation of chargeable gains, be the whole amount calculated in accordance with that subsection, and, accordingly, no reduction shall be made on account of expenditure incurred by that person or of any other matter whatsoever.

(4) Where subsection (1) above applies in relation to mineral royalties receivable under a mineral lease or agreement by a person not chargeable to corporation tax in respect of those royalties, then, in so far as the amount of income tax paid, by deduction or otherwise, by him in respect of those mineral royalties in any year of assessment exceeds the amount of income tax for which he is liable in respect of those royalties by virtue of subsection (1)(*a*) above—

(*a*) the amount of the excess shall in the first instance be set against the tax for which he is chargeable by virtue of subsection (1)(*b*) above; and
(*b*) on the making of a claim in that behalf, he shall be entitled to repayment of tax in respect of the balance of that excess.

(5) In this section references to mineral royalties refer only to royalties receivable on or after 6th April 1970, and the expression "mineral royalties" means so much of any rents, tolls, royalties and other periodical payments in the nature of rent payable under a mineral lease or agreement as relates to the winning and working of minerals; and the Board may by regulations—

(*a*) provide whether, and to what extent, payments made under a mineral lease or agreement and relating both to the winning and working of minerals and to other matters are to be treated as mineral royalties; and
(*b*) provide for treating the whole of such payments as mineral royalties in cases where the extent to which they relate to matters other than the winning and working of minerals is small.

(6) In this section—

"minerals" means all minerals and substances in or under land which are ordinarily worked for removal by underground or surface working but excluding water, peat, topsoil and vegetation; and
"mineral lease or agreement" means—

(*a*) a lease, profit à prendre, licence or other agreement conferring a right to win and work minerals in the United Kingdom;
(*b*) a contract for the sale, or a conveyance, of minerals in or under land in the United Kingdom; and
(*c*) a grant of a right under section 1 of the Mines (Working Facilities and Support) Act 1966, other than an ancillary right within the meaning of that Act.

(7) In the application of this section to Northern Ireland—

(*a*) references to mineral royalties include references to periodical payments—

(i) of compensation under section 29 or 35 of the Mineral Development Act (Northern Ireland) 1969 ("the 1969 Act") or under section 4 of the Petroleum (Production) Act (Northern Ireland) 1964 ("the 1964 Act"); and
(ii) made as mentioned in section 37 of the 1969 Act or under section 55(4)(*b*) of that Act or under section 11 of the 1964 Act (payments in respect of minerals to persons entitled to a share of royalties under section 13(3) of the Irish Land Act 1903); and

(*b*) in its application to any such payments as are mentioned in paragraph (*a*) above, references to the mineral lease or agreement under which mineral royalties are payable shall be construed as references to the enactment under which the payments are made.

(8) In any case where, before the commencement of this section, for the purposes of the 1979 Act or of corporation tax on chargeable gains, a person was treated as if there had accrued to him in any year of assessment or accounting period ending before 6th April 1988 a chargeable gain equal to the relevant fraction, determined in accordance with section 29(3)(*b*) of the Finance Act 1970, of the total of the mineral royalties receivable by him under that lease or agreement in that year or period, subsection (1)(*b*) above shall have effect in relation to any mineral royalties receivable by him under that lease or agreement in any later year or period with the substitution for the reference to one-half of a reference to the relevant fraction as so determined.

Former enactments.—Sub-s. (1): FA 1970, s. 29(1), (3); FA 1971, Sch. 9, para. 4.
Sub-s. (2): FA 1970, s. 29(2).
Sub-s. (3): FA 1970, s. 29(3).
Sub-ss. (4)–(7): FA 1970, s. 29(4), (6)–(9).

123. Foreign dividends

(1) In this section—
   (a) "foreign dividends" means any interest, dividends or other annual payments payable out of or in respect of the stocks, funds, shares or securities of any body of persons not resident in the United Kingdom (but not including any such payment to which section 348 or 349(1) applies) and references to dividends shall be construed accordingly;
   (b) "relevant foreign dividends" means foreign dividends payable out of or in respect of stocks, funds, shares or securities which are not held in a recognised clearing system;
   (c) "banker" includes a person acting as a banker; and
   (d) references to coupons include, in relation to any dividends, warrants for or bills of exchange purporting to be drawn or made in payment of those dividends.

(2) Where relevant foreign dividends are entrusted to any person in the United Kingdom for payment to any persons in the United Kingdom, they shall be assessed and charged to income tax under Schedule D by the Board, and Parts III and IV of Schedule 3 shall apply in relation to the income tax to be so assessed and charged.

(3) Where—
   (a) a banker or any other person in the United Kingdom, by means of coupons received from any other person or otherwise on his behalf, obtains payment of any foreign dividends [and either—
      (i) the payment of those dividends was not entrusted to any person in the United Kingdom, or
      (ii) the stocks, funds, shares or securities in respect of which those dividends are paid are held in a recognised clearing system]¹, or
   (b) any banker in the United Kingdom sells or otherwise realises coupons for foreign dividends, and pays over the proceeds to any person or carries them to his account, or
   (c) any dealer in coupons in the United Kingdom purchases any such coupons otherwise than from a banker or another dealer in coupons,

tax under Schedule D shall extend, in the cases mentioned in paragraph (a) above, to the dividends, and, in the cases mentioned in paragraphs (b) and (c) above, to the proceeds of the sale or other realisation, and income tax shall be assessed and charged and paid under this subsection in accordance with Parts III and IV of Schedule 3.

(4) In the cases mentioned in subsections (2) and (3) above, no tax shall be chargeable if it is proved, on a claim in that behalf made to the Board, that the person owning the stocks, funds, shares or securities and entitled to the dividends or proceeds is not resident in the United Kingdom.

(5) Where stocks, funds, shares or securities are held under a trust, and the person who is the beneficiary in possession under the trust is the sole beneficiary in possession and can, by means either of the revocation of the trust or the exercise of any power under the trust, call upon the trustees at any time to transfer the stocks, funds, shares or securities to him absolutely free from the trust, that person shall, for the purposes of subsection (4) above, be deemed to be the person owning the stocks, funds, shares or securities.

(6) Where any income of any person is by virtue of any provision of the Tax Acts (and in particular, but without prejudice to the generality of the preceding words, Chapter III of Part XVII) to be deemed to be income of any other person, that income is not exempt from tax by virtue of subsection (4) above by reason of the first mentioned person not being resident in the United Kingdom.

Former enactments.—TA 1970, s. 159; FA 1986, s. 48(2)–(5).
Cross references.—See FA 1989, Sch. 11, para. 18 (disapplication of this section in relation to foreign deep gain securities).
Amendments.—¹ Words in sub-s. (3)(a) substituted by FA 1988, s. 76(3), (6) with respect to payments obtained after the passing of FA 1988. FA 1988 was passed on 29 July 1988.

124. Interest on quoted Eurobonds

(1) Section 349(2) shall not apply to interest paid on any quoted Eurobond where—
   (a) the person by or through whom the payment is made is not in the United Kingdom; or
   (b) the payment is made by or through a person who is in the United Kingdom but either of the conditions mentioned in subsection (2) below is satisfied.

(2) The conditions are—
   (a) that it is proved, on a claim in that behalf made to the Board, that the person who is

the beneficial owner of the quoted Eurobond and is entitled to the interest is not resident in the United Kingdom;

(b) that the quoted Eurobond is held in a recognised clearing system.

(3) In a case falling within subsection (1)(b) above the person by or through whom the payment is made shall deliver to the Board—

(a) on demand by the Board an account of the amount of any such payment; and
(b) not later than 12 months after making any such payment, and unless within that time he delivers an account with respect to the payment under paragraph (a) above, a written statement specifying his name and address and describing the payment.

(4) Where by virtue of any provision of the Tax Acts interest paid on any quoted Eurobond is deemed to be income of a person other than the person who is the beneficial owner of the quoted Eurobond, subsection (2)(a) above shall apply as if it referred to that other person.

(5) Subsections (3) to (6) of section 123 shall apply in relation to interest on quoted Eurobonds as they apply to foreign dividends but with the following modifications—

(za) subsection (3)(a)(i) shall have effect in relation to quoted Eurobonds not held in a recognised clearing system as if the words "made by or" were inserted immediately before the words "entrusted to any person in the United Kingdom".][1]

(a) subsection (4) shall apply as if it required a claim to have been made on or before the event by virtue of which tax would otherwise be chargeable; and
(b) paragraph 6(1) of Schedule 3 shall apply with the omission of paragraphs (a) and (b).

(6) In this section—

"quoted Eurobond" means a security which—

(a) is issued by a company;
(b) is quoted on a recognised stock exchange;
(c) is in bearer form; and
(d) carries a right to interest; and

"recognised clearing system" means any system for clearing quoted Eurobonds [or relevant foreign securities][2] which is for the time being designated for the purposes of this section by order made by the Board, as a recognised clearing system.

["relevant foreign securities" means any of the following, that is to say—

(a) any such stocks, funds, shares or securities as give rise to foreign dividends, within the meaning of section 123; and
(b) any such securities as give rise to overseas public revenue dividends, within the meaning of Part III.][3]

(7) An order under subsection (6) above—

(a) may contain such transitional and other supplemental provisions as appear to the Board to be necessary or expedient; and
(b) may be varied or revoked by a subsequent order so made.

Former enactment.—FA 1984, s. 35(1)–(3), (5)–(8).
Cross references.—See FA 1989, s. 116 (interest paid after 31 March 1989 to a relevant Netherlands Antilles subsidiary to be utilised by the subsidiary for a specified purpose to be paid gross).
Amendments.—[1] Sub-s. (5)(za) inserted by FA 1988, s. 76(4), (6) with respect to payments obtained after the passing of FA 1988. FA 1988 was passed on 29 July 1988.
[2] Words in the definition of "recognised clearing system" in sub-s. (6) inserted by FA 1988, s. 76(5), (6).
[3] The definition of "relevant foreign securities" in sub-s. (6) added by *ibid.*

125. Annual payments for non-taxable consideration

(1) Any payment to which this subsection applies shall be made without deduction of income tax, shall not be allowed as a deduction in computing the income or total income of the person by whom it is made and shall not be a charge on income for the purposes of corporation tax.

(2) Subject to the following provisions of this section, subsection (1) above applies to any payment which—

(a) is an annuity or other annual payment charged with tax under Case III of Schedule D, not being interest; and
(b) is made under a liability incurred for consideration in money or money's worth all or any of which is not required to be brought into account in computing for the purposes of income tax or corporation tax the income of the person making the payment.

(3) Subsection (1) above does not apply to—

(a) any payment which in the hands of the recipient is income falling within [subsection (1)(a) or (c) of section 674A or 683 or subsection (6) of section 683 (including that subsection as it applies in relation to section 674A(1))][1];
(b) any payment made to an individual under a liability incurred in consideration of his surrendering, assigning or releasing an interest in settled property to or in favour of a person having a subsequent interest;
(c) any annuity granted in the ordinary course of a business of granting annuities; or
(d) any annuity charged on an interest in settled property and granted at any time before 30th March 1977 by an individual to a company whose business at that time consisted wholly or mainly in the acquisition of interests in settled property or which was at that time carrying on life assurance business in the United Kingdom.

(4) In the application of this section to Scotland the references in subsection (3) above to settled property shall be construed as references to property held in trust.

(5) Subsection (1) above applies to a payment made after 5th April 1988 irrespective of when the liability to make it was incurred.

Former enactment.—FA 1977, s. 48.
Cross references.—See FA 1989, s. 59 (this section to apply to covenanted subscriptions to certain charities notwithstanding enjoyment of certain benefits by the covenantor in return for the subscription).
Amendments.—[1] Words in sub-s. (3)(a) substituted by FA 1989, s. 109(2).

126. Treasury securities issued at a discount

(1) Where a security to which this section applies is issued at a discount, tax shall not be charged in respect of the discount under Case III of Schedule D; but the discount shall not for that reason be regarded as annual profits or gains chargeable to tax under Case VI of Schedule D.

(2) This section applies to all securities issued by the Treasury after 6th March 1973 [except—

(a) Treasury bills,
(b) relevant deep discount securities, and
(c) deep gain securities.][1]

[(3) For the purposes of subsection (2) above—

(a) a relevant deep discount security is a security falling within paragraph 1(1)(dd) of Schedule 4 to this Act, and
(b) a deep gain security is a security which is a deep gain security for the purposes of Schedule 11 to the Finance Act 1989.][2]

Former enactment.—FA 1973, s. 27.
Cross references.—See FA 1989, s. 95(5)–(7) (this section not to apply in the case of certain disposals, transfers or redemptions).
Amendments.—[1] Sub-s. (2)(a) (and the word "except" preceding it), (b), (c) substituted for the words "except Treasury bills" by FA 1989, s. 95(2), (4) for disposals, transfers or redemptions after 13 March 1989.
[2] Sub-s. (3) inserted by FA 1989, s. 95(3), (4) for disposals, transfers or redemptions after 13 March 1989.

127. Enterprise allowance

(1) This section applies to—

(a) payments known as enterprise allowance and made [(whether before or after the coming into force of section 25 of the Employment Act 1988)][1] in pursuance of arrangements under section 2(2)(d) of the Employment and Training Act 1973; and
(b) corresponding payments made in Northern Ireland by the Department of Economic Development.

(2) Any such payment which would (apart from this section) be charged to tax under Case I or II of Schedule D shall be charged to tax under Case VI of that Schedule.

(3) Nothing in subsection (2) above shall prevent such a payment—

(a) being treated for the purposes of section 623(2)(c) or 833(4)(c) as immediately derived from the carrying on or exercise of a trade, profession or vocation; . . .[2]
(b) . . .[2]

Former enactment.—FA 1986, s. 41.
Amendments.—[1] Words in sub-s. (1)(*a*) substituted for the words "by the Manpower Services Commission" by the Employment Act 1988, Sch. 3, para. 15.
[2] Sub-s. (3)(*b*) and the preceding word "or" repealed by FA 1989, Sch. 17, Pt. V.

128. Commodity and financial futures etc.: losses and gains

Any gain arising to any person in the course of dealing in commodity or financial futures or in qualifying options, which apart from this section would constitute profits or gains chargeable to tax under Schedule D otherwise than as the profits of a trade, shall not be chargeable to tax under that Schedule.

In this section "commodity or financial futures" and "qualifying options" have the same meaning as in section 72 of the Finance Act 1985, and the reference to a gain arising in the course of dealing in commodity or financial futures includes any gain which is regarded as arising in the course of such dealing by virtue of subsection (2A) of that section.

Former enactments.—FA 1985, s. 72(1), (2); F(No. 2)A 1987, s. 81(1).

129. Stock lending

(1) Subject to subsection (4) below, this section applies where a person ("A") has contracted to sell securities and, to enable him to fulfil the contract, he enters into an arrangement under which—

  (*a*) another person ("B") is to transfer securities to A or his nominee; and
  (*b*) in return securities of the same kind and amount are to be transferred (whether or not by A or his nominee) to B or his nominee.

(2) Subject to subsection (4) below, this section also applies where, to enable B to make the transfer to A or his nominee, B enters into an arrangement under which—

  (*a*) another person ("C") is to transfer securities to B or his nominee; and
  (*b*) in return securities of the same kind and amount are to be transferred (whether or not by B or his nominee) to C or his nominee.

(3) Any transfer made in pursuance of an arrangement mentioned in subsection (1) or (2) above shall not be taken into account for the purposes of the Tax Acts in computing the profits or losses of any trade carried on by the transferor or transferee.

(4) The Treasury may provide by regulations that this section or any provision of it or section 149B(9) of the 1979 Act does not apply unless such conditions as are specified in the regulations are fulfilled; and the conditions may relate to the capacity in which any person involved in any arrangement is acting, the Board's approval of any such person or of the arrangement, the nature of the securities or otherwise.

(5) In this section "securities" includes stocks and shares.

(6) This section applies to transfers made after such date as is specified for this purpose by regulations made under section 61 of the Finance Act 1986 or, if no such regulations have been made before 6th April 1988, under this section.

Former enactment.—FA 1986, s. 61.
Cross references.—See CGTA 1979, s. 142A(4A)(*a*) (securities transferred by trustees of a premiums trust fund in pursuance of an arrangement mentioned in sub-s. (1) or (2) above to be treated, where certain requirements are not fulfilled, as remaining within the premiums trust fund for valuation purpose),
s. 149B(9) (any disposal and acquisition made under an arrangement mentioned in sub-s. (1) or (2) above to be disregarded for CGT, subject to regulations under sub-s. (4) above);
FA 1989, Sch. 11, para. 10(4), (5) (deep gain securities transferred by trustees of Lloyd's underwriters' premiums trust fund).

130. Meaning of "investment company" for purposes of Part IV

In this Part of this Act "investment company", means any company whose business consists wholly or mainly in the making of investments and the principal part of whose income is derived therefrom, but includes any savings bank or other bank for savings except any which, for the purposes of the Trustee Savings Bank Act 1985, is a successor or a further successor to a trustee savings bank.

Former enactments.—TA 1970, s. 304(5); FA 1980, Sch. 11, para. 1; Trustee Savings Bank Act 1981, Sch. 6, para. 1; Trustee Savings Bank Act 1985, Sch. 2, para. 6(6).

PART V
PROVISIONS RELATING TO THE SCHEDULE E CHARGE

CHAPTER I
SUPPLEMENTARY CHARGING PROVISIONS OF GENERAL APPLICATION

Miscellaneous provisions

131. Chargeable emoluments

(1) Tax under Case I, II or III of Schedule E shall, except as provided to the contrary by any provision of the Tax Acts, be chargeable on the full amount of the emoluments falling under that Case, subject to such deductions only as may be authorised by the Tax Acts, and the expression "emoluments" shall include all salaries, fees, wages, perquisites and profits whatsoever.

(2) Tax under Case III of Schedule E shall be chargeable whether or not tax is chargeable in respect of the same office or employment under Case I or II of that Schedule, but shall not be chargeable on any emoluments falling under Case I or II . . .[1].

Former enactment.—TA 1970, s. 183.
Amendments.—[1] Words in sub-s. (2) repealed by FA 1989, s. 42(1), (2) and Sch. 17, Pt. IV.

132. Place of performance, and meaning of emoluments received in the U.K.

(1) Where a person ordinarily performs the whole or part of the duties of his office or employment in the United Kingdom, then, for the purposes of Cases I and II of Schedule E, his emoluments for any period of absence from the office or employment shall be treated as emoluments for duties performed in the United Kingdom, except in so far as it is shown that, but for that absence, they would have been emoluments for duties performed outside the United Kingdom.

(2) Where an office or employment is in substance one the duties of which fall in the chargeable period to be performed outside the United Kingdom, then, for the purposes of Cases I and II of Schedule E, there shall be treated as so performed any duties performed in the United Kingdom the performance of which is merely incidental to the performance of the other duties outside the United Kingdom.

(3) Subsection (2) above shall not be construed as affecting any question under section 193(1) or paragraph 3 of Schedule 12 as to where any duties are performed or whether a person is absent from the United Kingdom.

(4) For the purposes of Cases I and II of Schedule E, but subject to section 194(7) and paragraph 5 of Schedule 12, the following duties shall be treated as performed in the United Kingdom, namely—

(*a*) the duties of any office or employment under the Crown which is of a public nature and the emoluments of which are payable out of the public revenue of the United Kingdom or of Northern Ireland; and

(*b*) any duties which a person performs on a vessel engaged on a voyage not extending to a port outside the United Kingdom, or which a person resident in the United Kingdom performs on a vessel or aircraft engaged on a voyage or journey beginning or ending in the United Kingdom or on a part beginning or ending in the United Kingdom of any other voyage or journey.

(5) For the purposes of Case III of Schedule E, emoluments shall be treated as received in the United Kingdom if they are paid, used or enjoyed in, or in any manner or form transmitted or brought to, the United Kingdom, and subsections (6) to (9) of section 65 shall apply for the purposes of this subsection as they apply for the purposes of subsection (5) of that section.

Former enactments.—Sub-ss. (1), (2): TA 1970, s. 184(1), (2).
Sub-s. (3): FA 1977, Sch. 7, para. 9.
Sub-s. (4): TA 1970, s. 184(3); FA 1977, s. 31(3); FA 1986, s. 34(7).
Sub-s. (5): TA 1970, s. 184(4).

133. Voluntary pensions

(1) Where—
- (*a*) a person has ceased to hold any office or employment, and
- (*b*) a pension or annual payment is paid to him, or to his widow or child, or to any relative or dependant of his, by the person under whom he held the office or by whom he was employed, or by the successors of that person, and
- (*c*) that pension or annual payment is paid otherwise than by or on behalf of a person outside the United Kingdom,

then, notwithstanding that the pension or payment is paid voluntarily or is capable of being discontinued, it shall be deemed to be income for the purposes of assessment to tax, and shall be assessed and charged under Schedule E.

(2) For the avoidance of doubt, it is hereby declared that the expressions "annuity" and "pension" in Schedule E include respectively an annuity and a pension which is paid voluntarily or is capable of being discontinued.

Former enactment.—TA 1970, s. 182.
Cross references.—See FA 1989, s. 41(1)(*b*) (a pension or annual payment chargeable to income tax under this section to be charged in the year in which it accrued irrespective of when it is paid).

134. Workers supplied by agencies

(1) Subject to the provisions of this section, where—
- (*a*) an individual ("the worker") renders or is under an obligation to render personal services to another person ("the client") and is subject to, or to the right of, supervision, direction or control as to the manner in which he renders those services; and
- (*b*) the worker is supplied to the client by or through a third person ("the agency") and renders or is under an obligation to render those services under the terms of a contract between the worker and the agency ("the relevant contract"); and
- (*c*) remuneration receivable under or in consequence of that contract would not, apart from this section, be chargeable to income tax under Schedule E,

then, for all the purposes of the Income Tax Acts, the services which the worker renders or is under an obligation to render to the client under that contract shall be treated as if they were the duties of an office or employment held by the worker, and all remuneration receivable under or in consequence of that contract shall be treated as emoluments of that office or employment and shall be assessable to income tax under Schedule E accordingly.

(2) Subsection (1)(*b*) above includes cases in which the third person is an unincorporated body of which the worker is a member.

(3) Subsection (1) above shall apply whether or not the worker renders or is under an obligation to render the services in question as a partner in a firm or a member of an unincorporated body; and where, in any case in which that subsection applies, the worker is a partner in a firm or a member of such a body, remuneration receivable under or in consequence of the relevant contract shall be treated for all the purposes of the Income Tax Acts as income of the worker and not as income of the firm or body.

(4) For the purposes of this section, any remuneration which the client pays or provides by reason of the worker being a person who renders or is under an obligation to render the services in question shall be treated as receivable in consequence of the relevant contract.

(5) Subsection (1) above shall not apply—
- (*a*) if the services in question are services as an actor, singer, musician or other entertainer or as a fashion, photographic or artist's model; or
- (*b*) if the services in question are rendered wholly in the worker's own home or at other premises which are neither under the control or management of the client nor premises at which the worker is required, by reason of the nature of the services, to render them; or
- (*c*) if in rendering the services the worker is or would be a sub-contractor within the meaning of section 560.

(6) Where an individual enters into arrangements with another person with a view to the rendering of personal services by the individual, being arrangements such that, if and when he renders any such services as a result of the arrangements, those services will be treated under subsection (1) above as if they were the duties of an office or employment held by him, then for all purposes of the Income Tax Acts any remuneration receivable under or in consequence of the arrangements shall be treated as emoluments of an office or employment held by the individual and shall be assessable to income tax under Schedule E accordingly.

(7) In this section "remuneration", in relation to an individual, does not include anything

in respect of which he would not have been chargeable to tax under Schedule E if it had been receivable in connection with an office or employment held by him but, subject to that, includes every form of payment and all perquisites, benefits and profits whatsoever.

Former enactment.—F(No. 2)A 1975, s. 38(1)–(6), (8).
Cross references.—See TMA 1970, s. 16A(1) (agency workers).

Shareholdings, loans etc.

135. Gains by directors and employees from share options

(1) Subject to section 185, where a person realises a gain by the exercise, or by the assignment or release, of a right to acquire shares in a body corporate obtained by that person as a director or employee of that or any other body corporate, he shall be chargeable to tax under Schedule E on an amount equal to the amount of his gain, as computed in accordance with this section.

(2) Without prejudice to section 185, where tax may by virtue of this section become chargeable in respect of any gain which may be realised by the exercise of a right which is not capable of being exercised more than seven years after it is obtained, tax shall not be chargeable under any other provision of the Tax Acts in respect of the receipt of the right.

(3) Subject to section 136(4)—
   (a) the gain realised by the exercise of any such right at any time shall be taken to be the difference between the amount that a person might reasonably expect to obtain from a sale in the open market at that time of the shares acquired and the amount or value of the consideration given whether for them or for the grant of the right; and
   (b) the gain realised by the assignment or release of any such right shall be taken to be the difference between the amount or value of the consideration for the assignment or release and the amount or value of the consideration given for the grant of the right;
(a just apportionment being made of any entire consideration given for the grant of the right to acquire those shares and other shares or otherwise for the grant of the right to acquire those shares and for something besides).

(4) For the purposes of subsection (3) above, neither the consideration given for the grant of the right nor any such entire consideration as is mentioned in that subsection shall be taken to include the performance of any duties in or in connection with the office or employment by reason of which the right was granted, and no part of the amount or value of the consideration given for the grant shall be deducted more than once under that subsection.

(5) Where such a right as is mentioned in subsection (1) above is obtained as mentioned therein and is capable of being exercised later than seven years after it is obtained, and the receipt of the right is chargeable to tax under any other provision of the Tax Acts, then—
   (a) the tax so charged shall be deducted from any tax which is chargeable under subsection (1) above by reference to the gain realised by the exercise, assignment or release of that right; and
   (b) for the purpose of any such charge to tax in relation to the receipt of the right, the value of the right shall be taken to be not less than the market value at the time the right is obtained—
       (i) of the shares which may be acquired by the exercise of the right, or
       (ii) of shares for which shares so acquired may be exchanged,
   rreduced by the amount or value (or, if variable, the least amount or value) of the consideration for which the shares may be so acquired.

(6) Subject to subsection (7) below, a person shall, in the case of a right granted by reason of his office or employment, be chargeable to tax under this section in respect of a gain realised by another person—
   (a) if the right was granted to that other person, or
   (b) if the other person acquired the right otherwise than by or under an assignment made by way of a bargain at arm's length, or if the two are connected persons at the time when the gain is realised,
but in a case within paragraph (b) above the gain realised shall be treated as reduced by the amount of any gain realised by a previous holder on an assignment of the right.

(7) A person shall not be chargeable to tax by virtue of subsection (6)(b) above in respect of

any gain realised by another person if the first-mentioned person was divested of the right by operation of law on his bankruptcy or otherwise, but the other person shall be chargeable to tax in respect of the gain under Case VI of Schedule D.

(8) In any case where—

(a) a person has obtained any such right to acquire shares as is mentioned in subsection (1) above ("the first right"); and

(b) as to any of the shares to which the first right relates, he omits or undertakes to omit to exercise the right or grants or undertakes to grant to another a right to acquire the shares or any interest in them; and

(c) in consideration for or otherwise in connection with that omission, grant or undertaking, he receives any benefit in money or money's worth;

he shall be treated for the purposes of this section and section 136 as realising a gain by the assignment or release of the first right, so far as it relates to the shares in question, for a consideration equal to the amount or value of the benefit referred to in paragraph (c) above.

(9) Where subsection (8) above has had effect on any occasion, nothing in that subsection affects the application of this section in relation to a gain realised on a subsequent occasion, except that on that subsequent occasion so much of the consideration given for the grant of the first right as was deducted on the first occasion shall not be deducted again.

Former enactments.—Sub-s. (1): TA 1970, s. 186(1); FA 1984, s.38.
Sub-s. (2): TA 1970, s. 186(2); FA 1972, s. 77(1); FA 1984, s. 38.
Sub-ss. (3), (4): TA 1970, s. 186(3).
Sub-s. (5): FA 1972, s. 77(1)–(3).
Sub-ss. (6), (7): TA 1970, s. 186(4), (5).
Sub-ss. (8), (9): TA 1970, s. 186(5A), (5B); FA 1986, s. 26(1).
Construction.—CGTA 1979, s. 32A(3) to be construed as one with this section; see CGTA 1979, s. 32A(6).

136. Provisions supplementary to section 135

(1) If a right to acquire shares in a body corporate is assigned or released in whole or in part for a consideration which consists of or comprises another right to acquire shares in that or any other body corporate, that other right shall not be treated as consideration for the assignment or release, but section 135 and this section shall apply in relation to it as they apply in relation to the right assigned or released and as if the consideration for its acquisition—

(a) did not include the value of the right assigned or released, but

(b) did include the amount or value of the consideration given for the grant of the right assigned or released so far as that has not been offset by any valuable consideration for the assignment or release other than the consideration consisting of the other right.

(2) If—

(a) as a result of two or more transactions a person ceases to hold a right to acquire shares in a body corporate and he or a connected person comes to hold another right to acquire shares in that or any other body corporate (whether or not acquired from the person to whom the other right was assigned), and

(b) any of those transactions was effected under arrangements to which two or more persons holding rights in respect of which tax may be chargeable under this section were parties,

those transactions shall be treated for the purposes of subsection (1) above as a single transaction whereby the one right is assigned for a consideration which consists of or comprises the other right.

(3) Subsection (2) above applies in relation to two or more transactions whether they involve an assignment preceding, coinciding with or subsequent to an acquisition.

(4) In the case of a right to acquire shares granted before 3rd May 1966—

(a) the amount of the gain realised at any time by the exercise, or by the assignment or release, of the right shall not exceed the difference between the market value of those shares at that time and their market value on 3rd May 1966 (and no gain shall be treated as so realised unless the later value exceeds the earlier value); and

(b) subsection (2) of section 135 shall not affect tax chargeable under Case I of Schedule E in respect of the receipt of the right, but the amount, if any, on which tax is so chargeable shall be taken into account under subsection (3)(a) and (b) of that section in relation to the gain realised by the exercise or by the assignment or release, of the right as if that amount formed part (in addition to any other amount) of the consideration for the grant of the right.

(5) For the purposes of this section and section 135—

(a) references to the release of a right include references to agreeing to the restriction of the exercise of the right;

(b) "director" means—

(i) in relation to a body corporate the affairs of which are managed by a board of directors or similar body, a member of that board or similar body;

(ii) in relation to a body corporate the affairs of which are managed by a single director or similar person, that director or person;

(iii) in relation to a body corporate the affairs of which are managed by the members themselves, a member of the body corporate;

and includes any person who is to be or has been a director;

(c) "employee", in relation to a body corporate, includes any person taking part in the management of the affairs of the body corporate who is not a director, and includes a person who is to be or has been an employee; and

(d) in so far as the context permits, "shares" includes stock;

and this section and section 135 shall apply in relation to any securities issued by a body corporate as they apply to shares in that body corporate.

(6) Where in any year of assessment a body corporate grants a right in respect of which tax may become chargeable under section 135, or allots or transfers any shares in pursuance of such a right, or receives notice of the assignment of such a right or provides any benefit in money or money's worth—

(a) for the assignment or for the release in whole or in part of such a right; or

(b) for or in connection with an omission or undertaking to omit to exercise such a right; or

(c) for or in connection with the grant or undertaking to grant a right to acquire shares or an interest in shares to which such a right relates;

it shall deliver particulars thereof in writing to the inspector not later than 30 days after the end of that year.

Former enactments.—Sub-s. (1): TA 1970, s. 186(6).
Sub-ss. (2), (3): TA 1970, s. 186(7).
Sub-s. (4): TA 1970, s. 186(8).
Sub-s. (5)(a): TA 1970, s. 186(10)(a).
Sub-s. (5)(b), (c): TA 1970, ss. 186(10)(c), 224(1).
Sub-s. (5)(d): TA 1970, s. 186(10)(d).
Sub-s. (6): TA 1970, s. 186(11); FA 1986, s. 26(2).

137. Payment of tax under section 135 by instalments

(1) In any case where—

(a) for any year of assessment a person is chargeable to tax under Schedule E, by virtue of section 135, on an amount equal to a gain realised by the exercise of a right to acquire shares which was obtained before 6th April 1984; and

(b) the shares acquired in the exercise of that right were acquired for a consideration which, subject to subsection (2) below, was not less than the market value (determined as for the purposes of the 1979 Act) of shares of the same class at the time the right was granted or, if the right was granted before 6th April 1982, 90 per cent. of that market value; and

(c) following an assessment for the year in which that right was exercised ("the relevant year") an amount of tax chargeable by virtue of section 135 in respect of the amount referred to in paragraph (a) above and exceeding £250 is payable to the collector pursuant to regulations under section 203; and

(d) the person concerned makes an election in accordance with subsection (3) below,

he shall be entitled to pay tax by instalments in accordance with subsection (4) below.

(2) Shares which are acquired for a consideration less than that required by paragraph (b) of subsection (1) above by reason only of a diminution in the market value of shares of that class (determined as for the purposes of the 1979 Act) which is attributable solely to the share capital of the company issuing the shares being varied after the right to acquire the shares was granted, shall for the purposes of that paragraph be regarded as having been acquired for a consideration not less than that required by that paragraph.

(3) An election under this section shall be made by notice to the inspector before the expiry of the period of 60 days beginning immediately after the end of the relevant year.

(4) Where an election has been made under this section the tax referred to in subsection (1)(c) above shall, subject to subsection (5) and (6) below, be paid in five equal instalments as follows—

(a) the first shall be due and payable at the expiry of the period of 14 days beginning on the date on which application for the tax is made pursuant to regulations under section 203;
(b) the fifth shall be due and payable on the last day of the fifth year following the end of the relevant year; and
(c) the second, third and fourth instalments shall be due on such dates as will secure, so far as may be, that the interval between any two consecutive dates is the same.

(5) In any case where the date which, apart from this subsection, would be the due date for the fifth instalment of tax under subsection (4) above is earlier than the due date referred to in paragraph (a) of that subsection, all five instalments shall be due on the later date.

(6) Tax which, by virtue of an election under this section, is not yet due and payable in accordance with subsection (4) above may nevertheless be paid at any time and shall become due and payable forthwith if the person who made the election becomes bankrupt under the law of any part of the United Kingdom.

(7) Subject to any other provision of the Income Tax Acts requiring income of any description to be treated as the highest part of a person's income, for the purposes of paragraph (c) of subsection (1) above in determining what tax is chargeable on a person by virtue of section 135 in respect of the amount referred to in paragraph (a) of that subsection, that amount shall be treated as the highest part of his income for the relevant year.

Former enactments.—FA 1982, s. 40; FA 1984, s. 39(7), (8).

138. Share acquisitions by directors and employees

(1) Subject to section 185 and the following provisions of this section, where a person has acquired or acquires shares or an interest in shares in a body corporate in pursuance of a right conferred on him or opportunity offered to him as a director or employee of that or any other body corporate, and not in pursuance of an offer to the public—

(a) if the market value of the shares at the end of the period mentioned in subsection (9) below exceeds their market value at the time of the acquisition, he shall be chargeable to tax under Schedule E for the year of assessment in which that period ends on an amount equal, except as provided by subsection (8) below, to the excess (or, if his interest is less than the full beneficial ownership, such part of that amount as corresponds to his interest);
(b) if he receives, by virtue of his ownership of or interest in the shares, any benefit not received by the majority of persons who—

(i) hold shares forming part of the ordinary share capital of the same body corporate; and
(ii) have acquired the shares otherwise than as mentioned above;

and the benefit is not otherwise chargeable to income tax, he shall be chargeable to tax under Schedule E for the year of assessment in which he receives the benefit on an amount equal to the value of the benefit;

and any amount chargeable under this subsection shall be treated as earned income, whether or not it would otherwise fall to be so treated.

(2) Subsection (1) above does not apply if the acquisition—

(a) was made in pursuance of arrangements under which employees of a body corporate receive as part of their emoluments shares or interests in shares in that body or in a body controlling it to an extent determined in advance by reference to the profits of either body; and
(b) where the arrangements were made or modified after 22nd March 1973, was of shares or an interest in shares which satisfy the conditions set out in subsection (4)(a) below and the arrangements satisfy the condition set out in subsection (4)(b) below.

(3) Subsection (1)(a) above does not apply if—

(a) the acquisition was an acquisition of shares in a body and either of the following conditions was satisfied immediately after the acquisition, namely—

(i) that the shares were not subject to such restrictions as are specified in subsection (6) below, and were not exchangeable for shares subject to such restrictions, and the majority of

the available shares of the same class was acquired otherwise than as mentioned in subsection (1) above; or

(ii) that the shares were not subject to such restrictions as are specified in paragraph (a) or (b) of subsection (6) below and were not exchangeable for shares subject to such restrictions, and the majority of the available shares of the same class was acquired by persons who were or had been employees or directors of, or of a body controlled by, that body and who were together able as holders of the shares to control that body; or

(b) the acquisition was an acquisition after 5th April 1984 of an interest in shares which consists of units in an authorised unit trust and—

(i) prior to the acquisition the unit trust was approved by the Board for the purposes of this section and, at the time of the acquisition, continues to be so approved, and

(ii) the condition set out in subsection (7) below is fulfilled with respect to the body corporate (in that subsection referred to as "the relevant company") directorship of or employment by which gave rise to the right or opportunity by virtue of which the acquisition was made; or

(c) the acquisition took place before 6th April 1981.

(4) The conditions referred to in subsection (2)(b) above are as follows—

(a) that the shares—

(i) are not subject to such restrictions as will or may result in the person acquiring the shares or an interest in the shares obtaining a benefit through an increase, subsequent to the acquisition, of the value or the value to him of the shares or interest; and

(ii) cannot (whether by one transaction or a series of transactions) be exchanged for or converted into shares which are subject to such restrictions; and

(iii) are either shares of a class quoted on a recognised stock exchange or are shares in a company which is not under the control of another company;

(b) that the arrangements allow every full-time employee of the company concerned who—

(i) has been a full-time employee of that company for a continuous period of not less than five years, and

(ii) is chargeable to tax in respect of his employment under Case I of Schedule E, and

(iii) is not less than 25 years old,

to acquire shares or interests in shares of the same class on similar terms.

(5) For the purposes of subsection (3)(a) above—

(a) shares in a body are available shares if they are not held by or for the benefit of an associated company of that body; and

(b) shares are exchangeable for other shares if (whether by one transaction or a series of transactions) they can be exchanged for or converted into the other shares.

(6) The restrictions referred to in subsection (3)(a) above are—

(a) restrictions not attaching to all shares of the same class; or

(b) restrictions ceasing or liable to cease at some time after the acquisition; or

(c) restrictions depending on the shares being or ceasing to be held by directors or employees of any body corporate (other than such restrictions imposed by a company's articles of association as require shares to be disposed of on ceasing to be so held).

(7) The condition referred to in subsection (3)(b) above is fulfilled with respect to the relevant company if, for no continuous period of one month or more, throughout which any director or employee of the relevant company either—

(a) has, by virtue of his office or employment, any such right or opportunity as is referred to in subsection (1) above to acquire units in the unit trust, or

(b) retains any beneficial interest in any units in the unit trust which he acquired in pursuance of such a right or opportunity,

do investments in the relevant company and in any other company in relation to which the relevant company is an associated company make up more than 10 per cent. by value of the investments subject to the trusts of the unit trust.

(8) The amount on which or on part of which the person making the acquisition is chargeable to tax under subsection (1)(a) above ("the chargeable amount") shall, in the following cases, be reduced as follows, that is to say—

(a) where, in accordance with the terms on which the acquisition of the shares was made, the consideration for the acquisition is subsequently increased, the chargeable amount shall be reduced by an amount equal to the increase; and

(b) where, in accordance with those terms, the shares are subsequently disposed of for a consideration which is less than their market value at the time of the disposal, the chargeable amount shall be reduced so as to be equal to the excess of that consideration over the market value of the shares at the time of the acquisition;

and similarly where the interest acquired is less than the full beneficial ownership, and such assessments, alterations of assessments or repayments of tax shall be made as may be necessary to give effect to the reduction.

(9) The period referred to in subsection (1)(a) above is a period ending at the earliest of the following times—

(a) the expiration of seven years from the acquisition of the shares or interest in the shares;
(b) the time when the person making the acquisition ceases to have any beneficial interest in the shares;
(c) in relation only to a person who acquires shares, the time when by reason of their ceasing to be subject to such restrictions as are specified in subsection (6) above either of the conditions in subsection (3)(a) above would be satisfied in relation to the shares if they had been acquired at that time;

and for the purposes of subsection (1)(a) and paragraph (b) above a person whose beneficial interest in shares is reduced shall be treated as ceasing to have an interest in such part of the shares as is proportionate to the reduction.

(10) Subsection (11) below applies where—

(a) a person has acquired shares or an interest in shares as mentioned in subsection (1) above (and the shares which he acquires or in which he acquires an interest are in subparagraphs (b) and (c) and subsection (11) below referred to as "the original shares"); and
(b) the circumstances of his acquisition of the original shares are such that the application of subsection (1)(a) above is not excluded; and
(c) after 18th March 1986 by virtue of his holding of the original shares or the interest in them he acquires (whether or not for consideration) additional shares or an interest in additional shares (and the shares which he so acquires or in which he so acquires an interest are in subsection (11) below referred to as "the additional shares").

(11) Where this subsection applies—

(a) the additional shares or, as the case may be, the interest in them shall be treated as having been acquired as mentioned in subsection (1) above and in circumstances falling within subsection (10)(b) above and, for the purposes of subsection (9)(a) above, as having been acquired at the same time as the original shares or the interest in them;
(b) for the purposes of subsections (1)(a) and (8) above, the additional shares and the original shares shall be treated as one holding of shares and the market value of the shares comprised in that holding at any time shall be determined accordingly (the market value of the original shares at the time of acquisition being attributed proportionately to all the shares in the holding); and
(c) for the purposes of those subsections, any consideration given for the acquisition of the additional shares or the interest in them shall be taken to be an increase falling within subsection (8)(a) above in the consideration for the original shares or the interest in them.

(12) Subsection (1)(b) above does not apply where the benefit is received by virtue of a person's ownership of or of an interest in shares which were acquired before 6th April 1972.

Former enactments.—Sub-s. (1)(a): FA 1972, s. 79(1), (4).
Sub-s. (1)(b): FA 1972, s. 79(1), (7).
Sub-s. (2)(a): FA 1972, s. 79(2)(b), (3)(b), (8).
Sub-s. (2)(b): FA 1973, Sch. 8, para. 1.
Sub-s. (3)(a): FA 1972, s. 79(2)(c); FA 1973, Sch. 8, para. 4(1)(a)Sub-s. (3)(b): FA 1972, s. 79(2)(bb); FA 1984, s. 40(1).
Sub-s. (3)(c): FA 1972, s. 79(6).
Sub-s. (4)(a): FA 1973, Sch. 8, paras. 1(b), (3); FA 1974, s. 20(2).
Sub-s. (4)(b): FA 1973, Sch. 8, para. 2.
Sub-s. (5): FA 1972, s. 79(2)(c); FA 1973, Sch. 8, para. 4(1)(a).
Sub-s. (6): FA 1972, s. 79(2A); FA 1973, Sch. 8, para. 4(1)(b).
Sub-s. (7): FA 1972, s. 79(2B); FA 1984, s. 40(2).
Sub-ss. (8), (9): FA 1972, s. 79(5), (6); FA 1973, Sch. 8, para. 4(1)(c); FA 1986, s. 26(4).
Sub-ss. (10), (11): FA 1972, s. 79(5A), (5B); FA 1986, s. 26(3), (6).
Sub-s. (12): FA 1972, s. 79(3)(a); FA 1974, s. 20(1)(b).
Construction.—CGTA 1979, s. 32A(4) to be construed as one with this section; see CGTA 1979, s. 32A(6).
Cross references.—See FA 1988, s. 88(1) and Sch. 14, Pt. VI (repeal of FA 1972, s. 79 where an acquisition of shares is made after 25 October 1987),
s. 88(2)–(4) (transitional provisions with respect to this section when it ceases to have effect).
Amendments.—This section repealed by FA 1988, s. 88(1) and Sch. 14, Pt. VI in relation to acquisition after 25 October 1987. It is retained here because of the transitional provisions in FA 1988, s. 88.

139. Provisions supplementary to section 138

(1) Where—

(a) a director or employee of a body corporate acquires shares in pursuance of an opportunity to acquire shares of that class offered to directors and employees of the body in their capacity as such ("the discount offer"); and

(b) the discount offer is made in conjunction with an offer to the public ("the main offer") under which shares of the same class may be acquired on the same terms, except that a discount in price is offered to directors and employees; and

(c) the director or employee is chargeable to tax under Schedule E on an amount equal to the discount in the price of the shares acquired by him; and

(d) at least 75 per cent. of the aggregate number of shares of the class in question which are acquired in pursuance of the discount offer and the main offer taken together are shares acquired in pursuance of the main offer,

he shall be treated for the purposes of section 138(1) as acquiring the shares in pursuance of an offer to the public.

(2) Where a director or employee acquires an interest in shares, subsection (1) above shall apply as if the references in that subsection to the acquisition of shares were references to the acquisition of an interest in shares.

(3) For the purposes of section 138 and this section, where a person acquires any shares or an interest in shares in a body corporate in pursuance of a right conferred on him or opportunity offered to him as a person connected with a director or employee of that or any other body corporate, the shares or interest shall be deemed to be acquired by the director or employee, and section 32A(4) of the 1979 Act shall apply with the necessary modifications; and where that person receives a benefit as mentioned in section 138(1)(b) the benefit shall be deemed to be received by the director or employee.

(4) For the purposes of section 138, a person who disposes of shares or an interest in shares otherwise than by a bargain at arm's length with a person who is not connected with him shall be deemed not to cease to have a beneficial interest in the shares.

(5) Where in any year of assessment a person acquires shares or an interest in shares as mentioned in section 138(1) (disregarding subsections (1) and (2) above), the body from which the shares are or the interest is acquired shall deliver to the inspector within 30 days of the end of that year particulars in writing of the shares and the acquisition.

(6) The Board may by notice require the managers or trustees of any unit trust scheme which is an authorised unit trust approved by the Board for the purposes of section 138 to furnish to the Board within such time as they may direct (but not being less than 30 days) such information as the Board think necessary for the purposes of enabling them to determine—

(a) whether the condition in subsection (7) of that section is being or has at any time been fulfilled; and

(b) the liability to tax of any unit holder whose rights were acquired as mentioned in subsection (1) of that section.

(7) Subject to subsection (9) below, in determining for the purposes of section 138 (including any valuation made for those purposes) whether shares which, or interests in which, have been acquired or are or are to be acquired by any person are subject to any restrictions, there shall be regarded as a restriction attaching to the shares any contract, agreement, arrangement or condition by which his freedom to dispose of the shares or any interest in them or to exercise any right conferred by them is restricted or by which such a disposal or exercise may result in any disadvantages to him or a person connected with him, except where the restriction is imposed as a condition of a loan which is not a related loan as defined by subsection (8) below.

This subsection does not apply where the person acquired the shares before 19th October 1972.

(8) A loan made to any person is a related loan for the purposes of subsection (7) above if—

(a) it is made, arranged, guaranteed or in any way facilitated by—

(i) the body corporate of which he is a director or employee, or

(ii) an associated company of that body, or

(iii) if that body or an associated company of it is a close company, any person having a material interest in the close company; or

(b) it is made to a person connected with another person and would have been such a loan if it had been made to that other person;

but a loan made by the body corporate, associated company or person mentioned in para-

graph (a) above is not a related loan if that body, company or person carries on a business of making personal loans and the loan is made in the ordinary course of that business.

(9) For the purposes of section 138(3)(a), shares acquired by any person shall not, by virtue of subsection (7) above, be regarded as subject to any restriction by reason only of any contract, agreement, arrangement or condition providing for the disposal of the shares, when that person ceases to hold the office or employment by virtue of which he acquired the shares, to a person nominated in accordance with the contract, agreement, arrangement or condition if he is required to dispose of them at a price not exceeding their market value.

(10) Any reference in subsection (7) above to a contract, agreement, arrangement or condition does not include a reference to so much of any contract, agreement, arrangement or condition as contains provisions similar in purpose and effect to any of the provisions of the Model Rules set out in the Model Code for Securities Transactions by Directors of Listed Companies issued by the Stock Exchange in November 1984.

(11) In section 138 and this section—

"associated company" has the meaning given by section 416;
"control" has the meaning given by section 840;
"director" includes a person who is to be a director;
"employee" includes a person who is to be an employee;
"full-time", in relation to an employee, means required to devote substantially the whole of his time to service as an employee;
"shares" includes stock and securities and references to an interest in any shares include references to the proceeds of sale of part of the shares; and
"units", in relation to an authorised unit trust, means an entitlement to a share in the investments subject to that trust.

(12) For the purposes of section 138 and this section, section 168(11) shall apply for determining whether a person has a material interest in a company, but with the omission of the words following "417(3)".

(13) If, on a person ceasing to have a beneficial interest in any shares, he acquires, after 18th March 1986, other shares or an interest in other shares and the circumstances are such that, for the purposes of sections 78 to 81 of the 1979 Act (reorganisations etc.) the shares in which he ceases to have a beneficial interest constitute original shares and the other shares constitute a new holding—

(a) section 78 of that Act (which equates the original shares with the new holding) shall apply for the purposes of this section and section 138;
(b) if any such consideration is given for the new holding as is mentioned in section 79(1) of that Act, it shall be treated for the purposes of this section and section 138 as an increase falling within section 138(8)(a) in the consideration for the shares; and
(c) if any such consideration is received for the disposal of the original shares as is mentioned in section 79(2) of the 1979 Act—

(i) the consideration shall be apportioned among the shares comprised in the new holding, and
(ii) the amount which, apart from this paragraph, would at any subsequent time be the market value of any of those shares shall be taken to be increased by the amount of the consideration apportioned to them;

and in paragraphs (a) to (c) above "the original shares" shall be construed in accordance with sections 78 to 81 of the 1979 Act.

(14) In any case where section 138(1) applies and the acquisition was an acquisition of units in an authorised unit trust—

(a) any reference in section 138(1)(a), (8) or (9) or subsection (4) above or section 32A(4) of the 1979 Act to shares shall be construed as references to units; and
(b) any reference in those provisions to an interest in shares shall be omitted.

Former enactments.—Sub-ss. (1), (2): FA 1972, s. 79(1A), (1B); FA 1984, s. 41(1).
Sub-ss. (3), (4): FA 1972, s. 79(10), (11).
Sub-s. (5): FA 1972, Sch. 12, para. 3; FA 1984, s. 41(2).
Sub-s. (6): FA 1972, Sch. 12, para. 3A; FA 1984, s. 40(4).
Sub-ss. (7)–(9): FA 1973, Sch. 8, paras. 5–7; FA 1982, s. 41.
Sub-s. (10): FA 1982, s. 41; FA 1986, s. 23(4).
Sub-ss. (11), (12): FA 1972, Sch. 12, paras. 6, 8; FA 1973, Sch. 8, para. 35.
Sub-s. (13): FA 1972, s. 79(6A); FA 1986, s. 26(5).
Sub-s. (14): FA 1972, s. 79(4A); FA 1984, s 40(3).

Cross references.—See FA 1988, s. 88(1) and Sch. 14, Pt VI (repeal of FA 1972, s. 79 and Sch. 12 where an acquisition of shares is made after 25 October 1987).
Amendments.—This section repealed by FA 1988, Sch. 14, Pt. VI in relation to acquisitions after 25 October 1987. It is retained here because of the transitional provisions in FA 1988, s. 88.

140. Further interpretation of sections 135 to 139

(1) For the purposes of section 135, 136, 138 or 139, a right to acquire shares is obtained by a person as a director or employee (within the meaning of the section in question) of a body corporate—

(a) if it is granted to him by reason of his office or employment as such a director or employee who is chargeable to tax in respect of that office or employment under Case I of Schedule E; or

(b) if the right is assigned to him and was granted by reason of any such office or employment of his to some other person;

and paragraph (a) above shall apply to a right granted by reason of a person's office or employment after he has ceased to hold it if it would apply to a right so granted in the last chargeable period in which he did hold it.

(2) For those purposes any question whether a person is connected with another shall be determined in accordance with section 839.

(3) For those purposes—

"market value" has the same meaning as, for the purposes of the 1979 Act, it has by virtue of section 150 of that Act; and

"securities" has the meaning given by section 254(1).

Former enactments.—Sub-s. (1): TA 1970, s. 186(9); FA 1972, Sch. 12, para. 7.
Sub-s. (2): TA 1970, s. 186(10)(b); FA 1972, Sch. 12, para. 9.
Sub-s. (3): TA 1970, s. 186(10); FA 1972, ss. 77(3), 79(12), Sch. 12, para. 6.
Cross references.—See FA 1988, Sch. 14, Pt. VI (repeal of FA 1972, Sch. 12 where an acquisition of shares is made after 25 October 1987).

Vouchers etc.

141. Non-cash vouchers

(1) Subject to the following provisions of this section and section 157(3), where a non-cash voucher provided for an employee by reason of his employment is received by the employee, then, for the purposes of the Income Tax Acts—

(a) he shall be treated as having received in the relevant year of assessment an emolument from his employment of an amount equal to the expense incurred by the person providing the voucher in or in connection with the provision of the voucher and the money, goods or services for which it is capable of being exchanged; and

(b) any money, goods or services obtained by the employee or any other person in exchange for the voucher shall be disregarded;

and the expense incurred as mentioned in paragraph (a) above by the person providing the voucher is referred to below as "the chargeable expense".

(2) In subsection (1)(a) above "the relevant year of assessment" means—

(a) in relation to a cheque voucher, the year of assessment in which the voucher is handed over in exchange for money, goods or services (a voucher which is posted being treated as handed over at the time of posting); and

(b) in relation to any other non-cash voucher, the year of assessment in which the chargeable expense is incurred or, if later, the year of assessment in which the voucher is received by the employee.

(3) There shall be deductible under section 198, 201 or 332(3) from the amount taxable under subsection (1) above such amounts, if any, as would have been so deductible if the cost of the goods or services in question had been incurred by the employee out of his emoluments.

(4) The chargeable expense shall be treated as reduced by any part of that expense made good to the person incurring it by the employee.

(5) Where a non-cash voucher provided for an employee by reason of his employment is appropriated to him (whether by attaching it to a card held for him or in any other way),

subsections (1) and (2) above shall have effect as if the employee had received the voucher at the time when it was so appropriated.

(6) [Subsection (1)][1] above shall not apply in relation to a transport voucher provided for an employee of a passenger transport undertaking under arrangements in operation on 25th March 1982 and intended to enable that employee or a relation of his to obtain passenger transport services provided by—

    (*a*) his employer;
    (*b*) a subsidiary of his employer;
    (*c*) a body corporate of which his employer is a subsidiary; or
    (*d*) another passenger transport undertaking.

[(6A) Subsection (1) above shall not apply in relation to a non-cash voucher to the extent that it is used by the employee to obtain the use of a car parking space at or near his place of work.][2]

[(6B) Subsection (1) above shall not apply in relation to any non-cash voucher to the extent that it is used to obtain entertainment (including hospitality of any kind) for the employee or a relation of his, if—

    (*a*) the person providing the non-cash voucher is neither his employer nor a person connected with his employer;
    (*b*) neither his employer nor a person connected with his employer has directly or indirectly procured the provision of the entertainment; and
    (*c*) the entertainment is not provided either in recognition of particular services which have been performed by him in the course of his employment or in anticipation of particular services which are to be so performed by him;

and section 839 shall apply for determining whether persons are connected for the purposes of this subsection.][3]

(7) In this section—

    "cheque voucher" means a cheque provided for an employee and intended for use by him wholly or mainly for payment for particular goods or services or for goods or services of one or more particular classes; and, in relation to a cheque voucher, references to a voucher being exchanged for goods or services shall be construed accordingly;
    "passenger transport undertaking" means an undertaking whose business consists wholly or mainly in the carriage of passengers and includes a subsidiary of such an undertaking;
    "subsidiary" means a wholly owned subsidiary within the meaning of section 736(5)(*b*) of the Companies Act 1985;
    "transport voucher" means any ticket, pass or other document or token intended to enable a person to obtain passenger transport services (whether or not in exchange for it) and, in relation to a transport voucher, references to a voucher being exchanged for services shall be construed as references to it being exchanged for, or otherwise being used to procure, services; and
    "non-cash voucher" does not include a cash voucher within the meaning of section 143 but, subject to that, means any voucher, stamp or similar document or token capable of being exchanged (whether singly or together with other such vouchers, stamps, documents or tokens and whether immediately or only after a time) for money, goods or services (or for any combination of two or more of those things) and includes a transport voucher and a cheque voucher.

Former enactments.—Sub-ss. (1), (2): F(No. 2)A 1975, s. 36(1); FA 1982, s. 44(2).
Sub-s. (3): F(No. 2)A 1975, s. 36(2); FA 1982, s. 44(3).
Sub-s. (4): F(No. 2)A 1975, s. 36(2A); FA 1981, s. 70(2).
Sub-s. (5): F(No. 2)A 1975, s. 36(3).
Sub-s. (6): F(No. 2)A 1975, s. 36(3A); FA 1982, s. 44(4).
Sub-s. (7): F(No. 2)A 1975, s. 36(4); FA 1982, s. 44(5); Companies Consolidation (Consequential Provisions) Act 1985, Sch. 2.
Cross references.—See FA 1988, s. 47(2)–(4) (amendments to F(No. 2)A 1975, s. 36 effective for the year 1987–88).
Amendments.—[1] Words in sub-s. (6) substituted by FA 1988, s. 46(1), (5).
[2] Sub-s. (6A) inserted by *ibid*.
[3] Sub-s. (6B) inserted by FA 1988, s. 47(1), (4).

142. Credit-tokens

(1) Subject to the provisions of this section and section 157(3), where a credit-token is provided for an employee by reason of his employment, then, for the purposes of the Income Tax Acts—

    (*a*) on each occasion on which the employee uses the credit-token to obtain money, goods or services he shall be treated as having received an emolument from his employment of an amount equal to the expense incurred by the person providing the credit-token in or in connection with the provision of the money, goods or services obtained; and

(b) any money, goods or services obtained by the employee by use of the credit-token shall be disregarded.

(2) There shall be deductible under section 198, 201 or 332(3) from the amount taxable under subsection (1) above such amounts, if any, as would have been so deductible if the cost of the goods or services in question had been incurred by the employee out of his emoluments.

(3) The expense incurred by the person providing the credit-token as mentioned in subsection (1)(a) above shall be treated as reduced by any part of that expense made good to that person by the employee.

[(3A) Subsection (1) above shall not apply in relation to a credit-token to the extent that it is used by the employee to obtain the use of a car parking space at or near his place of work.][1]

[(3B) Subsection (1) above shall not apply in relation to any credit-token to the extent that it is used to obtain entertainment (including hospitality of any kind) for the employee or a relation of his, if—

(a) the person providing the credit-token is neither his employer nor a person connected with his employer;

(b) neither his employer nor a person connected with his employer has directly or indirectly procured the provision of the entertainment; and

(c) the entertainment is not provided either in recognition of particular services which have been performed by him in the course of his employment or in anticipation of particular services which are to be so performed by him;

and section 839 shall apply for determining whether persons are connected for the purposes of this subsection.][2]

(4) In this section "credit-token" means a card, token, document or other thing given to a person by another person who undertakes—

(a) that on the production of it (whether or not some other action is also required) he will supply money, goods and services (or any of them) on credit; or

(b) that where, on the production of it to a third party (whether or not some other action is also required) the third party supplies money, goods and services (or any of them), he will pay the third party for them (whether or not taking any discount or commission);

but does not include a non-cash voucher or a cash voucher.

(5) For the purposes of subsection (4) above, the use of an object to operate a machine provided by the person giving the object, or by a third party, shall be treated as production of the object to that person or, as the case may be, third party.

Former enactments.—Sub-s. (1): F(No. 2)A 1975, s. 36A(1)(b), (c); FA 1981, s. 71(1); FA 1982, s. 45(2).
Sub-s. (2): F(No. 2)A 1975, s. 36A(2); FA 1981, s. 71(1).
Sub-s. (3): F(No. 2)A 1975, s. 36A(3); FA 1981, s. 71(1); FA 1982, s. 45(2).
Sub-s. (4): F(No. 2)A 1975, s. 36A(4), (4B); FA 1981, s. 71(1); FA 1982, s. 45(3).
Sub-s. (5): F(No. 2)A 1975, s. 36A(4A); FA 1981, s. 71(1); FA 1982, s. 45(3).
Cross references.—See FA 1988, s. 48(2), (3) (amendments to F(No. 2)A 1975, s. 36A effective for the year 1987–88).
Amendments.—[1] Sub-s. (3A) inserted by FA 1988, s. 46(2), (5).
[2] Sub-s. (3B) inserted by FA 1988, s. 48(1), (3).

143. Cash vouchers taxable under P.A.Y.E.

(1) Where a cash voucher provided for an employee by reason of his employment is received by the employee, then, subject to subsection (5) below, for the purposes of the Income Tax Acts (and in particular section 203)—

(a) he shall be treated as being paid by his employer, at the time when he receives the voucher, an emolument of his employment equal to the sum of money for which the voucher is capable of being exchanged as mentioned in subsection (3) below; and

(b) any money obtained by the employee or any other person in exchange for the voucher shall be disregarded.

(2) Where a cash voucher provided for an employee by reason of his employment is appropriated to him (whether by attaching it to a card held for him or in any other way), subsections (1) and (5) of this section shall have effect as if the employee had received the voucher at the time when it was so appropriated.

(3) In this section "cash voucher" (subject to subsection (4) below) means any voucher, stamp or similar document capable of being exchanged (whether singly or together with such other vouchers, stamps or documents, and whether immediately or only after a time) for a sum of money greater than, equal to or not substantially less than the expense incurred in providing the voucher by the person who provides it (whether or not it is also capable of being exchanged for goods or services), except that it does not include—

(*a*) any document intended to enable a person to obtain payment of the sum mentioned in the document, being a sum which if paid to him directly would not have been chargeable to income tax under Schedule E; or
(*b*) a savings certificate the accumulated interest payable in respect of which is exempt from tax (or would be so exempt if certain conditions were satisfied).

(4) Where—

(*a*) a voucher, stamp or similar document is capable of being exchanged (as mentioned above) for a sum of money substantially less than the expense incurred in providing the voucher by the person who provides it, and
(*b*) the difference or part of the difference represents the cost to that person of providing benefits in connection with sickness, personal injury or death,

then, in determining whether the voucher, stamp or document is a cash voucher within the meaning of this section, the expense incurred by him in providing it shall be treated as reduced by that difference or part.

(5) Subsection (1) above shall not apply to a cash voucher received by an employee if, at the time when the voucher is received, the scheme under which it was issued is a scheme approved by the Board for the purposes of this subsection; and the Board shall not approve a scheme for those purposes unless satisfied that it is practicable for income tax in respect of all payments made in exchange for vouchers issued under the scheme to be deducted in accordance with regulations under section 203.

Former enactments.—Sub-ss. (1)–(4): F(No. 2)A 1975, s. 37(1)–(4).
Sub-s. (5): F(No. 2)A 1975, s. 37(5); FA 1976, s. 71(2).

144. Supplementary provisions

(1) If a person furnishes to the inspector a statement of the cases and circumstances in which non-cash vouchers or credit-tokens are provided for any employees (whether his own or those of anyone else) and the inspector is satisfied that no additional tax is payable under section 141 or 142 by reference to the vouchers or tokens mentioned in the statement, the inspector shall notify the person accordingly and nothing in those sections shall apply to the provision of those vouchers or tokens or their use.

(2) The inspector may, if in his opinion there is reason to do so, by notice served on the person to whom the notificiation under subsection (1) above was given, revoke the notification, either as from the date of its making or as from such later date as may be specified in the notice under this subsection; and all such income tax becomes chargeable, and all such returns are to be made by that person and by the employees in question, as would have been chargeable or would have had to be made in the first instance if the notification under subsection (1) above had never been given or, as the case may be, it had ceased to have effect on the specified date.

(3) For the purposes of sections 141 and 142 where a person incurs expense in or in connection with the provision by him of non-cash vouchers or credit-tokens for two or more employees as members of a group or class, the expense incurred in respect of any one of them shall be taken to be such part of that expense as is just and reasonable.

(4) For the purposes of sections 141, 142 and 143 and this section—

(*a*) a non-cash voucher, cash voucher or credit-token provided for an employee by his employer shall be deemed to be provided for him by reason of his employment; and
(*b*) any reference to a non-cash voucher, cash voucher or credit-token being provided for or received by an employee includes a reference to it being provided for or received by a relation of his.

(5) In sections 141, 142, 143 and this section—

"cash voucher" has the meaning given by section 143(3);
"credit-token" has the meaning given by section 142(4);
"employee" means the holder of any office or employment the emoluments in respect of

which fall to be assessed under Schedule E; and related expressions shall be construed accordingly;

"non-cash voucher" has the meaning given by section 141(7); and

"relation", with respect to an employee, means his spouse, parent or child, the spouse of his child and any dependant of that employee.

Former enactments.—Sub-ss. (1), (2): F(No. 2)A 1975, ss. 36(5A), 36A(6), (7); FA 1981, s. 71(1); FA 1982, s. 44(6).
Sub-s. (3): F(No. 2)A 1975, ss. 36(5)(b), 36A(5).
Sub-s. (4): F(No. 2)A 1975, ss. 36(5)(c), (d), 36A(5), 37(6); FA 1981, s. 70(5)(b).
Sub-s. (5): F(No. 2)A 1975, ss. 36(4), 36A(4B), 37(3), (6); FA 1982, ss. 44(5), 45(3).

Living accommodation

145. Living accommodation provided for employee

(1) Subject to the provisions of this section, where living accommodation is provided for a person in any period by reason of his employment, and is not otherwise made the subject of any charge to him by way of income tax, he is to be treated for the purposes of Schedule E as being in receipt of emoluments of an amount equal to the value to him of the accommodation for the period, less so much as is properly attributable to that provision of any sum made good by him to those at whose cost the accommodation is provided.

(2) The value of the accommodation to the employee in any period is the rent which would have been payable for the period if the premises had been let to him at an annual rent equal to their annual value as ascertained under section 837; but for a period in which those at whose cost the accommodation is provided pay rent at an annual rate greater than the annual value as so ascertained, the value of the accommodation to the employee is an amount equal to the rent payable by them for the period.

(3) From any amount to be treated as emoluments under subsection (1) above there are deductible under section 198 or 332(3) such amounts (if any) as would have been so deductible if the accommodation had been paid for by the employee out of his emoluments.

(4) Subject to subsection (5) below, subsection (1) above does not apply to accommodation provided for the employee in any of the following cases—

(a) where it is necessary for the proper performance of the employee's duties that he should reside in the accommodation;

(b) where the accommodation is provided for the better performance of the duties of his employment, and his is one of the kinds of employment in the case of which it is customary for employers to provide living accommodation for employees;

(c) where there is a special threat to his security, special security arrangements are in force and he resides in the accommodation as part of those arrangements;

and in any such case there is no charge to tax under Schedule E (either by virtue of this section or under section 131 or otherwise) in respect of a liability for rates on the premises being discharged for or on behalf of the employee or the employee being reimbursed for the discharge of that liability.

(5) If the accommodation is provided by a company and the employee is a director of the company or of an associated company, then, except in a case where paragraph (c) of subsection (4) above applies, no exemption is given by virtue of that subsection unless, for each employment of his which is employment as director of the company or an associated company, the following conditions are fulfilled, that is—

(a) he has no material interest in the company, and

(b) either his employment is as a full-time working director or the company is non-profit-making (meaning that neither does it carry on a trade nor do its functions consist wholly or mainly in the holding of investments or other property) or is established for charitable purposes only.

(6) If by reason of a person's employment accommodation is provided for others being members of his family or household, he is to be treated under subsections (1) to (3) above as if it were accommodation provided for him.

(7) For the purposes of this section, living accommodation provided for an employee, or for members of his family or household, by his employer is deemed to be provided by reason of his employment unless—

(a) the employer is an individual, and it can be shown that he makes the provision in the normal course of his domestic, family or personal relationships; or

(b) the accommodation is provided by a local authority for an employee of theirs, and it can be shown that the terms on which it is provided are no more favourable than those on which similar accommodation is provided by the authority for persons who are not their employees but are otherwise similarly circumstanced.

(8) For the purposes of this section—

(a) a company is associated with another if one has control of the other or both are under the control of the same person; and
(b) the expressions "employment", "family or household", "director", "full-time working director", "material interest" and (in relation to a body corporate) "control" shall be construed in accordance with subsections (2), (4) and (8) to (12) of section 168 as if this section were included in Chapter II of this Part.

Former enactment.—FA 1977, s. 33(1)–(8).

146. Additional charge in respect of certain living accommodation

(1) This section applies where—

(a) living accommodation is provided for a person in any period, by reason of his employment;
(b) by virtue of section 145 he is treated for the purposes of Schedule E as being in receipt of emoluments of an amount calculated by reference to the value to him of that accommodation, or would be so treated if there were disregarded any sum made good by him to those at whose cost the accommodation is provided; and
(c) the cost of providing the accommodation exceeds £75,000.

(2) Where this section applies, the employee shall be treated for the purposes of Schedule E as being in receipt of emoluments (in addition to those which he is treated as receiving by virtue of section 145) of an amount equal to the additional value to him of the accommodation for the period, less so much of any rent paid by the employee, in respect of the accommodation, to the person providing it as exceeds the value to the employee of the accommodation for the period (as determined under section 145).

(3) The additional value of the accommodation to the employee in any period is the rent which would have been payable for that period if the premises had been let to him at an annual rent equal to the appropriate percentage of the amount by which the cost of providing the accommodation exceeds £75,000.

(4) For the purposes of this section, the cost of providing any living accommodation shall be taken to be the aggregate of—

(a) the amount of any expenditure incurred in acquiring the estate or interest in the property held by a relevant person; and
(b) the amount of any expenditure incurred by a relevant person before the year of assessment in question on improvements to the property.

(5) The aggregate amount mentioned in subsection (4) above shall be reduced by the amount of any payment made by the employee to a relevant person, so far as that amount represents a reimbursement of any such expenditure as is mentioned in paragraph (a) or (b) of that subsection or represents consideration for the grant to the employee of a tenancy of the property.

(6) Subject to subsection (8) below, where throughout the period of six years ending with the date when the employee first occupied the property, any estate or interest in the property was held by a relevant person (whether or not it was the same estate, interest or person throughout), the additional value shall be calculated as if in subsection (4) above—

(a) the amount referred to in paragraph (a) were the market value of that property as at that date; and
(b) the amount referred to in paragraph (b) did not include expenditure on improvements made before that date.

(7) In this section, "relevant person" means any of the following—

(a) the person providing the accommodation;
(b) where the person providing the accommodation is not the employee's employer, that employer;
(c) any person, other than the employee, who is connected with a person falling within paragraph (a) or (b) above.

(8) Subsection (6) above does not apply where the employee first occupied the property before 31st March 1983.

(9) Any amount which is deductible, by virtue of section 145(3), from an amount to be treated as emoluments under that section may, to the extent to which it exceeds the amount of those emoluments, be deductible from the amount to be treated as emoluments under this section.

(10) For the purposes of this section, living accommodation shall be treated as provided for a person by reason of his employment if it is so treated for the purposes of section 145; and "employment" has the same meaning in this section as in that.

(11) In this section—

"the appropriate percentage" means the rate [applicable for the purposes of section 160][1] as at the beginning of the year of assessment in question;

"property", in relation to any living accommodation, means the property consisting of that accommodation;

"market value", in relation to any property, means the price which that property might reasonably be expected to fetch on a sale in the open market with vacant possession, no reduction being made, in estimating the market value, on account of any option in respect of the property held by the employee, or a person connected with him, or by any of the persons mentioned in subsection (7) above; and

"tenancy" includes a sub-tenancy;

and section 839 shall apply for the purposes of this section.

Former enactments.—FA 1977, s. 33A; FA 1983, s. 21(1).
Amendments.—[1] Words in the definition of "the appropriate percentage" substituted for the words "prescribed by the Treasury under section 160(5)" by FA 1989, s. 179(5) with effect from an appointed day.

147. Occupation of Chevening House

Section 145 shall not apply in relation to the occupation of Chevening House or any other premises held on the trusts of the trust instrument set out in the Schedule to the Chevening Estate Act 1959 by a person nominated in accordance with those trusts.

Former enactments.—FA 1973, s. 43; FA 1977, Sch. 8, para. 4.

Payments on retirement, sick pay etc.

148. Payments on retirement or removal from office or employment

(1) Subject to the provisions of this section and section 188, tax shall be charged under Schedule E in respect of any payment to which this section applies which is made to the holder or past holder of any office or employment, or to his executors or administrators, whether made by the person under whom he holds or held the office or employment or by any other person.

(2) This section applies to any payment (not otherwise chargeable to tax) which is made, whether in pursuance of any legal obligation or not, either directly or indirectly in consideration or in consequence of, or otherwise in connection with, the termination of the holding of the office or employment or any change in its functions or emoluments, including any payment in commutation of annual or periodical payments (whether chargeable to tax or not) which would otherwise have been so made.

(3) For the purposes of this section and section 188, any payment made to the spouse or any relative or dependant of a person who holds or has held an office or employment, or made on behalf of or to the order of that person, shall be treated as made to that person, and any valuable consideration other than money shall be treated as a payment of money equal to the value of that consideration at the date when it is given.

(4) Any payment which is chargeable to tax by virtue of this section shall be treated as income received on the following date, that is to say—

(*a*) in the case of a payment in commutation of annual or other periodical payments, the date on which the commutation is effected; and

(*b*) in the case of any other payment, the date of the termination or change in respect of which the payment is made;

and shall be treated as emoluments of the holder or past holder of the office or employment assessable to tax under Schedule E; and any such payment shall be treated for all the purposes of the Income Tax Acts as earned income.

(5) In the case of the death of any person who, if he had not died, would have been chargeable to tax in respect of any such payment, the tax which would have been so

chargeable shall be assessed and charged upon his executors or administrators and shall be a debt due from and payable out of his estate.

(6) This section shall not apply to any payment made in pursuance of an obligation incurred before 6th April 1960.

(7) Where any payment chargeable to tax under this section is made to any person in any year of assessment, it shall be the duty of the person by whom it is made to deliver particulars thereof in writing to the inspector not later than 30 days after the end of that year.

Former enactment.—TA 1970, s. 187.

149. Sick pay

(1) Where a person holding an employment is absent from work for any period by reason of sickness or disability, any sums which—

(a) are paid to, or to the order or for the benefit of, that person (or a member of his family or household) in respect of any such absence from work; and

(b) are, by reason of his employment, paid as a result of any arrangements entered into by his employer,

shall be chargeable to income tax under Schedule E as emoluments of the employment ...[1] if, apart from this section, they would not be so chargeable ...[1].

(2) Where the funds for making payments under any arrangements are attributable partly to contributions made by the employer and partly to contributions made by the persons employed by him, subsection (1) above shall apply only to such part of the sums paid as a result of the arrangements as it is just and reasonable to regard as attributable to the employer's contributions.

(3) In this section "employment" means an office or employment the emoluments of which fall to be assessed under Schedule E and related expressions shall be construed accordingly; and the reference to a person's family or household is to his spouse, his sons and daughters and their spouses, his parents and his dependants.

Former enactment.—FA 1981, s. 30(1), (2), (4).
Amendments.—[1] Words in sub-s. (1) repealed by FA 1989, s. 39(1), (3) and Sch. 17, Pt. IV.

150. Job release scheme allowances, maternity pay and statutory sick pay

The following payments shall be charged to income tax under Schedule E by virtue of this section if they would not otherwise be, that is to say—

(a) allowances paid under a scheme of the kind described in the Job Release Act 1977, being a scheme which provides for the payment of allowances for periods beginning earlier than one year before the date on which the recipient attains pensionable age, as defined in that Act;

(b) maternity pay (whether paid during the subsistence of a contract of employment or not) within the meaning of section 33 of the Employment Protection (Consolidation) Act 1978 or, in Northern Ireland, Article 15 of the Industrial Relations (No. 2) (Northern Ireland) Order 1976;

(c) payments of statutory sick pay within the meaning of section 1 of the Social Security and Housing Benefits Act 1982 or, in Northern Ireland, Article 3 of the Social Security (Northern Ireland) Order 1982; and

(d) payments of statutory maternity pay under Part V of the Social Security Act 1986 or, in Northern Ireland, under Part VI of the Social Security (Northern Ireland) Order 1986.

Former enactments.—TA 1970, s. 219A; FA 1982, s. 31(1); Social Security Act 1986, Sch. 10, para. 71.

151. Income support etc

(1) Subject to the following provisions of this section, payments to any person of income support under the Social Security Act 1986 in respect of any period shall be charged to income tax under Schedule E if during that period—

(a) his right to income support is subject to the condition specified in section 20(3)(d)(i) of that Act (availability for employment); or

(b) he is one of a married or unmarried couple and section 23 of that Act (trade disputes) applies to him but not to the other person;

(2) In this section "married couple" and "unmarried couple" have the same meaning as in Part II of the Social Security Act 1986.

(3) Where the amount of income support paid to any person in respect of any week or part of a week exceeds the taxable maximum for that period as defined below, the excess shall not be taxable.

(4) Where payments of unemployment benefit and payments of income support are made to any person in respect of the same week or part of a week, the amount taxable in respect of that period in respect of those payments shall not exceed the taxable maximum for that period within the meaning of subsection (3) above.

(5) For the purposes of subsections (3) and (4) above, the taxable maximum in respect of a week shall be determined in accordance with subsections (6) to (8) below and the taxable maximum in respect of part of a week shall be equal to one-sixth of the taxable maximum in respect of a week multiplied by the number of days in the part.

(6) Where the income support is paid to one of a married or unmarried couple in a case not falling within subsection (1)(b) above, the taxable maximum in respect of a week shall be equal to the aggregate of—
    (a) the weekly rate specified for the week in question in relation to unemployment benefit in paragraph 1 of Part I of Schedule 4 to the Social Security Act 1975; and
    (b) the increase for an adult dependant specified for that week in paragraph 1(a) of Part IV of that Schedule.

(7) Where the income support is paid to one of a married or unmarried couple in a case falling within subsection (1)(b) above, the taxable maximum in respect of a week shall—
    (a) if the applicable amount (within the meaning of Part II of the Social Security Act 1986) consists only of an amount in respect of them, be equal to one half of that amount; and
    (b) if the applicable amount includes other amounts, be equal to one half of the portion of it which is included in respect of them.

(8) Where the income support is paid to a person who is not one of a married or unmarried couple, the taxable maximum in respect of a week shall be equal to the weekly rate referred to in subsection (6)(a) above.

(9) In its application to Northern Ireland this section shall have effect as if—
    (a) for the references to the Social Security Act 1986, to Part II of that Act and to sections 20(3)(d)(i) and 23 of that Act there were substituted respectively references to the Social Security (Northern Ireland) Order 1986, Part III of that Order and Articles 21(3)(d)(i) and 24 of that Order; and
    (b) for the references to paragraph 1 of Part 1 of Schedule 4 to the Social Security Act 1975 and paragraph 1(a) of Part IV of that Schedule there were substituted respectively references to paragraph 1 of Part I of Schedule 4 to the Social Security (Northern Ireland) Act 1975 and paragraph 1(a) of Part IV of that Schedule.

Former enactments.—Sub-s. (1): FA 1987, s. 29(2).
Sub-s. (2): FA 1987, s. 29(2), Sch. 3, para. 1(2).
Sub-ss. (3), (4): FA 1987, s. 29(3), (4).
Sub-ss. (5)–(8): FA 1987, Sch. 3, paras. 1(1), 2–4.
Sub-s. (9): FA 1987, s. 29(5).
Cross references.—See FA 1989, s. 41(1)(c) (income support chargeable to income tax under this section to be charged in the year in which it accrues irrespective of when it is paid).

152. Notification of amount taxable under section 151

(1) A benefit officer may by notice notify a person who is taxable in respect of any unemployment benefit or income support of the amount on which he is taxable and any such notification shall state the date on which it is issued and shall inform the person to whom it is given that he may object to the notification by notice given within 60 days after the date of issue of the notification.

(2) Where—
    (a) no objection is made to a notification of an amount under subsection (1) above within the period specified in that subsection (or such further period as may be allowed by virtue of subsection (5) below); or
    (b) an objection is made but is withdrawn by the objector by notice,
that amount shall not be questioned in any appeal against any assessment in respect of income including that amount.

(3) Where—

(a) an objection is made to a notification of an amount under subsection (1) above within the period specified in that subsection (or such further period as may be allowed by virtue of subsection (5) below), and

(b) the benefit officer and the objector come to an agreement that the amount notified should be varied in a particular manner, and

(c) the officer confirms the agreement to vary in writing,

then, subject to subsection (4) below, that amount as so varied shall not be questioned in any appeal against any assessment in respect of income including that amount.

(4) Subsection (3) above shall not apply if, within 60 days from the date when the agreement was come to, the objector gives notice to the benefit officer that he wishes to repudiate or resile from the agreement.

(5) An objection to a notification may be made later than 60 days after the date of the issue of the notification if, on an application for the purpose—

(a) a benefit officer is satisfied that there was a reasonable excuse for not objecting within that time, and

(b) the objection was made thereafter without unreasonable delay, and

(c) the officer gives consent in writing;

and if the officer is not so satisfied he shall refer the application for determination—

(i) by the General Commissioners for the division in which the objector ordinarily resides or,

(ii) in a case where an appeal has been made against an assessment in respect of income including the amount in question, the General Commissioners or the Special Commissioners having jurisdiction in that appeal.

(6) Where a benefit officer has notified an amount to a person under subsection (1) above, he may by another notice notify the person of an alteration in the amount previously notified and, if he does so, the original notification shall be cancelled and this section shall apply to such a subsequent notification as it applies to the original notification.

(7) In this section "benefit officer" means the appropriate officer, in Great Britain, of the Department of Employment or of the Department of Health and Social Security, as the case may be, or, in Northern Ireland, of the Department of Health and Social Services.

Former enactments.—FA 1981, s. 28; FA 1987, Sch. 3, para. 6.

CHAPTER II

[EMPLOYEES EARNING £8,500 OR MORE AND DIRECTORS][1]

Amendments.—[1] Heading substituted by FA 1989, s. 53(2)(*a*).

Expenses

153. Payments in respect of expenses

(1) Subject to the provisions of this Chapter, where in any year a person is employed in [employment to which this Chapter applies][1] and by reason of his employment there are paid to him in respect of expenses any sums which, apart from this section, are not chargeable to tax as his income, those sums are to be treated as emoluments of the employment and accordingly chargeable to income tax under Schedule E.

(2) Subsection (1) above is without prejudice to any claim for deductions under section 198, 201 or 332(3).

(3) The reference in subsection (1) above to sums paid in respect of expenses includes any sums put at the employee's disposal by reason of his employment and paid away by him.

Former enactment.—FA 1976, s. 60.
Amendments.—[1] Words in sub-s. (1) substituted by FA 1989, s. 53(2)(*b*).

Benefits in kind

154. General charging provision

(1) Subject to section 163, where in any year a person is employed in [employment to which this Chapter applies][1] and—

(*a*) by reason of his employment there is provided for him, or for others being members of his family or household, any benefit to which this section applies; and
(*b*) the cost of providing the benefit is not (apart from this section) chargeable to tax as his income,

there is to be treated as emoluments of the employment, and accordingly chargeable to income tax under Schedule E, an amount equal to whatever is the cash equivalent of the benefit.

(2) The benefits to which this section applies are accommodation (other than living accommodation), entertainment, domestic or other services, and other benefits and facilities of whatsoever nature (whether or not similar to any of those mentioned above in this subsection), excluding however—

(*a*) any benefit consisting of the right to receive, or the prospect of receiving, any sums which would be chargeable to tax under section 149; and
(*b*) any benefit chargeable under section 157, 158, 160 or 162;

and subject to the exceptions provided for by section 155.

(3) For the purposes of this section and sections 155 and 156, the persons providing a benefit are those at whose cost the provision is made.

Former enactments.—FA 1976, s. 61; FA 1977, Sch. 8, para. 5; FA 1981, s. 30(3).
Amendments.—[1] Words in sub-s. (1) substituted by FA 1989, s. 53(2)(*b*).

155. Exceptions from the general charge

(1) Where the benefit of a car is taxable under section 157, section 154 does not apply to any benefit in connection with the car other than a benefit in connection with the provision of a driver for the car.

[(1A) Section 154 does not apply to a benefit consisting in the provision for the employee of a car parking space at or near his place of work.][1]

(2) Section 154 does not apply where the benefit consists in provision for the employee, in

premises occupied by the employer or others providing it, of accommodation, supplies or services used by the employee solely in performing the duties of his employment.

(3) Where living accommodation is provided by reason of a person's employment—

(a) alterations and additions to the premises concerned which are of a structural nature, and

(b) repairs to the premises of a kind which, if the premises were let under a lease to which section 11 of the Landlord and Tenant Act 1985 (repairing obligations) applies, would be the obligation of the lessor under the covenants implied by subsection (1) of that section,

are not benefits to which section 154 applies.

(4) Section 154 does not apply to a benefit consisting in the provision by the employee's employer for the employee himself, or for the spouse, children or dependants of the employee, of any pension, annuity, lump sum, gratuity or other like benefit to be given on the employee's death or retirement.

(5) Section 154 does not apply to a benefit consisting in the provision by the employee's employer of meals in any canteen in which meals are provided for the staff generally.

(6) Section 154 does not apply where the benefit consists—

(a) in providing the employee with medical treatment outside the United Kingdom (including providing for him to be an in-patient) in a case where the need for the treatment arises while the employee is outside the United Kingdom for the purpose of performing the duties of his employment; or

(b) in providing insurance for the employee against the cost of such treatment in such a case;

and for the purpose of this subsection, medical treatment includes all forms of treatment for, and all procedures for diagnosing, any physical or mental ailment, infirmity or defect.

[(7) Section 154 does not apply to a benefit consisting in the provision of entertainment (including hospitality of any kind) for the employee, or for members of his family or household, if—

(a) the person providing the benefit is neither his employer nor a person connected with his employer;

(b) neither his employer nor a person connected with his employer has directly or indirectly procured its provision; and

(c) it is not provided either in recognition of particular services which have been performed by the employee in the course of his employment or in anticipation of particular services which are to be so performed by him;

and section 839 shall apply for determining whether persons are connected for the purposes of this subsection.][2]

Former enactments.—Sub-s. (1): FA 1976, s. 62(1); FA 1980, s. 48(1).
Sub-s. (2): FA 1976, s. 62(3).
Sub-s. (3): FA 1976, s. 62(4); FA 1977, Sch. 8, para. 6; Housing (Consequential Provisions) Act 1985, Sch. 2, para. 31.
Sub-s. (4): FA 1976, s. 62(6).
Sub-s. (5): FA 1976, s. 62(7).
Sub-s. (6): FA 1976, s. 62(8); FA 1981, s. 72(1).
Cross references.—See FA 1988, s. 49(2), (3) (amendments to FA 1976, s. 62 effective for the year 1987–88).
Amendments.—[1] Sub-s. (1A) inserted by FA 1988, s. 46(3), (5).
[2] Sub-s. (7) added by FA 1988, s. 49(1), (3).

---

156. Cash equivalents of benefits charged under section 154

(1) The cash equivalent of any benefit chargeable to tax under section 154 is an amount equal to the cost of the benefit, less so much (if any) of it as is made good by the employee to those providing the benefit.

(2) Subject to the following subsections, the cost of a benefit is the amount of any expense incurred in or in connection with its provision, and (here and in those subsections) includes a proper proportion of any expense relating partly to the benefit and partly to other matters.

(3) Where the benefit consists in the transfer of an asset by any person, and since that person acquired or produced the asset it has been used or has depreciated, the cost of the benefit is deemed to be the market value of the asset at the time of transfer.

(4) Where the asset referred to in subsection (3) above is not a car and before the transfer a person (whether or not the transferee) has been chargeable to tax in respect of the asset in

accordance with subsection (5) below, the amount which under subsection (3) above is deemed to be the cost of the benefit shall (if apart from this subsection it would be less) be deemed to be—

(a) the market value of the asset at the time when it was first applied (by those providing the benefit in question) for the provision of any benefit for a person, or for members of his family or household, by reason of his employment, less

(b) the aggregate of the amounts taken into account as the cost of the benefit in charging tax in accordance with subsection (5) below in the year or years up to and including that in which the transfer takes place.

(5) Where the benefit consists in an asset being placed at the employee's disposal, or at the disposal of others being members of his family or household, for his or their use (without any transfer of the property in the asset), or of its being used wholly or partly for his or their purposes, then the cost of the benefit in any year is deemed to be—

(a) the annual value of the use of the asset ascertained under subsection (6) below; plus

(b) the total of any expense incurred in or in connection with the provision of the benefit excluding—

(i) the expense of acquiring or producing it incurred by the person to whom the asset belongs; and

(ii) any rent or hire charge payable for the asset by those providing the benefit.

(6) Subject to subsection (7) below, the annual value of the use of the asset, for the purposes of subsection (5) above—

(a) in the case of land, is its annual value determined in accordance with section 837; and

(b) in any other case is 20 per cent. of its market value at the time when it was first applied (by those providing the benefit in question) in the provision of any benefit for a person, or for members of his family or household, by reason of his employment.

(7) Where there is payable, by those providing the benefit, any sum by way of rent or hire-charge for the asset, the annual amount of which is equal to, or greater than, the annual value of the use of the asset as ascertained under subsection (6) above, that amount shall be substituted for the annual value in subsection (5)(a) above.

(8) From the cash equivalent there are deductible in each case under section 198, 201 or 332(3) such amounts (if any) as would have been so deductible if the cost of the benefit had been incurred by the employee out of his emoluments.

(9) In the case of assets first applied before 6th April 1980 by those providing the benefit in question in the provision of any benefit for a person, or for members of his family or household, by reason of his employment—

(a) subsection (4) above shall not have effect; and

(b) in subsection (6)(b) above for the words "20 per cent." there shall be substituted the words "10 per cent.".

Former enactments.—Sub-ss. (1)–(3): FA 1976, s. 63(1)–(3).
Sub-s. (4): FA 1976, s. 63(3A); FA 1980, s. 49(2).
Sub-s. (5): FA 1976, s. 63(4); FA 1980, s. 51(1)(a).
Sub-s. (6): FA 1976, s. 63(5)(a), (c); FA 1980, s. 49(3).
Sub-s. (7): FA 1976, s. 63(6); FA 1980, s. 51(1)(b).
Sub-s. (8): FA 1976, s. 63(8).
Sub-s. (9): FA 1980, s. 49(4).

157. Cars available for private use

(1) Where in any year in the case of a person employed in [employment to which this Chapter applies][1], a car is made available (without any transfer of the property in it) either to himself or to others being members of his family or household, and—

(a) it is so made available by reason of his employment and it is in that year available for his or their private use; and

(b) the benefit of the car is not (apart from this section) chargeable to tax as the employee's income,

there is to be treated as emoluments of the employment, and accordingly chargeable to income tax under Schedule E, an amount equal to whatever is the cash equivalent of that benefit in that year.

(2) Subject to the provisions of this section, the cash equivalent of that benefit is to be ascertained—

(a) from Tables A and B in Part I of Schedule 6, in the case of cars with an original market value of up to £19,250; and
(b) from Table C in that Part in the case of cars with an original market value of more than that amount;

the equivalent in each case being shown in the second or third column of the applicable Table by reference to the age of the car at the end of the relevant year of assessment.

(3) Where in any year the benefit of a car is chargeable to tax under this section as the employee's income he shall not be taxable—

(a) under Schedule E in respect of the discharge of any liability of his in connection with the car;
(b) under section 141 or 142 in respect of any non-cash voucher or credit-token to the extent that it is used by him—

(i) for obtaining money which is spent on goods or services in connection with the car; or
(ii) for obtaining such goods or services;

(c) under section 153 in respect of any payment made to him in respect of expenses incurred by him in connection with the car.

(4) The Treasury may by order taking effect from the beginning of any year beginning after it is made—

(a) increase or further increase the money sum specified in subsection (2)(a) above;
(b) with or without such an increase, substitute for any of the three Tables a different Table of cash equivalents;
(c) increase or further increase the money sum specified in paragraph 1(1) of Part II of Schedule 6.

(5) Part II of Schedule 6 has effect—

(a) with respect to the application of the Tables in Part I; and
(b) for the reduction of the cash equivalent under this section in cases where the car has not been available for the whole of the relevant year, or the use of it has been preponderantly business use, or the employee makes any payment for the use of it.

Former enactments.—Sub-s. (1): FA 1976, s. 64(1).
Sub-s. (2): FA 1976, s. 64(2); S.I. 1985 No. 1598.
Sub-s. (3): FA 1976, s. 64(2A); FA 1981, s. 68(3); FA 1982, s. 46(2).
Sub-s. (4): FA 1976, s. 64(4); FA 1980, s. 51(2).
Sub-s. (5): FA 1976, s. 64(5).
Amendments.—[1] Words in sub-s. (1) substituted by FA 1989, s. 53(2)(b).

158. Car fuel

(1) Where in any year in the case of a person employed in [employment to which this Chapter applies][1] fuel is provided by reason of his employment for a car which is made available as mentioned in section 157, an amount equal to whatever is the cash equivalent of that benefit in that year shall be treated as emoluments of the employment and, accordingly, shall be chargeable to income tax under Schedule E.

(2) Subject to the provisions of this section, the cash equivalent of that benefit shall be ascertained from Table A below where the car has an internal combustion engine with one or more reciprocating pistons and from Table B below in the case of other cars; and for the purposes of Table A below a car's cylinder capacity is the capacity of its engine calculated as for the purposes of the Vehicles (Excise) Act 1971 or the Vehicles (Excise) Act (Northern Ireland) 1972.

TABLE A

Cylinder capacity of car in cubic centimetres	Cash equivalent
1,400 or less	£480
More than 1,400 but not more than 2,000	£600
More than 2,000	£900

TABLE B

Original market value of car	Cash equivalent
Less than £6,000	£480
£6,000 or more but less than £8,500	£600
£8,500 or more	£900

(3) Without prejudice to the generality of subsection (1) above, fuel is provided for a car if—

(a) any liability in respect of the provision of fuel for the car is discharged;

(b) a non-cash voucher or a credit-token is used to obtain fuel for the car or money which is spent on such fuel;

(c) any sum is paid in respect of expenses incurred in providing fuel for the car.

In this subsection "non-cash voucher" and "credit-token" have the meanings given by section 141(7) and 142(4) respectively.

(4) The Treasury may by order taking effect from the beginning of any year beginning after it is made substitute a different Table for either of the Tables in subsection (2) above.

(5) Where paragraph 2 or 3 of Part II of Schedule 6 applies to reduce the cash equivalent of the benefit of the car for which the fuel is provided, the same reduction shall be made to the cash equivalent of the benefit of the fuel ascertained under subsection (2) above.

(6) If in the relevant year—

(a) the employee is required to make good to the person providing the fuel the whole of the expense incurred by him in or in connection with the provision of fuel for his private use and he does so; or

(b) the fuel is made available only for business travel;

the cash equivalent is nil.

Former enactments.—Sub-s. (1): FA 1976, s. 64A(1); FA 1981, s. 69(1); FA 1982, s. 46(4).
Sub-s. (2): FA 1976, s. 64A(2); FA 1981, s. 69(1); S.I. 1986 No. 702.
Sub-ss. (3)–(6): FA 1976, s. 64A(3)–(6); FA 1981, s. 69(1).
Amendments.—[1] Words in sub-s. (1) substituted by FA 1989, s. 53(2)(b).

159. Pooled cars

(1) This section applies to any car in the case of which the inspector is satisfied (whether on a claim under this section or otherwise) that it has for any year been included in a car pool for the use of the employees of one or more employers.

(2) A car is to be treated as having been so included for a year if—

(a) in that year it was made available to, and actually used by, more than one of those employees and, in the case of each of them, it was made available to him by reason of his employment but it was not in that year ordinarily used by one of them to the exclusion of the others; and

(b) in the case of each of them any private use of the car made by him in that year was merely incidental to his other use of it in the year; and

(c) it was in that year not normally kept overnight on or in the vicinity of any residential premises where any of the employees was residing, except while being kept overnight on premises occupied by the person making the car available to them.

(3) Where this section applies to a car, then for the year in question the car is to be treated under sections 154 and 157 as not having been available for the private use of any of the employees.

(4) A claim under this section in respect of a car for any year may be made by any one of the employees mentioned in subsection (2)(a) above (referred to below as "the employees concerned") or by the employer on behalf of all of them.

(5) On an appeal against the decision of the inspector on a claim under this section all the employees concerned may take part in the proceedings, and the determination of the body of Commissioners or county court appealed to shall be binding on all those employees, whether or not they have taken part in the proceedings.

(6) Where an appeal against the decision of the inspector on a claim under this section has been determined, no appeal against the inspector's decision on any other such claim in respect of the same car and the same year shall be entertained.

Former enactment.—FA 1976, s. 65.

160. Beneficial loan arrangements

(1) Where in the case of a person employed in [employment to which this Chapter applies]¹ there is outstanding for the whole or part of a year a loan (whether to the employee himself or a relative of his) of which the benefit is obtained by reason of his employment and—
   (a) no interest is paid on the loan for that year; or
   (b) the amount of interest paid on it for the year is less than interest at the official rate,
there is to be treated as emoluments of the employment, and accordingly chargeable to income tax under Schedule E, an amount equal to whatever is the cash equivalent of the benefit of the loan for that year.

(2) Where in the case of a person employed in [employment to which this Chapter applies]¹—
   (a) there is in any year released or written off the whole or part of a loan (whether to the employee himself or a relative of his, and whether or not such a loan as is mentioned in subsection (1) above), and
   (b) the benefit of that loan was obtained by reason of his employment,
then there is to be treated as emoluments of the employment, and accordingly chargeable to income tax under Schedule E, an amount equal to that which is released or written off.

[(3) Where—
   (a) there was outstanding, at any time when a person was in employment to which this Chapter applies, the whole or part of a loan to him (or a relative of his) the benefit of which was obtained by reason of his employment, and
   (b) that employment has terminated or ceased to be employment to which this Chapter applies,
subsection (2) above applies as if the employment had not terminated or, as the case may be, had not ceased to be employment to which this Chapter applies.]²

(4) Part I of Schedule 7 has effect as to what is meant by the benefit of a loan obtained by reason of a person's employment; the cash equivalent of the benefit is to be ascertained in accordance with Part II of that Schedule; and Part III of that Schedule has effect for excluding from the operation of subsection (1) above loans on which interest is eligible for relief under subsection (1) of section 353 or which would be so eligible apart from subsection (2) of that section.

(5) In this section, sections 161 and 162 and Schedule 7—
   (a) "loan" includes any form of credit;
   (b) references to a loan include references to any other loan applied directly or indirectly towards the replacement of the first-mentioned loan;
   (c) references to making a loan include arranging, guaranteeing or in any way facilitating a loan (related expressions being construed accordingly); and
   (d) references to the official rate of interest are to the [rate applicable under section 178 of the Finance Act 1989]³.

(6) For the purposes of this section and section 161, a person is a relative of another person if he or she is—
   (a) the spouse of that other; or
   (b) a parent or remoter forebear, child or remoter issue, or brother or sister of that other or of the spouse of that other; or
   (c) the spouse of a person falling within paragraph (b) above.

(7) Subject to section 161, this section applies to loans whether made before or after this Act is passed.

Former enactments.—Sub-s. (1): FA 1976, s. 66(1).
Sub-s. (2): FA 1976, s. 66(3).
Sub-s. (3): FA 1976, s. 66(6).
Sub-s. (4): FA 1976, s. 66(8); FA 1982, s. 26(9)(a).
Sub-ss. (5)–(7): FA 1976, s. 66(9)–(11).
Note.—For the purposes of this section the official rate of interest prescribed by the Income Tax (Official Rate of Interest on Beneficial Loans) Orders is—
   10·5 per cent. from 6 December 1987: S.I. 1987 No. 1988.
   9·5 per cent. from 6 May 1988: S.I. 1988 No. 757.
   12 per cent. from 6 August 1988: S.I. 1988 No. 1279.
   13·5 per cent. from 6 October 1988: S.I. 1988 No. 1622.
   14·5 per cent. from 6 January 1989: S.I. 1988 No. 2186.
   15·5 per cent. from 6 July 1989: S.I. 1989 No. 1001.
Amendments.—¹ Words in sub-ss. (1), (2) substituted by FA 1989, s. 53(2)(b).
² Sub-s. (3) substituted by FA 1989, s. 53(2)(c).
³ Words in sub-s. (5)(d) substituted for the words "rate prescribed from time to time by the Treasury by order" by FA 1989, s. 179(1)(g).

161. Exceptions from section 160

(1) There is no charge to tax under section 160(1) if the cash equivalent does not exceed £200 or (for a year in which there are two or more loans outstanding) the total of all the cash equivalents does not exceed that amount.

(2) Where the amount of interest paid on a loan for the year in which it is made is not less than interest at the official rate applying for that year for the purposes of section 160 and the loan is made—

(*a*) for a fixed and unvariable period; and
(*b*) at a fixed and unvariable rate of interest,

subsection (1) of that section shall not apply to the loan in any subsequent year by reason only of an increase in the official rate since the year in which the loan was made.

(3) Where a loan was made at any time before 6th April 1978—

(*a*) for a fixed and unvariable period; and
(*b*) at a fixed and unvariable rate of interest,

section 160(1) shall not apply to the loan if it is shown that the rate of interest is not less than such rate as could have been expected to apply to a loan on the same terms (other than as to the rate of interest) made at that time between persons not connected with each other (within the meaning of section 839) dealing at arm's length.

(4) If the employee shows that he derived no benefit from a loan made to a relative of his, section 160(1) and (2) above shall not apply to that loan.

(5) Section 160(2) does not apply where the amount released or written off is chargeable to income tax as income of the employee apart from that section, except—

(*a*) where it is chargeable only by virtue of section 148; or
(*b*) to the extent that the amount exceeds the sums previously falling to be treated as the employee's income under section 677.

(6) On the employee's death—

(*a*) a loan within subsection (1) of section 160 ceases to be outstanding for the purposes of the operation of that subsection; and
(*b*) no charge arises under subsection (2) of that section by reference to any release or writing-off which takes effect on or after the death.

(7) Section 160(2) does not apply to benefits received in pursuance of arrangements made at any time with a view to protecting the holder of shares acquired before 6th April 1976 from a fall in their market value.

Former enactments.—Sub-s. (1): FA 1976, s. 66(2); FA 1980, s. 50(1).
Sub-ss. (2), (3): FA 1980, s. 50(2), (3).
Sub-ss. (4), (5): FA 1976, s. 66(4), (5).
Sub-s. (6): FA 1976, s. 66(7).
Sub-s. (7): FA 1976, s. 66(11)(*b*).

162. Employee shareholdings

(1) Where [after 6th April 1976][1]—

(*a*) a person employed or about to be employed in [employment to which this Chapter applies][2] ("the employee"), or a person connected with him, acquires shares in a company (whether the employing company or not); and
(*b*) the shares are acquired at an under-value in pursuance of a right or opportunity available by reason of his employment,

section 160(1) and Schedule 7 apply as if the employee had the benefit of an interest-free loan obtained by reason of his employment ("the notional loan").

(2) The provisions of this section have effect subject to sections 185 and 186; and in this section—

(*a*) references to shares being acquired at an under-value are references to shares being acquired either without payment for them at the time or being acquired for an amount then paid which is less than the market value of fully paid up shares of that class (in either case with or without obligation to make payment or further payment at some later time); and
(*b*) any reference, in relation to any shares, to the under-value on acquisition is a reference to the market value of fully paid up shares of that class less any payment then made for the shares.

(3) The amount initially outstanding of the notional loan is so much of the under-value on acquisition as is not chargeable to tax as an emolument of the employee; and—

(a) the loan remains outstanding until terminated under subsection (4) below; and
(b) payments or further payments made for the shares after the initial acquisition go to reduce the amount outstanding of the notional loan.

(4) The notional loan terminates on the occurrence of any of the following events—

(a) the whole amount of it outstanding is made good by means of payments or further payments made for the shares; or
(b) the case being one in which the shares were not at the time of acquisition fully paid up, any outstanding or contingent obligation to pay for them is released, transferred or adjusted so as no longer to bind the employee or any person connected with him; or
(c) the shares are so disposed of by surrender or otherwise that neither he nor any such person any longer has a beneficial interest in the shares; or
(d) the employee dies.

(5) If the notional loan terminates as mentioned in subsection (4)(b) or (c) above, there is then for the year in which the event in question occurs the same charge to income tax on the employee, under section 160(2) [(and where appropriate section 160(3))]³, as if an amount equal to the then outstanding amount of the notional loan had been released or written off from a loan within that section.

(6) Where after 6th April 1976 shares are acquired, whether or not at an under-value but otherwise as mentioned in subsection (1) above, and—

(a) the shares are subsequently disposed of by surrender or otherwise so that neither the employee nor any person connected with him any longer has a beneficial interest in them; and
(b) the disposal is for a consideration which exceeds the then market value of the shares,

then for the year in which the disposal is effected the amount of the excess is treated as emoluments of the employee's employment and accordingly chargeable to income tax under Schedule E.

[(7) If at the time of the event giving rise to a charge by virtue of subsection (6) above the employment in question has terminated, that subsection shall apply as if it had not.]⁴

(8) No charge arises under subsection (6) above by reference to any disposal effected after the death of the employee, whether by his personal representatives or otherwise.

(9) This section applies in relation to acquisition and disposal of an interest in shares less than full beneficial ownership (including an interest in the proceeds of sale of part of the shares but not including a share option) as it applies in relation to the acquisition and disposal of shares, subject to the following modifications—

(a) for references to the shares acquired there shall be substituted references to the interest in shares acquired;
(b) for the reference to the market value of the shares acquired there shall be substituted a reference to the proportion corresponding to the size of the interest of the market value of the shares in which the interest subsists;
(c) for the reference to shares of the same class as those acquired there shall be substituted a reference to shares of the same class as those in which the interest subsists; and
(d) for the reference to the market value of fully paid up shares of that class there shall be substituted a reference to the proportion of that value corresponding to the size of the interest.

(10) In this section—

(a) "shares" includes stock and also includes securities as defined in section 254(1);
(b) "acquisition" in relation to shares includes receipt by way of allotment or assignment or otherwise howsoever;
(c) any reference to payment for shares includes giving any consideration in money or money's worth or making any subscription, whether in pursuance of a legal liability or not;
(d) "market value" has the same meaning as, for the purposes of the 1979 Act, it has by virtue of section 150 of that Act;

and section 839 applies for the purposes of this section.

(11) This section, in respect of any shares or any interest in shares, operates only to include an amount in emoluments so far as any amount corresponding to it, and representing the same benefit, does not otherwise fall to be so included under the Tax Acts.

Former enactments.—Sub-s. (1): FA 1976, s. 67(1), (3).
Sub-s. (2)(*a*): FA 1976, s. 67(2).
Sub-ss. (2)(*b*), (3): FA 1976, s. 67(4).
Sub-ss. (4)–(10): FA 1976, s. 67(5)–(11); CGTA 1979, Sch. 7, para. 8.
Sub-s. (11): FA 1976, s. 67(12).
Construction.—CGTA 1979, s. 32A(2) to be construed as one with this section; see CGTA 1979, s. 32A(6).
Amendments.—¹ Words in sub-s. (1) inserted by FA 1988, Sch. 13, para. 3.
² Words in sub-s. (1) substituted by FA 1989, s. 53(2)(*b*).
³ Words in sub-s. (5) inserted by FA 1989, s. 53(2)(*d*).
⁴ Sub-s. (7) substituted by FA 1989, s. 53(2)(*e*).

163. Expenses connected with living accommodation

(1) This section applies where, in the case of a person employed in [employment to which this Chapter applies]¹, living accommodation is provided by reason of the employment and, accordingly, a charge to tax would arise in his case under section 145 but for the case being one of those specified in subsection (4) of that section.

(2) Where, by reason of expenditure incurred in one or more of the following, that is to say,—

(*a*) heating, lighting or cleaning the premises concerned;
(*b*) repairs to the premises, their maintenance or decoration;
(*c*) the provision in the premises of furniture or other appurtenances or effects which are normal for domestic occupation;

or by reason of such expenditure being reimbursed to the employee, an amount falls to be included in the emoluments of his employment, that amount shall not exceed the limit specified in subsection (3) below.

(3) That limit is—

(*a*) 10 per cent. of the net amount of the emoluments of the employment or, if the accommodation is provided for a period of less than a year, so much of that percentage of the net amount as is attributable to the period; less
(*b*) where the expenditure is incurred by a person other than the employee, so much as is properly attributable to the expenditure of any sum made good by the employee to that other.

(4) The net amount of the emoluments of a person's employment for the purposes of subsection (3) above is the amount of those emoluments (leaving out of account the expenditure in question) after—

(*a*) any capital allowance; and
(*b*) any deductions allowable under section 198, 199, 201, 332(3), 592(7), 594 or 619(1)(*a*);

and, for the purposes of this subsection, in the case of employment by a company there shall be taken into account, as emoluments of the employment, the emoluments of any employment by an associated company.

(5) For the purposes of subsection (4) above, a company is an associated company of another if one of them has control of the other or both are under the control of the same person.

Former enactments.—FA 1976, s. 63A; FA 1977, s. 34.
Amendments.—¹ Words in sub-s. (1) substituted by FA 1989, s. 53(2)(*b*).

164. Director's tax paid by employer

(1) Subject to the provisions of this Chapter, where in any year a person ("the recipient") is employed as a director of a company and—

(*a*) a payment of, or on account of, income assessable to income tax under Schedule E as emoluments of that employment is made to him in circumstances in which the person making the payment is required, by regulations made under section 203, to deduct an amount of income tax on making the payment; and
(*b*) the whole of that amount is not so deducted but is, or any part of it is, accounted for to the Board by someone other than the recipient;

the amount so accounted for to the Board, less so much (if any) as is made good by the recipient to that other person or so deducted, shall be treated as emoluments of the employment and accordingly chargeable to income tax under Schedule E.

(2) A person shall not be treated, for the purposes of subsection (1) above, as employed as a director of a company if he has no material interest in the company and either paragraph (*a*) or paragraph (*b*) of section 167(5) is satisfied.

(3) Where an amount treated as emoluments of a person's employment, by subsection (1) above, is accounted for to the Board at a time when the employment has come to an end, those emoluments shall be treated, for the purposes of the Income Tax Acts, as having arisen in the year in which the employment ended; but that subsection shall not apply in relation to any amount accounted for to the Board after the death of the director in question.

Former enactments.—FA 1976, s. 66A; FA 1983, s. 22.

165. Scholarships

(1) Nothing in section 331 shall be construed as conferring on any person other than the person holding the scholarship in question any exemption from the charge to tax under section 154.

(2) For the purposes of this Chapter, any scholarship provided for a member of a person's family or household shall, without prejudice to any other provision of this Chapter, be taken to have been provided by reason of that person's employment if it is provided under arrangements entered into by, or by any person connected with, his employer (whether or not those arrangements require the employer or connected person to contribute directly or indirectly to the cost of providing the scholarship).

(3) Section 154 does not apply to a benefit consisting in a payment in respect of a scholarship—

(*a*) provided from a trust fund or under a scheme; and
(*b*) held by a person receiving full-time instruction at a university, college, school or other educational establishment; and
(*c*) which would not be regarded, for the purposes of this Chapter, as provided by reason of a person's employment were subsection (2) above and section 168(3) to be disregarded;

if, in the year in which the payment is made, not more than 25 per cent. of the total amount of the payments made from that fund, or under that scheme, in respect of scholarships held as mentioned in paragraph (*b*) above is attributable to relevant scholarships.

(4) This section does not have effect in relation to any payment if—

(*a*) it is made in respect of a scholarship awarded before 15th March 1983, and
(*b*) the first payment in respect of the scholarship was made before 6th April 1984; and
(*c*) in relation to payments made after 5th April 1989, the person holding the scholarship is receiving full-time instruction at the university, college, school or other educational establishment at which he was receiving such instruction on —

(i) 15th March 1983, in a case where the first payment in respect of the scholarship was made before that date; or
(ii) the date on which the first such payment was made, in any other case.

(5) For the purposes of subsection (4)(*c*) above, a payment made before 6th April 1989 in respect of any period beginning on or after that date shall be treated as made at the beginning of that period.

(6) In this section—

(*a*) "scholarship" includes an exhibition, bursary or other similar educational endowment;
(*b*) "relevant scholarship" means a scholarship which is provided by reason of a person's employment (whether or not that employment is [employment to which this Chapter applies][1]); and for the purposes of this definition "employment" includes an office or employment whose emoluments do not fall to be assessed under Schedule E but would fall to be so assessed if the employee were resident, and ordinarily resident, and all the duties of the employment were performed wholly, in the United Kingdom;

and section 839 applies for the purposes of this section.

Former enactments.—Sub-s. (1): FA 1976, s. 62A(1); FA 1983, s. 20(1).
Sub-s. (2): FA 1976, s. 62A(2); FA 1983, s. 20(1).
Sub-s. (3): FA 1976, s. 62A(3); FA 1983, s. 20(1); FA 1984, s. 31(3).
Sub-s. (4): FA 1983, s. 20(2), (3); FA 1984, s. 31(3).
Sub-s. (5): FA 1983, s. 20(3A); FA 1984, s. 31(3).
Sub-s. (6): FA 1976, s. 62A(4); FA 1983, s. 20(1); FA 1984, s. 31(2).
Amendments.—[1] Words in sub-s. (6)(*b*) substituted by FA 1989, s. 53(2)(*b*).

General supplementary provisions

166. Notice of nil liability under this Chapter

(1) If a person furnishes to the inspector a statement of the cases and circumstances in which payments of a particular character are made, or benefits or facilities of a particular kind are provided, for any employees (whether his own or those of anyone else), and the inspector is satisfied that no additional tax is payable under this Chapter by reference to the payments, benefits or facilities mentioned in the statement, the inspector shall notify the person accordingly; and then nothing in this Chapter applies to those payments, or to the provision of those benefits or facilities, or otherwise for imposing any additional charge to income tax.

(2) The inspector may, if in his opinion there is reason to do so, by notice served on the person to whom notification under subsection (1) above was given, revoke the notification, either as from the date of its making or from such later date as may be specified in the notice under this subsection; and then all such income tax becomes chargeable, and all such returns are to be made by that person and by the employees in question as would have been chargeable or would have had to be made in the first instance if the notification under subsection (1) had never been given or, as the case may be, it had ceased to have effect on the specified date.

(3) In relation to a notification given before 6th April 1988, the reference in subsection (2) above to income tax includes a reference to income tax chargeable under the corresponding enactments in force before that date, and accordingly, where the notification is revoked for any period before that date, that subsection has effect in relation to years of assessment before the year 1988–89.

(4) The validity of any notification given under section 199 of the 1970 Act which was continued in force by paragraph 14 of Schedule 9 to the Finance Act 1976 shall not be affected by the repeal of that paragraph by this Act but shall continue in force as if made under subsection (1) above in relation to tax liability under sections 153 to 156; and subsection (2) above shall apply accordingly.

Former enactment.—FA 1976, s. 70, Sch. 9, para. 14(2)–(4).

[167. Employment to which this Chapter applies

(1) This Chapter applies—
   (a) to employment as a director of a company (but subject to subsection (5) below), and
   (b) to employment with emoluments at the rate of £8,500 a year or more.

(2) For this purpose emoluments are to be calculated—
   (a) on the basis that they include all such amounts as come, or would but for section 157(3) come, into charge under this Chapter or section 141, 142, 143 or 145, and
   (b) without any deduction under section 198, 201 or 332(3).

(3) Where a person is employed in two or more employments by the same employer and either—
   (a) the total of the emoluments of those employments (applying this section) is at the rate of £8,500 a year or more; or
   (b) this Chapter applies (apart from this subsection) to one or more of those employments,
this Chapter shall apply to all the employments.

(4) All employees of a partnership or body over which an individual or another partnership or body has control are to be treated for the purposes of this section (but not for any other purpose) as if the employment were an employment by the individual or by that other partnership or body as the case may be.

(5) This Chapter shall not apply to a person's employment by reason only of its being employment as a director of a company (without prejudice to its application by virtue of subsection (1)(b) or (3) above) if he has no material interest in the company and either—
   (a) his employment is as a full-time working director; or
   (b) the company is non-profit making (meaning that neither does it carry on a trade nor do its functions consist wholly or mainly in the holding of investments or other property) or is established for charitable purposes only.][1]

Former enactments.—Sub-s. (1): FA 1976, s. 69(1); FA 1977, s. 35(1); FA 1978, s. 23(1). Sub-s. (2): FA 1976, s. 69(2); FA 1977, s. 35(1); FA 1981, s. 71(2); FA 1982, s. 46(2).

Sub-s. (3): FA 1976, s. 69(3); FA 1977, s.35(1); FA 1978, s. 23(1).
Sub-ss. (4), (5): FA 1976, s. 69(4), (5); FA 1977, s. 35(1).
Amendments.—¹ This section substituted by FA 1989, s. 53(1).

168. Other interpretative provisions

(1) The following provisions of this section apply for the interpretation of expressions used in this Chapter.

(2) Subject to section 165(6)(*b*), "employment" means an office or employment the emoluments of which fall to be assessed under Schedule E; and related expressions shall be construed accordingly.

(3) For the purposes of this Chapter—
   (*a*) all sums paid to an employee by his employer in respect of expenses, and
   (*b*) all such provision as is mentioned in this Chapter which is made for an employee, or for members of his family or household, by his employer,

are deemed to be paid to or made for him or them by reason of his employment, except any such payment or provision made by the employer, being an individual, as can be shown to have been made in the normal course of his domestic, family or personal relationships.

(4) References to members of a person's family or household are to his spouse, his sons and daughters and their spouses, his parents and his servants, dependants and guests.

(5) As respects cars, the following definitions apply—
   (*a*) "car" means any mechanically propelled road vehicle except—
      (i) a vehicle of a construction primarily suited for the conveyance of goods or burden of any description,
      (ii) a vehicle of a type not commonly used as a private vehicle and unsuitable to be so used,
      (iii) a motor cycle as defined in section 190(4) of the Road Traffic Act 1972, and
      (iv) an invalid carriage as defined in section 190(5) of that Act;
   (*b*) the age of a car at any time is the interval between the date of its first registration and that time;
   (*c*) "business travel" means travelling which a person is necessarily obliged to do in the performance of the duties of his employment;
   (*d*) the date of a car's first registration is the date on which it was first registered—
      (i) in Great Britain, under the Vehicles (Excise) Act 1971 or corresponding earlier legislation; or
      (ii) elsewhere, under the corresponding legislation of any country or territory;
   (*e*) the original market value of a car is the inclusive price which it might reasonably have been expected to fetch if sold in the United Kingdom singly in a retail sale in the open market immediately before the date of its first registration ("inclusive price" meaning the price inclusive of customs or excise duty, of any tax chargeable as if it were a duty of customs, and of value added tax and car tax); and
   (*f*) "private use", in relation to a car made available to any person, or to others being members of his family or household, means any use otherwise than for his business travel.

(6) For the purposes of this Chapter—
   (*a*) a car made available in any year to an employee, or to others being members of his family or household, by reason of his employment is deemed to be available in that year for his or their private use unless the terms on which the car is made available prohibit such use and no such use is made of the car in that year;
   (*b*) a car made available to an employee, or to others being members of his family or household, by his employer is deemed to be made available to him or them by reason of his employment (unless the employer is an individual and it can be shown that the car was made so available in the normal course of his domestic, family or personal relationships).

(7) For the purposes of section 156, the market value of an asset at any time is the price which it might reasonably have been expected to fetch on a sale in the open market at that time.

(8) Subject to subsection (9) below, "director" means—
   (*a*) in relation to a company whose affairs are managed by a board of directors or similar body, a member of that board or similar body;

(b) in relation to a company whose affairs are managed by a single director or similar person, that director or person; and
(c) in relation to a company whose affairs are managed by the members themselves, a member of the company,

and includes any person in accordance with whose directions or instructions the directors of the company (as defined above) are accustomed to act.

(9) A person is not under subsection (8) above to be deemed to be a person in accordance with whose directions or instructions the directors of the company are accustomed to act by reason only that the directors act on advice given by him in a professional capacity.

(10) "Full-time working director" means a director who is required to devote substantially the whole of his time to the service of the company in a managerial or technical capacity.

(11) A person shall be treated as having a material interest [in a company if he, either on his own or with one or more associates, or if any associate of his with or without such other associates,—][1]

[(a) is the beneficial owner of, or able, directly or through the medium of other companies, or by any other indirect means to control, more than 5 per cent. of the ordinary share capital of the company, or][1]

[(b) in the case of a close company, possesses, or is entitled to acquire, such rights as would, in the event of the winding-up of the company or in any other circumstances, give an entitlement to receive more than 5 per cent. of the assets which would then be available for distribution among the participators.]][1]

In this subsection "associate" has the same meaning as in section 417(3), except that for this purpose "relative" in that subsection has the meaning given by section 160(6) [, and "participator" has the meaning given by section 417(1)]][2].

(12) "Control", in relation to a body corporate or partnership, has the meaning given to it by section 840; and the definition of "control" in that section applies (with the necessary modifications) in relation to an unincorporated association as it applies in relation to a body corporate.

(13) "Year" means year of assessment (except where the expression is used with reference to the age of a car).

Former enactments.—FA 1976, s. 72(1)–(12); FA 1980, s. 51(3).
Amendments.—[1] Sub-s. (11)(a) (and the preceding words), (b) substituted by FA 1989, Sch. 12, para. 8 in relation to accounting periods beginning after 31 March 1989.
[2] Words in sub-s. (11) added by *ibid*.

CHAPTER III

PROFIT-RELATED PAY

Preliminary

169. Interpretation

(1) In this Chapter—

"employment" means an office or employment whose emoluments fall to be assessed under Schedule E, and related expressions have corresponding meanings;

"employment unit" means an undertaking, or that part of an undertaking, to which a profit-related pay scheme relates;

"pay" (except in the expression "profit-related pay") means emoluments paid under deduction of tax pursuant to section 203, reduced by any amounts included in them by virtue of Chapter II of Part V;

"profit period" means an accounting period by reference to which any profit-related pay is calculated;

"profit-related pay" means emoluments from an employment which are paid in accordance with a profit-related pay scheme;

"profit-related pay scheme" means a scheme providing for the payment of emoluments calculated by reference to profits;

"profits", or "losses", in relation to a profit period, means the amount shown in the account prepared for that period in accordance with the relevant profit-related pay scheme as the profit, or as the case may be the loss, on ordinary activities after taxation;

"registered scheme" means a profit-related pay scheme registered under this Chapter;

"scheme employer" means the person on whose application a profit-related pay scheme is or may be registered under this Chapter.

(2) References in this Chapter to the employees to whom a profit-related pay scheme relates are references to the employees who will receive any payments of profit-related pay under the scheme.

Former enactment.—F(No. 2)A 1987, s. 1.

170. Taxation of profit-related pay

Former enactment.—F(No. 2)A 1987, s. 2.
Amendments.—This section repealed by FA 1989, s. 42(4) and Sch. 17, Pt. IV.

The relief

171. Relief from tax

(1) One half of any profit-related pay to which this section applies shall be exempt from income tax.

(2) This section applies to any profit-related pay paid to an employee by reference to a profit period and in accordance with a registered scheme, but only so far as it does not exceed the lower of the two limits specified in the following provisions of this section.

(3) The first of the limits referred to in subsection (2) above is one fifth of the aggregate of—

(*a*) the pay (but not any profit-related pay) paid to the employee in the profit period in respect of his employment in the employment unit concerned (or, if the employee is eligible to receive profit-related pay by reference to part only of the period, so much of his pay, but not any profit-related pay, as is paid in that part); and
(*b*) the profit-related pay paid to him by reference to that period in respect of that employment.

(4) The second of the limits referred to in subsection (2) above is [£4,000][1] (or, if the profit period is less than 12 months, or the employee is eligible to receive profit-related pay by reference to part only of the profit period, a proportionately reduced amount).

Former enactment.—F(No. 2)A 1987, s. 3.
Amendments.—[1] Amount in sub-s. (4) substituted for "£3,000" by FA 1989, Sch. 4, paras. 1,2 in relation to profit-related pay paid by reference to profit periods beginning after 31 March 1989.

172. Exceptions from tax

(1) Profit-related pay shall not be exempt from income tax by virtue of section 171 if—

(*a*) it is paid to an employee in respect of his employment in an employment unit during a time when he also has another employment; and

(*b*) he receives in respect of that other employment during that time profit-related pay which is exempt from income tax by virtue of that section.

(2) Subject to subsection (3) below, profit-related pay in respect of which no secondary Class I contributions under Part I of the Social Security Act 1975 or Part I of the Social Security (Northern Ireland) Act 1975 are payable shall not be exempt from income tax by virtue of section 171.

(3) Subsection (2) above shall not apply to profit-related pay in respect of which no Class 1 contributions are payable only because the employee's earnings are below the lower earnings limit for such contributions.

Former enactment.—F(No. 2)A 1987, s. 4.

Registration

173. Persons who may apply for registration

(1) Where the emoluments of all the employees to whom a profit-related pay scheme relates are paid by the same person, an application to register the scheme under this Chapter may be made to the Board by that person.

(2) Where subsection (1) above does not apply to a profit-related pay scheme, no application to register it may be made unless all the persons who pay emoluments to employees to whom the scheme relates are bodies corporate which are members of the same group; and in that case an application may be made by the parent company of the group.

(3) In subsection (2) above—

"group" means a body corporate and its 51 per cent. subsidiaries, and
"parent company" means that body corporate; and

in applying for the purposes of this section the definition of "51 per cent. subsidiary" in section 838, any share capital of a registered industrial and provident society (within the meaning of section 486) shall be treated as ordinary share capital.

Former enactment.—F(No. 2)A 1987, s. 5.

174. Excluded employments

(1) No application may be made to register a scheme under this Chapter if any employment to which the scheme relates is—

(*a*) employment in an office under the Crown or otherwise in the service of the Crown; or
(*b*) employment by an excluded employer.

(2) For the purposes of this section "excluded employer" means—

(*a*) a person in an employment within subsection (1) above;
(*b*) a body under the control of the Crown, or of one or more persons acting on behalf of the Crown;
(*c*) a local authority;
(*d*) a body under the control of one or more local authorities, or of the Crown (or one or more persons acting on behalf of the Crown) and one or more local authorities.

(3) For the purposes of this section a person has control of a body only if one or more of the following conditions is satisfied—

(*a*) in the case of a body whose affairs are managed by its members, he has the power to appoint more than half of the members;
(*b*) in the case of a body having a share capital, he holds more than half of its issued share capital;

(c) in the case of a body whose members vote in general meeting, he has the power to exercise more than half of the votes exercisable in general meeting;
(d) the articles of association or other rules regulating the body give him the power to secure that the affairs of the body are conducted in accordance with his wishes.

(4) For the purposes of this section a person shall be taken to possess rights and powers possessed by—

(a) a person appointed by him to an office by virtue of which the rights or powers are exercisable; or
(b) a body which he controls;

including rights and powers which such an officer or body is taken to possess by virtue of this subsection.

(5) Subsections (3) and (4) above apply with the necessary modifications for the purpose of determining whether persons together have control of a body.

Former enactment.—F(No. 2)A 1987, s. 6.

175. Applications for registration

(1) An application for the registration of a profit-related pay scheme under this Chapter—
    (a) shall be in such form as the Board may prescribe;
    (b) shall contain a declaration by the applicant that the scheme complies with the requirements of Schedule 8;
    (c) shall contain an undertaking by the applicant that the emoluments paid to any employee to whom the scheme relates and to whom minimum wage legislation applies will satisfy that legislation without taking account of profit-related pay;
    (d) shall specify the profit period or periods to which the scheme relates;
    (e) shall be supported by such information as the Board may require.

(2) An application for the registration of a profit-related pay scheme under this Chapter shall be accompanied by a report by an independent accountant, in a form prescribed by the Board, to the effect that in his opinion—
    (a) the scheme complies with the requirements of Schedule 8;
    (b) the books and records maintained and proposed to be maintained by the applicant are adequate for the purpose of enabling the documents required by section 180(1) to be produced.

(3) ...[1]

(4) In subsection (1) above "minimum wage legislation" means the provisions relating to remuneration in Part II of the Wages Act 1986, the Wages Councils (Northern Ireland) Order 1982, the Agricultural Wages Act 1948, the Agricultural Wages (Scotland) Act 1949 and the Agricultural Wages (Regulation) (Northern Ireland) Order 1977.

Former enactment.—F(No. 2)A 1987, s. 7.
Amendments.—Sub-s. (3) repealed by FA 1989, Sch. 4, para. 10(2)(a) and Sch. 17, Pt. IV.

176. Registration

(1) If an application for registration of a profit-related pay scheme under this Chapter is made more than three months ...[1] before the beginning of the profit period, or the first of the profit periods, to which the scheme relates, then subject to subsection (2) below, the Board shall register the scheme before the beginning of that period.

(2) If the Board are not satisfied that an application made as mentioned in subsection (1) above complies with the requirements of this Chapter, they may within 30 days after the day on which they receive the application—
    (a) refuse the application; or
    (b) by notice to the applicant either require him to amend the application or require him to give them such further information as may be specified in the notice, and in either case to do so within such time, not exceeding 30 days after the day on which the notice is given, as may be so specified.

(3) If a notice under subsection (2) above is complied with and the Board are satisfied that the application complies with the requirements of this Chapter, the Board shall register the scheme before the beginning of the profit period.

(4) If a notice under subsection (2) above is complied with but the Board remain not satisfied that the application complies with the requirements of this Chapter, the Board shall refuse the application.

(5) If a notice under subsection (2) above is not complied with but the Board are before the beginning of the profit period satisfied that the application complies with the requirements of this Chapter, the Board may register the scheme before the beginning of the period; but if they do not do so, the application shall be regarded as having been refused.

(6) If an application for registration of a profit-related pay scheme under this Chapter is made within the period of three months before the beginning of the profit period, or the first of the profit periods, to which the scheme relates, then—

(a) if before the beginning of the profit period the Board are satisfied that the application complies with the requirements of this Chapter, they shall register the scheme before the beginning of the period; but
(b) in any other case, the application shall be regarded as having been refused.

(7) After registering a scheme under this Chapter, the Board shall by notice inform the applicant that they have done so.

(8) The Board shall give notice to the applicant if they refuse his application under subsection (2) or (4) above.

(9) For the purposes of this section an application does not comply with the requirements of this Chapter if the scheme to which it relates does not comply with the requirements of Schedule 8.

Former enactment.—F(No. 2)A 1987, s. 8.
Amendments.—[1] Words in sub-s. (1) repealed by FA 1989, Sch. 4, para. 10(2)(a) and Sch. 17, Pt. IV.

177. Change of scheme employer

(1) Where—

(a) a scheme employer ceases to fulful the conditions which section 173 requires to be fulfilled by an applicant for registration of the scheme; and
(b) he is succeeded by a person who would be eligible to apply for registration to the scheme; and
(c) there is otherwise no other material change in the employment unit or in the circumstances relating to the scheme;

the scheme employer and his successor may make a joint written application to the Board under this section for the amendment of the registration of the scheme.

(2) If on receiving an application under this section the Board are satisfied—

(a) that the conditions in subsection (1)(a), (b) and (c) above are fulfilled; and
(b) that, apart from the change of scheme employer, there would be no grounds for cancelling the registration of the scheme,

the Board shall amend the registration of the scheme by substituting the successor for the previous scheme employer.

(3) An application under this section shall be made before the end of the period of one month beginning with the date of the succession.

(4) Where the Board amend the registration of a scheme under this section, this Chapter shall (subject to any necessary modifications) have effect as if the successor had been the scheme employer throughout.

(5) The Board shall give notice to the applicants if they refuse an application under this section.

Former enactment.—F(No. 2)A 1987, s. 9.

[177A. Death of scheme employer

(1) Where a scheme employer has died, his personal representatives may make a written application to the Board under this section for the amendment of the registration of the scheme.

(2) If on receiving an application under this section the Board are satisfied that, apart from the death of the scheme employer, there would be no grounds for cancelling the registration

of the scheme, the Board shall amend the registration of the scheme by substituting the personal representatives for the deceased scheme employer.

(3) An application under this section shall be made before the end of the period of one month beginning with the date of the grant of probate or letters of administration or, in Scotland, confirmation of executors.

(4) Where the Board amend the registration of a scheme under this section, this Chapter shall (subject to any necessary modifications) have effect as if the personal representatives had been the scheme employer throughout.

(5) The Board shall give notice to the personal representatives if they refuse an application under this section.][1]

Amendments.—[1] This section inserted by FA 1989, Sch. 4, paras. 1, 3.

[177B. Alteration of scheme's terms

(1) The alteration of the terms of a registered scheme shall not of itself invalidate the registration of the scheme.

(2) Subsection (1) above is without prejudice to the power of cancellation conferred on the Board by section 178(3A); but the power conferred by section 178(3A) shall not be exercisable by virtue of an alteration registered in accordance with this section.

(3) Where the terms of a registered scheme have been altered, the scheme employer may apply to the Board for the registration of the alteration.

(4) An application under subsection (3) above—

(*a*) shall be in such form as the Board may prescribe;
(*b*) shall be made within the period of one month beginning with the day on which the alteration is made;
(*c*) shall contain a declaration by the applicant that the alteration is within subsection (8) below and that the scheme as altered complies with the requirements of Schedule 8 (either as that Schedule had effect when the scheme was registered, or as it then had effect but subject to one or more subsequent amendments specified in the declaration);
(*d*) shall be accompanied by a report by an independent accountant, in a form prescribed by the Board, to the effect that in his opinion the alteration is within subsection (8) below and the scheme as altered complies with the requirements of Schedule 8 (either as that Schedule had effect when the scheme was registered, or as it then had effect but subject to one or more subsequent amendments specified in the report).

(5) The Board shall not more than three months after the day on which they receive an application under subsection (3) above either register the alteration or refuse the application; and in either case they shall give notice of their decision to the applicant.

(6) Subject to subsection (7) below, the Board shall register an alteration on an application under subsection (3) above.

(7) The Board may refuse an application under subsection (3) above if they are not satisfied—

(*a*) that the application complies with the requirements of subsection (4) above, or
(*b*) that the declaration referred to in subsection (4)(*c*) above is true.

(8) An alteration is within this subsection if—

(*a*) it relates to a term which is not relevant to the question whether the scheme complies with the requirements of Schedule 8; or
(*b*) it relates to a term identifying any person (other than the scheme employer) who pays the emoluments of employees to whom the scheme relates; or
(*c*) it consists of the addition of a term making provision for an abbreviated profit period of the kind referred to in paragraph 10(3) of Schedule 8; or
(*d*) it amends the provisions by reference to which the employees to whom the scheme relates may be identified, and does so only for the purposes of profit periods which begin after the date on which the alteration is made; or
(*e*) it relates to a provision of a kind referred to in paragraph 13(4) or (5) or 14(3), (4) or (5) of Schedule 8 (as those provisions have effect at the time of the application for registration of the alteration), and has effect only for the purposes of profit periods beginning after the date on which the alteration is made; or
(*f*) it amends the provisions as to when payments will be made to employees, and does

so only for the purposes of profit periods beginning after the date on which the alteration is made; or

(g) the scheme did not comply with the requirements of Schedule 8 when it was registered, and the alteration—

(i) is made in order to bring the scheme into compliance with the requirements of that Schedule (either as it had effect when the scheme was registered or as it has effect at the time of the application for registration of the alteration), and

(ii) is made for the purposes of the first and any subsequent profit period to which the scheme relates, and

(iii) is made within two years of the beginning of the first profit period, and

(iv) does not invalidate (in whole or in part) any payment of profit-related pay already made under the scheme.][1]

Amendments.—[1] This section inserted by FA 1989, Sch. 4, paras. 1, 3.

178. Cancellation of registration

(1) If after a scheme has been registered under this Chapter it appears to the Board—

(a) that the scheme has not been or will not be administered in accordance with [its terms or in accordance with][1] this Chapter in relation to a profit period; or

(b) that the circumstances relating to the scheme have during a profit period become such that (if it were not registered) an application to register it under this Chapter would be excluded by section 174; or

(c) in the case of a scheme which employs (as the method of determining the distributable pool for a profit period) the method described as method B in paragraph 14 of Schedule 8, that losses were incurred in a profit period or in the preceding period of 12 months; or

(d) that the undertaking given in compliance with section 175(1)(c) has not been complied with in relation to employment at any time during a profit period;

the Board may cancel the registration and, subject to [subsections (5) and (5A)][2] below, the cancellation shall have effect from the beginning of that profit period.

(2) If after a scheme has been registered under this Chapter it appears to the Board—

(a) that at the time of registration the scheme did not comply with the requirements of Schedule 8 or that the application did not comply with the requirements of this Chapter; . . .[4]

(b) . . .[4]

the Board may cancel the registration with effect from the beginning of the profit period (or first profit period) to which the scheme related.

(3) If after a scheme has been registered under this Chapter the scheme employer fails to comply with the requirements of section 180 in relation to a profit period, the Board may cancel the registration with effect from the beginning of that profit period.

[(3A) Where the terms of a registered scheme have been altered, then, subject to section 177B(2), the Board may cancel the registration of the scheme with effect from the beginning of the profit period during which the alteration took effect or with effect from the beginning of any later profit period.][3]

[(3B) If after an alteration of the terms of a scheme has been registered under section 177B it appears to the Board—

(a) that the application for registration of the alteration did not comply with the requirements of subsection (4) of that section, or

(b) that the declaration referred to in subsection (4)(c) of that section was false,

the Board may cancel the registration of the scheme with effect from the beginning of the profit period during which the alteration took effect or with effect from the beginning of any later profit period.][3]

(4) If the scheme employer by notice requests the Board to cancel the registration of the scheme with effect from the beginning of a profit period specified in the notice, the Board shall comply with the request.

(5) Where—

(a) the scheme employer has given to the Board in accordance with section 181(3) notice of a change in the employment unit, or in the circumstances relating to the scheme, which is a ground for cancellation of the registration of the scheme by virtue of subsection (1)(a) or (b) above, and

(b) the Board are satisfied that the change is not brought about with a view to the registration of a new scheme, and
(c) in the notice the scheme employer requests the Board to cancel the registration of the scheme with effect from the date of the change,

then, if the notice is given before the end of the period of one month beginning with that day, the Board shall comply with the request.

[(5A) Where—
(a) the scheme employer has died, and
(b) his personal representatives by notice request the Board to cancel the registration of the scheme with effect from the date of death,

then, if the notice is given before the end of the period of one month beginning with the date of the grant of probate or letters of administration or, in Scotland, confirmation of executors, the Board shall comply with the request.]³

(6) The Board shall give notice to the scheme employer of the cancellation of a scheme's registration.

Former enactment.—F(No. 2)A 1987, s. 10.
Amendments.—¹ Words in sub-s. (1)(a) inserted by FA 1988, Sch. 13, para. 4.
² Words in sub-s. (1) substituted by FA 1989, Sch. 4, para. 4(1), (2).
³ Sub-ss. (3A), (3B), (5A) inserted by FA 1989, Sch 4, para. 4(1), (3), (4).
⁴ Sub-s. (2)(b) and the word "or" preceding it repealed by FA 1989, Sch. 4, para. 10(2)(a) and Sch. 17, Pt. IV.

Administration

179. Recovery of tax from scheme employer

(1) This section applies where—
(a) payments of profit-related pay are made to an employee in accordance with a registered scheme; and
(b) in consequence of the relief given by this Chapter in respect of registered schemes, less income tax is deducted from the payments in accordance with section 203 than would have been deducted if the scheme had not been registered; and
(c) the registration of the scheme is subsequently cancelled with effect from a time before that relevant for the purposes of the relief.

(2) Where this section applies, an amount equal to the shortfall in the deductions made in accordance with section 203 shall be payable by the scheme employer to the Board; and regulations under that section may include provision as to the collection and recovery of any such amount.

[(3) Where—
(a) the scheme employer has died, but
(b) his personal representatives have not been substituted for him as the scheme employer by virtue of section 177A,

the reference in subsection (2) above to the scheme employer shall be construed as a reference to the personal representatives.]¹

[(4) Where—
(a) a payment to which this section applies was made by a person other than the scheme employer, and
(b) the scheme employer is not resident in the United Kingdom,

then in relation to that payment the reference in subsection (2) above to the scheme employer shall include a reference to the person by whom the payment was made.]¹

Former enactment.—F(No. 2)A 1987, s. 11.
Amendments.—¹ Sub-ss. (3), (4) added by FA 1989, Sch. 4, para. 5.

180. Annual returns etc.

(1) After every profit period of a registered scheme, the scheme employer shall, within the period allowed by subsection (2) below, send to the Board—
(a) a return in such form and containing such information as the Board may prescribe; and
(b) a report by an independent accountant in such form and containing such information

as the Board may prescribe and stating that in his opinion the terms of the scheme have been complied with in respect of the profit period.

(2) Subject to subsection (3) below, the period allowed for complying with subsection (1) above is—

(a) seven months from the end of the profit period if the employment unit to which the scheme relates is an undertaking or part of an undertaking of a public company; and
(b) ten months from the end of the profit period in any other case.

(3) If before the end of the period allowed by subsection (2) above the scheme employer gives the Board notice that an extension of three months has been allowed under section 242(3) of the Companies Act 1985, or under Article 250(3) of the Companies (Northern Ireland) Order 1986, in relation to a financial year of the employer which corresponds with the profit period in question, then the period allowed by subsection (2) above shall be correspondingly extended.

(4) In subsection (2)(a) above, "public company" has the meaning given by section 1(3) of the Companies Act 1985 or Article 12(3) of the Companies (Northern Ireland) Order 1986.

[(5) Where—

(a) the scheme employer has died, but
(b) his personal representatives have not been substituted for him as the scheme employer by virtue of section 177A,

the reference in subsection (1) above to the scheme employer shall be construed as a reference to the personal representatives.][1]

Former enactment.—F(No. 2)A 1987, s. 12.
Amendments.—[1] Sub-s. (5) added by FA 1989, Sch. 4, para. 6.

181. Other information

(1) The Board may by notice require any person to give them, within a period of 30 days or such longer period as may be specified in the notice, any information which is so specified and which—

(a) that person has or can reasonably be required to obtain; and
(b) the Board consider they need to have in order to perform their functions under this Chapter.

(2) Without prejudice to the generality of subsection (1)(b) above, the Board may in particular require a person under subsection (1) to give them—

(a) information to enable them to determine whether the registration of a scheme should be cancelled;
(b) information to enable them to determine the liability to tax of any person who is or has been an employee to whom a registered scheme relates or who pays or has paid emoluments to such an employee;
(c) information about the administration of a profit-related pay scheme which is or has been a registered scheme;
(d) information about any change of person paying emoluments to employees to whom a registered scheme relates.

(3) The scheme employer of a registered scheme shall by notice inform the Board without delay if he becomes aware of anything that is or may be a ground for cancellation of the registration of the scheme.

[(4) Where the scheme employer has died, his personal representatives shall inform the Board of his death by notice given before the end of the period of one month beginning with the date of the grant of probate or letters of administration or, in Scotland, confirmation of executors.][1]

Former enactment.—F(No. 2)A 1987, s. 13.
Amendments.—[1] Sub-s. (4) added by FA 1989, Sch. 4, para. 7.

182. Appeals

(1) An appeal to the Special Commissioners may be made by a scheme employer—

(a) against a refusal by the Board under section 176(2) or (4) of an application for registration of the scheme;

(b) against a refusal by the Board of an application under section 177;
[(bb) against a refusal by the Board of an application under section 177B(3);][1]
(c) against the cancellation by the Board of the registration of the scheme.

[(1A) An appeal to the Special Commissioners may be made by the personal representatives of a scheme employer against a refusal by the Board of an application under section 177A.][1]

(2) An appeal under this section shall be made by notice given to the Board within 30 days of the day on which the [appellant][2] was notified of the refusal or, as the case may be, the cancellation.

Former enactment.—F(No. 2)A 1987, s. 15.
Amendments.—[1] Sub-ss. (1)(bb), (1A) inserted by FA 1989, Sch. 4, para. 8(1), (2), (3).
[2] Word in sub-s. (2) substituted by FA 1989, Sch. 4, para. 8(1), (4).

Supplementary

183. Partnerships

For the purposes of this Chapter the members of a partnership which is a scheme employer shall be treated as a single continuing body of persons notwithstanding any change in their identity.

Former enactment.—F(No. 2)A 1987, s. 16.

184. Independent accountants

(1) For the purposes of this Chapter, "independent accountant", in relation to a profit-related pay scheme, means a person who—

(a) is within section 389(1)(a) or (b) of the Companies Act 1985 or Article 397(1)(a) or (b) of the Companies (Northern Ireland) Order 1986 (qualification for appointment as auditor); and
(b) is not excluded by subsections (2) to (5) below.

(2) A person is not an independent accountant in relation to a profit-related pay scheme if—

(a) he is the employer of employees to whom the scheme relates; or
(b) he is a partner or an employee of, or partner of an employee of, a person within subsection (3) below; or
(c) he is an employee of a person within paragraph (b) above.

(3) The persons within this subsection are—

(a) any person having employees to whom the scheme relates;
(b) any body corporate which is the subsidiary or holding company of a body corporate within paragraph (a) above or a subsidiary of such a body's holding company.

(4) For the purposes of this section—

(a) an auditor of a company is not to be regarded as an employee of it; and
(b) "holding company" and "subsidiary" are to be construed in accordance with section 736 of the Companies Act 1985 or Article 4 of the Companies (Northern Ireland) Order 1986.

(5) A body corporate cannot be an independent accountant in relation to a scheme.

(6) For the purposes of this Chapter, "independent accountant", in relation to a scheme, includes a Scottish firm all the partners of which are independent accountants in relation to the scheme.

Former enactment.—F(No. 2)A 1987, s. 17.

CHAPTER IV

OTHER EXEMPTIONS AND RELIEFS

Share option and profit sharing schemes

185. Approved share option schemes

(1) The provisions of this section shall apply where, in accordance with the provisions of an approved share option scheme, an individual obtains a right to acquire shares in a body corporate by reason of his office or employment as a director or employee of that or any other body corporate and he obtains that right—

    (*a*) in the case of a savings-related share option scheme, on or after 15th November 1980; or

    (*b*) in the case of any other share option scheme, on or after 6th April 1984.

(2) Subject to subsections (4) and (6) below, tax shall not be chargeable under any provision of the Tax Acts in respect of the receipt of the right.

(3) Subject to subsections (4) and, except where paragraph 27(3) of Schedule 9 applies, (5) below, if he exercises the right in accordance with the provisions of the scheme at a time when it is approved—

    (*a*) tax shall not be chargeable under any provision of the Tax Acts in respect of the exercise nor under [section 78 or 79 of the Finance Act 1988 in respect of the shares][1];

    (*b*) section 29A(1) of the 1979 Act (assets deemed to be acquired at market value) shall not apply in calculating the consideration for the acquisition of the shares by him or for any corresponding disposal of them to him.

(4) Subsections (2) and (3) above shall not apply in respect of a right, obtained by a person under a scheme which is a savings-related share option scheme, which is exercised within three years of its being obtained by virtue of a provision included in a scheme pursuant to paragraph 21 of Schedule 9.

(5) Subsection (3) above shall not apply in relation to the exercise by any person of a right in accordance with the provisions of a scheme which is not a savings-related share option scheme if—

    (*a*) the period beginning with his obtaining the right and ending with his exercising it is less than three, or greater than ten, years; or

    (*b*) the right is exercised within three years of the date on which he last exercised (in circumstances in which subsection (3) above applied) any right obtained under the scheme or under any other approved share option scheme which is not a savings-related share option scheme (any such right exercised on the same day being disregarded).

(6) Where, in the case of a right obtained by a person under a scheme which is not a savings-related share option scheme, the aggregate of—

    (*a*) the amount or value of any consideration given by him for obtaining the right, and

    (*b*) the price at which he may acquire the shares by exercising the right,

is less than the market value, at the time he obtains the right, of the same quantity of issued shares of the same class, he shall be chargeable to tax under Schedule E for the year of assessment in which he obtains the right on the amount of the difference; and that amount so chargeable shall be treated as earned income, whether or not it would otherwise fall to be so treated.

(7) For the purposes of section 32(1)(*a*) of the 1979 Act (computation of chargeable gains: allowable expenditure) the consideration given for shares acquired in the exercise of the right shall be taken to have included that part of any amount on which income tax is payable in accordance with subsection (6) above which is attributable to the shares disposed of.

This subsection applies whether or not the exercise is in accordance with the provisions of the scheme and whether or not the scheme is approved at the time of the exercise.

(8) Where a person is chargeable to tax under subsection (6) above on any amount (the "amount of the discount") and subsequently, in circumstances in which subsection (3) above does not apply—

    (*a*) he is chargeable to tax under section 135, the amount of the gain on which he is chargeable to tax under that section shall be reduced by that part of the amount of the discount which is attributable to the shares in question; or

(b) he is treated by virtue of section 162 as having had the benefit of a notional interest-free loan, the amount of the notional loan initially outstanding shall be reduced by that part of the amount of the discount which is attributable to the shares in question.

(9) Where the provisions of a scheme which is not a savings-related share option scheme are approved in pursuance of an application made under paragraph 1 of Schedule 10 to the Finance Act 1984 before 1st January 1985 (and the approval has not been withdrawn), this section shall apply in relation to any right obtained before 1st July 1985 as if the scheme containing those provisions had been approved under that Schedule during the period beginning with the date on which that right was obtained and ending with the date on which those provisions were actually so approved.

(10) In this section "savings-related share option scheme" has the meaning given by Schedule 9.

Former enactments.—Sub-s. (1): FA 1980, s. 47(1); FA 1984, s. 38(1).
Sub-s. (2): FA 1980, s. 47(1)(a); FA 1984, s. 38(2).
Sub-s. (3): FA 1980, s. 47(1)(b); FA 1981, s. 90(3)(a); FA 1984, s. 38(3)(a).
Sub-s. (4): FA 1980, s. 47(2).
Sub-s. (5): FA 1984, s. 38(4).
Sub-s. (6): FA 1984, s. 38(5).
Sub-s. (7): FA 1984, s. 38(6).
Sub-s. (8)(a): FA 1984, s. 38(7)(a), (8).
Sub-s. (8)(b): FA 1984, s. 38(7)(b), (9).
Sub-s. (9): FA 1984, Sch. 10, para. 1(5).
Construction.—CGTA 1979, s. 32A(5) to be construed as one with this section; see CGTA 1979, s. 32A(6).
Cross references.—See CGTA 1979, s. 144A(4) (release of a right acquired under sub-s. (1) of this section for a right to acquire shares in another company);
FA 1988, s. 89(b)(ii), (iii) (amendments to FA 1980, s. 47(1)(b), FA 1984, s. 38(3)(a) in relation to acquisition of shares after 25 October 1987).
Amendments.—[1] Words in sub-s. (3)(a) substituted by FA 1988, s. 89 in relation to acquisitions after 25 October 1987.

186. Approved profit sharing schemes

(1) The provisions of this section apply where, after 5th April 1979, the trustees of an approved profit sharing scheme appropriate shares—

(a) which have previously been acquired by the trustees, and
(b) as to which the conditions in Part II of Schedule 9 are fulfilled,

to an individual who participates in the scheme ("the participant").

(2) Notwithstanding that, by virtue of such an appropriation of shares as is mentioned in subsection (1) above, the beneficial interest in the shares passes to the participant to whom they are appropriated—

(a) the value of the shares at the time of the appropriation shall be treated as not being income of his chargeable to tax under Schedule E; and
(b) he shall not be chargeable to income tax under that Schedule by virtue of [section 78 or 79 of the Finance Act 1988 in respect of the shares][1] or by virtue of section 162 in any case where the shares are appropriated to him at an under-value within the meaning of that section.

(3) Subject to the provisions of this section and paragraph 4 of Schedule 10, if, in respect of or by reference to any of a participant's shares, the trustees become or the participant becomes entitled, before the release date, to receive any money or money's worth ("a capital receipt"), the participant shall be chargeable to income tax under Schedule E for the year of assessment in which the entitlement arises on the appropriate percentage (determined as at the time the trustees become or the participant becomes so entitled) of so much of the amount or value of the receipt as exceeds the appropriate allowance for that year, as determined under subsection (12) below.

(4) If the trustees dispose of any of a participant's shares at any time before the release date or, if it is earlier, the date of the participant's death, then, subject to subsections (6) and (7) below, the participant shall be chargeable to income tax under Schedule E for the year of assessment in which the disposal takes place on the appropriate percentage of the locked-in value of the shares at the time of the disposal.

(5) Subject to paragraphs 5 and 6(6) of Schedule 10, the locked-in value of a participant's shares at any time is—

(a) if prior to that time he has become chargeable to income tax by virtue of subsection

(3) above on a percentage of the amount or value of any capital receipt which is referable to those shares, the amount by which their initial market value exceeds the amount or value of that capital receipt or, if there has been more than one such receipt, the aggregate of them; and

(*b*) in any other case, their initial market value.

(6) Subject to subsection (7) below, if, on a disposal of shares falling within subsection (4) above, the proceeds of the disposal are less than the locked-in value of the shares at the time of the disposal, subsection (4) above shall have effect as if that locked-in value were reduced to an amount equal to the proceeds of the disposal.

(7) If, at any time prior to the disposal of any of a participant's shares, a payment was made to the trustees to enable them to exercise rights arising under a rights issue, then, subject to subsection (8) below, subsections (4) and (6) above shall have effect as if the proceeds of the disposal were reduced by an amount equal to that proportion of that payment or, if there was more than one, of the aggregate of those payments which, immediately before the disposal, the market value of the shares disposed of bore to the market value of all the participant's shares held by the trustees at that time.

(8) For the purposes of subsection (7) above—

(*a*) no account shall be taken of any payment to the trustees if or to the extent that it consists of the proceeds of a disposal of rights arising under a rights issue; and

(*b*) in relation to a particular disposal the amount of the payment or, as the case may be, of the aggregate of the payments referred to in that subsection shall be taken to be reduced by an amount equal to the total of the reduction (if any) previously made under that subsection in relation to earlier disposals;

and any reference in subsection (7) or paragraph (*a*) above to the rights arising under a rights issue is a reference to rights conferred in respect of a participant's shares, being rights to be allotted, on payment, other shares or securities or rights of any description in the same company.

(9) If at any time the participant's beneficial interest in any of his shares is disposed of, the shares in question shall be treated for the purposes of the relevant provisions as having been disposed of at that time by the trustees for (subject to subsection (10) below) the like consideration as was obtained for the disposal of the beneficial interest; and for the purposes of this subsection there is no disposal of the participant's beneficial interest if and at the time when—

(*a*) in England and Wales or Northern Ireland, that interest becomes vested in any person on the insolvency of the participant or otherwise by operation of law, or

(*b*) in Scotland, that interest becomes vested in a judicial factor, in a trustee on the participant's sequestrated estate or in a trustee for the benefit of the participant's creditors.

(10) If—

(*a*) a disposal of shares falling with subsection (4) above is a transfer to which paragraph 2(2)(*c*) of Schedule 9 applies, or

(*b*) the Board is of opinion that any other disposal falling within that sub-paragraph is not at arm's length and accordingly direct that this subsection shall apply, or

(*c*) a disposal of shares falling within that sub-paragraph is one which is treated as taking place by virtue of subsection (9) above and takes place within the period of retention,

then for the purposes of the relevant provisions the proceeds of the disposal shall be taken to be equal to the market value of the shares at the time of the disposal.

(11) Where the trustees of an approved scheme acquire any shares as to which the requirements of Part II of Schedule 9 are fulfilled and, within the period of 18 months beginning with the date of their acquisition, those shares are appropriated in accordance with the scheme, section 686 shall not apply to income consisting of dividends on those shares received by the trustees; and, for the purpose of determining whether any shares are appropriated within that period, shares which were acquired at an earlier time shall be taken to be appropriated before shares of the same class which were acquired at a later time.

(12) For the purposes of subsection (3) above, "the appropriate allowance", in relation to any year of assessment, means a sum which, subject to a maximum of £100, is the product of multiplying £20 by 1 plus the number of years which fall within the period of five years immediately preceding the year in question and in which shares were appropriated to the participant under the scheme; and if in any year (and before the release date) the trustees become or the participant becomes entitled, in respect of or by reference to any of his shares,

to more than one capital receipt, the receipts shall be set against the appropriate allowance for that year in the order in which they are received.

(13) Schedule 10 shall have effect with respect to profit sharing schemes.

Former enactments.—Sub-s. (1): FA 1978, s. 53(1).
Sub-s. (2): FA 1978, s. 53(3).
Sub-s. (3): FA 1978, s. 56(1); FA 1982, s. 42(1).
Sub-s. (4): FA 1978, s. 55(1).
Sub-ss. (5)–(7): FA 1978, s. 55(2)–(4).
Sub-s. (8): FA 1978, s. 55(5), (9).
Sub-ss. (9), (10): FA 1978, s. 55(7), (8).
Sub-s. (11): FA 1978, s. 53(6).
Sub-s. (12): FA 1978, s. 56(6); FA 1980, s. 46(6); FA 1982, s. 42(2); FA 1985, s. 45(4).
Cross references.—See CGTA 1979, s. 144A(2)(*a*) (for capital gains tax, no deduction to be made from the consideration for disposal of shares by reason only that an amount determined under this section is chargeable to income tax under sub-s. (3) or (4) above),
s. 144A(2)(*b*) (any charge to income tax by virtue of sub-s. (3) above to be disregarded in determining whether a distribution is a capital distribution),
s. 144A(2)(*c*) (part disposal of a holding of shares or other securities acquired at different times),
s. 144A(2)(*d*) (a gain accruing on an appropriation of shares to which sub-s. (11) above applies not to be a chargeable gain);
FA 1988, s. 89(*b*)(i) (amendment to FA 1978, s. 53(3)(*b*) in relation to acquisition of shares after 25 October 1987).
Amendments.—[1] Words in sub-s. (2)(*b*) substituted by FA 1988, s. 89 in relation to acquisitions after 25 October 1987.

187. Interpretation of sections 185 and 186 and Schedules 9 and 10

(1) In sections 185 and 186, this section and Schedules 9 and 10 "the relevant provisions" means those sections (including this section) and Schedules.

(2) For the purposes of the relevant provisions, except where the context otherwise requires—

"appropriate percentage" shall be construed in accordance with paragraph 3 of Schedule 10;
"approved", in relation to a scheme, means approved under Schedule 9;
"associated company" has the same meaning as in section 416, except that, for the purposes of paragraph 23 of Schedule 9, subsection (1) of that section shall have effect with the omission of the words "or at any time within one year previously";
"bonus date" has the meaning given by paragraph 17 of Schedule 9;
"capital receipt" means money or money's worth to which the trustees of or a participant in a profit sharing scheme become or becomes entitled as mentioned in section 186(3), but subject to paragraph 4 of Schedule 10;
"certified contractual savings scheme" has the meaning given by section 326;
"control" has the same meaning as in section 840;
"grantor", in relation to any scheme, means the company which has established the scheme;
"group scheme" and, in relation to such a scheme, "participating company" have the meanings given by paragraph 1(3) and (4) of Schedule 9;
"initial market value", in relation to shares in a profit sharing scheme, has the meaning given by paragraph 30(4) of Schedule 9;
"locked-in value", in relation to any shares, shall be construed in accordance with section 186(5);
"market value" has the same meaning as in Part VIII of the 1979 Act;
"new holding" has the meaning given by section 77(1)(*b*) of the 1979 Act;
"participant", in relation to a profit sharing scheme, means an individual to whom the trustees of the scheme have appropriated shares;
"participant's shares", in relation to a participant in a profit sharing scheme, means, subject to paragraph 5(4) of Schedule 10, shares which have been appropriated to the participant by the trustees;
"pensionable age" has the meaning given by Schedule 20 to the Social Security Act 1975;
"period of retention" has the meaning given by paragraph 2 of Schedule 10;
"release date", in relation to any of the shares of a participant in a profit sharing scheme, means the fifth anniversary of the date on which they were appropriated to him;
"relevant amount", in relation to a participant in a profit sharing scheme, means an amount which is [not less than £2,000 and not more than £6,000][1] but which, subject to that, is 10 per cent. of his salary (determined under subsection (5) below) for the year of assessment in question or the preceding year of assessment, whichever is the greater;
"relevant requirements" has the meaning given by paragraph 1 of Schedule 9;
"savings-related share option scheme" has the meaning given by paragraph 1 of Schedule 9;

"scheme" means a savings-related share option scheme, a share option scheme which is not a savings-related share option scheme or a profit sharing scheme, as the context may require;
"shares" includes stock;
"the trustees", in relation to an approved profit sharing scheme or the shares of a participant in such a scheme, means the body of persons for the establishment of which the scheme must provide as mentioned in paragraph 30 of Schedule 9; and
"the trust instrument", in relation to an approved profit sharing scheme, means the instrument referred to in paragraph 30(1)(c) of Schedule 9.

(3) For the purposes of the application of the relevant provisions in relation to any share option scheme or profit sharing scheme, a person has a material interest [in a company if he, either on his own or with one or more associates, or if any associate of his with or without such other associates,—]²

[(a) is the beneficial owner of, or able, directly or through the medium of other companies, or by any other indirect means to control, more than 25 per cent. or, in the case of a share option scheme which is not a savings-related share option scheme, more than 10 per cent., of the ordinary share capital of the company, or]²

[(b) where the company is a close company, possesses, or is entitled to acquire, such rights as would, in the event of the winding-up of the company or in any other circumstances, give an entitlement to receive more than 25 per cent., or in the case of a share option scheme which is not a savings-related share option scheme more than 10 per cent., of the assets which would then be available for distribution among the participants.]²

In this subsection "associate" has the meaning given by section 417(3) and (4) [and "participator" has the meaning given by section 417(1)]³.

(4) Subsection (3) above shall have effect subject to the provisions of Part VI of Schedule 9.

(5) For the purposes of subsection (2) above, a participant's salary for a year of assessment means such of the emoluments of the office or employment by virtue of which he is entitled to participate in a profit sharing scheme as are liable to be paid in that year under deduction of tax pursuant to section 203 after deducting therefrom amounts included by virtue of Chapter II of this Part.

(6) Section 839 shall apply for the purposes of the relevant provisions.

(7) For the purposes of the relevant provisions a company is a member of a consortium owning another company if it is one of a number of companies which between them beneficially own not less than three-quarters of the other company's ordinary share capital and each of which beneficially owns not less than one-twentieth of that capital.

(8) Where the disposal referred to in section 186(4) is made from a holding of shares which were appropriated to the participant at different times, then, in determining for the purposes of the relevant provisions—

(a) the initial market value and the locked-in value of each of those shares, and
(b) the percentage which is the appropriate percentage in relation to each of those shares,

the disposal shall be treated as being of shares which were appropriated earlier before those which were appropriated later.

(9) Any of the relevant provisions with respect to—

(a) the order in which any of a participant's shares are to be treated as disposed of for the purposes of those provisions, or
(b) the shares in relation to which an event is to be treated as occurring for any such purpose,

shall have effect in relation to a profit sharing scheme notwithstanding any direction given to the trustees with respect to shares of a particular description or to shares appropriated to the participant at a particular time.

(10) In the relevant provisions "workers' cooperative" means a registered industrial and provident society, within the meaning of section 486, which is a cooperative society and the rules of which include provisions which secure—

(a) that the only persons who may be members of it are those who are employed by, or by a subsidiary of, the society and those who are the trustees of its profit sharing scheme; and
(b) that, subject to any provision about qualifications for membership which is from time

to time made by the members of the society by reference to age, length of service or other factors of any description, all such persons may be members of the society;

and in this subsection "cooperative society" has the same meaning as in section 1 of the Industrial and Provident Societies Act 1965 or, as the case may be, the Industrial and Provident Societies (Northern Ireland) Act 1969.

Former enactments.—Sub-s. (2): FA 1978, ss. 53(2), 54(2), (4)(*b*), (6), 56(1), 57(1), (4), 61(1), Sch. 9, paras. 1, 16; FA 1980, s. 46(4), Sch. 10, paras. 5(*b*), 8, 26(1); FA 1982, s. 40(8); FA 1983, s. 25(1); FA 1984, Sch. 10, para. 15(1), (2); FA 1985, s. 45(2).
Sub-s. (3): TA 1970, s. 285(6); FA 1978, Sch. 9, para. 11(3)(*b*); FA 1980, Sch. 10, para. 26(2); FA 1984, Sch. 10, para 4(4).
Sub-s. (4): FA 1987, s. 33(2).
Sub-s. (5): FA 1978, s. 61(4); FA 1983, s. 25(2).
Sub-s. (6): FA 1978, Sch. 9, para. 16; FA 1980, Sch. 10, para. 26(4); FA 1984, Sch. 10, para. 15(3).
Sub-s. (7): FA 1978, Sch. 9, para. 17; FA 1980, Sch. 10, para. 26(5); FA 1984, Sch. 10, para. 15(4); FA 1986, s. 23(5).
Sub-s. (8): FA 1978, s. 55(6).
Sub-s. (9): FA 1978, s. 61(2).
Sub-s. (10): FA 1978, Sch. 9, para. 18; FA 1986, s. 24(1).
Cross references.—See CGTA 1979, s. 144A(2)(*a*) (for capital gains tax, no deduction to be made from the consideration for disposal of shares by reason only that an amount determined under this section is chargeable to income tax under s. 186(3) or (4) of this Act), s. 144A(2)(*c*) (part disposal of a holding of shares or other securities acquired at different times).
Amendments.—[1] Words in sub-s. (2) in the definition of "relevant amount" substituted by FA 1989, s. 63.
[2] Sub-s. (3)(*a*) (and the preceding words), (*b*) substituted by FA 1989, Sch. 12, para. 9 in relation to accounting periods beginning after 31 March 1989.
[3] Words in sub-s. (3) added by *ibid*.

Retirement benefits etc.

188. Exemptions from section 148

(1) Tax shall not be charged by virtue of section 148 in respect of the following payments, that is to say—

(*a*) any payment made in connection with the termination of the holding of an office or employment by the death of the holder, or made on account of injury to or disability of the holder of an office or employment;
(*b*) any sum chargeable to tax under section 313;
(*c*) a benefit provided in pursuance of a retirement benefits scheme within the meaning of Chapter II of Part IX of the 1970 Act or Chapter I of Part XIV of this Act or of an agreement as described in section 220(2) of the 1970 Act, where under section 220 of that Act or section 595 of this Act the holder of the office or employment was chargeable to tax in respect of sums paid, or treated as paid, with a view to the provision of the benefit;
(*d*) a benefit paid in pursuance of any such scheme or fund as was described in section 221(1) and (2) of the 1970 Act or as is described in section 596(1);
(*e*) any terminal grant, gratuity or other lump sum paid under any Royal Warrant, Queen's Order, or Order in Council relating to members of Her Majesty's forces, and any payment made in commutation of annual or other periodical payments authorised by any such Warrant or Order;
(*f*) a payment of benefit under any superannuation scheme administered by the government of an overseas territory within the Commonwealth, or of compensation for loss of career, interruption of service or disturbance made in connection with any change in the constitution of any such overseas territory to persons who, before the change, were employed in the public services of that territory;

and references in paragraph (*f*) above to an overseas territory, to the government of such a territory, and to employment in the public service of such a territory shall be construed as if they occurred in the Overseas Development and Cooperation Act 1980, and sections 10(2) and 13(1) and (2) of that Act (which relate to the construction of such references) shall apply accordingly.

(2) Subsection (1)(*d*) above shall not apply to any compensation paid for loss of office or employment or for loss or diminution of emoluments unless the loss or diminution is due to ill-health; but this subsection shall not be taken to apply to any payment properly regarded as a benefit earned by past service.

(3) Tax shall not be charged by virtue of section 148 in respect of any payment in the case of which the following conditions are satisfied—

(*a*) that the payment is in respect of an office or employment in which the holder's service included foreign service; and
(*b*) that the foreign service comprised either—

(i) in any case, three-quarters of the whole period of service down to the relevant date, or

(ii) where the period of service down to the relevant date exceeded ten years, the whole of the last ten years, or

(iii) where the period of service down to the relevant date exceeded 20 years, one-half of that period, including any ten of the last 20 years.

(4) Tax shall not be charged by virtue of section 148 in respect of a payment of an amount not exceeding [£30,000][1] ("the exempt sum") and, subject to subsection (5) below, in the case of a payment which exceeds that amount shall be charged only in respect of the excess.

(5) Where two or more payments in respect of which tax is chargeable by virtue of section 148, or would be so chargeable apart from subsection (4) above, are made to or respect of the same person in respect of the same office or employment, or in respect of different offices or employments held under the same employer or under associated employers, sub-section (4) above shall apply as if those payments were a single payment of an amount equal to that aggregate amount; and the amount of any one payment chargeable to tax shall be ascertained as follows, that is to say—

(a) where the payments are treated as income of different chargeable periods, the exempt sum shall be deducted from a payment treated as income of an earlier period before any payment treated as income of a later period; and

(b) subject to that, the exempt sum shall be deducted rateably from the payments according to their respective amounts.

(6) The person chargeable to tax by virtue of section 148 in respect of any payment may make a claim for such relief in respect of the payment as is applicable thereto under Schedule 11.

(7) For the purposes of this section and Schedule 11 offices or employments in respect of which payments to which section 148 applies are made shall be treated as held under associated employers if, on the date which is the relevant date in relation to any of those payments, one of those employers is under the control of the other or of a third person who controls or is under the control of the other on that or any other such date.

In this subsection "control" has the meaning given by section 840.

(8) In this section—

(a) "the relevant date" and "foreign service" have the same meaning as in Schedule 11; and

(b) references to an employer or to a person controlling or controlled by an employer include references to his successors.

Former enactments.—Sub-s. (1): TA 1970, s. 188(1); FA 1970, Sch. 5, Pt. III, para. 12(1); FA 1971, Sch. 6, para. 24.
Sub-s. (2): FA 1972, s. 73.
Sub-s. (3): TA 1970, s. 188(2)(b); FA 1974, s. 21(3).
Sub-ss. (4), (5): TA 1970, s. 188(3); FA 1981, s. 31(1).
Sub-ss. (6)–(8): TA 1970, s. 188(4)–(6).
Amendments.—[1] Amount in sub-s. (4) substituted for "£25,000" by FA 1988, s. 74(1), (3) in relation to any payment treated by s. 148(4) of this Act as income received on or after 6 April 1988 unless a notice is given under Sch. 11, para. 12 of this Act.

189. Lump sum benefits on retirement

A lump sum paid to a person [(whether on his retirement from an office or employment or otherwise)][1] shall not be chargeable to income tax under Schedule E if—

(a) it is paid in pursuance of any such scheme or fund as was described in section 221(1) and (2) of the 1970 Act or as is described in section 596(1) and is neither a payment of compensation to which section 188(2) applies nor a payment chargeable to tax under section 600; or

(b) it is a benefit paid in pursuance of any such scheme or arrangement as was referred to in section 220 of the 1970 Act or a retirement benefits scheme within the meaning of section 611 of this Act and the person to whom it is paid was chargeable to tax under section 220 of the 1970 Act or section 595 of this Act in respect of sums paid, or treated as paid, with a view to the provision of the benefit; or

(c) it is paid under approved personal pension arrangements (within the meaning of Chapter IV of Part XIV).

Former enactments.—FA 1973, s. 14; FA 1987, Sch. 2, para. 3.
Cross references.—See FA 1988, s. 57 (amendments to FA 1973, s. 14 effective for the year 1987–88 and previous years).

Amendments.—¹ Words substituted by FA 1988, s. 57 and this section as so amended is deemed always to have had effect.

190. Payments to Members of Parliament, Representatives to the European Parliament and others

Grants and payments made—

(a) in pursuance of a resolution of the House of Commons to a person ceasing to be a Member of that House on a dissolution of Parliament, or
(b) under section 13 of the Parliamentary Pensions etc. Act 1984 (grants to persons ceasing to hold certain Ministerial and other offices), or
(c) under section 3 of the European Parliament (Pay and Pensions) Act 1979 (resettlement grants to persons ceasing to be Representatives),

shall be exempt from income tax under Schedule E as emoluments, but without prejudice to their being taken into account, to the extent permitted by section 188(4), under section 148.

Former enactments.—FA 1972, s. 72; FA 1984, s. 29.

191. Job release scheme allowances not to be treated as income

(1) A payment on account of an allowance to which this section applies shall not be treated as income for any purposes of the Income Tax Acts.

(2) This section applies to any allowance paid since the beginning of 1977 by the Secretary of State or the Department of Economic Development under any scheme of the kind described in the Job Release Act 1977, being a scheme which provides for the payment of allowances for periods beginning not earlier than one year before the date on which the recipient attains pensionable age as defined in that Act.

Former enactment.—FA 1977, s. 30.

Foreign emoluments and earnings, pensions and certain travel facilities

192. Relief from tax for foreign emoluments

(1) In this Part "foreign emoluments" means the emoluments of a person not domiciled in the United Kingdom from an office or employment under or with any person, body of persons or partnership resident outside, and not resident in, the United Kingdom, but shall be taken not to include the emoluments of a person resident in the United Kingdom from an office or employment under or with a person, body of persons or partnership resident in the Republic of Ireland.

(2) Where the duties of an office or employment are performed wholly outside the United Kingdom and the emoluments from the office or employment are foreign emoluments, the emoluments shall be excepted from Case I of Schedule E.

(3) If it appears to the Board on a claim made by the holder of an office or employment that out of any foreign emoluments from the office or employment he has made payments in circumstances corresponding to those in which the payments would have reduced his liability to income tax, the Board may allow those payments as a deduction in computing the amount of the emoluments.

(4) Subject to subsection (2) above, there shall be allowed in charging tax on foreign emoluments from an office or employment under Case I or II of Schedule E for the year of assessment 1988–89 a deduction equal to one-quarter of the emoluments in any case where—

(a) the holder of the office or employment was in that year of assessment not resident in the United Kingdom or was not resident in the United Kingdom for at least two of the preceding ten years of assessment ; and
(b) he—
(i) held an office or employment the emoluments of which were foreign emoluments chargeable under Case I or II of Schedule E at any time in the period beginning with 6th April 1983 and ending with 13th March 1984, or
(ii) in fulfilment of an obligation incurred before 14th March 1984, performed duties of such an office or employment in the United Kingdom before 1st August 1984,

and he held such an office or employment in the year 1984–85 and in each subsequent year of assessment.

(5) Paragraph 2(2) and (3) of Schedule 12 shall have effect with the necessary modifications in relation to the amount of emoluments to be excepted under subsection (2) above as they have effect in relation to the amount of emoluments in respect of which a deduction is allowed under section 193(1), and, subject to that, for the purposes of subsections (2) and (4) above the amount of any emoluments shall be taken to be the amount remaining after any capital allowance and after any deductions under subsection (3) above or section 193(4), 194(1), 195(7), 198, 199, 201, 332, 592 or 594.

Former enactments.—Sub-s. (1): TA 1970, s. 181(1), Sch. 12, Pt. III, para. 3(3); FA 1974, s. 21(1), (6).
Sub-s. (2): FA 1974, Sch. 2, para. 4.
Sub-s. (3): FA 1974, Sch. 2, para. 6.
Sub-s. (4): FA 1974, Sch. 2, para. 3(1), (2); FA 1984, s. 30(9)–(12).
Sub-s. (5): FA 1974, Sch. 2, para. 5; FA 1977, ss. 31(2), 32(8).

---

193. Foreign earnings and travel expenses

(1) Where in any year of assessment—

(*a*) the duties of an office or employment are performed wholly or partly outside the United Kingdom; and
(*b*) any of those duties are performed in the course of a qualifying period (within the meaning of Schedule 12) which falls wholly or partly in that year and consists of at least 365 days;

then, in charging tax under Case I of Schedule E on the amount of the emoluments from that employment attributable to that period, or to so much of it as falls in that year of assessment, there shall be allowed a deduction equal to the whole of that amount.

Schedule 12 shall have effect for the purpose of supplementing this subsection.

(2) Subsections (3) and (4) below apply where a person ("the employee") who is resident and ordinarily resident in the United Kingdom holds an office or employment ("the overseas employment") the duties of which are performed wholly outside the United Kingdom and the emoluments from which are not foreign emoluments.

(3) For the purposes of section 198(1) there shall be treated as having been necessarily incurred in the performance of the duties of the overseas employment expenses of the employee in travelling from any place in the United Kingdom to take up the overseas employment and in travelling to any place in the United Kingdom on its termination; and if travel is partly for a purpose mentioned in this subsection and partly for another purpose this subsection applies only to such part of the expenses as is properly attributable to the former purpose.

(4) Where, for the purpose of enabling the employee to perform the duties of the overseas employment—

(*a*) board and lodging outside the United Kingdom is provided for him and the cost of it is borne by or on behalf of his employer; or
(*b*) he incurs expenses out of the emoluments of the employment on such board and lodging for himself and those expenses are reimbursed by or on behalf of his employer,

there shall be allowed, in charging tax under Case I of Schedule E on the emoluments from that employment, a deduction of an amount equal to so much of that cost, or, as the case may be, those expenses as falls to be included in those emoluments.

Where board and lodging is partly for the purpose mentioned in this subsection and partly for another purpose, this subsection applies only to such part of the cost or expenses as is properly attributable to the former purpose.

(5) Subsection (6) below applies where a person resident and ordinarily resident in the United Kingdom—

(*a*) holds two or more offices or employments the duties of one or more of which are performed wholly or partly outside the United Kingdom; and
(*b*) travels from one place having performed there duties of one office or employment to another place for the purpose of performing duties of another office or employment (the emoluments from which are not foreign emoluments);

and either or both of those places is outside the United Kingdom.

(6) For the purposes of section 198(1) expenses incurred by such a person on such travel shall be treated as having been necessarily incurred in the performance of the duties which

he is to perform at his destination; and if travel is partly for the purpose of performing those duties and partly for another purpose this subsection applies only to such part of the expenses as is properly attributable to the former purpose.

(7) References in the Income Tax Acts (including any provision of this Act, but without prejudice to any express reference to subsection (3) above) to section 198 and to deductions allowable under sections 198, 199, 201 or 332 shall be construed as including a reference to subsection (3) above and to deductions allowable under that subsection.

Former enactments.—Sub-s. (1): FA 1977, Sch. 1, paras. 1, 11.
Sub-s. (2): FA 1977, s. 32(1).
Sub-s. (3): FA 1977, s. 32(2); FA 1986, s. 34(2).
Sub-ss. (4)–(6): FA 1977, s. 32(3)–(5).
Sub-s. (7): FA 1977, s. 32(8).

194. Other foreign travel expenses

(1) Where—

(*a*) travel facilities are provided for any journey to which this subsection applies and the cost of them is borne by or on behalf of the employer; or

(*b*) expenses are incurred out of the emoluments of any office or employment mentioned in subsection (2), (3) or (5) below on any such journey and those expenses are reimbursed by or on behalf of the employer,

there shall be allowed, in charging tax under Case I of Schedule E on the emoluments from that office or employment, a deduction of an amount equal to so much of that cost or, as the case may be, those expenses as falls to be included in those emoluments.

(2) Subsection (1) above applies where a person is absent from the United Kingdom for a continuous period of 60 days or more for the purpose of performing the duties of one or more offices or employments and applies to travel of the following descriptions between any place in the United Kingdom and the place of performance of any of those duties outside the United Kingdom, that is to say—

(*a*) any journey by his spouse or any child of his—

(i) accompanying him at the beginning of the period of absence; or
(ii) to visit him during that period;

(*b*) any return journey following a journey of a kind described in paragraph (*a*) above;

but that subsection does not extend to more than two outward and two return journeys by the same person in any year of assessment.

For the purposes of this subsection "child" includes a stepchild and an illegitimate child but does not include a person who is aged 18 or over at the beginning of the outward journey.

(3) Where a person holds an office or employment the duties of which are performed partly outside the United Kingdom, subsection (1) above applies, subject to subsection (4) below, to any journey by him—

(*a*) from any place in the United Kingdom to the place of performance of any of those duties outside the United Kingdom;

(*b*) from the place of performance of any of those duties outside the United Kingdom to any place in the United Kingdom.

(4) Subsection (1) does not apply by virtue of subsection (3) unless the duties concerned can only be performed outside the United Kingdom and the journey is made wholly and exclusively for the purpose—

(*a*) where the journey falls within subsection (3)(*a*), of performing the duties concerned; or

(*b*) where the journey falls within subsection (3)(*b*), of returning after performing the duties concerned.

(5) Where a person is absent from the United Kingdom for the purposes of performing the duties of one or more offices or employments, subsection (1) above applies, subject to subsection (6) below, to—

(*a*) any journey by him from the place of performance of any of those duties outside the United Kingdom to any place in the United Kingdom;

(*b*) any return journey following a journey of a kind described in paragraph (*a*) above.

(6) Subsection (1) does not apply by virtue of subsection (5) unless the duties concerned can only be performed outside the United Kingdom and the absence mentioned in sub-

section (5) was occasioned wholly and exclusively for the purpose of performing the duties concerned.

(7) For the purpose of applying this section in a case where the duties of the office or employment or (as the case may be) any of the offices or employments are performed on a vessel, in section 132(4)(*b*) the words from "or which" to the end shall be ignored.

(8) In such a case as is mentioned in subsection (7) above, subsection (4) above shall have effect as if "the duties concerned" in paragraphs (*a*) and (*b*) read "the duties concerned, or those duties and other duties of the office or employment".

(9) Where apart from this subsection a deduction in respect of any cost or expenses is allowable under a provision of this section or section 193 and a deduction in respect of the same cost or expenses is also allowable under another provision of this section or section 193 or of any other enactment, a deduction in respect of the cost or expenses may be made under either, but not both, of those provisions.

(10) References in the Income Tax Acts (including any provision of this Act, but without prejudice to any express reference to subsection (1) above) to section 198 and to deductions allowable under sections 198, 199, 201 or 332 shall be construed as including a reference to subsection (1) above and to deductions allowable under that subsection.

Former enactments.—Sub-s. (1): FA 1977, s. 32(7); FA 1986, s. 34(5).
Sub-s. (2): FA 1977, s. 32(6); FA 1986, s. 34(3).
Sub-ss. (3)–(6): FA 1977, s. 32(6A)–(6D); FA 1986, s. 34(4).
Sub-ss. (7)–(9): FA 1977, s. 32(7A)–(7C); FA 1986, s. 34(6).
Sub-s. (10): FA 1977, s. 32(8).

195. Travel expenses of employees not domiciled in the United Kingdom

(1) Subject to subsection (2) below, this section applies in the case of an office or employment in respect of which a person ("the employee") who is not domiciled in the United Kingdom is in receipt of emoluments for duties performed in the United Kingdom.

(2) This section does not apply unless subsection (3) below is satisfied in respect of a date on which the employee arrives in the United Kingdom to perform duties of the office or employment; and where subsection (3) is so satisfied, this section applies only for a period of five years beginning with that date.

(3) This subsection is satisfied in respect of a date if the employee—

(*a*) was not resident in the United Kingdom in either of the two years of assessment immediately preceding the year of assessment in which the date falls; or
(*b*) was not in the United Kingdom for any purpose at any time during the period of two years ending with the day immediately preceding the date.

(4) Where subsection (3) above is satisfied (by virtue of paragraph (*a*) of that subsection) in respect of more than one date in any year of assessment, only the first of those dates is relevant for the purposes of this section.

(5) Subsection (7) below applies to any journey by the employee—

(*a*) from his usual place of abode to any place in the United Kingdom in order to perform any duties of the office or employment there; or
(*b*) to his usual place of abode from any place in the United Kingdom after performing such duties there.

(6) Where the employee is in the United Kingdom for a continuous period of 60 days or more for the purpose of performing the duties of one or more offices or employments in the case of which this section applies, subsection (7) below applies to any journey by his spouse, or any child of his, between his usual place of abode and the place of performance of any of those duties in the United Kingdom, if the journey—

(*a*) is made to accompany him at the beginning of that period or to visit him during it; or
(*b*) is a return journey following a journey falling within paragraph (*a*) above;

but subsection (7) as it applies by virtue of this subsection does not extend to more than two journeys to the United Kingdom and two return journeys by the same person in any year of assessment.

(7) Subject to subsection (8) below, where—

(*a*) travel facilities are provided for any journey to which this subsection applies and the cost of them is borne by or on behalf of a person who is an employer in respect of any office or employment in the case of which this section applies; or (*b*) expenses are incurred out of the emoluments of any office or employment in the case of which this section applies on such a journey and those expenses are reimbursed by or on behalf of the employer;

there shall be allowed, in charging tax under Case I or II of Schedule E on the emoluments from the office or employment concerned, a deduction of an amount equal to so much of that cost or, as the case may be, those expenses as falls to be included in those emoluments.

(8) If a journey is partly for a purpose mentioned in subsection (5) or (6) above and partly for another purpose, only so much of the cost or expenses referred to in subsection (7) as is properly attributable to the former purpose shall be taken into account in calculating any deduction made under subsection (7) as it applies by virtue of subsection (5) or, as the case may be, (6).

(9) For the purposes of this section a person's usual place of abode is the country (outside the United Kingdom) in which he normally lives.

(10) In subsection (6) above "child" includes a step-child and an illegitimate child but does not include a person who is aged 18 or over at the beginning of the journey to the United Kingdom.

(11) References in the Income Tax Acts (including any provision of this Act, but without prejudice to any express reference to subsection (7) above) to section 198 and to deductions allowable under section 198, 199, 201 or 332 shall be construed as including a reference to subsection (7) above and to deductions allowable under it.

(12) Where apart from this subsection a deduction in respect of any cost or expenses is allowable under a provision of this section and a deduction in respect of the same cost or expenses is also allowable under another provision of this section or of any other enactment, a deduction in respect of the cost or expenses may be made under either, but not both, of those provisions.

(13) Where by virtue of subsection (3) of section 38 of the Finance Act 1986 any provision of section 37 of that Act applied in the case of any employee at any time during the year 1984–85 or 1985–86 (and that section applied to him immediately before 6th April 1988), this section shall apply in his case for the years 1988–89 to 1990–91 as if the following were substituted for subsections (2) to (4)—

"(2) This section does not apply after 5th April 1991.".

Former enactments.—Sub-ss. (1)–(12): FA 1986, s. 37.
Sub-s. (13): FA 1986, s. 38(4).

196. Foreign pensions

A deduction of one-tenth of its amount shall be allowed in charging any pension or annuity to tax under paragraph 4 of Schedule E.

Former enactment.—FA 1974, s. 22(3).

197. Leave travel facilities for the armed forces

(1) No charge to tax under Schedule E shall arise in respect of travel facilities provided for members of the naval, military or air forces of the Crown going on, or returning from, leave.

(2) Subsection (1) above applies whether the charge would otherwise have arisen under section 131, 141 or 154 and applies not only to travel vouchers and warrants for particular journeys but also to allowances and other payments for and in respect of leave travel, whether or not a warrant was available.

Former enactment.—FA 1977, s. 37(1), (2).

[197A. Car parking facilities

Any expenditure incurred in paying or reimbursing expenses in connection with the provision for, or use by, a person holding an office or employment of a car parking space at or near his place of work shall not be regarded as an emolument of the office or employment for any purpose of Schedule E.][1]

Amendments.—This section inserted by FA 1988, s. 46(4), (5).

Other expenses, subscriptions etc.

198. Relief for necessary expenses

(1) If the holder of an office or employment is necessarily obliged to incur and defray out of the emoluments of that office or employment the expenses of travelling in the performance of the duties of the office or employment, or of keeping and maintaining a horse to enable him to perform those duties, or otherwise to expend money wholly, exclusively and necessarily in the performance of those duties, there may be deducted from the emoluments to be assessed the expenses so necessarily incurred and defrayed.

(2) Subject to subsection (3) below, where the emoluments for any duties do not fall within Case I or II of Schedule E, then in relation to those or any other emoluments of the office or employment, subsection (1) above and Chapter II of Part I of the 1968 Act and Chapter I of Part III of the Finance Act 1971 (capital allowances in respect of machinery and plant) shall apply as if the performance of those duties did not belong to that office or employment.

(3) There may be deducted from any emoluments chargeable under Case III of Schedule E the amount of—

   (*a*) any expenses defrayed out of those emoluments, and
   (*b*) any other expenses defrayed in the United Kingdom in the chargeable period or in an earlier chargeable period in which the holder of the office or employment has been resident in the United Kingdom,

being in either case expenses for which a deduction might have been made under subsection (1) above from emoluments of the office or employment if they had been chargeable under Case I of Schedule E for the chargeable period in which the expenses were incurred; but a deduction shall not be made twice, whether under this subsection or otherwise, in respect of the same expenses from emoluments of the office or employment.

(4) No deduction shall be made under this section in respect of expenditure incurred by a Member of the House of Commons in, or in connection with, the provision or use of residential or overnight accommodation to enable him to perform his duties as such a Member in or about the Palace of Westminster or his constituency.

Former enactments.—TA 1970, s. 189; FA 1971, s. 47(1)(ii); FA 1984, s. 28(2)(*a*).

199. Expenses necessarily incurred and defrayed from official emoluments

(1) Subject to the provisions of subsection (2) below, where the Treasury are satisfied with respect to any class of persons in receipt of any salary, fees or emoluments payable out of the public revenue that such persons are obliged to lay out and expend money wholly, exclusively and necessarily in the performance of the duties in respect of which such salary, fees or emoluments are payable, the Treasury may fix such sum as in the opinion of the Treasury represents a fair equivalent of the average annual amount laid out and so expended by persons of that class, and in charging income tax on that salary or those fees or emoluments there shall be deducted from the amount thereof the sums so fixed by the Treasury.

(2) If any such person would, but for the provisions of subsection (1) above, be entitled to deduct a larger amount than the sum so fixed, that amount may be deducted instead of the sum so fixed.

Former enactments.—TA 1970, s. 191; Minister for the Civil Service Order 1971, S.I. 1971 No. 2099.

200. Expenses of Members of Parliament

An allowance—

   (*a*) which is paid to a Member of the House of Commons; and
   (*b*) for which provision is made by resolution of that House, and
   (*c*) which is expressed to be in respect of additional expenses necessarily incurred by the Member in staying overnight away from his only or main residence for the purpose of performing his parliamentary duties, either in the London area, as defined in such a resolution, or in his constituency,

shall not be regarded as income for any purpose of the Income Tax Acts.

Former enactment.—FA 1984, s. 28(1).

201. Fees and subscriptions to professional bodies, learned societies etc.

(1) Subject to the provisions of this section, the following may be deducted from the emoluments of any office or employment to be assessed to tax, if defrayed out of those emoluments, that is to say—

(*a*) any fee or contribution mentioned in subsection (2) below, and
(*b*) any annual subscription paid to a body of persons approved for the purposes of this section by the Board.

(2) The fees and contributions referred to in subsection (1)(*a*) above are—

(*a*) the fee payable in respect of the retention of a name in the Register of Architects;
(*b*) the fee payable in respect of the retention of a name in the dentists register or in a roll or record kept for a class of ancillary dental workers;
(*c*) the fee payable in respect of the retention of a name in either of the registers of ophthalmic opticians or in the register of dispensing opticians;
(*d*) the annual fee payable by a registered patent agent;
(*e*) the fee payable in respect of the retention of a name in the register of pharmaceutical chemists;
(*f*) the fee and contribution to the Compensation Fund or Guarantee Fund payable on the issue of a solicitor's practising certificate; and
(*g*) the annual fee payable by a registered veterinary surgeon or by a person registered in the Supplementary Veterinary Register.

(3) The Board may, on the application of the body, approve for the purposes of this section any body of persons not of a mainly local character whose activities are carried on otherwise than for profit and are solely or mainly directed to all or any of the following objects—

(*a*) the advancement or spreading of knowledge (whether generally or among persons belonging to the same or similar professions or occupying the same or similar positions);
(*b*) the maintenance or improvement of standards of conduct and competence among the members of any profession;
(*c*) the indemnification or protection of members of any profession against claims in respect of liabilities incurred by them in the exercise of their profession.

(4) If the activities of a body approved for the purposes of this section are to a significant extent directed to objects other than those mentioned in subsection (3) above, the Board may determine that such specified part only of any annual subscription paid to the body may be deducted under this section as corresponds to the extent to which its activities are directed to objects mentioned in that subsection; and in doing so the Board shall have regard to all relevant circumstances and, in particular, to the proportions of the body's expenditure attributable to the furtherance of objects so mentioned and other objects respectively.

(5) A fee, contribution or subscription shall not be deducted under this section from the emoluments of any office or employment unless—

(*a*) the fee is payable in respect of a registration (or retention of a name in a roll or record) or certificate which is a condition, or one of alternative conditions, of the performance of the duties of the office or employment or, as the case may be, the contribution is payable on the issue of such a certificate; or
(*b*) the subscription is paid to a body the activities of which, so far as they are directed to the objects mentioned in subsection (3) above, are relevant to the office or employment, that is to say, the performance of the duties of the office or employment is directly affected by the knowledge concerned or involves the exercise of the profession concerned.

(6) Any approval given and any determination made under this section may be withdrawn, and any such determination varied, so as to take account of any change of circumstances; and where a body is approved for the purposes of this section in pursuance of an application made before the end of any year of assessment, a deduction may be made under this section in respect of a subscription paid to the body in that year, whether the approval is given before or after the end of the year.

(7) Any body aggrieved by the failure of the Board to approve the body for the purposes of this section, or by their withdrawal of the approval, or by any determination made by them under this section or the variation of or refusal to withdraw or vary such a determination may, by notice given to the Board within 30 days from the date on which the body is notified of their decision, require the matter to be determined by the Special Commissioners, and the Special Commissioners shall thereupon hear and determine the matter in like manner as an appeal.

Former enactment.—TA 1970, s. 192.

202. Donations to charity: payroll deduction scheme

(1) This section applies where an individual ("the employee") is entitled to receive payments from which income tax falls to be deducted by virtue of section 203 and regulations under that section, and the person liable to make the payments ("the employer") withholds sums from them.

(2) If the conditions mentioned in subsections (3) to (7) below are fulfilled the sums shall, in assessing tax under Schedule E, be allowed to be deducted as expenses incurred in the year of assessment in which they are withheld.

(3) The sums must be withheld in accordance with a scheme which is (or is of a kind) approved by the Board at the time they are withheld and which either contains provisions falling within subsection (4)(*a*) below, or contains provisions falling within subsection (4)(*a*) below and provisions falling within subsection (4)(*b*) below.

(4) The provisions are that—

(*a*) the employer is to pay sums withheld to a person ("the agent") who is approved by the Board at the time they are withheld, and the agent is to pay them to a charity or charities;
(*b*) the employer is to pay sums withheld directly to a charity which (or charities each of which) is at the time the sums are withheld approved by the Board as an agent for the purpose of paying sums to other charities.

(5) The sums must be withheld in accordance with a request by the employee that they be paid to a charity or charities in accordance with a scheme approved (or of a kind approved) by the Board.

(6) The sums must constitute gifts by the employee to the charity or charities concerned, must not be paid by the employee under a covenant, and must fulfil any conditions set out in the terms of the scheme concerned.

(7) The sums must not in any year of assessment exceed [£480][1] in the case of any employee (however many offices or employments he holds or has held).

(8) The circumstances in which the Board may grant or withdraw approval of schemes (or kinds of schemes) or of agents shall be such as are prescribed by the Treasury by regulations; and the circumstances so prescribed (whether relating to the terms of schemes or the qualifications of agents or otherwise) shall be such as the Treasury think fit.

(9) The Treasury may by regulations make provision—

(*a*) that a participating employer or agent shall comply with any notice which is served on him by the Board and which requires him within a prescribed period to make available for the Board's inspection documents of a prescribed kind or records of a prescribed kind;
(*b*) that a participating employer or agent shall in prescribed circumstances furnish to the Board information of a prescribed kind;
(*c*) for, and with respect to, appeals to the Special Commissioners against the Board's refusal to grant, or their withdrawal of, approval of any scheme (or any kind of scheme) or agent;
(*d*) generally for giving effect to subsections (1) to (7) above.

In this subsection "prescribed" means prescribed by the regulations.

(10) For the purposes of subsection (9) above a person is a participating employer or agent if he is an employer or agent who participates, or has at any time participated, in a scheme under this section.

(11) In this section "charity" has the same meaning as in section 506.

Former enactments.—Sub-ss. (1)–(7): FA 1986, s. 27(1)–(7); FA 1987, s. 32.
Sub-ss. (8)–(10): FA 1986, s. 28(1)–(5).
Sub-s. (11): FA 1986, s. 27(8).
Amendments.—[1] Amount in sub-s. (7) substituted by FA 1989, s. 58.

CHAPTER V

ASSESSMENT, COLLECTION, RECOVERY AND APPEALS

[202A. Assessment on receipts basis

(1) As regards any particular year of assessment—

(*a*) income tax shall be charged under Cases I and II of Schedule E on the full amount of the emoluments received in the year in respect of the office or employment concerned;
(*b*) income tax shall be charged under Case III of Schedule E on the full amount of the emoluments received in the United Kingdom in the year in respect of the office or employment concerned.

(2) Subsection (1) above applies—

(*a*) whether the emoluments are for that year or for some other year of assessment;
(*b*) whether or not the office or employment concerned is held at the time the emoluments are received or (as the case may be) received in the United Kingdom.

(3) Where subsection (1) above applies in the case of emoluments received, or (as the case may be) received in the United Kingdom, after the death of the person who held the office or employment concerned, the charge shall be a charge on his executors or administrators; and accordingly income tax—

(*a*) shall be assessed and charged on the executors or administrators, and
(*b*) shall be a debt due from and payable out of the deceased's estate.

(4) Section 202B shall have effect for the purposes of subsection (1)(*a*) above.][1]

Cross references.—See FA 1989, s. 39(3) (income tax to be charged in accordance with this section where foreign emoluments for earlier years are received in the year 1989–90 or subsequently),
s. 40(2) (income tax to be charged in accordance with this section where emoluments for later years have been paid before the year 1989–90),
s. 40(4) (income tax to be charged in accordance with this section where foreign emoluments for later years are received before the year 1989–90).
Amendments.—[1] This section inserted by FA 1989, s. 37 and applies where the year of assessment mentioned in sub-s. (1) above is 1989–90 or a subsequent year even if the emoluments concerned are for a year before 1989–90. However, this section does not apply in the case of an employee who died before 6 April 1989.

[202B. Receipts basis: meaning of receipt

(1) For the purposes of section 202A(1)(*a*) emoluments shall be treated as received at the time found in accordance with the following rules (taking the earlier or earliest time in a case where more than one rule applies)—

(*a*) the time when payment is made of or on account of the emoluments;
(*b*) the time when a person becomes entitled to payment of or on account of the emoluments;
(*c*) in a case where the emoluments are from an office or employment with a company, the holder of the office or employment is a director of the company and sums on account of the emoluments are credited in the company's accounts or records, the time when sums on account of the emoluments are so credited;
(*d*) in a case where the emoluments are from an office or employment with a company, the holder of the office or employment is a director of the company and the amount of the emoluments for a period is determined before the period ends, the time when the period ends;
(*e*) in a case where the emoluments are from an office or employment with a company, the holder of the office or employment is a director of the company and the amount of the emoluments for a period is not known until the amount is determined after the period has ended, the time when the amount is determined.

(2) Subsection (1)(*c*), (*d*) or (*e*) above applies whether or not the office or employment concerned is that of director.

(3) Paragraph (*c*), (*d*) or (*e*) of subsection (1) above applies if the holder of the office or employment is a director of the company at any time in the year of assessment in which the time mentioned in the paragraph concerned falls.

(4) For the purposes of the rule in subsection (1)(*c*) above, any fetter on the right to draw the sums is to be disregarded.

(5) In subsection (1) above "director" means—

(*a*) in relation to a company whose affairs are managed by a board of directors or similar body, a member of that board or similar body,

(*b*) in relation to a company whose affairs are managed by a single director or similar person, that director or person, and

(*c*) in relation to a company whose affairs are managed by the members themselves, a member of the company.

(6) In subsection (1) above "director", in relation to a company, also includes any person in accordance with whose directions or instructions the company's directors (as defined in subsection (5) above) are accustomed to act; and for this purpose a person is not to be deemed to be a person in accordance with whose directions or instructions the company's directors are accustomed to act by reason only that the directors act on advice given by him in a professional capacity.

(7) Subsections (1) to (6) above shall have effect subject to subsections (8) to (11) below.

(8) In a case where section 141(1)(*a*), 142(1)(*a*), 143(1)(*a*) or 148(4) treats a person as receiving or being paid an emolument or emoluments at a particular time, for the purposes of section 202A(1)(*a*) the emolument or emoluments shall be treated as received at that time; and in such a case subsections (1) to (6) above shall not apply.

(9) In a case where section 145(1) treats a person as receiving emoluments, for the purposes of section 202A(1)(*a*) the emoluments shall be treated as received in the period referred to in section 145(1); and in such a case subsections (1) to (6) above shall not apply.

(10) In a case where section 154(1), 157(1), 158(1), 160(1), 160(2), 162(6) or 164(1) treats an amount as emoluments, for the purposes of section 202A(1)(*a*) the emoluments shall be treated as received in the year referred to in section 154(1) or the other provision concerned; and in such a case subsections (1) to (6) above shall not apply.

(11) In a case where—

(*a*) emoluments take the form of a benefit not consisting of money, and

(*b*) subsection (8), (9) or (10) above does not apply,

for the purposes of section 202A(1)(*a*) the emoluments shall be treated as received at the time when the benefit is provided; and in such a case subsections (1) to (6) above shall not apply.][2]

Cross references.—See FA 1989, s. 38(1) (application of this section for the purposes of FA 1989, s. 38(1)(*d*) (Schedule E: unpaid emoluments)),

s. 43(12) (application of this section for the purposes of FA 1989, s. 43 (Schedule D: computation)),

s. 44(11) (application of this section for the purposes of FA 1989, s. 44 (investment and insurance companies: computation)).

Amendments.—[1] This section inserted by FA 1989, s. 37 and applies where the year of assessment mentioned in s. 202A(1) above is 1989–90 or a subsequent year even if the emoluments concerned are for a year before 1989–90. However, this section does not apply in the case of an employee who died before 6 April 1989.

203. Pay as you earn

(1) On the making of any payment of, or on account of, any income assessable to income tax under Schedule E, income tax shall, subject to and in accordance with regulations made by the Board under this section, be deducted or repaid by the person making the payment, notwithstanding that when the payment is made no assessment has been made in respect of the income and notwithstanding that the income is in whole or in part income for some year of assessment other than the year during which the payment is made.

(2) The Board shall make regulations with respect to the assessment, charge, collection and recovery of income tax in respect of all income assessable thereto under Schedule E, and those regulations may, in particular, include provision—

(*a*) for requiring any person making any payment of, or on account of, any such income, when he makes the payment, to make a deduction or repayment of income tax calculated by reference to tax tables prepared by the Board, and for rendering persons who are required to make any such deduction or repayment accountable to, or, as the case may be, entitled to repayment from, the Board;

(*b*) for the production to and inspection by persons authorised by the Board of wages sheets and other documents and records for the purpose of satisfying themselves that income tax has been and is being deducted, repaid and accounted for in accordance with the regulations;

(*c*) for the collection and recovery, whether by deduction from any such income paid in any later year or otherwise, of income tax in respect of any such income which has not been deducted or otherwise recovered during the year;

[(*d*) for requiring the payment of interest on sums due to the Board which are not paid by the due date, for determining the date (being not less than 14 days after the end of the year of assessment in respect of which the sums are due) from which such interest is to be calculated and for enabling the repayment of remission of such interest;
(*dd*) for requiring the payment of interest on sums due from the Board and for determining the date (being not less than one year after the end of the year of assessment in respect of which the sums are due) from which such interest is to be calculated;][1]
(*e*) for the assessment and charge of income tax by the inspector in respect of income to which this section applies; and
(*f*) for appeals with respect to matters arising under the regulations which would otherwise not be the subject of an appeal;

and any such regulations shall have effect notwithstanding anything in the Income Tax Acts.

(3) The deductions of income tax required to be made by regulations under subsection (2)(*a*) above may be required to be made at the basic rate or other rates in such cases or classes of cases as may be provided for by the regulations.

[(3A) Regulations under this section may include provision for income tax in respect of any of a person's income for the year 1989–90 or any earlier year of assessment to be collected and recovered (whether by deduction from income assessable under Schedule E or otherwise) from the person's spouse if—

(*a*) the income was income to which section 279 applied, and
(*b*) the tax has not been deducted or otherwise recovered before 6th April 1990.][3]

(4) ...[4]

(5) Regulations under this section shall not affect any right of appeal to the General or Special Commissioners which a person would have apart from the regulations.

(6) The tax tables referred to in subsection (2)(*a*) above shall be constructed with a view to securing that so far as possible—

(*a*) the total income tax payable in respect of any income assessable under Schedule E for any year of assessment is deducted from such income paid during that year; and
(*b*) the income tax deductible or repayable on the occasion of any payment of, or on account of, any such income is such that the total net income tax deducted since the beginning of the year of assessment bears to the total income tax payable for the year the same proportion that the part of the year which ends with the date of the payment bears to the whole year.

(7) In subsection (6) above references to the total income tax payable for the year shall be construed as references to the total income tax estimated to be payable for the year in respect of the income in question, subject to a provisional deduction for allowances and reliefs, and subject also, if necessary, to an adjustment for amounts overpaid or remaining unpaid on account of income tax in respect of income assessable under Schedule E for any previous year.

(8) For the purpose of estimating the total income tax payable as mentioned in subsection (6)(*a*) above, it may be assumed in relation to any payment of, or on account of, income assessable under Schedule E that the income paid in the part of the year of assessment which ends with the making of the payment will bear to the income for the whole of that year the same proportion as that part of the year bears to the whole year.

[(9) Interest required to be paid by regulations under subsection (2) above shall be paid without any deduction of income tax and shall not be taken into account in computing any income, profits or losses for any tax purposes.][2]

Former enactments.—TA 1970, s. 204; FA 1971, Sch. 6, para. 25; F(No. 2)A 1987, s. 92.
Cross references.—See TMA 1970, s. 98A(1)(*a*) (regulations under this section in respect of special penalties in the case of certain returns);
FA 1988, s. 130(7)(*a*) (company migration: provisions to secure payment of tax due under this section by a migrating company),
s. 130(9) (company migration: provisions to secure payment of tax due by a migrating company in relation to any time before 6 April 1988);
Amendments.—[1] Sub-s. (2)(*d*), (*dd*) substituted for sub-s. (2)(*d*) by FA 1988, s. 128(1).
[2] Sub-s. (9) added by FA 1988, s. 128(2).
[3] Sub-s. (3A) inserted by FA 1988, Sch. 3, para. 4.
[4] Sub-s. (4) repealed by FA 1989, s. 45(3) and Sch. 17, Pt. IV.

[203A. PAYE: meaning of payment

(1) For the purposes of section 203 and regulations under it a payment of, or on account of, any income assessable to income tax under Schedule E shall be treated as made at the time found in accordance with the following rules (taking the earlier or earliest time in a case where more than one rule applies)—

    (*a*) the time when the payment is actually made;
    (*b*) the time when a person becomes entitled to the payment;
    (*c*) in a case where the income is income from an office or employment with a company, the holder of the office or employment is a director of the company and sums on account of the income are credited in the company's accounts or records, the time when sums on account of the income are so credited;
    (*d*) in a case where the income is income from an office or employment with a company, the holder of the office or employment is a director of the company and the amount of the income for a period is determined before the period ends, the time when the period ends;
    (*e*) in a case where the income is income from an office or employment with a company, the holder of the office or employment is a director of the company and the amount of the income for a period is not known until the amount is determined after the period has ended, the time when the amount is determined.

(2) Subsection (1)(*c*), (*d*) or (*e*) above applies whether or not the office or employment concerned is that of director.

(3) Paragraph (*c*), (*d*) or (*e*) of subsection (1) above applies if the holder of the office or employment is a director of the company at any time in the year of assessment in which the time mentioned in the paragraph concerned falls.

(4) For the purposes of the rule in subsection (1)(*c*) above, any fetter on the right to draw the sums is to be disregarded.

(5) Subsections (5) and (6) of section 202B shall apply for the purposes of subsection (1) above as they apply for the purposes of section 202B(1).][1]

Amendments.—[1] This section inserted by FA 1989, s. 45(1), (2), (4), (5) and has effect to determine whether anything occurring after 26 July 1989 constitutes a payment for the purposes of this section, but subject to FA 1989, s. 45(5).

204. PAYE repayments

Without prejudice to the generality of section 203, regulations under that section may provide that no repayment of income tax shall be made under that section to any person if at any time—

    (*a*) he has claimed unemployment benefit in respect of a period including that time; or
    (*b*) he has claimed a payment of income support under the Social Security Act 1986 or the Social Security (Northern Ireland) Order 1986 in respect of a period including that time and his right to that income support is subject to the condition specified in section 20(3)(*d*)(i) of that Act or, in Northern Ireland, Article 21(3)(*d*)(i) of that Order (availability for employment); or
    (*c*) he is disqualified at the time from receiving unemployment benefit by virtue of section 19 of the Social Security Act 1975 or of section 19 of the Social Security (Northern Ireland) Act 1975 (loss of employment due to stoppage of work) or would be so disqualified if he otherwise satisfied the conditions for entitlement;

and such regulations may make different provision with respect to persons falling within paragraph (*c*) above from that made with respect to other persons.

Former enactments.—FA 1981, s. 29; FA 1987, Sch. 3, para. 7.

205. Assessments unnecessary in certain circumstances

(1) Subject to the provisions of this section, no assessment under Schedule E need be made on a person in respect of income of his assessable to income tax under that Schedule for any year of assessment if the total net tax deducted in the year in question from that income is the same as it would have been if all the relevant circumstances had been known to all parties throughout the year, and deductions and repayments had throughout the year been made accordingly, and had been so made by reference to cumulative tax tables.

(2) In subsection (1) above—

(a) "cumulative tax tables" means tax tables prepared under section 203 which are so framed as to require the tax which is to be deducted or repaid on the occasion of each payment made in the year to be ascertained by reference to a total of emoluments paid in the year up to the time of making that payment; and

(b) references to the total net tax deducted shall be construed as references to the total income tax deducted during the year by virtue of regulations made under section 203, less any income tax repaid by virtue of any such regulations.

(3) Nothing in this section shall be construed as preventing an assessment being made on a person in respect of his income assessable under Schedule E, and, without prejudice to the generality of the preceding provisions of this subsection, an assessment shall be made in respect of the income of a person so assessable for any year of assessment if the person assessable requires an assessment to be made by notice given to the inspector within five years from the end of the year of assessment.

Former enactment.—TA 1970, s. 205.

206. Additional provision for certain assessments

Where an assessment to income tax under Schedule E is made as respects income which—

(a) has been taken into account in the making of deductions or repayments of tax under section 203, and

(b) was received not less than 12 months before the beginning of the year of assessment in which the assessment is made,

then, if the assessment is made after the expiration of the period of 12 months immediately following the year of assessment for which it is made, it shall be made in accordance with the practice generally prevailing at the expiration of that period.

Former enactment.—TA 1970, s. 206.

207. Disputes as to domicile or ordinary residence

Where a dispute arises under paragraph 1 of Schedule E or under section 192 whether a person is or has been ordinarily resident or domiciled in the United Kingdom, the question shall be referred to and determined by the Board; but any person who is aggrieved by their decision on the question may, by notice to that effect given to them within three months from the date on which notice is given to him, make an application to have the question heard and determined by the Special Commissioners, and where such an application is so made, the Special Commissioners shall hear and determine the question in like manner as an appeal.

Former enactment.—TA 1970, s. 207.

PART VI
COMPANY DISTRIBUTIONS, TAX CREDITS ETC.

CHAPTER I
TAXATION OF COMPANY DISTRIBUTIONS

208. U.K. company distributions not generally chargeable to corporation tax

Except as otherwise provided by the Corporation Tax Acts, corporation tax shall not be chargeable on dividends and other distributions of a company resident in the United Kingdom, nor shall any such dividends or distributions be taken into account in computing income for corporation tax.

Former enactment.—TA 1970, s. 239.

CHAPTER II

MATTERS WHICH ARE DISTRIBUTIONS FOR THE PURPOSES OF THE CORPORATION TAX ACTS

209. Meaning of "distribution"

(1) The following provisions of this Chapter, together with section 418, shall, subject to section 339(6) and to any other express exceptions, have effect with respect to the meaning of "distribution" and for determining the persons to whom certain distributions are to be treated as made, but references in the Corporation Tax Acts to distributions of a company shall not apply to distributions made in respect of share capital in a winding up.

(2) In the Corporation Tax Acts "distribution", in relation to any company, means—

(*a*) any dividend paid by the company, including a capital dividend;

(*b*) subject to subsections (5) and (6) below, any other distribution out of assets of the company (whether in cash or otherwise) in respect of shares in the company, except so much of the distribution, if any, as represents repayment of capital on the shares or is, when it is made, equal in amount or value to any new consideration received by the company for the distribution;

(*c*) subject to section 230, any redeemable share capital or any security issued by the company in respect of shares in or securities of the company otherwise than wholly for new consideration, or such part of any redeemable share capital or any security so issued as is not properly referable to new consideration;

(*d*) any interest or other distribution out of assets of the company in respect of securities of the company, where they are securities under which the consideration given by the company for the use of the principal thereby secured represents more than a reasonable commercial return for the use of that principal, except so much, if any, of any such distribution as represents that principal and so much as represents a reasonable commercial return for the use of that principal;

(*e*) any interest or other distribution out of assets of the company in respect of securities of the company (except so much, if any, of any such distribution as represents the principal thereby secured and except so much of any distribution as falls within paragraph (*d*) above), where the securities are—

(i) securities issued as mentioned in paragraph (*c*) above, but excluding securities issued before 6th April 1965 in respect of shares and securities issued before 6th April 1972 in respect of securities; or

(ii) securities convertible directly or indirectly into shares in the company or securities issued after 5th April 1972 and carrying any right to receive shares in or securities of the company, not being (in either case) securities quoted on a recognised stock exchange nor issued on terms which are reasonably comparable with the terms of issue of securities so quoted; or

(iii) securities under which the consideration given by the company for the use of the principal secured is to any extent dependent on the results of the company's business or any part of it; or

(iv) securities issued by the company ("the issuing company") and held by a company not resident in the United Kingdom where the issuing company is a 75 per cent. subsidiary of the other company or both are 75 per cent. subsidiaries of a third company which is not resident in the United Kingdom; or

(v) securities issued by the company ("the issuing company") and held by a company not resident in the United Kingdom ("the non-resident company") where less than 90 per cent. of the share capital of the issuing company is directly owned by a company resident in the United Kingdom and both the issuing company and the non-resident company are 75 per cent. subsidiaries of a third company which is resident in the United Kingdom; or

(vi) securities which are connected with shares in the company, and for this purpose securities are so connected if, in consequence of the nature of the rights attaching to the securities or shares and in particular of any terms or conditions attaching to the right to transfer the shares or securities, it is necessary or advantageous for a person who has, or disposes of or acquires, any of the securities also to have, or to dispose of or to acquire, a proportionate holding of the shares;

(*f*) any such amount as is required to be treated as a distribution by subsection (4) below or section 210.

(3) Without prejudice to section 254(11), no amount shall be regarded for the purposes of subsection (2)(*d*) and (*e*) above as representing the principal secured by a security issued after 5th April 1972 in so far as it exceeds any new consideration which has been received by the company for the issue of the security.

(4) Where on a transfer of assets or liabilities by a company to its members or to a company by its members, the amount or value of the benefit received by a member (taken according to its market value) exceeds the amount or value (so taken) of any new consideration given by him, the company shall, subject to subsections (5) and (6) below, be treated as making a distribution to him of an amount equal to the difference.

(5) Subsection (4) above shall not apply where the company and the member receiving the benefit are both resident in the United Kingdom and either the former is a subsidiary of the latter or both are subsidiaries of a third company also so resident; and any amount which would apart from this subsection be a distribution shall not constitute a distribution by virtue of subsection (2)(*b*) above.

(6) No transfer of assets (other than cash) or of liabilities between one company and another shall constitute, or be treated as giving rise to, a distribution by virtue of subsection (2)(*b*) or (4) above if they are companies—

(*a*) both of which are resident in the United Kingdom and neither of which is a 51 per cent. subsidiary of a company not so resident; and
(*b*) which, neither at the time of the transfer nor as a result of it, are under common control.

For the purposes of this subsection two companies are under common control if they are under the control of the same person or persons, and for this purpose "control" shall be construed in accordance with section 416.

(7) The question whether one body corporate is a subsidiary of another for the purpose of subsection (5) above shall be determined as a question whether it is a 51 per cent. subsidiary of that other, except that that other shall be treated as not being the owner—

(*a*) of any share capital which it owns directly in a body corporate, if a profit on a sale of the shares would be treated as a trading receipt of its trade; or
(*b*) of any share capital which it owns indirectly, and which is owned directly by a body corporate for which a profit on the sale of the shares would be a trading receipt; or
(*c*) of any share capital which it owns directly or indirectly in a body corporate not resident in the United Kingdom.

(8) For the purposes of subsection (2)(*c*) above—

(*a*) the value of any redeemable share capital shall be taken to be the amount of the share capital together with any premium payable on redemption, or in a winding up, or in any other circumstances; and
(*b*) the value of any security shall be taken to be the amount of the principal thereby secured (including any premium payable at maturity or in a winding up, or in any other circumstances);

and in determining the amount of the distribution constituted by the issue of any redeemable share capital or any security, the capital or security shall be taken at that value.

Former enactments.—Sub-s. (1): TA 1970, s. 233(1); FA 1980, s. 45(2).
Sub-s. (2)(*a*), (*b*), (*c*): TA 1970, s. 233(2)(*a*), (*b*), (*c*); FA 1972, Sch. 22, paras. 1, 2(1).
Sub-s. (2)(*d*): TA 1970, s. 233(2)(*d*)(iii); FA 1972, Sch. 22, para. 3(2).
Sub-s. (2)(*e*), (*f*): TA 1970, s. 233(2)(*d*), (*e*); FA 1970, Sch. 4, para. 6; FA 1972, Sch. 22, para. 3(1).
Sub-s. (3): FA 1972, Sch. 22, para. 3(3).
Sub-ss. (4), (5): TA 1970, s. 233(3); FA 1972, Sch. 22, para. 4(3).
Sub-s. (6): FA 1972, Sch. 22, para. 4(1), (2).
Sub-s. (7): TA 1970, s. 233(4).
Sub-s. (8): FA 1972, Sch. 22, para. 2(2).

210. Bonus issue following repayment of share capital

(1) Where a company—

(*a*) repays any share capital or has done so at any time after 6th April 1965, and
(*b*) at or after the time of that repayment issues any share capital as paid up otherwise than by the receipt of new consideration,

the amount so paid up shall, except as provided by any provision of the Corporation Tax Acts, be treated as a distribution made in respect of the shares on which it is paid up, except in so far as that amount exceeds the amount or aggregate amount of share capital so repaid less any amounts previously so paid up and treated by virtue of this subsection as distributions.

(2) Subsection (1) above shall not apply where the repaid share capital consists of fully paid preference shares—

(a) if those shares existed as issued and fully paid preference shares on 6th April 1965 and throughout the period from that date until the repayment those shares continued to be fully paid preference shares, or
(b) if those shares were issued after 6th April 1965 as fully paid preference shares wholly for new consideration not derived from ordinary shares and throughout the period from their issue until the repayment those shares continued to be fully paid preference shares.

(3) Except in relation to a company within paragraph D of section 704, subsection (1) above shall not apply if the issue of share capital mentioned in paragraph (b) of that subsection—

(a) is of share capital other than redeemable share capital; and
(b) takes place after 5th April 1973 and more than ten years after the repayment of share capital mentioned in paragraph (a) of that subsection.

(4) In this section—

"ordinary shares" means shares other than preference shares;
"preference shares" means shares—

(a) which do not carry any right to dividends other than dividends at a rate per cent. of the nominal value of the shares which is fixed, and
(b) which carry rights in respect of dividends and capital which are comparable with those general for fixed-dividend shares quoted on the Stock Exchange; and

"new consideration not derived from ordinary shares" means new consideration other than consideration—

(a) consisting of the surrender, transfer or cancellation of ordinary shares of the company or any other company or consisting of the variation of rights in ordinary shares of the company or any other company, or
(b) derived from a repayment of share capital paid in respect of ordinary shares of the company or of any other company.

Former enactments.—Sub-ss. (1), (2): TA 1970, s. 234(1), (2).
Sub-s. (3): FA 1972, Sch. 22, para. 5(2), (3).
Sub-s. (4): TA 1970, s. 234(3); FA 1973, s. 54.

211. Matters to be treated or not to be treated as repayments of share capital

(1) Where—

(a) a company issues any share capital as paid up otherwise than by the receipt of new consideration, or has done so after 6th April 1965; and
(b) any amount so paid up does not fall to be treated as a qualifying distribution or, where the issue took place before 6th April 1973, did not fall to be treated as a distribution;

then, except as otherwise provided by any provision of the Corporation Tax Acts, for the purposes of sections 209 and 210, distributions afterwards made by the company in respect of shares representing that share capital shall not be treated as repayments of share capital, except to the extent to which those distributions, together with any relevant distributions previously so made, exceed the amounts so paid up (then or previously) on such shares after 6th April 1965 and not falling to be treated as qualifying distributions or, where the share capital was issued before 6th April 1973, as distributions.

(2) Except in relation to a company within paragraph D of section 704, subsection (1) above shall not prevent a distribution being treated as a repayment of share capital if it is made—

(a) more than ten years after the issue of share capital mentioned in paragraph (a) of that subsection; and
(b) in respect of share capital other than redeemable share capital.

(3) In subsection (1) above "relevant distribution" means so much of any distribution made in respect of shares representing the relevant share capital as apart from that subsection would be treated as a repayment of share capital, but by virtue of that subsection cannot be so treated.

(4) For the purposes of subsection (1) above all shares of the same class shall be treated as representing the same share capital, and where shares are issued in respect of other shares,

or are directly or indirectly converted into or exchanged for other shares, all such shares shall be treated as representing the same share capital.

(5) Where share capital is issued at a premium representing new consideration, the amount of the premium is to be treated as forming part of that share capital for the purpose of determining under this Chapter whether any distribution made in respect of shares representing the share capital is to be treated as a repayment of share capital.

(6) Subsection (5) above shall not have effect in relation to any part of the premium after that part has been applied in paying up share capital.

(7) Subject to subsection (5) above, premiums paid on redemption of share capital are not to be treated as repayments of capital.

Former enactments.—Sub-s. (1): TA 1970, s. 235(1); FA 1972, Sch. 22, para. 6(1), (3).
Sub-s. (2): FA 1972, Sch. 22, para. 6(2).
Sub-ss. (3)–(7): TA 1970, s. 235(2)–(5).

CHAPTER III

MATTERS WHICH ARE NOT DISTRIBUTIONS FOR THE PURPOSES OF THE CORPORATION TAX ACTS

Payments of interest

212. Interest etc. paid in respect of certain securities

(1) Any interest or other distribution—

(*a*) which is paid out of the assets of a company ("the borrower") to another company which is within the charge to corporation tax; and

(*b*) which is so paid in respect of securities of the borrower which fall within any of sub-paragraphs (i) to (iii) and (vi) of paragraph (*e*) of section 209(2); and

(*c*) which does not fall within paragraph (*d*) of section 209(2),

shall not be a distribution for the purposes of the Corporation Tax Acts unless the application of this subsection is excluded by subsection (2) or (3) below.

(2) Subsection (1) above does not apply in the case of any interest or other distribution which is paid in respect of a security of the borrower falling within section 209(2)(*e*)(iii) if—

(*a*) the principal secured does not exceed £100,000; and

(*b*) the borrower is under an obligation to repay the principal and interest before the expiry of the period of five years beginning on the date on which the principal was paid to the borrower; and

(*c*) that obligation either was entered into before 9th March 1982 or was entered into before 1st July 1982 pursuant to negotiations which were in progress on 9th March 1982; and

(*d*) where the period for repayment of either principal or interest is extended after 8th March 1982 (but paragraph (*b*) above still applies), the interest or other distribution is paid within the period which was applicable immediately before that date;

and for the purposes of paragraph (*c*) above negotiations shall not be regarded as having been in progress on 9th March 1982 unless, before that date, the borrower had applied to the lender for a loan and had supplied the lender with any documents required by him to support the application.

(3) Subsection (1) above does not apply in a case where the company to which the interest or other distribution is paid is entitled under any enactment, other than section 208, to an exemption from tax in respect of that interest or distribution.

Former enactment.—FA 1982, s. 60(1)–(4).

Demergers

213. Exempt distributions

(1) The provisions of this section and sections 214 to 218 have effect for facilitating certain transactions whereby trading activities carried on by a single company or group are divided so as to be carried on by two or more companies not belonging to the same group or by two or more independent groups.

(2) References in the Corporation Tax Acts to distributions of a company shall not apply to any distribution—

(*a*) which falls within subsection (3) below, and

(*b*) in respect of which the conditions specified in subsections (4) to (12) below are satisfied;

and any such distribution is referred to in this section as an "exempt distribution".

(3) The following distributions fall within this subsection—

(*a*) a distribution consisting of the transfer to all or any of its members by a company ("the distributing company") of shares in one or more companies which are its 75 per cent. subsidiaries;

(*b*) a distribution consisting of the transfer by a company ("the distributing company") to one or more other companies ("the transferee company or companies") of—

(i) a trade or trades; or
(ii) shares in one or more companies which are 75 per cent. subsidiaries of the distributing company,

and the issue of shares by the transferee company or companies to all or any of the members of the distributing company;

and in this section and sections 214 to 217 references to a relevant company are to the distributing company, to each subsidiary whose shares are transferred as mentioned in paragraph (*a*) or (*b*)(ii) above and to each transferee company mentioned in paragraph (*b*) above.

(4) Each relevant company must be resident in the United Kingdom at the time of the distribution.

(5) The distributing company must at the time of the distribution be either a trading company or a member of a trading group and each subsidiary whose shares are transferred as mentioned in subsection (3)(*a*) or (*b*)(ii) above must at that time be either a trading company or the holding company of a trading group.

(6) In a case within subsection (3)(1)(*a*) above—
(*a*) the shares must not be redeemable, must constitute the whole or substantially the whole of the distributing company's holding of the ordinary share capital of the subsidiary and must confer the whole or substantially the whole of the distributing company's voting rights in the subsidiary; and
(*b*) subject to subsections (7) and (12)(*b*) below, the distributing company must after the distribution be either a trading company or the holding company of a trading group.

(7) Subsection (6)(*b*) above does not apply if the transfer relates to two or more 75 per cent. subsidiaries of the distributing company and that company is dissolved without there having been after the distribution any net assets of the company available for distribution in a winding up or otherwise.

(8) In a case within subsection (3)(*b*) above—
(*a*) if a trade is transferred the distributing company must either not retain any interest or retain only a minor interest in that trade;
(*b*) if shares in a subsidiary are transferred those shares must constitute the whole or substantially the whole of the distributing company's holding of the ordinary share capital of the subsidiary and must confer the whole or substantially the whole of the distributing company's voting rights in the subsidiary;
(*c*) the only or main activity of the transferee company or each transferee company after the distribution must be the carrying on of the trade or the holding of the shares transferred to it;
(*d*) the shares issued by the transferee company or each transferee company must not be redeemable, must constitute the whole or substantially the whole of its issued ordinary share capital and must confer the whole or substantially the whole of the voting rights in that company; and
(*e*) subject to subsections (9) and (12)(*b*) below, the distributing company must after the distribution be either a trading company or the holding company of a trading group.

(9) Subsection (8)(*e*) above does not apply if there are two or more transferee companies each of which has a trade or shares in a separate 75 per cent. subsidiary of the distributing company transferred to it and the distributing company is dissolved without there having been after the distribution any net assets of the company available for distribution in a winding up or otherwise.

(10) The distribution must be made wholly or mainly for the purpose of benefiting some or all of the trading activities which before the distribution are carried on by a single company or group and after the distribution will be carried on by two or more companies or groups.

(11) The distribution must not form part of a scheme or arrangements the main purpose or one of the main purposes of which is—
(*a*) the avoidance of tax (including stamp duty); or
(*b*) without prejudice to paragraph (*a*) above, the making of a chargeable payment, as defined by section 214, or what would be such a payment if any of the companies mentioned in that section were an unquoted company; or
(*c*) the acquisition by any person or persons other than members of the distributing company of control of that company, of any other relevant company or of any company which belongs to the same group as any such company; or
(*d*) the cessation of a trade or its sale after the distribution.

In paragraph (c) above "group" means a company which has one or more 51 per cent. subsidiaries together with that or those subsidiaries.

(12) Where the distributing company is a 75 per cent. subsidiary of another company—

(a) the group (or, if more than one, the largest group) to which the distributing company belongs at the time of the distribution must be a trading group;
(b) subsections (6)(b) and (8)(e) above shall not apply; and
(c) the distribution must be followed by one or more other distributions falling within subsection (3)(a) or (b)(ii) above which satisfy the conditions of this section and result in members of the holding company of the group (or, if more than one, the largest group) to which the distributing company belonged at the time of the distribution becoming members of—

(i) the transferee company or each transferee company to which a trade was transferred by the distributing company; or
(ii) the subsidiary or each subsidiary whose shares were transferred by the distributing company; or
(iii) a company (other than that holding company) of which the company or companies mentioned in sub-paragraph (i) or (ii) above are 75 per cent. subsidiaries.

Former enactment.—FA 1980, s. 117, Sch. 18, paras. 1–8, 23.

214. Chargeable payments connected with exempt distributions

(1) If within five years after the making of an exempt distribution there is a chargeable payment—

(a) the amount or value of the payment shall be treated as income chargeable to tax under Case VI of Schedule D;
(b) unless the payment is a transfer of money's worth, sections 349(1) and 350 shall apply to the payment as if it were an annual sum payable otherwise than out of profits or gains charged to income tax;
(c) the payment shall be regarded as a distribution for the purposes of sections 337(2), [and 338(2)(a)][1]; and
(d) the payment shall not (if it otherwise would) be treated as a repayment of capital for the purposes of section 210 or 211.

(2) In this section "a chargeable payment" means any payment made otherwise than for bona fide commercial reasons or forming part of a scheme or arrangement the main purpose or one of the main purposes of which is the avoidance of tax (including stamp duty), being a payment which—

(a) a company concerned in an exempt distribution makes directly or indirectly to a member of that company or of any other company concerned in that distribution; and
(b) is made in connection with, or with any transaction affecting, the shares in that or any such company; and
(c) is not a distribution or exempt distribution or made to another company which belongs to the same group as the company making the payment.

(3) Where a company concerned in an exempt distribution is an unquoted company subsection (2)(a) above shall have effect as if any reference to the making of a payment by, or to a member of, a company concerned in the exempt distribution included a reference to the making of a payment by or to any other person in pursuance of a scheme or arrangements made with the unquoted company or, if the unquoted company is—

(a) under the control of five or fewer persons; and
(b) not under the control of (and only of) a company which is not itself under the control of five or fewer persons,

with any of the persons mentioned in paragraph (a) above.

(4) References in this section to a company concerned in an exempt distribution are to any relevant company and to any other company which was connected with any such company for the whole or any part of the period beginning with the exempt distribution and ending with the making of the payment which is in question under this section.

(5) For the purposes of subsection (4) above and this subsection a company shall be deemed to have been connected in the period referred to in that subsection with each company to which a company connected with it was connected in that period.

(6) References in this section to a payment include references to a transfer of money's worth including the assumption of a liability.

Former enactments.—Sub-s. (1): FA 1980, Sch. 18, para. 14.
Sub-ss. (2)–(6): FA 1980, Sch. 18, para 13.
Amendments.—[1] Words in sub-s. (1)(c) substituted for the words "338(2)(a) and 427(4) and paragraph 3 of Schedule 19" by FA 1989, Sch. 12, para. 10 in relation to accounting periods beginning after 31 March 1989 except in any case where s. 427(4) of this Act has effect by virtue of s. 103(2) of this Act.

215. Advance clearance by Board of distributions and payments

(1) A distribution shall be treated as an exempt distribution in any case in which, before the distribution is made, the Board have, on the application of the distributing company, notified that company that the Board are satisfied that it will be such a distribution.

(2) A payment shall not be treated as a chargeable payment in any case in which, before the payment is made, the Board have, on the application of the person intending to make it, notified him that they are satisfied that it will be made for bona fide commercial reasons and will not form part of any scheme or arrangements the main purpose, or one of the main purposes, of which is the avoidance of tax (including stamp duty).

(3) A company which becomes or ceases to be connected with another company may make an application under subsection (2) above as respects any payments that may be made by it at any time after becoming or ceasing to be so connected (whether or not there is any present intention to make any payments); and where a notification is given by the Board on such an application no payment to which the notification relates shall be treated as a chargeable payment by reason only of the company being or having been connected with the other company.

(4) References in subsections (2) and (3) above to a payment shall be construed as in section 214.

(5) Any application under this section shall be in writing and shall contain particulars of the relevant transactions and the Board may, within 30 days of the receipt of the application or of any further particulars previously required under this subsection, by notice require the applicant to furnish further particulars for the purposes of enabling the Board to make their decision; and if any such notice is not complied with within 30 days or such longer period as the Board may allow, the Board need not proceed further on the application.

(6) The Board shall notify their decision to the applicant within 30 days of receiving the application or, if they give a notice under subsection (5) above, within 30 days of the notice being complied with.

(7) If the Board notify the applicant that they are not satisfied as mentioned in subsection (1) or (2) above or do not notify their decision to the applicant within the time required by subsection (6) above, the applicant may within 30 days of the notification or of that time require the Board to transmit the application, together with any notice given and further particulars furnished under subsection (5) above, to the Special Commissioners; and in that event any notification by the Special Commissioners shall have effect for the purposes of this section as if it were a notification by the Board.

(8) If any particulars furnished under this section do not fully and accurately disclose all facts and circumstances material for the decision of the Board or the Special Commissioners, any resulting notification that the Board or Commissioners are satisfied as mentioned in subsection (1) or (2) above shall be void.

Former enactments.—Sub-ss. (1)–(4): FA 1980, Sch. 18, para. 17.
Sub-ss. (5)–(8): FA 1980, Sch. 18, para 18.

216. Returns

(1) Where a company makes an exempt distribution it shall within 30 days after the distribution make a return to the inspector giving particulars of the distribution and of the circumstances by reason of which it is exempt.

(2) Where within five years after the making of an exempt distribution a person makes a chargeable payment which consists of a transfer of money's worth, he shall within 30 days after the transfer make a return to the inspector giving particulars—

(a) of the transaction effecting the transfer;
(b) of the name and address of the recipient or each recipient and the value of what is transferred to him or each of them; and
(c) if the transfer is accompanied by a chargeable payment consisting of a payment of money, of that payment.

(3) Subject to subsection (4) below, where within five years after the making of an exempt distribution a person makes a payment or a transfer of money's worth which would be a chargeable payment but for the fact that it is made for bona fide commercial reasons and does not form part of any such scheme or arrangements as are mentioned in section 214(2), that person shall within 30 days after making the payment or transfer make a return to the inspector giving particulars—

(*a*) in the case of a transfer, of the transaction by which it is effected;
(*b*) of the name and address of the recipient or each recipient and the amount of the payment made, or the value of what is transferred, to him or each of them; and
(*c*) of the circumstances by reason of which the payment or transfer is not a chargeable payment.

(4) Subsection (3) above does not apply where the payment or transfer is one in relation to which a notification under section 215(3) has effect.

Former enactments.—Sub-s. (1): FA 1980, Sch. 18, para. 19.
Sub-ss. (2)–(4): FA 1980, Sch. 18, para. 20.

217. Information

(1) Where a distribution falling within section 213(3) has been made and the inspector has reason to believe that it may form part of any such scheme or arrangements as are mentioned in section 213(11), he may by notice require any relevant company or any person controlling any such company to furnish him within such time, not being less than 30 days, as may be specified in the notice with—

(*a*) a declaration in writing stating whether or not, according to information which the company or that person has or can reasonably obtain, any such scheme or arrangements exist or have existed;
(*b*) such other information as the inspector may reasonably require for the purposes of section 213(11) and the company or that person has or can reasonably obtain.

(2) If the inspector has reason to believe that a person has not delivered an account or made a return which he is required to deliver or make by virtue of section 214(1)(*b*) or 216(2) or (3) in respect of any payment or transfer, he may by notice require that person to furnish him within such time, not being less than 30 days, as may be specified in the notice with such information relating to the payment or transfer as he may reasonably require for the purposes of section 214.

(3) If the inspector has reason to believe that a payment or transfer has been made within five years after the making of an exempt distribution and that the payment or transfer is a chargeable payment by reason of the existence of any such scheme or arrangements as are mentioned in section 214(3), he may by notice require the person making the payment or transfer or, if that person is a company, any person controlling it to furnish him within such time, not being less than 30 days, as may be specified in the notice with—

(*a*) a declaration in writing stating whether or not, according to information which that person has, or can reasonably obtain, any such scheme or arrangements exist or have existed;
(*b*) such other information as the inspector may reasonably require for the purposes of section 214 and that person has or can reasonably obtain.

(4) Any recipient of a chargeable payment and any person on whose behalf such a payment is received shall, if so required by the inspector, state whether the payment received by him or on his behalf is received on behalf of any person other than himself and, if so, the name and address of that person.

Former enactments.—Sub-s. (1): FA 1980, Sch. 18, para. 21.
Sub-ss. (2)–(4): FA 1980, Sch. 18, para. 22.

218. Interpretation of sections 213 to 217

(1) In sections 213 to 217—
  "chargeable payment" has the meaning given by section 214(2);
  "control" shall be construed in accordance with section 416(2) to (6);
  "distributing company" has the meaning given by section 213(3);
  "exempt distribution" has the meaning given by section 213(2);

"group", except in section 213(11)(c), means a company which has one or more 75 per cent. subsidiaries together with that or those subsidiaries;

"holding company" means a company whose business (disregarding any trade carried on by it) consists wholly or mainly of the holding of shares or securities of one or more companies which are its 75 per cent. subsidiaries;

"member", where the reference is to a member of a company, does not, except in section 214(2)(a), include a person who is a member otherwise than by virtue of holding shares forming part of the company's ordinary share capital;

"relevant company" has the meaning given by section 213(3);

"shares" includes stock;

"trade", except in subsection (3) below, does not include dealing in shares, securities, land, trades or commodity futures and "trading activities" shall be construed accordingly;

"trading company" means a company whose business consists wholly or mainly of the carrying on of a trade or trades;

"trading group" means a group the business of whose members, taken together, consists wholly or mainly in the carrying on of a trade or trades; and

"unquoted company" means a company which does not satisfy the condition that its shares or some class thereof (disregarding debenture or loan stock, preferred shares or preferred stock) are listed in the Official List of the Stock Exchange and are dealt in on the Stock Exchange regularly or from time to time, so however that this definition does not apply to a company under the control of (and only of) one or more companies to which this definition does not apply.

(2) In determining for the purposes of section 213(3) to (9) whether a company whose shares are transferred by the distributing company is a 75 per cent. subsidiary of the distributing company there shall be disregarded any share capital of the first-mentioned company which is owned indirectly by the distributing company.

(3) In determining for the purposes of sections 213 to 217 whether one company is a 75 per cent. subsidiary of another, the other company shall be treated as not being the owner of—

(a) any share capital which it owns directly in a body corporate if a profit on a sale of the shares would be treated as a trading receipt of its trade; or

(b) any share capital which it owns indirectly and which is owned directly by a body corporate for which a profit on the sale of the shares would be a trading receipt.

(4) Section 839 applies for the purposes of sections 213 to 217.

Former enactment.—FA 1980, Sch. 18, para. 23.

Purchase of own shares

219. Purchase by unquoted trading company of own shares

(1) References in the Corporation Tax Acts to distributions of a company shall not include references to a payment made by a company on the redemption, repayment or purchase of its own shares if the company is an unquoted trading company or the unquoted holding company of a trading group and either—

(a) the redemption, repayment or purchase is made wholly or mainly for the purpose of benefiting a trade carried on by the company or by any of its 75 per cent. subsidiaries, and does not form part of a scheme or arrangement the main purpose or one of the main purposes of which is—

(i) to enable the owner of the shares to participate in the profits of the company without receiving a dividend, or

(ii) the avoidance of tax; and

the conditions specified in sections 220 to 224, so far as applicable, are satisfied in relation to the owner of the shares; or

(b) the whole or substantially the whole of the payment (apart from any sum applied in paying capital gains tax charged on the redemption, repayment or purchase) is applied by the person to whom it is made in discharging a liability of his for inheritance tax charged on a death and is so applied within the period of two years after the death;

and in sections 220 to 224—

"the purchase" means the redemption, repayment or purchase referred to in subsection (1)(a) above; and

"the vendor" means the owner of the shares at the time it is made.

(2) Where, apart from this subsection, a payment falls within subsection (1)(*b*) above, subsection (1) above shall not apply to the extent that the liability in question could without undue hardship have been discharged otherwise than through the redemption, repayment or purchase of shares in the company or another unquoted company which is a trading company or the holding company of a trading group.

Former enactments.—FA 1982, s. 53(1)–(3); FA 1986, s. 100.

220. Conditions as to residence and period of ownership

(1) The vendor must be resident and ordinarily resident in the United Kingdom in the year of assessment in which the purchase is made and if the shares are held through a nominee the nominee must also be so resident and ordinarily resident.

(2) The residence and ordinary residence of trustees shall be determined for the purposes of this section as they are determined under section 52 of the 1979 Act for the purposes of that Act.

(3) The residence and ordinary residence of personal representatives shall be taken for the purposes of this section to be the same as the residence and ordinary residence of the deceased immediately before his death.

(4) The references in this section to a person's ordinary residence shall be disregarded in the case of a company.

(5) The shares must have been owned by the vendor throughout the period of five years ending with the date of the purchase.

(6) If at any time during that period the shares were transferred to the vendor by a person who was then his spouse living with him then, unless that person is alive at the date of the purchase but is no longer the vendor's spouse living with him, any period during which the shares were owned by that person shall be treated for the purposes of subsection (5) above as a period of ownership by the vendor.

(7) Where the vendor became entitled to the shares under the will or on the intestacy of a previous owner or is the personal representative of a previous owner—

(*a*) any period during which the shares were owned by the previous owner or his personal representatives shall be treated for the purposes of subsection (5) above as a period of ownership by the vendor, and
(*b*) that subsection shall have effect as if it referred to three years instead of five.

(8) In determining whether the condition in subsection (5) above is satisfied in a case where the vendor acquired shares of the same class at different times—

(*a*) shares acquired earlier shall be taken into account before shares acquired later, and
(*b*) any previous disposal by him of shares of that class shall be assumed to be a disposal of shares acquired later rather than of shares acquired earlier.

(9) If for the purposes of capital gains tax the time when shares were acquired would be determined under any provision of Chapter II of Part IV of the 1979 Act (reorganisation of share capital, conversion of securities, etc.) then, unless the shares were allotted for payment or were comprised in share capital to which section 249 applies, it shall be determined in the same way for the purposes of this section.

Former enactment.—FA 1982, Sch. 9, paras. 1, 2.

221. Reduction of vendor's interest as shareholder

(1) If immediately after the purchase the vendor owns shares in the company, then, subject to section 224, the vendor's interest as a shareholder must be substantially reduced.

(2) If immediately after the purchase any associate of the vendor owns shares in the company then, subject to section 224, the combined interests as shareholders of the vendor and his associates must be substantially reduced.

(3) The question whether the combined interests as shareholders of the vendor and his associates are substantially reduced shall be determined in the same way as is (under the following subsections) the question whether a vendor's interest as a shareholder is substantially reduced, except that the vendor shall be assumed to have the interests of his associates as well as his own.

(4) Subject to subsection (5) below, the vendor's interest as a shareholder shall be taken to be substantially reduced if and only if the total nominal value of the shares owned by him immediately after the purchase, expressed as a fraction of the issued share capital of the company at that time, does not exceed 75 per cent. of the corresponding fraction immediately before the purchase.

(5) The vendor's interest as a shareholder shall not be taken to be substantially reduced where—

(*a*) he would, if the company distributed all its profits available for distribution immediately after the purchase, be entitled to a share of those profits, and
(*b*) that share, expressed as a fraction of the total of those profits, exceeds 75 per cent. of the corresponding fraction immediately before the purchase.

(6) In determining for the purposes of subsection (5) above the division of profits among the persons entitled to them, a person entitled to periodic distributions calculated by reference to fixed rates or amounts shall be regarded as entitled to a distribution of the amount or maximum amount to which he would be entitled for a year.

(7) In subsection (5) above "profits available for distribution" has the same meaning as it has for the purposes of Part VIII of the Companies Act 1985, except that for the purposes of that subsection the amount of the profits available for distribution (whether immediately before or immediately after the purchase) shall be treated as increased—

(*a*) in the case of every company, by £100, and
(*b*) in the case of a company from which any person is entitled to periodic distributions of the kind mentioned in subsection (6) above, by a further amount equal to that required to make the distribution to which he is entitled in accordance with that subsection;

and where the aggregate of the sums payable by the company on the purchase and on any contemporaneous redemption, repayment or purchase of other shares of the company exceeds the amount of the profits available for distribution immediately before the purchase, that amount shall be treated as further increased by an amount equal to the excess.

(8) References in this section to entitlement are, except in the case of trustees and personal representatives, references to beneficial entitlement.

Former enactments.—Sub-s. (1): FA 1982, Sch. 9, para. 3(1).
Sub-ss. (2), (3): FA 1982, Sch. 9, para. 4.
Sub-ss. (4)–(6): FA 1982, Sch. 9, para. 3(2)–(4).
Sub-s. (7): FA 1982, para. 3(5), (6); Companies Consolidation (Consequential Provisions) Act 1985, Sch. 2.
Sub-s. (8): FA 1982, Sch. 9, para. 3(7).

222. Conditions applicable where purchasing company is member of group

(1) Subject to section 224, where the company making the purchase is immediately before the purchase a member of a group and—

(*a*) immediately after the purchase the vendor owns shares in one or more other members of the group (whether or not he then owns shares in the company making the purchase), or
(*b*) immediately after the purchase the vendor owns shares in the company making the purchase and immediately before the purchase he owned shares in one or more other members of the group,

the vendor's interest as a shareholder in the group must be substantially reduced.

(2) In subsections (5) to (7) below "relevant company" means the company making the purchase and any other member of the group in which the vendor owns shares immediately before or immediately after the purchase, but subject to subsection (4) below.

(3) Subject to section 224, where the company making the purchase is immediately before the purchase a member of a group and at that time an associate of the vendor owns shares in any member of the group, the combined interests as shareholders in the group of the vendor and his associates must be substantially reduced.

(4) The question whether the combined interests as shareholders in the group of the vendor and his associates are substantially reduced shall be determined in the same way as is (under the following subsections) the question whether a vendor's interest as a shareholder in a group is substantially reduced, except that the vendor shall be assumed to have the interests of his associates as well as his own (and references in subsections (5) to (7) below to a relevant company shall be construed accordingly).

(5) The vendor's interest as a shareholder in the group shall be ascertained by—

(a) expressing the total nominal value of the shares owned by him in each relevant company as a fraction of the issued share capital of the company,
(b) adding together the fractions so obtained, and
(c) dividing the result by the number of relevant companies (including any in which he owns no shares).

(6) Subject to subsection (7) below, the vendor's interest as a shareholder in the group shall be taken to be substantially reduced if and only if it does not exceed 75 per cent. of the corresponding interest immediately before the purchase.

(7) The vendor's interest as a shareholder in the group shall not be taken to be substantially reduced if—

(a) he would, if every member of the group distributed all its profits available for distribution immediately after the purchase (including any profits received by it on a distribution by another member), be entitled to a share of the profits of one or more of them, and
(b) that share, or the aggregate of those shares, expressed as a fraction of the aggregate of the profits available for distribution of every member of the group which is—

(i) a relevant company, or
(ii) a 51 per cent. subsidiary of a relevant company,

exceeds 75 per cent. of the corresponding fraction immediately before the purchase.

(8) Subsections (6) and (7) of section 221 shall apply for the purposes of subsection (7) above as they apply for the purposes of subsection (5) of that section.

(9) Subject to the following subsections, in this section "group" means a company which has one or more 51 per cent. subsidiaries, but is not itself a 51 per cent. subsidiary of any other company, together with those subsidiaries.

(10) Where the whole or a significant part of the business carried on by an unquoted company ("the successor company") was previously carried on by—

(a) the company making the purchase, or
(b) a company which is (apart from this subsection) a member of a group to which the company making the purchase belongs,

the successor company and any company of which it is a 51 per cent. subsidiary shall be treated as being a member of the same group as the company making the purchase (whether or not, apart from this subsection, the company making the purchase is a member of a group).

(11) Subsection (10) above shall not apply if the successor company first carried on the business there referred to more than three years before the time of the purchase.

(12) For the purposes of this section a company which has ceased to be a 51 per cent. subsidiary of another company before the time of the purchase shall be treated as continuing to be such a subsidiary if at that time there exist arrangements under which it could again become such a subsidiary.

Former enactments.—Sub-ss. (1), (2): FA 1982, Sch. 9, para. 5(1), (2).
Sub-s. (3): FA 1982, Sch. 9, para. 6(1), (2).
Sub-s. (4): FA 1982, Sch. 9, para. 6(3).
Sub-ss. (5)–(8): FA 1982, Sch. 9, para. 5(3)–(6).
Sub-s. (9): FA 1982, Sch. 9, paras. 5(7), 6(4).
Sub-ss. (10)–(12): FA 1982, Sch. 9, para. 5(8)–(10).

223. Other conditions

(1) Subject to section 224, the vendor must not immediately after the purchase be connected with the company making the purchase or with any company which is a member of the same group as that company.

In this subsection "group" has the same meaning as it has for the purposes of section 222.

(2) Subject to section 224, the purchase must not be part of a scheme or arrangement which is designed or likely to result in the vendor or any associate of his having interests in any company such that, if he had those interests immediately after the purchase, any of the conditions in sections 221 and 222 and subsection (1) above could not be satisfied.

(3) A transaction occurring within one year after the purchase shall be deemed for the purposes of subsection (2) above to be part of a scheme or arrangement of which the purchase is also part.

Former enactments.—Sub-s. (1): FA 1982, Sch. 9, para. 7.
Sub-ss. (2), (3): FA 1982, Sch. 9, para. 8.

224. Relaxation of conditions in certain cases

Where—
    (*a*) any of the conditions in sections 221 to 223 which are applicable are not satisfied in relation to the vendor, but
    (*b*) he proposed or agreed to the purchase in order that the condition in section 221(2) or 222(3) could be satisfied in respect of the redemption, repayment or purchase of shares owned by a person of whom he is an associate,
then, to the extent that that result is produced by virtue of the purchase, section 219(1)(*a*) shall have effect as if the conditions in sections 221 to 223 were satisfied in relation to the vendor.

Former enactment.—FA 1982, Sch. 9, para. 9.

225. Advance clearance of payments by Board

(1) A payment made by a company on the redemption, repayment or purchase of its own shares shall be deemed—
    (*a*) to be one to which section 219 applies if, before it is made, the Board have on the application of the company notified the company that they are satisfied that the section will apply; and
    (*b*) to be one to which section 219 does not apply if, before it is made, the Board have on the application of the company notified the company that they are satisfied that the section will not apply.

(2) An application under this section shall be in writing and shall contain particulars of the relevant transactions; and the Board may, within 30 days of the receipt of the application or of any further particulars previously required under this subsection, by notice require the applicant to furnish further particulars for the purpose of enabling the Board to make their decision.

(3) If a notice under subsection (2) above is not complied with within 30 days or such longer period as the Board may allow, the Board need not proceed further on the application.

(4) The Board shall notify their decision to the applicant within 30 days of receiving the application or, if they give a notice under subsection (2) above, within 30 days of the notice being complied with.

(5) If particulars furnished under this section do not fully and accurately disclose all facts and circumstances material for the decision of the Board, any resulting notification by the Board shall be void.

Former enactment.—FA 1982, Sch. 9, para 10.

226. Returns and information

(1) A company which treats a payment made by it as one to which section 219 applies shall within 60 days after making the payment make a return to the inspector giving particulars of the payment and of the circumstances by reason of which that section is regarded as applying to it.

(2) Where a company treats a payment made by it as one to which section 219(1)(*a*) applies, any person connected with the company who knows of any such scheme or arrangement affecting the payment as is mentioned in section 223(2) shall, within 60 days after he first knows of both the payment and the scheme or arrangement, give a notice to the inspector containing particulars of the scheme or arrangement.

(3) Where the inspector has reason to believe that a payment treated by the company making it as one to which section 219(1)(*a*) applies may form part of a scheme or arrangement of the kind referred to therein or in section 223(2), he may by notice require the company or any person who is connected with the company to furnish him within such time, not being less than 60 days, as may be specified in the notice with—
    (*a*) a declaration in writing stating whether or not, according to information which the

company or that person has or can reasonably obtain, any such scheme or arrangement exists or has existed, and

(b) such other information as the inspector may reasonably require for the purposes of the provision in question and the company or that person has or can reasonably obtain.

(4) The recipient of a payment treated by the company making it as one to which section 219 applies, and any person on whose behalf such a payment is received, shall if so required by the inspector state whether the payment received by him or on his behalf is received on behalf of any person other than himself and, if so, the name and address of that person.

Former enactments.—Sub-ss. (1), (2): FA 1982, Sch. 9, para. 11.
Sub-ss. (3), (4): FA 1982, Sch. 9, para. 12.

227. Associated persons

(1) Any question whether a person is an associate of another in relation to a company shall be determined for the purposes of sections 219 to 226 and 228 in accordance with the following provisions of this section.

(2) A husband and wife living together are associates of one another, a person under the age of 18 is an associate of his parents, and his parents are his associates.

(3) A person connected with a company is an associate of the company and of any company controlled by it, and the company and any company controlled by it are his associates.

(4) Where a person connected with one company has control of another company, the second company is an associate of the first.

(5) Where shares in a company are held by trustees (other than bare trustees) then in relation to that company, but subject to subsection (8) below, the trustees are associates of—

(a) any person who directly or indirectly provided property to the trustees or has made a reciprocal arrangement for another to do so,
(b) any person who is, by virtue of subsection (2) above, an associate of a person within paragraph (a) above, and
(c) any person who is or may become beneficially entitled to a significant interest in the shares;

and any such person is an associate of the trustees.

(6) Where shares in a company are comprised in the estate of a deceased person, then in relation to that company the deceased's personal representatives are associates of any person who is or may become beneficially entitled to a significant interest in the shares, and any such person is an associate of the personal representatives.

(7) Where one person is accustomed to act on the directions of another in relation to the affairs of a company, then in relation to that company the two persons are associates of one another.

(8) Subsection (5) above shall not apply to shares held on trusts which—

(a) relate exclusively to an exempt approved scheme as defined in Chapter I of Part XIV, or
(b) are exclusively for the benefit of the employees, or the employees and directors, of the company referred to in that subsection or of companies in a group to which that company belongs, or their dependants (and are not wholly or mainly for the benefit of directors or their relatives);

and for the purposes of this subsection "group" means a company which has one or more 51 per cent. subsidiaries, together with those subsidiaries.

(9) For the purposes of subsections (5) and (6) above a person's interest is significant if its value exceeds 5 per cent. of the value of all the property held on the trusts or, as the case may be, comprised in the estate concerned, excluding any property in which he is not and cannot become beneficially entitled to an interest.

Former enactment.—FA 1982, Sch. 9, para. 14.

228. Connected persons

(1) Any question whether a person is connected with a company shall be determined for the purposes of sections 219 to 227 in accordance with the following provisions of this section.

(2) A person is connected with a company if he directly or indirectly possesses or is entitled to acquire more than 30 per cent. of—
  (a) the issued ordinary share capital of the company, or
  (b) the loan capital and issued share capital of the company, or
  (c) the voting power in the company.

(3) Where a person—
  (a) acquired or became entitled to acquire loan capital of a company in the ordinary course of a business carried on by him, being a business which includes the lending of money, and
  (b) takes no part in the management or conduct of the company,

his interest in that loan capital shall be disregarded for the purposes of subsection (2) above.

(4) A person is connected with a company if he directly or indirectly possesses or is entitled to acquire such rights as would, in the event of the winding up of the company or in any other circumstances, entitle him to receive more than 30 per cent. of the assets of the company which would then be available for distribution to equity holders of the company; and for the purposes of this subsection—
  (a) the persons who are equity holders of the company, and
  (b) the percentage of the assets of the company to which a person would be entitled,

shall be determined in accordance with paragraphs 1 and 3 of Schedule 18, taking references in paragraph 3 to the first company as references to an equity holder and references to a winding up as including references to any other circumstances in which assets of the company are available for distribution to its equity holders.

(5) A person is connected with a company if he has control of it.

(6) References in this section to the loan capital of a company are references to any debt incurred by the company—
  (a) for any money borrowed or capital assets acquired by the company, or
  (b) for any right to receive income created in favour of the company, or
  (c) for consideration the value of which to the company was (at the time when the debt was incurred) substantially less than the amount of the debt (including any premium thereon).

(7) For the purposes of this section a person shall be treated as entitled to acquire anything which he is entitled to acquire at a future date or will at a future date be entitled to acquire.

(8) For the purposes of this section a person shall be assumed to have the rights or powers of his associates as well as his own.

Former enactment.—FA 1982, Sch. 9, para. 15.

229. Other interpretative provisions

(1) In sections 219 to 228—

"control" has the meaning given by section 840;
"holding company" means a company whose business (disregarding any trade carried on by it) consists wholly or mainly of the holding of shares or securities of one or more companies which are its 75 per cent. subsidiaries;
"personal representatives" means persons responsible for administering the estate of a deceased person;
"quoted company" means a company whose shares (or any class of whose shares) are listed in the official list of a stock exchange;
"shares" includes stock;
"trade" does not include dealing in shares, securities, land or futures and "trading activities" shall be construed accordingly;
"trading company" means a company whose business consists wholly or mainly of the carrying on of a trade or trades;
"trading group" means a group the business of whose members, taken together, consists wholly or mainly of the carrying on of a trade or trades, and for this purpose "group" means a company which has one or more 75 per cent. subsidiaries together with those subsidiaries; and
"unquoted company" means a company which is neither a quoted company nor a 51 per cent. subsidiary of a quoted company.

(2) References in sections 219 to 228 to the owner of shares are references to the beneficial owner except where the shares are held on trusts (other than bare trusts) or are comprised in the estate of a deceased person, and in such a case are references to the trustees or, as the case may be, to the deceased's personal representatives.

(3) References in sections 219 to 228 to a payment made by a company include references to anything else that is, or would but for section 219 be, a distribution.

Former enactment.—FA 1982, Sch. 9, para. 16.

Stock dividends

230. Stock dividends: distributions

Any share capital to which section 249 applies and which is issued by a company . . .[1] as mentioned in subsection (4), (5) or (6) of that section . . .[1] (read . . .[1] with subsection (3) of that section)—

(*a*) shall, notwithstanding section 209(2)(*c*), not constitute a distribution within the meaning of section 209(2); and
(*b*) for purposes of sections 210 and 211 shall not be treated as issued "as paid up otherwise than by the receipt of new consideration".

Former enactment.—F(No. 2)A 1975, Sch. 8, para. 6.
Amendments.—[1] Words repealed by FA 1989, Sch. 17, Pt. V in relation to accounting periods beginning after 31 March 1989.

CHAPTER IV

TAX CREDITS

231. Tax credits for certain recipients of qualifying distributions

(1) Subject to sections 95(1)(*b*) and 247, where a company resident in the United Kingdom makes a qualifying distribution and the person receiving the distribution is another such company or a person resident in the United Kingdom, not being a company, the recipient of the distribution shall be entitled to a tax credit equal to such proportion of the amount or value of the distribution as corresponds to the rate of advance corporation tax in force for the financial year in which the distribution is made.

(2) Subject to section 241(5), a company resident in the United Kingdom which is entitled to a tax credit in respect of a distribution may claim to have the amount of the credit paid to it if—

(*a*) the company is wholly exempt from corporation tax or is only not exempt in respect of trading income; or

(*b*) the distribution is one in relation to which express exemption is given (otherwise than by section 208), whether specifically or by virtue of a more general exemption from tax, under any provision of the Tax Acts.

(3) A person, not being a company resident in the United Kingdom, who is entitled to a tax credit in respect of a distribution may claim to have the credit set against the income tax chargeable on his income under section 3 or on his total income for the year of assessment in which the distribution is made and [subject to subsections (3A) to (3D) below][1] where the credit exceeds that income tax, to have the excess paid to him.

[(3A) Subject to subsection (3B) below, where it appears to the inspector that, in any accounting period of a company at the end of which it is a close investment-holding company—

(*a*) arrangements relating to the distribution of the profits of the company exist or have existed the main purpose of which or one of the main purposes of which is to enable payments, or payments of a greater amount, to be made to any one or more individuals under subsection (3) above in respect of such an excess as is mentioned in that subsection, and

(*b*) by virtue of those arrangements, any eligible person—

(i) receives a qualifying distribution consisting of a payment made by the company on the redemption, repayment or purchase of its own shares, or

(ii) receives any other qualifying distribution in respect of shares in or securities of the company, where the amount or value of the distribution is greater than might in all the circumstances have been expected but for the arrangements,

the entitlement of the eligible person to have paid to him under subsection (3) above all or part of a tax credit in respect of any distribution made by the company in the period shall be restricted to such extent as appears to the inspector to be just and reasonable.][2]

[(3B) Subsection (3A) above does not apply in relation to a tax credit in respect of a dividend paid by a company in any accounting period in respect of its ordinary share capital if—

(*a*) throughout the period, the company's ordinary share capital consisted of only one class of shares, and

(*b*) no person waived his entitlement to any dividend which would have become payable by the company in the period or failed to receive any dividend which had become due and payable to him by the company in the period.][2]

[(3C) In subsection (3A) above—

"arrangements" means arrangements of any kind whether in writing or not,

"close investment-holding company" has the meaning given by section 13A, and

"eligible person", in relation to a qualifying distribution, means an individual resident in the United Kingdom who would (apart from subsection (3A) above) be entitled to have paid to him under subsection (3) above all or part of a tax credit in respect of the distribution.][2]

[(3D) In determining under subsection (3) above whether a person is entitled to have any excess of tax credit paid to him in a case where subsection (3A) above applies, tax credits shall be set against income tax in the order that results in the greatest payment in respect of the excess.][2]

(4) Where a distribution mentioned in subsection (1) above is, or falls to be treated as, or under any provision of the Tax Acts is deemed to be, the income of a person other than the recipient, that person shall be treated for the purposes of this section as receiving the distribution (and accordingly the question whether he is entitled to a tax credit in respect of it shall be determined by reference to where he, and not the actual recipient, is resident); . . .[3]

(5) . . .[4]

Former enactment.—FA 1972, ss. 86, 110(1).
Cross references.—See FA 1989, Sch. 12, para. 1 (administrative provisions relating to close companies).
Amendments.—[1] Words in sub-s. (3) inserted by FA 1989, s. 106(1).
[2] Sub-ss. (3A)–(3D) inserted by FA 1989, s. 106 in relation to distributions made in accounting periods beginning after 31 March 1989.
[3] Words in sub-s (4) repealed by FA 1989, Sch. 17, Pt. IV with effect in accordance with FA 1989, ss. 110, 111. The repealed words read—
  "and where any such distribution is income of a United Kingdom trust the trustees shall be entitled to a tax credit in respect of it if no other person falls to be treated for the purposes of this section as receiving the distribution".
[4] Sub-s. (5) repealed by FA 1989, Sch. 17, Pt. IV with effect in accordance with FA 1989, ss. 110, 111. The repealed sub-s. (5) read—
  "(5) In subsection (4) above "United Kingdom trust" means a trust administered under the law of any part of the United Kingdom, not being a trust the general administration of which is ordinarily carried on outside the United Kingdom and the trustees, or a majority of the trustees, of which are resident or ordinarily resident outside the United Kingdom."

232. Tax credits for non-U.K. residents

(1) An individual who, having made a claim in that behalf, is entitled to relief under Chapter I of Part VII by virtue of section 278(2) in respect of any year of assessment shall be entitled to a tax credit in respect of any qualifying distribution received by him in that year to the same extent as if he were resident in the United Kingdom.

(2) Where a qualifying distribution is income of a fund to which section 615(2)(b) or (c) applies the persons entitled to receive the income shall be entitled to a tax credit in respect of the distribution to the same extent as a recipient mentioned in section 231(1).

(3) Where a qualifying distribution is income of, or of the government of, any sovereign power or of any international organisation, that power, government or organisation shall be entitled to a tax credit in respect of the distribution to the same extent as a recipient mentioned in section 231(1).

In this subsection "international organisation" means an organisation of which two or more sovereign powers, or the governments of two or more sovereign powers, are members; and if in any proceedings a question arises whether a person is within this subsection, a certificate issued by or under the authority of the Secretary of State stating any fact relevant to that question shall be conclusive evidence of that fact.

Former enactment.—FA 1972, s. 98(1), (3), (4).

233. Taxation of certain recipients of distributions and in respect of non-qualifying distributions

(1) Where in any year of assessment the income of any person, not being a company resident in the United Kingdom, includes a distribution in respect of which that person is not entitled to a tax credit—

(a) no assessment shall be made on that person in respect of income tax at the basic rate on the amount or value of the distribution;

(b) that person's liability under any assessment made in respect of income tax at a higher rate on the amount or value of the distribution or on any part of the distribution shall be reduced by a sum equal to income tax at the basic rate on so much of the distribution as is assessed at that higher rate;

(c) the amount or value of the distribution shall be treated for the purposes of sections 348 and 349(1) as not brought into charge to income tax.

(2) Where a person has paid tax ("the tax paid") in respect of excess liability on, or on any part of, a non-qualifying distribution, then if, apart from this subsection, he would be liable to pay an amount of tax in respect of excess liability on, or on any part of, a repayment of the share capital or of the principal of the security which constituted that non-qualifying distribution, he shall be so liable only to the extent (if any) to which that amount exceeds the amount of the tax paid.

In this subsection—

"excess liability" means the excess of liability to income tax over what it would be if all income tax were charged at the basic rate to the exclusion of any higher rate;

"non-qualifying distribution" means a distribution which is not a qualifying distribution.

Former enactment.—FA 1972, s. 87(5), (6).

234. Information relating to distributions

(1) Without prejudice to subsections (3) and (4) below but subject to section 95(1)(c), a company which makes a qualifying distribution shall, if the recipient so requests in writing, furnish to him a statement in writing showing the amount or value of the distribution and (whether or not the recipient is a person entitled to a tax credit in respect of the distribution) the amount of the tax credit to which a recipient who is such a person is entitled in respect of that distribution.

(2) The duty imposed by subsection (1) above shall be enforceable at the suit or instance of the person requesting the information.

(3) Every warrant or cheque or other order drawn or made, or purporting to be drawn or made, in payment of any dividend or interest distributed by any company, being a company within the meaning of the Companies Act 1985 or the Companies (Northern Ireland) Order 1986, or a company created by letters patent or by or in pursuance of an Act, shall have annexed to itself or be accompanied by a statement in writing showing—

(a) in the case of interest which is not a qualifying distribution—

(i) the gross amount which, after deduction of the income tax appropriate thereto, corresponds to the net amount actually paid;
(ii) the rate and the amount of income tax appropriate to such gross amount, and
(iii) the net amount actually paid;

(b) in the case of a dividend or interest which is a qualifying distribution, each of the following amounts—

(i) the amount of the dividend or interest paid, and
(ii) (whether or not the recipient is a person entitled to a tax credit in respect of that distribution) the amount of the tax credit to which a recipient who is such a person is entitled in respect of that distribution.

(4) If a company fails to comply with the provisions of subsection (3) above, the company shall in respect of each offence incur a penalty of [£60][1] except that the aggregate amount of any penalties imposed under this subsection on any company in respect of offences connected with any one distribution of dividends or interest shall not exceed [£600][1].

(5) Where a company makes a distribution which is not a qualifying distribution it shall make a return to the inspector—

(a) within 14 days from the end of the accounting period in which the distribution is made; or
(b) if the distribution is made on a date not falling in an accounting period, within 14 days from that date.

(6) A return under subsection (5) above shall contain—

(a) particulars of the transaction giving rise to the distribution; and
(b) the name and address of the person, or each of the persons, receiving the distribution, and the amount or value of the distribution received by him or by each of them.

(7) Where it is not in the circumstances apparent whether a transaction gives rise to a distribution in respect of which a return is required to be made under subsection (5) above, the company shall—

(a) within the time within which such a return would be required to be made if the transaction did give rise to such a distribution, make a return to the inspector containing particulars of the transaction in question; and
(b) if required by a notice served on the company by the inspector, furnish him with the time specified in the notice with such further information in relation to the transaction as he may reasonably require.

(8) If it appears to the inspector that particulars of any transaction ought to have been and have not been included in a return under subsection (5) or (7) above, he may by a notice served on the company require the company to furnish him within the time specified in the notice with such information relating thereto as he may reasonably require.

(9) Any power which the inspector may exercise under [paragraphs 2 to 4 of Schedule 12 to the Finance Act 1989 for the purposes of the relevant provisions (as defined in paragraph 1 of that Schedule)][2] may be exercised by him for the purposes of subsections (5) to (8) above.

Former enactments.—Sub-ss. (1), (2): TA 1970, s. 232(4); FA 1972, Sch. 24, para. 18.
Sub-ss. (3), (4): TA 1970, s. 242; FA 1972, Sch. 24, para. 19; Companies Consolidation (Consequential Provisions) Act 1985, Sch. 2; Companies Consolidation (Consequential Provisions) (Northern Ireland) Order 1986, S.I. 1986 No. 1032.

Sub-ss. (5)–(9): FA 1972, Sch. 21.
Amendments.—[1] Amounts in sub-s. (4) substituted for "£10" and "£100" respectively by FA 1989, s. 170(2), (6) in relation to things done or omitted after 26 July 1989.
[2] Words in sub-s. (9) substituted by FA 1989, Sch.12, para. 11.

235. Distributions of exempt funds etc.

(1) Where a person entitled to a tax credit in respect of a distribution to which this section applies is, by reason of any exemption from tax, entitled to recover tax and his holding (together with any associated holding) of any one class of the shares, securities or rights by virtue of which he is entitled to the distribution amounts to not less than 10 per cent. thereof, subsection (3) below shall apply to the income represented by any part of the distribution which is not a part—
  (a) to which profits arising after the date of acquisition are attributable in accordance with section 236; or
  (b) in relation to which the date of acquisition is earlier than 6th April 1965.

(2) For the purposes of this section and section 236, the date of acquisition, in relation to any part of a distribution or profits attributable to it, is the date on which the shares, securities or rights by virtue of which a person is entitled to that part were acquired by him.

(3) Where this subsection applies to any income—
  (a) the exemption from tax shall not extend to that income; and
  (b) it shall be treated for the purposes of sections 348 and 349(1) as not brought into charge to income tax; and
  (c) no amount of interest shall be deducted from or set off against it under section 353.

(4) Where, by virtue of this section, an exemption from tax does not apply to any income represented by a distribution or part of a distribution, the person entitled to the income shall be liable to tax or, as the case may be, additional tax, on it at a rate equal to the additional rate in force at the time the distribution is made and shall be assessable to income tax or corporation tax accordingly.

(5) This section applies to any qualifying distribution except any amount which is treated as such in accordance with section 209(3) or sections 210 and 211.

Former enactment.—FA 1973, s. 22.

236. Provisions supplementary to section 235

(1) Section 235 shall be construed in accordance with the following provisions of this section.

(2) Two or more holdings are associated if they were acquired by persons acting in concert or under arrangements made by any person.

(3) There shall be attributed—
  (a) to the distributions made by a company at any time (whether before or after the passing of this Act) in respect of any class of shares, securities or rights such of its relevant profits arising after the date of acquisition and before that time as remain after allowing for earlier distributions made in respect of that or any other class of shares, securities or rights, and for distributions made at or to be made after that time in respect of other classes of shares, securities or rights; and
  (b) to any part of a distribution made at any time to which a person is entitled by virtue of any part of his holding of any class of shares, securities or rights, such proportion of the profits attributable under paragraph (a) above to the distributions made at that time in respect of that class as corresponds to that part of his holding.

(4) For the purposes of subsection (3) above profits arising in part of an accounting period shall be taken to be a proportionate part of the profits arising in the whole of the accounting period except where a different method of arriving at the profits arising in that part can be shown to be fair and reasonable.

(5) For the purposes of this section the relevant profits of a company are, subject to subsection (6) below, its profits computed on a commercial basis after allowing for any provision properly made for corporation tax; and the computation shall be made without regard to any capital gains or losses or to any such amount as is mentioned in section 235(5), and—
  (a) shall include franked investment income received from any company not related to the first-mentioned company; and
  (b) shall exclude group income and franked investment income received from a company related to the first-mentioned company.

(6) There shall be treated as included in the relevant profits of a company the appropriate portion of the relevant profits of any company related to it.

(7) For the purposes of this section a company ("the owned company") is related to another company ("the owning company") if—
   (a) the owning company owns not less than 10 per cent. of any one class of shares in the owned company; or
   (b) any company related to the owning company owns not less than 10 per cent. of any one class of shares in the owned company;

and the appropriate proportion of the relevant profits of a related company is that proportion of those profits which the owning company would receive by virtue of the shares, securities or rights owned by it, if all the relevant profits of the owned company were distributed and, so far as received directly or indirectly by a company related to the owning company, were distributed by that related company, no account being taken of any profits arising at a time when the owned company was not related to the owning company.

Former enactment.—FA 1973, Sch. 10.

237. Disallowance of reliefs in respect of bonus issues

(1) This section has effect where any person ("the recipient") receives an amount treated as a distribution by virtue of section 209(3) or 210 or 211(1); and in this section—
   (a) any such distribution is referred to as a bonus issue; and
   (b) "relevant tax credit" in relation to a bonus issue means the tax credit to which the recipient becomes entitled in respect of the bonus issue.

(2) Subject to subsection (6) below, if the recipient is entitled by reason of—
   (a) any exemption from tax, or
   (b) the setting-off of losses against profits or income,

to recover tax in respect of any distribution received by him, no account shall be taken for the purposes of any such exemption or set-off of any bonus issue or relevant tax credit received by him.

(3) Subject to subsection (6) below, where, by virtue of this section, no account is to be taken for the purposes of any exemption from tax of any bonus issue and the relevant tax credit, the person entitled to that issue and that credit shall be liable to tax or, as the case may be, additional tax, on them at a rate equal to the additional rate in force at the time the bonus issue is made and shall be assessable to income tax or corporation tax accordingly.

(4) Subject to subsection (6) below, a bonus issue and the relevant tax credit shall be treated for the purposes of sections 241 and 244 as not being franked investment income.

(5) Subject to subsection (6) below—
   (a) the relevant tax credit relating to a bonus issue shall not be available to set against any income tax which the recipient is entitled to deduct under section 348 or with which he is chargeable by virtue of section 349(1), and
   (b) no interest may be deducted or set off under section 353 from or against so much of a person's income as consists of bonus issues and relevant tax credits.

(6) Nothing in subsections (2) to (5) above shall affect the proportion (if any) of any bonus issue made in respect of any shares or securities which, if it were declared as a dividend, would represent a normal return to the recipient on the consideration provided by him for the relevant shares or securities, that is to say, those in respect of which the bonus issue was made and, if those securities are derived from shares or securities previously acquired by the recipient, the shares or securities which were previously acquired; nor shall anything in those subsections affect the like proportion of the relevant tax credit relating to that bonus issue.

(7) For the purposes of subsection (6) above—
   (a) if the consideration provided by the recipient for any of the relevant shares or securities was in excess of their market value at the time he acquired them, or if no consideration was provided by him for any of the relevant shares or securities, the recipient shall be taken to have provided for those shares or securities consideration equal to their market value at the time he acquired them; and
   (b) in determining whether an amount received by way of dividend exceeds a normal return, regard shall be had to the length of time previous to the receipt of that amount since the recipient first acquired any of the relevant shares or securities and to any dividends and other distributions made in respect of them during that time.

Former enactment.—FA 1973, s. 23.

CHAPTER V
ADVANCE CORPORATION TAX AND FRANKED INVESTMENT INCOME

238. Interpretation of terms and collection of ACT

(1) In this Chapter—

"franked investment income" means income of a company resident in the United Kingdom which consists of a distribution in respect of which the company is entitled to a tax credit (and which accordingly represents income equal to the aggregate of the amount or value of the distribution and the amount of that credit), but subject to section 247(2);

"franked payment" means the sum of the amount or value of a qualifying distribution and such proportion of that amount or value as corresponds to the rate of advance corporation tax in force for the financial year in which the distribution is made, but subject to section 247(2);

"surplus advance corporation tax" has the meaning given by section 239(3);

"surplus of franked investment income" means any such excess as is mentioned in subsection (3) of section 241 (calculated without regard to franked investment income which by virtue of subsection (5) of that section cannot be used to frank distributions);

"tax credit" means a tax credit under section 231;

and references to any accounting or other period in which a franked payment is made are references to the period in which the distribution in question is made.

(2) References in this Chapter to distributions or payments received by a company apply to any received by another person on behalf of or in trust for the company but not to any received by the company on behalf of or in trust for another person.

(3) References in this Chapter to using franked investment income to frank distributions of a company shall be construed in accordance with section 241(5).

(4) References in this Chapter to an amount of profits on which corporation tax falls finally to be borne are references to the amount of those profits after making all deductions and giving all reliefs that for the purposes of corporation tax are made or given from or against those profits, including deductions and reliefs which under any provision are treated as reducing them for those purposes.

(5) Schedule 13 shall have effect for the purpose of regulating the time and manner in which advance corporation tax is to be accounted for and paid.

Former enactments.—Sub-s. (1): FA 1972, ss. 84(3), 88(1), 89(6), 110(1).
Sub-ss. (2)–(4): FA 1972, s. 110(2)–(4).
Sub-s. (5): FA 1972, s. 84(5).

239. Set-off of ACT against liability to corporation tax

(1) Subject to section 497 and subsection (2) below, advance corporation tax paid by a company (and not repaid) in respect of any distribution made by it in an accounting period shall be set against its liability to corporation tax on any profits charged to corporation tax for that accounting period and shall accordingly discharge a corresponding amount of that liability.

(2) The amount of advance corporation tax to be set against a company's liability for any accounting period under subsection (1) above shall not exceed the amount of advance corporation tax that would have been payable (apart from section 241) in respect of a distribution made at the end of that period of an amount which, together with the advance corporation tax so payable in respect of it, is equal to the company's profits charged to corporation tax for that period.

(3) Where in the case of any accounting period of a company there is an amount of surplus advance corporation tax, the company may, within two years after the end of that period, claim to have the whole or any part of that amount treated for the purposes of this section (but not of any further application of this subsection) as if it were advance corporation tax paid in respect of distributions made by the company in any of its accounting periods beginning in the six years preceding that period (but so that the amount which is the subject of the claim is set, so far as possible, against the company's liability for a more recent

accounting period before a more remote one) and corporation tax shall, so far as may be required, be repaid accordingly.

In this subsection "surplus advance corporation tax", in relation to any accounting period of a company, means advance corporation tax which cannot be set against the company's liability to corporation tax for that period because the company has no profits charged to corporation tax for that period or because of subsection (2) above or section 797(4).

(4) Where in the case of any accounting period of a company there is an amount of surplus advance corporation tax which has not been dealt with under subsection (3) above, that amount shall be treated for the purposes of this section (including any further application of this subsection) as if it were advance corporation tax paid in respect of distributions made by the company in the next accounting period.

(5) Effect shall be given to subsections (1) and (4) above as if on a claim in that behalf by the company and, for that purpose, a return made by the company under section 11 of the Management Act containing particulars of advance corporation tax or surplus advance corporation tax which falls to be dealt with under those subsections shall be treated as a claim.

(6) For the purposes of this section the profits of a company charged to corporation tax for any period shall be taken to be the amount of its profits for that period on which corporation tax falls finally to be borne.

(7) This section has effect subject to . . .[1] the following provisions of this Chapter.

Former enactments.—Sub-ss. (1)–(6): FA 1972, s. 85(1)–(6); FA 1974, Sch. 7, para. 3(1); FA 1984, s. 52(1), 53(2); F(No. 2)A 1987, s. 74(2).
Sub-s. (7): FA 1972, Sch. 16, para. 7.
Sub-s. (8): FA 1972, s. 85(7).
Cross references.—See FA 1989, s. 157(2)–(4), (6) (interest on corporation tax for an earlier period where surplus ACT from a later period is carried back after 13 March 1989, but subject to s. 157(6)—see below),
s. 157(6) (FA 1989, s. 157 not to have effect in relation to corporation tax for accounting periods ending after an appointed day).
Amendments.—[1] Words in sub-s. (7) repealed by FA 1989, Sch. 17, Pt. V.

240. Set-off of company's surplus ACT against subsidiary's liability to corporation tax

(1) Where a company ("the surrendering company") has paid an amount of advance corporation tax in respect of a dividend or dividends paid by it in an accounting period and the advance corporation tax has not been repaid, it may, on making a claim, surrender the benefit of the whole or any part of that amount—

(*a*) to any company which was a subsidiary of the surrendering company throughout that accounting period, or

(*b*) in such proportions as the surrendering company may determine, to any two or more companies which were subsidiaries of the surrendering company throughout that period.

(2) Subject to subsections (4) and (5) below, where the benefit of any amount of advance corporation tax ("the surrendered amount") is surrendered under this section to a subsidiary, then—

(*a*) if the advance corporation tax mentioned in subsection (1) above was paid in respect of one dividend only or of dividends all of which were paid on the same date, the subsidiary shall be treated for the purposes of section 239 as having paid an amount of advance corporation tax equal to the surrendered amount in respect of a distribution made by it on the date on which the dividend or dividends were paid;

(*b*) if the advance corporation tax mentioned in subsection (1) above was paid in respect of dividends paid on different dates, the subsidiary shall be treated for the purposes of section 239 as having paid an amount of advance corporation tax equal to the appropriate part of the surrendered amount in respect of a distribution made by it on each of those dates.

(3) For the purposes of paragraph (*b*) of subsection (2) above "the appropriate part of the surrendered amount", in relation to any distribution treated as made on the same date as that on which a dividend was paid, means such part of that amount as bears to the whole of it the same proportion as the amount of that dividend bears to the total amount of the dividends mentioned in that paragraph.

(4) No advance corporation tax which a subsidiary is treated as having paid by virtue of subsection (2) above shall be set against the subsidiary's liability to corporation tax under

subsection (3) of section 239; but in determining for the purposes of subsections (3) and (4) of that section what (if any) amount of surplus advance corporation tax there is in any accounting period of a subsidiary, an amount so treated as having been paid shall be set against its liability to corporation tax before any advance corporation tax paid in respect of any distribution made by the subsidiary.

(5) No advance corporation tax which a subsidiary is treated as having paid by virtue of subsection (2) above shall be set against the subsidiary's liability to corporation tax for any accounting period in which, or in any part of which, it was not a subsidiary of the surrendering company [unless throughout that period or part both companies were subsidiaries of a third company][1].

(6) Any claim under this section shall be made within six years after the end of the accounting period to which it relates and shall require the consent, notified to the inspector in such form as the Board may require, of the subsidiary or subsidiaries concerned.

(7) No amount of advance corporation tax which has been dealt with under section 239(3) shall be available for the purposes of a claim under this section; and no amount of advance corporation tax the benefit of which has been surrendered under this section shall be treated for the purposes of that section as advance corporation tax paid by the surrendering company.

(8) A payment made by a subsidiary to a surrendering company in pursuance of an agreement between them as respects the surrender of the benefit of an amount of advance corporation tax, being a payment not exceeding that amount—

(*a*) shall not be taken into account in computing profits or losses of either company for corporation tax purposes; and
(*b*) shall not for any of the purposes of the Corporation Tax Acts be regarded as a distribution or a charge on income.

(9) References in this section to dividends shall be construed as including references to distributions made on the redemption, repayment or purchase by a company of its own shares, and references to the payment of dividends shall be construed accordingly.

(10) References in this section to a company apply only to bodies corporate resident in the United Kingdom; and, subject to subsection (11) below, for the purposes of this section the question whether one body corporate is the subsidiary of another shall be determined as a question whether it is a 51 per cent. subsidiary of that other, except that that other shall be treated as not being the owner—

(*a*) of any share capital which it owns directly in a body corporate if a profit on the sale of the shares would be treated as a trading receipt of its trade; or
(*b*) of any share capital which it owns indirectly, and which is owned directly by a body corporate for which a profit on the sale of the shares would be a trading receipt; or
(*c*) of any share capital which it owns directly or indirectly in a body corporate not resident in the United Kingdom.

(11) Notwithstanding that, apart from this subsection, one company ("the subsidiary company") would at any time, by virtue of subsection (10) above, be a subsidiary of another company ("the parent company") for the purposes of this section, the subsidiary company shall not be treated at that time as a subsidiary for those purposes—

(*a*) if arrangements are in existence by virtue of which any person has or could obtain, or any persons together have or could obtain, control of the subsidiary company but not of the parent company; and
(*b*) unless the following conditions are also fulfilled, namely—

(i) that the parent company is beneficially entitled to more than 50 per cent. of any profits available for distribution to equity holders of the subsidiary company; and
(ii) that the parent company would be beneficially entitled to more than 50 per cent. of any assets of the subsidiary company available for distribution to its equity holders on a winding up.

In this subsection "control" has the meaning given by section 840 and "arrangements" means arrangements of any kind, whether in writing or not.

(12) Where by virtue of any enactment a Minister of the Crown or Northern Ireland department has power to give directions to a statutory body as to the disposal of assets belonging to, or to a subsidiary of, that body, the existence of that power shall not be regarded as constituting (or as having at any time constituted) an arrangement within the meaning of subsection (11) above.

(13) Schedule 18 shall have effect for the purposes of subsection (11)(*b*) above, subject to the following modifications—

(*a*) for any reference to section 413(7) to (10) there shall be substituted a reference to subsection (11)(*b*) above; and

(*b*) paragraph 7(1) shall be omitted and for any reference to the relevant accounting period there shall be substituted a reference to the accounting period current at the time in question.

Former enactments.—Sub-s. (1): FA 1972, s. 92(1); FA 1973, Sch. 13, para. 2.
Sub-s. (2): FA 1972, s. 92(2); FA 1973, Sch. 13, paras. 3, 4.
Sub-s. (3): FA 1972, s. 92(3).
Sub-s. (4): FA 1972, s. 92(3A); FA 1973, Sch. 13, para. 5.
Sub-s. (5): FA 1972, s. 92(4).
Sub-s. (6): FA 1972, s. 92(5); FA 1973, Sch. 13, para. 6.
Sub-s. (7): FA 1972, s. 92(6).
Sub-s. (8): FA 1972, s. 92(7).
Sub-s. (9): FA 1972, s. 92(7A); FA 1982, s. 55.
Sub-s. (10): FA 1972, s. 92(8); FA 1973, Sch. 13, para. 7.
Sub-s. (11): FA 1972, s. 92(9), (10); FA 1973, s. 32(6), Sch. 13, para. 8; FA 1981, s. 47.
Sub-s. (12): FA 1981, s. 47.
Sub-s. (13): FA 1972, s. 92(11); FA 1973, Sch. 13, para. 8.
Cross references.—See FA 1989, s. 157(1), (6) (reckonable date for the purpose of calculating interest on corporation tax becoming payable as a result of a claim under this section made after 13 March 1989, but subject to s. 157(6)—see below),
s. 157(6) (FA 1989, s. 157 not to have effect in relation to corporation tax for accounting periods ending after an appointed day).
Amendments.—[1] Words in sub-s. (5) inserted by FA 1989, s. 97 in relation to accounting periods ending after 13 March 1989.

241. Calculation of ACT where company receives franked investment income

(1) Where in any accounting period a company receives franked investment income the company shall not be liable to pay advance corporation tax in respect of qualifying distributions made by it in that period unless the amount of the franked payments made by it in that period exceeds the amount of that income.

(2) If in an accounting period there is such an excess, advance corporation tax shall be payable on an amount which, when the advance corporation tax payable thereon is added to it, is equal to the excess.

(3) If the amount of franked investment income received by a company in an accounting period exceeds the amount of the franked payments made by it in that period the excess shall be carried forward to the next accounting period and treated for the purposes of this section (including any further application of this subsection) as franked investment income received by the company in that period.

(4) Without prejudice to section 238(5), Schedule 13 shall apply for the purpose of regulating the manner in which effect is to be given to subsections (1) to (3) above.

(5) No franked investment income shall be used to frank distributions of a company (that is to say, used in accordance with this section and Schedule 13 so as to relieve the company from, or obtain repayment of, advance corporation tax for which the company would otherwise be liable) if the amount of the tax credit comprised in it has been paid under subsection (2) of section 231; and no payment shall be made under that subsection in respect of the tax credit comprised in franked investment income which has been so used.

Former enactment.—FA 1972, s. 89(1)–(5).

242. Set-off of losses etc. against surplus of franked investment income

(1) Where a company has a surplus of franked investment income for any accounting period—

(*a*) the company may, on making a claim for the purpose, require that the amount of the surplus shall for all or any of the purposes mentioned in subsection (2) below be treated as if it were a like amount of profits chargeable to corporation tax; and

(*b*) subject to subsection (4) below, the provisions mentioned in subsection (2) below shall apply in accordance with this section to reduce the amount of the surplus for purposes of section 241(3); and

(*c*) the company shall be entitled to have paid to it the amount of the tax credit comprised in the amount of franked investment income by which the surplus is so reduced.

(2) The purposes for which a claim may be made under subsection (1) above are those of—

(a) the setting of trading losses against total profits under section 393(2);
(b) the deduction of charges on income under section 338 or paragraph 5 of Schedule 4;
(c) the deduction of expenses of management under section 75 or 76;
(d) the setting of certain capital allowances against total profits under section 74(3) of the 1968 Act;
(e) the setting of losses against income under section 573(2).

(3) Where a company makes a claim under this section for any accounting period, the reduction falling to be made in profits of that accounting period shall be made, as far as may be, in profits chargeable to corporation tax rather than in the amount treated as profits so chargeable under this section.

(4) Where a claim under this section relates to section 393(2) or 573(2) of this Act or to section 74(3) of the 1968 Act and an accounting period of the company falls partly before and partly within the time mentioned in that subsection, then—

(a) the restriction imposed by section 393(3) or 573(3) of this Act or by section 74(4) of the 1968 Act on the amount of the relief shall be applied only to any relief to be given apart from this section, and shall be applied without regard to any amount treated as profits of the accounting period under this section; but
(b) relief under this section shall be given only against a part of the amount so treated proportionate to the part of the accounting period falling within that time.

(5) Where—

(a) on a claim made under this section for any accounting period relief is given in respect of the whole or part of any loss incurred in a trade, or of any amount which could be treated as a loss under section 393(9); and
(b) in a later accounting period the franked payments made by the company exceed its franked investment income;

then (unless the company has ceased to carry on the trade or to be within the charge to corporation tax in respect of it) the company shall, for the purposes of section 393(1), be treated as having, in the accounting period ending immediately before the beginning of the later accounting period mentioned in paragraph (b) above, incurred a loss equal to whichever is the lesser of —

(i) the excess referred to in paragraph (b) above; and
(ii) the amount in respect of which relief was given as mentioned in paragraph (a) above or so much of that amount as remains after deduction of any part of it dealt with under this subsection in relation to an earlier accounting period.

(6) Subject to subsection (7) below, subsection (5) above shall apply, with the necessary adaptations—

(a) in relation to relief given in respect of management expenses; and
(b) in relation to relief given in respect of capital allowances; and
(c) in relation to relief given in respect of losses under section 573(2);

as it applies in relation to relief given in respect of a loss (the reference to the company ceasing to be within the charge to corporation tax in respect of the trade being construed as a reference to its ceasing to be within that charge at all, and as respects the relief mentioned in paragraph (c) above, the reference to the purposes of section 393(1) being construed as a reference to the purposes of corporation tax on chargeable gains).

(7) Any amount which may be dealt with under subsection (5) above as a loss shall be so dealt with rather than under subsection (6) above, except in so far as the company concerned otherwise elects.

(8) The time limits for claims under this section shall be as follows—

(a) if and so far as the purpose for which the claim is made is the setting of trading losses against total profits under section 393(2), two years from the end of the accounting period in which the trading loss is incurred;
(b) if and so far as the purpose for which the claim is made is the deduction of charges on income under section 338 or paragraph 5 of Schedule 4 or of expenses of management under section 75 or 76, six years from the end of the accounting period in which the charges were paid or the expenses of management were incurred;
(c) if and so far as the purpose for which the claim is made is the setting of capital allowances against total profits under section 74(3) of the 1968 Act, two years from the end of the accounting period for which the capital allowances fall to be made;
(d) if and so far as the purpose for which the claim is made is the setting of a loss against

income under section 573(2), two years from the end of the accounting period in which the loss was incurred.

(9) For the purposes of a claim under this section for any accounting period, the surplus of franked investment income for that accounting period shall be calculated without regard to the part, if any, carried forward from an earlier accounting period; and for the purposes of subsection (5) above franked investment income which by virtue of section 241(5) cannot be used to frank distributions of a company shall be left out of account.

Former enactments.—Sub-s. (1): TA 1970, s. 254(1); FA 1972, Sch. 15, Pt. I.
Sub-s. (2): TA 1970, s. 254(2); FA 1972, Sch. 15, Pt I; FA 1981, s. 37(2); FA 1984, Sch. 9, para. 13.
Sub-s. (3): TA 1970, s. 254(3); FA 1972, Sch. 15, Pt. I.
Sub-s. (4): TA 1970, s. 254(4); FA 1972, Sch. 15. Pt. I; FA 1981, s. 37(3).
Sub-s. (5): TA 1970, s. 254(5); FA 1972, Sch. 15, Pt. I.
Sub-ss. (6), (7): TA 1970, s. 254(6); FA 1972, Sch. 15, Pt. I; FA 1981, s. 37(4).
Sub-s. (8): TA 1970, s. 254(7); FA 1972, Sch. 15, Pt. I; FA 1981, s. 37(5); FA 1984, Sch. 9, para. 13.
Sub-s. (9): TA 1970, s. 254(8); FA 1972, Sch. 15, Pt. I.

243. Set-off of loss brought forward, or terminal loss

(1) Where a company has a surplus of franked investment income for any accounting period, the company, instead of or in addition to making a claim under section 242, may on making a claim for the purpose require that the surplus shall be taken into account for relief under section 393(1) or 394, up to the amount of franked investment income for the accounting period which, if chargeable to corporation tax, would have been so taken into account by virtue of section 393(8); and (subject to the restriction to that amount of franked investment income) the following subsections shall have effect where the company makes a claim under this section for any accounting period.

(2) The amount to which the claim relates shall for the purposes of the claim be treated as trading income of the accounting period.

(3) The reduction falling to be made in trading income of an accounting period shall be made as far as possible in trading income chargeable to corporation tax rather than in the amount treated as trading income so chargeable under this section.

(4) If the claim relates to section 393(1), section 242(5) shall apply in relation to it.

(5) If the claim relates to section 394 and an accounting period of the company falls partly outside the three years mentioned in subsection (1) of that section, then—

(*a*) the restriction imposed by subsection (2) of that section on the amount of the reduction that may be made in the trading income of that period shall be applied only to any relief to be given apart from this section, and shall be applied without regard to any amount treated as trading income of the accounting period by virtue of this section, but

(*b*) relief under this section shall be given only against a part of the amount so treated proportionate to the part of the accounting period falling within the three years in question.

(6) The time limits for claims under this section shall be as follows—

(*a*) if and so far as the purpose for which the claim is made is the allowance of relief under section 393(1), six years from the end of the accounting period for which the claim is made,

(*b*) if and so far as the purpose for which the claim is made is the allowance of relief under section 394, six years from the time when the company ceases to carry on the trade.

(7) For the purposes of a claim under this section for any accounting period the surplus of franked investment income for that period shall be calculated without regard to the part, if any, carried forward from an earlier accounting period.

Former enactments.—TA 1970, s. 255; FA 1972, Sch. 15, Pt. I.

244. Further provisions relating to claims under section 242 or 243

(1) Without prejudice to section 242(9) or 243(7), the surplus of franked investment income for an accounting period for which a claim is made under either of those sections shall be

calculated without regard to any part of that surplus which, when the claim is made, has been used to frank distributions made by the company in a later accounting period.

(2) Where in consequence of a claim under either section 242 or section 243 for any accounting period a company is entitled to payment of a sum in respect of tax credit—

(a) an amount equal to that sum shall be deducted from any advance corporation tax which apart from this subsection would fall, under section 239, to be set against the company's liability to corporation tax for the next accounting period or the benefit of which could be surrendered under section 240; and

(b) if that amount exceeds that advance corporation tax or there is no such advance corporation tax, that excess or that amount (as the case may be) shall be carried forward and similarly deducted in relation to the following accounting period and so on.

Former enactments.—FA 1972, s. 90(2), (3) FA 1973, Sch. 13, para. 9.

245. Calculation etc. of ACT on change of ownership of company

(1) This section applies if—

(a) within any period of three years there is both a change in the ownership of a company and (either earlier or later in that period, or at the same time) a major change in the nature or conduct of a trade or business carried by the company; or

(b) at any time after the scale of the activities in a trade or business carried on by a company has become small or negligible, and before any considerable revival of the trade or business, there is a change in the ownership of the company.

(2) Sections 239 and 241 and Schedule 13 shall apply to an accounting period in which the change of ownership occurs as if the part ending with the change of ownership, and the part after, were two separate accounting periods; and for that purpose the profits of the company charged to corporation tax for the accounting period (as defined in section 239(6)) shall be apportioned between those parts.

(3) No advance corporation tax paid by the company in respect of distributions made in an accounting period beginning before the change of ownership shall be treated under section 239(4) as paid by it in respect of distributions made in an accounting period ending after the change of ownership; and this subsection shall apply to an accounting period in which the change of ownership occurs as if the part ending with the change of ownership, and the part after, were two separate accounting periods.

(4) In subsection (1) above "a major change in the nature or conduct of a trade or business" includes—

(a) a major change in the type of property dealt in, or services or facilities provided, in the trade or business; or

(b) a major change in customers, outlets or markets of the trade or business; or

(c) a change whereby the company ceases to be a trading company and becomes an investment company or vice versa; or

(d) where the company is an investment company, a major change in the nature of the investments held by the company;

and this section applies even if the change is the result of a gradual process which began outside the period of three years mentioned in subsection (1)(a) above.

(5) In this section—

"trading company" means a company whose business consists wholly or mainly of the carrying on of a trade or trades;

"investment company" means a company (other than a holding company) whose business consists wholly or mainly in the making of investments and the principal part of whose income is derived therefrom;

"holding company" means a company whose business consists wholly or mainly in the holding of shares or securities of companies which are its 90 per cent. subsidiaries and which are trading companies.

(6) Subsection (3) above applies to advance corporation tax which a company is treated as having paid by virtue of section 240 as it applies to advance corporation tax which it has actually paid.

(7) Sections 768(8) and (9) and 769 shall apply also for the purposes of this section and as if

in subsection (3) of section 769 the reference to the benefit of the losses were a reference to the benefit of advance corporation tax.

Former enactments.—FA 1972, s. 101; F(No. 2)A 1987, s. 74(5).

[245A. Restriction on application of section 240 in certain circumstances

(1) This section applies if—

(a) there is a change in the ownership of a company ("the relevant company");

(b) by virtue of section 240 the relevant company is treated as having paid an amount of advance corporation tax in respect of a distribution made by it at any time before the change; and

(c) within the period of six years beginning three years before the change, there is a major change in the nature or conduct of a trade or business of the company which is for the purposes of section 240 the surrendering company in relation to that amount.

(2) No advance corporation tax which the relevant company is treated by virtue of section 240 as having paid in respect of a distribution made by it in an accounting period beginning before the change of ownership shall be treated under section 239(4) as paid by it in respect of distributions made in an accounting period ending after the change of ownership; and this subsection shall apply to an accounting period in which the change of ownership occurs as if the part ending with the change of ownership, and the part after, were two separate accounting periods.

(3) Subsections (4) and (5) of section 245 shall apply for the purposes of this section and as if the reference in subsection (4) of section 245 to the period of three years mentioned in subsection (1)(a) of that section were a reference to the period mentioned in subsection (1)(c) above.

(4) Sections 768(8) and (9) and 769 shall apply also for the purposes of this section and as if in subsection (3) of section 769 the reference to the benefit of losses were a reference to the benefit of advance corporation tax.]

Amendments.—¹ This section inserted by FA 1989, s. 98 and has effect where the change in the ownership of the relevant company occurs after 13 March 1989.

[245B. Restriction on set-off where asset transferred after change in ownership of company

(1) Subsection (4) below applies if—

(a) there is a change of ownership of a company ("the relevant company");

(b) any advance corporation tax paid by the relevant company in respect of distributions made by it in an accounting period beginning before the change is treated under section 239(4) as paid by it in respect of distributions made by it in an accounting period ending after the change;

(c) after the change the relevant company acquires an asset from another company in such circumstances that section 273(1) of the Taxes Act 1970 applies to the acquisition; and

(d) a chargeable gain accrues to the relevant company on the disposal of the asset within the period of three years beginning with the change of ownership.

(2) Subsection (1)(b) above shall apply to an accounting period in which the change of ownership occurs as if the part ending with the change of ownership, and the part after, were two separate accounting periods.

(3) For the purposes of subsection (1)(d) above an asset acquired by the relevant company as mentioned in subsection (1)(c) above shall be treated as the same as an asset owned at a later time by that company if the value of the second asset is derived in whole or in part from the first asset, and in particular where the second asset is a freehold, and the first asset was a leasehold and the lessee has acquired the reversion.

(4) In relation to the accounting period in which the chargeable gain accrues to the relevant company ("the relevant period"), section 239 shall have effect as if the limit imposed by subsection (2) of that section on the amount of advance corporation tax to be set against the relevant company's liability to corporation tax were reduced by whichever is the lesser of—

(a) the amount of advance corporation tax that would have been payable (apart from section 241) in respect of a distribution made at the end of the relevant period of an

amount which, together with the advance corporation tax so payable in respect of it, is equal to the chargeable gain, and
(b) the amount of surplus advance corporation tax in relation to the accounting period which by virtue of subsection (2) above is treated for the purposes of subsection (1)(b) above as ending with the change of ownership.

(5) Sections 768(8) and (9) and 769 shall apply also for the purposes of this section and as if in subsection (3) of section 769 the reference to the benefit of losses were a reference to the benefit of advance corporation tax.][1]

Amendments.—[1] This section inserted by FA 1989, s. 98 and has effect where the change in the ownership of the relevant company occurs after 13 March 1989.

246. Charge of ACT at previous rate until new rate fixed, and changes of rate

(1) If, at the beginning of any financial year, the basic rate percentage for the appropriate year of assessment has not been determined (whether under the Provisional Collection of Taxes Act 1968 or otherwise), then, subject to subsection (2) below, advance corporation tax in respect of distributions made in that financial year shall be payable under Schedule 13 and may be assessed under the Schedule according to the rate of advance corporation tax fixed for the previous financial year.

(2) Subsection (1) above does not apply with respect to any distribution made in a financial year after—
   (a) the date on which is determined the basic rate percentage for the appropriate year of assessment; or
   (b) 5th August in that year,
whichever is the earlier.

(3) If a rate of advance corporation tax for any financial year is not fixed, under section 14(3) or any other enactment, or if advance corporation tax for any financial year is charged otherwise than as it has been paid or assessed, the necessary adjustment shall be made by discharge or repayment of tax or by a further assessment.

(4) In subsections (1) and (2) above "the basis rate percentage for the appropriate year of assessment", in relation to a financial year, means the percentage at which income tax at the basic rate is charged for the year of assessment which begins on 6th April in that financial year.

(5) Where different rates of advance corporation tax are in force in different parts of an accounting period, the maximum set-off permitted for that accounting period under section 239(2) shall be determined by apportioning the profits of the company charged to corporation tax for that period (as defined in section 239(6)) between the different parts of the period, calculating the maximum for each part as if it were a separate accounting period and aggregating the result.

(6) Where the rate of advance corporation tax for any financial year differs from the rate last fixed—
   (a) any advance corporation tax payable in respect of a distribution made in that financial year on or before 5th April shall be calculated according to the rate last fixed and—
      (i) the definition of "franked payment" in section 238(1), and
      (ii) section 231(1) and Schedule 13,
   shall have effect in relation to the distribution as if the rate for that year were the same as the rate last fixed;
   (b) if a distribution is made on or before 5th April in an accounting period which extends beyond 5th April in that year and another distribution is made, or franked investment income is received, in that period after that date, then—
      (i) the company's liability for advance corporation tax,
      (ii) the amount of any such tax, and
      (iii) the amount of any surplus of franked investment income,
   for that accounting period, shall be determined under section 241 and Schedule 13 as if

the part of the accounting period ending with, and the part of it beginning after, that date were separate accounting periods.

Former enactments.—Sub-ss. (1)–(3): FA 1986, s. 17(2)–(4).
Sub-s. (4): FA 1986, s. 17(1).
Sub-ss. (5), (6): FA 1972, s. 103(4), (5); FA 1973, Sch. 14, para. 5; F(No. 2)A 1987, s. 74(5).

construed (so that if the two companies are members of the same group in the surrendering company's accounting period, they must under that section also be members of the same group in any corresponding accounting period of the claimant company);

(c) references in section 408 to profits, and amounts to be set off against the profits, shall be so construed (so that an amount apportioned under subsection (2) above to a component accounting period may fall to be reduced under subsection (2) of that section).

(4) Subsections (2) and (3) above shall apply with the necessary modifications where a company begins or ceases to fulfil the conditions for relief for a consortium, either as a surrendering company or as a claimant company, as it applies where two companies become or cease to be members of the same group except that, in a case where—

(a) the surrendering company is owned by a consortium and two or more members of the consortium claim relief in respect of losses or other amounts of the surrendering company, or

(b) the claimant company is owned by a consortium and claims relief in respect of losses or other amounts of two or more members of the consortium,

the basis of apportionment which is adopted under subsection (2) above in relation to the losses or other amounts or, as the case may be, the total profits of the true accounting period of the company owned by the consortium shall be the same on each of the claims.

(5) In subsection (6) below—

"the primary claim" means a consortium claim made in respect of the loss or other amount of a relevant accounting period of a company owned by a consortium;
"the principal surrendering company" means that company; and
"the principal accounting period" means that accounting period.

(6) In any case where—

(a) the company making the primary claim or, if that claim is made by virtue of section 406(2), the company which is the link company for the purposes of that subsection was not a member of the consortium throughout the whole of the principal accounting period; and

(b) on or after the date on which the primary claim is made, a consortium claim is made which—

(i) is in respect of the loss or other amount of an accounting period of a surrendering company (being a company owned by the consortium referred to in paragraph (a) above, other than the principal surrendering company); and

(ii) is made by the company making the primary claim or, in a case where it or the primary claim is made by virtue of section 406(2), is made by any member of the group in question other than the company making the primary claim;

and the accounting period to which the claim relates falls, in whole or in part, within the principal accounting period; and

(c) at any time during the principal accounting period the surrendering company is a member of the same group of companies as the principal surrendering company;

no relief shall be allowed on the primary claim, or, as the case may be, any relief which was so allowed shall be withdrawn.

(7) In any case where—

(a) a company ("the principal claimant company") owned by a consortium makes a consortium claim ("the principal claim") in respect of the loss or other amount of an accounting period of a member of the consortium or, if the principal claim is made by virtue of section 406(5), of a company which, in relation to that member of the consortium, is a group member, within the meaning of that section; and

(b) the member of the consortium concerned (whether as the surrendering company or the link company, within the meaning of section 406) was not a member of the consortium throughout the whole of that accounting period; and

(c) on or after the date on which the principal claim is made, a consortium claim is made—

(i) by a company, other than the principal claimant company, which is owned by the consortium and which is a member of the same group of companies as the principal claimant company; and

(ii) which relates to the loss or other amount of an accounting period of the consortium member referred to in paragraph (b) above or of a company which in relation to that consortium member is a group member, within the meaning of section 406;

relief derived from a subsequent accounting period is to be set off shall include any group relief for that first-mentioned accounting period.

Former enactments.—Sub-ss. (1)(*a*), (*b*): TA 1970, s. 260(1), (2).
Sub-s. (2)(*a*): TA 1970, s. 260(3)(*a*), (*d*).
Sub-s. (2)(*b*): TA 1970, s. 260(3)(*b*).
Sub-s. (3): TA 1970, s. 260(4).

408. Corresponding accounting periods

(1) For the purposes of group relief an accounting period of the claimant company which falls wholly or partly within an accounting period of the surrendering company corresponds to that accounting period.

(2) If an accounting period of the surrendering company and a corresponding accounting period of the claimant company do not coincide—

(*a*) the amount which may be set off against the total profits of the claimant company for the corresponding accounting period shall be reduced by applying the fraction—

$$\frac{A}{B}$$

(if that fraction is less than unity); and
(*b*) the total profits of the claimant company for the corresponding accounting period shall be reduced by applying the fraction—

$$\frac{A}{C}$$

(if that fraction is less than unity);

where—

A is the length of the period common to the two accounting periods;
B is the length of the accounting period of the surrendering company;
C is the length of the corresponding accounting period of the claimant company.

Former enactment.—TA 1970, s. 261.

409. Companies joining or leaving group or consortium

(1) Subject to the following provisions of this section, group relief shall be given if, and only if, the surrendering company and the claimant company are members of the same group, or fulfil the conditions for relief for a consortium, throughout the whole of the surrendering company's accounting period to which the claim relates, and throughout the whole of the corresponding accounting period of the claimant company.

(2) Where on any occasion two companies become or cease to be members of the same group, then, for the purposes specified in subsection (3) below, it shall be assumed as respects each company that—

(*a*) on that occasion (unless a true accounting period of the company begins or ends then) an accounting period of the company ends and a new one begins, the new accounting period to end with the end of the true accounting period (unless before then there is a further break under this subsection); and
(*b*) the losses or other amounts of the true accounting period are apportioned to the component accounting periods; and
(*c*) the amount of total profits for the true accounting period of the company against which group relief may be allowed in accordance with section 407(1) is also apportioned to the component accounting periods;

and an apportionment under this subsection shall be on a time basis according to the respective lengths of the component accounting periods except that, if it appears that that method would work unreasonably or unjustly, such other method shall be used as appears just and reasonable.

(3) Where the one company is the surrendering company and the other company is the claimant company—

(*a*) references in section 403 to accounting periods, to profits, and to losses, allowances, expenses of management or charges on income of the surrendering company shall be construed in accordance with subsection (2) above;
(*b*) references in subsection (1) above and section 408 to accounting periods shall be so

eligible for relief of a relevant accounting period of a consortium company, a group member may make any consortium claim which could be made by the link company; and the fraction which is appropriate under section 403(9) where a group member is the claimant company shall be the same as that which would be appropriate if the link company were the claimant company.

(3) A group member may not, by virtue of subsection (2) above, make a consortium claim in respect of the loss or other amount of any accounting period of a consortium company unless the claimant company was a member of the group concerned throughout the whole of the accounting period or, as the case may be, each accounting period of the link company which, if that company were making the claim, would be a corresponding accounting period in relation to that accounting period of the consortium company.

(4) The maximum amount of relief which, in the aggregate, may be claimed by group members and the link company by consortium claims relating to the loss or other amount of a relevant accounting period of a consortium company shall not exceed the relief which could have been claimed by the link company (disregarding any deficiency of profits) if subsections (2) and (3) above had not been enacted.

(5) Subject to subsections (6) to (8) below, where a group member has for a relevant accounting period a loss or other amount available for relief, a consortium company may make any claim in respect of that loss or other amount which it could make if the group member were a member of the consortium at all times when the link company was such a member, but not at any other time.

(6) The fraction which is appropriate under section 403(9) in relation to a consortium claim made by virtue of subsection (5) above shall be the same as that which would be appropriate if the link company were the surrendering company, except that the accounting period in respect of which the member's share in the consortium is to be ascertained shall be that of the group member which is in fact the surrendering company.

(7) A consortium company may not, by virtue of subsection (5) above, make a consortium claim in respect of the loss or other amount of any accounting period of a group member unless the group member was a member of the group in question throughout the whole of that accounting period.

(8) For any accounting period of a consortium company ("the claimant company's accounting period") the maximum amount of relief which, in the aggregate, may be claimed by that company by consortium claims relating to the losses or other amounts of accounting periods of the link company and group members shall not exceed that fraction of the total profits of the claimant company's accounting period which would be brought into account under section 403(9)(*b*) on a consortium claim in respect of which—

    (*a*) the link company was the surrendering company; and
    (*b*) the link company's accounting period was the same as the claimant company's accounting period.

Former enactments.—Sub-s. (1): FA 1985, Sch 9, paras. 5(1), 6(1).
Sub-ss. (2)–(4): FA 1985, Sch. 9, para. 5(2)–(4).
Sub-ss. (5)–(8): FA 1985, Sch. 9, para. 6(2)–(5).

407. Relationship between group relief and other relief

(1) Group relief for an accounting period shall be allowed as a deduction against the claimant company's total profits for the period—

    (*a*) before reduction by any relief derived from a subsequent accounting period, but
    (*b*) as reduced by any other relief from tax (including relief in respect of charges on income under section 338(1)) determined on the assumption that the company makes all relevant claims under section 393(2) of this Act and section 74(3) of the 1968 Act (set-off of capital allowances against total profits).

(2) For the purposes of this section "relief derived from a subsequent accounting period" means—

    (*a*) relief under section 393(2) or 394 in respect of a loss incurred in an accounting period after the accounting period the profits of which are being computed; and
    (*b*) relief under section 74(3) of the 1968 Act in respect of capital allowances falling to be made for an accounting period after the accounting period the profits of which are being computed.

(3) The reductions to be made in total profits of an accounting period against which any

(iii) the paying of those charges by the company is its main activity or one of its main activities.

Former enactment.—F(No. 2)A 1987, s. 63.

405. Claims relating to losses etc. of members of both group and consortium

(1) For the purposes of a consortium claim in respect of the loss or other amount of any relevant accounting period of a group/consortium company, that loss or other amount shall be treated as reduced (or, as the case may be, extinguished) by first deducting therefrom the potential relief attributable to group claims.

(2) Subject to subsection (3) below, in relation to the loss or other amount of a relevant accounting period of a group/consortium company, the potential relief attributable to group claims is the aggregate amount of group relief that would be claimed if every company which, as a member of the same group of companies as the group/consortium company, could make a group claim in respect of that loss or other amount made such a claim for an amount which, when set against the claimant company's total profits for its corresponding accounting period, would equal those profits.

(3) Where for any accounting period another member of the group of companies of which the group/consortium company is a member has a loss or other amount available for relief and one or more group claims is or are in fact made in respect of that loss or other amount, account shall be taken of the relief so claimed before determining (in relation to the loss or other amount of the group/consortium company) the potential relief attributable to group claims under subsection (2) above.

(4) In any case where—
   (a) a consortium claim is made by a group/consortium company in respect of a loss or other amount of an accounting period of a member of the consortium, and
   (b) the corresponding accounting period of the group/consortium company is a relevant accounting period,

the total profits of the corresponding accounting period of the group/consortium company against a fraction of which that loss or other amount may be set off (in accordance with section 403(9)(b)) shall be treated as reduced (or as the case may be extinguished) by deducting therefrom the potential relief available to the group/consortium company by way of group claims.

(5) Subject to subsection (6) below, in relation to a relevant accounting period of a group/consortium company, the potential relief available to the company by way of group claims is the maximum amount of group relief that could be claimed by the company for that accounting period on group claims relating to the losses or other amounts available for relief of other members of the group of companies of which the group/consortium company is a member.

(6) Where another member of the group of companies of which the group/consortium company is a member in fact makes one or more group claims in respect of losses or other amounts of other members of the group, account shall be taken of the relief already claimed by that company in determining the potential relief available to the group/consortium company by way of group claims under subsection (5) above.

Former enactments.—Sub-ss. (1)–(3): FA 1985, Sch. 9, para. 2.
Sub-ss. (4)–(6): FA 1985, Sch. 9, para. 3.

406. Claims relating to losses etc. of consortium company or group member

(1) In this section—
   (a) "link company" means a company which is a member of a consortium and is also a member of a group of companies; and
   (b) "consortium company", in relation to a link company, means a company owned by the consortium of which the link company is a member; and
   (c) "group member", in relation to a link company, means a company which is a member of the group of which the link company is also a member but is not itself a member of the consortium of which the link company is a member.

(2) Subject to subsections (3) and (4) below, where the link company could (disregarding any deficiency of profits) make a consortium claim in respect of the loss or other amount

404. Limitation of group relief in relation to certain dual resident companies

(1) Notwithstanding any other provision of this Chapter, no loss or other amount shall be available for set off by way of group relief in accordance with section 403 if, in the material accounting period of the company which would otherwise be the surrendering company, that company is for the purposes of this section a dual resident investing company.

(2) In this section "the material accounting period" means, according to the kind of group relief which would be appropriate, the accounting period—

(*a*) in which the loss is incurred; or
(*b*) for which the capital allowances fall to be made; or
(*c*) for which the expenses of management are disbursed; or
(*d*) for which the amount is paid by way of charges on income;

but subsection (1) above does not have effect unless the material accounting period begins on or after 1st April 1987.

(3) In Schedule 17—

(*a*) Part I has effect where an accounting period of a company in which it is a dual resident investing company begins before and ends on or after 1st April 1987 and references in subsections (1) and (2) above to the material accounting period shall be construed accordingly; and
(*b*) Part II has effect with respect to the time at which certain interest and other payments are to be treated as paid.

(4) A company is for the purposes of this section a dual resident company in any accounting period in which—

(*a*) it is resident in the United Kingdom; and
(*b*) it is also within a charge to tax under the laws of a territory outside the United Kingdom—

(i) because it derives its status as a company from those laws; or
(ii) because its place of management is in that territory; or
(iii) because under those laws it is for any other reason regarded as a resident in that territory for the purposes of that charge.

(5) In any accounting period throughout which it is not a trading company, a dual resident company is for the purposes of this section an investing company.

(6) In any accounting period of a dual resident company in which it is a trading company, the company is nevertheless for the purposes of this section an investing company if—

(*a*) in that period it carries on a trade of such a description that its main function or one of its main functions consists of all or any of the following, namely—

(i) acquiring and holding, directly or indirectly, shares, securities or investments of any other description, including interests in companies (resident outside, as well as in, the United Kingdom) with which the dual resident company is connected, within the terms of section 839;
(ii) making payments which, by virtue of any enactment, are charges on income for the purposes of corporation tax;
(iii) making payments (of interest or other sums) which are similar to those referred to in sub-paragraph (ii) above but which are deductible in computing the profits of the company for the purposes of corporation tax;
(iv) obtaining funds (by borrowing or in any other manner whatsoever) for the purpose of, or otherwise in connection with, any of the activities referred to in sub-paragraphs (i) to (iii) above; or

(*b*) it does not fall within paragraph (*a*) above, but in that accounting period it carries on all or any of the activities referred to in sub-paragraphs (i) to (iv) of that paragraph and does so—

(i) to an extent which does not appear to be justified by any trade which it does carry on; or
(ii) for a purpose which does not appear to be appropriate to any such trade; or

(*c*) in that period—

(i) the amount paid by the company by way of charges on income exceeds its profits of the period, determined as mentioned in section 403(8); and
(ii) those charges include an amount which falls to be treated as a charge on income by virtue of section 78(2) or paragraph 5(2) of Schedule 4; and

(2) Subsection (1) above shall not apply to so much of a loss as is excluded from subsection (2) of section 393 by subsection (5) of that section or by section 397.

(3) Subject to the provisions of this Chapter, if for any accounting period any capital allowances fall to be made to the surrendering company which—

   (a) are to be given by discharge or repayment of tax, and
   (b) are to be available primarily against a specified class of income,

so much of the amount of those allowances (exclusive of any carried forward from an earlier period) as exceeds its income of the relevant class arising in that accounting period (before deduction of any losses of any other period or of any capital allowances) may be set off for purposes of corporation tax against the total profits of the claimant company for its corresponding accounting period.

(4) Subject to the provisions of this Chapter, if for any accounting period the surrendering company (being an investment company) may under subsection (1) of section 75 deduct as expenses of management any amount disbursed for that accounting period, so much of that amount (exclusive of any amount deductible only by virtue of subsection (3) of that section) as exceeds the company's profits of that accounting period may be set off for purposes of corporation tax against the total profits of the claimant company (whether an investment company or not) for its corresponding accounting period.

(5) The surrendering company's profits of the period shall be determined for the purposes of subsection (4) above without any deduction under section 75 and without regard to any deduction falling to be made in respect of losses or allowances of any other period.

(6) References in subsections (4) and (5) above to section 75 do not include references to that section as applied by section 76 to companies carrying on life assurance business.

(7) Subject to the provisions of this Chapter and section 494(4), if in any accounting period the surrendering company has paid any amount by way of charges on income, so much of that amount as exceeds its profits of the period may be set off for the purposes of corporation tax against the total profits of the claimant company for its corresponding accounting period.

(8) The surrendering company's profits of the period shall be determined for the purposes of subsection (7) above without regard to any deduction falling to be made in respect of losses or allowances of any other period, or to expenses of management deductible only by virtue of section 75(3).

(9) In applying any of the preceding subsections in the case of a consortium claim—

   (a) where the claimant company is a member of a consortium, only a fraction of the loss referred to in subsection (1) above, or of the excess referred to in subsection (3), (4) or (7) above, as the case may be, may be set off under the subsection in question;
   (b) where the surrendering company is a member of a consortium that loss or excess shall not be set off under the subsection in question against more than a fraction of the total profits of the claimant company;

and that fraction shall be equal to that member's share in the consortium in the accounting period referred to in section 402(4), subject to any further reduction under section 408(2) and subject also to sections 405(4) and 406(2) and (6).

(10) Where a company owned by a consortium—

   (a) has in any relevant accounting period incurred such a loss as is referred to in subsection (1) above, and
   (b) has profits (of whatever description) of that accounting period against which that loss could be set off under section 393(2),

the amount of that loss which is available to any member of the consortium on a consortium claim shall be determined on the assumption that the company owned by the consortium has made a claim under section 393(2) requiring the loss to be so set off.

(11) Where the company referred to in subsection (10) above is a group/consortium company, the amount of the loss shall be determined under that subsection before any reduction is made under section 405(1) to (3).

Former enactments.—Sub-ss. (1), (2): TA 1970, s. 259(1).
Sub-ss. (3)–(8): TA 1970, s. 259(2)–(7).
Sub-s. (9): TA 1970, s. 259(8); FA 1981, s. 40(3).
Sub-ss. (10), (11): FA 1985, Sch. 9, para. 4.
Cross references.—See FA 1971, s. 48(4A) (disapplication of sub-s. (3) of this section in cases where a non-trading company leases plant to a non-trader).

CHAPTER IV
GROUP RELIEF

402. Surrender of relief between members of groups and consortia

(1) Subject to and in accordance with this Chapter and section 492(8), relief for trading losses and other amounts eligible for relief from corporation tax may, in the cases set out in subsections (2) and (3) below, be surrendered by a company ("the surrendering company") and, on the making of a claim by another company ("the claimant company") may be allowed to the claimant company by way of a relief from corporation tax called "group relief".

(2) Group relief shall be available in a case where the surrendering company and the claimant company are both members of the same group.

A claim made by virtue of this subsection is referred to as a "group claim".

(3) Group relief shall also be available in the case of a surrendering company and a claimant company either where one of them is a member of a consortium and the other is—

    (*a*) a trading company which is owned by the consortium and which is not a 75 per cent. subsidiary of any company; or

    (*b*) a trading company—

        (i) which is a 90 per cent. subsidiary of a holding company which is owned by the consortium; and

        (ii) which is not a 75 per cent. subsidiary of a company other than the holding company; or

    (*c*) a holding company which is owned by the consortium and which is not a 75 per cent. subsidiary of any company;

or, in accordance with section 406, where one of them is a member of a group of companies and the other is owned by a consortium and another company is a member of both the group and the consortium.

A claim made by virtue of this subsection is referred to as "a consortium claim".

(4) A consortium claim shall not be made if the share in the consortium of the member in the relevant accounting period of the surrendering company (or, where that company is a trading company falling within subsection (3)(*b*) above, its holding company) is nil or if a profit on a sale of the share capital of the other company or its holding company which the member owns would be treated as a trading receipt of that member.

(5) Subject to the provisions of this Chapter, two or more claimant companies may make claims relating to the same surrendering company, and to the same accounting period of that surrendering company.

(6) A payment for group relief—

    (*a*) shall not be taken into account in computing profits or losses of either company for corporation tax purposes, and

    (*b*) shall not for any of the purposes of the Corporation Tax Acts be regarded as a distribution or a charge on income;

and in this subsection "a payment for group relief" means a payment made by the claimant company to the surrendering company in pursuance of an agreement between them as respects an amount surrendered by way of group relief, being a payment not exceeding that amount.

Former enactments.—Sub-ss. (1), (2): TA 1970, s. 258(1).
Sub-ss. (3), (4): TA 1970, s. 258(2); FA 1981, s. 40(2); FA 1985, Sch. 9, paras. 5, 6.
Sub-ss. (5), (6): TA 1970, s. 258(3), (4).

403. Losses etc. which may be surrendered by way of group relief

(1) Subject to the provisions of this Chapter, if in any accounting period the surrendering company has incurred a loss, computed as for the purposes of section 393(2), in carrying on a trade, the amount of the loss may be set off for the purposes of corporation tax against the total profits of the claimant company for its corresponding accounting period.

extent to which it is replaced by money lent, or a payment made, out of public funds or by shares subscribed for, whether for money or money's worth, by a Minister of the Crown.

(10) In this section—
"body corporate" means any body corporate which is a company for the purposes of corporation tax;
"group" means a company having one or more 51 per cent. subsidiaries and that or those subsidiaries; and
"Minister of the Crown" includes a Northern Ireland department.

Former enactment.—FA 1981, s. 48.
Cross references.—See the British Steel Act 1988, s. 11(3), (5), (6) (restriction of tax losses under this section not to apply to British Steel Corporation in relation to any reduction in or extinguishment of its public dividend capital).

401. Relief for pre-trading expenditure

(1) Where a person incurs expenditure for the purposes of a trade, profession or vocation before the time when he begins to carry it on and the expenditure—

(*a*) is incurred not more than [five][1] years before that time; and
(*b*) is not allowable as a deduction in computing his profits or gains from the trade, profession or vocation for the purposes of Case I or II of Schedule D but would have been so allowable if incurred after that time,

the expenditure shall be treated for the purposes of corporation tax as incurred on the day on which the trade, profession or vocation is first carried on by him and for the purposes of relief under Chapter I of this Part as if it were the amount of a loss sustained by him in the trade, profession or vocation in the year of assessment in which it is set up and commenced.

(2) A claim for relief under the Income Tax Acts in respect of an amount treated as a loss by virtue of subsection (1) above shall be made separately from any claim for relief under those Acts in respect of any other loss.

Former enactments.—FA 1980, s. 39(1), (2), (4); FA 1982, s. 50.
Amendments.—[1] Word in sub-s. (1)(*a*) substituted for the word "three" by FA 1989, s. 114 where the time when the person begins to carry on the trade etc. falls after 31 March 1989.

400. Write-off of government investment

(1) Where any amount of government investment in a body corporate is written-off on or after 6th April 1988, an amount equal to the amount written-off shall be set off against the body's tax losses as at the end of the accounting period ending last before the write-off date and, to the extent to which that amount exceeds those losses, against the body's tax losses as at the end of the next accounting period and so on.

(2) For the purposes of subsection (1) above a body's tax losses as at the end of an accounting period are—

    (*a*) any losses which under section 393(1) are or, if a claim had been made under that subsection, would be available for relief against its trading income for the next accounting period;
    (*b*) in the case of an investment company, any expenses of management or charges on income which under section 75(3) are available for carry forward to the next accounting period;
    (*c*) any allowances which under section 74(2) of the 1968 Act are available for carry forward to the next accounting period;
    (*d*) any amount paid by way of charges on income so far as it exceeds the company's profit for the period and is not taken into account under 75(3) or 393(9); and
    (*e*) any allowable losses available under 345 so far as not allowed in that or a previous accounting period.

(3) The set off to be made under subsection (1) above for any accounting period shall be made first against the amounts in paragraphs (*a*) to (*d*) of subsection (2) above and, so far as it cannot be so made, against the amount in paragraph (*e*) of that subsection.

(4) For the purposes of subsection (1) above there shall be excluded from a body's tax losses as at the end of the accounting period ending last before the write-off date any amounts in respect of which a claim has been made before the write-off date under section 393(2) or 402 of this Act or section 74(3) of the 1968 Act but the body's tax losses as at the end of any subsequent accounting period shall be determined as if no such claim had been made on or after that date.

(5) Any amount that could be set off under subsection (1) above against a body's tax losses as at the end of an accounting period (or could be so set off if that body then had any such losses) may be set off against the tax losses of any other body corporate which at the end of that period is a member of the same group as the first-mentioned body, or partly against the tax losses of one member of that group and partly against those of the other or any of the others, as may be just and reasonable.

(6) Expenditure shall not be treated for the purposes of section 84 of the 1968 Act or section 42 of the 1979 Act as met by the Crown by reason only of the writing-off of any government investment in the body in question and a sum shall not by reason only of any such writing-off be treated as not having been deductible in computing the profits or gains of that body for the purposes of Case I or II of Schedule D.

(7) For the purposes of this section an amount of government investment in a body corporate is written-off—

    (*a*) if its liability to repay any money lent to it out of public funds by a Minister of the Crown is extinguished;
    (*b*) if any of its shares for which a Minister of the Crown has subscribed out of public funds are cancelled; or
    (*c*) if its commencing capital debt is reduced otherwise than by being paid off or its public dividend capital is reduced otherwise than by being repaid (including, in either case, a reduction to nil);

and the amount written-off and the write-off date are the amount in respect of which the liability is extinguished and the date on which it is extinguished, the amount subscribed for the shares that are cancelled and the date of cancellation or the amount of reduction in the commencing capital debt or public dividend capital and the date of the reduction, as the case may be.

(8) In subsection (7) above "commencing capital debt" means any debt to a Minister of the Crown assumed as such under an enactment and "public dividend capital" means any amount paid by a Minister of the Crown under an enactment in which that amount is so described or under an enactment corresponding to an enactment in which a payment made on similar terms to another body is so described.

(9) This section shall not have effect in relation to any amount written-off if and to the

(9) For the purposes of subsection (8) above a trade shall not be treated as discontinued if, under section 343(2), it is not to be treated as discontinued for the purpose of capital allowances and charges.

(10) Where at any time there has been a change in the persons engaged in carrying on a trade, this section shall, notwithstanding subsection (8) above, apply to any person who was engaged in carrying on the trade immediately before and immediately after the change as if the trade were the same before and after without any discontinuance, and as if—

(*a*) a husband and his wife were the same person, and
(*b*) a husband or his wife were the same person as any company of which either the husband or the wife has control, or of which the two of them have control;

and accordingly relief from income tax or from corporation tax may be restricted under this section by reference to losses some of which are incurred in years of assessment and some, computed without regard to capital allowances, are incurred in a company's chargeable periods.

In this subsection "control" has the same meaning as in Part XI.

Former enactments.—TA 1970, s. 180; FA 1986, s. 56(7), Sch. 13, para. 2(5).

398. Transactions in deposits with and without certificates or in debts

Where a person sustains a loss on the exercise or disposal of a right to receive any amount, being a right to which section 56(2) applies, in a case where—

(*a*) if a profit had arisen from that exercise or disposal, that profit would have been chargeable to tax by virtue of section 56(2), and
(*b*) he is chargeable to tax under Schedule C or D in respect of interest payable on that amount,

then the amount of that interest shall be included in the amounts against which he may claim to set off the amount of his loss under section 392 or, as the case may be, 396.

Former enactments.—FA 1973, s. 26(2); FA 1974, s. 30(2).

399. Dealings in commodity futures etc.: withdrawal of loss relief

(1) If, apart from section 72(1) of the Finance Act 1985 or section 128 above, gains arising to any person in the course of dealing in commodity or financial futures or in qualifying options would constitute, for the purposes of the Tax Acts, profits or gains chargeable to tax under Schedule D otherwise than as the profits of a trade, then any loss arising in the course of that dealing shall not be allowable against profits or gains which are chargeable to tax under Schedule D.

(2) Relief shall not be given to any person under section 380, 381 or 393(2) in respect of a loss sustained in a trade of dealing in commodity futures if—

(*a*) the loss was sustained in a trade carried on in partnership and that person or one or more of the other partners was a company; and
(*b*) a scheme has been effected or arrangements have been made (whether by the partnership agreement or otherwise) such that the sole or main benefit that might be expected to accrue to that person from his interest in the partnership was the obtaining of a reduction in tax liability by means of any such relief.

(3) Where relief has been given in a case to which subsection (2) above applies it shall be withdrawn by the making of an assessment under Case VI of Schedule D.

(4) Subsection (2) above does not apply where the scheme was effected or the arrangements were made wholly before 6th April 1976.

(5) In this section "commodity futures", "financial futures" and "qualifying options" have the same meanings as in section 72 of the Finance Act 1985, and the reference in subsection (1) to a loss arising in the course of dealing in commodity or financial futures includes any loss which is regarded as arising in the course of such dealing by virtue of subsection (2A) of that section.

Former enactments.—Sub-s. (1): FA 1985, s. 72(1); F (No. 2) A 1987, s. 81(1).
Sub-ss. (2)–(4): FA 1978, s. 31.
Sub-s (5): FA 1985, s. 72(2); F (No. 2) A 1987, s. 81(1).

CHAPTER III
LOSS RELIEF: MISCELLANEOUS PROVISIONS

397. Restriction of relief in case of farming and market gardening

(1) Any loss incurred in a trade of farming or market gardening shall be excluded from section 380 if in each of the prior five years a loss was incurred in carrying on that trade; and where a loss is so excluded any related capital allowance shall also be excluded from that section.

(2) Any loss incurred in any accounting period by a company in carrying on a trade of farming or market gardening shall be excluded from section 393(2) if a loss, computed without regard to capital allowances, was incurred in carrying on that trade in that accounting period, and in each of the chargeable periods wholly or partly comprised in the prior five years.

(3) Subsections (1) and (2) above shall not restrict relief for any loss or for any capital allowance, if it is shown by the claimant—

(*a*) that the whole of the farming or market gardening activities in the year next following the prior five years are of such a nature, and carried on in such a way, as would have justified a reasonable expectation of the realisation of profits in the future if they had been undertaken by a competent farmer or market gardener, but
(*b*) that, if that farmer or market gardener had undertaken those activities at the beginning of the prior period of loss, he could not reasonably have expected the activities to become profitable until after the end of the year next following the prior period of loss.

(4) Subsections (1) and (2) above shall not restrict relief where the carrying on of the trade forms part of, and is ancillary to, a larger trading undertaking.

(5) In this section—

"basis year", in relation to any capital allowance, shall be construed in accordance with section 383(5)(*a*);
"chargeable period", in relation to a company, means any accounting period, or any basis period ending before its first accounting period, "basis period" having the meaning given by section 72 of the 1968 Act;
"prior five years"—

(*a*) in relation to a loss incurred in a year of assessment, means the last five years of assessment before that year, and
(*b*) in relation to a loss incurred in a company's accounting period, means the last five years before the beginning of the accounting period;

"prior period of loss" means the prior five years, except that, if losses were incurred in the trade in successive years of assessment or chargeable periods amounting in all to a period longer than five years (and ending when the prior five years end), it means that longer period, and in applying this definition to a chargeable period of a company "losses" means losses computed without regard to capital allowances; and
"farming" and "market gardening" shall be construed in accordance with the definitions of those terms in section 832, but as if those definitions were not restricted to activities in the United Kingdom.

(6) For the purposes of this section, a capital allowance is related to a loss incurred in a trade if it falls to be made in taxing that trade and its basis year is the year of assessment in which the loss was incurred.

(7) In ascertaining for the purposes of this section whether a loss was incurred in any part of the prior five years or earlier, the rules applicable to Case I of Schedule D shall be applied; and in this section "loss computed without regard to capital allowances" means, in relation to a chargeable period of a company, a loss so ascertained, but so that, notwithstanding section 73(2) of the 1968 Act, no account shall be taken of any allowance or charge under any of the Capital Allowances Acts.

(8) Subsections (1) and (2) above shall not restrict relief for any loss or capital allowance if the trade was set up and commenced within the prior five years, and, for the purposes of this subsection, a trade shall be treated as discontinued, and a new trade set up, in any event which under any of the provisions of the Tax Acts is to be treated as equivalent to the permanent discontinuance or setting up of a trade.

period in which the loss is incurred and must be so made notwithstanding that relief cannot be given in respect of the loss until after the end of that period of six years.

Former enactment.—TA 1970, s. 179.

(6) A claim under this section must be made within six years from the time when the company ceases to carry on the trade.

Former enactments.—Sub-s. (1): TA 1970, s. 178(1).
Sub-s. (2): TA 1970, s. 178(1) (proviso).
Sub-ss. (3)–(6): TA 1970, s. 178(2)–(5).

395. Leasing contracts and company reconstructions

(1) Subject to the provisions of this section, if—

(*a*) under a contract entered into on or after 6th March 1973 a company ("the first company") incurs capital expenditure on the provision of machinery or plant which the first company lets to another person by another contract (a "leasing contract"); and

(*b*) apart from this subsection, the first company would be entitled to claim relief under subsection (1) or (2) of section 393 in respect of losses incurred on the leasing contract; and

(*c*) in the accounting period for which a first-year allowance, within the meaning of Chapter I of Part III of the Finance Act 1971, in respect of the expenditure referred to in paragraph (*a*) above is made to the first company, arrangements are in existence by virtue of which, at some time during or after the expiry of that accounting period, a successor company will be able to carry on any part of the first company's trade which consists of or includes the performance of all or any of the obligations which, apart from the arrangements, would be the first company's obligations under the leasing contract;

then, in the accounting period specified in paragraph (*c*) above and in any subsequent accounting period, the first company shall not be entitled to claim relief as mentioned in paragraph (*b*) above except in computing its profits (if any) arising under the leasing contract.

(2) For the purposes of this section a company is a successor of the first company if the circumstances are such that—

(*a*) section 343 applies in relation to the first company and the other company as the predecessor and the successor within the meaning of that section; or

(*b*) the two companies are connected with each other within the terms of section 839.

(3) For the purposes of this section losses incurred on a leasing contract and profits arising under such a contract shall be computed as if the performance of the leasing contract were a trade begun to be carried on by the first company, separately from any other trade which it may carry on, at the commencement of the letting under the leasing contract.

(4) In determining whether the first company would be entitled to claim relief as mentioned in subsection (1)(*b*) above, any losses incurred on the leasing contract shall be treated as incurred in a trade carried on by that company separately from any other trade which it may carry on.

(5) In this section "arrangements" means arrangements of any kind whether in writing or not.

Former enactments.—FA 1973, ss. 30, 32(6).

Case VI losses

396. Case VI losses

(1) Subject to subsection (2) below, where in any accounting period a company incurs a loss in a transaction in respect of which the company is within the charge to corporation tax under Case VI of Schedule D, the company may make a claim requiring that the loss be set off against the amount of any income arising from transactions in respect of which the company is assessed to corporation tax under that Case for the same or any subsequent accounting period; and the company's income in any accounting period from such transactions shall then be treated as reduced by the amount of the loss, or by so much of that amount as cannot be relieved under this section against income of an earlier accounting period.

(2) This section shall not apply to a loss incurred in a transaction falling within section 34, 35 or 36.

(3) A claim under this section must be made within six years after the end of the accounting

(*b*) in any later accounting period to which the loss or any part of it is carried forward under subsection (1) above relief in respect thereof cannot be given, or cannot wholly be given, because the amount of the trading income of the trade is insufficient,

any interest or dividends on investments which would fall to be taken into account as trading receipts in computing that trading income but for the fact that they have been subjected to tax under other provisions shall be treated for the purposes of subsection (1) above as if they were trading income of the trade.

(9) Where in an accounting period the charges on income paid by a company—
   (*a*) exceed the amount of the profits against which they are deductible, and
   (*b*) include payments made wholly and exclusively for the purposes of a trade carried on by the company,

then, up to the amount of that excess or of those payments, whichever is the less, the charges on income so paid shall in computing a loss for the purposes of subsection (1) above be deductible as if they were trading expenses of the trade.

(10) In this section references to a company carrying on a trade refer to the company carrying it on so as to be within the charge to corporation tax in respect of it.

(11) A claim under subsection (1) above must be made within six years after the end of the accounting period in which the loss is incurred, and must be so made notwithstanding that relief cannot be given in respect of the loss until after the end of that period of six years; and a claim under subsection (2) above must be made within two years from the end of the accounting period in which the loss is incurred.

Former enactments.—Sub-ss. (1)–(3): TA 1970, s. 177(1)–(3).
Sub-s. (4): TA 1970, s. 177(3A); FA 1971, Sch. 8, para. 16(6); FA 1972, s. 67(2)(*c*); FA 1985, s. 60.
Sub-ss. (5)–(11): TA 1970, s 177(4)–(10).

394. Terminal losses

(1) Where a company ceasing to carry on a trade after 5th April 1988 has in any accounting period falling wholly or partly within the previous 12 months incurred a loss in the trade, the company may make a claim requiring that the loss be set off for the purposes of corporation tax against trading income from the trade in accounting periods falling wholly or partly within the three years preceding those 12 months (or within any less period throughout which the company has carried on the trade); and, subject to subsections (2) to (6) below and to any relief for earlier losses, the trading income of any of those periods shall be then treated as reduced by the amount of the loss, or by so much of that amount as cannot be relieved under this subsection against income of a later accounting period.

(2) Relief under subsection (1) above shall not be given in respect of any loss in so far as the loss has been or can be otherwise taken into account so as to reduce or relieve any charge to tax.

(3) Where a loss is incurred in an accounting period falling partly outside the 12 months mentioned in subsection (1) above, relief shall be given under that subsection in respect of a part only of that loss proportionate to the part of the period falling within those 12 months; and the amount of the reduction which may be made under that subsection in the trading income of an accounting period falling partly outside the three years there mentioned shall not exceed a part of that income proportionate to the part of the period falling within those three years.

(4) A claim for relief under this section may require that capital allowances in respect of the trade, being allowances which fall to be made to the company by way of discharge or repayment of tax, and to be so made for an accounting period falling wholly or partly within the 12 months ending when the company ceases to carry on the trade, shall (so far as they cannot be otherwise taken into account so as to reduce or relieve any charge to corporation tax) be added to the loss incurred by the company in that accounting period or, if the company has not incurred a loss in the period, shall be treated as a loss so incurred.

For the purposes of this subsection the allowances for any period shall not be treated as including amounts carried forward from an earlier period.

(5) Subsections (7) to (10) of section 393 shall apply for the purposes of this section as they apply for the purposes of subsection (1) of that section; and relief shall not be given under this section in respect of a loss incurred in a trade so as to interfere with any relief under section 338 in respect of payments made wholly and exclusively for the purposes of that trade.

CHAPTER II

LOSS RELIEF: CORPORATION TAX

Trade etc. losses

393. Losses other than terminal losses

(1) Where in any accounting period a company carrying on a trade incurs a loss in the trade, the company may make a claim requiring that the loss be set off for the purposes of corporation tax against any trading income from the trade in succeeding accounting periods; and (so long as the company continues to carry on the trade) its trading income from the trade in any succeeding accounting period shall then be treated as reduced by the amount of the loss, or by so much of that amount as cannot, on that claim or on a claim (if made) under subsection (2) below, be relieved against income or profits of an earlier accounting period.

(2) Subject to section 492(2), where in any accounting period ending after 5th April 1988 a company carrying on a trade incurs a loss in the trade, then (subject to subsection (5) below) the company may make a claim requiring that the loss be set off for the purposes of corporation tax against profits (of whatever description) of that accounting period and, if the company was then carrying on the trade and the claim so requires, of preceding accounting periods ending within the time specified in subsection (3) below; and, subject to that subsection and to any relief for an earlier loss, the profits of any of those periods shall then be treated as reduced by the amount of the loss, or by so much of that amount as cannot be relieved under this subsection against profits of a later accounting period.

(3) The time referred to in subsection (2) above is a time equal in length to the accounting period in which the loss is incurred; but the amount of the reduction which may be made under that subsection in the profits of an accounting period falling partly before that time shall not exceed a part of those profits proportionate to the part of the period falling within that time.

(4) Where a company incurs a loss in a trade in an accounting period for which one or more first-year allowances fall to be made to it under Chapter I of Part III of the Finance Act 1971 in respect of expenditure on the provision for the purposes of the trade of machinery or plant, subsections (2) and (3) above shall have effect in relation to so much of the loss as does not exceed the allowance or allowances which are so made as if the time specified in subsection (3) above were a period of three years ending immediately before the accounting period in which the loss is incurred.

(5) Subsection (2) above shall not apply to trades falling within Case V of Schedule D; and, except in so far as it represents an excess in respect of expenditure incurred before the year 1960–61 of capital allowances over balancing charges, a loss incurred in a trade in any accounting period shall not be relieved under that subsection unless the trade is one carried on in the exercise of functions conferred by or under any enactment (including an enactment contained in a local or private Act), or it is shown that for that accounting period the trade was being carried on on a commercial basis and with a view to the realisation of gain in the trade or in any larger undertaking of which the trade formed part.

This subsection has effect without prejudice to section 397.

(6) For the purposes of subsection (5) above, the fact that a trade was being carried on at any time so as to afford a reasonable expectation of gain shall be conclusive evidence that it was then being carried on with a view to the realisation of gain; and where in an accounting period there is a change in the manner in which a trade is being carried on, it shall for those purposes be treated as having throughout the accounting period been carried on in the way in which it was being carried on by the end of that period.

(7) The amount of a loss incurred in a trade in an accounting period shall be computed for the purposes of this section in the same way as trading income from the trade in that period would have been computed.

(8) For the purposes of this section "trading income" means, in relation to any trade, the income which falls or would fall to be included in respect of the trade in the total profits of the company; but where—

(*a*) in an accounting period a company incurs a loss in a trade in respect of which it is within the charge to corporation tax under Case I or V of Schedule D, and this section against tax for any year of assessment may be the subject of a separate claim made not later than six years after that year of assessment.

Former enactment.—TA 1970, s. 176.

by him in the occupation of the woodlands as they apply to a terminal loss sustained in a trade.

Former enactments.—TA 1970, s. 174(7)–(13); FA 1986, Sch. 13, para. 27; FA 1971, Sch. 8, para. 16.
Note.—See **Prospective Legislation Notes** (Commercial Woodlands).

390. Treatment of interest as a loss for purposes of carry-forward and carry-back

Where—

(*a*) a payment of interest eligible for relief under section 353 is money wholly and exclusively laid out or expended for the purposes of a trade, profession or vocation the profits of which are chargeable to tax under Case I or II of Schedule D, and
(*b*) full effect cannot be given to such relief in respect of the payment by reason of a want or deficiency of income of the year of assessment in which the payment is made,

the amount unallowed may be carried forward to succeeding years of assessment as if it were a loss carried forward under section 385, or may be treated for the purposes of sections 388 and 389 as a loss sustained at the date of payment.

Former enactments.—TA 1970, s. 175; FA 1972, Sch. 11, para. 3; FA 1974, Sch. 1, para. 28.

391. Losses from trade etc. carried on abroad

(1) Subject to the following provisions of this section, sections 380 to 386 and 388 and 389, so far as applicable, shall apply in relation to a loss incurred by any person in the carrying on of a trade, profession or vocation chargeable in accordance with section 65(3) as they apply to a loss incurred in a trade, profession or vocation chargeable to tax under Case I or II of Schedule D.

(2) Relief shall not be given by virtue of subsection (1) above except on income falling within section 65(2) or (3), 192(2), (3) or (4) or 196.

Former enactments.—Sub-s. (1): FA 1974, s. 23(2)(*a*); FA 1978, s. 30(7)(*b*).
Sub-s. (2): FA 1974, s. 23(4); FA 1984, s. 30(13).

Case VI losses

392. Case VI losses

(1) Where in any year of assessment a person sustains a loss in any transaction, whether he was engaged therein solely or in partnership, being a transaction of such a nature that, if any profits had arisen therefrom, he would have been liable to be assessed to income tax in respect thereof under Case VI of Schedule D, he may make a claim requiring—

(*a*) that the amount of the loss sustained by him shall, as far as may be, be deducted from or set off against the amount of any profits or gains arising from any transaction in respect of which he is assessed for that year under that Case, and
(*b*) that any portion of the loss for which relief is not so given shall, as far as may be, be carried forward and deducted from or set off against the amount of any profits or gains arising from any transaction in respect of which he is assessed to income tax under that Case for any subsequent year of assessment.

(2) In the application of this section to a loss sustained by a partner in a partnership, "the amount of any profits or gains arising from any transaction in respect of which he is assessed" shall be taken to mean in respect of any year such portion of the amount on which the partnership is assessed under Case VI of Schedule D in respect of any transaction as falls to be taken into account in computing his total income for that year.

(3) Any relief under this section by way of the carrying forward of the loss shall be given as far as possible from the first subsequent assessment in respect of any profits or gains arising from any transaction in respect of which he is assessed under Case VI of Schedule D for any year, and, so far as it cannot be so given, then from the next such assessment, and so on.

(4) This section does not apply to any loss sustained in a transaction falling within section 34, 35 or 36.

(5) So far as a claim under this section concerns the amount of the loss for any year of assessment, it must be made within six years after the year of assessment in question; but the question whether any and if so how much relief on that amount should be given under

beginning of the third year of assessment preceding that in which the discontinuance occurs, carried on the trade, profession or vocation in partnership—

(a) in section 388(1) "the amount of profits or gains on which he has been charged to income tax" shall be taken to mean, in respect of any year or part of a year for which the partnership was assessed in respect of the trade, profession or vocation, such portion of the amount of the profits or gains on which the partnership has been, or is treated by virtue of section 388(5) as having been, charged to income tax in respect of it for that year or part of a year as would be required to be included in a return of his total income for that year;

(b) any reduction in the amount of his terminal loss which falls to be made under section 388(5) by reason of profits or gains having been applied by the partnership in any such year or part of a year in making any payment shall be limited to the same proportion of the profits or gains brought into charge which were so applied; and

(c) if he was carrying on the trade, profession or vocation immediately before the discontinuance, the amounts to be included in his terminal loss by virtue of section 388(6)(b) or (d) shall be such part only of the amounts therein mentioned (in so far as they have not otherwise been taken into account so as to reduce or relieve any charge to tax) as would fall to his share on a division made according to the shares in which the partners were then entitled to the profits of the trade, profession or vocation.

(4) For all purposes of this section and section 388 a trade, profession or vocation shall be treated as discontinued, and a new one as set up and commenced, when it is so treated for the purposes of section 113; but—

(a) a person who continues to be engaged in carrying it on immediately after such a discontinuance shall not be entitled to relief in respect of any terminal loss on that discontinuance; and

(b) on any discontinuance, a person not continuing to be so engaged may be given relief in respect of a terminal loss against profits or gains on which he was charged in respect of the same trade, profession or vocation for a period before a previous discontinuance, if he has been continuously engaged in carrying it on between the two discontinuances, and, in his case, if the previous discontinuance occurred within 12 months before the other—

(i) it shall be disregarded for the purposes of paragraphs (a) and (c) of section 388(6), except that those paragraphs shall be taken to include any amount on which relief could have been allowed to him as for a loss sustained before the previous discontinuance by virtue of section 385(5)(c), so far as it is referable to a period within those 12 months; and

(ii) paragraph (d) of section 388(6) shall be taken to include the whole amount of the allowances in question instead of the fraction there mentioned.

(5) Where a trade, profession or vocation is being carried on by any persons in partnership immediately before it is permanently discontinued, relief under section 388 given to one of them on the discontinuance shall not, in relation to a claim made by another of them by virtue of paragraph (c) of section 385(5), be taken to affect the non-effective amount of any allowances within the meaning of that paragraph.

(6) Subject to subsection (7) below, a claim for relief under section 388 may require that, in so far as they have not been otherwise taken into account so as to reduce or relieve any charge to tax, capital allowances in respect of the trade under Part I of the 1968 Act or Chapter I of Part III of the Finance Act 1971, being allowances which—

(a) fall to be made to the claimant by way of discharge or repayment of tax, and

(b) fall to be so made for the year of assessment in which the discontinuance occurs or the preceding year of assessment,

shall be added to the terminal loss sustained by him (or, if he has not sustained a terminal loss computed in accordance with the provisions of this section and section 388, shall be treated as a terminal loss so sustained), and the allowances to be taken into account for this purpose may include allowances arising before a previous discontinuance.

(7) For the purposes of subsection (6) above—

(a) there shall be taken into account such fraction only of the allowances for the preceding year of assessment referred to in that subsection as the part of that year beginning 12 months before the discontinuance giving rise to the claim is of a year; and

(b) the allowances for any year shall not be treated as including any amounts carried forward from an earlier year.

(8) Where a person occupying woodlands has elected to be charged to income tax in respect thereof under Schedule D, this section and section 388 shall apply to a terminal loss sustained

(3) Any relief under this section shall be given as far as possible from the assessment for a later rather than an earlier year.

(4) Where—

(*a*) a claim under this section is made in respect of a terminal loss sustained in a trade, and

(*b*) relief cannot be given, or cannot be wholly given, against the profits or gains of the trade charged to income tax under Schedule D for any year because the amount of those profits or gains is insufficient,

any relevant interest or dividends arising in that year shall be treated for the purposes of the application of this section as if they were profits or gains on which the person carrying on the trade was assessed under Case I of Schedule D in respect of that trade for that year of assessment, and relief shall be given accordingly by repayment or otherwise.

For the purposes of this subsection "any relevant interest or dividends" means interest or dividends which would fall to be taken into account as trading receipts in computing the profits or gains of the trade for the purpose of assessment under Case I of Schedule D but for the fact that they have been subjected to tax under other provisions of the Income Tax Acts.

(5) The profits or gains on which a person or partnership has been charged to income tax for any year of assessment shall be treated for the purposes of any relief under this section from the assessment for that year as reduced by the amount of those profits or gains applied in making any payment from which income tax was deducted, but was not accounted for because the payment was made out of profits or gains brought into charge to income tax; and the like reduction shall be made in the amount of the terminal loss for which relief may be given under this section from the assessments for earlier years unless the payment was one which, if not made out of profits or gains brought into charge to income tax—

(*a*) could have been assessed to income tax under section 350, and

(*b*) if so assessed, could have been treated as a loss by virtue of section 387.

(6) The question whether a person has sustained any and, if so, what terminal loss in a trade, profession or vocation shall be determined for the purposes of this section by taking the amounts (if any) of the following, in so far as they have not otherwise been taken into account so as to reduce or relieve any charge to tax—

(*a*) the loss sustained by him in the trade, profession or vocation in the year of assessment in which it is permanently discontinued;

(*b*) the relevant capital allowances for that year of assessment;

(*c*) the loss sustained by him in the trade, profession or vocation in the part of the preceding year of assessment beginning 12 months before the discontinuance; and

(*d*) the same fraction of the relevant capital allowances for that preceding year of assessment as the part thereof beginning 12 months before the discontinuance is of a year.

(7) In subsection (6) above "the relevant capital allowances" means, in relation to any year of assessment, any capital allowances falling to be made in taxing the trade, profession or vocation for that year, excluding amounts carried forward from an earlier year; and for the purposes of paragraphs (*a*) and (*c*) of that subsection the amount of a loss shall, subject to the provisions of this section, be computed in the same way as profits or gains under the provisions of the Income Tax Acts applicable to Cases I and II of Schedule D.

Former enactments.—Sub-ss. (1), (2): TA 1970, s. 174(1).
Sub-ss. (3)–(7): TA 1970, s. 174(2)–(6).

389. Supplementary provisions relating to carry-back of terminal losses

(1) Sections 387, 458 and 474 shall apply to the computation of losses, or of profit or loss, for any purpose of this section or section 388 as they apply to any such computation for the corresponding purposes of section 385.

(2) Where on the permanent discontinuance of a trade which consists of or includes the working of a mine, oil well or other source of mineral deposits within the meaning of Schedule 13 to the Finance Act 1986, a claim for relief is made both under section 388 above and section 15(1) of the 1968 Act (carry-back of balancing allowances), the balancing allowance in respect of which the claim is made under section 15(1) shall be left out of account for the purposes of section 388(6), but relief under section 388 shall be given in priority to relief under section 15(1).

(3) Where a person claiming relief under section 388 on a discontinuance has, since the

been so allotted, his total income for any year of assessment throughout which he is the beneficial owner of the shares, and throughout which the company carries on the business, includes any income derived by him from the company, whether by way of dividends on those shares or otherwise;

then, subject to subsection (2) below, section 385 (except subsection (5)) shall apply as if the income so derived were profits or gains on which that individual was assessed under Schedule D in respect of that business for that year.

(2) Where under section 385 as applied by subsection (1) above a loss falls to be deducted from or set off against any income for any year of assessment, the deduction or set-off shall be made in the first place against that part, if any, of the income in respect of which the individual has been, or is liable to be, assessed to tax for that year.

(3) This section, in its application to the year of assessment in which a business is transferred, shall have effect as if, for the reference in subsection (1)(*b*) to the year of assessment throughout which the individual is the beneficial owner of the shares and the business is carried on by the company, there were substituted a reference to the period from the date of the transfer to the following 5th April.

(4) Where a change to which subsection (5) of section 385 applies has occurred before a transfer to which this section applies, paragraph (*a*), but not paragraph (*c*), of that subsection shall for the purposes of this section apply in relation to the earlier change as it applies for the purposes of that section.

Former enactment.—TA 1970, s. 172.

387. Carry-forward as losses of amounts taxed under section 350

(1) Subject to the provisions of this section, where under section 350 a person has been assessed to income tax in respect of a payment made wholly and exclusively for the purposes of a trade, profession or vocation, the amount on which tax has been paid under that assessment shall be treated for the purposes of sections 385 and 386 as though it were a loss sustained in that trade, profession or vocation, and relief in respect of the loss shall be allowed accordingly.

(2) Relief shall not be allowed by virtue of this section in respect of any payment, or part of a payment, which is not ultimately borne by the person assessed, or which is charged to capital.

(3) This section shall not apply—
   (*a*) to any payment falling within section 349(2);
   (*b*) to any payment falling within section 349 by virtue of section 43(1);
   (*c*) to any such payment of rent as is referred to in section 120(4);
   (*d*) to any capital sum paid in respect of any patent rights assessed under section 349(1) by virtue of section 524;
   (*e*) to any payment of, or on account of, copyright royalties to which section 536 applies [or royalties in respect of a right in a design to which section 537B applies][1]; or
   (*f*) to any payment to which section 349(1) applies by virtue of section 737.

Former enactments.—Sub-ss. (1), (2): TA 1970, s. 173(1), (2).
Sub-s. (3)(*a*): TA 1970, s. 173(3)(*aa*); FA 1970, Sch. 4, para. 9(6).
Sub-s. (3)(*b*)–(*f*): TA 1970, s. 173(3)(*a*)–(*e*).
Amendments.—[1] Words in sub-s. (3)(*e*) inserted by the Copyright, Designs and Patents Act 1988, Sch. 7, para. 36(4).

388. Carry-back of terminal losses

(1) Where a trade, profession or vocation is permanently discontinued in the year 1988–89 or any later year, and any person then carrying it on, either alone or in partnership, has sustained therein a loss to which this section applies ("a terminal loss"), that person may, subject to the provisions of this section and of section 389, make a claim requiring that the amount of the terminal loss shall, as far as may be, be deducted from or set off against the amount of profits or gains on which he has been charged to income tax under Schedule D in respect of the trade, profession or vocation for the three years of assessment last preceding that in which the discontinuance occurs; and there shall be made all such reductions of assessments or repayments of tax as may be necessary to give effect to the claim.

(2) Relief shall not be given in respect of the same matter both under this section and under some other provision of the Income Tax Acts.

respect of a loss carried forward under this section because the amount of the profits or gains of the trade assessed under Case I of Schedule D for that year is insufficient, any interest or dividends being interest or dividends—

(*a*) on investments arising in that year, and
(*b*) which would fall to be taken into account as trading receipts in computing the profits or gains of the trade for the purposes of assessment under that Case but for the fact that they have been subjected to tax under other provisions of the Income Tax Acts,

shall be treated for the purposes of the application of this section as if they were profits or gains on which the person carrying on the trade was assessed under that Case in respect of that trade for that year of assessment, and relief shall be given accordingly by repayment or otherwise.

(5) Where there is in any year of assessment a change on which a trade, profession or vocation is treated under section 113 as permanently discontinued, and a person engaged in carrying it on immediately before the change continues to be so engaged immediately thereafter, then—

(*a*) the trade, profession or vocation carried on by him immediately before and that carried on immediately after the change shall, notwithstanding the discontinuance, be treated as the same for the purposes of this section, except as respects the computation of profits or gains and losses; and
(*b*) in respect of a loss sustained by him in the trade, profession or vocation in the part of that year before the change, relief shall be given under this section from the assessment relating to the part of the year after the change as if it were an assessment for a subsequent year; and
(*c*) for the purposes of this section, there shall be treated as a loss so sustained in the part of the year before the change his share of the non-effective amount (if any) of any capital allowances falling to be made in taxing the trade, profession or vocation for that part of that year.

For the purposes of paragraph (*c*) above—

(i) the persons engaged in carrying on the trade, profession or vocation immediately before the change shall be treated as entitled to capital allowances in the shares in which they are then entitled to the profits of the trade, profession or vocation, and
(ii) "the non-effective amount" means, in relation to any such allowances, the amount to which, because of an insufficiency of profits or gains, effect cannot be given in taxing the trade, profession or vocation.

(6) Where a loss is sustained by a person in the occupation of woodlands, and that person, if he had made a profit, would by reason of his election under [paragraph 4 of Schedule 6 to the Finance Act 1988][1] have been chargeable for the following year to income tax under Schedule D computed on the amount of that profit, this section shall apply so as to give relief in respect of that loss in the same manner, and to the same extent, as if it were a loss sustained in a trade.

(7) In so far as relief in respect of any loss has been given to any person under this section, that person shall not be entitled to claim relief in respect of that loss under any other provision of the Income Tax Acts.

(8) So far as a claim under this section concerns the amount of the loss for any year of assessment it must be made within six years after the year of assessment in question, but the question whether any and if so how much relief on that amount should be given under this section against tax for any year of assessment may be the subject of a separate claim made not later than six years after that year of assessment.

Former enactments.—Sub-ss. (1), (2): TA 1970, s. 171(1).
Sub-ss. (3)–(8): TA 1970, s. 171(2)–(7).
Note.—See **Prospective Legislation Notes** (Commercial Woodlands).
Cross references.—See FA 1988, Sch. 6, para. 6(4), (9) (amendment to TA 1970, s. 171(5) effective from 15 March 1988).
Amendments.—[1] Words in sub-s. (6) substituted by FA 1988, Sch. 6, para. 6(8), (9) with effect from 15 March 1988.

386. Carry-forward where business transferred to a company

(1) Where—

(*a*) a business carried on by any individual, or any individuals in partnership, has been transferred to a company in consideration solely or mainly of the allotment of shares in the company to that individual or those individuals; and
(*b*) in the case of any individual to whom, or to whose nominee or nominees, shares have

above shall have effect in relation to the trade as regards that part of that year as if any reference to the manner of carrying on the trade for or by the end of that year were a reference to the manner of carrying it on for or by the end of that part of that year.

(5) Where in any year of assessment there is a change in the persons engaged in carrying on a trade, then, for the purposes of the application of subsections (1) to (4) above in the case of any person who, being engaged in carrying on the trade immediately before the change, continues to be so engaged immediately after it, the trade carried on by that person immediately before the change shall be treated as continuing to be carried on by him notwithstanding the change, whether or not it falls to be treated for any other purpose as having been discontinued on the change.

(6) There shall be disregarded for the purposes of section 383 any allowances made to an individual under Chapter I of Part III of the Finance Act 1971 in respect of expenditure incurred on the provision of machinery or plant for leasing in the course of a trade unless—

(a) the trade is carried on by him (alone or in partnership) for a continuous period of at least six months in, or beginning or ending in, the year of the loss (as defined in section 383); and
(b) he devotes substantially the whole of his time to carrying it on (alone or in partnership) throughout that year or if it is set up or permanently discontinued (or both) in that year, for a continuous period of at least six months beginning or ending in that year.

(7) Subsection (6) above shall apply also to expenditure incurred by an individual on the provision for the purposes of a trade carried on by him (alone or in partnership) of an asset which is not to be leased if payments in the nature of royalties or licence fees are to accrue from rights granted by him in connection with that asset.

(8) Where relief has been given in a case to which subsection (6) above applies it shall be withdrawn by the making of an assessment under Case VI of Schedule D.

(9) For the purposes of subsection (1) above, the fact that a trade was being carried on at any time so as to afford a reasonable expectation of profit shall be conclusive evidence that it was then being carried on with a view to the realisation of profits.

(10) Subsections (1) to (5) and (9) above—

(a) apply to professions and vocations as they apply to trades, with references to a commercial basis construed accordingly; and
(b) have effect without prejudice to section 397;

and subsection (6) above is without prejudice to section 41 of the Finance Act 1976.

Former enactments.—Sub-s. (1): TA 1970, s. 170(1).
Sub-s. (2): TA 1970, s. 170 (proviso).
Sub-ss. (3)–(5): TA 1970, s. 170(2)–(4).
Sub-s. (6): FA 1980, s. 70(1), (5).
Sub-s. (7): FA 1980, s. 70(2), (5).
Sub-s. (8): FA 1980, s. 70(4).
Sub-ss. (9), (10): TA 1970, s. 170(5), (6); FA 1980, s. 70(6).

385. Carry-forward against subsequent profits

(1) Where a person has, in any trade, profession or vocation carried on by him either alone or in partnership, sustained a loss (to be computed in the same way as profits or gains under the provisions of the Income Tax Acts applicable to Cases I and II of Schedule D) in respect of which relief has not been wholly given either under section 380 or under any other provision of those Acts, he may make a claim requiring that any portion of the loss for which relief has not been so given shall be carried forward and, as far as may be, deducted from or set off against the amount of profits or gains on which he is assessed to income tax under Schedule D in respect of that trade, profession or vocation for subsequent years of assessment.

(2) In the application of this section to a loss sustained by a partner in a partnership, "the amount of profits or gains on which he is assessed" shall, in respect of any year, be taken to mean such portion of the amount on which the partnership is assessed to income tax under Schedule D in respect of the trade, profession or vocation as he would be required to include in a return of his total income for that year.

(3) Any relief under this section shall be given as far as possible from the first subsequent assessment, and so far as it cannot be so given, then from the next assessment, and so on.

(4) Where in any year of assessment relief cannot be given, or cannot be wholly given, in

apart from any deficiency of income, relief might have been given under either section separately, and the total amount for which relief is to be given to all the partners under those sections in respect of any allowances shall not in any event exceed the amount of the allowances to which effect has not been given apart from those sections.

(9) Where a person claiming relief under section 380 or 381 has, since the end, where the claim is under section 380, of the year for which the claim is made, or, where the claim is under section 381, of the year of loss, carried on the trade in question in partnership, effect shall not be given to this section in relation to that claim except with the written consent of, or of the personal representatives of, every other person who has been engaged in carrying on the trade between the end of that year and the making of the claim.

(10) Where the claim is for a loss sustained before an event treated as the permanent discontinuance of the trade, subsection (9) above shall not require the consent of any person as having been so engaged since that discontinuance, or as the personal representative of such a person.

(11) Relief from tax may be given by virtue of this section by reference to capital allowances for a year of assessment before the passing of any Act granting income tax for that year, as if income tax had been granted for the year without alteration; but if relief given to a person by virtue of this section for any year of assessment is affected by a subsequent alteration of the law, or by any discontinuance of the trade or other event occurring after the end of the year, any necessary adjustment may be made, and so much of any repayment of tax as exceeded the amount repayable in the events that happened may, if not otherwise made good, be assessed under Case VI of Schedule D and recovered from that person accordingly.

(12) This section applies (with any necessary adaptations)—

(*a*) in the case of a claim under section 380, in relation to a profession, vocation or employment and in relation to the occupation of woodlands the profits or gains of which are assessable under Schedule D by virtue of an election under [paragraph 4 of Schedule 6 to the Finance Act 1988][1] ; and

(*b*) in relation to a claim under section 381, in relation to a profession or vocation,

as it applies in relation to a trade.

Former enactments.—Sub-ss. (1), (2): TA 1970, s. 169(1), (2); FA 1978, s. 30(7)(*a*).
Sub-s. (3): TA 1970, s. 169(3).
Sub-s. (4): TA 1970, s. 169(3); FA 1978, s. 30(7)(*a*), (8)(*a*).
Sub-s. (5): TA 1970, s. 169(4); FA 1978, s. 30(7)(*a*).
Sub-s. (6): TA 1970, s. 169(5).
Sub-s. (7): TA 1970, s. 169(6); FA 1978, s. 30(7)(*a*), (8)(*b*).
Sub-s. (8): TA 1970, s. 169(7); FA 1978, s. 30(7)(*a*).
Sub-s. (9): TA 1970, s. 169(8); FA 1978, s. 30(7)(*a*), (8)(*c*).
Sub-ss. (10), (11): TA 1970, s. 169(8), (9).
Sub-s. (12): TA 1970, s. 169(10); FA 1978, s. 30(10).
Note.—See **Prospective Legislation Notes** (Commercial Woodlands).
Cross references.—See FA 1988, Sch. 6, para. 6(4), (9) (amendment to TA 1970, s. 169(10) effective from 15 March 1988).
Amendments.—[1] Words in sub-s. (12)(*a*) substituted by FA 1988, Sch. 6, para. 6(8), (9) with effect from 15 March 1988.

384. Restrictions on right of set-off

(1) Subject to subsection (2) below, a loss (including any amount in respect of capital allowances which, by virtue of section 383, is to be treated as a loss) shall not be available for relief under section 380 unless it is shown that, for the year of assessment in which the loss is claimed to have been sustained, the trade was being carried on on a commercial basis and with a view to the realisation of profits in the trade or, where the carrying on of the trade formed part of a larger undertaking, in the undertaking as a whole.

(2) Subsection (1) above shall not apply—

(*a*) to a loss made, or an allowance in respect of expenditure incurred, by any person in the exercise of functions conferred by or under any enactment (including an enactment contained in a local or private Act); or
(*b*) to an allowance in respect of expenditure incurred before 6th April 1960.

(3) Where during a year of assessment there is a change in the manner in which a trade is being carried on, it shall be treated for the purposes of this section as having been carried on throughout the year in the way in which it was being carried on by the end of the year.

(4) Subject to subsection (5) below, where a trade is (or falls to be treated as being) carried on for a part only of a year of assessment by reason of its being (or falling to be treated as being) set up and commenced, or discontinued, or both, in that year, subsections (1) to (3)

(if any) of capital allowances for earlier years which is carried forward to that year and would, without the balancing charges, be non-effective in that year.

(3) In the case of a claim under section 380, where the capital allowances taken into account by virtue of this section are those for the year of assessment for which the claim is made or for the preceding year (the year of loss being the basis year for that year itself, or the claim being made by way of carry-forward of the loss by virtue of section 380(2)) relief shall not be given by reference to those allowances in respect of an amount greater than the amount non-effective in the year for which the claim is made, or, in the case of allowances for the preceding year, the amount non-effective in both years.

(4) In the case of a claim under section 381, where the capital allowances taken into account by virtue of this section are those for the year of loss, relief shall not be given by reference to those allowances in respect of an amount greater than the amount non-effective in that year.

(5) For the purposes of this section—

(*a*) where the end of the basis period for a year of assessment (as defined in section 72 of the 1968 Act) falls in, or coincides with the end of, any year of assessment, that year is the basis year for the first-mentioned year of assessment, but so that, if a year of assessment would under the foregoing provision be the basis year both for that year itself and for another year of assessment, it shall be the basis year for the year itself and not for the other year;
(*b*) any reference to the capital allowances or balancing charges for a year of assessment shall be construed as a reference to those falling to be made in taxing the trade for that year (but not including, in the case of allowances, any part of the allowances for an earlier year carried forward under section 70(4) of the 1968 Act);
(*c*) any reference to an amount of capital allowances non-effective in a year shall be construed as referring to the amount to which, by reason of an insufficiency of profits or gains, effect cannot be given in taxing the trade for the year; and
(*d*) effect shall be deemed to be given in taxing the trade to allowances carried forward from an earlier year before it is given to allowances arising in a later year.

(6) Where, on a claim made by virtue of this section, relief is not given under section 380 or 381 for the full amount of the loss determined as mentioned in subsection (1) above, the relief shall be referred as far as may be to the loss sustained by the claimant in the trade rather than to the capital allowances in respect of the trade.

(7) Subject to subsection (8) below, where for any year of assessment relief is given under section 380 or 381 by reference to any capital allowances, then, for all the purposes of the Income Tax Acts, effect shall be deemed to have been given to those allowances up to the amount in respect of which relief is so given, as if (in accordance with section 70(2) of the 1968 Act) a deduction in respect thereof had been allowed in taxing the trade for that year, or—

(*a*) where relief is given under section 380, in the case of allowances for the following year, in taxing the trade for that following year;
(*b*) where relief is given under section 381, in the case of allowances for any later year, in taxing the trade for that later year;

and any relief previously given for a subsequent year on the basis that effect had not been given to the allowances as aforesaid shall be adjusted where necessary by an assessment.

(8) Where in any year of assessment a trade is permanently discontinued, or is treated for the purposes of section 113 as permanently discontinued, and, immediately before the discontinuance, the trade was being carried on in partnership, then, notwithstanding subsection (7) above, for the purposes of any claim for relief made by virtue of section 385(5)(*c*) or 388 and relating to that discontinuance, effect shall not be deemed to have been given either—

(*a*) to any part of the capital allowances falling to be made in taxing the trade for that year by reason of relief given under section 380 or 381 by reference to those allowances; or
(*b*) to any part of the capital allowances falling to be made in taxing the trade for the preceding year by reason of relief so given by reference to them, in so far as that relief must be referred to the part of the allowances apportionable to the part of the year within 12 months of the discontinuance on an apportionment made by reference to the comparative lengths of the two parts of the year;

but where the same partner claims relief both under section 380 or 381 and under section 385(5) or 388 in respect of the same allowances, the total amount for which relief is to be given to him by reference thereto shall not exceed the greater of the amounts for which,

(5) Relief shall not be given under subsection (1) above in respect of a loss sustained by an individual in a trade if—

(a) at the time when it is first carried on by him he is married to and living with another individual who has previously carried on the trade; and
(b) the loss is sustained in a year of assessment later than the third year of assessment after that in which the trade was first carried on by the other individual.

(6) For the purposes of this section an individual carries on a trade whether he does so solely or in partnership; and (except as respects the computation of profits or gains and losses) an individual continues to carry on the same trade notwithstanding a change in the persons engaged in carrying it on if he is engaged in carrying it on immediately before and immediately after the change.

(7) This section applies, with the necessary modifications, in relation to a profession or vocation as it applies in relation to a trade.

Former enactments.—Sub-s. (1): FA 1978, s. 30(1).
Sub-s. (2): FA 1978, s. 30(2); Oil Taxation Act 1975, s. 13.
Sub-s (3): FA 1978, s. 30(3).
Sub-ss. (4)–(6): FA 1978, s. 30(4)–(6).
Sub-s. (7): FA 1978, s. 30(10).

382. Provisions supplementary to sections 380 and 381

(1) A claim for relief under section 380 or 381 may require that the relief be given only by reference to the income of the person sustaining the loss, without extending to the income of that person's wife or husband.

(2) Subject to any requirement under subsection (1) above, relief under section 380 or 381 shall be given in respect of a loss sustained by any person by treating the loss as reducing first his income of the corresponding class, then his other income, then the income of the corresponding class of that person's wife or husband, then the other income of the wife or husband.

For the purposes of this subsection "income of the corresponding class" means earned or unearned income according as income arising during the same period as the loss to the person sustaining it from profits or gains of the same trade, profession, vocation or employment would have been that person's earned or unearned income.

(3) Where relief under section 380 or 381 has been given to a person for any year of assessment, he shall not be entitled, in computing the amount of the assessment for any subsequent year, to a deduction of any portion of the amount in respect of which such relief has been obtained.

(4) For the purposes of sections 380 and 381, the amount of a loss sustained in a trade, (including the occupation of woodlands in a case where section 380(4) applies), profession or vocation shall be computed in like manner as the profits or gains arising or accruing from the trade, profession or vocation are computed under the provisions of the Income Tax Acts applicable to Case I or II of Schedule D.

Former enactments.—Sub-s. (1): TA 1970, s. 168(3); FA 1971, s. 16(2)(a); FA 1978, s. 30(7)(a).
Sub-s (2): TA 1970, s. 168(4); FA 1978, s. 30(7)(a).
Sub-ss. (3), (4): TA 1970, s. 168(5), (7), (8); FA 1978, s. 30(7)(a); FA 1987, Sch. 15, para. 2(11).
Note.—See **Prospective Legislation Notes** (Married Couples).

383. Extension of right of set-off to capital allowances

(1) Subject to the provisions of this section, any claim made under section 380 or 381 for relief in respect of a loss sustained by the claimant in any trade in any year of assessment ("the year of loss") may require the amount of that loss to be determined as if an amount equal to the capital allowances for the year of assessment for which the year of loss is the basis year were to be deducted in computing the profits or gains or losses of the trade in the year of loss; and a claim may be so made notwithstanding that apart from those allowances the claimant has not sustained a loss in the trade in the year of loss.

(2) Capital allowances for any year of assessment shall be taken into account by virtue of this section only if and so far as they are not required to offset balancing charges for the year; and, for the purposes of this subsection, the capital allowances for a year of assessment shall be treated as required to offset balancing charges for the year up to the amount on which the balancing charges fall to be made after deducting from that amount the amount

PART X
LOSS RELIEF AND GROUP RELIEF

CHAPTER I
LOSS RELIEF: INCOME TAX

Trade etc. losses

380. Set-off against general income

(1) Where any person sustains a loss in any trade, profession, vocation or employment carried on by him either solely or in partnership, he may, by notice given within two years after the year of assessment, make a claim for relief from income tax on an amount of his income equal to the amount of the loss.

(2) Subject to section 492(2), relief may be given under subsection (1) above in respect of a person's loss sustained in the last preceding year of assessment in any trade, profession, vocation or employment still carried on by him in the year for which the claim is made, in so far as relief in respect of that loss has not already been given under that subsection or otherwise; and where relief is claimed by virtue of this subsection it shall be given in priority to any relief under that subsection in respect of a loss sustained in the year for which the relief is claimed.

(3) Where there is in any year of assessment a change on which a trade, profession or vocation is treated under section 113(1) as permanently discontinued, and a person engaged in carrying it on immediately before the change continues to be so engaged immediately afterwards, it shall, notwithstanding the discontinuance, be treated as the same trade, profession or vocation for the purposes of subsection (2) above, except as respects the computation of profits or gains and losses.

(4) This section applies in relation to losses sustained in the occupation of woodlands in respect of which a person has elected under [paragraph 4 of Schedule 6 to the Finance Act 1988][1] to be charged to income tax under Schedule D as it applies in relation to losses sustained in a trade.

Former enactments.—Sub-s. (1): TA 1970, s. 168(1).
Sub-s. (2): TA 1970, s. 168(2); Oil Taxation Act 1975, s. 13.
Sub-s. (3): TA 1970, s. 168(6).
Sub-s. (4): TA 1970, s. 168(8).
Note.—See **Prospective Legislation Notes** (Commercial Woodlands).
Cross references.—See FA 1988, Sch. 6, para. 6(4), (9) (amendment to TA 1970, s. 168(8) effective from 15 March 1988).
Amendments.—[1] Words in sub-s. (4) substituted by FA 1988, Sch. 6, para. 6(8), (9) with effect from 15 March 1988.

381. Further relief for individuals for losses in early years of trade

(1) Where an individual carrying on a trade sustains a loss in the trade in—
   (a) the year of assessment in which it is first carried on by him; or
   (b) any of the next three years of assessment;

he may, by notice given within two years after the year of assessment in which the loss is sustained, make a claim for relief under this section.

(2) Subject to section 492 and this section, relief shall be given under subsection (1) above from income tax on an amount of the claimant's income equal to the amount of the loss, being income for the three years of assessment last preceding that in which the loss is sustained, taking income for an earlier year before income for a later year.

(3) Relief shall not be given for the same loss or the same portion of a loss both under subsection (1) above and under any other provision of the Income Tax Acts.

(4) Relief shall not be given under subsection (1) above in respect of a loss sustained in any period unless it is shown that the trade was carried on throughout that period on a commercial basis and in such a way that profits in the trade (or, where the carrying on of the trade forms part of a larger undertaking, in the undertaking as a whole) could reasonably be expected to be realised in that period or within a reasonable time thereafter.

379. Interpretation of sections 369 to 378

In sections 369 to 378—

"prescribed", except in section 376(4) and (5), means prescribed by the Board;
"qualifying borrower" has the meaning given by section 376(1) to (3);
"qualifying lender" has the meaning given by section 376(4) to (6);
"regulations", except in sections 378(1) and (2), means regulations made by the Board under section 378;
"relevant loan interest" has the meaning given by section 370(1).

Former enactments.—FA 1982, ss. 26(3), 28(5), (7), Sch. 7, paras. 1, 4(1)(*a*), 13(1), 14(1).

(8) A building society is by virtue of this subsection specified for the purposes of this section; and the Treasury may by order specify any other qualifying lender or class of qualifying lender for the purposes of this section.

(9) The giving of a notice under subsection (2)(*a*) or (*b*) above does not affect the right of the qualifying lender and the qualifying borrower to vary, by agreement, the terms on which interest or capital or both is to be repaid.

(10) In this section—

"loan agreement" means an agreement governing the terms of payment of interest and repayment of capital of a loan the interest on which is relevant loan interest; and
"combined payment" means one of a number of regular payments which are attributable in part to repayment of capital and in part to payment of interest.

Former enactments.—Sub-ss. (1)–(3): FA 1982, s 28(1)–(3).
Sub-s (4): FA 1982, s. 28(4); FA 1984, s. 23(2).
Sub-s. (5): FA 1982, s. 28(4).
Sub-s. (6): FA 1982, s. 28(4A); FA 1984, s. 23(3).
Sub-s. (7): FA 1982, s. 28(4).
Sub-ss. (8)–(10): FA 1982, s. 28(5)–(7).

378. Supplementary regulations

(1) The Treasury may by regulations make provision for the application of sections 369 to 377 in relation to—

(*a*) a housing association which is for the time being approved for the purposes of section 488 and which borrows or has borrowed from a qualifying lender on the security of a freehold or leasehold estate of that association on land in the United Kingdom; and
(*b*) a self-build society which is for the time being approved for the purposes of section 489 and which borrows or has borrowed from a qualifying lender on the security of a freehold or leasehold estate of that society on land in the United Kingdom.

(2) Regulations under subsection (1) above—

(*a*) may contain such modifications of the provisions of sections 369 to 377, and
(*b*) may make the application of any of those provisions subject to such special conditions,

as appear to the Treasury to be appropriate.

(3) The Board may by regulations make provision—

(*a*) for the purposes of any provision of sections 369 to 377 which relates to any matter or thing to be specified by or done in accordance with regulations;
(*b*) for the application of those sections in relation to loan interest paid by personal representatives and trustees;
(*c*) with respect to the furnishing of information by borrowers or lenders, including, in the case of lenders, the inspection of books, documents and other records on behalf of the Board;
(*d*) for, and with respect to, appeals to the General Commissioners or the Special Commissioners against the refusal of the Board to issue a notice under section 374(1)(*b*) or the issue of a notice under section 375(6) or (7); and
(*e*) generally for giving effect to sections 369 to 377.

(4) In this section—

(*a*) references to a self-build society are references to a self-build society within the meaning of Part I of the Housing Associations Act 1985 or, in Northern Ireland, Part VII of the Housing (Northern Ireland) Order 1981; and
(*b*) in its application to Scotland—

(i) "a freehold or leasehold estate" means any interest in land, and
(ii) any reference to a loan on the security of such an estate is a reference to a loan upon a heritable security within the meaning of section 9(8)(*a*) of the Conveyancing and Feudal Reform (Scotland) Act 1970.

Former enactments.—FA 1982, s. 28(4); FA 1984, s. 56(2); Housing (Consequential Provisions) Act 1985, Sch. 2, para 54(2).

377. Variation of terms of repayment of certain loans

(1) If relevant loan interest payable by a qualifying borrower—

    (*a*) is payable under a loan agreement requiring combined payments, and
    (*b*) is payable to a qualifying lender who, in accordance with subsection (5) below, is specified for the purposes of this section, and
    (*c*) is interest on a loan made before 1st April 1983, or if it is interest in respect of which the Board notified an earlier date to the lender under paragraph 2(5) of Schedule 7 to the Finance Act 1982, before that earlier date,

then, subject to subsection (2) below, the terms of repayment are by virtue of this section varied in accordance with subsection (3) below.

(2) Subsection (1) above does not apply to any combined payments unless—

    (*a*) the qualifying lender concerned has, in accordance with regulations, given notice to the qualifying borrower that this section is to apply to combined payments which the borrower is required to make under the loan agreement; and
    (*b*) the qualifying borrower has not, in accordance with regulations, given notice to the qualifying lender that he wishes to continue with combined payments which, allowing for any sums he is entitled to deduct by virtue of section 369, do not exceed the combined payments which he would have been required to make but for the provisions of that section.

(3) Where subsection (1) applies, the amount of any combined payment payable by the qualifying borrower concerned which includes a payment of relevant loan interest shall be determined by the lender so as to secure, so far as practicable—

    (*a*) that the principal and interest are repaid over the period which is for the time being agreed between the lender and the borrower; and
    (*b*) that, unless there is a change in that period or in the basic rate of income tax or in the rate of interest charged by the lender, the amount of each net payment due from the borrower to the lender will be of the same amount;

and for the purposes of paragraph (*b*) above "net payment" means a payment which, so far as it is a payment of interest, consists of interest from which the sum provided for by section 369(1) has been deducted.

(4) Where the qualifying borrower gives a notice under subsection (2)(*b*) above, the amount of any combined payment payable by him which includes a payment of relevant loan interest and the period over which the principal and interest on the loan are to be repaid shall be determined by the lender so as to secure, so far as practicable, that, unless there is a change in the basic rate of income tax or in the rate of interest charged by the lender—

    (*a*) the amount of each net payment as defined in subsection (3) above which is due from the borrower to the lender will be of the same amount; and
    (*b*) the amount of each such payment does not exceed what, apart from section 369, would have been the amount of the combined payment payable by the borrower on the effective date of the notice under subsection (2)(*a*) above, less tax at the basic rate for the year of assessment in which that effective date falls on so much of that combined payment as would have consisted of interest.

(5) Nothing in this section or in the loan agreement shall prevent the borrower from making, at such time or times as he chooses, additional repayments of capital of any amount so as to secure that the principal and interest on the loan are repaid within a period which is not shorter than that referred to in subsection (3)(*a*) above.

(6) For the purposes of subsection (4)(*b*) above the effective date of a notice under subsection (2)(*a*) above is the date which, in accordance with regulations, is the due date for the first combined payment which, in consequence of that notice and the notice under subsection (2)(*b*) above, is a net payment for the purposes of subsection (3)(*b*) above.

(7) The repeal by this Act of section 28 of the Finance Act 1982 shall not affect the variation of any agreement in pursuance of that section before 26th July 1984 and accordingly, where the borrower gave a notice under subsection (2)(*b*) of that section, the maximum amount of any combined payment payable under the agreement as so varied which includes a payment of relevant loan interest shall continue to be the amount which would, apart from section 369, have been the first combined payment payable by the borrower after the date referred to in subsection (1)(*c*) above less tax at the basic rate for the year 1983–84 on so much of that combined payment as would have consisted of interest (subject to any change in the basic rate of income tax or in the rate of interest charged by the lender); and subsection (5) above shall apply in relation to any agreement as so varied.

(b) the disclosure is made for the purposes of any civil or criminal proceedings concerned with the loan to which the disclosure relates.

Former enactments.—Sub-ss. (1)–(4): FA 1982, Sch. 7, para. 8.
Sub-s. (5): FA 1982, Sch. 7, para. 9(1).
Sub-ss. (6), (7): FA 1982, Sch. 7, para. 10(1), (2).
Sub-s. (8): FA 1982, Sch. 7, para. 11.
Sub-ss. (9), (10): FA 1982, Sch. 7, para. 12.

376. Qualifying borrowers and qualifying lenders

(1) Subject to subsection (2) below, an individual is a qualifying borrower with respect to the interest on any loan.

(2) In relation to interest paid at a time when the borrower or the borrower's husband or wife holds an office or employment in respect of the emoluments of which he or she would but for some special exemption or immunity from tax be chargeable to tax under Case I, II or III of Schedule E, the borrower is not a qualifying borrower.

(3) In subsection (2) above references to the borrower's husband or wife do not include references to a separated husband or wife, and for this purpose "separated" has the meaning given by section 367(1).

(4) The following bodies are qualifying lenders:—

(a) a building society;
(b) a local authority;
(c) the Bank of England;
(d) the Post Office;
(e) a company which is authorised under section 3 or 4 of the Insurance Companies Act 1982 to carry on in the United Kingdom any of the classes of business specified in Schedule 1 to that Act;
(f) any company to which property and rights belonging to a trustee savings bank were transferred by section 3 of the Trustee Savings Bank Act 1985;
(g) a registered friendly society or branch, within the meaning of the Friendly Societies Act 1974 or the Friendly Societies Act (Northern Ireland) 1970;
(h) a development corporation within the meaning of the New Towns Act 1981 or the New Towns (Scotland) Act 1968;
(j) the Commission for the New Towns;
(k) the Housing Corporation;
[(ka) Housing for Wales;][1]
(l) the Northern Ireland Housing Executive;
(m) the Scottish Special Housing Association;
(n) the Development Board for Rural Wales;
(o) the Church of England Pensions Board;
(p) any of the following which is prescribed under subsection (5) below, namely, an institution authorised under the Banking Act 1987, a company which is authorised as mentioned in paragraph (e) above to carry on in the United Kingdom any of the classes of business specified in Schedule 2 to the Insurance Companies Act 1982, and a 90 per cent. subsidiary of any such institution or company or of a company within paragraph (e) above and any other body whose activities and objects appear to the Treasury to qualify it for inclusion in this paragraph.

(5) The Treasury may by order prescribe for the purposes of subsection (4) above generally or in relation to any specified description of loan any of the bodies referred to in paragraph (p) of subsection (4) above; and a body which is prescribed by such an order shall become a qualifying lender generally or, as the case may be, in relation to such description of loan as is specified in the order with effect from such date as may be so specified.

(6) Without prejudice to subsection (4) above, in relation to interest to which section 370(3) applies, the person who, as a qualifying lender for the purposes of Part II of the Housing Subsidies Act 1967 or Part VIII of the Housing (Northern Ireland) Order 1981, was the lender in relation to the loan referred to in section 370(3) shall also be a qualifying lender.

Former enactments.—Sub-ss. (1)–(3): FA 1982, Sch. 7 para. 13.
Sub-s. (4): FA 1982, Sch. 7, para 14(1); Insurance Companies Act 1982, Sch. 5, para. 28(b); FA 1983, s. 17(3); Trustee Savings Bank Act 1985, Sch. 2, para. 7(1); Banking Act 1987, Sch 6, para 13.
Sub-s. (5): FA 1982, Sch. 7, para 14(2); FA 1973, s. 17(4); FA 1985, s. 37(4).
Sub-s (6): FA 1982, Sch. 7, para. 15.
Amendments.—[1] Sub-s. (4)(ka) inserted by the Housing Act 1988, Sch. 17, para. 115.

375. Interest ceasing to be relevant loan interest etc.

(1) If at any time—

(a) the interest on a loan ceases to be relevant loan interest; or
(b) a person making payments of relevant loan interest ceases to be a qualifying borrower;

the borrower shall give notice of the fact to the lender.

(2) Without prejudice to subsection (3) below, in relation to a payment of interest—

(a) which is due after the time referred to in subsection (1) above and before the date on which notice is given under that subsection, and
(b) from which a deduction was made as mentioned in section 369(1),

section 369 shall have effect as if the payment were a payment of relevant loan interest made by a qualifying borrower.

(3) Nothing in subsection (2) above entitles the borrower to any relief from tax or other benefit and, accordingly, where the amount of any such relief or other benefit which is allowed by virtue of that subsection exceeds that which ought to have been allowed, he shall be liable to make good the excess and an inspector may make such assessments as may in his judgment be required for recovering the excess.

(4) The Management Act shall apply to an assessment under subsection (3) above as if it were an assessment to tax for the year of assessment in which the relief was given and as if—

(a) the assessment were among those specified in sections 55(1) (recovery of tax not postponed) and 86(2) (interest on overdue tax) of that Act; and
(b) the sum charged by the assessment were tax specified in paragraph 3 of the Table in section 86(4) of that Act (reckonable date).

(5) If, as a result of receiving a notice under subsection (1) above or otherwise, a qualifying lender has reason to believe that any interest is not longer relevant loan interest or that a borrower is no longer a qualifying borrower, the lender shall furnish the Board with such information as is in his possession with respect to those matters.

(6) Where it appears to the Board that any of the provisions of sections 370 to 373 is not or may not be fulfilled with respect to any interest, or that a qualifying borrower has or may have ceased to be a qualifying borrower, they shall give notice of that fact to the lender and the borrower specifying the description of relevant loan interest concerned or, as the case may be, that the borrower has or may have ceased to be a qualifying borrower.

(7) Section 369 shall not apply to any payment of relevant loan interest of a description to which a notice under subsection (6) above relates and which becomes due or is made after such date as may be specified in the notice and before such date as may be specified in a further notice given by the Board to the lender and the borrower.

(8) In any case where—

(a) section 369 applies to any relevant loan interest by virtue of a notice under section 374(1)(b), and
(b) the relevant date specified in the notice is earlier than the date from which the interest begins to be paid under deduction of tax, and
(c) a payment of that interest was made on or after the relevant date but not under deduction of tax,

regulations may provide for a sum to be paid by the Board of an amount equal to that which the borrower would have been able to deduct from that payment by virtue of section 369 if it had been made after the relevant date.

(9) No obligation as to secrecy imposed by statute or otherwise on persons employed in relation to Inland Revenue shall prevent information relating to any loan in respect of which an option notice has been given as mentioned in section 370(3)(a) from being disclosed to the Secretary of State or the Department of the Environment for Northern Ireland, or to an officer of either of them authorised to receive such information, in connection with the exercise by the Secretary of State or that Department of any of his or its functions in relation to any such loan.

(10) Subsection (9) above extends only to disclosure by or under the authority of the Inland Revenue; and information which is disclosed to any person by virtue of that subsection shall not be further disclosed to any other person unless—

(a) it could have been disclosed to that other person in accordance with that subsection; or

357, the interest on the loans falls to be treated for the purposes of that section as payable on one loan; but, notwithstanding that each of those loans is accordingly a limited loan for the purposes of this section, none of the interest on any of them is relevant loan interest unless each of the loans was made by the same qualifying lender.

(5) Where the condition in paragraph (*a*) or (*b*) of subsection (2) above is fulfilled and, if subsection (3) or (4) above also applies, the condition in that subsection is also fulfilled only so much of the interest as (apart from section 353(2)) would be eligible for relief under section 353 is relevant loan interest.

(6) Where a loan on which interest is payable by the borrower was made jointly to the borrower and another person who is not the borrower's husband or wife, the interest on the loan is not relevant loan interest unless—

(*a*) each of the persons to whom the loan was made is a qualifying borrower; and
(*b*) in relation to each of them considered separately, the whole of that interest is relevant loan interest, in accordance with sections 370 to 372 and this section.

(7) In subsection (6) above references to the borrower's husband or wife do not include references to a separated husband or wife, and for this purpose "separated" has the meaning given by section 367(1).

Former enactments.—Sub-ss. (1)–(3): FA 1982, Sch. 7, para. 5(1)–(3); FA 1985, s. 37(2).
Sub-s. (4): FA 1982, Sch. 7, para. 5(3A); FA 1983, s. 17(2).
Sub-s. (5): FA 1982, Sch. 7, para. 5(4); FA 1983, s. 17(2); FA 1985, s. 37(3).
Sub-ss. (6), (7): FA 1982, Sch. 7, para. 6(1), (2).
Amendments.—[1] Words in sub-ss. (1), (3), (4) inserted by FA 1988, s. 42(3)(*d*), (4) with effect from 1 August 1988.

374. Conditions for application of section 369

(1) Section 369 does not apply to any relevant loan interest unless—

(*a*) in the case of a loan of a description specified by regulations for the purposes of this paragraph, the borrower or, in the case of joint borrowers, each of them has given notice to the lender in the prescribed form certifying—
  (i) that he is a qualifying borrower; and
  (ii) that the interest is relevant loan interest; and
  (iii) such other matters as may be prescribed; or

(*b*) the Board have given notice to the lender and the borrower that the interest may be paid under deduction of tax; or
(*c*) it is interest to which section 370(3) applies; or
(*d*) the loan to which the interest relates is of a description specified by regulations for the purposes of this paragraph and was made—
  (i) if sub-paragraph (2) of paragraph 2 of Schedule 7 to the Finance Act 1982 applied to interest on the loan which became due on or after a date earlier than 6th April 1983, being a date specified by the Board in pursuance of sub-paragraph (5) of that paragraph, before that earlier date; or
  (ii) if the qualifying lender is a building society or a local authority, before 1st April 1983; or
  (iii) if sub-paragraphs (i) and (ii) above do not apply and the interest falls within section 370(2), before 6th April 1983.

(2) Where notice has been given as mentioned in paragraph (*a*) or (*b*) of subsection (1) above, section 369 applies to any relevant loan interest to which the notice relates and which becomes due on or after the relevant date, as defined by subsection (3) below; and in a case falling within paragraph (*c*) or (*d*) of subsection (1) above, section 369 applies to the relevant loan interest referred to in that paragraph.

(3) In subsection (2) above "the relevant date" means—

(*a*) in the case of a notice under subsection (1)(*a*) above, the date the notice is given, and
(*b*) in the case of a notice under subsection (1)(*b*) above, a date specified in the notice as being the relevant date (which may be earlier than the date so specified as the date from which the interest may be paid under deduction of tax).

Former enactments.—Sub-s. (1)(*a*)–(*c*): FA 1982, Sch. 7, para 7(1)(*a*)–(*c*).
Sub-s. (1)(*d*): FA 1982, Sch. 7, para. 7(1)(*d*), (4), (5).
Sub-ss. (2), (3): FA 1982, Sch. 7, para. 7(2), (3).

(*a*) to the use of other land or another caravan or house-boat wholly or partly as that person's only or main residence, and
(*b*) to the disposal of the land, caravan, house-boat or dwelling to which the first loan relates,

then, in relation to interest payable within 12 months from the making of the other loan, the condition in section 355(1) shall be treated as continuing to be fulfilled.

(2) If in a case falling within subsection (1) above the interest on the first loan is interest to which section 370(2) applies and a direction is given under section 354(6) extending the period within which section 354 applies to that loan, subsection (1) above shall have effect in relation to that case as if for the reference to 12 months there were substituted a reference to such longer period as is specified in the direction.

(3) If in a case falling within subsection (1) above the interest on the first loan is interest to which section 370(3) applies and, having regard to the circumstances of that case, it appears to the Board reasonable to do so, they may direct that, in relation to that case, subsection (1) above shall have effect as if for the reference to 12 months there were substituted a reference to such longer period as meets the circumstances of the case.

Former enactment.—FA 1982, Sch. 7, para. 3(4)–(6).

372. Home improvement loans

(1) Notwithstanding anything in section 370(2), interest on a home improvement loan (other than interest to which section 370(3) applies) is not relevant loan interest unless—

(*a*) the qualifying lender to whom the interest is payable is a building society or a local authority or the Northern Ireland Housing Executive; or
(*b*) the qualifying lender to whom the interest is payable has given notice to the Board in accordance with regulations that he is prepared to have those home improvement loans in respect of which he is the lender and which were made after such date as he may specify in the notice brought within the tax deduction scheme.

(2) A qualifying lender may not specify a date in a notice under subsection (1) above which is earlier than the earliest date on which paragraph 2 of Schedule 7 to the Finance Act 1982 applied, or, if that paragraph did not apply, section 370 applies to interest on any loan (whether or not a home improvement loan) made by him.

(3) In this section "home improvement loan" means a loan made to defray money applied wholly in improving or developing land or buildings on land or in paying off another loan which was itself to defray money so applied.

(4) Section 354(2) shall apply for the purposes of this section as it applies for the purposes of sections 354 and 355.

Former enactments.—FA 1982, Sch. 7, para. 4; FA 1983, s. 17(1).

373. Loans in excess of the qualifying maximum, and joint borrowers

(1) The provisions of this section have effect in relation to a loan where, by virtue of section [356A, section][1] 357(1) or section 365(3), only part of the interest on the loan would (apart from section 353(2)) be eligible for relief under section 353; and in this section any such loan is referred to as a "limited loan".

(2) None of the interest on a limited loan is relevant loan interest unless—

(*a*) the loan is made on or after 6th April 1987; or
(*b*) the qualifying lender to whom the interest is payable has given notice to the Board in accordance with regulations that he is prepared to have limited loans of a description which includes that limited loan brought within the tax deduction scheme.

(3) If in a case where subsection (2) above applies [section 356D(6) or][1] section 357(1) requires an earlier loan to be taken into account for the purpose of determining that part of the limited loan interest on which would (apart from section 353(2)) be eligible for relief under section 353, none of the interest on the limited loan is relevant loan interest unless that earlier loan was made by the same qualifying lender as the limited loan.

(4) The reference in subsection (1) above to a loan only part of the interest on which would (apart from section 353(2)) be eligible for relief under section 353 includes a reference to each of two or more loans if, by virtue of [section 356D(7) or][1] subsection (3)(*b*) of section

any amount so recovered shall be treated for the purposes of the Tax Acts in like manner as the payment of relevant loan interest to which it relates.

Former enactments.—Sub-ss. (1), (2): FA 1982, s. 26(1), (2).
Sub-ss. (3)–(5): FA 1982, s. 26(4)–(6).
Sub-s. (6): FA 1982, s. 26(7).

370. Relevant loan interest

(1) Subject to this section and sections 371 to 376, in this Part "relevant loan interest" means interest which is paid and payable in the United Kingdom to a qualifying lender and to which subsection (2) or (3) below applies.

(2) Subject to subsection (4) below, this subsection applies to interest if, disregarding section 353(2)—

(a) it is interest falling within section 354(1) or 365; and
(b) apart from section 74(o) and, where applicable, section [356A,][1] 357 or 365(3), the whole of the interest either would be eligible for relief under section 353 or would be taken into account in a computation of profits or gains or losses for the purposes of Case I, II or VI of Schedule D for any year of assessment; and
(c) except in the case of interest falling within section 365, at the time the interest is paid, the condition in either section 355(1) or 356(1) is fulfilled with respect to the land, caravan or house-boat to which the loan concerned relates.

(3) This subsection applies to interest which is payable on a loan—

(a) in respect of which there was in force on 31st March 1983—

(i) an option notice given under section 24(2) of the Housing Subsidies Act 1967 (option mortgages) other than one falling within section 27(3)(b) of the Finance Act 1982; or
(ii) an option notice given under Article 142(2) of the Housing (Northern Ireland) Order 1981 (option mortgages in Northern Ireland) other than one falling within section 27(4)(b) of the Finance Act 1982; and

(b) which relates to a dwelling in respect of which, at the time the interest is paid, the condition in section 355(1) is fulfilled.

(4) Subsection (2) above does not apply to interest payable on a loan the only security for which is a contract of insurance on human life or a contract to pay an annuity on human life.

(5) In determining whether subsection (2) above applies to any interest, sections 354(1) and 365 shall each have effect as if the words "or the Republic of Ireland" were omitted.

(6) In determining whether subsection (2)(c) above applies to any interest, section 355(1) shall have effect as if—

(a) in paragraph (a) after the word "used", where it first occurs, there were inserted the words "wholly or to a substantial extent"; and
(b) paragraph (b) and the word "or" immediately preceding it were omitted.

(7) In determining for the purposes of subsection (3)(b) above whether the condition in section 355(1) is for the time being fulfilled with respect to any dwelling—

(a) subsection (1) of that section shall have effect as if for the words from "section 354" to "used" (where it first occurs) there were substituted the words "interest shall not be relevant loan interest for the purposes of section 369 unless the dwelling to which the loan relates is at the time the interest is paid used wholly or partly" and paragraph (b) and the word "or" immediately preceding it were omitted; and
(b) subsection (3) of that section shall have effect as if for "land, caravan or house-boat" there were substituted "dwelling".

Former enactments.—Sub-ss. (1)–(3): FA 1982, Sch. 7, para. 2(1)–(3).
Sub-s. (4): FA 1982, Sch. 7, para. 2(7).
Sub-ss. (5)–(7): FA 1982, Sch. 7, para. 3(1)–(3).
Amendments.—[1] Number in sub-s. (2)(b) inserted by FA 1988, s. 42(3)(c), (4) with effect from 1 August 1988.

371. Second loans

(1) Where at a time when interest on a loan ("the first loan") is relevant loan interest, the borrower raises another loan to defray money to be applied as mentioned in section 354(1) with a view—

(*b*) interest on that debt or liability shall not be taken into account in that computation for any year of assessment for which the interest so paid could have been taken into account but for the relief.

(5) For the purposes of subsections (3) and (4) above, all interest capable of being taken into account in such a computation as is mentioned in those subsections which is payable by any person on money advanced to him on current account, whether advanced on one or more accounts or by the same or separate banks or other persons, shall be treated as interest payable on the same debt.

(6) References in subsections (3) and (4) above to relief given or an amount taken into account are references to relief given or an amount taken into account on a claim or in an assessment which has been finally determined.

Former enactment.—FA 1972, Sch. 10, paras. 1–6.

Mortgage interest relief at source

Cross references.—See FA 1988, s. 43(3) (interest paid by a housing association or a self-build society on a home improvement loan made after 5 April 1988 not to be relevant loan interest for the purposes of tax relief under the following provisions),
s. 44(6) (interest paid by a housing association or a self-build society on a loan for residence of dependent relative or former spouse made after 5 April 1988 not to be relevant loan interest for the purposes of tax relief under the following provisions).

369. Mortgage interest payable under deduction of tax

(1) If a person who is a qualifying borrower makes a payment of relevant loan interest to which this section applies, he shall be entitled, on making the payment, to deduct and retain out of it a sum equal to income tax thereon at the basic rate for the year of assessment in which the payment becomes due.

(2) Where a sum is deducted under subsection (1) above from a payment of relevant loan interest—

(*a*) the person to whom the payment is made shall allow the deduction on receipt of the residue;
(*b*) the borrower shall be acquitted and discharged of so much money as is represented by the deduction as if the sum had been actually paid; and
(*c*) the sum deducted shall be treated as income tax paid by the person to whom the payment is made.

(3) Where payments of relevant loan interest to which this section applies become due in any year, the borrower shall be charged with tax at the basic rate for that year on an amount of income equal, subject to subsection (4) below, to the deduction which, in computing his total income, falls to be made on account of those payments.

(4) In any case where—

(*a*) payments of relevant loan interest to which this section applies become due in any year; and
(*b*) the total income of the borrower for that year is such that he cannot benefit from any or, as the case may be, the full amount of the relevant personal reliefs to which he is entitled;

so much of that full amount as cannot be deducted from his total income shall be deducted from the amount of income on which he is chargeable to tax by virtue of subsection (3) above.

(5) In subsection (4) above "relevant personal relief" means any relief to which the borrower concerned is entitled under Chapter I of Part VII other than—

(*a*) relief under section 266 which is given either by deduction by virtue of subsection (5) of that section or in accordance with paragraph 6 of Schedule 14; and
(*b*) relief under section 273;

and for the purposes of subsection (4) above the full amount of those reliefs means the amount of them determined without regard to section 276.

(6) Any person by whom a payment of relevant loan interest to which this section applies is received shall be entitled to recover from the Board, in accordance with regulations, an amount which by virtue of subsection (2)(*c*) above is treated as income tax paid by him; and

that person, or of his spouse, if the mother is widowed or living apart from her husband, or, in consequence of dissolution or annulment of marriage, a single woman;

"house-boat" means a boat or similar structure designed or adapted for use as a place of permanent habitation;

"large caravan" means one which has either or both of the following dimensions—

  (a) an overall length (excluding any draw bar) exceeding 22 feet;
  (b) an overall width exceeding seven feet six inches;

where "overall length" and "overall width" have the meanings given in Regulation 3 of the Motor Vehicles (Construction and Use) Regulations 1966;

"separated" means separated under an order of a court of competent jurisdiction or by deed of separation or in such circumstances that the separation is likely to be permanent; and

"street works" means any works for the sewering, levelling, paving, metalling, flagging, channelling and making good of a road, and includes the provision of proper means for lighting a road.

(2) Sections 354(1) and 360 to 364 do not apply to a loan unless it is made—

  (a) in connection with the application of money, and
  (b) on the occasion of, or within what is in the circumstances a reasonable time from, the application of the money;

and those sections do not apply to a loan the proceeds of which are applied for some other purpose before being applied as mentioned in those sections.

(3) For the purposes of sections 354 to 364, the giving of credit for any money due from the purchaser under any sale shall be treated as the making of a loan to defray money applied by him in making the purchase.

(4) Where part only of a debt fulfils the conditions required under sections 354 to 364 for interest on the debt to be eligible for relief under section 353, such proportion of the interest shall be treated as eligible for relief under that section as is equal to the portion of the debt fulfilling those conditions at the time of the application of the money in question.

(5) In sections [356A to 357][1] references to the qualifying maximum for the year of assessment are references to such sum as Parliament may determine for the purpose for that year.

Former enactments.—Sub-s. (1): FA 1972, Sch. 9, paras. 5A, 9; FA 1974, Sch. 1, paras. 3, 4(4).
Sub-s. (2): FA 1972, Sch. 9, para. 2; FA 1974, Sch. 1, para. 23.
Sub-s. (3): FA 1972, Sch. 9, para. 14; FA 1974, Sch. 1, para. 23.
Sub-s. (4): FA 1972, Sch. 9, para. 15; FA 1974, Sch. 1, paras. 1, 23.
Sub-s. (5): FA 1972, Sch. 9, para. 5(1A); FA 1984, s. 22(1)(c).
Note.—The qualifying maximum for the year 1989–90 is £30,000; see FA 1989, s. 43.
Amendments.—[1] Numbers in sub-s. (5) substituted by FA 1988, s. 42(3)(b), (4) with effect from 1 August 1988.

368. Exclusion of double relief etc.

(1) Interest in respect of which relief is given under section 353 shall not be allowable as a deduction for any other purpose of the Income Tax Acts.

(2) Relief shall not be given under section 353 against income chargeable to corporation tax, and shall not be given against any other income of a company, except where both of the following conditions are satisfied, that is to say—

  (a) that the company is not resident in the United Kingdom; and
  (b) that the interest cannot be taken into account in computing corporation tax chargeable on the company.

(3) Where interest on any debt or liability is taken into account in the computation of profits or gains or losses for the purposes of Case I or II of Schedule D no relief shall be given under section 353—

  (a) in respect of the payment of that interest; or
  (b) in respect of interest on the same debt or liability which is paid in any year of assessment for which that computation is relevant.

(4) Where relief is given under section 353 in respect of the interest paid in any year of assessment on any debt or liability—

  (a) that interest shall not be taken into account in the computation of profits or gains or losses for the purposes of Case I or II of Schedule D for any year of assessment; and

Former enactments.—Sub-s. (1): FA 1974, Sch. 1, para. 17(1); FA 1975, Sch. 12, para. 19(2); FA 1986, s. 100.
Sub-s. (2): FA 1974, Sch. 1, para. 18.
Sub-ss. (3), (4): FA 1974, Sch. 1, paras. 20, 21; FA 1975, Sch. 12, para. 19(3), (4); FA 1986, s. 100.

365. Loan to buy life annuity

(1) Subject to the following provisions of this section, interest is eligible for relief under section 353 if it is interest on a loan in respect of which the following conditions are satisfied—

(*a*) that the loan was made as part of a scheme under which not less than nine-tenths of the proceeds of the loan were applied to the purchase by the person to whom it was made of an annuity ending with his life or with the life of the survivor of two or more persons ("the annuitants") who include the person to whom the loan was made;
(*b*) that at the time the loan was made the person to whom it was made or each of the annuitants had attained the age of 65 years;
(*c*) that the loan was secured on land in the United Kingdom or the Republic of Ireland and the person to whom it was made or one of the annuitants owns an estate or interest in that land; and
(*d*) that, if the loan was made after 26th March 1974, the person to whom it was made or each of the annuitants uses the land on which it was secured as his only or main residence at the time the interest is paid.

(2) Interest is not eligible for relief by virtue of this section unless it is payable by the person to whom the loan was made or by one of the annuitants.

(3) If the loan was made after 26th March 1974 interest on it is eligible for relief by virtue of this section only to the extent that the amount on which it is payable does not exceed the qualifying maximum for the year of assessment; and if the interest is payable by two or more persons the interest payable by each of them is so eligible only to the extent that the amount on which it is payable does not exceed such amount as bears to the qualifying maximum for the year of assessment the same proportion as the interest payable by him bears to the interest payable by both or all of them.

Former enactments.—FA 1974, Sch. 1, para. 24; FA 1984, s. 22(3).

366. Information

(1) A person who claims relief under section 353 in respect of any payment of interest shall furnish to the inspector a statement in writing by the person to whom the payment is made, showing—

(*a*) the date when the debt was incurred;
(*b*) the amount of the debt when incurred;
(*c*) the interest paid in the year of assessment for which the claim is made (or, in the case of relief by virtue of section 355(4) or 364(2), the year of assessment for which the claim would be made but for an insufficiency of income); and
(*d*) the name and address of the debtor.

(2) Where any such interest as is mentioned in section 353 is paid, the person to whom it is paid shall, if the person who pays it so requests in writing, furnish him with such statement as regards that interest as is mentioned in subsection (1) above; and the duty imposed by this subsection shall be enforceable at the suit or instance of the person making the request.

(3) Subsections (1) and (2) above do not apply to interest paid to a building society, or to a local authority.

Former enactments.—Sub-s. (1): FA 1972, Sch. 10, para. 7; FA 1974, Sch. 1, para. 25(1).
Sub-ss. (2), (3): FA 1972, Sch. 10, paras. 8, 9.

367. Provisions supplementary to sections 354 to 366

(1) In sections 354 to 366 as they apply throughout the United Kingdom and in relation to the Republic of Ireland—

"caravan" has the meaning given by section 29(1) of the Caravan Sites and Control of Development Act 1960;
"dependent relative" means, in relation to any person, a relative of his, or of his spouse, who is incapacitated by old age or infirmity from maintaining himself, or the mother of

(*a*) he receives consideration of that amount or value for the sale, exchange or assignment of any part of the ordinary share capital of the company or of his share or shares in the co-operative or of his interest in the partnership, or of any consideration of that amount or value by way of repayment of any part of that ordinary share capital or of his share or shares in the co-operative; or

(*b*) the close company, co-operative, employee-controlled company or partnership repays that amount of a loan or advance from him or the partnership returns that amount of capital to him; or

(*c*) he receives consideration of that amount or value for assigning any debt due to him from the close company, co-operative, employee-controlled company or partnership;

and where a sale or assignment is not a bargain made at arm's length, the sale or assignment shall be deemed to be for a consideration of an amount equal to the market value of what is disposed of.

(3) In the application of this section to Scotland for the word "assignment" wherever it occurs there shall be substituted the word "assignation".

(4) Section 360, or, as the case may be, 361(2) or (4) or 362(2) and subsections (1) to (3) above, shall apply to a loan within section 360(1)(*c*), 361(1)(*c*) or (3)(*b*) or 362(1)(*c*) as if it, and any loan it replaces, were one loan, and so that—

(*a*) references to the application of the proceeds of the loan were references to the application of the proceeds of the original loan; and

(*b*) any restriction under subsection (1) above which applies to any loan which has been replaced shall apply to the loan which replaces it.

(5) In this section and sections 361 and 362—

"co-operative" means a common ownership enterprise or a co-operative enterprise as defined in section 2 of the Industrial Common Ownership Act 1976; and

"subsidiary" has the same meaning as for the purposes of section 2 of that Act.

Former enactments.—Sub-s. (1): FA 1974, Sch. 1, para. 13; FA 1981, s. 25(4); FA 1983, s. 24(2)(*a*).
Sub-s. (2): FA 1974, Sch. 1, para. 14(1); FA 1981, s. 25(4); FA 1983, s. 24(2)(*a*).
Sub-s. (3): FA 1974, Sch. 1, para. 14(2).
Sub-s. (4): FA 1974, Sch. 1, para. 15; FA 1981, s. 25(4); FA 1983, s. 24(2)(*b*).
Sub-s. (5): FA 1974, Sch. 1, para. 10A(2); FA 1981, s. 25(3).

364. Loan to pay inheritance tax

(1) Interest is eligible for relief under section 353 if it is interest on a loan to the personal representatives of a deceased person, the proceeds of which are applied—

(*a*) in paying, before the grant of representation or confirmation, capital transfer tax or inheritance tax payable on the delivery of the personal representatives' account and attributable to the value of personal property to which the deceased was beneficially entitled immediately before his death and which vests in the personal representatives or would vest in them if the property were situated in the United Kingdom; or

(*b*) in paying off another loan interest on which would have been eligible for that relief by virtue of this section if the loan had not been paid off (on the assumption, if the loan was free of interest, that it carried interest);

and the interest is paid in respect of a period ending within one year from the making of the loan within paragraph (*a*) above.

(2) If or to the extent that any relief in respect of interest eligible for it under subsection (1) above cannot be given against income of the year in which the interest is paid because of an insufficiency of income in that year, it may instead be given against income of the preceding year of assessment, and so on; and if or to the extent that it cannot be so given it may instead be given against income of the year following that in which the interest is paid, and so on.

(3) Sufficient evidence of the amount of capital transfer tax or inheritance tax paid as mentioned in subsection (1)(*a*) above and of any statements relevant to its computation may be given by the production of a document purporting to be a certificate from the Board.

(4) For the purposes of subsections (1) to (3) above—

(*a*) references to capital transfer tax or inheritance tax include any interest payable on that tax; and

(*b*) references to interest in respect of a period ending within a given time apply whether or not interest continues to run after that time.

"trading company" means a company whose business consists wholly or mainly of the carrying on of a trade or trades;

"trading group" means a group the business of whose members taken together consists wholly or mainly of the carrying on of a trade or trades, and for this purpose "group" means a company which has one or more 75 per cent. subsidiaries together with those subsidiaries; and

"unquoted company" means a company none of whose shares are listed in the Official List of the Stock Exchange.

Former enactments.—Sub-s. (1): FA 1974, Sch. 1, para. 10A(1); FA 1981, s. 25(3).
Sub-s (2): FA 1974, Sch. 1, para. 10B; FA 1981, s. 25(3), (6).
Sub-s (3): FA 1974, Sch. 1, para. 10C; FA 1983, s. 24(1).
Sub-ss. (4)–(6): FA 1974, Sch. 1, para. 10D(1)–(3); FA 1983, s. 24(1); FA 1984, s. 24(2), (3).
Sub-s. (7): FA 1974, Sch. 1, para. 10D(3A); FA 1983, s. 24(1); FA 1984, s. 24(4).
Sub-s. (8): FA 1974, Sch. 1, para. 10D(4); FA 1983, s. 24(1).
Note.—See **Prospective Legislation Notes** (Married Couples).
Cross references.—See FA 1988, Sch. 6, para. 3(3)(b)(i), (4)(b), (5), (7) (interest paid after 14 March 1988 in relation to commercial woodlands not eligible for relief under this section),
Sch. 6, para. 3(3)(b)(ii), (4)(b), (7) (interest paid after 14 March 1988 in relation to commercial woodlands not eligible for relief under FA 1974, Sch. 1, para. 10C).
Amendments.—[1] Words "or his spouse" in sub-s. (4)(d) and words "or whose spouses" in sub-s. (5) repealed by FA 1988, Sch. 3, para. 15(1), (2) and Sch. 14, Pt. VIII in relation to payments of interest made after 5 April 1990 unless the proceeds of the loan were used before that date to defray money applied as mentioned in sub-s. (3) above.
[2] Sub-ss. (6), (7) substituted by the following sub-s. (6) by FA 1988, Sch. 3, para. 15(1), (2) in relation to payments of interest made after 5 April 1990 unless the proceeds of the loan were used before that date to defray money applied as mentioned in sub-s. (3) above—

"(6) Where an individual owns beneficially more than 10 per cent. of the issued ordinary share capital of, or voting power in, a company, the excess shall be treated for the purposes of subsection (5) above as being owned by an individual who is not a full-time employee of the company."

362. Loan to buy into partnership

(1) Subject to sections 363 to 365, interest is eligible for relief under section 353 if it is interest on a loan to an individual to defray money applied—

(a) in purchasing a share in a partnership; or

(b) in contributing money to a partnership by way of capital or premium, or in advancing money to a partnership, where the money contributed or advanced is used wholly for the purposes of the trade, profession or vocation carried on by the partnership; or

(c) in paying off another loan interest on which would have been eligible for relief under that section had the loan not been paid off (on the assumption, if the loan was free of interest, that it carried interest);

and the conditions stated in subsection (2) below are satisfied.

(2) The conditions referred to in subsection (1) above are—

(a) that, throughout the period from the application of the proceeds of the loan until the interest was paid, the individual has been a member of the partnership otherwise than as a limited partner; and

(b) that he shows that in that period he has not recovered any capital from the partnership, apart from any amount taken into account under section 363(1).

Former enactments.—Sub-s. (1): FA 1974, Sch. 1, para. 11(1).
Sub-s. (2): FA 1974, Sch. 1, para. 12; FA 1981, s. 25(2).
Cross references.—See FA 1988, Sch. 6, para. 3(3)(b)(i), (4)(b), (5), (7) (interest paid after 14 March 1988 in relation to commercial woodlands not eligible for relief under this section),
Sch. 6, para. 3(3)(b)(ii), (4)(b), (7) (interest paid after 14 March 1988 in relation to commercial woodlands not eligible for relief under FA 1974, Sch. 1, paras. 11, 12).

363. Provisions supplementary to sections 360 to 362

(1) If at any time after the application of the proceeds of the loan the individual has recovered any amount of capital from the close company, co-operative, employee-controlled company or partnership without using that amount in repayment of the loan, he shall be treated for the purposes of sections 353, 360, 361 and 362 as if he had at that time repaid that amount out of the loan, so that out of the interest otherwise eligible for relief (or, where section 367(4) applies, out of the proportion so eligible) and payable for any period after that time there shall be deducted an amount equal to interest on the amount of capital so recovered.

(2) The individual shall be treated as having recovered an amount of capital from the close company, co-operative, employee-controlled company or partnership if—

(2) The conditions referred to in subsection (1) above are—

(a) that the loan was made after 10th March 1981;
(b) that, when the interest is paid, the body continues to be a co-operative; and
(c) that in the period from the application of the proceeds of the loan to the payment of the interest the individual has worked for the greater part of his time as an employee of the body or of a subsidiary of the body; and
(d) that he shows that in that period he has not recovered any capital from the body apart from any taken into account under section 363(1).

(3) Subject to sections 362 to 365, interest is eligible for relief under section 353 if it is interest on a loan to an individual to defray money applied—

(a) in acquiring any part of the ordinary share capital of an employee-controlled company; or
(b) in paying off another loan, interest on which would have been eligible for relief under section 353 had the loan not been paid off (on the assumption, if it was free of interest, that it carried interest);

and the conditions stated in subsection (4) below are satisfied.

(4) The conditions referred to in subsection (3) above are that—

(a) the company is, throughout the period beginning with the date on which the shares are acquired and ending with the date on which the interest is paid—
   (i) an unquoted company resident in the United Kingdom and not resident elsewhere; and
   (ii) a trading company or the holding company of a trading group;
(b) the shares are acquired before, or not later than 12 months after, the date on which the company first becomes an employee-controlled company;
(c) during the year of assessment in which the interest is paid the company either—
   (i) first becomes an employee-controlled company; or
   (ii) is such a company throughout a period of at least nine months;
(d) the individual *or his spouse*[1] is a full-time employee of the company throughout the period beginning with the date on which the proceeds of the loan are applied and ending with the date on which the interest is paid or, if at that date he has ceased to be such an employee, ending with whichever is the later of—
   (i) the date on which he ceased to be such an employee;
   (ii) the date 12 months before the payment of the interest; and
(e) the individual shows that in the period from the application of the proceeds of the loan to the payment of the interest he has not recovered any capital from the company, apart from any amount taken into account under section 363(1).

(5) For the purposes of this section a company is employee-controlled at any time when more than 50 per cent.—

(a) of the issued ordinary share capital of the company, and
(b) of the voting power in the company,

is beneficially owned by persons who, *or whose spouses*[1], are full-time employees of the company.

(6) Where an individual owns beneficially, or he and his spouse together own beneficially, more than 10 per cent. of the issued ordinary share capital of, or voting power in, a company, the excess shall be treated for the purposes of subsection (5) above as being owned by an individual who is neither a full-time employee of the company nor the spouse of such an employee.[2]

(7) Where an individual and his spouse are both full-time employees of the company, subsection (6) above shall apply in relation to them with the omission of the words "or he and his spouse together own beneficially".[2]

(8) In this section—

"full-time employee", in relation to a company, means a person who works for the greater part of his time as an employee or director of the company or of a 51 per cent. subsidiary of the company;
"holding company" means a company whose business (disregarding any trade carried on by it) consists wholly or mainly of the holding of shares or securities of one or more companies which are its 75 per cent. subsidiaries;

(5) In subsection (4) above "employee benefit trust" has the same meaning as in paragraph 7 of Schedule 8, except that in its application for this purpose paragraph 7(5)(*b*) shall have effect as if it referred to the day on which the Finance Act 1989 was passed instead of to 14th March 1989.

(6) This subsection applies in relation to an individual if at any time on or after the day on which the Finance Act 1989 was passed—

(*a*) the individual, either on his own or with any one or more of his associates, or
(*b*) any associate of his, with or without other such associates,

has been the beneficial owner of, or able (directly or through the medium of other companies or by any other indirect means) to control, more than 5 per cent. of the ordinary share capital of the company.

(7) Sub-paragraphs (9) to (12) of paragraph 7 of Schedule 8 shall apply for the purposes of subsection (6) above in relation to an individual as they apply for the purposes of that paragraph in relation to an employee.

(8) In relation to any loan made before 14th November 1986, where the individual is interested in any shares or obligations of the company which are subject to any trust, or are part of the estate of a deceased person, subsection (2)(*c*) above shall have effect as if for the reference to the trustee or trustees of the settlement concerned or, as the case may be, the personal representative of the deceased there were substituted a reference to any person (other than the individual) interested in the settlement or estate, but subject to subsection (9) below.

(9) Subsection (8) above shall not apply so as to make an individual an associate as being entitled or eligible to benefit under a trust—

(*a*) if the trust relates exclusively to an exempt approved scheme as defined in section 592; or
(*b*) if the trust is exclusively for the benefit of the employees, or the employees and directors, of the company or their dependants (and not wholly or mainly for the benefit of directors or their relatives), and the individual in question is not (and could not as a result of the operation of the trust become), either on his own or with his relatives, the beneficial owner of more than 5 per cent. of the ordinary share capital of the company;

and in applying paragraph (*b*) above any charitable trusts which may arise on the failure or determination of other trusts shall be disregarded.

(10) In this section "participator" has the meaning given by section 417(1) and "relative" means husband or wife, parent or remoter forebear, child or remoter issue or brother or sister.][1]

Note.—FA 1989 was passed on 27 July 1989.
Amendments.—[1] This section inserted by FA 1989, s. 48(2) and Sch. 12, para. 13 in relation to accounting periods beginning after 31 March 1989. In relation to accounting periods beginning on or before 31 March 1989, sub-s. (1) reads—

"(1) For the purposes of section 360(2)(*a*) an individual shall be treated as having a material interest in a company—

(*a*) if he, either on his own or with one or more of his associates, or if any associate of his with or without other such associates, is the beneficial owner of, or able (directly or through the medium of other companies or by any other indirect means) to control, more than 5 per cent. of the ordinary share capital of the company, or
(*b*) if, on an amount equal to the whole distributable income of the company falling to be apportioned under Part XI for the purpose of computing total income, more than 5 per cent. of that amount could be apportioned to him together with his associates (if any), or to any associate of his, or any such associates taken together."

361. Loan to buy interest in co-operative or employee-controlled company

(1) Subject to the following provisions of this section and sections 363 and 364, interest is eligible for relief under section 353 if it is interest on a loan to an individual to defray money applied—

(*a*) in acquiring a share or shares in a body which is a co-operative as defined by section 363(5); or
(*b*) in lending money to any such body which is used wholly and exclusively for the purposes of the business of that body or of a subsidiary of that body; or
(*c*) in paying off another loan interest on which would have been eligible for relief under section 353 had the loan not been paid off (on the assumption, if it was free of interest, that it carried interest);

and the conditions in subsection (2) below are satisfied.

(3) The conditions secondly referred to in subsection (1) above are—

  (*a*) that, when the interest is paid, the company continues to satisfy any of the conditions of section 424(4) and the individual holds any part of the ordinary share capital of the company; and
  (*b*) that in the period from the application of the proceeds of the loan to the payment of the interest the individual has worked for the greater part of his time in the actual management or conduct of the company or of an associated company of the company; and
  (*c*) that he shows in the period from the application of the proceeds of the loan to the payment of the interest he has not recovered any capital from the company, apart from any amount taken into account under section 363(1).

[(3A) Interest shall not be eligible for relief under section 353 by virtue of paragraph (*a*) of subsection (1) above in respect of shares acquired on or after 14th March 1989 if at any time the person by whom they are acquired, or that person's husband or wife, makes a claim for relief in respect of them under Chapter III of Part VII.][1]

[(4) Subject to section 360A, in this section expressions to which a meaning is assigned by Part XI have that meaning.][2]

Former enactments.—Sub-s. (1): FA 1974, Sch. 1, para. 9(1); FA 1982, s. 49(2).
Sub-s. (2): FA 1974, Sch. 1, para. 10(1); FA 1980, s. 28(1)(*b*), (*c*); FA 1982, s. 49(3).
Sub-s (3): FA 1974, Sch. 1, para. 10(2); FA 1982, s. 49(3).
Sub-s (4): FA 1974, Sch. 1, para. 16; FA 1987, ss. 33(3), 37(2).
Cross references.—See FA 1988, Sch. 6, para. 3(3)(*b*)(i), (4)(*b*), (5), (7) (interest paid after 14 March 1988 in relation to commercial woodlands not eligible for relief under this section),
Sch. 6, para. 3(3)(*b*)(ii), (4)(*b*), (7) (interest paid after 14 March 1988 in relation to commercial woodlands not eligible for relief under FA 1974, Sch. 1, para. 9(1)).
Amendments.—[1] Sub-s. (3A) inserted by FA 1989, s. 47.
[2] Sub-s. (4) substituted by FA 1989, s. 48(1).
[3] Words in sub-s. (1)(*a*) substituted for the words "satisfying any of the conditions of section 424(4)" by FA 1989, Sch. 12, para. 12 in relation to interest paid after 26 July 1989; and accordingly s. 424(4) of this Act continues to have effect until that date.
[4] Words in sub-ss. (2)(*a*), (3)(*a*) substituted for the words "satisfy any of the conditions of section 424(4)" by *ibid*.

[360A. Meaning of "material interest" in section 360

(1) For the purposes of section 360(2)(*a*) an individual shall be treated as having a material interest in a company if he, either on his own or with one or more associates, or if any associate of his with or without such other associates,—

  (*a*) is the beneficial owner of, or able, directly or through the medium of other companies, or by any other indirect means to control, more than 5 per cent. of the ordinary share capital of the company, or
  (*b*) possesses, or is entitled to acquire, such rights as would, in the event of the winding-up of the company or in any other circumstances, give an entitlement to receive more than 5 per cent. of the assets which would then be available for distribution among the participators.

(2) Subject to the following provisions of this section, in subsection (1) above "associate", in relation to an individual, means—

  (*a*) any relative or partner of the individual;
  (*b*) the trustee or trustees of a settlement in relation to which the individual is, or any relative of his (living or dead) is or was, a settlor ("settlement" and "settlor" having the same meaning as in section 681(4)); and
  (*c*) where the individual is interested in any shares or obligations of the company which are subject to any trust, or are part of the estate of a deceased person, the trustee or trustees of the settlement concerned or, as the case may be, the personal representative of the deceased.

(3) In relation to any loan made after 5th April 1987, there shall be disregarded for the purposes of subsection (2)(*c*) above—

  (*a*) the interest of the trustees of an approved profit sharing scheme (within the meaning of section 187) in any shares which are held by them in accordance with the scheme and have not yet been appropriated to an individual; and
  (*b*) any rights exercisable by those trustees by virtue of that interest.

(4) In relation to any loan made on or after the day on which the Finance Act 1989 was passed, where the individual has an interest in shares or obligations of the company as a beneficiary of an employee benefit trust, the trustees shall not be regarded as associates of his by reason only of that interest unless subsection (6) below applies in relation to him.

359. Loan to buy machinery or plant

(1) Where an individual is a member of a partnership which, under section 44 of the 1968 Act, is entitled to a capital allowance or liable to a balancing charge for any year of assessment in respect of machinery or plant belonging to the individual, any interest paid by him in the basis period (as defined in section 72 of that Act) for that year on a loan to defray money applied as capital expenditure on the provision of that machinery or plant is eligible for relief under section 353, except interest falling due and payable more than three years after the end of the year of assessment in which the debt was incurred.

(2) Where the machinery or plant is in use partly for the purposes of the trade, profession or vocation carried on by the partnership and partly for other purposes, such part only of the interest is eligible for relief under section 353 as is just and reasonable to attribute to the purposes of the trade, profession or vocation, having regard to all the relevant circumstances and, in particular, to the extent of the use for those other purposes.

(3) Where the holder of an office or employment—

(a) is under Chapter II of Part I of the 1968 Act or Chapter I of Part III of the Finance Act 1971 entitled to a capital allowance or liable to a balancing charge, (or would be so entitled or liable but for some contribution made by the employer), for any year of assessment in respect of machinery or plant belonging to him and in use for the purposes of the office or employment; and

(b) pays interest in that year on a loan to defray money applied as capital expenditure on the provision of that machinery or plant;

the interest so paid is eligible for relief under section 353 unless it is interest falling due and payable more than three years after the end of the year of assessment in which the debt was incurred.

(4) Where the machinery or plant is in use partly for the purposes of the office or employment and partly for other purposes, such part only of the interest is eligible for relief under section 353 as it is just and reasonable to attribute to the purposes of the office or employment, having regard to all the relevant circumstances and, in particular, to the extent of the use for those other purposes.

Former enactments.—Sub-s. (1): FA 1972, Sch. 9, para. 10; FA 1974, Sch. 1, para. 1.
Sub-s. (2): FA 1972, Sch. 9, para. 11; FA 1974, Sch. 1, para. 1.
Sub-s. (3): FA 1972, Sch. 9, para. 12; FA 1974, Sch. 1, para. 1.
Sub-s. (4): FA 1972, Sch. 9, para. 13; FA 1972, Sch. 1, para. 1.

360. Loan to buy interest in close company

(1) Subject to the following provisions of this section and sections 361 to 364, interest is eligible for relief under section 353 if it is interest on a loan to an individual to defray money applied—

(a) in acquiring any part of the ordinary share capital of a close company [complying with section 13A(2)][3]; or

(b) in lending money to such a close company which is used wholly and exclusively for the purposes of the business of the company or of any associated company of it which is a close company satisfying any of those conditions; or

(c) in paying off another loan interest on which would have been eligible for relief under section 353 had the loan not been paid off (on the assumption, if the loan was free of interest, that it carried interest);

and either the conditions stated in subsection (2) below or those stated in subsection (3) below are satisfied.

(2) The conditions first referred to in subsection (1) above are—

(a) that, when the interest is paid, the company continues to [comply with section 13A(2)][4] and the individual has a material interest in the company; and

(b) that he shows that in the period from the application of the proceeds of the loan to the payment of the interest he has not recovered any capital from the company, apart from any amount taken into account under section 363(1); and

(c) that, if the company exists wholly or mainly for the purpose of holding investments or other property, no property held by the company is used as a residence by the individual;

but the condition in paragraph (c) above shall not apply in a case where the individual has worked for the greater part of his time in the actual management or conduct of the business of the company, or of an associated company of the company.

the amount on which interest is payable under the loan shall be treated for the purposes of this section as being such part only of that amount as bears to the whole thereof the same proportion as the amount of interest paid by the borrower bears to the whole of the interest paid on the loan.

(3) For the purposes of this section—

(a) any interest payable on a loan made to the borrower's husband or wife shall be treated as payable on a loan made to the borrower; and
(b) where interest is payable on more than one loan made or treated as made to the borrower and the loans were made simultaneously it shall be treated as payable on one loan.

(4) Where section 354 continues to apply to a loan by virtue of section 354(5)(a), this section shall also continue to have effect in relation to the loan as if section 354 applied to it by virtue of section 355(1)(a).

(5) References in this section to the borrower's husband or wife do not include references to a separated husband or wife.

(6) In determining whether the amount on which interest is payable under a loan exceeds the limit in subsection (1) above, no account shall be taken of so much (if any) of that amount as consists of interest which has been added to capital and does not exceed £1000.

Former enactments.—Sub-s. (1): FA 1974, Sch. 1, para. 5(1), (2)(a); FA 1977, Sch. 8, para. 8(2); FA 1984, s. 22(1)(a), (b).
Sub-s. (2): FA 1974, Sch. 1, para. 5(3); FA 1977, Sch. 8, para. 8(3).
Sub-s. (3): FA 1974, Sch. 1, para. 5(4).
Sub-s. (4): FA 1974, Sch. 1, para. 6(1A); FA 1984, s. 22(2).
Sub-s. (5): FA 1974, Sch. 1, para. 5(5).
Sub-s. (6): FA 1974, Sch. 1, para. 5(6); FA 1982, s. 25(2).
Amendments.—[1] Words in sub-s. (1) substituted by FA 1988, s. 42(2), (4) with effect from 1 August 1988.
[2] Words in sub-s. (1) inserted by *ibid*.
[3] Sub-ss. (1A), (1B), (1C) inserted by *ibid*.
[4] Words "or of a dependent relative or former or separated spouse of his" in sub-s. (2)(a) repealed by FA 1988, s. 44(1) and Sch. 14, Pt. IV in relation to interest paid after 5 April 1988 on loans for a dependent relative's etc. residence, subject to certain qualifications in s. 44(2), (3), (5).

358. Relief where borrower deceased

(1) Where any interest paid by persons as the personal representatives of a deceased person or as the trustees of a settlement made by his will would, on the assumptions required by this section, be eligible for relief under section 353 by virtue of section 354 above and, in a case where subsection (3) below applies, one of the conditions in subsection (4) below is satisfied, that interest shall be so eligible notwithstanding sections 354 to 357.

(2) For the purposes of subsection (1) above it shall be assumed that the deceased would have survived and been the borrower.

(3) If, at his death,—

(a) the land, caravan or house-boat concerned was used as his only or main residence, or
(b) it was used by him as a residence or was intended to be used in due course as his only or main residence and, in either case, he resided in job-related living accommodation;

that shall be assumed for the purposes of subsection (1) above to have continued to be the case.

(4) The conditions referred to in subsection (1) above are—

(a) that, at the time the interest is paid, the land, caravan or house-boat concerned is used as the only or main residence of the deceased's widow or widower . . .[1];
(b) that, at that time, it is used by the deceased's widow or widower as a residence or is intended to be used in due course as his or her only or main residence and, in either case, he or she resides in job-related living accommodation.

(5) In this section "personal representatives" has the meaning given by section 701; and subsections (3) to (6) of section 356 apply in relation to this section as they apply in relation to that.

Former enactments.—FA 1974, Sch. 1, para. 8; FA 1977, Sch. 8, para. 10.
Amendments.—[1] Words "or of any dependent relative of the deceased" in sub-s. (4)(a) repealed by FA 1988, s. 44(4) and Sch. 14, Pt. IV in relation to interest paid after 5 April 1988, subject to certain qualifications in s. 44(4), (5).

that loan were reduced by the amount of any earlier loan; and if that amount is equal to or exceeds the limit, none of the interest paid on the later loan is eligible for relief.

(7) for the purposes of subsection (6) above, where interest is paid on more than one loan made simultaneously to one person it shall be treated as paid on one loan.

(8) Subject to section 356B, where a loan is made jointly to more than one person by whom qualifying interest is payable in relation to a residence under the loan, the amount on which qualifying interest is payable in relation to the residence under the loan by each of the persons shall be treated for the purposes of section 356A as being such amount as is produced by dividing the whole of the amount on which qualifying interest is payable in relation to the residence under the loan by the number of persons by whom qualifying interest is so payable.

(9) Where section 354 continues to apply to a loan by virtue of section 354(5)(*a*), then sections 356A to 356C and this section shall also continue to have effect as if section 354 applied to it by virtue of section 355(1)(*a*).

(10) In determining whether the amount on which interest is payable exeeds any limit under section 356A, no account shall be taken of so much (if any) of that amount as consists of interest which has been added to capital and which does not exceed £1,000.][1]

Amendments.—[1] This section inserted by FA 1988, s. 42(1), (4) with effect from 1 August 1988.

357. Limit on amount of loan eligible for relief by virtue of section 354

(1) [Subject to subsection (1A) below, where section 356A does not have effect with respect to a payment of interest because of section 356C (2) or (7) and the payment is of interest][1] on a loan ("the limited loan") which (apart from this subsection) is eligible for relief under section 353 by virtue of section 355(1)(*a*) or 356(1) [the payment of interest][2] shall be so eligible for relief only to the extent that the amount on which it is payable does not exceed the following limit, that is to say, the qualifying maximum for the year of assessment reduced by the amount on which interest is payable by the borrower under any earlier loans so eligible for relief, so that—

(*a*) if the amount on which interest is payable under the limited loan exceeds the limit, so much only of that interest is eligible for relief as bears to the whole of that interest the same proportion as that part of that amount which does not exceed the limit bears to the whole of that amount; and

(*b*) if the amount on which interest is payable under any earlier loans is equal to or exceeds the qualifying maximum for the year of assessment, none of the interest on the limited loan is eligible for relief.

[(1A) Where section 356A does not have effect with respect to a payment of interest made by a person in relation to land, or a caravan or house-boat, used or to be used as his only or main residence because of section 356C(2), subsection (1) above shall have effect with respect to the payment of interest as if the reference to the qualifying maximum for the year of assessment were a reference to the amount specified in subsection (1B) below.][3]

[(1B) The amount referred to in subsection (1A) above is the lesser of £30,000 and the amount on which interest was payable by the person in relation to the land, caravan or house-boat immediately before 1st August 1988.][3]

[(1C) Where subsection (2) of section 356C applies in the case of a person by virtue of subsection (3) of that section, for the purposes of subsection (1B) above the amount on which interest is payable by him under the loan referred to in section 356C(3) for the first day for which interest is so payable shall be treated as the amount on which interest is payable by him under the loan immediately before 1st August 1988.][3]

(2) Where a loan on which interest is payable by the borrower was made jointly to the borrower and another person, not being the borrower's husband or wife, then, if—

(*a*) the land, caravan or house-boat concerned is used as the main or only residence of that other person, . . .[4], and

(i) that other person owns an estate or interest in the land or the property in the caravan or house-boat, and

(ii) that other person pays part of the interest payable on the loan; or

(*b*) that other person falls within sub-paragraphs (i) and (ii) of paragraph (*a*) above and is by virtue of section 356 entitled to claim relief under section 353 in respect of that part of the interest, and where a payment is made under such a loan the references in subsection (2) above to 1st August 1988 shall be treated as references to the first day for which qualifying interest is payable in relation to the residence under the loan (or where there is more than one such loan the latest such day).

(4) Subject to subsection (5) below, where by virtue of subsection (2) above sections 356A and 356B do not have effect with respect to payments of qualifying interest made by a person for any period in relation to a residence under one loan those sections shall not have effect with respect to payments of qualifying interest for that period in relation to the residence made by that person or his spouse under any other loan.

(5) Where all the persons by whom qualifying interest is payable in relation to a residence have made a joint election for the purpose, sections 356A and 356B shall have effect with respect to all payments of qualifying interest made by any person in relation to the residence notwithstanding that they would otherwise be payments with respect to which those sections would not have effect.

(6) An election under subsection (5) above—

    (*a*) shall have effect for the period in which it is made and subsequent periods,
    (*b*) shall be irrevocable, and
    (*c*) shall be in such form, and be made in such manner, as the Board may prescribe.

(7) Sections 356A and 356B shall not have effect with respect to payments of qualifying interest if the interest is qualifying interest only by reason of its being paid in relation to a residence used or to be used as the only or main residence of a dependent relative or former or separated spouse of the person by whom the payment is made.

(8) In this section references to a spouse do not include references to a separated spouse.][1]

Amendments.—[1] This section inserted by FA 1988, s. 42(1), (4) with effect from 1 August 1988.

[356D. Provisions supplementary to sections 356A to 356C

(1) In sections 356A to 356C and this section "qualifying interest" means interest which (apart from those sections or section 357) is eligible for relief under section 353 by virtue of section 355(1)(*a*) or 356(1).

(2) In sections 356A to 356C and this section "residence" means a building, or part of a building, occupied or intended to be occupied as a separate residence, or a caravan or houseboat; but a building, or part of a building, which is designed for permanent use as a single residence shall be treated as a single residence notwithstanding that it is temporarily divided into two or more parts which are occupied or intended to be occupied as separate residences.

(3) In sections 356A to 356C and this section "period", with respect to qualifying interest payable by a person in relation to a residence, means a period commencing with—

    (*a*) any day which is the first day for which qualifying interest is payable in relation to the residence by that or any other person (whether or not qualifying interest was payable by any person in relation to the residence for any earlier day),
    (*b*) any day immediately following a day which is the last day for which qualifying interest is payable in relation to the residence by any other person (whether or not qualifying interest is payable by any person in relation to the residence for any later day), or
    (*c*) the first day of a year of assessment,

and ending with either the day immediately preceding the next day such as is mentioned in paragraph (*a*), (*b*) or (*c*) above or (if sooner) the day which is the last day for which qualifying interest is payable in relation to the residence by that person.

(4) In section 356A references to the qualifying maximum during a period are references to the qualifying maximum for the year of assessment in which the period falls.

(5) Where because of section 356A the full amount of qualifying interest paid by a person for a period is not eligible for relief, the part of that interest that is eligible for relief shall be such as bears to the whole of it the same proportion as the part of the amount on which qualifying interest is payable by him for the period that does not exceed the limit under that section in his case bears to the whole of that amount.

(6) Where a person pays qualifying interest on more than one loan, the limit under section 356A in his case shall have effect in relation to qualifying interest paid on a later loan as if

relation to a husband and wife for a year of assessment, subsections (1) to (3) above shall not apply in relation to them for the year but they may jointly elect—

(*a*) that qualifying interest payable or paid by one of them for the year (or a period within the year), or such part of that interest as may be specified in the election, shall be treated for the purposes of sections 353 to 356A and 369 to 379 (and section 287(7)) as payable or paid by the other, and

(*b*) that the sharer's limit under section 356A for the year (or period) in the case of one of them shall be reduced by such amount as may be specified in the election and the sharer's limit under that section for the year (or period) in the case of the other shall be correspondingly increased.

(5) An election under subsection (4) above—

(*a*) shall be made before the end of the period of twelve months beginning with the end of the first year of assessment for which it is made or such longer period as the Board may in any particular case allow,

(*b*) shall, subject to subsection (6) below, have effect if made for the year 1988–89 not only for that year but also for the year 1989–90, and

(*c*) shall be in such form, and be made in such manner, as the Board may prescribe.

(6) Where a husband and wife have made an election under subsection (4) above for the year 1988–89 they may give, for the year 1989–90, a notice to withdraw that election; and, if they do so, the election shall not have effect for the year 1989–90.

(7) A notice of withdrawal under subsection (6) above—

(*a*) shall be in such form, and be given in such manner, as the Board may prescribe,

(*b*) shall not be given after 5th April 1991 or such later date as the Board may in any particular case allow, and

(*c*) shall not prejudice the making of a fresh election for 1989–90.

(8) Where—

(*a*) a husband and wife are not separated,

(*b*) the husband pays interest in relation to a residence used or to be used as his only or main residence, and

(*c*) his wife pays interest in relation to some other residence used or to be used as her only or main residence,

the residence which was purchased first shall be treated for the purposes of sections 355(1)(*a*) and 356 as used or to be used as the only or main residence of both of them and the other residence shall be treated as used or to be used as the only or main residence of neither.][1]

Note.—See **Prospective Legislation Notes** (Married Couples).
Amendments.—[1] This section inserted by FA 1988, s. 42(1), (4) with effect from 1 August 1988.

[356C. Payments to which sections 356A and 356B apply

(1) Subject to subsection (2) below, sections 356A and 356B shall have effect with respect to payments of qualifying interest made on or after 1st August 1988.

(2) Subject to subsection (5) below, those sections shall not have effect with respect to a payment of qualifying interest made by a person in relation to a residence if—

(*a*) the payment is made under a loan made before 1st August 1988,

(*b*) qualifying interest was payable in relation to the residence for 1st August 1988 by someone other than the person making the payment or his spouse,

(*c*) qualifying interest has been payable in relation to the residence by the person making the payment or his spouse throughout the time beginning with 1st August 1988 and ending with the date of the payment, and

(*d*) someone other than the person making the payment or his spouse owns an estate or interest or property in the residence at each point during that time and at each such point at least one such person is a person by whom qualifying interest is payable in relation to the residence at some point during that time.

(3) For the purposes of subsection (2) above a loan made on or after 1st August 1988 shall be treated as made before that date if it is proved by written evidence—

(*a*) that the loan was made in pursuance of an offer made before that date and that the offer either was in writing or was evidenced by a note or memorandum made by the lender before that date, and

(*b*) that the loan was used to defray money applied in pursuance of a binding contract entered into before that date;

[356A. Limit on relief for home loans: residence basis

(1) Where all the qualifying interest payable for any period in relation to a residence is payable by one person, it shall be eligible for relief only to the extent that the amount on which it is payable does not exceed the qualifying maximum during the period.

(2) Where qualifying interest is payable for any period in relation to a residence by more than one person, the interest paid by each of them shall be eligible for relief only to the extent that the amount on which it is payable by him does not exceed the sharer's limit for the period in his case.

(3) Subject to the following provisions of this section and section 356B, in this section and section 356B "the sharer's limit", in relation to a person by whom qualifying interest is payable for a period in relation to a residence, means the amount arrived at by dividing the amount of the qualifying maximum during the period by the number of persons by whom qualifying interest is payable for the period in relation to the residence.

(4) Subsection (5) below applies where—

(*a*) in the case of any person by whom qualifying interest is payable for any period in relation to a residence the sharer's limit for the period exceeds the amount on which the interest is payable by him, and
(*b*) the amount which (apart from that subsection) would be the sharer's limit for the period in the case of any other person by whom qualifying interest is payable for the period in relation to the residence falls short of the amount on which qualifying interest is so payable by him.

(5) Where this subsection applies—

(*a*) the sharer's limit for the period in the case of the person mentioned in subsection (4)(*a*) above shall be reduced by the amount of the excess, and
(*b*) the sharer's limit for the period in the case of any person such as is mentioned in subsection (4)(*b*) above shall be increased in accordance with subsections (6) to (8) below.

(6) Where there is only one other person by whom qualifying interest is payable for the period in relation to the residence, the sharer's limit in his case shall be increased by the amount of the excess.

(7) Where there is more than one other person by whom qualifying interest is payable for the period in relation to the residence, the sharer's limit in the case of each of them shall be increased by such part of the excess as bears to the whole of it the same proportion as any shortfall in his case bears to the aggregate of any shortfalls in the case of each of them.

(8) In subsection (7) above "shortfall" means the amount by which what would be the sharer's limit in the case of a person (apart from subsection (5) above) falls short of the amount on which qualifying interest is payable by him.][1]

Amendments.—[1] This section inserted by FA 1988, s. 42(1), (4) with effect from 1 August 1988.

[356B. Residence basis: married couples

(1) Subject to subsections (2) and (4) below, qualifying interest payable or paid by a married woman who is not separated from her husband shall be treated for the purposes of sections 353 to 356A and 369 to 379 as payable or paid by her husband (and not by her).

(2) Where—

(*a*) qualifying interest is payable, or treated by subsection (1) above as payable, for a period in relation to a residence by a married man who is not separated from his wife, and
(*b*) qualifying interest is also payable for the period in relation to the residence by one or more persons other than the man and his wife,

then for the purposes of section 356A(2) and (3) qualifying interest shall be treated as payable by the wife for the period in relation to the residence (whether or not it actually is).

(3) The application of subsection (2) above in the case of a husband and wife shall not give rise to a separate sharer's limit for the period in question in the case of the wife; but the limit arrived at under subsection (3) of section 356A for the period in the case of the husband shall be increased by the amount which (apart from this subsection) would be the limit arrived at under that subsection in the case of the wife.

(4) Where an application under section 283 or an election under section 287 is in force in

(*a*) is, at the time the interest is paid, used by the borrower as a residence or, if it is paid less than 12 months after the date on which the loan is made, is so used by him within 12 months after that date; or

(*b*) is intended at that time to be used in due course as his only or main residence;

and at that time he resides in living accommodation which is for him job-related.

[(1A) Subsection (1) above shall not apply where the interest is paid on a home improvement loan (as defined in section 355(2B)) unless the loan was made before 6th April 1988; and section 355(2C) shall have effect for the purposes of this subsection as for those of section 355(2A).]¹

(2) A borrower for whom there are two or more properties falling within subsection (1) above may not by virtue of this section claim relief for any period under section 353 in respect of more than one of them.

(3) Subject to subsections (4) and (5) below, living accommodation is job-related for a person if—

(*a*) it is provided for him by reason of his employment, or for his spouse by reason of her employment, in any of the following cases—

(i) where it is necessary for the proper performance of the duties of the employment that the employee should reside in that accommodation;
(ii) where the accommodation is provided for the better performance of the duties of the employment, and it is one of the kinds of employment in the case of which it is customary for employers to provide living accommodation for employees;
(iii) where, there being a special threat to the employee's security, special security arrangements are in force and the employee resides in the accommodation as part of those arrangements; or

(*b*) under a contract entered into at arm's length and requiring him or his spouse to carry on a particular trade, profession or vocation, he or his spouse is bound—

(i) to carry on that trade, profession or vocation on premises or other land provided by another person (whether under a tenancy or otherwise); and
(ii) to live either on those premises or on other premises provided by that other person.

(4) If the living accommodation is provided by a company and the employee is a director of that or an associated company, subsection (3)(*a*)(i) or (ii) above shall not apply unless—

(*a*) the company of which the employee is a director is one in which he or she has no material interest; and
(*b*) either—

(i) the employment is as a full-time working director, or
(ii) the company is non-profit making, that is to say, it does not carry on a trade nor do its functions consist wholly or mainly in the holding of investments or other property, or
(iii) the company is established for charitable purposes only.

(5) Subsection (3)(*b*) above does not apply if the living accommodation concerned is in whole or in part provided by—

(*a*) a company in which the borrower or his spouse has a material interest; or
(*b*) any person or persons together with whom the borrower or his spouse carries on a trade or business in partnership.

(6) For the purposes of this section—

(*a*) a company is an associated company of another if one of them has control of the other or both are under the control of the same person; and
(*b*) "employment", "director", "full-time working director", "material interest" and "control", in relation to a body corporate, have the same meanings as they have for the purposes of Chapter II of Part V.

Former enactments.—Sub-ss. (1)–(3)(*a*): FA 1974, Sch. 1, para. 4A(1)–(3); FA 1977, s. 36(1).
Sub-s. (3)(*b*): FA 1974, Sch. 1, para. 4A(3A); FA 1984, s. 25.
Sub-s. (4): FA 1974, Sch. 1, para. 4A(4), (5); FA 1977, s. 36(1).
Sub-s. (5): FA 1974, Sch. 1, para. 4A(3B); FA 1984, s. 25.
Sub-s. (6): FA 1974, Sch. 1, para. 4A(6).
Amendments.—¹ Sub-s. (1A) inserted by FA 1988, s. 43(2) in relation to interest paid after 5 April 1988.

(2) If it appears to the Board reasonable to do so, having regard to all the circumstances of a particular case, they may direct that in relation to that case subsection (1) above shall have effect as if for the references to 12 months there were substituted references to such longer period as meets the circumstances of that case.

[(2A) Section 354 shall not apply by virtue of subsection (1)(*a*) above where the interest is paid on a home improvement loan unless the loan was made before 6th April 1988.][2]

[(2B) In subsection (2A) above "home improvement loan" means—

(*a*) a loan to defray money applied in improving or developing land or buildings on land, otherwise than by the erection of a new building (which is not part of an existing residence) on land which immediately before the improvement or development began had no building on it, or
(*b*) a loan replacing (whether directly or indirectly) a loan within paragraph (*a*) above.][2]

[(2C) Where it is proved by written evidence that a loan made on or after 6th April 1988 was made in pursuance of an offer made by the lender before that date and that the offer either was in writing or was evidenced by a note or memorandum made by the lender before that date, the loan shall be deemed for the purposes of subsection (2A) above to have been made before that date.][2]

(3) The land, caravan or house-boat does not fall within subsection (1)(a) above by reason of its being used as the only or main residence of a dependent relative of the borrower unless it is provided rent-free and without any other consideration.[4]

(4) Relief under section 353 for interest eligible for it by virtue of section 354 in a case where it is eligible only because the land, caravan or house-boat referred to in it falls under subsection (1)(*b*) above shall be given only against income from the letting of that or any other land, caravan or house-boat, but may, if and to the extent that such income for the year of assessment is insufficient, be given against such income for the following year, and so on, provided the first-mentioned land, caravan or house-boat continues to fall under that subsection.

(5) Subsection (1)(*a*) of section 354 shall not apply—

(*a*) where the seller and purchaser are husband and wife and either sells to the other, or
(*b*) where the purchaser, or the wife or husband of the purchaser, has since 15th April 1969 disposed of an estate or interest in the land, or the property in the caravan or house-boat, in question, and it appears that the main purpose of the disposal and purchase was to obtain relief in respect of interest on the loan, or
(*c*) where the purchasers are the trustees of a settlement, and the seller is the settlor, or the wife or husband of the settlor, and it appears that the main purpose of the purchase is to obtain relief in respect of interest on the loan, or
(*d*) where the purchaser is directly or indirectly purchasing from a person who is connected with him, and the price substantially exceeds the value of what is acquired;

and subsection (1)(*b*) of that section shall not apply where the person spending the money is connected with the person who directly or indirectly receives the money, and the money substantially exceeds the value of the work done.

For the purposes of this subsection—

(i) references to a husband and wife are references to a husband and his wife living with him; and
(ii) one person is connected with another if he is so connected within the terms of section 839.

Former enactments.—Sub-ss. (1)–(3): FA 1974, Sch. 1, para. 4(1)–(3).
Sub-s. (4): FA 1974, Sch. 1, para. 7; FA 1977, Sch. 8, para. 9.
Sub-s. (5): FA 1972, Sch. 9, para. 8.
Amendments.—[1] Words in sub-s. (1) inserted by FA 1988, s. 42(3)(*a*), (4).
[2] Sub-ss. (2A), (2B), (2C) inserted by FA 1988, s. 43(1) in relation to interest paid after 5 April 1988.
[3] Words "or of a dependent relative or former or separated spouse of his" in sub-s. (1)(*a*) repealed by FA 1988, s. 44(1) and Sch. 14, Pt. IV in relation to interest paid after 5 April 1988 on loans for a dependent relative's etc residence, subject to certain qualifications in s. 44(2), (3), (5).
[4] Sub-s. (3) repealed by FA 1988, Sch. 14, Pt. IV in relation to interest paid after 5 April 1988, subject to certain qualifications in s. 44(2), (3), (5).

356. Job-related accommodation

(1) Section 355(1) shall not prevent relief being given under section 353 in a case where the land, caravan or house-boat in question—

(3) Interest is eligible for relief under section 353 in the case of a caravan only if the caravan—

>   (*a*) is a large caravan, or
>   (*b*) taken with the land on which it stands, is for the time being a rateable hereditament for the purposes of a relevant enactment and the owner or the wife or husband of the owner has as occupier of the caravan duly paid rates under the relevant enactment for the period in which the interest was paid.

In this subsection—

> "relevant enactment" means the General Rate Act 1967, any corresponding enactment in force in Scotland or the Republic of Ireland or the Rates (Northern Ireland) Order 1977; and
> "hereditament", in relation to Scotland, means lands and heritages.

(4) References in this section and in section 355 to an estate or interest do not include references—

>   (*a*) to a rentcharge or, in Scotland, a superiority or the interest of a creditor in a contract of ground annual; or
>   (*b*) to the interest of a chargee or mortgagee or, in Scotland, the interest of a creditor in a charge or security of any kind over land.

(5) Where this section applies to a loan by reason of the land, caravan or house-boat concerned being used as a person's only or main residence, and the borrower raises another loan to defray money to be applied as mentioned in subsection (1) above with a view to the use of other land or another caravan or house-boat as that person's only or main residence and the disposal of the first-mentioned land, caravan or house-boat, then in relation to interest payable within 12 months from the making of the other loan, this section—

>   (*a*) shall continue to apply to the first-mentioned loan, whether or not the first-mentioned land, caravan or house-boat continues to be so used; and
>   (*b*) shall apply to the other loan to the same extent (if any) as if no interest were payable on the first-mentioned loan.

(6) If it appears to the Board reasonable to do so, having regard to all the circumstances of a particular case, they may direct that in relation to that case subsection (5) above shall have effect as if for the reference to 12 months there were substituted a reference to such longer period as meets the circumstances of that case.

(7) Where interest is payable by the tenant occupier of any property to the landlord in pursuance of arrangements whereby money advanced at interest by the landlord is applied by the tenant in purchasing the landlord's estate or interest, or in the case of a caravan or house-boat the property in the caravan or house-boat, but that estate or interest or property is not to pass to the tenant until some time after the interest begins to be payable, this section and section 355(5) shall have effect in relation to the tenant as if he were the owner of the landlord's estate, interest or property.

Former enactments.—Sub-s. (1): FA 1972, Sch. 9, paras. 1, 5, 5A; FA 1974, Sch. 1, paras. 1–3; FA 1983, s. 17(5).
Sub-s. (2)(*a*): FA 1972, Sch. 9, para. 3.
Sub-s. (2)(*b*): FA 1972, Sch. 9, para. 4.
Sub-s. (3): FA 1972, Sch. 9, para. 5; FA 1974, Sch. 1, para. 1.
Sub-s. (4): FA 1972, Sch. 9, para. 6.
Sub-s. (5): FA 1974, Sch. 1, para. 6(1).
Sub-s. (6): FA 1974, Sch. 1, para. 6(2).
Sub-s. (7): FA 1972, Sch. 9, para. 7.

355. Matters excluded from section 354

(1) Subject to the following provisions of this section and sections 356 to 358, section 354 shall not apply unless the land, caravan or house-boat in question—

>   (*a*) is at the time the interest is paid used as the only or main residence of the person by whom it is paid ("the borrower") . . .[3] or, if the interest is paid less than 12 months after the date on which the loan is made, is so used within 12 months after that date; or
>   (*b*) is, in any period of 52 weeks comprising the time at which the interest is payable and falling wholly or partly within the year of assessment, let at a commercial rent for more than 26 weeks and, when not so let, either available for letting at such a rent or used as mentioned in paragraph (*a*) above or prevented from being so available or used by any works of construction or repair;

and shall in a case within paragraph (*a*) above apply only within the limit imposed by section [356A or][1] 357.

statement in writing showing the gross amount of the payment, the amount of tax deducted, and the actual amount paid.

(2) The duty imposed by subsection (1) above shall be enforceable at the suit or instance of the person requesting the statement.

Former enactments.—TA 1970, s. 55; FA 1973, s. 17(4); FA 1986, s. 29(3).

Relief for payments of interest (excluding MIRAS)

353. General provision

(1) Where a person pays in any year of assessment—

(*a*) annual interest chargeable to tax under Case III of Schedule D; or
(*b*) interest payable in the United Kingdom or the Republic of Ireland on an advance from a bank carrying on a bona fide banking business in the United Kingdom or the Republic of Ireland or from a person bona fide carrying on a business as a member of the Stock Exchange or bona fide carrying on the business of a discount house in the United Kingdom or the Republic of Ireland;

and the interest is stated in sections 354 to 365 to be eligible for relief under this section, then, if he makes a claim to the relief and subject to the following provisions of this section, sections 354 to 368 and section 237(5)(*b*), the amount of the interest shall be deducted from or set off against his income for that year of assessment, and income tax shall be discharged or repaid accordingly.

(2) This section does not apply to a payment of relevant loan interest to which section 369 applies.

(3) Relief under this section shall not be given in respect of—

(*a*) interest on a debt incurred by overdrawing an account or by debiting the account of any person as the holder of a credit card or under similar arrangements; or
(*b*) where interest is paid at a rate in excess of a reasonable commercial rate, so much of the interest as represents the excess.

Former enactments.—Sub-s. (1): FA 1972, s. 75(1), (6), (7); FA 1973, s. 23(6); FA 1974, s. 19(1)(*a*), (*d*); FA 1976, s. 49(5).
Sub-s. (2) FA 1982, s. 26(1).
Sub-s. (3): FA 1972, s. 75(1A), (2); FA 1974, s. 19(1)(*b*).
Cross references.—See FA 1988, Sch. 6, para. 3(3)(*b*), (4)(*b*), (5) , (7) (interest paid after 14 March 1988 in relation to commercial woodlands not eligible for relief under this section),
Sch. 6, para. 3(3)(*b*)(ii), (4)(*b*), (7) (interest paid after 14 March 1988 in relation to commercial woodlands not eligible for relief under FA 1972, s. 75).

354. Loans to buy land etc.

(1) Subject to sections 355 to 358 and subsections (2) to (6) below, interest is eligible for relief under section 353 if it is paid by a person for the time being owning an estate or interest in land, or the property in a caravan or house-boat, in the United Kingdom or the Republic of Ireland on a loan to defray money applied—

(*a*) in purchasing that estate, interest or property, or another estate, interest or property absorbed into, or given up to obtain, that estate, interest or property; or
(*b*) in improving or developing the land, or buildings on the land; or
(*c*) in paying off another loan, if interest on that other loan would have been eligible for relief under section 353 had the loan not been paid off (on the assumption, if the loan was free of interest, that it carried interest) or would have been so eligible apart from section 353(2).

(2) In this section and section 355—

(*a*) references to money applied in improving or developing land or buildings include references to payments in respect of maintenance or repairs incurred by reason of dilapidation attributable to a period before the estate or interest was acquired, but otherwise do not include references to payments in respect of maintenance or repairs, or any of the other payments mentioned in section 25(1); and
(*b*) references to money applied in improving or developing land include references to expenditure incurred or defrayed directly or indirectly in respect of street works, other than works of maintenance or repair, for any highway or road, or in Scotland any right of way, adjoining or serving the land.

and chargeable with income tax at the basic rate on the payment, or on so much thereof as is not made out of profits or gains brought into charge to income tax.

(2) In section 349(1) any reference to a payment or sum as being not payable, or not wholly payable, out of profits or gains brought into charge to income tax shall be construed as a reference to it as being payable wholly or in part out of a source other than profits or gains brought into charge; and any such reference elsewhere in the Tax Acts shall be construed accordingly.

(3) All the provisions of the Income Tax Acts relating to persons who are to be chargeable with income tax, to income tax assessments, and to the collection and recovery of income tax, shall, so far as they are applicable, apply to the charge, assessment, collection and recovery of income tax under this section.

(4) Section 349 and this section have effect subject to the provisions of Schedule 16 which has effect for the purpose of regulating the time and manner in which companies resident in the United Kingdom—

(*a*) are to account for and pay income tax in respect of payments from which tax is deductible under section 349, and
(*b*) are to be repaid income tax in respect of payments received by them;

and for that purpose the Board may by regulations modify, supplement or replace any of the provisions of Schedule 16; and references in this Act and in any other enactment to any of those provisions shall be construed as including references to any such regulations.

(5) Without prejudice to the generality of subsection (4) above, regulations under that subsection may, in relation to income tax for which a company is liable to account, modify any provision of Parts II to VI of the Management Act or apply any such provision with or without modifications.

(6) Regulations under this section may—

(*a*) make different provision for different descriptions of companies and for different circumstances and may authorise the Board, where in their opinion there are special circumstances justifying it, to make special arrangements as respects income tax for which a company is liable to account or the repayment of income tax borne by a company;
(*b*) include such transitional and other supplemental provisions as appear to the Board to be expedient or necessary.

(7) The Board shall not make any regulations under this section unless a draft of them has been laid before and approved by a resolution of the House of Commons.

Former enactments.—Sub-s. (1): TA 1970, ss. 53(2), 54(3); FA 1971, Sch. 6, para. 21.
Sub-s. (2): TA 1970, s. 56.
Sub-s. (3): TA 1970, ss. 53(3), 54(3).
Sub-s. (4): TA 1970, ss. 53(4), 54(3); FA 1972, ss. 104, 108(1), Sch. 24, para. 16.
Sub-ss. (5)–(7): FA 1972, s. 108(2)–(4).
Cross references.—See FA 1988, s. 130(7)(*b*) (company migration: provisions to secure payment by a migrating company of income tax in respect of payments under sub-s. (4)(*a*) above),
s. 130(9) (company migration: provisions to secure payment by a migrating company of income tax in respect of payments in relation to any time before 6 April 1988);
FA 1989, Sch. 11, para. 18 (disapplication of this section in relation to redemption proceeds of deep gain securities).

351. Small maintenance payments

Former enactments.—Sub-ss. (1), (2): TA 1970, s. 65(1), (1A); FA 1982, s. 33(2); Income Tax (Small Maintenance Payments) Order 1986, S.I. 1986 No. 328.
Sub-s. (3): TA 1970, s. 65(2).
Sub-ss. (4), (5): TA 1970, s. 65(3), (4).
Sub-s. (6): TA 1970, s. 65(5); FA 1982, s. 33(3).
Sub-s. (7): TA 1970, s. 65(6); FA 1982, s. 33(4).
Sub-s. (8): TA 1970, s. 65(7).
Cross references.—See FA 1988, s. 36(6) (this section not to apply to any payment in relation to which ss. 347A, 347B of this Act apply),
s. 36(6) (TA 1970, s. 65 not to apply to any payment in relation to which TA 1970, ss. 51A and 51B apply).
Amendments.—This section repealed by FA 1988, Sch. 14, Pt IV in relation to payments made after 5 April 1989 and in relation to orders and variations made after 5 April 1989.

352. Certificates of deduction of tax

(1) A person making any payment which is subject to deduction of income tax by virtue of section 339, 348, 349 or 687 shall, if the recipient so requests in writing, furnish him with a

discharged of so much money as is represented by the deduction, as if that sum had been actually paid; and

(d) the deduction shall be treated as income tax paid by the person to whom the payment is made.

(2) Subject to any provision to the contrary in the Income Tax Acts, where—

(a) any royalty or other sum paid in respect of the user of a patent; or

(b) any rent, royalty or other payment which, by section 119 or 120, is declared to be subject to deduction of income tax under this section or section 349 as if it were a royalty or other sum paid in respect of the user of a patent;

is paid wholly out of profits or gains brought into charge to income tax, the person making the payment shall be entitled on making the payment to deduct and retain out of it a sum representing the amount of the income tax thereon.

(3) This section does not apply to ...[1] any payment to which section 687 applies.

Former enactments.—TA 1970, ss. 52, 65(2); FA 1971, Sch. 6, para. 20(c); FA 1973, s. 17(1).
Cross references.—See FA 1989, Sch. 11, para. 18 (disapplication of this section in relation to redemption proceeds of deep gain securities).
Amendments.—[1] Words in sub-s. (3) repealed by FA 1988, Sch. 14, Pt IV in relation to payments made after 5 April 1989.

349. Payments not out of profits or gains brought into charge to income tax, and annual interest

(1) Where—

(a) any annuity or other annual payment charged with tax under Case III of Schedule D, not being interest; or

(b) any royalty or other sum paid in respect of the user of a patent; or

(c) any rent, royalty or other payment which, by section 119 or 120, is declared to be subject to deduction of income tax under this section or section 348 as if it were a royalty or other sum paid in respect of the user of a patent,

is not payable or not wholly payable out of profits or gains brought into charge to income tax, the person by or through whom any payment thereof is made shall, on making the payment, deduct out of it a sum representing the amount of income tax thereon.

This subsection does not apply to any payment to which section 687 applies.

(2) Subject to subsection (3) below and to any other provision to the contrary in the Income Tax Acts, where any yearly interest of money chargeable to tax under Case III of Schedule D is paid—

(a) otherwise than in a fiduciary or representative capacity, by a company or local authority; or

(b) by or on behalf of a partnership of which a company is a member; or

(c) by any person to another person whose usual place of abode is outside the United Kingdom;

the person by or through whom the payment is made shall, on making the payment, deduct out of it a sum representing the amount of income tax thereon for the year in which the payment is made.

(3) Subsection (2) above does not apply—

(a) to interest payable in the United Kingdom on an advance from a bank carrying on a bona fide banking business in the United Kingdom; or

(b) to interest paid by such a bank in the ordinary course of that business; or

(c) to any payment to which section 124 applies; or

(d) to any payment to which section 369 or 479(1) applies;

...[1]

Former enactments.—Sub-s. (1): TA 1970, s. 53(1); FA 1971, Sch. 6, para. 21; FA 1973, s. 17(1).
Sub-ss. (2), (3): TA 1970, ss. 54(1), (2), 65(2); FA 1971, Sch. 6, para. 22; FA 1982, s. 26(1); FA 1984, ss. 27(2), 35(1).
Cross references.—See FA 1989, s. 116(1)(b) (interest payments made after 31 March 1989 to Netherlands Antilles subsidiaries to be made gross if used by them for certain purposes);
Sch. 11 para. 18 (disapplication of this section in relation to redemption proceeds of deep gain securities).
Amendments.—[1] Words in sub-s. (3) repealed by FA 1988, Sch. 14, Pt. IV in relation to payments made after 5 April 1989.

350. Charge to tax where payments made under section 349

(1) Where any payment within section 349 is made by or through any person, that person shall forthwith deliver to the inspector an account of the payment, and shall be assessable

(ii) the party to whom or for whose benefit the payment is made has not remarried, and

(*d*) is not a payment in respect of which relief from tax is available to the person making the payment under any provision of the Income Tax Acts other than this section.

(2) Notwithstanding section 347A(1)(*a*) but subject to subsections (3) and (4) below, a person making a claim for the purpose shall be entitled, in computing his total income for a year of assessment, to deduct an amount equal to the aggregate amount of any qualifying maintenance payments made by him which fall due in that year.

(3) The amount which may be deducted under this section by a person in computing his total income for a year of assessment shall not exceed the amount of the difference between the higher (married person's) relief and the lower (single person's) relief under subsection (1) of section 257 as it applies for the year to a person not falling within subsection (2) or (3) of that section.

(4) Where qualifying maintenance payments falling due in a year of assessment are made by a person who also makes other maintenance payments attracting relief for that year, subsection (3) above shall apply as if the limit imposed by it were reduced by an amount equal to the aggregate amount of those other payments.

(5) the reference in subsection (4) above to other maintenance payments attracting relief for a year is a reference to periodical payments which—

(*a*) are made under an order made by a court (whether in the United Kingdom or elsewhere) or under a written or oral agreement, and
(*b*) are made by a person—

(i) as one of the parties to a marriage (including a marriage which has been dissolved or annulled) to or for the benefit of the other party to the marriage and for the maintenance of the other party, or
(ii) to any person under 21 years of age for his own benefit, maintenance or education, or
(iii) to any person for the benefit, maintenance or education of a person under 21 years of age,

and in respect of which the person making them is entitled otherwise than under this section to make a deduction in computing his income for the year.

(6) The reference in subsection (1) above to a married couple living together shall be construed in accordance with section 282(1), but section 282(2) shall not apply for the purposes of this section.

(7) In this section—

"child of the family", in relation to the parties to a marriage, means a person under 21 years of age—

(*a*) who is a child of both those parties, or
(*b*) who (not being a person who has been boarded out with them by a public authority or voluntary organisation) has been treated by both of them as a child of their family;

"periodical payment" does not include an instalment of a lump sum."

Note.—See **Prospective Legislation Notes** (Married Couples).
Cross references.—See FA 1988, s. 36(2), (3) (insertion of ss. 51A and 51B in TA 1970 which contain provisions (with necessary modifications) similar to the provisions of s. 347A above and this section).
Amendments.—[1] This section inserted by FA 1988, s. 36(1), (3)–(5) in relation to any payment falling due after 14 March 1988 unless made in pursuance of an existing obligation as defined.

348. Payments out of profits or gains brought into charge to income tax: deduction of tax

(1) Subject to any provision to the contrary in the Income Tax Acts, where any annuity or other annual payment charged with tax under Case III of Schedule D, not being interest, is payable wholly out of profits or gains brought into charge to income tax—

(*a*) the whole of the profits or gains shall be assessed and charged with income tax on the person liable to the annuity or other annual payment, without distinguishing the annuity or other annual payment; and
(*b*) the person liable to make the payment, whether out of the profits or gains charged with income tax or out of any annual payment liable to deduction, or from which a deduction has been made, shall be entitled on making the payment to deduct and retain out of it a sum representing the amount of income tax thereon; and
(*c*) the person to whom the payment is made shall allow the deduction on receipt of the residue of the payment, and the person making the deduction shall be acquitted and

PART IX

ANNUAL PAYMENTS AND INTEREST

Cross references.—See FA 1988, s. 43(3) (interest paid by a housing association or a self-build society on a home improvement loan made after 5 April 1988 not to be relevant loan interest for the purposes of this Part), s. 44(6) (interest paid by a housing association or a self-build society on a loan for residence of dependent relative or former spouse made after 5 April 1988 not to be relevant loan interest for the purposes of this Part).

Annual payments

[347A. General rule

(1) A payment to which this section applies shall not be a charge on the income of the person liable to make it, and accordingly—

(*a*) his income shall be computed without any deduction being made on account of the payment, and
(*b*) the payment shall not form part of the income of the person to whom it is made or of any other person.

(2) This section applies to any annual payment made by an individual which would otherwise be within the charge to tax under Case III of Schedule D except—

(*a*) a payment of interest;
(*b*) a covenanted payment to charity (within the meaning given by section 660(3));
(*c*) a payment made for bona fide commercial reasons in connection with the individual's trade, profession or vocation; and
(*d*) a payment to which section 125(1) applies.

(3) This section applies to a payment made by personal representatives (within the meaning given in section 701(4)) where—

(*a*) the deceased would have been liable to make the payment if he had died, and
(*b*) this section would have applied to the payment if he had made it.

(4) A maintenance payment arising outside the United Kingdom shall not be within the charge to tax under Case V of Schedule D if, because of this section, it would not have been within the charge to tax under Case III had it arisen in the United Kingdom; and for this purpose "maintenance payment" means a periodical payment (not being an instalment of a lump sum) which satisfies the conditions set out in paragraphs (a) and (b) of section 347B(5).

(5) No deduction shall be made under section 65(1)(*b*) on account of an annuity or other annual payment which would not have been within the charge to tax under Case III of Schedule D if it had arisen in the United Kingdom.][1]

(6) References in subsection (2) above to an individual include references to a Scottish partnership in which at least one partner is an individual.

Cross references.—See FA 1988, s. 36(2), (3) (insertion of ss. 51A and 51B in TA 1970 which contain provisions (with necessary modifications) similar to the provisions of this section and s. 347B below).
Amendments.—[1] This section inserted by FA 1988, s. 36(1), (3)–(5) in relation to any payment falling due after 14 March 1988 unless made in pursuance of an existing obligation as defined.

[347B. Qualifying maintenance payments

(1) In this section "qualifying maintenance payment" means a periodical payment which—

(*a*) is made under an order made by a court in the United Kingdom, or under a written agreement the proper law of which is the law of a part of the United Kingdom,
(*b*) is made by one of the parties to a marriage (including a marriage which has been dissolved or annulled) either—

(i) to or for the benefit of the other party and for the maintenance of the other party, or
(ii) to the other party for the maintenance by the other party of any child of the family,

(*c*) is due at a time when—

(i) the two parties are not a married couple living together, and

and a company paying any amount under paragraph (*b*) above shall be entitled to recover a sum of that amount from the company to which the chargeable gain accrued, and so far as it is not so recovered, to recover from any company which is for the time being a member of the group and which has while a member of the group owned the asset disposed of or any part of it (or where that asset is an interest or right in or over another asset, owned either asset or any part of it) such proportion of the amount unrecovered as is just having regard to the value of the asset at the time when the asset, or an interest or right in or over it, was disposed of by that company.

(4) Any reference in subsection (3) above to an amount of tax includes a reference to any interest paid under section 87A of the Management Act on that amount.

(5) Section 272 of the 1970 Act shall apply for the interpretation of this section as it applies for the interpretation of sections 273 to 281 of that Act.

(6) In relation to any chargeable gains accruing in accounting periods ending on or before the day, not being earlier than 31st March 1992, appointed by order by the Treasury for the purposes of this section, this section shall have effect—

    (*a*) with the substitution for the words in subsection (2) after "above" of the words "is the date when the tax becomes payable by the company"; and
    (*b*) with the omission of subsection (4).

Former enactments.—Sub-ss. (1)–(4): TA 1970, s. 277; F(No. 2)A 1987, Sch. 6, para. 3.
Sub-s. (5): TA 1970, s. 272.

(b) the distribution constitutes such a disposal of assets;

and that person is referred to below as "the shareholder".

(2) If the corporation tax assessed on the company for the accounting period in which the chargeable gains accrues included any amount in respect of chargeable gains, and any of the tax assessed on the company for that period is not paid within six months from the date determined under subsection (3) below, the shareholder may by an assessment made within two years from that date be assessed and charged (in the name of the company) to an amount of that corporation tax—

(a) not exceeding the amount or value of the capital distribution which the shareholder has received or become entitled to receive; and
(b) not exceeding a proportion equal to the shareholder's share of the capital distribution made by the company of corporation tax on the amount of that gain at the rate in force when the gain accrued.

(3) The date referred to in subsection (2) above is whichever is the later of—

(a) the date when the tax becomes due and payable by the company; and
(b) the date when the assessment was made on the company.

(4) Where the shareholder pays any amount of tax under this section, he shall be entitled to recover from the company a sum equal to that amount together with any interest paid by him under section 87A of the Management Act on that amount.

(5) The provisions of this section are without prejudice to any liability of the shareholder in respect of a chargeable gain accruing to him by reference to the capital distribution as constituting a disposal of an interest in shares in the company.

(6) With respect to chargeable gains accruing in accounting periods ending on or before the day, not being earlier than 31st March 1992, appointed by order by the Treasury for the purposes of this section, this section shall have effect—

(a) with the substitution for the words in subsection (3) after "above" of the words "is the date when the tax becomes payable by the company"; and
(b) with the omission of the words in subsection (4) from "together" to the end of the subsection.

(7) In this section "capital distribution" has the same meaning as in section 72(5)(b) of the 1979 Act and "connected with" shall be construed in accordance with section 839.

Former enactments.—TA 1970, s. 266; CGTA 1979, Sch. 7; F(No. 2)A 1987, Sch. 6, para. 1.

347. Tax on one member of group recoverable from another member

(1) If at any time a chargeable gain accrues to a company which at that time is a member of a group of companies and any of the corporation tax assessed on the company for the accounting period in which the chargeable gain accrues is not paid within six months from the date determined under subsection (2) below by the company, then, if the tax so assessed included any amount in respect of chargeable gains—

(a) a company which was at the time when the gain accrued the principal company of the group; and
(b) any other company which in any part of the period of two years ending with that time was a member of that group of companies and owned the asset disposed of or any part of it, or where that asset is an interest or right in or over another asset, owned either asset or any part of either asset;

may at any time within two years from the date determined under subsection (2) below be assessed and charged (in the name of the company to whom the chargeable gain accrued) to an amount of that corporation tax not exceeding corporation tax on the amount of that gain at the rate in force when the gain accrued.

(2) The date referred to in subsection (1) above is whichever is the later of—

(a) the date when the tax becomes due and payable by the company; and
(b) the date when the assessment is made on the company.

(3) A company paying any amount of tax under subsection (1) above shall be entitled to recover a sum of that amount—

(a) from the company to which the chargeable gain accrued, or
(b) if that company is not the company which was the principal company of the group at the time when the chargeable gain accrued, from that principal company,

other security was incurred, the person who was the creditor was carrying on a trade of lending money.

Former enactments.—TA 1970, s. 253; FA 1986, s. 42, Sch. 10, para. 2.

Chargeable gains

345. Computation of chargeable gains

(1) Subject to the provisions of this section and sections 400 and 435, the amount to be included in respect of chargeable gains in a company's total profits for any accounting period shall be the total amount of chargeable gains accruing to the company in the accounting period after deducting any allowable losses accruing to the company in the period and, so far as they have not been allowed as a deduction from chargeable gains accruing in any previous accounting period, any allowable losses previously accruing to the company while it has been within the charge to corporation tax.

(2) Except as otherwise provided by the Corporation Tax Acts, the total amount of the chargeable gains to be included in respect of chargeable gains in a company's total profits for any accounting period shall for purposes of corporation tax be computed in accordance with the principles applying for capital gains tax, all questions—

(*a*) as to the amounts which are or are not to be taken into account as chargeable gains or as allowable losses, or in computing gains or losses, or charged to tax as a person's gain; or

(*b*) as to the time when any such amount is to be treated as accruing,

being determined in accordance with the provisions relating to capital gains tax as if accounting periods were years of assessment.

(3) Subject to subsection (4) below, where the enactments relating to capital gains tax contain any reference to income tax or to the Income Tax Acts the reference shall, in relation to a company, be construed as a reference to corporation tax or to the Corporation Tax Acts; but—

(*a*) this subsection shall not affect the references to income tax in section 33(2) of the 1979 Act (exclusion of expenditure by reference to hypothetical income tax); and

(*b*) in so far as those enactments operate by reference to matters of any specified description, account shall for corporation tax be taken of matters of that description which are confined to companies, but not of any which are confined to individuals.

(4) The 1979 Act as extended by this section shall not be affected in its operation by the fact that capital gains tax and corporation tax are distinct taxes but, so far as is consistent with the Corporation Tax Acts, shall apply in relation to capital gains tax and corporation tax on chargeable gains as if they were one tax, so that, in particular, a matter which in a case involving two individuals is relevant for both of them in relation to capital gains tax shall in a like case involving an individual and a company be relevant for him in relation to that tax and for it in relation to corporation tax.

(5) Where assets of a company are vested in a liquidator under section 145 of the Insolvency Act 1986 or Article 498 of the Companies (Northern Ireland) Order 1986 or otherwise, this section and the enactments applied by this section shall apply as if the assets were vested in, and the acts of the liquidator in relation to the assets were the acts of, the company (acquisitions from or disposals to him by the company being disregarded acccordingly).

Former enactments.—Sub-s. (1): TA 1970, s. 265(1).
Sub-s. (2): TA 1970, s. 265(2).
Sub-s. (3): TA 1970, s. 265(3)(*a*), (*c*); CGTA 1979, Sch. 7.
Sub-s. (4): TA 1970, s. 265(4); CGTA 1979, Sch. 7; Companies Consolidation (Consequential Provisions) Act 1985, Sch. 2; Companies Consolidation (Consequential Provisions) (Northern Ireland) Order 1986, S.I. 1986 No. 1032.
Sub-s. (5): TA 1970, s. 265(5).

346. Capital distribution of chargeable gains: recovery of tax from shareholder

(1) This section applies where a person who is connected with a company resident in the United Kingdom receives or becomes entitled to receive in respect of shares in the company any capital distribution from the company, other than a capital distribution representing a reduction of capital, and—

(*a*) the capital so distributed derives from the disposal of assets in respect of which a chargeable gain accrued to the company; or

owning the share capital are conducted in accordance with his or their wishes, be regarded as owned by the person or body of persons having that power.

(3) For the purposes of subsection (2) above—
   (a) references to ownership shall be construed as references to beneficial ownership;
   (b) a company shall be deemed to be a subsidiary of another company if and so long as not less than three-quarters of its ordinary share capital is owned by that other company, whether directly or through another company or other companies, or partly directly and partly through another company or other companies;
   (c) the amount of ordinary share capital of one company owned by a second company through another company or other companies, or partly directly and partly through another company or other companies, shall be determined in accordance with section 838(5) to (10); and
   (d) where any company is a subsidiary of another company, that other company shall be considered as its parent company unless both are subsidiaries of a third company.

(4) In determining, for the purposes of section 343, whether or to what extent a trade belongs at different times to the same persons, persons who are relatives of one another and the persons from time to time entitled to the income under any trust shall respectively be treated as a single person, and for this purpose "relative" means husband, wife, ancestor, lineal descendant, brother or sister.

(5) For the purposes of section 343(4), relevant assets are—
   (a) assets which were vested in the predecessor immediately before it ceased to carry on the trade, which were not transferred to the successor and which, in a case where the predecessor was the predecessor on a previous application of section 343, were not by virtue of subsection (9) of that section apportioned to a trade carried on by the company which was the successor on that application; and
   (b) consideration given to the predecessor by the successor in respect of the change of company carrying on the trade;

and for the purposes of paragraph (b) above the assumption by the successor of any liabilities of the predecessor shall not be treated as the giving of consideration to the predecessor by the successor.

(6) For the purposes of section 343(4), relevant liabilities are liabilities which were outstanding and vested in the predecessor immediately before it ceased to carry on the trade, which were not transferred to the successor and which, in a case where the predecessor was the predecessor on a previous application of section 343, were not by virtue of subsection (9) of that section apportioned to a trade carried on by the company which was the successor on that application; but a liability representing the predecessor's share capital, share premium account, reserves or relevant loan stock is not a relevant liability.

(7) For the purposes of section 343(4)—
   (a) the value of assets (other than money) shall be taken to be the price which they might reasonably be expected to have fetched on a sale in the open market immediately before the predecessor ceased to carry on the trade; and
   (b) the amount of liabilities shall be taken to be their amount at that time.

(8) Where the predecessor transferred a liability to the successor but the creditor concerned agreed to accept settlement of part of the liability as settlement of the whole, the liability shall be treated for the purposes of subsection (6) above as not having been transferred to the successor except as to that part.

(9) A liability representing the predecessor's share capital, share premium account, reserves or relevant loan stock shall, for the purposes of subsection (6) above, be treated as not doing so if, in the period of one year ending with the day on which the predecessor ceased to carry on the trade, the liability arose on a conversion of a liability not representing its share capital, share premium account, reserves or relevant loan stock.

(10) Where a liability of the predecessor representing its relevant loan stock is not a relevant liability for the purposes of section 343(4) but is secured on an asset of the predecessor not transferred to the successor, the value of the asset shall, for the purposes of section 343(4), be reduced by an amount equal to the amount of the liability.

(11) In this section "relevant loan stock" means any loan stock or similar security (whether secured or unsecured) except any in the case of which subsection (12) below applies.

(12) This subsection applies where, at the time the liability giving rise to the loan stock or

company ceasing or beginning to carry them on, to be treated as a separate trade, such apportionments of receipts, expenses, assets or liabilities shall be made as may be just.

(10) Where, by virtue of subsection (9) above, any item falls to be apportioned and, at the time of the apportionment, it appears that it is material as respects the liability to tax (for whatever period) of two or more companies, any question which arises as to the manner in which the item is to be apportioned shall be determined, for the purposes of the tax of all those companies—

(*a*) in a case where the same body of General Commissioners have jurisdiction with respect to all those companies, by those Commissioners, unless all the companies agree that it shall be determined by the Special Commissioners;
(*b*) in a case where different bodies of Commissioners have jurisdiction with respect to those companies, by such of those bodies as the Board may direct, unless all the companies agree that it shall be determined by the Special Commissioners; and
(*c*) in any other case, by the Special Commissioners,

and any such Commissioners shall determine the question in like manner as if it were an appeal except that all those companies shall be entitled to appear and be heard by the Commissioners who are to make the determination or to make representations to them in writing.

(11) Any relief obtainable under this section by way of discharge or repayment of tax shall be given on the making of a claim.

(12) In the application of this section to any case in relation to which subsection (4) above does not apply—

(*a*) subsection (9) above shall have effect with the substitution for the words following "separate trade" of the words "any necessary apportionment shall be made of receipts or expenses"; and
(*b*) subsection (10) above shall have effect with the substitution for "item" of "sum".

Former enactments.—Sub-s. (1): TA 1970, s. 252(1).
Sub-s. (2): TA 1970, s. 252(2), (2A); FA 1971, Sch. 8, para. 16(5); FA 1986, s. 56(7), Sch. 13, para. 2; F(No. 2)A 1987, s. 64(2).
Sub-s. (3): TA 1970, s. 252(3)–(7).
Sub-s. (4): TA 1970, s. 252(3A); FA 1986, s. 42(2), (3), Sch. 10, para. 1(2).
Sub-ss. (5)–(8): TA 1970, s. 252(4)–(7).
Sub-s. (9): TA 1970, s. 252(8); FA 1986, Sch. 10, para. 1(3).
Sub-ss. (10), (11): TA 1970, s. 252(9), (10).
Sub-s. (12): FA 1986, s. 42(2), (3).
Cross references.—See TMA 1970, s. 58(3)(*b*), FA 1988, ss 134(4), 135(2) (with effect from 3 April 1989, by virtue of FA 1988 (Commencement) Order 1989, S.I. 1989 No. 473, proceedings under sub-s. (10) of this section to be in Northern Ireland if the place given by certain rules in relation to the parties to the proceedings is in Northern Ireland).

344. Company reconstructions: supplemental

(1) For the purposes of section 343—

(*a*) a trade carried on by two or more persons shall be treated as belonging to them in the shares in which they are entitled to the profits of the trade;
(*b*) a trade or interest in a trade belonging to any person as trustee (otherwise than for charitable or public purposes) shall be treated as belonging to the persons for the time being entitled to the income under the trust; and
(*c*) a trade or interest in a trade belonging to a company shall, where the result of so doing is that subsection (1) or (7) of section 343 has effect in relation to an event, be treated in any of the ways permitted by subsection (2) below.

(2) For the purposes of section 343, a trade or interest in a trade which belongs to a company engaged in carrying it on may be regarded—

(*a*) as belonging to the persons owning the ordinary share capital of the company and as belonging to them in proportion to the amount of their holdings of that capital, or
(*b*) in the case of a company which is a subsidiary company, as belonging to a company which is its parent company, or as belonging to the persons owning the ordinary share capital of that parent company, and as belonging to them in proportion to the amount of their holdings of that capital,

and any ordinary share capital owned by a company may, if any person or body of persons has the power to secure by means of the holding of shares or the possession of voting power in or in relation to any company, or by virtue of any power conferred by the articles of association or other document regulating any company, that the affairs of the company

(ii) everything done to or by the predecessor had been done to or by the successor (but so that no sale or transfer which on the transfer of the trade is made to the successor by the predecessor of any assets in use for the purpose of the trade shall be treated as giving rise to any such allowance or charge).

The preceding provisions of this subsection shall not apply if the successor is a dual resident investing company (within the meaning of section 404) which begins to carry on the trade after 31st March 1987.

(3) The predecessor shall not be entitled to relief under section 394, except as provided by subsection (6) below; and, subject to subsection (4) below and to any claim made by the predecessor under section 393(2), the successor shall be entitled to relief under section 393(1), as for a loss sustained by the successor in carrying on the trade, for any amount for which the predecessor would have been entitled to claim relief if it had continued to carry on the trade.

(4) Where the amount of relevant liabilities exceeds the value of relevant assets, the successor shall be entitled to relief by virtue of subsection (3) above only if, and only to the extent that, the amount of that excess is less than the amount mentioned in that subsection.

This subsection does not apply where the predecessor ceased to carry on the trade or part of a trade before 19th March 1986 nor, in a case where subsection (7) below applies, in relation to any earlier event, within the meaning of that subsection, which occurred before that date (but without prejudice to its application in relation to any later event which occurred on or after that date).

(5) Any securities, within the meaning of section 731, which at the time when the predecessor ceases to carry on the trade form part of the trading stock belonging to the trade shall be treated for the purposes of that section as having been sold at that time in the open market by the predecessor and as having been purchased at that time in the open market by the successor.

(6) On the successor ceasing to carry on the trade—

(*a*) if the successor does so within four years of succeeding to it, any relief which might be given to the successor under section 394 on its ceasing to carry on the trade may, so far as it cannot be given to the successor, be given to the predecessor as if the predecessor had incurred the loss (including any amount treated as a loss under subsection (4) of that section); and

(*b*) if the successor ceases to carry on the trade within one year of succeeding to it, relief may be given to the predecessor under that section in respect of any loss incurred by it (or amount treated as such a loss under subsection (4) of that section);

but for the purposes of that section, as it applies by virtue of this subsection to the giving of relief to the predecessor, the predecessor shall be treated as ceasing to carry on the trade when the successor does so.

(7) Where the successor ceases to carry on the trade within the period taken for the comparison under subsection (1)(*a*) above and on its doing so a third company begins to carry on the trade, then no relief shall be given to the predecessor by virtue of subsection (6) above by reference to that event, but, subject to that, subsections (2) to (6) above shall apply both in relation to that event (together with the new predecessor and successor) and to the earlier event (together with the original predecessor and successor), but so that—

(*a*) in relation to the earlier event "successor" shall include the successor at either event; and

(*b*) in relation to the later event "predecessor" shall include the predecessor at either event;

and if the conditions of this subsection are thereafter again satisfied, it shall apply again in like manner.

(8) Where, on a company ceasing to carry on a trade, another company begins to carry on the activities of the trade as part of its trade, then that part of the trade carried on by the successor shall be treated for the purposes of this section as a separate trade, if the effect of so treating it is that subsection (1) or (7) above has effect on that event in relation to that separate trade; and where, on a company ceasing to carry on part of a trade, another company begins to carry on the activities of that part as its trade or part of its trade, the predecessor shall for purposes of this section be treated as having carried on that part of its trade as a separate trade if the effect of so treating it is that subsection (1) or (7) above has effect on that event in relation to that separate trade.

(9) Where under subsection (8) above any activities of a company's trade fall, on the

(*b*) where the corporation tax charged on the company's income included in those profits falls to be calculated or reduced in accordance with section 13, it shall be so calculated or reduced in accordance with such rate or fraction fixed or proposed for the penultimate year as is applicable under that section.

(3) If, before the affairs of the company are completely wound up, any of the rates or fractions mentioned in subsection (2) above has been fixed or proposed for the final year, that subsection shall have effect in relation to that rate or fraction as if for the references to the penultimate year there were substituted references to the final year.

(4) An assessment on the company's profits for an accounting period which falls after the commencement of the winding-up shall not be invalid because made before the end of the accounting period.

(5) In making an assessment after the commencement of the winding-up of the company but before the date when its affairs are completely wound up, the inspector may, with the concurrence of the liquidator, act on an assumption as to when that date will fall, so far as it governs section 12(7).

(6) The assumption of the wrong date shall not alter the company's final and penultimate year, and, if the right date is later, an accounting period shall end on the date assumed, and a new accounting period shall begin and section 12(7) shall thereafter apply as if that new accounting period began with the commencement of the winding-up.

(7) References in this section to a rate or fraction fixed or proposed are references to a rate or fraction fixed by an Act passed before the completion of the winding-up or, if not so fixed, proposed by a Budget resolution (and without regard to any subsequent Act); except that if a rate or fraction so fixed is proposed to be altered by a Budget resolution any such reference to it is a reference to it as proposed to be so altered.

In this subsection "Budget resolution" means a resolution of the House of Commons for fixing any such rate or fraction as is mentioned in this section.

(8) Where the winding-up commenced before the company's final year, paragraphs (*a*) and (*b*) of subsection (2) (but not subsection (3)) above shall apply in relation to the company's profits arising at any time in its penultimate year.

(9) Any assessment made by virtue of section 8(4) shall be subject to any such adjustment by discharge or repayment of tax or by a further assessment as may be required to give effect to this section.

Former enactments.—Sub-s. (1): TA 1970, s. 245(1).
Sub-ss. (2), (3): TA 1970, s. 245(2), (3); FA 1974, s. 37(1).
Sub-ss. (4)–(6): TA 1970, s. 245(4)–(6).
Sub-ss. (7)–(9): TA 1970, s. 245(7)–(9); FA 1974, s. 37(1).

343. Company reconstructions without a change of ownership

(1) Where, on a company ("the predecessor") ceasing to carry on a trade, another company ("the successor") begins to carry it on, and—

(*a*) on or at any time within two years after that event the trade or an interest amounting to not less than a three-fourths share in it belongs to the same persons as the trade or such an interest belonged to at some time within a year before that event; and

(*b*) the trade is not, within the period taken for the comparison under paragraph (*a*) above, carried on otherwise than by a company which is within the charge to tax in respect of it;

then the Corporation Tax Acts shall have effect subject to subsections (2) to (6) below.

In paragraphs (*a*) and (*b*) above references to the trade shall apply also to any other trade of which the activities comprise the activities of the first mentioned trade.

(2) The trade shall not be treated as permanently discontinued nor a new trade as set up and commenced for the purpose of the allowances and charges provided for by the Capital Allowances Acts; but—

(*a*) there shall be made to or on the successor in accordance with those Acts all such allowances and charges as would, if the predecessor had continued to carry on the trade, have fallen to be made to or on it; and

(*b*) the amount of any such allowance or charge shall be computed as if—

(i) the successor had been carrying on the trade since the predecessor began to do so, and

(c) the person carrying on the trade and the person entitled to the interest are both bodies of persons, and some other person has control over both of them.

In this subsection references to a body of persons include references to a partnership and "control" has the meaning given by section 840.

(3) For the purposes of subsection (1) above the company paying the interest shall be treated as carrying on any trade carried on by a 75 per cent. subsidiary of it (both being bodies corporate) if the subsidiary (as well as the company making the payment) is resident in the United Kingdom.

(4) In determining for the purposes of this section whether one company is a 75 per cent. subsidiary of another that other company shall be treated as not being the owner—
   (a) of any share capital which it owns directly in a body corporate if a profit on a sale of the shares would be treated as a trading receipt of its trade; or
   (b) of any share capital which it owns indirectly, and which is owned directly by a body corporate for which a profit on the sale of the shares would be a trading receipt; or
   (c) of any share capital which it owns directly or indirectly in a body corporate not resident in the United Kingdom.

Former enactments.—TA 1970, 249(1)–(4); FA 1982, s. 64(1).

341. Payments of interest etc. between related companies

(1) This section applies where—
   (a) the relationship between two companies is as mentioned in subsection (2) below;
   (b) one of the companies makes to the other a payment which, for the purposes of corporation tax, is a charge on income of the company making it; and
   (c) in the hands of the company receiving it, the payment is chargeable to tax under Case III of Schedule D.

(2) The relationship between two companies which is referred to in subsection (1)(a) above is—
   (a) that one company controls the other; or
   (b) that another person controls both companies; or
   (c) that one company is a 51 per cent. subsidiary of the other; or
   (d) that both companies are 51 per cent. subsidiaries of another company;

and section 840 applies for the purposes of this section.

(3) In a case where this section applies, the payment referred to in subsection (1)(b) above shall be treated for the purposes of corporation tax as received by the company to which it is paid on the same day as that on which it is for those purposes treated as paid by the company paying it.

(4) Subject to subsection (5) below, where the payment referred to in subsection (1)(b) above is a "relevant payment" for the purposes of Schedule 16, it shall be treated for the purposes of that Schedule as received on the same day as that on which, by virtue of subsection (3) above, it is treated as received for the purposes of corporation tax; and the reference in paragraph 5(1) of that Schedule to the accounting period in which the payment is received shall be construed accordingly.

(5) Subsection (4) above does not apply if the day on which the payment would be treated as received apart from that subsection falls within the same accounting period (of the receiving company) as the day on which it would be treated as received under that subsection.

Former enactment.—F(No. 2)A 1987, s. 60.

342. Tax on company in liquidation

(1) In this section references to a company's final year are references to the financial year in which the affairs of the company are completely wound up, and references to a company's penultimate year are references to the last financial year preceding its final year.

(2) Subject to subsection (3) below—
   (a) corporation tax shall be charged on the profits of the company arising in the winding-up in its final year at the rate of corporation tax fixed or proposed for the penultimate year; but

(4) Where, with a view to securing relief under section 338 a company makes a payment subject to such a deduction as is mentioned in subsection (3) above, then, whether or not it proves to be a qualifying donation, the payment—

(a) shall be treated as a relevant payment for the purposes of Schedule 16; and
(b) shall in the hands of the recipient (whether a charity or not) be treated for the purposes of this Act as if it were an annual payment.

(5) In any accounting period of a company, the maximum amount allowable under section 338 by virtue of subsection (2)(b) of that section in respect of qualifying donations made by the company shall be a sum equal to 3 per cent. of the dividends paid on the company's ordinary share capital in that accounting period.

(6) A covenanted donation to charity shall not be regarded for the purposes of the definition of "charges on income" in section 338, or for any of the other purposes of the Corporation Tax Acts, as being, by reason of any provision of this Act, a distribution.

(7) Notwithstanding anything in any other provision of the Tax Acts, a covenanted donation to charity made by a company shall not be a charge on income for the purposes of section 338 unless the company—

(a) deducts out of it a sum representing the amount of income tax on it; and
(b) accounts for that tax in accordance with Schedule 16;

and any such payment from which a deduction is made as mentioned in paragraph (a) above shall be treated as a relevant payment for the purposes of Schedule 16, whether or not it would otherwise fall to be so treated.

(8) In this section "covenanted donation to charity" means a payment under a disposition or covenant made by the company in favour of a charity whereby the like annual payments (of which the donation is one) become payable for a period which may exceed three years and is not capable of earlier termination under any power exercisable without the consent of the persons for the time being entitled to the payments.

(9) For the purposes of this section "charity" includes [each of the bodies mentioned in section 507, and in subsections (1) to (5) above includes][1] any Association of a description specified in section 508, but, subject to that, in this section "charity" has the same meaning as in section 506.

Former enactments.—Sub-s. (1): FA 1986, s. 29(1), (2).
Sub-s. (2): FA 1986, s. 29(1).
Sub-ss. (3)–(5): FA 1986, s. 29(3)–(5).
Sub-s. (6): TA 1970, s. 248(8); FA 1972, Sch. 24, para. 20.
Sub-s. (7): TA 1970, s. 248(8A); FA 1986, s. 30(2).
Sub-s. (8): TA 1970, s. 248(9); FA 1980, s. 55(3).
Sub-s. (9): FA 1981, s. 49; FA 1983, s. 46(3); FA 1986, s. 29(6).
Amendments.—[1] Words in sub-s. (9) substituted by FA 1989, s. 60(2), (4) in respect of payments due after 13 March 1989.

340. Charges on income: interest payable to non-residents

(1) A payment of interest by a company is one to which section 338(4)(c) applies if the company is carrying on a trade and—

(a) under the terms of the contract under which the interest is payable, the interest is to be paid, or may be required to be paid, outside the United Kingdom; and
(b) the interest is in fact paid outside the United Kingdom; and
(c) either—
  (i) the liability to pay the interest was incurred wholly or mainly for the purposes of activities of the company's trade carried on outside the United Kingdom; or
  (ii) the interest is payable in a currency other than sterling and, subject to subsection (2) below, the liability to pay the interest was incurred wholly or mainly for the purposes of activities of that trade, wherever carried on.

(2) Subsection (1)(c)(ii) above does not apply where—

(a) the trade is carried on by a body of persons over whom the person entitled to the interest has control; or
(b) the person entitled to the interest is a body of persons over whom the person carrying on the trade has control; or

(b) it is a payment of interest on a quoted Eurobond falling within section 124; or
(c) the payment is a payment of interest falling within section 340; or
(d) the payment is one payable out of income brought into charge to tax under Case IV or V of Schedule D.

(5) No such payment made by a company as is mentioned in subsection (3) above shall be treated as a charge on income if—

(a) the payment, not being interest, is charged to capital or the payment is not ultimately borne by the company; or
(b) the payment is not made under a liability incurred for a valuable and sufficient consideration (and, in the case of a company not resident in the United Kingdom, incurred wholly and exclusively for the purposes of a trade carried on by it in the United Kingdom through a branch or agency), and is not a covenanted donation to charity (within the meaning of section 339).

(6) No such payment of interest as is mentioned in subsection (3) above made by a company shall be treated as a charge on income unless—

(a) the company exists wholly or mainly for the purpose of carrying on a trade; or
(b) the payment of interest is wholly and exclusively laid out or expended for the purposes of a trade carried on by the company; or
(c) the company is an investment company, within the meaning of section 130 and including an authorised unit trust; or
(d) the payment of interest would, on the assumptions made below, be eligible for relief under section 353 by virtue of section 354 if it were made by an individual.

For the purposes of paragraph (d) above, it shall be assumed that if the land concerned is occupied by the company the conditions of section 355(1) are satisfied if the land either—

(i) is not used as a residence; or
(ii) is used as an individual's main or only residence;

but the limit imposed by section 357 shall apply only in a case falling within paragraph (ii) above and shall then apply without regard to any loan made in connection with any other land.

(7) Any payment to which section 125(1) applies shall not be a charge on income for the purposes of corporation tax.

Former enactments.—Sub-s. (1): TA 1970, s. 248(1); FA 1986, s. 29.
Sub-s. (2): TA 1970, s. 248(2)(a).
Sub-s. (3): TA 1970, s. 248(3); FA 1973, s. 54(1)(a); FA 1981, s. 38(1).
Sub-s. (4)(a): TA 1970, s. 248(4); FA 1972, Sch. 24, para. 20.
Sub-s. (4)(b): TA 1970, s. 248(4)(aa); FA 1984, s. 35(4).
Sub-s. (4)(c), (d): TA 1970, s. 248(4)(b), (c).
Sub-s. (5): TA 1970, s. 248(5); FA 1981, s. 38(2).
Sub-s. (6): TA 1970, s. 248(6); FA 1974, Sch. 1, para. 27.
Sub-s. (7): FA 1977, s. 48(1).
Cross references.—See FA 1989, s. 116(1)(a) (interest payments to Netherlands Antilles subsidiaries made after 31 March 1989 for certain purposes to be made gross).

339. Charges on income: donations to charity

(1) A qualifying donation is a payment made by a company to a charity, other than—

(a) a covenanted payment to charity, as defined in section 660(3); and
(b) a payment which is deductible in computing profits or any description of profits for purposes of corporation tax.

(2) A qualifying donation shall not constitute a charge on the income of the company unless a claim is made by the company and the company is resident in the United Kingdom and is not a close company.

(3) A payment made by a company is not a qualifying donation unless, on the making of it, the company deducts out of it a sum representing the amount of income tax on it.

PART VIII

TAXATION OF INCOME AND CHARGEABLE GAINS OF COMPANIES

Taxation of income

337. Companies beginning or ceasing to carry on a trade

(1) Where a company begins or ceases to carry on a trade, or to be within the charge to corporation tax in respect of a trade, the company's income shall be computed as if that were the commencement or, as the case may be, discontinuance of the trade, whether or not the trade is in fact commenced or discontinued.

(2) Subject to subsection (3) below and to any other provision of the Corporation Tax Acts which expressly authorises such a deduction, no deduction shall be made in computing income from any source—

(*a*) in respect of dividends or other distributions; nor
(*b*) in respect of any yearly interest, annuity or other annual payment or in respect of any such other payments as are mentioned in section 348(2), but not including sums which are, or but for any exemption would be, chargeable under Schedule A.

(3) In computing income from a trade, subsection (2)(*b*) above shall not prevent the deduction of yearly interest payable in the United Kingdom on an advance from a bank carrying on a bona fide banking business in the United Kingdom.

Former enactment.—TA 1970, s. 251.

338. Allowance of charges on income and capital

(1) Subject to sections 339, 494 and 787, in computing the corporation tax chargeable for any accounting period of a company any charges on income paid by the company in the accounting period, so far as paid out of the company's profits brought into charge to corporation tax, shall be allowed as deductions against the total profits for the period as reduced by any other relief from tax, other than group relief.

(2) Subject to the following subsections, to section 339 and to any other express exceptions, "charges on income" means for the purposes of corporation tax—

(*a*) payments of any description mentioned in subsection (3) below, not being dividends or other distributions of the company; and
(*b*) payments which are qualifying donations (within the meaning of section 339);

but no payment which is deductible in computing profits or any description of profits for purposes of corporation tax shall be treated as a charge on income.

(3) Subject to subsections (4) to (6) below, the payments referred to in subsection (2)(*a*) above are—

(*a*) any yearly interest (whether charged to revenue or capital), annuity or other annual payment and any such other payments as are mentioned in section 348(2) but not including sums which are or, but for any exemption would be, chargeable under Schedule A; and
(*b*) any other interest (whether charged to revenue or capital) payable in the United Kingdom on an advance from a bank carrying on a bona fide banking business in the United Kingdom, or from a person who in the opinion of the Board is bona fide carrying on business as a member of the Stock Exchange or bona fide carrying on the business of a discount house in the United Kingdom;

and for the purposes of this section any interest payable by a company as mentioned in paragraph (*b*) above shall be treated as paid on its being debited to the company's account in the books of the person to whom it is payable.

(4) No such payment as is mentioned in subsection (3)(*a*) above made by a company to a person not resident in the United Kingdom shall be treated as a charge on income unless the company is so resident and either—

(*a*) the company deducts income tax from the payment in accordance with section 349, and accounts under Schedule 16 for the tax so deducted, or

CHAPTER V
RESIDENCE OF INDIVIDUALS

334. Commonwealth citizens and others temporarily abroad

Every Commonwealth citizen or citizen of the Republic of Ireland—

(*a*) shall, if his ordinary residence has been in the United Kingdom, be assessed and charged to income tax notwithstanding that at the time the assessment or charge is made he may have left the United Kingdom, if he has so left the United Kingdom for the purpose only of occasional residence abroad, and

(*b*) shall be charged as a person actually residing in the United Kingdom upon the whole amount of his profits or gains, whether they arise from property in the United Kingdom or elsewhere, or from any allowance, annuity or stipend, or from any trade, profession, employment or vocation in the United Kingdom or elsewhere.

Former enactments.—TA 1970, s. 49; British Nationality Act 1981, s. 51(1), (2).

335. Residence of persons working abroad

(1) Where—

(*a*) a person works full-time in one or more of the following, that is to say, a trade, profession, vocation, office or employment; and

(*b*) no part of the trade, profession or vocation is carried on in the United Kingdom and all the duties of the office or employment are performed outside the United Kingdom;

the question whether he is resident in the United Kingdom shall be decided without regard to any place of abode maintained in the United Kingdom for his use.

(2) Where an office or employment is in substance one of which the duties fall in the year of assessment to be performed outside the United Kingdom there shall be treated for the purposes of this section as so performed any duties performed in the United Kingdom the performance of which is merely incidental to the performance of the other duties outside the United Kingdom.

Former enactment.—TA 1970, s. 50.

336. Temporary residents in the United Kingdom

(1) A person shall not be charged to income tax under Schedule D as a person residing in the United Kingdom, in respect of profits or gains received in respect of possessions or securities out of the United Kingdom, if—

(*a*) he is in the United Kingdom for some temporary purpose only and not with any view or intent of establishing his residence there, and

(*b*) he has not actually resided in the United Kingdom at one time or several times for a period equal in the whole to six months in any year of assessment,

but if any such person resides in the United Kingdom for such a period he shall be so chargeable for that year.

(2) For the purposes of Cases I, II and III of Schedule E, a person who is in the United Kingdom for some temporary purpose only and not with the intention of establishing his residence there shall not be treated as resident in the United Kingdom if he has not in the aggregate spent at least six months in the United Kingdom in the year of assessment, but shall be treated as resident there if he has.

Former enactment.—TA 1970, s. 51.

(e) provide that plans and plan managers must be such as are approved by the Board;
(f) specify the circumstances in which approval may be granted and withdrawn.

(4) The regulations may include provision—

(a) that in prescribed circumstances—

(i) an investor under a plan shall cease to be, and be treated as not having been, entitled to relief from tax in respect of the investments; and
(ii) he or the plan manager concerned (depending on the terms of the regulations) shall account to the Board for tax from which relief has already been given on the basis that the investor was so entitled;

(b) that an investor under a plan or the plan manager concerned (depending on the terms of the regulations) shall account to the Board for tax from which relief has been given in circumstances such that the investor was not entitled to it;

(c) adapting, or modifying the effect of, any enactment relating to income tax in order to—

(i) secure that investors under plans are entitled to relief from tax in respect of investments;
(ii) secure that investors under plans cease to be, and are treated as not having been, so entitled;
(iii) secure that investors under plans or plan managers account for tax as mentioned in paragraph (a) or (b) above;

(d) that a person who is, or has at any time been, either an investor under a plan or a plan manager—

(i) shall comply with any notice which is served on him by the Board and which requires him within a prescribed period to make available for the Board's inspection documents (of a prescribed kind) relating to a plan or to investments which are or have been held under it;
(ii) shall, within a prescribed period of being required to do so by the Board, furnish to the Board information (of a prescribed kind) about a plan or about investments which are or have been held under it;

(e) generally for the purpose of bringing plans into existence, and generally for the purpose of the administration of plans and the administration of income tax and corporation tax in relation to them.

(5) In this section "prescribed" means prescribed by the regulations.

Former enactment.—FA 1986, Sch. 8.
Cross references.—See CGTA 1979, s. 149D(2) (extension of the application of sub-ss. (2) to (5) of this section in relation to capital gains tax).

(2) In this section "scholarship" includes an exhibition, bursary or any other similar educational endowment.

Former enactment.—TA 1970, s. 375(1), (2).

332. Expenditure and houses of ministers of religion

(1) Subsection (2) below applies where an interest in any premises belongs to a charity or any ecclesiastical corporation and (in right of that interest)—
   (a) the persons from time to time holding any full-time office as clergyman or minister of any religious denomination, or
   (b) any particular person holding such an office,

have or has a residence in those premises from which to perform the duties of the office.

(2) In the case of such a clergyman or minister, for the purposes of income tax with which he may be chargeable under Schedule E, there shall be disregarded—
   (a) the making good to him, in consequence of his being the holder of his office, of statutory amounts payable in connection with the premises or statutory deductions falling to be made in connection therewith, except in so far as an amount or deduction is properly attributable to a part of the premises in respect of which he receives rent;
   (b) the payment on his behalf, except as aforesaid, of such a statutory amount; and
   (c) unless he is in [employment to which Chapter II of Part V applies][1], the value to him of any expenses incurred in connection with the provision in the premises of living accommodation for him, being expenses incurred in consequence of his being the holder of his office.

(3) In assessing the income tax chargeable (whether under Schedule E or any other Schedule) upon a clergyman or minister of any religious denomination, the following deductions may be made from any profits, fees or emoluments of his profession or vocation—
   (a) any sums of money paid or expenses incurred by him wholly, exclusively and necessarily in the performance of his duty as a clergyman or minister;
   (b) such part of the rent (not exceeding one-quarter) as the inspector by whom the assessment is made may allow, paid by him in respect of a dwelling-house any part of which is used mainly and substantially for the purposes of his duty as such clergyman or minister; and
   (c) in respect of expenses borne by him in the maintenance, repairs, insurance or management of any premises in which, in right of such an interest as is mentioned in subsection (1) above, he has such a residence as is mentioned in that subsection, such part of the expenses as, together with any deduction allowable in respect of such expenses under paragraph (a) above, is equal to one-quarter of the amount of the expenses.

On an appeal to the General Commissioners or Special Commissioners, the Commissioners shall have jurisdiction to review the inspector's decision under paragraph (b) above.

(4) In this section "statutory amount" and "statutory deduction" mean an amount paid and a deduction made in pursuance of any provision contained in or having the force of an Act.

Former enactments.—TA 1970, s. 194; FA 1977, Sch. 8, paras. 2, 3; FA 1987, Sch. 15, para. 2(12).
Amendments.—[1] Words in sub-s. (2)(c) substituted by FA 1989, s. 53(2)(f).

333. Personal equity plans

(1) The Treasury may make regulations providing that an individual who invests under a plan shall be entitled to relief from income tax in respect of the investments.

(2) The regulations shall set out the conditions subject to which plans are to operate and the extent to which investors are to be entitled to relief from tax.

(3) In particular, the regulations may—
   (a) specify the description of individuals who may invest and the kind of investments they may make;
   (b) specify maximum investment limits and minimum periods for which investments are to be held;
   (c) provide that investments are to be held by persons ("plan managers") on behalf of investors;
   (d) specify how relief from tax is to be claimed by, and granted to, investors or plan managers on their behalf;

without deduction of tax by virtue of that subsection and of the persons to whom they were paid, except that particulars shall not be required of any case where the total of such sums paid to any person in that year did not exceed £15.

(7) An agreement designating a fund for the purposes of subsection (1) above may provide for incidental and consequential matters, including arrangements for giving effect to subsection (1)(*a*) above by provisional repayments of tax deducted at source, and may be determined by the Board or the investment manager of the fund by one year's notice expiring at the end of any year of assessment.

(8) The reference to the Accountant General is a reference to the Accountant General of the Supreme Court of England and Wales in the relation to money in the Supreme Court of Judicature of Northern Ireland, or money in a county court in Northern Ireland, and in relation to investments representing such money, includes a reference to the Accountant General of the Supreme Court of Judicature of Northern Ireland or any other person by whom such funds are held.

Former enactments.—Sub-s. (1): TA 1970, s. 413(1), (2); Administration of Justice Act 1982, s. 46(2).
Sub-ss. (2)–(4): FA 1985, Sch. 23, para. 8(5), (6); FA 1986, Sch. 17, para. 1(1).
Sub-ss. (5)–(8): TA 1970, s. 413(3)–(6); Judicature (Northern Ireland) Act 1978, Sch. 5; Supreme Court Act 1981, s 1; Administration of Justice Act 1982, s. 46(2).

329. Interest on damages for personal injuries

(1) The following interest shall not be regarded as income for any income tax purpose—

(*a*) any interest on damages in respect of personal injuries to a plaintiff or any other person, or in respect of a person's death, which is included in any sum for which judgment is given by virtue of a provision to which this paragraph applies; and
(*b*) any interest on damages or solatium in respect of personal injuries sustained by a pursuer or by any other person, decree for payment of which is included in any interlocutor by virtue of section 1 of the Interest on Damages (Scotland) Act 1958.

(2) The provisions to which subsection (1)(*a*) above applies are—

(*a*) section 3 of the Law Reform (Miscellaneous Provisions) Act 1934;
(*b*) section 17 of the Law Reform (Miscellaneous Provisions) Act (Northern Ireland) 1937;
(*c*) section 35A of the Supreme Court Act 1981;
(*d*) section 69 of the County Courts Act 1984;
(*e*) section 33A of the Judicature (Northern Ireland) Act 1978; and
(*f*) Article 45A of the County Courts (Northern Ireland) Order 1980.

(3) A payment in satisfaction of a cause of action, including a payment into court, shall not be regarded as income for any income tax purpose to the extent to which it is in respect of interest which would fall within subsection (1) above if included in a sum for which a judgment is given or if decree for payment of it were included in an interlocutor.

(4) In this section "personal injuries" includes any disease and any impairment of a person's physical or mental condition.

Former enactments.—Sub-s. (1): TA 1970, s. 375A(1); FA 1971, s. 19; Administration of Justice Act 1982, s. 74.
Sub-s. (2): TA 1970, s. 375A(1B); Administration of Justice Act 1982, s. 74; County Courts Act 1984, Sch. 2, para. 37.
Sub-s. (3): TA 1970, s. 375A(1A); FA 1981, s. 39.
Sub-s. (4): TA 1970, s. 375A(2); FA 1971, s. 19.

330. Compensation for National-Socialist persecution

Annuities and pensions payable under any special provision for victims of National-Socialist persecution which is made by the law of the Federal Republic of Germany or any part of it or of Austria shall not be regarded as income for any income tax purpose.

Former enactments.—TA 1970, s. 377; FA 1986, s. 51.

331. Scholarship income

(1) Income arising from a scholarship held by a person receiving full-time instruction at a university, college, school or other educational establishment shall be exempt from income tax, and no account shall be taken of any such income in computing the amount of income for income tax purposes.

(*a*) governed by regulations made under section 12 of the National Debt Act 1958 or section 52 of the Finance Act 1969; and

(*b*) providing for periodical contributions by individuals for a specified period, and the repayment in accordance with the regulations of contributions together with any additional sum by way of bonus or interest, and

(*c*) certified by the Treasury as qualifying for exemption under this section.

(3) In this section "certified contractual savings scheme" means, in relation to a building society, a scheme—

(*a*) providing for periodical contributions by individuals for a specified period, being contributions by way of investment in shares in the building society, and

(*b*) certified by the Treasury as corresponding to a scheme certified under subsection (2) above, and as qualifying for exemption under this section.

Former enactment.—TA 1970, s. 415(1)–(3), (5).
Construction.—CGTA 1979, s. 149B(4) to be construed as one with this section; see CGTA 1979, s. 149B(4); FA 1988, Sch. 12, para. 7(*a*) (building societies change of status: continuation of tax exemption under this section where contractual savings schemes are in operation before change of status).

327. Disabled person's vehicle maintenance grant

A grant made under paragraph 2 of Schedule 2 to the National Health Service Act 1977 or section 46(3) of the National Health Service (Scotland) Act 1978 (cost of maintenance etc. of vehicles belonging to disabled persons) or under Article 30 of the Health and Personal Social Services (Northern Ireland) Order 1972 to any person owning a vehicle shall not be treated as income for any purpose of the Income Tax Acts.

Former enactments.—FA 1972, s. 70; National Health Service Act 1977, Sch. 15, para. 57; National Health Service (Scotland) Act 1978, Sch. 16, para. 37.

328. Funds in court

(1) If any common investment fund established under section 42 of the Administration of Justice Act 1982 is for the time being designated for the purposes of this subsection by an agreement between the Board and the investment manager of the fund—

(*a*) subject to subsection (2) below, the investment manager shall be entitled to exemption from income tax in respect of so much of the income derived from that fund or any investment thereof as is paid by him by way of dividend on the shares into which the fund is divided; and

(*b*) dividends on those shares shall be paid without deduction of income tax and shall be chargeable under Case III of Schedule D.

A claim for exemption under paragraph (*a*) shall be made to the Board.

(2) Where the income or part of the income derived in a year of assessment from the fund or its investments consists of interest on securities, the income or part (as the case may be) shall for the purposes of subsection (1)(*a*) above be calculated by treating it as the amount it would be apart from section 714(5), but reduced by an amount (if any) equal to the excess of A over B.

(3) In subsection (2) above—

A is the total amount of allowances to which, by virtue of section 714(4), the investment manager of the fund is entitled in the year of assessment in respect of all securities comprised in the fund; and

B is the total amount of annual profits or gains which, by virtue of section 714(2), he is treated as receiving in the year of assessment in respect of those securities.

(4) In subsections (2) and (3) above "interest" and "securities" have the same meanings as in sections 710 and 711.

(5) Where at any time by virtue of subsection (1) above the income of any person from any source becomes chargeable to income tax as provided by that subsection, not having previously been chargeable by direct assessment on that person, section 66(3) shall apply as if the source of that income were a new source of income acquired by that person at that time.

(6) The Accountant General and any other person authorised to invest in a fund designated for the purposes of subsection (1) above shall as respects each year of assessment furnish to the Board, at such time and in such manner as they may direct, particulars of any sums paid

(a) employment by a designated allied headquarters shall be treated for the purposes of subsection (2) above as if it were service as a member of a visiting force of a designated country; and

(b) the emoluments paid by a designated allied headquarters to persons employed by such a headquarters shall be exempt from income tax.

(7) The exemption conferred by subsection (6)(b) above shall cease to apply to British citizens, British Dependent Territories citizens and British Overseas citizens if it becomes unnecessary that it should so apply for the purpose of giving effect to any agreement between parties to the North Atlantic Treaty.

(8) For the purposes of this section—

"allied headquarters" means any international military headquarters established under the North Atlantic Treaty, and

"designated" means designated for the purpose in question by or under any Order in Council made for giving effect to any international agreement.

Former enactments.—TA 1970, s. 367; British Nationality Act 1981, s. 51(3)(a).
Construction.—CGTA 1979, s. 18(5) to be construed as one with sub-s. (2) of this section and sub-ss. (4)–(8) to apply accordingly; see CGTA 1979, s. 18(5).

324. Designated international organisations

(1) The Treasury may by order designate for the purposes of this section—

(a) any international organisation—

(i) if one of its members is the United Kingdom or any of the Communities; and

(ii) if the agreement under which that member became a member provides for exemption from tax, in relation to the organisation, of the kind for which provision is made by this section; or

(b) any of the Communities or the European Investment Bank.

(2) Where an organisation has been so designated, a person not resident in the United Kingdom shall not be liable to income tax in respect of income from any security issued by the organisation if he would not be liable but for the fact that—

(a) the security or income is issued, made payable or paid in the United Kingdom or in sterling; or

(b) the organisation maintains an office or other place of business in the United Kingdom.

Former enactments.—FA 1984, s. 126(1), (2), (3)(a), (4); FA 1985, s. 96(1).

325. Interest on deposits with National Savings Bank

Where the total income of an individual for the year of assessment includes, or would but for this section include, any sums paid or credited in respect of interest on deposits with the National Savings Bank, other than investment deposits, those sums shall be disregarded for all purposes of the Income Tax Acts, other than the furnishing of information, if or in so far as they do not exceed £70; and for this purpose the question whether or how far those sums exceed £70 shall, where by virtue of section 279 a woman's income is deemed to be her husband's, be determined separately as regards the part of his income which is his by virtue of that section and the part which is his apart from that section.

Former enactments.—TA 1970, s. 414; FA 1977, s. 29; FA 1980, s. 59.
Note.—See **Prospective Legislation Notes** (Married Couples).

326. Interest etc. under contractual savings schemes

(1) Any terminal bonus, or interest or other sum, payable under a certified contractual savings scheme—

(a) in respect of money raised under section 12 of the National Loans Act 1968, or

(b) in respect of shares in a building society,

shall be disregarded for all purposes of the Income Tax Acts.

(2) In this section "certified contractual savings scheme" means, except in relation to a building society, a scheme—

(a) is not a British citizen, a British Dependent Territories citizen or a British Overseas citizen, and
(b) is not engaged in any trade, profession, vocation or employment in the United Kingdom, otherwise than as such a consular officer or employee, and
(c) either is a permanent employee of that state or was not ordinarily resident in the United Kingdom immediately before he became a consular officer or employee in the United Kingdom of that state;

then any income of his falling within Case IV or V of Schedule D shall be exempt from income tax, and he shall be treated as not resident in the United Kingdom for the purposes of sections 48 and 123(4).

(2) Without prejudice to section 321, the income arising from a person's employment in the United Kingdom as a consular employee of any foreign state to which this section applies shall be exempt from income tax, except in the case of a person who is not a national of that state but is a British citizen, a British Dependent Territories citizen or a British Overseas citizen.

(3) For the purposes of this section "consular employee" includes any person employed, for the purposes of the official business of a consular officer, at any consulate or consular establishment or at any other premises used for those purposes.

(4) This section shall apply to any foreign state to which Her Majesty by Order in Council directs that it shall apply for the purpose of giving effect to any consular convention or other arrangement with that state making similar provision in the case of Her Majesty's consular officers or employees in that state.

(5) An Order in Council under subsection (4) above—
(a) may limit the operation of this section in relation to any state in such manner as appears to Her Majesty to be necessary or expedient having regard to the arrangement with that state;
(b) may be made so as to have effect from a date earlier than the making of the Order or the passing of this Act (but not earlier than the coming into force of the arrangement with regard to which it is made); and
(c) may contain such transitional provisions as appear to Her Majesty to be necessary or expedient;

and any statutory instrument under this section shall be subject to annulment in pursuance of a resolution of the House of Commons.

Former enactments.—TA 1970, s. 374(1), (3)–(7); British Nationality Act 1981, s. 51(3)(a).

323. Visiting forces

(1) The emoluments paid by the government of any designated country to any member of a visiting force of that country who is not a British citizen, a British Dependent Territories citizen or a British Overseas citizen shall be exempt from income tax.

(2) A period during which a member of a visiting force to whom subsection (1) above applies is in the United Kingdom by reason solely of his being a member of that force shall not be treated for the purposes of income tax either as a period of residence in the United Kingdom or as creating a change of his residence or domicile.

(3) Subsection (2) above shall not affect the operation of section 278 in relation to any person for any year of assessment.

(4) In subsections (1) and (2) above references to a visiting force shall apply to a civilian component of such a force as they apply to the force itself; and those subsections shall be construed as one with the Visiting Forces Act 1952, but so that, for the purposes of this section, references to a designated country shall be substituted in that Act for references to a country to which a provision of that Act applies.

(5) For the purpose of conferring on persons attached to any designated allied headquarters the like benefits as are conferred by subsections (1) and (2) above on members of a visiting force or civilian component, any members of the armed forces of a designated country shall, while attached to any such headquarters, be deemed to constitute a visiting force of that country, and there shall be a corresponding extension of the class of persons who may be treated as members of a civilian component of such a visiting force.

(6) In the case of persons of any category for the time being agreed between Her Majesty's government in the United Kingdom and the other members of the North Atlantic Council—

320. Commonwealth Agents-General and official agents etc.

(1) An Agent-General who is resident in the United Kingdom shall be entitled to the same immunity from income tax as that to which the head of a mission so resident is entitled under the Diplomatic Privileges Act 1964.

(2) Any person having or exercising any employment to which this subsection applies (not being a person employed in any trade, business or other undertaking carried on for the purposes of profit) shall be entitled to the same immunity from income tax as that to which a member of the staff of a mission is entitled under the Diplomatic Privileges Act 1964.

(3) The employments to which subsection (2) above applies are the employment in the United Kingdom as—

(*a*) a member of the personal staff of any Agent-General; or
(*b*) an official agent for, or for any state or province of, any of the countries for the time being mentioned in Schedule 3 to the British Nationality Act 1981 or the Republic of Ireland; or
(*c*) an official agent for any self-governing colony,

of a person certified by the High Commissioner of the country in question or, as the case may be, by the Agent-General for the state, province or self-governing colony in question to be ordinarily resident outside the United Kingdom and to be resident in the United Kingdom solely for the purpose of the performance of his duties as such member or official agent.

(4) In this section—

"Agent-General" means the Agent-General for any state or province of a country within subsection (3)(*b*) above or for any self-governing colony;
"High Commissioner" includes the head of the mission of a country within subsection (3)(*b*) above by whatever name called;
"mission" has the same meaning as in the Diplomatic Privileges Act 1964, and references to the head of a mission and a member of the staff of a mission shall be construed in accordance with that Act;
"self-governing colony" means any colony certified by a Secretary of State to be a self-governing colony.

Former enactments.—TA 1970, s. 372; British Nationality Act 1981, Sch. 7.
Construction.—CGTA 1979, s. 18(6), (7) to be construed as one with this section; see CGTA 1979, s. 18(8).

321. Consuls and other official agents

(1) Income arising from any office or employment to which this section applies shall be exempt from income tax, and no account shall be taken of any such income in estimating the amount of income for any income tax purposes.

(2) The offices and employments to which this section applies are the following, that is to say—

(*a*) the office of a consul in the United Kingdom in the service of any foreign state; and
(*b*) the employment of an official agent in the United Kingdom for any foreign state, not being an employment exercised by a Commonwealth citizen or a citizen of the Republic of Ireland or exercised in connection with any trade, business or other undertaking carried on for the purposes of profit.

(3) In this section—

"consul" means a person recognised by Her Majesty as being a consul-general, consul, vice-consul or consular agent; and
"official agent" means a person, not being a consul, who is employed on the staff of any consulate, official department or agency of a foreign state, not being a department or agency which carries on any trade, business or other undertaking for the purposes of profit.

Former enactments.—TA 1970, s. 373; British Nationality Act 1981, s. 51(1), (2).

322. Consular officers and employees

(1) Where a consular officer or employee in the United Kingdom of any foreign state to which this section applies—

Command Paper laid before Parliament in August 1950, becomes payable out of moneys provided by Parliament by way of bounty to a person who, having served in the armed forces of the Crown, voluntarily undertakes to serve for a further period shall not be regarded as income for any income tax purpose.

Former enactments.—TA 1970, s. 366; Transfer of Functions (Minister for the Civil Service and the Treasury) Order 1981, S.I. 1981 No. 1670.

317. Victoria Cross and other awards

The following shall be disregarded for all the purposes of the Income Tax Acts—

(*a*) annuities and additional pensions paid to holders of the Victoria Cross;
(*b*) annuities and additional pensions paid to holders of the George Cross;
(*c*) annuities paid to holders of the Albert Medal or of the Edward Medal;
(*d*) additional pensions paid to holders of the Military Cross;
(*e*) additional pensions paid to holders of the Distinguished Flying Cross;
(*f*) additional pensions paid to holders of the Distinguished Conduct Medal;
(*g*) additional pensions paid to holders of the Conspicuous Gallantry medal;
(*h*) additional pensions paid to holders of the Distinguished Service Medal;
(*i*) additional pensions paid to holders of the Military Medal;
(*j*) additional pensions paid to holders of the Distinguished Flying Medal;

where paid by virtue of holding the award.

Former enactments.—TA 1970, s. 368; FA 1980, s. 26.

318. Other pensions in respect of death due to war service etc.

(1) Payments of pensions or allowances to which this section applies shall not be treated as income for any purposes of the Income Tax Acts.

(2) This section applies to—

(*a*) any pension or allowance payable by or on behalf of the Department of Health and Social Security under so much of any Order in Council, Royal Warrant, order or scheme as relates to death due to—

(i) service in the armed forces of the Crown or war-time service in the merchant navy, or
(ii) war injuries;

(*b*) any pension or allowance at similar rates and subject to similar conditions which is payable by the Ministry of Defence in respect of death due to peacetime service in the armed forces of the Crown before 3rd September 1939; and
(*c*) any pension or allowance which is payable under the law of a country other than the United Kingdom and is of a character substantially similar to a pension or allowance falling within paragraph (*a*) or (*b*) above.

(3) Where a pension or allowance falling within subsection (2) above is withheld or abated by reason of the receipt of another pension or allowance not falling within that subsection, there shall be treated as falling within that subsection so much of the other pension or allowance as is equal to the pension or allowance that is withheld or, as the case may be, to the amount of the abatement.

Former enactment.—F(No. 2)A 1979, s. 9.

319. Crown servants: foreign service allowance

Where any allowance to any person in the service of the Crown is certified by the Treasury to represent compensation for the extra cost of having to live outside the United Kingdom in order to perform his duties, that allowance shall not be regarded as income for any income tax purpose.

Former enactments.—TA 1970, s. 369; Transfer of Functions (Minister for the Civil Service and the Treasury) Order 1981, S.I. 1981 No. 1670.

315. Wounds and disability pensions

(1) Income from wounds and disability pensions to which this subsection applies shall be exempt from income tax and shall not be reckoned in computing income for any purposes of the Income Tax Acts.

(2) Subsection (1) above applies to—

(*a*) wounds pensions granted to members of the naval, military or air forces of the Crown;
(*b*) retired pay of disabled officers granted on account of medical unfitness attributable to or aggravated by naval, military or air-force service;
(*c*) disablement or disability pensions granted to members, other than commissioned officers, of the naval, military or air forces of the Crown on account of medical unfitness attributable to or aggravated by naval, military or air-force service;
(*d*) disablement pensions granted to persons who have been employed in the nursing services of any of the naval, military or air forces of the Crown on account of medical unfitness attributable to or aggravated by naval, military or air-force service; and
(*e*) injury and disablement pensions payable under any scheme made under the Injuries in War (Compensation) Act 1914, the Injuries in War Compensation Act 1914 (Session 2) and the Injuries in War (Compensation) Act 1915 or under any War Risks Compensation Scheme for the Mercantile marine.

(3) Where the amount of any retired pay or pensions to which subsection (1) above applies is not solely attributable to disablement or disability, the relief conferred by that subsection shall extend only to such part as is certified by the Secretary of State for Social Services, after consultation with the appropriate government department, to be attributable to disablement or disability.

Former enactment.—TA 1970, s. 365.

316. Allowances, bounties and gratuities

(1) Where, under the scheme relating to men in the Armed Forces of the Crown announced on behalf of His Majesty's Government in the United Kingdom on 15th April 1946 or under any other scheme certified by the Treasury to make analogous provision for classes of persons to whom the first-mentioned scheme does not apply, a person who has served in the armed forces of the Crown at any time during the continuance in force of the Emergency Powers (Defence) Act 1939 voluntarily undertakes to serve therein for a further period, any sum payable to him in pursuance of the scheme out of moneys provided by Parliament by way of gratuity at the end of his further period of service shall not be regarded as income for any income tax purposes.

(2) Where, under the scheme relating to members of the Women's Royal Naval Service, the Auxiliary Territorial Service and the Women's Auxiliary Air Force announced on behalf of His Majesty's Government in the United Kingdom on 20th November 1946, or under any other scheme certified by the Treasury to make analogous provision for classes of persons to whom the first-mentioned scheme does not apply, a woman who has served in or with the armed forces of the Crown at any time during the continuance in force of the Emergency Powers (Defence) Act 1939 voluntarily undertakes to serve in or with those forces for a further period, any sum payable to her in pursuance of the scheme out of moneys provided by Parliament by way of gratuity at the end of her further period of service shall not be regarded as income for any income tax purposes.

(3) Any allowance payable out of the public revenue to or in respect of any class of persons, being members of the armed forces of the Crown, as respects which the Treasury certifies either—

(*a*) that it is payable to the persons in question in lieu of food or drink normally supplied in kind to members of the armed forces, or
(*b*) that it is payable in respect of the persons in question as a contribution to the expenses of a mess,

shall not be regarded as income for any income tax purposes.

(4) The sums known as training expenses allowances payable out of the public revenue to members of the reserve and auxiliary forces of the Crown, and the sums payable by way of bounty out of the public revenue to such members in consideration of their undertaking prescribed training and attaining a prescribed standard of efficiency, shall not be treated as income for any income tax purpose.

(5) Any sum which, in pursuance of the scheme as to service emoluments contained in the

CHAPTER IV

SPECIAL PROVISIONS

313. Taxation of consideration for certain restrictive undertakings

[(1) Where an individual who holds, has held, or is about to hold, an office or employment gives in connection with his holding that office or employment an undertaking (whether absolute or qualified, and whether legally valid or not) the tenor or effect of which is to restrict him as to his conduct or activities, any sum to which this section applies shall be treated as an emolument of the office or employment, and accordingly shall be chargeable to tax under Schedule E, for the year of assessment in which it is paid.][1]

[(2) This section applies to any sum which—

(*a*) is paid, in respect of the giving of the undertaking or its total or partial fulfilment, either to the individual or to any other person; and

(*b*) would not, apart from this section, fall to be treated as an emolument of the office or employment.][1]

[(3) Where the individual has died before the payment of any sum to which this section applies, subsections (1) and (2) above shall have effect as if that sum had been paid immediately before his death.][1]

[(4) Where valuable consideration otherwise than in the form of money is given in respect of the giving of the undertaking or its total or partial fulfilment, subsections (1) to (3) above shall have effect as if a sum had instead been paid equal to the value of that consideration.][1]

(6) In this section—

(*a*) "office or employment" means any office or employment whatsoever such that the emoluments thereof, if any, are or would be chargeable to income tax under Case I or II of Schedule E; and

(*b*) references to the giving of valuable consideration do not include references to the mere assumption of an obligation to make over or provide valuable property, rights or advantages, but do include references to the doing of anything in or towards the discharge of such an obligation.

Former enactments.—Sub-ss. (1)–(3): TA 1970, s. 34(1); FA 1971, Sch. 6, para. 15.
Sub-ss. (4)–(6): TA 1970, s. 34(2), (4), (5).
Cross references.—See FA 1988, s. 73(2) (notwithstanding anything in s. 74 of this Act (deductions not allowable), any sum to which this section applies to be an allowable deduction from the profits or gains of a trade etc.),
s. 73(3) (any sum to which this section applies to be treated as management expenses in the case of investment companies).
Amendments.—[1] Sub-ss. (1)–(4) substituted for sub-ss. (1)–(5) by FA 1988, s. 73 in relation to sums paid or treated as paid in respect of the giving of, or the total or partial fulfilment of, undertakings given after 8 June 1988.

314. Divers and diving supervisors

(1) Where the duties of any employment which are performed by a person in the United Kingdom or a designated area consist wholly or mainly—

(*a*) of taking part, as a diver, in diving operations concerned with the exploration or exploitation of the seabed, its subsoil and their natural resources; or

(*b*) of acting, in relation to any such diving operations, as a diving supervisor,

the Income Tax Acts shall have effect as if the performance by that person of those duties constituted the carrying on by him of a trade within Case I of Schedule D; and accordingly Schedule E shall not apply to the emoluments from the employment so far as attributable to his performance of those duties.

(2) In this section "designated area" means any area designated under section 1(7) of the Continental Shelf Act 1964.

Former enactment.—FA 1978, s. 29(1), (2).

and "the 1984 Regulations" means the Petroleum (Production) (Landward Areas) Regulations 1984.

(2) Section 839 applies for the purposes of this Chapter other than section 291.

(3) References in this Chapter to a disposal of shares include references to a disposal of an interest or right in or over the shares and an individual shall be treated for the purposes of this Chapter as disposing of any shares which he is treated by virtue of section 86(1) of the 1979 Act as exchanging for other shares.

(4) References in this Chapter to the reduction of any amount include references to its reduction to nil.

(5) For the purposes of this Chapter—

(*a*) in relation to shares issued after 18th March 1986, the market value at any time of any asset shall be taken to be the price which it might reasonably be expected to fetch on a sale at that time in the open market free from any interest or right which exists by way of security in or over it;

(*b*) in relation to shares issued before 19th March 1986, "market value" shall be construed in accordance with section 150 of the 1979 Act.

(6) References in this Chapter to relief given to an individual in respect of eligible shares, and to the withdrawal of such relief, include respectively references to relief given to him in respect of those shares at any time after he has disposed of them and references to the withdrawal of such relief at any such time.

(7) In relation to any case falling within section 289(1)(*d*), any reference in that section to any licence being held by, or granted to, any person shall be read as including a reference to such a licence being held by, or (as the case may be) granted to, that person together with one or more other persons.

(8) The Treasury may by order amend any of the definitions set out in subsection (1) above which relate to licences under the Petroleum (Production) Act 1934 or the Petroleum (Production) Act (Northern Ireland) 1964.

Former enactments.—Sub-s. (1): FA 1981, s. 67; FA 1983, Sch. 5, para 20(1), (2); Companies Consolidation (Consequential Provisions) Act 1985, Sch. 2; FA 1985, s. 44(6); FA 1986, Sch. 9, para. 21(1), (2).
Sub-ss. (2)–(4): FA 1981, s. 67(2)–(4); FA 1983, Sch. 5, para. 20(1).
Sub-ss. (5)–(8): FA 1983, Sch. 5, para. 20(3)–(6); FA 1986, Sch. 9, para. 21(3).

(6) Section 306(6) shall not apply in relation to any certificate issued by the managers of an approved fund for the purposes of subsection (4) above.

Former enactments.—Sub-s. (1): FA 1983, Sch. 5, para. 19(1).
Sub-s. (2): FA 1983, Sch. 5, para. 19A; FA 1986, Sch. 9, para. 20.
Sub-ss. (3)–(6): FA 1983, Sch. 5, para. 19(2)–(5).
Amendments.—[1] Sub-ss. (2A), (2B), (3) substituted for sub-s. (3) by FA 1988, s. 53 in relation to approved funds closing after 15 March 1988.

312. Interpretation of Chapter III

(1) In this Chapter—

"associate" has the meaning given in subsections (3) and (4) of section 417 except that in those subsections "relative" shall not include a brother or sister;

"appraisal licence" means an appraisal licence incorporating the model clauses set out in Schedule 4 to the 1984 Regulations or a Northern Ireland licence granted for the five year renewal term and includes in either case any modified appraisal licence;

"control", except in sections 291(7), 308(2) and 309(6)(*a*), shall be construed in accordance with section 416(2) to (6);

"debenture" has the meaning given by section 744 of the Companies Act 1985;

"development licence" means a development licence incorporating the model clauses set out in Schedule 5 to the 1984 Regulations or a Northern Ireland licence granted for the 30 year renewal term and includes in either case any modified development licence;

"director" shall be construed in accordance with section 417(5);

"exploration licence" means an exploration licence incorporating the model clauses set out in Schedule 3 to the 1984 Regulations or a Northern Ireland licence granted for the initial term and includes in either case any modified exploration licence;

"fixed-rate preference share capital" means share capital consisting of shares which—

(*a*) are issued for consideration which is or includes new consideration; and
(*b*) do not carry any right either to conversion into shares or securities of any other description or to the acquisition of any additional shares or securities; and
(*c*) do not carry any right to dividends other than dividends which—

  (i) are of a fixed amount or at a fixed rate per cent. of the nominal value of the shares, and
  (ii) represent no more than a reasonable commercial return on the new consideration received by the company in respect of the issue of the shares; and

(*d*) on repayment do not carry any rights to an amount exceeding that new consideration except in so far as those rights are reasonably comparable with those general for fixed dividend shares listed in the Official List of the Stock Exchange;

"modified appraisal licence", "modified development licence" and "modified exploration licence" mean, respectively, any appraisal licence, development licence or exploration licence in which any of the relevant model clauses have been modified or excluded by the Secretary of State or in Northern Ireland the Department of Economic Development;

"new consideration" has the same meaning as in Part VI;

"Northern Ireland licence" means a licence granted under the Petroleum (Production) Act (Northern Ireland) 1964 and incorporating the model clauses set out in Schedule 2 to the Petroleum Production (Licences) Regulations (Northern Ireland) 1965, and in relation to such a licence the references above to "the initial term", "the 30 year renewal term" and "the five year renewal term" shall be construed in accordance with Clause 2 of Schedule 2 to those Regulations;

"oil" and "oil extraction activities" have the same meanings as they have in Chapter V of Part XII;

"oil exploration" means searching for oil;

"ordinary shares" means shares forming part of a company's ordinary share capital;

"the relevant period" has the meaning given in section 289(12);

"research and development" means any activity which is intended to result in a patentable invention (within the meaning of the Patents Act 1977) or in a computer program;

"the relief" and "relief", except where the reference is to relief under Chapter II of Part IV of the Finance Act 1981, means relief under section 289 (and includes relief under Schedule 5 to the Finance Act 1983), and references to the amount of the relief shall be construed in accordance with section 289(5); and

"unquoted company" means a company none of whose shares, stocks or debentures are listed in the Official List of the Stock Exchange or dealt in on the Unlisted Securities Market;

(*e*) in subsection (7) for "300, 301 or 303(3)" of "58 or 59(4) of the Finance Act 1981".

(11) In any case where this section has effect in accordance with subsection (10) above and the qualifying company has one or more subsidiaries—

(*a*) subsection (3) above shall, where the inspector has notified the subsidiary that relief has been given in respect of shares in the company of which it is a subsidiary, apply to the subsidiary as respects any transfer of its shares as it applies to the company as respects any transfer of shares in the company; and
(*b*) subsections (5) and (6) above shall have effect in relation to any such arrangements as are mentioned in paragraph (*c*) of subsection (2) of section 308 (as that subsection has effect by virtue of subsection (6) of that section) as they have effect in relation to any such arrangement as is mentioned in section 289(11).

Former enactments.—Sub-ss. (1), (2): FA 1983, Sch. 5, para. 15(1), (2).
Sub-s. (3): FA 1983, Sch. 5, para. 15A(1); FA 1986, Sch. 9, para. 15.
Sub-s. (4): FA 1983, Sch. 5, paras. 15(3), 15A(2); FA 1986, Sch. 9, para. 15.
Sub-ss. (5), (6): FA 1983, Sch. 5, paras. 15(4), (5), 18(4); FA 1986, Sch. 9, para. 19(2).
Sub-ss. (7)–(9): FA 1981, s. 63(7)–(9); FA 1983, Sch. 5, para. 15(6).
Sub-ss. (10), (11): FA 1981, Sch. 12, paras. 6, 7; FA 1983, s. 26(2).

311. Nominees, bare trustees and approved investment funds

(1) Shares subscribed for, issued to, held by or disposed of for an individual by a nominee shall be treated for the purposes of this Chapter as subscribed for, issued to, held by or disposed of by that individual.

(2) Where eligible shares issued after 18th March 1986 are held on a bare trust for two or more beneficiaries, this Chapter shall have effect (with the necessary modifications) as if—

(*a*) each beneficiary had subscribed as an individual for all of those shares; and
(*b*) the amount subscribed by each beneficiary was equal to the total amount subscribed on the issue of those shares divided by the number of beneficiaries.

[(2A) Subsection (2B) below applies where an individual claims relief in respect of eligible shares in a company and—

(*a*) the shares have been issued to the managers of an approved fund as nominee for the individual;
(*b*) the fund has closed, that is to say, no further investments in the fund are to be accepted; and
(*c*) the amounts which the managers have, as nominee for the individual, subscribed for eligible shares issued within six months after the closing of the fund represent not less than 90 per cent. of his investment in the fund;

and in this section "the managers of an approved fund" means the person or persons having the management of an investment fund approved for the purposes of this section by the Board.][1]

[(2B) In any case where this subsection applies, subsections (5) to (7) of section 289 and subsections (1) to (3) and (6) of section 304 shall have effect as if—

(*a*) any reference to the year of assessment or other period in which the shares are issued were a reference to the year of assessment or other period in which the fund closes; and
(*b*) any reference to the time of the issue of the shares, or the time of the subscription for the shares, were a reference to the time of the closing of the fund.][1]

(3) Section 290(1) shall not apply where the amount is subscribed as nominee for an individual by the managers of an approved fund.][1]

(4) Where an individual claims relief in respect of eligible shares in a company which have been issued to the managers of an approved fund as nominee for that individual, section 306(2) shall apply as if it required—

(*a*) the certificate referred to in that section to be issued by the company to the managers;
(*b*) the claim for relief to be accompanied by a certificate issued by the managers, in such form as the Board may authorise, certifying that the managers hold certificates issued to them by the companies concerned, for the purposes of sections 306(2), in respect of the holdings of eligible shares shown on the managers' certificate.

(5) The managers of an approved fund may be required by a notice given to them by an inspector or other officer of the Board to deliver to the officer, within the time limited by the notice, a return of the holdings of eligible shares shown on certificates issued by them in accordance with subsection (4) above in the year of assessment to which the return relates.

knowledge of the matter, that section 294 may have effect to deny relief in respect of those shares;

the company or (as the case may be) that person or (where it so appears to each of them) both the company and that person shall give notice to the inspector setting out the particulars of the case.

(4) If the inspector has reason to believe that a person has not given a notice which he is required to give under subsection (1) or (2) above in respect of any event, or under subsection (3) above in respect of any particular case, the inspector may by notice require that person to furnish him within such time (not being less than 60 days) as may be specified in the notice with such information relating to the event or case as the inspector may reasonably require for the purposes of this Chapter.

(5) Where relief is claimed in respect of shares in a company and the inspector has reason to believe that it may not be due by reason of any such arrangement or scheme as is mentioned in section 289(11), 291(10), 293(8) or 308(2)(*e*), he may by notice require any person concerned to furnish him within such time (not being less than 60 days) as may be specified in the notice with—

(*a*) a declaration in writing stating whether or not, according to the information which that person has or can reasonably obtain, any such arrangement or scheme exists or has existed;
(*b*) such other information as the inspector may reasonably require for the purposes of the provision in question and as that person has or can reasonably obtain.

(6) References in subsection (5) above to the person concerned are references, in relation to sections 289(11), 291(10) and 308(2)(*e*), to the claimant and, in relation to sections 289(11), 293(8) and 308(2)(*e*), to the company and any person controlling the company.

(7) Where relief has been given in respect of shares in a company—

(*a*) any person who receives from the company any payment or asset which may constitute value received (by him or another) for the purposes of sections 300, 301 and 303(3); and
(*b*) any person on whose behalf such a payment or asset is received,

shall, if so required by the inspector, state whether the payment or asset received by him or on his behalf is received on behalf of any person other than himself and, if so, the name and address of that person.

(8) Where relief has been claimed in respect of shares in a company, any person who holds or has held shares in the company and any person on whose behalf any such shares are or were held shall, if so required by the inspector, state whether the shares which are or were held by him or on his behalf are or were held on behalf of any person other than himself and, if so, the name and address of that person.

(9) No obligation as to secrecy imposed by statute or otherwise shall preclude the inspector from disclosing to a company that relief has been given or claimed in respect of a particular number or proportion of its shares.

(10) This section shall have effect in relation to relief under Chapter II of Part IV of the Finance Act 1981 as it has effect in relation to relief under this Chapter but with the substitution—

(*a*) in subsection (1) for "291, 299, 300 or 304(2) to (6)" of "54, 57, 58 and 60(6) of the Finance Act 1981";
(*b*) for subsection (3) of the following subsection—

"(3) Where the company is notified by the inspector that relief has been given in respect of any shares issued by the company on a specified date, then, if any shares in the company (whether or not shares in respect of which relief has been given) are transferred at any time in the period of five years beginning with that date, the company shall within 60 days of—

(*a*) coming to know of the transfer; or
(*b*) receiving the notification from the inspector,

whichever is the later, give a notice to the inspector containing particulars of the transfer.";

(*c*) in subsection (5) for references to sections 289(11), 291(10), 293(8) and 308(2)(*e*) of references to sections 54(9), 55(8) and 59(1) of the 1981 Act;
(*d*) in subsection (6) for "289(11), 293(10) and 308(2)(*e*)" and "289(11), 293(8) and 308(2)(*e*)" of "54(9) and 59(1) of the Finance Act 1981" and "55(8) and 59(1) of that Act", respectively;

(2) The shares issued by the qualifying company may, instead of or as well as being issued for the purpose mentioned in subsection (1)(*a*) of section 289, be issued for the purpose of raising money for a qualifying trade which is being carried on by a subsidiary or which a subsidiary intends to carry on; and, where shares are so issued, subsections (8), (9), (12)(*b*)(ii) and (13) of that section shall have effect as if references to the company were or, as the case may be, included references to the subsidiary.

(3) In relation to a qualifying trade carried on by a subsidiary the reference in section 297(2)(*g*) to another person shall not include a reference to the company of which it is a subsidiary.

(4) In section 303(1) references to the company (except the first) shall include references to a company which during the relevant period is a subsidiary of the company whether it becomes a subsidiary before or after the redemption, repayment, repurchase or payment referred to in that subsection.

(5) In subsections (2), (4) and (6) of section 291, references to the company (except, in each subsection, the first such reference) include references to a company which is during the relevant period a subsidiary of that company—

(*a*) whether it becomes a subsidiary before, during or after the year of assessment in respect of which the individual concerned claims relief; or
(*b*) whether or not it is such a subsidiary while he is such an employee, partner or director as is mentioned in subsection (2) or while he has or is entitled to acquire such capital or voting power or rights as are mentioned in subsections (4) and (6).

(6) Without prejudice to the provisions of section 291 (as it has effect in accordance with subsection (5) above), an individual shall be treated as connected with a company if—

(*a*) he has at any time in the relevant period had control (within the meaning of section 840) of another company which has since that time and before the end of the relevant period become a subsidiary of the company; or
(*b*) he directly or indirectly possesses or is entitled to acquire any loan capital of a subsidiary of that company.

(7) Section 291(5) and (8) shall apply for the purposes of this section.

(8) In sections 300(1) and 303(3) references to the receipt of value from the company shall include references to the receipt of value from any company which during the relevant period is a subsidiary of that company, whether it becomes a subsidiary before or after the individual concerned receives any value from it, and other references to the company in sections 300 and 301 and in section 303(6) shall be construed accordingly.

Former enactments.—Sub-s. (1): FA 1983, Sch. 5, para. 17(2).
Sub-ss. (2)–(4): FA 1983, Sch. 5, para. 18(1)–(3); F(No. 2)A 1983, Sch. 1, para. 9.
Sub-ss. (5)–(7): FA 1981, Sch. 12, para. 2; FA 1982, s. 52(2); FA 1983, Sch. 5, para. 18(5).
Sub-s. (8): FA 1981, Sch. 12, para. 4; FA 1982, s. 52(3); FA 1983, Sch. 5, para. 18(5).
Cross references.—See FA 1988, s. 50 and Sch. 4, para. 11 (modification of this section in relation to shares issued after the passing of FA 1988 and before the end of 1993 for financing private rented housing; FA 1988 was passed on 29 July 1988).

310. Information

(1) Where an event occurs by reason of which any relief given to an individual falls to be withdrawn by virtue of sections 291, 299, 300 or 304(2) to (6), the individual shall within 60 days of his coming to know of the event give a notice to the inspector containing particulars of the event.

(2) Where an event occurs by reason of which any relief in respect of any shares in a company falls to be withdrawn by virtue of section 289(11), 293, 297, 300, 302 or 303—

(*a*) the company; and
(*b*) any person connected with the company who has knowledge of that matter;

shall within 60 days of the event or, in the case of a person within paragraph (*b*) above, of his coming to know of it, give a notice to the inspector containing particulars of the event or payment.

(3) Where—

(*a*) a company has issued a certificate under section 306(2) in respect of any eligible shares in the company; and
(*b*) it appears to the company, or to any person connected with the company who has

less than 90 per cent. of any profits of the subsidiary which are available for distribution to the equity holders of the subsidiary;

(*d*) that no person other than the qualifying company or another of its subsidiaries has control of the subsidiary within the meaning of section 840; and

(*e*) that no arrangements are in existence by virtue of which the conditions in paragraphs (*a*) to (*d*) above could cease to be satisfied.

(3) The conditions shall not be regarded as ceasing to be satisfied by reason only of the subsidiary or the qualifying company being wound up, or dissolved without winding up, if—

(*a*) it is shown that the winding up or dissolution is for bona fide commercial reasons and not part of a scheme or arrangement the main purpose or one of the main purposes of which is the avoidance of tax; and

(*b*) the net assets, if any, of the subsidiary or, as the case may be, the qualifying company are distributed to its members or dealt with as bona vacantia before the end of the relevant period, or in the case of a winding up, the end (if later) of three years from the commencement of the winding up.

(4) The conditions shall not be regarded as ceasing to be satisfied by reason only of the disposal by the qualifying company or (as the case may be) by another subsidiary, within the relevant period, of all its interest in the subsidiary if it is shown that the disposal is for bona fide commercial reasons and not part of a scheme or arrangement the main purpose or one of the main purposes of which is the avoidance of tax.

(5) For the purposes of this section—

(*a*) a subsidiary of a qualifying company is a property managing subsidiary if it exists wholly, or substantially wholly, for the purpose of holding and managing property used by the qualifying company, or by any of its subsidiaries, for the purposes of—

(i) research and development from which it is intended that a qualifying trade to be carried on by the company or any of its subsidiaries will be derived; or

(ii) one or more qualifying trades so carried on;

(*b*) a subsidiary is a dormant subsidiary if it has no profits for the purposes of corporation tax and no part of its business consists in the making of investments; and

(*c*) the persons who are equity holders of a subsidiary and the percentage of the assets of a subsidiary to which an equity holder would be entitled shall be determined in accordance with paragraphs 1 and 3 of Schedule 18, taking references in paragraph 3 to the first company as references to an equity holder and references to a winding up as including references to any other circumstances in which assets of the subsidiary are available for distribution to its equity holders.

(6) In relation to shares issued before 19th March 1986 this section shall have effect subject to the following modifications—

(*a*) the following paragraph shall be substituted for subsection (1)(*b*)—

"(*b*) the subsidiary or each subsidiary was incorporated in the United Kingdom and is a company falling within section 293(2)(*a*).";

(*b*) the following subsection shall be substituted for subsection (2)—

"(2) The conditions referred to in subsection (1)(*a*) above are—

(*a*) that the qualifying company possesses all the issued share capital of, and all the voting power in, the subsidiary; and

(*b*) that no other person has control of the subsidiary within the meaning of section 840; and

(*c*) that no arrangements are in existence by virtue of which the conditions in paragraphs (*a*) and (*b*) above could cease to be satisfied."; and

(*c*) subsections (4) and (5) shall be omitted.

Former enactments.—Sub-ss. (1)–(5): FA 1983, Sch. 5, para. 17(1)–(1D); FA 1986, Sch. 9, para. 18; FA 1987, Sch. 15, para. 15(2).
Sub-s. (6): FA 1981, s. 65(2); FA 1983, Sch. 5, para. 17(1)(*b*); FA 1986, Sch. 9, para. 1(2).
Cross references.—See FA 1988, s. 50 and Sch. 4, para. 11 (modification of this section in relation to shares issued after the passing of FA 1988 and before the end of 1993 for financing private rented housing; FA 1988 was passed on 29 July 1988).

309. Further provisions as to subsidiaries

(1) Where a qualifying company has one or more subsidiaries in the relevant period, this Chapter shall have effect subject to subsections (2) to (8) below.

withdrawing relief in respect of any of those shares shall be made by reason of any subsequent event unless it occurs at a time when he is connected with the company within the meaning of section 291.

(5) Subsection (2) above is without prejudice to section 36 of the Management Act ([fraudulent or negligent conduct][1]).

(6) In its application to an assessment made by virtue of this section, section 86 of the Management Act (interest on overdue tax) shall have effect as if the reckonable date were—

   (*a*) in the case of relief withdrawn by virtue of section 289(11)—

      (i) so far as effect has been given to the relief in accordance with regulations under section 203, 5th April in the year of assessment in which effect was so given;
      (ii) so far as effect has not been so given, the date on which the relief was granted.

   (*b*) in the case of relief withdrawn by virtue of section 291, 293, 297, 302, 303(1) or 305 in consequence of any event after the grant of the relief, the date of that event;
   (*c*) in the case of relief withdrawn by virtue of section 299(1) in consequence of a disposal after the grant of the relief, the date of the disposal;
   (*d*) in the case of relief withdrawn by virtue of section 300 in consequence of a receipt of value after the grant of the relief, the date of the receipt.

(7) For the purposes of subsection (6) above the date on which the relief is granted is the date on which a repayment of tax for giving effect to the relief was made or, if there was no such repayment, the date on which the inspector issued a notice to the claimant showing the amount of tax payable after giving effect to the relief.

(8) Where a company has ceased to be a qualifying company in consequence of the operation of section 294, subsection (6) above shall apply as if the relief was withdrawn in consequence of an event which occurred at the time when the company so ceased to be a qualifying company.

(9) Subsections (1) to (7) above apply in relation to relief under Chapter II of Part IV of the Finance Act 1981 as they apply in relation to relief under this Chapter (or Schedule 5 to the Finance Act 1983) but—

   (*a*) with the substitution for references to sections 299 (in both places), 291, 289(11), 293, 297, 302, 303(1), 305 and 300 of this Act of references respectively to sections 57, 54, 59(1), 53(7), 54, 55, 56, 59(2) and 58 of the Finance Act 1981; and
   (*b*) with the omission of subsection (6)(*a*)(i).

Former enactments.—Sub-s. (1): FA 1983, Sch. 5, para. 14(1), (1A); FA 1987, s. 42(5).
Sub-ss. (2)–(5): FA 1981, s. 62(2)–(5); FA 1983, Sch. 5, para. 14(2).
Sub-s. (6)(*a*): FA 1981, s. 62(6)(*d*); FA 1983, Sch. 5, para. 14(2).
Sub-s. (6)(*b*)–(*d*): FA 1981, s. 62(6)(*a*)–(*c*); FA 1983, Sch. 5, para. 14(2); F(No. 2)A 1983, Sch. 1, para. 8; FA 1986, Sch. 9, para. 14.
Sub-s. (7): FA 1981, s. 62(7).
Sub-s. (8): FA 1983, Sch. 5, para. 5A(10); FA 1986, Sch. 9, para. 6.
Amendments.—[1] Words in sub-s. (5) substituted for the words "fraud and wilful default) and section 37 of that Act (neglect)" by FA 1989, s. 149(4)(*b*), (7) but without affecting the making of assessment for years before 1983–84 or for accounting periods ending before 1 April 1983.

308. Application to subsidiaries

(1) A qualifying company may, in the relevant period, have one or more subsidiaries if—

   (*a*) the conditions mentioned in subsection (2) below are satisfied in respect of the subsidiary or, as the case may be, each subsidiary and, except as provided by subsection (3) below, continue to be so satisfied until the end of the relevant period; and
   (*b*) the subsidiary or, as the case may be, each subsidiary exists wholly, or substantially wholly, for the purpose of carrying on one or more qualifying trades or is a property managing, or dormant, subsidiary.

(2) The conditions referred to are—

   (*a*) that the qualifying company, or another of its subsidiaries, possesses not less than 90 per cent. of the issued share capital of, and not less than 90 per cent. of the voting power in, the subsidiary;
   (*b*) that the qualifying company, or another of its subsidiaries, would in the event of a winding up of the subsidiary or in any other circumstances be beneficially entitled to receive not less than 90 per cent. of the assets of the subsidiary which would then be available for distribution to the equity holders of the subsidiary;
   (*c*) that the qualifying company or another of its subsidiaries is beneficially entitled to not

(2) A claim for relief in respect of eligible shares in a company shall not be allowed unless it is accompanied by a certificate issued by the company in such form as the Board may direct and certifying that the conditions for the relief, so far as applying to the company and the trade, are satisfied in relation to those shares.

(3) Before issuing a certificate for the purposes of subsection (2) above a company shall furnish the inspector with a statement to the effect that it satisfies the conditions for the relief, so far as they apply in relation to the company and the trade, and has done so at all times since the beginning of the relevant period.

(4) No such certificate shall be issued without the authority of the inspector or where the company, or a person connected with the company, has given notice to the inspector under section 310(2).

(5) Any statement under subsection (3) above shall contain such information as the Board may reasonably require, shall be in such form as the Board may direct and shall contain a declaration that it is correct to the best of the company's knowledge and belief.

(6) Where a company has issued a certificate for the purposes of subsection (2) above, or furnished a statement under subsection (3) above and—

(a) the certificate or statement is made fraudulently or negligently; or
(b) the certificate was issued in contravention of subsection (4) above;

the company shall be liable to a penalty not exceeding [£3,000][1].

(7) For the purposes of regulations made under section 203 no regard shall be had to the relief unless a claim for it has been duly made and admitted.

(8) No application shall be made under section 55(3) or (4) of the Management Act (application for postponement of payment of tax pending appeal) on the ground that the applicant is entitled to the relief unless a claim for the relief has been duly made by him.

(9) For the purposes of section 86 of the Management Act (interest on overdue tax), tax charged by an assessment—

(a) shall be regarded as due and payable notwithstanding that relief from the tax (whether by discharge or repayment) is subsequently given on a claim for the relief; but
(b) shall, unless paid earlier or due and payable later, be regarded as paid on the date of the making of the claim on which the relief is given;

and section 91 of that Act (effect on interest of reliefs) shall not apply in consequence of any discharge or repayment for giving effect to the relief.

(10) For the purposes of the provisions of the Management Act relating to appeals against decisions on claims, the refusal of the inspector to authorise the issue of a certificate under subsection (2) above shall be taken to be a decision refusing a claim made by the company. This subsection shall not apply in relation to shares issued before 19th March 1986.

Former enactments.—Sub-ss. (1)–(9): FA 1981, s. 61(6); FA 1983, Sch. 5, para. 13(1)–(9). Sub-s. (10): FA 1983, Sch. 5, para. 13(10); FA 1986, Sch. 9, paras. 1(2), 13.
Cross references.—See FA 1988, s. 50 and Sch. 4, paras. 10, 16 (modification of this section in relation to shares issued after the passing of FA 1988 and before the end of 1993 for financing private rented housing, subject to the modification not applying to certain housing; FA 1988 was passed on 29 July 1988).
Amendments.—[1] Amount in sub-s. (6) substituted for the words "£250 or, in the case of fraud, £500" by FA 1989, s. 170(3), (6) in relation to things done or omitted after 26 July 1989.

---

307. Withdrawal of relief

(1) Where any relief has been given which is subsequently found not to have been due, it shall be withdrawn by the making of an assessment to tax under Case VI of Schedule D for the year of assessment for which the relief was given; but where by virtue of section 289(6) relief has been given for each of two consecutive years of assessment, any withdrawal of relief shall be made for the first of those years before being made for the second.

(2) Subject to subsections (3) to (7) below, any assessment for withdrawing relief which is made by reason of an event occurring after the date of the claim may be made within six years after the end of the year of assessment in which that event occurs.

(3) No assessment for withdrawing relief in respect of shares issued to any person shall be made by reason of any event occurring after his death.

(4) Where a person has, by a disposal or disposals to which section 299(1)(b) applies, disposed of all the ordinary shares issued to him by a company, no assessment for

her husband at a time when she is living with him or to a disposal made at such a time by him to her; but where shares issued to one of them have been transferred to the other by a transaction inter vivos—

(*a*) that subsection shall apply on the disposal of the shares by the transferee to a third person; and
(*b*) if at any time the husband and wife are divorced or cease to live together and any of those shares have not been disposed of by the transferee before that time, any assessment for withdrawing relief in respect of those shares shall be made on the transferee.

(6) Where a husband and wife are divorced or cease to live together, then, if any relief given in respect of shares for which either of them has subscribed and which were issued while they were married and living together falls to be withdrawn by virtue of a subsequent disposal of those shares by the person who subscribed for them, any assessment for withdrawing that relief shall be made on the person making the disposal and shall be made by reference to the reduction of tax flowing from the amount of the relief regardless of any allocation of that relief under section 280 or of any allocation of the reduction under section 284.

Former enactments.—Sub-s. (1): FA 1983, Sch. 5, para. 12(1).
Sub-ss. (2)–(6): FA 1981, s. 60(4)–(7); FA 1983, Sch. 5, para. 12(2), (3); FA 1987, s. 42(4).
Note.—See **Prospective Legislation Notes** (Married Couples).

305. Reorganisation of share capital

(1) Where shares in respect of which relief has been given and not withdrawn have by virtue of any such allotment, otherwise than for payment, as is mentioned in section 77(2)(*a*) of the 1979 Act fallen to be treated under section 78 of that Act as the same asset as a new holding—

(*a*) a disposal of the whole or part of the new holding shall be treated for the purposes of this Part as a disposal of the whole or a corresponding part of those shares; and
(*b*) the new holding shall be treated for the purposes of section 299(3) as shares in respect of which relief has been given and not withdrawn.

(2) Where—

(*a*) there is, by virtue of any such allotment for payment as is mentioned in section 77(2)(*a*) of the 1979 Act, a reorganisation affecting ordinary shares in respect of which relief has been given; and
(*b*) immediately before the reorganisation the relief had not been withdrawn; and
(*c*) the amount of relief (or, where the relief has been reduced, the amount remaining) and the market value of the shares immediately before the reorganisation, exceeds their market value immediately after the reorganisation;

the relief shall be reduced by an amount equal to whichever is the smaller of those excesses.

(3) Subsection (2) above shall also apply where—

(*a*) an individual who has received, or become entitled to receive, in respect of any ordinary shares in a company, a provisional allotment of shares in or debentures of the company disposes of his rights; and
(*b*) subsection (2) above would have applied (apart from this subsection) had those rights not been disposed of but an allotment of shares or debentures made to him.

(4) This section has effect in relation to reorganisations occurring after 18th March 1986.

Former enactments.—FA 1983, Sch. 5, para. 16A(1), (3), (4); FA 1986, Sch. 9, para. 17(1), (2).
Cross references.—See CGTA 1979, s. 149C(9) (treatment, for the purposes of capital gains tax, of the reduction referred to in sub-s. (2) above in the computation of gain or loss accruing to an individual on the disposal, after 18 March 1986, of any of the alloted shares or debentures).

306. Claims

(1) A claim for relief in respect of eligible shares issued by a company in any year of assessment shall be made—

(*a*) not earlier than the end of the period of four months mentioned in section 289(8)(*a*), (*b*) or (*c*), as the case may be; and
(*b*) not later than two years after the end of that year of assessment or, if that period of four months ended after the end of that year, not later than two years after the end of that period.

(8) Subsection (1) above does not apply in relation to the redemption of any share capital for which the redemption date was fixed before 15th March 1983.

(9) Where—
 (a) a company issues share capital ("the original shares") of nominal value equal to the authorised minimum (within the meaning of the Companies Act 1985) for the purposes of complying with the requirements of section 117 of that Act (public company not to do business unless requirements as to share capital complied with); and
 (b) after the registrar of companies has issued the company with a certificate under section 117, it issues eligible shares;
subsection (1) above shall not apply in relation to any redemption of any of the original shares within 12 months of the date on which those shares were issued.
In relation to companies incorporated under the law of Northern Ireland references in this subsection to the Companies Act 1985 and to section 117 of that Act shall have effect as references to the Companies (Northern Ireland) Order 1986 and to Article 127 of that Order.

(10) Where relief to which an individual is entitled in respect of eligible shares issued after 18th March 1986 is reduced by virtue of this section, effect shall be given to the reduction by apportioning it as between any such eligible shares held by him in such a way as appears to the inspector, or on appeal to the Commissioners concerned, to be just and reasonable.

(11) In relation to shares issued before 19th March 1986, subsection (1)(b) above shall have effect with the omission of the words "withdrawn or reduced by virtue of section 299 or".

Former enactments.—Sub-s. (1): FA 1983, Sch. 5, para. 10(1); FA 1986, Sch. 9, para. 11(2).
Sub-ss. (2)–(7): FA 1981, s. 59(3)–(8); FA 1983, Sch. 5, para. 10(2).
Sub-ss. (8), (9): FA 1983, Sch. 5, para. 10(3), (4); Companies Consolidation (Consequential Provisions) Act 1985, Sch. 2; FA 1987, Sch. 15, para. 15(1).
Sub-s. (10): FA 1983, Sch. 5, para. 10(5A); FA 1986, Sch. 9, para. 11(3).
Sub-s. (11): FA 1986, Sch. 9, para. 1(2).

304. Husband and wife

(1) In the case of any amount subscribed by a married woman for eligible shares issued to her at a time—
 (a) when she is living with her husband; and
 (b) which falls in a year of assessment for which his income includes (or, if there were any, would include) any of hers,
the deduction under section 289(5) shall, subject to Chapter II of this Part and subsections (2) to (5) below, be made from his total income, and references in this Chapter to the relief to which an individual is entitled in respect of any shares shall be construed accordingly.

(2) The limits in section 290 shall apply jointly to a husband and wife as respects amounts subscribed for shares at a time—
 (a) when they are married and living together; and
 (b) which falls in a year of assessment for which his income includes (or, if there were any, would include) any of hers;
but if the husband dies or they are divorced or cease to live together before the end of any such year those limits shall apply to the wife as respects amounts subscribed by her for shares issued in the remainder of the year as if it were a separate year of assessment.

(3) Where an application under section 283(1) or an election under section 287(1) is in force for a year of assessment in which shares are issued for which amounts have been subscribed both by the husband and the wife, then, if section 290(2) requires a restriction to be placed on the relief given on a claim or claims in respect of those amounts, the available relief shall be divided between the husband and wife in proportion to the amounts which have been respectively subscribed by them for the shares to which the claim or claims relate and which would, apart from the restriction, be eligible for the relief.

(4) Subsections (2) and (3) above shall apply in relation to the limit of £5,000 imposed by section 289(7) as it applies in relation to the limit of £40,000 imposed by section 290(2); and for this purpose the reference in subsection (3) above to a division in proportion to the amounts subscribed by the husband and wife shall be construed as a reference to a division in proportion to the aggregate amounts of the relevant deductions sought by each of them in their claims under section 289(6).

(5) Subsection (1) of section 299 shall not apply to a disposal made by a married woman to

and that individual is that person or one of those persons.

(4) For the purposes of subsection (2) above—

(*a*) the persons to whom a trade belongs and, where a trade belongs to two or more persons, their respective shares in that trade shall be determined in accordance with section 344(1)(*a*) and (*b*), (2) and (3); and
(*b*) any interest, rights or powers of a person who is an associate of another person shall be treated as those of that other person.

(5) In this section—

"subsidiary" means a subsidiary of a kind which a qualifying company may have by virtue of sections 308 and 309; and
"trade" includes any business, profession or vocation, and references to a trade previously carried on include references to part of such a trade.

Former enactments.—FA 1983, Sch. 5, para. 9; F(No. 2)A 1983, Sch. 1, para. 6.
Cross references.—See FA 1988, s. 50 and Sch. 4, para. 9 (modification of this section in relation to shares issued after the passing of FA 1988 and before the end of 1993 for financing private rented housing; FA 1988 was passed on 29 July 1988).

303. Value received by persons other than claimants

(1) The relief to which an individual is entitled in respect of any shares in a company shall be reduced in accordance with subsection (2) below if at any time in the relevant period the company repays, redeems or repurchases any of its share capital which belongs to any member other than—

(*a*) that individual; or
(*b*) another individual whose relief is thereby withdrawn or reduced by virtue of section 299 or reduced by virtue of section 300(2)(*a*);

or makes any payment to any such member for giving up his right to any of the company's share capital on its cancellation or extinguishment.

(2) Where subsection (1) above applies, the amount of relief to which an individual is entitled shall be reduced by the amount receivable by the member or, if greater, the nominal value of the share capital in question; and where, apart from this subsection, two or more individuals would be entitled to relief the reduction shall be made in proportion to the amounts of relief to which they would, apart from this subsection, have been entitled.

(3) Where at any time in the relevant period a member of a company receives or is entitled to receive any value from the company within the meaning of this subsection, then, for the purposes of section 291(4) in its application to any subsequent time—

(*a*) the amount of the company's issued ordinary share capital; and
(*b*) the amount of the part of that capital which consists of the shares which (within the meaning of section 291) the individual directly or indirectly possesses or is entitled to acquire, and the amount of the part consisting of the remainder,

shall each be treated as reduced in accordance with subsection (4) below.

(4) The amount of each of the parts mentioned in subsection (3)(*b*) above shall be treated as equal to such proportion of that amount as the amount subscribed for that part less the relevant value bears to the amount subscribed; and the amount of the issued share capital shall be treated as equal to the sum of the amounts treated under this subsection as the amount of those parts respectively.

(5) In subsection (4) above "the relevant value", in relation to each of the parts there mentioned, means the value received by the member or members entitled to the shares of which that part consists.

(6) For the purposes of subsection (3) above a member of a company receives or is entitled to receive value from the company in any case in which an individual would receive value from the company by virtue of section 300(2)(*d*), (*e*), (*f*), (*g*) or (*h*) (but treating as excepted from paragraph (*h*) all payments made for full consideration) and the value received shall be determined as for the purposes of that section.

(7) For the purposes of subsection (6) above a person shall be treated as entitled to receive anything which he is entitled to receive at a future date or will at a future date be entitled to receive.

(2) Where relief to which an individual is entitled in respect of eligible shares issued after 18th March 1986 is reduced by virtue of section 300, effect shall be given to the reduction by apportioning it, as between any such eligible shares held by him, in such a way as appears to the inspector, or on an appeal to the Commissioners concerned, to be just and reasonable.

(3) For the purposes of section 300(2)(*d*) a company shall be treated as having released or waived a liability if the liability is not discharged within 12 months of the time when it ought to have been discharged.

(4) For the purposes of section 300(2)(*e*) there shall be treated as if it were a loan made by the company to the individual—

(*a*) the amount of any debt (other than an ordinary trade debt) incurred by the individual to the company; and
(*b*) the amount of any debt due from the individual to a third person which has been assigned to the company.

(5) In this section and section 300, "an ordinary trade debt" means any debt for goods or services supplied in the ordinary course of a trade or business where the credit given does not exceed six months and is not longer than that normally given to the customers of the person carrying on the trade or business.

(6) In this section and section 300—

(*a*) any reference to a payment or transfer to an individual includes a reference to a payment or transfer made to him indirectly or to his order or for his benefit; and
(*b*) any reference to an individual includes a reference to an associate of his and any reference to the company includes a reference to any person connected with the company.

(7) Section 300 shall apply in relation to shares issued before 19th March 1986 with the omission—

(*a*) in subsection (2)(*e*) of the words "which has not been repaid in full before the issue of the shares in respect of which relief is claimed"; and
(*b*) in subsection (4)(*c*) of the words "reduced by the amount of any repayment made before the issue of the shares in respect of which relief is claimed".

Former enactments.—Sub-s. (1): FA 1981, s. 58(5); FA 1983, Sch. 5, para. 8(2).
Sub-s. (2): FA 1983, Sch. 5, para. 8(4); FA 1986, Sch. 9, para. 10(4).
Sub-ss. (3)–(6): FA 1981, s. 58(6)–(9); FA 1983, Sch. 5, para. 8(2); FA 1986, Sch. 9, para. 10(3); FA 1987, Sch. 15, para. 14(2).
Sub-s. (7): FA 1986, Sch. 9, paras. 1(2), 10(3).

---

302. Replacement capital

(1) An individual is not entitled to relief in respect of any shares in a company where—

(*a*) at any time in the relevant period, the company or any of its subsidiaries—

(i) begins to carry on as its trade or as part of its trade a trade which was previously carried on at any time in that period otherwise than by the company or any of its subsidiaries; or
(ii) acquires the whole, or greater part, of the assets used for the purposes of a trade previously so carried on; and

(*b*) subsection (2) below applies in relation to that individual.

(2) This subsection applies in relation to an individual where—

(*a*) any person or group of persons to whom an interest amounting in the aggregate to more than a half share in the trade (as previously carried on) belonged, at any time in the relevant period, is or are a person or group of persons to whom such an interest in the trade carried on by the company belongs or has, at any such time, belonged; or
(*b*) any person or group of persons who control or, at any such time, have controlled the company is or are a person or group of persons who, at any such time, controlled another company which previously carried on the trade;

and the individual is that person or one of those persons.

(3) An individual is not entitled to relief in respect of any shares in a company where—

(*a*) the company comes to acquire all of the issued share capital of another company, at any time in the relevant period; and
(*b*) any person or group of persons who control or have, at any such time, controlled the company is or are a person or group of persons who, at any such time, controlled that other company;

(2) For the purposes of this section an individual receives value from the company if the company—

(*a*) repays, redeems or repurchases any of its share capital or securities which belong to the individual or makes any payment to him for giving up his right to any of the company's share capital or any security on its cancellation or extinguishment;
(*b*) repays any debt owed to the individual other than a debt which was incurred by the company—

(i) on or after the date on which he subscribed for the shares in respect of which the relief is claimed; and
(ii) otherwise than in consideration of the extinguishment of a debt incurred before that date;

(*c*) makes to the individual any payment for giving up his right to any debt (other than a debt in respect of a payment of the kind mentioned in section 291(3)(*a*) or (*e*) or an ordinary trade debt) on its extinguishment;
(*d*) releases or waives any liability of the individual to the company or discharges, or undertakes to discharge, any liability of his to a third person;
(*e*) makes a loan or advance to the individual which has not been repaid in full before the issue of the shares in respect of which relief is claimed;
(*f*) provides a benefit or facility for the individual;
(*g*) transfers an asset to the individual for no consideration or for consideration less than its market value or acquires an asset from him for consideration exceeding its market value; or
(*h*) makes to him any other payment except a payment of the kind mentioned in section 291(3)(*a*), (*b*), (*c*), (*d*) or (*e*) or a payment in discharge of an ordinary trade debt.

(3) For the purposes of this section an individual also receives value from the company if he receives in respect of ordinary shares held by him any payment or asset in a winding up or in connection with a dissolution of the company, being a winding up or dissolution falling within section 293(6).

(4) The value received by an individual is—

(*a*) in a case within paragraph (*a*), (*b*) or (*c*) of subsection (2) above, the amount receivable by the individual or, if greater, the market value of the shares, securities or debt in question;
(*b*) in a case within paragraph (*d*) of that subsection, the amount of the liability;
(*c*) in a case within paragraph (*e*) of that subsection, the amount of the loan or advance reduced by the amount of any repayment made before the issue of the shares in respect of which relief is claimed;
(*d*) in a case within paragraph (*f*) of that subsection, the cost to the company of providing the benefit or facility less any consideration given for it by the individual;
(*e*) in a case within paragraph (*g*) of that subsection, the difference between the market value of the asset and the consideration (if any) given for it;
(*f*) in a case within paragraph (*h*) of that subsection, the amount of the payment; and
(*g*) in a case within subsection (3) above, the amount of the payment or, as the case may be, the market value of the asset.

(5) For the purposes of this section an individual also receives value from the company if any person who would, for the purposes of section 291, be treated as connected with the company—

(*a*) purchases any of its share capital or securities which belong to the individual; or
(*b*) makes any payment to him for giving up any right in relation to any of the company's share capital or securities;

and the value received by the individual is the amount receivable by the individual or, if greater, the market value of the shares or securities in question.

Former enactments.—Sub-s. (1): FA 1983, Sch. 5, para. 8(1); FA 1986, Sch. 9, para. 10(2).
Sub-ss. (2)–(4): FA 1981, s. 58(2)–(4); FA 1983, Sch. 5, para. 8(2); FA 1986, Sch. 9, para. 10(3).
Sub-s. (5): FA 1983, Sch. 5, para. 8(3); F(No. 2)A 1983, Sch. 1, para. 5.

301. Provisions supplementary to section 300

(1) Where by virtue of section 300 any relief is withheld or withdrawn in the case of an individual to whom ordinary shares in a company have been issued at different times before 19th March 1986 the relief shall be withheld or withdrawn in respect of shares issued earlier rather than in respect of shares issued later.

passing of FA 1988 and before the end of 1993 for financing private rented housing; FA 1988 was passed on 29 July 1988).

299. Disposal of shares

(1) Where an individual disposes of any eligible shares before the end of the relevant period, then—

(a) if the disposal is otherwise than by way of a bargain made at arm's length, he shall not be entitled to any relief in respect of those shares; and
(b) in any other case, the amount of relief to which he is entitled in respect of those shares shall be reduced by the amount or value of the consideration which he receives for them.

(2) Where after 18th March 1986 an option, the exercise of which would bind the grantor to purchase any shares, is granted to an individual during the relevant period, the individual shall not be entitled to any relief in respect of the shares to which the option relates.

(3) Where an individual holds ordinary shares of any class in a company and the relief has been given (and not withdrawn) in respect of some shares of that class but not others, any disposal by him of ordinary shares of that class in the company, and any option of the kind mentioned in subsection (2) above, shall be treated for the purposes of this section as relating—

(a) first, to those (if any) in respect of which relief has been given (and not withdrawn) under Chapter II of Part IV of the Finance Act 1981 rather than to others; and
(b) then, to those in respect of which relief has been given (and not withdrawn) under this Chapter (or Schedule 5 to the Finance Act 1983).

(4) Where the relief has been given (and not withdrawn) to an individual in respect of shares of any class in a company which have been issued to him at different times, any disposal by him of shares of that class shall, subject to subsection (3) above, be treated for the purposes of this section as relating to those issued earlier rather than to those issued later.

(5) Where shares in respect of which the relief was given have by virtue of any such allotment as is mentioned in section 77(2)(a) of the 1979 Act (not being an allotment for payment) fallen to be treated under section 78 of that Act as the same asset as a new holding—

(a) a disposal of the whole or part of the new holding shall be treated for the purposes of this section as a disposal of the whole or a corresponding part of those shares; and
(b) the new holding shall be treated for the purposes of subsection (3) above as shares in respect of which the relief has been given.

(6) For the purposes of this section—

(a) shares in a company shall not be treated as being of the same class unless they would be so treated if dealt with on the Stock Exchange; and
(b) references to a disposal of shares include references to the grant of an option (after 18th March 1986) the exercise of which would bind the grantor to sell the shares.

Former enactments.—Sub-s. (1): FA 1983, Sch. 5, para. 7(1).
Sub-s. (2): FA 1983, Sch. 5, para. 7(1A); FA 1986, Sch. 9, para. 9(2), (6).
Sub-s. (3): FA 1983, Sch. 5, para. 7(2); F(No. 2)A 1983, Sch. 1, para. 4(2); FA 1986, Sch. 9, para. 9(3).
Sub-s. (4): FA 1983, Sch. 5, para. 7(2A); F(No. 2)A 1983, Sch. 1, para. 4(3); FA 1986, Sch. 9, para. 9(4).
Sub-s. (5): FA 1981, s. 57(4); FA 1983, Sch. 5, para. 7(3); F(No. 2)A 1983, Sch. 1, para. 4(4).
Sub-s. (6): FA 1983, Sch. 5, para. 7(4); F(No. 2)A 1983, Sch. 1, para. 4(5); FA 1986, Sch. 9, para. 9(5).
Cross references.—See CGTA 1979, s. 149C(4) (application of this section for capital gains tax purposes).

300. Value received from company

(1) Subject to section 299, where an individual who subscribes for eligible shares in a company—

(a) has, before the issue of the shares but within the relevant period, received any value from the company; or
(b) after their issue but before the end of the relevant period, receives any such value;

the amount of the relief to which he is entitled in respect of the shares shall be reduced by the value received; but the value received shall be disregarded to the extent to which relief under Schedule 5 to the Finance Act 1983 or under this Chapter has been reduced on its account.

298. Provisions supplementary to sections 293 and 297

(1) For the purposes of sections 293(9) and 297 a person has a controlling interest in a trade—

(a) in the case of a trade carried on by a company, if—

(i) he controls the company;
(ii) the company is a close company and he or an associate of his is a director of the company and the beneficial owner of, or able directly or through the medium of other companies or by any other indirect means to control, more than 30 per cent. of the ordinary share capital of the company; or
(iii) not less than half of the trade could in accordance with section 344(2) be regarded as belonging to him;

(b) in any other case, if he is entitled to not less than half of the assets used for, or the income arising from, the trade.

(2) For the purposes of subsection (1) above, there shall be attributed to any person any rights or powers of any other person who is an associate of his.

(3) References in this section and section 297 to a trade shall be construed without regard to so much of the definition of "trade" in section 832(1) as relates to adventures or concerns in the nature of trade; but the foregoing provisions do not affect the construction of references in section 297(2)(g) or subsection (1) above to a trade carried on by a person other than the company and those references shall be construed as including a reference to any business, profession or vocation.

(4) The Treasury may by order amend section 297 and this section, except in relation to shares issued before 19th March 1986, in such manner as they consider expedient.

(5) In section 297—

"film" means an original master negative of a film, an original master film disc or an original master film tape;
"oil rig" means any ship which is an offshore installation for the purposes of the Mineral Workings (Offshore Installations) Act 1971;
"pleasure craft" means any ship of a kind primarily used for sport or recreation;
"property development" means the development of land, by a company which has, or at any time has had, an interest in the land (within the meaning of section 294(5)), with the sole or main object of realising a gain from disposing of the land when developed; and
"sound recording" means, in relation to a film, its sound track, original master audio disc or, as the case may be, original master audio tape.

(6) Section 297 shall have effect in relation to shares issued before 19th March 1986 subject to the following modifications—

(a) in subsection (2) the words "or those activities when taken together amount" shall be omitted;
(b) subsection (2)(h) shall not apply unless the shares were issued after 19th March 1985;
(c) subsection (2)(j) shall not apply unless the shares were issued after 13th March 1984;
(d) in subsection (3) the words in paragraph (a) "to members of the general public for their use or consumption" and paragraph (c) shall be omitted; and
(e) subsections (6) and (7) shall be omitted;

and in relation to shares issued after 18th March 1986 section 297(2) shall have effect with the omission of paragraphs (h) and (j).

(7) Section 297(2) shall have effect so far as it relates to oil extraction only in relation to shares issued after 25th July 1986.

(8) Section 297(4) shall have effect in relation to shares issued before 17th March 1987 with the omission of paragraph (a)(ii), together with the word "or" immediately before it, (but not the word "and" at the end of it) and the words in paragraph (b) "in that period" in the second place where they appear.

Former enactments.—Sub-ss. (1)–(3): FA 1981, s. 56(8)–(10); FA 1983, Sch. 5, paras. 5(9), 6(2)–(7); FA 1986, Sch. 9, paras. 1(2), 8(4).
Sub-s. (4): FA 1983, Sch. 5, para. 6(8); FA 1986, Sch. 9, paras. 1(2), 8(4).
Sub-s. (5): FA 1983, Sch. 5, para. 6(2B), (10); FA 1984, s. 37(2); FA 1985, s. 44(5); FA 1986, Sch. 9, para. 4.
Sub-s. (6): FA 1984, s. 37(3); FA 1985, s. 44(7); FA 1986, Sch. 9, para. 1(2).
Sub-s. (7): FA 1986, Sch. 9, para. 8(5).
Sub-s. (8): FA 1987, s. 43(2).
Cross references.—See FA 1988, s. 50 and Sch. 4, para. 8 (this section not to apply in relation to shares issued after the

(*a*) the company carrying on the trade is engaged in research and development throughout the relevant period; and
(*b*) all royalties and licence fees received by it in that period are attributable to research and development which it has carried out.

(6) A trade shall not be treated as failing to comply with this section by reason only of its consisting of letting ships, other than oil rigs or pleasure craft, on charter if—

(*a*) every ship let on charter by the company carrying on the trade is beneficially owned by the company;
(*b*) every ship beneficially owned by the company is registered in the United Kingdom; and
(*c*) throughout the relevant period the company is solely responsible for arranging the marketing of the services of its ships; and
(*d*) the conditions mentioned in subsection (7) below are satisfied in relation to every letting on charter by the company;

but where any of the requirements mentioned in paragraphs (*a*) to (*d*) above are not satisfied in relation to any lettings of such ships, the trade shall not thereby be treated as failing to comply with this section if those lettings and any other activity of a kind falling within subsection (2) above do not, when taken together, amount to a substantial part of the trade.

(7) The conditions are that—

(*a*) the letting is for a period not exceeding 12 months and no provision is made at any time (whether in the lease or otherwise) for extending it beyond that period otherwise than at the option of the lessee;
(*b*) during the period of the letting there is no provision in force (whether made in the lease or otherwise) for the grant of a new letting to end, otherwise than at the option of the lessee, more than 12 months after that provision is made;
(*c*) the letting is by way of a bargain made at arm's length between the company and a person who is not connected with it;
(*d*) under the terms of the charter the company is responsible as principal—

  (i) for taking, throughout the period of the charter, management decisions in relation to the ship, other than those of a kind generally regarded by persons engaged in trade of the kind in question as matters of husbandry; and
  (ii) for defraying all expenses in connection with the ship throughout that period, or substantially all such expenses, other than those directly incidental to a particular voyage or to the employment of the ship during that period; and

(*e*) no arrangements exist by virtue of which a person other than the company may be appointed to be responsible for the matters mentioned in paragraph (*d*) above on behalf of the company;

but this subsection shall have effect, in relation to any letting between the company in question and its subsidiary, or between it and another company of which it is a subsidiary or between it and a company which is a subsidiary of the same company of which it is a subsidiary, as if paragraph (*c*) were omitted.

(8) The trade must, during the relevant period, be conducted on a commercial basis and with a view to the realisation of profits.

(9) A trade which consists to any substantial extent of oil extraction activities shall, if it would be a qualifying trade were it not for subsection (2)(*d*) above, be treated as a qualifying trade for the purposes of section 289(1)(*d*).

Former enactments.—Sub-s. (1): FA 1983, Sch. 5, para. 6(1).
Sub-s. (2)(*a*)–(*g*): FA 1983, Sch. 5, para. 6(2); FA 1986, Sch. 9, para. 8(2).
Sub-s. (2)(*h*): FA 1985, s. 44(3).
Sub-s. (2)(*j*): FA 1984, s. 37(1).
Sub-s. (3): FA 1981, s. 56(3), Sch. 11; FA 1983, Sch. 5, para. 6(4); FA 1986, Sch. 9, para. 8(4).
Sub-s. (4): FA 1983, Sch. 5, para. 6(2A); FA 1984, s. 37(2); FA 1987, s. 43.
Sub-s. (5): FA 1983, Sch. 5, para. 6(2AA); FA 1985, s. 44(4).
Sub-ss. (6), (7): FA 1983, Sch. 5, para. 6(2B), (2C); FA 1984, s. 37(2); FA 1986, Sch. 9, para. 8(3).
Sub-s. (8): FA 1983, Sch. 5, para. 6(3).
Sub-s. (9): FA 1983, Sch. 5, para. 2B(7); FA 1986, Sch. 9, para. 4.
Cross references.—See FA 1988, s. 50 and Sch. 4, para. 8 (this section not to apply in relation to shares issued after the passing of FA 1988 and before the end of 1993 for financing private rented housing; FA 1988 was passed on 29 July 1988).

(2) Subject to subsection (9) below, the trade must not at any time in the relevant period consist of one or more of the following activities if that activity amounts, or those activities when taken together amount, to a substantial part of the trade—

(a) dealing in commodities, shares, securities, land or futures;
(b) dealing in goods otherwise than in the course of an ordinary trade of wholesale or retail distribution;
(c) banking, insurance, money-lending, debt-factoring, hire-purchase financing or other financial activities;
(d) oil extraction activities;
(e) leasing (including letting ships on charter or other assets on hire) or receiving royalties or licence fees;
(f) providing legal or accountancy services;
(g) providing services or facilities for any trade carried on by another person which consists to any substantial extent of activities within any of paragraphs (a) to (f) above and in which a controlling interest is held by a person who also has a controlling interest in the trade carried on by the company;
(h) property development;
(j) farming.

(3) For the purposes of subsection (2)(b) above—

(a) a trade of wholesale distribution is one in which the goods are offered for sale and sold to persons for resale by them, or for processing and resale by them, to members of the general public for their use or consumption;
(b) a trade of retail distribution is one in which the goods are offered for sale and sold to members of the general public for their use or consumption;
(c) a trade is not an ordinary trade of wholesale or retail distribution if—

(i) it consists to a substantial extent of dealing in goods of a kind which are collected or held as an investment or of that activity and any other activity of a kind falling within subsection (2) above, taken together; and
(ii) a substantial proportion of those goods are held by the company for a period which is significantly longer than the period for which a vendor would reasonably be expected to hold them while endeavouring to dispose of them at their market value; and

(d) in determining whether a trade is an ordinary trade of wholesale or retail distribution regard shall be had to the extent to which it has the following features, that is to say—

(i) the goods are bought by the trader in quantities larger than those in which he sells them;
(ii) the goods are bought and sold by the trader in different markets;
(iii) the trader employs staff and incurs expenses in the trade in addition to the cost of the goods and, in the case of a trade carried on by a company, in addition to any remuneration paid to any person connected with it;
(iv) there are purchases or sales from or to persons who are connected with the trader;
(v) purchases are matched with forward sales or vice versa;
(vi) the goods are held by the trader for longer than is normal for goods of the kind in question;
(vii) the trade is carried on otherwise than at a place or places commonly used for wholesale or retail trade;
(viii) the trader does not take physical possession of the goods;

those features in sub-paragraphs (i) to (iii) being regarded as indications that the trade is such an ordinary trade and those in sub-paragraphs (iv) to (viii) being regarded as indications of the contrary.

(4) A trade shall not be treated as failing to comply with this section by reason only of its consisting to a substantial extent of receiving royalties or licence fees if—

(a) the company carrying on the trade is engaged throughout the relevant period in—

(i) the production of films; or
(ii) the production of films and the distribution of films produced by it in the relevant period; and

(b) all royalties and licence fees received by it in that period are in respect of films produced by it in that period or sound recordings in relation to such films or other products arising from such films.

(5) A trade shall not be treated as failing to comply with this section by reason only that at any time after 19th March 1985 it consists to a substantial extent of receiving royalties or licence fees if—

whether by way of a further assessment or the discharge or repayment of tax or otherwise, shall be made as is required in consequence.

(7) Where the relief obtainable under subsection (6) above requires a discharge or repayment of tax, it shall be given on a claim to the Board and such a claim may be made at any time.

Former enactments.—FA 1983, Sch. 5, paras. 5A(1)–(9), 5B, 5C; FA 1986, Sch. 9, paras. 1(2), 7.
Cross references.—See FA 1988, s. 50 and Sch. 4, para. 7 (this section not to apply in relation to shares issued after the passing of FA 1988 and before the end of 1993 for financing private rented housing; FA 1988 was passed on 29 July 1988).

296. Section 294 disapplied where amounts raised total £50,000 or less

(1) Where a company raises any amount through the issue of eligible shares, section 294—

(a) shall not have effect to deny relief in relation to those shares if the aggregate of that amount and of all other amounts (if any) so raised within the period of 12 months ending with the date of that issue does not exceed £50,000; and
(b) where that aggregate exceeds £50,000, shall have effect to deny relief only in relation to the excess.

(2) Where—

(a) at any time within the relevant period, the company in question or any of its subsidiaries carries on any trade or part of a trade in partnership, or as a party to a joint venture, with one or more other persons; and
(b) that other person, or at least one of those other persons, is a company;

each reference to £50,000 in subsection (1)(a) and (b) above shall have effect as if it were a reference to—

$$\frac{£50,000}{1+A}$$

where A is the total number of companies (apart from the company in question or any of its subsidiaries) which are members of any such partnership or parties to any such joint venture during the relevant period.

(3) Where section 294, as read with this section, requires a restriction to be placed on the relief given on claims in respect of shares issued to two or more individuals, the available relief shall be divided between them in proportion to the amounts which have been respectively subscribed by them for the shares to which their claims relate and which would, apart from the restrictions, be eligible for the relief.

(4) A claimant who is dissatisfied with the manner in which the available relief is divided under this section between him and any other claimant or claimants may apply to the appropriate Commissioners who shall, after giving the other claimant or claimants an opportunity to appear and be heard or to make representations in writing, determine the question for all the claimants in the same way as an appeal.

(5) In this section "the appropriate Commissioners" means—

(a) in a case where the same body of General Commissioners has jurisdiction with respect to all the claimants, those Commissioners, unless all the claimants agree that the question should be determined by the Special Commissioners;
(b) in a case where different bodies of General Commissioners have jurisdiction with respect to the claimants, such of those bodies as the Board may direct, unless all the claimants agree that the question should be determined by the Special Commissioners;
(c) in any other case, the Special Commissioners.

(6) In calculating the aggregate mentioned in subsection (1)(a) above in respect of any period of 12 months which begins on or before 18th March 1986, any amount raised by the issue of eligible shares on or before that date shall be disregarded.

Former enactments.—FA 1983, Sch. 5, paras. 5A(1)–(9), 5B, 5C; FA 1986, Sch. 9, paras. 1(2), 7.
Cross references.—See FA 1988, s. 50 and Sch. 4, para. 7 (this section not to apply in relation to shares issued after the passing of FA 1988 and before the end of 1993 for financing private rented housing; FA 1988 was passed on 29 July 1988).

297. Qualifying trades

(1) Subject to section 298(6) and (7) below, a trade is a qualifying trade if it complies with the requirements of this section.

(apart from this subsection) as is equal to the fraction of the assets of the partnership to which the company would be entitled if the partnership were dissolved at that time.

(8) Where a qualifying company has one or more subsidiaries, the company and its subsidiaries ("the group") shall be treated as a single company for the purposes of this section and sections 295 and 296; but any debt owed by, or liability of, one member of the group to another shall be disregarded for those purposes.

(9) The Treasury may by order amend subsection (1) above by substituting a different fraction for the fraction for the time being specified there.

Former enactments.—FA 1983, Sch. 5, paras. 5A(1)–(9), 5B, 5C; FA 1986, Sch. 9, paras. 1(2), (7).
Cross references.—See FA 1988, s. 50 and Sch. 4, para. 7 (this section not to apply in relation to shares issued after the passing of FA 1988 and before the end of 1993 for financing private rented housing; FA 1988 was passed on 29 July 1988).
Amendments.—[1] Sub-s. (5A) inserted by FA 1988, s. 52 in relation to valuations which fall to be made after the passing of FA 1988. FA 1988 was passed on 29 July 1988.

295. Valuation of interests in land for purposes of section 294(1)(*b*)

(1) For the purposes of section 294(1)(*b*), the value of the interests in land held by a company immediately after the issue of the shares in question ("the original interests") shall be adjusted by—

(*a*) adding—

(i) the cost of any interests in land subsequently acquired by the company ("the later interests"); and
(ii) any expenditure (whenever payable) incurred by the company wholly and exclusively in enhancing the value of any of the original or later interests;

(*b*) deducting any consideration received by the company on the disposal of any of the original or later interests or on the grant by the company of any interest in land out of any of those interests;
(*c*) deducting any consideration otherwise derived by the company from its ownership of any of the original or later interests.

(2) Any sum which is received by a company by way of rent, or which is attributable to the use of any premises by the company, shall be disregarded for the purposes of subsection (1)(*c*) above.

(3) For the purposes of this section—

(*a*) the cost of an interest in land acquired by a company shall be taken to be the amount or value of the consideration given by the company, or on its behalf, wholly and exclusively for the acquisition of the interest;
(*b*) consideration shall be brought into account without any discount for the postponement of the right to receive any part of it; and
(*c*) the grant of an interest in land out of any of the original interests shall be treated as a disposal of the original interest in question.

(4) Where—

(*a*) the interest of a company as lessee under a lease ("the lease") falls to be valued at any time for the purposes of section 294 or the cost of acquiring that interest falls to be calculated for the purposes of this section; and
(*b*) the aggregate amount of the rent payable by the lessee under the lease before the end of the relevant period exceeds that which would be so payable under a lease of the premises at a full market rent (but otherwise on the same terms and conditions as the lease);

the value of the company's interest at that time shall be calculated on the assumption that the aggregate amount payable as mentioned in paragraph (*b*) above is a nominal amount and, where the interest was acquired after the issue of the shares in question, it shall be assumed that the company paid the appropriate premium when acquiring the interest.

(5) In determining, for the purposes of this section, the consideration for the disposal or acquisition of an interest in land, no account shall be taken in the first instance of any contingent liability assumed by the company or by any other person.

(6) If it is subsequently shown to the satisfaction of the Board that a contingent liability which was not taken into account in determining the consideration for a disposal or acquisition has become enforceable and is being or had been enforced, such adjustment,

(11) In subsections (9) and (10) above references to a company's trade include references to the trade of any of its subsidiaries.

Former enactments.—Sub-s. (1): FA 1983, Sch. 5, para. 5(1); FA 1986, Sch. 9, para. 6(2).
Sub-s. (2): FA 1983, Sch. 5, para 5(2); F(No. 2)A 1983, Sch. 1, para. 3(*a*).
Sub-s. (3): FA 1983, Sch. 5, para. 5(3).
Sub-s. (4): FA 1983, Sch. 5, para. 5(3A); FA 1986, Sch. 9, para. 6(3).
Sub-ss. (5)–(8): FA 1983, Sch. 5, para. 5(4)–(7); Insolvency Act 1986, Sch. 14.
Sub-s. (9): FA 1983, Sch. 5, para. 5(8); FA 1986, Sch. 9, para. 6(4).
Sub-ss. (10), (11): FA 1983, Sch. 5, para. 5(10), (11); F(No. 2)A 1983, Sch 1, para. 3(*b*); FA 1986, Sch. 9, para. 6(4).
Cross references.—See FA 1988, s. 50 and Sch. 4, para. 6 (modification of this section in relation to shares issued after the passing of FA 1988 and before the end of 1993 for financing private rented housing; FA 1988 was passed on 29 July 1988).

294. Companies with interests in land

(1) Subject to section 296, a company is not a qualifying company in relation to shares issued after 18th March 1986 if at any time during the relevant period—

(*a*) the value of the interests in land held by the company at that time; or
(*b*) where lower, the value of the interests in land which were held by the company immediately after the issue of the shares (adjusted in accordance with section 295);

is greater than half the value of the company's assets as a whole.

(2) For the purposes of this section, the value of the interests in land held by a company on any date shall be arrived at by first aggregating the market value on that date of each of those interests and then deducting—

(*a*) the amount of any debts of the company which are secured on any of those interests (including any debt secured by a floating charge on property which comprises any of those interests);
(*b*) the amount of any unsecured debts of the company which do not fall due for payment before the expiry of the period of 12 months beginning with that date; and
(*c*) the amount paid up in respect of those shares of the company (if any) which carry a present or future preferential right to the company's assets on its winding up.

(3) For the purposes of this section, the value of a company's assets as a whole shall be arrived at by first aggregating the market value of each of those assets and then deducting the amount of the debts and liabilities of the company.

(4) For the purposes of subsection (3) above, the amount paid up in respect of those shares of a company (if any) which carry a present or future preferential right to the company's assets on its winding up shall be treated as a debt of the company, but otherwise a company's share capital, share premium account and reserves shall not be treated for those purposes as debts or liabilities of the company.

(5) In this section "interest in land" means any estate or interest in land, any right in or over land or affecting the use or disposition of land, and any right to obtain such an estate, interest or right from another which is conditional on that other's ability to grant the estate, interest or right in question, except that it does not include—

(*a*) the interest of a creditor (other than a creditor in respect of a rentcharge) whose debt is secured by way of a mortgage, an agreement for a mortgage or a charge of any kind over land; or
(*b*) in Scotland, the interest of a creditor in a charge or security of any kind over land.

[(5A) For the purposes of this section, the value of an interest in any building or other land shall be adjusted by deducting the market value of any machinery or plant which is so installed or otherwise fixed in or to the building or other land as to become, in law, part of it.][1]

(6) In arriving at the value of any interest in land for the purposes of this section—

(*a*) it shall be assumed that there is no source of mineral deposits in the land of a kind which it would be practicable to exploit by extracting them from underground otherwise than by means of opencast mining or quarrying; and
(*b*) any borehole on the land shall be disregarded if it was made in the course of oil exploration.

(7) Where a company is a member of a partnership which holds any interest in land—

(*a*) that interest shall, for the purposes of this section and sections 295 and 296, be treated as an interest in land held by the company; but
(*b*) its value at any time shall, for those purposes, be taken to be such fraction of its value

293. Qualifying companies

(1) Subject to section 294, a company is a qualifying company if it is incorporated in the United Kingdom and complies with the requirements of this section.

(2) The company must, throughout the relevant period, be an unquoted company which is resident in the United Kingdom and not resident elsewhere, and be—

(*a*) a company which exists wholly, or substantially wholly, for the purpose of carrying on wholly or mainly in the United Kingdom one or more qualifying trades; or
(*b*) a company whose business consists wholly of—
  (i) the holding of shares or securities of, or the making of loans to, one or more qualifying subsidiaries of the company; or
  (ii) both the holding of such shares or securities, or the making of such loans, and the carrying on wholly or mainly in the United Kingdom of one or more qualifying trades.

(3) In this section "qualifying subsidiary", in relation to a company, means a subsidiary of that company of a kind which may be held by virtue of sections 308 and 309.

(4) Where a company has one or more qualifying subsidiaries, it shall not be a qualifying company in relation to shares issued after 18th March 1986 if the qualifying trade or trades carried on by the company and its subsidiaries, taken as a whole, are not carried out wholly or mainly in the United Kingdom.

(5) Without prejudice to the generality of subsection (2) above, but subject to subsection (6) below, a company ceases to comply with that subsection if before the end of the relevant period a resolution is passed, or an order is made, for the winding up of the company (or, in the case of a winding up otherwise than under the Insolvency Act 1986 or the Companies (Northern Ireland) Order 1986, any other act is done for the like purpose) or the company is dissolved without winding up.

(6) A company shall not be regarded as ceasing to comply with subsection (2) above if it does so by reason of being wound up or dissolved without winding up and—

(*a*) it is shown that the winding up or dissolution is for bona fide commercial reasons and not part of a scheme or arrangement the main purpose or one of the main purposes of which is the avoidance of tax; and
(*b*) the company's net assets, if any, are distributed to its members or dealt with as bona vacantia before the end of the relevant period or, in the case of a winding up, the end (if later) of three years from the commencement of the winding up.

(7) The company's share capital must not, at any time in the relevant period, include any issued shares that are not fully paid up.

(8) Subject to sections 308 and 309, the company must not at any time in the relevant period—

(*a*) control (or together with any person connected with it control) another company or be under the control of another company (or another company and any other person connected with that other company); or
(*b*) be a 51 per cent. subsidiary of another company or itself have a 51 per cent. subsidiary;

and no arrangements must be in existence at any time in that period by virtue of which the company could fall within paragraph (*a*) or (*b*) above.

(9) A company is not a qualifying company in relation to shares issued before 19th March 1986 if—

(*a*) an individual has acquired a controlling interest in the company's trade after 5th April 1983; and
(*b*) at any time in the period mentioned in subsection (10) below he has, or has had, a controlling interest in another trade; and
(*c*) the trade carried on by the company or a substantial part of it—
  (i) is concerned with the same or similar types of property or parts thereof or provides the same or similar services or facilities as the other trade, or
  (ii) serves substantially the same or similar outlets or markets as the other trade.

Section 298(1) and (2) shall apply for the purposes of this subsection.

(10) The period referred to in subsection (9) above is the period beginning two years before and ending three years after—

(*a*) the date on which the shares were issued; or
(*b*) if later, the date on which the company began to carry on the trade.

(7) An individual is connected with a company if he has control of it within the meaning of section 840.

(8) For the purposes of this section an individual shall be treated as entitled to acquire anything which he is entitled to acquire at a future date or will at a future date be entitled to acquire, and there shall be attributed to any person any rights or powers of any other person who is an associate of his.

(9) In determining for the purposes of this section whether an individual is connected with a company, no debt incurred by the company by overdrawing an account with a person carrying on a business of banking shall be treated as loan capital of the company if the debt arose in the ordinary course of that business.

(10) Where an individual subscribes for shares in a company with which he is not connected (either within the meaning of this section or by virtue of section 309(6)(*b*)) he shall nevertheless be treated as connected with it if he subscribes for the shares as part of any arrangement which provides for another person to subscribe for shares in another company with which that or any other individual who is a party to the arrangement is connected (within the meaning of this section or by virtue of section 309(6)(*b*)).

Former enactments.—Sub-s. (1): FA 1983, Sch. 5, para. 4(1), (5); F(No. 2)A 1983, Sch. 1, para. 2; FA 1986, Sch. 9, para. 5.
Sub-ss. (2)–(8): FA 1983, Sch. 5, para. 4(2); FA 1981, s. 54(2)–(8).
Sub-ss. (9), (10): FA 1983, Sch. 5, para. 4(3), (4).
Cross references.—See FA 1988, s. 50 and Sch. 4, para. 4 (modification of this section in relation to shares issued after the passing of FA 1988 and before the end of 1993 for financing private rented housing; Finance Act 1988 was passed on 29 July 1988).

292. Parallel trades

(1) An individual is not entitled to relief in respect of any shares in a company which are issued after 18th March 1986 where, at the date mentioned in subsection (2) below—

   (*a*) he is one of a group of persons—

      (i) who control the company; or
      (ii) to whom belongs an interest amounting in the aggregate to more than a half share in the trade carried on by the company;

   (*b*) he is also an individual, or one of a group of persons—

      (i) controlling another company; or
      (ii) to whom belongs an interest amounting in the aggregate to more than a half share in another trade; and

   (*c*) the trade carried on by the company, or a substantial part of it—

      (i) is concerned with the same or similar types of property or parts thereof or provides the same or similar services or facilities; and
      (ii) serves substantially the same or similar outlets or markets;

as the other trade or (as the case may be) the trade carried on by the other company.

(2) The date mentioned in subsection (1) above is—

   (*a*) the date on which the shares are issued; or
   (*b*) if later, the date on which the company begins to carry on the trade.

(3) For the purposes of subsection (1) above—

   (*a*) the persons to whom a trade belongs, and (where a trade belongs to two or more persons) their respective shares in that trade, shall be determined in accordance with section 344(1)(*a*) and (*b*), (2) and (3); and
   (*b*) any interest, rights or powers of a person who is an associate of another person shall be treated as those of that other person.

(4) For the purposes of this section—

   (*a*) references to a company's trade include references to the trade of any of its subsidiaries; and
   (*b*) "trade" in the expressions "another trade", "other trade" and "trade carried on by the other company" includes any business, profession or vocation.

Former enactments.—FA 1983, Sch. 5, para. 10A; FA 1986, Sch. 9, para. 12.
Cross references.—See FA 1988, s. 50 and Sch. 4 para. 5 (this section not to apply in relation to shares issued after the passing of FA 1988 and before the end of 1993 for financing private rented housing; Finance Act 1988 was passed on 29 July 1988).

291. Individuals qualifying for relief

(1) Subject to section 292, an individual qualifies for the relief if he—
  (*a*) subscribes for the eligible shares on his own behalf,
  (*b*) is resident and ordinarily resident in the United Kingdom at the time when they are issued, and
  (*c*) is not at any time in the relevant period connected with the company;

and, in relation to shares issued after 5 April 1986, an individual who is at any time performing duties which are treated by virtue of section 132(4)(*a*) as performed in the United Kingdom shall be treated for the purposes of this section as resident and ordinarily resident in the United Kingdom at that time.

(2) An individual is connected with the company if he, or an associate of his, is—
  (*a*) an employee of the company or of a partner of the company;
  (*b*) a partner of the company; or
  (*c*) subject to subsection (3) below, a director of the company or of another company which is a partner of that company.

(3) An individual is not connected with a company by reason only that he, or an associate of his, is a director unless he or his associate (or a partnership of which he or his associate is a member) receives a payment from the company during the period of five years beginning with the date on which the shares are issued or is entitled to receive such a payment in respect of that period or any part of it; but for that purpose there shall be disregarded—
  (*a*) any payment or reimbursement of travelling or other expenses wholly, exclusively and necessarily incurred by him or his associate in the performance of his duties as a director of the company;
  (*b*) any interest which represents no more than a reasonable commercial return on money lent to the company;
  (*c*) any dividend or other distribution which does not exceed a normal return on the investment;
  (*d*) any payment for the supply of goods which does not exceed their market value; and
  (*e*) any reasonable and necessary remuneration which—
    (i) is paid for services rendered to the company in the course of a trade or profession (not being secretarial or managerial services or services of a kind provided by the company itself); and
    (ii) is taken into account in computing the profits or gains of the trade or profession under Case I or II of Schedule D or would be so taken into account if it fell in a period on the basis of which those profits or gains are assessed under that Schedule.

(4) An individual is connected with the company if he directly or indirectly possesses or is entitled to acquire more than 30 per cent. of—
  (*a*) the issued ordinary share capital of the company; or
  (*b*) the loan capital and issued share capital of the company; or
  (*c*) the voting power in the company.

(5) For the purposes of subsection (4)(*b*) above the loan capital of a company shall be treated as including any debt incurred by the company—
  (*a*) for any money borrowed or capital assets acquired by the company; or
  (*b*) for any right to receive income created in favour of the company; or
  (*c*) for consideration the value of which to the company was (at the time when the debt was incurred) substantially less than the amount of the debt (including any premium thereon).

(6) An individual is connected with the company if he directly or indirectly possesses or is entitled to acquire such rights as would, in the event of the winding up of the company or in any other circumstances, entitle him to receive more than 30 per cent. of the assets of the company which would then be available for distribution to equity holders of the company, and for the purposes of this subsection—
  (*a*) the persons who are equity holders of the company, and
  (*b*) the percentage of the assets of the company to which the individual would be entitled,

shall be determined in accordance with paragraphs 1 and 3 of Schedule 18, taking references in paragraph 3 to the first company as references to an equity holder and references to a winding up as including references to any other circumstances in which assets of the company are available for distribution to its equity holders.

the reference to £500,000 in subsection (1) above shall have effect as if it were a reference to—

$$\frac{£500{,}000}{1 + A,}$$

where A is the total number of companies (apart from the company in question or any of its subsidiaries) which, during the relevant period, are members of any such partnership or parties to any such joint venture.

(5) Where this section precludes the giving of relief on claims in respect of shares issued to two or more individuals, the available relief shall be divided between them in proportion to the amounts which have been respectively subscribed by them for the shares to which their claims relate and which would, apart from this section, be eligible for relief.

(6) Where—
   (a) in the case of a company falling within subsection (2)(a) of section 293, the qualifying trade or each of the qualifying trades is a trade to which subsection (7) below applies;
   (b) in the case of a company falling within subsection (2)(b)(i) of that section, the subsidiary or each of the subsidiaries is a dormant subsidiary or exists wholly, or substantially wholly, for the purpose of carrying on one or more qualifying trades which or each of which is a trade to which subsection (7) below applies; or
   (c) in the case of a company falling within subsection (2)(b)(ii) of that section, the requirements mentioned in each of paragraphs (a) and (b) above are satisfied,

subsections (1) and (4) above shall have effect as if for the amount there specified there were substituted £5 million.

(7) This subsection applies to a trade if it consists, wholly or substantially wholly, of operating or letting ships, other than oil rigs or pleasure craft, and—
   (a) every ship operated or let by the company carrying on the trade is beneficially owned by the company;
   (b) every ship beneficially owned by the company is registered in the United Kingdom;
   (c) throughout the relevant period the company is solely responsible for arranging the marketing of the services of its ships; and
   (d) the conditions mentioned in section 297(7) are satisfied in relation to every letting by the company.

(8) Where—
   (a) any of the requirements mentioned in paragraphs (a) to (c) of subsection (7) above are not satisfied in relation to any ships; or
   (b) any of the conditions referred to in paragraph (d) of that subsection are not satisfied in relation to any lettings,

the trade shall not thereby be precluded from being a trade to which that subsection applies if the operation or letting of those ships, or, as the case may be, those lettings do not amount to a substantial part of the trade.

(9) The Treasury may by order amend any of the foregoing provisions of this section by substituting a different amount for the amount for the time being specified there.

(10) Where—
   (a) the issue of the eligible shares is made in pursuance of a prospectus published, or an offer in writing made, before 15th March 1988;
   (b) the shares are issued after that date and before 6th April 1988; and
   (c) subsection (6) above does not apply,

subsections (1) and (4) above shall have effect as if for the amount there specified there were substituted £1 million.

(11) In this section—
   "let" means let on charter and "letting" shall be construed accordingly;
   "oil rig" and "pleasure craft" have the same meanings as in section 297;
   "prospectus" has the meaning given by section 744 of the Companies Act 1985 or Article 2(3) of the Companies (Northern Ireland) Order 1986].[1]

Cross references.—See FA 1988, s. 50 and Sch.4, para. 3 (modification of this section in relation to shares issued after the passing of FA 1988 and before the end of 1993 for financing private rented housing; FA 1988 was passed on 29 July 1988),
s. 51(2) (amendments to FA 1983, Sch. 5 effective for the year 1987–88 and previous years).
Amendments.—[1] This section inserted by FA 1988, s. 51(1)(b) and deemed always to have had effect.

assessment in which the shares are issued or, if the period mentioned in subsection (8)(*a*) above ends in a later year, the end of that later year.

Former enactments.—Sub-s. (1)(*a*): FA 1983, s. 26(1), Sch. 5, para. 2(1); FA 1986, s. 40(2).
Sub-s. (1)(*b*): FA 1983, Sch. 5, paras. 2(1)(*b*), 2A(2); FA 1985, s. 44(2); FA 1986, Sch. 9, para. 3(*b*).
Sub-s. (1)(*c*): FA 1983, Sch. 5, paras. 2(1)(*b*), 2A(2); FA 1985, s. 44(2), (7).
Sub-s. (1)(*d*): FA 1983, Sch. 5, paras. 2(1)(*b*), 2A(2); FA 1985, s. 44(2); FA 1986, Sch. 9, para. 4.
Sub-s. (2): FA 1983, Sch. 5, paras. 2(1)(*c*)–(*e*), 2B(2); FA 1985, s. 44(2); FA 1986, Sch. 9, para. 4.
Sub-s. (3): FA 1983, Sch. 5, paras. 2(1)(*a*), 2B(3); FA 1985, s. 44(2); FA 1986, Sch. 9, para. 4.
Sub-ss. (4), (5): FA 1983, Sch. 5, para. 2(2), (3).
Sub-ss. (6), (7): FA 1983, Sch. 5, para. 2(4A), (4B); FA 1987, s. 42(1).
Sub-s. (8)(*a*): FA 1983, Sch. 5, para. 2(4).
Sub-s. (8)(*b*): FA 1983, Sch. 5, paras. 2(4), 2A(3); FA 1985, s. 44(2); FA 1986, Sch. 9, para. 3(*c*).
Sub-s. (8)(*c*): FA 1983, Sch. 5, paras. 2(4), 2B(4); FA 1985, s. 44(2); FA 1986, Sch. 9, para. 4.
Sub-s. (9): FA 1983, Sch. 5, paras. 2(5), 2A(4), 2B(5); FA 1985, s. 44(2); FA 1986, Sch. 9, paras. 3(*d*), 4.
Sub-s. (10): FA 1983, Sch. 5, para. 2(6).
Sub-s. (11): FA 1983, Sch. 5, para. 11.
Sub-s. (12): FA 1983, Sch. 5, paras. 2(7), 2A(5), 2B(6); FA 1985, s. 44(2); FA 1986, Sch. 9, paras. 2, 4.
Sub-s. (13): FA 1983, Sch. 5, para. 2(8).
Sub-ss. (14), (15): FA 1983, Sch. 5, para. 2(9), (10); FA 1981, s. 52(7), (8); FA 1987, s. 42(2).
Cross references.—See FA 1988, s. 50 and Sch. 4, para. 2 (modification of this section in relation to shares issued after the passing of FA 1988 and before the end of 1993 for financing private rented housing; FA 1988 was passed on 29 July 1988),
Sch. 3, para. 12(2), (3) (claim for relief from 1989–90 income in accordance with sub-s. (6) by a spouse subscribing for shares in 1990–91 when the law about aggregation of income of married couples is abolished).
Amendments.—[1] Words in sub-s. (12)(*b*) substituted by FA 1988, s. 51(1)(*a*).
[2] Words in sub-s. (14) repealed by FA 1988, Sch. 14, Pt. IV.

290. Minimum and maximum subscriptions

(1) Subject to section 311(3), the relief shall not be given in respect of any amount subscribed by an individual for eligible shares issued to him by any company in any year of assessment unless the amount or total amount subscribed by him for the eligible shares issued to him by the company in that year is £500 or more.

(2) No more than £40,000 may be deducted by way of relief under section 289 from the total income of an individual for a year of assessment.

Former enactments.—FA 1983, Sch. 5, para. 3; FA 1987, s. 42(3).
Cross references.—See FA 1988, Sch. 3, para. 12(2), (3) (claim for relief from 1989–90 income in accordance with s. 289(6) above by a spouse subscribing for shares in 1990–91 when the law about aggregation of income of married couples is abolished).

[290A. Restriction of relief where amounts raised exceed permitted maximum

(1) Where—

(*a*) a company raises any amount through the issue of eligible shares after 15th March 1988; and
(*b*) the aggregate of that amount and of all other amounts (if any) so raised within the period mentioned in subsection (2) below exceeds £500,000,

the relief shall not be given in respect of the excess.

(2) The period referred to in subsection (1) above is—

(*a*) the period of 6 months ending with the date of the issue of the shares; or
(*b*) the period beginning with the preceding 6th April and ending with the date of that issue,

whichever is the longer.

(3) In determining the aggregate mentioned in subsection (1) above, no account shall be taken of any amount—

(*a*) which is subscribed by a person other than an individual who qualifies for relief; or
(*b*) as respects which relief is precluded by section 290 or this section.

(4) Where—

(*a*) at any time within the relevant period, the company in question or any of its subsidiaries carries on any trade or part of a trade in partnership, or as a party to a joint venture, with one or more other persons; and
(*b*) that other person, or at least one of those other persons, is a company,

(*b*) the claimant so requests in his claim for relief;

the relief shall be given partly by way of deduction from the claimant's total income for the year of assessment in which the shares are issued and partly by way of deduction from his total income for the preceding year of assessment.

(7) A deduction from the claimant's total income for the year of assessment preceding that in which the shares are issued shall be of such amount as may be specified in the claim; but

(*a*) that amount shall not exceed one half of the total relief in respect of the shares; and
(*b*) the aggregate of that amount and the amounts of any other deductions made by virtue of subsection (6) above from the claimant's total income for the year of assessment preceding that in which the shares are issued shall not exceed £5,000.

(8) The relief shall be given on a claim and shall not be allowed—

(*a*) in a case falling within subsection (1)(*a*)—
    (i) unless and until the company has carried on the trade for four months; and
    (ii) if the company is not carrying on that trade at the time when the shares are issued, unless the company begins to carry it on within two years after that time;
(*b*) in a case falling within subsection (1)(*b*) or (*c*) unless and until the company or (as the case may be) the subsidiary has carried on the research and development for four months;
(*c*) in a case falling within subsection (1)(*d*) unless and until the company has carried on the exploration for four months.

(9) A claim for relief may be allowed—

(*a*) under subsection (1)(*a*), (*c*) or (*d*) at any time after the trade, the research and development or the exploration (as the case may be) has been carried on by the company for four months;
(*b*) under subsection (1)(*b*) at any time after the research and development has been carried on for four months;

if the conditions for the relief are then satisfied.

(10) In the case of a claim allowed before the end of the relevant period, the relief shall be withdrawn if by reason of any subsequent event it appears that the claimant was not entitled to the relief allowed.

(11) An individual is not entitled to relief in respect of any shares unless the shares are subscribed for and issued for bona fide commercial purposes and not as part of a scheme or arrangement the main purpose, or one of the main purposes of which, is the avoidance of tax.

(12) In this Chapter "the relevant period", in relation to relief in respect of any eligible shares issued by a company, means—

(*a*) as respects sections 291, 299, 300, 302 and 303, the period beginning with the incorporation of the company (or, if the company was incorporated more than two years before the date on which the shares were issued, beginning two years before that date) and ending five years after the issue of the shares; and
(*b*) as respects [sections 290A, 293][1], 294, 297, 308 and 309, the period beginning with the date on which the shares were issued and ending either—
    (i) three years after that date; or
    (ii) in a case falling within subsection (1)(*a*), where the company was not at that date carrying on a qualifying trade, three years after the date on which it subsequently began to carry on such a trade.

(13) Where by reason of its being wound up, or dissolved without winding up, the company carries on the qualifying trade for a period shorter than four months, subsection (8)(*a*) above shall have effect as if it referred to that shorter period but only if it is shown that the winding up or dissolution was for bona fide commercial reasons and not as part of a scheme or arrangement the main purpose or one of the main purposes of which was the avoidance of tax.

(14) The relief shall be treated for the purposes of section 835(5) as a deduction to be made under Chapter I of this Part after all other deductions under that Chapter and shall be disregarded for the purposes of calculating relief under section 550(2), . . .[2] and paragraphs 4 and 16 of Schedule 11 where an election has effect under paragraph 12 of that Schedule.

(15) Where effect is given to a claim for relief by repayment of tax, section 824 shall have effect in relation to the repayment as if the time from which the 12 months mentioned in subsections (1)(*b*) and (3)(*a*) of that section are to be calculated were the end of the year of

CHAPTER III

RELIEF FOR INVESTMENT IN CORPORATE TRADES: THE BUSINESS EXPANSION SCHEME

Cross references.—See FA 1988, s. 50 and Sch. 4 (modification of this Chapter in relation to shares issued after the passing of FA 1988 and before the end of 1993 for financing private rented housing).

289. The relief

(1) This Chapter has effect for affording relief from income tax where an individual who qualifies for the relief subscribes for eligible shares in a qualifying company, and either—

(*a*) those shares are issued to him after 5 April 1983 for the purpose of raising money for a qualifying trade which is being carried on by the company or which it intends to carry on; or

(*b*) those shares are issued to him after 18th March 1986 for the purpose of raising money—

(i) for research and development which is being carried on by the company or by any subsidiary of the company on the date on which the shares are issued, or begins so to be carried on immediately thereafter, and from which it is intended that a qualifying trade (to be so carried on) will be derived; or

(ii) both for any such research and development and the resulting trade; or

(*c*) those shares are issued to him after 5 April 1985 and before 19th March 1986 for the purpose of raising money—

(i) for research and development which is being carried on at the time when the shares are issued, or begins immediately thereafter, and from which the company intends to derive a qualifying trade which will be carried on by it; or

(ii) both for any such research and development and the resulting trade; or

(*d*) those shares are issued to him after the passing of the Finance Act 1986 (25th July 1986) for the purpose of raising money for oil exploration which—

(i) is being carried on by the company, or by any subsidiary of the company, on the date on which the shares are issued; or

(ii) begins so to be carried on immediately thereafter;

and from which it is intended that a qualifying trade (to be so carried on) will be derived.

(2) Subsection (1)(*d*) above shall not apply unless—

(*a*) throughout the period of three years beginning with the date on which the shares were issued the company, or any subsidiary of the company, holds an exploration licence which was granted to it, or to another such subsidiary;

(*b*) the exploration is carried out solely within the area to which the licence applies; and

(*c*) on the date on which the shares are issued, neither the company nor any subsidiary of the company holds an appraisal licence or a development licence relating to that area or any part of that area.

(3) Where, at any time after the issue of the shares but before the end of the period mentioned in subsection (2)(*a*) above, the company, or any subsidiary of the company, comes to hold an appraisal licence or development licence which relates to the area, or any part of the area, to which the exploration licence relates, the exploration licence and that other licence shall be treated for the purposes of subsection (2)(*a*) above as a single exploration licence.

(4) In this Chapter "eligible shares" means new ordinary shares which, throughout the period of five years beginning with the date on which they are issued, carry no present or future preferential right to dividends or to a company's assets on its winding up and no present or future preferential right to be redeemed.

(5) Subject to subsection (6) below, the relief in respect of the amount subscribed by an individual for any eligible shares shall be given as a deduction of that amount from his total income for the year of assessment in which the shares are issued, and references in this Chapter to the amount of the relief are references to the amount of that deduction.

(6) If—

(*a*) the shares are issued before 6th October in a year of assessment; and

(*a*) if under that provision it is (or is in the first instance) to reduce the wife's earned income, or is to be deducted or set off in respect of payments made by her or, in the case of relief under Chapter III of this Part, in respect of a payment made by her as a subscription for shares, it shall be treated as reducing her earnings and as not reducing any other income; and

(*b*) in any other case, it shall be treated as not reducing the wife's earnings.

(8) Subsection (7) above shall not affect the giving of any relief under section 388 for a year of assessment for which no election under this section was in force.

(9) Income tax charged on the wife's earnings under subsection (3)(*a*) above shall, whether or not an application under section 283 is in force, be assessed and recovered as if she were a single woman, and any repayment of tax assessed in pursuance of this subsection shall be made to her.

(10) Where subsection (4) of section 284 applies for the purposes of subsections (1) to (3) of that section, it shall apply also for the purposes of this section; but, subject to that, nothing in this section shall be taken to affect the provisions of the Management Act as to returns.

Former enactments.—Sub-s. (1): FA 1971, s. 23(1).
Sub-s. (2): FA 1971, Sch. 4, para. 1; F(No. 2)A 1979, Sch. 2, para. 5; FA 1987, s. 27(2).
Sub-s. (3): FA 1971, Sch. 4, para. 2.
Sub-s. (4): FA 1971, Sch. 4, para. 3(1), (2).
Sub-s. (5): FA 1971, Sch. 4, para. 3(3); F(No. 2)A 1975, s. 31(5); FA 1987, s. 26(5)(*c*).
Sub-s. (6): FA 1971, Sch. 4, para. 3(4).
Sub-s. (7): FA 1971, Sch. 4, para. 4; FA 1981, s. 60(2); FA 1983, Sch. 5, para. 12.
Sub-ss. (8)–(10): FA 1971, Sch. 4, paras. 5, 7.
Note.—See **Prospective Legislation Notes** (Married Couples).

288. Elections under section 287

(1) An election under section 287 ("an election") must be made in such form and manner as the Board may prescribe and must be made not earlier than six months before the beginning of the year of assessment for which it is made nor later than 12 months after the end of that year or such later time as the Board may in any particular case allow.

(2) An election for any year of assessment shall, unless revoked, have effect for any subsequent year of assessment.

(3) An election in force for any year may be revoked by notice in such form and manner as the Board may prescribe and any such notice must be given jointly by the husband and the wife not later than 12 months after the end of that year or such later time as the Board may in any particular case allow.

(4) An election or revocation of an election under this section that could have been made jointly with a person who has died may, within the time permitted by this section, be made jointly with his personal representatives.

Former enactments.—FA 1971, s. 23(2)–(5); FA 1976, s. 36(10).
Note.—See **Prospective Legislation Notes** (Married Couples).

(2) A notice under subsection (1) above shall not be deemed to be validly served on the inspector unless it specifies the names and addresses of the woman's executors or administrators.

(3) Where a notice under subsection (1) above has been duly served on a woman's executors or administrators and on the inspector—

(*a*) it shall be the duty of the Board to exercise such powers as they may then or thereafter be entitled to exercise under section 285 in connection with any assessment made on or before the date when the service of the notice is completed, being an assessment in respect of any of the income to which the notice relates; and
(*b*) the assessments (if any) which may be made after that date shall in all respects, and in particular as respects the persons assessable and the tax payable, be the assessments which would have fallen to be made if—

(i) an application for separate assessment under section 283(1) had been in force in respect of the year of assessment in question; and
(ii) all assessments previously made had been made accordingly.

(4) In the application of this section to Scotland, the reference to the date of the grant of probate or letters of administration shall be construed as a reference to the date of confirmation.

Former enactment.—TA 1970, s. 41.
Note.—See **Prospective Legislation Notes** (Married Couples).

Separate taxation

287. Separate taxation of wife's earnings

(1) Where a man and his wife living with him jointly so elect or have elected for any year of assessment, the wife's earnings and their other income shall be chargeable to income tax as provided in the following provisions of this section.

(2) References in this section to the wife's earnings are references to any earned income of hers other than—

(*a*) income arising in respect of any pension, superannuation or other allowance, deferred pay or compensation for loss of office given in respect of the husband's past services in any office or employment; or
(*b*) any payment of benefit under the Social Security Acts except a Category A retirement pension (exclusive of any increase under section 10 of the Social Security Pensions Act 1975 or Article 12 of the Social Security Pensions (Northern Ireland) Order 1975), unemployment benefit or invalid care allowance.

In this subsection "the Social Security Acts" means the Social Security Acts 1975 and the Social Security (Northern Ireland) Acts 1975.

(3) In charging the income of the husband and wife in accordance with section 279—

(*a*) the wife's earnings shall be charged to income tax as if she were a single woman with no other income; and
(*b*) the husband's other income shall be charged to income tax as if the wife's earnings were nil.

(4) Subject to subsections (5) and (6) below, the reliefs to be given under Chapter I of this Part shall be determined as if the husband and the wife were not married and—

(*a*) the wife's earnings were her only income; and
(*b*) the husband's income included all income of the wife, other than her earnings;

and accordingly the reliefs to be given under that Chapter in respect of the income chargeable under either paragraph (*a*) or paragraph (*b*) of subsection (3) above shall not reduce the tax or the income chargeable under the other of those paragraphs.

(5) No relief shall be given to either the husband or the wife under section 257(2) or (3) or 259.

(6) References in Chapter I of this Part to the claimant shall be construed as including the wife.

(7) Notwithstanding anything to the contrary in the Income Tax Acts, where any amount is under any provision of those Acts to be deducted from or set off against income in respect of any payments, loss or capital allowance, then—

(2) The same consequences as respects—

  (a) the imposition of a liability to pay, and the recovery of, the tax, with or without interest; and
  (b) priority for the tax in bankruptcy, or in the administration of the estate of a deceased person; and
  (c) appeals to the General or Special Commissioners, and the stating of cases for the opinion of the High Court; and
  (d) the ultimate incidence of the liability imposed,

shall follow on the service of a notice under subsection (1) above on a woman, or on her trustee, guardian, curator, receiver or committee, or on her executors or administrators, as would have followed on the making on her, or on her trustee, guardian, curator, receiver or committee, or on her executors or administrators, as the case may be, of the potential assessment, being an assessment which—

  (i) was made on the day of the service of the notice, and
  (ii) charged the same amount of income tax as is required to be paid by the notice, and
  (iii) fell to be made, and was made, by the authority who made the original assessment, and
  (iv) was made by that authority to the best of their judgment,

and the provisions of the Income Tax Acts relating to the matters specified in paragraphs (a) to (d) above shall, with the necessary adaptations, have effect accordingly.

(3) Where an appeal against the original assessment has been heard in whole or in part by the Special Commissioners, any appeal from the notice under subsection (1) above shall be an appeal to the Special Commissioners, and where an appeal against the orginal assessment has been heard in whole or in part by the General Commissioners for any division, any appeal from the notice shall be an appeal to the General Commissioners for that division.

(4) Where a notice is given under subsection (1) above—

  (a) income tax up to the amount required to be paid by the notice shall cease to be recoverable under the original assessment, and
  (b) where the tax charged by the original assessment carried interest under section 86 of the Management Act, such adjustment shall be made of the amount payable under that section in relation to that assessment, and such repayment shall be made of any amounts previously paid under that section in relation thereto, as are necessary to secure that the total sum, if any, paid or payable under that section in relation to that assessment is the same as it would have been if the amount which ceases to be recoverable had never been charged.

(5) Where the amount payable under a notice given under subsection (1) above is reduced as the result of an appeal, or of the stating of a case for the opinion of the High Court—

  (a) the Board shall, if in the light of that result they are satisfied that the original assessment was excessive, cause such relief to be given by way of repayment or otherwise as appears to them to be just, but
  (b) subject to any relief so given, a sum equal to the reduction in the amount payable under the notice shall again become recoverable under the original assessment.

(6) The Board and the inspector shall have the like powers of obtaining information with a view to the giving of, and otherwise in connection with, a notice under subsection (1) above as they would have had with a view to the making of, and otherwise in connection with, the potential assessment if the necessary conditions had been fulfilled for the making of such an assessment.

Former enactment.—TA1970, s. 40.
Note.—See **Prospective Legislation Notes** (Married Couples).

286. Right of husband to disclaim liability for tax on deceased wife's income

(1) Where a woman dies who at any time before her death was a married woman living with her husband, he or, if he is dead, his executors or administrators, may, not later than two months from the date of the grant of probate or letters of administration in respect of her estate or, with the consent of her executors or administrators, at any later date, serve on her executors or administrators and on the inspector a notice declaring that, to the extent permitted by this section, he disclaims or they disclaim responsibility for unpaid income tax in respect of all income of hers for any year of assessment or part of a year of assessment during which he was her husband and she was living with him.

284. Effect of separate assessment on personal reliefs

(1) Where, by virtue of an application under section 283(1), income tax for any year of assessment is to be assessable and chargeable on the incomes of a husband and wife as if they were not married, the total relief given to the husband and the wife by way of personal reliefs shall be the same as if the application had not had effect with respect to the year and, subject to subsections (2) and (3) below, the reduction of tax flowing from the personal reliefs shall be allocated to the husband and the wife—

(*a*) so far as it flows from relief under section 273 or Chapter III of this Part, to the husband or the wife according as he or she made the payment giving rise to the relief;
(*b*) . . .[1]
(*c*) as to the balance, in proportion to the amounts of tax which would have been payable by them respectively if no personal reliefs had been allowable.

(2) Subject to subsection (3) below, the amount of reduction of tax allocated to the wife by virtue of subsection (1) above shall not be less than the reduction resulting from section 279(5) in the tax chargeable in respect of her earned income, and the amount of reduction of tax allocated to the husband shall be correspondingly reduced.

(3) Where the amount of reduction of tax allocated to the husband under subsection (1) above exceeds the tax chargeable on the income of the husband for the year of assessment, the balance shall be applied to reduce the tax chargeable on the income of the wife for that year; and where the amount of reduction of tax allocated to the wife under that subsection exceeds the tax chargeable on her income for the year of assessment, the balance shall be applied to reduce the tax chargeable on the income of the husband for that year.

(4) Returns of the total incomes of the husband and the wife may be made for the purposes of this section either by the husband or by the wife, but, if the Board are not satisfied with any such return, they may obtain a return from the wife or the husband, as the case may be.

(5) In this section "personal reliefs" means the reliefs provided for by Chapters I and III of this Part.

Former enactments.—Sub-s. (1): TA 1970, s. 39(1)(*c*)–(*e*); FA 1971, Sch. 6, para. 19; FA 1978, s. 19(5); FA 1981, s. 60(2); FA 1983, Sch. 5, para. 12.
Sub-s. (2): TA 1970, s. 39(1); FA 1971, Sch. 6, para. 19.
Sub-ss. (3), (4): TA 1970, s. 39(2), (3).
Sub-s. (5): TA 1970, s. 39(1); FA 1981, s. 60(2); FA 1983, Sch. 5, para. 12.
Note.—See **Prospective Legislation Notes** (Married Couples).
Amendments.—[1] Sub-s. (1)(*b*) repealed by FA 1988, Sch. 14, Pt. IV.

285. Collection from wife of tax assessed on husband but attributable to her income

(1) Where—

(*a*) an assessment to income tax ("the original assessment") is made on a man, or on a man's trustee, guardian, curator, receiver or committee, or on a man's executors or administrators; and
(*b*) the Board are of opinion that, if an application for separate assessment under section 283(1) had been in force with respect to the year for which the assessment is made, an assessment ("the potential assessment") in respect of, or of part of, the same income would have fallen to be made on, or on the trustee, guardian, curator, receiver or committee of, or on the executors or administrators of, a woman who is that man's wife, or was his wife in that year of assessment; and
(*c*) the whole or part of the amount payable under the original assessment has remained unpaid at the expiration of 28 days from the time when it became due;

the Board may serve on her, or, if she is dead, on her executors or administrators, or, if the potential assessment could in the event referred to in paragraph (*b*) above have been made on her trustee, guardian, curator, receiver or committee, on her or on her trustee, guardian, curator, receiver or committee, a notice—

(i) giving particulars of the original assessment, and of the amount remaining unpaid thereunder, and
(ii) giving particulars, to the best of their judgment, of the potential assessment,

and requiring the person on whom the notice is served to pay the amount which would have been payable under the potential assessment if it conformed with those particulars, or the amount remaining unpaid under the original assessment, whichever is the less.

FA 1988 (Commencement) Order 1989, S.I. 1989 No. 473, proceedings under sub-s. (4) above to be in Northern Ireland if the place given by certain rules in relation to the parties to the proceedings is in Northern Ireland).
Amendments.—[1] Words in sub-s. (4) substituted for the words "Great Britain" by FA 1988, s. 134(3), (4) with effect from 3 April 1989 by virtue of FA 1988 (Commencement) Order 1989, S.I. 1989 No. 473.

282. Construction of references to married women living with their husbands

(1) A married woman shall be treated for income tax purposes as living with her husband unless—

(*a*) they are separated under an order of a court of competent jurisdiction, or by deed of separation, or
(*b*) they are in fact separated in such circumstances that the separation is likely to be permanent.

(2) Where a married woman is living with her husband and either—

(*a*) one of them is, and the other is not, resident in the United Kingdom for a year of assessment, or
(*b*) both of them are resident in the United Kingdom for a year of assessment, but one of them is, and the other is not, absent from the United Kingdom throughout that year,

the same consequences shall follow for income tax purposes as would have followed if, throughout that year of assessment, they had been in fact separated in such circumstances that the separation was likely to be permanent.

(3) Where subsection (2) above applies and the net aggregate amount of income tax falling to be borne by the husband and the wife for the year is greater than it would have been but for that subsection, the Board shall cause such relief to be given (by the reduction of such assessments on the husband or the wife or the repayment of such tax paid, by deduction or otherwise, by the husband or the wife, as the Board may direct) as will reduce that net aggregate amount by the amount of the excess.

Former enactment.—TA 1970, s. 42.
Note.—See **Prospective Legislation Notes** (Married Couples).

Separate assessments

283. Option for separate assessment

(1) If, within six months before the 6th July in any year of assessment for which his income would include any of hers, a husband or a wife makes an application for the purpose in such manner and form as the Board may prescribe, income tax for that year shall be assessed, charged and recovered on the income of the husband and on the income of the wife as if they were not married, and all the provisions of the Income Tax Acts with respect to the assessment, charge and recovery of income tax shall, save as otherwise provided by those Acts, apply as if they were not married.

(2) Notwithstanding an application under subsection (1) above the income of the husband and the wife shall be treated as one in estimating total income; and the amount of tax payable by each of them shall be ascertained by first dividing between them, in proportion to the amounts of their respective incomes, the amount that would be payable by them if no reliefs were given under Chapter I or III of this Part and then applying section 284 to give effect to those reliefs.

(3) Subject to subsection (4) below, an application duly made by a husband or wife under subsection (1) above shall have effect, not only as respects the year of assessment for which it is made, but also for any subsequent year of assessment.

(4) A person who has made any such application for any year of assessment may give, for any subsequent year of assessment, a notice to withdraw that application, and where such a notice is given, the application shall not have effect with respect to the year for which the notice is given or any subsequent year.

(5) A notice of withdrawal under subsection (4) above shall be in such form, and be given in such manner, as may be prescribed by the Board, and shall not be valid unless it is given within the period allowed by law for making, for the year for which the notice is given, applications similar to that to which the notice relates.

Former enactments.—Sub-s. (1): TA 1970, s. 38(1); FA 1976, s. 36(3).
Sub-s. (2): TA 1970, s. 38(2); FA 1971, Sch. 6, para. 18; FA 1981, s. 60(2); FA 1983, Sch. 5, para. 12.
Sub-ss. (3)–(5): TA 1970, s. 38(3)–(5).
Note.—See **Prospective Legislation Notes** (Married Couples).

(ii) section 289 but only in respect of amounts subscribed by her for shares issued in the part of the year of assessment mentioned in subsection (1) above; and
(iii) section 353 so far as applicable to interest paid in the part of the year mentioned in subsection (1) above.

Former enactments.—FA 1976, s. 36(7), (8); FA 1981, s. 60(3); FA 1983, s. 15(2), Sch. 5, para. 12; FA 1987, s. 26(6).
Note.—See **Prospective Legislation Notes** (Married Couples).
Amendments.—[1] Number in sub-s. (2)(*b*)(i) repealed by FA 1988, Sch. 14, Pt. IV.

281. Tax repayments to wives

(1) Where in any year of assessment tax has been deducted under section 203 from the earned income of a wife and, apart from this section, a repayment of tax for that year would fall to be made to her husband in consequence of an assessment under Schedule E, so much of the repayment as is attributable to the tax so deducted shall be made to her and not to him.

(2) The amount of a repayment attributable to tax deducted as mentioned in subsection (1) above is the excess (if any) of the total net tax so deducted in the year of assessment over the tax chargeable on the wife's relevant earned income included in her husband's total income for that year after allowing—

(*a*) any relief for that year under section 266 in respect of any payment made by her of the kind mentioned in paragraph 5 of Schedule 14; and
(*b*) any relief for that year to which her husband is entitled under any other provision of the Income Tax Acts to the extent to which it cannot be allowed because his income, exclusive of her earned income, is insufficient;

but that amount shall not exceed the aggregate of the amounts repayable for that year in respect of the total net tax deducted in that year under section 203 from the income of the wife and the income of her husband.

(3) Where in consequence of an assessment under Schedule E any amount is repayable under this section to the wife of the person on whom the assessment is made the inspector shall notify both of them of his determination of that amount and, subject to subsection (4) below, an appeal shall lie against the determination as if it were a decision on a claim.

(4) Any appeal under subsection (3) above shall be to the General Commissioners for the division in which the spouses reside or, if they reside in different divisions, for the division in which one of them resides, as the Board may direct, or, if neither of them resides in [the United Kingdom][1], to the Special Commissioners; and on any such appeal by one of the spouses the other shall have the same rights as an appellant, including any right to require the statement of a case for the opinion of the court.

(5) The Board may make regulations—

(*a*) modifying subsection (2) above in relation to such cases as may be specified in the regulations;
(*b*) modifying section 824 in relation to cases in which a repayment falls to be made under this section.

(6) This section does not apply to any repayment for a year of assessment—

(*a*) for which the husband is chargeable to income tax at a rate or rates higher than the basic rate; or
(*b*) for which any earned income of the wife has been assessed otherwise than under Schedule E.

(7) For the purposes of this section earned income of a wife has the same meaning as for the purposes of subsection (6) of section 257 and relevant earned income of a wife means so much of her earned income as exceeds the relief available in respect of it under that subsection.

(8) References in this section to the total net tax deducted in any year under section 203 are references to the total income tax deducted during that year by virtue of regulations made under that section less any income tax repaid by virtue of any such regulations.

Former enactment.—FA 1978, s. 22(1)–(4), (6)–(9).
Note.—See **Prospective Legislation Notes** (Married Couples).
Cross references.—See TMA 1970, s. 58(3)(*b*), FA 1988, ss. 134(4), 135(2) (with effect from 3 April 1989 by virtue of

CHAPTER II
TAXATION OF INCOME OF SPOUSES

General rules

279. Aggregation of wife's income with husband's

(1) Subject to the provisions of this Chapter, a woman's income chargeable to income tax shall, so far as it is income for—
  (*a*) a year of assessment; or
  (*b*) any part of a year of assessment, being a part beginning with 6th April,
during which she is a married woman living with her husband, be deemed for income tax purposes to be his income and not to be her income.

(2) The question whether there is any income of hers chargeable to income tax for any year of assessment and, if so, what is to be taken to be the amount thereof for income tax purposes shall not be affected by the provisions of subsection (1) above.

(3) Any tax falling to be assessed in respect of any income which, under subsection (1) above, is to be deemed to be the income of a woman's husband shall, instead of being assessed on her, or on her trustee, guardian, curator, receiver or committee, or on her executors or administrators, be assessable on him or, in the appropriate cases, on his trustee, guardian, curator, receiver or committee, or on his executors or administrators.

(4) Nothing in subsection (3) above shall affect the operation of section 111.

(5) Any deduction from a man's total income made under section 257(6) and (7) shall be treated as reducing the earned income of his wife.

(6) References in this section to a woman's income include references to any sum which, apart from the provisions of this section, would fall to be included in computing her total income, and this subsection has effect in relation to any such sum notwithstanding that some enactment (including, except so far as the contrary is expressly provided, an enactment passed after the passing of this Act) requires that that sum should not be treated as income of any person other than her.

(7) For the purposes of sections 380 and 381 of this Act and section 71 of the 1968 Act (set off of capital allowances against general income), subsection (1)(*b*) above shall have effect as if the words "being a part beginning with 6th April" were omitted.

Former enactments.—TA 1970, s. 37; FA 1971, Sch. 6, para. 17; FA 1976, s. 36(2), (9); FA 1978, s. 30(7)(*e*).
Note.—See **Prospective Legislation Notes** (Married Couples).
Cross references.—See FA 1988, Sch. 3, para. 25 (transitional provisions for the operation of sub-s. (1) above for a year of assessment earlier than 1990–91 in the case of a married woman),
  Sch. 3, para. 29 (time limits for assessments for fraud etc from the year 1990–91).

280. Transfer of reliefs

(1) Where during any part of a year of assessment a husband and wife are living together but his income for that year does not or, if there were any, would not include any of hers, then if either of them—
  (*a*) would, if he or she had sufficient income for that year, be entitled to have any amount deducted from or set off against it under a provision to which this subsection applies, and
  (*b*) makes a claim in that behalf,
that amount or, as the case may be, so much of it as cannot be deducted from or set off against his or her own income for that year shall instead be deducted from and set off against the income for that year of the other spouse.

(2) Subsection (1) above applies—
  (*a*) in the case of the husband, to any provision of Chapter I of this Part and sections 289 and 353;
  (*b*) in the case of the wife, to—
    (i) any provision of that Chapter except sections 257(1)(*b*), (2)(*b*) and (3)(*b*), . . .[1], 259 and 262;

(b) in computing the amount of his income subject to income tax charged in the United Kingdom, the income eligible for double taxation relief shall be disregarded; and

(c) in computing his total income from all sources, including income which is not subject to income tax charged in the United Kingdom, income eligible for double taxation relief shall be included, and the income tax which would be chargeable on that total income shall be computed without regard to the double taxation relief available in respect of the income eligible for double taxation relief;

and, accordingly, where this subsection applies, the amount of the tax chargeable in respect of the income eligible for double taxation relief shall not be affected by subsections (2) and (3) above.

(6) Subsection (5) shall not operate so as to make the tax payable by an individual for a year of assessment higher than it would have been if the double taxation relief had not been available.

(7) In subsection (5) above "income eligible for double taxation relief" means any dividends, interest, royalties or other profits which are chargeable to income tax but in respect of which relief (other than credit) is available under an Order in Council under section 788 so as to limit the rate of income tax so chargeable (but not so as to confer an exemption and make it income which is not subject to income tax charged in the United Kingdom).

(8) Any claim which an individual is entitled to make by virtue of subsection (2) above shall be made to the Board.

Former enactments.—Sub-ss. (1)–(3): TA 1970, s. 27(1), (2); British Nationality Act 1981, s. 51(1), (2).
Sub-s. (4): FA 1976, Sch. 4, para. 18(3).
Sub-ss. (5)–(8): TA 1970, s. 27(3)–(5).
Note.—See **Prospective Legislation Notes**.

(2) Notwithstanding subsection (1) above, relief under section 273 may be given to the extent that the deduction from tax provided for by that section can be made from so much of the income tax with which the claimant is chargeable as exceeds what would be the amount of that tax if all income tax were chargeable at the basic rate to the exclusion of any other rate.

Former enactments.—TA 1970, s. 25; FA 1971, s. 33(5).

277. Partners

(1) Subject to subsection (2) below, the following persons having joint interests, that is to say—

   (*a*) coparceners, joint tenants, or tenants in common of the profits of any property, and
   (*b*) joint tenants, or tenants of land or tenements in partnership, being in the actual and joint occupation thereof in partnership, who are entitled to the profits thereof in shares, and
   (*c*) partners carrying on a trade, profession or vocation together who are entitled to the profits thereof in shares,

may claim any relief under this Chapter according to their respective shares and interests, and any such claims which are proved may be dealt with in the same manner as in the case of several interests.

(2) The income of a partner from a partnership carrying on any trade, profession or vocation shall be deemed to be the share to which he is entitled during the year to which the claim relates in the partnership profits, such profits being estimated according to the provisions of the Income Tax Acts.

Former enactment.—TA 1970, s. 26.

278. Non-residents

(1) Subject to the provisions of this section, no relief under this Chapter shall be given in the case of any individual who is not resident in the United Kingdom.

(2) Subject to subsection (3) below, subsection (1) above shall not apply in the case of any individual who satisfies the Board that he or she—

   (*a*) is a Commonwealth citizen or a citizen of the Republic of Ireland; or
   (*b*) is a person who is or who has been employed in the service of the Crown, or who is employed in the service of any missionary society or in the service of any territory under Her Majesty's protection; or
   (*c*) is resident in the Isle of Man or the Channel Islands; or
   (*d*) has previously resided within the United Kingdom, and is resident abroad for the sake of his or her health, or the health of a member of his or her family resident with him or her; or
   (*e*) is a widow whose late husband was in the service of the Crown.

(3) No relief under this Chapter shall be given so as to reduce the amount of the income tax payable by the individual below the amount which results from applying the fraction—

$$\frac{A}{B}$$

to the amount which would have been payable by him by way of income tax if the tax were chargeable on his total income from all sources (including income which is not subject to income tax charged in the United Kingdom) where—

   A is the amount of his income subject to income tax charged in the United Kingdom; and
   B is the amount of his total income.

(4) Subsection (3) above shall have effect as if the amount of any relief to which an individual is entitled under section 266(4) were an amount by which his liability to income tax is reduced.

(5) For the purposes of subsection (3) above as it applies to an individual whose income includes income eligible for double taxation relief—

   (*a*) in computing the amount of the income tax payable by the individual, the tax chargeable in respect of the income eligible for double taxation relief shall be disregarded;

section 268 or 269 applies has been issued, require the body, within such time, not being less than 30 days, as may be specified in the notice—

(*a*) to furnish such particulars; or
(*b*) to make available for inspection by an officer authorised by the Board such books and other documents in the possession or under the control of the body;

as the Board or officer may reasonably require for the purposes of those sections or this section.

Former enactment.—FA 1975, Sch. 1.

273. Payments securing widows' and children's annuities

Subject to sections 274, 617(3) and 619(6), if the claimant is, under any Act of Parliament or under the terms or conditions of his employment, liable to the payment of any sum, or to the deduction from his salary or stipend of any sum, for the purpose of securing a deferred annuity to his widow or provision for his children after his death, he shall be entitled to a deduction from the amount of income tax with which he is chargeable equal to income tax at the basic rate on the amount of the sum paid by him or deducted from his salary or stipend.

Former enactments.—TA 1970, s. 20(1)(*b*), (3)(*c*); FA 1987, Sch. 15, para. 2(4).
Note.—See **Prospective Legislation Notes** (Married Couples).

274. Limits on relief under sections 266 and 273

(1) The aggregate of the premiums or other sums in respect of which relief is given to any person under section 266 shall not exceed £1,500 in any year of assessment or one-sixth of that person's total income, whichever is the greater.

(2) The aggregate of the relief given under sections 266 and 273 in respect of premiums or sums payable for securing any benefits other than capital sums on death shall not exceed the amount of the income tax calculated at the appropriate rate on £100.

(3) In subsection (2) above "the appropriate rate"—

(*a*) in relation to premiums to which section 266 applies, means [12·5 per cent.][1];
(*b*) in relation to other payments, means the basic rate of income tax.

(4) War insurance premiums shall not be taken into account in calculating the limits of one-sixth of total income or of £100 mentioned in this section.

In this subsection "war insurance premiums" means any additional premium or other sum paid in order to extend an existing life insurance policy to risks arising from war or war service abroad, and any part of any premium or other sum paid in respect of a life insurance policy covering those risks, or either of them, which appears to the inspector to be attributable to those risks, or either of them.

Former enactments.—Sub-s. (1): TA 1970, s. 21(1); FA 1976, Sch. 4, para. 21.
Sub-s. (2): TA 1970, s. 21(3); FA 1975, Sch. 2, para. 6.
Sub-s. (3): TA 1970, s. 21(4); FA 1975, Sch. 2, para. 6; FA 1976, Sch. 4, para. 21; FA 1980, s. 29; FA 1987, Sch. 15, para. 2(5).
Sub-s. (4): TA 1970, s. 21(5).
Amendments.—[1] "12·5 per cent." in sub-s. (3)(*a*) substituted by FA 1988, s. 29 with effect from 6 April 1989.

Supplemental

275. Meaning of "relative"

Former enactment.—TA 1970, s. 23.
This section repealed by FA 1988, Sch. 14, Pt. IV.

276. Effect on relief of charges on income

(1) Where any of the claimant's income is income the income tax on which (at the basic rate) he is entitled to charge against any other person, or to deduct, retain or satisfy out of any payment, he shall not be entitled to relief under this Chapter in respect of that income, except to the extent, if any, that the relief would exceed tax at the basic rate on that income.

later than six years after the end of the year of assessment in which the event happens, to repayment of the excess.

Former enactments.—FA 1975, s. 9(1)–(4); FA 1976, Sch. 4, para. 19(3).

271. Deemed surrender in cases of certain loans

(1) Where—
    (*a*) under section 547 a gain arising in connection with a policy or contract would be treated as forming part of an individual's total income; and
    (*b*) the policy was issued in respect of an insurance made after 26th March 1974 or the contract was made after that date; and
    (*c*) any sum is at any time after the making of the insurance or contract lent to or at the direction of that individual by or by arrangement with the body issuing the policy or, as the case may be, the body with which the contract was made;
then, subject to subsection (2) below, the same results shall follow under section 268 to 270 as if at the time the sum was lent there had been a surrender of part of the rights conferred by the policy or contract and the sum had been paid as consideration for the surrender (and if the policy is a qualifying policy, whether or not the premiums under it are eligible for relief under section 266, those results shall follow under section 269, whether or not a gain would be treated as arising on the surrender).

(2) Subsection (1) above does not apply—
    (*a*) in relation to a policy if—
        (i) it is a qualifying policy; and
        (ii) either interest at a commercial rate is payable on the sum lent or the sum is lent to a full-time employee of the body issuing the policy for the purpose of assisting him in the purchase or improvement of a dwelling used or to be used as his only or main residence; or
    (*b*) in relation to a contract if and to the extent that interest on the sum lent is eligible for relief under section 353 by virtue of section 365.

Former enactments.—FA 1975, Sch. 2, para. 16(1), (3); FA 1976, s. 35.

272. Collection of sums payable under sections 268 and 269

(1) Any body by whom a policy to which section 268 or 269 applies has been issued shall, within 30 days of the end of each period of 12 months ending with 31st March in every year, make a return to the collector of the sums which, in that period, have become payable by it under either of those sections.

(2) Any sum which is to be included in a return made under subsection (1) above shall be due at the time by which the return is to be made and shall be paid without being demanded.

(3) Where any sum which was or ought to have been included in such a return is not paid by the end of the period for which the return was to be made, it may be recovered by an assessment as if it were income tax for the year of assessment in which that period ends; and where it appears to the inspector that a sum which ought to have been so included had not been included or that a return is not correct he may make such an assessment to the best of his judgment.

(4) All the provisions of the Income Tax Acts relating to the assessment and collection of tax, interest on unpaid tax, appeals and penalties shall, with the necessary modifications, apply in relation to sums due under this section; and for the purposes of those provisions so far as they relate to interest on unpaid tax, a sum assessed in pursuance of this section shall be treated as having been payable when it would have been payable had it been included in a return under subsection (1) above.

(5) Where, on an appeal against an assessment made in pursuance of this section, it is determined that a greater sum has been assessed than was payable, the excess, if paid, shall be repaid.

(6) Where a body has paid a sum which is payable under section 268 or 269 it shall give within 30 days to the person by whom the sum is, under section 270(4), treated as received a statement specifying that sum and showing how it has been arrived at.

(7) The Board or an inspector may, by notice served on the body by whom a policy to which

269. Surrender etc. of policies after four years

(1) Where a policy of life insurance to which this section applies has been issued and, in the fifth or any later year from the making of the insurance in respect of which it was issued, either of the following events happens, that is to say—

    (*a*) the surrender of the whole or part of the rights conferred by the policy; and
    (*b*) the falling due (otherwise than on death or maturity) of a sum payable in pursuance of a right conferred by the policy to participate in profits;

then, if either of those events has happened before, the body by whom the policy was issued shall pay to the Board, out of the sums payable by reason of the surrender, or, as the case may be, out of the sum falling due, a sum determined in accordance with the following provisions of this section.

(2) The sum payable under subsection (1) above shall, subject to the following provisions of this section, be equal to the applicable percentage of the lower of the following—

    (*a*) the total of the premiums which are payable in that year under the policy; and
    (*b*) the sums payable by reason of the surrender or, as the case may be, the sum falling due;

and the percentage to be applied for this purpose shall be a percentage equal to that mentioned in section 266(5)(*a*) as in force for the year of assessment in which the event happens.

(3) Where, after a sum has become payable under subsection (1) above, and within the same year from the making of the insurance, another such event happens as is mentioned therein, the sums payable under that subsection in respect of both or all of the events shall not exceed the applicable percentage of the total mentioned in subsection (2)(*a*) above.

(4) Where, on the happening of an event in the fifth or any later year from the making of the insurance, any sum is payable under subsection (1) of section 268 as applied by subsection (6) of that section as well as under subsection (1) above, subsection (2) above shall apply as if the sums or sum mentioned in paragraph (*b*) thereof were reduced by the sum payable under that section.

(5) This section applies to any policy of life insurance which is a qualifying policy unless—

    (*a*) it is a policy in respect of the premiums on which relief under section 266 is not available by virtue of subsection (3)(*c*) of that section; or
    (*b*) it is a policy issued in the course of an industrial insurance business; or
    (*c*) it was issued in respect of an insurance made before 27th March 1974.

Former enactments.—FA 1975, s. 8; FA 1976, Sch. 4, para. 19(2) FA 1984, s. 72(5).

270. Provisions supplementary to sections 268 and 269

(1) Where on the happening of an event in relation to a policy of life insurance a sum is payable under section 268 or 269, relief under section 266 in respect of the relevant premiums paid under the policy shall be reduced by the sum so payable or, as the case may be, by so much of the sum as does not exceed the amount of that relief (or as does not exceed so much of that amount as remains after any previous reduction under this section).

(2) For the purposes of this section the relevant premiums are—

    (*a*) in relation to a sum payable under section 268, the premiums payable under the policy up to the happening of the event by reason of which the sum is payable; and
    (*b*) in relation to a sum payable under section 269, the premiums payable in the year (from the making of the insurance) in which the event happens by reason of which the sum is payable.

(3) Where the relevant premiums are payable in more than one year of assessment the reduction in relief under this section shall, so far as possible, reduce relief for an earlier year of assessment before reducing relief for a later one.

(4) Any sum paid under section 268 or 269 by reason of any event shall be treated—

    (*a*) as between the parties, as received by the person by whom the premiums under the policy were paid; and
    (*b*) for the purposes of section 266, as a sum paid by that person in satisfaction of his liability resulting from the reduction of relief under this section;

and where that sum exceeds that liability he shall be entitled, on a claim made by him not

the body by whom the policy was issued shall pay to the Board, out of the sums payable by reason of the surrender or, as the case may be, out of the sum falling due or out of the fund available to pay the sums which will be due on death or on the maturity of the policy, a sum determined in accordance with the following provisions of this section, unless the body is wound up and the event is a surrender or conversion effected in connection with the winding-up.

(2) The sum payable under subsection (1) above shall, subject to the following provisions of this section, be equal to the lower of the following, that is to say—

(a) the appropriate percentage of the premiums payable under the policy up to the happening of the event; and
(b) the surrender value of the policy at the time of the happening of the event less the complementary percentage of the premiums mentioned in paragraph (a) above.

(3) If the event is one of those mentioned below, the sum payable to the Board shall not exceed the following limit, that is to say—

(a) if it is the surrender of part of the rights conferred by the policy, the value of the rights surrendered at the time of the surrender;
(b) if it is the conversion of the policy into a partly paid-up policy, the surrender value at the time of the conversion, of so much of the policy as is paid up; and
(c) if it is the falling due of a sum, that sum.

(4) If the event was preceded by the happening of such an event as is mentioned in subsection (1) above, subsection (2) above shall apply—

(a) as if the lower of the amounts mentioned therein were reduced by the sum paid under this section in respect of the earlier event; and
(b) if the earlier event was such an event as is mentioned in paragraph (a) or (c) of subsection (3) above, as if the surrender value of the policy were increased by the amount which, under that paragraph, limited or might have limited the sum payable under this section in respect of the earlier event.

(5) For the purposes of this section the appropriate percentage, in relation to any event, is the percentage equal to the following fraction of the percentage found by doubling that mentioned in section 266(5)(a) as in force for the year of assessment in which the event happened, that is to say—

(a) if the event happens in the first two of the four years mentioned in subsection (1) above, three-sixths;
(b) if it happens in the third of those years, two-sixths; and
(c) if it happens in the last of those years, one-sixth;

and the complementary percentage, in relation to any event, is 100 per cent. less the appropriate percentage.

(6) Where the annual amount of the premiums payable under a policy of life insurance is at any time increased (whether under the policy or by any contract made after its issue) so as to exceed by more than 25 per cent.—

(a) if the insurance was made on or before 26th March 1974, the annual amount as at that date, or
(b) in the case of any other insurance, the first annual amount so payable,

the additional rights attributable to the excess shall be treated for the purposes of this section as conferred by a new policy issued in respect of an insurance made at that time, and the excess shall be treated as premiums payable under the new policy.

(7) This section applies to any policy of life insurance which is a qualifying policy unless—

(a) it is a policy in respect of the premiums on which relief under section 266 is not available by virtue of subsection (3)(c) of that section; or
(b) it is a policy of life insurance issued in connection with an approved scheme, as defined in Chapter I of Part XIV;

and in relation to a policy of life insurance issued in respect of an insurance made before 27th March 1974 applies only in accordance with subsection (6) above.

Former enactments.—FA 1975, s. 7; FA 1976, Sch. 4, para. 19(1); FA 1984, s. 72(5).

(8) Where the individual is not resident in the United Kingdom but is entitled to relief by virtue of section 278(2), subsection (4) above shall not apply but (subject to section 278(3)) the like relief shall be given to him under paragraph 6 of Schedule 14.

(9) Subsections (5) and (8) above shall apply in relation to an individual who is not resident in the United Kingdom but is a member of the armed forces of the Crown or the wife (but not the husband) of such a member as if the individual were so resident.

(10) Subsection (3)(*b*) above shall not apply—

> (*a*) to any policy of life insurance having as its sole object the provision on an individual's death or disability of a sum substantially the same as any amount then outstanding under a mortgage of his residence, or of any premises occupied by him for the purposes of a business, being a mortgage the principal amount secured by which is repayable by instalments payable annually or at shorter regular intervals; or
> (*b*) to any policy of life insurance issued in connection with an approved scheme as defined in Chapter I of Part XIV.

In the application of this subsection to Scotland, for any reference to a mortgage there shall be substituted a reference to a heritable security within the meaning of the Conveyancing (Scotland) Act 1924 (but including a security constituted by ex facie absolute disposition or assignation).

(11) Subsection (3)(*a*) and (*d*) above shall not affect premiums payable—

> (*a*) under policies or contracts made in connection with any superannuation or bona fide pension scheme for the benefit of the employees of any employer, or of persons engaged in any particular trade, profession, vocation or business, or for the benefit of the wife or widow of any such employee or person or of his children or other dependants, or
> (*b*) under policies taken out by teachers in the schools known in the year 1918 as secondary schools, pending the establishment of a superannuation or pension scheme for those teachers.

(12) Schedule 14 shall have effect for the purpose of modifying, for certain cases, and supplementing the provisions of this section.

Former enactments.—Sub-s. (1): TA 1970, s. 19(1); FA 1976, Sch. 4, para. 3(1).
Sub-s. (2): TA 1970, s. 19(2); FA 1976, s. 36(5), Sch. 4, para. 3(2); Insurance Companies Act 1982, Sch. 5, para. 10.
Sub-s. (3)(*a*): TA 1970, s. 19(3)(*a*).
Sub-s. (3)(*b*): TA 1970, s. 19(4).
Sub-s. (3)(*c*): FA 1984, s. 72(1).
Sub-s. (3)(*d*): TA 1970, s. 19(3)(*b*).
Sub-ss. (4), (5): FA 1976, Sch. 4, paras. 4(1), 5; FA 1978, Sch. 3, para. 2; FA 1980, s. 29(2)(*b*).
Sub-s. (6): FA 1978, Sch. 3, para. 11.
Sub-s. (7): FA 1978, Sch. 3, para 12; FA 1981, s. 33.
Sub-s. (8): FA 1976, Sch. 4, para. 4(2).
Sub-s. (9): FA 1976, Sch. 4, para. 5A; FA 1978, Sch. 3, para. 5; Armed Forces Act 1981, Sch. 3, para. 1.
Sub-s. (10): TA 1970, s. 19(4)(*a*), (*c*); FA 1971, Sch. 3, para. 11.
Sub-s. (11): TA 1970, s. 19(3)(i), (ii).
Note.—See **Prospective Legislation Notes** (Married Couples).
Amendments.—[1] "12·5 per cent." in sub-s. (5)(*a*) substituted by FA 1988, s. 29 with effect from 6 April 1989.

267. Qualifying policies

Schedule 15, Part I of which contains the basic rules for determining whether or not a policy is a qualifying policy, Part II of which makes provision for the certification etc. of policies as qualifying policies and Part III of which modifies Parts I and II in their application to certain policies issued by non-resident companies, shall have effect for the purpose of determining whether or not a policy is a qualifying policy; and, accordingly, any reference in this Act to a qualifying policy shall be construed in accordance with that Schedule.

268. Early conversion or surrender of life policies

(1) Where a policy of life insurance to which this section applies has been issued and, within four years from the making of the insurance in respect of which it was issued, any of the following events happens, that is to say—

> (*a*) the surrender of the whole or part of the rights conferred by the policy;
> (*b*) the falling due (otherwise than on death) of a sum payable in pursuance of a right conferred by the policy to participate in profits; and
> (*c*) the conversion of the policy into a paid-up or partly paid-up policy;

266. Life assurance premiums

(1) Subject to the provisions of this section, sections 274 and 619(6) and Schedules 14 and 15, an individual who pays any such premium as is specified in subsection (2) below or makes a payment falling within subsection (7) below shall (without making any claim) be entitled to relief under this section.

(2) The premiums referred to in subsection (1) above are any premiums paid by an individual under a policy of insurance or contract for a deferred annuity, where—

    (*a*) the payments are made to—

        (i) any insurance company legally established in the United Kingdom or any branch in the United Kingdom of an insurance company lawfully carrying on in the United Kingdom life assurance business (as defined in section 431); or

        (ii) underwriters being members of Lloyd's who comply with the requirements set forth in section 83 of the Insurance Companies Act 1982; or

        (iii) a registered friendly society; or

        (iv) in the case of a deferred annuity, the National Debt Commissioners; and

    (*b*) the insurance or, as the case may be, the deferred annuity is on the life of the individual or on the life of his spouse; and

    (*c*) the insurance or contract was made by him or his spouse.

(3) Subject to subsections (7), (10) and (11) below, no relief under this section shall be given—

    (*a*) except in respect of premiums payable under policies for securing a capital sum on death, whether in conjunction with any other benefit or not;

    (*b*) in respect of premiums payable under any policy issued in respect of an insurance made after 19th March 1968 unless the policy is a qualifying policy;

    (*c*) in respect of premiums payable under any policy issued in respect of an insurance made after 13th March 1984, except where the relief relates to part only of any such payment as falls within subsection (6) below;

    (*d*) in respect of premiums payable during the period of deferment in respect of a policy of deferred assurance.

(4) Subject to subsections (6) to (8) below, relief under this section in respect of any premiums paid by an individual in a year of assessment shall be given by making good to the person to whom they are paid any deficiency arising from the deductions authorised under subsection (5) below; and this section and Schedule 14 shall have effect in relation to any premium or part of a premium which is paid otherwise than in the year of assessment in which it becomes due and payable as if it were paid in that year.

(5) Subject to the provisions of Schedule 14—

    (*a*) an individual resident in the United Kingdom who is entitled to relief under this section in respect of any premium may deduct from any payment in respect of the premium and retain an amount equal to [12·5 per cent.]¹ of the payment; and

    (*b*) the person to whom the payment is made shall accept the amount paid after the deduction in discharge of the individual's liability to the same extent as if the deduction had not been made and may recover the deficiency from the Board.

(6) Where—

    (*a*) a person is entitled to relief under this section in respect of part only of a payment made to a registered friendly society; and

    (*b*) the insurance or contract was made by the society in the course of tax exempt life or endowment business (as defined in section 466(2)),

subsection (4) above shall not apply with respect to that relief but there shall be deducted from his total income an amount equal to one-half of that part of the payment.

(7) Where a person makes a payment to a trade union as defined in section 28(1) of the Trade Union and Labour Relations Act 1974, and part of that payment is attributable to the provision of superannuation, life insurance or funeral benefits, he shall be entitled to relief under this section in respect of that part of the payment, but—

    (*a*) subsection (4) above shall not apply; and

    (*b*) there shall be deducted from his total income an amount equal to one-half of that part of the payment.

This subsection shall also apply in relation to any payment made to an organisation of persons in police service but only where the annual amount of the part of the payment attributable to the provision of the benefits in question is £20 or more.

section . . .¹ 259, and, in that case, the marriage shall also be disregarded for the purposes of any claim for that year under section 257.

Former enactment.—TA 1970, s. 15.
Note.—See **Prospective Legislation Notes** (Married Couples).
Amendments.—¹ Words repealed by FA 1988, Sch. 14, Pt. IV.

262. Widow's bereavement allowance

[Where a man dies in the year 1989–90 and for that year he is entitled to the higher (married person's) relief under section 257(1), or would be so entitled but for an election under section 261 or 287, his widow shall be entitled—

(*a*) for that year of assessment, to a deduction from her total income of an amount equal to the amount referred to in section 259(2), and
(*b*) (unless she marries again before the beginning of it) for the year 1990–91, to a deduction from her total income of an amount equal to the amount specified in section 257A(1) for that year.]¹

Former enactments.—TA 1970, s. 15A; FA 1980, ss. 23, 24(6); FA 1983, s. 15(1).
Note.—See **Prospective Legislation Notes** (Married Couples).
Amendments.—¹ This section substituted by FA 1988, Sch. 3, para. 7(1), (2).

263. Dependent relatives

Former enactments.—Sub-ss. (1), (2): TA 1970, s. 16(1), (2); FA 1973, s. 12(2).
Sub-s (3): TA 1970, s. 16(2A); F(No. 2)A 1979, Sch. 2, para. 2.
Sub-ss. (4), (5), (6): TA 1970, ss. 11(4), (5), 16(3); FA 1973, s. 12(2).
Sub-s. (7): TA 1970, s. 16(4).
Amendments.—This section repealed by FA 1988, s. 25(3) and Sch. 14, Pt. IV.

264. Claimant depending on services of a son or daughter

Former enactments.—TA 1970, s. 17; FA 1971, Sch. 6, para. 11; FA 1978, s. 19(5).
Amendments.—This section repealed by FA 1988, s. 25(3) and Sch. 14, Pt IV.

265. Relief for blind persons

(1) Subject to subsection (3) below, if the claimant proves—

(*a*) that he is a married man who for the year of assessment has his wife living with him, and that one of them was, and the other was not, a registered blind person for the whole or part of the year; or
(*b*) that, not being such a married man, he was a registered blind person for the whole or part of the year,

he shall be entitled to a deduction of £540 from his total income.

(2) Subject to subsection (3) below, if the claimant proves—

(*a*) that he is a married man who for the year of assessment has his wife living with him, and
(*b*) that he was a registered blind person for the whole or part of the year and his wife was also a registered blind person for the whole or part of the year,

he shall be entitled to a deduction of £1,080 from his total income.

(3) . . .¹

(4) In this section "registered blind person" means a person registered as a blind person in a register compiled under section 29 of the National Assistance Act 1948 or, in the case of a person ordinarily resident in Scotland or in Northern Ireland, a person who is a blind person within the meaning of section 64(1) of that Act.

Former enactments.—Sub-s. (1): TA 1970, s. 18(1); FA 1978, s. 19(6); FA 1981, s. 23(2); FA 1987, s. 28.
Sub-s. (2): TA 1970, s. 18(2)(*a*), (*b*); FA 1981, s. 23(3); FA 1987, s. 28.
Sub-s. (3): TA 1970, s. 18(5); FA 1978, s. 19(5).
Sub-s. (4): TA 1970, s. 18(6); FA 1987, Sch. 15, para. 2(3).
Note.—See **Prospective Legislation Notes** (Prospective Amendments and Married Couples).
Amendments.—¹ Sub-s. (3) repealed by FA 1988, Sch. 14, Pt. IV.

over the age of 16 at the commencement of the year which begins with his 16th birthday and over the age of 18 at the commencement of the year which begins with his 18th birthday.

Former enactments.—Sub-ss. (1), (2): TA 1970, s. 14(1), (2); FA 1976, s. 36(4); F(No. 2)A 1979, Sch. 1, para. 2(2); FA 1980, s. 24(6); FA 1987, s. 26(5).
Sub-s. (3): TA 1970, s. 14(3); F(No. 2)A 1979, Sch. 1, para. 2(3).
Sub-s. (4): TA 1970, s. 14(4); FA 1976, s. 36(4).
Sub-ss. (5)–(9): TA 1970, s. 14(5)–(9); F(No. 2)A 1979, Sch. 1, para. 2(4); FA 1987, Sch. 15, para. 2(2).
Note.—See **Prospective Legislation Notes** (Married Couples).
Amendments.—[1] Words in sub-s. (2) substituted by FA 1988, s. 30.
[2] Sub-s. (4A) inserted by FA 1988, s. 30 with effect from the year 1989–90.

260. Apportionment of relief under section 259

(1) Where for any year of assessment two or more individuals are entitled to relief under section 259 in connection with the same child—

  (*a*) the amount referred to in subsection (2) of that section shall be apportioned between them; and
  (*b*) the deduction to which each of them is entitled under that section shall, subject to subsection (2) below, be equal to so much of that amount as is apportioned to him.

(2) Where for any year of assessment amounts are apportioned to an individual under this section in respect of two or more children, the deduction to which he is entitled for that year under section 259 shall be equal to the sum of those amounts or the amount referred to in subsection (2) of that section, whichever is the less.

(3) Any amount required to be apportioned under this section shall be apportioned between the individuals concerned in such proportions as may be agreed between them or, in default of agreement, in proportion to the length of the periods for which the child in question is resident with them respectively in the year of assessment; and where the proportions are not so agreed, the apportionment shall be made by such body of General Commissioners, being the General Commissioners for a division in which one of the individuals resides, as the Board may direct, or, if none of the individuals resides in [the United Kingdom][1], by the Special Commissioners.

(4) Where a claim is made under section 259 and it appears that, if the claim is allowed, an apportionment will be necessary under this section, the Board may if they think fit direct that the claim itself shall be dealt with by any specified body of Commissioners which could under this section be directed to make the apportionment and that the same Commissioners shall also make any apportionment which proves to be necessary; and where a direction is given under this subsection no other body of Commissioners shall have jurisdiction to determine the claim.

(5) The Commissioners making any apportionment under this section shall hear and determine the case in like manner as an appeal, but any individual who is, or but for the provisions of this section would be, entitled to relief in connection with the child shall be entitled to appear and be heard by the Commissioners or to make representations to them in writing.

(6) For the purposes of this section an individual shall not be regarded as entitled to relief under section 259 for any year of assessment in connection with the same child as another individual if there is another child in connection with whom he, and he is alone, is entitled to relief under that section for that year.

Former enactments.—TA 1970, s. 14A; F(No. 2)A 1979, Sch. 1, para. 3; FA 1980, s. 24(6).
Cross references.—See TMA 1970, s. 58(3)(*b*), FA 1988, ss. 134(4), 135(2) (with effect from 3 April 1989, by virtue of FA 1988 (Commencement) Order 1989, S.I. 1989 No. 473, proceedings under sub-s. (3) of this section to be in Northern Ireland if the place given by certain rules in relation to the parties to the proceedings is in Northern Ireland).
Amendments.—[1] Words in sub-s. (3) substituted for the words "Great Britain" by FA 1988, s. 134(3), (4) with effect from 3 April 1989 by virtue of FA 1988 (Commencement) Order 1989, S.I. 1989 No. 473.

261. Claims under sections 258 and 259 for year of marriage

A man who becomes married during a year of assessment may by notice to the inspector elect that his marriage be disregarded for the purposes of any claim for that year under

Sub-s. (3): TA 1970, s. 12(1)(iii).
Sub-s. (4): TA 1970, s. 12(2).
Amendments.—This section repealed by FA 1988, s. 25(3) and Sch. 14, Pt. IV.

259. Additional relief in respect of children

(1) This section applies—

(*a*) to any individual who is not entitled for the year of assessment to the higher (married persons) relief under section 257(1); and
(*b*) to any married man who is entitled for the year of assessment to that higher relief but whose wife was throughout that year totally incapacitated by physical or mental infirmity.

(2) Subject to subsections (3) [to (4A)]¹ below and to section 260, if the claimant, being a person to whom this section applies, proves in the case of a year of assessment that a qualifying child is resident with him for the whole or part of the year, he shall be entitled to a deduction from his total income of an amount equal to the difference between the higher (married persons) relief and the lower (single persons) relief under subsection (1) of section 257 as it applies to persons not falling within subsection (2) or (3) of that section.

(3) A claimant is entitled to only one deduction under subsection (2) above for any year of assessment irrespective of the number of qualifying children resident with him in that year.

(4) A person to whom this section applies by virtue of subsection (1)(*a*) above shall not be entitled to relief under this section for a year of assessment during any part of which that person is married and living with his or her spouse unless the child in connection with whom the relief is claimed is resident with that person during a part of the year in which that person is not married and living with his or her spouse.

[(4A) Where—

(*a*) a man and a woman who are not married to each other live together as husband and wife for the whole or any part of a year of assessment, and
(*b*) apart from this subsection each of them would on making a claim be entitled to a deduction under subsection (2) above,

neither of them shall be entitled to such a deduction except in respect of the youngest of the children concerned (that is to say, the children in respect of whom either would otherwise be entitled to a deduction).]²

(5) For the purposes of this section a qualifying child means, in relation to any claimant and any year of assessment, a child who—

(*a*) is born in, or is under the age of 16 years at the commencement of, the year or, being over that age at the commencement of that year, is receiving full-time instruction at any university, college, school or other educational establishment; and
(*b*) is a child of the claimant or, not being such a child, is born in, or is under the age of 18 years at the commencement of, the year and maintained for the whole or part of that year by the claimant at his own expense.

(6) In subsection (5)(*a*) above the reference to a child receiving full-time instruction at an educational establishment includes a reference to a child undergoing training by any person ("the employer") for any trade, profession or vocation in such circumstances that the child is required to devote the whole of his time to the training for a period of not less than two years.

For the purposes of a claim in connection with a child undergoing training, the inspector may require the employer to furnish particulars with respect to the training of the child in such form as may be prescribed by the Board.

(7) If any question arises under this section whether a child is receiving full-time instruction at an educational establishment, the Board may consult the Secretary of State or the Department of Education for Northern Ireland.

(8) In subsection (5)(*b*) above the reference to a child of the claimant includes a reference to a stepchild of his, an illegitimate child of his if he has married the other parent after the child's birth and an adopted child of his if the child was under the age of 18 years when he was adopted.

(9) Notwithstanding anything in section 9 of the Family Law Reform Act 1969 or section 5 of the Age of Majority Act (Northern Ireland) 1969 or any rule of law in Scotland, for the purposes of subsection (5) above a child whose birthday falls on 6 April shall be taken to be

such a case subsection (2) or (3), as the case may be, shall apply as if the sums mentioned in it were reduced by [one half][3] of the excess of that total income over £9,800.

(6) If the total income of the claimant includes any earned income of his wife, the deduction to be allowed under this section shall be increased by the amount of that earned income or by [£2,785][1], whichever is the less.

(7) For the purposes of subsection (6) above—

(a) any earned income of the claimant's wife arising in respect of any pension, superannuation or other allowance, deferred pay or compensation for loss of office, given in respect of his past services in any office or employment, shall be deemed not to be earned income of his wife; and
(b) no payment of benefit under the Social Security Acts 1975 or the Social Security (Northern Ireland) Acts 1975 except—

(i) a Category A retirement pension (exclusive of any increase under section 10 of the Social Security Pensions Act 1975 or Article 12 of the Social Security Pensions (Northern Ireland) Order 1975);
(ii) unemployment benefit, and
(iii) invalid care allowance,

shall be treated as earned income.

(8) Subsection (1) above shall have effect in relation to any claim by a man who becomes married in the year of assessment for which the claim is made and has not previously in that year been entitled to relief under paragraph (a) of that subsection, as if the sum specified in that paragraph were reduced, for each month of that year ending before the date of the marriage, by one-twelfth of the amount by which it exceeds the sum specified in paragraph (b) of that subsection.

In this subsection "month" means a month beginning with the 6th day of a month of the calendar year.

(9) If the retail prices index for the month of December preceding a year of assessment is higher than it was for the previous December, then, unless Parliament otherwise determines, this section shall apply for that year as if for each amount specified in subsections (1) to (6) above as they applied for the previous year (whether by virtue of this subsection or otherwise) there were substituted an amount arrived at by increasing the amount for the previous year by the same percentage as the percentage increase in the retail prices index, and if—

(a) in the case of an amount specified in subsection (5) above, the result is not a multiple of £100, rounding it up to the nearest amount which is such a multiple;
(b) in the case of any other amount, the increase is not a multiple of £10, rounding the increase up to the nearest amount which is such a multiple.

(10) Subsection (9) above shall not require any change to be made in the amounts deductible or repayable under section 203 between the beginning of a year of assessment and [18th May][4] in that year.

(11) The Treasury shall in each year of assessment make an order specifying the amounts which by virtue of subsection (9) above will be treated as specified for the following year of assessment in subsections (1) to (6) above.

Former enactments.—Sub-s. (1): TA 1970, s. 8(1) FA 1971, Sch. 6, para. 5; Income Tax (Indexation) Order 1987, S.I. 1987 No. 434.
Sub-s. (2): TA 1970, s. 8(1A); F(No. 2)A 1975, s. 31(1); FA 1977, s. 22(1)(c), S.I. 1987 No. 434.
Sub-ss. (3), (4): FA 1987, s. 26(1)–(3).
Sub-s. (5): TA 1970, s. 8(1B); F(No. 2)A 1975, s. 31(1); FA 1987, s. 26(5), S.I. 1987 No. 434.
Sub-ss. (6), (7): TA 1970, s. 8(2); FA 1971, Sch. 6, para. 5; F(No. 2)A 1979, Sch. 2, para. 1; FA 1981, s. 27(9); FA 1987, s. 27(1); S.I. 1987 No. 434.
Sub-s. (8): TA 1970, s. 8(3); FA 1970, s. 14(1)(a)(iv).
Sub-ss. (9)–(11): FA 1980, s. 24(5), (7), (9); FA 1987, s. 26(7).
Note.—See **Prospective Legislation Notes** (Married Couples).
Cross references.—See FA 1988, s. 38 (maintenance payments under existing obligations: 1989–90 onwards);
Amendments.—[1] Amounts in sub-ss. (1)–(3), (5), (6) substituted by the Income Tax (Indexation) Order 1989, S.I. 1989 No 467.
[2] Age in sub-s. (3) substituted by FA 1989, s. 31.
[3] Fraction in sub-s. (5) substituted by *ibid*.
[4] Date in sub-s. (10) substituted for "5th May" by virtue of FA 1989, s. 32 for the year 1989–90.

258. Widower's or widow's housekeeper

Former enactments.—Sub-ss. (1), (2): TA 1970, s. 12(1)(i), (ii), (iv); FA 1971, s. 15(5), Sch. 6, para. 7; FA 1978, s. 19(2)(b).

PART VII

GENERAL PROVISIONS RELATING TO TAXATION OF INCOME OF INDIVIDUALS

CHAPTER I

PERSONAL RELIEFS

The reliefs

256. General

An individual who makes a claim in that behalf or, in the case of relief under section 266, who satisfies the conditions of that section, shall be entitled to such relief as is specified in sections 257 to 274, subject however to the provisions of sections 275 to 278 and 287 and 288.

Former enactments.—TA 1970, s. 5; FA 1971, Sch. 4, para. 3; F(No. 2)A 1975, s. 31(3); FA 1976, Sch. 4, paras. 3(1), 18(1).
Note.—See **Prospective Legislation Notes** (Married Couples).

257. Personal relief

(1) Subject to the provisions of this section and section 261, the claimant shall be entitled—

(*a*) if he proves—

(i) that for the year of assessment he has his wife living with him, or
(ii) that his wife is wholly maintained by him during the year of assessment, and that he is not entitled in computing the amount of his income for that year for income tax purposes to make any deduction in respect of the sums paid for the maintenance of his wife,

to a deduction of [£4,375][1] from his total income;
(*b*) in any other case, to a deduction of [£2,785][1] from his total income.

(2) Subject to the provisions of this section, subsection (1) above shall have effect—

(*a*) in relation to a claim by a person who proves that he or his wife was at any time within the year of assessment of the age of 65 or upwards, as if the sum specified in paragraph (*a*) were [£5,385][1]; and
(*b*) in relation to a claim by a person who proves that he was at any time within the year of assessment of the age of 65 or upwards, as if the sum specified in paragraph (*b*) were [£3,400][1];

and for the purposes of this subsection a person who would have been of the age of 65 or upwards within the year of assessment if he had not died in the course of it shall be treated as having been of that age within that year.

(3) Subject to the provisions of this section, subsection (1) above shall have effect—

(*a*) in relation to a claim by a person who proves that he or his wife was at any time within the year of assessment of the age of [75][2] or upwards, as if the sum specified in paragraph (*a*) were [£5,565][1]; and
(*b*) in relation to a claim by a person who proves that he was at any time within the year of assessment of the age of [75][2] or upwards, as if the sum specified in paragraph (*b*) were [£3,540][1];

and for the purposes of this subsection, a person who would have been of the age of [75][2] or upwards within the year of assessment if he had not died in the course of it shall be treated as having been of that age within that year.

(4) For any year of assessment for which a person is entitled to increased personal relief by virtue of subsection (3) above, he shall not be entitled to increased relief under subsection (2) above.

(5) Where the claimant's total income for the year of assessment exceeds [£11,400][1], subsections (2) and (3) above shall not apply except in a case where the deduction to be allowed under subsection (1) above will be increased by virtue of this subsection; and in

(2) Subsection (1) above shall apply with the necessary modifications to a dividend partly at a gross rate or of a gross amount and shall apply to any distribution other than a dividend as it applies to a dividend.

Former enactments.—FA 1972, Sch. 23, para. 18; FA 1976, s. 46(1).

distributed out of assets of the company (whether in cash or otherwise) in respect of shares in or securities of another company in the group.

(4) Nothing in subsections (2) and (3) above shall require a company to be treated as making a distribution to any other company which is in the same group and is resident in the United Kingdom.

(5) Where share capital has been issued at a premium representing new consideration, any part of that premium afterwards applied in paying up share capital shall be treated as new consideration also for that share capital, except in so far as the premium has been taken into account under section 211(5) so as to enable a distribution to be treated as a repayment of share capital.

(6) Subject to subsection (7) below, no consideration derived from the value of any share capital or security of a company, or from voting or other rights in a company, shall be regarded for the purposes of this Part as new consideration received by the company unless the consideration consists of—

    (*a*) money or value received from the company as a qualifying distribution;
    (*b*) money received from the company as a payment which for those purposes constitutes a repayment of that share capital or of the principal secured by the security; or
    (*c*) the giving up of the right to the share capital or security on its cancellation, extinguishment or acquisition by the company.

(7) No amount shall be regarded as new consideration by virtue of subsection (6)(*b*) or (*c*) above in so far as it exceeds any new consideration received by the company for the issue of the share capital or security in question or, in the case of share capital which constituted a qualifying distribution on issue, the nominal value of that share capital.

(8) Where two or more companies enter into arrangements to make distributions to each other's members, all parties concerned (however many) may for the purposes of this Part be treated as if anything done by any one of those companies had been done by any of the others.

(9) A distribution shall be treated under this Part as made, or consideration as provided, out of assets of a company if the cost falls on the company.

(10) References in this Part to issuing share capital as paid up apply also to the paying up of any issued share capital.

(11) Where securities are issued at a price less than the amount repayable on them, and are not quoted on a recognised stock exchange, the principal secured shall not be taken for the purposes of this Part to exceed the issue price, unless the securities are issued on terms reasonably comparable with the terms of issue of securities so quoted.

(12) For the purposes of this Part a thing is to be regarded as done in respect of a share if it is done to a person as being the holder of the share, or as having at a particular time been the holder, or is done in pursuance of a right granted or offer made in respect of a share; and anything done in respect of shares by reference to share holdings at a particular time is to be regarded as done to the then holders of the shares or the personal representatives of any share holder then dead.

This subsection shall apply in relation to securities as it applies in relation to shares.

Former enactments.—Sub-s. (1): TA 1970, s. 237(1), (3), (5); FA 1972, Sch. 22, para. 10(4).
Sub-ss. (2)–(4): FA 1972, Sch. 22, para. 10(1)–(3).
Sub-s. (5): TA 1970, s. 237(1).
Sub-ss. (6), (7): FA 1972, Sch. 22, para 8.
Sub-s. (8): FA 1972, Sch. 22, para. 9.
Sub-s. (9): TA 1970, s. 237(2).
Sub-s. (10): TA 1970, s. 237(4).
Sub-s. (11): TA 1970, s. 237(6).
Sub-s. (12): TA 1970, s. 237(7).

255. "Gross rate" and "gross amount" of distributions to include ACT

(1) Where any right or obligation created before 6th April 1973 is expressed by reference to a dividend at a gross rate or of a gross amount, that right or obligation shall continue to have effect, in relation to a dividend payable on or after that date, as if the reference were to a dividend of an amount which, when there is added to it such proportion thereof as corresponds to the rate of advance corporation tax in force on that date, that is to say, 6th April 1973, is equal to a dividend at that gross rate or of that gross amount.

(5) The Management Act shall apply to any assessment under this section for recovering a payment of tax credit or interest on such a payment as if it were an assessment to income tax for the year of assessment, or in the case of a company, corporation tax for the accounting period, in respect of which the payment was claimed, and as if that payment represented a loss of tax to the Crown; and any sum charged by any such assessment shall, subject to any appeal against the assessment, be due within 14 days after the issue of the notice of assessment.

Former enactments.—FA 1972, s. 102; F(No. 2)A 1987, s. 88(5)–(7).
Cross references.—See FA 1989, s. 157 (transitional provisions in respect of a charge of interest on corporation tax assessed under sub-s. (1) above for the period from 14 March 1989 to an appointed date).

253. Power to modify or replace section 234(5) to (9) and Schedule 13

(1) The Board may by regulations—

(a) modify, supplement or replace any of the provisions of subsections (5) to (9) of section 234 for the purpose of requiring companies resident in the United Kingdom to make returns and give information to the inspector in respect of distributions made by them, whether before or after the passing of this Act, which are not qualifying distributions;
(b) modify, supplement or replace any of the provisions of Schedule 13 for the purpose of regulating the time and manner in which advance corporation tax is to be accounted for and paid or the manner in which effect is to be given to section 241(1) to (3);

and references in this Act and in any other enactment to section 234(5) to (9) and to Schedule 13 shall be construed as including references to any such regulations.

(2) Without prejudice to the generality of subsection (1) above, regulations under that subsection may, in relation to advance corporation tax, modify any provision of Parts II to VI of the Management Act or apply any such provision with or without modifications.

(3) Regulations under this section may—

(a) make different provision for different descriptions of companies and for different circumstances and may authorise the Board, where in their opinion there are special circumstances justifying it, to make special arrangements as respects advance corporation tax or the repayment of income tax borne by a company or the payment to a company of amounts in respect of any tax credit to which it is entitled;
(b) include such transitional and other supplemental provisions as appear to the Board to be expedient or necessary.

(4) The Board shall not make any regulations under this section unless a draft of them has been laid before and approved by a resolution of the House of Commons.

Former enactment.—FA 1972, s. 108.

254. Interpretation of Part VI

(1) In this Part, except where the context otherwise requires—

"new consideration" means, subject to subsections (5) and (6) below, consideration not provided directly or indirectly out of the assets of the company, and in particular does not include amounts retained by the company by way of captitalising a distribution;
"security" includes securities not creating or evidencing a charge on assets, and interest paid by a company on money advanced without the issue of a security for the advance, or other consideration given by a company for the use of money so advanced, shall be treated as if paid or given in respect of a security issued for the advance by the company;
"share" includes stock, and any other interest of a member in a company;

and in this section "a 90 per cent. group" means a company and all of its 90 per cent. subsidiaries.

(2) In this Part, the expression "in respect of shares in the company" and "in respect of securities of the company", in relation to a company which is a member of a 90 per cent. group, mean respectively in respect of shares in that company or any other company in the group and in respect of securities of that company or any other company in the group.

(3) Without prejudice to section 209(2)(b) as extended by subsection (2) above, in relation to a company which is a member of a 90 per cent. group, "distribution" includes anything

(3) In subsection (2) above—

"the relevant cash dividend", in a case falling within subsection (2)(*a*)(i) above, means the cash dividend mentioned in section 249(1)(*a*) or, in a case falling within subsection (2)(*a*)(ii) above, means the cash dividend there mentioned (subject to subsection (4) below);

"the relevant date", in the case of share capital listed in the Stock Exchange Daily Official List, means the date of first dealing and, in the case of share capital not so listed, means the due date of issue; and

"market value", in relation to any share capital in a company, means, subject to the provisions applied by subsections (5) and (6) below, the price which that share capital might reasonably be expected to fetch on a sale in the open market.

(4) Where, in a case falling within subsection (2)(*a*)(ii) above, the company on the occasion on which it issues the share capital in question also issues a dividend in cash ("the accompanying cash dividend") in respect of the shares in the company in respect of which that share capital is issued, "the relevant cash dividend" means the cash dividend mentioned in subsection (2)(*a*)(ii) above reduced by the amount of the accompanying cash dividend.

(5) Section 150(3) of the 1979 Act (market value of shares or securities listed in the Stock Exchange Daily Official List) shall apply for the purposes of subsection (3) above as it applies for the purposes of that Act.

(6) In the case of shares or securities which are not quoted on a recognised stock exchange at the time when their market value for the purposes of subsection (2) above falls to be determined, subsection (3) of section 152 of the 1979 Act shall apply with respect to the determination of their market value for those purposes as it applies with respect to a determination falling within subsection (1) of that section.

Former enactments.—Sub-s. (1): F(No. 2)A 1975, s. 34(8)(*a*)–(*d*).
Sub-s. (2): F(No. 2)A 1975, Sch. 8, para 1(1)–(3).
Sub-s. (3): F(No. 2)A 1975, Sch. 8, paras. 1(4), 2(1).
Sub-s. (4): F(No. 2)A 1975, Sch. 8, para. 1(5).
Sub-ss. (5), (6): F(No. 2)A 1975, Sch. 8, para. 2(2), (3); CGTA 1979, Sch. 7.

Supplemental

252. Rectification of excessive set-off etc. of ACT or tax credit

(1) If an inspector discovers that—

(*a*) any set-off of advance corporation tax under section 239, or

(*b*) any set-off or payment of tax credit,

ought not to have been made, or is or has become excessive, the inspector may make any such assessments as may in his judgment be required for recovering any tax that ought to have been paid or any payment of tax credit that ought not to have been made and generally for securing that the resulting liabilities to tax (including interest on unpaid tax) of the persons concerned are what they would have been if only such set-offs or payments had been made as ought to have been made.

(2) In any case where—

(*a*) interest has been paid under section 826 on a payment of tax credit; and

(*b*) interest ought not to have been paid on that payment, either at all or to any extent,

an assessment under this section may be made for recovering any interest that ought not to have been paid.

(3) Where—

(*a*) an assessment is made under this section to recover tax credit paid to a company in respect of franked investment income received by the company in an accounting period; and

(*b*) more than one payment of tax credit has been made in respect of that period,

any sum recovered shall as far as possible be treated as relating to a payment of tax credit made later rather than to a payment made earlier.

(4) Subsections (2) and (3) above shall have effect in relation to payments of tax credit claimed in respect of accounting periods ending after such day as may be appointed for the purpose of those subsections by order made by the Treasury, not being earlier than 31st March 1992.

periods of three months ending with 31st March, 30th June, 30th September or 31st December which falls within that period;
(b) each part of the accounting period which is not a complete quarter and ends on the first (or only), or begins immediately after the last (or only), of those dates which falls within the accounting period;
(c) if none of those dates falls within the accounting period, the whole accounting period.

(3) A return for any period for which a return is required to be made under this section (a "return period") shall be made within 30 days from the end of that period.

(4) No return need be made under this section by a company for any period in which it has issued no relevant share capital.

(5) The return made by a company for any return period shall state—
(a) the date on which any relevant share capital issued by it in the period was issued and, if different, the date on which the company was first required to issue it;
(b) particulars of the terms on which any such share capital so issued by it was issued; and
(c) what is, in relation to any such share capital so issued, the appropriate amount in cash.

(6) If it appears to the inspector that a company ought to have, but has not, made a return for any return period, he may (notwithstanding subsection (4) above) by notice require the company to make a return for that period within such time (not being less than 30 days) as may be specified in the notice; and a return required to be made under this subsection shall, if such be the case, state that no relevant share capital was issued in the period in question.

(7) As regards any share capital included in a return made under this section by a company, the inspector may by notice require the company to furnish him within such time (not being less than 30 days) as may be specified in the notice with such further information relating thereto as he may reasonably require for the purposes of sections 230 and 249, this section and section 251 . . .[1].

Former enactments.—Sub-s. (1): F(No. 2)A 1975, Sch. 8, para. 7(1).
Sub-ss. (2), (3): F(No. 2)A 1975, Sch. 8, para. 7(2).
Sub-ss. (4)–(7): F(No. 2)A 1975, Sch 8, para. 7(3)–(6).
Amendments.—[1] Words in sub-s. (7) repealed by FA 1989, Sch. 17, Pt. V.

251. Interpretation of sections 249 and 250

(1) For the purposes of sections 249 and 250—
(a) "bonus share capital", in relation to a company, means share capital issued by the company otherwise than wholly for new consideration or such part of any share capital so issued as is not properly referable to new consideration;
(b) "due date of issue", in relation to any share capital issued by a company, means the earliest date on which the company was required to issue that share capital;
(c) an option to receive either a dividend in cash or additional share capital is conferred on a person not only where he is required to choose one or the other, but also where he is offered the one subject to a right, however expressed, to choose the other instead, and a person's abandonment of, or failure to exercise, such a right is to be treated as an exercise of the option;

and in section 254 the definition of "security" (in subsection (1)) and subsections (5) and (11) shall not apply.

(2) In sections 249 and 250 "the appropriate amount in cash", in relation to any share capital to which section 249 applies—
(a) in a case where that share capital was issued—
(i) in consequence of the exercise of an option such as is mentioned in section 249(1)(a); or
(ii) in a quantity which is determined by or determines the amount of a dividend in cash payable in respect of share capital in the company of a different class,

and where the relevant cash dividend is not substantially greater nor substantially less than the market value of that share capital on the relevant date, means the amount of the relevant cash dividend or, in a case in which section 249(3) applies, a due proportion of that amount;
(b) in a case where paragraph (a) above does not apply, means the market value of that share capital on the relevant date or, in a case in which section 249(3) applies, a due proportion of that market value.

(5) Where a company issues any share capital to the personal representatives of a deceased person as such during the administration period, the amount of income which, if the case had been one in which an individual was beneficially entitled to that share capital, that individual would have been treated under subsection (4) above as having received shall be deemed for the purposes of Part XVI to be part of the aggregate income of the estate of the deceased.

This subsection shall be construed as if it were contained in Part XVI.

(6) Where a company issues any share capital to trustees in respect of any shares in the company held by them (or by them and one or more other persons) in a case in which a dividend in cash paid to the trustees in respect of those shares would have been to any extent income to which section 686 applies, then—

(*a*) there shall be ascertained the amount of income which, if the case had been one in which an individual was beneficially entitled to that share capital, that individual would have been treated under subsection (4) above as having received; and

(*b*) income of that amount shall be treated as having arisen to the trustees on the due date of issue and as if it had been chargeable to income tax at the basic rate; and

(*c*) paragraphs (*a*) to (*c*) of subsection (4) above shall, with the substitution of "income" for "total income" and with all other necessary modifications, apply to that income as they apply to income which an individual is treated as having received under that subsection.

(7) This section does not apply to—

(*a*) any share capital of which the due date of issue is earlier than 6th April 1975; or

(*b*) any share capital issued by a company in respect of shares in the company which confer on the holder a right to convert or exchange them into or for shares in the company of a class which is not a relevant class for the purposes of subsection (1)(*b*) above where the due date of issue of the share capital so issued precedes the earlier of the following dates, namely—

(i) the day next after the earliest date after 5th August 1975 on which conversion or exchange of the shares could be effected by an exercise of that right; and

(ii) 6th April 1976 or, in the case of share capital issued by an investment trust, 6th April 1977.

(8) Where, in a case within subsection (4) above, the share capital in question is issued in respect of shares in the company issued before 6th April 1975 which confer on the holder a right to convert or exchange them into or for shares of a different class, this section shall not apply to so much (if any) of any bonus share capital issued by the company after 5th April 1976 in connection with an exercise of that right as would have been issued if that right had been exercised so as to effect the conversion or exchange of the shares on the earliest possible date after 5th April 1975; and subsections (5) and (6) above shall, where applicable, have effect accordingly.

(9) Where any bonus share capital falling within subsection (1)(*b*) above is after 5th April 1975 converted into or exchanged for shares in the company in question of a different class, then—

(*a*) this section shall not apply to any shares in the company issued, in connection with the conversion or exchange, in consideration of the cancellation, extinguishment or acquisition by the company of that bonus share capital; but

(*b*) section 230(*a*) and (*b*) shall apply to any shares in the company issued, in connection with the conversion or exchange, in consideration of the cancellation, extinguishment or acquisition by the company of so much of that bonus share capital as caused an individual to be treated under subsection (4) above as having received an amount of income on the due date of issue (or would have done so if the case had been one in which an individual was beneficially entitled to that share capital).

Former enactments.—Sub-ss. (1)–(6): F(No. 2)A 1975, s. 34(1)–(6).
Sub-ss. (7)–(9): F(No. 2)A 1975, s. 34(9)–(11).
Amendments.—[1] Words in sub-s. (3) repealed by FA 1989, Sch. 17, Pt. V.

250. Returns

(1) A company shall for each of its accounting periods make, in accordance with this section, returns to the inspector of all share capital to which section 249 applies ("relevant share capital") and which was issued by it in that period.

(2) A return shall be made for—

(*a*) each complete quarter falling within the accounting period, that is to say, each of the

in connection with that section and, subject to the provisions of such regulations, an election under that section ("the election") shall be made by notice to the inspector which shall set out the facts necessary to show that the companies are entitled to make the election.

(2) The election shall not have effect in relation to dividends or other payments paid less than three months after the giving of the notice and before the inspector is satisfied that the election is validly made, and has so notified the companies concerned; but shall be of no effect if within those three months the inspector notifies the companies concerned that the validity of the election is not established to his satisfaction.

(3) The companies concerned shall have the like right of appeal against any decision that the validity of the election is not established as the company paying the dividends or other payments would have if it were an assessment made on that company, and Part V of the Management Act shall apply accordingly.

(4) The election shall cease to be in force if at any time the companies cease to be entitled to make the election, and on that happening each company shall forthwith notify the inspector.

(5) Either of the companies making the election may at any time give the inspector notice revoking the election; and any such notice shall have effect from the time it is given.

(6) The Board shall not make any regulations under subsection (1) above unless a draft of them has been laid before and approved by a resolution of the House of Commons.

Former enactments.—Sub-s. (1): TA 1970, s. 257(1); FA 1972, s. 91(3).
Sub-ss. (2), (3): TA 1970, s. 257(2).
Sub-ss. (4), (5): TA 1970, s. 257(3), (4).
Sub-s. (6): FA 1972, s. 91(3).

Stock dividends

249. Stock dividends treated as income

(1) Subject to subsections (7) to (9) below, this section applies to any of the following share capital, that is to say—

(*a*) any share capital issued by a company resident in the United Kingdom in consequence of the exercise by any person of an option conferred on him to receive in respect of shares in the company (whether the last-mentioned shares were issued before or after the coming into force of this section) either a dividend in cash or additional share capital; and
(*b*) any bonus share capital issued by a company so resident in respect of any shares in the company of a relevant class (whether the last-mentioned shares were issued before or after the coming into force of this section).

(2) For the purposes of subsection (1)(*b*) above a class of shares is a relevant class if—

(*a*) shares of that class carry the right to receive bonus share capital in the company of the same or a different class; and
(*b*) that right is conferred by the terms on which shares of that class were originally issued or by those terms as subsequently extended or otherwise varied.

(3) Where a company issues any share capital in a case in which two or more persons are entitled thereto, the following provisions of this section . . .[1] shall have effect as if the company had issued to each of those persons separately a part of that share capital proportionate to his interest therein on the due date of issue.

(4) Subject to the following provisions of this section, where a company issues any share capital in a case in which an individual is beneficially entitled to that share capital, that individual shall be treated as having received on the due date of issue income of an amount which, if reduced by an amount equal to income tax on that income at the basic rate for the year of assessment in which that date fell, would be equal to the appropriate amount in cash, and—

(*a*) no assessment shall be made on the individual in respect of income tax at the basic rate on that income but he shall be treated as having paid tax at the basic rate on it or, if his total income is reduced by any deductions, on so much of it as is part of his total income as so reduced;
(*b*) no repayment shall be made of income tax treated by virtue of paragraph (*a*) above as having been paid; and
(*c*) that income shall be treated for the purposes of sections 348 and 349(1) as not brought into charge to income tax.

and that accounting period falls, in whole or in part, in the accounting period referred to in paragraph (*a*) above;

no relief shall be allowed on the principal claim or, as the case may be, any relief which was so allowed shall be withdrawn.

(8) Where any relief which has been allowed is withdrawn by virtue of subsection (6) or (7) above, all such adjustments shall be made, whether by way of assessment or otherwise, as may be necessary in consequence of that withdrawal.

Former enactments.—Sub-ss. (1)–(4): TA 1970, s. 262; FA 1984, s. 47(1).
Sub-ss. (5), (6): FA 1985, Sch. 9, para. 7(1), (2).
Sub-s. (7): FA 1985, Sch. 9, para. 8(1), (2).
Sub-s. (8): FA 1985, Sch. 9, para. 7(3), 8(3).

410. Arrangements for transfer of company to another group or consortium

(1) If, apart from this section, two companies ("the first company" and "the second company") would be treated as members of the same group of companies and—

(*a*) in an accounting period one of the two companies has trading losses or other amounts eligible for relief from corporation tax which it would, apart from this section, be entitled to surrender by way of group relief; and

(*b*) arrangements are in existence by virtue of which, at some time during or after the expiry of that accounting period—

(i) the first company or any successor of it could cease to be a member of the same group of companies as the second company and could become a member of the same group of companies as a third company; or
(ii) any person has or could obtain, or any persons together have or could obtain, control of the first company but not of the second; or
(iii) a third company could begin to carry on the whole or any part of a trade which, at any time in that accounting period, is carried on by the first company and could do so either as a successor of the first company or as a successor of another company which is not a third company but which, at some time during or after the expiry of that accounting period, has begun to carry on the whole or any part of that trade;

then, for the purposes of this Chapter, the first company shall be treated as not being a member of the same group of companies as the second company.

(2) If a trading company is owned by a consortium or is a 90 per cent. subsidiary of a holding company which is owned by a consortium and—

(*a*) in any accounting period the trading company or a member of the consortium has trading losses or other amounts eligible for relief from corporation tax which it would, apart from this section, be entitled to surrender by way of group relief; and

(*b*) arrangements are in existence by virtue of which—

(i) the trading company or any successor of it could, at some time during or after the expiry of that accounting period, become a 75 per cent. subsidiary of a third company; or
(ii) any person who owns, or any persons who together own, less than 50 per cent. of the ordinary share capital of the trading company has or together have, or could at some time during or after the expiry of that accounting period obtain, control of the trading company; or
(iii) any person, other than a holding company of which the trading company is a 90 per cent. subsidiary, either alone or together with connected persons, holds or could obtain, or controls or could control the exercise of not less than 75 per cent. of the votes which may be cast on a poll taken at a general meeting of that trading company in that accounting period or in any subsequent accounting period; or
(iv) a third company could begin to carry on, at some time during or after the expiry of that accounting period, the whole or any part of a trade which, at any time in that accounting period, is carried on by the trading company and could do so either as a successor of the trading company or as a successor of another company which is not a third company but which, at some time during or after the expiry of that accounting period, has begun to carry on the whole or any part of that trade;

then, for the purposes of this Chapter, the trading company shall be treated as though it did not (as the surrendering company or the claimant company) fall within section 402(3).

(3) In any case where a trading company is a 90 per cent. subsidiary of a holding company which is owned by a consortium, any reference in subsection (2) above to the trading

company, other than a reference in paragraph (*b*)(iv), shall be construed as including a reference to the holding company.

(4) In this section "third company" means a company which, apart from any provision made by or under any such arrangements as are specified in paragraph (*b*) of either subsection (1) or subsection (2) above, is not a member of the same group of companies as the first company or, as the case may be, the trading company or the holding company to which subsection (2) above applies.

(5) In subsections (1) and (2) above—

"arrangements" means arrangements of any kind whether in writing or not;
"connected persons" shall be construed in accordance with section 839; and
"control" has the meaning assigned by section 840.

(6) For the purposes of subsections (1) and (2) above a company is the successor of another if it carries on a trade which, in whole or in part, the other company has ceased to carry on and the circumstances are such that—

(*a*) section 343 applies in relation to the two companies as the predecessor and the successor within the meaning of that section; or
(*b*) the two companies are connected with each other within the meaning of section 839.

(7) Where by virtue of any enactment a Minister of the Crown or Northern Ireland department has power to give directions to a statutory body as to the disposal of assets belonging to, or to a subsidiary of, that body, the existence of that power shall not be regarded as constituting or as having at any time constituted an arrangement within the meaning of this section.

Former enactments.—Sub-ss. (1)–(6): FA 1973, ss. 29, 32(6); FA 1981, s. 40(6).
Sub-s. (7): FA 1981, s. 47.

411. Exclusion of double allowances

(1) Relief shall not be given more than once in respect of the same amount, whether by giving group relief and by giving some other relief (in any accounting period) to the surrendering company, or by giving group relief more than once.

(2) In accordance with subsection (1) above, two or more claimant companies cannot, in respect of any one loss or other amount for which group relief may be given, and whatever their accounting periods corresponding to that of the surrendering company, obtain in all more relief than could be obtained by a single claimant company whose corresponding accounting period coincided with the accounting period of the surrendering company.

(3) Subject to subsections (4) and (5) below, if claims for group relief relating to the same accounting period of the same surrendering company are made by two or more claimant companies which themselves are members of a group of companies, and—

(*a*) all the claims so made are admissible only by virtue of subsection (2) and (3) of section 409, and
(*b*) there is a part of the surrendering company's accounting period during which none of those claimant companies is a member of the same group as the surrendering company,

those claimant companies shall not obtain in all more relief than could be obtained by a single claimant company which was not a member of the same group as the surrendering company during that part of the surrendering company's accounting period (but was a member during the remainder of that accounting period).

(4) If companies which are members of different groups make claims falling within subsection (3) above, that subsection shall apply separately in relation to the companies in each group.

(5) For the purposes of subsection (3) above, there shall be left out of account a claim made by a company if—

(*a*) the claimant company joins or leaves a group of companies at the same time as the surrendering company; and
(*b*) both before and after that time either the claimant company is a 75 per cent. subsidiary of the surrendering company or the surrendering company is a 75 per cent. subsidiary of the claimant company or both companies are 75 per cent. subsidiaries of another company.

(6) Subject to subsection (7) below, if claims as respects two or more surrendering companies

which themselves are members of a group of companies are made by a claimant company for group relief to be set off against its total profits for any one accounting period, and—

(*a*) all the claims so made are admissible only by virtue of subsections (2) and (3) of section 409, and
(*b*) there is a part of the claimant company's accounting period during which none of the surrendering companies by reference to which the claims are made is a member of the same group as the claimant company,

the claimant company shall not obtain in all more relief to be set off against its profits for the accounting period than it could obtain on a claim as respects a single surrendering company (with unlimited losses and other amounts eligible for relief) which was not a member of the same group as the claimant company during that part of the claimant company's accounting period (but was a member during the remainder of that accounting period).

(7) If claims falling within subsection (6) above are made as respects surrendering companies which are members of different groups, that subsection shall apply separately in relation to claims as respects the surrendering companies in each group.

(8) For the purposes of subsection (6) above there shall be left out of account a claim made as respects a surrendering company if—

(*a*) the surrendering company joins or leaves the group of companies concerned at the same time as the claimant company; and
(*b*) both before and after that time either the surrendering company is a 75 per cent. subsidiary of the claimant company or the claimant company is a 75 per cent. subsidiary of the surrendering company or both companies are 75 per cent. subsidiaries of another company.

(9) References in subsections (3) to (6) above to claims for group relief do not include references to consortium claims.

(10) Without prejudice to the provisions of section 87(3) of the 1968 Act, any reference in Part I of that Act to an allowance made includes a reference to an allowance which would be made but for the granting of group relief, or but for that and but for an insufficiency of profits or other income against which to make it.

Former enactments.—Sub-ss. (1), (2): TA 1970, s. 263(1), (2).
Sub-s. (3): TA 1970, s. 263(3); FA 1985, Sch. 9, para. 9.
Sub-ss. (4), (5): TA 1970, s. 263(3A), (3B); FA 1985, Sch. 9, para. 10.
Sub-s. (6): TA 1970, s. 263(4); FA 1985, Sch. 9, para. 11.
Sub-ss. (7), (8): TA 1970, s. 263(4A), (4B); FA 1985, Sch. 9, para. 12.
Sub-s. (9): TA 1970, s. 263(5); FA 1985, Sch. 9, para. 13.
Sub-s. (10): TA 1970, s. 263(6).

412. Claims and adjustments

(1) A claim for group relief—

(*a*) need not be for the full amount available,
(*b*) shall require the consent of the surrendering company notified to the inspector in such form as the Board may require,
(*c*) must be made within two years from the end of the surrendering company's accounting period to which the claim relates.

(2) A consortium claim shall require the consent of each member of the consortium, notified to the inspector in such form as the Board may require, in addition to the consent of the surrendering company.

(3) If the inspector discovers that any group relief which has been given is or has become excessive he may make an assessment to corporation tax under Case VI of Schedule D in the amount which ought in his opinion to be charged.

(4) Subsection (3) above is without prejudice to the making of an assessment under section 29(3)(*c*) of the Management Act and to the making of all such adjustments by way of discharge or repayment of tax or otherwise as may be required where a claimant company has obtained too much relief, or a surrendering company has forgone relief in respect of a corresponding amount.

Former enactments.—TA 1970, s. 264; FA 1981, s. 40(4).

413. Interpretation of Chapter IV

(1) The following provisions of this section have effect for the interpretation of this Chapter.

(2) In this Chapter—
"claimant company" has the meaning given by section 402(1);
"consortium claim" means a claim for group relief made by virtue of section 402(3);
"group claim" means a claim for group relief made by virtue of section 402(2);
"group/consortium company" means a company which is both a member of a group of companies and a company owned by a consortium;
"group relief" has the meaning given by section 402(1);
"relevant accounting period" means an accounting period beginning after 31st July 1985; and
"surrendering company" has the meaning given by section 402(1).

(3) For the purposes of this Chapter—
(a) two companies shall be deemed to be members of a group of companies if one is the 75 per cent. subsidiary of the other or both are 75 per cent. subsidiaries of a third company;
(b) "holding company" means a company the business of which consists wholly or mainly in the holding of shares or securities of companies which are its 90 per cent. subsidiaries and which are trading companies; and
(c) "trading company" means a company the business of which consists wholly or mainly in the carrying on of a trade or trades.

(4) In applying for the purposes of this Chapter the definition of "75 per cent. subsidiary" in section 838, any share capital of a registered industrial and provident society shall be treated as ordinary share capital.

(5) References in this Chapter to a company apply only to bodies corporate resident in the United Kingdom; and in determining for the purposes of this Chapter whether one company is a 75 per cent. subsidiary of another, the other company shall be treated as not being the owner—
(a) of any share capital which it owns directly in a body corporate if a profit on a sale of the shares would be treated as a trading receipt of its trade; or
(b) of any share capital which it owns indirectly, and which is owned directly by a body corporate for which a profit on a sale of the shares would be a trading receipt; or
(c) of any share capital which it owns directly or indirectly in a body corporate not resident in the United Kingdom.

(6) References to a company being owned by a consortium shall be construed in accordance with paragraph (a) below except for the purposes of the definition of "group/consortium company" in subsection (2) above and of sections 403(10), 406(1)(b) and 409(5), (6) and (7), and for those purposes shall be construed in accordance with paragraph (b) below—
(a) a company is owned by a consortium if three-quarters or more of the ordinary share capital of the company is beneficially owned between them by companies of which none beneficially owns less than one-twentieth of that capital;
(b) a company is owned by a consortium if—
(i) it is either such a trading company as is referred to in paragraph (a) or (b) of subsection (3) of section 402 or such a holding company as is referred to in paragraph (c) of that subsection, and
(ii) three-quarters or more of the ordinary share capital of the company or, in the case of a company within section 402(3)(b), of its holding company is beneficially owned between them by companies of which none beneficially owns less than one-twentieth of that capital;

and the companies which so own three-quarters or more of that ordinary share capital are in this Chapter called the members of the consortium.

(7) Notwithstanding that at any time a company ("the subsidiary company") is a 75 per cent. subsidiary or a 90 per cent. subsidiary of another company ("the parent company") it shall not be treated at that time as such a subsidiary for the purposes of this Chapter unless, additionally at that time—

(a) the parent company is beneficially entitled to not less than 75 per cent. or, as the case may be, 90 per cent. of any profits available for distribution to equity holders of the subsidiary company; and
(b) the parent company would be beneficially entitled to not less than 75 per cent. or, as

the case may be, 90 per cent. of any assets of the subsidiary company available for distribution to its equity holders on a winding-up.

(8) Subject to subsection (9) below, for the purposes of this Chapter, a member's share in a consortium, in relation to an accounting period of the surrendering company, shall be whichever is the lowest in that period of the following percentages, namely—

(*a*) the percentage of the ordinary share capital of the surrendering or claimant company which is beneficially owned by that member;
(*b*) the percentage to which that member is beneficially entitled of any profits available for distribution to equity holders of the surrendering or claimant company; and
(*c*) the percentage to which that member would be beneficially entitled of any assets of the surrendering or claimant company available for distribution to its equity holders on a winding-up;

and if any of those percentages have fluctuated in that accounting period, the average percentage over the period shall be taken for the purposes of this subsection.

(9) In any case where the surrendering or claimant company is a subsidiary of a holding company which is owned by a consortium, for references in subsection (8) above to the surrendering or claimant company there shall be substituted references to the holding company.

(10) Schedule 18 shall have effect for supplementing this section.

Former enactments.—Sub-s. (2): TA 1970, s. 258; FA 1985, Sch. 9, para. 1.
Sub-ss. (3)–(5): TA 1970, s. 258(5)–(7).
Sub-s (6): TA 1970, s. 258(8); FA 1984, s. 46(2); FA 1985, Sch. 9, para. 1(*a*).
Sub-ss. (7)–(10): FA 1973, s. 28(2)–(5); FA 1981, s. 40(5).

PART XI

CLOSE COMPANIES

CHAPTER I

INTERPRETATIVE PROVISIONS

414. Close companies

(1) For the purposes of the Tax Acts, a "close company" is one which is under the control of five or fewer participators, or of participators who are directors, except that the expression does not apply—

(*a*) to a company not resident in the United Kingdom;
(*b*) to a registered industrial and provident society within the meaning of section 486(12) or to a building society;
(*c*) to a company controlled by or on behalf of the Crown, and not otherwise a close company; or
(*d*) to a company falling within section 415 or subsection (5) below.

[(2) Subject to section 415 and subsection (5) below, a company resident in the United Kingdom (but not falling within subsection (1)(*b*) above) is also a close company if five or fewer participators, or participators who are directors, together possess or are entitled to acquire—

(*a*) such rights as would, in the event of the winding-up of the company ("the relevant company") on the basis set out in subsection (2A) below, entitle them to receive the greater part of the assets of the relevant company which would then be available for distribution among the participators, or
(*b*) such rights as would in that event so entitle them if any rights which any of them or any other person has as a loan creditor (in relation to the relevant company or any other company) were disregarded.][1]

[(2A) In the notional winding-up of the relevant company, the part of the assets available for distribution among the participators which any person is entitled to receive is the aggregate of—

(*a*) any part of those assets which he would be entitled to receive in the event of the winding-up of the company, and
(*b*) any part of those assets which he would be entitled to receive if—

(i) any other company which is a participator in the relevant company and is entitled to receive any assets in the notional winding-up were also wound up on the basis set out in this subsection, and
(ii) the part of the assets of the relevant company to which the other company is entitled were distributed among the participators in the other company in proportion to their respective entitlement to the assets of the other company available for distribution among the participators.][1]

[(2B) In the application of subsection (2A) above to the notional winding-up of the other company and to any further notional winding-up required by paragraph (*b*) of that subsection (or by any further application of that paragraph), references to "the relevant company" shall have effect as references to the company concerned.][1]

[(2C) In ascertaining under subsection (2) above whether five or fewer participators, or participators who are directors, together possess or are entitled to acquire rights such as are mentioned in paragraph (*a*) or (*b*) of that subsection—

(*a*) a person shall be treated as a participator in or director of the relevant company if he is a participator in or director of any other company which would be entitled to receive assets in the notional winding-up of the relevant company on the basis set out in subsection (2A) above, and
(*b*) except in the application of subsection (2A) above, no account shall be taken of a participator which is a company unless the company possesses or is entitled to acquire the rights in a fiduciary or representative capacity.][1]

[(2D) Subsections (4) to (6) of section 416 apply for the purposes of subsections (2) and (2A) above as they apply for the purposes of subsection (2) of that section.][1]

(3) ...²

(4) For the purposes of this section—

(a) a company is to be treated as controlled by or on behalf of the Crown if, but only if, it is under the control of the Crown or of persons acting on behalf of the Crown, independently of any other person, and
(b) where a company is so controlled, it shall not be treated as being otherwise a close company unless it can be treated as a close company as being under the control of persons acting independently of the Crown.

(5) A company is not to be treated as a close company—

(a) if—

(i) it is controlled by a company which is not a close company, or by two or more companies none of which is a close company; and
(ii) it cannot be treated as a close company except by taking as one of the five or fewer participators requisite for its being so treated a company which is not a close company;

(b) if it cannot be treated as a close company except by virtue of [paragraph (a) of subsection (2) above or paragraph (c) of section 416(2) and it would not be a close company if the references in those paragraphs]³ to participators did not include loan creditors who are companies other than close companies.

(6) References in subsection (5) above to a close company shall be treated as applying to any company which, if resident in the United Kingdom, would be a close company.

(7) If shares in any company ("the first company") are held on trust for an exempt approved scheme as defined in section 592, then, unless the scheme is established wholly or mainly for the benefit of persons who are, or are dependants of, directors or employees or past directors or employees of—

(a) the first company; or
(b) an associated company of the first company; or
(c) a company which is under the control of any director or associate of a director of the first company or of two or more persons each of whom is such a director or associate; or
(d) a close company;

the persons holding the shares shall, for the purposes of subsection (5) above, be deemed to be the beneficial owners of the shares and, in that capacity, to be a company which is not a close company.

Former enactments.—Sub-s. (1): TA 1970, s. 282(1).
Sub-ss. (2), (3): TA 1970, s. 282(2); FA 1972, Sch. 17, para. 1.
Sub-s. (4): TA 1970, s. 282(3).
Sub-ss. (5), (6): TA 1970, s. 282(4), (5); FA 1972, Sch. 17, para. 1.
Sub-s. (7): FA 1971, s. 25(6).
Amendments.—¹ Sub-ss. (2) to (2D) substituted for sub-s. (2) by FA 1989, s. 104(1), (4) with effect from 1 April 1989.
² Sub-s. (3) repealed by FA 1989, s. 104(2), (4) and Sch. 17, Pt. V with effect from 1 April 1989.
³ Words in sub-s. (5)(b) substituted by FA 1989, s. 104(3), (4) with effect from 1 April 1989.

415. Certain quoted companies not to be close companies

(1) Subject to the following provisions of this section, a company is not to be treated as being at any time a close company if—

(a) shares in the company carrying not less than 35 per cent. of the voting power in the company (and not being shares entitled to a fixed rate of dividend, whether with or without a further right to participate in profits) have been allotted unconditionally to, or acquired unconditionally by, and are at that time beneficially held by, the public, and
(b) any such shares have within the preceding 12 months been the subject of dealings on a recognised stock exchange, and the shares have within those 12 months been quoted in the official list of a recognised stock exchange.

(2) Subsection (1) above shall not apply to a company at any time when the total percentage of the voting power in the company possessed by all of the company's principal members exceeds 85 per cent.

(3) For the purposes of subsection (1) above shares in a company shall be deemed to be beneficially held by the public if, and only if, they—

(a) fall within subsection (4) below, and
(b) are not within the exceptions in subsection (5) below,

and a corresponding construction shall be given to the reference to shares which have been allotted unconditionally to, or acquired unconditionally by, the public.

(4) Shares shall fall within this subsection (as being beneficially held by the public)—
   (a) if beneficially held by a company resident in the United Kingdom which is not a close company, or by a company not so resident which would not be a close company if it were so resident, or
   (b) if held on trust for an exempt approved scheme as defined in section 592, or
   (c) if they are not comprised in a principal member's holding.

(5) Shares shall not be deemed to be held by the public if they are held—
   (a) by any director or associate of a director of the company, or
   (b) by any company which is under the control of any such director or associate, or of two or more persons each of whom is such a director or associate, or
   (c) by any associated company of the company, or
   (d) as part of any fund the capital or income of which is applicable or applied wholly or mainly for the benefit of, or of the dependants of, the employees or directors, or past employees or directors, of the company, or of any company within paragraph (b) or (c) above.

References in this subsection to shares held by any person include references to any shares the rights or powers attached to which could, for the purposes of section 416, be attributed to that person under subsection (5) of that section.

(6) For the purposes of this section—
   (a) a person is a principal member of a company if he possesses a percentage of the voting power in the company of more than 5 per cent. and, where there are more than five such persons, if he is one of the five persons who possess the greatest percentages or if, because two or more persons possess equal percentages of the voting power in the company, there are no such five persons, he is one of the six or more persons (so as to include those two or more who possess equal percentages) who possess the greatest percentages, and
   (b) a principal member's holding consists of the shares which carry the voting power possessed by him.

(7) In arriving at the voting power which a person possesses, there shall be attributed to him any voting power which, for the purposes of section 416, would be attributed to him under subsection (5) or (6) of that section.

(8) In this section "shares" include stock.

Former enactments.—Sub-ss. (1)–(3): TA 1970, s. 283(1)–(3).
Sub-s. (4)(a): TA 1970, s. 283(4)(a).
Sub-s. (4)(b): TA 1970, s. 283(4)(bb); FA 1970, Sch. 5, Pt. III, para. 12(3).
Sub-s. (4)(c): TA 1970, s. 283(4)(c).
Sub-ss. (5)–(8): TA 1970, s. 283(5)–(8).

416. Meaning of "associated company" and "control"

(1) For the purposes of this Part, ...[1], a company is to be treated as another's "associated company" at a given time if, at that time or at any other time within one year previously, one of the two has control of the other, or both are under the control of the same person or persons.

(2) For the purposes of this Part, a person shall be taken to have control of a company if he exercises, or is able to exercise or is entitled to acquire, direct or indirect control over the company's affairs, and in particular, but without prejudice to the generality of the preceding words, if he possesses or is entitled to acquire—
   (a) the greater part of the share capital or issued share capital of the company or of the voting power in the company; or
   (b) such part of the issued share capital of the company as would, if the whole of the income of the company were in fact distributed among the participators (without regard to any rights which he or any other person has as a loan creditor), entitle him to receive the greater part of the amount so distributed; or
   (c) such rights as would, in the event of the winding-up of the company or in any other circumstances, entitle him to receive the greater part of the assets of the company which would then be available for distribution among the participators.

(3) Where two or more persons together satisfy any of the conditions of subsection (2) above, they shall be taken to have control of the company.

(4) For the purposes of subsection (2) above a person shall be treated as entitled to acquire anything which he is entitled to acquire at a future date, or will at a future date be entitled to acquire.

(5) For the purposes of subsections (2) and (3) above, there shall be attributed to any person any rights or powers of a nominee for him, that is to say, any rights or powers which another person possesses on his behalf or may be required to exercise on his direction or behalf.

(6) For the purposes of subsections (2) and (3) above, there may also be attributed to any person all the rights and powers of any company of which he has, or he and associates of his have, control or any two or more such companies, or of any associate of his or of any two or more associates of his, including those attributed to a company or associate under subsection (5) above, but not those attributed to an associate under this subsection; and such attributions shall be made under this subsection as will result in the company being treated as under the control of five or fewer participators if it can be so treated.

Former enactments.—Sub-s. (1): TA 1970, s. 302(1); FA 1972, Sch. 24, para. 21.
Sub-ss. (2)–(4): TA 1970, s. 302(2)–(4); FA 1972, Sch. 17, para. 5.
Sub-ss. (5), (6): TA 1970, s. 302(5), (6).
Amendments.—[1] Words in sub-s. (1) repealed by FA 1989, Sch. 17, Pt V in relation to accounting periods beginning after 31 March 1989.

417. Meaning of "participator", "associate", "director" and "loan creditor"

(1) For the purposes of this Part, a "participator" is, in relation to any company, a person having a share or interest in the capital or income of the company, and, without prejudice to the generality of the preceding words, includes—

(a) any person who possesses, or is entitled to acquire, share capital or voting rights in the company;
(b) any loan creditor of the company;
(c) any person who possesses, or is entitled to acquire, a right to receive or participate in distributions of the company (construing "distributions" without regard to section 418) or any amounts payable by the company (in cash or in kind) to loan creditors by way of premium on redemption; and
(d) any person who is entitled to secure that income or assets (whether present or future) of the company will be applied directly or indirectly for his benefit.

In this subsection references to being entitled to do anything apply where a person is presently entitled to do it at a future date, or will at a future date be entitled to do it.

(2) The provisions of subsection (1) above are without prejudice to any particular provision of this Part requiring a participator in one company to be treated as being also a participator in another company.

(3) For the purposes of this Part "associate" means, in relation to a participator—

(a) any relative or partner of the participator;
(b) the trustee or trustees of any settlement in relation to which the participator is, or any relative of his (living or dead) is or was, a settlor ("settlement" and "settlor" having here the same meaning as in section 681(4)); and
(c) where the participator is interested in any shares or obligations of the company which are subject to any trust, or are part of the estate of a deceased person—

(i) the trustee or trustees of the settlement concerned or, as the case may be, the personal representatives of the deceased; and
(ii) if the participator is a company, any other company interested in those shares or obligations;

and has a corresponding meaning in relation to a person other than a participator.

(4) In subsection (3) above "relative" means husband or wife, parent or remoter forebear, child or remoter issue, or brother or sister.

(5) For the purposes of this Part "director" includes any person occupying the position of director by whatever name called, any person in accordance with whose directions or instructions the directors are accustomed to act, and any person who—

(a) is a manager of the company or otherwise concerned in the management of the company's trade or business, and
(b) is, either on his own or with one or more associates, the beneficial owner of, or able, directly or through the medium of other companies or by any other indirect means, to control 20 per cent. or over of the ordinary share capital of the company.

(6) In subsection (5)(*b*) above the expression "either on his own or with one or more associates" requires a person to be treated as owning or, as the case may be, controlling what any associate owns or controls, even if he does not own or control share capital on his own.

(7) Subject to subsection (9) below, for the purposes of this Part "loan creditor", in relation to a company, means a creditor in respect of any debt incurred by the company—

    (*a*) for any money borrowed or capital assets acquired by the company; or
    (*b*) for any right to receive income created in favour of the company; or
    (*c*) for consideration the value of which to the company was (at the time when the debt was incurred) substantially less than the amount of the debt (including any premium thereon);

or in respect of any redeemable loan capital issued by the company.

(8) Subject to subsection (9) below, a person who is not the creditor in respect of any debt or loan capital to which subsection (7) above applies but nevertheless has a beneficial interest therein shall, to the extent of that interest, be treated for the purposes of this Part as a loan creditor in respect of that debt or loan capital.

(9) A person carrying on a business of banking shall not be deemed to be a loan creditor in respect of any loan capital or debt issued or incurred by the company for money lent by him to the company in the ordinary course of that business.

Former enactments.—Sub-ss. (1), (2): TA 1970, s. 303(1), (2).
Sub-s. (3): TA 1970, s. 303(3); FA 1970, Sch. 5, Pt. III, para. 12(4); FA 1987, s. 37(1).
Sub-ss. (4)–(6): TA 1970, s. 303(4)–(6).
Sub-ss. (7), (9): TA 1970, s. 303(7).
Sub-s. (8): TA 1970, s. 303(8); FA 1972, Sch. 17, para. 7.

Additional matters to be treated as distributions

418. "Distribution" to include certain expenses of close companies

(1) Subject to such exceptions as are mentioned in section 209(1), in the Corporation Tax Acts "distribution", in relation to a close company, includes, unless otherwise stated, any such amount as is required to be treated as a distribution by subsection (2) below.

(2) Subject to subsection (3) below, where a close company incurs expense in or in connection with the provision for any participator of living or other accommodation, of entertainment, of domestic or other services, or of other benefits or facilities of whatever nature, the company shall be treated as making a distribution to him of an amount equal to so much of that expense as is not made good to the company by the participator.

(3) Subsection (2) above shall not apply to expense incurred in or in connection with the provision—

    (*a*) for a person employed in [employment to which Chapter II of Part V applies][1] of such benefits as are mentioned in any of sections 154 to 165; or
    (*b*) of living accommodation for any person if the accommodation is (within the meaning of section 145) provided by reason of his employment; or
    (*c*) for the spouse, children or dependants of a person employed by the company of any pension, annuity, lump sum, gratuity or other like benefit to be given on that person's death or retirement.

(4) The amount of the expense to be taken into account under subsection (2) above as a distribution shall be the same as would under Chapter II of Part V be the cash equivalent of the resultant benefit to the participator.

(5) Subsection (2) above shall not apply if the company and the participator are both resident in the United Kingdom and—

    (*a*) one is a subsidiary of the other or both are subsidiaries of a third company also so resident, and
    (*b*) the benefit to the participator arises on or in connection with a transfer of assets or liabilities by the company to him, or to the company by him.

(6) The question whether one body corporate is a subsidiary of another for the purposes of subsection (5) above shall be determined as a question whether it is a 51 per cent. subsidiary of that other, except that that other shall be treated as not being the owner—

    (*a*) of any share capital which it owns directly in a body corporate if a profit on a sale of the shares would be treated as a trading receipt of its trade; or

(*b*) of any share capital which it owns indirectly, and which is owned directly by a body corporate for which a profit on a sale of the shares would be a trading receipt; or
(*c*) of any share capital which it owns directly or indirectly in a body corporate not resident in the United Kingdom.

(7) Where each of two or more close companies makes a payment to a person who is not a participator in that company, but is a participator in another of those companies, and the companies are acting in concert or under arrangements made by any person, then each of those companies and any participator in it shall be treated as if the payment made to him had been made by that company.

This subsection shall apply, with any necessary adaptations, in relation to the giving of any consideration, and to the provision of any facilities, as it applies in relation to the making of a payment.

(8) For the purposes of this section any reference to a participator includes an associate of a participator, and any participator in a company which controls another company shall be treated as being also a participator in that other company.

Former enactments.—Sub-s. (1): TA 1970, s. 284(1).
Sub-s. (2): TA 1970, s. 284(2).
Sub-s. (3)(*a*): TA 1970, s. 284(2)(*a*); FA 1976, Sch. 9, para. 15.
Sub-s. (3)(*b*): TA 1970, s. 284(2)(*aa*); FA 1980, s. 51(4).
Sub-s. (3)(*c*): TA 1970, s. 284(2)(*b*); FA 1976, Sch. 9, para. 15; FA 1977, s. 35(4).
Sub-s. (4): TA 1970, s. 284(3); FA 1976, Sch. 9, para. 16.
Sub-ss. (5)–(8): TA 1970, s. 284(4)–(7).
Amendments.—[1] Words in sub-s. (3)(*a*) substituted by FA 1989, s. 53(2)(*f*).

CHAPTER II

CHARGES TO TAX IN CONNECTION WITH LOANS

419. Loans to participators etc.

(1) Subject to the following provisions of this section and section 420, where a close company, otherwise than in the ordinary course of a business carried on by it which includes the lending of money, makes any loan or advances any money to an individual who is a participator in the company or an associate of a participator, there shall be assessed on and recoverable from the company, as if it were an amount of corporation tax chargeable on the company for the accounting period in which the loan or advance is made, an amount equal to such proportion of the amount of the loan or advance as corresponds to the rate of advance corporation tax in force for the financial year in which the loan or advance is made.

In relation to a loan or advance made in an accounting period ending after the day, not being earlier than 31st March 1992, appointed by order by the Treasury for the purpose of this provision, this subsection shall have effect with the substitution for "assessed on and recoverable" of "due".

(2) For the purposes of this section the cases in which a close company is to be regarded as making a loan to any person include a case where—

(a) that person incurs a debt to the close company; or
(b) a debt due from that person to a third party is assigned to the close company;

and then the close company shall be regarded as making a loan of an amount equal to the debt.

(3) Tax shall be assessable by virtue of this section whether or not the whole or any part of the loan or advance in question has been repaid at the time of the assessment; and tax assessed by virtue of this section shall, subject to any appeal against the assessment, be due within 14 days after the issue of the notice of assessment.

The preceding provisions of this subsection shall not apply in relation to a loan or advance made in an accounting period ending after the day, not being earlier than 31st March 1992, appointed by order by the Treasury for the purpose of this provision, but in relation to any such loan or advance tax due by virtue of this section shall be due and payable within 14 days after the end of the accounting period in which the loan or advance was made.

(4) Where a close company has made a loan or advance which gave rise to a charge to tax on the company under subsection (1) above and the loan or advance or any part of it is repaid to the company, relief shall be given from that tax, or a proportionate part of it, by discharge or repayment.

Relief under this subsection shall be given on a claim, which must be made within six years from the end of the financial year in which the repayment is made.

(5) Where, under arrangements made by any person otherwise than in the ordinary course of a business carried on by him—

(a) a close company makes a loan or advance which, apart from this subsection, does not give rise to any charge on the company under subsection (1) above, and
(b) some person other than the close company makes a payment or transfers property to, or releases or satisfies (in whole or in part) a liability of, an individual who is a participator in the company or an associate of a participator,

then, unless in respect of the matter referred to in paragraph (b) above there falls to be included in the total income of the participator or associate an amount not less than the loan or advance, this section shall apply as if the loan or advance had been made to him.

(6) In subsections (1) and (5)(b) above the references to an individual shall apply also to a company receiving the loan or advance in a fiduciary or representative capacity, and to a company not resident in the United Kingdom.

(7) For the purposes of this section any participator in a company which controls another company shall be treated as being also a participator in that other company.

Former enactments.—Sub-s (1): TA 1970, s. 286(1); FA 1972, Sch. 17, para. 3(2); F(No. 2)A 1987, s. 90(3).
Sub-s. (2): TA 1970, s. 286(2).
Sub-s. (3): TA 1970, s. 286(4); FA 1986, s. 43(1); F(No. 2)A 1987, s. 90(3).
Sub-s. (4): TA 1970, s. 286(5); FA 1972, Sch. 17, para. 3(4); FA 1976, s. 44; FA 1986, s. 43(2).
Sub-ss. (5)–(7): TA 1970, s. 286(7)–(9).
Cross references.—See FA 1989, Sch. 12, para. 1(a) (administrative provisions relating to close companies).

420. Exceptions from section 419

(1) Section 419(2)(*a*) shall not apply to a debt incurred for the supply by the close company of goods or services in the ordinary course of its trade or business unless the credit given exceeds six months or is longer than that normally given to the company's customers.

(2) Section 419(1) shall not apply to a loan made to a director or employee of a close company, or of an associated company of the close company, if—

(*a*) neither the amount of the loan, nor that amount when taken together with any other outstanding loans which—

(i) were made by the close company or any of its associated companies to the borrower or the wife or husband of the borrower; and
(ii) if made before 31st March 1971, were made for the purpose of purchasing a dwelling which was or was to be the borrower's only or main residence;

exceeds £15,000 and the outstanding loans falling within sub-paragraph (ii) above do not together exceed £10,000; and

(*b*) the borrower works full-time for the close company or any of its associated companies; and

(*c*) the borrower does not have a material interest in the close company or in any associated company of the close company;

but if the borrower acquires such a material interest at a time when the whole or part of any such loan made after 30th March 1971 remains outstanding the close company shall be regarded as making to him at that time a loan of an amount equal to the sum outstanding.

Section 168(11) shall apply for the purpose of determining whether a person has, for the purpose of this subsection, a material interest in a company, but with the omission of the words following "417(3)".

Former enactments.—Sub-s. (1): TA 1970, s. 286(2).
Sub-s. (2): TA 1970, s. 286(3), (9); FA 1971, s. 25(5); FA 1972, Sch. 17, para. 3(3).
Note.—See **Prospective Legislation Notes** (Married Couples).
Cross references.—See FA 1989, Sch. 12, para. 1(*a*) (administrative provisions relating to close companies).

421. Taxation of borrower when loan under section 419 released etc.

(1) Subject to the following provisions of this section, where a company is assessed or liable to be assessed under section 419 in respect of a loan or advance and releases or writes off the whole or part of the debt in respect of it, then—

(*a*) for the purpose of computing the total income of the person to whom the loan or advance was made, a sum equal to the amount so released or written off shall be treated as income received by him after deduction of income tax from a corresponding gross amount;

(*b*) no repayment of income tax shall be made in respect of that income and no assessment shall be made on him in respect of income tax at the basic rate on that income;

(*c*) the income included by virtue of paragraph (*a*) above in his total income shall, notwithstanding that paragraph, be treated for the purposes of sections 348 and 349(1) as not brought into charge to income tax;

(*d*) for the purpose of determining whether any or what amount of tax is, by virtue of paragraph (*a*) above, to be taken into account as having been deducted from a gross amount in the case of an individual whose total income is reduced by any deductions so much only of that gross amount shall be taken into account as is part of his total income as so reduced.

(2) If the loan or advance referred to in subsection (1) above was made to a person who has since died, or to trustees of a trust which has come to an end, this section, instead of applying to the person to whom it was made, shall apply to the person from whom the debt is due at the time of release or writing off (and if it is due from him as personal representative, within the meaning of Part XVI, the amount treated as received by him shall accordingly be included for the purposes of that Part in the aggregate income of the estate) and subsection (1) above shall apply accordingly with the necessary modifications.

(3) This section shall not have effect in relation to a loan or advance made to a person if any sum falls in respect of the loan or advance to be included in his income by virtue of section 677, except so far as the amount released or written off exceeds the sums previously falling to be so included (without the addition for income tax provided for by subsection (6) of that section).

(4) This section shall be construed as one with section 419.

Former enactments.—Sub-s. (1): TA 1970, s. 287(1); FA 1971, Sch. 6, para. 32; FA 1978, Sch. 2, para. 4.
Sub-s. (2): TA 1970, s. 287(2); FA 1971, Sch. 6, para. 32.
Sub-ss. (3), (4): TA 1970, s. 287(3), (4).
Cross references.—See FA 1989, Sch. 12, para. 1(a) (administrative provisions relating to close companies).

422. Extension of section 419 to loans by companies controlled by close companies

(1) Subject to subsection (4) below, where a company which is controlled by a close company makes a loan which, apart from this section, does not give rise to a charge under subsection (1) of section 419, that section and section 420 shall apply as if the loan had been made by the close company.

(2) Subject to subsection (4) below, where a company which is not controlled by a close company makes a loan which, apart from this section, does not give rise to a charge under subsection (1) of section 419 and a close company subsequently acquires control of it, that section and section 420 shall apply as if the loan had been made by the close company immediately after the time when it acquired control.

(3) Where two or more close companies together control the company that makes or has made the loan, subsections (1) and (2) above shall have effect—

(a) as if each of them controlled that company; and
(b) as if the loan had been made by each of those close companies,

but the loan shall be apportioned between those close companies in such proportion as may be appropriate having regard to the nature and amount of their respective interests in the company that makes or has made the loan.

(4) Subsections (1) and (2) above do not apply if it is shown that no person has made any arrangements (otherwise than in the ordinary course of a business carried on by him) as a result of which there is a connection—

(a) between the making of the loan and the acquisition of control; or
(b) between the making of the loan and the provision by the close company of funds for the company making the loan;

and the close company shall be regarded as providing funds for the company making the loan if it directly or indirectly makes any payment or transfers any property to, or releases or satisfies (in whole or in part) a liability of, the company making the loan.

(5) Where, by virtue of this section, sections 419 and 420 have effect as if a loan made by one company had been made by another, any question under those sections or section 421 whether—

(a) the compnay making the loan did so otherwise than in the ordinary course of a business carried on by it which includes the lending of money;
(b) the loan or any part of it has been repaid to the company;
(c) the company has released or written off the whole or part of the debt in respect of the loan,

shall be determined by reference to the company that makes the loan.

(6) This section shall be construed as one with section 419 and section 420 and in this section—

(a) "loan" includes advance; and
(b) references to a company making a loan include references to cases in which the company is, or if it were a close company would be, regarded as making a loan by virtue of section 419(2).

Former enactments.—TA 1970, s. 287A; FA 1970, s. 44(2).
Cross references.—See FA 1989, Sch. 12, para. 1(a) (administrative provisions relating to close companies).

CHAPTER III

APPORTIONMENT OF UNDISTRIBUTED INCOME ETC.

Cross references.—See FA 1989, Sch. 12, para. 1(*b*) (administrative provisions relating to close companies).
Amendments.—This Chapter repealed by FA 1989, s.103(1) and Sch. 17, Pt. V in relation to accounting periods beginning after 31 March 1989, subject to FA 1989, s. 103(2).

423. Apportionment of certain income, deductions and interest

(1) Subject to section 424, there shall, for the purposes of this Chapter, be apportioned by the inspector among the participators in a close company—

  (a) the income of the company for any accounting period; and
  (b) as if it were the income of the company for an accounting period, any amount—

    (i) which was deducted in respect of annual payments made by the company in arriving at its distributable income for that period, and
    (ii) which in the case of an individual would not have been deductible or would (apart from section 683(3)) have been treated as his income in computing his total income; and

  (c) as if it were the income of the company for an accounting period, any interest paid by the company in that period.

(2) Any amount apportionable under any paragraph of subsection (1) above shall be in addition to the amount (if any) which may be apportioned under any other provision of that subsection.

(3) Any amount apportioned to a close company under this section, or by one or more sub-apportionments under this subsection, shall be further apportioned among the participators in that company.

(4) If any amount of interest apportionable by virtue of paragraph (c) of subsection (1) above is interest paid to a participator in the close company or is (apart from that paragraph) treated for the purposes of income tax as the income of such a participator, the amount so apportionable to that participator shall be reduced by the first-mentioned amount (and without requiring the reduction to be reflected in the amount apportioned to any other person).

(5) In determining for the purposes of this Chapter the person to whom any amount is to be apportionable by virtue of subsection (1)(c) above, any interest which any person possesses as a loan creditor shall be disregarded (but without prejudice to the making of an apportionment to him in any other capacity).

(6) Subject to paragraph 10 of Schedule 19, this section shall, notwithstanding the winding up of a company, or the passing of any resolution or the making of any order or anything else done for the purpose of winding up a company, continue to apply as if the company were not being wound up.

(7) Schedule 19, which makes provision for determining the relevant income and distributions of a company for an accounting period and whether there is any such excess as is mentioned in section 424(1), shall have effect for the purpose of supplementing this Chapter.

Former enactments.—Sub-s. (1)(*a*): FA 1972, Sch. 16, para. 1(1); F(No. 2)A 1987, s. 61(3).
Sub-s. (1)(*b*): FA 1972, Sch. 16, para. 3(1); FA 1980, s. 56(4); F(No. 2)A 1987, s. 61(4).
Sub-s. (1)(*c*): FA 1972, Sch. 16, para. 3A(1); FA 1974, Sch. 1, para. 26; F(No. 2)A 1987, s. 61(4).
Sub-s. (2): FA 1972, Sch. 16, para. 3(3), 3A(5); FA 1974, Sch. 1, para. 26.
Sub-s. (3): FA 1977, Sch. 16, para. 1(4); F(No. 2)A 1987, s. 61(3).
Sub-ss. (4), (5): FA 1972, Sch. 16, para. 3A(4), (6); FA 1974, Sch. 1, para. 26.
Sub-s. (6): FA 1972, Sch. 16, para. 1(5).
Sub-s. (7): FA 1972, Sch. 16, para. 1(2).

424. Exclusions from section 423

(1) Subject to the following provisions of this Chapter, an apportionment shall not be made under subsection (1)(a) of section 423 of any relevant income of a company unless—

  (a) its relevant income for the accounting period exceeds its distributions for that period; and
  (b) if the company is a trading company or a member of a trading group by virtue of paragraph 7(2)(a) of Schedule 19, that excess is more than £1,000;

and the amount apportioned shall be the amount of that excess.

(2) Subject to paragraphs 10(5) and 11(2) of Schedule 19, there may be apportioned under

section 423(1)(a), if the inspector sees reason for it, the whole of the relevant income for an accounting period of a close company which is not a trading company whether or not there is any such excess as is mentioned in subsection (1) above.

(3) Subsection (1)(b) of section 423 does not apply to annual payments which consist of interest or are made wholly and exclusively for the purposes of the company's trade.

(4) Subsection (1)(c) of section 423 does not apply to a company—
   (a) if it is a trading company, or
   (b) if it is a member of a trading group, or
   (c) if more than 75 per cent. of its income is of one or more of the following descriptions, that is—
      (i) estate or trading income;
      (ii) interest, and dividends or other distributions, received from a 51 per cent. subsidiary of it (both companies being bodies corporate) if the subsidiary is itself within paragraph (a) or (b) above or this paragraph;

and for the purposes of paragraph (c) above no account shall be taken of any deduction from the company's profits for charges on income, expenses of management or other amounts which can be deducted from or set off against or treated as reducing profits of more than one description.

(5) In determining for the purposes of subsection (4)(c)(ii) above whether one body corporate is a 51 per cent. subsidiary of another, that other shall be treated as not being the owner—
   (a) of any share capital which it owns directly or indirectly in a body corporate not resident in the United Kingdom, or
   (b) of any share capital which it owns indirectly and which is owned directly by a body corporate for which a profit on the sale of the shares would be a trading receipt.

(6) Subsection (1)(c) of section 423 shall not apply to interest which—
   (a) would be eligible for relief under section 353 if paid by an individual; or
   (b) is money wholly and exclusively laid out or expended for the purposes of a trade carried on by the company.

Former enactments.—Sub-s. (1): FA 1972, Sch. 16, paras. 1(2), (3), 3(3), 3A(5); FA 1974, Sch. 1, para. 26.
Sub-s. (2): FA 1972, Sch. 16, para. 2.
Sub-s. (3): FA 1972, Sch. 16, para. 3(2).
Sub-s. (4): FA 1972, Sch. 16, para. 3A(2); FA 1974, Sch. 1, para. 26.
Sub-s. (5): FA 1972, Sch. 16, para. 3A(7); FA 1974, Sch. 1, para. 26.
Sub-s. (6): FA 1972, Sch. 16, para. 3A(3); FA 1974, Sch. 1, para. 26.

425. Manner of apportionment

(1) Subject to the provisions of this section, any apportionment under section 423, including any sub-apportionment of an amount directly or indirectly apportioned to a company, shall be made according to the respective interests in the company in question of the participators.

(2) In determining for the purposes of this section the respective interests of the participators, the inspector may, if it seems proper to him to do so, attribute to each participator an interest corresponding to his interest in the assets of the company available for distribution among the participators in the event of a winding up or in any other circumstances.

(3) Where income of a company which is not a trading company is apportioned under section 423, the inspector may, if it seems proper to him to do so, treat a loan creditor as having an interest for the purposes of this section to the extent to which the income to be apportioned, or assets representing it, has or have been expended or applied, or is or are available to be expended or applied, in redemption, repayment or discharge of the loan capital or debt (including any premium thereon) in respect of which he is a loan creditor.

Former enactment.—FA 1972, Sch. 16, para. 4.

426. Charge to income tax where apportionment is to an individual

(1) Where a sum has been apportioned under section 423 to an individual (whether by an original apportionment or a sub-apportionment), income tax shall be assessed and charged in respect of that sum in accordance with the following provisions of this section and sections 427 and 428.

(2) Where a sum has been so apportioned to an individual—
   (a) it shall be treated for the purpose of computing his total income as income received by him

at the end of the accounting period to which the apportionment relates and, subject to section 833(3), shall be deemed to be the highest part of his total income;

(b) no assessment shall be made on the individual in respect of income tax at the basic rate on that sum (nor, in the case mentioned in section 427(1), in respect of income tax at any other rate) but he shall be treated as having paid income tax at the basic rate on that sum or, if his total income is reduced by any deductions, on so much of that sum as is part of his total income as so reduced;

(c) no repayment shall be made of the income tax treated by virtue of paragraph (b) above as having been paid; and

(d) the sum so apportioned shall be treated for the purposes of sections 348 and 349(1) as not brought into charge to income tax.

(3) Where a sum is so apportioned to the personal representatives of a deceased person it shall be treated, in ascertaining the aggregate income of the estate for the purposes of Part XVI, as having been received as mentioned in paragraph (a) of subsection (2) above, and paragraphs (b) to (d) of that subsection shall apply accordingly with the necessary modifications.

Former enactment.—FA 1972, Sch. 16, para. 5(1)–(3).

427. Reduction of charge under section 426 in certain cases

(1) No individual shall be assessed to income tax by virtue of any apportionment unless the sum or, where there is a sub-apportionment, the aggregate sum on which he is so assessable amounts at least to—

(a) £1,000; or
(b) 5 per cent. of the amount apportioned;

whichever is the less.

(2) Where an apportionment is made by virtue of section 424(2), an individual shall not be charged to tax on a sum treated in consequence of the apportionment or any sub-apportionment as being his income except in so far as it exceeds the amount which, apart from the apportionment, falls in respect of distributions made by the company for the accounting period to be included in his total income.

(3) Where as a result of a company or companies making covenanted payments to charity a sum or sums are apportioned by virtue of section 423(1)(b) and form part of the total income of an individual for any year of assessment, then, except in so far as any such sum is referable to a payment which, if made by the individual, would be treated by virtue of section 683(1) as the income of the individual for the purposes of excess liability, his total income for that year and the total amount assessable for that year in respect of that sum or those sums shall be reduced by the amount of that sum or those sums.

In this subsection "covenanted payments to charity" has the same meaning as in section 683.

(4) Where the income of a company for any accounting period has been apportioned under section 423 of this Act or 296 of the 1970 Act and the distributions of the company for a later accounting period for which it is a close company—

(a) consist of or include a distribution of all or any of the apportioned income; and
(b) exceed the company's relevant income for that later period,

then, if any individual who was charged to tax under section 426 or section 297 of the 1970 Act in respect of any of the apportioned income is entitled to any of that income on that subsequent distribution, there shall be deemed not to form part of his income for the purposes of excess liability an amount of the income subsequently distributed (or of the excess mentioned in paragraph (b) above if it is less) equal to such fraction as corresponds to—

(i) the fraction of the apportioned income in respect of which he was charged to tax; or
(ii) the fraction to which he is entitled of the subsequent distribution of that income,

whichever is the smaller.

(5) In this section "excess liability" means the excess of liability to income tax over what it would be if all income tax were chargeable at the basic rate to the exclusion of any higher rate.

Former enactments.—Sub-s. (1): FA 1972, Sch. 16, para. 5(4); FA 1984, s. 32.
Sub-s. (2): FA 1972, Sch. 16, para. 5(5).
Sub-s. (3): FA 1972, Sch. 16, para. 5(5A); FA 1980, s. 56(5); FA 1986, s. 32(3).
Sub-s. (4): FA 1972, Sch. 16, para. 5(6); FA 1973, Sch. 9, para. 1(3).
Sub-s. (5): FA 1972, Sch. 16, para. 5(5A), (6A); FA 1973, Sch. 9, para. 1(3); FA 1978, Sch. 2, para 16(*b*); FA 1986, s. 32(3).

Cross references.—See FA 1988, s. 102(2)(*a*) (taxation of capital gains at income tax rates; the higher rate not to apply to the amount deemed under sub-s. (4) above not to form part of income);
FA 1989, s. 98(2) (sub-ss. (4), (5) to have effect in cases where the subsequent distribution referred to in sub-s. (4) of this section is made before 1 April 1992).

428. Increase of apportioned sum etc. by reference to ACT

(1) For the purposes of sections 426 and 427—

(a) the sum apportioned to any person;
(b) the amount mentioned in section 427(1)(b); and
(c) the amount to be excluded from a person's income in accordance with section 427(4),

shall respectively be taken to consist of the aggregate of that sum or amount and such proportion of it as corresponds to the appropriate rate of advance corporation tax; but paragraphs (a) and (b) above shall not apply in the case of any apportionment so far as made by virtue of section 423(1)(b) or (c).

(2) For the purposes of paragraphs (a) and (b) of subsection (1) above, the appropriate rate of advance corporation tax is the rate applicable to a distribution made at the end of the accounting period to which the apportionment relates, and for the purposes of paragraph (c) of that subsection the appropriate rate of advance corporation tax is the rate applicable to the distribution mentioned in section 427(4)(a).

Former enactments.—FA 1972, Sch. 16, para. 5(7), (8); FA 1974, Sch. 1, para. 26.

429. Payment and collection of income tax

(1) Any income tax chargeable under section 426 in respect of a sum apportioned to a participator shall be assessed on the participator and, subject to the provisions of this section, all the provisions of the Income Tax Acts relating to assessment and the collection and recovery of tax shall with any necessary modifications apply to tax chargeable under that section.

(2) If the whole or any part of the tax assessed on the participator is not paid within 30 days from the date on which the assessment became final and conclusive or by 1st December in the year next following the year of assessment, whichever is the later, a notice of liability to tax under this section may be served on the company and the tax or the part remaining unpaid, as the case may be, shall be payable by the company upon service of the notice.

(3) Where a notice of liability is served under subsection (2) above, any interest due on the tax assessed on the participator and not paid by him, and any interest accruing due on that tax after the date of service, shall be payable by the company.

(4) Where a notice of liability is served on the company and the relevant tax and any interest payable by the company under subsection (3) above is not paid by the company before the expiry of three months from the date of service, that tax and interest may, without prejudice to the right of recovery from the company, be recovered from the participator.

(5) Where, in consequence of a sub-apportionment, subsections (1) to (4) above apply in relation to a participator in a company other than the company in relation to which the original apportionment was made, references in those subsections to the company shall be taken as references to the company in relation to which the original apportionment was made.

Former enactments.—FA 1977, Sch. 16, para. 6; FA 1976, s. 45; FA 1980, s. 61(4).

430. Consequences of apportionment: ACT

(1) This section has effect where the income of a company is apportioned under section 423(1)(a); and in this section "the apportioned amount" means the aggregate of the amount of that income which is so apportioned (subject to subsection (2) below) and such proportion of the amount as corresponds to the rate of advance corporation tax applicable to a distribution made at the end of the accounting period to which the apportionment relates ("the relevant period").

(2) Where a company issues to a close company any share capital to which section 249 applies, the amount of the company's income apportioned under section 423(1)(a) shall, for the purposes of the definition of "apportioned amount" in subsection (1) above, be treated as reduced by an amount equal to the appropriate amount in cash (within the meaning of section 251(2)).

(3) If in the relevant period the company has a surplus of franked investment income, the surplus (so far as not already reduced in consequence of a claim under section 242 or 243 or of being used

to frank distributions made by the company in a subsequent accounting period) shall be treated for all purposes as reduced by a sum equal to the apportioned amount or, if that is greater, as extinguished.

(4) If in the relevant period the company has no such surplus (so far as not already reduced as mentioned in subsection *(3)* above) or the apportioned amount exceeds that surplus (so far as not already so reduced), subsections *(5)* to *(7)* below shall have effect in relation to a sum equal to the advance corporation tax comprised in a franked payment made at the end of the relevant period of an amount equal to the apportioned amount or to that excess, as the case may be.

(5) If, apart from this section, surplus advance corporation tax of a later accounting period could by virtue of subsection *(3)* of section 239 be set against the company's liability to corporation tax for the relevant period, that advance corporation tax shall not be so set except to such extent, if any, as would be possible if the sum mentioned in subsection *(4)* above had been advance corporation tax available to be so set against that liability for the relevant period and had, so far as permitted by that section, already been set against that liability.

(6) If the sum mentioned in subsection *(4)* above exceeds the amount that could, if it were advance corporation tax available for the purpose, be set as mentioned in subsection *(5)* above against the company's liability for the relevant period—

   (a) there shall be deducted from the excess an amount equal to the advance corporation tax, if any, that could by virtue of subsection *(3)* of section 239 be set against the company's liability to corporation tax for earlier accounting periods after taking into account advance corporation tax so set in consequence of a claim already made under that subsection; and
   (b) if no such claim has already been made, advance corporation tax shall not by virtue of any such claim be set against the company's liability to corporation tax for any such earlier accounting periods except to such extent, if any, as would be possible if an amount equal to any deduction under paragraph *(a)* above had been advance corporation tax available to be so set and had, so far as permitted by section 239, already been set against that liability.

(7) Any excess of the sum mentioned in subsection *(4)* above remaining after the deduction mentioned in subsection *(6)(a)* above—

   (a) shall be assessed on and recoverable from the company as if it were advance corporation tax payable by the company in respect of a distribution made by it at the end of the relevant period; and
   (b) shall carry interest as if it were advance corporation tax so payable; and
   (c) shall be treated as surplus advance corporation tax of the relevant period falling to be dealt with in accordance with section 239(4).

(8) Tax assessed by virtue of subsection *(7)(a)* above shall, subject to any appeal against the assessment, be due within 14 days after the issue of the notice of assessment.

(9) Subsection *(7)(c)* above shall not be construed as authorising any sum to be carried forward to a later accounting period in any case in which section 245 would prevent the carry-forward of advance corporation tax.

(10) Section 238 shall apply for the interpretation of this section as it applies for the interpretation of Chapter V of Part VI.

Former enactments.—Sub-s. (1): FA 1972, Sch. 16, para. 7(1).
Sub-s. (2): F(No. 2)A 1975, Sch. 8, para. 3(4).
Sub-ss. (3)–(6): FA 1972, Sch. 16, para. 7(2)–(5).
Sub-s. (7)(*a*): FA 1972, Sch. 16, para. 7(6)(*a*).
Sub-s. (7)(*b*): FA 1972, Sch. 16, para. 7(6)(*aa*); F(No. 2)A 1975, s. 46(6).
Sub-s. (7)(*c*): FA 1972, Sch.16, para. 7(6)(*b*).
Sub-ss. (8), (9): FA 1972, Sch. 16, para. 7(8), (9).

PART XII

SPECIAL CLASSES OF COMPANIES AND BUSINESSES

CHAPTER I

INSURANCE COMPANIES, UNDERWRITERS AND
CAPITAL REDEMPTION BUSINESS

Insurance companies: general

431. Interpretative provisions relating to insurance companies

(1) This section has effect for the interpretation of this Chapter.

(2) Unless the context otherwise requires—

"annuity business" means the business of granting annuities on human life;
"general annuity business" means any annuity business which is not pension business, and "pension business" shall be construed in accordance with subsections (3) and (4) below;
"annuity fund" means, where an annuity fund is not kept separately from the life assurance fund of an insurance company, such part of the life assurance fund as represents the liability of the company under its annuity contracts, as stated in its periodical returns;
"insurance company" means a company to which Part II of the Insurance Companies Act 1982 applies;
"life assurance business" includes annuity business;
"offshore income gain" has the same meaning as in Chapter V of Part XVII;
"overseas life insurance company" means an insurance company having its head office outside the United Kingdom but carrying on life assurance business through a branch or agency in the United Kingdom; and
"periodical return", in relation to an insurance company, means a return deposited with the Secretary of State under Part II of the Insurance Companies Act 1982.
[" policy holders' fraction" and "shareholders' fraction" shall be construed in accordance with section 89 of the Finance Act 1989.][2]

(3) Subject to section 439, any division to be made between general annuity business, pension business and other life assurance business shall be made on the principle of—

(a) referring to pension business any premiums falling within subsection (4) below, together with the incomings, outgoings and liabilities referable to those premiums and the policies and contracts under which they are or have been paid;

(b) allocating to general annuity business all other annuity business;

and references to "pension fund" and "general annuity fund" shall be construed accordingly, whether or not any such funds are kept separate from the insurance company's life assurance fund.

(4) The premiums to be referred to pension business are those payable under contracts falling within one or other of the following descriptions, that is to say—

(a) any contract with an individual who is, or would but for an insufficiency of profits or gains be, chargeable to income tax in respect of relevant earnings (as defined in section 623(1) and (2)) from a trade, profession, vocation, office or employment carried on or held by him (being a contract approved by the Board under section 620), or any substituted contract within the meaning of section 622(3);

(b) any contract (including a contract of insurance) entered into for the purposes of, and made with the persons having the management of, an exempt approved scheme as defined in Chapter I of Part XIV, being a contract so framed that the liabilities undertaken by the insurance company under the contract correspond with liabilities against which the contract is intended to secure the scheme;

(c) any contract made under approved personal pension arrangements within the meaning of Chapter IV of Part XIV;

(d) any annuity contract entered into for the purposes of—

(i) a scheme which is approved or is being considered for approval under Chapter I of Part XIV;

[(ii) a scheme which is a relevant statutory scheme for the purposes of Chapter I of Part XIV;][1] or
(iii) a fund to which section 608 applies,

being a contract which is approved by the Board and made with the persons having the management of the scheme or fund (or those persons and a member of or contributor to the scheme or fund) and by means of which relevant benefits as defined by section 612(1) (but no other benefits) are secured;
(*e*) any annuity contract approved by the Board which is entered into in substitution for a contract within paragraph (*d*) above;
(*f*) any contract with the trustees or other persons having the management of a scheme approved under section 620 or, subject to subsection (5) below, of a superannuation fund which was approved under section 208 of the 1970 Act, being a contract which—

(i) was entered into for the purposes only of that scheme or fund or, in the case of a fund part only of which was approved under section 208, for the purposes only of that part of that fund, and
(ii) (in the case of a contract entered into or varied after 1st August 1956) is so framed that the liabilities undertaken by the insurance company under the contract correspond with liabilities against which the contract is intended to secure the scheme or fund (or the relevant part of the fund).

(5) Subsection (4)(*c*) above shall not apply to premiums payable under a contract where the fund in question was approved under section 208 of the 1970 Act unless—

(*a*) immediately before 6th April 1980 premiums paid under the contract with the trustees or other persons having the management of the fund fell within section 323(4) of that Act (premiums referable to pension business); and
(*b*) the terms on which benefits are payable from the fund have not been altered since that time; and
(*c*) section 608 applies to the fund.

(6) In subsections (3) to (5) above "premium" includes any consideration for an annuity.

Former enactments.—Sub-s. (1): TA 1970, s. 323(1); FA 1973, s. 40(7); FA 1982, s. 58(7).
Sub-s. (2): TA 1970, s. 323(2); FA 1970, Sch. 5, Pt. III, para. 11(4); Secretary of State for Trade and Industry Order 1970, S.I. 1970 No. 1537; Insurance Companies Act 1973, s. 54(2); Insurance Companies Act 1982, Sch. 5, para. 10(*b*).
Sub-s. (3): TA 1970, s. 323(3); FA 1970, Sch. 5, Pt. III, para. 11(5); FA 1981, s. 41.
Sub-s. (4)(*a*): TA 1970, s. 323(4)(*a*); FA 1970, Sch. 5, Pt. III, para. 11(3); FA 1978, s. 26(5).
Sub-s. (4)(*b*): TA 1970, s. 323(4)(*aa*); FA 1970, Sch. 5, Pt. III, para. 11(1).
Sub-s. (4)(*c*): TA 1970, s. 323(4)(*ab*); F(No. 2)A 1987, s. 39(3).
Sub-s. (4)(*d*), (*e*): TA 1970, s. 323(4)(*ac*), (*ad*); F(No. 2)A 1987, Sch. 3, para. 16.
Sub-s. (4)(*f*): TA 1970, s. 323(4)(*b*).
Sub-s. (5): FA 1980, s. 36(5).
Sub-s. (6): TA 1970, s. 323(4).
Amendments.—[1] Sub-s. (4)(*d*)(ii) substituted by FA 1989, Sch. 6, paras. 1, 2, 18(1) with effect from 14 March 1989.
[2] Words in sub-s. (2) added by FA 1989, Sch. 8, para. 1.

432. Separation of different classes of business

(1) Where an insurance company carries on life assurance business in conjunction with insurance business of any other class, the life assurance business shall, for the purposes of the Corporation Tax Acts, be treated as a separate business from any other class of business carried on by the company.

(2) Where an insurance company carries on both ordinary life assurance business and industrial life assurance business, the business of each such class shall, for the purposes of the Corporation Tax Acts, be treated as though it were a separate business, and section 76 shall apply separately to each such class of business.

Former enactment.—TA 1970, s. 307.

433. Profits reserved for policy holders and annuitants

Where the profits of an insurance company in respect of its life assurance business are, for the purposes of this Act, computed in accordance with the provisions of this Act applicable to Case I of Schedule D, such part of those profits as belongs or is allocated to, or is reserved for, or expended on behalf of, policy holders or annuitants shall be excluded in making the computation, but if any profits so excluded as being reserved for policy holders or annuitants cease at any time to be so reserved and are not allocated to or expended on behalf of policy holders or annuitants, those profits shall be treated as profits of the company for the accounting period in which they ceased to be so reserved.

Former enactment.—TA 1970, s. 309.
Cross references.—See FA 1989, s. 82(5)–(8) (calculation of the profits of life assurance business with respect to periods of account beginning before 14 March 1989).
Amendments.—This section repealed by FA 1989, s. 84(5)(*a*), Sch. 8, para. 2 and Sch. 17, Pt. IV with effect from 14 March 1989, but subject to FA 1989, s. 84(6).

434. Franked investment income etc.

(1) Section 208 shall not prevent franked investment income of a company resident in the United Kingdom which carries on life assurance business from being taken into account as part of the profits in computing trading income in accordance with the provisions applicable to Case I of Schedule D.

(2) In ascertaining for the purposes of section 393 or 394 whether and to what extent a company has incurred a loss on its life assurance business, any profits derived from the investments of its life assurance fund (including franked investment income of a company so resident) shall be treated as part of the profits of that business.

[(3) Subject to sections 437 and 438, the policy holders' fraction of the franked investment income from investments held in connection with a company's life assurance business shall not be used under Chapter V of Part VI to frank distributions made by the company and, accordingly, for the purposes of that Chapter (other than the application of franked investment income under section 241), in relation to any unrelieved income of a company falling within subsection (1) above, the surplus of franked investment income for any accounting period means the aggregate of—
  (*a*) the policy holders' fraction of that franked investment income; and
  (*b*) the amount determined under section 241(3) on the basis that the reference therein to franked investment income is a reference only to the shareholders' fraction of that income.]¹

[(3A) The policy holders' fraction of the franked investment income from investments held in connection with a company's life assurance business shall be left out of account in determining, under subsection (7) of section 13, the franked investment income forming part of the company's profits for the purposes of that section.]¹

(4)–(5) . . .²

(6) For the purposes of section 239 the profits charged to corporation tax for any accounting period (as defined in subsection (6) of that section) shall be reduced by deducting therefrom [the policy holders' fraction thereof]³.

(7) For the purposes of subsection [(3)]⁴ above "unrelieved income" means income which has not been excluded from charge to tax by virtue of any provision and against which [disregarding relief under section 242]⁵ no relief has been allowed by deduction or set-off.

(8) Where subsection (3) or (6) above would deny to a company any relief to which it would have been entitled if it had been charged to tax in respect of its life assurance business under Case I of Schedule D, corresponding relief shall be afforded to the company by repayment of, or set-off against, corporation tax or by payment of tax credit comprised in franked investment income from investments held in connection with that business.

Former enactments.—Sub-ss. (1), (2): TA 1970, s. 308(1), (2).
Sub-s. (3): TA 1970, s. 310(5); FA 1972, Sch. 18, para. 2(3).
Sub-ss. (4), (5): TA 1970, s. 310(6).
Sub-s. (6): FA 1972, Sch. 18, para. 2(4); F(No. 2)A 1987, s. 75(1)(*b*).
Sub-s. (7): TA 1970, s. 310(7); FA 1984, s. 18(5).
Sub-s. (8): FA 1972, Sch. 18, para. 2(5).
Amendments.—¹ Sub-ss. (3), (3A) substituted for sub-s. (3) by FA 1989, s. 84(5)(*b*) and Sch. 8, para. 3 and, subject to FA 1989, s. 84(6), has effect with respect to accounting periods beginning after 31 December 1989 including the 1990 component period as defined in FA 1989, s. 84(3). Previously sub-s. (3) read—

"(3) Any such part of the franked investment income from investments held in connection with a company's life assurance business as is specified in subsection (4) below ("the specified part") shall not be used under Chapter V of Part VI to frank distributions made by the company."

² Sub-ss. (4), (5) repealed by *ibid* and Sch. 17, Pt. IV. They read—

"(4) Subject to subsection (5) below, the specified part shall be, in the case of any unrelieved income, the same fraction of it as the fraction which, on a computation of the profits of the company in respect of its life assurance business in accordance with the provisions applicable to Case I of Schedule D (whether or not the company is in fact charged to tax under that Case for the relevant accounting period or periods), would be connoted by the words in section 433 "such part of those profits as belongs or is allocated to, or is reserved for, or expended on behalf of, policy holders or annuitants.

(5) If the income exceeds the profits as computed in accordance with the provisions applicable to Case I of Schedule D other than section 433, the specified part shall be that fraction of the income so far as not exceeding the profits, together with the amount of the excess."

[3] Words in sub-s. (6) substituted by *ibid*. The original words read—

"such fraction thereof as is equal to the fraction of the profits of the company in respect of its life assurance business which under section 433 is excluded from the computation of those profits or would be so excluded if the profits were computed in accordance with the provisions applicable to Case I of Schedule D."

[4] Number in sub-s. (7) substituted for "(4)" by *ibid*.
[5] Words in sub-s. (7) inserted by *ibid*.

[434A. Limitations on loss relief and group relief

(1) In the case of a company carrying on life assurance business, no relief shall be allowable under Chapter II (loss relief) or Chapter IV (group relief) of Part X against the policy holders' fraction of the relevant profits for any accounting period.

(2) For the purposes of subection (1) above, the relevant profits of a company for an accounting period are the total profits of its life assurance business, less any deduction due under section 76, but before allowing any relief under Chapter II or Chapter IV of Part X.][1]

Amendments.—[1] This section inserted by FA 1989, s. 84(5)(*b*) and Sch. 8, para. 4 and, subject to FA 1989, s. 84(6), has effect with respect to accounting periods beginning after 31 December 1989 including the 1990 component period as defined in FA 1989, s. 84(3).

435. Taxation of gains reserved for policy holders and annuitants

(1) This section has effect in relation to any accounting period of an insurance company carrying on life assurance business and for the purposes of this section—

(a) the life assurance gains are such part of the amount to be included, in accordance with section 345, in the company's total profits as is attributable to gains from investments held in connection with the company's life assurance business;

(b) the policy holders' share of the life assurance gains or of the relevant reliefs is such fraction thereof as is equal to the fraction of the profits of the company in respect of its life assurance business which, under section 433, is excluded from the computation of those profits or would be so excluded if the profits were computed in accordance with the provisions applicable to Case I of Schedule D; and

(c) the relevant reliefs are such of the sums to be deducted from or set off against the company's profits as are deducted from or set off against the life assurance gains.

(2) Corporation tax charged on so much of the policy holders' share of the life assurance gains as remains after setting against it the amounts referred to in subsection (3)(c) below shall be calculated on the basis of a rate of corporation tax of 30 per cent.

(3) For the purposes of this section there shall be ascertained the policy holders' share and the remainder ("the residual part") of the life assurance gains and of the relevant reliefs; and—

(a) the residual part of the relevant reliefs shall be set against the residual part of those gains; and

(b) if the residual part of the relevant reliefs exceeds the residual part of those gains, the excess (or so much of it as does not, together with the policy holders' share of the relevant reliefs, exceed the policy holders' share of those gains) shall be added to the policy holders' share of the relevant reliefs; and

(c) the policy holders' share of the relevant reliefs, with any addition made under paragraph (b) above, shall be set against the policy holders' share of the life assurance gains.

Former enactments.—Sub-s. (1): FA 1974, s. 26(1), (4).
Sub-ss. (2), (3): FA 1974, s. 26(2), (3); F(No. 2)A 1987, s. 75(2), (3).
Amendments.—This section repealed by FA 1989, s. 84(5)(*b*), Sch. 8, para. 5 and Sch. 17, Pt. IV with effect, subject to FA 1989, s. 84(6), with respect to accounting periods beginning after 31 December 1989 including the 1990 component period as defined in FA 1989, s. 84(3).

436. Annuity business and pension business: separate charge on profits

(1) Subject to the provisions of this section, profits arising to an insurance company from general annuity business or pension business shall be treated as income within Schedule D, and be chargeable under Case VI of that Schedule, and for that purpose—

(*a*) the business of each such class shall be treated separately, and
(*b*) subject to paragraph (*a*) above, and to subsection (3) below, the profits therefrom shall be computed in accordance with the provisions of this Act applicable to Case I of Schedule D.

(2) Subsection (1) above shall not apply to an insurance company charged to corporation

tax in accordance with the provisions applicable to Case I of Schedule D in respect of the profits of its ordinary life assurance business.

(3) In making the computation referred to in subsection (1) above—

(a) [sections 82 and 83 of the Finance Act 1989][1] shall apply with the necessary modifications and in particular with the omission of all references to policy holders (other than holders of policies referable to pension business);

(b) ...[2]

(c) there may be set off against the profits any loss, to be computed on the same basis as the profits, which has arisen from pension business or general annuity business in any previous accounting period or year of assessment;

(d) where the computation in question is of profits arising to an insurance company from pension business—

    (i) group income shall not be taken into account as part of those profits, and

    (ii) annuities shall be deductible notwithstanding section 337(2);

and the company shall not be entitled to treat as paid out of profits or gains brought into charge to income tax any part of the annuities paid by the company which is referable to pension business; and

(e) distributions which are not qualifying distributions shall not be taken into account where the computation in question is of the profits arising to an insurance company or overseas life insurance company from general annuity business or pension business.

(4) Section 396 shall not be taken to apply to a loss incurred by a company on its general annuity business or pension business.

(5) Nothing in section 128 or 399(1) shall affect the operation of this section.

Former enactments.—Sub-ss. (1), (2): TA 1970, s. 312(1); FA 1970, Sch. 5, Pt. III, para. 11(3).
Sub-s. (3): TA 1970, ss. 312(2), 314(5); FA 1970, Sch. 5, Pt. III, para. 11(6)(a), (b); FA 1972, Sch. 18, para. 5(1)(a).
Sub-s. (4): TA 1970, s. 312(3); FA 1970, Sch. 5, Pt. III, para. 11(3).
Sub-s. (5): FA 1985, s. 72(7).
Cross references.—See FA 1989, s. 43(13) (sub-s. (1)(b) above to be read as if after the words "this Act" were included the words "FA 1989, s. 43").
Amendments.—[1] Words in sub-s. (3)(a) substituted for the words "section 433" by FA 1989, s. 84(4), (5)(a) and Sch. 8, para. 6 with effect from 14 March 1989, but subject to FA 1989, s. 84(6).
[2] Sub-s. (3)(b) repealed by FA 1989, s. 87(4) and Sch. 17, Pt. IV with respect to accounting periods beginning after 31 December 1989, but subject to FA 1989, ss. 84(1)–(3), 87(5) in relation to a straddling period as defined in those provisions and subject also to FA 1989, s. 84(6). Sub-s. (3)(b) read—

"(b) no deduction shall be allowed in respect of any expenses of management deductible under section 76;".

437. General annuity business

(1) In the case of a company carrying on general annuity business, the annuities paid by the company, so far as referable to that business and so far as they do not exceed the taxed income of the part of the annuity fund so referable, shall be treated as charges on income.

(2) In computing under section 436 the profits arising to an insurance company from general annuity business—

(a) taxed income, group income and income attributable to offshore income gains shall not be taken into account as part of those profits; and

(b) of the annuities paid by the company and referable to general annuity business—

    (i) those which under subsection (1) above are treated as charges on income shall not be deductible, and

    (ii) those which are not so treated shall (notwithstanding section 337(2)) be deductible.

(3) In subsections (1) and (2) above "taxed income" means income charged to corporation tax otherwise than under section 436, and franked investment income.

(4) Subject to subsection (5) below, franked investment income which is taken into account under subsection (2) above to enable annuities referable to general annuity business to be treated as charges on income shall not be used under Chapter V of Part VI to frank distributions made by the company.

(5) For the purposes of subsection (4) above there shall be deducted from the amount of the franked investment income of the company arising in any accounting period and taken into account under subsection (1) above—

(a) the amount of any profit arising in that accounting period to the company from general annuity business and computed under section 436; and

(b) the amount of any group income arising in that accounting period to the company and referable to its general annuity business.

(6) A company which is not resident in the United Kingdom but carries on through a branch or agency there any general annuity business shall not be entitled to treat any part of the annuities paid by it which are referable to that business as paid out of profits or gains brought into charge to income tax.

Former enactments.—Sub-s. (1): TA 1970, s. 313(1).
Sub-s. (2)(*a*): TA 1970, s. 313(2)(*a*); FA 1985, Sch. 25, para. 7.
Sub-s. (2)(*b*): TA 1970, s. 313(2)(*b*).
Sub-s. (3): TA 1970, s. 313(3).
Sub-s. (4): TA 1970, s. 313(4); FA 1972, Sch. 18, para. 3.
Sub-ss. (5), (6): TA 1970, s. 313(5), (6).

438. Pension business: exemption from tax

(1) Exemption from corporation tax shall be allowed in respect of income from, and chargeable gains in respect of, investments and deposits of so much of an insurance company's life assurance fund and separate annuity fund, if any, as is referable to pension business.

(2) The exemption from tax conferred by subsection (1) above shall not exclude any sums from being taken into account as receipts in computing profits or losses for any purpose of the Corporation Tax Acts.

(3) Subject to subsection (6) below, the exclusion by section 208 from the charge to corporation tax of franked investment income shall not prevent such income being taken into account as part of the profits in computing under section 436 income from pension business.

(4) If in the case of any company the income referred to in subsection (1) above includes a distribution in respect of which the company is entitled to a tax credit, the company may, subject to subsections (5) and (6) below, claim to have the amount of that credit paid to it.

(5) If the company is resident in the United Kingdom (so that the distribution and the tax credit in question constitute franked investment income of that company), no franked investment income comprising any tax credit which is paid under subsection (4) above shall, subject to subsection (6) below, be used under Chapter V of Part VI to frank the company's distributions.

(6) If for any accounting period there is, apart from this subsection, a profit arising to an insurance company from pension business and computed under section 436, and the company so elects as respects all or any part of its franked investment income arising in that period, being an amount of franked investment income not exceeding the amount of that profit, subsections (3) to (5) above shall not apply to the franked investment income to which the election relates.

(7) An election under subsection (6) above shall be made by notice given to the inspector not later than two years after the end of the accounting period to which the election relates or within such longer period as the Board may by notice allow.

(8) Nothing in sections 431(4)(*c*) or 643(2) of this Act or section 149B(1)(*h*) of the 1979 Act shall be construed as affording relief in respect of any sums to be brought into account under this section.

Former enactments.—Sub-s. (1): TA 1970, s. 314(1); FA 1970, Sch. 5, Pt. III, para. 11(3), (6)(*c*).
Sub-s. (2): TA 1970, s. 314(2).
Sub-s. (3): TA 1970, s. 314(3)(*a*); FA 1970, Sch. 5, Pt. III, para. 11(3).
Sub-ss. (4), (5): FA 1972, Sch. 18, para. 4(1), (2).
Sub-ss. (6), (7): TA 1970, s. 314(4); FA 1970, Sch. 5, Pt. III, para. 11(3); FA 1972, Sch. 18, para. 4(2).
Sub-s. (8): F(No. 2)A 1987, s. 39(3).

439. Restricted government securities

(1) This section applies where for any accounting period—

(*a*) any division falls to be made between the pension business and any other kind of long-term business of an insurance company, and
(*b*) any of the income or gains or losses of the company for that period relate to restricted government securities;

and where this section applies section 431(3) shall have effect subject to the provisions of this section.

(2) All income, gains or losses of the company which relate to restricted government securities shall be referred to its pension business.

(3) Where the division of the other income, gains or losses of the company is made by reference to the liabilities at any time in the accounting period which are referable to pension business or to two or more kinds of business including pension business, those liabilities shall be treated as reduced by the appropriate amount.

(4) In subsection (3) above "the appropriate amount" means—

(*a*) in a case in which the total liabilities of the company at the time in question which are referable to long-term business are less than the market value at that time of the investments and deposits held by the company relating to all such business, such proportion of the market value of the restricted government securities held by the company at that time as those liabilities bear to the market value of those investments and deposits, and

(*b*) in any other case, the market value of the restricted government securities at that time.

(5) In this section—

"long-term business" has the same meaning as in section 1(1) of the Insurance Companies Act 1982;

"restricted government securities" means, subject to the following provisions of this section, government securities issued on the condition that, except in such circumstances as may be specified in the conditions of issue, they are to be held by insurance companies against and applied solely towards meeting pension business liabilities.

(6) Subject to subsection (7) below, the following Treasury Stock, namely—

(*a*) 2 per cent. Index-linked Treasury Stock 1996;
(*b*) 2 per cent. Index-linked Treasury Stock 2006;
(*c*) $2\frac{1}{2}$ per cent. Index-linked Treasury Stock 2011;

are not restricted government securities for the purposes of this section.

(7) If any of the index-linked stock referred to in subsection (6) above was on 27th March 1982 held by an insurance company against and applied solely towards meeting the liabilities of the company's pension business, then—

(*a*) if and so long as the stock continues to be so held by that company, it shall continue to be treated as restricted government securities for the purposes of this section; and

(*b*) if the stock ceases to be restricted government securities otherwise than by virtue of being actually disposed of or redeemed, on the day on which it so ceases the stock shall be deemed for the purposes of corporation tax, including (subject to subsection (8) below) corporation tax on chargeable gains, to have been disposed of and immediately re-acquired at its market value on that date.

(8) For the purposes of sections 67 and 68 of the 1979 Act (gilt-edged securities)—

(*a*) in ascertaining the date on which securities were acquired, no account shall be taken of any deemed disposal and re-acquisition resulting from subsection (7)(*b*) above; and

(*b*) so long as any index-linked stock continues, by virtue of subsection (7)(*a*) above, to be treated as restricted government securities for the purposes of this section, it shall be regarded as being stock of a different kind from the index-linked stock referred to in subsection (6) above which is not so treated.

Former enactments.—Sub-ss. (1)–(5): FA 1981, s. 41; Insurance Companies Act 1982, Sch. 5, para. 25.
Sub-s. (6): FA 1982, s. 58(1), (3).
Sub-s. (7)(*a*), (*b*): FA 1982, s. 58(4); FA 1982, s. 58(5).
Sub-s. (8): FA 1982, s. 58(6).

440. Identification or exchange of long term assets

(1) The provisions of this section apply to any insurance company which carries on or has carried on long term business, and shall have effect for all purposes of the Corporation Tax Acts.

(2) Subject to subsection (4) below, a profit or loss shall not be taken to arise in respect of any asset of the company by reason only that at any time after the base date the asset was or is exchanged for other assets of the company so as to become or cease to be part of the long term assets.

(3) Subject to subsection (5) below, if an asset of the company which has at any time after 29th April 1975 been exchanged as mentioned in subsection (2) above is—

  (a) within the period of one year beginning with the date of that exchange ("the relevant exchange") exchanged again for other assets of the company so as to cease to be or, as the case may be, become part of the long term assets; or
  (b) within the period of six months beginning with the date of the relevant exchange disposed of by the company,

then any income arising in respect of the asset after the relevant exchange, and any profit, gain or loss accruing to the company on a disposal of the asset made after the relevant exchange, shall be treated as if the relevant exchange had not taken place.

(4) If an insurance company to which this section applies by notice given to the inspector so elects, then, where in the relevant period any relevant asset of the company was or is exchanged as mentioned in subsection (2) above—

  (a) that subsection shall not apply in relation to that asset as regards that exchange; and
  (b) the company shall be treated as if the asset had been disposed of at market value by the company at the time of the exchange.

In this and the following subsection—

  "the relevant period", in relation to a notice under this subsection, means the period of six years from the end of the accounting period of the company in which the notice is given;
  "relevant asset", in relation to an insurance company, means an asset of the company such that, if it were sold, the proceeds would be taken into account in any computation of profits of the company in accordance with the provisions of this Act applicable to Case I of Schedule D.

(5) Where an insurance company has given a notice under subsection (4) above, subsection (3) above shall, as regards relevant assets disposed of by the company in the relevant period, have effect as if paragraph (b) and the reference to any profit, gain or loss accruing to the company on a disposal made after the relevant exchange were omitted.

(6) If at any time after the base date an insurance company to which this section applies disposed or disposes of an asset which—

  (a) was or is part of the long term assets at the time of the disposal, but without having been continuously part of those assets since its acquisition by the company; or
  (b) was or is not part of the long term assets at the time of the disposal, but without having been continuously not part of those assets since its acquisition by the company,

the asset shall be treated, in a case falling within paragraph (a) above, as if it had been continuously part of the long term assets from the time of its acquisition by the company to the time of the disposal, or, in a case falling within paragraph (b) above, as if it had been continuously not part of the long term assets from the time of its acquisition by the company to the time of its disposal; and if the disposal is one as respects which subsection (3) above applies, this subsection shall apply as if the relevant exchange (within the meaning of that subsection) had not taken place.

(7) Without prejudice to subsection (6) above, if—

  (a) an insurance company to which this section applies disposes of an asset which, since its acquisition by the company, has on one or more occasions (whether after the base date or not) been exchanged for other assets of the company; and
  (b) as regards that occasion or one or more of those occasions the company was assessed to income tax or corporation tax in an amount computed by reference to the value of the asset at the time of the exchange,

then, in computing for any purpose of the Corporation Tax Acts the profit, gain or loss (if any) arising on the disposal, the asset shall be deemed to have been acquired by the company on the occasion or latest of the occasions mentioned in paragraph (b) above at a cost equal to the value by reference to which the company was so assessed as regards that occasion.

(8) There shall be made such assessments, reductions of assessments or, on a claim in that behalf, repayments of tax as may in any case be required in order to give effect to subsection (3) or (4) above.

(9) In this section, unless the context otherwise requires, "asset" includes part of an asset and any reference to a disposal of part of an asset includes a reference to a part disposal of an asset within the meaning of section 19(2)(b) of the 1979 Act; and where part of an asset is exchanged or disposed of as mentioned in any of subsections (2) to (7) above, that

subsection shall have effect as if that part of the asset and the part not exchanged or disposed of were separate assets.

(10) For the purposes of this section—

"the base date", in relation to an insurance company, means the last day of the financial year of the company which ended next after 7th December 1973;

"financial year" has the meaning given by section 96 of the Insurance Companies Act 1982;

"long term assets", in relation to an insurance company, means assets representing the fund or funds maintained by the company in respect of its long term business; and

"long term business" has the meaning given by section 1(1) of the Insurance Companies Act 1982.

Former enactments.—F(No. 2)A 1975, s. 42; CGTA 1979, Sch. 7; FA 1987, Sch. 15, para. 8.

441. Foreign life assurance funds

(1) Corporation tax under Cases IV and V on income arising from investments of the foreign life assurance fund of an insurance company shall be computed as in the case mentioned in section 65(4), that is to say, by reference to the amount of income received in the United Kingdom; and this subsection shall apply notwithstanding that that section relates only to income tax.

(2) Where any of the following securities, namely—

(a) securities issued by the Treasury with the condition that the interest thereon shall not be liable to income tax so long as it is shown, in manner directed by the Treasury, that the securities are in the beneficial ownership of persons who are not ordinarily resident in the United Kingdom; or

(b) securities issued by the Treasury with the condition that—

(i) so long as the securities are in the beneficial ownership of persons who are not ordinarily resident in the United Kingdom, the interest thereon shall be exempt from income tax, and

(ii) so long as the securities are in the beneficial ownership of persons who are neither domiciled nor ordinarily resident in the United Kingdom, neither the capital thereof nor the interest thereon shall be liable to any taxation present or future; or

(c) securities to which section 581 applies;

for the time being form part of the investments of the foreign life assurance fund of an insurance company, the income arising from those securities, if applied for the purposes of that fund or reinvested so as to form part of that fund, shall not be liable to tax.

(3) Where any income arising abroad from the investments of the foreign life assurance fund of an insurance company has been remitted to the United Kingdom and invested, as part of the investments of that fund, in any such securities as are mentioned in subsection (2) above, that income shall not be liable to tax and any tax paid thereon shall, if necessary, be repaid to the company on the making of a claim.

(4) Any securities issued by the Treasury in pursuance of the power conferred by section 60(1) of the Finance Act 1940 with a modified form of the condition specified in subsection (2)(b) above shall, save in so far as the terms of the issue otherwise provide, be deemed for the purposes of subsections (2) and (3) above to be such securities as are mentioned in subsection (2) above.

(5) Where income arising from the investments of the foreign life assurance fund of an insurance company has been relieved from tax in pursuance of the provisions of this section, a corresponding reduction shall be made—

(a) in the relief granted under section 76 in respect of expenses of management; and

(b) in any amount on which [in respect of its general annuity business only][1] the company is chargeable to tax by virtue of section 436.

(6) In this section "foreign life assurance fund"—

(a) means any fund representing the amount of the liability of an insurance company in respect of its life assurance business with policy holders and annuitants residing outside the United Kingdom whose proposals were made to, or whose annuity contracts were granted by, the company at or through a branch or agency outside the United Kingdom; and

(b) where such a fund is not kept separately from the life assurance fund, means such part of the life assurance fund as represents the liability of the company under such policies and contracts, such liability being estimated in the same manner as it is estimated for the purpose of the company's periodical return.

(7) Where this section has effect in relation to income arising from investments of any part of an insurance company's life assurance fund, it shall have the like effect in relation to chargeable gains accruing from the disposal of any such investments, and losses so accruing shall not be allowable losses.

(8) For the purposes of this section, an offshore income gain accruing to an insurance company carrying on life assurance business shall, if it accrues in respect of investments held in connection with that business, be treated as if it were income from investments held in connection with that business.

(9) Where any payment is made by the Export Credits Guarantee Department—

(a) under any agreement entered into under arrangements made by the Secretary of State in pursuance of section 11 of the Export Guarantees and Overseas Investment Act 1978, and
(b) in respect of any income—
  (i) which cannot be transferred to the United Kingdom, and
  (ii) which arises from investments of the foreign life assurance fund of an insurance company,

then, to the extent of the payment, this section shall apply in relation to the income as if it had been received in the United Kingdom (and accordingly cannot be received again in the United Kingdom).

Former enactments.—Sub-ss. (1)–(7): TA 1970, s. 315(1)–(6), (9); CGTA 1979, Sch. 7.
Sub-s. (8): FA 1984, s. 99(1).
Sub-s. (9): FA 1972, s. 124(2)(b).
Amendments.—[1] Words in sub-s. (5)(b) inserted by FA 1989, s. 84(4), (5)(b) and Sch. 8, para. 7 with effect, subject to FA 1989, s. 84(6), in relation to accounting periods beginning after 31 December 1989 including the 1990 component period as defined in FA 1989, s. 84(2), (3).

442. Overseas business of U.K. companies

(1) Subsections (2) and (3) below apply where a company resident in the United Kingdom carries on insurance business outside the United Kingdom through a branch or agency and—

(a) that business, or part of it, together with the whole assets of the company used for the purposes of that business or part (or together with the whole of those assets other than cash), is transferred to a company not resident in the United Kingdom;
(b) the business or part is so transferred wholly or partly in exchange for shares, or for shares and loan stock, issued by the transferee company to the transferor company; and
(c) the shares so issued, either alone or taken together with any other shares in the transferee company already held by the transferor company, amount in all to not less than one quarter of the ordinary share capital of the transferee company.

(2) In making any computation in accordance with the provisions of this Act applicable to Case I of Schedule D of the profits or losses of the transferor company for the accounting period in which the transfer occurs, there shall be disregarded any profit or loss in respect of any asset transferred which, apart from this subsection, would fall to be taken into account in making that computation.

(3) Where by virtue of subsection (2) above any profit or loss is disregarded in making any computation otherwise than for the purposes of section 76(2) the profit or loss shall be treated for the purposes of the 1979 Act as a chargeable gain or allowable loss accruing to the transferor company on the transfer.

(4) Where at any time a company resident in the United Kingdom—

(a) which carries on insurance business wholly outside the United Kingdom, and
(b) the whole or part of whose ordinary share capital is beneficially owned by one or more companies resident in the United Kingdom,

ceases to be resident in the United Kingdom, the profits or losses of the company in respect of that business for the accounting period ending at that time shall be computed for tax purposes without regard to the whole, or, as the case may be, a corresponding part of any profit or loss in respect of any asset which, apart from this subsection, would fall to be calculated in accordance with section 100(1)(*b*) and taken into account in making that computation.

Former enactments.—FA 1977, s. 45(1)–(4); CGTA 1979, Sch. 7.

443. Life policies carrying rights not in money

Where any investments or other assets are or have been, in accordance with a policy issued in the course of life assurance business carried on by an insurance company, transferred to the policy holder on or after 6th April 1967, the policy holder's acquisition of the assets, and the disposal of them to him, shall be deemed to be for a consideration equal to the market value of the assets for the purposes of computing income in accordance with Case I or VI of Schedule D.

Former enactment.—FA 1970, s. 321(1)(*b*), (2).

444. Life policies issued before 5th August 1965

(1) This section applies in relation to policies of life assurance issued before 5th August 1965 by a company carrying on life assurance business, being policies which—
  (*a*) provide for benefits consisting to any extent of investments of a specified description or of a sum of money to be determined by reference to the value of such investments, but
  (*b*) do not provide for the deduction from those benefits of any amount by reference to tax chargeable in respect of chargeable gains.

(2) Where—
  (*a*) the investments of the company's life assurance fund, so far as referable to those policies, consist wholly or mainly of investments of the description so specified, and
  (*b*) on the company becoming liable under any of those policies for any such benefits (including benefits to be provided on the surrender of a policy), a chargeable gain accrues to the company from the disposal, in meeting or for the purpose of meeting that liability, of investments of that description forming part of its life assurance fund, or would so accrue if the liability were met by or from the proceeds of such a disposal,

then the company shall be entitled as against the person receiving the benefits to retain out of those benefits a part not exceeding in amount or value corporation tax, at the rate specified in subsection (3) below, in respect of the chargeable gain referred to in paragraph (*b*) above, computed without regard to any amount retained under this subsection.

(3) The amount to be retained under subsection (2) above shall, subject to subsection (4) below, be computed by reference to the rate of corporation tax for the time being in force or, if no rate of corporation tax has yet been fixed for the financial year, the rate last in force.

(4) In so far as the chargeable gain represents or would represent a gain belonging or allocated to, or reserved for, policy holders, the amount to be retained shall be computed by reference to a rate of tax not exceeding 37.5 per cent.

Former enactment.—TA 1970, s. 322.

Provisions applying only to overseas life insurance companies

445. Charge to tax on investment income

(1) Any income of an overseas life insurance company from the investments of its life assurance fund (excluding the pension fund and general annuity fund, if any), wherever received, shall, to the extent provided in this section, be deemed to be profits comprised in Schedule D and shall be charged to corporation tax under Case III of Schedule D.

(2) In subsection (1) above "income" shall not include—
  (*a*) distributions which are not qualifying distributions or income attributable to offshore income gains; or
  (*b*) annual profits or gains chargeable to tax by virtue of section 714(2) or 716(3).

(3) Qualifying distributions received from companies resident in the United Kingdom shall be brought into account under this section notwithstanding their exclusion from the charge to corporation tax.

(4) A portion only of the income from the investments of the life assurance fund (excluding

the pension fund and general annuity fund, if any) shall be charged in accordance with subsection (1) above, and for any accounting period that portion shall be determined by the formula—

$$\frac{A \times B}{C}$$

where—

A is the total income from those investments for that period;

B is the average of the liabilities for that period to policy holders resident in the United Kingdom and to policy holders resident abroad whose proposals were made to the company at or through its branch or agency in the United Kingdom; and

C is the average of the liabilities for that period to all the company's policy holders;

but any reference in this subsection to liabilities does not include liabilities in respect of general annuity and pension business.

(5) For the purposes of subsection (4) above the average of any liabilities for an accounting period shall be taken as one half of the aggregate of the liabilities at the beginning and end of the valuation period which coincides with that accounting period or in which that accounting period falls.

(6) For the purposes of this section the liabilities of an insurance company attributable to any business at any time shall be ascertained by reference to the net liabilities of the company as valued by an actuary for the purposes of the relevant periodical return.

(7) Section 73 shall not apply to tax in respect of income to which subsection (1) above applies.

(8) In the case of an overseas life insurance company—

(*a*) in computing for the purposes of this section the income from the investments of the life assurance fund of the company, any interest, dividends and other payments whatsoever to which section 48 or 123(4) extends shall be included notwithstanding the exemption from tax conferred by those sections respectively; and

(*b*) where in computing that income any interest on any securities issued by the Treasury is excluded by virtue of a condition of the issue of those securities regulating the treatment of the interest on them for tax purposes, the relief under section 76 shall be reduced so as to bear to the amount of relief which would be granted but for the provisions of this paragraph the same proportion as the amount of that income, excluding that interest, bears to the amount of that income including that interest.

Former enactments.—Sub-s. (1): TA 1970, s. 316(1); FA 1970, Sch. 5, Pt. III, para. 11(6)(*d*).
Sub-s. (2): TA 1970, s. 316(1A); FA 1972, Sch. 18, para. 5(1)(*b*); FA 1985, Sch. 23, para. 20(1), Sch. 25, para. 8.
Sub-s. (3): TA 1970, s. 316(2); FA 1972, Sch. 18, para. 5(2).
Sub-s. (4): TA 1970, s. 316(3); FA 1970, Sch. 5, Pt. III, para. 11(6)(*d*), (*e*).
Sub-ss. (5)–(7): TA 1970, s. 316(4)–(6).
Sub-s. (8): TA 1970, s. 328(3).

446. Annuity business

(1) Nothing in the Corporation Tax Acts shall prevent the qualifying distributions of companies resident in the United Kingdom from being taken into account as part of the profits in computing, under section 436, the profits arising from pension business and general annuity business to an overseas life insurance company.

(2) Any charge to tax under section 436 for any accounting period on profits arising to an overseas life insurance company from general annuity business shall extend only to a portion of the profits arising from that business and that portion shall be determined by the formula—

$$\frac{A \times B}{C}$$

where—

A is the total amount of those profits;

B is the average of the liabilities attributable to that business for the relevant accounting period in respect of contracts with persons resident in the United Kingdom or contracts with persons resident abroad whose proposals were made to the company at or through its branch or agency in the United Kingdom; and

C is the average of the liabilities attributable to that business for that accounting period in respect of all contracts.

(3) For the purposes of subsection (2) above, the average of any liabilities for an accounting period shall be taken as one half of the aggregate of the liabilities at the beginning and end of the valuation period which coincides with that accounting period or in which that accounting period falls.

(4) For the purposes of this section the liabilities of an insurance company attributable to general annuity business at any time shall be ascertained by reference to the net liabilities of the company as valued by an actuary for the purposes of the relevant periodical return.

Former enactments.—Sub-s. (1): TA 1970, s. 318(1); FA 1970, Sch. 5, Pt. III, para. 11(3); FA 1972, Sch. 18, para. 5(2). Sub-ss. (2)–(4): TA 1970, s. 318(2)–(4).

447. Set-off of income tax and tax credits against corporation tax

(1) For the purposes of subsection (3) of section 11 as it applies to life insurance companies, the amount of the income tax referred to in that subsection which shall be available for set-off under that subsection in an accounting period shall be limited in accordance with subsections (2) to (4) below.

(2) If the company is chargeable to corporation tax for an accounting period in accordance with section 445 in respect of the income from the investments of its life assurance fund, the amount of income tax available for set-off against any corporation tax assessed for that period on that income shall not exceed an amount equal to income tax at the basic rate on the portion of income from investments which is chargeable to corporation tax by virtue of subsection (4) of that section.

(3) If the company is chargeable to corporation tax for an accounting period in accordance with section 446 on a proportion of the total amount of the profits arising from its general annuity business, the amount of income tax available for set-off against any corporation tax assessed for that period on those profits shall not exceed an amount equal to income tax at the basic rate on the like proportion of the income from investments included in computing those profits.

(4) Where an overseas life insurance company receives a distribution in respect of which it is entitled to a tax credit the company may claim to have that credit set off against any corporation tax assessed on the company under section 445 or 446 for the accounting period in which the distribution is received, but the restriction in subsections (2) and (3) above on the amount of income tax that may be set off against corporation tax so assessed shall apply to the aggregate of that income tax and of the tax credit that can be so set off by virtue of this subsection.

Former enactments.—Sub-ss. (1)–(3): TA 1970, s. 319; FA 1971, Sch. 6, para. 39. Sub-s. (4): FA 1972, Sch. 18, para 6.

448. Qualifying distributions and tax credits

(1) Where an overseas life insurance company receives a qualifying distribution made by a company resident in the United Kingdom and relief in respect of the distribution is not available or is not claimed under arrangements specified in an Order in Council made under section 788, the overseas life insurance company shall be deemed for the purposes of sections 76(3) and (4), 434(8), 436, 438 and 445 to 447 to be entitled to such a tax credit in respect of the distribution as it would be entitled to under section 231 if it were resident in the United Kingdom; and accordingly the distribution shall be treated for the purposes of those provisions as representing income equal to the aggregate of the amount or value of the distribution and the amount of that credit.

(2) Where under subsection (1) above an overseas life insurance company is deemed to be entitled to a tax credit in respect of a distribution, it may claim to have the income represented by the distribution set, subject to subsection (3) below, against its profits chargeable to tax under section 436 or against its income chargeable to tax in accordance with section 445 or partly against the one and partly against the other; but to the extent that any income is so set the tax credit included in it shall not be payable and shall not be set against corporation tax under section 447(4).

(3) The amounts that an overseas life insurance company may by virtue of subsection (2) above set against profits or income of any description shall not exceed the amount of the profits or income of that description and shall be further limited as follows—

    (a) the amount set against profits arising from general annuity business shall not exceed a portion of the company's income from investments referable to that business, and that portion shall be determined by the same formula as determines under section 446 the portion of those profits which is chargeable to tax; and

(b) the amount set against profits from pension business shall not exceed such of its income referable to that business as is represented by distributions in respect of which the company is deemed to be entitled to a tax credit by virtue of this section, and shall not reduce any other income.

(4) Where by virtue of a set-off under this section income or profits of any description are reduced by any amount, that amount shall be left out of account in determining the amount of income tax which is available for set-off against corporation tax under section 11(3).

(5) A claim under this section in respect of a distribution shall not prevent the making of a subsequent claim for relief in respect of that distribution under arrangements specified in an Order in Council made under section 788; but where such a subsequent claim is made the claim under this section shall be deemed never to have been made, and no adjustment (whether by additional assessments or otherwise) to which the subsequent claim gives rise shall be out of time if it is made within 12 months after the making of the subsequent claim.

Former enactment.—FA 1973, s. 40(2)–(6).

449. Double taxation agreements

(1) This section applies to an overseas life insurance company if, by virtue of arrangements specified in an Order in Council made under section 788, no charge to corporation tax under Case III of Schedule D arises under section 445 in respect of any income of the company from the investments of its life assurance fund (excluding the pension fund and general annuity fund, if any).

(2) For the purposes of section 242 so much of any relevant distributions as is received in any year of assessment by an overseas life insurance company to which this section applies in respect of the portion of the investments of its life assurance fund (excluding the pension fund and general annuity fund, if any) attributable to the business of its branch or agency in the United Kingdom shall be deemed to be franked investment income of that company, and accordingly the company may make a claim under subsection (1) of section 242 for any of the purposes specified in subsection (2) of that section.

(3) In subsection (2) above "relevant distributions" means distributions in respect of which the company receiving them is entitled to a tax credit.

Former enactments.—TA 1970, s. 320; FA 1972, Sch. 18, para. 5(2); FA 1970, Sch. 5, Pt. III, para. 6(d).

Underwriters

450. Assessment, set-off of losses and reinsurance

(1) Income tax, for any year of assessment, on the profits or gains arising from a member's underwriting business or from assets forming part of a premiums trust fund shall be computed on the profits or gains of that year of assessment; but for this purpose and all other purposes of the Income Tax Acts—

(a) the profits or gains arising in any year of assessment from a member's underwriting business shall be taken to be those arising in the corresponding underwriting year; and
(b) the profits or gains arising from assets forming part of a premiums trust fund shall be taken to be those allocated under the rules or practice of Lloyd's to the corresponding underwriting year.

[(2) The aggregate for any year of assessment of—

(a) the profits or gains arising to a member from his underwriting business; and
(b) the profits or gains arising to him from assets forming part of a premiums trust fund,

shall be chargeable to tax under Case I of Schedule D; but nothing in this subsection shall affect the manner in which the amount of those profits or gains is to be computed.][1]

[(2A) Schedule 19A shall have effect with respect to the assessment and collection of tax charged under Case I of Schedule D in accordance with this section.][1]

(3) Relief under section 380 in respect of a loss sustained by a member in his underwriting business in any year of assessment shall not be given under subsection (2) of that section but may, if the member so claims and he was a member in the preceding year of assessment, be

given against his income for that preceding year, so far as it cannot be given against the income for the year in which the loss was sustained and can be given after any relief for a loss sustained in that preceding year.

(4) In any case where a member has taken out an insurance against losses in his underwriting business—

(*a*) any premium paid by him on that insurance shall be deducted as an expense in computing the profits or gains arising from that business; and

[(*b*) any insurance money payable to him under that insurance in respect of a loss shall be taken into account as a trading receipt in computing those profits or gains for the year of assessment which corresponds to the underwriting year in which the loss arose;][2]

[(5) Subsection (5A) below applies where—

(*a*) in accordance with the rules or practice of Lloyd's and in consideration of the payment of a premium, one member agrees with another to meet liabilities arising from the latter's business for an underwriting year so that the accounts of the business for that year may be closed; and

(*b*) the member by whom the premium is payable is a continuing member, that is, a member not only of the syndicate as a member of which he is liable to pay the premium ("the reinsured syndicate") but also of the syndicate as a member of which the other member is entitled to receive it ("the reinsurer syndicate").][3]

[(5A) In any case where this subsection applies—

(*a*) in computing for the purposes of income tax the profits or gains of the continuing member's business as a member of the reinsured syndicate, the amount of the premium shall be deductible as an expense of his only to the extent that it is shown not to exceed a fair and reasonable assessment of the value of the liabilities in respect of which it is payable; and

(*b*) in computing for those purposes the profits or gains of his business as a member of the reinsurer syndicate, those profits or gains shall be reduced by an amount equal to any part of a premium which, by virtue of paragraph (*a*) above, is not deductible as an expense of his as a member of the reinsured syndicate;

and the assessment referred to above shall be taken to be fair and reasonable only if it is arrived at with a view to producing the result that a profit does not accrue to the member to whom the premium is payable but that he does not suffer a loss.][3]

(6) The cost of acquisition and the consideration for the disposal of assets forming part of a premiums trust fund shall be left out of account in computing the profits or gains or losses of a member's underwriting business for the purposes of Schedule D (and accordingly shall not be excluded for the purposes of capital gains tax under section 31 or 33 of the 1979 Act).

Former enactments.—Sub-s. (1): FA 1973, Sch. 16, para. 2.
Sub-s. (2): FA 1973, Sch. 16, para. 16.
Sub-s. (3): FA 1973, Sch. 16, para. 3.
Sub-s. (4): FA 1973, Sch. 16, para. 4.
Sub-s. (5): F(No. 2)A 1987, s. 70.
Sub-s. (6): FA 1973, Sch. 16, para. 5; CGTA 1979, Sch. 7.
Cross references.—See FA 1988, s. 58(2)–(5) (amendments to FA 1973, s. 39 and Sch. 16 and insertion of new Schedule 16A effective for the years 1986–87 and 1987–88),
s. 58(3)(*b*) and Sch. 14 Pt. IV (repeal of FA 1973, Sch. 16, para. 16 effective from the year 1986–87),
s. 59(2), (3) (amendments to FA 1973, Sch. 16, para. 4 effective for the years 1985–86, 1986–87 and 1987–88),
s. 60(2), (3) (amendments to F(No. 2)A 1987 s. 70 effective for the years 1985–86, 1986–87 and 1987–88);
FA 1989, Sch. 11, para. 10(7)(*a*) (application of sub-s. (1)(*b*) of this section to Lloyd's underwriter's income from deep gain securities).
Amendments.—[1] Sub-ss. (2), (2A) substituted for sub-s. (2) by FA 1988, s. 58(1), (5).
[2] Sub-s. (4)(*b*) substituted by FA 1988, s. 59(1), (3).
[3] Sub-ss. (5), (5A) substituted for sub-s. (5) by FA 1988, s. 60(1), (3)(*a*) in relation to premiums payable in connection with the closing of underwriting accounts in the year 1988–89.

451. Regulations

(1) The Board may by regulations provide—

[(*a*) for the assessment and collection of tax charged in accordance with section 450 (so far as not provided for by Schedule 19A);][1]

[(*aa*) for making, in the event of any changes in the rules or practice of Lloyd's, such amendments of that Schedule as appear to the Board to be expedient having regard to those changes;][1]

(*b*) for modifying the provisions of section 450 in relation to syndicates continuing for more than two years after the end of an underwriting year;

(*c*) for giving credit for foreign tax.

[(1A) Regulations under subsection (1) above may make provision [with respect to any year or years of assessment; and the year (or any of the years) may be the one in which the regulations are made or any year falling before or after that year.]³]²

[(1B) But the regulations may not make provision with respect to any year of assessment which precedes the next but one preceding the year of assessment in which the regulations are made.]⁴

(2) The Treasury may by regulations modify any of the provisions specified in paragraphs (a) to (c) below in their application to companies permitted by the Council of Lloyd's to act as underwriting agents at Lloyd's—

(a) section 11 of the Management Act (return of profits);
(b) section 87A of that Act (interest on overdue corporation tax); and
(c) section 10(1) of this Act.

(3) Regulations under subsection (2) above shall not have effect with respect to accounting periods ending on or before such day, not being earlier than 31st March 1992, as the Treasury may by order appoint for the purposes of that subsection.

(4) Regulations made under paragraph 17(1)(b) of Schedule 16 to the Finance Act 1973 which are in force immediately before the coming into operation of this Act shall continue in force notwithstanding the repeal of that paragraph by this Act, and shall be deemed to have been made under this section.

Former enactments.—Sub-s. (1): FA 1973, Sch. 16, para. 17(1)(a), (c), (e).
Sub-ss. (2), (3): F(No. 2)A 1987, Sch. 6, para. 8.
Sub-s. (4): FA 1973, Sch. 16, para. 17(1)(b).
Cross references.—See FA 1988, s. 61(4), (5) (amendments to FA 1973, Sch. 16, para. 17(1) effective for the years 1986–87 and 1987–88).
Amendments.—¹ Sub-s. (1)(a), (aa) substituted for sub-s. (1)(a) by FA 1988, s. 61(1)(b), (5).
² Sub-s. (1A) inserted by FA 1988, s. 61(1)(c), (5).
³ Words in sub-s. (1A) substituted by FA 1989, s. 92(1).
⁴ Sub-s. (1B) inserted by FA 1989, s. 92(2).

452. Special reserve funds

(1) If in the case of Lloyd's—

(a) arrangements are made for the setting up in relation to each underwriting member of such a special reserve fund as is referred to in the following provisions of this section and sections 453 to 456; and
(b) the arrangements comply with the requirements of this section and sections 453 to 455, are approved by the Board and are certified by the Secretary of State to be in the public interest;

then, subject to section 456(4), the provisions of this section and sections 453 to 456 relating to taxation shall have effect in relation to any underwriting member.

(2) The arrangements must provide for the setting up, in relation to the underwriter, of a special reserve fund vested in trustees who have control over it and power to invest the capital thereof and to vary the investments.

(3) Where part of the business of the underwriter is carried on through an underwriting agent and part is not so carried on, or where different parts of his business are carried on through different underwriting agents, the arrangements may provide for separate special reserve funds being constituted in relation to the different parts of his business.

(4) The arrangements must provide—

(a) for the income arising from the investments of the underwriter's special reserve fund or funds being held on trust for the underwriter, his personal representatives or assigns; and
(b) that, on the underwriter ceasing to carry on his business, the capital of his special reserve fund or funds, so far as not required for giving effect to the requirements of section 453, shall be paid over to the underwriter or his personal representatives or assigns.

(5) The arrangements must be such as to secure that if, for an underwriting year corresponding to a year of assessment during the whole or any part of which the underwriter continues to carry on his business (subject to section 456(4)), the underwriter makes a profit from his business, he has the right to make, into his special reserve fund or funds, payments ("permissible payments") the gross amount of which is not in the aggregate greater than £7,000 or 50 per cent. of the profit, whichever is the less, or such less sum as may be specified in the arrangements.

(6) The amount of any permissible payment shall be notified to the inspector not later than 12 months after the date at which the accounts of the business for that underwriting year are deemed by the Board to be closed for the purposes of the arrangements, and no permissible payment shall be made more than 30 days after the date on which the inspector has notified his agreement in writing or, if later, 30 days after the expiration of those 12 months.

(7) Where the underwriter carries on his business during part only of the year of assessment referred to in subsection (5) above, the maximum gross amount of the permissible payments shall be reduced by the application thereto of the proportion which the part of that year of assessment for which he is entitled to profits from the business bears to a full year.

(8) In subsection (5) above "profit" means a profit computed in the manner in which the profits or gains of the business of the underwriting year in question would fall to be computed under [in accordance with section 450][1] if—

(a) income arising from ...[2], his special reserve fund or funds and any other fund required or authorised by the rules of Lloyd's or required by the underwriting agent through whom the business or any part thereof is carried on, to be kept in connection with the business fell to be taken into account; and

(b) all shares of the profits of the business and all charges related to those profits or to the income mentioned in paragraph (a) above, being shares and charges payable to persons other than the underwriter and not otherwise taken into account, fell to be deducted.

[In paragraph (a) above "income" includes—

(a) annual profits or gains chargeable to tax by virtue of section 714(2) or 716(3),
(b) amounts treated as income chargeable to tax by virtue of paragraph 4 of Schedule 4, and
(c) amounts treated as income chargeable to tax by virtue of paragraph 4 of Schedule 11 to the Finance Act 1989.][3]

Former enactments.—Sub-s. (1): TA 1970, Sch. 10, para. 1; Secretary of State for Trade and Industry Order 1970, S.I. 1970 No. 1537.
Sub-ss. (2), (3): TA 1970, Sch. 10, para. 5.
Sub-s. (4)(a), (b): TA 1970, Sch. 10, para 6; TA 1970, Sch. 10, para 10.
Sub-s. (5): TA 1970, Sch. 10, para. 7(1), (2).
Sub-s. (6): TA 1970, Sch. 10, para. 7(1)(a); FA 1973, Sch. 16, paras. 8, 10.
Sub-s. (7): TA 1970, Sch. 10, para. 7(1)(b); Secretary of State for Trade and Industry Order 1970, S.I. 1970 No. 1537.
Sub-s. (8): TA 1970, Sch. 10, para. 7(3); FA 1985, Sch. 23, para. 29.
Cross references.—See FA 1988, s. 61(2), (5) and Sch. 14, Pt. IV (amendments to TA 1970, Sch. 10, para. 7(3) effective for the years 1986–87 and 1987–88).
Amendments.—[1] Words in sub-s. (8) substituted by FA 1988, s. 61(1)(d), (5).
[2] Words in sub-s. (8)(a) repealed by FA 1988, s. 61(1)(d), (5) and Sch. 14, Pt IV.
[3] Words in sub-s. (8) substituted by FA 1989, s. 96(1), (4) where a disposal of a deep discount security or a transfer or a redemption of a deep gain security occurs after 13 March 1989.

453. Payments into premiums trust fund on account of losses

(1) The arrangements must be such as to secure that, if it is certified that the underwriter has sustained a loss in his business for an underwriting year subsequent to that which corresponds to the first year of assessment to which section 452(5) applies, there shall be made into his premiums trust fund, out of the capital of his special reserve fund or funds, payments the gross amount of which is equal in the aggregate to the certified amount of the loss.

(2) If the capital of the underwriter's special reserve fund or funds, reduced by so much thereof as represents sums paid into it or them as a consequence of a profit for a year later than the year of the loss, is less than the net amount of the payments required to be made by subsection (1) above, those payments shall be reduced so that the net amount thereof is equal to the capital of the fund or funds as so reduced.

(3) In this section—

(a) "loss" means a loss computed in the manner in which the profits or gains of the business of the underwriting year in question would fall to be computed under section 452(8); and
(b) where, under any arrangement between the underwriter and another person which provides for the sharing of losses, any amount is paid to the underwriter by that person as that person's share of a loss for that year, the loss (as so computed) shall be reduced by that amount.

(4) In this section "certified" means certified by a certificate of the inspector, but—

(a) no certificate shall be given by the inspector until 30 days have elapsed from the date on which he has given notice to the underwriter or his personal representatives stating his intention to give a certificate and stating the amount which he proposes to specify as the amount of the loss;

(b) the underwriter or his personal representatives may, on giving notice to the inspector within that 30 day period, appeal to the Special Commissioners;

(c) where notice is so given by the underwriter or his personal representatives, the inspector shall not without the consent of the underwriter or his personal representatives give any certificate until after the hearing of the appeal; and

(d) on the hearing of the appeal, the Special Commissioners may direct the inspector not to give a certificate or to give it with such an amount specified as the amount of the loss as may be specified in the direction.

(5) The arrangements may authorise the making of payments pursuant to subsection (1) above on a provisional basis before the amount of the loss has been finally ascertained and certified by the inspector.

(6) The amount so withdrawn shall not exceed such proportion of the estimated loss as may be specified in the arrangements.

(7) When the amount of the loss has been certified by the inspector such adjustments shall be made by repayment to the underwriter's special reserve fund or funds, or by further withdrawal of sums for payment into the underwriter's premiums trust fund, as will secure that the net amount withdrawn from the underwriter's special reserve fund or funds in respect of the loss is that required pursuant to subsection (1) above; and no tax consequences shall ensue on the withdrawal of sums in respect of a loss until the amount of the loss has been so certified and any such adjustments have been made.

Former enactments.—Sub-ss. (1), (2): TA 1970, Sch. 10, para. 8(1).
Sub-ss. (3), (4): TA 1970, Sch. 10, para. 8(2), (3).
Sub-ss. (5)–(7): TA 1970, Sch. 10, para. 9.

454. Income tax consequences on payments into and out of special reserve fund

(1) Where such a payment as is mentioned in section 452(5) is made into a special reserve fund of an underwriter by reason of the making by him of a profit for an underwriting year—

(a) subject to subsection (2) below, the payment shall be deemed to be an annual payment chargeable to income tax by way of deduction and payable and paid in the year of assessment corresponding to that underwriting year; and

(b) the sum actually paid shall be deemed for the purposes of sections 452 to 456 and for all income tax purposes to be a net amount corresponding to a gross amount from which income tax has been duly deducted.

(2) Subsection (1)(a) above—

(a) shall not reduce any income other than income derived from the underwriter's underwriting business or from any deposit made or assets held on trust in connection with that business; and

(b) subject to paragraph (a) above, shall reduce income other than investment income before reducing investment income.

(3) Where such a payment as is mentioned in section 453(1) is made out of a special reserve fund of an underwriter into a premiums trust fund of his by reason that he has sustained a loss for an underwriting year then, subject to section 453(7)—

(a) the payment shall be deemed for all income tax purposes—

(i) to be an annual payment chargeable to income tax by way of deduction and paid out of profits or gains brought into charge to income tax; and
(ii) to have been payable and paid to the underwriter; and
(iii) to have been payable and paid to him on the last day of the year of assessment corresponding to that underwriting year or, if he ceased to carry on his business before that day, on the last day on which he carried on his business; and

(b) the sum actually paid shall be deemed for the purposes of sections 452 to 456 and for all income tax purposes to be a net amount corresponding to a gross amount from which income tax has been duly deducted for the year of assessment in which the payment is so deemed to have been payable and paid.

(4) Where such a payment as is mentioned in section 453(1) is made out of a special reserve fund of an underwriter by reason that he has sustained a loss, relief in respect of the loss

shall, so far as possible, be given by treating the loss as reducing the income represented by the payment.

(5) Where the underwriter ceases to carry on his business before his death and under so much of the arrangements as gives effect to section 452(4)(*b*) a sum is paid to him or his personal representatives or assigns—

  (*a*) the payment shall be deemed for all income tax purposes—

   (i) to be an annual payment chargeable to income tax by way of deduction and paid out of profits or gains brought into charge to income tax; and
   (ii) to have been payable and paid to the underwriter; and
   (iii) to have been payable and paid to him on the last day on which he carried on his business; and

  (*b*) the sum actually paid shall be deemed for the purposes of sections 452 to 456 and for all income tax purposes to be a net amount corresponding to a gross amount from which income tax has been duly deducted.

(6) Neither the arrangements, nor any disposition, trust, covenant, agreement or arrangement entered into for the purposes of the arrangements, shall be treated as included in the expression "settlement" for the purposes of Chapter III or IV of Part XV.

Former enactments.—Sub-s. (1): TA 1970, Sch. 10, para. 11(1)(*a*), (*b*).
Sub-s. (2): TA 1970, Sch. 10, para. 11(i), (ii); FA 1973, Sch. 16, paras. 8, 11.
Sub-s. (3): TA 1970, Sch. 10, para. 11(2).
Sub-s. (4): TA 1970, Sch. 10, para. 11(2A); FA 1973, Sch. 16, paras. 8, 12.
Sub-s. (5): TA 1970, Sch. 10, para. 11(3).
Sub-s. (6): TA 1970, Sch. 10, para 11(4).

455. Income tax consequences on death of underwriter

(1) In this section "the lower limit" means the limit which would be imposed by section 452(5) if the words "£5,000 or 35 per cent. of that profit, whichever is the less" stood in that subsection in place of the words "£7,000 or 50 per cent. of that profit, whichever is the less".

(2) Where an underwriter dies while carrying on his business and, after giving effect to the requirements of section 453, his special reserve fund or funds include an amount which represents an excess in the payments made into the fund or funds for any underwriting year over the lower limit—

  (*a*) he shall be deemed for all income tax purposes to have received in the year of assessment corresponding to that underwriting year a payment of that amount—

   (i) which was an annual payment chargeable to income tax by way of deduction and paid out of profits or gains brought into charge to income tax, and
   (ii) which was payable in the year of assessment in which it is deemed to have been paid, and

  (*b*) the payment (to that actual amount) shall be deemed for the purposes of sections 452 to 456 and for all income tax purposes to be a net amount corresponding to a gross amount from which tax has been duly deducted.

(3) Where, to give effect to the requirements of section 453 as to the meeting of a loss, any withdrawal was made at any time from the capital of the underwriter's special reserve fund or funds, the amount withdrawn shall be regarded for the purposes of subsection (2) above—

  (*a*) as having been met out of payments made into the fund or funds for underwriting years before that in which the loss was incurred, and as having been met before any withdrawal to meet a loss for a later underwriting year; and
  (*b*) as having been met out of so much of the payments made for any underwriting year as was not in excess of the lower limit, rather than out of such part of the payments made for any underwriting year as was in excess of the lower limit; and
  (*c*) subject to that, as having been met out of payments in excess of the lower limit for a later year rather than out of payments in excess of the lower limit for an earlier year;

and, where payments have been made into the underwriter's special reserve fund or funds for any underwriting year in excess of the lower limit, his fund or funds shall be deemed at all subsequent times to include an amount representing that excess except to the extent that any withdrawal is, under the provisions of this subsection, to be regarded as having been met out of that amount.

(4) Any tax chargeable by virtue of this section shall be assessed and charged upon the underwriter's personal representatives and tax so charged shall be a debt due from and

payable out of his estate; and, notwithstanding section 34(1) of the Management Act (which requires assessments to be made not later than six years after the end of the year to which they relate), assessments in respect of tax so chargeable may be made at any time not later than three years after the end of the year of assessment in which the underwriter died.

(5) References in this section to payments made into a special reserve fund or funds for any underwriting year are references to payments made, as described in section 452(5), by reference to the profits made for that underwriting year.

Former enactment.—TA 1970, Sch. 10, para 12.

456. Unearned income, variation of arrangements and cancellation of approval etc.

(1) So much of an underwriter's income as is attributable to payments from his special reserve fund or to such an excess as is mentioned in section 455 shall (so far as remaining after allowing for any relief by which it is reduced) be treated as unearned income if, but only if, his income from his underwriting business falls to be so treated.

(2) Where, as a result of a change in the circumstances in which an underwriting business is carried on, an underwriter's income from the business falls to be treated as unearned income, the change shall be disregarded for the purposes of subsection (1) above except to the extent that the special reserve fund represents payments made into it after the change; and for this purpose any amount withdrawn after the change to give effect to the requirements of section 453 shall, so far as possible and notwithstanding section 455(3), be regarded as having been met by payments into the fund made after the change.

(3) The arrangements may from time to time be varied with the consent of the Board and the Secretary of State.

(4) If, after giving notice of their intention so to do to the Council of Lloyd's, the Board or the Secretary of State cancel the approval or certificate which they have or he has given with respect to the arrangements, section 452(5) to (9) shall not apply, in the case of any underwriter, to any year of assessment after the year of assessment in which the approval or certificate is cancelled.

Former enactments.—Sub-ss. (1), (2): TA 1970, Sch. 10, para. 12A; FA 1973, Sch. 16, paras. 8, 13.
Sub-s. (3): TA 1970, Sch. 10, para. 13; Secretary of State for Trade and Industry Order 1970, S.I. 1970 No. 1537.
Sub-s. (4): TA 1970, Sch. 10, para. 14(*b*); Lloyd's Act 1982, Ch. XIV, s. 15(2); Secretary of State for Trade and Industry Order 1970, S.I. 1970 No. 1537.

457. Interpretation of sections 450 to 456

(1) In sections 450 to 456—

> "arrangements" means any such arrangements as are referred to in section 452(1);
> "business", in relation to an underwriter, means his underwriting business as a member of Lloyd's, whether carried on personally or through an underwriting agent, and does not include any other business carried on by him, and in particular, where he is himself an underwriting agent, does not include his business as such an agent;
> "member" means an underwriting member of Lloyd's;
> "net amount" and "gross amount", in relation to any payment, mean respectively the sum actually paid and the sum which, after deduction of income tax, is equal to the sum actually paid;
> "premiums trust fund" means such a trust fund as is referred to in section 83 of the Insurance Companies Act 1982;
> "underwriting year" means the calendar year.

(2) For the purpose of construing any reference in sections 450 to 456 to the year of assessment which corresponds to an underwriting year or to the underwriting year which corresponds to a year of assessment, an underwriting year and a year of assessment shall be deemed to correspond to each other if the underwriting year ends in the year of assessment.

Former enactments.—TA 1970, Sch. 10, para. 16; FA 1973, Sch. 16, paras. 1, 14; FA 1987, Sch. 15, para. 2(23).

Capital redemption business

458. Capital redemption business

(1) Where any person carries on capital redemption business in conjunction with business of any other class, the capital redemption business shall, for the purposes of the Corporation Tax Acts (including the provisions about corporation tax on chargeable gains) and the Income Tax Acts, be treated as a separate business from any other class of business carried on by that person.

(2) In ascertaining whether and to what extent any person has incurred a loss on his capital redemption business for the purposes of section 380 or sections 393 and 394—

    (*a*) any profits derived from investments held in connection with the capital redemption business (including franked investment income of a company resident in the United Kingdom) shall be treated as part of the profits of that business, and

    (*b*) in determining whether any, and if so what, relief can be given under section 385(4) in the case of capital redemption business, the loss which may be carried forward under subsection (1) of that section shall be similarly computed.

(3) In this section "capital redemption business" means the business (not being life assurance business or industrial assurance business) of effecting and carrying out contracts of insurance, whether effected by the issue of policies, bonds or endowment certificates or otherwise, whereby, in return for one or more premiums paid to the insurer, a sum or a series of sums is to become payable to the insured in the future.

(4) This section shall not apply to any capital redemption business in so far as it consists of carrying out contracts of insurance effected before 1st January 1938.

Former enactment.—TA 1970, s. 324.

CHAPTER II

FRIENDLY SOCIETIES, TRADE UNIONS AND EMPLOYERS' ASSOCIATIONS

Unregistered friendly societies

459. Exemption from tax

An unregistered friendly society whose income does not exceed £160 a year shall, on making a claim, be entitled to exemption from income tax and corporation tax (whether on income or chargeable gains).

Former enactment.—TA 1970, s. 331.

Registered friendly societies

460. Exemption from tax in respect of life or endowment business

(1) Subject to subsection (2) below, a registered friendly society shall, on making a claim, be entitled to exemption from income tax and corporation tax (whether on income or chargeable gains) on its profits arising from life or endowment business.

(2) Subsection (1) above—

(*a*) shall not, subject to section 462, exempt a friendly society registered after 31st December 1957 which at any time in the period of three months ending 3rd May 1966 entered into any transaction in return for a single premium, being a transaction forming part of its life or endowment business;

(*b*) shall not apply to profits arising from pension business;

(*c*) shall not apply to profits arising from life or endowment business consisting—

(i) where the profits relate to contracts made after 31st August 1987, of the assurance of gross sums under contracts under which the total premiums payable in any period of 12 months exceed £100 or of the granting of annuities of annual amounts exceeding £156;

(ii) where the profits relate to contracts made after 13th March 1984 but before 1st September 1987, of the assurance of gross sums exceeding £750 or of the granting of annuities of annual amounts exceeding £156;

(iii) where the profits relate to contracts made before 14th March 1984, of the assurance of gross sums exceeding £500 or of the granting of annuities of annual amounts exceeding £104; and

(*d*) as respects other life or endowment business ("tax exempt life or endowment business"), has effect subject to the following provisions of this Chapter.

(3) In determining for the purposes of subsection (2)(*c*)(i) above the total premiums payable in any period of 12 months—

(*a*) where those premiums are payable more frequently than annually, there shall be disregarded an amount equal to 10 per cent. of those premiums; and

(*b*) so much of any premium as is charged on the ground that an exceptional risk of death is involved shall be disregarded;

and in applying the limit of £156 in subsection (2)(*c*)(i) above, any bonus or addition declared upon an annuity shall be disregarded.

(4) In applying the limits referred to in subsection (2)(*c*)(ii) and (iii) above, any bonus or addition which either is declared upon an assurance of a gross sum or annuity or accrues upon such an assurance by reference to an increase in the value of any investments shall be disregarded.

(5) A registered friendly society is within this subsection if its rules make no provision for it to carry on life or endowment business consisting of the assurance of gross sums exceeding £2,000 or of the granting of annuities of annual amounts exceeding £416.

(6) In the case of a registered friendly society within subsection (5) above—

(*a*) subsection (2)(*c*)(iii) above shall have effect with the substitution of references to £2,000 and £416 respectively for the references to £500 and £104; and

(b) references in this Chapter to tax exempt life or endowment business shall be construed accordingly.

(7) Where at any time a registered friendly society within subsection (5) above amends its rules so as to cease to be within that subsection, any part of its life or endowment business consisting of business which—

(a) relates to contracts made before that time; and
(b) immediately before that time was tax exempt life or endowment business,

shall thereafter continue to be tax exempt life or endowment business for the purposes of this Chapter.

(8) Where at any time a registered friendly society not within subsection (5) above amends its rules so as to bring itself within that subsection, any part of its life or endowment business consisting of business which—

(a) related to contracts made before that time; and
(b) immediately before that time was not tax exempt life or endowment business,

shall thereafter continue not to be tax exempt life or endowment business for the purposes of this Chapter.

(9) Where at any time a registered friendly society not within subsection (5) above acquires by way of transfer of engagements or amalgamation from another registered friendly society any life or endowment business consisting of business which—

(a) relates to contracts made before that time; and
(b) immediately before that time was tax exempt life or endowment business,

that business shall thereafter continue to be tax exempt life or endowment business for the purposes of this Chapter.

(10) Where at any time a registered friendly society within subsection (5) above acquires by way of transfer of engagements or amalgamation from another registered friendly society any life or endowment business consisting of business which—

(a) relates to contracts made before that time; and
(b) immediately before that time was not tax exempt life or endowment business,

that business shall thereafter continue not to be tax exempt life or endowment business for the purposes of this Chapter.

(11) Where at any time a registered friendly society ceases by virtue of section 84 of the Friendly Societies Act 1974 or by virtue of section 72 of the Friendly Societies Act (Northern Ireland) 1970 (conversion into company) to be registered under that Act, any part of its life or endowment business consisting of business which—

(a) relates to contracts made before that time; and
(b) immediately before that time was tax exempt life or endowment business,

shall thereafter continue to be tax exempt life or endowment business for the purposes of this Chapter.

(12) For the purposes of the Corporation Tax Acts any part of a company's business which continues to be tax exempt life or endowment business by virtue of subsection (11) above shall be treated as a separate business from any other business carried on by the company.

Former enactments.—Sub-s. (1): TA 1970, s. 332(1); FA 1974, s. 27(1)(a).
Sub-s. (2)(a): TA 1970, s. 333(1).
Sub-s. (2)(b): TA 1970, s. 332(2)(aa); F(No. 2)A 1987, Sch. 2, para. 2(1).
Sub-s. (2)(c): TA 1970, s. 332(2)(a); FA 1984, s. 73(2); FA 1987, s. 30(2).
Sub-s. (2)(d): TA 1970, s. 332(2)(b).
Sub-ss. (3), (4): TA 1970, s. 332(3); Friendly Societies Act 1984, s. 2(4); FA 1987, s. 30(3).
Sub-s. (5): TA 1970, s. 332(4); F(No. 2)A 1975, s. 52(1); FA 1984, s. 73(3).
Sub-s. (6): TA 1970, s. 332(5); F(No. 2)A 1975, s. 52(1); FA 1984, s. 73(3).
Sub-ss. (7)–(10): TA 1970, s. 332(6)–(9); F(No. 2)A 1975, s. 52(1).
Sub-s. (11): TA 1970, s. 332(10); FA 1976, s. 48(1).
Sub-s. (12): TA 1970, s. 332(12)(a); FA 1976, s. 48(1).

461. Taxation in respect of other business

(1) Subject to the following provisions of this section, a registered friendly society other than a society to which subsection (2) below applies shall, on making a claim, be entitled to exemption from income tax and corporation tax (whether on income or chargeable gains) on its profits other than those arising from life or endowment business.

(2) This subsection applies to any society registered after 31st May 1973 unless—

(a) its business is limited to the provision, in accordance with the rules of the society, of benefits for or in respect of employees of a particular employer or such other group of persons as is for the time being approved for the purposes of this section by the registrar; or

(b) it was registered before 27th March 1974 and its rules limit the aggregate amount which may be paid by a member by way of contributions and deposits to not more than £1 per month or such greater amount as the registrar may authorise for the purposes of this section;

and also applies to any society registered before 1st June 1973 with respect to which a direction under subsection (8) below is in force.

(3) If a society to which subsection (2) above applies, after 26th March 1974 or such later date as may be specified in a direction under this section, makes a payment to a member in respect of his interest in the society and the payment is made otherwise than in the course of life or endowment business and exceeds the aggregate of any sums paid by him to the society by way of contributions or deposits, after deducting from that aggregate the amount of—

(a) any previous payment so made to him by the society after that date, and
(b) any earlier repayment of such sums paid by him,

the excess shall be treated for the purposes of corporation tax and income tax as a qualifying distribution.

(4) Where a registered friendly society—

(a) at any time ceases by virtue of section 84 of the Friendly Societies Act 1974 or by virtue of section 72 of the Friendly Societies Act (Northern Ireland) 1970 (conversion into company) to be registered under that Act; and
(b) immediately before that time was exempt from income tax or corporation tax on profits arising from any business carried on by it other than life or endowment business,

the company into which the society is converted shall be so exempt on its profits arising from any part of that business which relates to contracts made before that time so long as there is no increase in the scale of benefits which it undertakes to provide in the course of carrying on that part of its business.

(5) For the purposes of the Corporation Tax Acts any part of a company's business in respect of the profits from which the company is exempt by virtue of subsection (4) above shall be treated as a separate business from any other business carried on by the company.

(6) If—

(a) a friendly society registered before 1st June 1973 begins after 26th March 1974 to carry on business other than life or endowment business or, in the opinion of the registrar, begins to carry on business other than life or endowment business on an enlarged scale or of a new character; and
(b) it appears to the registrar, having regard to the restrictions imposed by this section on friendly societies registered later, that for the protection of the revenue it is expedient to do so;

he may serve a notice on the society referring to the provisions of this subsection and stating that he is considering the question whether, for the protection of the revenue, it is expedient to give a direction that subsection (2) above shall apply to the society as from the date of the notice.

(7) The registrar shall consider any representations or undertakings made or offered to him by the society within the period of one month from service of the notice, and if the society so requests shall afford it an opportunity of being heard by him not later than three weeks after the end of that period.

(8) If, after consideration of any such representations or undertakings, the registrar remains of the opinion that it is expedient to do so, he shall direct that subsection (2) above shall apply to the society as from the date of the notice, but subject to any further direction given by him cancelling that direction.

(9) A friendly society may, within one month from the giving of a direction under subsection (8) above, appeal against it to the court to which or person to whom it might appeal under section 92 of the Friendly Societies Act 1974 or section 81 of the Friendly Societies Act (Northern Ireland) 1970 against cancellation of its registration.

(10) For the purposes of this section a registered friendly society formed on the amalgamation of two or more friendly societies shall be treated as registered before 1st June 1973 if at the

time of the amalgamation subsection (2) above did not apply to any of the societies amalgamated, but otherwise shall be treated as registered at that time.

Former enactments.—Sub-s. (1): TA 1970, s. 332(1); FA 1974, s. 27(1)(*a*).
Sub-s. (2): FA 1974, s. 27(2).
Sub-s. (3): FA 1974, s. 27(1)(*b*).
Sub-ss. (4), (5): TA 1970, s. 332(11), (12)(*b*); FA 1976, s. 48(1).
Sub-ss. (6)–(10): FA 1974, s. 27(3)–(7); FA 1985, s. 41(10); FA 1987, Sch. 15, para. 6.

462. Conditions for tax exempt business

(1) Subject to subsections (2) to (4) below, section 460(1) shall not apply to so much of the profits arising from tax exempt life or endowment business as is attributable to a policy which, by virtue of paragraph 6(2) of Schedule 15—

(*a*) is not a qualifying policy; and
(*b*) would not be a qualifying policy if all policies with other friendly societies were left out of account.

(2) Section 460(2)(*a*) and subsection (1) above shall not withdraw exemption under section 460(1) for profits arising from any part of a life or endowment business relating to contracts made not later than 3rd May 1966.

(3) If, with respect to a policy issued in respect of an insurance made on or after 1st June 1984 and before 19th March 1985 for the assurance of a gross sum, there is or has been an infringement of any of the conditions in paragraph 3(2) to (11) of Schedule 15, section 460(1) shall not apply to so much as is attributable to that policy of the profits of the registered friendly society or branch concerned which arise from tax exempt life or endowment business.

(4) Nothing in subsection (3) above shall be taken to affect the status of a policy as a qualifying policy.

Former enactments.—Sub-s. (1): TA 1970, s. 334(1); FA 1985, s. 41(6).
Sub-ss. (2)–(4): TA 1970, s. 336; FA 1985, Sch. 10, Pt. II.

463. Life or endowment business: application of the Corporation Tax Acts

Subject to section 460(1), the Corporation Tax Acts shall apply to the life or endowment business carried on by registered friendly societies in the same way as they apply to mutual life assurance business carried on by insurance companies, so however that the Treasury may by regulations provide that those Acts as so applied shall have effect subject to such modifications and exceptions as may be prescribed by the regulations, and those regulations may in particular require any part of any business to be treated as a separate business.

Former enactment.—TA 1970, s. 335(1).

464. Maximum benefits payable to members

(1) Subject to subsections (2) and (3) below, a member of a registered friendly society or branch shall not be entitled to have at any time outstanding contracts with any one or more such societies or branches (taking together all such societies or branches throughout the United Kingdom) for the assurance of—

(*a*) more than £750 by way of gross sum under tax exempt life or endowment business;
(*b*) more than £156 by way of annuity under tax exempt life or endowment business.

In any case where the member's outstanding contracts were all made before 14th March 1984 this subsection shall have effect with the substitution for "£750" and "£156" of "£2,000" and "£416" respectively.

(2) Subsection (1)(*a*) above shall not apply as respects sums assured under contracts made after 31st August 1987.

(3) With respect to contracts for the assurance of gross sums under tax exempt life or endowment business, a member of a registered friendly society or branch shall not be entitled to have outstanding with any one or more such societies or branches (taking together all such societies or branches throughout the United Kingdom) contracts under which the total premiums payable in any period of 12 months exceed £100 unless all those contracts were entered into before 1st September 1987.

(4) In applying the limit in subsection (3) above, the premiums under any contract for an annuity which was made before 1st June 1984 by a new society shall be brought into account as if the contract were for the assurance of a gross sum.

(5) In applying the limits in this section there shall be disregarded—

(*a*) any bonus or addition which either is declared upon assurance of a gross sum or annuity or accrues upon such an assurance by reference to an increase in the value of any investments;
(*b*) any approved annuities as defined in section 620(9) or any policy of insurance or annuity contract by means of which the benefits to be provided under an occupational pension scheme as defined in section 51(3)(*a*) of the Social Security Act 1973 are secured;
(*c*) any increase in a benefit under a friendly society contract, as defined in section 6 of the Decimal Currency Act 1969, resulting from the adoption of a scheme prescribed or approved in pursuance of subsection (3) of that section; and
(*d*) so far as concerns the total premiums payable in any period of 12 months—

(i) 10 per cent. of the premiums payable under any contract under which the premiums are payable more frequently than annually; and
(ii) £10 of the premiums payable under any contract made before 1st September 1987 by a society which is not a new society; and
(iii) so much of any premium as is charged on the ground that an exceptional risk of death is involved.

(6) In applying the limits in this section in any case where a member has outstanding with one or more society or branch one or more contracts made after 13th March 1984 and one or more contracts made on or before that date, any contract for an annuity which was made before 1st June 1984 by a new society shall be regarded not only as a contract for the annual amount concerned but also as a contract for the assurance of a gross sum equal to 75 per cent. of the total premiums which would be payable under the contract if it were to run for its full term or, as the case may be, if the member concerned were to die at the age of 75 years.

(7) A registered friendly society or branch may require a member to make and sign a statutory declaration that the total amount assured under outstanding contracts entered into by that member with any one or more registered friendly societies or branches (taking together all such societies or branches throughout the United Kingdom) does not exceed the limits applicable by virtue of this section and that the total premiums under those contracts do not exceed those limits.

Former enactments.—Friendly Societies Act 1974, s. 64(1), (2), (2A), (6); FA 1985, s. 41(1), (2); FA 1984, s. 73(5), (6); S.I. 1976 No. 598; Friendly Societies Act 1984, s. 2; FA 1987, s. 30(4), (5), (7).

465. Old societies

(1) In this section "old society" means a friendly society which is not a new society.

(2) This section applies if, on or after 19th March 1985, an old society—

(*a*) begins to carry on tax exempt life or endowment business; or
(*b*) in the opinion of the Board begins to carry on such business on an enlarged scale or of a new character.

(3) If it appears to the Board, having regard to the restrictions placed on qualifying policies issued by new societies by paragraphs 3(1)(*b*) and (*c*) and 4(3)(*b*) of Schedule 15, that for the protection of the revenue it is expedient to do so, the Board may give a direction to the old society under subsection (4) below.

(4) A direction under this subsection is that (and has the effect that) the old society to which it is given is to be treated for the purposes of this Act as a new society with respect to business carried on after the date of the direction.

(5) An old society to which a direction is given may, within 30 days of the date on which it is given, appeal against the direction to the Special Commissioners on the ground that—

(*a*) it has not begun to carry on business as mentioned in subsection (2) above; or
(*b*) that the direction is not necessary for the protection of the revenue.

Former enactment.—FA 1985, Sch. 10, Pt. III.

466. Interpretation of Chapter II

(1) In this Chapter "life or endowment business" means any business within any of paragraphs (1), (2), (4) and (5) of Schedule 1 to the Friendly Societies Act 1974 or paragraphs 1, 2, 4 and 5 of Schedule 1 to the Friendly Societies Act (Northern Ireland) 1970, any pension business and any other life assurance business, but—

    (*a*) shall not include the issue of a policy affording provision for sickness or other infirmity (whether bodily or mental) unless—

        (i) it also affords assurance for a gross sum independent of sickness or other infirmity; and

        (ii) not less than 60 per cent. of the amount of the premiums is attributable to the provision afforded during sickness or other infirmity; and

        (iii) there is no bonus or addition which may be declared or accrue upon the assurance of the gross sum;

    (*b*) shall not include the assurance of any annuity the consideration for which consists of sums obtainable on the maturity, or on the surrender, of any other policy of assurance issued by the friendly society, being a policy of assurance forming part of the tax exempt life or endowment business of the friendly society.

(2) In this Chapter—

"life assurance business" means the issue of, or the undertaking of liability under, policies of assurance upon human life, or the granting of annuities upon human life, not being industrial assurance business;

"new society" means a friendly society which was registered after 3rd May 1966 or which was registered in the period of three months ending on that date but which at no time earlier than that date carried on any life or endowment business;

"pension business" shall be construed in accordance with section 431;

"policy", in relation to life or endowment business, includes an instrument evidencing a contract to pay an annuity upon human life;

"registrar" means the Chief Registrar of Friendly Societies or, in the application of this Chapter to Scotland, the assistant registrar for Scotland or, in the application of this Chapter to Northern Ireland, the Registrar of Friendly Societies for Northern Ireland;

"tax exempt life or endowment business" has, subject to subsections (7) to (11) of section 460, the meaning given by subsection (2)(*d*) of that section, that is to say, it means (subject to those subsections) life or endowment business other than business profits arising from which are excluded from subsection (1) of that section by subsection (2)(*b*) or (*c*) of that section (read, where appropriate, with subsection (6) of that section);

and references in sections 460 to 465 and this subsection to a friendly society include references to any branch of that friendly society.

(3) It is hereby declared that for the purposes of this Chapter (except where provision to the contrary is made) a registered friendly society formed on the amalgamation of two or more friendly societies is to be treated as different from the amalgamated societies.

(4) A registered friendly society formed on the amalgamation of two or more friendly societies shall, for the purposes of this Chapter, be treated as registered not later than 3rd May 1966 if at the time of the amalgamation—

    (*a*) all the friendly societies amalgamated were registered friendly societies eligible for the exemption conferred by section 460(1); and

    (*b*) at least one of them was not a new society;

or, if the amalgamation took place before 19th March 1985, the society was treated as registered not later than 3rd May 1966 by virtue of the proviso to section 337(4) of the 1970 Act.

Former enactments.—Sub-ss. (1), (2): TA 1970, ss. 335(1), 337(1)–(3); FA 1974, s. 27(8); FA 1985, s. 41(7)(*b*)–(*e*); Friendly Societies Act 1974, s. 64(8), Sch. 9, para. 23; F(No. 2)A 1987, Sch. 2, para. 2(2); F(No. 2)A 1975, s. 52(2). Sub-ss. (3), (4): TA 1970, s. 337(4); FA 1985, s. 41(7)(*e*).

Trade unions and employers' associations

467. Exemption for trade unions and employers' associations

(1) A trade union which is precluded by Act of Parliament or by its rules from assuring to any person a sum exceeding £3,000 by way of gross sum or £625 by way of annuity shall on making a claim be entitled—

    (*a*) to exemption from income tax and corporation tax in respect of its income which is not trading income and which is applicable and applied for the purpose of provident benefits;

(*b*) to exemption from tax in respect of chargeable gains which are applicable and applied for the purpose of provident benefits.

(2) In this section "provident benefits" includes any payment, expressly authorised by the rules of the trade union, which is made to a member during sickness or incapacity from personal injury or while out of work, or to an aged member by way of superannuation, or to a member who has met with an accident, or has lost his tools by fire or theft, and includes a payment in discharge or aid of funeral expenses on the death of a member or the wife of a member or as provision for the children of a deceased member.

(3) In determining for the purposes of this section whether a trade union is by Act of Parliament or its rules precluded from assuring to any person a sum exceeding £625 by way of annuity, there shall be disregarded any approved annuities (as defined in section 620(9)).

(4) In this section "trade union" means—

(*a*) any trade union the name of which is entered in the list of trade unions maintained by the Registrar of Friendly Societies under section 8 of the Trade Union and Labour Relations Act 1974;

(*b*) any employers' association the name of which is entered in the list of employers' associations maintained by the Registrar of Friendly Societies under section 8 of the Trade Union and Labour Relations Act 1974 and which on 30th September 1971 was a registered trade union for the purposes of section 338 of the 1970 Act; and

(*c*) the Police Federation for England and Wales, the Police Federation for Scotland, the Police Federation for Northern Ireland and any other organisation of persons in police service which has similar functions.

Former enactments.—Sub-ss. (1)–(3): TA 1970, s. 338(1)–(3); FA 1982, s. 36(1); FA 1974, s. 28(1)(*b*); FA 1987, s. 31. Sub-s. (4)(*a*)–(*c*): FA 1974, s. 28(1)(*a*); F(No. 2)A 1975, s. 53; FA 1977, s. 47.
Note.—See **Prospective Legislation Notes** (Married Couples).

CHAPTER III

UNIT TRUST SCHEMES, DEALERS IN SECURITIES ETC.

Unit trust schemes

468. Authorised unit trusts

(1) In respect of income arising to the trustees of an authorised unit trust, and for the purposes of the provisions relating to relief for capital expenditure, the Tax Acts shall have effect as if—

   (a) the trustees were a company resident in the United Kingdom; and
   (b) the rights of the unit holders were shares in the company.

(2) The Tax Acts shall also have effect as if the aggregate amount shown in the accounts of the trust as income available for payment to unit holders or for investment were dividends on the shares referred to in subsection (1) above paid to them in proportion to their rights, the date of payment, in the case of income not paid to unit holders, being taken to be—

   (a) the date or latest date provided by the terms of the authorised unit trust for any distribution in respect of the distribution period in question;
   (b) if no date is so provided, the last day of the distribution period.

This subsection shall not apply to any authorised unit trust which is also an approved personal pension scheme (within the meaning of Chapter IV of Part XIV).

(3) References in the Corporation Tax Acts to a body corporate shall be construed in accordance with subsections (1) and (2) above, and section 234(3) and (4) shall apply with any necessary modifications.

(4) Section 75 shall apply in relation to an authorised unit trust whether or not it is an investment company within the meaning of section 130; and sums periodically appropriated for managers' remuneration shall be treated for the purposes of section 75 as sums disbursed as expenses of management.

(5) Subsection (1) above shall not apply in relation to an authorised unit trust under the terms of which the funds of the trust cannot be invested in such a way that income can arise to the trustees which will be chargeable to tax in the hands of the trustees otherwise than—

   (a) under Schedule C as profits arising from United Kingdom public revenue dividends, or
   (b) under Case III of Schedule D;

and in this subsection "United Kingdom public revenue dividends" means public revenue dividends payable in the United Kingdom (whether they are also payable outside the United Kingdom or not) out of the public revenue of the United Kingdom.

(6) In this section—

   "authorised unit trust" means, as respects an accounting period, a unit trust scheme in the case of which an order under section 78 of the Financial Services Act 1986 is in force during the whole or part of that accounting period;
   "distribution period" means a period beginning on or after 1st April 1987 over which income from the investments subject to the trusts is aggregated for the purposes of ascertaining the amount available for distribution to unit holders;
   "unit holder" means a person entitled to a share of the investments subject to the trusts of a unit trust scheme; and
   "unit trust scheme" has the same meaning as in section 469.

Former enactments.—TA 1970, ss. 354, 358; FA 1980, s. 60; FA 1987, ss. 38, 40(1); F(No. 2)A 1987, s. 40(1).
Cross references.—See FA 1989, s. 80(1), (2) (provisions in respect of sub-s. (5) of this section in its application to gilt unit trusts as regards distribution periods beginning after 31 December 1989 or beginning on or before and ending after 31 December 1989).

[468A. Certified unit trusts

(1) For the purposes of sections 468B and 468C "certified unit trust" means, as respects an accounting period, a unit trust scheme in the case of which—

(a) an order under section 78 of the Financial Services Act 1986 is in force during the whole or part of that accounting period, and
(b) a certificate under section 78(8) of that Act, certifying that the scheme complies with the conditions necessary for it to enjoy the rights conferred by the UCITS directive, has been issued before or at any time during that accounting period.

(2) In this section—

"the UCITS directive" means the directive of the Council of the European Communities, dated 20th December 1985, on the co-ordination of laws, regulations and administrative provisions relating to undertakings for collective investment in transferable securities (no. 85/611/EEC), and
"unit trust scheme" has the same meaning as in section 469.][1]

Amendments.—[1] This section inserted by FA 1989, s. 78.

[468B. Certified unit trusts: corporation tax

(1) This section has effect as regards an accounting period of the trustees of a certified unit trust ending after 31st December 1989.

(2) Subject to subsection (3) below, the rate of corporation tax for a financial year shall be deemed to be the rate at which income tax at the basic rate is charged for the year of assessment which begins on 6th April in the financial year concerned.

(3) Where the period begins before 1st January 1990, subsection (2) above shall only apply for the purpose of computing corporation tax chargeable for so much of the period as falls in the financial year 1990 and subsection (4) below shall apply for the purpose of computing corporation tax chargeable for so much of the period as falls in the financial year 1989.

(4) So much of the period as falls after 31st December 1989 and before 1st April 1990 shall be deemed to fall in a financial year for which the rate of corporation tax is the rate at which income tax at the basic rate is charged for the year 1989–90.

(5) Where the period begins after 31st December 1989, section 338 shall have effect as if any reference to interest of any description were a reference to interest of that description on borrowing of a relevant description.

(6) For the purposes of subsection (5) above borrowing is of a relevant description if it is borrowing in respect of which there has been no breach during the accounting period of the duties imposed on the manager of the scheme by regulations under section 81 of the Financial Services Act 1986 with respect to borrowing by the trustees of the scheme.

(7) The Treasury may by regulations provide that for subsection (6) above (as it has effect for the time being) there shall be substituted a subsection containing a different definition of what constitutes borrowing of a relevant description for the purposes of subsection (5) above.

(8) Regulations under subsection (7) above may contain such supplementary, incidental, consequential or transitional provision as the Treasury think fit.

(9) In this section "certified unit trust" has the meaning given by section 468A.][1]

Amendments.—[1] This section inserted by FA 1989, s. 78.

[468C. Certified unit trusts: distributions

(1) Subsection (2) below applies where—

(a) as regards a distribution period ending after 31st December 1989 a dividend is treated by virtue of section 468(2) as paid to a unit holder (whether or not income is in fact paid to the unit holder),
(b) the dividend is treated as paid by the trustees of a unit trust scheme which is a certified unit trust as respects the accounting period in which the distribution period falls, and
(c) on the date of payment the unit holder is within the charge to corporation tax and not a dual resident.

(2) For the purpose of computing corporation tax chargeable in the case of the unit holder the payment shall be deemed—

(a) to be an annual payment, and not a dividend or other distribution, and
(b) to have been received by the unit holder after deduction of income tax at the basic

rate, for the year of assessment in which the date of payment falls, from a corresponding gross amount.

(3) Subsection (2) above shall not apply where the rights in respect of which the dividend is treated as paid are held by the trustees of a unit trust scheme which on the date of payment is a fund of funds.

(4) Where the unit holder is on the date of payment the manager of the scheme, subsection (2) above shall not apply in so far as the rights in respect of which the dividend is treated as paid are rights held by him in the ordinary course of his business as manager of the scheme.

(5) Subsection (2) above shall not apply to so much of the payment as is attributable to income of the trustees arising before 1st January 1990.

(6) In this section—

"certified unit trust" has the meaning given by section 468A,
"distribution period" has the same meaning as in section 468,
"dual resident" means a person who is resident in the United Kingdom and falls to be regarded for the purposes of any arrangements having effect by virtue of section 788 as resident in a territory outside the United Kingdom,
"fund of funds" means a unit trust scheme the sole object of which is to enable the unit holders to participate in or receive profits or income arising from the acquisition, holding, management or disposal of units in unit trust schemes, and
"unit trust scheme" has the same meaning as in section 469.][1]

Amendments.—[1] This section inserted by FA 1989, s. 78.

[468D. Funds of funds: distributions

(1) Subsection (2) below applies where—

(a) as regards a distribution period ending after 31st December 1989 a dividend is treated by virtue of section 468(2) as paid to a unit holder (whether or not income is in fact paid to the unit holder),
(b) the dividend is treated as paid by the trustees of a unit trust scheme which on the date of payment is a fund of funds, and
(c) on the date of payment the unit holder is within the charge to corporation tax and not a dual resident.

(2) For the purpose of computing corporation tax chargeable in the case of the unit holder the payment shall be deemed—

(a) to be an annual payment, and not a dividend or other distribution, and
(b) to have been received by the unit holder after deduction of income tax at the basic rate, for the year of assessment in which the date of payment falls, from a corresponding gross amount.

(3) Where the unit holder is on the date of payment the manager of the scheme, subsection (2) above shall not apply in so far as the rights in respect of which the dividend is treated as paid are rights held by him in the ordinary course of his business as manager of the scheme.

(4) Subsection (2) above shall not apply to so much of the payment as is attributable to income of the trustees arising before 1st January 1990.

(5) In this section—

"distribution period" has the same meaning as in section 468,
"dual resident" and "fund of funds" have the same meanings as in section 468C,
"unit trust scheme" has the same meaning as in section 469.][1]

Amendments.—[1] This section inserted by FA 1989, s. 79.

469. Other unit trusts

(1) This section applies to—

(a) any unit trust scheme that is not an authorised unit trust; and
(b) any authorised unit trust to which, by virtue of subsection (5) of section 468, that section does not apply,

except where the trustees of the scheme are not resident in the United Kingdom.

(2) Income arising to the trustees of the scheme shall be regarded for the purposes of the Tax Acts as income of the trustees (and not as income of the unit holders); and the trustees (and not the unit holders) shall be regarded as the persons to or on whom allowances or charges are to be made under the provisions of those Acts relating to relief for capital expenditure.

(3) For the purposes of the Tax Acts the unit holders shall be treated as receiving annual payments (made by the trustees under deduction of tax) in proportion to their rights.

This subsection shall not apply to any authorised unit trust which is also an approved personal pension scheme (within the meaning of Chapter IV of Part XIV).

(4) The total amount of those annual payments in respect of any distribution period shall be the amount which, after deducting income tax at the basic rate in force for the year of assessment in which the payments are treated as made, is equal to the aggregate amount shown in the accounts of the scheme as income available for payment to unit holders or for investment.

(5) The date on which the annual payments are treated as made shall be the date or latest date provided by the terms of the scheme for any distribution in respect of the distribution period in question, except that, if—

(*a*) the date so provided is more than 12 months after the end of the period; or
(*b*) no date is so provided,

the date on which the payments are treated as made shall be the last day of the period.

[(5A) Subsection (5B) below applies where for any year of assessment—

(*a*) the trustees are (or, apart from this subsection, would be) chargeable under section 350 with tax on payments treated as made by them under subsection (3) above, and
(*b*) there is an uncredited surplus in the case of the scheme.][1]

[(5B) Where this subsection applies, the amount on which the trustees would otherwise be so chargeable shall be reduced—

(*a*) if the surplus is greater than that amount, to nil, or
(*b*) if it is not, by an amount equal to the surplus.][1]

[(5C) For the purposes of subsections (5A) and (5B) above whether there is an uncredited surplus for a year of assessment in the case of a scheme (and, if so, its amount) shall be ascertained by—

(*a*) determining, for each earlier year of assessment in which the income on which the trustees were chargeable to tax by virtue of subsection (2) above exceeded the amount treated by subsection (3) above as annual payments received by the unit holders, the amount of the excess,
(*b*) aggregating the amounts determined in the case of the scheme under paragraph (*a*) above, and
(*c*) deducting from that aggregate the total of any reductions made in the case of the scheme under subsection (5B) above for earlier years of assessment.][1]

[(5D) The references in subsection (5C)(*a*) above to subsections (2) and (3) above include references to subsections (2) and (3) of section 354A of the 1970 Act.][1]

(6) In this section "distribution period" has the same meaning as in section 468, but—

(*a*) if the scheme does not make provision for distribution periods, then for the purposes of this section its distribution periods shall be taken to be successive periods of 12 months the first of which began with the day on which the scheme took effect; and
(*b*) if the scheme makes provision for distribution periods of more than 12 months, then for the purposes of this section each of those periods shall be taken to be divided into two (or more) distribution periods, the second succeeding the first after 12 months (and so on for any further periods).

(7) In this section "unit trust scheme" has the same meaning as in the Financial Services Act 1986, except that the Treasury may by regulations provide that any scheme of a description specified in the regulations shall be treated as not being a unit trust scheme for the purposes of this section.

(8) Regulations under this section may contain such supplementary and transitional provisions as appear to the Treasury to be necessary or expedient.

(9) Sections 686 and 687 shall not apply to a scheme to which this section applies.

(10) Section 720(5) shall not apply in relation to profits or gains treated as received by the trustees of a scheme to which this section applies if or to the extent that those profits or gains represent accruals of interest (within the meaning of Chapter II of Part XVII) which are treated as income in the accounts of the scheme.

(11) This section shall have effect in relation to distribution periods beginning on or after 6th April 1987.

Former enactments.—TA 1970, s. 354A; FA 1987, s. 39; F(No. 2)A 1987, s. 40(1).
Amendments.—Sub-ss. (5A)–(5D) inserted by FA 1988, s. 71.

470. Transitional provisions relating to unit trusts

(1) Any transitional provisions contained in an order made under section 40(5) of the Finance Act 1987 appointing a day for the coming into force of subsections (1) and (2) of that section and made in connection therewith shall after the coming into force of this section have effect for the purposes of this Act as they had effect for the purposes of that section, with such modifications if any as may be necessary.

(2) If such an order as is mentioned in subsection (1) above has not been made before the coming into force of this Act, section 468 shall have effect with the substitution for the definition of "authorised unit trust" contained in subsection (6) of the following definition—

"authorised unit trust" means, as respects any accounting period, a unit trust scheme in the case of which an order under section 17 of the Prevention of Frauds (Investments) Act 1958 or under section 16 of the Prevention of Frauds (Investments) Act (Northern Ireland) 1940 is in force during the whole or some part of that accounting period";

and sections 468 and 832 shall have effect with the omission of the definition of "unit trust scheme".

(3) If such an order as is mentioned in subsection (1) above has not been made before the coming into force of this Act, subsection (2) above shall cease to have effect on such day as the Board may by order appoint; and an order under this subsection may contain such transitional provisions as appear to the Board to be necessary or expedient.

Former enactment.—FA 1987, s. 40(5).
Note.—The day appointed under sub-s. (3) of this section is 29 April 1988; the Income and Corporation Taxes Act 1988 (Appointed Day) Order 1988, S.I. 1988 No. 745.

Dealers in securities, banks and insurance businesses

471. Exchange of securities in connection with conversion operations, nationalisation etc.

(1) If—
   (a) any securities to which a person who is carrying on a trade which consists wholly or partly in dealing in securities is beneficially entitled are exchanged for other securities; and
   (b) the exchange is one to which this section applies;

then, whether or not any additional consideration is given for the exchange but subject to subsection (2) below, that person shall be treated for tax purposes (except as regards any tax payable in respect of dividends or interest), both at the time of the exchange and thereafter, as if the exchange had not taken place, and in that case the produce of any subsequent realisation of any of the securities received by him under the exchange (together with any additional consideration, or the appropriate part of any additional consideration, received by him under the exchange) shall be treated as the produce of the realisation of the corresponding securities surrendered by or transferred from him under the exchange, or of a corresponding part thereof, as the case may be.

(2) Subsection (1) above shall not apply to any person who gives notice to the inspector not later than two years after the end of the chargeable period in which the exchange takes place that he desires not to be treated as mentioned in that subsection.

(3) The exchanges to which this section applies are—
   (a) any exchange effected under any arrangement carried out under section 2 of the National Loans Act 1939 or section 14 of the National Loans Act 1968 if the Treasury direct, in pursuance of that arangement, that this section shall apply to exchanges thereunder;

(b) any exchange of securities effected by section 1 of the Bank of England Act 1946; and
(c) any exchange of securities effected in pursuance of any enactment passed after 5th April 1946 which provides for the compulsory acquisition of any securities and the issue of other securities in lieu thereof, if the Treasury direct that this section shall apply to exchanges of securities effected in pursuance of that enactment.

(4) In this section "securities" includes shares, stock, bonds, debentures and debenture stock.

Former enactment.—TA 1970, s. 326.

472. Distribution of securities issued in connection with nationalisation etc.

(1) Where—

(a) in pursuance of any enactment passed after 5th April 1946 any securities are issued to any body corporate as, or as part of, the consideration for the compulsory acquisition of any property under that enactment; and
(b) that body corporate is wound up or the capital thereof is reduced or any bonds, debentures or debenture stock thereof are redeemed, and, in or in connection with the winding up, reduction of capital or redemption, all or any of the securities so issued are distributed to holders of securities of the body corporate ("the distributed securities"); and
(c) the Treasury direct that this section shall apply in relation to the distribution;

any person ("the dealer") who is carrying on a trade which consists wholly or partly in dealing in securities and is beneficially entitled to any securities ("the relevant securities") to the holders of which the distribution is made shall, in relation to that distribution, be treated for tax purposes in the manner specified in subsections (2) and (3) below, unless he gives notice to the inspector not later than two years after the end of the chargeable period in which the distribution takes place that he desires not to be so treated in relation to that distribution.

(2) If the result of the winding up, reduction of capital or redemption of bonds, debentures or debenture stock is that the relevant securities to which the dealer is beneficially entitled are wholly extinguished without his receiving anything in respect thereof except the distributed securities, he shall be treated for tax purposes (except as regards any tax payable in respect of dividends or interest), both then and thereafter, as if neither the extinction nor the distribution had taken place but as if the produce of any subsequent realisation of any of the distributed securities were the produce of the realisation of the relevant securities or a corresponding part thereof, as the case may be.

(3) In any other case—

(a) the dealer shall be treated as having acquired the distributed securities at a cost equal to such proportion of the cost to him of the relevant securities as may be specified in the direction of the Treasury referred to in subsection (1) above and the question whether he has made any, and if so what, profit or suffered any, and if so what, loss on any subsequent realisation of the distributed securities shall be determined accordingly; and
(b) in considering whether he has, either as the result of the winding up, reduction of capital or redemption of bonds, debentures or debenture stock and the distribution of the securities, or on any subsequent realisation of any of the relevant securities, made any, and if so what, profit or suffered any, and if so what, loss in connection with the relevant securities, the distributed securities shall be left out of account and the cost to him of the relevant securities shall be deemed to be reduced by the amount of the cost at which, under paragraph (a) above, he is taken to have acquired the distributed securities.

(4) In this section "securities" includes shares, stock, bonds, debentures and debenture stock.

Former enactment.—TA 1970, s. 327.

473. Conversion etc. of securities held as circulating capital

(1) Subsections (3) and (4) below shall have effect where a transaction to which this section applies occurs in relation to any securities ("the original holding")—

(a) to which a person carrying on a banking business, an insurance business or a business consisting wholly or partly in dealing in securities is beneficially entitled; and

(b) which are such that a profit on their sale would form part of the trading profits of that business.

(2) This section applies to any transaction which, if the securities were not such as are mentioned in subsection (1)(b) above—

(a) would result in the original holding being equated with a new holding by virtue of sections 77 to 86 of the 1979 Act (capital gains tax roll-over relief in cases of conversion etc.); or
(b) would be treated by virtue of section 84 of that Act (compensation stock) as an exchange for a new holding which does not involve a disposal of the original holding;

but does not apply to any transaction in relation to which section 471 applies or would apply if the person concerned had not given a notice under that section.

(3) Subject to subsection (4) below, in making any computation in accordance with the provisions of this Act applicable to Case I of Schedule D of the profits or losses of the business—

(a) the transaction shall be treated as not involving any disposal of the original holding, and
(b) the new holding shall be treated as the same asset as the original holding.

(4) Where under the transaction the person concerned receives or becomes entitled to receive any consideration in addition to the new holding, subsection (3) above shall have effect as if references to the original holding were references to the proportion of it which the market value of the new holding at the time of the transaction bears to the aggregate of that value and the market value at that time (or, if it is cash, the amount) of the consideration.

(5) Subsections (3) and (4) above shall have effect with the necessary modifications in relation to any computation made for the purposes of section 76(2) in a case where securities held by the company concerned are equated with a new holding by virtue of any of sections 77 to 86 of the 1979 Act or are treated as not disposed of by virtue of section 84 of that Act.

(6) In this section "securities" includes shares, any security within the meaning of section 82 of the 1979 Act and any rights, interests or options which by virtue of section 86(7), 93 or 139 of that Act are treated as shares for the purposes of sections 77 to 86 of that Act.

(7) In determining for the purposes of subsection (2)(a) above whether a transaction would result in the original holding being equated with a new holding by virtue of section 85 or 86 of the 1979 Act the reference in section 87(1) of that Act to capital gains tax shall be construed as a reference to income tax.

Former enactments.—FA 1977, s. 46; CGTA 1979, Sch. 7.

474. Treatment of tax-free income

(1) Where a banking business, an insurance business or a business consisting wholly or partly in dealing in securities is carried on in the United Kingdom by a person not resident there, then—

(a) in computing for any of the purposes of the Tax Acts the profits arising from, or loss sustained in, the business, and
(b) in the case of an insurance business, also in computing the profits or loss from pension business and general annuity business under section 436,

all interest, dividends and other payments whatsoever to which section 48 or 123(4) extends shall be included notwithstanding the exemption from tax conferred by those sections respectively.

In this subsection "securities" includes stocks and shares.

(2) Where a banking business, an insurance business or a business consisting wholly or partly in dealing in securities—

(a) is carried on in the United Kingdom by a person not ordinarily resident there, and
(b) in making any such computation as is referred to in subsection (1) above with respect to that business, any interest on any securities issued by the Treasury is excluded by virtue of a condition of the issue thereof regulating the treatment of the interest on those securities for tax purposes,

then any expenses attributable to the acquisition or holding of, or to any transaction in, the securities (but not including in those expenses any interest on borrowed money), and any profits or losses so attributable, shall also be excluded in making that computation.

Former enactments.—TA 1970, s. 328(1), (2); FA 1970, Sch. 5, Pt. III, para. 11(6)(*f*).

475. Tax-free Treasury securities: exclusion of interest on borrowed money

(1) This section has effect where paragraphs (*a*) and (*b*) of section 474(2) apply to a business for any accounting period or year of assessment.

(2) Up to the amount determined under this section ("the amount ineligible for relief"), interest on money borrowed for the purposes of the business—

(*a*) shall be excluded in any computation under the Tax Acts of the profits (or losses) arising from the business or, where subsection (6) below applies, arising from any annuity business forming part of the life assurance business, and
(*b*) shall be excluded from the definition of "charges on income" in section 338.

(3) Subject to subsection (4) below, in determining the amount ineligible for relief, account shall be taken of all money borrowed for the purposes of the business which is outstanding in the accounting or basis period, up to the total cost of the tax-free Treasury securities held for the purpose of the business in that period.

(4) Where the person carrying on the business is a company, account shall not be taken of any borrowed money carrying interest which, apart from subsection (2) above, does not fall to be included in the computations under paragraph (*a*) of that subsection, and is not to be treated as a charge on income for the purposes of the Corporation Tax Acts.

(5) Subject to subsection (6) below, the amount ineligible for relief shall be equal to a year's interest on the amount of money borrowed which is to be taken into account under subsection (3) above at a rate equal to the average rate of interest in the accounting or basis period on money borrowed for the purposes of the business, except that in the case of a period of less than 12 months interest shall be taken for that shorter period instead of for a year.

(6) Where relief for expenses of management is to be granted to an insurance company for any accounting period, and that relief falls to be reduced under section 445(8)(*b*) (by applying the fraction which is investment income of the life assurance fund other than income from tax-free Treasury securities divided by that total investment income)—

(*a*) the amount ineligible for relief shall be a fraction of the amount of interest in the accounting period on money borrowed for the purposes of the business; and
(*b*) that fraction shall be the fraction which is income from tax-free Treasury securities divided by total investment income of the life assurance fund (that is to say, one minus the fraction to be applied under section 445(8)(*b*)).

(7) In this section "tax-free Treasury securities" means securities issued by the Treasury with a condition regulating the treatment of the interest thereon for income tax or corporation tax purposes such that interest on the securities is excluded in computing the income or profits.

(8) For the purposes of this section the cost of a holding of tax-free Treasury securities which has fluctuated in the accounting or basis period shall be the average cost of acquisition of the initial holding, and of any subsequent acquisitions in the accounting or basis period, applied to the average amount of the holding in the accounting or basis period, and this subsection shall be applied separately to securities of different classes.

(9) In this section "accounting or basis period" means the company's accounting period or the period by reference to which the profits or gains arising in the year of assessment are to be computed.

Former enactment.—TA 1970, s. 329.

CHAPTER IV

BUILDING SOCIETIES, BANKS, SAVINGS BANKS, INDUSTRIAL AND PROVIDENT SOCIETIES AND OTHERS

476. Building societies: regulations for payment of tax

(1) The Board may by regulations make provision with respect to any year of assessment requiring building societies, on such sums as may be determined in accordance with the regulations (including sums paid or credited before the beginning of the year but not previously brought into account under this subsection), to account for and pay an amount representing income tax calculated in part at the basic rate and in part at the reduced rate determined for the year of assessment concerned under section 483(1)(*a*); and in this section and section 477 such sums are referred to as "aggregate rate sums".

(2) Regulations under subsection (1) may contain such incidental and consequential provisions as appear to the Board to be appropriate, including provisions requiring the making of returns.

(3) For any year of assessment to which regulations under subsection (1) above apply, dividends or interest payable in respect of shares in, or deposits with or loans to, a building society shall be dealt with for the purposes of corporation tax as follows—

> (*a*) in computing for any accounting period ending in the year of assessment the income of the society from the trade carried on by it, there shall be allowed as a deduction the actual amount paid or credited in the accounting period of any such dividends or interest, together with any amount accounted for and paid by the society in respect thereof as representing income tax;
> (*b*) in computing the income of a company which is paid or credited in the year of assessment with any such dividends or interest which are aggregate rate sums, the company shall—
>> (i) be treated as having received an amount which, after deduction of income tax, is equal to the amount paid or credited, and
>> (ii) be entitled to a set-off or repayment of income tax accordingly;
>
> (*c*) no part of any such dividends or interest paid or credited in the year of assessment shall be treated as a distribution of the society or as franked investment income of any company resident in the United Kingdom.

(4) Nothing in section 326 shall be taken as affecting subsection (3)(*a*) above and that paragraph shall apply to any terminal bonus paid by the society under a certified contractual savings scheme as if it were a dividend on a share in the society.

(5) Except in so far as regulations under subsection (1) above otherwise provide, for any year of assessment to which such regulations apply—

> (*a*) notwithstanding anything in sections 348 to 350, income tax shall not be deducted from any dividends or interest payable in that year in respect of shares in or deposits with or loans to a building society;
> (*b*) subject to subsections (3)(*b*), (6) and (7) of this section, no repayment of income tax and no assessment to income tax shall be made in respect of any such dividends or interest to or on the person receiving or entitled to the dividends or interest;
> (*c*) any amounts paid or credited in respect of any such dividends or interest shall in computing the total income of an individual entitled thereto be treated as income for that year received by him after deduction of income tax from a corresponding gross amount;
> (*d*) subject to section 7(1), the amounts so paid or credited (and no more) shall, in applying sections 348 and 349(1) to other payments, be treated as profits or gains which have been brought into charge to income tax.

(6) Subsection (5)(*b*) above shall not prevent an assessment in respect of income tax at a rate other than the basic rate.

(7) Subsection (5)(*b*) above shall not apply to sums which are payable to exempt pension funds and which are aggregate rate sums; but the amounts paid or credited in respect of such sums shall be treated as paid or credited after deduction of income tax from a corresponding gross amount.

In this subsection "exempt pension fund" means any fund or scheme in the case of which provision is made by section 592(2), 613(4), 614(1), (2) or (3), 620(6) or 643(2) for exempting the whole or part of its income from income tax.

(8) For the purpose of determining whether any or what amount of tax is, by virtue of subsection (5)(*c*) above, to be taken into account as having been deducted from a gross amount in the case of an individual whose total income is reduced by any deductions, so much only of that gross amount shall be taken into account as is part of his total income as so reduced.

(9) Notwithstanding anything in sections 348 to 350, for any year of assessment to which regulations under subsection (1) above apply income tax shall not be deducted upon payment to the society of any interest on advances, being interest payable in that year.

(10) Subsection (9) above shall not apply to any payment of relevant loan interest to which section 369 applies.

(11) In this section "dividend" has the meaning given by regulations under subsection (1) above, but any sum which is paid by a building society by way of dividend and which is not an aggregate rate sum shall be treated for the purposes of Schedule D as paid by way of interest.

Former enactments.—Sub-ss. (1), (2): TA 1970, s. 343(1A); FA 1985, s. 40(3); FA 1986, s. 47(1).
Sub-s. (3): TA 1970, s. 343(2); FA 1972, Sch. 24, para. 22; FA 1985, s. 40(4); FA 1986, s. 47(2).
Sub-s. (4): TA 1970, s. 415(4).
Sub-s. (5)(*a*): TA 1970, s. 343(3)(*a*); FA 1985, s. 40(5).
Sub-s. (5)(*b*): TA 1970, s. 343(*b*); FA 1971, Sch. 6, para. 40(*c*).
Sub-s. (5)(*c*): TA 1970, s. 343(*c*); FA 1971, Sch. 6, para. 40(*d*).
Sub-s. (5)(*d*): TA 1970, s. 343(3)(*d*); FA 1971, Sch. 6, para. 40(*e*).
Sub-s. (6): TA 1970, s. 343(3)(*i*); FA 1971, Sch. 6, para. 40(*f*).
Sub-s. (7): FA 1975, s. 6; FA 1986, s. 47(4)(*b*); F(No. 2)A 1987, s. 39(4).
Sub-s. (8): TA 1970, s. 343(3); FA 1970, Sch. 6, para. 40(*f*).
Sub-s. (9): TA 1970, s. 343(4); FA 1985, s. 40(6).
Sub-s. (10): FA 1982, s. 26(1).
Sub-s. (11): TA 1970, s. 343(7); FA 1985, s. 40(7); FA 1986, s. 47(3).
Note.—For the year 1989–90 the reduced rate for the purposes of this section is 21·75 per cent; the Income Tax (Reduced and Composite Rate) Order 1988, S.I. 1988 No. 2145.
Cross references.—See FA 1988, s. 130(7)(*c*)(i), (9) (company migration: provisions for securing payment by migrating company of tax under regulations under sub-s. (1) above and TA 1970, s. 343(1A)).

477. Investments becoming or ceasing to be relevant building society investments

(1) Where a building society investment which is a source of income of any person ("the lender") is not a relevant building society investment but at any time becomes such an investment, section 67 shall apply as if the investment were a source of income which the lender ceased to possess immediately before that time.

(2) Where a building society investment which is a source of income of any person ceases at any time to be a relevant building society investment, section 66(3) shall apply as if the investment were a new source of income acquired by him immediately after that time.

(3) In this section "building society investment" does not include a quoted Eurobond (as defined in section 124(1)) but, subject to that, means any share in, deposit with or loan to a building society; and for the purposes of this section a building society investment is relevant if dividends or interest payable in respect of it are aggregate rate sums.

Former enactment.—FA 1986, s. 47(5), (6), (8).

478. Building societies: time for payment of tax

(1) This section shall apply, in place of the provisions of section 10, with respect to any accounting period ending before 6th April 1990 of a building society to which section 344 of the 1970 Act applied immediately before the coming into force of this Act.

(2) Where this section applies to a building society, then—

(*a*) corporation tax assessed on the society for any accounting period shall be paid within 30 days from the date of the issue of the notice of assessment, except that if the society's basis period for the year 1965–66 did not extend into the year 1966, the tax shall not be payable before the like time after the last day of the accounting period as 1st January 1966 is after the last day of that basis period; but
(*b*) if corporation tax has not become payable by the society for an accounting period by the like time from the beginning of that period as there is between the beginning of the society's basis period for the year 1965–66 and 1st January 1966, the society shall at that

time from the beginning of the accounting period make a provisional payment of tax computed on the amount on which the society is chargeable to corporation tax for the accounting period last ended with such adjustments, if any, as may be required for periods of different length or as may be agreed between the society and the inspector.

(3) References in subsection (2) above to a society's basis period for the year 1965–66 are references to the period by reference to which the society was assessed to income tax for that year under arrangements entered into under section 445 of the Income Tax Act 1952.

(4) Where, by virtue of subsection (2)(*a*) above, corporation tax assessed on a building society in respect of a 1989 accounting period would, apart from this subsection, be payable by a date which is earlier than the end of the period of two months from the end of that accounting period, the tax shall be payable within that period of two months.

(5) If, apart from this subsection, the date on which, under subsection (2)(*b*) above, a building society would be required to make a provisional payment of corporation tax for a 1989 accounting period would fall before the end of the period of two months from the end of that accounting period, that date shall be postponed until the end of that period of two months.

(6) With respect to a 1989 accounting period of a building society to which subsection (4) above applies, in section 825(8)(*b*) of this Act and paragraph 5(*c*) in the second column of the Table in section 86(4) of the Management Act (the reckonable date for interest on overdue tax), the reference to the time limit imposed by subsection (2)(*a*) above shall be construed as a reference to the limit imposed by subsection (4) above.

(7) In subsections (4) to (6) above a "1989 accounting period" means an accounting period ending in the year 1989–90.

Former enactments.—Sub-ss. (1)–(3): TA 1970, s. 344; F(No. 2)A 1975, s. 44(2); FA 1987, s. 36(2). Sub-ss. (4)–(7): FA 1987, Sch. 6, Pt. II.

479. Interest paid on deposits with banks etc.

(1) Any deposit-taker making a payment of interest in respect of a relevant deposit shall be liable to account for and pay an amount representing income tax on that payment, calculated by applying the composite rate (determined in accordance with section 483) to the grossed-up amount of the payment, that is to say, to the amount which after deduction of tax at the composite rate would be equal to the amount actually paid.

(2) Where in relation to any payment of interest a deposit-taker is liable to account for and pay an amount under subsection (1) above—

(*a*) subject to subsection (3) below, no assessment to income tax shall be made on, and no repayment of income tax shall be made to, the person receiving or entitled to the payment in respect of it;
(*b*) the payment shall, in computing the total income of the person entitled to it, be treated as income for that year received by him after deduction of income tax at the basic rate from a corresponding gross amount; and
(*c*) the payment (and no more) shall, in applying sections 348 and 349 to other payments, be treated as profits or gains which have been brought into charge to income tax.

(3) Subsection (2)(*a*) above shall not prevent an assessment in respect of income tax at a rate other than the basic rate.

(4) For the purpose of determining whether any or what amount of tax is, by virtue of subsection (2)(*b*) above, to be taken into account as having been deducted from a gross amount in the case of an individual whose total income is reduced by any deductions, so much only of that gross amount shall be taken into account as is part of his total income as so reduced.

(5) Any payment of interest in respect of which an amount is payable under subsection (1) above shall be a relevant payment for the purposes of Schedule 16 whether or not the deposit-taker making the payment is resident in the United Kingdom.

(6) Schedule 16 shall apply in relation to any payment which is a relevant payment by virtue of subsection (5) above—

(*a*) with the substitution for any reference to a company of a reference to a deposit-taker;
(*b*) as if any amount payable under subsection (1) above were payable as income tax;
(*c*) as if paragraph 5 applied only in relation to payments received by the deposit-taker

and falling to be taken into account in computing his income chargeable to corporation tax; and

(*d*) as if in paragraph 7 the reference to section 7(2) included a reference to sections 11(3) and 349(1).

(7) In relation to any deposit-taker who is not a company, Schedule 16 shall have effect as if—

(*a*) paragraph 5 were omitted; and
(*b*) references to accounting periods were references to periods for which the deposit-taker makes up his accounts.

Former enactments.—Sub-s. (1): FA 1984, s. 27(1).
Sub-ss. (2)–(4): FA 1984, Sch. 8, para. 4.
Sub-ss. (5)–(7): FA 1984, Sch. 8, para. 5.
Note.—For the year 1989–90 the composite rate for the purposes of this section is 21·75 per cent; the Income Tax (Reduced Composite Rate) Order 1988, S.I. 1988 No. 2145.
Cross references.—See FA 1988, s. 130(7)(*c*)(ii), (9) (company migration: provisions for securing payment by migrating company of tax under this section and FA 1984, s. 27 and Sch. 8, paras. 4, 5).

480. Deposits becoming or ceasing to be composite rate deposits

(1) Where a deposit which is a source of income of any person ("the lender") is not a composite rate deposit but at any time becomes such a deposit, section 67 shall apply as if the deposit were a source of income which the lender ceased to possess immediately before it became a composite rate deposit.

(2) Section 67 shall apply in relation to a deposit which became a composite rate deposit on 6th April 1985 with the omission from subsection (1)(*b*) of the words from "and shall" to "this provision".

(3) Where a deposit which is a source of income of any person ceases to be a composite rate deposit, section 66(3) shall apply as if the deposit were a new source of income acquired by him immediately after it ceased to be a composite rate deposit.

(4) For the purposes of this section a deposit is at any time a composite rate deposit if, were the person holding it to make a payment of interest in respect of it at that time, he would be liable to account for and pay an amount on that payment under section 479(1).

Former enactment.—FA 1984, Sch. 8, para. 6(5)–(8).

481. "Deposit-taker", "deposit" and "relevant deposit"

(1) In this section "the relevant provisions" means sections 479 and 480, this section and section 482.

(2) In the relevant provisions "deposit-taker" means any of the following—

(*a*) the Bank of England;
(*b*) any institution authorised under the Banking Act 1987 or municipal bank within the meaning of that Act;
(*c*) the Post Office;
(*d*) any company to which property and rights belonging to a trustee savings bank were transferred by section 3 of the Trustee Savings Bank Act 1985;
(*e*) any bank formed under the Savings Bank (Scotland) Act 1819; and
(*f*) any person or class of person who receives deposits in the course of his business or activities and which is for the time being prescribed by order made by the Treasury for the purposes of this paragraph.

(3) In the relevant provisions "deposit" means a sum of money paid on terms under which it will be repaid with or without interest and either on demand or at a time or in circumstances agreed by or on behalf of the person making the payment and the person to whom it is made.

(4) For the purposes of the relevant provisions a deposit is a relevant deposit if, but only if—

(*a*) the person who is beneficially entitled to any interest in respect of the deposit is an individual or, where two or more persons are so entitled, all of them are individuals; or
(*b*) in Scotland, the person who is so entitled is a partnership all the partners of which are individuals; or

(c) the person entitled to any such interest receives it as a personal representative in his capacity as such;

and the deposit is not prevented from being a relevant deposit by subsection (5) below.

(5) A deposit is not a relevant deposit if—

   (a) a qualifying certificate of deposit has been issued in respect of it or it is a qualifying time deposit;
   (b) it is a debt on a debenture ("debenture" having the meaning given in section 744 of the Companies Act 1985) issued by the deposit-taker;
   (c) it is a loan made by a deposit-taker in the ordinary course of his business or activities;
   (d) it is a debt on a security which is listed on a recognised stock exchange;
   (e) it is a general client account deposit;
   (f) it forms part of a premiums trust fund (within the meaning of section 457) of an underwriting member of Lloyd's;
   (g) it is made by a Stock Exchange money broker (recognised by the Bank of England) in the course of his business as such a broker;
   (h) in the case of a deposit-taker resident in the United Kingdom for the purposes of income tax or corporation tax, it is held at a branch of his situated outside the United Kingdom;
   (j) in the case of a deposit-taker who is not so resident, it is held otherwise than at a branch of his situated in the United Kingdom; or
   (k) the appropriate person has declared in writing to the deposit-taker liable to pay interest in respect of the deposit that—

      (i) at the time when the declaration is made, the person who is beneficially entitled to the interest is not, or, as the case may be, all the persons who are so entitled are not, ordinarily resident in the United Kingdom;
      (ii) in a case falling within subsection (4)(c) above the deceased was, immediately before his death, not ordinarily resident in the United Kingdom.

(6) The Treasury may by order make amendments in this section and sections 479(2) to (7), 480 and 482 providing for deposits of a kind specified in the order to be or, as the case may be, not to be relevant deposits in relation to all deposit-takers or such deposit-takers or classes of deposit-takers as may be so specified.

Former enactments.—Sub-s. (2): FA 1984, Sch. 8, para. 2(1); FA 1985, s. 38(2); Banking Act 1987, Sch. 6, para. 16; FA 1987, Sch. 15, para. 16(2).
Sub-ss. (3)–(5): FA 1984, Sch. 8, para. 3(1)–(3); FA 1985, s. 38(3), (4).
Sub-s. (6): FA 1984, Sch. 8, para. 3A(1); FA 1985, s. 38(7).

482. Supplementary provisions

(1) For the purposes of sections 479, 480 and 481 and this section, any amount which is credited as interest in respect of a relevant deposit shall be treated as a payment of interest.

(2) A declaration under section 481(5)(k) shall—

   (a) if made under sub-paragraph (i), contain an undertaking by the person making it that if the person, or any of the persons in respect of whom it is made, becomes ordinarily resident in the United Kingdom he will notify the deposit-taker accordingly; and
   (b) in any case, be in such form as may be prescribed or authorised, and contain such information as may reasonably be required, by the Board.

(3) A deposit-taker shall, on being so required by notice given to him by an inspector, make all declarations which have been made to him under section 481(5) available for inspection by the inspector or by a named officer of the Board.

(4) Where a notice has been given to a deposit-taker under subsection (3) above, the declarations shall be made available within such time as may be specified in the notice, and the person to whom they are to be made available may take copies of or extracts from them.

(5) A deposit-taker shall treat every deposit made with him as a relevant deposit unless satisfied that it is not a relevant deposit, but where he has satisfied himself that a deposit is not a relevant deposit he shall be entitled to continue to so treat it until such time as he is in possession of information which can reasonably be taken to indicate that the deposit is or may be a relevant deposit.

(6) In section 481(5)—

"appropriate person", in relation to a deposit, means any person who is beneficially entitled to any interest in respect of the deposit or entitled to receive any such interest as a personal representative in his capacity as such or to whom any such interest is payable;

"general client account deposit" means a deposit, held by the deposit-taker in a client account (other than one which is identified by the deposit-taker as one in which sums are held only for one or more particular clients of the person whose account it is) in respect of which that person is required by provision made under any enactment to make payments representing interest to some or all of the clients for whom, or on whose account, he received the sums deposited in the account;

"qualifying certificate of deposit" means a certificate of deposit, as defined in section 56(5), which is issued by a deposit-taker and under which—

(a) the amount payable by the deposit-taker, exclusive of interest, is not less than £50,000 (or, for a deposit denominated in foreign currency, not less than the equivalent of £50,000 at the time when the deposit is made); and

(b) the obligation of the deposit-taker to pay that amount arises after a period of not less than seven days beginning with the date on which the deposit is made; and

"qualifying time deposit" means a deposit which is made by way of loan for an amount which is not less than £50,000 (or, for a deposit denominated in foreign currency, not less than the equivalent of £50,000 at the time when the deposit is made) and on terms which—

(a) prevent repayment of the deposit before the expiry of the period of seven days beginning with the date on which the deposit is made, but which require repayment at the end of a specified period;

(b) do not make provision for the transfer of the right to repayment; and

(c) prevent partial withdrawals of, or additions to, the deposit.

In relation to deposits made before 20th May 1986 this subsection shall have effect with the substitution for "seven" of "28" (in both places).

(7) For the purposes of section 481(5)(h) and (j) a deposit is held at a branch of a deposit-taker if it is recorded in his books as a liability of that branch.

(8) A certificate of deposit, as defined in section 56(5), which was issued before 13th March 1984 on terms which provide for interest to be payable on the deposit at any time after 5th April 1985 (whether or not interest is payable on it before that date) shall, if it is not a qualifying certificate of deposit, be treated for the purposes of section 481(5) as if it were a qualifying certificate of deposit.

(9) Any deposit which was made before 6th July 1984 but which is not a qualifying time deposit shall, where it is made on terms which—

(a) do not make provision for the transfer of the right to repayment;
(b) prevent partial withdrawals of, or additions to, the deposit; and
(c) require—

(i) the deposit-taker to repay the sum at the end of a specified period which ends after 5th April 1985; or
(ii) in a case where interest is payable only at the time of repayment of the deposit, the deposit-taker to repay the sum on demand or on notice;

be treated for the purposes of section 481(5) as if it were a qualifying time deposit.

(10) An order under section 481(2)(f) may prescribe a person or class of person in relation to all relevant deposits or only in relation to relevant deposits of a kind specified in the order.

(11) The Board may by regulations make provision—

(a) requiring any declaration under section 481(5)(k)(i) which does not give the address of the person making it, to be supported by a certificate given by the deposit-taker concerned—

(i) in such form as may be prescribed or authorised by the Board; and
(ii) containing such information as may reasonably be required by the Board; and

(b) generally for giving effect to sections 479 to 481 and this section.

(12) Regulations under subsection (11) above or an order under section 481(6) may contain such incidental and consequential provision as appears to the Board or the Treasury, as the case may be, to be appropriate.

Former enactments.—Sub-s. (1): FA 1984, Sch. 8, para. 1(2).
Sub-s. (2): FA 1984, Sch. 8, para. 3(4), 4A); FA 1985, s. 38(5).
Sub-ss. (3)–(7): FA 1984, Sch. 8, para. 3(5)–(9); FA 1985, s. 38(6); Income Tax (Composite Rate) (Relevant Deposits) Order 1986, S.I. 1986 No. 771.

TA 1988, s. 482   *Income and Corporation Taxes Act 1988: Pt. XII*   1158

Sub-s. (8): FA 1984, Sch. 8, para. 6(2).
Sub-s. (9): FA 1984, Sch. 9, para. 6(3).
Sub-s. (10): FA 1984, Sch. 8, para. 2(2); FA 1985, s. 38(2).
Sub-s. (11): FA 1984, Sch. 8, para. 3A(2); FA 1985, s. 38(7).
Sub-s. (12): FA 1984, Sch. 8, para. 3A(3); FA 1985, s. 38(7).

483. Determination of reduced rate for building societies and composite rate for banks etc.

(1) In every year of assessment the Treasury shall by order determine a rate which shall, for the following year of assessment, be—
   (*a*) the reduced rate for the purposes of section 476; and
   (*b*) the composite rate for the purposes of section 479.

(2) The order made under subsection (1) above in each year of assessment shall—
   (*a*) be made before 31st December in that year; and
   (*b*) be based only on information relating to periods before the end of the year of assessment in which the order is made.

(3) Whenever they exercise their powers under this section the Treasury shall aim at securing that (assuming for the purposes of this subsection that the amounts payable by building societies under section 476 and by deposit-takers under section 479 are income tax) the total income tax becoming payable to, and not being repayable by, the Crown is (when regard is had to the operation of those sections) as nearly as may be the same in the aggregate as it would have been if those sections had not been enacted.

(4) If the order made under section 26 of the Finance Act 1984 in the year 1987–88 is made in pursuance of subsection (4) of that section, that order shall, notwithstanding that that subsection is not re-enacted by this Act, apply for the purposes of sections 476 and 479 for the year 1988–89.

(5) For the purposes of enabling the Treasury to comply with the requirements of subsection (3) above, the Board may by notice require any deposit-taker (within the meaning of section 481) or building society to furnish to the Board such information about its depositors as the Board may reasonably require for those purposes.

In this subsection "depositors", in relation to a building society, includes shareholders.

Former enactments.—Sub-ss. (1)–(4): FA 1984, s. 26(1)–(4).
Sub-s. (5): FA 1984, s. 26(7), (9).
Note.—For the year 1989–90 the reduced rate for the purposes of s. 476 and the composite rate for the purposes of s. 479 is 21·75 per cent; the Income Tax (Reduced and Composite Rate) Order 1988, S.I. 1988 No. 2145.

484. Savings banks: exemption from tax

(1) Any savings bank other than a savings bank which is the successor or further successor to an existing trustee savings bank shall on making a claim be entitled to exemption from income tax and corporation tax in respect of the income of its funds to the extent that such income is applied in the payment or credit of interest to any depositor; but, subject to section 325, any such interest shall be chargeable under Case III of Schedule D.

(2) Any gain or loss accruing to a savings bank which is the successor to an existing trustee savings bank on a disposal of an exempt investment held by that existing bank on 21st November 1979, may, if that existing bank has so elected, be computed by reference to the cost of the investment instead of by reference to its market value on the latter date and, in the case of a loss, without any restriction under section 270(4) of the 1970 Act.

(3) In subsection (2) above the reference to an election is a reference to an election under paragraph 2(3) of Schedule 11 to the Finance Act 1980 (under which the election must have been by notice in writing given to the Board within two years after 21st November 1979, and has effect in relation to all exempt investments held by the bank on that date).

(4) Where a savings bank which is the successor to an existing trustee savings bank holds investments which include both exempt investments held by the existing bank on 21st November 1979 and other investments of the same class, any investments of that class which are disposed of by the successor shall be treated for the purposes of subsection (2) above as consisting of the other investments rather than of the exempt investments held on that date.

(5) In this section references to exempt investments held by an existing trustee savings bank on 21st November 1979 are to investments on the disposal of which immediately before that

date no chargeable gain or allowable loss would have accrued to the bank by virtue of section 67 of the 1979 Act (gilt-edged securities held for more than a year).

(6) In this section "successor" and "existing", in relation to a trustee savings bank, have the meanings given by section 1 of the Trustee Savings Bank Act 1985, and "further successor" has the meaning given by paragraph 9 of Schedule 2 to that Act.

Former enactments.—Sub-s. (1): TA 1970, s. 339; FA 1980, Sch. 11, para. 5; Trustee Savings Bank Act 1985, Sch. 2, para. 6(5), (6).
Sub-ss. (2)–(5): FA 1980, Sch. 11, para. 2(3)–(6); Trustee Savings Bank Act 1985, Sch. 2, para. 6(3).
Sub-s. (6): Trustee Savings Bank Act 1985, s. 1(1); Sch. 2, para. 9(1).

485. Savings banks: supplemental

(1) Where the business of a trustee savings bank has been transferred to another trustee savings bank after 21st November 1979 and before the day which was the vesting day for the purposes of the Trustee Savings Bank Act 1985—

(*a*) any exempt investment which was held on that date by the first bank and was transferred with the business shall be treated for the purposes of section 484 in its application to any savings bank which is the successor to the second bank as if it had been held on that date by the second bank but without prejudice to any election made in respect of the investment by the first bank under sub-paragraph (3) of paragraph 2 of Schedule 11 to the Finance Act 1980; and

(*b*) the cost of the investment shall be taken for the purposes of that sub-paragraph as equal to the cost of the investment to the first bank.

(2) Where the business of a trustee savings bank was transferred to another trustee savings bank before 21st November 1979 the cost of any exempt investment held by the second bank on that date which—

(*a*) was transferred to it with the business; and
(*b*) was an exempt investment on the date of the transfer,

shall be taken for the purposes of section 484(2) in its application to any savings bank which is the successor to the second bank as equal to the cost of the investment to the first bank.

(3) In this section references to exempt investments held by a trustee savings bank on 21st November 1979 or the date of the transfer are to investments on the disposal of which immediately before that date no chargeable gain or allowable loss would have accrued to the bank by virtue of section 67 of the 1979 Act (gilt-edged securities held for more than a year) or, in the case of a transfer which took place before that section came into force, section 41 of the Finance Act 1969 (which was re-enacted by section 67 of the 1979 Act).

Former enactments.—FA 1980, Sch. 11, paras. 3, 4, 6(2)–(4); Trustee Savings Bank Act 1985, Sch. 2, para. 6(7).

486. Industrial and provident societies and co-operative associations

(1) Notwithstanding anything in the Tax Acts, share interest or loan interest paid by a registered industrial and provident society shall not be treated as a distribution; and, subject to subsection (7) below and section 487(3), any share or loan interest paid in an accounting period of the society—

(*a*) shall be deductible in computing, for the purposes of corporation tax, the income of the society for that period from the trade carried on by the society, or
(*b*) if the society is not carrying on a trade, shall be treated for those purposes as a charge on the income of the society.

(2) Notwithstanding anything in sections 348 to 350, any share interest or loan interest paid by a registered industrial and provident society, except any to which subsection (3) below applies, shall be paid without deduction of income tax.

(3) This subsection applies to any share interest or loan interest payable to a person whose usual place of abode is not within the United Kingdom, and in any such case section 349(2) shall apply to the payment as it applies to a payment of yearly interest, and income tax shall be deducted accordingly.

(4) Any share interest or loan interest paid by a registered industrial and provident society shall be chargeable under Case III of Schedule D.

(5) Where at any time, by virtue of this section, the income of a person from any source, not having previously been chargeable by direct assessment on that person, becomes so

chargeable, section 66(3) shall apply as if the source of that income were a new source of income acquired by that person at that time.

(6) Every registered industrial and provident society shall, within three months after the end of any accounting period of the society, deliver to the inspector a return showing—

(a) the name and place of residence of every person to whom the society has by virtue of this section paid without deduction of income tax sums amounting to more than £15 in that period; and
(b) the amount so paid in that period to each of those persons.

(7) If for any accounting period a return under subsection (6) above is not duly made by a registered industrial and provident society, share and loan interest paid by the society in that period shall not be deductible in computing its income, or be treated as a charge on income.

(8) If in the course of, or as part of, a union or amalgamation of two or more registered industrial and provident societies, or a transfer of engagements from one registered industrial and provident society to another, there is a disposal of an asset by one society to another, both shall be treated for the purposes of corporation tax in respect of chargeable gains as if the asset were acquired from the society making the disposal for a consideration of such amount as would secure that neither a gain nor a loss would accrue to that society on the disposal.

(9) Subsections (1) and (8) above shall have effect as if references to a registered industrial and provident society included any co-operative association established and resident in the United Kingdom, and having as its object or primary object to assist its members in the carrying on of agricultural or horticultural businesses on land occupied by them in the United Kingdom or in the carrying on of businesses consisting in the catching or taking of fish or shellfish.

(10) It is hereby declared that, in computing, for the purposes of any provision of the Tax Acts relating to profits or gains chargeable under Case I of Schedule D ("the tax computation"), any profits or gains of—

(a) any registered industrial and provident society which does not sell to persons not members thereof: or
(b) any registered industrial and provident society the number of the shares in which is not limited by its rules or practice;

there are to be deducted as expenses any sums which—

(i) represent a discount, rebate, dividend or bonus granted by the company to members or other persons in respect of amounts paid or payable by or to them on account of their transactions with the company, being transactions which are taken into account in the tax computation; and
(ii) are calculated by reference to those amounts or to the magnitude of those transactions and not by reference to the amount of any share or interest in the capital of the company.

(11) No dividends or bonus deductible in computing income as mentioned in subsection (10) above shall be regarded as a distribution.

(12) In this section—

"co-operative association" means a body of persons having a written constitution from which the Minister is satisfied, having regard to the provision made as to the manner in which the income of the body is to be applied for the benefit of its members and all other relevant provisions, that the body is in substance a co-operative association;
"the Minister" means—

the Minister of Agriculture, Fisheries and Food, as regards England and Wales;
the Secretary of State, as regards Scotland; and
the Department of Agriculture for Northern Ireland, as regards Northern Ireland;

"registered industrial and provident society" means a society registered or deemed to be registered under the Industrial and Provident Societies Act 1965 or under the Industrial and Provident Societies Act (Northern Ireland) 1969;
"share interest" means any interest, dividend, bonus or other sum payable to a shareholder of the society by reference to the amount of his holding in the share capital of the society;
"loan interest" means any interest payable by the society in respect of any mortgage, loan, loan stock or deposit;

and references to the payment of share interest or loan interest include references to the crediting of such interest.

Former enactments.—TA 1970, ss. 340, 345; Credit Unions Act 1979, s. 25(2); Northern Ireland Constitution Act 1973, Sch. 5, para. 8.
Cross references.—See FA 1985, s. 68(7), (7A)(*b*), (*f*) (modification of indexation allowance with respect to disposals of assets after 31 March or 5 April 1985);
FA 1988, Sch. 8, para. 1 (capital gains: re-basing to 1982 of assets held on 31 March 1982).

487. Credit unions

(1) Subject to subsection (2) below, in computing for the purposes of corporation tax the income of a credit union for any accounting period—

(*a*) neither the activity of the credit union in making loans to its members nor in placing on deposit or otherwise investing from time to time its surplus funds shall be regarded as the carrying on of a trade or part of a trade; and
(*b*) interest received by the credit union on loans made by it to its members shall not be chargeable to tax under Case III of Schedule D or otherwise.

(2) Paragraph (*b*) of subsection (1) above shall not apply to an accounting period of a credit union for which the credit union is obliged to make a return under section 486(6) and has not done so within three months after the end of that accounting period or such longer period as the inspector shall allow.

(3) No share interest, loan interest or annuity or other annual payment paid or payable by a credit union in any accounting period shall be deductible in computing for the purposes of corporation tax the income of the credit union for that period from any trade carried on by it or be treated for those purposes as a charge on income.

(4) A credit union shall not be regarded as an investment company for the purposes of section 75 above or section 306 of the 1970 Act (capital allowances).

(5) In this section—

"credit union" means a society registered as a credit union under the Industrial and Provident Societies Act 1965 or the Credit Unions (Northern Ireland) Order 1985;
"share interest" and "loan interest" have the same meaning as in section 486;
"surplus funds", in relation to a credit union, means funds not immediately required for its purposes;

and references to the payment of share interest or loan interest include references to the crediting of such interest.

Former enactments.—TA 1970, s. 340A; Credit Unions Act 1979, s. 25(1); Credit Unions (Northern Ireland) Order 1985, S.I. 1985 No. 1205.

488. Co-operative housing associations

(1) Where a housing association makes a claim in that behalf for any year or part of a year of assessment during which the association was approved for the purposes of this section—

(*a*) rent to which the association was entitled from its members for the year or part shall be disregarded for tax purposes; and
(*b*) any yearly interest payable by the association for the year or part shall be treated for tax purposes as payable not by the association but severally by the members of the association who during the year or part were tenants of property of the association, in the proportion which the rents payable by those members for the year or part bear to the aggregate of the rents to which the association was entitled for the year or part from the properties to which the interest relates; and
(*c*) each member of the association shall be treated for the purposes of section 354 as if he were the owner of the association's estate or interest in the property of which he is the tenant.

(2) Where the property, or any of the properties, to which any such interest as is mentioned in paragraph (*b*) of subsection (1) above relates is for any period not subject to a tenancy—

(*a*) that paragraph shall not apply in relation to so much of the interest as is attributable to the property not subject to a tenancy; and
(*b*) for the purposes of that paragraph as it applies in relation to a tenant of any other property to which the interest relates, the association shall be deemed to have received,

in respect of the property not subject to a tenancy, rent at the rate payable therefor when it was last let by the association.

(3) In computing the income of the association no payments shall be deductible under section 25(3) to (7) in so far as attributable to a period as respects which a claim under subsection (1) above has effect.

(4) Where a claim under subsection (1) above has effect, any adjustment of the liability to tax of a member or of the association which is required in consequence of the claim may be made by an assessment or by repayment or otherwise, as the case may require.

(5) Where a housing association makes a claim in that behalf for an accounting period or part of an accounting period during which it was approved for the purposes of this section, the housing association shall be exempt from corporation tax on chargeable gains accruing to it in the accounting period or part on the disposal by way of sale of any property which has been or is being occupied by a tenant of the housing association.

(6) References in this section to the approval of an association shall be construed as references to approval—
    (*a*) by the Secretary of State in the case of a housing association in Great Britain;
    (*b*) by the Head of the Department of the Environment for Northern Ireland in the case of a housing association in Northern Ireland;
and an association shall not be approved unless the approving authority is satisfied—
    (i) that the association is, or is deemed to be, duly registered under the Industrial and Provident Societies Act 1965 or the Industrial and Provident Societies Act (Northern Ireland) 1969, and is a housing association within the meaning of the Housing Associations Act 1985 or Article 114 of the Housing (Northern Ireland) Order 1981;
    (ii) that the rules of the association restrict membership to persons who are tenants or prospective tenants of the association, and preclude the granting or assignment (or, in Scotland, the granting or assignation) of tenancies to persons other than members; and
    (iii) that the association satisfies such other requirements as may be prescribed by the approving authority, and will comply with such conditions as may for the time being be so prescribed.

(7) An approval given for the purposes of this section shall have effect as from such date (whether before or after the giving of the approval) as may be specified by the approving authority and shall cease to have effect if revoked.

(8) The Secretary of State as respects Great Britain, or the Head of the Department of the Environment for Northern Ireland as respects Northern Ireland, may make regulations for the purpose of carrying out the provisions of this section; and, from the coming into operation of regulations under this subsection prescribing requirements or conditions for the purposes of subsection (6)(iii) above, "prescribed" in subsection (6)(iii) above shall mean prescribed by or under such regulations.

The power to make regulations under this subsection shall be exercisable by the Secretary of State by statutory instrument and by the Head of the Department of the Environment for Northern Ireland by statutory rule for the purposes of the Statutory Rules (Northern Ireland) Order 1979.

(9) A claim under this section shall be made to the inspector, and shall be made not later than two years after the end of the year of assessment or accounting period to which, or to a part of which, it relates.

Section 42 of the Management Act shall not apply to a claim under this section.

(10) Subject to subsection (11) below, no claim under this section shall have effect unless it is proved that during the year or accounting period, or part thereof, to which the claim relates—
    (*a*) no property belonging to the association making the claim was let otherwise than to a member of the association;
    (*b*) no property let by the association, and no part of such property, was occupied, whether solely or as joint occupier, by a person not being a member of the association;
    (*c*) the association making the claim satisfies the conditions specified in subsection (6)(i) and (ii) above and has complied with the conditions prescribed under subsection (6)(iii) for the time being in force; and
    (*d*) any covenants required to be included in grants of tenancies by those conditions have been observed.

For the purposes of paragraph (*b*) above occupation by any other person in accordance with the will, or the provisions applicable on the intestacy, of a deceased member, shall be treated during the first six months after the death as if it were occupation by a member.

(11) Where the Board are satisfied that the requirements of subsection (10) above are substantially complied with they may direct that the claim shall have effect; but if subsequently information comes to the knowledge of the Board which satisfies them that the direction was not justified they may revoke the direction and thereupon the liability of all persons concerned to tax for all relevant years or accounting periods shall be adjusted by the making of assessments or otherwise.

(12) A claim under this section shall be in such form and contain such particulars as may be prescribed by the Board, and, without prejudice to the generality of this provision, the required particulars may include an authority granted by all members of the association for any relevant information contained in any return made by a member under the provisions of the Income Tax Acts to be used by the Board in such manner as the Board may think fit for determining whether the claim ought to be allowed.

Former enactments.—TA 1970, s. 341; FA 1972, Sch. 11, para. 6; Housing (Consequential Provisions) Act 1985, Sch. 2, para. 18(2); Secretary of State for the Environment Order 1970, S.I. 1970 No. 1681; Northern Ireland Constitution Act 1973, Sch. 5, para. 7(1); Statutory Rules (Northern Ireland) Order 1979, S.I. 1979 No. 1573; Building Societies and Tax (Northern Ireland Consequential Amendments) Order 1981, S.I. 1981 No. 157.

489. Self-build societies

(1) Where a self-build society makes a claim in that behalf for any year or part of a year of assessment during which the society was approved for the purposes of this section, rent to which the society was entitled from its members for the year or part shall be disregarded for tax purposes.

(2) Where a claim under subsection (1) above has effect, any adjustment of the society's liability to tax which is required in consequence of the claim may be made by an assessment or by repayment or otherwise, as the case may require.

(3) Where a self-build society makes a claim in that behalf for an accounting period or part during which it was approved for the purposes of this section, the society shall be exempt from corporation tax on chargeable gains accruing to it in the accounting period or part thereof on the disposal of any land to a member of the society.

(4) References in this section to the approval of a self-build society are references to its approval by the Secretary of State, and the Secretary of State shall not approve a self-build society for the purposes of this section unless he is satisfied—

(*a*) that the society is, or is deemed to be, duly registered under the Industrial and Provident Societies Act 1965; and
(*b*) that the society satisfies such other requirements as may be prescribed by or under regulations under subsection (6) below and will comply with such conditions as may for the time being be so prescribed.

(5) An approval given for the purposes of this section shall have effect as from such date (whether before or after the giving of the approval) as may be specified by the Secretary of State and shall cease to have effect if revoked by him.

(6) The Secretary of State may by statutory instrument make regulations for the purpose of carrying out the provisions of this section; and a statutory instrument containing any such regulations shall be subject to annulment in pursuance of a resolution of the House of Commons.

(7) Section 42 of the Management Act shall not apply to a claim under this section, but such a claim shall be made to the inspector and shall be made not later than two years after the end of the year of assessment or accounting period to which, or to a part of which, it relates.

(8) Subject to subsection (9) below, no claim under this section shall have effect unless it is proved that during the year or accounting period, or part thereof, to which the claim relates—

(*a*) no land owned by the society was occupied, in whole or in part and whether solely or as joint occupier, by a person who was not, at the time of his occupation, a member of the society; and
(*b*) the society making the claim satisfies the condition specified in paragraph (*a*) of subsection (4) above and has complied with the conditions prescribed under paragraph (*b*) of that subsection and for the time being in force;

and for the purposes of paragraph (*a*) above, occupation by any other person in accordance with the will, or the provisions applicable on the intestacy, of a deceased member, shall be treated during the first six months after the death as if it were occupation by a member.

(9) Notwithstanding the provisions of subsection (8) above, where, on a claim under this section, the Board are satisfied that the requirements of paragraphs (*a*) and (*b*) of that subsection are substantially complied with, they may direct that the claim shall have effect; but if, subsequently, information comes to the knowledge of the Board which satisfies them that the direction was not justified, they may revoke the direction and thereupon the liability of the society to tax for all relevant years or accounting periods shall be adjusted by the making of assessments or otherwise.

(10) A claim under this section shall be in such form and contain such particulars as may be prescribed by the Board.

(11) In this section—

"self-build society" has the same meaning as in the Housing Associations Act 1985 or, in Northern Ireland, Part VII of the Housing (Northern Ireland) Order 1981; and

"rent" includes any sums to which a self-build society is entitled in respect of the occupation of any of its land under a licence or otherwise.

(12) In the application of this section to Northern Ireland—

(*a*) any reference in subsections (4) and (5) above to the Secretary of State shall be construed as a reference to the Department of the Environment for Northern Ireland;

(*b*) the reference in subsection (4)(*a*) to the Industrial and Provident Societies Act 1965 shall be construed as a reference to the Industrial and Provident Societies Act (Northern Ireland) 1969; and

(*c*) for subsection (6) there shall be substituted the following subsection—

"(6) The Department of the Environment for Northern Ireland may by statutory rule for the purpose of the Statutory Rules (Northern Ireland) Order 1979 make regulations for the purpose of carrying out the provisions of this section; and a statutory rule containing any such regulations shall be subject to negative resolution within the meaning of section 41(6) of the Interpretation Act (Northern Ireland) 1954".

Former enactments.—TA 1970, s. 341A; Housing Act 1974, s. 120; FA 1984, s. 56(1); Housing (Consequential Provisions) Act 1985, Sch. 2, para. 18(3).

490. Companies carrying on a mutual business or not carrying on a business

(1) Subject to subsection (2) below, where a company carries on any business of mutual trading or mutual insurance or other mutual business the provisions of the Tax Acts relating to distributions shall apply to distributions made by the company notwithstanding that they are made to persons participating in the mutual activities of that business and derive from those activities, but shall so apply only to the extent to which the distributions are made out of profits of the company which are brought into charge to corporation tax or out of franked investment income (including group income).

(2) In the case of a company carrying on any mutual life assurance business, the provisions of the Tax Acts relating to distributions shall not apply to distributions made to persons participating in the mutual activities of that business and derived from those activities; but if the business includes annuity business, the annuities payable in the course of that business shall not be treated as charges on the income of the company to any greater extent than if the business were not mutual but were being carried on by the company with a view to the realisation of profits for the company.

(3) Subject to subsections (1) and (2) above, the fact that a distribution made by a company carrying on any such business is derived from the mutual activities of that business and the recipient is a person participating in those activities shall not affect the character which the payment or other receipt has for purposes of corporation tax or income tax in the hands of the recipient.

(4) Where a company does not carry on, and never has carried on, a trade or a business of holding investments, and is not established for purposes which include the carrying on of a trade or of such a business, the provisions of the Tax Acts relating to distributions shall apply to distributions made by the company only to the extent to which the distributions are made out of profits of the company which are brought into charge to corporation tax or out of franked investment income.

Former enactment.—TA 1970, s. 346.

491. Distribution of assets of body corporate carrying on mutual business

(1) Where any person receives any money or money's worth—

(*a*) forming part of the assets of a body corporate, other than assets representing capital; or

(*b*) forming part of the consideration for the transfer of the assets of a body corporate, other than assets representing capital, as part of a scheme of amalgamation or reconstruction which involves the winding up of the body corporate; or

(*c*) consisting of the consideration for a transfer or surrender of a right to receive anything falling under paragraph (*a*) of (*b*) above, being a receipt not giving rise to any charge to tax on the recipient apart from this section,

and the body corporate has at any time carried on a trade which consists of or includes the conducting of any mutual business (whether confined to members of the body corporate or not), and is being or has been wound up or dissolved, the provisions of this section shall apply to the receipt.

(2) If a transfer or surrender of a right under subsection (1)(*c*) above is not at arm's length, the person making the transfer or surrender shall, for the purposes of this section, be deemed then to have received consideration equal to the value of the right.

(3) If in respect of a payment of any amount made to the body corporate for the purposes of its mutual business any deduction has been allowed for the purposes of tax in computing the profits or gains or losses of a trade, then—

(*a*) if at the time of the receipt the recipient is the person, or one of the persons, carrying on that trade, the amount or value of the receipt shall be treated for the purposes of tax as a trading receipt of that trade; and

(*b*) if at the time of the receipt the recipient is not the person, or one of the persons, carrying on that trade, but was the person, or one of the persons, carrying on that trade when any payment was made to the body corporate for the purposes of its mutual business in respect of which a deduction was allowed for the purposes of tax in computing the profits or gains or losses of the trade, the recipient shall, subject to subsection (6) below, be charged under Case VI of Schedule D for the chargeable period in which the receipt falls on an amount equal to the amount or value of the receipt.

(4) Subsection (3)(*a*) above applies notwithstanding that, as a result of a change in the persons carrying on the trade, the profits or gains are under section 113 or 337(1) determined as if it had been permanently discontinued and a new trade set up and commenced.

(5) Where an individual is chargeable to tax by virtue of subsection (3)(*b*) above and the profits or gains of the trade there mentioned fell to be treated as earned income for the purposes of the Income Tax Acts, the sums in respect of which he is so chargeable shall also be treated for those purposes as earned income.

(6) If the trade mentioned in subsection (3)(*b*) above was permanently discontinued before the time of the receipt, then in computing the charge to tax under subsection (3)(*b*) above there shall be deducted from the amount or value of the receipt—

(*a*) any loss, expense or debit (not being a loss, expense or debit arising directly or indirectly from the discontinuance itself) which, if the trade had not been discontinued, would have been deducted in computing for tax purposes the profits or gains or losses of the person by whom it was carried on before the discontinuance, or would have been deducted from or set off against those profits as so computed, and

(*b*) any capital allowance to which the person who carried on the trade was entitled immediately before the discontinuance and to which effect has not been given by way of relief before discontinuance.

(7) Relief shall not be given under subsection (6) above or under section 105(1) in respect of any loss, expense, debit or allowance if and so far as it has been so given by reference to another charge to tax under this section or under section 103.

(8) For the purposes of subsection (1) above assets representing capital consist of—

(*a*) assets representing any loan or other capital subscribed, including income derived from any investment of any part of that capital, but not including profits from the employment of that capital for the purposes of the mutual business of the body corporate;

(*b*) assets representing any profits or gains charged to tax as being profits or gains of any

part of the trade carried on by the body corporate which does not consist of the conducting of any mutual business;
(c) (so far as not comprised in paragraphs (a) and (b) above) assets representing taxed income from any investments.

(9) In this section "mutual business" includes any business of mutual insurance or mutual trading.

(10) Subsections (3) to (7) above shall apply with any necessary modifications—
   (a) to a profession or vocation; and
   (b) to the occupation of woodlands the profits or gains of which are assessable under Schedule D;
as they apply to a trade.

(11) It is hereby declared that the description of trades in subsection (1) above does not include any trade all the profits or gains of which are chargeable to tax and, in particular, does not include such a trade carried on by any registered industrial and provident society.

Former enactment.—TA 1970, s. 347.
Note.—See **Prospective Legislation Notes** (Commercial Woodlands).

CHAPTER V

PETROLEUM EXTRACTION ACTIVITIES

492. Treatment of oil extraction activities etc. for tax purposes

(1) Where a person carries on as part of a trade—

(*a*) any oil extraction activities; or
(*b*) any of the following activities, namely, the acquisition, enjoyment or exploitation of oil rights; or
(*c*) activities of both those descriptions,

those activities shall be treated for all purposes of income tax, and for the purposes of the charge of corporation tax on income, as a separate trade, distinct from all other activities carried on by him as part of the trade.

(2) Relief in respect of a loss incurred by a person shall not be given under section 380 or 381 against income arising from oil extraction activities or from oil rights ("ring fence income") except to the extent that the loss arises from such activities or rights.

(3) Relief in respect of a loss incurred by a person shall not be given under section 393(2) against his ring fence profits except to the extent that the loss arises from oil extraction activities or from oil rights.

(4) In any case where—

(*a*) in any chargeable period a person incurs a loss in activities ("separate activities") which, for that or any subsequent chargeable period, are treated by virtue of subsection (1) above as a separate trade for the purposes specified in that subsection; and
(*b*) in any subsequent chargeable period any of his trading income is derived from activities ("related activities") which are not part of the separate activities but which, apart from subsection (1) above, would together with those activities constitute a single trade,

then, notwithstanding anything in that subsection, the amount of the loss may be set off, in accordance with section 385 or 393(1), against so much of his trading income in any subsequent chargeable period as is derived from the related activities.

(5) Subject to subsection (7) below, a capital allowance which is to be given to any person by discharge or repayment of tax shall not to any extent be given effect under section 71 of the 1968 Act by deduction from or set off against his ring fence income.

(6) Subject to subsection (7) below, a capital allowance which is to be given to any person by discharge or repayment of tax shall not to any extent be given effect under section 74 of the 1968 Act by deduction from or set off against his ring fence profits.

(7) Subsection (5) or (6) above shall not apply to a capital allowance which falls to be made to a company for any accounting period in respect of an asset used in the relevant accounting period by a company associated with it and so used in carrying on oil extraction activities.

For the purposes of this subsection, the relevant accounting period is that in which the allowance in question first falls to be made to the company (whether or not it can to any extent be given effect in that period under section 74(1) of the 1968 Act).

(8) On a claim for group relief made by a claimant company in relation to a surrendering company, group relief shall not be allowed against the claimant company's ring fence profits except to the extent that the claim relates to losses incurred by the surrendering company that arose from oil extraction activities or from oil rights.

Former enactments.—Oil Taxation Act 1975, s. 13; FA 1984, s. 79(5); FA 1978, s. 30(7)(*d*); FA 1982, s. 136(1).

493. Valuation of oil disposed of or appropriated in certain circumstances

(1) Where a person disposes of any oil in circumstances such that the market value of that oil in a particular month falls to be taken into account under section 2 of the Oil Taxation Act 1975 ("the 1975 Act"), otherwise than by virtue of paragraph 6 of Schedule 3 to that Act, in computing for the purposes of petroleum revenue tax the assessable profit or allowable loss accruing to him in any chargeable period from an oil field (or as would so fall but for section 10 of that Act), then—

(*a*) for all purposes of income tax, and
(*b*) for the purposes of the charge of corporation tax on income,

the disposal of the oil and its acquisition by the person to whom it was disposed of shall be treated as having been for a consideration equal to the market value of the oil as so taken into account under section 2 of that Act (or as would have been so taken into account under that section but for section 10 of that Act).

(2) Where a person makes a relevant appropriation of any oil without disposing of it and does so in circumstances such that the market value of that oil in a particular month falls to be taken into account under section 2 of the 1975 Act in computing for the purposes of petroleum revenue tax the assessable profit or allowable loss accruing to him in any chargeable period from an oil field (or would so fall but for section 10 of that Act), then for all the purposes of income tax and for the purposes of the charge of corporation tax on income, he shall be treated—

(*a*) as having, at the time of the appropriation—

(i) sold the oil in the course of the separate trade consisting of activities falling within section 492(1)(*a*) or (*b*); and
(ii) bought it in the course of the separate trade consisting of activities not so falling; and

(*b*) as having so sold and bought it at a price equal to its market value as so taken into account under section 2 of the 1975 Act (or as would have been so taken into account under that section but for section 10 of that Act).

In this subsection "relevant appropriation" has the meaning given by section 12(1) of the 1975 Act.

(3) Where—

(*a*) a person disposes otherwise than in a sale at arm's length (as defined in paragraph 1 of Schedule 3 to the 1975 Act) of oil acquired by him in the course of oil extraction activities carried on by him or by virtue of oil rights held by him, and
(*b*) subsection (1) above does not apply in relation to the disposal,

then, for all purposes of income tax and for the purposes of the charge of corporation tax on income, the disposal of the oil and its acquisition by the person to whom it was disposed of shall be treated as having been for a consideration equal to the market value of the oil in the calendar month in which the disposal was made.

(4) If a person appropriates oil acquired by him in the course of oil extraction activities carried on by him or by virtue of oil rights held by him and the appropriation is to refining or to any use except for production purposes of an oil field, within the meaning of Part I of the 1975 Act, then, unless subsection (2) above applies, for all purposes of income tax and for the purposes of the charge of corporation tax on income—

(*a*) he shall be treated as having, at the time of the appropriation, sold and bought the oil as mentioned in subsection (2)(*a*)(i) and (ii) above; and
(*b*) that sale and purchase shall be deemed to have been at a price equal to the market value of the oil in the calendar month in which it was appropriated.

(5) For the purposes of subsections (3) and (4) above—

(*a*) "calendar month" means a month of the calendar year; and
(*b*) paragraph 2 of Schedule 3 to the 1975 Act shall apply as it applies for the purposes of Part I of that Act, but with the following modifications, that is to say—

(i) for sub-paragraph (2)(*f*) there shall be substituted—

"(*f*) the contract is for the sale of the whole quantity of oil of which the market value falls to be ascertained for the purposes of section 493(3) or (4) of the Income and Corporation Taxes Act 1988 and of no other oil; and for the avoidance of doubt it is hereby declared that the terms as to payment which are to be implied in the contract shall be those which are customarily contained in contracts for sale at arm's length of oil of the kind in question."; and

(ii) sub-paragraphs (3) and (4) shall be omitted.

Former enactments.—Oil Taxation Act 1975, s. 14; FA 1985, s. 53; FA 1987, Sch. 11, para. 6.

494. Charges on income

(1) Section 338 shall have effect subject to the folowing provisions of this section.

(2) Interest paid by a company shall not be allowable under section 338 as a deduction against the company's ring fence profits except—

> (*a*) to the extent that it was payable in respect of money borrowed by the company which is shown to have been used to meet expenditure incurred by the company in carrying on oil extraction activities or in acquiring oil rights otherwise than from a connected person or to have been appropriated to meeting expenditure to be so incurred by the company; and
>
> (*b*) in the case of interest paid by the company to a company associated with it, to the extent that (subject always to paragraph (*a*) above) the rate at which it was payable did not exceed what, having regard to all the terms on which the money was borrowed and the standing of the borrower, was a reasonable commercial rate.

Section 839 shall apply for the purposes of this subsection.

(3) Where a company pays to a company associated with it a charge on income not consisting of a payment of interest, the charge shall not be allowable to any extent under section 338 against the first-mentioned company's ring fence profits.

(4) In any case where—

> (*a*) such of the charges on income which are paid by a company and allowable under section 338 as, by virtue of subsections (2) and (3) above, are not allowable against the company's ring fence profits exceed the remaining part of its profits (the company's "non-oil profits"), and
>
> (*b*) the amount of that excess is greater than the amount (if any) by which the total of the charges on income which are allowable to the company under that section exceeds the total of the company's profits,

then, for the purpose of enabling the company to surrender the excess referred to in paragraph (*a*) above by way of group relief, section 403(7) shall have effect as if in that subsection—

> (i) the reference to the amount paid by the surrendering company by way of charges on income were a reference to so much of that amount as is allowable only against the company's non-oil profits; and
>
> (ii) the reference to the surrendering company's profits were a reference to its non-oil profits alone.

Former enactments.—Oil Taxation Act 1975, s. 15; FA 1984, s. 79(5); FA 1982, s. 136(2).

495. Regional development grants

(1) Subsection (2) below applies in any case where—

> (*a*) a person has incurred expenditure (by way of purchase, rent or otherwise) on the acquisition of an asset in a transaction to which paragraph 2 of Schedule 4 to the 1975 Act applies (transactions between connected persons and otherwise than at arm's length), and
>
> (*b*) the expenditure incurred by the other person referred to in that paragraph in acquiring, bringing into existence or enhancing the value of the asset as mentioned in that paragraph has been or is to be met by a regional development grant and, in whole or in part, falls to be taken into account under Chapter I of Part I, or under Part II, of the 1968 Act (industrial buildings and structures and scientific research) or Chapter I of Part III of the Finance Act 1971 (machinery or plant).

(2) Where this subsection applies, for the purposes of the charge of income tax or corporation tax on the income arising from those activities of the person referred to in paragraph (*a*) of subsection (1) above which are treated by virtue of section 492(1) as a separate trade for those purposes, the expenditure referred to in that paragraph shall be treated as reduced by the amount of the regional development grant referred to in paragraph (*b*) of that subsection.

(3) Subsections (4) to (6) below apply where—

> (*a*) expenditure incurred by any person in relation to an asset in any relevant period ("the initial period") has been or is to be met by a regional development grant; and
>
> (*b*) notwithstanding the provisions of section 137 of the Finance Act 1982 and subsections

(1) and (2) above, in determining that person's liability to income tax or corporation tax for the initial period the whole or some part of that expenditure falls to be taken into account under Chapter I of Part I, or under Part II, of the 1968 Act or Chapter I of Part III of the Finance Act 1971; and

(c) in a relevant period subsequent to the initial period either expenditure on the asset becomes allowable under section 3 or 4 of the 1975 Act or the proportion of any such expenditure which is allowable is different as compared with the initial period;

and in subsections (4) to (6) below the subsequent relevant period referred to in paragraph (c) above is referred to as "the adjustment period".

(4) Where this subsection applies—

(a) there shall be redetermined for the purposes of subsections (5) and (6) below the amount of the expenditure referred to in subsection (3)(a) above which would have been taken into account as mentioned in subsection (3)(b) if the circumstances referred to in subsection (3)(c) had existed in the initial period; and

(b) according to whether the amount as so redetermined is greater or less than the amount actually taken into account as mentioned in subsection (3)(b), the difference is in subsections (5) and (6) below referred to as the increase or the reduction in the allowance.

(5) If there is an increase in the allowance, then, for the purposes of the provisions referred to in subsection (3)(b) above, an amount of capital expenditure equal to the increase shall be deemed to have been incurred by the person concerned in the adjustment period on an extension of or addition to the asset referred to in subsection (3)(a) above.

(6) If there is a reduction in the allowance, then, for the purpose of determining the liability to income tax or corporation tax of the person concerned, he shall be treated as having received in the adjustment period, as income of the trade in connection with which the expenditure referred to in subsection (3)(a) above was incurred, a sum equal to the amount of the reduction in the allowance.

(7) In this section—

"regional development grant" means a grant made under the provisions of Part II of the Industrial Development Act 1982 or Part I of the Industry Act 1972 or such grant made under an enactment of the Parliament of Northern Ireland or Measure of the Northern Ireland Assembly as has been or may be declared by the Treasury under section 84 or 95 of the 1968 Act to correspond to a grant made under those provisions; and

"relevant period" means an accounting period of a company or a year of assessment.

Former enactments.—FA 1982, ss. 137(4)–(6), 138; Industrial Development Act 1982, Sch. 2, para. 18.

496. Tariff receipts

(1) Any sum which—

(a) constitutes a tariff receipt of a person who is a participator in an oil field, and
(b) constitutes consideration in the nature of income rather than capital, and
(c) would not, apart from this subsection, be treated for the purposes of this Chapter as a receipt of the separate trade referred to in section 492(1),

shall be so treated for those purposes.

(2) To the extent that they would not otherwise be so treated, the activities of a participator in an oil field or a person connected with him in making available an asset in a way which gives rise to tariff receipts of the participator shall be treated for the purposes of this Chapter as oil extraction activities.

(3) In determining for the purposes of subsection (1) above whether any sum constitutes a tariff receipt of a person who is a participator, no account shall be taken of any sum which—

(a) is in fact received or receivable by a person connected with the participator, and
(b) constitutes a tariff receipt of the participator,

but in relation to the person by whom such a sum is actually received, subsection (1) above shall have effect as if he were a participator and as if the condition in paragraph (a) of that subsection were fulfilled.

(4) References in this section to a person connected with a participator include references to a person with whom the person is associated within the meaning of paragraph 11 of Schedule 2 to the Oil Taxation Act 1983.

Former enactment.—Oil Taxation Act 1983, s. 11.

497. Restriction on setting ACT against income from oil extraction activities etc.

(1) Section 239 shall have effect subject to the following provisions of this section; and in those provisions any reference to a company's ring fence income shall be construed, except in relation to relief under section 380 of this Act and section 71 of the 1968 Act, as a reference to the company's ring fence profits.

(2) Where advance corporation tax is paid by a company ("the distributing company") in respect of any distribution made by it to a company associated with it and resident in the United Kingdom or, where subsection (3) below applies, in respect of any distribution consisting of a dividend on a redeemable preference share—

  (*a*) that advance corporation tax shall not be set against the distributing company's liability to corporation tax on any ring fence income of the distributing company; and
  (*b*) if the benefit of any amount of that advance corporation tax is surrendered under section 240 to a subsidiary of the distributing company, the corresponding amount of advance corporation tax which under that section the subsidiary is treated for the purposes of section 239 as having paid shall not be set against the subsidiary's liability to corporation tax on any ring fence income of the subsidiary.

(3) Subject to subsection (4) below, this subsection applies in relation to the payment of a dividend on redeemable preference shares if the dividend is paid on or after 17th March 1987 and—

  (*a*) at the time the shares are issued, or
  (*b*) at the time the dividend is paid,

the company paying the dividend is under the control of a company resident in the United Kingdom, and in this subsection "control" shall be construed in accordance with section 416.

(4) Subsection (3) above does not apply if or to the extent that it is shown that the proceeds of the issue of the redeemable preference shares–

  (*a*) were used to meet expenditure incurred by the company issuing them in carrying on oil extraction activities or in acquiring oil rights otherwise than from a connected person; or
  (*b*) were appropriated to meeting expenditure to be so incurrred by that company;

and section 839 applies for the purposes of this subsection.

(5) Where in the case of any accounting period of a company there is an amount of advance corporation tax which because of subsection (2) above is not available to be set against the company's liability to corporation tax for that period on ring fence income of the company, section 239(2) shall as regards that period have effect as if the reference to the company's profits charged to corporation tax for that period were a reference to the company's profits so charged exclusive of any ring fence income.

(6) For the purposes of subsections (2) to (4) above, shares in a company are redeemable preference shares either if they are so described in the terms of their issue or if, however they are described, they fulfil the condition in paragraph (*a*) below and either or both of the conditions in paragraphs (*b*) and (*c*) below—

  (*a*) that, as against other shares in the company, they carry a preferential entitlement to a dividend or to any assets in a winding up or both;
  (*b*) that, by virtue of the terms of their issue, the exercise of a right by any person or the existence of any arrangements, they are liable to be redeemed, cancelled or repaid, in whole or in part;
  (*c*) that, by virtue of any material arrangements, the holder has a right to require another person to acquire the shares or is obliged in any circumstances to dispose of them or another person has a right or is in any circumstances obliged to acquire them.

(7) For the purposes of paragraph (*a*) of subsection (6) above, shares are to be treated as carrying a preferential entitlement to a dividend as against other shares if, by virtue of any arrangements, there are circumstances in which a minimum dividend will be payable on those shares but not on others; and for the purposes of paragraph (*c*) of that subsection arrangements relating to shares are material arrangements if the company which issued the shares or a company associated with that company is a party to the arrangements.

Former enactments.—Oil Taxation Act 1975, s. 16; FA 1987, s. 46; F(No. 2)A 1987, s. 76(2), (3).

498. Limited right to carry back surrendered ACT

(1) In any case where,—

(*a*) on a date not earlier than 17th March 1987, a company which is the surrendering company for the purposes of section 240 paid a dividend; and

(*b*) at no time in the accounting period of the surrendering company in which that dividend was paid was the surrendering company under the control of a company resident in the United Kingdom (construing "control" in accordance with section 416); and

(*c*) under section 240(1) the benefit of the advance corporation tax paid in respect of that dividend was surrendered to a subsidiary of the surrendering company; and

(*d*) that advance corporation tax is not such that the restriction in paragraph (*a*) or paragraph (*b*) of section 497(2) applies with respect to it; and

(*e*) in one or more of the accounting periods of the subsidiary beginning in the six years preceding the accounting period in which falls the date referred to in paragraph (*a*) above, the subsidiary has a liability to corporation tax in respect of profits which consist of or include ring fence profits,

sections 239 and 240 shall have effect subject to subsections (3) to (7) below.

(2) Where the conditions in subsection (1) above are fulfilled, the subsidiary to which the benefit of the advance corporation tax is surrendered is in the following provisions of this section referred to as a "qualifying subsidiary"; and in those provisions—

(*a*) "the surrendering company" has the same meaning as in section 240;

(*b*) "surrendered advance corporation tax" means advance corporation tax which, by virtue of section 240(2), a qualifying subsidiary is treated as having paid in respect of a distribution made on a particular date; and

(*c*) "the principal accounting period" means the accounting period of the qualifying subsidiary in which that date falls.

(3) So much of section 240(4) as would prevent surrendered advance corporation tax being set against a qualifying subsidiary's liability to corporation tax under section 239(3) shall not apply, but section 239(3) shall instead have effect subject to the following provisions of this section.

(4) Surrendered advance corporation tax may not under section 239(3) be set against a qualifying subsidiary's liability to corporation tax for an accounting period earlier than the principal accounting period unless throughout—

(*a*) that period,

(*b*) the principal accounting period, and

(*c*) any intervening accounting period,

the qualifying subsidiary was carrying on activities which, under and for the purposes specified in section 492, constitute a separate trade.

(5) Subject to subsection (6) below, for each accounting period of the surrendering company in which is paid a dividend the advance corporation tax on which gives rise, under section 240, to surrendered advance corporation tax, the total amount of that surrendered advance corporation tax in respect of which claims may be made under section 239(3) (whether by one qualifying subsidiary of the surrendering company or by two or more taken together) shall not exceed whichever of the following limits is appropriate to the accounting period of the surrendering company—

(*a*) for periods ending on or after 17th March 1987 and before 1st April 1989, £10 million;

(*b*) for periods ending on or after 1st April 1989 and before 1st April 1991, £15 million;

(*c*) for later periods, £20 million.

(6) In any case where an accounting period of the surrendering company is less than 12 months, the amount which is appropriate to it under subsection (5)(*a*) to (*c*) above shall be proportionately reduced.

(7) The amount of surrendered advance corporation tax of the principal accounting period which, on a claim under section 239(3), may be treated as if it were advance corporation tax paid in respect of distributions made by the qualifying subsidiary concerned in any earlier accounting period shall not exceed the amount of advance corporation tax that would have been payable in respect of a distribution made at the end of that earlier period of an amount

which, together with the advance corporation tax so payable in respect of it, would equal the qualifying subsidiary's ring fence profits of that period.

(8) In determining the amount (if any) of advance corporation tax which may be repayable—

(*a*) under section 17(3) of the 1975 Act, or
(*b*) under section 127(5) of the Finance Act 1981,

any advance corporation tax in respect of a distribution actually made on or after 17th March 1987 shall be left out of account.

Former enactments.—FA 1987, s. 44; F(No. 2)A 1987, s. 76(4).

499. Surrender of ACT where oil extraction company etc. owned by a consortium

(1) In any case where—

(*a*) a company (in this section referred to as "the consortium company") is owned by a consortium consisting of two members only, each of which owns 50 per cent. of the issued share capital of the company; and
(*b*) the consortium company carries on a trade consisting of or including activities falling within section 492(1)(*a*) to (*c*); and
(*c*) all of the issued share capital of the consortium company is of the same class and carries the same rights as to voting, dividends and distribution of assets on a winding up,

section 240 shall have effect, subject to the following provisions of this section, as if the company were a subsidiary of each member of the consortium.

(2) This section has effect with respect to advance corporation tax paid by either member of the consortium in respect of a dividend paid by it on or after 17th March 1987; and, in relation to a surrender under section 240 of the benefit of the advance corporation tax paid in respect of such a dividend—

(*a*) "surrendered advance corporation tax" means advance corporation tax which, by virtue of section 240(2), the consortium company is treated as having paid; and
(*b*) "the notional distribution date" means the date of the distribution in respect of which the surrendered advance corporation tax is treated as paid.

(3) No surrender under section 240 of the benefit of advance corporation tax may be made by virtue of this section—

(*a*) unless the conditions in paragraphs (*a*) to (*c*) of subsection (1) above are fulfilled throughout that accounting period of the consortium company in which falls the notional distribution date; or
(*b*) if arrangements are in existence by virtue of which any person could cause one or more of those conditions to cease to be fulfilled at some time during that or any later accounting period.

(4) In the application of section 239 in relation to surrendered advance corporation tax resulting from a surrender by either one of the consortium members under section 240, the reference in section 239(2) to the consortium company's profits charged to corporation tax shall be construed as a reference to one half of so much of those profits as consists of ring fence profits.

(5) So much of any surplus advance corporation tax as consists of or includes surrendered advance corporation tax shall not be treated under section 239(4) as if it were advance corporation tax paid in respect of distributions made by the consortium company in a later accounting period unless the conditions in paragraphs (*a*) to (*c*) of subsection (1) above are fulfilled throughout that later period.

(6) In any case where—

(*a*) as a result of a surrender by one of the consortium members, the consortium company is treated as paying an amount of surrendered advance corporation tax which exceeds the limit applicable under section 239(2) (as modified by subsection (4) above), and
(*b*) that excess falls to be treated under section 239(4) as advance corporation tax paid by the consortium company in respect of distributions made in a later accounting period,

then, for the purposes of the application of section 239(2) (as modified by subsection (4) above) in relation to that later accounting period, the excess of the surrendered advance corporation tax shall be treated as resulting from a surrender by that one of the consortium members referred to in paragraph (*a*) above.

(7) Where section 240 has effect as mentioned in subsection (2) above, subsection (11) of

that section shall have effect with the omission of paragraph (*b*) (and the word "and" immediately preceding it).

(8) Notwithstanding the provisions of subsection (1) above the consortium company shall not be regarded as a subsidiary for the purposes of section 498.

Former enactments.—FA 1987, s. 45; F(No. 2)A 1987, s. 76(5).

500. Deduction of PRT in computing income for corporation tax purposes

(1) Where a participator in an oil field has paid any petroleum revenue tax with which he was chargeable for a chargeable period, then, in computing for corporation tax the amount of his income arising in the relevant accounting period from oil extraction activities or oil rights, there shall be deducted an amount equal to that petroleum revenue tax.

(2) There shall be made all such adjustments of assessments to corporation tax as are required in order to give effect to subsection (1) above.

(3) For the purposes of subsection (1) above, the relevant accounting period, in relation to any petroleum revenue tax paid by a company, is—

 (*a*) the accounting period of the company in or at the end of which the chargeable period for which that tax was charged ends; or
 (*b*) if that chargeable period ends after the accounting period of the company in or at the end of which the trade giving rise to the income referred to above is permanently discontinued, that accounting period.

(4) If some or all of the petroleum revenue tax in respect of which a deduction has been made under subsection (1) above is subsequently repaid, that deduction shall be reduced or extinguished accordingly; and any additional assessment to corporation tax required in order to give effect to this subsection may be made at any time not later than six years after the end of the accounting period in which the first-mentioned tax was repaid.

(5) In this section "chargeable period" has the same meaning as in Part I of the 1975 Act.

Former enactments.—Oil Taxation Act 1975, s. 17; FA 1981, s. 120.

501. Interest on repayment of PRT

Where any amount of petroleum revenue tax paid by a participator in an oil field is, under any provision of Part I of the 1975 Act, repaid to him with interest, the amount of the interest paid to him shall be disregarded in computing the amount of his income for the purposes of corporation tax.

Former enactment.—Oil Taxation Act 1975, s. 18.

502. Interpretation of Chapter V

(1) In this Chapter—

 "the 1975 Act" means the Oil Taxation Act 1975;
 "oil" means any substance won or capable of being won under the authority of a licence granted under either the Petroleum (Production) Act 1934 or the Petroleum (Production) Act (Northern Ireland) 1964, other than methane gas won in the course of operations for making and keeping mines safe;
 "oil extraction activities" means any activities of a person—

  (*a*) in searching for oil in the United Kingdom or a designated area or causing such searching to be carried out for him; or
  (*b*) in extracting or causing to be extracted for him oil at any place in the United Kingdom or a designated area under rights authorising the extraction and held by him or, if the person in question is a company, by the company or a company associated with it; or
  (*c*) in transporting or causing to be transported for him as far as dry land in the United Kingdom oil extracted at any such place not on dry land under rights authorising the extraction and so held; or
  (*d*) in effecting or causing to be effected for him the initial treatment or initial storage of oil won from any oil field under rights authorising its extraction and so held;

"oil field" has the same meaning as in Part I of the 1975 Act;
"oil rights" means rights to oil to be extracted at any place in the United Kingdom or a designated area, or to interests in or to the benefit of such oil;
"participator" has the same meaning as in Part I of the 1975 Act; and
"ring fence income" means income arising from oil extraction activities or oil rights; and
"ring fence profits" has the same meaning as in section 79(5) of the Finance Act 1984 or, in any case where that subsection does not apply, means ring fence income.

(2) For the purposes of subsection (1) above—

(*a*) "designated area" means an area designated by Order in Council under section 1(7) of the Continental Shelf Act 1964;
(*b*) "initial treatment" has the same meaning as in Part I of the 1975 Act; and
(*c*) the definition of "initial storage" in section 12(1) of the 1975 Act shall apply but, in its application for those purposes in relation to the person mentioned in subsection (1)(*d*) above and to oil won from any one oil field shall have effect as if the reference to the maximum daily production rate of oil for the field as there mentioned were a reference to that person's share of that maximum daily production rate, that is to say, a share thereof proportionate to his share of the oil won from that field.

(3) For the purposes of this Chapter two companies are associated with one another if—

(*a*) one is a 51 per cent. subsidiary of the other;
(*b*) each is a 51 per cent. subsidiary of a third company; or
(*c*) one is owned by a consortium of which the other is a member.

Section 413(6) shall apply for the purposes of paragraph (*c*) above.

(4) Without prejudice to subsection (3) above, for the purposes of this Chapter, two companies are also associated with one another if one has control of the other or both are under the control of the same person or persons; and in this subsection "control" shall be construed in accordance with section 416.

Former enactments.—Oil Taxation Act 1975, ss. 17(4), 18(2), 19; FA 1984, s. 79(5), (10); FA 1986, s. 54.

CHAPTER VI

MISCELLANEOUS BUSINESSES AND BODIES

503. Letting of furnished holiday accommodation treated as a trade

(1) Subject to the following provisions of this section, for the purposes of sections 5(2), 380 to 390, 393, 394, 401, 623(2)(c), 644(2)(c) and 833(4)(c) and of Chapter I of Part III of the Finance Act 1971—

    (a) the commercial letting of furnished holiday accommodation in the United Kingdom in respect of which the profits or gains are chargeable under Case VI of Schedule D shall be treated as a trade; and

    (b) all such lettings made by a particular person or partnership or body of persons shall be treated as one trade.

(2) In their application by virtue of subsection (1) above sections 390(1) and 401(1) shall have effect as if for the references in those sections to Case I of Schedule D there were substituted references to Case VI of that Schedule.

(3) No relief shall be given to an individual under section 381 as it has effect by virtue of subsection (1) above, in respect of a loss sustained in any year of assessment, if any of the accommodation in respect of which the trade is carried on in that year was first let by him as furnished accommodation more than three years before the beginning of that year of assessment.

(4) Relief shall not be given for the same loss or the same portion of a loss both under any provision of Chapters I and II of Part X except sections 391, 392, 395 and 396, as those Chapters apply by virtue of this section, and under any other provision of the Tax Acts.

(5) In computing the profits or gains arising from the commercial letting of furnished holiday accommodation which are chargeable to tax under Case VI of Schedule D, such expenditure may be deducted as would be deductible if the letting were a trade and those profits or gains were accordingly to be computed in accordance with the rules applicable to Case I of that Schedule.

(6) Where there is a letting of accommodation only part of which is holiday accommodation such apportionments shall be made for the purposes of this section as appear to the inspector, or on appeal the Commissioners, to be just and reasonable.

(7) Where a person has been charged to income tax or corporation tax otherwise than in accordance with the provisions of this section, such assessment, reduction or discharge of an assessment or, where a claim for repayment is made, such repayment, shall be made as may be necessary to give effect to those provisions.

Former enactments.—Sub-s. (1): FA 1984, Sch. 11, para. 1; F(No. 2)A 1987, Sch. 2, para. 6.
Sub-ss. (2)–(4): FA 1984, Sch. 11, para. 2.
Sub-s. (5): FA 1984, Sch. 11, para. 3.
Sub-ss. (6), (7): FA 1984, Sch. 11, paras. 6, 7.

504. Supplementary provisions

(1) This section has effect for the purposes of section 503.

(2) A letting—

    (a) is a commercial letting if it is let on a commercial basis and with a view to the realisation of profits; and

    (b) is of furnished accommodation if the tenant is entitled to the use of furniture.

(3) Accommodation shall not be treated as holiday accommodation for the purposes of this section unless—

    (a) it is available for commercial letting to the public generally as holiday accommodation for periods which amount, in the aggregate, to not less than 140 days;

    (b) the periods for which it is so let amount in the aggregate to at least 70 days; and

    (c) for a period comprising at least seven months (which need not be continuous but includes any months in which it is let as mentioned in paragraph (b) above) it is not normally in the same occupation for a continuous period exceeding 31 days.

(4) Any question whether accommodation let by any person other than a company is, at any time in a year of assessment, holiday accommodation shall be determined—

(a) if the accommodation was not let by him as furnished accommodation in the preceding year of assessment but is so let in the following year of assessment, by reference to the 12 months beginning with the date on which he first so let it in the year of assessment;
(b) if the accommodation was let by him as furnished accommodation in the preceding year of assessment but is not so let in the following year of assessment, by reference to the 12 months ending with the date on which he ceased so to let it in the year of assessment; and
(c) in any other case, by reference to the year of assessment.

(5) Any question whether accommodation let by a company is at any time in an accounting period holiday accommodation shall be determined—

(a) if the accommodation was not let by it as furnished accommodation in the period of 12 months immediately preceding the accounting period but is so let in the period of 12 months immediately following the accounting period, by reference to the 12 months beginning with the date in the accounting period on which it first so let it;
(b) if the accommodation was let by it as furnished accommodation in the period of 12 months immediately preceding the accounting period but is not so let by it in the period of 12 months immediately following the accounting period, by reference to the 12 months ending with the date in the accounting period on which it ceased so to let it;
(c) in any other case, by reference to the period of 12 months ending with the last day of the accounting period.

(6) Where, in any year of assessment or accounting period, a person lets furnished accommodation which is treated as holiday accommodation for the purposes of this section in that year or period ("the qualifying accommodation"), he may make a claim under this subsection, within two years after that year or period, for averaging treatment to apply for that year or period to that and any other accommodation specified in the claim which was let by him as furnished accommodation during that year or period and would fall to be treated as holiday accommodation in that year or period if subsection (3)(b) above were satisfied in relation to it.

(7) Where a claim is made under subsection (6) above in respect of any year of assessment or accounting period, any such other accommodation shall be treated as being holiday accommodation in that year or period if the number of days for which the qualifying accommodation and any other such accommodation was let by the claimant as mentioned in subsection (3)(a) above during the year or period amounts on average to at least 70.

(8) Qualifying accommodation may not be specified in more than one claim in respect of any one year of assessment or accounting period.

(9) For the purposes of this section a person lets accommodation if he permits another person to occupy it, whether or not in pursuance of a lease; and "letting" and "tenant" shall be construed accordingly.

Former enactment.—FA 1984, s. 50(2)–(9).

505. Charities: general

(1) Subject to subsections (2) and (3) below, the following exemptions shall be granted on a claim in that behalf to the Board—

(a) exemption from tax under Schedules A and D in respect of the rents and profits of any lands, tenements, hereditaments or heritages belonging to a hospital, public school or almshouse, or vested in trustees for charitable purposes, so far as the same are applied to charitable purposes only;
(b) ...[1]
(c) exemption—

(i) from tax under Schedule C in respect of any interest, annuities, dividends or shares of annuities,
(ii) from tax under Schedule D in respect of any yearly interest or other annual payment, and
(iii) from tax under Schedule F in respect of any distribution,

where the income in question forms part of the income of a charity, or is, according to rules or regulations established by Act of Parliament, charter, decree, deed of trust or will, applicable to charitable purposes only, and so far as it is applied to charitable purposes only;

(d) exemption from tax under Schedule C in respect of any interest, annuities, dividends or shares of annuities which are in the names of trustees and are applicable solely towards the repairs of any cathedral, college, church or chapel, or of any building used solely for the purposes of divine worship, so far as the same are applied to those purposes;

(e) exemption from tax under Schedule D in respect of the profits of any trade carried on by a charity, if the profits are applied solely to the purposes of the charity and either—

   (i) the trade is exercised in the course of the actual carrying out of a primary purpose of the charity; or
   (ii) the work in connection with the trade is mainly carried out by beneficiaries of the charity.

(2) Any payment which—

   (a) is received by a charity from another charity; and
   (b) is not made for full consideration in money or money's worth; and
   (c) is not chargeable to tax apart from this subsection; and
   (d) is not, apart from this subsection, of a description which (on a claim) would be eligible for relief from tax by virtue of any provision of subsection (1) above;

shall be chargeable to tax under Case III of Schedule D but shall be eligible for relief from tax under subsection (1)(c) above as if it were an annual payment.

(3) If in any chargeable period of a charity—

   (a) its relevant income and gains are not less than £10,000; and
   (b) its relevant income and gains exceed the amount of its qualifying expenditure; and
   (c) the charity incurs, or is treated as incurring, non-qualifying expenditure;

relief shall not be available under either subsection (1) above or section 145 of the 1979 Act for so much of the excess as does not exceed the non-qualifying expenditure incurred in that period.

(4) In relation to a chargeable period of less than 12 months, subsection (3) above shall have effect as if the amount specified in paragraph (a) of that subsection were proportionately reduced.

(5) In subsection (3) above "relevant income and gains" means—

   (a) income which apart from subsection (1) above would not be exempt from tax together with any income which is taxable notwithstanding that subsection; and
   (b) gains which apart from section 145 of the 1979 Act would be chargeable gains together with any gains which are chargeable gains notwithstanding that section.

(6) Where by virtue of subsection (3) above there is an amount of a charity's relevant income and gains for which relief under subsection (1) above and section 145 of the 1979 Act is not available, the charity may, by notice to the Board, specify which items of its relevant income and gains are, in whole or in part, to be attributed to that amount, and, for this purpose, all covenanted payments to charity (within the meaning of section 660(3)) shall be treated as a single item; and if within 30 days of being required to do so by the Board, a charity does not give notice under this subsection, the items of its relevant income and gains which are to be attributed to the amount in question shall be such as the Board may determine.

(7) Where it appears to the Board that two or more charities acting in concert are engaged in transactions of which the main purpose or one of the main purposes is the avoidance of tax (whether by the charities or by any other person), the Board may by notice given to the charities provide that, for such chargeable periods as may be specified in the notice, subsection (3) above shall have effect in relation to them with the omission of paragraph (a).

(8) An appeal may be brought against a notice under subsection (7) above as if it were notice of the decision of the Board on a claim made by the charities concerned.

Former enactments.—Sub-s. (1): TA 1970, s. 360(1).
Sub-s. (2): FA 1986, s. 30(1).
Sub-ss. (3)–(5): FA 1986, s. 31(1), (2), (3)(c), (d).
Sub-ss. (6)–(8): FA 1986, s. 31(7)–(9).
Cross references.—See FA 1988, Sch. 14, Pt. V (repeal of TA 1970, s. 360(1)(b) from 6 April 1988).
Amendments.—[1] Sub-s. (1)(b) repealed by FA 1988, Sch. 14, Pt. V.

506. Qualifying expenditure and non-qualifying expenditure

(1) In this section, section 505 and Schedule 20—

"charity" means any body of persons or trust established for charitable purposes only;
"qualifying expenditure", in relation to a chargeable period of a charity, means, subject to subsection (3) below, expenditure incurred in that period for charitable purposes only; and
"non-qualifying expenditure" means expenditure which is not qualifying expenditure.

(2) For the purposes of section 505 and subsection (1) above, where expenditure which is not actually incurred in a particular chargeable period properly falls to be charged against the income of that chargeable period as being referable to commitments (whether or not of a contractual nature) which the charity has entered into before or during that period, it shall be treated as incurred in that period.

(3) A payment made (or to be made) to a body situated outside the United Kingdom shall not be qualifying expenditure by virtue of this section unless the charity concerned has taken such steps as may be reasonable in the circumstances to ensure that the payment will be applied for charitable purposes.

(4) If in any chargeable period a charity—

(*a*) invests any of its funds in an investment which is not a qualifying investment, as defined in Part I of Schedule 20; or
(*b*) makes a loan (not being an investment) which is not a qualifying loan, as defined in Part II of that Schedule;

then, subject to subsection (5) below, the amount so invested or lent in that period shall be treated for the purposes of this section as being an amount of expenditure incurred by the charity, and, accordingly, as being non-qualifying expenditure.

(5) If, in any chargeable period, a charity which has in that period made an investment or loan falling within subsection (4) above—

(*a*) realises the whole or part of that investment; or
(*b*) is repaid the whole or part of that loan;

any further investment or lending in that period of the sum realised or repaid shall, to the extent that it does not exceed the sum originally invested or lent, be left out of account in determining the amount which, by virtue of subsection (4) above, is treated as non-qualifying expenditure incurred in that period.

(6) If the aggregate of the qualifying and non-qualifying expenditure incurred by a charity in any chargeable period exceeds the relevant income and gains of that period, Part III of Schedule 20 shall have effect to treat, in certain cases, some or all of that excess as non-qualifying expenditure incurred in earlier periods.

Former enactments.—Sub-s. (1): TA 1970, s. 360(3); FA 1986, s. 31(1)(*a*), (*c*), Sch. 7, para. 1(1).
Sub-ss. (2), (3): FA 1986, Sch. 7, para. 1(2), (3).
Sub-ss. (4)–(6): FA 1986, s. 31(4)–(6).

507. The National Heritage Memorial Fund, the Historic Buildings and Monuments Commission for England and the British Museum

(1) There shall on a claim in that behalf to the Board be allowed in the case of—

(*a*) the Trustees of the National Heritage Memorial Fund;
(*b*) the Historic Buildings and Monuments Commission for England;
[(*c*) the Trustees of the British Museum;][1]
[(*d*) the Trustees of the British Museum (Natural History);][1]

such exemption from tax as falls to be allowed under section 505 in the case of a charity the whole income of which is applied to charitable purposes.

(2) ...[2]

Former enactments.—Sub-s. (1): FA 1980, s. 118(1); FA 1983, s. 46(1).
Sub-s. (2): TA 1970, s. 363(*a*), (*b*).
Cross references.—See FA 1989, s. 59(6)(*b*), (7) (covenanted subscriptions due after 13 March 1989 in favour of the bodies mentioned in this section exempt from tax notwithstanding certain benefits accruing to the covenantor).
Amendments.—[1] Sub-s. (1)(*c*), (*d*) inserted by FA 1989, s. 60(1), (4) in relation to accounting periods ending after 13 March 1989.
[2] Sub-s. (2) repealed by FA 1989, Sch. 17, Pt. IV.

508. Scientific research organisations

(1) Where—

(a) an Association which has as its object the undertaking of scientific research which may lead to or facilitate an extension of any class or classes of trade is approved for the purposes of this section by the Secretary of State; and

(b) the memorandum of association or other similar instrument regulating the functions of the Association precludes the direct or indirect payment or transfer to any of its members of any of its income or property by way of dividend, gift, division, bonus or otherwise howsoever by way of profit;

there shall, on a claim in that behalf to the Board, be allowed in the case of the Association such exemption from tax as falls to be allowed under section 505 in the case of a charity the whole income of which is applied to charitable purposes.

(2) The condition specified in paragraph (b) of subsection (1) above shall not be deemed not to be complied with in the case of any Association by reason only that the memorandum or other similar instrument regulating its functions does not prevent the payment to its members of reasonable remuneration for goods, labour or power supplied, or for services rendered, of reasonable interest for money lent, or of reasonable rent for any premises.

(3) In this section "scientific research" means any activities in the fields of natural or applied science for the extension of knowledge.

Former enactments.—TA 1970, s. 362; Secretary of State for Trade and Industry Order 1970, S.I. 1970 No. 1537.
Cross references.—See CGTA 1979, s. 149B(6)(b) (an Association within this section exempt from tax in respect of all chargeable gains).

509. Reserves of marketing boards and certain other statutory bodies

(1) Where a body established by or under any enactment and having as its object, or one of its objects, the marketing of an agricultural product or the stabilising of the price of an agricultural product is required, by or under any scheme or arrangements approved by or made with a Minister of the Crown or government department, to pay the whole or part of any surplus derived from its trading operations or other trade receipts into a reserve fund satisfying the conditions specified in subsection (2) below, then, in computing for the purposes of tax the profits or gains or losses of the body's trade—

(a) there shall be allowed as deductions any sums so required to be paid by the body into the reserve fund out of the profits or gains of the trade, and

(b) there shall be taken into account as trading receipts any sums withdrawn by the body from the fund, except so far as they are so required to be paid to a Minister or government department, or are distributed to producers of the product in question or refunded to persons paying any levy or duty.

(2) The conditions to be satisfied by the reserve fund are as follows—

(a) that no sum may be withdrawn from the fund without the authority or consent of a Minister of the Crown or government department; and

(b) that where money has been paid to the body by a Minister of the Crown or government department in connection with arrangements for maintaining guaranteed prices, or in connection with the body's trading operations, and is repayable to that Minister or department, sums afterwards standing to the credit of the fund are required as mentioned in subsection (1) above to be applied in whole or in part in repaying the money; and

(c) that the fund is reviewed by a Minister of the Crown at intervals fixed by or under the scheme or arrangements in question, and any amount by which it appears to the Minister to exceed the reasonable requirements of the body is withdrawn therefrom.

(3) In this section references to a Minister of the Crown or government department include references to a Head of a Department or a Department in Northern Ireland, and references to producers of a product include references to producers of one type or quality of a product from another.

Former enactments.—TA 1970, s. 348; FA 1971, s. 28(1).

510. Agricultural societies

(1) Profits or gains arising to an agricultural society from any exhibition or show held for the purposes of the society shall be exempt from tax if applied solely to the purposes of the society.

(2) In this section "agricultural society" means any society or institution established for the purpose of promoting the interests of agriculture, horticulture, livestock breeding or forestry.

Former enactment.—TA 1970, s. 361.

511. The Electricity Council and Boards, the Northern Ireland Electricity Service and the Gas Council

(1) For the purposes of the Corporation Tax Acts, the Electricity Council shall be treated as carrying on a trade, and those Acts shall have effect as if the trade carried on by the Central Electricity Authority at any time before 1st January 1958 had been the trade of the Electricity Council.

(2) For the purposes of the Corporation Tax Acts—

(a) any trade carried on by a Board shall be treated as if it were part of the trade carried on by the Electricity Council;
(b) subject to paragraph (c) below, any property, rights or liabilities of a Board shall be treated as property, rights or liabilities of the Electricity Council, and anything done by or to a Board shall be deemed to have been done by or to the Electricity Council;
(c) any rights, liabilities or things done—

   (i) of, by or to the Electricity Council against, to or by a Board, or
   (ii) of, by or to a Board against, to or by the Electricity Council or any other Board,

shall be left out of account;

and corporation tax shall be charged accordingly.

(3) For the purposes of the operation of the Corporation Tax Acts in accordance with subsections (1) and (2) above, the Electricity Council shall be deemed to have been in existence as from 1st April 1948, and anything done by, to or in relation to the Central Electricity Authority shall be treated as if it had been done by, to or in relation to the Electricity Council.

(4) The Corporation Tax Acts shall have effect as if the trade carried on at any time before 1st April 1973 by any predecessor of the Northern Ireland Electricity Service had been carried on by the Service; and for that purpose the Service shall be deemed to have been in existence as from the time when the predecessor began to carry on its trade and anything done by, to or in relation to the predecessor shall be treated as if it had been done by, to or in relation to the Service.

(5) In subsection (4) above references to a predecessor of the Northern Ireland Electricity Service are references to any body whose functions were transferred to the Service on the 1st April 1973, and references to the trade of a predecessor are references to its activities in the discharge of the functions that were so transferred.

(6) In subsections (1) and (2) above "Board" means—

(a) any Area Board established by or under the provisions of the Electricity Act 1947; and
(b) in relation to any time on or after 1st January 1958, the Central Electricity Generating Board.

(7) The Corporation Tax Acts shall apply in relation to the trade of the Gas Council as if before the beginning of April 1962 it had consisted of the trades of the Area Boards (within the meaning of the Gas Act 1948), and (without prejudice to the generality of the foregoing) allowances and balancing charges shall be made to or on the Gas Council accordingly by reference to the capital expenditure of Area Boards and to the allowances made to Area Boards in respect of that expenditure.

Former enactments.—Sub-ss. (1)–(3): TA 1970, s. 349(1)–(3).
Sub-ss. (4), (5): FA 1981, s. 50(3), (4).
Sub-s. (6): TA 1970, s. 349(4).
Sub-s. (7): TA 1970, s. 350(3).

512. Atomic Energy Authority and National Radiological Protection Board

(1) The United Kingdom Atomic Energy Authority and the National Radiological Protection Board shall be entitled to exemption from income tax and corporation tax—

(a) under Schedules A, . . .[1] and C;

(b) under Schedule D in respect of any yearly interest or other annual payment received by the Authority or Board;
(c) under Schedule F in respect of distributions received by the Authority or Board.

(2) Income arising from investments or deposits held for the purposes of any pension scheme provided and maintained by the Authority shall be treated for the purposes of this section as if that income and the source thereof belonged to the Authority.

Former enactment.—TA 1970, s. 351.
Cross references.—See FA 1988, Sch. 14, Pt. V (repeal of the reference to Schedule B in TA 1970, s. 351(1)(a) with effect from 6 April 1988).
Amendments.—[1] The reference to Schedule B in sub-s. (1)(a) repealed by FA 1988, Sch. 14, Pt. V.

513. British Airways Board and National Freight Corporation

(1) Subject to subsection (2) below, the successor company in which the property, rights, liabilities and obligations of the British Airways Board are vested by the Civil Aviation Act 1980 shall be treated for all purposes of corporation tax as if it were the same person as the British Airways Board; and the successor company to which the undertaking of the National Freight Corporation is transferred by the Transport Act 1980 shall be treated for those purposes as if it were the same person as the National Freight Corporation.

(2) The transfer by the Civil Aviation Act 1980 from the British Airways Board to the successor company of liability for any loan made to the Board shall not affect any direction in respect of the loan which has been given by the Treasury under section 581.

(3) A successor company shall not by virtue of subsection (1) above be regarded as a body falling within section 272(5) of the 1970 Act.

Former enactment.—FA 1980, s. 119.

514. Funds for reducing the National Debt

Where any property is held upon trust in accordance with directions which are valid and effective under section 9 of the Superannuation and other Trust Funds (Validation) Act 1927 (which provides for the validation of trust funds for the reduction of the national debt), any income arising from that property or from any accumulation of any such income, and any profits of any description otherwise accruing to the property and liable to be accumulated under the trust, shall be exempt from income tax.

Former enactment.—TA 1970, s. 364.

515. Signatories to Operating Agreement for INMARSAT

(1) An overseas signatory to the Operating Agreement made pursuant to the Convention on the International Maritime Satellite Organisation which came into force on 16th July 1979 shall be exempt from income tax and corporation tax in respect of any payment received by that signatory from the Organisation in accordance with that Agreement.

(2) In this section "an overseas signatory" means a signatory other than one designated for the purposes of the Agreement by the United Kingdom in accordance with the Convention.

Former enactment.—TA 1970, s. 63.

516. Government securities held by non-resident central banks

(1) Tax shall not be chargeable on dividends (within the meaning of Schedule C) paid out of the public revenue of the United Kingdom where they are income of any bank or issue department of a bank to which this subsection for the time being applies.

(2) Subsection (1) above shall not prevent any such dividends being taken into account in computing profits or gains or losses of a business carried on in the United Kingdom.

(3) A bank or issue department of a bank to which this subsection for the time being applies shall be exempt from tax in respect of chargeable gains accruing to it.

(4) Her Majesty may by Order in Council direct that subsection (1) or (3), or both, shall apply to any bank, or to its issue department, if it appears to Her Majesty that the bank is not resident in the United Kingdom and is entrusted by the government of a territory

outside the United Kingdom with the custody of the principal foreign exchange reserves of that territory.

(5) No recommendation shall be made to Her Majesty in Council to make an order under this section unless a draft of the order has been laid before the House of Commons and has been approved by resolution of that House.

Former enactment.—TA 1970, s. 370.

517. Issue departments of the Reserve Bank of India and the State Bank of Pakistan

There shall be exempt from tax any profits or income arising or accruing to the issue department of the Reserve Bank of India constituted under an Act of the Indian legislature called the Reserve Bank of India Act 1934, or to the issue department of the State Bank of Pakistan constituted under certain orders made under section 9 of the Indian Independence Act 1947.

Former enactment.—TA 1970, s. 371.

518. Harbour reorganisation schemes

(1) This section has effect where the trade of any body corporate other than a limited liability company is transferred to a harbour authority by or under a certified harbour reorganisation scheme which provides also for the dissolution of the transferor.

(2) For the purposes of the Corporation Tax Acts, the trade shall not be treated as permanently discontinued, nor shall a new trade be treated as set up and commenced.

(3) The transferee shall be entitled to relief from corporation tax under section 393(1), as for a loss sustained by it in carrying on the transferred trade or any trade of which it comes to form part, for any amount which, if the transferor had continued to carry it on, would have been available to the transferor for carry-forward against chargeable profits of succeeding accounting periods, but subject to any claim made by the transferor under section 393(2).

(4) There shall be made to or on the transferee in accordance with the provisions of the Capital Allowances Acts all such allowances and charges as would, if the transferor had continued to carry on the trade, have fallen to be made to or on it under those Acts and the amount of any such allowance or charge shall be computed as if the transferee had been carrying on the trade since the transferor had begun to do so and as if everything done to or by the transferor had been done to or by the transferee.

(5) No sale or transfer which on the transfer of the trade is made by the transferor to the transferee of any assets in use for the purposes of the trade shall be treated as giving rise to any such allowance or charge as is mentioned in subsection (4) above.

(6) The transferor shall not be entitled to relief under section 394 in respect of the trade.

(7) The transferee shall be entitled to relief from corporation tax in respect of chargeable gains for any amount for which the transferor would have been entitled to claim relief in respect of allowable losses if it had continued to carry on the trade.

(8) Where part only of such trade is transferred to a harbour authority by or under a certified harbour organisation scheme, and the transferor continues to carry on the remainder of the trade, or any such trade is, by or under a certified harbour reorganisation scheme which provides also for the dissolution of the transferor, transferred in parts to two or more harbour authorities, this section shall apply as if the transferred part, or each of the transferred parts, had at all times been a separate trade.

(9) Where a part of any trade is to be treated by virtue of subsection (8) above as having been a separate trade over any period there shall be made any necessary adjustments of accounting periods, and such apportionments as may be just of receipts, expenses, allowances or charges.

Subsection (10) of section 343 shall apply to any apportionment under this subsection as it applies to an apportionment under subsection (9) of that section.

(10) In this section—

"harbour authority" has the same meaning as in the Harbours Act 1964;
"harbour reorganisation scheme" means any statutory provision providing for the

management by a harbour authority of any harbour or group of harbours in the United Kingdom, and "certified", in relation to any harbour reorganisation scheme, means certified by a Minister of the Crown or government department as so providing with a view to securing, in the public interest, the efficient and economical development of the harbour or harbours in question;

"limited liability company" means a company having a limit on the liability of its members;

"statutory provision" means any enactment, or any scheme, order or other instrument having effect under an enactment, and includes an enactment confirming a provisional order; and

"transferor", in relation to a trade, means the body from whom the trade is transferred, whether or not the transfer is effected by that body.

Former enactments.—Sub-ss. (1)–(7): TA 1970, s. 352(1)–(6); FA 1971, Sch. 8, para. 16; FA 1986, s. 56(7)(a), Sch. 13, para. 2(5)(a).
Sub-ss. (8), (9): TA 1970, s. 352(8), (9).
Sub-s. (10): TA 1970, s. 352(11).

519. Local authorities

(1) A local authority in the United Kingdom—

    (a) shall be exempt from all charge to income tax in respect of its income;

    (b) shall be exempt from corporation tax;

and so far as the exemption from income tax conferred by this subsection calls for repayment of tax, effect shall be given thereto by means of a claim.

(2) Subsection (1) above shall apply to a local authority association as it applies to a local authority.

(3) In this Act "local authority association" means any incorporated or unincorporated association—

    (a) of which all the constituent members are local authorities, groups of local authorities or local authority associations, and

    (b) which has for its object or primary object the protection and furtherance of the interests in general of local authorities or any description of local authorities;

and for this purpose, if a member of an association is a representative of or appointed by any authority, group of authorities or association, that authority, group or association (and not he) shall be treated as a constituent member of the association.

(4) In this Act "local authority" means—

    (a) any authority having power to make or determine a rate;

    (b) any authority having power to issue a precept, requisition or other demand for the payment of money to be raised out of a rate;

and in this subsection "rate" means a rate the proceeds of which are applicable for public local purposes and which is leviable by reference to the value of land or other property.

Former enactments.—Sub-ss. (1)–(3): TA 1970, s. 353(1), (4).
Sub-s. (4): FA 1974, s. 52.

PART XIII

MISCELLANEOUS SPECIAL PROVISIONS

CHAPTER I

INTELLECTUAL PROPERTY

Patents and know-how

520. Allowances for expenditure on purchase of patent rights: post-31st March 1986 expenditure

(1) Subject to subsection (3) below, where a person incurs capital expenditure after 31st March 1986 on the purchase of patent rights, allowances and charges shall, in accordance with subsections (4) and (6) below, be made to and on him in respect of that expenditure.

(2) No allowance shall be made to a person under subsection (1) above in respect of any expenditure unless—

(*a*) the allowance falls in accordance with section 528(1) to be made to him in taxing his trade; or
(*b*) any income receivable by him in respect of the rights would be liable to tax.

(3) For the purposes of this section and section 521 any expenditure incurred for the purposes of a trade by a person about to carry it on shall be treated as if it had been incurred by that person on the first day on which he does carry it on, unless, before that first day, he has sold all the rights on the purchase of which the expenditure was incurred.

(4) For any chargeable period for which a person within subsection (1) above has qualifying expenditure which exceeds any disposal value to be brought into account by him in accordance with section 521(2) there shall be made to him—

(*a*) except where paragraph (*b*) or (*c*) below applies, a writing-down allowance of an amount equal, subject to subsection (5) below, to—

(i) 25 per cent. of the excess; or
(ii) a proportionately reduced percentage of the excess if the period is part only of a year, or if, in a case where the period is a year of assessment and the allowance falls to be made in taxing a trade, the trade has been carried on for part only of that year;

(*b*) if an allowance falls to be made to that person in taxing his trade and the period is the chargeable period related to the permanent discontinuance of the trade, a balancing allowance equal to the whole of the excess; and
(*c*) if paragraph (*b*) above does not apply but the period is the chargeable period in which the last of the relevant patent rights comes to an end without any of those rights being revived, a balancing allowance equal to the whole of the excess.

(5) For the purposes of subsection (4)(*c*) above the "relevant patent rights" at any time are those—

(*a*) on the purchase of which the person concerned has incurred capital expenditure which has been taken into account in determining his qualifying expenditure for any chargeable period; and
(*b*) which he has not wholly disposed of.

(6) For any chargeable period for which a person's qualifying expenditure is less than the disposal value which he is to bring into account, there shall be made on him a balancing charge and the amount on which the charge is made shall be an amount equal to the difference.

Former enactments.—Sub-ss. (1), (2): TA 1970, s. 378(1); FA 1985, s. 64(1).
Sub-s. (3): TA 1970, s. 378(2)(*c*); FA 1985, s. 64(2)(*b*).
Sub-ss. (4)–(6): FA 1985, Sch. 18, Pt. I, para. 1.

521. Provisions supplementary to section 520

(1) For the purposes of section 520(4) to (6), a person's qualifying expenditure for a chargeable period is the aggregate of the following amounts—

(a) any capital expenditure incurred by him on the purchase of patent rights, being expenditure incurred during the chargeable period or its basis period or at any previous time, other than expenditure which, or any part of which, has formed part of his qualifying expenditure for any previous chargeable period; and
(b) if, for the chargeable period immediately preceding the chargeable period in question, there was an excess of qualifying expenditure over disposal value, the balance of that excess after deducting any writing-down allowance under section 520(4)(a) made by reference to that excess.

(2) If, in any chargeable period or its basis period, a person sells the whole or any part of any patent rights on the purchase of which he has incurred capital expenditure, then, for the purposes of section 520(4) to (6) and subsection (1) above, he is required to bring into account for that chargeable period disposal value equal, subject to subsections (3) and (4) below, to the net proceeds to him of that sale.

(3) The disposal value to be brought into account by any person in respect of any patent rights as a result of one or more sales falling within subsection (2) above shall not (or, as the case may be, shall not in the aggregate) exceed the capital expenditure incurred by him on the purchase of those rights.

(4) Where the person mentioned in subsection (3) above has acquired the patent rights as a result of a transaction which was, or a series of transactions each of which was, between persons who are connected with each other within the terms of section 839, that subsection shall have effect as if it referred to the capital expenditure on the purchase of the rights incurred by whichever party to that transaction or to any of those transactions incurred the greatest such expenditure.

(5) Where a person incurs capital expenditure on the purchase of patent rights and either—
(a) he and the seller are connected with each other . . .[1], or
(b) it appears with respect to the sale, or with respect to transactions of which the sale is one, that the sole or main benefit which, but for this subsection, might have been expected to accrue to the parties was the obtaining of an allowance under section 520(4),

there shall be disregarded for the purposes of section 520(4) and (6) and subsection (1) above so much (if any) of that expenditure as exceeds [the relevant amount determined in accordance with subsection (6) below][2].

[(6) The relevant amount referred to in subsection (5) above is—
(a) in a case in which, by virtue of subsections (2) to (4) above, a disposal value falls to be brought into account by reason of the sale, an amount equal to that disposal value,
(b) in a case in which no disposal value falls to be brought into account as mentioned in paragraph (a) above, but the seller receives on the sale a capital sum in respect of which he is chargeable to tax in accordance with section 524, an amount equal to that sum,
(c) in any other case, an amount equal to whichever of the following is the smallest—
 (i) the price which the rights would have fetched if sold in the open market,
 (ii) where capital expenditure was incurred by the seller on acquiring the rights, the amount of that expenditure,
 (iii) where capital expenditure was incurred by any person connected with the seller on acquiring the rights, the amount of the expenditure incurred by that person.][3]

[(7) Section 839 (connected persons) shall apply for the purposes of this section.][3]

Former enactment.—FA 1985, Sch. 18, Pt. I, paras. 2–4.
Amendments.—[1] Words "within the terms of section 839" in sub-s. (5)(a) repealed by FA 1989, Sch. 13, para. 27(1), (2)(a), (4) and Sch. 17, Pt. VI in relation to expenditure incurred after 26 July 1989.
[2] Words in sub-s. (5) substituted by FA 1989, Sch. 13, para. 27(1), (2)(b), (4) in relation to expenditure incurred after 26 July 1989. The original words read—
 "the disposal value to be brought into account by virtue of subsections (2) to (4) above by reason of the sale".
[3] Sub-ss. (6), (7) added by FA 1989, Sch. 13, para. 27(1), (3), (4) in relation to expenditure incurred after 26 July 1989.

522. Allowances for expenditure on purchase of patent rights: pre-1st April 1986 expenditure

(1) Subject to subsection (2) below, where a person incurred capital expenditure before 1st April 1986 on the purchase of patent rights, there shall, subject to and in accordance with the following provisions of this Chapter, be made to him writing-down allowances in respect of that expenditure during the writing-down period.

(2) No writing-down allowance shall be made to a person under subsection (1) above in respect of any expenditure unless—

(*a*) the allowance falls in accordance with section 528(1) to be made to him in taxing his trade; or
(*b*) any income receivable by him in respect of the rights would be liable to tax.

(3) Subject to subsections (4) to (6) below, the writing-down period referred to in subsection (1) above is 17 years beginning with the chargeable period related to the expenditure.

(4) Where the rights are purchased for a specified period, subsection (3) above shall have effect with the substitution for the reference to 17 years of a reference to 17 years or the number of years comprised within that period, whichever is the less.

(5) Where the rights purchased begin one complete year or more after the commencement of the patent and subsection (4) above does not apply, subsection (3) above shall have effect with the substitution for the reference to 17 years of a reference to 17 years less the number of complete years which, when the rights began, have elapsed since the commencement of the patent or, if 17 complete years have so elapsed, of a reference to one year.

(6) Any expenditure incurred for the purposes of a trade by a person about to carry it on shall be treated for the purposes of subsections (3) to (5) above as if it had been incurred by that person on the first day on which he does carry it on, unless, before that first day, he has sold all the rights on the purchase of which the expenditure was incurred.

(7) Subsections (2) and (3) of section 75 of the 1968 Act (effect of providing for writing-down allowances during a writing-down period of a specified length) shall apply to this section as they apply to the provisions specified in subsection (1) of that section.

Former enactments.—TA 1970, s. 378; FA 1985, s. 64(1).

523. Lapses of patent rights, sales etc.

(1) Where a person incurred capital expenditure before 1st April 1986 on the purchase of patent rights and, before the end of the writing-down period under section 522, any of the following events occurs, that is to say—

(*a*) the rights come to an end without being subsequently revived; or
(*b*) he sells all those rights or so much of them as he still owns; or
(*c*) he sells part of those rights and the net proceeds of the sale (so far as they consist of capital sums) are not less than the amount of the capital expenditure remaining unallowed,

no writing-down allowance shall be made to that person for the chargeable period related to the event or for any subsequent chargeable period.

(2) Where a person incurred capital expenditure before 1st April 1986 on the purchase of patent rights and, before the end of the writing-down period under section 522, either of the following events occurs, that is to say—

(*a*) the rights come to an end without being subsequently revived, or
(*b*) he sells all those rights, or so much of them as he still owns, and the net proceeds of the sale (so far as they consist of capital sums) are less than the amount of the capital expenditure remaining unallowed,

there shall, subject to and in accordance with the following provisions of this Chapter, be made to him for the chargeable period related to the event an allowance ("a balancing allowance") equal, if the event is the rights coming to an end, to the amount of the capital expenditure remaining unallowed and, if the event is a sale, to the amount of the capital expenditure remaining unallowed less the net proceeds of the sale.

(3) Where—

(*a*) a person who incurred capital expenditure before 1st April 1986 on the purchase of patent rights sells all or any part of those rights, and
(*b*) the net proceeds of the sale (so far as they consist of capital sums) exceed the amount of the capital expenditure remaining unallowed, if any,

there shall, subject to and in accordance with the following provisions of this Chapter, be made on him for the chargeable period related to the sale a charge ("a balancing charge") on an amount equal to the excess or, where the amount of the capital expenditure remaining unallowed is nil, to those net proceeds.

(4) Where a person who incurred capital expenditure before 1st April 1986 on the purchase of patent rights sells a part of those rights and subsection (3) above does not apply, the amount of any writing-down allowance made in respect of that expenditure for the

chargeable period related to the sale or any subsequent chargeable period shall be the amount arrived at by—
> (a) subtracting the net proceeds of the sale (so far as they consist of capital sums) from the amount of the expenditure remaining unallowed at the time of the sale, and
> (b) dividing the result by the number of complete years of the writing-down period which remained at the beginning of the chargeable period related to the sale,

and so on for any subsequent sales.

(5) References in this section to the amount of any capital expenditure remaining unallowed shall, in relation to any event, be construed as references to the amount of that expenditure less any writing-down allowances made in respect thereof for chargeable periods before that related to the event, and less also the net proceeds of any previous sale by the person who incurred the expenditure of any part of the rights acquired by the expenditure, so far as those proceeds consist of capital sums.

(6) Notwithstanding anything in subsections (1) to (5) above—
> (a) no balancing allowance shall be made in respect of any expenditure incurred before 1st April 1986 unless a writing-down allowance has been, or, but for the happening of the event giving rise to the balancing allowance, could have been, made in respect of that expenditure, and
> (b) the total amount on which a balancing charge is made in respect of any expenditure incurred before 1st April 1986 shall not exceed the total writing-down allowances actually made in respect of that expenditure, less, if a balancing charge has previously been made in respect of that expenditure, the amount on which that charge was made.

Former enactments.—TA 1970, s. 379; FA 1985, s. 64(2)(c).

524. Taxation of receipts from sale of patent rights

(1) Subject to subsection (2) below, where a person resident in the United Kingdom sells all or any part of any patent rights and the net proceeds of the sale consist wholly or partly of a capital sum, he shall, subject to the provisions of this Chapter, be charged to tax under Case VI of Schedule D, for the chargeable period in which the sum is received by him and successive chargeable periods, being charged in each period on the same fraction of the sum as the period is of six years (or such less fraction as has not already been charged).

(2) If the person by notice served on the inspector not later than two years after the end of the chargeable period in which the sum was received, elects that the whole of the sum shall be charged to tax for that chargeable period, it shall be charged to tax accordingly.

(3) Subject to subsection (4) below, where a person not resident in the United Kingdom sells all or any part of any patent rights and the net proceeds of the sale consist wholly or partly of a capital sum, and the patent is a United Kingdom patent, then, subject to the provisions of this Chapter—
> (a) he shall be chargeable to tax in respect of that sum under Case VI of Schedule D; and
> (b) section 349(1) shall apply to that sum as if it was an annual sum payable otherwise than out of profits or gains charged to income tax; and
> (c) all other provisions of the Tax Acts shall, save as therein otherwise provided, have effect accordingly.

(4) If, not later than two years after the end of the year of assessment in which the sum is paid, the person to whom it is paid, by notice to the Board, elects that the sum shall be treated for the purpose of income tax for that year and each of the five succeeding years as if one-sixth thereof, and no more, were included in his income chargeable to tax for all those years respectively, it shall be so treated, and all such repayments and assessments of tax for each of those years shall be made as are necessary to give effect to the election, but—
> (a) the election shall not affect the amount of tax which is to be deducted and assessed under section 349(1) and 350; and
> (b) where any sum is deducted under section 349(1), any adjustments necessary to give effect to the election shall be made by way of repayment of tax; and
> (c) those adjustments shall be made year by year and as if one-sixth of the sum deducted had been deducted in respect of tax for each year, and no repayment of, or of any part of, that portion of the tax deducted which is to be treated as deducted in respect of tax for any year shall be made unless and until it is ascertained that the tax ultimately falling to be paid for that year is less than the amount of tax paid for that year.

(5) In subsections (3) and (4) above, "tax" shall mean income tax or, in subsection (3) in a

case where the seller of the patent rights, being a company, would be within the charge to corporation tax in respect of any proceeds of the sale not consisting of a capital sum, corporation tax.

(6) Where subsection (3) applies to charge a company to corporation tax in respect of a sum paid to it, subsection (4) shall not apply, but the company may, by notice given to the Board not later than two years after the end of the accounting period in which the sum is paid, elect that the sum shall be treated as arising rateably in the accounting periods ending not later than six years from the beginning of that in which the sum is paid (being accounting periods during which the company remains within the charge to corporation tax in respect of any proceeds of the sale not consisting of a capital sum), and there shall be made all such repayments of tax and assessments to tax as are necessary to give effect to any such election.

(7) Subject to subsections (8) and (9) below, where the person selling all or any part of any patent rights ("the seller") acquired the rights sold, or the rights out of which they were granted, by purchase and the price paid by him consisted wholly or partly of a capital sum, the preceding provisions of this section shall apply as if any capital sum received by him when he sells the rights were reduced by the amount of that sum.

(8) Where between the purchase and the sale the seller has sold part of the rights acquired by him and the net proceeds of that sale consist wholly or partly of a capital sum, the amount of the reduction falling to be made under subsection (7) above in respect of the subsequent sale shall be itself reduced by the amount of that sum.

(9) Nothing in subsections (7) and (8) above shall affect the amount of income tax which is to be deducted and assessed under section 349(1) and (3) by virtue of subsection (3) above, and, where any sum is deducted under section 349(1), any adjustment necessary to give effect to the provisions of this subsection shall be made by way of repayment of tax.

(10) A claim for relief under this section shall be made to the Board.

Former enactments.—Sub-s. (1), (2): TA 1970, s. 380(1).
Sub-ss. (3), (4): TA 1970, s. 380(2).
Sub-ss. (5), (6): TA 1970, s. 380(3).
Sub-ss. (7)–(9): TA 1970, s. 380(4).
Sub-s. (10): TA 1970, s. 380(5).

525. Capital sums: death, winding up or partnership change

(1) Where a person on whom, by reason of the receipt of a capital sum, a charge falls or would otherwise fall to be made under section 524 dies or, being a body corporate, commences to be wound up—

(*a*) no sums shall be charged under that section on that person for any chargeable period subsequent to that in which the death takes place or the winding up commences; and
(*b*) the amount falling to be charged for the chargeable period in which the death occurs or the winding up commences shall, subject to subsection (2) below, be increased by the total amounts which, but for the death or winding up, would have fallen to be charged for subsequent chargeable periods.

(2) In the case of a death the personal representatives may, by notice served on the inspector not later than 30 days after notice has been served on them of the charge falling to be made by virtue of subsection (1) above, require that the income tax payable out of the estate of the deceased by reason of the increase provided for by that subsection shall be reduced so as not to exceed the total amount of income tax which would have been payable by him or out of his estate by reason of the operation of section 524 in relation to that sum, if, instead of the amount falling to be charged for the year in which the death occurs being increased by the whole amount of the sums charged for subsequent years, the several amounts falling to be charged for the years beginning with that in which the capital sum was received and ending with that in which the death occurred had each been increased by that whole amount divided by the number of those years.

(3) Where, under section 79 of the 1968 Act (succession to trades) as applied by section 532, a charge under section 524 falls to be made on two or more persons jointly as being the persons for the time being carrying on a trade, and that trade is discontinued, subsection (1) above shall have effect in relation to the discontinuance as it has effect where a body corporate commences to be wound up.

(4) Where subsection (3) above applies—

(*a*) the additional sum which, under subsection (1) above, falls to be charged for the chargeable period in which the discontinuance occurs shall be apportioned among the members of the partnership immediately before the discontinuance, according to their respective interests in the partnership profits before the discontinuance, and each partner (or, if he is dead, his personal representatives) shall be charged separately for his proportion; and

(b) each partner (or, if he is dead, his personal representatives) shall have the same right to require a reduction of the total income tax payable by him or out of his estate by reason of the increase as would have been exercisable by the personal representatives under subsection (2) above in the case of a death, and that subsection shall have effect accordingly, but as if references to the amount of income tax which would have been payable by the deceased or out of his estate in the event therein mentioned were a reference to the amount of income tax which would in that event have fallen to be paid or borne by the partner in question or out of his estate.

(5) In this section any references to income tax paid or borne or payable or falling to be paid or borne by a person include, in cases where the income of a wife is deemed to be income of the husband, references to the income tax paid or borne, or payable or falling to be paid or borne, by his wife or her husband, as the case may be.

Former enactments.—Sub-ss. (1), (2): TA 1970, s. 381(1).
Sub-ss. (3), (4): TA 1970, s. 381(2).
Sub-s. (5): TA 1970, s. 381(3).
Note.—See **Prospective Legislation Notes** (Married Couples).

526. Relief for expenses

(1) Where—

(a) a person, otherwise than for the purposes of a trade carried on by him, pays any fees or incurs any expenses in connection with the grant or maintenance of a patent, or the obtaining of an extension of a term of a patent, or a rejected or abandoned application for a patent, and

(b) those fees or expenses would, if they had been paid or incurred for the purposes of a trade, have been allowable as a deduction in estimating the profits or gains of that trade,

there shall be made to him, for the chargeable period in which those expenses were paid or incurred, an allowance equal to the amount thereof.

(2) Where a patent is granted in respect of any invention, an allowance equal to so much of the net amount of any expenses incurred by an individual who, whether alone or in conjunction with any other person, actually devised the invention as is properly ascribable to the devising thereof (not being expenses in respect of which, or of assets representing which, an allowance falls to be made under any other provision of the Income Tax Acts) shall be made to that individual for the year of assessment in which the expenses were incurred.

Former enactment.—TA 1970, s. 382.

527. Spreading of royalties over several years

(1) Where a royalty or other sum to which section 348 or 349(1) applies is paid in respect of the user of a patent, and that user extended over a period of six complete years or more, the person receiving the payment may on the making of a claim require that the income tax or corporation tax payable by him by reason of the receipt of that sum shall be reduced so as not to exceed the total amount of income tax or corporation tax which would have been payable by him if that royalty or sum had been paid in six equal instalments at yearly intervals, the last of which was paid on the date on which the payment was in fact made.

(2) Subsection (1) above shall apply in relation to a royalty or other sum where the period of the user is two complete years or more but less than six complete years as it applies to the royalties and sums mentioned in that subsection, but with the substitution for the reference to six equal instalments of a reference to so many equal instalments as there are complete years comprised in that period.

(3) In this section any reference to the income tax payable by a person includes, in cases where the income of a wife is deemed to be the income of the husband, references to the income tax payable by his wife or her husband, as the case may be.

(4) Nothing in this section shall apply to any sum to which section 349(1) applies by virtue of section 524(3)(b).

Former enactment.—TA 1970, s. 384.
Note.—See **Prospective Legislation Notes** (Married Couples).

528. Manner of making allowances and charges

(1) An allowance or charge under section 520, 522 or 523 shall be made to or on a person in taxing his trade if—

    (*a*) he is carrying on a trade the profits or gains of which are, or, if there were any, would be, chargeable to tax under Case I of Schedule D for the chargeable period for which the allowance or charge is made, and

    (*b*) at any time in that chargeable period or its basis period the patent rights in question, or other rights out of which they were granted, were or were to be used for the purposes of that trade.

(2) Where an allowance falls to be made to a person for any year of assessment under section 520, 522, 523 or 526 as those provisions apply for the purposes of income tax, and the allowance is not to be made in taxing a trade—

    (*a*) the amount of the allowance shall be deducted from or set off against his income from patents for that year of assessment, and

    (*b*) if the amount to be allowed is greater than the amount of his income from patents for that year of assessment, the balance shall be deducted from or set off against his income from patents for the next year of assessment, and so on for subsequent years of assessment, and tax shall be discharged or repaid accordingly.

Relief shall be given under this subsection on the making of a claim.

(3) Where an allowance falls to be made to a company for any accounting period under section 520, 522, 523 or 526 as those provisions apply for the purposes of corporation tax, and is not to be made in taxing a trade—

    (*a*) the allowance shall, as far as may be, be given effect by deducting the amount of the allowance from the company's income from patents of the accounting period;

    (*b*) where the allowance cannot be given full effect under paragraph (*a*) above in that period by reason of a want or deficiency of income from patents, then (so long as the company remains within the charge to corporation tax) the amount unallowed shall be carried forward to the succeeding accounting period, and shall be treated for the purposes of that paragraph, and of any further application of this paragraph, as the amount of a corresponding allowance for that period.

(4) Effect shall be given to any balancing charge under section 520 or 523 which is not to be made in taxing a trade—

    (*a*) if a charge to income tax, by making the charge under Case VI of Schedule D;

    (*b*) if a charge to corporation tax, by treating the amount on which the charge is to be made as income from patents.

Former enactments.—TA 1970, s. 385; FA 1985, s. 64(2)(*d*)–(*f*).

529. Patent income to be earned income in certain cases

(1) Subject to subsection (2) below, any income from patent rights arising to an individual where the patent was granted for an invention actually devised by him, whether alone or jointly with any other person, shall be treated for all purposes as earned income.

(2) Where any part of the rights in question or of any rights out of which they were granted has at any time belonged to any other person, so much only of that income shall be treated as earned income as is not properly attributable to the rights which have belonged to that other person.

Former enactment.—TA 1970, s. 383.

530. Disposal of know-how

(1) Subject to section 531, where after 31st March 1986 a person—

    (*a*) acquires know-how for use in a trade carried on by him, or

    (*b*) acquires know-how, and thereafter sets up and commences a trade in which it is used,

allowances and charges shall, in accordance with subsections (2) and (3) below, be made to and on him in respect of his expenditure on the acquisition, so far as not otherwise deducted for the purposes of corporation tax or income tax.

(2) For any chargeable period for which a person within subsection (1) above has qualifying expenditure which exceeds any disposal value to be brought into account by him in accordance with subsection (5) below, there shall be made to him—

    (*a*) unless the period is the chargeable period related to the permanent discontinuance of the trade, a writing-down allowance of an amount equal to—

        (i) 25 per cent. of the excess, or
        (ii) a proportionately reduced percentage of the excess if the period is part only of a year, or if the period is a year of assessment but the trade had been carried on for part only of the year; and

    (*b*) if the period is the chargeable period related to the permanent discontinuance of the trade, a balancing allowance equal to the whole of the excess.

(3) For any chargeable period for which a person's qualifying expenditure is less than the disposal value which he is to bring into account, there shall be made on him a balancing charge and the amount on which the charge is made shall be an amount equal to the difference.

(4) For the purposes of subsections (2) and (3) above a person's qualifying expenditure for a chargeable period is the aggregate of the following amounts—

    (*a*) any capital expenditure incurred by him on the acquisition of know-how, being expenditure incurred during the chargeable period or its basis period or at any previous time, other than expenditure which, or any part of which, has formed part of his qualifying expenditure for any previous chargeable period; and
    (*b*) if, for the chargeable period immediately preceding the chargeable period in question, there was an excess of qualifying expenditure over disposal value, the balance of that excess after deducting any writing-down allowance under subsection (2)(*a*) above made by reference to that excess.

(5) If, in any chargeable period or its basis period, a person sells any know-how on the acquisition of which for use in a trade carried on by him he has incurred expenditure falling within subsection (1) above, then, for the purposes of subsections (2) to (4) above, he is required to bring into account for that chargeable period disposal value equal to the net proceeds to him of that sale.

(6) Subject to section 531, where after 19th March 1968 and before 1st April 1986 a person—

    (*a*) acquired know-how for use in a trade carried on by him, or
    (*b*) acquired know-how, and thereafter sets up and commences a trade in which it is used,

writing-down allowances in respect of his expenditure on the acquisition, so far as not otherwise deducted for the purposes of corporation tax or income tax, shall be made in taxing the trade during a writing-down period of six years beginning with the chargeable period related to the expenditure; and if during that period he ceases to carry on the trade, an allowance equal to the amount of that expenditure then unallowed shall be made in taxing the trade for the chargeable period related to the discontinuance.

(7) For the purposes of subsections (1) and (6) above, a person incurring expenditure on know-how before the setting up and commencement of the trade in which it is used shall be treated as incurring it on that setting up and commencement.

(8) Subsection (2) of section 75 of the 1968 Act (effect of providing writing-down allowances during writing-down period of a specified length) shall apply to subsection (6) above as it applies to the provisions specified in subsection (1) of that section.

Former enactments.—Sub-s. (1): TA 1970, s. 386(1); FA 1985, s. 65(1).
Sub-ss. (2)–(5): FA 1985, Sch. 18, Pt. II, paras. 5–7.
Sub-s. (6): TA 1970, s. 386(1); FA 1985, s. 65(1).
Sub-s. (7): TA 1970, s. 386(1).
Sub-s. (8): TA 1970, s. 386(9); FA 1985, s. 65(2).

531. Provisions supplementary to section 530

(1) Subject to subsection (7) below, where, after 19th March 1968, a person disposes of know-how which has been used in a trade carried on by him, and continues to carry on the trade after the disposal, the amount or value of any consideration received by him for the disposal shall—

(*a*) if it is received in respect of the disposal of know-how after 31st March 1986, so far as it is not brought into account as disposal value under section 530(5), nor is chargeable to tax as a revenue or income receipt;

(*b*) in any other case, so far as it is not chargeable to tax as a revenue or income receipt,

be treated for all purposes as a trading receipt.

(2) Subject to subsection (3) below, where, after 19th March 1968, a person disposes of a trade or part of a trade and, together with that trade or part, of know-how used in it, any consideration received by him for the know-how shall be dealt with in relation both to him and to the person acquiring the know-how, if that person provided the consideration, and for the purposes of corporation tax, income tax and capital gains tax, as a payment for goodwill.

(3) Subsection (2) above shall not apply—

(*a*) to either of the persons concerned if they so elect by notice given jointly to the inspector within two years of the disposal, or

(*b*) to the person acquiring the know-how if the trade in question was, before the acquisition, carried on wholly outside the United Kingdom;

and where know-how is disposed of with a trade or part of a trade, but that subsection is excluded in relation to the person acquiring it, section 530(1) and (6) shall apply as if that person had acquired it for use in a trade previously carried on by him.

(4) Subject to subsections (5) and (7) below, any consideration received by a person for the disposal of know-how shall—

(*a*) if it is received in respect of the disposal of know-how after 31st March 1986 and is not brought into account as disposal value under section 530(5), or

(*b*) if it is neither chargeable to tax under subsection (1) above or otherwise as a revenue or income receipt, nor dealt with in relation to him as a payment for goodwill as mentioned in subsection (2) above, (whether the disposal took place before or after 31st March 1986),

be treated as a profit or gain chargeable to tax under Case VI of Schedule D.

(5) Where the person concerned has incurred expenditure wholly and exclusively in the acquisition or disposal of the know-how, the amount which would apart from this subsection be treated as a profit or gain chargeable to tax under Case VI of Schedule D shall be reduced by the amount of that expenditure; but a deduction shall not be twice made in respect of the same expenditure, whether under this subsection or otherwise.

(6) Where subsection (4) above has effect in the case of an individual who devised the know-how in question, whether alone or jointly with any other person, the amount in respect of which he is chargeable to tax by virtue of that subsection shall be treated for all purposes as earned income.

(7) Subsections (1) and (3) to (6) above and section 530(1) and (6) shall not apply on any sale of know-how where the buyer is a body of persons over whom the seller has control, or the seller is a body of persons over whom the buyer has control, or both the seller and the buyer are bodies of persons and some other person has control over both of them; and subsection (2) above shall apply in any such case with the omission of the words "Subject to subsection (3) below".

In this subsection references to a body of persons include references to a partnership.

(8) Where in connection with any disposal of know-how a person gives an undertaking (whether absolute or qualified, and whether legally valid or not) the tenor or effect of which is to restrict his or another's activities in any way, any consideration received in respect of the giving of the undertaking or its total or partial fulfilment shall be treated for the purposes of this section as consideration received for the disposal of the know-how.

Former enactments.—Sub-s. (1): TA 1970, s. 386(2); FA 1985, s. 65(3)(*a*).
Sub-ss. (2), (3): TA 1970, s. 386(3).
Sub-s. (4): TA 1970, s. 386(4); FA 1985, s. 65(3)(*b*).
Sub-s. (5)–(7): TA 1970, s. 386(4)–(6).
Sub-s. (8): TA 1970, s. 386(8); FA 1985, Sch. 18, Pt. II, para. 8.

532. Application of the 1968 Act

(1) Subject to subsection (2) below, the Tax Acts shall have effect as if sections 520 to 531, this section and section 533 were contained in Part I of the 1968 Act, and any reference in the Tax Acts to any capital allowance to be given "by way of discharge or repayment of tax and to be available or available primarily against a specified class of income" shall include

a reference to any capital allowance given in accordance with subsection (2) or (3) of section 528.

(2) Schedule 7 to the 1968 Act (special provisions as to controlled sales) shall not (by virtue of subsection (1) above) apply with respect to expenditure incurred after 31st March 1986 on the purchase of patent rights.

(3) Subject to subsection (2) above, in Part I of the 1968 Act, as applied by virtue of subsection (1) above to patent rights, the sum referred to in paragraph 4(1)(*a*) of Schedule 7 to that Act (special provisions as to controlled sales) is the amount of any capital expenditure on the acquisition of the patent rights remaining unallowed, computed in accordance with the provisions of section 523.

(4) The reference in section 82(1) of the 1968 Act (certain payments not to be treated as capital expenditure) to any expenditure or sum in the case of which a deduction of income tax falls or may fall to be made under sections 348 to 350 does not include a sum in the case of which such a deduction falls or may fall to be so made by virtue of section 524(3)(*b*).

(5) In Part I of the 1968 Act as so applied to know-how—
>   (*a*) references in that Part to property and its purchase or sale include references to know-how and its acquisition or disposal;
>   (*b*) section 78, together with Schedule 7 to that Act (special provisions as to controlled sales), shall be omitted.

Former enactments.—TA 1970, s. 387; FA 1985, s. 64(2)(*h*).

533. Interpretation of sections 520 to 532

(1) In sections 520 to 532—
>   "income from patents" means—
>   >   (*a*) any royalty or other sum paid in respect of the user of a patent; and
>   >   (*b*) any amount on which tax is payable for any chargeable period by virtue of section 520(6), 523(3), 524 or 525;
>
>   "the commencement of the patent" means, in relation to a patent, the date as from which the patent rights become effective;
>   "patent rights" means the right to do or authorise the doing of anything which would, but for that right, be an infringement of a patent;
>   "United Kingdom patent" means a patent granted under the laws of the United Kingdom.

(2) Subject to subsection (3) below, in sections 520 to 532 any reference to the sale of part of patent rights includes a reference to the grant of a licence in respect of the patent in question, and any reference to the purchase of patent rights includes a reference to the acquisition of a licence in respect of a patent.

(3) If a licence granted by a person entitled to any patent rights is a licence to exercise those rights to the exclusion of the grantor and all other persons for the whole of the remainder of the term for which the right subsists, the grantor shall be treated for the purposes of sections 520 to 532 as thereby selling the whole of the rights.

(4) Where, under sections 46 to 49 of the Patents Act 1949[, sections 55 to 59 of the Patents Act 1977][1] or any corresponding provisions of the law of any country outside the United Kingdom, an invention which is the subject of a patent is made, used, or exercised or vended by or for the service of the Crown or the government of the country concerned, sections 520 to 532 shall have effect as if the making, user, exercise or vending of the invention had taken place in pursuance of a licence, and any sums paid in respect thereof shall be treated accordingly.

(5) Expenditure incurred in obtaining a right to acquire in the future patent rights as respects any invention in respect of which the patent has not yet been granted shall be deemed for all the purposes of sections 520 to 532 to be expenditure on the purchase of patent rights, and if the patent rights are subsequently acquired the expenditure shall be deemed for those purposes to have been expenditure on the purchase of those rights.

(6) Any sum received from a person which by virtue of subsection (5) above is deemed to be expenditure incurred by him on the purchase of patent rights shall be deemed to be proceeds of a sale of patent rights.

(7) In sections 530 and 531 "know-how" means any industrial information and techniques likely to assist in the manufacture or processing of goods or materials, or in the working of a

mine, oil-well or other source of mineral deposits (including the searching for, discovery or testing of deposits or the winning of access thereto), or in the carrying out of any agricultural, forestry or fishing operations.

Former enactments.—Sub-ss. (1)–(6): TA 1970, s. 388; FA 1985, s. 64(2)(*g*).
Sub-s. (7): TA 1970, s. 386(7); FA 1985, Sch. 18, Pt. II, para. 8.
Amendments.—Words in sub-s. (4) inserted by FA 1988, Sch. 13, para. 5.

Copyright and public lending right

534. Relief for copyright payments etc.

(1) Where—

(*a*) an author of a literary, dramatic, musical or artistic work assigns the copyright in the work wholly or partially, or grants any interest in the copyright by licence; and
(*b*) the consideration for the assignment or grant consists wholly or partially of a payment to which this section applies, being a payment the whole amount of which would, but for this section, be included in computing the amount of his profits or gains for a single year of assessment; and
(*c*) the author was engaged on the making of the work for a period of more than 12 months;

he may, on making a claim, require that effect shall be given to the following provisions of this section in connection with that payment.

(2) If the period for which he was engaged on the making of the work does not exceed 24 months, then, for all income tax purposes, one-half only of the amount of the payment shall be treated as having become receivable on the date on which it actually became receivable, and the remaining half shall be treated as having become receivable 12 months before that date.

(3) If the period for which he was engaged on the making of the work exceeds 24 months, then, for all income tax purposes, one-third only of the amount of the payment shall be treated as having become receivable on the date on which it actually became receivable, and one-third shall be treated as having become receivable 12 months, and one-third 24 months, before that date.

(4) This section applies to—

(*a*) a lump sum payment, including an advance on account of royalties which is not returnable, and
(*b*) any payment of or on account of royalties or sums payable periodically,

except that it shall not by virtue of paragraph (*b*) above apply to payments in respect of the copyright in any work which only become receivable more than two years after its first publication.

(5) A claim under this section with respect to any payment to which it applies by virtue only of subsection (4)(*b*) above shall have effect as a claim with respect to all such payments in respect of the copyright in the same work which are receivable by the claimant, whether before or after the claim; and such a claim may be made at any time not later than 5th April next following the expiration of eight years after the work's first publication.

(6) A claim cannot be made under this section in respect of a payment if a prior claim has been made under section 535 as respects that payment.

(7) In this section—

(*a*) "author" includes a joint author; and
(*b*) any reference to the first publication of a work is a reference to the first occasion on which the work or a reproduction of it is published, performed or exhibited.

Former enactment.—TA 1970, s. 389.

535. Relief where copyright sold after ten years or more

(1) Where not less than ten years after the first publication of the work the author of a literary, dramatic, musical or artistic work assigns the copyright in the work wholly or partially, or grants any interest in the copyright by licence, and—

(*a*) the consideration for the assignment or grant consists wholly or partially of a lump sum payment the whole amount of which would, but for this section, be included in computing the amount of his profits or gains for a single year of assessment, and

(b) the copyright or interest is not assigned or granted for a period of less than two years,

he may by making a claim require that effect shall be given to the following provisions of this section in connection with that payment.

(2) Except where the copyright or interest is assigned or granted for a period of less than six years, the amount of the payment shall for income tax purposes be treated as becoming receivable in six equal instalments at yearly intervals the first of which becomes receivable on the date when the payment actually became receivable.

(3) Where the copyright or interest is assigned or granted for a period of less than six years, the amount of the payment shall for income tax purposes be treated as becoming receivable in a number of equal instalments at yearly intervals the first of which becomes receivable on the date when the payment actually became receivable, the number being the number of whole years in that period.

(4) Subject to subsection (5) below, if the author dies, any instalment which under this section would, but for the death, be treated as becoming receivable after the death shall for income tax purposes be treated as becoming receivable on the date when the last instalment before the death is to be treated as becoming receivable.

(5) If the personal representatives so elect—

(a) the total amount of income tax which would have been payable by the deceased or out of his estate in respect of the payment if the copyright or interest had been assigned or granted for a period beginning with the date when the first instalment is treated as becoming receivable and ending with the day before the death shall be computed, and

(b) the income tax payable out of the estate by reason of the provisions of subsection (4) above shall be reduced so as not to exceed the amount at (a) above.

The references in this subsection to the income tax payable by a person include, in cases where the income of a wife is deemed to be the income of the husband, references to the income tax payable by his wife or her husband, as the case may be.

(6) If—

(a) the payment would, apart from this section, have been taken into account in assessing the profits or gains of a profession or vocation, and

(b) the profession or vocation is permanently discontinued (otherwise than on death) after the date on which the payment actually became receivable,

any instalment which under this section would, but for the discontinuance, be treated as receivable on a date after the discontinuance shall for income tax purposes be treated as becoming receivable when the last instalment before the discontinuance is to be treated as becoming receivable, unless the author elects to be treated (for all purposes) as if the copyright or interest had been assigned or granted for a period beginning with the date when the first instalment is treated as becoming receivable and ending with the day before the discontinuance.

(7) Notice of any election under subsection (5) or (6) above shall be served on the inspector within two years of the death, or as the case may be of the discontinuance.

(8) In any case where—

(a) but for this section, the payment would be included in computing any profits or gains chargeable to tax under Case VI of Schedule D, and

(b) any amount would be deductible from that payment in computing those profits or gains (whether under the general provisions relating to Case VI or under section 105(1)),

the amount which, under this section, is to be treated as receivable in instalments shall be the amount of the payment after that deduction, and effect shall not be given to that deduction in any other way.

(9) A claim cannot be made under this section in respect of a payment if a prior claim has been made under section 534 as respects that payment.

(10) Where it is necessary, in order to give effect to a claim or election under this section, or as a result of the claim or election, to make any adjustment by way of an assessment on any person, the assessment shall not be out of time if it is made within one year of the final determination of the claim or, as the case may be, within one year from the giving of notice of the election.

(11) In this section—

"author" includes a joint author;
"lump sum payment" includes an advance on account of royalties which is not returnable;

and any reference to the first publication of a work is a reference to the first occasion on which the work or a reproduction of it is published, performed or exhibited.

Former enactment.—TA 1970, s. 390.
Note.—See **Prospective Legislation Notes** (Married Couples).

536. Taxation of royalties where owner abroad

(1) Subject to the provisions of this section, where the usual place of abode of the owner of a copyright is not within the United Kingdom, section 349(1) shall apply to any payment of or on account of any royalties or sums paid periodically for or in respect of that copyright as it applies to annual payments not payable out of profits or gains brought into charge to income tax.

(2) In subsection (1) above—

["copyright" does not include copyright in—

(i) a cinematograph film or video recording, or
(ii) the sound-track of such a film or recording, so far as it is not separately exploited; and][1]

"owner of a copyright" includes a person who, notwithstanding that he has assigned a copyright to some other person, is entitled to receive periodical payments in respect of that copyright;

and the reference to royalties or sums paid periodically for or in respect of a copyright does not include royalties or sums paid in respect of copies of works which are shown on a claim to have been exported from the United Kingdom for distribution outside the United Kingdom.

(3) Subject to subsection (4) below, where any payment to which subsection (1) above applies is made through an agent resident in the United Kingdom and that agent is entitled as against the owner of the copyright to deduct any sum by way of commission in respect of services rendered, the amount of the payment shall for the purposes of section 349(1) be taken to be diminished by the sum which the agent is so entitled to deduct.

(4) Where the person by or through whom the payment is made does not know that any such commission is payable or does not know the amount of any such commission, any income tax deducted by or assessed and charged on him shall be computed in the first instance on, and the account to be delivered of the payment shall be an account of, the total amount of the payment without regard being had to any diminution thereof, and in that case, on proof of the facts on a claim, there shall be made to the agent on behalf of the owner of the copyright such repayment of income tax as is proper in respect of the sum deducted by way of commission.

(5) The time of the making of a payment to which subsection (1) above applies shall, for all tax purposes, be taken to be the time when it is made by the person by whom it is first made and not the time when it is made by or through any other person.

(6) Any agreement for the making of any payment to which subsection (1) above applies in full and without deduction of income tax shall be void.

Former enactment.—TA 1970, s. 391.
Amendments.—[1] The definition of "copyright" in sub-s. (2) substituted by the Copyright, Designs and Patents Act 1988, Sch. 7, para. 36(5) with effect from 1 August 1989 by virtue of the Copyright, Designs and Patents Act 1988 (Commencement No. 1) Order 1989, S.I. 1989 No. 816. The original definition read—

""copyright" does not include a copyright in any dramatic work being a cinematograph production, or in any artistic work being a photograph intended to be used for the purposes of the exhibition of pictures or other optical effects by means of a cinematograph or other similar apparatus; and".

537. Public lending right

Sections 534, 535 and 536 shall have effect in relation to public lending right as they have effect in relation to copyright.

Former enactment.—FA 1983, s. 27.

[*Designs*][1]

[537A. Relief for payments in respect of designs

(1) Where the designer of a design in which design right subsists assigns that right, or the author of a registered design assigns the right in the design, wholly or partially, or grants an interest in it by licence, and—

    (*a*) the consideration for the assignment or grant consists, in whole or in part, of a payment to which this section applies, the whole amount of which would otherwise be included in computing the amount of his profits or gains for a single year of assessment, and

    (*b*) he was engaged in the creation of the design for a period of more than 12 months,

he may, on making a claim, require that effect shall be given to the following provisions in connection with that payment.

(2) If the period for which he was engaged in the creation of the design does not exceed 24 months, then, for all income tax purposes, one-half only of the amount of the payment shall be treated as having become receivable on the date on which it actually became receivable and the remaining half shall be treated as having become receivable 12 months before that date.

(3) If the period for which he was engaged in the creation of the design exceeds 24 months, then, for all income tax purposes, one-third only of the amount of the payment shall be treated as having become receivable on the date on which it actually became receivable, and one-third shall be treated as having become receivable 12 months, and one-third 24 months, before that date.

(4) This section applies to—

    (*a*) a lump sum payment, including an advance on account of royalties which is not returnable, and

    (*b*) any other payment of or on account of royalties or sums payable periodically which does not only become receivable more than two years after articles made to the design or, as the case may be, articles to which the design is applied are first made available for sale or hire.

(5) A claim under this section with respect to any payment to which it applies by virtue only of subsection (4)(*b*) above shall have effect as a claim with respect to all such payments in respect of rights in the design in question which are receivable by the claimant, whether before or after the claim; and such a claim may be made at any time not later than 5th April next following the expiration of eight years after articles made to the design or, as the case may be, articles to which the design is applied were first made available for sale or hire.

(6) In this section—

    (*a*) "designer" includes a joint designer, and

    (*b*) any reference to articles being made available for sale or hire is to their being so made available anywhere in the world by or with the licence of the design right owner or, as the case may be, the proprietor of the registered design.

Amendments.—[1] This section inserted by the Copyright, Designs and Patents Act 1988, Sch. 7, para. 36(6) with effect from 1 August 1989 by virtue of the Copyright, Designs and Patents Act 1988 (Commencement No. 1) Order 1989, S.I. 1989 No. 816.

[537B. Taxation of design royalties where owner abroad

(1) Where the usual place of abode of the owner of a right in a design is not within the United Kingdom, section 349(1) shall apply to any payment of or on account of any royalties or sums paid periodically for or in respect of that right as it applies to annual payments not payable out of profits or gains brought into charge to income tax.

(2) In subsection (1) above—

    (*a*) "right in a design" means design right or the right in a registered design,

    (*b*) the reference to the owner of a right includes a person who, notwithstanding that he has assigned the right to some other person, is entitled to receive periodical payments in respect of the right, and

    (*c*) the reference to royalties or other sums paid periodically for or in respect of a right does not include royalties or sums paid in respect of articles which are shown on a claim to have been exported from the United Kingdom for distribution outside the United Kingdom.

(3) Where a payment to which subsection (1) above applies is made through an agent resident in the United Kingdom and that agent is entitled as against the owner of the right to deduct any sum by way of commission in respect of services rendered, the amount of the payment shall for the purposes of section 349(1) be taken to be diminished by the sum which the agent is entitled to deduct.

(4) Where the person by or through whom the payment is made does not know that any such commission is payable or does not know the amount of any such commission, any income tax deducted by or assessed and charged on him shall be computed in the first instance on, and the account to be delivered of the payment shall be an account of, the total amount of the payment without regard being had to any diminution thereof, and in that case, on proof of the facts on a claim, there shall be made to the agent on behalf of the owner of the right such repayment of income tax as is proper in respect of the sum deducted by way of commission.

(5) The time of the making of a payment to which subsection (1) above applies shall, for all tax purposes, be taken to be the time when it is made by the person by whom it is first made and not the time when it is made by or through any other person.

(6) Any agreement for the making of any payment to which subsection (1) above applies in full and without deduction of income tax shall be void.][1]

Amendments.—[1] This section inserted by the Copyright, Designs and Patents Act 1988, Sch. 7, para. 36(6) with effect from 1 August 1989 by virtue of the Copyright, Designs and Patents Act 1988 (Commencement No. 1) Order 1989, S.I. 1989 No. 816.

Artists' receipts

538. Relief for painters, sculptors and other artists

(1) Where the artist obtains any sum for the sale of a painting, sculpture or other work of art, or by way of commission or fee for the creation of the work of art, and—

(*a*) he was engaged on the making of the work of art for a period of more than 12 months, or

(*b*) he was engaged for a period of more than 12 months in making a number of works of art for an exhibition, and the work is one of them,

he may, by making a claim, require that effect shall be given to the following provisions of this section as respects that sum.

(2) If the period for which he was engaged on the making of the work does not exceed 24 months, then, for all income tax purposes, one-half only of the amount of the payment shall be treated as having become receivable on the date on which it actually became receivable, and the remaining half shall be treated as having become receivable 12 months before that date.

(3) If the period for which he was engaged on the making of the work exceeds 24 months, then, for all income tax purposes, one-third only of the amount of the payment shall be treated as having become receivable on the date on which it actually became receivable, and one-third shall be treated as having become receivable 12 months, and one-third 24 months, before that date.

Former enactment.—TA 1970, s. 392.

CHAPTER II

LIFE POLICIES, LIFE ANNUITIES AND CAPITAL REDEMPTION POLICIES

539. Introductory

(1) This Chapter shall have effect for the purposes of imposing, in the manner and to the extent therein provided, charges to tax, . . .², in respect of gains to be treated in accordance with this Chapter as arising in connection with policies of life insurance, contracts for life annuities and capital redemption policies.

(2) Nothing in this Chapter shall apply—

(a) to any policy of life insurance having as its sole object the provision on an individual's death or disability of a sum substantially the same as any amount then outstanding under a mortgage of his residence, or of any premises occupied by him for the purposes of a business, being a mortgage the principal amount secured by which is repayable by instalments payable annually or at shorter regular intervals; or

(b) to any policy of life insurance issued in connection with an approved scheme, as defined in Chapter I of Part XIV; or

(c) to a policy of insurance which constitutes, or is evidence of, a contract for the time being approved under section 621.

In the application of this subsection to Scotland, for the reference to a mortgage there shall be substituted a reference to a heritable security within the meaning of the Conveyancing (Scotland) Act 1924 (but including a security constituted by ex facie absolute disposition or assignation).

(3) In this Chapter—

"assignment", in relation to Scotland, means an assignation;

"capital redemption policy" means any insurance effected in the course of a capital redemption business as defined in section 458(3); and

"life annuity" means any annuity to which sections 656 and 657 apply and any annuity the contract for which is made on or after 1st June 1984 by a friendly society or branch thereof in the course of life or endowment business as defined in section 466.

(4) For the purposes of this Chapter the falling due of a sum payable in pursuance of a right conferred by a policy or contract to participate in profits shall be treated as the surrender of rights conferred by the policy or contract.

(5) This Chapter shall have effect only as respects policies of life insurance issued in respect of insurances made after 19th March 1968, contracts for life annuities entered into after that date, and capital redemption policies effected after that date.

(6) A policy of life insurance issued in respect of an insurance made on or before 19th March 1968 shall be treated for the purposes of subsection (5) above and the following provisions of this Chapter as issued in respect of one made after that date if it is varied after that date so as to increase the benefits secured or to extend the term of the insurance.

(7) A variation effected before the end of the year 1968 shall be disregarded for the purposes of subsection (6) above if its only effect was to bring into conformity with paragraph 2 of Schedule 9 to the Finance Act 1968 (which is re-enacted, as amended, by paragraph 2 of Schedule 15 to this Act) a policy previously conforming therewith except as respects the amount guaranteed on death, and no increase was made in the premiums payable under the policy.

(8) Subsections (1) to (7) above do not apply in relation to section 554.

[(9) A policy of life insurance issued in respect of an insurance made before 14th March 1989 shall be treated for the purposes of sections 540(5A), 547(8) and 548(3A) as issued in respect of one made on or after that date if it is varied on or after that date so as to increase the benefits secured or to extend the term of the insurance; and any exercise of rights conferred by the policy shall be regarded for this purpose as a variation.]¹

Former enactments.—Sub-s. (1): TA 1970, s. 393(1); FA 1971, Sch. 6, para. 41; FA 1972, Sch. 24, para. 23.
Sub-s. (2)(a), (b): TA 1970, s. 393(2)(a), (c); FA 1971, Sch. 3, para. 11.
Sub-s. (2)(c): TA 1970, s. 393(2A); FA 1971, Sch. 2, para. 6.
Sub-s. (3): TA 1970, s. 393(3); FA 1985, s. 41(8).
Sub-s. (4): FA 1975, Sch. 2, para. 15.

Sub-ss. (5)–(7): TA 1970, s. 393(4), (5).
Amendments.—¹ Sub-s. (9) added by FA 1989, Sch. 9, paras. 1, 2, 8 with effect from 14 March 1989.
² Words in sub-s. (1) repealed by FA 1989, Sch. 17, Pt. V in relation to accounting periods beginning after 31 March 1989.

540. Life policies: chargeable events

(1) Subject to the provisions of this section, in this Chapter "chargeable event" means, in relation to a policy of life insurance—

(*a*) if it is not a qualifying policy, any of the following—

(i) any death giving rise to benefits under the policy;
(ii) the maturity of the policy;
(iii) the surrender in whole of the rights conferred by the policy;
(iv) the assignment for money or money's worth of those rights; and
(v) an excess of the reckonable aggregate value mentioned in subsection (2) of section 546 over the allowable aggregate amount mentioned in subsection (3) of that section, being an excess occurring at the end of any year (as defined in subsection (4) of that section) except, if it ends with another chargeable event, the final year; and

(*b*) if it is a qualifying policy (whether or not the premiums thereunder are eligible for relief under section 266), any of the above events, but—

(i) in the case of death or maturity, only if the policy is converted into a paid-up policy before the expiry of ten years from the making of the insurance, or, if sooner, of three-quarters of the term for which the policy is to run if not ended by death or disability;
(ii) in the case of a surrender or assignment or such an excess as is mentioned in paragraph (*a*)(v) above, only if it is effected or occurs within that time, or the policy has been converted into a paid-up policy within that time.

(2) The maturity of a policy is not a chargeable event in relation thereto if—

(*a*) a new policy is issued in consequence of the exercise of an option conferred by the maturing policy, and
(*b*) the whole of the sums becoming payable under the maturing policy are retained by the company with whom the insurance was made and applied in the payment of one or more premiums under the new policy,

unless the circumstances are such that the person making the insurance in respect of which the new policy is issued was an infant when the former policy was issued, and the former policy was one securing a capital sum payable either on a specified date falling not later than one month after his attaining 25 or on the anniversary of the policy immediately following his attainment of that age.

(3) Except as provided by section 544, no event is a chargeable event in relation to a policy issued in respect of an insurance made before 26th June 1982 if the rights conferred by the policy have at any time before that date and before the event been assigned for money or money's worth and are not at the time of the event held by the original beneficial owner.

(4) No account shall be taken for the purposes of [subsections (1) and (3) above]¹ of any assignment effected by way of security for a debt, or on the discharge of a debt secured by the rights or share concerned, or of any assignment between spouses living together.

(5) Where subsection (1)(*b*) applies to a policy which has been varied so as to increase the premiums payable thereunder, it shall so apply as if the references in subsection (1)(*b*)(i) to the making of the insurance and the term of the policy were references respectively to the taking effect of the variation and the term of the policy as from the variation.

[(5A) Sub-paragraphs (i) and (ii) of subsection (1)(*b*) above shall not apply in relation to a policy issued in respect of an insurance made on or after 14th March 1989 if, immediately before the happening of the event, the rights conferred by the policy were in the beneficial ownership of a company, or were held on trusts created, or as security for a debt owed, by a company.]²

(6) This section has effect subject to paragraph 20 of Schedule 15.

Former enactments.—Sub-s. (1): TA 1970, s. 394(1), (2); FA 1975, Sch. 2, para. 9(1), (2).
Sub-s. (2): TA 1970, s. 394(3); FA 1984, s. 75(1).
Sub-s. (3): TA 1970, s. 394(4); FA 1983, s. 18(1); FA 1975, Sch. 2, para. 10.
Sub-ss. (4), (5): TA 1970, s. 394(5), (6); FA 1975, Sch. 2, para. 10.
Sub-s. (6): FA 1982, s. 34.
Amendments.—¹ Words in sub-s. (4) substituted by FA 1989, Sch. 9, paras. 1, 3, 8.
² Sub-s. (5A) inserted by *ibid* with effect from 14 March 1989.

541. Life policies: computation of gain

(1) On the happening of a chargeable event in relation to any policy of life insurance, there shall be treated as a gain arising in connection with the policy—

    (*a*) if the event is a death, the excess (if any) of the surrender value of the policy immediately before the death, plus the amount or value of any relevant capital payments, over the sum of the following—

        (i) the total amount previously paid under the policy by way of premiums; and
        (ii) the total amount treated as a gain by virtue of paragraph (*d*) below on the previous happening of chargeable events;

    (*b*) if the event is the maturity of the policy, or the surrender in whole of the rights thereby conferred, the excess (if any) of the amount or value of the sum payable or other benefits arising by reason of the event, plus the amount or value of any relevant capital payments, over the sum of the following—

        (i) the total amount previously paid under the policy by way of premiums; and
        (ii) the total amount treated as a gain by virtue of paragraph (*d*) below on the previous happening of chargeable events;

    (*c*) if the event is an assignment, the excess (if any) of the amount or value of the consideration, plus the amount or value of any relevant capital payments or of any previously assigned share in the rights conferred by the policy, over the sum of the following—

        (i) the total amount previously paid under the policy by way of premiums; and
        (ii) the total amount treated as a gain by virtue of paragraph (*d*) below on the previous happening of chargeable events;

    (*d*) if the event is the occurrence of such an excess as is mentioned in section 540(1)(*a*)(v), the amount of the excess.

(2) Where, in a case falling within subsection (1)(*b*) above, a right to periodical payments arises by reason of the event, there shall be treated as payable by reason thereof an amount equal to the capital value of those payments at the time the right arises.

(3) Where, in a case falling within subsection (1)(*c*) above, the assignment is between persons who are connected with each other within the meaning of section 839, the assignment shall be deemed to have been made for a consideration equal to the market value of the rights or share assigned.

(4) Where there is an assignment, otherwise than for money or money's worth, of all the rights conferred by the policy, the calculations required to be made by section 546 shall be made, in the first instance, without regard to any surrender or assignment of part of or a share in those rights which takes place after the assignment, and any gain treated as arising under subsection (1)(*d*) above on the calculation so made shall be treated as arising to the assignor.

[(4A) Where, immediately before the happening of the chargeable event, the rights conferred by a qualifying endowment policy are held as security for a debt owed by a company, then, if—

    (*a*) the conditions in subsection (4B) below are satisfied,
    (*b*) the amount of the debt exceeds the total amount previously paid under the policy by way of premiums, and
    (*c*) the company makes a claim for the purpose within two years after the end of the accounting period in which the chargeable event happens,

this section shall have effect as if the references in subsection (1)(*a*) and (*b*) to that total amount were references to the amount of the debt.][1]

[(4B) The conditions referred to in subsection (4A) above are—

    (*a*) that, throughout the period beginning with the making of the insurance and ending immediately before the happening of the chargeable event, the rights conferred by the policy have been held as security for a debt owed by the company;
    (*b*) that the capital sum payable under the policy in the event of death during the term of the policy is not less than the amount of the debt when the insurance was made;
    (*c*) that any sum payable under the policy by reason of the chargeable event is applied in repayment of the debt (except to the extent that its amount exceeds the amount of the debt);
    (*d*) that the debt was incurred to defray money applied—

        (i) in purchasing an estate or interest in land to be occupied by the company for the purposes of a trade carried on by it, or

(ii) for the purpose of the construction, extension or improvement (but not the repair or maintenance) of buildings which are or are to be so occupied.]¹

[(4C) If the amount of the debt is higher immediately before the happening of the chargeable event than it was at some earlier time during the period mentioned in subsection (4B)(*a*) above, the amount to be taken into account for the purposes of subsection (1) above shall be the lowest amount at which it stood during that period.]¹

[(4D) If during the period mentioned in subsection (4B)(*a*) above the company incurs a debt by borrowing in order to repay another debt, subsections (4B) and (4C) above shall have effect as if, where appropriate, references to either debt included references to the other.]¹

(5) In this section—

   (*a*) "relevant capital payments" means, in relation to any policy, any sum or other benefit of a capital nature, other than one attributable to a person's disability, paid or conferred under the policy before the happening of the chargeable event; and
   (*b*) references in this subsection and (in relation to premiums) in subsection (1) above to "the policy" include references to any related policy, that is to say, to any policy in relation to which the policy is a new policy within the meaning of paragraph 17 of Schedule 15, and any policy in relation to which that policy is such a policy, and so on; [and]²
   [(*c*) "qualifying endowment policy" means a policy which is a qualifying policy by virtue of paragraph 2 of Schedule 15;]²

and the provisions of this section are subject to paragraph 20 of Schedule 15.

(6) There shall be disregarded for the purposes of this section any amount which was treated under section 72(9) of the Finance Act 1984 as an additional premium.

Former enactments.—Sub-s. (1): TA 1970, s. 395(1); FA 1975, Sch. 2, para. 11(1).
Sub-ss. (2), (3): TA 1970, s. 395(2), (3).
Sub-s. (4): TA 1970, s. 395(3A); FA 1975, Sch. 2, para. 11(2).
Sub-s. (5): TA 1970, s. 395(4); FA 1975, Sch. 2, para. 10; FA 1982, s. 34.
Sub-s. (6): FA 1984, s. 72(9).
Amendments.—¹ Sub-ss. (4A)–(4D) inserted by FA 1989, Sch. 9, paras. 4, 8 with effect from 14 March 1989.
² Sub-s. (5)(*c*) inserted by *ibid*.

542. Life annuity contracts: chargeable events

(1) Subject to subsections (2) and (3) below, in this Chapter "chargeable event" means, in relation to any contract for a life annuity—

   (*a*) the surrender in whole of the rights conferred by the contract, or
   (*b*) the assignment for money or money's worth of those rights, or
   (*c*) an excess of the reckonable aggregate value mentioned in subsection (2) of section 546 over the allowable aggregate amount mentioned in subsection (3) of that section, being an excess occurring at the end of any year (as defined in subsection (4) of that section) except, if it ends with another chargeable event, the final year.

(2) Where the terms of a contract provide for the payment of a capital sum as an alternative, in whole or in part, to payments by way of annuity, the taking of the capital sum shall be treated for the purposes of this section and section 543 as a surrender in whole or in part of the rights conferred by the contract, and where the terms of the contract provide for the payment of a capital sum on death and the contract was made on or after 10th December 1974, the death shall be treated for those purposes as a surrender in whole of the rights conferred by the contract.

(3) Except as provided by section 544, an event referred to in subsection (1) above is not a chargeable event in relation to any contract made before 26th June 1982 if the rights conferred by the contract have at any time before that date and before the event been assigned for money or money's worth and are not at the time of the event held by the original beneficial owner.

(4) Subsection (4) of section 540 shall, with any necessary modifications, apply for the purposes of this section as it applies for the purposes of that section.

Former enactments.—Sub-ss. (1), (2): TA 1970, s. 396(1); FA 1975, Sch. 2, paras. 9(3), 12.
Sub-ss. (3), (4): TA 1970, s. 396(2), (3); FA 1975, Sch. 2, para. 12; FA 1983, s. 18(2).

543. Life annuity contracts: computation of gain

(1) On the happening of a chargeable event in relation to any contract for a life annuity, there shall be treated as a gain arising in connection with the contract—

(a) if the event is the surrender in whole of the rights conferred by the contract, the excess (if any) of the amount payable by reason of the event plus the amount or value of any relevant capital payments over the sum of the following—

    (i) the total amount previously paid under the contract, whether by way of premiums or as lump sum consideration, reduced, if before the happening of the event one or more payments have been made on account of the annuity, by the capital element in that payment or payments, as determined in accordance with section 656; and
    (ii) the total amount treated as a gain by virtue of paragraph (c) below on the previous happening of chargeable events;

(b) if the event is an assignment, the excess (if any) of the amount or value of the consideration, plus the amount or value of any relevant capital payments or of any previously assigned share in the rights conferred by the contract, over the sum of the following—

    (i) the amount specified in paragraph (a)(i) above; and
    (ii) any amount treated as a gain by virtue of paragraph (c) below on the previous happenings of chargeable events;

(c) if the event is the occurrence of such an excess as is mentioned in section 542(1), the amount of the excess.

(2) Subsection (3) of section 541 shall apply for the purposes of subsection (1) above as it applies for the purposes of subsection (1)(c) of that section, and subsection (4) of that section shall apply for the purposes of this section with the substitution of references to the contract for references to the policy.

(3) In this section "relevant capital payments" means, in relation to any contract, any sum or other benefit of a capital nature paid or conferred under the contract before the happening of the chargeable event.

Former enactments.—TA 1970, s. 397; FA 1975, Sch. 2, para. 13.

544. Second and subsequent assignment of life policies and contracts

(1) In this section "assigned policy" means a policy of life assurance—

    (a) which was issued in respect of an insurance made before 26th June 1982; and
    (b) the rights conferred by which have been assigned for money or money's worth before that date; and
    (c) in relation to which an event occurring on or after that date would not, apart from this section, be a chargeable event.

(2) In this section "assigned contract" means a contract for a life annuity—

    (a) which was made before 26th June 1982; and
    (b) the rights conferred by which have been assigned for money or money's worth before that date; and
    (c) in relation to which an event occurring on or after that date would not, apart from this section, be a chargeable event.

(3) In any case where after 23rd August 1982—

    (a) the rights conferred by an assigned policy or, as the case may be, an assigned contract are again assigned for money or money's worth; or
    (b) a payment is made by way of premium or as lump sum consideration under the policy or contract; or
    (c) subject to subsections (5) and (7) below, a sum is lent by or by arrangement with the body issuing the policy or, as the case may be, the body with which the contract was made;

section 540(3) shall cease to apply to the policy or section 542(3) shall cease to apply to the contract, as the case may be.

(4) No account shall be taken for the purposes of subsection (3)(a) above of any assignment effected by way of security for a debt, or on the discharge of a debt secured by the rights concerned, or of an assignment between spouses living together.

(5) Subsection (3)(c) above does not apply unless—

    (a) the policy was issued in respect of an insurance made after 26th March 1974 or, as the case may be, the contract was entered into after that date; and
    (b) the sum concerned is lent to or at the direction of the individual who, in accordance with subsection (6) below, is at the time of the loan the chargeable individual.

(6) The individual who is at any time the chargeable individual for the purposes of subsection (5)(*b*) above shall be determined as follows—

  (*a*) if at the time the rights conferred by the policy or contract are vested in an individual as beneficial owner or are held on trusts created by an individual (including such trusts as are referred to in section 547(1)(*a*)), that individual is the chargeable individual; and
  (*b*) if at that time those rights are held as security for a debt owned by an individual, that individual is the chargeable individual.

(7) Subsection (3)(*c*) above does not apply in relation to a policy if—

  (*a*) it is a qualifying policy; and
  (*b*) either interest at a commercial rate is payable on the sum lent or the sum is lent to a full-time employee of the body issuing the policy for the purpose of assisting him in the purchase or improvement of a dwelling-house to be used as his only or main residence.

(8) Where section 540(3) or 542(3) ceases to apply to an assigned policy or assigned contract by virtue of paragraph (*c*) of subsection (3) above, the lending of the sum concerned shall be regarded for the purposes of the Income Tax Acts (other than that paragraph) as taking place immediately after the time at which section 540(3) or, as the case may be, 542(3) ceases so to apply.

Former enactments.—Sub-ss. (1), (2): FA 1983, Sch. 4, para. 1.
Sub-s. (3): FA 1983, s. 18(3), Sch. 4, para. 2(1).
Sub-s. (4): FA 1983, Sch. 4, para. 2(2).
Sub-ss. (5)–(7): FA 1983, Sch. 4, para. 2(3).
Sub-s. (8): FA 1983, Sch. 4, para. 2(4).

545. Capital redemption policies

(1) Subject to subsection (2) below, in this Chapter "chargeable event" means, in relation to a capital redemption policy, any of the following—

  (*a*) the maturity of the policy, except where the sums payable on maturity are annual payments chargeable to tax under Schedule D;
  (*b*) the surrender in whole of the rights conferred by the policy;
  (*c*) the assignment for money or money's worth of those rights; and
  (*d*) an excess of the reckonable aggregate value mentioned in subsection (2) of section 546 over the allowable aggregate amount mentioned in subsection (3) of that section, being an excess occurring at the end of any year (as defined in subsection (4) of that section), except, if it ends with another chargeable event, the final year.

(2) Subsection (4) of section 540 shall apply for the purposes of this section as it applies for purposes of that section.

(3) The provisions of section 541, except subsection (3), shall, so far as appropriate and subject to subsection (4) below, apply to capital redemption policies as they apply to policies of life assurance.

(4) Where a chargeable event happens in relation to a capital redemption policy which has previously been assigned for money or money's worth, section 541 shall have effect in relation thereto as if, for the references to the total amount previously paid under the policy by way of premiums, there were substituted references to the amount or value of the consideration given for the last such assignment, plus the total amount of the premiums paid under the policy since that assignment.

Former enactments.—TA 1970, s. 398; FA 1975, Sch. 2, paras. 9(4), 14.

546. Calculation of certain amounts for purposes of sections 540, 542 and 545

(1) For the purposes of sections 540, 542 and 545, there shall be calculated as at the end of each year—

  (*a*) the value, as at the time of surrender or assignment, of any part of or share in the rights conferred by the policy or contract which has been assigned or surrendered during the period ending with the end of that year and beginning with the commencement of the first year which falls wholly after 13th March 1975; and
  (*b*) the appropriate portion of any payment made up to the end of that period by way of premium or as a lump sum consideration;

and the appropriate portion of any payment shall be one-twentieth for the year in which it is made, increased by a further one-twentieth for each of the subsequent years, up to a maximum of nineteen, but excluding therefrom any such one-twentieth for any year before that first year.

(2) The reckonable aggregate value referred to in those sections shall be—
   (a) the sum of the values calculated under subsection (1) above; less
   (b) the sum of the values so calculated for a previous year and brought into account on the previous happening of a chargeable event.

(3) The allowable aggregate amount referred to in those sections shall be—
   (a) the aggregate of the appropriate portions calculated under subsection (1) above;
less
   (b) the aggregate of the appropriate portions so calculated for a previous year and brought into account on the previous happening of a chargeable event.

(4) In this section "year" means the 12 months beginning with the making of the insurance or contract and any subsequent period of 12 months; except that—
   (a) death, the maturity of the policy or the surrender of the rights conferred by the policy or contract shall be treated as ending the final year; and
   (b) if the final year would by virtue of paragraph (a) above begin and end in the same year of assessment, the final year and the year preceding it shall together be one year.

(5) There shall be disregarded for the purposes of this section any amount which was treated under section 72(9) of the Finance Act 1984 as an additional premium.

Former enactments.—Sub-s. (1): FA 1975, Sch. 2, para. 9(5), (8).
Sub-ss. (2), (3): FA 1975, Sch. 2, para. 9(6), (7).
Sub-s. (4): FA 1975, Sch. 2, para. 9(9).
Sub-s. (5): FA 1984, s. 72(9)(c).

547. Method of charging gain to tax

(1) Where under section 541, 543 or 545 a gain is to be treated as arising in connection with any policy or contract—
   (a) if, immediately before the happening of the chargeable event in question, the rights conferred by the policy or contract were vested in an individual as beneficial owner, or were held on trusts created by an individual (including trusts arising under section 11 of the Married Women's Property Act 1882, section 2 of the Married Women's Policies of Assurance (Scotland) Act 1880 or section 4 of the Law Reform (Husband and Wife) Act (Northern Ireland) 1964 or as security for a debt owed by an individual, the amount of the gain shall be deemed to form part of that individual's total income for the year in which the event happened;
   [(b) if, immediately before the happening of that event, those rights were in the beneficial ownership of a company, or were held on trusts created, or as security for a debt owed, by a company, the amount of the gain shall be deemed to form part of the company's income (chargeable under Case VI of Schedule D) for the accounting period in which the event happened;][1]
   (c) if, immediately before the happening of that event, those rights were vested in personal representatives, within the meaning of Part XVI, the amount of the gain shall be deemed for the purposes of that Part to be part of the aggregate income of the estate of the deceased.

(2) Nothing in subsection (1) above shall apply to any amount which is chargeable to tax apart from that subsection.

(3) Where, immediately before the happening of a chargeable event, the rights conferred by any policy or contract were vested beneficially in two or more persons, or were held on trusts created, or as security for a debt owed, by two or more persons, subsection (1)(a) and (b) above shall have effect in relation to each of those persons as if he had been the sole owner, settlor or debtor, but with references to the amount of the gain construed as references to the part of it proportionate to his share in the rights at the time of the event or, as the case may require, when the trusts were created.

(4) References in subsections (1) and (3) above to the rights conferred by a policy or contract are, in the case of an assignment of a share only in any rights, references to that share.

(5) Subject to subsections (6) and (7) below and section 550, where by virtue of subsection (1) above, a sum is included in an individual's total income—
   (a) no assessment shall be made on him in respect of income tax at the basic rate on that sum but he shall be treated as having paid income tax at the basic rate on that sum or, if

his total income is reduced by any deductions, on so much of that sum as is part of his total income as so reduced;

(b) no repayment shall be made of the income tax treated by virtue of paragraph (a) above as having been paid; and

(c) the sum so included shall be treated for the purposes of sections 348 and 349(1) as not brought into charge to income tax.

(6) Where under section 543 a gain is to be treated as arising in connection with a contract for a life annuity made after 26th March 1974—

(a) this section shall have effect, in relation to the gain, as if subsection (5) were omitted; and

(b) the gain shall be chargeable to tax under Case VI of Schedule D; but

(c) any relief under section 550 shall be computed as if this subsection had not been enacted.

(7) Where under section 541 or 543 a gain is to be treated as arising in connection with a policy issued by a friendly society in the course of tax exempt life or endowment business, this section shall have effect in relation to the gain as if subsection (5) were omitted, but any relief under section 550 shall be computed as if this subsection had not been enacted.

[(8) Subsection (1)(b) above shall not have effect as respects—

(a) a policy of life insurance issued in respect of an insurance made before 14th March 1989,

(b) a contract for a life annuity made before that date, or

(c) a capital redemption policy issued in respect of an insurance made before that date, or issued by a company resident in the United Kingdom in respect of an insurance made on or after that date.][1]

Former enactments.—Sub-ss. (1), (2): TA 1970, s. 399(1); FA 1972, Sch. 24, para. 24.
Sub-ss. (3), (4): TA 1970, s. 399(2), (3).
Sub-s. (5): TA 1970, s. 399(4); FA 1971, Sch. 6, para 42.
Sub-s. (6): FA 1975, Sch. 2, para. 17.
Sub-s. (7): FA 1985, s. 41(9); FA 1987, s. 30(8).
Cross references.—See FA 1988, s. 102(3) (taxation of capital gains at income tax rates: the higher rate not to apply to the whole of the amount which is deemed to be included in the total income by virtue of sub-s. (1)(a) above).
Amendments.—[1] Sub-s. (1)(b) substituted by FA 1989, Sch. 9, paras. 1, 5, 8 in relation to chargeable events in accounting periods beginning after 31 March 1989.
[2] Sub-s. (8) inserted by *ibid.*

548. Deemed surrender of certain loans

(1) Where—

(a) under section 547 a gain arising in connection with a policy or contract would be treated as forming part of an individual's total income [or the income of a company][1]; and

(b) the policy was issued in respect of an insurance made after 26th March 1974 or the contract was made after that date; and

(c) any sum is at any time after the making of the insurance or contract lent to or at the direction of that individual [or company][1] by or by arrangement with the body issuing the policy or, as the case may be, the body with which the contract was made;

then, subject to [subsections (3) and (3A)][2] below, the same results shall follow under this Chapter as if at the time the sum was lent there had been a surrender of part of the rights conferred by the policy or contract and the sum had been paid as consideration for the surrender.

(2) If the whole or any part of the sum is repaid the repayment shall be treated, for the purpose of computing any gain arising on the happening, at the end of the final year, of a chargeable event, as a payment of a premium or lump sum consideration.

(3) Subsections (1) and (2) above do not apply in relation—

(a) to a policy if—

(i) it is a qualifying policy; and

(ii) either interest at a commercial rate is payable on the sum lent or the sum is lent to a full-time employee of the body issuing the policy for the purpose of assisting him in the purchase or improvement of a dwelling used or to be used as his only or main residence;

(b) to a contract if and to the extent that interest on the sum lent is eligible for relief under section 353 by virtue of section 365.

[(3A) Subsections (1) and (2) do not apply where the rights conferred by the policy or contract are in the beneficial ownership of a company, or are held on trusts created, or as security for a debt owed, by a company, if the policy was issued in respect of an insurance made before 14th March 1989 or the contract was made before that date.]³

(4) In this section "final year" has the same meaning as in section 546.

Former enactments.—FA 1975, Sch. 2, para. 16; FA 1976, s. 35.
Amendments.—¹ Words in sub-s. (1)(*a*), (*c*) inserted by FA 1989, Sch. 9, paras. 1, 6, 8 with effect from 14 March 1989.
² Words in sub-s. (1) substituted by *ibid*.
³ Sub-s. (3A) inserted by *ibid*.

549. Certain deficiencies allowable as deductions

(1) Subject to subsections (2) below, where such an excess as is mentioned in section 541(1)(*a*) or (*b*) or 543(1)(*a*)—
   (*a*) would be treated as a gain arising in connection with a policy or contract, and
   (*b*) would form part of an individual's total income for the year of assessment in which the final year ends,
a corresponding deficiency occurring at the end of the final year shall be allowable as a deduction from his total income for that year of assessment, so far as it does not exceed the total amount treated as a gain by virtue of section 541(1)(*d*) or 543(1)(*c*) on the previous happenings of chargeable events.

(2) Except where the deficiency mentioned in subsection (1) above occurs in connection with a contract for a life annuity made after 26th March 1974, the deduction allowable under that subsection shall be made only for the purposes of ascertaining the individual's excess liability, that is to say, the excess (if any) of his liability to income tax over what it would be if all income tax were chargeable at the basic rate to the exclusion of any higher rate.

(3) In this section "final year" has the same meaning as in section 546.

Former enactments.—FA 1975, Sch. 2, para. 19; F(No. 2)A 1975, s. 40.
Cross references.—See FA 1988, s. 102(2)(*b*) (taxation of capital gains at income tax rates: higher rate exemption in respect of the amount deducted under sub-s. (2) above).

550. Relief where gain charged at a higher rate

(1) The following provisions of this section shall have effect for the purposes of giving relief, on a claim in that behalf being made by him to the Board, in respect of any increase in an individual's liability to tax which is attributable to one or more amounts being included in his total income for a year of assessment by virtue of section 547(1)(*a*).

(2) Where one amount only is so included, there shall be computed—
   (*a*) the tax which would be chargeable in respect of the amount if relief under this section were not available and it constituted the highest part of the claimant's total income for the year, and
   (*b*) the tax (if any) which would be chargeable in respect of the amount if calculated, in accordance with subsection (3) below, by reference to its appropriate fraction;
and the relief shall consist of a reduction or repayment of tax equal to the difference between the two amounts of tax so computed, or, if tax would not be chargeable on a calculation by reference to the appropriate fraction, of a reduction or repayment of the tax equal to the tax computed under paragraph (*a*) above.

(3) In subsection (2) above "appropriate fraction" means, in relation to any amount, such a sum as bears thereto the same proportion as that borne by one to the number of complete years for which the policy or contract has run before the happening of the chargeable event; and the computation required by paragraph (*b*) of that subsection shall be made by applying to the amount in question such rate or rates of income tax, other than the basic rate, as would apply if it were reduced to that fraction and, as so reduced, still constituted the highest part of the claimant's total income for the year.

(4) For the purposes of subsection (3) above the number of years for which a policy of life insurance has run before the happening of a chargeable event shall be calculated, where appropriate, from the issue of the earliest related policy, meaning, any policy in relation to which the policy is a new policy within the meaning of paragraph 17 of Schedule 15, any policy in relation to which that policy is such a policy, and so on.

(5) Where a chargeable event on the happening of which an amount is included in an individual's total income by virtue of section 547(1)(*a*) follows the happening of another chargeable event in relation to the same policy or contract, and each of those events is such an excess as is mentioned in section 540(1)(*a*)(*v*), 542(1) or 545(1)(*d*), subsection (3) and (4) above shall have effect in relation to that amount as if the number of complete years referred to in subsection (3) were the number of complete years elapsing between that other event (or, if more that one, the last of them) and the first-mentioned event.

(6) Where by virtue of section 547(1)(*a*) two or more amounts are included in an individual's total income for any year of assessment, subsections (2) and (3) above shall apply as if they together constituted a single amount, but with the appropriate fraction of the whole determined by adding together the appropriate fractions of the individual amounts.

(7) A provision of this section requiring tax to be calculated as if an amount constituted the highest part of a claimant's total income shall apply notwithstanding any other provision of the Income Tax Acts directing any other amount to be treated as the highest part thereof, but, for the purposes of this section, a claimant's total income shall be deemed not to include any amount in respect of which he is chargeable to tax under section 34, 35, 36 or 148.

Former enactments.—Sub-ss. (1)–(4): TA 1970, s. 400(1)–(3); FA 1971, Sch. 6, para. 43.
Sub-s. (5): FA 1975, Sch. 2, para. 18.
Sub-ss. (6), (7): TA 1970, s. 400(4), (5); FA 1971, Sch. 6, para. 43.
Cross references.—See FA 1988, s. 102(3) (taxation of capital gains at income tax rates: top slicing relief in respect of capital gains tax).

551. Right of individual to recover tax from trustees

(1) Where—

   (*a*) an amount is included in an individual's income by virtue of section 547(1)(*a*), and
   (*b*) the rights or share in question were held immediately before the happening of the chargeable event on trust,

the individual shall be entitled to recover from the trustees, to the extent of any sums, or to the value of any benefits, received by them by reason of the event, an amount equal to that (if any) by which the tax with which he is chargeable for the year of assessment in question, reduced by the amount of any relief available under section 550 in respect of the amount so included, exceeds the tax with which he would have been chargeable for the year if that amount had not been so included.

(2) Where, for the purposes of relief under section 550, two or more amounts are to be treated as one, the reduction required by subsection (1) above on account of the relief available in respect of any of them shall consist of a proportionate part of the relief available in respect of their aggregate.

(3) An individual may require the Board to certify any amount recoverable by him by virtue of this section, and the certificate shall be conclusive evidence of the amount.

Former enactment.—TA 1970, s. 401.

552. Information: duty of insurers

(1) Subject to subsections (2) to (5) below, where a chargeable event within the meaning of this Chapter has happened in relation to any policy or contract, the body by or with whom the policy or contract was issued, entered into or effected shall, within three months of the event or, if it is a death or an assignment, within three months of their receiving written notification thereof, deliver to the inspector a certificate specifying—

   (*a*) the name and address of the policy holder;
   (*b*) the nature of the event, and the date on which it happened;
   (*c*) as may be required for computing the gain to be treated as arising by virtue of this Chapter—

      (i) the surrender value of the policy, or the sum payable, or other benefits to be conferred, by the body in question by reason of the event;
      (ii) the amount or value of any relevant capital payments;
      (iii) the amounts previously paid under the policy or contract by way of premiums or otherwise by way of consideration for an annuity; and
      (iv) the capital element in any payment previously made on account of an annuity;

   (*d*) the number of years relevant for computing the appropriate fraction of the gain for the purposes of section 550(3).

(2) Subsection (1) above shall not apply where—

(a) the body in question are satisfied that no gain is to be treated as arising by reason of the event, or
(b) the amount of the surrender value or sum, or the value of the other benefits, referred to in paragraph (c)(i) of that subsection, together with the amount or value of any payments within paragraph (c)(ii) of that subsection, does not exceed £500, [or]¹
[(c) the event is a chargeable event only because of section 540(5A).]¹

but the inspector may by notice require a like certificate in any such case, and it shall be the duty of the body to deliver the certificate within 30 days of receipt of the notice.

(3) Where the chargeable event is an assignment of all the rights conferred by the policy or contract the certificate shall also specify any such excess as is mentioned in section 540(1)(a)(v), 542(1) or 545(1)(d) which has occurred since the relevant date, the date on which it occurred and the value of the part of or share in the rights which have been surrendered or assigned since the relevant date.

(4) Where the chargeable event is the occurrence of such an excess as is mentioned in section 540(1)(a)(v), 542(1) or 545(1)(d), subsections (1) and (2) above shall apply with the omission of paragraph (b) of subsection (2) and the certificate shall also specify the value of the part of or share in the rights surrendered or assigned in any year since the relevant date and the amounts paid by way of premiums in any year since the relevant date.

(5) In subsections (3) and (4) above—
"year" has the same meaning as in section 546(4); and
"the relevant date", in relation to any certificate, means the date of the chargeable event in respect of which the last certificate under this section was delivered or, if none was delivered, the commencement of the policy or contract.

Former enactments.—Sub-ss. (1), (2): TA 1970, s. 402.
Sub-ss. (3)–(5): FA 1975, Sch. 2, para. 20.
Amendments.—¹ Sub-s. (2)(c) and the preceding word "or" inserted by FA 1989, Sch. 9, paras. 1, 7, 8 with effect from 14 March 1989.

553. Non-resident policies and off-shore capital redemption policies

(1) If, in the case of a substitution of policies falling within paragraph 25(1) or (3) of Schedule 15, the new policy is a qualifying policy, section 540 shall have effect with the following modifications—
(a) the surrender of the rights conferred by the old policy shall not be a chargeable event (within the meaning of that section); and
(b) the new policy shall be treated as having been issued in respect of an insurance made on the day referred to in paragraph 26 of that Schedule.

(2) If at any time neither the conditions in sub-paragraph (3) nor those in sub-paragraph (4) of paragraph 24 of Schedule 15 are fulfilled with respect to a new non-resident policy which has previously become a qualifying policy, then, from that time onwards, this Chapter shall apply in relation to the policy as if it were not a qualifying policy.

(3) Subject to subsection (5) below, on the happening of a chargeable event in relation to a new non-resident policy or a new offshore capital redemption policy, the amount which, apart from this subsection, would by virtue of section 541 be treated as a gain arising in connection with the policy shall be reduced by multiplying it by the fraction—

$$\frac{A}{B}$$

where
A is the number of days on which the policy holder was resident in the United Kingdom in the period for which the policy has run before the happening of the chargeable event; and
B is the number of days in that period.

(4) The calculation of the number of days in the period referred to in subsection (3) above shall be made in like manner as is provided in section 550(4), substituting a reference to the number of days for the reference to the number of years.

(5) If, on the happening of the chargeable event referred to in subsection (3) above or at any time during the period referred to in that subsection, the policy is or was held by a trustee resident outside the United Kingdom or by two or more trustees any of whom is or was so resident, no reduction shall be made under that subsection unless—
(a) the policy was issued in respect of an insurance made on or before 19th March 1985; and

    (*b*) on that date the policy was held by a trustee who was so resident or, as the case may be, by two or more trustees any of whom was so resident.

(6) Subject to subsection (7) below, where, under section 541, a gain (reduced in accordance with subsection (3) above) is to be treated as arising in connection with a new non-resident policy or a new offshore capital redemption policy—

  (*a*) section 547 shall have effect, in relation to the gain, as if subsection (5) were omitted; and
  (*b*) the gain shall be chargeable to tax under Case VI of Schedule D;

but any relief under section 550 shall be computed as if this subsection had not been enacted.

(7) Paragraphs (*a*) and (*b*) of subsections (6) above do not apply to a gain arising in connection with a new non-resident policy if the conditions in either sub-paragraph (3) or sub-paragraph (4) of paragraph 24 of Schedule 15 are fulfilled at all times between the date on which the policy was issued and the date on which the gain is treated as arising.

(8) Where a claim is made under section 550 in respect of the amount of a gain treated as arising in connection with a new non-resident policy or a new offshore capital redemption policy (with or without other amounts), the "appropriate fraction" which, in accordance with subsection (2) of that section, is to be applied to that amount shall be modified by deducting from the number of complete years referred to in subsection (3) of that section any complete years during which the policy holder was not resident in the United Kingdom.

(9) Subsection (5) of section 550 shall not apply in relation to a new non-resident policy or a new offshore capital redemption policy.

(10) In this section—

  "chargeable event" has, subject to subsection (1) above, the meaning given by section 540 or, as the case may be, 545;
  "new non-resident policy" has the meaning given by paragraph 24 of Schedule 15; and
  "new offshore capital redemption policy" means a capital redemption policy, as defined in section 539(3), which—

    (*a*) is issued in respect of an insurance made after 22nd February 1984; and
    (*b*) is so issued by a company resident outside the United Kingdom.

Former enactments.—FA 1984, s. 76(5), Sch. 15, Pt. III; FA 1985, s. 51.

554. Borrowings on life policies to be treated as income in certain cases

(1) Where—

  (*a*) under any contract or arrangements made on or after 7th April 1949, provision is made for the making to any person, at intervals until the happening of an event or contingency dependent on human life, of payments by way of loan; and
  (*b*) under the contract or arrangements, the loans are secured upon a policy of life assurance which assures moneys payable on the happening of such an event or contingency and need not be repaid until the policy moneys become payable; and
  (*c*) the amount of the moneys payable on the happening of the event or contingency is made by the policy to increase by reference to the length of a period ending on the happening of that event or contingency;

the payments made by way of loan shall be treated for tax purposes as annual payments falling within Case III of Schedule D, or, if they are made to a person residing in the United Kingdom and the contract or arrangements were made outside the United Kingdom, as income from a possession out of the United Kingdom and, for income tax, as falling within section 65(1).

(2) The amount of the moneys payable under a policy of life assurance shall not be deemed for the purposes of this section to be made to increase by reference to the length of a period ending on the happening of an event or contingency dependent on human life by reason only that those moneys are to increase from time to time if profits are made by the person liable under the policy.

(3) This section shall not apply to any payments by way of loan if the Board are satisfied as respects those payments that it is not one of the objects of the contract or arrangements under which the payments are made that the recipient of them should enjoy the advantages which would, apart from any question of liability to tax, be enjoyed by a person in receipt of payments of the same amounts paid at the same times by way of annuity.

Former enactment.—TA 1970, s. 405.

CHAPTER III

ENTERTAINERS AND SPORTSMEN

555. Payment of tax

(1) Where a person who is an entertainer or sportsman of a prescribed description performs an activity of a prescribed description in the United Kingdom ("a relevant activity"), this Chapter shall apply if he is not resident in the United Kingdom in the year of assessment in which the relevant activity is performed.

(2) Where a payment is made (to whatever person) and it has a connection of a prescribed kind with the relevant activity, the person by whom it is made shall on making it deduct out of it a sum representing income tax and shall account to the Board for the sum.

(3) Where a transfer is made (to whatever person) and it has a connection of a prescribed kind with the relevant activity, the person by whom it is made shall account to the Board for a sum representing income tax.

(4) The sums mentioned in subsections (2) and (3) above shall be such as are calculated in accordance with prescribed rules but shall in no case exceed the relevant proportion of the payment concerned or of the value of what is transferred, as the case may be; and "relevant proportion" here means a proportion equal to the basic rate of income tax for the year of assessment in which the payment or, as the case may be, the transfer is made.

(5) In this Chapter—
  (*a*) references to a payment include references to a payment by way of loan of money; and
  (*b*) references to a transfer do not include references to a transfer of money but, subject to that, include references to a temporary transfer (as by way of loan) and to a transfer of a right (whether or not a right to receive money).

(6) This section shall not apply to payments or transfers of such a kind as may be prescribed.

(7) Regulations may—
  (*a*) make provision enabling the Board to serve notices requiring persons who make payments or transfers to which subsection (2) or (3) above applies to furnish to the Board particulars of a prescribed kind in respect of payments or transfers;
  (*b*) make provision requiring persons who make payments or transfers to which subsection (2) or (3) above applies to make, at prescribed times and for prescribed periods, returns to the Board containing prescribed information about payments or transfers and the income tax for which those persons are accountable in respect of them;
  (*c*) make provision for the collection and recovery of such income tax, provision for assessments and claims to be made in respect of it, and provision for the payment of interest on it;
  (*d*) adapt, or modify the effect of, any enactment relating to income tax for the purpose of making any such provision as is mentioned in paragraphs (*a*) to (*c*) above.

(8) Where in accordance with subsections (2) to (7) above a person pays a sum to the Board, they shall treat it as having been paid on account of a liability of another person to income tax or corporation tax; and the liability and the other person shall be such as are found in accordance with prescribed rules.

(9) Where the sum exceeds the liability concerned, the Board shall pay such of the sum as is appropriate to the other person mentioned in subsection (8) above.

(10) Where no liability is found as mentioned in subsection (8) above, the Board shall pay the sum to the person to whom the payment or transfer to which subsection (2) or (3) above applies, and which gave rise to the payment of the sum concerned to the Board, was made.

(11) In construing references to a sum in subsections (8) to (10) above, anything representing interest shall be ignored.

Former enactments.—Sub-s. (1): FA 1986, Sch. 11, para. 1.
Sub-s. (2): FA 1986, Sch. 11, para. 2(1).
Sub-s. (3): FA 1986, Sch. 11, para. 2(3).
Sub-s. (4): FA 1986, Sch. 11, para. 2(2), (4).
Sub-s. (5): FA 1986, Sch. 11, para. 2(5), (6).
Sub-s. (6): FA 1986, Sch. 11, para. 2(7).

Sub-s. (7): FA 1986, Sch. 11, para. 3(1).
Sub-ss. (8)–(11): FA 1986, Sch. 11, para. 4.
Cross references.—See FA 1988, s. 130(7)(*c*)(iii), (9) (company migration: provisions for securing payment by migrating company of tax under this section and FA 1986, Sch. 11, paras. 1–4).

556. Activity treated as trade etc. and attribution of income

(1) Where a payment is made (to whatever person) and it has a connection of the prescribed kind with the relevant activity, the activity shall be treated for the purposes of the Tax Acts as performed in the course of a trade, profession or vocation exercised by the entertainer or sportsman within the United Kingdom, to the extent that (apart from this subsection) it would not be so treated.

This subsection shall not apply where the relevant activity is performed in the course of an office or employment.

(2) Where a payment is made to a person who fulfils a prescribed description but is not the entertainer or sportsman and the payment has a connection of the prescribed kind with the relevant activity—

(*a*) the entertainer or sportsman shall be treated for the purposes of the Tax Acts as the person to whom the payment is made; and
(*b*) the payment shall be treated for those purposes as made to him in the course of a trade, profession or vocation exercised by him within the United Kingdom (whether or not he would be treated as exercising such a trade, profession or vocation apart from this paragraph).

(3) Regulations may provide—

(*a*) for the deduction, in computing any profits or gains of the entertainer or sportsman arising from the payment, of expenses incurred by other persons in relation to the payment;
(*b*) that any liability to tax (whether of the entertainer or sportsman or of another person) which would, apart from subsection (2) above, arise in relation to the payment shall not arise or shall arise only to a prescribed extent.

(4) References in this section to a payment include references to a transfer.

(5) This section shall not apply unless the payment or transfer is one to which section 555(2) or (3) applies, and subsections (2) and (3) above shall not apply in such circumstances as may be prescribed.

Former enactments.—Sub-s. (1): FA 1986, Sch. 11, para. 6(1), (3).
Sub-ss. (2), (3): FA 1986, Sch. 11, para. 7(2), (3).
Sub-s. (4): FA 1986, Sch. 11, paras. 6(4), 7(6).
Sub-s. (5): FA 1986, Sch. 11, paras. 6(2), 7(5).

557. Charge on profits or gains

(1) Where income tax is chargeable under Case I or II of Schedule D on the profits or gains arising from payment (made to whatever person) and the payments have a connection of the prescribed kind with relevant activities of the entertainer or sportsman, such tax shall be charged—

(*a*) as if those payments were received in the course of one trade, profession or vocation exercised by the entertainer or sportsman within the United Kingdom separately from any other trade, profession or vocation exercised by him; and
(*b*) for each of assessment, on the full amount of the profits or gains arising in the year from those payments.

(2) Regulations may—

(*a*) provide for the apportionment of profits or gains between different trades, professions or vocations of the entertainer or sportsman;
(*b*) provide for the apportionment between different years of assessment of the profits or gains arising from relevant activities of the entertainer or sportsman;
(*c*) provide for losses sustained in any trade, profession or vocation of the entertainer or sportsman to be deducted from or set off against the profits or gains of another trade, profession or vocation of the entertainer or sportsman;
(*d*) provide that prescribed provisions of the Tax Acts about losses, or about expenditure, shall not apply (or shall apply with prescribed modifications) in prescribed circumstances relating to the entertainer or sportsman.

(3) References in subsection (2)(*a*) and (*c*) above to a trade, profession or vocation of the entertainer or sportsman include references to that first mentioned in subsection (1)(*a*) above as well as to any other exercised by him.

(4) References in this section to a payment include references to a transfer.

(5) This section shall not apply in the case of a payment or transfer unless it is one to which section 555(2) or (3) applies.

Former enactment.—FA 1986, Sch. 11, para. 8.

558. Supplementary provisions

(1) A payment to which subsection (2) of section 555 applies shall be treated for the purposes of the Tax Acts as not diminished by the sum mentioned in that subsection.

(2) Regulations may provide that for the purposes of the Tax Acts the value of what is transferred by a transfer to which section 555(3) applies shall be calculated in accordance with prescribed rules.

(3) In particular, rules may include provision for the calculation of an amount representing the actual worth of what is transferred, for that amount to be treated as a net amount corresponding to a gross amount from which income tax at the basic rate has been deducted, and for the gross amount to be taken to be the value of what is transferred.

(4) No obligation as to secrecy imposed by statute or otherwise shall preclude the Board or an authorised officer of the Board from disclosing to any person who appears to the Board to have an interest in the matter information which may be relevant to determining whether section 555(2) or (3) applies to a payment or transfer.

(5) Regulations may make provision generally for giving effect to this Chapter, and may make different provision for different cases or descriptions of case.

(6) In this Chapter—
 "regulations" means regulations made by the Treasury; and
 "prescribed" means prescribed by regulations.

Former enactments.—Sub-ss. (1)–(3): FA 1986, Sch. 11, para. 9.
Sub-s. (4): FA 1986, Sch. 11, para. 5.
Sub-s. (5): FA 1986, Sch. 11, paras. 10, 11(2).
Sub-s. (6): FA 1986, Sch. 11, para. 11(1), (3).

CHAPTER IV

SUB-CONTRACTORS IN THE CONSTRUCTION INDUSTRY

559. Deductions on account of tax etc. from payments to certain sub-contractors

(1) Subject to subsection (2) below, where a contract relating to construction operations is not a contract of employment but—

(*a*) one party to the contract is a sub-contractor; and
(*b*) another party to the contract ("the contractor") either is a sub-contractor under another such contract relating to all or any of the construction operations or is a person to whom section 560(2) applies,

this section shall apply to any payments which are made under the contract and are so made by the contractor to—

(i) the sub-contractor;
(ii) a person nominated by the sub-contractor or the contractor; or
(iii) a person nominated by a person who is a sub-contractor under another such contract relating to all or any of the construction operations.

(2) Subsection (1) above shall not apply to any payment made under the contract in question if the person to whom it is made or, if it is made to a nominee, each of the following persons, that is to say, the nominee, the person who nominated him and the person for whose labour (or, where that person is a company, for whose employees' or officers' labour) the payment is made, is excepted from this section in relation to those payments by virtue of section 561.

(3) Subsection (2) above does not apply to so much of any payment made under the contract in question to a person falling within subsection (4) of section 561 as exceeds, or in aggregate with other payments specified in regulations made under subsection (5) of that section exceeds, the limit prescribed by those regulations.

(4) On making a payment to which this section applies the contractor shall deduct from it a sum equal to [25 per cent.][1] of so much of the payment as is not shown to represent the direct cost to any other person of materials used or to be used in carrying out the construction operations to which the contract under which the payment is to be made relates; and the sum so deducted shall be paid to the Board and shall be treated for the purposes of income tax or, as the case may be, corporation tax—

(*a*) as not diminishing the payment; but
(*b*) subject to subsection (5) below, as being income tax or, as the case may be, corporation tax paid in respect of the profits or gains of the trade, profession or vocation of the person for whose (or for whose employees' or officers') labour the contractor makes the payment.

(5) Where a sum deducted and paid to the Board under subsection (4) above is more than sufficient to discharge the liability to income tax of the person referred to in paragraph (*b*) of that subsection in respect of the profits or gains mentioned in that paragraph, so much of the excess as is required to discharge any liability of that person for Class 4 contributions shall be treated as being, for the purposes of the Social Security Act, Class 4 contributions paid in respect of the profits or gains so mentioned.

(6) References in section 1(1) of the Preferential Payments (Bankruptcies and Arrangements) Act (Northern Ireland) 1964 to sums due on account of tax deductions for any period shall be construed as including references to any amounts due from any person in respect of deductions required to be made by him under this section.

(7) For the purposes of this Chapter a payment (including a payment by way of loan) that has the effect of discharging an obligation under a contract relating to construction operations shall be taken to be made under the contract; and if—

(*a*) the obligation is to make a payment to a person within subsection (1)(i) to (iii) above, but
(*b*) the payment discharging that obligation is made to a person not within those paragraphs,

the payment shall for those purposes be taken to be made to the first-mentioned person.

(8) In this section—

"Class 4 contributions" means Class 4 contributions within the meaning of the Social

Security Act 1975 or, as the case may be, the Social Security (Northern Ireland) Act 1975; and
"the Social Security Act" means whichever of those Acts is the one under which the contribution in question is payable.

Former enactments.—Sub-ss. (1)–(3): F(No. 2)A 1975, ss. 69(1), 70A(2); FA 1982, Sch. 8, para. 5.
Sub-ss. (4), (5): F(No. 2)A 1975, s. 69(4), (5); FA 1987, s. 23.
Sub-s. (6): F(No. 2)A 1975, ss. 69(7), 71(6).
Sub-s. (7): FA 1972, s. 71(5); FA 1982, Sch. 8, para. 6.
Sub-s. (8): F(No. 2)A 1975, s. 69(10).
Cross references.—See TMA 1970, s. 7(4)(*b*) (duty to notify inspector of taxes of liability to tax in respect of income consisting of a payment under this section);
FA 1988, s. 130(7)(*d*), (9) (company migration: provisions for securing payment by migrating company of tax under sub-s. (4) above and F(No. 2)A 1975, s. 69).
Amendments.—[1] Percentage in sub-s. (4) substituted for "27 per cent" by FA 1988, s. 28 in relation to payments made after 30 October 1988.

560. Persons who are sub-contractors or contractors for purposes of Chapter IV

(1) For the purposes of this Chapter a party to a contract relating to construction operations is a sub-contractor if, under the contract—

(*a*) he is under a duty to the contractor to carry out the operations, or to furnish his own labour (that is to say, in the case of a company, the labour of employees or officers of the company) or the labour of others in the carrying out of the operations or to arrange for the labour of others to be furnished in the carrying out of the operations; or

(*b*) he is answerable to the contractor for the carrying out of the operations by others, whether under a contract or under other arrangements made or to be made by him.

(2) This subsection applies to the following persons, that is to say—

(*a*) any person carrying on a business which includes construction operations;
(*b*) any local authority;
(*c*) any development corporation or new town commission;
(*d*) the Commission for the New Towns;
(*e*) the Housing Corporation, [Housing for Wales][1] a housing association, a housing trust, the Scottish Special Housing Association, and the Northern Ireland Housing Executive;
(*f*) a person carrying on a business at any time if—

(i) his average annual expenditure on construction operations in the period of three years ending with the end of the last period of account before that time exceeds £250,000, or
(ii) where he was not carrying on the business at the beginning of that period of three years, one-third of his total expenditure on construction operations for the part of that period during which he has been carrying on the business exceeds £250,000;

and in paragraph (*f*) "period of account" means a period for which an account is made up in relation to the business in question.

(3) Where section 559(1)(*b*) begins to apply to any person in any period of account by virtue of his falling within subsection (2)(*f*) above, it shall continue to apply to him until he satisfies the Board that his expenditure on construction operations has been less than £250,000 in each of three successive years beginning in or after that period of account.

(4) Where the whole or part of a trade is transferred by a company ("the transferor") to another company ("the transferee") and section 343 has effect in relation to the transfer, then in determining for the purposes of this section the amount of expenditure incurred by the transferee—

(*a*) the whole or, as the case may be, a proportionate part of any expenditure incurred by the transferor at a time before the transfer shall be treated as if it had been incurred at that time by the transferee; and
(*b*) where only a part of the trade is transferred the expenditure shall be apportioned in such manner as appears to the Board, or on appeal to the Commissioners, to be just and reasonable.

(5) In this section—

"development corporation" has the same meaning as in the New Towns Act 1981 or the New Towns (Scotland) Act 1968;
"housing association" has the same meaning as in the Housing Associations Act 1985 or the Housing (Northern Ireland) Order 1981;

"housing trust" has the same meaning as in the Housing Associations Act 1985; and "new town commission" has the same meaning as in the New Towns Act (Northern Ireland) 1965.

Former enactments.—Sub-s. (1): F(No. 2)A 1975, s. 69(2).
Sub-s. (2)(*a*)–(*e*): F(No. 2)A 1975, s. 69(3).
Sub-s. (2)(*f*): F(No. 2)A 1975, s. 69(3A); FA 1980, Sch. 8, para. 1.
Sub-ss. (3), (4): F(No. 2)A 1975, s. 69(3B), (3C); FA 1980, Sch. 8, para. 1.
Sub-s. (5): F(No. 2)A 1975, s. 71(3); New Towns Act 1981, Sch. 12, para. 16;
Housing (Consequential Provisions) Act 1985, Sch. 2, para. 28.
Amendments.—[1] Words in sub-s. (2)(*e*) inserted by the Housing Act 1988, Sch. 17, para. 116.

561. Exceptions from section 559

(1) Subject to the provisions of regulations under subsection (5) below or section 566(2), a person is excepted from section 559 in relation to payments made under a contract if a certificate under this section has been issued to that person and is in force when the payment is made, but—

(*a*) where the certificate has been issued to a person who becomes a partner in a firm, that person is not excepted in relation to payments made under contracts under which the firm or, where a person has nominated the firm to receive payments, the person who has nominated the firm is a sub-contractor; and

(*b*) where a certificate has been issued to a person as a partner in a firm, that person is excepted in relation only to payments made under contracts under which the firm or, where a person has nominated the firm to receive payments, the person who has nominated the firm, is a sub-contractor.

(2) If the Board are satisfied, on the application of an individual or a company, that—

(*a*) where the application is for the issue of a certificate to an individual (otherwise than as a partner in a firm), he satisfies the conditions set out in section 562;

(*b*) where the application is for the issue of a certificate to a person as a partner in a firm, that person satisfies the conditions set out in section 563 if he is an individual or, if a company, the conditions set out in section 565 and, in either case, the firm itself satisfies the conditions set out in section 564;

(*c*) where the application is for the issue of a certificate to a company, the company satisfies the conditions set out in section 565 and, if the Board have given a direction under subsection (4) below, each of the persons to whom any of the conditions set out in section 562 applies in accordance with the direction satisfies the conditions which so apply to him,

the Board shall issue to that individual or company a certificate excepting that individual or company (or, in a case falling within paragraph (*b*) above, that individual or company as a partner in the firm specified in the certificate) from section 559.

(3) References in subsection (2) above to an individual, a company or a firm satisfying conditions set out in section 562, 563, 564 or 565 include, in relation to a condition which may, by virtue of a provision of that section, be treated as being satisfied, references to that individual, company or firm being treated as satisfying that condition.

(4) This subsection applies to the holder of a certificate in force under this section if it was issued to him on the basis—

(*a*) that the condition in subsection (3) of section 562 was inapplicable to him by reason of paragraph (*b*) of that subsection; or

(*b*) that he satisfied that condition by virtue of subsection (7) of that section.

(5) The Board may make regulations securing that a person to whom subsection (4) above applies shall not be excepted from subsection (1) above in relation to a payment to the extent that the amount of the payment, or the aggregate amount of the payment and such other payments as may be prescribed by the regulations, exceeds a limit so prescribed.

(6) Where it appears to the Board, on an application made under subsection (2) above by a company, that the company—

(*a*) was incorporated on a date within the period of three years ending with the date of the application; or

(*b*) has not carried on business continuously throughout that period; or

(*c*) has carried on business continuously throughout that period but the business has not at all times in that period consisted of or included the carrying out of construction operations; or

(d) does not at the date of the application hold a certificate which is then in force under this section;

the Board may direct that the conditions set out in section 562 or such of them as are specified in the direction shall apply to the directors of the company and, if the company is a close company, to the persons who are the beneficial owners of shares in the company or to such of those directors or persons as are so specified as if each of them were an applicant for a certificate under this section (not being a certificate to the holder of which section 561(4) would apply).

In this subsection "director" has the same meaning as in Chapter II of Part V.

(7) Where it appears to the Board that there has been a change in the control of a company holding or applying for a certificate, the Board may make any such direction as is referred to in subsection (6) above.

(8) The Board may at any time cancel a certificate which has been issued to a person and is in force under this section if it appears to them that—

(a) it was issued on information which was false;
(b) if an application for the issue of a certificate under this section to that person were made at that time, the Board would refuse to issue a certificate;
(c) that person has permitted the certificate to be misused; or
(d) in the case of a certificate issued to a company, there has been a change in the control of the company and information with respect to that change has not been furnished in accordance with regulations under section 566(2);

and may by notice require that person to deliver the certificate to the Board within the time specified in the notice.

Section 840 shall apply for the purposes of paragraph (d) above.

(9) A person aggrieved by the refusal of an application for a certificate under this section or the cancellation of such a certificate may, by notice given to the Board within 30 days after the refusal or, as the case may be, cancellation, appeal to the General Commissioners or, if he so elects in the notice, to the Special Commissioners; and the jurisdiction of the Commissioners on such an appeal shall include jurisdiction to review any relevant decision taken by the Board in the exercise of their functions under this section.

(10) If any person, for the purpose of obtaining a certificate under this section—

(a) makes any statement, or furnishes any document, which he knows to be false in a material particular; or
(b) recklessly makes any statement, or furnishes any document, which is false in a material particular,

he shall be liable on summary conviction to a fine not exceeding £5,000.

(11) A person to whom a certificate is issued under this section or a voucher is given as required by regulations under section 566(2)(j) shall take all reasonable steps to ensure its safety; and any person who, without lawful authority or lawful excuse—

(a) disposes of any such certificate or voucher or any form supplied by the Board in connection with regulations made by virtue of section 566(2)(e); or
(b) possesses such a certificate, voucher or form or any document purporting to be such a certificate, voucher or form,

shall be liable on summary conviction to a fine not exceeding £5,000.

(12) Notwithstanding any enactment prescribing the period within which summary proceedings may be commenced, proceedings for an offence under subsection (10) or (11) above may be commenced at any time within three years from the commission of the offence.

(13) Without prejudice to section 843(3), this section shall come into force on 6th April 1988 to the exclusion of the provisions of section 70 of the Finance (No. 2) Act 1975 which are re-enacted in this section, but any offence committed before that date shall not be punishable under this section and neither this subsection nor any other provision of this Act shall prevent any such offence from being punishable as if this Act had not been passed.

Former enactments.—F(No. 2)A 1975, ss. 70(1)–(6), (9)–(11), 70A(1), (2), 71(4); FA 1982, Sch. 8, paras. 3, 5; F(No. 2)A 1987, s. 93.

562. Conditions to be satisfied by individuals

(1) In the case of an application for the issue of a certificate under section 561 to an individual (otherwise than as a partner in a firm) the following conditions are required to be satisfied by that individual.

(2) The applicant must be carrying on a business in the United Kingdom which satisfies the following conditions, that is to say—

(*a*) the business consists of or includes the carrying out of construction operations or the furnishing or arranging for the furnishing of labour in carrying out construction operations;
(*b*) the business is, to a substantial extent, carried on by means of an account with a bank;
(*c*) the business is carried on with proper records and in particular with records which are proper having regard to the obligations referred to in subsections (8) to (12) below; and
(*d*) the business is carried on from proper premises and with proper equipment, stock and other facilities.

(3) Unless the applicant—

(*a*) is the holder of a certificate in force under section 561 (other than a holder to whom section 561(4) applies), or
(*b*) supplies the Board with a guarantee by such person, for such amount and in such form as may be prescribed in regulations made by the Board,

he must throughout the period of three years ending with the date of his application for a certificate under section 561, have been employed in the United Kingdom as the holder of an office or employment or as a person carrying on a trade, profession or vocation.

(4) The applicant must not be receiving full-time education or full-time training.

(5) An applicant shall be treated as satisfying the condition in subsection (3) above if—

(*a*) he satisfies the Board that he has been employed as mentioned in that subsection throughout a period of three years beginning not more than six years before the date of his application and ending on a date before that date;
(*b*) he satisfies the Board either—

(i) that he has not been so employed throughout the whole of the period between those dates, or
(ii) that he has not been so employed during any part of that period other than a part for which he specifies he has been so employed; and

(*c*) where the applicant states that he has been outside the United Kingdom for the whole or part of the period mentioned in paragraph (*b*) above, he satisfies the Board of that fact by such evidence as may be prescribed in regulations made by the Board.

(6) The Board may for the purposes of subsections (3) and (5) above treat a person as having been employed as mentioned in subsection (3) above throughout a period of three years if during a period of three years he has been so employed except for a period or periods not exceeding six months or six months in aggregate.

(7) If the applicant satisfies the Board that he has during any period within six years before the date of his application attended a school or other establishment for the purpose of receiving full-time education or full-time training, this section shall have effect as if that period were one during which he was employed as mentioned in subsection (3) above.

(8) The applicant must, subject to subsection (10) below, have complied with all obligations imposed on him by or under the Tax Acts or the Management Act in respect of periods ending within the qualifying period and with all requests to supply to an inspector accounts of, or other information about, any business of his in respect of periods so ending.

(9) An applicant who at any time in the qualifying period had control of a company shall be taken not to satisfy the condition in subsection (8) above unless the company has satisfied that condition in relation to periods ending at a time within that period when he had control of it; and for this purpose "control" has the meaning given by section 840.

(10) An applicant or company that has failed to comply with such an obligation or request as is referred to in subsection (8) above shall nevertheless be treated as satisfying that condition as regards that obligation or request if the Board are of the opinion that the failure is minor and technical and does not give reason to doubt that the conditions mentioned in subsection (13) below will be satisfied.

(11) An applicant who must satisfy the Board under subsection (5) above that he has been

outside the United Kingdom for the whole or part of the period mentioned in subsection (5)(*b*) above must also satisfy them by such evidence as may be prescribed in regulations made by the Board that he has complied with any obligations imposed under the tax laws of any country in which he was living during that period which are comparable to the obligations mentioned in subsection (8) above.

(12) The applicant must, if any contribution has at any time during the qualifying period become due from him under Part I of the Social Security Act 1975 or Part I of the Social Security (Northern Ireland) Act 1975, have paid the contribution when it became due.

(13) There must be reason to expect that the applicant will, in respect of periods ending after the end of the qualifying period, comply with such obligations as are referred to in subsections (8) to (12) above and with such requests as are referred to in subsection (8) above.

(14) In this section "the qualifying period" means—

(*a*) in relation to a person who is within subsection (5) above, the period starting at the beginning of the last period of three years before his application throughout which he has been employed as mentioned in subsection (3) above (or is by virtue of subsection (6) above treated as having been so employed) and ending on the date of his application; and
(*b*) in the case of any other person, the period of three years ending with the date of his application.

Former enactments.—Sub-s. (2): F(No. 2)A 1975, Sch. 12, Pt. I, para. 1.
Sub-s. (3): F(No. 2)A 1975, Sch. 12, Pt. I, para. 2(1); FA 1982, Sch. 8, para. 7.
Sub-s. (4): F(No. 2)A 1975, Sch. 12, Pt. I, para. 2A; FA 1982, Sch. 8, para. 10.
Sub-s. (5): F(No. 2)A 1975, Sch 12, Pt. I, para. 2(2); FA 1980, Sch. 8, para. 4(3); FA 1982, Sch. 8, para. 8.
Sub-s. (6): F(No. 2)A 1975, Sch 12, Pt. I, para. 2(3); FA 1980, Sch. 8, para. 4(3).
Sub-s. (7): F(No. 2)A 1975, Sch. 12, Pt. I, para. 2(5); FA 1982, Sch. 8, para. 9.
Sub-s. (8): F(No. 2)A 1975, Sch. 12, Pt. I, para. 3(1); FA 1982, Sch. 8, para. 11.
Sub-s. (9): F(No. 2)A 1975, Sch. 12, Pt. I, para. 3(1A); FA 1982, Sch. 8, para. 12.
Sub-s. (10): F(No. 2)A 1975, Sch. 12, Pt. I, para. 3(2); FA 1980, Sch. 8, para. 7; FA 1982, Sch. 8, para. 13.
Sub-s. (11): F(No. 2)A 1975, Sch 12, Pt. I, para. 3(3); FA 1980, Sch. 8, para. 6(1).
Sub-s. (12): F(No. 2)A 1975, Sch. 12, Pt. I, para. 4.
Sub-s. (13): F(No. 2)A 1975, Sch. 12, Pt. I, para. 7.
Sub-s. (14): F(No. 2)A 1975, Sch. 12, Pt. I, para. 2(4); FA 1980, Sch. 8, para. 4(3).

563. Conditions to be satisfied by partners who are individuals

(1) In the case of an application for the issue of a certificate under section 561 to an individual who is a partner in a firm, the following conditions are required to be satisfied by that individual.

(2) The partner, unless he is the holder of a certificate in force under section 561 (other than a holder to whom section 561(4) applies), must throughout the period of three years ending with the date of his application for a certificate under section 561 have been employed in the United Kingdom as the holder of an office or employment or as a person carrying on a trade, profession or vocation.

(3) A partner who has not fulfilled the condition in subsection (2) above shall nevertheless be treated as satisfying that condition if—

(*a*) he satisfies the Board that he has been employed as mentioned in that subsection throughout a period of three years beginning not more than six years before the date of his application and ending on a date before that date;
(*b*) he satisfies the Board either—
  (i) that he has not been so employed throughout the whole of the period between those dates, or
  (ii) that he has not been so employed during any part of that period other than a part for which he specifies he has been so employed; and
(*c*) where the partner states that he has been outside the United Kingdom for the whole or part of the period mentioned in paragraph (*b*) above, he satisfies the Board of that fact by such evidence as may be prescribed in regulations made by the Board.

(4) The Board may for the purposes of this paragraph treat a person as having been employed as mentioned in subsection (2) above throughout a period of three years if during a period of three years he has been so employed except for a period or periods not exceeding six months or six months in aggregate.

(5) The partner must, subject to subsection (6) below, have complied with all obligations imposed on him by or under the Income Tax Acts or the Management Act in respect of

periods ending within the qualifying period and with all requests to supply to an inspector accounts of, or other information about, any business of his in respect of periods so ending.

(6) A partner who has failed to comply with such an obligation or request as is referred to in subsection (5) above shall nevertheless be treated as satisfying that condition as regards that obligation or request if the Board are of the opinion that the failure is minor and technical and does not give reason to doubt that the conditions mentioned in subsection (9) below will be satisfied.

(7) A partner who must satisfy the Board under subsection (3) above that he has been outside the United Kingdom for the whole or part of the period mentioned in subsection (3)(*b*) above must also satisfy them by such evidence as may be prescribed in regulations made by the Board that he has complied with any obligations imposed under the tax laws of any country in which he was living during that period which are comparable to the obligations mentioned in subsection (5) above.

(8) The partner must, if any contribution has at any time during the qualifying period become due from him under Part I of the Social Security Act 1975 or Part I of the Social Security (Northern Ireland) Act 1975, have paid the contribution when it became due.

(9) There must be reason to expect that the partner will, in respect of periods ending after the end of the qualifying period, comply with such obligations as are referred to in subsections (5) to (8) above and with such requests as are referred to in subsection (5) above.

(10) In this section "the qualifying period" means—

(*a*) in relation to a person who is within subsection (3) above, the period starting at the beginning of the last period of three years before his application throughout which he has been employed as mentioned in subsection (2) above (or is by virtue of subsection (4) above treated as having been so employed) and ending on the date of his application, and
(*b*) in the case of any other person, the period of three years ending with the date of his application.

Former enactments.—Sub-s. (2): F(No. 2)A 1975, Sch. 12, Pt. II, para. 1(1); FA 1982, Sch. 8, para. 14.
Sub-ss. (3), (4): F(No. 2)A 1975, Sch. 12, Pt. II, para. 1(2), (3); FA 1980, Sch. 8, paras. 4, 5.
Sub-s. (5): F(No. 2)A 1975, Sch. 12, Pt. II, para. 2(1).
Sub-s. (6): F(No. 2)A 1975, Sch. 12, Pt. II, para. 2(2); FA 1980, Sch. 8, para. 7.
Sub-s. (7): F(No. 2)A 1975, Sch. 12, Pt. II, para. 2(3); FA 1980, Sch. 8, para. 6.
Sub-ss. (8), (9): F(No. 2)A 1975, Sch. 12, Pt. II, paras. 3, 4.
Sub-s. (10): F(No. 2)A 1975, Sch. 12, Pt. II, para. 1(4); FA 1980, Sch. 8, para. 5.

564. Conditions to be satisfied by firms

(1) In the case of an application for the issue of a certificate under section 561 to an individual or a company as a partner in a firm the following conditions are required to be satisfied by the firm.

(2) The firm's business must be carried on in the United Kingdom and must satisfy the conditions mentioned in section 562(2)(*a*) to (*d*).

(3) Subject to subsection (4) below, any income tax or corporation tax which became due from any partner in the firm in respect of the firm's business at any time in the period of three years ending with the date of the application for a certificate under section 561 must have been paid when the tax was demanded.

(4) Where the obligation referred to in subsection (3) above has not been complied with in the case of any firm, the firm shall nevertheless be treated as satisfying that condition as regards that tax if the Board are of the opinion that the failure is minor and technical and does not give reason to doubt that the conditions mentioned in subsection (5) below will be satisfied.

(5) There must be reason to expect that income tax or corporation tax becoming due in respect of the firm's business in respect of periods ending after the end of the period referred to in subsection (3) above will be paid when it is demanded.

Former enactments.—Sub-ss. (2)–(4): F(No. 2)A 1975, Sch. 12, Pt. III, paras. 1, 2; FA 1980, Sch. 8, para. 7.
Sub-s. (5): F(No. 2)A 1975, Sch. 12, Pt. III, para. 5.

565. Conditions to be satisfied by companies

(1) In the case of an application for the issue of a certificate under section 561 to a company (whether as a partner in a firm or otherwise), the following conditions are required to be satisfied by the company.

(2) The company must be carrying on (whether or not in partnership) a business in the United Kingdom and that business must satisfy the conditions mentioned in section 562(2)(*a*) to (*d*).

(3) The company must, subject to subsection (4) below, have complied with all obligations imposed on it by or under the Tax Acts or the Management Act in respect of periods ending within the qualifying period and with all requests to supply to an inspector accounts of, or other information about, the business of the company in respect of periods so ending.

(4) A company which has failed to comply with such an obligation or request as is referred to in subsection (3) above shall nevertheless be treated as satisfying this condition as regards that obligation or request if the Board are of the opinion that the failure is minor and technical and does not give reason to doubt that the conditions mentioned in subsection (8) below will be satisfied.

(5) The company must, if any contribution has at any time during the qualifying period become due from the company under Part I of the Social Security Act 1975 or Part I of the Social Security (Northern Ireland) Act 1975 have paid the contribution when it became due.

(6) The company must have complied with any obligations imposed on it by the following provisions of the Companies Act 1985, in so far as those obligations fell to be complied with within the qualifying period, that is to say—

   (*a*) sections 227 and 241 (contents, laying and delivery of annual accounts);
   (*b*) section 287 (registered office and notification of changes therein);
   (*c*) section 288(2) (return of directors and secretary and notification of changes therein);
   (*d*) sections 363, 364 and 365 (annual returns);
   (*e*) section 691 (registration of constitutional documents and list of directors and secretary of oversea company);
   (*f*) section 692 (notification of changes in constitution or directors or secretary of oversea company);
   (*g*) section 693 (oversea company to state its name and country of incorporation);
   (*h*) section 699 (obligations of companies incorporated in Channel Islands or Isle of Man);
   (*j*) Chapter II of Part XXIII (accounts of oversea company).

(7) The company must have complied with any obligations imposed on it by the following provisions of the Companies (Northern Ireland) Order 1986, in so far as those obligations fell to be complied with within the qualifying period, that is to say—

   (*a*) Articles 235, 247 and 249 (annual accounts, documents included in annual accounts and laying and delivery of accounts);
   (*b*) Article 295 (registered office and notification of changes therein);
   (*c*) Article 296(2) (return of directors and secretary and notification of changes therein);
   (*d*) Articles 371, 372 and 373 (annual returns);
   (*e*) Article 641 (registration of constitutional documents and list of directors and secretary of oversea company);
   (*f*) Article 642 (notification of changes in constitution or directors or secretary of oversea company);
   (*g*) Article 643 (oversea company to state its name and country of incorporation);
   (*h*) Article 649 (accounts of oversea company).

(8) There must be reason to expect that the company will, in respect of periods ending after the end of the qualifying period, comply with all such obligations as are referred to in subsections (2) to (7) above and with such requests as are referred to in subsection (3) above.

(9) In this section "qualifying period" means the period of three years ending with the date of the company's application for a certificate under section 561.

Former enactments.—Sub-ss. (2)–(4): F(No. 2)A 1975, Sch. 12, Pt. IV, paras. 1, 2(1), (2); FA 1980, Sch. 8, para. 7; FA 1982, Sch. 8, para. 15.
Sub-s. (5): F(No. 2)A 1975, Sch. 12, Pt. IV, para. 3.
Sub-ss. (6), (7): F(No. 2)A 1975, Sch. 12, Pt. IV, para. 6; Companies Consolidation (Consequential Provisions) Act 1985, Sch. 2; Companies Consolidation (Consequential Provisions) (Northern Ireland) Order 1986, SI 1986 No. 1032; FA 1987, Sch. 15, para. 8.
Sub-s. (8): F(No. 2)A 1975, Sch. 12, Pt. IV, para. 7.
Sub-s. (9): F(No. 2)A 1975, Sch. 12, Pt. IV, para. 2(3).

566. General powers to make regulations under Chapter IV

(1) The Board shall make regulations with respect to the collection and recovery, whether by assessment or otherwise, of sums required to be deducted from any payments under section 559 and for the giving of receipts by persons receiving the payments to persons making them; and those regulations may include any matters with respect to which regulations may be made under section 203.

(2) The Board may make regulations—

(*a*) prescribing the period for which certificates under section 561 are to be issued and the form of such certificates;
(*b*) providing for the renewal of such certificates;
(*c*) providing for the issue, renewal or cancellation of such certificates or the giving of directions under section 561(6) by inspectors on behalf of the Board;
(*d*) requiring the furnishing of information with respect to changes in the control of a company holding or applying for such a certificate;
(*e*) requiring the production of such certificates to such persons and in such circumstances as may be specified in the regulations and providing for the completion and return to the Board of forms certifying such production;
(*f*) requiring the surrender to the Board of such certificates in such circumstances as may be specified in the regulations;
(*g*) requiring persons who make payments under contracts relating to construction operations to keep such records and to make to the Board such returns relating to payments so made by them as may be specified in the regulations, and requiring persons who hold such certificates to keep such records relating to payments so made to them as may be so specified;
(*h*) with respect to the production, copying and removal of, and the making of extracts from, any records kept by virtue of any such requirement as is referred to in paragraph (*g*) above and with respect to rights of access to or copies of any such records which are removed;
(*j*) requiring vouchers for payments made under contracts relating to construction operations to persons who hold such certificates to be obtained by the person making, and given by the person receiving, the payment, prescribing the form of the vouchers, and requiring their production or surrender to the Board in such circumstances as may be specified in the regulations; and
(*k*) excluding payments from the operation of section 561 where, in such circumstances as may be specified in the regulations, the requirements of regulations relating to the production of certificates or the obtaining, production or surrender of vouchers have not been complied with;

and any such regulations may make different provision for different circumstances.

Section 840 shall apply for the purposes of paragraph (*d*) above.

Former enactments.—Sub-s. (1): F(No. 2)A 1975, s. 69(6).
Sub-s. (2): F(No. 2)A 1975, s. 70(7); FA 1982, Sch. 8, para. 4; F(No. 2)A 1987, s. 93(5), (6).
Cross references.—See TMA 1970, s. 98A(*b*) (special penalties in the case of matters under sub-s. (1) of this section).

567. Meaning of "construction operations"

(1) In this Chapter "construction operations" means operations of any description specified in subsection (2) below, not being operations of any description specified in subsection (3) below; and references to construction operations shall be taken—

(*a*) except where the context otherwise requires, as including references to the work of individuals participating in the carrying out of such operations; and
(*b*) except in the case of offshore installations, as not including references to operations carried out or to be carried out otherwise than in the United Kingdom.

(2) The following operations are, subject to subsection (3) below, construction operations for the purposes of this Chapter—

(*a*) construction, alteration, repair, extension, demolition or dismantling of buildings or structures (whether permanent or not), including offshore installations;
(*b*) construction, alteration, repair, extension or demolition of any works forming, or to form, part of the land, including (without prejudice to the foregoing) walls, roadworks, power-lines, telecommunication apparatus, aircraft runways, docks and harbours, railways, inland waterways, pipe-lines, reservoirs, water-mains, wells, sewers, industrial plant and installations for purposes of land drainage, coast protection or defence;

(c) installation in any building or structure of systems of heating, lighting, air-conditioning, ventilation, power supply, drainage, sanitation, water supply or fire protection;
(d) internal cleaning of buildings and structures, so far as carried out in the course of their construction, alteration, repair, extension or restoration;
(e) operations which form an integral part of, or are preparatory to, or are for rendering complete, such operations as are previously described in this subsection, including site clearance, earth-moving, excavation, tunnelling and boring, laying of foundations, erection of scaffolding, site restoration, landscaping and the provision of roadways and other access works;
(f) painting or decorating the internal or external surfaces of any building or structure.

(3) The following operations are not construction operations for the purposes of this Chapter—
(a) drilling for, or extraction of, oil or natural gas;
(b) extraction (whether by underground or surface working) of minerals; tunnelling or boring, or construction of underground works, for this purpose;
(c) manufacture of building or engineering components or equipment, materials, plant or machinery, or delivery of any of these things to site;
(d) manufacture of components for systems of heating, lighting, air-conditioning, ventilation, power supply, drainage, sanitation, water supply or fire protection, or delivery of any of these things to site;
(e) the professional work of architects or surveyors, or of consultants in building, engineering, interior or exterior decoration or in the laying-out of landscape;
(f) the making, installation and repair of artistic works, being sculptures, murals and other works which are wholly artistic in nature;
(g) signwriting and erecting, installing and repairing signboards and advertisements;
(h) the installation of seating, blinds and shutters;
(j) the installation of security systems, including burglar alarms, closed circuit television and public address systems.

(4) In this section "offshore installations" means installations which are maintained, or are intended to be established, for underwater exploitation or exploration to which the Mineral Workings (Offshore Installations) Act 1971 applies.

(5) The Treasury may by order—
(a) include in subsection (2) above any description of operations as to which they are satisfied that it is a normal activity of the construction industry and that its inclusion in that subsection is necessary for achieving the object of section 559;
(b) include in subsection (3) above any description of operations as to which they are satisfied that it cannot properly be considered a normal activity of the construction industry and ought to be excluded from subsection (2) above.

(6) An order under subsection (5) above shall not have effect unless a draft of the instrument containing it has been laid before and approved by a resolution of the House of Commons.

Former enactments.—Sub-s. (1): F(No. 2)A 1975, s. 71(8).
Sub-s. (2): F(No. 2)A 1975, Sch. 13, Pt. I; Telecommunications Act 1984, Sch. 4, para. 62.
Sub-s. (3): F(No. 2)A 1975, Sch. 13, Pt. II; Income Tax (Construction Operations) Order 1980, S.I. 1980 No. 1171.
Sub-s (4): F(No. 2)A 1975, s. 71(8), Sch. 13, Pt. I.
Sub-ss. (5), (6): F(No. 2)A 1975, s. 71(9), (10).

CHAPTER V
SCHEMES FOR RATIONALIZING INDUSTRY

568. Deductions from profits of contributions paid under certified schemes

(1) Notwithstanding anything contained in section 74 but subject to the following provisions of this Chapter, where a person pays, wholly and exclusively for the purposes of a trade in respect of which he is chargeable under Case I of Schedule D, a contribution in furtherance of a scheme which is for the time being certified by the Secretary of State under this section, the contribution shall, in so far as it is paid in furtherance of the primary object of the scheme, be allowed to be deducted as an expense in computing the profits or gains of that trade.

(2) The Secretary of State shall certify a scheme under this section if he is satisfied—

(*a*) that the primary object of the scheme is the elimination of redundant works or machinery or plant from use in an industry in the United Kingdom; and
(*b*) that the scheme is in the national interest and in the interests of that industry as a whole; and
(*c*) that such number of persons engaged in that industry as are substantially representative of the industry are liable to pay contributions in furtherance of the primary object of the scheme by agreement between them and the body of persons carrying out the scheme.

References in this subsection to an industry in the United Kingdom shall include references to the business carried on by owners of ships or of a particular class of ships, wherever that business is carried on, and, in relation to that business, references in this subsection to works or machinery or plant shall include references to ships.

(3) The Secretary of State shall cancel any certificate granted under this section if he ceases to be satisfied as to any of the matters referred to in subsection (2) above.

(4) The Secretary of State may at any time require the body of persons carrying out a scheme certified under this section to produce any books or documents of whatever nature relating to the scheme and, if the requirement is not complied with, he may cancel the certificate.

(5) In this section and in section 569 "contribution", in relation to a scheme, does not include a sum paid by a person by way of loan or subscription of share capital, or in consideration of the transfer of assets to him, or by way of a penalty for contravening or failing to comply with the scheme.

Former enactments.—TA 1970, s. 406; Secretary of State for Trade and Industry Order 1970, S.I. 1970 No. 1537.

569. Repayment of contributions

(1) In the event of the repayment, whether directly or by way of distribution of assets on a winding up or otherwise, of a contribution or any part of a contribution which has been allowed to be deducted under section 568, the deduction of the contribution, or so much of it as has been repaid, shall be deemed to be an unauthorised deduction in respect of which an assessment shall be made, and, notwithstanding the provisions of the Tax Acts requiring assessments to be made within six years after the end of the chargeable period to which they relate, any such assessment and any consequential assessment may be made at any time within three years after the end of the chargeable period in which the repayment was made.

(2) For the purposes of this section, a sum received by any person by way of repayment of contributions shall be deemed to be by way of repayment of the last contribution paid by him, and, if the sum exceeds the amount of that contribution, by way of repayment of the penultimate contribution so paid, and so on.

Former enactments.—TA 1970, s. 407; FA 1971, Sch. 6, para. 45.

570. Payments under certified schemes which are not repayments of contributions

(1) Subject to the provisions of this section, where, under any scheme which is for the time being certified or has at any time been certified by the Secretary of State under section 568, any payment (not being a payment made by way of repayment of contributions) is made to

a person carrying on a trade to which the scheme relates, that payment shall be treated for the purposes of the Tax Acts as a trading receipt of the trade, and shall accordingly be taken into account in computing the profits or gains of the trade for those purposes.

(2) Where on a claim it is shown in accordance with the provisions of Part II of Schedule 21 that the payments which have been made under such a scheme in respect of a trade (not being payments made by way of repayment of contributions) have been made wholly or partly in respect of damage in respect of which no relief may be given under the Tax Acts, then, subject to and in accordance with the provisions of that Schedule—

(a) relief shall be given in respect of those payments by reducing the amounts which are to be treated as trading receipts of the trade under subsection (1) above; but
(b) where such relief is given, section 568 shall, in relation to contributions subsequently paid under the scheme in respect of the trade, have effect subject to the modifications specified in Part III of that Schedule.

(3) The provisions of this section and Schedule 21 shall apply in relation to any payment made to a person who has ceased to carry on a trade to which any such scheme as is mentioned in subsection (1) above relates as they apply in relation to payments made to a person carrying on such a trade, subject to the modification that so much of that payment as falls to be treated as a trading receipt by virtue of those provisions shall be deemed for the purposes of those provisions to have been made to him on the last day on which he was engaged in carrying on the trade.

(4) In determining for the purposes of this section and of Schedule 21—

(a) whether any trade has ceased to be carried on; or
(b) whether any contribution is paid in respect of a trade in respect of which a payment has been made; or
(c) whether any payment is made in respect of a trade in respect of which a contribution has been paid,

no regard shall be had to any event which, by virtue of any of the provisions of section 113 or section 337(1), is to be treated as effecting a discontinuance of a trade.

Former enactment.—TA 1970, s. 408.

571. Cancellation of certificates

(1) Where any certificate granted with respect to a scheme under section 568 is cancelled by the Secretary of State, and any deductible contributions paid in furtherance of the scheme have not been repaid at the expiration of one year from the cancellation, the body of persons carrying out the scheme shall, for the chargeable period in which that year expires, be charged to tax under Case VI of Schedule D upon the aggregate amount of the deductible contributions which have not been repaid at that time.

(2) The charge to tax under subsection (1) above shall not be made if the total amount of any contributions, other than deductible contributions, which have been paid under the scheme and have not been repaid before that time is greater than the available resources of the scheme, and shall not in any case be made upon an amount greater than the excess, if any, of those resources over that total amount.

(3) In subsection (2) above "the available resources", in relation to any scheme, means a sum representing the total funds held for the purposes of the scheme at the expiration of one year from the cancellation of the certificate plus a sum representing any funds held for the purposes of the scheme which, during that year, have been applied otherwise than in accordance with the provisions of the scheme as in force when the certificate was granted.

(4) Where the body of persons carrying out a scheme are charged to tax by virtue of subsection (1) above, and, after the expiration of one year from the cancellation of the certificate, any deductible contribution paid in furtherance of the scheme is repaid, the amount upon which the charge is made shall on the making of a claim be reduced by the amount repaid, and all such repayments of tax shall be made as are necessary to give effect to the provisions of this subsection.

(5) In this section "contribution" includes a part of a contribution, and "deductible contribution" means a contribution allowed to be deducted under section 568, any reduction under Part III of Schedule 21 being left out of account.

(6) For the purposes of this section, a sum received by any person by way of repayment of contributions shall be deemed to be by way of repayment of the last contribution paid by

him, and, if the sum exceeds the amount of that contribution, by way of repayment of the penultimate contribution so paid, and so on.

Former enactment.—TA 1970, s. 409.

572. Application to statutory redundancy schemes

(1) Sections 569 to 571 and Schedule 21 shall, subject to the adaptations specified in subsection (2) below, apply in relation to a statutory redundancy scheme as they apply in relation to a scheme certified under section 568.

(2) The adaptations referred to above are as follows, that is to say—

(*a*) for any reference to a contribution allowed to be deducted under section 568 there shall be substituted a reference to a contribution allowed to be deducted under any provision of the Tax Acts other than that section;

(*b*) any provision that section 568 shall, in relation to contributions, have effect subject to modifications, shall be construed as a provision that so much of any provision of the Tax Acts other than that section as authorises the deduction of contributions shall, in relation to the contributions in question, have effect subject to the modifications in question;

(*c*) for any reference to the cancellation of a certificate with respect to a scheme there shall be substituted a reference to the scheme ceasing to have effect; and

(*d*) for any reference to the provisions of the scheme as in force when the certificate was granted there shall be substituted a reference to the provisions of the scheme as in force when the contributions were first paid thereunder.

(3) In this section "statutory redundancy scheme" means a scheme for the elimination or reduction of redundant works, machinery or plant, or for other similar purposes, to which effect is given by or under any Act, whether passed before or after this Act.

Former enactment.—TA 1970, s. 410.

CHAPTER VI

OTHER PROVISIONS

Relief for losses on unquoted shares in trading companies

573. Relief for companies

(1) Subsection (2) below has effect where a company which has subscribed for shares in a qualifying trading company incurs an allowable loss (for the purpose of corporation tax on chargeable gains) on the disposal of the shares in any accounting period and the company disposing of the shares—

    (*a*) is an investment company on the date of the disposal and either—

        (i) has been an investment company for a continuous period of six years ending on that date; or
        (ii) has been an investment company for a shorter continuous period ending on that date and has not before the beginning of that period been a trading company or an excluded company; and

    (*b*) was not associated with, or a member of the same group as, the qualifying trading company at any time in the period beginning with the date when it subscribed for the shares and ending with the date of the disposal.

(2) The company disposing of the shares may, within two years after the end of the accounting period in which the loss was incurred, make a claim requiring that the loss be set off for the purposes of corporation tax against income—

    (*a*) of that accounting period; and
    (*b*) if the company was then an investment company and the claim so requires, of preceding accounting periods ending within the time specified in subsection (3) below;

and, subject to any relief for an earlier loss, the income of any of those periods shall then be treated as reduced by the amount of the loss or by so much of it as cannot be relieved under this subsection against income of a later accounting period.

(3) The time referred to in subsection (2) above is the period of 12 months ending immediately before the accounting period in which the loss is incurred; but the amount of the reduction which may be made under that subsection in the income of an accounting period falling partly before that time shall not exceed a part of that income proportionate to the part of the accounting period falling within that time.

(4) Relief under subsection (2) above shall be given before any deduction for charges on income, expenses of management or other amounts which can be deducted from or set against or treated as reducing profits of any description; and where relief is given under that subsection in respect of the amount of a loss no deduction shall be made in respect of that amount for the purposes of corporation tax on chargeable gains.

(5) For the purposes of subsection (1)(*b*) above companies are associated with each other if one controls the other or both are under the control of the same person or persons; and section 416(2) to (6) shall apply for the purposes of this subsection.

(6) For the purposes of this section a company subscribes for shares in another company if they are issued to it by that other company in consideration of money or money's worth.

Former enactments.—Sub-ss. (1)–(5): FA 1981, s. 36(1)–(5).
Sub-s. (6): FA 1981, s. 36(6); FA 1980, s. 37(3).

574. Relief for individuals

(1) Where an individual who has subscribed for shares in a qualifying trading company incurs an allowable loss (for capital gains tax purposes) on the disposal of the shares in any year of assessment, he may, by notice given within two years after that year, make a claim for relief from income tax on an amount of his income equal to the amount of the loss; and where such relief is given in respect of the amount of a loss no deduction shall be made in respect of that amount under the 1979 Act.

(2) The following provisions shall have effect as respects relief under this section—

(*a*) relief may, by notice given within two years after a year of assessment, be claimed for that year in respect of a loss incurred in the preceding year of assessment so far as relief under this section in respect of that loss has not already been given in that year, and relief claimed by virtue of this paragraph shall be given in priority to any relief in respect of a loss incurred in the year for which the relief is claimed;

(*b*) a claim for relief may require it to be given only by reference to the income of the individual without extending to the income of his spouse;

(*c*) subject to paragraph (*b*) above, relief shall be given by treating the loss as reducing first the earned income of the individual, then his other income, then the earned income of his spouse and then his spouse's other income;

(*d*) the relief shall be given in priority to relief under section 380 or 381.

(3) For the purposes of this section—

(*a*) an individual subscribes for shares if they are issued to him by the company in consideration of money or money's worth; and

(*b*) an individual shall be treated as having subscribed for shares if his spouse did so and transferred them to him by a transaction inter vivos.

Former enactment.—FA 1980, s. 37(1)–(4).
Note.—See **Prospective Legislation Notes** (Married Couples).

575. Exclusion of relief under section 573 or 574 in certain cases

(1) Sections 573 and 574 do not apply unless the disposal is—

(*a*) by way of a bargain made at arm's length for full consideration; or
(*b*) by way of a distribution in the course of dissolving or winding up the company; or
(*c*) a deemed disposal under section 22(2) of the 1979 Act (claim that value of asset has become negligible).

(2) Where a person disposes of shares ("the new shares") which by virtue of section 78 of the 1979 Act (reorganisation etc. treated as not involving disposal) are identified with other shares ("the old shares") previously held by him, relief shall not be given under section 573 or 574 on the disposal of the new shares unless—

(*a*) relief under section 573 or 574 could (or if this section had been in force could) have been given on a disposal of the old shares if he had incurred an allowable loss in disposing of them as mentioned in subsection (1)(*a*) above on the occasion of the disposal that would have occurred but for section 78 of the 1979 Act; or

(*b*) he gave new consideration for the new shares;

but in a case within paragraph (*b*) above the amount of relief under section 573 or 574 on the disposal of the new shares shall not exceed the amount or value of the new consideration taken into account as a deduction in computing the loss incurred on their disposal.

(3) Where the shares are the subject of an exchange or arrangement of the kind mentioned in section 85 or 86 of the 1979 Act (company reconstructions etc.) which by reason of section 87 of that Act involves a disposal of the shares, section 573 or 574 shall not apply to any allowable loss incurred on the disposal.

Former enactments.—FA 1980, s. 37(6)–(8); FA 1981, s. 36(6).

576. Provisions supplementary to sections 573 to 575

(1) Where a person holds shares in a company which constitute a holding and comprise—

(*a*) shares for which he has subscribed ("qualifying shares"); and
(*b*) shares which he has acquired otherwise than by subscription,

any question whether a disposal by him of shares forming part of the holding is of qualifying shares shall be determined by treating that and any previous disposal by him out of the holding as relating to shares acquired later rather than earlier; and if a disposal by him is of qualifying shares forming part of a holding and he makes a claim under section 573 or 574 in respect of a loss incurred on their disposal, the amount of relief under that section on the disposal shall not exceed the sums that would be allowed as deductions in computing the loss if the shares had not been part of the holding.

(2) Where a claim is made under section 573 or 574 in respect of a loss accruing on the disposal of shares, section 26 of the 1979 Act (value-shifting) shall have effect in relation to the disposal as if for the references in subsections (1)(*b*) and (4) to a tax-free benefit there were substituted references to any benefit whether tax-free or not.

(3) There shall be made all such adjustments of corporation tax on chargeable gains or capital gains tax, whether by way of assessment or by way of discharge or repayment of tax, as may be required in consequence of relief being given under section 573 or 574 in respect of an allowable loss or in consequence of the whole or part of such a loss in respect of which a claim is made not being relieved under that section.

(4) For the purposes of sections 573 to 575 and this section a qualifying trading company is a company none of whose shares have at any time in the relevant period been quoted on a recognised stock exchange and which—

(a) either—

(i) is a trading company on the date of the disposal; or
(ii) has ceased to be a trading company at a time which is not more than three years before that date and has not since that time been an excluded company or an investment company; and

(b) either—

(i) has been a trading company for a continuous period of six years ending on that date or at that time; or
(ii) has been a trading company for a shorter continuous period ending on that date or at that time and has not before the beginning of that period been an excluded company or an investment company; and

(c) has been resident in the United Kingdom throughout the period from its incorporation until that date.

(5) In sections 573 to 575 and this section—

"excluded company" means a company—

(a) which has a trade which consists wholly or mainly of dealing in shares, securities, land, trades or commodity futures or is not carried on on a commercial basis and in such a way that profits in the trade can reasonably be expected to be realised; or
(b) which is the holding company of a group other than a trading group; or
(c) which is a building society or a registered industrial and provident society as defined in section 486(12);

"group" means a company which has one or more 51 per cent. subsidiaries together with that or those subsidiaries;
"holding" means a holding within the meaning of section 65 of the 1979 Act;
"holding company" means a company whose business consists wholly or mainly in the holding of shares or securities of one or more companies which are its 51 per cent. subsidiaries;
"investment company" has the meaning given by section 130 except that it does not include the holding company of a trading group;
"new consideration" means consideration in money or money's worth other than consideration of the kind excluded by the first proviso to section 79(1) of the 1979 Act;
"relevant period" means the period ending with the date on which the shares in question are disposed of and beginning with the incorporation of the company, or, if later, one year before the date on which the shares were subscribed for;
"shares" includes stock but except in the definition of "excluded company" does not include shares or stock not forming part of a company's ordinary share capital;
"spouse" refers to one of two spouses who are living together (construed in accordance with section 155(2) of the 1979 Act);
"trading company" means a company other than an excluded company which is—

[(a) a company whose business consists wholly or mainly of the carrying on of a trade or trades;][1]
(b) the holding company of a trading group;

"trading group" means a group the business of whose members, taken together, consists wholly or mainly in the carrying on of a trade or trades, but for the purposes of this definition any trade carried on by a subsidiary which is an excluded company or not resident in the United Kingdom shall be treated as not constituting a trade.

Former enactments.—Sub-ss. (1)–(3): FA 1980, s. 37(9)–(11); FA 1981, s. 36(6).
Sub-s. (4): FA 1980, s. 37(5); FA 1981, s. 36(6).
Sub-s. (5): FA 1980, s. 37(12); FA 1981, s. 36(6), (7); F(No. 2)A 1987, s. 71.
Amendments.—[1] Para. (a) in the definition of "trading company" substituted by FA 1989, Sch. 12, para. 14 in relation to disposals after 31 March 1989.

Miscellaneous

577. Business entertaining expenses

(1) Subject to the provisions of this section—

(*a*) no deduction shall be made in computing profits or gains chargeable to tax under Schedule A or Schedule D for any expenses incurred in providing business entertainment, and such expenses shall not be included in computing any expenses of management in respect of which relief may be given under the Tax Acts;

(*b*) no deduction for expenses so incurred shall be made from emoluments chargeable to tax under Schedule E; and

(*c*) for the purposes of Chapter II of Part I of the 1968 Act and Chapter I of Part III of the Finance Act 1971, the use of any asset for providing business entertainment shall be treated as use otherwise than for the purposes of trade.

(2) ...[1]

(3) The expenses to which paragraph (*a*) of subsection (1) above applies include, in the case of any person, any sums paid by him to, or on behalf of, or placed by him at the disposal of a member of his staff exclusively for the purpose of defraying expenses incurred or to be incurred by him in providing business entertainment, but where—

(*a*) any such sum falls to be included in his emoluments chargeable to tax under Schedule E; and

(*b*) the deduction or inclusion of that sum as mentioned in that paragraph falls to be disallowed in whole or in part by virtue of this section;

paragraph (*b*) of that subsection shall not preclude the deduction of any expenses defrayed out of that sum.

(4) ...[1]

(5) For the purposes of this section "business entertainment" means entertainment (including hospitality of any kind) provided by a person, or by a member of his staff, in connection with a trade carried on by that person, but does not include anything provided by him for bona fide members of his staff unless its provision for them is incidental to its provision also for others.

(6) ...[1]

(7) In this section—

(*a*) any reference to expenses incurred in, or to the use of an asset for, providing entertainment includes a reference to expenses incurred in, or to the use of an asset for, providing anything incidental thereto;

(*b*) references to a trade include references to any business, profession or vocation; and

(*c*) references to the members of a person's staff are references to persons employed by that person, directors of a company or persons engaged in the management of a company being for this purpose deemed to be persons employed by it.

(8) This section shall apply in relation to the provision of a gift as it applies in relation to the provision of entertainment, except that it shall not by virtue of this subsection apply in relation to the provision for any person of a gift consisting of an article incorporating a conspicuous advertisement for the donor, being an article—

(*a*) which is not food, drink, tobacco or a token or voucher exchangeable for goods; and

(*b*) the cost of which to the donor, taken together with the cost to him of any other such articles given by him to that person in the same year, does not exceed £10.

(9) Subsection (8) above shall not preclude the deduction, in computing profits or gains under Case I or II of Schedule D, of expenditure incurred in making a gift to a body of persons or trust established for charitable purposes only; and for the purposes of this subsection the Historic Buildings and Monuments Commission for England and the Trustees of the National Heritage Memorial Fund shall each be treated as such a body of persons.

(10) Nothing in this section shall be taken as precluding the deduction of expenses incurred in, or any claim for capital allowances in respect of the use of an asset for, the provision by any person of anything which it is his trade to provide, and which is provided by him in the ordinary course of that trade for payment or, with the object of advertising to the public generally, gratuitously.

Former enactments.—Sub-ss. (1)–(8): TA 1970, s. 411(1)–(8); FA 1971, s. 50(8); FA 1985, s. 43.
Sub-s. (9): FA 1980, ss. 54, 118(3); FA 1983, s. 46(3)(*b*).

Sub-s. (10): TA 1970, s. 411(9).
Amendments.—[1] Sub-ss. (2), (4), (6) repealed by FA 1988, s. 72 and Sch. 14, Pt. IV in relation to entertainment provided after 14 March 1988 unless provided under a contract entered into before 15 March 1988.

578. Housing grants

(1) Where, under any enactment relating to the giving of financial assistance for the provision, maintenance or improvement of housing accommodation or other residential accommodation, a payment is made to a person by way of grant or other contribution towards expenses incurred, or to be incurred, by that or any other person, the payment shall not be treated as a receipt in computing income for any tax purpose.

(2) Subsection (1) above shall not apply to a payment in so far as it is made in respect of an expense giving rise to a deduction in computing income for any tax purpose.

Former enactment.—TA 1970, s. 376.

579. Statutory redundancy payments

(1) Any redundancy payment, and the corresponding amount of any other employer's payment, shall be exempt from income tax under Schedule E.

(2) Where a redundancy payment or other employer's payment is made in respect of employment wholly in a trade, profession or vocation carried on by the employer, and within the charge to tax, the amount of the redundancy payment or the corresponding amount of the other employer's payment shall (if not otherwise so allowable) be allowable as a deduction in computing for the purposes of Schedule D the profits or gains or losses of the trade, profession or vocation, but—

(*a*) if it is so allowed by virtue of this section the amount of the rebate recoverable shall (if it is not otherwise to be so treated) be treated as a receipt to be brought into account in computing those profits or gains; and

(*b*) if the employer's payment was made after the discontinuance of the trade, profession or vocation the net amount so deductible shall be treated as if it were a payment made on the last day on which the trade, profession or vocation was carried on.

(3) Where a redundancy payment or other employer's payment is made in respect of employment wholly in a business carried on by the employer and expenses of management of the business are eligible for relief under section 75 or 76—

(*a*) the amount by which the redundancy payment, or the corresponding amount of the other employer's payment, exceeds the recoverable rebate shall (if not otherwise so allowable) be allowable as expenses of management eligible for relief under that section, and

(*b*) if the employer's payment was made after the discontinuance of the business the net amount so allowable shall be treated as if it were expenses of management incurred on the last day on which the business was carried on.

(4) Where a redundancy payment or other employer's payment is made in respect of employment wholly in maintaining or managing property the expenses of maintaining or managing which were eligible for relief under the provisions of section 25(1) or 28—

(*a*) the amount by which the redundancy payment or the corresponding amount of the other employer's payment exceeds the recoverable rebate shall (if not otherwise allowable under those provisions) be treated for the purposes of those provisions as a payment made by the employer in respect of the maintenance or management of the property, or of such part of it as he may elect; and

(*b*) if the employer's payment was made after the latest time when it could be taken into account for the purposes of relief under those provisions as a payment in respect of the maintenance or management of the property or any part of it, it shall be treated as having been made at that time.

(5) Relief shall not be given under subsections (2), (3) and (4) above, or otherwise, more than once in respect of any employer's payment, and if the employee was being employed in such a way that different parts of his remuneration fell for tax purposes to be treated in different ways—

(*a*) the amount by which the redundancy payment or the corresponding amount of the other employer's payment exceeds the recoverable rebate shall be apportioned to the different capacities in which the employee was employed; and

(*b*) subsections (2), (3) and (4) above shall apply separately to the employment in those capacities, and by reference to the apportioned part of that amount, instead of by reference to the full amount of the employer's payment, and the full amount of the rebate.

(6) Where the Minister pays a sum under section 106 of the Employment Protection (Consolidation) Act 1978 or section 42 of the Contracts of Employment and Redundancy Payments Act (Northern Ireland) 1965 in respect of an employer's payment this section shall apply as if—

(*a*) that sum had been paid on account of that redundancy or other employer's payment, and

(*b*) so far as the employer has reimbursed the Minister, it had been so paid by the employer.

Former enactments.—TA 1970, s. 412(1)–(6); Employment Protection (Consolidation) Act 1978, Sch. 16, para. 9(1).

580. Provisions supplementary to section 579

(1) In section 579—

(*a*) "redundancy payment", "employer's payment" and "rebate" have the same meaning as in the Employment Protection (Consolidation) Act 1978 ("the 1978 Act") or Part III of the Contracts of Employment and Redundancy Payments Act (Northern Ireland) 1965 ("the 1965 Act");

(*b*) references to the corresponding amount of an employer's payment (other than a redundancy payment) are references to the amount of that employer's payment so far as not in excess of the amount of the relevant redundancy payment (and so that, where in consequence of section 104(2) of the 1978 Act or section 40(2) of the 1965 Act there is no relevant redundancy payment, the corresponding amount of an employer's payment is nil);

(*c*) "the Minister" in relation to the 1978 Act means the Secretary of State and in relation to the 1965 Act means the Department of Health and Social Services.

(2) For the purposes of subsection (1) above "relevant redundancy payment" shall be construed in accordance with paragraph 8 of Schedule 6 to the 1978 Act or paragraph 8 of Schedule 6 to the 1965 Act.

(3) In section 579(1) the reference to tax under Schedule E does not include a reference to tax under section 148 and accordingly payments exempted by section 579(1) may be taken into account under section 148.

Former enactments.—TA 1970, s. 412(7), (8); Employment Protection (Consolidation) Act 1978, Sch. 16, para. 9(2); Northern Ireland Constitution Act 1973, Sch. 5.

581. Borrowing in foreign currency by local authorities and statutory corporations

(1) If the Treasury direct that this section shall apply to any securities issued by a local authority and expressed in a currency other than sterling, interest on those securities—

(*a*) shall be paid without deduction of income tax, and

(*b*) so long as the beneficial owner is not resident in the United Kingdom, shall be exempt from income tax (but not corporation tax).

(2) Where for repayment of the principal amount due under the securities there is an option between sterling and one or more currencies other than sterling, that subsection shall be applicable to the securities if the option is exercisable only by the holder of the securities, and shall not be applicable to the securities in any other case.

(3) Where any income of any person is by virtue of any provision of the Income Tax Acts to be deemed to be income of any other person, that income shall not be exempt from tax by virtue of this section by reason of the first-mentioned person not being resident in the United Kingdom.

(4) This section shall have effect in relation to any securities issued by or loan made to a statutory corporation as it has effect in relation to any securities issued by a local authority, the references to the beneficial owner or holder of the securities being for this purpose read, in the case of such a loan, as references to the person for the time being entitled to repayment or eventual repayment of the loan.

(5) In subsection (4) above "statutory corporation" means—

(*a*) a corporation incorporated by an Act; or

(*b*) any other corporation, being a corporation to which functions in respect of the carrying on of an undertaking are entrusted by an Act or by an order made under or confirmed by an Act;

but, save as is provided by paragraph (b) above, does not include any company within the meaning of the Companies Act 1985 or the Companies (Northern Ireland) Order 1986.

(6) In relation to securities issued before 6th April 1982 subsections (1) and (2) above shall have effect with the substitution for references to sterling of references to a currency of a country which at the time of the issue was specified in Schedule 1 to the Exchange Control Act 1947.

Former enactments.—Sub-ss. (1)–(3), (6): TA 1970, s. 416(1)–(3); FA 1982, s. 64(2).
Sub-ss. (4), (5): FA 1975, s. 12; FA 1987, Sch. 15, para. 7.

582. Funding bonds issued in respect of interest on certain debts

(1) Where any funding bonds are issued to a creditor in respect of any liability to pay interest on any debts to which this section applies—

 (a) the issue of the bonds shall be treated for all the purposes of the Tax Acts as if it were the payment of an amount of that interest equal to the value of the bonds at the time of their issue, and
 (b) the redemption of the bonds shall not be treated for those purposes as the payment of any amount of that interest.

(2) Where an issue of bonds is treated by virtue of subsection (1) above as if it were the payment of an amount of interest, and any person by or through whom the bonds are issued would be required by virtue of any provision of the Tax Acts to deduct income tax from that amount of interest if it had been actually paid by or through him, the following provisions shall have effect—

 (a) subject to paragraph (b) below, any such person—
  (i) shall retain bonds the value of which at the time of their issue is equal to income tax on that amount of interest at the basic rate for the year of assessment in which the bonds are issued, and
  (ii) shall be acquitted in respect of any such retention in the same way as if he had deducted such tax from the interest, and
  (iii) shall be chargeable with that tax accordingly, but may tender the bonds retained in satisfaction thereof;
 (b) where the Board are satisfied that it is impracticable to retain bonds on account of income tax under paragraph (a) above—
  (i) they may relieve any such person from the obligation to retain bonds and account for income tax under that paragraph, on his furnishing to them a statement of the names and addresses of the persons to whom the bonds have been issued and the amount of the bonds issued to each such person; and
  (ii) tax in respect of the amount of interest treated by virtue of this section as having been paid by the issue of the bonds shall be charged under Case VI of Schedule D for the chargeable period in which the bonds are issued on the persons receiving or entitled to the bonds.

(3) This section applies to any debt incurred, whether in respect of any money borrowed or otherwise, by any government, public authority or public institution whatsoever, or by any body corporate whatsoever.

(4) For the purposes of this section "funding bonds" includes any bonds, stocks, shares, securities or certificates of indebtedness.

Former enactments.—TA 1970, s. 417; FA 1971, Sch. 6, para. 47.

583. Inter-American Development Bank

A person not resident in the United Kingdom shall not be liable to income tax in respect of income from any security issued by the Inter-American Development Bank if he would not be liable but for the fact that—

 (a) the security or income is issued, made payable or paid in the United Kingdom or in sterling; or
 (b) the Bank maintains an office or other place of business in the United Kingdom.

Former enactment.—FA 1976, s. 131(2).

584. Relief for unremittable overseas income

(1) Where a person is chargeable to tax by reference to the amount of any income arising in a territory outside the United Kingdom ("overseas income"), then for the purposes of tax this section shall apply to the overseas income in so far as—

   (a) he is prevented from transferring the amount of the overseas income to the United Kingdom, either by the laws of that territory or any executive action of its government or by the impossibility of obtaining foreign currency in that territory; and
   (b) he has not realised the overseas income outside that territory for a consideration in sterling or a consideration in some other currency which he is not prevented from transferring to the United Kingdom.

Overseas income to which this section applies is referred to below as unremittable.

(2) Subject to subsection (3) below, where a person so chargeable gives notice of his desire to be assessed in accordance with this subsection, then, in the first instance, account shall not be taken of the overseas income to the extent to which he shows to the satisfaction of the Board that the following conditions are satisfied with respect to it, that is to say—

   (a) that it is unremittable; and
   (b) that subsection (1)(a) above would continue to apply notwithstanding any reasonable endeavours on his part,

and tax shall be assessed and charged on all persons concerned and for all periods accordingly; but, on the Board ceasing, as respects any part of the income, to be satisfied that those conditions are satisfied, such assessments, reductions of assessments and repayments of tax shall be made as may be necessary to take account of it, and of any tax payable in respect of it under the law of the territory where it arises, according to their value at the date when, in the opinion of the Board, those conditions cease to be satisfied with respect to it, and may be so made at any time not later than six years after that date.

(3) Where the tax chargeable is corporation tax, subsection (2) above shall have effect as if—

   (a) for the word "assessed" in the second place where it occurs, there were substituted "assessable";
   (b) for the words from "on the Board ceasing" to "take account" there were substituted "on the said conditions ceasing to be satisfied as respects any part of the income, it shall be treated as income arising on the date when those conditions cease to be satisfied with respect to it and account shall be taken"; and
   (c) for the words from "the date" onwards there were substituted "that date".

(4) Where a company becomes chargeable to corporation tax in respect of income from any source by virtue of subsections (2) and (3) above after it has ceased to possess that source of income, the income shall be chargeable under Case VI of Schedule D.

(5) Where under an agreement entered into under arrangements made by the Secretary of State in pursuance of section 11 of the Export Guarantees and Overseas Investment Act 1978 any payment is made by the Export Credit Guarantee Department in respect of any income which cannot be transferred to the United Kingdom, then, to the extent of the payment, the income shall be treated as income with respect to which the conditions mentioned in subsection (2) above are not satisfied (and accordingly cannot cease to be satisfied).

(6) Any notice under subsection (2) above shall be delivered to the inspector before an assessment made by reference to that income otherwise than in accordance with that subsection has become final and conclusive; and there shall be made all such assessments, reductions of assessments or repayments of tax as may be required by reason of any such notice.

(7) In the case of the death of a person who, if he had not died, would, under subsection (2) above, have become chargeable to any income tax, the tax which would have been so chargeable shall be assessed and charged upon his executors or administrators, and shall be a debt due from and payable out of his estate.

(8) Subject to subsections (2) and (3) above, the amount of any unremittable overseas income shall be determined by reference to the generally recognised market value in the

United Kingdom (if any), or, in the absence of any such value, according to the official rate of exchange of the territory where the income arises.

(9) Any appeal against an assessment which involves a question as to the operation of this section shall be made to the Special Commissioners and not to the General Commissioners.

(10) This section shall have effect as respects any accounting period in which the conditions in subsection (2) above cease to be satisfied in relation to any income, being an accounting period ending on or before such day, not being earlier than 31st March 1992, as the Treasury may by order appoint for the purposes of this section, with the omission of subsections (3) and (4).

Former enactments.—Sub-ss. (1)–(4): TA 1970, s. 418(1), (2), (2A), (2B); F(No. 2)A 1987, Sch. 6, para. 6.
Sub-s. (5): FA 1972, s. 124(2)(*a*).
Sub-ss. (6)–(9): TA 1970, s. 418(3)–(6); F(No. 2)A 1987, Sch. 6, para. 6.
Sub-s. (10): F(No. 2)A 1987, Sch. 6, para. 6(5).

585. Relief from tax on delayed remittances

(1) A person charged or chargeable for any year of assessment in respect of income from any source with tax which (apart from this section) falls to be computed under Case IV or V of Schedule D, or under Case III of Schedule E, on the amount of income received in the United Kingdom in the basis year for that year of assessment, may by making a claim require that the following provisions of this section shall apply, on showing that the following conditions are satisfied, that is to say—

(*a*) that of the income so received all or part arose before the basis year but he was unable to transfer it to the United Kingdom before that year; and
(*b*) subject to subsection (2) below, that that inability was due to the laws of the territory where the income arose, or to executive action of its government, or to the impossibility of obtaining foreign currency in that territory; and
(*c*) that the inability was not due to any want of reasonable endeavours on his part.

(2) For the purposes of this section, where in any year of assessment a person is granted a pension or increase of pension retrospectively, the amount paid in respect of any previous year of assessment by virtue of the grant shall be treated as income arising in that previous year, whenever it is paid, and he shall be treated as having possessed the source of income from the time as from which the grant has effect; and subsection (1)(*b*) above shall not apply in relation to any amount so paid, except as respects the period after it becomes payable.

(3) Where a person claims that the provisions of this section shall apply for any year of assessment as respects the income from any source, then for the purposes of income tax—

(*a*) there shall be deducted from the income received in the United Kingdom in the basis year for that year the amount as respects which the conditions in paragraphs (*a*), (*b*) and (*c*) of subsection (1) above are satisfied, so far as applicable; but
(*b*) the part (if any) of that amount arising in each previous year of assessment shall be treated as if it were income received in the United Kingdom in the basis year for that previous year.

(4) Nothing in this section shall alter the year which is to be taken as the basis year for computing tax chargeable for any year of assessment under Case IV or V of Schedule D, and where under subsection (3)(*b*) above income is treated as received in the United Kingdom in a year which is the basis year for two years of assessment, it shall not by reason thereof be taken into account except in the year in which it arose.

(5) Where—

(*a*) a person makes a claim under this section for any year of assessment as respects income from any source chargeable under Case IV or V of Schedule D, and
(*b*) that year is the basis year for computing the tax with which he is chargeable on the income from that source both for that and for the succeeding year of assessment,

tax shall not be chargeable for either of those years of assessment on the amount referred to in paragraph (*a*) of subsection (3) above (without however being charged a second time by virtue of paragraph (*b*) of that subsection).

(6) No claim under this section shall be made in respect of any income more than six years after the end of the year of assessment in which the income is received in the United Kingdom.

(7) There shall be made all such adjustments, whether by way of repayment of tax, assessment or otherwise, as may be necessary to give effect to this section, and

notwithstanding anything in the Income Tax Acts, any adjustment to give effect to a claim under this section may be made at any time.

(8) A person's executors or administrators may make any claim under this section which he might have made, if he had not died, and after a person's death—

(*a*) any tax paid by him and repayable by virtue of a claim under this section (whoever made the claim) shall be repaid to his executors or administrators; and
(*b*) any additional tax chargeable by virtue of such a claim shall be assessed and charged upon his executors or administrators and shall be a debt due from and payable out of his estate.

(9) In this section "basis year" means—

(*a*) in relation to tax chargeable for any year of assessment under Case IV or V of Schedule D in respect of income from any source, the year by reference to which the amount of the income chargeable finally falls to be computed; and
(*b*) in relation to tax chargeable for any year of assessment under Case III of Schedule E, that year of assessment;

and any reference in this section to a source of income includes a part of a source.

Former enactment.—TA 1970, s. 419.

586. Disallowance of deductions for war risk premiums

(1) In computing the amount of the profits or gains of any person for any tax purpose, no sum shall be deducted in respect of any payment made by him to which this section applies.

(2) No payment to which this section applies shall be included in computing the expenses of management in respect of which relief may be given under section 75 or 76.

(3) Subject to subsections (4) and (5) below, this section applies to any payment made by any person under any contract or arrangement under which that person is, in the event of war damage, entitled or eligible, either absolutely or conditionally, to or for any form of indemnification, whether total or partial, and whether by way of a money payment or not, in respect of that war damage.

(4) Where the payment is made in respect of the right or eligibility mentioned in subsection (3) above and also in respect of other matters, the deduction or inclusion of so much of the payment as is properly attributable to the other matters shall not be disallowed by virtue only of subsection (1) or (2) above.

(5) This section shall not apply to any payment made under any contract of marine insurance, or any contract of insurance of an aircraft, or any contract of insurance of goods in transit.

(6) In this section "war damage" means loss or damage arising from action taken by an enemy of Her Majesty, or action taken in combating such an enemy or in repelling an imagined attack by such an enemy, or action taken in anticipation of or in consequence of an attack by such an enemy.

Former enactment.—TA 1970, s. 420.

587. Disallowance of certain payments in respect of war injuries to employees

(1) In computing the amount of the profits or gains, or total income, of any person for any tax purpose, no sum shall be deducted in respect of any payment made by him to which this section applies.

(2) No payment to which this section applies shall be included in computing—

(*a*) the expenses of management in respect of which relief may be given under section 75 or 76; or
(*b*) the expenses of management or supervision in respect of which relief may be given under section 121.

(3) Subject to subsections (4) and (5) below, this section applies—

(*a*) to any payments by way of benefit made by any person to, or to the personal representatives or dependants of, any employees of his on account of their incapacity, retirement or death owing to war injuries, whether sustained in the United Kingdom or elsewhere; and

(b) to any payments made by any person by way of premium or contribution under any policy, agreement, scheme or arrangement providing for the payment of benefits to, or to the personal representatives or dependants of, any employees of his on account of their incapacity, retirement or death owing to such war injuries.

(4) This section shall not apply to any payment (whether by way of benefit or by way of premium or contribution) which is payable under any policy, agreement, scheme or arrangement made before 3rd September 1939, except to the extent that the amount of the payment is increased by any variation of the terms of that policy, agreement, scheme or arrangement made on or after that date.

(5) This section shall not apply to any payment by way of benefit if, in the opinion of the Board, that payment was made under an established practice which was such that the same or a greater payment would have been made if the incapacity, retirement or death had not been due to war injuries.

(6) Where a person makes a payment by way of benefit to which this section applies and, in the opinion of the Board, there is an established practice under which a smaller payment would have been made if the incapacity, retirement or death had not been due to war injuries, the deduction or inclusion of an amount equal to that smaller payment shall not be disallowed by virtue only of subsection (1) or (2) above.

(7) Where a person makes a payment to which this section applies by way of premium or contribution, and the policy, agreement, scheme or arrangement provides for the payment of any benefit in the event of incapacity, retirement or death not due to war injuries, the deduction or inclusion of so much of the payment of premium or contribution as, in the opinion of the Board, is properly attributable to benefit payable in the event of incapacity, retirement or death not due to war injuries shall not be disallowed by virtue only of subsection (1) or (2) above.

(8) In this section "war injuries" means physical injuries—
  (a) caused by—
    (i) the discharge of any missile (including liquids and gas);
    (ii) the use of any weapon, explosive or other noxious thing; or
    (iii) the doing of any other injurious act,
either by the enemy or in combating the enemy or in repelling an imagined attack by the enemy; or
  (b) caused by the impact on any person or property of any enemy aircraft, or any aircraft belonging to, or held by any person on behalf of, or for the benefit of, Her Majesty or any allied power, or any part of, or anything dropped from, any such aircraft.

Former enactment.—TA 1970, s. 421.

588. Training courses for employees

(1) Where, on or after 6th April 1987, a person (in this section referred to as the "employer") incurs expenditure in paying or reimbursing relevant expenses incurred in connection with a qualifying course of training which—
  (a) is undertaken by a person (in this section referred to as the "employee") who is the holder or past holder of any office or employment under the employer; and
  (b) is undertaken with a view to retraining the employee,
the employee shall not thereby be regarded as receiving any emolument which forms part of his income for any purpose of Schedule E.

(2) Section 589 shall have effect to determine for the purposes of this section—
  (a) what is a qualifying course of training;
  (b) whether such a course is undertaken by an employee with a view to retraining; and
  (c) what are relevant expenses in relation to such a course.

(3) Subject to subsection (4) below, where—
  (a) an employer incurs expenditure in paying or reimbursing relevant expenses as mentioned in subsection (1) above; and
  (b) that subsection has effect in relation to the income of the employee for the purposes of Schedule E;
then, if and so far as that expenditure would not, apart from this subsection, be so deductible, it shall be deductible in computing for the purposes of Schedule D the profits or gains of the

trade, profession or vocation of the employer for the purposes of which the employee is or was employed.

(4) If the employer carries on a business, the expenses of management of which are eligible for relief under section 75, subsection (3) above shall have effect as if for the words from "in computing" onwards there were substituted "as expenses of management for the purposes of section 75".

(5) In any case where—

   (*a*) an employee's liability to tax for any year of assessment is determined (by assessment or otherwise) on the assumption that subsection (1) above applies in his case and, subsequently, there is a failure to comply with any provision of section 589(3) and (4); or
   (*b*) an employer's liability to tax for any year is determined (by assessment or otherwise) on the assumption that, by virtue only of subsection (3) above (or subsections (3) and (4) above), he is entitled to a deduction on account of any expenditure and, subsequently, there is such a failure as is referred to in paragraph (*a*) above;

an assessment under section 29(3) of the Management Act of an amount due in consequence of the failure referred to above may be made at any time not later than six years after the end of the chargeable period in which the failure occurred.

(6) Where an event occurs by reason of which there is a failure to comply with any provision of section 589(3) and (4), the employer of the employee concerned shall within 60 days of coming to know of the event give a notice to the inspector containing particulars of the event.

(7) If the inspector has reason to believe that an employer has not given a notice which he is required to give under subsection (6) above in respect of any event, the inspector may by notice require the employer to furnish him within such time (not less than 60 days) as may be specified in the notice with such information relating to the event as the inspector may reasonably require for the purposes of this section.

Former enactment.—FA 1987, s. 35(1)–(7).

589. Qualifying courses of training etc.

(1) Subject to subsection (2) below, a course is a qualifying course of training if—

   (*a*) it provides a course of training designed to impart or improve skills or knowledge relevant to, and intended to be used in the course of, gainful employment (including self-employment) of any description; and
   (*b*) the course is entirely devoted to the teaching or practical application of the skills or knowledge (or to both such teaching and practical application); and
   (*c*) the duration of the course does not exceed one year; and
   (*d*) all teaching and practical application forming part of the course takes place within the United Kingdom.

(2) A course shall not be regarded as a qualifying course of training in relation to a particular employee unless—

   (*a*) he attends the course on a full-time or substantially full-time basis; and
   (*b*) he is employed by the employer full-time throughout the period of two years ending at the time when he begins to undertake the course or, if it is earlier, at the time he ceases to be employed by him; and
   (*c*) the opportunity to undertake the course, on similar terms as to payment or reimbursement of relevant expenses, is available either generally to holders or past holders of offices or employment under the employer or to a particular class or classes of such holders or past holders.

(3) An employee shall not be regarded as undertaking a course with a view to retraining unless—

   (*a*) he begins to undertake the course of training while he is employed by the employer or within the period of one year after he ceases to be so employed; and
   (*b*) he ceases to be employed by the employer not later than the end of the period of two years beginning at the end of the qualifying course of training.

(4) An employee shall not be regarded as having undertaken a course with a view to retraining if, any time within the period of two years beginning at the time when he ceased to be employed as mentioned in subsection (3)(*b*) above, he is again employed by the employer.

(5) Where an employee undertakes a qualifying course of training, the relevant expenses consist of—

(*a*) fees for attendance at the course;
(*b*) fees for any examination which is taken during or at the conclusion of the course;
(*c*) the cost of any books which are essential for a person attending the course, and
(*d*) travelling expenses falling within subsection (6) below.

(6) The travelling expenses referred to in subsection (5)(*d*) above are those which would be deductible under section 198—

(*a*) on the assumption that attendance at the course is one of the duties of the employee's office or employment; and
(*b*) if the employee has in fact ceased to be employed by the employer, on the assumption that he continues to be employed by him.

(7) Any reference in this section to an employee being employed by an employer is a reference to the employee holding office or employment under the employer.

Former enactment.—FA 1987, Sch. 5.

PART XIV
PENSION SCHEMES, SOCIAL SECURITY BENEFITS, LIFE ANNUITIES ETC.
CHAPTER I
RETIREMENT BENEFIT SCHEMES

Cross references.—See FA 1989, Sch. 6, Pts. II, III (new provisions in relation to retirement benefits schemes and additional voluntary contributions schemes approved before 27 July 1989).

Approval of schemes

590. Conditions for approval of retirement benefit schemes

(1) Subject to section 591, the Board shall not approve any retirement benefits scheme for the purposes of this Chapter unless the scheme satisfies all of the conditions set out in subsection (2) below.

(2) The conditions are—
   (a) that the scheme is bona fide established for the sole purpose of providing relevant benefits in respect of service as an employee, being benefits payable to, or to the widow, children or dependants or personal representatives of, the employee;
   (b) that the scheme is recognised by the employer and employees to whom it relates, and that every employee who is, or has a right to be, a member of the scheme has been given written particulars of all essential features of the scheme which concern him;
   (c) that there is a person resident in the United Kingdom who will be responsible for the discharge of all duties imposed on the administrator of the scheme under this Chapter;
   (d) that the employer is a contributor to the scheme;
   (e) that the scheme is established in connection with some trade or undertaking carried on in the United Kingdom by a person resident in the United Kingdom;
   (f) that in no circumstances, whether during the subsistence of the scheme or later, can any amount be paid by way of repayment of an employee's contributions under the scheme.

(3) Subject to subsection (1) above, the Board shall approve a retirement benefits scheme for the purposes of this Chapter if the scheme satisfies all the conditions of this subsection, that is to say—
   (a) that any benefit for an employee is a pension on retirement at a specified age not earlier than 60 or, if the employee is a woman, 55, and not later than 70, which does not exceed one-sixtieth of the employee's final remuneration for each year of service up to a maximum of 40;
   (b) that any benefit for any widow of an employee is a pension payable on his death after retirement such that the amount payable to the widow by way of pension does not exceed two-thirds of any pension or pensions payable to the employee;
   (c) that no other benefits are payable under the scheme;
   (d) that no pension is capable in whole or in part of surrender, commutation or assignment, except in so far as the scheme allows an employee on retirement to obtain, by commutation of his pension, a lump sum or sums not exceeding in all three-eightieths of his final remuneration . . .[1] for each year of service up to a maximum of 40.
   [(e) that, in the case of any employee who is a member of the scheme by virtue of two or more relevant associated employments, the amount payable by way of pension in respect of service in any one of them may not, when aggregated with any amount payable by way of pension in respect of service in the other or others, exceed the relevant amount;][2]
   [(f) that, in the case of any employee who is a member of the scheme by virtue of two or more relevant associated employments, the amount payable by way of commuted pension in respect of service in any one of them may not, when aggregated with any amount payable by way of commuted pension in respect of service in the other or others, exceed the relevant amount;][2]
   [(g) that, in the case of any employee in relation to whom the scheme is connected with another scheme which is (or other schemes each of which is) an approved scheme, the amount payable by way of pension under the scheme may not, when aggregated with any amount payable by way of pension under the other scheme or schemes, exceed the relevant amount;][2]
   [(h) that, in the case of any employee in relation to whom the scheme is connected with another scheme which is (or other schemes each of which is) an approved scheme, the amount payable by way of commuted pension may not, when aggregated with any amount payable by way of commuted pension under the other scheme or schemes, exceed the relevant amount.][2]

(4) The conditions set out in subsections (2) and (3) above are in this Chapter referred to as "the prescribed conditions".

(5) If in the opinion of the Board the facts concerning any scheme or its administration cease to warrant the continuance of their approval of the scheme, they may at any time by notice to the administrator withdraw their approval on such grounds, and from such date (which shall not be earlier than the date when those facts first ceased to warrant the continuance of their approval or 17th March 1987, whichever is the later), as may be specified in the notice.

(6) Where an alteration has been made in a retirement benefits scheme, no approval given as regards the scheme before the alteration shall apply after the date of the alteration unless the alteration has been approved by the Board.

[(7) Subsections (8) to (10) below apply where the Board are considering whether a retirement benefits scheme satisfies or continues to satisfy the prescribed conditions.][3]

[(8) For the purpose of determining whether the scheme, so far as it relates to a particular class or description of employees, satisfies or continues to satisfy the prescribed conditions, that scheme shall be considered in conjunction with—

(a) any other retirement benefits scheme (or schemes) which relates (or relate) to employees of that class or description and which is (or are) approved for the purposes of this Chapter,
(b) any other retirement benefits scheme (or schemes) which relates (or relate) to employees of that class or description and which is (or are) at the same time before the Board in order for them to decide whether to give approval for the purposes of this Chapter,
(c) any section 608 scheme or schemes relating to employees of that class or description, and
(d) any relevant statutory scheme or schemes relating to employees of that class or description.][3]

[(9) If those conditions are satisfied in the case of both or all of those schemes taken together, they shall be taken to be satisfied in the case of the scheme mentioned in subsection (7) above (as well as the other or others).][3]

[(10) If those conditions are not satisfied in the case of both or all of those schemes taken together, they shall not be taken to be satisfied in the case of the scheme mentioned in subsection (7) above.][3]

[(11) The reference in subsection (8)(c) above to a section 608 scheme is a reference to a fund to which section 608 applies.][3]

Former enactments.—Sub-s. (1): FA 1970, s. 19(1); FA 1971, s. 21(2).
Sub-s. (2): FA 1970, s. 19(2).
Sub-ss. (3), (4): FA 1970, s. 19(2A), (2B); FA 1971, s. 21(3); F(No. 2)A 1987, Sch. 3, para. 1.
Sub-s. (5): FA 1970, s. 19(3); F(No. 2)A 1987, Sch. 3, para. 2.
Sub-s. (6): FA 1970, s. 19(4); FA 1971, Sch. 3, para. 12(1).
Sub-s. (7): FA 1970, s. 19(5).
Note.—See **Prospective Legislation Notes** (Married Couples).
Amendments.—[1] Words in sub-s. (3)(d) repealed by FA 1989, Sch. 6, paras. 3(1), (2), 18(2) and Sch. 17, Pt. IV in relation to a scheme not approved by the Board before 27 July 1989; but if the scheme came into existence before 14 March 1989, the repeal does not affect an employee who became a member of the scheme before 1 June 1989. The repealed words read—

"(disregarding any excess of that remuneration over the permitted maximum)".

[2] Sub-s. (3)(e) to (h) substituted by FA 1989, Sch. 6, paras. 3(1), (3), 18(2) in relation to a scheme not approved by the Board before 27 July 1989; but if the scheme came into existence before 14 March 1989, the repeal does not affect an employee who became a member of the scheme before 1 June 1989. The substituted words read—

"In paragraph (d) above "the permitted maximum" means £100,000 or such other sum as may for the time being be specified in an order made by the Treasury."

[3] Sub-ss. (7) to (11) substituted for sub-s. (7) by FA 1989, Sch. 6, paras. 3(1), (4), 18(3) and have effect where determination is made after 26 July 1989. The original sub-s (7) read—

"(7) For the purpose of determining whether a retirement benefits scheme, so far as it relates to a particular class or description of employees, satisfies or continues to satisfy the prescribed conditions—

(a) that scheme shall be considered in conjunction with any other retirement benefits scheme or schemes relating to employees of that class or description, and
(b) if those conditions are satisfied in the case of both or all of those schemes taken together, they shall be taken to be satisfied in the case of each of them, but otherwise those conditions shall be taken to be satisfied in the case of none of them."

[590A. Section 590: supplementary provisions

(1) For the purposes of section 590(3)(*e*) and (*f*) two or more employments are relevant associated employments if they are employments in the case of which—

(*a*) there is a period during which the employee has held both or all of them,
(*b*) the period counts under the scheme in the case of both or all of them as a period in respect of which benefits are payable, and
(*c*) the period is one during which both or all of the employers in question are associated.

(2) For the purposes of section 590(3)(*g*) and (*h*) the scheme is connected with another scheme in relation to an employee if—

(*a*) there is a period during which he has been the employee of two persons who are associated employers,
(*b*) the period counts under both schemes as a period in respect of which benefits are payable, and
(*c*) the period counts under one scheme by virtue of service with one employer and under the other scheme by virtue of service with the other employer.

(3) For the purposes of subsections (1) and (2) above, employers are associated if (directly or indirectly) one is controlled by the other or if both are controlled by a third person.

(4) In subsection (3) above the reference to control, in relation to a body corporate, shall be construed—

(*a*) where the body corporate is a close company, in accordance with section 416, and
(*b*) where it is not, in accordance with section 840.][1]

Amendments.—[1] This section inserted by FA 1989, Sch. 6, paras. 4, 18(2) in relation to a scheme not approved by the Board before 27 July 1989; but if the scheme came into existence before 14 March 1989, the repeal does not affect an employee who became a member of the scheme before 1 June 1989.

[590B. Section 590: further supplementary provisions

(1) For the purposes of section 590(3)(*e*) the relevant amount, in relation to an employee, shall be found by applying the following formula—

$$\frac{A \times C}{60}$$

(2) For the purposes of section 590(3)(*f*) the relevant amount, in relation to an employee, shall be found by applying the following formula—

$$\frac{3 \times A \times C}{80}$$

(3) For the purposes of section 590(3)(*g*) the relevant amount, in relation to an employee, shall be found by applying the following formula—

$$\frac{B \times C}{60}$$

(4) For the purposes of section 590(3)(*h*) the relevant amount, in relation to an employee, shall be found by applying the following formula—

$$\frac{3 \times B \times C}{80}$$

(5) For the purposes of this section A is the aggregate number of years service (expressing parts of a year as a fraction), subject to a maximum of 40, which, in the case of the employee, count for the purposes of the scheme at the time the benefits in respect of service in the employment become payable.

(6) But where the same year (or part of a year) counts for the purposes of the scheme by virtue of more than one of the relevant associated employments it shall be counted only once in calculating the aggregate number of years service for the purposes of subsection (5) above.

(7) For the purposes of this section B is the aggregate number of years service (expressing parts of a year as a fraction), subject to a maximum of 40, which, in the case of the employee, count for the purposes of any of the following—

(*a*) the scheme, and
(*b*) the other scheme or schemes with which the scheme is connected in relation to him

at the time the benefits become payable.

(8) But where the same year (or part of a year) counts for the purposes of more than one scheme it shall be counted only once in calculating the aggregate number of years service for the purpose of subsection (7) above.

(9) For the purposes of this section C is the permitted maximum in relation to the year of assessment in which the benefits in question become payable, that is, the figure found for that year by virtue of subsections (10) and (11) below.

(10) For the years 1988–89 and 1989–90 the figure is £60,000.

(11) For any subsequent year of assessment the figure is the figure found for that year, for the purposes of section 590C, by virtue of section 590C(4) and (5).]¹

Amendments.—¹ This section inserted by FA 1989, Sch. 6, paras. 4, 18(2) in relation to a scheme not approved by the Board before 27 July 1989; but if the scheme came into existence before 14 March 1989, the repeal does not affect an employee who became a member of the scheme before 1 June 1989.

[590C. Earnings cap

(1) In arriving at an employee's final remuneration for the purposes of section 590(3)(*a*) or (*d*), any excess of what would be his final remuneration (apart from this section) over the permitted maximum for the year of assessment in which his participation in the scheme ceases shall be disregarded.

(2) In subsection (1) above "the permitted maximum", in relation to a year of assessment, means the figure found for that year by virtue of subsections (3) and (4) below.

(3) For the years 1988–89 and 1989–90 the figure is £60,000.

(4) For any subsequent year of assessment the figure is also £60,000, subject to subsection (5) below.

(5) If the retail prices index for the month of December preceding a year of assessment falling within subsection (4) above is higher than it was for the previous December, the figure for that year shall be an amount arrived at by—

    (*a*) increasing the figure for the previous year of assessment by the same percentage as the percentage increase in the retail prices index, and

    (*b*) if the result is not a multiple of £600, rounding it up to the nearest amount which is such a multiple.

(6) The Treasury shall in the year of assessment 1989–90, and in each subsequent year of assessment, make an order specifying the figure which is by virtue of this section the figure for the following year of assessment.]¹

Amendments.—¹ This section inserted by FA 1989, Sch. 6, paras. 4, 18(2) in relation to a scheme not approved by the Board before 27 July 1989; but if the scheme came into existence before 14 March 1989, this section does not affect an employee who became a member of the scheme before 1 June 1989.

591. Discretionary approval

(1) The Board may, if they think fit having regard to the facts of a particular case, and subject to such conditions, if any, as they think proper to attach to the approval, approve a retirement benefits scheme for the purposes of this Chapter notwithstanding that it does not satisfy one or more of the prescribed conditions; but this subsection has effect subject to subsection (5) below.

(2) The Board may in particular approve by virtue of this section a scheme—

    (*a*) which exceeds the limits imposed by the prescribed conditions as respects benefits for less than 40 years; or

    (*b*) which provides pensions for the widows of employees on death in service, or for the children or dependants of employees; or

    (*c*) which provides on death in service a lump sum of up to four times the employee's final remuneration (exclusive of any refunds of contributions); or

    (*d*) which allows benefits to be payable on retirement within ten years of the specified age, or on earlier incapacity; or

    (*e*) which provides for the return in certain contingencies of employees' contributions; or

    (*f*) which relates to a trade or undertaking carried on only partly in the United Kingdom and by a person not resident in the United Kingdom; or

(g) which provides in certain contingencies for securing relevant benefits (but no other benefits) by means of an annuity contract approved by the Board and made with an insurance company of the employee's choice; or

(h) to which the employer is not a contributor and which provides benefits additional to those provided by a scheme to which he is a contributor.

(3) In subsection (2)(g) above "insurance company" means a company to which Part II of the Insurance Companies Act 1982 applies.

(4) In applying this section to a scheme which was in existence on 6th April 1980, the Board shall exercise their discretion, in such cases as appear to them to be appropriate, so as to preserve—

(a) benefits earned or rights arising out of service before 6th April 1980; and
(b) any rights to death-in-service benefits conferred by rules of the scheme in force on 26th February 1970.

(5) The Board shall not approve a scheme by virtue of this section if to do so would be inconsistent with regulations made [by the Board][1] for the purposes of this section.

(6) Regulations made [by the Board][1] for the purposes of this section may restrict the Board's discretion to approve a scheme by reference to the benefits provided by the scheme, the investments held for the purposes of the scheme, the manner in which the scheme is administered or any other circumstances whatever.

Former enactments.—Sub-s. (1): FA 1970, s. 20(1); F(No. 2)A 1987, Sch. 3, para. 3(2).
Sub-s. (2): FA 1970, s. 20(2); FA 1971, s. 21(4); FA 1981, s. 32; F(No. 2)A 1987, Sch. 3, para. 3(3), (4).
Sub-s. (3): FA 1970, s. 20(2A); FA 1981, s. 32; Insurance Companies Act 1982.
Sub-s. (4): FA 1970, s. 20(3); FA 1987, Sch. 15, para. 3.
Sub-ss. (5), (6): FA 1970, s. 20(4), (5); F(No. 2)A 1987, Sch. 3, para. 3(5).
Amendments.—Words in sub-ss. (5), (6) inserted by FA 1988, Sch. 13, para. 6.

Tax reliefs

592. Exempt approved schemes

(1) This section has effect as respects—

(a) any approved scheme which is shown to the satisfaction of the Board to be established under irrevocable trusts; or
(b) any other approved scheme as respects which the Board, having regard to any special circumstances, direct that this section shall apply;

and any scheme which is for the time being within paragraph (a) or (b) above is in this Chapter referred to as an "exempt approved scheme".

(2) Exemption from income tax shall, on a claim being made in that behalf, be allowed in respect of income derived from investments or deposits if, or to such extent as the Board are satisfied that, it is income from investments or deposits held for the purposes of the scheme.

(3) Exemption from income tax shall, on a claim being made in that behalf, be allowed in respect of underwriting commissions if, or to such extent as the Board are satisfied that, the underwriting commissions are applied for the purposes of the schemes and would, but for this subsection, be chargeable to tax under Case VI of Schedule D.

(4) Any sum paid by an employer by way of contribution under the scheme shall, for the purposes of Case I or II of Schedule D and of sections 75 and 76, be allowed to be deducted as an expense, or expense of management, incurred in the chargeable period in which the sum is paid.

(5) The amount of an employer's contributions which may be deducted under subsection (4) above shall not exceed the amount contributed by him under the scheme in respect of employees in a trade or undertaking in respect of the profits of which the employer is assessable to tax (that is to say, to United Kingdom income tax or corporation tax).

(6) A sum not paid by way of ordinary annual contribution shall for the purposes of subsection (4) above be treated, as the Board may direct, either as an expense incurred in the chargeable period in which the sum is paid, or as an expense to be spread over such period of years as the Board think proper.

(7) Any contribution paid under the scheme by an employee shall, in assessing tax under Schedule E, be allowed to be deducted as an expense incurred in the year of assessment in which the contribution is paid.

(8) [Subject to subsection (8A) below,][1] the amount allowed to be deducted by virtue of subsection (7) above in respect of contributions paid by an employee in a year of assessment (whether under a single scheme or under two or more schemes) shall not exceed 15 per cent., or such higher percentage as the Board may in a particular case prescribe, of his remuneration for that year.

[(8A) Where an employee's remuneration for a year of assessment includes remuneration in respect of more than one employment, the amount allowed to be deducted by virtue of subsection (7) above in respect of contributions paid by the employee in that year by virtue of any employment (whether under a single scheme or under two or more schemes) shall not exceed 15 per cent, or such higher percentage as the Board may in a particular case prescribe, of his remuneration for the year in respect of that employment.][2]

[(8B) In arriving at an employee's remuneration for a year of assessment for the purposes of subsection (8) or (8A) above, any excess of what would be his remuneration (apart from this subsection) over the permitted maximum for that year shall be disregarded.][2]

[(8C) In subsection (8B) above "permitted maximum", in relation to a year of assessment, means the figure found for that year by virtue of subsections (8D) and (8E) below.][2]

[(8D) For the year of assessment 1989–90 the figure is £60,000.][2]

[(8E) For any subsequent year of assessment the figure is the figure found for that year, for the purposes of section 590C, by virtue of section 590C(4) and (5).][2]

(9) Relief shall not be given under section 266 or 273 in respect of any payment in respect of which an allowance can be made under subsection (7) above.

(10) Subsection (2) of section 468 and subsection (3) of section 469 shall not apply to any authorised unit trust which is also an exempt approved scheme if the employer is not a contributor to the exempt approved scheme and that scheme provides benefits additional to those provided by another exempt approved scheme to which he is a contributor.

(11) Nothing in this section shall be construed as affording relief in respect of any sums to be brought into account under section 438.

(12) This section has effect only as respects income arising or contributions paid at a time when the scheme is an exempt approved scheme.

Former enactments.—FA 1970, s. 21(1)–(9); FA 1971, s. 21(5); F(No. 2)A 1987, Sch. 3, paras. 4, 5.
Cross references.—See CGTA 1979, s. 149B(1)(*j*) (an authorised unit trust to which sub-s. (10) above applies exempt from tax in respect of gains on disposal of units).
Amendments.—[1] Words in sub-s. (8) inserted by FA 1989, Sch. 6, para. 5(1), (2).
[2] Sub-ss. (8A) to (8E) inserted by FA 1989, Sch. 6, paras. 5(1), (3), (4), 18(4) with effect from the year 1989–90 unless their effect is nullified by regulations.

593. Relief by way of deductions from contributions

(1) Relief under section 592(7) shall be given in accordance with subsections (2) and (3) below in such cases and subject to such conditions as the Board may prescribe by regulations under section 612(3) in respect of schemes—

    (*a*) to which employees, but not their employers, are contributors; and
    (*b*) which provide benefits additional to benefits provided by schemes to which their employers are contributors.

(2) An employee who is entitled to relief under section 592(7) in respect of a contribution may deduct from the contribution when he pays it, and may retain, an amount equal to income tax at the basic rate on the contribution.

(3) The administrator of the scheme—

    (*a*) shall accept the amount paid after the deduction in discharge of the employee's liability to the same extent as if the deduction had not been made; and
    (*b*) may recover an amount equal to the deduction from the Board.

(4) Regulations under subsection (3) of section 612 may, without prejudice to the generality of that subsection—

    (*a*) provide for the manner in which claims for the recovery of a sum under subsection (3)(*b*) above may be made;
    (*b*) provide for the giving of such information, in such form, as may be prescribed by or under the regulations;
    (*c*) provide for the inspection by persons authorised by the Board of books, documents and other records.

Former enactments.—FA 1970, Sch. 5, Pt. II, para. 6A; F(No. 2)A 1987, Sch. 3, para. 12.

594. Exempt statutory schemes

(1) Any contribution paid by any officer or employee under a [relevant][1] statutory scheme established under a public general Act shall, in assessing tax under Schedule E, be allowed to be deducted as an expense incurred in the year of assessment in which the contribution is paid; and relief shall not be given under section 266 or 273 in respect of any contribution allowable as a deduction under this section.

(2) [Subject to subsection (3) below,][2] the amount allowed to be deducted by virtue of subsection (1) above in respect of contributions paid by a person in a year of assessment (whether under a single scheme or under two or more schemes) shall not exceed 15 per cent., or such higher percentage as the Board may in a particular case prescribe, of his remuneration for that year.

[(3) Where a person's remuneration for a year of assessment includes remuneration in respect of more than one office or employment, the amount allowed to be deducted by virtue of subsection (1) above in respect of contributions paid by the person in that year by virtue of any office or employment (whether under a single scheme or under two or more schemes) shall not exceed 15 per cent, or such higher percentage as the Board may in a particular case prescribe, of his remuneration for the year in respect of that office or employment.][3]

[(4) In arriving at a person's remuneration for a year of assessment for the purposes of subsection (2) or (3) above, any excess of what would be his remuneration (apart from this subsection) over the permitted maximum for that year shall be disregarded.][3]

[(5) In subsection (4) above "permitted maximum", in relation to a year of assessment, means the figure found for that year by virtue of subsections (6) and (7) below.][3]

[(6) For the year 1989–90 the figure is £60,000.][3]

[(7) For any subsequent year of assessment the figure is the figure found for that year, for the purposes of section 590C, by virtue of section 590C(4) and (5).][3]

Former enactments.—FA 1970, s. 22; FA 1972, s. 74(3); F(No. 2)A 1987, Sch. 3, para. 6.
Amendments.—[1] Word in sub-s. (1) inserted by FA 1989, Sch. 6, paras. 6(1), (2), 18(1) with effect from 14 March 1989.
[2] Words in sub-s. (2) inserted by FA 1989, Sch. 6, paras. 6(1), (3), 18(4).
[3] Sub-ss. (3) to (7) inserted by FA 1989, Sch. 6, paras. 6(1), (4), (5), 18(4) with effect from the year 1989–90 unless their effect is nullified by regulations.

Charge to tax in certain cases

595. Charge to tax in respect of certain sums paid by employer etc.

(1) Subject to the provisions of this Chapter, where, pursuant to a retirement benefits scheme, the employer in any year of assessment pays a sum with a view to the provision of any relevant benefits for any employee of that employer, then (whether or not the accrual of the benefits is dependent on any contingency)—

(*a*) the sum paid, if not otherwise chargeable to income tax as income of the employee, shall be deemed for all purposes of the Income Tax Acts to be income of that employee for that year of assessment and assessable to tax under Schedule E; and
(*b*) where the payment is made under such an insurance or contract as is mentioned in section 266, relief, if not otherwise allowable, shall be given to that employee under that section in respect of the payment to the extent, if any, to which such relief would have been allowable to him if the payment had been made by him and the insurance or contract under which the payment is made had been made with him.

(2) . . .[1]

(3) . . .[1]

(4) Where the employer pays any sum as mentioned in subsection (1) above in relation to more than one employee, the sum so paid shall, for the purpose of that subsection, be apportioned among those employees by reference to the separate sums which would have had to be paid to secure the separate benefits to be provided for them respectively, and the part of the sum apportioned to each of them shall be deemed for that purpose to have been paid separately in relation to that one of them.

(5) Any reference in this section to the provision for an employee of relevant benefits

includes a reference to the provision of benefits payable to that employee's wife or widow, children, dependants or personal representatives.

Former enactment—FA 1970, s. 23(1)–(5).
Amendments.—[1] Sub-ss. (2), (3) repealed by FA 1989, Sch. 6, paras. 7, 18(5) and Sch. 17, Pt. IV with retrospective effect from the year 1988–89.

596. Exceptions from section 595

(1) [Section 595(1) shall not][1] apply where the retirement benefits scheme in question is—
  (a) an approved scheme, or
  (b) a [relevant][2] statutory scheme, or
  (c) a scheme set up by a government outside the United Kingdom for the benefit, or primarily for the benefit of, its employees.

(2) [Section 595(1) shall not][1] apply for any year of assessment—
  (a) where the employee performs the duties of his employment in such circumstances that no tax is chargeable under Case I or II of Schedule E in respect of the emoluments of his employment (or would be so chargeable were there such emoluments), or
  (b) where the emoluments from the employment are foreign emoluments within the meaning of section 192 and the Board are satisfied, on a claim made by the employee, that the retirement benefits scheme in question corresponds to such a scheme as is mentioned in paragraph (a), (b) or (c) of subsection (1) above.

(3) Where, in respect of the provision for an employee of any relevant benefits—
  (a) a sum has been deemed to be income of his by virtue . . .[3] of subsection (1) . . .[3] of section 595, and
  (b) subsequently, the employee proves to the satisfaction of the Board that—
    (i) no payment in respect of, or in substitution for, the benefits has been made, and
    (ii) some event has occurred by reason of which no such payment will be made,
and makes application for relief under this subsection within six years from the time when that event occurred,
the Board shall give relief in respect of tax on that sum by repayment or otherwise as may be appropriate; and if the employee satisfies the Board as mentioned above in relation to some particular part, but not the whole, of the benefits, the Board may give such relief as may seem to them just and reasonable.

Former enactments.—FA 1970, s. 24; FA 1974, s. 21(7).
Amendments.—[1] Words in sub-ss. (1), (2) substituted by FA 1989, Sch. 6, paras. 8(1), (2)(a), (3), 18(5) with retrospective effect from the year 1988–89.
[2] Words in sub-s. (1)(b) inserted by FA 1989, Sch. 6, paras. 8(1), (2)(b), 18(1) with effect from 14 March 1989.
[3] Words in sub-s. (3)(a) repealed by FA 1989, Sch. 6, paras. 8(1), (4), 18(6) and Sch. 17, Pt. IV where a sum has been deemed to be income of a person by virtue of s. 595(2) of this Act after 5 April 1988.

[596A. Charge to tax: benefits under non-approved schemes

(1) Where in any year of assessment a person receives a benefit provided under a retirement benefits scheme which is not of a description mentioned in section 596(1)(a), (b) or (c), tax shall be charged in accordance with the provisions of this section.

(2) Where the benefit is received by an individual, he shall be charged to tax under Schedule E for that year.

(3) Where the benefit is received by a person other than an individual, the administrator of the scheme shall be charged to tax under Case VI of Schedule D for that year.

(4) The amount to be charged to tax is—
  (a) in the case of a cash benefit, the amount received, and
  (b) in the case of a benefit in kind, an amount equal to whatever is the cash equivalent of the benefit.

(5) In the case of the charge under Case VI of Schedule D, the rate of tax is 40 per cent. or such other rate (whether higher or lower) as may for the time being be specified by the Treasury by order.

(6) Tax shall not be charged under this section in the case of a benefit which is chargeable to tax under Schedule E by virtue of section 19(1)1.

(7) But where the amount chargeable to tax by virtue of section 19(1)1 is less than the amount which would be chargeable to tax under this section—
  (a) subsection (6) above shall not apply, and

(*b*) the amount chargeable to tax under this section shall be reduced by the amount chargeable to tax by virtue of section 19(1)1.

(8) Tax shall not be charged under this section to the extent that the benefit received is attributable to the payment of a sum—

(*a*) which is deemed to be the income of a person by virtue of section 595(1), and
(*b*) in respect of which that person has been assessed to tax.

(9) For the purpose of subsection (8) above the provision of a benefit shall be presumed not to be attributable to the payment of such a sum as is mentioned in that subsection unless the contrary is shown.][1]

Amendments.—[1] This section inserted by FA 1989, Sch. 6, paras. 9, 18(7) in relation to payments made and benefits provided after 26 July 1989.

[596B. Section 596A: supplementary provisions

(1) For the purposes of section 596A the cash equivalent of a benefit in kind is—

(*a*) in the case of a benefit other than living accommodation, the amount which would be the cash equivalent of the benefit under Chapter II of Part V if it were chargeable under the appropriate provision of that Chapter (treating any sum made good by the recipient as made good by the employee), and
(*b*) in the case of living accommodation, an amount equal to the value of the accommodation to the recipient determined in accordance with the following provisions of this section less so much of any sum made good by him to those at whose cost the accommodation is provided as is properly attributable to the provision of the accommodation.

(2) Where the cost of providing the accommodation does not exceed £75,000, the value of the accommodation to the recipient in any period is the rent which would have been payable for the period if the premises had been let to him at an annual rent equal to their annual value as ascertained under section 837.

(3) But for a period in which those at whose cost the accommodation is provided pay rent at an annual rate greater than the annual value as so ascertained, the value of the accommodation to the recipient is an amount equal to the rent payable by them for the period.

(4) Where the cost of providing the accommodation does exceed £75,000, the value of the accommodation to the recipient shall be taken to be the aggregate of the value of the accommodation to him determined in accordance with subsections (2) and (3) above and the additional value of the accommodation to him determined in accordance with subsections (5) and (6) below.

(5) The additional value of the accommodation to the recipient in any period is the rent which would have been payable for that period if the premises had been let to him at an annual rent equal to the appropriate percentage of the amount by which the cost of providing the accommodation exceeds £75,000.

(6) Where throughout the period of six years ending with the date when the recipient first occupied the property any estate or interest in the property was held by a relevant person (whether or not it was the same estate, interest or person throughout), the additional value shall be calculated as if in subsection (7) below—

(a) the amount referred to in paragraph (a) were the market value of that property as at that date, and
(b) the amount referred to in paragraph (b) did not include expenditure on improvements made before that date.

(7) For the purposes of this section, the cost of providing any living accommodation shall be taken to be the aggregate of—

(a) the amount of any expenditure incurred in acquiring the estate or interest in the property held by a relevant person, and
(b) the amount of any expenditure incurred by a relevant person before the year of assessment in question on improvements to the property.

(8) The aggregate amount mentioned in subsection (7) above shall be reduced by the amount of any payment made by the recipient to a relevant person, so far as that amount represents a reimbursement of any such expenditure as is mentioned in paragraph (a) or (b) of that subsection or represents consideration for the grant to the recipient of a tenancy of the property.

(9) For the purposes of this section, any of the following persons is a relevant person—

(a) the person providing the accommodation;
(b) any person, other than the recipient, who is connected with a person falling within paragraph (a) above.

(10) In this section—

"the appropriate percentage" means the rate applicable for the purposes of section 160 as at the beginning of the year of assessment in question;
"market value", in relation to any property, means the price which that property might reasonably be expected to fetch on a sale in the open market with vacant possession, no reduction being made, in estimating the market value, on account of any option in respect of the property held by the recipient, or a person connected with him, or by any of the persons mentioned in subsection (9) above;
"property", in relation to any living accommodation, means the property consisting of that living accommodation;
"tenancy" includes a sub-tenancy;

and section 839 shall apply for the purposes of this section.][1]

Amendments.—[1] This section inserted by FA 1989, Sch. 6, paras. 9, 18 (7) in relation to payments made and benefits provided after 26 July 1989.

597. Charge to tax: pensions

(1) Subject to subsection (2) below, all pensions paid under any scheme which is approved or is being considered for approval under this Chapter shall be charged to tax under Schedule E, and section 203 shall apply accordingly.

(2) As respects any scheme which is approved or is being considered for approval under this Chapter, the Board may direct that, until such date as the Board may specify, pensions under the scheme shall be charged to tax as annual payments under Case III of Schedule D, and tax shall be deductible under sections 348 and 349 accordingly.

Former enactment.—FA 1970, Sch. 5, Pt. II, para. 1.
Cross references.—See FA 1989, s. 41 (1) (d) (a pension chargeable to income tax under this section to be charged in the year of assessment in which it accrues irrespective of when it is paid).

598. Charge to tax: repayment of employee's contributions

(1) Subject to the provisions of this section, tax shall be charged under this section on any repayment to an employee during his lifetime of any contributions (including interest on contributions, if any) if the payment is made under—

   (a) a scheme which is or has at any time been an exempt approved scheme, or
   (b) a [relevant][1] statutory scheme established under a public general Act.

(2) Where any payment is chargeable to tax under this section, the administrator of the scheme shall be charged to income tax under Case VI of Schedule D and, subject to subsection (3) below, the rate of tax shall be 10 per cent.

(3) The Treasury may by order from time to time increase or decrease the rate of tax under subsection (2) above.

(4) The tax shall be charged on the amount paid or, if the rules permit the administrator to deduct the tax before payment, on the amount before deduction of tax, and the amount so charged to tax shall not be treated as income for any other purpose of the Tax Acts.

(5) Subsection (1)(a) above shall not apply in relation to a contribution made after the scheme ceases to be an exempt approved scheme (unless it again becomes an exempt approved scheme).

(6) This section shall not apply where the employee's employment was carried on outside the United Kingdom.

(7) In relation to a statutory scheme, "employee" in this section includes any officer.

Former enactments.—FA 1970, Sch. 5, Pt. II, paras. 2, 3; FA 1971, Sch. 3, para. 7; F(No. 2)A 1987, Sch. 3, para. 9.
Note.—The rate of tax under sub-s. (2) changed by virtue of sub-s. (3) as follows—
   20 per cent. from 6 April 1988: S.I. 1988 No. 504.
Amendments.—[1] Word in sub-s. (1)(b) inserted by FA 1989, Sch. 6, paras. 10, 18(1) with effect from 14 March 1989.

---

599. Charge to tax: commutation of entire pension in special circumstances

(1) Where a scheme to which this section applies contains a rule allowing, in special circumstances, a payment in commutation of an employee's entire pension, and any pension is commuted, whether wholly or not, under the rule, tax shall be charged on the amount by which the sum receivable exceeds—

   (a) the largest sum which would have been receivable in commutation of any part of the pension if the scheme had secured that the aggregate value of the relevant benefits payable to an employee on or after retirement, excluding any pension which was not commutable, could not exceed three-eighties of his final remuneration (disregarding any excess of that remuneration over the permitted maximum) for each year of service up to a maximum of 40; or
   (b) the largest sum which would have been receivable in commutation of any part of the pension under any rule of the scheme authorising the commutation of part (but not the

whole) of the pension, or which would have been so receivable but for those special circumstances;

whichever gives the lesser amount chargeable to tax.

(2) This section applies to—
    (a) a scheme which is or has at any time been an approved scheme, or
    (b) a [relevant][1] statutory scheme established under a public general Act.

(3) Where any amount is chargeable to tax under this section the administrator of the scheme shall be charged to income tax under Case VI of Schedule D on that amount, and section 598(2), (3) and (4) shall apply as they apply to tax chargeable under that section.

(4) This section shall not apply where the employee's employment was carried on outside the United Kingdom.

(5) In relation to a statutory scheme, "employee" in this section includes any officer.

(6) In applying paragraph (a) or (b) of subsection (1) above—
    (a) the same considerations shall be taken into account, including the provisions of any other relevant scheme, as would have been taken into account by the Board in applying section 590; and
    (b) where the scheme has ceased to be an approved scheme, account shall only be taken of the rules in force when the scheme was last an approved scheme.

(7) Where the pension has been secured by means of an annuity contract with an insurance company and the sum receivable is payable under that contract by the insurance company, the references to the administrator of the scheme in subsection (3) above and in section 598(2) and (4) as applied by that subsection are to be read as references to the insurance company.

(8) In subsection (7) above "insurance company" means—
    (a) a person authorised under section 3 or 4 of the Insurance Companies Act 1982 to carry on long term business and acting through a branch or agency in the United Kingdom; or
    (b) a society registered as a friendly society under the Friendly Societies Act 1974 or the Friendly Societies Act (Northern Ireland) 1970.

(9) In relation to payments made under schemes approved or established before 17th March 1987 to employees who became members before that date, subsection (1)(a) above shall have effect with the omission of the words "(disregarding any excess of that remuneration over the permitted maximum)".

[(10) In subsection (1)(a) above "the permitted maximum" means, as regards a charge to tax arising under this section in a particular year of assessment, the figure found for that year by virtue of subsections (11) and (12) below.][2]

[(11) For the years 1988–89 and 1989–90 the figure is £60,000.][2]

[(12) For any subsequent year of assessment the figure is the figure found for that year, for the purposes of section 590C, by virtue of section 590C(4) and (5).][2]

Former enactments.—FA 1970, Sch. 5, Pt. II, paras. 2, 3; FA 1971, Sch. 3, para. 7; F(No. 2)A 1987, Sch. 3, para. 9.
Amendments.—[1] Word in sub-s. (2)(b) inserted by FA 1989, Sch. 6, paras 11(1), (2), 18(1) with effect from 14 March 1989.
[2] Sub-ss. (10), (11), (12) inserted by FA 1989, Sch. 6, paras. 11(1), (3), 18(8) where the charge to tax under this section arises after 13 March 1989, but not where the scheme came into existence before 14 March 1989 and the employee became a member of it before 1 June 1989.

[599A. Charge to tax: payments out of surplus funds

(1) This subsection applies to any payment which is made to or for the benefit of an employee or to his personal representatives out of funds which are or have been held for the purposes of—
    (a) a scheme which is or has at any time been an exempt approved scheme, or
    (b) a relevant statutory scheme established under a public general Act,
and which is made in pursuance of duty to return surplus funds.

(2) On the making of a payment to which subsection (1) above applies, the administrator of the scheme shall be charged to income tax under Case VI of Schedule D at the relevant rate on such amount as, after deduction of tax at that rate, would equal the amount of the payment.

(3) Subject to subsection (4) below, the relevant rate shall be 35 per cent.

(4) The Treasury may by order from time to time increase or decrease the relevant rate.

(5) Where a payment made to or for the benefit of an employee is one to which subsection (1) applies, it shall be treated in computing the total income of the employee for the year in which it is made as income for that year which is—
   (a) received by him after deduction of income tax at the basic rate from a corresponding gross amount, and
   (b) chargeable to income tax under Case VI of Schedule D.

(6) But, subject to subsection (7) below, no assessment to income tax shall be made on, and no repayment of income tax shall be made to, the employee.

(7) Subsection (6) above shall not prevent an assessment in respect of income tax at a rate other than the basic rate.

(8) Subsection (5) above applies whether or not the employee is the recipient of the payment.

(9) Any payment chargeable to tax under this section shall not be chargeable to tax under section 598, 599 or 600 or under the Regulations mentioned in paragraph 8 of Schedule 3 to the Finance Act 1971.

(10) In this section—

"employee", in relation to a relevant statutory scheme, includes any officer;
references to any payment include references to any transfer of assets or other transfer of money's worth.][1]

Amendments.—[1] This section inserted by FA 1989, Sch. 6, paras. 12, 18(9) in relation to payments made after 26 July 1989.

600. Charge to tax: unauthorised payments to or for employees

(1) This section applies to any payment to or for the benefit of an employee, otherwise than in course of payment of a pension, being a payment made out of funds which are ...[1] held for the purposes of a scheme which is ...[2] approved for the purposes of—
   (a) this Chapter;
   (b) Chapter II of Part II of the Finance Act 1970; or
   (c) section 208 or Chapter II of Part IX of the 1970 Act.

(2) If the payment [is not expressly authorised by the rules of the scheme or by virtue of paragraph 33 of Schedule 6 to the Finance Act 1989][3] the employee (whether or not he is the recipient of the payment) shall be chargeable to tax on the amount of the payment under Schedule E for the year of assessment in which the payment is made.

(3) Any payment chargeable to tax under this section shall not be chargeable to tax under section 598 or 599 or under the Regulations mentioned in paragraph 8 of Schedule 3 to the Finance Act 1971.

(4) References in this section to any payment include references to any transfer of assets or other transfer of money's worth.

Former enactment.—FA 1971, Sch. 3, para 9.
Amendments.—[1] Words "or have been" in sub-s. (1) repealed by FA 1989, Sch. 6, paras. 13(1), (2), 18(9) and Sch. 17, Pt. IV in relation to payments made after 26 July 1989.
[2] Words "or has at any time been" repealed by *ibid.*
[3] Words in sub-s. (2) substituted for sub-s/ (2)(a), (b) by FA 1989, Sch. 6, paras. 13(1), (3), 18(9) in relation to payments made after 26 July 1989. Sub-s. (2)(a), (b) read—
   "(a) is not expressly authorised by the rules of the scheme, or
   (b) is made at a time when the scheme is not approved for the purposes of any of the enactments mentioned in subsection (1) above, and would not have been expressly authorised by the rules of the scheme when it was last so approved."

601. Charge to tax: payments to employers

(1) Subsection (2) below applies where a payment is made to an employer out of funds which are or have been held for the purposes of a scheme which is or has at any time been an exempt approved scheme and whether or not the payment is made in pursuance of Schedule 22.

(2) An amount equal to 40 per cent. of the payment shall be recoverable by the Board from the employer.

(3) Subsection (2) above does not apply to any payment—
   (a) to the extent that, if this section had not been enacted, the employer would have been exempt, or entitled to claim exemption, from income tax or corporation tax in respect of the payment; or

(b) made before the scheme became an exempt approved scheme; or
(c) of any prescribed description; or
(d) made in pursuance of the winding-up of the scheme where the winding-up commenced on or before 18th March 1986; or
(e) made in pursuance of an application which—

    (i) was made to the Board on or before that date and was not withdrawn before the making of the payment, and
    (ii) sought the Board's assurance that the payment would not lead to a withdrawal of approval under section 19(3) of the Finance Act 1970;

(4) Subsection (2) above does not apply where the employer is a charity (within the meaning of section 506).

(5) Where any payment is made or becomes due to an employer out of funds which are or have been held for the purposes of a scheme which is or has at any time been an exempt approved scheme then—

    (a) if the scheme relates to a trade, profession or vocation carried on by the employer, the payment shall be treated for the purposes of the Tax Acts as a receipt of that trade, profession or vocation receivable when the payment falls due or on the last day on which the trade, profession or vocation is carried on by the employer, whichever is the earlier;
    (b) if the scheme does not relate to such a trade, profession or vocation, the employer shall be charged to tax on the amount of the payment under Case VI of Schedule D.

This subsection shall not apply to a payment which fell due before the scheme became an exempt approved scheme or to a payment to which subsection (2) above applies or would apply but for subsection (3)(a) or (4) above.

(6) In this section—

    (a) references to any payment include references to any transfer of assets or other transfer of money's worth; and
    (b) "prescribed" means prescribed by regulations made by the Treasury.

Former enactments.—FA 1986, Sch. 12, para. 1; FA 1970, Sch. 5, Pt. II, para. 4; FA 1971, Sch. 3, para. 12(5).

602. Regulations relating to surpluses

(1) In relation to an amount recoverable as mentioned in section 601(2), the Treasury may by regulations make any of the provisions mentioned in subsection (2) below; and for this purpose the amount shall be treated as if it were—

    (a) an amount of income tax chargeable on the employer under Case VI of Schedule D for the year of assessment in which the payment is made; or
    (b) where the employer is a company, an amount of corporation tax chargeable on the company for the accounting period in which the payment is made.

(2) The provisions are—

    (a) provision requiring the administrator of the scheme or the employer (or both) to furnish to the Board, in respect of the amount recoverable and of the payment concerned, information of a prescribed kind;
    (b) provision enabling the Board to serve a notice or notices requiring the administrator or employer (or both) to furnish to the Board, in respect of the amount and payment, particulars of a prescribed kind;
    (c) provision requiring the administrator to deduct out of the payment the amount recoverable and to account to the Board for it;
    (d) provision as to circumstances in which the employer may be assessed in respect of the amount recoverable;
    (e) provision that, in a case where the employer has been assessed in respect of an amount recoverable but has not paid it (or part of it) within a prescribed period, the administrator may be assessed and charged (in the employer's name) in respect of the amount (or part unpaid);
    (f) provision that, in a case where the amount recoverable (or part of it) has been recovered from the administrator by virtue of an assessment in the employer's name, the administrator is entitled to recover from the employer a sum equal to the amount (or part);
    (g) provision enabling the employer or administrator (as the case may be) to appeal against an assessment made on him in respect of the amount recoverable;
    (h) provision as to when any sum in respect of the amount recoverable is payable to the

Board by the administrator or employer and provision requiring interest to be paid on any sum so payable;

(*j*) provision that an amount paid to the Board by the adminstrator shall be treated as paid on account of the employer's liability under section 601(2).

(3) For the purpose of giving effect to any provision mentioned in subsection (2)(*c*) to (*j*) above, regulations under this section may include provision applying (with or without modifications) provisions of the enactments relating to income tax and corporation tax.

(4) Subject to any provision of regulations under this section—

(*a*) a payment to which section 601(2) applies shall not be treated as a profit or gain brought into charge to income tax or corporation tax and shall not be treated as part of the employer's income for any purpose of this Act; and
(*b*) the amount recoverable shall not be subject to any exemption or reduction (by way of relief, set-off or otherwise) or be available for set-off against other tax.

(5) If the employer is a company and a payment to which section 601(1) and (2) applies is made at a time not otherwise within an accounting period of the company, an accounting period of the company shall for the purposes of subsection (1)(*b*) above be treated as beginning immediately before the payment is made.

Former enactments.—FA 1986, Sch. 12, paras. 2(1)(i), (2), (4)–(6).

603. Reduction of surpluses

Schedule 22 (which provides for the reduction of certain pension fund surpluses) shall have effect.

Supplementary provisions

604. Application for approval of a scheme

(1) An application for the approval for the purposes of this Chapter of any retirement benefits scheme shall be made in writing by the administrator of the scheme to the Board before the end of the first year of assessment for which approval is required, and shall be accompanied by—

(*a*) two copies of the instrument or other document constituting the scheme; and
(*b*) two copies of the rules of the scheme and, except where the application is being sought on the setting up of the scheme, two copies of the accounts of the scheme for the last year for which such accounts have been made up; and
(*c*) such other information and particulars (including copies of any actuarial report or advice given to the administrator or employer in connection with the setting up of the scheme) as the Board may consider relevant.

(2) The form in which an application for approval is to be made, or in which any information is to be given, in pursuance of this section may be prescribed by the Board.

Former enactments.—FA 1970, Sch. 5, Pt. II, paras. 6, 7, 8, 9; F(No. 2)A 1987, Sch. 3, paras. 11, 13–15.

605. Information

(1) In the case of every approved scheme, the administrator of the scheme, and every employer who pays contributions under the scheme, shall, within 30 days from the date of a notice from the inspector requiring them so to do—

(*a*) furnish to the inspector a return containing such particulars of contributions paid under the scheme as the notice may require;
(*b*) prepare and deliver to the inspector a return containing particulars of all payments under the scheme, being—
  (i) payments by way of return of contributions (including interest on contributions, if any);
  (ii) payments by way of commutation of, or in lieu of, pensions, or other lump sum payments;
  (iii) other payments made to an employer;
(*c*) furnish to the inspector a copy of the accounts of the scheme up to the last date previous to the notice to which such accounts have been made up together with such other information and particulars (including copies of any actuarial report or advice given to

the administrator or employer in connection with the conduct of the scheme during the period to which the accounts relate) as the inspector considers relevant.

(2) Where benefits provided for an employee under an approved scheme or a [relevant][1] statutory scheme have been secured by means of an annuity contract with an insurance company (within the meaning given by section 599(8)), the insurance company shall, within 30 days from the date of a notice from the inspector requiring it to do so, prepare and deliver to the inspector a return containing particulars of—

    (*a*) any payments under the contract by way of commutation of, or in lieu of, a pension, or any other lump sum payments under the contract; and
    (*b*) any payments made under the contract to the employer.

(3) It shall be the duty of every employer—

    (*a*) if there subsists in relation to any of his employees a retirement benefits scheme to which he contributes and which is neither an approved scheme nor a [relevant][1] statutory scheme, to deliver particulars of that scheme to the Board within three months beginning with the date on which the scheme first comes into operation in relation to any of his employees, and
    (*b*) when required to do so by notice given by the Board, to furnish within the time limited by the notice such particulars as the Board may require with regard to—

        (i) any retirement benefits scheme relating to the employer which is neither an approved scheme nor a [relevant][1] statutory scheme; and
        (ii) the employees of his to whom any such scheme relates.

(4) It shall be the duty of the administrator of a retirement benefits scheme which is neither an approved scheme nor a [relevant][1] statutory scheme, when required to do so by notice given by the Board, to furnish within the time limited by the notice such particulars as the Board may require with regard to the scheme.

Former enactments.—FA 1970, Sch. 5, Pt. II, paras. 6, 7, 8, 9; F(No. 2)A 1987, Sch. 3, paras. 11, 13–15.
Amendments.—[1] Word in sub-ss. (2), (3)(*a*), (*b*)(i), (4) inserted by FA 1989, Sch. 6, paras. 14, 18(1) with effect from 14 March 1989.

606. Responsibilities of administrator of scheme, and employer

(1) If the administrator of a retirement benefits scheme defaults or cannot be traced or dies, the employer shall be responsible in his place for the discharge of all duties imposed on the administrator under this Chapter and shall be liable for any tax due from him in his capacity as administrator.

This subsection does not apply if the employer is not a contributor to the scheme.

(2) No liability incurred under this Chapter by the administrator of a scheme, or by an employer, shall be affected by the termination of the scheme or by it ceasing to be an approved scheme, or to be an exempt approved scheme.

(3) References in this section to the employer include, where the employer is resident outside the United Kingdom, references to any branch or agent of the employer in the United Kingdom, and in this subsection "branch or agent" has the meaning given by section 118(1) of the Management Act.

(4) This section does not apply for the purposes of sections 602 and 603 and Schedule 22.

Former enactments.—FA 1970, Sch. 5, Pt. II, paras. 6, 7, 8, 9; F(No. 2)A 1987, Sch. 3, paras. 11, 13–15.

607. Pilots' benefit fund

(1) The Board may, if they think fit, and subject to such conditions as they think proper to attach to the approval, approve a pilots' benefit fund for the purposes of this Chapter as if it were a retirement benefits scheme and notwithstanding that it does not satisfy one or more of the conditions set out in section 590(2) and (3).

(2) If a fund is approved by virtue of this section—

    (*a*) sections 592, 597 to 600 and 604 to 606 shall have effect in relation to the fund with the modifications specified in subsection (3) below;
    (*b*) pensions paid out of the fund and any sums chargeable to tax in connection with the fund under section 600 shall be treated for the purposes of the Income Tax Acts as earned income; and

612. Other interpretative provisions, and regulations for purposes of this Chapter

(1) In this Chapter, except where the context otherwise requires—

"administrator", in relation to a retirement benefits scheme, means the person or persons having the management of the scheme;

"approved scheme" means a retirement benefits scheme for the time being approved by the Board for the purposes of this Chapter;

"director" in relation to a company includes—

    (*a*) in the case of a company the affairs of which are managed by a board of directors or similar body, a member of that board or body,

    (*b*) in the case of a company the affairs of which are managed by a single director or similar person, that director or person,

    (*c*) in the case of a company the affairs of which are managed by the members themselves, a member of that company;

and includes a person who is to be or has been a director;

"employee"—

    (*a*) in relation to a company, includes any officer of the company, any director of the company and any other person taking part in the management of the affairs of the company, and

    (*b*) in relation to any employer, includes a person who is to be or has been an employee;

and "employer" and other cognate expressions shall be construed accordingly;

"exempt approved scheme" has the meaning given by section 592(1);

"final remuneration" means the average annual remuneration of the last three years' service;

"pension" includes annuity;

"the permitted maximum" has the meaning given by section 590(3);

"relevant benefits" means any pension, lump sum, gratuity or other like benefit given or to be given on retirement or on death, or in anticipation of retirement, or, in connection with past service, after retirement or death, or to be given on or in anticipation of or in connection with any change in the nature of the service of the employee in question, except that it does not include any benefit which is to be afforded solely by reason of the disablement by accident of a person occurring during his service or of his death by accident so occurring and for no other reason;

"remuneration" does not include—

    (*a*) anything in respect of which tax is chargeable under Schedule E and which arises from the acquisition or disposal of shares or an interest in shares or from a right to acquire shares; or

    (*b*) anything in respect of which tax is chargeable by virtue of section 148;

"service" means service as an employee of the employer in question and other expressions, including "retirement", shall be construed accordingly; and

"statutory scheme" means a retirement benefits scheme established by or under any enactment—

    (*a*) the particulars of which are set out in any enactment, or in any regulations made under any enactment, or

    (*b*) which has been approved as an appropriate scheme by a Minister or government department (including the head of a Northern Ireland department or a Northern Ireland department).

(2) Any reference in this Chapter to the provision of relevant benefits, or of a pension, for employees of an employer includes a reference to the provision of relevant benefits or a pension by means of a contract between the administrator or the employer or the employee and a third person; and any reference to pensions or contributions paid, or payments made, under a scheme includes a reference to pensions or contributions paid, or payments made, under such a contract entered into for the purposes of the scheme.

(3) The Board may make regulations generally for the purpose of carrying the preceding provisions of this Chapter into effect.

Former enactments.—Sub-s. (1): FA 1970, s. 26(1); FA 1971, Sch. 3, para. 12(4); Northern Ireland Constitution Act 1973, Sch. 5, para. 8; FA 1986, Sch. 12, para. 1(10); F(No. 2)A 1987, Sch. 3, para. 7.
Sub-s. (2): FA 1970, s. 26(2); F(No. 2)A 1987, Sch. 3, para. 8.
Sub-s. (3): FA 1970, Sch. 5, Pt. II, para. 10; FA 1971, Sch. 3, para. 13(3).

CHAPTER II
OTHER PENSION FUNDS AND SOCIAL SECURITY BENEFITS AND CONTRIBUTIONS

613. Parliamentary pension funds

(1) The salary of a Member of the House of Commons shall, for all the purposes of the Income Tax Acts, be treated as reduced by the amounts deducted in pursuance of section 1 of the House of Commons Members' Fund Act 1939; but a Member shall not by reason of any such deduction be entitled to relief under any other provision of the Income Tax Acts.

(2) In subsection (1) above the reference to salary shall be construed as mentioned in subsection (3) of section 1 of the House of Commons Members' Fund Act 1939, the reference to amounts deducted includes a reference to amounts required to be set aside under that subsection, and "deduction" shall be construed accordingly.

(3) Periodical payments granted out of the House of Commons Members' Fund (including periodical payments granted out of sums appropriated from that Fund or out of the income from those sums) shall be charged to income tax under Schedule E.

(4) The respective trustees of—

(a) the House of Commons Members' Fund established under section 1 of that Act of 1939;
(b) the Parliamentary Contributory Pension Fund;
(c) the Members' Contributory Pension (Northern Ireland) Fund constituted under section 3(2) of the Ministerial Salaries and Members' Pensions Act (Northern Ireland) 1965; and
(d) the Assembly Contributory Pension Fund constituted under the Assembly Pensions (Northern Ireland) Order 1976;

shall be entitled to exemption from income tax in respect of all income derived from those Funds or any investment of those Funds.

A claim under this subsection shall be made to the Board.

Former enactments.—Sub-ss. (1)–(3): TA 1970, s. 211(1), (4).
Sub-s. (4): TA 1970, s. 211(2); FA 1981, s. 50(1); Parliamentary and Other Pensions Act 1987, Sch. 3, para. 2(1).
Cross references.—See CGTA 1979, s. 149B(1)(b) (sub-s. (4) exemption to apply also to capital gains tax).

614. Exemptions and reliefs in respect of income from investments etc. of certain pension schemes

(1) All income receivable from any source whatsoever for the purposes of any supplementary scheme under section 158 of the Social Security Act 1975 or section 149 of the Social Security (Northern Ireland) Act 1975, or under the enactments replaced by those sections, by the body charged with the administration of the scheme shall be exempt from income tax.

(2) Any interest or dividends received by the person in whom is vested any of the Family Pension Funds mentioned in section 273 of the Government of India Act 1935, and having effect as a scheme made under section 2 of the Overseas Pensions Act 1973, on sums forming part of that fund shall be exempt from income tax.

(3) Income derived from investments or deposits of any fund referred to in paragraph (b), (c), (d) or (f) of subsection (2) of section 615 shall not be charged to income tax, and any income tax deducted from any such income shall be repaid by the Board to the persons entitled to receive the income.

(4) In respect of income derived from investments or deposits of the Overseas Service Pensions Fund established pursuant to section 7(1) of the Overseas Aid Act 1966, the Board shall give by way of repayment such relief from income tax as is necessary to secure that the income is exempt to the like extent (if any) as if it were income of a person not domiciled, ordinarily resident or resident in the United Kingdom.

(5) In respect of dividends and other income derived from investments, deposits or other property of a superannuation fund to which section 615(3) applies the Board shall give by way of repayment such relief from income tax as is necessary to secure that the income is

exempt to the like extent (if any) as if it were income of a person not domiciled, ordinarily resident or resident in the United Kingdom.

(6) A claim under this section shall be made to the Board.

Former enactments.—Sub-s. (1): TA 1970, s. 212(1); Social Security (Consequential Provisions) Act 1975, Sch. 2, para. 38.
Sub-s. (2): TA 1970, s. 213(1); Overseas Pensions Act 1973, s. 2.
Sub-s. (3): TA 1970, ss. 214(2), 216(2); FA 1973, s. 53(1).
Sub-s. (4): TA 1970, s. 217(2), (4).
Sub-s. (5): TA 1970, s. 218(1).
Sub-s. (6): TA 1970, ss. 212(3), 213(1), 214(3), 216(2), 217(2), 218(1); FA 1987, Sch. 15, para. 2(13).
Cross references.—See CGTA 1979, s. 149B(1)(*b*), (*c*) (sub-ss. (1), (2) exemption to apply also to capital gains tax).

615. Exemption from tax in respect of certain pensions

(1) A pension to which this subsection applies shall not be liable to charge to income tax if it is the income of a person who satisfies the Board that he is not resident in the United Kingdom.

A claim under this subsection shall be made to the Board.

(2) Subsection (1) above applies to any of the following pensions—

(*a*) a pension paid under the authority of the Pensions (India, Pakistan and Burma) Act 1955 (which has effect, by virtue of subsection (3) of section 2 of the Overseas Pensions Act 1973, as a scheme made under that section);
(*b*) a pension paid out of any fund established in the United Kingdom by the government of any country which is, or forms part of, a country to which this paragraph applies, an associated state, a colony, a protectorate, a protected state or a United Kingdom trust territory, or by a government constituted for two or more such countries, if the fund was established for the sole purpose of providing pensions, whether contributory or not, payable in respect of service under that government;
(*c*) a pension paid out of the fund formed under the Overseas Superannuation Scheme (formerly known as the Colonial Superannuation Scheme);
(*d*) a pension paid under section 1 of the Overseas Pensions Act 1973, whether or not paid out of a fund established under a scheme made under that section;
(*e*) so much of any pension paid to or in respect of any person—

(i) under an order made under section 2 of the Overseas Service Act 1958 and having effect as if it were a scheme under section 2 of the Overseas Pensions Act 1973 or under a pension scheme originally provided and maintained under such an order and having such effect, or
(ii) under section 4(2) of the Overseas Service Act 1958, which has effect as if it were a scheme under section 2 of the Overseas Pensions Act 1973,

as may be certified by the Secretary of State to be attributable to the employment of that person in the public services of an overseas territory;
(*f*) a pension paid out of the fund established under the name "the Central African Pension Fund" by section 24 of the Federation of Rhodesia and Nyasaland (Dissolution) Order in Council 1963;
(*g*) a pension paid out of the Overseas Service Pensions Fund established under section 7(1) of the Overseas Aid Act 1966.

(3) Where an annuity is paid from a superannuation fund to which this subsection applies to a person who is not resident in the United Kingdom, income tax shall not be deducted from any payment of the annuity or accounted for under section 349(1) by the trustees or other persons having the control of the fund.

(4) Subsection (1) above shall not apply to so much of any pension falling within paragraph (*a*) or (*d*) of subsection (2) above as is paid by virtue of the application to the pension of the Pensions (Increase) Acts.

(5) Paragraph (*b*) of subsection (2) above applies to any country mentioned in Schedule 3 to the British Nationality Act 1981 except Australia, Canada, New Zealand, India, Sri Lanka and Cyprus.

(6) Subsection (3) above applies to any superannuation fund which—

(*a*) is bona fide established under irrevocable trusts in connection with some trade or undertaking carried on wholly or partly outside the United Kingdom;
(*b*) has for its sole purpose the provision of superannuation benefits in respect of persons' employment in the trade or undertaking wholly outside the United Kingdom; and

(c) is recognised by the employer and employed persons in the trade or undertaking;

and for the purposes of this subsection duties performed in the United Kingdom the performance of which is merely incidental to the performance of other duties outside the United Kingdom shall be treated as performed outside the United Kingdom.

(7) In this section—

"pension" includes a gratuity or any sum payable on or in respect of death or, in the case of a pension falling within subsection (2)(g) above, ill-health, and a return of contributions with or without interest thereon or any other addition thereto;

"overseas territory" means any territory or country outside the United Kingdom;

"the Pensions (Increase) Acts" means the Pensions (Increase) Act 1971 and any Act passed after that Act for purposes corresponding to the purposes of that Act;

"United Kingdom trust territory" means a territory administered by the government of the United Kingdom under the trusteeship system of the United Nations.

(8) In this section—

(a) references to a government constituted for two or more countries include references to any authority established for the purpose of providing or administering services which are common to, or relate to matters of common interest to, two or more countries;

(b) any reference to employment in the public services of an overseas territory shall be construed as if it occurred in the Overseas Development and Cooperation Act 1980 and section 10(2) of that Act shall apply accordingly; and

(c) any reference to an enactment or order having effect as if it were a scheme constituted under section 2 of the Overseas Pensions Act 1973 includes a reference to a scheme made under that section and certified by the Secretary of State for the purpose of the 1970 Act or this Act to correspond to that enactment or order.

Former enactments.—Sub-s. (1): TA 1970, ss. 214(1), (3), 215(1), (2), 216(1), 217(1).
Sub-s. (2)(a): TA 1970, s. 214(1)(a); Overseas Pensions Act 1973, s. 2(3); FA 1973, s. 53(1).
Sub-s. (2)(b): TA 1970, s. 214(1)(b).
Sub-s (2)(c), (d): TA 1970, s. 214(1)(c), (d); FA 1973, s. 53(1).
Sub-s. (2)(e): TA 1970, s. 215(1); Overseas Pensions Act 1973, s. 2(3); FA 1973, s. 53(2).
Sub-s. (2)(f): TA 1970, s. 216(1), (4).
Sub-s. (2)(g): TA 1970, s. 217(1), (4).
Sub-s. (3): TA 1970, s. 218(3).
Sub-s. (4): TA 1970, s. 214(1); FA 1973, s. 53(1).
Sub-s. (5): TA 1970, s. 214(6); British Nationality Act 1981, Sch. 7; FA 1987, Sch. 15, para. 2(14).
Sub-s. (6): TA 1970, s. 218(4).
Sub-s. (7): TA 1970, ss. 214(5), 215(3), 216(4), 217(4); Pensions (Increase) Act 1971.
Sub-s. (8)(a): TA 1970, s. 214(5).
Sub-s. (8)(b): TA 1970, s. 215(3).
Sub-s. (8)(c): FA 1973, s. 53(2).
Cross references.—See CGTA 1979, s. 149B(1)(c) (capital gains tax exemption in respect of certain funds mentioned in this section).

616. Other overseas pensions

(1) If and so long as provision is made by double taxation relief arrangements for a pension of a description specified in subsection (2) below to be exempt from tax in the United Kingdom and, by reason of Her Majesty's Government in the United Kingdom having assumed responsibility for the pension, payments in respect of it are made under section 1 of the Overseas Pensions Act 1973, then, to the extent that those payments are made to, or to the widow or widower of, an existing pensioner, the provision made under the arrangements shall apply in relation to the pension, exclusive of any statutory increases in it, as if it continued to be paid by the government which had responsibility for it before that responsibility was assumed by Her Majesty's Government in the United Kingdom.

(2) The pensions referred to in subsection (1) above are pensions paid by—

(a) the Government of Malawi for services rendered to that Government or to the Government of the Federation of Rhodesia and Nyasaland in the discharge of governmental functions;

(b) the Government of Trinidad and Tobago in respect of services rendered to that Government in the discharge of governmental functions;

(c) the Government of the Republic of Zambia for services rendered to that Government or to the Government of Northern Rhodesia or to the Government of the Federation of Rhodesia and Nyasaland in the discharge of governmental functions.

(3) If—

(a) immediately before 6th April 1973 a person resident in the United Kingdom was entitled to receive a pension as or as the widow or widower of an existing pensioner, and

(b) by reason of Her Majesty's Government in the United Kingdom having assumed responsibility for the pension, payments in respect of it are made under section 1 of the Overseas Pensions Act 1973,

then, if and so long as the pension is received by that person or, where that person is an existing pensioner, by his or her widow or widower, the provisions of this Act shall apply in relation to it, exclusive of any statutory increases in it, as if it continued to be paid by the government or other body or fund which had responsibility for it before that responsibility was assumed by Her Majesty's Government in the United Kingdom.

(4) In this section—

"double taxation relief arrangements" means arrangements specified in an Order in Council making any such provisions as are referred to in section 788;
"existing pensioner", in relation to a pension, means a person by virtue of whose service the pension is payable and who retired from that service before 6th April 1973; and
"statutory increases", in relation to a pension, means so much (if any) of the pension as is paid by virtue of the application to it of any provision of the Pensions (Increase) Act 1971;

and in this subsection "pension" has the same meaning as in section 1 of the Overseas Pensions Act 1973.

Former enactment.—FA 1973, s. 53(3)–(5), (9).

617. Social security benefits and contributions

(1) Payments of benefit under Chapters I to III of Part II of the Social Security Act 1975, Part II of the Social Security Pensions Act 1975, Chapters I to III of Part II of the Social Security (Northern Ireland) Act 1975 or Part III of the Social Security Pensions (Northern Ireland) Order 1975, except—

(a) sickness benefit, invalidity benefit, attendance allowance, mobility allowance, severe disablement allowance, maternity allowance, widow's payments, child's special allowance and guardian's allowance; and
(b) so much of any benefit as is attributable to an increase in respect of a child,

shall be charged to income tax under Schedule E.

(2) The following payments shall not be treated as income for any purpose of the Income Tax Acts—

(a) payments of income support, family credit or housing benefit under the Social Security Act 1986 or the Social Security (Northern Ireland) Order 1986 other than payments of income support which are taxable by virtue of section 151;
[(aa) payments by way of an allowance under section 70 of the Social Security Act 1975 and section 70 of the Social Security (Northern Ireland) Act 1975;][1]
(b) payments of child benefit; and
(c) payments excepted by subsection (1) above from the charge to tax imposed by that subsection.

(3) Subject to subsection (4) and (5) below, no relief or deduction shall be given or allowed in respect of any contribution paid by any person under—

(a) Part I of the Social Security Act 1975, or
(b) Part I of the Social Security (Northern Ireland) Act 1975.

(4) Subsection (3) above shall not apply to any secondary Class I contributions within the meaning of the Social Security Act 1975 or the Social Security (Northern Ireland) Act 1975 which is allowable as a deduction in computing profits or gains, in computing expenses of management under section 75 or under that section as applied by section 76 or in computing expenses of management or supervision under section 121.

(5) An individual making a claim in that behalf shall be entitled, in computing his total income for any year of assessment, to deduct one-half of any amount (as finally settled) which is determined under subsection (2) of section 9 of the Social Security Act 1975 or of the Social Security (Northern Ireland) Act 1975 and which he is liable to pay in respect of that year by way of Class 4 contributions under either of those sections.

(6) Until such day as may be appointed by the Secretary of State by order made by statutory instrument, subsection (1)(a) above shall have effect with the omission of the words "widow's payments".

Former enactments.—Sub-s. (1): TA 1970, s. 219(1)(*a*); FA 1971, s. 18(1)(*a*); F(No. 2)A 1979, Sch. 1, para. 4(1), Sch. 2, para. 3; Social Security (Consequential Provisions) Act 1975, Sch. 2, para. 39(*a*); FA 1981, s. 27(1); FA 1982, s. 30(1); Health and Social Security Act 1984, Sch. 4, para. 2.
Sub-s. (2): TA 1970, s. 219(2); FA 1987, s. 29(1).
Sub-s. (3): TA 1970, s. 219(3); Social Security (Consequential Provisions) Act 1975, Sch. 2, para. 39.
Sub-s. (4): TA 1970, s. 219(3); Social Security (Consequential Provisions) Act 1975, Sch. 2, para. 39(*b*).
Sub-s. (5): FA 1985, s. 42(1).
Sub-s. (6): TA 1970, s. 219(1); Social Security (Consequential Provisions) Act 1975, Sch. 2, para. 39(*a*); Social Security Act 1986, Sch. 10, para. 101.
Cross references.—See FA 1989, s. 41(1)(*e*) (a benefit chargeable to income tax under sub-s. (1) of this section to be charged in the year of assessment in which it accrues irrespective of when it is paid).
Amendments.—[1] Sub-s. (2)(*aa*) inserted by the Social Security Act 1988, Sch. 4, para. 1 with effect from 6 April 1988 by virtue of the Social Security Act 1988 (Commencement No. 1) Order 1988, S.I. 1988 No. 520.

CHAPTER III

RETIREMENT ANNUITIES

618. Termination of relief under this Chapter, and transitional provisions

(1) Nothing in this Chapter shall apply in relation to—

(a) a contract made or trust scheme established on or after [1st July][1] 1988; or

(b) a person by whom contributions are first paid on or after that date under a trust scheme established before that date.

(2) Subject to subsection (4) below, the terms of a contract made, or the rules of a trust scheme established, on or after 17th March 1987 and before [1st July][1] 1988 and approved by the Board under section 620 shall have effect (notwithstanding anything in them to the contrary) as if they did not allow the payment to the individual by whom the contract is made, or an individual paying contributions under the scheme, of a lump sum exceeding £150,000 or such other sum as may for the time being be specified in an order under section 635(4).

(3) Subject to subsection (5) below, the rules of a trust scheme established before 17th March 1987 and approved by the Board under section 620 shall have effect (notwithstanding anything in them to the contrary) as if they did not allow the payment to any person first paying contributions under the scheme on or after 17th March 1987 of a lump sum such as is mentioned in subsection (2) above.

(4) Subsection (2) above shall not apply—

(a) to a contract if, before the end of January 1988, the persons by and to whom premiums are payable under it jointly give notice to the Board that subsection (2) is not to apply; or

(b) to a scheme if, before the end of January 1988, the trustees or other persons having the management of the scheme give notice to the Board that subsection (2) is not to apply;

and where notice is given to the Board under this subsection, the contract or scheme shall, with effect from the date with effect from which it was approved, cease to be approved.

(5) Subsection (3) above shall not apply in the case of any person paying contributions under a scheme if, before the end of January 1988, he and the trustees or other persons having the management of the scheme jointly give notice to the Board that subsection (3) is not to apply; and where notice is given to the Board, the scheme shall cease to be approved in relation to the contributor with effect from the date on which he first paid a contribution under it or (if later) the date with effect from which it was approved.

Former enactment.—FA 1987, s. 54.
Cross references.—See FA 1988, s. 54(2)(a), (b) (amendments to F(No. 2)A 1987, s. 54(1), (3) deemed always to have had effect).
Amendments.—[1] Date in sub-ss. (1)(a), (2) substituted by FA 1988, s. 54(2)(a)(i), (ii), (3) and deemed always to have had effect.

---

619. Exemption from tax in respect of qualifying premiums

(1) Where in any year of assessment an individual is (or would but for an insufficiency of profits or gains be) chargeable to income tax in respect of relevant earnings from any trade, profession, vocation, office or employment carried on or held by him, and pays a qualifying premium, then—

(a) relief from income tax shall be given under this section in respect of that qualifying premium, but only on a claim made for the purpose, and where relief is to be so given, the amount of that premium shall, subject to the provisions of this section, be deducted from or set off against his relevant earnings for the year of assessment in which the premium is paid; and

(b) any annuity payable to the same or another individual shall be treated as earned income of the annuitant to the extent to which it is payable in return for any amount on which relief is so given.

Paragraph (b) above applies only in relation to the annuitant to whom the annuity is made payable by the terms of the annuity contract under which it is paid.

(2) Subject to the provisions of this section and section 626, the amount which may be deducted or set off in any year of assessment (whether in respect of one or more qualifying

premiums, and whether or not including premiums in respect of a contract approved under section 621) shall not be more than 17½ per cent. of the individual's net relevant earnings for that year.

(3) Subject to the provisions of this section, the amount which may be deducted or set off in any year of assessment in respect of qualifying premiums paid under a contract approved under section 621 (whether in respect of one or more such premiums) shall not be more than 5 per cent. of the individual's net relevant earnings for that year.

(4) An individual who pays a qualifying premium in a year of assessment (whether or not a year for which he has relevant earnings) may before the end of that year elect that the premium shall be treated as paid—
   (a) in the last preceding year of assessment; or
   (b) if he had no net relevant earnings in the year referred to in paragraph (a) above, in the last preceding year of assessment but one;
and where an election is made under this subsection in respect of a premium the other provisions of this Chapter shall have effect as if the premium had been paid in the year specified in the election and not in the year in which it was actually paid.

(5) Where relief under this section for any year of assessment is claimed and allowed (whether or not relief then falls to be given for that year), and afterwards there is made any assessment, alteration of an assessment, or other adjustment of the claimant's liability to tax, there shall be made also such adjustments, if any, as are consequential thereon in the relief allowed or given under this section for that or any subsequent year of assessment.

(6) Where relief under this section is claimed and allowed for any year of assessment in respect of any payment, relief shall not be given in respect of it under any other provision of the Income Tax Acts for the same or a later year of assessment nor (in the case of a payment under an annuity contract) in respect of any other premium or consideration for an annuity under the same contract; and references in the Income Tax Acts to relief in respect of life assurance premiums shall not be taken to include relief under this section.

(7) If any person, for the purpose of obtaining for himself or any other person any relief from or repayment of tax under this section, knowingly makes any false statement or false representation, he shall be liable to a penalty not exceeding [£3,000][1].

Former enactments.—Sub-s. (1): TA 1970, ss. 226(1), (4), 227(1).
Sub-ss. (2), (3): TA 1970, s. 227(1A), (1B); FA 1971, s. 20(2); FA 1980, s. 31(1), (2).
Sub-s. (4): TA 1970, s. 227(1BB); FA 1980, s. 33(2).
Sub-ss. (5)–(7): TA 1970, s. 227(10), (11), (13).
Amendments.—[1] Amount in sub-s. (7) substituted for "£500" by FA 1989, s. 170(4)(a), (6) in relation to things done or omitted after 26 July 1989.

620. Qualifying premiums

(1) In this Chapter "qualifying premium" means, subject to subsection (5) below, a premium or other consideration paid by an individual—
   (a) under an annuity contract for the time being approved by the Board under this section as having for its main object the provision for the individual of a life annuity in old age, or
   (b) under a contract for the time being approved under section 621.

(2) Subject to subsection (3) and (4) below, the Board shall not approve a contract under this section unless it appears to them to satisfy the conditions that it is made by the individual with a person lawfully carrying on in the United Kingdom the business of granting annuities on human life, and that it does not—
   (a) provide for the payment by that person during the life of the individual of any sum except sums payable by way of annuity to the individual; or
   (b) provide for the annuity payable to the individual to commence before he attains the age of 60 or after he attains the age of 75; or
   (c) provide for the payment by that person of any other sums except sums payable by way of annuity to the individual's widow or widower and any sums which, in the event of no annuity becoming payable either to the individual or to a widow or widower, are payable by way of return of premiums, by way of reasonable interest on premiums or by way of bonuses out of profits; or
   (d) provide for the annuity, if any, payable to a widow or widower of the individual to be of a greater annual amount than that paid or payable to the individual; or
   (e) provide for the payment of any annuity otherwise than for the life of the annuitant;

and that it does include provision securing that no annuity payable under it shall be capable in whole or in part of surrender, commutation or assignment.

(3) A contract shall not be treated as not satisfying the requirements of subsection (2) above by reason only that it—

> (*a*) gives the individual the right to receive, by way of commutation of part of the annuity payable to him, a lump sum not exceeding three times the annual amount of the remaining part of the annuity, taking, where the annual amount is or may be different in different years, the initial annual amount, and
> (*b*) makes any such right depend on the exercise by the individual of an election at or before the time when the annuity first becomes payable to him.

(4) The Board may, if they think fit, and subject to any conditions they think proper to impose, approve, under this section, a contract otherwise satisfying the preceding conditions, notwithstanding that the contract provides for one or more of the following matters—

> (*a*) for the payment after the individual's death of an annuity to a dependant not the widow or widower of the individual;
> (*b*) for the payment to the individual of an annuity commencing before he attains the age of 60, if the annuity is payable on his becoming incapable through infirmity of body or mind of carrying on his own occupation or any occupation of a similar nature for which he is trained or fitted;
> (*c*) if the individual's occupation is one in which persons customarily retire before attaining the age of 60, for the annuity to commence before he attains that age;
> (*d*) for the annuity payable to any person to continue for a term certain (not exceeding ten years), notwithstanding his death within that term, or for the annuity payable to any person to terminate, or be suspended, on marriage (or re-marriage) or in other circumstances;
> (*e*) in the case of an annuity which is to continue for a term certain, for the annuity to be assignable by will, and in the event of any person dying entitled to it, for it to be assignable by his personal representatives in the distribution of the estate so as to give effect to a testamentary disposition, or to the rights of those entitled on intestacy, or to an appropriation of it to a legacy or to a share or interest in the estate.

(5) Subject to section 621(5), section 619 and subsections (1) to (4) above shall apply in relation to a contribution under a trust scheme approved by the Board as they apply in relation to a premium under an annuity contract so approved, with the modification that, for the condition as to the person with whom the contract is made, there shall be substituted a condition that the scheme—

> (*a*) is established under the law of any part of, and administered in, the United Kingdom; and
> (*b*) is established for the benefit of individuals engaged in or connected with a particular occupation (or one or other of a group of occupations), and for the purpose of providing retirement annuities for them, with or without subsidiary benefits for their families or dependants; and
> (*c*) is so established under irrevocable trusts by a body of persons comprising or representing a substantial proportion of the individuals so engaged in the United Kingdom, or of those so engaged in England, Wales, Scotland or Northern Ireland;

and with the necessary adaptations of other references to the contract or the person with whom it is made.

(6) Exemption from income tax shall be allowed in respect of income derived from investments or deposits of any fund maintained for the purpose mentioned in subsection (5)(*b*) above under a scheme for the time being approved under that subsection.

(7) The Board may at any time, by notice given to the persons by and to whom premiums are payable under any contract for the time being approved under this section, or to the trustees or other persons having the management of any scheme so approved, withdraw that approval on such grounds and from such date as may be specified in the notice.

(8) Nothing in sections 4 and 6 of the Policies of Assurance Act 1867 (obligations of assurance companies in respect of notices of assignment of policies of life assurance) shall be taken to apply to any contract approved under this section.

(9) For the purposes of any provision applying this subsection "approved annuities" means—

> (*a*) annuities under contracts approved by the Board under this section, being annuities payable wholly in return for premiums or other consideration paid by a person who (when

the premiums or other consideration are or is payable) is, or would but for an insufficiency of profits or gains be, chargeable to tax in respect of relevant earnings from a trade, profession, vocation, office or employment carried on or held by him; and
(*b*) annuities or lump sums under approved personal pension arrangements within the meaning of Chapter IV of this Part.

Former enactments.—Sub-s. (1): TA 1970, s. 226(1)(*b*); FA 1971, s. 20(1).
Sub-ss. (2), (3): TA 1970, ss. 226(2), 226A(5); FA 1971, s. 20(3); FA 1976, s. 30(2).
Sub-s. (4): TA 1970, ss. 226(3), 226A(5).
Sub-ss. (5)–(7): TA 1970, s. 226(5)–(7).
Sub-ss. (8), (9): TA 1970, s. 226(12), (13); F(No. 2)A 1987, Sch. 2, para. 1.
Cross references.—See CGTA 1979, s. 149B(1)(*d*) (capital gains tax exemption in respect of a fund maintained for the purpose mentioned in sub-s. (5)(*b*) above).

621. Other approved contracts

(1) The Board may approve under this section—

(*a*) a contract the main object of which is the provision of an annuity for the wife or husband of the individual, or for any one or more dependants of the individual,
(*b*) a contract the sole object of which is the provision of a lump sum on the death of the individual before he attains the age of 75.

(2) The Board shall not approve the contract unless it appears to them that it is made by the individual with a person lawfully carrying on in the United Kingdom the business of granting annuities on human life.

(3) The Board shall not approve a contract under subsection (1)(*a*) above unless it appears to them to satisfy all the following conditions, that is to say—

(*a*) that any annuity payable to the wife or husband or dependant of the individual commences on the death of the individual,
(*b*) that any annuity payable to the individual commences at a time after the individual attains the age of 60, and, unless the individual's annuity is one to commence on the death of a person to whom an annuity would be payable under the contract if that person survived the individual, cannot commence after the time when the individual attains the age of 75;
(*c*) that the contract does not provide for the payment by the person contracting with the individual of any sum, other than any annuity payable to the individual's wife or husband or dependant, or to the individual, except, in the event of no annuity becoming payable under the contract, any sums payable by way of return of premiums, by way of reasonable interest on premiums or by way of bonuses out of profits;
(*d*) that the contract does not provide for the payment of any annuity otherwise than for the life of the annuitant;
(*e*) that the contract does include provision securing that no annuity payable under it shall be capable in whole or in part of surrender, commutation or assignment.

(4) The Board may, if they think fit, and subject to any conditions that they think proper to impose, approve a contract under subsection (1)(*a*) above notwithstanding that, in one or more respects, they are not satisfied that the contract complies with the provisions of paragraphs (*a*) to (*e*) of subsection (3) above.

(5) The main purpose of a trust scheme, or part of a trust scheme, within section 620(5) may be to provide annuities for the wives, husbands and dependants of the individuals, or lump sums payable on death and in that case—

(*a*) approval of the trust scheme shall be subject to subsections (1) to (4) above with any necessary modifications, and not subject to section 620(2) to (4);
(*b*) the provisions of this Chapter shall apply to the scheme or part of the scheme when duly approved as they apply to a contract approved under this section; and
(*c*) section 620(6) shall apply to any duly approved trust scheme, or part of a trust scheme.

(6) Except as otherwise provided in this Chapter (and in particular except in section 620), any reference in the Tax Acts to a contract or scheme approved under that section shall include a reference to a contract or scheme approved under this section.

Former enactments.—TA 1970, s. 226A(1)–(4), (6), (7); FA 1971, Sch. 2, para. 1; FA 1976, s. 30(2).
Cross references.—See CGTA 1979, s. 149B(1)(*d*) (capital gains tax exemption in respect of a fund maintained for the purpose mentioned in sub-s. (5) above under an approved scheme).

622. Substituted retirement annuity contracts

(1) The Board may, if they think fit, and subject to any conditions they think proper to impose, approve an annuity contract under section 620 notwithstanding that the contract provides that the individual by whom it is made—

(*a*) may agree with the person with whom it is made that a sum representing the value of the individual's accrued rights under it should be applied as the premium or other consideration either under another annuity contract made between them and approved by the Board under section 620, or under personal pension arrangements made between them and approved by the Board under Chapter IV of this Part; or

(*b*) may require the person with whom it is made to pay such a sum to such other person as the individual may specify, to be applied by that other person as the premium or other consideration either under an annuity contract made between the individual and him and approved by the Board under section 620, or under personal pension arrangements made between the individual and him and approved by the Board under Chapter IV of this Part.

(2) References in subsection (1) above to the individual by whom the contract is made include references to any widow, widower or dependant having accrued rights under the contract.

(3) Where in pursuance of any such provision as is mentioned in subsection (1) above of an annuity contract approved under section 620, or of a corresponding provision of a contract approved under section 621(1)(*a*), a sum representing the value of accrued rights under one contract ("the original contract") is paid by way of premium or other consideration under another contract ("the substituted contract"), any annuity payable under the substituted contract shall be treated as earned income of the annuitant to the same extent that an annuity payable under the original contract would have been so treated.

Former enactments.—FA 1978, s. 26(1)–(3); F(No. 2)A 1987, Sch. 2, para. 4.

623. Relevant earnings

(1) For the purposes of this Chapter, a married woman's relevant earnings shall not be treated as her husband's relevant earnings, notwithstanding that her income chargeable to tax is treated as his income.

(2) Subject to subsection (1) above, "relevant earnings", in relation to any individual, means, for the purposes of this Chapter, any income of his chargeable to tax for the year of assessment in question, being either—

(*a*) income arising in respect of remuneration from an office or employment held by him other than a pensionable office or employment; or

(*b*) income from any property which is attached to or forms part of the emoluments of any such office or employment held by him; or

(*c*) income which is chargeable under . . .[1] Schedule D and is immediately derived by him from the carrying on or exercise by him of his trade, profession or vocation either as an individual or, in the case of a partnership, as a partner personally acting therein; or

(*d*) income treated as earned income by virtue of section 529;

but does not include any remuneration as director of a company whose income consists wholly or mainly of investment income [(that is to say, income which, if the company were an individual, would not be earned income)][2] being a company of which he is a controlling director.

(3) For the purposes of this Chapter, an office or employment is a pensionable office or employment if, and only if, service in it is service to which a sponsored superannuation scheme relates (not being a scheme under which the benefits provided in respect of that service are limited to a lump sum payable on the termination of the service through death or disability before the age of 75 or some lower age); but references to a pensionable office or employment apply whether or not the duties are performed wholly or partly in the United Kingdom or the holder is chargeable to tax in respect of it.

(4) Service in an office or employment shall not for the purposes of subsection (3) above be treated as service to which a sponsored superannuation scheme relates by reason only of the fact that the holder of the office or employment might (though he does not) participate in the scheme by exercising or refraining from exercising an option open to him by virtue of that service.

(5) For the purposes of relief under section 619, an individual's relevant earnings are those earnings before giving effect to any capital allowances, other than deductions allowable in

computing profits or gains, but after taking into account the amounts on which charges fall to be made under any of the Capital Allowances Acts; and references to income in the following provisions of this section (other than references to total income) shall be construed similarly.

(6) Subject to the following provisions of this section "net relevant earnings" means, in relation to an individual, the amount of his relevant earnings for the year of assessment in question, less the amount of any deductions falling to be made from the relevant earnings in computing for the purposes of income tax his total income for that year, being—

    (a) deductions which but for section 74(m), (p) or (q) could be made in computing his profits or gains; or
    (b) deductions in respect of relief under Schedule 9 of the Finance Act 1981 (stock relief); or
    (c) deductions in respect of losses or capital allowances arising from activities profits or gains of which would be included in computing relevant earnings of the individual or of the individual's wife or husband.

(7) Where in any year of assessment for which an individual claims and is allowed relief under section 619—

    (a) there falls to be made in computing the total income of the individual or that of his wife or her husband a deduction in respect of any such loss or allowance of the individual as is mentioned in subsection (6)(c) above; and
    (b) the deduction or part of it falls to be so made from income other than relevant earnings,

the amount of the deduction made from that other income shall be treated as reducing the individual's net relevant earnings for subsequent years of assessment (being deducted as far as may be from those of the immediately following year, whether or not he claims or is entitled to claim relief under this section for that year, and so far as it cannot be so deducted, then from those of the next year, and so on).

(8) An individual's net relevant earnings for any year of assessment are to be computed without regard to any relief which falls to be given for that year under section 619 either to that individual or to that individual's wife or husband.

(9) An individual's relevant earnings, in the case of partnership profits, shall be taken to be his share of the partnership income, estimated in accordance with the Income Tax Acts, but the amount to be included in respect of those earnings in arriving at his net relevant earnings shall be his share of that income after making therefrom all such deductions (if any) in respect of payments made by the partnership or of relief given to the partnership under Schedule 9 of the Finance Act 1981 (stock relief) or in respect of capital allowances falling to be made to the partnership as would be made in computing the tax payable in respect of that income.

Former enactments.—Sub-ss. (1)–(4): TA 1970, s. 226(8)–(10); FA 1976, s. 30(2); FA 1972, Sch. 24, para. 17.
Sub-ss. (5)–(7): TA 1970, s. 227(4), (5)(a), (aa), (b), (6); FA 1971, Sch. 8, para. 16; FA 1980, s. 33(3); FA 1981, s. 35; FA 1986, s. 56(7), Sch. 13, para. 2.
Sub-ss. (8), (9): TA 1970, s. 227(8), (9); FA 1980, s. 33(4); FA 1981, s. 35.
Note.—See **Prospective Legislation Notes** [(Married Couples)].
Cross references.—See FA 1988, Sch. 14, Pt. V (repeal of the reference to Schedule B in TA 1970, s. 226(9)(c) with effect from 6 April 1988).
Amendments.—[1] Words in sub-s. (2)(c) repealed by FA 1988, Sch. 14, Pt. V.
[2] Words in sub-s. (2) substituted by FA 1989, Sch. 12, para. 15 in relation to accounting periods beginning after 31 March 1989.

624. Sponsored superannuation schemes and controlling directors

(1) In section 623 "a sponsored superannuation scheme" means a scheme or arrangement—

    (a) relating to service in particular offices or employments, and
    (b) having for its objects or one of its objects to make provision in respect of persons serving in those offices or employments against future retirement or partial retirement, against future termination of service through death or disability, or against similar matters,

being a scheme or arrangement under which any part of the cost of the provision so made is or has been borne otherwise than by those persons by reason of their service (whether it is the cost or part of the cost of the benefits provided, or of paying premiums or other sums in order to provide those benefits, or of administering or instituting the scheme or arrangement).

(2) For the purposes of subsection (1) above a person shall be treated as bearing by reason of his service the cost of any payment made or agreed to be made in respect of his service, if that payment or the agreement to make it is treated under the Income Tax Acts as increasing

his income, or would be so treated if he were chargeable to tax under Case I of Schedule E in respect of his emoluments from that service.

(3) In section 623 "controlling director" means a director of a company, the directors of which have a controlling interest in the company, who is the beneficial owner of, or able either directly or through the medium of other companies or by any other indirect means to control, more than 5 per cent. of the ordinary share capital of the company; and for the purposes of this definition—

"company" means one within the Companies Act 1985 or the Companies (Northern Ireland) Order 1986; and
"director" means—

(a) in relation to a body corporate the affairs of which are managed by a board of directors or similar body, a member of that board or similar body;
(b) in relation to a body corporate the affairs of which are managed by a single director or similar person, that director or person;
(c) in relation to a body corporate the affairs of which are managed by the members themselves, a member of the body corporate;

and includes any person who is to be or has been a director.

Former enactments.—Sub-ss. (1), (2): TA 1970, s. 226(11).
Sub-s. (3): TA 1970, ss. 224(1), 226(9).

625. Carry-forward of unused relief under section 619

(1) Where—

(a) in any year of assessment an individual is (or would but for an insufficiency of profits or gains be) chargeable to income tax in respect of relevant earnings from any trade, profession, vocation, office or employment carried on or held by him, but
(b) there is unused relief for that year, that is to say, an amount which would have been deducted from or set off against the individual's relevant earnings for that year under subsection (1) of section 619 if—

(i) he had paid a qualifying premium in that year; or
(ii) the qualifying premium or premiums paid by him in that year had been greater;

then, subject to section 655(1)(b), relief may be given under that section, up to the amount of the unused relief, in respect of so much of any qualifying premium or premiums paid by the individual in any of the next six years of assessment as exceeds the maximum applying for that year under subsection (2) of that section.

(2) Relief by virtue of this section shall be given for an earlier year rather than a later year, the unused relief taken into account in giving relief for any year being deducted from that available for giving relief in subsequent years and unused relief derived from an earlier year being exhausted before unused relief derived from a later year.

(3) Where a relevant assessment to tax in respect of a year of assessment becomes final and conclusive more than six years after the end of that year and there is an amount of unused relief for that year which results from the making of the assessment—

(a) that amount shall not be available for giving relief by virtue of this section for any of the six years following that year, but
(b) the individual may, within the period of six months beginning with the date on which the assessment becomes final and conclusive, elect that relief shall be given under section 619, up to that amount, in respect of so much of any qualifying premium or premiums paid by him within that period as exceeds the maximum applying under subsection (2) of that section for the year of assessment in which they were paid;

and to the extent to which relief in respect of any premium or premiums is given by virtue of this subsection it shall not be given by virtue of subsection (1) above.

(4) In this section "a relevant assessment to tax" means an assessment on the individual's relevant earnings or on the profits or gains of a partnership from which the individual derives relevant earnings.

Former enactments.—TA 1970, s. 227A; FA 1980, s. 32(1).

626. Modification of section 619 in relation to persons over 50

In the case of an individual whose age at the beginning of a year of assessment is within a range specified in the first column of the Table set out below, section 619(2) shall have effect for that year with the substitution for the reference to $17\frac{1}{2}$ per cent. of a reference to the relevant percentage specified in the second column of the Table.

TABLE

Age range	Percentage
51 to 55	20
56 to 60	$22\frac{1}{2}$
61 or more	$27\frac{1}{2}$

Former enactments.—TA 1970, s. 228; F(No. 2)A 1987, s. 54(2).

627. Lloyd's underwriters

(1) Where for any year of assessment an individual—

(a) is chargeable to income tax in respect of relevant earnings derived from Lloyd's underwriting activities; and

(b) there is an amount of unused relief attributable to those earnings,

the individual may, subject to subsection (2) below, elect that there shall be treated as paid in that year any qualifying premium paid by him in the next year of assessment but two.

(2) An election under this section shall not have effect in relation to so much of any qualifying premium as exceeds the amount of unused relief referred to in subsection (1)(b) above.

(3) Any election under this section shall be made before the end of the year of assessment in which the premium is paid.

(4) Where an election is made under this section the provisions of this Chapter, other than section 619(4), shall have effect as if the premium or, as the case may be, the part of the premium in question had been paid in the year specified in the election and not in the year in which it was actually paid.

(5) In this section—

"unused relief" has the same meaning as in section 625; and
"relevant earnings derived from Lloyd's underwriting activities" means relevant earnings as an underwriting member of Lloyd's or by way of commission calculated by reference to the profits of Lloyd's underwriting business.

Former enactment.—FA 1982, s. 37.

628. Partnership retirement annuities

(1) Where a person ("the former partner") has ceased to be a member of a partnership on retirement, because of age or ill-health or on death and, under—

(a) the partnership agreement; or

(b) an agreement replacing the partnership agreement or supplementing it or supplementing an agreement replacing it; or

(c) an agreement made with an individual who acquires the whole or part of the business carried on by the partnership;

annual payments are made for the benefit of the former partner or his widow or a dependant of his and are for the purposes of income tax income of the person for whose benefit they are made, the payments shall be treated as earned income of that person, except to the extent that they exceed the limit specified in subsection (2) below.

(2) The limit mentioned in subsection (1) above is 50 per cent. of the average of the amounts which, in the best three of the relevant years of assessment, were the former partner's shares of the relevant profits or gains; and for this purpose—

(a) the former partner's share in any year of the relevant profits or gains is, subject to subsection (3) below, so much of the relevant profits or gains as fell to be included in a return of his income for that year; and

(b) the relevant profits or gains are the profits or gains of any trade, profession or vocation on which the partnership or any other partnership of which the former partner was a member was assessed to income tax; and

(c) the relevant years of assessment are the last seven years of assessment in which he was required to devote substantially the whole of his time to acting as a partner in the partnership or those partnership; and
(d) the best three of the relevant years of assessment are those three of them in which the amounts of his shares of the relevant profits were highest;

but where, in any of the relevant years, the circumstances were such that any of the profits or gains of a partnership were not assessable to income tax, paragraphs (a), (b) and (d) above shall apply as they would apply had those profits or gains been so assessable.

(3) If the retail prices index for the month of December in the last of the seven years referred to in paragraph (c) of subsection (2) above is higher than it was for the month of December in any of the other years referred to in that paragraph, the amount which, for that other year, was the former partner's share of the relevant profits or gains shall be treated for the purposes of that subsection as increased by the same percentage as the percentage increase in that index.

(4) If the retail prices index for the month of December preceding a year of assessment after that in which the former partner ceased to be a member of the partnership is higher than it was for the month of December in the year of assessment in which he ceased to be such a member, the amount which under subsection (2) above is the limit for the first-mentioned year of assessment shall be treated as increased by the same percentage as the percentage increase in that index.

(5) Where the former partner ceased to be a member of the partnership before the year 1974–75, subsection (4) above shall have effect as if he had ceased to be a member in that year.

Former enactments.—FA 1974, s. 16; FA 1982, s. 39(1); FA 1980, s. 34(3).

629. Annuity premiums of Ministers and other officers

(1) For the purposes of this Chapter so much of any salary which—
(a) is payable to the holder of a qualifying office who is also a Member of the House of Commons, and
(b) is payable for a period in respect of which the holder is not a participant in relation to that office in arrangements contained in the Parliamentary pension scheme but is a participant in relation to his membership of the House of Commons in any such arrangements, or for any part of such a period,

as is equal to the difference between a Member's pensionable salary and the salary which (in accordance with any such resolution as is mentioned in subsection (3)(a) below) is payable to him as a Member holding that qualifying office shall be treated as remuneration from the office of Member and not from the qualifying office.

(2) In this section—
"Member's pensionable salary" means a Member's ordinary salary under any resolution of the House of Commons which, being framed otherwise than as an expression of opinion, is for the time being in force relating to the remuneration of Members or, if the resolution provides for a Member's ordinary salary thereunder to be treated for pension purposes as being at a higher rate, a notional yearly salary at that higher rate;
"qualifying office" means an office mentioned in section 2(2)(b), (c) or (d) of the Parliamentary and other Pensions Act 1987;
"the Parliamentary pension scheme" has the same meaning as in that Act;

and without prejudice to the power conferred by virtue of paragraph 13 of Schedule 1 to that Act, regulations under section 2 of that Act may make provision specifying the circumstances in which a person is to be regarded for the purposes of this section as being or not being a participant in relation to his Membership of the House of Commons, or in relation to any office, in arrangements contained in the Parliamentary pension scheme.

(3) In subsection (2) above "a Member's ordinary salary", in relation to any resolution of the House of Commons, means—

(a) if the resolution provides for salary to be paid to Members at different rates according to whether or not they are holders of particular offices, or are in receipt of salaries or pensions as the holders or former holders of particular offices, a Member's yearly salary at the higher or highest rate; and
(b) in any other case, a Member's yearly salary at the rate specified in or determined under the resolution.

Former enactments.—TA 1970, s. 229; Parliamentary and Other Pensions Act 1972, s. 32(1); Parliamentary and Other Pensions and Salaries Act 1976, s. 1(3); Parliamentary and Other Pensions Act 1987, Sch. 3, para. 2(2).

CHAPTER IV

PERSONAL PENSION SCHEMES

Cross references.—See FA 1989, Sch. 7, Pt. II (new provisions in respect of personal pension schemes approved before 27 July 1989).

Preliminary

630. Interpretation

In this Chapter—

"approved"—

(a) in relation to a scheme, means approved by the Board under this Chapter; and
(b) in relation to arrangements, means made in accordance with a scheme which is for the time being, and was when the arrangements were made, an approved scheme;

but does not refer to cases in which approval has been withdrawn;

"authorised insurance company" means either—

(a) a person authorised under section 3 or 4 of the Insurance Companies Act 1982 to carry on long term business and acting through a branch or office in the United Kingdom; or
(b) a society registered as a friendly society under the Friendly Societies Act 1974 or the Friendly Societies Act (Northern Ireland) 1970;

"member", in relation to a personal pension scheme, means an individual who makes arrangements in accordance with the scheme;

"personal pension arrangements" means arrangements made by an individual in accordance with a personal pension scheme;

"personal pension scheme" means a scheme whose sole purpose is the provision of annuities or lump sums under arrangements made by individuals in accordance with the scheme;

"scheme administrator" means the person referred to in section 638(1);

[and references to an employee or to an employer include references to the holder of an office or to the person under whom an office is held.][1]

Former enactment.—F(No. 2)A 1987, s. 18.
Amendments.—[1] Words inserted by FA 1988, s. 55(1), (4) with effect from 1 July 1988.

631. Approval of schemes

(1) An application to the Board for their approval of a personal pension scheme shall be in such form, shall contain such information, and shall be accompanied by such documents, in such form, as the Board may prescribe.

(2) The Board may at their discretion grant or refuse an application for approval of a personal pension scheme, but their discretion shall be subject to the restrictions set out in sections 632 to 638.

(3) The Board shall give notice to the applicant of the grant or refusal of an application; and in the case of a refusal the notice shall state the grounds for the refusal.

(4) If an amendment is made to an approved scheme without being approved by the Board, their approval of the scheme shall cease to have effect.

Former enactment.—F(No. 2)A 1987, s. 19.

Restrictions on approval

632. Establishment of schemes

(1) The Board shall not approve a personal pension scheme established by any person other than—

(a) a person who is authorised under Chapter III of Part I of the Financial Services Act 1986 to carry on investment business and who carries on business of a kind mentioned in subsection (2) below;
(b) a building society within the meaning of the Building Societies Act 1986;

(c) an institution authorised under the Banking Act 1987;
   (d) a recognised bank or licensed institution within the meaning of the Banking Act 1979.

(2) The kinds of business referred to in subsection (1)(a) above are—
   (a) issuing insurance policies or annuity contracts;
   (b) managing unit trust schemes authorised under section 78(1) of the Financial Services Act 1986.

(3) Subsection (1) above shall not apply in relation to a scheme approved by the Board by virtue of section 620(5) if it was established before [1st July][1] 1988.

(4) The Treasury may by order amend this section as it has effect for the time being.

Former enactment.—F(No. 2)A 1987, s. 20.
Cross references.—See FA 1988, s. 54(2)(a)(iii), (3) (amendment to F(No. 2)A 1987, s. 20(3) deemed always to have had effect).
Amendments.—[1] Date in sub-s. (3) substituted by FA 1988, s. 54(2)(a)(iii), (3) and deemed always to have had effect.

633. Scope of benefits

(1) The Board shall not approve a personal pension scheme which makes provision for any benefit other than—
   (a) the payment of an annuity satisfying the conditions in section 634;
   (b) the payment to a member of a lump sum satisfying the conditions in section 635;
   (c) the payment after the death of a member of an annuity satisfying the conditions in section 636;
   (d) the payment on the death of a member of a lump sum satisfying either the conditions in section 637(1) or those in section 637(2).

(2) Subsection (1) above shall not prevent the approval of a scheme which makes provision for insurance against a risk relating to the non-payment of contributions.

Former enactment.—F(No. 2)A 1987, s. 21.

634. Annuity to member

(1) The annuity must be payable by an authorised insurance company which may be chosen by the member.

(2) Subject to subsection (3) below, the annuity must not commence before the member attains the age of 50 or after he attains the age of 75.

(3) The annuity may commence before the member attains the age of 50 if—
   (a) it is payable on his becoming incapable through infirmity of body or mind of carrying on his own occupation or any occupation of a similar nature for which he is trained or fitted; or
   (b) the Board are satisfied that his occupation is one in which persons customarily retire before that age.

(4) Subject to subsection (5) below, the annuity must be payable to the member for his life.

(5) The annuity may continue for a term certain not exceeding ten years, notwithstanding the member's death within that term; and for this purpose an annuity shall be regarded as payable for a term certain notwithstanding that it may terminate, after the death of the member and before expiry of that term, on the happening of any of the following—
   (a) the marriage of the annuitant;
   (b) his attaining the age of 18;
   (c) the later of his attaining that age and ceasing to be in full-time education.

(6) The annuity must not be capable of assignment or surrender, except that an annuity for a term certain may be assigned by will or by the annuitant's personal representatives in the distribution of his estate so as to give effect to a testamentary disposition, or to the rights of those entitled on an intestacy, or to an appropriation of it to a legacy or to a share or interest in the estate.

Former enactment.—F(No. 2)A 1987, s. 22.

635. Lump sum to member

(1) The lump sum must be payable only if the member so elects on or before the date on which an annuity satisfying the conditions in section 634 is first payable to him under the arrangements made in accordance with the scheme.

(2) The lump sum must be payable when that annuity is first payable.

[(3) The lump sum must not exceed one quarter of the difference between—

(a) the total value, at the time when the lump sum is paid, of the benefits provided for by the arrangements made by the member in accordance with the scheme, and
(b) the value, at that time, of such of the member's rights under the scheme as are protected rights for the purposes of the Social Security Act 1986 or the Social Security (Northern Ireland) Order 1986.][1]

. . .[2]

(5) The right to payment of the lump sum must not be capable of assignment or surrender.

Former enactment.—F(No. 2)A 1987, s. 23.
Amendments.—[1] Sub-s. (3) substituted by FA 1989, Sch. 7, paras. 1, 2 in relation to the approval of a scheme after 26 July 1989 except as regards arrangements made by a member before 27 July 1989 in accordance with a scheme coming into existence before that date. Previously sub-s (3) read—

"(3) The lump sum must not exceed one quarter of the total value, at the time when the lump sum is paid, of the benefits for the member provided for by the arrangements made by him in accordance with the scheme."
[2] Sub-s. (4) repealed by *ibid* and Sch. 17, Pt. IV. It read—

"(4) The lump sum must not exceed £150,000 or such other sum as may for the time being be specified in an order made by the Treasury."

636. Annuity after death of member

(1) The annuity must be payable by an authorised insurance company which may be chosen by the member or by the annuitant.

(2) The annuity must be payable to the surviving spouse of the member, or to a person who was at the member's death a dependant of his.

(3) The aggregate annual amount (or, if that amount varies, the aggregate of the initial annual amounts) of all annuities to which this section applies and which are payable under the same personal pension arrangements shall not exceed—

(a) where before his death the member was in receipt of an annuity under the arrangements, the annual amount (or, if it varied, the highest annual amount) of that annuity; or
(b) where paragraph (a) does not apply, the highest annual amount of the annuity that would have been payable under the arrangements to the member (ignoring any entitlement of his to commute part of it for a lump sum) if it had vested on the day before his death.

(4) Subject to subsections (5) to (9) below, the annuity must be payable for the life of the annuitant.

(5) Where the annuity is payable to the surviving spouse of the member and at the time of the member's death the surviving spouse is under the age of 60, the annuity may be deferred to a time not later than—

(a) the time when the surviving spouse attains that age; or
(b) where the member's annuity is payable to the surviving spouse for a term certain as mentioned in section 634(5) and the surviving spouse attains the age of 60 before the time when the member's annuity terminates, that time.

(6) The annuity may cease to be payable on the marriage of the annuitant.

(7) Where the annuity is payable to the surviving spouse of the member, it may cease before the death of the surviving spouse if—

(a) the member was survived by one or more dependants under the age of 18 and at the time of the member's death the surviving spouse was under the age of 45; and
(b) at some time before the surviving spouse attains that age no such dependant remains under the age of 18.

(8) Where the annuity is payable to a person who is under the age of 18 when it is first payable, it must cease to be payable either—

(a) on his attaining that age; or
(b) on the later of his attaining that age and ceasing to be in full-time education,

unless he was a dependant of the member otherwise than by reason only that he was under the age of 18.

(9) The annuity may continue for a term certain not exceeding ten years, notwithstanding the original annuitant's death within that term; and for this purpose an annuity shall be regarded as payable for a term certain notwithstanding that it may terminate, after the death of the original annuitant and before the expiry of that term, on the happening of any of the following—

  (a) the marriage of the annuitant to whom it is payable;
  (b) his attaining the age of 18;
  (c) the later of his attaining that age and ceasing to be in full-time education.

(10) The annuity must not be capable of assignment or surrender, except that an annuity for a term certain may be assigned by will or by the annuitant's personal representatives in the distribution of his estate so as to give effect to a testamentary disposition, or to the rights of those entitled on an intestacy, or to an appropriation of it to a legacy or to a share or interest in the estate.

Former enactment.—F(No. 2)A 1987, s. 24.

637. Lump sum on death of member

(1) The lump sum—
  (a) must be payable by an authorised insurance company; and
  (b) must be payable on the death of the member before he attains the age of 75.

(2) The lump sum—
  (a) must be payable only if no annuity satisfying the conditions in either section 634 or section 636 has become payable; and
  (b) subject to subsection (3) below, must represent no more than the return of contributions together with reasonable interest on contributions or bonuses out of profits.

(3) To the extent that contributions are invested in units under a unit trust scheme, the lump sum referred to in subsection (2) above may represent the sale or redemption price of the units.

Former enactments.—Sub-s. (1): F(No. 2)A 1987, s. 25.
Sub-ss. (2), (3); F(No. 2)A 1987, s. 26.

638. Other restrictions on approval

(1) The Board shall not approve a personal pension scheme unless they are satisfied that there is a person resident in the United Kingdom who will be responsible for the management of the scheme.

(2) The Board shall not approve a personal pension scheme unless it makes such provision for the making, acceptance and application of transfer payments as satisfies any requirements imposed by or under regulations made by the Board.

(3) The Board shall not approve a personal pension scheme unless it makes provision, in relation to arrangements made in accordance with the scheme, for ensuring that—

  (a) the aggregate amount of the contributions that may be made in a year of assessment by the member and an employer of his under the arrangements, together with the aggregate amounts of such contributions under other approved personal pension arrangements made by that member, does not exceed the permitted maximum for that year; and
  (b) any excess is repaid to the member to the extent of his contributions and otherwise to his employer.

(4) In subsection (3) above "the permitted maximum" for a year of assessment means an amount equal to the aggregate of—

  (a) the relevant percentage of the member's net relevant earnings for the year; and
  (b) so much of any relief given under section 639(1) for that year as is given by virtue of section 642;

and references in subsection (3) to contributions by the member do not include references to contributions treated by virtue of section 649(3) as paid by him.

(5) In subsection (4) above "the relevant percentage" means 17.5 per cent. or, in a case where section 640(2) applies, the relevant percentage there specified.

(6) The Board shall not approve a personal pension scheme which permits the acceptance of contributions other than—

(a) contributions by members;
(b) contributions by employers of members;
(c) minimum contributions paid by the Secretary of State under Part I of the Social Security Act 1986 or by the Department of Health and Social Services for Northern Ireland under Part II of the Social Security (Northern Ireland) Order 1986.

[(7) The Board shall not approve a personal pension scheme which permits the acceptance of minimum contributions paid as mentioned in subsection (6)(c) above in respect of an individual's service as director of a company, if his emoluments as such are within section 644(5).][1]

[(8) A personal pension scheme which permits the acceptance of minimum contributions paid as mentioned in subsection (6)(c) above in respect of an individual's service in an office or employment to which section 645 applies may be approved by the Board only if—

(a) the scheme does not permit the acceptance of contributions from the individual or from the person who is his employer in relation to that office or employment; or
(b) at the time when the minimum contributions are paid the individual is not serving in an office or employment to which section 645 applies.][1]

Former enactments.—Sub-s. (1): F(No. 2)A 1987, s. 27.
Sub-s. (2): F(No. 2)A 1987, s. 28(1).
Sub-ss. (3)–(5): F(No. 2)A 1987, s. 29.
Sub-ss. (6), (7): F(No. 2)A 1987, s. 30.
Amendments.—[1] Sub-ss. (7), (8) substituted for sub-s. (7) by FA 1988, s. 55(2), (4) with effect from 1 July 1988.

Tax reliefs

639. Member's contributions

(1) A contribution paid by an individual under approved personal pension arrangements made by him shall, subject to the provisions of this Chapter, be deducted from or set off against any relevant earnings of his for the year of assessment in which the payment is made.

Except where subsections (2) to (4) below apply, relief under this subsection in respect of a contribution shall be given only on a claim made for the purpose.

(2) In such cases and subject to such conditions as the Board may prescribe in regulations, relief under subsection (1) above shall be given in accordance with subsections (3) and (4) below.

(3) An individual who is entitled to such relief in respect of a contribution may deduct from the contribution when he pays it, and may retain, an amount equal to income tax at the basic rate on the contribution.

(4) The scheme administrator—

(a) shall accept the amount paid after the deduction in discharge of the individual's liability to the same extent as if the deduction had not been made; and
(b) may recover an amount equal to the deduction from the Board.

(5) Regulations under this section may make provision for carrying subsections (3) and (4) above into effect and, without prejudice to the generality of that, may provide—

(a) for the manner in which claims for the recovery of a sum under subsection (4)(b) may be made;
(b) for the giving of such information, in such form, as may be prescribed by or under the regulations;
(c) for the inspection by persons authorised by the Board of books, documents and other records.

(6) Where relief under this section for any year of assessment is claimed and allowed (whether or not it then falls to be given for that year), and afterwards an assessment, alteration of an assessment, or other adjustment of the claimant's liability to tax is made, there shall also be made such consequential adjustments in the relief allowed or given under this section for that or any subsequent year as are appropriate.

(7) Where relief under this section is claimed and allowed for any year of assessment in respect of a contribution, relief shall not be given in respect of it under any other provision of the Income Tax Acts for the same or any subsequent year, nor (in the case of a contribution under an annuity contract) in respect of any other premium or consideration for an annuity under the same contract.

(8) References in the Income Tax Acts to relief in respect of life assurance premiums shall not be taken to include relief under this section.

Former enactments.—Sub-s. (1): F(No. 2)A 1987, ss. 31, 46.
Sub-ss. (2)–(5): F(No. 2)A 1987, s. 45.
Sub-s. (6): F(No. 2)A 1987, s. 48.
Sub-s. (7), (8): F(No. 2)A 1987, s. 49.

640. Maximum amount of deductions

(1) The maximum amount that may be deducted or set off in any year of assessment by virtue of section 639(1) shall be 17.5 per cent. of the individual's net relevant earnings for that year.

(2) In the case of an individual whose age at the beginning of the year of assessment is within a range specified in the first column of the following table, subsection (1) above shall have effect with the substitution for 17.5 per cent. of the relevant percentage specified in the second column.

[36 to 45	20 per cent.
46 to 50	25 per cent.
51 to 55	30 per cent.
56 to 60	35 per cent.
61 or more	40 per cent.][1]

(3) Without prejudice to subsection (1) above, the maximum amount that may be deducted or set off in any year of assessment in respect of contributions paid by an individual to secure benefits satisfying the conditions in section 637(1) shall be 5 per cent. of the individual's net relevant earnings for that year.

(4) Where personal pension arrangements are made by an employee whose employer makes contributions under the arrangements, the maximum amount that may be deducted or set off in any year of assessment shall be reduced by the amount of the employer's contributions in the year.

(5) Any minimum contributions treated by virtue of section 649(3) as paid by the individual in respect of whom they are paid shall be disregarded for the purposes of this section.

Former enactment.—F(No. 2)A 1987, s. 32.
Amendments.—[1] The Table in sub-s. (2) substituted by FA 1989, Sch. 7, paras. 1, 3.

[640A. Earnings cap

(1) In arriving at an individual's net relevant earnings for a year of assessment for the purposes of section 640 above, any excess of what would be his net relevant earnings for the year (apart from this subsection) over the allowable maximum for the year shall be disregarded.

(2) In subsection (1) above "the allowable maximum" means, as regards a particular year of assessment, the figure found for that year by virtue of subsections (3) and (4) below.

(3) For the year of assessment 1989–90 the figure is £60,000.

(4) For the year of assessment 1990–91 and any subsequent year of assessment the figure is the figure found for that year, for the purposes of section 590C, by virtue of section 590C(4) and (5).][1]

Amendments.—[1] This section inserted by FA 1989, Sch. 7, paras. 1, 4.

641. Carry-back of contributions

(1) An individual who pays a contribution under approved personal pension arrangements in a year of assessment (whether or not a year for which he has relevant earnings) may elect that the contribution, or part of it, shall be treated as paid—

(a) in the year of assessment preceding that year; or
(b) if he had no net relevant earnings in that preceding year of assessment, in the year of assessment before that.

(2) Where for any year of assessment an individual—

(a) has relevant earnings as an underwriting member of Lloyd's or by way of commission calculated by reference to the profits of Lloyd's underwriting business; and
(b) there is an amount of unused relief attributable to those earnings,

the individual may elect that there shall be treated as paid in that year so much of any contributions paid by him under approved personal pension arrangements in the next year of assessment but two as does not exceed the amount of the unused relief.

(3) Subject to section 655(2), references in subsection (2) above to an amount of unused relief attributable to the earnings mentioned in subsection (2)(a) are to an amount which could have been deducted from or set off against those earnings under section 639(1) if—

(a) the individual had paid contributions under approved personal pension arrangements in the year of assessment for which he has the earnings; or
(b) any such contributions paid by him in that year had been greater.

(4) An election under this section must be made not later than three months after the end of the year of assessment in which the contributions treated as paid in another year are actually paid.

(5) Where an election is made under this section in respect of a contribution or part of a contribution, the other provisions of this Chapter shall have effect as if the contribution or part had been paid in the year specified in the election and not in the year in which it was actually paid.

Former enactment.—F(No. 2)A 1987, s. 33.

642. Carry-forward of relief

(1) Where—

(a) for any year of assessment an individual has relevant earnings from any trade, profession, vocation, office or employment carried on or held by him, and
(b) there is an amount of unused relief for that year,

relief may be given under section 639(1), up to the amount of the unused relief, in respect of so much of any contributions paid by him under approved personal pension arrangements in any of the next six years of assessment as exceeds the maximum applying for that year under section 640.

(2) In this section, references to an amount of unused relief for any year are to an amount which could have been deducted from or set off against the individual's relevant earnings for that year under section 639(1) if—

(a) the individual had paid contributions under approved personal pension arrangements in that year; or
(b) any such contributions paid by him in that year had been greater.

(3) Relief by virtue of this section shall be given for an earlier year rather than a later year, the unused relief taken into account in giving relief for any year being deducted from that available for giving relief in subsequent years and unused relief derived from an earlier year being exhausted before unused relief derived from a later year.

(4) Where a relevant assessment to tax in respect of a year of assessment becomes final and conclusive more than six years after the end of that year and there is an amount of unused relief for that year which results from the making of the assessment—

(a) that amount shall not be available for giving relief by virtue of this section for any of the six years following that year; but
(b) the individual may, within the period of six months beginning with the date on which the assessment becomes final and conclusive, elect that relief shall be given under section 639(1), up to that amount, in respect of so much of any contributions paid by him under approved personal pension arrangements within that period as exceeds the maximum applying under section 640 for the year of assessment in which they are paid;

and to the extent to which relief in respect of any contributions is given by virtue of this subsection it shall not be given by virtue of subsection (1) above.

(5) In this section "a relevant assessment to tax" means an assessment on the individual's

relevant earnings or on the profits or gains of a partnership from which the individual derives relevant earnings.

Former enactment.—F(No. 2)A 1987, s. 34.

643. Employer's contributions and personal pension income etc

(1) Where contributions are paid by an employer under approved personal pension arrangements made by his employee, those contributions shall not be regarded as emoluments of the employment chargeable to tax under Schedule E.

(2) Income derived by a person from investments or deposits held by him for the purposes of an approved personal pension scheme shall be exempt from income tax.

(3) An annuity payable under approved personal pension arrangements shall be treated as earned income of the annuitant.

(4) Subsection (3) above applies only in relation to the annuitant to whom the annuity is made payable by the terms of the arrangements.

Former enactments.—Sub-s. (1): F(No. 2)A 1987, s. 38.
Sub-s. (2): F(No. 2)A 1987, s. 39(1).
Sub-ss. (3), (4): F(No. 2)A 1987, s. 41(1), (2).

644. Meaning of "relevant earnings"

(1) In this Chapter, "relevant earnings", in relation to an individual, means any income of his which is chargeable to tax for the year of assessment in question and is within subsection (2) below.

(2) Subject to subsections (3) to [(6F)]¹ below, income is within this subsection if it is—

(*a*) emoluments chargeable under Schedule E from an office or employment held by the individual;
(*b*) income from any property which is attached to or forms part of the emoluments of an office or employment held by him;
(*c*) income which is chargeable under Schedule D and is immediately derived by him from the carrying on or exercise by him of his trade, profession or vocation (either as an individual or as a partner acting personally in a partnership);
(*d*) income treated as earned income by virtue of section 529.

(3) Where section 645 applies to an office or employment held by the individual, neither emoluments from the office or employment nor income from any property which is attached to it or forms part of its emoluments are within subsection (2) above.

(4) The following are not income within subsection (2) above—

(*a*) anything in respect of which tax is chargeable under Schedule E and which arises from the acquisition or disposal of shares or an interest in shares or from a right to acquire shares;
(*b*) anything in respect of which tax is chargeable by virtue of section 148.

(5) Emoluments of an individual as director of a company are not income within subsection (2) above if—

(*a*) the income of the company consists wholly or mainly of investment income; and
(*b*) the individual, either alone or together with any other persons who are or have been at any time directors of the company, controls the company;

and section 840 shall apply for the purposes of this subsection.

(6) For the purposes of subsection (5) above—

"director" includes any person occupying the position of director by whatever name called; and
["investment income" means income which, if the company were an individual, would not be earned income.]³

[(6A) Emoluments of an individual as an employee of a company are not income within subsection (2) above if—

(*a*) he is a controlling director of the company at any time in the year of assessment in question or has been a controlling director of the company at any time in the ten years immediately preceding that year of assessment, and
(*b*) any of subsections (6B) to (6E) below applies in his case.]²

[(6B) This subsection applies in the case of the individual if—

(a) at any time in the year of assessment in question he is in receipt of benefits under a relevant superannuation scheme, and
(b) the benefits are payable in respect of past service with the company.]²

[(6C) This subsection applies in the case of the individual if—

(a) at any time in the year of assessment in question he is in receipt of benefits under a personal pension scheme,
(b) the scheme has received a transfer payment relating to him from a relevant superannuation scheme, and
(c) the transfer payment is in respect of past service with the company.]²

[(6D) This subsection applies in the case of the individual if—

(a) at any time in the year of assessment in question he is in receipt of benefits under a relevant superannuation scheme,
(b) the benefits are payable in respect of past service with another company,
(c) the emoluments are for a period during which the company mentioned in subsection (6A) above has carried on a trade or business previously carried on by the other company, and
(d) the other company carried on the trade or business at any time during the period of service in respect of which the benefits are payable.]²

[(6E) This subsection applies in the case of the individual if—

(a) at any time in the year of assessment in question he is in receipt of benefits under a personal pension scheme,
(b) the scheme has received a transfer payment relating to him from a relevant superannuation scheme,
(c) the transfer payment is in respect of past service with another company,
(d) the emoluments are for a period during which the company mentioned in subsection (6A) above has carried on a trade or business previously carried on by the other company, and
(e) the other company carried on the trade or business at any time during the period of service in respect of which the transfer payment was made.]²

[(6F) For the purposes of subsections (6A) to (6E) above—

(a) a person is a controlling director of a company if he is a director (as defined by section 612(1)), and he is within paragraph (b) of section 417(5), in relation to the company;
(b) "relevant superannuation scheme" has the same meaning as in section 645(1);
(c) references to benefits payable in respect of past service with a company include references to benefits payable partly in respect of past service with the company; and
(d) references to a transfer payment in respect of past service with a company include references to a transfer payment partly in respect of past service with the company.]²

(7) For the purposes of this Chapter, a married woman's relevant earnings shall not be treated as her husband's relevant earnings, notwithstanding that her income chargeable to tax is treated as his income.

Former enactment.—F(No. 2)A 1987, s. 35.
Note.—See **Prospective Legislation Notes** (Married Couples).
Amendments.—¹ Number in sub-s. (2) substituted by FA 1989, Sch. 7, paras. 1, 5.
² Sub-ss. (6A) to (6F) inserted by *ibid.*
³ Definition of "investment income" in sub-s. (6) substituted by FA 1989, Sch. 12, para. 16.

645. Earnings from pensionable employment

(1) This section applies to an office or employment held by an individual if—

(a) service in it is service to which a relevant superannuation scheme relates; and
(b) the individual is a participant in the scheme; and
(c) [subsection (4) below does not apply]¹ to his participation in the scheme.

(2) This section applies whether or not the duties of the office or employment are performed wholly or partly in the United Kingdom or the individual is chargeable to tax in respect of it.

(3) In subsection (1) above "a relevant superannuation scheme" means a scheme or arrangement—

(a) the object or one of the objects of which is the provision, in respect of persons serving

in particular offices or employments, of relevant benefits within the meaning of section 612;...[2]
 (b) which is established by a person other than the individual; [and][3]
 (c) which is of a description mentioned in section 596(1)(a), (b) or (c).][3]

(4) This subsection applies to an individual's participation in a scheme if the scheme provides no benefits in relation to him other than—
 (a) an annuity payable to his surviving spouse or a dependant of his;
 (b) a lump sum payable on his death in service.

[(4A) Where the emoluments from an office or employment held by an individual are foreign emoluments within the meaning of section 192, this section shall have effect with the substitution of the following for paragraph (c) of subsection (3) above—

 "(c) which corresponds to a scheme of a description mentioned in section 596(1)(a), (b) or (c)."][4]

(5) ...[2]

Former enactment.—F(No. 2)A 1987, s. 36.
Amendments.—[1] Words in sub-s. (1)(c) substituted by FA 1989, Sch. 7, paras. 1, 6.
[2] Sub-s. (5) and the word "and" in sub-s. (3)(a) repealed by *ibid* and Sch. 17, Pt. IV.
[3] Sub-s. (3)(c) and the preceding word "and" inserted by FA 1989, Sch 7, paras. 1, 6.
[4] Sub-s. (4A) inserted by *ibid*.

646. Meaning of "net relevant earnings"

(1) Subject to subsections (3) to (7) below [and section 646A][1], in this Chapter "net relevant earnings", in relation to an individual, means the amount of his relevant earnings for the year of assessment in question, less the amount of any deductions within subsection (2) below which fall to be made from the relevant earnings in computing for the purposes of income tax his total income for that year.

(2) Deductions are within this subsection if they are—
 (a) deductions which but for section 74(m), (p) or (q) could be made in computing the profits or gains of the individual;
 (b) deductions made by virtue of section 198, 201 or 332(3);
 (c) deductions in respect of relief under Schedule 9 to the Finance Act 1981 (stock relief);
 (d) deductions in respect of losses or capital allowances, being losses or capital allowances arising from activities profits or gains of which would be included in computing relevant earnings of the individual or the individual's wife or husband.

(3) For the purposes of this section, an individual's relevant earnings shall be taken to be those earnings before giving effect to any capital allowances, other than deductions allowable in computing profits or gains, but after taking into account the amounts on which charges fall to be made under the 1968 Act (including the enactments which under this Act or the 1970 Act are to be treated as contained in Part I of the 1968 Act); and in subsections (4) and (5) below, references to income (other than references to total income) shall be construed similarly.

(4) In the case of an individual's partnership profits, the amount to be included in arriving at his net relevant earnings shall be his share of the partnership income (estimated in accordance with the Income Tax Acts) after making from it any such deductions in respect of—
 (a) payments made by the partnership;
 (b) relief given to the partnership under Schedule 9 to the Finance Act 1981; or
 (c) capital allowances falling to be made to the partnership,
as would be made in computing the tax payable in respect of that income.

(5) Where, in a year of assessment for which an amount is deducted or set off under section 639(1) against the net relevant earnings of an individual—
 (a) a deduction in respect of such a loss or allowance of the individual as is mentioned in subsection (2)(d) above falls to be made in computing the total income of the individual or the individual's wife or husband; and
 (b) the deduction or part of it falls to be so made from income other than relevant earnings;
the amount of the deduction made from that other income shall be treated as reducing the

individual's net relevant earnings for subsequent years of assessment in accordance with subsection (6) below.

(6) The deduction shall be made so far as possible from the individual's net relevant earnings for the first of the subsequent years of assessment (whether or not he is entitled to relief under section 639(1) for that year), and than, so far as it cannot be so made, from those of the next year, and so on.

(7) An individual's net relevant earnings for any year of assessment shall be computed without regard to any deduction or set off under section 639(1) which falls to be made for that year in respect of the individual or the individual's wife or husband.

Former enactment.—F(No. 2)A 1987, s. 37.
Note.—See **Prospective Legislation Notes** (Married Couples).
Amendments.—[1] Words in sub-s. (1) inserted by FA 1989, Sch. 7, para. 7.

[646A. Earnings from associated employments

(1) This section applies where in the year of assessment in question—

(a) an individual holds two or more offices or employments which are associated in that year,
(b) one or more of them is an office or employment to which section 645 applies ("pensionable job"), and
(c) one or more of them is an office or employment to which that section does not apply ("non-pensionable job").

(2) Where the emoluments for that year from the pensionable job (or jobs) are equal to or exceed the allowable maximum for that year, section 646(1) shall have effect in the case of the individual as if the references to relevant earnings were references to relevant earnings not attributable to the non-pensionable job (or jobs).

(3) Where the allowable maximum for that year exceeds the emoluments for that year from the pensionable job (or jobs), the individual's net relevant earnings, so far as attributable to the non-pensionable job (or jobs), shall not be greater than the amount of the excess.

(4) For the purposes of this section two or more offices or employments held by an individual in a year of assessment are associated in that year if the employers in question are associated at any time during it.

(5) For the purposes of subsection (4) above, employers are associated if (directly or indirectly) one is controlled by the other or if both are controlled by a third person.

(6) In subsection (5) above the reference to control, in relation to a body corporate, shall be construed—

(a) where the body corporate is a close company, in accordance with section 416, and
(b) where it is not, in accordance with section 840.

(7) In this section "the allowable maximum" has the same meaning as in section 640A(1).][1]

Amendments.—[1] This section inserted by FA 1989, Sch. 7, para. 8.

Charge to tax

647. Unauthorised payments

(1) This section applies to any payment within subsection (2) below which is made—

(a) out of funds which are or have been held for the purposes of a personal pension scheme which is or has at any time been approved; and
(b) to or for the benefit of an individual who has made personal pension arrangements in accordance with the scheme.

(2) A payment is within this subsection if—

(a) it is not expressly authorised by the rules of the scheme; or
(b) it is made at a time when the scheme or the arrangements are not approved and it would not have been expressly authorised by the rules of the scheme or by the arrangements when the scheme, or as the case may be the arrangements, were last so approved.

(3) The individual referred to in subsection (1)(b) above, whether or not he is the recipient of the payment, shall be chargeable to tax under Schedule E on the amount of the payment for the year of assessment in which the payment is made.

(4) This section applies to a transfer of assets or other transfer of money's worth as it applies to a payment, and in relation to such a transfer the reference in subsection (3) above to the amount of the payment shall be read as a reference to the value of the transfer.

Former enactment.—F(No. 2)A 1987, s. 44.

648. Contributions under unapproved arrangements

Where contributions are paid by an employer under personal pension arrangements made by his employee than, if those arrangements are not approved arrangements and the contributions are not otherwise chargeable to income tax as income of the employee, the contributions shall be regarded for all the purposes of the Income Tax Acts as emoluments of the employment chargeable to tax under Schedule E.

Former enactment.—F(No. 2)A 1987, s. 53.

Miscellaneous

649. Minimum contributions under Social Security Act 1986

(1) Where under Part I of the Social Security Act 1986 the Secretary of State pays minimum contributions for the purposes of approved personal pension arrangements, the amount of the employee's share of those contributions shall, instead of being the amount provided for in that Part, be the grossed-up equivalent of the amount so provided for.

(2) For the purposes of this section—

"the employee's share" of minimum contributions is so much of the contributions as is attributable to the percentage mentioned in paragraph (*a*) of the definition of "rebate percentage" in section 3(3) of the Social Security Act 1986;

"the grossed-up equivalent" of an amount is such sum as, after deduction of income tax at the basic rate in force for the year of assessment for which the contributions are paid, is equal to that amount.

(3) The employee's share of minimum contributions paid for a year of assessment by the Secretary of State for the purposes of approved personal pension arrangements shall be treated for the purposes of income tax—

(*a*) as the income for that year of the individual in respect of whom it is paid; and
(*b*) as contributions paid in that year by that individual under those arrangements.

(4) The Board may make regulations—

(*a*) providing for the recovery by the Secretary of State from the Board, in such circumstances as may be prescribed by the regulations, of any increase attributable to this section in the sums paid by the Secretary of State out of the National Insurance Fund;
(*b*) requiring the Secretary of State to give the Board such information as may be so prescribed about minimum contributions paid by the Secretary of State;
(*c*) prescribing circumstances in which this section or any provision of it shall not apply;
(*d*) making such provision as appears to the Board to be necessary or expedient for the purposes of supplementing the provisions of this section.

(5) Any payment received by the Secretary of State by virtue of this section shall be paid into the National Insurance Fund.

(6) In relation to Northern Ireland, this section shall have effect as if—

(*a*) references to the Secretary of State were references to the Department of Health and Social Services for Northern Ireland;
(*b*) references to Part I and section 3(3) of the Social Security Act 1986 were references to Part II and Article 5(3) of the Social Security (Northern Ireland) Order 1986; and
(*c*) references to the National Insurance Fund were references to the Northern Ireland National Insurance Fund.

Former enactment.—F(No. 2)A 1987, s. 42.

650. Withdrawal of approval

(1) If in the opinion of the Board the facts concerning an approved personal pension scheme or its administration or arrangements made in accordance with it do not warrant the continuance of their approval of the scheme, they may at any time by notice given to the scheme administrator withdraw their approval of the scheme.

(2) If in the opinion of the Board the facts concerning any approved personal pension arrangements do not warrant the continuance of their approval in relation to the arrangements, they may at any time by notice given to the individual who made them and to the scheme administrator withdraw their approval in relation to the arrangements.

(3) Without prejudice to the generality of subsection (2) above, the Board may withdraw their approval in relation to any personal pension arrangements if they are of the opinion that securing the provision of benefits under the arrangements was not the sole purpose of the individual in making them.

(4) A notice under subsection (1) or (2) above shall state the grounds on which, and the date from which, approval is withdrawn.

(5) The Board may not withdraw their approval from a date earlier than the date when the facts were first such that they did not warrant the continuance of their approval (so, however, that in a case within subsection (3) above their approval may be withdrawn from the day the arrangements in question were made).

Former enactment.—F(No. 2)A 1987, s. 43.

651. Appeals

(1) Where the Board—

  (*a*) refuse an application by notice under section 631; or
  (*b*) withdraw an approval by notice under section 650;

the person to whom the notice is given may appeal to the Special Commissioners against the refusal or, as the case may be, the withdrawal.

(2) An appeal under this section shall be made by notice stating the grounds for the appeal and given to the Board before the end of the period of 30 days beginning with the day on which the notice of refusal or withdrawal was given to the appellant.

(3) On an appeal under this section against the withdrawal of an approval, the Special Commissioners may, instead of allowing or dismissing the appeal, order that the withdrawal shall have effect from a date other than that determined by the Board.

(4) The bringing of an appeal under this section shall not affect the validity of the decision appealed against pending the determination of the proceedings.

Former enactment.—F(No. 2)A 1987, s. 47.

652. Information about payments

(1) An inspector may give a notice to a scheme administrator requiring him to provide the inspector with—

  (*a*) such particulars as the notice may require relating to contributions paid under approved personal pension arrangements made in accordance with the scheme;
  (*b*) such particulars as the notice may require relating to payments by way of return of contributions;
  (*c*) copies of such accounts as the notice may require.

(2) A person to whom a notice is given under this section shall comply with the notice within the period of 30 days beginning with the day on which it is given.

Former enactment.—F(No. 2)A 1987, s. 50.

653. Information penalties

A person who knowingly makes a false statement or false representation on making an application under section 631 or for the purpose of obtaining for himself or any other person any relief from or repayment of tax under this Chapter shall be liable to a penalty not exceeding [£3,000][1].

Former enactment.—F(No. 2)A 1987, s. 51(1).
Amendments.—[1] Amount substituted for "£500" by FA 1989, s. 170(4)(*b*), (6) in relation to things done or omitted after 26 July 1989.

654. Remuneration of Ministers and other officers

(1) This section applies to any salary—

(a) payable to the holder of a qualifying office who is also a Member of the House of Commons; and

(b) payable for a period in respect of which the holder is not a participant in relation to that office in arrangements contained in the Parliamentary pension scheme but is a participant in relation to his membership of the House of Commons in any such arrangements, or for any part of such a period.

(2) So much of any salary to which this section applies as is equal to the difference between a Member's pensionable salary and the salary which (in accordance with any such resolution as is mentioned in subsection (4)(a) below) is payable to him as a Member holding that qualifying office, shall be treated for the purposes of this Chapter as remuneration from the office of Member and not from the qualifying office.

(3) In this section—

"Member's pensionable salary" means a Member's ordinary salary under any resolution of the House of Commons which, being framed otherwise than as an expression of opinion, is for the time being in force relating to the remuneration of Members or, if the resolution provides for a Member's ordinary salary thereunder to be treated for pension purposes as being at a higher rate, a notional yearly salary at that higher rate;

"qualifying office" means an office mentioned in paragraph (b), (c) or (d) of subsection (2) of section 2 of the Parliamentary and other Pensions Act 1987;

"the Parliamentary pension scheme" has the same meaning as in that Act;

and, without prejudice to the power conferred by virtue of paragraph 13 of Schedule 1 to that Act, regulations under section 2 of that Act may make provision specifying the circumstances in which a person is to be regarded for the purposes of this section as being or not being a participant in relation to his membership of the House of Commons, or in relation to any office, in arrangements contained in the Parliamentary pension scheme.

(4) In subsection (3) above "a Member's ordinary salary", in relation to any resolution of the House of Commons, means—

(a) if the resolution provides for salary to be paid to Members at different rates according to whether or not they are holders of particular offices or are in receipt of salaries or pensions as the holders or former holders of particular offices, a Member's yearly salary at the higher or highest rate; and

(b) in any other case, a Member's yearly salary at the rate specified in or determined under the resolution.

Former enactment.—F(No. 2)A 1987, s. 52.

655. Transitional provisions

(1) Where approved personal pension arrangements are made by an individual who pays qualifying premiums within the meaning of section 620(1)—

(a) the amount that may be deducted or set off by virtue of section 639(1) in any year of assessment shall be reduced by the amount of any qualifying premiums which are paid in the year by the individual and in respect of which relief is given for the year under section 619(1)(a); and

(b) the relief which, by virtue of section 625, may be given under section 619 by reference to the individual's unused relief for any year shall be reduced by the amount of any contributions paid by him in that year under the approved personal pension arrangements.

(2) Where an individual elects under section 641 that a contribution or part of a contribution shall be treated as paid in the year of assessment [1985–86, 1986–87 or 1987–88][1], the payment shall be treated as the payment of a qualifying premium for the purposes of Chapter III of this Part; and in such a case references in section 641 to an amount of unused relief shall be construed in accordance with section 625.

(3) The references in section 642 to unused relief for any year are, for years of assessment before [1988–89][1], references to unused relief within the meaning of section 625.

(4) The Board shall not grant any application under section 631 so as to approve a scheme with effect from a date earlier than [1st July][1] 1988.

(5) The Board may by regulations make provisions for applications for approval of personal pension schemes to be granted provisionally . . .[2], notwithstanding that the Board have not

satisfied themselves that the schemes comply with the requirements of sections 632 to 638; and such regulations may, in particular, provide—

(a) for the contents and form of certificates or other documents which the Board may require the applicant to give them before they grant an application provisionally;

(b) for the making of such amendments of the rules of the scheme after the provisional grant of an application as are necessary to enable the scheme to comply with the requirements of sections 632 to 638, and for those amendments to have effect as from the date of approval of the scheme;

(c) for the withdrawal of approval of the scheme as from that date if it does not comply with the requirements of sections 632 to 638 and such amendments as are mentioned in paragraph (b) above are not made;

and may make such supplementary provision as appears to the Board to be necessary or expedient.

Former enactments.—Sub-ss. (1)–(3): F(No. 2)A 1987, s. 55.
Sub-ss. (4), (5): F(No. 2)A 1987, s. 56.
Cross references.—See FA 1988, s. 54(1), (2)(b), (c), (3) (amendments to F(No. 2)A 1987, ss. 55(2), (3), 56(1), (2) deemed always to have had effect).
Amendments.—[1] Dates in sub-ss. (2), (3), (4) substituted by FA 1988, s. 54(1), (2)(b), (c), (3) and deemed always to have had effect.
[2] Words in sub-s. (5) repealed by FA 1989, Sch. 7, paras. 1, 9 and Sch. 17, Pt. IV.

CHAPTER V

PURCHASED LIFE ANNUITIES

656. Purchased life annuities other than retirement annuities

(1) Subject to section 657, a purchased life annuity shall, for the purposes of the provisions of the Tax Acts relating to tax on annuities and other annual payments, be treated as containing a capital element and, to the extent of the capital element, as not being an annual payment or in the nature of an annual payment; but the capital element in such an annuity shall be taken into account in computing profits or gains or losses for other purposes of the Tax Acts in any circumstances in which a lump sum payment would be taken into account.

(2) Where, in the case of any purchased life annuity to which this section applies, the amount of any annuity payment (but not the term of the annuity) depends on any contingency other than the duration of a human life or lives—

    (*a*) the capital element shall be determined by reference—

        (i) to the amount or value of the payments made or other consideration given for the grant of the annuity ("the purchase price"); and
        (ii) to the expected term of the annuity, as at the date when the first annuity payment began to accrue, expressed in years (and any odd fraction of a year), and determined by reference to the prescribed tables of mortality;

and in head (ii) above "term" means the period from the date when the first annuity payment begins to accrue to the date when the last payment becomes payable;
    (*b*) the capital element in any annuity payment made in respect of a period of 12 months shall be a fraction—

$$\frac{1}{E}$$

of the purchase price, where E is the expected term referred to in paragraph (*a*)(ii) above;
    (*c*) the capital element in any annuity payment made in respect of a period of less than, or more than, 12 months shall be the amount at (*b*) above reduced or, as the case may be, increased, in the same proportion as the length of that period bears to a period of 12 months;
    (*d*) subsection (3) below shall not apply but paragraphs (*a*) and (*b*) of subsection (4) below shall apply as they apply to that subsection.

(3) Subject to subsection (2) above, in the case of any purchased life annuity to which this section applies—

    (*a*) the capital element shall be determined by reference to the amount or value of the payments made or other consideration given for the grant of the annuity; and
    (*b*) the proportion which the capital element in any annuity payment bears to the total amount of that payment shall be constant for all payments on account of the annuity; and
    (*c*) where neither the term of the annuity nor the amount of any annuity payment depends on any contingency other than the duration of a human life or lives, that proportion shall be the same proportion which the total amount or value of the consideration for the grant of the annuity bears to the actuarial value of the annuity payments as determined in accordance with subsection (4) below; and
    (*d*) where either the term of the annuity or the amount of any annuity payment (but not both) depends on any contingency other than the duration of a human life or lives, that proportion shall be such as may be just, having regard to paragraph (*c*) above and to the contingencies affecting the annuity; and
    (*e*) where both the term of the annuity and the amount of any annuity payment depend on any contingency other than the duration of a human life or lives, that proportion shall be such as may be just, having regard to subsection (2) above and to the contingencies affecting the annuity.

(4) For the purposes of subsection (3) above—

    (*a*) an entire consideration given for the grant of an annuity and for some other matter shall be apportioned as appears just (but so that a right to a return of premiums or other consideration for an annuity shall not be treated for this purpose as a distinct matter from the annuity);
    (*b*) where it appears that the amount or value of the consideration purporting to be given

for the grant of an annuity has affected, or has been affected by, the consideration given for some other matter, the aggregate amount or value of those considerations shall be treated as one entire consideration given for both and shall be apportioned under paragraph (*a*) above accordingly; and

(*c*) the actuarial value of any annuity payments shall be taken to be their value as at the date when the first of those payments begins to accrue, that value being determined by reference to the prescribed tables of mortality and without discounting any payment for the time to elapse between that date and the date it is to be made.

(5) Where a person making a payment on account of any life annuity has been notified in the prescribed manner of any decision as to its being or not being a purchased life annuity to which this section applies or as to the amount of the capital element (if any), and has not been notified of any alteration of that decision, the notice shall be conclusive as to those matters for the purpose of determining the amount of income tax which he is entitled or required to deduct from the payment, or for which he is chargeable in respect of it.

(6) Where a person making a payment on account of a purchased life annuity to which this section applies has not been notified in the prescribed manner of the amount of the capital element, the amount of income tax which he is entitled or required to deduct from the payment, or for which he is chargeable in respect of it, shall be the same as if the annuity were not a purchased life annuity to which this section applies.

Former enactments.—Sub-s. (1): TA 1970, s. 230(1).
Sub-s. (2): TA 1970, s. 230(2A); FA 1970, Sch. 4, para. 8.
Sub-s. (3)(*a*)–(*c*): TA 1970, s. 230(2)(*a*)–(*c*).
Sub-s. (3)(*d*), (*e*): TA 1970, s. 230(2)(*d*), (2A); FA 1970, Sch. 4, para 8.
Sub-ss. (4)–(6): TA 1970, s. 230(3)–(5).

657. Purchased life annuities to which section 656 applies

(1) For the purposes of section 656—

"life annuity" means an annuity payable for a term ending with (or at a time ascertainable only by reference to) the end of a human life, whether or not there is provision for the annuity to end during the life on the expiration of a fixed term or on the happening of any event or otherwise, or to continue after the end of the life in particular circumstances; and

"purchased life annuity" means a life annuity granted for consideration in money or money's worth in the ordinary course of a business of granting annuities on human life.

(2) Section 656 does not apply—

(*a*) to any annuity which would, apart from that section, be treated for the purposes of the provisions of the Tax Acts relating to tax on annuities and other annual payments as consisting to any extent in the payment or repayment of a capital sum;

(*b*) to any annuity where the whole or part of the consideration for the grant of the annuity consisted of sums satisfying the conditions for relief under section 266, 273 or 619 or to any annuity payable under a substituted contract within the meaning of section 622(3);

(*c*) to any annuity purchased in pursuance of any direction in a will, or to provide for an annuity payable by virtue of a will or settlement out of income of property disposed of by the will or settlement (whether with or without resort to capital);

(*d*) to any annuity purchased under or for the purposes of any sponsored superannuation scheme (as defined in section 624) or any scheme approved under section 620 or in pursuance of any obligation imposed, or offer or invitation made, under or in connection with any such scheme or to any other annuity purchased by any person in recognition of another's services (or past services) in any office or employment; or

(*e*) to any annuity payable under approved personal pension arrangements within the meaning of Chapter IV of this Part.

Former enactments.—TA 1970, s. 230(6), (7); FA 1978, s. 26(4); F(No. 2)A 1987, s. 41(3).

658. Supplementary

(1) Any question whether an annuity is a purchased life annuity to which section 656 applies, or what is the capital element in such an annuity, shall be determined by the inspector; but a person aggrieved by the inspector's decision on any such question may appeal within the prescribed time to the Special Commissioners.

(2) Save as otherwise provided in this Chapter, the procedure to be adopted in giving effect to this Chapter shall be such as may be prescribed.

(3) The Board may make regulations for prescribing anything which is to be prescribed under this Chapter, and the regulations may apply for the purposes of this Chapter or of the regulations any provision of the Income Tax Acts, with or without modifications.

(4) Regulations under subsection (3) above may in particular make provision as to the time limit for making any claim for relief from or repayment of tax under this Chapter and as to all or any of the following matters, that is to say—

(*a*) as to the information to be furnished in connection with the determination of any question whether an annuity is a purchased life annuity to which section 656 applies or what is the capital element in an annuity, and as to the persons who may be required to furnish any such information;

(*b*) as to the manner of giving effect to the decision on any such question, and (notwithstanding anything in section 348) as to the making of assessments for the purpose on the person entitled to the annuity; and

(*c*) as to the extent to which the decision on any such question is to be binding, and the circumstances in which it may be reviewed.

(5) If any person, for the purpose of obtaining for himself or for any other person any relief from or repayment of tax under this Chapter, knowingly makes any false statement or false representation, he shall be liable to a penalty not exceeding [£3,000][1].

Former enactment.—TA 1970, s. 231.
Amendments.—[1] Amount in sub-s. (5) substituted for "£500" by FA 1989, s. 170(4)(*c*), (6) in relation to things done or omitted after 26 July 1989.

CHAPTER VI
MISCELLANEOUS

659. Financial futures and traded options

For the purposes of sections 592(2), 608(2)(*a*), 613(4), 614(3) and (4), 620(6) and 643(2) of this Act and section 149B(1)(*g*) and (*h*) and (2) of the 1979 Act, a contract entered into in the course of dealing in financial futures or traded options shall be regarded as an investment; and in this section "traded option" means an option which is for the time being quoted on a recognised stock exchange or on the London International Financial Futures Exchange.

Former enactments.—FA 1984, s. 45; FA 1987, Sch. 2, para. 5.

PART XV
SETTLEMENTS

CHAPTER I
DISPOSITIONS FOR SHORT PERIODS

660. Dispositions for period which cannot exceed six years

(1) Subject to subsection (2) below, any income which by virtue or in consequence of any disposition made, directly or indirectly, by any person (other than a disposition made for valuable and sufficient consideration), is payable to or applicable for the benefit of any other person for a period which cannot exceed six years shall be deemed for all the purposes of the Income Tax Acts to be the income of the person, if living, by whom the disposition was made, and not to be the income of any other person.

(2) Subsection (1) above shall not apply in relation to income which is payable as a covenanted payment to charity.

(3) In this Chapter, unless the context otherwise requires—

"disposition" includes any trust, covenant, agreement or arrangement, and

"a covenanted payment to charity" means a payment made under a covenant made otherwise than for consideration in money or money's worth in favour of a body of persons or trust established for charitable purposes only whereby the like annual payments (of which the payment in question is one) become payable for a period which may exceed three years and is not capable of earlier termination under any power exercisable without the consent of the persons for the time being entitled to the payments.

(4) For the purposes of subsection (3) above [the bodies mentioned in section 507][1] shall each be treated as a body of persons established for charitable purposes only.

Former enactments.—Sub-s. (1): TA 1970, s. 434(1); FA 1980, s. 55(1)(*a*).
Sub-s. (2): TA 1970, s. 434(1A); FA 1980, s. 55(1)(*b*); FA 1987, Sch. 15, para. 2(16).
Sub-s. (3): TA 1970, s. 434(2); FA 1980, s. 55(1)(*c*).
Sub-s. (4): FA 1980, s. 118(3); FA 1983, s. 46(3)(*a*).
Amendments.—[1] Words in sub-s. (4) substituted by FA 1989, s. 60(3), (4) in relation to payments due after 13 March 1989.

661. Adjustments between disponor and trustees

(1) Where, by virtue of this Chapter, any income tax becomes chargeable on and is paid by the person by whom a disposition was made, that person shall be entitled—

(*a*) to recover from any trustee or other person to whom the income is payable by virtue or in consequence of the disposition the amount of the tax so paid; and

(*b*) for that purpose to require an inspector to furnish to him a certificate specifying the amount of the income in respect of which he has so paid tax and the amount of the tax so paid;

and any certificate so furnished shall be conclusive evidence of the facts appearing thereby.

(2) Where any person obtains in respect of any allowance or relief a repayment of income tax in excess of the amount of the repayment to which he would but for the provisions of this Chapter have been entitled, an amount equal to the excess shall be paid by him to the trustee or other person to whom the income is payable by virtue or in consequence of the disposition, or, where there are two or more such persons, shall be apportioned among those persons as the case may require.

If any question arises as to the amount of any payment or as to any apportionment to be made under this subsection, that question shall be decided by the General Commissioners whose decision thereon shall be final.

(3) Subject to section 833(3), any income which is deemed by virtue of this Chapter to be the income of any person shall be deemed to be the highest part of his income.

Former enactment.—TA 1970, s. 435.

662. Application of Chapter I to dispositions by two or more disponors

(1) In the case of any disposition where there is more than one person who made the disposition, this Chapter shall, subject to the provisions of this section, have effect in relation to each person who made the disposition as if he were the only person who had made it.

(2) In the case of any such disposition, references in this Chapter to income payable or applicable by virtue or in consequence of the disposition include, in relation to any person making the disposition, only—

(*a*) income from property which that person has provided directly or indirectly for the purposes of the disposition ("the settled property"); and
(*b*) income from property representing the settled property; and
(*c*) income from so much of any property which represents both the settled property and other property as, on a just apportionment, represents the settled property; and
(*d*) income provided directly or indirectly by that person.

(3) In this section references to property which represents other property include references to property which represents accumulated income from that other property.

Former enactment.—TA 1970, s. 436.

CHAPTER II

SETTLEMENTS ON CHILDREN

663. The general rule

(1) Where, by virtue or in consequence of any settlement to which this Chapter applies and during the life of the settlor, any income is paid to or for the benefit of a child of the settlor in any year of assessment, the income shall, if at the time of the payment the child was unmarried and below the age of 18, be treated for all the purposes of the Income Tax Acts as the income of the settlor for that year and not as the income of any other person.

(2) Where an offshore income gain (within the meaning of Chapter V of Part XVII) accrues in respect of a disposal of assets made by a person holding them as trustee for a person who would be absolutely entitled as against the trustee but for being an infant, the income which by virtue of section 761(1) is treated as arising by reference to that gain shall for the purposes of this Chapter be deemed to be paid to the infant; and in this subsection, in relation to Scotland, "infant" means pupil or minor.

(3) This Chapter applies to every settlement, wheresoever it was made or entered into, and whether it was made or entered into before or after the passing of this Act, except a settlement made or entered into before 22nd April 1936 which immediately before that date was irrevocable.

Paragraph 10 of Schedule 30 shall have effect as respects certain earlier settlements on children.

(4) Income paid to or for the benefit of a child of a settlor shall not be treated as provided in subsection (1) above for any year of assessment in which the aggregate amount of the income paid to or for the benefit of that child, which, but for this subsection, would be so treated by virtue of subsection (1) above, does not exceed £5.

(5) This Chapter shall not apply in relation to any income arising under a settlement in any year of assessment for which the settlor is not chargeable to income tax as a resident in the United Kingdom, and references in this Chapter to income shall be construed accordingly.

Former enactments.—Sub-s. (1): TA 1970, s. 437(1); FA 1971, s. 16(2)(*b*).
Sub-s. (2): FA 1984, s. 100(3).
Sub-s. (3): TA 1970, s. 437(2).
Sub-s. (4): TA 1970, s. 437(3); FA 1971, s. 16(2)(*d*).
Sub-s. (5): TA 1970, s. 437(5).

664. Accumulation settlements

(1) Subject to the provisions of this section, for the purposes of this Chapter—

 (*a*) income which, by virtue or in consequence of a settlement to which this Chapter applies, is so dealt with that it, or assets representing it, will or may become payable or applicable to or for the benefit of a child of the settlor in the future (whether on fulfilment of a condition, or the happening of a contingency, or as the result of the exercise of a power or discretion conferred on any person, or otherwise) shall be deemed to be paid to or for the benefit of that child; and
 (*b*) any income so dealt with which is not required by the settlement to be allocated, at the time when it is so dealt with, to any particular child or children of the settlor shall be deemed to be paid in equal shares to or for the benefit of each of the children to or for the benefit of whom or any of whom the income or assets representing it will or may become payable or applicable.

(2) Where any income is dealt with as mentioned in subsection (1) above by virtue or in consequence of a settlement to which this Chapter applies, being a settlement which, at the time when the income is so dealt with, is an irrevocable settlement—

 (*a*) subsection (1) above shall not apply to that income unless and except to the extent that that income consists of, or represents directly or indirectly, sums paid by the settlor which are allowable as deductions in computing his total income; and
 (*b*) subject to subsection (3) below, any sum whatsoever paid thereafter by virtue or in consequence of the settlement, or any enactment relating thereto, to or for the benefit of a child of the settlor, being a child who at the time of the payment is unmarried and below the age of 18, shall be deemed for the purposes of section 663 to be paid as income.

(3) Subsection (2)(*b*) above shall not apply if and to the extent that the sum paid as mentioned in that paragraph together with any other sums previously so paid (whether to that child or to any other child who, at the time of the payment, was unmarried and below the age of 18) exceeds the aggregate amount of the income which, by virtue or in consequence of the settlement, has been paid to or for the benefit of a child of the settlor, or dealt with as mentioned in subsection (1) above, since the date when the settlement took effect or the date when it became irrevocable, whichever is the later.

Former enactments.—Sub-s. (1): TA 1970, s. 438(1).
Sub-s. (2): TA 1970, s. 438(2); FA 1971, s. 16(2)(*c*).
Sub-s. (3): TA 1970, s. 438(2)(*b*); FA 1971, s. 16(2)(*c*); FA 1987, Sch. 15, para. 2(17).

665. Meaning of "irrevocable"

(1) For the purposes of this Chapter, a settlement shall not be deemed to be irrevocable if its terms provide—

(*a*) for the payment to the settlor or, during the life of the settlor, to the wife or husband of the settlor for his or her benefit, or for the application for the benefit of the settlor or, during the life of the settlor, of the wife or husband of the settlor, of any income or assets in any circumstances whatsoever during the life of the settlor's child; or
(*b*) for the determination of the settlement by the act or on the default of any person; or
(*c*) for the payment of any penalty by the settlor in the event of his failing to comply with the provisions of the settlement.

In this section "the settlor's child", in relation to any settlement, means any child of the settlor to or for the benefit of whom any income, or assets representing it, is or are or may be payable or applicable by virtue or in consequence of the settlement.

(2) For the purposes of this Chapter, a settlement shall not be deemed to be revocable by reason only—

(*a*) that it contains a provision under which any income or assets will or may become payable to or applicable for the benefit of the settlor, or the wife or husband of the settlor, on the bankruptcy of the settlor's child or in the event of an assignment of or charge on that income or those assets being executed by the settlor's child; or
(*b*) that it provides for the determination of the settlement by the act or on the default of any person in such a manner that the determination will not, during the lifetime of the settlor's child, benefit the settlor or the wife or husband of the settlor; or
(*c*) in the case of a settlement to which section 33 of the Trustee Act 1925 applies, that it directs income to be held for the benefit of the settlor's child on protective trusts, unless the trust period is a period less than the life of the child or the settlement specifies some event on the happening of which the child would, if the income were payable during the trust period to him absolutely during that period, be deprived of the right to receive all or part of the income.

Former enactment.— TA 1970, s. 439(1).

666. Interest paid by trustees

(1) Where interest is paid by the trustees of a settlement to which this Chapter applies there shall be deemed for the purposes of this Chapter to be paid to or for the benefit of a child of the settlor who at the time of the payment is unmarried and below the age of 18 (in addition to any other amount deemed to be so paid) an amount equal to a fraction—

$$\frac{B}{A}$$

of the interest, where—

A is the whole of the income arising under the settlement in the year of assessment, less any expenses of the trustees of the settlement paid in that year which, in the absence of any express provision of the settlement, would be properly chargeable to income, and
B is such part of A as is paid to or for the benefit of any child of the settlor who is unmarried and below the age of 18.

(2) This section shall not apply to interest in respect of which relief from tax is allowable under any provision of the Income Tax Acts or to interest payable to the settlor or the wife or husband of the settlor (if living with the settlor).

(3) Nothing in this section shall be construed as affecting the liability to tax of the person receiving or entitled to the interest.

(4) For the purpose of this section "income arising under the settlement" has the meaning given by section 681, which for that purpose shall be deemed to apply in relation to settlements to which this Chapter applies as it applies in relation to settlements to which Chapter III of this Part applies.

(5) In this section the reference to the trustees' expenses excludes sums mentioned in section 682(1)(*a*).

Former enactments.—Sub-s. (1): TA 1970, s. 440(1); FA 1971, s. 16(2)(*c*).
Sub-ss. (2), (3): TA 1970, s. 440(2), (3).
Sub-ss. (4), (5): TA 1970, s. 440(4).

667. Adjustments between disponor and trustees

(1) Where, by virtue of this Chapter, any income tax becomes chargeable on and is paid by the person by whom a settlement was made or entered into, that person shall be entitled—

(*a*) to recover from any trustee or other person to whom the income is payable by virtue or in consequence of the settlement the amount of the tax so paid; and
(*b*) for that purpose to require an inspector to furnish to him a certificate specifying the amount of income in respect of which he has so paid tax and the amount of the tax so paid,

and any certificate so furnished shall be conclusive evidence of the facts appearing thereby.

(2) Where any person obtains in respect of any allowance or relief a repayment of income tax in excess of the amount of the repayment to which he would but for the provisions of this Chapter have been entitled, an amount equal to the excess shall be paid by him to the trustee or other person to whom the income is payable by virtue or in consequence of the settlement, or, where there are two or more such persons, shall be apportioned among those persons as the case may require.

If any question arises as to the amount of any payment or as to any apportionment to be made under this subsection, that question shall be decided by the General Commissioners whose decision thereon shall be final.

(3) Subject to section 833(3), any income which is deemed by virtue of this Chapter to be the income of any person shall be deemed to be the highest part of his income.

Former enactment.—TA 1970, s. 441.

668. Application of Chapter II to settlements by two or more settlors

(1) In the case of any settlement where there is more than one settlor, this Chapter shall, subject to the provisions of this section, have effect in relation to each settlor as if he were the only settlor.

(2) In the case of any such settlement, only the following can, for the purposes of this Chapter, be taken into account, in relation to any settlor, as income paid by virtue or in consequence of the settlement to or for the benefit of a child of the settlor, that is to say—

(*a*) income originating from that settlor; and
(*b*) in a case in which section 664(2)(*b*) applies, any sums which are under that paragraph to be deemed to be paid as income.

(3) In applying section 664(2)(*b*) to any settlor—

(*a*) the references to sums paid by virtue or in consequence of the settlement or any enactment relating thereto include only sums paid out of property originating from that settlor or income originating from that settlor; and
(*b*) the reference to income which by virtue or in consequence of the settlement has been paid to or for the benefit of a child of the settlor or dealt with as mentioned in section 664(1) includes only income originating from that settlor.

(4) References in this section to property originating from a settlor are references to—

(*a*) property which that settlor has provided directly or indirectly for the purposes of the settlement; and
(*b*) property representing that property; and
(*c*) so much of any property which represents both property provided as mentioned in

paragraph (*a*) above and other property as, on a just apportionment, represents the property so provided.

(5) References in this section to income originating from a settlor are references to—
  (*a*) income from property originating from that settlor; and
  (*b*) income provided directly or indirectly by that settlor.

(6) In subsections (4) and (5) above—
  (*a*) references to property or income which a settlor has provided directly or indirectly include references to property or income which has been provided directly or indirectly by another person in pursuance of reciprocal arrangements with that settlor but do not include references to property or income which that settlor has provided directly or indirectly in pursuance of reciprocal arrangements with another person; and
  (*b*) references to property which represents other property include references to property which represents accumulated income from that other property.

Former enactments.—Sub-ss. (1): TA 1970, s. 442(1).
Sub-ss. (2), (3): TA 1970, s. 442(2).
Sub-ss. (4)–(6): TA 1970, s. 442(3)–(5).

669. Power to obtain information under Chapter II

An inspector may by notice require any party to a settlement to furnish him within such time as he may direct (not being less that 28 days) with such particulars as he thinks necessary for the purposes of this Chapter.

Former enactments.—TA 1970, s. 443; FA 1971, Sch. 6, para. 62.

670. Interpretation of Chapter II

In this Chapter—
  "child" includes a stepchild and an illegitimate child;
  "settlement" includes any disposition, trust, covenant, agreement, arrangement or transfer of assets;
  "settlor", in relation to a settlement, includes any person by whom the settlement was made or entered into directly or indirectly, and in particular (but without prejudice to the generality of the preceding words of this definition) includes any person who has provided or undertaken to provide funds directly or indirectly for the purpose of the settlement, or has made with any other person a reciprocal arrangement for that other person to make or enter into the settlement;
  "income", except in the phrase (occurring in section 663(1)) "be treated for all the purposes of the Income Tax Acts as the income of the settlor for that year and not as the income of any other person", includes any income chargeable to income tax by deduction or otherwise and any income which would have been so chargeable if it had been received in the United Kingdom by a person resident and ordinarily resident in the United Kingdom.

Former enactment.—TA 1970, s. 444(1), (2).

CHAPTER III
REVOCABLE SETTLEMENTS ETC.

671. Revocable settlements allowing release of obligation

(1) If and so long as the terms of any settlement (wherever made) are such that—

(*a*) any person has or may have power, whether immediately or in the future, and whether with or without the consent of any other person, to revoke or otherwise determine the settlement or any provision thereof and, in the event of the exercise of the power, the settlor or the wife or husband of the settlor will or may cease to be liable to make any annual payments payable by virtue or in consequence of any provision of the settlement; or

(*b*) the settlor or the wife or husband of the settlor may, whether immediately or in the future, cease, on the payment of a penalty, to be liable to make any annual payments payable by virtue or in consequence of any provision of the settlement,

any sums payable by the settlor or the wife or husband of the settlor by virtue or in consequence of that provision of the settlement in any year of assessment shall be treated for all the purposes of the Income Tax Acts as the income of the settlor for that year and not as the income of any other person.

(2) Where any such power as is referred to in subsection (1)(*a*) above cannot be exercised—

(*a*) in the case of a covenanted payment to charity (as defined by section 660(3)), within the period of three years, or

(*b*) in any other case, within the period of six years,

from the time when the first of the annual payments so referred to becomes payable, and the like annual payments are payable in each year throughout that period, subsection (1)(*a*) above shall not apply so long as that power cannot be exercised.

(3) In subsections (1) and (2) above—

(*a*) the references to a power to revoke or otherwise determine a settlement or any provision thereof shall be deemed to include references to any power to diminish the amount of any payments which are or may be payable under the settlement or any provision thereof and to any power to diminish the amount of any annual payments which the settlor or the wife or husband of the settlor is or may be liable to make by virtue or in consequence of any provision of the settlement;

(*b*) the references to the settlor or the wife or husband of the settlor ceasing to be liable to make any annual payments payable by virtue or in consequence of any provision of the settlement shall be deemed to include references to a diminution of the amount of any such annual payments which the settlor or the wife or husband of the settlor is or may be liable to make;

but the sums to be treated under subsections (1) and (2) above as the income of the settlor for any year of assessment and not as the income of any other person shall, where those subsections would not apply but for paragraph (*b*) above, be such part only of the sums payable as mentioned in that paragraph by the settlor or the wife or husband of the settlor in that year as corresponds to the diminution mentioned in that paragraph.

Former enactments.—Sub-s. (1): TA 1970, s. 445(1).
Sub-s. (2): TA 1970, s. 445(1), (1A); FA 1980, s. 55(2).
Sub-s. (3): TA 1970, s. 445(2).

672. Revocable settlements allowing reversion of property

(1) If and so long as the terms of any settlement (wherever made) are such that—

(*a*) any person has or may have power, whether immediately or in the future, and whether with or without the consent of any other person, to revoke or otherwise determine the settlement or any provision thereof; and

(*b*) in the event of the exercise of the power, the settlor or the wife or husband of the settlor will or may become beneficially entitled to the whole or any part of the property then comprised in the settlement or of the income arising from the whole or any part of the property so comprised,

any income arising under the settlement from the property comprised in the settlement in any year of assessment or from a corresponding part of that property, or a corresponding part of any such income, as the case may be, shall, subject to subsection (2) below, be treated for all the purposes of the Income Tax Acts as the income of the settlor for that year and not as the income of any other person.

(2) Where any such power cannot be exercised within six years from the time when any particular property first becomes comprised in the settlement, subsection (1) above shall not apply to income arising under the settlement from that property, or from property representing that property, so long as the power cannot be exercised.

(3) In subsection (1) above the references to a power to revoke or otherwise determine a settlement or any provision thereof shall be deemed to include references to—

(a) any power to diminish the property comprised in the settlement; and
(b) any power to diminish the amount of any payments which are or may be payable under the settlement or any provision thereof to any person other than the settlor and the wife or husband of the settlor.

Former enactments.—Sub-ss. (1), (2): TA 1970, s. 446(1).
Sub-s. (3): TA 1970, s. 446(2).

673. Settlements where settlor retains an interest

(1) If and so long as the settlor has an interest in any income arising under or property comprised in a settlement (wherever made), any income so arising during the life of the settlor in any year of assessment shall, to the extent to which it is not distributed, be treated for all the purposes of the Income Tax Acts as the income of the settlor for that year and not as the income of any other person except that—

(a) if and so long as that interest is an interest neither in the whole of the income arising under the settlement nor in the whole of the property comprised in the settlement, the amount of income to be treated as the income of the settlor by virtue of this subsection shall be such part of the income which, but for this paragraph, would be so treated as is proportionate to the extent of that interest; and
(b) where it is shown that any amount of the income which is not distributed in any year of assessment consists of income which falls to be treated as the income of the settlor for that year by virtue of section 671 or 672, that amount shall be deducted from the amount of income which, but for this paragraph, would be treated as his for that year by virtue of this subsection.

(2) Subject to subsection (3) below, the settlor shall, for the purpose of subsection (1) above, be deemed to have an interest in income arising under or property comprised in a settlement if any income or property which may at any time arise under or be comprised in that settlement is, or will or may become, payable to or applicable for the benefit of the settlor or the wife or husband of the settlor in any circumstances whatsoever.

(3) The settlor shall not be deemed to have an interest in any income arising under or property comprised in a settlement—

(a) if and so long as that income or property cannot become payable or applicable as mentioned in subsection (2) above except in the event of—

(i) the bankruptcy of some person who is or may become beneficially entitled to that income or property; or
(ii) any assignment of or charge on that income or property being made or given by some such person; or
(iii) in the case of a marriage settlement, the death of both the parties to the marriage and of all or any of the children of the marriage; or
(iv) the death under the age of 25 or some lower age of some person who would be beneficially entitled to that income or property on attaining that age; or

(b) if and so long as some person is alive and under the age of 25 during whose life that income or property cannot become payable or applicable as mentioned in subsection (2) above except in the event of that person becoming bankrupt or assigning or charging his interest in that income or property.

Former enactments.—Sub-s. (1): TA 1970, s. 447(1).
Sub-ss. (2), (3): TA 1970, s. 447(2).

674. Settlements: discretionary power for benefit of settlor etc.

(1) This section applies to any settlement (wherever made) if and so long as the terms of the settlement are such that any person has or may have power, exercisable at his discretion, whether immediately or in the future, and whether with or without the consent of any person—

   (*a*) to pay or apply to or for the benefit of the settlor or the wife or husband of the settlor the whole or any part of the income or property which may at any time arise under or be comprised in the settlement; or
   (*b*) to secure the payment or application to or for the benefit of the settlor or the wife or husband of the settlor of the whole or any part of that income or property.

(2) Subject to subsections (3) and (4) below, any income arising in any year of assessment under a settlement to which this section applies or, as the case may be, any income so arising from the property comprised in any such settlement or from a corresponding part of that property, or a corresponding part of any such income, shall (so far as it is not so treated apart from this section) be treated for all the purposes of the Income Tax Acts as the income of the settlor for that year and not as the income of any other person.

(3) Where the power mentioned in subsection (1) of this section cannot be exercised within six years from the time when any income or class of income first arises under the settlement or from the time when any particular property first becomes comprised in the settlement, then, so long as the power cannot be exercised, subsection (2) above shall not apply to any income arising under the settlement or, as the case may be, any income of that class or income from that property or property representing that property.

(4) Where, under section 673(3), the settlor is not deemed to have an interest in any income arising under or property comprised in the settlement, subsection (2) above shall not apply to that income or, as the case may be, to income arising from that property.

Former enactments.—Sub-ss. (1), (2): TA 1970, s. 448(1).
Sub-ss. (3), (4): TA 1970, s. 448(2), (3).

[674A. Other settlements where settlor retains interest in settled property

(1) Where, during the life of the settlor, income arising under a settlement is, under the settlement and in the events that occur, payable to or applicable for the benefit of any person other than the settlor, then, unless, under the settlement and in those events, the income—

   (*a*) consists of annual payments made under a partnership agreement to or for the benefit of a former member, or the widow or dependants of a deceased former member, of the partnership, being payments made under a liability incurred for full consideration; or
   (*b*) is of a kind excluded from subsection (1) of section 683 by subsection (6) or (9) of that section; or
   (*c*) is income arising under a settlement made by one party to a marriage by way of provision for the other after the dissolution or annulment of the marriage, or while they are separated under an order of a court or under a separation agreement or in such circumstances that the separation is likely to be permanent, being income payable to or applicable for the benefit of that other party; or
   (*d*) is income from property of which the settlor has divested himself absolutely by the settlement; or
   (*e*) consists of covenanted payments to charity (as defined by section 660(3)); or
   (*f*) is income which, by virtue of any provision of the Income Tax Acts other than this section, is to be treated for all the purposes of those Acts as income of the settlor;

the income shall be treated for all purposes of the Income Tax Acts as the income of the settlor and not as the income of any other person.

(2) Subsections (6) to (10) of section 683 shall apply in relation to subsection (1) above as they apply in relation to subsection (1) of that section.

(3) Subsections (1), (2), (3) and (for the year 1990–91 and subsequent years of assessment) (4A) to (4C) of section 685 shall have effect for the purposes of this section as they have effect for the purposes of section 683, but with the omission from subsections (1) and (2) of the words "in the case of a settlement made after 6th April 1965".

(4) For the year 1990–91 and subsequent years of assessment subsection (1)(*a*) above shall have effect with the insertion after the word "widow" of the word "widower".

(5) This section applies in relation to income—

(*a*) which arises on or after 14th March 1989 under a settlement made on or after that day, or
(*b*) which arises on or after 6th April 1990 under a settlement made before 14th March 1989, so far as it is payable to or applicable for the benefit of the settlor's husband or wife,

except income consisting of annual payments made under an obligation which is an existing obligation for the purposes of section 36(3) of the Finance Act 1988.]¹

Amendments.—¹ This section inserted by FA 1989, s. 109(1).

675. Provisions supplementary to sections 671 to 674

(1) Tax chargeable by virtue of section 671, 672, 673, [674 or 674A]¹ shall be charged under Case VI of Schedule D.

(2) In computing the liability to income tax of a settlor chargeable by virtue of any of those sections the same deductions and reliefs shall be allowed as would have been allowed if the income treated as his by virtue of that section had been received by him.

(3) Where, by virtue of any of those secitons, any income tax becomes chargeable on and is paid by a settlor, he shall be entitled—
(*a*) to recover from any trustee, or other person to whom income arises under the settlement, the amount of the tax so paid; and
(*b*) for that purpose to require an inspector to furnish to him a certificate specifying the amount of income in respect of which he has so paid tax and the amount of tax so paid.

Any certificate so furnished shall be conclusive evidence of the facts stated therein.

(4) Where any person obtains, in respect of any allowance or relief, a repayment of income tax in excess of the amount of the repayment to which he would, but for section 671, 672, 673, [674 or 674A]¹, have been entitled, an amount equal to the excess shall be paid by him to the trustee or other person to whom income arises under the settlement, or, where there are two or more such persons, shall be apportioned among those persons as the case may require.

If any question arises as to the amount of any payment or as to any apportionment to be made under this subsection, that question shall be decided by the General Commissioners whose decision thereon shall be final.

(5) Subject to section 833(3), any income which is treated by virtue of section 671, 672, 673, [674 or 674A]¹ as income of a settlor shall be deemed for the purpose of this section to be the highest part of his income.

Former enactment.—TA 1970, s. 449.
Amendments.—¹ Words in sub-ss. (1), (4), (5) substituted by FA 1989, s. 109(3).

676. Disallowance of deduction from total income of certain sums paid by settlor

(1) Where, by virtue or in consequence of any settlement to which this section applies, the settlor pays directly or indirectly in any year of assessment to the trustees of the settlement any sums which would, but for this subsection, be allowable as deductions in computing his total income for that year, those sums shall not be so allowable to the extent to which the aggregate amount thereof falls within the amount of income arising under the settlement in that year which has not been distributed, less—
(*a*) so much of any income arising under the settlement in that year which has not been distributed as is shown to consist of income which has been treated as the income of the settlor by virtue of section 671, 672, [674 or 674A]¹, and
(*b*) the amount of income so arising in that year which is treated as the income of the settlor by virtue of section 673.

(2) For the purposes of subsection (1) above, any sum paid in any year of assessment by the settlor to any body corporate connected with the settlement in that year shall be treated as if it had been paid to the trustees of the settlement in that year by virtue or in consequence of the settlement.

(3) No relief shall be given under any of the provisions of the Income Tax Acts on account of tax paid in respect of so much of any income arising under a settlement in any year of assessment as is equal to the aggregate amount of any sums paid by the settlor in that year which are not allowable as deductions by virtue of this section.

(4) This section shall apply to any settlement (wherever made) made after 26th April 1938, and where income arising under any settlement (wherever made) made on or before that date is treated as the income of the settlor by virtue of section 671 or 672 but ceases to be so treated by reason of any variation of the terms of the settlement made after that date, or would have been so treated but for such a variation, this section shall apply to that settlement as from the date when the variation takes effect.

(5) In this section, references to sums paid by a settlor include references to sums paid by the wife or husband of the settlor.

Former enactment.—TA 1970, s. 450.
Amendments.—[1] Words in sub-s. (1)(a) substituted by FA 1989, s. 109(3).

677. Sums paid to settlor otherwise than as income

(1) Any capital sum paid directly or indirectly in any year of assessment by the trustees of a settlement to which this section applies to the settlor shall—

(a) to the extent to which the amount of that sum falls within the amount of income available up to the end of that year, be treated for all the purposes of the Income Tax Acts as the income of the settlor for that year;
(b) to the extent to which the amount of that sum is not by virtue of this subsection treated as his income for that year and falls within the amount of the income available up to the end of the next following year, be treated for those purposes as the income of the settlor for the next following year;

and so on for each subsequent year up to a maximum of ten subsequent years, taking the reference in pararaph (b) to the year mentioned in paragraph (a) as a reference to that and any other year before the subsequent year in question.

(2) For the purposes of subsection (1) above, the amount of income available up to the end of any year shall, in relation to any capital sum paid as mentioned in that subsection, be taken to be the aggregate amount of income arising under the settlement in that year and any previous year which has not been distributed, less—

(a) the amount of that income taken into account under that subsection in relation to that sum in any previous year or years; and
(b) the amount of any other capital sums paid to the settlor in any year before that sum was paid; and
(c) so much of any income arising under the settlement in that year and any previous year which has not been distributed as is shown to consist of income which has been treated as income of the settlor by virtue of section 671, 672, 674, [674A][1] or 683; and
(d) any income arising under the settlement in that year and any previous year which has been treated as the income of the settlor by virtue of section 673; and
(e) any sums paid by virtue or in consequence of the settlement, to the extent that they are not allowable, by virtue of section 676, as deductions in computing the settlor's income for that year or any previous year; and
(f) any sums paid by virtue or in consequence of the settlement in that year or any previous year which have been treated as the income of the settlor by virtue of section 664(2)(b); and
(g) any sums included in the income arising under the settlement as amounts which have been or could have been apportioned to a beneficiary as mentioned in section 681(1)(b); and
(h) an amount equal to the sum of tax at the basic rate and tax at the additional rate on—

(i) the aggregate amount of income arising under the settlement in that year and any previous year which has not been distributed, less
(ii) the aggregate amount of the income and sums referred to in paragraphs (c), (d), (e), (f) and (g) above.

(3) Where any amount is included in a person's income by virtue of section 421 in respect of any loan or advance, there shall be a corresponding reduction in the amount (if any) afterwards falling to be so included in respect of it by virtue of this section.

(4) Where the capital sum paid to the settlor is a sum paid by way of loan, then—

(a) if the whole of it is repaid, no part of that sum shall by virtue of subsection (1) above be treated as the settlor's income for any year of assessment after that in which the repayment occurs; and
(b) if one or more capital sums have previously been paid to him by way of loan and wholly repaid, the amount of that capital sum shall be treated as equal to its excess, if any,

over so much of the sum or sums previously paid as has already fallen to be treated as his income by virtue of that subsection.

(5) Where the capital sum paid to the settlor is a sum paid by way of complete repayment of a loan, then, if an amount not less than that sum is thereafter lent by the settlor to the trustees of the settlement, no part of that sum shall by virtue of subsection (1) above be treated as his income for any year of assessment after that in which the further loan is made.

(6) Where the whole or any part of any sum is treated by virtue of this section as income of the settlor for any year, it shall be treated as income of such an amount as, after deduction of both tax at the basic rate and tax at the additional rate for that year, would be equal to that sum or that part of that sum.

(7) Tax chargeable by virtue of this section shall be charged under Case VI of Schedule D; and there shall be set off against the tax charged on any amount treated by virtue of this section as income of the settlor for any year an amount equal to—

(a) the sum of tax at the basic rate and tax at the additional rate for that year on the amount so treated as his income; or
(b) so much of that sum as is equal to the tax charged,

whichever is the less.

(8) In computing the liability to income tax of a settlor chargeable by virtue of this section, the same deductions and reliefs shall be allowed as would have been allowed if the amount treated as his income by virtue of this section had been received by him as income.

(9) This section applies to any settlement wherever made, and whether made before or after the passing of this Act, and in this section—

(a) "capital sum" means, subject to subsection (10) below—
   (i) any sum paid by way of loan or repayment of a loan; and
   (ii) any other sum paid otherwise than as income, being a sum which is not paid for full consideration in money or money's worth,

but does not include any sum which could not have become payable to the settlor except in one of the events specified in section 673(3); and

(b) references to sums paid to the settlor include references to sums paid to the wife or husband of the settlor or to the settlor (or the husband or wife of the settlor) jointly with another person.

(10) For the purposes of this section there shall be treated as a capital sum paid to the settlor by the trustees of the settlement any sum which—

(a) is paid by them to a third party at the settlor's direction or by virtue of the assignment by him of his right to receive it where the direction or assignment was given or made on or after 6th April 1981; or
(b) is otherwise paid or applied by them for the benefit of the settlor,

and which would not apart from this subsection be treated as a capital sum paid to him.

Former enactments.—Sub-s. (1): TA 1970, s. 451(1); FA 1981, s. 42(2)(a), (b); FA 1982, s. 63(3).
Sub-s. (2)(a): TA 1970, s. 451(2)(aa); FA 1981, s. 42(3)(a).
Sub-s. (2)(b)–(e): TA 1970, s. 451(2)(a)–(d); FA 1981, s. 42(3)(b).
Sub-s. (2)(f), (g): TA 1970, s. 451(2)(dd), (ddd); FA 1981, s. 42(3)(c).
Sub-s. (2)(h): TA 1970, s. 451(2)(e); FA 1971, Sch. 6, para. 64; FA 1973, s. 16(7)(a); FA 1981, s. 42(3)(d).
Sub-s. (3): TA 1970, s. 451(3).
Sub-ss. (4), (5): TA 1970, s. 451(3A), (3B); FA 1981, s. 42(4).
Sub-s. (6): TA 1970, s. 451(5); FA 1971, Sch. 6, para. 64; FA 1973, s. 16(7)(b).
Sub-s. (7): TA 1970, s. 451(6); FA 1981, s. 42(5).
Sub-s. (8): TA 1970, s. 451(7).
Sub-s. (9): TA 1970, s. 451(8); FA 1981, s. 42(6).
Sub-s. (10): TA 1970, s. 451(9); FA 1981, s. 42(7), (8).
Amendments.—[1] Number in sub-s. (2)(c) inserted by FA 1989, s. 109(4).

678. Capital sums paid by body connected with settlement

(1) Where—

(a) a capital sum is paid after 5th April 1981 to the settlor in a year of assessment by any body corporate connected with the settlement in that year; and
(b) an associated payment has been or is made directly or indirectly to that body by the trustees of the settlement,

the capital sum shall, in accordance with subsection (2) below, be treated for the purposes of section 677 as having been paid to the settlor by the trustees of the settlement.

(2) A capital sum to which subsection (1) above applies shall—

(a) to the extent to which the amount of that sum falls within the total of the associated payment or payments made up to the end of the year of assessment in which it is paid, be treated as having been paid to the settlor in that year;
(b) to the extent to which the amount of that sum is not treated as paid to the settlor in that year and falls within the total of the associated payment or payments made up to the end of the next following year (less what was taken into account under this subsection in relation to that sum in the previous year), be treated as having been paid to the settlor in the next following year,

and so on for each subsequent year, taking the references in paragraph (b) to the year mentioned in paragraph (a) as references to that and any other year before the subsequent year in question.

(3) In this section "associated payment", in relation to any capital sum paid to the settlor by a body corporate, means—

(a) any capital sum paid to that body by the trustees of the settlement; and
(b) any other sum paid or asset transferred to that body by those trustees which is not paid or transferred for full consideration in money or money's worth,

being a sum paid or asset transferred in the five years ending or beginning with the date on which the capital sum is paid to the settlor.

(4) For the purposes of this section any capital sum paid by a body corporate, and any associated payment made to a body corporate, at a time when it is, within the meaning of section 416, associated with another body corporate may be treated as paid by or made to that other body corporate.

(5) In this section "capital sum" has the same meaning as in section 677; and any question whether a capital sum has been paid to the settlor by a body corporate or to a body corporate by the trustees shall be determined in the same way as any question under that section whether a capital sum has been paid to the settlor by the trustees.

(6) Subsection (1) above does not apply to any sum paid to the settlor by way of loan or repayment of a loan if—

(a) the whole of the loan is repaid within 12 months of the date on which it was made; and
(b) the period for which amounts are outstanding in respect of loans made to the settlor by that or any other body corporate connected with the settlement, or by him to that or any other such body, in any period of five years does not exceed 12 months.

(7) Where a capital sum is paid to the settlor in a year of assessment by a body corporate connected with the settlement in that year it shall be assumed until the contrary is shown that an associated payment of an amount not less than that of the capital sum has been made to that body by the trustees of the settlement.

Former enactments.—TA 1970, s. 451A; FA 1981, s. 43(2).

679. Application of Chapter III to settlements by two or more settlors

(1) In the case of any settlement where there is more than one settlor, this Chapter shall, subject to the provisions of this section, have effect in relation to each settlor as if he were the only settlor.

(2) In this Chapter—

(a) references to the property comprised in a settlement include, in relation to any settlor, only property originating from that settlor, and
(b) references to income arising under the settlement include, in relation to any settlor, only income originating from that settlor.

(3) In considering for the purposes of this Chapter, in relation to any settlor, whether any, and if so, how much, of the income arising under the settlement has been distributed, any sums paid partly out of income originating from that settlor and partly out of other income must (so far as not apportioned by the terms of the settlement) be apportioned evenly over all that income.

(4) References in sections 671(1) and 676 to sums payable by virtue or in consequence of any provision of the settlement or sums paid by virtue or in consequence of the settlement include, in relation to any settlor, only sums payable or paid by that settlor.

(5) References in this section to property originating from a settlor are references to—
 (a) property which that settlor has provided directly or indirectly for the purposes of the settlement; and
 (b) property representing that property; and
 (c) so much of any property which represents both property so provided and other property as, on a just apportionment, represents the property so provided.

(6) References in this section to income originating from a settlor are references to—
 (a) income from property originating from that settlor; and
 (b) so much of any such income of a body corporate as is mentioned in section 681(1)(b) as corresponds to property originating from the settlor which is comprised in the settlement; and
 (c) income provided directly or indirectly by that settlor.

(7) In subsections (5) and (6) above—
 (a) references to property or income which a settlor has provided directly or indirectly include references to property or income which has been provided directly or indirectly by another person in pursuance of reciprocal arrangements with that settlor, but do not include references to property or income which that settlor has provided directly or indirectly in pursuance of reciprocal arrangements with another person; and
 (b) references to property which represents other property include references to property which represents accumulated income from that other property.

Former enactment.—TA 1970, s. 452.

680. Power to obtain information for purposes of Chapter III

An inspector may by notice require any person, being a party to a settlement, to furnish him within such time as he may direct (not being less than 28 days) with such particulars as he thinks necessary for the purposes of any of the provisions of this Chapter.

Former enactments.—TA 1970, s. 453; FA 1971, Sch. 6, para. 65.

681. Interpretation of Chapter III

(1) In this Chapter, "income arising under a settlement" includes—
 (a) any income chargeable to income tax by deduction or otherwise, and any income which would have been so chargeable if it had been received in the United Kingdom by a person domiciled, resident and ordinarily resident in the United Kingdom; . . .[1]
 (b) . . .[1]
but, where the settlor is not domiciled, or not resident, or not ordinarily resident, in the United Kingdom in any year of assessment, does not include income arising under the settlement in that year in respect of which the settlor, if he were actually entitled thereto, would not be chargeable to income tax by deduction or otherwise by reason of his not being so domiciled, resident or ordinarily resident.

(2) . . .[1]

(3) . . .[1]

(4) In this Chapter—
 "settlement" includes any disposition, trust, covenant, agreement or arrangement, and
 "settlor", in relation to a settlement, means any person by whom the settlement was made;

and a person shall be deemed for the purposes of this Chapter to have made a settlement if he has made or entered into the settlement directly or indirectly, and, in particular, but without prejudice to the generality of the preceding words, if he has provided or undertaken to provide funds directly or indirectly for the purpose of the settlement, or has made with any other person a reciprocal arrangement for that other person to make or enter into the settlement.

(5) For the purposes of this Chapter, a body corporate shall be deemed to be connected with a settlement in any year of assessment if at any time in that year—

(a) it is a close company (or only not a close company because it is not resident in the United Kingdom) and the participators then include the trustees of the settlement; or
(b) it is controlled (within the meaning of section 840) by a company falling within paragraph (a) above.

(6) The provisions of this Chapter shall be in addition to and not in derogation of any other provisions of this Act.

Former enactments.—Sub-ss. (1), (2): TA 1970, s. 451(1); FA 1972, Sch. 24, para. 26; FA 1981, s. 44(1).
Sub-s. (3): TA 1970, s. 454(1A); FA 1981, s. 44(1).
Sub-s. (4): TA 1970, s. 454(3).
Sub-s. (5): TA 1970, s. 454(4); FA 1981, s. 44(2).
Sub-s. (6): TA 1970, s. 454(6).
Amendments.—[1] Sub-ss. (1)(b), (2), (3) and the word "and" at the end of sub-s. (1)(a) repealed by FA 1989, Sch. 17, Pt. V in relation to the income of bodies corporate for accounting periods beginning after 31 March 1989.

682. Ascertainment of undistributed income

(1) For the purposes of this Chapter, income arising under a settlement in any year of assessment shall be deemed not to have been distributed if and to the extent that it exceeds the aggregate amount of—

(a) the sums, excluding all payments of interest, paid in that year by the trustees of the settlement to any persons (not being a body corporate connected with the settlement and not being the trustees of another settlement made by the settlor or the trustees of the settlement) in such manner that they fall to be treated in that year, otherwise than by virtue of section 677, as the income of those persons for the purposes of income tax, or would fall to be so treated if those persons were domiciled, resident and ordinarily resident in the United Kingdom and the sums had been paid to them there, and
(b) subject to subsections (2) to (5) below, any expenses of the trustees of the settlement paid in that year which, in the absence of any express provision of the settlement, would be properly chargeable to income, in so far as such expenses are not included in the sums mentioned in paragraph (a) above, and
(c) in a case where the trustees of the settlement are trustees for charitable purposes, the amount by which any income arising under the settlement in that year in respect of which exemption from tax may be granted under section 505 exceeds the aggregate amount of any such sums or expenses as are mentioned in paragraphs (a) and (b) above paid in that year which are properly chargeable to that income.

(2) Subsection (1)(b) above shall apply to any interest paid by the trustees of the settlement subject to subsections (3) to (6) below.

(3) If no sums within subsection (1)(a) were paid to any person other than the settlor, or the wife or husband of the settlor, the whole of any interest paid by the trustees of the settlement shall be excluded from subsection (1)(b) above.

(4) If any sum was so paid, there shall be excluded from subsection (1)(b) above a fraction—

$$\frac{A-B}{A}$$

of any interest paid by the trustees of the settlement where—

A is the whole of the income arising under the settlement in the year of assessment, less the sums referred to in subsection (1)(b) above apart from subsections (2), (3) and (5) of this section; and
B is so much of the sums within subsection (1)(a) above as is paid to persons other than the settlor, or the wife or husband of the settlor.

(5) Subsections (2) to (4) above shall not apply to interest in respect of which relief from tax is allowable under any provision of the Income Tax Acts or to interest payable to the settlor or the wife or husband of the settlor if living with the settlor.

(6) Nothing in subsections (2) to (5) above shall be construed as affecting the liability to tax of the person receiving or entitled to the interest.

Former enactments.—Sub-s. (1): TA 1970, s. 455.
Sub-ss. (2)–(6): TA 1970, s. 456.

CHAPTER IV

LIABILITY TO HIGHER RATE AND ADDITIONAL RATE TAX

Liability of settlors

683. Settlements made after 6th April 1965

(1) Where, during the life of the settlor, income arising under a settlement made after 6th April 1965 is, under the settlement and in the events that occur, payable to or applicable for the benefit of any person other than the settlor, then, unless, under the settlement and in those events, the income either—

(*a*) consists of annual payments made under a partnership agreement to or for the benefit of a former member, or the widow or dependants of a deceased former member, of the partnership, being payments made under a liability incurred for full consideration; or

(*b*) is excluded by subsection (3), (6) or (9) below; or

(*c*) is income arising under a settlement made by one party to a marriage by way of provision for the other after the dissolution or annulment of the marriage, or while they are separated under an order of a court or under a separation agreement or in such circumstances that the separation is likely be permanent, being income payable to or applicable for the benefit of that other party; or

(*d*) is income from property of which the settlor has divested himself absolutely by the settlement; or

(*e*) is income which, by virtue of some provision of the Income Tax Acts not contained in this Chapter, is to be treated for the purposes of those Acts as income of the settlor;

the income shall, for the purposes of excess liability, be treated as the income of the settlor and not as the income of any other person.

(2) In subsection (1) above "excess liability" means the excess of liability to income tax over what it would be if all income tax were charged at the basic rate to the exclusion of any higher rate.

(3) Subject to subsection (4) below, subsection (1) above shall not apply to so much of an individual's income as consists of covenanted payments to charity.

(4) If at least £1,000 of an individual's income for any year of assessment consists of covenanted payments to charity which, in the hands of the charities receiving them, constitute income for which, by virtue of subsection (3) of section 505, relief is not available under subsection (1) of that section, so much of the individual's income as consists of those payments shall not be excluded from the operation of subsection (1) above by virtue of subsection (3) above.

(5) If, for any chargeable period of a charity—

(*a*) the income of the charity includes two or more covenanted payments to charity; and

(*b*) only a part of the aggregate of those payments constitutes income for which, by virtue of subsection (3) of section 505 relief is not available under subsection (1) of that section,

each of the payments which make up the aggregate shall be treated for the purposes of subsection (4) above as apportioned rateably between the part of the aggregate referred to in paragraph (*b*) above and the remainder.

(6) Subsection (1) above shall not apply to income consisting of annual payments made by an individual, in connection with the acquisition by him of the whole or part of a business—

(*a*) to or for the benefit of the individual from whom it is acquired or, if he is dead, to or for the benefit of his widow or dependants, or

(*b*) if the acquisition was from a partnership, to or for the benefit of a former member, or the widow or dependants of a deceased former member, of that or any preceding partnership, or to or for the benefit of an individual from whom the business or part was acquired by that or any preceding partnership or, if he is dead, to or for the benefit of the widow or dependants of such an individual;

being payments made under a liability incurred for full consideration.

(7) Payments made in respect of any individual under a liability incurred in connection with an acquisition from a partnership shall only be excluded from the operation of subsection (1) above by virtue of subsection (6)(*b*) above if, and to the extent that, they are

made in substitution for, or matched by reductions in, other payments which would themselves be excluded from its operation.

(8) Where the right of a former member of a partnership to payments falling due not more than ten years after he ceased to be a member of that partnership has devolved on his death, subsections (1)(*a*) and (6) above shall apply to the payments as they would apply if he had not died.

(9) Where for any year of assessment there is made to or for the benefit of a former member, or the widow or a dependant of a deceased former member, of a partnership an annual payment which—

    (*a*) is excluded from the operation of subsection (1) above by virtue of paragraph (*a*) of that subsection or by virtue of subsection (6) above; and
    (*b*) falls short of the limit applying for that year under section 628;

any additional annual payment made to or for the benefit of that person shall, notwithstanding that it is not made under a liability incurred for full consideration, be excluded from the operation of subsection (1) above to the extent to which it makes good that shortfall.

(10) For the purposes of this section—

    (*a*) "former member", in relation to a partnership, means an individual who has ceased to be a member of that partnership on retirement or death;
    (*b*) a partnership becomes a "preceding partnership" of another if it transfers its business or part of its business to another and one or more individuals are member of both, and any preceding partnership of the transferor by reference to any part of the business transferred shall also become a preceding partnership of the transferee;
    (*c*) "covenanted payments to charity" has the meaning given by section 660(3).

Former enactments.—Sub-ss. (1), (2): TA 1970, s. 457(1); FA 1971, Sch. 6, para. 67; FA 1978, Sch. 2, para. 12; FA 1980, s. 56(1); FA 1986, s. 32(1).
Sub-s. (3): TA 1970, s. 457(1A); FA 1980, s. 56(2); FA 1985, s. 49(1); FA 1986, s. 32(1).
Sub-ss. (4), (5): TA 1970, s. 457(1B), (1C); FA 1986, s. 32(2).
Sub-ss. (6)–(8): TA 1970, s. 457(2)–(4).
Sub-s. (9): TA 1970, s. 457(4A); FA 1980, s. 34(4).
Sub-s. (10): TA 1970, s. 457(5); FA 1980, s. 56(3).
Cross references.—See FA 1988, s. 102(1), (2)(*c*) (taxation of capital gains at income tax rates: higher rate not to apply to the beneficiary mentioned in sub-s. (1) above).

684. Settlements made before 7th April 1965 but after 9th April 1946

(1) Where, during the life of the settlor, income arising under a settlement made before 7th April 1965, but after 9th April 1946, is, under the settlement and in the events that occur, payable to or applicable for the benefit of any person other than the settlor, then, unless under the settlement and in those events, the income either—

    (*a*) is payable to an individual for his own use; or
    (*b*) is applicable for the benefit of an individual named in that behalf in the settlement or of two or more individuals so named; or
    (*c*) is applicable for the benefit of a child or children of an individual named in that behalf in the settlement; or
    (*d*) is income from property of which the settlor has divested himself absolutely by the settlement; or
    (*e*) is income which, by virtue of some provision of the Income Tax Acts not contained in this Chapter, is to be treated for the purposes of those Acts as income of the settlor;

the income shall, for the purposes of excess liability, be treated as the income of the settlor and not as the income of any other person.

(2) In subsection (1) above "excess liability" means the excess of liability to income tax over what it would be if all income tax were charged at the basic rate to the exclusion of any higher rate.

(3) The exceptions provided for by paragraphs (*a*), (*b*) and (*c*) of subsection (1) above shall not apply where the named individual or individuals or, in the case of paragraph (*c*), either the named individual or the child or any of the children in question, is in the service of the settlor or accustomed to act as the solicitor or agent of the settlor.

Former enactments.—TA 1970, s. 458(1); FA 1971, Sch. 6, para. 68; FA 1978, Sch. 2, para. 13.
Cross references.—See FA 1988, s. 102(1), (2)(*c*) (taxation of capital gains at income tax rates: higher rate not to apply to the beneficiary mentioned in sub-s. (1) above).

685. Provisions supplementary to sections 683 and 684

(1) For the purposes of section 683 and 684, the settlor shall not be deemed to have divested himself absolutely of any property if that property or any derived property is, or will or may become, in any circumstances whatsoever, payable to or applicable for the benefit of the settlor or, in the case of a settlement made after 6th April 1965, the wife or husband of the settlor.

(2) For those purposes, the settlor shall not be deemed not to have divested himself absolutely of any property by reason only that the property or any derived property may become payable to or applicable for the benefit of the settlor, or, in the case of a settlement made after 6th April 1965, the wife or husband of the settlor, in the event of—

   (a) the bankruptcy of some person who is or may become beneficially entitled to the property or any of the derived property; or
   (b) an assignment of or charge on the property or any of the derived property being made or given by some such person; or
   (c) in the case of a marriage settlement, the death of both parties to the marriage and of all or any of the children of the marriage; or
   (d) the death under the age of 25 or some lower age of some person who would be beneficially entitled to the property or the derived property on attaining that age.

(3) In subsections (1) and (2) above "derived property", in relation to any property, means income from that property or any other property directly or indirectly representing proceeds of, or of income from, that property or any income therefrom.

(4) In sections 683 and 684 and this section "income arising under a settlement", "settlement" and "settlor" have the meanings assigned to them for the purposes of Chapter III of this Part by section 681.

(5) Section 679 shall have effect in relation to sections 683 and 684 and this section as it has effect in relation to Chapter III of this Part.

Former enactments.—Sub-ss. (1)–(3): TA 1970, ss. 457(6), 458(2).
Sub-ss. (4), (5): TA 1970, s. 459.
Note.—See **Prospective Legislation Notes**.

Liability of trustees

686. Liability to additional rate tax of certain income of discretionary trusts

(1) So far as income arising to trustees is income to which this section applies it shall, in addition to being chargeable to income tax at the basic rate, be chargeable at the additional rate.

(2) This section applies to income arising to trustees in any year of assessment so far as it—

   (a) is income which is to be accumulated or which is payable at the discretion of the trustees or any other person (whether or not the trustees have power to accumulate it); and
   (b) is neither (before being distributed) the income of any person other than the trustees nor treated for any of the purposes of the Income Tax Acts as the income of a settlor; and
   [(c) is not income arising under a trust established for charitable purposes only or income from investments, deposits or other property held—
      (i) for the purposes of a fund or scheme established for the sole purpose of providing relevant benefits within the meaning of section 612; or
      (ii) for the purposes of a personal pension scheme (within the meaning of secton 630) which makes provision only for benefits such as are mentioned in section 633; and][1]
   (d) exceeds the income applied in defraying the expenses of the trustees in that year which are properly chargeable to income (or would be so chargeable but for any express provisions of the trust).

(3) . . .[2]

(4) . . .[2]

(5) For the purposes of this section sums paid or credited to trustees in any year of assessment in respect of dividends or interest payable in respect of shares in or deposits with or loans to a building society being sums in respect of which the society is required to account for and pay an amount in accordance with regulations under section 476(1) shall be

treated as income for that year received by the trustees after deduction of income tax from a corresponding gross amount.

In this subsection expressions used in section 476 have the same meanings as in that section.

(6) In this section "trustees" does not include personal representatives; but where personal representatives, on or before the completion of the administration of the estate, pay to trustees any sum representing income which, if personal representatives were trustees within the meaning of this section, would be income to which this section applies, that sum shall be deemed to be paid to the trustees as income and to have borne income tax at the basic rate.

This subsection shall be construed as if it were contained in Part XVI.

Former enactments.—FA 1973, s. 16(1)–(6); FA 1986, s. 47(4)(a).
Cross references.—See FA 1988, s. 100(2) (rate of capital gains tax in respect of gains accruing to trustees of discretionary trusts).
Amendments.—[1] Sub-s. (2)(c) substituted by FA 1988, s. 55(3), (4) with effect from 1 July 1988.
[2] Sub-ss. (3), (4) repealed by FA 1989, Sch. 17, Pt. V in relation to accounting periods beginning after 31 March 1989.

687. Payments under discretionary trusts

(1) Where, in any year of assessment, trustees make a payment to any person in the exercise of a discretion exercisable by them or any person other than the trustees, then, if the sum paid is for all the purposes of the Income Tax Acts income of the person to whom it is paid (but would not be his income apart from the payment), the following provisions of this section shall apply with respect to the payment in lieu of section 348 or 349(1).

(2) The payment shall be treated as a net amount corresponding to a gross amount from which tax has been deducted at a rate equal to the sum of the basic rate and the additional rate in force for the year in which the payment is made; and the sum treated as so deducted shall be treated—

(a) as income tax paid by the person to whom the payment is made; and
(b) so far as not set off under the following provisions of this section, as income tax assessable on the trustees.

(3) The following amounts, so far as not previously allowed, shall be set against the amount assessable (apart from this subsection) on the trustees in pursuance of subsection (2)(b) above—

(a) the amount of any tax on income arising to the trustees and charged at the additional as well as at the basic rate in pursuance of section 686;
(b) ...[2]
(c) ...[2]
(d) an amount of tax in respect of income found on a claim made by the trustees to have been available to them for distribution at the end of the year 1972–73, which shall be taken to be two-thirds of the net amount of that income;
(e) the amount of any tax on income arising to the trustees by virtue of section 761(1) and charged at a rate equal to the sum of the basic rate and the additional rate by virtue of section 764; and
(f) the amount of any tax on annual profits or gains treated as received by trustees by virtue of section 714(2) or 716(3) of this Act or paragraph 2(2) or (3) of Schedule 22 to the Finance Act 1985 and charged at a rate equal to the sum of the basic rate and the additional rate by virtue of section 720(5) of this Act or paragraph 8(1) of Schedule 23 to that Act;
(g) the amount of any tax on income which arose to the trustees by virtue of section 38(2) of the Finance Act 1974 (development gains) and charged at a rate equal to the basic rate and the additional rate in pursuance of section 43(1) of that Act;
[(h) the amount of any tax on an amount which is treated as income of the trustees by virtue of paragraph 4 of Schedule 4 and is charged to tax at a rate equal to the sum of the basic rate and the additional rate by virtue of paragraph 17 of that Schedule;][1]
[(i) the amount of any tax on an amount which is treated as income of the trustees by virtue of paragraph 4 of Schedule 11 to the Finance Act 1989 and is charged to tax at a rate equal to the sum of the basic rate and the additional rate by virtue of paragraph 10 of that Schedule;][1]

but tax on any income represented by amounts paid or credited as mentioned in section 686(5) shall be taken into account under paragraph (a) above only on production of a certificate from the building society concerned specifying those amounts and stating that an amount representing income tax on that income calculated at the basic rate has been or will be accounted for.

(4) In this section "trustees" does not include personal representatives within the meaning of section 701(4).

Former enactments.—Sub-ss. (1), (2): FA 1973, s. 17(1), (2).
Sub-s. (3): FA 1973, s. 17(3)(*a*)–(*d*), (*f*), (*g*); FA 1974, Sch. 7, para. 8; F(No. 2)A 1975, s. 34(6); FA 1984, s. 100(2); FA 1985, Sch. 23, para. 8(3).
Sub-s. (4): FA 1973, s. 17(5).
Amendments.—[1] Sub-s. (3)(*h*), (*i*) inserted by FA 1989, s. 96(2), (4) and apply where there is a disposal of a deep discount security or a transfer or a redemption of a deep gain security after 13 March 1989.
[2] Sub-s. (3)(*b*), (*c*) repealed by FA 1989, Sch. 17, Pt. V in relation to accounting periods beginning after 31 March 1989.

688. Schemes for employees and directors to acquire shares

Where under a scheme set up to comply with section 153(4)(*b*) of the Companies Act 1985 or Article 163(4)(*b*) of the Companies (Northern Ireland) Order 1986 (financial assistance for company employees and salaried directors acquiring shares) trustees receive interest from such employees or directors then, if and so far as the scheme requires an equivalent amount to be paid by way of interest by the trustees to the company, the trustees shall be exempt from tax under Case III of Schedule D on that interest received by them.

Former enactments.—TA 1970, s. 64A; FA 1970, Sch. 4, para. 9(5); Companies Consolidation (Consequential Provisions) Act 1985, Sch. 2.

689. Recovery from trustees of discretionary trusts of higher rate tax due from beneficiaries

(1) The provisions of this section shall have effect in relation to the excess amount of the income tax due from any person ("the beneficiary") to whom, or for whose benefit, any income or any capital may in the discretion of some other person be paid or applied under a trust.

(2) In this section "the excess amount" means so much of the income tax payable in respect of the beneficiary's income as exceeds what would be the amount thereof if all income tax were chargeable at the basic rate to the exclusion of any higher rate.

(3) If the whole or part of the excess amount of the income tax charged in respect of the income of the beneficiary is not paid before the expiry of six months from the date when it became due and payable, the Board may at any time thereafter, so long as the excess amount or any part thereof remains unpaid, cause to be served on the trustees of the trust a notice that the excess amount or any part thereof remains unpaid.

(4) Where such a notice is served in accordance with the provisions of this section on the trustees of the trust, it shall be the duty of the trustees, as soon as may be, and if necessary from time to time, to pay to the Board in or towards satisfaction of the excess amount or any part thereof from time to time remaining unpaid any income or capital which, by virtue of any exercise of the discretion under the trust, the beneficiary may become entitled to receive or to have applied for his benefit.

(5) Any payments made out of income by trustees on account of tax in respect of which a notice under this section has been served shall be deemed for all the purposes of the Income Tax Acts to represent income paid to the beneficiary.

(6) Any sum which the trustees are liable to pay by virtue of this section shall be recoverable from them as a debt due to the Crown.

(7) Where there are two or more trustees under the trust, a notice under this section shall be deemed to have been validly served upon the trustees if served upon any one of them, but nothing in this section shall render a trustee personally liable for anything done by him in good faith and in ignorance of the fact that such a notice has been served.

Former enactments.—TA 1970, s. 36; FA 1971, Sch. 6, para. 16; FA 1978, Sch. 2, para. 3.

CHAPTER V

MAINTENANCE FUNDS FOR HISTORIC BUILDINGS

690. Schedule 4 directions

In this Chapter "a Schedule 4 direction" means a direction under paragraph 1 of Schedule 4 to the Inheritance Tax Act 1984 (maintenance funds for historic buildings); and any reference in this Chapter to paragraph 1 or Schedule 4 is a reference to that paragraph or that Schedule, as the case may be.

Note.—For the Inheritance Tax Act 1984, Sch. 4, see *Butterworths Orange Tax Handbook.*

691. Certain income not to be income of settlor etc.

(1) This section applies to any settlement in relation to which a Schedule 4 direction has effect.

(2) The trustees of the settlement may elect that this subsection shall have effect in relation to any year of assessment, and if they do so—

   (*a*) any income arising in that year from the property comprised in the settlement which, apart from this subsection, would be treated by virtue of this Part as income of the settlor shall not be so treated; and
   (*b*) no sum applied in that year out of the property for the purposes mentioned in paragraph 3(1)(*a*)(i) of Schedule 4 (maintenance etc. of qualifying property) shall be treated for any purposes of the Income Tax Acts as the income of any person—

      (i) by virtue of any interest of that person in, or his occupation of, the qualifying property in question; or
      (ii) by virtue of section 677.

(3) Where income arising from the property comprised in the settlement in a year of assessment for which no election is made under subsection (2) above is treated by virtue of this Part as income of the settlor, paragraph (*b*) of that subsection shall have effect in relation to any sums in excess of that income which are applied in that year as mentioned in that paragraph.

(4) Any election under subsection (2) above shall be by notice to the Board in such form as the Board may require and shall be made within two years of the end of the year of assessment to which it relates.

(5) Where—

   (*a*) for part of a year of assessment a Schedule 4 direction has effect and circumstances obtain by virtue of which income arising from property comprised in the settlement is treated as income of a settlor under this Part; and
   (*b*) for the remainder of that year either no such direction has effect, or no such circumstances obtain, or both,

subsections (1) to (4) above shall apply as if each of those parts were a separate year of assessment and separate elections may be made accordingly.

Former enactments.—Sub-s. (1): FA 1977, s. 38(1); FA 1982, Sch. 10, para. 1; IHTA 1984, Sch. 8, para. 8.
Sub-s. (2): FA 1977, s. 38(2); FA 1980, s. 88(7); FA 1987, Sch. 15, para. 10.
Sub-ss. (3), (4): FA 1977, s. 38(3), (4).
Sub-s. (5): FA 1977, s. 38(5); FA 1982, Sch. 10, para. 1(3); IHTA 1984, Sch. 8, para. 8.
Note.—For the Inheritance Tax Act 1984, Sch. 4, see *Butterworths Orange Tax Handbook.*

692. Reimbursement of settlor

(1) This section applies to income arising from settled property in respect of which a Schedule 4 direction has effect if the income—

   (*a*) is treated by virtue of this Part as income of the settlor, and
   (*b*) is applied in reimbursing the settlor for expenditure incurred by him for a purpose within paragraph 3(1)(*a*)(i) of Schedule 4,

and if that expenditure is (or would apart from the reimbursement be) deductible in computing the profits of a trade carried on by the settlor.

(2) Income to which this section applies shall not be treated as reducing the expenditure deductible in computing the profits referred to in subsection (1) above, and shall not be regarded as income of the settlor otherwise than by virtue of this Part.

Former enactments.—FA 1982, s. 61; IHTA 1984, Sch. 8, para. 21.
Note.—For the Inheritance Tax Act 1984, Sch. 4, see *Butterworths Orange Tax Handbook*.

693. Severance of settled property for certain purposes

Where settled property in respect of which a Schedule 4 direction has effect constitutes part only of the property comprised in a settlement, it and the other property shall be treated as comprised in separate settlements for the purposes of sections 27 and 380 to 387 and this Part.

Former enactments.—FA 1982, s. 62(1), (2); IHTA 1984, Sch. 8, para. 22.
Note.—For the Inheritance Tax Act 1984, Sch. 4, see *Butterworths Orange Tax Handbook*.

694. Trustees chargeable to income tax at 30 per cent. in certain cases

(1) If in the case of a settlement in respect of which a Schedule 4 direction has effect—

(*a*) any of the property comprised in the settlement (whether capital or income) is applied otherwise than as mentioned in paragraph 3(1)(*a*)(i) or (ii) of Schedule 4; or
(*b*) any of that property on ceasing to be comprised in the settlement devolves otherwise than on any such body or charity as is mentioned in paragraph 3(1)(*a*)(ii) of that Schedule; or
(*c*) the direction ceases to have effect;

then, unless subsection (6) below applies, income tax shall be charged under this section in respect of the settlement.

(2) Subject to subsection (3) below, tax chargeable under this section shall be charged . . .[1] on the whole of the income which has arisen in the relevant period from the property comprised in the settlement and has not been applied (or accumulated and then applied) as mentioned in paragraph 3(1)(*a*)(i) or (ii) of Schedule 4.

In this subsection "the relevant period" means, if tax has become chargeable under this section in respect of the settlement on a previous occasion, the period since the last occasion and, in any other case, the period since the settlement took effect.

[(2A) The rate at which tax is charged under this section shall be equivalent to the higher rate of income tax for the year of assessment during which the charge arises, reduced by the sum of the basic and additional rates for that year.][2]

(3) Tax shall not be chargeable under this section in respect of income which by virtue of Chapters I to IV of this Part is treated as income of the settlor; but where income arising in any year of assessment is exempted by this subsection any sums applied in that year as mentioned in paragraph 3(1)(*a*)(i) or (ii) of Schedule 4 shall be treated as paid primarily out of that income and only as to the excess, if any, out of income not so exempted.

(4) Tax charged under this section shall be in addition to any tax chargeable apart from this section and—

(*a*) the persons assessable and chargeable with tax under this section shall be the trustees of the settlement; and
(*b*) all the provisions of the Income Tax Acts relating to assessments and to the collection and recovery of income tax shall, so far as applicable, apply to the charge, assessment, collection and recovery of tax under this section.

(5) Tax shall also be chargeable in accordance with subsections (1) to (4) above if—

(*a*) any of the property comprised in a settlement to which subsection (1) above applies, on ceasing at any time to be comprised in the settlement, devolves on any such body or charity as is referred to in paragraph (*b*) of that subsection, and
(*b*) at or before that time an interest under the settlement is or has been acquired for a consideration in money or money's worth by that or another such body or charity;

but for the purposes of this subsection any acquisition from another such body or charity shall be disregarded.

(6) Tax shall not be chargeable under this section in respect of a settlement on an occasion when the whole of the property comprised in it is transferred tax-free into another settlement; but on the first occasion on which tax becomes chargeable under this section in

respect of a settlement ("the current settlement") comprising property which was previously comprised in another settlement or settlements and has become comprised in the current settlement as a result of, or of a series of, tax-free transfers, the relevant period for the purposes of subsection (2) above shall, as respects that property, be treated as having begun—

(*a*) on the last occasion on which tax became chargeable under this section in respect of the other settlement or any of the other settlements; or

(*b*) if there has been no such occasion, when the other settlement or the first of the other settlements took effect.

(7) For the purposes of subsection (6) above, property is transferred tax-free from one settlement into another if either—

(*a*) it ceases to be comprised in the first-mentioned settlement and becomes comprised in the other settlement in circumstances such that by virtue of paragraph 9(1) of Schedule 4 there is (or, but for paragraph 9(4), there would be) no charge to capital transfer tax or inheritance tax in respect of the property; or

(*b*) both immediately before and immediately after the transfer it is property in respect of which a Schedule 4 direction has effect.

Former enactments.—Sub-ss. (1), (2): FA 1980, s. 52(1), (2); FA 1982, Sch. 10, para. 2(2), (3); IHTA 1984, Sch. 8, para. 17.
Sub-ss. (3)–(6): FA 1980, s. 52(3)–(6); IHTA 1984, Sch. 8, para. 17.
Sub-s. (7): FA 1980, s. 52(7); FA 1982, Sch. 10, para. 2(4); IHTA 1984, Sch. 8, para. 17.
Note.—For the Inheritance Tax Act 1984, Sch. 4, see *Butterworths Orange Tax Handbook*.
Amendments.—[1] Words in sub-s. (2) repealed by FA 1988, s. 24(3) and Sch. 14, Pt. IV.
[2] Sub-s. (2A) inserted by FA 1988, s. 24(3).

PART XVI
ESTATES OF DECEASED PERSONS IN COURSE OF ADMINISTRATION

695. Limited interests in residue

(1) The following provisions of this section shall have effect in relation to a person who, during the period commencing on the death of a deceased person and ending on the completion of the administration of his estate ("the administration period") or during a part of that period, has a limited interest in the residue of the estate or in a part thereof.

(2) When any sum has been paid during the administration period in respect of that limited interest, the amount of that sum shall, subject to subsection (3) below, be deemed for all tax purposes to have been paid to that person as income for the year of assessment in which that sum was paid or, in the case of a sum paid in respect of an interest that has ceased, for the last year of assessment in which it was subsisting.

(3) On the completion of the administration of the estate—

(*a*) the aggregate amount of all sums paid before, or payable on, the completion of the administration in respect of that limited interest shall be deemed to have accrued due to that person from day to day during the administration period or the part of that period during which he had that interest, as the case may be, and to have been paid to him as it accrued due; and

(*b*) the amount deemed to have been paid to that person by virtue of paragraph (*a*) above in any year of assessment shall be deemed for all tax purposes to have been paid to him as income for that year; and

(*c*) where the amount which is deemed to have been paid to that person as income for any year by virtue of this subsection is less or greater than the amount deemed to have been paid to him as income for that year by virtue of subsection (2) above, such adjustments shall be made as are provided in section 700.

(4) Any amount which is deemed to have been paid to that person as income for any year by virtue of this section shall—

(*a*) in the case of a United Kingdom estate, be deemed to be income of such an amount as would after deduction of income tax for that year be equal to the amount deemed to have been so paid, and to be income which has borne income tax at the basic rate; and

(*b*) in the case of a foreign estate, be deemed to be income of the amount deemed to have been so paid, and shall be chargeable to income tax under Case IV of Schedule D as if it were income arising from securities in a place out of the United Kingdom.

(5) Where—

(*a*) a person has been charged to income tax for any year by virtue of this section in respect of an amount deemed to have been paid to him as income in respect of an interest in a foreign estate ("the deemed income"), and

(*b*) any part of the aggregate income of that estate for that year has borne United Kingdom income tax by deduction or otherwise ("the aggregate income"),

the tax so charged on him shall, on proof of the facts on a claim, be reduced by an amount bearing the same proportion thereto as the amount of the deemed income which has borne United Kingdom income tax, less the tax so borne, bears to the amount of the aggregate income, less the tax so borne.

(6) Where relief has been given under subsection (5) above, such part of the amount in respect of which he has been charged to income tax as corresponds to the proportion mentioned in that subsection shall, for the purpose of computing his total income, be deemed to represent income of such an amount as would after deduction of income tax be equal to that part of the amount charged.

Former enactments.—TA 1970, s. 426; FA 1971, Sch. 6, para. 52.

696. Absolute interests in residue

(1) The following provisions of this section shall have effect in relation to a person who, during the administration period or during a part of that period, has an absolute interest in the residue of the estate of a deceased person or in a part thereof.

(2) There shall be ascertained in accordance with section 697 the amount of the residuary income of the estate for each whole year of assessment, and for each broken part of a year of assessment, during which—

  (a) the administration period was current, and
  (b) that person had that interest;

and the amount so ascertained in respect of any year or part of a year or, in the case of a person having an absolute interest in a part of a residue, a proportionate part of that amount, is in this Part referred to as the "residuary income" of that person for that year of assessment.

(3) When any sum or sums has or have been paid during the administration period in respect of that absolute interest, the amount of that sum or the aggregate amount of those sums shall, subject to subsection (5) below, be deemed for all tax purposes to have been paid to that person as income to the extent to which, and for the year or years of assessment for which, he would have been treated for those purposes as having received income if he had had a right to receive in each year of assessment—

  (a) in the case of a United Kingdom estate, his residuary income for that year less income tax at the basic rate for that year; and
  (b) in the case of a foreign estate, his residuary income for that year;

and that sum or the aggregate of those sums had been available for application primarily in or towards satisfaction of those rights as they accrued and had been so applied.

(4) In the case of a United Kingdom estate, any amount which is deemed to have been paid to that person as income for any year by virtue of subsection (3) above shall be deemed to be income of such an amount as would, after deduction of income tax for that year, be equal to the amount deemed to have been so paid, and to be income that has borne income tax at the basic rate.

(5) On the completion of the administration of the estate—

  (a) the amount of the residuary income of that person for any year of assessment shall be deemed for all tax purposes to have been paid to him as income for that year, and in the case of a United Kingdom estate shall be deemed to have borne income tax at the basic rate; and
  (b) where the amount which is deemed to have been paid to that person as income for any year by virtue of this subsection is less or greater than the amount deemed to have been paid to him as income for that year by virtue of subsection (3) above, such adjustments shall be made as are provided in section 700.

(6) In the case of a foreign estate, any amount which is deemed to have been paid to that person as income for any year by virtue of this section shall be deemed to be income of that amount and shall be chargeable to income tax under Case IV of Schedule D as if it were income arising from securities in a place out of the United Kingdom.

(7) Where—

  (a) a person has been charged to income tax for any year by virtue of this section in respect of an amount deemed to have been paid to him as income in respect of an interest in a foreign estate ("the deemed income"), and
  (b) any part of the aggregate income of that estate for that year has borne United Kingdom income tax by deduction or otherwise ("the aggregate income"),

the tax so charged on him shall, on proof of the facts on a claim, be reduced by an amount bearing the same proportion thereto as the amount of the deemed income which has borne United Kingdom income tax bears to the amount of the aggregate income.

(8) For the purposes of any charge to corporation tax under this section, the residuary income of a company shall be computed in the first instance by reference to years of assessment, and the residuary income for any such year shall be apportioned between the accounting periods (if more than one) comprising that year.

Former enactments.—TA 1970, s. 427; FA 1971, Sch. 6, para. 53.

697. Supplementary provisions as to absolute interests in residue

(1) The amount of the residuary income of an estate for any year of assessment shall be ascertained by deducting from the aggregate income of the estate for that year—

  (a) the amount of any annual interest, annuity or other annual payment for that year which is a charge on residue and the amount of any payment made in that year in respect of any such expenses incurred by the personal representatives as such in the management of the assets of the estate as, in the absence of any express provision in a will, would be properly chargeable to income, but excluding any such interest, annuity or payment allowed or allowable in computing the aggregate income of the estate; and

(b) the amount of any of the aggregate income of the estate for that year to which a person has on or after assent become entitled by virtue of a specific disposition either for a vested interest during the administration period or for a vested or contingent interest on the completion of the administration.

(2) In the event of its appearing, on the completion of the administration of an estate in the residue of which, or in a part of the residue of which, a person had an absolute interest at the completion of the administration, that the aggregate of the benefits received in respect of that interest does not amount to as much as the aggregate for all years of the residuary income of the person having that interest, his residuary income for each year shall be reduced for the purpose of section 696 by an amount bearing the same proportion thereto as the deficiency bears to the aggregate for all years of his residuary income.

(3) In subsection (2) above "benefits received" in respect of an absolute interest means the following amounts in respect of all sums paid before, or payable on, the completion of the administration in respect of that interest, that is to say—

(a) as regards a sum paid before the completion of the administration, in the case of a United Kingdom estate such an amount as would, after deduction of income tax for the year of assessment in which that sum was paid, be equal to that sum, or in the case of a foreign estate the amount of that sum; and

(b) as regards a sum payable on the completion of the administration, in the case of a United Kingdom estate such an amount as would, after deduction of income tax for the year of assessment in which the administration is completed, be equal to that sum, or in the case of a foreign estate the amount of that sum.

(4) In the application of subsection (2) above to a residue or a part of a residue in which a person other than the person having an absolute interest at the completion of the administration had an absolute interest at any time during the administration period, the aggregates mentioned in that subsection shall be computed in relation to those interests taken together, and the residuary income of that other person also shall be subject to reduction under that subsection.

Former enactments.—TA 1970, s. 428; FA 1971, Sch. 6, para. 54.

698. Special provisions as to certain interests in residue

(1) Where the personal representatives of a deceased person have as such a right in relation to the estate of another deceased person such that, if that right were vested in them for their own benefit, they would have an absolute or limited interest in the residue of that estate or in a part of that residue, they shall be deemed to have that interest notwithstanding that that right is not vested in them for their own benefit, and any amount deemed to be paid to them as income by virtue of this Part shall be treated as part of the aggregate income of the estate of the person whose personal representatives they are.

(2) Where different persons have successively during the administration period absolute interests in the residue of the estate of a deceased person or in a part of such residue, sums paid during that period in respect of the residue or of that part, as the case may be, shall be treated for the purposes of this Part as having been paid in respect of the interest of the person who first had an absolute interest in that residue or that part up to the amount of—

(a) in the case of a United Kingdom estate, the aggregate for all years of that person's residuary income less income tax at the basic rate; or

(b) in the case of a foreign estate, the aggregate for all years of that person's residuary income;

and, as to any balance up to a corresponding amount, in respect of the interest of the person who next had an absolute interest in that residue or part, and so on.

(3) Where, upon the exercise of a discretion, any of the income of the residue of the estate of a deceased person for any period (being the administration period or a part of the administration period) would, if the residue had been ascertained at the commencement of that period, be properly payable to any person, or to another in his right, for his benefit, whether directly by the personal representatives or indirectly through a trustee or other person—

(a) the amount of any sum paid pursuant to an exercise of the discretion in favour of that person shall be deemed for all tax purposes to have been paid to that person as income for the year of assessment in which it was paid; and

(b) section 695(4) to (6) shall have effect in relation to an amount which is deemed to have been paid as income by virtue of paragraph (a) above.

Former enactments.—TA 1970, s. 429; FA 1981, Sch. 6, para. 55.

699. Relief from higher rate tax for inheritance tax on accrued income

(1) Where any income, having accrued before the death of any person, is taken into account both—

(a) in determining the value of his estate for the purposes of any inheritance tax chargeable on his death; and
(b) in ascertaining for the purposes of this Part the residuary income of his estate for any year of assessment;

then, in ascertaining the excess liability of any person having an absolute interest in the residue of that or any other estate or part thereof, that residuary income shall be treated as reduced by an amount calculated in accordance with the following provisions of this section.

(2) In subsection (1) above "excess liability" means the excess of liability to income tax over what it would be if all income tax were chargeable at the basic rate to the exclusion of any higher rate.

(3) The amount of the reduction shall be an amount which, after deduction of income tax for the year of assessment in question, would be equal to the amount of inheritance tax attributable to so much of the income taken into account as mentioned in subsection (1) above as exceeds any liabilities so taken into account.

(4) The amount of any income accruing before the death of any person and taken into account in estimating the value of an estate shall (whether or not the income was valued separately or its amount known at the date of the death) be taken to be the actual amount so accruing less income tax at the basic rate for the year of assessment in which the death occurred.

(5) The amounts agreed between the persons liable for inheritance tax and the Board, or determined in the proceedings between them, as being respectively the value of an estate and the amount of any inheritance tax payable shall be conclusive for the purposes of this section; and evidence of those amounts and of any facts relevant to their computation may be given by the production of a document purporting to be a certificate from the Board.

(6) In this section—

(a) references to liabilities taken into account in ascertaining the amount of the residuary income of an estate include references to liabilities allowed or allowable in computing its aggregate income; and
(b) references to inheritance tax include references to capital transfer tax.

Former enactments.—TA 1970, s. 430; FA 1971, Sch. 6, para 56; FA 1975, Sch. 12, para. 16; FA 1978, Sch. 2, para. 11; FA 1986, s. 100.
Cross references.—See FA 1988, s. 102(2)(d) (taxation of capital gains at income tax rates: sub-s. (1) above to apply to capital gains as it applies to income).

700. Adjustments and information

(1) Where on the completion of the administration of an estate any amount is deemed by virtue of this Part to have been paid to any person as income for any year of assessment and—

(a) that amount is greater than the amount that has previously been deemed to have been paid to him as income for that year by virtue of this Part; or
(b) no amount has previously been so deemed to have been paid to him as income for that year;

an assessment may be made upon him for that year and tax charged accordingly or, on a claim being made for the purpose, any relief or additional relief to which he may be entitled shall be allowed accordingly.

(2) Where on the completion of the administration of an estate any amount is deemed by virtue of this Part to have been paid to any person as income for any year of assessment, and

that amount is less than the amount that has previously been so deemed to have been paid to him, then—

(a) if an assessment has already been made upon him for that year, such adjustments shall be made in that assessment as may be necessary for the purpose of giving effect to the provisions of this Part which take effect on the completion of the administration, and any tax overpaid shall be repaid; and
(b) if—

(i) any relief has been allowed to him by reference to the amount which has been previously deemed by virtue of this Part to have been paid to him as income for that year, and
(ii) the amount of that relief exceeds the amount of relief which could have been given by reference to the amount which, on the completion of the administration, is deemed to have been paid to him as income for that year,

the relief so given in excess may, if not otherwise made good, be charged under Case VI of Schedule D and recovered from that person accordingly.

(3) Notwithstanding anything in the Tax Acts, the time within which an assessment may be made for the purposes of this Part, or an assessment may be adjusted for those purposes, or a claim for relief may be made by virtue of this Part, shall not expire before the end of the third year following the year of assessment in which the administration of the estate in question was completed.

(4) An inspector may by notice require any person being or having been a personal representative of a deceased person, or having or having had an absolute or limited interest in the residue of the estate of a deceased person or in a part of such residue, to furnish him within such time as he may direct (not being less than 28 days) with such particulars as he thinks necessary for the purposes of this Part.

Former enactments.—TA 1970, s. 431; FA 1971, Sch. 6, para. 57.

701. Interpretation

(1) The following provisions of this section shall have effect for the purpose of the interpretation of sections 695 to 700.

(2) A person shall be deemed to have an absolute interest in the residue of the estate of a deceased person, or in a part of such residue, if and so long as the capital of the residue or of that part would, if the residue had been ascertained, be properly payable to him, or to another in his right, for his benefit, or is properly so payable, whether directly by the personal representatives or indirectly through a trustee or other person.

(3) A person shall be deemed to have a limited interest in the residue of the estate of a deceased person, or in a part of such residue, during any period, being a period during which he has not an absolute interest in the residue or in that part, where the income of the residue or of that part for that period would, if the residue had been ascertained at the commencement of that period, be properly payable to him, or to another in his right, for his benefit, whether directly by the personal representatives or indirectly through a trustee or other person.

(4) "Personal representatives" means, in relation to the estate of a deceased person, his personal representatives as defined in relation to England and Wales by section 55 of the Administration of Estates Act 1925, and persons having in relation to the deceased under the law of another country any functions corresponding to the functions for administration purposes under the law of England and Wales of personal representatives as so defined; and references to "personal representatives as such" shall be construed as references to personal representatives in their capacity as having such functions.

(5) "Specific disposition" means a specific devise or bequest made by a testator, and includes the disposition of personal chattels made by section 46 of the Administration of Estates Act 1925 and any disposition having, whether by virtue of any enactment or otherwise, under the law of another country an effect similar to that of a specific devise or bequest under the law of England and Wales.

Real estate included (either by a specific or general description) in a residuary gift made by the will of a testator shall be deemed to be a part of the residue of his estate and not to be the subject of a specific disposition.

(6) Subject to subsection (7) below, "charges on residue" means, in relation to the estate of a deceased person, the following liabilities, properly payable thereout and interest payable in respect of those liabilities, that is to say—

(a) funeral, testamentary and administration expenses and debts, and
(b) general legacies, demonstrative legacies, annuities and any sum payable out of residue to which a person is entitled under the law of intestacy of any part of the United Kingdom or any other country, and
(c) any other liabilities of his personal representatives as such.

(7) Where, as between persons interested under a specific disposition or in a general or demonstrative legacy or in an annuity and persons interested in the residue of the estate, any such liabilities as are mentioned in subsection (6) above fall exclusively or primarily upon the property that is the subject of the specific disposition or upon the legacy or annuity, only such part (if any) of those liabilities as falls ultimately upon the residue shall be treated as charges on residue.

(8) References to the aggregate income of the estate of a deceased person for any year of assessment shall be construed as references to the aggregate income from all sources for that year of the personal representatives of the deceased as such, treated as consisting of—
(a) any such income which is chargeable to United Kingdom income tax by deduction or otherwise, such income being computed at the amount on which that tax falls to be borne for that year; and
(b) any such income which would have been so chargeable if it had arisen in the United Kingdom to a person resident and ordinarily resident there, such income being computed at the full amount thereof actually arising during that year, less such deductions as would have been allowable if it had been charged to United Kingdom income tax;

but excluding any income from property devolving on the personal representatives otherwise than as assets for payment of the debts of the deceased.

This subsection has effect subject to sections 249(5), 421(2), . . .[1] and 547(1)(*c*).

(9) "United Kingdom estate" means, as regards any year of assessment, an estate the income of which comprises only income which either—
(a) has borne United Kingdom income tax by deduction, or
(b) in respect of which the personal representatives are directly assessable to United Kingdom income tax,

not being an estate any part of the income of which is income in respect of which the personal representatives are entitled to claim exemption from United Kingdom income tax by reference to the fact that they are not resident, or not ordinarily resident, in the United Kingdom.

(10) "Foreign estate" means, as regards any year of assessment, an estate which is not a United Kingdom estate.

(11) In a case in which different parts of the estate of a deceased person are the subjects respectively of different residuary dispositions, this Part shall have effect in relation to each of those parts with the substitution—
(a) for references to the estate of references to that part of the estate; and
(b) for references to the personal representatives of the deceased as such of references to his personal representatives in their capacity as having the functions referred to in subsection (4) above in relation to that part of the estate.

(12) In this Part—
(a) references to sums paid include references to assets that are transferred or that are appropriated by a personal representative to himself, and to debts that are set off or released;
(b) references to sums payable include references to assets as to which an obligation to transfer or a right of a personal representative to appropriate to himself is subsisting on the completion of the administration and to debts as to which an obligation to release or set off, or a right of a personal representative so to do in his own favour, is then subsisting; and
(c) references to amount shall be construed, in relation to such assets as are referred to in paragraph (a) or (b) above, as references to their value at the date on which they were transferred or appropriated, or at the completion of the administration, as the case may require, and, in relation to such debts as are so referred to, as references to the amount thereof.

(13) In this Part references to the administration period shall be construed in accordance with section 695(1).

(14) In relation to so much of any residuary income for any year of assessment which has

borne income tax at a rate equal to the sum of the basic rate and the additional rate for that year, section 696(3) shall have effect with the substitution for paragraph (*a*) of the following paragraph—

"(*a*) in the case of a United Kingdom estate—

(i) in the first instance, as regards so much of his residuary income for that year as has borne income tax at the basic rate for that year, that much of that income less income tax at that rate; and

(ii) subject to sub-paragraph (i), as regards so much of his residuary income for that year as has borne income tax at a rate equal to the sum of the basic rate and the additional rate for that year, that much of that income less income tax at the sum of those rates; and";

and the references in sections 696(4) and (5)(*a*) and 698(2)(*a*) to income tax at the basic rate shall have effect as references to income tax at a rate equal to that sum.

Former enactments.—Sub-ss. (1)–(12): TA 1970, s. 432; FA 1972, Sch. 24, para. 25; F(No 2)A 1975, s. 34(5). Sub-s (13): TA 1970, s. 426(1).
Sub-s (14): FA 1974, Sch. 7, para. 9(3)–(5).
Amendments.—[1] Number in sub-s. (8) repealed by FA 1989, Sch. 17, Pt. V.

702. Application to Scotland

For the purpose of the application of this Part to Scotland—

(*a*) any reference to the completion of the administration of an estate shall be construed as a reference to the date at which, after discharge of, or provision for, liabilities falling to be met out of the deceased's estate (including, without prejudice to the generality of the foregoing, debts, legacies immediately payable, prior rights of surviving spouse on intestacy and legal rights of surviving spouse or children), the free balance held in trust for behoof of the residuary legatees has been ascertained;

(*b*) for paragraph (*b*) of section 697(1) the following paragraph shall be substituted—

"(*b*) the amount of any of the aggregate income of the estate for that year to which a person has become entitled by virtue of a specific disposition";

(*c*) "real estate" means heritable estate, and

(*d*) "charge on residue" shall include, in addition to the liabilities specified in section 701(6), any sums required to meet claims in respect of prior rights by surviving spouse or in respect of legal rights by surviving spouse or children.

Former enactments.—TA 1970, s. 433; FA 1987, Sch 15, para. 2(15).

PART XVII

TAX AVOIDANCE

CHAPTER I

CANCELLATION OF TAX ADVANTAGES FROM CERTAIN
TRANSACTIONS IN SECURITIES

703. Cancellation of tax advantage

(1) Where—

(*a*) in any such circumstances as are mentioned in section 704, and
(*b*) in consequence of a transaction in securities or of the combined effect of two or more such transactions,

a person is in a position to obtain, or has obtained, a tax advantage, then unless he shows that the transaction or transactions were carried out either for bona fide commercial reasons or in the ordinary course of making or managing investments, and that none of them had as their main object, or one of their main objects, to enable tax advantages to be obtained, this section shall apply to him in respect of that transaction or those transactions.

(2) For the purposes of this Chapter a tax advantage obtained or obtainable by a person shall be deemed to be obtained or obtainable by him in consequence of a transaction in securities or of the combined effect of two or more such transactions, if it is obtained or obtainable in consequence of the combined effect of the transaction or transactions and the liquidation of a company.

(3) Where this section applies to a person in respect of any transaction or transactions, the tax advantage obtained or obtainable by him in consequence thereof shall be counteracted by such of the following adjustments, that is to say an assessment, the nullifying of a right to repayment or the requiring of the return of a repayment already made (the amount to be returned being chargeable under Case VI of Schedule D and recoverable accordingly), or the computation or recomputation of profits or gains, or liability to tax, on such basis as the Board may specify by notice served on him as being requisite for counteracting the tax advantage so obtained or obtainable.

(4) Where, by virtue of an assessment under subsection (3) above to counteract a tax advantage obtained in circumstances falling within paragraph D or paragraph E of section 704 and consisting of the avoidance of a charge to income tax, income tax has been paid by any person on an amount specified in the assessment and it appears to the Board that, as a result of that payment, it is just and reasonable in the circumstances that an amount should be treated as having been paid by way of advance corporation tax, the Board shall serve a notice under subsection (5) below on every company which appears to them to be concerned in the transaction or transactions in consequence of which the tax advantage was obtained.

(5) A notice under this subsection—

(*a*) shall provide that, for the purposes of section 239 (but not for the purposes of entitling any person to a tax credit under section 231), such company or each of such companies as may be specified in the notice is to be treated as having paid, on such date as may be so specified, such amount of advance corporation tax as may be so specified in relation to that company;
(*b*) shall specify the amount which is equal to income tax at the basic rate on the amount on which income tax has been paid as mentioned in subsection (4) above; and
(*c*) may contain such supplementary or incidental directions as appear to the Board to be appropriate;

but the total amount of advance corporation tax which, by virtue of paragraph (*a*) above, a notice under this subsection may treat as having been paid shall not exceed the amount specified in accordance with paragraph (*b*) above.

(6) If, in a case falling within subsection (4) above, it does not appear to the Board that any amount should be treated as having been paid by way of advance corporation tax, the Board shall serve on every company which appears to them to be concerned in the transaction or transactions in consequence of which the tax advantage was obtained in a notice informing

the company of the Board's decision that no amount is to be treated as having been paid by way of advance corporation tax.

(7) In the case of a man and his wife living with him (whether or not she is separately assessed to tax), this Chapter shall, subject to subsection (8) below, be treated as applying to him in respect of any transaction or transactions as it would apply if any property, rights or liabilities of the wife were his property, rights or liabilities in relation to which she had acted only as nominee for him, and shall be treated as applying to the wife in respect of any transaction or transactions as it would apply if any property, rights or liabilities of the man were her property, rights or liabilities in relation to which he had acted only as nominee for her.

(8) No adjustment made under subsection (3) above by reference to any transaction or transactions to counteract any tax advantage shall by virtue of subsection (7) above be so made that a person bears more tax than if the transaction or transactions had not had as a consequence that any relief or increased relief from, or repayment or increased repayment of, income tax, or any deduction in computing profits or gains, was obtained or obtainable, or that the way in which receipts accrued was such that the recipient did not pay or bear tax on them.

(9) The Board shall not give a notice under subsection (3) above until they have notified the person in question that they have reason to believe that this section may apply to him in respect of a transaction or transactions specified in the notification; and if within 30 days of the issue of the notification that person, being of opinion that this section does not so apply to him, makes a statutory declaration to that effect stating the facts and circumstances upon which his opinion is based, and sends it to the Board, then subject to subsection (10) below, this section shall not apply to him in respect of the transaction or transactions.

(10) If, when a statutory declaration has been sent to the Board under subsection (9) above, they see reason to take further action in the matter—

(*a*) the Board shall send to the tribunal a certificate to that effect, together with the statutory declaration, and may also send therewith a counter-statement with reference to the matter;

(*b*) the tribunal shall take into consideration the declaration and the certificate, and the counter-statement, if any, and shall determine whether there is or is not a prime facie case for proceeding in the matter, and if they determine that there is no such case this section shall not apply to the person in question in respect of the transaction or transactions;

but any such determination shall not affect the operation of this section in respect of transactions which include that transaction or some or all of those transactions and also include another transaction or other transactions.

(11) Any notice or notification under subsection (3) or subsection (9) above, or under section 708, concerning the application of this section to a person who has died may be given or issued to his personal representatives, and the provisions of this Chapter relating to the making of a statutory declaration, to rights of appeal and to the giving of information shall be construed accordingly.

(12) This section applies whether the tax advantage in question relates to a chargeable period ending before or after the commencement of this Act, but nothing in this section shall authorise the making of an assessment later than six years after the chargeable period to which the tax advantage relates; and no other provision contained in the Tax Acts shall be construed as limiting the powers conferred by this section.

Former enactments.—Sub-ss (1)–(3): TA 1970, s. 460(1)–(3).
Sub-ss. (4)–(6): TA 1970, s. 460(4), (4A), (4B); FA 1973, Sch. 11, para. 1.
Sub-ss. (7)–(12): TA 1970, s. 460(5)–(9).
Note.—See **Prospective Legislation Notes** (Married Couples).

704. The prescribed circumstances

The circumstances mentioned in section 703(1) are—

A. That in connection with the distribution of profits of a company, or in connection with the sale or purchase of securities being a sale or purchase followed by the purchase or sale of the same or other securities, the person in question receives an abnormal amount by way of dividend, and the amount so received is taken into account for any of the following purposes—

(*a*) any exemption from tax, or
(*b*) the setting-off of losses against profits or income, or

(c) the giving of group relief, or
(d) the application of franked investment income in calculating a company's liability to pay advance corporation tax, or
(e) the application of a surplus of franked investment income under section 242 or 243, or
(f) the computation of profits or gains out of which are made payments falling within section 348 or 349(1), or
(g) the deduction from or set-off against income of interest under section 353.

OR

B.—(1) That in connection with the distribution of profits of a company, or in connection with the sale or purchase of securities being sale or purchase followed by the purchase or sale of the same or other securities, the person in question becomes entitled—
　(a) in respect of securities held or sold by him, or
　(b) in respect of securities formerly held by him (whether sold by him or not),
to a deduction in computing profits or gains by reason of a fall in the value of the securities resulting from the payment of a dividend thereon or from any other dealing with any assets of a company.

(2) Where a company in the circumstances mentioned in sub-paragraph (1) above becomes entitled to a deduction as there mentioned, section 703 shall apply in relation to any tax advantage obtained or obtainable in consequence of that deduction by another company by way of group relief as if obtained or obtainable by the other company in circumstances falling within sub-paragraph (1) above.

OR

C.—(1) That the person in question receives, in consequence of a transaction whereby any other person—
　(a) subsequently receives, or has received, an abnormal amount by way of dividend; or
　(b) subsequently becomes entitled, or has become entitled, to a deduction as mentioned in paragraph B(1) above,
a consideration which either—
　(i) is, or represents the value of, assets which are (or apart from anything done by the company in question would have been) available for distribution by way of dividend, or
　(ii) is received in respect of future receipts of the company, or
　(iii) is, or represents the value of, trading stock of the company,
and the person in question so receives the consideration that he does not pay or bear tax on it as income.

(2) The assets mentioned in sub-paragraph (1) above do not include assets which (while of a description which under the law of the country in which the company is incorporated is available for distribution by way of dividend) are shown to represent a return of sums paid by subscribers on the issue of securities.

OR

D.—(1) That in connection with the distribution of profits of a company to which this paragraph applies, the person in question so receives as is mentioned in paragraph C(1) above such a consideration as is therein mentioned.

(2) The companies to which this paragraph applies are—
　(a) any company under the control of not more than five persons, and
　(b) any other company which does not satisfy the conditions that its shares or stocks or some class thereof (disregarding debenture stock, preferred shares or preferred stock), are authorised to be dealt in on the Stock Exchange, and are so dealt in (regularly or from time to time),
so, however, that this paragraph does not apply to a company under the control of one or more companies to which this paragraph does not apply.

(3) Subsections (2) to (6) of section 416 shall apply for the purposes of this paragraph.

OR

E.—(1) That in connection with the transfer directly or indirectly of assets of a company to which paragraph D above applies to another such company, or in connection with any transaction in securities in which two or more companies to which paragraph D above applies are concerned, the person in question receives non-taxable consideration which is or represents the value of assets available for distribution by such a company, and which consists of any share capital or any security (as defined by section 254(1)) issued by such a company.

(2) So far as sub-paragraph (1) above relates to share capital other than redeemable share capital, it shall not apply unless and except to the extent that the share capital is repaid (in a winding-up or otherwise), and, where section 703 applies to a person by virtue of sub-paragraph (1) above on the repayment of any share capital, any assessment to tax under subsection (3) of that section shall be an assessment to tax for the year in which the share capital is repaid.

(3) In this paragraph—

> "assets available for distribution" means assets which are, or apart from anything done by the company in question would have been, available for distribution by way of dividend, or trading stock of the company;
> "non-taxable", in relation to a person receiving consideration, means that the recipient does not pay or bear tax on it as income (apart from the provisions of this Chapter);
> "share" includes stock and any other interest of a member in a company;

and the reference in sub-paragraph (2) above to the repayment of share capital include references to any distribution made in respect of any shares in a winding-up or dissolution of the company.

Former enactments.—TA 1970, s. 461; FA 1973, s. 54, Sch. 11, para. 2(*a*), (*b*).

705. Appeals against Board's notices under section 703

(1) Any person to whom notice has been given under section 703(3) may within 30 days by notice to the Board appeal to the Special Commissioners on the grounds that section 703 does not apply to him in respect of the transaction or transactions in question, or that the adjustments directed to be made are inappropriate.

(2) If he or the Board are dissatisfied with the determination of the Special Commissioners he or they may, on giving notice to the clerk to the Special Commissioners within 30 days after the determination, require the appeal to be re-heard by the tribunal, and the Special Commissioners shall transmit to the tribunal any document in their possession which was delivered to them for the purposes of the appeal.

(3) Where notice is given under subsection (2) above, the tribunal shall re-hear and determine the appeal and shall have and exercise the same powers and authorities in relation to the appeal as the Special Commissioners might have and exercise, and the determination of the tribunal thereon shall be final and conclusive.

(4) Section 56 of the Management Act (statement of case for opinion of High Court etc.) shall apply with the necessary modifications in the case of any such rehearing and determination as it applies in the case of appeals to the General or Special Commissioners.

(5) On an appeal under subsections (1) to (3) above the Special Commissioners or the tribunal shall have power to cancel or vary a notice under subsection (3) of section 703 or to vary or quash an assessment made in accordance with such a notice, but the bringing of an appeal or the statement of a case shall not affect the validity of a notice given or of any other thing done in pursuance of that subsection pending the determination of the proceedings.

(6) A company on which a notice has been served under section 703(5) or (6) may within 30 days by notice to the Board appeal to the Special Commissioners on the ground that it is just and reasonable in the circumstances that the company should be treated, for the purposes specified in section 703(6), as having paid an amount of advance corporation tax or, as the case may require, a greater amount of advance corporation tax than is specified in the notice.

(7) Notwithstanding that a company on which a notice has been served as mentioned in subsection (6) above has made no appeal under that subsection, the company—

> (*a*) shall be entitled, to the same extent as the appellant, to receive notice of, and to appear and be heard in, any proceedings arising from the notice referred to in subsection (6) above, whether the proceedings are before the Special Commissioners, by way of further appeal or otherwise;
> (*b*) if it does appear, shall be treated as a party to the proceedings and as having the same rights in respect of those proceedings and any decision made therein as the appellant; and

(c) whether or not it so appears, shall be bound by any order made in any such proceedings;

and no agreement under section 54 of the Management Act (settling of appeals by agreement) shall have effect except with the consent of each company which, by virtue of this subsection, would have been entitled to appear and be heard on the appeal if it had been proceeded with.

(8) On an appeal under subsection (6) above, the Special Commissioners—
  (a) may cancel or vary any notice served under section 703(5), or
  (b) if no such notice was served, may by order make any provision which could have been made by the Board in such a notice.

Former enactments.—Sub-ss. (1)–(5): TA 1970, s. 462.
Sub-ss. (6)–(8): TA 1970, s. 462A; FA 1973, Sch. 11, para. 3.

706. The tribunal

For the purposes of this Chapter the tribunal shall consist of—
  (a) a chairman, appointed by the Lord Chancellor, and
  (b) two or more persons appointed by the Lord Chancellor as having special knowledge of and experience in financial or commercial matters.

Former enactments.—TA 1970, s. 463; FA 1982, Sch. 21, para. 3(1).
Cross references.—See FA 1989, s. 182(3)(d) (criminal liability of the tribunal appointed under this section for disclosure of information).

707. Procedure for clearance in advance

(1) The following provisions shall have effect where in pursuance of this section a person furnishes to the Board particulars of a transaction or transactions effected or to be effected by him, that is to say—
  (a) if the Board are of opinion that the particulars, or any further information furnished in pursuance of this paragraph, are not sufficient for the purposes of this section, they shall within 30 days of the receipt thereof notify to that person what further information they require for those purposes, and unless that further information is furnished to the Board within 30 days from the notification, or such further time as the Board may allow, they shall not be required to proceed further under this section;
  (b) subject to paragraph (a) above, the Board shall within 30 days of the receipt of the particulars, or, where that paragraph has effect, of all further information required, notify that person whether or not they are satisfied that the transaction or transactions as described in the particulars were or will be such that no notice under section 703(3) ought to be given in respect of it or them;

and, subject to the following provisions of this section, if the Board notify him that they are so satisfied, section 703 shall not apply to him in respect of that transaction or those transactions.

(2) If the particulars, and any further information given under this section with respect to any transaction or transactions, are not such as to make full and accurate disclosure of all facts and considerations relating thereto which are material to be known to the Board, any notification given by the Board under this section shall be void.

(3) In no event shall the giving of a notification under this section with respect to any transaction or transactions prevent section 703 applying to a person in respect of transactions which include that transaction or all or some of those transactions and also include another transaction or other transactions.

Former enactment.—TA 1970, s. 464.

708. Power to obtain information

Where it appears to the Board that by reason of any transaction or transactions a person may be a person to whom section 703 applies, the Board may by notice served on him require him, within such time not less than 28 days as may be specified in the notice, to furnish information in his possession with respect to the transaction or any of the transactions, being information as to matters, specified in the notice, which are relevant to the question whether a notice under section 703(3) should be given in respect of him.

Former enactment.—TA 1970, s. 465.

709. Meaning of "tax advantage" and other expressions

(1) In this Chapter "tax advantage" means a relief or increased relief from, or repayment or increased repayment of, tax, or the avoidance or reduction of a charge to tax or an assessment to tax or the avoidance of a possible assessment thereto, whether the avoidance or reduction is effected by receipts accruing in such a way that the recipient does not pay or bear tax on them, or by a deduction in computing profits or gains.

(2) In this Chapter—

"company" includes any body corporate;
"securities"—

(*a*) includes shares and stock, and
(*b*) in relation to a company not limited by shares (whether or not it has a share capital) includes also a reference to the interest of a member of the company as such, whatever the form of that interest;

"trading stock" has the same meaning as in section 100(1);
"transaction in securities" includes transactions, of whatever description, relating to securities, and in particular—

(i) the purchase, sale or exchange of securities;
(ii) the issuing or securing the issue of, or applying or subscribing for, new securities;
(iii) the altering, or securing the alteration of, the rights attached to securities;

and references to dividends include references to other qualifying distributions and to interest.

(3) In section 704—

(*a*) references to profits include references to income, reserves or other assets;
(*b*) references to distribution include references to transfer or realisation (including application in discharge of liabilities); and
(*c*) references to the receipt of consideration include references to the receipt of any money or money's worth.

(4) For the purposes of section 704 an amount received by way of dividend shall be treated as abnormal if the Board, the Special Commissioners or the tribunal, as the case may be, are satisfied—

(*a*) in the case of a dividend at a fixed rate, that it substantially exceeds the amount which the recipient would have received if the dividend had accrued from day to day and he had been entitled only to so much of the dividend as accrued while he held the securities, so however that an amount shall not be treated as abnormal by virtue only of this paragraph if during the six months beginning with the purchase of the securities the recipient does not sell or otherwise dispose of, or acquire an option to sell, any of those securities or any securities similar to those securities; or
(*b*) in any case, that it substantially exceeds a normal return on the consideration provided by the recipient for the relevant securities, that is to say, the securities in respect of which the dividend was received and, if those securities are derived from securities previously acquired by the recipient, the securities which were previously acquired.

(5) For the purposes of subsection (4)(*a*) above securities shall be deemed to be similar if they entitle their holders to the same rights against the same persons as to capital and interest and the same remedies for the enforcement of those rights, notwithstanding any difference in the total nominal amounts of the respective securities or in the form in which they are held or the manner in which they can be transferred, and for those purposes rights guaranteed by the Treasury shall be treated as rights against the Treasury.

(6) For the purposes of subsection (4)(*b*) above—

(*a*) if the consideration provided by the recipient for any of the relevant securities was in excess of their market value at the time he acquired them, or if no consideration was provided by him for any of the relevant securities, the recipient shall be taken to have provided for those securities consideration equal to their market value at the time he acquired them; and
(*b*) in determining whether an amount received by way of dividend exceeds a normal return, regard shall be had to the length of time previous to the receipt of that amount

that the recipient first acquired any of the relevant securities and to any dividends and other distributions made in respect of them during that time.

Former enactments.—Sub-s. (1): TA 1970, s. 466(1); FA 1973, Sch. 11, para. 4.
Sub-ss. (2)–(6): TA 1970, s. 467; FA 1973, Sch. 11, para. 5.

CHAPTER II

TRANSFERS OF SECURITIES

Transfers with or without accrued interest: introductory

Cross references.—See FA 1989, Sch. 11, para. 17 (provisions which apply to transfer of deep gain securities).

710. Meaning of "securities", "transfer" etc. for purposes of sections 711 to 728

(1) This section has effect for the interpretation of sections 711 to 728.

(2) "Securities" does not include shares in a company but, subject to subsection (3) below, includes any loan stock or similar security—
   (*a*) whether of the government of the United Kingdom, any other government, any public or local authority in the United Kingdom or elsewhere, or any company or other body; and
   (*b*) whether or not secured, whether or not carrying a right to interest of a fixed amount or at a fixed rate per cent. of the nominal value of the securities, and whether or not in bearer form.

(3) "Securities" does not include—
   (*a*) securities on which the whole of the return is a distribution by virtue of section 209(2)(*e*)(iv) and (v);
   (*b*) national savings certificates (including Ulster Savings Certificates);
   (*c*) war savings certificates;
   (*d*) certificates of deposit (within the meaning of section 56(5));
   (*e*) any security which fulfils the following conditions, namely, it is redeemable, the amount payable on its redemption exceeds its issue price, and no return other than the amount of that excess is payable on it.

(4) Securities are to be taken to be of the same kind if they are treated as being of the same kind by the practice of a recognised stock exchange or would be so treated if dealt with on such a stock exchange.

(5) "Transfer", in relation to securities, means transfer by way of sale, exchange, gift or otherwise.

(6) Where an agreement for the transfer of securities is made, they are transferred, and the person to whom they are agreed to be transferred becomes entitled to them, when the agreement is made and not on a later transfer made pursuant to the agreement; and "entitled", "transfer" and cognate expressions shall be construed accordingly.

(7) A person holds securities—
   (*a*) at a particular time if he is entitled to them at the time;
   (*b*) on a day if he is entitled to them throughout the day or he becomes and does not cease to be entitled to them on the day.

(8) A person acquires securities when he becomes entitled to them.

(9) Where—
   (*a*) one individual holds securities at a particular time, and
   (*b*) any interest on them would, if it became payable at that time, be treated for the purposes of the Tax Acts as part of another individual's income,

then, for the purposes of section 715(1)(*b*) and section 715(2)(*b*) so far as relating to section 715(1)(*b*), each of them shall be treated as holding at that time the securities which the other holds as well as those which he actually holds.

(10) Where in Scotland two or more persons carry on a trade or business in partnership, any partnership dealings shall be treated as dealings by the partners and not by the firm as such and the partners as being entitled to securities held by the firm.

(11) The nominal value of securities is—
   (*a*) where the interest on them is expressed to be payable by reference to a given value, that value; and
   (*b*) in any other case, the price of the securities when they were issued.

(12) Where apart from this subsection the nominal value of securities would be a value ("the foreign value") expressed in a currency other than sterling, then, for the purposes of

section 715, their nominal value on a particular day is the sterling equivalent on that day of the foreign value.

For the purposes of this subsection the sterling equivalent of a value on a particular day is the sterling equivalent calculated by reference to the London closing rate of exchange for that day.

(13) Where there is a conversion of securities then,—

(a) the person who was entitled to them immediately before the conversion shall be treated as transferring them on the day of the conversion (if there is no actual transfer); and

(b) the interest period in which the conversion is made shall be treated as ending on the day on which it would have ended had the conversion not been made.

In this subsection "conversion" means a conversion within the meaning of section 82 of the 1979 Act.

(14) In relation to an underwriting member of Lloyd's, "business" and "premiums trust fund" have the meanings given by section 457.

Former enactments.—Sub-ss. (1)–(4): FA 1985, Sch. 23, para. 1.
Sub-s. (5): FA 1985, Sch. 23, para. 2(2).
Sub-s. (6): FA 1985, Sch. 23, para. 2(3), (4).
Sub-s. (7): FA 1985, Sch. 23, para. 2(5), (6).
Sub-s. (8): FA 1985, Sch. 23, para. 2(7).
Sub-s. (9): FA 1985, Sch. 23, para. 2(8), (9).
Sub-s. (10): FA 1985, Sch. 23, para. 2(10).
Sub-s. (11): FA 1985, Sch. 23, para. 5.
Sub-s. (12): FA 1985, Sch. 23, para. 10(6), (7).
Sub-s. (13): FA 1985, Sch. 23, para. 14(1), (3), (4).
Sub-s. (14): FA 1985, Sch. 23, para. 21.
Cross references.—See CGTA 1979, s. 33A (computation of gain for capital gains tax purposes where there is a transfer of securities within the meaning of this section);
FA 1989, Sch. 11, para. 17 (provisions which apply to transfer of deep gain securities).

711. Meaning of "interest", "transfers with or without accrued interest" etc.

(1) This section has effect for the interpretation of sections 710 and 712 to 728.

(2) An interest payment day, in relation to securities, is a day on which interest on them is payable; and, in a case where a particular payment of interest may be made on one of a number of days, the interest is for the purposes of this subsection payable on the first of those days.

(3) Subject to subsection (4) below, the following are interest periods in relation to securities—

(a) the period beginning with the day following that on which they are issued and ending with the first interest payment day to fall;

(b) the period beginning with the day following one interest payment day and ending with the next to fall.

(4) A period which would (apart from this subsection) be an interest period exceeding 12 months ("a long period") is not an interest period, but the following shall apply to it—

(a) the period of 12 months beginning with the day on which it begins is an interest period;

(b) each successive period (if any) of 12 months falling within it is an interest period;

(c) any period of it which remains after applying paragraphs (a) and (b) above is an interest period.

(5) Securities are transferred with accrued interest if they are transferred with the right to receive interest payable on—

(a) the settlement day, if that is an interest payment day; or

(b) the next (or first) interest payment day to fall after the settlement day, in any other case;

and they are transferred without accrued interest if they are transferred without that right.

(6) Where section 710(13), 715(3), 720(4), 721(1) or 722(1) or (2) applies, the transfer shall be treated as made with accrued interest if the person treated as making the transfer was entitled to receive in respect of the securities interest payable on—

(a) the settlement day, if that is an interest payment day; or

(b) the next (or first) interest payment day to fall after that day, in any other case;

and they shall be treated as transferred without accrued interest if he was not so entitled.

(7) The interest applicable to securities for an interest period is, subject to subsection (8) below, the interest payable on them on the interest payment day with which the period ends.

(8) In the case of a period which is an interest period by virtue only of subsection (4) above or section 725(9)—

(a) the interest applicable to securities for the period is the interest payable on them on the interest payment day with which the long or straddling period concerned ends; and
(b) section 713(6) shall have effect as if the references to the period were to the long or straddling period concerned.

(9) "Interest" includes dividends and any other return (however described) except a return consisting of an amount by which the amount payable on a security's redemption exceeds its issue price.

Former enactments.—Sub-ss. (1)–(5): FA 1985, Sch. 23, para. 3(1)–(5).
Sub-s. (6): FA 1985, Sch. 23, paras. 7(2), 12(2), 13(3), 14(2), 31(2).
Sub-ss. (7)–(9): FA 1985, Sch. 23, para. 3(6)–(8).
Cross references.—See CGTA 1979, s. 33A (computation of gain for capital gains tax purposes where there is a transfer of securities with or without accrued interest within the meaning of this section).

712. Meaning of "settlement day" for purposes of sections 711 to 728

(1) This section has effect to determine, for the purposes of sections 711 and 713 to 728, the settlement day in relation to a transfer of securities.

(2) Where the securities are transferred in accordance with the rules of a recognised market, the settlement day is the day on which the transferee agrees to settle or, if he may settle on one of a number of days, the day on which he settles; and, where they are transferred otherwise, subsections (3) to (5) below apply.

(3) Where the consideration for the transfer is money alone, and the transferee agrees to pay the whole of it on or before the next (or first) interest payment day to fall after an agreement for transfer is made, the settlement day is the day on which he agrees to make the payment or, if payment may be made on one of a number of days, or on a number of different days, the latest of them to fall.

(4) Where there is no consideration for the transfer, or the transfer is a transfer by virtue of sections 710(13), 715(3), 717(8), 720(4), 721 and 722, the settlement day is the day on which the securities are transferred.

(5) In any other case, the settlement day is such day as an inspector decides; and the jurisdiction of the General Commissioners or the Special Commissioners on any appeal shall include jurisdiction to review such a decision of the inspector.

Former enactments.—FA 1985, Sch. 23, para. 4; FA 1986, Sch. 17, para. 3(2).

Transfers with or without accrued interest: charge to tax and reliefs

713. Deemed sums and reliefs

(1) Subject to sections 714 to 728, this section applies whether the securities in question are transferred before, on or after 6th April 1988; and in this section references to a period are references to the interest period in which the settlement day falls.

(2) If securities are transferred with accrued interest—

(a) the transferor shall be treated as entitled to a sum on them in the period of an amount equal to the accrued amount; and
(b) the transferee shall be treated as entitled to relief on them in the period of the same amount.

(3) If securities are transferred without accrued interest—

(a) the transferor shall be treated as entitled to relief on them in the period of an amount equal to the rebate amount; and
(b) the transferee shall be treated as entitled to a sum on them in the period of the same amount.

(4) In subsection (2) above "the accrued amount" means—

(a) if the securities are transferred under an arrangement by virtue of which the transferee accounts to the transferor separately for the consideration for the securities and for gross interest accruing to the settlement day, an amount equal to the amount (if any) of gross interest so accounted for; and

(b) in any other case, an amount equal to the accrued proportion of the interest applicable to the securities for the period.

(5) In subsection (3) above "the rebate amount" means—

(a) if the securities are transferred under an arrangement by virtue of which the transferor accounts to the transferee for gross interest accruing from the settlement day to the next interest payment day, an amount equal to the amount (if any) of gross interest so accounted for; and

(b) in any other case, an amount equal to the rebate proportion of the interest applicable to the securities for the period.

(6) In this section—

(a) the accrued proportion is—

$$\frac{A}{B}$$

(b) the rebate proportion is—

$$\frac{B-A}{B}$$

where—

A is the number of days in the period up to (and including) the settlement day, and
B is the number of days in the period.

(7) For the purposes of subsection (2) above, in a case where the interest on the securities is payable in a currency other than sterling the accrued amount is to be determined as follows—

(a) if subsection (4)(a) above applies and the sterling equivalent of the amount of gross interest there mentioned is shown in an agreement for transfer, the accrued amount is the sterling equivalent so shown;

(b) if subsection (4)(a) applies but paragraph (a) above does not, or if subsection (4)(b) above applies, the accrued amount is the sterling equivalent on the settlement day of the amount found by virtue of subsection (4)(a) or (b) (as the case may be).

(8) For the purposes of subsection (3) above, in a case where the interest on the securities is payable in a currency other than sterling the rebate amount is to be determined as follows—

(a) if subsection (5)(a) above applies and the sterling equivalent of the amount of gross interest there mentioned is shown in an agreement for transfer, the rebate amount is the sterling equivalent so shown;

(b) if subsection (5)(a) applies but paragraph (a) above does not, or if subsection (5)(b) above applies, the rebate amount is the sterling equivalent on the settlement day of the amount found by virtue of subsection (5)(a) or (b) (as the case may be).

(9) For the purposes of subsections (7) and (8) above the sterling equivalent of an amount on a particular day is the sterling equivalent calculated by reference to the London closing rate of exchange for that day.

Former enactments.—Sub-ss. (1)–(6): FA 1985, s. 73.
Sub-ss. (7), (8): FA 1985, Sch. 23, para. 10(1)–(3).
Sub-s. (9): FA 1985, sch. 23, para. 10(7).
Cross references.—See CGTA 1979, s. 33A (computation of gain for capital gains tax purposes where there is a transfer of securities and provisions of this section apply).

714. Treatment of deemed sums and reliefs

(1) Subsection (2) below applies if a person is treated as entitled under section 713 to a sum on securities of a particular kind in an interest period, and either—

(a) he is not treated as entitled under that section to relief on securities of that kind in the period; or

(b) the sum (or total sum) to which he is treated as entitled exceeds the amount (or total amount) of relief to which he is treated as entitled under that section on securities of that kind in the period.

(2) The person shall be treated as receiving on the day the period ends annual profits or gains whose amount is (depending on whether subsection (1)(a) or (1)(b) above applies) equal to the sum (or total sum) to which he is treated as entitled or equal to the amount of

the excess; and the profits or gains shall be chargeable to tax under Case VI of Schedule D for the chargeable period in which they are treated as received.

(3) Subsection (4) below applies if a person is treated as entitled under section 713 to relief on securities of a particular kind in an interest period, and either—

(a) he is not treated as entitled under that section to a sum on securities of that kind in the period; or
(b) the amount (or total amount) of relief to which he is treated as entitled exceeds the sum (or total sum) to which he is treated as entitled under that section on securities of that kind in the period.

(4) The person shall be entitled to an allowance whose amount is (depending on whether subsection (3)(a) or (3)(b) above applies) equal to the amount (or total amount) of relief to which he is treated as entitled or equal to the amount of the excess; and subsection (5) below shall apply.

(5) Any amount to which the person is entitled by way of interest which—

(a) falls due on the securities at the end of the interest period, and
(b) is taken into account in computing tax charged for the chargeable period in which the interest period ends,

shall for the purposes of the Tax Acts be treated as reduced by the amount of the allowance; but if the period is one which does not end with an interest payment day, he shall be treated as becoming, in the next interest period, entitled under section 713 to relief on the securities of an amount equal to the amount of the allowance.

(6) Where, but for this subsection, a company would by virtue of subsection (2) above be treated as receiving profits or gains on a day which does not fall within an accounting period of the company, the profits or gains shall instead be treated as received by the company on the latest day of the interest period which does so fall.

Former enactment.—FA 1985, s. 74.

715. Exceptions from sections 713 and 714

(1) Section 713(2)(a) or (3)(a) (as the case may be) does not apply—

(a) if the transferor carries on a trade and the transfer falls to be taken into account for the purposes of the Tax Acts in computing the profits or losses of that trade;
(b) if the transferor is an individual and on no day in the year of assessment in which the interest period ends or the previous year of assessment the nominal value of securities held by him exceeded £5,000;
(c) if the securities transferred form part of the estate of a deceased person, the transferor is that person's personal representative and on no day in the year of assessment in which the interest period ends or the previous year of assessment the nominal value of securities held by him as the deceased's personal representative exceeded £5,000;
(d) where—

(i) if the transferor became entitled to any interest on the securities transferred and applied it for charitable purposes only, exemption could be granted under section 505(1)(c) in respect of the interest;
(ii) if the transferor became entitled to any interest on the securities transferred and applied it for the purposes mentioned in paragraph (d) of section 505(1), exemption could be granted under that paragraph in respect of the interest;

(e) if the securities transferred are held on a disabled person's trusts, the transferor is trustee of the settlement and on no day in the year of assessment in which the interest period ends or the previous year of assessment the nominal value of securities held by him as trustee of the settlement exceeded £5,000;
(f) if the transferor does not fulfil the residence requirement for the chargeable period in which the transfer is made and is not a non-resident United Kingdom trader in that period;
(g) if the transferor is not ordinarily resident in the United Kingdom during the chargeable period in which the transfer occurs and, if he became entitled in the period to any interest on the securities transferred, it would not be liable to income tax by virtue of section 47;
(h) if the securities transferred are FOTRA securities, the transferor is not domiciled in the United Kingdom at any time in the chargeable period in which the transfer occurs,

and he is either not ordinarily resident in the United Kingdom during that period or a non-resident United Kingdom trader in that period;

(*j*) if the transferor is an individual who, if he became entitled in the year of assessment in which the transfer occurs to any interest on the securities transferred, would be liable, in respect of the interest, to tax chargeable under Case IV or V of Schedule D and computed on the amount of sums received in the United Kingdom; or

(*k*) where, if the transferor became entitled to any interest on the securities transferred, exemption could be allowed under section 592(2) in respect of the interest.

(2) Section 713(2)(*b*) or (3)(*b*) (as the case may be) does not apply if—

(*a*) the transferee carries on a trade, and if at the time he acquired the securities he were to transfer them that transfer would fall to be taken into account for the purposes of the Tax Acts in computing the profits or losses of that trade; or

(*b*) any provision of subsection (1) above except paragraph (*a*) would apply if "transferor" read "transferee".

(3) If securities held on charitable trusts cease to be subject to charitable trusts the trustees shall be treated for the purposes of sections 710 to 728 as transferring the securities (in their capacity as charitable trustees) to themselves (in another capacity) at the time when the securities cease to be so subject.

(4) For the purposes of this section a person fulfils the residence requirement for a chargeable period if he is resident in the United Kingdom during any part of the period or is ordinarily resident in the United Kingdom during the period.

(5) For the purposes of this section a person is a non-resident United Kingdom trader in a chargeable period if during any part of it he is (though neither resident during any part of it nor ordinarily resident during it) carrying on a trade in the United Kingdom through a branch or agency and the securities transferred—

(*a*) were situated in the United Kingdom and used or held for the purposes of the branch or agency at or before the time of the transfer (where the person concerned is a transferor); or

(*b*) were so situated at the time of the transfer and were acquired for use by or for the purposes of the branch or agency (where the person concerned is a transferee);

but the provisions of this subsection relating to the situation of the securities in the United Kingdom do not apply where the person concerned is a company.

(6) In any case where securities are transferred without accrued interest to a person ("the seller") and a contract is made for the sale by the seller of securities of that kind ("the seller's contract") and the seller's contract or any contract under which the securities are transferred to the seller is one in the case of which section 737 has effect and in relation to which the seller is the dividend manufacturer, then—

(*a*) where the nominal value of the securities subject to the seller's contract is greater than or equal to that of the securities transferred, the seller shall not be treated as entitled to any sum to which, but for this subsection, he would be treated as entitled under section 713(3)(*b*) on the securities transferred;

(*b*) where the nominal value of the securities subject to the seller's contract is less than that of the securities transferred, any sum (or the aggregate of any sums) to which he is treated as entitled under section 713(3)(*b*) on the securities transferred shall be reduced by the amount of any part of the sum (or aggregate) attributable to securities ("relevant securities") of a nominal value equal to that of the securities subject to the seller's contract;

and for the purposes of sections 710 to 728 the securities which the seller contracts to sell shall not be treated as transferred by him (though treated as transferred to the person to whom he contracts to sell).

(7) In determining for the purposes of subsection (6)(*b*) above which of the securities transferred are relevant securities, those transferred to the seller earlier must be chosen before those transferred to him later.

(8) For the purposes of this section—

"disabled person's trusts" means trusts falling within paragraph 5(1) of Schedule 1 to the 1979 Act;

"branch or agency" has the meaning given by section 12(3) of the 1979 Act;

"FOTRA securities" means securities issued with the condition mentioned in section 22(1) of the Finance (No. 2) Act 1931 (securities free of tax for residents abroad) as modified by virtue of section 60(1) of the Finance Act 1940;

Former enactments.—Sub-s. (1)(*a*)–(*c*): FA 1985, s. 75(1)(*a*)–(*c*).
Sub-s. (1)(*d*): FA 1985, Sch. 23, para. 30(1), (4).
Sub-s. (1)(*e*)–(*j*): FA 1985, s. 75(1)(*d*)–(*h*).
Sub-s. (1)(*k*): FA 1985, Sch. 23, para. 32(1).
Sub-s. (2): FA 1985, s. 75(2), Sch. 23, paras. 30(2), (5), 32(2).
Sub-s. (3): FA 1985, Sch. 23, para. 31(1).
Sub-ss. (4), (5): FA 1985, s. 75(3), (4).
Sub-ss. (6), (7): FA 1985, Sch. 23, para. 43; FA 1986, Sch. 17, para. 5.
Sub-s. (8): FA 1985, s. 75(5), (6).

716. Transfer of unrealised interest

(1) This section applies where securities are transferred (whether before or after 6th April 1988) with the right to receive interest ("unrealised interest") payable on them on an interest payment day falling before the settlement day.

(2) Where the settlement day falls within an interest period, section 714 shall (subject to subsection (5) below) apply as if the transferor were entitled under section 713 to a sum on them in the period of an amount equal to the unrealised interest (in addition to any other sum to which he may be treated as so entitled).

(3) Where the settlement day falls after the end of the last interest period in relation to the securities, the transferor shall be treated as receiving on the settlement day annual profits or gains of an amount equal to the unrealised interest; and the profits or gains shall be chargeable to tax under Case VI of Schedule D for the chargeable period in which they are treated as received.

(4) Where the transferee receives the unrealised interest, and but for this subsection it would be taken into account in computing tax charged for the chargeable period in which the interest is received, it shall for the purposes of the Tax Acts be left out of account.

(5) Section 715 shall apply for the purposes of this section as if—

  (*a*) in subsection (1)—

    (i) the reference to section 713(2)(*a*) or (3)(*a*) were a reference to subsection (2) or (3) above; and
    (ii) references to the year of assessment in which the interest period ends were references to the year in which the settlement day falls; and

  (*b*) in subsection (2) the reference to section 713(2)(*b*) or (3)(*b*) were a reference to subsection (4) above.

Paragraph (*b*) above does not apply where the securities in question were transferred before 19th March 1986.

(6) Where the unrealised interest is payable in a currency other than sterling its amount is for the purposes of this section the sterling equivalent on the settlement day of the amount it would be apart from this subsection; and for this purpose the sterling equivalent is to be calculated by reference to the London closing rate of exchange for the day.

Former enactments.—Sub-ss. (1)–(4): FA 1985, Sch. 23, para. 15(1)–(4).
Sub-s. (5): FA 1985, Sch. 23, para. 15(5); FA 1986, Sch. 17, para. 2(2).
Sub-s. (6): FA 1985, Sch. 23, para. 15(8).
Construction.—CGTA 1979, s. 33A(5)(*a*) to be construed as one with this section; see CGTA 1979, s. 33A(5).
Cross references.—See CGTA 1979, s. 33A (computation of gain for capital gains tax purposes where there is a transfer of securities and provisions of this section apply).

717. Variable interest rate

(1) This section applies to securities other than securities falling within subsection (2) or (4) below.

(2) Securities fall within this subsection if their terms of issue provide that throughout the period from issue to redemption (whenever redemption might occur) they are to carry interest at a rate which falls into one, and one only, of the following categories—

  (*a*) a fixed rate which is the same throughout the period;
  (*b*) a rate which bears to a standard published base rate the same fixed relationship throughout the period;

(c) a rate which bears to a published index of prices the same fixed relationship throughout the period.

(3) In subsection (2)(c) above "published index of prices" means the retail prices index or any similar general index of prices which is published by, or by an agent of, the government of any territory outside the United Kingdom.

(4) Securities fall within this subsection if they are deep discount securities and the rate of interest for each (or their only) interest period is equal to or less than the yield to maturity.

(5) In subsection (4) above "deep discount securities" and "yield to maturity" have the same meanings as in Schedule 4; and for the purposes of that subsection the rate of interest for an interest period is, in relation to securities, the rate of return (expressed as a percentage) attributable to the interest applicable to them for the interest period.

(6) Subsections (7) to (11) below apply if securities to which this section applies are transferred at any time between the time they are issued and the time they are redeemed.

(7) If the securities are transferred without accrued interest they shall be treated for the purposes of sections 710 to 728 as transferred with accrued interest.

(8) The person entitled to the securities immediately before they are redeemed shall be treated for the purposes of those sections as transferring them with accrued interest on the day they are redeemed.

(9) Where there is a transfer as mentioned in subsection (6) above or by virtue of subsection (8) above, section 713 shall have effect with the omission of subsection (2)(b) and with the substitution for subsections (3) to (6) of the following subsection—

"(3) In subsection (2) above "the accrued amount" means such amount (if any) as an inspector decides is just and reasonable; and the jurisdiction of the General Commissioners or the Special Commissioners on any appeal shall include jurisdiction to review such a decision of the inspector.".

(10) Subsection (11) below applies where there is a transfer by virtue of subsection (8) above and the settlement day in relation to the transfer falls after the end of a period which would (by virtue of section 711(3) and (4) and apart from this subsection) be the only or last interest period in relation to the securities.

(11) For the purposes of sections 710 to 728 the period beginning with the day following that interest period and ending with the settlement day shall be treated as an interest period in relation to the securities; and section 711(4) shall not apply to it.

Former enactments.—FA 1985, Sch. 23, paras. 15A, 15B, 15C; FA 1986, Sch. 17, para. 3.

718. Interest in default

(1) This section applies where, because of any failure to fulfil the obligation to pay interest on securities, the value (on a day mentioned in section 711(7) or (8)(a), as the case may be) of the right to receive the interest payable on them on that day is less than the interest so payable.

(2) Section 711(7) or (8)(a), as the case may be, shall be construed as if the reference to that interest were to an amount equal to that value.

Former enactments.—FA 1985, Sch. 23, paras. 15A, 15B, 15C; FA 1986, Sch. 17, para. 3.

719. Unrealised interest in default

(1) Where securities are transferred as mentioned in section 716(1) and, because of any failure to fulfil the obligation to pay interest on them, the value (on the day of the transfer) of the right to receive the unrealised interest is less than the amount of the unrealised interest, section 716 shall have effect as modified by subsections (2) to (4) below.

(2) In subsections (2) and (3) for "the unrealised interest" there shall be substituted "amount A".

(3) For subsection (4) there shall be substituted—

"(4) Where the transferee receives an amount by way of the unrealised interest (amount B) and that amount falls to be taken into account in computing tax charged for the chargeable period in which it is received, it shall for the purposes of the Tax Acts be treated as reduced by an amount (amount C) equal to—

(a) nil, if the amounts have been previously received by the transferee by way of the unrealised interest and their aggregate is equal to or greater than the value (on the day of the transfer to the transferee) of the right to receive the unrealised interest;
(b) amount B, if that value is equal to or greater than amount B (aggregated with other amounts previously so received, if any);
(c) that value, if no amount has been previously so received and that value is less than amount B; or
(d) so much of that value as exceeds the aggregate of amounts previously so received, in any other case.".

(4) The following shall be substituted for subsection (6)—

"(6) In this section "amount A" means, in a case where the transferor acquired the securities on or after 28th February 1986 with the right to receive unrealised interest—

(a) an amount equal to amount D less amount E; or
(b) if amount D is equal to or less than amount E, nil.

(7) In this section "amount A" means, in a case not falling within subsection (6) above, an amount equal to amount D.

(8) In this section "amount D" means an amount equal to the value (on the day of the transfer by the tranferor) of the right to receive the unrealised interest.

(9) In this section "amount E" means, in a case where the transferor (as transferee) has received in respect of the securities an amount or amounts falling within subsection (4) above—

(a) an amount equal to amount F less the total received; or
(b) if amount F is equal to or less than the total received, nil.

(10) In this section "amount E" means, in any other case, an amount equal to amount F.

(11) In this section "amount F" means an amount equal to the value (on the day of the transfer to the transferor) of the right to receive the unrealised interest.

(12) In determining for the purposes of this section which securities of a particular kind a person has transferred, he is to be taken to have transferred securities of that kind which he acquired later before securities of that kind which he acquired earlier.

(13) Where the unrealised interest is payable in a currency other than sterling—

(a) any amount received by way of the interest is for the purposes of this section the sterling equivalent on the day it is received of the amount it would be apart from this subsection; and
(b) the value (on the day of a transfer) of the right to receive the interest is for the purposes of this section the sterling equivalent (on that day) of the value it would be apart from this subsection;

and for this purpose the sterling equivalent is to be calculated by reference to the London closing rate of exchange for the day concerned."

Former enactments.—FA 1985, Sch. 23, paras. 15A, 15B, 15C; FA 1986, Sch. 17, para. 3.
Construction.—CGTA 1979, s. 33A(5)(*b*) to be construed as one with this section; see CGTA 1979, s. 33A(5).

Transfers with or without accrued interest: supplemental

720. Nominees, trustees etc.

(1) Where securities are transferred by or to a person as nominee for another person, or as trustee for another person absolutely entitled as against the trustee, or for any person who would be so entitled but for being an infant or other person under disability, or for two or more persons who are or would be jointly so entitled, sections 713, 715 and 716 shall apply as if references to the transferor or the transferee (as the case may be) were to the person or persons for whom the nominee or trustee disposes or acquires.

(2) It is hereby declared that for the purposes of subsection (1) above—

(a) securities are transferred by a person as trustee for another person absolutely entitled as against the trustee if that other person has immediately before the transfer the exclusive right to direct how the securities shall be dealt with, subject only to satisfying any outstanding charge, lien or other right of the trustee to resort to the securities for payment of duty, taxes, costs or other outgoings; and

(b) securities are transferred to a person as trustee for another person so entitled if that other person has that right immediately after the transfer.

(3) An underwriting member of Lloyd's shall be treated for the purposes of sections 710 to 728 as absolutely entitled as against the trustees to the securities forming part of his premiums trust fund, his special reserve fund (if any) and any other trust fund required or authorised by the rules of Lloyd's or required by the underwriting agent through whom his business or any part of it is carried on, to be kept in connection with the business.

(4) Where a person who is entitled to securities becomes trustee of them, he shall be treated for the purposes of sections 710 to 728 as transferring them (in a capacity other than trustee) to himself (in his capacity as trustee), or to himself and any other trustees, at the time he becomes trustee.

(5) Annual profits or gains which by virtue of 714(2) or 716(3) are treated as received in a year of assessment by trustees shall be chargeable to income tax at a rate equal to the sum of the basic rate and the additional rate for that year.

This subsection does not apply where the profits or gains are treated as received by the investment manager of a common investment fund for the time being designated as mentioned in section 328(1).

(6) In any case where—

(a) a trustee of a settlement is treated as receiving annual profits or gains under section 714(2), or

(b) a trustee of a settlement who is resident or domiciled outside the United Kingdom throughout any chargeable period in which an interest period (or part of it) falls would, at the end of the interest period, have been treated under section 714(2) as receiving annual profits or gains or annual profits or gains of a greater amount if he had been resident or domiciled in the United Kingdom during a part of each such chargeable period,

Chapters II to IV of Part XV shall have effect as if the amount which the trustee is or would be treated as receiving were income (within Chapter II) or income arising under the settlement (within Chapter III or IV).

(7) In any case where income of a trustee of a settlement who is resident or domiciled outside the United Kingdom throughout any chargeable period in which an interest period (or part of it) falls consists of interest which—

(a) falls due at the end of the interest period; and

(b) would have been treated under section 714(5) as reduced by an allowance or an allowance of a greater amount if he had been resident or domiciled in the United Kingdom during a part of each such chargeable period;

then, for the purposes of Chapters II to IV of Part XV, the interest shall be treated as being reduced by the amount of the allowance or by the additional amount (as the case may be).

(8) In subsections (6) and (7) above—

(a) "settlement" means settlement within the meaning of Chapter II, III or IV of Part XV (as the case may be); and

(b) references to a trustee of a settlement are, where there is no trustee of the settlement, to any person entitled to securities comprised in the settlement.

Former enactments.—Sub-s. (1): FA 1985, Sch. 23, paras. 6(1), 15(6).
Sub-s. (2): FA 1985, Sch. 23, para. 6(2).
Sub-s. (3): FA 1985, Sch. 23, para. 22.
Sub-s. (4): FA 1985, Sch. 23, para. 7(1).
Sub-s. (5): FA 1985, Sch. 23, para. 8(1), (2), (4); FA 1986, Sch. 17, para. 1(1).
Sub-s. (6): FA 1985, Sch. 23, para. 9(1), (2).
Sub-s. (7): FA 1985, Sch. 23, para. 9(3), (4).
Sub-s. (8): FA 1985, Sch. 23, para. 9(5).

721. Death

(1) Where an individual who is entitled to securities dies, he shall be treated for the purposes of sections 710 to 728 as transferring the securities to his personal representatives immediately before his death.

(2) Where the securities are transferred with accrued interest by the personal representatives to a legatee in the interest period in which the individual died—

(*a*) section 713 shall not apply to the transfer, and
(*b*) the transfer of the securities which the individual is treated as making by virtue of subsection (1) above shall be treated as made to the legatee (and not to the personal representatives).

(3) In subsection (2) above "legatee" includes any person taking (whether beneficially or as trustee) under a testamentary disposition or on an intestacy or partial intestacy, including any person taking by virtue of an appropriation by the personal representatives in or towards satisfaction of a legacy or other interest or share in the deceased's property.

(4) In the case of an individual who dies in an interest period, section 714(2) shall have effect as if the reference to the day the period ends were to the day he dies.

(5) Subsections (1) to (4) above do not apply where the individual concerned is an underwriting member of Lloyd's and the securities concerned form part of a premiums trust fund, a special reserve fund or any other trust fund required or authorised by the rules of Lloyd's or required by the underwriting agent through whom the individual's business or any part of it is carried on, to be kept in connection with the business.

(6) In a case where subsection (5) above applies the deceased's personal representatives shall be treated for the purposes of sections 710 to 728 as the transferor or transferee in relation to transfers of securities as to which the deceased was the transferor or transferee (as the case may be) in the interest period in which he died.

Former enactments.—Sub-ss. (1)–(4): FA 1985, Sch. 23, para. 12(1), (3)–(5).
Sub-ss. (5), (6): FA 1985, Sch. 23, para. 27.

722. Trading stock

(1) Where securities acquired by a person otherwise than as trading stock of a trade carried on by him are appropriated by him for the purposes of the trade as trading stock (whether on the commencement of the trade or otherwise), he shall be treated for the purposes of sections 710 to 728 as transferring them otherwise than in the course of the trade and re-acquiring them in the course of the trade on the day the appropriation is made.

(2) Where securities forming part of the trading stock of a person's trade are appropriated by him for any other purpose, or are retained by him on his ceasing to carry on the trade, he shall be treated for the purposes of sections 710 to 728 as transferring them in the course of the trade and re-acquiring them otherwise than in the course of the trade on the day the appropriation is made or (as the case may be) he ceases to carry on the trade.

Former enactment.—FA 1985, Sch. 23, para. 13(1), (2).

723. Foreign securities: delayed remittances

(1) This section applies where in an interest period a person is treated as entitled to a sum or sums under section 713(2)(*a*) in respect of a transfer or transfers of securities of a particular kind which are situated outside the United Kingdom.

(2) Subject to subsection (3) below, the amount of any annual profits or gains which the person is treated under section 714 as receiving on the day the period ends in respect of securities of that kind shall be reduced—

(*a*) if the amount of the sum or aggregate of the sums exceeds the amount of the profits or gains, to nil; or
(*b*) in any other case, by the amount of the sum or aggregate.

(3) No reduction shall be made unless the person makes a claim and shows that the conditions in subsection (5) below are, so far as applicable, satisfied in the chargeable period in which the profits or gains are treated as received.

(4) The claimant (or his personal representatives) shall be charged to tax under Case VI of Schedule D on the amount of the reduction for the chargeable period in which the conditions in subsection (5) below cease to be satisfied.

(5) The conditions are—

(*a*) that the claimant was unable to remit the proceeds of the transfer or transfers to the United Kingdom;
(*b*) that the inability was due to the laws of the territory in which the securities are

situated, or to the executive action of its government, or to the impossibility of obtaining foreign currency in that territory; and

(c) that the inability was not due to any want of reasonable endeavours on the part of the claimant.

(6) No claim under this section shall be made in respect of a transfer more than six years after the end of the interest period in which the transfer occurred.

(7) The personal representatives of a deceased person may make any claim which he might have made under this section if he had not died.

(8) For the purposes of this section the place where securities are situated shall be determined in accordance with section 18(4) of the 1979 Act.

Former enactment.—FA 1985, Sch. 23, para. 11.

724. Insurance companies

(1) The references in section 715(1)(a) and (2)(a) to computing the profits or losses of a trade shall not be taken as applying to a computation of income for the purposes of section 76(2).

(2) Where an insurance company carrying on life assurance business is treated as receiving annual profits or gains under section 714(2) or 716(3) in respect of securities held as investments in connection with that business, the profits or gains shall be treated for the purposes of section 434(3) to (5) as if they were income from investments held in connection with that business.

(3) Section 713(2)(a) or (3)(a) (as the case may be) shall not apply if the transferor is an insurance company and—

(a) the transfer falls to be taken into account in computing its profits or losses for the purposes of section 436; or
(b) if the company became entitled to any interest on the securities transferred, it would by virtue of section 441(1) be liable, in respect of the interest, to tax computed by reference to the amount of income received in the United Kingdom; or
(c) if the company became entitled to any interest on the securities transferred and applied the interest for the purposes of its foreign life assurance fund, it would by virtue of section 441(2) not be liable to tax in respect of the interest.

(4) Section 713(2)(b) or (3)(b) (as the case may be) shall not apply if subsection (3) above would apply if in that subsection "transferor" read "transferee".

(5) Where an overseas life insurance company (within the meaning of section 431) is entitled to an allowance under section 714(4), section 714(5) and (6) shall not apply but subsections (6) and (7) below shall apply.

(6) If the company is treated under section 714(2) as receiving annual profits or gains in an accounting period, the profits or gains shall be treated as reduced by any amount ("the deductible amount") equal to the allowance or aggregate of the allowances, as the case may be, to which the company is entitled under section 714(4) in relation to an interest period or periods ending in the accounting period.

(7) Where the deductible amount exceeds the amount of those annual profits or gains, the company may claim to have the excess treated as reducing any annual profits or gains the company is treated as receiving under section 714(2) in the company's next accounting period or, if there is still an excess, the one after (and so on for future accounting periods).

(8) Subsections (5) to (7) above do not apply to an overseas life insurance company if, by virtue of arrangements specified in an Order in Council under section 788, no charge to corporation tax under Case III of Schedule D arises under section 445 in respect of any income of the company.

Former enactments.—Sub-ss. (1), (2): FA 1985, Sch. 23, paras. 16, 17.
Sub-s. (3): FA 1985, Sch. 23, paras. 18(1), 19(1), (4).
Sub-s. (4): FA 1985, Sch. 23, paras. 18(2), 19(2), (5).
Sub-ss. (5)–(8): FA 1985, Sch. 23, para. 20(2)–(6).

725. Lloyd's underwriters

(1) The securities forming part of a premiums trust fund at the beginning of 1st January of any year shall be treated for the purposes of sections 710 to 728 as transferred on that day to

the trustees of the fund, and in relation to such a transfer, the settlement day is the day preceding that of the transfer (notwithstanding section 712).

(2) The securities shall be treated as transferred with accrued interest if the trustees are entitled to receive in respect of them interest payable on—
   (*a*) the day of the transfer, if that is an interest payment day, or
   (*b*) the next (or first) interest payment day to fall after that day, in any other case;
and they shall be treated as transferred without accrued interest if they are not so entitled.

(3) Subsections (1) and (2) above do not apply as regards securities if the day preceding 1st January concerned is an interest payment day in relation to them.

(4) The securities forming part of a premiums trust fund at the end of 31st December of any year shall be treated for the purposes of sections 710 to 728 as transferred on that day by the trustees of the fund, and in relation to such a transfer, the settlement day is the day of the transfer (notwithstanding section 712).

(5) The securities shall be treated as transferred with accrued interest if the trustees are entitled to receive in respect of them interest payable on the next (or first) interest payment day to fall after the day of the transfer, and they shall be treated as transferred without accrued interest if they are not so entitled.

(6) Subsections (4) and (5) above do not apply as regards securities if 31st December concerned is an interest payment day in relation to them.

(7) Where securities are transferred by or to the trustees of a premiums trust fund, subsections (8) and (9) below shall have effect in relation to the trustees, though not in relation to the transferee or transferor (unless in turn constituting trustees of such a fund).

(8) In subsection (9) below "straddling period" means a period which would (by virtue of section 711(3) and (4) and apart from subsection (9)) be in relation to the securities an interest period beginning on or before and ending after 31st December of any year.

(9) For the purposes of sections 710 to 728 a straddling period is not an interest period, but—
   (*a*) the period beginning with the day on which the straddling period begins and ending with 31st December concerned is an interest period; and
   (*b*) the period beginning with the day following 31st December concerned and ending with the day with which the straddling period ends is an interest period.

[(10) Subsection (11) below applies where the following state of affairs exists at the beginning of 1st January of any year or the end of 31st December of any year—
   (*a*) securities have been transferred by the trustees of a premiums trust fund in pursuance of an arrangement mentioned in section 129(1) or (2),
   (*b*) the transfer was made to enable another person to fulfil a contract or to make a transfer,
   (*c*) securities have not been transferred in return, and
   (*d*) section 129(3) applies to the transfer made by the trustees.][1]

[(11) The securities transferred by the trustees shall be treated for the purposes of subsections (1) to (6) above as if they formed part of the premiums trust fund at the beginning of 1st January concerned or the end of 31st December concerned (as the case may be).][1]

Former enactments.—Sub-s. (1): FA 1985, Sch. 23, para. 24(1), (2).
Sub-ss. (2), (3): FA 1985, Sch. 23, para. 24(3), (4).
Sub-ss. (4)–(6): FA 1985, Sch. 23, para. 25.
Sub-ss. (7)–(9): FA 1985, Sch. 23, para. 26.
Amendments.—[1] Sub-ss. (10), (11) inserted by FA 1989, s. 91(1), (3) where the transfer by trustees of a premiums trust fund is made after the date specified in TA 1988, s. 129(6).

726. Building societies

(1) Subsections (2) to (5) below apply where securities are transferred and the interest which falls due on them either before the settlement day or at the end of the interest period in which the settlement day falls is subject to the provisions of regulations under section 476(1) but would not on being paid (to whatever person) be a gross payment within the meaning of those regulations ("a gross payment").

(2) Section 713(4) shall be construed as if the following were substituted for paragraphs (*a*) and (*b*)—

   "(*a*) if the securities are transferred under an arrangement by virtue of which the transferee accounts to the transferor separately for the consideration for the securities and for an amount equal to the grossed up equivalent of the interest (if any) accruing to the settlement day, an amount equal to that amount; and

(b) in any other case, an amount equal to the accrued proportion of the grossed up equivalent of the interest applicable to the securities for the period.".

(3) Section 713(5) shall be construed as if the following were substituted for paragraphs (a) and (b)—

"(a) if the securities are transferred under an arrangement by virtue of which the transferor accounts to the transferee for an amount equal to the grossed up equivalent of the interest (if any) accruing from the settlement day to the next interest payment day, an amount equal to that amount; and

(b) in any other case, an amount equal to the rebate proportion of the grossed up equivalent of the interest applicable to the securities for the period.".

(4) Section 716 shall be construed as if in subsections (2) and (3) "the unrealised interest" read "the grossed up equivalent of the unrealised interest".

(5) In calculating the grossed up equivalent of interest for the purposes of sections 713(4)(b) and (5)(b) and 716(2) and (3) of this Act (as substituted or amended as mentioned in this section) and section 33A(5)(c) of the 1979 Act, the interest shall be treated as if it would, on being paid, not be a gross payment.

(6) For the purposes of the provisions mentioned in subsection (5) above, the grossed up equivalent of interest is to be calculated by adding to the interest a sum found by applying the formula—

$$\frac{S}{I+S} = R$$

where—

S is the sum to be found;
I is the interest; and
R is the basic rate of income tax (expressed as a fraction) for the year of assessment in which the interest is payable.

(7) Where a sum is both interest mentioned in section 714(5), 720(7) or 742(6) and dividends or interest in the case of which section 476(3)(b) or (5)(c) applies—

(a) in calculating the deduction of income tax as mentioned in section 476(3)(b) or (5)(c) any reduction mentioned in section 714(5), 720(7) or 742(6) shall be disergarded; and
(b) the amount which is treated as reduced as mentioned in section 714(5), 720(7) or 742(6) shall be the amount the person concerned is treated as receiving by virtue of section 476(3)(b) or (5)(c) (rather than the interest which falls due).

Former enactments.—Sub-ss. (1)–(6): FA 1985, Sch. 23, para. 32A; FA 1986, Sch. 17, para. 4.
Sub-s. (7): FA 1985, Sch. 23, para. 32B; FA 1986, Sch. 17, para. 4.
Construction.—CGTA 1979, s. 33A(5)(c) to be construed as one with this section; see CGTA 1979, s. 33A(5).

727. Stock lending

(1) The effect of section 129(3) shall be disregarded in construing section 715(1)(a) and (2)(a).

(2) Where securities are transferred in circumstances such that by virtue of section 149B(9) of the 1979 Act (capital gains tax exemption) any disposal and acquisition are disregarded for the purposes of capital gains tax, sections 713(2) and (3) and 716 shall not apply.

Former enactments.—FA 1985, Sch. 23, para. 32C; FA 1986, Sch. 17, para. 4.

728. Information

(1) In order to obtain for the purposes of sections 710 to 727 particulars relating to securities, an inspector may by notice require a return under subsection (2) or (3) below.

(2) A member of the Stock Exchange, other than a market maker, may be required to make a return giving, in relation to any transactions effected by him in the course of his business in the period specified in the notice, such particulars as may be so specified.

In relation to transactions before 27th October 1986 this subsection shall have effect with the substitution of "jobber" for "market maker".

(3) A person (other than a member of the Stock Exchange), who acts as an agent or broker in the United Kingdom in transactions in securities, may be required to make a return giving, in relation to any such transactions effected by him in the period specified in the notice, such particulars as may be so specified.

(4) No person shall be required under subsection (2) or (3) above to include in a return particulars of any transaction effected more than three years before the service of the notice requiring him to make the return.

(5) In order to obtain for the purposes of sections 710 to 727 particulars relating to securities, the Board or an inspector may by notice require any person in whose name any securities are registered to state whether or not he is the beneficial owner of those securities and, if he is not the beneficial owner of them or any of them, to furnish the name and address of the person or persons on whose behalf the securities are registered in his name.

(6) In this section "market maker", in relation to securities, means a person who—

(*a*) holds himself out at all normal times in compliance with the rules of the Stock Exchange as willing to buy and sell securities of the kind concerned at a price specified by him; and
(*b*) is recognised as doing so by the Council of the Stock Exchange.

(7) The Board may by regulations provide that—

(*a*) subsections (2), (3) and (6)(*a*) above shall have effect as if references to the Stock Exchange were to any recognised investment exchange (within the meaning of the Financial Services Act 1986) or to any of those exchanges specified in the regulations; and
(*b*) subsection (6)(*b*) shall have effect as if the reference to the Council of the Stock Exchange were to the investment exchange concerned.

(8) Regulations under subsection (7) above shall apply in relation to transactions effected on or after such day as may be specified in the regulations.

Former enactments.—FA 1985, Sch. 23, para. 44(1)–(5A); FA 1986, Sch. 17, para. 18(6).

Other transfers of securities

729. Sale and repurchase of securities

(1) Where the owner of any securities ("the owner") agrees to sell or transfer those securities and by the same or any collateral agreement—

(*a*) agrees to buy back or re-acquire the securities, or
(*b*) acquires an option, which he subsequently exercises, to buy back or re-acquire the securities,

then, if the result of the transaction is that any interest becoming payable in respect of the securities is receivable otherwise than by the owner, the following provisions shall have effect—

(i) the interest so payable shall, whether it would or would not have been chargeable to tax apart from the provisions of this section, be deemed for all the purposes of the Tax Acts to be the income of the owner and not to be the income of any other person; and
(ii) if the securities are of such a character that the interest payable in respect thereof may be paid without deduction of tax, the owner shall be chargeable to tax under Case VI of Schedule D in respect of the interest which is so deemed to be his income, but shall be entitled to credit for any tax which that income is shown to have borne.

(2) In relation to corporation tax—

(*a*) subject to the provisions of the Tax Acts about distributions, interest deemed under subsection (1)(i) above to be the income of the owner shall be chargeable under Case VI of Schedule D, and
(*b*) subsection (1)(ii) above shall not apply.

(3) The references in subsection (1) above to buying back or re-acquiring the securities shall be deemed to include references to buying or acquiring similar securities, so, however, that where similar securities are bought or acquired, the owner shall be under no greater liability to tax than he would have been under if the original securities had been bought back or re-acquired.

(4) Where any person carrying on a trade which consists wholly or partly in dealing in

securities agrees to buy or acquire any securities, and by the same or any collateral agreement—

(a) agrees to sell back or re-transfer the securities, or
(b) acquires an option, which he subsequently exercises, to sell back or re-transfer the securities,

then, if the result of the transaction is that any interest becoming payable in respect of the securities is receivable by him, no account shall be taken of the transaction in computing for any of the purposes of the Tax Acts the profits arising from or loss sustained in the trade.

(5) Subsection (4) above shall have effect, subject to any necessary modifications, as if references to selling back or re-transferring the securities included references to selling or transferring similar securities.

(6) This section shall not apply to any income to which section 786(4) applies.

(7) Subsections (1) and (2) above shall not apply where—

(a) the securities are Eurobonds or foreign government stock; and
(b) the owner of the securities carries on a trade which consists wholly or partly in dealing in securities and the person who agrees to buy or acquire the securities carries on such a trade.

(8) Subsection (4) above shall not apply where—

(a) the securities are Eurobonds or foreign government stock; and
(b) the person from whom the person there mentioned agrees to buy or acquire the securities carries on a trade which consists wholly or partly in dealing in securities.

(9) In subsections (7) and (8) above—

"Eurobond" has the same meaning as in section 732(5); and
"foreign government stock" means stock which is issued by a government other than that of the United Kingdom and is denominated in a currency other than sterling.

(10) For the purposes of this section—

(a) "interest" includes a dividend;
(b) "securities" includes stocks and shares, except securities which are securities for the purposes of sections 710 to 728; and
(c) securities shall be deemed to be similar if they entitle their holders to the same rights against the same persons as to capital and interest and the same remedies for the enforcement of those rights, notwithstanding any difference in the total nominal amounts of the respective securities or in the form in which they are held or the manner in which they can be transferred.

(11) The Board may by notice require any person to furnish them within such time as they may direct (not being less than 28 days), in respect of all securities of which he was the owner at any time during the period specified in the notice, such particulars as they consider necessary for the purposes of this section and for the purpose of discovering whether tax has been borne in respect of the interest on all those securities.

(12) In any case where the owner agrees to sell or transfer before such day as the Board may by order appoint for the purposes of this section or the person referred to in subsection (4) above agreed to buy or acquire before that day—

(a) subsections (1) and (2) above shall not apply if the owner's agreement to sell or transfer constitutes a transfer to which section 713(2)(a) applies; and
(b) subsection (10)(b) above shall have effect with the omission of the words "except securities which are securities for the purposes of sections 710 to 728".

Former enactments.—Sub-ss. (1)–(6): TA 1970, s. 469(1)–(6); FA 1971, Sch. 6, para. 70.
Sub-ss. (7)–(9): TA 1970, s. 469(6A), (6B), (6C); FA 1986, Sch. 18, para. 1(1).
Sub-s. (10): TA 1970, s. 469(7); FA 1986, Sch. 18, para. 1(4).
Sub-s. (11): TA 1970, s. 469(8).
Sub-s. (12): FA 1986, Sch. 18, para. 1(5).
Note.—The day appointed under sub-s. (12) above is 9 June 1988: TA 1988 (Appointed Day No. 2) Order 1988, S.I. 1988 No. 1002.

730. Transfers of income arising from securities

(1) Where in any chargeable period the owner of any securities ("the owner") sells or transfers the right to receive any interest payable (whether before or after the sale or transfer) in respect of the securities without selling or transferring the securities, then, for

all the purposes of the Tax Acts, that interest, whether it would or would not be chargeable to tax apart from the provisions of this section—

(a) shall be deemed to be the income of the owner or, in a case where the owner is not the beneficial owner of the securities and some other person ("a beneficiary") is beneficially entitled to the income arising from the securities, the income of the beneficiary, and
(b) shall be deemed to be the income of the owner or beneficiary for that chargeable period, and
(c) shall not be deemed to be the income of any other person.

(2) For the purposes of subsection (1) above, in the case of a sale or other realisation the proceeds of which are chargeable to tax under Schedule C or under section 123(3) the interest so deemed to be the income of the owner or beneficiary shall be deemed to be equal in amount to the amount of those proceeds.

(3) Nothing in subsection (1) above shall affect any provision of this Act authorising or requiring the deduction of income tax—

(a) from any interest which, under that subsection, is deemed to be the income of the owner or beneficiary, or
(b) from the proceeds of any subsequent sale or other realisation of the right to receive that interest;

but the proceeds of any such subsequent sale or other realisation shall not, for any of the purposes of the Tax Acts, be deemed to be the income of the seller or the person on whose behalf the right is otherwise realised.

(4) Where—

(a) the securities are of such a character that the interest payable in respect thereof may be paid without deduction of income tax, and
(b) the owner or beneficiary does not show that the proceeds of any sale or other realisation of the right to receive the interest which is deemed to be his income by virtue of this section have been charged to tax under Schedule C or under section 123(3),

then the owner or beneficiary shall be chargeable to tax under Case VI of Schedule D in respect of that interest, but shall be entitled to credit for any tax which that interest is shown to have borne.

(5) For the purposes of subsection (4) above, in any case where, if the interest had been chargeable under Case IV or Case V of Schedule D, the computation of tax would have been made by reference to the amount received in the United Kingdom, the tax under Case VI shall be computed on the full amount of the sums which have been or will be received in the United Kingdom in the year of assessment or any subsequent year in which the owner remains the owner of the securities.

(6) In relation to corporation tax, subsections (4) and (5) above shall not apply but, subject to the provisions of the Tax Acts about distributions, the owner or beneficiary shall, in respect of any interest which is deemed to be his income by virtue of this section, be chargeable to corporation tax under Case VI of Schedule D unless he shows that the proceeds of any sale or other realisation of the right to receive that interest have been charged to tax under Schedule C or under section 123(3).

(7) In this section—

"interest" includes dividends, annuities and shares of annuities, and
"securities" includes stocks and shares.

(8) The Board may by notice require any person to furnish them within such time as they may direct (not being less than 28 days), in respect of all securities of which he was the owner at any time during the period specified in the notice, with such particulars as they consider necessary for the purposes of this section and for the purpose of discovering whether—

(a) tax has been borne in respect of the interest on all those securities; or
(b) the proceeds of any sale or other realisation of the right to receive the interest on the securities have been charged to tax under Schedule C or section 123(3).

Former enactments.—TA 1970, s. 470; FA 1971, Sch. 6, para. 71.

Purchase and sale of securities

731. Application and interpretation of sections 732 to 734

(1) In this section "the relevant provisions" means sections 732, 733, 734 and this section.

(2) Subject to subsections (3) to (10) below, the relevant provisions relate to cases of a purchase by a person ("the first buyer") of any securities and their subsequent sale by him, the result of the transaction being that interest becoming payable in respect of the securities ("the interest") is receivable by the first buyer.

(3) The relevant provisions do not relate to cases where—

    (*a*) the time elapsing between the purchase by the first buyer and his taking steps to dispose of the securities exceeded six months, or

    (*b*) that time exceeded one month and it is shown to the satisfaction of the Board that the purchase and sale were each effected at the current market price, and that the sale was not effected in pursuance of an agreement or arrangement made before or at the time of the purchase.

The jurisdiction of the General Commissioners or Special Commissioners on any appeal shall include jurisdiction to review any relevant decision taken by the Board in the exercise of their functions under this subsection.

(4) The reference in subsection (3) above to the first buyer taking steps to dispose of the securities shall be construed—

    (*a*) if he sold them in the exercise of an option he had acquired, as a reference to his acquisition of the option,

    (*b*) in any other case, as a reference to his selling them.

(5) For the purposes of the relevant provisions, a sale of securities similar to, and of the like nominal amount as, securities previously bought ("the original securities") shall be equivalent to a sale of the original securities and subsection (4) above shall apply accordingly; and where the first buyer bought parcels of similar securities at different times a subsequent sale of any of the securities shall, so far as may be, be related to the last to be bought of the parcels, and then to the last but one, and so on.

(6) A person shall be under no greater liability to tax by virtue of subsection (5) above than he would have been under if instead of selling the similar securities he had sold the original securities.

(7) Where at the time when a trade is, or is deemed to be, set up and commenced any securities form part of the trading stock belonging to the trade, those securities shall be treated for the purposes of this section—

    (*a*) as having been sold at that time in the open market by the person to whom they belonged immediately before that time, and

    (*b*) as having been purchased at that time in the open market by the person thereafter engaged in carrying on the trade.

(8) Subject to subsection (7) above, where there is a change in the persons engaged in carrying on a trade which is not a change on which the trade is deemed to be discontinued, the provisions of this section shall apply in relation to the person so engaged after the change as if anything done to or by his predecessor had been done to or by him.

(9) For the purposes of the relevant provisions—

"interest" includes a qualifying distribution and any dividend which is not a qualifying distribution, and in applying references to interest in relation to a qualifying distribution—

    (*a*) "gross interest" means the qualifying distribution together with the tax credit to which the recipient of the distribution is entitled in respect of it; and

    (*b*) "net interest" means the qualifying distribution exclusive of any such tax credit;

"person" includes any body of persons, and references to a person entitled to any exemption from tax include, in a case of an exemption expressed to apply to income of a trust or fund, references to the persons entitled to make claims for the granting of that exemption;

"securities" includes stocks and shares, except securities which are securities for the purposes of sections 710 to 728.

(10) For the purposes of the relevant provisions, securities shall be deemed to be similar if they entitle their holders to the same rights against the same persons as to capital and

interest and the same remedies for the enforcement of those rights, notwithstanding any difference in the total nominal amounts of the respective securities or in the form in which they are held or the manner in which they can be transferred; and for the purposes of this subsection, rights guaranteed by the Treasury shall be treated as rights against the Treasury.

Former enactments.—Sub-ss. (1)–(8): TA 1970, s. 471(1)–(5).
Sub-ss. (9)–(10): TA 1970, s. 471(6), FA 1973, Sch. 11, para. 6; FA 1986, Sch. 18, para. 2(1).

732. Dealers in securities

(1) Subject to the provisions of this section, if the first buyer is engaged in carrying on a trade which consists of or comprises dealings in securities, then, in computing for any of the purposes of the Tax Acts the profits arising from or loss sustained in the trade, the price paid by him for the securities shall be reduced by the appropriate amount in respect of the interest, as determined in accordance with section 735.

(2) Subsection (1) above shall not apply if the subsequent sale is carried out by the first buyer after 26th October 1986 in the ordinary course of his business as a market maker in securities of the kind concerned.

(3) Subsection (1) above shall not apply if the purchase of the securities by the first buyer and their resale, or as the case may be the subsequent sale of similar securities, constitute a transaction which is to be left out of account in computing profits or losses by virtue of section 729(4), or a transaction which would fall to be so left out of account apart from section 729(8).

(4) Subsection (1) above shall not apply if the securities are overseas securities bought by the first buyer on a stock exchange outside the United Kingdom in the ordinary course of his trade as a dealer in securities and the following conditions are satisfied, namely—

(*a*) the interest is brought into account in computing for the purposes of the Tax Acts the profits arising from or loss sustained in the trade, and
(*b*) where credit against tax would fall to be allowed in respect of the interest under section 788 or 790, the first buyer elects that credit shall not be so allowed.

In this subsection "overseas securities" means securities of the government of, or of a body of persons resident in, any country or territory outside the United Kingdom and the Republic of Ireland.

(5) Subsection (1) above shall not apply if the securities are Eurobonds brought by the first buyer in the ordinary course of his trade as a dealer in Eurobonds; and in this subsection "Eurobond" means a security—

(*a*) which is neither preference stock nor preference share capital; and
(*b*) which is issued in bearer form; and
(*c*) which carries a right to interest either at a fixed rate or at a rate bearing a fixed relationship to a standard published base rate; and
(*d*) which does not carry a right to any other form of benefit, whether in the nature of interest, participation in profits or otherwise; and
(*e*) the interest on which is payable without any deduction in respect of income tax or of any tax of a similar character imposed by the laws of a territory outside the United Kingdom;

but, notwithstanding anything in paragraph (*d*) above, a security is not prevented from being a Eurobond by reason only that it carries a right to convert into a security of another description or to subscribe for further securities (whether of the same description or not).

(6) For the purposes of subsection (2) above a person is a market maker in securities of a particular kind if he—

(*a*) holds himself out at all normal times in compliance with the rules of the Stock Exchange as willing to buy and sell securities of that kind at a price specified by him; and
(*b*) is recognised as doing so by the Council of the Stock Exchange.

Former enactments.—TA 1970, s. 472; FA 1982, s. 57; FA 1986, Sch. 18, paras. 1, 3.

733. Persons entitled to exemptions

(1) If the first buyer is entitled under any enactment to an exemption from tax which, apart from this subsection, would extend to the interest, then the exemption shall not extend to an

amount equal to the appropriate amount in respect of the interest, as determined in accordance with section 735.

(2) If the first buyer is so entitled and any annual payment is payable by him out of the interest, the annual payment shall be deemed as to the whole thereof to be paid out of profits or gains not brought into charge to income tax, and section 349(1) shall apply accordingly.

Former enactment.—TA 1970, s. 473.

734. Persons other than dealers in securities

(1) If the first buyer carries on a trade not falling within section 732, then in ascertaining whether any or what repayment of income tax is to be made to him under section 380 or 381 by reference to any loss sustained in the trade and the amount of his income for the year of assessment his income for which includes the interest, there shall be left out of account—

  (a) the appropriate amount in respect of the interest, as determined in accordance with section 735, and
  (b) any tax paid on that amount.

(2) Where the first buyer is a company which does not carry on a trade falling within section 732—

  (a) the appropriate amount in respect of the interest, as determined in accordance with section 735(2), and
  (b) any tax paid in respect of or deducted from that amount,

shall be disregarded except that, for the purposes of corporation tax on chargeable gains, the appropriate proportion of the net interest receivable by the first buyer as mentioned in section 735(2) shall be treated as if it were a capital distribution within the meaning of section 72(5)(b) of the 1979 Act received in respect of the holding of the securities concerned.

(3) In applying references in this section to interest in relation to a qualifying distribution, references to any tax paid on or in respect of an amount shall be construed as references to so much of any related tax credit as is attributable to that amount; and for this purpose "related tax credit", in relation to an amount, means the tax credit to which the recipient of the distribution of which that amount is a proportion is entitled.

Former enactments.—TA 1970, s. 474; FA 1973, Sch. 11, para. 7; FA 1978, s. 30(7); CGTA 1979, Sch. 7.

735. Meaning of "appropriate amount in respect of" interest

(1) For the purposes of section 732 the appropriate amount in respect of the interest is the appropriate proportion of the net interest receivable by the first buyer.

(2) For the purposes of sections 733 and 734 the appropriate amount in respect of the interest is the gross amount corresponding with the appropriate proportion of the net interest receivable by the first buyer.

(3) For the purposes of this section the appropriate proportion is the proportion which—

  (a) the period beginning with the date on which the securities were first listed in The Stock Exchange Daily Official List at a price excluding the value of the interest payment last payable before the interest receivable by the first buyer, and ending with the day before the day on which the first buyer bought the securities,

bears to—

  (b) the period beginning with that date and ending with the day before the first date after the purchase by the first buyer on which the securities are quoted in that List at a price excluding the value of the interest receivable by the first buyer.

(4) Where the interest receivable by the first buyer was the first interest payment payable in respect of the securities, paragraphs (a) and (b) of subsection (3) above shall have effect with the substitution, for references to the date on which the securities were first quoted as mentioned in paragraph (a), of the beginning of the period for which the interest was payable; except that where the capital amount of the securities was not fully paid at the beginning of that period and one or more instalments of capital were paid during that period—

  (a) the interest shall be treated as divided into parts, calculated by reference to the amount of the interest attributable to the capital paid at or before the beginning of that period and the amount thereof attributable to each such instalment, and

(b) treating each of those parts as interest payable for that period or, where the part was calculated by reference to any such instalment, as interest payable for the part of that period beginning with the payment of the instalment, there shall be calculated, in accordance with the preceding provisions of this section, the amount constituting the appropriate proportion of each part, and
(c) the appropriate proportion of the interest for the purposes of this section shall be the proportion thereof constituted by the sum of those amounts.

(5) In relation to securities not listed in the Stock Exchange Daily Official List, subsection (3) above shall have effect with the substitution for the periods therein mentioned of such periods as in the opinion of the Commissioners having jurisdiction in the matter, correspond therewith in the case of the securities in question.

Former enactments.—TA 1970, s. 475; FA 1973, Sch. 21, para. 7.

Miscellaneous provisions relating to securities

736. Company dealing in securities: distribution materially reducing value of holding

(1) Subsection (2) below applies where a company has, as a dealing company, a holding in another company resident in the United Kingdom (being a body corporate), and—
  (a) the holding amounts to, or is an ingredient in a holding amounting to, 10 per cent. of all holdings of the same class in that company, and
  (b) a distribution is, or two or more distributions are, made in respect of the holding, and
  (c) the value (at any accounting date or immediately before realisation or appropriation) of any security comprised in the holding is materially reduced below the value of the security at the time when it was acquired, and the whole or any part of this reduction is attributable to any distribution falling within paragraph (b) above;

and in relation to any security comprised in the holding, the company having the holding is in subsection (2) below referred to as "the dealing company" and so much of any reduction in the value of the security as is attributable to any distribution falling within paragraph (b) above is in that subsection referred to as "the relevant reduction".

(2) Where this subsection applies, an amount equal to the relevant reduction in the value of a security comprised in the holding—
  (a) shall, if and so long as the security is not realised or appropriated as mentioned below, be added to the value of the security for the purposes of any valuation;
  (b) shall be treated, on any realisation of the security in the course of trade, as a trading receipt of the dealing company or, in the event of a partial realisation, shall be so treated to an appropriate extent, and
  (c) shall be treated as a trading receipt of the dealing company if the security is appropriated in such circumstances that a profit on the sale of the security would no longer form part of the dealing company's trading profits.

(3) References in this section to a holding in a company refer to a holding of securities by virtue of which the holder may receive distributions made by the company, but so that—
  (a) a company's holdings of different classes in another company shall be treated as separate holdings, and
  (b) holdings of securities which differ in the entitlements or obligations they confer or impose shall be regarded as holdings of different classes.

(4) For the purposes of subsection (2) above—
  (a) all a company's holdings of the same class in another company are to be treated as ingredients constituting a single holding, and
  (b) a company's holding of a particular class shall be treated as an ingredient in a holding amounting to 10 per cent. of all holdings of that class if the aggregate of that holding and other holdings of that class held by connected persons amounts to 10 per cent. of all holdings of that class;

and section 839 shall have effect in relation to paragraph (b) above as if, in subsection (7) of that section, after the words "or exercise control of" in each place where they occur there were inserted the words "or to acquire a holding in".

(5) Where this section applies in relation to a distribution which consists of or includes interest to which section 732 applies, any reduction under that section in the price paid for the securities in respect of which the distribution is made shall be adjusted in such manner as seems appropriate to the Board to take account of subsection (2) above.

(6) For the purposes of this section "security" includes a share or other right and a company is a "dealing company" in relation to a holding if a profit on a sale of the holding would be taken into account in computing the company's trading profits.

Former enactment.—TA 1970, s. 476.

737. Manufactured dividends: treatment of tax deducted

(1) Subject to the provisions of this section, where—

(*a*) under a contract for the sale of securities one of the parties to the contract ("the dividend manufacturer") is required to pay to the other the amount of a periodical payment of interest on the securities, and
(*b*) the dividend manufacturer does not satisfy the following condition, that is to say, that he is entitled to that payment of interest either as the registered holder of the securities or from a person from whom the dividend manufacturer purchased them,

section 350(1) and Schedule 16 shall apply as if the payment by the dividend manufacturer were an annual payment made, after due deduction of tax, wholly out of a source other than profits or gains brought into charge to income tax.

(2) Subsection (1) of this section shall not apply where otherwise than by virtue of section 476(5)(*a*) the interest in question is payable without deduction of tax or where, under the rules of the stock exchange governing the transaction, the payment required to be made in respect of the interest is of the amount of the interest before deduction of tax.

(3) If for any chargeable period the liability to tax of a market maker is determined on the footing that any excess of his payments in respect of interest on securities over his receipts in respect thereof, being payments made or receipts accrued in pursuance of a contract for the sale or purchase of the securities, is to be treated for all the purposes of the Tax Acts as an annual payment made by him, then as respects that chargeable period subsection (1) above shall not apply to him if he sold or purchased the securities in the ordinary course of his business as a market maker in securities of the kind concerned.

(4) Where the dividend manufacturer is resident in the United Kingdom and purchased the securities (otherwise than through a broker) from a person not so resident, then paragraph (*b*) of subsection (1) above shall have effect as if after the word "say" there were inserted the word "either" and as if for the words from "either as" to the end of the paragraph there were inserted the words "as the registered holder of the securities or that he shows that he acquired the securities, directly or indirectly, from a person who was so entitled to the payment".

(5) Where the dividend manufacturer in relation to such a contract as is mentioned in paragraph (*a*) of subsection (1) above is not resident in the United Kingdom, and the sale is effected through a broker, that subsection shall not apply; but unless the broker shows either—

(*a*) that the dividend manufacturer was entitled to the payment of interest as the registered holder of the securities, or
(*b*) that the dividend manufacturer acquired the securities, directly or indirectly, from a person who was so entitled to the payment,

section 350(1) shall apply as if the payment through the broker of the amount of the payment of interest were an annual payment by the broker made, after due deduction of tax, wholly out of such a source as is mentioned in subsection (1) above.

(6) In this section—

"broker", in relation to securities, means a member of the Stock Exchange who carries on business in the United Kingdom and is not, at the time the contract is made, a market maker in securities of the kind concerned;
"market maker", in relation to securities of a particular kind, means a person who—

(*a*) holds himself out at all normal times in compliance with the rules of the Stock Exchange as willing to buy and sell securities of that kind at a price specified by him; and
(*b*) is recognised as doing so by the Council of the Stock Exchange;

"securities" includes shares and stock;

and references to a periodical payment of interest include references to a qualifying distribution and any dividend which is not a qualifying distribution.

(7) In the application of this section in a case where the references in subsection (1) above

to a periodical payment of interest are construed as references to a qualifying distribution, subsection (2) above shall be omitted.

(8) Where it appears to the Board that by reason of any transaction or transactions a person may by virtue of this section have incurred any liability to tax, the Board may by notice served on him require him, within such time not less than 28 days as may be specified in the notice, to furnish information in his possession with respect to the transaction or any of the transactions, being information as to matters, specified in the notice, which are relevant to the question whether he has incurred any such liability.

Former enactments.—TA 1970, s. 477; FA 1973, Sch. 11, para. 8; FA 1982, s. 59(1); FA 1986, Sch. 18, paras. 5, 6.

Supplemental

738. Power to amend sections 732, 735 and 737

(1) The Board may by regulations provide for all or any of the following—

(*a*) that section 732(2) shall not apply unless the subsequent sale is carried out in compliance with further conditions specified in the regulations;
(*b*) that section 732(6) shall have effect as if the reference to the Stock Exchange in paragraph (*a*) were to any recognised investment exchange or to any of those exchanges specified in the regulations, and as if the reference to the Council of the Stock Exchange in paragraph (*b*) were to the investment exchange concerned;
(*c*) that for section 735(3) and (5) (which refer to the Stock Exchange Daily Official List) there shall be substituted such provisions as the Board think fit to take account of recognised investment exchanges.

Regulations under this subsection shall apply where the subsequent sale is carried out by the first buyer on or after such day as is specified in the regulations.

(2) The Board may by regulations provide that section 737(6) shall have effect—

(*a*) as if references to the Stock Exchange in the definition of "broker" and in paragraph (*a*) of the definition of "market maker" were to any recognised investment exchange or to any of those exchanges specified in the regulations; and
(*b*) as if the reference to the Council of the Stock Exchange in paragraph (*b*) of the definition of "market maker" were to the investment exchange concerned.

(3) The Board may by regulations substitute for subsection (3) of section 737 a provision that subsection (1) of that section shall not apply to such persons and in such circumstances as are specified in the substituted provision, and make such incidental and consequential provisions (which may include the amendment of other provisions of section 737) as appear to the Board to be appropriate.

(4) Regulations under subsections (2) and (3) above shall apply where the contract for the sale of securities is made on or after such day as is specified in the regulations.

(5) In this section "recognised investment exchange" means a recognised investment exchange within the meaning of the Financial Services Act 1986.

Former enactment.—Sub-s. (1): FA 1986, Sch. 18, para. 4.
Sub-s. (2): FA 1986, Sch. 18, para. 6(5).
Sub-s. (3): FA 1986, Sch. 18, para. 9(1)(*a*), (*c*).
Sub-s. (4): FA 1986, Sch. 18, para. 6(6), 9(2).
Sub-s. (5): FA 1986, Sch. 18, para. 10(2).

CHAPTER III

TRANSFER OF ASSETS ABROAD

739. Prevention of avoidance of income tax

(1) Subject to section 747(4)(*b*), the following provisions of this section shall have effect for the purpose of preventing the avoiding by individuals ordinarily resident in the United Kingdom of liability to income tax by means of transfer of assets by virtue or in consequence of which, either alone or in conjunction with associated operations, income becomes payable to persons resident or domiciled outside the United Kingdom.

(2) Where by virtue or in consequence of any such transfer, either alone or in conjunction with associated operations, such an individual has, within the meaning of this section, power to enjoy, whether forthwith or in the future, any income of a person resident or domiciled outside the United Kingdom which, if it were income of that individual received by him in the United Kingdom, would be chargeable to income tax by deduction or otherwise, that income shall, whether it would or would not have been chargeable to income tax apart from the provisions of this section, be deemed to be income of that individual for all purposes of the Income Tax Acts.

(3) Where, whether before or after any such transfer, such an individual receives or is entitled to receive any capital sum the payment of which is in any way connected with the transfer or any associated operation, any income which, by virtue or in consequence of the transfer, either alone or in conjunction with associated operations, has become the income of a person resident or domiciled outside the United Kingdom shall, whether it would or would not have been chargeable to income tax apart from the provisions of this section, be deemed to be income of that individual for all purposes of the Income Tax Acts.

(4) In subsection (3) above "capital sum" means, subject to subsection (5) below—

(*a*) any sum paid or payable by way of loan or repayment of a loan, and
(*b*) any other sum paid or payable otherwise than as income, being a sum which is not paid or payable for full consideration in money or money's worth.

(5) For the purposes of subsection (3) above, there shall be treated as a capital sum which an individual receives or is entitled to receive any sum which a third person receives or is entitled to receive at the individual's direction or by virtue of the assignment by him of his right to receive it.

(6) Income shall not by virtue of subsection (3) above be deemed to be that of an individual for any year of assessment by reason only of his having received a sum by way of loan if that sum has been wholly repaid before the beginning of that year.

Former enactments.—TA 1970, s. 478(1), (2), (2A), (2B); FA 1981, s. 46(3), (4).
Cross references.—See FA 1989, s. 110(8) (residence of trustees), s. 111(8) (residence of personal representatives).

740. Liability of non-transferors

(1) This section has effect where—

(*a*) by virtue or in consequence of a transfer of assets, either alone or in conjunction with associated operations, income becomes payable to a person resident or domiciled outside the United Kingdom; and
(*b*) an individual ordinarily resident in the United Kingdom who is not liable to tax under section 739 by reference to the transfer receives a benefit provided out of assets which are available for the purpose by virtue or in consequence of the transfer or of any associated operations.

(2) Subject to the provisions of this section, the amount or value of any such benefit as is mentioned in subsection (1) above, if not otherwise chargeable to income tax in the hands of the recipient, shall—

(*a*) to the extent to which it falls within the amount of relevant income of years of assessment up to and including the year of assessment in which the benefit is received, be treated for all the purposes of the Income Tax Acts as the income of the individual for that year;

(*b*) to the extent to which it is not by virtue of this subsection treated as his income for that year and falls within the amount of relevant income of the next following year of assessment, be treated for those purposes as his income for the next following year,

and so on for subsequent years, taking the reference in paragraph (*b*) to the year mentioned in paragraph (*a*) as a reference to that and any other year before the subsequent year in question.

(3) Subject to subsection (7) below and section 744(1), the relevant income of a year of assessment, in relation to an individual, is any income which arises in that year to a person resident or domiciled outside the United Kingdom and which by virtue or in consequence of the transfer or associated operations referred to in subsection (1) above can directly or indirectly be used for providing a benefit for the individual or for enabling a benefit to be provided for him.

(4) Income tax chargeable by virtue of this section shall be charged under Case VI of Schedule D.

(5) An individual who is domiciled outside the United Kingdom shall not, in respect of any benefit not received in the United Kingdom, be chargeable to tax under this section by reference to relevant income which is such that if he had received it he would not, by reason of his being so domiciled, have been chargeable to income tax in respect of it; and subsections (6) to (9) of section 65 shall apply for the purposes of this subsection as they would apply for the purposes of subsection (5) of that section if the benefit were income arising from possessions outside the United Kingdom.

(6) Where—

(*a*) the whole or part of the benefit received by an individual in a year of assessment is a capital payment within the meaning of section 80 or 81(2) of the Finance Act 1981 (chargeable gains: non-resident and migrant settlements) (because not falling within the amount of relevant income referred to in paragraph (*a*) of subsection (2) above); and
(*b*) chargeable gains are by reason of that payment treated under either of those sections as accruing to him in that or a subsequent year,

paragraph (*b*) of that subsection shall apply in relation to any year of assessment ("a year of charge") after one in which chargeable gains have been so treated as accruing to him as if a part of the amount or value of the benefit corresponding to the amount of those gains had been treated under that subsection as his income for a year of assessment before the year of charge.

(7) This section applies irrespective of when the transfer or associated operations referred to in subsection (1) above took place, but applies only to relevant income arising on or after 10th March 1981.

Former enactment.—FA 1981, s. 45(1)–(6), (9).
Cross references.—See FA 1989, s. 110(9) (residence of trustees),
s. 111(7) (residence of personal representatives).

741. Exemption from sections 739 and 740

Sections 739 and 740 shall not apply if the individual shows in writing or otherwise to the satisfaction of the Board either—

(*a*) that the purpose of avoiding liability to taxation was not the purpose or one of the purposes for which the transfer or associated operations or any of them were effected; or
(*b*) that the transfer and any associated operations were bona fide commercial transactions and were not designed for the purpose of avoiding liability to taxation.

The jurisdiction of the Special Commissioners on any appeal shall include jurisdiction to review any relevant decision taken by the Board in exercise of their functions under this section.

Former enactments.—TA 1970, s. 478(3); FA 1981, s. 45(7).

742. Interpretation of sections 739 to 741

(1) For the purposes of sections 739 to 741 "an associated operation" means, in relation to any transfer, an operation of any kind effected by any person in relation to any of the assets

transferred or any assets representing, whether directly or indirectly, any of the assets transferred, or to the income arising from any such assets, or to any assets representing, whether directly or indirectly, the accumulations of income arising from any such assets.

(2) An individual shall, for the purposes of section 739, be deemed to have power to enjoy income of a person resident or domiciled outside the United Kingdom if—

(*a*) the income is in fact so dealt with by any person as to be calculated, at some point of time, and whether in the form of income or not, to enure for the benefit of the individual; or

(*b*) the receipt or accrual of the income operates to increase the value to the individual of any assets held by him or for his benefit; or

(*c*) the individual receives or is entitled to receive, at any time, any benefit provided or to be provided out of that income or out of moneys which are or will be available for the purpose by reason of the effect or successive effects of the associated operations on that income and on any assets which directly or indirectly represent that income; or

(*d*) the individual may, in the event of the exercise or successive exercise of one or more powers, by whomsoever exercisable and whether with or without the consent of any other person, become entitled to the beneficial enjoyment of the income; or

(*e*) the individual is able in any manner whatsoever, and whether directly or indirectly, to control the application of the income.

(3) In determining whether an individual has power to enjoy income within the meaning of subsection (2) above—

(*a*) regard shall be had to the substantial result and effect of the transfer and any associated operations, and

(*b*) all benefits which may at any time accrue to the individual (whether or not he has rights at law or in equity in or to those benefits) as a result of the transfer and any associated operations shall be taken into account irrespective of the nature or form of the benefits.

(4) Subsection (5) below applies where a person resident or domiciled outside the United Kingdom throughout any chargeable period in which an interest period (or part of it) falls would, at the end of the interest period, have been treated under section 714(2) as receiving annual profits or gains or annual profits or gains of a greater amount if he had been resident or domiciled in the United Kingdom during a part of each such chargeable period.

(5) Sections 739 to 741 shall have effect as if the amount which the person would be treated as receiving or the additional amount (as the case may be) were income becoming payable to him; and, accordingly, any reference in those sections to income of (or payable or arising to) such a person shall be read as including a reference to such an amount.

(6) Where income of a person resident or domiciled outside the United Kingdom throughout any chargeable period in which an interest period (or part of it) falls consists of interest—

(*a*) which falls due at the end of the interest period, and

(*b*) which would have been treated under section 714(5) as reduced by an allowance or an allowance of a greater amount if he had been resident or domiciled in the United Kingdom during a part of each such chargeable period,

then for the purposes of sections 739 to 741, the interest shall be treated as being reduced by the amount of the allowance or by the additional amount (as the case may be).

(7) In subsections (4) to (6) above "interest period" has the meaning given by section 711.

(8) For the purposes of sections 739 to 741, any body corporate incorporated outside the United Kingdom shall be treated as if it were resident outside the United Kingdom whether it is so resident or not.

(9) For the purposes of sections 739 to 741—

(*a*) a reference to an individual shall be deemed to include the wife or husband of the individual;

(*b*) "assets" includes property or rights of any kind and "transfer", in relation to rights, includes the creation of those rights;

(*c*) "benefits" includes a payment of any kind;

(*d*) . . .[1]

(*e*) references to assets representing any assets, income or accumulations of income include references to shares in or obligations of any company to which, or obligations of any other person to whom, those assets, that income or those accumulations are or have been transferred.

(10) ...¹

Former enactments.—Sub-ss. (1)–(3): TA 1970, s. 478(4)–(6); FA 1972, Sch. 24, para. 27; FA 1981, ss. 45(7), 46(5).
Sub-ss. (4)–(7): FA 1985, Sch. 23, para. 39.
Sub-ss. (8)–(10): TA 1970, s. 478(7)–(9); FA 1972, Sch. 24, para. 7; FA 1981, s. 46(5).
Amendments.—¹ Sub-ss. (9)(*d*), (10) repealed by FA 1989, Sch. 17, Pt. V in relation to accounting periods beginning after 31 March 1989.

743. Supplemental provisions

(1) Income tax at the basic rate shall not be charged by virtue of section 739 in respect of income which has borne tax at the basic rate by deduction or otherwise but, subject to that, income tax so chargeable shall be charged under Case VI of Schedule D.

(2) In computing the liability to income tax of an individual chargeable by virtue of section 739, the same deductions and reliefs shall be allowed as would have been allowed if the income deemed to be his by virtue of that section had actually been received by him.

(3) An individual who is domiciled outside the United Kingdom shall not be chargeable to tax in respect of any income deemed to be his by virtue of that section if he would not, by reason of his being so domiciled, have been chargeable to tax in respect of it if it had in fact been his income.

(4) Where an individual has been charged to income tax on any income deemed to be his by virtue of section 739 and that income is subsequently received by him, it shall be deemed not to form part of his income again for the purposes of the Income Tax Acts.

(5) In any case where an individual has for the purposes of that section power to enjoy income of a person abroad by reason of his receiving any such benefit as is referred to in section 742(2)(*c*), then notwithstanding anything in subsection (1) above, the individual shall be chargeable to income tax by virtue of section 739 for the year of assessment in which the benefit is received on the whole of the amount or value of that benefit except in so far as it is shown that the benefit derives directly or indirectly from income on which he has already been charged to tax for that or a previous year of assessment.

Former enactments.—TA 1970, s. 480; FA 1971, Sch. 6, para. 72; FA 1981, s. 46(7).

744. No duplication of charge

(1) No amount of income shall be taken into account more than once in charging tax under the provisions of sections 739 and 740; and where there is a choice as to the persons in relation to whom any amount of income can be so taken into account—

(*a*) it shall be so taken into account in relation to such of them, and if more than one in such proportions respectively, as appears to the Board to be just and reasonable; and
(*b*) the jurisdiction of the Special Commissioners on any appeal against an assessment charging tax under those provisions shall include jurisdiction to review any relevant decision taken by the Board under this subsection.

(2) In subsection (1) above references to an amount of income taken into account in charging tax are—

(*a*) in the case of tax which under section 739 is charged on income, to the amount of that income;
(*b*) in the case of tax charged under that section by virtue of section 743(5), to an amount of the income out of which the benefit is provided equal to the amount or value of the benefit charged;
(*c*) in the case of tax charged under section 740, to the amount of relevant income taken into account under subsection (2) of that section in charging the benefit.

Former enactment.—FA 1981, s. 46(1), (2).

745. Power to obtain information

(1) The Board may by notice require any person to furnish them within such time as they may direct (not being less than 28 days) with such particulars as they think necessary for the purposes of this Chapter.

(2) The particulars which a person must furnish under this section, if he is required by such a notice so to do, include particulars—

(*a*) as to transactions with respect to which he is or was acting on behalf of others;
(*b*) as to transactions which in the opinion of the Board it is proper that they should investigate for the purposes of this Chapter notwithstanding that, in the opinion of the person to whom the notice is given, no liability to tax arises under this Chapter; and
(*c*) as to whether the person to whom the notice is given has taken or is taking any, and if so what, part in any, and if so what, transactions of a description specified in the notice.

(3) Notwithstanding anything in subsection (2) above, a solicitor shall not be deemed for the purposes of paragraph (*c*) of that subsection to have taken part in a transaction by reason only that he has given professional advice to a client in connection with that transaction, and shall not, in relation to anything done by him on behalf of his client, be compellable under this section, except with the consent of his client, to do more than state that he is or was acting on behalf of a client, and give the name and address of the client and also—

(*a*) in the case of anything done by the solicitor in connection with the transfer of any asset by or to an individual ordinarily resident in the United Kingdom to or by any such body corporate as is mentioned in subsection (4) below, or in connection with any associated operation in relation to any such transfer, the names and addresses of the transferor and the transferee or of the persons concerned in the associated operations, as the case may be;
(*b*) in the case of anything done by the solicitor in connection with the formation or management of any such body corporate as is mentioned in subsection (4) below, the name and address of the body corporate;
(*c*) in the case of anything done by the solicitor in connection with the creation, or with the execution of the trusts, of any settlement by virtue or in consequence of which income becomes payable to a person resident or domiciled outside the United Kingdom, the names and addresses of the settlor and of that person.

(4) The bodies corporate mentioned in subsection (3) above are bodies corporate resident or incorporated outside the United Kingdom which are, or if resident in the United Kingdom would be, close companies, but not [companies whose business consists wholly or mainly of the carrying on of a trade or trades][1].

(5) Nothing in this section shall impose on any bank the obligation to furnish any particulars of any ordinary banking transactions between the bank and a customer carried out in the ordinary course of banking business, unless the bank has acted or is acting on behalf of the customer in connection with the formation or management of any such body corporate as is mentioned in subsection (4) above or in connection with the creation, or with the execution of the trusts, of any such settlement as is mentioned in subsection (3)(*c*) above.

(6) In this section "settlement" and "settlor" have the meanings given by section 681(4).

Former enactments.—TA 1970, s. 481; FA 1972, Sch. 24, para. 28; FA 1981, s. 45(8).
Amendments.—[1] Words in sub-s. (4) substituted by FA 1989, Sch. 12, para. 17.

746. Persons resident in the Republic of Ireland

In relation to amounts which by virtue of any provision of section 34, 35 or 36 would, in the case of a person resident in the Republic of Ireland and not resident in the United Kingdom, be included in his income if he were not resident in the Republic of Ireland, sections 739, 742(1) to (3), 743 and 745 shall apply—

(*a*) as if his income included those amounts; and
(*b*) as if references to an individual included references to any person (and so that in accordance with section 9 those sections then apply for corporation tax as well as for income tax);

but section 741 shall not apply in any such case.

Former enactment.—TA 1970, s. 479.

CHAPTER IV

CONTROLLED FOREIGN COMPANIES

747. Imputation of chargeable profits and creditable tax of controlled foreign companies

(1) If the Board have reason to believe that in any accounting period a company—

(*a*) is resident outside the United Kingdom, and
(*b*) is controlled by persons resident in the United Kingdom, and
(*c*) is subject to a lower level of taxation in the territory in which it is resident,

and the Board so direct, the provisions of this Chapter shall apply in relation to that accounting period.

(2) A company which falls within paragraphs (*a*) to (*c*) of subsection (1) above is in this Chapter referred to as a "controlled foreign company".

(3) Where, by virtue of a direction under subsection (1) above, the provisions of this Chapter apply in relation to an accounting period of a controlled foreign company, the chargeable profits of that company for that period and its creditable tax (if any) for that period shall each be apportioned in accordance with section 752 among the persons (whether resident in the United Kingdom or not) who had an interest in that company at any time during that accounting period.

(4) Where, on such an apportionment of a controlled foreign company's chargeable profits for an accounting period as is referred to in subsection (3) above, an amount of those profits is apportioned to a company resident in the United Kingdom then, subject to subsection (5) below—

(*a*) a sum equal to corporation tax at the appropriate rate on that apportioned amount of profits, less the portion of the controlled foreign company's creditable tax for that period (if any) which is apportioned to the resident company, shall be assessed on and recoverable from the resident company as if it were an amount of corporation tax chargeable on that company; and
(*b*) if, apart from this paragraph, section 739 would deem any sum forming part of the company's chargeable profits for that accounting period to be the income of an individual for the purposes of the Income Tax Acts, that section shall not apply to such portion of that sum as corresponds to the portion of those chargeable profits which is apportioned to companies which are resident in the United Kingdom and which, by virtue of paragraph (*a*) above, have a liability to tax in respect thereof;

and for the purposes of paragraph (*a*) above "the appropriate rate" means the rate of corporation tax applicable to profits of that accounting period of the resident company in which ends the accounting period of the controlled foreign company to which the direction under subsection (1) above relates or, if there is more than one such rate, the average rate over the whole of that accounting period of the resident company.

(5) Tax shall not, by virtue of subsection (4) above, be assessed and recoverable from a company resident in the United Kingdom unless, on the apportionment in question, the aggregate of—

(*a*) the amount of the controlled foreign company's chargeable profits for the accounting period in question which is apportioned to the resident company, and
(*b*) any amounts of those chargeable profits which are apportioned to persons who are connected or associated with the resident company,

is at least 10 per cent. of the total of those chargeable profits.

(6) In relation to a company resident outside the United Kingdom—

(*a*) any reference in this Chapter to its chargeable profits for an accounting period is a reference to the amount which, on the assumptions in Schedule 24, would be the amount of the total profits of the company for that period on which, after allowing for any deductions available against those profits, corporation tax would be chargeable; and
(*b*) any reference in this Chapter to profits does not include a reference to chargeable gains but otherwise (except as provided by paragraph (*a*) above) has the same meaning as it has for the purposes of corporation tax.

Former enactment.—FA 1984, s. 82.
Cross references.—See TMA 1970, s. 55(6A) (appeals by UK controlled foreign companies against tax assessment and liability).

748. Limitations on direction-making power

(1) No direction may be given under section 747(1) with respect to an accounting period of a controlled foreign company if—

(a) in respect of that period the company pursues, within the meaning of Part 1 of Schedule 25, an acceptable distribution policy; or
(b) throughout that period the company is, within the meaning of Part II of that Schedule, engaged in exempt activities; or
(c) the public quotation condition set out in Part III of that Schedule is fulfilled with respect to that period; or
(d) the chargeable profits of the accounting period do not exceed £20,000 or, if the accounting period is less than 12 months, a proportionately reduced amount.

(2) Without prejudice to any right of appeal, nothing in subsection (1) above prevents the Board from giving a direction with respect to an accounting period after the end of that period but before it is known whether the company has paid such a dividend as establishes that it is pursuing an acceptable distribution policy in respect of the profits arising in that period.

(3) Notwithstanding that none of paragraphs (a) to (d) of subsection (1) above applies to an accounting period of a controlled foreign company, no direction may be given under section 747(1) with respect to that accounting period if it appears to the Board that—

(a) in so far as any of the transactions the results of which are reflected in the profits arising in that accounting period, or any two or more of those transactions taken together, achieved a reduction in United Kingdom tax, either the reduction so achieved was minimal or it was not the main purpose or one of the main purposes of that transaction or, as the case may be, of those transactions taken together to achieve that reduction, and
(b) it was not the main reason or, as the case may be, one of the main reasons for the company's existence in that accounting period to achieve a reduction in United Kingdom tax by a diversion of profits from the United Kingdom,

and Part IV of Schedule 25 shall have effect with respect to the preceding provisions of this subsection.

Former enactment.—FA 1984, s. 83.

749. Residence and interest

(1) Subject to subsections (2) and (4) below, in any accounting period in which a company is resident outside the United Kingdom, it shall be regarded for the purposes of this Chapter as resident in that territory in which, throughout that period, it is liable to tax by reason of domicile, residence or place of management.

(2) If, in the case of any company, there are in any accounting period two or more territories falling within subsection (1) above, the company shall in that accounting period be regarded for the purposes of this Chapter as resident in only one of them, namely—

(a) if, throughout the accounting period, the company's place of effective management is situated in one of those territories only, in that territory; and
(b) if, throughout the accounting period, the company's place of effective management is situated in two or more of those territories, in that one of them in which, at the end of the accounting period, the greater amount of the company's assets is situated; and
(c) if neither paragraph (a) nor paragraph (b) above applies, in that one of the territories falling within subsection (1) above in which, at the end of the accounting period, the greater amount of the company's assets is situated; and
(d) if paragraph (a) above does not apply and neither paragraph (b) nor paragraph (c) above produces one, and only one, of those territories, in that one of them which may be specified in a direction under section 747(1) relating to that accounting period.

(3) If, in the case of any company, there is in any accounting period no territory falling within subsection (1) above, then, for the purposes of this Chapter, it shall be conclusively presumed that the company is in that accounting period resident in a territory in which it is subject to a lower level of taxation.

(4) In any case where it becomes necessary for the purposes of subsection (2) above to determine in which of two or more territories the greater amount of a company's assets is situated at the end of an accounting period, account shall be taken only of those assets which, immediately before the end of that period, are situated in those territories and the amount of them shall be determined by reference to their market value at that time.

(5) For the purposes of this Chapter, the following persons have an interest in a controlled foreign company—

(*a*) any person who possesses, or is entitled to acquire, share capital or voting rights in the company,
(*b*) any person who possesses, or is entitled to acquire, a right to receive or participate in distributions of the company or any amounts payable by the company (in cash or in kind) to loan creditors by way of premium on redemption,
(*c*) any person who is entitled to secure that income or assets (whether present or future) of the company will be applied directly or indirectly for his benefit, and
(*d*) any other person who, either alone or together with other persons, has control of the company,

and for the purposes of paragraph (*b*) above the definition of "distribution" in Part VI shall be construed without any limitation to companies resident in the United Kingdom.

(6) References in subsection (5) above to being entitled to do anything apply where a person is presently entitled to do it at a future date, or will at a future date be entitled to do it; but a person whose entitlement to secure that any income or assets of the company will be applied as mentioned in paragraph (*c*) of that subsection is contingent upon a default of the company or any other person under any agreement shall not be treated as falling within that paragraph unless the default has occurred.

(7) Without prejudice to subsection (5) above, the Board may, if they think it appropriate, treat a loan creditor of a controlled foreign company as having an interest in the company for the purposes of this Chapter.

Former enactment.—FA 1984, s. 84.

750. Territories with a lower level of taxation

(1) Without prejudice to subsection (3) of section 749, a company which, by virtue of subsection (1) or subsection (2) of that section, is to be regarded as resident in a particular territory outside the United Kingdom shall be considered to be subject to a lower level of taxation in that territory if the amount of tax ("the local tax") which is paid under the law of that territory in respect of the profits of the company which arise in any accounting period is less than one-half of the corresponding United Kingdom tax on those profits.

(2) For the purposes of this Chapter, the amount of the corresponding United Kingdom tax on the profits arising in an accounting period of a company resident outside the United Kingdom is the amount of corporation tax which, on the assumptions set out in Schedule 24 and subject to subsection (3) below, would be chargeable in respect of the chargeable profits of the company for that accounting period.

(3) In determining the amount of corporation tax which, in accordance with subsection (2) above, would be chargeable in respect of the chargeable profits of an accounting period of a company resident outside the United Kingdom—

(*a*) it shall be assumed for the purposes of Schedule 24—

(i) that a direction has been given under section 747(1) in respect of that period; and
(ii) that the Board have made any declaration which they could have made under sub-paragraph (3) of paragraph 11 of that Schedule and of which they gave notice as mentioned in that sub-paragraph; and

(*b*) there shall be disregarded so much of any relief from corporation tax in respect of income as would be attributable to the local tax and would fall to be given by virtue of any provision of Part XVIII other than section 810; and
(*c*) there shall be deducted from what would otherwise be the amount of that corporation tax—

(i) any amount which (on the assumptions set out in Schedule 24) would fall to be set off against corporation tax by virtue of section 7(2); and
(ii) any amount of income tax or corporation tax actually charged in respect of any of those chargeable profits.

(4) The references in subsection (3)(c) above to an amount falling to be set off or an amount actually charged do not include so much of any such amount as has been or falls to be repaid to the company whether on the making of a claim or otherwise.

Former enactment.—FA 1984, s. 85.

751. Accounting periods and creditable tax

(1) For the purposes of this Chapter, an accounting period of a company resident outside the United Kingdom shall begin—

   (a) whenever the company comes under the control of the persons resident in the United Kingdom;
   (b) whenever the company, not being the subject of an earlier direction under section 747(1), commences to carry on business; and
   (c) whenever an accounting period of the company ends without the company then ceasing either to carry on business or to have any source of income whatsoever.

(2) For the purposes of this Chapter, an accounting period of a company resident outside the United Kingdom shall end if and at the time when—

   (a) the company ceases to be under the control of persons resident in the United Kingdom; or
   (b) the company becomes, or ceases to be, liable to tax in a territory; or
   (c) the company ceases to have any source of income whatsoever;

and for the purposes of paragraph (b) above "liable to tax" means liable to tax by reason of domicile, residence or place of management.

(3) Without prejudice to subsections (1) and (2) above, subsections (3), (5) and (7) of section 12 shall apply for the purposes of this Chapter as they apply for the purposes of corporation tax, but with the omission of so much of those provisions as relates to a company coming or ceasing to be within the charge to corporation tax.

(4) Where it appears to the Board that the beginning or end of any accounting period of a company resident outside the United Kingdom is uncertain, a direction under section 747(1) may specify as an accounting period of the company such period, not exceeding 12 months, as appears to the Board to be appropriate, and that period shall be treated for the purposes of this Chapter as an accounting period of the company unless the direction is subsequently amended under subsection (5) below.

(5) If, on further facts coming to the knowledge of the Board after the making of a direction (including facts emerging on an appeal against notice of the making of the direction), it appears to the Board that any accounting period specified in the direction is not the true accounting period, the Board shall amend the direction so as to specify the true period.

(6) In this Chapter, in relation to an accounting period of a controlled foreign company in respect of which a direction is given under section 747(1), the creditable tax means the aggregate of—

   (a) the amount of any relief from corporation tax in respect of income which (on the assumptions set out in Schedule 24 and assuming the company to be liable for corporation tax on the chargeable profits of that accounting period) would fall to be given to the company by virtue of any provision of Part XVIII in respect of foreign tax attributable to any income which is brought into account in determining those chargeable profits; and
   (b) any amount which (on those assumptions) would fall to be set off against corporation tax on those chargeable profits by virtue of section 7(2); and
   (c) the amount of any income tax or corporation tax actually charged in respect of the chargeable profits of that accounting period, less any of that tax which has been or falls to be repaid to the company, whether on the making of a claim or otherwise.

Former enactment.—FA 1984, s. 86.

752. Apportionment of chargeable profits and creditable tax

(1) Where a direction has been given under section 747(1) in respect of an accounting period of a controlled foreign company, then, subject to subsections (2) and (3) below, the apportionment of the company's chargeable profits and creditable tax (if any) for that period shall be made among, and according to the respective interests of, the persons who at any time during that period had interests in the company.

(2) In determining for the purposes of this Chapter the respective interests of persons who (in accordance with section 749) have interests in a controlled foreign company, the Board may, if it seems to them just and reasonable to do so, attribute to each of those persons an interest corresponding to his interest in the assets of the company available for distribution among those persons in the event of a winding up or in any other circumstances.

(3) Where the controlled foreign company is not a trading company, the Board may, if it seems to them just and reasonable to do so, treat a loan creditor as having for the purposes of this section an interest in the company to the extent to which the income of the company has been, or is available to be, expended in redemption, repayment or discharge of the loan capital or debt (including any premium thereon) in respect of which he is a loan creditor.

(4) Subject to subsections (5) and (7) below, as between persons each of whom has an unvarying holding of shares of the same class throughout a particular accounting period of a controlled foreign company, the amount of the company's chargeable profits and creditable tax which is apportioned to each of them by virtue of his holding of those shares shall be in direct proportion to the numbers of shares comprised in their holdings; and similar principles shall apply in relation to an apportionment among other persons each of whom holds an interest of the same description in the controlled foreign company.

(5) Where the same interest in a controlled foreign company is held directly by one person and indirectly by another or others (as in a case where one company has a shareholding in the controlled foreign company and the first company is controlled by a third company or by two or more persons together) then, subject to subsection (6) below, the Board, in apportioning the company's chargeable profits and creditable tax—

(*a*) may treat that interest as held solely by a person who holds that interest indirectly or, as the case may be, by two or more persons (the "holders") who, taken together, hold that interest indirectly, and
(*b*) in particular, if that person or one or more of those holders is resident in the United Kingdom, may treat the interest as held solely by that one or, as the case may be, those holders.

(6) In any case where the same interest is held directly by one person and indirectly by another and the circumstances are as set out in any of paragraphs (*a*) to (*c*) below, the Board shall treat the interest as held solely by the company which is described in the paragraph concerned as "the assessable company"—

(*a*) where the interest is held directly by a company resident in the United Kingdom, that company is the assessable company; and
(*b*) where the interest is held directly by a person resident outside the United Kingdom and indirectly by only one company resident in the United Kingdom, that company is the assessable company; and
(*c*) where the interest is held directly by a person resident outside the United Kingdom and indirectly by two or more companies resident in the United Kingdom, the assessable company is that one of the companies which so holds the interest by virtue of holding directly an interest in a foreign holding company;

and for the purposes of paragraph (*c*) above a foreign holding company is a company resident outside the United Kingdom which holds directly or indirectly the interest in the controlled foreign company.

(7) Without prejudice to subsection (5) above, in any case where an interest in a controlled foreign company is held in a fiduciary or representative capacity in such circumstances that there is or are an identifiable beneficiary or beneficiaries, the Board may treat the interest as held by that beneficiary or, as the case may be, as apportioned among those beneficiaries; and any such apportionment shall be made on such basis as seems to the Board to be just and reasonable.

(8) Subject to the preceding provisions of this section, the apportionment of the chargeable profits and creditable tax of a controlled foreign company for any accounting period shall be made on such basis as seems to the Board to be just and reasonable.

Former enactment.—FA 1984, s. 87.

753. Notices and appeals

(1) Where the Board have given a direction under section 747(1) with respect to an accounting period of a controlled foreign company, notice of the making of the direction shall be given to every company resident in the United Kingdom which appears to the

Board to have had an interest in the controlled foreign company at any time during that period.

(2) A notice under subsection (1) above shall—

(a) specify the date on which the direction was made and the controlled foreign company to which it relates;

(b) specify the accounting period to which the direction relates and the amount of the chargeable profits and creditable tax computed for that period;

(c) specify the reliefs (if any) which it has been assumed that the company has claimed by virtue of paragraph 4(1) of Schedule 24;

(d) specify, in a case where paragraph (d) of subsection (2) of section 749 applies, the territory which, by virtue of that paragraph, was specified in the direction and, in any other case, specify the territory (if any) in which, by virtue of that section, the Board consider that the company is to be regarded as resident for the purposes of this Chapter;

(e) inform the recipient of the notice of the right of appeal conferred on him by subsection (4) below and of the right to give notice under paragraph 4(2) of Schedule 24; and

(f) specify any declaration with respect to the accounting period concerned which was made prior to or at the same time as the notice by virtue of paragraph 11(3) of Schedule 24 or paragraph 3(2) of Schedule 25;

and, in the case of a notice given after the direction concerned has been amended by virtue of section 751(5), the notice shall specify the date of the amendment and (so far as paragraphs (b) and (c) above are concerned) shall relate to the position resulting from the amendment.

(3) Where, by virtue of section 751(5), the Board have amended a direction so as to specify a revised accounting period, notice of the making of the amendment shall be given to every company which was previously given notice of the making of the direction; and a notice under this subsection—

(a) shall identify the direction which is amended and state the effect of the amendment, including the extent to which the matters specified in the notice of the making of the direction are superseded; and

(b) shall contain the provisions required, by virtue of paragraphs (b) to (f) of subsection (2) above, to be included in a notice under subsection (1) above.

(4) Any company to which notice is given under subsection (1) or subsection (3) above may, by giving notice of appeal to the Board within 60 days of the date of the notice given to the company, appeal to the Special Commissioners against that notice on all or any of the following grounds—

(a) that the direction should not have been given or, where the direction has been amended, that the amendment should not have been made;

(b) that the amount of chargeable profits or creditable tax specified in the notice is incorrect;

(c) that the company did not have an interest in the controlled foreign company concerned at any time during the accounting period in question;

(d) that, if the notice specifies a declaration made by virtue of subparagraph (3) of paragraph 11 of Schedule 24, the condition for the making of that declaration in subparagraph (5) of that paragraph was not fulfilled; and

(e) that, if the notice specifies a declaration made by virtue of paragraph 3(2) of Schedule 25, the condition for the making of that declaration was not fulfilled;

and the notice of appeal shall specify the grounds of appeal, but on the hearing of the appeal the Special Commissioners may allow the appellant to put forward any ground not specified in the notice and take it into consideration if satisfied that the omission was not wilful or unreasonable.

(5) If, after the time at which notice is given under subsection (1) above with respect to an accounting period of a controlled foreign company, the Board make a declaration by virtue of—

(a) paragraph 11(3) of Schedule 24; or

(b) paragraph 3(2) of Schedule 25,

then, unless the effect of the declaration is such that a notice (which, among other matters, will specify the declaration) will be required to be given under subsection (3) above, the Board shall give notice specifying the declaration to every company which was previously given notice of the making of the direction; and subsection (4) above shall apply in relation to a notice under this subsection as it applies in relation to a notice under subsection (3) above but with the omission of paragraphs (a) to (c).

(6) If it appears to the inspector that the amount of the chargeable profits or creditable tax specified in a notice under subsection (1) or subsection (3) above is incorrect, he shall give notice of the revised amount to every company to which notice was given under subsection (1) or subsection (3) above and, except where the revised amount results from—

(*a*) an appeal under this section, or
(*b*) a notice given to the Board under paragraph 4(2) of Schedule 24 or by virtue of paragraph 12 of that Schedule,

any company to which notice is given under this subsection may, by giving notice of appeal to the Board within 60 days of the date of the notice given to the company, appeal to the Special Commissioners against the revised amount specified in the notice.

(7) The jurisdiction of the Special Commissioners on an appeal under this section shall include jurisdiction to review any decision of the Board or the inspector which is relevant to a ground of the appeal.

(8) The Board may make regulations—

(*a*) as respects the conduct of appeals under this section;
(*b*) entitling any person who has received, or is connected or associated with a person who has received, a notice under subsection (1) above with respect to a particular accounting period of a controlled foreign company to appear on an appeal brought by another person who has received such a notice; and
(*c*) with respect to the joinder of appeals brought by different persons with respect to the same direction or the same amount of chargeable profits or creditable tax.

Former enactment.—FA 1984, s. 88.
Cross references.—See TMA 1970, s. 55(6A) (appeals by UK controlled foreign companies against tax assessments and liability).

754. Assessment, recovery and postponement of tax

(1) Subject to the following provisions of this section, the provisions of section 747(4)(*a*) relating to assessment and recovery of a sum as if it were an amount of corporation tax shall be taken as applying, subject to the provisions of the Taxes Acts, and to any necessary modifications, all enactments applying generally to corporation tax, including those relating to the assessing, collecting and receiving of corporation tax, those conferring or regulating a right of appeal and those concerning administration, penalties, interest on unpaid tax and priority of tax in cases of insolvency under the law of any part of the United Kingdom.

(2) For the purposes of the Taxes Acts, any sum assessable and recoverable under section 747(4)(*a*) shall be regarded as corporation tax which falls to be assessed for the accounting period in which ends that one of the controlled foreign company's accounting periods the chargeable profits of which give rise to that sum; and a notice of assessment relating to such a sum shall (in addition to any other matter required to be contained in such a notice) specify separately—

(*a*) the total amount of those chargeable profits and of any creditable tax which has been apportioned to persons falling within each of paragraphs (*a*) to (*d*) of subsection (5), or within subsection (7), of section 749, and
(*b*) where there is more than one class of shares in the controlled foreign company, the total amount apportioned to persons holding shares of each class,

but such a notice shall not identify any particular person (other than the person assessed) as having an interest of any description in the controlled foreign company.

(3) On an appeal against an assessment to tax under section 747(4)(*a*), the jurisdiction of the Special Commissioners shall include jurisdiction to review any relevant decision taken by the Board under section 752 in connection with the apportionment of chargeable profits or creditable tax.

(4) No appeal may be brought against an assessment to tax under section 747(4)(*a*) on a ground on which an appeal has or could have been brought under section 753(4) or (6).

(5) Schedule 26 shall have effect with respect to the reliefs which may be claimed by a company resident in the United Kingdom which has a liability for tax in respect of an amount of chargeable profits; and no reliefs other than those provided for by that Schedule shall be allowed against any such liability.

(6) In any case where—

(*a*) the whole or any part of the tax assessed on a company ("the assessable company") by virtue of section 752(6) is not paid before the date on which it is due and payable in accordance with this Act or, as the case may be, the Management Act; and

(b) the Board serve a notice of liability to tax under this subsection on another company ("the responsible company") which is resident in the United Kingdom and holds or has held (whether directly or indirectly) the same interest in the controlled foreign company as is or was held by the assessable company,

the tax assessed on the assessable company or, as the case may be, so much of it as remains unpaid shall be payable by the responsible company upon service of the notice.

(7) Where a notice of liability is served under subsection (6) above—

(a) any interest due on the tax assessed on the assessable company and not paid; and
(b) any interest accruing due on that tax after the date of service,

shall be payable by the responsible company.

(8) In any case where—

(a) a notice of liability is served on the responsible company under subsection (6) above, and
(b) the relevant tax and any interest payable by the responsible company under subsection (7) above is not paid by that company before the expiry of the period of three months beginning on the date of service of the notice,

that tax and interest may, without prejudice to the right of recovery from the responsible company, be recovered from the assessable company.

(9) In this section "the Taxes Acts" has the same meaning as in the Management Act.

Former enactments.— FA 1984, s. 89(1)–(4), (7)–(11).

755. Information relating to controlled foreign companies

(1) Where it appears to the Board that a company resident outside the United Kingdom (in this section referred to as a "foreign subsidiary") may be a controlled foreign company, the Board may, by notice given to any company which appears to them to be a controlling company of the foreign subsidiary, require that company to give to the Board, within such time (not being less than 30 days) as may be specified in the notice, such particulars (which may include details of documents) as may be so specified with respect to any matter concerning the foreign subsidiary, being particulars required by the Board for the purposes of this Chapter as being relevant to the affairs of the controlling company, the foreign subsidiary or any connected or associated company.

(2) In this section "controlling company", in relation to a foreign subsidiary or any other company, means a company which is resident in the United Kingdom and has, alone or together with other persons so resident, control of the foreign subsidiary or, as the case may be, that other company.

(3) The Board may by notice given to a company which appears to them to be a controlling company in relation to a foreign subsidiary require that company to make available for inspection any relevant books, accounts, or other documents or records whatsoever of the company itself or, subject to subsection (6) below, of any other company, including the foreign subsidiary, in relation to which it appears to the Board to be a controlling company.

(4) In subsection (3) above "relevant" means relevant to—

(a) the computation of any profits of the foreign subsidiary; or
(b) the question whether a direction should be given under section 747(1) with respect to the foreign subsidiary or a connected or associated company or whether any such direction should be amended; or
(c) any question as to the amount of the chargeable profits or creditable tax for any accounting period of the foreign subsidiary or a connected or associated company; or
(d) any question as to the sum which, in accordance with section 747(4)(a), should be assessed on and recoverable from any person.

(5) In subsections (1) and (4) above "connected or associated company" means a controlled foreign company with which the foreign subsidiary or the controlling company is connected or associated.

(6) In any case where—

(a) under subsection (3) above a company is by notice required to make available for inspection any books, accounts, documents or records of a company other than itself, and

(b) it appears to the Board, on the application of the company, that the circumstances are such that the requirement ought not to have effect,

the Board shall direct that the company need not comply with the requirement.

(7) If, on an application under subsection (6) above, the Board refuse to give a direction under that subsection, the company concerned may, by notice given to the Board within 30 days after the refusal, appeal to the Special Commissioners who, if satisfied that the requirement in question ought in the circumstances not to have effect, may determine accordingly.

Former enactment.—FA 1984, s. 90(1)–(7).

756. Interpretation and construction of Chapter IV

(1) In this Chapter "trading company" means a company whose business consists wholly or mainly of the carrying on of a trade or trades.

(2) For the purposes of this Chapter—

(a) section 839 applies; and
(b) subsection (10) of section 783 applies as it applies for the purposes of that section.

(3) The following provisions of Part XI apply for the purposes of this Chapter as they apply for the purposes of that Part—

(a) section 416; and
(b) section 417(7) to (9);

but, in the application of subsection (6) of section 416 for the purposes of this Chapter, for the words "five or fewer participators" there shall be substituted the words "persons resident in the United Kingdom".

Former enactment.—FA 1984, s. 91.

CHAPTER V

OFFSHORE FUNDS

Material interests in non-qualifying offshore funds

757. Disposal of material interests in non-qualifying offshore funds

(1) This Chapter applies to a disposal by any person of an asset if—

(a) at the time of the disposal, the asset constitutes a material interest in an offshore fund which is or has at any material time been a non-qualifying offshore fund; or

(b) at the time of the disposal, the asset constitutes an interest in a company resident in the United Kingdom or in a unit trust scheme, the trustees of which are at that time resident in the United Kingdom and at a material time after 31st December 1984 the company or unit trust scheme was a non-qualifying offshore fund and the asset constituted a material interest in that fund;

and for the purpose of determining whether the asset disposed of falls within paragraph (b) above, section 78 of the 1979 Act (equation of original shares and new holding) shall have effect as it has effect for the purposes of that Act.

(2) Subject to the following provisions of this section and section 758, there is a disposal of an asset for the purposes of this Chapter if there would be such a disposal for the purposes of the 1979 Act.

(3) Notwithstanding anything in paragraph (b) of subsection (1) of section 49 of the 1979 Act (general provisions applicable on death: no deemed disposal by the deceased) where a person dies and the assets of which he was competent to dispose include an asset which is or has at any time been a material interest in a non-qualifying offshore fund, then, for the purposes of this Chapter, other than section 758—

(a) immediately before the acquisition referred to in paragraph (a) of that subsection, that interest shall be deemed to be disposed of by the deceased for such a consideration as is mentioned in that subsection; but

(b) nothing in this subsection affects the determination, in accordance with subsection (1) above, of the question whether that deemed disposal is one to which this Chapter applies.

(4) Subject to subsection (3) above, section 49 of the 1979 Act applies for the purposes of this Chapter as it applies for the purposes of that Act, and the reference in that subsection to the assets of which a deceased person was competent to dispose shall be construed in accordance with subsection (10) of that section.

(5) Notwithstanding anything in section 85 of the 1979 Act (exchange of securities for those in another company) in any case where—

(a) the company which is company B for the purposes of subsection (1) of that section is or was at a material time a non-qualifying offshore fund and the company which is company A for those purposes is not such a fund, or

(b) under section 86 of that Act (reconstruction or amalgamation involving issue of securities) persons are to be treated, in consequence of an arrangement, as exchanging shares, debentures or other interests in or of an entity which is or was at a material time a non-qualifying offshore fund for assets which do not constitute interests in such a fund;

then, subsection (3) of section 85 of that Act (which applies provisions of that Act treating transactions as not being disposals and equating original shares with a new holding in certain cases) shall not apply for the purposes of this Chapter.

(6) In any case where, apart from subsection (5) above, section 85(3) of the 1979 Act would apply, the exchange concerned of shares, debentures or other interests in or of a non-qualifying offshore fund shall for the purposes of this Chapter constitute a disposal of interests in the offshore fund for a consideration equal to their market value at the time of the exchange.

(7) For the purposes of this section—

(a) a material time, in relation to the disposal of an asset, is the earliest date on which any relevant consideration was given for the acquisition of the asset or, if that date is earlier than 1st January 1984, any time on or after 1st January 1984; and (*b*) "relevant consideration" means consideration which, assuming the application to the disposal of Chapter II of Part II of the 1979 Act, would fall to be taken into account in determining the amount of the gain or loss accruing on the disposal, whether that consideration was given by or on behalf of the person making the disposal or by or on behalf of a predecessor in title of his whose acquisition cost represents, directly or indirectly, the whole or any part of the acquisition cost of the person making the disposal.

Former enactments.—Sub-s. (1): FA 1984, s. 92(1), (7).
Sub-ss. (2)–(7): FA 1984, s. 92(2)–(6), (8).

758. Offshore funds operating equalisation arrangements

(1) For the purposes of this Chapter, an offshore fund operates equalisation arrangements if, and at a time when, arrangements are in existence which have the result that where—

(*a*) a person acquires by way of initial purchase a material interest in the fund at some time during a period relevant to the arrangements; and
(*b*) the fund makes a distribution for a period which begins before the date of his acquisition of that interest;

the amount of that distribution which is paid to him (assuming him still to retain that interest) will include a payment of capital which is debited to an account maintained under the arrangements ("the equalisation account") and which is determined by reference to the income which had accrued to the fund at the date of his acquisition.

(2) For the purposes of this section, a person acquires an interest in an offshore fund by way of initial purchase if—

(*a*) his acquisition is by way of subscription for or allotment of new shares, units or other interests issued or created by the fund; or
(*b*) his acquisition is by way of direct purchase from the persons concerned with the management of the fund and their sale to him is made in their capacity as managers of the fund.

(3) Without prejudice to section 757(1), this Chapter applies, subject to the following provisions of this section, to a disposal by any person of an asset if—

(*a*) at the time of the disposal, the asset constitutes a material interest in an offshore fund which at that time is operating equalisation arrangements; and
(*b*) the fund is not and has not at any material time (within the meaning of section 757(7)) been a non-qualifying offshore fund; and
(*c*) the proceeds of the disposal do not fall to be taken into account as a trading receipt.

(4) This Chapter does not, by virtue of subsection (3) above, apply to a disposal if—

(*a*) it takes place during such a period as is mentioned in subsection (1)(*a*) above; and
(*b*) throughout so much of that period as precedes the disposal, the income of the offshore fund concerned has been of such a nature as is referred to in paragraph 3(1) of Schedule 27.

(5) An event which, apart from section 78 of the 1979 Act (reorganisations etc.), would constitute a disposal of an asset shall constitute such a disposal for the purpose of determining whether, by virtue of subsection (3) above, there is a disposal to which this Chapter applies.

(6) The reference in subsection (5) above to section 78 of the 1979 Act includes a reference to that section as applied by section 85 of that Act (exchange of securities) [and a reference to section 78][1] as applied by section 82 of that Act (conversion of securities).

Former enactment.—FA 1984, s. 93.
Amendments.—[1] Words in sub-s. (6) substituted by FA 1989, s. 81 where a conversion of securities occurs after 13 March 1989.

759. Material interests in offshore funds

(1) In this Chapter references to a material interest in an offshore fund are references to such an interest in any of the following, namely—

(*a*) a company which is resident outside the United Kingdom;
(*b*) a unit trust scheme the trustees of which are not resident in the United Kingdom; and
(*c*) any arrangements which do not fall within paragraph (*a*) or (*b*) above, which take effect by virtue of the law of a territory outside the United Kingdom and which, under

that law, create rights in the nature of co-ownership (without restricting that expression to its meaning in the law of any part of the United Kingdom);

and any reference in this Chapter to an offshore fund is a reference to any such company, unit trust scheme or arrangements in which any person has an interest which is a material interest.

(2) Subject to the following provisions of this section, a person's interest in a company, unit trust scheme or arrangements is a material interest if, at the time when he acquired the interest, it could reasonably be expected that, at some time during the period of seven years beginning at the time of his acquisition, he would be able to realise the value of the interest (whether by transfer, surrender or in any other manner).

(3) For the purposes of subsection (2) above, a person is at any time able to realise the value of an interest if at that time he can realise an amount which is reasonably approximate to that portion which the interest represents (directly or indirectly) of the market value at that time of the assets of the company or, as the case may be, of the assets subject to the scheme or arrangements.

(4) For the purposes of subsections (2) and (3) above—

(*a*) a person is able to realise a particular amount if he is able to obtain that amount either in money or in the form of assets to the value of that amount; and

(*b*) if at any time an interest in an offshore fund has a market value which is substantially greater than the portion which the interest represents, as mentioned in subsection (3) above, of the market value at that time of the assets concerned, the ability to realise such a market value of the interest shall not be regarded as an ability to realise such an amount as is referred to in that subsection.

(5) An interest in a company, scheme or arrangements is not a material interest if—

(*a*) it is an interest in respect of any loan capital or debt issued or incurred for money which, in the ordinary course of a business of banking, is lent by a person carrying on that business; or

(*b*) it is a right arising under a policy of insurance.

(6) Shares in a company falling within subsection (1)(*a*) above (an "overseas company") do not constitute a material interest if—

(*a*) the shares are held by a company and the holding of them is necessary or desirable for the maintenance and development of a trade carried on by the company or a company associated with it; and

(*b*) the shares confer at least 10 per cent. of the total voting rights in the overseas company and a right, in the event of a winding-up, to at least 10 per cent. of the assets of that company remaining after the discharge of all liabilities having priority over the shares; and

(*c*) not more than ten persons hold shares in the overseas company and all the shares in that company confer both voting rights and a right to participate in the assets on a winding-up; and

(*d*) at the time of its acquisition of the shares, the company had such a reasonable expectation as is referred to in subsection (2) above by reason only of the existence of—

(i) an arrangement under which, at some time within the period of seven years beginning at the time of acquisition, that company may require the other participators to purchase its shares; or

(ii) provisions of either an agreement between the participators or the constitution of the overseas company under which the company will be wound up within a period which is, or is reasonably expected to be, shorter than the period referred to in subsection (2) above; or

(iii) both such an arrangement and such provisions;

and in this paragraph "participators" means the persons holding shares falling within paragraph (*c*) above.

(7) For the purposes of subsection (6)(*a*) above, a company is associated with another company if one of them has control of the other within the meaning of section 416 or both of them are under the control, within the meaning of that section, of the same person or persons.

(8) An interest in a company falling within subsection (1)(*a*) above is not a material interest at any time when the following conditions are satisfied, namely—

(*a*) that the holder of the interest has the right to have the company wound up; and

(*b*) that, in the event of a winding up, the holder is, by virtue of the interest and any other interest which he then holds in the same capacity, entitled to more than 50 per cent. of the assets remaining after the discharge of all liabilities having priority over the interest or interests concerned.

(9) The market value of any asset for the purposes of this Chapter shall be determined in like manner as it would be determined for the purposes of the 1979 Act except that, in the case of an interest in an offshore fund for which there are separate published buying and selling prices, section 150(4) of that Act (meaning of "market value" in relation to rights of unit holders in a unit trust scheme) shall apply with any necessary modifications for determining the market value of the interest for the purposes of this Chapter.

Former enactment.—FA 1984, s. 94.

760. Non-qualifying offshore funds

(1) For the purposes of this Chapter, an offshore fund is a non-qualifying fund except during an account period of the fund in respect of which the fund is certified by the Board as a distributing fund.

(2) An offshore fund shall not be certified as a distributing fund in respect of any account period unless, with respect to that period, the fund pursues a full distribution policy, within the meaning of Part I of Schedule 27.

(3) Subject to Part II of that Schedule, an offshore fund shall not be certified as a distributing fund in respect of any account period if, at any time in that period—

   (*a*) more than 5 per cent. by value of the assets of the fund consists of interests in other offshore funds; or
   (*b*) subject to subsections (4) and (5) below, more than 10 per cent. by value of the assets of the fund consists of interests in a single company; or
   (*c*) the assets of the fund include more than 10 per cent. of the issued share capital of any company or of any class of that share capital; or
   (*d*) subject to subsection (6) below, there is more than one class of material interest in the offshore fund and they do not all receive proper distribution benefits, within the meaning of subsection (7) below.

(4) For the purposes of subsection (3)(*b*) above, in any account period the value, expressed as a percentage of the value of all the assets of an offshore fund, of that portion of the assets of the fund which consists of an interest in a single company shall be determined as at the most recent occasion (whether in that account period or an earlier one) on which the fund acquired an interest in that company for consideration in money or money's worth; but for this purpose there shall be disregarded any occasion—

   (*a*) on which the interest acquired constituted the "new holding" for the purposes of section 78 of the 1979 Act (equation of original shares and new holding), including that section as applied by any later provision of Chapter II of Part IV of that Act (reorganisation of share capital etc.); and
   (*b*) on which no consideration fell to be given for the interest acquired, other than the interest which constituted the "original shares" for the purposes of that section.

(5) Except for the purpose of determining the total value of the assets of an offshore fund, an interest in a company shall be disregarded for the purposes of subsection (3)(*b*) above if—

   (*a*) the company carries on (in the United Kingdom or elsewhere) a banking business providing current or deposit account facilities in any currency for members of the public and bodies corporate; and
   (*b*) the interest consists of a current or deposit account provided in the normal course of the company's banking business.

(6) There shall be disregarded for the purposes of subsection (3)(*d*) above any interests in an offshore fund—

   (*a*) which are held solely by persons employed or engaged in or about the management of the assets of the fund; and
   (*b*) which carry no right or expectation to participate, directly or indirectly, in any of the profits of the fund; and
   (*c*) which, on a winding up or on redemption, carry no right to receive anything other than the return of the price paid for the interests.

(7) If in any account period of an offshore fund there is more than one class of material

interests in the fund, the classes of interest do not, for the purposes of subsection (3)(*d*) above, all receive proper distribution benefits unless, were each class of interests and the assets which that class represents interests in and assets of a separate offshore fund, each of those separate funds would, with respect to that period, pursue a full distribution policy, within the meaning of Part I of Schedule 27.

(8) For the purposes of this Chapter, an account period of an offshore fund shall begin—

(*a*) whenever the fund begins to carry on its activities; and
(*b*) whenever an account period of the funds ends without the fund then ceasing to carry on its activities.

(9) For the purposes of this Chapter, an account period of an offshore fund shall end on the first occurrence of any of the following—

(*a*) the expiration of 12 months from the beginning of the period;
(*b*) an accounting date of the fund or, if there is a period for which the fund does not make up accounts, the end of that period; and
(*c*) the fund ceasing to carry on its activities.

(10) For the purposes of this Chapter—

(*a*) an account period of an offshore fund which is a company falling within section 759(1)(*a*) shall end if, and at the time when, the company ceases to be resident outside the United Kingdom; and
(*b*) an account period of an offshore fund which is a unit trust scheme falling within section 759(1)(*b*) shall end if, and at the time when, the trustees of the scheme become resident in the United Kingdom.

(11) The provisions of Part III of Schedule 27 shall have effect with respect to the procedure for and in connection with the certification of an offshore fund as a distributing fund, and the supplementary provisions in Part IV of that Schedule shall have effect.

Former enactment.—FA 1984, s. 95.

Charge to tax of offshore income gains

761. Charge to income tax or corporation tax of offshore income gain

(1) If a disposal to which this Chapter applies gives rise in accordance with section 758 and Schedule 28 to an offshore income gain, then, subject to the provisions of this section, the amount of that gain shall be treated for all the purposes of the Tax Acts as—

(*a*) income arising at the time of the disposal to the person making the disposal, and
(*b*) constituting profits or gains chargeable to tax under Case VI of Schedule D for the chargeable period in which the disposal is made.

(2) Subject to subsection (3) below, sections 2 and 12 of the 1979 Act (persons chargeable to tax in respect of chargeable gains) and section 11(2)(*b*) shall have effect in relation to income tax or corporation tax in respect of offshore income gains as they have effect in relation to capital gains tax or corporation tax in respect of chargeable gains.

(3) In the application of section 12 of the 1979 Act in accordance with subsection (2) above, paragraphs (*a*) and (*b*) of subsection (1) of that section (which define the assets on the disposal of which chargeable gains are taxable) shall have effect with the omission of the words "situated in the United Kingdom and".

(4) In a case where section 12 of the 1979 Act has effect as modified by subsection (3) above, section 11 shall have effect as if, in subsection (2)(*b*), the words "situated in the United Kingdom" were omitted.

(5) In the case of individuals resident or ordinarily resident but not domiciled in the United Kingdom, section 14 of the 1979 Act (which provides for taxation on a remittance basis) shall have effect in relation to income tax chargeable by virtue of subsection (1) above on an offshore income gain as it has effect in relation to capital gains tax in respect of gains accruing to such individuals from the disposal of assets situated outside the United Kingdom.

(6) A charity shall be exempt from tax in respect of an offshore income gain if the gain is applicable and applied for charitable purposes; but if property held on charitable trusts ceases to be subject to charitable trusts and that property represents directly or indirectly an offshore income gain, the trustees shall be treated as if they had disposed of and immediately reacquired that property for a consideration equal to its market value, any gain (calculated

in accordance with Schedule 28) accruing being treated as an offshore income gain not accruing to a charity.

In this subsection "charity" has the same meaning as in section 506 and "market value" has the same meaning as in the 1979 Act.

(7) In any case where—

(*a*) a disposal to which this Chapter applies is a disposal of settled property, within the meaning of the 1979 Act, and

(*b*) for the purposes of the 1979 Act, the general administration of the trusts is ordinarily carried on outside the United Kingdom and the trustees or a majority of them for the time being are not resident or not ordinarily resident in the United Kingdom,

subsection (1) above shall not apply in relation to any offshore income gain to which the disposal gives rise.

Former enactments.—FA 1984, s. 96; FA 1987, Sch. 15, para. 16(1).

762. Offshore income gains accruing to persons resident or domiciled abroad

(1) Section 15 of the 1979 Act (chargeable gains accruing to certain non-resident companies) shall have effect in relation to offshore income gains subject to the following modifications—

(*a*) for any reference to a chargeable gain there shall be substituted a reference to an offshore income gain;

(*b*) for the reference in subsection (7) to capital gains tax there shall be substituted a reference to income tax or corporation tax; and

(*c*) paragraphs (*b*) and (*c*) of subsection (5) and subsection (8) shall be omitted.

(2) Subject to subsections (3) and (4) below, sections 80 to 84 of the Finance Act 1981 (gains of non-resident settlements) shall have effect in relation to offshore income gains subject to the following modifications—

(*a*) for any reference to chargeable gains, other than the reference in section 80(5), there shall be substituted a reference to offshore income gains;

(*b*) in section 80(2) for the words "tax under section 4(1) of the Capital Gains Tax Act 1979" there shall be substituted the words "income tax by virtue of section 761 of the Taxes Act";

(*c*) in section 80(6) the reference to tax shall be construed as a reference to income tax or corporation tax; and

(*d*) sections 80(8) and 83(6) shall be omitted.

(3) In section 80(5) of the Finance Act 1981, both as it applies apart from subsection (2) above and as applied by subsection (2) above, the reference to chargeable gains shall be construed as including a reference to offshore income gains.

(4) If, in any year of assessment—

(*a*) under subsection (3) of section 80 of the Finance Act 1981, as it applies apart from subsection (2) above, a chargeable gain falls to be attributed to a beneficiary, and

(*b*) under that subsection, as applied by subsection (2) above, an offshore income gain also falls to be attributed to him,

subsection (4) of that section (gains attributed in proportion to capital payments received) shall have effect as if it required offshore income gains to be attributed before chargeable gains.

(5) Subject to subsection (6) below, for the purpose of determining whether an individual ordinarily resident in the United Kingdom has a liability for income tax in respect of an offshore income gain which arises on a disposal to which this Chapter applies where the disposal is made by a person resident or domiciled outside the United Kingdom—

(*a*) sections 739 and 740 shall apply as if the offshore income gain arising to the person resident or domiciled outside the United Kingdom constituted income becoming payable to him, and

(*b*) any reference in those sections to income of (or payable or arising to) such a person accordingly includes a reference to the offshore income gain arising to him by reason of the disposal to which this Chapter applies.

(6) To the extent that an offshore income gain is treated, by virtue of subsection (1) or subsection (2) above, as having accrued to any person resident or ordinarily resident in the United Kingdom, that gain shall not be deemed to be the income of any individual for the purposes of section 739 or 740 or any provision of Part XV.

Former enactment.—FA 1984, s. 97.

763. Deduction of offshore income gain in determining capital gain

(1) The provisions of this section apply where a disposal to which this Chapter applies gives rise to an offshore income gain; and, if that disposal also constitutes the disposal of the interest concerned for the purposes of the 1979 Act, then that disposal is in the following provisions of this section referred to as "the 1979 Act disposal".

(2) So far as relates to an offshore income gain which arises on a material disposal (within the meaning of Part I of Schedule 28), subsections (3) and (4) below shall have effect in relation to the 1979 Act disposal in substitution for section 31(1) of that Act (deduction of consideration chargeable to tax on income).

(3) Subject to the following provisions of this section, in the computation under Chapter II of Part II of the 1979 Act of any gain accruing on the 1979 Act disposal, a sum equal to the offshore income gain shall be deducted from the sum which would otherwise constitute the amount or value of the consideration for the disposal.

(4) Where the 1979 Act disposal is of such a nature that, by virtue of section 35 of that Act (part disposals) an apportionment falls to be made of certain expenditure, no deduction shall be made by virtue of subsection (3) above in determining, for the purposes of the fraction in subsection (2) of that section, the amount or value of the consideration for the disposal.

(5) If the 1979 Act disposal forms part of a transfer to which section 123 of that Act applies (roll-over relief on transfer of business in exchange wholly or partly for shares) then, for the purposes of subsection (4) of that section (determination of the amount of the deduction from the gain on the old assets) "B" in the fraction in that subsection (the value of the whole of the consideration received by the transferor in exchange for the business) shall be taken to be what it would be if the value of the consideration other than shares so received by the transferor were reduced by a sum equal to the offshore income gain.

(6) Where the disposal to which this Chapter applies constitutes such a disposal by virtue of section 757(6) or 758(5), the 1979 Act shall have effect as if an amount equal to the offshore income gain to which the disposal gives rise were given (by the person making the exchange concerned) as consideration for the new holding, within the meaning of section 79 of that Act (consideration given or received for new holding on a reorganisation).

(7) In any case where—

(*a*) a disposal to which this Chapter applies by virtue of subsection (3) of section 758 is made otherwise than to the offshore fund concerned or the persons referred to in subsection (2)(*b*) of that section; and
(*b*) subsequently, a distribution which is referable to the asset disposed of is paid either to the person who made the disposal or to a person connected with him; and
(*c*) the disposal gives rise (in accordance with Part II of Schedule 28) to an offshore income gain;

then, for the purposes of the Tax Acts, the amount of the first distribution falling within paragraph (*b*) above shall be taken to be reduced or, as the case may be, extinguished by deducting therefrom an amount equal to the offshore income gain referred to in paragraph (*c*) above and, if that amount exceeds the amount of that first distribution, the balance shall be set against the second and, where necessary, any later distribution falling within paragraph (*b*) above, until the balance is exhausted.

(8) Section 839 shall apply for the purposes of subsection (7)(*b*) above.

Former enactment.—FA 1984, s. 98.

764. Offshore income gains of trustees

Income arising in a year of assessment by virtue of section 761(1) to trustees shall be chargeable to income tax at a rate equal to the sum of the basic rate and the additional rate for that year.

Former enactment.—FA 1984, s. 100(1).

CHAPTER VI

MISCELLANEOUS

Migration etc. of company

765. Migration etc. of companies

(1) Subject to the provisions of this section, all transactions of the following classes shall be unlawful unless carried out with the consent of the Treasury, that is to say—

(*a*) ...[1]
(*b*) ...[1]
(*c*) for a body corporate [resident in the United Kingdom][2] to cause or permit a body corporate not [resident in the United Kingdom][2] over which it has control to create or issue any shares or debentures; or
(*d*) except for the purpose of enabling a person to be qualified to act as a director, for a body corporate so resident to transfer to any person, or cause or permit to be transferred to any person, any shares or debentures of a body corporate not so resident over which it has control, being shares or debentures which it owns or in which it has an interest.

(2) Nothing in subsection (1)(*c*) above shall apply to the giving to the bankers of the body corporate not resident in the United Kingdom of any security for the payment of any sum due or to become due from it to them by reason of any transaction entered into with it by them in the ordinary course of their business as bankers.

(3) Nothing in subsection (1)(*c*) above shall apply to the giving by the body corporate not resident in the United Kingdom to an insurance company of any security for the payment of any sum due or to become due from that body corporate to that company by reason of any transaction entered into with that body corporate by that company in the ordinary course of that company's business by way of investment of its funds.

(4) Any consent granted by the Treasury under this section—

(*a*) may be given either specially (that is to say, so as to apply only to specified transactions of or relating to a specified body corporate) or generally (that is to say, so as not only so to apply); and
(*b*) may, if given generally, be revoked by the Treasury; and
(*c*) may in any case be absolute or conditional; and
(*d*) shall be published in such a way as to give any person entitled to the benefit of it an adequate opportunity of getting to know of it, unless in the opinion of the Treasury publication is not necessary for that purpose.

Former enactment.—TA 1970, s. 482(1)–(4).
Cross references.—See FA 1988, s. 105(6) and Sch. 14, Pt. IV (amendments to TA 1970, s. 482 effective from 15 March 1988).
Amendments.—[1] Sub-s. (1)(*a*), (*b*) repealed by FA 1988, s. 105(6), (7) and Sch. 14, Pt. IV with effect from 15 March 1988 but the repeal does not affect an application for Treasury consent made before that date or a consent already granted.
[2] Words in sub-s. (1)(*c*) substituted by FA 1988, s. 105(6), (7) with effect from 15 March 1988.

766. Offences under section 765

(1) Any person who, whether within or outside the United Kingdom, does or is a party to the doing of any act which to his knowledge amounts to or results in, or forms part of a series of acts which together amount to or result in, or will amount to or result in, something which is unlawful under section 765(1) shall be guilty of an offence under this section.

(2) In any proceedings in respect of such an offence against a director of the body corporate in question (that is to say, the body corporate which is or was resident in the United Kingdom) or against any person who was purporting to act in that capacity—

(*a*) it shall be presumed that he was a party to every act of that body corporate unless he proves that it was done without his consent or connivance; and
(*b*) it shall, unless the contrary is proved, be presumed that any act which in fact amounted to or resulted in, or formed part of a series of acts which together amounted to or resulted in or would amount to or result in, something which is unlawful under section 765(1) was to his knowledge such an act.

(3) Any person who is guilty of an offence under this section shall be liable on conviction on indictment—

(a) to imprisonment for not more than two years or to a fine, or to both; or
(b) where the person in question is a body corporate which is or was resident in the United Kingdom, to a fine not exceeding an amount equal to three times the corporation tax, capital gains tax and income tax paid or payable which is attributable to the income, profits or gains (including chargeable gains) arising in the 36 months immediately preceding the commission of the offence, or £10,000, whichever is the greater;

and proceedings in respect of such an offence alleged to have been committed by a person may be taken before the appropriate court in the United Kingdom having jurisdiction in the place where that person is for the time being.

(4) No proceedings for an offence under this section shall be instituted, in England or Wales, except by or with the consent of the Attorney General, or in Northern Ireland, except by or with the consent of the Attorney General for Northern Ireland.

Former enactments.—Sub-ss. (1)–(2): TA 1970, s. 482(5).
Sub-s. (3): TA 1970, s. 482(6).
Sub-s. (4): TA 1970, s. 482(11).

767. Interpretation and commencement of sections 765 and 766

(1)–(4) . . .[1]

(5) In this section and in sections 765 and 766—

"share", "debenture" and "director" have, in relation to any body corporate, the meanings respectively assigned to them by Part XXVI of the Companies Act 1985 in relation to a company;
"control" (except in the expression "central management and control") has, in relation to a body corporate, the meaning given by section 840;
"transfer", in relation to shares or debentures, includes a transfer of any beneficial interest therein;
"insurance company" means a body corporate lawfully carrying on business as an insurer, whether in the United Kingdom or elsewhere; and
"funds" in relation to an insurance company means the funds held by it in connection with that business;

. . .[1]

(6) This section and sections 765 and 766 shall come into force on 6th April 1988 to the exclusion of section 482 of the 1970 Act (which is re-enacted by those sections); but any offence committed before 6th April 1988 shall not be punishable under section 766 and neither this subsection nor any other provision of this Act shall prevent any such offence from being punishable as if this Act had not been passed.

Former enactments.—Sub-ss. (1)–(2): TA 1970, s. 482(7).
Sub-ss. (3)–(5): TA 1970, s. 482(8)–(10).
Sub-s. (6): TA 1970, s. 482(12).
Amendments.—[1] Sub-ss. (1)–(4) and words in sub-s. (5) repealed by FA 1988, Sch. 14, Pt. IV with effect from 15 March 1988.

Change in ownership of company

768. Change in ownership of company: disallowance of trading losses

(1) If—

(a) within any period of three years there is both a change in the ownership of a company and (either earlier or later in that period, or at the same time) a major change in the nature or conduct of a trade carried on by the company, or
(b) at any time after the scale of the activities in a trade carried on by a company has become small or negligible, and before any considerable revival of the trade, there is a change in the ownership of the company,

no relief shall be given under section 393 by setting a loss incurred by the company in an accounting period beginning before the change of ownership against any income or other profits of an accounting period ending after the change of ownership.

(2) In applying this section to the accounting period in which the change of ownership occurs, the part ending with the change of ownership, and the part after, shall be treated as

two separate accounting periods, and the profits or losses of the accounting period shall be apportioned to the two parts.

(3) The apportionment under subsection (2) above shall be on a time basis according to the respective lengths of those parts except that if it appears that that method would work unreasonably or unjustly such other method shall be used as appears just and reasonable.

(4) In subsection (1) above "major change in the nature or conduct of a trade" includes—

(*a*) a major change in the type of property dealt in, or services or facilities provided, in the trade; or
(*b*) a major change in customers, outlets or markets of the trade;

and this section applies even if the change is the result of a gradual process which began outside the period of three years mentioned in subsection (1)(*a*) above.

(5) In relation to any relief available under section 343 to a successor company, subsection (1) above shall apply as if any loss sustained by a predecessor company had been sustained by a successor company and as if the references to a trade included references to the trade as carried on by a predecessor company.

(6) Where relief in respect of a company's losses has been restricted under this section then, notwithstanding section 87(3) of the 1968 Act, in applying the provisions of that Act about balancing charges to the company by reference to any event after the change of ownership of the company, any allowance or deduction falling to be made in taxing the company's trade for any chargeable period before the change of ownership shall be disregarded unless the profits or gains of that chargeable period or of any subsequent chargeable period before the change of ownership were sufficient to give effect to the allowance or deduction.

(7) In applying subsection (6) above it shall be assumed that any profits or gains are applied in giving effect to any such allowance or deduction in preference to being set off against any loss which is not attributable to such an allowance or deduction.

(8) Where the operation of this section depends on circumstances or events at a time after the change of ownership (but not more than three years after), an assessment to give effect to the provisions of this section shall not be out of time if made within six years from that time, or the latest of those times.

(9) Any person in whose name any shares, stock or securities of a company are registered shall, if required by notice by an inspector given for the purposes of this section, state whether or not he is the beneficial owner of those shares or securities and, if not the beneficial owner of those shares or securities of any of them, shall furnish the name and address of the person or persons on whose behalf those shares, stock or securities are registered in his name.

Former enactment.—TA 1970, s. 483(1)–(7).

769. Rules for ascertaining change in ownership of company

(1) For the purposes of section 768 there is a change in the ownership of a company—

(*a*) if a single person acquires more than half the ordinary share capital of the company; or
(*b*) if two or more persons each acquire a holding of 5 per cent. or more of the ordinary share capital of the company, and those holdings together amount to more than half the ordinary share capital of the company; or
(*c*) if two or more persons each acquire a holding of the ordinary share capital of the company, and the holdings together amount to more than half the ordinary share capital of the company, but disregarding a holding of less than 5 per cent. unless it is an addition to an existing holding and the two holdings together amount to 5 per cent. or more of the ordinary share capital of the company.

(2) In applying subsection (1) above—

(*a*) the circumstances at any two points of time with not more than three years between may be compared, and a holder at the later time may be regarded as having acquired whatever he did not hold at the earlier time, irrespective of what he has acquired or disposed of in between;
(*b*) to allow for any issue of shares or other reorganisation of capital, the comparison may be made in terms of percentage holdings of the total ordinary share capital at the respective times, so that a person whose percentage holding is greater at the later time may be regarded as having acquired a percentage holding equal to the increase;

(c) to decide for the purposes of subsection (1)(b) or (c) above if any person has acquired a holding of at least 5 per cent., or a holding which makes at least 5 per cent. when added to an existing holding, acquisitions by, and holdings of, two or more persons who are connected persons within the meaning of section 839 shall be aggregated as if they were acquisitions by, and holdings of, one and the same person;
(d) any acquisition of shares under the will or on the intestacy of a deceased person and, if it is shown that the gift is unsolicited and made without regard to the provisions of section 768, any gift of shares, shall be left out of account.

(3) Where, because persons, whether company members or not, possess extraordinary rights or powers under the articles of association or under any other document regulating the company, ownership of the ordinary share capital may not be an appropriate test of whether there has been a major change in the persons for whose benefit the losses may ultimately enure, then, in considering whether there has been a change in the ownership of the company for the purposes of section 768, holdings of all kinds of share capital, including preference shares, or of any particular category of share capital, or voting power or any other special kind of power, may be taken into account instead of ordinary share capital.

(4) Where section 768 has operated to restrict relief by reference to a change of ownership taking place at any time, no transaction or circumstances before that time shall be taken into account in determining whether there is any subsequent change of ownership.

(5) A change in the ownership of a company shall be disregarded for the purposes of section 768 if—

(a) immediately before the change the company is the 75 per cent. subsidiary of another company, and
(b) (although there is a change in the direct ownership of the company) that other company continues after the change to own the first-mentioned company as a 75 per cent. subsidiary.

[(6) If there is a change in the ownership of a company, including a change occurring by virtue of the application of this subsection but not a change which is to be disregarded under subsection (5) above, then—

(a) in a case falling within subsection (1)(a) above, the person mentioned in subsection (1)(a) shall be taken for the purposes of this section to acquire at the time of the change any relevant assets owned by the company;
(b) in a case falling within subsection (1)(b) above but not within subsection (1)(a) above, each of the persons mentioned in subsection (1)(b) shall be taken for the purposes of this section to acquire at the time of the change the appropriate proportion of any relevant assets owned by the company; and
(c) in any other case, each of the persons mentioned in paragraph (c) of subsection (1) above (other than any whose holding is disregarded under that paragraph) shall be taken for the purposes of this section to acquire at the time of the change the appropriate proportion of any relevant assets owned by the company.][1]

[(6A) In subsection (6) above—

"the appropriate proportion", in relation to one of two or more persons mentioned in subsection (1)(b) or (c) above, means a proportion corresponding to the proportion which the percentage of the ordinary share capital acquired by him bears to the percentage of that capital acquired by all those persons taken together; and
"relevant assets", in relation to a company, means—

(a) any ordinary share capital of another company, and
(b) any property or rights which under subsection (3) above may be taken into account instead of ordinary share capital of another company.][1]

[(6B) Notwithstanding that at any time a company ("the subsidiary company") is a 75 per cent. subsidiary of another company ("the parent company") it shall not be treated at that time as such a subsidiary for the purposes of this section unless, additionally, at that time—

(a) the parent company would be beneficially entitled to not less than 75 per cent. of any profits available for distribution to equity holders of the subsidiary company; and
(b) the parent company would be beneficially entitled to not less than 75 per cent. of any assets of the subsidiary company available for distribution to its equity holders on a winding-up.][1]

[(6C) Schedule 18 shall apply for the purposes of subsection (6B) above as it applies for the purposes of section 413(7).][1]

(7) For the purposes of this section—

(a) references to ownership shall be construed as references to beneficial ownership, and references to acquisition shall be construed accordingly;
(b) ...[2]
(c) ...[2]
(d) "shares" includes stock.

(8) If any acquisition of ordinary share capital or other property or rights taken into account in determining that there has been a change of ownership of a company was made in pursuance of a contract of sale or option or other contract, or the acquisition was made by a person holding such a contract, then the time when the change in the ownership of the company took place shall be determined as if the acquisition had been made when the contract was made with the holder or when the benefit of it was assigned to him so that, in the case of a person exercising an option to purchase shares, he shall be regarded as having purchased the shares when he acquired the option.

Former enactment.—TA 1970, s. 484.
Amendments.—[1] Sub-ss. (6) to (6C) substituted for sub-s. (6) by FA 1989, s. 100 where the change of ownership of a company would be treated as occurring after 13 March 1989.
[2] Sub-s. (7)(b), (c) repealed by *ibid* and Sch. 17, Pt. IV.

Transactions between associated persons

770. Sales etc. at an undervalue or overvalue

(1) Subject to the provisions of this section and section 771, where any property is sold and—

(a) the buyer is a body of persons over whom the seller has control or the seller is a body of persons over whom the buyer has control or both the buyer and the seller are bodies of persons over whom the same person or persons has or have control; and
(b) the property is sold at a price ("the actual price") which is either—

(i) less than the price which it might have been expected to fetch if the parties to the transaction had been independent persons dealing at arm's length ("the arm's length price"), or
(ii) greater than the arm's length price,

then, in computing for tax purposes the income, profits or losses of the seller where the actual price was less than the arm's length price, and of the buyer where the actual price was greater than the arm's length price, the like consequences shall ensue as would have ensued if the property had been sold for the arm's length price.

(2) Subsection (1) above shall not apply—

(a) in any case where—

(i) the actual price is less than the arm's length price, and
(ii) the buyer is resident in the United Kingdom and is carrying on a trade there, and
(iii) the price of the property falls to be taken into account as a deduction in computing the profits or gains or losses of that trade for tax purposes; or

(b) in any case where—

(i) the actual price is greater than the arm's length price, and
(ii) the seller is resident in the United Kingdom and is carrying on a trade there, and
(iii) the price of the property falls to be taken into account as a trading receipt in computing the profits or gains or losses of that trade for tax purposes; or

(c) in relation to any transaction in relation to which section 493(1) or (3) applies; or
(d) in relation to any other sale, unless the Board so direct.

(3) Where a direction is given under subsection (2)(d) above all such adjustments shall be made, whether by assessment, repayment of tax or otherwise, as are necessary to give effect to the direction.

Former enactments.—Sub-s. (1): TA 1970, s. 485(1), (2); FA 1975, s. 17(2).
Sub-s. (2): TA 1970, s. 485(1), (2), (3); OTA 1975, s. 14(6).
Sub-s. (3): TA 1970, s. 485(3).

771. Transactions by petroleum companies

(1) For the purposes of this section a company is a petroleum company if—

(a) its activities include any relevant activities; or

(b) it is associated with a company whose activities include any relevant activities and its own activities include the ownership, operation or management of ships or pipelines (as defined in section 65 of the Pipelines Act 1962) used for transporting or conveying petroleum or petroleum products.

(2) "Relevant activities" means any of the following—

(a) the acquisition or disposal of petroleum or of rights to acquire or dispose of petroleum;
(b) the importation into or exportation from the United Kingdom of petroleum products or the acquisition or disposal of rights to such importation or exportation;
(c) the acquisition otherwise than for importation into the United Kingdom of petroleum products outside the United Kingdom or the disposal outside the United Kingdom of petroleum products not exported from the United Kingdom by the company making the disposal;
(d) the refining or processing of crude petroleum; and
(e) the extraction of petroleum, either under rights authorising it or under contractual or other arrangements with persons by whom such rights are exercisable.

(3) Section 770(2) shall have effect with the omission of paragraphs (a) and (b) in any case where—

(a) either party to the transaction is a petroleum company or both are petroleum companies; and
(b) the activities of either or both are or include activities—
  (i) the profits from which are or would be chargeable to overseas tax for which credit could be given under section 790 or in pursuance of arrangements having effect by virtue of section 788; or
  (ii) which are exploration or exploitation activities within the meaning of section 830; and
(c) the transaction is part of such activities or is connected with them.

(4) Where both the buyer and the seller are resident in the United Kingdom and the Board, in pursuance of this section, direct that section 770(1) is to apply to the computation of the income, profits or losses of the one, the direction may extend the application of that subsection to the computation of the income, profits or losses of the other, and where it does so adjustments shall be made under section 770(3) accordingly.

(5) Where any property is sold and either the buyer or the seller is a petroleum company or both are petroleum companies, then if—

(a) the sale is part of a transaction or series of transactions (whether or not between the same persons) and its terms are affected by those of the remainder of the transaction or transactions; or
(b) what is sold is petroleum extracted under rights exercisable by a company other than the buyer, and not less than 20 per cent. of that company's ordinary share capital was at the time of the sale owned directly or indirectly by one or more of the following, that is to say, the buyer and any companies associated with the buyer;

section 770 shall apply in relation to the sale as if in subsection (1) of that section paragraph (a) were omitted.

(6) Where a petroleum company was a party to a sale of property, then, in determining for the purposes of section 770 what price the property might have been expected to fetch had the parties to the transaction been independent persons dealing at arm's length and what consequences would have ensued in computing the income, profits or losses of the seller or the buyer for tax purposes if the property had been sold for that price, it shall be assumed—

(a) that the terms of the transaction would have been such as might have been expected to secure both to the buyer and to the seller a reasonable profit from transactions of the same kind carried out on similar terms over a reasonable period; and
(b) that the seller would not have been compelled by law or by executive action of any government to demand a price fixed by law or such action or a price not less than one so fixed; and
(c) that, if the transaction was part of a transaction or series of transactions (whether or not between the same persons), its terms would not have been affected by those of the remainder of the transaction or transactions; and
(d) in a case where the whole of the property sold is not delivered by the seller within 12 months after the date of the sale—
  (i) that such part of the property as is delivered within that time would have fetched a price equal to that which it might have been expected to fetch if sold under a contract

for the sale of that part and of no other property, being a contract made at the date of the sale; and

(ii) that such part of the property not so delivered as is delivered in any calendar month would have fetched a price equal to that which it might have been expected to fetch if sold under a contract for the sale of that part and of no other property, being a contract made at the material time in that month;

and no regard shall be had to the terms of similar transactions which were capable of being varied.

In this subsection "calendar month" means a month of the calendar year and "material time", in relation to a calendar month, means noon on the middle day of the month which, in the case of a month containing an even number of days, shall be taken to be the last day of the first half of the month.

(7) In this section—

"petroleum" includes any mineral oil or relative hydrocarbon and, except in the expression "crude petroleum", includes natural gas;

"petroleum products" means products derived from petroleum and wholly or substantially of a hydrocarbon nature.

(8) For the purposes of this section—

(*a*) two companies are associated with one another if one is under the control of the other or both are under the control of the same person or persons, and "control" has the meaning given by section 840;

(*b*) any question whether ordinary share capital is owned by a company directly or indirectly shall be determined as for the purposes of section 838;

(*c*) rights are exercisable by a company if they are exercisable by that company alone or jointly with another company or companies.

Former enactments.—OTA 1975, s. 20(1), Sch. 9, paras. 1–6, 7(1), (2)(*a*)–(*c*); FA 1987, Sch. 11, para. 7.

772. Information for purposes of section 770, and appeals

(1) The Board may, by notice given to any body corporate, require it to give to the Board, within such time (not being less than 30 days) as may be specified in the notice, such particulars (which may include details of relevant documents) as may be so specified of any related transaction which appears to the Board—

(*a*) to be, or to be connected with, a transaction with respect to which the Board might give a direction under section 770; or

(*b*) to be relevant for determining whether such a direction could or should be given in any case; or

(*c*) to be relevant for determining for the purposes of that section what price any property sold would have fetched had the sale been one between independent persons dealing at arm's length.

(2) For the purposes of a notice under subsection (1) above, a transaction is a related transaction if, but only if, it is one to which the body corporate to which the notice is given, or a body corporate associated with that body, was a party; and for the purposes of this subsection two bodies corporate are associated with one another if one is under the control of the other or both are under the control of the same person or persons.

(3) Where, in the case of a transaction with respect to which it appears to the Board that a direction under section 770 might be given—

(*a*) one of the parties is a body corporate resident outside the United Kingdom and a 51 per cent. subsidiary of a body corporate ("the parent body") resident in the United Kingdom; and

(*b*) the other party is, or is a 51 per cent. subsidiary of, the parent body,

the Board may, by notice given to the parent body, require it to make available for inspection any books, accounts or other documents or records whatsoever of the parent body or, subject to subsection (4) below, of any body of persons over which it has control which relate to that transaction, to any other transaction (of whatever nature) in the same assets, or to transactions (of whatever nature) in assets similar to those to which the first-mentioned transaction related.

(4) If, in a case in which under subsection (3) above the parent body is by notice required to make available for inspection any books, accounts, documents or records of a body of

persons resident outside the United Kingdom over which the parent body has control, it appears to the Board, on the application of the parent body, that the circumstances are such that the requirement ought not to have effect, the Board shall direct that the parent body need not comply with the requirement.

(5) If, on an application under subsection (4) above, the Board refuse to give a direction under that subsection, the parent body may, by notice given to the Board within 30 days after the refusal, appeal to the Special Commissioners who, if satisfied that the requirement in question ought in the circumstances not to have effect, may determine accordingly.

(6) Where it appears to the Board that a body of persons may be a party to a transaction or transactions with respect to which a direction under section 770 might be given, then, for the purpose of assisting the Board to determine whether such a direction should be given, an inspector specifically authorised in that behalf by the Board may, at any reasonable time, on production if so required of his authority—

(a) enter any premises used in connection with the relevant trade carried on by that body of persons (that is to say, the trade in the course of which the transaction or transactions were effected),
(b) inspect there any books, accounts or other documents or records whatsoever relating to that trade which he considers it necessary for him to inspect for that purpose, and
(c) require any such books, accounts or other documents or records to be produced to him there for inspection.

(7) An inspector's authority for entering any premises under subsection (6) above shall state the name of the inspector and the name of the body of persons carrying on the trade in connection with which the premises are used.

(8) If and so far as the question in dispute on an appeal to the General Commissioners or, in Northern Ireland, to a county court against an assessment to tax arises from a direction of the Board under section 770 the question shall be referred to and determined by the Special Commissioners.

Former enactments.—FA 1975, s. 17(3)–(8); OTA 1975, s. 20(2), (3).

773. Interpretation of sections 770 and 771

(1) Nothing in sections 770 and 771 shall be construed as affecting the operation of any of the provisions of the 1968 Act or of Chapter I of Part III of the Finance Act 1971.

(2) In sections 770 and 772—

"body of persons" includes a partnership, and
"control" has the meaning given by section 840;

and, for the purposes of this section, a sale shall be deemed to take place at the time of completion or when possession is given, whichever is the earlier.

(3) In determining for the purposes of sections 770 and 771 whether any person (alone or with others) has control over a body of persons—

(a) there shall be attributed to him any rights or powers of a nominee for him, that is to say, any rights or powers which another possesses on his behalf or may be required to exercise on his direction or behalf;
(b) there may also be attributed to him any rights or powers of a person with whom he is connected (within the meaning of section 839 but omitting subsections (5) to (7) and the exception in subsection (4)), including any rights or powers of a nominee for such a person, that is to say, any rights or powers which another possesses on behalf of such a person or may be required to exercise on his direction or behalf.

(4) Sections 770, 771, except subsection (5)(b), and 772 and this section shall, with the necessary adaptations, have effect in relation to lettings and hirings of property, grants and transfers of rights, interests or licences and the giving of business facilities of whatever kind as they have effect in relation to sales, and the references in those sections to sales, sellers, buyers and prices shall be deemed to be extended accordingly.

Former enactments.—TA 1970, s. 485(4)–(6); FA 1975, s. 17(1), (10); OTA 1975, Sch. 9, para. 7(2)(d).

774. Transactions between dealing company and associated company

(1) Subject to the provisions of this section, where—

(*a*) a dealing company becomes entitled to a deduction, in computing the profits or gains of the company for tax purposes for any period, in respect of the depreciation in the value of any right subsisting against an associated company, being a non-dealing company; or
(*b*) a dealing company makes any payment to such an associated company, being a payment in respect of which the dealing company is entitled to a deduction in computing its profits or gains for tax purposes for any period;

and the depreciation or payment is not brought into account in computing the profits or gains of the non-dealing company, that company shall be deemed to have received on the last day of the period income of an amount equal to the amount of the deduction and shall be chargeable in respect thereof under Case VI of Schedule D.

(2) Where the non-dealing company is carrying on a trade, the income referred to in subsection (1) above shall, if the company so elects, not be so chargeable but shall be deemed to have been a receipt of the trade, or, if the company is carrying on more than one trade, to have been a receipt of such one of the trades as the company may choose.

(3) Where the non-dealing company is carrying on, or was formed to carry on a trade, then if—

(*a*) either—

(i) the right subsisting against it was a right to the repayment of moneys lent for meeting expenditure which has proved (in whole or in part) abortive, or
(ii) the payment to the company was made for meeting such expenditure, and

(*b*) that expenditure is such that the company is not entitled in respect of it to any allowance or deduction in computing losses or gains,

subsection (1) above shall not apply in so far as the expenditure proved abortive.

(4) For the purposes of this section—

(*a*) "company" includes any body corporate;
(*b*) "dealing company" means a company dealing in securities, land or buildings and includes any company whose profits on the sale of securities, land or buildings are part of its trading profits;
(*c*) "non-dealing company" means any company which is not a dealing company;
(*d*) two or more companies shall be treated as associated companies if one has control of the other or others, or any person has control of both or all of them;
(*e*) references to a company ("the first company") having control of another company ("the second company") shall be construed as references to the first company having control of the second company either by itself or in conjunction with any person having control over the first company, and "control" has the meaning given by section 840;
(*f*) "securities" includes shares and stock.

(5) Where it appears to the Board that by reason of any transaction or transactions a person may by virtue of this section have incurred any liability to tax, the Board may by notice served on him require him, within such time not less than 28 days as may be specified in the notice, to furnish information in his possession with respect to the transaction or any of the transactions, being information as to matters, specified in the notice, which are relevant to the question whether he has incurred any such liability to tax.

Former enactment.—TA 1970, s. 486.

Other provisions

775. Sale by individual of income derived from his personal activities

(1) Subject to subsection (7) below, this section has effect where—

(*a*) transactions or arrangements are effected or made to exploit the earning capacity of an individual in any occupation by putting some other person in a position to enjoy all or any part of the profits or gains or other income, or of the receipts, derived from the individual's activities in that occupation, or anything derived directly or indirectly from any such income or receipts; and
(*b*) as part of, or in connection with, or in consequence of, the transactions or arrangements any capital amount is obtained by the individual for himself or for any other person; and

(c) the main object or one of the main objects of the transactions was the avoidance or reduction of liability to income tax.

(2) Any such capital amount shall for all the purposes of the Income Tax Acts be treated as being earned income of the individual which arises when the capital amount is receivable, and which is chargeable to tax under Case VI of Schedule D.

(3) In this section—
   (a) references to any occupation are references to any activities of any of the kinds pursued in any profession or vocation, irrespective of whether the individual is engaged in a profession or vocation, or is employed by or holds office under some other person; and
   (b) references in subsection (1) above to income or receipts include references to payments for any description of copyright or licence or franchise or other right deriving its value from the activities, including past activities, of the individual.

(4) This section shall not apply to a capital amount obtained from the disposal—
   (a) of assets (including any goodwill) of a profession or vocation, or of a share in a partnership which is carrying on a profession or vocation, or
   (b) of shares in a company,

in so far as the value of what is disposed of, at the time of disposal, is attributable to the value of the profession or vocation as a going concern, or as the case may be to the value of the company's business, as a going concern.

(5) If the value of the profession, vocation or business as a going concern is derived to a material extent from prospective income or receipts derived directly or indirectly from the individual's activities in the occupation, and for which, when all capital amounts are disregarded, the individual will not have received full consideration, whether as a partner in a partnership or as an employee or otherwise, subsection (4) above shall not exempt the part of the capital amount so derived.

(6) In subsections (4) and (5) above references to the company's business include references to the business of any other company in which it holds shares directly or indirectly.

(7) Where on any occasion an individual obtains a capital amount consisting of any property or right which derives substantially the whole of its value from the activities of the individual, or (as in the case where the individual acquires a stock option and subsequently exercises the stock option) there are two or more occasions on which an individual obtains a capital amount consisting of any such property or right, then—
   (a) tax under this section shall not be charged on any such occasion, but
   (b) without prejudice to the generality of the provisions of this section or section 777, tax under this section shall be charged on the occasion when the capital amount, or any such capital amount, is sold or otherwise realised, and shall be so charged by reference to the proceeds of sale or the realised value.

(8) For the purposes of subsection (1)(b) above the cases where an individual obtains any capital amount for some other person include cases where the individual has put some other person in a position to receive the capital amount by providing that other person with something of value derived, directly or indirectly, from the individual's activities in the occupation.

(9) This section shall apply to all persons, whether resident in the United Kingdom or not, if the occupation of the individual is carried on wholly or partly in the United Kingdom.

Former enactment.—TA 1970, s. 487(1)–(7).

776. Transactions in land: taxation of capital gains

(1) This section is enacted to prevent the avoidance of tax by persons concerned with land or the development of land.

(2) This section applies wherever—
   (a) land, or any property deriving its value from land, is acquired with the sole or main object of realising a gain from disposing of the land; or
   (b) land is held as trading stock; or
   (c) land is developed with the sole or main object of realising a gain from disposing of the land when developed;

and any gain of a capital nature is obtained from the disposal of the land—

(i) by the person acquiring, holding or developing the land, or by any connected person, or

(ii) where any arrangement or scheme is effected as respects the land which enables a gain to be realised by any indirect method, or by any series of transactions, by any person who is a party to, or concerned in, the arrangement or scheme;

and this subsection applies whether any such person obtains the gain for himself or for any other person.

(3) Where this section applies, the whole of any such gain shall for all the purposes of the Tax Acts be treated—

(*a*) as being income which arises when the gain is realised; and which constitutes profits or gains chargeable to tax under Case VI of Schedule D for the chargeable period in which the gain is realised; and

(*b*) subject to the following provisions of this section, as being income of the person by whom the gain is realised.

(4) For the purposes of this section—

(*a*) land is disposed of if, by any one or more transactions, or by any arrangement or scheme, whether concerning the land or property deriving its value from the land, the property in the land, or control over the land, is effectually disposed of; and

(*b*) references in subsection (2) above to the acquisition or development of property with the sole or main object of realising the gain from disposing of the land shall be construed accordingly.

(5) For those purposes—

(*a*) where, whether by a premature sale or otherwise, a person directly or indirectly transmits the opportunity of making a gain to another person, that other person's gain is obtained for him by the first-mentioned person; and

(*b*) any number of transactions may be regarded as constituting a single arrangement or scheme if a common purpose can be discerned in them, or if there is other sufficient evidence of a common purpose.

(6) For the purposes of this section, such method of computing a gain shall be adopted as is just and reasonable in the circumstances, taking into account the value of what is obtained for disposing of the land, and allowing only such expenses as are attributable to the land disposed of; and in applying this subsection—

(*a*) where a freehold is acquired and the reversion is retained on disposal, account may be taken of the way in which the profits or gains under Case I of Schedule D of a person dealing in land are computed in such a case; or

(*b*) account may be taken of the adjustments to be made in computing such profits or gains under subsections (2) and (3) of section 99.

In the application of this subsection to Scotland, "freehold" means the estate or interest of the proprietor of the *dominium utile* or, in the case of property other than feudal property, of the owner, and "reversion" means the interest of the landlord in property subject to a lease.

(7) Subsection (2)(*c*) above shall not apply to so much of any gain as is fairly attributable to the period, if any, before the intention to develop the land was formed, and which would not fall under paragraph (*a*) or (*b*) of that subsection; and in applying this subsection account shall be taken of the treatment under Case I of Schedule D of a person who appropriates land as trading stock.

(8) If all or any part of the gain accruing to any person is derived from value, or an opportunity of realising a gain, provided directly or indirectly by some other person, whether or not put at the disposal of the first-mentioned person, subsection (3)(*b*) above shall apply to the gain, or that part of it, with the substitution of that other person for the person by whom the gain was realised.

(9) This section shall not apply to a gain accruing to an individual which by virtue of sections 101 to 105 of the 1979 Act (private residences) is exempt from capital gains tax, or which would be so exempt but for the provisions of section 103(3) of that Act (residences acquired partly with a view to making a gain).

(10) Where—

(*a*) there is a disposal of shares in—

(i) a company which holds land as trading stock; or

(ii) a company which owns directly or indirectly 90 per cent. or more of the ordinary share capital of another company which holds land as trading stock; and

(b) all the land so held is disposed of—
   (i) in the normal course of its trade by the company which held it, and
   (ii) so as to procure that all opportunity of profit in respect of the land arises to that company,

then this section shall not by virtue of subsection (2)(i) above apply to any gain to the holder of shares as being a gain on property deriving value from that land (but without prejudice to any liability under subsection (2)(ii) above).

(11) Where a person who considers that paragraph (a) or (c) of subsection (2) above may apply as respects a gain of a capital nature which that person has obtained from the disposal of land, or which he would obtain from a proposed disposal of land, supplies to the inspector to whom he makes his return of income written particulars showing how the gain has arisen or would arise—
   (a) the inspector shall, within 30 days from his receipt of the particulars, notify that person whether or not he is satisfied that, in the circumstances as described in the particulars, the gain will not, or would not, be chargeable to tax on that person under this section; and
   (b) if the inspector notifies that person that he is so satisfied, the gain shall not be chargeable on that person under this section.

(12) If the particulars given under this section with respect to the gain are not such as to make full and accurate disclosure of all facts and considerations relating thereto which are material to be known to the inspector, any notification given by the inspector under subsection (11) above shall be void.

(13) In this section—
   (a) references to the land include references to all or any part of the land, and "land" includes buildings, and any estate or interest in land or buildings;
   (b) references to property deriving its value from land include—
      (i) any shareholding in a company, or any partnership interest, or any interest in settled property, deriving its value directly or indirectly from land, and
      (ii) any option, consent or embargo affecting the disposition of land;

and for the purposes of this section any question whether a person is connected with another shall be determined in accordance with section 839.

(14) This section shall apply to all persons, whether resident in the United Kingdom or not, if all or any part of the land in question is situated in the United Kingdom.

Former enactments.—TA 1970, s. 488; CGTA 1979, Sch. 7.

777. Provisions supplementary to sections 775 and 776

(1) This section has effect to supplement sections 775 and 776, and those sections and this section are together referred to as the relevant provisions.

(2) In applying the relevant provisions account shall be taken of any method, however indirect, by which—
   (a) any property or right is transferred or transmitted; or
   (b) the value of any property or right is enhanced or diminished;

and accordingly the occasion of the transfer or transmission of any property or right, however indirect, and the occasion when the value of any property or right is enhanced, may be an occasion when, under sections 775 and 776, tax becomes chargeable.

(3) Subsection (2) above applies in particular—
   (a) to sales, contracts and other transactions made otherwise than for full consideration or for more than full consideration; and
   (b) to any method by which any property or right, or the control of any property or right, is transferred or transmitted by assigning share capital or other rights in a company or any partnership or interest in settled property; and
   (c) to the creation of any option or consent or embargo affecting the disposition of any property or right, and to the consideration given for the option, or for the giving of the consent or the release of the embargo; and
   (d) to the disposal of any property or right on the winding up, dissolution or termination of any company, partnership or trust.

(4) In ascertaining for the purposes of the relevant provisions the intentions of any person,

the objects and powers of any company, partners or trustees, as set out in any memorandum, articles of association or other document, shall not be conclusive.

(5) In order to ascertain whether and to what extent the value of any property or right is derived from any other property or right, value may be traced through any number of companies, partnerships and trusts, and the property held by any company, partnership or trust shall be attributed to the shareholders, partners or beneficiaries at each stage in such manner as is appropriate in the circumstances.

(6) In applying the relevant provisions—

    (*a*) any expenditure or receipt or consideration or other amount may be apportioned by such method as is just and reasonable in the circumstances;
    (*b*) all such valuations shall be made as are appropriate to give effect to sections 775 and 776.

(7) For the purposes of the relevant provisions (and in particular for the purpose of the reference in section 775 to an individual putting some other person in a position to enjoy income or receipts) partners, or the trustees of settled property, or personal representatives, may be regarded as persons distinct from the individuals or other persons who are for the time being partners or trustees or personal representatives.

(8) Where a person is assessed to tax under the relevant provisions in respect of consideration receivable by another person—

    (*a*) he shall be entitled to recover from that other person any part of that tax which he has paid; and
    (*b*) if any part of that tax remains unpaid at the expiration of six months from the date when it became due and payable, it shall be recoverable from that other person as though he were the person assessed, but without prejudice to the right to recover it from the person actually assessed;

and for the purposes of paragraph (*a*) above the Board or an inspector shall on request furnish a certificate specifying the amount of income in respect of which tax has been paid, and the amount of tax so paid; and the certificate shall be conclusive evidence of any facts stated in it.

For the purposes of this subsection any income which a person is treated as having by virtue of sections 775 and 776 shall, subject to section 833(3), be treated as the highest part of his income.

(9) If it appears to the Board that any person entitled to any consideration or other amount taxable under section 775 and 776 is not resident in the United Kingdom, the Board may direct that section 349(1) shall apply to any payment forming part of that amount as if it were an annual payment charged with tax under Case III of Schedule D, but without prejudice to the final determination of the liability of that person, including any liability under subsection (8)(*b*) above.

(10) Sections 775 and 776 have effect subject to Part XV and to any other provision of the Tax Acts deeming income to belong to a particular person.

(11) Where under section 776(2)(*c*) any person is charged to tax on the realisation of a gain, and the computation of the gain proceeded on the footing that the land or some other property was appropriated at any time as trading stock, that land or other property shall be treated on that footing also for the purposes of section 122 of the 1979 Act (property becoming or ceasing to be stock in trade).

(12) Where under section 775(1)(*b*) or 776(8) the person charged to tax is a person other than the person for whom the capital amount was obtained or the person by whom the gain was realised, and the tax has been paid, then, for the purposes of sections 31 and 33 of the 1979 Act (profits taxable as income excluded from tax on capital gains), the person for whom the capital amount was obtained or the person by whom the gain was realised shall be regarded as having been charged to that tax.

(13) For the purposes of the relevant provisions—

    "capital amount" means any amount, in money or money's worth, which, apart from the sections 775 and 776, does not fall to be included in any computation of income for purposes of the Tax Acts, and other expressions including the word "capital" shall be construed accordingly;
    "company" includes any body corporate; and
    "share" includes stock;

and any amount in money or money's worth shall not be regarded as having become receivable by some person until that person can effectively enjoy or dispose of it.

Former enactments.—TA 1970, s. 489; CGTA 1979, Sch. 7.

778. Power to obtain information

(1) The Board or an inspector may by notice require any person to furnish them within such time as the Board or the inspector may direct (not being less than 30 days) with such particulars as the Board or the inspector think necessary for the purposes of sections 775 and 776.

(2) The particulars which a person must furnish under this section, if he is required by a notice from the Board or the inspector so to do, include particulars—

(*a*) as to transactions or arrangements with respect to which he is or was acting on behalf of others;
(*b*) as to transactions or arrangements which in the opinion of the Board or the inspector should properly be investigated for the purposes of sections 775 and 776 notwithstanding that, in the opinion of the person to whom the notice is given, no liability to tax arises under those sections; and
(*c*) as to whether the person to whom the notice is given has taken or is taking any, and if so what, part in any, and if so what, transactions or arrangements of a description specified in the notice.

(3) Notwithstanding anything in subsection (2) above, a solicitor—

(*a*) shall not be deemed for the purposes of paragraph (*c*) of that subsection to have taken part in any transaction or arrangement by reason only that he has given professional advice to a client in connection with the transaction or arrangement, and
(*b*) shall not, in relation to anything done by him on behalf of a client, be compellable under this section, except with the consent of his client, to do more than state that he is or was acting on behalf of a client, and give the name and address of his client.

Former enactment.—TA 1970, s. 490.

779. Sale and lease-back: limitation on tax reliefs

(1) If land or any estate or interest in land is transferred from one person to another and—

(*a*) as a result of a lease of the land or any part of the land granted at that time or subsequently by the transferee to the transferor, or
(*b*) as a result of any other transaction or series of transactions affecting the land or any estate or interest in the land,

the transferor, or any person who is associated with the transferor, becomes liable at the time of the transfer or subsequently to pay any rent under a lease of the land or any part of the land, this section shall apply to all rent due under the lease from the transferor, or from any person who is associated with the transferor.

(2) If—

(*a*) land or any estate or interest in land is transferred from one person to another, and
(*b*) as a result of any transaction or series of transactions affecting the land or any estate or interest in the land, the transferor, or any person who is associated with the transferor, becomes liable at the time of the transfer or subsequently to make any payment (other than rent under a lease) for which any relevant tax relief is available, being a payment by way of rentcharge on the land or any part of the land or a payment in any other way connected with the land,

then this section shall apply to all such payments under the rentcharge or other transaction due from the transferor, or from any person who is associated with the transferor.

(3) The references in subsections (1) and (2) above to the transfer of an estate or interest in land include references to—

(*a*) the granting of a lease or any other transaction involving the creation of a new estate or interest in the land;
(*b*) the transfer of the lessee's interest under a lease by surrender or forfeiture of the lease; and
(*c*) any transaction or series of transactions affecting land or an estate or interest in land, such that some person is the owner, or one of the owners, before and after the carrying

out of the transaction or transactions, but another person becomes or ceases to become one of the owners;

and in relation to any such transaction or series of transactions any person who is an owner before the carrying out of the transaction or transactions, and is not the sole owner thereafter, shall be regarded for the purposes of this section as a transferor.

(4) A deduction by way of any relevant tax relief, being a deduction in respect of rent or of any other payment to which this section applies, shall not exceed the commercial rent for the period for which the rent or other payment is made of the land in respect of which that payment is made.

(5) If—

(*a*) under subsection (4) above part of a payment which would otherwise be allowable as a deduction by way of any relevant tax relief is not so allowable, and
(*b*) one or more subsequent payments are made by the transferor, or a person who is associated with the transferor, under the lease or other transaction,

that part of the first-mentioned payment may be carried forward and treated for the purposes of any such deduction by way of tax relief as if it were made at the time when the next of those subsequent payments was made, and so made for the period for which that subsequent payment was made.

(6) For the purposes of subsection (4) above—

(*a*) if more than one payment is made for the same period the payments shall be taken together;
(*b*) if payments are made for periods which overlap, the payments shall be apportioned, and the apportioned payments which belong to the common part of the overlapping periods shall be taken together;
(*c*) the preceding references to payments include references to parts of payments which under subsection (5) above are treated as if made at a time subsequent to that at which they were made, and to the extent that a part of a payment so carried forward under that subsection is not so allowable as a deduction by way of tax relief, it may again be carried forward under that subsection;
(*d*) so much of any payment as is in respect of services or the use of assets or rates usually borne by the tenant shall be excluded, and in determining the amount to be so excluded provisions in any lease or agreement fixing the payments or parts of payments which are in respect of services or the use of assets may be overridden.

(7) A payment made for a period all of which falls more than one year after the payment is made shall be treated for the purposes of this section as made for that period of one year beginning with the date on which the payment was made, and a payment for a period part of which falls after the end of that year shall be treated for those purposes as if a corresponding part of the payment was made for that year (and no part for any later period).

(8) For the purpose of making a comparison under subsection (4) above between a payment consisting of rent under a lease ("the actual lease"), or such payments taken together, and the commercial rent of the land, "commercial rent" shall mean the rent which might be expected to be paid under a lease of the land negotiated in the open market at the time when the actual lease was created, being a lease which is of the same duration as the actual lease, which is, as respects liability for maintenance and repairs, subject to the terms and conditions of the actual lease and which provides for rent payable at uniform intervals and—

(*a*) at a uniform rate, or
(*b*) if the rent payable under the actual lease is rent at a progressive rate (and such that the amount of rent payable for any year is never less than the amount payable for any previous year), a rent which progresses by gradations proportionate to those provided by the actual lease.

(9) For the purpose of making a comparison under subsection (4) above between a payment which does not consist of rent under a lease (or such a payment taken together with other payments) and the commercial rent of the land, "commercial rent" shall mean the rent which might be expected to be paid under a tenant's repairing lease negotiated in the open market at the time when the transaction was effected under which the payment or payments became due, being—

(*a*) where the period over which payments are to be made under that transaction is not less than 200 years, or the obligation to make such payments is perpetual, a lease for 200 years; and

(b) where that period is less than 200 years, a lease which is of the same duration as that period.

(10) In this section references to rent under a lease include references to rent which the person entitled to the lease is under subsection (4), (5) or (6) of section 37 or under section 87 treated, for any purpose, as paying in respect of land comprised in the lease, and such rent shall be treated for the purposes of this section as having been paid from day to day as it has become due.

(11) For the purposes of this section the following persons shall be deemed to be associated with one another, that is—

(a) the transferor in any such transaction as is described in subsection (1) or (2) above, and the transferor in another such transaction, if those two persons are acting in concert, or if the two transactions are in any way reciprocal, and any person who is an associate of either of those associated transferors;
(b) any two or more bodies corporate participating in, or incorporated for the purposes of, a scheme for the reconstruction of any body or bodies corporate or for the amalgamation of any two or more bodies corporate;
(c) any persons who are associates as defined in section 783(10).

(12) In this section—

"asset" means any description of property or rights other than land or an interest in land;
"lease" includes an underlease, sublease or any tenancy or licence, and any agreement for a lease, underlease, sublease or tenancy or licence and, in the case of land outside the United Kingdom, any interest corresponding to a lease as so defined; and in relation to such land, expressions in this section relating to interests in land and their disposition shall be construed accordingly;
"rent" includes any payment made under a lease; and
"tenant's repairing lease" means a lease where the lessee is under an obligation to maintain and repair the whole, or substantially the whole, of the premises comprised in the lease.

(13) For the purposes of this section the following are deductions by way of relevant tax relief, that is to say—

(a) a deduction in computing profits or gains chargeable under Schedule A allowable by virtue of sections 25, 26 and 28 to 31 and Schedule 1;
(b) a deduction in computing profits or gains or losses of a trade, profession or vocation for the purposes of tax;
(c) a deduction in computing profits or gains chargeable under Case VI of Schedule D, or in computing any loss for which relief is allowable under section 392 or 396;
(d) allowance of a payment under section 75 or 76;
(e) a deduction from emoluments to be assessed under Schedule E made in pursuance of section 198(1) or allowable in computing losses in an employment for tax purposes;
(f) a deduction allowable for tax purposes in computing profits or gains or losses arising from woodlands.

(14) This section shall not apply if the transfer described in subsection (1) or (2) above was on or before 14th April 1964.

Former enactment.—TA 1970, s. 491.

780. Sale and lease-back: taxation of consideration received

(1) If, in any case where a person ("the lessee") who is a lessee of land under a lease having not more than 50 years to run ("the original lease") is entitled in respect of the rent under the lease to a deduction by way of tax relief which is a relevant tax relief for the purposes of section 779—

(a) the lessee assigns the original lease to another person, or surrenders it to his landlord, for a consideration which apart from this section would not be taxable otherwise than as capital in the hands of the lessee, and
(b) there is granted or assigned to the lessee another lease ("the new lease") of or including the whole or any part of the land which was the subject of the original lease for a term not exceeding 15 years;

then, subject to the following provisions of this section, the provisions of this Act providing for deductions or allowances by way of tax relief in respect of payments of rent shall apply in relation to the rent under the new lease, and for the purposes of the Tax Acts a proportion of the consideration received by the lessee shall be treated not as a capital receipt but in accordance with subsection (3) below.

(2) For the purposes of this section—

(*a*) if the aggregate of the rent payable under the new lease in respect of any rental period ending on a date falling before the 15th anniversary of the date on which the term of the new lease begins is greater than the aggregate of the rent payable under the new lease in respect of the period of equal duration beginning on the day following that date, then unless the term of the new lease would be treated as ending on an earlier date by virtue of paragraph (*b*) below, that term shall be treated as ending on that date;
(*b*) if under the terms of the new lease—

(i) the lessor or the lessee has power to determine the new lease at a time before the expiry of the term for which it was granted, or
(ii) the lessee has power to vary his obligations under the new lease so as to reduce the rent which he would otherwise have to pay or in any other manner beneficial to him,

then, unless the term of the new lease would be treated as ending on an earlier date by virtue of paragraph (*a*) above, that term shall be treated as ending on the earliest date with effect from which, in exercise of that power, the lessor or the lessee could determine the new lease or, as the case may be, the lessee could so vary his obligations;

and in any case where a rentcharge payable by the lessee is secured on the whole or any part of the property which is the subject of the new lease, the rent payable under the new lease shall be treated for the purposes of paragraphs (*a*) and (*b*) above as equal to the aggregate of the rentcharge and the rent payable under the terms of that lease.

(3) Subject to the following provisions of this section, the proportion of the consideration received by the lessee as mentioned in subsection (1) above, or of any instalment of that consideration, which for the purposes of the Tax Acts is to be treated not as a capital receipt but in accordance with this subsection shall be determined by the formula—

$$\frac{16-N}{15}$$

where N is the term of the new lease expressed in years or, if that term is less than a year, where N is 1; and that proportion shall be treated for the purposes of the Tax Acts—

(*a*) as a receipt of a trade, profession or vocation, if the rent payable by the lessee under the new lease is allowable as a deduction in computing profits or gains or losses of a trade, profession or vocation for the purposes of tax and if the consideration is received by the lessee in the course of that trade, profession or vocation; and
(*b*) in any other case, as a profit or gain chargeable under Case VI of Schedule D.

(4) In any case where the property which is the subject of the new lease does not include the whole of the property which was the subject of the original lease, the consideration received by the lessee shall be treated for the purposes of subsection (3) above as reduced to that portion of the consideration which is reasonably attributable to such part of the property which was the subject of the original lease as consists of, or is included in, the property which is the subject of the new lease.

(5) ...[1]

(6) Where by agreement with his landlord, the lessee varies the terms of the original lease in such a manner that, in return for such a consideration as is specified in subsection (1)(*a*) above, the lessee undertakes to pay, during a period ending not later than 15 years after the date on which the consideration, or if the consideration is paid in instalments, the last such instalment, is paid to the lessee, a rent greater than that payable under the original lease, he shall be treated for the purposes of this section—

(*a*) as having surrendered the original lease for that consideration, and
(*b*) as having been granted a new lease for a term not exceeding 15 years but otherwise on the terms of the original lease as so varied.

(7) References in this section to the lessee (other than in subsection (1)(*a*) above) include references to a person who is a partner or associate of the lessee or an associate of a partner of the lessee; and for the purposes of this section the expression "associate" shall be construed in accordance with section 783(10).

(8) Subject to subsection (7) above, expressions used in this section have the meanings

assigned to them by section 24, and in subsection (2)(*a*) above "rental period" means a period in respect of which a payment of rent falls to be made, and for the purposes of that subsection, in a case where the rental period is a quarter or a month, each such period shall be treated as of equal duration.

(9) The preceding provisions of this section shall not apply if the lessee had, before 22nd June 1971, a right enforceable at law or in equity to the grant of the new lease, but in any case where, apart from this subsection, those provisions would apply, no part of the rent paid under the new lease shall be treated as a payment of capital, and the provisions of this Act providing for deductions or allowances by way of tax relief in respect of payments of rent shall apply accordingly.

Former enactment.—FA 1972, s. 80.
Amendments.—[1] Sub-s. (5) repealed by FA 1988, s. 76 and Sch. 14, Pt. IV.

781. Assets leased to traders and others

(1) Subject to section 782, where—

(*a*) a deduction by way of tax relief which is one of the kinds listed in subsection (4) below is allowable in respect of a payment made under a lease of an asset of any description, and

(*b*) before, at or after the time when the payment is made, either—

(i) the person who made the payment has obtained or obtains a capital sum in respect of the lessee's interest in the lease, or

(ii) the lessor's interest in the lease, or any other interest in the asset, has belonged to an associate of the person who made the payment, and that associate has obtained a capital sum in respect of that interest,

the person obtaining that sum shall be charged under Case VI of Schedule D for the chargeable period in which the sum is obtained with tax on an amount equal to the amount of the payment in respect of which tax relief is so allowed.

(2) A person shall not be assessed to tax under subsection (1) above on any amount to the extent to which it exceeds the capital sum by reference to which he is so assessed.

(3) Subsection (1) above shall not apply to payments under a lease created on or before 14th April 1964.

(4) The kinds of deductions by way of tax relief to which subsection (1) above applies are as follows—

(*a*) a deduction in computing profits or gains or losses of a trade, profession or vocation for the purposes of tax;

(*b*) a deduction in computing profits or gains chargeable under Case VI of Schedule D, or in computing any loss for which relief is allowable under section 392 or 396;

(*c*) allowance of a payment under section 75 or 76;

(*d*) a deduction from emoluments to be assessed under Schedule E made in pursuance of section 198(1) or allowable in computing losses in an employment for tax purposes;

(*e*) a deduction allowable for tax purposes in computing profits or gains or losses arising from woodlands.

(5) Where—

(*a*) the deduction by way of tax relief mentioned in subsection (1)(*a*) above is a deduction in computing, for income tax purposes, profits or gains or losses of a trade, profession or vocation, or arising from woodlands, and

(*b*) any part of the payments made under the lease by the person obtaining the capital sum is a payment in respect of which a deduction is not allowed for the reason that the whole or any part of the period in which the payment would fall to be allowed is not a period on the profits or gains of which income tax falls to be computed in respect of the trade, profession or vocation,

for the reference in subsection (2) above to the amount of the capital sum there shall be substituted a reference to that amount after deducting the amount of the payment in respect of which a deduction is not allowed for that reason.

(6) So far as in respect of a capital sum any part of a payment allowed as a deduction by way of tax relief of a kind to which this section applies is taken into account in making an assessment under subsection (1) above, that part of the payment shall be left out of account in determining whether any and if so what amount should be assessed by reference to any

other capital sum; and the order in which this subsection is applied shall be the order in which the capital sums are obtained.

(7) There shall be made all such adjustments of tax, whether by way of making assessments or by repayment of tax, as are required after the making of any such payment as is described in subsection (1) above to give effect to the charge under that subsection in respect of a sum obtained before the making of the payment.

(8) Notwithstanding anything in the Tax Acts limiting the time within which an assessment may be made or a claim for relief may be admitted any such adjustment may be made, by making an assessment or otherwise, at any time not more than six years from the end of the chargeable period in which the payment was made.

(9) This section shall not apply if the capital sum obtained in respect of the lessee's interest in a lease constituting a hire-purchase agreement for machinery or plant is a sum which is required to be brought into account as the whole or part of the disposal value of the machinery or plant under section 45(2) of the Finance Act 1971.

Former enactments.—TA 1970, s. 492(1)–(5), (7)–(9); FA 1971, Sch. 8, para. 16(7).

782. Leased assets: special cases

(1) This section shall apply, and section 781 shall not apply, to payments—

(*a*) which are allowable by way of deductions in computing the profits or gains or losses of a trade, and
(*b*) which are made under a lease of an asset which at any time before the creation of the lease was used for the purposes—

(i) of that trade; or
(ii) of another trade carried on by the person who at that time or later was carrying on the first-mentioned trade;

and when so used was owned by the person carrying on the trade in which it was being used.

(2) Subject to the following provisions of this section, the deduction allowable in computing the profits or gains or losses of the trade for the purposes of tax as respects any such payment shall not exceed the commercial rent of the asset for the period for which the payment was made.

(3) If under subsection (2) above part of a payment which would otherwise be allowable as a deduction is not so allowable, and one or more subsequent payments are made by the same person under the same lease, that part of the first-mentioned payment may be carried forward and treated for the purposes of computing the profits or gains or losses of the trade for the purposes of tax as if it were made at the time when the next of those subsequent payments was made, and so made for the period for which that subsequent payment was made.

(4) For the purposes of subsection (2) above—

(*a*) if more than one payment is made for the same period the payments shall be taken together;
(*b*) if the payments are made for periods which overlap, the payments shall be apportioned, and the apportioned payments which belong to the common part of the overlapping periods shall be taken together;
(*c*) the preceding references to payments include references to parts of payments which under subsection (3) above are treated as if made at a time subsequent to that at which they were made;

and to the extent that a part of a payment carried forward under subsection (3) above is not allowable as a deduction it may again be carried forward under that subsection.

(5) A payment made for a period all of which falls more than one year after the payment is made shall be treated for the purposes of this section as made for that period of one year beginning with the date on which the payment is made, and a payment for a period part of which falls after the end of that year shall be treated for those purposes as if a corresponding part of the payment was made for that year (and no part for any later period).

(6) For the purpose of making a comparison under subsection (2) above between a payment, or payments taken together, and the commercial rent of the asset, "commercial rent" shall mean the rent which might at the relevant time be expected to be paid under a lease of the asset for the remainder of the anticipated normal working life of the asset, being a rent

payable at uniform intervals and at a uniform rate which would afford a reasonable return for its market value at the relevant time, having regard to the terms and conditions of the lease; and in this subsection—

"anticipated normal working life" means, in the case of any asset, the period which might be expected, when the asset is first put into use, to be going to elapse before it is finally put out of use as being unfit for further use, it being assumed that the asset is going to be used in the normal manner and to the normal extent, and is going to be so used throughout that period; and

"the relevant time" means the time when the lease was created under which the payment was made with which the commercial rent is to be compared.

(7) If the asset is used at the same time partly for the purposes of the trade and partly for other purposes the commercial rent as defined in subsection (6) above shall be determined by reference to what would be paid for such a partial use of the asset.

(8) This section shall not apply in relation to payments made under a lease created on or before 14th April 1964.

(9) In this section references to the person carrying on a trade are references to the person carrying on the trade for the time being, and where at any time a person succeeds to a trade which until that time was carried on by another person, and by virtue of section 113 or 337(1) the trade is to be treated as discontinued, the trade shall, nonetheless, be treated as the same trade for the purposes of this section.

(10) In this section references to a trade include references to a profession or vocation.

Former enactments.—TA 1970, s. 493; FA 1971, Sch. 8, para. 16(8).

783. Leased assets: supplemental

(1) References in section 781 to a sum obtained in respect of the lessee's interest in a lease of an asset, or in respect of any other interest in an asset include—

(*a*) in the case of a lessee's interest, references to sums representing the consideration in money or money's worth obtained on a surrender of the rights to the lessor, or on an assignment of the lease, or on creating a sublease or any other interest out of the lease; and

(*b*) references to any insurance moneys payable in respect of the asset, so far as payable to the owner of the interest in the asset.

(2) Such references also include references to sums representing money or money's worth obtained by the person entitled to the interest by a transaction or series of transactions disposing of the asset, or of an interest in the asset, and in particular transactions which comprise arrangements under which the rights of the lessee under a lease of the asset are merged in any way with the rights of the lessor, or with any other rights as respects the asset, so far as the money or money's worth so obtained is attributable to the rights of the lessee under the lease.

(3) References in section 781 to sums obtained in respect of any interest in an asset include references to money or money's worth so obtained in any transaction (including a transaction of the kind described in subsection (1) or (2) above) by way of consideration received by a person who is an associate of the person entitled to the interest in the asset.

(4) If an interest in the asset is disposed of by any person to a person who is his associate, the person disposing of the interest shall (unless in fact he obtains a greater sum) be treated for the purposes of section 781 as having obtained in respect of the interest—

(*a*) the value of the interest in the open market; or

(*b*) the value of the interest to the person to whom it is, in effect, transferred;

whichever is the greater.

(5) For the purposes of subsections (3) and (4) above a disposition may be direct or indirect and may be effected by any such transaction as is described in subsection (2) above.

(6) For the purposes of sections 781 and 784 and this section any sum obtained by any persons carrying on a trade, profession or vocation in partnership in respect of an interest in an asset which is and continues to be used for the purposes of the trade, profession or vocation shall be regarded as apportionable between them in the shares in which they are then entitled to the profits of the trade, profession or vocation.

(7) Subject to subsection (6) above, for those purposes a sum obtained by persons jointly

entitled to an interest in an asset shall be apportionable according to their respective interests in the rights.

(8) For those purposes, any payment in respect of which a deduction is allowable by way of tax relief which is made by persons carrying on a trade, profession or vocation in partnership shall be apportioned in such manner as may be just.

(9) Where under this section any sum or payment falls to be apportioned and, at the time of the apportionment, it appears that it is material as respects the liability to tax (for whatever period) of two or more persons, any question which arises as to the manner in which the sum or payment is to be apportioned shall be determined, for the purposes of tax of all those persons—

(*a*) in a case where the same body of General Commissioners have jurisdiction with respect to all those persons, by those Commissioners unless all those persons agree that it shall be determined by the Special Commissioners;
(*b*) in a case where different bodies of Commissioners have jurisdiction with respect to those persons, by such of those bodies as the Board may direct unless all those persons agree that it shall be determined by the Special Commissioners; and
(*c*) in any other case, by the Special Commissioners;

and any such Commissioners shall determine the question in like manner as if it were an appeal, except that all those persons shall be entitled to appear and be heard by the Commissioners who are to make the determination or to make representations to them in writing.

(10) For the purposes of this section and in construing the expressions "associate" and "associated" in section 781 and this section, the following persons shall be deemed to be associated with each other, that is to say—

(*a*) any individual and that individual's husband or wife, and any relative, or husband or wife of a relative, of that individual or that individual's husband or wife ("relative" meaning, for this purpose, brother, sister, ancestor or lineal descendant);
(*b*) any person in his capacity of trustee of a settlement and any individual who in relation to the settlement is a settlor, and any person associated with that individual ("settlement" and "settlor" having, for this purpose, the meanings given by section 670(2));
(*c*) any person and a body of persons of which that person, or persons associated with him, or that person and persons associated with him, has or have control;
(*d*) any two or more bodies of persons associated with the same person by virtue of paragraph (*c*) above;
(*e*) in relation to a disposal by joint owners, the joint owners and any person associated with any of them.

(11) In subsection (10) above "body of persons" includes a partnership and "control" has the meaning given by section 840.

Former enactment.—TA 1970, s. 494.
Cross references.—See TMA 1970, s. 58(3)(*b*), FA 1988, s. 134(4) (with effect from an appointed day, proceedings under sub-s. (9) above to be in Northern Ireland if the place given by certain rules in relation to the parties to the proceedings is in Northern Ireland).

784. Leased assets subject to hire-purchase agreements

(1) In the application of section 781 to a lease which constitutes a hire-purchase agreement, for the reference in subsection (2) of that section to the amount of the capital sum there shall, where that capital sum was obtained in respect of the lessee's interest in the lease constituting the hire-purchase agreement, be substituted references to the amount of the capital sum (adjusted, if necessary, under subsection (5) of that section) after deducting any capital expenditure which was incurred by the person obtaining the capital sum in providing the lessee's interest.

(2) In subsection (1) above "capital expenditure which was incurred by the person obtaining the capital sum in providing the lessee's interest" means—

(*a*) so much of any payment made under the lease by the person obtaining the capital sum (or, where the capital sum was obtained by the personal representatives of a deceased person, so made by that deceased person) as is not a payment in respect of which a deduction is allowable by way of tax relief which is one of the kinds listed in subsection (4) of section 781, plus
(*b*) where the lessee's interest was assigned to the person obtaining the capital sum, any capital payment made by that person as consideration for the assignment.

(3) If the amount to be deducted in pursuance of subsection (1) above exceeds the amount of the capital sum from which it is to be deducted, no charge shall arise under section 781(1) in respect of the capital sum.

(4) If the capital sum represents the consideration for part only of the lessee's interest in the lease which constitutes a hire-purchase agreement, the amount to be deducted under subsection (1) above shall be such proportion of the capital expenditure which is still unallowed as is reasonable having regard to the degree to which the capital expenditure has contributed to the value of what is disposed of in return for the capital sum.

(5) If more than one capital sum is, or is to be regarded as, obtained by the same person in respect of the lessee's interest in the lease which constitutes a hire-purchase agreement, then, so far as in respect of one of those capital sums any deduction is made in respect of capital expenditure in pursuance of subsection (1) above that capital expenditure shall be left out of account in applying subsections (1) and (3) above to any other such capital sum; and the order in which this subsection is applied shall be the order in which the capital sums are obtained.

(6) In this section—

"hire-purchase agreement" means an agreement, other than a conditional sale agreement, under which—

(a) goods are bailed or, in Scotland, hired in return for periodical payments by the person to whom they are bailed or hired, and
(b) the property in the goods will pass to that person if the terms of the agreement are complied with and one or more of the following occurs—

(i) the exercise of an option to purchase by that person;
(ii) the doing of any other specified act by any party to the agreement;
(iii) the happening of any other specified event; and

"conditional sale agreement" means an agreement for the sale of goods under which the purchase price or part of it is payable by instalments, and the property in the goods is to remain in the seller (notwithstanding that the buyer is to be in possession of the goods) until such conditions as to the payment of instalments or otherwise as may be specified in the agreement are fulfilled.

Former enactments.—TA 1970, s. 495; Consumer Credit Act 1974, Sch. 4, para. 29.

785. Meaning of "asset", "capital sum" and "lease" for purposes of sections 781 to 784

In sections 781 to 784—

"asset" means any description of property or rights other than land or an interest in land;
"capital sum" means any sum of money, or any money's worth, except so far as it or any part of it is to be treated for the purposes of tax as a receipt to be taken into account in computing the profits or gains or losses of a trade, profession or vocation, or profits or gains or losses arising from woodlands, or is, apart from section 781, chargeable under Case VI of Schedule D; and
"lease", in relation to an asset, means any kind of agreement or arrangement under which payments are made for the use of, or otherwise in respect of, an asset, and includes, in particular, any agreement or arrangement all or any of the payments under which represent instalments of, or payments towards, a purchase price.

Former enactment.—TA 1970, s. 492(6).

786. Transactions associated with loans or credit

(1) This section applies as respects any transaction effected with reference to the lending of money or the giving of credit, or the varying of the terms on which money is lent or credit is given, or which is effected with a view to enabling or facilitating any such arrangement concerning the lending of money or the giving of credit.

(2) Subsection (1) above has effect whether the transaction is effected between the lender or creditor and the borrower or debtor, or between either of them and a person connected with the other or between a person connected with one and a person connected with the other.

(3) If the transaction provides for the payment of any annuity or other annual payment, not being interest, being a payment chargeable to tax under Case III of Schedule D, the payment shall be treated for all the purposes of the Tax Acts as if it were a payment of annual interest.

(4) If the transaction is one by which the owner of any securities or other property carrying a right to income ("the owner") agrees to sell or transfer the property ("the relevant property"), and by the same or any collateral agreement—

(a) the purchaser or transferee ("the buyer"), or a person connected with him, agrees that at a later date he will sell or transfer the same or any other property to the owner or a person connected with him; or

(b) the owner or a person connected with him acquires an option which he subsequently exercises, to buy or acquire the same or any other property from the buyer or a person connected with the buyer;

then, without prejudice to the liability of any other person, the owner shall be chargeable to tax under Case VI of Schedule D on an amount equal to any income which arises from the relevant property at any time before the repayment of the loan or the termination of the credit.

(5) If under the transaction a person assigns, surrenders or otherwise agrees to waive or forego income arising from any property (without a sale or transfer of the property) then, without prejudice to the liability of any other person, he shall be chargeable to tax under Case VI of Schedule D on a sum equal to the amount of income assigned, surrendered, waived or foregone.

(6) If credit is given for the purchase price of any property, and the rights attaching to the property are such that, during the subsistence of the debt, the purchaser's rights to income from the property are suspended or restricted, he shall be treated for the purposes of subsection (5) above as if he had surrendered a right to income of an amount equivalent to the income which he has in effect foregone by obtaining the credit.

(7) The amount of any income payable subject to deduction of income tax shall be taken for the purposes of subsection (5) above as the amount before deduction of tax.

(8) References in this section to connected persons shall be construed in accordance with section 839.

Former enactment.—TA 1970, s. 496.

787. Restriction of relief for payments of interest

(1) Relief shall not be given to any person under any provision of the Tax Acts in respect of any payment of interest if a scheme has been effected or arrangements have been made (whether before or after the time when the payment is made) such that the sole or main benefit that might be expected to accrue to that person from the transaction under which the interest is paid was the obtaining of a reduction in tax liability by means of any such relief.

(2) In this section "relief" means relief by way of deduction in computing profits or gains or deduction or set off against income or total profits.

(3) Where the relief is claimed by virtue of section 403(7) any question under this section as to what benefit might be expected to accrue from the transaction in question shall be determined by reference to the claimant company and the surrendering company taken together.

Former enactment.—FA 1976, s. 38.

PART XVIII

DOUBLE TAXATION RELIEF

CHAPTER I

THE PRINCIPAL RELIEFS

788. Relief by agreement with other countries

(1) If Her Majesty by Order in Council declares that arrangements specified in the Order have been made with the government of any territory outside the United Kingdom with a view to affording relief from double taxation in relation to—

(a) income tax,
(b) corporation tax in respect of income or chargeable gains, and
(c) any taxes of a similar character to those taxes imposed by the laws of that territory,

and that it is expedient that those arrangements should have effect, then those arrangements shall have effect in accordance with subsection (3) below.

(2) Without prejudice to the generality of subsection (1) above, if it appears to Her Majesty to be appropriate, the arrangements specified in an Order in Council under this section may include provisions with respect to the exchange of information necessary for carrying out the domestic laws of the United Kingdom and the laws of the territory to which the arrangements relate concerning taxes covered by the arrangements including, in particular, provisions about the prevention of fiscal evasion with respect to those taxes; and where arrangements do include any such provisions, the declaration in the Order in Council shall state that fact.

(3) Subject to the provisions of this Part, the arrangements shall, notwithstanding anything in any enactment, have effect in relation to income tax and corporation tax in so far as they provide—

(a) for relief from income tax, or from corporation tax in respect of income or chargeable gains; or
(b) for charging the income arising from sources, or chargeable gains accruing on the disposal of assets, in the United Kingdom to persons not resident in the United Kingdom; or
(c) for determining the income or chargeable gains to be attributed—

(i) to persons not resident in the United Kingdom and their agencies, branches or establishments in the United Kingdom; or
(ii) to persons resident in the United Kingdom who have special relationships with persons not so resident; or

(d) for conferring on persons not resident in the United Kingdom the right to a tax credit under section 231 in respect of qualifying distributions made to them by companies which are so resident.

(4) The provisions of Chapter II of this Part shall apply where arrangements which have effect by virtue of this section provide that tax payable under the laws of the territory concerned shall be allowed as a credit against tax payable in the United Kingdom.

(5) For the purposes of this section and, subject to section 795(3), Chapter II of this Part in its application to relief under this section, any amount of tax which would have been payable under the law of a territory outside the United Kingdom but for a relief to which this subsection applies given under the law of that territory shall be treated as having been payable; and references in this section and that Chapter to double taxation, to tax payable or chargeable, or to tax not chargeable directly or by deduction shall be construed accordingly.

This subsection applies—

(a) to any relief given with a view to promoting industrial, commercial, scientific, educational or other development in a territory outside the United Kingdom, being a relief with respect to which provision is made in the arrangements in question for double taxation relief; and

(b) to any relief provided under and in accordance with the arrangements, where the latter expressly contemplate that the relief is to fall within this subsection.

(6) Except in the case of a claim for an allowance by way of credit in accordance with Chapter II of this Part, a claim for relief under subsection (3)(a) above shall be made to the Board.

(7) Where—

(a) under any arrangements which have effect by virtue of this section, relief may be given, either in the United Kingdom or in the territory with the government of which the arrangements are made, in respect of any income or chargeable gains, and

(b) it appears that the assessment to income tax or corporation tax made in respect of the income or chargeable gains is not made in respect of the full amount thereof, or is incorrect having regard to the credit, if any, which falls to be given under the arrangements,

any such assessments may be made as are necessary to ensure that the total amount of the income or chargeable gains is assessed, and the proper credit, if any, is given in respect thereof, and, where the income is, or the chargeable gains are, entrusted to any person in the United Kingdom for payment, any such assessment may be made on the recipient of the income or gains, and, in the case of an assessment in respect of income, may be assessed under Case VI of Schedule D.

(8) Any arrangements to which effect is given under this section may include provision for relief from tax for periods before the passing of this Act, or before the making of the arrangements, and provisions as to income or chargeable gains which is or are not subject to double taxation, and the preceding provisions of this section shall have effect accordingly.

(9) Any Order in Council made under this section revoking an earlier such Order in Council may contain such transitional provisions as appear to Her Majesty to be necessary or expedient.

(10) Before any Order in Council proposed to be made under this section is submitted to Her Majesty in Council, a draft of the Order shall be laid before the House of Commons, and the Order shall not be so submitted unless an Address is presented to Her Majesty by that House praying that the Order be made.

Former enactments.—TA 1970, s. 497(1)–(8); FA 1972, ss. 98(2), 100(1); FA 1976, s. 50(2); FA 1987, s. 70(1).
Cross references.—See FA 1989, s. 115 (double taxation tax credits).

789. Arrangements made under old law

(1) Notwithstanding section 793(2), any arrangements made in relation to the profits tax under section 347 of the Income Tax Act 1952 or any earlier enactment corresponding to that section shall, except in so far as arrangements made after the passing of the Finance Act 1965 provide otherwise, have effect in relation to corporation tax and income and gains chargeable to corporation tax as they are expressed to have effect in relation to the profits tax and profits chargeable to the profits tax, with the substitution of accounting periods for chargeable accounting periods (and not as they had effect in relation to income tax).

(2) In so far as any arrangements made before 30th March 1971 provide for the exemption of any income from surtax they shall have effect, unless otherwise modified by subsequent arrangements, as if they provided for that income to bear income tax at the basic rate and to be disregarded for the purpose of computing total income, except in so far as the computation affects the matters mentioned in section 835(5).

(3) Any reference in the Tax Acts (including this Part) to arrangements under or by virtue of section 788 includes a reference to arrangements having effect by virtue of this section.

Former enactments.—TA 1970, s. 497(9), (10); FA 1971, Sch. 6, para. 74; FA 1972, s. 100(1).

790. Unilateral relief

(1) To the extent appearing from the following provisions of this section, relief from income tax and corporation tax in respect of income and chargeable gains shall be given in respect of tax payable under the law of any territory outside the United Kingdom by allowing that tax as a credit against income tax or corporation tax, notwithstanding that there are not for the time being in force any arrangements under section 788 providing for such relief.

(2) Relief under subsection (1) above is referred to in this Part as "unilateral relief".

(3) Unilateral relief shall be such relief as would fall to be given under Chapter II of this

Part if arrangements with the government of the territory in question containing the provisions specified in subsections (4) to (10) below were in force by virtue of section 788, but subject to any particular provision made with respect to unilateral relief in that Chapter; and any expression in that Chapter which imports a reference to relief under arrangements for the time being having effect by virtue of that section shall be deemed to import also a reference to unilateral relief.

(4) Credit for tax paid under the law of the territory outside the United Kingdom and computed by reference to income arising or any chargeable gain accruing in that territory shall be allowed against any United Kingdom income tax or corporation tax computed by reference to that income or gain (profits from, or remuneration for, personal or professional services performed in that territory being deemed for this purpose to be income arising in that territory).

(5) Subsection (4) above shall have effect subject to the following modifications, that is to say—

(*a*) where the territory is the Isle of Man or any of the Channel Islands, the limitation to income or gains arising in the territory shall not apply;

(*b*) where arrangements with the government of the territory are for the time being in force by virtue of section 788, credit for tax paid under the law of the territory shall not be allowed by virtue of subsection (4) above in the case of any income or gains if any credit for that tax is allowable under those arrangements in respect of that income or those gains; and

(*c*) credit shall not be allowed by virtue of subsection (4) above for overseas tax on a dividend paid by a company resident in the territory unless—

(i) the overseas tax is directly charged on the dividend, whether by charge to tax, deduction of tax at source or otherwise, and the whole of it represents tax which neither the company nor the recipient would have borne if the dividend had not been paid; or
(ii) the dividend is paid to a company within subsection (6) below; or
(iii) the dividend is paid to a company to which section 802(1) applies and is a dividend of the kind described in that subsection.

(6) Where a dividend paid by a company resident in the territory is paid to a company resident in the United Kingdom which either directly or indirectly controls, or is a subsidiary of a company which directly or indirectly controls—

(*a*) not less than 10 per cent. of the voting power in the company paying the dividend; or
(*b*) less than 10 per cent. of the voting power in the company paying the dividend if—

(i) it has been reduced below that percentage on or after 1st April 1972; or
(ii) it has been acquired on or after that date in exchange for voting power in another company in respect of which relief under this subsection by virtue of paragraph (*a*) above was due prior to the exchange;

and the company receiving the dividend shows that the conditions specified in subsection (7) below are satisfied;

any tax in respect of its profits paid under the law of the territory by the company paying the dividend shall be taken into account in considering whether any, and if so what, credit is to be allowed in respect of the dividend.

In this subsection references to one company being a subsidiary of another are to be construed in accordance with section 792(2).

(7) The conditions referred to in subsection (6)(*b*) above are as follows—

(*a*) that the reduction below the 10 per cent. limit (and any further reduction) or, as the case may be, the exchange (and any reduction thereafter) could not have been prevented by any reasonable endeavours on the part of the company receiving the dividend and was due to a cause or causes not reasonably foreseeable by it when control of the relevant voting power was acquired; and

(*b*) no reasonable endeavours on the part of that company could have restored or, as the case may be, increased the voting power to not less than 10 per cent.

(8) In subsection (7) above references to the company receiving the dividend include references—

(*a*) to any company of which it is a subsidiary within the meaning of section 792(2); and
(*b*) where prior to the reduction or exchange the voting power in question was controlled otherwise than directly by the company receiving the dividend, to each other company relevant for determining whether that voting power was controlled as required by subsection (6)(*a*) above.

(9) In subsection (7) above "the relevant voting power" means the voting power by virtue of which relief was due under subsection (6)(*a*) above prior to the reduction or exchange or, where control of the whole of that voting power was not acquired at the same time, that part of the voting power of which control was last acquired.

(10) In any case in which relief in respect of a dividend is due by virtue of subsection (6)(*b*) above, there shall be taken into account, as if it were tax payable under the law of the territory in which the company paying the dividend is resident, any tax that would be so taken into account under section 801 if the company paying the dividend and the company receiving it were related to each other within the meaning of section 801(5).

(11) Where—

(*a*) unilateral relief may be given in respect of any income or chargeable gain, and
(*b*) it appears that the assessment to income tax or corporation tax made in respect of the income or chargeable gain is not made in respect of the full amount thereof, or is incorrect having regard to the credit, if any, which falls to be given by way of unilateral relief,

any such assessments may be made as are necessary to ensure that the total amount of the income or chargeable gain is assessed, and the proper credit, if any, is given in respect thereof, and, where the income is, or the chargeable gain is, entrusted to any person in the United Kingdom for payment, any such assessment may be made on the recipient of the income or gain, and, in the case of an assessment in respect of income, may be assessed under Case VI of Schedule D.

(12) In this section and in Chapter II of this Part in its application to unilateral relief, references to tax payable or paid under the law of a territory outside the United Kingdom include only references—

(*a*) to taxes which are charged on income and which correspond to United Kingdom income tax, and
(*b*) to taxes which are charged on income or chargeable gains and which correspond to United Kingdom corporation tax;

but for this purpose tax under the law of any such territory shall not be treated as not corresponding to income tax or corporation tax by reason only that it is payable under the law of a province, state or other part of a country, or is levied by or on behalf of a municipality or other local body.

Former enactments.—Sub-ss. (1), (2): TA 1970, s. 498(1); FA 1972, s. 100(1).
Sub-s. (3): TA 1970, s. 498(2).
Sub-ss. (4), (5): TA 1970, s. 498(3); FA 1972, s. 100(1).
Sub-ss. (6)–(10): TA 1970, s. 498(4); FA 1971, s. 26(3); FA 1972, s. 83(1)–(5).
Sub-ss. (11), (12): TA 1970, s. 498(5), (6); FA 1972, s. 100(1).

791. Power to make regulations for carrying out section 788

The Board may from time to time make regulations generally for carrying out the provisions of section 788 or any arrangements having effect thereunder, and may in particular by those regulations provide—

(*a*) for securing that relief from taxation imposed by the laws of the territory to which any such arrangements relate does not enure for the benefit of persons not entitled to such relief; and
(*b*) for authorising, in cases where tax deductible from any payment has, in order to comply with any such arrangements, not been deducted, and it is discovered that the arrangements did not apply to that payment, the recovery of the tax by assessment on the person entitled to the payment or by deduction from subsequent payments.

Former enactment.—TA 1970, s. 517.

CHAPTER II

RULES GOVERNING RELIEF BY WAY OF CREDIT

General

792. Interpretation of credit code

(1) In this Chapter, except where the context otherwise requires—

"arrangements" means any arrangements having effect by virtue of section 788;
"foreign tax" means, in relation to any territory, arrangements with the government of which have effect by virtue of section 788, any tax chargeable under the laws of that territory for which credit may be allowed under the arrangements;
"the United Kingdom taxes" means income tax and corporation tax;
"underlying tax" means, in relation to any dividend, tax which is not chargeable in respect of that dividend directly or by deduction; and
"unilateral relief" means relief under section 790.

(2) For the purposes of this Chapter one company is a subsidiary of another if the other company controls, directly or indirectly, not less than 50 per cent. of the voting power in the first company.

(3) Any reference in this Chapter to foreign tax shall be construed in relation to credit to be allowed under any arrangements as a reference only to tax chargeable under the laws of the territory with the government of which the arrangements were made.

Former enactment.—TA 1970, s. 500.

793. Reduction of United Kingdom taxes by amount of credit due

(1) Subject to the provisions of this Chapter, where under any arrangements credit is to be allowed against any of the United Kingdom taxes chargeable in respect of any income or chargeable gain, the amount of the United Kingdom taxes so chargeable shall be reduced by the amount of the credit.

(2) Nothing in subsection (1) above authorises the allowance of credit against any United Kingdom tax against which credit is not allowable under the arrangements.

Former enactments.—TA 1970, s. 501; FA 1972, s. 100(1).

794. Requirement as to residence

(1) Subject to subsection (2) below, credit shall not be allowed under any arrangements against any of the United Kingdom taxes for any chargeable period unless the person in respect of whose income or chargeable gains the United Kingdom tax is chargeable is resident in the United Kingdom for that period.

(2) Credit may be allowed by way of unilateral relief—

(a) for tax paid under the law of the Isle of Man or any of the Channel Islands, if the person in question is, for the chargeable period in question, resident either in the United Kingdom or in the Isle of Man or any of the Channel Islands, as the case may be;

(b) for tax paid under the law of any territory and computed by reference to income from an office or employment the duties of which are performed wholly or mainly in that territory, against income tax chargeable under Schedule E and computed by reference to that income, if the person in question is for the year of assessment in question resident either in the United Kingdom or that territory; and

(c) for tax paid under the law of any territory in respect of interest on a loan where the following conditions are fulfilled, namely—

(i) that the person in question is a company which, for the chargeable period in question, carries on a banking business in the United Kingdom through a branch or agency;

(ii) that the loan was made by the company through the branch or agency in the United Kingdom;

amount, in relation to spared tax which is referable to the whole or any part of the foreign loan interest, is an amount which does not exceed—

(a) 15 per cent. of the interest to which the spared tax is referable, computed without regard to any increase under subsection (3) above; or
(b) if it is less, the amount of that spared tax for which, in accordance with any arrangements applicable to the case in question, credit falls to be given as mentioned in subsection (1)(c) above.

(5) If in a case where this section applies—

(a) the foreign tax referred to in subsection (1)(c) above is or includes an amount of tax which is not spared tax; and
(b) the amount of tax exceeds—

(i) the amount of the credit which, by virtue of this Chapter (but disregarding subsection (6) below), is allowed for that foreign tax against income tax or corporation tax; or
(ii) if it is less, 15 per cent. of the foreign loan interest, computed without regard to any increase or reduction under this section,

then, for the purposes of income tax or corporation tax, the amount which, apart from this subsection, would be the amount of the foreign loan interest shall be treated as reduced by a sum equal to the excess.

(6) Where this section applies, the amount of the credit for foreign tax referred to in subsection (1)(c) above which, in accordance with this Chapter, is to be allowed against income tax or corporation tax—

(a) shall be limited by treating the amount of the foreign loan interest (as increased or reduced under subsection (3) or (5) above) as reduced (or further reduced) for the purposes of this Chapter by an amount equal to so much of the lender's financial expenditure in relation to the loan concerned as is properly attributable to the period for which the interest is paid; and
(b) shall not exceed 15 per cent. of the foreign loan interest, computed without regard to paragraph (a) above or to any increase under subsection (3) above or any reduction under subsection (5) above.

(7) For the purposes of this section the lender's financial expenditure in relation to a loan is the aggregate of—

(a) the financial expenses (consisting of interest or similar sums) incurred by the lender in or in connection with the provision of the loan, so far as those expenses consist of payments which either are charges on income for the purposes of corporation tax or are deductible in computing profits of the lender which are brought into charge to income tax or corporation tax; and
(b) where the loan is financed by the issue of securities at a discount by the lender, so much of the amount of the discount as either constitutes such a charge as is mentioned in paragraph (a) above or is deductible as mentioned in that paragraph; and
(c) so much as it is just and reasonable to attribute to the loan of any interest or other return foregone by a person connected or associated with the lender in connection with the provision of funds to the lender, either interest free or in other circumstances more favourable to the lender than if the parties were at arm's length; and
(d) any other sum, whether paid by way of refund of tax or interest or by way of commission, which—

(i) is paid by the lender or a person connected or associated with him;
(ii) is paid directly or indirectly to the borrower or a person connected or associated with him;
(iii) is deductible as mentioned in paragraph (a) above;
(iv) would not, apart from this paragraph, be taken into account in determining the amount of the foreign loan interest; and
(v) it is reasonable to regard as referable to the loan or the foreign loan interest (or both).

(8) In a case where the amount of the lender's financial expenditure in relation to a loan is not readily ascertainable, that amount shall be taken, subject to subsection (9) below, to be such sum as it is just and reasonable to attribute to the financing of the loan, having regard, in particular, to any market rates of interest by reference to which the rate of interest on the loan is determined.

(9) The Board may by regulations supplement subsection (8) above—

(a) by specifying matters to be taken into account in determining such a just and reasonable attribution as is referred to in that subsection; and
(b) by making provision with respect to the determination of market rates of interest for the purposes of that subsection;

and any such regulations may make different provision for different cases.

(10) For the purposes of this section—

(a) section 839 applies; and
(b) subsection (10) of section 783 applies as it applies for the purposes of that section.

(11) Where the loan on which the foreign loan interest is payable was made pursuant to an agreement entered into before 1st April 1987, this section shall have effect subject to the following modifications in relation to interest payable before 1st April 1989—

(a) in subsection (1) in paragraph (a) the words "in a territory" shall be inserted after "resident" and the words following paragraph (c) shall be omitted;
(b) subsection (2) shall be omitted;
(c) in subsection (5) for paragraph (b) there shall be substituted—

"(b) that amount of tax exceeds the amount of the credit which, by virtue of this Chapter and in particular subsection (6) below, is allowed for that foreign tax against income tax or corporation tax;" and

(d) for subsections (6) to (10) there shall be substituted—

"(6) Where this section applies, the amount of the credit for foreign tax referred to in subsection (1)(c) above which, in accordance with this Chapter, is to be allowed against income tax or corporation tax shall not exceed 15 per cent. of the foreign loan interest, computed without regard to any increase under subsection (3) or any reduction under subsection (5) above.";

but subject to that, this section applies whether the loan was made before or after the passing of this Act.

Former enactments.—FA 1982, s. 65; F(No. 2)A 1987, s. 67.

Tax underlying dividends

799. Computation of underlying tax

(1) Where in the case of any dividend arrangements provide for underlying tax to be taken into account in considering whether any and if so what credit is to be allowed against the United Kingdom taxes in respect of the dividend, the tax to be taken into account by virtue of that provision shall be so much of the foreign tax borne on the relevant profits by the body corporate paying the dividend as is properly attributable to the proportion of the relevant profits represented by the dividend.

(2) Where under the foreign tax law the dividend has been increased for tax purposes by an amount to be set off against the recipient's own tax under that law or, to the extent that it exceeds his own tax thereunder, paid to him, then, from the amount of the underlying tax to be taken into account under subsection (1) above there is to be subtracted the amount of that increase.

(3) For the purposes of subsection (1) above the relevant profits, subject to subsection (4) below, are—

(a) if the dividend is paid for a specified period, the profits of that period;
(b) if the dividend is not paid for a specified period, but is paid out of specified profits, those profits; and
(c) if the dividend is paid neither for a specified period nor out of specified profits, the profits of the last period for which accounts of the body corporate were made up which ended before the dividend became payable.

(4) If, in a case falling under paragraph (a) or (c) of subsection (3) above, the total dividend exceeds the profits available for distribution of the period mentioned in that paragraph the relevant profits shall be the profits of that period plus so much of the profits available for distribution of preceding periods (other than profits previously distributed or previously treated as relevant profits for the purposes of this section or section 506 of the 1970 Act) as is equal to the excess; and for the purposes of this subsection the profits of the most recent preceding period shall first be taken into account, then the profits of the next most recent preceding period, and so on.

Former enactments.—TA 1970, s. 506; FA 1976, s. 50(3).

800. Dividends paid between related companies but not covered by arrangements

Where—

(*a*) arrangements provide, in relation to dividends of some classes but not in relation to dividends of other classes, that underlying tax is to be taken into account in considering whether any, and if so what, credit is to be allowed against the United Kingdom taxes in respect of the dividends; and

(*b*) a dividend is paid which is not of a class in relation to which the arrangements so provide;

then, if the dividend is paid to a company which controls directly or indirectly, or is a subsidiary of a company which controls directly or indirectly, not less than 10 per cent. of the voting power in the company paying the dividend, credit shall be allowed as if the dividend were a dividend of a class in relation to which the arrangements so provide.

Former enactments.—TA 1970, s. 507; FA 1971, s. 26(4).

801. Dividends paid between related companies: relief for U.K. and third country taxes

(1) Where a company resident outside the United Kingdom ("the overseas company") pays a dividend to a company resident in the United Kingdom ("the United Kingdom company") and the overseas company is related to the United Kingdom company, then for the purpose of allowing credit under any arrangements against corporation tax in respect of the dividend, there shall be taken into account, as if it were tax payable under the law of the territory in which the overseas company is resident—

(*a*) any United Kingdom income tax or corporation tax payable by the overseas company in respect of its profits; and

(*b*) any tax which, under the law of any other territory, is payable by the overseas company in respect of its profits.

(2) Where the overseas company has received a dividend from a third company and the third company is related to the overseas company, then, subject to subsection (4) below, there shall be treated for the purposes of subsection (1) above as tax paid by the overseas company in respect of its profits any underlying tax payable by the third company, to the extent that it would be taken into account under this Part if the dividend had been paid by a company resident outside the United Kingdom to a company resident in the United Kingdom and arrangements had provided for underlying tax to be taken into account.

(3) Where the third company has received a dividend from a fourth company and the fourth company is related to the third company, then, subject to subsection (4) below, tax payable by the fourth company shall similarly be treated for the purposes of subsection (2) above as tax paid by the third company; and so on for successive companies each of which is related to the one before.

(4) Subsections (2) and (3) above are subject to the following limitations—

(*a*) no tax shall be taken into account in respect of a dividend paid by a company resident in the United Kingdom except United Kingdom corporation tax and any tax for which that company is entitled to credit under this Part; and

(*b*) no tax shall be taken into account in respect of a dividend paid by a company resident outside the United Kingdom to another such company unless it could have been taken into account under the other provisions of this Part had the other company been resident in the United Kingdom.

(5) For the purposes of this section a company is related to another company if that other company—

(*a*) controls directly or indirectly, or

(*b*) is a subsidiary of a company which controls directly or indirectly,

not less than 10 per cent. of the voting power in the first-mentioned company.

Former enactments.—TA 1970, s. 508; FA 1971, s. 26(2).

802. U.K. insurance companies trading overseas

(1) Subject to subsection (2) below, where—
 (a) a company resident in the United Kingdom is charged to tax under Case I of Schedule D in respect of any insurance business carried on by it, and
 (b) that business or any part of it is carried on through a branch or agency in a territory outside the United Kingdom,

then, in respect of dividends referable to that business which are paid to the company by companies resident in that territory, any tax payable by those companies in respect of their profits under the law of that or any other territory outside the United Kingdom, and any United Kingdom income tax or corporation tax so payable, shall, in considering whether any and if so what credit is to be allowed under any arrangements, be taken into account as tax so payable under the law of the first-mentioned territory is taken into account in a case falling within section 799.

(2) Credit shall not be allowed to a company by virtue of subsection (1) above for any financial year in respect of a greater amount of dividends paid by companies resident in any overseas territory than is equal to any excess of—
 (a) the relevant fraction of the company's total income in that year from investments (including franked investment income and group income) so far as referable to the business referred to in subsection (1) above;

over

 (b) the amount of the dividends so referable which are paid to it in the year by companies resident in that territory and in respect of which credit may, apart from subsection (1) above, be allowed to it for underlying tax.

(3) For the purposes of subsection (2) above the relevant fraction, in relation to any overseas territory, is—

$$\frac{A}{B}$$

where—

 A is the company's local premium income in the financial year so far as referable to the business referred to in subsection (1) above;
 B is the company's total premium income in the financial year so far as referable to that business;

and premium income shall be deemed to be local premium income in so far as it consists of premiums under contracts entered into at or through a branch or agency in that territory by persons not resident in the United Kingdom.

Former enactment.—TA 1970, s. 509.

803. Underlying tax reflecting interest on loans

(1) This section applies in a case where—
 (a) a bank or a company connected with a bank makes a claim for an allowance by way of credit in accordance with this Chapter; and
 (b) the claim relates to underlying tax on a dividend paid by the overseas company, within the meaning of section 801; and
 (c) that underlying tax is or includes tax payable under the law of a territory outside the United Kingdom on or by reference to interest on a loan made in the course of its business by that overseas company or by such third, fourth or successive company as is referred to in subsection (2) or (3) of that section; and
 (d) if the company which made the loan had been resident in the United Kingdom, then, in determining its liability to corporation tax, expenditure related to the earning of the interest on the loan would be deductible in computing the profits of the company brought into charge to tax.

(2) In a case where this section applies, the amount of the credit for that part of the foreign tax which consists of the tax referred to in subsection (1)(c) above shall not exceed an amount determined under subsection (3) below.

(3) The amount referred to in subsection (2) above is a sum equal to corporation tax, at the rate in force at the time the foreign tax referred to in paragraph (c) of subsection (1) above was chargeable, on so much of the interest on the loan as exceeds the amount of the lender's

relevant expenditure which is properly attributable to the period for which that interest is paid.

(4) In subsection (3) above—

(*a*) "interest", subject to subsection (5) below, has the meaning assigned to it by section 798(2); and

(*b*) "the lender's relevant expenditure" means the amount which, if the company referred to in subsection (1)(*d*) above were resident in the United Kingdom (and liable to tax accordingly) would be its financial expenditure in relation to the loan, as determined in accordance with section 798(6) to (10).

(5) If, in accordance with subsection (6) or subsection (8) below, the amount of the dividend would be treated for the purposes of corporation tax as increased or reduced by any amount, then the amount which, apart from this subsection, would be the amount of the interest referred to in subsection (3) above shall be taken to be increased or reduced by the same amount as the dividend is so treated as increased or reduced.

(6) If, in a case where this section applies, the underlying tax is or includes an amount of spared tax, then, for the purposes of corporation tax, the amount which apart from this subsection would be the amount of the dividend shall be treated as increased by an amount equal to so much of that spared tax as does not exceed the permitted amount; but nothing in this subsection prejudices the operation of section 795 in relation to foreign tax which is not spared tax.

(7) In this section—

(*a*) "spared tax" has the same meaning as in section 798; and

(*b*) the permitted amount, in relation to spared tax which is referable to the whole or any part of the interest referred to in subsection (1)(*c*) above, is an amount which does not exceed—

(i) 15 per cent. of the interest to which that spared tax is referable; or

(ii) if it is less, the amount of that spared tax which under any arrangements is to be taken into account for the purpose of allowing credit against corporation tax in respect of the dividend concerned.

(8) If, in a case where this section applies—

(*a*) the underlying tax is or includes an amount of tax which is not spared tax, and

(*b*) that amount of tax exceeds 15 per cent. of the interest to which it is referable,

then, for the purposes of corporation tax, the amount which would apart from this subsection be the amount of the dividend shall be treated as reduced by a sum equal to the excess.

(9) Where this section applies, the amount of the credit referred to in paragraph (*a*) of subsection (1) above which is referable to the underlying tax payable as mentioned in paragraph (*c*) of that subsection shall not exceed 15 per cent. of so much of the interest referred to in that paragraph as is included in the relevant profits of the company paying the dividend; and for the purposes of this subsection—

(*a*) "relevant profits" has the same meaning as, by virtue of section 799, it has for the purposes of the computation of underlying tax; and

(*b*) the amount of the interest shall be determined without making any deduction in respect of any foreign tax.

(10) In subsection (1) above "bank" means a company carrying on, in the United Kingdom or elsewhere—

(*a*) a banking business; or

(*b*) another business which includes the making of loans where the circumstances of the business are such that, in determining the liability of the company to corporation tax, expenditure related to the earning of the interest on those loans is deductible in computing the profits brought into charge to tax;

and section 839 applies for the purposes of subsection (1) above.

(11) Where the loan referred to in subsection (1)(*c*) was made pursuant to an agreement entered into before 1st April 1987, subsections (2) to (5) above shall not apply in relation to tax payable as mentioned in subsection (1)(*c*) above by reference to interest payable before 1st April 1989, but subject to that, this section applies whenever the loan referred to in subsection (1)(*c*) was made.

Former enactments.—FA 1982, s. 66; F(No. 2)A 1987, s. 68.

Miscellaneous rules

804. Relief against income tax in respect of income arising in years of commencement

(1) Subject to the provisions of this section, credit for overseas tax paid in respect of any income arising in the years of commencement shall be allowed under this Part against United Kingdom income tax chargeable for any year of assessment in respect of that income if it would have been so allowed but for the fact that credit for that overseas tax had been allowed against the United Kingdom income tax chargeable in respect of that income for a previous year of assessment.

(2) The amount of credit to be allowed in respect of any income by virtue of this section for any year of assessment shall not exceed the difference between—

(*a*) the total credit allowable against income tax in respect of that income under this Part (including this section) for all years of assessment for which credit is so allowable; and
(*b*) the amount of credit which was in fact so allowed in respect of that income for any earlier year or years of assessment.

(3) The total credit so allowable in respect of any income for all those years of assessment shall be taken to be the amount of the overseas tax charged on that income, adjusted where the number of the United Kingdom periods of assessment exceeds the number of foreign periods of assessment, in the proportion which the former number bears to the latter, a period for which part only of the income is charged to tax being counted not as one period but as a fraction equal to the proportion which that part of the income bears to the whole of the income.

(4) Where the same income is charged to different overseas taxes for different foreign periods of assessment, subsection (3) above, so far as it relates to the adjustment of overseas tax, shall be applied separately to each of the overseas taxes, and the total credit allowable shall be the aggregate of those taxes after the making of any adjustments in accordance with that subsection as so applied.

(5) Where credit against income tax for any year of assessment is allowed by virtue of subsection (1) above in respect of any income ("the original income") and subsequently by reason of the enactments relating to cessations, income arising in a non-basis period from the same source as the original income is not assessed to income tax, then if the amount of credit allowed against income tax in respect of the original income under this Part (including this section) for all years of assessment for which credit is so allowable exceeds the aggregate of the following amounts—

(*a*) the amount of the credit against income tax which would have been allowed apart from subsection (1) above for all those years in respect of the original income; and
(*b*) the amount of the overseas tax for which, under this Part, credit would have been allowable against income tax in respect of income arising in the non-basis period from the same source as the original income,

the person chargeable in respect of income (if any) from the same source in the year of assessment following the non-basis period shall be treated as having received in that year a payment chargeable under Case VI of Schedule D of an amount such that income tax thereon at the basic rate is equal to the excess.

(6) Any payment which a person is treated by virtue of subsection (5) above as having received shall not on that account constitute income of his for any of the purposes of the Income Tax Acts other than that subsection and in particular no part thereof shall constitute profits or gains brought into charge to income tax for the purposes of section 348.

(7) Any claim for relief by way of credit under subsection (1) above against income tax for any year of assessment shall be made within six years of the end of that year or, where there is more than one year of assessment in respect of which such relief may be given, within six years of the end of the later of them.

(8) In this section—

"overseas tax" means tax under the law of a territory outside the United Kingdom;
"non-basis period" means a period the income arising in which is, by reason only of the operation of the enactments relating to cessations, not chargeable to United Kingdom income tax for any year of assessment;
"United Kingdom period of assessment" and "foreign period of assessment", in relation to any income, mean respectively a year or other period for which under the relevant law the income falls to be charged to the relevant tax;
"years of commencement", in relation to income from any source, means the first three

years of assessment for which income from that source falls to be assessed to income tax, and also, in the case of profits or gains chargeable to tax under Case I or II of Schedule D, the whole of any period falling partly within those years such that the profits or gains arising in the period fall to be assessed to income tax for a year of assessment later than those years;

references to the enactments relating to cessations are references to sections 63, 67 and 113; and

references to income arising in any year include, in relation to income the income tax on which is to be computed by reference to the amount of income received in the United Kingdom, references to income received in that year.

Former enactments.—TA 1970, s. 510; FA 1971, Sch. 6, para. 75.

805. Elections against credit

Credit shall not be allowed under any arrangements against the United Kingdom taxes chargeable in respect of any income or chargeable gains of any person if he elects that credit shall not be allowed in respect of that income or those gains.

Former enactments.—TA 1970, s. 511; FA 1972, s. 100(1).

806. Time limit for claims etc.

(1) Subject to subsection (2) below and section 804(7), any claim for an allowance under any arrangements by way of credit for foreign tax in respect of any income or chargeable gain shall be made not later than six years from the end of the chargeable period for which the income or the gain falls to be charged to income tax or corporation tax, or would fall to be so charged if any income tax or corporation tax were chargeable in respect of the income or gain.

(2) Where the amount of any credit given under the arrangements is rendered excessive or insufficient by reason of any adjustment of the amount of any tax payable either in the United Kingdom or under the laws of any other territory, nothing in the Tax Acts limiting the time for the making of assessments or claims for relief shall apply to any assessment or claim to which the adjustment gives rise, being an assessment or claim made not later than six years from the time when all such assessments, adjustments and other determinations have been made, whether in the United Kingdom or elsewhere, as are material in determining whether any and if so what credit falls to be given.

Former enactment.—TA 1970, s. 512.

CHAPTER III

MISCELLANEOUS PROVISIONS

807. Sale of securities with or without accrued interest

(1) In any case where—
    (*a*) a person is treated under section 714(2) as receiving annual profits or gains on the day an interest period ends; and
    (*b*) assuming that, in the chargeable period in which the day falls, he were to become entitled to any interest on the securities concerned, he would be liable in respect of the interest to tax chargeable under Case IV or V of Schedule D; and
    (*c*) he is liable under the law of a territory outside the United Kingdom to tax in respect of interest payable on the securities at the end of the interest period or he would be so liable if he were entitled to that interest,

credit of an amount equal to the relevant proportion of the profits or gains shall be allowed against any United Kingdom income tax or corporation tax computed by reference to the profits or gains, and shall be treated as if it were allowed under section 790(4).

In this subsection the relevant proportion is the rate of tax to which the person is or would be liable as mentioned in paragraph (*c*) above.

(2) In any case where—
    (*a*) a person is entitled to credit against United Kingdom tax under section 790(4) or any corresponding provision of arrangements under section 788; and
    (*b*) the tax is computed by reference to income consisting of interest which falls due on securities at the end of an interest period and which is treated as reduced by virtue of section 714(5);

then the amount of that credit shall be a proportion of the amount it would be apart from this subsection, and the proportion is to be found by applying the formula—

$$\frac{I-R}{I}$$

where—

I is the amount of the interest; and

R is the amount by which it is treated as reduced.

(3) Where the person entitled to the credit is an individual, subsection (2) above does not apply unless the interest arises from securities to which the person either became or ceased to be entitled during the interest period.

(4) Where section 811(1) applies to any income and, if credit were allowable in respect of it the credit would be reduced by virtue of subsection (2) above, section 811(1) shall have effect in relation to the income as if the reference to any sum paid in respect of tax on it were a reference to the amount which would be the amount of the credit if it were allowable and subsection (2) above applied.

(5) Sections 710 and 711 shall apply for the interpretation of this section.

Former enactments.—Sub-ss. (1), (2): FA 1985, Sch. 23, para. 37.
Sub-ss. (3)–(5): FA 1985, Sch. 23, para. 38(1)–(3).

808. Restriction on deduction of interest or dividends from trading income

In the case of a person not resident in the United Kingdom who carries on in the United Kingdom a banking business, an insurance business or a business consisting wholly or partly in dealing in securities, receipts of interest or dividend which have been treated as tax-exempt under arrangements having effect by virtue of section 788 are not to be excluded from trading income or profits of the business so as to give rise to losses to be set off (under section 393 or 436) against income or profits.

In this section "securities" includes stocks and shares.

Former enactment.—FA 1976, s. 50(1).

809. Relief in respect of discretionary trusts

(1) In any case where—

(*a*) a payment made by trustees falls to be treated as a net amount in accordance with 687(2) and the income arising under the trust includes any taxed overseas income, and

(*b*) the trustees certify that—

(i) the income out of which the payment was made was or included taxed overseas income of an amount and from a source stated in the certificate, and

(ii) that amount arose to them not earlier than six years before the end of the year of assessment in which the payment was made;

then the person to whom the payment was made may claim that the payment, up to the amount so certified, shall be treated for the purposes of this Part as income received by him from that source and so received in the year in which the payment was made.

(2) In subsection (1) above "taxed overseas income", in relation to any trust, means income in respect of which the trustees are entitled to credit for overseas tax under this Part.

Former enactment.—FA 1973, s. 18.

810. Postponement of capital allowances to secure double taxation relief

(1) Where—

(*a*) a person chargeable to tax under Schedule D in respect of a trade is liable to overseas tax in respect of any income arising from the trade, being overseas tax for which relief may be given by way of credit, repayment or set off under the preceding provisions of this Part, and

(*b*) the conditions specified in subsection (2) below are satisfied,

he may, in claiming the relief in respect of that income, claim a postponement under this section of the relevant capital allowances operating to reduce that income for the purposes of tax for any chargeable period.

(2) The conditons are—

(*a*) that the law under which the overseas tax is chargeable provides for deductions or allowances to be given corresponding to capital allowances, but on a different basis such that they operate to reduce the income in question (if at all) to a less extent than the capital allowances to which the claim relates, but are calculated to operate to a greater extent than the corresponding capital allowances to reduce income arising subsequently; and

(*b*) that the relief falling to be so given in respect of the income in question is less than it would be if the capital allowances to which the claim relates operated to reduce the income to the same extent only as the deductions or allowances so provided for.

(3) Where a person claims a postponement under this section of capital allowances for any chargeable period, then—

(*a*) for the purposes of making the assessment for that period, the amount of those allowances shall be reduced by such amount as may be necessary to secure that they operate to reduce the income only to the extent mentioned in subsection (2)(*b*) above (or such less amount as the claimant may require); and

(*b*) for the purpose of making the assessment for the following period that amount shall be added to the amount of the allowances for that period, and shall be deemed to be part of those allowances or, if there are no such allowances for that period, shall be deemed to be the allowances for that period.

(4) For the purposes of any claim under this section—

(*a*) there shall be taken into account such only of the relevant capital allowances, and the deductions or allowances operating to reduce the income in question for purposes of the overseas tax, as are calculated to give relief in respect of the same expenditure or the same assets; and

(*b*) no account shall be taken of expenditure incurred or treated for the purposes of Chapter I of Part III of the Finance Act 1971 as incurred on or after 27th October 1970.

(5) In this section "overseas tax" means tax chargeable under the laws of any territory outside the United Kingdom, and "relevant capital allowances", in relation to any trade, means capital allowances falling to be made in taxing the trade.

(6) This section applies (with any necessary adaptations) in relation to a profession,

employment, vocation or office, and in relation to the occupation of woodlands the profits or gains of which are assessable under Schedule D, as it applies in relation to a trade.

Former enactments.—TA 1970, s. 515; FA 1971, s. 54(1); FA 1982, s. 78.
Note.—See **Prospective Legislation Notes** (Commercial Woodlands).

811. Deduction for foreign tax where no credit allowable

(1) For the purposes of the Tax Acts, the amount of any income arising in any place outside the United Kingdom shall, subject to subsection (2) below, be treated as reduced by any sum which has been paid in respect of tax on that income in the place where the income has arisen (that is to say, tax payable under the law of a territory outside the United Kingdom).

(2) Subsection (1) above—

(*a*) shall not apply to income the tax on which is to be computed by reference to the amount of income received in the United Kingdom; and
(*b*) shall not affect section 278(3); and
(*c*) shall not affect the liability to tax of an overseas life insurance company for any accounting period for which a charge to corporation tax under Case III of Schedule D arises under section 445 in respect of any of its income from the investments of its life assurance fund (excluding the pension fund and general annuity fund, if any) or for which such a charge would arise if there were such income;

and this section has effect subject to section 795(2).

Former enactments.—TA 1970, s. 516; FA 1973, s. 40(1); FA 1987, Sch. 15, para. 2(19).

812. Withdrawal of right to tax credit of certain non-resident companies connected with unitary states

(1) In any case where—

(*a*) a company has, or is an associated company of a company which has, a qualifying presence in a unitary state, and
(*b*) at any time when it or its associated company has such a qualifying presence, the company is entitled by virtue of arrangements having effect under section 788(1) to a tax credit in respect of qualifying distributions made to it by companies which are resident in the United Kingdom which is equal to one half of the tax credit to which an individual resident in the United Kingdom would be entitled in respect of such distributions,

then, notwithstanding anything to the contrary in the arrangements, the company shall not be entitled to claim under section 231(3) to have that tax credit set against the income tax chargeable on its income for the year of assessment in which the distribution is made or, where the credit exceeds that income tax, to have the excess paid to it.

(2) In this section and sections 813 and 814, "unitary state" means a province, state or other part of a territory outside the United Kingdom with the government of which the arrangements referred to in subsection (1) above have been made which, in taxing the income or profits of companies from sources within that province, state or other part, takes into account, or is entitled to take into account, income, receipts, deductions, outgoings or assets of such companies, or associated companies of such companies, arising, expended or situated, as the case may be, outside that territory and which has been prescribed under subsection (6) below as a unitary state for the purposes of this subsection.

(3) A company shall be treated as having a qualifying presence in a unitary state if it is a member of a group and, in any period for which members of the group make up their accounts ending after the relevant date, $7\frac{1}{2}$ per cent. or more in value of the property, payroll or sales of such members situated in, attributable to or derived from the territory outside the United Kingdom, of which that state is a province, state or other part, are situated in, attributable to or derived from that state.

(4) For the purposes of subsection (3) above—

(*a*) $7\frac{1}{2}$ per cent. or more in value of such property, payroll or sales as are referred to in that subsection shall be treated as being situated in, attributable to or derived from the state there referred to, unless, on making any claim under section 231(3), the claimant proves otherwise to the satisfaction of the Board; and
(*b*) the value of the property, payroll or sales of a company shall be taken to be the value as shown in its accounts for the period in question and for this purpose the value of any

property consisting of an interest in another member of the group or of any sales made to another such member shall be disregarded.

(5) Except where the context otherwise requires, in this section and sections 813 to 815—

(a) "arrangements" means the arrangements referred to in subsection (1) above;
(b) "group" and "member of a group" shall be construed in accordance with section 272(1) of the 1970 Act with the omission of the restriction in paragaph (a) of that subsection and the substitution of the words "51 per cent." for the words "75 per cent." wherever they occur;
(c) section 839 applies;
(d) section 416 applies with the substitution of the words "six years" for "one year" in subsection (1); and
(e) "the relevant date" means the earliest of the following dates—

(i) the date on which this section comes into force;
(ii) the earliest date on which a distribution could have been made in relation to which the provisions of this section and sections 813 and 814 are applied by an order under this section;
(iii) the earliest date on which a distribution could have been made in relation to which the provisions of section 54 of the Finance Act 1985 were applied by an order under that section.

(6) The Treasury may by order prescribe those provinces, states or other parts of a territory outside the United Kingdom which are to be treated as unitary states for the purposes of subsection (2) above, but no province, state or other part of such a territory shall be so prescribed which only takes into account such income, receipts, deductions, outgoings or assets as are mentioned in that subsection—

(a) if the associated company was incorporated under the law of the territory; or
(b) for the purpose of granting relief in taxing dividends received by companies.

(7) The Treasury may by order prescribe that for subsections (3) and (4) above (or for those subsections as they have effect at any time) there shall be substituted either the following provisions—

"(3) A company shall be treated as having a qualifying presence in a unitary state if it is subject to tax in such a state for any period ending after the relevant date for which that state charges tax.

(4) For the purposes of subsection (3) above a company shall be regarded as subject to tax in a unitary state if it is liable there to a tax charged on its income or profits by whatever name called and shall be treated as so charged unless it proves otherwise to the satisfaction of the Board.";

or the following provisions—

"(3) A company shall be treated as having a qualifying presence in a unitary state if it has its principal place of business in such a state at any time after the relevant date.

(4) For the purposes of subsection (3) above—

(a) a company shall be treated as having its principal place of business in a unitary state unless it proves otherwise to the satisfaction of the Board; and
(b) the principal place of business of a company shall include both the place where central management and control of the company is exercised and the place where the immediate day-to-day management of the company as a whole is exercised.".

(8) The provisions of this section and sections 813 to 815 shall come into force on such date as the Treasury may by order appoint and the Treasury may in the order prescribe that those provisions shall apply in relation to distributions made, in accounting periods ending after 5th April 1988, before the date on which the order is made.

(9) No order shall be made under this section unless a draft of it has been laid before and approved by a resolution of the House of Commons.

Former enactments.—Sub-s. (1): FA 1985, s. 54(1), (3).
Sub-s. (2): FA 1985, Sch. 13, para. 5(1).
Sub-ss. (3), (4): FA 1985, s. 54(4), (5).
Sub-s. (5): FA 1985, s. 54(6), Sch. 13, para. 5.
Sub-s. (6): FA 1985, s. 54(7)(b), Sch. 13, para. 5(1).
Sub-s. (7): FA 1985, s. 54(7)(c).
Sub-s. (8): FA 1985, s. 54(7)(a).
Sub-s. (9): FA 1985, s. 54(8).

813. Recovery of tax credits incorrectly paid

(1) Where—

   (a) section 812 applies so as to withdraw the entitlement of a company to claim to have a tax credit in respect of a qualifying distribution set against the income tax chargeable on its income and to have the excess of the credit over that income tax paid to it; and
   (b) the company ("the recipient company") has either had that excess paid to it, or has received an additional amount in accordance with arrangements made under Regulation 2(1) of the Double Taxation Relief (Taxes on Income) (General) (Dividend) Regulations 1973;

the recipient company shall be liable to a fine for the violation of the provisions of section 812 equal to twice the amount of the excess or the additional amount, as the case may be.

(2) Any fine payable under subsection (1) above—

   (a) shall be payable to the Board;
   (b) shall be treated as having become payable at the date when the excess or additional amount was paid to the recipient company; and
   (c) may be recovered in accordance with subsections (3) to (7) below;

and any such fine is referred to below as "the recoverable amount".

(3) The recoverable amount may be assessed and recovered as if it were unpaid tax and section 30 of the Management Act (recovery of overpayment of tax etc.) shall apply accordingly.

(4) Any amount which may be assessed and recovered as if it were unpaid tax by virtue of this section shall carry interest at the rate of 9 per cent. per annum from the date when it was payable in accordance with subsection (1) above until the date it is paid.

(5) It is hereby declared that this section applies to a recoverable amount which is paid without the making of an assessment (but is paid after it is due) and that, where the recoverable amount is charged by any assessment (whether or not any part of it has been paid when the assessment is made), this section applies in relation to interest running before, as well as after, the making of the assessment.

(6) Where the recoverable amount is not paid by the recipient company within six months from the date on which it became payable—

   (a) the recoverable amount may at any time within six years from the date on which it became payable be assessed and recovered as if it were unpaid tax due from any person who—
      (i) is or was at any time prior to the expiration of that six year period connected with the recipient company, or
      (ii) would have been connected on the assumption that all the facts and circumstances relating to the recipient company at the time the excess or additional amount, as the case may be, was paid continued to apply for six years thereafter,

   and section 30 of the Management Act shall apply accordingly; and

   (b) as respects its accounting periods beginning with that in which the excess or additional amount referred to in subsection (1) above was paid and ending with that following that in which the recoverable amount is paid in accordance with the provisions of this section, the company which made the qualifying distribution in respect of which the recipient company received the excess or additional amount shall not be entitled—
      (i) to set any advance corporation tax paid by it against its liability to corporation tax for such periods in accordance with section 239; nor
      (ii) to surrender the benefit of the whole or any part of any amount of advance corporation tax to a subsidiary in accordance with section 240 in such periods.

(7) Where a recoverable amount is assessed and recovered from a person connected with the recipient company in accordance with subsection (6)(a) above, that person shall be liable for the interest payable in accordance with subsection (4) above, and until the interest is so paid, subsection (6)(b) above shall apply as if the words "the interest due in accordance with subsection (4) above is paid" were substituted for the words "the recoverable amount is paid in accordance with the provisions of this section".

(8) Interest payable under this section shall be paid without any deduction of income tax and shall not be allowed as a deduction in computing any income, profits or losses for any tax purposes.

(9) Where under the law in force in a territory outside the United Kingdom interest is

payable subject to a deduction in respect of taxation and such deduction applies to an amount of interest paid in accordance with subsection (4) above, the reference to the rate of 9 per cent. per annum in that subsection shall be deemed to be a reference to such rate of interest as after such deduction shall be equal to the rate of 9 per cent. per annum.

Former enactment.—FA 1985, Sch. 13, para. 1.

814. Arrangements to avoid section 812

(1) In any case where arrangements are made, whether before or after the coming into force of this section, as a result of which interest is paid or a discount is allowed by or through a person who is resident in the United Kingdom, or carries on business in the United Kingdom through a branch or agency, and it is reasonable to suppose that, if such payment or allowance had not been made, a qualifying distribution would have been made by that person, or by another company resident in the United Kingdom to a company which has, or is an associated company of a company which has, a qualifying presence in a unitary state at the time when the payment or allowance is made, then—

(*a*) no person who receives that payment or allowance shall be entitled to relief from income tax or corporation tax thereon by virtue of arrangements having effect under section 788(1); and

(*b*) the payment or allowance shall not be allowed as a deduction in computing any income, profits or losses for any tax purposes.

(2) Without prejudice to the generality of subsection (1) above, where a payment or allowance is not of itself a payment or allowance to which that subsection applies, but is made in conjunction with other payments of whatever nature and taken together with those payments has substantially similar effect to a distribution, then, for the purposes of subsection (1) above it shall be treated as a payment or allowance within that subsection.

(3) Any company which has received such a payment of interest as is referred to in subsection (1) above, from which income tax has not been deducted by the person making the payment, and has a qualifying presence in a unitary state at the time of the payment, shall be treated for the purposes of section 813 as a company—

(*a*) from which the entitlement to claim payment of the excess of a tax credit over the income tax chargeable on its income has been withdrawn by section 812(1), and

(*b*) which has had paid to it such an excess in an amount equal to the income tax which should have been deducted from the payment of interest.

Former enactment.—FA 1985, Sch. 13, para. 3.

815. Power to inspect documents

Where it appears to the Board that the provisions of sections 812 to 814 may apply to a company resident outside the United Kingdom ("the foreign parent"), the Board may, by notice given to the foreign parent or any associated company of the foreign parent, require that company within such time (not being less than 30 days) as may be specified in the notice to make available for inspection any books, accounts or other documents or records whatsoever of that company where in the opinion of the Board it is proper that they should inspect such documents for the purposes of ascertaining whether those provisions apply to the foreign parent or such associated company notwithstanding that in the opinion of the person to whom the notice is given those provisions do not apply to that company or any associated company of that company.

Former enactment.—FA 1985, Sch. 13, para. 4(1).

816. Disclosure of information

(1) Where under the law in force in any territory outside the United Kingdom provision is made for the allowance, in respect of the payment of United Kingdom income tax or corporation tax, of relief from tax payable under that law, the obligation as to secrecy imposed by the Tax Acts upon persons employed in relation to Inland Revenue shall not prevent the disclosure to the authorised officer of the government of the territory in question of such facts as may be necessary to enable the proper relief to be given under that law.

Section 790(12) shall apply for the interpretation of this subsection as it applies for the interpretation of that section.

(2) Where any arrangements have effect by virtue of section 788, the obligation as to secrecy imposed by any enactment shall not prevent the Board, or any authorised officer of the Board, from disclosing to any authorised officer of the government with which the arrangements are made such information as is required to be disclosed under the arrangements.

(3) Where a person beneficially entitled to income from any securities as defined by section 24 of the Management Act (information as to income from securities) is resident in a territory to which arrangements having effect under section 788 with respect to income tax or corporation tax relate, section 24(3) of that Act shall not exempt any bank from the duty of disclosing to the Board particulars relating to the income of that person.

(4) The obligation as to secrecy imposed by any enactments with regard to income tax or corporation tax shall not prevent the disclosure, to any authorised officer of any country to which a declaration made under section 514 of the 1970 Act (agreements about shipping etc.) relates, of such facts as may be necessary to enable relief to be duly given in accordance with the arrangements specified in the declaration.

Former enactments.—TA 1970, s. 518; FA 1972, s. 100(1).

PART XIX

SUPPLEMENTAL

Miscellaneous

817. Deductions not to be allowed in computing profits or gains

(1) In arriving at the amount of profits or gains for tax purposes—

(*a*) no other deductions shall be made than such as are expressly enumerated in the Tax Acts; and
(*b*) no deduction shall be made on account of any annuity or other annual payment (not being interest) to be paid out of such profits or gains in regard that a proportionate part of income tax is allowed to be deducted on making any such payment.

(2) In arriving at the amount of profits or gains from any property described in the Tax Acts, or from any office or employment, no deduction shall be made on account of diminution of capital employed, or of loss sustained, in any trade or in any profession, employment or vocation.

Former enactment.—TA 1970, s. 519.

818. Arrangements for payments of interest less tax or of fixed net amount

(1) It is hereby declared that any provision made before or after the passing of this Act, whether orally or in writing, for the payment of interest "less tax", or using words to that effect, is to be construed, in relation to interest payable without deduction of tax, as if the words "less tax", or the equivalent words, were not included.

(2) In relation to interest on which the recipient is chargeable to tax under Case III of Schedule D, and which is payable without deduction of tax, any provision, made before or after the passing of this Act, whether orally or in writing, and however worded, for the payment of interest at such a rate ("the gross rate") as shall, after the deduction of income tax, be equal to a stated rate, shall be construed as if it were a provision requiring the payment of interest at the gross rate.

Former enactments.—TA 1970, s. 425; FA 1971, Sch. 6, para. 51.

819. Old references to standard rate tax

(1) Where any provision, however worded, contained in an instrument (of whatever nature) made on or after 3rd September 1939 or in a will or codicil taking effect on or after that date provides for the payment, whether periodically or otherwise—

(*a*) of a stated amount free of income tax other than surtax; or
(*b*) of an amount which, after deduction of income tax at the standard rate, is equal to a stated amount;

it shall have effect as follows.

(2) If it is such a provision as is mentioned in subsection (1)(*a*) above it shall have effect as if it provided for the payment of the stated amount free of income tax other than such as exceeds the amount to which the person to whom the payment is made would be liable if all income tax were charged at the basic rate to the exclusion of any higher rate.

(3) If it is such a provision as is mentioned in subsection (1)(*b*) above it shall have effect as if it provided for the payment of an amount which after deduction of income tax at the basic rate is equal to the stated amount.

(4) Any instrument however worded conferring on any person a right to receive a dividend or interest the amount of which depends on the standard rate of income tax shall have effect as if instead of referring to the standard rate it referred to the basic rate.

(5) Any reference in a statutory instrument made under the Tax Acts to the standard rate of income tax shall have effect as if it were a reference to the basic rate.

Former enactments.—FA 1971, Sch. 7, paras. 2–4; FA 1978, Sch. 2, para. 14.

820. Application of Income Tax Acts from year to year

In order to ensure the collection in due time of income tax which may be granted for any year commencing on 6th April, all such provisions contained in the Income Tax Acts as were in force on the preceding day shall have full force and effect with respect to tax which may be so granted, in the same manner as if that tax had been actually granted by Act of Parliament and those provisions had been applied thereto by the Act.

Former enactment.—TA 1970, s. 520.

821. Under-deductions from payments made before passing of annual Act

(1) Where, in any year of assessment, any half-yearly or quarterly payments have been made on account of any interest, dividends or other annual profits or gains, previously to the passing of the Act imposing income tax for that year, and tax has not been charged thereon or deducted therefrom or has not been charged thereon or deducted therefrom at the rate ultimately imposed for that year—

 (*a*) the amount not so charged or deducted shall be charged under Schedule D in respect of those payments, as profits or gains not charged by virtue of any other Schedule, under Case VI of Schedule D; and
 (*b*) the agents entrusted with the payment of the interest, dividends or other annual profits or gains shall furnish to the Board a list containing the names and addresses of the persons to whom payments have been made and the amount of those payments, upon a requisition made by the Board in that behalf.

(2) Any person liable to pay any rent, interest or annuity, or to make any other annual payment—

 (*a*) shall be authorised—
  (i) to make any deduction on account of income tax for any year of assessment which he has failed to make previously to the passing of the Act imposing the tax for that year, or
  (ii) to make up any deficiency in any such deduction which has been so made,
 on the occasion of the next payment of the rent, interest or annuity or making of the other annual payment after the passing of the Act so imposing the tax, in addition to any other deduction which he may be by law authorised to make; and
 (*b*) shall also be entitled, if there is no future payment from which the deduction may be made, to recover the sum which might have been deducted as if it were a debt due from the person as against whom the deduction could originally have been made if the Act imposing the tax for the year had been in force.

(3) Subsection (2) above shall apply with respect to—

 (*a*) any payment for or in respect of copyright to which section 536 applies or of public lending right to which that section applies by virtue of section 537; and
 [(*aa*) any payment for or in respect of a right in a design to which section 537B applies; and][1]
 (*b*) any royalty or other sum paid in respect of the user of a patent; and
 (*c*) any rent, royalty or other payment which by section 119 or 120 is declared to be subject to deduction of tax under section 348 or 349 as if it were a royalty or other sum paid in respect of the user of a patent;

as it applies with respect to any rent, interest, annuity or other annual payment.

(4) In this section "interest" and "dividends" do not include any interest or dividend which is a distribution.

Former enactments.—TA 1970, s. 521; FA 1972, Sch. 24, para. 29; FA 1983, s. 27.
Amendments.—[1] Sub-s. (3)(*aa*) inserted by the Copyright, Design and Patents Act 1988, Sch. 7, para. 36(7) with effect from 1 August 1989 by virtue of the Copyright, Design and Patents Act 1988 (Commencement No. 1) Order 1989, S.I. 1989 No. 816.

822. Over-deductions from interest on loan capital etc. made before passing of annual Act

(1) If in any year of assessment ("the year") a resolution having statutory effect under the Provisional Collection of Taxes Act 1968 provides for the charging of income tax at a basic rate lower than that charged for the previous year, the following provisions of this section shall have effect with respect to deductions in respect of income tax by any body corporate, from payments of interest (not being a distribution) on any of its securities.

(2) Any deduction which was made before the expiration of one month from the passing of the resolution and which would, if the tax had been renewed at the rate imposed for the previous year, have been a legal deduction, shall be deemed to be a deduction rendered legal by section 2 of the Provisional Collection of Taxes Act 1968 and that section shall, subject to this section, apply accordingly.

(3) Any over-deduction to be made good under that section may be made good by a reduction of the amount of tax deducted from the next payment of like nature made on the security in question after the passing of the Act imposing the tax for the year.

(4) Any amount made good under section 2 of the Provisional Collection of Taxes Act 1968 shall—

(*a*) in the case of an over-deduction which is made good under subsection (3) above, enure to the benefit of the person entitled to the payment on the occasion of which the over-deduction is made good; and
(*b*) in any other case, enure to the benefit of the person entitled to the security in question at the date when the amount is made good,

irrespective, in either case, of whether or not he is the person who was entitled to the payment, or to the security at the date when the original deduction was made.

(5) Subsection (3) above shall not authorise the retention of any part of the amount over-deducted for more than one year from the passing of the Act imposing the tax for the year.

Former enactments.—TA 1970, s. 522; FA 1971, Sch. 6, para. 76; FA 1972, Sch. 24, para. 30.

823. Adjustments of reliefs where given at different times

Where under the provisions of the Income Tax Acts an individual—

(*a*) is entitled to claim relief from income tax (other than relief in respect of life insurance premiums), by repayment or otherwise, in respect of—

(i) any amount which is paid or borne by him out of his income or which is allowable or may be deducted from his income; or
(ii) any reduction of an assessment relating to his income or any part of his income; or
(iii) any adjustment or set-off with regard to a loss; and

(*b*) claims that relief for any year of assessment,

any relief granted shall not extend so as to make the total income tax paid or payable by him for that year less than it would have been if the amount in respect of which relief is claimed had been deducted in computing his total income for the year and the amount of any other deductions or reliefs to which he is entitled for that year had been determined accordingly.

Former enactment.—TA 1970, s. 523.

824. Repayment supplements: individuals and others

(1) Subject to the provisions of this section, where—

[(*a*) in the case of income tax or surtax paid by or on behalf of an individual for a year of assessment for which he was resident in the United Kingdom, a repayment of the tax . . .[5] is made by the Board or an inspector after the end of the 12 months following that year of assessment; or][1]
[(*b*) in the case of the special charge under Part IV of the Finance Act 1968, a repayment of the charge . . .[5] is made by the Board or an inspector,][1]

the repayment shall be increased under this section by an amount (a "repayment supplement") equal to interest on the amount repaid at the [rate applicable under section 178 of the Finance Act 1989][7] for the period (if any) between the relevant time and the end of the tax month in which the order for the repayment is issued.

[(1A) In relation to so much (if any) of the last-mentioned period as preceded 6th April 1974, subsection (1) above shall have effect as if the rate of interest specified in it were 6 per cent. per annum (instead of the rate so specified or any other rate in force by virtue of subsection (6) below or section 47(7) of the Finance (No. 2) Act 1975).][2]

(2) [Subsections (1) *and (1A)*][3] above shall with the necessary modifications apply to a payment of the whole or part of a tax credit as [they apply to a repayment falling within subsection (1)][3] of income tax paid in the year of assessment to which the tax credit relates.

[(2A) Subsection (1) above shall apply to a repayment made in consequence of a claim under section 228 of the Income Tax Act 1952 (relief in respect of income accumulated under trusts) as if the repayment were of income tax paid by the claimant for the year of assessment in which the contingency mentioned in that section happened.]²

(3) For the purposes of subsection (1) above—
   (*a*) if the repayment is of tax that was paid after the end of the 12 months following the year of assessment for which it was payable, the relevant time is the end of the year of assessment in which that tax was paid;
   [(*aa*) if the repayment is of the special charge, the relevant time, as regards so much of the charge as was paid before the end of the year 1969–70, is the end of that year, and, as regards so much of the charge as was paid in any later year of assessment, is the end of the year of assessment in which it was paid;]²
   (*b*) in any other case, the relevant time is the end of the 12 months mentioned in that subsection;
and, subject to subsection (5) below, where a repayment to which subsection (1) above applies is of tax paid in two or more years of assessment, the repayment shall as far as possible be treated for the purposes of this subsection as a repayment of tax paid in a later rather than an earlier year among those years.

(4) For the purposes of subsections (1) and (3) above, income tax deducted by virtue of regulations made under section 203 from a person's emoluments during any year of assessment shall (without prejudice to subsection (5) below) be treated as paid by him for that and no other year of assessment.

(5) Where in consequence of an assessment under Schedule E for any year of assessment there is made by the Board or an inspector a repayment of income tax . . .⁵, being an amount which takes account of tax overpaid or remaining unpaid for one or more earlier years of assessment, then—
   (*a*) the repayment shall for the purposes of this subsection be attributable to such of the years in question, and in such proportions, as may be determined in accordance with regulations made under and for the purposes of this subsection by the Board; . . .⁶
   . . .⁶

(6) [*Without prejudice to subsection (1A) above,*]⁴ the Treasury may by order from time to time increase or decrease the rate of interest by reference to which—
   (*a*) repayment supplements are calculated under subsection (1) above; and
   (*b*) repayment supplements are calculated under section 47 of the Finance (No 2) Act 1975.

(7) A repayment supplement shall not be payable under this section in respect of a repayment or payment made in consequence of an order or judgment of a court having power to allow interest on the repayment or payment, or in respect of a repayment of a post-war credit within the meaning of the Income Tax (Repayment of Post-War Credits) Act 1959.

(8) A repayment supplement paid to any person under this section or under section 47 of the Finance (No. 2) Act 1975 shall not be income of that person for any tax purposes.

(9) Subsections (1) to (8) above shall apply in relation to a partnership, [the trustees of a settlement]⁸ [or personal representatives (within the meaning of section 111 of the Finance Act 1989)]⁹ as they apply in relation to an individual.

(10) In this section—
   "tax month" means the period beginning with the 6th day of any calendar month and ending with the 5th day of the following calendar month;
   . . .¹⁰

Former enactments.—Sub-s. (1): F(No. 2)A 1975, s. 47(1)(*a*); Income Tax (Interest on Unpaid Tax and Repayment Supplement) (No. 2) Order 1987, S.I. 1987 No. 898.
Sub-s. (2): F(No. 2)A 1975, s. 47(3)(*a*).
Sub-s. (3): F(No. 2)A 1975, s. 47(4)(*a*), (*c*).
Sub-ss. (4)–(8): F(No. 2)A 1975, s. 47(5)–(9).
Sub-ss. (9), (10): F(No. 2)A 1975, s. 47(11), (12).
Notes.—For the purposes of sub-s. (1) above, the rate of interest prescribed by the Income Tax (Interest on Unpaid Tax and Repayment Supplement) Orders is—
   8·25 per cent. from 6 December 1987: S.I. 1987 No. 1988.
   7·75 per cent. from 6 May 1988: S.I. 1988 No. 756.
   9·75 per cent. from 6 August 1988: S.I. 1988 No. 1278.
   10·75 per cent. from 6 October 1988: S.I. 1988 No. 1621.
   11·5 per cent. from 6 January 1989: S.I. 1988 No. 2185.
   12·25 per cent. from 6 July 1989: S.I. 1989 No. 1000.
See **Prospective Legislation Notes**.

Amendments.—¹ Sub-s. (1)(*a*), (*b*) substituted by FA 1988, Sch. 13, para. 7.
² Sub-ss. (1A), (2A), (3)(*aa*) inserted by *ibid.*
³ Words in sub-s. (2) substituted by *ibid.*
⁴ Words in sub-s. (6) inserted by *ibid.*
⁵ Words "of not less than £25" in sub-ss. (1)(*a*), (*b*), (5) repealed by FA 1989, s. 158(2)(*b*), (5) and Sch. 17, Pt. VIII with effect from an appointed day.
⁶ Sub-s. (5)(*b*) and the preceding word "and" repealed by *ibid.* It read—

"(*b*) subsection (1) and (3) above shall have effect in relation to so much of the repayment as is by virtue of paragraph (*a*) above attributed to any particular year of assessment as if in subsection (1) the words "of not less than £25" were omitted."

⁷ Words in sub-s. (1) substituted by FA 1989, s. 179(1)(*a*)(vii).
⁸ Words in sub-s. (9) substituted by FA 1989, s. 110(5).
⁹ Words in sub-s. (9) substituted by FA 1989, s. 111(4).
¹⁰ Definition of "United Kingdom estate" in sub-s. (10) repealed by FA 1989, Sch. 17, Pt. IV.
Sub-s. (1A), words "and (1A)" in sub-s. (2) and words "Without prejudice to subsection (1A) above" in sub-s. (6) repealed by FA 1989, Sch. 17, Pt. X with effect from an appointed day.

825. Repayment supplements: companies

(1) This section applies to the following payments made to a company in connection with any accounting period for which the company was resident in the United Kingdom ("the relevant accounting period"), that is to say—

(*a*) a repayment of corporation tax paid by the company for that accounting period (including advance corporation tax paid in respect of distributions made by the company in that accounting period . . .⁵); or
(*b*) a repayment of income tax in respect of a payment received by the company in that accounting period on which the company bore income tax by deduction; or
(*c*) a payment of the whole or part of the tax credit comprised in any franked investment income received by the company in that accounting period.

(2) Subject to the following provisions of this section, where a payment . . .³ to which this section applies is made by the Board or an inspector after the end of the 12 months beginning with the material date, the payment shall be increased under this section by an amount (a "repayment supplement") equal to interest on the amount paid at the [rate applicable under section 178 of the Finance Act 1989]⁴ for each complete tax month contained in the period (if any) beginning with the relevant date and ending at the end of the tax month in which the order for the payment is issued.

*[(2A) In relation to any complete tax month beginning before 6th April 1974 which is contained in the last-mentioned period, subsection (2) above shall have effect as if the rate of interest specified in it were 6 per cent. per annum (instead of the rate so specified or any other rate in force by virtue of subsection (5) below or section 48(6) of the Finance (No. 2) Act 1975).]*¹

(3) For the purposes of subsection (2) above—

(*a*) if the payment is a repayment of corporation tax that was paid on or after the first anniversary of the material date, the relevant date is the anniversary of the material date that occurs next after the date on which that tax was paid;
(*b*) in any other case, the relevant date is the first anniversary of the material date;

and where a payment to which this section applies is a repayment of corporation tax paid by a company on different dates, the payment shall as far as possible be treated for the purposes of this subsection as a repayment of tax paid on a later rather than an earlier date among those dates.

(4) For the purposes of this section—

(*a*) a repayment of corporation tax made in consequence of a claim by a company under section 239(3) to have the whole or any part of an amount of surplus advance corporation tax arising in the case of any accounting period treated as if it were advance corporation tax paid in respect of distributions made by the company in any earlier accounting period shall be treated as a repayment of corporation tax paid for the accounting period in the case of which that amount of surplus advance corporation tax arose; and
(*b*) a repayment of income tax or corporation tax made on a claim under subsection (4) of section 419 shall be treated as if it were a repayment of corporation tax paid for the accounting period in which the repayment of, or of the part in question of, the loan or advance mentioned in that subsection was made.

(5) [*Without prejudice to subsection (2A) above,*]² the Treasury may by order from time to time increase or decrease the rate of interest by reference to which repayment supplements are calculated under subsection (2) above.

(6) A repayment supplement shall not be payable under this section in respect of a payment

made in consequence of an order or judgment of a court having power to allow interest on the payment.

(7) A repayment supplement paid under this section shall be disregarded for all purposes of income tax and corporation tax.

(8) In this section—

"tax month" means the period beginning with the 6th day of any calendar month and ending with the 5th day of the following calendar month;

"the material date" in relation to a payment to which this section applies, means the last date on which corporation tax on any of the profits of the company in question arising in the relevant accounting period could have been paid—

    (a) in a case where section 10(1) applies, within the nine months there mentioned;
    (b) in a case where section 478 applies, within the time limit imposed by subsection (2)(a) of that section, but subject to subsection (6) of that section.

(9) This section has effect subject to section 826(8).

Former enactments.—Sub-ss. (1), (2): F(No. 2)A 1975, s. 48(1), (2); Income Tax (Interest on Unpaid Tax and Repayment Supplement) (No. 2) Order 1987, S.I. 1987 No. 898.
Sub-ss. (3)–(8): F(No. 2)A 1975, s. 48(4)–(9).
Notes.—For the purposes of sub-s. (2) above, the rate of interest prescribed by the Income Tax (Interest on Unpaid Tax and Repayment Supplement) Orders is—
    8·25 per cent. from 6 December 1987: S.I. 1987 No. 1988.
    7·75 per cent. from 6 May 1988: S.I. 1988 No. 756.
    9·75 per cent. from 6 August 1988: S.I. 1988 No. 1278.
    10·75 per cent. from 6 October 1988: S.I. 1988 No. 1621.
    11·5 per cent. from 6 January 1989: S.I. 1988 No. 2185.
    12·25 per cent. from 6 July 1989: S.I. 1989 No. 1000.
See **Prospective Legislation Notes.**
Amendments.—[1] Sub-s. (2A) inserted by FA 1988, Sch. 13, para. 8.
[2] Words in sub-s. (5) inserted by *ibid.*
[3] Words "of not less than £100" in sub-s. (2) repealed by FA 1989, s. 158(2), (5) and Sch. 17, Pt. VIII with effect from an appointed day.
[4] Words in sub-s. (2) substituted by FA 1989, s. 179(1)(a)(vii).
[5] Words in sub-s. (1)(a) repealed by FA 1989, Sch. 17, Pt. V in relation to accounting periods beginning after 31 March 1989.
Sub-s. (2A) and the words "Without prejudice to subsection (2A) above" in sub-s. (5) repealed by FA 1989, Sch. 17, Pt X with effect from an appointed day.

826. Interest on tax overpaid

(1) In any case where—

    (a) a repayment falls to be made of corporation tax paid by a company for an accounting period which ends after the appointed day; or
    (b) a repayment of income tax falls to be made in respect of a payment received by a company in such an accounting period; or
    (c) a payment falls to be made to a company of the whole or part of the tax credit comprised in any franked investment income received by the company in such an accounting period,

then, from the material date until [the order for repayment or payment is issued][2], the repayment or payment shall carry interest at the [rate applicable under section 178 of the Finance Act 1989][1].

(2) In relation to corporation tax paid by a company for an accounting period, the material date for the purposes of this section is the date on which corporation tax was paid or, if it is later, the date on which corporation tax for that accounting period became (or, as the case may be, would have become) due and payable in accordance with section 10.

(3) In relation to a repayment of income tax falling within subsection (1)(b) above or a payment of the whole or part of a tax credit falling within subsection (1)(c) above, the material date is the date on which corporation tax became (or, as the case may be, would have become) due and payable for the accounting period in which the payment referred to in subsection (1)(b) above or, as the case may be, the franked investment income referred to in subsection (1)(c) above was received by the company.

(4) For the purposes of this section a repayment of tax made on a claim under section 419(4) shall be treated as if it were a repayment of corporation tax for the accounting period in which the repayment of, or of the part in question of, the loan or advance mentioned in section 419(4) was made but, in relation to such a repayment of tax, the material date for the purposes of this section is—

    (a) the date on which the loan or advance (or part thereof) is repaid; or
    (b) if it is later, the date on which the tax which is to be repaid was in fact paid.

(5) Interest paid under this section shall be paid without any deduction of income tax and shall not be brought into account in computing any profits or income.

(6) Where a repayment of corporation tax is a repayment of tax paid by a company on different dates, the repayment shall so far as possible be treated for the purposes of this section as a repayment of tax paid on a later rather than an earlier date among those dates.

(7) In any case where—
  (a) there is in any accounting period of a company ("the later period") an amount of surplus advance corporation tax, as defined in section 239(3); and
  (b) pursuant to a claim under section 239(3), the whole or any part of that amount is treated for the purposes of section 239 as discharging liability for an amount of corporation tax for an earlier accounting period ("the earlier period"); and
  (c) a repayment falls to be made of corporation tax made for the earlier period,
then, in determining the amount of interest (if any) payable under this section on the repayment of corporation tax for the earlier period, no account shall be taken of any increase in the amount of the repayment resulting from section 239(3) except so far as concerns interest for any time after the date on which any corporation tax for the later period became due and payable (as mentioned in subsection (2) above).

(8) In consequence of the preceding provisions of this section, no repayment supplement (within the meaning of section 825) shall be paid in respect of any repayment of tax or payment of tax credit where the relevant accounting period (within the meaning of that section) ends after the appointed day.

(9) In this section "the appointed day" means such day or days, not being earlier than 31st March 1992, as the Treasury may by order appoint for the purposes of this section.

Former enactment.—F(No. 2)A 1987, s. 87.
Amendments.—[1] Words in sub-s. (1) substituted by FA 1989, s. 179(1)(c)(ii).
[2] Words in sub-s. (1) substituted by FA 1989, s. 180(6), (7) and deemed always to have had effect.

827. VAT penalties etc.

(1) Where, under Chapter II of Part I of the Finance Act 1985 (value added tax), a person is liable to make a payment by way of—
  (a) penalty under any of sections 13 to 17; or
  (b) interest under section 18; or
  (c) surcharge under section 19;
the payment shall not be allowed as a deduction in computing any income, profits or losses for any tax purposes.

(2) A sum paid to any person by way of supplement under section 20 of the Finance Act 1985 (VAT repayment supplements) shall be disregarded for all purposes of corporation tax and income tax.

Former enactment.—FA 1986, s. 53.
Note.—For the Finance Act 1985, Pt. I, Ch. II, see *Butterworths Orange Tax Handbook*.

828. Orders and regulations made by the Treasury or the Board

(1) Subject to subsection (2) below, any power of the Treasury or the Board to make any order or regulations under this Act or under any other provision of the Tax Acts (including enactments passed after this Act) shall be exercisable by statutory instrument.

(2) Subsection (1) above shall not apply in relation to any power conferred by section 124(6) or 841(1)(b) or paragraph 15(4) of Schedule 3 [or section 178(5) of the Finance Act 1989][1].

(3) Subject to subsection (4) below and to any other provision to the contrary, any statutory instrument containing any order or regulations made by the Treasury or the Board under this Act or under any other provision of the Tax Acts (including enactments passed after this Act) shall be subject to annulment in pursuance of a resolution of the House of Commons.

(4) Subsection (3) above shall not apply in relation to an order or regulations made under section 1(6), 257(11), 324, 376(5), 377(8), [590C(6)][2], 658(3) or 791 or paragraph 7 of Schedule 14 or—
  (a) if any other Parliamentary procedure is expressly provided;
  (b) if the order in question is an order appointing a day for the purposes of any provision of the Tax Acts, being a day as from which the provision will have effect, with or without amendments, or will cease to have effect.

Former enactments.—Sub-s. (1): TA 1970, ss. 65(5), 204, 231(3), 341(8), 341A(6), 343(1A); FA 1970, s. 29(6), Sch. 5, paras. 2(3), 10; FA 1972, ss. 91(3), 108(4); FA 1973, Sch. 16, para. 17(2); F(No. 2)A 1975, ss. 47(10), 48(6), 69(9), 70(8), 70A(3); FA 1976, ss. 64(4), 64A(4), Sch. 4, para. 16(2); FA 1980, s. 24(9), Sch. 10, para. 13(3); FA 1982, ss. 28(5), 29(1), (3), Sch. 7, para. 14(2); FA 1983, Sch. 5, paras. 5A(8), 6(8); FA 1984, ss. 26(1), 88(8), 126(1), Sch. 8, paras. 2(1)(ƒ), 3A; FA 1986, ss. 26, 27(7), 55, Sch. 11, para. 2, Sch. 16, para. 6(7).
Sub-s. (3): TA 1970, ss. 65(5), 204, 341A(6), 343(1A), 374(1A), (5); FA 1970, s. 29(6), Sch. 5, paras. 2(3), 10; FA 1973, Sch. 16, para. 17(2); F(No. 2)A 1975, ss. 69(9), 70(8), 70A(3); FA 1976, ss. 64(4), 64A(4); FA 1982, s. 29(1), (3); FA 1983, Sch. 5, paras. 5A(8), 6(9); FA 1984, ss. 26(6), 88(7), Sch. 8, paras. 2(1), 3A; FA 1986, ss. 26, 27(7), 55, Sch. 11, para. 2, Sch. 16, para. 6(7).
Amendments.—[1] Words in sub-s. (2) added by FA 1989, s. 178(6).
[2] Number in sub-s. (4) inserted by FA 1989, Sch. 6, para. 16.

829. Application of Income Tax Acts to public departments and avoidance of exempting provisions

(1) Subject to subsections (2) and (3) below, all the provisions of the Income Tax Acts relating to the assessment, charge, deduction and payment of income tax shall apply in relation to public offices and departments of the Crown.

(2) Nothing in those provisions of the Income Tax Acts shall require the payment by any such office or department of any tax which would be ultimately borne by the Crown.

(3) Subsection (1) above shall not apply to public offices and departments of any country, state, province or colony within section 320(3)(*b*) or (*c*) and nothing in subsection (1) above shall exempt any government from taxation to which it is liable in connection with any office or department by virtue of section 25 of the Finance Act 1925 (liability in respect of trading operations of Dominion governments and others).

(4) No letters patent granted or to be granted by the Crown to any person, city, borough or town corporate of any liberty, privilege or exemption from subsidies, tolls, taxes, assessments or aids, and no statute which grants any salary, annuity or pension to any person free of any taxes, deductions or assessments, shall be construed or taken to exempt any person, city, borough or town corporate, or any inhabitant of any city, borough or town corporate, from income tax, and all non-obstantes in any such letters patent or statute made or to be made to the contrary effect shall be void.

Former enactment.—TA 1970, ss. 524, 525(1).

830. Territorial sea and designated areas

(1) The territorial sea of the United Kingdom shall for all purposes of income tax and corporation tax (including the following provisions of this section) be deemed to be part of the United Kingdom.

(2) In this section—
   (*a*) "exploration or exploitation activities" means activities carried on in connection with the exploration or exploitation of so much of the seabed and subsoil and their natural resources as is situated in the United Kingdom or a designated area;
   (*b*) "exploration or exploitation rights" means rights to assets to be produced by exploration or exploitation activities or to interests in or to the benefit of such assets; and
   (*c*) "designated area" means an area designated by Order in Council under section 1(7) of the Continental Shelf Act 1964.

(3) Any profits or gains from exploration or exploitation activities carried on in a designated area or from exploration or exploitation rights shall be treated for the purposes of income tax or corporation tax as profits or gains from activities or property in the United Kingdom.

(4) Any profits or gains arising to any person not resident in the United Kingdom from exploration or exploitation activities or rights shall for the purposes of corporation tax be treated as profits or gains of a trade carried on by that person in the United Kingdom through a branch or agency.

(5) Any emoluments from an office or employment in respect of duties performed in a designated area in connection with exploration or exploitation activities shall be treated for the purposes of income tax as emoluments in respect of duties performed in the United Kingdom.

Former enactment.—FA 1973, s. 38(1).

Interpretation

831. Interpretation of this Act

(1) In this Act, except so far as the context otherwise requires—

(*a*) "the Corporation Tax Acts" means the enactments relating to the taxation of the income and chargeable gains of companies and of company distributions (including provisions relating also to income tax); and
(*b*) "the Income Tax Acts" means the enactments relating to income tax, including any provisions of the Corporation Tax Acts which relate to income tax.

(2) In this Act "the Tax Acts", except so far as the context otherwise requires, means this Act and all other provisions of the Income Tax Acts and the Corporation Tax Acts.

(3) In this Act—

"the Management Act" means the Taxes Management Act 1970;
"the 1968 Act" means the Capital Allowances Act 1968;
"the 1970 Act" means the Income and Corporation Taxes Act 1970; and
"the 1979 Act" means the Capital Gains Tax Act 1979.

(4) Section 1 of the Family Law Reform Act 1987, the paragraph inserted in Schedule 1 to the Interpretation Act 1978 by paragraph 73 of Schedule 2 to that Act and section 1(3) of the Law Reform (Parent and Child) (Scotland) Act 1986 (legal equality of illegitimate children) shall be disregarded in construing references in this Act to a child or to children (however expressed).

(5) This Act, so far as it relates to capital gains tax, shall be construed as one with the 1979 Act.

(6) Any reference in this Act to a section, Part or Schedule is a reference to that section, Part or Schedule of or to this Act, unless the context otherwise requires.

Former enactments.—Sub-ss. (1), (2): TA 1970, s. 526(1), (2); FA 1987, Sch. 15, para. 12.
Sub-s. (5): TA 1970, s. 540(2).

832. Interpretation of the Tax Acts

(1) In the Tax Acts, except in so far as the context otherwise requires—

"Act" includes an Act of the Parliament of Northern Ireland and a Measure of the Northern Ireland Assembly;
"additional rate", in relation to [any year of assessment for which income tax is charged, means 10 per cent. or such other rate as Parliament may determine][1];
"authorised unit trust" has the meaning given by section 468(6);
"basic rate", in relation to the charging of income tax for any year of assessment, means the rate of income tax determined in pursuance of section 1(2)(*a*), and any reference to the basic rate limit shall be construed in accordance with section 1(3);
"the Board" means the Commissioners of Inland Revenue;
"body of persons" means any body politic, corporate or collegiate, and any company, fraternity, fellowship and society of persons whether corporate or not corporate;
"building society" means a building society within the meaning of the Building Societies Act 1986;
"capital allowance" means any allowance under the Capital Allowances Acts;
"the Capital Allowances Acts" means the 1968 Act, Chapter I of Part III of the Finance Act 1971 and Part III of Schedule 13 and Schedule 15 to the Finance Act 1986 (including enactments which under this Act or the 1970 Act are to be treated as contained in Part I of the 1968 Act);
"chargeable gain" has the same meaning as in the 1979 Act;
"chargeable period" means an accounting period of a company or a year of assessment;
"close company" has the meaning given by sections 414 and 415;
"collector" means any collector of taxes;
"company" means, subject to subsection (2) below, any body corporate or unincorporated association but does not include a partnership, a local authority or a local authority association;
"distribution" has the meaning given by Part VI with section 418;
"farm land" means land in the United Kingdom wholly or mainly occupied for the purposes of husbandry, but excluding any dwelling or domestic offices, and excluding market garden land, and "farming" shall be construed accordingly;

"franked investment income" shall be construed in accordance with section 238, but subject to section 247(1);

"franked payment" shall be construed in accordance with section 238, but subject to section 247(1);

"group income" has the meaning given by section 247(2);

"higher rate", in relation to the charging of income tax for any year of assessment, means any rate of income tax determined in pursuance of section 1(2)(b), ...[2]

"industrial assurance business" has the meaning given by section 1(2) of the Industrial Assurance Act 1923 or Article 3(1) of the Industrial Assurance (Northern Ireland) Order 1979;

"inspector" means any inspector of taxes;

"interest" means both annual or yearly interest and interest other than annual or yearly interest;

"local authority" and "local authority association" have the meanings given by section 519;

"market garden land" means land in the United Kingdom occupied as a nursery or garden for the sale of the produce (other than land used for the growth of hops) and "market gardening" shall be construed accordingly;

"notice" means notice in writing;

"ordinary share capital", in relation to a company, means all the issued share capital (by whatever name called) of the company, other than capital the holders of which have a right to a dividend at a fixed rate but have no other right to share in the profits of the company;

"preference dividend" means a dividend payable on a preferred share or preferred stock at a fixed rate per cent. or, where a dividend is payable on a preferred share or preferred stock partly at a fixed rate per cent. and partly at a variable rate, such part of that dividend as is payable at a fixed rate per cent.;

"qualifying distribution" has the meaning given by section 14(2);

"qualifying policy" means a policy of insurance which is a qualifying policy for the purposes of Chapter I of Part VII;

"the rate of advance corporation tax" means the rate referred to in section 14(3);

"recognised clearing system" has the meaning given by section 124(6);

"surplus of franked investment income" has the meaning given by section 238;

"tax credit" means a tax credit under section 231;

"trade" includes every trade, manufacture, adventure or concern in the nature of trade;

"Ulster Savings Certificates" means savings certificates issued or treated as issued under section 15 of the Exchequer and Financial Provisions Act (Northern Ireland) 1950;

"unit holder" has the meaning given by section 468(6);

"unit trust scheme" has the meaning given by section 469;

"year of assessment" means, with reference to any income tax, the year for which such tax was granted by any Act granting income tax;

"the year 1988-89" means the year of assessment beginning on 6th April 1988, and any corresponding expression in which two years are similarly mentioned means the year of assessment beginning on 6th April in the first-mentioned of those two years;

and a source of income is within the charge to corporation tax or income tax if that tax is chargeable on the income arising from it, or would be so chargeable if there were any such income, and references to a person, or to income, being within the charge to tax, shall be similarly construed.

(2) The definition of "company" is subject to section 468, and does not apply in the following provisions of this Act, that is to say—

Chapter I of Part XVII;
sections 774 to 777;
section 839;
paragraph 15 of Schedule 3;

(and also does not apply where the context otherwise requires because some other definition of "company" applies).

(3) Except so far as the context otherwise requires, in the Tax Acts, and in any enactment passed after 12th March 1970 which by any express provision is to be construed as one with the Tax Acts, the Corporation Tax Acts or the Income Tax Acts, "tax", where neither income tax nor corporation tax is specified, means either of those taxes.

(4) Subsection (3) above is without prejudice to the provisions of section 9 which apply income tax law for certain purposes of corporation tax, and accordingly the employment of

"income tax" rather than "tax" in any provision of the Tax Acts is not a conclusive indication that that provision is not applied to corporation tax by that section.

(5) In the Tax Acts any reference to a child, however expressed, shall be construed as including a reference to an adopted child.

This subsection does not apply for the purposes of paragraph 10 of Schedule 30.

Former enactments.—Sub-s. (1): TA 1970, ss. 526(5), 527(1); FA 1971, s. 32(1), (1D), Sch. 8, para. 16(3); FA 1972, s. 93(6), Sch. 24, para. 3; FA 1974, Sch. 4, para. 10; FA 1976, Sch. 4, para. 11; CGTA 1979, Sch. 7; F(No. 2)A 1979, Sch. 2, para. 4; FA 1981, s. 34(5); Building Societies Act 1986, Sch. 18, para. 7; FA 1987, Sch. 15, para. 2(20).
Sub-s. (2): TA 1970, s. 526(6).
Sub-ss. (3), (4): TA 1970, ss. 526(3), (4).
Sub-s. (5): TA 1970, s. 526(5A); FA 1987, Sch. 15, para. 2(21).
Amendments.—[1] Words in the definition of "additional rate" in sub-s. (1) substituted by FA 1988, s. 24(4).
[2] Words in the definition of "higher rate" in sub-s. (1) repealed by FA 1988, Sch. 14, Pt. IV.

833. Interpretation of Income Tax Acts

(1) In the Income Tax Acts references to profits or gains shall not include references to chargeable gains.

(2) References in the Income Tax Acts to the retail prices index are references to the general index of retail prices (for all items) published by the Department of Employment; and if that index is not published for a month which is relevant for the purposes of any provision of those Acts that provision shall be construed as referring to any substituted index or index figures published by that Department.

(3) For the purposes of any provision of the Income Tax Acts (other than section 550 . . .[1]) requiring income of any description to be treated as the highest part of a person's income, his income shall be calculated without regard to—

(a) any payment chargeable to tax by virtue of section 148; or
(b) any amount included in his total income by virtue of section 547(1)(a); . . .[1]
(c) . . .[1]

(4) Subject to subsections (5) and (6) below, in the Income Tax Acts "earned income" means, in relation to any individual—

(a) any income arising in respect of—

(i) any remuneration from any office or employment held by the individual, or
(ii) any pension, superannuation or other allowance, deferred pay or compensation for loss of office, given in respect of the past services of the individual or of the husband or parent of the individual in any office or employment, or given to the individual in respect of past services of any deceased person, whether the individual or husband or parent of the individual shall have contributed to such pension, superannuation allowance or deferred pay or not; and

(b) any income from any property which is attached to or forms part of the emoluments of any office or employment held by the individual; and
(c) any income which is charged under Schedule . . .[1] or D and is immediately derived by the individual from the carrying on or exercise by him of his trade, profession or vocation, either as an individual or, in the case of a partnership, as a partner personally acting in the partnership.

In cases where the income of a wife is deemed to be income of the husband, any reference in this subsection to the individual includes either the husband or the wife.

(5) Without prejudice to the generality of the provisions of subsection (4) above, in the Income Tax Acts, except so far as is otherwise expressly provided, "earned income" also includes, in relation to any individual—

(a) any income arising in respect of Civil List pensions granted under the Civil List Act 1837 as amended by any subsequent enactment; and
(b) any annuity, pension or annual payment to which section 58(2) or 133 applies; and
(c) any payments chargeable to income tax under Schedule E by virtue of section 150, 151 or 617;
(d) any sum payable by way of annuity to an individual by virtue of a scheme under section 27 of the Agriculture Act 1967 (grants for relinquishing occupation of uncommercial agricultural units), unless the annuity was granted to the individual by reason of his having relinquished occupation before attaining the age of 55; and
(e) income which is earned income by virtue of section 529.

(6) The provisions of this section are without prejudice to any other provision of the Income Tax Acts directing income to be treated as earned income.

Former enactments.—Sub-s. (1): CGTA 1979, s. 155(5).
Sub-s. (2): FA 1980, s. 24(8).
Sub-s. (3): TA 1970, s. 529.
Sub-s. (4): TA 1970, s. 530(1).
Sub-s. (5): TA 1970, ss. 383, 530(2); FA 1981, s. 27(10); FA 1982, s. 31(2); FA 1987, Sch. 3, para. 5.
Sub-s. (6): TA 1970, s. 530(3).
Note.—See **Prospective Legislation Notes** (Married Couples).
Cross references.—See FA 1988, Sch. 14, Pt. V (repeal of the reference to Schedule B in TA 1970, s. 530(1)(c) with effect from 6 April 1988).
Amendments.—[1] Words in sub-ss. (3), (4)(c) repealed by FA 1988, Sch. 14, Pts. IV, V.

834. Interpretation of the Corporation Tax Acts

(1) For the purposes of the Corporation Tax Acts, except in so far as the context otherwise requires—

"accounting date" means the date to which a company makes up its accounts and "period of account" means the period for which it does so;

"accounting period" shall be construed in accordance with section 12;

"allowable loss" does not include, for the purposes of corporation tax in respect of chargeable gains, a loss accruing to a company in such circumstances that if a gain accrued the company would be exempt from corporation tax in respect of it;

"branch or agency" means any factorship, agency, receivership, branch or management;

"charges on income" has the meaning given by section 338;

"the financial year 1988" means the financial year beginning with April 1988, and similarly with references embodying other dates;

"group relief" has the meaning given by section 402.

(2) Section 6(4) shall also apply for the purposes of the following provisions of this Act, that is to say—

Chapter II of Part X except section 395;
sections 75 and 76;
section 490;
sections 768 and 769;

and also for sections 73 and 74 of the 1968 Act.

(3) For all the purposes of the Corporation Tax Acts dividends shall be treated as paid on the date when they become due and payable, except in so far as section 468(1) makes other provision as to amounts treated under that section as dividends.

(4) Except as otherwise provided by the Corporation Tax Acts, any apportionment to different periods which falls to be made under those Acts shall be made on a time basis according to the respective lengths of those periods.

Former enactments.—TA 1970, s. 527; FA 1980, s. 45(2).

835. "Total income" in the Income Tax Acts

(1) In the Income Tax Acts "total income", in relation to any person, means the total income of that person from all sources estimated in accordance with the provisions of the Income Tax Acts.

(2) Any person who, on his own behalf or on behalf of another person, delivers a statement of the amount of his or that other person's total income shall observe the rules and directions contained in section 836.

(3) Where deductions reduce a person's total income and the order in which they are made or in which income of different descriptions is reduced thereby may affect his liability to income tax the deductions shall be made and treated as reducing income in accordance with subsections (4) and (5) below.

(4) Subject to any express provisions of the Income Tax Acts, any deductions allowable in computing a person's total income or to be made from a person's total income shall be treated as reducing income of different descriptions in the order which will result in the greatest reduction of his liability to income tax.

(5) Deductions from total income under Chapter I of Part VII shall be made after any other

deductions and shall not affect the amount to be taken as a person's total income for the purposes of section 257(5) or 274...[1].

(6) In estimating the total income of any person—
  (a) any income which is chargeable with income tax by way of deduction at the basic rate in force for any year or which for the purposes of Schedule F comprises an amount equal to a tax credit calculated by reference to the rate of advance corporation tax in force for any year shall be deemed to be income of that year; and
  (b) any deductions which are allowable on account of sums payable under deduction of income tax at the basic rate in force for any year out of the property or profits of that person shall be allowed as deductions in respect of that year;

notwithstanding that the income or sums, as the case may be, accrued or will accrue in whole or in part before or after that year.

(7) Where an assessment has become final and conclusive for the purposes of income tax for any year of assessment—
  (a) that assessment shall also be final and conclusive in estimating total income; and
  (b) no allowance or adjustment of liability, on the ground of diminution of income or loss, shall be taken into account in estimating total income unless that allowance or adjustment has previously been made on an application under the special provisions of the Income Tax Acts relating thereto.

(8) Subsection (7) above shall apply in relation to—
  (a) any relief under section 353;
  (b) any relief by reason of the operation of an election for the herd basis under Schedule 5; and
  (c) any allowance under Part I of the 1968 Act or Chapter I of Part III of the Finance Act 1971 to be given by way of discharge or repayment of tax and to be available or available primarily against a specified class of income (that is to say, any capital allowance to which section 71 of the 1968 Act applies, or as provided by section 532 of this Act, any capital allowance to which section 528(2) of this Act applies);

as it applies in relation to allowances or adjustments on the ground of diminution of income or loss.

Former enactments.—Sub-ss. (1), (2): TA 1970, s. 528(1), (2); FA 1971, Sch. 6, para. 78; FA 1972, Sch. 24, para. 32.
Sub-ss. (3)–(5): FA 1971, s. 34; F(No. 2)A 1975, s. 31(4).
Sub-ss. (6)–(8): TA 1970, s. 528(3)–(5); FA 1971, Sch. 6, para. 78; FA 1972, Sch. 11, para. 8.
Note.—See **Prospective Legislation Notes** (Married Couples).
Amendments.—[1] Words in sub-s. (5) repealed by FA 1988, Sch. 14, Pt IV.

836. Returns of total income

The following rules and directions shall be observed in delivering returns of total income under section 835(2)—

  First—Declaration of the amount of profits or gains returned, or for which the person in question has been or is liable to be assessed.
  Second—Declaration of the amount of rents, interest, annuities or other annual payments, in respect of which the person in question is liable to allow the tax, with the names of the respective persons by whom such payments are to be made, distinguishing the amount of each payment.
  Third—Declaration of the amount of annuities or other annual payments (not being interest) to be made out of the property or profits or gains assessed on the person in question, distinguishing each source.
  Fourth—Statement of the amount of income derived according to the three preceding declarations.
  Fifth—Statement of any tax which the person in question may be entitled to deduct, retain or charge against any other person.

Former enactment.—TA 1970, Sch. 13.

837. "Annual value" of land

(1) For the purposes of, and subject to, the provisions of the Tax Acts which apply this section, the annual value of land shall be taken to be the rent which might reasonably be expected to be obtained on a letting from year to year if the tenant undertook to pay all usual tenant's rates and taxes, and if the landlord undertook to bear the costs of the repairs and

insurance, and the other expenses, if any, necessary for maintaining the subject of the valuation in a state to command that rent.

(2) Section 23 of the General Rate Act 1967 (adjustment of gross value by reference to provision of or payment for services etc.) shall apply for the purpose of subsection (1) above, and in relation to land in Scotland or Northern Ireland shall apply as if it extended to the whole of the United Kingdom.

(3) Where any question arises as to the annual value of land it shall be determined by the General Commissioners and those Commissioners shall hear and determine the question in like manner as an appeal.

Former enactment.—TA 1970, s. 531.

838. Subsidiaries

(1) For the purposes of the Tax Acts a body corporate shall be deemed to be—
   (a) a "51 per cent. subsidiary" of another body corporate if and so long as more than 50 per cent. of its ordinary share capital is owned directly or indirectly by that other body corporate;
   (b) a "75 per cent. subsidiary" of another body corporate if and so long as not less than 75 per cent. of its ordinary share capital is owned directly or indirectly by that other body corporate;
   (c) a "90 per cent. subsidiary" of another body corporate if and so long as not less than 90 per cent. of its ordinary share capital is owned directly by that other body corporate.

(2) In subsection (1)(a) and (b) above "owned directly or indirectly" by a body corporate means owned, whether directly or through another body corporate or other bodies corporate or partly directly and partly through another body corporate or other bodies corporate.

(3) In this section references to ownership shall be construed as references to beneficial ownership.

(4) For the purposes of this section the amount of ordinary share capital of one body corporate owned by a second body corporate through another body corporate or other bodies corporate, or partly directly and partly through another body corporate or other bodies corporate, shall be determined in accordance with the following provisions of this section.

(5) Where, in the case of a number of bodies corporate, the first directly owns ordinary share capital of the second and the second directly owns ordinary share capital of the third, then for the purposes of this section, the first shall be deemed to own ordinary share capital of the third through the second, and, if the third directly owns ordinary share capital of a fourth, the first shall be deemed to own ordinary share capital of the fourth through the second and third, and the second shall be deemed to own ordinary share capital of the fourth through the third and so on.

(6) In this section—
   (a) any number of bodies corporate of which the first directly owns ordinary share capital of the next and the next directly owns ordinary share capital of the next but one, and so on, and, if they are more than three, any three or more of them, are referred to as "a series";
   (b) in any series—
      (i) that body corporate which owns ordinary share capital of another through the remainder is referred to as the "first owner";
      (ii) that other body corporate the ordinary share capital of which is so owned is referred to as "the last owned body corporate";
      (iii) the remainder, if one only, is referred to as "an intermediary" and, if more than one, are referred to as "a chain of intermediaries";
   (c) a body corporate in a series which directly owns ordinary share capital of another body corporate in the series is referred to as "an owner"; and
   (d) any two bodies corporate in a series of which one owns ordinary share capital of the other directly, and not through one or more of the other bodies corporate in the series, are referred to as being directly related to one another.

(7) Where every owner in a series owns the whole of the ordinary share capital of the body corporate to which it is directly related, the first owner shall be deemed to own through the intermediary or chain of intermediaries the whole of the ordinary share capital of the last owned body corporate.

(8) Where one of the owners in a series owns a fraction of the ordinary share capital of the body corporate to which it is directly related, and every other owner in the series owns the whole of the ordinary share capital of the body corporate to which it is directly related, the first owner shall be deemed to own that fraction of the ordinary share capital of the last owned body corporate through the intermediary or chain of intermediaries.

(9) Where—

(a) each of two or more of the owners in a series owns a fraction, and every other owner in the series owns the whole, of the ordinary share capital of the body corporate to which it is directly related; or
(b) every owner in a series owns a fraction of the ordinary share capital of the body corporate to which it is directly related;

the first owner shall be deemed to own through the intermediary or chain of intermediaries such fraction of the ordinary share capital of the last owned body corporate as results from the multiplication of those fractions.

(10) Where the first owner in any series owns a fraction of the ordinary share capital of the last owned body corporate in that series through the intermediary or chain of intermediaries in that series, and also owns another fraction or other fractions of the ordinary share capital of the last owned body corporate, either—

(a) directly, or
(b) through an intermediary or intermediaries which is not a member or are not members of that series, or
(c) through a chain or chains of intermediaries of which one or some or all are not members of that series, or
(d) in a case where the series consists of more than three bodies corporate, through an intermediary or intermediaries which is a member or are members of the series, or through a chain or chains of intermediaries consisting of some but not all of the bodies corporate of which the chain of intermediaries in the series consists;

then, for the purpose of ascertaining the amount of the ordinary share capital of the last owned body corporate owned by the first owner, all those fractions shall be aggregated and the first owner shall be deemed to own the sum of those fractions.

Former enactment.—TA 1970, s. 532.
Cross references.—See TA 1970, s. 272(1D)(d) (extension of sub-s. (1)(a) of this section for the purposes of definition of groups of companies).

839. Connected persons

(1) For the purposes of, and subject to, the provisions of the Tax Acts which apply this section, any question whether a person is connected with another shall be determined in accordance with the following provisions of this section (any provision that one person is connected with another being taken to mean that they are connected with one another).

(2) A person is connected with an individual if that person is the individual's wife or husband, or is a relative, or the wife or husband of a relative, of the individual or of the individual's wife or husband.

(3) A person, in his capacity as trustee of a settlement, is connected with any individual who in relation to the settlement is a settlor, with any person who is connected with such an individual and with a body corporate which, under section 681 is deemed to be connected with that settlement ("settlement" and "settlor" having for the purposes of this subsection the meanings given by subsection (4) of that section).

(4) Except in relation to acquisitions or disposals of partnership assets pursuant to bona fide commercial arrangements, a person is connected with any person with whom he is in partnership, and with the wife or husband or relative of any individual with whom he is in partnership.

(5) A company is connected with another company—

(a) if the same person has control of both, or a person has control of one and persons connected with him, or he and persons connected with him, have control of the other; or
(b) if a group of two or more persons has control of each company, and the groups either consist of the same persons or could be regarded as consisting of the same persons by treating (in one or more cases) a member of either group as replaced by a person with whom he is connected.

(6) A company is connected with another person if that person has control of it or if that person and persons connected with him together have control of it.

(7) Any two or more persons acting together to secure or exercise control of a company shall be treated in relation to that company as connected with one another and with any person acting on the directions of any of them to secure or exercise control of the company.

(8) In this section—

"company" includes any body corporate or unincorporated association, but does not include a partnership, and this section shall apply in relation to any unit trust scheme as if the scheme were a company and as if the rights of the unit holders were shares in the company;

"control" shall be construed in accordance with section 416; and

"relative" means brother, sister, ancestor or lineal descendant.

In relation to any period during which section 470(2) has effect the reference above to a unit trust scheme shall be construed as a reference to a unit trust scheme within the meaning of the Prevention of Fraud (Investments) Act 1958 or the Prevention of Fraud (Investments) Act (Northern Ireland) 1940.

Former enactment.—TA 1970, s. 533.

840. Meaning of "control" in certain contexts

For the purposes of, and subject to, the provisions of the Tax Acts which apply this section, "control", in relation to a body corporate, means the power of a person to secure—

(a) by means of the holding of shares or the possession of voting power in or in relation to that or any other body corporate; or

(b) by virtue of any powers conferred by the articles of association or other document regulating that or any other body corporate,

that the affairs of the first-mentioned body corporate are conducted in accordance with the wishes of that person, and, in relation to a partnership, means the right to a share of more than one-half of the assets, or of more than one-half of the income, of the partnership.

Former enactment.—TA 1970, s. 534.

841. Recognised stock exchange and recognised investment exchanges

(1) In the Tax Acts "recognised stock exchange" means—

(a) the Stock Exchange; and

(b) any such stock exchange outside the United Kingdom as is for the time being designated for the purposes of this section as a recognised stock exchange by order made by the Board.

(2) An order made by the Board under this section—

(a) may designate a stock exchange by name, or by reference to any class or description of stock exchanges including a class or description framed by reference to any authority or approval given in a country outside the United Kingdom;

(b) may contain such transitional and other supplemental provisions as appear to the Board to be necessary or expedient;

(c) may be varied or revoked by a subsequent order so made.

(3) The Board may by regulations make provision securing that enactments in the Tax Acts containing references to the Stock Exchange have effect, for such purposes and subject to such modifications as may be prescribed by the regulations, in relation to all other recognised investment exchanges (within the meaning of the Financial Services Act 1986), or in relation to such of those exchanges as may be prescribed.

Former enactments.—TA 1970, s. 535; FA 1973, Sch. 21, para 9; F(No. 2) A 1987, s. 73.

842. Investment trusts

(1) In the Tax Acts "investment trust" means, as respects any accounting period, a company which is not a close company and which is approved for the purposes of this section for that accounting period by the Board, and the Board shall not approve any company unless it is shown to their satisfaction—

[(aa) that the company is resident in the United Kingdom; and][1]

(a) that the company's income is derived wholly or mainly from shares or securities; and

(b) subject to subsection (2) below, that no holding in a company, other than an investment trust or a company which would qualify as an investment trust but for paragraph (c) below, represents more than 15 per cent. by value of the investing company's investments; and

[(c) that the shares making up the company's ordinary share capital (or, if there are such shares of more than one class, those of each class) are quoted on the Stock Exchange; and]²

(d) that the distribution as dividend of surpluses arising from the realisation of investments is prohibited by the company's memorandum or articles of association; and

(e) that the company does not retain in respect of any accounting period more than 15 per cent. of the income it derives from shares and securities.

[(1A) For the purposes of paragraph (b) of subsection (1) above and the other provisions of this section having effect in relation to that paragraph—

(a) holdings in companies which are members of a group (whether or not including the investing company) and are not excluded from that paragraph shall be treated as holdings in a single company; and

(b) where the investing company is a member of a group, money owed to it by another member of the group shall be treated as a security of the latter held by the investing company and accordingly as, or as part of, the holding of the investing company in the company owing the money;

and for the purposes of this subsection "group" means a company and all companies which are its 51 per cent. subsidiaries.]¹

(2) Subsection (1)(b) above shall not apply—

(a) to a holding in a company acquired before 6th April 1965 which on that date represented not more than 25 per cent. by value of the investing company's investments; or

(b) to a holding in a company which, when it was acquired, represented not more than 15 per cent. by value of the investing company's investments;

so long as no addition is made to the holding.

(3) For the purposes of subsection (2) above—

(a) "holding" means the shares or securities (whether of one class or more than one class) held in any one company; and

(b) an addition is made to a holding whenever the investing company acquires shares or securities of that one company, otherwise than by being allotted shares or securities without becoming liable to give any consideration, and if an addition is made to a holding that holding is acquired when the addition or latest addition is made to the holding; and

(c) where in connection with a scheme of reconstruction or amalgamation, a company issues shares or securities to persons holding shares or securities in a second company in respect of and in proportion to (or as nearly as may be in proportion to) their holdings in the second company, without those persons becoming liable to give any consideration, a holding of the shares or securities in the second company and a corresponding holding of the shares or securities so issued shall be regarded as the same holding.

(4) In this section "company" and "shares" shall be construed in accordance with sections 64, 93 and 155(1) of the 1979 Act.

Former enactments.—TA 1970, s. 359; FA 1973, s. 54; CGTA 1979, Sch. 7.
Cross references.—See FA 1988, s. 117(2) (TA 1970, s. 359 as amended by FA 1972, s. 93 to apply where companies' accounting periods end before 6 April 1988).
Amendments.—¹ Sub-s. (1)(aa), (1A) inserted by FA 1988, s. 117(1), (4) for companies' accounting periods ending after 5 April 1988.
² Sub-s. (1)(c) substituted by *ibid.*

Commencement, savings, repeals etc

843. Commencement

(1) Except as otherwise provided by the following provisions of this section, this Act shall come into force in relation to tax for the year 1988–89 and subsequent years of assessment, and for companies' accounting periods ending after 5th April 1988.

(2) Except as otherwise provided by the following provisions of this section, such of the provisions of this Act as relate to capital gains tax (including the provisions of Part XVIII

as applied to capital gains tax by section 10 of the 1979 Act) shall come into force in relation to that tax for the year 1988-89 and subsequent years of assessment.

(3) The following provisions of this Act, that is to say—

(a) so much of any provision as authorises the making of any Order in Council or regulations or other instrument;
(b) so much of any provision as relates to the making of a return, the furnishing of a certificate or the giving of any other information, including any such provision which imposes a duty on the Board or an officer of the Board as well as any such provision which imposes a duty on any other person;
(c) so much of any provision as imposes any penalty;
(d) except where the tax concerned is all tax for years of assessment before the year 1988-89 or accounting periods ending before 6th April 1988, so much of any other provision as confers any power or imposes any duty the exercise or performance of which operates or may operate in relation to tax for more than one chargeable period,

shall come into force for all purposes on 6th April 1988 to the exclusion of the corresponding enactments repealed by this Act.

(4) This section has effect except as otherwise provided by any other provision of this Act, and in particular except as provided by sections 96, 380 to 384, 393, 394, 400, 703 and 812.

844. Savings, transitional provisions, consequential amendments and repeals

(1) Schedule 29, which makes amendments to other enactments consequential on the passing of this Act, shall have effect.

(2) Schedule 29, section 843 and this section are without prejudice to the provisions of the Interpretation Act 1978 as respects the effect of repeals.

(3) Schedule 30 which contains savings and transitional provisions shall have effect.

(4) The enactments mentioned in Schedule 31 are hereby repealed to the extent specified in the third column of that Schedule.

(5) Subject to subsection (6) below, section 843(3), Schedule 30 and to any other provision of this Act by which any provision is brought into force to the exclusion of the corresponding enactments repealed by this Act, those repeals shall come into force in accordance with subsections (1) and (2) of section 843.

(6) No provision mentioned in subsection (5) above shall be taken as bringing a repeal into force except to the extent that the repealed enactment is being superseded.

845. Short title

This Act may be cited as the Income and Corporation Taxes Act 1988.

SCHEDULES

SCHEDULE 1

Section 31

RESTRICTIONS ON SCHEDULE A DEDUCTIONS

Expenditure before 1964–65: deductions from rents

1.—(1) Except as provided by sub-paragraphs (2) and (3) below, no payment shall be deductible under sections 25 and 26 if made before the beginning of the year 1964–65.

(2) Where, by virtue of paragraph 1(2) of Schedule 2 to the 1970 Act, any amount fell to be treated as a payment in relation to premises made by a person in the year 1964–65 in respect of dilapidation attributable to that year, the amount shall be similarly treated for the purposes of sections 25 and 26.

(3) If the amount of any loss was treated, by virtue of paragraph 1(3) of that Schedule, as if it were a payment such as is mentioned in section 72(1) of the 1970 Act made by any person in respect of any premises in and in respect of any year, it shall be treated for the purposes of sections 25 and 26 as if it were a payment such as is mentioned in section 25(1) made by that person in respect of those premises in and in respect of that year.

(4) A deduction falling to be made by virtue of sub-paragraph (3) above shall be made notwithstanding anything in sections 392(3) and 396(1); and relief shall not be given under either of those sections in respect of the loss insofar as a deduction in respect of it is given under this paragraph.

Former enactment.—TA 1970, Sch. 2, para. 1.

Expenditure before 1964–65: deductions from other receipts

2.—(1) Subject to sub-paragraph (2) below, no payment shall be deductible under section 28 if made before the beginning of the year 1964–65.

(2) Sub-paragraph (1) above shall not prevent the deduction of a payment in so far as a loss in respect thereof was carried forward to the year 1964–65 by virtue of section 346 of the Income Tax Act 1952 (Case VI losses).

(3) Paragraph 1(4) above shall apply in the case of a deduction falling to be made by virtue of sub-paragraph (2) above as it applies in the case of one falling to be made by virtue of paragraph 1(3) above.

Former enactment.—TA 1970, Sch. 2, para. 2.

Expenditure on sea walls before 1964–65

3.—(1) Section 30 shall not apply in relation to expenditure incurred before the beginning of the year 1964–65 except in accordance with sub-paragraphs (2) and (3) below.

(2) Subject to sub-paragraph (3) below, section 30 shall apply in relation to expenditure which, by virtue of paragraph 3(1) of Schedule 2 to the 1970 Act, was treated as if—

(*a*) it had been incurred in the year of assessment following that in which it was actually incurred, and

(*b*) in so far as it was incurred in repairing an embankment, it had been incurred in making it,

as if it had been incurred in that year and in making that embankment.

(3) If, by virtue of the proviso to paragraph 3(1) of Schedule 2 to the 1970 Act, any expenditure fell to be treated for the purposes of sections 71 to 77 of that Act as if it were an amount paid by any person in and in respect of the year 1964–65 in respect of the maintenance of premises preserved or protected by an embankment, it shall be similarly treated for the purposes of sections 25 to 31.

Former enactment.—TA 1970, Sch. 2, para. 3.

SCHEDULE 2

Section 39(3)

PREMIUMS ETC. TAXABLE UNDER SCHEDULES A AND D: SPECIAL RELIEF FOR INDIVIDUALS

Former enactment.—TA 1970, Sch. 3, paras. 1–6.
Amendments.—This Schedule repealed by FA 1988, s. 75 and Sch. 14, Pt. IV.

SCHEDULE 3

Section 44(2)

MACHINERY FOR ASSESSMENT, CHARGE AND PAYMENT OF INCOME TAX UNDER SCHEDULE C AND, IN CERTAIN CASES, SCHEDULE D

PART I
PUBLIC REVENUE DIVIDENDS ETC. PAYABLE TO THE BANK OF ENGLAND OR THE BANK OF IRELAND OR ENTRUSTED FOR PAYMENT TO THE BANK OF ENGLAND, THE BANK OF IRELAND OR THE NATIONAL DEBT COMMISSIONERS

1. The Bank of England and the Bank of Ireland as respects the dividends and the profits attached thereto payable to them out of the public revenue of the United Kingdom, or payable out of any public revenue and entrusted to them for payment and distribution, and the National Debt Commissioners, as respects the dividends payable by them or of which they have the distribution, shall, when any payment becomes due, deliver to the Board true accounts, in books provided for the purpose, of—

(*a*) the amounts of the dividends and profits attached thereto payable to the Bank, and
(*b*) all dividends entrusted to the Bank or the National Debt Commissioners for payment to the persons entitled thereto, and
(*c*) the amount of income tax chargeable thereon at the basic rate in force at the time of payment, without any other deduction than is allowed by the Income Tax Acts.

Former enactments.—TA 1970, Sch. 5, para. 1; FA 1971, Sch. 6, para. 80.

2.—(1) In the case of dividends and profits attached thereto payable to the Bank of England out of the public revenue of the United Kingdom, the Bank of England shall set apart the income tax in respect of the amount payable to them.

(2) In the case of dividends and profits attached thereto entrusted to the Bank of England for payment and distribution, dividends payable by the Bank of Ireland at its principal office in Belfast, and dividends payable by the National Debt Commissioners or of which the National Debt Commissioners have the distribution—

(*a*) the Bank of England, the Bank of Ireland and the National Debt Commissioners respectively shall, before any payment is made by them, retain the amount of the income tax for the purposes of the Income Tax Acts, and
(*b*) the retaining of the amount shall be deemed to be a payment of the income tax by the persons entitled to the dividends, and shall be allowed by them on the receipt of the residue thereof, and
(*c*) the Bank of England, the Bank of Ireland and the National Debt Commissioners respectively shall be acquitted and discharged of a sum equal to the amount retained as though that sum had been actually paid.

(3) In relation to dividends payable to the Bank of Ireland out of the public revenue of the United Kingdom, and public revenue dividends which are entrusted to the Bank of Ireland for payment and distribution and are not payable by that Bank out of its principal office in Belfast, the following provisions shall have effect—

(*a*) the money which, apart from this sub-paragraph, would be issuable to the Bank of Ireland under section 14 of the National Debt Act 1870, or otherwise payable to the Bank of Ireland for the purpose of dividends on securities of the United Kingdom government entered in the register of the Bank of Ireland in Dublin, shall be issued and paid to the Bank of England; and
(*b*) the Bank of England shall set apart and retain out of moneys so issued and paid to them the amount of the income tax on the dividends payable to the Bank of Ireland, and on the dividends on the securities of the United Kingdom government entered in the register of the Bank of Ireland in Dublin; and
(*c*) the Bank of England shall pay to the Bank of Ireland the residue of moneys so issued and paid to them, to be applied by the Bank of Ireland to the payment of the dividends; and
(*d*) the retaining of the amount shall be deemed to be a payment of the income tax by the persons entitled to the dividends, and shall be allowed by them on the receipt of the

residue thereof, and the Bank of England and the Bank of Ireland shall be acquitted and discharged of a sum equal to the amount retained as though that sum had been actually paid.

Former enactment.—TA 1970, Sch. 5, para. 2.

3. Money set apart or retained under paragraph 2 above, and the amount of any tax charged on the trading profits of the Bank of England or the Bank of Ireland, shall be paid into the general account of the Board at the Bank of England or the Bank of Ireland.

Former enactment.—TA 1970, Sch. 5, para. 3.

4. No deduction of income tax under this Part of this Schedule shall be made from any dividends payable in respect of stock, securities or annuities standing in the name of the official custodian for charities, nor from any dividends in respect of which there is given to the Bank of England a certificate from the Charity Commissioners that the dividends are subject only to charitable trusts and are exempt from tax.

Former enactment.—TA 1970, Sch. 5, para. 4.

PART II
PUBLIC REVENUE DIVIDENDS PAYABLE BY PUBLIC OFFICES AND DEPARTMENTS

5. Where any payment is made of public revenue dividends payable by any public office or department of the Crown, the appropriate officer shall retain the income tax charged and pay the same into the general account of the Board at the Bank of England or the Bank of Ireland.

Former enactment.—TA 1970, Sch. 5, para. 5.

PART III
OTHER PUBLIC REVENUE DIVIDENDS, FOREIGN DIVIDENDS AND PROCEEDS OF COUPONS

6.—(1) The following persons are chargeable persons for the purposes of this Part of this Schedule—

(*a*) every person (other than the National Debt Commissioners or the Bank of England or the Bank of Ireland) who is entrusted with the payment of any dividends which are payable out of the public revenue of Northern Ireland, or which are payable to any persons in the United Kingdom out of any public revenue other than that of the United Kingdom or Northern Ireland;
(*b*) every person in the United Kingdom who is entrusted with the payment of any foreign dividends;
(*c*) every banker or other person in the United Kingdom who obtains payment of any dividends in such circumstances that the dividends are chargeable to tax under Schedule C, or in the case of foreign dividends, under Schedule D; and
(*d*) every banker in the United Kingdom who sells or otherwise realises coupons, and every dealer in coupons in the United Kingdom who purchases coupons, in such manner that the proceeds of the sale or realisation are chargeable to tax under Schedule C, or in the case of foreign dividends, under Schedule D.

(2) Every chargeable person shall deliver to the Board—

(*a*) on demand by the Board, true and perfect accounts of the amount of all such dividends or proceeds; and
(*b*) not later than 12 months after paying any dividends or effecting any other transaction in respect of which he is a chargeable person, and unless within that time he delivers an account with respect to the dividends or proceeds in question under sub-paragraph (*a*) above, a written statement specifying his name and address and describing those dividends or proceeds.

Former enactments.—Sub-para. (1): TA 1970, Sch. 5, para. 6(*a*), (*b*).
Sub-para. (2): TA 1970, Sch. 5, para. 6(i), (ii).

7. The Board shall have all necessary powers in relation to the examining, auditing,

checking and clearing of the books and accounts of dividends or proceeds delivered under paragraph 6 above, and shall assess and charge the dividends or proceeds at the basic rate of tax in force at the time of payment, but reduced by the amount of the exemptions (if any) allowed by them, and shall give notice of the amount so assessed and charged to the chargeable person.

Former enactments.—TA 1970, Sch. 5, para. 7; FA 1971, Sch. 6, para. 80.

8. The chargeable person shall out of moneys in his hands pay the income tax on the dividends or proceeds on behalf of the persons entitled thereto, and shall be acquitted in respect of all such payments, and the provisions of the Income Tax Acts shall apply as in the case of dividends payable out of the public revenue of the United Kingdom and entrusted to the Bank of England for payment and distribution.

Former enactment.—TA 1970, Sch. 5, para. 8.

9. The chargeable person shall pay the income tax into the general account of the Board at the Bank of England or the Bank of Ireland within 30 days of the date of the issue of the notice of assessment, and in default of payment it shall be recovered from him in the same manner as other tax assessed and charged on him may be recovered.

Former enactments.—TA 1970, Sch. 5, para. 9; F(No. 2)A 1975, s. 44(3).

10.—(1) Subject to sub-paragraph (2) below, a chargeable person who does all such things as are necessary to enable the tax to be assessed and paid shall receive as remuneration an allowance, to be calculated by reference to the amount of the dividends or proceeds paid from which tax has been deducted, and to be fixed by the Treasury at a rate not being less than 68p for every £1,000 of that amount.

(2) Sub-paragraph (1) above shall not apply to any person entrusted with the payment of dividends payable out of the public revenue of Northern Ireland.

Former enactments.—TA 1970, Sch. 5, para. 10; Decimal Currency Act 1969, s. 10(1).

11. Nothing in paragraphs 6 to 10 above shall impose on any banker the obligation to disclose any particulars relating to the affairs of any person on whose behalf he may be acting.

Former enactment.—TA 1970, Sch. 5, para. 11.

12. Where income tax in respect of the proceeds of the sale or realisation of any coupon has been accounted for under this Part of this Schedule by any banker or dealer, and the coupon has been subsequently paid in such manner that income tax has been deducted from the payment under any of the provisions of this Schedule, the tax so deducted shall be repaid.

A claim under this paragraph shall be made to the Board.

Former enactment.—TA 1970, Sch. 5, para. 12.

13.—(1) Without prejudice to the generality of paragraph 7 above, the Board may, by notice served on any chargeable person, require that person within such time as may be specified in the notice to make available at his premises for inspection by an officer authorised by the Board all such books and other documents in the possession or control of that person as the officer may reasonably require for the purpose of determining whether any accounts delivered by that person under paragraph 6 above are correct and complete.

(2) The Board may grant a certificate exempting any chargeable person from the provisions of sub-paragraph (1) above, and while the certificate is in force the powers conferred by that sub-paragraph shall not be exercisable in relation to that person; and any such certificate may be revoked at any time by the Board, and may contain such terms and conditions as they think proper.

Former enactment.—TA 1970, Sch. 5, para. 13.

14. In this Part of this Schedule—
"dividends" includes foreign dividends, and
"foreign dividends" has the meaning given by section 123.

Former enactment.—TA 1970, Sch. 5, paras. 6(c), 14.

PART IV
INTEREST PAYABLE OUT OF THE PUBLIC REVENUE OF THE REPUBLIC OF IRELAND ETC.

15.—(1) Any person who is entrusted with the payment of any interest, dividends or other annual payments which are payable to any persons in the United Kingdom out of the public revenue of the Republic of Ireland, or out of or in respect of the stocks, funds, shares or securities of any Republic of Ireland company, society, adventure or concern, shall be relieved from the obligation imposed on him under the preceding provisions of this Schedule to pay income tax thereon on behalf of the persons entitled thereto as regards any such interest, dividends or other annual payments in respect of which he furnishes to the Board, in such form and subject to such conditions as they may prescribe, a list containing—
   (a) a full description of the interest, dividends or other annual payments, and
   (b) the name and address of each person who is entitled thereto, and
   (c) the amount thereof to which each such person is entitled.

(2) Any person entrusted with payment who, by virtue of sub-paragraph (1) above, is relieved from the obligation to pay income tax on interest, dividends or other annual payments, shall be entitled to the like remuneration to which, if he had paid tax thereon, he would have been entitled under paragraph 10 above.

(3) Any interest, dividends or other annual payments in respect of which the person entrusted with payment is relieved from the obligation to pay income tax by virtue of sub-paragraph (1) above, shall be assessable and chargeable under Case IV or V of Schedule D, as the case may be.

(4) The Board may make such regulations as may be necessary for the purposes of this paragraph.

(5) This paragraph shall apply to—
   (a) any banker or other person in the United Kingdom who obtains payment of any such interest, dividends or other annual payments as is or are mentioned in sub-paragraph (1) above; and
   (b) to any person who would, apart from this paragraph, be obliged to pay income tax in respect of the proceeds of the sale or other realisation of any coupon for any such interest, dividends or other annual payments,

as it applies to any person entrusted with the payment of any such interest, dividends or other annual payments, with the substitution in a case falling within paragraph (b) above, of references to the proceeds of the sale or other realisation for references to such interest, dividends or other annual payments.

In this sub-paragraph "coupon" has the same meaning as in section 123.

Former enactments.—TA 1970, Sch. 12, Pt. III, para. 6; FA 1987, Sch. 15, para. 2(23).

SCHEDULE 4

Section 57

DEEP DISCOUNT SECURITIES

Interpretation

1.—(1) For the purposes of this Schedule—

(*a*) "adjusted issue price", in relation to any security in a particular income period, is the aggregate of the issue price of the security and the income elements for all previous income periods;

(*b*) "the amount payable on redemption" does not include any amount payable by way of interest;

(*c*) "a deep discount", in relation to any redeemable security, means a discount which—

(i) represents more than 15 per cent. of the amount payable on redemption of that security; or

(ii) is 15 per cent. or less, but exceeds half Y per cent. of the amount so payable (where Y is the number of complete years between the date of issue of the security and the redemption date);

(*d*) subject to sub-paragraph (2) below, "a deep discount security" means any redeemable security which has been issued by a company, after 13th March 1984, at a deep discount, other than—

(i) a share in the company;

(ii) a security in respect of which the amount payable on redemption is determined by reference to the movement of the retail prices index or any similar general index of prices which is published by, or by an agent of, the government of any territory outside the United Kingdom; or

(iii) a security the whole or part of which, by virtue of section 209(2)(*c*), is a "distribution";

[(*dd*) "a deep discount security" also means any redeemable security which has been issued by a public body (at whatever time) at a deep discount, other than—

(i) a security such as is mentioned in paragraph (*d*)(ii) above;

(ii) a security falling within sub-paragraph (5), (6) or (7) below;][1].

(*e*) "a discount" means any amount by which the issue price of a redeemable security is less than the amount payable on redemption of that security;

(*f*) "income period" means—

(i) in the case of a security carrying a right to interest, any period to which a payment of interest which falls to be made in respect of the security is attributable; and

(ii) in any other case, any year ending immediately before the anniversary of the issue of the security or any period of less than a year which begins on the issue or on such an anniversary and ends on the redemption date;

(*g*) "the redemption date" in relation to any redeemable security, means the earliest date on which, under the terms on which the security is issued, the holder of the security will be entitled to require it to be redeemed by the company [or the public body][2] which issued it;

(*h*) "yield to maturity", in relation to any security, means a rate (expressed as a percentage) such that if a sum equal to the issue price of the security were to be invested at that rate on the assumption that—

(i) the rate would be applied on a compounding basis at the end of each income period; and

(ii) the amount of any interest attributable to an income period would be deducted after applying the rate,

the value of that sum at the redemption date would be equal to the amount payable on redemption of the security; and

(*j*) "chargeable security" has the meaning given by paragraph 2(5) below.

(2) Where securities which were issued on or before 13th March 1984 have been exchanged at any time after that date for new securities which would be deep discount securities but for this sub-paragraph, the new securities shall not be treated as deep discount securities if—

(*a*) the old securities would not have been deep discount securities if they had been issued after 13th March 1984;
(*b*) the date which is the redemption date in relation to the new securities is not later than the date which was the redemption date in relation to the old securities; and
(*c*) the amount payable on redemption of the new securities does not exceed the amount which would have been payable on redemption of the old securities.

[This sub-paragraph applies only in the case of securities issued by a company.][2]

(3) For the purposes of this Schedule, a security comprised in any letter of allotment or similar instrument shall be treated as issued unless the right to the security conferred by the letter or instrument remains provisional until accepted, and there has been no acceptance.

[(4) For the purposes of this Schedule a public body is any of the following which is not a company—

(*a*) a government, whether of the United Kingdom or elsewhere;
(*b*) a public or local authority, whether in the United Kingdom or elsewhere.][1]

[(5) A security falls within this sub-paragraph if it is a gilt-edged security and—

(*a*) it was issued before 14th March 1989, or
(*b*) it was issued on or after that date but was issued under the same prospectus as any gilt-edged security issued before that date.][1]

[(6) A security falls within this sub-paragraph if it is a gilt-edged security and—

(*a*) it was issued under a prospectus under which no securities were issued before 14th March 1989,
(*b*) it was issued otherwise than on the occasion of the original issue under the prospectus, and
(*c*) all the securities issued on the occasion of the original issue under the prospectus are gilt-edged securities which are not deep discount securities.][1]

[(7) A security falls within this sub-paragraph if it is not a gilt-edged security and was issued (at whatever time) under the same prospectus as any other security which was issued before the security in question and which is not a deep discount security.][1]

[(8) For the purposes of this Schedule "gilt-edged security" has the same meaning as it has for the purposes of the 1979 Act.][1]

Former enactments.—Sub-para. (1)(*a*): FA 1984, Sch. 9, para. 1(7); FA 1985, Sch. 11, paras. 1(6), 4.
Sub-paras. (1)(*b*)–(*e*): FA 1984, s. 36(2), (5); FA 1985, Sch. 11, para. 1(6).
Sub-para. (1)(*f*): FA 1984, Sch. 9, para. 1(7); FA 1985, Sch. 11, paras. 1(6), 4.
Sub-para. (1)(*g*): FA 1984, s. 36(2), (5); FA 1985, Sch. 11, para. 1(6).
Sub-para. (1)(*h*): FA 1984, Sch. 9, para. 1(7); FA 1985, Sch. 11, paras. 1(6), 4.
Sub-para. (1)(*j*): FA 1985, Sch. 11, para. 1(5).
Sub-paras. (2), (3): FA 1984, s. 36(3), (4); FA 1985, Sch. 11, para. 1(6).
Amendments.—[1] Sub-paras. (1)(*dd*), (4) to (8) inserted by FA 1989, Sch. 10, paras. 1, 2(1), (2), (5).
[2] Words in sub-paras. (1)(*g*), (2) inserted by FA 1989, Sch. 10, paras. 1, 2(3), (4).

Charge to tax after acquisition of certain securities

2.—(1) This sub-paragraph applies to deep discount securities issued by a company on or after 19th March 1985 where one or both of the following applies—

(*a*) immediately before the issue the assets held by the company included relevant securities with a value equal to at least 75 per cent. of the value of all the assets held by it;
(*b*) the terms of issue of the deep discount securities are determined by the company by reference to (though not necessarily in such a way that they reflect) the terms of issue of relevant securities which are held by the company when the deep discount securities are issued or which it intends to acquire later.

(2) This sub-paragraph applies to deep discount securities issued by a company where—

(*a*) sub-paragraph (1) above would apply if the references to relevant securities included references to United Kingdom corporate bonds; and
(*b*) the company acquired those bonds on or after their issue (by another company) in circumstances where sub-paragraph (1) above would have applied if they had been deep discount securities.

(3) This sub-paragraph applies to deep discount securities of a particular kind issued by a company and in the case of which—

(*a*) neither of the preceding sub-paragraphs applies; and
(*b*) at any time in the first income period of the securities of that kind the assets held by

the company include relevant securities with a value equal to at least 75 per cent. of the value of all the assets held by it.

(4) This sub-paragraph applies to deep discount securities issued by a company where either—

(*a*) they are issued on a conversion to which section 82 of the 1979 Act applies of old securities; or
(*b*) they are issued by a company in exchange for old securities in circumstances in which section 85(3) of the 1979 Act applies or are treated as so issued by virtue of section 86(1) of that Act;

and in this sub-paragraph "old securities" means deep discount securities to which sub-paragraph (1), (2) or (3) above or this sub-paragraph applies, except that securities to which sub-paragraph (3) above applies are not old securities unless sub-paragraph (3)(*b*) has been fulfilled in their case by the time the conversion or exchange concerned takes place.

(5) In the following provisions of this Schedule "chargeable security" means a deep discount security to which any of the preceding sub-paragraphs applies.

(6) In this paragraph—

"relevant securities" means securities within the meaning of section 710, but excluding United Kingdom corporate bonds;
"terms of issue" includes terms relating to amounts payable on redemption or by way of interest, or to times of payment of such amounts; and
"value" in relation to assets means the price they might reasonably be expected to fetch on a sale in the open market.

(7) For the purposes of this paragraph—

(*a*) a company holds assets if it has a beneficial interest in them and acquires them if it acquires such an interest in them; and
(*b*) securities are of the same kind if they are treated as being of the same kind by the practice of a stock exchange, or would be so treated if dealt with on a stock exchange.

(8) In this paragraph "United Kingdom corporate bonds" means securities—

(*a*) issued by a company resident in the United Kingdom at the time of issue;
(*b*) the debt on which represents and has at all times represented a normal commercial loan, as defined in paragraph 1(5) of Schedule 18; and
(*c*) which are expressed in sterling and in respect of which no provision is made for conversion into, or redemption in, a currency other than sterling.

(9) For the purposes of sub-paragraph (8)(*c*) above—

(*a*) a security shall not be regarded as expressed in sterling if the amount of sterling falls to be determined by reference to the value at any time of any other currency or asset; and
(*b*) a provision for redemption in a currency other than sterling but at the rate of exchange prevailing at redemption shall be disregarded.

Former enactment.—FA 1985, Sch. 11, para. 1.

3.—(1) Where a person acquires a chargeable security, the chargeable amount shall be treated as income chargeable to tax under Case III or IV (as the case may be) of Schedule D on each of the following occasions—

(*a*) the end of each income period to fall within the period of ownership;
(*b*) the end of any income period which ends but does not begin in the period of ownership.

(2) In sub-paragraph (1) above "the chargeable amount" means—

(*a*) where paragraph (*a*) applies, an amount equal to the income element for the income period;
(*b*) where paragraph (*b*) applies, an amount equal to the income element for the part of the income period falling within the period of ownership.

(3) The income chargeable shall (notwithstanding anything in sections 64 to 67) be taken into account in computing tax charged for the year of assessment in which the occasion concerned occurs.

Former enactment.—FA 1985, Sch. 11, para. 2(1)–(3).
Cross references.—See CGTA 1979, s. 132A (computation of gains on disposal of deep discount securities).

Charge to tax on disposal of securities

4.—(1) On the disposal by any person of any deep discount security—

(*a*) an amount which represents the accrued income attributable to the period between his acquisition and disposal of the security (the "period of ownership"), less any amount or amounts treated as income by virtue of paragraph 3 above, shall be treated as income chargeable to tax under Case III or, as may be, Case IV of Schedule D; and

(*b*) the tax shall (notwithstanding anything in sections 64 to 67 but subject to sub-paragraph (5) below) be computed on the income so arising from any disposal made in the year of assessment.

(2) The amount which represents the accrued income attributable to any period of ownership is the aggregate of the income elements for each income period or part of an income period in the period of ownership.

(3) In relation to any security, the income element for any income period shall be determined by applying the formula—

$$\frac{A \times B}{100} - C$$

where—

A is the adjusted issue price;
B is the yield to maturity; and
C is the amount of interest (if any) attributable to the income period.

(4) The income element for any period (the "short period") falling within an income period shall be determined by applying the formula—

$$\frac{P}{Y} \times I$$

where—

I is the income element for the income period in which the short period falls;
P is the number of days in the short period; and
Y is the number of days in that income period.

(5) Where—

(*a*) by virtue of sub-paragraph (1) above income tax is chargeable under Case IV of Schedule D, and

(*b*) the person making the disposal satisfies the Board, on a claim in that behalf, that he is not domiciled in the United Kingdom, or that, being a British subject or a citizen of the Republic of Ireland, he is not ordinarily resident in the United Kingdom,

the tax shall be computed on the amounts, if any, received in the United Kingdom in the year of assessment in question in respect of the sum mentioned in sub-paragraph (1)(*a*) above (any such amounts being treated as income arising when they are received in the United Kingdom).

(6) For the purposes of sub-paragraph (5) above—

(*a*) there shall be treated as received in the United Kingdom all amounts paid, used or enjoyed in, or in any manner or form transmitted or brought to, the United Kingdom; and

(*b*) subsections (6) to (9) of section 65 shall apply as they apply for the purposes of subsection (5) of that section.

(7) Sections 348 to 350 and 123 shall not apply to so much of the proceeds of redemption of a deep discount security as represents income chargeable to tax under Case III or, as may be, Case IV of Schedule D.

[(8) In the case of a deep discount security issued by a public body, this paragraph applies where a disposal is made on or after 14th March 1989 (whatever the date of acquisition).][1]

Former enactments.—Sub-para. (1): FA 1984, Sch. 9, para. 1(1)(*a*), (*b*); FA 1985, Sch. 11, para. 2(4). Sub-paras. (2)–(7): FA 1984, Sch. 9, para. 1(2)–(6), (9).
Cross references.—See CGTA 1979, s. 132A (computation of gains on disposal of deep discount securities).
Amendments.—[1] Sub-para. (8) inserted by FA 1989, Sch. 10, paras. 1, 3.

Deduction of income element from total profits of company and allowance as charge on income

5.—(1) In computing the corporation tax chargeable for any accounting period of a company which has issued any deep discount security, the income element in respect of that security

respect of the security in question for any income period in which the security is at any time beneficially owned by a person mentioned in that sub-paragraph.

(3) ...[1]

(4) In this paragraph—

"associate" has the meaning given in section 417(3) and (4);
"control" shall be construed in accordance with section 416(2) to (6); and
"participator" means a person who is, in relation to a company, a participator for the purposes of Part XI (by virtue of section 417) other than a person who is a participator for those purposes by virtue only of his holding a deep discount security issued by the company.

(5) In determining whether a person who carries on a business of banking is a participator in a company for the purposes of this paragraph, there shall be disregarded any securities of the company acquired by him in the ordinary course of his business.

Former enactments.—FA 1984, Sch. 9, para. 6; FA 1985, Sch. 11, para. 2(7).
Amendments.—[1] Sub-para. (3) repealed by FA 1989, Sch. 17, Pt. V in relation to accounting periods beginning after 31 March 1989.

Early redemption

11.—(1) Where any deep discount security [issued by a company][1] is redeemed before the redemption date by the company which issued it, paragraphs 4, 5, 7(1) and (2) and 8 to 10 above shall have effect subject to the provisions of this paragraph.

(2) The accrued income attributable to the period between the acquisition of the security by the person who, immediately before its redemption, was the beneficial owner of the security and its redemption shall be the amount paid to him on redemption of the security less the issue price of the security or, in a case where he did not acquire it on its issue, less the aggregate of—

(*a*) the issue price; and
(*b*) the accrued income attributable to the period beginning with the issue, and ending with his acquisition, of the security;

and, if in either case paragraph 3 above applies, less also an amount equal to the chargeable amount (within the meaning of that paragraph).

(3) The deduction allowed under paragraph 5(1) above in relation to the accounting period in which the deep discount security is redeemed shall be the amount paid by the company on redemption less the aggregate of—

(*a*) the issue price of the security; and
(*b*) the accrued income attributable to the period beginning with the issue of the security and ending with the last income period to end in or with the accounting period of the company which precedes that in which the security is redeemed.

(4) Where paragraph 9 or 10 above has applied to the deep discount security at any time, the amount mentioned in sub-paragraph (3)(*b*) above shall not include any linked income element (within the meaning of that paragraph).

(5) Where the aggregate mentioned in sub-paragraph (3) above exceeds the amount paid by the company on redemption of the security, the amount of the excess or, if it is less, the amount mentioned in paragraph (*b*) of that sub-paragraph shall be treated as income of the company—

(*a*) arising in the accounting period in which the security is redeemed; and
(*b*) chargeable to tax under Case VI of Schedule D.

(6) Where a resolution is passed, an order made or any other act takes place for the winding up of a company which has issued a deep discount security before the security is redeemed, this paragraph shall have effect in relation to any payment made in respect of the security in the course of the winding up as if the payment were made on redemption.

Former enactments.—FA 1984, Sch. 9, para. 7; FA 1985, Sch. 11, para. 2(7).
Amendments.—[1] Words in sub-para. (1) inserted by FA 1989, Sch. 10, paras. 1, 4.

[**11A.** Where any deep discount security issued by a public body is redeemed before the redemption date by the body which issued it, paragraph 4 above shall have effect subject to paragraph 11(2) above (ignoring the words following paragraph (*b*)).][1]

Amendments.—[1] This paragraph inserted by FA 1989, Sch. 10, paras. 1, 5.

Identification of securities disposed of

12. The rules contained in section 88 of the Finance Act 1982 (identification, for the purposes of capital gains tax, of securities disposed of) shall apply for the purposes of this Schedule as they apply for the purposes of capital gains tax.

Former enactment.—FA 1984, Sch. 9, para. 11(1).

Information

13.—(1) Every company which issues deep discount securities shall cause to be shown on the certificate of each such security the income element for each income period between the date of issue of the security and the redemption date.

(2) Every company which issues a chargeable security to which paragraph 2(1), (2) or (4) above applies shall cause to be shown on the certificate of each such security the fact that tax is chargeable under paragraph 3 above.

[(3) Every public body which issues deep discount securities on or after 1st August 1989 shall cause to be shown on the certificate of each such security the income element for each income period between the date of issue of the security and the redemption date.][1]

Former enactments.—FA 1984, Sch. 9, para. 1(8); FA 1985, Sch. 11, para. 3.
Amendments.—[1] Sub-para. (3) inserted by FA 1989, Sch. 10, paras. 1, 6.

Charities

14. A charity shall be exempt from income tax in respect of an amount which (apart from this paragraph) is chargeable to income tax by virtue of this Schedule if the amount is applicable and applied for charitable purposes.

In this paragraph "charity" has the same meaning as in section 506.

Former enactments.—FA 1984, Sch. 9, para. 12; FA 1987, Sch. 15, para. 16(3).

[*Retirement benefit schemes*][1]

[**15.**—(1) In a case where—

(*a*) paragraph 4 above would apply (apart from this paragraph) to a disposal of a security, and
(*b*) immediately before the disposal was made the security was held for the purposes of an exempt approved scheme (within the meaning of Chapter I of Part XIV),

that paragraph shall not apply to the disposal.

(2) Sub-paragraph (1) above shall not apply unless the disposal is made on or after 14th March 1989.][1]

Amendments.—[1] This paragraph inserted by FA 1989, Sch. 10, paras. 1, 7.

[*Stock lending*][1]

[**16.**—(1) In a case where—

(*a*) a security is the subject of a transfer which falls within section 129(3), and
(*b*) the transfer constitutes a disposal to which (apart from this paragraph) paragraph 4 above would apply,

that paragraph shall not apply to the disposal.

(2) Sub-paragraph (1) above shall not apply unless the disposal is made on or after 14th March 1989.][1]

Amendments.—[1] This paragraph inserted by FA 1989, Sch. 10, paras. 1, 7.

[*Trustees*][1]

[**17.**—(1) Where on the disposal by trustees of a deep discount security an amount is treated as income chargeable to tax by virtue of paragraph 4(1) above, the rate at which it is chargeable shall be a rate equal to the sum of the basic rate and the additional rate for the year of assessment in which the disposal is made.

(2) Where the trustees are trustees of a scheme to which section 469 applies, sub-paragraph (1) above shall not apply if or to the extent that the amount is treated as income in the accounts of the scheme.

(3) Sub-paragraph (1) above shall not apply unless the disposal is made on or after 14th March 1989.][1]

Amendments.—[1] This paragraph inserted by FA 1989, Sch. 10, paras. 1, 7.

[*Underwriters*][1]

[**18.**—(1) An underwriting member of Lloyd's shall be treated for the purposes of this Schedule as absolutely entitled as against the trustees to the securities forming part of his premiums trust fund, his special reserve fund (if any) and any other trust fund required or authorised by the rules of Lloyd's, or required by the underwriting agent through whom his business or any part of it is carried on, to be kept in connection with the business.

(2) Sub-paragraph (1) above applies where a disposal is made on or after 14th March 1989 (whatever the date of acquisition).

(3) Where a security forms part of a premiums trust fund at the end of 31st December of any relevant year, for the purposes of this Schedule the trustees of the fund shall be deemed to dispose of the security at that time; and for this purpose relevant years are 1989 and subsequent years.

(4) Where a security forms part of a premiums trust fund at the beginning of 1st January of any relevant year, for the purposes of this Schedule the trustees of the fund shall be deemed to acquire the security at that time; and for this purpose relevant years are 1990 and subsequent years.

(5) Sub-paragraph (6) below applies where the following state of affairs exists at the beginning of 1st January of any year or the end of 31st December of any year—

  (*a*) securities have been transferred by the trustees of a premiums trust fund in pursuance of an arrangement mentioned in section 129(1) or (2),
  (*b*) the transfer was made to enable another person to fulfil a contract or to make a transfer,
  (*c*) securities have not been transferred in return, and
  (*d*) section 129(3) applies to the transfer made by the trustees.

(6) The securities transferred by the trustees shall be treated for the purposes of sub-paragraphs (3) and (4) above as if they formed part of the premiums trust fund at the beginning of 1st January concerned or the end of 31st December concerned (as the case may be).

(7) Paragraph 7 above shall have effect subject to sub-paragraph (3) above.

(8) Paragraph 7(2) above shall not apply where—

  (*a*) the deceased was an underwriting member of Lloyd's who died on or after 14th March 1989, and
  (*b*) immediately before his death the security concerned formed part of a premiums trust fund, a special reserve fund or any other trust fund required or authorised by the rules of Lloyd's, or required by the underwriting agent through whom the deceased's business or any part of it was carried on, to be kept in connection with the business.

(9) In a case where an amount treated as income chargeable to tax by virtue of paragraph 4(1) above constitutes profits or gains mentioned in section 450(1)—

  (*a*) section 450(1)(*b*) shall apply; and
  (*b*) paragraph 4(1)(*b*) above shall not apply.

(10) For the purpose of computing income tax for the year 1987–88 sub-paragraph (9) above shall have effect as if—

  (*a*) the reference to section 450(1) were to paragraph 2 of Schedule 16 to the Finance Act 1973, and
  (*b*) the reference to section 450(1)(*b*) were to paragraph 2(*b*) of that Schedule.

(11) In this paragraph "business" and "premiums trust fund" have the meanings given by section 457.][1]

Cross references.—See CGTA 1979, s. 132A(5), (6) (extension of sub-paras. (3), (4) above for the purposes of CGT).
Amendments.—[1] This paragraph inserted by FA 1989, Sch. 10, paras. 1, 7.

[Gilts: special rules][1]

[**19.**—(1) In a case where—

(*a*) securities have been issued by a public body under a prospectus under which no securities were issued before 14th March 1989,
(*b*) some of the securities issued under the prospectus are gilt-edged securities which are would-be deep discount securities,
(*c*) some of the securities issued under the prospectus are gilt-edged securities which are not would-be deep discount securities, and
(*d*) there is a time when the aggregate nominal value of the securities falling within paragraph (*b*) above (at that time) exceeds the aggregate nominal value of the securities falling within paragraph (*c*) above (at that time),

sub-paragraph (2) below shall apply in relation to any gilt-edged security which has been or is issued under the prospectus at any time (whether before, at or after the time mentioned in paragraph (*d*) above).

(2) As regards any event occurring in relation to the security after the time mentioned in sub-paragraph (1)(*d*) above, paragraphs 4, 7, 8, 11A, 12 and 14 to 18 above shall have effect as if—

(*a*) the security were a deep discount security,
(*b*) it had been issued as such (whatever the time it was issued), and
(*c*) it had been acquired as such (whatever the time it was acquired).

(3) For the purposes of sub-paragraph (1) above a would-be deep discount security is a security which would be a deep discount security apart from paragraph 1(6) above.

(4) For the purposes of sub-paragraph (2) above events, in relation to a security, include anything constituting a disposal for the purposes of the 1979 Act, the death of a person competent to dispose of the security, a disposal mentioned in paragraph 18(3) above, and an acquisition mentioned in paragraph 18(4) above.][1]

Cross references.—See FA 1989, s. 95(5), (7) (Treasury securities issued at a discount).
Amendments.—[1] This paragraph inserted by FA 1989, Sch. 10, paras. 1, 7.

[Non-gilts: special rules][1]

[**20.**—(1) In a case where—

(*a*) all the securities issued by a public body on the occasion of the original issue under a particular prospectus (whatever the time of the issue) are neither gilt-edged securities nor deep discount securities,
(*b*) some of the securities issued under the prospectus are not gilt-edged securities but are new would-be deep discount securities, and
(*c*) there is a time when the aggregate nominal value of the securities falling within paragraph (*b*) above (at that time) exceeds the aggregate nominal value of the securities which (looking at the state of affairs at that time) have been issued under the prospectus and are neither gilt-edged securities nor new would-be deep discount securities,

sub-paragraph (2) below shall apply in relation to any security which is not a gilt-edged security but which has been or is issued under the prospectus at any time (whether before, at or after the time mentioned in paragraph (*c*) above).

(2) As regards any event occurring in relation to the security after the time mentioned in sub-paragraph (1)(*c*) above, paragraphs 4, 7, 8, 11A, 12 and 14 to 18 above shall have effect as if—

(*a*) the security were a deep discount security,
(*b*) it had been issued as such (whatever the time it was issued), and
(*c*) it had been acquired as such (whatever the time it was acquired).

(3) For the purposes of sub-paragraph (1) above a new would-be deep discount security is a security which—

(*a*) would be a deep discount security apart from paragraph 1(7) above, and
(*b*) was issued on or after 14th March 1989.

(4) For the purposes of sub-paragraph (2) above events, in relation to a security, include anything constituting a disposal for the purposes of the 1979 Act, the death of a person competent to dispose of the security, a disposal mentioned in paragraph 18(3) above, and an acquisition mentioned in paragraph 18(4) above.][1]

Amendments.—[1] This paragraph inserted by FA 1989, Sch. 10, paras. 1, 7.

SCHEDULE 5

Section 97

TREATMENT OF FARM ANIMALS ETC. FOR PURPOSES OF CASE I OF SCHEDULE D

Farming: the general rule

1.—(1) Subject to the provisions of this Schedule, in computing profits or gains under Case I of Schedule D, animals kept by a farmer for the purposes of his farming shall be treated as trading stock.

(2) Animals forming part of production herds with respect to which an election under paragraph 2 below has effect shall not be so treated, but shall be treated instead in accordance with the rules set out in paragraph 3 below.

(3) An election under paragraph 2 below is referred to in this Schedule as "an election for the herd basis".

Former enactment.—TA 1970, Sch. 6, para. 1.

Farming: election for the herd basis

2.—(1) An election for the herd basis shall apply to all production herds of a particular class kept by the farmer making the election, including herds which he has ceased to keep before, or first begins to keep after, the making of the election.

(2) An election for the herd basis must be made in writing to the inspector, and must specify the class of herds to which it relates.

(3) Subject to paragraphs 6 and 12 below, an election for the herd basis made by any farmer shall be valid only if it is made not later than two years after the end of—

(*a*) the first chargeable period for which he is chargeable under Case I of Schedule D to tax in respect of the profits or gains of his farming, or is given relief under section 380 or 393(2) in respect of his farming, being profits or gains or relief the amount of which is computed by reference to the facts of a period during the whole or some part of which he kept a production herd of the class in question; or
(*b*) the first period for which an account is made up for his farming.

(4) An election for the herd basis made by any farmer shall be irrevocable and, subject to paragraph 6 below, shall have effect—

(*a*) in a case within sub-paragraph (3)(*a*) above, for the first chargeable period referred to in that sub-paragraph and all subsequent chargeable periods; and
(*b*) in a case within sub-paragraph (3)(*b*) above, for the first chargeable period for which the profits or gains or losses of his farming are computed by reference to the facts of the first period for which an account is made up for his farming.

Former enactments.—TA 1970, Sch. 6, para. 2; FA 1973, s. 35; FA 1984, s. 48(6)–(9).

3.—(1) Where an election for the herd basis has effect, the consequences for the purposes of computing profits or gains under Case I of Schedule D shall be as provided by this paragraph.

(2) The initial cost of the herd and, subject to the provisions of this paragraph as to replacements, the cost of any animal added to the herd shall not be deducted as an expense and the value of the herd shall not be brought into account.

(3) Where an animal which has theretofore been treated as part of the farmer's trading stock is added to the herd otherwise than by way of replacement, there shall be included as a trading receipt—

(*a*) in the case of an animal bred by the farmer, a sum equal to the cost of breeding it and rearing it to maturity; and
(*b*) in any other case, a sum equal to the initial cost to the farmer of acquiring the animal, together with any cost incurred by him in rearing it to maturity.

(4) Where an animal (the "first animal") forming part of the herd dies, or ceases to form part of the herd, and is replaced in the herd by another animal (the "second animal")—

(a) any proceeds of sale of the first animal shall be included as a trading receipt; and
(b) the cost of the second animal, except in so far as that cost consists of such costs as are allowable apart from the provisions of this Schedule as deductions in computing profits or gains of farming under Case I of Schedule D, shall, subject to sub-paragraphs (5) and (6) below, be deducted as an expense.

(5) Where the second animal is of better quality than the first animal, the amount deducted shall not exceed the amount which it would have been necessary to expend in order to acquire an animal of the same quality as the first animal.

(6) Where the first animal was slaughtered by the order of any Ministry, government department or local or public authority under the law relating to diseases of animals, and the second animal is of worse quality, the amount included as a trading receipt shall not exceed the amount allowable as a deduction.

(7) Where the herd is sold as a whole, and another production herd of the same class is acquired, sub-paragraphs (1) to (6) above shall apply as though there had been sold from, and replaced in, the original herd a number of animals equal to the number in the original herd or in the newly acquired herd, whichever is the less.

(8) Subject to sub-paragraph (9) below, if (either all at once or over a period not exceeding 12 months) either—
(a) the whole of a herd is sold in circumstances in which sub-paragraph (7) above does not apply, or
(b) a part of a herd is sold on a substantial reduction being made in the number of animals in the herd,
any profit or loss arising from the transaction shall not be taken into account.

(9) Where within five years of the sale the seller acquires or begins to acquire another production herd of the class in question or, as the case may be, acquires or begins to acquire animals to replace the part of the herd in question—
(a) sub-paragraphs (4) to (7) above shall apply to the acquisition or replacement, except that, if the sale was one which the seller was compelled to effect by causes wholly beyond his control, the amount included as a trading receipt in respect of any animal sold which is replaced by an animal of worse quality shall not exceed the amount allowable as a deduction in respect of that animal of worse quality; and
(b) for the purpose of the application of those sub-paragraphs, the proceeds of sale of the animals comprised in the original herd or part of a herd shall be brought into account as if they had been respectively received at the times of the corresponding acquisitions.

(10) If an animal forming part of the herd is sold, and none of sub-paragraphs (4) to (9) above applies, any profit or loss arising from the transaction shall be included or deducted, as the case may be; and for the purposes of this sub-paragraph, that profit or loss shall be computed by comparing with the proceeds of sale—
(a) in the case of an animal bred by the farmer, the cost of breeding it and rearing it to maturity; and
(b) in any other case, a sum equal to the initial cost to the farmer of acquiring the animal (or in the case of an animal acquired otherwise than for valuable consideration, its market value when the farmer acquired it) together, in both cases, with any cost incurred by him in rearing it to maturity.

(11) Where the herd is sold as a whole, and another production herd of the same class is acquired, and the number of animals in the newly acquired herd is less than the number in the original herd, then, if the difference is not substantial, sub-paragraphs (8) and (9) above shall not apply, and sub-paragraph (10) above shall apply to a number of animals in the original herd equal to the difference.

(12) The preceding provisions of this paragraph shall apply in relation to the death or destruction of animals as they apply in relation to their sale, as if any insurance or compensation moneys received by reason of the death or destruction were proceeds of sale, and any reference in this paragraph to the proceeds of sale of an animal includes a reference to any proceeds of sale of its carcase or any part of its carcase.

Former enactment.—TA 1970, Sch. 6, para. 3.

Farming: provisions applicable to special cases

4. A farmer who, having kept a production herd of a particular class, ceases altogether to keep herds of that class for a period of at least five years shall, as respects production herds kept by him after the end of that period, be treated as if he had never kept any production herds of that class before the end of that period.

Former enactment.—TA 1970, Sch. 6, para. 4.

5.—(1) Where a farmer transfers to another person all or any of the animals which form part of a production herd otherwise than by way of sale or by way of sale but for a price other than that which they would have fetched if sold in the open market, and either—

(*a*) the transferor is a body of persons over whom the transferee has control or the transferee is a body of persons over whom the transferor has control or both the transferor and the transferee are bodies of persons and some other person has control over both of them; or
(*b*) it appears with respect to the transfer, or with respect to transactions of which the transfer is one that the sole or main benefit, or one of the main benefits, which (apart from the provisions of this paragraph) might have been expected to accrue to the parties or any of them was a benefit resulting from—

(i) the obtaining of a right to make an election for the herd basis, or
(ii) such an election having effect or ceasing to have effect, or
(iii) such an election having a greater effect or a less effect;

the like consequences shall ensue, in relation to all persons concerned, for the purpose of computing profits or gains under Case I of Schedule D as would have ensued if the animals had been sold for the price which they would have fetched if sold in the open market.

(2) In this paragraph "body of persons" includes a partnership, and "control" has the meaning given by section 840.

Former enactment.—TA 1970, Sch. 6, para. 5.

6.—(1) Where the whole or a substantial part of a production herd kept by a farmer for the purposes of his farming is slaughtered by the order of any Ministry, government department or local or public authority under the law relating to the diseases of animals in such circumstances that compensation is payable in respect of it, an election for the herd basis thereupon made by the farmer in relation to that herd and any other production herds of the same class so kept by him shall, subject to sub-paragraph (2) below, be valid notwithstanding that it is not made within the time required by paragraph 2(3) above.

(2) An election for the herd basis made by virtue of sub-paragraph (1) above shall, subject to sub-paragraph (3) below, only be valid if made not later than two years after the end of the first chargeable period for which the tax chargeable on the farmer in respect of the profits or gains of his farming finally falls to be computed by reference to the facts of a period in which the compensation is relevant.

(3) If that first chargeable period is the second year of assessment within the meaning of section 62 and notice is given under subsection (2) of that section, then for the purposes of income tax (but not corporation tax), the election shall be valid if made not later than the giving of that notice.

(4) An election for the herd basis made by virtue of sub-paragraph (1) above shall, notwithstanding paragraph 2(4) above, have effect only for the chargeable period mentioned in sub-paragraph (2) above and subsequent chargeable periods except that for the purposes of income tax (but not corporation tax) the election shall have effect for earlier chargeable periods for the purposes of any claim under section 380 which is made by the farmer for relief in respect of his farming, if the relief falls to be computed wholly or partly by reference to the facts of a period in which the compensation is relevant.

(5) For the purposes of this paragraph, compensation shall be deemed to be relevant in any period if, but only if, it falls (or would but for an election under this paragraph fall) to be taken into account as a trading receipt in computing the profits or gains or losses of that or an earlier period.

Former enactment.—TA 1970, Sch. 6, para. 6.

Exclusion of working animals, and interpretation of preceding provisions

7. Nothing in this Schedule applies to any animals kept wholly or mainly for the work they do in connection with the carrying on of the farming.

Former enactment.—TA 1970, Sch. 6, para. 7.

8.—(1) In this Schedule "herd" includes a flock, and any other collection of animals however named.

(2) For the purposes of this Schedule, immature animals kept in a herd shall not be treated as forming part of the herd unless—

    (*a*) the land on which the herd is kept is such that animals which die or cease to form part of the herd cannot be replaced except by animals bred and reared on that land; and
    (*b*) the immature animals in question are bred in the herd, are maintained in the herd for the purpose of replacement, and are necessarily maintained for that purpose;

and references in this Schedule to herds shall be construed accordingly.

(3) References in this Schedule to an animal being added to a herd include references to an immature animal which is kept in the herd becoming a mature animal except that not more immature animals shall be treated as forming part of a herd than are required to prevent a fall in the numbers of the herd.

(4) Female animals shall be treated for the purposes of this Schedule as becoming mature when they produce their first young.

(5) In this Schedule "a production herd" means, in relation to a farmer, a herd of animals of the same species (irrespective of breed) kept by him wholly or mainly for the sake of the products which they produce for him to sell, being products obtainable from the living animal.

In this sub-paragraph "products obtainable from the living animal" means—

    (*a*) the young of the animal, or
    (*b*) any other product obtainable from the animal, not being a product obtainable only by slaughtering the animal itself.

(6) For the purposes of this Schedule, production herds kept by a farmer shall be deemed to be of the same class if, and only if, all the animals kept in the herds are of the same species (irrespective of breed) and the products produced for him to sell for the sake of which (either wholly or mainly) the herds are kept by him are of the same kinds in the case of all the herds; and elections for the herd basis shall be framed accordingly.

(7) Any reference in this Schedule to profits or gains chargeable to tax under Schedule D includes a reference to profits or gains which would be so chargeable if there were any such profits or gains for the chargeable period in question.

Former enactment.—TA 1970, Sch. 6, para. 8.

Application of preceding provisions to trades other than farming, creatures other than animals, and animals and creatures kept singly

9.—(1) The preceding provisions of this Schedule shall, with the necessary adaptations, apply in relation to trades other than farming, and trades consisting only in part of farming as they apply in relation to farming, and references to farmers shall be construed accordingly.

(2) Those provisions shall (both in relation to farming and in relation to other trades) apply in relation to living creatures other than animals as they apply in relation to animals.

(3) Laying birds shall be treated for the purposes of this Schedule as becoming mature when they first lay.

(4) The provisions of this Schedule shall (both in relation to farming and in relation to other trades) apply, with the necessary adaptations, in relation to animals or other creatures kept singly as they apply in relation to herds.

(5) Nothing in this Schedule shall apply in relation to any animal or other creature kept wholly or mainly for public exhibition or for racing or other competitive purposes.

Former enactment.—TA 1970, Sch. 6, para. 9.

Supplemental and saving

10. Where an election for the herd basis is made, every person carrying on any farming or other trade affected by the election shall, if required to do so by notice from the inspector, make and deliver to the inspector, within the time specified in the notice, such returns as to, and as to the products of, the animals or other creatures kept by him for the purposes of the trade as may be required by the notice.

Former enactment.—TA 1970, Sch. 6, para. 10.

11. Where an election for the herd basis has effect for any chargeable period after an assessment for that period has become final and conclusive, any such assessment or, on a claim therefor, repayment of tax shall be made as may be necessary to give effect to the election.

Former enactment.—TA 1970, Sch. 6, para. 11.

12. The validity of an election for the herd basis in force immediately before the commencement of this Schedule and made in pursuance of—

   (*a*) section 35 of the Finance Act 1973 on or after 25th July 1973 and before 6th April 1976, or

   (*b*) section 48(6) to (9) of the Finance Act 1984,

shall not be affected by the repeal of those sections by this Act.

Former enactments.—FA 1973, s. 35; FA 1984, s. 48(6)–(9).

SCHEDULE 6

Section 157

TAXATION OF DIRECTORS AND OTHERS IN RESPECT OF CARS

[PART 1][1]

TABLES OF FLAT RATE CASH EQUIVALENTS

TABLE A

Cars with an original market value up to £19,250 and having a cylinder capacity

Cylinder capacity of car in cubic centimetres	Age of car at end of relevant year of assessment	
	Under 4 years	4 years or more
1,400 or less	£1,400	£950
More than 1,400 but not more than 2,000	£1,850	£1,250
More than 2,000	£2,950	£1,950

TABLE B

Cars with an original market value up to £19,250 and not having a cylinder capacity

Original market value of car	Age of car at end of relevant year of assessment	
	Under 4 years	4 years or more
Less than £6,000	£1,400	£950
£6,000 or more but less than £8,500	£1,850	£1,250
£8,500 or more but not more than £19,250	£2,950	£1,950

TABLE C

Cars with an original market value of more than £19,250

Original market value of car	Age of car at end of relevant year of assessment	
	Under 4 years	4 years or more
More than £19,250 but not more than £29,000	£3,850	£2,600
More than £29,000	£6,150	£4,100

Amendments.—[1] This Part substituted by FA 1989, s. 49.

PART II

SUPPLEMENTARY PROVISIONS

Application of Tables A and B

1.—(1) In the case of cars with an original market value of £19,250 or less, Table A applies to those having an internal combustion engine with one or more reciprocating pistons, and Table B applies to other cars.

(2) A car's cylinder capacity is the cylinder capacity of its engine calculated as for the purposes of the Vehicles (Excise) Act 1971 or the Vehicles (Excise) Act (Northern Ireland) 1972.

Former enactments.—FA 1976, Sch. 7, Pt. II, para. 1;
Income Tax (Cash Equivalents of Car Benefits) Order 1985, S.I. 1985 No. 1598.

Reduction for periods when car not available for use

2.—(1) If, for any part of the relevant year, the car was unavailable, the cash equivalent is to be reduced by an amount which bears to the full amount of the equivalent (ascertained under Part I of this Schedule) the same proportion as the number of days in the year on which the car was unavailable bears to 365.

(2) The car is to be treated as being unavailable on any day if—

(*a*) it was not made available to the employee until after that day, or it had ceased before that day to be available to him; or

(*b*) it was incapable of being used at all throughout a period of not less than 30 consecutive days of which that day was one.

Former enactment.—FA 1976, Sch. 7, Pt. II, para. 2.

Car used preponderantly for business purposes

3.—(1) The cash equivalent derived from Table A, B or C is to be reduced (or, where paragraph 2 above applies, further reduced) by half if it is shown to the inspector's satisfaction that the employee was required by the nature of his employment to make and made use of the car preponderantly for business travel, which means that such travel must have amounted to at least 18,000 miles in the relevant year.

(2) In relation to a car which for part of the year was unavailable in the sense of paragraph 2 above, the figure of 18,000 is proportionately reduced.

Former enactments.—FA 1976, Sch. 7, Pt. II, para. 3; FA 1980, s. 48(2).

Reduction for employee paying for use of car

4. If in the relevant year the employee was required, as a condition of the car being available for his private use, to pay any amount of money (whether by way of deduction from his emoluments or otherwise) for that use, the cash equivalent—

(*a*) is to be reduced (or, if already reduced under the foregoing paragraphs, further reduced) by the amount so paid by the employee in or in respect of the year; or

(*b*) if that amount exceeds the equivalent shown in the applicable Table in Part I of this Schedule, is nil.

Former enactment.—FA 1976, Sch. 7, Pt. II, para. 4.
Note.—See **Prospective Legislation Notes** (Commercial Woodlands).

Cars with insubstantial business use and additional cars

5.—(1) The cash equivalent derived from Table A, B or C is to be increased by half if in the relevant year—

(*a*) the car was not used for the employee's business travel; or

(*b*) its use for such travel did not amount to more than 2,500 miles.

(2) In relation to a car which for part of the year was unavailable in the sense of paragraph 2 above, the figure of 2,500 is proportionately reduced.

(3) Without prejudice to sub-paragraph (1) above, if in any year a person is taxable under section 157 in respect of two or more cars which are made available concurrently, there shall be increased by half the cash equivalent derived from Table A, B or C in respect of each of those cars other than the one which in the period for which they are concurrently available is used to the greatest extent for the employee's business travel.

(4) In paragraphs 2 to 4 above references to the cash equivalent which is to be reduced shall be construed as references to the cash equivalent after any increase under this paragraph.

Former enactments.—FA 1976, Sch. 7, Pt. II, para. 5; FA 1980, s. 48(3); FA 1981, s. 68(6).
Note.—See **Prospective Legislation Notes** (Commercial Woodlands).

SCHEDULE 7
Section 160

TAXATION OF BENEFIT FROM LOANS OBTAINED BY REASON OF EMPLOYMENT

PART I
MEANING OF "OBTAINED BY REASON OF EMPLOYMENT"

1.—(1) Subject to sub-paragraph (5) below, the benefit of a loan is obtained by reason of a person's employment if, in relation to that person, it is of a class described in sub-paragraphs (2), (3) or (4) below.

(2) A loan made by his employer.

(3) A loan made by a company—
   (*a*) over which his employer had control;
   (*b*) by which his employer (being a company) was controlled; or
   (*c*) which was controlled by a person by whom his employer (being a company) was controlled.

(4) A loan made in any case where—
   (*a*) his employer was, or had control over, or was controlled by, a close company; and
   (*b*) the loan was made by a person having a material interest in that close company or, that company being controlled by another company, in that other company.

(5) Sub-paragraph (2) above does not apply to a loan made by his employer, being an individual, and shown to have been made in the normal course of his domestic, family or personal relationships.

Former enactments.—Sub-paras. (1), (2): FA 1976, Sch. 8, para. 1(1).
Sub-para. (3): FA 1976, Sch. 8, para. 2.
Sub-para. (4): FA 1976, Sch. 8, para. 3.
Sub-para. (5): FA 1976, Sch. 8, para. 1(2).

2. In paragraph 1 above—
   (*a*) references to a loan being made by any person include references to his assuming the rights and liabilities of the person who originally made the loan and to his arranging, guaranteeing or in any way facilitating the continuation of a loan already in existence;
   (*b*) "employer" includes a prospective employer; and
   (*c*) "company", except in the expression "close company", includes a partnership.

Former enactment.—FA 1976, Sch. 8, para. 4.

PART II
CALCULATION OF CASH EQUIVALENT OF LOAN BENEFIT

General

3.—(1) The cash equivalent for any year of the benefit obtained from a loan is—

   (*a*) the amount of interest (calculated in accordance with paragraph 4 or 5 below) which would have been payable for that year had interest at the official rate been payable on the loan, less

   (*b*) the amount of interest actually paid on the loan for that year.

(2) Where an assessment for any year in respect of a loan has been made or determined on the footing that the whole or part of the interest payable on the loan for that year was not in fact paid, but it is subsequently paid, then on a claim in that behalf, the cash equivalent for that year shall be recalculated so as to take that payment into account and the assessment shall be adjusted accordingly.

(3) All the loans between the same lender and borrower for which a cash equivalent falls to be ascertained and which are outstanding at any time, as to any amount, in any year are to be treated for the purposes of this Schedule as a single loan.

Former enactment.—FA 1976, Sch. 8, para. 5.

Normal method of calculation (averaging)

4. In the absence of a requirement or election that paragraph 5 below should apply, the amount of interest at the official rate payable on a loan for any year ("the relevant year") shall be ascertained as follows—

  (*a*) take half the aggregate of—

   (i) the maximum amount of the loan outstanding on 5th April preceding the relevant year or, if it was made in that year, on the date on which it was made, and
   (ii) the maximum amount of the loan outstanding on 5th April in the relevant year or, if the loan was discharged in that year, the date of discharge;

  (*b*) multiply that figure by the number of whole months during which the loan was outstanding in that year, and divide by 12;
  (*c*) multiply the result by the official rate of interest in force during the period when the loan was outstanding in that year or, if the official rate changed during that period, the average rate during that period ascertained by reference to the number of days in the period and the number of days for which each rate was in force.

For the purposes of this paragraph, months begin on the sixth day of the calendar month.

Former enactment.—FA 1976, Sch. 8, para. 6.
Note.—The official rate of interest prescribed by the Income Tax (Official Rate of Interest on Beneficial Loans) Orders is—
  10·5 per cent. from 6 December 1987: S.I. 1987 No. 1988.
  9·5 per cent. from 6 May 1988: S.I. 1988 No. 757.
  12 per cent. from 6 August 1988: S.I. 1988 No. 1279.
  13·5 per cent. from 6 October 1988: S.I. 1988 No. 1622.
  14·5 per cent. from 6 January 1989: S.I. 1988 No. 2186.
  15·5 per cent. from 6 July 1989: S.I. 1989 No. 1001.

Election for alternative method of calculation

5.—(1) For any year of assessment ("the relevant year") the alternative method of calculation set out in this paragraph applies if—

  (*a*) the inspector so requires, by notice given to the employee, for the purpose of any assessment to income tax (or the adjustment of any such assessment in consequence of an appeal); or
  (*b*) the employee so elects, by notice given to the inspector within the time allowed by sub-paragraph (2) below.

(2) An election by the employee must be made—

  (*a*) in a case where an assessment including the emoluments in question has been made on the basis of the normal method of calculation, within the time allowed for appealing against that assessment or such further time as the inspector may allow;
  (*b*) where no such assessment has been made, within six years after the end of the relevant year of assessment.

(3) The alternative method of calculating the amount of interest at the official rate payable on a loan for the relevant year is as follows—

  (*a*) take each period in the relevant year during which the official rate of interest remains the same;
  (*b*) for each such period take for each day in the period the maximum amount outstanding of the loan on that day, and add those amounts together;
  (*c*) multiply that sum by the official rate in force during the period divided by 365; and
  (*d*) add together the resulting figures for each period in the relevant year.

Former enactment.—FA 1976, Sch. 8, para. 7.
Note.—The official rate of interest prescribed by the Income Tax (Official Rate of Interest on Beneficial Loans) Orders is—
  10·5 per cent. from 6 December 1987: S.I. 1987 No. 1988.
  9·5 per cent. from 6 May 1988: S.I. 1988 No. 757.
  12 per cent. from 6 August 1988: S.I. 1988 No. 1279.
  13·5 per cent. from 6 October 1988: S.I. 1988 No. 1622.
  14·5 per cent. from 6 January 1989: S.I. 1989 No. 2186.
  15·5 per cent. from 6 July 1989: S.I. 1988 No. 1001.

PART III
EXCEPTIONS WHERE INTEREST ELIGIBLE FOR RELIEF

6. Interest is eligible for relief for the purposes of this Part of this Schedule if it is eligible for relief under section 353 or would be eligible for such relief apart from subsection (2) of that section.

Former enactments.—FA 1976, Sch. 8, para. 8(1); FA 1982, s. 26(9)(*b*).

7. Section 160(1) does not apply to a loan in any year—

(*a*) for which interest is paid on the loan and the whole of that interest is eligible for relief, or

(*b*) for which no interest is paid on the loan but had interest been paid on it at the official rate the whole of that interest would have been eligible for relief.

Former enactment.—FA 1976, Sch. 8, para. 9.
Note.—The official rate of interest prescribed by the Income Tax (Official Rate of Interest on Beneficial Loans) Orders is—
    10·5 per cent. from 6 December 1987: S.I. 1987 No. 1988.
    9·5 per cent. from 6 May 1988: S.I. 1988 No. 757.
    12 per cent. from 6 August 1988: S.I. 1988 No. 1279.
    13·5 per cent. from 6 October 1988: S.I. 1988 No. 1622.
    14·5 per cent. from 6 January 1989: S.I. 1988 No. 2186.
    15·5 per cent. from 6 July 1989: S.I. 1989 No. 1001.

8. Where for any year interest is paid on a loan and part of that interest is eligible for relief, the calculation of the cash equivalent under Part II of this Schedule is modified as follows—

(*a*) where paragraph 4 applies, the maximum amounts referred to in sub-paragraph (*a*)(i) and (ii) of that paragraph shall be proportionately reduced by reference to the proportion which so much of that interest paid for that year as is not eligible for relief bears to the whole of the interest so paid;

(*b*) where paragraph 5 applies, the maximum amounts referred to in sub-paragraph (3)(*b*) of that paragraph shall be proportionately reduced by reference to the proportion which so much of the interest paid on each such amount for the day in question as is not eligible for relief bears to the whole of the interest so paid; and

(*c*) the amount of interest eligible for relief shall be left out of account in ascertaining for the purposes of paragraph 3(1)(*b*) above the amount of interest paid for that year.

Former enactment.—FA 1976, Sch. 8, para. 10.

9.—(1) Where for any year—

(*a*) no interest is paid on a loan, but

(*b*) had interest been paid on it at the official rate part of that interest would have been eligible for relief,

then the calculation of the cash equivalent under Part II of this Schedule shall be modified as provided by paragraph 8(*a*) or (*b*) above with the substitution for the references to the amounts of interest paid or not eligible for relief of references to the amounts (ascertained in accordance with the following provisions of this paragraph) which would have been paid or would not have been eligible for relief.

(2) For the purposes of paragraph 8(*a*) above as applied by this paragraph, the whole amount of interest at the official rate which would have been paid for any year shall be taken to be the amount payable for that year calculated in accordance with paragraph 4 above (disregarding paragraph 8); and the amount of that interest which would not have been eligible for relief shall be ascertained—

(*a*) by finding that amount on the assumption that the amount referred to in paragraph 4(*a*)(i) was the amount outstanding for the whole year;

(*b*) by finding that amount on the assumption that the amount referred to in paragraph 4(*a*)(ii) was the amount outstanding for the whole year; and

(*c*) by adding together the resulting figures and dividing by 2.

(3) For the purposes of paragraph 8(*b*) above as applied by this paragraph, the amount of interest which would have been paid and the amount of it which would not have been eligible for relief shall be ascertained on the assumption that interest at the official rate was paid daily throughout the year on the maximum amount outstanding on each day.

Former enactment.—FA 1976, Sch. 8, para. 11.
Note.—The official rate of interest prescribed by the Income Tax (Official Rate of Interest on Beneficial Loans) Orders is—
  10·5 per cent. from 6 December 1987: S.I. 1987 No. 1988.
  9·5 per cent. from 6 May 1988: S.I. 1988 No. 757.
  12 per cent. from 6 August 1988: S.I. 1988 No. 1279.
  13·5 per cent. from 6 October 1988: S.I. 1988 No. 1622.
  14·5 per cent. from 6 January 1989: S.I. 1988 No. 2186.
  15·5 per cent. from 6 July 1989: S.I. 1989 No. 1001.

10.—(1) If—

(*a*) a person has a loan on which no interest is paid and of which the benefit was obtained by reason of his or any other person's employment ("the employer's loan"); and

(*b*) that person or his wife or her husband has another loan which was made later than, or at the same time as, the employer's loan and interest on which is, in whole or in part, eligible for relief;

then, for the purposes of determining whether, had interest been paid on the employer's loan at the official rate, the whole or any part of that interest would have been eligible for relief, sections 354(5) and (6), 355(1) to (4), 356 to 358 and 360 to 365 shall have effect as if the employer's loan were made after any other loan which falls within paragraph (*b*) above and which, in the context of the application of sections 354(1) to (4) and 355(5), relates to the same land, caravan or house boat as does the employer's loan.

(2) Where such a loan is made as is mentioned in paragraph (*b*) of sub-paragraph (1) above, sections 354(5) and (6), 355(1) to (4), 356 to 358 and 360 to 365 have effect in accordance with that sub-paragraph with respect to so much of the interest referred to therein as would be paid on and after the day on which the loan is made; and paragraph 9(3) above shall have effect for the purpose of determining how much of that interest would have been eligible for relief.

Former enactments.—FA 1976, Sch. 8, para. 12; F(No. 2)A 1983, s. 4.
Note.—The official rate of interest prescribed by the Income Tax (Official Rate of Interest on Beneficial Loans) Orders is—
  10·5 per cent. from 6 December 1987: S.I. 1987 No. 1988.
  9·5 per cent. from 6 May 1988: S.I. 1988 No. 757.
  12 per cent. from 6 August 1988: S.I. 1988 No. 1279.
  13·5 per cent. from 6 October 1988: S.I. 1988 No. 1622.
  14·5 per cent. from 6 January 1989: S.I. 1988 No. 2186.
  15·5 per cent. from 6 July 1989: S.I. 1989 No. 1001.

11.—(1) Where in any year a person has, alone or together with his wife or her husband, two or more loans—

(*a*) on which no interest is paid, and

(*b*) which, assuming the application of sections 354(1) to (4) and 355(5), would relate, in the context of those sections, to the same land, caravan or house boat,

then, for the purpose of determining whether, had interest been paid on any of those loans, it would, in whole or in part, have been eligible for relief, it shall be assumed in the first instance that those loans constitute a single loan (equal in amount to the aggregate of the actual loans) and to the extent that, had interest been paid on that single loan, it would have been eligible for relief, the relief shall then be attributed first to the earliest of the actual loans and, if all the relief is not thereby attributed, the balance shall be attributed to the next in time and so on with any of the balance remaining until the relief is wholly attributed.

(2) Nothing in sub-paragraph (1) above affects the operation of paragraph 10 above in relation to the priority which it gives to a loan falling within sub-paragraph (1)(*b*) of that paragraph, but any question which of two or more loans falling within sub-paragraph (1) above is the earlier shall be determined without regard to that paragraph.

Former enactments.—FA 1976, Sch. 8, para. 13; F(No. 2)A 1983, s. 4.

12. References in paragraphs 10 and 11 above to a husband or wife do not include references to a separated husband or wife.

Former enactments.—FA 1976, Sch. 8, para. 14; F(No. 2)A 1983, s. 4.

SCHEDULE 8

Section 176(9)

PROFIT-RELATED PAY SCHEMES: CONDITIONS FOR REGISTRATION

Form

1. The terms of the scheme must be set out in writing.

Former enactment.—F(No. 2)A 1987, Sch. 1, para. 1.

Employer and employment unit

2. The scheme must identify the scheme employer.

Former enactment.—F(No. 2)A 1987, Sch. 1, para. 2.

3. If the scheme employer does not pay the emoluments of all the employees to whom the scheme relates, the scheme must identify each of the persons who pays the emoluments of any of those employees.

Former enactment.—F(No. 2)A 1987, Sch. 1, para. 3.

4.—(1) The scheme must identify the undertaking to which the scheme relates and that undertaking must be one which is carried on with a view to profit.

(2) The references in sub-paragraph (1) above to an undertaking include references to part of an undertaking; and the provisions of a scheme identifying part of an undertaking must do so in such a way as to distinguish it, otherwise than by name only, from other parts of the undertaking.

Former enactment.—F(No. 2)A 1987, Sch. 1, para. 4.

Employees

5. The scheme must contain provisions by reference to which the employees to whom the scheme relates may be identified.

Former enactment.—F(No. 2)A 1987, Sch. 1, para. 5.

6. The scheme must contain provisions ensuring that no payments are made under it by reference to a profit period if the employees to whom the scheme relates constitute less than 80 per cent. of all the employees in the employment unit at the beginning of that profit period, but for this purpose any person who is at that time within paragraph 7 or 8 below shall not be counted.

Former enactment.—F(No. 2)A 1987, Sch. 1, para. 6.

7.—(1) The scheme must contain provisions ensuring that no payments are made under it to any person who is employed in the employment unit by a company and who has . . .[1] a material interest in the company.

(2) For the purposes of this paragraph a person shall be treated as having a material interest [in a company if he, either on his own or with one or more associates, or if any associate of his with or without such other associates,—][4]

   [(*a*) is the beneficial owner of, or able, directly or through the medium of other companies, or by any other indirect means to control, more than 25 per cent. of the ordinary share capital of the company, or][4]
   [(*b*) in the case of a close company, possesses, or is entitled to acquire, such rights as would, in the event of the winding-up of the company or in any other circumstances, give an entitlement to receive more than 25 per cent. of the assets which would then be available for distribution among the participators.][4]

(3) In this paragraph—

"associate" has the same meaning as in section 417(3) and (4) [, but subject to sub-paragraph (4) below][2]; ...[5]

"control" has the meaning given by section 840; [and][6]

["participator" has the meaning given by section 417(1);][6]

and the definition of "control" in section 840 applies (with the necessary modifications) in relation to a company which is an unincorporated association as it applies in relation to one that is not.

[(4) For the purposes of this paragraph, where an employee of a company has an interest in shares or obligations of the company as a beneficiary of an employee benefit trust, the trustees shall not be regarded as associates of his by reason only of that interest unless sub-paragraph (8) below applies in relation to him.][3]

[(5) A trust is an employee benefit trust for the purposes of this paragraph if—

(a) all or most of the employees of the company are eligible to benefit under it, and
(b) none of the property subject to it has been disposed of on or after 14th March 1989 (whether by sale, loan or otherwise) except in the ordinary course of management of the trust or in accordance with sub-paragraph (6) below.][3]

[(6) Property is disposed of in accordance with this sub-paragraph if—

(a) it is applied for the benefit of—

(i) individual employees or former employees of the company,
(ii) spouses, former spouses, widows or widowers of employees or former employees of the company,
(iii) relatives, or spouses of relatives, of persons within sub-paragraph (i) or (ii) above, or
(iv) dependants of persons within sub-paragraph (i) above,

(b) it is applied for charitable purposes, or
(c) it is transferred to the trustees of an approved profit sharing scheme (within the meaning of section 187), of another employee benefit trust, or of a qualifying employee share ownership trust (within the meaning of Schedule 5 to the Finance Act 1989),

and the property applied or transferred consists of any of the ordinary share capital of the company or of money paid outright.][3]

[(7) In sub-paragraph (6)(a)(iii) above "relative" means parent or remoter forebear, child or remoter issue, brother, sister, uncle, aunt, nephew or niece.][3]

[(8) This sub-paragraph applies in relation to an employee if at any time on or after 14th March 1989—

(a) the employee, either on his own or with any one or more of his associates, or
(b) any associate of his, with or without other such associates,

has been the beneficial owner of, or able (directly or through the medium of other companies or by any other indirect means) to control, more than 25 per cent. of the ordinary share capital of the company.][3]

[(9) Where—

(a) on or after 14th March 1989 an employee of a company, or an associate of his, receives a payment ("the relevant payment") from the trustees of an employee benefit trust, and
(b) at any time during the period of three years ending with the day on which the relevant payment is received, the property subject to the trust consists of or includes any part of the ordinary share capital of the company,

the employee or associate shall be treated for the purposes of sub-paragraph (8) above as if he were the beneficial owner of the appropriate percentage of the ordinary share capital of the company on the day on which the relevant payment is received (in addition to any percentage of that share capital of which he is actually the beneficial owner on that day).][3]

[(10) For the purposes of sub-paragraph (9) above, the appropriate percentage is—

$$\frac{A \times 100}{B}$$

where—

A is the smaller of—

(a) the aggregate of the relevant payment and any other payments received by the employee or associates of his from the trustees of the trust during the period of 12 months ending with the day on which the relevant payment is received, and

(b) the aggregate of the distributions made to the trustees of the trust by the company in respect of its ordinary share capital during the period of three years ending with the day on which the relevant payment is received; and

B is the aggregate of—
(a) any distributions made by the company in respect of its ordinary share capital during the period of 12 months ending with the day on which the relevant payment is received,
(b) any distributions so made during the period of 12 months immediately preceding that mentioned in paragraph (a) above, and
(c) any distributions so made during the period of 12 months immediately preceding that mentioned in paragraph (b) above,

divided by the number of the periods mentioned in paragraphs (a) to (c) above in which distributions were so made.][3]

[(11) Where—
(a) an employee or associate is treated by sub-paragraph (9) above as if he were the beneficial owner of a percentage of the ordinary share capital of a company by reason of receiving the relevant payment from the trustees of a trust, and
(b) that employee, or an associate of his, has, during the period of 12 months ending with the day on which the relevant payment is received, received one or more payments from trustees of another employee benefit trust or trusts satisfying the requirement in paragraph (b) of sub-paragraph (9) above,

that sub-paragraph shall have effect in relation to the employee or associate mentioned in paragraph (a) above as if he had received the payment from the trustees of the trust or of each of the trusts mentioned in paragraph (b) above (or where more than one payment has been received from the trustees of a trust, the last of the payments) on the day on which the relevant payment is received.][3]

[(12) In sub-paragraphs (8) to (11) above "associate", in relation to an employee, does not include the trustees of an employee benefit trust by reason only that the employee has an interest in shares or obligations of the trust.][3]

Former enactment.—F(No. 2)A 1987, Sch. 1, para. 7.
Cross references.—See FA 1989, Sch. 5, para. 16(6) (extension of the application of this paragraph to employee share ownership trusts).
Amendments.—[1] Words in sub-para. (1) repealed by FA 1989, Sch. 4, para. 9(1), (2) and Sch. 17, Pt IV.
[2] Words in the definition of "associate" in sub-para. (3) inserted by FA 1989, Sch. 4, para. 9(1), (3).
[3] Sub-paras. (4) to (12) added by FA 1989, Sch. 4, para. 9(1), (4).
[4] Sub-para. (2)(a), (b) and the preceding words substituted by FA 1989, Sch. 12, para. 18 in relation to accounting periods beginning after 31 March 1989.
[5] Word "and" in sub-para. (3) repealed by *ibid* and Sch. 17, Pt V.
[6] Definition of "participator" in sub-para. (3) inserted by FA 1989, Sch. 12, para. 18.

8. The persons within this paragraph are any of the following employees who are excluded by the scheme from receiving any payment of profit-related pay—
(a) those who are not required under the terms of their employment to work in the employment unit for 20 hours or more a week;
(b) those who have not been employed by a relevant employer for a minimum period (of not more than three years) specified in the scheme;

and for this purpose "relevant employer" means the scheme employer or any person who pays the emoluments of any of the employees to whom the scheme relates.

Former enactment.—F(No. 2)A 1987, Sch. 1, para. 8.

Profit periods

9. The scheme must identify the accounting period or periods by reference to which any profit-related pay is to be calculated.

Former enactment.—F(No. 2)A 1987, Sch. 1, para. 9.

10.—(1) Subject to sub-paragraphs (2) and (3) below, any such accounting period must be a period of 12 months.

(2) If the scheme is a replacement scheme, the first of two profit periods may be a period of less than 12 months, but the scheme may not provide for more than two profit periods.

(3) The scheme may make provision for a profit period to be abbreviated where registration of the scheme is cancelled with effect from a day after the beginning of the period; and a

scheme making such provision may exclude the operation of all or any of the provisions of paragraph 13(4) and (5) or (as the case may be) paragraph 14(3)(*b*), (4) and (5) below in relation to the determination of the distributable pool for an abbreviated period.

(4) For the purposes of this paragraph, a scheme is a replacement scheme if—

(*a*) it succeeds another scheme (or two or more other schemes) registration of which was cancelled under section 178(1)(*a*) on the ground of a change in the employment unit or in the circumstances relating to the scheme; and
(*b*) that change occurred not more than three months before the beginning of the first (or only) profit period of the new scheme, and the Board are satisfied that it was not brought about with a view to the registration of the new scheme or in circumstances satisfying the conditions in section 177(1)(*a*), (*b*) and (*c*); and
(*c*) not less than one half of the employees to whom the new scheme relates were employees to whom the previous scheme (or any of the previous schemes) related at the time of that change.

Former enactment.—F(No. 2)A 1987, Sch. 1, para. 10.

Distributable pool

11. The scheme must contain provisions by reference to which the aggregate sum that may be paid to employees in respect of a profit period ("the distributable pool") may be determined.

Former enactment.—F(No. 2)A 1987, Sch. 1, para. 11.

12. Except where the scheme is a replacement scheme (within the meaning of paragraph 10 above), the provisions for the determination of the distributable pool must employ either the method specified in paragraph 13 below ("method A") or the method specified in paragraph 14 below ("method B").

Former enactment.—F(No. 2)A 1987, Sch. 1, para. 12.

13.—(1) Method A is that the distributable pool is equal to a . . .[1] percentage of the profits of the employment unit in the profit period.

[(1A) That percentage must be a fixed percentage specified in the scheme and, if the scheme relates to more than one period, must be the same for each period.][3]

(2) . . .[2].

(3) . . .[2].

(4) Notwithstanding sub-paragraph (1) above, a scheme employing method A may include provision for disregarding profits in the profit period so far as they exceed 160 per cent. (or such greater percentage as may be specified in the scheme) of—

(*a*) if the profit period is the first or only period to which the scheme relates, the profits for [a base year specified in the scheme][4];
(*b*) in any other case, the profits for the previous profit period.

(5) Notwithstanding sub-paragraph (1) above, a scheme employing method A may include provision to the effect that there shall be no distributable pool if the profits in the profit period are less than an amount specified in, or ascertainable by reference to, the scheme; but that amount [must not exceed the profits for a base year specified in the scheme][4].

[(6) The base year referred to in sub-paragraph (4)(*a*) and sub-paragraph (5) above must be a period of 12 months ending at a time within the period of two years immediately preceding the profit period, or the first of the profit periods, to which the scheme relates.][5]

[(7) Any provision included in a scheme by virtue of sub-paragraph (4) or (5) above may take effect either from the scheme's first profit period or from any later profit period determined in accordance with the scheme.][6]

Former enactment.—F(No. 2)A 1987, Sch. 1, para. 13.
Amendments.—[1] Word in sub-para. (1) repealed by FA 1989, Sch. 4, para. 10(2)(*a*) and Sch. 17, Pt. IV.
[2] Sub-paras. (2), (3) repealed by FA 1989, Sch. 4, para. 10(1), (2)(*a*) and Sch. 17, Pt. IV.
[3] Sub-para. (1A) inserted by FA 1989, Sch. 4, para. 10(2)(*b*)(i).
[4] Words in sub-paras. (4)(*a*), (5) substituted by FA 1989, Sch. 4, para. 10(2)(*b*)(ii), (iii).
[5] Sub-para. (6) substituted by FA 1989, Sch. 4, para. 10(2)(*b*)(iv).
[6] Sub-para. (7) added by FA 1989, Sch. 4, para. 11.

14.—(1) Method B is that the distributable pool is—

(*a*) if the profit period is the first or only profit period to which the scheme relates, a percentage of a notional pool of an amount specified in the scheme;
(*b*) in any other case, a percentage of the distributable pool for the previous profit period.

(2) ...[1]

(3) The percentage referred to in sub-paragraph (1) above must be either—

(*a*) that arrived at by expressing the profits in the profit period as a percentage of the profits in the preceding period of 12 months; or
(*b*) the percentage mentioned in paragraph (*a*) above reduced (if it is more than 100) or increased (if it is less than 100) by a specified fraction of the difference between it and 100;

and the reference in paragraph (*b*) above to a specified fraction is a reference to a fraction of not more than one half specified in the scheme.

(4) Notwithstanding sub-paragraph (1) above, a scheme employing method B may include provision for disregarding profits in the profit period so far as they exceed 160 per cent. (or such greater percentage as may be specified in the scheme) of the profits in the preceding period of 12 months.

(5) Notwithstanding sub-paragraph (1) above, a scheme employing method B may include provision to the effect that there shall be no distributable pool if the profits in the profit period are less than an amount ...[3] ascertainable by reference to, the scheme; but that amount [must not exceed the profits in the period of 12 months immediately preceding the first or only profit period to which the scheme relates][2].

(6) Where by virtue of a provision of the kind described in sub-paragraph (5) above there is no distributable pool for a profit period, any comparison required in accordance with sub-paragraph (1)(*b*) to be made with the distributable pool for that period shall be made with what would have been the pool but for sub-paragraph (5).

(7) ...[1]

[(8) Any provision included in a scheme by virtue of sub-paragraph (3)(*b*), (4) or (5) above may take effect either from the scheme's first profit period or from any later profit period determined in accordance with the scheme.][4]

Former enactment.—F(No. 2)A 1987, Sch. 1, para. 14.
Amendments.—[1] Sub-paras. (2), (7) repealed by FA 1989, Sch. 4, para. 10(1), (2)(*a*) and Sch. 17, Pt. IV.
[2] Words in sub-para. (5) substituted by FA 1989, Sch. 4, para. 10(2)(*c*).
[3] Words in sub-para. (5) repealed by FA 1989, Sch. 4, para. 12 and Sch. 17, Pt. IV.
[4] Sub-para. (8) added by FA 1989, Sch. 4, para. 13.

15. If the scheme is a replacement scheme (within the meaning of paragraph 10 above), it must provide for the distributable pool for a profit period to be equal to a specified percentage of the profits for the period.

Former enactment.—F(No. 2)A 1987, Sch. 1, para. 15.

Payment from distributable pool etc.

16. The scheme must provide for the whole of the distributable pool to be paid to employees in the employment unit.

Former enactment.—F(No. 2)A 1987, Sch. 1, para. 16.

17. The scheme must make provision as to when payments will be made to employees.

Former enactment.—F(No. 2)A 1987, Sch. 1, para. 17.

18.—(1) The provisions of the scheme must be such that employees participate in the scheme on similar terms.

(2) For the purposes of sub-paragraph (1) above, the fact that the payments to employees vary according to the levels of their remuneration, the length of their service or similar factors shall not be regarded as meaning that they do not participate on similar terms.

Former enactment.—F(No. 2)A 1987, Sch. 1, para. 18.

Ascertainment of profits

19.—(1) The scheme must provide for the preparation of a profit and loss account in respect of—

(*a*) each profit period of the employment unit; and
(*b*) any other period the profits for which must be ascertained for the purposes of this Chapter.

(2) The profit and loss account must give a true and fair view of the profit or loss of the employment unit for the period to which it relates.

(3) Subject to sub-paragraph (2) above, the requirements of Schedule 4 to the Companies Act 1985 shall apply (with any necessary modifications) to a profit and loss account prepared for the purposes of the scheme as they apply to a profit and loss account of a company for a financial year.

(4) Notwithstanding the preceding provisions of this paragraph, a profit and loss account prepared for the purposes of the scheme must not make any deduction, in arriving at the profits or losses of the employment unit, for the remuneration of any person excluded from the scheme by virtue of paragraph 7 above.

[(4A) In sub-paragraph (4) above "remuneration", in relation to a person, includes fees and percentages, any sums paid by way of expenses allowance (insofar as those sums are charged to income tax), any contributions paid in respect of him under any pension scheme and the estimated value of any other benefits received by him otherwise than in cash.][1]

(5) Notwithstanding the preceding provisions of this paragraph, if the scheme so provides in relation to any of the items listed in sub-paragraph (6) below, a profit and loss account prepared for the purposes of the scheme may, in arriving at the profits or losses of the employment unit—

(*a*) leave the item out of account notwithstanding that Schedule 4 to the Companies Act 1985 requires it to be taken into account; or
(*b*) take the item into account notwithstanding that Schedule 4 to the Companies Act 1985 requires it to be left out of account.

(6) The items referred to in sub-paragraph (5) above are—

(*a*) interest receivable and similar income;
(*b*) interest payable and similar charges;
(*c*) goodwill;
(*d*) tax on profit or loss on ordinary activities (but not any penalty under the Taxes Acts);
(*e*) research and development costs;
[(*f*) profit-related pay payable under the scheme, and profit-related pay payable under any other registered scheme if it is one to which paragraph 21 below applies;][2]
[(*ff*) secondary Class 1 contributions under Part I of the Social Security Act 1975 or Part I of the Social Security (Northern Ireland) Act 1975 in respect of profit-related pay payable under the scheme;][2]
(*g*) extraordinary income;
(*h*) extraordinary charges;
(*j*) extraordinary profit or loss;
(*k*) tax on extraordinary profit or loss.

(7) References in this paragraph to Schedule 4 to the Companies Act 1985 shall be construed, in relation to Northern Ireland, as references to Schedule 4 to the Companies (Northern Ireland) Order 1986.

Former enactment.—F(No. 2)A 1987, Sch. 1, para. 19.
Amendments.—[1] Sub-para. (4A) inserted by FA 1989, Sch. 4, para. 14(1), (2).
[2] Sub-para. (6)(*f*), (*ff*) substituted for sub-para. (6)(*f*) by FA 1989, Sch. 4, para. 14(1), (3).

20.—(1) The scheme must provide that, in preparing a profit and loss account for the purposes of this Schedule, no changes may be made from the accounting policies used in preparing accounts for any earlier period relevant for those purposes, or in the methods of applying those policies, if the effect of the changes (either singly or taken together) would be that the amount of profits (or losses) differed by more than 5 per cent. from what would be that amount if no changes were made.

(2) Sub-paragraph (1) above has effect subject to paragraph 19(2) above.

Former enactment.—F(No. 2)A 1987, Sch. 1, para. 20.

[*Parts of undertakings*]¹

[**21.**—(1) This paragraph shall apply to a scheme if the employment unit is a part of an undertaking, and the scheme states that the profits or losses of the unit are for the purposes of the scheme to be taken to be equivalent to those of the whole undertaking (which must be identified by the scheme).

(2) Where this paragraph applies to a scheme, this Schedule shall have effect as if any reference to the profits or losses of the employment unit were a reference to the profits or losses of the undertaking of which it forms part.]¹

Amendments.—¹ This paragraph inserted by FA 1989, Sch. 4, para. 15.

[**22.**—(1) Where paragraph 21 above applies to a scheme, the scheme must contain provisions ensuring that no payments are made under it by reference to a profit period unless, at the beginning of that profit period,—

(*a*) there is at least one other registered scheme which relates to employees employed in the same undertaking as that of which the employment unit forms part, and

(*b*) the number of the employees to whom the scheme relates does not exceed 33 per cent. of the number of the employees to whom that other scheme relates (or if there is more than one other scheme, the aggregate number of the employees to whom they relate).

(2) Another registered scheme shall be disregarded for the purposes of sub-paragraph (1) above—

(*a*) if paragraph 21 above applies to it, or

(*b*) if, by virtue of provisions of the kind described in paragraph 6 above, no payments could be made under it by reference to the profit period concerned.

(3) Where paragraph 21 above applies to two or more schemes relating to employment units which are parts of the same undertaking, an employee to whom another scheme relates shall not be counted for the purposes of sub-paragraph (1)(*b*) above in connection with more than one of those schemes.]¹

Amendments.—¹ This paragraph inserted by FA 1989, Sch. 4, para. 15.

SCHEDULE 9

Sections 185, 186, 187

APPROVED SHARE OPTION SCHEMES AND PROFIT SHARING SCHEMES

Cross references.—See CGTA 1979, s. 144A(1) (notwithstanding anything in a profit sharing scheme approved under this Schedule, for the purposes of capital gains tax a participant in the scheme to be treated as absolutely entitled to his shares against the trustees),
s. 144A(2) (computation of gains on disposal or part disposal of shares in schemes approved under this Schedule).

PART I
GENERAL

1.—(1) Subject to the provisions of this Schedule, on the application of a body corporate ("the grantor") which has established a share option scheme or a profit sharing scheme, the Board shall approve the scheme if they are satisfied that it fulfils such requirements of Part II and this Part as apply in relation to the scheme in question, and the requirements of Part III, IV or V of this Schedule; and in this Schedule—

"the relevant requirements" means, in relation to any scheme, the requirements of this Schedule by reference to which the scheme is approved; and

"savings-related share option scheme" means a scheme in relation to which the relevant requirements include the requirements of Part III of this Schedule.

(2) An application under sub-paragraph (1) above shall be made in writing and contain such particulars and be supported by such evidence as the Board may require.

(3) Where the grantor has control of another company or companies, the scheme may be expressed to extend to all or any of the companies of which it has control and in this Schedule a scheme which is expressed so to extend is referred to as a "group scheme".

(4) In relation to a group scheme the expression "participating company" means the grantor or any other company to which for the time being the scheme is expressed to extend.

Former enactments.—Sub-para. (1): FA 1978, Sch. 9, para. 1(1)(*a*); FA 1980, Sch. 10, para. 1(1)(*a*); FA 1984, Sch. 10, para 1(1).
Sub-para. (2): FA 1978, Sch. 9, para. 1(5); FA 1980, Sch. 10, para. 1(2); FA 1984, Sch. 10, para. 1(2).
Sub-para. (3): FA 1978, Sch. 9, para. 1(2); FA 1980, Sch. 10, para. 1(3); FA 1984, Sch. 10, para. 1(3).
Sub-para. (4): FA 1978, Sch. 9, para. 1(2); FA 1980, Sch. 10, para. 1(3); FA 1984, Sch. 10, para. 1(4).

2.—(1) The Board shall not approve a scheme under this Schedule if it appears to them that it contains features which are neither essential nor reasonably incidental to the purpose of providing for employees and directors benefits in the nature of rights to acquire shares or, in the case of a profit sharing scheme, in the nature of interests in shares.

(2) A profit sharing scheme shall not be approved under paragraph 1 above unless the Board are satisfied that, whether under the terms of the scheme or otherwise, every participant in the scheme is bound in contract with the grantor—

(*a*) to permit his shares to remain in the hands of the trustees throughout the period of retention; and

(*b*) not to assign, charge or otherwise dispose of his beneficial interest in his shares during that period; and

(*c*) if he directs the trustees to transfer the ownership of his shares to him at any time before the release date, to pay to the trustees before the transfer takes place a sum equal to income tax at the basic rate on the appropriate percentage of the locked-in value of the shares at the time of the direction; and

(*d*) not to direct the trustees to dispose of his shares at any time before the release date in any other way except by sale for the best consideration in money that can reasonably be obtained at the time of the sale or, in the case of redeemable shares in a workers' cooperative, by redemption.

(3) The Board must be satisfied in the case of a savings-related share option scheme or a profit sharing scheme—

(*a*) that there are no features of the scheme (other than any which are included to satisfy requirements of this Schedule) which have or would have the effect of discouraging any description of employees or former employees who fulfil the conditions in paragraph 26(1) or, as the case may be, 36(1) below from actually participating in the scheme; and

(b) where the grantor is a member of a group of companies, that the scheme does not and would not have the effect of conferring benefits wholly or mainly on directors of companies in the group or on those employees of companies in the group who are in receipt of the higher or highest levels of remuneration.

(4) For the purposes of sub-paragraph (3) above "a group of companies" means a company and any other companies of which it has control.

Former enactments.—Sub-para. (1): FA 1978, Sch. 9, para. 1(1)(*b*); FA 1980, Sch. 10, para. 1(1)(*b*); FA 1984, Sch. 10, para. 1(1); FA 1987, Sch. 15, para. 13.
Sub-para. (2): FA 1978, s. 54(1); FA 1986, s. 24(3)(*a*).
Sub-paras. (3), (4): FA 1978, Sch. 9, para. 2(3), (4); FA 1980, Sch. 10, para. 1(1)(*aa*), (*ab*), (1A); FA 1983, s. 25(5); FA 1984, s. 39(2).
Cross references.—See CGTA 1979, s. 144A(1) (notwithstanding anything in sub-para. (2) above, a participant in a profit sharing scheme to be treated as absolutely entitled to his shares as against the trustees).

3.—(1) If, at any time after the Board have approved a share option scheme, any of the relevant requirements ceases to be satisfied or the grantor fails to provide information requested by the Board under paragraph 6 below, the Board may withdraw the approval with effect from that time or such later time as the Board may specify; but where rights obtained under a savings-related share option scheme before the withdrawal of approval from the scheme under this paragraph are exercised after the withdrawal, section 185(3) shall apply in respect of the exercise as if the scheme were still approved.

(2) If at any time after the Board have approved a profit sharing scheme—

(*a*) a participant is in breach of any of his obligations under paragraph 2(2)(*a*), (*c*) and (*d*) above; or

(*b*) there is, with respect to the operation of the scheme, any contravention of any of the relevant requirements, Schedule 10, the scheme itself or the terms of the trust referred to in paragraph 30(1)(*c*) below; or

(*c*) any shares of a class of which shares have been appropriated to the participants receive different treatment in any respect from the other shares of that class, in particular, different treatment in respect of—

(i) the dividend payable;
(ii) repayment;
(iii) the restrictions attaching to the shares; or
(iv) any offer of substituted or additional shares, securities or rights of any description in respect of the shares; or

(*d*) the Board cease to be satisfied that the scheme complies with the requirements of paragraph 2(3) above or paragraph 36 below; or

(*e*) the trustees, the grantor or, in the case of a group scheme, a company which is or has been a participating company fail or fails to furnish any information which they are or it is required to furnish under paragraph 6 below,

the Board may, subject to sub-paragraph (3) below, withdraw the approval with effect from that time or from such later time as the Board may specify.

(3) It shall not be a ground for withdrawal of approval of a profit sharing scheme that shares which have been newly issued receive, in respect of dividends payable with respect to a period beginning before the date on which the shares were issued, treatment which is less favourable than that accorded to shares issued before that date.

Former enactments.—Sub-para. (1): FA 1980, Sch. 10, para. 3(1); FA 1984, Sch. 10, para. 2(1).
Sub-para. (2): FA 1978, Sch. 9, para. 3(1); FA 1983, s. 25(6).
Sub-para. (3): FA 1978, Sch. 9, para. 3(3).

4. If an alteration is made in the scheme at any time after the Board have approved the scheme, the approval shall not have effect after the date of the alteration unless the Board have approved the alteration.

Former enactments.—FA 1978, Sch. 9, para. 3(2); FA 1980, Sch. 10, para. 3(2); FA 1984, Sch. 10, para. 2(2).

5. If aggrieved—

(*a*) in any case, by the failure of the Board to approve the scheme or to approve an alteration in the scheme or by the withdrawal of approval; or

(b) in the case of a savings-related share option scheme, by the failure of the Board to decide that a condition subject to which the approval has been given is satisfied; or
(c) in the case of a profit sharing scheme, by the failure of the Board to approve an alteration in the terms of the trust referred to in paragraph 30(1)(c) below;

the grantor may, by notice given to the Board within 30 days from the date on which it is notified of the Board's decision, require the matter to be determined by the Special Commissioners, and the Special Commissioners shall hear and determine the matter in like manner as an appeal.

Former enactments.—FA 1978, Sch. 9, para. 4; FA 1980, Sch. 10, para. 4; FA 1984, Sch. 10, para. 3.

6. The Board may by notice require any person to furnish them, within such time as the Board may direct (not being less than 30 days), with such information as the Board think necessary for the performance of their functions under the relevant provisions and as the person to whom the notice is addressed has or can reasonably obtain, including in particular information—

(a) to enable the Board to determine—

(i) whether to approve a scheme or withdraw an approval already given; or
(ii) the liability to tax, including capital gains tax, of any person who has participated in a scheme; and

(b) in relation to the administration of a scheme and any alteration of the terms of a scheme.

Former enactments.—FA 1978, s. 53(7); FA 1980, Sch. 10, para. 25; FA 1984, Sch. 10, para. 14.

PART II
REQUIREMENTS GENERALLY APPLICABLE

7. The provisions of this Part apply in relation to all schemes unless otherwise stated.

8. The scheme must not provide for any person to be eligible to participate in it, that is to say, to obtain and exercise rights under it, or in the case of a profit sharing scheme to have shares appropriated to him, at any time when he has, or has within the preceding 12 months had, a material interest in a close company which is—

(a) a company shares in which, in the case of a profit sharing scheme, are to be appropriated or, in the case of a share option scheme, may be acquired pursuant to the exercise of rights obtained under the scheme; or
(b) a company which has control of such a company or is a member of a consortium which owns such a company.

In determining whether a company is a close company for the purposes of this paragraph, sections 414(1)(a) and 415 shall be disregarded.

Former enactments.—FA 1978, Sch. 9, para. 11(1), (2); FA 1980, Sch. 10, para.23; FA 1984, Sch. 10, para. 4(1)(b), (3).

9.—(1) A share option scheme must provide for directors and employees to obtain rights to acquire shares ("scheme shares") which satisfy the requirements of paragraphs 10 to 14 below.

(2) In the case of a profit sharing scheme, the shares to be acquired by the trustees as mentioned in paragraph 30 below ("scheme shares") must satisfy the requirements of paragraphs 10 to 12 and 14 below.

Former enactments.—FA 1978, Sch. 9, para. 1(1), (3); FA 1980, Sch. 10, para. 5(a); FA 1984, Sch. 10, para. 6.

10. Scheme shares must form part of the ordinary share capital of—

(a) the grantor; or
(b) a company which has control of the grantor; or
(c) a company which either is, or has control of, a company which—

(i) is a member of a consortium owning either the grantor or a company having control of the grantor; ...[1]
(ii) ...[1]

Former enactments.—FA 1978, Sch. 9, para. 5; FA 1980, Sch. 10, para. 15; FA 1984, Sch. 10, para. 7.
Amendments.—[1] Para. (c)(ii) and the preceding word "and" repealed by FA 1989, s. 64 and Sch. 17, Pt. IV.

11. Scheme shares must be—
   (*a*) shares of a class quoted on a recognised stock exchange; or
   (*b*) shares in a company which is not under the control of another company; or
   (*c*) shares in a company which is under the control of a company (other than a company which is, or would if resident in the United Kingdom be, a close company), whose shares are quoted on a recognised stock exchange.

Former enactments.—FA 1978, Sch. 9, para. 6; FA 1980, s. 46(10), Sch. 10, para. 16; FA 1984, Sch. 10, para. 8.

12.—(1) Scheme shares must be—
   (*a*) fully paid up;
   (*b*) not redeemable; and
   (*c*) not subject to any restrictions other than restrictions which attach to all shares of the same class or a restriction authorised by sub-paragraph (2) below.

Sub-paragraph (*b*) above does not apply, in the case of a profit sharing scheme, in relation to shares in a workers' cooperative.

(2) Except as provided below, the shares may be subject to a restriction imposed by the company's articles of association—
   (*a*) requiring all shares held by directors or employees of the company or of any other company of which it has control to be disposed of on ceasing to be so held; and
   (*b*) requiring all shares acquired, in pursuance of rights or interests obtained by such directors or employees, by persons who are not (or have ceased to be) such directors or employees to be disposed of when they are acquired.

(3) A restriction is not authorised by sub-paragraph (2) above unless—
   (*a*) any disposal required by the restriction will be by way of sale for a consideration in money on terms specified in the articles of association; and
   (*b*) the articles also contain general provisions by virtue of which any person disposing of shares of the same class (whether or not held or acquired as mentioned in sub-paragraph (2) above) may be required to sell them on terms which are the same as those mentioned in paragraph (*a*) above.

(4) In the case of a profit sharing scheme, except in relation to redeemable shares in a workers' cooperative, nothing in sub-paragraph (2) above authorises a restriction which would require a person, before the release date, to dispose of his beneficial interest in shares the ownership of which has not been transferred to him.

Former enactments.—FA 1978, Sch. 9, para. 7; FA 1980, Sch. 10, para. 17; FA 1984, Sch. 10, para. 9; FA 1986, ss. 22, 24(2).

13.—(1) In determining, in the case of a share option scheme, for the purposes of paragraph 12(1)(*c*) above whether scheme shares which are or are to be acquired by any person are subject to any restrictions, there shall be regarded as a restriction attaching to the shares any contract, agreement, arrangement or condition by which his freedom to dispose of the shares or of any interest in them or of the proceeds of their sale or to exercise any right conferred by them is restricted or by which such a disposal or exercise may result in any disadvantage to him or to a person connected with him.

(2) Sub-paragraph (1) does not apply to so much of any contract, agreement, arrangement or condition as contains provisions similar in purpose and effect to any of the provisions of the Model Rules set out in the Model Code for Securities Transactions by Directors of Listed Companies issued by the Stock Exchange in November 1984.

[(3) In the case of schemes other than savings-related share option schemes, sub-paragraph (1) above does not apply in relation to any terms of a loan making provision about how it is to be repaid or the security to be given for it.][1]

Former enactments.—FA 1980, Sch. 10, para. 18; FA 1982, s. 41; FA 1984, Sch. 10, para. 10; FA 1986, s. 23(4).
Cross references.—See FA 1988, s. 69(2) (amendment to FA 1984, Sch. 10, para. 10 effective for the year 1987–88 and previous years).
Amendments.—[1] Sub-para. (3) added by FA 1988, s. 69(1) and deemed always to have had effect.

14.—(1) Except where scheme shares are shares in a company the ordinary share capital of which consists of shares of one class only, the majority of the issued shares of the same class either must be employee-control shares or must be held by persons other than—
   (*a*) persons who acquired their shares in pursuance of a right conferred on them or an

opportunity afforded to them as a director or employee of the grantor or any other company and not in pursuance of an offer to the public;

(*b*) trustees holding shares on behalf of persons who acquired their beneficial interests in the shares as mentioned in sub-paragraph (*a*) above; and

(*c*) in a case where the shares fall within sub-paragraph (*c*), but not within sub-paragraph (*a*), of paragraph 11 above, companies which have control of the company whose shares are in question or of which that company is an associated company.

(2) In its application to a profit sharing scheme, sub-paragraph (1) above shall have effect with the addition after the words "ordinary share capital of which" of the words "at the time of the acquisition of the shares by the trustees".

(3) For the purposes of this paragraph, shares in a company are employee-control shares if—

(*a*) the persons holding the shares are, by virtue of their holding, together able to control the company; and

(*b*) those persons are or have been employees or directors of the company or of another company which is under the control of the company.

Former enactments.—FA 1978, Sch. 9, para. 8; FA 1980, s. 46(11), Sch. 10, para. 19; FA 1984, Sch. 10, para. 11; FA 1986, s. 23(3).

15.—(1) Except in the case of a profit sharing scheme, the scheme may provide that if any company ("the acquiring company")—

(*a*) obtains control of a company whose shares are scheme shares as a result of making a general offer—

(i) to acquire the whole of the issued ordinary share capital of the company which is made on a condition such that if it is satisfied the person making the offer will have control of the company; or

(ii) to acquire all the shares in the company which are of the same class as the scheme shares;

(*b*) obtains control of a company whose shares are scheme shares in pursuance of a compromise or arrangement sanctioned by the court under section 425 of the Companies Act 1985 or Article 418 of the Companies (Northern Ireland) Order 1986; or

(*c*) becomes bound or entitled to acquire shares in a company whose shares are scheme shares under sections 428 to 430 of that Act or Articles 421 to 423 of that Order,

any participant in the scheme may at any time within the appropriate period, by agreement with the acquiring company, release his rights under the scheme (in this paragraph referred to as "the old rights") in consideration of the grant to him of rights (in this paragraph referred to as "the new rights") which are equivalent to the old rights but relate to shares in a different company (whether the acquiring company itself or some other company falling within paragraph 10(*b*) or (*c*) above).

(2) In sub-paragraph (1) above "the appropriate period" means—

(*a*) in a case falling within paragraph (*a*), the period of six months beginning with the time when the person making the offer has obtained control of the company and any condition subject to which the offer is made is satisfied;

(*b*) in a case falling within paragraph (*b*), the period of six months beginning with the time when the court sanctions the compromise or arrangement; and

(*c*) in a case falling within paragraph (*c*), the period during which the acquiring company remains bound or entitled as mentioned in that paragraph.

(3) The new rights shall not be regarded for the purposes of this paragraph as equivalent to the old rights unless—

(*a*) the shares to which they relate satisfy the conditions specified, in relation to scheme shares, in paragraphs 10 to 14 above; and

(*b*) the new rights will be exercisable in the same manner as the old rights and subject to the provisions of the scheme as it had effect immediately before the release of the old rights; and

(*c*) the total market value, immediately before the release, of the shares which were subject to the participant's old rights is equal to the total market value, immediately after the grant, of the shares in respect of which the new rights are granted to the participant; and

(*d*) the total amount payable by the participant for the acquisition of shares in pursuance of the new rights is equal to the total amount that would have been payable for the acquisition of shares in pursuance of the old rights.

(4) Where any new rights are granted pursuant to a provision included in a scheme by virtue of this paragraph they shall be regarded—

(*a*) for the purpose of section 185 and this Schedule; and
(*b*) for the purposes of the subsequent application (by virtue of a condition complying with sub-paragraph (3)(*b*) above) of the provisions of the scheme,

as having been granted at the time when the corresponding old rights were granted.

(5) Where a scheme which was approved before 1st August 1987 is altered before 1st August 1989 so as to include such a provision as is mentioned above ("an exchange provision"), the scheme as altered may by virtue of this and the following sub-paragraphs apply that provision to rights obtained under the scheme before the date on which the alteration takes effect.

(6) If an exchange provision is applied as mentioned in sub-paragraph (5) above in a case where, on or after 17th March 1987 but before the date on which the alteration takes effect, an event has occurred by reason of which a person holding rights under the scheme would be able to take advantage of the exchange provision—

(*a*) the scheme may permit a person who held rights under the scheme immediately before that event to take advantage of the exchange provision; and
(*b*) in a case where rights then held would otherwise, by reason of the event, have ceased to be exercisable, the scheme may provide that the exchange provision shall apply as if the rights were still exercisable.

(7) The application of an exchange provision as mentioned in sub-paragraph (5) or (6) above shall not itself be regarded for the purposes of this Schedule as the acquisition of a right.

(8) Sub-paragraphs (5) and (6) above have effect subject to paragraph 4 above.

Former enactments.—Sub-paras. (1)–(4): FA 1980, Sch. 10, para. 10A; FA 1984, Sch. 10, para. 4A; FA 1987, Sch. 4, paras. 1, 2; F(No. 2)A 1987, s. 59.
Cross references.—See CGTA 1979, s. 144A(4) (transaction involving exchange of old rights for new rights to be treated for capital gains tax purposes as if the new rights were the same assets as the old rights).

PART III
REQUIREMENTS APPLICABLE TO SAVINGS-RELATED SHARE OPTION SCHEMES

16.—(1) The scheme must provide for the scheme shares to be paid for with money not exceeding the amount of repayments made and any interest paid to them under a certified contractual savings scheme which has been approved by the Board for the purposes of this Schedule.

(2) Where the Board are satisfied that—

(*a*) a person has entered into a certified contractual savings scheme before 15th November 1980, and
(*b*) he has obtained rights under a scheme established before that date to acquire shares in a company of which he is an employee or director (or a company of which such a company has control) using repayments made under the certified contractual savings scheme;

then, repayments and interest paid under the certified contractual savings scheme shall be treated as repayments and interest paid, under a scheme approved by the Board for the purposes of this Schedule under sub-paragraph (1) above, and, accordingly, may be used for the purchase of shares under a savings-related share option scheme approved under this Schedule.

(3) The repayments and interest to which sub-paragraph (2) above applies shall not exceed the repayments and interest to which the participant would have been entitled if the terms of the scheme had corresponded to those of a certified contractual savings scheme approved by the Board under sub-paragraph (1) above.

Former enactments.—Sub-para. (1): FA 1980, Sch. 10, para. 5(*b*).
Sub-paras. (2), (3): FA 1980, Sch. 10, para. 24.

17. Subject to paragraphs 18 to 21 below, the rights obtained under the scheme must not be capable of being exercised before the bonus date, that is to say, the date on which repayments under the certified contractual savings scheme are due; and for the purposes of this paragraph and paragraph 16 above—

(a) repayments under a certified contractual savings scheme may be taken as including or as not including a bonus;
(b) the time when repayments are due shall be, where repayments are taken as including the maximum bonus, the earliest date on which the maximum bonus is payable and, in any other case, the earliest date on which a bonus is payable under the scheme; and
(c) the question what is to be taken as so included must be required to be determined at the time when rights under the scheme are obtained.

Former enactment.—FA 1980, Sch. 10, para. 6.

18. The scheme must provide that if a person who has obtained rights under the scheme dies before the bonus date the rights must be exercised, if at all, within 12 months after the date of his death and if he dies within six months after the bonus date the rights may be exercised within 12 months after the bonus date.

Former enactment.—FA 1980, Sch. 10, para. 7.

19. The scheme must provide that if a person who has obtained rights under it ceases to hold the office or employment by virtue of which he is eligible to participate in the scheme by reason of—

(a) injury or disability or redundancy within the meaning of the Employment Protection (Consolidation) Act 1978; or
(b) retirement on reaching pensionable age or any other age at which he is bound to retire in accordance with the terms of his contract of employment,

then the rights must be exercised, if at all, within six months of his so ceasing and, if he so ceases for any other reason within three years of obtaining the rights, they may not be exercised at all except pursuant to such a provision of the scheme as is mentioned in paragraph 21(1)(e) below; and in relation to the case where he so ceases for any other reason more than three years after obtaining the rights the scheme must either provide that the rights may not be exercised or that they must be exercised, if at all, within six months of his so ceasing.

Former enactments.—FA 1980, Sch. 10, para. 8; FA 1986, s. 23(3).

20. The scheme must provide that where a person who has obtained rights under it continues to hold the office or employment by virtue of which he is eligible to participate in the scheme after the date on which he reaches pensionable age, he may exercise the rights within six months of that date.

Former enactments.—FA 1980, Sch. 10, para. 9; Companies Consolidation (Consequential Provisions) Act 1985, Sch. 2; Companies Consolidation (Consequential Provisions) (Northern Ireland) Order 1986, S.I. 1986 No. 1032.

21.—(1) The scheme may provide that—

(a) if any person obtains control of a company whose shares are scheme shares as a result of making a general offer falling within paragraph 15(a)(i) or (ii) above, rights obtained under the scheme to acquire shares in the company may be exercised within six months of the time when the person making the offer has obtained control of the company and any condition subject to which the offer is made has been satisfied;
(b) if under section 425 of the Companies Act 1985 or Article 418 of the Companies (Northern Ireland) Order 1986 (power to compromise with creditors and members) the court sanctions a compromise or arrangement proposed for the purposes of or in connection with a scheme for the reconstruction of a company whose shares are scheme shares or its amalgamation with any other company or companies, rights obtained under the share option scheme to acquire shares in the company may be exercised within six months of the court sanctioning the compromise or arrangement;
(c) if any person becomes bound or entitled, under sections 428 to 430 of that Act of 1985 or Articles 421 to 423 of that Order of 1986 (power to acquire shares of shareholders dissenting from schemes or contract approved by majority), to acquire shares in a company shares in which are scheme shares, rights obtained under the scheme to acquire shares in the company may be exercised at any time when that person remains so bound or entitled;
(d) if a company whose shares are scheme shares passes a resolution for voluntary winding up, rights obtained under a scheme to acquire shares in the company may be exercised within six months of the passing of the resolution; and

(e) if a person ceases to hold an office or employment by virtue of which he is eligible to participate in the scheme by reason only that—

(i) that office or employment is in a company of which the grantor ceases to have control; or
(ii) that office or employment relates to a business or part of a business which is transferred to a person who is neither an associated company of the grantor nor a company of which the grantor has control;

rights under the scheme held by that person may be exercised within six months of his so ceasing.

(2) For the purposes of this paragraph a person shall be deemed to have obtained control of a company if he and others acting in concert with him have together obtained control of it.

(3) Where a scheme which has been approved before 1st August 1986 has been or is altered before 1st August 1988 so as to include such a provision as is specified in sub-paragraph (1)(e) above, the scheme as altered may by virtue of this sub-paragraph apply that provision to rights obtained under the scheme before the date on which the alteration takes effect, and where that provision is so applied in relation to such rights—

(a) the scheme may permit a person having such rights to take advantage of the provision notwithstanding that under the scheme he would otherwise be unable to exercise those rights after he has ceased to hold the office or employment in question; and
(b) if, before the date on which the alteration takes effect, a person who held such rights on 18th March 1986 ceases, in either of the circumstances set out in sub-paragraph (1)(e) above, to hold an office or employment by virtue of which he was eligible to participate in the scheme, then, so far as concerns the rights so held, the scheme may permit him to take advantage of the provision in question as if the alteration had been made immediately before he ceased to hold that office or employment; and
(c) the application of the provision shall not itself be regarded as the acquisition of a right for the purposes of this Schedule.

This sub-paragraph has effect subject to paragraph 4 above.

Former enactments.—FA 1980, Sch. 10, para. 10; FA 1986, s. 25(4), (8), (9).

22. Except as provided in paragraph 18 above, rights obtained by a person under the scheme must not be capable—

(a) of being transferred by him, or
(b) of being exercised later than six months after the bonus date.

Former enactment.—FA 1980, Sch. 10, para. 11.

23. No person shall be treated for the purposes of paragraph 19 or 21(1)(e) above as ceasing to hold an office or employment by virtue of which he is eligible to participate in the scheme until he ceases to hold an office or employment in the grantor or in any associated company or company of which the grantor has control.

Former enactments.—FA 1980, Sch. 10, para. 12; FA 1986, s. 25(5).

24.—(1) The scheme must provide for a person's contributions under the certified contractual savings scheme to be of such amount as to secure as nearly as may be repayment of an amount equal to that for which shares may be acquired in pursuance of rights obtained under the scheme; and for this purpose the amount of repayment under the certified contractual savings scheme shall be determined as mentioned in paragraph 17 above.

(2) The scheme must not—

(a) permit the aggregate amount of a person's contributions under certified contractual savings schemes linked to savings-related share option schemes approved under this Schedule to exceed [£150][1] monthly, nor
(b) impose a minimum on the amount of a person's contributions which exceeds £10 monthly.

(3) The Treasury may by order amend sub-paragraph (2) above by substituting for any amount for the time being specified in that sub-paragraph such amount as may be specified in the order.

Former enactments.—Sub-para. (1): FA 1980, Sch. 10, para. 13(1).
Sub-para. (2), (3): FA 1980, Sch. 10, para. 13(2), (3); FA 1984, s. 39(5).
Amendments.—[1] Amount in sub-para. (2)(*a*) substituted for "£100" by FA 1989, s. 62(1), (2), (4) with effect from an appointed day.

25. The price at which scheme shares may be acquired by the exercise of a right obtained under the scheme—

(*a*) must be stated at the time the right is obtained, and
(*b*) must not be manifestly less than [80 per cent.][1] of the market value of shares of the same class at that time or, if the Board and the grantor agree in writing, at such earlier time or times as may be provided in the agreement,

but the scheme may provide for such variation of the price as may be necessary to take account of any variation in the share capital of which the scheme shares form part.

Former enactment.—FA 1980, Sch. 10, para. 14.
Amendments.—[1] Percentage in para. (*b*) substituted by FA 1989, s. 62(1), (3).

26.—(1) Subject to paragraph 8 above, every person who—

(*a*) is a full-time employee or a full-time director of the grantor or, in the case of a group scheme, a participating company, and
(*b*) has been such an employee or director at all times during a qualifying period not exceeding five years, and
(*c*) is chargeable to tax in respect of his office or employment under Case I of Schedule E,

must be eligible to participate in the scheme, that is to say, to obtain and exercise rights under it, on similar terms, and those who do participate in the scheme must actually do so on similar terms.

(2) For the purposes of sub-paragraph (1) above, the fact that the rights to be obtained by the persons participating in a scheme vary according to the levels of their remuneration, the length of their service or similar factors shall not be regarded as meaning that they are not eligible to participate in the scheme on similar terms or do not actually do so.

(3) Except as provided by paragraph 19 above or pursuant to such a provision as is referred to in paragraph 21(1)(*e*) above, a person must not be eligible to participate in the scheme at any time unless he is at that time a director or employee of the grantor or, in the case of a group scheme, of a participating company.

Former enactments.—Sub-paras. (1), (2): FA 1980, Sch. 10, para. 20; FA 1984, s. 39(6); FA 1986, s. 25(7).
Sub-para. (3): FA 1980, Sch. 10, para. 21; FA 1986, s. 25(6).

PART IV
REQUIREMENTS APPLICABLE TO OTHER SHARE OPTION SCHEMES

27.—(1) A person must not be eligible to obtain rights under the scheme at any time unless he is at that time a full-time director or qualifying employee of the grantor or, in the case of a group scheme, of a participating company, but the scheme may provide that a person may exercise rights under it after he has ceased to be a full-time director or qualifying employee.

(2) The scheme must not permit any person obtaining rights under it to transfer any of them but may provide that, if a person who has obtained rights under it dies before exercising them, they may be exercised after, but not more than one year after, the date of his death.

(3) Where the scheme contains the provisions permitted by sub-paragraph (2) above and any rights are exercised—

(*a*) after the death of the person who obtained them; but
(*b*) before the expiry of the period of ten years beginning with his obtaining them;

subsection (3) of section 185 shall apply with the omission of the reference to subsection (5) of that section.

(4) In sub-paragraph (1) above "qualifying employee", in relation to a company, means an employee of the company (other than one who is a director of the company or, in the case of a group scheme, of a participating company) who is required, under the terms of his employment, to work for the company for at least 20 hours a week.

Former enactments.—Sub-para. (1): FA 1984, Sch. 10, para. 4(1)(*a*), (2).
Sub-paras. (2), (3): FA 1984, Sch. 10, para. 12.
Sub-para. (4): FA 1984, Sch. 10, para. 15(1).

28.—(1) The scheme must provide that no person shall obtain rights under it which would, at the time they are obtained, cause the aggregate market value of the shares which he may acquire in pursuance of rights obtained under the scheme or under any other share option scheme, not being a savings-related share option scheme, approved under this Schedule and established by the grantor or by any associated company of the grantor (and not exercised) to exceed or further exceed the appropriate limit.

(2) The appropriate limit is the greater of—
   (*a*) £100,000; or
   (*b*) if there were relevant emoluments for the preceding year of assessment, four times the amount of the relevant emoluments for the current or preceding year of assessment (whichever of those years gives the greater amount); or
   (*c*) if there were no relevant emoluments for the preceding year of assessment, four times the amount of the relevant emoluments for the period of 12 months beginning with the first day during the current year of assessment in respect of which there are relevant emoluments.

(3) For the purposes of sub-paragraph (1) above, the market value of shares shall be calculated as at the time when the rights in relation to those shares were obtained or, in a case where an agreement relating to them has been made under paragraph 29 below, such earlier time or times as may be provided in the agreement.

(4) For the purposes of sub-paragraph (2) above, the relevant emoluments are such of the emoluments of the office or employment by virtue of which the person in question is eligible to participate in the scheme as are liable to be paid under deduction of tax pursuant to section 203 after deducting amounts included by virtue of Chapter II of Part V.

Former enactment.—FA 1984, Sch. 10, para. 5.

29. The price at which scheme shares may be acquired by the exercise of a right obtained under the scheme—
   (*a*) must be stated at the time the right is obtained, and
   (*b*) must not be manifestly less than the market value of shares of the same class at that time or, if the Board and the grantor agree in writing, at such earlier time or times as may be provided in the agreement, but the scheme may provide for such variation of the price as may be necessary to take account of any variation in the share capital of which the scheme shares form part.

Former enactment.—FA 1984, Sch. 10, para. 13.

PART V
REQUIREMENTS APPLICABLE TO PROFIT SHARING SCHEMES

30.—(1) The scheme must provide for the establishment of a body of persons resident in the United Kingdom ("the trustees")—
   (*a*) who, out of moneys paid to them by the grantor or, in the case of a group scheme, a participating company, are required by the scheme to acquire shares in respect of which the conditions in paragraphs 10 to 12 and 14 above are fulfilled; and
   (*b*) who are under a duty to appropriate shares acquired by them to individuals who participate in the scheme, not being individuals who are ineligible by virtue of paragraph 8 or 35 of this Schedule; and
   (*c*) whose functions with respect to shares held by them are regulated by a trust which is constituted under the law of a part of the United Kingdom and the terms of which are embodied in an instrument which complies with the provisions of paragraphs 31 to 34 below.

(2) If at any time after the Board have approved the scheme, an alteration is made in the terms of the trust referred to in sub-paragraph (1)(*c*) above, the approval shall not have effect after the date of the alteration unless the Board have approved the alteration.

(3) The scheme must provide that the total of the initial market values of the shares appropriated to any one participant in a year of assessment will not exceed the relevant amount.

(4) In this Part of this Schedule "initial market value", in relation to a participant's shares, means the market value of those shares determined—

(*a*) except where paragraph (*b*) below applies, on the date on which the shares were appropriated to him; and

(*b*) if the Board and the trustees agree in writing, on or by reference to such earlier date or dates as may be provided for in the agreement.

Former enactments.—Sub-para. (1): FA 1978, Sch. 9, para. 1(3).
Sub-para. (2): FA 1978, Sch. 9, para. 3(2).
Sub-para. (3): FA 1978, Sch. 9, para. 1(4); FA 1983, s. 25(1).
Sub-para. (4): FA 1978, s. 53(4).

31. The trust instrument shall provide that, as soon as practicable after any shares have been appropriated to a participant, the trustees will give him notice of the appropriation—

(*a*) specifying the number and description of those shares; and
(*b*) stating their initial market value.

Former enactment.—FA 1978, Sch. 9, para. 12.

32.—(1) The trust instrument must contain a provision prohibiting the trustees from disposing of any shares, except as mentioned in paragraph 1(1)(*a*), (*b*) or (*c*) of Schedule 10, during the period of retention (whether by transfer to the participant or otherwise).

(2) The trust instrument must contain a provision prohibiting the trustees from disposing of any shares after the end of the period of retention and before the release date except—

(*a*) pursuant to a direction given by or on behalf of the participant or any person in whom the beneficial interest in his shares is for the time being vested; and
(*b*) by a transaction which would not involve a breach of the participant's obligations under paragraph 2(2)(*c*) or (*d*) above.

Former enactments.—FA 1978, Sch. 9, para. 13; FA 1980, s. 46(13).

33. The trust instrument must contain a provision requiring the trustees—

(*a*) subject to their obligations under paragraph 7 of Schedule 10 and to any such direction as is mentioned in paragraph 4(2) of that Schedule to pay over to the participant any money or money's worth received by them in respect of or by reference to any of his shares other than money's worth consisting of new shares within the meaning of paragraph 5 of that Schedule; and
(*b*) to deal only pursuant to a direction given by or on behalf of the participant or any person in whom the beneficial interest in his shares is for the time being vested with any right conferred in respect of any of his shares to be allotted other shares, securities or rights of any description.

Former enactment.—FA 1978, Sch. 9, para. 14.

34. The trust instrument must impose an obligation on the trustees—

(*a*) to maintain such records as may be necessary to enable the trustees to carry out their obligations under paragraph 7 of Schedule 10; and
(*b*) where the participant becomes liable to income tax under Schedule E by reason of the occurrence of any event, to inform him of any facts relevant to determining that liability.

Former enactment.—FA 1978, Sch. 9, para. 15.

35.—(1) An individual shall not be eligible to have shares appropriated to him under the scheme at any time unless he is at that time or was within the preceding 18 months a director or employee of the grantor or, in the case of a group scheme, of a participating company.

(2) An individual shall not be eligible to have shares appropriated to him under the scheme at any time if in that year of assessment shares have been appropriated to him under another approved scheme established by the grantor or by—

(*a*) a company which controls or is controlled by the grantor or which is controlled by a company which also controls the grantor, or
(*b*) a company which is a member of a consortium owning the grantor or which is owned in part by the grantor as a member of a consortium.

Former enactments.—Sub-para. (1): FA 1978, Sch. 9, para. 9.
Sub-para. (2): FA 1978, Sch. 9, para. 10.

36.—(1) Subject to paragraphs 8 and 35 above, every person who at any time—

(*a*) is a full-time employee or a full-time director of the grantor or, in the case of a group scheme, a participating company, and

(*b*) has been such an employee or director at all times during a qualifying period, not exceeding five years, ending at that time, and

(*c*) is chargeable to tax in respect of his office or employment under Case I of Schedule E,

must then be eligible (subject to paragraphs 8 and 35 of this Schedule) to participate in the scheme on similar terms and those who do participate must actually do so on similar terms.

(2) For the purposes of sub-paragraph (1) above, the fact that the number of shares to be appropriated to the participants in a scheme varies by reference to the levels of their remuneration, the length of their service or similar factors shall not be regarded as meaning that they are not eligible to participate in the scheme on similar terms or do not actually do so.

Former enactments.—FA 1978, Sch. 9, para. 2; FA 1983, s. 25(4).

PART VI
MATERIAL INTEREST TEST

Interests under trusts

37.—(1) This paragraph applies in a case where—

(*a*) the individual ("the beneficiary") was one of the objects of a discretionary trust; and

(*b*) the property subject to the trust at any time consisted of or included any shares or obligations of the company.

(2) If neither the beneficiary nor any relevant associate of his had received any benefit under the discretionary trust before 14th November 1986, then, as respects any time before that date, the trustees of the settlement concerned shall not be regarded, by reason only of the matters referred to in sub-paragraph (1) above, as having been associates (as defined in section 417(3) and (4)) of the beneficiary.

(3) If, on or after 14th November 1986—

(*a*) the beneficiary ceases to be eligible to benefit under the discretionary trust by reason of—

(i) an irrevocable disclaimer or release executed by him under seal; or

(ii) the irrevocable exercise by the trustees of a power to exclude him from the objects of the trust; and

(*b*) immediately after he so ceases, no relevant associate of his is interested in the shares or obligations of the company which are subject to the trust; and

(*c*) during the period of 12 months ending with the date when the beneficiary so ceases, neither the beneficiary nor any relevant associate of his received any benefit under the trust,

the beneficiary shall not be regarded, by reason only of the matters referred to in sub-paragraph (1) above, as having been interested in the shares or obligations of the company as mentioned in section 417(3)(*c*) at any time during the period of 12 months referred to in paragraph (*c*) above.

(4) In sub-paragraphs (2) and (3) above "relevant associate" has the meaning given to "associate" by subsection (3) or section 417 but with the omission of paragraph (*c*) of that subsection.

(5) Sub-paragraph (3)(*a*)(i) above, in its application to Scotland, shall be construed as if the words "under seal" were omitted.

Former enactment.—FA 1987, Sch. 4, para. 6.

Options etc.

38.—(1) For the purposes of section 187(3)(*a*) a right to acquire shares (however arising) shall be taken to be a right to control them.

(2) Any reference in sub-paragraph (3) below to the shares attributed to an individual is a reference to the shares which, in accordance with section 187(3)(*a*), fall to be brought into account in his case to determine whether their number exceeds a particular percentage of the company's ordinary share capital.

(3) In any case where—

(a) the shares attributed to an individual consist of or include shares which he or any other person has a right to acquire; and

(b) the circumstances are such that, if that right were to be exercised, the shares acquired would be shares which were previously unissued and which the company is contractually bound to issue in the event of the exercise of the right;

then, in determining at any time prior to the exercise of that right whether the number of shares attributed to the individual exceeds a particular percentage of the ordinary share capital of the company, that ordinary share capital shall be taken to be increased by the number of unissued shares referred to in paragraph (b) above.

(4) This paragraph has effect as respects any time after 5th April 1987.

Former enactment.—FA 1987, Sch. 4, para. 7.

Shares held by trustees of approved profit sharing schemes

39. In applying section 187(3), as respects any time before or after the passing of this Act, there shall be disregarded—

(a) the interest of the trustees of an approved profit sharing scheme in any shares which are held by them in accordance with the scheme and have not yet been appropriated to an individual; and

(b) any rights exercisable by those trustees by virtue of that interest.

Former enactment.—FA 1987, Sch. 4, para. 8.

[Shares subject to an employee benefit trust][1]

[**40.**—(1) Where an individual has an interest in shares or obligations of the company as a beneficiary of an employee benefit trust, the trustees shall not be regarded as associates of his by reason only of that interest unless sub-paragraph (3) below applies in relation to him.

(2) In this paragraph "employee benefit trust" has the same meaning as in paragraph 7 of Schedule 8.

(3) This sub-paragraph applies in relation to an individual if at any time on or after 14th March 1989—

(a) the individual, either on his own or with any one or more of his associates, or

(b) any associate of his, with or without other such associates,

has been the beneficial owner of, or able (directly or through the medium of other companies or by any other indirect means) to control, more than 25 per cent., or in the case of a share option scheme which is not a savings-related share option scheme more than 10 per cent., of the ordinary share capital of the company.

(4) Sub-paragraphs (9) to (12) of paragraph 7 of Schedule 8 shall apply for the purposes of this paragraph in relation to an individual as they apply for the purposes of that paragraph in relation to an employee.][1]

Amendments.—[1] This paragraph inserted by FA 1989, s. 65.

SCHEDULE 10

Section 186

FURTHER PROVISIONS RELATING TO PROFIT SHARING SCHEMES

Cross references.—See CGTA 1979, s. 144A(2) (computation of gains on disposal or part disposal of shares in a profit sharing scheme).

Limitations on contractual obligations of participants

1.—(1) Any obligation placed on the participant by virtue of paragraph 2(2) of Schedule 9 shall not prevent the participant from—

(*a*) directing the trustees to accept an offer for any of his shares ("the original shares") if the acceptance or agreement will result in a new holding being equated with the original shares for the purposes of capital gains tax; or

(*b*) directing the trustees to agree to a transaction affecting his shares or such of them as are of a particular class, if the transaction would be entered into pursuant to a compromise, arrangement or scheme applicable to or affecting—

(i) all the ordinary share capital of the company in question or, as the case may be, all the shares of the class in question; or

(ii) all the shares, or all the shares of the class in question, which are held by a class of shareholders identified otherwise than by reference to their employment or their participation in an approved scheme; or

(*c*) directing the trustees to accept an offer of cash, with or without other assets, for his shares if the offer forms part of a general offer which is made to holders of shares of the same class as his or of shares in the same company and which is made in the first instance on a condition such that if it is satisfied the person making the offer will have control of that company, within the meaning of section 416; or

(*d*) agreeing after the expiry of the period of retention to sell the beneficial interest in his shares to the trustees for the same consideration as, in accordance with sub-paragraph (*d*) of paragraph 2(2) of Schedule 9, would be required to be obtained for the shares themselves.

(2) No obligation placed on the participant by virtue of paragraph 2(2)(*c*) of Schedule 9 shall be construed as binding his personal representatives to pay any sum to the trustees.

(3) If, in breach of his obligation under paragraph 2(2)(*b*) of Schedule 9 a participant assigns, charges or otherwise disposes of the beneficial interest in any of his shares, then, as respects those shares, he shall be treated for the purposes of the relevant provisions as if at the time they were appropriated to him he was ineligible to participate in the scheme; and paragraph 6 below shall apply accordingly.

Former enactments.—Sub-para. (1): FA 1978, s. 54(2); CGTA 1979, Sch. 7.
Sub-para. (2): FA 1978, s. 54(1A); FA 1980, s. 46(2).
Sub-para. (3): FA 1978, s. 54(3).

The period of retention

2. For the purposes of any of the relevant provisions, "the period of retention", in relation to any of a participant's shares, means the period beginning on the date on which they are appropriated to him and ending on the second anniversary of that date or, if it is earlier—

(*a*) the date on which the participant ceases to be a director or employee of the grantor or, in the case of a group scheme, a participating company by reason of injury or disability or on account of his being dismissed by reason of redundancy, within the meaning of the Employment Protection (Consolidation) Act 1978 or the Contracts of Employment and Redundancy Payments Act (Northern Ireland) 1965; or

(*b*) the date on which the participant reaches pensionable age; or

(*c*) the date of the participant's death; [or][1]

(*d*) in a case where the participant's shares are redeemable shares in a workers' cooperative, the date on which the participant ceases to be employed by, or by a subsidiary of, the cooperative.

For the purposes of sub-paragraph (*a*) above, in the case of a group scheme, the participant shall not be treated as ceasing to be a director or employee of a participating company until such times as he is no longer a director or employee of any of the participating companies.

Former enactments.—FA 1978, s. 54(4), (5); Employment Protection (Consolidation) Act 1978, Sch. 15, para. 4; FA 1980, s. 46(3); FA 1986, s. 24(3).
Amendments.—[1] Word in para (c) inserted by FA 1988, Sch. 13, para. 9.

The appropriate percentage

3. Subject to paragraph 6(4) below, for the purposes of any of the relevant provisions charging an individual to income tax under Schedule E by reason of the occurrence of an event relating to any of his shares, any reference to "the appropriate percentage" in relation to those shares shall be determined according to the time of that event, as follows—

(a) if the event occurs before the fourth anniversary of the date on which the shares were appropriated to the participant and paragraph (c) below does not apply, the appropriate percentage is 100 per cent.;
(b) if the event occurs on or after the fourth anniversary and before the fifth anniversary of the date on which the shares were appropriated to the participant and paragraph (c) below does not apply, the appropriate percentage is 75 per cent.;
(c) if the participant—

(i) ceases to be a director or employee of the grantor or, in the case of a group scheme, a participating company as mentioned in paragraph 2(a) above, or
(ii) reaches pensionable age,

and the event occurs before the fifth anniversary of the date on which the shares were appropriated to him, the appropriate percentage is 50 per cent.

Former enactments.—FA 1978, s. 54(7); FA 1980, s. 46(5); FA 1985, s. 43(3).

Capital receipts

4.—(1) Money or money's worth is not a capital receipt for the purposes of section 186(3) if or, as the case may be, to the extent that—

(a) it constitutes income in the hands of the recipient for the purposes of income tax; or
(b) it consists of the proceeds of a disposal falling within section 186(4); or
(c) it consists of new shares within the meaning of paragraph 5 below.

(2) If, pursuant to a direction given by or on behalf of the participant or any person in whom the beneficial interest in the participant's shares is for the time being vested, the trustees—

(a) dispose of some of the rights arising under a rights issue, as defined in section 186(8), and
(b) use the proceeds of that disposal to exercise other such rights,

the money or money's worth which constitutes the proceeds of that disposal is not a capital receipt for the purposes of section 186(3).

(3) If, apart from this sub-paragraph, the amount or value of a capital receipt would exceed the sum which, immediately before the entitlement to the receipt arose, was the locked-in value of the shares to which the receipt is referable, section 186(3) shall have effect as if the amount or value of the receipt were equal to that locked-in value.

(4) Section 186(3) does not apply in relation to a capital receipt if the entitlement to it arises after the death of the participant to whose shares it is referable.

Former enactment.—FA 1978, s. 56(2)–(5).

Company reconstructions

5.—(1) This paragraph applies where there occurs in relation to any of a participant's shares ("the original holding") a transaction which results in a new holding being equated with the original holding for the purposes of capital gains tax; and any such transaction is referred to below as a "company reconstruction".

(2) Where an issue of shares of any of the following descriptions (in respect of which a charge to income tax arises) is made as part of a company reconstruction, those shares shall be treated for the purposes of this paragraph as not forming part of the new holding, that is to say—

(a) redeemable shares or securities issued as mentioned in section 209(2)(c);
(b) share capital issued in circumstances such that section 210(1) applies; and
(c) share capital to which section 249 applies.

(3) In this paragraph—

"corresponding shares", in relation to any new shares, means those shares in respect of which the new shares are issued or which the new shares otherwise represent;

"new shares" means shares comprised in the new holding which were issued in respect of, or otherwise represent, shares comprised in the original holding; and

"original holding" has the meaning given by sub-paragraph (1) above.

(4) Subject to the following provisions of this paragraph, in relaton to a profit sharing scheme, references in the relevant provisions to a participant's shares shall be construed, after the time of the company reconstruction, as being or, as the case may be, as including references to any new shares, and for the purposes of the relevant provisions—

(a) a company reconstruction shall be treated as not involving a disposal of shares comprised in the original holding;
(b) the date on which any new shares are to be treated as having been appropriated to the participant shall be that on which the corresponding shares were appropriated; and
(c) the conditions in paragraphs 10 to 12 and 14 of Schedule 9 shall be treated as fulfilled with respect to any new shares if they were (or were treated as) fulfilled with respect to the corresponding shares.

(5) In relation to shares comprised in the new holding, section 186(5) shall apply as if the references in that subsection to the initial market value of the shares were references to their locked-in value immediately after the company reconstruction, which shall be determined as follows—

(a) ascertain the aggregate amount of locked-in value immediately before the reconstruction of those shares comprised in the original holding which had at that time the same locked-in value; and
(b) distribute that amount *pro rata* among—
  (i) such of those shares as remains in the new holding, and
  (ii) any new shares in relation to which those shares are the corresponding shares, according to their market value immediately after the date of their reconstruction;

and section 186(5)(a) shall apply only to capital receipts after the date of the reconstruction.

(6) For the purposes of the relevant provisions if, as part of a company reconstruction, trustees become entitled to a capital receipt, their entitlement to the capital receipt shall be taken to arise before the new holding comes into being and, for the purposes of sub-paragraph (5) above, before the date on which the locked-in value of any shares comprised in the original holding falls to be ascertained.

(7) In the context of a new holding, any reference in this paragraph to shares includes securities and rights of any description which form part of the new holding for the purposes of Chapter II of Part IV of the 1979 Act.

Former enactments.—FA 1978, s. 57; CGTA 1979, Sch. 7.

Excess or unauthorised shares

6.—(1) This paragraph applies in any case where—

(a) the total amount of the initial market value of all the shares which are appropriated to an individual in any one year of assessment (whether under a single approved profit sharing scheme or under two or more such schemes) exceeds the relevant amount; or
(b) the trustees of an approved profit sharing scheme appropriate shares to an individual at a time when he is ineligible to participate in the scheme by virtue of paragraph 8 or 35 of Schedule 9.

(2) In this paragraph—

"excess shares" means any share which caused the relevant amount to be exceeded and any share appropriated after that amount was exceeded; and

"unauthorised shares" means any share appropriated as mentioned in sub-paragraph (1)(b) above.

(3) For the purposes of sub-paragraph (1)(a) above, if a number of shares is appropriated to an individual at the same time under two or more approved profit sharing schemes, the same proportion of the shares appropriated at that time under each scheme shall be regarded as being appropriated before the relevant amount is exceeded.

(4) For the purposes of any of the relevant provisions charging an individual to income tax under Schedule E by reason of the occurrence of an event relating to any of his shares—

(*a*) the appropriate percentage in relation to excess or unauthorised shares shall in every case be 100 per cent.; and
(*b*) without prejudice to section 187(8), the event shall be treated as relating to shares which are not excess or unauthorised shares before shares which are.

(5) Excess or unauthorised shares which have not been disposed of before the release date or, if it is earlier, the date of the death of the participant whose shares they are, shall be treated for the purposes of the relevant provisions as having been disposed of by the trustees immediately before the release date or, as the case may require, the date of the participant's death, for a consideration equal to their market value at that time.

(6) The locked-in value at any time of any excess or unauthorised shares shall be their market value at that time.

(7) Where there has been a company reconstruction to which paragraph 5 above applies, a new share (within the meaning of that paragraph) shall be treated as an excess or unauthorised share if the corresponding share (within the meaning of that paragraph) or, if there was more than one corresponding share, each of them was an excess or unauthorised share.

Former enactments.—FA 1978, s. 58; FA 1983, s. 25(1).

PAYE deduction of tax

7.—(1) Subject to sub-paragraphs (4) and (5) below, where the trustees of an approved profit sharing scheme receive a sum of money which constitutes (or forms part of)—

(*a*) the proceeds of a disposal of shares falling within section 186(4), or
(*b*) a capital receipt,

in respect of which a participant in the scheme is chargeable to income tax under Schedule E in accordance with section 186, the trustees shall pay out of that sum of money to the company specified in sub-paragraph (3) below an amount equal to that on which income tax is so payable; and the company shall then pay over that amount to the participant but in so doing shall make a P.A.Y.E. deduction.

(2) Where a participant disposes of his beneficial interest in any of his shares to the trustees of the scheme and the trustees are deemed by virtue of section 186(9) to have disposed of the shares in question, this paragraph shall apply as if the consideration payable by the trustees to the participant on the disposal had been received by the trustees as the proceeds of disposal of shares falling within section 186(4).

(3) The company to which the payment mentioned in sub-paragraph (1) above is to be made is the company—

(*a*) of which the participant is an employee or director at the time the trustees receive the sum of money referred to in that sub-paragraph, and
(*b*) whose employees are at that time eligible (subject to the terms of the scheme and Schedule 9) to be participants in the approved profit sharing scheme concerned,

and if there is more than one company which falls within paragraphs (*a*) and (*b*) above, such one of those companies as the Board may direct.

(4) Where the trustees of an approved profit sharing scheme receive a sum of money to which sub-paragraph (1) above applies but—

(*a*) there is no company which falls within paragraphs (*a*) and (*b*) of sub-paragraph (3) above, or
(*b*) the Board is of opinion that it is impracticable for the company which falls within those paragraphs (or, as the case may be, any of them) to make a P.A.Y.E. deduction and accordingly direct that this sub-paragraph shall apply,

then, in paying over to the participant the proceeds of the disposal or the capital receipt, the trustees shall make a P.A.Y.E. deduction in respect of an amount equal to that on which income tax is payable as mentioned in sub-paragraph (1) above as if the participant were a former employee of the trustees.

(5) Where the trustees of an approved profit sharing scheme receive a sum of money to which sub-paragraph (1) above applies and the Board direct that this sub-paragraph shall apply—

(*a*) the trustees shall make the payment mentioned in that sub-paragraph to the company specified in the Board's direction; and
(*b*) that company shall pay over that amount to the participant but in so doing shall make a P.A.Y.E. deduction, and for that purpose if the participant is not an employee of that company he shall be treated as a former employee;

but no such direction shall be given except with the consent of the trustees, the company or companies (if any) specified in sub-paragraph (3) above and the company specified in the direction.

(6) Where, in accordance with this paragraph any person is required to make a P.A.Y.E. deduction in respect of any amount, that amount shall be treated for the purposes of section 203 and any regulations made under that section as an amount of income payable to the recipient and assessable to income tax under Schedule E, and, accordingly, such deduction shall be made as is required by those regulations.

(7) Where, in connection with a transfer of a participant's shares to which sub-paragraph (*c*) of paragraph 2(2) of Schedule 9 applies, the trustees receive such a sum as is referred to in that sub-paragraph, that sum shall be treated for the purposes of the Income Tax Acts—

(*a*) as a sum deducted by the trustees pursuant to a requirement to make a P.A.Y.E. deduction under sub-paragraph (4) above; and
(*b*) as referable to the income tax to which, as a result of the transfer, the participant is chargeable by virtue of section 186(4).

(8) Unless the Board otherwise direct, in the application of this paragraph to a sum of money which constitutes or forms part of the proceeds of a disposal of, or a capital receipt referable to, excess or unauthorised shares (within the meaning of paragraph 6 above), the trustees shall determine the amount of the payment mentioned in sub-paragraph (1) above or, as the case may be, the amount of the P.A.Y.E. deduction to be made under sub-paragraph (4) above as if the shares were not excess or unauthorised shares.

Former enactments.—FA 1978, s. 59; FA 1980, s. 46(8); FA 1987, Sch. 15, para. 11(3).

SCHEDULE 11

Section 188

RELIEF AS RESPECTS TAX ON PAYMENTS ON RETIREMENT OR REMOVAL FROM OFFICE OR EMPLOYMENT

PART I
GENERAL PROVISIONS

Preliminary

1. Relief shall be allowed in accordance with the following provisions of this Schedule in respect of tax chargeable by virtue of section 148, where a claim is made under section 188(6).

Former enactment.—TA 1970, Sch. 8, para. 1.

2.—(1) A person shall not be entitled to relief under this Schedule in so far as such relief, together with any personal relief allowed to him, would reduce the amount of income on which he is chargeable below the amount of income tax on which he is entitled to charge against any other person, or to deduct, retain or satisfy out of any payment which he is liable to make to any other person.

(2) In sub-paragraph (1) above "personal relief" means relief under Chapter I of Part VII.

Former enactment.—TA 1970, Sch. 8, para. 2.

Relief by reduction of sums chargeable

3. In computing the charge to tax in respect of a payment chargeable to tax under section 148, being a payment made in respect of an office or employment in which the service of the holder includes foreign service, there shall be deducted from the payment a sum which bears to the amount which would be chargeable to tax apart from this paragraph the same proportion as the length of the foreign service bears to the length of the service before the relevant date.

Former enactment.—TA 1970, Sch. 8, para. 6.

Relief by reduction of tax

4.—*(1) Subject to sub-paragraph (2) below, in the case of any payment in respect of which tax is chargeable under section 148, the following relief shall be allowed by way of deduction from the tax chargeable by virtue of that section, that is to say, there shall be ascertained—*

(a) the amount of tax which would be chargeable apart from this paragraph in respect of the income of the holder or past holder of the office or employment for the chargeable period of which the payment is treated as income;
(b) the amount of tax which would have been so chargeable if the payment had not been made;

and the amount to be deducted shall be half the difference between the amount ascertained at (a) and the amount ascertained at (b).

(2) In the case of a payment which exceeds £50,000, this paragraph applies as if it were a payment of £50,000 exactly.

Former enactments.—TA 1970, Sch. 8, para. 7; FA 1981, s. 31(3); FA 1982, s. 43(1).
Amendments.—This paragraph repealed by FA 1988, s. 74(2), (3) and Sch. 14, Pt. IV in relation to any payment treated by s. 148(4) of this Act as income received after 5 April 1988 unless a notice is given in relation to it under para. 12 of this Schedule.

5.—*(1) Subject to sub-paragraph (2) below, in the case of a payment which exceeds £50,000 and in respect of which tax is chargeable under section 148, the following relief shall be allowed by way of deduction from the tax chargeable by virtue of that section, that is to say, there shall be ascertained—*

(a) the amount of tax which would be chargeable apart from this paragraph and paragraph 4 above in respect of the income of the holder or past holder of the office or employment for the chargeable period of which the payment is treated as income; and
(b) the amount of tax which would have been so chargeable if the amount of the payment had been £50,000 exactly;

and the amount to be deducted shall be one-quarter of the difference between the amount ascertained at (a) and the amount ascertained at (b).

(2) In the case of a payment which exceeds £75,000, this paragraph applies as if it were a payment of £75,000 exactly.

(3) Any relief allowed by virtue of this paragraph shall be in addition to that allowed by virtue of paragraph 4 above.

Former enactments.—TA 1970, Sch. 8, para. 7A; FA 1982, s. 43(1).
Amendments.—This paragraph repealed by FA 1988, s. 74(2), (3) and Sch. 14, Pt. IV in relation to any payment treated by s. 148(4) of this Act as income received after 5 April 1988 unless a notice is given in relation to it under para. 12 of this Schedule.

6. Where tax is chargeable under section 148 in respect of two or more payments to or in respect of the same person in respect of the same office or employment and is so chargeable for the same chargeable period, those payments shall be treated for the purposes of paragraphs 4 and 5 above as a single payment of an amount equal to their aggregate amount.

Former enactments.—TA 1970, Sch. 8, para. 10; FA 1986, s. 45(2).
Amendments.—This paragraph repealed by FA 1988, s. 74(2), (3) and Sch. 14, Pt. IV in relation to any payment treated by s. 148(4) of this Act as income received after 5 April 1988 unless a notice is given in relation to it under para. 12 of this Schedule.

7. Where tax is chargeable under section 148 in respect of two or more payments to or in respect of the same person in respect of different offices or employments and is so chargeable for the same chargeable period, paragraphs 4 to 6 above shall apply as if those payments were made in respect of the same office or employment.

Former enactment.—TA 1970, Sch. 8, para. 11.
Amendments.—This paragraph repealed by FA 1988, s. 74(2), (3) and Sch. 14, Pt. IV in relation to any payment treated by s. 148(4) of this Act as income received after 5 April 1988 unless a notice is given in relation to it under para. 12 of this Schedule.

Supplemental

8. Any reference in this Schedule to the emoluments of an office or employment is a reference to those emoluments exclusive of any payment chargeable to tax under section 148; and in calculating for any purpose of this Schedule the amount of such emoluments—

(a) there shall be included any balancing charge to which the holder of the office or employment is liable under section 33 of the 1968 Act or under Chapter I of Part III of the Finance Act 1971 ("the 1971 Act"), and
(b) there shall be deducted any allowances under Chapter II of Part I of the 1968 Act or Chapter I of Part III of the 1971 Act, and any allowances for expenses under section 198 or 201, to which he is entitled,

and any such charges or allowances for a chargeable period shall, for the purpose of ascertaining the amount of the emoluments for any year of service, be treated as accruing from day to day, and shall be apportioned in respect of time accordingly.

Former enactments.—TA 1970, Sch. 8, para. 14; FA 1971, Sch. 8, para. 16.

9. In this Schedule "the relevant date" means, in relation to a payment not being a payment in commutation of annual or other periodical payments, the date of the termination or change in respect of which it is made and, in relation to a payment in commutation of annual or other periodical payments, the date of the termination or change in respect of which those payments would have been made.

Former enactment.—TA 1970, Sch. 8, para. 15.

10. In this Schedule, "foreign service", in relation to an office or employment, means—

(a) service before the year 1974–75 such that tax was not chargeable in respect of the emoluments of the office or employment—

(i) in the case of the year 1956–57 or any subsequent chargeable period, under Case I of Schedule E;

(ii) in the case of any preceding year of assessment, under Schedule E; or

(b) service after the year 1973–74 such that the emoluments from the office or employment were not chargeable under Case I of Schedule E (or would not have been so chargeable, had there been any) or that a deduction equal to their whole amount was or would have been allowable under paragraph 1 of Schedule 2 to the Finance Act 1974, paragraph 1 of Schedule 7 to the Finance Act 1977 or section 193(1) in charging them.

Former enactments.—TA 1970, Sch. 8, para. 16; FA 1974, s. 21(4); FA 1977, s. 31(3).

11. Any reference in this Schedule to the amount of tax to which a person is or would be chargeable is a reference to the amount of tax to which he is or would be chargeable either by assessment or by deduction.

Former enactment.—TA 1970, Sch. 8, para. 17.

PART II

PAYMENTS IN PURSUANCE OF PRE-10TH MARCH 1981 OBLIGATIONS

12. Where a payment is made in pursuance of an obligation incurred before 10th March 1981, the person chargeable to tax in respect of it may, by notice given to the inspector within six years after the year of assessment in which the payment is made, elect that Part I of this Schedule shall have effect in relation to the payment subject to the modifications contained in the following provisions of this Part, and those provisions shall have effect accordingly (and not otherwise).

Former enactment.—FA 1981, s. 31(7).

13. The following paragraphs shall be inserted immediately before paragraph 3—

"**2A.** In computing the charge to tax in respect of a payment chargeable to tax under section 148, not being a payment of compensation for loss of office, there shall be deducted from the payment a sum equal to the amount (if any) by which the standard capital superannuation benefit for the office or employment in respect of which the payment is made exceeds £10,000.

2B.—(1) In this Schedule "the standard capital superannuation benefit", in relation to an office or employment, means a sum arrived at as follows, that is to say—

(a) there shall be ascertained the average for one year of the holder's emoluments from the office or employment for the last three years of his service before the relevant date (or for the whole period of his service if less than three years);

(b) one-twentieth of the amount ascertained at (a) shall be multiplied by the whole number of complete years of the service of the holder in the office or employment; and

(c) there shall be deducted from the product at (b) a sum equal to the amount, or, as the case may be, to the value at the relevant date, of any lump sum (not chargeable to tax) received or receivable by the holder in respect of the office or employment in pursuance of any such scheme or fund as was described in section 221(1) and (2) of the 1970 Act or is described in section 596.

(2) In sub-paragraph (1)(c) above the reference to a lump sum receivable by the holder includes a reference to a lump sum that would be receivable by him if he had exercised or refrained from exercising (with any necessary consent) any option or other right conferred on him by the rules of the scheme or fund.

2C. Where tax is chargeable under section 148 in respect of two or more payments to which paragraph 2A above applies, being payments made to or in respect of the same person in respect of the same office or employment or in respect of different offices or employments held under the same employer or under associated employers, then—

(a) paragraph 2A above shall apply as if those payments were a single payment of an amount equal to their aggregate amount and, where they are made in respect of different offices or employments, as if the standard capital superannuation benefit were an amount equal to the sum of the standard capital superannuation benefits for those offices or employments, and

(b) where the payments are treated as income of different chargeable periods, the relief to be granted under that paragraph in respect of a payment chargeable for any such period shall be the amount by which the relief computed in accordance with the preceding provision in respect of that payment and any payments chargeable for previous chargeable periods exceeds the relief in respect of the last mentioned payments;

and where the standard capital superannuation benefit for an office or employment in respect of which two or more of the payments are made is not the same in relation to each of those payments, it shall be treated for the purpose of this paragraph as equal to the higher or highest of those benefits."

Former enactments.—TA 1970, Sch. 8, paras. 3, 4, 5; FA 1970, Sch. 5, Pt. III, para. 12(6); FA 1971, Sch. 3, para. 12(6); FA 1978, s. 24(1), (2).

14. In paragraph 3, after the words "from the payment" there shall be inserted the words "(in addition to any deduction allowed under the preceding provisions of this Schedule)".

Former enactment.—TA 1970, Sch. 8, para. 6.

15. In paragraph 4(1), for the words following sub-paragraph (*b*) there shall be substituted the following words—

"(*c*) the difference between the respective amounts of tax which would be so chargeable on the assumptions—

(i) that the appropriate fraction only of the payment (after deducting any relief applicable thereto under the preceding provisions of this Schedule) had been made, and

(ii) that no part of the payment had been made,

and disregarding, in each case, any other emoluments of the office or employment,

and the amount to be deducted shall be the difference between the amount ascertained at (*a*) and the sum of the amount ascertained at (*b*) and the appropriate multiple of the difference ascertained at (*c*)."

Former enactment.—TA 1970, Sch. 8, para. 7.

16. The following paragraphs shall be inserted after paragraph 5—

"**5A.**—(1) Where the income of the holder or past holder of the office or employment for the chargeable period of which the payment is treated as income includes income, income tax on which he is entitled to charge against any other person, or to deduct, retain or satisfy out of any payment which he is liable to make to any other person, the amounts referred to in sub-paragraphs (*a*) to (*c*) of paragraph 4 above shall be calculated as if that tax were not chargeable in respect of that income.

(2) Where for any year of assessment an individual claims relief under paragraph 4 above, and also under section 550 or Schedule 2, or under both that section and that Schedule, then, in computing the relief under paragraph 4 above, his income shall be deemed to include—

(*a*) in respect of any amount which would otherwise be included therein by virtue of section 547(1)(*a*), no greater amount than the appropriate fraction thereof within the meaning of section 550, and

(*b*) in respect of any chargeable sum within the meaning of Schedule 2 (including two or more sums treated for the purposes of paragraph 3 of that Schedule as one chargeable sum), no greater amount than the balance (if any) of the yearly equivalent thereof remaining after the making of any deduction required by that paragraph.

5B. In this Schedule "the appropriate fraction" (except in paragraph 5A(2)(*a*)) and "the appropriate multiple", in relation to any payment, mean respectively—

(*a*) where the payment is not a payment of compensation for loss of office, one-sixth and six, and

(*b*) where the payment is a payment of compensation for loss of office, one divided by the relevant number of years of unexpired service, and that number of years,

and for the purposes of this paragraph "the relevant number of years of unexpired service" means the number of complete years taken into account in calculating the amount of the payment, being years for which the holder of the office or employment would have been entitled (otherwise than by virtue of arrangements made in contemplation of his retirement or removal or of any relevant change in the functions or emoluments of the office or employment) to retain the office or employment or its full emoluments, and where the period so taken into account is less than one complete year or exceeds an exact number of years, it shall be treated for the purposes of this paragraph as one complete year or as the next higher number of complete years, as the case may be."

Former enactment.—TA 1970, Sch. 8, paras. 8, 9.

17. The following proviso shall be added at the end of paragraph 6—

"Provided that, where the appropriate fraction and the appropriate multiple are not the same for each of the payments, the calculations of relief under paragraph 4 above shall be made separately in relation to each payment or payments having a different appropriate fraction and multiple, and in any such calculation—

(*a*) any payment for which the appropriate multiple is lower shall be left out of account for all the purposes of that paragraph, and

(*b*) in ascertaining the difference at (*c*) of that paragraph it shall be assumed that the appropriate fraction only of any payment for which the appropriate multiple is higher had been made,

and the relief to be allowed shall be the sum of the reliefs so calculated in respect of the payments respectively."

Former enactment.—TA 1970, Sch. 8, para. 10.

18. The following words shall be added at the end of paragraph 7—

"and as if any emoluments of any of those offices or employments were emoluments of the same office or employment."

Former enactment.—TA 1970, Sch. 8, para. 11.

19. The following paragraph shall be inserted after paragraph 8—

"**8A.** In this Schedule "payment of compensation for loss of office" means a payment made—

(*a*) in pursuance of an order of a court in proceedings for wrongful dismissal or otherwise for breach of contract of employment, or by way of settlement of such proceedings or of a claim in respect of which such proceedings could have been brought, or

(*b*) by way of compensation for the extinguishment of any right the infringement of which would be actionable in such proceedings,

and any question whether, and to what extent, a payment is or is not a payment of compensation for loss of office shall be determined according to all the circumstances and not (or not exclusively) by reference to the terms on which it is expressed to be made."

Former enactment.—TA 1970, Sch. 8, para. 13.

SCHEDULE 12
Section 193

FOREIGN EARNINGS

1. This Schedule shall have effect for the purpose of supplementing the provisions of section 193(1).

Emoluments eligible for relief

2.—(1) This paragraph has effect where a deduction falls to be allowed under section 193(1) in respect of the emoluments from an employment ("the relevant employment") for a year of assessment in which the duties of—

(*a*) the relevant employment; or

(*b*) any other employment or employments held by the person concerned which are associated with the relevant employment,

are not performed wholly outside the United Kingdom.

(2) The amount of the [emoluments for the year of assessment from the relevant employment in respect of which such a deduction is allowed][1] shall not exceed such proportion of the emoluments for that year from the relevant employment and the other employment or employments (if any) as is shown to be reasonable having regard to the nature of and time devoted to the duties performed outside and in the United Kingdom respectively and to all other relevant circumstances.

(3) For the purposes of this paragraph an employment is associated with another if they are with the same person or with persons associated with each other and—

(*a*) a company is associated with another company if one of them has control of the other within the meaning of section 416 or both of them are under the control within the meaning of that section of the same persons or persons,

(*b*) an individual or partnership is associated with another person (whether or not a company) if one of them has control of the other within the meaning of section 840 or both are under the control within the meaning of that section of the same person or persons;

but paragraph (*b*) above shall not be construed as requiring an individual to be treated in any circumstances as under the control of another person.

Former enactment.—FA 1977, Sch. 7, para. 4(1), (2), (5).
Amendments.—[1] Words in sub-para. (2) substituted by FA 1989, s. 42(1), (5).

Qualifying periods

3.—(1) For the purposes of section 193(1) a qualifying period is a period of consecutive days which either—

(*a*) consists entirely of days of absence from the United Kingdom; or

(*b*) consists partly of such days and partly of days included by virtue of sub-paragraph (2) below.

(2) Where, in the case of any person, a period consisting entirely of days of absence from the United Kingdom ("the relevant period") comes to an end and there have previously been one or more qualifying periods, the relevant period and the (or, if more than one, the last) qualifying period together with the intervening days between those periods shall be treated as a single qualifying period provided that—

(*a*) there are no more than 62 intervening days, and

(*b*) the number of days in the resulting period which are not days of absence from the United Kingdom does not exceed one-sixth of the total number of days in that period.

[(2A) In relation to emoluments from employment as a seafarer, sub-paragraph (2) above shall have effect—

(*a*) as if the number of days specified in paragraph (*a*) were 90 instead of 62, and

(*b*) as if the fraction specified in paragraph (*b*) were one quarter instead of one sixth;

and for the purposes of this sub-paragraph "employment as a seafarer" means employment consisting of the performance of duties on a ship (or of such duties and of others incidental to them).][1]

(3) For the purposes of section 193(1) the emoluments from an employment attributable to a qualifying period include any emoluments from that employment for a period of leave immediately following that period but not so as to make any emoluments for one year of assessment emoluments for another.

Former enactment.—FA 1977, Sch. 7, para. 1(2), (3), (4).
Amendments.—[1] Sub-para. (2A) inserted by FA 1988, s. 67 with effect from the year 1988–89; but the relevant period and the earlier qualifying period referred to in sub-para. (2) above shall not be treated as a single period if none of the intervening days falls after 5 April 1988.

Supplementary

4. For the purposes of this Schedule a person shall not be regarded as absent from the United Kingdom on any day unless he is so absent at the end of it.

Former enactment.—FA 1977, Sch. 7, para. 6.

5. Notwithstanding section 132(4)(*b*), there shall be treated for the purposes of section 193(1) and this Schedule as performed outside the United Kingdom any duties which a person performs on a vessel or aircraft engaged on—

(*a*) a voyage or journey beginning or ending outside the United Kingdom (but exclusive of any part of it which begins and ends in the United Kingdom); or
(*b*) any part beginning or ending outside the United Kingdom of a voyage or journey which begins and ends in the United Kingdom;

and for the purposes of this paragraph any area designated under section 1(7) of the Continental Shelf Act 1964 shall be treated as part of the United Kingdom.

Former enactment.—FA 1977, Sch. 7, para. 7.

6. Where an employment is in substance one the duties of which fall in the year of assessment to be performed in the United Kingdom, then, for the purposes of section 193(1), there shall be treated as so performed any duties performed outside the United Kingdom the performance of which is merely incidental to the performance of other duties in the United Kingdom.

Former enactment.—FA 1977, Sch. 7, para. 8.

7. In this Schedule references to an employment include references to an office.

Former enactment.—FA 1977, Sch. 7, para. 11.

SCHEDULE 13

Sections 238(5), 241(4)

COLLECTION OF ADVANCE CORPORATION TAX

Duty to make returns

1.—(1) A company shall for each of its accounting periods make, in accordance with this Schedule, returns to the collector of the franked payments made and franked investment income received by it in that period and of the advance corporation tax (if any) payable by it in respect of those payments.

(2) A return shall be made for—

(*a*) each complete quarter falling within the accounting period, that is to say, each of the periods of three months ending with 31st March, 30th June, 30th September or 31st December which falls within that period:

(*b*) each part of the accounting period which is not a complete quarter and ends on the first (or only), or begins immediately after the last (or only), of those dates which falls within the accounting period;

(*c*) if none of those dates falls within the accounting period, the whole accounting period.

(3) A return for any period for which a return is required to be made under this paragraph ("a return period") shall be made within 14 days from the end of that period.

(4) Subject to paragraphs 4(2) and 7(3) below, no return need be made under this Schedule by a company for any period in which it has made no franked payments.

Former enactment.—FA 1972, Sch. 14, para. 1.

Contents of return

2.—(1) Subject to paragraph 7(2) below, the return made by a company for any return period shall show—

(*a*) the amount of the franked payments made by it in that period;
(*b*) the amount of franked investment income, if any, received by it in that period, and
(*c*) if any advance corporation tax is payable in respect of those payments, the amount thereof.

(2) The return shall specify whether any amount of franked payments is included under paragraph (*a*) of sub-paragraph (1) above in consequence of the giving of a notice under section 247(3) and, if so, the amount so included.

(3) For the purposes of paragraph (*b*) of sub-paragraph (1) above the amount of franked investment income received by a company in a return period shall be treated as including the excess, if any, of—

(*a*) any surplus of franked investment income carried forward to the accounting period for which the return is made; and
(*b*) any amount of franked investment income received by the company in that accounting period but before the beginning of the return period,

over the amount of any franked payments made by the company in that accounting period but before the beginning of the return period.

(4) For the purposes of paragraph (*c*) of sub-paragraph (1) above advance corporation tax shall be payable in respect of franked payments made in a return period if—

(*a*) the amount shown under paragraph (*a*) of that sub-paragraph exceeds the amount shown under paragraph (*b*) of that sub-paragraph, or
(*b*) no amount is shown under paragraph (*b*) of that sub-paragraph;

and the amount of that tax shall be calculated at the rate of advance corporation tax in force for the financial year in which the return period ends on an amount which, when that tax is added to it, is equal to that excess or, if no amount is shown under sub-paragraph (1)(*b*) above, to the amount shown under sub-paragraph (1)(*a*) above.

Former enactment.—FA 1972, Sch. 14, para. 2.

Payment of tax

3.—(1) Subject to paragraph 7(2) below, advance corporation tax in respect of franked payments required to be included in a return under this Schedule shall be due at the time by which the return for that period is to be made, and advance corporation tax so due shall be payable without the making of any assessment.

(2) Advance corporation tax which has become so due may be assessed on the company (whether or not it has been paid when the assessment is made) if that tax, or any part of it, is not paid on or before the due date.

(3) If it appears to the inspector that there is a franked payment which ought to have been and has not been included in a return, or if the inspector is dissatisfied with any return, he may make an assessment on the company to the best of his judgment; and any advance corporation tax due under an assessment made by virtue of this sub-paragraph shall be treated for the purposes of interest on unpaid tax as having been payable at the time when it would have been payable if a correct return had been made.

Former enactment.—FA 1972, Sch. 14, para. 3.

Receipt of franked investment income after payment of advance corporation tax

4.—(1) This paragraph shall have effect where—

(*a*) a return has been made of franked payments made in any return period falling within an accounting period and advance corporation tax has been paid in respect of those payments; and
(*b*) the company receives franked investment income after the end of the return period but before the end of the accounting period.

(2) The company shall make a return under paragraph 1 above for the return period in which the franked investment income is received whether or not it has made any franked payments in that period, and, subject to sub-paragraph (3) below, shall be entitled to repayment of any advance corporation tax paid (and not repaid) in respect of franked payments made in the accounting period in question.

(3) If no franked payments were made by the company in the return period for which a return is made by virtue of sub-paragraph (2) above the amount of the repayment shall not exceed the amount of the tax credit comprised in the franked investment income received; and in any other case the repayment shall not exceed the amount of the tax credit comprised in so much of that franked investment income, if any, as exceeds the amount of the franked payments made in that return period.

Former enactment.—FA 1972, Sch. 14, para. 4.

Claims for set-off in respect of franked investment income received by a company

5. Where under paragraph 2 or 4 above franked investment income received by a company falls to be taken into account in determining—

(*a*) whether advance corporation tax is payable or repayable; or
(*b*) the amount of such tax which is payable or repayable,

the inclusion of that franked investment income in the appropriate return shall be treated as a claim by the company to have it so taken into account, and any such claim shall be supported by such evidence as the inspector may reasonably require.

Former enactment.—FA 1972, Sch. 14, para. 5.

6.—(1) Where a claim has been made under paragraph 5 above no proceedings for collecting tax which would fall to be discharged if the claim were allowed shall be instituted pending the final determination of the claim, but this sub-paragraph shall not affect the date when the tax is due.

(2) When the claim is finally determined any tax underpaid in consequence of sub-paragraph (1) above shall be paid.

(3) Where proceedings are instituted for collecting tax assessed, or interest on tax assessed, under any provision of this Schedule, effect shall not be given to any claim made after the institution of the proceedings so as to affect or delay the collection or recovery of the tax charged by the assessment or of interest thereon, until the claim has been finally determined.

(4) When the claim is finally determined any tax overpaid in consequence of sub-paragraph (3) above shall be repaid.

(5) References in this paragraph to proceedings for the collection of tax include references to proceedings by way of distraint or poinding for tax.

Former enactment.—FA 1972, Sch. 14, para. 6.

Qualifying distributions which are not payments and payments of uncertain nature

7.—(1) This paragraph applies to—
   (*a*) any qualifying distribution which is not a payment; and
   (*b*) any payment in respect of which the company making it would be liable to pay advance corporation tax if, but only if, it amounted to or involved a qualifying distribution and it is not in the circumstances clear whether or how far it does so.

(2) No amount shall be shown in respect of the qualifying distribution or payment under paragraph 2(1)(*a*) or (*c*) above and paragraph 3(1) above shall not apply to the payment of advance corporation tax in respect thereof.

(3) Particulars of the qualifying distribution or payment shall be given separately in the return for the return period in which it is made and if, apart from that distribution or payment, no franked payment is made in that period, a return containing those particulars shall be made for that period under paragraph 1 above.

(4) Any advance corporation tax payable in respect of the qualifying distribution or payment shall be assessed on the company and shall be so assessed without regard to any franked investment income received by the company but—
   (*a*) relief shall be given from the tax assessed (by discharge thereof) to the extent, if any, to which that tax exceeds the tax that would have been payable if the amount of the franked payment comprising the qualifying distribution or payment, calculated on the amount or value thereof shown in the assessment, had been included in the return under sub-paragraph (1)(*a*) of paragraph 2 above and the tax had been calculated in accordance with sub-paragraph (4) of that paragraph; and
   (*b*) for the purposes of the application of sub-paragraph (3) of that paragraph to any subsequent return period, the amount of that franked payment shall be taken to be the amount so calculated.

Former enactment.—FA 1972, Sch. 14, para. 7.

Items included in error

8. Where any item has been included in a return under this Schedule as a franked payment made or as franked investment income received by a company but that item should have been included in a return or claim under Schedule 16, the inspector may make any such assessments, adjustments or set-offs as may be required for securing that the resulting liabilities to tax (including interest on unpaid tax) whether of the company or of any other person are the same as they would have been if the item had been included in the right return or claim.

Former enactment.—FA 1972, Sch. 14, para. 8.

Qualifying distribution made otherwise than in an accounting period

9. Where a company makes a qualifying distribution on a date which does not fall within an accounting period the company shall make a return of that distribution within 14 days from that date, and the advance corporation tax in respect thereof shall be due at the time by which the return is to be made, except where the distribution is not a payment in which case the advance corporation tax shall be assessed on the company.

Former enactment.—FA 1972, Sch. 14, para. 9.

Assessments and due date of tax

10.—(1) All the provisions of the Corporation Tax Acts as to the time within which an assessment may be made, so far as they refer or relate to the accounting period for which an assessment is made, or the accounting period to which an assessment relates, shall apply in relation to an assessment under this Schedule notwithstanding that, under this Schedule, the assessment may be said to relate to a quarter or other period which is not an accounting period; and the provisions of [section 36]¹ of the Management Act as to the circumstances in which an assessment may be made out of time shall apply accordingly on the footing that any such assessment relates to the accounting period in which the quarter or other period ends or, in the case of an assessment under paragraph 9 above, to an accounting period ending on the date on which the distribution is made.

(2) Advance corporation tax assessed on a company under this Schedule shall be due within 14 days after the issue of the notice of assessment (unless due earlier under paragraph 3(1) or 9 above).

(3) Sub-paragraph (2) above has effect subject to any appeal against the assessment, but no such appeal shall affect the date when tax is due under paragraph 3(1) or 9 above.

(4) On the determination of an appeal against an assessment under this Schedule any tax overpaid shall be repaid.

(5) Any tax assessable under any one or more of the provisions of this Schedule may be included in one assessment if the tax so included is all due on the same date.

Former enactment.—FA 1972, Sch. 14, para. 10.
Amendments.—¹ Words in sub-para. (1) substituted by FA 1989, s. 149(3)(c).

SCHEDULE 14

Section 266(12)

PROVISIONS ANCILLARY TO SECTION 266

PART I
MODIFICATION OF SECTION 266 IN CERTAIN CASES

Husband and wife

1.—(1) The references in section 266 to an individual's spouse shall include any person who was that individual's spouse at the time the insurance or contract was made, unless the marriage was dissolved before 6th April 1979.

(2) Where an election under section 287 is in force, the relief to which either the husband or the wife is entitled under section 266 in respect of an insurance or contract on the life of the other or made by the other shall not be affected by section 287(4), (5) or (6).

(3) Where throughout a year of assessment a woman is a married woman living with her husband, then—

(*a*) if no election under section 283 is in force, section 274 and paragraph 6 below shall apply as if any relief to which the wife is entitled under section 266 were relief to which the husband is entitled; and

(*b*) if such an election is in force, section 274 and paragraph 6 below shall apply separately to the amounts paid by each of them, but as if for the limit specified in that section there were substituted, in relation to each of them, a limit of £750 or one-twelfth of their total income, whichever is the greater, plus any amount by which the payments in respect of which relief can be given to the other fall short of the limit so substituted.

Former enactment.—FA 1976, Sch. 4, paras. 8, 9, 10.
Note.—See **Prospective Legislation Notes** (Married Couples).

Premiums payable to friendly societies and industrial assurance companies

2.—(1) This paragraph applies to—

(*a*) a policy issued in the course of an industrial assurance business; and
(*b*) a policy issued by a registered friendly society in the course of tax exempt life or endowment business (as defined in section 466).

(2) Subject to paragraph 3(2) below, if a policy to which this paragraph applies was issued before the passing of the Finance Act 1976 (29th July 1976), section 266 shall have effect in relation to it as if subsections (2)(*b*), (3)(*a*), (*b*) and (*d*) were omitted; and if a policy to which this paragraph applies was issued after the passing of that Act, subsection (2)(*b*) of that section shall have effect in relation to it as if it permitted the insurance to be on the life of the individual's parent or grandparent or, subject to sub-paragraph (3) below, on the life of the individual's child or grandchild.

(3) Relief may be given in respect of premiums under a policy of insurance on the life of an individual's child or grandchild which was or is issued after the passing of the Finance Act 1976 (29th July 1976), as if subsection (3)(*d*) of section 266 were omitted, but may be given only if the annual amount of the premiums, together with that of any relevant premiums, does not exceed £52 if the policy was issued in respect of an insurance made before 25th March 1982 or £64 in any other case.

(4) For the purposes of sub-paragraph (3) above, a relevant premium, in relation to an insurance made at any time on the life of an individual's child or grandchild, is any premium under a policy of insurance on the same life, where the insurance is made at the same time or earlier, whether it is made by the individual or any other person.

(5) In this paragraph "child" includes a step-child and an illegitimate child whose parents have married each other after his birth, and "grandchild", "parent" and "grandparent" have corresponding meanings.

Former enactments.—TA 1970, s. 10; FA 1976, Sch. 14, para. 11; Tax, Consumer Credit and Judicature (Northern Ireland Consequential Amendments) Order 1979, S.I. 1979 No. 1576; FA 1982, s. 35(2), (4).

3.—(1) Where a policy is issued or a contract is made by a registered friendly society or a policy to which paragraph 2 above applies is issued by an industrial assurance company, section 266(4), (5) and (8) shall apply in relation to premiums payable under the policy or contract subject to the following provisions of this paragraph.

(2) References to the deductions authorised under section 266(5) shall be construed as including references to any amount retained by or refunded to the person paying the premium under any scheme made by the society or company in accordance with regulations made under this paragraph.

(3) The appropriate authority may make regulations authorising—

(*a*) the adoption by registered friendly societies and industrial assurance companies of any prescribed scheme for securing that in the case of policies or contracts to which the scheme applies amounts equal to [12·5 per cent.][1] of the premiums payable are retained by or refunded to the person paying the premiums or that, in the case of such policies or contracts issued or made before 6th April 1979, the amounts expressed as the amounts of the premiums payable are treated as amounts arrived at by deducting [12·5 per cent.][1] from the amounts payable and that the amounts of the capital sums assured or guaranteed are treated as correspondingly increased; or

(*b*) the adoption by any such society or company of any special scheme for that purpose which may, in such circumstances as may be prescribed, be approved by the appropriate authority.

(4) Increases treated as made in pursuance of regulations under this paragraph shall not be treated as variations of a policy or contract and shall be disregarded for the purposes of paragraph 2(3) above, sections 268(6), 460, 461(1) and 464 of, and paragraph 7 of Schedule 15 to, this Act . . .[2]

(5) The regulations may include such adaptations and modifications of the enactments relating to friendly societies or industrial assurance companies and such other incidental and supplementary provisions as appear to the appropriate authority necessary or expedient for the purpose of enabling such societies or companies to adopt the schemes authorised by the regulations.

(6) Subsections (4), (5) and (7) to (11) of section 6 of the Decimal Currency Act 1969 shall, with the necessary modifications, apply in relation to regulations made under this paragraph.

Former enactments.—FA 1976, Sch. 4, para. 13; FA 1978, Sch. 3, para. 7; FA 1980, s. 29(2)(*c*); FA 1987, Sch. 15, para. 9.
Amendments.—[1] "12·5 per cent." in sub-para. (3)(*a*) substituted by FA 1988, s. 29 with effect from 6 April 1989.
[2] Words "and section 100 of the Stamp Act 1891 and the heading 'Policy of Life Insurance' in Schedule 1 to that Act" in sub-para. (4) repealed by FA 1989, Sch. 17, Pt. IX.

PART II
SUPPLEMENTARY PROVISIONS AS TO RELIEF UNDER SECTION 266

4.—(1) Where it appears to the Board that the relief (if any) to which a person is entitled under section 266 has been exceeded or might be exceeded unless the premiums payable by him under any policy or contract were paid in full, they may, by notice to that person and to the person to whom the payments are made, exclude the application of subsection (5) of that section in relation to any payments due or made after such date as may be specified in the notice and before such date as may be specified in a further notice to those persons.

(2) Where the application of section 266(5) is so excluded in relation to any payments, the relief (if any) to which the person by whom the payments are made is entitled under section 266 shall be given to him under paragraph 6 below.

Former enactments.—FA 1976, Sch. 4, para. 14; FA 1978, Sch. 3, paras. 2, 8.

5. Where a person is entitled to relief under section 266 in respect of a payment to which section 595 applies, section 266(5) shall not apply but the like relief shall be given to him under paragraph 6 below.

Former enactments.—FA 1976, Sch. 4, para. 14A; FA 1978, Sch. 3, para. 9.

6.—(1) Where in any year of assessment the relief to which a person is entitled under section 266, otherwise than in accordance with subsections (6) and (7) of that section, has not been fully given in accordance with that section and the preceding provisions of this Schedule, he may claim relief for the difference, and relief for the difference shall then be given by a payment made by the Board or by discharge or repayment of tax or partly in one such manner and partly in another; and where relief so given to any person exceeds that to which he is entitled under section 266, he shall be liable to make good the excess and an inspector may make such assessments as may in his judgment be required for recovering the excess.

(2) The Management Act shall apply to any assessment under this paragraph as if it were an assessment to tax for the year of assessment in which the relief was given and as if—

(*a*) the assesssment were among those specified in sections 55(1) (recovery of tax not postponed) and 86(2) (interest on overdue tax) of that Act; and
(*b*) the sum charged by the assessment were tax specified in paragraph 3 of the Table in section 86(4) of that Act (reckonable date).

Former enactment.—FA 1976, Sch. 4, para. 15.

7.—(1) The Board may make regulations for carrying into effect section 266(4), (5), (8) and (9) and the preceding provisions of this Schedule and paragraphs 9 and 10 of Schedule 15 ("the relevant provisions").

(2) Regulations under this paragraph may, without prejudice to the generality of sub-paragraph (1) above, provide—

(*a*) for the furnishing of such information by persons by whom premiums are payable as may be necessary for determining whether they are entitled to make deductions under section 266(5) and for excluding the operation of that subsection in relation to payments made by persons who fail to comply with the regulations;
(*b*) for rounding to a multiple of one penny any payment which, after a deduction authorised under section 266(5), is not such a multiple;
(*c*) for the manner in which claims for the recovery of any sum under section 266(5)(*b*) may be made;
(*d*) for the furnishing of such information by persons by or to whom premiums are payable as appears to the Board necessary for deciding such claims and for exercising their powers under paragraph 4 or 6 above; and
(*e*) for requiring persons to whom premiums are paid to make available for inspection by an officer authorised by the Board such books and other documents in their possession or under their control as may reasonably be required for the purposes of determining whether any information given by those persons for the purposes of the relevant provisions is correct and complete.

(3) The following provisions of the Management Act, that is to say—

(*a*) section 29(3)(*c*) (excessive relief);
(*b*) section 30 (recovery of tax repaid in consequence of fraud or negligence etc.);
(*c*) section 88 (interest); and
(*d*) section 95 (incorrect return or accounts);

shall apply in relation to the payment of a sum claimed under section 266(5)(*b*) to which the claimant was not entitled as if it had been income tax repaid as a relief which was not due.

Former enactments.—FA 1976, Sch. 4, para. 16; FA 1978, Sch. 3, para. 10.

8.—(1) A policy of life insurance issued in respect of an insurance made on or before 19th March 1968 shall be treated for the purposes of section 266(3)(*b*) as issued in respect of one made after that date if varied after that date so as to increase the benefits secured or to extend the term of the insurance.

(2) A variation effected before the end of the year 1968 shall be disregarded for the purposes of sub-paragraph (1) above if its only effect was to bring into conformity with paragraph 2 of Schedule 9 to the Finance Act 1968 (qualifying conditions for endowment policies, and now re-enacted as paragraph 2 of Schedule 15 to this Act) a policy previously conforming therewith except as respects the amount guaranteed on death, and no increase was made in the premiums payable under the policy.

(3) A policy which was issued in the course of industrial assurance business in respect of an insurance made after 13th March 1984 shall be treated for the purposes of section 266(3)(*c*) and this paragraph as issued in respect of an insurance made on or before that date if—

(*a*) the proposal form for the policy was completed on or before that date; and
(*b*) on or before 31st March 1984 the policy was prepared for issue by the company or society concerned; and
(*c*) on or before 31st March 1984 and in accordance with the normal business practice of the company or society a permanent record of the preparation of the policy was made in

any book or by any other means kept or instituted by the company or society for the purpose.

(4) For the purposes of section 266(3)(*c*) a policy of life insurance which was issued in respect of an insurance made on or before 13th March 1984 shall be treated as issued in respect of an insurance made after that date if the policy is varied after that date so as to increase the benefits secured or to extend the term of the insurance.

(5) If a policy of life insurance which was issued as mentioned in sub-paragraph (4) above confers on the person to whom it was issued an option to have another policy substituted for it or to have any of its terms changed, then, for the purposes of that sub-paragraph and section 266(3)(*c*), any change in the terms of the policy which is made in pursuance of the option shall be deemed to be a variation of the policy.

(6) In any case where—

(*a*) one policy is replaced by another in such circumstances that the provisions of paragraph 20 of Schedule 15 apply; and
(*b*) the earlier policy was issued in respect of an insurance made or or before 13th March 1984; and
(*c*) the later policy confers on the life or lives assured thereby benefits which are substantially equivalent to those which would have been enjoyed by the life or lives assured under the earlier policy, if that policy had continued in force;

then, for the purposes of section 266(3)(*c*), the insurance in respect of which the later policy is issued shall be deemed to have been made before 13th March 1984; and in this sub-paragraph "the earlier policy" and "the later policy" have the same meaning as in paragraph 20 of Schedule 15.

(7) In any case where—

(*a*) there is a substitution of policies falling within paragraph 25(1) or (3) of Schedule 15; and
(*b*) the old policy was issued in respect of an insurance made on or before 13th March 1984;

then, for the purposes of section 266(3)(*c*), the insurance in respect of which the new policy is issued shall be deemed to have been made before 13th March 1984; and in this sub-paragraph "the old policy" and "the new policy" have the same meaning as in paragraph 17 of Schedule 15.

Former enactments.—Sub-para. (1), (2): TA 1970, s.19(5).
Sub-paras. (3)–(7): FA 1984, s. 72(2)–(4), (6), (7).

SCHEDULE 15

Section 267

QUALIFYING POLICIES

PART I
QUALIFYING CONDITIONS

General rules applicable to whole life and term assurances

1.—(1) Subject to the following provisions of this Part of this Schedule, if a policy secures a capital sum which is payable only on death, or one payable either on death or on earlier disability, it is a qualifying policy if—

  (*a*) it satisfies the conditions appropriate to it under sub-paragraphs (2) to (5) below, and
  (*b*) except to the extent permitted by sub-paragraph (7) below, it does not secure any other benefits.

(2) If the capital sum referred to in sub-paragraph (1) above is payable whenever the event in question happens, or if it happens at any time during the life of a specified person—

  (*a*) the premiums under the policy must be payable at yearly or shorter intervals, and either—

    (i) until the happening of the event or, as the case may require, until the happening of the event or the earlier death of the specified person, or
    (ii) until the time referred to in sub-paragraph (i) above or the earlier expiry of a specified period ending not earlier than ten years after the making of the insurance; and

  (*b*) the total premiums payable in any period of 12 months must not exceed—

    (i) twice the amount of the total premiums payable in any other such period, or
    (ii) one-eighth of the total premiums which would be payable if the policy were to continue in force for a period of ten years from the making of the insurance, or, in a case falling within sub-paragraph (ii) of paragraph (*a*) above, until the end of the period referred to in that sub-paragraph.

(3) If the capital sum referred to in sub-paragraph (1) above is payable only if the event in question happens before the expiry of a specified term ending more than ten years after the making of the insurance, or only if it happens both before the expiry of such a term and during the life of a specified person—

  (*a*) the premiums under the policy must be payable at yearly or shorter intervals, and either—

    (i) until the happening of the event or the earlier expiry of that term or, as the case may require, until the happening of the event or, if earlier, the expiry of the term or the death of the specified person, or
    (ii) as in sub-paragraph (i) above, but with the substitution for references to the term of references to a specified shorter period being one ending not earlier than ten years after the making of the insurance or, if sooner, the expiry of three-quarters of that term; and

  (*b*) the total premiums payable in any period of 12 months must not exceed—

    (i) twice the amount of the total premiums payable in any other such period, or
    (ii) one-eighth of the total premiums which would be payable if the policy were to continue in force for the term referred to in sub-paragraph (i) of paragraph (*a*) above, or, as the case may require, for the shorter period referred to in sub-paragraph (ii) of that paragraph.

(4) If the capital sum referred to in sub-paragraph (1) above is payable only if the event in question happens before the expiry of a specified term ending not more than ten years after the making of the insurance, or only if it happens both before the expiry of such a term and during the life of a specified person, the policy must provide that any payment made by reason of its surrender during the period is not to exceed the total premiums previously paid under the policy.

(5) Except where—

(a) the capital sum referred to in sub-paragraph (1) above is payable only in the circumstances mentioned in sub-paragraph (3) or (4) above; and
(b) the policy does not provide for any payment on the surrender in whole or in part of the rights conferred by it; and
(c) the specified term mentioned in sub-paragraph (3) or, as the case may be, (4) above ends at or before the time when the person whose life is insured attains the age of 75 years;

the capital sum, so far as payable on death, must not be less than 75 per cent. of the total premiums that would be payable if the death occurred at the age of 75 years, the age being, if the sum is payable on the death of the first to die of two persons, that of the older of them, if on the death of the survivor of them, that of the younger of them, and in any other case, that of the person on whose death it is payable; and if the policy does not secure a capital sum in the event of death occurring before the age of 16 or some lower age, it must not provide for the payment in that event of an amount exceeding the total premiums previously paid under it.

(6) In determining for the purposes of sub-paragraph (5) above whether a capital sum is less than 75 per cent. of the total premiums, any amount included in the premiums by reason of their being payable otherwise than annually shall be disregarded, and if the policy is issued in the course of an industrial assurance business, 10 per cent. of the premiums payable under the policy shall be treated as so included.

(7) Notwithstanding sub-paragraph (1)(b) above, if a policy secures a capital sum payable only on death, it may also secure benefits (including benefits of a capital nature) to be provided in the event of a person's disability; and no policy is to be regarded for the purposes of that provision as securing other benefits by reason only of the fact that—

(a) it confers a right to participate in profits, or
(b) it provides for a payment on the surrender in whole or in part of the rights conferred by the policy, or
(c) it gives an option to receive payments by way of annuity, or
(d) it makes provision for the waiver of premiums by reason of a person's disability, or for the effecting of a further insurance or insurances without the production of evidence of insurability.

(8) In applying sub-paragraph (2) or (3) above to any policy—

(a) no account shall be taken of any provision for the waiver of premiums by reason of a person's disability, and
(b) if the term of the policy runs from a date earlier, but not more than three months earlier, than the making of the insurance, the insurance shall be treated as having been made on that date, and any premium paid in respect of the period before the making of the insurance, or in respect of that period and a subsequent period, as having been payable on that date.

(9) References in this paragraph to a capital sum payable on any event include references to any capital sum, or series of capital sums, payable by reason of that event but where what is so payable is either an amount consisting of one sum or an amount made up of two or more sums, the 75 per cent. mentioned in sub-paragraph (5) above shall be compared with the smaller or smallest amount so payable; and a policy secures a capital sum payable either on death or on disability notwithstanding that the amount payable may vary with the event.

(10) In relation to any policy issued in respect of an insurance made before 1st April 1976 this paragraph shall have effect—

(a) with the omission of sub-paragraphs (5) and (6) and in sub-paragraph (9) the words "but where what is so payable is either an amount consisting of one sum or an amount made up of two or more sums, the 75 per cent. mentioned in sub-paragraph (5) above shall be compared with the smaller or smallest amount so payable"; and
(b) with the substitution, for sub-paragraph (7)(b), of—

"(b) it carries a guaranteed surrender value;".

Former enactments.—Sub-paras. (1)–(5): TA 1970, Sch. 1, para. 1(1)–(4A); FA 1975, Sch. 2, para. 4(2), (3).
Sub-para. (6): FA 1975, Sch. 2, para. 4(4).
Sub-paras. (7)–(9): TA 1970, Sch. 1, para. 1(5)–(7); FA 1975, Sch. 2, para. 4(5), (6).
Sub-para. (10): FA 1975, Sch. 2, para. 4(1).

General rules applicable to endowment assurances

2.—(1) Subject to the following provisions of this Part of this Schedule, a policy which secures a capital sum payable either on survival for a specified term or on earlier death, or earlier death or disability, including a policy securing the sum on death only if occurring after the attainment of a specified age not exceeding 16, is a qualifying policy if it satisfies the following conditions—

(a) the term must be one ending not earlier than ten years after the making of the insurance;

(b) premiums must be payable under the policy at yearly or shorter intervals, and—
  (i) until the happening of the event in question; or
  (ii) until the happening of that event, or the earlier expiry of a specified period shorter than the term but also ending not earlier than ten years after the making of the insurance; or
  (iii) if the policy is to lapse on the death of a specified person, until one of those times or the policy's earlier lapse;

(c) the total premiums payable under the policy in any period of 12 months must not exceed—
  (i) twice the amount of the total premiums payable in any other such period, or
  (ii) one-eighth of the total premiums which would be payable if the policy were to run for the specified term;

(d) the policy—
  (i) must guarantee that the capital sum payable on death, or on death occurring after the attainment of a specified age not exceeding 16, will, whenever that event may happen, be equal to 75 per cent. at least of the total premiums which would be payable if the policy were to run for that term, disregarding any amounts included in those premiums by reason of their being payable otherwise than annually, except that if, at the beginning of that term, the age of the person concerned exceeds 55 years, the capital sum so guaranteed may, for each year of the excess, be less by 2 per cent. of that total than 75 per cent. thereof, the person concerned being, if the capital sum is payable on the death of the first to die of two persons, the older of them, if on the death of the survivor of them, the younger of them and in any other case the person on whose death it is payable; and
  (ii) if it is a policy which does not secure a capital sum in the event of death before the attainment of a specified age not exceeding 16, must not provide for the payment in that event of an amount exceeding the total premiums previously paid thereunder; and

(e) the policy must not secure the provision (except by surrender in whole or in part of the rights conferred by the policy) at any time before the happening of the event in question of any benefit of a capital nature other than a payment falling within paragraph (d)(ii) above, or benefits attributable to a right to participate in profits or arising by reason of a person's disability.

(2) For the purposes of sub-paragraph (1)(d)(i) above, 10 per cent. of the premiums payable under any policy issued in the course of industrial assurance business shall be treated as attributable to the fact that they are not paid annually.

(3) Sub-paragraphs (8) and (9) of paragraph 1 above shall, with any necessary modifications, have effect for the purposes of this paragraph as they have effect for the purposes of that paragraph.

(4) In relation to any policy issued in respect of an insurance made before 1st April 1976 this paragraph shall have effect with the omission in sub-paragraph (1)(d)(i) of the words from "except that if" to the end, and in sub-paragraph (1)(e) of the words "in whole or in part of the rights conferred by the policy".

Former enactment.—Sub-paras. (1)–(3): TA 1970, Sch. 1, para. 2; FA 1975, Sch. 2, para. 4(7), (8). Sub-para. (4): FA 1975, Sch. 2, para. 4(1).

Special types of policy

(i) Friendly Society policies

3.—(1) Paragraphs 1 and 2 above do not apply to a policy issued by a registered friendly society in the course of tax exempt life or endowment business in respect of an insurance made or varied on or after 19th March 1985, but such a policy shall not be a qualifying policy unless—

(a) in the case of a policy for the assurance of a gross sum or annuity, the conditions in sub-paragraph (2) are fulfilled with respect to it; and

(b) in the case of a policy for the assurance of a gross sum, the conditions in sub-paragraphs (5) to (11) below are fulfilled with respect to it; and

(c) in the case of a policy issued by a new society, the contract for the insurance was made by a member of the society over the age of 18.

(2) The conditions referred to in sub-paragraph (1) above are as follows—

(a) subject to sub-paragraph (3) below, the period (the "term" of the policy) between—

(i) the making of the insurance or, where the contract provides for the term to begin on a date not more than three months earlier than the making of the insurance, that date, and

(ii) the time when the gross sum assured is payable (or, as the case may be, when the first instalment of the annuity is payable),

shall be not less than ten years, and must not, on any contingency other than the death, or retirement on grounds of ill health, of the person liable to pay the premiums or whose life is insured, become less than ten years;

(b) subject to sub-paragraph (4) below, the premiums payable under the policy shall be premiums of equal or rateable amounts payable at yearly or shorter intervals over the whole term of the policy of assurance, or over the whole term of the policy of assurance apart from any period after the person liable to pay the premiums or whose life is insured attains a specified age, being an age which he will attain at a time not less than ten years after the beginning of the term of the policy of assurance;

(c) until the expiration of three-quarters of the term of the policy of assurance, or of ten years from the beginning of the term, whichever is the shorter, the policy may not be surrendered to the friendly society for consideration exceeding the amount of the premiums paid, except that if a surrender value is prescribed by section 24 of the Industrial Assurance Act 1923 or section 3 of the Industrial Assurance and Friendly Societies Act 1929 or by Article 30 or 35 of and Schedule 7 to the Industrial Assurance (Northern Ireland) Order 1979, the limit on the consideration shall be either that value or the amount of the premiums paid whichever is the greater.

(3) Notwithstanding sub-paragraph (2)(a) above, the policy—

(a) may provide for a payment to a person of an age not exceeding 18 years at any time not less than five years from the beginning of the term of the policy if the premium or premiums payable in any period of 12 months in the term of the policy do not exceed £13;

(b) may provide for a payment at any time not less than five years from the beginning of the term of the policy, if it is one of a series of payments falling due at intervals of not less than five years, and the amount of any payment, other than the final payment, does not exceed four-fifths of the premiums paid in the interval before its payment.

For the purposes of paragraph (a) above, if the term begins on a date earlier than the making of the insurance, any premium paid in respect of a period before the making of the insurance, or in respect of that period and a subsequent period, shall be treated as having been payable on that date.

(4) Notwithstanding sub-paragraph (2)(b) above, the policy—

(a) may allow a payment at any time after the expiration of one-half of the term of the policy of assurance, or of ten years from the beginning of the term, whichever is the earlier, being a payment in commutation of the liability to pay premiums falling due after that time;

(b) may allow the person liable to pay the premiums to commute any liability for premiums where he ceases to reside in the United Kingdom or gives satisfactory proof of intention to emigrate;

(c) may allow any liability for premiums to be discharged in consideration of surrendering a sum which has become payable on the maturity of any other policy of assurance issued by the same friendly society to the person liable to pay the premiums, or to his parent, where that other policy of assurance is issued as part of the friendly society's tax exempt life or endowment business; and

(d) may make provision for the waiver of premiums by reason of a person's disability.

(5) Where the policy secures a capital sum which is payable only on death or only on death occurring after the attainment of a specified age not exceeding 16, that capital sum must be not less than 75 per cent. of the total premiums which would be payable if the death of the relevant beneficiary occurred at the age of 75.

(6) Where the policy secures a capital sum which is payable only on survival for a specified term, that capital sum must be not less than 75 per cent. of the total premiums which would be payable if the policy were to run for that term.

(7) Where the policy secures a capital sum which is payable on survival for a specified term

or on earlier death, or on earlier death or disability (including a policy securing the sum on death only if occurring after the attainment of a specified age not exceeding 16), the capital sum payable on death, whenever that event occurs, must be not less than 75 per cent. of the total premiums which would be payable if the policy were to run for that term, except that if, at the beginning of that term, the age of the relevant beneficiary exceeds 55, that capital sum may, for each year of the excess, be less by 2 per cent. of that total than 75 per cent. thereof.

(8) For the purposes of sub-paragraphs (5) to (7) above—

(*a*) "the relevant beneficiary" means—

(i) if the capital sum concerned is payable on the death of the first to die of two persons, the older of them;
(ii) if that capital sum is payable on the death of the survivor of two persons, the younger of them; and
(iii) in any other case, the person on whose death that capital sum is payable; and

(*b*) in determining the total premiums payable in any circumstances—

(i) where those premiums are payable otherwise than annually, and the policy is issued by a new society, there shall be disregarded an amount equal to 10 per cent. of those premiums;
(ii) where the policy is issued by a society other than a new society, there shall be disregarded an amount equal to £10 for each year for which account is taken of those premiums; and
(iii) so much of any premium as is charged on the ground that an exceptional risk of death is involved shall be disregarded; and

(*c*) in determining the capital sum payable on any event, there shall be disregarded any provision of the policy under which, on the ground referred to in paragraph (*b*)(iii) above, any sum may become chargeable as a debt against that capital sum.

(9) If the policy does not secure a capital sum in the event of death occurring before the age of 16 or some lower age, it must not provide for the payment in that event of an amount exceeding the total premiums previously paid under it.

(10) References in this paragraph to a capital sum payable on any event include references to a capital sum or series of capital sums payable by reason of that event, but where what is so payable is either an amount consisting of one sum or an amount made up to two or more sums, any reference in sub-paragraphs (5) to (7) above to 75 per cent. of the total premiums payable in any circumstances shall be compared with the smaller or smallest amount so payable; and for the purposes of those sub-paragraphs a policy secures a capital sum payable either on death or on disability notwithstanding that the amount may vary with the event.

(11) For the purposes of sub-paragraphs (5) to (7) and (10) above, in the case of a policy which provides for any such payments as are referred to in sub-paragraph (3) above ("interim payments"), the amount of the capital sum which is payable on any event shall be taken to be increased—

(*a*) in the case of a policy which secures such a capital sum as is referred to in sub-paragraph (5) above, by the total of the interim payments which would be payable if the death of the relevant beneficiary (within the meaning of that sub-paragraph) occurred at the age of 75; and
(*b*) in the case of a policy which secures such a capital sum as is referred to in sub-paragraph (6) or (7) above, by the total of the interim payments which would be payable if the policy were to run for the specified term referred to in that sub-paragraph.

Former enactments.—TA 1970, ss. 334(2)–(4), 337(5)(*a*), Sch. 1, para. 3; the Tax, Consumer Credit and Judicature (Northern Ireland Consequential Amendments) Order 1979, S.I. 1979 No. 1576; FA 1985, s. 41(4), (6), Sch. 10, Pt. I.

4.—(1) The provisions of this paragraph have effect notwithstanding anything in paragraph 3 above.

(2) In determining whether a policy—

(*a*) which affords provision for sickness or other infirmity (whether bodily or mental), and
(*b*) which also affords assurance for a gross sum independent of sickness or other infirmity, and
(*c*) under which not less than 60 per cent. of the amount of the premiums is attributable to the provision referred to in paragraph (*a*) above,

is a qualifying policy, the conditions referred to in paragraph 3(1)(*b*) above shall be deemed to be fulfilled with respect to it.

(3) A policy shall cease to be a qualifying policy—

(*a*) if it falls within sub-paragraph (1) of paragraph 3 above and there is such a variation of its terms that any of the conditions referred to in that sub-paragraph ceases to be fulfilled; or

(*b*) if—

(i) for any purpose it falls within paragraph (1) of Schedule 1 to the Friendly Societies Act 1974 or paragraph (1) of Schedule 1 to the Friendly Societies Act (Northern Ireland) 1970,
(ii) it was issued by a new society, and
(iii) the rights conferred by it are surrendered in whole or in part.

Former enactments.—TA 1970, Sch. 1, para. 4; FA 1985, Sch. 10, Pt. I.

5. Section 466 shall apply for the interpretation of paragraphs 3 and 4 above as it applies for the interpretation of sections 460 to 465.

Former enactments.—TA 1970, s. 337(1)(*b*); FA 1985, s. 41(7)(*a*).

6.—(1) A policy which was issued by any friendly society, or branch of a friendly society, in the course of tax exempt life or endowment business (as defined in section 466) in respect of insurances made before 19th March 1985 and which has not been varied on or after that date is a qualifying policy notwithstanding that it does not comply with the conditions specified in paragraph 1 or 2 above.

(2) Notwithstanding paragraphs 3 to 5 or sub-paragraph (1) above, if, on or after 19th March 1985, a person becomes in breach of the limits in section 464, the policy effected by that contract which causes those limits to be exceeded shall not be a qualifying policy; and in any case where—

(*a*) the limits in that section are exceeded as a result of the aggregation of the sums assured or premiums payable under two or more contracts, and
(*b*) at a time immediately before one of those contracts was entered into (but not immediately after it was entered into) the sums assured by or, as the case may be, the premiums payable under the contract or contracts which were then in existence did not exceed the limits in that section,

only those policies effected by contracts made after that time shall be treated as causing the limits to be exceeded.

Former enactments.—Sub-para. (1): TA 1970, Sch. 1, para. 3; FA 1985, s. 41(4).
Sub-para. (2): Friendly Societies Act 1974, s. 64(2B); FA 1985, s. 41(1); FA 1987, s. 30(6).

(ii) Industrial assurance policies

7.—(1) A policy issued in the course of an industrial assurance business, and not constituting a qualifying policy by virtue of paragraph 1 or 2 above, is nevertheless a qualifying policy if—

(*a*) the sums guaranteed by the policy, together with those guaranteed at the time the assurance is made by all other policies issued in the course of such a business to the same person and not constituting qualifying policies apart from this paragraph, do not exceed £1,000;
(*b*) it satisfies the conditions with respect to premiums specified in paragraph 1(2) above;
(*c*) except by reason of death or surrender, no capital sum other than one falling within paragraph (*d*) below can become payable under the policy earlier than ten years after the making of the assurance; and
(*d*) where the policy provides for the making of a series of payments during its term—

(i) the first such payment is due not earlier than five years after the making of the assurance, and the others, except the final payment, at intervals of not less than five years, and
(ii) the amount of any payment, other than the final payment, does not exceed fourfifths of the premiums paid in the interval before its payment; or

(*e*) the policy was issued before 6th April 1976, or was issued before 6th April 1979 and is in substantially the same form as policies so issued before 6th April 1976.

(2) For the purposes of this paragraph, the sums guaranteed by a policy do not include any bonuses, or in the case of a policy providing for a series of payments during its term, any of those payments except the first, or any sum payable on death during the term by reference to one or more of those payments except so far as that sum is referable to the first such payment.

Former enactments.—TA 1970, Sch. 1, para. 4; FA 1976, Sch. 4, para. 12.

8. Where a policy issued in respect of an insurance made after 1st April 1976 in the course of an industrial assurance business is not a qualifying policy by virtue of paragraph 1 or 2 above but is a policy with respect to which the conditions in paragraph 7(1)(*b*) and (*c*) above are satisfied, it shall be a qualifying policy whether or not the condition in paragraph 7(1)(*a*) above is satisfied with respect to it; but where that condition is not satisfied, relief under section 266 in respect of premiums paid under the policy shall be given only on such amount (if any) as would have been the amount of those premiums had that condition been satisfied.

Former enactments.—FA 1975, Sch. 2, para. 7; FA 1976, Sch. 4, para. 19(4).

(iii) Family income policies and mortgage protection policies

9.—(1) The following provisions apply to any policy which is not a qualifying policy apart from those provisions, and the benefits secured by which consist of or include the payment on or after a person's death of—

(*a*) one capital sum which does not vary according to the date of death, plus a series of capital sums payable if the death occurs during a specified period, or
(*b*) a capital sum, the amount of which is less if the death occurs in a later part of a specified period than if it occurs in an earlier part of that period.

(2) A policy falling within sub-paragraph (1)(*a*) above is a qualifying policy if—

(*a*) it would be one if it did not secure the series of capital sums there referred to, and the premiums payable under the policy were such as would be chargeable if that were in fact the case, and
(*b*) it would also be one if it secured only that series of sums, and the premiums thereunder were the balance of those actually so payable.

(3) A policy falling within sub-paragraph (1)(*b*) above is a qualifying policy if—

(*a*) it would be one if the amount of the capital sum there referred to were equal throughout the period to its smallest amount, and the premiums payable under the policy were such as would be chargeable if that were in fact the case, and
(*b*) it would also be one if it secured only that capital sum so far as it from time to time exceeds its smallest amount, and the premiums payable thereunder were the balance of those actually so payable.

Former enactment.—TA 1970, Sch. 1, para. 5.

Other special provisions

(i) Short-term assurances

10. A policy which secures a capital sum payable only on death or payable either on death or on earlier disability shall not be a qualifying policy if the capital sum is payable only if the event in question happens before the expiry of a specified term ending less than one year after the making of the insurance.

Former enactment.—FA 1976, Sch. 4, para. 2.

(ii) Personal accident insurance

11.—(1) A policy which evidences a contract of insurance to which sub-paragraph (3) below applies shall not be a qualifying policy unless it also evidences a contract falling within Class I or Class III in Schedule 1 to the Insurance Companies Act 1982.

(2) A policy which evidences a contract of insurance to which sub-paragraph (4) below applies shall not be a qualifying policy unless it also evidences a contract falling within section 83(2)(*a*) of the Insurance Companies Act 1974.

(3) This sub-paragraph applies to contracts of insurance issued in respect of insurances

made on or after 25th March 1982 against risks of persons dying as a result of an accident or an accident of a specified class, not being contracts which—

(*a*) are expressed to be in effect for a period of not less than five years or without limit of time; and
(*b*) either are not expressed to be terminable by the insurer before the expiration of five years from their taking effect or are expressed to be so terminable before the expiration of that period only in special circumstances therein mentioned.

(4) This sub-paragraph applies to contracts of insurance issued in respect of insurances made before 25th March 1982 against risks of persons dying as a result of an accident or an accident of a specified class, not being contracts falling within section 83(2)(*b*) of the Insurance Companies Act 1974.

Former enactments.—FA 1976, Sch. 4, para. 2A; FA 1978, Sch. 3, para. 4; FA 1982, s. 35(1); Insurance Companies Act 1982, Sch. 5, para. 17.

(iii) Exceptional mortality risk

12. For the purpose of determining whether any policy is a qualifying policy, there shall be disregarded—

(*a*) so much of any premium thereunder as is charged on the grounds that an exceptional risk of death is involved; and
(*b*) any provision under which, on those grounds, any sum may become chargeable as a debt against the capital sum guaranteed by the policy on death.

Former enactment.—TA 1970, Sch. 1, para. 6.

(iv) Connected policies

13. Subject to paragraph 14 below, where the terms of any policy provide that it is to continue in force only so long as another policy does so, neither policy is a qualifying policy unless, if they had constituted together a single policy issued in respect of an insurance made at the time of the insurance in respect of which the first-mentioned policy was issued, that single policy would have been a qualifying policy.

Former enactment.—TA 1970, Sch. 1, para. 7.

14.—(1) A policy shall not be a qualifying policy if the policy is connected with another policy and the terms of either policy provide benefits which are greater than would reasonably be expected if any policy connected with it were disregarded.

(2) For the purposes of this paragraph a policy is connected with another policy if they are at any time simultaneously in force and either of them is issued with reference to the other, or with a view to enabling the other to be issued on particular terms or facilitating its being issued on those terms.

(3) In this paragraph "policy" means a policy effected in the course of long term business, as defined in section 1 of the Insurance Companies Act 1982, and includes any such policy issued outside the United Kingdom.

(4) Where any person issues a policy—

(*a*) which by virtue of this paragraph is not a qualifying policy, or
(*b*) the issue of which causes another policy to cease by virtue of this paragraph to be a qualifying policy,

he shall within three months of issuing the policy give notice of that fact to the Board.

(5) The Board may, by notice, require any person who is, or appears to them to be, concerned in the issue of any such policy as is mentioned in sub-paragraph (4) above, to furnish them within such time (not being less than 30 days) as may be specified in the notice with such particulars as they think necessary for the purposes of this paragraph and as the person to whom the notice is addressed has or can reasonably obtain; but no solicitor shall be deemed for the purposes of this sub-paragraph to have been concerned in the issue of a policy by reason only that he has given professional advice to a client in connection with that policy.

(6) This paragraph shall apply to policies issued in respect of insurances made before 23rd August 1983 in accordance with sub-paragraphs (7) and (8) below.

(7) Where—

(a) a policy is issued in respect of an insurance made before 23rd August 1983, and
(b) a policy is issued in respect of an insurance made on or after that date which is connected with it within the meaning of this paragraph,

sub-paragraphs (1) to (6) above shall apply to the policy issued in respect of an insurance made before that date.

(8) Sub-paragraphs (1) to (7) above shall apply to policies issued in respect of insurances made before 23rd August 1983 (other than policies which, disregarding this paragraph, fall within sub-paragraph (7)) with the substitution—

(a) in sub-paragraph (1) for the words "and the terms of either policy" of the words "the terms of which";
(b) in sub-paragraph (3) for the words from "long term business" to "1982" of the words "ordinary long-term insurance business within the meaning of section 83(2) of the Insurance Companies Act 1974 (as enacted) or, in relation to a policy made after 25th March 1982, section 96(1) of the Insurance Companies Act 1982"; and
(c) in sub-paragraphs (6) and (7) for the words "23rd August 1983" of the words "26th March 1980".

(9) In any case where payments made—

(a) after 22nd August 1983, and
(b) by way of premium or other consideration in respect of a policy issued in respect of an insurance made before that date,

exceed £5 in any period of 12 months, the policy shall be treated for the purposes of this paragraph as if it were issued in respect of an insurance made after 22nd August 1983; but nothing in this paragraph shall apply with respect to any premium paid in respect of it before that date.

(10) Sub-paragraphs (8) and (9) above do not apply in relation to policies issued in the course of industrial assurance business.

Former enactments.—FA 1980, s. 30; FA 1982, s. 35(3); FA 1984, s. 74.

(v) Premiums paid out of sums due under previous policies

15.—(1) Where, in the case of a policy under which a single premium only is payable, liability for the payment of that premium is discharged in accordance with sub-paragraph (2) below, the policy is a qualifying policy notwithstanding anything in paragraph 1(2) or (3) or paragraph 2(1)(b) or (c) above; and where, in the case of any other policy, liability for the payment of the first premium thereunder, or of any part of that premium, is so discharged, the premium or part shall be disregarded for the purposes of paragraphs 1(2)(b) and (3)(b) and 2(1)(c) above.

(2) Liability for the payment of a premium is discharged in accordance with this sub-paragraph if it is discharged by the retention by the company with which the insurance is made of the whole or a part of any sum which has become payable on the maturity of, or on the surrender more than ten years after its issue of the rights conferred by, a policy—

(a) previously issued by the company to the person making the insurance, or, if it is made by trustees, to them or any predecessors in office; or
(b) issued by the company when the person making the insurance was an infant, and securing a capital sum payable either on a specified date falling not more than one month after his attaining 25, or on the anniversary of the policy immediately following his attainment of that age,

being, unless it is a policy falling within paragraph (b) above and the premium in question is a first premium only, a policy which was itself a qualifying policy, or which would have been a qualifying policy had it been issued in respect of an insurance made after 19th March 1968.

Former enactment.—TA 1970, Sch. 1, para. 8.

(vi) Additional premiums under section 72(9) of the Finance Act 1984

16. In determining whether a policy is a qualifying policy, no account shall be taken of any amount recovered, as if it were an additional premium, in pursuance of section 72(9) of the Finance Act 1984.

Former enactment.—FA 1984, s. 72(9)(a).

(vii) Substitutions and variations

17.—(1) Subject to paragraph 19 below, where one policy ("the new policy") is issued in substitution for, or on the maturity of and in consequence of an option conferred by, another policy ("the old policy"), the question whether the new policy is a qualifying policy shall, to the extent provided by the rules in sub-paragraph (2) below, be determined by reference to both policies.

(2) The rules (for the purposes of which, the question whether the old policy was a qualifying policy shall be determined in accordance with this Part of this Schedule, whatever the date of the insurance in respect of which it was issued), are as follows—

(*a*) if the new policy would apart from this paragraph be a qualifying policy but the old policy was [not][1], the new policy is not a qualifying policy unless the person making the insurance in respect of which it is issued was an infant when the old policy was issued, and the old policy was one securing a capital sum payable either on a specified date falling not later than one month after his attaining 25 or on the anniversary of the policy immediately following his attainment of that age;

(*b*) if the new policy would apart from this paragraph be a qualifying policy, and the old policy was also a qualifying policy, the new policy is a qualifying policy unless—

(i) it takes effect before the expiry of ten years from the making of the insurance in respect of which the old policy was issued, and
(ii) subject to sub-paragraph (4) below, the highest total of premiums payable thereunder for any period of 12 months expiring before that time is less than one half of the highest total paid for any period of 12 months under the old policy, or under any related policy issued less than ten years before the issue of the new policy ("related policy" meaning any policy in relation to which the old policy was a new policy within the meaning of this paragraph, any policy in relation to which that policy was such a policy, and so on);

(*c*) if the new policy would not apart from this paragraph be a qualifying policy, and would fail to be so by reason only of paragraph 1(2) or (3) or 2(1)(*a*), (*b*) or (*c*) above, it is nevertheless a qualifying policy if the old policy was a qualifying policy and—

(i) the old policy was issued in respect of an insurance made more than ten years before the taking effect of the new policy, and, subject to sub-paragraph (4) below, the premiums payable for any period of 12 months under the new policy do not exceed the smallest total paid for any such period under the old policy; or
(ii) the old policy was issued outside the United Kingdom, and the circumstances are as specified in sub-paragraph (3) below.

(3) The circumstances are—

(*a*) where the new policy referred to in sub-paragraph (2)(*c*) above is issued after 22nd February 1984, that the policy holder under the new policy became resident in the United Kingdom during the 12 months ending with the date of its issue;

(*b*) where paragraph (*a*) above does not apply, that the person in respect of whom the new insurance is made became resident in the United Kingdom during the 12 months ending with the date of its issue;

(*c*) that the issuing company certify that the new policy is in substitution for the old, and that the old was issued either by a branch or agency of theirs outside the United Kingdom or by a company outside the United Kingdom with whom they have arrangements for the issue of policies in substitution for ones held by persons coming to the United Kingdom; and

(*d*) that the new policy confers on the holder benefits which are substantially equivalent to those which he would have enjoyed if the old policy had continued in force.

(4) Where the new policy is one issued on or after 1st April 1976 then, in determining under sub-paragraph (2) above whether that policy would or would not (apart from sub-paragraphs (1) to (3) above) be a qualifying policy, there shall be left out of account so much of the first premium payable thereunder as is accounted for by the value of the old policy.

Former enactments.—Sub-paras. (1), (2): TA 1970, Sch. 1, para. 9(1), (2).
Sub-para. (3): TA 1970, Sch. 1, para. 9(3); FA 1984, s. 76(3), (6).
Sub-para. (4): FA 1975, Sch. 2, para. 5.
Amendments.—[1] Word in sub-para. (2)(*a*) inserted by FA 1988, Sch. 13, para. 10.

18.—(1) Subject to paragraph 19 below and to the provisions of this paragraph, where the terms of a policy are varied, the question whether the policy after the variation is a qualifying policy shall be determined in accordance with the rules in paragraph 17 above, with references in those rules to the new policy and the old policy construed for that purpose as references respectively to the policy after the variation and the policy before the variation, and with any other necessary modifications.

(2) In applying any of those rules by virtue of this paragraph, the question whether a policy after a variation would be a qualifying policy apart from the rule shall be determined as if any reference in paragraphs [1, 2, 3(5) to (11), 4 to 9][1], 12 and 13 above to the making of an insurance, or to a policy's term, were a reference to the taking effect of the variation or, as the case may be, to the term of the policy as from the variation.

(3) This paragraph does not apply by reason of—

   (a) any variation which, whether or not of a purely formal character, does not affect the terms of a policy in any significant respect, or

   (b) any variation effected before the end of the year 1968 for the sole purpose of converting into a qualifying policy any policy issued (but not one treated, by virtue of paragraph 8(1) and (2) of Schedule 14, as issued) in respect of an insurance made after 19th March 1968.

Former enactment.—TA 1970, Sch. 1, para. 10.
Amendments.—[1] Numbers in sub-para. (2) substituted by FA 1988, Sch. 13, para. 11.

19.—(1) The following provisions of this paragraph shall have effect for determining for the purposes of this Schedule whether a policy has been varied or whether a policy which confers on the person to whom it is issued an option to have another policy substituted for it or to have any of its terms changed is a qualifying policy.

(2) If the policy is one issued in respect of an insurance made before 1st April 1976—

   (a) any such option shall, until it is exercised, be disregarded in determining whether the policy is a qualifying policy; and

   (b) any change in the terms of the policy which is made in pursuance of such an option shall be deemed to be a variation of the policy.

(3) If the policy is one issued in respect of an insurance made on or after 1st April 1976, the policy shall not be a qualifying policy unless it satisfies the conditions applicable to it under this Schedule before any such option is exercised and—

   (a) each policy that might be substituted for it in pursuance of such an option would satisfy those conditions under the rules of paragraph 17 above; and

   (b) the policy would continue to satisfy those conditions under the rules of that paragraph as applied by paragraph 18 above if each or any of the changes capable of being made in pursuance of such an option had been made and were treated as a variation;

and it shall not be treated as being varied by reason only of any change made in pursuance of such an option.

Former enactment.—FA 1975, Sch. 2, para. 3.

20.—(1) Where, as a result of a variation in the life or lives for the time being assured, a qualifying policy ("the earlier policy") is replaced by a new policy ("the later policy") which in accordance with the rules in paragraph 17 above is also a qualifying policy, then, subject to sub-paragraph (2) below, for the purposes of—

   (a) sections 268 to 270 and 540 and 541; and

   (b) any second or subsequent application of this paragraph;

the later policy and the earlier policy shall be treated as a single policy issued in respect of an insurance made at the time of the making of the insurance in respect of which the earlier policy was issued; and, accordingly, so long as the later policy continues to be a qualifying policy, the single policy shall also be treated as a qualifying policy for those purposes.

(2) Sub-paragraph (1) above does not apply unless—

   (a) any sum which would otherwise become payable by the insurer on or in connection with the coming to an end of the earlier policy is retained by the insurer and applied in the discharge of some or all of the liability for any premium becoming due under the later policy; and

   (b) no consideration in money or money's worth (other than the benefits for which provision is made by the later policy) is receivable by any person on or in connection with the coming to an end of the earlier policy or the coming into existence of the later policy.

(3) Any sum which is applied as mentioned in sub-paragraph (2)(a) above—

   (a) shall be left out of account in determining, for the purposes of sections 268 to 270 and 540 and 541, the total amount which at any time has been paid by way of premiums under the single policy referred to in sub-paragraph (1) above; and (*b*) shall not be regarded, in relation to that single policy, as a relevant capital payment, within the meaning of section 541.

(4) This paragraph applies where the later policy comes into existence on or after 25th March 1982.

Former enactment.—FA 1982, s. 34.

PART II
CERTIFICATION OF QUALIFYING POLICIES

Policies issued in respect of insurances made on or after 1st April 1976 or varied on or after that date

21.—(1) A policy of life insurance issued in respect of an insurance made on or after 1st April 1976 or varied on or after that date (other than one to which paragraph 22(2)(*c*) below applies) shall not be a qualifying policy unless—

(*a*) it is certified by the Board as being a qualifying policy; or
(*b*) it conforms with a form which at the time the policy is issued or varied is either—

 (i) a standard form certified by the Board as a standard form of qualifying policy; or
 (ii) a form varying from a standard form so certified in no other respect than by making such additions thereto as are, at the time the policy is issued, certified by the Board as compatible with a qualifying policy when made to that standard form and satisfy any conditions subject to which they are so certified;

and any certificate issued in pursuance of paragraph (*a*) above shall be conclusive evidence that the policy is a qualifying policy.

(2) In issuing a certificate in pursuance of sub-paragraph (1) above the Board may disregard any provision of the policy, standard form or addition which appears to them insignificant.

(3) Where the Board refuse to certify a policy as being a qualifying policy, the person to whom it is issued may appeal to the General Commissioners or, if he so elects, to the Special Commissioners.

(4) Sub-paragraphs (1) to (3) above do not apply in relation to such a policy as is mentioned in paragraphs 3 to 6 above.

Former enactments.—FA 1975, Sch. 2, para. 1; FA 1987, Sch. 15, para. 7.

22.—(1) A body which issues or which, after 5th April 1979, has issued any policy of life insurance (other than one to which sub-paragraph (2)(*c*) below applies)—

(*a*) which is certified by the Board as being a qualifying policy; or
(*b*) which conforms with such a form as is mentioned in paragraph 21(1)(*b*) above, and is in the opinion of the body issuing it a qualifying policy,

shall, within three months of receipt of a request in writing by the policy holder, give to the policy holder a duly authenticated certificate to that effect, specifying in the certificate the name of the policy holder, the name of the person whose life is assured, the reference number or other means of identification allocated to the policy, the reference number of the relevant Inland Revenue certificate (if any), the capital sum or sums assured and the amounts and dates for payment of the premiums.

(2) Subject to sub-paragraph (3) below, where a policy of life insurance is varied after 5th April 1979, and, after the variation—

(*a*) it is certified by the Board as a qualifying policy, or
(*b*) it conforms with such a form as is referred to in sub-paragraph (1) above and is in the opinion of the body by whom it was issued a qualifying policy, or
(*c*) in the case of a policy issued in respect of an insurance made before 1st April 1976, it is in the opinion of the body by whom it was issued a qualifying policy,

that body shall, within three months of receipt of a request in writing by the policy holder, give to the policy holder a like certificate with respect to the policy as varied.

(3) Sub-paragraph (2) above shall not apply by reason of—

(*a*) any variation which, whether or not of a purely formal character, does not affect the terms of a policy in any significant respect; or
(*b*) any variation of a policy issued in respect of an insurance made on or before 19th March 1968, other than a variation by virtue of which the policy falls, under paragraph

8(1) and (2) of Schedule 14, to be treated as issued in respect of an insurance made after that date.

Former enactments.—Sub-para. (1): TA 1970, Sch. 1, para. 11(1): FA 1975, Sch. 2, para. 2(1); FA 1976, s. 33(1); FA 1978, Sch. 3, para. 13(1)(*a*), (*b*).
Sub-para. (2): TA 1970, Sch. 1, para. 11(2); FA 1975, Sch. 2, para. 2(2); FA 1976, s. 33(2); FA 1978, Sch. 3, para. 13(1)(*b*).
Sub-para. (3): TA 1970, Sch. 1, para. 11(3).

PART III
POLICIES ISSUED BY NON-RESIDENT COMPANIES

23. In this Part—
   (*a*) any reference to a paragraph is a reference to that paragraph of this Schedule; and
   (*b*) "the old policy" and "the new policy" have the same meanings as in paragraph 17.

Former enactment.—FA 1984, Sch. 15, Pt. II, para. 1.

24.—(1) This paragraph applies to a policy of life insurance—
   (*a*) which is issued in respect of an insurance made after 17th November 1983; and
   (*b*) which is so issued by a company resident outside the United Kingdom;
and in the following provisions of this paragraph such a policy is referred to as "a new non-resident policy" and the company by which it is issued is referred to as "the issuing company".

(2) Notwithstanding anything in paragraph 21—
   (*a*) a new non-resident policy shall not be certified under sub-paragraph (1)(*a*) of that paragraph, and
   (*b*) a new non-resident policy which conforms with such a form as is mentioned in sub-paragraph (1)(*b*) of that paragraph shall not be a qualifying policy,
until such time as the conditions in either sub-paragraph (3) or sub-paragraph (4) below are fulfilled with respect to it.

(3) The conditions first referred to in sub-paragraph (2) above are—
   (*a*) that the issuing company is lawfully carrying on in the United Kingdom life assurance business (as defined in section 431(2)); and
   (*b*) that the premiums under the policy are payable to a branch in the United Kingdom of the issuing company, being a branch through which the issuing company carries on its life assurance business; and
   (*c*) the premiums under the policy form part of those business receipts of the issuing company which arise through that branch.

(4) The conditions secondly referred to in sub-paragraph (2) above are—
   (*a*) that the policy holder is resident in the United Kingdom; and
   (*b*) that the income of the issuing company from the investments of its life assurance fund is, by virtue of section 445, charged to corporation tax under Case III of Schedule D;
and expressions used in paragraph (*b*) above have the same meaning as in section 445(1).

Former enactments.—FA 1975, Sch. 2, para. 1A; FA 1984, Sch. 15, Pt. I.

25.—(1) In the application of paragraph 17 in any case where—
   (*a*) the old policy was issued in respect of an insurance made after 17th November 1983 and could not be a qualifying policy by virtue of paragraph 24, and
   (*b*) the new policy is not a new non-resident policy as defined in that paragraph,
the rules for the determination of the question whether the new policy is a qualifying policy shall apply with the modifications in sub-paragraph (2) below.

(2) The modifications are the following—
   (*a*) if, apart from paragraph 24, the old policy and any related policy (within the meaning of paragraph 17(2)(*b*)) of which account falls to be taken would have been, or would have been capable of being certified as, a qualifying policy under paragraph 21, that policy shall be assumed to have been a qualifying policy for the purposes of paragraph 17(2); and
   (*b*) if, apart from this paragraph, the new policy would be, or would be capable of being certified as, a qualifying policy, it shall not be such a policy or, as the case may be, be

capable of being so certified unless the circumstances are as specified in paragraph 17(3); and

(c) in paragraph 17(3)(b) the words "either by a branch or agency of theirs outside the United Kingdom or" shall be omitted.

(3) In the application of paragraph 17 in any case where—

(a) the old policy is a qualifying policy which was issued in respect of an insurance made on or before 17th November 1983 but, if the insurance had been made after that date, the policy could not have been a qualifying policy by virtue of paragraph 24, and

(b) the new policy is issued after that date and is not a new non-resident policy, as defined in paragraph 24,

the rules for the determination of the question whether the new policy is a qualifying policy shall apply with the modification in sub-paragraph (2)(c) above.

Former enactment.—FA 1984, Sch. 15, Pt. II, para. 2.

26. If, in the case of a substitution of policies falling within paragraph 25(1) or (3), the new policy confers such an option as results in the application to it of paragraph 19(3), the new policy shall be treated for the purposes of paragraph 19(3) as having been issued in respect of an insurance made on the same day as that on which was made the insurance in respect of which the old policy was issued.

Former enactment.—FA 1984, Sch. 15, Pt. II, para. 3.

27.—(1) For the purposes of Part I and paragraphs 21 and 24, a policy of life insurance which was issued—

(a) in respect of an insurance made on or before 17th November 1983, and

(b) by a company resident outside the United Kingdom,

shall be treated as issued in respect of an insurance made after that date if the policy is varied after that date so as to increase the benefits secured or to extend the term of the insurance.

(2) If a policy of life insurance which was issued as mentioned in sub-paragraph (1)(a) and (b) above confers on the person to whom it is issued an option to have another policy substituted for it or to have any of its terms changed, then for the purposes of that sub-paragraph any change in the terms of the policy which is made in pursuance of the option shall be deemed to be a variation of the policy.

Former enactment.—FA 1984, Sch. 15, Pt. II, para. 4.

SCHEDULE 16

Section 350(4)

COLLECTION OF INCOME TAX ON COMPANY PAYMENTS WHICH ARE NOT DISTRIBUTIONS

Interpretation

1. In this Schedule "relevant payment" means any payment to which section 350(4)(*a*) applies.

Former enactment.—FA 1972, Sch. 20, para. 1.

Duty to make returns

2.—(1) A company shall for each of its accounting periods make, in accordance with this Schedule, returns to the collector of the relevant payments made by it in that period and of the income tax for which it is accountable in respect of those payments.

(2) A return shall be made for—

  (*a*) each complete quarter falling within the accounting period, that is to say, each of the periods of three months ending with 31st March, 30th June, 30th September and 31st December which falls within that period;
  (*b*) each part of the accounting period which is not a complete quarter and ends on the first (or only), or begins immediately after the last (or only), of those dates which falls within the accounting period;
  (*c*) if none of those dates falls within the accounting period, the whole accounting period.

(3) A return for any period for which a return is required to be made under this paragraph shall be made within 14 days from the end of that period.

Former enactment.—FA 1972, Sch. 20, para. 2.

Contents of returns

3. The return made by a company for any period shall show—

  (*a*) the amount of any relevant payments made by the company in that period; and
  (*b*) the income tax in respect of those payments for which the company is accountable.

Former enactment.—FA 1972, Sch. 20, para. 3.

Payment of tax

4.—(1) Subject to sub-paragraph (4) below, income tax in respect of any payment required to be included in a return under this Schedule shall be due at the time by which the return is to be made, and income tax so due—

  (*a*) shall be payable by the company without the making of any assessment; and
  (*b*) may be assessed on the company (whether or not it has been paid when the assessment is made) if it, or any part of it, is not paid on or before the due date.

(2) If it appears to the inspector that there is a relevant payment which ought to have been and has not been included in a return, or if the inspector is dissatisfied with any return, he may make an assessment on the company to the best of his judgment; and any income tax due under an assessment made by virtue of this sub-paragraph shall be treated for the purposes of interest on unpaid tax as having been payable at the time when it would have been payable if a correct return had been made.

(3) Where a payment has been included in a return under Schedule 13 by virtue of paragraph 7(1)(*b*) of that Schedule and it becomes apparent that the payment is not a qualifying distribution but a relevant payment—

  (*a*) sub-paragraph (1)(*a*) above shall not apply to that payment; and
  (*b*) income tax shall be assessed in respect of it on the company.

Former enactment.—FA 1972, Sch. 20, para. 4.

Set-off of income tax borne on company income against tax payable

5.—(1) Where in any accounting period a company receives any payment on which it bears income tax by deduction the company may claim to have the income tax thereon set against any income tax which it is liable to pay under this Schedule in respect of payments made by it in that period.

(2) Any such claim shall be included in a return made under paragraph 2 above for the accounting period in question and (where necessary) income tax paid by the company under this Schedule for that accounting period and before the claim is allowed shall be repaid accordingly.

Former enactment.—FA 1972, Sch. 20, para. 5.

6.—(1) Where a claim has been made under paragraph 5 above no proceedings for collecting tax which would fall to be discharged if the claim were allowed shall be instituted pending the final determination of the claim, but this sub-paragraph shall not affect the date when the tax is due.

(2) When the claim is finally determined any tax underpaid in consequence of sub-paragraph (1) above shall be paid.

(3) Where proceedings are instituted for collecting tax assessed, or interest on tax assessed, under any provision of paragraph 4 above, effect shall not be given to any claim made after the institution of the proceedings so as to affect or delay the collection or recovery of the tax charged by the assessment or of interest thereon, until the claim has been finally determined.

(4) When the claim is finally determined any tax overpaid in consequence of sub-paragraph (3) above shall be repaid.

(5) References in this paragraph to proceedings for the collection of tax include references to proceedings by way of distraint or poinding for tax.

Former enactment.—FA 1972, Sch. 20, para. 6.

7. Income tax set against other tax under paragraph 5 above shall be treated as paid or repaid, as the case may be, and the same tax shall not be taken into account both under this Schedule and under section 7(2).

Former enactment.—FA 1972, Sch. 20, para. 7.

Items included in error

8. Where any item has been included in a return or claim under this Schedule as a relevant payment but should have been included in a return under Schedule 13, the inspector may make such assessments, adjustments or set-offs as may be required for securing that the resulting liabilities to tax (including interest on unpaid tax) whether of the company or of any other person are the same as they would have been if the item had been included in the right return.

Former enactment.—FA 1972, Sch. 20, para. 8.

Relevant payment made otherwise than in accounting period

9. Where a company makes a relevant payment on a date which does not fall within an accounting period the company shall make a return of that payment within 14 days from that date, and the income tax for which the company is accountable in respect of that payment shall be due at the time by which the return is to be made.

Former enactment.—FA 1972, Sch. 20, para. 9.

Assessments and due date of tax

10.—(1) All the provisions of the Income Tax Acts as to the time within which an assessment may be made, so far as they refer or relate to the year of assessment for which an assessment is made, or the year to which an assessment relates, shall apply in relation to any assessment under this Schedule notwithstanding that, under this Schedule, the assessment may be said to relate to a quarter or other period which is not a year of assessment, and the provisions of [section 36][1] of the Management Act as to the circumstances in which an assessment may be made out of time shall apply accordingly on the footing that any such assessment relates to the year of assessment in which the quarter or other period ends.

(2) Income tax assessed on a company under this Schedule shall be due within 14 days after the issue of the notice of assessment (unless due earlier under paragraph 4(1) or 9 above).

(3) Sub-paragraph (2) above has effect subject to any appeal against the assessment, but no such appeal shall affect the date when tax is due under paragraph 4(1) or 9 above.

(4) On the determination of an appeal against an assessment under this Schedule any tax overpaid shall be repaid.

(5) Any tax assessable under any one or more of the provisions of this Schedule may be included in one assessment if the tax so included is all due on the same date.

Former enactment.—FA 1972, Sch. 20, para. 10.
Amendments.—[1] Words in sub-para. (1) substituted by FA 1989, s. 149(3)(*d*).

Saving

11. Nothing in paragraphs 1 to 10 above shall be taken to prejudice any powers conferred by the Income Tax Acts for the recovery of income tax by means of an assessment or otherwise; and any assessment in respect of tax payable under paragraph 9 above shall be treated for the purposes of the provisions mentioned in paragraph 10(1) above as relating to the year of assessment in which the payment is made.

Former enactment.—FA 1972, Sch. 20, para. 11.

SCHEDULE 17

Section 404

DUAL RESIDENT INVESTING COMPANIES

PART I
DIVISION OF ACCOUNTING PERIODS COVERING 1ST APRIL 1987

1.—(1) This Part of this Schedule has effect in the circumstances set out in section 404(3)(*a*).

(2) In this Part of this Schedule—

(*a*) "the straddling period" means the accounting period of the dual resident investing company which begins before and ends on or after 1st April 1987; and
(*b*) "dual resident investing company" has the same meaning as in section 404.

(3) It shall be assumed for the purposes of this Chapter (except section 404(3) to (6)) and Part II of this Schedule—

(*a*) that an accounting period of the company ends on 31st March 1987; and
(*b*) that a new accounting period begins on 1st April 1987, the new accounting period to end with the end of the straddling period.

(4) In this Part of this Schedule "the component accounting periods" means the two accounting periods referred to in sub-paragraph (3) above.

Former enactment.—F(No. 2)A 1987, Sch. 4, para. 1.

2. Subject to paragraph 5 below, for the purposes referred to in paragraph 1(3) above, the losses and other amounts of the straddling period of a dual resident investing company, excluding any such excess of charges on income as is referred to in section 403(7), shall be apportioned to the component accounting periods on a time basis according to their lengths.

Former enactment.—F(No. 2)A 1987, Sch. 4, para. 2.

3. If, in the straddling period of a dual resident investing company, the company has paid any amount by way of charges on income, then, for the purposes referred to in paragraph 1(3) above, the excess of that amount referred to in section 403(7) shall be apportioned to the component accounting periods—

(*a*) according to the dates on which, subject to paragraph 6 below, the interest or other payments giving rise to those charges were paid (or were treated as paid for the purposes of section 338); and
(*b*) in proportion to the amounts of interest or other payments paid (or treated as paid) on those dates.

Former enactment.—F(No. 2)A 1987, Sch. 4, para. 3.

PART II
EARLY PAYMENTS OF INTEREST ETC. AND CHARGES ON INCOME

Interpretation

4. In this Part of this Schedule—

(*a*) a "1986 accounting period" means an accounting period which begins or ends (or begins and ends) in the financial year 1986;
(*b*) a "post-1986 accounting period" means an accounting period which begins on or after 1st April 1987; and
(*c*) "dual resident investing company" has the same meaning as in section 404.

Former enactment.—F(No. 2)A 1987, Sch. 4, para. 4.

Early payment of interest etc.

5.—(1) If the conditions in sub-paragraph (2) or (3) below are fulfilled and if the Board so direct, this paragraph applies in relation to a 1986 accounting period of a dual resident investing company.

(2) The conditions in this sub-paragraph are applicable only if the company is carrying on a trade in the 1986 accounting period, and those conditions are—

   (*a*) that in that accounting period the company has incurred a loss, computed as for the purposes of section 393(2), in carrying on that trade; and
   (*b*) that in that period the company has made a payment falling within section 404(6)(*a*)(iii); and
   (*c*) that the payment referred to in paragraph (*b*) above either did not fall due in that period or would not have fallen due in that period but for the making, on or after 5th December 1986, of arrangements varying the due date for payment.

(3) The conditions in this sub-paragraph are applicable only if the company is an investment company in the 1986 accounting period, and those conditions are—

   (*a*) that for that accounting period the company has (apart from this paragraph) such an excess as is referred to in section 403(4); and
   (*b*) that one or more of the sums which for that accounting period may be deducted as expenses of management under section 75(1) either did not fall due in that period or would not have fallen due in that period but for the making, on or after 5th December 1986, of arrangements varying the due date for payment.

(4) The Board shall not give a direction under this paragraph with respect to a 1986 accounting period of a dual resident investing company unless it appears to the Board that the sole or main benefit that might be expected to accrue from the early payment or, as the case may be, from the arrangements was that (apart from this paragraph) the company would, for that period, have an amount or, as the case may be, a larger amount available for surrender by way of group relief.

(5) If this paragraph applies in relation to a 1986 accounting period of a dual resident investing company which is carrying on a trade then, for the purposes of this Chapter and, where appropriate, any apportionment under paragraph 2 above—

   (*a*) the loss (if any) of the company for that period shall be computed (as mentioned in section 403(1)) as if any payment falling within sub-paragraph (2)(*b*) above had not been made in that period; and
   (*b*) the loss (if any) of the company for its first post-1986 accounting period shall be computed as if any such payment were made in that period.

(6) If this paragraph applies in relation to a 1986 accounting period of a dual resident investing company which is an investment company, then, for the purposes referred to in sub-paragraph (5) above—

   (*a*) the amount which may be deducted as expenses of management for that period, as mentioned in section 403(4), shall be computed as if any sum falling within sub-paragraph (3)(*b*) above had not been disbursed; and
   (*b*) the amount which may be so deducted as expenses of managment for the first of the company's post-1986 accounting periods shall be computed as if any such sum were disbursed in that period.

Former enactment.—F(No. 2)A 1987, Sch. 4, para. 5.

Early payment of charges on income

6.—(1) If, in the case of a dual resident investing company, either of the following conditions is fulfilled—

   (*a*) that any interest or other payment which is, or is treated as, a charge on income falls due in a post-1986 accounting period but is paid (or treated for the purposes of section 338 as paid) in a 1986 accounting period, or
   (*b*) that, on or after 5th December 1986, arrangements have been made such that any such interest or other payment which, but for the arrangements, would have fallen due in a post-1986 accounting period, fell due in a 1986 accounting period,

the interest or other payment shall, if the Board so direct, be treated for the purposes of this Chapter and, where appropriate, paragraph 3 above as paid in the post-1986 accounting period referred to in paragraph (*a*) or, as the case may be, paragraph (*b*) above.

(2) The Board shall not give a direction under this paragraph unless it appears to them that

the sole or main benefit that might be expected to accrue from the early payment or, as the case may be, from the arrangements was that (apart from the direction) the interest or other payment would be attributed or apportioned to a 1986 accounting period rather than a post-1986 accounting period, so that, for the 1986 accounting period, the dual resident investing company would have an amount or, as the case may be, a larger amount available for surrender by way of group relief.

Former enactment.—F(No. 2)A 1987, Sch. 4, para. 6.

Appeals

7. Notice of the giving of a direction under paragraph 5 or 6 above shall be given to the dual resident investing company concerned; and any company to which such a notice is given may, by giving notice of appeal to the Board within 60 days of the date of the notice given to the company, appeal to the Special Commissioners against the direction on either or both of the following grounds—

(*a*) that the conditions applicable to the company under paragraph 5(2) or (3) above are not fulfilled or, as the case may be, that neither of the conditions in paragraph 6(1) above is fulfilled;

(*b*) that the sole or main benefit that might be expected to accrue from the early payment or, as the case may be, the arrangements was not that stated in paragraph 5(4) or, as the case may be, paragraph 6(2) above.

Former enactment.—F(No. 2)A 1987, Sch. 4, para. 7.

PART III
GENERAL

8.—(1) Parts I and II of this Schedule have effect in priority to section 409 and, accordingly, each of the component accounting periods resulting from the operation of Part I of this Schedule shall be regarded as a true accounting period for the purposes of that section.

(2) References in this Schedule to this Chapter do not include any provision of this Schedule.

Former enactment.—F(No. 2)A 1987, Sch. 4, para. 8.

SCHEDULE 18

Section 413(10)

Cross references.—See TA 1970, s. 272(1F) (this Schedule to apply with certain modifications for the purposes of TA 1970, s. 272(1D), (1E) (definitions of groups of companies)).

GROUP RELIEF: EQUITY HOLDERS AND PROFITS OR ASSETS AVAILABLE FOR DISTRIBUTION

1.—(1) For the purposes of section 413(7) to (9) and this Schedule, an equity holder of a company is any person who—

(*a*) holds ordinary shares in the company, or
(*b*) is a loan creditor of the company in respect of a loan which is not a normal commercial loan,

and any reference in that section to profits or assets available for distribution to a company's equity holders does not include a reference to any profits or assets available for distribution to any equity holder otherwise than as an equity holder.

(2) For the purposes of sub-paragraph (1)(*a*) above "ordinary shares" means all shares other than fixed-rate preference shares.

(3) In this Schedule "fixed-rate preference shares" means share which—

(*a*) are issued for consideration which is or includes new consideration; and
[(*b*) do not carry any right either to conversion into shares or securities of any other description except—

 (i) shares to which sub-paragraph (5A) below applies,
 (ii) securities to which sub-paragraph (5B) below applies, or
 (iii) shares or securities in the company's quoted parent company,

or to the acquisition of any additional shares or securities;][1]
(*c*) do not carry any right to dividends other than dividends which—

 (i) are of a fixed amount or at a fixed rate per cent. of the nominal value of the shares, and
 (ii) represent no more than a reasonable commercial return on the new consideration received by the company in respect of the issue of the shares; and

(*d*) on repayment do not carry any rights to an amount exceeding that new consideration except in so far as those rights are reasonably comparable with those general for fixed dividend shares listed in the Official List of the Stock Exchange.

(4) Subsection (7) of section 417 shall apply for the purposes of sub-paragraph (1)(*b*) above as it applies for the purposes of Part XI, but with the omission of the reference to subsection (9) of that section.

(5) In sub-paragraph (1)(*b*) above "normal commercial loan" means a loan of or including new consideration and—

[(*a*) which does not carry any right either to conversion into shares or securities of any other description except—

 (i) shares to which sub-paragraph (5A) below applies,
 (ii) securities to which sub-paragraph (5B) below applies, or
 (iii) shares or securities in the company's quoted parent company,

or to the acquisition of any additional shares or securities;][1]
(*b*) which does not entitle that loan creditor to any amount by way of interest which depends to any extent on the results of the company's business or any part of it or on the value of any of the company's assets or which exceeds a reasonable commercial return on the new consideration lent; and
(*c*) in respect of which the loan creditor is entitled, on repayment, to an amount which either does not exceed the new consideration lent or is reasonably comparable with the amount generally repayable (in respect of an equal amount of new consideration) under the terms of issue of securities listed in the Official List of the Stock Exchange.

[(5A) This sub-paragraph applies to any shares which—

(*a*) satisfy the requirements of sub-paragraph (3)(*a*), (*c*) and (*d*) above, and (*b*) do not carry any rights either to conversion into shares or securities of any other description, except shares or securities in the company's quoted parent company, or to the acquisition of any additional shares or securities.]²

[(5B) This sub-paragraph applies to any securities representing a loan of or including new consideration and—

(*a*) which satisfies the requirements of sub-paragraph (5)(*b*) and (*c*) above, and
(*b*) which does not carry any such rights as are mentioned in sub-paragraph (5A)(*b*) above.]²

[(5C) For the purposes of sub-paragraphs (3) and (5) to (5B) above a company ("the parent company") is another company's "quoted parent company" if and only if—

(*a*) the other company is a 75 per cent. subsidiary of the parent company,
(*b*) the parent company is not a 75 per cent. subsidiary of any company, and
(*c*) the parent company's ordinary shares (or, if its ordinary share capital is divided into two or more classes, its ordinary shares of each class) are quoted on a recognised stock exchange or dealt in on the Unlisted Securities Market;

and in this sub-paragraph "ordinary shares" means shares forming part of ordinary share capital.]²

[(5D) In the application of sub-paragraphs (3) and (5) to (5B) above in determining for the purposes of sub-paragraph (5C)(*a*) above who are the equity holders of the other company (and, accordingly, whether section 413(7) prevents the other company from being treated as a 75 per cent. subsidiary of the parent company for the purposes of sub-paragraph (5C)(*a*)), it shall be assumed that the parent company is for the purposes of sub-paragraphs (3) and (5) to (5B) above the other company's quoted parent company.]²

(6) Notwithstanding anything in sub-paragraphs (1) to (5) above but subject to sub-paragraph (7) below, where—

(*a*) any person has, directly or indirectly, provided new consideration for any shares or securities in the company, and
(*b*) that person, or any person connected with him, uses for the purposes of his trade assets which belong to the company and in respect of which there is made to the company—

(i) a first-year allowance within the meaning of Chapter I of Part III of the Finance Act 1971 ("the 1971 Act") in respect of expenditure incurred by the company on the provision of machinery or plant;
(ii) a writing-down allowance within the meaning of Chapter II of Part I of the 1968 Act or, as the case may be, Chapter I of Part III of the 1971 Act in respect of expenditure incurred by the company on the provision of machinery or plant; or
(iii) an allowance under section 91 of the 1968 Act in respect of expenditure incurred by the company on scientific research;

then, for the purposes of this Schedule, that person, and no other, shall be treated as being an equity holder in respect of those shares or securities and as being beneficially entitled to any distribution of profits or assets attributable to those shares or securities.

(7) In any case where sub-paragraph (6) above applies in relation to a bank in such circumstances that—

(*a*) the only new consideration provided by the bank as mentioned in paragraph (*a*) of that sub-paragraph is provided in the normal course of its banking business by way of a normal commercial loan as defined in sub-paragraph (5) above; and
(*b*) the cost to the company concerned of assets falling within paragraph (*b*) of that sub-paragraph which are used as mentioned in that paragraph by the bank or a person connected with the bank is less than the amount of that new consideration,

references in sub-paragraph (6) above, other than the reference in paragraph (*a*), to shares or securities in the company shall be construed as references to so much only of the loan referred to paragraph (*a*) above as is equal to the cost referred to in paragraph (*b*) above.

(8) In this paragraph "new consideration" has the same meaning as in section 254 and any question whether one person is connected with another shall be determined in accordance with section 839.

Former enactments.—FA 1973, Sch. 12, para. 1; FA 1987, Sch. 15, para. 5.
Amendments.—¹ Sub-paras. (3)(*b*), (5)(*a*) substituted by FA 1989, s. 101 and in their application (by virtue of FA 1989, s. 138) for the purposes of TA 1970, s. 272(1D), (1E) are deemed to have come into force on 14 March 1989.
² Sub-paras. (5A)–(5D) inserted by *ibid*.

2.—(1) Subject to the following provisions of this Schedule, for the purposes of section

413(7) to (9) the percentage to which one company is beneficially entitled of any profits available for distribution to the equity holders of another company means the percentage to which the first company would be so entitled in the relevant accounting period on a distribution in money to those equity holders of—

(*a*) an amount of profits equal to the total profits of the other company which arise in that accounting period (whether or not any of those profits are in fact distributed); or

(*b*) if there are no profits of the other company in that accounting period, profits of £100;

and in the following provisions of this Schedule that distribution is referred to as "the profit distribution".

(2) For the purposes of the profit distribution, it shall be assumed that no payment is made by way of repayment of share capital or of the principal secured by any loan unless that payment is a distribution.

(3) Subject to sub-paragraph (2) above, where an equity holder is entitled as such to a payment of any description which, apart from this sub-paragraph, would not be treated as a distribution, it shall nevertheless be treated as an amount to which he is entitled on the profit distribution.

Former enactment.—FA 1973, Sch. 12, para. 2.

3.—(1) Subject to the following provisions of this Schedule, for the purposes of section 413(7) to (9) the percentage to which one company would be beneficially entitled of any assets of another company available for distribution to its equity holders on a winding-up means the percentage to which the first company would be so entitled if the other company were to be wound up and on that winding-up the value of the assets available for distribution to its equity holders (that is to say, after deducting any liabilities to other persons) were equal to—

(*a*) the excess, if any, of the total amount of the assets of the company, as shown in the balance sheet relating to its affairs as at the end of the relevant accounting period, over the total amount of those of its liabilities as so shown which are not liabilities to equity holders as such; or

(*b*) if there is no such excess or if the company's balance sheet is prepared to a date other than the end of the relevant accounting period, £100.

(2) In the following provisions of this Schedule a winding-up on the basis specified in sub-paragraph (1) above is referred to as "the notional winding-up".

(3) If, on the notional winding-up, an equity holder would be entitled as such to an amount of assets of any description which, apart from this sub-paragraph, would not be treated as a distribution of assets, it shall nevertheless be treated, subject to sub-paragraph (4) below, as an amount to which the equity holder is entitled on the distribution of assets on the notional winding up.

(4) If an amount ("the returned amount") which corresponds to the whole or any part of the new consideration provided by an equity holder of a company for any shares or securities in respect of which he is an equity holder is applied by the company, directly or indirectly, in the making of a loan to, or in the acquisition of any shares or securities in, the equity holder or any person connected with him, then, for the purposes of this Schedule—

(*a*) the total amount referred to in sub-paragraph (1)(*a*) above shall be taken to be reduced by a sum equal to the returned amount; and

(*b*) the amount of assets to which the equity holder is beneficially entitled on the notional winding-up shall be taken to be reduced by a sum equal to the returned amount.

(5) In sub-paragraph (4) above "new consideration" has the same meaning as in section 254 and any question whether one person is connected with another shall be determined in accordance with section 839.

Former enactment.—FA 1973, Sch. 12, para. 3.

4.—(1) This paragraph applies if any of the equity holders—

(*a*) to whom the profit distribution is made, or

(*b*) who is entitled to participate in the notional winding-up,

holds, as such an equity holder, any shares or securities which carry rights in respect of dividend or interest or assets on a winding-up which are wholly or partly limited by reference to a specified amount or amounts (whether the limitation takes the form of the capital by reference to which a distribution is calculated or operates by reference to an amount of profits or otherwise).

(2) Where this paragraph applies there shall be determined—

(a) the percentage of profits to which, on the profit distribution, the first company referred to in paragraph 2(1) above would be entitled, and

(b) the percentage of assets to which, on the notional winding-up, the first company referred to in paragraph 3(1) above would be entitled,

if, to the extent that they are limited as mentioned in sub-paragraph (1) above, the rights of every equity holder falling within that sub-paragraph (including the first company concerned if it is such an equity holder) had been waived.

(3) If, on the profit distribution, the percentage of profits determined as mentioned in sub-paragraph (2)(a) above is less than the percentage of profits determined under paragraph 2(1) above without regard to that sub-paragraph, the lesser percentage shall be taken for the purposes of section 413(7) to (9) to be the percentage of profits to which, on the profit distribution, the first company referred to in paragraph 2(1) above would be entitled as mentioned in that paragraph.

(4) If, on the notional winding-up, the percentage of assets determined as mentioned in sub-paragraph (2)(b) above is less than the percentage of assets determined under paragraph 3(1) above without regard to that sub-paragraph, the lesser percentage shall be taken for the purposes of section 413(7) to (9) to be the percentage to which, on the notional winding-up, the first company mentioned in paragraph 3(1) above would be entitled of any assets of the other company available for distribution to its equity holders on a winding-up.

Former enactment.—FA 1973, Sch. 12, para. 4.

5.—(1) This paragraph applies if, at any time in the relevant accounting period, any of the equity holders—

(a) to whom the profit distribution is made, or

(b) who is entitled to participate in the notional winding-up,

holds, as such an equity holder, any shares or securities which carry rights in respect of dividend or interest or assets on a winding-up which are of such a nature, (as, for example, if any shares will cease to carry a right to a dividend at a future time) that if the profit distribution or the notional winding-up were to take place in a different accounting period the percentage to which, in accordance with paragraphs 1 to 4 above, that equity holder would be entitled of profits on the profit distribution or of assets on the notional winding-up would be different from the percentage determined in the relevant accounting period.

(2) Where this paragraph applies, there shall be determined—

(a) the percentage of profits to which, on the profit distribution, the first company referred to in paragraph 2(1) above would be entitled, and

(b) the percentage of assets to which, on the notional winding-up, the first company referred to in paragraph 3(1) above would be entitled,

if the rights of the equity holders in the relevant accounting period were the same as they would be in the different accounting period referred to in sub-paragraph (1) above.

(3) If in the relevant accounting period an equity holder holds, as such, any shares or securities in respect of which arrangements exist by virtue of which, in that or any subsequent accounting period, the equity holder's entitlement to profits on the profit distribution or to assets on the notional winding-up could be different as compared with his entitlement if effect were not given to the arrangements, then for the purposes of this paragraph—

(a) it shall be assumed that effect would be given to those arrangements in a later accounting period, and

(b) those shares or securities shall be treated as though any variation in the equity holder's entitlement to profits or assets resulting from giving effect to the arrangements were the result of the operation of such rights attaching to the share or securities as are referred to in sub-paragraph (1) above.

In this sub-paragraph "arrangements" means arrangements of any kind whether in writing or not.

(4) Sub-paragraphs (3) and (4) of paragraph 4 above shall apply for the purposes of this paragraph as they apply for the purposes of that paragraph and, accordingly, references therein to sub-paragraphs (2)(a) and (2)(b) of that paragraph shall be construed as references to sub-paragraphs (2)(a) and (2)(b) of this paragraph.

(5) In any case where paragraph 4 above applies as well as this paragraph, that paragraph shall be applied separately (in relation to the profit distribution and the notional winding-up)—

  (*a*) on the basis specified in sub-paragraph (2) above, and
  (*b*) without regard to that sub-paragraph,

and sub-paragraphs (3) and (4) of that paragraph shall apply accordingly in relation to the percentages so determined as if for the word "lesser" there were substituted the word "lowest".

Former enactment.—FA 1973, s. 32(6), Sch. 12, para. 5.

6. For the purposes of section 413(7) to (9) and paragraphs 2 to 5 above—

  (*a*) the percentage to which one company is beneficially entitled of any profits available for distribution to the equity holders of another company, and
  (*b*) the percentage to which one company would be beneficially entitled of any assets of another company on a winding-up,

means the percentage to which the first company is, or would be, so entitled either directly or through another body corporate or other bodies corporate or partly directly and partly through another body corporate or other bodies corporate.

Former enactment.—FA 1973, Sch. 12, para. 6.

7.—(1) In this Schedule "the relevant accounting period" means—

  (*a*) in a case falling within subsection (7) of section 413, the accounting period current at the time in question; and
  (*b*) in a case falling within subsection (8) of that section, the accounting period in relation to which the share in the consortium falls to be determined.

(2) For the purposes of this Schedule, a loan to a company shall be treated as a security, whether or not it is a secured loan, and, if it is a secured loan, regardless of the nature of the security.

Former enactment.—FA 1973, Sch. 12, para. 7.

SCHEDULE 19

Section 423

APPORTIONMENT OF INCOME OF CLOSE COMPANIES

PART I
DETERMINATION OF RELEVANT INCOME AND DISTRIBUTIONS

Amendments.—This Schedule repealed by FA 1989, s. 103 and Sch. 17, Pt. V in relation to accounting periods beginning after 31 March 1989 except that Part I of the Schedule continues to have effect in any case where the subsequent distribution referred to in s. 427(4) of this Act is made before 1 April 1992.

Relevant income

1.—*(1) Subject to the provisions of this Part of this Schedule, the relevant income of a company for an accounting period is—*

(a) in the case of a company which is a trading company or a member of a trading group, so much of its distributable income, other than trading income, for that period as can be distributed without prejudice to the requirements of the company's business;

(b) in the case of a company not within paragraph (a) above whose distributable income for that period consists of or includes estate or trading income—

  (i) so much of the estate or trading income as can be distributed without prejudice to the requirements of the company's business so far as concerned with the activities or assets giving rise to estate or trading income; and

  (ii) its distributable income, if any, other than estate or trading income;

(c) in the case of any other company, its distributable income for that period.

(2) In arriving at the relevant income for any accounting period—

(a) where under sub-paragraph (1) above regard is to be had to the requirements of a company's business, regard shall be had not only to the current requirements of the business but also to such other requirements as may be necessary or advisable for the maintenance and development of that business but, for this purpose, the provisions of paragraph 8 below shall apply;

(b) the amount of the estate or trading income shall be taken as the amount included in respect of it in the distributable income.

(3) In arriving at the relevant income for any accounting period of a company which is a trading company or a member of a trading group, regard shall be had not only to the current requirements of the company's business and to such requirements as may be necessary or advisable for the maintenance and development of that business as fall within sub-paragraph (2)(a) above, but also to any other requirements necessary or advisable for the acquisition of a trade or of a controlling interest in a trading company or in a company which is a member of a trading group by virtue of paragraph 7(2)(a) below; but, for this purpose, paragraph 9 below shall apply.

(4) For the purposes of sub-paragraph (3) above, the acquisition of a controlling interest in a company means the acquisition, whether on a single occasion or otherwise, of such ordinary share capital of that company as enables the acquiring company to exercise the greater part of the voting power in that company.

(5) For the purposes of sub-paragraph (3) above, the requirements of a company's business which are necessary or advisable for such an acquisition as is mentioned in that sub-paragraph include such requirements as are necessary or advisable for—

(a) the redemption or repayment of any share or loan capital or debt (including any premium thereon) issued or incurred in or towards payment for that acquisition, or issued or incurred for the purpose of raising money to be applied in or towards payment therefor, or

(b) meeting any obligation of the company in respect of that acquisition,

so far as any sum so expended or applied, or intended to be expended or applied, does not fall to be treated for the purposes of this Chapter as a distribution by the company.

Former enactments.—Sub-para. (1): FA 1972, Sch. 16, para. 8(1); FA 1980, Sch. 9, para. 1.
Sub-para. (2): FA 1972, Sch. 16, para. 8(2).
Sub-paras. (3)–(5): FA 1972, Sch. 16, para. 8(3)–(5); FA 1978, Sch. 5, para. 1.

Maximum amount of relevant income

2.—*(1) Subject to paragraphs 10 and 12 below, the relevant income of a company shall in no case be taken to exceed the company's distributable investment income for the accounting period plus 50 per cent. of the estate or trading income for the period.*

(2) In the application of sub-paragraph (1) above to a company which is a trading company or a member of a trading group, the trading income shall be disregarded; and in the application of that sub-paragraph to a trading company, the estate income—

(a) if it is less than the appropriate fraction of the relevant maximum amount, shall be treated as reduced by one-half of the amount required to make it up to that fraction of the relevant maximum amount; or
(b) if it is less than the appropriate fraction of the relevant minimum amount, shall be disregarded;

and in this sub-paragraph the appropriate fraction is—

$$\frac{A}{A+B}$$

where—

A is the amount of the estate income, and
B is the amount of the trading income.

(3) The relevant maximum and minimum amounts referred to above shall be determined as follows—

(a) where the company has no associated company in the accounting period, those amounts are £75,000 and £25,000 respectively;
(b) where the company has one or more associated companies in the accounting period—

(i) the relevant maximum amount is—

$$\frac{£75,000}{1+X}$$

(ii) the relevant minimum amount is—

$$\frac{£25,000}{1+X}$$

where X is the number of those associated companies.

(4) In applying sub-paragraphs (2) and (3) above to any accounting period of a trading company, an associated company shall be disregarded if—

(a) it was not a trading company, or has not carried on any trade, at any time in that accounting period; or
(b) where it was an associated company during part only of that accounting period, it was not a trading company, or has not carried on any trade, at any time in that part of that accounting period;

and for the purposes of this paragraph a company is to be treated as an associated company of another at a given time if at that time one of the two has control of the other or both are under the control of the same person or persons.

(5) In determining how many associated companies a trading company has in an accounting period or whether a trading company has an associated company in an accounting period, an associated company shall be counted even if it was an associated company for part only of the accounting period, and two or more associated companies shall be counted even if they were associated companies for different parts of the accounting period.

(6) For an accounting period of less than 12 months the relevant maximum and minimum amounts determined in accordance with sub-paragraphs (1) to (5) above shall be proportionately reduced.

Former enactments.—Sub-para. (1): FA 1972, Sch. 16, para. 9(1).
Sub-para. (2): FA 1972, Sch. 16, para. 9(2); FA 1980, Sch. 9, para. 2.
Sub-para. (3): FA 1972, Sch. 16, para. 9(3); FA 1978, s. 35(1).
Sub-para. (4): FA 1972, Sch. 16, para. 9(4); FA 1978, s. 35(2).
Sub-para. (5), (6): FA 1972, Sch. 16, para. 9(5), (6).

Distributions

3.—*(1)* For the purposes of this Chapter the distributions of a company for an accounting period shall, subject to sub-paragraphs (2) to (4) and paragraph 12 below, be taken to consist of—

  (a) any dividends which are declared in respect of the period and are paid during the period or within a reasonable time thereafter;
  (b) all distributions made in the period except dividends which, in relation to any previous period, would fall under paragraph (a) above; and
  (c) anything that would be a distribution but for section 213 or 219 (or both).

(2) Where a period of account is not an accounting period, dividends which, if it were an accounting period, would be treated under sub-paragraph (1)(a) above as distributions for that accounting period shall be apportioned to any accounting period or part of an accounting period falling within the period of account in proportion to the distributable income of each such period or part.

(3) For the purposes of determining whether there is any such excess as is referred to in section 424(1), no account shall be taken of a distribution which, in relation to the company making it, is a bonus distribution unless—

  (a) it is made to a person other than a close company, or
  (b) it is made to a close company and the share capital or security of which it consists is subsequently distributed, by that or any other close company, by a distribution falling within section 14(2)(b) to a person other than a close company.

(4) Where a bonus distribution has occurred and, by virtue of paragraph (a) or paragraph (b) of sub-paragraph (3) above, it falls to be taken into account for the purpose of determining whether there is any such excess as is referred to in section 424(1), no account shall be taken for that purpose of a qualifying distribution which consists of the repayment of the share capital or, as the case may be, the principal of the security, which constituted the bonus distribution.

(5) In sub-paragraphs (3) and (4) above "bonus distribution" means a distribution which in relation to the company making it is a distribution by virtue only of paragraph (c) of section 209(2).

Former enactments.—Sub-para. (1)(*a*), (*b*): FA 1972, Sch. 16, para. 10(1); F(No. 2)A 1975, Sch. 8, para. 4.
Sub-para. (1)(*c*): FA 1982, s. 56(1).
Sub-para. (2): FA 1972, Sch. 16, para. 10(1).
Sub-paras. (3)–(5): FA 1972, Sch. 16, para. 10A; FA 1973, Sch. 9, para. 3.

Distributable income and estate or trading income

4.—*(1)* For the purposes of this Chapter, the distributable income of a company for an accounting period shall be the amount of its distributable profits for the period exclusive of the part attributable to chargeable gains; and for the purposes of this sub-paragraph—

  (a) the distributable profits of a company for an accounting period shall be the aggregate of the following amounts, that is to say—

   (i) the amount of any profits on which corporation tax falls finally to be borne, less the amount of that tax;
   (ii) an amount equal to the qualifying distributions comprised in any franked investment income, other than franked investment income against which relief is given under section 242 or 243; and
   (iii) an amount equal to any group income;

  (b) the part of a company's distributable profits attributable to chargeable gains shall be taken to be the amount of the chargeable gains on which corporation tax is finally borne less the amount of that tax; and
  (c) the amount on which corporation tax falls finally to be borne (but not the amount of that tax) shall be computed as if section 242 did not include subsection (5) or (6) of that section (and as if section 243 did not apply section 242(5));

and for the purposes of sub-paragraph (a)(ii) above relief under section 242 or 243 shall be treated as having been given first against franked investment income which is not trading income and secondly, so far as it cannot be so given, against franked investment income which is trading income.

(2) For the purposes of this Chapter, the distributable investment income of a company for an accounting period shall be the amount of the distributable income, exclusive of the part attributable to estate or trading income, and less whichever is the smaller of—

(a) 10 per cent. of the estate or trading income; and
(b) £1,000 or, if the company is a trading company or a member of a trading group, £3,000 or (in either case) if the accounting period is of less than 12 months, a proportionately reduced amount.

Former enactments.—Sub-para. (1): FA 1972, Sch. 16, para. 10(2); FA 1980, Sch. 9, para 3.
Sub-para. (2): FA 1972, Sch. 16, para. 10(3); FA 1978, s.35(3); FA 1980, s. 44(2).

5.—(1) For the purposes of this Chapter, "estate or trading income" means estate income and trading income.

(2) For those purposes "estate income" means income which is chargeable to tax under Schedule A or Schedule B, and income (other than yearly or other interest) which is chargeable to tax under Schedule D, and which arises from the ownership or occupation of land (including any interest in or right over land) or from the letting furnished of any building or part of a building, but does not include trading income.

(3) For those purposes "trading income" means income which is not investment income for the purposes of paragraph 7(1) below; and, where the following conditions are satisfied with respect to a close company, that is to say—

(a) that its activities consist wholly or mainly of the carrying on of a trade; and
(b) that the trade consists wholly or mainly of one or more of the following, that is to say, life assurance business (within the meaning of section 431), insurance business of any other class, banking, money lending, financing of hire-purchase or similar transactions, or dealing in securities;

its income incidental to that trade shall also be trading income.

(4) For the purposes of sub-paragraph (3) above income of a company is incidental to its trade if, and only if—

(a) it is derived from investments (other than investments in a 51 per cent. subsidiary) or is interest on a debt; and
(b) any profit on the sale of the investments would be a trading receipt, and the debt, if proved to be a bad debt, would be allowed as a deduction in computing the company's trading income for the purposes of corporation tax.

Former enactments.—Sub-paras. (1), (2): FA 1972, Sch. 16, para. 10(4), (4A); FA 1980, Sch. 9, para. 4.
Sub-para. (3): FA 1972, Sch. 16, para 10(5); FA 1980, Sch. 9, para. 5.
Sub-para. (4): FA 1972, Sch. 16, para. 10(6).

6.—(1) The amount for part of an accounting period of any description of income referred to in paragraph 4 or 5 above shall be a proportionate part of the amount for the whole period.

(2) In determining the amount for any period of any description of income referred to in paragraph 4 or 5 above, any deduction from the company's profits for charges on income, expenses of management or other amounts which can be deducted from or set against or treated as reducing profits of more than one description shall be treated as made—

(a) first, from the company's income charged to corporation tax other than estate or trading income;
(b) secondly, so far as it cannot be made under paragraph (a) above, from the company's estate or trading income so charged;
(c) thirdly, so far as it cannot be made under paragraph (a) or (b) above, from the amount included in the company's profits in respect of chargeable gains.

(3) In the application of sub-paragraph (2) above to a company which is a trading company or a member of a trading group there shall be substituted for paragraph (b) the following paragraphs—

"(b) secondly, so far as it cannot be made under (a) above, from the company's estate income so charged;
(bb) thirdly, so far as it cannot be made under (a) or (b) above, from the company's trading income so charged;"

and in paragraph (c) for "thirdly" there shall be substituted "fourthly", and for "(a) or (b)" there shall be substituted "(a), (b) or (bb)".

Former enactments.—Sub-para. (1): FA 1972, Sch. 16, para. 10(7).
Sub-para. (2)(a): FA 1972, Sch 16, para. 10(8)(a).
Sub-para. (2)(b), (c): FA 1972, Sch. 16, para. 10(8)(b), (c); FA 1985, Sch. 25, para. 9.
Sub-para (3): FA 1972, Sch. 16, para. 10(9); FA 1980, Sch. 9, para. 6; FA 1987, Sch. 15, para. 4.

Meaning of "trading company" and "member of a trading group"

7.—*(1)* For the purposes of this Chapter, a "trading company" is any company which exists wholly or mainly for the purpose of carrying on a trade, and any other company whose income does not consist wholly or mainly of investment income, that is to say, income which, if the company were an individual, would not be earned income; but for this purpose any amount which is apportioned to a company under section 423(1) shall be deemed to be income of the company and to be investment income.

(2) Subject to sub-paragraph (3) below, for the purposes of this Chapter, a company is to be treated as a member of a trading group if, but only if—

(a) it exists wholly or mainly for the purpose of co-ordinating the administration of a group of two or more companies each of which is under its control and exists wholly or mainly for the purpose of carrying on a trade; or

(b) it is under the control of another company resident in the United Kingdom and not itself under the control of a third company, and it exists wholly or mainly for the purpose of a trade or trades carried on by that other company or by a group which, consisting of that other company and a company or companies also under its control and resident in the United Kingdom, exists wholly or mainly for the purpose of carrying on that trade or trades.

(3) A company shall not be treated as a member of a trading group by reason only of any company having the control of another if that control is exercised through a company which is not resident in the United Kingdom or through a company whose control depends on holding a profit on the sale of which would be treated as a trading receipt of the company.

Former enactment.—FA 1972, Sch. 16, para. 11.

Requirements of a company's business

8.—*(1)* For the purposes of paragraph 1(2) above there shall be regarded as income available for distribution and not as having been applied, or as being applicable, to the current requirements of a company's business, or to such other requirements as may be necessary or advisable for the maintenance and development of that business—

(a) any sum expended or applied, or intended to be expended or applied, out of the income of the company—

(i) in or towards payment for the business, undertaking or property which the company was formed to acquire or which was the first business, undertaking or property of a substantial character in fact acquired by the company, or

(ii) in redemption or repayment of any share or loan capital or debt (including any premium thereon) issued or incurred in or towards payment for any such business, undertaking or property, or issued or incurred for the purpose of raising money applied or to be applied in or towards payment therefor, or

(iii) in meeting any obligations of the company in respect of the acquisition of any such business, undertaking or property, or

(iv) in redemption or repayment of any share or loan capital or debt (including any premium thereon) issued or incurred otherwise than for adequate consideration; and

(b) any sum expended or applied, or intended to be expended or applied, in pursuance or in consequence of any fictitious or artificial transactions; and

(c) in the case of a company which is neither a trading company nor a member of a trading group, any sum expended or applied, or available to be expended or applied, out of the income of the company in or towards the redemption, repayment or discharge of any loan capital or debt (including any premium thereon) in respect of which any person is a loan creditor of the company; and

(d) in the case of a company which is neither a trading company nor a member of a trading group, any sum expended or applied, or available to be expended or applied, out of the income of the company in or towards the acquisition of an estate or interest in land or the construction or extension of a building, not being a construction or extension which constitutes an improvement or development of farm land or market garden land.

Sub-paragraph (d) above does not apply where the acquisition, construction or extension concerned was made in pursuance of a contract entered into before 24th March 1973.

(2) For the purposes of sub-paragraph (1)(a)(iv) above, share or loan capital or debt shall be deemed to be issued or incurred otherwise than for adequate consideration if—

(a) it is issued or incurred for consideration the value of which to the company is substantially less than the amount of the capital or debt (including any premium thereon); or

(b) it is issued or incurred in or towards, or for the purpose of raising money applied or to be

applied in or towards, the redemption or repayment of any share or loan capital or debt which itself was issued or incurred for such consideration as is mentioned in paragraph *(a)* above or which represents, directly or indirectly, any share or loan capital or debt which itself was issued or incurred for such consideration.

(3) In relation to any loan capital or debt mentioned in sub-paragraph *(1)(c)* above which was issued or incurred by the company for money borrowed by it for the purpose of financing expenditure on any acquisition, construction or extension falling within sub-paragraph *(1)(d)* above, the expression "loan creditor" in sub-paragraph *(1)(c)* above shall be construed as if, in the definition of that expression in subsections *(7)* to *(9)* of section 417, subsection *(9)* were omitted.

(4) References in sub-paragraphs *(1)(a)* and *(2)(b)* above to the redemption or repayment of a company's share capital shall be construed as including references to the purchase by the company of its own shares.

(5) References in sub-paragraphs *(1)* to *(4)* above to money applied or to be applied for any purpose shall be deemed to include references to money applied or to be applied in or towards the replacement of that money.

Former enactments.—Sub-para. (1): FA 1972, Sch. 16, para. 12(1); FA 1973, Sch. 9, para. 4(2), (4).
Sub-para. (2): FA 1972, Sch. 16, para. 12(2).
Sub-para. (3): FA 1972, Sch. 16, para. 12(2A); FA 1973, Sch. 9, para. 4(3).
Sub-para. (4): FA 1972, Sch. 16, para. 12(2B); FA 1982, s. 56(2).
Sub-para. (5): FA 1972, Sch. 16, para. 12(3).

9.—*(1)* Paragraph *1(3)* above shall not apply to—

(a) the acquisition of a trade, or of an asset to be used in a trade, or of an interest in any such asset, which at the date of the acquisition or at any time within one year previously was owned by an associated company of the acquiring company; or
(b) the intended acquisition of a trade, or of such an asset or interest as is referred to in paragraph *(a)* above, which, at the end of the accounting period for which the acquiring company's relevant income is to be ascertained, is owned by a company which is then an associated company of the acquiring company;

and, where the trade, asset or interest was, or is, in part owned as mentioned above, paragraph *1(3)* above shall not apply with respect to that part.

(2) Paragraph *1(3)* above shall not apply to—

(a) the acquisition of shares which at the date of the acquisition or at any time within one year previously were owned by an associated company of the acquiring company or by a person who then had control of the acquiring company; or
(b) the intended acquisition of shares which at the end of the accounting period for which the acquiring company's relevant income is to be ascertained are owned by a company which is then an associated company of the acquiring company or by a person who has control of the acquiring company;

and where shares were, or are, in part owned as mentioned above, paragraph *1(3)* above shall not apply with respect to that part.

(3) Paragraph *1(3)* above shall not apply to—

(a) the acquisition of shares in a company which immediately before the acquisition or at any time within one year previously was an associated company of the acquiring company; or
(b) the intended acquisition of shares in a company which, at the end of the accounting period for which the acquiring company's relevant income is to be ascertained, is an associated company of the acquiring company.

(4) Section 416(1)—

(a) shall not apply for the purposes of paragraph *(a)* of sub-paragraphs *(1)*, *(2)* and *(3)* above; and
(b) shall apply for the purposes of paragraph *(b)* of each of those sub-paragraphs with the omission of the words "or at any time within one year previously".

(5) For the purposes of paragraph *(a)* of sub-paragraphs *(1)*, *(2)* and *(3)* above, another company is an associated company of the acquiring company if—

(a) the acquiring company controlled that other company or that other company controlled the acquiring company either at the date of the acquisition of the trade, asset or interest or at any time within one year previously; or
(b) a person who had control of the acquiring company at that date also controlled that other company either at that date or at any time within one year previously.

(6) In ascertaining for the purposes of sub-paragraphs (2) and (5) above or for the purposes of section 416(1) as it applies it for the purposes of paragraph (b) of sub-paragraphs (1), (2) and (3) above, whether any person has control of a company—

(a) there shall be left out of account for the purposes of section 416(2)(c) the rights of another company as loan creditor in respect of a debt incurred or redeemable loan capital issued in connection with the acquisition from that company of any trade, any asset to be used in a trade, or any interest in any such asset;
(b) section 417(3)(a) shall have effect as if the reference to a partner of a participator were omitted;
(c) section 417(3)(a) and (b) shall have effect as if the expression "relative" did not have the meaning assigned to it by section 417(4) but meant husband or wife or, in the case of a director of the company, husband or wife or any child or remoter issue who is an infant; and
(d) section 417(3)(c) shall have effect as if the reference to any other person interested were a reference (and a reference only) to the trustees or to the personal representatives as defined in section 701.

(7) For the purposes of this paragraph the time of acquisition of a trade, asset or interest, or shares, acquired under a contract shall be—

(a) the time at which the contract is made, or
(b) if it is conditional (and in particular if it is conditional on the exercise of an option), the time at which the condition is satisfied,

and not, if different, the time at which the trade, asset, interest or shares is or are conveyed or transferred.

(8) For the purposes of paragraph 1(3) above there shall be regarded as income available for distribution and not as having been applied, or as being applicable, to such requirements of a company's business as may be necessary or advisable for such an acquisition as is mentioned in paragraph 1(3) above any sum expended or applied, or intended to be expended or applied, as mentioned in paragraph 8(1)(a)(iv) or (b) above; and paragraph 8(2) and (5) above shall apply for the purposes of this sub-paragraph as they apply for the purposes of paragraph 8.

Former enactments.—FA 1972, Sch. 16, para. 12A; FA 1978, Sch. 5, para. 2.

Cessations and liquidations

10.—*(1) Where a close company ceases to carry on the trade, or the business of holding investments, in which its activities wholly or mainly consisted, the relevant income of the company for any accounting period in which that event occurs, or which ends in or within the 12 months ending with that event, shall be calculated as if—*

(a) paragraph 1(1)(a) and (b)(i) above referred respectively to the whole of the company's distributable income other than trading income and to the whole of the estate or trading income and not to so much thereof as can be distributed without prejudice to the requirements there mentioned, and paragraphs 1(2)(a) and 8 above were omitted;
(b) in paragraph 2(1) above the words "50 per cent. of" were omitted.

(2) Where sub-paragraph (1) above applies for an accounting period and the company could not make distributions without prejudice to the claims of creditors (excluding those mentioned in sub-paragraph (3) below), the excess mentioned in section 424(1) shall be disregarded to the extent to which the company could not make distributions up to the amount of its relevant income without prejudice to those claims.

(3) Subject to sub-paragraph (4) below, the creditors to be excluded for the purposes of sub-paragraph (2) above are all participators and associates of participators, and all creditors in respect of debts originally created in favour of or due to a person who was then a participator or associate of a participator.

(4) A creditor is not to be excluded in respect of any debt which either—

(a) arose in the ordinary course of the company's trade or the company's business of holding investments and also in the ordinary course of a trade or profession of the creditor or, as the case may be, of the participator or associate who was the original creditor; or
(b) is a debt for remuneration chargeable to income tax under Schedule E; or
(c) is a debt for any rent or other payment due for the use of—

[(i) tangible property,
(ii) copyright in a literary, dramatic, musical or artistic work within the meaning of Part I of the Copyright, Designs and Patents Act 1988 (or any similar right under the law of a country to which that Part does not extend), or

    (iii) *design right,]*[1]

    and not representing more than a reasonable commercial consideration for that use.

  (5) Where sub-paragraph (1) above applies for any accounting period, there shall be disregarded for the purposes of any apportionment made by virtue of section 424(2) so much of the relevant income of the company for that period as is equal to the amount which would be disregarded under sub-paragraph (2) above.

  (6) Where a resolution is passed or an order is made for the winding up of a close company, or where any other act is done for a like purpose in the case of a winding up otherwise than under the Insolvency Act 1986, sub-paragraphs (1) to (5) above shall apply for any accounting period ending in or with the 12 months ending with the passing of the resolution or other event, or for any later accounting period, as they apply, in a case falling within sub-paragraph (1) above, for an accounting period in which a close company ceases to carry on a trade.

Former enactments.—Sub-para. (1): FA 1972, Sch. 16, para. 13(1); FA 1980, Sch. 9, para. 7.
Sub-para. (2): FA 1972, Sch. 16, para. 13(2).
Sub-paras. (3), (4): FA 1972, Sch. 16, para. 13(3).
Sub-paras. (5), (6): FA 1972, Sch. 16, para. 13(4), (5); Companies Consolidation (Consequential Provisions) Act 1985, Sch. 2.
Amendments.—[1] Sub-para. (4)(*c*)(i), (ii), (iii) substituted by the Copyright, Designs and Patents Act 1988, Sch. 7, para. 36(8) with effect from 1 August 1989 by virtue of the Copyright, Designs and Patents Act 1988 (Commencement No. 1) Order 1989, S.I. 1989 No. 816. The original words read—

    "tangible property or of copyright in a literary, dramatic, musical or artistic work within the meaning of the Copyright Act 1956 (or any corresponding right under the law of a country to which that Act does not extend),".

Legal restrictions on distributions

11.—*(1) Subject to paragraph 12 below, where a company is subject to any restriction imposed by law as regards the making of distributions, the excess mentioned in section 424(1) shall be disregarded to the extent to which the company could not make distributions up to the amount of its relevant income without contravening that restriction.*

  (2) Except where paragraph 10(1) above applies, there shall be disregarded for the purposes of any apportionment made by virtue of section 424(2) so much of the relevant income of the company as is equal to any amount which would be disregarded under sub-paragraph (1) above.

Former enactments.—FA 1972, Sch. 16, para. 14; F(No. 2)A 1975, Sch. 8, para. 3(3).

Stock dividends

12.—*(1) Where a company issues to a close company any relevant share capital, sub-paragraphs (2) and (3) below shall apply as regards that share capital, and in this paragraph—*

    "the relevant accounting period" means the accounting period of the close company in which the due date of issue falls;
    "relevant share capital" means share capital to which section 249 applies; and
    "appropriate amount in cash" has the meaning given by section 251(2).

  (2) The relevant income of the close company for the relevant accounting period, as determined under paragraph 1 above, and the amount which, under paragraph 2 above (read, where appropriate, with paragraph 10 above) the relevant income of the close company for that period cannot exceed, shall each be increased by an amount equal to the appropriate amount in cash (or, if it would otherwise be nil, be treated as equal to the appropriate amount in cash).

  (3) The amount, if any, which would otherwise be disregarded under paragraph 11(1) above shall be reduced by an amount equal to the appropriate amount in cash.

  (4) Where a close company issues any relevant share capital in a case falling within section 249(4), (5) or (6) or sub-paragraph (1) above (read in each case with section 249(3)), the company shall be treated for the purposes of paragraph 3(1) and (2) above—

    (a) as if a dividend of an amount equal to the appropriate amount in cash had been paid on the due date of issue; and
    (b) where, in relation to that share capital, "the appropriate amount in cash" has the meaning given by section 251(2)(a), as if that dividend had been declared in respect of the accounting period (if any) in respect of which the relevant cash dividend (as defined in section 251(3)) was declared.

Former enactment.—F(No. 2)A 1975, Sch. 8, paras. 3, 4.

PART II
PROCEDURE

Amendments.—This Part of this Schedule repealed by FA 1989, s. 103 and Sch. 17, Pt. V in relation to accounting periods beginning after 31 March 1989.

[SCHEDULE 19A][1]

Amendments.—[1] This Schedule inserted by FA 1988, s. 58(4)(a), (5) and Sch. 5.

UNDERWRITERS: ASSESSMENT AND COLLECTION OF TAX

Preliminary

1.—(1) In this Schedule—

"agent", in relation to a syndicate and a year of assessment, means—

(a) the person who was acting as underwriting agent for that syndicate at the end of the corresponding underwriting year; or
(b) such other person as may be determined in accordance with regulations made by the Board by statutory instrument;

"closing year", in relation to a year of assessment, means the year of assessment next but one following that year;
"inspector" includes any officer of the Board;
"profits" includes gains;
"syndicate" means a syndicate of underwriting members of Lloyd's formed for an underwriting year;
"syndicate profit or loss", in relation to a syndicate, means the aggregate amount of the profits or losses arising to all the members of the syndicate (taken together), and "syndicate profits" and "syndicate losses" shall be construed accordingly.

(2) References in this Schedule to profits or losses arising to a member of a syndicate are references to profits or losses which—

(a) arise to him in his capacity as such a member, whether from his underwriting business or from assets forming part of a premiums trust fund; and
(b) are chargeable or, as the case may be, allowable under Case I of Schedule D.

(3) Regulations under this paragraph may make provision with respect to the year of assessment next but one preceding the year of assessment in which they are made.

Returns by agent

2.—(1) An inspector may, at any time after the end of the closing year for a year of assessment, by notice in writing to the agent require him to deliver to the inspector, on or before the final day determined under sub-paragraph (2) below, a return of the syndicate profit or loss for the year of assessment—

(a) containing such information as may be required in pursuance of the notice; and
(b) accompanied by such accounts, statements and reports as may be so required; and
(c) in the case of a syndicate profit, containing a statement of the amount of tax which would be payable on that profit if the whole of it were charged to tax at the basic rate of income tax for that year.

(2) The final day for the delivery of any return required by a notice under sub-paragraph (1) above is whichever is the later of—

(a) the 1st September next following the end of the closing year for the year of assessment; and
(b) the end of the period of three months beginning on the day following that on which the notice was served.

(3) If the agent, having been required by a notice under sub-paragraph (1) above to deliver a return, fails to deliver the return on or before the final day for its delivery, he shall be liable to a penalty equal to the prescribed amount multiplied by the number of days on which the failure continues; and in this sub-paragraph "the prescribed amount" means £10 for each fifty members of the syndicate (counting any number of members left over as fifty).

(4) If the agent fraudulently or negligently delivers an incorrect return under sub-paragraph (1) above, he shall be liable to a penalty not exceeding the prescribed amount multiplied by the number of members of the syndicate; and in this sub-paragraph "the prescribed amount" means [£3,000][1].

(5) In relation to a return required by a notice under sub-paragraph (1) above—

(a) any reference in sub-paragraph (2) or (3) above to the delivery of the return is a reference to its delivery together with the accompanying documents referred to in sub-paragraph (1) above; and

(*b*) the reference in sub-paragraph (4) above to the return being incorrect includes a reference to any of those documents being incorrect.

Amendments.—[1] Amount in sub-para. (4) substituted for the words "£500 in the case of fraud and £250 in the case of negligence" by FA 1989, s. 170(5), (6) in relation to things done or omitted after 26 July 1989.

Payments on account of tax

3.—(1) In the case of a syndicate profit for a year of assessment, the agent shall, on or before the 1st January next following the end of the closing year for that year—

(*a*) pay to the collector, on account of the liabilities to tax of the members of the syndicate, the amount stated in his return for that year under paragraph 2(1)(*c*) above; and

(*b*) deliver to the inspector a return apportioning, between those members, the amount so paid.

(2) Where an amount is paid to the collector under sub-paragraph (1)(*a*) above for a year of assessment, the following provisions shall apply as between each member of the syndicate and the agent—

(*a*) where the member's proportion of the amount so paid exceeds the amount deducted by the agent in accounting to the member for his share of the syndicate profit for that year, the amount of the excess shall be paid by the member to the agent; and

(*b*) where the amount so deducted exceeds that proportion, the amount of the excess shall be paid by the agent to the member.

(3) Where an amount is paid to the collector under sub-paragraph (1)(*a*) above for a year of assessment, the following provisions shall apply as respects the liability to tax for that year of each member of the syndicate—

(*a*) where the amount in which the member is charged to tax exceeds his proportion of the amount so paid, the amount of the excess shall be the amount of tax due and payable; and

(*b*) where that proportion exceeds the amount in which the member is so charged, the amount of the excess shall be treated as tax overpaid.

(4) Any amount which is payable under sub-paragraph (1)(*a*) above shall carry interest at the [rate applicable under section 178 of the Finance Act 1989][1] from the date when it becomes payable until payment, whether or not that date is a non-business day within the meaning of the Bills of Exchange Act 1882; and—

(*a*) ...[2]

(*b*) section 90 of that Act (disallowance of relief for interest on tax),

shall apply for the purposes of this sub-paragraph as ...[3] for the purposes of any provision of Part IX of that Act.

Amendments.—[1] Words in sub-para. (4) substituted by FA 1989, s. 179(1)(*b*)(iii).
[2] Sub-para. (4)(*a*) repealed by FA 1989, Sch. 17, Pt. X.
[3] Words in sub-para. (4) repealed by *ibid*.

Determinations by inspector

4.—(1) If the inspector is satisfied that a return under paragraph 2(1) above affords correct and complete information concerning the syndicate profit or loss for a year of assessment, he shall determine that profit or loss accordingly.

(2) If for a year of assessment the inspector is dissatisfied with a return under paragraph 2(1) above, or there is no such return, the inspector shall determine the syndicate profit or loss for that year to the best of his judgment.

(3) If the inspector discovers that a determination under sub-paragraph (1) or (2) above—

(*a*) understates the syndicate profits for the year of assessment; or
(*b*) overstates the syndicate losses for that year,

he may, by a determination under this sub-paragraph, vary the first-mentioned determination accordingly.

(4) Notice of a determination under this paragraph shall be served on the agent and shall state the time within which any appeal against the determination may be made under paragraph 5 below.

(5) After notice of a determination under this paragraph has been served on the agent, the determination shall not be altered except in accordance with the express provisions of the Taxes Acts.

Appeals

5.—(1) The agent may appeal against a determination under paragraph 4 above by a notice of appeal in writing given to the inspector within thirty days after the date of the notice of determination.

(2) An appeal under this paragraph shall be to the General Commissioners, except that the agent may elect (in accordance with section 46(1) of the Taxes Management Act 1970) to bring the appeal before the Special Commissioners instead of the General Commissioners; and subsections (5) to (5E) of section 31 of that Act shall apply for the purposes of an election under this sub-paragraph as they apply for the purposes of an election under subsection (4) of that section.

Modification of determinations pending appeal

6.—(1) Where the agent appeals against a determination under paragraph 4 above, then, for the purpose of establishing, in the event of a member of the syndicate appealing against an assessment made on him, the amount of tax the payment of which should, pending the determination of that appeal, be postponed under section 55 of the Taxes Management Act 1970, that section shall apply to the first-mentioned appeal with the modifications specified in sub-paragraph (2) below.

(2) The modifications are as follows—

(*a*) any reference to the notice of assessment shall be construed as a reference to the notice of determination;

(*b*) any reference to the appellant believing that he is overcharged to tax by the assessment shall be construed as a reference to him believing that the determination overstates the syndicate profits, or understates the syndicate losses, for the year of assessment, and any reference to the appellant having grounds for so believing, or there being reasonable grounds for so believing, shall be construed accordingly;

(*c*) any reference to a determination of the amount of tax the payment of which should be postponed pending the determination of the appeal shall be construed as a reference to a direction that the determination shall, pending the determination of the appeal, have effect for the purpose stated in sub-paragraph (1) above as if the syndicate profits there stated were reduced, or the syndicate losses there stated were increased, by such amount as may be specified in the direction, and any reference to an amount of tax so determined, or to the amount of tax which should be so postponed, shall be construed accordingly; and

(*d*) subsections (2) and (9) and, in subsection (6), paragraphs (*a*) and (*b*) and the word "and" immediately preceding paragraph (*a*) shall be omitted.

Apportionments of syndicate profit or loss

7.—(1) Where a determination of a syndicate profit or loss for a year of assessment is made, varied or modified (whether under the foregoing provisions of this Schedule or on appeal), the inspector may, by notice in writing to the agent, require him to make to the inspector, within the specified period, a return apportioning, between the members of the syndicate, the syndicate profit or loss as stated in the determination as so made, varied or modified.

(2) If the agent, having been required by a notice under sub-paragraph (1) above to deliver a return within the specified period, fails to deliver the return within that period, he shall be liable to a penalty equal to the prescribed amount multiplied by the number of days on which the failure continues; and in this sub-paragraph "the prescribed amount" means £5 for each fifty members of the syndicate (counting any number of members left over as fifty).

(3) In this paragraph "the specified period" means such period, not being less than thirty days and beginning with the day following the date of the notice under sub-paragraph (1) above, as may be specified in that notice.

Individual members: effect of determinations

8.—(1) A determination of a syndicate profit or loss for a year of assessment (whether as originally made or as varied or modified) shall, for the purpose of determining the liability to tax of each member of the syndicate, be conclusive against that member that the syndicate profit or loss for that year is as there stated.

(2) Where a determination of a syndicate profit or loss for a year of assessment is varied or

modified at any time after the issue of a notice of assessment assessing any member of the syndicate to tax—

(*a*) section 31 of the Taxes Management Act 1970 (right of appeal) and section 55 of that Act (postponement of tax) shall have effect, in relation to that member, as if any reference to the date of the notice of assessment, or the date of the issue of the notice of assessment, were a reference to the date of the variation or modification; and

(*b*) in the case of a variation, an assessment which gives effect to the determination as varied shall not be out of time if it is made within one year of the date of the variation.

(3) Sub-paragraph (2)(*b*) above shall not apply in the case of a variation under paragraph 4(3) above which is made later than six years after the end of the closing year.

Assessment of individual members: time limits

9. For the purposes of sections 36 [and 40][2] of the Taxes Management Act 1970 (extension of time in cases of [fraudulent or negligent conduct][1]), anything done or omitted to be done by the agent shall be deemed to have been done or omitted to be done by each member of the syndicate.

Amendments.—[1] Words substituted by FA 1989, s. 149(4)(*a*)(iii).
[2] Words substituted by FA 1989, s. 149(6).

Supplemental: penalties

10. ...[1]

Amendments.—[1] This paragraph repealed by FA 1989, Sch. 17, Pt. VIII.

Supplemental: interest

11.—(1) Interest charged under paragraph 3(4) above shall be treated for the purposes of the enactments mentioned in section 69 of the Taxes Management Act 1970 (interest on tax) as if it were tax charged and due and payable under an assessment.

(2) References to section 86 of that Act in sections 70(2) and 92 of that Act (evidence, and remission of interest in certain cases) shall include a reference to paragraph 3(4) above.

SCHEDULE 20

Section 506

CHARITIES: QUALIFYING INVESTMENTS AND LOANS

PART I
QUALIFYING INVESTMENTS

1. Investments specified in any of the following paragraphs of this Part of this Schedule are qualifying investments for the purposes of section 506.

Former enactment.—FA 1986, Sch. 7, para. 2.

2. Any investment falling within Part I, Part II, apart from paragraph 13 (mortgages etc.) or Part III of Schedule 1 to the Trustee Investments Act 1961.

Former enactment.—FA 1986, Sch. 7, para. 3.

3. Any investment in a common investment fund established under section 22 of the Charities Act 1960 or section 25 of the Charities Act (Northern Ireland) 1964 or in any similar fund established for the exclusive benefit of charities by or under any enactment relating to any particular charities or class of charities.

Former enactment.—FA 1986, Sch. 7, para. 4.

4. Any interest in land, other than an interest held as security for a debt of any description.

Former enactment.—FA 1986, Sch. 7, para. 5.

5. Shares in, or securities of, a company which are quoted on a recognised stock exchange, or which are dealt in on the Unlisted Securities Market.

Former enactment.—FA 1986, Sch. 7, para. 6.

6. Units, or other shares of the investments subject to the trusts, of a unit trust scheme within the meaning of the Financial Services Act 1986.

Former enactment.—FA 1986, Sch. 7, para. 7.

7.—(1) Deposits with an institution authorised under the Banking Act 1987 in respect of which interest is payable at a commercial rate.

(2) A deposit mentioned in sub-paragraph (1) above is not a qualifying investment if it is made as part of an arrangement under which a loan is made by the authorised institution to some other person.

Former enactments.—FA 1986, Sch. 7, para. 8; Banking Act 1987, Sch. 6, para. 24.

8. Certificates of deposit as defined in section 56(5).

Former enactment.—FA 1986, Sch. 7, para. 9.

9.—(1) Any loan or other investment as to which the Board are satisfied, on a claim made to them in that behalf, that the loan or other investment is made for the benefit of the charity and not for the avoidance of tax (whether by the charity or any other person).

(2) The reference in sub-paragraph (1) above to a loan includes a loan which is secured by a mortgage or charge of any kind over land.

Former enactment.—FA 1986, Sch. 7, para. 10.

PART II
QUALIFYING LOANS

10. For the purposes of section 506, a loan which is not made by way of investment is a qualifying loan if it consists of—

  (*a*) a loan made to another charity for charitable purposes only; or
  (*b*) a loan to a beneficiary of the charity which is made in the course of carrying out the purposes of the charity; or
  (*c*) money placed on current account with an institution authorised under the Banking Act 1987 otherwise than as part of such an arrangement as is mentioned in paragraph 7(2) above; or
  (*d*) any other loan as to which the Board are satisfied, on a claim made to them in that behalf, that the loan is made for the benefit of the charity and not for the avoidance of tax (whether by the charity or by some other person).

Former enactments.—FA 1986, Sch. 7, para. 11; Banking Act 1987, Sch. 6, para. 24.

PART III
ATTRIBUTION OF EXCESS NON-QUALIFYING EXPENDITURE TO EARLIER CHARGEABLE PERIODS

11. This Part of this Schedule applies in the circumstances specified in subsection (6) of section 506 and in this Part—

  (*a*) "the primary period" means the chargeable period of the charity concerned in which there is such an excess as is mentioned in that subsection;
  (*b*) "unapplied non-qualifying expenditure" means so much of the excess referred to in that subsection as does not exceed the non-qualifying expenditure of the primary period; and
  (*c*) "earlier period", in relation to an amount of unapplied non-qualifying expenditure, means any chargeable period of the charity concerned which ended not more than six years before the end of the primary period.

Former enactment.—FA 1986, Sch. 7, para. 12.

12.—(1) So much of the unapplied non-qualifying expenditure as is not shown by the charity to be the expenditure of non-taxable sums received by the charity in the primary period shall be treated in accordance with paragraph 13 below as non-qualifying expenditure of earlier periods.

(2) In sub-paragraph (1) above "non-taxable sums" means donations, legacies and other sums of a similar nature which, apart from section 505(1) of this Act and section 145 of the 1979 Act, are not within the charge to tax.

Former enactment.—FA 1986, Sch. 7, para. 13.

13.—(1) Where, in accordance with paragraph 12 above, an amount of unapplied non-qualifying expenditure ("the excess expenditure") falls to be treated as non-qualifying expenditure of earlier periods—

  (*a*) it shall be attributed only to those earlier periods (if any) which, apart from the attribution, (but taking account of any previous operation of this paragraph) the relevant income and gains exceed the aggregate of the qualifying and non-qualifying expenditure incurred in that period; and
  (*b*) the amount to be attributed to any such earlier period shall not be greater than the excess of that period referred to in paragraph (*a*) above.

(2) Where there is more than one earlier period to which the excess expenditure can be attributed in accordance with sub-paragraph (1) above, it shall be attributed to later periods in priority to earlier periods.

(3) In so far as any of the excess expenditure cannot be attributed to earlier periods in accordance with this paragraph, it shall be disregarded for the purposes of section 506(6) (and this Part of this Schedule).

Former enactment.—FA 1986, Sch. 7, para. 14.

14. All such adjustments shall be made, whether by way of the making of assessments or otherwise, as may be required in consequence of the provisions of this Part of this Schedule.

Former enactment.—FA 1986, Sch. 7, para. 15.

SCHEDULE 21

Sections 570 and 572

TAX RELIEF IN CONNECTION WITH SCHEMES FOR RATIONALIZING INDUSTRY AND OTHER REDUNDANCY SCHEMES

PART I
PRELIMINARY

1.—(1) In this Schedule—

"scheme" means a scheme which is for the time being certified or has at any time been certified by the Secretary of State under section 568;

"payment" means a payment made under a scheme, being a payment made to a person carrying on a trade to which the scheme relates and not being a payment made by way of repayment of contributions;

"the person chargeable" means, in relation to any such payment, the person liable to pay any tax which may fall to be paid by reason of the receipt of the payment;

"damage" includes any loss, liability, expense or other burden, and references to the amount of any damage are references to the sum which would be fair compensation for that damage;

"contribution" includes part of a contribution, and "deductible contribution" means a contribution allowed to be deducted under section 568, any reduction under Part III of this Schedule being left out of account; and

"asset" includes part of an asset.

(2) For the purposes of this Schedule, a sum received by any person by way of repayment of contributions shall be deemed to be by way of repayment of the last contribution paid by him, and, if the sum exceeds the amount of that contribution, by way of repayment of the penultimate contribution so paid, and so on.

Former enactment.—TA 1970, Sch. 11, para. 1.

PART II
RELIEF IN RESPECT OF CERTAIN PAYMENTS

2. The question whether any, and if so, what, relief is to be given shall be determined separately in relation to each payment made under the scheme in respect of the trade, but for the purpose of determining that question regard shall be had, as provided by the following provisions of this Part of this Schedule, to the sum ("the total payment") produced by adding the amount of the payment to the amount of any payments previously so made.

Former enactment.—TA 1970, Sch. 11, para. 2.

3. No relief shall be given in respect of the payment unless the person chargeable shows—

(*a*) the amount of the damage in respect of which the total payment has been made; and

(*b*) how much of that amount is referable to damage in respect of which no relief may be given under the Tax Acts.

Former enactment.—TA 1970, Sch. 11, para. 3.

4. No relief shall be given in respect of the payment unless the total payment, or the amount of the damage in respect of which the total payment has been made, whichever is the smaller, exceeds the aggregate amount of the deductible contributions which have been paid in furtherance of the scheme in respect of the trade in question before the payment is made, exclusive of any contributions which have been repaid before the payment is made.

Former enactment.—TA 1970, Sch. 11, para. 4.

5. The amount of the reduction to be made in respect of the payment shall be arrived at by—

(*a*) ascertaining the sum which bears to the excess mentioned in paragraph 4 above the same proportion that the amount mentioned in paragraph 3(*b*) above bears to the amount mentioned in paragraph 3(*a*); and

(*b*) deducting from that sum the total amount of any reductions which have been or fall to be made under this Schedule in respect of payments previously made under the scheme in respect of the trade.

Former enactment.—TA 1970, Sch. 11, para. 5.

6.—(1) For the purposes of this Schedule, and subject to sub-paragraph (2) below, damage shall be deemed to be damage in respect of which relief may be given under the Tax Acts if and only if—

(*a*) the damage is attributable to any of the following events, that is to say, the demolition, destruction or putting out of use of any asset, or the disposition or termination of an interest in any asset, and, by reason of that event, an allowance falls to be made under Chapter I or Chapter II of Part I of the 1968 Act in taxing the trade; or

(*b*) the damage consists of any loss, liability, expense or other burden in respect of which an allowance may be made in computing the profits or gains of the trade for the purposes of the Tax Acts.

(2) Where an allowance under Chapter I of Part I of the 1968 Act in respect of any damage falls to be reduced in the proportion specified in section 3(4) of that Act, only a proportionately reduced amount of the damage shall be treated as being referable to damage in respect of which relief may be given under the Tax Acts.

(3) Where any event occurs which would give rise to an allowance under the Tax Acts in respect of any asset in taxing, or computing the profits or gains of, a trade but for any of the following matters, that is to say—

(*a*) that there are no profits or gains against which the allowance could be made, or

(*b*) that account is required to be taken of allowances previously made or deemed to have been made in respect of the asset; or

(*c*) that account is required to be taken of any sum which falls to be written off the expenditure incurred on the asset for the purpose of determining whether any and if so what allowance may be given by reason of the event; or

(*d*) that account is required to be taken of any sum falling to be taken into account as sale, insurance, salvage or compensation moneys, the like consequences shall ensue under this Schedule as if an allowance had fallen to be made by reason of that event.

(4) Where any damage is attributable to a permanent change in the purposes for which an asset is used, or the temporary or permanent putting out of use of an asset, the question whether the damage is damage in respect of which relief may be given under the Tax Acts shall be determined as if the damage had been attributable to a sale of the asset on the date upon which the change or putting out of use took place.

Former enactment.—TA 1970, Sch. 11, para. 6.

PART III
EXCLUSION OF RELIEF IN RESPECT OF CONTRIBUTIONS PAID AFTER RELIEF HAS BEEN GIVEN UNDER PART II

7. The provisions of this Part of this Schedule shall have effect where—

(*a*) a contribution is paid under a scheme in respect of a trade; and

(*b*) before the contribution is paid, payments have been made under the scheme to the person carrying on the trade; and

(*c*) reductions have been made, under Part II of this Schedule, in the amounts which, by reason of those payments, are to be treated as trading receipts of the trade.

Former enactment.—TA 1970, Sch. 11, para. 7.

8. There shall be ascertained—

(*a*) the total amount of those reductions; and

(*b*) the sum by which that total would have been decreased if the contribution, and any previous contributions to which this Part of this Schedule applies, had been paid before any of the payments were made.

Former enactment.—TA 1970, Sch. 11, para. 8.

9. For the purpose of determining what deduction is to be made in respect of the contribution under section 568, the contribution shall be deemed to be reduced by the sum specified in paragraph 8(*b*) above, but—

(*a*) for the purpose of the application of paragraph 8 above in relation to contributions subsequently paid under the scheme in respect of the trade, the total amount of the reductions referred to in that paragraph shall be treated as decreased by that sum; and
(*b*) for the purpose of the application of paragraph 5 above in relation to payments subsequently made under the scheme in respect of the trade, the total amount of the reductions referred to in that paragraph shall be treated as decreased by that sum.

Former enactment.—TA 1970, Sch. 11, para. 9.

10. When two or more contributions are paid at the same time, the provisions of this Part of this Schedule shall have effect as if they were a single contribution.

Former enactment.—TA 1970, Sch. 11, para. 10.

SCHEDULE 22

Section 603

REDUCTION OF PENSION FUND SURPLUSES

1.—(1) The Board may make regulations providing for this Schedule to apply, as from a prescribed date, in relation to any exempt approved scheme which is of a prescribed kind.

(2) The Board may make regulations providing for prescribed provisions of this Schedule to apply, as from a prescribed date, in prescribed circumstances, and subject to any prescribed omissions or modifications, in relation to any exempt approved scheme of another prescribed kind.

(3) In this Schedule "prescribed" means prescribed by regulations made by the Board.

Former enactment.—FA 1986, Sch. 12, para. 4.

2.—(1) The administrator of a scheme in relation to which this Schedule applies shall, in prescribed circumstances and at a prescribed time, either produce to the Board a written valuation such as is mentioned in sub-paragraph (2) below or give to the Board a certificate such as is mentioned in sub-paragraph (3) below.

(2) The valuation must be a valuation of the assets held for the purposes of the scheme and the liabilities of the scheme, must be determined in accordance with prescribed principles and fulfil prescribed requirements, and must be signed by a person with qualifications of a prescribed kind.

(3) The certificate must state whether or not the value of the assets (as determined in accordance with prescribed principles) exceeds the value of the liabilities (as so determined) by a percentage which is more than a prescribed maximum, must be in a prescribed form, and must be signed by a person with qualifications of a prescribed kind.

Former enactment.—FA 1986, Sch. 12, para. 5.

3.—(1) Subject to paragraph 4(4) below, where a valuation produced under paragraph 2 shows, or a certificate given under that paragraph states, that the value of the assets exceeds the value of the liabilities by a percentage which is more than the prescribed maximum, the administrator of the scheme shall within a prescribed period submit to the Board for their approval proposals which comply with sub-paragraph (2) below.

(2) The proposals must be proposals for reducing (or, subject to paragraph (*b*) below, eliminating) the excess in a way or ways set out in the proposals and falling within sub-paragraph (3) below; and they must be such as to secure that—

(*a*) by the end of a prescribed period the percentage (if any) by which the value of the assets exceeds the value of the liabilities is no more than the prescribed maximum; and
(*b*) if the way, or one of the ways, set out in the proposals falls within sub-paragraph (3)(*a*) below, there remains an excess which is of a level not less than the prescribed minimum.

(3) Subject to sub-paragraph (4) below, the permitted ways of reducing or eliminating the excess are—

(*a*) making payments to an employer;
(*b*) suspending for a period (of five years or less) set out in the proposals an employer's obligation to pay contributions under the scheme or reducing for such a period the amount of an employer's contributions under the scheme;
(*c*) suspending for a period (of five years or less) set out in the proposals the obligation of employees to pay contributions under the scheme or reducing for such a period the amount of employees' contributions under the scheme;
(*d*) improving existing benefits provided under the scheme;
(*e*) providing new benefits under the scheme;
(*f*) such other ways as may be prescribed.

(4) In prescribed circumstances sub-paragraph (3) above shall apply subject to such omissions or modifications as may be prescribed.

(5) Subject to paragraph 4(4) below, if the administrator of the scheme fails to submit proposals to the Board within the period mentioned in sub-paragraph (1) above, or if the

proposals submitted to them within that period are not approved by the Board within a further prescribed period, paragraph 7 below shall apply.

Former enactment.—FA 1986, Sch. 12, para. 6.

4.—(1) Where a valuation has been produced under paragraph 2 above, the Board may serve on the administrator of the scheme a notice requiring him to furnish the Board, within a prescribed period, with such particulars relating to the valuation as may be specified in the notice.

(2) Where a certificate has been given under paragraph 2 above, the Board may serve on the administrator of the scheme a notice requiring him to produce to the Board, within a prescribed period, a written valuation such as is mentioned in paragraph 2(2) above.

(3) Where a valuation has been produced in compliance with a notice served under sub-paragraph (2) above, the Board may serve on the administrator of the scheme a further notice requiring him to furnish the Board, within a prescribed period, with such particulars relating to the valuation as may be specified in the notice.

(4) Where a notice is served on the administrator of a scheme under sub-paragraph (1) or (2) above, paragraph 3(1) and (5) above shall cease to apply.

Former enactment.—FA 1986, Sch. 12, para. 7.

5.—(1) Where particulars have been furnished under paragraph 4 above, or a valuation has been produced under that paragraph, the Board shall, within a prescribed period, serve on the administrator of the scheme a notice—

(*a*) stating that they accept the valuation produced under paragraph 2 or, as the case may be, 4 above; or

(*b*) stating that they do not accept the valuation so produced, and specifying their estimate of the value of the liabilities of the scheme at the relevant time and their estimate of the value of the assets held for the purposes of the scheme at that time.

(2) For the purposes of sub-paragraph (1)(*b*) above, the relevant time is the time specified in the valuation produced under paragraph 2 or 4 above as the time by reference to which the values of the assets and liabilities are determined.

(3) Where—

(*a*) in a case falling within sub-paragraph (1)(*a*) above, the valuation shows that the value of the assets exceeds the value of the liabilities by a percentage which is more than the prescribed maximum; or

(*b*) in a case falling within sub-paragraph (1)(*b*) above, the value of the assets as estimated by the Board exceeds the value of the liabilities as so estimated by a percentage which is more than the prescribed maximum;

the administrator of the scheme shall within a prescribed period submit to the Board for their approval proposals which comply with paragraph 3(2) to (4) above.

(4) If the administrator of the scheme fails to submit proposals to the Board within the period mentioned in sub-paragraph (3) above, or if proposals submitted to them within that period are not approved by the Board within a further prescribed period, paragraph 7 below shall apply.

Former enactment.—FA 1986, Sch. 12, para. 8.

6.—(1) Where proposals are submitted to the Board under paragraph 3(1) or 5(3) above and they approve them within the further prescribed period mentioned in paragraph 3(5) or 5(4) above, the administrator of the scheme shall carry out the proposals within the period mentioned in paragraph 3(2) above.

(2) If the administrator fails to carry out the proposals within that period, paragraph 7 below shall apply.

Former enactment.—FA 1986, Sch. 12, para. 9.

7.—(1) Where this paragraph applies the Board may specify a percentage equivalent to the fraction—

$$\frac{A}{B}$$

where—

A represents their estimate of the value of the liabilities of the scheme at the relevant time increased by a prescribed percentage; and

B represents their estimate of the value of the assets held for the purposes of the scheme at that time.

(2) For the purposes of this paragraph the relevant time is the time specified—

(*a*) in the valuation produced or certificate given under paragraph 2 above; or

(*b*) where a valuation has been produced under paragraph 4 above, in that valuation,

as the time by reference to which the values of the assets and liabilities are determined.

(3) Where a percentage has been so specified—

(*a*) section 592(2) shall apply only to that percentage of any income derived in the relevant period from the assets held for the purposes of the scheme;

(*b*) section 592(3) shall apply only to that percentage of any underwriting commissions applied in the relevant period for the purposes of the scheme;

(*c*) section 56 shall by virtue of subsection (3)(*b*) of that section not apply only to that percentage of any profits or gains arising to the scheme in the relevant period; and

(*d*) section 149B(1)(*g*) of the 1979 Act (capital gains tax exemption) shall apply only to that percentage of any gain accruing on the disposal in the relevant period of any of those assets.

(4) Sub-paragraphs (5) to (8) below shall apply where a percentage has been so specified, securities are transferred in the relevant period, and the transferor or transferee is such that, if he became entitled to any interest on them, exemption could be allowed under section 592(2).

(5) Section 715(1)(*k*) shall not apply.

(6) Where, in consequence of sub-paragraph (5) above, section 713(2)(*a*) or (3)(*b*) applies, the sum concerned shall be treated as reduced by an amount equal to the specified percentage of itself.

(7) Where, in consequence of sub-paragraph (5) above, section 713(2)(*b*) or (3)(*a*) applies, the relief concerned shall be treated as reduced by an amount equal to the specified percentage of itself.

(8) For the purposes of section 714(5), the amount of interest falling to be reduced by the amount of the allowance shall be treated as the amount found after applying section 592(2).

(9) In sub-paragraphs (4) to (8) above expressions which also appear in sections 710 to 728 have the same meanings as in those sections.

(10) In this paragraph "the relevant period" means the period beginning at the relevant time and ending when it is proved to the satisfaction of the Board that the value of the assets (as determined in accordance with prescribed principles) exceeds the value of the liabilities (as so determined) by a percentage which is no more than the prescribed maximum.

Former enactment.—FA 1986, Sch. 12, para. 10.

8.—(1) The Board may make regulations providing that an appeal may be brought against a notice under paragraph 5(1)(*b*) above as if it were notice of the decision of the Board on a claim made by the administrator of the scheme concerned.

(2) Regulations under this paragraph may include—

(*a*) provision that bringing an appeal shall suspend the operation of paragraph 5(3) and (4) above; and

(*b*) other provisions consequential on the provision that an appeal may be brought (including provisions modifying this Schedule).

Former enactment.—FA 1986, Sch. 12, para. 11.

SCHEDULE 23
Section 609

OCCUPATIONAL PENSION SCHEMES: SCHEMES APPROVED BEFORE 23RD JULY 1987

Cross references.—[1] See FA 1989, Sch. 6, para. 20(2) (notwithstanding the effect of anything in this Schedule, certain rules to apply in arriving at relevant annual remuneration for the purposes of calculating benefits of an employee joining after 31 May 1989 a retirement benefits scheme coming into existence before 14 March 1989).

Preliminary

1.—(1) This Schedule shall be deemed to have come into force on 17th March 1987 and, subject to sub-paragraphs (2) and (3) below, applies in relation to any retirement benefits scheme approved by the Board before the passing of the Finance (No. 2) Act 1987 (23rd July 1987).

[(2) The Board may by regulations provide that, in circumstances prescribed in the regulations, this Schedule or any provision of it shall not apply or shall apply with such modifications as may be so prescribed.][1]

[(2A) Regulations under sub-paragraph (2) above—

(*a*) may include provision authorising the Board to direct that this Schedule or any provision of it shall not apply in any particular case where in the opinion of the Board the facts are such that its application would not be appropriate;

(*b*) may take effect (and may authorise any direction given under them to take effect) as from 17th March 1987 or any later date;

(*c*) may make such supplementary provision as appears to the Board to be necessary or expedient.][1]

(3) This Schedule shall not apply to a retirement benefits scheme if, before the end of 1987, the administrator of the scheme gave notice to the Board that it is not to apply.

(4) Where a notice is given to the Board under sub-paragraph (3) above, the scheme shall, with effect from 17th March 1987 or (if later) the date with effect from which it was approved, cease to be approved.

Former enactment.—F(No. 2)A 1987, Sch. 3, para. 18.
Note.—Reference should be made to the Occupational Pension Schemes (Transitional Provisions) Regulations 1988, S.I. 1988 No. 1436 made under sub-para. (2) above which contain regulations disapplying or applying with modifications certain paragraphs of this Schedule. The Regulations are not printed as statutory instruments are outside the scope of this work.
Amendments.—[1] Sub-paras. (2), (2A) substituted for sub-para. (2) by FA 1988, s. 56.

Accelerated accrual

2.—(1) This paragraph applies where an employee becomes a member of the scheme on or after 17th March 1987.

(2) Notwithstanding anything to the contrary in the rules of the scheme, they shall have effect as if they did not allow the provision for the employee of a pension exceeding one-thirtieth of his relevant annual remuneration for each year of service up to a maximum of 20.

Former enactment.—F(No. 2)A 1987, Sch. 3, para. 19.

3.—(1) This paragraph applies where an employee becomes a member of the scheme on or after 17th March 1987 and the scheme allows him to commute his pension or part of it for a lump sum or sums.

(2) If the employee's full pension (that is, the pension before any commutation) is equal to or less than a basic rate commutable pension, the rules of the scheme shall have effect (notwithstanding anything in them to the contrary) as if they did not allow him to obtain by way of commutation a lump sum or sums exceeding in all a basic rate lump sum.

(3) If the employee's full pension is greater than a basic rate commutable pension but less than a maximum rate commutable pension, the rules of the scheme shall have effect

(notwithstanding anything in them to the contrary) as if they did not allow him to obtain by way of commutation a lump sum or sums exceeding in all the aggregate of—

(*a*) a basic rate lump sum, and
(*b*) an amount equal to the relevant percentage of the difference between a basic rate lump sum and a maximum rate lump sum.

(4) In this paragraph, as it applies in relation to an employee—

(*a*) a "basic rate commutable pension" means a pension of one-sixtieth of his relevant annual remuneration for each year of service up to a maximum of 40;
(*b*) a "maximum rate commutable pension" means a pension of one-thirtieth of his relevant annual remuneration for each year of service up to a maximum of 20;
(*c*) a "basic rate lump sum" means a lump sum of three-eighteths of his relevant annual remuneration for each year of service up to a maximum of 40;
(*d*) a "maximum rate lump sum" means a lump sum of such amount as may be determined by or under regulations made by the Board for the purposes of this paragraph and paragraph 4 below;
(*e*) "the relevant percentage" means the difference between a basic rate commutable pension and the employee's full pension expressed as a percentage of the difference between a basic rate commutable pension and a maximum rate commutable pension.

Former enactment.—F(No. 2)A 1987, Sch. 3, para. 20.
Cross references.—See FA 1989, Sch. 6, para. 23(2) (new rules for commutation of pension for a lump sum).

4.—(1) This paragraph applies where an employee becomes a member of the scheme on or after 17th March 1987 and the scheme provides a lump sum or sums for him otherwise than by commutation of his pension or part of it.

(2) If the employee's pension is equal to or less than a basic rate non-commutable pension, the rules of the scheme shall have effect (notwithstanding anything in them to the contrary) as if they did not allow the payment to him, otherwise than by way of commutation, of a lump sum or sums exceeding in all a basic rate lump sum.

(3) If the employee's pension is greater than a basic rate non-commutable pension but less than a maximum rate non-commutable pension the rules of the scheme shall have effect (notwithstanding anything in them to the contrary) as if they did not allow the payment to him, otherwise than by way of commutation, of a lump sum or sums exceeding in all the aggregate of—

(*a*) a basic rate lump sum, and
(*b*) an amount equal to the relevant percentage of the difference between a basic rate lump sum and a maximum rate lump sum.

(4) In this paragraph, as it applies in relation to an employee—

(*a*) a "basic rate non-commutable pension" means a pension of one-eightieth of his relevant annual remuneration for each year of service up to a maximum of 40,
(*b*) a "maximum rate non-commutable pension" means a pension of one-fortieth of his relevant annual remuneration for each year of service up to a maximum of 20,
(*c*) "basic rate lump sum" and "maximum rate lump sum" have the same meanings as in paragraph 3 above, and
(*d*) "the relevant percentage" means the difference between a basic rate non-commutable pension and the employee's actual pension expressed as a percentage of the difference between a basic rate non-commutable pension and a maximum rate non-commutable pension.

Former enactment.—F(No. 2)A 1987, Sch. 3, para. 21.
Cross references.—See FA 1989, Sch. 6, para. 24(2) (new rules for accelerated accrual of lump sum benefits).

Final remuneration

5.—(1) This paragraph applies where an employee who is a member of the scheme retires on or after 17th March 1987.

(2) The rules of the scheme shall have effect as if they provided that in determining the employee's relevant annual remuneration for the purpose of calculating benefits, no account should be taken of anything excluded from the definition of "remuneration" in section 612(1).

(3) In the case of an employee—

(*a*) whose employer is a company and who at any time in the last ten years of his service is a controlling director of the company, or

(b) whose relevant annual remuneration for the purpose of calculating benefits, so far as the remuneration is ascertained by reference to years beginning on or after 6th April 1987, would (apart from this Schedule) exceed the permitted maximum,

the rules of the scheme shall have effect as if they provided that his relevant annual remuneration must not exceed his highest average annual remuneration for any period of three or more years ending within the period of ten years which ends with the date on which his service ends.

(4) In the case of an employee within paragraph (b) of sub-paragraph (3) above who retires before 6th April 1991, the rules of the scheme shall have effect as if they provided that his relevant annual remuneration must not exceed the higher of—

(a) the average annual remuneration referred to in that sub-paragraph, and
(b) his remuneration (within the meaning given by section 612(1)) assessable to income tax under Schedule E for the year of assessment 1986–87.

(5) For the purposes of this paragraph a person is a controlling director of a company if—

(a) he is a director (as defined in section 612), and
(b) he is within paragraph (b) of section 417(5),

in relation to the company.

Former enactment.—F(No. 2)A 1987, Sch. 3, para. 22.

Lump sums

6.—(1) This paragraph applies where an employee becomes a member of the scheme on or after 17th March 1987.

(2) If the rules of the scheme allow the employee to obtain, (by commutation of his pension or otherwise), a lump sum or sums calculated by reference to his relevant annual remuneration, they shall have effect as if they included a rule that in calculating a lump sum any excess of that remuneration over the permitted maximum should be disregarded.

Former enactment.—F(No. 2)A 1987, Sch. 3, para. 23.

Additional voluntary contributions

7.—(1) This paragraph applies where—

(a) the rules of the scheme make provision for the payment by employees of voluntary contributions, and
(b) on or after 8th April 1987 an employee enters into arrangements to pay such contributions.

(2) Notwithstanding anything in the rules of the scheme, they shall have effect as if they did not allow the payment to the employee of a lump sum in commutation of a pension if or to the extent that the pension is secured by the voluntary contributions.

Former enactment.—F(No. 2)A 1987, Sch. 3, para. 24.

8.—*(1) This paragraph applies where an employee who is a member of the scheme ("the main scheme") is also a member of an approved scheme ("the voluntary scheme") which provides additional benefits to supplement those provided by the main scheme and to which no contributions are made by any employer of his.*

(2) Any rules of the main scheme imposing a limit on the amount of a benefit provided for the employee shall have effect (notwithstanding anything in them to the contrary) as if they provided for the limit to be reduced by the amount of any like benefit provided for the employee by the voluntary scheme.

Former enactment.—F(No. 2)A 1987, Sch. 3, para. 25.
Amendments.—This paragraph repealed by FA 1989, Sch. 6, paras. 17, 18(10) and Sch. 17, Pt. IV in relation to benefits provided after 26 July 1989.

Supplementary

9. In this Schedule "relevant annual remuneration" means final remuneration or, if the scheme provides for benefits to be calculated by reference to some other annual remuneration, that other annual remuneration.

Former enactment.—F(No. 2)A 1987, Sch. 3, para. 26.

SCHEDULE 24
Section 747(6)

ASSUMPTIONS FOR CALCULATING CHARGEABLE PROFITS, CREDITABLE TAX AND CORRESPONDING UNITED KINGDOM TAX OF FOREIGN COMPANIES

General

1.—(1) The company shall be assumed to be resident in the United Kingdom.

(2) Nothing in sub-paragraph (1) above requires it to be assumed that there is any change in the place or places at which the company carries on its activities.

(3) For the avoidance of doubt, it is hereby declared that, if any sums forming part of the company's profits for an accounting period have been received by the company without any deduction of or charge to tax by virtue of section 47 of 48 the effect of the assumption in sub-paragraph (1) above is that those sums are to be brought within the charge to tax for the purposes of calculating the company's chargeable profits or corresponding United Kingdom tax.

(4) In any case where—
(a) it is at any time necessary for any purpose of Chapter IV of Part XVII to determine the chargeable profits of the company for an accounting period, and
(b) at that time no direction has been given under section 747(1) with respect to that or any earlier accounting period of the company,

it shall be assumed, for the purpose of any of the following provisions of this Schedule which refer to the first accounting period in respect of which a direction is given under that section, that such a direction has been given for that period (but not for any earlier period).

(5) Nothing in this Schedule affects any liability for, or the computation of, corporation tax in respect of a trade which is carried on by a company resident outside the United Kingdom through a branch or agency in the United Kingdom.

Former enactment.—FA 1984, Sch. 16, para. 1.

2.—(1) The company shall be assumed to have become resident in the United Kingdom (and, accordingly, within the charge to corporation tax) at the beginning of the first accounting period in respect of which a direction is given under section 747(1) and that United Kingdom residence shall be assumed to continue throughout subsequent accounting periods of the company (whether or not a direction is given in respect of all or any of them) until the company ceases to be controlled by persons resident in the United Kingdom.

(2) Except in so far as the following provisions of this Schedule otherwise provide, for the purposes of calculating a company's chargeable profits or corresponding United Kingdom tax for any accounting period which is not the first such period referred to in sub-paragraph (1) above (and, in particular, for the purpose of applying any relief which is relevant to two or more accounting periods), it shall be assumed that a calculation of chargeable profits or, as the case may be, corresponding United Kingdom tax has been made for every previous accounting period throughout which the company was, by virtue of sub-paragraph (1) above, assumed to have been resident in the United Kingdom.

Former enactment.—FA 1984, Sch. 16, para. 2.

3. The company shall be assumed not to be a close company.

Former enactment.—FA 1984, Sch. 16, para. 3.

4.—(1) Subject to sub-paragraph (2) below, where any relief under the Corporation Tax Acts is dependent upon the making of a claim or election, the company shall be assumed to have made that claim or election which would give the maximum amount of relief and to have made that claim or election within any time limit applicable to it.

(2) If, by notice given to the Board at any time not later than the expiry of the time for the making of an appeal under section 753 or within such longer period as the Board may in any particular case allow, the United Kingdom resident company which has or, as the case may

be, any two or more United Kingdom resident companies which together have, a majority interest in the company so request, the company shall be assumed—

(*a*) not to have made any claim or election specified in the notice; or
(*b*) to have made a claim or election so specified, being different from one assumed by sub-paragraph (1) above but being one which (subject to compliance with any time limit) could have been made in the case of a company within the charge to corporation tax; or
(*c*) to have disclaimed or required the postponement, in whole or in part, of an allowance if (subject to compliance with any time limit) a company within the charge to corporation tax could have disclaimed the allowance or, as the case may be, required such a postponement.

(3) For the purposes of this paragraph, a United Kingdom resident company has, or two or more United Kingdom resident companies together have, a majority interest in the company if on the apportionment of the company's chargeable profits for the relevant accounting period under section 747(3) more than half of the amount of those profits—

(*a*) which are apportioned to all United Kingdom resident companies, and
(*b*) which give rise to an assessment on any such companies under subsection (4)(*a*) of that section,

are apportioned to the United Kingdom resident company or companies concerned.

(4) In sub-paragraph (3) above, "the relevant accounting period" means the accounting period or, as the case may be, the first accounting period in which the relief in question is or would be available in accordance with sub-paragraph (1) above.

Former enactment.—FA 1984, Sch. 16, para. 4.

Group relief etc.

5. The company shall be assumed to be neither a member of a group of companies nor a member of a consortium for the purposes of any provision of the Tax Acts.

Former enactment.—FA 1984, Sch. 16, para. 5.

6.—(1) In relation to section 247 it shall be assumed—

(*a*) that the conditions for the making of an election under subsection (1) are not fulfilled with respect to dividends paid or received by the company; and
(*b*) that the conditions for the making of an election under subsection (4) are not fulfilled with respect to payments made or received by the company.

(2) References in sub-paragraph (1) above to dividends or payments received by the company apply to any received by another person on behalf of or in trust for the company, but not to any received by the company on behalf of or in trust for another person.

Former enactment.—FA 1984, Sch. 16, para. 6.

7. The company shall be assumed not to be a subsidiary to which the benefit of any advance corporation tax may be surrendered under section 240.

Former enactment.—FA 1984, Sch. 16, para. 7.

Company reconstructions

8. Without prejudice to the operation of section 343 in a case where the company is the predecessor, within the meaning of that section, and a company resident in the United Kingdom is the successor, within the meaning of that section—

(*a*) the assumption that the company is resident in the United Kingdom shall not be regarded as requiring it also to be assumed that the company is within the charge to tax in respect of a trade for the purposes of that section, and
(*b*) except in so far as the company is actually within that charge (by carrying on the trade through a branch or agency in the United Kingdom), it shall accordingly be assumed that the company can never be the successor, within the meaning of that section, to another company (whether resident in the United Kingdom or not).

Former enactment.—FA 1984, Sch. 16, para. 8.

Losses in pre-direction accounting periods

9.—(1) Subject to sub-paragraph (2) below, this paragraph applies in any case where the company incurred a loss in trade in an accounting period—

(a) which precedes the first accounting period in respect of which a direction is given under section 747(1) ("the starting period"); and
(b) which ended less than six years before the beginning of the starting period; and
(c) in which the company was not resident in the United Kingdom;

and in this paragraph any such accounting period is referred to as a "pre-direction period".

(2) This paragraph does not apply in any case where a declaration is made under paragraph 11(3) below specifying an accounting period of the company which begins before, or is the same as, the first pre-direction period in which the company incurred a loss as mentioned in sub-paragraph (1) above.

(3) If a claim is made for the purpose by the United Kingdom resident company or companies referred to in paragraph 4(2) above, the chargeable profits (if any) of the company for accounting periods beginning with that pre-direction period which is specified in the claim and in which a loss is incurred as mentioned in sub-paragraph (1) above shall be determined (in accordance with the provisions of this Schedule other than this paragraph) on the assumption that that pre-direction period was the first accounting period in respect of which a direction was given under section 747(1).

(4) A claim under sub-paragraph (3) above shall be made by notice given to the Board within 60 days of the date of the notice under subsection (1) or subsection (3) of section 753 relating to the starting period or within such longer period as the Board may in any particular case allow.

(5) For the purposes of a claim under sub-paragraph (3) above, it shall be assumed that Chapter IV of Part XVII was in force before the beginning of the first of the pre-direction periods.

(6) In determining for the purposes of this paragraph which accounting period of the company is the starting period, no account should be taken of the effect of any declaration under paragraph 11(3) below.

Former enactment.—FA 1984, Sch. 16, para. 9.

Capital allowances

10.—(1) Subject to paragraphs 11 and 12 below, if, in an accounting period falling before the beginning of the first accounting period in respect of which a direction is given under section 747(1), the company incurred any capital expenditure on the provision of machinery or plant for the purposes of its trade, that machinery or plant shall be assumed, for the purposes of Chapter I of Part III of the Finance Act 1971, to have been provided for purposes wholly other than those of the trade and not to have been brought into use for the purposes of that trade until the beginning of that first accounting period, and paragraph 7 of Schedule 8 to that Act (expenditure treated as equivalent to market value at the time the machinery or plant is brought into use) shall apply accordingly.

(2) This paragraph shall be construed as one with Chapter I of Part III of the Finance Act 1971.

Former enactments.—FA 1984, Sch. 16, para. 10; FA 1985, Sch. 14, para. 16.

11.—(1) This paragraph applies in any case where it appears to the Board that the reason why no direction was given under section 747(1) in respect of an accounting period which precedes the starting period was that the effect of any allowance which would be assumed for that preceding period by virtue of this Schedule would be such that—

(a) the company would not have been considered to be subject in that accounting period to a lower level of taxation in the territory in which it was resident; or
(b) the company would have had no chargeable profits for that accounting period; or
(c) the chargeable profits of the company for that accounting period would not have exceeded £20,000 or such smaller amount as was appropriate in accordance with section 748(1)(d).

(2) In this paragraph "the starting period" means the first accounting period in respect of which a direction is given under section 747(1) and, in a case where a claim is made under sub-paragraph (3) of paragraph 9 above, no account shall be taken of the effect of that sub-

paragraph in determining which accounting period is the starting period for the purposes of this paragraph.

(3) If, in a case where this paragraph applies, the Board so declare by notice given to every company to which, in accordance with section 753(1), notice of the making of the direction relating to the starting period is required to be given, the chargeable profits of that period and every subsequent accounting period and the corresponding United Kingdom tax for every subsequent accounting period shall be determined (in accordance with the provisions of this Schedule other than this paragraph) on the assumption that the accounting period specified in the declaration was the first accounting period in respect of which a direction was given and, accordingly, as if allowances had been assumed in respect of that accounting period and any subsequent accounting period which precedes the starting period.

(4) Nothing in sub-paragraph (3) above affects the operation of paragraph 9(3) above in a case where the accounting period specified in a claim under paragraph 9(3) above begins before the period specified in a declaration under sub-paragraph (3) above.

(5) Subject to sub-paragraph (6) below, the Board shall not make a declaration under sub-paragraph (3) above with respect to an accounting period which precedes the starting period unless the facts are such that—

(a) assuming the company to have been subject in that period to a lower level of taxation in the territory in which it was resident, and
(b) assuming the company to have had in that period chargeable profits of such an amount that the condition in section 748(1)(d) would not be fulfilled,

a direction could have been given in respect of that period under section 747(1).

(6) In its application to a company falling within section 749(3), sub-paragraph (5) above shall have effect with the omission of paragraph (a).

(7) In this paragraph "allowance" means an allowance under Chapter I of Part I of the 1968 Act or Chapter I of Part III of the Finance Act 1971.

Former enactment.—FA 1984, Sch. 16, para. 11.

Unremittable overseas income

12. For the purposes of the application of section 584 to the company's income it shall be assumed—

(a) that any reference in paragraph (a) or paragraph (b) of subsection (1) of that section to the United Kingdom is a reference to both the United Kingdom and the territory in which the company is in fact resident; and
(b) that a notice under subsection (2) of that section (expressing a wish to be assessed in accordance with that subsection) may be given on behalf of the company by the United Kingdom resident company or companies referred to in paragraph 4(2) above.

Former enactment.—FA 1984, Sch. 16, para. 13.

SCHEDULE 25
Section 748

CASES EXCLUDED FROM DIRECTION-MAKING POWERS

PART I
ACCEPTABLE DISTRIBUTION POLICY

1. The provisions of this Part of this Schedule have effect for the purposes of paragraph (*a*) of subsection (1) of section 748.

Former enactment.—FA 1984, Sch. 17, para. 1.

2.—(1) Subject to sub-paragraph (2) below, a controlled foreign company pursues an acceptable distribution policy in respect of a particular accounting period if, and only if—

(*a*) a dividend which is not paid out of specified profits is paid for that accounting period or for some other period which, in whole or in part, falls within that accounting period; and

(*b*) the dividend is paid during, or not more than eighteen months after the expiry of, the period for which it is paid or at such later time as the Board may, in any particular case, allow; and

(*c*) the dividend is paid at a time when the company is not resident in the United Kingdom (whether or not it is at that time a controlled foreign company); and

(*d*) the proportion of the dividend or, if there is more than one, of the aggregate of those dividends which is paid to persons resident in the United Kingdom represents at least 50 per cent. of the company's available profits for the accounting period referred to in paragraph (*a*) above or, where sub-paragraph (4) or (5) below applies, of the appropriate portion of those profits;

and for the purposes of this sub-paragraph a dividend which is not paid for a specified period shall be treated as paid for the period or periods the profits of which are, in relation to the dividend, the relevant profits for the purposes of section 799.

(2) In the case of a controlled foreign company which is not a trading company, sub-paragraph (1) above shall have effect with the substitution of 90 per cent. for 50 per cent.

(3) For the purposes of this Part of this Schedule, a dividend represents those profits of the controlled foreign company in question which in relation to that dividend are the relevant profits for the purposes of section 799 and, accordingly, where those profits are the profits of a period which falls partly within and partly outside an accounting period of that company, the necessary apportionment shall be made to determine what proportion of those profits is attributable to that accounting period.

(4) This sub-paragraph applies where—

(*a*) throughout the accounting period in question all the issued shares of the controlled foreign company are of a single class, and

(*b*) at the end of that accounting period some of those shares are held by persons resident outside the United Kingdom, and

(*c*) at no time during that accounting period does any person have an interest in the company other than an interest derived from the issued shares of the company;

and in a case where this sub-paragraph applies the appropriate portion for the purposes of sub-paragraph (1)(*d*) above is the fraction of which the denominator is the total number of the issued shares of the company at the end of the accounting period in question and, subject to sub-paragraph 8 below, the numerator is the number of those issued shares by virtue of which persons resident in the United Kingdom have interests in the company at that time.

(5) This sub-paragraph applies where—

(*a*) throughout the accounting period in question there are only two classes of issued shares of the controlled foreign company and, of those classes, one ("non-voting shares") consists of non-voting fixed-rate preference shares and the other ("voting shares") consists of shares which carry the right to vote in all circumstances at general meetings of the company; and

(*b*) at the end of that accounting period some of the issued shares of the company are held by persons resident outside the United Kingdom; and

(c) at no time during that accounting period does any person have an interest in the company other than an interest derived from non-voting or voting shares;

and in a case where this sub-paragraph applies the appropriate portion of the profits referred to in sub-paragraph (1)(d) above is the amount determined in accordance with sub-paragraph (6) below.

(6) The amount referred to in sub-paragraph (5) above is that given by the formula—

$$\frac{P \times Q}{R} + \frac{(X-P) \times Y}{Z}$$

where—

P is the amount of any dividend falling within (a) and (b) of sub-paragraph (1) above which is paid in respect of the non-voting shares or, if there is more than one such dividend, of the aggregate of them;

Q is, subject to sub-paragraph (8) below, the number of the non-voting shares by virtue of which persons resident in the United Kingdom have interests in the company at the end of the accounting period in question;

R is the total number at that time of the issued non-voting shares;

X is the available profits for the accounting period in question;

Y is, subject to sub-paragraph (8) below, the number of voting shares by virtue of which persons resident in the United Kingdom have interests in the company at the end of that accounting period; and

Z is the total number at that time of the issued voting shares.

(7) For the purposes of sub-paragraph (5)(a) above, non-voting fixed-rate preference shares are shares—

(a) which are fixed-rate preference shares as defined in paragraph 1 of Schedule 18; and
(b) which either carry no right to vote at a general meeting of the company or carry such a right which is contingent upon the non-payment of a dividend on the shares and which has not in fact become exercisable at any time prior to the payment of a dividend for the accounting period in question.

(8) In any case where the immediate interests held by persons resident in the United Kingdom who have indirect interests in a controlled foreign company at the end of a particular accounting period do not reflect the proportion of the shares or, as the case may be, shares of a particular class in the company by virtue of which they have those interests (as in the case where they hold, directly or indirectly, part of the shares in a company which itself holds, directly or indirectly, some or all of the shares in the controlled foreign company) the number of those shares shall be treated as reduced for the purposes of sub-paragraph (4) or (6) above, as the case may be, to such number as may be appropriate having regard to—

(a) the immediate interests held by the persons resident in the United Kingdom; and
(b) any intermediate shareholdings between those interests and the shares in the controlled foreign company.

(9) The definition of "profits" in section 747(6)(b) does not apply to any reference in this paragraph to specified profits or to relevant profits for the purposes of section 799.

Former enactments.—FA 1984, Sch. 17, para. 2; F(No. 2)A 1987, s. 65(2).

3.—(1) Subject to sub-paragraphs (2) and (5) below, for the purposes of this Part of this Schedule, the available profits of a controlled foreign company for any accounting period shall be ascertained by—

(a) determining what would be the relevant profits of that period for the purposes of section 799 if a dividend were paid for that period; and
(b) deducting so much of those relevant profits as consists of an excess of capital profits over capital losses.

(2) If, for any accounting period of the controlled foreign company which is of less than 12 months duration, the available profits, as ascertained under sub-paragraph (1) above, are less than the chargeable profits (determined on the additional assumptions in section 750(3)(a)) then, if the Board so declare, for the purposes of this Part of this Schedule the available profits for the accounting period shall be those chargeable profits.

(3) The definition of "profits" in section 747(6)(b) does not apply to the reference in sub-paragraph (1)(a) above to relevant profits for the purposes of section 799.

(4) In sub-paragraph (1)(b) above "capital profits" means gains—

(a) which accrue on the disposal of assets; and

(b) which, if the company were within the charge to corporation tax in respect of the activities giving rise to those disposals, would not be taken into account as receipts in computing the company's income or profits or gains or losses for the purposes of the Income Tax Acts;

and the expression "capital losses' shall be construed accordingly.

(5) In any case where—

(a) a controlled foreign company pays a dividend for any period out of specified profits, and

(b) those profits represent dividends received by the company, directly or indirectly, from another controlled foreign company,

so much of those specified profits as is equal to the dividend referred to in paragraph (a) above shall be left out of account in determining, for the purposes of this Part of this Schedule, the available profits of the controlled foreign company referred to in that paragraph for any accounting period.

Former enactment.—FA 1984, Sch. 17, para. 3.

4.—(1) For the purposes of this Part of this Schedule, where—

(a) a controlled foreign company pays a dividend ("the initial dividend") to another company which is also not resident in the United Kingdom, and

(b) that other company or another company which is related to it pays a dividend ("the subsequent dividend") to a United Kingdom resident, and

(c) the subsequent dividend is paid at a time when the company paying it is not resident in the United Kingdom; and

(d) the subsequent dividend is paid out of profits which are derived, directly or indirectly, from the whole or part of the initial dividend,

so much of the initial dividend as is respresented by the subsequent dividend shall be regarded as paid to the United Kingdom resident.

(2) For the purposes of this paragraph, one company is related to another if the other—

(a) controls directly or indirectly, or

(b) is a subsidiary of a company which controls directly or indirectly,

at least 10 per cent. of the voting power in the first-mentioned company; and where one company is so related to another and that other is so related to a third company, the first company is for the purposes of this paragraph related to the third, and so on where there is a chain of companies, each of which is related to the next.

Former enactments.—FA 1984, Sch. 17, para. 4; F(No. 2)A 1987, s. 65(3).

PART II
EXEMPT ACTIVITIES

5.—(1) The provisions of this Part of this Schedule have effect for the purposes of paragraph (b) of subsection (1) of section 748.

(2) In the case of a controlled foreign company—

(a) which is, by virtue of section 749(3), presumed to be resident in a territory in which it is subject to a lower level of taxation, and

(b) the business affairs of which are, throughout the accounting period in question, effectively managed in a territory outside the United Kingdom other than one in which companies are liable to tax by reason of domicile, residence or place of management,

referemces in the following provisions of this Part of this Schedule to the territory in which that company is resident shall be construed as references to the territory falling within paragraph (b) above, or, if there is more than one, to that one of them which may be notified to the Board by the United Kingdom resident company or companies referred to in paragraph 4(2) of Schedule 24.

Former enactment.—FA 1984, Sch. 17, para. 5.

6.—(1) Throughout an accounting period a controlled foreign company is engaged in exempt activities if, and only if, each of the following conditions is fulfilled—

(a) that, throughout that accounting period, the company has a business establishment in the territory in which it is resident; and

cent. of its gross income during the accounting period in question is derived directly from companies which it controls and which, throughout that period—

(a) are resident in the territory in which the holding company is resident; and

(b) are not themselves holding companies, but otherwise are, in terms of this Schedule, engaged in exempt activities;

and a holding company to which this sub-paragraph applies is in this Part of this Schedule referred to as a "local holding company".

(4) This sub-paragraph applies to a company which is a holding company, but not a local holding company, if at least 90 per cent. of its gross income during the accounting period in question is derived directly from companies which it controls and which, throughout that period—

(a) are local holding companies; or

(b) are not themselves holding companies (whether local or not), but otherwise are, in terms of this Schedule, engaged in exempt activities.

(5) Any reference in sub-paragraph (3) or (4) above to a company which a holding company controls includes a reference to a trading company in which the holding company holds the maximum amount of ordinary share capital which is permitted under the law of the territory—

(a) in which the trading company is resident; and

(b) from whose laws the trading company derives its status as a company.

(6) The following provisions of this Part of this Schedule have effect in relation to sub-paragraphs (1) to (4) above.

Former enactment.—FA 1984, Sch. 17, para. 6.

7.—(1) For the purposes of paragraph 6(1)(a) above, a "business establishment", in relation to a controlled foreign company, means premises—

(a) which are, or are intended to be, occupied and used with a reasonable degree of permanence; and

(b) from which the company's business in the territory in which it is resident is wholly or mainly carried on.

(2) For the purposes of sub-paragraph (1) above the following shall be regarded as premises—

(a) an office, shop, factory or other building or part of a building; or

(b) a mine, an oil or gas well, a quarry or any other place of extraction of natural resources; or

(c) a building site or the site of a construction or installation project;

but such a site as is referred to in paragraph (c) above shall not be regarded as premises unless the building work or the project, as the case may be, has a duration of at least twelve months.

Former enactment.—FA 1984, Sch. 17, para. 7.

8.—(1) Subject to sub-paragraph (4) below, the condition in paragraph 6(1)(b) above shall not be regarded as fulfilled unless—

(e) dealing in securities in the capacity of a broker, as defined in paragraph 9(2) above;
(f) dealing in commodity or financial futures; and
(g) insurance business which is long-term business or general business, as defined in section 1 of the Insurance Companies Act 1982.

(2) In a case where the gross trading receipts of a company include an amount in respect of the proceeds of sale of any description of property or rights, the cost to the company of the purchase of that property or those rights shall be a deduction in calculating the company's gross trading receipts for the purposes of paragraph 6(2)(b) above.

(3) In the case of a controlled foreign company engaged in a banking or other business falling within sub-paragraph (1)(c) above—

(a) no payment of interest received from a company resident in the United Kingdom shall be regarded for the purposes of paragraph 6(2)(b) above as a receipt derived directly or indirectly from connected or associated persons, but
(b) it shall be conclusively presumed that the condition in paragraph 6(2)(b) above is not fulfilled if, at any time during the accounting period in question, the amount by which the aggregate value of the capital interests in the company held directly or indirectly by—

   (i) the persons who have control of the company, and
   (ii) any person connected or associated with those persons,

exceeds the value of the company's fixed assets is 15 per cent. or more of the amount by which the company's outstanding capital exceeds that value.

(4) For the purposes of this paragraph, in relation to a controlled foreign company—

(a) "capital interest" means an interest in the issued share capital or reserves of the company or in a loan to or deposit with the company or the liability of a guarantor under a guarantee given to or for the benefit of the company;
(b) except in the case of the liability of a guarantor, the value of a capital interest is its value as shown in the company's accounts;
(c) in the case of the liability of a guarantor, the value shall be taken to be the market value of the benefit which the controlled foreign company derives from the provision of the guarantee;
(d) the value of the company's fixed assets means the value, as shown in the company's accounts, of the plant, premises and trade investments employed in the company's business; and
(e) "outstanding capital" means the total value of all the capital interests in the company, less the value, as shown in the company's accounts, of any advances made by the company to persons resident outside the United Kingdom and falling within paragraph (i) or paragraph (ii) of sub-paragraph (3)(b) above.

(5) For the purposes of sub-paragraph (4) above—

(a) "trade investments", in relation to a controlled foreign company, means securities any profit on the sale of which would not be brought into account as a trading receipt in computing the chargeable profits of an accounting period in which that profit arose; and
(b) the reference in paragraph (e) to advances made to a person by the controlled foreign company includes, in the case of a company which is a person resident outside the United Kingdom and falling within paragraph (i) or paragraph (ii) of sub-paragraph (3)(b) above, any securities of that company which are held by the controlled foreign company but are not trade investments, as defined in paragraph (a) above;

and in this sub-paragraph "securities" includes stocks and shares.

(6) In the application of paragraph 6(2)(b) above in the case of a controlled foreign company engaged in insurance business of any kind—

(a) the reference to gross trading receipts which are derived directly or indirectly from connected or associated persons is a reference to those which, subject to sub-paragraph (7) below, are attributable, directly or indirectly, to liabilities undertaken in relation to any of those persons or their property;
(b) the only receipts to be taken into account are commissions and premiums received under insurance contracts;
(c) so much of any such commission or premium as is returned is not to be taken into account; and
(d) when a liability under an insurance contract is reinsured, in whole or in part, the amount of the premium which is attributable, directly or indirectly, to that liability shall be treated as reduced by so much of the premium under the reinsurance contract as is attributable to that liability.

(7) In determining, in relation to a controlled foreign company to which sub-paragraph (6)

above applies, the gross trading receipts referred to in paragraph (*a*) of that sub-paragraph, there shall be left out of account any receipts under a local reinsurance contract which are attributable to liabilities which—

(*a*) are undertaken under an insurance contract made in the territory in which the company is resident; and
(*b*) are not reinsured under any contract other than a local reinsurance contract; and
(*c*) relate either to persons who are resident in that territory and are neither connected nor associated with the company or to property which is situated there and belongs to persons who are not so connected or associated;

and in paragraph (*a*) above "insurance contract" does not include a reinsurance contract.

(8) In sub-paragraph (7) above "local reinsurance contract" means a reinsurance contract—
(*a*) which is made in the territory in which the controlled foreign company is resident; and
(*b*) the parties to which are companies which are resident in that territory.

(9) For the purposes of sub-paragraphs (7) and (8) above, any question as to the territory in which a company is resident shall be determined in accordance with section 749 and, where appropriate, paragraph 5(2) above; and, for the purpose of the application of those provisions in accordance with this sub-paragraph, the company shall be assumed to be a controlled foreign company.

Former enactment.—FA 1984, Sch. 17, para. 11.

12.—(1) Subject to sub-paragraph (2) below, in paragraphs 6 and 8(3) above and sub-paragraphs (4) and (5) below "holding company" means—
(*a*) a company the business of which consists wholly or mainly in the holding of shares or securities of companies which are either local holding companies and its 90 per cent. subsidiaries or trading companies and either its 51 per cent. subsidiaries or companies falling within paragraph 6(5) above; or
(*b*) a company which would fall within paragraph (*a*) above if there were disregarded so much of its business as consists in the holding of property or rights of any description for use wholly or mainly by companies which it controls and which are resident in the territory in which it is resident.

(2) In determining whether a company is a holding company for the purposes of paragraph 6(3) above (and, accordingly, whether the company is or may be a local holding company), sub-paragraph (1) above shall have effect with the omission from paragraph (*a*) thereof of the words "either local holding companies and its 90 per cent. subsidiaries or".

(3) In its application for the purposes of this paragraph, section 838 shall have effect with the omission of—
(*a*) in subsection (1)(*a*), the words "or indirectly"; and
(*b*) subsection (2).

(4) For the purposes of sub-paragraph (3) or (4), as the case may be, of paragraph 6 above, as it applies in relation to a holding company part of whose business consists of activities other than the holding of shares or securities or the holding of property or rights as mentioned in paragraph (*a*) or (*b*) of sub-paragraph (1) above, the company's gross income during any accounting period shall be determined as follows—
(*a*) there shall be left out of account so much of what would otherwise be the company's gross income as is derived from any activity which, if it were the business in which the company is mainly engaged, would be such that paragraph 6(2) above would apply to the company; and
(*b*) to the extent that the receipts of the company from any other activity include receipts from the proceeds of sale of any description of property or rights, the cost to the company of the purchase of that property or those rights shall (to the extent that the cost does not exceed the receipts) be a deduction in calculating the company's gross income, and no other deduction shall be made in respect of that activity.

(5) For the purposes of sub-paragraphs (3) and (4) of paragraph 6 above, so much of the income of a holding company as—
(*a*) is derived directly from another company which it controls and which is not a holding company but otherwise is, in terms of this Schedule, engaged in exempt activities, and
(*b*) was or could have been paid out of any non-trading income of that other company which is derived directly or indirectly from a third company connected or associated with it,

shall be treated, in relation to the holding company, as if it were not derived directly from companies which it controls.

(6) The reference in sub-paragraph (5) above to the non-trading income of a company is a reference to so much of its income as, if the company were carrying on its trade in the United Kingdom, would not be within the charge to corporation tax under Case I of Schedule D.

Former enactment.—FA 1984, Sch. 17, para. 12.

PART III
THE PUBLIC QUOTATION CONDITION

13.—(1) The provisions of this Part of this Schedule have effect for the purposes of section 748(1)(*c*).

(2) Subject to paragraph 14 below, a controlled foreign company fulfils the public quotation condition with respect to a particular accounting period if—

(*a*) shares in the company carrying not less than 35 per cent. of the voting power in the company (and not being shares entitled to a fixed rate of dividend, whether with or without a further right to participate in profits) have been allotted unconditionally to, or acquired unconditionally by, the public and, throughout that accounting period, are beneficially held by the public; and
(*b*) within the period of 12 months ending at the end of the accounting period, any such shares have been the subject of dealings on a recognised stock exchange situated in the territory in which the company is resident; and
(*c*) within that period of 12 months the shares have been quoted in the official list of such a recognised stock exchange.

Former enactment.—FA 1984, Sch. 17, para. 13.

14.—(1) The condition in paragraph 13(2) above is not fulfilled with respect to an accounting period of a controlled foreign company if at any time in that period the total percentage of the voting power in the company possessed by all of the company's principal members exceeds 85 per cent.

(2) For the purposes of paragraph 13(2) above shares in a controlled foreign company shall be deemed to be beneficially held by the public if they are held by any person other than—

(*a*) a person connected or associated with the company; or
(*b*) a principal member of the company;

and a corresponding construction shall be given to the reference to shares which have been allotted unconditionally to, or acquired unconditionally by, the public.

Former enactment.—FA 1984, Sch. 17, para. 14.

15.—(1) References in this Part of this Schedule to shares held by any person include references to any shares the rights or powers attached to which could, for the purposes of section 416, be attributed to that person under subsection (5) of that section.

(2) For the purposes of this Part of this Schedule—

(*a*) a person is a principal member of a controlled foreign company if he possesses a percentage of the voting power in the company of more than 5 per cent. and—

(i) where there are more than five such persons, if he is one of the five persons who possess the greatest percentages, or
(ii) if, because two or more persons possess equal percentages of the voting power in the company, there are no such five persons, he is one of six or more persons (so as to include those two or more who possess the equal percentages) who possess the greatest percentages; and

(*b*) a principal member's holding consists of the shares which carry the voting power possessed by him.

(3) In arriving at the voting power which a person possesses, there shall be attributed to him any voting power which, for the purposes of section 416, would be attributed to him under subsection (5) or (6) of that section.

(4) In this Part of this Schedule "shares" include "stock".

Former enactment.—FA 1984, Sch. 17, para. 15.

PART IV
REDUCTIONS IN UNITED KINGDOM TAX AND DIVERSION OF PROFITS

16.—(1) The provisions of this Part of this Schedule have effect for the purposes of section 748(3).

(2) Any reference in paragraphs 17 and 18 below to a transaction—

   (*a*) is a reference to a transaction reflected in the profits arising in an accounting period of a controlled foreign company; and
   (*b*) includes a reference to two or more such transactions taken together.

Former enactment.—FA 1984, Sch. 17, para. 16.

17.—(1) A transaction achieves a reduction in United Kingdom tax if, had the transaction not been effected, any person—

   (*a*) would have been liable for any such tax or for a greater amount of any such tax; or
   (*b*) would not have been entitled to a relief from or repayment of any such tax or would have been entitled to a smaller relief from or repayment of any such tax.

(2) In this Part of this Schedule and section 748(3) "United Kingdom tax" means income tax, corporation tax or capital gains tax.

Former enactment.—FA 1984, Sch. 17, para. 17.

18. It is the main purpose or one of the main purposes of a transaction to achieve a reduction in United Kingdom tax if this is the purpose or one of the main purposes—

   (*a*) of the controlled foreign company concerned; or
   (*b*) of a person who has an interest in that company at any time during the accounting period concerned.

Former enactment.—FA 1984, Sch. 17, para. 18.

19.—(1) The existence of a controlled foreign company achieves a reduction in United Kingdom tax by a diversion of profits from the United Kingdom in an accounting period if it is reasonable to suppose that, had neither the company nor any company related to it been in existence—

   (*a*) the whole or a substantial part of the receipts which are reflected in the controlled foreign company's profits in that accounting period would have been received by a company or individual resident in the United Kingdom; and
   (*b*) that company or individual or any other person resident in the United Kingdom either—

      (i) would have been liable for any United Kingdom tax or for a greater amount of any such tax; or
      (ii) would not have been entitled to a relief from or repayment of any such tax or would have been entitled to a smaller relief from or repayment of any such tax.

(2) For the purposes of sub-paragraph (1) above, a company is related to a controlled foreign company if—

   (*a*) it is resident outside the United Kingdom; and
   (*b*) it is connected or associated with the controlled foreign company; and
   (*c*) in relation to any company or companies resident in the United Kingdom, it fulfils or could fulfil, directly or indirectly, substantially the same functions as the controlled foreign company.

(3) Any reference in sub-paragraph (1) above to a company resident in the United Kingdom includes a reference to such a company which, if the controlled foreign company in question were not in existence, it is reasonable to suppose would have been established.

Former enactment.—FA 1984, Sch. 17, para. 19.

SCHEDULE 26

Section 754(5)

RELIEFS AGAINST LIABILITY FOR TAX IN RESPECT OF CHARGEABLE PROFITS

Trading losses and group relief etc.

1.—(1) In any case where—

(*a*) an amount of chargeable profits is apportioned to a company resident in the United Kingdom, and

(*b*) the company is entitled, or would on the making of a claim be entitled, in computing its profits for the appropriate accounting period, to a deduction in respect of any relevant allowance, and

(*c*) for the appropriate accounting period the company has no profits against which a deduction could be made in respect of that allowance or, as the case may be, the amount of that allowance exceeds the profits against which a deduction falls to be made in respect of it,

then, on the making of a claim, a sum equal to corporation tax at the appropriate rate on so much of the relevant allowance or, as the case may be, of the excess of it referred to in paragraph (*c*) above as is specified in the claim shall be set off against the company's liability to tax under section 747(4)(*a*) in respect of the chargeable profits apportioned to it.

(2) In this paragraph—

(*a*) "the appropriate accounting period" means the accounting period for which, by virtue of section 754(2), the company is regarded as assessed to corporation tax in respect of the chargeable profits concerned; and

(*b*) "the appropriate rate" means the rate of corporation tax applicable to profits of the appropriate accounting period or, if there is more than one such rate, the average rate over the whole accounting period.

(3) In this paragraph "relevant allowance" means—

(*a*) any loss to which section 393(2) applies;
(*b*) any charge on income to which section 338(1) applies;
(*c*) any expenses of management to which section 75(1) applies;
(*d*) so much of any allowance to which section 74 of the 1968 Act applies as falls within subsection (3) of that section; and
(*e*) any amount available to the company by way of group relief.

(4) In any case where, for the appropriate accounting period, an amount would have been available to the company by way of group relief if a claim had been made under section 412, such a claim may be made for the purposes of this paragraph at any time before the end of the accounting period following that in which the assessment under section 747(4)(*a*) is made, notwithstanding that the period of two years referred to in section 412(1)(*c*) has expired.

(5) Where, by virtue of sub-paragraph (1) above, a sum is set off against a liability to tax, so much of the relevant allowance as gives rise to the amount set off shall be regarded for the purposes of the Tax Acts as having been allowed as a deduction against the company's profits in accordance with the appropriate provisions of those Acts.

(6) In its application to a claim under this paragraph, section 43 of the Management Act (time limit for making claims) shall have effect as if, in subsection (2)—

(*a*) any reference to an assessment to income tax were a reference to an assessment under section 747(4)(*a*); and
(*b*) any reference to a year of assessment were a reference to an accounting period.

Former enactment.—FA 1984, Sch. 18, para. 1.

Advance corporation tax

2.—(1) In any case where—

(*a*) an amount of chargeable profits is apportioned to a company resident in the United Kingdom, and

(b) the company has an amount of advance corporation tax which, apart from this paragraph, would, in relation to the appropriate accounting period, be surplus advance corporation tax for the purposes of section 239(3),

then, on the making of a claim, so much of that advance corporation tax as is specified in the claim and does not exceed the relevant maximum shall be set against the company's liability to tax under section 747(4)(a) in respect of the chargeable profits apportioned to it, to the extent that that liability has not or could not have been relieved by virtue of paragraph 1 above.

(2) So much of any advance corporation tax as, by virtue of this paragraph, is set against the company's liability to tax under section 747(4)(a) in respect of chargeable profits shall be regarded for the purposes of the Tax Acts as not being surplus advance corporation tax within the meaning of section 239.

(3) In this paragraph "the appropriate accounting period" has the same meaning as in paragraph 1 above and "the relevant maximum", in relation to the liability to tax referred to in sub-paragraph (1) above, is the amount of advance corporation tax that would have been payable (apart from section 241) in respect of a distribution made at the end of the appropriate accounting period of an amount which, together with the advance corporation tax in respect of it, is equal to—

(a) that amount of the chargeable profits apportioned to the company on which it is chargeable to corporation tax for that accounting period,

less

(b) any amount which, for that accounting period, is to be regarded, by virtue of paragraph 1(5) above, as having been allowed as a deduction against the company's profits.

Former enactment.—FA 1984, Sch. 18, para. 2.

Gains on disposal of shares in controlled foreign companies

3.—(1) This paragraph applies in any case where—

(a) a direction has been given under subsection (1) of section 747 in respect of an accounting period of a controlled foreign company ("the direction period"); and
(b) the company's chargeable profits for the direction period have been apportioned among the persons in subsection (3) of that section; and
(c) a company resident in the United Kingdom ("the claimant company") disposes of—

(i) shares in the controlled foreign company, or
(ii) shares in another company which, in whole or in part, give rise to the claimant company's interest in the controlled foreign company,

being, in either case, shares acquired before the end of the direction period; and
(d) by virtue of the apportionment referred to in paragraph (b) above, a sum is, under section 747(4)(a), assessed on and recoverable from the claimant company as if it were an amount of corporation tax; and
(e) the claimant company makes a claim for relief under this paragraph;

and in this paragraph the disposal mentioned in paragraph (c) above is referred to as "the relevant disposal".

(2) Subject to the following provisions of this paragraph, in the computation under Chapter II of Part II of the 1979 Act of the gain accruing on the relevant disposal, the appropriate fraction of the sum referred to in sub-paragraph (1)(d) above shall be allowable as a deduction; but to the extent that any sum has been allowed as a deduction under this sub-paragraph it shall not again be allowed as a deduction on any claim under this paragraph (whether made by the claimant company or another company).

(3) In relation to the relevant disposal, the appropriate fraction is—

$$\frac{A}{B}$$

where—

A is the average market value in the direction period of the shares disposed of, and
B is the average market value in that period of the interest in the controlled foreign company which, in the case of the claimant company, was taken into account in the apportionment referred to in sub-paragraph (1)(b) above.

(4) Where, before the relevant disposal—

(*a*) a dividend is paid by the controlled foreign company, and
(*b*) the profits out of which the dividend is paid are those from which the chargeable profits referred to in sub-paragraph (1)(*b*) above are derived, and
(*c*) at least one of the two conditions in sub-paragraph (5) below is fulfilled,

this paragraph does not apply in relation to a sum assessed and recoverable in respect of so much of the chargeable profits as corresponds to the profits which the dividend represents.

(5) The conditions referred to in sub-paragraph (4) above are—

(*a*) that the effect of the payment of the dividend is such that the value of the shares disposed of by the relevant disposal is less after the payment than it was before it; and
(*b*) that, in respect of a dividend paid or payable on the shares disposed of by the relevant disposal, the claimant company is, by virtue of paragraph 4(2) below, entitled under Part XVIII to relief (by way of underlying tax) by reference to sums which include the sum referred to in sub-paragraph (1)(*d*) above.

(6) A claim for relief under this paragraph shall be made before the expiry of the period of three months beginning—

(*a*) at the end of the accounting period in which the relevant disposal occurs; or
(*b*) if it is later, on the date on which the assessment to tax for which the claimant company is liable by virtue of section 747(4)(*a*) becomes final and conclusive.

(7) In identifying for the purposes of this paragraph shares in a company with shares of the same class which are disposed of by the relevant disposal, shares acquired at an earlier time shall be deemed to be disposed of before shares acquired at a later time.

Former enactment.—FA 1984, Sch. 18, para. 3.

Dividends from the controlled foreign company

4.—(1) This paragraph applies in any case where—

(*a*) a direction has been given under subsection (1) of section 747 in respect of an accounting period of a controlled foreign company, and
(*b*) the company's chargeable profits for that period have been apportioned among the persons referred to in subsection (3) of that section, and
(*c*) the controlled foreign company pays a dividend in whole or in part out of the total profits from which (in accordance with subsection (6)(*a*) of that section) those chargeable profits are derived.

(2) Subject to paragraphs 5 and 6 below, where this paragraph applies, the aggregate of the sums assessed on and recoverable from companies resident in the United Kingdom in accordance with section 747(4)(*a*) in respect of the chargeable profits referred to in sub-paragraph (1)(*b*) above shall be treated for the purposes of Part XVIII as if it were an amount of tax paid in respect of the profits concerned under the law of the territory in which the controlled foreign company was resident and, accordingly, as underlying tax for the purposes of Chapter II of that Part.

(3) In the following provisions of this paragraph and in paragraphs 5 and 6 below, the aggregate of the sums which, under sub-paragraph (2) above, fall to be treated as underlying tax is referred to as the "gross attributed tax".

(4) If, in the case of a person who receives the dividend, section 796 or section 797 has the effect of reducing the amount which (apart from that section) would have been the amount of the credit for foreign tax which is to be allowed to that person, then, for the purposes of sub-paragraph (5) below, the amount of that reduction shall be determined and so much of it as does not exceed the amount of the foreign tax, exclusive of underlying tax, for which credit is to be allowed in respect of the dividend is in that sub-paragraph referred to as "the wasted relief".

(5) Except for the purpose of determining the amount of the wasted relief, the gross attributed tax shall be treated as reduced by the aggregate of the wasted relief arising in the case of all the persons falling within sub-paragraph (4) above and, on the making of a claim by any of the companies referred to in sub-paragraph (2) above—

(*a*) the amount of tax assessed on and recoverable from the company in accordance with section 747(4)(*a*) in respect of the chargeable profits referred to in sub-paragraph (1)(*b*) above shall, where appropriate, be reduced; and
(*b*) all such adjustments (whether by repayment of tax or otherwise) shall be made as are appropriate to give effect to any reduction under paragraph (*a*) above.

Former enactment.—FA 1984, Sch. 18, para. 4.

5.—(1) In so far as any provision of—

(a) arrangements having effect by virtue of section 788, or
(b) section 790,

makes relief which is related to foreign dividends received by a company resident in the United Kingdom conditional upon that company either having a particular degree of control of the company paying the dividend or being a subsidiary of another company which has that degree of control, that condition shall be treated as fulfilled in considering whether any such company is by virtue of paragraph 4(2) above entitled to relief under Part XVIII in respect of any of the gross attributed tax.

(2) Notwithstanding anything in paragraph 4(2) above, in section 795(2)(b) the expression "underlying tax" does not include gross attributed tax.

(3) In a case where the controlled foreign company pays a dividend otherwise than out of specified profits and, on the apportionment referred to in paragraph 4(1) above, less than the whole of the chargeable profits of the controlled foreign company concerned is apportioned to companies which are resident in the United Kingdom and liable for tax thereon as mentioned in section 747(4)(a)—

(a) the gross attributed tax shall be regarded as attributable to a corresponding proportion of the profits in question, and in this sub-paragraph the profits making up that proportion are referred to as "taxed profits";
(b) so much of the dividend as is received by, or by a successor in title of, any such company shall be regarded as paid primarily out of taxed profits; and
(c) so much of the dividend as is received by any other person shall be regarded as paid primarily out of profits which are not taxed profits.

(4) The reference in sub-paragraph (3)(b) above to a successor in title of a company resident in the United Kingdom is a reference to a person who is such a successor in respect of the whole or any part of that interest in the controlled foreign company by virtue of which an amount of its chargeable profits was apportioned to that company.

Former enactment.—FA 1984, Sch. 18, para. 5.

6.—(1) in any case where—

(a) on a claim for relief under paragraph 3 above, the whole or any part of any sum has been allowed as a deduction on a disposal of shares in any company; and
(b) that sum forms part of the gross attributed tax in relation to a dividend paid by that company; and
(c) a person receiving the dividend in respect of the shares referred to in paragraph (a) above ("the primary dividend") or any other relevant dividend is, by virtue of paragraph 4(2) above, entitled under Part XVIII to relief (by way of underlying tax) by reference to the whole or any part of the gross attributed tax;

the amount which, apart from this paragraph, would be available by way of any such relief to the person referred to in paragraph (c) above shall be reduced or, as the case may be, extinguished by deducting therefrom the amount allowed by way of relief as mentioned in paragraph (a) above.

(2) For the purposes of sub-paragraph (1)(c) above, in relation to the primary dividend, another dividend is a relevant dividend if—

(a) it is a dividend in respect of shares in a company which is resident outside the United Kingdom; and
(b) it represents profits which, directly or indirectly, consist of or include the primary dividend.

Former enactment.—FA 1984, Sch. 18, para. 6.

SCHEDULE 27

Section 760

DISTRIBUTING FUNDS

PART I

THE DISTRIBUTION TEST

Requirements as to distributions

1.—(1) For the purposes of this Chapter, an offshore fund pursues a full distribution policy with respect to an account period if—

(*a*) a distribution is made for that account period or for some other period which, in whole or in part, falls within that account period; and
(*b*) subject to Part II of this Schedule, the amount of the distribution which is paid to the holders of material and other interests in the fund—

(i) represents at least 85 per cent. of the income of the fund for that period, and
(ii) is not less than 85 per cent. of the fund's United Kingdom equivalent profits for that period; and

(*c*) the distribution is made during that account period or not more than six months, or such longer period as the Board may in any particular case allow, after the expiry of it; and
(*d*) the form of the distribution is such that, if any sum forming part of it were received in the United Kingdom by a person resident there and did not form part of the profits of a trade, profession or vocation, that sum would fall to be chargeable to tax under Case IV or V of Schedule D;

and any reference in this sub-paragraph to a distribution made for an account period includes a reference to any two or more distributions so made or, in the case of paragraph (*b*), the aggregate of them.

(2) Subject to sub-paragraph (3) below, with respect to any account period for which—

(*a*) there is no income of the fund, and
(*b*) there are no United Kingdom equivalent profits of the fund,

the fund shall be treated as pursuing a full distribution policy notwithstanding that no distribution is made as mentioned in sub-paragraph (1) above.

(3) For the purposes of this Chapter, an offshore fund shall be regarded as not pursuing a full distribution policy with respect to an account period for which the fund does not make up accounts.

(4) For the purposes of this paragraph—

(*a*) where a period for which an offshore fund makes up accounts includes the whole or part of two or more account periods of the fund, then, subject to paragraph (*c*) below, income shown in those accounts shall be apportioned between those account periods on a time basis according to the number of days in each period which are comprised in the period for which the accounts are made up;
(*b*) where a distribution is made for a period which includes the whole or part of two or more account periods of the fund, then, subject to sub-paragraph (5) below, the distribution shall be apportioned between those account periods on a time basis according to the number of days in each period which are comprised in the period for which the distribution is made;
(*c*) where a distribution is made out of specified income but is not made for a specified period, that income shall be attributed to the account period of the fund in which it in fact arose and the distribution shall be treated as made for that account period; and
(*d*) where a distribution is made neither for a specified period nor out of specified income, then, subject to sub-paragraph (5) below, it shall be treated as made for the last account period of the fund which ended before the distribution was made.

(5) If, apart from this sub-paragraph, the amount of a distribution made, or treated by virtue of sub-paragraph (4) above as made, for an account period would exceed the income of that period, then, for the purposes of this paragraph—

(*a*) if the amount of the distribution was determined by apportionment under sub-paragraph (4)(*b*) above, the excess shall be re-apportioned, as may be just and reasonable, to any other account period which, in whole or in part, falls within the period for which the distribution was made or, if there is more than one such period, between those periods; and

(b) subject to paragraph (a) above, the excess shall be treated as an additional distribution or series of additional distributions made for preceding account periods in respect of which the distribution or, as the case may be, the aggregate distributions would otherwise be less than the income of the period, applying the excess to later account periods before earlier ones, until it is exhausted.

(6) In any case where—

(a) for a period which is or includes an account period, an offshore fund is subject to any restriction as regards the making of distributions, being a restriction imposed by the law of any territory outside the United Kingdom; and

(b) the fund is subject to that restriction by reason of an excess of losses over profits (applying the concepts of "profits" and "losses" in the sense in which and to the extent to which they are relevant for the purposes of the law in question);

then in determining for the purposes of the preceding provisions of this paragraph the amount of the fund's income for that account period, there shall be allowed as a deduction any amount which, apart from this sub-paragraph, would form part of the income of the fund for that account period and which cannot be distributed by virtue of the restriction.

Former enactments.—FA 1984, Sch. 19, para 1; F(No. 2)A 1987, s. 66(1).

Funds operating equalisation arrangements

2.—(1) In the case of an offshore fund which throughout any account period operates equalisation arrangements, on any occasion in that period when there is a disposal to which this sub-paragraph applies, the fund shall be treated for the purposes of this Part of this Schedule as making a distribution of an amount equal to so much of the consideration for the disposal as, in accordance with this paragraph, represents income accrued to the date of the disposal.

(2) Sub-paragraph (1) above applies to a disposal—

(a) which is a disposal of a material interest in the offshore fund concerned; and

(b) which is a disposal to which this Chapter applies (whether by virtue of section 758(3) or otherwise) or is one to which this Chapter would apply if subsections (5) and (6) of that section applied generally and not only for the purpose of determining whether, by virtue of subsection (3) of that section, there is a disposal to which this Chapter applies; and

(c) which is not a disposal with respect to which the conditions in subsection (4) of that section are fulfilled; and

(d) which is a disposal to the fund itself or to the persons concerned in the management of the fund ("the managers") in their capacity as such.

(3) On a disposal to which sub-paragraph (1) above applies, the part of the consideration which represents income accrued to the date of the disposal is, subject to sub-paragraph (4) and paragraph 4(4) below, the amount which would be credited to the equalisation account of the offshore fund concerned in respect of accrued income if, on the date of the disposal, the material interest which is disposed of were acquired by another person by way of initial purchase.

(4) If, after the beginning of the period by reference to which the accrued income referred to in sub-paragraph (3) above is calculated, the material interest disposed of by a disposal to which sub-paragraph (1) above applies was acquired by way of initial purchase (whether or not by the person making the disposal)—

(a) there shall be deducted from the amount which, in accordance with sub-paragraph (3) above, would represent income accrued to the date of the disposal, the amount which on that acquisition was credited to the equalisation account of the fund in respect of accrued income; and

(b) if in that period there has been more than one such acquisition of that material interest by way of initial purchase, the deduction to be made under this sub-paragraph shall be the amount so credited to the equalisation account on the latest such acquisition prior to the disposal in question.

(5) Where, by virtue of this paragraph, an offshore fund is treated for the purposes of this Part of this Schedule as making a distribution on the occasion of a disposal, the distribution shall be treated for those purposes—

(a) as complying with paragraph 1(1)(d) above; and

as a distributing fund in respect of its account period or, as the case may be, each of its account periods which comprises the whole or any part of the account period of the primary fund;

then, in determining whether anything in section 760(3)(*a*) to (*c*) prevents the primary fund being certified as mentioned in paragraph (*b*) above, the interests of the primary fund in that other fund shall be left out of account except for the purposes of determining the total value of the assets of the primary fund.

(2) In this Part of this Schedule an offshore fund falling within sub-paragraph (1)(*c*) above is referred to as a "qualifying fund".

(3) In a case falling within sub-paragraph (1) above—

(*a*) section 760(3)(*a*) to (*c*) shall have effect in relation to the primary fund with the modification in paragraph 7 below (in addition to that provided for by sub-paragraph (1) above); and

(*b*) Part I of this Schedule shall have effect in relation to the primary fund with the modification in paragraph 8 below.

Former enactment.—FA 1984, Sch. 19, para. 6.

7. The modification referred to in paragraph 6(3)(*a*) above is that, in any case where—

(*a*) at any time in the account period referred to in paragraph 6(1) above, the assets of the primary fund include an interest in an offshore fund or in any company (whether an offshore fund or not); and

(*b*) that interest falls to be taken into account in determining whether anything in section 760(3)(*a*) to (*c*) prevents the primary fund being certified as a distributing fund in respect of that account period; and

(*c*) at any time in that account period the assets of the qualifying fund include an interest in the offshore fund or company referred to in paragraph (*a*) above;

for the purposes of the application in relation to the primary fund of section 760(3)(*a*) to (*c*), at any time when the assets of the qualifying fund include the interest referred to in paragraph (*c*) above, the primary fund's share of that interest shall be treated as an additional asset of the primary fund.

Former enactment.—FA 1984, Sch. 19, para. 7.

8.—(1) The modification referred to in paragraph 6(3)(*b*) above is that, in determining whether the condition in paragraph 1(1)(*b*)(ii) above is fulfilled with respect to the account period of the primary fund referred to in paragraph 6(1) above, the United Kingdom equivalent profits of the primary fund for that period shall be treated as increased by the primary fund's share of the excess income (if any) of the qualifying fund which is attributable to that period.

(2) For the purposes of this paragraph, the excess income of the qualifying fund for any account period of that fund is the amount (if any) by which its United Kingdom equivalent profits for that account period exceed the amount of the distributions made for that period, as determined for the purposes of the application of paragraph 1(1) above to the qualifying fund.

(3) If an account period of the qualifying fund coincides with an account period of the primary fund, then the excess income (if any) of the qualifying fund for that period is the excess income which is attributable to that period of the primary fund.

(4) In a case where sub-paragraph (3) above does not apply, the excess income of the qualifying fund which is attributable to an account period of the primary fund is the appropriate fraction of the excess income (if any) of the qualifying fund for any of its account periods which comprises the whole or any part of the account period of the primary fund and, if there is more than one such account period of the qualifying fund, the aggregate of the excess income (if any) of each of them.

(5) For the purposes of sub-paragraph (4) above, the appropriate fraction is—

$$\frac{A}{B}$$

where—

A is the number of days in the account period of the primary fund which are also days in an account period of the qualifying fund; and

B is the number of days in that account period of the qualifying fund or, as the case may be, in each of those account periods of that fund which comprises the whole or any part of the account period of the primary fund.

Former enactment.—FA 1984, Sch. 19, para. 8.

9.—(1) The references in paragraphs 7 and 8(1) above to the primary fund's share of—
   (a) an interest forming part of the assets of the qualifying fund, or
   (b) the excess income (as defined in paragraph 8 above) of the qualifying fund,
shall be construed as references to the fraction specified in sub-paragraph (2) below of that interest or excess income.

(2) In relation to any account period of the primary fund, the fraction referred to in sub-paragraph (1) above is—

$$\frac{C}{D}$$

where—
   C is the average value of the primary fund's holding of interests in the qualifying fund during that period; and
   D is the average value of all the interests in the qualifying fund held by any persons during that period.

Former enactment.—FA 1984, Sch. 19, para. 9.

Offshore funds investing in trading companies

10.—(1) In any case where the assets of an offshore fund for the time being include an interest in a trading company, as defined in sub-paragraph (2) below, the provisions of section 760(3) have effect subject to the modifications in sub-paragraphs (3) and (4) below.

(2) In this paragraph "trading company" means a company whose business consists wholly of the carrying on of a trade or trades and does not to any extent consist of—
   (a) dealing in commodities, as defined in paragraph 4(2) above, or dealing, as so defined, in currency, securities, debts or other assets of a financial nature; or
   (b) banking or money-lending.

(3) In the application of section 760(3)(b) to so much of the assets of an offshore fund as for the time being consists of interests in a single trading company, for the words "10 per cent." there shall be substituted the words "20 per cent.".

(4) In the application of section 760(3)(c) to an offshore fund the assets of which for the time being include any issued share capital of a trading company or any class of that share capital, for the words "more than 10 per cent." there shall be substituted the words "50 per cent. or more".

Former enactment.—FA 1984, Sch. 19, para. 10.

Offshore funds with wholly-owned subsidiaries

11.—(1) In relation to an offshore fund which has a wholly-owned subsidiary which is a company the provisions of section 760(3) and Part I of this Schedule shall have effect subject to the modifications in sub-paragraph (3) below.

(2) Subject to sub-paragraph (3) below, for the purposes of this paragraph, a company is a wholly-owned subsidiary of an offshore fund if and so long as the whole of the issued share capital of the company is—
   (a) in the case of an offshore fund falling within section 759(1)(a), directly and beneficially owned by the fund; and
   (b) in the case of an offshore fund falling within section 759(1)(b), directly owned by the trustees of the fund for the benefit of the fund; and
   (c) in the case of an offshore fund falling within section 759(1)(c), owned in a manner which, as near as may be, corresponds either to paragraph (a) or paragraph (b) above.

(3) In the case of a company which has only one class of issued share capital, the reference in sub-paragraph (2) above to the whole of the issued share capital shall be construed as a reference to at least 95 per cent. of that share capital.

(4) The modifications referred to in sub-paragraph (1) above are that, for the purposes of section 760(3) and Part I of this Schedule—

(*a*) that percentage of the receipts, expenditure, assets and liabilities of the subsidiary which is equal to the percentage of the issued share capital of the company concerned which is owned as mentioned in sub-paragraph (2) above shall be regarded as the receipts, expenditure, assets and liabilities of the fund; and
(*b*) there shall be left out of account the interest of the fund in the subsidiary and any distributions or other payments made by the subsidiary to the fund or by the fund to the subsidiary.

Former enactments.—FA 1984, Sch. 19, para. 11; FA 1986, s. 50.

Offshore funds with interests in dealing and management companies

12.—(1) Section 760(3)(*c*) shall not apply to so much of the assets of an offshore fund as consists of issued share capital of a company which is either—

(*a*) a wholly-owned subsidiary of the fund which falls within sub-paragraph (2) below; or
(*b*) a subsidiary management company of the fund, as defined in sub-paragraph (3) below.

(2) A company which is a wholly-owned subsidiary of an offshore fund is one to which sub-paragraph (1)(*a*) above applies if—

(*a*) the business of the company consists wholly of dealing in material interests in the offshore fund for the purposes of and in connection with the management and administration of the business of the fund; and
(*b*) the company is not entitled to any distribution in respect of any material interest for the time being held by it;

and paragraph 11(2) above shall apply to determine whether a company is, for the purposes of this paragraph, a wholly-owned subsidiary of an offshore fund.

(3) A company in which an offshore fund has an interest is for the purposes of sub-paragraph (1)(*b*) above a subsidiary management company of the fund if—

(*a*) the company carries on no business other than providing services falling within sub-paragraph (4) below either for the fund alone or for the fund and for any other offshore fund which has an interest in the company; and
(*b*) the company's remuneration for the services which it provides to the fund is not greater than it would be if it were determined at arm's length between the fund and a company in which the fund has no interest.

(4) The services referred to in sub-paragraph (3) above are—

(*a*) holding property (of any description) which is occupied or used in connection with the management or administration of the fund; and
(*b*) providing administrative, management and advisory services to the fund.

(5) In determining, in accordance with sub-paragraph (3) above, whether a company in which an offshore fund has an interest is a subsidiary management company of that fund—

(*a*) every business carried on by a wholly-owned subsidiary of the company shall be treated as carried on by the company; and
(*b*) no account shall be taken of so much of the company's business as consists of holding its interests in a wholly-owned subsidiary; and
(*c*) any reference in sub-paragraph (3)(*b*) above to the company shall be taken to include a reference to a wholly-owned subsidiary of the company.

(6) Any reference in sub-paragraph (5) above to a wholly-owned subsidiary of a company is a reference to another company the whole of the issued share capital of which is for the time being directly and beneficially owned by the first company.

Former enactment.—FA 1984, Sch. 19, para. 12.

Disregard of certain investments forming less than 5 per cent. of a fund

13.—(1) In any case where—

(*a*) in any account period of an offshore fund, the assets of the fund include a holding of issued share capital (or any class of issued share capital) of a company; and
(*b*) that holding is such that by virtue of section 760(3)(*c*) the fund could not (apart from this paragraph) be certified as a distributing fund in respect of that account period;

then, if the condition in sub-paragraph (3) below is fulfilled, that holding shall be disregarded for the purposes of section 760(3)(*c*).

(2) In this paragraph any holding falling within sub-paragraph (1) above is referred to as an "excess holding".

(3) The condition referred to in sub-paragraph (1) above is that at no time in the account period in question does that portion of the fund which consists of—

(a) excess holdings, and
(b) interests in other offshore funds which are not qualifying funds,

exceed 5 per cent. by value of all the assets of the fund.

Former enactments.—FA 1984, Sch. 19, para. 12A; FA 1986, s. 50.

Power of Board to disregard certain breaches of conditions

14.—If, in the case of any account period of an offshore fund ending after the passing of the Finance (No. 2) Act 1987 (23rd July 1987), it appears to the Board that there has been a failure to comply with any of the conditions in paragraphs (a) to (c) of section 760(3) (as modified, where appropriate, by the preceding provisions of this Part of this Schedule) but the Board are satisfied—

(a) that the failure occurred inadvertently; and
(b) that the failure was remedied without unreasonable delay,

the Board may disregard the failure in determining whether to certify the fund as a distributing fund in respect of that account period.

Former enactments.—FA 1984, Sch. 19, para. 12B; F(No. 2)A 1987, s. 66(2).

PART III
CERTIFICATION PROCEDURE

Application for certification

15.—(1) The Board shall, in such manner as they think appropriate, certify an offshore fund as a distributing fund in respect of an account period if—

(a) an application in respect of that period is made under this paragraph; and
(b) the application is accompanied by the accounts of the fund for, or for a period which includes, the account period to which the application relates; and
(c) there is furnished to the Board such information as they may reasonably require for the purposes of determining whether the fund should be so certified; and
(d) they are satisfied that nothing in section 760(2) or (3) prevents the fund being so certified.

(2) An application under this paragraph shall be made to the Board by the fund or by a trustee or officer thereof on behalf of the fund and may be so made—

(a) before the expiry of the period of six months beginning at the end of the account period to which the application relates; or
(b) at such later time as the Board may in any particular case allow.

(3) In any case where, on an application under this paragraph, the Board determine that the offshore fund concerned should not be certified as a distributing fund in respect of the account period to which the application relates, they shall give notice of that fact to the fund.

(4) If at any time it appears to the Board that the accounts accompanying an application under this paragraph in respect of any account period of an offshore fund or any information furnished to the Board in connection with such an application is or are not such as to make full and accurate disclosure of all facts and considerations relevant to the application, they shall give notice to the fund accordingly, specifying the period concerned.

(5) Where a notice is given by the Board under sub-paragraph (4) above, any certification by them in respect of the account period in question shall be void.

Former enactment.—FA 1984, Sch. 19, para. 13.

Appeals

16.—(1) An appeal to the Special Commissioners—

(a) against such a determination as is referred to in paragraph 15(3) above, or (*b*) against a notification under paragraph 15(4) above,

may be made by the offshore fund or by a trustee or officer thereof on behalf of the fund, and shall be so made by notice specifying the grounds of appeal and given to the Board within 90 days of the date of the notice under paragraph 15(3) or (4), as the case may be.

(2) The jurisdiction of the Special Commissioners on an appeal under this paragraph shall include jurisdiction to review any decision of the Board which is relevant to a ground of the appeal.

Former enactment.—FA 1984, Sch. 19, para. 14.

PART IV
SUPPLEMENTARY

Assessment: effect of non-certification

17. No appeal may be brought against an assessment to tax on the ground that an offshore fund should have been certified as a distributing fund in respect of an account period of the fund.

Former enactment.—FA 1984, Sch. 19, para. 15.

18.—(1) Without prejudice to paragraph 17 above, in any case where no application has been made under paragraph 15 above in respect of an account period of an offshore fund, any person who is assessed to tax for which he would not be liable if the offshore fund were certified as a distributing fund in respect of that period may by notice in writing require the Board to take action under this paragraph with a view to determining whether the fund should be so certified.

(2) Subject to sub-paragraphs (3) and (5) below, if the Board receive a notice under sub-paragraph (1) above, they shall by notice invite the offshore fund concerned to make an application under paragraph 15 above in respect of the period in question.

(3) Where sub-paragraph (2) above applies, the Board shall not be required to give notice under that sub-paragraph before the expiry of the account period to which the notice is to relate nor if an application under paragraph 15 above has already been made; but where notice is given under that sub-paragraph, an application under paragraph 15 above shall not be out of time under paragraph 15(2)(*a*) above if it is made within 90 days of the date of that notice.

(4) If an offshore fund to which notice is given under sub-paragraph (2) above does not, within the time allowed by sub-paragraph (3) above or, as the case may be, paragraph 15(2)(*a*) above, make an application under paragraph 15 above in respect of the account period in question, the Board shall proceed to determine the question of certification in respect of that period as if such an application had been made.

(5) Where the Board receive more than one notice under sub-paragraph (1) above with respect to the same account period of the same offshore fund, their obligations under sub-paragraphs (2) and (4) above shall be taken to be fulfilled with respect to each of those notices if they are fulfilled with respect to any one of them.

(6) Notwithstanding anything in sub-paragraph (5) above, for the purpose of a determination under sub-paragraph (4) above with respect to an account period of an offshore fund, the Board shall have regard to accounts and other information furnished by all persons who have given notice under sub-paragraph (1) above with respect to that account period; and paragraph 15 above shall apply as if accounts and information so furnished had been furnished in compliance with sub-paragraph (1) of that paragraph.

(7) Without prejudice to sub-paragraph (5) above, in any case where—

(*a*) at a time after the Board have made a determination under sub-paragraph (4) above that an offshore fund should not be certified as a distributing fund in respect of an account period, notice is given under sub-paragraph (1) above with respect to that period; and
(*b*) the person giving that notice furnishes the Board with accounts or information which had not been furnished to the Board at the time of the earlier determination;

the Board shall reconsider their previous determination in the light of the new accounts or information and, if they consider it appropriate, may determine to certify the fund accordingly.

(8) Where any person has given notice to the Board under sub-paragraph (1) above with

respect to an account period of an offshore fund and no application has been made under paragraph 15 above with respect to that period—

(a) the Board shall notify that person of their determination with respect to certification under sub-paragraph (4) above; and
(b) paragraph 16 above shall not apply in relation to that determination.

Former enactment.—FA 1984, Sch. 19, para. 16.

Postponement of tax pending determination of question as to certification

19.—(1) In any case where—

(a) an application has been made under paragraph 15 above with respect to an account period of an offshore fund and that application has not been finally determined; or
(b) paragraph (a) above does not apply but notice has been given under paragraph 18(1) above in respect of an account period of an offshore fund and the Board have not yet given notice of their decision as to certification under paragraph 18(4) above;

any person who has been assessed to tax and considers that, if the offshore fund were to be certified as a distributing fund in respect of the account period in question, he would be overcharged to tax by the assessment may, by notice given to the inspector within 30 days after the date of the issue of the notice of assessment, apply to the General Commissioners for a determination of the amount of tax the payment of which should be postponed pending the determination of the question whether the fund should be so certified.

(2) A notice of application under sub-paragraph (1) above shall state the amount in which the applicant believes that he is over-charged to tax and his grounds for that belief.

(3) Subsections (3A) onwards of section 55 of the Management Act (recovery of tax not postponed) shall apply with any necessary modifications in relation to an application under sub-paragraph (1) above as if it were an application under subsection (3) of that section and as if the determination of the question as to certification (whether by the Board or on appeal) were the determination of an appeal.

Former enactment.—FA 1984, Sch. 19, para. 17.

Information as to decisions on certification etc.

20. No obligation as to secrecy imposed by statute or otherwise shall preclude the Board or an inspector from disclosing to any person appearing to have an interest in the matter—

(a) any determination of the Board or (on appeal) the Special Commissioners whether an offshore fund should or should not be certified as a distributing fund in respect of any account period; or
(b) the content and effect of any notice given by the Board under paragraph 15(4) above.

Former enactment.—FA 1984, Sch. 19, para. 18.

SCHEDULE 28

Section 761(1)

COMPUTATION OF OFFSHORE INCOME GAINS

PART I
DISPOSALS OF INTERESTS IN NON-QUALIFYING FUNDS

Interpretation

1. In this Part of this Schedule "material disposal" means a disposal to which this Chapter applies, otherwise than by virtue of section 758.

Former enactment.—FA 1984, Sch. 20, para. 1.

Calculation of unindexed gain

2.—(1) Where there is a material disposal, there shall first be determined for the purposes of this Part of this Schedule the amount (if any) which, in accordance with the provisions of this paragraph, is the unindexed gain accruing to the person making the disposal.

(2) Subject to section 757(3) to (6) and paragraph 3 below, the unindexed gain accruing on a material disposal is the amount which would be the gain on that disposal for the purposes of the 1979 Act if it were computed—

(*a*) without regard to any charge to income tax or corporation tax by virtue of section 761; and
(*b*) without regard to any indexation allowance on the disposal under Chapter III of Part III of the Finance Act 1982.

Former enactment.—FA 1984, Sch. 20, para. 2.

3.—(1) If the amount of any chargeable gain or allowable loss which (apart from section 763) would accrue on the material disposal would fall to be determined in a way which, in whole or in part, would take account of the indexation allowance on an earlier disposal to which paragraph 2 of Schedule 13 to the Finance Act 1982 (disposals on a no gain/no loss basis) applies, the unindexed gain on the material disposal shall be computed as if—

(*a*) no indexation allowance had been available on any such earlier disposal; and
(*b*) subject to that, neither a gain nor a loss had accrued to the person making such an earlier disposal.

(2) If the material disposal forms part of a transfer to which section 123 of the 1979 Act (roll-over relief on transfer of business) applies, the unindexed gain accruing on the disposal shall be computed without regard to any deduction which falls to be made under that section in computing a chargeable gain.

(3) If the material disposal is made otherwise than under a bargain at arm's length and a claim for relief is made in respect of that disposal under section [126 or 147A of the Capital Gains Tax Act 1979 (relief for gifts), the claim][1] shall not affect the computation of the unindexed gain accruing on the disposal.

(4) Where, in the case of an insurance company carrying on life assurance business, a profit arising from general annuity business and attributable to a material disposal falls (or would but for the reference to offshore income gains in section 437(2) fall) to be taken into account in the computation under section 436, the unindexed gain, if any, accruing to the company on the disposal shall be computed as if section 31(1) of the 1979 Act (exclusion of certain sums in computing chargeable gain) did not apply.

(5) Notwithstanding section 29 of the 1979 Act (losses determined in like manner as gains) if, apart from this sub-paragraph, the effect of any computation under the preceding provisions of this Part of this Schedule would be to produce a loss, the unindexed gain on the material disposal shall be treated as nil; and accordingly for the purposes of this Part of this Schedule no loss shall be treated as accruing on a material disposal.

(6) Section 431 has effect in relation to sub-paragraph (4) above as if it were included in Chapter I of Part XII.

Former enactment.—FA 1984, Sch. 20, para. 3.
Amendments.—¹ Words in sub-para. (3) substituted by FA 1989, s. 124(2), (3) and Sch. 14, para. 6(6) in relation to disposals after 13 March 1989, subject to certain exceptions; see FA 1989, s. 124(3).

Gains since 1st January 1984

4.—(1) This paragraph applies where—

(*a*) the interest in the offshore fund which is disposed of by the person making a material disposal was acquired by him before 1st January 1984; or

(*b*) he is treated by virtue of any provision of sub-paragraphs (3) and (4) below as having acquired the interest before that date.

(2) Where this paragraph applies, there shall be determined for the purposes of this Part of this Schedule the amount which would have been the gain on the material disposal—

(*a*) on the assumption that, on 1st January 1984, the interest was disposed of and immediately reacquired for a consideration equal to its market value at that time; and

(*b*) subject to that, on the basis that the gain is computed in like manner as, under paragraphs 2 and 3 above, the unindexed gain on the material disposal is determined;

and that amount is in paragraph 5 below referred to as the "post-1983 gain" on the material disposal.

(3) Where the person making the material disposal acquired the interest disposed of—

(*a*) on or after 1st January 1984, and

(*b*) in such circumstances that, by virtue of any enactment other than section 86(5) of or Schedule 13 to the Finance Act 1982 (indexation provisions), he and the person from whom he acquired it ("the previous owner") fell to be treated for the purposes of the 1979 Act as if his acquisition were for a consideration of such an amount as would secure that, on the disposal under which he acquired it, neither a gain nor a loss accrued to the previous owner,

the previous owner's acquisition of the interest shall be treated as his acquisition of it.

(4) If the previous owner acquired the interest disposed of on or after 1st January 1984 and in circumstances similar to those referred to in sub-paragraph (3) above, his predecessor's acquisition of the interest shall be treated for the purposes of this paragraph as the previous owner's acquisition, and so on back through previous acquisitions in similar circumstances until the first such acquisition before 1st January 1984 or, as the case may be, until an acquisition on a material disposal on or after that date.

Former enactment.—FA 1984, Sch. 20, para. 4.

The offshore income gain

5.—(1) Subject to sub-paragraph (2) below, a material disposal gives rise to an offshore income gain of an amount equal to the unindexed gain on that disposal.

(2) In any case where—

(*a*) paragraph 4 above applies, and

(*b*) the post-1983 gain on the material disposal is less than the unindexed gain on the disposal,

the offshore income gain to which the disposal gives rise is an amount equal to the post-1983 gain.

Former enactment.—FA 1984, Sch. 20, para. 5.

PART II
DISPOSALS INVOLVING AN EQUALISATION ELEMENT

6.—(1) Subject to paragraph 7 below, a disposal to which this Chapter applies by virtue of section 758(3) gives rise to an offshore income gain of an amount equal to the equalisation element relevant to the asset disposed of.

(2) Subject to sub-paragraphs (4) to (6) below, the equalisation element relevant to the asset disposed of by a disposal falling within sub-paragraph (1) above is the amount which would be credited to the equalisation account of the offshore fund concerned in respect of accrued income if, on the date of the disposal, the asset which is disposed of were acquired by another person by way of initial purchase.

(3) In the following provisions of this Part of this Schedule, a disposal falling within sub-paragraph (1) above is referred to as a "disposal involving an equalisation element".

(4) Where the asset disposed of by a disposal involving an equalisation element was acquired by the person making the disposal after the beginning of the period by reference to which the accrued income referred to in sub-paragraph (2) above is calculated, the amount which, apart from this sub-paragraph, would be the equalisation element relevant to that asset shall be reduced by the following amount, that is to say—

(*a*) if that acquisition took place on or after 1st January 1984, the amount which, on that acquisition, was credited to the equalisation account of the offshore fund concerned in respect of accrued income or, as the case may be, would have been so credited if that asquisition had been an acquisition by way of initial purchase; and

(*b*) in any other case, the amount which would have been credited to that account in respect of accrued income if that acquisition had been an acquisition by way of initial purchase taking place on 1st January 1984.

(5) In any case where—

(*a*) the asset disposed of by a disposal involving an equalisation element was acquired by the person making the disposal at or before the beginning of the period by reference to which the accrued income referred to in sub-paragraph (2) above is calculated, and

(*b*) that period began before 1st January 1984 and ends after that date,

the amount which, apart from this sub-paragraph, would be the equalisation element relevant to that asset shall be reduced by the amount which would have been credited to the equalisation account of the offshore fund concerned in respect of accrued income if the acquisition referred to in paragraph (*a*) above had been an acquisition by way of initial purchase taking place on 1st January 1984.

(6) Where there is a disposal involving an equalisation element, then, to the extent that any amount which was or would be credited to the equalisation account of the offshore fund in respect of accrued income, as mentioned in any of sub-paragraphs (2) to (5) above, represents profits from dealing in commodities, within the meaning of paragraph 4 of Schedule 27, one half of that accrued income shall be left out of account in determining under those sub-paragraphs the equalisation element relevant to the asset disposed of by that disposal.

Former enactment.—FA 1984, Sch. 20, para. 6.

7.—(1) For the purposes of this Part of this Schedule, there shall be determined, in accordance with paragraph 8 below, the Part I gain (if any) on any disposal involving an equalisation element.

(2) Notwithstanding anything in paragraph 6 above—

(*a*) if there is no Part I gain on a disposal involving an equalisation element, that disposal shall not give rise to an offshore income gain; and

(*b*) if, apart from this paragraph, the offshore income gain on a disposal involving an equalisation element would exceed the Part I gain on that disposal, the offshore income gain to which that disposal gives rise shall be reduced to an amount equal to that Part I gain.

Former enactment.—FA 1984, Sch. 20, para. 7.

8.—(1) On a disposal involving an equalisation element, the Part I gain is the amount (if any) which, by virtue of Part I of this Schedule (as modified by sub-paragraphs (2) to (5) below), would be the offshore income gain on that disposal if it were a material disposal within the meaning of that Part.

(2) For the purposes only of the application of Part I of this Schedule to determine the Part I gain (if any) on a disposal involving an equalisation element, subsections (5) and (6) of section 758 shall have effect as if, in subsection (5), the words "by virtue of subsection (3) above" were omitted.

(3) If a disposal involving an equalisation element is one which, by virtue of any enactment other than section 86(5)(*b*) of or Schedule 13 to the Finance Act 1982, is treated for the purposes of the 1979 Act as one on which neither a gain nor a loss accrues to the person making the disposal, then, for the purpose only of determining the Part I gain (if any) on the disposal, that enactment shall be deemed not to apply to it (but without prejudice to the application of that enactment to any earlier disposal).

(4) In any case where a disposal involving an equalisation element is made by a company which has made an election under Schedule 6 to the Finance Act 1983 (indexation: election

for pooling) and the asset disposed of consists of or includes securities which, by virtue of paragraph 3(3) of that Schedule, are to be treated for the purposes of the 1979 Act as a single asset or part of a single asset, then, for the purpose only of determining the Part I gain (if any) on the disposal—

(*a*) the reference in paragraph 2(2)(*b*) above to an indexation allowance under Chapter III of Part III of the Finance Act 1982 shall be construed as including a reference to an indexation allowance under Schedule 6 to the Finance Act 1983; and

(*b*) if some of the securities comprised in the asset disposed of were acquired by the company making the disposal before 1st January 1984 and some were not, paragraph 4(2) above shall not apply and paragraph 5 above shall have effect with the omission of sub-paragraph (2) (together with the reference to it in sub-paragraph (1)).

(5) The reference in sub-paragraph (4)(*b*) above to securities acquired before 1st January 1984 includes a reference to securities which, by virtue of any provision of paragraph 4 above, are treated as so acquired.

Former enactment.—FA 1984, Sch. 20, para. 8.

SCHEDULE 29

Section 844

CONSEQUENTIAL AMENDMENTS

The Capital Allowances Acts

1. The Capital Allowances Act 1968 and Part III of the Finance Act 1971 shall apply in relation to a trade, profession or vocation chargeable in accordance with section 65(3) as they apply to one chargeable to tax under Case I or II of Schedule D.

2. No allowance shall be made under Chapter I of Part III of the Finance Act 1971 in respect of any expenditure incurred by a Member of the House of Commons in or in connection with the provision or use of residential or overnight accommodation to enable him to perform his duties as such a Member in or about the Palace of Westminster or his constituency.

10.—(1) The Taxes Management Act 1970, as amended by the Finance (No. 2) Act 1987, shall have effect, after the day appointed under section 95 of the 1987 Act for the purposes of the provision in question, subject to the following amendments.

(2) In section 11(8) for "286" there shall be substituted "419".

(3) In section 30(2A) and (3A) for "87 of the Finance (No. 2) Act 1987" there shall be substituted "826 of the principal Act".

(4) In section 87A—

   (*a*) in subsection (1) for "243(4)" there shall be substituted "10";
   (*b*) in subsection (3) for the words from "266" to "Taxes Act" there shall be substituted "346(2) or 347(1) of the principal Act, section 267(3C) or 278(5) of the Income and Corporation Taxes Act 1970";
   (*c*) in subsection (4), in paragraph (*a*) for "85 of the Finance Act 1972" there shall be substituted "239 of the principal Act", and in paragraph (*b*) for "85" there shall be substituted "239"; and
   (*d*) in subsection (5) for the words from "subsection" to "1972" there shall be substituted "section 252(5) of the principal Act".

(5) In section 89 for "87 of the Finance (No. 2) Act 1987" there shall be substituted "826 of the principal Act".

(6) In section 91(2A) for "90 of the Finance (No. 2) Act 1987" there shall be substituted "10 of the principal Act".

(7) In section 94(8) for the words from "subsection (3)" to "1972" there shall be substituted "section 239(3) of the principal Act";

(8) In section 109—

   (*a*) in subsection (3) for "286" and "(4)" there shall be substituted "419" and "(3)";
   (*b*) in subsection (3A) for "(5)" and "286" (twice) there shall be substituted "(4)" and "419".

The Social Security Acts

14. In section 9(1) of the Social Security Act 1975 and the Social Security (Northern Ireland) Act 1975 (Class IV contributions) the reference to profits or gains chargeable to income tax under Case I or II of Schedule D shall be taken to include a reference to profits or gains consisting of a payment of enterprise allowance (within the meaning of section 127 of this Act) chargeable to income tax under Case VI of Schedule D.

Translation of references to enactments repealed and re-enacted

32. In the enactments specified in Column 1 of the following Table for the words set out or referred to in Column 2 there shall be substituted the words set out in the corresponding entry in Column 3.

Enactment amended	Words to be omitted	Words to be substituted
In the Income and Corporation Taxes Act 1970 c. 10 Section 278(3A)(*a*)	262(2) of this Act	409(2) of the Taxes Act 1988

Note.—See **Prospective Legislation Notes** (Taxes Management Provisions).

SCHEDULE 30

Section 844

TRANSITIONAL PROVISIONS AND SAVINGS

Corporation tax payment dates

1.—(1) In this paragraph, an "old company" means a company to which section 244 of the 1970 Act applied in respect of the last accounting period ending before 17th March 1987.

(2) In relation to an old company—

(*a*) "the company's section 244 interval" means the interval after the end of an accounting period of the company which, in accordance with section 244 of the 1970 Act, was the period within which corporation tax assessed for that period was required to be paid; and
(*b*) "the period of reduction" means the number of whole days which are comprised in a period equal to one-third of the difference between nine months and the company's section 244 interval.

(3) Subject to sub-paragraph (6) below, with respect to the first accounting period of an old company beginning on or after 17th March 1987, section 243(4) of the 1970 Act and section 10(1) of this Act (time for payment of corporation tax) shall have effect as if for the reference to nine months there were substituted a reference to a period which is equal to the company's section 244 interval less the period of reduction.

(4) Subject to sub-paragraph (6) below, with respect to any accounting period of an old company which begins—

(*a*) after the accounting period referred to in sub-paragraph (3) above, but
(*b*) before the second anniversary of the beginning of that period,

section 10(1) of this Act shall have effect as if for the reference to nine months there were substituted a reference to a period equal to the previous payment interval less the period of reduction.

(5) In relation to any accounting period of an old company falling within sub-paragraph (4) above, "the previous payment interval" means the interval after the end of the immediately preceding accounting period within which corporation tax for that preceding period is required to be paid by virtue of section 243(4) of the 1970 Act or section 10(1) of this Act, as modified by this paragraph.

(6) If the accounting period referred to in sub-paragraph (3) above or any accounting period falling within sub-paragraph (4) above is less than 12 months, the sub-paragraph in question shall have effect in relation to that accounting period as if for the reference in that sub-paragraph to the period of reduction there were substituted a reference to the number of whole days comprised in a period which bears to the period of reduction the same proportion as that accounting period bears to 12 months.

(7) With respect to any accounting period of an old company which falls within sub-paragraph (3) or (4) above, section 86(4) of the Management Act (interest on overdue tax) shall have effect as if, in paragraph 5(*a*) of the Table (the reckonable date in relation to corporation tax), the reference to the nine months mentioned in section 243(4) of the 1970 Act or section 10(1) of this Act were a reference to the period which, under sub-paragraphs (3) to (6) above, is substituted for those nine months.

(8) In section 88(5)(*e*) of the Management Act (the date when corporation tax ought to have been paid) for the words from "where section 244(1)" to "the interval" there shall be substituted "in the case of an accounting period in respect of which section 10(1) of the principal Act applies as modified by sub-paragraph 1(3) or (4) of Schedule 30 to that Act, at the end of the period which, under that sub-paragraph, is substituted for the period of nine months".

(9) With respect to any accounting period of an old company which falls within sub-paragraph (3) or (4) above, section 825 shall have effect as if, in subsection (8) in paragraph (*a*) of the definition of "the material date", the reference to the nine months mentioned in section 10(1) were a reference to the period which, under sub-paragraphs (1) to (8) above is substituted for those nine months.

Duration of leases

2.—(1) Subject to sub-paragraph (2) and paragraph 3 below, section 38 has effect—

(*a*) as respects a lease granted after 12th June 1969; and
(*b*) so far as it relates to section 34(5), as respects a variation or waiver the contract for which is entered into after that date.

(2) So far as relates to relief under—

(*a*) section 385 or 393; or
(*b*) section 380(1) as applied by subsection (2) of that section; or
(*c*) section 25(1);

given by setting a loss against, or making a deduction from, income of—

(i) the year 1988–89 or any subsequent year of assessment, or
(ii) a company's accounting period ending after 5th April 1988,

section 38 shall be deemed to have had effect as from the passing of the Finance Act 1963, and as respects leases granted at any time.

(3) Notwithstanding section 31 or any other enactment governing the order in which reliefs are given, in applying sub-paragraph (2) above it shall be assumed that all relief which could not be affected by the operation of that sub-paragraph was given (for all years of assessment and accounting periods before or after the passing of this Act) before relief which could be affected by the operation of that sub-paragraph.

(4) All such adjustments shall be made, whether by way of assessment or discharge of repayment of tax, as are required to give effect to section 38 with this paragraph.

Note.—FA 1963 referred to in sub-para. (2) above was passed on 31 July 1963.

3.—(1) Sections 24 and 38 shall have effect subject to the modifications set out in sub-paragraphs (2) to (4) below in relation to any lease granted after 12th June 1969 and before 25th August 1971 and, so far as section 38 relates to section 34(5), in relation to any variation or waiver the contract for which was entered into between those dates, except to the extent that section 38 affects the computation of the profits or gains or losses of a trade, profession or vocation or relates to relief under—

(*a*) section 25(1);
(*b*) section 385 or 393;
(*c*) subsection (1) of section 380 as applied by subsection (2) of that section; or
(*d*) section 779(5).

(2) In section 24, in subsection (1), in the definition of "premium", the words from "or to" to "landlord", and subsections (3) and (4) shall be omitted.

(3) In subsection (1) of section 38 the following paragraph shall be inserted before paragraph (*a*)—

"(*aa*) where the terms of the lease include provision for the determination of the lease by notice given by the landlord, the lease shall not be treated as granted for a term longer than one ending at the earliest date on which it could be determined by notice so given;";

and sub-paragraph (ii) of paragraph (*a*) and paragraph (*c*) shall be omitted.

(4) In subsection (2) of that section for the words "Subsection (1)" there shall be substituted the words "Subsection (1)(*a*)", and subsection (4) of that section shall be omitted.

4.—(1) Where section 38 does not have effect, the following provisions of this paragraph shall apply in ascertaining the duration of a lease for the purposes of sections 34 to 36.

(2) Subject to sub-paragraph (4) below, where the terms of the lease include provision for the determination of the lease by notice given either by the landlord or by the tenant, the lease shall not be treated as granted for a term longer than one ending at the earliest date on which it could be determined by notice.

(3) Subject to sub-paragraph (4) below, where any of the terms of the lease (whether relating to forfeiture or to any other matter) or any other circumstances render it unlikely that the lease will continue beyond a date falling before the expiration of the term of the lease, the lease shall not be treated as having been granted for a term longer than one ending on that date.

(4) Where the duration of a lease falls to be ascertained after the date on which the lease has for any reason come to an end, the duration shall be taken to have extended from its commencement to that date, and where the duration falls to be ascertained at a time when

the lease is subsisting the preceding provisions of this paragraph shall be applied in accordance with circumstances prevailing at that time.

(5) In relation to Scotland, "term" in this paragraph, where referring to the duration of a lease, means "period".

(6) This paragraph shall be construed as one with Part II.

Repeal of section 136 of the Income Tax Act 1952: allowance of annual value of land as a business expense

5.—(1) This paragraph has effect for allowing deductions by reference to those which would have fallen to be made if section 136 of the Income Tax Act 1952 had applied for the years 1963–64 and 1964–65.

(2) Subject to the provisions of this paragraph, an allowance under this paragraph shall be made to the person ("the occupier") carrying on a trade where land which was occupied by him at any time before the end of the year 1962–63 for the purposes of the trade permanently ceases to be occupied by him for those purposes.

(3) The amount of the allowance shall be the excess of—

(*a*) the aggregate of any deductions in respect of the annual value of the land which, by virtue of section 136; would have been made in computing the profits or gains of the trade for the years 1963–64 and 1964–65 but for section 29(1) of the Finance Act 1963 and the repeal by that Act of section 136;

over

(*b*) the aggregate of any deductions relating to the land made in computing the profits or gains of the trade for those years, being—

(i) deductions permitted by section 29(2) of the Finance Act 1963, so far as made in respect of the period in respect of which the deductions mentioned in paragraph (*a*) above would have been made; or

(ii) deductions in respect of rent from which an amount representing tax was deducted under section 173 of the Income Tax Act 1952, so far as made in respect of that period.

(4) The allowance shall be made by—

(*a*) treating the amount of it as rent paid for the land by the occupier (in addition to any actual rent), becoming due from day to day during the period defined in sub-paragraph (5) below; and

(*b*) allowing deductions accordingly in computing the profits or gains of the trade chargeable under Case I of Schedule D for any chargeable period the profits or gains for which fall to be computed by reference to a period including the period defined in sub-paragraph (5) below or any part thereof.

(5) The period referred to in sub-paragraph (4) above is that ending when the land permanently ceases to be occupied by the occupier for the purposes of the trade, and of a duration, equal to the aggregate of—

(*a*) the number of months and fractions of months during which the land was occupied by him for the purposes of the trade in so much of the period by reference to which the profits or gains of the trade for the year 1963–64 fell to be computed as fell before the beginning of that year; and

(*b*) the number of months and fractions of months during which the land was so occupied in so much of the period by reference to which the profits or gains of the trade for the year 1964–65 fell to be computed as fell before the beginning of the year 1963–64.

(6) No allowance shall be made under this paragraph where the date on which the land permanently ceases to be occupied by the occupier for the purposes of the trade—

(*a*) falls within a chargeable period in which he permanently ceases to carry on the trade; or

(*b*) where the occupier is not a company, falls within a year of assessment and also within a period by reference to which the profits or gains of the trade for that year of assessment fall to be computed.

(7) Where, by reason of a change in the persons carrying on the trade, the trade falls to be treated for any of the purposes of the Income Tax Acts as permanently discontinued, a person engaged in carrying on the trade immediately before the change occurred who continues to be so engaged immediately after it occurred shall be treated for the purposes of this paragraph as not having been in occupation of the land at any time before it occurred.

(8) Where there has been a change in the persons carrying on the trade, but by virtue of section 113 of this Act or section 17(1) of the Finance Act 1954 (company reconstructions

before introduction of corporation tax), the trade does not by reason of the change fall to be treated for any of the purposes of the Income Tax Acts as permanently discontinued, this paragraph (including this sub-paragraph) shall apply as if any occupation of the land before the change occurred by the persons carrying on the trade immediately before it occurred were occupation by the persons carrying on the trade immediately after it occurred.

(9) Where section 343(1) applies, then for the purposes of this paragraph any occupation of land for the purposes of the trade by the predecessor shall be treated as having been the occupation of the successor.

Subsection (6) of that section shall apply to this sub-paragraph as it applies to subsections (2) to (5) of that section, and in this paragraph "predecessor" and "successor" have the same meaning as in that section.

(10) Where section 518 has effect, then for the purposes of this paragraph any occupation of land for the purposes of the trade by the transferor shall be treated as having been the occupation of the transferee.

This sub-paragraph shall be construed as one with section 518.

(11) Sub-paragraph 1 to 10 above shall apply in relation to a profession or vocation as they apply in relation to a trade, but as if the reference in sub-paragraph (4) to Case I of Schedule D were a reference to Case II of that Schedule.

(12) For the purposes of this paragraph, any occupation of land by the London Transport Board which was by virtue of paragraph 6 of Schedule 3 to the Finance Act 1970 immediately before the commencement of this Act treated as occupation by another body, shall continue to be so treated by virtue of this sub-paragraph.

Loss relief etc.

6.—(1) The substitution of this Act for the corresponding enactments repealed by this Act shall not alter the effect of any provision enacted before this Act (whether or not there is a corresponding provision in this Act) so far as it determines whether and to what extent—

(*a*) losses or expenditure incurred in, or other amounts referable to, a chargeable period earlier than those to which this Act applies may be taken into account for any tax purposes in a chargeable period to which this Act applies; or

(*b*) losses or expenditure incurred in, or other amounts referable to, a chargeable period to which this Act applies may be taken into account for any tax purposes in a chargeable period earlier than those to which this Act applies.

(2) Without prejudice to sub-paragraph (1) above, the repeals made by this Act shall not affect the following enactments (which are not re-enacted)—

(*a*) section 27(4) of the Finance Act 1952 (restrictions on removal of six year time limit on carry forward of trading losses);
(*b*) section 29(3) of the Finance Act 1953 (Isles of Scilly);
(*c*) section 17 of, and Schedule 3 to, the Finance Act 1954 (company reconstructions before corporation tax) so far as in force by virtue of the saving in Part IV of Schedule 22 to the Finance Act 1965, and section 80(8) of the Finance Act 1965 (which amends Schedule 3 to the Finance Act 1954);
(*d*) section 82(4) of the Finance Act 1965 (losses allowable against chargeable gains);
(*e*) section 85 of the Finance Act 1965 (carry forward of surplus of franked investment income: dividends paid out of pre-1966–67 profits) and the enactments amending that section;
(*f*) paragraph 25 of Schedule 15 to the Finance Act 1965 (continuity of elections for purposes of corporation tax);
(*g*) paragraph 7 of Schedule 16 to the Finance Act 1965 (overseas trade corporations);

in so far as those enactments may be relevant to tax for any chargeable period to which this Act applies.

7.—(1) This paragraph shall apply with respect to claims for group relief in respect of any amount which is attributable—

(*a*) to writing-down allowances, within the meaning of Chapter II of Part I of the 1968 Act, or, as the case may require, Chapter I of Part III of the Finance Act 1971, in respect of expenditure incurred by the surrendering company on the provision of machinery or plant; or
(*b*) to initial allowances under section 56 of the 1968 Act (expenditure in connection with mines etc.) in respect of expenditure incurred by the surrendering company and falling within section 52(1) of that Act of 1971 (works in a development area or in Northern Ireland); or

(*c*) to allowances under section 91 of the 1968 Act in respect of expenditure incurred by the surrendering company on scientific research;

where the expenditure is incurred under a contract entered into by the surrendering company before 6th March 1973.

(2) Notwithstanding anything in section 410(1) to (6) or 413(7) to (10) or in Schedule 18 but subject to sub-paragraph (5) below, group relief may be claimed in respect of any such amount as is referred to in sub-paragraph (1) above if—

  (*a*) immediately before 6th March 1973—

    (i) the surrendering company and the company claiming relief were members of a group of companies, and
    (ii) throughout the period beginning on that date and ending at the end of the accounting period in respect of which the claim is made, there is no reduction in the rights of the parent company with respect to the matters specified in section 413(7)(*a*) and (*b*); or

  (*b*) immediately before 6th March 1973 the company claiming relief was a member of a consortium and, throughout the period beginning on that date and ending at the end of the accounting period in respect of which the claim is made, there is—

    (i) no variation in the percentage of the ordinary share capital of the company owned by the consortium which is beneficially owned by that member, and
    (ii) no reduction in the rights of that member (in respect of the company owned by the consortium) with respect to the matters specified in section 413(7)(*a*) and (*b*);

and in either case no such arrangements as are specified in section 410(1) or (2) have come into existence after 5th March 1973 with respect to any of the companies concerned and no variation is made in any such arrangements which are in existence on that date with respect to any of those companies.

(3) For the purposes of sub-paragraph (2)(*a*) above, "the parent company" means the company of which another member of the group referred to in that sub-paragraph was, immediately before 6th March 1973, a 75 per cent. subsidiary, and the rights of the parent company referred to in that paragraph are—

  (*a*) if the parent company is either the surrendering company or the company claiming relief, its rights in the other company; and
  (*b*) in any other case, its rights in both the surrendering company and the company claiming relief.

(4) For the purposes of this paragraph an amount which the claimant company claims by way of group relief shall be treated as attributable to an allowance falling within any of paragraphs (*a*) to (*c*) of sub-paragraph (1) above to the extent that that amount would not have been available for surrender by the surrendering company if no such allowance had been available to the surrendering company in respect of the expenditure concerned.

(5) Sub-paragraph (2) above shall not apply if, during the period referred to in that sub-paragraph—

  (*a*) there is a major change in the nature or conduct of a trade or business carried on by the relevant company; or
  (*b*) the relevant company sets up and commences a trade or business which it did not carry on immediately before 6th March 1973.

(6) In sub-paragraph (5) above—

  "a major change in the nature or conduct of a trade or business" has the same meaning as in section 245(1); and
  "the relevant company" means, if the machinery or plant to which the allowance relates was brought into use on or before 6th March 1978, the company claiming group relief and in any other case either that company or the company which if sub-paragraph (5) did not apply would be the surrendering company.

(7) This paragraph shall be construed as if it were contained in Chapter IV of Part X.

Capital allowances

8. Without prejudice to paragraphs 6 and 7 above, where a person is, immediately before the commencement of this Act, entitled to a capital allowance by virtue of any enactment repealed by this Act, he shall not cease to be so entitled by reason only of that repeal, notwithstanding that the enactment in question is not re-enacted by this Act; and accordingly the provisions of this Act shall apply, with any necessary modifications, so far as may be necessary to give effect to any such entitlement.

Social security benefits

9.—(1) In relation to any period before regulations containing the first schemes under section 20 of the Social Security Act 1986 and Article 21 of the Social Security (Northern Ireland) Order 1986 providing for income support come into force—

(a) the repeal by this Act of sections 27 and 28 of the Finance Act 1981 shall not have effect;

(b) sections 151 and 152 of this Act shall not have effect;

(c) section 204 of this Act shall have effect with the substitution for paragraph (b) of the following paragraph—

"(b) he has claimed a payment of supplementary allowance under the Supplementary Benefits Act 1976 or the Supplementary Benefits (Northern Ireland) Order 1977 in respect of a period including that time and his right to the allowance is subject to any condition contained in section 5 of the said Act of 1976 or, in Northern Ireland, Article 7 of the said Order (requirements as to registration and availability for employment)"

and with the addition at the end of the following—

"(2) Any reference in this section to section 5 of the Supplementary Benefits Act 1976 or to Article 7 of the Supplementary Benefits (Northern Ireland) Order 1977 includes a reference to that section or Article as amended by any other enactment including an enactment passed or made after the passing of this Act"; and

(d) section 617(2) of this Act shall have effect with the substitution for paragraph (a) of the following paragraphs—

"(a) payments of benefit under the Supplememtary Benefits Act 1976 or the Supplementary Benefits (Northern Ireland) Order 1977 other than payments of supplementary allowance which are taxable by virtue of section 27 of the Finance Act 1981;

(aa) payments by way of an allowance under section 70 of the Social Security Act 1975 or section 70 of the Social Security (Northern Ireland) Act 1975;".

(2) In relation to any period before regulations containing the first schemes under section 20 of the Social Security Act 1986 and Article 21 of the Social Security (Northern Ireland) Order 1986 providing for family credit come into force, section 617(2) of this Act shall have effect with the addition after paragraph (b) of the following paragraph—

"(bb) payments in respect of family income supplement under the Family Income Supplements Act 1970 or the Family Income Supplements Act (Northern Ireland) 1970;".

Children's settlements: irrevocable dispositions made before 22nd April 1936

10.—(1) Sub-paragraph (2) below applies to any disposition which—

(a) was made, directly or indirectly, by any person ("the settlor") after 5th April 1914 and before 22nd April 1936, and

(b) immediately before 22nd April 1936, was an irrevocable settlement within the meaning of Chapter II of Part XV.

(2) Subject to the provisions of this paragraph, any income which, by virtue or in consequence of any disposition to which this sub-paragraph applies, is payable to or applicable for the benefit of a child of the settlor for some period less than the life of the child, shall, if and so long as the child is an infant and unmarried, be deemed for all purposes of the Income Tax Acts to be the income of the settlor, if living and not to be the income of any other person.

(3) Sub-paragraph (2) above shall not apply as regards any income—

(a) which is derived from capital which, at the end of the period during which that income is payable to or applicable for the benefit of the child, is required by the disposition to be held on trust absolutely for, or to be transferred to, the child; or

(b) which is payable to or applicable for the benefit of a child during the whole period of the life of the settlor.

(4) Income shall not be deemed for the purposes of this paragraph, to be payable to or applicable for the benefit of a child for some period less than its life by reason only that the disposition contains a provision for the payment to some other person of the income in the event of the bankruptcy of the child, or of an assignment thereof, or a charge thereon, being executed by the child.

(5) In this paragraph, unless the context otherwise requires—

"child" includes a step-child or an illegitimate child, and

"disposition" includes any trust, covenant, agreement or arrangement.

(6) Sections 661 and 662 shall apply as if this paragraph were contained in Chapter I of Part XV, and this paragraph, notwithstanding that it is referred to in Chapter II of that Part, shall not be construed as one with that Chapter.

Pre-1959 settlements

11.—(1) Where, in the case of any settlement made before 16th April 1958, any sums payable by the settlor or by the wife or husband of the settlor would, by virtue only of section 671(3), fall to be treated as the income of the settlor and not as the income of any other person, the sums shall not be so treated if—

(*a*) no power by reason of which they would fall to be so treated has been exercised after 15th April 1958, or is or can become exercisable after 5th April 1959, or such later date as the Board may in any particular case allow, and

(*b*) neither the settlor nor the wife or husband of the settlor has received or is entitled to any consideration or benefit in connection with the fulfilment of the condition set out in paragraph (*a*) above,

or if the settlement was entered into in connection with any judicial separation or any agreement between spouses to live separate and apart, or with the dissolution or annulment of a marriage.

(2) Where, in the case of any settlement made before 16th April 1958, any income arising under the settlement would, by virtue only of section 672(3), fall to be treated as the income of the settlor and not as the income of any other person, the income shall not be so treated if—

(*a*) no power by reason of which it would fall to be so treated has been exercised after 15th April 1958 or is or can become exercisable after 5th April 1959, or such later date as the Board may in any particular case allow; and

(*b*) neither the settlor nor the wife or husband of the settlor has received or is entitled to any consideration or benefit in connection with the fulfilment of the condition set out in paragraph (*a*) above.

12. Where, in the case of any settlement made before 9th July 1958, any income arising under the settlement would, by virtue only of section 674, fall to be treated as the income of the settlor and not as the income of any other person, it shall not be so treated if—

(*a*) no power by reason of which it would fall to be so treated has been exercised after 8th July 1958, or is or can become exercisable after 5th April 1959, or such later date as the Board may in any particular case allow; and

(*b*) neither the settlor nor the wife or husband of the settlor has received or is entitled to any consideration or benefit in connection with the fulfilment of the condition set out in paragraph (*a*) above.

General powers of amendment in Acts relating to overseas countries

13. Where under any Act passed before this Act and relating to a country or territory outside the United Kingdom there is a power to affect Acts passed or in force before a particular time, or instruments made or having effect under such Acts, and the power would but for the passing of this Act, have included power to change the law which is reproduced in, or is made or has effect under, this Act, then that power shall include power to make such provision as will secure the like change in the law reproduced in, or made or having effect under, this Act notwithstanding that it is not an Act passed or in force before that time.

Double taxation agreements

14. The repeal by this Act of section 16 of the Finance (No. 2) Act 1979 shall not prejudice the effect of any Order in Council which gives effect to arrangements contained in the Convention mentioned in that section and is made under section 497 of the 1970 Act.

Securities

15. The repeal by this Act of Schedule 22 to the Finance Act 1985 shall not affect the continued operation of paragraph 6 of that Schedule in relation to the holding of securities by any person at any time during the year (within the meaning of that Schedule).

Building societies

16. Any enactment relating to building societies contained in this Act which re-enacts an enactment which was an existing enactment for the purposes of section 121 of the Building Societies Act 1986 shall continue to be an existing enactment for those purposes.

Pension business

17. Any reference to pension business in any enactment (other than an enactment repealed by this Act) which immediately before the commencement of this Act was such a reference by virtue of paragraph 11(3) of Part III of Schedule 5 to the Finance Act 1970 shall not be affected by the repeal by this Act of that paragraph and accordingly the business in question shall continue to be known as pension business.

Stock relief

18. Schedule 9 to the Finance Act 1981 shall continue to have effect in relation to any relief to which paragraph 9 or 17(1) of that Schedule applied immediately before the commencement of this Act notwithstanding the repeal by this Act of that Schedule.

Schedule E emoluments

19. The repeal by this Act of section 21 of the Finance Act 1974 shall not affect the taxation of emoluments which if that section had been in force before 1973–74 would have fallen within Case I or Case II of Schedule E, and, accordingly, any such emoluments shall not be chargeable under Case III of Schedule E.

Unitary states

20. The repeal by this Act of section 54 of and Schedule 13 to the Finance Act 1985 shall not prevent the Treasury making an order under subsection (7) of section 54 exercising the powers conferred on the Treasury by that subsection in relation to distributions made in chargeable periods ending before 6th April 1988 and, accordingly, subsections (7) and (8) of section 54 shall continue to have effect in later chargeable periods for that purpose.

Continuity and construction of references to old and new law

21.—(1) The continuity of the operation of the Tax Acts and of the law relating to chargeable gains shall not be affected by the substitution of this Act for the enactments repealed by this Act and earlier enactments repealed by and corresponding to any of those enactments ("the repealed enactments").

(2) Any reference, whether express or implied, in any enactment, instrument or document (including this Act and any Act amended by this Act) to, or to things done or falling to be done under or for the purposes of, any provision of this Act shall, if and so far as the nature of the reference permits, be construed as including, in relation to the times, years or periods, circumstances or purposes in relation to which the corresponding provision in the repealed enactments has or had effect, a reference to, or as the case may be to things done or falling to be done under or for the purposes of, that corresponding provision.

(3) Any reference, whether express or implied, in any enactment, instrument or document (including the repealed enactments and enactments, instruments and documents passed or made after the passing of this Act) to, or to things done or falling to be done under or for the purposes of, any of the repealed enactments shall, if and so far as the nature of the reference permits, be construed as including, in relation to the times, years or periods, circumstances or purposes in relation to which the corresponding provision in this Act has effect, a reference to, or as the case may be to things done or falling to be done under or for the purposes of, that corresponding provision.

(4) Any reference to Case VIII of Schedule D, whether a specific reference or one imported by more general words, in any enactment, instrument or document shall, in relation to the chargeable periods to which section 843(1) applies, be construed as a reference to Schedule A, and for the purposes of sub-paragraph (2) above, Schedule A in this Act shall be treated as corresponding to Case VIII of Schedule D in the repealed enactments, and any provision of this Act or of any Act passed after 12th March 1970 and before this Act referring to Schedule A shall be construed accordingly.

BRITISH STEEL ACT 1988

(1988 Chapter 35)

11. Corporation tax

(1) Subject to subsection (2), the successor company shall be treated for all purposes of corporaton tax as if it were the same person as the Corporation.

(2) The successor company shall not by virtue of subsection (1) be regarded as a body falling within section 272(5) of the Income and Corporation Taxes Act 1970 (bodies established for carrying on industries or undertakings under national ownership or control).

(3) Section 400(1) of the Income and Corporation Taxes Act 1988 (write-off of government investment: restriction of tax losses) shall not have effect in relation to any reduction in the Corporation's public dividend capital under section 2(1) above or its extinguishment by virtue of section 2(3) above; but instead the Secretary of State may, with the consent of the Treasury, direct that such amount as is specified in the direction shall be set off against the successor company's tax losses as at the end of the accounting period ending last before the date of the direction.

(4) No direction shall be given by the Secretary of State under subsection (3) above at a time when the successor company has ceased to be wholly owned by the Crown.

(5) For the purposes of subsection (3) above the successor company's tax losses as at the end of the accounting period there mentioned are those referred to in paragraphs (*a*) to (*e*) of subsection (2) of the said section 400; and subsections (3) to (5) of that section shall have effect in relation to any set-off under subsection (3) above as if—

(*a*) any reference to subsection (1) of that section were a reference to subsection (3) above; and

(*b*) the reference in subsection (4) of that section to the write-off date were a reference to the date of the direction under subsection (3) above.

(6) Subsection (6) of the said section 400 shall apply in relation to any such reduction or extinguishment of the Corporation's public dividend capital as is mentioned in subsection (3) above as if the reference to the body in question were a reference to the Corporation.

(7) Where any debentures are issued in pursuance of section 3 above, any annual payment secured by those debentures shall be treated for all purposes of corporation tax as if it were a charge on income of the successor company.

(8) The vesting in the successor company by virtue of section 1 above of liability for a loan made to the Corporation shall not affect any direction given by the Treasury in respect of the loan under section 416 of the Income and Corporation Taxes Act 1970 (borrowing in foreign currency).

(9) In this section "accounting period" has the same meaning as in the Income and Corporation Taxes Act 1988.

FINANCE ACT 1988
(1988 Chapter 39)

ARRANGEMENT OF SECTIONS

PART I
CUSTOMS AND EXCISE

Duties of excise: rates

Sections 1–4 (not printed)

Duties of excise: other provisions

Sections 5–7 (not printed)

Management

Sections 8–12 (see Orange Book)

PART II
VALUE ADDED TAX

Exemptions

Sections 13–22 (see Orange Book)

PART III
INCOME TAX, CORPORATION TAX AND CAPITAL GAINS TAX

CHAPTER I
GENERAL

Tax rates and personal reliefs

Section
23. *Charge and basic rate of income tax for 1988–89.* (spent)
24. *Higher and additional rates of income tax.* (spent/amending)
25. *Personal reliefs.* (amending)
26. *Charge and rate of corporation tax for financial year 1988.* (spent)
27. *Corporation tax: small companies.* (spent)
28. *Deduction rate for sub-contractors in construction industry.* (amending)
29. *Life assurance premium relief.* (amending)
30. *Additional relief in respect of children.* (amending)
31. Non-residents' personal reliefs.

Married couples

32. Abolition of aggregation of income.
33. Personal allowance and married couple's allowance.
34. Jointly held property.
35. Minor and consequential provisions.

Annual payments

36. Annual payments.
37. Maintenance payments under existing obligations: 1988–89.

Section
38. Maintenance payments under existing obligations: 1989–90 onwards.
39. Maintenance payments under existing obligations: election for new rules.
40. Provisions supplementary to sections 37 to 39.

Relief for interest

41. *Qualifying maximum for loans.* (spent)
42. *Home loans: restriction of relief.* (amending)
43. Home improvement loans.
44. Loans for residence of dependent relative etc.

Benefits in kind

45. *Car benefits.* (amending)
46. *Car parking facilities.* (amending)
47. Entertainment: non-cash vouchers.
48. Entertainment: credit tokens.
49. Entertainment of directors and higher-paid employees.

Business expansion scheme

50. Private rented housing.
51. Restriction of relief.
52. *Valuation of interests in land.* (amending)
53. *Approved investment funds.* (amending)

Pensions etc.

54. Personal pension schemes: commencement.
55. *Personal pension schemes: other amendments.* (amending)
56. *Occupational pension schemes.* (amending)
57. Lump sum benefits paid otherwise than on retirement.

Underwriters

58. Assessment and collection.
59. Reinsurance: general.
60. Reinsurance to close.
61. Minor and consequential amendments.

Oil licences

62. Disposals of oil licences relating to undeveloped areas.
63. Allowance of certain drilling expenditure etc. in determining chargeable gains.
64. Interpretation of sections 62 and 63.

Miscellaneous

65. Commercial woodlands.
66. Company residence.
67. *Seafarers: foreign earnings.* (amending)
68. Priority share allocations for employees etc.
69. Share options: loans.
70. *Charities: payroll deduction scheme.* (amending)
71. *Unit trusts: relief on certain payments.* (amending)
72. Entertainment of overseas customers.
73. Consideration for certain restrictive undertakings.
74. *Payments on termination of office or employment etc.* (amending)
75. *Premiums for leases etc.* (amending)
76. *Foreign dividends etc., quoted Eurobonds and recognised clearing systems.* (amending)

CHAPTER II

UNAPPROVED EMPLOYEE SHARE SCHEMES

Preliminary

77. Scope of Chapter.

Section

Charges to tax

78. Charge where restrictions removed etc.
79. Charge for shares in dependent subsidiaries.
80. Charge on special benefits.

Miscellaneous

81. Changes in interest.
82. Company reorganisations etc.
83. Connected persons etc.
84. Capital gains tax.
85. Information.

Supplementary

86. Meaning of "dependent subsidiary".
87. Other interpretation provisions.
88. Transitional provisions.
89. Consequential amendments.

CHAPTER III
CAPITAL ALLOWANCES

90. *Buildings or structures sold by exempt bodies.* (amending)
91. *Sales without change of control.* (amending)
92. Successions to trades between connected persons.
93. *Safety at sports grounds.* (amending)
94. *Quarantine premises.* (amending)
95. Dwelling-houses let on assured tenancies.

CHAPTER IV
CAPITAL GAINS

Re-basing to 1982

96. Assets held on 31st March 1982.
97. Deferred charges on gains before 31st March 1982.

Unification of rates of tax on income and capital gains

98. Rates of capital gains tax.
99. Husband and wife.
100. Accumulation and discretionary settlements.
101. *Underwriters.* (amending).
102. Other special cases.
103. Commencement of sections 98 to 102.

Married couples

104. Married couples.

Company migration

105. Deemed disposal of assets on company ceasing to be resident in U.K.
106. Deemed disposal of assets on company ceasing to be liable to U.K. tax.
107. Postponement of charge on deemed disposal.

Miscellaneous

108. *Annual exempt amount for 1988–89.* (spent)
109. Gains arising from certain settled property.
110. *Retirement relief.* (amending)
111. Dependent relative's residence.
112. *Roll-over relief.* (amending)
113. Indexation: building societies etc.
114. Indexation: groups and associated companies.
115. *Transfers within a group.* (amending)
116. *Personal equity plans.* (amending)

Section
117. Definition of "investment trust".
118. *Amendments of Finance Act 1985 s. 68.* (amending)

CHAPTER V
MANAGEMENT
Assessment

119. *Current year assessments.* (amending)

Returns of income and gains

120. *Notice of liability to income tax.* (amending)
121. *Notice of liability to corporation tax.* (amending)
122. *Notice of liability to capital gains tax.* (amending)

Other returns and information

123. *Three year time limit.* (amending)
124. *Returns of fees, commissions etc.* (amending)
125. *Other payments and licences etc.* (amending)

Production of accounts, books etc.

126. *Production of documents relating to a person's tax liability.* (amending)
127. Production of computer records etc.

Interest and penalties

128. *Interest on overdue or overpaid PAYE.* (amending)
129. *Two or more tax-geared penalties in respect of same tax.* (amending)

Company migration

130. Provisions for securing payment by company of outstanding tax.
131. Penalties for failure to comply with section 130.
132. Liability of other persons for unpaid tax.

Appeals etc.

133. *Jurisdiction of General Commissioners.* (amending)
134. General Commissioners for Northern Ireland.
135. *Cases stated in Northern Ireland.* (amending)

PART IV
MISCELLANEOUS AND GENERAL
Inheritance tax

Sections 136–137 (see Orange Book)

Petroleum revenue tax

Sections 138–139 (not printed)

Stamp duty and stamp duty reserve tax

Sections 140–144 (see Orange Book)

Miscellaneous

145. Building societies: change of status.
146. Post-consolidation amendments.
147. Interpretation etc.
148. Repeals.
149. Short title.

SCHEDULES:

Schedule 1—*Alcoholic liquor duties.* (not printed)
Schedule 2—*Vehicles excise duty.* (not printed)

Schedule 3—Married couples: minor and consequential provisions.
          Part I   Amendments of the Taxes Act 1988.
          Part II   Other provisions.
Schedule 4—Business expansion scheme: private rented housing.
          Part I   Modifications made by section 50.
          Part II   Dwelling-houses to which section 50 does not apply.
Schedule 5—Underwriters: assessment and collection of tax.
Schedule 6—Commercial woodlands.
Schedule 7—Exceptions to rule in section 66(1).
Schedule 8—Capital gains: assets held on 31st March 1982.
Schedule 9—Deferred charges on gains before 31st March 1982.
Schedule 10—Gains arising from certain settled property.
Schedule 11—Capital gains indexation: groups and associated companies.
Schedule 12—Building societies: change of status.
Schedule 13—Post-consolidation amendments.
          Part I   Amendments of the Taxes Act 1988.
          Part II   Amendments of other enactments.
Schedule 14—Repeals.
          Part I   *Customs and excise.* (not printed)
          Part II   *Vehicles excise duty.* (not printed)
          Part III   *Value added tax.* (see Orange Book)
          Part IV   Income and corporation tax: general.
          Part V   Commercial woodlands.
          Part VI   Unapproved employee share schemes.
          Part VII   Capital gains: general.
          Part VIII   Married couples.
          Part IX   Tax appeals etc. in Northern Ireland.
          Part X   *Inheritance tax.* (see Orange Book)
          Part XI   *Stamp duty.* (see Orange Book)

An Act to grant certain duties, to alter other duties, and to amend the law relating to the National Debt and the Public Revenue, and to make further provision in connection with Finance.
[29th July 1988]

PART III
INCOME TAX, CORPORATION TAX AND CAPITAL GAINS TAX
CHAPTER I
GENERAL

Tax rates and personal reliefs

31. Non-residents' personal reliefs

(1) For the year 1990–91 and subsequent years of assessment section 278 of the Taxes Act 1988 (which with certain exceptions denies relief under Chapter I of Part VII to non-residents) shall have effect with the following amendments.

(2) In subsection (2)(*e*) (exception for widows of Crown servants) after the word "husband" there shall be inserted the words ", or a widower whose late wife,".

(3) After subsection (2) there shall be inserted—

"(2A) Notwithstanding subsection (2) above, no relief shall be given under section 257D in a case where the husband is not resident in the United Kingdom."

(4) Subsections (3) to (7) shall be omitted.

Married couples

32. Abolition of aggregation of income

Section 279 of the Taxes Act 1988 (which treats the income of a woman living with her husband as his income for income tax purposes) shall not have effect for the year 1990–91 or any subsequent year of assessment.

33. Personal allowance and married couple's allowance

The Taxes Act 1988 shall have effect for the year 1990–91 and subsequent years of assessment with the substitution of the following sections for section 257—

"**257. Personal allowance**

(1) The claimant shall be entitled to a deduction from his total income of [£2,785][1].

(2) If the claimant proves that he is at any time within the year of assessment of the age of 65 or upwards, he shall be entitled to a deduction from his total income of [£3,400][1] (instead of the deduction provided for by subsection (1) above).

(3) If the claimant proves that he is at any time within the year of assessment of the age of [75][1] or upwards, he shall be entitled to a deduction from his total income of [£3,540][1] (instead of the deduction provided for by subsection (1) or (2) above).

(4) For the purposes of subsections (2) and (3) above a person who would have been of or over a specified age within the year of assessment if he had not died in the course of it shall be treated as having been of that age within that year.

(5) In relation to a claimant whose total income for the year of assessment exceeds [£11,400][1], subsections (2) and (3) above shall apply as if the amounts specified in them were reduced by [one half][1] of the excess (but not so as to reduce those amounts below that specified in subsection (1) above).

Amendments.—[1] Amounts etc. in sub-ss. (1), (2), (3), (5) substituted by FA 1989, s. 33(1)–(5).

257A. Married couple's allowance

(1) If the claimant proves that for the whole or any part of the year of assessment he is a married man whose wife is living with him, he shall be entitled to a deduction from his total income of [£1,590][1].

(2) If the claimant proves that for the whole or any part of the year of assessment he is a married man whose wife is living with him, and that either of them is at any time within that year of the age of 65 or upwards, he shall be entitled to a deduction from his total income of [£1,985][1] (instead of the deduction provided for by subsection (1) above).

(3) If the claimant proves that for the whole or any part of the year of assessment he is a married man whose wife is living with him, and that either of them is at any time within that year of the age of [75][1] or upwards, he shall be entitled to a deduction from his total income of [£2,025][1] (instead of the deduction provided for by subsection (1) or (2) above).

(4) For the purposes of subsections (2) and (3) above a person who would have been of or over a specified age within the year of assessment if he had not died in the course of it shall be treated as having been of that age within that year.

(5) In relation to a claimant whose total income for the year of assessment exceeds [£11,400][1], subsections (2) and (3) above shall apply as if the amounts specified in them were reduced by—

(a) [one half][1] of the excess, less
(b) any reduction made in his allowance under section 257 by virtue of subsection (5) of that section,

(but not so as to reduce the amounts so specified below the amount specified in subsection (1) above).

(6) A man shall not be entitled by virtue of this section to more then one deduction for any year of assessment; and in relation to a claim by a man who becomes married in the year of assessment and has not previously in the year been entitled to relief under this section, this section shall have effect as if the amounts specified in subsections (1) to (3) above were reduced by one twelfth for each month of the year ending before the date of the marriage.

In this subsection "month" means a month beginning with the 6th day of a month of the calendar year.

Amendments.—[1] Amounts etc. in sub-ss. (1), (2), (3), (5) substituted by FA 1989, s. 33(1), (6)–(9).

257B. Transfer of relief under section 257A

(1) Where—

(a) a man is entitled to relief under section 257A, but
(b) the amount which he is entitled to deduct from his total income by virtue of that section exceeds what is left of his total income after all other deductions have been made from it,

his wife shall be entitled to a deduction from her total income of an amount equal to the excess.

(2) In determining for the purposes of subsection (1)(b) above the amount that is left of a person's total income for a year of assessment after other deductions have been made from it, there shall be disregarded any deduction made—

(a) on account of any payments of relevant loan interest which become due in that year and to which section 369 applies, or
(b) under section 289, [or][1]
[(c) on account of any payments to which section 593(2) or 639(3) applies,][1] [or][2]
[(d) on account of any payments to which section 54(5) of the Finance Act 1989 applies.][2]

(3) This section shall not apply for a year of assessment unless the claimant's husband has given to the inspector written notice that it is to apply; and any such notice—

(a) shall be given not later than six years after the end of the year of assessment to which it relates,
(b) shall be in such form as the Board may determine, and
(c) shall be irrevocable.

Amendments.—¹ Sub-s. (2)(c) and the preceding word "or" inserted by FA 1989, s. 33(1), (10).
² Sub-s. (2)(d) and the preceding word "or" inserted by FA 1989, s. 57(4).

257C. Indexation of amounts in sections 257 and 257A

(1) If the retail prices index for the month of December preceding a year of assessment is higher than it was for the previous December, then, unless Parliament otherwise determines, sections 257 and 257A shall apply for that year as if for each amount specified in them as they applied for the previous year (whether by virtue of this section or otherwise) there were substituted an amount arrived at by increasing the amount for the previous year by the same percentage as the percentage increase in the retail prices index, and—

  (a) if in the case of an amount specified in sections 257(5) and 257A(5) the result is not a multiple of £100, rounding it up to the nearest amount which is such a multiple;
  (b) if in the case of any other amount the increase is not a multiple of £10, rounding the increase up to the nearest amount which is such a multiple.

(2) Subsection (1) above shall not require any change to be made in the amounts deductible or repayable under section 203 between the beginning of a year of assessment and 5th May in that year.

(3) The Treasury shall in each year of assessment make an order specifying the amounts which by virtue of subsection (1) above will be treated as specified for the following year of assessment in sections 257 and 257A.

(4) This section shall have effect in relation to reliefs for the year 1990–91 (as well as for later years); and for that purpose it shall be assumed that sections 257 and 257A applied for the year 1989–90 as they apply, apart from this section, for the year 1990–91.

257D. Transitional relief: husband with excess allowances

(1) Where—

  (a) a husband and wife are living together for the whole or any part of the year 1990–91 and section 279 (but not section 287) applied in relation to them for the whole or any part of the year 1989–90, and
  (b) the deductions which the husband was entitled to make from his total income for the year 1989–90 under this Chapter exceed the aggregate mentioned in subsection (2) below,

the wife shall be entitled to a deduction from her total income for the year 1990–91 of an amount equal to the excess.

(2) The aggregate referred to in subsection (1) above is the aggregate of—

  (a) the husband's total income for the year 1990–91, and
  (b) the deductions which the wife is entitled to make from her total income for that year under this Chapter (apart from this section).

(3) Where—

  (a) a husband and wife are living together for the whole or any part of the year 1990–91 and for part of the year 1989–90 but section 279 did not apply in relation to them for any part of the year 1989–90, and
  (b) the deductions which the husband was entitled to make from his total income for the year 1989–90 under this Chapter, apart from section 257(6), exceed his total income for the year 1990–91,

then, subject to subsection (4) below, the wife shall be entitled to a deduction from her total income for the year 1990–91 of an amount equal to the excess.

(4) If the deductions which the wife is entitled to make from her total income for the year 1990–91 under this Chapter (apart from this section) exceed the lesser of—

  (a) her total income for the year 1989–90, and
  (b) the deductions which she was entitled to make from her total income for that year under this Chapter, apart from section 259, section 262 and section 280,

the deduction provided for by subsection (3) above shall be reduced by an amount equal to the excess.

(5) Where—

  (a) a husband and wife are living together for the whole or any part of the year 1991–92 or any subsequent year of assessment ("the year in question"), and

(b) they were also living together throughout the immediately preceding year of assessment and the wife made a deduction from her total income for that year under this section, and

(c) the deductions which the wife is entitled to make from her total income under this Chapter (apart from this section) are either no greater for the year in question than for the immediately preceding year, or greater by a margin which does not exceed the deduction referred to in paragraph (b) above, and

(d) the deductions which the husband is entitled to make from his total income for the year in question under this Chapter, apart from section 257A and section 265, exceed his total income for that year,

the wife shall be entitled to a deduction from her total income for that year.

(6) The amount of that deduction shall be equal to—

(a) the deduction referred to in subsection (5)(b) above, reduced where applicable by an amount equal to the margin referred to in subsection (5)(c), or

(b) the excess referred to in subsection (5)(d),

whichever is less.

(7) In determining for the purposes of subsection (5)(b) above whether the wife made a deduction from her total income for the immediately preceding year of assessment under this section, and the amount of any such deduction, it shall be assumed that a deduction under this section is made after all other deductions (except any deduction under section 289).

(8) In determining for the purposes of this section a person's total income for a year of assessment there shall be disregarded any deduction made—

(a) on account of any payments of relevant loan interest which become due in that year and to which section 369 applies, or

(b) under this Chapter or under section 289, [or][1]

[(c) on account of any payments to which section 593(2) or 639(3) applies,][1] [or][2]

[(d) on account of any payments to which section 54(5) of the Finance Act 1989 applies][2];

and in determining for the purposes of subsection (1)(b) above the deductions which a man was entitled to make under this Chapter for the year 1989–90, any application under section 283 shall be disregarded.

(9) This section shall not apply for a year of assessment unless the claimant's husband has given to the inspector written notice that it is to apply; and any such notice—

(a) shall be given not later than six years after the end of the year of assessment to which it relates,

(b) shall be in such form as the Board may determine, and

(c) shall be irrevocable.

(10) A notice given under subsection (9) above in relation to a year of assessment shall have effect also as a notice under section 257B(3) (and, where it is relevant, under section 265(5)).

Amendments.—[1] Sub-s. (8)(c) and the preceding word "or" inserted by FA 1989, s. 33(1), (10).
[2] Sub-s. (8)(d) and the preceding word "or" inserted by FA 1989, s. 57(4).

257E. Transitional relief: the elderly

(1) This section shall apply in relation to a claimant for any year of assessment for the whole or any part of which he has his wife living with him if he proves—

(a) that for the year 1989–90 he was entitled to relief by virtue of section 257(2)(a) of this Act (as it had effect for that year) and that his entitlement was due to her age and not to his (he being under the age of 65 throughout that year), or

(b) that for the year 1989–90 he was entitled to relief by virtue of section 257(3)(a) of this Act (as it had effect for that year) and that his entitlement was due to her age and not to his (he being under the age of [75][1] throughout that year),

and, in either case, that the amount of that relief exceeded the aggregate amount of any relief to which he would be entitled for the year 1990–91 under sections 257 and 257A (apart from this section).

(2) Where this section applies, section 257 shall have effect—

(a) in a case within subsection (1)(a) above, as if for the amount specified in subsection (1) of that section there were substituted [£3,400][1], and

(b) in a case within subsection (1)(b) above, as if for the amounts specified in subsections (1) and (2) of that section there were substituted [£3,540][1].

(3) Section 257(5) shall have effect in relation to section 257(1) as modified by this section as it has effect in relation to section 257(2) and (3); and in all cases the reference in section 257(5) to the amount specified in section 257(1) is a reference to the amount specified apart from this section.

(4) The references in section 257C to the amounts specified in section 257 are references to the amounts specified apart from this section.

(5) In determining for the purposes of this section the amount of any reliefs to which a person was entitled for the year 1989–90, any application under section 283 shall be disregarded.

Amendments.—[1] Age and amounts in sub-ss. (1)(b), (2)(a), (b) substituted by FA 1989, s. 33(1), (11)–(13).

257F. Transitional relief: separated couples

If the claimant proves—

(a) that he and his wife ceased to live together before 6th April 1990 but that ever since they ceased to live together they have continued to be married to one another and she has been wholly maintained by him, and

(b) that he is not entitled to make any deduction in respect of the sums paid for her maintenance in computing for income tax purposes the amount of his income for the year to which the claim relates, and

(c) that he was entitled to a deduction for the year 1989–90 by virtue of section 257(1)(a) of this Act (as it had effect for that year) and, if the claim relates to a year later than 1990–91, that he has been entitled by virtue of this section to a deduction under section 257A for each intervening year,

sections 257A and 257E (but not section 257B or section 257D) shall have effect for the year to which the claim relates as if his wife were living with him."

34. Jointly held property

The Taxes Act 1988 shall have effect for the year 1990–91 and subsequent years of assessment with the insertion of the following sections after section 282—

"282A. Jointly held property

(1) Subject to the following provisions of this section, income arising from property held in the names of a husband and his wife shall for the purposes of income tax be regarded as income to which they are beneficially entitled in equal shares.

(2) Subsection (1) above shall not apply to income to which neither the husband nor the wife is beneficially entitled.

(3) Subsection (1) above shall not apply to income—

(a) to which either the husband or the wife is beneficially entitled to the exclusion of the other, or

(b) to which they are beneficially entitled in unequal shares,

if a declaration relating to it has effect under section 282B.

(4) Subsection (1) above shall not apply to—

(a) earned income, or

(b) income which is not earned income but to which section 111 applies.

(5) Subsection (1) above shall not apply to income to which the husband or the wife is beneficially entitled if or to the extent that it is treated by virtue of any other provision of the Income Tax Acts as the income of the other of them or of a third party.

(6) References in this section to a husband and his wife are references to a husband and wife living together.

282B. Jointly held property: declarations

(1) The declaration referred to in section 282A(3) is a declaration by both the husband and the wife of their beneficial interests in—

(*a*) the income to which the declaration relates, and
(*b*) the property from which that income arises.

(2) Subject to the following subsections, a declaration shall have effect under this section in relation to income arising on or after the date of the declaration; but a declaration made before 6th June 1990 shall also have effect in relation to income arising before that date.

(3) A declaration shall not have effect under this section unless notice of it is given to the inspector, in such form and manner as the Board may prescribe, within the period of 60 days beginning with the date of the declaration.

(4) A declaration shall not have effect under this section in relation to income from property if the beneficial interests of the husband and the wife in the property itself do not correspond to their beneficial interests in the income.

(5) A declaration having effect under this section shall continue to have effect unless and until the beneficial interests of the husband and wife in either the income to which it relates, or the property from which the income arises, cease to accord with the declaration."

35. Minor and consequential provisions

Schedule 3 to this Act (which makes provision consequential on sections 32 and 33 above and other minor amendments relating to the treatment for income tax purposes of husbands, wives, widowers and widows) shall have effect.

Annual payments

36. Annual payments

(1) . . .

(2) The following sections shall be inserted at the beginning of Part II of the Taxes Act 1970—

"**51A. General rule**

(1) A payment to which this section applies shall not be a charge on the income of the person liable to make it, and accordingly—

(*a*) his income shall be computed without any deduction being made on account of the payment, and
(*b*) the payment shall not form part of the income of the person to whom it is made or of any other person.

(2) This section applies to any annual payment made by an individual which would otherwise be within the charge to tax under Case III of Schedule D except—

(*a*) a payment of interest;
(*b*) a covenanted payment to charity (within the meaning given by section 434(2) below);
(*c*) a payment made for bona fide commercial reasons in connection with the individual's trade, profession or vocation; and
(*d*) a payment to which section 48(1) of the Finance Act 1977 applies.

(3) This section applies to a payment made by personal representatives (within the meaning given in section 432(4) below) where—

(*a*) the deceased would have been liable to make the payment if he had not died, and
(*b*) this section would have applied to the payment if he had made it.

(4) A maintenance payment arising outside the United Kingdom shall not be within the charge to tax under Case V of Schedule D if, because of this section, it would not have been within the charge to tax under Case III had it arisen in the United Kingdom; and for this purpose "maintenance payment" means a periodical payment (not being an instalment of a lump sum) which satisfies the conditions set out in paragraphs (*a*) and (*b*) of section 51B(5) below.

(5) No deduction shall be made under section 122(1)(*b*) below on account of an annuity or other annual payment which would not have been within the charge to tax under Case III of Schedule D if it had arisen in the United Kingdom.

(6) References in subsection (2) above to an individual include references to a Scottish partnership in which at least one partner is an individual.

51B. Qualifying maintenance payments

(1) In this section "qualifying maintenance payment" means a periodical payment which—

   (*a*) is made under an order made by a court in the United Kingdom, or under a written agreement the proper law of which is the law of a part of the United Kingdom,
   (*b*) is made by one of the parties to a marriage (including a marriage which has been dissolved or annulled) either—

      (i) to or for the benefit of the other party and for the maintenance of the other party, or
      (ii) to the other party for the maintenance by the other party of any child of the family,

   (*c*) is due at a time when—

      (i) the two parties are not a married couple living together, and
      (ii) the party to whom or for whose benefit the payment is made has not remarried, and

   (*d*) is not a payment in respect of which relief from tax is available to the person making the payment under any provision of the Income Tax Acts other than this section.

(2) Notwithstanding section 51A(1)(*a*) above but subject to subsections (3) and (4) below, a person making a claim for the purpose shall be entitled, in computing his total income for the year 1987–88, to deduct an amount equal to the aggregate amount of any qualifying maintenance payments made by him which fall due in that year.

(3) The amount which may be deducted under this section by a person in computing his total income for the year 1987–88 shall not exceed £1,370.

(4) Where qualifying maintenance payments falling due in the year 1987–88 are made by a person who also makes other maintenance payments attracting relief for that year, subsection (3) above shall apply as if the limit imposed by it were reduced by an amount equal to the aggregate amount of those other payments.

(5) The reference in subsection (4) above to other maintenance payments attracting relief for the year 1987–88 is a reference to periodical payments which—

   (*a*) are made under an order made by a court (whether in the United Kingdom or elsewhere) or under a written or oral agreement, and
   (*b*) are made by a person—

      (i) as one of the parties to a marriage (including a marriage which has been dissolved or annulled) to or for the benefit of the other party to the marriage and for the maintenance of the other party, or
      (ii) to any person under 21 years of age for his own benefit, maintenance or education, or
      (iii) to any person for the benefit, maintenance or education of a person under 21 years of age,

and in respect of which the person making them is entitled otherwise than under this section to make a deduction in computing his income for the year.

(6) The reference in subsection (1) above to a married couple living together shall be construed in accordance with section 42(1) above, but section 42(2) above shall not apply for the purposes of this section.

(7) In this section—

   "child of the family", in relation to the parties to a marriage, means a person under 21 years of age—

      (*a*) who is a child of both those parties, or
      (*b*) who (not being a person who has been boarded out with them by a public authority or voluntary organisation) has been treated by both of them as a child of their family;

   "periodical payment" does not include an instalment of a lump sum."

(3) This section shall have effect in relation to any payment falling due on or after 15th March 1988 unless it is made in pursuance of an existing obligation.

(4) In subsection (3) above "existing obligation" means a binding obligation—

   (*a*) under an order made by a court (whether in the United Kingdom or elsewhere) before

15th March 1988, or before the end of June 1988 on an application made on or before 15th March 1988;

(*b*) under a deed executed or written agreement made before 15th March 1988 and received by an inspector before the end of June 1988;

(*c*) under an oral agreement made before 15th March 1988, written particulars of which have been received by an inspector before the end of June 1988; or

(*d*) under an order made by a court (whether in the United Kingdom or elsewhere) on or after 15th March 1988, or under a written agreement made on or after that date, where the order or agreement replaces, varies or supplements an order or agreement within this subsection;

but subject to subsection (5) below.

(5) An obligation within subsection (4)(*d*) above is an existing obligation only if—

(*a*) it is an obligation to make periodical payments (not being instalments of a lump sum) which are made by a person—

(i) as one of the parties to a marriage (including a marriage which has been dissolved or annulled) to or for the benefit of the other party to the marriage and for the maintenance of the other party, or

(ii) to any person under 21 years of age for his own benefit, maintenance or education, or

(iii) to any person for the benefit, maintenance or education of a person under 21 years of age, and

(*b*) the order or agreement replaced, varied or supplemented provided for such payments to be made for the benefit, maintenance or, as the case case may be, education of the same person.

(6) Section 351 of the Taxes Act 1988 and section 65 of the Taxes Act 1970 shall not apply to any payment in relation to which this section has effect.

Note.—Sub-s. (1) enacts TA 1988, ss. 347A, 347B.

37. Maintenance payments under existing obligations: 1988–89

(1) This section applies to any annual payment due in the year 1988–89 which—

(*a*) is made in pursuance of an existing obligation under an order made by a court (whether in the United Kingdom or elsewhere) or under a written or oral agreement,

(*b*) is made by one of the parties to a marriage (including a marriage which has been dissolved or annulled) either—

(i) to or for the benefit of the other party and for the maintenance of the other party, or

(ii) to the other party for the maintenance by the other party of any child of the family,

(*c*) is due at a time when—

(i) the two parties are not a married couple living together, and

(ii) the party to whom or for whose benefit the payments are made has not remarried, and

(*d*) is within the charge to tax under Case III or Case V of Schedule D, and is not by virtue of Part XV of the Taxes Act 1988 treated for any purpose as the income of the person making it.

(2) On making a claim for the purpose a person chargeable to tax in respect of payments to which this section applies shall be entitled, in computing his total income for the year 1988–89, to deduct an amount equal to the aggregate amount of the payments, or £1,490, whichever is less.

38. Maintenance payments under existing obligations: 1989–90 onwards

(1) This section applies to any annual payment due in the year 1989–90 or any subsequent year of assessment which—

(*a*) is made in pursuance of an existing obligation under an order made by a court (whether in the United Kingdom or elsewhere) or under a written or oral agreement,

(*b*) is made by an individual—

(i) as one of the parties to a marriage (including a marriage which has been dissolved or annulled) to or for the benefit of the other party to the marriage and for the maintenance of the other party, or

(ii) to any person under 21 years of age for his own benefit, maintenance or education, or

(iii) to any person for the benefit, maintenance or education of a person under 21 years of age, and

(c) is (apart from this section) within the charge to tax under Case III or Case V of Schedule D, and is not by virtue of Part XV of the Taxes Act 1988 treated for any purpose as the income of the person making it.

(2) A payment to which this section applies shall not be a charge on the income of the person liable to make it, but—

(a) that person shall be entitled, on making a claim for the purpose, to make a deduction of an amount determined in accordance with subsection (3) below in computing his total income for the year of assessment in which the payment falls due, and
(b) the payment shall form part of the income of the recipient, but subject to subsections (4) and (5) below.

(3) The amount which a person may deduct under subsection (2)(a) above in computing his total income for a year of assessment shall be equal to the aggregate amount of the payments made by him which fall due in that year and to which this section applies, except that it shall not in any event exceed the aggregate amount of any payments due in the year 1988–89—

(a) which satisfy the conditions in paragraphs (a), (b) and (c) of subsection (1) above, and
(b) in respect of which he was entitled to make a deduction in computing his income for that year.

(4) The amount which, by virtue of subsection (2)(b) above, is treated as forming part of a person's income for a year of assessment by reason of payments made by another person ("the payer") shall not exceed the aggregate amount of any payments made by the payer which—

(a) formed part of the same recipient's income for the year 1988–89, and
(b) satisfy the conditions in paragraphs (a), (b) and (c) of subsection (1) above.

(5) The amount which, by virtue of subsection (2)(b) above, would apart from this subsection be treated as forming part of a person's income for a year of assessment by reason of payments within subsection (6) below shall, if he makes a claim for the purpose, be reduced by the amount of the difference between the higher (married person's) relief and the lower (single person's) relief under subsection (1) of section 257 of the Taxes Act 1988 as it applies for that year to a person not falling within subsection (2) or (3) of that section.

(6) The payments referred to in subsection (5) above are payments which—

(a) are made by one of the parties to a marriage (including a marriage which has been dissolved or annulled) either—

(i) to or for the benefit of the other party and for the maintenance of the other party, or
(ii) to the other party for the maintenance by the other party of any child of the family, and

(b) are due at a time when—

(i) the two parties are not a married couple living together, and
(ii) the party to whom or for whose benefit the payments are made has not remarried.

(7) A payment to which this section applies shall be made without deduction of income tax.

(8) A payment to which this section applies shall be within the charge to tax under Case III or (if it arises outside the United Kingdom) Case V of Schedule D; and tax chargeable under Case III shall, notwithstanding anything in sections 64 to 67 of the Taxes Act 1988, be computed on the payments falling due in the year of assessment, so far as paid in that or any other year.

(9) No deduction shall be made under section 65(1)(b) of the Taxes Act 1988 on account of a payment to which this section applies.

Note.—See **Prospective Legislation Notes** (Married Couples).

39. Maintenance payments under existing obligations: election for new rules

(1) If an election is duly made for the purpose by any person, section 36 above shall have effect in relation to all payments made by him—

    (*a*) to which section 37 or section 38 above would apply apart from the election, and
    (*b*) which fall due in a year of assessment for which the election has effect;

and accordingly sections 37 and 38 shall not apply to the payments.

(2) An election under subsection (1) above—

    (*a*) shall be made in such form and manner as the Board may prescribe,
    (*b*) shall be made not later than twelve months after the end of the first year of assessment for which it is to have effect,
    (*c*) shall have effect for any subsequent year of assessment, and
    (*d*) shall be irrevocable.

(3) A person making an election under subsection (1) above shall, before the end of the period of 30 days beginning with the day on which it is made, give notice of it to every recipient of a payment affected by the election.

40. Provisions supplementary to sections 37 to 39

(1) In sections 37 to 39 above—

"child of the family", in relation to the parties to a marriage, means a person under 21 years of age—

    (*a*) who is a child of both those parties, or
    (*b*) who (not being a person who has been boarded out with them by a public authority or voluntary organisation) has been treated by both of them as a child of their family;

"existing obligation" has the same meaning as in section 36(3) above.

(2) The references in sections 38(2)(*b*) and (4) and 39(3) above to the recipient of a payment are, in a case of the kind described in sections 37(1)(*b*)(i) and 38(1)(*b*)(i), references to the other party there mentioned.

(3) The references in sections 37 and 38 above to a married couple living together shall be construed in accordance with section 282(1) of the Taxes Act 1988, but section 282(2) shall not apply for the purposes of those sections.

Note.—See Prospective Legislation Notes (Married Couples).

Relief for interest

43. Home improvement loans

(1) ...

(2) ...

(3) Interest paid by a housing association on a home improvement loan made on or after 6th April 1988 shall not be relevant loan interest for the purposes of Part IX of the Taxes Act 1988; and for the purposes of this subsection—

    (*a*) "housing association" means a housing association for the time being approved for the purposes of section 488 of that Act or a self-build society for the time being approved for the purposes of section 489,
    (*b*) "home improvement loan" has the same meaning as in subsection (2B) of section 355 of that Act, and
    (*c*) subsection (2C) of that section shall have effect as it does for the purposes of subsection (2A) of that section.

Notes.—Sub-s. (1) amends TA 1988, s. 355.
Sub-s. (2) amends TA 1988, s. 356.

44. Loans for residence of dependent relative etc.

(1) In section 355(1)(*a*) and 357(2)(*a*) of the Taxes Act 1988 the words "or of a dependent relative or former or separated spouse of his," shall not have effect in relation to payments of interest made on or after 6th April 1988.

(2) Subsection (1) above shall not apply where the interest is paid on a loan made before 6th April 1988 if interest paid on it at a relevant time was eligible for relief under section 353 of the Taxes Act 1988 only because the land, caravan or house-boat concerned was used as the only or main residence of the same dependent relative or former or separated spouse.

(3) In subsection (2) above "relevant time" means—

(*a*) the last time when interest was paid on the loan before 6th April 1988, or
(*b*) if no interest was paid on it before that date, any time within the period of 12 months (or any longer period substituted in relation to the case under section 355(2) of the Taxes Act 1988) after the date on which the loan was made;

but paragraph (*b*) above shall not apply if at any time after the date on which the loan was made and before the date on which the land, caravan or house-boat was first used as mentioned in subsection (2) above, the land, caravan or house-boat was used for any other purpose.

(4) In section 358(4)(*a*) of the Taxes Act 1988 (relief where borrower deceased) the words "or of any dependent relative of the deceased" shall not have effect in relation to payments of interest made on or after 6th April 1988 unless—

(*a*) the deceased died before that date, and
(*b*) the land, caravan or house-boat was used as the only or main residence of the dependent relative before that date.

(5) Where it is proved by written evidence that a loan made on or after 6th April 1988 was made in pursuance of an offer made by the lender before that date and that the offer either was in writing or was evidenced by a note or memorandum made by the lender before that date, the loan shall be deemed for the purposes of this section to have been made before that date.

(6) Interest paid by a housing association shall not be relevant loan interest for the purposes of Part IX of the Taxes Act 1988 where by virtue of this section it would not be relevant loan interest if paid by a member of the association; and in this subsection "housing association" means a housing association for the time being approved for the purposes of section 488 of that Act or a self-build society for the time being approved for the purposes of section 489.

Benefits in kind

47. Entertainment: non-cash vouchers

(1) In section 141 of the Taxes Act 1988 (non-cash vouchers), after subsection (6A) there shall be inserted—

"(6B) Subsection (1) above shall not apply in relation to any non-cash voucher to the extent that it is used to obtain entertainment (including hospitality of any kind) for the employee or a relation of his, if—

(*a*) the person providing the non-cash voucher is neither his employer nor a person connected with his employer;
(*b*) neither his employer nor a person connected with his employer has directly or indirectly procured the provision of the entertainment; and
(*c*) the entertainment is not provided either in recognition of particular services which have been performed by him in the course of his employment or in anticipation of particular services which are to be so performed by him;

and section 839 shall apply for determining whether persons are connected for the purposes of this subsection."

(2) In subsection (1) of section 36 of the Finance (No. 2) Act 1975 (vouchers other than cash vouchers), for the words "Subject to subsection (2) below" there shall be substituted the words "Subject to the provisions of this section".

(3) The provision set out in subsection (1) above shall be inserted after subsection (3A) of that section as subsection (3B) with the substitution—

(*a*) for the reference to section 839 of the Taxes Act 1988 of a reference to section 533 of the Taxes Act 1970; and
(*b*) for any reference to a non-cash voucher of a reference to a voucher.

(4) The amendment made by subsection (1) above shall have effect for the year 1988–89 and subsequent years of assessment; and the amendments made by subsections (2) and (3) above shall have effect for the year 1987–88.

48. Entertainment: credit tokens

(1) In section 142 of the Taxes Act 1988 (credit-tokens), after subsection (3A) there shall be inserted—

"(3B) Subsection (1) above shall not apply in relation to any credit-token to the extent that it is used to obtain entertainment (including hospitality of any kind) for the employee or a relation of his, if—

    (a) the person providing the credit-token is neither his employer nor a person connected with his employer;
    (b) neither his employer nor a person connected with his employer has directly or indirectly procured the provision of the entertainment; and
    (c) the entertainment is not provided either in recognition of particular services which have been performed by him in the course of his employment or in anticipation of particular services which are to be so performed by him;

and section 839 shall apply for determining whether persons are connected for the purposes of this subsection."

(2) The provision set out in subsection (1) above shall be inserted after subsection (3) of section 36A of the Finance (No. 2) Act 1975 (credit-tokens) as subsection (3A) with the substitution for the reference to section 839 of the Taxes Act 1988 of a reference to section 533 of the Taxes Act 1970.

(3) The amendment made by subsection (1) above shall have effect for the year 1988–89 and subsequent years of assessment; and the amendment made by subsection (2) above shall have effect for the year 1987–88.

49. Entertainment of directors and higher-paid employees

(1) At the end of section 155 of the Taxes Act 1988 (benefits in kind for persons in director's or higher-paid employment: exceptions from the general charge) there shall be added—

"(7) Section 154 does not apply to a benefit consisting in the provision of entertainment (including hospitality of any kind) for the employee, or for members of his family or household, if—

    (a) the person providing the benefit is neither his employer nor a person connected with his employer;
    (b) neither his employer nor a person connected with his employer has directly or indirectly procured its provision; and
    (c) it is not provided either in recognition of particular services which have been performed by the employee in the course of his employment or in anticipation of particular services which are to be so performed by him;

and section 839 shall apply for determining whether persons are connected for the purposes of this subsection."

(2) The provision set out in subsection (1) above shall be added at the end of section 62 of the Finance Act 1976 as subsection (9) with the substitution—

    (a) for the reference to section 154 of the Taxes Act 1988 of a reference to section 61 of the 1976 Act; and
    (b) for the reference to section 839 of the Taxes Act 1988 of a reference to section 533 of the Taxes Act 1970.

(3) The amendment made by subsection (1) above shall have effect for the year 1988–89 and subsequent years of assessment; and the amendment made by subsection (2) above shall have effect for the year 1987–88.

Business expansion scheme

50. Private rented housing

(1) Where eligible shares in a company are issued for the purpose of raising money for qualifying activities—

    (a) which are being carried on by the company or any of its subsidiaries; or
    (b) which the company or any of its subsidiaries intends to carry on,

Chapter III of Part VII of the Taxes Act 1988 (relief for investment in new corporate trades: the business expansion scheme) shall apply in relation to the company with the modifications set out in Part I of Schedule 4 to this Act.

(2) In this section and Chapter III (as so modified) "qualifying activities", in relation to a company by which eligible shares are issued or any subsidiary of such a company, means activities which—

(*a*) consist of or are connected with the provision and maintenance of dwelling-houses to which this section applies which the company or subsidiary lets, or intends to let, on qualifying tenancies; and
(*b*) are, during the period beginning with the date on which the shares are issued and ending four years after that date, conducted on a commercial basis and with a view to the realisation of profits.

(3) This section applies to any dwelling-house which is not precluded from being a dwelling-house to which this section applies by Part II of Schedule 4 to this Act; and in this section and that Part of that Schedule—

(*a*) references to a company or subsidiary do not include references to a company or subsidiary which is a registered housing association within the meaning of the Housing Associations Act 1985 or Part VII of the Housing (Northern Ireland) Order 1981;
(*b*) "qualifying tenancy" means any tenancy which is—

(i) for the purposes of the Housing Act 1988, an assured tenancy other than an assured shorthold tenancy;
(ii) for the purposes of the Housing (Scotland) Act 1988, an assured tenancy other than a short assured tenancy; or
(iii) in Northern Ireland, a tenancy which complies with such requirements or conditions as may be prescribed by regulations made by the Department of the Environment for Northern Ireland,

and is not a tenancy which falls within subsection (4) below; and
(*c*) expressions which are also used in Chapter III have the same meanings as in that Chapter.

(4) A tenancy falls within this subsection if—

(*a*) it is a tenancy granted in consideration of a premium within the meaning of Schedule 3 to the Capital Gains Tax Act 1979; or
(*b*) any option to purchase in relation to the dwelling-house has been granted to the tenant or an associate of his;

and in this subsection any reference to the tenant includes, in the case of a joint tenancy, a reference to either or any of the joint tenants.

(5) Regulations under subsection (3) above shall be made by statutory rule for the purposes of the Statutory Rules (Northern Ireland) Order 1979 and shall be subject to negative resolution within the meaning of section 41(6) of the Interpretation Act (Northern Ireland) 1954.

(6) This section and Schedule 4 to this Act shall have effect in relation to shares issued after the passing of this Act and before the end of 1993.

51. Restriction of relief

(1) The Taxes Act 1988 shall have effect, and be deemed always to have had effect, with the following amendments, namely—

(*a*) in section 289(12)(*b*), the substitution of the words "sections 290A, 293" for the words "sections 293"; and
(*b*) the insertion after section 290 of the following section—

"290A. Restriction of relief where amounts raised exceed permitted maximum

(1) Where—

(*a*) a company raises any amount through the issue of eligible shares after 15th March 1988; and
(*b*) the aggregate of that amount and of all other amounts (if any) so raised within the period mentioned in subsection (2) below exceeds £500,000,

the relief shall not be given in respect of the excess.

(2) The period referred to in subsection (1) above is—

(*a*) the period of 6 months ending with the date of the issue of the shares; or
(*b*) the period beginning with the preceding 6th April and ending with the date of that issue,

whichever is the longer.

(3) In determining the aggregate mentioned in subsection (1) above, no account shall be taken of any amount—

(a) which is subscribed by a person other than an individual who qualifies for relief; or
(b) as respects which relief is precluded by section 290 or this section.

(4) Where—

(a) at any time within the relevant period, the company in question or any of its subsidiaries carries on any trade or part of a trade in partnership, or as a party to a joint venture, with one or more other persons; and
(b) that other person, or at least one of those other persons, is a company,

the reference to £500,000 in subsection (1) above shall have effect as if it were a reference to—

$$\frac{£500,000}{1+A,}$$

where A is the total number of companies (apart from the company in question or any of its subsidiaries) which, during the relevant period, are members of any such partnership or parties to any such joint venture.

(5) Where this section precludes the giving of relief on claims in respect of shares issued to two or more individuals, the available relief shall be divided between them in proportion to the amounts which have been respectively subscribed by them for the shares to which their claims relate and which would, apart from this section, be eligible for relief.

(6) Where—

(a) in the case of a company falling within subsection (2)(a) of section 293, the qualifying trade or each of the qualifying trades is a trade to which subsection (7) below applies;
(b) in the case of a company falling within subsection (2)(b)(i) of that section, the subsidiary or each of the subsidiaries is a dormant subsidiary or exists wholly, or substantially wholly, for the purpose of carrying on one or more qualifying trades which or each of which is a trade to which subsection (7) below applies; or
(c) in the case of a company falling within subsection (2)(b)(ii) of that section, the requirements mentioned in each of paragraphs (a) and (b) above are satisfied,

subsections (1) and (4) above shall have effect as if for the amount there specified there were substituted £5 million.

(7) This subsection applies to a trade if it consists, wholly or substantially wholly, of operating or letting ships, other than oil rigs or pleasure craft, and—

(a) every ship operated or let by the company carrying on the trade is beneficially owned by the company;
(b) every ship beneficially owned by the company is registered in the United Kingdom;
(c) throughout the relevant period the company is solely responsible for arranging the marketing of the services of its ships; and
(d) the conditions mentioned in section 297(7) are satisfied in relation to every letting by the company.

(8) Where—

(a) any of the requirements mentioned in paragraphs (a) to (c) of subsection (7) above are not satisfied in relation to any ships; or
(b) any of the conditions referred to in paragraph (d) of that subsection are not satisfied in relation to any lettings,

the trade shall not thereby be precluded from being a trade to which that subsection applies if the operation or letting of those ships, or, as the case may be, those lettings do not amount to a substantial part of the trade.

(9) The Treasury may by order amend any of the foregoing provisions of this section by substituting a different amount for the amount for the time being specified there.

(10) Where—

(a) the issue of the eligible shares is made in pursuance of a prospectus published, or an offer in writing made, before 15th March 1988;
(b) the shares are issued after that date and before 6th April 1988; and

(c) subsection (6) above does not apply,

subsections (1) and (4) above shall have effect as if for the amount there specified there were substituted £1 million.

(11) In this section—

"let" means let on charter and "letting" shall be construed accordingly;
"oil rig" and "pleasure craft" have the same meanings as in section 297;
"prospectus" has the meaning given by section 744 of the Companies Act 1985 or Article 2(3) of the Companies (Northern Ireland) Order 1986."

(2) Schedule 5 to the Finance Act 1983 shall be deemed always to have had effect as if—

(a) in paragraph 2(7), for the words "paragraph 5" there had been substituted the words "paragraphs 3A, 5"; and
(b) the provisions set out in subsection (1)(b) above had been inserted, with any necessary modifications, after paragraph 3 as paragraph 3A.

Pensions etc.

54. Personal pension schemes: commencement

(1) In section 56(1) of the Finance (No. 2) Act 1987 and section 655(4) of the Taxes Act 1988 (personal pension schemes not to be approved with effect from date earlier than 4th January 1988) for "4th January" there shall be substituted "1st July".

(2) In consequence of the amendment made by subsection (1) above—

(a) the same amendment shall be made in—

(i) section 54(1) of the Act of 1987 and section 618(1) of the Act of 1988 (no retirement annuity relief for contracts made or trust schemes established on or after 4th January 1988);
(ii) section 54(3) of the Act of 1987 and section 618(2) of the Act of 1988 (limit on lump sums under contracts made or schemes established before 4th January 1988); and
(iii) section 20(3) of the Act of 1987 and section 632(3) of the Act of 1988 (removal of restriction from certain schemes established before 4th January 1988);

(b) in section 55 of the Act of 1987 and section 655 of the Act of 1988 (transitional provisions: carry back and carry forward)—

(i) in subsection (2), for "1984–85, 1985–86 or 1986–87" there shall be substituted "1985–86, 1986–87 or 1987–88"; and
(ii) in subsection (3), for "1987–88" there shall be substituted "1988–89"; and

(c) in section 56(2) of the Act of 1987 and section 655(5) of the Act of 1988 (provisional approval where application made before 1st August 1989) for "August 1989" there shall be substituted "February 1990".

(3) The amendments made by this section shall be deemed always to have had effect.

57. Lump sum benefits paid otherwise than on retirement

(1) In section 14 of the Finance Act 1973 and section 189 of the Taxes Act 1988 (lump sum benefits paid on retirement not chargeable to income tax under Schedule E), for the words "on his retirement from an office or employment" there shall be substituted the words "(whether on his retirement from an office or employment or otherwise)".

(2) The amendment made by this section shall be deemed always to have had effect.

Underwriters

58. Assessment and collection

(1) For subsection (2) of section 450 of the Taxes Act 1988 (underwriters) there shall be substituted—

"(2) The aggregate for any year of assessment of—

(a) the profits or gains arising to a member from his underwriting business; and
(b) the profits or gains arising to him from assets forming part of a premiums trust fund,

shall be chargeable to tax under Case I of Schedule D; but nothing in this subsection shall affect the manner in which the amount of those profits or gains is to be computed.

(2A) Schedule 19A shall have effect with respect to the assessment and collection of tax charged under Case I of Schedule D in accordance with this section."

(2) Section 39 of the Finance Act 1973 shall be renumbered as subsection (1) of that section and after that provision as so renumbered there shall be inserted—

"(2) Schedule 16A to this Act shall have effect with respect to the assessment and collection of tax charged under Case I of Schedule D in accordance with Schedule 16 to this Act."

(3) In Schedule 16 to that Act (underwriters)—

(a) the subsection (2) set out in subsection (1) above shall be inserted after paragraph 2 as paragraph 2A; and
(b) paragraph 16 (assessment on agent) shall cease to have effect.

(4) The provisions set out in Schedule 5 to this Act shall be inserted—

(a) after Schedule 19 to the Taxes Act 1988 as Schedule 19A; and
(b) after Schedule 16 to the Finance Act 1973 as Schedule 16A.

(5) Subsections (1) and (4)(a) above shall have effect for the year 1988–89 and subsequent years of assessment; and subsections (2), (3) and (4)(b) above shall have effect for the years 1986–87 and 1987–88.

59. Reinsurance: general

(1) In subsection (4) of section 450 of the Taxes Act 1988 (underwriters), for paragraph (b) there shall be substituted—

"(b) any insurance money payable to him under that insurance in respect of a loss shall be taken into account as a trading receipt in computing those profits or gains for the year of assessment which corresponds to the underwriting year in which the loss arose;".

(2) The amendment set out in subsection (1) above shall also be made in paragraph 4 of Schedule 16 to the Finance Act 1973 (underwriters).

(3) Subsection (1) above shall have effect for the year 1988–89 and subsequent years of assessment; and subsection (2) above shall have effect for the years 1985–86, 1986–87 and 1987–88.

60. Reinsurance to close

(1) For subsection (5) of section 450 of the Taxes Act 1988 (underwriters) there shall be substituted—

"(5) Subsection (5A) below applies where—

(a) in accordance with the rules or practice of Lloyd's and in consideration of the payment of a premium, one member agrees with another to meet liabilities arising from the latter's business for an underwriting year so that the accounts of the business for that year may be closed; and
(b) the member by whom the premium is payable is a continuing member, that is, a member not only of the syndicate as a member of which he is liable to pay the premium ("the reinsured syndicate") but also of the syndicate as a member of which the other member is entitled to receive it ("the reinsurer syndicate").

(5A) In any case where this subsection applies—

(a) in computing for the purposes of income tax the profits or gains of the continuing member's business as a member of the reinsured syndicate, the amount of the premium shall be deductible as an expense of his only to the extent that it is shown not to exceed a fair and reasonable assessment of the value of the liabilities in respect of which it is payable; and
(b) in computing for those purposes the profits or gains of his business as a member of the reinsurer syndicate, those profits or gains shall be reduced by an amount equal to any part of a premium which, by virtue of paragraph (a) above, is not deductible as an expense of his as a member of the reinsured syndicate;

and the assessment referred to above shall be taken to be fair and reasonable only if it is arrived at with a view to producing the result that a profit does not accrue to the member to whom the premium is payable but that he does not suffer a loss."

(2) The provisions set out in subsection (1) above, but renumbered as subsections (1) and (2) and with the substitution, in the provision renumbered as subsection (1), of the words "subsection (2)" for the words "subsection (5A)", shall also be substituted for subsections (1) to (4) of section 70 of the Finance (No. 2) Act 1987 (underwriters); and in subsection (5) of that section, for the word "underwriter" there shall be substituted the word "member".

(3) In this section—

(*a*) subsection (1) shall have effect in relation to premiums payable in connection with the closing of accounts of a member's business for an underwriting year ending in the year 1988–89 or any subsequent year of assessment; and
(*b*) subsection (2) shall have effect in relation to premiums payable in connection with the closing of accounts of a member's business for an underwriting year ending in the year 1985–86, 1986–87, or 1987–88.

61. Minor and consequential amendments

(1) . . .

(2) In Schedule 10 to the Taxes Act 1970, in paragraph 7(3), for the words "Case I of Schedule D" there shall be substituted the words "in accordance with Schedule 16 to Finance Act 1973" and the words "the investments forming part of the premiums trust fund of the underwriter" shall cease to have effect.

(3) In section 87 of the Finance Act 1972, at the beginning of subsection (3) there shall be inserted the words "Except as provided by Schedule 16 to Finance Act 1973 (underwriters)".

(4) In Schedule 16 to the Finance Act 1973—

(*a*) in sub-paragraph (1) of paragraph 17, for paragraph (*a*) there shall be substituted—

"(*a*) for the assessment and collection of tax charged in accordance with the preceding provisions of this Schedule (so far as not provided for by Schedule 16A to this Act);
(*aa*) for making, in the event of any changes in the rules or practice of Lloyd's, such amendments of that Schedule as appear to the Board to be expedient having regard to those changes;";

(*b*) after that sub-paragraph, there shall be inserted—

"(1A) Regulations under this paragraph may make provision with respect to the year of assessment next but one preceding the year of assessment in which they are made."

(5) Subsection (1) above shall have effect for the year 1988–89 and subsequent years of assessment; and subsections (2) to (4) above shall have effect for the years 1986–87 and 1987–88.

Note.—Sub-s. (1) amends TA 1988, ss. 20, 451, 452.

Oil licences

62. Disposals of oil licences relating to undeveloped areas

(1) If, at the time of the material disposal of a licence, the licence relates to an undeveloped area, then, to the extent that the consideration for the disposal consists of—

(*a*) another licence which at that time relates to an undeveloped area or an interest in another such licence, or
(*b*) an obligation to undertake exploration work or appraisal work in an area which is or forms part of the licensed area in relation to the licence disposed of,

the value of that consideration shall be treated as nil for the purposes of the Capital Gains Tax Act 1979 (in this section referred to as "the 1979 Act") and the appropriate legislation relating to capital allowances.

(2) For the purposes of this section a "material disposal" is a disposal (which includes a part disposal) which occurred or occurs before or after the passing of this Act, other than,—

(*a*) so far as concerns the 1979 Act, a disposal which is made otherwise than by way of a bargain at arm's length; and
(*b*) so far as concerns the appropriate legislation relating to capital allowances, a disposal in relation to which Schedule 7 to the Capital Allowances Act 1968 (sales between connected persons etc.) has effect.

(3) If a material disposal of a licence which, at the time of the disposal, relates to an undeveloped area is part of a larger transaction under which one party makes to another material disposals of two or more licences, each of which at the time of the disposal relates to an undeveloped area, the reference in subsection (1)(*b*) above to the licensed area in relation to the licence disposed of shall be construed as a reference to the totality of the licensed areas in relation to those two or more licences.

(4) Where a claim is made under section 68(5)(*b*) of the Finance Act 1985 (claims to substitute, for indexation purposes, a 1982 market value for cost on certain disposals between 1st April 1985 and 5th April 1988) for the purpose of computing the indexation allowance on a material disposal of a licence which, at the time of the disposal, relates to an undeveloped area and, accordingly, it is assumed for that purpose that, on 31st March 1982, the licence concerned was sold and immediately reacquired, then, for that purpose, section 34 of the 1979 Act (effect of capital allowances on allowable expenditure) shall apply in relation to any capital allowance—

(*a*) made in respect of the expenditure actually incurred in providing the licence, and
(*b*) so made for an accounting period ending on or after 1st April 1982,

as if the allowance (or, if the accounting period begins before that date, a time-apportioned part of the allowance) were made in respect of expenditure which, on that assumption, was incurred in reacquiring the asset on 31st March 1982.

(5) In relation to a material disposal of a licence which at the time of the disposal relates to an undeveloped area, being a disposal—

(*a*) which is a part disposal of the licence in question, and
(*b*) part but not the whole of the consideration for which falls within paragraph (*a*) or paragraph (*b*) of subsection (1) above,

section 35 of the 1979 Act (apportionment of expenditure etc. on part disposals) shall not apply unless the amount or value of the part of the consideration which does not fall within one of those paragraphs is less than the aggregate of the amounts which, if the material disposal were a disposal of the whole of the licence rather than a part disposal, would be—

(i) the relevant allowable expenditure, as defined in section 86 of the Finance Act 1982 (indexation allowance on certain disposals); and
(ii) the indexation allowance on the disposal.

(6) Where section 35 of the 1979 Act has effect in relation to such a disposal as is referred to in subsection (5) above, it shall have effect as if, for subsection (2) thereof, there were substituted the following subsection—

"(2) The apportionment shall be made by reference to—

(*a*) the amount or value of the consideration for the disposal on the one hand (call that amount or value A), and
(*b*) the aggregate referred to in subsection (5) of section 62 of the Finance Act 1988 on the other hand (call that aggregate C),

and the fraction of the said sums allowable as a deduction in computing the amount of the gain (if any) accruing on the disposal shall be—

$$\frac{A}{C},$$

and the remainder shall be attributed to the part of the property which remains undisposed of."

(7) In the case of a material disposal—

(*a*) which falls within subsection (5) above, and
(*b*) in respect of which a claim is made under section 68(5)(*b*) of the Finance Act 1985,

the claim shall be treated also as having effect for the purpose of determining the indexation allowance referred to in sub-paragraph (ii) of subsection (5) above on the notional material disposal of the whole of the licence referred to in that subsection.

63. Allowance of certain drilling expenditure etc. in determining chargeable gains

(1) On the disposal of a licence, whether occurring before or after the passing of this Act, relevant qualifying expenditure incurred by the person making the disposal—

(*a*) in searching for oil anywhere in the licensed area, or (*b*) in ascertaining the extent or characteristics of any oil-bearing area the whole or part of which lies in the licensed area or what the reserves of oil of any such oil-bearing area are,

shall be treated as expenditure falling within section 32(1)(*b*) of the Capital Gains Tax Act 1979 (enhancement expenditure reflected in the state or nature of the asset at the time of disposal).

(2) Expenditure incurred as mentioned in subsection (1) above is relevant expenditure if, and only if,—

(*a*) it is expenditure of a capital nature on scientific research; and
(*b*) either it was allowed or allowable under section 91 of the Capital Allowances Act 1968 (capital expenditure on scientific research) for a chargeable period which, or the basis year for which, began before the date of the disposal or it would have been so allowable if the trading condition had been fulfilled; and
(*c*) the disposal is an occasion by virtue of which section 92 of that Act (termination of user of assets representing scientific research expenditure of a capital nature) applies in relation to the expenditure or would apply if the trading condition had been fulfilled and the expenditure had been allowed accordingly.

(3) In subsection (2) above and subsection (4) below, the expression "if the trading condition had been fulfilled" means, in relation to expenditure of a capital nature on scientific research, if, after the expenditure was incurred but before the disposal concerned was made, the person incurring the expenditure had set up and commenced a trade connected with that research; and in subsection (2)(*b*) above—

(*a*) "chargeable period" has the same meaning as in section 91 of the Capital Allowances Act 1968; and
(*b*) "basis year" has the same meaning as in subsection (3)(*c*) of that section.

(4) Relevant expenditure is qualifying expenditure only to the extent that it does not exceed the trading receipt which, by reason of the disposal,—

(*a*) is treated as accruing under section 92(2) of the Capital Allowances Act 1968; or
(*b*) would be treated as so accruing if the trading condition had been fulfilled and the expenditure had been allowed accordingly.

(5) On the disposal of a licence, sections 31 and 34 of the Capital Gains Tax Act 1979 (which include provisions under which set off is given for balancing charges) shall apply in relation to any such trading receipt as is mentioned in subsection (4)(*a*) above as if it were a balancing charge falling to be made by reference to the disposal.

(6) Where, on the disposal of a licence, subsection (1) above has effect in relation to any relevant qualifying expenditure which had not in fact been allowed or become allowable as mentioned in subsection (2)(*b*) above,—

(*a*) no allowance shall be made in respect of that expenditure under section 91 of the Capital Allowances Act 1968; and
(*b*) no deduction shall be allowed in respect of it under section 92(3) of that Act.

(7) Where, on the disposal of a licence which is a part disposal, subsection (1) above has effect in relation to any relevant qualifying expenditure, then, for the purposes of section 35 of the Capital Gains Tax Act 1979 (part disposals), that expenditure shall be treated as wholly attributable to what is disposed of (and, accordingly, shall not be apportioned as mentioned in that section).

64. Interpretation of sections 62 and 63

(1) For the purposes of section 62 above, a licence relates to an undeveloped area at any time if—

(*a*) for no part of the licensed area has consent for development been granted to the licensee by the Secretary of State on or before that time; and
(*b*) for no part of the licensed area has a programme of development been served on the licensee or approved by the Secretary of State on or before that time.

(2) Subsections (4) and (5) of section 36 of the Finance Act 1983 (meaning of "development") shall have effect in relation to subsection (1) above as they have effect in relation to subsection (2) of that section.

(3) In relation to a licence under the Petroleum (Production) Act (Northern Ireland) 1964

any reference in subsection (1) above to the Secretary of State shall be construed as a reference to the Department of Economic Development.

(4) In relation to a material disposal, within the meaning of section 62 above, of a licence under which the buyer acquires an interest in the licence only so far as it relates to part of the licensed area, any reference in subsection (1) or subsection (3) of that section or subsection (1) above to the licensed area shall be construed as a reference only to that part of the licensed area to which the buyer's acquisition relates.

(5) In sections 62 and 63 above and the preceding provisions of this section "oil", "licence", "licensee" and, subject to subsection (4) above, "licensed area" have the meaning assigned by section 12(1) of the Oil Taxation Act 1975.

(6) In section 62 above—

(a) "exploration work", in relation to any area, means work carried out for the purpose of searching for oil anywhere in that area;
(b) "appraisal work", in relation to any area, means work carried out for the purpose of ascertaining the extent or characteristics of any oil-bearing area the whole or part of which lies in the area concerned or what the reserves of oil of any such oil-bearing area are;
(c) "the appropriate legislation relating to capital allowances" means—

(i) Chapter III of Part I and Part II of the Capital Allowances Act 1968; and
(ii) section 55 of and Schedules 13 and 14 to the Finance Act 1986 (new code of allowances for capital expenditure on mineral extraction); and

(d) any reference to section 68(5)(b) of the Finance Act 1985 is a reference to that section as it had effect before the amendment made by Schedule 8 to this Act.

Miscellaneous

65. Commercial woodlands

Schedule 6 to this Act (which abolishes the charge to tax under Schedule B and makes other provision with respect to the occupation of commercial woodlands) shall have effect.

66. Company residence

(1) Subject to the provisions of Schedule 7 to this Act, a company which is incorporated in the United Kingdom shall be regarded for the purposes of the Taxes Acts as resident there; and accordingly, if a different place of residence is given by any rule of law, that place shall no longer be taken into account for those purposes.

(2) For the purposes of the Taxes Acts, a company which—

(a) is no longer carrying on any business; or
(b) is being wound up outside the United Kingdom,

shall be regarded as continuing to be resident in the United Kingdom if it was so regarded for those purposes immediately before it ceased to carry on business or, as the case may be, before any of its activities came under the control of a person exercising functions which, in the United Kingdom, would be exercisable by a liquidator.

(3) In this section "the Taxes Acts" has the same meaning as in the Taxes Management Act 1970.

(4) This section and Schedule 7 to this Act shall be deemed to have come into force on 15th March 1988.

68. Priority share allocations for employees etc.

(1) Where—

(a) there is an offer to the public of shares in a company at a fixed price or by tender, and
(b) a director or employee (whether of that company or of any other company or person) is entitled by reason of his office or employment to an allocation of the shares, in priority to members of the public, . . .[3], and
(c) the conditions set out in subsection (2) below are satisfied,

any benefit derived by the director or employee from his entitlement shall not be treated as an emolument of his office or employment.

[(1A) Where the price payable by the director or employee is less than the fixed price or the lowest price successfully tendered, subsection (1) above shall not apply to the benefit represented by the difference in price.]¹

(2) The conditions referred to in subsection (1) above are—

[(*a*) that the aggregate number of shares subject to the offer that may be allocated as mentioned in subsection (1)(*b*) above does not exceed the limit specified in subsection (2A) below or, as the case may be, either of the limits specified in subsection (2B) below]²;
(*b*) that all the persons entitled to such an allocation are entitled to it on similar terms;
(*c*) that those persons are not restricted wholly or mainly to persons who are directors or whose remuneration exceeds a particular level.

[(2A) Except where subsection (2B) below applies, the limit relevant for the purposes of subsection (2)(*a*) above is 10 per cent. of the shares subject to the offer (including the shares that may be allocated as mentioned in subsection (1)(*b*) above).]¹

(2B) Where the offer is part of arrangements which include one or more other offers to the public of shares of the same class, the limits relevant for the purposes of subsection (2)(*a*) above are—

(*a*) 40 per cent. of the shares subject to the offer (including the shares that may be allocated as mentioned in subsection (1)(*b*) above), and
(*b*) 10 per cent. of all the shares of the class in question (including the shares that may be so allocated) that are subject to any of the offers forming part of the arrangements.]¹

(3) For the purposes of subsection (2)(*b*) above the fact that different provision is made for persons according to the levels of their remuneration, the length of their service or similar factors shall not be regarded as meaning that they are not entitled to an allocation on similar terms.

(4) Section 29A(1) of the Capital Gains Tax Act 1979 (assets deemed to be acquired at market value) shall not apply to any acquisition in relation to which subsection (1) above applies.

(5) In this section "director" includes a person who is to be, or has ceased to be, a director and "employee" includes a person who is to be, or has ceased to be, an employee.

(6) This section shall apply to offers made on or after 23rd September 1987.

Amendments.—¹ Sub-ss. (1A), (2A), (2B) inserted by FA 1989, s. 66 in relation to offers made after 10 October 1988.
² Sub-s. (2)(*a*) substituted by *ibid*.
³ Words in sub-s. (1) repealed by *ibid* and Sch. 17, Pt. IV in relation to offers made after 10 October 1988.

69. Share options: loans

(1) . . .

(2) Paragraph 10 of Schedule 10 to the Finance Act 1984 (approved share option schemes: cases where scheme shares are subject to restrictions) shall be deemed always to have had effect with the addition of the following sub-paragraph after sub-paragraph (2)—

"(3) Sub-paragraph (1) above does not apply in relation to any terms of a loan making provision about how it is to be repaid or the security to be given for it."

Note.—Sub-s. (1) amends TA 1988, Sch. 9, para. 13.

72. Entertainment of overseas customers

(1) Subsection (2) of section 577 of the Taxes Act 1988 (which excepts the entertainment of overseas customers from the general rule that entertainment expenses are not deductible for tax purposes) shall not have effect in relation to entertainment provided on or after 15th March 1988.

(2) Subsection (1) above shall not apply where the expenses incurred or the assets used in providing the entertainment were incurred or used under a contract entered into before 15th March 1988.

73. Consideration for certain restrictive undertakings

(1) . . .

(2) Notwithstanding anything in section 74 of the Taxes Act 1988, any sum to which section 313 of that Act applies, and which is paid or treated as paid by a person carrying on a trade,

profession or vocation, may be deducted as an expense in computing the profits or gains of the trade, profession or vocation for the purposes of tax.

(3) Any sum to which section 313 of the Taxes Act 1988 applies, and which is paid or treated as paid by an investment company, shall for the purposes of section 75 of that Act be treated as an expense of management.

(4) This section has effect in relation to sums paid or treated as paid in respect of the giving of, or the total or partial fulfilment of, undertakings given on or after 9th June 1988.

Notes.—Sub-s. (1) amends TA 1988, s. 313.

CHAPTER II

UNAPPROVED EMPLOYEE SHARE SCHEMES

Preliminary

77. Scope of Chapter

(1) Subject to subsections (2) and (3) below, this Chapter shall apply where, on or after 26th October 1987, a person acquires shares or an interest in shares in a company in pursuance of a right conferred on him or an opportunity offered to him by reason of his office as a director of, or his employment by, that or any other company.

(2) This Chapter shall not apply in relation to an acquisition by a person who is not chargeable to tax under Case I of Schedule E in respect of the office or employment in question.

(3) This Chapter shall not apply where the acquisition is made in pursuance of an offer to the public.

Charges to tax

78. Charge where restrictions removed etc.

(1) The person acquiring the shares or interest in shares shall be chargeable to tax if—

(*a*) a chargeable event occurs in relation to the shares at a time when he has not ceased to have a beneficial interest in them, and
(*b*) the shares are shares in a company which was not a dependent subsidiary at the time of the acquisition and is not a dependent subsidiary at the time of the chargeable event.

(2) Subject to subsections (4) and (5) below, any of the following events is a chargeable event in relation to shares in a company for the purposes of this section if it increases, or but for the occurrence of some other event would increase, the value of the shares—

(*a*) the removal or variation of a restriction to which the shares are subject;
(*b*) the creation or variation of a right relating to the shares;
(*c*) the imposition of a restriction on other shares in the company or the variation of a restriction to which such other shares are subject;
(*d*) the removal or variation of a right relating to other shares in the company.

(3) A charge by virtue of this section shall be a charge under Schedule E, for the year of assessment in which the chargeable event occurs, on the amount by which the value of the shares is increased by the chargeable event or the amount by which it would be increased but for the occurrence of some other event (or, if the interest of the person chargeable is less than full beneficial ownership, on an appropriate part of that amount).

(4) An event is not a chargeable event in relation to shares in a company for the purposes of this section unless the person who acquired the shares or interest has been a director or employee of—

(*a*) that company, or
(*b*) (if it is different) the company as a director or employee of which he acquired the shares or interest, or
(*c*) an associated company of a company within paragraph (*a*) or (*b*) above,

at some time during the period of seven years ending with the date on which the event occurs.

(5) An event is not a chargeable event for the purposes of this section if it consists of—

(*a*) the removal of a restriction to which all shares of a class are subject from all those shares,
(*b*) the variation of such a restriction in the case of all those shares,
(*c*) the creation of a right relating to all shares of a class,
(*d*) the variation of such a right in the case of all those shares,
(*e*) the imposition of a restriction on all shares of a class, or
(*f*) the removal of a right relating to all shares of a class from all those shares,

and any of the conditions in subsection (6) below is satisfied.

(6) The conditions referred to in subsection (5) above are—

(a) that at the time of the event the majority of the company's shares of the same class as those which, or an interest in which, the person acquired are held otherwise than by or for the benefit of—
    (i) directors or employees of the company,
    (ii) an associated company of the company, or
    (iii) directors or employees of any such associated company;

(b) that at the time of the event the company is employee-controlled by virtue of holdings of shares of that class;

(c) that at the time of the event the company is a subsidiary which is not a dependent subsidiary and its shares are of a single class.

(7) References in this section to restrictions to which shares are subject, or to rights relating to shares, include references to restrictions imposed or rights conferred by any contract or arrangement or in any other way.

79. Charge for shares in dependent subsidiaries

(1) The person acquiring the shares or interest in shares shall be chargeable to tax if the shares are shares in a company which—

(a) was a dependent subsidiary at the time of the acquisition, or

(b) was not a dependent subsidiary at that time but becomes a dependent subsidiary before the person making the acquisition ceases to have any beneficial interest in the shares,

and there is a chargeable increase in the value of the shares.

(2) There is a chargeable increase in the value of shares in a case within subsection (1)(a) above if the value of the shares at the earlier of—

(a) the expiration of seven years from the time of the acquisition, and

(b) the time when the person making the acquisition ceases to have any beneficial interest in the shares,

exceeds their value at the time of the acquisition.

(3) Subject to subsection (7) below, there is a chargeable increase in the value of shares in a case within subsection (1)(b) above if the value of the shares at the earlier or earliest of—

(a) the expiration of seven years from the time when the company becomes a dependent subsidiary, and

(b) the time when the person making the acquisition ceases to have any beneficial interest in the shares, and

(c) if the company ceases to be a dependent subsidiary, the time when it does so,

exceeds their value at the time when the company becomes a dependent subsidiary.

(4) A charge by virtue of this section shall be a charge under Schedule E, for the year of assessment which includes the end of the period for which the chargeable increase is determined, on an amount equal to that increase (or, if the interest of the person chargeable is less than full beneficial ownership, on an appropriate part of that amount).

(5) Where, in accordance with the terms on which the acquisition was made, the consideration for the acquisition is subsequently increased, the amount chargeable to tax by virtue of this section shall be reduced by an amount equal to the increase in the consideration.

(6) Where, in accordance with those terms, the person making the acquisition subsequently ceases to have a beneficial interest in the shares by a disposal made for a consideration which is less than the value of the shares or his interest in them at the time of the disposal, the amount on which tax is chargeable by virtue of this section shall be reduced so as to be equal to the excess of that consideration over the value of the shares or interest at the time of the acquisition.

(7) In a case within subsection (1)(b) above there is no chargeable increase in the value of shares in a company unless the person who acquired the shares or interest has been a director or employee of—

(a) that company, or

(b) (if it is different) the company as a director or employee of which he acquired the shares or interest, or

(c) an associated company of a company within paragraph (a) or (b) above,

at some time during the period of seven years ending with the time when the company becomes a dependent subsidiary.

80. Charge on special benefits

(1) Subject to subsections (5) and (6) below, the person acquiring the shares or interest in shares shall be chargeable to tax if he receives a special benefit by virtue of his ownership of or interest in the shares.

(2) A benefit is a "special benefit" for the purposes of subsection (1) above unless—

(a) it is received in respect of all shares of the same class as those which, or an interest in which, the person acquired, and
(b) any of the conditions in subsection (3) below is satisfied.

(3) The conditions referred to in subsection (2) above are—

(a) that when the benefit is received the majority of the company's shares of the class concerned are held otherwise than by or for the benefit of—

(i) directors or employees of the company,
(ii) an associated company of the company, or
(iii) directors or employees of any such associated company;

(b) that when the benefit is received the company is employee-controlled by virtue of holdings of shares of the class concerned;
(c) that when the benefit is received the company is a subsidiary which is not a dependent subsidiary and its shares are of a single class.

(4) A charge by virtue of this section shall be a charge under Schedule E, for the year of assessment in which the benefit is received, on an amount equal to the value of the benefit.

(5) Subsection (1) above shall apply only if the person receiving the benefit has been a director or employee of—

(a) the company referred to in that subsection, or
(b) (if it is different) the company as a director or employee of which he acquired the shares or interest, or
(c) an associated company of a company within paragraph (a) or (b) above,

at some time during the period of seven years ending with the date on which the benefit is received.

(6) A benefit shall not be chargeable by virtue of this section if it is chargeable to income tax apart from this section.

Miscellaneous

81. Changes in interest

Where a person's interest in shares is increased or reduced he shall be treated for the purposes of this Chapter as acquiring or disposing of a separate interest proportionate to the increase or reduction.

82. Company reorganisations etc.

(1) Subsection (2) below applies where—

(a) a person has acquired shares or an interest in shares as mentioned in section 77 above (those shares being referred to in subsection (2) below as "the originally-acquired shares"); and
(b) by virtue of his holding of those shares or the interest in them he acquires (whether or not for consideration) additional shares or an interest in additional shares (those shares being referred to in subsection (2) below as "the additional shares").

(2) Where this subsection applies—

(a) the additional shares or the interest in them shall be treated for the purposes of this Chapter as having been acquired as mentioned in section 77 above and as having been acquired at the same time as the originally-acquired shares or the interest in them;
(b) for the purposes of section 79 above, the additional shares and the originally-acquired

shares shall be treated as one holding of shares and the value of the shares comprised in that holding at any time shall be determined accordingly (the value of the originally-acquired shares at the time of acquisition being attributed proportionately to all the shares in the holding); and

(c) for the purposes of that section, any consideration given for the acquisition of the additional shares or the interest in them shall be taken to be an increase falling within subsection (5) of that section in the consideration for the original acquisition.

(3) If, on a person ceasing to have a beneficial interest in any shares, he acquires other shares or an interest in other shares and the circumstances are such that, for the purposes of sections 78 to 81 of the Capital Gains Tax Act 1979 (reorganisations etc.) the shares in which he ceases to have a beneficial interest constitute "original shares" and the other shares constitute a "new holding"—

(a) section 78 of that Act (which equates the original shares and the new holding) shall apply for the purposes of this Chapter; and
(b) if any such consideration is given for the new holding as is mentioned in section 79(1) of that Act, it shall be treated for the purposes of this Chapter as an increase falling within section 79(5) above in the consideration for the shares; and
(c) if any such consideration is received for the disposal of the original shares as is mentioned in section 79(2) of that Act, the consideration shall be apportioned among the shares comprised in the new holding and the amount which, apart from this paragraph, would at any subsequent time be the value of any of those shares shall be taken to be increased by the amount of the consideration apportioned to them.

83. Connected persons etc.

(1) For the purposes of this Chapter, where a person acquires shares or an interest in shares in a company in pursuance of a right conferred on him or opportunity offered to him as a person connected with a director or employee of that or any other company, the shares or interest shall be deemed to be acquired by the director or employee.

(2) For the purposes of this Chapter, where a person who acquires shares or an interest in shares disposes of the shares or interest otherwise than by a bargain at arm's length with a person who is not connected with him, he shall be deemed to continue to have a beneficial interest in the shares until there is a disposal of the shares or interest by such a bargain.

(3) Subsection (2) above shall not apply where shares, or an interest in shares, in a company are disposed of to the company in accordance with the terms on which the acquisition was made.

(4) Where a person who has made an acquisition as mentioned in subsection (1) above receives a benefit in the circumstances described in section 80 above, the benefit shall be treated for the purposes of that section as received by the person deemed by that subsection to have made the acquisition; and where at a time when a person is deemed by subsection (2) above to continue to have a beneficial interest in shares another person receives a benefit in such circumstances, the benefit shall be treated for those purposes as received by him.

84. Capital gains tax

Where an amount is chargeable to tax under this Chapter on a person who acquires shares or an interest in shares, then on the first disposal of the shares (whether by him or another person) after his acquisition, section 32(1)(a) of the Capital Gains Tax Act 1979 (expenditure allowable in computation of chargeable gains) shall apply as if a sum equal to the amount chargeable had formed part of the consideration given by the person making the disposal for his acquisition of the shares; and this section shall apply with the appropriate modifications in a case to which section 83 above applies.

85. Information

(1) Where in any year of assessment a person acquires shares, or an interest in shares, in a company in the circumstances described in section 77(1) above, that company and (if it is different) the company as a director or employee of which he acquires the shares or interest shall give written particulars of the acquisition to the inspector within 30 days of the end of the year.

(2) Where—

(a) there occurs in relation to shares in a company an event which is a chargeable event for the purposes of section 78 above, or

(b) a person receives a special benefit (within the meaning given for the purposes of section 80(1) above) in respect of shares, or an interest in shares, in a company,

the company, and (if it is different) the company as a director or employee of which the person who acquired the shares or an interest in the shares made the acquisition, shall within 60 days give to the inspector written particulars of the event or benefit and of the shares concerned.

(3) ...

Note.—Sub-s. (3) amends TMA 1970, s. 98.

Supplementary

86. Meaning of "dependent subsidiary"

(1) For the purposes of this Chapter a company which is a subsidiary is a dependent subsidiary throughout a period of account of the company unless—

(a) the whole or substantially the whole of the company's business during the period of account (taken as a whole) is business carried on with persons who are not members of the same group as the company,
(b) during the period of account either there is no increase in the value of the company as a result of intra-group transactions, or any such increase in value does not exceed 5 per cent. of the value of the company at the beginning of the period (or a proportionately greater or smaller percentage in the case of a period which is longer or shorter than a year),
(c) the directors of the principal company of the group give to the inspector, not later than two years after the end of the period of account, a certificate that in their opinion the conditions mentioned in paragraphs (a) and (b) above are satisfied in relation to the period of account, and
(d) there is attached to the certificate a report addressed to those directors by the auditors of the subsidiary that the auditors—

(i) have enquired into the state of affairs of the company with particular reference to the conditions mentioned in paragraphs (a) and (b) above, and
(ii) are not aware of anything to indicate that the opinion expressed by the directors in their certificate is unreasonable in all the circumstances.

(2) For the purposes of subsection (1)(a) above business carried on with any subsidiary of the company concerned shall be treated as carried on with a person who is not a member of the same group as the company unless the whole or substantially the whole of the business of that or any other subsidiary of the company during the company's period of account (taken as a whole) is carried on with members of the group other than the company and its subsidiaries.

(3) In this section—

"group" means a principal company and all its subsidiaries;
"intra-group transactions" means transactions between companies which are members of the same group on terms which are not such as might be expected to be agreed between persons acting at arm's length (other than any payment for group relief, within the meaning given in section 402(6) of the Taxes Act 1988);
"period of account", in relation to a company, means the period for which it makes up its accounts;
"principal company" means a company of which another company is a subsidiary and which is not itself a subsidiary of another company.

87. Other interpretation provisions

(1) In this Chapter, except where the context otherwise requires,—

"associated company" has the same meaning as, by virtue of section 416 of the Taxes Act 1988, it has for the purposes of Part XI of that Act;
"director" includes a person who is to be, or who has ceased to be, a director;
"employee" includes a person who is to be, or who has ceased to be, an employee;
"shares" includes stock and also includes securities as defined in section 254(1) of the Taxes Act 1988;
"subsidiary" means 51 per cent. subsidiary;
"value", in relation to shares or a benefit, means the amount which the person holding

the shares or receiving the benefit might reasonably expect to obtain from a sale in the open market;

and references to an interest in any shares include references to an interest in the proceeds of sale of part of the shares.

(2) For the purposes of this Chapter a company is "employee-controlled" by virtue of shares of a class if—

(a) the majority of the company's shares of that class (other than any held by or for the benefit of an associated company) are held by or for the benefit of employees or directors of the company or a company controlled by the company, and
(b) those directors and employees are together able as holders of the shares to control the company.

(3) Sections 839 (connected persons) and 840 (control) of the Taxes Act 1988 shall apply for the purposes of this Chapter.

(4) Where a right to acquire shares or an interest in shares in a company is assigned to a person and the right was conferred on some other person by reason of the assignee's office as a director of, or his employment by, that or any other company, the assignee shall be treated for the purposes of this Chapter as acquiring the shares or interest in pursuance of a right conferred on him by reason of that office or employment.

88. Transitional provisions

(1) Section 138 of the Taxes Act 1988 and section 79 of the Finance Act 1972 shall not apply to an acquisition of shares, or of an interest in shares, made on or after 26th October 1987.

(2) Where—

(a) tax is chargeable by virtue of section 138(1)(a) of the Taxes Act 1988 or section 79(4) of the Finance Act 1972 by reference to the market value, after 26th October 1987, of shares in a company which is not a dependent subsidiary on that date, and
(b) that market value is greater than the market value of the shares on 26th October 1987,

the amount on which tax is chargeable (and the question whether any tax is chargeable) shall be determined by reference to the market value on 26th October 1987 (and for this purpose "market value" has the same meaning as in section 138 of the Taxes Act 1988).

(3) Subject to subsection (4) below, this Chapter, with the omission of sections 79 and 80, shall have effect where shares, or an interest in shares, in a company which is not a dependent subsidiary on 26th October 1987 have been acquired before that date as it has effect (apart from this section) where shares or an interest in shares are acquired on or after that date.

(4) In relation to shares which were, or an interest in which was, acquired before 26th October 1987 the removal or variation of a restriction to which the shares are subject shall not be a chargeable event for the purposes of section 78 above if, because of paragraph 7 of Schedule 8 to the Finance Act 1973, the restriction would not have been regarded as one to which the shares were subject for the purposes of section 79(2)(c) of the Finance Act 1972.

89. Consequential amendments

In relation to acquisitions of shares or interests in shares on or after 26th October 1987—

(a) for the words from "section 138(1)(a)" to "value of the shares" in section 185(3)(a) (approved share option schemes) and section 186(2)(b) (approved profit sharing schemes) of the Taxes Act 1988, and
(b) for the words from "section 79(4)" to "value of the shares" in—

(i) section 53(3)(b) of the Finance Act 1978 (approved profit sharing schemes),
(ii) section 47(1)(b) of the Finance Act 1980 (savings-related share option schemes), and
(iii) section 38(3)(a) of the Finance Act 1984 (approved share option schemes),

there shall be substituted the words "section 78 or 79 of the Finance Act 1988 in respect of the shares".

CHAPTER III
CAPITAL ALLOWANCES

92. Successions to trades between connected persons

(1) For paragraph 13 of Schedule 8 to the Finance Act 1971 (successions to trades between connected persons) there shall be substituted—

"**13.**—(1) Where at any time a person ('the successor') succeeds to a trade which was until that time carried on by another person ('the predecessor') and—

  (*a*) the two persons are connected with each other;
  (*b*) each of them is within the charge to tax in the United Kingdom on the profits of the trade; and
  (*c*) the successor is not a dual resident investing company within the meaning of section 404 of the Taxes Act,

those persons may, by notice in writing given to the inspector not later than two years after that time, elect that the provisions of this paragraph shall have effect.

(2) In the event of such an election—

  (*a*) for the purpose of making allowances and charges under Chapter I of Part III of this Act, any machinery or plant which—

    (i) immediately before the time when the succession took place, belonged to the predecessor and was in use for the purposes of the trade; and
    (ii) immediately after that time, belonged to the successor and was in use for those purposes,

shall (notwithstanding any actual sale or transfer) be treated as sold by the predecessor to the successor at a price which does not give rise to a balancing allowance or a balancing charge; and
  (*b*) allowances and charges shall be made under that Chapter to or on the successor as if everything done to or by the predecessor had been done to or by the successor.

(3) The predecessor and the successor are connected with each other for the purposes of this paragraph if—

  (*a*) they are connected with each other within the meaning of section 839 of the Taxes Act;
  (*b*) one of them is a partnership and the other has the right to a share in that partnership;
  (*c*) one of them is a body corporate and the other has control over that body;
  (*d*) both of them are partnerships and some other person has the right to a share in both of them; or
  (*e*) both of them are bodies corporate, or one of them is a partnership and the other is a body corporate, and (in either case) some other person has control over both of them.

(4) All such assessments and adjustments of assessments shall be made as may be necessary to give effect to this paragraph.

(5) In this paragraph 'control' shall be construed in accordance with section 840 of the Taxes Act; and any reference to the right to a share in a partnership is a reference to the right to a share of the assets or income of that partnership."

(2) This section shall have effect in relation to successions occurring after the passing of this Act.

95. Dwelling-houses let on assured tenancies

(1) In relation to any capital expenditure which—

  (*a*) is expenditure on the construction of a building which is or includes a dwelling-house; and
  (*b*) is expenditure to which subsection (2) or (3) below applies,

Schedule 12 to the Finance Act 1982 (capital allowances for dwelling-houses let on assured tenancies) shall have effect, after the coming into force of Part I of the Housing Act 1988, as if any qualifying tenancy of the dwelling-house were an assured tenancy within the meaning of section 56 of the Housing Act 1980.

(2) This subsection applies to any expenditure incurred—

(a) by an approved company; or
(b) by a person who sells or sold the relevant interest in the building to an approved company before any of the dwelling-houses comprised in it are or were used,

if it is incurred before 15th March 1988 or consists of the payment of sums under a contract entered into before that date.

(3) This subsection applies to any expenditure incurred before 1st April 1992 by an approved company which, before 15th March 1988, bought or contracted to buy the relevant interest in the building.

(4) For the purposes of this section, "qualifying tenancy" means a tenancy (whenever created) which for the purposes of the Housing Act 1988 is an assured tenancy other than an assured shorthold tenancy.

(5) In this section—

(a) "approved company" means a company which was on 15th March 1988 an approved body; and
(b) expressions which are also used in Schedule 12 to the Finance Act 1982 have the same meanings as in that Schedule;

and paragraph 10 of that Schedule (expenditure on repair of buildings) shall apply for the purposes of this section as it applies for the purposes of that Schedule.

CHAPTER IV
CAPITAL GAINS

Re-basing to 1982

96. Assets held on 31st March 1982

(1) This section applies to a disposal on or after 6th April 1988 of an asset which was held on 31st March 1982 by the person making the disposal.

(2) Subject to the following provisions of this section, in computing for the purpose of capital gains tax the gain or loss accruing on the disposal it shall be assumed that the asset was on 31st March 1982 sold by the person making the disposal, and immediately re-acquired by him, at its market value on that date.

(3) Subject to subsection (5) below, subsection (2) above shall not apply to a disposal—

(*a*) where a gain would accrue on the disposal to the person making the disposal if that subsection did apply, and either a smaller gain or a loss would so accrue if it did not,
(*b*) where a loss would so accrue if that subsection did apply, and either a smaller loss or a gain would accrue if it did not,
(*c*) where, either on the facts of the case or by virtue of Schedule 5 to the Capital Gains Tax Act 1979, neither a gain nor a loss would accrue if that subsection did not apply, or
(*d*) where neither a gain nor a loss would accrue by virtue of any of the specified enactments.

(4) Where in the case of a disposal of an asset—

(*a*) the effect of subsection (2) above would be to substitute a loss for a gain or a gain for a loss, but
(*b*) the application of subsection (2) is excluded by subsection (3),

it shall be assumed in relation to the disposal that the asset was acquired by the person making the disposal for a consideration such that, on the disposal, neither a gain nor a loss accrues to him.

(5) If a person so elects, disposals made by him (including any made by him before the election) shall fall outside subsection (3) above (so that subsection (2) above is not excluded by that subsection).

(6) An election by a person under subsection (5) above shall be irrevocable and shall be made by notice in writing to the inspector at any time before 6th April 1990 or at any time during the period beginning with the day of the first relevant disposal and ending—

(*a*) two years after the end of the year of assessment or accounting period in which the disposal is made, or
(*b*) at such later time as the Board may allow;

and "the first relevant disposal" means the first disposal to which this section applies which is made by the person making the election.

(7) An election made by a person under subsection (5) above in one capacity does not cover disposals made by him in another capacity.

(8) All such adjustments shall be made, whether by way of discharge or repayment of tax, the making of assessments or otherwise, as are required to give effect to an election under subsection (5) above.

(9) Schedule 8 to this Act (which contains provisions supplementary to this section) shall have effect; and in subsection (3)(*d*) above "specified enactments" means the enactments specified in paragraph 1(3) of that Schedule.

Cross references.—See FA 1989, Sch. 15, para. 3(1)(*a*), (2) (reduction of 1982 value where sub-s. (2) above applies in relation to a disposal after 5 April 1989).

97. Deferred charges on gains before 31st March 1982

Schedule 9 to this Act (which provides for the reduction of a deferred charge to tax where the charge is wholly or partly attributable to an increase in the value of an asset before 31st March 1982) shall have effect.

Unification of rates of tax on income and capital gains

98. Rates of capital gains tax

(1) Subject to the provisions of this section and sections 99 and 100 below, the rate of capital gains tax in respect of gains accruing to a person in a year of assessment shall be equivalent to the basic rate of income tax for the year.

(2) If income tax is chargeable at the higher rate in respect of any part of the income of an individual for a year of assessment, the rate of capital gains tax in respect of gains accruing to him in the year shall be equivalent to the higher rate.

(3) If no income tax is chargeable at the higher rate in respect of the income of an individual for a year of assessment, but the amount on which he is chargeable to capital gains tax exceeds the unused part of his basic rate band, the rate of capital gains tax on the excess shall be equivalent to the higher rate of income tax for the year.

(4) The reference in subsection (3) above to the unused part of an individual's basic rate band is a reference to the amount by which the basic rate limit exceeds his total income (as reduced by any deductions made in accordance with the Income Tax Acts).

99. Husband and wife

(1) Where—
   (a) gains accrue to a woman in a year of assessment during which she is a married woman living with her husband, and
   (b) if her chargeable amount were added to, and constituted the highest part of, her husband's chargeable amount for the year, capital gains tax would be chargeable on it or any part of it at a rate equivalent to the higher rate of income tax for the year,
the rate of capital gains tax on her chargeable amount or that part of it shall be equivalent to the higher rate.

(2) For the purposes of this section a person's chargeable amount for a year of assessment is the amount on which he is (or would apart from section 45 of the Capital Gains Tax Act 1979 be) chargeable to capital gains tax for the year.

(3) In relation to a year of assessment for which an application under section 45(2) of the Capital Gains Tax Act 1979 (separate assessment) has effect, the amounts of tax payable by the husband and by the wife shall be determined by—
   (a) aggregating the amounts that would be payable by each of them apart from this subsection, and
   (b) dividing that aggregate between them in proportion to their chargeable amounts for the year.

(4) This section shall apply in relation to a part of a year of assessment, being a part beginning with 6th April, as it applies in relation to a whole year (except that references to a husband's chargeable amount are references to his chargeable amount for the whole year).

(5) This section shall have effect for the years 1988–89 and 1989–90 only.

Note.—See **Prospective Legislation Notes**.

100. Accumulation and discretionary settlements

(1) The rate of capital gains tax in respect of gains accruing to trustees of an accumulation or discretionary settlement in a year of assessment shall be equivalent to the sum of the basic and additional rates of income tax for the year.

(2) For the purposes of subsection (1) above a trust is an accumulation or discretionary settlement where—
   (a) all or any part of the income arising to the trustees in the year of assessment is income to which section 686 of the Taxes Act 1988 (liability to income tax at the additional rate) applies, or
   (b) all the income arising to the trustees in the year of assessment is treated as the income of the settlor, but that section would apply to it if it were not so treated, or
   (c) all the income arising to the trustees in the year of assessment is applied in defraying

expenses of the trustees in that year, but that section would apply to it if it were not so applied, or

(*d*) no income arises to the trustees in the year of assessment, but that section would apply if there were income arising to the trustees and none of it were treated as the income of the settlor or applied as mentioned in paragraph (*c*) above.

102. Other special cases

(1) References in section 98 above to income tax chargeable at the higher rate include references to tax chargeable by virtue of section 683(1) or 684(1) of the Taxes Act 1988 (settlements) in respect of excess liability (that is, liability to income tax over what it would be if all income tax were charged at the basic rate to the exclusion of any higher rate); and where for any year of assessment income is treated by virtue of either of those provisions as the income of a person for the purposes of excess liability then, whether or not he is chargeable to tax otherwise than at the basic rate, it shall also be treated as his income for the purposes of section 98(4) above.

(2) Where for any year of assessment—

(*a*) ...[1]

(*b*) by virtue of section 549(2) of that Act (gains under life policy or life annuity contract) a deduction of an amount is made from a person's total income for those purposes,

(*c*) by virtue of section 683(1) or 684(1) of that Act an amount of a person's income is treated as not being his income for those purposes, or

(*d*) by virtue of section 699(1) of that Act (income accruing before death) the residuary income of an estate is treated as reduced so as to reduce a person's income by any amount for the purposes of excess liability,

section 98(4) above shall have effect as if his income for the year were reduced by that amount.

(3) Where by virtue of section 547(1)(*a*) of that Act (gains from insurance policies etc.) a person's total income for a year of assessment is deemed to include any amount or amounts—

(*a*) section 98(4) above shall have effect as if his total income included not the whole of the amount or amounts concerned but only the appropriate fraction within the meaning of section 550(3), and

(*b*) if relief is given under section 550 of that Act and the calculation required by section 550(2)(*b*) does not involve the higher rate of income tax, section 98(2) and (3) above shall have effect as if no income tax were chargeable at the higher rate in respect of his income.

(4) Nothing in subsection (1) above shall be taken to reduce, and nothing in subsections (2) and (3) above shall be taken to increase, the amount of the deduction which a person is entitled to make from his total income by virtue of any provision of Chapter 1 of Part VII of the Taxes Act 1988 which limits any allowance by reference to the level of his total income.

Amendments.—[1] Sub-s. (2)(*a*) repealed by FA 1989, Sch. 17, Pt. V in relation to accounting periods beginning after 31 March 1989.

103. Commencement of sections 98 to 102

Subject to section 99(5) above, sections 98 to 102 above shall have effect for the year 1988–89 and subsequent years of assessment.

Married couples

104. Married couples

(1) In the Capital Gains Tax Act 1979—

(*a*) section 4(2) (losses of one spouse deductible from gains of other),

(*b*) section 45 (assessment and charge of wife's gains on husband), and

(*c*) paragraphs 2 and 3 of Schedule 1 (special rules for annual exemption in case of married couple),

shall cease to have effect.

(2) Subsection (1) above shall have effect in relation to the year 1990–91 and subsequent years of assessment.

(3) Where—

(*a*) a claim under section 13 of the Capital Gains Tax Act 1979 (enforced delay in remitting gains from disposals of foreign assets) is made by a man in respect of chargeable gains accruing to his wife before 6th April 1990, and

(b) by virtue of that section the amount of the gains falls to be assessed to capital gains tax as if it were an amount of gains accruing in the year 1990–91 or a subsequent year of assessment,

it shall be assessed not on the claimant (or his personal representatives) but on the person to whom the gains accrued (or her personal representatives).

Company migration

105. Deemed disposal of assets on company ceasing to be resident in U.K.

(1) This section and section 107 below apply to a company if, at any time ("the relevant time"), the company ceases to be resident in the United Kingdom otherwise than in pursuance of a Treasury consent.

(2) The company shall be deemed for all purposes of the Capital Gains Tax Act 1979—

(a) to have disposed of all its assets, other than assets excepted from this subsection by subsection (4) below, immediately before the relevant time; and
(b) immediately to have reacquired them,

at their market value at that time.

(3) Section 115 of the Capital Gains Tax Act 1979 (roll-over relief) shall not apply where the company—

(a) has disposed of the old assets, or of its interest in those assets, before the relevant time; and
(b) acquires the new assets, or its interest in those assets, after that time,

unless the new assets are excepted from this subsection by subsection (4) below.

(4) If at any time after the relevant time the company carries on a trade in the United Kingdom through a branch or agency—

(a) any assets which, immediately after the relevant time, are situated in the United Kingdom and are used in or for the purposes of the trade, or are used or held for the purposes of the branch or agency, shall be excepted from subsection (2) above; and
(b) any new assets which, after that time, are so situated and are so used or so held shall be excepted from subsection (3) above;

and references in this subsection to assets situated in the United Kingdom include references to exploration or exploitation assets and to exploration or exploitation rights.

(5) In this section—

"branch or agency" has the same meaning as in the Capital Gains Tax Act 1979;
"designated area", "exploration or exploitation activities" and "exploration or exploitation rights" have the same meanings as in section 38 of the Finance Act 1973;
"exploration or exploitation assets" means assets used or intended for use in connection with exploration or exploitation activities carried on in the United Kingdom or a designated area;
"the old assets" and "the new assets" have the same meanings as in section 115 of the 1979 Act;
"Treasury consent" means a consent under section 765 of the Taxes Act 1988 or section 482 of the Taxes Act 1970 (restrictions on the migration etc. of companies) given for the purposes of subsection (1)(a) of that section;

and a company shall not be regarded for the purposes of this section as ceasing to be resident in the United Kingdom by reason only that it ceases to exist.

(6) In section 765 of the Taxes Act 1988 and section 482 of the Taxes Act 1970, in subsection (1), paragraphs (a) and (b) shall cease to have effect and in paragraph (c) for the words "so resident" there shall be substituted the words "resident in the United Kingdom"; but nothing in this subsection shall affect the operation of either section in relation to—

(a) an application for a Treasury consent made before the date of the coming into force of this section; or
(b) such a consent granted on an application so made.

(7) This section and sections 106 and 107 below shall be deemed to have come into force on 15th March 1988.

106. Deemed disposal of assets on company ceasing to be liable to U.K. tax

(1) This section and section 107 below apply to a company if, at any time ("the relevant time"), the company, while continuing to be resident in the United Kingdom, becomes a company which falls to be regarded for the purposes of any double taxation relief arrangements—

   (*a*) as resident in a territory outside the United Kingdom; and
   (*b*) as not liable in the United Kingdom to tax on gains arising on disposals of assets of descriptions specified in the arrangements ("prescribed assets").

(2) The company shall be deemed for all purposes of the Capital Gains Tax Act 1979—

   (*a*) to have disposed of all its prescribed assets immediately before the relevant time; and
   (*b*) immediately to have reacquired them,

at their market value at that time.

(3) Section 115 of the Capital Gains Tax Act 1979 (roll-over relief) shall not apply where the new assets are prescribed assets and the company—

   (*a*) has disposed of the old assets, or of its interest in those assets, before the relevant time; and
   (*b*) acquires the new assets, or its interest in those assets, after that time.

(4) In this section—

   "double taxation relief arrangements" means arrangements having effect by virtue of section 497 of the Taxes Act 1970 or section 788 of the Taxes Act 1988 (as extended, in either case, to capital gains tax by section 10 of the Capital Gains Tax Act 1979);
   "the old assets" and "the new assets" have the same meanings as in section 115 of the 1979 Act.

107. Postponement of charge on deemed disposal

(1) If—

   (*a*) immediately after the relevant time, a company to which this section applies by virtue of section 105 or 106 above ("the company") is a 75 per cent. subsidiary of another company ("the principal company") which is resident in the United Kingdom; and
   (*b*) the principal company and the company so elect, by notice in writing given to the inspector within two years after that time,

the Capital Gains Tax Act 1979 shall have effect in accordance with the following provisions.

(2) Any allowable losses accruing to the company on a deemed disposal of foreign assets shall be set off against the chargeable gains so accruing and—

   (*a*) that disposal shall be treated as giving rise to a single chargeable gain equal to the aggregate of those gains after deducting the aggregate of those losses; and
   (*b*) the whole of that gain shall be treated as not accruing to the company on that disposal but an equivalent amount ("the postponed gain") shall be brought into account in accordance with subsections (3) and (4) below.

(3) If at any time within six years after the relevant time the company disposes of any assets ("relevant assets") the chargeable gains on which were taken into account in arriving at the postponed gain, there shall be deemed to accrue to the principal company as a chargeable gain on that occasion the whole or the appropriate proportion of the postponed gain so far as not already taken into account under this subsection or subsection (4) below.

In this subsection "the appropriate proportion" means the proportion which the chargeable gain taken into account in arriving at the postponed gain in respect of the part of the relevant assets disposed of bears to the aggregate of the chargeable gains so taken into account in respect of the relevant assets held immediately before the time of the disposal.

(4) If at any time after the relevant time—

   (*a*) the company ceases to be a 75 per cent. subsidiary of the principal company on the disposal by the principal company of ordinary shares of the company;
   (*b*) after the company has ceased to be such a subsidiary otherwise than on such a disposal, the principal company disposes of such shares; or
   (*c*) the principal company ceases to be resident in the United Kingdom,

there shall be deemed to accrue to the principal company as a chargeable gain on that occasion the whole of the postponed gain so far as not already taken into account under this subsection or subsection (3) above.

(5) If at any time—

(a) the company has allowable losses which have not been allowed as a deduction from chargeable gains; and

(b) a chargeable gain accrues to the principal company under subsection (3) or (4) above,

then, if and to the extent that the principal company and the company so elect, by notice in writing given to the inspector within two years after that time, those losses shall be allowed as a deduction from that gain.

(6) In this section—

"deemed disposal" means a disposal which, by virtue of section 105(2) or, as the case may be, section 106(2) above, is deemed to have been made;

"foreign assets" means any assets of the company which, immediately after the relevant time, are situated outside the United Kingdom and are used in or for the purposes of a trade carried on outside the United Kingdom;

"ordinary share" means a share in the ordinary share capital of the company;

"the relevant time" has the meaning given by section 105(1) or, as the case may be, section 106(1) above.

(7) For the purposes of this section a company is a 75 per cent. subsidiary of another company if and so long as not less than 75 per cent. of its ordinary share capital is owned directly by that other company.

Miscellaneous

109. Gains arising from certain settled property

Schedule 10 to this Act (taxation of gains arising from settled property in which the settlor or his spouse has an interest) shall have effect.

111. Dependent relative's residence

(1) Section 105 of the Capital Gains Tax Act 1979 shall not apply to disposals on or after 6th April 1988.

(2) Subsection (1) above shall not have effect where, on 5th April 1988 or at any earlier time during the period of ownership of the individual making the disposal, the dwelling-house or part in question was the sole residence (provided rent-free and without any other consideration) of a dependent relative of his.

(3) If in a case within subsection (2) above the dwelling-house or part ceases, whether before 6th April 1988 or later, to be the sole residence (provided as mentioned above) of the dependent relative, any subsequent period of residence beginning on or after that date by that or any other dependent relative shall be disregarded for the purposes of section 105(2) of the Capital Gains Tax Act 1979.

113. Indexation: building societies etc.

(1) The provisions specified in subsection (2) below (which provide for an indexation allowance on the disposal of assets) shall not apply in the case of—

(a) shares in a building society within the meaning of the Building Societies Act 1986, or

(b) shares in a registered industrial and provident society as defined in section 486 of the Taxes Act 1988.

(2) The provisions referred to in subsection (1) above are—

(a) in the Finance Act 1982, sections 86(4) and 87 and, in Schedule 13, paragraphs 1 to 7, 8(2)(c) and 10(3); and

(b) in the Finance Act 1985, section 68(4) to (8) and, in Schedule 19, paragraphs 1(3), 2, 5, 7(3), 8(1)(b) and (c), 11 to 15, 18, 22 and 23.

(3) This section shall apply to disposals on or after 4th July 1987.

114. Indexation: groups and associated companies

Schedule 11 to this Act (which makes provision removing or restricting indexation allowance in the case of certain disposals by companies of debts or shares) shall have effect.

117. Definition of "investment trust"

(1) . . .

(2) The repeal by the Finance (No. 2) Act 1987 of section 93 of the Finance Act 1972 shall be treated as not having extended to subsection (6) of that section (amendment of definition of "investment trust" in section 359 of the Taxes Act 1970).

(3) . . .

(4) Subsections (1) and (3) above shall have effect for companies' accounting periods ending after 5th April 1988 and subsection (2) above shall have effect for companies' accounting periods ending on or before that date.

Note.—Sub-s. (1) amends TA 1988, s. 842.
Sub-s. (3) amends the Companies Act 1985, s. 266 and the Companies (Northern Ireland) Order 1986, art. 274.

CHAPTER V

MANAGEMENT

Production of accounts, books etc.

127. Production of computer records etc.

(1) Any provision made by or under the Taxes Acts which requires a person—

(*a*) to produce, furnish or deliver any document or cause any document to be produced, furnished or delivered; or

(*b*) to permit the Board, or an inspector or other officer of the Board—

(i) to inspect any document, or
(ii) to make or take extracts from or copies of or remove any document,

shall have effect as if any reference in that provision to a document were a reference to a document within the meaning of Part I of the Civil Evidence Act 1968; and, accordingly, any reference in such a provision to a copy of a document shall be construed in accordance with section 10(2) of that Act.

(2) In connection with tax, a person authorised by the Board to exercise the powers conferred by this subsection—

(*a*) shall be entitled at any reasonable time to have access to, and inspect and check the operation of, any computer and any associated apparatus or material which is or has been in use in connection with any document to which this subsection applies; and
(*b*) may require—

(i) the person by whom or on whose behalf the computer is or has been so used, or
(ii) any person having charge of, or otherwise concerned with the operation of, the computer, apparatus, or material,

to afford him such reasonable assistance as he may require for the purposes of paragraph (*a*) above.

(3) Subsection (2) above applies to any document, within the meaning of Part I of the Civil Evidence Act 1968, which a person is or may be required by or under any provision of the Taxes Acts—

(*a*) to produce, furnish or deliver, or cause to be produced, furnished or delivered; or
(*b*) to permit the Board, or an inspector or other officer of the Board, to inspect, make or take extracts from or copies of or remove.

(4) Any person who—

(*a*) obstructs a person authorised under subsection (2) above in the exercise of his powers under paragraph (*a*) of that subsection, or
(*b*) fails to comply within a reasonable time with a requirement under paragraph (*b*) of that subsection,

shall be liable to a penalty not exceeding £500.

(5) In the application of this section to Scotland and Northern Ireland, references in this section to Part I of the Civil Evidence Act 1968 and section 10(2) of that Act shall be construed—

(*a*) in the case of Scotland, as references to Part III of the Law Reform (Miscellaneous Provisions) (Scotland) Act 1968 and section 17(4) of that Act respectively, and
(*b*) in the case of Northern Ireland, as references to Part I of the Civil Evidence Act (Northern Ireland) 1971 and section 6(2) of that Act respectively.

(6) This section shall be construed as if it were contained in the Taxes Management Act 1970.

Company migration

130. Provisions for securing payment by company of outstanding tax

(1) The requirements of subsections (2) and (3) below must be satisfied before a company ceases to be resident in the United Kingdom otherwise than in pursuance of a Treasury consent.

(2) The requirements of this subsection are satisfied if the company gives to the Board—

  (*a*) notice of its intention to cease to be resident in the United Kingdom, specifying the time ("the relevant time") when it intends so to cease;
  (*b*) a statement of the amount which, in its opinion, is the amount of the tax which is or will be payable by it in respect of periods beginning before that time; and
  (*c*) particulars of the arrangements which it proposes to make for securing the payment of that tax.

(3) The requirements of this subsection are satisfied if—

  (*a*) arrangements are made by the company for securing the payment of the tax which is or will be payable by it in respect of periods beginning before the relevant time; and
  (*b*) those arrangements as so made are approved by the Board for the purposes of this subsection.

(4) If any question arises as to the amount which should be regarded for the purposes of subsection (3) above as the amount of the tax which is or will be payable by the company in respect of periods beginning before the relevant time, that question shall be referred to the Special Commissioners, whose decision shall be final.

(5) If any information furnished by the company for the purpose of securing the approval of the Board under subsection (3) above does not fully and accurately disclose all facts and considerations material for the decision of the Board under that subsection, any resulting approval of the Board shall be void.

(6) In this section "Treasury consent" means a consent under section 765 of the Taxes Act 1988 (restrictions on the migration etc. of companies) given for the purposes of subsection (1)(*a*) of that section.

(7) In this section and sections 131 and 132 below any reference to the tax payable by a company includes a reference to—

  (*a*) any amount of tax which it is liable to pay under regulations made under section 203 of the Taxes Act 1988 (PAYE);
  (*b*) any income tax which it is liable to pay in respect of payments to which section 350(4)(*a*) of that Act (company payments which are not distributions) applies;
  (*c*) any amount representing income tax which it is liable to pay under—

    (i) regulations made under section 476(1) of that Act (building societies);
    (ii) section 479 of that Act (interest paid on deposits with banks etc.); or
    (iii) section 555 of that Act (entertainers and sportsmen);

  (*d*) any amount which it is liable to pay under section 559(4) of that Act (sub-contractors in the construction industry); and
  (*e*) any amount which it is liable to pay under paragraph 4 of Schedule 15 to Finance Act 1973 (territorial extension of charge of tax).

(8) In this section and section 132 below any reference to the tax payable by a company in respect of periods beginning before any particular time includes a reference to any interest on the tax so payable, or on tax paid by it in respect of such periods, which it is liable to pay in respect of periods beginning before or after that time.

(9) In this section and sections 131 and 132 below any reference to a provision of the Taxes Act 1988 shall be construed, in relation to any time before 6th April 1988, as a reference to the corresponding enactment repealed by that Act.

(10) This section and sections 131 and 132 below shall be deemed to have come into force on 15th March 1988.

131. Penalties for failure to comply with section 130

(1) If a company fails to comply with section 130 above at any time, it shall be liable to a penalty not exceeding the amount of tax which is or will be payable by it in respect of periods beginning before that time and which has not been paid at that time.

(2) If, in relation to a company ("the migrating company"), any person does or is party to the doing of any act which to his knowledge amounts to or results in, or forms part of a series of acts which together amount to or result in, or will amount to or result in, the migrating company failing to comply with section 130 above at any time and either—

    (*a*) that person is a person to whom subsection (3) below applies; or
    (*b*) the act in question is a direction or instruction given (otherwise than by way of advice given by a person acting in a professional capacity) to persons to whom that subsection applies,

that person shall be liable to a penalty not exceeding the amount of tax which is or will be payable by the migrating company in respect of periods beginning before that time and which has not been paid at that time.

(3) This subsection applies to the following persons, namely—

    (*a*) any company which has control of the migrating company; and
    (*b*) any person who is a director of the migrating company or of a company which has control of the migrating company.

(4) In any proceedings against any person to whom subsection (3) above applies for the recovery of a penalty under subsection (2) above—

    (*a*) it shall be presumed that he was party to every act of the migrating company unless he proves that it was done without his consent or connivance; and
    (*b*) it shall, unless the contrary is proved, be presumed that any act which in fact amounted to or resulted in, or formed part of a series of acts which together amounted to or resulted in, or would amount to or result in, the migrating company failing to comply with section 130 above was to his knowledge such an act.

(5) References in this section to a company failing to comply with section 130 above are references to the requirements of subsections (2) and (3) of that section not being satisfied before the company ceases to be resident in the United Kingdom otherwise than in pursuance of a Treasury consent; and in this subsection "Treasury consent" has the same meaning as in that section.

(6) In this section and section 132 below "director", in relation to a company—

    (*a*) has the meaning given by subsection (8) of section 168 of the Taxes Act 1988 (read with subsection (9) of that section); and
    (*b*) includes any person falling within subsection (5) of section 417 of that Act (read with subsection (6) of that section);

and any reference to a person having control of a company shall be construed in accordance with section 416 of that Act.

132. Liability of other persons for unpaid tax

(1) This section applies where—

    (*a*) a company ("the migrating company") ceases to be resident in the United Kingdom at any time; and
    (*b*) any tax which is payable by the migrating company in respect of periods beginning before that time is not paid within six months from the time when it becomes payable.

(2) The Board may, at any time before the end of the period of three years beginning with the time when the amount of the tax is finally determined, serve on any person to whom subsection (3) below applies a notice—

    (*a*) stating particulars of the tax payable, the amount remaining unpaid and the date when it became payable; and
    (*b*) requiring that person to pay that amount within thirty days of the service of the notice.

(3) This subsection applies to the following persons, namely—

    (*a*) any company which is, or within the relevant period was, a member of the same group as the migrating company; and
    (*b*) any person who is, or within the relevant period was, a controlling director of the migrating company or of a company which has, or within that period had, control over the migrating company.

(4) Any amount which a person is required to pay by a notice under this section may be

recovered from him as if it were tax due and duly demanded of him; and he may recover any such amount paid by him from the migrating company.

(5) A payment in pursuance of a notice under this section shall not be allowed as a deduction in computing any income, profits or losses for any tax purposes.

(6) In this section—

"controlling director", in relation to a company, means a director of the company who has control of it;

"group" has the meaning which would be given by section 272 of the Taxes Act 1970 if in that section references to residence in the United Kingdom were omitted and for references to 75 per cent. subsidiaries there were substituted references to 51 per cent. subsidiaries;

"the relevant period" means—

(*a*) where the time when the migrating company ceases to be resident in the United Kingdom is less than twleve months after 15th March 1988, the period beginning with that date and ending with that time;

(*b*) in any other case, the period of twelve months ending with that time.

134. General Commissioners for Northern Ireland

(1) ...

(2) ...

(3) In sections 260(3) and 281(4) of the Taxes Act 1988 (and the corresponding enactments repealed by that Act) and in section 11(4) of the Taxes Act 1970 (Special Commissioners to act instead of General Commissioners where taxpayers not resident in Great Britain) for the words "Great Britain" there shall be substituted the words "the United Kingdom".

(4) This section and section 135 below shall come into force on such day as the Lord Chancellor may by order made by statutory instrument appoint.

(5) Subject to the following provisions of this section, the preceding provisions of this section and section 135(2) below shall not affect any proceedings instituted before the day appointed under subsection (4) above.

(6) Subject to subsection (8) below, where—

(*a*) before the day appointed under subsection (4) above proceedings in Northern Ireland have been instituted before the Special Commissioners but not determined by them, and

(*b*) the proceedings might have been instituted before the General Commissioners if they had been proceedings in Great Britain,

they shall be transferred to the General Commissioners; and subsection (3) of section 58 of the Taxes Management Act 1970 shall apply for the purposes of this subsection as for those of that section (the reference to proceedings in Great Britain being construed accordingly).

(7) Section 44 of that Act shall apply in relation to proceedings transferred to the General Commissioners under subsection (6) above as it applies to proceedings instituted before them; and in the case of an appeal so transferred a notice of election under rule 3 or 5 of Schedule 3 to that Act may be given at any time before the end of the period of thirty days beginning with the day appointed under subsection (4) above.

(8) Subsection (6) above shall not apply in relation to proceedings if—

(*a*) before the end of that period an election that the proceedings be not transferred is made by any of the parties to the proceedings and written notice of the election is given to the other parties to the proceedings, or

(*b*) they are proceedings under section 100 of the Taxes Management Act 1970 (recovery of penalties);

but subsections (5A) to (5E) of section 31 of that Act shall apply in relation to an election under paragraph (*a*) of this subsection in respect of an appeal against an assessment or the decision of an inspector on a claim as they apply in relation to an election under subsection (4) of that section.

(9) The Lord Chancellor may by order made by statutory instrument make provision supplementing or modifying the effect of subsections (5) to (8) above; and an order under this subsection shall be subject to annulment in pursuance of a resolution of either House of Parliament.

1988, s. 134 Finance Act 1988 : Pt. III 1640

Notes.—Sub-s. (1) amends TMA 1970, s. 2.
Sub-s. (2) repeals TMA 1970, ss. 58(1), 59.

135. Cases stated in Northern Ireland

Note.—This section amends TMA 1970, s. 58.

PART IV

MISCELLANEOUS AND GENERAL

Miscellaneous

145. Building societies: change of status

Schedule 12 to this Act (which makes provision in connection with the transfer of a building society's business to a company in accordance with the Building Societies Act 1986) shall have effect.

146. Post-consolidation amendments

The enactments specified in Schedule 13 to this Act shall have effect subject to the amendments specified in that Schedule (being amendments to correct errors in the Taxes Act 1988 and in the amendments made by the Finance Act 1987 for the purposes of the consolidation effected by the Taxes Act 1988).

147. Interpretation etc.

(1) In this Act "the Taxes Act 1970" means the Income and Corporation Taxes Act 1970 and "the Taxes Act 1988" means the Income and Corporation Taxes Act 1988.

(2) ...

(3) Part III of this Act, so far as it relates to income tax, shall be construed as one with the Income Tax Acts, so far as it relates to corporation tax, shall be construed as one with the Corporation Tax Acts and, so far as it relates to capital gains tax, shall be construed as one with the Capital Gains Tax Act 1979.

Note.—Sub-s. (2) is not relevant to this Handbook.

148. Repeals

The enactments specified in Schedule 14 to this Act (which include unnecessary enactments) are hereby repealed to the extent specified in the third column of that Schedule, but subject to any provision at the end of any Part of that Schedule.

149. Short title

This Act may be cited as the Finance Act 1988.

SCHEDULES

SCHEDULE 3

Section 35

MARRIED COUPLES: MINOR AND CONSEQUENTIAL PROVISIONS

PART I

AMENDMENTS OF THE TAXES ACT 1988

Introductory

1. The Taxes Act 1988 shall have effect subject to the following amendments.

Additional relief in respect of children

5.—(1) For the year 1990–91 and subsequent years of assessment section 259 (additional relief in respect of children) shall have effect with the following amendments.

(2) For subsection (1) there shall be substituted—

"(1) This section applies to—

(a) any woman who is not throughout the year of assessment married and living with her husband;

(b) any man who is neither married and living with his wife for the whole or any part of the year, nor entitled to a deduction from his total income by virtue of section 257F; and

(c) any man who for the whole or any part of the year is married to and living with a wife who is totally incapacitated by physical or mental infirmity throughout the year."

(3) In subsection (2), for the words "the difference between" onwards there shall be substituted the words "that specified in section 257A(1) for the year".

(4) For subsection (4) there shall be substituted—

"(4) A woman shall not be entitled to relief under this section for a year of assessment during any part of which she is married and living with her husband unless the child in respect of whom the relief is claimed is resident with her during a part of the year when she is not married and living with her husband."

6. For the year 1990–91 and subsequent years of assessment the following section shall be substituted for section 261 (year of marriage)—

"**261. Claims under section 259 for year of marriage**

A man (but not a woman) who becomes married during a year of assessment may by notice to the inspector elect that his marriage shall be disregarded for the purposes of any claim that he makes for that year under section 259, and, in that case, the marriage shall also be disregarded for the purposes of any claim that he makes for that year under section 257A."

Widow's bereavement allowance

7.—(1) The section set out in sub-paragraph (2) below shall have effect in substitution for section 262 (widow's bereavement allowance) in relation to deaths occurring during the year 1989–90, and the section set out in sub-paragraph (3) below shall have effect in substitution for that section in relation to deaths occurring during the year 1990–91 or any subsequent year of assessment.

(3) The section second referred to in sub-paragraph (1) above is—

"**262. Widow's bereavement allowance**

Where a married man whose wife is living with him dies, his widow shall be entitled—

(a) for the year of assessment in which the death occurs, to a deduction from her total income of an amount equal to the amount specified in section 257A(1) for that year, and

(b) (unless she marries again before the beginning of it) for the next following year of assessment, to a deduction of an amount equal to the amount specified in section 257A(1) for that year."

Blind person's allowance

8. For the year 1990–91 and subsequent years of assessment the following section shall be substituted for section 265—

"265. Blind person's allowance

(1) If the claimant proves that he is a registered blind person for the whole or any part of the year of assessment, he shall be entitled to a deduction of £540 from his total income.

(2) Where—

   (*a*) a person entitled to relief under subsection (1) above is a married man whose wife is living with him for the whole or any part of the year of assessment, but
   (*b*) the amount which he is entitled to deduct from his total income by virtue of that subsection exceeds what is left of his total income after all other deductions have been made from it,

his wife shall be entitled to a deduction from her total income of an amount equal to the excess.

(3) In determining for the purposes of subsection (2)(*b*) above the amount that is left of a person's total income for a year of assessment after other deductions have been made from it, there shall be disregarded any deduction made—

   (*a*) on account of any payments of relevant loan interest which become due in that year and to which section 369 applies, or
   (*b*) under section 257A or section 289, [or][1]
   [(*c*) on account of any payments to which section 593(2) or 639(3) applies,][1] [or][2]
   [(*d*) on account of any payments to which section 54(5) of the Finance Act 1989 applies.][2]

(4) Subsections (2) and (3) above shall have effect where a wife is entitled to relief under subsection (1) above as they have effect where the husband is entitled to that relief, but with the appropriate modifications (and in particular the omission from subsection (3) of the reference to section 257A).

(5) Subsections (2) to (4) above shall not apply for a year of assessment unless the person entitled to relief under subsection (1) has given to the inspector written notice that they are to apply; and any such notice—

   (*a*) shall be given not later than six years after the end of the year of assessment to which it relates,
   (*b*) shall be in such form as the Board may determine, and
   (*c*) shall be irrevocable.

(6) A notice given under subsection (5) above in relation to a year of assessment by a husband shall have effect also as a notice under section 257B(3).

(7) In this section "registered blind person" means a person registered as a blind person in a register compiled under section 29 of the National Assistance Act 1948 or, in the case of a person ordinarily resident in Scotland or Northern Ireland, a person who is a blind person within the meaning of section 64(1) of that Act."

Amendments.—[1] Sub-s. (3)(*c*) and the preceding word "or" inserted by FA 1989, s. 33(1), (10).
[2] Sub-s. (3)(*d*) and the preceding word "or" inserted by FA 1989, s. 57(4).

Life assurance premiums

9. For the year 1990–91 and subsequent years of assessment section 266 (life assurance premiums) shall have effect with the substitution—

   (*a*) in subsection (9), of the word "spouse" for the words "wife (but not the husband)", and
   (*b*) in subsection (11)(*a*), of the words "spouse, widow, widower or children or other dependants of any such employee or person," for the word "wife" onwards.

Payments securing annuities

10. For the year 1990–91 and subsequent years of assessment the following section shall be substituted for section 273 (payments securing annuities)—

"**273. Payments securing annuities**

Subject to sections 274, 617(3) and 619(6), if the claimant is, under any Act of Parliament or under any terms and conditions of employment, liable to the payment of any sum, or to the deduction from any salary or stipend of any sum, for the purpose of securing a deferred annuity to a widow or widower of the claimant or provision for the claimant's children after the claimant dies, the claimant shall be entitled to a deduction from the amount of income tax on which he or she is chargeable equal to income tax at the basic rate on the amount of the sum which he or she has paid or which has been deducted from his or her salary or stipend."

Married couples living together

11. For the year 1990–91 and subsequent years of assessment the following section shall be substituted for section 282 (construction of references to married women living with their husbands)—

"**282. Construction of references to husband and wife living together**

A husband and wife shall be treated for income tax purposes as living together unless—

(*a*) they are separated under an order of a court of competent jurisdiction, or by deed of separation, or
(*b*) they are in fact separated in such circumstances that the separation is likely to be permanent."

Business expansion scheme

12.—(1) For the year 1990–91 and subsequent years of assessment section 304 (business expansion scheme: husband and wife) shall have effect—

(*a*) with the omission of subsections (1) to (4), and
(*b*) with the substitution of the following subsections for subsections (5) and (6)—

"(5) Subsection (1) of section 299 shall not apply to a disposal made by a married man to his wife or a married woman to her husband at a time when they are living together; but where shares issued to one of them have been transferred to the other by a transaction inter vivos that subsection shall apply on the disposal of the shares by the transferee to a third person and any assessment for withdrawing relief in respect of the shares shall be made on the transferee.

(6) If any relief given for the year 1989–90 or any earlier year of assessment in respect of shares for which a married man or married woman has subscribed and which were issued while they were living together falls to be withdrawn in the year 1990–91 or any subsequent year of assessment by virtue of a disposal of those shares by the person who subscribed for them, any assessment for withdrawing that relief shall be made on the person making the disposal and shall be made by reference to the reduction of tax flowing from the amount of the relief regardless of any allocation of that relief under section 280 or of any allocation of the reduction under section 284 for the year of assessment for which the relief was given."

(2) Sub-paragraph (3) below applies where—

(*a*) an amount is subscribed for shares in the year 1990–91 by one of a married couple who are living together,
(*b*) the couple were married and living together throughout the year 1989–90, and
(*c*) the subscriber claims that relief in respect of the amount be given partly by way of deduction from total income for the year 1989–90 in accordance with section 289(6).

(3) Where this sub-paragraph applies—

(*a*) the deduction shall be made from the husband's total income (references in Chapter II of Part VII to the relief to which an individual is entitled in respect of any shares being construed accordingly), and
(*b*) the limits in sections 289(7) and 290 shall apply jointly to the husband and wife for the year 1989–90 as respects the amount subscribed.

Qualifying maintenance payments

13. For the year 1990–91 and subsequent years of assessment section 347B(3) (qualifying maintenance payments) shall have effect with the substitution of the words "specified in section 257A(1) for the year" for the words "of the difference between" onwards.

Home loans

14. For the year 1990–91 and subsequent years of assessment the following section shall be substituted for section 356B—

"**356B. Residence basis: married couples**

(1) A husband and wife who are not separated may jointly elect—

(*a*) that qualifying interest payable or paid by one of them for a year of assessment (or a period within a year), or such part of that interest as may be specified in the election, shall be treated for the purposes of sections 353 to 356A and 369 to 379 as payable or paid by the other, and
(*b*) that the sharer's limit under section 356A for the year (or period) in the case of one of them shall be reduced by such amount as may be specified in the election and the sharer's limit under that section for the year (or period) in the case of the other shall be correspondingly increased.

(2) An election under subsection (1) above—

(*a*) shall be made before the end of the period of twelve months beginning with the end of the first year of assessment for which it is made or such longer period as the Board may in any particular case allow,
(*b*) shall, subject to subsection (4) below, have effect not only for the year of assessment for which it is made but also for subsequent years of assessment, and
(*c*) shall be in such form, and be made in such manner, as the Board may prescribe.

(3) Where a husband and wife have made an election under subsection (1) above for any year of assessment either of them may give, for any subsequent year, a notice to withdraw that election; and, if he or she does so, the election shall not have effect (in relation to either of them) for the year for which the notice is given or any subsequent year.

(4) A notice of withdrawal under subsection (3) above—

(*a*) shall be in such form, and be given in such manner, as the Board may prescribe,
(*b*) shall not be given after the end of the period of twelve months beginning with the end of the year of assessment for which it is given or such longer period as the Board may in any particular case allow, and
(*c*) shall not prejudice the making of a fresh election for any subsequent year.

(5) Where—

(*a*) a husband and wife are not separated,
(*b*) the husband pays interest in relation to a residence used or to be used as his only or main residence, and
(*c*) the wife pays interest in relation to some other residence used or to be used as her only or main residence,

the residence which was purchased first shall be treated for the purposes of sections 355(1)(*a*) and 356 as used or to be used as the only or main residence of both of them and the other residence shall be treated as used or to be used as the only or main residence of neither."

Loans for shares in employee-controlled company

15.—(1) In section 361 (relief for interest on loans to acquire shares in employee-controlled company)—

(*a*) the words "or his spouse" in subsection (4)(*d*) and ", or whose spouses," in subsection (5) shall cease to have effect, and
(*b*) the following subsection shall be substituted for subsections (6) and (7)—

"(6) Where an individual owns beneficially more than 10 per cent. of the issued ordinary share capital of, or voting power in, a company, the excess shall be treated for the purposes of subsection (5) above as being owned by an individual who is not a full-time employee of the company."

(2) Sub-paragraph (1) above shall have effect in relation to payments of interest made on or after 6th April 1990 unless the proceeds of the loan were used before that date to defray money applied as mentioned in section 361(3).

(3) Interest paid on a loan made on or after 6th April 1990 to defray money applied in paying off another loan shall not be eligible for relief by virtue of paragraph (*b*) of subsection (3) of section 361 unless—

(a) the proceeds of the loan paid off were used on or after 6th April 1990 to defray money applied as mentioned in that subsection, or

(b) those proceeds were so used before that date but interest on the loan paid off would have been eligible for relief had they been so used on or after that date.

Close company loans

16.—(1) In section 420(2)(a)(i) (exception from charge in case where close company loans to borrower and spouse do not exceed £15,000) the words "or the wife or husband of the borrower" shall cease to have effect.

(2) This paragraph shall apply where the loan first mentioned in section 420(2) is made on or after 6th April 1990.

Trade unions and employers' associations

17.—(1) In section 467(2) (tax exemption in respect of income of trade unions and employers' associations applied for provident benefits) for the word "wife" there shall be substituted the word "spouse".

(2) This paragraph shall apply for any chargeable period beginning on or after 6th April 1990.

Retirement benefit schemes

18.—(1) In section 590 (conditions for approval of retirement benefit schemes)—

(a) after the word "widow," in subsection (2)(a) there shall be inserted the word "widower," and

(b) after the word "widow" in both places where it occurs in subsection (3)(b) there shall be inserted the words "or widower".

(2) This paragraph shall have effect on and after 6th April 1990.

Partnership retirement annuities

19. For the year 1990–91 and subsequent years of assessment section 628(1) (partnership retirement annuities) shall have effect with the substitution of the words "a widow, widower or dependant of the former partner" for the words "his widow or a dependant of his".

20.—(1) For the year 1990–91 and subsequent years of assessment section 683 (settlements) shall have effect with the following amendments.

(2) In subsection (1)(a), after the word "widow" there shall be inserted the word ", widower".

(3) In subsection (6)(a), for the words "he is dead, to or for the benefit of his widow" there shall be substituted the words "that individual is dead, to or for the benefit of that individual's widow, widower".

(4) In subsection (6)(b), after the word "widow", in the first place where it occurs, there shall be inserted the word ", widower" and for the words "he is dead" onwards there shall be substituted the words "such an individual is dead, to or for the benefit of that individual's widow, widower or dependants."

(5) In subsection (9), after the word "widow" there shall be inserted the word ", widower".

Earned income

21. For the year 1990–91 and subsequent years of assessment section 833(4)(a) (meaning of "earned income") shall have effect with the substitution of the word "spouse" for the word "husband", in both places where it occurs.

Total income

22. For the year 1990–91 and subsequent years of assessment section 835(5) (meaning of "total income") shall have effect with the insertion of ", 257A(5)" after "257(5)".

PART II
OTHER PROVISIONS

Capital allowances

23. Where—

(a) before 6th April 1990, a woman was entitled to the relevant interest, within the meaning of section 11 of the Capital Allowances Act 1968, in relation to expenditure incurred on the construction of a building or structure (whether she was entitled to it when the expenditure was incurred or acquired it afterwards);

(*b*) for a chargeable period ending before that date, an allowance such as is mentioned in section 3(6) of that Act (allowances relating to capital expenditure on industrial buildings etc.) was made to the woman's husband in respect of her relevant interest; and

(*c*) on or after that date, there occurs an event such as is mentioned in section 3(1) of that Act (events giving rise to a balancing allowance or a balancing charge) in respect of which the woman is entitled to all or part of any sale, insurance, salvage or compensation moneys,

the allowance shall be treated, for the purposes of section 3(6) of that Act (amount of balancing charge not to exceed amount of allowances given), as having been made to the woman.

24. Where—

(*a*) before 6th April 1990, a woman was entitled to the relevant interest, within the meaning of paragraph 3 of Schedule 15 to the Finance Act 1986, in relation to expenditure falling within paragraph 1(1) of that Schedule (expenditure on the construction of agricultural buildings, etc.) whether she was entitled to it when the expenditure was incurred or acquired it afterwards;

(*b*) for a chargeable period ending before that date, an allowance under paragraph 1(1) of that Schedule (writing-down allowances) was made to the woman's husband in respect of her relevant interest; and

(*c*) on or after that date, there occurs an event which is a balancing event for the purposes of that Schedule and in respect of which the woman is entitled to all or part of any sale, insurance, salvage or compensation moneys,

the allowance shall be treated, for the purposes of paragraph 6(6) of that Schedule (amount of balancing charge not to exceed amount of allowances given), as having been made to the woman.

The transition

25. The operation of section 279(1) of the Taxes Act 1988 for a year of assessment earlier than the year 1990–91 in the case of a married woman shall not affect the question whether there is any income of hers chargeable to income tax for the year 1990–91 or any subsequent year of assessment or, if there is, what is to be taken to be its amount for income tax purposes.

Returns

26. Where a man is required under section 8 of the Taxes Management Act 1970 to deliver a return which is—

(*a*) so far as relates to certain sources of income, a return of income chargeable to income tax for the year 1990–91, and

(*b*) so far as relates to the remaining sources of income, a return of income chargeable to income tax for the year 1989–90,

the same particulars shall be included in the return as would have been required had section 279 of the Taxes Act 1988 not been repealed by this Act.

27. Where a man delivers a return such as is mentioned in paragraph 26 above, the reference in sections 93(2) and 95(2) of the Taxes Management Act 1970 (penalties) to tax charged on or payable by him shall include a reference to tax charged on or payable by his wife in respect of any income of hers.

28. Where a woman is liable to a penalty under section 93(1) or 95(1) of the Taxes Management Act 1970, section 93(2) or 95(2) shall apply as if the reference to tax charged on or payable by her included a reference to any tax which is charged on or payable by her husband by virtue of section 279 of the Taxes Act 1988.

Time limits for assessments

29. Where—

(a) for the purpose of making good to the Crown a loss of tax wholly or partly attributable to fraud, wilful default or neglect, an assessment to income tax has been made on a woman for the year 1990–91 or any subsequent year of assessment, and

(b) the woman's income for an earlier year was treated as that of her husband by virtue of section 279 of the Taxes Act 1988,

assessments to income tax for the earlier year may be made on him if they could have been made in accordance with section 37 of the Taxes Management Act 1970 had the assessment mentioned in sub-paragraph (a) above been made on him.

Amendments.—This paragraph repealed by FA 1989, Sch. 17, Pt. VIII, subject to FA 1989, s. 149(7).

Transfers of allowances

30. For the year 1990–91 and subsequent years of assessment the Taxes Management Act 1970 shall have effect with the insertion of the following section after section 37—

"**37A. Effect of assessment where allowances transferred**

Where an assessment is made on any person for the purpose of making good a loss of tax wholly or partly attributable to [fraudulent or negligent conduct][1], the fact that the person's total income for any year of assessment is assessed as greater than it was previously taken to be shall not affect the validity of any deduction made from the total income of the person's spouse by virtue of section 257B, 257D or 265 of the principal Act; and where any such deduction has been made in such a case, the total amount which the first-mentioned person is entitled to deduct from total income for the year in question shall be correspondingly reduced."

Amendments.—[1] Words substituted by FA 1989, s. 149(4)(a)(i).

Class 4 social security contributions

31. For the year 1990–91 and subsequent years of assessment Schedule 2 to the Social Security Act 1975 and the Social Security (Northern Ireland) Act 1975 (Class 4 contributions) shall have effect with the substitution of the following for paragraph 3(3)—

"(3) Where in a year for which a person claims and is allowed relief by virtue of sub-paragraph (1) above there falls to be made in computing his total income for income tax purposes a deduction in respect of any loss in any relevant trade, profession or vocation—

(*a*) the amount of the deduction shall, as far as may be, be treated for the purpose of the charge to Class 4 contributions as reducing the person's profits or gains for that year of any relevant trade, profession or vocation, and

(*b*) any excess shall be treated for that purpose as reducing such profits or gains for subsequent years (being deducted as far as may be from those of the immediately following year, whether or not the person claims or is entitled to claim relief under this paragraph for that year, and, so far as it cannot be so deducted, then from those of the next year, and so on)."

Annual payments

32. Section 36 of this Act shall have effect in relation to a payment which is due from a husband to his wife or from a wife to her husband at a time after 5th April 1990 when they are living together, notwithstanding that the payment is made in pursuance of an obligation which is an existing obligation for the purposes of subsection (3) of that section.

Maintenance payments

33. For the year 1990–91 and subsequent years of assessment section 38(5) of this Act shall have effect with the substitution of the words "specified in section 257A(1) of the Taxes Act 1988 for the year" for the words "of the difference between" onwards.

SCHEDULE 4

Section 50

BUSINESS EXPANSION SCHEME: PRIVATE RENTED HOUSING

PART I
MODIFICATIONS MADE BY SECTION 50

Preliminary

1. The modifications of Chapter III of Part VII of the Taxes Act 1988 (relief for investment in new corporate trades: the business expansion scheme) made by section 50 of this Act are as follows.

The relief

2.—(1) In subsection (1) of section 289 (relief under the business expansion scheme), for paragraph (*a*) there shall be substituted—

"(*a*) those shares are issued to him after the passing of the Finance Act 1988 and before the end of 1993 for the purpose of raising money for qualifying activities which are being carried on by the company or which it intends to carry on;".

(2) In subsection (8) of that section, for paragraph (*a*) there shall be substituted—

"(*a*) in a case falling within subsection (1)(*a*) unless and until the company has carried on the activities for four months;".

(3) For subsection (9) of that section there shall be substituted—

"(9) A claim for relief may be allowed under subsection (1)(*a*) at any time after the activities have been carried on by the company for four months, if the conditions for the relief are then satisfied."

(4) In subsection (12)(*b*) of that section, for the words from "either" onwards there shall be substituted the words "four years after that date".

(5) Subsection (13) of that section shall be omitted.

Restriction of relief where amounts raised exceed permitted maximum

3.—(1) In subsection (1) of section 290A (restriction of relief where amounts raised exceed permitted maximum), for "£500,000" there shall be substituted "£5 million".

(2) In subsection (4) of that section, for the words "any trade or part of a trade" there shall be substituted the words "any qualifying activities" and for "£500,000", in both places, there shall be substituted "£5 million".

(3) Subsections (6) to (8), (10) and (11) of that section shall be omitted.

Individuals qualifying for relief

4. In section 291 (individuals qualifying for relief), after subsection (1) there shall be inserted—

"(1A) An individual is connected with the company if—

(*a*) he, or an associate of his, occupies or is a tenant of a dwelling-house in which the company holds an interest; and
(*b*) the interest held by the company is superior to any interest in the dwelling-house held by the individual.".

Parallel trades

5. Section 292 (parallel trades) shall be omitted.

Qualifying companies

6.—(1) For subsection (2) of section 293 (qualifying companies) there shall be substituted—

"(2) The company must, throughout the relevant period, be an unquoted company which is resident in the United Kingdom and not resident elsewhere, and be—

(*a*) a company which exists wholly, or substantially wholly, for the purpose of carrying on activities which do not include, to any substantial extent, activities which are not qualifying activities; or

(b) a company whose activities consist wholly of—

(i) the holding of shares or securities of, or the making of loans to, one or more qualifying subsidiaries of the company; or

(ii) both the holding of such shares or securities, or the making of such loans, and the carrying on of activities which do not include, to any substantial extent, activities which are not qualifying activities."

(2) Subsections (4) and (9) to (11) of that section shall be omitted.

Companies with interests in land etc.

7. The following shall be omitted, namely—

(a) section 294 (companies with interests in land);
(b) section 295 (valuation of interests in land for purposes of section 294(1)(b)); and
(c) section 296 (section 294 disapplied where amounts raised total £50,000 or more).

Qualifying trades etc.

8. The following shall also be omitted, namely—

(a) section 297 (qualifying trades); and
(b) section 298 (provisions supplementary to sections 293 and 297).

Replacement capital

9.—(1) In subsection (1) of section 302 (replacement capital), for the words "carry on as its trade or as part of its trade a trade which was" there shall be substituted the words "carry on, as its activities or as part of its activities, activities which were" and for the words "of a trade" there shall be substituted the words "of activities".

(2) In subsection (2) of that section, for the words "the trade", in each place where they occur, there shall be substituted the words "the activities".

(3) In subsection (4) of that section, for paragraph (a) there shall be substituted—

"(a) the persons to whom activities belong and, where activities belong to two or more persons, their respective shares in those activities shall be determined in accordance with section 344(1)(a) and (b), (2) and (3) (those provisions having effect for this purpose with any necessary modifications);"

(4) In subsection (5) of that section, the definition of "trade" shall be omitted.

Claims

10. In subsections (2) and (3) of section 306 (claims), for the words "the trade" there shall be substituted the words "the activities".

Subsidiaries

11. In subsection (1) of section 308 (application to subsidiaries), for paragraph (b) there shall be substituted—

"(b) the subsidiary or, as the case may be, each subsidiary is a dormant subsidiary or exists wholly, or substantially wholly, for the purpose of carrying on activities which do not include, to any substantial extent, activities which are not qualifying activities;".

12. In subsection (2) of section 309 (further provisions as to subsidiaries), for the words "a qualifying trade which is" there shall be substituted the words "qualifying activities which are" and for the words "subsections (8), (9), (12)(b)(ii) and (13)" there shall be substituted the words "subsections (8) and (9)".

PART II
DWELLING-HOUSES TO WHICH SECTION 50 DOES NOT APPLY

Expensive dwelling-houses

13.—(1) Section 50 of this Act does not apply to a dwelling-house the market value of which exceeds—

(a) in the case of a dwelling-house in Greater London, £125,000;
(b) in any other case, £85,000.

(2) The market value of a dwelling-house at any date ("the valuation date") shall be taken to be the price which, at the relevant date, it might reasonably have been expected to fetch on a sale in the open market—

(*a*) on the assumptions as to state mentioned in sub-paragraph (3) below; and
(*b*) on the assumptions as to title mentioned in sub-paragraph (4) below;

and in this paragraph "the relevant date" means the date of the issue of the shares or, if later, the date when the company or any of its subsidiaries first acquired an interest in the dwelling-house (or the land which comprises the dwelling-house).

(3) The assumptions as to state are that, at the relevant date—

(*a*) the dwelling-house was in the same state as at the valuation date; and
(*b*) that the locality in which the dwelling-house is situated was in the same state, so far as concerns the other premises situated in that locality and the occupation and use of those premises, the transport services and other facilities available in the locality, and other matters affecting the amenities of the locality, as at that date.

(4) The assumptions as to title are—

(*a*) where the dwelling-house is in England and Wales or Northern Ireland and is a house, that the vendor was selling for an estate in fee simple with vacant possession and that the dwelling-house was to be conveyed with the same rights and subject to the same burdens as it would be if conveyed in pursuance of the right to buy legislation;
(*b*) where the dwelling-house is in England and Wales or Northern Ireland and is a flat, that the vendor was granting a lease with vacant possession for a term of 125 years at a rent of £10 per annum and that the grant was to be made with the same rights and subject to the same burdens as it would be if made in pursuance of that legislation; and
(*c*) where the dwelling-house is in Scotland, that it was available with vacant possession and with no heritable security constituted over any interest in it.

(5) In sub-paragraph (4) above "the right to buy legislation" means—

(*a*) in relation to a dwelling-house in England and Wales, Part V of the Housing Act 1985;
(*b*) in relation to a dwelling-house in Northern Ireland, Chapter I of Part II of the Housing (Northern Ireland) Order 1983;

and "flat" and "house" have the same meanings as in that legislation.

(6) The Treasury may by order amend sub-paragraph (1) above by substituting a different amount for any amount for the time being specified there.

Unfit and sub-standard dwelling-houses

14. Section 50 of this Act does not apply to—

(*a*) a dwelling-house in England and Wales which is unfit for human habitation within the meaning of section 604 of the Housing Act 1985 or does not have all the standard amenities within the meaning of section 508 of that Act;
(*b*) a dwelling-house in Scotland which does not meet the tolerable standard described, for the purposes of the Housing (Scotland) Act 1987, by section 86 of that Act or does not have all the standard amenities described in the first column of Part I of Schedule 18 to that Act; or
(*c*) a dwelling-house in Northern Ireland which is unfit for human habitation within the meaning of Article 46 of the Housing (Northern Ireland) Order 1981 or does not have all the standard amenities within the meaning of Article 59 of the Housing (Northern Ireland) Order 1983.

Dwelling-houses already let etc.

15.—(1) Section 50 of this Act does not apply to a dwelling-house if—

(*a*) before the relevant date, the company or any of its subsidiaries had entered into arrangements for letting the whole or any part of the dwelling-house;
(*b*) at that date, the whole or any part of the dwelling-house was let; or
(*c*) after that date, the whole or any part of the dwelling-house has been let otherwise than on a qualifying tenancy.

(2) In this paragraph—

"let" includes let under a licence and "letting" shall be construed accordingly;

"the relevant date" means the date when the company or any of its subsidiaries first acquired an interest in the dwelling-house (or the land which comprises the dwelling-house).

Dwelling-houses already qualifying for relief

16.—(1) Section 50 of this Act does not apply to a dwelling-house if—

(a) a certificate has been issued under section 306(2) of the Taxes Act 1988 (as modified by paragraph 10 above) by some other company ("the other company"); and

(b) at any time after the issue of the shares to which that certificate related, the conditions mentioned in sub-paragraph (2) below were satisfied in relation to the dwelling-house (or a dwelling-house the whole or any part of which has been converted into or consists of the whole or any part of the dwelling-house).

(2) The conditions referred to in sub-paragraph (1) above are satisfied in relation to a dwelling-house at any time if, at that time—

(a) the dwelling-house is a dwelling-house to which section 50 of this Act applies in relation to the other company or any of its subsidiaries; and

(b) an interest in the dwelling-house is owned by that company or any such subsidiary.

Dwelling-houses qualifying for capital allowances

17. Section 50 of this Act does not apply to a dwelling-house in respect of which the company is entitled to capital allowances under paragraph 2 of Schedule 12 to the Finance Act 1982.

Interpretation of certain expressions: Scotland

18. In the application of the above provisions of this Part to Scotland, references to acquiring an interest shall be construed, if there is a contract to acquire the interest, as references to entering into that contract and for the purposes of paragraph 16(2)(b) above, a company or subsidiary shall be regarded as owning an interest during the period between its entering into such a contract as regards that interest and its acquiring the interest.

SCHEDULE 5
Section 58

UNDERWRITERS: ASSESSMENT AND COLLECTION OF TAX

Note.—This Schedule inserts FA 1973, Sch. 16A and TA 1988, Sch. 19A. See TA 1988, Sch. 19A where the provisions as amended from time to time are fully reproduced.

SCHEDULE 6

Section 65

COMMERCIAL WOODLANDS

Preliminary

1. In this Schedule "commercial woodlands" means woodlands in the United Kingdom which are managed on a commercial basis and with a view to the realisation of profits.

Abolition of charge under Schedule B

2.—(1) The charge to tax under Schedule B in respect of the occupation of commercial woodlands is hereby abolished.

(2) In any case where, as respects an accounting period of a company which begins before and ends on or after 6th April 1988, the charge to tax under Schedule B has effect in relation to one part of that period but does not have effect in relation to the other part—

(*a*) the income deemed to arise to the company for that period from the occupation of the woodlands concerned shall be apportioned between those parts; and
(*b*) so much of that income as is apportioned to the part beginning on 6th April 1988 shall not be regarded as income arising to the company for that period.

(3) This paragraph shall be deemed to have come into force on 6th April 1988.

Abolition of Schedule D election etc.

3.—(1) Section 54 of the Taxes Act 1988 and section 111 of the Taxes Act 1970 (which confer on a person occupying commercial woodlands the right to elect to be assessed and charged to tax in respect of them under Schedule D instead of under Schedule B) shall cease to have effect.

(2) Subject to paragraph 5(1) below, profits or gains or losses which arise to a person from the occupation of commercial woodlands on or after 15th March 1988 shall not be regarded for any purposes as profits or gains or losses chargeable under Schedule D.

(3) Subject to paragraph 5(1) below—

(*a*) interest which is paid by a company on or after 15th March 1988 shall not be treated as a charge on income for the purposes of corporation tax; and
(*b*) interest which is paid by any person on or after that date and—

(i) is stated in section 360(1), 361(3) or 362 of the Taxes Act 1988 (loans to buy interest in close company, interest in employee-controlled company or into partnership) to be eligible for relief under section 353 of that Act; or
(ii) is stated in any of the corresponding enactments repealed by that Act to be eligible for relief under section 75 of the Finance Act 1972,

shall not be so eligible,

if the relevant business consists of the occupation of commercial woodlands.

(4) Where part only of the relevant business consists of the occupation of commercial woodlands—

(*a*) interest falling within paragraph (*a*) of sub-paragraph (3) above shall not be treated as a charge on income for the purposes of corporation tax; and
(*b*) interest falling within paragraph (*b*) of that sub-paragraph shall not be eligible for relief under section 353 of the Taxes Act 1988 or section 75 of the Finance Act 1972,

to such extent as may be just and reasonable having regard to all the circumstances of the case and, in particular, to the proportion which that part of that business bears to the whole.

(5) In this paragraph "the relevant business" means—

(*a*) in relation to interest paid on or after 15th March 1988 by a company which is not a member of a group, the business carried on by the company;
(*b*) in relation to interest paid on or after that date by a company which is a member of a group, the business carried on by the group; and
(*c*) in relation to interest falling within paragraph (*b*) of sub-paragraph (3) above, the business carried on by the close company, employee-controlled company or partnership concerned;

and for the purposes of this paragraph two or more businesses carried on by a company, group or partnership shall be regarded as a single business.

(6) For the purposes of this paragraph a company shall be deemed to be a member of a group with one or more other companies if the relationship between that company and the other company or, as the case may be, each of the other companies is as mentioned in section 341(2) of the Taxes Act 1988 or section 60(2) of the Finance (No. 2) Act 1987 (payments of interest between related companies).

(7) This paragraph shall be deemed to have come into force on 15th March 1988.

Transitional provisions

4.—(1) Where this paragraph applies in relation to a person's occupation of any commercial woodlands—

(*a*) that person; or
(*b*) in the event of his death, any other person who occupies them by virtue of any disposition (whether effected by will, under the law relating to intestacy or otherwise) of property comprised in his estate immediately before his death,

may elect to be assessed and charged to tax in respect of them under Schedule D; and the reference in this sub-paragraph to a disposition includes a reference to a disposition as varied under section 142 of the Inheritance Tax Act 1984.

(2) This paragraph applies in relation to a person's occupation of any commercial woodlands if—

(*a*) he had entered into a contract or made arrangements before 15th March 1988 for his occupation of them;
(*b*) he was occupying them on that date; or
(*c*) he is or was occupying them after that date and the requirements of sub-paragraph (3) below are satisfied with respect to the land which comprises them;

and in this sub-paragraph and sub-paragraph (3) below "arrangements" does not include arrangements which are not evidenced by an instrument or other document made before that date.

(3) The requirements of this sub-paragraph are satisfied with respect to any land which comprises commercial woodlands if, before 15th March 1988, the person who is or was occupying them after that date—

(*a*) had entered into a contract or made arrangements for the afforestation (including the replanting) of the land; or
(*b*) had made an application for a grant under section 1 of the Forestry Act 1979 or section 2(1)(*e*) of the Forestry Act (Northern Ireland) 1953 with respect to the land;

and for the purposes of paragraph (*b*) above an application shall be treated as made when it was received by the Forestry Commissioners or, in Northern Ireland, by the Department of Agriculture.

(4) Subject to sub-paragraph (5) below, an election under sub-paragraph (1) above—

(*a*) shall be made by notice in writing given to the inspector not later than two years after the end of the chargeable period to which the election relates;
(*b*) shall have effect not only in relation to that period but also, so long as the person by whom it is made continues to occupy the woodlands, in relation to subsequent chargeable periods; and
(*c*) shall extend to all woodlands on the same estate.

(5) An election made under sub-paragraph (1) above in respect of any commercial woodlands shall not have effect in relation to any chargeable period if before the beginning of that period a relevant grant has been made with respect to any land which comprises woodlands on the same estate.

(6) For the purposes of sub-paragraphs (4) and (5) above, woodlands shall be treated as being on a separate estate if the person occupying them so elects by notice in writing given to the inspector not later than two years after the time when they are planted or replanted.

(7) An election under section 111 of the Taxes Act 1970 made before 15th March 1988 in respect of any commercial woodlands by a person who, on that date, was occupying those woodlands shall have effect as if made under sub-paragraph (1) above.

(8) In this paragraph and paragraph 5 below "relevant grant" means a grant under section 1 of the Forestry Act 1979 or section 2(1)(*e*) of the Forestry Act (Northern Ireland) 1953 which—

(a) is made on terms and conditions first published after 15th March 1988; and
(b) is not made by way of supplement to a grant made on terms and conditions first published before that date.

(9) This paragraph shall be deemed to have come into force on 15th March 1988 and shall cease to have effect on 6th April 1993.

Note.—See **Prospective Legislation Notes** (Commercial Woodlands).
Cross references.—See FA 1989, s. 120(4) (forestry land: abolition of agricultural buildings allowances).

5.—(1) For any chargeable period in relation to which an election made under paragraph 4(1) above by any person has effect in respect of any commercial woodlands—

(a) any profits or gains or losses which arise to him before 6th April 1993 from the occupation of those woodlands shall for all purposes be regarded as profits or gains or losses of a trade chargeable under Schedule D;
(b) in computing those profits or gains or losses, no account shall be taken of any relevant grant and no deduction shall be made for any expenditure in respect of which any such grant was made; and
(c) the occupation of those woodlands shall not be taken into account under paragraph 3(3) or (4) above as respects any interest paid before that date.

(2) In any case where, as respects an accounting period of a company which begins before and ends on or after 6th April 1993, sub-paragraph (1) above has effect in relation to one part of that period but does not have effect in relation to the other part—

(a) the profits or gains or losses arising to the company for that period from the occupation of the woodlands concerned shall be apportioned between those parts; and
(b) such of those profits or gains or losses as are apportioned to the part beginning on 6th April 1993 shall not be regarded as profits or gains or losses arising to the company for that period.

(3) In any case where—

(a) sub-paragraph (1) above, as it applies for income tax purposes, has effect for a year of assessment as respects a person's occupation of any commercial woodlands;
(b) that year of assessment is the final year of assessment for which that sub-paragraph, as it so applies, has effect as respects that person's occupation of those woodlands; and
(c) there is an interval between the end of the relevant basis period and the beginning of the next following year of assessment;

then, for the purpose of calculating any capital allowances which fall to be made in taxing his occupation of those woodlands, the interval shall be deemed to form part of that basis period.

(4) In sub-paragraph (3) above—

"basis period" has the meaning given by section 72 of the Capital Allowances Act 1968;
"the relevant basis period", in relation to a year of assessment, means—

(a) except where that year of assessment is in relation to the occupation by the person of the woodlands concerned a year of loss within the meaning of section 383 of the Taxes Act 1988, the basis period for that year of assessment;
(b) in the excepted case, the basis period for the next following year of assessment.

(5) Sub-paragraph (1) above shall be deemed to have come into force on 15th March 1988 and shall cease to have effect on 6th April 1993.

Note.—See **Prospective Legislation Notes** (Commercial Woodlands).

Consequential amendments

6.—(1) . . .

(2) In section 67(1) of the Taxes Act 1970 (Schedule A), in paragraph 3 of Schedule A (exceptions), after paragraph (a) there shall be inserted—

"(aa) to any profits or gains arising from a person's occupation of any woodlands which are managed on a commercial basis and with a view to the realisation of profits, or".

(3) In section 110 of the Taxes Act 1970 (farming and the commercial occupation of land), in subsection (3), for the proviso there shall be substituted—

"Provided that nothing in this subsection shall apply in relation to the occupation of land which comprises woodlands or is being prepared for use for forestry purposes.";

but the amendment made by this sub-paragraph shall not apply in relation to land which is being prepared for use for forestry purposes if the requirements of paragraph 4(3) above are satisfied with respect to it.

(4) In sections 168(8), 169(10) and 171(5) of the Taxes Act 1970, for the words "section 111 of this Act" there shall be substituted the words "paragraph 4 of Schedule 6 to the Finance Act 1988".

(5) . . .

(6) . . .

(7) In section 53 of the Taxes Act 1988 (farming and the commercial occupation of land), for subsection (4) there shall be substituted—

"(4) Subsection (3) above shall not apply in relation to the occupation of land which comprises woodlands or is being prepared for use for forestry purposes.";

but the amendment made by this sub-paragraph shall not apply in relation to land which is being prepared for use for forestry purposes if the requirements of paragraph 4(3) above are satisfied with respect to it.

(8) . . .

(9) Sub-paragraphs (1), (4) and (8) above shall be deemed to have come into force on 15th March 1988; and sub-paragraphs (2), (3) and (5) to (7) above shall be deemed to have come into force on 6th April 1988.

Notes.—Sub-para. (1) amends CAA 1968, ss. 69, 85.
Sub-para. (5) amends CGTA 1979, s. 113.
Sub-para. (6) amends TA 1988, s. 15.
Sub-para. (8) amends TA 1988, ss. 380, 383, 385.

SCHEDULE 7

Section 66

EXCEPTIONS TO RULE IN SECTION 66(1)

Cases where rule does not apply

1.—(1) Subject to sub-paragraphs (2) and (3) below, section 66(1) of this Act shall not apply in relation to a company which, immediately before the commencement date—

    (*a*) was carrying on business;
    (*b*) was not resident in the United Kingdom, having ceased to be so resident in pursuance of a Treasury consent; and
    (*c*) where that consent was a general consent, was taxable in a territory outside the United Kingdom.

(2) If at any time on or after the commencement date a company falling within sub-paragraph (1) above—

    (*a*) ceases to carry on business; or
    (*b*) where the Treasury consent there referred to was a general consent, ceases to be taxable in a territory outside the United Kingdom,

section 66(1) of this Act shall apply in relation to the company after that time or after the end of the transitional period, whichever is the later.

(3) If at any time on or after the commencement date a company falling within sub-paragraph (1) above becomes resident in the United Kingdom, section 66(1) of this Act shall apply in relation to the company after that time.

2.—(1) Subject to sub-paragraphs (2) and (3) below, section 66(1) of this Act shall not apply in relation to a company which—

    (*a*) carried on business at any time before the commencement date;
    (*b*) ceases to be resident in the United Kingdom at any time on or after that date in pursuance of a Treasury consent; and
    (*c*) is carrying on business immediately after that time.

(2) If at any time after it ceases to be resident in the United Kingdom a company falling within sub-paragraph (1) above ceases to carry on business, section 66(1) of this Act shall apply in relation to the company after that time or after the end of the transitional period, whichever is the later.

(3) If at any time after it ceases to be resident in the United Kingdom a company falling within sub-paragraph (1) above becomes resident in the United Kingdom, section 66(1) of this Act shall apply in relation to the company after that time.

Cases where rule does not apply until end of transitional period

3.—(1) Subject to sub-paragraph (2) below, in relation to a company which—

    (*a*) carried on business at any time before the commencement date;
    (*b*) was not resident in the United Kingdom immediately before that date; and
    (*c*) is not a company falling within paragraph 1(1) above,

section 66(1) of this Act shall not apply until after the end of the transitional period.

(2) If at any time on or after the commencement date a company falling within sub-paragraph (1) above becomes resident in the United Kingdom, section 66(1) of this Act shall apply in relation to the company after that time.

4.—(1) Subject to sub-paragraph (2) below, in relation to a company which—

    (*a*) carried on business at any time before the commencement date;
    (*b*) ceases to be resident in the United Kingdom at any time on or after that date in pursuance of a Treasury consent; and
    (*c*) is not a company falling within paragraph 2(1) above,

section 66(1) of this Act shall not apply until after the end of the transitional period.

(2) If at any time after it ceases to be resident in the United Kingdom a company falling within sub-paragraph (1) above becomes resident in the United Kingdom, section 66(1) of this Act shall apply in relation to the company after that time.

Supplemental

5.—(1) In this Schedule—

"the commencement date" means the date of the coming into force of this Schedule;
"general consent" means a consent under any section to which sub-paragraph (2) below applies given generally within the meaning of subsection (4) of that section;
"taxable" means liable to tax on income by reason of domicile, residence or place of management;
"the transitional period" means the period of five years beginning with the commencement date;
"Treasury consent" means a consent under any section to which sub-paragraph (2) below applies given for the purposes of subsection (1)(*a*) of that section.

(2) This sub-paragraph applies to the following sections (restrictions on the migration etc. of companies), namely—

section 765 of the Taxes Act 1988;
section 482 of the Taxes Act 1970;
section 468 of the Income Tax Act 1952; and
section 36 of the Finance Act 1951.

(3) Any question which arises under any of the provisions of this Schedule shall be determined without regard to the provision made by section 66(1) of this Act.

SCHEDULE 8

Section 96

CAPITAL GAINS: ASSETS HELD ON 31st MARCH 1982

Previous no gain/no loss disposals

1.—(1) Where—

(a) a person makes a disposal, not being a no gain/no loss disposal, of an asset which he acquired after 31st March 1982, and
(b) the disposal by which he acquired the asset and any previous disposal of the asset after 31st March 1982 was a no gain/no loss disposal,

he shall be treated for the purposes of section 96 of this Act as having held the asset on 31st March 1982.

(2) For the purposes of this paragraph a no gain/no loss disposal is one on which by virtue of any of the enactments specified in sub-paragraph (3) below neither a gain nor a loss accrues to the person making the disposal.

(3) The enactments mentioned in sub-paragraph (2) above are—

(a) sections 44, 56, 123A, 146(3), 147(4), 148 and 149A of the Capital Gains Tax Act 1979;
(b) sections 267, 273, 340(7), 342, 342A, 342B, 343(5) and 352(7) of the Taxes Act 1970;
(c) section 148 of the Finance Act 1982;
(d) section 7 of the Finance (No. 2) Act 1983;
(e) paragraph 2 of Schedule 2 to the Trustee Savings Banks Act 1985;
[(ee) section 130(3) of the Transport Act 1985;][1]
(f) section 486(8) of the Taxes Act 1988; and
(g) paragraph 4 of Schedule 12 to this Act.

2.—(1) Sub-paragraph (2) below applies where a person makes a disposal of an asset acquired by him on or after 6th April 1988 in circumstances in which either of the relevant enactments applied.

(2) Where this sub-paragraph applies—

(a) an election under subsection (5) of section 96 of this Act by the person making the disposal shall not cover the disposal, but
(b) the making of such an election by the person from whom the asset was acquired shall cause the disposal to fall outside subsection (3) of that section (so that subsection (2) of that section is not excluded by it) whether or not the person making the disposal makes such an election.

(3) Where the person from whom the asset was acquired by the person making the disposal himself acquired it on or after 6th April 1988 in circumstances in which either of the relevant enactments applied, an election made by him shall not have the effect described in sub-paragraph (2)(b) above but an election made by—

(a) the last person by whom the asset was acquired after 5th April 1988 otherwise than in such circumstances, or
(b) if there is no such person, the person who held the asset on 5th April 1988,

shall have that effect.

(4) In this paragraph "the relevant enactments" means—

(a) section 273 of the Taxes Act 1970, and
(b) section 44 of the Capital Gains Tax Act 1979.

Amendments.—[1] Sub-para. (3)(ee) inserted by FA 1989, Sch. 15, para. 4(2) and deemed always to have had effect.

Capital allowances

3. If under section 96 of this Act it is to be assumed that any asset was on 31st March 1982 sold by the person making the disposal and immediately re-acquired by him, sections 34 and 39 of the Capital Gains Tax Act 1979 shall apply in relation to any capital allowance or renewals allowance made in respect of the expenditure actually incurred by him in providing the asset as if it were made in respect of expenditure which, on that assumption, was incurred by him in re-acquiring the asset on 31st March 1982.

Part disposals

4. Where, in relation to a disposal to which section 96(2) of this Act applies, section 35 of the Capital Gains Tax Act 1979 has effect by reason of an earlier disposal made after 31st March 1982 and before 6th April 1988, the sums to be apportioned under section 35 shall for the purposes of the later disposal be ascertained on the assumption stated in section 96(2) of this Act.

Assets derived from other assets

5. Section 96 of this Act shall have effect with the necessary modifications in relation to a disposal of an asset which on 31st March 1982 was not itself held by the person making the disposal, if its value is derived from another asset of which account is to be taken in relation to the disposal under section 36 of the Capital Gains Tax Act 1979.

Group transactions

6. In relation to disposals to which section 96(2) of this Act applies, section 280 of the Taxes Act 1970 (depreciatory transactions effected on or after 6th April 1965) shall have effect with the substitution in subsections (1) and (5) of the words "31st March 1982" for the words "6th April 1965".

Close companies

7. In relation to disposals to which section 96(2) of this Act applies, section 75(1) of the Capital Gains Tax Act 1979 (close company transferring assets at an undervalue after 6th April 1965) shall have effect with the substitution of the words "31st March 1982" for the words "6th April 1965".

Apportionment of pre-1965 gains and losses

10. In a case where because of paragraph 11 of Schedule 5 to the Capital Gains Tax Act 1979 (which apportions gains and losses partly attributable to ownership before 6th April 1965) only part of a gain or loss is a chargeable gain or allowable loss, subsection (3)(*a*) and (*b*) of section 96 of this Act shall have effect as if the amount of the gain or loss that would accrue if subsection (2) did not apply were equal to that part.

Elections under section 96(5) : excluded disposals

12.—(1) An election under section 96(5) of this Act shall not cover disposals such as are specified in sub-paragraph (2) below.

(2) The disposals mentioned in sub-paragraph (1) above are disposals of, or of an interest in,—

(*a*) plant or machinery,
(*b*) an asset which the person making the disposal has at any time held for the purposes of or in connection with—

(i) a trade consisting of the working of a source of mineral deposits, or
(ii) where a trade involves (but does not consist of) such working, the part of the trade which involves such working, or

(*c*) a licence under the Petroleum (Production) Act 1934 or the Petroleum (Production) Act (Northern Ireland) 1964;

but a disposal does not fall within paragraph (*a*) or (*b*) above unless a capital allowance in respect of any expenditure attributable to the asset has been made to the person making the disposal or would have been made to him had he made a claim.

(3) Where the person making the disposal acquired the asset on a no gain/no loss disposal, the references in sub-paragraph (2) above to that person are references to the person making the disposal, the person who last acquired the asset otherwise than on a no gain/no loss disposal or any person who subsequently acquired the asset on such a disposal.

(4) In this paragraph—

(*a*) "source of mineral deposits" shall be construed in accordance with Schedule 13 to the Finance Act 1986, and
(*b*) references to a no gain/no loss disposal shall be construed in accordance with paragraph 1 above.

Elections under section 96(5) : groups of companies

13.—(1) A company may not make an election under section 96(5) of this Act at a time when it is a member but not the principal company of a group unless the company did not become a member of the group until after the relevant time.

(2) Subject to sub-paragraph (3) below, an election under section 96(5) of this Act by a company which is the principal company of a group shall have effect also as an election by any other company which at the relevant time is a member of the group.

(3) Sub-paragraph (2) above shall not apply in relation to a company which, in some period after 5th April 1988 and before the relevant time, is not a member of the group if—

(a) during that period the company makes a disposal to which section 96 of this Act applies, and
(b) the period during which an election under subsection (5) of that section could be made expires without such an election having been made.

(4) Sub-paragraph (2) above shall apply in relation to a company notwithstanding that the company ceases to be a member of the group at any time after the relevant time except where—

(a) the company is an outgoing company in relation to the group, and
(b) the election relating to the group is made after the company ceases to be a member of the group.

(5) In relation to a company which is the principal company of a group the reference in [subsection (6)]¹ of section 96 of this Act to the first relevant disposal is a reference to the first disposal to which that section applies by a company which is—

(a) a member of the group but not an outgoing company in relation to the group, or
(b) an incoming company in relation to the group.

Amendments.—¹ Words in sub-para. (5) substituted by FA 1989, Sch. 15, para. 5 and deemed always to have had effect.

14.—(1) In paragraph 13 above "the relevant time", in relation to a group of companies, is—

(a) the first time when any company which is then a member of the group, and is not an outgoing company in relation to the group, makes a disposal to which section 96 of this Act applies,
(b) the time immediately following the first occasion when a company which is an incoming company in relation to the group becomes a member of the group,
(c) the time when an election is made by the principal company,

whichever is earliest.

(2) In paragraph 13 above and this paragraph—

"incoming company", in relation to a group of companies, means a company which—

(a) makes its first disposal to which section 96 of this Act applies at a time when it is not a member of the group, and
(b) becomes a member of the group before the end of the period during which an election under subsection (5) of that section could be made in relation to it and at a time when no such election has been made, and

"outgoing company", in relation to a group of companies, means a company which ceases to be a member of the group before the end of the period during which an election under section 96(5) of this Act could be made in relation to it and at a time when no such election has been made.

(3) Section 272 of the Taxes Act 1970 shall have effect for the purposes of paragraph 13 above and this paragraph as for those of sections 272 to 281 of that Act.

SCHEDULE 9

Section 97

DEFERRED CHARGES ON GAINS BEFORE 31st MARCH 1982

Reduction of deduction or gain

1. Where this Schedule applies—

(*a*) in a case within paragraph 2 below, the amount of the deduction referred to in that paragraph, and
(*b*) in a case within paragraph 3 below, the amount of the gain referred to in that paragraph,

shall be one half of what it would be apart from this Schedule.

Charges rolled-over or held-over

2.—(1) Subject to sub-paragraph (2) below, this Schedule applies on a disposal, not being a no gain/no loss disposal, of an asset on or after 6th April 1988 if—

(*a*) the person making the disposal acquired the asset after 31st March 1982,
(*b*) a deduction falls to be made by virtue of any of the enactments specified in sub-paragraph (3) below from the expenditure which is allowable in computing the amount of any gain accruing on the disposal, and
(*c*) the deduction is attributable (whether directly or indirectly and whether in whole or in part) to a chargeable gain accruing on the disposal before 6th April 1988 of an asset acquired before 31st March 1982 by the person making that disposal.

(2) This Schedule does not apply where, by reason of the previous operation of this Schedule, the amount of the deduction is less than it otherwise would be.

(3) The enactments referred to in sub-paragraph (1) above are—

(*a*) section 21(4) and (5) of the Capital Gains Tax Act 1979 (roll-over where replacement asset acquired after receipt of compensation or insurance money);
(*b*) section 111A of that Act (roll-over where replacement land acquired on compulsory acquisition of other land);
(*c*) section 115 of that Act (roll-over where replacement asset acquired on disposal of business asset);
(*d*) section 123 of that Act (roll-over where shares acquired on disposal of business to company);
(*e*) section 126 of that Act (hold-over where business asset acquired by gift); and
(*f*) section 79 of the Finance Act 1980 (hold-over where asset acquired by gift).

Postponed charges

3.—(1) Subject to sub-paragraph (3) below [and to paragraph 1 of Schedule 15 to the Finance Act 1989][1], this Schedule applies where—

(*a*) by virtue of any of the enactments specified in sub-paragraph (2) below a gain is treated as accruing in consequence of an event occurring on or after 6th April 1988, and
(*b*) the gain is attributable (whether directly or indirectly and whether in whole or in part) to the disposal before 6th April 1988 of an asset acquired before 31st March 1982 by the person making that disposal.

(2) The enactments referred to in sub-paragraph (1) above are—

(*a*) section 268A of the Taxes Act 1970 (postponement of charge where securities acquired in exchange for business acquired by non-resident company);
(*b*) section 278(3) of that Act (charge on company leaving group in respect of asset acquired from another member of same group);
(*c*) section 84 of the Capital Gains Tax Act 1979 (postponement of charge where gilts acquired on compulsory acquisition of shares);
(*d*) section 111B(3) of that Act (postponement of charge where depreciating asset acquired on compulsory acquisition of land);
(*e*) section 117(2) of that Act (postponement of charge where depreciating asset acquired as replacement for business asset);
(*f*) section 79 of the Finance Act 1981 (activation of charge rolled over under section 79 of the Finance Act 1980 on emigration of donee); and

(g) paragraph 10 of Schedule 13 to the Finance Act 1984 (postponement of charge on reorganisation etc. involving acquisition of qualifying corporate bonds).

(3) Where a gain is treated as accruing by virtue of section 278(3) of the Taxes Act 1970 this Schedule applies only if the asset was acquired by the chargeable company (within the meaning of section 278) before 6th April 1988.

Amendments.—[1] Words in sub-para. (1) inserted by FA 1989, Sch. 15, para. 2 and deemed always to have had effect.

Previous no gain/no loss disposals

4. Where—

(a) a person makes a disposal of an asset which he acquired on or after 31st March 1982, and

(b) the disposal by which he acquired the asset and any previous disposal of the asset on or after 31st March 1982 was a no gain/no loss disposal,

he shall be treated for the purposes of paragraphs 2(1)(c) and 3(1)(b) above as having acquired the asset before 31st March 1982.

5.—(1) Sub-paragraph (2) below applies where—

(a) on or after 6th April 1988 a person makes a disposal of an asset which he acquired on or after 31st March 1982.

(b) the disposal by which he acquired the asset was a no gain/no loss disposal, and

(c) a deduction falling to be made as mentioned in paragraph (b) of sub-paragraph (1) of paragraph (2) above which was attributable as mentioned in paragraph (c) of that sub-paragraph was made—

  (i) on that disposal, or
  (ii) where one or more earlier no gain/no loss disposals of the asset have been made on or after 31st March 1982 and since the last disposal of the asset which was not a no gain/no loss disposal, on any such earlier disposal.

(2) Where this sub-paragaph applies the deduction shall be treated for the purposes of paragraph 2 above as falling to be made on the disposal mentioned in sub-paragraph (1)(a) above and not on the no gain/no loss disposal.

6. For the purposes of this Schedule "no gain/no loss disposal" has the same meaning as in paragraph 1 of Schedule 8 to this Act.

Assets derived from other assets

7. The references in paragraphs 2(1)(c) and 3(1)(b) above to the disposal of an asset acquired by a person before 31st March 1982 include references to the disposal of an asset which was not acquired by the person before that date if its value is derived from another asset which was so acquired and of which account is to be taken in relation to the disposal under section 36 of the Capital Gains Tax Act 1979.

Claims

8.—(1) No relief shall be given under this Schedule unless a claim is made—

(a) in the case of a gain treated as accruing by virtue of section 278(3) of the Taxes Act 1970 to a company which ceases to be a member of a group, within the period of two years beginning at the end of the accounting period which ends when the company ceases to be a member of the group,

(b) in any other case, within the period of two years beginning at the end of the year of assessment or accounting period in which the disposal in question is made, or the gain in question is treated as accruing,

or within such longer period as the Board may by notice in writing allow.

(2) A claim under sub-paragraph (1) above shall be supported by such particulars as the inspector may require for the purpose of establishing entitlement to relief under this Schedule and the amount of relief due.

SCHEDULE 10

Section 109

GAINS ARISING FROM CERTAIN SETTLED PROPERTY

Charge on settlor with interest in settlement

1.—(1) Subject to paragraphs 3 and 4 below, this paragraph applies where—

(*a*) in a year of assessment chargeable gains accrue to the trustees of a settlement from the disposal of any or all of the settled property,
(*b*) after making any deductions provided for by section 4(1) of the Capital Gains Tax Act 1979 in respect of disposals of the settled property there remains an amount on which the trustees would, disregarding section 5 (annual exemption) of that Act (and apart from this Schedule), be chargeable to tax for the year in respect of those gains, and
(*c*) at any time during the year the settlor has an interest in the settlement.

(2) Where this paragraph applies, the trustees shall not be chargeable to tax in respect of the gains concerned but instead chargeable gains of an amount equal to that referred to in sub-paragraph (1)(*b*) above shall be treated as accruing to the settlor in the year.

2.—(1) Subject to sub-paragraphs (2) and (3) below, for the purposes of paragraph 1(1)(*c*) above a settlor has an interest in a settlement if—

(*a*) any property which may at any time be comprised in the settlement or any income which may arise under the settlement is, or will or may become, applicable for the benefit of or payable to the settlor or the spouse of the settlor in any circumstances whatsoever, or
(*b*) the settlor, or the spouse of the settlor, enjoys a benefit deriving directly or indirectly from any property which is comprised in the settlement or any income arising under the settlement.

(2) A settlor does not have an interest in a settlement by virtue of paragraph (*a*) of sub-paragraph (1) above if and so long as none of the property which may at any time be comprised in the settlement and none of the income which may arise under the settlement can become applicable or payable as mentioned in that paragraph except in the event of—

(*a*) the bankruptcy of some person who is or may become beneficially entitled to that property or income;
(*b*) any assignment of or charge on that property or income being made or given by some such person;
(*c*) in the case of a marriage settlement, the death of both the parties to the marriage and of all or any of the children of the marriage; or
(*d*) the death under the age of 25 or some lower age of some person who would be beneficially entitled to that property or income on attaining that age.

(3) A settlor does not have an interest in a settlement by virtue of paragraph (*a*) of sub-paragraph (1) above if and so long as some person is alive and under the age of 25 during whose life none of the property which may at any time be comprised in the settlement and none of the income which may arise under the settlement can become applicable or payable as mentioned in that paragraph except in the event of that person becoming bankrupt or assigning or charging his interest in that property or income.

3.—(1) Paragraph 1 above does not apply where the settlor dies during the year.

(2) In a case where the settlor has an interest in the settlement only for either or both of the following reasons, namely—

(*a*) that property or income is, or will or may become, applicable for the benefit of or payable to the settlor's spouse, and
(*b*) that the settlor's spouse enjoys a benefit from property or income,

paragraph 1 above does not apply where the spouse dies, or the settlor and the spouse cease to be married, during the year.

4. Paragraph 1 above does not apply unless the settlor is, and the trustees are, either resident in the United Kingdom during any part of the year or ordinarily resident in the United Kingdom during the year.

Right of recovery

5.—(1) Where any tax becomes chargeable on and is paid by a person in respect of gains treated as accruing to him (or, if he is a married man, to his wife) under paragraph 1 above he shall be entitled—

(*a*) to recover the amount of the tax from any trustee of the settlement, and
(*b*) for that purpose to require an inspector to give him a certificate specifying—

(i) the amount of the gains accruing to the trustees in respect of which he has paid tax; and
(ii) the amount of tax paid;

and any such certificate shall be conclusive evidence of the facts stated in it.

(2) In order to ascertain for the purposes of sub-paragraph (1) above the amount of tax chargeable for any year by virtue of paragraph 1 above in respect of gains treated as accruing to any person, those gains shall be regarded as forming the highest part of the amount on which he is chargeable to capital gains tax for the year.

(3) Where for the year 1988–89 or 1989–90—

(*a*) section 99(1) of this Act applies in relation to a husband and wife, and
(*b*) gains are treated by virtue of paragraph 1 above as accruing to either of them, and
(*c*) tax at a rate equivalent to the higher rate of income tax is charged on the whole or part of the chargeable amount (within the meaning of section 99) of either of them,

sub-paragraphs (4) and (5) below shall have effect for ascertaining for the purposes of sub-paragraph (1) above the amount of tax chargeable for the year in respect of gains treated as accruing by virtue of paragraph 1 above.

(4) Those gains shall be regarded as having been taxed at a rate equivalent to the higher rate of income tax so far as their amount does not exceed the amount (or the aggregate of the amounts) on which tax was charged as mentioned in sub-paragraph (3)(*c*) above, and otherwise as having been taxed at a rate equivalent to the basic rate of income tax.

(5) In a case where—

(*a*) section 99(3) applies, and
(*b*) the chargeable amounts of both husband and wife include gains treated as accruing by virtue of paragraph 1 above,

the extent to which the gains treated as accruing to the husband and the gains treated as accruing to the wife are regarded as having been taxed at a rate equivalent to the higher rate of income tax shall be proportionate to the amounts of those gains.

Note.—See **Prospective Legislation Notes** (Married Couples).

Meaning of "settlor" etc.

6.—(1) For the purposes of this Schedule a person is a settlor in relation to a settlement if the settled property consists of or includes property originating from him.

(2) In this Schedule—

(*a*) references to settled property (and to property comprised in a settlement), in relation to any settlor, are references only to property originating from that settlor, and
(*b*) references to income arising under a settlement, in relation to any settlor, are references only to income originating from that settlor.

(3) References in this paragraph to property originating from a settlor are references to—

(*a*) property which that settlor has provided directly or indirectly for the purposes of the settlement,
(*b*) property representing that property, and
(*c*) so much of any property which represents both property so provided and other property as, on a just apportionment, represents the property so provided.

(4) References in this paragraph to income originating from a settlor are references to—

(*a*) income from property originating from that settlor, and
(*b*) income provided directly or indirectly by that settlor.

(5) In sub-paragraphs (3) and (4) above—

(*a*) references to property or income which a settlor has provided directly or indirectly include references to property or income which has been provided directly or indirectly by another person in pursuance of reciprocal arrangements with that settlor, but do not include references to property or income which that settlor has provided directly or indirectly in pursuance of reciprocal arrangements with another person, and

(b) references to property which represents other property include references to property which represents accumulated income from that other property.

Information

7.—(1) An inspector may by notice require any person who is or has been a trustee of, a beneficiary under, or a settlor in relation to, a settlement to give him within such time as he may direct, not being less than 28 days, such particulars as he thinks necessary for the purposes of this Schedule.

(2) ...

Note.—Sub-para. (2) amends TMA 1970, s. 98.

Shares in non-resident companies

8. The reference in paragraph 1(1)(a) above to gains accruing to trustees from the disposal of settled property includes a reference to gains treated as accruing to them under section 15 of the Capital Gains Tax Act 1979 (non-resident companies) and the reference in paragraph 1(1)(b) above to deductions in respect of disposals of the settled property includes a reference to deductions on account of losses treated under that section as accruing to the trustees.

Maintenance funds for historic buildings

9. Where the trustees of a settlement have elected that section 691(2) of the Taxes Act 1988 (certain income of maintenance funds for historic buildings not to be income of settlor etc.) shall have effect in the case of any settlement or part of a settlement in relation to a year of assessment, the preceding provisions of this Schedule shall not apply in relation to the settlement or part for the year.

Commencement

10. This Schedule shall have effect for the year 1988–89 and subsequent years of assessment.

SCHEDULE 11

Section 114

CAPITAL GAINS INDEXATION: GROUPS AND ASSOCIATED COMPANIES

Debts

1.—(1) Subject to sub-paragraph (3) below, where—

(*a*) there is a disposal by a company of a linked company debt on a security owed by another company, and
(*b*) the two companies are linked companies immediately before the disposal,

there shall be no indexation allowance on the disposal.

(2) Subject to sub-paragraph (3) below, where—

(*a*) there is a disposal by a company of a debt on a security owed by another company which is not a linked company debt on a security, and
(*b*) the two companies are linked companies immediately before the disposal,

then, in ascertaining any indexation allowance due on the disposal, RD as defined in section 87(2) of the Finance Act 1982 shall be taken as the retail prices index for the first month after the acquisition of the debt in which the two companies were linked companies (or, if later, March 1982).

(3) Where—

(*a*) there is a disposal by a company of a debt on a security owed by another company,
(*b*) the debt constituted or formed part of the new holding received by the company making the disposal on a reorganisation, and
(*c*) sub-paragraph (1) or (2) above would apply in relation to the disposal but for this sub-paragraph,

neither of those sub-paragraphs shall apply in relation to the disposal, but any indexation allowance which, apart from this sub-paragraph, would be due on the disposal shall be reduced by such amount as appears to the inspector, or on appeal the Commissioners concerned, to be just and reasonable.

(4) For the purposes of this paragraph a debt on a security owed by a company is a linked company debt on a security where immediately after its acquisition by the company making the disposal the two companies were linked companies.

2. Where—

(*a*) there is a disposal by a company of a debt on a security owed by any person,
(*b*) the company and that person are not linked companies immediately before the disposal, and
(*c*) the debt was incurred by that person as part of arrangements involving another company being put in funds,

paragraph 1 above shall have effect if and to the extent that it would if the debt were owed by that other company.

Shares

3.—(1) This paragraph applies—

(*a*) where there is a disposal by a company of—

(i) a holding of redeemable preference shares of another company, or
(ii) a holding of shares, other than redeemable preference shares, of another company which has at all times consisted entirely of, or has at any time included, linked company shares, or

(*b*) where—

(i) there is a disposal by a company of a holding of shares of another company which is not a holding falling within paragraph (*a*) above,
(ii) the holding constituted or formed part of the new holding received by the company making the disposal on a reorganisation, and

(iii) but for section 78 of the Capital Gains Tax Act 1979 that reorganisation (or in a case where the holding disposed of derives, in whole or in part, from assets which were original shares in relation to an earlier reorganisation, that reorganisation or any such earlier reorganisation) would have involved a disposal in relation to which paragraph 1 above would have applied or this paragraph would have applied by virtue of paragraph (*a*) above,

if the two companies are linked companies immediately before the disposal.

(2) Where this paragraph applies, any indexation allowance which, apart from this paragraph, would be due on the disposal shall be reduced by such amount as appears to the inspector, or on appeal the Commissioners concerned, to be just and reasonable.

(3) For the purposes of this paragraph shares of a company are linked company shares where—

(*a*) immediately after their acquisition by the company making the disposal the two companies were linked companies,
(*b*) their acquisition by the company making the disposal was wholly or substantially financed by one or more linked company loans or linked company funded subscriptions (or by a combination of such loans and subscriptions), and
(*c*) the sole or main benefit which might have been expected to accrue from that acquisition was the obtaining of an indexation allowance on a disposal of the shares.

(4) In sub-paragraph (3) above—

"linked company loan" means a loan made to the company making the disposal by another company where immediately after the acquisition of the shares by the company making the disposal the two companies were linked companies, and
"linked company funded subscription" means a subscription for shares in the company making the disposal by another company where—

(*a*) immediately after the acquisition of the shares by the company making the disposal those two companies were linked companies, and
(*b*) the subscription was wholly or substantially financed, either directly or indirectly, by one or more linked company subscription-financing loans.

(5) In sub-paragraph (4) above "linked company subscription-financing loan" means a loan made by a company to the subscribing company or any other company where immediately after the acquisition of the shares by the company making the disposal—

(*a*) the company making the loan, and
(*b*) the subscribing company, and
(*c*) where the company to which the loan was made was not the subscribing company, that company,

were linked companies.

Linked companies

4. For the purposes of this Schedule companies are linked companies if they are members of the same group or are associated with each other; and for the purposes of this paragraph—

(*a*) "group" means a company which has one or more 51 per cent. subsidiaries together with that subsidiary or those subsidiaries (section 838 (meaning of 51 per cent. subsidiary) of the Taxes Act 1988 having effect for the purposes of this paragraph as for those of the Tax Acts), and
(*b*) two companies are associated with each other if one controls the other or both are under the control of the same person or persons (section 416(2) to (6) (meaning of control) of the Taxes Act 1988 having effect for the purposes of this paragraph as for those of Part XI of that Act).

Supplementary

5. Where a disposal of a holding of shares follows one or more disposals of the same holding to which section 273(1) of the Taxes Act 1970 (which treats certain intra-group transactions as producing neither a gain nor a loss) applied, paragraph 3(3) to (5) above shall have effect as if the references to the company making the disposal were references to the company which last acquired the asset otherwise than on a disposal to which section 273(1) applied.

6.—(1) In this Schedule "redeemable preference shares" means shares in a company which are described as such in the terms of their issue or which fulfil the condition in paragraph (*a*) below and either or both of the conditions in paragraphs (*b*) and (*c*) below—

(*a*) that, as against other shares in the company, they carry a preferential entitlement to a dividend or to any assets in a winding up or both;
(*b*) that, by virtue of the terms of their issue, the exercise of a right by any person or the existence of any arrangements, they are liable to be redeemed, cancelled or repaid, in whole or in part;
(*c*) that, by virtue of any arrangements—

> (i) to which the company which issued the shares is a party, or
> (ii) where that company and another company are linked companies at the time of the issue, to which that other company is a party,

the holder has a right to require another person to acquire the shares or is obliged in any circumstances to dispose of them or another person has a right or is in any circumstances obliged to acquire them;

and for the purposes of paragraph (*a*) above shares are to be treated as carrying a preferential entitlement to a dividend as against other shares if, by virtue of any arrangements, there are circumstances in which a minimum dividend will be payable on those shares but not on others.

(2) In this Schedule the expressions "reorganisation", "original shares" and "new holding" have the meanings given by section 77 of the Capital Gains Tax Act 1979 except that, in a case where sections 78 and 79 of that Act apply in circumstances other than a reorganisation (within the meaning of section 77 of that Act) by virtue of any other provision of Chapter II of Part IV of that Act (conversion of securities, company reconstructions and amalgamations etc.), those expressions shall be construed as they fall to be construed in sections 78 and 79 as they so apply.

(3) In this Schedule—

> "holding", in relation to shares, means a number of shares which are to be regarded for the purposes of the Capital Gains Tax Act 1979 as indistinguishable parts of a single asset,
> "indexation allowance" has the same meaning as in Chapter III of Part III of the Finance Act 1982, and
> "security" has the same meaning as in section 82 of the Capital Gains Tax Act 1979.

Commencement

7. This Schedule shall apply to disposals on or after 15th March 1988.

SCHEDULE 12

Section 145

BUILDING SOCIETIES: CHANGE OF STATUS

Introductory

1. Paragraphs 2 to 7 below apply where there is a transfer of the whole of a building society's business to a company ("the successor company") in accordance with section 97 and the other applicable provisions of the Building Societies Act 1986.

Gilt-edged securities and other financial trading stock

2.—(1) For the purposes of section 100(1) of the Taxes Act 1988 (valuation of trading stock on discontinuance of trade) the society's financial trading stock shall be valued at an amount equal to its cost to the society.

(2) In computing for any corporation tax purpose the profits or gains of a trade carried on by the successor company, such of the assets comprised in the transfer as constituted the society's financial trading stock shall be regarded as acquired by the company at their cost to the society.

(3) In this paragraph "financial trading stock", in relation to a building society, means such of the assets held by the society by virtue of regulations under section 21(7) of the Building Societies Act 1986 (liquid assets etc.) as constitute trading stock for the purposes of section 100 of the Taxes Act 1988.

Capital allowances

3.—(1) For the purposes of the allowances and charges provided for by the Capital Allowances Act 1968 and by Part III of the Finance Act 1971 (capital allowances) the trade of the society shall not be treated as permanently discontinued and the trade of the successor company shall not be treated as a new trade set up and commenced by the successor company.

(2) There shall be made to or on the successor company in accordance with those Acts all such allowances and charges as would, if the society had continued to carry on the trade, have fallen to be made to or on it, and the amount of any such allowance or charge shall be computed as if the successor company had been carrying on the trade since the society began to do so and as if everything done to or by the society had been done to or by the successor company.

(3) No transfer of assets from the society to the successor company effected by section 97 of the Building Societies Act 1986 shall be treated as giving rise to any such allowance or charge.

Capital gains: assets acquired from society, etc.

4.—(1) Where the society and the successor company are not members of the same group at the time of the transfer—

(*a*) they shall be treated for the purposes of corporation tax on capital gains as if any asset disposed of as part of the transfer were acquired by the successor company for a consideration of such amount as would secure that on the disposal neither a gain nor a loss would accrue to the society, and

(*b*) if because of the transfer any company ceases to be a member of the same group as the society, that event shall not cause section 278 of the Taxes Act 1970 (which treats a company ceasing to be a member of a group as having sold and reacquired at the time of acquisition assets acquired from another member of the group) to have effect as respects any asset acquired by the company from the society or any other member of the same group.

(2) Where the society and the successor company are members of the same group at the time of the transfer but later cease to be so, that later event shall not cause section 278 to have effect as respects—

(*a*) any asset acquired by the successor company on or before the transfer from the society or any other member of the same group, or

(*b*) any asset acquired from the society or any other member of the same group by any company other than the successor company which is a member of the same group at the time of the transfer.

(3) Subject to sub-paragraph (5) below, where a company which is a member of the same group as the society at the time of the transfer—

(a) ceases to be a member of that group and becomes a member of the same group as the successor company, and
(b) subsequently ceases to be a member of that group,

section 278 shall have effect on that later event as respects any relevant asset acquired by the company otherwise than from the successor company as if it had been acquired from the successor company.

(4) In sub-paragraph (3) above "relevant asset" means any asset acquired by the company—

(a) from the society, or
(b) from any other company which is a member of the same group at the time of the transfer,

when the company and the society, or the company, the society and the other company, were members of the same group.

(5) Sub-paragraph (3) above shall not apply if the company which acquired the asset and the company from which it was acquired (one being a 75 per cent. subsidiary of the other) cease simultaneously to be members of the same group as the successor company but continue to be members of the same group as one another.

(6) For the purposes of this paragraph "group" shall be construed in accordance with section 272 of the Taxes Act 1970.

Cross references.—See FA 1985, s. 68(7), (7A)(f) (modification of indexation allowance with respect to disposals of assets after 1 April 1985).

Capital gains: shares, and rights to shares, in successor company

5.—(1) Where, in connection with the transfer, there are conferred on members of the society—

(a) any rights to acquire shares in the successor company in priority to other persons, or
(b) any rights to acquire shares in that company for consideration of an amount or value lower than the market value of the shares, or
(c) any rights to free shares in that company,

any such right so conferred on a member shall be regarded for the purposes of capital gains tax as an option (within the meaning of section 137 of the Capital Gains Tax Act 1979) granted to, and acquired by, him for no consideration and having no value at the time of that grant and acquisition.

(2) Where, in connection with the transfer, shares in the successor company are issued by that company, or disposed of by the society, to a member of the society, those shares shall be regarded for the purposes of capital gains tax—

(a) as acquired by the member for a consideration of an amount or value equal to the amount or value of any new consideration given by him for the shares (or, if no new consideration is given, as acquired for no consideration); and
(b) as having, at the time of their acquisition by the member, a value equal to the amount or value of the new consideration so given (or, if no new consideration is given, as having no value);

but this sub-paragraph is without prejudice to the operation of sub-paragraph (1) above, where applicable.

(3) Sub-paragraph (4) below applies in any case where—

(a) in connection with the transfer, shares in the successor company are issued by that company, or disposed of by the society, to trustees on terms which provide for the transfer of those shares to members of the society for no new consideration; and
(b) the circumstances are such that in the hands of the trustees the shares constitute settled property, within the meaning of the Capital Gains Tax Act 1979.

(4) Where this sub-paragraph applies, then, for the purposes of capital gains tax—

(a) the shares shall be regarded as acquired by the trustees for no consideration;
(b) the interest of any member in the settled property constituted by the shares shall be

regarded as acquired by him for no consideration and as having no value at the time of its acquisition;

(c) where a member becomes absolutely entitled as against the trustees to any of the settled property, both the trustees and the member shall be treated as if, on his becoming so entitled, the shares in question had been disposed of and immediately reacquired by the trustees, in their capacity as trustees within section 46(1) of the Capital Gains Tax Act 1979, for a consideration of such an amount as would secure that on the disposal neither a gain nor a loss would accrue to the trustees (and accordingly section 54 of that Act shall not apply in relation to that occasion); and

(d) on the disposal by a member of an interest in the settled property, other than the disposal treated as occurring for the purposes of paragraph (c) above, any gain accruing shall be a chargeable gain (and accordingly section 58(1) of the Capital Gains Tax Act 1979 shall not apply in relation to the disposal).

(5) Where, in connection with the transfer, the society disposes of any shares in the successor company, then, for the purposes of the Capital Gains Tax Act 1979, any gains arising on the disposal shall not be chargeable gains.

(6) In this paragraph—

"free shares", in relation to a member of the society, means any shares issued by the successor company, or disposed of by the society, to that member in connection with the transfer but for no new consideration;

"member", in relation to the society, means a person who is or has been a member of it, in that capacity, and any reference to a member includes a reference to a member of any particular class or description;

"new consideration" means consideration other than—

(a) consideration provided directly or indirectly out of the assets of the society; or
(b) consideration derived from a member's shares or other rights in the society.

(7) References in this paragraph to the case where a member becomes absolutely entitled to settled property as against the trustees shall be taken to include references to the case where he would become so entitled but for being an infant or otherwise under disability.

Distributions

6.—(1) Where, in connection with the transfer, qualifying benefits are conferred by the society or the successor company on members of the society, the conferring of those benefits shall not be regarded as either—

(a) the making of a distribution, within the meaning of the Corporation Tax Acts; or
(b) the payment or crediting of a dividend for the purposes of section 476 of the Taxes Act 1988 or any regulations under that section (building society interest etc.).

(2) Sub-paragraph (1) above does not preclude any qualifying benefit (and, in particular, any qualifying benefit which in the hands of the recipient would, apart from that sub-paragraph, constitute income for the purposes of income tax) from being a capital distribution for the purposes of section 72 of the Capital Gains Tax Act 1979, and in that section "distribution" shall be construed accordingly.

(3) In this paragraph "qualifying benefits" means—

(a) any such rights as are mentioned in paragraph 5(1)(a), (b) or (c) above, and any property obtained by the exercise of those rights;
(b) any shares issued or disposed of as mentioned in paragraph 5(2) above;
(c) any shares issued or disposed of, or to which a member becomes entitled, as mentioned in paragraph 5(3) or (4) above, and any interest in the settled property constituted by those shares;
(d) any payment in lieu of a qualifying benefit falling within paragraphs (a) to (c) above;
(e) any distribution made in pursuance of section 100(2)(b) of the Building Societies Act 1986.

(4) "Member" has the same meaning in this paragraph as in paragraph 5 above.

Contractual savings schemes

7. The following provisions, namely—

(a) section 326 of the Taxes Act 1988 (certain sums to be disregarded for income tax purposes), and
(b) section 149B(4) of the Capital Gains Tax Act 1979 (corresponding provision for capital gains tax purposes),

shall have effect in relation to any terminal bonus, or interest or other sum, payable after the transfer under a savings scheme which immediately before the transfer was a certified contractual savings scheme (within the meaning of section 326) in relation to the society notwithstanding that it ceased to be such a scheme by reason of the transfer.

Stamp duty

8. . . .

Note.—See Orange Book.

SCHEDULE 13

Section 146

POST-CONSOLIDATION AMENDMENTS
PART I
AMENDMENTS OF THE TAXES ACT 1988

15. The repeals made in section 47 of the Finance (No. 2) Act 1975 shall be treated as never having had effect.

PART II
AMENDMENTS OF OTHER ENACTMENTS

The Finance Act 1987 (c. 16)

24. The repeals made by the Finance Act 1987 in section 47 of the Finance (No. 2) Act 1975 shall be treated as never having had effect.

Commencement

25. The amendments made by paragraphs 16 to 23 of this Schedule shall be treated for the purposes of their commencement as if they had been made by the Taxes Act 1988.

SCHEDULE 14
Section 148

REPEALS

PART IV
INCOME AND CORPORATION TAX: GENERAL

Chapter	Short title	Extent of repeal
1988 c. 1.	The Income and Corporation Taxes Act 1988.	In section 278, in subsection (2), the words "Subject to subsection (3) below," and subsections (3) to (7).

4. The repeals in section 278 of the Income and Corporation Taxes Act 1988 have effect for the year 1990–91 and subsequent years of assessment.

PART V
COMMERCIAL WOODLANDS

Chapter	Short title	Extent of repeal
1968 c. 3	The Capital Allowances Act 1968.	In section 47, subsection (1)(*b*) and, in subsection (2), the words "(including woodlands)". In section 69, the definitions of "forestry land" and "forestry income". In section 70(7), the words from "and the occupation of woodlands" to "Schedule D". Section 79(3). Section 85(4). In section 87(5), the words "This subsection" onwards. In Schedule 9, in paragraph 4, the words "or the occupation of woodland in the United Kingdom".
1970 c. 10.	The Income and Corporation Taxes Act 1970.	Section 168(8). In section 169(10), the words from "and in relation to the occupation of woodlands" to "paragraph 4 of Schedule 6 to the Finance Act 1988". Section 171(5). Section 174(13). In section 238(4)(*b*), the words "or the occupation of woodlands" onwards. Section 347(8)(*b*). In section 515(6), the words from "and in relation to the occupation of woodlands" to "Schedule D".
1971 c. 68.	The Finance Act 1971.	Section 47(1)(*b*).
1988 c. 1.	The Income and Corporation Taxes Act 1988.	In section 6(4)(*b*), the words "or the occupation of woodlands" onwards. Section 380(4). In section 383(12)(*a*), the words from "and in relation to the occupation of woodlands" to "paragraph 4 of Schedule 6 to the Finance Act 1988". Section 385(6). Section 389(8) Section 491(10)(*b*). In section 810(6), the words from "and in relation to the occupation of woodlands" to "Schedule D".
1988 c. 39.	The Finance Act 1988.	In Schedule 6, paragraphs 4 and 5(1).

3. The ... repeals have effect from 6th April 1993.

PART VIII
MARRIED COUPLES

Chapter	Short title	Extent of repeal
1970 c. 9.	The Taxes Management Act 1970.	In section 8(3B), the words "or of his wife living with him". Section 11A(3). In section 13(1)(*c*), the words ", or is a married woman,". In section 29(8), the words "and 'return under Part II of this Act'" onwards. In section 93(1) the words from "or section 284(4)" to "wife)". In section 95(1)(*a*), the words from "or section 284(4)" to "wife)".
1975 c. 14.	The Social Security Act 1975.	In Schedule 2, paragraph 4.
1975 c. 15.	The Social Security (Northern Ireland) Act 1975.	In Schedule 2, paragraph 4.
1979 c. 14.	The Capital Gains Tax Act 1979.	Section 4(2). In section 5(6), the words "husbands and wives,". Section 45. In Schedule 1, paragraphs 2 and 3.
1980 c. 48.	The Finance Act 1980.	Section 77(4)(*b*) and (*d*).
1982 c. 39.	The Finance Act 1982.	In section 80(3)(*b*), the words "2(1) and".
1988 c. 1.	The Income and Corporation Taxes Act 1988.	In section 256, the words "and 287 and 288". Sections 279 to 281. Sections 283 to 288. Section 304(1) to (4). In section 325, the words "and for this purpose" onwards. Section 347B(6). In section 361, in subsection (4)(*d*) the words "or his spouse" and in subsection (5) the words ", or whose spouses,". Section 382(1) and (2). In section 420(2)(*a*)(i), the words "or the wife or husband of the borrower". Section 525(5). Section 527(3). In section 535(5), the second sentence. Section 574(2)(*b*) and (*c*). In section 623, subsection (1), in subsection (2) the words "Subject to subsection (1) above,", in subsection (6)(*c*) the words "or of the individual's wife or husband", in subsection (7)(*a*) the words "or that of his wife or her husband" and in subsection (8) the words "either" and "or to that individual's wife or husband". Section 644(7). In section 646, in subsections (2)(*d*), (5)(*a*) and (7) the words "or the individual's wife or husband". Section 703(7) and (8). In section 833(4), the second sentence. In Schedule 14, paragraph 1(2) and (3). In Schedule 29, in the Table in paragraph 32, the entries relating to sections 29(8), 93(1) and 95(1)(*a*) of the Taxes Management Act 1970 and paragraph 4 of Schedule 2 to the Social Security Act 1975 and those relating to the Social Security (Northern Ireland) Act 1975.
1988 c. 39.	The Finance Act 1988.	Section 40(3). In Schedule 10, in paragraph 5, in sub-paragraph (1), the words "(or, if he is a married man, to his wife)" and sub-paragraphs (3) to (5).

1. The repeals in section 361 of the Income and Corporation Taxes Act 1988 have effect in accordance with paragraph 15 of Schedule 3 to this Act.

2. The repeals in sections 382 and 574 of that Act have effect in relation to relief given for the year 1990–91 or a subsequent year of assessment.

3. The repeal in section 420(2) of that Act has effect in accordance with paragraph 16 of Schedule 3 to this Act.

4. The repeal in section 525 of that Act has effect in relation to tax paid or borne or payable or falling to be paid or borne for the year 1990–91 or a subsequent year of assessment.

5. The repeals in sections 527 and 535 of that Act have effect in relation to tax payable for the year 1990–91 or a subsequent year of assessment.

6. The remaining repeals have effect for the year 1990–91 and subsequent years of assessment.

PART IX

TAX APPEALS ETC. IN NORTHERN IRELAND

Chapter	Short title	Extent of repeal
1970 c. 9.	The Taxes Management Act 1970.	In section 2(6), the second sentence. In section 58, subsection (1), in subsection (2) the word "Special" and subsection (4). Section 59. In section 100(4), the words "(or, in Northern Ireland, the Special Commissioners)".
1975 c. 22.	The Oil Taxation Act 1975.	In section 20(2), the words "or, in Northern Ireland, to a county court". In Schedule 2, in the Table in paragraph 1(1), in the entry relating to section 58(3) of the Taxes Management Act 1970, the words "Omit the references to section 59 and,".
1975 c. 45.	The Finance (No. 2) Act 1975.	In section 45(3), the words "and section 59(6) (election for county court in Northern Ireland)" and the word "each".
1978 c. 23.	The Judicature (Northern Ireland) Act 1978.	In Schedule 5, in Part II, in the entry relating to the Taxes Management Act 1970, the words "and 59(5)".
S.I. 1980/ 397 (N.I. 3).	The County Courts (Northern Ireland) Order 1980.	In Schedule 1, in Part II, the entry relating to section 59(3) of the Taxes Management Act 1970.
1981 c. 35.	The Finance Act 1981.	In Schedule 17, in the Table in paragraph 18(1), in the entry relating to section 58(3) of the Taxes Management Act 1970, the words "Omit the reference to section 59 and".
1988 c. 1.	The Income and Corporation Taxes Act 1988.	In Schedule 29, in the Table in paragraph 32, the entry relating to section 58(3)(b) of the Taxes Management Act 1970.

Subject to any provision made by an order under subsection (9) of section 134 of this Act, these repeals come into force on the day appointed under subsection (4) of that section but do not affect any proceedings which by virtue of subsection (5) of that section are unaffected by subsections (1) to (3) of that section.

WATER ACT 1989

(1989 Chapter 15)

95. Tax provisions

(1) The Secretary of State may, for the purposes of section 2 of the Capital Allowances Act 1968 (writing-down allowance), by order make provision specifying—

(*a*) the amount to be taken for the purposes of subsection (3) of that section as the residue on the transfer date of any expenditure in relation to which any property vested in a successor company in accordance with a scheme under Schedule 2 to this Act is a relevant interest for the purposes of that section; and
(*b*) the part of the period mentioned in subsection (3) of that section which is to be treated, in relation to any such property, as unexpired on that date.

(2) For the purposes of Chapter I of Part III of the Finance Act 1971 (capital allowances in respect of machinery and plant) property which is vested in a successor company in accordance with a scheme under Schedule 2 to this Act shall be treated as if—

(*a*) it had been acquired by that company on the transfer date for the purposes for which it is used by that company on and after that date; and
(*b*) capital expenditure of such amount as may be specified for the purposes of this subsection in an order made by the Secretary of State had been incurred on that date by that company on the acquisition of the property for the purposes mentioned in paragraph (*a*) above.

(3) The Secretary of State shall not make an order under subsection (1) or (2) above in relation to any property of a successor company except with the consent of the Treasury and at a time when the company is wholly owned by the Crown; and the power to make such an order shall be exercisable by statutory instrument and shall include power to make different provision for different cases, including different provision in relation to different property or descriptions of property.

(4) Subject to subsection (5) below, for the purposes of the Capital Gains Tax Act 1979 ("the 1979 Act") the following securities of a successor company, that is to say—

(*a*) those issued to that company's nominated holding company in pursuance of section 83 above;
(*b*) those issued to that company's nominated holding company in pursuance of section 85 above, so far as they are not extinguished under section 86 above; and
(*c*) those not issued in pursuance of section 83 or 85 above which are—

(i) held by that holding company, or any of its nominees, on the transfer date; or
(ii) held by the Secretary of State, or any of his nominees, on that date and transferred to that holding company at any time when that holding company is wholly owned by the Crown,

shall, together, be deemed to have been acquired by the nominated holding company on the transfer date for a consideration equal to whatever is the market value of the successor company's undertaking immediately after the coming into force, on that date, of the scheme under Schedule 2 to this Act in accordance with which property, rights and liabilities of a water authority are transferred to the successor company.

(5) For the purposes of the 1979 Act—

(*a*) any loan which is a relevant loan for the purposes of section 85 above shall be disregarded in determining the market value referred to in subsection (4) above; and
(*b*) where an apportionment of the aggregate amount for which securities of any company are treated under that subsection as having been acquired by any company falls to be made between different securities, any debenture to which that subsection applies shall

be treated as having been acquired by that company for an amount equal to the principal sum payable under the debenture.

(6) Where—

(a) any debt owed to a water authority is transferred to its successor company in accordance with a scheme under Schedule 2 to this Act; and
(b) the authority would have been the original creditor in relation to that debt for the purposes of section 134 of the 1979 Act (disposal of debts),

the successor company shall be treated as the original creditor for those purposes.

(7) For the purposes of Part VI of the Income and Corporation Taxes Act 1988 (company distributions) any securities of a company issued in pursuance of section 83, 85 or 86 above shall be treated as having been issued for new consideration equal—

(a) in the case of a share, to its nominal value; and
(b) in the case of a debenture, to the principal sum payable under the debenture.

(8) Subsection (1) of section 400 of the Income and Corporation Taxes Act 1988 (write-off of government investment: restriction of tax losses) shall not have effect in relation to any extinguishment, at a time when the nominated holding company of a successor company is wholly owned by the Crown, of any liabilities of that holding company.

(9) Subsection (6) of the said section 400 shall apply in relation to any such extinguishment of liabilities as is mentioned in subsection (8) above as if the reference to the body in question were a reference to the company whose liabilities are extinguished.

(10) Where any debentures of any company are issued in pursuance of section 83, 85 or 86 above, any annual payment secured by those debentures shall be treated for all purposes of corporation tax as if it were a charge on income of that company.

(11) The vesting in accordance with a scheme under Schedule 2 to this Act in a successor company of any liability for a loan made to a water authority shall not affect any direction in respect of the loan which has been given, or has effect as if given, under section 581 of the Income and Corporation Taxes Act 1988 (income tax exemption for interest on foreign currency securities).

FINANCE ACT 1989

(1989 Chapter 26)

ARRANGEMENT OF SECTIONS

PART I
CUSTOMS AND EXCISE, VALUE ADDED TAX AND CAR TAX
CHAPTER I
CUSTOMS AND EXCISE

Hydrocarbon oil duties

Sections 1–2 (not printed)

Alcoholic liquor duties

Sections 3–5 (not printed)

Vehicles excise duty

Sections 6–14 (not printed)

General

Section
15. *Estimation of excise duty.* (not printed)
16. *Time limits for proceedings.* (see Orange Book)
17. *Disbursements in Port of London.* (not printed)

CHAPTER II
VALUE ADDED TAX

Zero-rating etc.

Sections 18–23 (see Orange Book)

Other provisions

Sections 24–26 (see Orange Book)

CHAPTER III
MISCELLANEOUS

27. *Relief from car tax where vehicle leased to the handicapped.* (not printed)
28. *Reliefs from duties and taxes for persons enjoying certain immunities and privileges.* (see Orange Book)
29. *Recovery of overpaid excise duty and car tax.* (not printed)

PART II
INCOME TAX, CORPORATION TAX AND CAPITAL GAINS TAX
CHAPTER I
GENERAL

Income tax rates and allowances

Section
30. Charge and rates of income tax for 1989–90.
31. Age allowance.
32. Operative date for PAYE.
33. Married couples.

Corporation tax rates etc.

34. Charge and rate of corporation tax for financial year 1989.
35. Corporation tax: small companies.

Receipts basis etc.

36. Schedule E: revised Cases.
37. Schedule E: assessment on receipts basis.
38. Schedule E: unpaid emoluments.
39. Schedule E: unremitted emoluments.
40. Schedule E: emoluments already paid.
41. Schedule E: pensions etc.
42. Schedule E: supplementary.
43. Schedule D: computation.
44. Investment and insurance companies: computation.
45. PAYE: meaning of payment.

Interest

46. Relief for interest.
47. Close company loans: business expansion scheme.
48. Close company loans: material interest.

Benefits in kind

49. Car benefits.
50. Security assets and services.
51. Assets used partly for security.
52. Security: supplementary.
53. Employees earning £8,500 or more and directors.

Medical insurance

54. Relief.
55. Eligible contracts.
56. Certification of contracts.
57. Medical insurance: supplementary.

Charities

58. Payroll deduction scheme.
59. Covenanted subscriptions.
60. British Museum and Natural History Museum.

Profit-related pay, share schemes etc.

61. Profit-related pay.
62. Savings-related share option schemes.
63. Profit sharing schemes.
64. Share option and profit sharing schemes: shares of consortium member.
65. Employee share schemes: material interest.
66. Priority share allocations for employees etc.

Section

Employee share ownership trusts

67. Tax relief.
68. Principal charges to tax.
69. Chargeable events.
70. Chargeable amounts.
71. Further charges to tax: borrowing.
72. Limit on chargeable amount.
73. Information.
74. Interpretation.

Pensions etc.

75. Retirement benefits schemes.
76. Non-approved retirement benefits schemes.
77. Personal pension schemes.

Unit trusts etc.

78. Certified unit trusts.
79. Funds of funds.
80. Gilt unit trusts.
81. Offshore funds operating equalisation arrangements.

Life assurance

82. Calculation of profits.
83. Receipts to be brought into account.
84. Interpretation of sections 85 to 89 and further provisions about insurance companies.
85. Charge of certain receipts of basic life assurance business.
86. Spreading of relief for acquisition expenses.
87. Management expenses.
88. Corporation tax: policy holders' fraction of profits.
89. Shareholders' and policy holders' fractions.
90. Life policies etc. held by companies.

Underwriters

91. Premiums trust funds: stock lending.
92. Regulations about underwriters etc.

Securities

93. Deep discount securities: amendments.
94. Deep gain securities.
95. Treasury securities issued at a discount.
96. Securities: miscellaneous.

Groups of companies

97. Set-off of ACT where companies remain in same group.
98. Restriction on set-off of ACT.
99. Dividends etc. paid by one member of a group to another.
100. Change in ownership of company.
101. Treatment of convertible shares or securities for purposes relating to group relief etc.
102. Surrender of company tax refund etc. within group.

Close companies

103. Repeal of apportionment provisions.
104. Meaning of "close company".
105. Small companies' rate not available to certain close companies.
106. Restriction on payment of tax credits.
107. Close companies: consequential amendments.

Settlements etc.

108. Outright gifts etc. between husband and wife.
109. Settlements where settlor retains interest in settled property.

Section
110. Residence of trustees.
111. Residence of personal representatives.

Miscellaneous

112. Security: trades etc.
113. Security: trades etc. (supplementary).
114. Relief for pre-trading expenditure.
115. Double taxation: tax credits.
116. Interest payments to Netherlands Antilles subsidiaries.

CHAPTER II
CAPITAL ALLOWANCES

117. Security.
118. Security: supplementary.
119. Expenditure on stands at sports grounds.
120. Forestry land: abolition of agricultural buildings allowances.
121. Miscellaneous amendments.

CHAPTER III
CAPITAL GAINS

Exemptions

122. Annual exempt amount for 1989-90.
123. Increase of chattel exemption.

Gifts

124. Relief for gifts.
125. Gifts to housing associations.

Non-residents etc.

126. Non-resident carrying on profession or vocation in the United Kingdom.
127. Non-residents: deemed disposals.
128. Non-residents: post-cessation disposals.
129. Non-residents: roll-over relief.
130. Exploration or exploitation assets: definition.
131. Exploration or exploitation assets: deemed disposals.
132. Dual resident companies: deemed disposal.
133. Dual resident companies: roll-over relief.
134. Non-payment of tax by non-resident companies.

Value shifting and groups of companies

135. Value shifting.
136. Value shifting: reductions attributable to distributions within a group.
137. Value shifting: transactions treated as a reorganisation of share capital.
138. Groups of companies.

Miscellaneous

139. Corporate bonds.
140. Collective investment schemes.
141. Re-basing to 1982 etc.

CHAPTER IV
MANAGEMENT

Information

142. Power to call for documents and information.
143. Power to call for papers of tax accountant.
144. Restrictions on powers under TMA ss. 20 and 20A.
145. Falsification etc. of documents.

Section
146. Entry with warrant to obtain documents.
147. Procedure where documents etc. are removed.
148. Interpretation.

Assessments, claims etc.

149. Assessments founded on fraudulent or negligent conduct.
150. Further assessments: claims etc.
151. Assessment of trustees etc.

Distress and poinding etc.

152. Distress for non-payment of tax.
153. Priority in cases of distraint by others.
154. Recovery of tax from debtor in Scotland.
155. Priority in cases of poinding etc. by others in Scotland.

Interest etc.

156. Interest on overdue tax.
157. Effect of certain claims on interest.
158. Small amounts of interest.
159. Interest on tax in case of failure or error.
160. Determinations under TMA s. 88.
161. Tax carrying interest under TMA ss. 86 and 88.

Penalties

162. Failure to make return.
163. Incorrect return, accounts etc.
164. Special returns, information etc.
165. Special penalties in the case of certain returns.
166. Assisting in preparation of incorrect return etc.
167. Determination of penalties.
168. Amendments consequential on section 167.
169. Time limits.
170. Up-rating of certain penalties.

PART III

MISCELLANEOUS AND GENERAL

Inheritance tax

Sections 171–172 (see Orange Book)

Stamp duty etc.

Sections 173–177 (see Orange Book)

Interest etc.

178. Setting of rates of interest.
179. Provisions consequential on section 178.
180. Repayment interest: period of accrual.

Miscellaneous

181. *Broadcasting: additional payments by programme contractors.* (not printed)
182. Disclosure of information.
183. *Government securities: redemption and transfer.* (not printed)
184. *National savings accounts.* (not printed)
185. *Winding up of Redemption Annuities Account.* (not printed)

General

186. Interpretation etc.

Section
187. Repeals.
188. Short title.

SCHEDULES:

Schedule 1—*Vehicles excise duty: rates.* (not printed)
Schedule 2—*Vehicles excise duty: special machines.* (not printed)
Schedule 3—*Value added tax: buildings and land.* (see Orange Book)
Schedule 4—Profit-related pay.
Schedule 5—Employee share ownership trusts.
Schedule 6—Retirement benefits schemes.
  Part I Amendments of Taxes Act.
  Part II Approved schemes: general.
  Part III Approved schemes: additional voluntary contributions.
Schedule 7—Personal pension schemes.
  Part I Amendments of Taxes Act.
  Part II Schemes approved before passing of this Act.
Schedule 8—Amendments of Chapter I of Part XII of Taxes Act 1988 (Insurance Companies).
Schedule 9—Life policies etc. held by companies.
Schedule 10—Deep discount securities: amendments.
Schedule 11—Deep gain securities.
Schedule 12—Close companies.
  Part I Administrative provisions.
  Part II Amendments connected with repeal of Chapter III of Part XI of Taxes Act 1988.
Schedule 13—Capital allowances: miscellaneous amendments.
Schedule 14—Capital gains tax: gifts etc.
Schedule 15—Capital gains: re-basing to 1982 etc.
Schedule 16—*Broadcasting: additional payments by programme contractors.* (not printed)
Schedule 17—Repeals.
  Part I *Customs and excise.* (not printed)
  Part II *Vehicles excise duty.* (not printed)
  Part III *Value added tax.* (see Orange Book)
  Part IV Income and corporation tax: general.
  Part V Close companies.
  Part VI Capital allowances.
  Part VII Capital gains.
  Part VIII Management.
  Part IX *Stamp duty: insurance.* (see Orange Book)
  Part X Rates of interest.
  Part XI *Broadcasting.* (not printed)
  Part XII *Government stock: redemption.* (not printed)
  Part XIII *National Savings.* (not printed).
  Part XIV Tithe redemption.

An Act to grant certain duties, to alter other duties, and to amend the law relating to the National Debt and the Public Revenue, and to make further provision in connection with Finance.
[27th July 1989]

PART II

INCOME TAX, CORPORATION TAX AND CAPITAL GAINS TAX

CHAPTER I

GENERAL

Income tax rates and allowances

30. Charge and rates of income tax for 1989–90

(1) Income tax shall be charged for the year 1989–90, and the basic rate of tax shall be 25 per cent.

(2) The higher rate at which income tax is charged for the year 1989–90 in respect of so much of an individual's total income as exceeds the basic rate limit (£20,700) shall be 40 per cent.

31. Age allowance

(1) in section 257 of the Taxes Act 1988—

(*a*) in subsection (3) (increased allowance for those aged 80 and over) for "80", wherever occurring, there shall be substituted "75", and
(*b*) in subsection (5) (age allowance withdrawn by two-thirds of amount by which income exceeds a specified limit) for "two-thirds" there shall be substituted "one half".

(2) This section shall have effect for the year 1989–90.

32. Operative date for PAYE

For the year 1989–90, sections 1(5) and 257(10) of the Taxes Act 1988 (which specify the date from which indexed changes in the basic rate limit and in allowances are to be brought into account for the purposes of PAYE) shall have effect as if for the reference to 5th May there were substituted a reference to 18th May.

33. Married couples

(1) Sections 257 to 257F and 265 of the Taxes Act 1988, as inserted for the year 1990–91 and subsequent years by the Finance Act 1988, shall be amended as follows.

(2) In section 257(1) for "£2,605" there shall be substituted "£2,785".

(3) In section 257(2) for "£3,180" there shall be substituted "£3,400".

(4) In section 257(3)—

(*a*) for "80" there shall be substituted "75", and
(*b*) for "£3,310" there shall be substituted "£3,540".

(5) In section 257(5)—

(*a*) for "£10,600" there shall be substituted "£11,400", and
(*b*) for "two-thirds" there shall be substituted "one half".

(6) In section 257A(1) for "£1,490" there shall be substituted "£1,590".

(7) In section 257A(2) for "£1,855" there shall be substituted "£1,985".

(8) In section 257A(3)—

(*a*) for "80" there shall be substituted "75", and
(*b*) for "£1,895" there shall be substituted "£2,025".

(9) In section 257A(5)—

(*a*) for "£10,600" there shall be substituted "£11,400", and
(*b*) for "two-thirds" there shall be substituted "one half".

(10) In sections 257B(2), 257D(8) and 265(3) after paragraph (*b*) there shall be inserted "or

(*c*) on account of any payments to which section 593(2) or 639(3) applies,".

(11) In section 257E(1)(*b*) for "80" there shall be substituted "75".

(12) In section 257E(2)(*a*) for "£3,180" there shall be substituted "£3,400".

(13) In section 257E(2)(*b*) for "£3,310" there shall be substituted "£3,540".

Corporation tax rates etc.

34. Charge and rate of corporation tax for financial year 1989

Corporation tax shall be charged for the financial year 1989 at the rate of 35 per cent.

35. Corporation tax: small companies

(1) For the financial year 1989—

(*a*) the small companies' rate shall be 25 per cent., and
(*b*) the fraction mentioned in section 13(2) of the Taxes Act 1988 (marginal relief for small companies) shall be one fortieth.

(2) In section 13(3) of that Act (limits of marginal relief), in paragraphs (*a*) and (*b*)—

(*a*) for "£100,000" there shall be substituted "£150,000", and
(*b*) for "£500,000" there shall be substituted "£750,000".

(3) Subsection (2) above shall have effect for the financial year 1989 and subsequent financial years; and where by virtue of that subsection section 13 of the Taxes Act 1988 has effect with different relevant maximum amounts in relation to different parts of a company's accounting period, then for the purposes of that section those parts shall be treated as if they were separate accounting periods and the profits and basic profits of the company for that period shall be apportioned between those parts.

Receipts basis etc.

36. Schedule E: revised Cases

(1) The Taxes Act 1988 shall be amended as follows.

(2) In paragraph 1 of section 19(1) the following Cases shall be substituted for Cases I, II and III—

"Case I: any emoluments for any year of assessment in which the person holding the office or employment is resident and ordinarily resident in the United Kingdom, subject however to section 192 if the emoluments are foreign emoluments (within the meaning of that section) and to section 193(1) if in the year of assessment concerned he performs the duties of the office or employment wholly or partly outside the United Kingdom;
Case II: any emoluments, in respect of duties performed in the United Kingdom, for any year of assessment in which the person holding the office or employment is not resident (or, if resident, not ordinarily resident) in the United Kingdom, subject however to section 192 if the emoluments are foreign emoluments (within the meaning of that section);
Case III: any emoluments for any year of assessment in which the person holding the office or employment is resident in the United Kingdom (whether or not ordinarily resident there) so far as the emoluments are received in the United Kingdom;".

(3) The following paragraph shall be inserted after paragraph 4 of section 19(1)—

"4A. Where (apart from this paragraph) emoluments from an office or employment would be for a year of assessment in which a person does not hold the office or employment, the following rules shall apply for the purposes of the Cases set out in paragraph 1 above—

(*a*) if in the year concerned the office or employment has never been held, the emoluments shall be treated as emoluments for the first year of assessment in which the office or employment is held;
(*b*) if in the year concerned the office or employment is no longer held, the emoluments shall be treated as emoluments for the last year of assessment in which the office or employment was held."

(4) Subsection (2) above shall apply where the year of assessment mentioned in the substituted Case I, II or III is 1989–90 or a subsequent year of assessment.

(5) Subsection (3) above shall apply where each of the years mentioned in the new paragraph 4A(*a*) or (*b*) (as the case may be) is 1989–90 or a subsequent year of assessment.

37. Schedule E: assessment on receipts basis

(1) The following sections shall be inserted immediately before section 203 of the Taxes Act 1988—

"202A. Assessment on receipts basis

(1) As regards any particular year of assessment—

(*a*) income tax shall be charged under Cases I and II of Schedule E on the full amount of the emoluments received in the year in respect of the office or employment concerned;
(*b*) income tax shall be charged under Case III of Schedule E on the full amount of the emoluments received in the United Kingdom in the year in respect of the office or employment concerned.

(2) Subsection (1) above applies—

(*a*) whether the emoluments are for that year or for some other year of assessment;
(*b*) whether or not the office or employment concerned is held at the time the emoluments are received or (as the case may be) received in the United Kingdom.

(3) Where subsection (1) above applies in the case of emoluments received, or (as the case may be) received in the United Kingdom, after the death of the person who held the office or employment concerned, the charge shall be a charge on his executors or administrators; and accordingly income tax—

(*a*) shall be assessed and charged on the executors or administrators, and
(*b*) shall be a debt due from and payable out of the deceased's estate.

(4) Section 202B shall have effect for the purposes of subsection (1)(*a*) above.

202B. Receipts basis: meaning of receipt

(1) For the purposes of section 202A(1)(*a*) emoluments shall be treated as received at the time found in accordance with the following rules (taking the earlier or earliest time in a case where more than one rule applies)—

(*a*) the time when payment is made of or on account of the emoluments;
(*b*) the time when a person becomes entitled to payment of or on account of the emoluments;
(*c*) in a case where the emoluments are from an office or employment with a company, the holder of the office or employment is a director of the company and sums on account of the emoluments are credited in the company's accounts or records, the time when sums on account of the emoluments are so credited;
(*d*) in a case where the emoluments are from an office or employment with a company, the holder of the office or employment is a director of the company and the amount of the emoluments for a period is determined before the period ends, the time when the period ends;
(*e*) in a case where the emoluments are from an office or employment with a company, the holder of the office or employment is a director of the company and the amount of the emoluments for a period is not known until the amount is determined after the period has ended, the time when the amount is determined.

(2) Subsection (1)(*c*), (*d*) or (*e*) above applies whether or not the office or employment concerned is that of director.

(3) Paragraph (*c*), (*d*) or (*e*) of subsection (1) above applies if the holder of the office or employment is a director of the company at any time in the year of assessment in which the time mentioned in the paragraph concerned falls.

(4) For the purposes of the rule in subsection (1)(*c*) above, any fetter on the right to draw the sums is to be disregarded.

(5) In subsection (1) above "director" means—

(*a*) in relation to a company whose affairs are managed by a board of directors or similar body, a member of that board or similar body,
(*b*) in relation to a company whose affairs are managed by a single director or similar person, that director or person, and
(*c*) in relation to a company whose affairs are managed by the members themselves, a member of the company.

(6) In subsection (1) above "director", in relation to a company, also includes any person in accordance with whose directions or instructions the company's directors (as defined in subsection (5) above) are accustomed to act; and for this purpose a person is not to be deemed to be a person in accordance with whose directions or instructions the company's directors are accustomed to act by reason only that the directors act on advice given by him in a professional capacity.

(7) Subsections (1) to (6) above shall have effect subject to subsections (8) to (11) below.

(8) In a case where section 141(1)(*a*), 142(1)(*a*), 143(1)(*a*) or 148(4) treats a person as receiving or being paid an emolument or emoluments at a particular time, for the purposes of section 202A(1)(*a*) the emolument or emoluments shall be treated as received at that time; and in such a case subsections (1) to (6) above shall not apply.

(9) In a case where section 145(1) treats a person as receiving emoluments, for the purposes of section 202A(1)(*a*) the emoluments shall be treated as received in the period referred to in section 145(1); and in such a case subsections (1) to (6) above shall not apply.

(10) In a case where section 154(1), 157(1), 158(1), 160(1), 160(2), 162(6) or 164(1) treats an amount as emoluments, for the purposes of section 202A(1)(*a*) the emoluments shall be treated as received in the year referred to in section 154(1) or the other provision concerned; and in such a case subsections (1) to (6) above shall not apply.

(11) In a case where—

(*a*) emoluments take the form of a benefit not consisting of money, and
(*b*) subsection (8), (9) or (10) above does not apply,

for the purposes of section 202A(1)(*a*) the emoluments shall be treated as received at the time when the benefit is provided; and in such a case subsections (1) to (6) above shall not apply."

(2) This section shall apply where the year of assessment mentioned in the new section 202A(1) is 1989–90 or a subsequent year of assessment, even if the emoluments concerned are for a year of assessment before 1989–90.

(3) This section shall not apply in the case of emoluments of an office or employment held by a person who died before 6 April 1989.

38. Schedule E: unpaid emoluments

(1) This section applies to emoluments of an office or employment if—

(*a*) they are emoluments for a year of assessment (a relevant year) before 1989–90,
(*b*) they fall within Case I or II of Schedule E as the Case applies for years before 1989–90,
(*c*) they have not been paid before 6th April 1989, and
(*d*) they have been received on or after 6th April 1989 and before 6th April 1991;

and section 202B of the Taxes Act 1988 shall apply for the purposes of paragraph (*d*) above as it applies for the purposes of section 202A(1)(*a*) of that Act.

(2) The emoluments shall be charged to income tax only by reference to the year of assessment in which they are received.

(3) Any adjustments consequential on this section (such as the amendment of assessments or the repayment or setting-off of tax paid) shall be made.

(4) This section shall not apply to emoluments of an office or employment held by a person who died before 6th April 1989.

(5) This section shall not apply if the only emoluments of the office or employment not paid before 6th April 1989 are emoluments for a period consisting of or falling within the period beginning with 5th March 1989 and ending with 5th April 1989.

(6) This section shall not apply unless—

(*a*) written notice that it is to apply is given to the inspector before 6th April 1991,
(*b*) the notice is given by or on behalf of the person who holds or held the office or employment concerned, and
(*c*) the notice states the amount of the emoluments falling within subsection (1) above.

(7) Subsection (8) below applies where emoluments of an office or employment have been

or fall to be computed by reference to the accounts basis as regards the year 1987–88 or years of assessment including that year.

(8) In deciding for the purposes of subsection (1)(*a*) above whether emoluments are emoluments for a particular year, the emoluments of the office or employment for the year or (as the case may be) years mentioned in subsection (7) above, and for the year 1988–89, shall be computed by reference to that basis.

(9) In deciding whether subsection (8) above applies in a particular case, any request to revoke the application of the accounts basis shall be ignored if—

   (*a*) it is made after 5th April 1989, or
   (*b*) it is made before 6th April 1989 otherwise than in writing.

(10) In the application of this section to emoluments of an office or employment under or with a person carrying on business as an authorised Lloyd's underwriting agent, the references in subsections (1)(*d*) and (6)(*a*) above to 6th April 1991 shall be construed as references to 6th April 1994.

(11) Subsection (10) above shall not apply unless the duties of the office or employment relate wholly or mainly to the underwriting agency business.

(12) The reference in subsection (10) above to an authorised Lloyd's underwriting agent is to a person permitted by the Council of Lloyd's to act as an underwriting agent at Lloyd's.

(13) If in a particular case it appears to the Board reasonable to do so they may direct that subsections (1)(*d*) and (6)(*a*) above shall have effect in relation to that case as if for the references to 6th April 1991 or (as the case may be) 6th April 1994 there were substituted references to such later date as they may specify in the direction.

(14) In this section "the accounts basis" means the basis commonly so called (under which emoluments for a year of assessment are computed by reference to the emoluments for a period other than the year of assessment).

39. Schedule E: unremitted emoluments

(1) This section applies to emoluments of an office or employment if—

   (*a*) they are emoluments for a year of assessment (a relevant year) before 1989–90,
   (*b*) they are received in the United Kingdom after 5th April 1989, and
   (*c*) had this Act not been passed they would have fallen within Case III of Schedule E.

(2) The emoluments shall be treated as if they were not emoluments for the relevant year.

(3) But they shall be treated as if they were emoluments for the year of assessment in which they are received in the United Kingdom and as if they fell within Case III as substituted by section 36 above; and accordingly income tax shall be charged, in accordance with section 202A of the Taxes Act 1988, by reference to the year of assessment in which the emoluments are received in the United Kingdom.

40. Schedule E: emoluments already paid

(1) Subsection (2) below applies to emoluments of an office or employment if—

   (*a*) they are emoluments for a year of assessment after 1988–89,
   (*b*) they have been paid before 6th April 1989, and
   (*c*) they fall within Case I or II of Schedule E as substituted by section 36 above.

(2) The emoluments shall be treated as if they were received, within the meaning of section 202B of the Taxes Act 1988, on 6th April 1989; and accordingly income tax shall be charged, in accordance with section 202A of that Act, by reference to the year 1989–90.

(3) Subsection (4) below applies to emoluments of an office or employment if—

   (*a*) they are emoluments for a year of assessment after 1988–89,
   (*b*) they have been received in the United Kingdom before 6th April 1989, and
   (*c*) they fall within Case III of Schedule E as substituted by section 36 above.

(4) The emoluments shall be treated as if they were received in the United Kingdom on 6th April 1989; and accordingly income tax shall be charged, in accordance with section 202A of the Taxes Act 1988, by reference to the year 1989–90.

41. Schedule E: pensions etc.

(1) This section applies in relation to the following pensions and other benefits—

(*a*) a pension, stipend or annuity chargeable to income tax under Schedule E by virtue of paragraph 2, 3 or 4 of section 19(1) of the Taxes Act 1988;

(*b*) a pension or annual payment chargeable to income tax under Schedule E by virtue of section 133 of that Act (voluntary pensions);

(*c*) income support chargeable to income tax under Schedule E by virtue of section 151 of that Act;

(*d*) a pension chargeable to income tax under Schedule E by virtue of section 597 of that Act (retirement benefit schemes);

(*e*) a benefit chargeable to income tax under Schedule E by virtue of section 617(1) of that Act (social security benefits).

(2) As regards any particular year of assessment income tax shall be charged on the amount of the pension or other benefit accruing in respect of the year; and this shall apply irrespective of when any amount is actually paid in respect of the pension or other benefit.

(3) This section shall apply where the year of assessment mentioned in subsection (2) above is 1989–90 or a subsequent year of assessment.

42. Schedule E: supplementary

(1) The Taxes Act 1988 shall be amended as follows.

(2) In section 131(2) (interaction of Cases) the words "for the same or another chargeable period" shall be omitted.

(3) In section 149(1) (sick pay chargeable as emoluments of employment for a certain period) the words "for that period" and the words "for that or any other period" shall be omitted.

(4) Section 170 (profit-related pay charged for year of assessment in which it is paid) shall cease to have effect.

(5) In paragraph 2(2) of Schedule 12 (foreign earnings) for the words from "emoluments from" to "year of assessment" there shall be substituted the words "emoluments for the year of assessment from the relevant employment in respect of which such a deduction is allowed".

(6) This section shall apply for the year 1989–90 and subsequent years of assessment.

43. Schedule D: computation

(1) Subsection (2) below applies where—

(*a*) a calculation is made of profits or gains which are to be charged under Schedule D and are for a period of account ending after 5th April 1989,

(*b*) relevant emoluments would (apart from that subsection) be deducted in making the calculation, and

(*c*) the emoluments are not paid before the end of the period of nine months beginning with the end of that period of account.

(2) The emoluments—

(*a*) shall not be deducted in making the calculation mentioned in subsection (1)(*a*) above, but

(*b*) shall be deducted in calculating profits or gains which are to be charged under Schedule D and are for the period of account in which the emoluments are paid.

(3) Subsections (4) and (5) below apply where—

(*a*) a calculation such as is mentioned in subsection (1)(*a*) above is made,

(*b*) the calculation is made before the end of the period of nine months beginning with the end of the period of account concerned,

(*c*) relevant emoluments would (apart from subsection (2) above) be deducted in making the calculation, and

(*d*) the emoluments have not been paid when the calculation is made.

(4) It shall be assumed for the purpose of making the calculation that the emoluments will not be paid before the end of that period of nine months.

(5) But the calculation shall be adjusted if—

(*a*) the emoluments are paid after the calculation is made but before the end of that period of nine months,
(*b*) a claim to adjust the calculation is made to the inspector, and
(*c*) the claim is made before the end of the period of two years beginning with the end of the period of account concerned.

(6) In the application of this section to the calculation of a person's profits or gains as an authorised Lloyd's underwriting agent—

(*a*) the references in subsections (1)(*c*), (3)(*b*), (4) and (5)(*a*) above to nine months shall be construed as references to three years and nine months, and
(*b*) the reference in subsection (5)(*c*) above to two years shall be construed as a reference to five years.

(7) The reference in subsection (5A) above to an authorised Lloyd's underwriting agent is to a person permitted by the Council of Lloyd's to act as an underwriting agent at Lloyd's.

(8) In a case where the period of account mentioned in subsection (1)(*a*) above begins before 6th April 1989 and ends before 6th April 1990, the references in subsections (1)(*c*), (3)(*b*), (4) and (5)(*a*) above to nine months shall be construed as references to eighteen months.

(9) In this section "period of account" means a period for which an account is made up.

(10) For the purposes of this section "relevant emoluments" are emoluments for a period after 5th April 1989 allocated either—

(*a*) in respect of particular offices or employments (or both), or
(*b*) generally in respect of offices or employments (or both).

(11) This section applies in relation to potential emoluments as it applies in relation to relevant emoluments, and for this purpose—

(*a*) potential emoluments are amounts or benefits reserved in the accounts of an employer, or held by an intermediary, with a view to their becoming relevant emoluments;
(*b*) potential emoluments are paid when they become relevant emoluments which are paid.

(12) In deciding for the purposes of this section whether emoluments are paid at any time after 5th April 1989, section 202B of the Taxes Act 1988 (time when emoluments are treated as received) shall apply as it applies for the purposes of section 202A(1)(*a*) of that Act, but reading "paid" for "received" throughout.

(13) In section 436(1)(*b*) of the Taxes Act 1988 (profits to be computed in accordance with provisions of that Act applicable to Case I of Schedule D) the reference to that Act shall be deemed to include a reference to this section.

44. Investment and insurance companies: computation

(1) Subsection (2) below applies where—

(*a*) a calculation is made for the purposes of corporation tax of the profits of an investment company for an accounting period ending after 5th April 1989,
(*b*) relevant emoluments would (apart from that subsection) be deducted in making the calculation, and
(*c*) the emoluments are not paid before the end of the period of nine months beginning with the end of the relevant period of account.

(2) The emoluments—

(*a*) shall not be deducted in making the calculation mentioned in subsection (1)(*a*) above, but
(*b*) shall be deducted in calculating for the purposes of corporation tax the profits of the company concerned for the accounting period in which the emoluments are paid.

(3) Subsections (4) and (5) below apply where—

(*a*) a calculation such as is mentioned in subection (1)(*a*) above is made,
(*b*) the calculation is made before the end of the period of nine months beginning with the end of the relevant period of account,
(*c*) relevant emoluments would (apart from subsection (2) above) be deducted in making the calculation, and
(*d*) the emoluments have not been paid when the calculation is made.

(4) It shall be assumed for the purpose of making the calculation that the emoluments will not be paid before the end of that period of nine months.

(2) Subject to the following provisions of this section, in subsection (1) above "associate", in relation to an individual, means—

(a) any relative or partner of the individual;
(b) the trustee or trustees of a settlement in relation to which the individual is, or any relative of his (living or dead) is or was, a settlor ("settlement" and "settlor" having the same meaning as in section 681(4)); and
(c) where the individual is interested in any shares or obligations of the company which are subject to any trust, or are part of the estate of a deceased person, the trustee or trustees of the settlement concerned or, as the case may be, the personal representative of the deceased.

(3) In relation to any loan made after 5th April 1987, there shall be disregarded for the purposes of subsection (2)(c) above—

(a) the interest of the trustees of an approved profit sharing scheme (within the meaning of section 187) in any shares which are held by them in accordance with the scheme and have not yet been appropriated to an individual; and
(b) any rights exercisable by those trustees by virtue of that interest.

(4) In relation to any loan made on or after the day on which the Finance Act 1989 was passed, where the individual has an interest in shares or obligations of the company as a beneficiary of an employee benefit trust, the trustees shall not be regarded as associates of his by reason only of that interest unless subsection (6) below applies in relation to him.

(5) In subsection (4) above "employee benefit trust" has the same meaning as in paragraph 7 of Schedule 8, except that in its application for this purpose paragraph 7(5)(b) shall have effect as if it referred to the day on which the Finance Act 1989 was passed instead of to 14th March 1989.

(6) This subsection applies in relation to an individual if at any time on or after the day on which the Finance Act 1989 was passed—

(a) the individual, either on his own or with any one or more of his associates, or
(b) any associate of his, with or without other such associates,

has been the beneficial owner of, or able (directly or through the medium of other companies or by any other indirect means) to control, more than 5 per cent. of the ordinary share capital of the company.

(7) Sub-paragraphs (9) to (12) of paragraph 7 of Schedule 8 shall apply for the purposes of subsection (6) above in relation to an individual as they apply for the purposes of that paragraph in relation to an employee.

(8) In relation to any loan made before 14th November 1986, where the individual is interested in any shares or obligations of the company which are subject to any trust, or are part of the estate of a deceased person, subsection (2)(c) above shall have effect as if for the reference to the trustee or trustees of the settlement concerned or, as the case may be, the personal representative of the deceased there were substituted a reference to any person (other than the individual) interested in the settlement or estate, but subject to subsection (9) below.

(9) Subsection (8) above shall not apply so as to make an individual an associate as being entitled or eligible to benefit under a trust—

(a) if the trust relates exclusively to an exempt approved scheme as defined in section 592; or
(b) if the trust is exclusively for the benefit of the employees, or the employees and directors, of the company or their dependants (and not wholly or mainly for the benefit of directors or their relatives), and the individual in question is not (and could not as a result of the operation of the trust become), either on his own or with his relatives, the beneficial owner of more than 5 per cent. of the ordinary share capital of the company;

and in applying paragraph (b) above any charitable trusts which may arise on the failure or determination of other trusts shall be disregarded.

(10) In this section "relative" means husband or wife, parent or remoter forebear, child or remoter issue or brother or sister."

Benefits in kind

49. Car benefits

(1) In Schedule 6 to the Taxes Act 1988 (taxation of directors and others in respect of cars) for Part I (tables of flat rate cash equivalents) there shall be substituted—

PART I

TABLES OF FLAT RATE CASH EQUIVALENTS

TABLE A

Cars with an original market value up to £19,250 and having a cylinder capacity

Cylinder capacity of car in cubic centimetres	Age of car at end of relevant year of assessment	
	Under 4 years	4 years or more
1400 or less	£1,400	£950
More than 1400 but not more than 2000	£1,850	£1,250
More than 2000	£2,950	£1,950

TABLE B

Cars with an original market value up to £19,250 and not having a cylinder capacity

Original market value of car	Age of car at end of relevant year of assessment	
	Under 4 years	4 years or more
Less than £6,000	£1,400	£950
£6,000 or more but less than £8,500	£1,850	£1,250
£8,500 or more but not more than £19,250	£2,950	£1,950

TABLE C

Cars with an original market value of more than £19,250

Original market value of car	Age of car at end of relevant year of assessment	
	Under 4 years	4 years or more
More than £19,250 but not more than £29,000	£3,850	£2,600
More than £29,000	£6,150	£4,100

(2) This section shall have effect for the year 1989–90 and subsequent years of assessment.

50. Security assets and services

(1) For the purposes of this section a security asset is an asset which improves personal security, and a security service is a service which improves personal security.

(2) In a case where—

   (*a*) a security asset or security service is provided for an employee by reason of his employment, or is used by an employee, and
   (*b*) the cost is wholly or partly borne by or on behalf of a person (the provider) other than the employee,

in charging tax under Schedule E on the emoluments from the employment a deduction shall be allowed of an amount equal to so much of the cost so borne as falls to be included in the emoluments of the employment.

(3) In a case where—

    (*a*) a security asset or security service is provided for or used by an employee,
    (*b*) expenses in connection with the provision or use are incurred out of the emoluments of the employment, and
    (*c*) the expenses are reimbursed by or on behalf of a person (the provider) other than the employee,

in charging tax under Schedule E on the emoluments from the employment a deduction shall be allowed of an amount equal to the amount of the expenses.

(4) Subsection (2) or (3) above shall not apply unless the asset or service is provided for or used by the employee to meet a threat which—

    (*a*) is a special threat to his personal physical security, and
    (*b*) arises wholly or mainly by virtue of the particular employment concerned.

(5) Subsection (2) or (3) above shall not apply unless the provider has the meeting of that threat as his sole object in wholly or partly bearing the cost or reimbursing the expenses (as the case may be).

(6) Subsection (2) or (3) above shall not apply in the case of a service unless the benefit resulting to the employee consists wholly or mainly of an improvement of his personal physical security.

(7) Subsection (2) or (3) above shall not apply in the case of an asset unless the provider intends the asset to be used solely to improve personal physical security.

51. Assets used partly for security

(1) In a case where—

    (*a*) apart from section 50(7) above, section 50(2) above would apply in the case of an asset, and
    (*b*) the provider intends the asset to be used partly to improve personal physical security,

section 50(2) shall nevertheless apply, but only so as to allow a deduction of the appropriate proportion of the amount there mentioned.

(2) For the purposes of subsection (1) above the appropriate proportion of the amount mentioned in section 50(2) above is such proportion of that amount as is attributable to the provider's intention that the asset be used to improve personal physical security.

(3) In a case where—

    (*a*) apart from section 50(7) above, section 50(3) above would apply in the case of an asset, and
    (*b*) the provider intends the asset to be used partly to improve personal physical security,

section 50(3) shall nevertheless apply, but only so as to allow a deduction of the appropriate proportion of the amount there mentioned.

(4) For the purposes of subsection (3) above the appropriate proportion of the amount mentioned in section 50(3) above is such proportion of that amount as is attributable to the provider's intention that the asset be used to improve personal physical security.

52. Security: supplementary

(1) If the provider intends the asset to be used solely to improve personal physical security, but there is another use for the asset which is incidental to improving personal physical security, that other use shall be ignored in construing section 50(7) above.

(2) The fact that an asset or service improves the personal physical security of any member of the employee's family or household, as well as that of the employee, shall not prevent section 50(2) or (3) above from applying.

(3) In sections 50 and 51 above and this section—

    (*a*) references to an asset do not include references to a car, a ship or an aircraft,
    (*b*) references to an asset or service do not include references to a dwelling, grounds appurtenant to a dwelling, or living accommodation,
    (*c*) references to an asset include references to equipment and a structure (such as a wall),
    (*d*) references to an employee are to a person who holds an employment, and
    (*e*) references to an employment include references to an office.

(4) For the purposes of sections 50 and 51 above and this section in their application to an

asset, it is immaterial whether or not the asset becomes affixed to land (whether constituting a dwelling or otherwise).

(5) For the purposes of sections 50 and 51 above and this section in their application to an asset, it is immaterial whether or not the employee is or becomes entitled to the property in the asset or (in the case of a fixture) an estate or interest in the land concerned.

(6) Sections 50 and 51 above and this section apply where expenditure is incurred on or after 6th April 1989 in or towards bearing a cost or in reimbursing expenses (as the case may be).

53. Employees earning £8,500 or more and directors

(1) For section 167 of the Taxes Act 1988 (which defines "director's or higher-paid enployment" for the purposes of Chapter II of Part V) there shall be substituted—

"**167. Employment to which this Chapter applies**

(1) This Chapter applies—

(*a*) to employment as a director of a company (but subject to subsection (5) below), and
(*b*) to employment with emoluments at the rate of £8,500 a year or more.

(2) For this purpose emoluments are to be calculated—

(*a*) on the basis that they include all such amounts as come, or would but for section 157(3) come, into charge under this Chapter or section 141, 142, 143 or 145, and
(*b*) without any deduction under section 198, 201 or 332(3).

(3) Where a person is employed in two or more employments by the same employer and either—

(*a*) the total of the emoluments of those employments (applying this section) is at the rate of £8,500 a year or more, or
(*b*) this Chapter applies (apart from this subsection) to one or more of those employments,

this Chapter shall apply to all the employments.

(4) All employees of a partnership or body over which an individual or another partnership or body has control are to be treated for the purposes of this section (but not for any other purpose) as if the employment were an employment by the individual or by that other partnership or body as the case may be.

(5) This Chapter shall not apply to a person's employment by reason only of its being employment as a director of a company (without prejudice to its application by virtue of subsection (1)(*b*) or (3) above) if he has no material interest in the company and either—

(*a*) his employment is as a full-time working director; or
(*b*) the company is non-profit making (meaning that neither does it carry on a trade nor do its functions consist wholly or mainly in the holding of investments or other property) or is established for charitable purposes only."

(2) In consequence of subsection (1) above—

(*a*) for the heading to Chapter II of Part V of the Taxes Act 1988 there shall be substituted "EMPLOYEES EARNING £8,500 OR MORE AND DIRECTORS";
(*b*) the words "employment to which this Chapter applies" shall be substituted for the words "director's or higher-paid employment" in sections 153(1), 154(1), 157(1), 158(1), 160(1) and (2), 162(1), 163(1) and 165(6)(*b*) of that Act;
(*c*) for section 160(3) of that Act there shall be substituted—

"(3) Where—

(*a*) there was outstanding, at any time when a person was in employment to which this Chapter applies, the whole or part of a loan to him (or a relative of his) the benefit of which was obtained by reason of his employment, and
(*b*) that employment has terminated or ceased to be employment to which this Chapter applies,

subsection (2) above applies as if the employment had not terminated or, as the case may be, had not ceased to be employment to which this Chapter applies.";

(*d*) in section 162(5) of that Act, after the words "section 160(2)" there shall be inserted the words "(and where appropriate section 160(3))";
(*e*) for section 162(7) of that Act there shall be substituted—

"(7) If at the time of the event giving rise to a charge by virtue of subsection (6) above the employment in question has terminated, that subsection shall apply as if it had not."

(f) the words "employment to which Chapter II of Part V applies" shall be substituted for the words from "director's" to "section 167)" in sections 332(2)(c) and 418(3)(a) of that Act;

(g) the words "employment to which Chapter II of Part V of the principal Act applies" shall be substituted for the words "director's or higher paid employment" in section 15(3)(a) of the Taxes Management Act 1970.

Medical insurance

54. Relief

(1) This section applies where—

(a) on or after 6th April 1990 an individual makes a payment in respect of a premium under a contract of private medical insurance (whenever issued),
(b) the contract meets the requirement in subsection (2) below as to the person or persons insured,
(c) at the time the payment is made the contract is an eligible contract,
(d) the individual making the payment does not make it out of resources provided by another person for the purpose of enabling it to be made, and
(e) the individual making the payment is not entitled to claim any relief or deduction in respect of it under any other provision of the Tax Acts.

(2) The requirement mentioned in subsection (1)(b) above is that the contract insures—

(a) an individual who at the time the payment is made is aged 60 or over and resident in the United Kingdom,
(b) individuals each of whom at that time is aged 60 or over and resident in the United Kingdom, or
(c) two individuals who are married to each other at that time, at least one of whom is aged 60 or over at that time, and each of whom is resident in the United Kingdom at that time.

(3) If the payment is made by an individual who at the time it is made is resident in the United Kingdom (whether or not he is the individual or one of the individuals insured by the contract) it shall be deducted from or set off against his income for the year of assessment in which it is made; but relief under this subsection shall be given only on a claim made for the purpose, except where subsections (4) to (6) below apply.

(4) In such cases and subject to such conditions as the Board may specify in regulations, relief under subsection (3) above shall be given in accordance with subsections (5) and (6) below.

(5) An individual who is entitled to such relief in respect of a payment may deduct and retain out of it an amount equal to income tax on it at the basic rate for the year of assessment in which it is made.

(6) The person to whom the payment is made—

(a) shall accept the amount paid after deduction in discharge of the individual's liability to the same extent as if the deduction had not been made, and
(b) may, on making a claim, recover from the Board an amount equal to the amount deducted.

(7) The Treasury may make regulations providing that in circumstances prescribed in the regulations—

(a) an individual who has made a payment in respect of a premium under a contract of private medical insurance shall cease to be and be treated as not having been entitled to relief under subsection (3) above; and
(b) he or the person to whom the payment was made (depending on the terms of the regulations) shall account to the Board for tax from which relief has been given on the basis that the individual was so entitled.

(8) Regulations under subsection (7) above may include provision adapting or modifying the effect of any enactment relating to income tax in order to secure the performance of any obligation imposed under paragraph (b) of that subsection.

(9) In this section—

(*a*) references to a premium, in relation to a contract of insurance, are to any amount payable under the contract to the insurer, and
(*b*) references to an individual who is resident in the United Kingdom at any time include references to an individual who is at that time performing duties which are treated by virtue of section 132(4)(*a*) of the Taxes Act 1988 as performed in the United Kingdom.

55. Eligible contracts

(1) This section has effect to determine whether a contract is at a particular time (the relevant time) an eligible contract for the purposes of section 54 above.

(2) A contract is an eligible contract at the relevant time if—

(*a*) it was entered into by an insurer who at the time it was entered into was a qualifying insurer and was approved by the Board for the purposes of this section,
(*b*) the period of insurance under the contract does not exceed one year (commencing with the date it was entered into),
(*c*) the contract is not connected with any other contract at the relevant time and has not been connected with any other contract at any time it was entered into,
(*d*) no benefit has been provided by virtue of the contract other than an approved benefit, and
(*e*) the contract meets one or more of the three conditions set out below.

(3) The first condition is that the contract is certified by the Board under section 56 below at the relevant time.

(4) The second condition is that, at the time the contract was entered into, it conformed with a standard form certified by the Board as a standard form of eligible contract.

(5) The third condition is that, at the time the contract was entered into, it conformed with a form varying from a standard form so certified in no other respect than by making additions—

(*a*) which were (at the time the contract was entered into) certified by the Board as compatible with an eligible contract when made to that standard form, and
(*b*) which (at that time) satisfied any conditions subject to which the additions were so certified.

(6) Where a contract is varied, and the relevant time falls after the time the variation takes effect, subsections (1) to (5) above shall have effect as if "entered into" read "varied" in each place where it occurs in subsections (4) and (5) above.

(7) For the purposes of this section a contract is connected with another contract at any time if—

(*a*) they are simultaneously in force at that time,
(*b*) either of them was entered into with reference to the other, or with a view to enabling the other to be entered into on particular terms, or with a view to facilitating the other being entered into on particular terms, and
(*c*) the terms on which either of them was entered into would have been significantly less favourable to the insured if the other had not been entered into.

(8) For the purposes of this section each of the following is a qualifying insurer—

(*a*) an insurer lawfully carrying on in the United Kingdom business of any of the classes specified in Part I of Schedule 2 to the Insurance Companies Act 1982;
(*b*) an insurer not carrying on business in the United Kingdom but carrying on business in another member State and being either a national of a member State or a company or partnership formed under the law of any part of the United Kingdom or another member State and having its registered office, central administration or principal place of business in a member State.

(9) For the purposes of this section a benefit is an approved benefit if it is provided in pursuance of a right of a description mentioned in section 56(3)(*a*) below.

56. Certification of contracts

(1) The Board shall certify a contract under this section if it satisfies the conditions set out in subection (3) below; and the certification shall be expressed to take effect from the time the conditions are satisfied, and shall take effect accordingly.

(2) The Board shall revoke a certification of a contract under this section if it comes to their notice that the contract has ceased to satisfy the conditions set out in subsection (3) below;

and the revocation shall be expressed to take effect from the time the conditions ceased to be satisfied, and shall take effect accordingly.

(3) The conditions referred to above are that—

> (*a*) the contract either provides indemnity in respect of all or any of the costs of all or any of the treatments, medical services and other matters for the time being specified in regulations made by the Treasury, or in addition to providing indemnity of that description provides cash benefits falling within rules for the time being so specified,
> (*b*) the contract does not confer any right other than such a right as is mentioned in paragraph (*a*) above or is for the time being specified in regulations made by the Treasury,
> (*c*) the premium under the contract is in the Board's opinion reasonable, and
> (*d*) the contract satisfies such other requirements as are for the time being specified in regulations made by the Treasury.

(4) The certification of a contract by the Board under this section shall cease to have effect if the contract is varied; but this is without prejudice to the application of the preceding provisions of this section to the contract as varied.

(5) Where the Board refuse to certify a contract under this section, or they revoke a certification, an appeal may be made to the Special Commissioners by—

> (*a*) the insurer, or
> (*b*) any person who (if the policy were certified) would be entitled to relief under section 54 above.

(6) Where a contract is certified under this section, or a certification is revoked or otherwise ceases to have effect, any adjustments resulting from the certification or from its revocation or ceasing to have effect shall be made.

(7) Subsection (6) above applies where a certification or revocation takes place on appeal as it applies in the case of any other certification or revocation.

(8) In this section the reference to a premium, in relation to a contract of insurance, is to any amount payable under the contract to the insurer.

57. Medical insurance: supplementary

(1) The Board may by regulations—

> (*a*) provide that a claim under section 54(3) or (6)(*b*) above shall be made in such form and manner, shall be made at such time, and shall be accompanied by such documents, as may be prescribed;
> (*b*) make provision, in relation to payments in respect of which a person is entitled to relief under section 54 above, for the giving by insurers in such circumstances as may be prescribed of certificates of payment in such form as may be prescribed to such persons as may be prescribed;
> (*c*) provide that a person who provides (or has at any time provided) insurance under contracts of private medical insurance shall comply with any notice which is served on him by the Board and which requires him within a prescribed period to make available for the Board's inspection documents (of a prescribed kind) relating to such contracts;
> (*d*) provide that persons of such a description as may be prescribed shall, within a prescribed period of being required to do so by the Board, furnish to the Board information (of a prescribed kind) about contracts of private medical insurance;
> (*e*) make provision with respect to the approval of insurers for the purposes of section 55 above and the withdrawal of approval for the purposes of that section;
> (*f*) make provision for and with respect to appeals against decisions of the Board with respect to the giving or withdrawal of approval of insurers for the purposes of section 55 above;
> (*g*) make provision with respect to the certification by the Board of standard forms of eligible contract and variations from standard forms of eligible contract certified by them;
> (*h*) make provision for and with respect to appeals against decisions of the Board with respect to the certification of standard forms of eligible contract or variations from standard forms of eligible contract certified by them;
> (*i*) provide that certification, or the revocation of a certification, under section 56 above shall be carried out in such form and manner as may be prescribed;
> (*j*) make provision with respect to appeals against decisions of the Board with respect to certification or the revocation of certification under section 56 above;
> (*k*) make provision generally as to administration in connection with sections 54 to 56 above.

(2) The words "Regulations under section 57 of the Finance Act 1989" shall be added at the end of each column in the Table in section 98 of the Taxes Management Act 1970 (penalties for failure to furnish information etc.).

(3) The following provisions of the Taxes Management Act 1970, namely—

(a) section 29(3)(c) (excessive relief),
(b) section 30 (tax repaid in error etc.),
(c) section 88 (interest), and
(d) section 95 (incorrect return or accounts),

shall apply in relation to the payment of an amount claimed under section 54(6)(b) above to which the claimant was not entitled as if it had been income tax repaid as a relief which was not due.

(4) In sections 257B(2), 257D(8) and 265(3) of the Taxes Act 1988 after paragraph (c) there shall be inserted "or

(d) on account of any payments to which section 54(5) of the Finance Act 1989 applies".

(5) In subsection (1) above—

"eligible contract" has the meaning given by section 55 above, and
"prescribed" means prescribed by or, in relation to form, under the regulations.

Charities

58. Payroll deduction scheme

(1) In section 202(7) of the Taxes Act 1988 (which limits to £240 the deductions attracting relief) for "£240" there shall be substituted "£480".

(2) This section shall have effect for the year 1989–90 and subsequent years of assessment.

59. Covenanted subscriptions

(1) In determining whether a payment made to a charity within subsection (2) below is—

(a) an annual payment for the purposes of the Tax Acts, or
(b) a payment to which section 125(1) of the Taxes Act 1988 applies, or
(c) a covenanted payment to charity within the meaning given by section 660(3) of that Act,

there shall be disregarded any consideration for the payment which is of a kind described in subsection (3) below.

(2) A charity is within this subsection if its sole or main purpose is—

(a) the preservation of property for the public benefit, or
(b) the conservation of wildlife for the public benefit.

(3) The consideration referred to in subsection (1) above is the right of admission—

(a) to view property the preservation of which is the sole or main purpose of the charity, or
(b) to observe wildlife the conservation of which is the sole or main purpose of the charity.

(4) In subsection (3) above "right of admission" refers to admission of the person making the payment (or of any member of his family who may be admitted because of the payment) either free of the charges normally payable for admission by members of the public, or on payment of a reduced charge.

(5) Subsection (1) above shall not apply unless the opportunity to make payments of the kind in question is available to members of the public.

(6) For the purposes of this section—

(a) "charity" means a body of persons or trust established for charitable purposes only, and
(b) the bodies mentioned in section 507 shall each be treated as having been so established.

(7) This section shall apply to payments due on or after 14th March 1989.

60. British Museum and Natural History Museum

(1) In subsection (1) of section 507 of the Taxes Act 1988 (which gives tax exemption to the National Heritage Memorial Fund and the Historic Buildings and Monuments Commission) after paragraph (*b*) there shall be inserted—

"(*c*) the Trustees of the British Museum;
(*d*) the Trustees of the British Museum (Natural History);"

and subsection (2) of that section (which gives partial tax exemption to those Trustees) shall cease to have effect.

(2) In section 339(9) of that Act, for the words from "the Trustees" (where those words first occur) to "History) and" there shall be substituted the words "each of the bodies mentioned in section 507, and in subsections (1) to (5) above includes".

(3) In section 660(4) of that Act, for the words from "the Trustees" to "England" there shall be substituted the words "the bodies mentioned in section 507".

(4) Subsection (1) above shall apply in relation to accounting periods ending on or after 14th March 1989, and subsections (2) and (3) above shall apply to payments due on or after that day.

Profit-related pay, share schemes etc.

61. Profit-related pay

Schedule 4 to this Act (which amends the provisions of the Taxes Act 1988 relating to profit-related pay) shall have effect.

62. Savings-related share option schemes

(1) Part III of Schedule 9 to the Taxes Act 1988 (requirements applicable to savings-related share option schemes) shall be amended as follows.

(2) In paragraph 24(2)(*a*) (scheme not to permit monthly amount of contributions linked to schemes to exceed £100), for "£100" there shall be substituted "£150".

(3) In paragraph 25(*b*) (requirement that price at which share may be acquired under scheme be not less than 90 per cent. of market value), for the words "90 per cent." there shall be substituted the words "80 per cent.".

(4) Subsection (2) above shall come into force on such day as the Treasury may by order made by statutory instrument appoint.

63. Profit sharing schemes

(1) In section 187(2) of the Taxes Act 1988, in the definition of "relevant amount" (limit on the value of shares that may be appropriated to a participant in a year of assessment), for the words "not less than £1,250 and not more than £5,000" there shall be substituted the words "not less than £2,000 and not more than £6,000".

(2) This section shall apply for the year 1989–90 and subsequent years of assessment.

64. Share option and profit sharing schemes: shares of consortium member

In paragraph 10 of Schedule 9 to the Taxes Act 1988, paragraph (*c*)(ii) (which requires a consortium member to hold not less than three-twentieths of share capital of grantor company etc. if member's shares are to qualify as scheme shares) shall cease to have effect.

65. Employee share schemes: material interest

In Schedule 9 to the Taxes Act 1988 the following paragraph shall be inserted after paragraph 39—

"Shares subject to an employee benefit trust

40.—(1) Where an individual has an interest in shares or obligations of the company as a beneficiary of an employee benefit trust, the trustees shall not be regarded as associates of his by reason only of that interest unless sub-paragraph (3) below applies in relation to him.

(2) In this paragraph "employee benefit trust" has the same meaning as in paragraph 7 of Schedule 8.

(3) This sub-paragraph applies in relation to an individual if at any time on or after 14th March 1989—

(*a*) the individual, either on his own or with any one or more of his associates, or
(*b*) any associate of his, with or without other such associates,

has been the beneficial owner of, or able (directly or through the medium of other companies or by any other indirect means) to control, more than 25 per cent., or in the case of a share option scheme which is not a savings-related share option scheme more than 10 per cent., of the ordinary share capital of the company.

(4) Sub-paragraphs (9) to (12) of paragraph 7 of Schedule 8 shall apply for the purposes of this paragraph in relation to an individual as they apply for the purposes of that paragraph in relation to an employee."

66. Priority share allocations for employees etc.

(1) In relation to offers made on or after 11th October 1988, section 68 of the Finance Act 1988 (which provides for the benefits derived from priority rights in share offers to be disregarded in certain circumstances) shall have effect with the following amendments.

(2) In subsection (1), the words from "at the fixed price" to "tendered" shall be omitted.

(3) After that subsection there shall be inserted—

"(1A) Where the price payable by the director or employee is less than the fixed price or the lowest price successfully tendered, subsection (1) above shall not apply to the benefit represented by the difference in price."

(4) In subsection (2), for paragraph (*a*) (priority shares not to exceed 10 per cent. of shares subject to the offer) there shall be substituted—

"(*a*) that the aggregate number of shares subject to the offer that may be allocated as mentioned in subsection (1)(*b*) above does not exceed the limit specified in subsection (2A) below or, as the case may be, either of the limits specified in subsection (2B) below".

(5) After subsection (2) there shall be inserted—

"(2A) Except where subsection (2B) below applies, the limit relevant for the purposes of subsection (2)(*a*) above is 10 per cent. of the shares subject to the offer (including the shares that may be allocated as mentioned in subsection (1)(*b*) above).

(2B) Where the offer is part of arrangements which include one or more other offers to the public of shares of the same class, the limits relevant for the purposes of subsection (2)(*a*) above are—

(*a*) 40 per cent. of the shares subject to the offer (including the shares that may be allocated as mentioned in subsection (1)(*b*) above), and
(*b*) 10 per cent. of all the shares of the class in question (including the shares that may be so allocated) that are subject to any of the offers forming part of the arrangements."

Employee share ownership trusts

67. Tax relief

(1) This section applies where—

(*a*) a company expends a sum in making a payment by way of contribution to the trustees of a trust which is a qualifying employee share ownership trust at the time the sum is expended,
(*b*) at that time, the company or a company which it then controls has employees who are eligible to benefit under the terms of the trust deed,
(*c*) at that time the company is resident in the United Kingdom,
(*d*) before the expiry of the expenditure period the sum is expended by the trustees for one or more of the qualifying purposes, and
(*e*) before the end of the claim period a claim for relief under this section is made.

(2) In such a case the sum—

(*a*) shall be deducted in computing for the purposes of Schedule D the profits or gains of a trade carried on by the company, or
(*b*) if the company is an investment company or a company in the case of which section

75 of the Taxes Act 1988 applies by virtue of section 76 of that Act, shall be treated as expenses of management.

(3) For the purposes of subsection (1)(b) above, the question whether one company is controlled by another shall be construed in accordance with section 840 of the Taxes Act 1988.

(4) For the purposes of subsection (1)(d) above each of the following is a qualifying purpose—

   (a) the acquisition of shares in the company which established the trust;
   (b) the repayment of sums borrowed;
   (c) the payment of interest on sums borrowed;
   (d) the payment of any sum to a person who is a beneficiary under the terms of the trust deed;
   (e) the meeting of expenses.

(5) For the purposes of subsection (1)(d) above the expenditure period is the period of nine months beginning with the day following the end of the period of account in which the sum is charged as an expense of the company, or such longer period as the Board may allow by notice given to the company.

(6) For the purposes of subsection (1)(e) above the claim period is the period of two years beginning with the day following the end of the period of account in which the sum is charged as an expense of the company.

(7) For the purposes of this section the trustees of an employee share ownership trust shall be taken to expend sums paid to them in the order in which the sums are received by them (irrespective of the number of companies making payments).

68. Principal charges to tax

(1) This section applies where a chargeable event (within the meaning of section 69 below) occurs in relation to the trustees of an employee share ownership trust.

(2) In such a case—

   (a) the trustees shall be treated as receiving, when the event occurs, annual profits or gains whose amount is equal to the chargeable amount (within the meaning of section 70 below),
   (b) the profits or gains shall be chargeable to tax under Case VI of Schedule D for the year of assessment in which the event occurs, and
   (c) the rate at which the tax is chargeable shall be a rate equal to the sum of the basic rate and the additional rate for the year of assessment in which the event occurs.

(3) If the whole or any part of the tax assessed on the trustees is not paid before the expiry of the period of six months beginning with the day on which the assessment becomes final and conclusive, a notice of liability to tax under this subsection may be served on a qualifying company and the tax or the part unpaid (as the case may be) shall be payable by the company on service of the notice.

(4) Where a notice of liability is served under subsection (3) above—

   (a) any interest which is due on the tax or the part (as the case may be) and has not been paid by the trustees, and
   (b) any interest accruing due on the tax or the part (as the case may be) after the date of service,

shall be payable by the company.

(5) Where a notice of liability is served under subsection (3) above and any amount payable by the company (whether on account of tax or interest) is not paid by the company before the expiry of the period of three months beginning with the date of service, the amount unpaid may be recovered from the trustees (without prejudice to the right to recover it instead from the company).

(6) For the purposes of this section each of the following is a qualifying company—

   (a) the company which established the employee share ownership trust;
   (b) any company falling within subsection (7) below.

(7) A company falls within this subsection if, before it is sought to serve a notice of liability on it under subsection (3) above—

   (a) it has paid a sum to the trustees, and

(*b*) the sum has been deducted as mentioned in section 67(2)(*a*) above or treated as mentioned in section 67(2)(*b*) above.

69. Chargeable events

(1) For the purposes of section 68 above each of the following is a chargeable event in relation to the trustees of an employee share ownership trust—

(*a*) the transfer of securities by the trustees, if the transfer is not a qualifying transfer;
(*b*) the transfer of securities by the trustees to persons who are at the time of the transfer beneficiaries under the terms of the trust deed, if the terms on which the transfer is made are not qualifying terms;
(*c*) the retention of securities by the trustees at the expiry of the period of seven years beginning with the date on which they acquired them;
(*d*) the expenditure of a sum by the trustees for a purpose other than a qualifying purpose.

(2) For the purposes of subsection (1)(*a*) above a transfer is a qualifying transfer if it is made to a person who at the time of the transfer is a beneficiary under the terms of the trust deed.

(3) For the purposes of subsection (1)(*a*) above a transfer is also a qualifying transfer if—

(*a*) it is made to the trustees of a scheme which at the time of the transfer is a profit sharing scheme approved under Schedule 9 to the Taxes Act 1988, and
(*b*) it is made for a consideration which is not less than the price the securities might reasonably be expected to fetch on a sale in the open market.

(4) For the purposes of subsection (1)(*b*) above a transfer of securities is made on qualifying terms if—

(*a*) all the securities transferred at the same time are transferred on similar terms,
(*b*) securities have been offered to all the persons who are beneficiaries under the terms of the trust deed when the transfer is made, and
(*c*) securities are transferred to all such beneficiaries who have accepted.

(5) For the purposes of subsection (1)(*d*) above each of the following is a qualifying purpose—

(*a*) the acquisition of shares in the company which established the trust;
(*b*) the repayment of sums borrowed;
(*c*) the payment of interest on sums borrowed;
(*d*) the payment of any sum to a person who is a beneficiary under the terms of the trust deed;
(*e*) the meeting of expenses.

(6) For the purposes of subsection (4) above, the fact that terms vary according to the levels of remuneration of beneficiaries, the length of their service, or similar factors, shall not be regarded as meaning that the terms are not similar.

(7) In ascertaining for the purposes of this section whether particular securities are retained, securities acquired earlier by the trustees shall be treated as transferred by them before securities acquired by them later.

(8) For the purposes of this section trustees—

(*a*) acquire securities when they become entitled to them (subject to the exceptions in subsection (9) below);
(*b*) transfer securities to another person when that other becomes entitled to them;
(*c*) retain securities if they remain entitled to them.

(9) The exceptions are these—

(*a*) if securities are issued to trustees in exchange in circumstances mentioned in section 85(1) of the Capital Gains Tax Act 1979, they shall be treated as having acquired them when they became entitled to the securities for which they are exchanged;
(*b*) if trustees become entitled to securities as a result of a reorganisation, they shall be treated as having acquired them when they became entitled to the original shares which those securities represent (construing "reorganisation" and "original shares" in accordance with section 77 of that Act).

(10) If trustees agree to take a transfer of securities, for the purposes of this section they shall be treated as becoming entitled to them when the agreement is made and not on a later transfer made pursuant to the agreement.

(11) If trustees agree to transfer securities to another person, for the purposes of this section

the other person shall be treated as becoming entitled to them when the agreement is made and not on a later transfer made pursuant to the agreement.

(12) For the purposes of this section the following are securities—

(*a*) shares;
(*b*) debentures.

70. Chargeable amounts

(1) This section has effect to determine the chargeable amount for the purposes of section 68 above.

(2) If the chargeable event falls within section 69(1)(*a*), (*b*) or (*c*) above the following rules shall apply—

(*a*) if the event constitutes a disposal of the securities by the trustees for the purposes of the Capital Gains Tax Act 1979, the chargeable amount is an amount equal to the sums allowable under section 32(1)(*a*) and (*b*) of that Act;
(*b*) if the event does not constitute such a disposal, the chargeable amount is an amount equal to the sums which would be so allowable had the trustees made a disposal of the securities for the purposes of that Act at the time the chargeable event occurs.

(3) If the chargeable event falls within section 69(1)(*d*) above the chargeable amount is an amount equal to the sum concerned.

71. Further charges to tax: borrowing

(1) This section applies where—

(*a*) a chargeable event (within the meaning of section 69 above) occurs in relation to the trustees of an employee share ownership trust,
(*b*) at the time the event occurs anything is outstanding in respect of the principal of an amount or amounts borrowed at any time by the trustees, and
(*c*) the chargeable event is one as regards which section 72(2)(*b*) below applies.

(2) In the following provisions of this section—

(*a*) "the initial chargeable event" means the event referred to in subsection (1)(*a*) above, and
(*b*) "the total outstanding amount" means the total amount outstanding, at the time the initial chargeable event occurs, in respect of the principal of an amount or amounts borrowed at any time by the trustees.

(3) If any of the total outstanding amount is repaid after the initial chargeable event occurs, a further chargeable event shall occur in relation to the trustees at the end of the year of assessment in which the repayment is made.

(4) In such a case—

(*a*) the trustees shall be treated as receiving, when the further event occurs, annual profits or gains whose amount is equal to the chargeable amount,
(*b*) the profits or gains shall be chargeable to tax under Case VI of Schedule D for the year of assessment at the end of which the further event occurs, and
(*c*) the rate at which the tax is chargeable shall be a rate equal to the sum of the basic rate and the additional rate for the year of assessment at the end of which the further event occurs.

(5) Subject to subsection (6) below, for the purposes of subsection (4) above the chargeable amount is an amount equal to the aggregate of the total outstanding amount repaid in the year of assessment.

(6) In a case where section 72(2)(*b*) below had effect in the case of the initial chargeable event, for the purposes of subsection (4) above the chargeable amount is an amount equal to the smaller of—

(*a*) the aggregate of the total outstanding amount repaid in the year of assessment, and
(*b*) an amount found by applying the formula $A - B - C$.

(7) For the purposes of subsection (6) above—

(*a*) A is the amount which would be the chargeable amount for the initial chargeable event apart from section 72(2) below,
(*b*) B is the chargeable amount for the initial chargeable event, and
(*c*) C is the amount (if any) found under subsection (8) below.

(8) If, before the further chargeable event occurs, one or more prior chargeable events have occurred in relation to the trustees by virtue of the prior repayment of any of the total outstanding amount found for the time the initial chargeable event occurs, the amount found under this subsection is an amount equal to the chargeable amount for the prior chargeable event or to the aggregate of the chargeable amounts for the prior chargeable events (as the case may be).

(9) In a case where—

(*a*) a chargeable event (within the meaning of section 69 above) occurs in relation to the trustees in circumstances mentioned in subsection (1) above,
(*b*) a sum falls to be included in the total outstanding amount found for the time the event occurs,
(*c*) another chargeable event (within the meaning of that section) occurs in relation to the trustees in circumstances mentioned in subsection (1) above, and
(*d*) the same sum or a part of it would (apart from this subsection) fall to be included in the total outstanding amount found for the time the event occurs,

the sum or part (as the case may be) shall not be included in the total outstanding amount found for the time the other chargeable event occurs.

(10) In ascertaining for the purposes of this section whether a repayment is in respect of a particular amount, amounts borrowed earlier shall be taken to be repaid before amounts borrowed later.

(11) Subsections (3) to (7) of section 68 above shall apply where tax is assessed by virtue of this section as they apply where tax is assessed by virtue of that section.

72. Limit on chargeable amount

(1) For the purposes of this section each of the following is a chargeable event in relation to the trustees of an employee share ownership trust—

(*a*) an event which is a chargeable event by virtue of section 69 above;
(*b*) an event which is a chargeable event by virtue of section 71 above.

(2) If a chargeable event (the event in question) occurs in relation to the trustees of an employee share ownership trust, the following rules shall apply—

(*a*) the amount which would (apart from this subsection) be the chargeable amount for the event in question shall be aggregated, for the purposes of paragraph (*b*) below, with the chargeable amounts for other chargeable events (if any) occurring in relation to the trustees before the event in question,
(*b*) if the amount which would (apart from this subsection) be the chargeable amount for the event in question (or the aggregate found under paragraph (*a*) above, if there is one) exceeds the deductible amount, the chargeable amount for the event in question shall be the amount it would be apart from this subsection less an amount equal to the excess, and
(*c*) section 70(2) and (3) and section 71(5) above shall have effect subject to paragraph (*b*) above.

(3) For the purposes of subsection (2) above the deductible amount (as regards the event in question) is an amount equal to the total of the sums falling within subsection (4) below.

(4) A sum falls within this subsection if it has been received by the trustees before the occurrence of the event in question and—

(*a*) it has been deducted as mentioned in section 67(2)(*a*) above, or treated as mentioned in section 67(2)(*b*) above, before the occurrence of that event, or
(*b*) it would fall to be so deducted or treated if a claim for relief under section 67 above had been made immediately before the occurrence of that event.

73. Information

(1) An inspector may by notice in writing require a return to be made by the trustees of an employee share ownership trust if they have at any time received a sum which has been deducted as mentioned in section 67(2)(*a*) above or treated as mentioned in section 67(2)(*b*) above.

(2) Where he requires such a return to be made the inspector shall specify the information to be contained in it.

(3) The information which may be specified is information the inspector needs for the purposes of sections 68 to 72 above, and may include information about—

(a) sums received (including sums borrowed) by the trustees;
(b) expenditure incurred by them;
(c) assets acquired by them;
(d) transfers of assets made by them.

(4) The information which may be required under subsection (3)(a) above may include the persons from whom the sums were received.

(5) The information which may be required under subsection (3)(b) above may include the purpose of the expenditure and the persons receiving any sums.

(6) The information which may be specified under subsection (3)(c) above may include the persons from whom the assets were acquired and the consideration furnished by the trustees.

(7) The information which may be included under subsection (3)(d) above may include the persons to whom assets were transferred and the consideration furnished by them.

(8) In a case where a sum has been deducted as mentioned in section 67(2)(a) above, or treated as mentioned in section 67(2)(b) above, the inspector shall send to the trustees to whom the payment was made a certificate stating—

(a) that a sum has been so deducted or so treated, and
(b) what sum has been so deducted or so treated.

(9) In the Table in section 98 of the Taxes Management Act 1970 (penalties for failure to comply with notices etc.) at the end of the first column there shall be inserted—

"Section 73 of the Finance Act 1989".

74. Interpretation

Schedule 5 to this Act shall have effect to determine whether, for the purposes of sections 67 to 73 above, a trust is at a particular time—

(a) an employee share ownership trust;
(b) a qualifying employee share ownership trust.

Pensions etc.

75. Retirement benefits schemes

Schedule 6 to this Act (which relates to retirement benefits schemes) shall have effect.

76. Non-approved retirement benefits schemes

(1) In computing the amount of the profits or gains to be charged under Case I or Case II of Schedule D, no sum shall be deducted in respect of any expenses falling within subsection (2) or (3) below; and no expenses falling within either of those subsections shall be treated for the purposes of section 75 of the Taxes Act 1988 (investment companies) as expenses of management.

(2) Expenses fall within this subsection if—

(a) they are expenses of providing benefits pursuant to a relevant retirement benefits scheme, and
(b) the benefits are not ones in respect of which a person is on receipt chargeable to income tax.

(3) Expenses fall within this subsection if—

(a) they are expenses of paying any sum pursuant to a relevant retirement benefits scheme with a view to the provision of any benefits, and
(b) the sum is not one which when paid is treated as the income of a person by virtue of section 595(1) of the Taxes Act 1988 (sum paid with a view to the provision of any relevant benefits for an employee).

(4) No sum shall be deducted in respect of any expenses falling within subsection (5) or (6) below—

(a) in computing the amount of the profits or gains to be charged under Case I or Case II of Schedule D, or
(b) by virtue of section 75 of the Taxes Act 1988,

unless the sum has actually been expended.

(5) Expenses fall within this subsection if—

(*a*) they are expenses of providing benefits pursuant to a relevant retirement benefits scheme, and
(*b*) the benefits are ones in respect of which a person is on receipt chargeable to income tax.

(6) Expenses fall within this subsection if—

(*a*) they are expenses of paying any sum pursuant to a relevant retirement benefits scheme with a view to the provision of any benefits, and
(*b*) the sum is one which when paid is treated as the income of a person by virtue of section 595(1) of the Taxes Act 1988.

(7) In this section—

"retirement benefits scheme" has the same meaning as in Chapter I of Part XIV of the Taxes Act 1988, and
references to a relevant retirement benefits scheme are references to a retirement benefits scheme which is not of a description mentioned in section 596(1)(*a*), (*b*) or (*c*) of the Taxes Act 1988.

(8) This section has effect in relation to expenses incurred on or after the day on which this Act is passed.

77. Personal pension schemes

Schedule 7 to this Act (which relates to personal pension schemes) shall have effect.

Unit trusts etc.

78. Certified unit trusts

The following sections shall be inserted after section 468 of the Taxes Act 1988—

"468A. Certified unit trusts

(1) For the purposes of sections 468B and 468C "certified unit trust" means, as respects an accounting period, a unit trust scheme in the case of which—

(*a*) an order under section 78 of the Financial Services Act 1986 is in force during the whole or part of that accounting period, and
(*b*) a certificate under section 78(8) of that Act, certifying that the scheme complies with the conditions necessary for it to enjoy the rights conferred by the UCITS directive, has been issued before or at any time during that accounting period.

(2) In this section—

"the UCITS directive" means the directive of the Council of the European Communities, dated 20th December 1985, on the co-ordination of laws, regulations and administrative provisions relating to undertakings for collective investment in transferable securities (no. 85/611/EEC), and
"unit trust scheme" has the same meaning as in section 469.

468B. Certified unit trusts: corporation tax

(1) This section has effect as regards an accounting period of the trustees of a certified unit trust ending after 31st December 1989.

(2) Subject to subsection (3) below, the rate of corporation tax for a financial year shall be deemed to be the rate at which income tax at the basic rate is charged for the year of assessment which begins on 6th April in the financial year concerned.

(3) Where the period begins before 1st January 1990, subsection (2) above shall only apply for the purpose of computing corporation tax chargeable for so much of the period as falls in the financial year 1990 and subsection (4) below shall apply for the purpose of computing corporation tax chargeable for so much of the period as falls in the financial year 1989.

(4) So much of the period as falls after 31st December 1989 and before 1st April 1990 shall be deemed to fall in a financial year for which the rate of corporation tax is the rate at which income tax at the basic rate is charged for the year 1989–90.

(5) Where the period begins after 31st December 1989, section 338 shall have effect as if

any reference to interest of any description were a reference to interest of that description on borrowing of a relevant description.

(6) For the purposes of subsection (5) above borrowing is of a relevant description if it is borrowing in respect of which there has been no breach during the accounting period of the duties imposed on the manager of the scheme by regulations under section 81 of the Financial Services Act 1986 with respect to borrowing by the trustees of the scheme.

(7) The Treasury may by regulations provide that for subsection (6) above (as it has effect for the time being) there shall be substituted a subsection containing a different definition of what constitutes borrowing of a relevant description for the purposes of subsection (5) above.

(8) Regulations under subsection (7) above may contain such supplementary, incidental, consequential or transitional provision as the Treasury think fit.

(9) In this section "certified unit trust" has the meaning given by section 468A.

468C. Certified unit trusts: distributions

(1) Subsection (2) below applies where—

(*a*) as regards a distribution period ending after 31st December 1989 a dividend is treated by virtue of section 468(2) as paid to a unit holder (whether or not income is in fact paid to the unit holder),
(*b*) the dividend is treated as paid by the trustees of a unit trust scheme which is a certified unit trust as respects the accounting period in which the distribution period falls, and
(*c*) on the date of payment the unit holder is within the charge to corporation tax and not a dual resident.

(2) For the purpose of computing corporation tax chargeable in the case of the unit holder the payment shall be deemed—

(*a*) to be an annual payment, and not a dividend or other distribution, and
(*b*) to have been received by the unit holder after deduction of income tax at the basic rate, for the year of assessment in which the date of payment falls, from a corresponding gross amount.

(3) Subsection (2) above shall not apply where the rights in respect of which the dividend is treated as paid are held by the trustees of a unit trust scheme which on the date of payment is a fund of funds.

(4) Where the unit holder is on the date of payment the manager of the scheme, subsection (2) above shall not apply in so far as the rights in respect of which the dividend is treated as paid are rights held by him in the ordinary course of his business as manager of the scheme.

(5) Subsection (2) above shall not apply to so much of the payment as is attributable to income of the trustees arising before 1st January 1990.

(6) In this section—

"certified unit trust" has the meaning given by section 468A,
"distribution period" has the same meaning as in section 468,
"dual resident" means a person who is resident in the United Kingdom and falls to be regarded for the purposes of any arrangements having effect by virtue of section 788 as resident in a territory outside the United Kingdom,
"fund of funds" means a unit trust scheme the sole object of which is to enable the unit holders to participate in or receive profits or income arising from the acquisition, holding, management or disposal of units in unit trust schemes, and
"unit trust scheme" has the same meaning as in section 469."

79. Funds of funds

The following section shall be inserted after section 468C of the Taxes Act 1988—

"**468D. Funds of funds: distributions**

(1) Subsection (2) below applies where—

(*a*) as regards a distribution period ending after 31st December 1989 a dividend is treated by virtue of section 468(2) as paid to a unit holder (whether or not income is in fact paid to the unit holder),

(*b*) the dividend is treated as paid by the trustees of a unit trust scheme which on the date of payment is a fund of funds, and
(*c*) on the date of payment the unit holder is within the charge to corporation tax and not a dual resident.

(2) For the purpose of computing corporation tax chargeable in the case of the unit holder the payment shall be deemed—

(*a*) to be an annual payment, and not a dividend or other distribution, and
(*b*) to have been received by the unit holder after deduction of income tax at the basic rate, for the year of assessment in which the date of payment falls, from a corresponding gross amount.

(3) Where the unit holder is on the date of payment the manager of the scheme, subsection (2) above shall not apply in so far as the rights in respect of which the dividend is treated as paid are rights held by him in the ordinary course of his business as manager of the scheme.

(4) Subsection (2) above shall not apply to so much of the payment as is attributable to income of the trustees arising before 1st January 1990.

(5) In this section—

"distribution period" has the same meaning as in section 468,
"dual resident" and "fund of funds" have the same meanings as in section 468C,
"unit trust scheme" has the same meaning as in section 469."

80. Gilt unit trusts

(1) Where, in the case of a certified unit trust and apart from this subsection, section 468(5) of the Taxes Act 1988 would apply as regards a distribution period beginning after 31st December 1989, section 468(5) shall not apply in the case of the trust as regards that period.

(2) Where by virtue of subsection (1) above the last distribution period as regards which section 468(5) applies in the case of a certified unit trust is one beginning on or before, and ending after, 31st December 1989, the trustees' liability to income tax in respect of any source of income chargeable under Case III of Schedule D shall be assessed as if they had ceased to possess the source of income on the last day of that distribution period.

(3) But where section 67 of the Taxes Act 1988 applies by virtue of subsection (2) above, it shall apply with the omission from subsection (1)(*b*) of the words from "and shall" to "this provision".

(4) For the purposes of this section "certified unit trust" means, as respects a distribution period, a unit trust scheme in the case of which—

(*a*) an order under section 78 of the Financial Services Act 1986 is in force during the whole or part of the accounting period in which the distribution period falls, and
(*b*) a certificate under section 78(8) of that Act, certifying that the scheme complies with the conditions necessary for it to enjoy the rights conferred by the UCITS directive, has been issued before or at any time during that accounting period.

(5) In this section—

"distribution period" has the same meaning as in section 468 of the Taxes Act 1988,
"the UCITS directive" means the directive of the Council of the European Communities, dated 20th December 1985, on the co-ordination of laws, regulations and administrative provisions relating to undertakings for collective investment in transferable securities (No. 85/611/EEC), and
"unit trust scheme" has the same meaning as in section 469 of the Taxes Act 1988.

81. Offshore funds operating equalisation arrangements

(1) In section 758 of the Taxes Act 1988 (offshore funds operating equalisation arrangements) in subsection (6) (reference to section 78 of the Capital Gains Tax Act 1979 not to include reference to it as applied by section 82) for the words "but not" there shall be substituted the words "and a reference to section 78".

(2) This section shall apply where a conversion of securities occurs on or after 14th March 1989; and "conversion of securities" here has the same meaning as in section 82 of the Capital Gains Tax Act 1979.

Life assurance

82. Calculation of profits

(1) Where the profits of an insurance company in respect of its life assurance business are, for the purposes of the Taxes Act 1988, computed in accordance with the provisions of that Act applicable to Case I of Schedule D, then, in calculating the profits for any period of account,—

(a) there shall be taken into account as an expense (so far as not so taken into account apart from this section) any amounts which, in respect of the period, are allocated to or expended on behalf of policy holders or annuitants; and

(b) if, at the end of the period, the company has an unappropriated surplus on valuation, as shown in its return for the purposes of the Insurance Companies Act 1982, then, subject to subsection (3) below, the closing liabilities of the period may include such amount, forming part of that surplus, as is required to meet the reasonable expectations of policy holders or annuitants with regard to bonuses or other additions to benefit of a discretionary nature.

(2) For the purposes of this section an amount is allocated to policy holders or annuitants if, and only if,—

(a) bonus payments are made to them; or

(b) reversionary bonuses are declared in their favour or a reduction is made in the premiums payable by them;

and the amount of the allocation is, in a case within paragraph (a) above, the amount of the payments and, in a case within paragraph (b) above, the amount of the liabilities assumed by the company in consequence of the declaration or reduction.

(3) The amount which, apart from this subsection, would be included in the closing liabilities of a period of account by virtue of subsection (1)(b) above shall be reduced or, as the case may be, extinguished by deducting therefrom the total of the amounts which,—

(a) for periods of account ending before 14th March 1989 have been excluded, by virtue of section 433 of the Taxes Act 1988, as being reserved for policy holders or annuitants, and

(b) have not before that date either been allocated to or expended on behalf of policy holders or annuitants or been treated as profits of an accounting period on ceasing to be so reserved.

(4) Where the closing liabilities of a period of account include an amount by virtue of subsection (1)(b) above, the like amount shall be included in the opening liabilities of the next following period of account.

(5) This section has effect with respect to periods of account ending on or after 14th March 1989; and the following provisions of this section shall apply for the purposes of the application of this section to any such period which begins before that date (in this section referred to as a "straddling period").

(6) For the purposes referred to in subsection (5) above, it shall be assumed that the straddling period consists of two separate periods of account,—

(a) the first beginning at the beginning of the straddling period and ending on 13th March 1989 (in this section referred to as "the first notional period"); and

(b) the second beginning on 14th March 1989 and ending at the end of the straddling period (in this section referred to as "the second notional period");

and any reference in subsection (7) or subsection (8) below to a time apportionment is a reference to an apportionment made by reference to the respective lengths of the two notional periods.

(7) To determine the profits of the first notional period and the amount excluded from the profits of that period by virtue of section 433 of the Taxes Act 1988, as being reserved for policy holders or annuitants,—

(a) in the first instance the profits of the straddling period and the amount so excluded from those profits shall be computed as if subsections (1) to (4) above did not apply with respect to any part of the straddling period; and

(b) there shall then be determined that part of the profits and the amount computed under paragraph (a) above which, on a time apportionment, is properly attributable to the first notional period.

(8) To determine the profits of the second notional period,—

(a) in the first instance the profits of the straddling period shall be computed as if subsections (1) to (4) above applied to the whole of the straddling period; and
(b) there shall then be determined that part of the profits computed under paragraph (a) above which, on a time apportionment, is properly attributable to the second notional period.

83. Receipts to be brought into account

(1) Where the profits of an insurance company in respect of its life assurance business are, for the purposes of the Taxes Act 1988, computed in accordance with the provisions of that Act applicable to Case I of Schedule D, then, so far as referable to that business, the following items, as brought into account for a period of account (and not otherwise), namely,—

(a) the company's investment income from the assets of its long-term business fund, and
(b) any increase in the value (whether realised or not) of those assets,

shall be taken into account as receipts of the period; and if for any period of account there is a reduction in the value referred to in paragraph (b) above (as brought into account for the period), that reduction shall be taken into account as an expense of that period.

(2) Except in so far as regulations made by the Treasury otherwise provide, in subsection (1) above "brought into account" means brought into account in the revenue account prepared for the purposes of the Insurance Companies Act 1982.

(3) Subject to subsection (5) below, this section has effect with respect to periods of account ending on or after 1st January 1990; and the following provisions of this section shall apply for the purposes of the application of this section to any such period which begins before that date (in this section referred to as a "straddling period").

(4) Subject to subsection (5) below, for the purposes referred to in subsection (3) above, it shall be assumed that the straddling period consists of two separate periods of account,—

(a) the first beginning at the beginning of the straddling period and ending on 31st December 1989 (in this section referred to as "the first notional period"); and
(b) the second beginning on 1st January 1990 and ending at the end of the straddling period (in this section referred to as "the second notional period");

and any reference in subsection (6) or subsection (7) below to a time apportionment is a reference to an apportionment made by reference to the respective lengths of the two notional periods.

(5) In the case of any company which, by notice in writing given to the inspector on or before 31st December 1992, so elects,—

(a) subsections (3) and (4)(b) above shall have effect as if for "1st January 1990" there were substituted "14th March 1989"; and
(b) subsection (4)(a) above shall have effect as if for "31st December" there were substituted "13th March".

(6) To determine the profits of the first notional period,—

(a) in the first instance the profits of the straddling period shall be computed as if subsections (1) and (2) above did not apply with respect to any part of that period; and
(b) there shall then be determined that part of the profits computed under paragraph (a) above which, on a time apportionment, is properly attributable to the first notional period.

(7) To determine the profits of the second notional period,—

(a) in the first instance the profits of the straddling period shall be computed as if subsections (1) and (2) above applied with respect to the whole of that period; and
(b) there shall then be determined that part of the profits computed under paragraph (a) above which, on a time apportionment, is properly attributable to the second notional period.

84. Interpretation of sections 85 to 89 and further provisions about insurance companies

(1) In sections 85 to 89 below "basic life assurance business" means life assurance business other than general annuity business and pension business.

(2) Any reference in the sections referred to in subsection (1) above or the following

provisions of this section to a straddling period is a reference to an accounting period which begins before 1st January 1990 and ends on or after that date.

(3) For the purposes of the sections referred to in subsection (1) above and for the purposes of subsection (5)(*b*) below it shall be assumed that a straddling period consists of two separate accounting periods—

(*a*) the first beginning at the beginning of the straddling period and ending on 31st December 1989; and
(*b*) the second beginning on 1st January 1990 and ending at the end of the straddling period;

and in those sections and subsection (5)(*b*) below the first of those two notional accounting periods is referred to as "the 1989 component period" and the second is referred to as "the 1990 component period".

(4) Chapter I of Part XII of the Taxes Act 1988 (insurance companies) shall have effect subject to the amendments in Schedule 8 to this Act, being—

(*a*) amendments relating to franked investment income, loss relief and group relief; and
(*b*) amendments consequential on or supplemental to sections 82 and 83 above and sections 85 to 89 below.

(5) Subject to subsection (6) below, in Schedule 8 to this Act,—

(*a*) paragraphs 2 and 6 shall be deemed to have come into force on 14th March 1989; and
(*b*) the remainder shall have effect with respect to accounting periods beginning on or after 1st January 1990 (including the 1990 component period).

(6) Nothing in subsection (5) above affects the operation, by virtue of any provision of sections 82 and 83 above and sections 85 to 89 below, of any enactment repealed or amended by Schedule 8 to this Act and, so long as the provisions of that Schedule do not have effect in relation to sections 434 and 435 of the Taxes Act 1988, nothing in subsection (5)(*a*) above affects the continuing operation of section 433 of that Act for the purpose only of determining the fraction of the profits referred to in subsection (6) of section 434 and subsection (1)(*b*) of section 435.

85. Charge of certain receipts of basic life assurance business

(1) Subject to subsection (2) below, where the profits of an insurance company in respect of its life assurance business are not charged under Case I of Schedule D, there shall be chargeable under Case VI of that Schedule any receipts referable to the company's basic life assurance business—

(*a*) which, if those profits were charged under Case I of Schedule D, would be taken into account in computing those profits; and
(*b*) which would not be within the charge to tax (except under Case I of Schedule D) apart from this section;

and for the purposes of paragraph (*a*) above, the provisions of section 83 above as to the manner in which any item is to be taken into account shall be disregarded.

(2) The receipts referred to in subsection (1) above do not include—

(*a*) any premium; or
(*b*) any sum received by virtue of a claim under an insurance contract (including a re-insurance contract); or
(*c*) any repayment or refund (in whole or in part) of a sum disbursed by the company as acquisition expenses falling within paragraphs (*a*) to (*c*) of subsection (1) of section 86 below; or
(*d*) any sum which is taken into account under section 76(1)(*a*) of the Taxes Act 1988 as a deduction from the amount treated as expenses of management of the company; or
(*e*) any sum which is not within the charge to tax (except under Case I of Schedule D) because of an exemption from tax.

(3) This section has effect with respect to the receipts of accounting periods beginning on or after 1st January 1990 (including the 1990 component period).

86. Spreading of relief for acquisition expenses

(1) For the purposes of this section, the acquisition expenses for any period of an insurance company carrying on life assurance business are such of the following expenses of management as are for that period attributable to the company's basic life assurance business,—

(*a*) commissions (however described), other than commissions in respect of industrial life assurance business carried on by the company,
(*b*) any other expenses of management which are disbursed solely for the purpose of the acquisition of business, and
(*c*) so much of any other expenses of management which are disbursed partly for the purpose of the acquisition of business and partly for other purposes as are properly attributable to the acquisition of business,

less any such repayments or refunds falling within section 76(1)(*c*) of the Taxes Act 1988 as are received in the period.

(2) The exclusion from paragraph (*a*) of subsection (1) above of commissions in respect of industrial life assurance business shall not prevent such commissions constituting expenses of management for the purposes of paragraph (*b*) or paragraph (*c*) of that subsection.

(3) Nothing in subsections (1) and (2) above applies to commissions (however described) in respect of insurances made before 14th March 1989, but without prejudice to the application of those subsections to any commission attributable to a variation on or after that date in a policy issued in respect of an insurance made before that date; and, for this purpose, the exercise of any rights conferred by a policy shall be regarded as a variation of it.

(4) In subsection (1) above "the acquisition of business" includes the securing on or after 14th March 1989 of the payment of increased or additional premiums in respect of a policy of insurance issued in respect of an insurance already made (whether before, on or after that date).

(5) In relation to any period, the expenses of management attributable to a company's basic life assurance business are expenses—

(*a*) which are disbursed for that period (disregarding any treated as so disbursed by section 75(3) of the Taxes Act 1988); and
(*b*) which, disregarding subsection (6) below, are deductible as expenses of management in accordance with sections 75 and 76 of the Taxes Act 1988.

(6) Notwithstanding anything in sections 75 and 76 of the Taxes Act 1988 but subject to subsection (7) below, only one-seventh of the acquisition expenses for any accounting period (in this section referred to as "the base period") shall be treated as deductible under those sections for the base period, and in subsections (8) and (9) below any reference to the full amount of the acquisition expenses for the base period is a reference to the amount of those expenses which would be deductible for that period apart from this subsection.

(7) In the case of the acquisition expenses for an accounting period or part of an accounting period falling wholly within 1990, subsection (6) above shall have effect as if for "one-seventh" there were substituted "five-sevenths"; and, in the case of the acquisition expenses for an accounting period or part of an accounting period falling wholly within 1991, 1992 or 1993, the corresponding substitution shall be "four-sevenths", "three-sevenths" or "two-sevenths" respectively.

(8) Where, by virtue of subsection (6) (and, where appropriate, subsection (7)) above, only a fraction of the full amount of the acquisition expenses for the base period is deductible under sections 75 and 76 of the Taxes Act 1988 for that period, then, subject to subsection (9) below, a further one-seventh of the full amount shall be so deductible for each succeeding accounting period after the base period until the whole of the full amount has become so deductible, except that, for any accounting period of less than a year, the fraction of one-seventh shall be proportionately reduced.

(9) For any accounting period for which the fraction of the full amount of the acquisition expenses for the base period which would otherwise be deductible in accordance with subsection (8) above exceeds the balance of those expenses which has not become deductible for earlier accounting periods, only that balance shall be deductible.

(10) This section has effect for accounting periods beginning on or after 1st January 1990 (including the 1990 component period).

87. Management expenses

(1) Section 76 of the Taxes Act 1988 shall be amended in accordance with subsections (2) and (3) below.

(2) In subsection (1), after paragraph (*b*) there shall be inserted "and

(*c*) there shall be deducted from the amount treated as the expenses of management for any accounting period any repayment or refund (in whole or in part) of a sum disbursed by the company (for that or any earlier period) as acquisition expenses; and

(d) the amount treated as expenses of management shall not include any amount in respect of expenses referable to general annuity business or pension business; and

(e) the amount of profits from which expenses of management may be deducted for any accounting period shall not exceed the net income and gains of that accounting period referable to basic life assurance business;

and for this purpose "net income and gains" means income and gains after deducting any reliefs or exemptions which fall to be applied before taking account of this section."

(3) For subsection (8) there shall be substituted—

"(8) In this section—

"acquisition expenses" means expenses falling within paragraphs (a) to (c) of subsection (1) of section 86 of the Finance Act 1989;
"basic life assurance business" has the meaning assigned by section 84(1) of that Act;

and other expressions have the same meaning as in Chapter I of Part XII."

(4) In consequence of the amendment made by subsection (2) above, section 436(3)(b) of the Taxes Act 1988 (no deduction of expenses of management in certain cases) shall cease to have effect.

(5) This section has effect with respect to accounting periods beginning on or after 1st January 1990; and, in relation to a straddling period, sections 75, 76 and 436 of the Taxes Act 1988—

(a) shall have effect in relation to the 1989 component period without regard to the amendments made by subsections (2) to (4) above; and

(b) shall have effect in relation to the 1990 component period as amended by those subsections.

(6) If, for the 1989 component period, there is an amount of expenses of management available to be carried forward to the 1990 component period under section 75(3)(a) of the Taxes Act 1988 (as applied by section 76 thereof),—

(a) that amount shall form a pool to which the following provisions of this section shall apply and to which section 75(3)(b) of that Act (in this subsection referred to as "the carry-forward provision") shall apply only to the extent specified in paragraph (c) below;

(b) if, for the 1990 component period or any subsequent accounting period, the amount which (disregarding the pool) may be deducted in respect of expenses of management is less than the amount of the profits from which, disregarding section 76(1)(e) of that Act (as set out in subsection (2) above), the expenses of management are deductible, paragraph (c) below shall apply for that period; and in that paragraph the difference between the amount which may be so deducted and that amount of profits is referred to as "the potential deficiency" for the period;

(c) where this paragraph applies for an accounting period (including the 1990 component period) the carry-forward provision shall be taken to have had effect to carry forward to the accounting period (as if disbursed as expenses for that period) so much of the pool as does not exceed the potential deficiency for the period and is permitted under section 76(2) of the Taxes Act 1988; and the amount of the pool shall be reduced accordingly.

(7) In the case of a company which has an accounting period beginning on 1st January 1990, subsection (6) above shall apply as if—

(a) any reference therein to the 1989 component period were a reference to the accounting period ending on 31st December 1989; and

(b) any reference therein to the 1990 component period were a reference to the accounting period beginning on 1st January 1990.

88. Corporation tax: policy holders' fraction of profits

(1) Subject to subsection (2) below, in the case of a company carrying on life assurance business, the rate of corporation tax chargeable for any financial year on the policy holders' fraction of its relevant profits for any accounting period shall be deemed to be the rate at which income tax at the basic rate is charged for the year of assessment which begins on 6th April in the financial year concerned.

(2) Subsection (1) above does not apply in relation to profits charged under Case I of Schedule D.

(3) For the purposes of subsection (1) above, the relevant profits of a company for an accounting period are the total profits of its life assurance business, less any deduction due under section 76 of the Taxes Act 1988, but before allowing any relief under Chapter II or Chapter IV of Part X of that Act.

(4) In determining for the purposes of section 13 of the Taxes Act 1988 (small companies' relief) the profits and basic profits (within the meaning of that section) of an accounting period of a company carrying on life assurance business, the policy holders' fraction of the company's relevant profits for that period shall be left out of account.

(5) This section has effect with respect to the profits of a company for accounting periods beginning on or after 1st January 1990 (including the 1990 component period); and, for this purpose, the profits of the 1990 component period shall be taken to be that portion of the profits of the straddling period which the length of the 1990 component period bears to the length of the straddling period.

89. Shareholders' and policy holders' fractions

(1) In relation to an accounting period of an insurance company carrying on life assurance business, any reference to the shareholders' fraction or the policy holders' fraction is a reference to the appropriate fraction determined, subject to subsections (7) and (8) below, by the formulae in subsection (2) below.

(2) The formulae referred to in subsection (1) above are—

(*a*) for the shareholders' fraction,

$$\frac{A}{A+B},$$

and
(*b*) for the policy holders' fraction,

$$\frac{B}{A+B},$$

where "A" and "B" are determined in accordance with the following provisions of this section.

(3) In the formulae in subsection (2) above "A" is the profits of the company for the accounting period in respect of its life assurance business, computed in accordance with the provisions of the Taxes Act 1988 applicable to Case I of Schedule D, and, if there are no such profits (or there is a loss), "A" is zero.

(4) Subject to subsection (6) below, in those formulae "B" is such a sum as, after deduction of corporation tax at the rate provided for by subsection (1) of section 88 above in relation to the policy holders' fraction of the company's relevant profits for the accounting period (within the meaning of that subsection), is equal to the excess (if any) for the corresponding period of account of—

(*a*) the aggregate of—

(i) the closing liabilities to policy holders referable to the company's basic life assurance business,
(ii) the sums paid to policy holders in the period in respect of claims referable to that business, and
(iii) any amounts allocated to policy holders in respect of that period which do not fall within sub-paragraph (i) or sub-paragraph (ii) above and which are referable to that business,

over
(*b*) the aggregate of the premiums receivable by the company for the period in respect of its basic life assurance business and the opening liabilities to policy holders referable to that business,

and, if there is no such excess, "B" is zero.

(5) The references in subsection (4) above to the opening and closing liabilities to policy holders are references to those liabilities including any such amount as is referred to in section 82(1)(*b*) above.

(6) In relation to an accounting period, references in subsection (4) above to the corresponding period of account are references,—

(a) if the accounting period coincides with a period of account, to that period; and
(b) in any other case, to the period of account in which the accounting period is comprised;

and, for the purpose of determining "B" in a case where paragraph (b) above applies, the aggregates referred to in paragraphs (a) and (b) of subsection (4) above shall each be proportionately reduced to reflect the length of the accounting period as compared with the length of the corresponding period of account.

(7) Subject to subsection (8) below, if in the case of any accounting period of a company both "A" and "B" in the formulae in subsection (2) above are zero,—

(a) the shareholders' fraction shall be taken to be the whole; and
(b) the policy holders' fraction shall be taken to be nil.

(8) In relation to an accounting period of an insurance company carrying on mutual life assurance business,—

(a) any reference to the shareholders' fraction is a reference to nil; and
(b) any reference to the policy holders' fraction is a reference to the whole.

90. Life policies etc. held by companies

Schedule 9 to this Act (which imposes tax on certain benefits relating to life policies, life annuities and capital redemption policies held by companies, and makes related provision) shall have effect.

Underwriters

91. Premiums trust funds: stock lending

(1) In section 725 of the Taxes Act 1988 (Lloyd's underwriters) the following subsections shall be inserted after subsection (9)—

"(10) Subsection (11) below applies where the following state of affairs exists at the beginning of 1st January of any year or the end of 31st December of any year—

(a) securities have been transferred by the trustees of a premiums trust fund in pursuance of an arrangement mentioned in section 129(1) or (2),
(b) the transfer was made to enable another person to fulfil a contract or to make a transfer,
(c) securities have not been transferred in return, and
(d) section 129(3) applies to the transfer made by the trustees.

(11) The securities transferred by the trustees shall be treated for the purposes of subsections (1) to (6) above as if they formed part of the premiums trust fund at the beginning of 1st January concerned or the end of 31st December concerned (as the case may be)."

(2) In section 142A of the Capital Gains Tax Act 1979 (assets in premiums trust fund) the following subsections shall be inserted after subsection (4)—

"(4A) Subsection (4B) below applies where the following state of affairs exists at the beginning of an accounting period or the end of an accounting period—

(a) securities have been transferred by the trustees of a premiums trust fund in pursuance of an arrangement mentioned in section 129(1) or (2) of the Taxes Act 1988 (stock lending),
(b) the transfer was made to enable another person to fulfil a contract or to make a transfer,
(c) securities have not been transferred in return, and
(d) the transfer made by the trustees constitutes a disposal which by virtue of section 149B(9) below is to be disregarded as there mentioned.

(4B) The securities transferred by the trustees shall be treated for the purposes of subsection (3) above as if they formed part of the premiums trust fund at the beginning concerned or the end concerned (as the case may be)."

(3) This section applies where the transfer by the trustees of a premiums trust fund is made after the date specified as mentioned in section 129(6) of the Taxes Act 1988.

92. Regulations about underwriters etc.

(1) In section 451(1A) of the Taxes Act 1988 (regulations about underwriters) for the words from "with respect to" to the end there shall be substituted the words "with respect to any

year or years of assessment; and the year (or any of the years) may be the one in which the regulations are made or any year falling before or after that year."

(2) The following subsection shall be inserted after section 451(1A) of that Act—

"(1B) But the regulations may not make provision with respect to any year of assessment which precedes the next but one preceding the year of assessment in which the regulations are made."

(3) In section 142A of the Capital Gains Tax Act 1979 (regulations about premiums trust funds) subsection (5)(c) shall be omitted and the following subsections shall be inserted after subsection (5)—

"(6) Regulations under subsection (5) above may make provision with respect to any year or years of assessment; and the year (or any of the years) may be the one in which the regulations are made or any year falling before or after that year.

(7) But the regulations may not make provision with respect to any year of assessment which precedes the next but one preceding the year of assessment in which the regulations are made."

(4) Subsection (5) below applies in the case of any provision of the Tax Acts, the Taxes Management Act 1970, the Capital Gains Tax Act 1979, or any other enactment relating to capital gains tax, which imposes a time limit for making a claim or an election or an application.

(5) The Board may by regulations provide that where the claim or election or application falls to be made by an underwriting member of Lloyd's or his spouse (or both) the provision shall have effect as if it imposed such longer time limit as is specified in the regulations.

(6) Regulations under subsection (5) above—

(*a*) shall be made by statutory instrument subject to annulment in pursuance of a resolution of the House of Commons;
(*b*) may make different provision for different provisions or different purposes.

(7) Regulations under subsection (5) above may make provision with respect to any year or years of assessment; and the year (or any of the years) may be the one in which the regulations are made or any year falling before or after that year.

Securities

93. Deep discount securities: amendments

Schedule 10 to this Act (which amends Schedule 4 to the Taxes Act 1988) shall have effect.

94. Deep gain securities

Schedule 11 to this Act (which contains provisions about securities capable of yielding a deep gain) shall have effect.

95. Treasury securities issued at a discount

(1) Section 126 of the Taxes Act 1988 (tax not to be charged on certain securities in respect of discount under Case III of Schedule D) shall be amended as mentioned in subsections (2) and (3) below.

(2) In subsection (2) (the securities affected) for the words "except Treasury bills" there shall be substituted the words "except—

(*a*) Treasury bills,
(*b*) relevant deep discount securities, and
(*c*) deep gain securities."

(3) The following subsection shall be inserted after subsection (2)—

"(3) For the purposes of subsection (2) above—

(*a*) a relevant deep discount security is a security falling within paragraph 1(1)(*dd*) of Schedule 4 to this Act, and
(*b*) a deep gain security is a security which is a deep gain security for the purposes of Schedule 11 to the Finance Act 1989."

(4) The preceding provisions of this section shall apply—

(*a*) in the case of a deep discount security, where there is a disposal (within the meaning of Schedule 4 to the Taxes Act 1988) on or after 14th March 1989;
(*b*) in the case of a deep gain security, where there is a transfer within the meaning of Schedule 11 to this Act, or a redemption, on or after 14th March 1989.

(5) Subsection (7) below applies where—

(*a*) by virtue of paragraph 19(2) of Schedule 4 to the Taxes Act 1988, a security falls to be treated as a deep discount security as there mentioned, and
(*b*) after the time mentioned in paragraph 19(1)(*d*) of that Schedule there is a disposal (within the meaning of that Schedule) of the security.

(6) Subsection (7) below also applies where—

(*a*) by virtue of paragraph 19(2) of Schedule 11 to this Act, a security falls to be treated as a deep gain security as there mentioned, and
(*b*) after the time mentioned in paragraph 19(1)(*d*) of that Schedule there is a transfer (within the meaning of that Schedule) or a redemption of the security.

(7) In a case where this subsection applies, section 126 of the Taxes Act 1988 shall not apply in the case of the disposal, transfer or redemption (as the case may be).

96. Securities: miscellaneous

(1) In section 452(8) of the Taxes Act 1988 (special reserve funds) for the words from "In paragraph (*a*) above" to the end there shall be substituted—

"In paragraph (*a*) above "income" includes—

(*a*) annual profits or gains chargeable to tax by virtue of section 714(2) or 716(3),
(*b*) amounts treated as income chargeable to tax by virtue of paragraph 4 of Schedule 4, and
(*c*) amounts treated as income chargeable to tax by virtue of paragraph 4 of Schedule 11 to the Finance Act 1989."

(2) In section 687 of the Taxes Act 1988 (payments under discretionary trusts) the following shall be inserted after subsection (3)(*g*)—

"(*h*) the amount of any tax on an amount which is treated as income of the trustees by virtue of paragraph 4 of Schedule 4 and is charged to tax at a rate equal to the sum of the basic rate and the additional rate by virtue of paragraph 17 of that Schedule;
(*i*) the amount of any tax on an amount which is treated as income of the trustees by virtue of paragraph 4 of Schedule 11 to the Finance Act 1989 and is charged to tax at a rate equal to the sum of the basic rate and the additional rate by virtue of paragraph 10 of that Schedule;".

(3) The following subsections shall be inserted at the end of section 132A of the Capital Gains Tax Act 1979 (deep discount securities)—

"(5) Where by virtue of paragraph 18(3) of Schedule 4 to the Taxes Act 1988 trustees are deemed for the purposes of that Schedule to dispose of a security at a particular time—

(*a*) they shall be deemed to dispose of the security at that time for the purposes of this Act, and
(*b*) the disposal deemed by paragraph (*a*) above shall be deemed to be at the market value of the security.

(6) Where by virtue of paragraph 18(4) of Schedule 4 to the Taxes Act 1988 trustees are deemed for the purposes of that Schedule to acquire a security at a particular time—

(*a*) they shall be deemed to acquire the security at that time for the purposes of this Act, and
(*b*) the acquisition deemed by paragraph (*a*) above shall be deemed to be at the market value of the security."

(4) The new paragraphs (*b*) and (*c*) inserted by subsection (1) above, and subsection (2) above, shall apply—

(*a*) in the case of a deep discount security, where there is a disposal (within the meaning of Schedule 4 to the Taxes Act 1988) on or after 14th March 1989;
(*b*) in the case of a deep gain security, where there is a transfer within the meaning of Schedule 11 to this Act, or a redemption, on or after 14th March 1989.

Groups of companies

97. Set-off of ACT where companies remain in same group

(1) In section 240 of the Taxes Act 1988 (set-off of company's ACT against subsidiary's liability to corporation tax) at the end of subsection (5) (set-off not to be made against subsidiary's liability to corporation tax for any accounting period in which, or in any part of which, it was not a subsidiary of the surrendering company) there shall be added the words "unless throughout that period or part both companies were subsidiaries of a third company".

(2) This section shall have effect in relation to accounting periods ending on or after 14th March 1989.

98. Restriction on set-off of ACT

(1) After section 245 of the Taxes Act 1988 there shall be inserted—

"**245A. Restriction on application of section 240 in certain circumstances**

(1) This section applies if—

    (*a*) there is a change in the ownership of a company ("the relevant company");
    (*b*) by virtue of section 240 the relevant company is treated as having paid an amount of advance corporation tax in respect of a distribution made by it at any time before the change; and
    (*c*) within the period of six years beginning three years before the change, there is a major change in the nature or conduct of a trade or business of the company which is for the purposes of section 240 the surrendering company in relation to that amount.

(2) No advance corporation tax which the relevant company is treated by virtue of section 240 as having paid in respect of a distribution made by it in an accounting period beginning before the change of ownership shall be treated under section 239(4) as paid by it in respect of distributions made in an accounting period ending after the change of ownership; and this subsection shall apply to an accounting period in which the change of ownership occurs as if the part ending with the change of ownership, and the part after, were two separate accounting periods.

(3) Subsections (4) and (5) of section 245 shall apply also for the purposes of this section and as if the reference in subsection (4) of section 245 to the period of three years mentioned in subsection (1)(*a*) of that section were a reference to the period mentioned in subsection (1)(*c*) above.

(4) Sections 768(8) and (9) and 769 shall apply also for the purposes of this section and as if in subsection (3) of section 769 the reference to the benefit of losses were a reference to the benefit of advance corporation tax.

245B. Restriction on set-off where asset transferred after change in ownership of company

(1) Subsection (4) below applies if—

    (*a*) there is a change in the ownership of a company ("the relevant company");
    (*b*) any advance corporation tax paid by the relevant company in respect of distributions made by it in an accounting period beginning before the change is treated under section 239(4) as paid by it in respect of distributions made by it in an accounting period ending after the change;
    (*c*) after the change the relevant company acquires an asset from another company in such circumstances that section 273(1) of the Taxes Act 1970 applies to the acquisition; and
    (*d*) a chargeable gain accrues to the relevant company on the disposal of the asset within the period of three years beginning with the change of ownership.

(2) Subsection (1)(*b*) above shall apply to an accounting period in which the change of ownership occurs as if the part ending with the change of ownership, and the part after, were two separate accounting periods.

(3) For the purposes of subsection (1)(*d*) above an asset acquired by the relevant company as mentioned in subsection (1)(*c*) above shall be treated as the same as an asset owned at a later time by that company if the value of the second asset is derived in whole or in part from the first asset, and in particular where the second asset is a freehold, and the first asset was a leasehold and the lessee has acquired the reversion.

(4) In relation to the accounting period in which the chargeable gain accrues to the

relevant company ("the relevant period"), section 239 shall have effect as if the limit imposed by subsection (2) of that section on the amount of advance corporation tax to be set against the relevant company's liability to corporation tax were reduced by whichever is the lesser of—

    (*a*) the amount of advance corporation tax that would have been payable (apart from section 241) in respect of a distribution made at the end of the relevant period of an amount which, together with the advance corporation tax so payable in respect of it, is equal to the chargeable gain, and

    (*b*) the amount of surplus advance corporation tax in relation to the accounting period which by virtue of subsection (2) above is treated for the purposes of subsection (1)(*b*) above as ending with the change of ownership.

(5) Sections 768(8) and (9) and 769 shall apply also for the purposes of this section and as if in subsection (3) of section 769 the reference to the benefit of losses were a reference to the benefit of advance corporation tax."

(2) This section shall have effect where the change in the ownership of the relevant company occurs on or after 14th March 1989.

99. Dividends etc. paid by one member of a group to another

(1) Section 247 of the Taxes Act 1988 (dividends etc. paid by one member of a group to another) shall be amended in accordance with this section.

(2) In subsection (1) for paragraph (*b*) there shall be substituted—

"(*b*) a trading or holding company which does not fall within subsection (1A) below and which is owned by a consortium the members of which include the receiving company,".

(3) After subsection (1) there shall be inserted—

"(1A) A company falls within this subsection if—

    (*a*) it is a 75 per cent. subsidiary of any other company, or

    (*b*) arrangements of any kind (whether in writing or not) are in existence by virtue of which it could become such a subsidiary."

(4) After subsection (8) there shall be inserted—

"(8A) Notwithstanding that at any time a company ("the subsidiary company") is a 51 per cent. subsidiary of another company ("the parent company") it shall not be treated at that time as such a subsidiary for the purposes of this section unless, additionally, at that time—

    (*a*) the parent company would be beneficially entitled to more than 50 per cent. of any profits available for distribution to equity holders of the subsidiary company; and

    (*b*) the parent company would be beneficially entitled to more than 50 per cent. of any assets of the subsidiary company available for distribution to its equity holders on a winding-up."

(5) For subsection (9)(*c*) there shall be substituted—

"(*c*) a company is owned by a consortium if 75 per cent. or more of the ordinary share capital of the company is beneficially owned between them by companies resident in the United Kingdom of which none—

    (i) beneficially owns less than 5 per cent. of that capital,

    (ii) would be beneficially entitled to less than 5 per cent. of any profits available for distribution to equity holders of the company, or

    (iii) would be beneficially entitled to less than 5 per cent. of any assets of the company available for distribution to its equity holders on a winding-up,

and those companies are called the members of the consortium."

(6) After subsection (9) there shall be inserted—

"(9A) Schedule 18 shall apply for the purposes of subsections (8A) and (9)(*c*) above as it applies for the purposes of section 413(7)."

(7) This section shall have effect in relation to dividends and other sums paid on or after the day on which this Act is passed.

100. Change in ownership of company

(1) Section 769 of the Taxes Act 1988 (which contains rules for determining whether for the purposes of sections 245 and 768 of that Act there is a change in the ownership of a company) shall be amended in accordance with this section.

(2) For subsection (6) there shall be substituted—

"(6) If there is a change in the ownership of a company, including a change occurring by virtue of the application of this subsection but not a change which is to be disregarded under subsection (5) above, then—

(a) in a case falling within subsection (1)(a) above, the person mentioned in subsection (1)(a) shall be taken for the purposes of this section to acquire at the time of the change any relevant assets owned by the company;
(b) in a case falling within subsection (1)(b) above but not within subsection (1)(a) above, each of the persons mentioned in subsection (1)(b) shall be taken for the purposes of this section to acquire at the time of the change the appropriate proportion of any relevant assets owned by the company; and
(c) in any other case, each of the persons mentioned in paragraph (c) of subsection (1) above (other than any whose holding is disregarded under that paragraph) shall be taken for the purposes of this section to acquire at the time of the change the appropriate proportion of any relevant assets owned by the company.

(6A) In subsection (6) above—

"the appropriate proportion", in relation to one of two or more persons mentioned in subsection (1)(b) or (c) above, means a proportion corresponding to the proportion which the percentage of the ordinary share capital acquired by him bears to the percentage of that capital acquired by all those persons taken together; and
"relevant assets", in relation to a company, means—

(a) any ordinary share capital of another company, and
(b) any property or rights which under subsection (3) above may be taken into account instead of ordinary share capital of another company.

(6B) Notwithstanding that at any time a company ("the subsidiary company") is a 75 per cent. subsidiary of another company ("the parent company") it shall not be treated at that time as such a subsidiary for the purposes of this section unless, additionally, at that time—

(a) the parent company would be beneficially entitled to not less than 75 per cent. of any profits available for distribution to equity holders of the subsidiary company; and
(b) the parent company would be beneficially entitled to not less than 75 per cent. of any assets of the subsidiary company available for distribution to its equity holders on a winding-up.

(6C) Schedule 18 shall apply for the purposes of subsection (6B) above as it applies for the purposes of section 413(7)."

(3) Subsection (7)(b) and (c) shall cease to have effect.

(4) This section shall have effect where the change of ownership of a company would be treated as occurring on or after 14th March 1989.

101. Treatment of convertible shares or securities for purposes relating to group relief etc.

(1) Paragraph 1 of Schedule 18 to the Taxes Act 1988 (which contains definitions relating to group relief) shall be amended in accordance with this section.

(2) For sub-paragraph (3)(b) there shall be substituted—

"(b) do not carry any right either to conversion into shares or securities of any other description except—

(i) shares to which sub-paragraph (5A) below applies,
(ii) securities to which sub-paragraph (5B) below applies, or
(iii) shares or securities in the company's quoted parent company,

or to the acquisition of any additional shares or securities;".

(3) For sub-paragraph (5)(a) there shall be substituted—

"(a) which does not carry any right either to conversion into shares or securities of any other description except—

(i) shares to which sub-paragraph (5A) below applies,
(ii) securities to which sub-paragraph (5B) below applies, or
(iii) shares or securities in the company's quoted parent company,

or to the acquisition of any additional shares or securities;".

(4) After sub-paragraph (5) there shall be inserted—

"(5A) This sub-paragraph applies to any shares which—

(*a*) satisfy the requirements of sub-paragraph (3)(*a*), (*c*) and (*d*) above, and
(*b*) do not carry any rights either to conversion into shares or securities of any other description, except shares or securities in the company's quoted parent company, or to the acquisition of any additional shares or securities.

(5B) This sub-paragraph applies to any securities representing a loan of or including new consideration and—

(*a*) which satisfies the requirements of sub-paragraph (5)(*b*) and (*c*) above, and
(*b*) which does not carry any such rights as are mentioned in sub-paragraph (5A)(*b*) above.

(5C) For the purposes of sub-paragraphs (3) and (5) to (5B) above a company ("the parent company") is another company's "quoted parent company" if and only if—

(*a*) the other company is a 75 per cent. subsidiary of the parent company,
(*b*) the parent company is not a 75 per cent. subsidiary of any company, and
(*c*) the parent company's ordinary shares (or, if its ordinary share capital is divided into two or more classes, its ordinary shares of each class) are quoted on a recognised stock exchange or dealt in on the Unlisted Securities Market;

and in this sub-paragraph "ordinary shares" means shares forming part of ordinary share capital.

(5D) In the application of sub-paragraphs (3) and (5) to (5B) above in determining for the purposes of sub-paragraph (5C)(*a*) above who are the equity holders of the other company (and, accordingly, whether section 413(7) prevents the other company from being treated as a 75 per cent. subsidiary of the parent company for the purposes of sub-paragraph (5C)(*a*)), it shall be assumed that the parent company is for the purposes of sub-paragraphs (3) and (5) to (5B) above the other company's quoted parent company."

(5) In sub-paragraph (6) for the words "to (5)" there shall be substituted the words "to (5D)".

(6) This section, so far as relating to Schedule 18 of the Taxes Act 1988 in its application (by virtue of section 138 below) for the purposes of subsections (1D) and (1E) of section 272 of the Taxes Act 1970, shall be deemed to have come into force on 14th March 1989.

102. Surrender of company tax refund etc. within group

(1) Subsection (2) below applies where—

(*a*) there falls to be made to a company ("the surrendering company") which is a member of a group throughout the appropriate period a tax refund relating to an accounting period of the company ("the relevant accounting period"), and
(*b*) another company ("the recipient company") which is a member of the same group throughout the appropriate period also has the relevant accounting period as an accounting period.

(2) Where this subsection applies the two companies may, at any time before the refund is made to the surrendering company, jointly give notice to the inspector in such form as the Board may require that subsection (4) below is to have effect in relation to the refund or to any part of the refund specified in the notice.

(3) In subsection (1) above—

"appropriate period" means the period beginning with the relevant accounting period and ending on the day on which the notice under subsection (2) above is given, and
"tax refund relating to an accounting period" means, in relation to a company—

(*a*) a repayment of corporation tax paid by the company for the period,
(*b*) a repayment of income tax in respect of a payment received by the company in the period, or
(*c*) a payment of the whole or part of the tax credit comprised in any franked investment income received by the company in the period.

(4) Subject to subsection (6) below, where this subsection has effect in relation to any refund or part of a refund—

(*a*) the recipient company shall be treated for all purposes of the Tax Acts as having paid on the relevant date an amount of corporation tax for the relevant accounting period equal to the amount of the refund or part, and
(*b*) there shall be treated for all those purposes as having been made to the surrendering company on the relevant date a repayment of corporation tax or income tax or a payment of tax credit (as the case may be) equal to the amount of the refund or part;

and where the refund is a repayment of corporation tax, any interest relating to it which has been paid by the surrendering company shall be treated as having been paid by the recipient company.

(5) In subsection (4) above "relevant date", in relation to a refund, means—

(*a*) in so far as it consists of a repayment of corporation tax paid by the surrendering company after the date on which it became due and payable under section 10 of the Taxes Act 1988, the day on which it was paid by that company, and
(*b*) otherwise, the date on which corporation tax for the relevant accounting period became due and payable.

(6) For the purpose of ascertaining the amount of any penalty to which the recipient company is liable under section 94(6) of the Taxes Management Act 1970, the corporation tax which the company is treated as having paid by subsection (4)(*a*) above shall be treated as paid on the day on which the notice under subsection (2) above is given (and not on the relevant date).

(7) A payment for a transferred tax refund—

(*a*) shall not be taken into account in computing profits or losses of either company for corporation tax purposes, and
(*b*) shall not for any of the purposes of the Corporation Tax Acts be regarded as a distribution or a charge on income;

and in this subsection "a payment for a transferred tax refund" means a payment made by the receiving company to the surrendering company in pursuance of an agreement between them as respects the giving of a notice under this section, being a payment not exceeding the amount of the refund in question.

(8) For the purposes of this section two companies are members of the same group if and only if they would be for the purposes of Chapter IV of Part X of the Taxes Act 1988.

(9) This section shall not apply unless the relevant accounting period ends after such day, not being earlier than 31st March 1992, as the Treasury may by order made by statutory instrument appoint.

Close companies

103. Repeal of apportionment provisions

(1) Except as provided by subsection (2) below, Chapter III of Part XI of the Taxes Act 1988 (apportionment of undistributed income etc. of close companies) shall not have effect in relation to accounting periods beginning after 31st March 1989.

(2) Section 427(4) of the Taxes Act 1988 (which gives relief to an individual where income apportioned to him in an earlier accounting period of a close company is included in a distribution received by him in a later accounting period), and section 427(5) of, and Part I of Schedule 19 to, that Act so far as they relate to section 427(4), shall continue to have effect in any case where the subsequent distribution referred to in section 427(4) is made before 1st April 1992.

104. Meaning of "close company"

(1) In section 414 of the Taxes Act 1988 for subsection (2) (further case in which a company is a close company for the purposes of the Tax Acts) there shall be substituted—

"(2) Subject to section 415 and subsection (5) below, a company resident in the United Kingdom (but not falling within subsection (1)(*b*) above) is also a close company if five or fewer participators, or participators who are directors, together possess or are entitled to acquire—

(*a*) such rights as would, in the event of the winding-up of the company ("the relevant company") on the basis set out in subsection (2A) below, entitle them to receive the greater part of the assets of the relevant company which would then be available for distribution among the participators, or

(b) such rights as would in that event so entitle them if any rights which any of them or any other person has as a loan creditor (in relation to the relevant company or any other company) were disregarded.

(2A) In the notional winding-up of the relevant company, the part of the assets available for distribution among the participators which any person is entitled to receive is the aggregate of—

(a) any part of those assets which he would be entitled to receive in the event of the winding-up of the company, and

(b) any part of those assets which he would be entitled to receive if—

(i) any other company which is a participator in the relevant company and is entitled to receive any assets in the notional winding-up were also wound up on the basis set out in this subsection, and

(ii) the part of the assets of the relevant company to which the other company is entitled were distributed among the participators in the other company in proportion to their respective entitlement to the assets of the other company available for distribution among the participators.

(2B) In the application of subsection (2A) above to the notional winding-up of the other company and to any further notional winding-up required by paragraph (b) of that subsection (or by any further application of that paragraph), references to "the relevant company" shall have effect as references to the company concerned.

(2C) In ascertaining under subsection (2) above whether five or fewer participators, or participators who are directors, together possess or are entitled to acquire rights such as are mentioned in paragraph (a) or (b) of that subsection—

(a) a person shall be treated as a participator in or director of the relevant company if he is a participator in or director of any other company which would be entitled to receive assets in the notional winding-up of the relevant company on the basis set out in subsection (2A) above, and

(b) except in the application of subsection (2A) above, no account shall be taken of a participator which is a company unless the company possesses or is entitled to acquire the rights in a fiduciary or representative capacity.

(2D) Subsections (4) to (6) of section 416 apply for the purposes of subsections (2) and (2A) above as they apply for the purposes of subsection (2) of that section."

(2) Subsection (3) of that section shall cease to have effect.

(3) In subsection (5)(b) of that section for the words from "paragraph (c)" to "that paragraph" there shall be substituted the words "paragraph (a) of subsection (2) above or paragraph (c) of section 416(2) and it would not be a close company if the references in those paragraphs".

(4) This section shall be deemed to have come into force on 1st April 1989.

105. Small companies' rate not available to certain close companies

(1) In section 13 of the Taxes Act 1988 (small companies' relief) in subsection (1) for the words "a company resident in the United Kingdom" there shall be substituted the words "a company which—

(a) is resident in the United Kingdom, and

(b) is not a close investment-holding company (as defined in section 13A) at the end of that period,".

(2) After that section there shall be inserted the following section—

"13A. Close investment-holding companies

(1) A close company is for the purposes of section 13(1) a "close investment-holding company" unless it complies with subsection (2) below.

(2) A company ("the relevant company") complies with this subsection in any accounting period if throughout that period it exists wholly or mainly for any one or more of the following purposes—

(a) the purpose of carrying on a trade or trades on a commercial basis,

(b) the purpose of making investments in land or estates or interests in land in cases where the land is, or is intended to be, let to persons other than—

(i) any person connected with the relevant company, or
(ii) any person who is the wife or husband of an individual connected with the relevant company, or is a relative, or the wife or husband of a relative, of such an individual or of the husband or wife of such an individual,

(c) the purpose of holding shares in and securities of, or making loans to, one or more companies each of which is a qualifying company or a company which—

(i) is under the control of the relevant company or of a company which has control of the relevant company, and
(ii) itself exists wholly or mainly for the purpose of holding shares in or securities of, or making loans to, one or more qualifying companies,

(d) the purpose of co-ordinating the administration of two or more qualifying companies,
(e) the purpose of a trade or trades carried on on a commercial basis by one or more qualifying companies or by a company which has control of the relevant company, and
(f) the purpose of the making, by one or more qualifying companies or by a company which has control of the relevant company, of investments as mentioned in paragraph (b) above.

(3) For the purposes of subsection (2) above, a company is a "qualifying company", in relation to the relevant company, if it—

(a) is under the control of the relevant company or of a company which has control of the relevant company, and
(b) exists wholly or mainly for either or both of the purposes mentioned in subsection (2)(a) or (b) above.

(4) Where a company is wound up, it shall not be treated as failing to comply with subsection (2) above in the accounting period that (by virtue of subsection (7) of section 12) begins with the time which is for the purposes of that subsection the commencement of the winding up, if it complied with subsection (2) above in the accounting period that ends with that time.

(5) In this section—

"control" shall be construed in accordance with section 416, and
"relative" has the meaning given by section 839(8).

(6) Section 839 shall apply for the purposes of this section."

(3) This section shall have effect in relation to accounting periods beginning after 31st March 1989.

106. Restriction on payment of tax credits

(1) In section 231 of the Taxes Act 1988 (tax credits for certain recipients of qualifying distributions) in subsection (3) after the words "made and" there shall be inserted the words "subject to subsections (3A) to (3D) below" and after that subsection there shall be inserted—

"(3A) Subject to subsection (3B) below, where it appears to the inspector that, in any accounting period of a company at the end of which it is a close investment-holding company—

(a) arrangements relating to the distribution of the profits of the company exist or have existed the main purpose of which or one of the main purposes of which is to enable payments, or payments of a greater amount, to be made to any one or more individuals under subsection (3) above in respect of such an excess as is mentioned in that subsection, and
(b) by virtue of those arrangements, any eligible person—

(i) receives a qualifying distribution consisting of a payment made by the company on the redemption, repayment or purchase of its own shares, or
(ii) receives any other qualifying distribution in respect of shares in or securities of the company, where the amount or value of the distribution is greater than might in all the circumstances have been expected but for the arrangements,

the entitlement of the eligible person to have paid to him under subsection (3) above all or part of a tax credit in respect of any distribution made by the company in the period shall be restricted to such extent as appears to the inspector to be just and reasonable.

(3B) Subsection (3A) above does not apply in relation to a tax credit in respect of a dividend paid by a company in any accounting period in respect of its ordinary share capital if—

(a) throughout the period, the company's ordinary share capital consisted of only one class of shares, and
(b) no person waived his entitlement to any dividend which would have become payable by the company in the period or failed to receive any dividend which had become due and payable to him by the company in the period.

(3C) In subsection (3A) above—

"arrangements" means arrangements of any kind whether in writing or not,
"close investment-holding company" has the meaning given by section 13A, and
"eligible person", in relation to a qualifying distribution, means an individual resident in the United Kingdom who would (apart from subsection (3A) above) be entitled to have paid to him under subsection (3) above all or part of a tax credit in respect of the distribution.

(3D) In determining under subsection (3) above whether a person is entitled to have any excess of tax credit paid to him in a case where subsection (3A) above applies, tax credits shall be set against income tax in the order that results in the greatest payment in respect of the excess."

(2) This section shall have effect in relation to distributions made by companies in accounting periods beginning after 31st March 1989.

107. Close companies: consequential amendments

Schedule 12 to this Act (in which Part I contains administrative provisions relating to close companies and Part II makes amendments connected with section 103 above) shall have effect.

Settlements etc.

108. Outright gifts etc. between husband and wife

(1) Section 685 of the Taxes Act 1988 (provisions supplementary to sections charging settlor to tax in excess of a basic rate on certain settlement income) shall be amended as follows.

(2) In subsection (3), after the word "above" there shall be inserted the words "and subsection (4B) below".

(3) At the end of subsection (4) there shall be added the words ", but subject to subsections (4A) and (4C) below".

(4) After subsection (4) there shall be inserted—

"(4A) References in section 683 to a settlement do not include references to an outright gift by one spouse to the other of property from which income arises unless—

(a) the gift does not carry a right to the whole of that income, or
(b) the property given is wholly or substantially a right to income.

(4B) For the purposes of subsection (4A) above a gift is not an outright gift if it is subject to conditions, or if the property given or any derived property is or will or may become, in any circumstances whatsoever, payable to or applicable for the benefit of the donor.

(4C) References in section 683 to a settlement do not include references to the irrevocable allocation of pension rights by one spouse to the other in accordance with the terms of a relevant statutory scheme (within the meaning of Chapter I of Part XIV)."

(5) This section shall have effect for the year 1990–91 and subsequent years of assessment.

109. Settlements where settlor retains interest in settled property

(1) After section 674 of the Taxes Act 1988 there shall be inserted—

"674A. Other settlements where settlor retains interest in settled property

(1) Where, during the life of the settlor, income arising under a settlement is, under the settlement and in the events that occur, payable to or applicable for the benefit of any

person other than the settlor, then, unless, under the settlement and in those events, the income—

(*a*) consists of annual payments made under a partnership agreement to or for the benefit of a former member, or the widow or dependants of a deceased former member, of the partnership, being payments made under a liability incurred for full consideration; or

(*b*) is of a kind excluded from subsection (1) of section 683 by subsection (6) or (9) of that section; or

(*c*) is income arising under a settlement made by one party to a marriage by way of provision for the other after the dissolution or annulment of the marriage, or while they are separated under an order of a court or under a separation agreement or in such circumstances that the separation is likely to be permanent, being income payable to or applicable for the benefit of that other party; or

(*d*) is income from property of which the settlor has divested himself absolutely by the settlement; or

(*e*) consists of covenanted payments to charity (as defined by section 660(3)); or

(*f*) is income which, by virtue of any provision of the Income Tax Acts other than this section, is to be treated for all the purposes of those Acts as income of the settlor;

the income shall be treated for all the purposes of the Income Tax Acts as the income of the settlor and not as the income of any other person.

(2) Subsections (6) to (10) of section 683 shall apply in relation to subsection (1) above as they apply in relation to subsection (1) of that section.

(3) Subsections (1), (2), (3) and (for the year 1990–91 and subsequent years of assessment) (4A) to (4C) of section 685 shall have effect for the purposes of this section as they have effect for the purposes of section 683, but with the omission from subsections (1) and (2) of the words "in the case of a settlement made after 6th April 1965".

(4) For the year 1990–91 and subsequent years of assessment subsection (1)(*a*) above shall have effect with the insertion after the word "widow" of the word "widower".

(5) This section applies in relation to income—

(*a*) which arises on or after 14th March 1989 under a settlement made on or after that day, or

(*b*) which arises on or after 6th April 1990 under a settlement made before 14th March 1989, so far as it is payable to or applicable for the benefit of the settlor's husband or wife,

except income consisting of annual payments made under an obligation which is an existing obligation for the purposes of section 36(3) of the Finance Act 1988."

(2) In section 125(3) of the Taxes Act 1988, in paragraph (*a*), for the words "section 683(1)(*a*) or (*c*) or (6)" there shall be substituted the words "subsection (1)(*a*) or (*c*) of section 674A or 683 or subsection (6) of section 683 (including that subsection as it applies in relation to section 674A(1))".

(3) In sections 675(1), (4) and (5) and 676(1)(*a*) of that Act, for the words "or 674" there shall be substituted the words "674 or 674A".

(4) In section 677(2)(*c*) of that Act, after "674" there shall be inserted "674A".

110. Residence of trustees

(1) Where the trustees of a settlement include at least one who is not resident in the United Kingdom as well as at least one who is, then for all the purposes of the Income Tax Acts—

(*a*) if the condition in subsection (2) below is satisfied, the trustee or trustees not resident in the United Kingdom shall be treated as resident there, and

(*b*) otherwise, the trustee or trustees resident in the United Kingdom shall be treated as not resident there (but as resident outside the United Kingdom).

(2) The condition referred to in subsection (1) above is that the settlor or, where there is more than one, any of them is at any relevant time—

(*a*) resident in the United Kingdom,
(*b*) ordinarily resident there, or
(*c*) domiciled there.

(3) For the purposes of subsection (2) above the following are relevant times in relation to a settlor—

(a) in the case of a settlement arising under a testamentary disposition of the settlor or on his intestacy, the time of his death, and

(b) in the case of any other settlement, the time or, where there is more than one, each of the times when he has provided funds directly or indirectly for the purposes of the settlement.

(4) For the purposes of this section "settlor", in relation to a settlement, includes any person who has provided or undertaken to provide funds directly or indirectly for the purposes of the settlement.

(5) In section 824(9) of the Taxes Act 1988 (repayment supplements), for the words "or a United Kingdom trust (as defined in section 231)," there shall be substituted the words "the trustees of a settlement".

(6) Subject to subsections (7) to (9) below, this section shall apply for the year 1989–90 and subsequent years of assessment.

(7) For the purpose of determining the residence of trustees at any time during the year 1989–90, the condition in subsection (2) above shall be regarded as not having been satisfied if none of the trustees of the settlement is resident in the United Kingdom at any time during the period beginning with 1st October 1989 and ending with 5th April 1990.

(8) This section shall not apply for any of the purposes of section 739 of the Taxes Act 1988 in relation to income payable before 15th June 1989, or for the purposes of subsection (3) of that section in relation to income payable on or after that date if—

(a) the capital sum there referred to is received, or the right to receive it is acquired, before that date, and

(b) that sum is wholly repaid, or the right to it waived, before 1st October 1989.

(9) This section shall not apply for any of the purposes of section 740 of the Taxes Act 1988 in relation to benefits received before 15th June 1989; and, in relation to benefits received on or after that date, "relevant income" for those purposes shall include income arising to trustees before 6th April 1989 notwithstanding that one or more of them was not resident outside the United Kingdom, unless they have been charged to tax in respect of it.

111. Residence of personal representatives

(1) Where the personal representatives of a deceased person include at least one who is not resident in the United Kingdom as well as at least one who is, then for all the purposes of the Income Tax Acts—

(a) if the condition in subsection (2) below is satisfied, the personal representative or representatives not resident in the United Kingdom shall be treated as resident there, and

(b) otherwise, the personal representative or representatives resident in the United Kingdom shall be treated as not resident there (but as resident outside the United Kingdom).

(2) The condition referred to in subsection (1) above is that the deceased person is at his death—

(a) resident in the United Kingdom,
(b) ordinarily resident there, or
(c) domiciled there.

(3) In this section "personal representatives" means—

(a) in relation to England and Wales, the deceased person's personal representatives as defined by section 55 of the Administration of Estates Act 1925;
(b) in relation to Scotland, his executor or the judicial factor on his estate;
(c) in relation to Northern Ireland, his personal representatives as defined by section 45(1) of the Administration of Estates Act (Northern Ireland) 1955; and
(d) in relation to another country or territory, the persons having in relation to him under its law any functions corresponding to the functions for administration purposes of personal representatives under the law of England and Wales.

(4) In section 824(9) of the Taxes Act 1988 (repayment supplements), for the words from "or, in" to "section 701)" there shall be substituted the words "or personal representatives (within the meaning of section 111 of the Finance Act 1989)".

(5) Subject to subsections (6) to (8) below, this section shall apply for the year 1989–90 and subsequent years of assessment.

(6) For the purpose of determining the residence of personal representatives at any time

during the year 1989–90, the condition in subsection (2) above shall be regarded as not having been satisfied if none of the personal representatives is resident in the United Kingdom at any time during the period beginning with 1st October 1989 and ending with 5th April 1990.

(7) This section shall not apply for any of the purposes of section 739 of the Taxes Act 1988 in relation to income payable before 15th June 1989, or for the purposes of subsection (3) of that section in relation to income payable on or after that date if—

(a) the capital sum there referred to is received, or the right to receive it is acquired, before that date, and
(b) that sum is wholly repaid, or the right to it waived, before 1st October 1989.

(8) This section shall not apply for any of the purposes of section 740 of the Taxes Act 1988 in relation to benefits received before 15th June 1989 and, in relation to benefits received on or after that date, "relevant income" for those purposes shall include income arising to personal representatives before 6th April 1989 notwithstanding that one or more of them was not resident outside the United Kingdom, unless they have been charged to tax in respect of it.

Miscellaneous

112. Security: trades etc.

(1) This section applies in computing, for the purposes of Case I or Case II of Schedule D, the profits or gains of a trade, profession or vocation carried on by an individual or by a partnership of individuals.

(2) In a case where this section applies, nothing in section 74(a) or (b) of the Taxes Act 1988 (deductions limited by reference to purposes of trade etc.) shall prevent the deduction of a sum in respect of expenditure incurred in connection with the provision for or use by the individual, or any of the individuals, of a security asset or security service.

(3) Subsection (2) above shall not apply unless the asset or service is provided or used to meet a threat which—

(a) is a special threat to the individual's personal physicial security, and
(b) arises wholly or mainly by virtue of the particular trade, profession or vocation concerned.

(4) Subsection (2) above shall not apply unless the person incurring the expenditure has as his sole object in doing so the meeting of that threat.

(5) Subsection (2) above shall not apply in the case of a service unless the benefit resulting to the individual consists wholly or mainly of an improvement of his personal physical security.

(6) Subsection (2) above shall not apply in the case of an asset unless the person incurring the expenditure intends the asset to be used solely to improve personal physical security.

(7) But in a case where—

(a) apart from subsection (6) above, subsection (2) above would apply in the case of an asset, and
(b) the person incurring the expenditure intends the asset to be used partly to improve personal physical security,

subsection (2) shall nevertheless apply, but only as regards the appropriate proportion of the expenditure there mentioned.

(8) For the purposes of subsection (7) above the appropriate proportion of the expenditure mentioned in subsection (2) above is such proportion of that expenditure as is attributable to the intention of the person incurring it that the asset be used to improve personal physical security.

113. Security: trades etc. (supplementary)

(1) For the purposes of section 112 above—

(a) a security asset is an asset which improves personal security,
(b) a security service is a service which improves personal security,
(c) references to an asset do not include references to a car, a ship or an aircraft,
(d) references to an asset or service do not include references to a dwelling or grounds appurtenant to a dwelling, and

(*e*) references to an asset include references to equipment and a structure (such as a wall).

(2) If the person incurring the expenditure intends the asset to be used solely to improve personal physical security, but there is another use for the asset which is incidental to improving personal physical security, that other use shall be ignored in construing section 112(6) above.

(3) The fact that an asset or service improves the personal physical security of any member of the family or household of the individual concerned, as well as that of the individual, shall not prevent section 112(2) above from applying.

(4) For the purposes of section 112 above in its application to an asset, it is immaterial whether or not the asset becomes affixed to land (whether constituting a dwelling or otherwise).

(5) For the purposes of section 112 above in its application to an asset, it is immaterial whether or not the individual concerned is or becomes entitled to the property in the asset or (in the case of a fixture) an estate or interest in the land concerned.

(6) Section 112 above applies where expenditure is incurred on or after 6th April 1989.

114. Relief for pre-trading expenditure

(1) In section 401(1) of the Taxes Act 1988 (which gives relief for expenditure incurred by a person within three years before he begins to carry on a trade, profession or vocation), for the word "three" there shall be substituted the word "five".

(2) This section shall have effect where the time when the person begins to carry on the trade, profession or vocation falls after the end of March 1989.

115. Double taxation: tax credits

(1) Where any arrangements having effect by virtue of section 788 of the Taxes Act 1988 provide—

(*a*) for persons who are resident outside the United Kingdom and who receive distributions from companies resident in the United Kingdom to be entitled to tax credits, and
(*b*) for the amount paid to such a person by way of tax credit to be determined by reference to the amount to which an individual resident in the United Kingdom would have been entitled, subject to a deduction calculated by reference to the aggregate of the amount or value of the distribution and the amount of the tax credit paid,

the arrangements shall be construed as providing for that deduction to be calculated by reference to the gross amount or value of the distribution and tax credit, without any allowance for the deduction itself.

(2) This section shall have effect in relation to payments made before the passing of this Act as well as those made after that time, except that it shall not affect—

(*a*) the judgment of any court given before 25th October 1988, or
(*b*) the law to be applied in proceedings on appeal to the Court of Appeal or the House of Lords where the judgment of the High Court or the Court of Session which is in issue was given before that date.

116. Interest payments to Netherlands Antilles subsidiaries

(1) A payment to which this section applies shall be treated for the purposes of—

(*a*) section 338 of the Taxes Act 1988 (payment of interest within section 124 of that Act to be a charge on income), and
(*b*) section 349 of that Act (such a payment to be made gross),

as if it were a payment of interest within section 124 of that Act (quoted Eurobonds).

(2) This section applies to a payment of interest if—

(*a*) it is made on or after 1st April 1989 by a relevant United Kingdom company to a relevant Netherlands Antilles subsidiary, and
(*b*) not later than 90 days after the payment is received by the subsidiary, it is applied by the subsidiary in paying interest on quoted Eurobonds issued by it before 26th July 1984 or in meeting expenses incurred in connection with the issue of quoted Eurobonds so issued.

(3) In subsection (2) above—

(*a*) "relevant Netherlands Antilles subsidiary" means a company which—

(i) at the time when the quoted Eurobonds were issued was resident in the Netherlands Antilles (including Aruba) and was a 90 per cent. subsidiary of a company resident in the United Kingdom, and
(ii) at the time when the payment is made is resident in the Netherlands Antilles (but not Aruba) and is a 90 per cent. subsidiary of the relevant United Kingdom company; and

(*b*) "relevant United Kingdom company" means a company which is resident in the United Kingdom and which is not a 51 per cent. subsidiary of a company not resident in the United Kingdom.

(4) For the purpose of determining whether a company is a relevant Netherlands Antilles subsidiary, its residence (whether before 1st April 1989 or at any later time) shall be ascertained in accordance with the terms of the arrangements made with the Government of the Kingdom of the Netherlands on behalf of the Government of the Netherlands Antilles which had effect by virtue of section 788 of the Taxes Act 1988 immediately before 1st April 1989.

(5) In this section "quoted Eurobond" has the same meaning as in section 124 of the Taxes Act 1988.

CHAPTER II
CAPITAL ALLOWANCES

117. Security

(1) This section applies where—

(a) an individual, or a partnership of individuals, carries on a trade, profession or vocation,
(b) expenditure is incurred by the individual or partnership in connection with the provision for or use by the individual, or any of the individuals, of a security asset,
(c) no sum in respect of the expenditure could be deducted in computing the profits or gains of the trade, profession or vocation for the purposes of Case I or Case II of Schedule D, and
(d) apart from this section, paragraph (a) or paragraph (b) (or both) of section 44(1) of the Finance Act 1971 (capital allowances) would not apply.

(2) In a case where this section applies, Chapter I of Part III of the Finance Act 1971 shall apply as if—

(a) the expenditure were capital expenditure incurred on the provision of machinery or plant wholly and exclusively for the purposes of the trade, profession or vocation concerned,
(b) in consequence of the expenditure being incurred, the machinery or plant belonged to the individual or partnership carrying on the trade, profession or vocation, and
(c) the disposal value of the machinery or plant were nil.

(3) Subsection (2) above shall not apply unless the asset is provided or used to meet a threat which—

(a) is a special threat to the individual's personal physical security, and
(b) arises wholly or mainly by virtue of the particular trade, profession or vocation concerned.

(4) Subsection (2) above shall not apply unless the person incurring the expenditure has as his sole object in doing so the meeting of that threat.

(5) Subsection (2) above shall not apply unless the person incurring the expenditure intends the asset to be used solely to improve personal physical security.

(6) But in a case where—

(a) apart from subsection (5) above, subsection (2) above would apply, and
(b) the person incurring the expenditure intends the asset to be used partly to improve personal physical security,

subsection (2) shall nevertheless apply, but only so as to treat the appropriate proportion of the expenditure there mentioned as capital expenditure incurred as there mentioned.

(7) For the purposes of subsection (6) above the appropriate proportion of the expenditure mentioned in subsection (2) above is such proportion of that expenditure as is attributable to the intention of the person incurring it that the asset be used to improve personal physical security.

118. Security: supplementary

(1) For the purposes of section 117 above—

(a) a security asset is an asset which improves personal security,
(b) references to an asset do not include references to a car, a ship or an aircraft,
(c) references to an asset do not include references to a dwelling or grounds appurtenant to a dwelling, and
(d) references to an asset include references to equipment and a structure (such as a wall).

(2) If the person incurring the expenditure intends the asset to be used solely to improve personal physical security, but there is another use for the asset which is incidental to improving personal physical security, that other use shall be ignored in construing section 117(5) above.

(3) The fact that an asset improves the personal physical security of any member of the

family or household of the individual concerned, as well as that of the individual, shall not prevent section 117(2) above from applying.

(4) For the purposes of section 117 above, it is immaterial whether or not the asset becomes affixed to land (whether constituting a dwelling or otherwise).

(5) Section 117 above applies where expenditure is incurred on or after 6th April 1989.

119. Expenditure on stands at sports grounds

(1) If a person carrying on a trade incurs expenditure, in respect of a regulated stand at a sports ground used by him for the purposes of his trade, in taking—

(a) steps necessary for compliance with the terms and conditions of a safety certificate issued for the stand, or
(b) steps specified in a letter or other document sent or given to him by or on behalf of the local authority for the area in which the ground is situated as steps the taking of which either would be taken into account by them in deciding what terms and conditions to include in a safety certificate to be issued for the stand or would lead to the amendment or replacement of a safety certificate issued or to be issued for it,

then, if an allowance or deduction in respect of the expenditure could not, apart from this section, be made in taxing the trade or computing the profits or gains arising from it, Chapter I of Part III of the Finance Act 1971 shall apply as if the expenditure were capital expenditure incurred on the provision of machinery or plant for the purposes of the trade, and as if the machinery or plant had, in consequence of his incurring the expenditure, belonged to him, and as if the disposal value of the machinery or plant were nil.

(2) In this section "local authority", "regulated stand", "safety certificate" and "sports ground" have the same meanings as in Part III of the Fire Safety and Safety of Places of Sport Act 1987.

(3) This section shall be construed as if contained in Chapter I of Part III of the Finance Act 1971.

(4) This section shall be deemed to have come into force on 1st January 1989.

120. Forestry land: abolition of agricultural buildings allowances

(1) This section applies to any allowance under—

(a) section 68 of the Capital Allowances Act 1968 (agricultural buildings allowances in respect of expenditure incurred before 1st April 1986); or
(b) Schedule 15 to the Finance Act 1986 (agricultural buildings allowances in respect of expenditure incurred on or after that date),

which would not fall to be made if that section or Schedule had been enacted without any reference to forestry land or the purposes of forestry; and any reference in this section to an allowance is a reference to an allowance to which this section applies.

(2) Subject to subsection (4) below, no allowance shall be made for a chargeable period beginning on or after 20th June 1989.

(3) Subject to subsection (4) below, any allowance which falls to be made—

(a) for the year of assessment 1989–90; or
(b) for an accounting period of a company beginning before and ending on or after 20th June 1989,

shall be apportioned (on a time basis according to their respective lengths) between the part of that year or period beginning on that date and the other part; and so much of any such allowance as is apportioned to the part beginning on that date shall not be made.

(4) Subsections (2) and (3) above shall not have effect in relation to an allowance which falls to be made for a chargeable period which begins before 6th April 1993 and is a period in relation to which an election under paragraph 4 of Schedule 6 to the Finance Act 1988 (commercial woodlands: Schedule D election for transitional period) has effect in respect of the relevant land.

(5) Any such allowance as is mentioned in subsection (4) above which, for an accounting period of a company ending on or after 6th April 1993, falls to be made otherwise than under paragraph 11(1) of Schedule 15 to the Finance Act 1986 shall be apportioned (on a time basis according to their respective lengths) between the part of that period beginning

on that date and the other part; and so much of any such allowance as is apportioned to the part beginning on that date shall not be made.

(6) In subsection (4) above "the relevant land", in relation to an allowance falling to be made in respect of any expenditure, means the land for the purposes of forestry on which that expenditure was incurred.

121. Miscellaneous amendments

(1) Schedule 13 to this Act (which makes miscellaneous amendments of the enactments relating to capital allowances) shall have effect.

(2) That Schedule shall be construed as one with Part I of the Capital Allowances Act 1968.

CHAPTER III
CAPITAL GAINS

Exemptions

122. Annual exempt amount for 1989–90

For the year 1989–90 section 5 of the Capital Gains Tax Act 1979 (annual exempt amount) shall have effect as if the amount specified in subsection (1A) were £5,000; and accordingly subsection (1B) of that section (indexation) shall not apply for that year.

123. Increase of chattel exemption

(1) In the following enactments, namely—

(*a*) section 128 of the Capital Gains Tax Act 1979 (chattel exemption by reference to consideration of £3,000),
(*b*) section 12(2)(*b*) of the Taxes Management Act 1970 (information about assets acquired), and
(*c*) section 25(7) of that Act (information about assets disposed of),

for "£3,000", in each place where it occurs, there shall be substituted "£6,000".

(2) This section applies to disposals on or after 6th April 1989 and accordingly, in relation to subsection (1)(*b*) above, to assets acquired on or after that date.

Gifts

124. Relief for gifts

(1) Section 79 of the Finance Act 1980 (which gives general relief for gifts and other disposals not at arm's length) shall cease to have effect.

(2) Schedule 14 to this Act (which extends relief for gifts of business assets, provides relief for gifts on which inheritance tax is chargeable, gifts for political parties, gifts of property of historic interest etc. or works of art and gifts to certain maintenance funds etc., and makes provision for payment of tax by instalments in the case of gifts where relief is not available) shall have effect.

(3) This section shall have effect in relation to disposals on or after 14th March 1989 (except that it shall not affect the operation of any enactment in relation to such a disposal in a case where the enactment operates in consequence of relief having been given under section 79 of the Finance Act 1980 in respect of a disposal made before that date).

125. Gifts to housing associations

(1) The following section shall be inserted in the Capital Gains Tax Act 1979 after section 146—

"**146A. Gifts to housing associations**

(1) Subsection (2) below shall apply where—

(*a*) a disposal of an estate or interest in land in the United Kingdom is made to a registered housing association otherwise than under a bargain at arm's length, and
(*b*) a claim for relief under this section is made by the transferor and the association.

(2) Section 29A(1) above (consideration deemed to be equal to market value) shall not apply; but if the disposal is by way of gift or for a consideration not exceeding the sums allowable as a deduction under section 32 above, then—

(*a*) the disposal and acquisition shall be treated for the purposes of this Act as being made for such consideration as to secure that neither a gain nor a loss accrues on the disposal, and
(*b*) where, after the disposal, the estate or interest is disposed of by the association, its acquisition by the person making the earlier disposal shall be treated for the purposes of this Act as the acquisition of the association.

(3) In this section "registered housing association" means a registered housing association

within the meaning of the Housing Associations Act 1985 or Part VII of the Housing (Northern Ireland) Order 1981."

(2) This section shall apply to disposals made on or after 14th March 1989.

Non-residents etc.

126. Non-resident carrying on profession or vocation in the United Kingdom

(1) For the year 1988–89, section 12 of the Capital Gains Tax Act 1979 (non-resident with United Kingdom branch or agency) shall have effect with the insertion of the following subsection after subsection (2)—

"(2A) In the case of a disposal made on or after 14th March 1989, this section shall apply as if references to a trade included references to a profession or vocation, but not so as to make a person chargeable to capital gains tax by virtue of a profession or vocation which he ceased to carry on in the United Kingdom through a branch or agency before 14th March 1989."

(2) For the year 1989–90 and subsequent years of assessment section 12 of the Capital Gains Tax Act 1979 shall have effect with the insertion of the following subsection after subsection (2)—

"(2A) This section shall apply as if references to a trade included references to a profession or vocation."

(3) Where immediately before 14th March 1989 a person is not resident and not ordinarily resident in the United Kingdom but is carrying on a profession or vocation in the United Kingdom through a branch or agency, he shall be deemed for all purposes of capital gains tax—

(a) to have disposed immediately before 14th March 1989 of every asset to which subsection (4) below applies, and
(b) immediately to have reacquired every such asset,

at its market value at the time of the deemed disposal.

(4) This subsection applies to any asset which was held by the person immediately before 14th March 1989 and which at the beginning of 14th March 1989 is a chargeable asset in relation to him by virtue of his carrying on the profession or vocation.

(5) For the purposes of subsection (4) above an asset is at the beginning of 14th March 1989 a chargeable asset in relation to the person if, were it to be disposed of at that time, any chargeable gains accruing to him on the disposal would be gains in respect of which he would be chargeable to capital gains tax under section 12(1) of the Capital Gains Tax Act 1979.

(6) In the case of a person carrying on a profession or vocation in the United Kingdom through a branch or agency, the charge to capital gains tax under section 12(1) of the Capital Gains Tax Act 1979 shall not apply in respect of chargeable gains accruing on the disposal of assets only used in or for the purposes of the profession or vocation before 14th March 1989 or only used or held for the purposes of the branch or agency before that date.

127. Non-residents: deemed disposals

(1) Where an asset ceases by virtue of becoming situated outside the United Kingdom to be a chargeable asset in relation to a person, he shall be deemed for all purposes of the Capital Gains Tax Act 1979—

(a) to have disposed of the asset immediately before the time when it became situated outside the United Kingdom, and
(b) immediately to have reacquired it,

at its market value at that time.

(2) Subsection (1) above does not apply—

(a) where the asset becomes situated outside the United Kingdom contemporaneously with the person there mentioned ceasing to carry on a trade in the United Kingdom through a branch or agency, or
(b) where the asset is an exploration or exploitation asset.

(3) Where an asset ceases to be a chargeable asset in relation to a person by virtue of his

ceasing to carry on a trade in the United Kingdom through a branch or agency, he shall be deemed for all purposes of the Capital Gains Tax Act 1979—

(a) to have disposed of the asset immediately before the time when he ceased to carry on the trade in the United Kingdom through a branch or agency, and
(b) immediately to have reacquired it,

at its market value at that time.

(4) Subsection (3) above does not apply to an asset which is a chargeable asset in relation to the person there mentioned at any time after he ceases to carry on the trade in the United Kingdom through a branch or agency and before the end of the chargeable period in which he does so.

(5) In this section—

"exploration or exploitation asset" means an asset used in connection with exploration or exploitation activities carried on in the United Kingdom or a designated area, and
"designated area" and "exploration or exploitation activities" have the same meanings as in section 38 of the Finance Act 1973.

(6) For the purposes of this section an asset is at any time a chargeable asset in relation to a person if, were it to be disposed of at that time, any chargeable gains accruing to him on the disposal—

(a) would be gains in respect of which he would be chargeable to capital gains tax under section 12(1) of the Capital Gains Tax Act 1979 (non-resident with United Kingdom branch or agency), or
(b) would form part of his chargeable profits for corporation tax purposes by virtue of section 11(2)(b) of the Taxes Act 1988 (non-resident companies).

(7) Subsection (1) above shall apply where an asset ceases to be situated in the United Kingdom on or after 14th March 1989.

(8) Subsection (3) above shall apply where a person ceases to carry on a trade in the United Kingdom through a branch or agency on or after 14th March 1989.

(9) This section shall apply as if references to a trade included references to a profession or vocation.

128. Non-residents: post-cessation disposals

(1) For the year 1988–89, section 12 of the Capital Gains Tax Act 1979 (non-resident with United Kingdom branch or agency) shall have effect with the insertion of the following subsection after subsection (1)—

"(1A) In the case of a disposal made on or after 14th March 1989, subsection (1) above only applies—

(a) if it is made at a time when the person is carrying on the trade in the United Kingdom through a branch or agency, or
(b) if he ceased to carry on the trade in the United Kingdom through a branch or agency before 14th March 1989."

(2) For the year 1989–90 and subsequent years of assessment, section 12 of the Capital Gains Tax Act 1979 shall have effect with the insertion of the following subsection after subsection (1)—

"(1A) Subsection (1) above does not apply unless the disposal is made at a time when the person is carrying on the trade in the United Kingdom through a branch or agency."

129. Non-residents: roll-over relief

(1) Section 115 of the Capital Gains Tax Act 1979 (roll-over relief) shall not apply in the case of a person if the old assets are chargeable assets in relation to him at the time they are disposed of, unless the new assets are chargeable assets in relation to him immediately after the time they are acquired.

(2) Subsection (1) above shall not apply where—

(a) the person acquires the new assets after he has disposed of the old assets, and
(b) immediately after the time they are acquired the person is resident or ordinarily resident in the United Kingdom.

(3) Subsection (2) above shall not apply where immediately after the time the new assets are acquired—

(a) the person is a dual resident, and
(b) the new assets are prescribed assets.

(4) This section shall apply where the disposal of the old assets or the acquisition of the new assets (or both) takes place on or after 14th March 1989.

(5) But where the acquisition of the new assets takes place before 14th March 1989 and the disposal of the old assets takes place on or after that date, this section shall not apply if the disposal of the old assets takes place within twelve months of the acquisition of the new assets or such longer period as the Board may by notice in writing allow.

(6) For the purposes of this section an asset is at any time a chargeable asset in relation to a person if, were it to be disposed of at that time, any chargeable gains accruing to him on the disposal—

(a) would be gains in respect of which he would be chargeable to capital gains tax under section 12(1) of the Capital Gains Tax Act 1979 (non-resident with United Kingdom branch or agency), or
(b) would form part of his chargeable profits for corporation tax purposes by virtue of section 11(2)(b) of the Taxes Act 1988 (non-resident companies).

(7) In this section—

"dual resident" means a person who is resident or ordinarily resident in the United Kingdom and falls to be regarded for the purposes of any double taxation relief arrangements as resident in a territory outside the United Kingdom;
"double taxation relief arrangements" means arrangements having effect by virtue of section 788 of the Taxes Act 1988 (as extended to capital gains tax by section 10 of the Capital Gains Tax Act 1979);
"prescribed asset", in relation to a dual resident, means an asset in respect of which, by virtue of the asset being of a description specified in any double taxation relief arrangements, he falls to be regarded for the purposes of the arrangements as not liable in the United Kingdom to tax on gains accruing to him on a disposal.

(8) In this section—

(a) "the old assets" and "the new assets" have the same meanings as in section 115 of the Capital Gains Tax Act 1979,
(b) references to disposal of the old assets include references to disposal of an interest in them, and
(c) references to acquisition of the new assets include references to acquisition of an interest in them or to entering into an unconditional contract for the acquisition of them.

130. Exploration or exploitation assets: definition

(1) In section 38 of the Finance Act 1973 (territorial extension) in subsection (3B) (definition of exploration or exploitation asset for purposes of that section)—

(a) in paragraph (a) the words "within the period of two years ending at the date of the disposal" shall be omitted, and
(b) in paragraph (b) for the words ", at some time within the period of two years ending at the date of the disposal, has" there shall be substituted the words "has at some time".

(2) This section shall apply where assets are disposed of on or after 14th March 1989.

131. Exploration or exploitation assets: deemed disposals

(1) Where an exploration or exploitation asset which is a mobile asset ceases to be chargeable in relation to a person by virtue of ceasing to be dedicated to an oil field in which he, or a person connected with him within the meaning of section 839 of the Taxes Act 1988, is or has been a participator, he shall be deemed for all purposes of the Capital Gains Tax Act 1979—

(a) to have disposed of the asset immediately before the time when it ceased to be so dedicated, and
(b) immediately to have reacquired it,

at its market value at that time.

(2) Where a person who is not resident and not ordinarily resident in the United Kingdom

ceases to carry on a trade in the United Kingdom through a branch or agency, he shall be deemed for all purposes of the Capital Gains Tax Act 1979—

(*a*) to have disposed immediately before the time when he ceased to carry on the trade in the United Kingdom through a branch or agency of every asset to which subsection (3) below applies, and
(*b*) immediately to have reacquired every such asset,

at its market value at that time.

(3) This subsection applies to any exploration or exploitation asset, other than a mobile asset, used in or for the purposes of the trade at or before the time of the deemed disposal.

(4) A person shall not be deemed by subsection (2) above to have disposed of an asset if, immediately after the time when he ceases to carry on the trade in the United Kingdom through a branch or agency, the asset is used in or for the purposes of exploration or exploitation activities carried on by him in the United Kingdom or a designated area.

(5) Where in a case to which subsection (4) above applies the person ceases to use the asset in or for the purposes of exploration or exploitation activities carried on by him in the United Kingdom or a designated area, he shall be deemed for all purposes of the Capital Gains Tax Act 1979—

(*a*) to have disposed of the asset immediately before the time when he ceased to use it in or for the purposes of such activities, and
(*b*) immediately to have reacquired it,

at its market value at that time.

(6) For the purposes of this section an asset is at any time a chargeable asset in relation to a person if, were it to be disposed of at that time, any chargeable gains accruing to him on the disposal—

(*a*) would be gains in respect of which he would be chargeable to capital gains tax under section 12(1) of the Capital Gains Tax Act 1979 (non-resident with United Kingdom branch or agency), or
(*b*) would form part of his chargeable profits for corporation tax purposes by virtue of section 11(2)(*b*) of the Taxes Act 1988 (non-resident companies).

(7) In this section—

(*a*) "exploration or exploitation asset" means an asset used in connection with exploration or exploitation activities carried on in the United Kingdom or a designated area;
(*b*) "designated area" and "exploration or exploitation activities" have the same meanings as in section 38 of the Finance Act 1973; and
(*c*) the expressions "dedicated to an oil field" and "participator" shall be construed as if this section were included in Part I of the Oil Taxation Act 1975.

(8) Subsection (1) above shall apply where an asset ceases to be dedicated as mentioned in that subsection on or after 14th March 1989.

(9) Subsection (2) above shall apply where a person ceases to carry on a trade in the United Kingdom through a branch or agency on or after 14th March 1989.

(10) Subsection (5) above shall apply where a person ceases to use an asset in or for the purposes of exploration or exploitation activities on or after 14th March 1989.

132. Dual resident companies: deemed disposal

(1) For the purposes of this section, a company is a dual resident company if it is resident in the United Kingdom and falls to be regarded for the purposes of any double taxation relief arrangements as resident in a territory outside the United Kingdom.

(2) Where an asset of a dual resident company becomes a prescribed asset, the company shall be deemed for all purposes of the Capital Gains Tax Act 1979—

(*a*) to have disposed of the asset immediately before the time at which it became a prescribed asset, and
(*b*) immediately to have reacquired it,

at its market value at that time.

(3) Subsection (2) above does not apply where the asset becomes a prescribed asset on the company becoming a company which falls to be regarded as mentioned in subsection (1) above.

(4) This section applies where an asset becomes a prescribed asset on or after 14th March 1989.

(5) In this section—

"double taxation relief arrangements" means arrangements having effect by virtue of section 788 of the Taxes Act 1988 (as extended to capital gains tax by section 10 of the Capital Gains Tax Act 1979);

"prescribed asset", in relation to a dual resident company, means an asset in respect of which, by virtue of the asset being of a description specified in any double taxation relief arrangements, the company falls to be regarded for the purposes of the arrangements as not liable in the United Kingdom to tax on gains accruing to it on a disposal.

133. Dual resident companies: roll-over relief

(1) Where a company is a dual resident company at the time it disposes of the old assets and at the time it acquires the new assets, and the old assets are not prescribed assets at the time of disposal, section 115 of the Capital Gains Tax Act 1979 (roll-over relief) shall not apply unless the new assets are not prescribed assets immediately after the time of acquisition.

(2) This section shall apply where the disposal of the old assets or the acquisition of the new assets (or both) takes place on or after 14th March 1989.

(3) But where the acquisition of the new assets takes place before 14th March 1989 and the disposal of the old assets takes place on or after that date, this section shall not apply if the disposal takes place within twelve months of the acquisition or such longer period as the Board may by notice in writing allow.

(4) In this section—

"dual resident company" means a company which is resident in the United Kingdom and falls to be regarded for the purposes of any double taxation relief arrangements as resident in a territory outside the United Kingdom;

"double taxation relief arrangements" means arrangements having effect by virtue of section 788 of the Taxes Act 1988 (as extended to capital gains tax by section 10 of the Capital Gains Tax Act 1979);

"prescribed asset", in relation to a dual resident company, means an asset in respect of which, by virtue of the asset being of a description specified in any double taxation relief arrangements, the company falls to be regarded for the purposes of the arrangements as not liable in the United Kingdom to tax on gains accruing to it on a disposal.

(5) In this section—

(*a*) "the old assets" and "the new assets" have the same meanings as in section 115 of the Capital Gains Tax Act 1979,
(*b*) references to disposal of the old assets include references to disposal of an interest in them, and
(*c*) references to acquisition of the new assets include references to acquisition of an interest in them or to entering into an unconditional contract for the acquisition of them.

134. Non-payment of tax by non-resident companies

(1) This section applies where—

(*a*) a chargeable gain has accrued to a company not resident in the United Kingdom (the taxpayer company) on the disposal of an asset on or after 14th March 1989,
(*b*) the gain forms part of its chargeable profits for corporation tax purposes by virtue of section 11(2)(*b*) of the Taxes Act 1988, and
(*c*) any of the corporation tax assessed on the company for the accounting period in which the gain accrued is not paid within six months from the time when it becomes payable.

(2) The Board may, at any time before the end of the period of three years beginning with the time when the amount of corporation tax for the accounting period in which the chargeable gain accrued is finally determined, serve on any person to whom subsection (4) below applies a notice—

(*a*) stating the amount which remains unpaid of the corporation tax assessed on the taxpayer company for the accounting period in which the gain accrued and the date when the tax became payable, and (*b*) requiring that person to pay the relevant amount within thirty days of the service of the notice.

(3) For the purposes of subsection (2) above the relevant amount is the lesser of—

(*a*) the amount which remains unpaid of the corporation tax assessed on the taxpayer company for the accounting period in which the gain accrued, and
(*b*) an amount equal to corporation tax on the amount of the chargeable gain at the rate in force when the gain accrued.

(4) This subsection applies to the following persons—

(*a*) any company which is, or within the relevant period was, a member of the same group as the taxpayer company, and
(*b*) any person who is, or within the relevant period was, a controlling director of the taxpayer company or of a company which has, or within that period had, control over the taxpayer company.

(5) Any amount which a person is required to pay by a notice under this section may be recovered from him as if it were tax due and duly demanded of him; and he may recover any such amount paid by him from the taxpayer company.

(6) A payment in pursuance of a notice under this section shall not be allowed as a deduction in computing any income, profits or losses for any tax purposes.

(7) In this section—

"director", in relation to a company, has the meaning given by subsection (6) of section 168 of the Taxes Act 1988 (read with subsection (9) of that section) and includes any person falling within subsection (5) of section 417 of that Act (read with subsection (6) of that section);
"controlling director", in relation to a company, means a director of the company who has control of it (construing control in accordance with section 416 of the Taxes Act 1988);
"group" has the meaning which would be given by section 272 of the Taxes Act 1970 if in that section references to residence in the United Kingdom were omitted and for references to 75 per cent. subsidiaries there were substituted references to 51 per cent. subsidiaries.

(8) In this section "the relevant period" means—

(*a*) where the time when the chargeable gain accrues is less than twelve months after 14th March 1989, the period beginning with that date and ending with that time;
(*b*) in any other case, the period of twelve months ending with that time.

Value shifting and groups of companies

135. Value shifting

(1) In section 26 of the Capital Gains Tax Act 1979 (value shifting: further provisions) in subsection (1)(*a*) (schemes whereby value of the asset disposed of is materially reduced) after the words "the asset" there shall be inserted the words "or a relevant asset" and at the end of that subsection there shall be inserted—

"(1A) For the purposes of this section, where the asset disposed of by a company ("the disposing company") consists of shares in, or securities of, another company, another asset is a relevant asset if, at the time of the disposal, it is owned by a company associated with the disposing company; but no account shall be taken of any reduction in the value of a relevant asset except in a case where—

(*a*) during the period beginning with the reduction in value and ending immediately before the disposal by the disposing company, there is no disposal of the asset to any person, other than a disposal falling within section 273(1) of the Taxes Act 1970 (transfers within a group: no gain/no loss),
(*b*) no disposal of the asset is treated as having occurred during that period by virtue of section 278 of the Taxes Act 1970 (company ceasing to be member of group), and
(*c*) if the reduction had not taken place but any consideration given for the relevant asset and any other material circumstances (including any consideration given before the disposal for the asset disposed of) were unchanged, the value of the asset disposed of would, at the time of the disposal, have been materially greater;

and in this subsection "securities" has the same meaning as in section 82 below."

(2) For subsection (7) of that section there shall be substituted—

"(7) References in this section, in relation to any disposal, to a reduction in the value of an asset, where the asset consists of shares owned by a company in another company, shall be interpreted in accordance with sections 26A to 26C below and, in those sections, the disposal, the asset and those companies are referred to respectively as "the section 26 disposal", "the principal asset", "the first company" and "the second company"."

(3) In subsection (8) of that section for the words "reference in subsection (1)(*a*)" there shall be substituted the words "references in subsections (1)(*a*) and (1A)".

(4) This section shall have effect in respect of any disposal of an asset on or after 14th March 1989.

136. Value shifting: reductions attributable to distributions within a group

(1) After section 26 of the Capital Gains Tax Act 1979 there shall be inserted—

"**26A. Value shifting: distributions within a group followed by a disposal of shares**

(1) The references in section 26 above to a reduction in the value of an asset, in the case mentioned in subsection (7) of that section, do not include a reduction attributable to the payment of a dividend by the second company at a time when it and the first company are associated, except to the extent (if any) that the dividend is attributable to chargeable profits of the second company and, in such a case, the tax-free benefit shall be ascertained without regard to any part of the dividend that is not attributable to such profits.

(2) Subsections (3) to (11) below apply for the interpretation of subsection (1) above.

(3) Chargeable profits shall be ascertained as follows—

(*a*) the distributable profits of any company are chargeable profits of that company to the extent that they are profits arising on a transaction caught by this section, and
(*b*) where any company makes a distribution attributable wholly or party to chargeable profits (including any profits that are chargeable profits by virtue of this paragraph) to another company, the distributable profits of the other company, so far as they represent that distribution or so much of it as was attributable to chargeable profits, are chargeable profits of the other company,

and for this purpose any loss or other amount to be set against the profits of a company in determining the distributable profits shall be set first against profits other than the profits so arising or, as the case may be, representing so much of the distribution as was attributable to chargeable profits.

(4) The distributable profits of a company are such profits computed on a commercial basis as, after allowing for any provision properly made for tax, the company is empowered, assuming sufficient funds, to distribute to persons entitled to participate in the profits of the company.

(5) Profits of a company ("company A") are profits arising on a transaction caught by this section where each of the following three conditions is satisfied.

(6) The first condition is that the transaction is—

(*a*) a disposal of an asset by company A to another company in circumstances such that company A and the other company are treated as mentioned in section 273(1) of the Taxes Act 1970 (transfers within a group: no gain/no loss), or
(*b*) an exchange, or a transaction treated for the purposes of section 85(2) and (3) below as an exchange, of shares in or debentures of a company held by company A for shares in or debentures of another company, being a company associated with company A immediately after the transaction, and is treated by virtue of section 85(3) below as a reorganisation of share capital, or
(*c*) a revaluation of an asset in the accounting records of company A.

In the following conditions the "asset with enhanced value" means (subject to section 26C below), in the paragraph (*a*) case, the asset acquired by the person to whom the disposal is made, in the paragraph (*b*) case, the shares in or debentures of the other company and, in the paragraph (*c*) case, the revalued asset.

(7) The second condition is that—

(*a*) during the period beginning with the transaction referred to in subsection (6) above and ending immediately before the section 26 disposal, there is no disposal of the asset with enhanced value to any person, other than a disposal falling within section 273(1) of the Taxes Act 1970, and

(b) no disposal of the asset with enhanced value is treated as having occurred during that period by virtue of section 278 of the Taxes Act 1970 (company ceasing to be member of group).

(8) The third condition is that, immediately after the section 26 disposal, the asset with enhanced value is owned by a person other than the company making that disposal or a company associated with it.

(9) The conditions in subsections (6) to (8) above are not satisfied if—

(a) at the time of the transaction referred to in subsection (6) above, company A carries on a trade and a profit on a disposal of the asset with enhanced value would form part of the trading profits, or

(b) by reason of the nature of the asset with enhanced value, a disposal of it could give rise neither to a chargeable gain nor to an allowable loss, or

(c) immediately before the section 26 disposal, the company owning the asset with enhanced value carries on a trade and a profit on a disposal of the asset would form part of the trading profits.

(10) The amount of chargeable profits of a company to be attributed to any distribution made by the company at any time in respect of any class of shares, securities or rights shall be ascertained by—

(a) determining the total of distributable profits, and the total of chargeable profits, that remains after allowing for earlier distributions made in respect of that or any other class of shares, securities or rights, and for distributions made at or to be made after that time in respect of other classes of shares, securities or rights, and

(b) attributing first to that distribution distributable profits other than chargeable profits.

(11) The amount of chargeable profits of a company to be attributed to any part of a distribution made at any time to which a person is entitled by virtue of any part of his holding of any class of shares, securities or rights, shall be such proportion of the chargeable profits as are attributable under subsection (10) above to the distributions made at that time in respect of that class as corresponds to that part of his holding.

26B. Value shifting: disposals within a group followed by a disposal of shares

(1) The references in section 26 above to a reduction in the value of an asset, in the case mentioned in subsection (7) of that section, do not include a reduction attributable to the disposal of any asset ("the underlying asset") by the second company at a time when it and the first company are associated, being a disposal falling within section 273(1) of the Taxes Act 1970 (transfers within group: no gain/no loss), except in a case within subsection (2) below.

(2) A case is within this subsection if the amount or value of the actual consideration for the disposal of the underlying asset—

(a) is less than the market value of the underlying asset, and
(b) is less than the cost of the underlying asset,

unless the disposal is effected for bona fide commercial reasons and does not form part of a scheme or arrangements of which the main purpose, or one of the main purposes, is avoidance of liability to corporation tax.

(3) For the purposes of subsection (2) above, the cost of an asset owned by a company is the aggregate of—

(a) any capital expenditure incurred by the company in acquiring or providing the asset, and
(b) any other capital expenditure incurred by the company in respect of the asset while owned by that company.

(4) For the purposes of this section, where the disposal of the underlying asset is a part disposal, the reference in subsection (2)(a) above to the market value of the underlying asset is to the market value of the asset acquired by the person to whom the disposal is made and the amounts to be attributed to the underlying asset under paragraphs (a) and (b) of subsection (3) above shall be reduced to the appropriate proportion of those amounts, that is—

(a) the proportion of capital expenditure in respect of the underlying asset properly attributed in the accounting records of the company to the asset acquired by the person to whom the disposal is made, or

(b) where paragraph (a) above does not apply, such proportion as appears to the inspector, or on appeal the Commissioners concerned, to be just and reasonable.

(5) Where by virtue of a distribution in the course of dissolving or winding up the second company the first company is treated as disposing of an interest in the principal asset, the exception mentioned in subsection (1) above does not apply.

26C. Value shifting: supplementary

(1) For the purposes of sections 26(1A) and 26A(7) to (9) above, subsections (2) to (6) below apply for the purpose of determining in the case of any asset ("the original asset") whether it is subsequently disposed of or treated as disposed of or owned or any other condition is satisfied in respect of it.

(2) References in sections 26(1A)(a) and (b) and 26A(7) to a disposal are to a disposal other than a part disposal.

(3) References to an asset are to the original asset or, where at a later time one or more assets are treated by virtue of subsections (5) or (6) below as the same as the original asset—

(a) if no disposal falling within paragraph (a) or (b) of section 26(1A) or, as the case may be, of 26A(7) has occurred, those references are to the asset so treated or, as the case may be, all the assets so treated, and

(b) in any other case, those references are to an asset or, as the case may be, all the assets representing that part of the value of the original asset that remains after allowing for earlier disposals falling within the paragraphs concerned,

references in this subsection to a disposal including a disposal which would fall within the paragraphs concerned but for subsection (2) above.

(4) Where by virtue of subsection (3) above those references are to two or more assets—

(a) those assets shall be treated as if they were a single asset,
(b) any disposal of any one of them is to be treated as a part disposal, and
(c) the reference in section 26(1A) to the asset owned at the time of the disposal by a company associated with the disposing company and the reference in section 26A(8) to the asset with enhanced value is to all or any of those assets.

(5) Where there is a part disposal of an asset, that asset and the asset acquired by the person to whom the disposal is made are to be treated as the same.

(6) Where the value of an asset is derived from any other asset in the ownership of the same or an associated company, in a case where assets have been merged or divided or have changed their nature or rights or interests in or over assets have been created or extinguished, the first asset is to be treated as the same as the second.

(7) For the purposes of section 26(1A) above, where account is to be taken under that subsection of a reduction in the value of a relevant asset and at the time of the disposal by the disposing company referred to in that subsection—

(a) references to the relevant asset are by virtue of this section references to two or more assets treated as a single asset, and
(b) one or more but not all of those assets are owned by a company associated with the disposing company,

the amount of the reduction in the value of the relevant asset to be taken into account by virtue of that subsection shall be reduced to such amount as appears to the inspector, or on appeal to the Commissioners concerned, to be just and reasonable.

(8) For the purposes of section 26A above, where—

(a) a dividend paid by the second company is attributable to chargeable profits of that company, and
(b) the condition in subsection (7), (8) or (9)(c) of that section is satisfied by reference to an asset, or assets treated as a single asset, treated by virtue of subsection (3)(b) above as the same as the asset with enhanced value,

the amount of the reduction in value of the principal asset shall be reduced to such amount as appears to the inspector, or on appeal to the Commissioners concerned, to be just and reasonable.

(9) For the purposes of sections 26 to 26B above and this section, companies are associated if they are members of the same group.

(10) Section 272(1) to (4) of the Taxes Act 1970 (groups of companies: definitions) applies for the purposes of sections 26 to 26B above and this section as it applies for the purposes of that section."

(2) This section shall have effect in respect of any disposal of an asset on or after 14th March 1989, but—

(*a*) no account shall be taken by virtue of section 26A of the Capital Gains Tax Act 1979 of any reduction in the value of an asset attributable to the payment of a dividend unless it is paid on or after that date, and
(*b*) no account shall be taken by virtue of section 26B of that Act of a reduction in the value of an asset attributable to the disposal of another asset unless the disposal took place on or after that date.

137. Value shifting: transactions treated as a reorganisation of share capital

(1) After section 26C of the Capital Gains Tax Act 1979 there shall be inserted—

"26D. Value shifting: transactions treated as a reorganisation of share capital

(1) Where—

(*a*) but for sections 78 and 85(3) below, section 26 above would have effect as respects the disposal by a company ("the disposing company") of an asset consisting of shares in or debentures of another company ("the original holding") in exchange for shares in or debentures of a further company which, immediately after the disposal, is not a member of the same group as the disposing company, and
(*b*) if section 26 above had effect as respects that disposal, any allowable loss or chargeable gain accruing on the disposal would be calculated as if the consideration for the disposal were increased by an amount,

the disposing company shall be treated for the purposes of section 79(2) below as receiving, on the reorganisation of share capital that is treated as occurring by virtue of section 85(3) below, that amount for the disposal of the original holding.

(2) For the purposes of subsection (1) above it shall be assumed that section 86 below has effect generally for the purposes of this Act, and in that subsection "group" has the same meaning as in sections 26 to 26C above."

(2) This section shall have effect where the reduction in value, by reason of which the amount referred to in section 26D(1)(*b*) of the Capital Gains Tax Act 1979 falls to be calculated, occurred on or after 14th March 1989.

138. Groups of companies

(1) In section 272 of the Taxes Act 1970 (groups of companies: definitions) in subsection (1), for paragraphs (*b*) and (*c*) there shall be substituted—

"(*b*) subsections (1A) to (1D) below apply to determine whether companies form a group and, where they do, which is the principal company of the group;".

(2) After that subsection there shall be inserted—

"(1A) Subject to subsections (1B) to (1D) below—

(*a*) a company (referred to below in this Chapter as the "principal company of the group") and all its 75 per cent. subsidiaries form a group and, if any of those subsidiaries have 75 per cent. subsidiaries, the group includes them and their 75 per cent. subsidiaries, and so on, but
(*b*) a group does not include any company (other than the principal company of the group) that is not an effective 51 per cent. subsidiary of the principal company of the group.

(1B) A company cannot be the principal company of a group if it is itself a 75 per cent. subsidiary of another company.

(1C) Where a company ("the subsidiary") is a 75 per cent. subsidiary of another company but those companies are prevented from being members of the same group by subsection (1A)(*b*) above, the subsidiary may, where the requirements of subsection (1A) above are satisfied, itself be the principal company of another group notwithstanding subsection

(1B) above unless this subsection enables a further company to be the principal company of a group of which the subsidiary would be a member.

(1D) A company cannot be a member of more than one group; but where, apart from this subsection, a company would be a member of two or more groups (the principal company of each group being referred to below as the "head of a group"), it is a member only of that group, if any, of which it would be a member under one of the following tests (applying earlier tests in preference to later tests)—

>   (*a*) it is a member of the group it would be a member of if, in applying subsection (1A)(*b*) above, there were left out of account any amount to which a head of a group is or would be beneficially entitled of any profits available for distribution to equity holders of a head of another group or of any assets of a head of another group available for distribution to its equity holders on a winding-up,
>   (*b*) it is a member of the group the head of which is beneficially entitled to a percentage of profits available for distribution to equity holders of the company that is greater than the percentage of those profits to which any other head of a group is so entitled,
>   (*c*) it is a member of the group the head of which would be beneficially entitled to a percentage of any assets of the company available for distribution to its equity holders on a winding-up that is greater than the percentage of those assets to which any other head of a group would be so entitled,
>   (*d*) it is a member of the group the head of which owns directly or indirectly a percentage of the company's ordinary share capital that is greater than the percentage of that capital owned directly or indirectly by any other head of a group (interpreting this paragraph as if it were included in section 838(1)(*a*) of the Taxes Act 1988).

(1E) For the purposes referred to in subsection (1) above, a company ("the subsidiary") is an effective 51 per cent. subsidiary of another company ("the parent") at any time if and only if—

>   (*a*) the parent is beneficially entitled to more than 50 per cent. of any profits available for distribution to equity holders of the subsidiary; and
>   (*b*) the parent would be beneficially entitled to more than 50 per cent. of any assets of the subsidiary available for distribution to its equity holders on a winding-up.

(1F) Schedule 18 to the Taxes Act 1988 (group relief: equity holders and profits or assets available for distribution) shall apply for the purposes of subsections (1D) and (1E) above as if the references to subsection (7), or subsections (7) to (9), of section 413 of that Act were references to subsections (1D) and (1E) above and as if, in paragraph 1(4), the words from "but" to the end and paragraph 7(1)(*b*) were omitted."

(3) In subsection (3) of that section for the words from "75 per cent. subsidiary of another company" to "is the principal company" there shall be substituted the words "member of another group, the first group and the other group shall be regarded as the same".

(4) In subsection (4) of that section—

>   (*a*) for the words "a company" there shall be substituted the words "a member of a group of companies", and
>   (*b*) for the words from "that company, or" to the end there shall be substituted the words "that or any other company ceasing to be a member of the group".

(5) In section 278 of that Act (deemed disposal of certain assets held by company leaving group) after subsection (3A) there shall be inserted—

"(3B) Where, apart from subsection (3C) below, a company ceasing to be a member of a group by reason only of the fact that the principal company of the group becomes a member of another group would be treated by virtue of subsection (3) above as selling an asset at any time, subsections (3C) to (3E) below shall apply.

(3C) The company in question shall not be treated as selling the asset at that time; but if—

>   (*a*) within six years of that time the company in question ceases at any time ("the relevant time") to satisfy the following conditions, and
>   (*b*) at the relevant time, the company in question, or a company in the same group as that company, owns otherwise than as trading stock the asset or property to which a chargeable gain has been carried forward from the asset on a replacement of business assets,

the company in question shall be treated for all the purposes of the Capital Gains Tax

Act 1979 as if, immediately after its acquisition of the asset, it had sold and immediately reacquired the asset at the value that, at the time of acquisition, was its market value.

(3D) Those conditions are—

> (a) that the company is a 75 per cent. subsidiary of one or more members of the other group referred to in subsection (3B) above, and
> (b) that the company is an effective 51 per cent. subsidiary of one or more of those members.

(3E) Any chargeable gain or allowable loss accruing to the company on that sale shall be treated as accruing at the relevant time.

(3F) Where—

> (a) by virtue of this section a company is treated as having sold an asset at any time, and
> (b) if at that time the company had in fact sold the asset at market value at that time, then, by virtue of section 26 of that Act, any allowable loss or chargeable gain accruing on the disposal would have been calculated as if the consideration for the disposal were increased by an amount,

subsections (3) and (3C) above shall have effect as if the market value at that time had been that amount greater."

(6) In section 97 of the Inheritance Tax Act 1984 (transfers within group, etc.)—

> (a) for the words "principal member" and "principal member's", wherever appearing, there shall be substituted "principal company" and "principal company's" respectively,
> (b) for subsection (2)(a) there shall be substituted—
>
>> "(a) section 272 of the Taxes Act 1970 (groups of companies: definitions) applies as for the purposes of sections 273 to 281 of that Act", and
>
> (c) the words from "and in this section" in subsection (2) to the end shall be omitted.

(7) Subject to the following provisions, this section shall be deemed to have come into force on 14th March 1989; but section 278(3E) of the Taxes Act 1970 shall have effect where the accounting period in which the company referred to in subsection (3B) of that section ceases to be a member of a group ends after the day appointed for the purposes of paragraph 4 of Schedule 6 to the Finance (No. 2) Act 1987.

(8) Where—

> (a) at the beginning of the commencement day a company ceases for the purposes of the group provisions to be a member of a group by reason only of the substitution for the old definition of the new definition, and
> (b) in consequence of ceasing to be such a member the company would, apart from this subsection, be treated by virtue of section 278(3) of the Taxes Act 1970 as selling an asset at any time,

the company in question shall not be treated as selling that asset at that time unless the conditions in subsection (9) below become satisfied, assuming for that purpose that the old definition applies.

(9) Those conditions are—

> (a) that for the purposes of section 278 of that Act the company in question ceases at any time ("the relevant time") to be a member of the group referred to in subsection (8)(a) above,
> (b) that, at the relevant time, the company in question, or an associated company also leaving that group at that time, owns otherwise than as trading stock the asset or property to which a chargeable gain has been carried forward from the asset on a replacement of business assets, and
> (c) that the time of acquisition referred to in section 278(1) of that Act fell within the period of six years ending with the relevant time.

(10) Where, under any compromise or arrangement agreed to on any date before 14th March 1989 in pursuance of section 425 of the Companies Act 1985 and sanctioned by the court, one company acquires at any time, directly or indirectly, an interest in ordinary share capital of another company and immediately after that time—

> (a) under the old definition the two companies are, by virtue of that acquisition, members of a group for the purposes of the group provisions, but
> (b) the second company is not an effective 51 per cent. subsidiary of the first company,

subsection (11) below applies; and in that subsection those companies and any other members of the group are referred to as "relevant companies".

(11) In respect of the period beginning with the time of acquisition and ending with—

(*a*) the expiry of the six months beginning with the date of the agreement, or
(*b*) if earlier, the date when, under the old definition, the other company ceases for the purposes of the group provisions to be a member of the group referred to in subsection (10)(*a*) above,

the old definition shall apply in relation to the relevant companies for the purposes of the group provisions and the commencement day in relation to those companies is the day following the end of that period.

(12) In subsections (8) to (11) above—

"arrangement" has the same meaning as in section 425 of the Companies Act 1985,
"commencement day", subject to subsection (11) above, is 14th March 1989,
"effective 51 per cent. subsidiary" has the meaning given by section 272(1E) of the Taxes Act 1970,
"group provisions" means sections 273 to 281 of that Act, and
"the new definition" means section 272 of that Act as amended by this section and "the old definition" means that section as it had effect on 13th March 1989,

and section 278(4) of that Act shall apply for the purposes of those subsections.

Miscellaneous

139. Corporate bonds

(1) In relation to disposals on or after 14th March 1989 Chapter III of Part II of the Finance Act 1984 shall have effect subject to the following provisions of this section (and, in relation to such disposals, those provisions shall be regarded as always having had effect).

(2) In subsection (2) of section 64 (which defines "corporate bond" for the purposes of that section and accordingly for the purposes of certain other enactments including, by virtue of section 64(1) of the Capital Gains Tax Act 1979, that Act) paragraph (*a*) shall be omitted.

(3) After subsection (3) of section 64 there shall be inserted—

"(3A) For the purposes of this section "corporate bond" also includes a security—

(*a*) which is not included in the definition in subsection (2) above, and
(*b*) which is a deep gain security for the purposes of Schedule 11 to the Finance Act 1989.

(3B) For the purposes of this section "corporate bond" also includes a security—

(*a*) which is not included in the definition in subsection (2) above, and
(*b*) which, by virtue of paragraph 21(2) of Schedule 11 to the Finance Act 1989, falls to be treated as a deep gain security as there mentioned.

(3C) For the purposes of this section "corporate bond" also includes a security—

(*a*) which is not included in the definition in subsection (2) above, and
(*b*) which, by virtue of paragraph 22(2) of Schedule 11 to the Finance Act 1989, falls to be treated as a deep gain security as there mentioned."

(4) After subsection (5) of section 64 there shall be inserted—

"(5A) Subject to subsection (6) below, for the purposes of this section and Schedule 13 to this Act a corporate bond which falls within subsection (3A) above is a qualifying corporate bond, whatever the date of its issue; and subsections (4) and (5) above shall not apply in the case of such a bond.

(5B) Subject to subsection (6) below, for the purposes of this section and Schedule 13 to this Act a corporate bond which falls within subsection (3B) above is a qualifying corporate bond as regards a disposal made after the time mentioned in paragraph 21(1)(*c*) of Schedule 11 to the Finance Act 1989, whatever the date of its issue; and subsections (4) and (5) above shall not apply in the case of such a bond.

(5C) Subject to subsection (6) below, for the purposes of this section and Schedule 13 to this Act a corporate bond which falls within subsection (3C) above is a qualifying corporate bond as regards a disposal made after the time the agreement mentioned in paragraph 22(1)(*b*) of Schedule 11 to the Finance Act 1989 is made, whatever the date of its issue; and subsections (4) and (5) above shall not apply in the case of such a bond."

(5) In subsection (6) of section 64, after the words "this Act" there shall be inserted the words "except in relation to a disposal by a person who (at the time of the disposal) is not a member of the same group as the company which issued the security".

(6) In paragraph 10(2) of Schedule 13—

(*a*) after paragraph (*b*) there shall be inserted—

"(*bb*) section 267 of the Taxes Act (company reconstructions and amalgamations); or", and

(*b*) the word "not" shall be inserted after the words "previous disposal".

140. Collective investment schemes

(1) In this section—

"collective investment scheme" has the same meaning as in the Financial Services Act 1986, and

"participant" shall be construed in accordance with that Act.

(2) Subsection (3) below applies in the case of arrangements which constitute a collective investment scheme and under which—

(*a*) the contributions of the participants, and the profits or income out of which payments are to be made to them, are pooled in relation to separate parts of the property in question, and

(*b*) the participants are entitled to exchange rights in one part for rights in another.

(3) If a participant exchanges rights in one such part for rights in another section 78 of the Capital Gains Tax Act 1979 (reorganisations etc.) shall not prevent the exchange constituting a disposal and acquisition for the purposes of that Act.

(4) The reference in subsection (3) above to section 78 of that Act—

(*a*) includes a reference to that section as applied by section 82 of that Act (conversion of securities), but

(*b*) does not include a reference to section 78 as applied by section 85 of that Act (exchange of securities for those in another company).

(5) Subsection (3) above shall apply where rights are exchanged on or after 14th March 1989.

(6) Section 78 of the Finance (No. 2) Act 1987 shall cease to have effect as regards any case where the question it mentions is determined in relation to a disposal made on or after 14th March 1989.

141. Re-basing to 1982 etc.

Schedule 15 to this Act (which makes further provision about charges etc. postponed from 31st March 1982 or before, assets held on that date and related matters) shall have effect.

CHAPTER IV

MANAGEMENT

Information

142. Power to call for documents and information

(1) Section 20 of the Taxes Management Act 1970 (power to call for documents of taxpayer and others) shall be amended in accordance with subsections (2) to (8) below.

(2) In subsection (1), for the words "a person" onwards there shall be substituted the words "a person—

(*a*) to deliver to him such documents as are in the person's possession or power and as (in the inspector's reasonable opinion) contain, or may contain, information relevant to—

(i) any tax liability to which the person is or may be subject, or
(ii) the amount of any such liability, or

(*b*) to furnish to him such particulars as the inspector may reasonably require as being relevant to, or to the amount of, any such liability."

(3) In subsection (2), for the words "a person" onwards there shall be substituted the words "a person—

(*a*) to deliver to a named officer of the Board such documents as are in the person's possession or power and as (in the Board's reasonable opinion) contain, or may contain, information relevant to—

(i) any tax liability to which the person is or may be subject, or
(ii) the amount of any such liability, or

(*b*) to furnish to a named officer of the Board such particulars as the Board may reasonably require as being relevant to, or to the amount of, any such liability."

(4) In subsection (3)—

(*a*) for the words "of the persons who in relation to the taxpayer are subject to this subsection" there shall be substituted the words "other person", and
(*b*) at the end there shall be added the words "; and the persons who may be required to deliver or make available a document under this subsection include the Director of Savings."

(5) Subsections (4) and (5) shall be omitted.

(6) In subsection (6)—

(*a*) for the words "under subsections (3) and (4)" there shall be substituted the words "for the purposes of this section", and
(*b*) the words "and in relation" onwards shall be omitted.

(7) For subsection (8) there shall be substituted—

"(8) Subject to subsection (8A) below, a notice under subsection (3) above shall name the taxpayer with whose liability the inspector (or, where section 20B(3) below applies, the Board) is concerned."

(8) After subsection (8B) there shall be inserted—

"(8C) In this section references to documents do not include—

(*a*) personal records (as defined in section 12 of the Police and Criminal Evidence Act 1984), or
(*b*) journalistic material (as defined in section 13 of that Act),

and references to particulars do not include particulars contained in such personal records or journalistic material.

(8D) Subject to subsection (8C) above, references in this section to documents and particulars are to those specified or described in the notice in question; and—

(*a*) the notice shall require documents to be delivered (or delivered or made available), or particulars to be furnished, within such time (which, except in the case of a notice under subsection (2) above, shall not be less than thirty days after the date of the notice) as may be specified in the notice; and

(b) the person to whom they are delivered, made available or furnished may take copies of them or of extracts from them."

(9) In section 12(3) of the National Savings Bank Act 1971, for the words "20(4)(b)" onwards there shall be substituted the words "20(3) of that Act (requirement to deliver or make available documents relating to liability of a taxpayer)."

(10) This section shall apply with respect to notices given on or after the day on which this Act is passed.

143. Power to call for papers of tax accountant

(1) In section 20A of the Taxes Management Act 1970 (power to call for papers of tax accountant) for the last sentence of subsection (1) there shall be substituted—

"(1A) The reference to documents in subsection (1) above does not include—

(a) personal records (as defined in section 12 of the Police and Criminal Evidence Act 1984), or
(b) journalistic material (as defined in section 13 of that Act).

(1B) Subject to subsection (1A) above, the reference to documents in subsection (1) above is to those specified or described in the notice in question; and—

(a) the notice shall require documents to be delivered within such time (which shall not be less than thirty days after the date of the notice) as may be specified in the notice; and
(b) the inspector may take copies of them or of extracts from them."

(2) This section shall apply with respect to notices given on or after the day on which this Act is passed.

144. Restrictions on powers under TMA ss. 20 and 20A

(1) Section 20B of the Taxes Management Act 1970 (restrictions on powers under sections 20 and 20A) shall be amended as follows.

(2) In subsection (1), after the word "question" there shall be inserted the words ", or to furnish the particulars in question".

(3) After that subsection there shall be inserted—

"(1A) Subject to subsection (1B) below, where a notice is given to any person under section 20(3) the inspector shall give a copy of the notice to the taxpayer to whom it relates.

(1B) If, on an application by the inspector, a General or Special Commissioner so directs, a copy of a notice under section 20(3) need not be given to the taxpayer to whom it relates; but such a direction shall not be given unless the Commissioner is satisfied that the inspector has reasonable grounds for suspecting the taxpayer of fraud."

(4) In subsection (2), after the words "deliver documents", in the first place where they occur, there shall be inserted the words "or furnish particulars".

(5) In subsection (5), for the words from "if" to "or company" there shall be substituted the words "does not oblige a person".

(6) In subsection (7), the words from "to a person" to "daughter" shall be omitted.

(7) For subsection (9) there shall be substituted—

"(9) Subject to subsections (11) and (12) below, a notice under section 20(3) or (8A)—

(a) does not oblige a person who has been appointed as an auditor for the purposes of any enactment to deliver or make available documents which are his property and were created by him or on his behalf for or in connection with the performance of his functions under that enactment, and
(b) does not oblige a tax adviser to deliver or make available documents which are his property and consist of relevant communications.

(10) In subsection (9) above "relevant communications" means communications between the tax adviser and—

(a) a person in relation to whose tax affairs he has been appointed, or
(b) any other tax adviser of such a person,

the purpose of which is the giving or obtaining of advice about any of those tax affairs; and in subsection (9) above and this subsection "tax adviser" means a person appointed to give advice about the tax affairs of another person (whether appointed directly by that other person or by another tax adviser of his).

(11) Subject to subsection (13) below, subsection (9) above shall not have effect in relation to any document which contains information explaining any information, return, accounts or other document which the person to whom the notice is given has, as tax accountant, assisted any client of his in preparing for, or delivering to, the inspector or the Board.

(12) Subject to subsection (13) below, in the case of a notice under section 20(8A) subsection (9) above shall not have effect in relation to any document which contains information giving the identity or address of any taxpayer to whom the notice relates or of any person who has acted on behalf of any such person.

(13) Subsection (9) above is not disapplied by subsection (11) or (12) above in the case of any document if—

(a) the information within subsection (11) or (12) is contained in some other document, and
(b) either—

(i) that other document, or a copy of it, has been delivered to the inspector or the Board, or
(ii) that other document has been inspected by an officer of the Board.

(14) Where subsection (9) above is disapplied by subsection (11) or (12) above in the case of a document, the person to whom the notice is given either shall deliver the document to the inspector or make it available for inspection by an officer of the Board or shall—

(a) deliver to the inspector (or, where subsection (3) above applies, the Board) a copy (which is photographic or otherwise by way of facsimile) of any parts of the document which contain the information within subsection (11) or (12), and
(b) if so required by the inspector (or, as the case may be, the Board), make available for inspection by a named officer of the Board such parts of the document as contain that information;

and failure to comply with any requirement under paragraph (b) above shall constitute a failure to comply with the notice."

(8) This section shall apply with respect to notices given on or after the day on which this Act is passed.

145. Falsification etc. of documents

(1) After section 20B of the Taxes Management Act 1970 there shall be inserted—

"20BB. Falsification etc. of documents

(1) Subject to subsections (2) to (4) below, a person shall be guilty of an offence if he intentionally falsifies, conceals, destroys or otherwise disposes of, or causes or permits the falsification, concealment, destruction or disposal of, a document which—

(a) he has been required by a notice under section 20 or 20A above, or
(b) he has been given an opportunity in accordance with section 20B(1) above,

to deliver, or to deliver or make available for inspection.

(2) A person does not commit an offence under subsection (1) above if he acts—

(a) with the written permission of a General or Special Commissioner, the inspector or an officer of the Board,
(b) after the document has been delivered or, in a case within section 20(3) or (8A) above, inspected, or
(c) after a copy has been delivered in accordance with section 20B(4) or (14) above and the original has been inspected.

(3) A person does not commit an offence under subsection (1)(a) above if he acts after the end of the period of two years beginning with the date on which the notice is given, unless before the end of that period the inspector or an officer of the Board has notified the person in writing that the notice has not been complied with to his satisfaction.

(4) A person does not commit an offence under subsection (1)(*b*) above if he acts—

(*a*) after the end of the period of six months beginning with the date on which an opportunity to deliver the document was given, or
(*b*) after an application for consent to a notice being given in relation to the document has been refused.

(5) A person guilty of an offence under subsection (1) above shall be liable—

(*a*) on summary conviction, to a fine not exceeding the statutory maximum;
(*b*) on conviction on indictment, to imprisonment for a term not exceeding two years or to a fine or to both."

(2) This section shall apply to any falsification, concealment, destruction or disposal of a document occurring on or after the day on which this Act is passed.

146. Entry with warrant to obtain documents

(1) Section 20C of the Taxes Management Act 1970 (entry with warrant to obtain documents) shall be amended as follows.

(2) In subsection (1)—

(*a*) for the words "any form of fraud" there shall be substituted the words "serious fraud", and
(*b*) for the words "has been" there shall be substituted the words "is being, has been or is about to be".

(3) After that subsection there shall be inserted—

"(1A) Without prejudice to the generality of the concept of serious fraud—

(*a*) any offence which involves fraud is for the purposes of this section an offence involving serious fraud if its commission had led, or is intended or likely to lead, either to substantial financial gain to any person or to serious prejudice to the proper assessment or collection of tax; and
(*b*) an offence which, if considered alone, would not be regarded as involving serious fraud may nevertheless be so regarded if there is reasonable ground for suspecting that it forms part of a course of conduct which is, or but for its detection would be, likely to result in serious prejudice to the proper assessment or collection of tax.

(1B) The powers conferred by a warrant under this section shall not be exercisable—

(*a*) by more than such number of officers of the Board as may be specified in the warrant;
(*b*) outside such times of day as may be so specified;
(*c*) if the warrant so provides, otherwise than in the presence of a constable in uniform."

(4) For subsections (3) to (5) there shall be substituted—

"(3) An officer who enters the premises under the authority of a warrant under this section may—

(*a*) take with him such other persons as appear to him to be necessary;
(*b*) seize and remove any things whatsoever found there which he has reasonable cause to believe may be required as evidence for the purposes of proceedings in respect of such an offence as is mentioned in subsection (1) above; and
(*c*) search or cause to be searched any person found on the premises whom he has reasonable cause to believe to be in possession of any such things;

but no person shall be searched except by a person of the same sex.

(4) Nothing in subsection (3) above authorises the seizure and removal of documents in the possession of a barrister, advocate or solicitor with respect to which a claim to professional privilege could be maintained.

(5) An officer of the Board seeking to exercise the powers conferred by a warrant under this section or, if there is more than one such officer, that one of them who is in charge of the search—

(*a*) if the occupier of the premises concerned is present at the time the search is to begin, shall supply a copy of the warrant endorsed with his name to the occupier;
(*b*) if at that time the occupier is not present but a person who appears to the officer to be in charge of the premises is present, shall supply such a copy to that person; and

(c) if neither paragraph (a) nor paragraph (b) above applies, shall leave such a copy in a prominent place on the premises.

(6) Where entry to premises has been made with a warrant under this section, and the officer making the entry has seized any things under the authority of the warrant, he shall endorse on or attach to the warrant a list of the things seized.

(7) Subsections (10) to (12) of section 16 of the Police and Criminal Evidence Act 1984 (return, retention and inspection of warrants) apply to a warrant under this section (together with any list endorsed on or attached to it under subsection (6) above) as they apply to a warrant issued to a constable under any enactment.

(8) Subsection (7) above extends to England and Wales only."

(5) This section shall apply with respect to warrants issued on or after the day on which this Act is passed.

147. Procedure where documents etc. are removed

(1) The following section shall be inserted after section 20C of the Taxes Management Act 1970—

"20CC. Procedure where documents etc. are removed

(1) An officer of the Board who removes anything in the exercise of the power conferred by section 20C above shall, if so requested by a person showing himself—

   (a) to be the occupier of premises from which it was removed, or
   (b) to have had custody or control of it immediately before the removal,

provide that person with a record of what he removed.

(2) The officer of the Board shall provide the record within a reasonable time from the making of the request for it.

(3) Where anything which has been removed by an officer of the Board as mentioned in subsection (1) above is of such a nature that a photograph or copy of it would be sufficient—

   (a) for use as evidence at a trial for an offence, or
   (b) for forensic examination or for investigation in connection with an offence,

it shall not be retained longer than is necessary to establish that fact and to obtain the photograph or copy.

(4) Subject to subsection (8) below, if a request for permission to be granted access to anything which—

   (a) has been removed by an officer of the Board, and
   (b) is retained by the Board for the purpose of investigating an offence,

is made to the officer in overall charge of the investigation by a person who had custody or control of the thing immediately before it was so removed or by someone acting on behalf of any such person, the officer shall allow the person who made the request access to it under the supervision of an officer of the Board.

(5) Subject to subsection (8) below, if a request for a photograph or copy of any such thing is made to the officer in overall charge of the investigation by a person who had custody or control of the thing immediately before it was so removed, or by someone acting on behalf of any such person, the officer shall—

   (a) allow the person who made the request access to it under the supervision of an officer of the Board for the purpose of photographing it or copying it, or
   (b) photograph or copy it, or cause it to be photographed or copied.

(6) Where anything is photographed or copied under subsection (5)(b) above the photograph or copy shall be supplied to the person who made the request.

(7) The photograph or copy shall be supplied within a reasonable time from the making of the request.

(8) There is no duty under this section to grant access to, or to supply a photograph or copy of, anything if the officer in overall charge of the investigation for the purposes of which it was removed has reasonable grounds for believing that to do so would prejudice—

   (a) that investigation;

(b) the investigation of an offence other than the offence for the purposes of the investigation of which the thing was removed; or

(c) any criminal proceedings which may be brought as a result of—

(i) the investigation of which he is in charge, or
(ii) any such investigation as is mentioned in paragraph (b) above.

(9) Any reference in this section to the officer in overall charge of the investigation is a reference to the person whose name and address are endorsed on the warrant concerned as being the officer so in charge."

(2) This section shall apply with respect to warrants issued on or after the day on which this Act is passed.

148. Interpretation

(1) Section 20D of the Taxes Management Act 1970 shall be amended as follows.

(2) In subsection (2), for the words "of returns or accounts to be made or delivered by the other" there shall be substituted the words "or delivery of any information, return, accounts or other document which he knows will be, or is or are likely to be, used".

(3) For subsection (3) there shall be substituted—

"(3) Without prejudice to section 127 of the Finance Act 1988, in sections 20 to 20CC above "document" has, subject to sections 20(8C) and 20A(1A), the same meaning as it has—

(a) in relation to England and Wales, in Part I of the Civil Evidence Act 1968,
(b) in relation to Scotland, in Part III of the Law Reform (Miscellaneous Provisions) (Scotland) Act 1968, and
(c) in relation to Northern Ireland, in Part I of the Civil Evidence Act (Northern Ireland) 1971."

(4) Subsection (3) above shall not affect the meaning of "business" in sections 20 and 20C of the Taxes Management Act 1970 before the coming into force of sections 142 and 146 above.

Assessments, claims etc.

149. Assessments founded on fraudulent or negligent conduct

(1) The following section shall be substituted for section 36 of the Taxes Management Act 1970—

"36. Fraudulent or negligent conduct

(1) An assessment on any person (in this section referred to as "the person in default") for the purpose of making good to the Crown a loss of tax attributable to his fraudulent or negligent conduct or the fraudulent or negligent conduct of a person acting on his behalf may be made at any time not later than twenty years after the end of the chargeable period to which the assessment relates.

(2) Where the person in default is an individual who carried on a trade or profession in partnership with another individual, or with other persons at least one of whom is an individual, at any time in the year for which the assessment is made, an assessment in respect of the profits or gains of the trade or profession for the purpose mentioned in subsection (1) above may be made not only on the person in default but also on his partner or, as the case may be, on any of his partners who is an individual.

(3) If the person on whom the assessment is made so requires, in determining the amount of the tax to be charged for any chargeable period in any assessment made for the purpose mentioned in subsection (1) above, effect shall be given to any relief or allowance to which he would have been entitled for that chargeable period on a claim or application made within the time allowed by the Taxes Acts."

(2) Sections 37 to 39 (special provisions as to "neglect") and section 41 (leave required for certain assessments) of the Taxes Management Act 1970 shall cease to have effect.

(3) The words "section 36" shall be substituted—

(a) for the words "sections 36, 37 and 39" in section 30(6) of the Taxes Management Act 1970 (tax repaid in error etc.),

(b) for the words "sections 37 to 39" in section 118(3) of that Act (effect under law of Scotland of assessment in partnership name),
(c) for the words "sections 36 and 39" in paragraph 10(1) of Schedule 13 to the Taxes Act 1988 (assessments to advance corporation tax), and
(d) for the words "sections 36 and 37" in paragraph 10(1) of Schedule 16 to that Act (assessments to income tax on company payments which are not distributions).

(4) The words "fraudulent or negligent conduct" shall be substituted—

(a) for the words "fraud, wilful default or neglect" in—

(i) section 37A of the Taxes Management Act 1970 (married couples),
(ii) section 40(2) of that Act (assessment on personal representatives), and
(iii) paragraph 9 of Schedule 16A to the Finance Act 1973 and of Schedule 19A to the Taxes Act 1988 (Lloyd's), and

(b) for the words "fraud and wilful default) and section 37 of that Act (neglect" in section 307(5) of the Taxes Act 1988 (assessments for withdrawing relief under Chapter III of Part VII of that Act).

(5) In section 105 of the Taxes Management Act 1970 (admissibility of evidence), for the words "fraud or default" and the words "fraud or wilful default" there shall be substituted the words "fraudulent conduct".

(6) In paragraph 9 of Schedule 16A to the Finance Act 1973 and of Schedule 19A to the Taxes Act 1988, for "37, 40 and 41" there shall be substituted "and 40".

(7) Nothing in this section shall affect the making of assessments—

(a) for years of assessment before the year 1983-84, or
(b) for accounting periods which ended before 1st April 1983.

150. Further assessments: claims etc.

(1) The following sections shall be inserted after section 43 of the Taxes Management Act 1970—

"**43A. Further assessments: claims etc.**

(1) This section applies where—

(a) by virtue of section 29(3) of this Act an assessment is made on any person for a chargeable period, and
(b) the assessment is not made for the purpose of making good to the Crown any loss of tax attributable to his fraudulent or negligent conduct or the fraudulent or negligent conduct of a person acting on his behalf.

(2) Without prejudice to section 43(2) above but subject to section 43B below, where this section applies—

(a) any relevant claim, election, application or notice which could have been made or given within the time allowed by the Taxes Acts may be made or given at any time within one year from the end of the chargeable period in which the assessment is made, and
(b) any relevant claim, election, application or notice previously made or given may at any such time be revoked or varied—

(i) in the same manner as it was made or given, and
(ii) by or with the consent of the same person or persons who made, gave or consented to it (or, in the case of any such person who has died, by or with the consent of his personal representatives),

except where by virtue of any enactment it is irrevocable.

(3) For the purposes of this section and section 43B below, a claim, election, application or notice is relevant in relation to an assessment for a chargeable period if—

(a) it relates to that chargeable period or is made or given by reference to an event occurring in that chargeable period, and
(b) it or, as the case may be, its revocation or variation has or could have the effect of reducing any of the liabilities mentioned in subsection (4) below.

(4) The liabilities referred to in subsection (3) above are—

(a) the increased liability to tax resulting from the assessment,
(b) any other liability to tax of the person concerned for—

(i) the chargeable period to which the assessment relates, or
(ii) any chargeable period which follows that chargeable period and ends not later than one year after the end of the chargeable period in which the assessment is made.

(5) Where a claim, election, application or notice is made, given, revoked or varied by virtue of subsection (2) above, all such adjustments shall be made, whether by way of discharge or repayment of tax or the making of assessments or otherwise, as are required to take account of the effect of the taking of that action on any person's liability to tax for any chargeable period.

(6) The provisions of this Act relating to appeals against decisions on claims shall apply with any necessary modifications to a decision on the revocation or variation of a claim by virtue of subsection (2) above.

43B. Limits on application of section 43A

(1) If the effect of the exercise by any person of a power conferred by section 43A(2) above—

(*a*) to make or give a claim, election, application or notice, or
(*b*) to revoke or vary a claim, election, application or notice previously made or given,

would be to alter the liability to tax of another person, that power may not be exercised except with the consent in writing of that other person or, where he has died, his personal representatives.

(2) Where—

(*a*) a power conferred by subsection (2) of section 43A above is exercised in consequence of an assessment made on a person, and
(*b*) the exercise of the power increases the liability to tax of another person,

that section shall not apply by reason of any assessment made because of that increased liability.

(3) In any case where—

(*a*) one or more relevant claims, elections, applications or notices are made, given, revoked or varied by virtue of the application of section 43A above in the case of an assessment, and
(*b*) the total of the reductions in liability to tax which, apart from this subsection, would result from the action mentioned in paragraph (*a*) above would exceed the additional liability to tax resulting from the assessment,

the excess shall not be available to reduce any liability to tax.

(4) Where subsection (3) above has the effect of limiting either the reduction in a person's liability to tax for more than one period or the reduction in the liability to tax of more than one person, the limited amount shall be apportioned between the periods or persons concerned—

(*a*) except where paragraph (*b*) below applies, in such manner as may be specified by the inspector by notice in writing to the person or persons concerned, or
(*b*) where the person concerned gives (or the persons concerned jointly give) notice in writing to the inspector within the relevant period, in such manner as may be specified in the notice given by the person or persons concerned.

(5) For the purposes of paragraph (*b*) of subsection (4) above the relevant period is the period of 30 days beginning with the day on which notice under paragraph (*a*) of that subsection is given to the person concerned or, where more than one person is concerned, the latest date on which such notice is given to any of them."

(2) This section shall apply in relation to any assessment notice of which is issued on or after the day on which this Act is passed.

151. Assessment of trustees etc.

(1) Income tax chargeable in respect of income arising to the trustees of a settlement, or to the personal representatives of a deceased person, may be assessed and charged on and in the name of any one or more of the relevant trustees or, as the case may be, the relevant personal representatives.

(2) In this section "the relevant trustees", in relation to any income, means the trustees to

whom the income arises and any subsequent trustees of the settlement, and "the relevant personal representatives" has a corresponding meaning.

(3) In this section "personal representatives" has the same meaning as in section 111 of this Act.

(4) This section shall be deemed always to have had effect.

Distress and poinding etc.

152. Distress for non-payment of tax

(1) Section 61 of the Taxes Management Act 1970 (distress) shall be amended as follows.

(2) In subsection (1), for the words "the collector shall" onwards there shall be substituted the words "the collector may distrain upon the goods and chattels of the person charged (in this section referred to as "the person in default")."

(3) In subsection (2), for the words from "a collector" to "Commissioners" there shall be substituted the words "a justice of the peace, on being satisfied by information on oath that there is reasonable ground for believing that a person is neglecting or refusing to pay a sum charged, may issue a warrant in writing authorising a collector to".

(4) In subsection (4), for the words "neglecting or refusing to pay" there shall be substituted the words "in default".

(5) In subsection (5)—

    (*a*) for the word "aforesaid" there shall be substituted the words "in default",
    (*b*) the words "within the said five days" shall be omitted,
    (*c*) for the words from "two or more inhabitants of the parish" to "sufficient persons" there shall be substituted the words "one or more independent persons appointed by the collector", and
    (*d*) the words from "The costs" to "the collector, and" shall be omitted.

(6) The following subsection shall be added after that subsection—

"(6) The Treasury may by regulations make provision with respect to—

    (*a*) the fees chargeable on or in connection with the levying of distress, and
    (*b*) the costs and charges recoverable where distress has been levied;

and any such regulations shall be made by statutory instrument which shall be subject to annulment in pursuance of a resolution of the House of Commons."

(7) This section shall come into force on such day as the Treasury may by order made by statutory instrument appoint.

153. Priority in cases of distraint by others

(1) Section 62 of the Taxes Management Act 1970 (priority of claim for tax) shall be amended as follows.

(2) In subsection (1)—

    (*a*) for the words from the beginning to "shall be" there shall be substituted the words "If at any time at which any goods or chattels belonging to any person (in this section referred to as "the person in default") are",
    (*b*) for the word "unless" there shall be substituted the words "the person in default is in arrears in respect of any such sums as are referred to in subsection (1A) below, the goods or chattels may not be so taken unless on demand made by the collector", and
    (*c*) for the words "arrears of tax" onwards there shall be substituted the words "such sums as have fallen due at or before the date of seizure."

(3) The following subsection shall be inserted after that subsection—

"(1A) The sums referred to in subsection (1) above are—

    (*a*) sums due from the person in default on account of deductions of income tax from emoluments paid during the period of twelve months next before the date of seizure, being deductions which the person in default was liable to make under section 203 of the principal Act (pay as you earn) less the amount of the repayments of income tax which he was liable to make during that period; and
    (*b*) sums due from the person in default in respect of deductions required to be made

by him for that period under section 559 of the principal Act (sub-contractors in the construction industry)."

(4) In subsection (2)—

(*a*) for the words from the beginning to "the collector shall" there shall be substituted the words "If the sums referred to in subsection (1) above are not paid within ten days of the date of the demand referred to in that subsection, the collector may",
(*b*) for the words "shall proceed" there shall be substituted the words "may proceed", and
(*c*) for the words "the tax charged and claimed" there shall be substituted the words "those sums".

154. Recovery of tax from debtor in Scotland

(1) Section 63 of the Taxes Management Act 1970 (recovery of tax in Scotland) shall be amended as follows.

(2) In subsection (3), for the words "which relates to" onwards there shall be substituted the words "insofar as it relates to sums due in respect of—

(*a*) deductions of income tax which any person specified in the application was liable to make under section 203 of the principal Act (pay as you earn); or
(*b*) deductions required to be made under section 559 of the principal Act (sub-contractors in the construction industry) by any person specified in the application."

(3) The following subsection shall be added after that subsection—

"(4) In this section references to amounts of tax due and references to sums due in respect of deductions include references to amounts which are deemed to be—

(*a*) amounts of tax which the person is liable to pay by virtue of the Income Tax (Employments) Regulations 1973; or
(*b*) amounts which the person is liable to pay by virtue of the Income Tax (Sub-Contractors in the Construction Industry) Regulations 1975."

155. Priority in cases of poinding etc. by others in Scotland

(1) Section 64 of the Taxes Management Act 1970 (priority of claim for tax in Scotland) shall be amended as follows.

(2) In subsection (1)—

(*a*) for the words from the beginning to "shall be" there shall be substituted the words "If at any time at which any moveable goods and effects belonging to any person (in this section referred to as "the person in default") are",
(*b*) for the word "unless" there shall be substituted the words "the person in default is in arrears in respect of any such sums as are referred to in subsection (1A) below, the goods and effects may not be so taken unless on demand made by the collector", and
(*c*) for the words "the tax so in arrear" onwards there shall be substituted the words "such sums as have fallen due at or before the date of poinding or, as the case may be, other diligence or assignation."

(3) The following subsection shall be inserted after that subsection—

"(1A) The sums referred to in subsection (1) above are—

(*a*) sums due from the person in default on account of deductions of income tax from emoluments paid during the period of twelve months next before the date of poinding, being deductions which the person in default was liable to make under section 203 of the principal Act (pay as you earn) less the amount of the repayments of income tax which he was liable to make during that period; and
(*b*) sums due from the person in default in respect of deductions required to be made by him for that period under section 559 of the principal Act (sub-contractors in the construction industry)."

(4) In subsection (2)—

(*a*) for the words from the beginning to "the tax claimed shall" there shall be substituted the words "If the sums referred to in subsection (1) above are not paid within ten days of the date of the demand referred to in that subsection, the sums shall", and
(*b*) for the words "proceeding at his instance" there shall be substituted the word "proceedings".

Interest etc.

156. Interest on overdue tax

(1) In section 86 of the Taxes Management Act 1970, for subsection (3) and the words in subsection (4) preceding the Table there shall be substituted—

"(3) For the purposes of this section—

(*a*) the reckonable date in relation to any tax charged by an assessment to income tax under Schedule E, and
(*b*) subject to subsection (3A) below, the reckonable date in relation to tax charged by any other assessment to which this section applies,

is the date on which the tax becomes due and payable.

(3A) Where an appeal has been made against an assessment and any of the tax charged by the assessment is due and payable on a date later than the date given by the Table in subsection (4) below, the reckonable date in relation to the tax so due and payable is the later of—

(*a*) the date given by that Table, and
(*b*) the date on which the tax would have been due and payable if there had been no appeal against the assessment (assuming in a case where the tax would not have been charged by the assessment if there had been no appeal that it was so charged).

(4) The Table referred to in subsection (3A) above is as follows—".

(2) In section 55 of that Act—

(*a*) in subsection (2), for the words "it were" onwards there shall be substituted the words "there had been no appeal.",
(*b*) in subsection (6), for paragraphs (*a*) and (*b*) there shall be substituted—

"(*a*) in the case of a determination made on an application under subsection (3) above, other than an application made by virtue of subsection (3A) above, the date on which any tax the payment of which is not so postponed is due and payable shall be determined as if the tax were charged by an assessment notice of which was issued on the date of that determination and against which there had been no appeal; and
(*b*) in the case of a determination made on an application under subsection (4) above—

(i) the date on which any tax the payment of which ceases to be so postponed is due and payable shall be determined as if the tax were charged by an assessment notice of which was issued on the date of that determination and against which there had been no appeal; and
(ii) any tax overpaid shall be repaid.", and

(*c*) for subsection (9) there shall be substituted—

"(9) On the determination of the appeal—

(*a*) the date on which any tax payable in accordance with that determination is due and payable shall, so far as it is tax the payment of which had been postponed, or which would not have been charged by the assessment if there had been no appeal, be determined as if the tax were charged by an assessment—

(i) notice of which was issued on the date on which the inspector issues to the appellant a notice of the total amount payable in accordance with the determination, and
(ii) against which there had been no appeal; and

(*b*) any tax overpaid shall be repaid."

(3) In section 56(9) of that Act, for the words "amount of" there shall be substituted the words "amount charged by".

(4) This section shall apply to tax charged by any assessment notice of which is issued after 30th July 1982.

157. Effect of certain claims on interest

(1) In relation to any tax charged by an assessment made under section 252(1) of the Taxes Act 1988 to recover corporation tax that becomes payable as a result of the making of a claim under section 240 of that Act, the reckonable date for the purposes of section 86 of the

Taxes Management Act 1970 (in this section referred to as "section 86") is the date which is given by paragraph 5 of the Table in subsection (4) of that section.

(2) Subsections (3) and (4) below apply in any case where—

(a) there is in any accounting period of a company (in this section referred to as "the later period") an amount of surplus advance corporation tax, as defined in subsection (3) of section 239 of the Taxes Act 1988, and

(b) pursuant to a claim under the said subsection (3), the whole or any part of that amount is treated for the purposes of the said section 239 as discharging liability for an amount of corporation tax for an earlier accounting period (in this section referred to as "the earlier period"), and

(c) if the claim under the said subsection (3) had not been made—

(i) an amount of corporation tax assessed for the earlier period would carry interest in accordance with section 86, or
(ii) an assessment could have been made under section 252(1) of that Act to recover corporation tax for the earlier period.

(3) In determining the amount of interest payable under section 86 on corporation tax unpaid for the earlier period, no account shall be taken of any reduction in the amount of that tax which results from section 239(3) of the Taxes Act 1988 except so far as concerns interest for any time after the day following the expiry of nine months from the end of the later period.

(4) Where, but for the claim under section 239(3) of the Taxes Act 1988, an assessment could have been made under section 252(1) of that Act to recover corporation tax for the earlier period, interest under section 86 shall be chargeable, in relation to any time not later than the day referred to in subsection (3) above, as if the claim had not been made and such an assessment had been made.

(5) In relation to interest charged under section 86 by virtue of subsection (4) above, section 69 of the Taxes Management Act 1970 shall have effect with the substitution for the words following paragraph (c) of the words "as if it were tax charged and due and payable under an assessment".

(6) In this section—

(a) subsection (1) above shall have effect where the claim under section 240 of the Taxes Act 1988 is made on or after 14th March 1989, and
(b) subsections (2) to (5) above shall have effect where the claim under section 239(3) of that Act is made on or after that date,

but this section shall not have effect in relation to corporation tax for any accounting period ending after the day which is the appointed day for the purposes of section 85 of the Finance (No. 2) Act 1987.

158. Small amounts of interest

(1) In the Taxes Management Act 1970—

(a) section 86(6) (remission of interest payable on overdue income tax, capital gains tax or corporation tax where interest would not exceed £30), and
(b) section 87(4) (no interest payable on overdue advance corporation tax or income tax on company payments where interest would not exceed £30),

shall cease to have effect.

(2) The words "of not less than £25" in—

(a) section 47(1) of the Finance (No. 2) Act 1975 (no repayment supplement where overdue repayment of capital gains tax less than £25), and
(b) section 824(1)(a) and (b) and (5) of the Taxes Act 1988 (no repayment supplement where overdue repayment of income tax etc. less than £25),

and the words "of not less than £100" in section 825(2) of the Taxes Act 1988 (no repayment supplement where overdue repayment of company tax less than £100) shall cease to have effect.

(3) Paragraph (a) of subsection (1) above shall have effect—

(a) in relation to income tax under Schedule E, where the demand for the tax is made on or after the appointed day, and

(b) in any other case, where the tax is charged by an assessment notice of which is issued on or after the appointed day.

(4) Paragraph (b) of that subsection shall have effect where the tax is charged by an assessment relating to an accounting period beginning on or after the appointed day.

(5) Subsection (2) above shall have effect in relation to repayments of tax made on or after the appointed day.

(6) In this section "the appointed day" means such day as the Treasury may by order made by statutory instrument appoint; and different days may be appointed for different enactments or for different purposes of the same enactment.

159. Interest on tax in case of failure or error

(1) Section 88 of the Taxes Management Act 1970 (interest on tax recovered to make good loss due to taxpayer's fault) shall be amended as follows.

(2) In subsection (1), for the words "the fraud, wilful default or neglect of any person" there shall be substituted the words—

"(a) a failure to give a notice, make a return or produce or furnish a document or other information required by or under the Taxes Acts, or
(b) an error in any information, return, accounts or other document delivered to an inspector or other officer of the Board,"

(3) The following subsection shall be added at the end—

"(7) In paragraph (a) of subsection (1) above the reference to a failure to do something includes, in relation to anything required to be done at a particular time or within a particular period, a reference to a failure to do it at that time or within that period; and, accordingly, section 118(2) of this Act shall not apply for the purposes of that paragraph."

(4) This section shall have effect in relation to failures occurring, and errors in any information or documents delivered, on or after the day on which this Act is passed.

160. Determinations under TMA s. 88

(1) In subsection (1) of section 88 of the Taxes Management Act 1970, for the words "shall carry" there shall be substituted the words "shall, if an inspector or the Board so determine, carry".

(2) The following section shall be inserted after that section—

"88A. Determinations under section 88

(1) Notice of a determination under section 88 above shall be served on the person liable to pay the interest to which it relates and shall specify—

(a) the date on which it is issued,
(b) the amount of the tax which carries interest and the assessment by which that tax was charged,
(c) the date when for the purposes of section 88 above that tax ought to have been paid, and
(d) the time within which an appeal against the determination may be made.

(2) After the notice of a determination under section 88 above has been served the determination shall not be altered except in accordance with this section.

(3) A determination under section 88 above may be made at any time—

(a) within six years after the end of the chargeable period for which the tax carrying the interest is charged (or, in the case of development land tax, of the financial year in which the liability for that tax arose), or
(b) within three years after the date of the final determination of the amount of that tax.

(4) An appeal may be brought against a determination under section 88 above and, subject to the following provisions of this section, the provisions of this Act relating to appeals shall have effect in relation to an appeal against such a determination as they have effect in relation to an appeal against an assessment to tax.

(5) On an appeal against a determination under section 88 above section 50(6) to (8) of this Act shall not apply but the Commissioners may—

(a) if it appears to them that the tax carries no interest under that section, set the determination aside,
(b) if the determination appears to them to be correct, confirm the determination, or
(c) if the determination appears to them to be incorrect as to the amount of tax or the date on which the tax ought to have been paid, revise the determination accordingly."

(3) In section 70 (certificates) of the Taxes Management Act 1970, for subsection (3) there shall be substituted—

"(3) A certificate of the inspector or any other officer of the Board that it has been determined that tax carries interest under section 88 of this Act, together with a certificate of the collector that payment of the interest has not been made to him, or, to the best of his knowledge and belief, to any other collector, or to any person acting on his behalf or on behalf of another collector, shall be sufficient evidence—

(a) that interest is chargeable on the tax from the date when for the purposes of section 88 of this Act the tax ought to have been paid, and
(b) that the sum mentioned in the certificate is unpaid and is due to the Crown;

and any document purporting to be such a certificate as is mentioned in this subsection shall be deemed to be such a certificate unless the contrary is proved."

(4) In section 113 of that Act (form of documents), the following subsection shall be inserted after subsection (1B)—

"(1C) Where an officer of the Board has decided that an amount of tax carries interest under section 88 of this Act and has taken the decisions needed for arriving at the date when for the purposes of that section that tax ought to have been paid, he may entrust to any other officer of the Board responsibility for completing the determination procedure, whether by means involving the use of a computer or otherwise, including responsibility for serving notice of the determination on the person liable to the interest."

(5) In section 114 of that Act (want of form not to invalidate), after the word "assessment", in each place where it occurs, there shall be inserted the words "or determination".

(6) In paragraph 5 of Schedule 3 to that Act (rules for assigning proceedings to Commissioners), the following entry shall be inserted in the first column after the entry relating to an appeal against an assessment to capital gains tax—

"An appeal against a determination under section 88 of this Act."

161. Tax carrying interest under TMA ss. 86 and 88

The following subsection shall be substituted for section 88(3) of the Taxes Management Act 1970—

"(3) Where it is finally determined that any tax carries interest under this section, the tax shall carry no interest under section 86 or 86A above (and, accordingly, any interest under either of those sections which has been paid before the final determination shall be set off against the amount of the interest under this section); and for the purposes of this subsection a determination that tax carries interest is not final until it can no longer be varied, whether by any Commissioners on appeal or by the order of any court."

Penalties

162. Failure to make return

(1) Section 93 of the Taxes Management Act 1970 (failure to comply with notice to make return for income tax or capital gains tax) shall be amended as follows.

(2) In subsection (1) (initial and daily penalties), for paragraphs (a) and (b) there shall be substituted—

"(a) to a penalty not exceeding £300, and
(b) if the failure continues after a penalty is imposed under paragraph (a) above, to a further penalty or penalties not exceeding £60 for each day on which the failure continues after the day on which the penalty under paragraph (a) above was imposed (but excluding any day for which a penalty under this paragraph has already been imposed)."

(3) The following subsection shall be substituted for subsection (2)—

"(2) If a failure by a person to comply with a notice such as is referred to in subsection (1) above continues after the end of the year of assessment following that during which it was served then, without prejudice to any penalty under subsection (1) above, he shall be liable to a penalty of an amount not exceeding so much of the tax with which he is charged (whether for one or for more than one year of assessment) in assessments—

(a) based wholly or partly on any income or chargeable gains that ought to have been included in the return required by the notice, and
(b) made after the end of the year next following the year of assessment in which the notice was served,

as is attributable to the income or chargeable gains that ought to have been so included."

(4) The following subsection shall be substituted for subsection (5)—

"(5) No penalty shall be imposed under subsection (1) above in respect of a failure at any time after the failure has been remedied."

(5) The following subsection shall be substituted for subsection (7)—

"(7) If the person on whom a notice is served proves that there was no income or chargeable gain to be included in the return, the penalty under this section shall not exceed £100."

(6) This section shall apply in relation to any failure to comply with a notice served on or after 6th April 1989.

163. Incorrect return, accounts etc.

(1) In—

(a) section 95(1) of the Taxes Management Act 1970 (incorrect return etc. for income tax or capital gains tax), and
(b) section 96(1) of that Act (incorrect return etc. for corporation tax),

for the words "the aggregate" onwards there shall be substituted the words "the amount of the difference specified in subsection (2) below."

(2) This section shall apply in relation to returns, statements, declarations or accounts delivered, made or submitted on or after the day on which this Act is passed.

164. Special returns, information etc.

(1) Section 98 of the Taxes Management Act 1970 (special returns, information etc.) shall be amended as follows.

(2) In subsection (1) (initial and daily penalties)—

(a) for the word "Where" there shall be substituted the words "Subject to section 98A below, where", and
(b) for the words "subsection (3)" onwards there shall be substituted the words "subsections (3) and (4) below—

(i) to a penalty not exceeding £300, and
(ii) if the failure continues after a penalty is imposed under paragraph (i) above, to a further penalty or penalties not exceeding £60 for each day on which the failure continues after the day on which the penalty under paragraph (i) above was imposed (but excluding any day for which a penalty under this paragraph has already been imposed)."

(3) In subsection (2) (maximum penalty for information given fraudulently or negligently)—

(a) for the word "Where" there shall be substituted the words "Subject to section 98A below, where", and
(b) for the words "£250, or, in the case of fraud, £500" there shall be substituted "£3,000".

(4) The following subsections shall be substituted for subsection (3)—

"(3) No penalty shall be imposed under subsection (1) above in respect of a failure within paragraph (a) of that subsection at any time after the failure has been remedied.

(4) No penalty shall be imposed under paragraph (ii) of subsection (1) above in respect of a failure within paragraph (b) of that subsection at any time after the failure has been remedied."

(5) In the Table—

(a) in the first column, in the entry relating to Part III of the Taxes Management Act 1970, the words ", except sections 16 and 24(2)" shall be omitted;

(b) the entries relating to sections 38(5) and 42 of the Taxes Act 1988 shall be moved from the second column to the appropriate place in the first column; and

(c) the entry relating to section 481(5)(k) of that Act shall be omitted from the first column and an entry relating to section 482(2) of that Act shall be inserted at the appropriate place in the second column.

(6) In consequence of the amendment made by subsection (5)(a) above section 16(6) of the Taxes Management Act 1970 shall cease to have effect.

(7) This section shall apply in relation to—

(a) any failure to comply with a notice or to furnish information, give a certificate or produce a document or record beginning on or after the day on which this Act is passed, and

(b) the furnishing, giving, producing or making of any incorrect information, certificate, document, record or declaration on or after that day.

165. Special penalties in the case of certain returns

(1) The following section shall be inserted after section 98 of the Taxes Management Act 1970—

"**98A. Special penalties in the case of certain returns**

(1) Regulations under section 203(2) (PAYE) or 566(1) (sub-contractors) of the principal Act may provide that this section shall apply in relation to any specified provision of the regulations.

(2) Where this section applies in relation to a provision of regulations, any person who fails to make a return in accordance with the provision shall be liable—

(a) to a penalty or penalties of the relevant monthly amount for each month (or part of a month) during which the failure continues, but excluding any month after the twelfth or for which a penalty under this paragraph has already been imposed, and

(b) if the failure continues beyond twelve months, without prejudice to any penalty under paragraph (a) above, to a penalty not exceeding so much of the amount payable by him in accordance with the regulations for the year of assessment to which the return relates as remained unpaid at the end of 19th April after the end of that year.

(3) For the purposes of subsection (2)(a) above, the relevant monthly amount in the case of a failure to make a return—

(a) where the number of persons in respect of whom particulars should be included in the return is fifty or less, is £100, and

(b) where that number is greater than fifty, is £100 for each fifty such persons and an additional £100 where that number is not a multiple of fifty.

(4) Where this section applies in relation to a provision of regulations, any person who fraudulently or negligently makes an incorrect return of a kind mentioned in the provision shall be liable to a penalty not exceeding the difference between—

(a) the amount payable by him in accordance with the regulations for the year of assessment to which the return relates, and

(b) the amount which would have been so payable if the return had been correct."

(2) In relation to a failure to make a return beginning before such day as the Treasury may by order made by statutory instrument appoint, section 98A(2) shall have effect with the substitution of the following paragraph for paragraph (a)—

"(a) to—

(i) a penalty not exceeding twelve times the relevant monthly amount, and
(ii) if the failure continues after a penalty is imposed under sub-paragraph (i) above, a further penalty or penalties of the relevant monthly amount for each month (or part of a month) during which the failure continues, but excluding any month after the twelfth or for which a penalty under this sub-paragraph has already been imposed,".

166. Assisting in preparation of incorrect return etc.

(1) The following section shall be substituted for section 99 of the Taxes Management Act 1970—

"**99. Assisting in preparation of incorrect return etc.**

Any person who assists in or induces the preparation or delivery of any information, return, accounts or other document which—

(*a*) he knows will be, or is or are likely to be, used for any purpose of tax, and
(*b*) he knows to be incorrect,

shall be liable to a penalty not exceeding £3,000."

(2) This section shall apply in relation to assistance and inducements occurring on or after the day on which this Act is passed.

167. Determination of penalties

The following sections shall be substituted for section 100 of the Taxes Management Act 1970—

"**100. Determination of penalties by officer of Board**

(1) Subject to subsection (2) below and except where proceedings for a penalty have been instituted under section 100D below or a penalty has been imposed by the Commissioners under section 53 of this Act, an officer of the Board authorised by the Board for the purposes of this section may make a determination imposing a penalty under any provision of the Taxes Acts and setting it at such amount as, in his opinion, is correct or appropriate.

(2) Subsection (1) above does not apply where the penalty is a penalty under—

(*a*) section 93(1) above as it has effect before the amendments made by section 162 of the Finance Act 1989 or section 93(1)(*a*) above as it has effect after those amendments,
(*b*) section 94(1) above as it has effect before the substitution made by section 83 of the Finance (No. 2) Act 1987,
(*c*) section 98(1) above as it has effect before the amendments made by section 164 of the Finance Act 1989 or section 98(1)(i) above as it has effect after those amendments, or
(*d*) paragraph (*a*)(i) of section 98A(2) above as it has effect by virtue of section 165(2) of the Finance Act 1989.

(3) Notice of a determination of a penalty under this section shall be served on the person liable to the penalty and shall state the date on which it is issued and the time within which an appeal against the determination may be made.

(4) After the notice of a determination under this section has been served the determination shall not be altered except in accordance with this section or on appeal.

(5) If it is discovered by an officer of the Board authorised by the Board for the purposes of this section that the amount of a penalty determined under this section is or has become insufficient the officer may make a determination in a further amount so that the penalty is set at the amount which, in his opinion, is correct or appropriate.

(6) In any case where—

(*a*) a determination under this section is of a penalty under section 94(6) above, and
(*b*) after the determination has been made it is discovered by an officer of the Board authorised by the Board for the purposes of this section that the amount which was taken into account as the relevant amount of tax is or has become excessive,

the determination shall be revised so that the penalty is set at the amount which is correct; and, where more than the correct amount has already been paid, the appropriate amount shall be repaid.

100A. Provisions supplementary to section 100

(1) Where a person who has incurred a penalty has died, a determination under section 100 above which could have been made in relation to him may be made in relation to his personal representatives, and any penalty imposed on personal representatives by virtue of this subsection shall be a debt due from and payable out of his estate.

(2) A penalty determined under section 100 above shall be due and payable at the end of the period of thirty days beginning with the date of the issue of the notice of determination.

(3) A penalty determined under section 100 above shall for all purposes be treated as if it were tax charged in an assessment and due and payable.

100B. Appeals against penalty determinations

(1) An appeal may be brought against the determination of a penalty under section 100 above and, subject to the following provisions of this section, the provisions of this Act relating to appeals shall have effect in relation to an appeal against such a determination as they have effect in relation to an appeal against an assessment to tax.

(2) On an appeal against the determination of a penalty under section 100 above section 50(6) to (8) of this Act shall not apply but—

(*a*) in the case of a penalty which is required to be of a particular amount, the Commissioners may—

(i) if it appears to them that no penalty has been incurred, set the determination aside,
(ii) if the amount determined appears to them to be correct, confirm the determination, or
(iii) if the amount determined appears to them to be incorrect, increase or reduce it to the correct amount,

(*b*) in the case of any other penalty, the Commissioners may—

(i) if it appears to them that no penalty has been incurred, set the determination aside,
(ii) if the amount determined appears to them to be appropriate, confirm the determination,
(iii) if the amount determined appears to them to be excessive, reduce it to such other amount (including nil) as they consider appropriate, or
(iv) if the amount determined appears to them to be insufficient, increase it to such amount not exceeding the permitted maximum as they consider appropriate.

(3) Without prejudice to section 56 of this Act, an appeal from a decision of the Commissioners against the amount of a penalty which has been determined under section 100 above or this section shall lie, at the instance of the person liable to the penalty, to the High Court or, in Scotland, to the Court of Session as the Court of Exchequer in Scotland; and on that appeal the court shall have the like jurisdiction as is conferred on the Commissioners by virtue of this section.

100C. Penalty proceedings before Commissioners

(1) An officer of the Board authorised by the Board for the purposes of this section may commence proceedings before the General or Special Commissioners for any penalty to which subsection (1) of section 100 above does not apply by virtue of subsection (2) of that section.

(2) Proceedings under this section shall be by way of information in writing, made to the Commissioners, and upon summons issued by them to the defendant (or defender) to appear before them at a time and place stated in the summons; and they shall hear and decide each case in a summary way.

(3) Any penalty determined by the Commissioners in proceedings under this section shall for all purposes be treated as if it were tax charged in an assessment and due and payable.

(4) An appeal against the determination of a penalty in proceedings under this section shall lie to the High Court or, in Scotland, the Court of Session as the Court of Exchequer in Scotland—

(*a*) by any party on a question of law, and
(*b*) by the defendant (or, in Scotland, the defender) against the amount of the penalty.

(5) On any such appeal the court may—

(*a*) if it appears that no penalty has been incurred, set the determination aside,
(*b*) if the amount determined appears to be appropriate, confirm the determination,
(*c*) if the amount determined appears to be excessive, reduce it to such other amount (including nil) as the court considers appropriate, or
(*d*) if the amount determined appears to be insufficient, increase it to such amount not exceeding the permitted maximum as the court considers appropriate.

100D. Penalty proceedings before court

(1) Where in the opinion of the Board the liability of any person for a penalty arises by reason of the fraud of that or any other person, proceedings for the penalty may be

instituted before the High Court or, in Scotland, the Court of Session as the Court of Exchequer in Scotland.

(2) Proceedings under this section which are not instituted (in England, Wales or Northern Ireland) under the Crown Proceedings Act 1947 by and in the name of the Board as an authorised department for the purposes of that Act shall be instituted—

(*a*) in England and Wales, in the name of the Attorney General,
(*b*) in Scotland, in the name of the Lord Advocate, and
(*c*) in Northern Ireland, in the name of the Attorney General for Northern Ireland.

(3) Any proceedings under this section instituted in England and Wales shall be deemed to be civil proceedings by the Crown within the meaning of Part II of the Crown Proceedings Act 1947 and any such proceedings instituted in Northern Ireland shall be deemed to be civil proceedings within the meaning of that Part of that Act as for the time being in force in Northern Ireland.

(4) If in proceedings under this section the court does not find that fraud is proved but consider that the person concerned is nevertheless liable to a penalty, the court may determine a penalty notwithstanding that, but for the opinion of the Board as to fraud, the penalty would not have been a matter for the court."

168. Amendments consequential on section 167

(1) In consequence of the amendment made by section 167 above the Taxes Management Act 1970 shall be amended in accordance with subsections (2) to (8) below.

(2) In section 20A (power to call for papers of tax accountant)—

(*a*) in subsection (1), for the words "awarded against him a penalty incurred by" there shall be substituted the words "a penalty imposed on",
(*b*) in subsection (2), for the word "award" in the first place where it occurs there shall be substituted the word "penalty" and for that word in the second place where it occurs there shall be substituted the word "imposition", and
(*c*) in subsection (4), for the words "award against" there shall be substituted the words "imposition on" and for the word "award" there shall be substituted the word "penalty".

(3) In section 53 (summary award of penalties by Commissioners)—

(*a*) in subsection (1), for the word "awarded" there shall be substituted the word "determined" and for the words "for its recovery" there shall be substituted the words "under section 100C of this Act",
(*b*) in subsection (2), for the words "award" and "decision" there shall be substituted the word "determination" and for the word "awarded" there shall be substituted the word "determined", and
(*c*) in subsection (3), for the word "awarded" there shall be substituted the word "determined".

(4) In section 102 (mitigation of penalties), for the words "recovery thereof" there shall be substituted the words "a penalty".

(5) In section 105 (evidence)—

(*a*) the following paragraph shall be substituted for paragraph (*a*) of subsection (1)—

"(*a*) pecuniary settlements may be accepted instead of a penalty being determined, or proceedings being instituted, in relation to any tax,",

(*b*) in paragraph (*b*) of subsection (2), for the words "sum" onwards there shall be substituted the words "tax due from him", and
(*c*) after that paragraph there shall be inserted the words "and

(*c*) any proceedings for a penalty or on appeal against the determination of a penalty."

(6) In section 112 (loss of documents etc.), the following subsection shall be added at the end—

"(3) The references in subsection (1) above to assessments to tax include references to determinations of penalties; and in its application to such determinations the proviso to that subsection shall have effect with the appropriate modifications."

(7) In section 113 (form of documents)—

(*a*) the following subsection shall be inserted after subsection (1C)—

"(1D) Where an officer of the Board has decided to impose a penalty under section 100 of this Act and has taken all other decisions needed for arriving at the amount of the penalty, he may entrust to any other officer of the Board responsibility for completing the determination procedure, whether by means involving the use of a computer or otherwise, including responsibility for serving notice of the determination on the person liable to the penalty.", and

(*b*) in subsection (3)—

(i) after the words "Every assessment," there shall be inserted the words "determination of a penalty,",
(ii) after the words "notice of assessment" there shall be inserted the words ", of determination", and
(iii) after the words "levying tax" there shall be inserted the words "or determining a penalty".

(8) In paragraph 5 of Schedule 3 (rules for assigning proceedings to Commissioners), for the words "section 100(4)" there shall be substituted the words "section 100C or an appeal under section 100B against the determination of a penalty".

(9) In section 41 of the Development Land Tax Act 1976 (administration of development land tax) the following subsection shall be inserted after subsection (1)—

"(1A) Nothing in sections 167 to 169 of the Finance Act 1989 shall apply to penalties relating to development land tax."

169. Time limits

(1) The following section shall be substituted for section 103 of the Taxes Management Act 1970—

"103. Time limits for penalties

(1) Subject to subsection (2) below, where the amount of a penalty is to be ascertained by reference to tax payable by a person for any period, the penalty may be determined by an officer of the Board, or proceedings for the penalty may be commenced before the Commissioners or a court—

(*a*) at any time within six years after the date on which the penalty was incurred, or
(*b*) at any later time within three years after the final determination of the amount of tax by reference to which the amount of the penalty is to be ascertained.

(2) Where the tax was payable by a person who has died, and the determination would be made in relation to his personal representatives, subsection (1)(*b*) above does not apply if the tax was charged in an assessment made later than six years after the end of the chargeable period for which it was charged.

(3) A penalty under section 99 of this Act may be determined by an officer of the Board, or proceedings for such a penalty may be commenced before a court, at any time within twenty years after the date on which the penalty was incurred.

(4) A penalty to which neither subsection (1) nor subsection (3) above applies may be so determined, or proceedings for such a penalty may be commenced before the Commissioners or a court, at any time within six years after the date on which the penalty was incurred or began to be incurred."

(2) The amendment made by subsection (1) above shall not affect the application of section 103(4) of the Taxes Management Act 1970 to proceedings under section 100 of that Act as it has effect before the amendment made by section 167 above.

170. Up-rating of certain penalties

(1) In section 23(8) of the Taxes Act 1988 (maximum penalty for agents failing to make certain payments on behalf of principals), for "£50" there shall be substituted "£300".

(2) In section 234(4) of that Act (penalty for failure to comply with provisions as to explanation of deduction from dividends etc.), for "£10" and "£100" there shall be substituted respectively "£60" and "£600".

(3) In section 306(6) of that Act (maximum penalty for false certificates or statements relating to investment in corporate trades), for the words "£250 or, in the case of fraud, £500" there shall be substituted "£3,000".

(4) In—

(*a*) section 619(7) of that Act (maximum penalty for false statements or representations relating to relief for qualifying premiums),
(*b*) section 653 of that Act (maximum penalty for statements or representations about personal pension schemes), and
(*c*) section 658(5) of that Act (maximum penalty for false statements or representations relating to purchased life annuities),

for "£500" there shall be substituted "£3,000".

(5) In paragraph 2(4) of Schedule 19A to that Act and Schedule 16A to the Finance Act 1973 (maximum penalty for incorrect return by Lloyd's agent), for the words "£500 in the case of fraud and £250 in the case of negligence" there shall be substituted "£3,000".

(6) This section shall apply in relation to things done or omitted on or after the day on which this Act is passed.

PART III

MISCELLANEOUS AND GENERAL

Inheritance tax

Interest etc.

178. Setting of rates of interest

(1) The rate of interest applicable for the purposes of an enactment to which this section applies shall be the rate which for the purposes of that enactment is provided for by regulations made by the Treasury under this section.

(2) This section applies to—

(*a*) section 8(9) of the Finance Act 1894,
(*b*) section 18 of the Finance Act 1896,
(*c*) section 61(5) of the Finance (1909–10) Act 1910,
(*d*) section 17(3) of the Law of Property Act 1925,
(*e*) section 73(6) of the Land Registration Act 1925,
(*f*) sections 86, 86A, 87, 87A and 88 of the Taxes Management Act 1970,
(*g*) paragraph 3 of Schedule 16A to the Finance Act 1973,
(*h*) paragraphs 15 and 16 of Schedule 2, and paragraph 8 of Schedule 5, to the Oil Taxation Act 1975,
(*i*) section 47 of the Finance (No. 2) Act 1975,
(*j*) paragraph 59 of Schedule 8 to the Development Land Tax Act 1976,
(*k*) sections 233 and 236(3) and (4) of the Inheritance Tax Act 1984,
(*l*) section 92 of the Finance Act 1986, and
(*m*) sections 160, 824, 825 and 826 of, and paragraph 3 of Schedule 19A to, the Taxes Act 1988.

(3) Regulations under this section may—

(*a*) make different provision for different enactments or for different purposes of the same enactment,
(*b*) either themselves specify a rate of interest for the purposes of an enactment or make provision for any such rate to be determined by reference to such rate or the average of such rates as may be referred to in the regulations,
(*c*) provide for rates to be reduced below, or increased above, what they otherwise would be by specified amounts or by reference to specified formulae,
(*d*) provide for rates arrived at by reference to averages to be rounded up or down,
(*e*) provide for circumstances in which alteration of a rate of interest is or is not to take place, and
(*f*) provide that alterations of rates are to have effect for periods beginning on or after a day determined in accordance with the regulations in relation to interest running from before that day as well as from or from after that day.

(4) The power to make regulations under this section shall be exercisable by statutory instrument which shall be subject to annulment in pursuance of a resolution of the House of Commons.

(5) Where—

(*a*) the rate provided for by regulations under this section as the rate applicable for the purposes of any enactment is changed, and
(*b*) the new rate is not specified in the regulations,

the Board shall by order specify the new rate and the day from which it has effect.

(6) In section 828(2) of the Taxes Act 1988 (powers to make orders which are not exercisable by statutory instrument) the words "or section 178(5) of the Finance Act 1989" shall be added at the end.

(7) Subsection (1) shall have effect for periods beginning on or after such day as the Treasury may by order made by statutory instrument appoint and shall have effect in relation to interest running from before that day as well as from or from after that day; and different days may be appointed for different enactments.

179. Provisions consequential on section 178

(1) The words "rate applicable under section 178 of the Finance Act 1989" shall be substituted—

  (*a*) for the words from "rate" to "annum" in—

    (i) section 18(1) of the Finance Act 1896,
    (ii) section 61(5) of the Finance (1909–10) Act 1910,
    (iii) section 17(3) of the Law of Property Act 1925,
    (iv) section 73(6) of the Land Registration Act 1925,
    (v) paragraphs 15(1) and 16 of Schedule 2, and paragraph 8(4) of Schedule 5, to the Oil Taxation Act 1975,
    (vi) section 47(1) of the Finance (No. 2) Act 1975, and
    (vii) sections 824(1) and 825(2) of the Taxes Act 1988,

  (*b*) for the words "prescribed rate" in—

    (i) sections 86(1), 86A(1), 87(1), 87A(1) and (5) and 88(1) of the Taxes Management Act 1970,
    (ii) paragraph 3(4) of Schedule 16A to the Finance Act 1973, and
    (iii) paragraph 3(4) of Schedule 19A to the Taxes Act 1988,

  (*c*) for the words "rate which" onwards in—

    (i) paragraph 59(1) of Schedule 8 to the Development Land Tax Act 1976, and
    (ii) section 826(1) of the Taxes Act 1988,

  (*d*) for the words "rate applicable under subsection (2) below" in section 233(1) of the Inheritance Tax Act 1984,

  (*e*) for the words "rate for the time being applicable under section 233(2)(*b*) above" in subsection (3), and the words "rate for the time being applicable under section 233(2)(*a*) above" in subsection (4), of section 236 of that Act,

  (*f*) for the words "appropriate rate" in section 92(2) of the Finance Act 1986, and

  (*g*) for the words "rate prescribed from time to time by the Treasury by order" in section 160(5)(*d*) of the Taxes Act 1988.

(2) In section 8(9) of the Finance Act 1894, for the words from "such interest" to "per cent." there shall be substituted the words "interest at such rate not exceeding that applicable under section 178 of the Finance Act 1989".

(3) In section 236(4) of the Inheritance Tax Act 1984, for the words "as if section 233(1)(*b*) above had applied" there shall be substituted the words "from the end of the period mentioned in section 233(1)(*b*) above".

(4) Any amendment made by subsection (1), (2) or (3) above shall have effect in relation to any period for which section 178(1) above has effect for the purposes of the enactment concerned.

(5) Section 146(11) of the Taxes Act 1988 shall have effect in relation to any year of assessment beginning after the day on which section 178(1) above has effect for the purposes of section 160 of that Act with the substitution of the words "applicable for the purposes of section 160" for the words "prescribed by the Treasury under section 160(5)".

180. Repayment interest: period of accrual

(1) In section 48(1) of the Finance Act 1975, after the words "carry interest" there shall be inserted the words "from the date on which the sums were paid until the order for repayment is issued".

(2) In—

  (*a*) paragraph 16 of Schedule 2 to the Oil Taxation Act 1975,
  (*b*) section 105(7) of the Finance Act 1980,
  (*c*) paragraph 13(4) and (5) of Schedule 16 to the Finance Act 1981, and
  (*d*) paragraph 10(4) of Schedule 19 to the Finance Act 1982,

for the word "repayment" there shall be substituted the words "the order for repayment is issued".

(3) In paragraph 59(1) of Schedule 8 to the Development Land Tax Act 1976, after the word "later," there shall be inserted the words "until the order for repayment is issued".

(4) In section 235(1) of the Inheritance Tax Act 1984 (and paragraph 19(3) of Schedule 4 to

the Finance Act 1975), after the word "made" there shall be inserted the words "until the order for repayment is issued".

(5) In section 92(2) of the Finance Act 1986, for the words "the time it was paid" there shall be substituted the words "the date on which the payment was made until the order for repayment is issued".

(6) In section 826(1) of the Taxes Act 1988, for the words "that repayment or payment is made" there shall be substituted the words "the order for repayment or payment is issued".

(7) The amendments made by this section shall be deemed always to have had effect.

Miscellaneous

182. Disclosure of information

(1) A person who discloses any information which he holds or has held in the exercise of tax functions is guilty of an offence if it is information about any matter relevant, for the purposes of those functions, to tax or duty in the case of any identifiable person.

(2) In this section "tax functions" means functions relating to tax or duty—

 (*a*) of the Commissioners, the Board and their officers,
 (*b*) of any person carrying out the administrative work of any tribunal mentioned in subsection (3) below, and
 (*c*) of any other person providing, or employed in the provision of, services to any person mentioned in paragraph (*a*) or (*b*) above.

(3) The tribunals referred to in subsection (2)(*b*) above are—

 (*a*) the General Commissioners and the Special Commissioners,
 (*b*) any value added tax tribunal,
 (*c*) any referee or board of referees appointed for the purposes of section 80(3) of the Taxes Management Act 1970 or under section 26(7) of the Capital Allowances Act 1968, and
 (*d*) any tribunal established under section 463 of the Taxes Act 1970 or section 706 of the Taxes Act 1988.

(4) A person who discloses any information which—

 (*a*) he holds or has held in the exercise of functions—

  (i) of the Comptroller and Auditor General and any member of the staff of the National Audit Office, or
  (ii) of the Parliamentary Commissioner for Administration and his officers,

 (*b*) is, or is derived from, information which was held by any person in the exercise of tax functions, and
 (*c*) is information about any matter relevant, for the purposes of tax functions, to tax or duty in the case of any identifiable person,

is guilty of an offence.

(5) Subsections (1) and (4) above do not apply to any disclosure of information—

 (*a*) with lawful authority,
 (*b*) with the consent of any person in whose case the information is about a matter relevant to tax or duty, or
 (*c*) which has been lawfully made available to the public before the disclosure is made.

(6) For the purposes of this section a disclosure of any information is made with lawful authority if, and only if, it is made—

 (*a*) by a Crown servant in accordance with his official duty,
 (*b*) by any other person for the purposes of the function in the exercise of which he holds the information and without contravening any restriction duly imposed by the person responsible,
 (*c*) to, or in accordance with an authorisation duly given by, the person responsible,
 (*d*) in pursuance of any enactment or of any order of a court, or
 (*e*) in connection with the institution of or otherwise for the purposes of any proceedings relating to any matter within the general responsibility of the Commissioners or, as the case requires, the Board,

and in this subsection "the person responsible" means the Commissioners, the Board, the Comptroller or the Parliamentary Commissioner, as the case requires.

(7) It is a defence for a person charged with an offence under this section to prove that at the time of the alleged offence—

(*a*) he believed that he had lawful authority to make the disclosure in question and had no reasonable cause to believe otherwise, or
(*b*) he believed that the information in question had been lawfully made available to the public before the disclosure was made and had no reasonable cause to believe otherwise.

(8) A person guilty of an offence under this section is liable—

(*a*) on conviction on indictment, to imprisonment for a term not exceeding two years or a fine or both, and
(*b*) on summary conviction, to imprisonment for a term not exceeding six months or a fine not exceeding the statutory maximum or both.

(9) No prosecution for an offence under this section shall be instituted in England and Wales or in Northern Ireland except—

(*a*) by the Commissioners or the Board, as the case requires, or
(*b*) by or with the consent of the Director of Public Prosecutions or, in Northern Ireland, the Director of Public Prosecutions for Northern Ireland.

(10) In this section—

"the Board" means the Commissioners of Inland Revenue,
"the Commissioners" means the Commissioners of Customs and Excise,
"Crown servant" has the same meaning as in the Official Secrets Act 1989, and
"tax or duty" means any tax or duty within the general responsibility of the Commissioners or the Board.

(11) In this section—

(*a*) references to the Comptroller and Auditor General include the Comptroller and Auditor General for Northern Ireland,
(*b*) references to the National Audit Office include the Northern Ireland Audit Office, and
(*c*) references to the Parliamentary Commissioner for Administration include the Health Service Commissioner for England, the Health Service Commissioner for Wales, the Health Service Commissioner for Scotland, the Northern Ireland Parliamentary Commissioner for Administration and the Northern Ireland Commissioner for Complaints.

(12) This section shall come into force on the repeal of section 2 of the Official Secrets Act 1911.

General

186. Interpretation etc.

(1) In this Act "the Taxes Act 1970" means the Income and Corporation Taxes Act 1970 and "the Taxes Act 1988" means the Income and Corporation Taxes Act 1988.

(2) Chapter II of Part I of this Act shall be construed as one with the Value Added Tax Act 1983.

(3) Part II of this Act, so far as it relates to capital gains tax, shall be construed as one with the Capital Gains Tax Act 1979.

187. Repeals

(1) The enactments specified in Schedule 17 to this Act (which include unnecessary enactments) are hereby repealed to the extent specified in the third column of that Schedule, but subject to any provision at the end of any Part of that Schedule.

(2) The repeal of the enactments specified in Part XIV of Schedule 17 shall come into force on such day as the Treasury may appoint by order made by statutory instrument; and different days may be appointed for different enactments.

188. Short title

This Act may be cited as the Finance Act 1989.

SCHEDULES
SCHEDULE 4
Section 61
PROFIT-RELATED PAY

1. The Taxes Act 1988 shall be amended in accordance with the following provisions of this Schedule.

2.—(1) In section 171(4) (limit on pay of which half may be exempt from tax) for "£3,000" there shall be substituted "£4,000".

(2) This paragraph shall have effect in relation to profit-related pay paid by reference to profit periods beginning on or after 1st April 1989.

3. After section 177 there shall be inserted—

"177A. Death of scheme employer

(1) Where a scheme employer has died, his personal representatives may make a written application to the Board under this section for the amendment of the registration of the scheme.

(2) If on receiving an application under this section the Board are satisfied that, apart from the death of the scheme employer, there would be no grounds for cancelling the registration of the scheme, the Board shall amend the registration of the scheme by substituting the personal representatives for the deceased scheme employer.

(3) An application under this section shall be made before the end of the period of one month beginning with the date of the grant of probate or letters of administration or, in Scotland, confirmation of executors.

(4) Where the Board amend the registration of a scheme under this section, this Chapter shall (subject to any necessary modifications) have effect as if the personal representatives had been the scheme employer throughout.

(5) The Board shall give notice to the personal representatives if they refuse an application under this section.

177B. Alteration of scheme's terms

(1) The alteration of the terms of a registered scheme shall not of itself invalidate the registration of the scheme.

(2) Subsection (1) above is without prejudice to the power of cancellation conferred on the Board by section 178(3A); but the power conferred by section 178(3A) shall not be exercisable by virtue of an alteration registered in accordance with this section.

(3) Where the terms of a registered scheme have been altered, the scheme employer may apply to the Board for the registration of the alteration.

(4) An application under subsection (3) above—

   (*a*) shall be in such form as the Board may prescribe;
   (*b*) shall be made within the period of one month beginning with the day on which the alteration is made;
   (*c*) shall contain a declaration by the applicant that the alteration is within subsection (8) below and that the scheme as altered complies with the requirements of Schedule 8 (either as that Schedule had effect when the scheme was registered, or as it then had effect but subject to one or more subsequent amendments specified in the declaration);
   (*d*) shall be accompanied by a report by an independent accountant, in a form prescribed by the Board, to the effect that in his opinion the alteration is within subsection (8) below and the scheme as altered complies with the requirements of Schedule 8 (either as that Schedule had effect when the scheme was registered, or as it then had effect but subject to one or more subsequent amendments specified in the report).

(5) The Board shall not more than three months after the day on which they receive an application under subsection (3) above either register the alteration or refuse the application; and in either case they shall give notice of their decision to the applicant.

(6) Subject to subsection (7) below, the Board shall register an alteration on an application under subsection (3) above.

(7) The Board may refuse an application under subsection (3) above if they are not satisfied—

(a) that the application complies with the requirements of subsection (4) above, or
(b) that the declaration referred to in subsection (4)(c) above is true.

(8) An alteration is within this subsection if—

(a) it relates to a term which is not relevant to the question whether the scheme complies with the requirements of Schedule 8; or
(b) it relates to a term identifying any person (other than the scheme employer) who pays the emoluments of employees to whom the scheme relates; or
(c) it consists of the addition of a term making provision for an abbreviated profit period of the kind referred to in paragraph 10(3) of Schedule 8; or
(d) it amends the provisions by reference to which the employees to whom the scheme relates may be identified, and does so only for the purposes of profit periods which begin after the date on which the alteration is made; or
(e) it relates to a provision of a kind referred to in paragraph 13(4) or (5) or 14(3), (4) or (5) of Schedule 8 (as those provisions have effect at the time of the application for registration of the alteration), and has effect only for the purposes of profit periods beginning after the date on which the alteration is made; or
(f) it amends the provisions as to when payments will be made to employees, and does so only for the purposes of profit periods beginning after the date on which the alteration is made; or
(g) the scheme did not comply with the requirements of Schedule 8 when it was registered, and the alteration—

(i) is made in order to bring the scheme into compliance with the requirements of that Schedule (either as it had effect when the scheme was registered or as it has effect at the time of the application for registration of the alteration), and
(ii) is made for the purposes of the first and any subsequent profit period to which the scheme relates, and
(iii) is made within two years of the beginning of the first profit period, and
(iv) does not invalidate (in whole or in part) any payment of profit-related pay already made under the scheme."

4.—(1) Section 178 (cancellation of registration) shall be amended as follows.

(2) In subsection (1) for the words "subsection (5)" there shall be substituted the words "subsections (5) and (5A)".

(3) After subsection (3) there shall be inserted—

"(3A) Where the terms of a registered scheme have been altered, then, subject to section 177B(2), the Board may cancel the registration of the scheme with effect from the beginning of the profit period during which the alteration took effect or with effect from the beginning of any later profit period.

(3B) If after an alteration of the terms of a scheme has been registered under section 177B it appears to the Board—

(a) that the application for registration of the alteration did not comply with the requirements of subsection (4) of that section, or
(b) that the declaration referred to in subsection (4)(c) of that section was false,

the Board may cancel the registration of the scheme with effect from the beginning of the profit period during which the alteration took effect or with effect from the beginning of any later profit period."

(4) After subsection (5) there shall be inserted—

"(5A) Where—

(a) the scheme employer has died, and
(b) his personal representatives by notice request the Board to cancel the registration of the scheme with effect from the date of death,

then, if the notice is given before the end of the period of one month beginning with the date of the grant of probate or letters of administration or, in Scotland, confirmation of executors, the Board shall comply with the request."

5. At the end of section 179 (recovery of tax) there shall be added—

"(3) Where—

(a) the scheme employer has died, but
(b) his personal representatives have not been substituted for him as the scheme employer by virtue of section 177A,

the reference in subsection (2) above to the scheme employer shall be construed as a reference to the personal representatives.

(4) Where—

(*a*) a payment to which this section applies was made by a person other than the scheme employer, and
(*b*) the scheme employer is not resident in the United Kingdom,

then in relation to that payment the reference in subsection (2) above to the scheme employer shall include a reference to the person by whom the payment was made."

6. At the end of section 180 (annual returns) there shall be added—

"(5) Where—

(*a*) the scheme employer has died, but
(*b*) his personal representatives have not been substituted for him as the scheme employer by virtue of section 177A,

the reference in subsection (1) above to the scheme employer shall be construed as a reference to the personal representatives."

7. At the end of section 181 (information) there shall be added—

"(4) Where the scheme employer has died, his personal representatives shall inform the Board of his death by notice given before the end of the period of one month beginning with the date of the grant of probate or letters of administration or, in Scotland, confirmation of executors."

8.—(1) Section 182 (appeals) shall be amended as follows.

(2) In subsection (1) after paragraph (*b*) there shall be inserted—

"(*bb*) against a refusal by the Board of an application under section 177B(3);".

(3) After subsection (1) there shall be inserted—

"(1A) An appeal to the Special Commissioners may be made by the personal representatives of a scheme employer against a refusal by the Board of an application under section 177A."

(4) In subsection (2) for the words "scheme employer" there shall be substituted the word "appellant".

9.—(1) Paragraph 7 of Schedule 8 (no payments for employees with material interest in company) shall be amended as follows.

(2) In sub-paragraph (1), the words ", or is an associate of a person who has," shall be omitted.

(3) In sub-paragraph (3), after the words "section 417(3) and (4)" there shall be inserted the words ", but subject to sub-paragraph (4) below".

(4) The following sub-paragraphs shall be added at the end—

"(4) For the purposes of this paragraph, where an employee of a company has an interest in shares or obligations of the company as a beneficiary of an employee benefit trust, the trustees shall not be regarded as associates of his by reason only of that interest unless sub-paragraph (8) below applies in relation to him.

(5) A trust is an employee benefit trust for the purposes of this paragraph if—

(*a*) all or most of the employees of the company are eligible to benefit under it, and
(*b*) none of the property subject to it has been disposed of on or after 14th March 1989 (whether by sale, loan or otherwise) except in the ordinary course of management of the trust or in accordance with sub-paragraph (6) below.

(6) Property is disposed of in accordance with this sub-paragraph if—

(*a*) it is applied for the benefit of—

(i) individual employees or former employees of the company,
(ii) spouses, former spouses, widows or widowers of employees or former employees of the company,
(iii) relatives, or spouses of relatives, of persons within sub-paragraph (i) or (ii) above, or
(iv) dependants of persons within sub-paragraph (i) above,

(*b*) it is applied for charitable purposes, or
(*c*) it is transferred to the trustees of an approved profit sharing scheme (within the

meaning of section 187), of another employee benefit trust, or of a qualifying employee share ownership trust (within the meaning of Schedule 5 to the Finance Act 1989),

and the property applied or transferred consists of any of the ordinary share capital of the company or of money paid outright.

(7) In sub-paragraph (6)(*a*)(iii) above "relative" means parent or remoter forebear, child or remoter issue, brother, sister, uncle, aunt, nephew or niece.

(8) This sub-paragraph applies in relation to an employee if at any time on or after 14th March 1989—

(*a*) the employee, either on his own or with any one or more of his associates, or
(*b*) any associate of his, with or without other such associates,

has been the beneficial owner of, or able (directly or through the medium of other companies or by any other indirect means) to control, more than 25 per cent. of the ordinary share capital of the company.

(9) Where—

(*a*) on or after 14th March 1989 an employee of a company, or an associate of his, receives a payment ("the relevant payment") from the trustees of an employee benefit trust, and
(*b*) at any time during the period of three years ending with the day on which the relevant payment is received, the property subject to the trust consists of or includes any part of the ordinary share capital of the company,

the employee or associate shall be treated for the purposes of sub-paragraph (8) above as if he were the beneficial owner of the appropriate percentage of the ordinary share capital of the company on the day on which the relevant payment is received (in addition to any percentage of that share capital of which he is actually the beneficial owner on that day).

(10) For the purposes of sub-paragraph (9) above, the appropriate percentage is—

$$\frac{A \times 100}{B}$$

where—

A is the smaller of—

(*a*) the aggregate of the relevant payment and any other payments received by the employee or associates of his from the trustees of the trust during the period of 12 months ending with the day on which the relevant payment is received, and
(*b*) the aggregate of the distributions made to the trustees of the trust by the company in respect of its ordinary share capital during the period of three years ending with the day on which the relevant payment is received; and

B is the aggregate of—

(*a*) any distributions made by the company in respect of its ordinary share capital during the period of 12 months ending with the day on which the relevant payment is received,
(*b*) any distributions so made during the period of 12 months immediately preceding that mentioned in paragraph (*a*) above, and
(*c*) any distributions so made during the period of 12 months immediately preceding that mentioned in paragraph (*b*) above,

divided by the number of the periods mentioned in paragraphs (*a*) to (*c*) above in which distributions were so made.

(11) Where—

(*a*) an employee or associate is treated by sub-paragraph (9) above as if he were the beneficial owner of a percentage of the ordinary share capital of a company by reason of receiving the relevant payment from the trustees of a trust, and
(*b*) that employee, or an associate of his, has, during the period of 12 months ending with the day on which the relevant payment is received, received one or more payments from trustees of another employee benefit trust or trusts satisfying the requirement in paragraph (*b*) of sub-paragraph (9) above,

that sub-paragraph shall have effect in relation to the employee or associate mentioned in paragraph (*a*) above as if he had received the payment from the trustees of the trust or of each of the trusts mentioned in paragraph (*b*) above (or where more than one payment has been received from the trustees of a trust, the last of the payments) on the day on which the relevant payment is received.

(12) In sub-paragraphs (8) to (11) above "associate", in relation to an employee, does not include the trustees of an employee benefit trust by reason only that the employee has an interest in shares or obligations of the trust."

10.—(1) Paragraphs 13(2) and 14(2) of Schedule 8 (which provide for a scheme's distributable pool to be at least 5 per cent. of the pay of all the employees to whom the scheme relates if profits remain unchanged) shall be omitted.

(2) In consequence of sub-paragraph (1) above—

(*a*) the following provisions shall be omitted—

section 175(3);
in section 176(1), the words "(but not more than six months)";
section 178(2)(*b*);
in paragraph 13(1) of Schedule 8, the word "fixed";
paragraph 13(3) of that Schedule;
paragraph 14(7) of that Schedule.

(*b*) in paragraph 13 of Schedule 8—

(i) after sub-paragraph (1) there shall be inserted—

"(1A) That percentage must be a fixed percentage specified in the scheme and, if the scheme relates to more than one period, must be the same for each period.";

(ii) in sub-paragraph (4)(*a*), for the words "the base year referred to in sub-paragraph (3) above" there shall be substituted the words "a base year specified in the scheme";
(iii) in sub-paragraph (5), for the words "must be" onwards there shall be substituted the words "must not exceed the profits for a base year specified in the scheme";
(iv) for sub-paragraph (6), there shall be substituted—

"(6) The base year referred to in sub-paragraph (4)(*a*) and sub-paragraph (5) above must be a period of 12 months ending at a time within the period of two years immediately preceding the profit period, or the first of the profit periods, to which the scheme relates";

(*c*) in paragraph 14(5) of that Schedule, for the words "must be" onwards there shall be substituted the words "must not exceed the profits in the period of 12 months immediately preceding the first or only profit period to which the scheme relates".

11. At the end of paragraph 13 of Schedule 8 (calculation of distributable pool by method A) there shall be added—

"(7) Any provision included in a scheme by virtue of sub-paragraph (4) or (5) above may take effect either from the scheme's first profit period or from any later profit period determined in accordance with the scheme."

12. In paragraph 14 of Schedule 8 (calculation of distributable pool by method B), in sub-paragraph (5) the words "specified in, or" shall be omitted.

13. At the end of paragraph 14 of Schedule 8 there shall be added—

"(8) Any provision included in a scheme by virtue of sub-paragraph (3)(*b*), (4) or (5) above may take effect either from the scheme's first profit period or from any later profit period determined in accordance with the scheme."

14.—(1) Paragraph 19 of Schedule 8 (profit and loss account for purposes of profit-related pay scheme) shall be amended as follows.

(2) After sub-paragraph (4) (account to make no allowance for remuneration of persons excluded from scheme) there shall be inserted—

"(4A) In sub-paragraph (4) above "remuneration", in relation to a person, includes fees and percentages, any sums paid by way of expenses allowance (insofar as those sums are charged to income tax), any contributions paid in respect of him under any pension scheme and the estimated value of any other benefits received by him otherwise than in cash."

(3) In sub-paragraph (6) (items which may be left out of account in arriving at profits or losses) for paragraph (*f*) there shall be substituted—

"(*f*) profit-related pay payable under the scheme, and profit-related pay payable under any other registered scheme if it is one to which paragraph 21 below applies;
(*ff*) secondary Class 1 contributions under Part I of the Social Security Act 1975 or

Part I of the Social Security (Northern Ireland) Act 1975 in respect of profit-related pay payable under the scheme;".

15. After paragraph 20 of Schedule 8 there shall be inserted—

"Parts of undertakings

21.—(1) This paragraph shall apply to a scheme if the employment unit is a part of an undertaking, and the scheme states that the profits or losses of the unit are for the purposes of the scheme to be taken to be equivalent to those of the whole undertaking (which must be identified by the scheme).

(2) Where this paragraph applies to a scheme, this Schedule shall have effect as if any reference to the profits or losses of the employment unit were a reference to the profits or losses of the undertaking of which it forms part.

22.—(1) Where paragraph 21 above applies to a scheme, the scheme must contain provisions ensuring that no payments are made under it by reference to a profit period unless, at the beginning of that profit period,—

(*a*) there is at least one other registered scheme which relates to employees employed in the same undertaking as that of which the employment unit forms part, and
(*b*) the number of the employees to whom the scheme relates does not exceed 33 per cent. of the number of the employees to whom that other scheme relates (or if there is more than one other scheme, the aggregate number of the employees to whom they relate).

(2) Another registered scheme shall be disregarded for the purposes of sub-paragraph (1) above—

(*a*) if paragraph 21 above applies to it, or
(*b*) if, by virtue of provisions of the kind described in paragraph 6 above, no payments could be made under it by reference to the profit period concerned.

(3) Where paragraph 21 above applies to two or more schemes relating to employment units which are parts of the same undertaking, an employee to whom another scheme relates shall not be counted for the purposes of sub-paragraph (1)(*b*) above in connection with more than one of those schemes."

SCHEDULE 5

Section 74

EMPLOYEE SHARE OWNERSHIP TRUSTS

Qualifying trusts

1. A trust is a qualifying employee share ownership trust at the time it is established if the conditions set out in paragraphs 2 to 11 below are satisfied in relation to the trust at that time.

General

2.—(1) The trust must be established under a deed (the trust deed).

(2) The trust must be established by a company (the founding company) which, at the time the trust is established, is resident in the United Kingdom and not controlled by another company.

Trustees

3.—(1) The trust deed must provide for the establishment of a body of trustees.

(2) The trust deed must—

   (*a*) appoint the initial trustees;
   (*b*) contain rules for the retirement and removal of trustees;
   (*c*) contain rules for the appointment of replacement and additional trustees.

(3) The trust deed must provide that at any time while the trust subsists (the relevant time)—

   (*a*) the number of trustees must not be less than three;
   (*b*) all the trustees must be resident in the United Kingdom;
   (*c*) the trustees must include one person who is a trust corporation, a solicitor, or a member of such other professional body as the Board may from time to time allow for the purposes of this paragraph;
   (*d*) most of the trustees must be persons who are not and have never been directors of any company which falls within the founding company's group at the relevant time;
   (*e*) most of the trustees must be persons who are employees of companies which fall within the founding company's group at the relevant time, and who do not have and have never had a material interest in any such company;
   (*f*) the trustees falling within paragraph (*e*) above must, before being appointed as trustees, have been selected by a majority of the employees of the companies falling within the founding company's group at the time of the selection or by persons elected to represent those employees.

(4) For the purposes of sub-paragraph (3) above a company falls within the founding company's group at a particular time if—

   (*a*) it is the founding company, or
   (*b*) it is at that time resident in the United Kingdom and controlled by the founding company.

Beneficiaries

4.—(1) The trust deed must contain provision as to the beneficiaries under the trust, in accordance with the following rules.

(2) The trust deed must provide that a person is a beneficiary at a particular time (the relevant time) if—

   (*a*) he is at the relevant time an employee or director of a company which at that time falls within the founding company's group,
   (*b*) at each given time in a qualifying period he was an employee or director of a company falling within the founding company's group at that given time, and
   (*c*) at that given time he worked as an employee or director of the company concerned at the rate of at least 20 hours a week (ignoring such matters as holidays and sickness).

(3) The trust deed may provide that a person is a beneficiary at a particular time (the relevant time) if—

(a) he has at each given time in a qualifying period been an employee or director of a company falling within the founding company's group at that given time,
(b) he has ceased to be an employee or director of the company or the company has ceased to fall within that group, and
(c) at the relevant time a period of not more than eighteen months has elapsed since he so ceased or the company so ceased (as the case may be).

(4) The trust deed may provide for a person to be a beneficiary if the person is a charity and the circumstances are such that—

(a) there is no person who is a beneficiary within any rule which is included in the deed and conforms with sub-paragraph (2) or (3) above, and
(b) the trust is in consequence being wound up.

(5) For the purposes of sub-paragraph (2) above a qualifying period is a period—

(a) whose length is not less than one year and not more than five years,
(b) whose length is specified in the trust deed, and
(c) which ends with the relevant time (within the meaning of that sub-paragraph).

(6) For the purposes of sub-paragraph (3) above a qualifying period is a period—

(a) whose length is equal to that of the period specified in the trust deed for the purposes of a rule which conforms with sub-paragraph (2) above, and
(b) which ends when the person or company (as the case may be) ceased as mentioned in sub-paragraph (3)(b) above.

(7) The trust deed must not provide for a person to be a beneficiary unless he falls within any rule which is included in the deed and conforms with sub-paragraph (2), (3) or (4) above.

(8) The trust deed must provide that, notwithstanding any other rule which is included in it, a person cannot be a beneficiary at a particular time (the relevant time) if—

(a) at that time he has a material interest in the founding company, or
(b) at any time in the period of one year preceding the relevant time he has had a material interest in that company.

(9) For the purposes of this paragraph a company falls within the founding company's group at a particular time if—

(a) it is at that time resident in the United Kingdom, and
(b) it is the founding company or it is at that time controlled by the founding company.

(10) For the purposes of this paragraph a charity is a body of persons established for charitable purposes only.

Trustees' functions

5.—(1) The trust deed must contain provision as to the functions of the trustees.

(2) The functions of the trustees must be so expressed that it is apparent that their general functions are—

(a) to receive sums from the founding company and other sums (by way of loan or otherwise);
(b) to acquire securities;
(c) to transfer securities or sums (or both) to persons who are beneficiaries under the terms of the trust deed;
(d) to transfer securities to the trustees of profit sharing schemes approved under Schedule 9 to the Taxes Act 1988, for a price not less than the price the securities might reasonably be expected to fetch on a sale in the open market;
(e) pending transfer, to retain the securities and to manage them (whether by exercising voting rights or otherwise).

Sums

6.—(1) The trust deed must require that any sum received by the trustees—

(a) must be expended within the relevant period,
(b) may be expended only for one or more of the qualifying purposes, and
(c) must, while it is retained by them, be kept as cash or be kept in an account with a bank or building society.

(2) For the purposes of sub-paragraph (1) above the relevant period is the period of nine months beginning with the day found as follows—

(*a*) in a case where the sum is received from the founding company, or a company which is controlled by that company at the time the sum is received, the day following the end of the period of account in which the sum is charged as an expense of the company from which it is received;
(*b*) in any other case, the day the sum is received.

(3) For the purposes of sub-paragraph (1) above each of the following is a qualifying purpose—

(*a*) the acquisition of shares in the founding company;
(*b*) the repayment of sums borrowed;
(*c*) the payment of interest on sums borrowed;
(*d*) the payment of any sum to a person who is a beneficiary under the terms of the trust deed;
(*e*) the meeting of expenses.

(4) The trust deed must provide that, in ascertaining for the purposes of a relevant rule whether a particular sum has been expended, sums received earlier by the trustees shall be treated as expended before sums received by them later; and a relevant rule is one which is included in the trust deed and conforms with sub-paragraph (1) above.

(5) The trust deed must provide that, where the trustees pay sums to different beneficiaries at the same time, all the sums must be paid on similar terms.

(6) For the purposes of sub-paragraph (5) above, the fact that terms vary according to the levels of remuneration of beneficiaries, the length of their service, or similar factors, shall not be regarded as meaning that the terms are not similar.

Securities

7.—(1) Subject to paragraph 8 below, the trust deed must provide that securities acquired by the trustees must be shares in the founding company which—

(*a*) form part of the ordinary share capital of the company,
(*b*) are fully paid up,
(*c*) are not redeemable, and
(*d*) are not subject to any restrictions other than restrictions which attach to all shares of the same class or a restriction authorised by sub-paragraph (2) below.

(2) Subject to sub-paragraph (3) below, a restriction is authorised by this sub-paragraph if—

(*a*) it is imposed by the founding company's articles of association,
(*b*) it requires all shares held by directors or employees of the founding company, or of any other company which it controls for the time being, to be disposed of on ceasing to be so held, and
(*c*) it requires all shares acquired, in pursuance of rights or interests obtained by such directors or employees, by persons who are not (or have ceased to be) such directors or employees to be disposed of when they are acquired.

(3) A restriction is not authorised by sub-paragraph (2) above unless—

(*a*) any disposal required by the restriction will be by way of sale for a consideration in money on terms specified in the articles of association, and
(*b*) the articles also contain general provisions by virtue of which any person disposing of shares of the same class (whether or not held or acquired as mentioned in sub-paragraph (2) above) may be required to sell them on terms which are the same as those mentioned in paragraph (*a*) above.

(4) The trust deed must provide that shares in the founding company may not be acquired by the trustees at a price exceeding the price they might reasonably be expected to fetch on a sale in the open market.

(5) The trust deed must provide that shares in the founding company may not be acquired by the trustees at a time when that company is controlled by another company.

8. The trust deed may provide that the trustees may acquire securities other than shares in the founding company—

(*a*) if they are securities issued to the trustees in exchange in circumstances mentioned in section 85(1) of the Capital Gains Tax Act 1979, or
(*b*) if they are securities acquired by the trustees as a result of a reorganisation, and the

original shares the securities represent are shares in the founding company (construing "reorganisation" and "original shares" in accordance with section 77 of that Act).

9.—(1) The trust deed must provide that—

(*a*) where the trustees transfer securities to a beneficiary, they must do so on qualifying terms;
(*b*) the trustees must transfer securities before the expiry of the period of seven years beginning with the date on which they acquired them.

(2) For the purposes of sub-paragraph (1) above a transfer of securities is made on qualifying terms if—

(*a*) all the securities transferred at the same time are transferred on similar terms,
(*b*) securities have been offered to all the persons who are beneficiaries under the terms of the trust deed when the transfer is made, and
(*c*) securities are transferred to all such beneficiaries who have accepted.

(3) For the purposes of sub-paragraph (2) above, the fact that terms vary according to the levels of remuneration of beneficiaries, the length of their service, or similar factors, shall not be regarded as meaning that the terms are not similar.

(4) The trust deed must provide that, in ascertaining for the purposes of a relevant rule whether particular securities are transferred, securities acquired earlier by the trustees shall be treated as transferred by them before securities acquired by them later; and a relevant rule is one which is included in the trust deed and conforms with sub-paragraph (1) above.

Other features

10. The trust deed must not contain features which are not essential or reasonably incidental to the purpose of acquiring sums and securities, transferring sums and securities to employees and directors, and transferring securities to the trustees of profit sharing schemes approved under Schedule 9 to the Taxes Act 1988.

Rules about acquisition etc.

11.—(1) The trust deed must provide that, for the purposes of the deed, the trustees—

(*a*) acquire securities when they become entitled to them;
(*b*) transfer securities to another person when that other becomes entitled to them;
(*c*) retain securities if they remain entitled to them.

(2) But if the deed provides as mentioned in paragraph 8 above, it must provide for the following exceptions to any rule which is included in it and conforms with sub-paragraph (1)(*a*) above, namely, that—

(*a*) if securities are issued to the trustees in exchange in circumstances mentioned in section 85(1) of the Capital Gains Tax Act 1979, they shall be treated as having acquired them when they became entitled to the securities for which they are exchanged;
(*b*) if the trustees become entitled to securities as a result of a reorganisation, they shall be treated as having acquired them when they became entitled to the original shares which those securities represent (construing "reorganisation" and "original shares" in accordance with section 77 of that Act).

(3) The trust deed must provide that—

(*a*) if the trustees agree to take a transfer of securities, for the purposes of the deed they become entitled to them when the agreement is made and not on a later transfer made pursuant to the agreement;
(*b*) if the trustees agree to transfer securities to another person, for the purposes of the deed the other person becomes entitled to them when the agreement is made and not on a later transfer made pursuant to the agreement.

Position after trust's establishment

12. A trust which was at the time it was established a qualifying employee share ownership trust shall continue to be one, except that it shall not be such a trust at any time when the requirements mentioned in paragraph 3(3)(*a*) to (*f*) above are not satisfied.

13. A trust is an employee share ownership trust at a particular time (the relevant time) if it was a qualifying employee share ownership trust at the time it was established; and it is immaterial whether or not it is a qualifying employee share ownership trust at the relevant time.

Interpretation

14. For the purposes of this Schedule the following are securities—

(*a*) shares;
(*b*) debentures.

15. For the purposes of this Schedule, the question whether one company is controlled by another shall be construed in accordance with section 840 of the Taxes Act 1988.

16.—(1) For the purposes of this Schedule a person shall be treated as having a material interest in a company if he, either on his own or with one or more of his associates, or if any associate of his with or without other such associates,—

(*a*) is the beneficial owner of, or able (directly or through the medium of other companies or by any other indirect means) to control, more than 5 per cent. of the ordinary share capital of the company, or
(*b*) possesses, or is entitled to acquire, such rights as would, in the event of the winding-up of the company or in any other circumstances, give an entitlement to receive more than 5 per cent. of the assets which would then be available for distribution among the participators.

(2) In this paragraph—

(*a*) "associate" has the same meaning as in section 417(3) and (4) of the Taxes Act 1988, but subject to sub-paragraph (3) below,
(*b*) "control" has the meaning given by section 840 of that Act, and
(*c*) "participator" has the same meaning as in Part XI of that Act.

(3) Where a person has an interest in shares or obligations of the company as a beneficiary of an employee benefit trust, the trustees shall not be regarded as associates of his by reason only of that interest unless sub-paragraph (5) below applies in relation to him.

(4) In sub-paragraph (3) above "employee benefit trust" has the same meaning as in paragraph 7 of Schedule 8 to the Taxes Act 1988, except that in its application for this purpose paragraph 7(5)(*b*) of that Schedule shall have effect as if it referred to the day on which this Act was passed instead of to 14th March 1989.

(5) This sub-paragraph applies in relation to a person if at any time on or after the day on which this Act was passed—

(*a*) he, either on his own or with any one or more of his associates, or
(*b*) any associate of his, with or without other such associates,

has been the beneficial owner of, or able (directly or through the medium of other companies or by any other indirect means) to control, more than 5 per cent. of the ordinary share capital of the company.

(6) Sub-paragraphs (9) to (12) of paragraph 7 of Schedule 8 to the Taxes Act 1988 shall apply for the purposes of sub-paragraph (5) above as they apply for the purposes of that paragraph.

SCHEDULE 6

Section 75

RETIREMENT BENEFITS SCHEMES

PART I
AMENDMENTS OF TAXES ACT

Preliminary

1. The Taxes Act 1988 shall be amended as mentioned in the following provisions of this Part of this Schedule.

Amendments

2. In section 431(4) (pension business of insurance companies) for paragraph (*d*)(ii) there shall be substituted—

"(ii) a scheme which is a relevant statutory scheme for the purposes of Chapter I of Part XIV;".

3.—(1) Section 590 (conditions for approval of schemes) shall be amended as follows.

(2) In subsection (3)(*d*) (condition to be satisfied as to lump sum) the words "(disregarding any excess of that remuneration over the permitted maximum)" shall be omitted.

(3) In subsection (3) for the words from "In paragraph (*d*) above" to the end there shall be substituted—

"(*e*) that, in the case of any employee who is a member of the scheme by virtue of two or more relevant associated employments, the amount payable by way of pension in respect of service in any one of them may not, when aggregated with any amount payable by way of pension in respect of service in the other or others, exceed the relevant amount;
(*f*) that, in the case of any employee who is a member of the scheme by virtue of two or more relevant associated employments, the amount payable by way of commuted pension in respect of service in any one of them may not, when aggregated with any amount payable by way of commuted pension in respect of service in the other or others, exceed the relevant amount;
(*g*) that, in the case of any employee in relation to whom the scheme is connected with another scheme which is (or other schemes each of which is) an approved scheme, the amount payable by way of pension under the scheme may not, when aggregated with any amount payable by way of pension under the other scheme or schemes, exceed the relevant amount;
(*h*) that, in the case of any employee in relation to whom the scheme is connected with another scheme which is (or other schemes each of which is) an approved scheme, the amount payable by way of commuted pension may not, when aggregated with any amount payable by way of commuted pension under the other scheme or schemes, exceed the relevant amount."

(4) For subsection (7) there shall be substituted—

"(7) Subsections (8) to (10) below apply where the Board are considering whether a retirement benefits scheme satisfies or continues to satisfy the prescribed conditions.

(8) For the purpose of determining whether the scheme, so far as it relates to a particular class or description of employees, satisfies or continues to satisfy the prescribed conditions, that scheme shall be considered in conjunction with—

(*a*) any other retirement benefits scheme (or schemes) which relates (or relate) to employees of that class or description and which is (or are) approved for the purposes of this Chapter,
(*b*) any other retirement benefits scheme (or schemes) which relates (or relate) to employees of that class or description and which is (or are) at the same time before the Board in order for them to decide whether to give approval for the purposes of this Chapter,
(*c*) any section 608 scheme or schemes relating to employees of that class or description, and

(*d*) any relevant statutory scheme or schemes relating to employees of that class or description.

(9) If those conditions are satisfied in the case of both or all of those schemes taken together, they shall be taken to be satisfied in the case of the scheme mentioned in subsection (7) above (as well as the other or others).

(10) If those conditions are not satisfied in the case of both or all of those schemes taken together, they shall not be taken to be satisfied in the case of the scheme mentioned in subsection (7) above.

(11) The reference in subsection (8)(*c*) above to a section 608 scheme is a reference to a fund to which section 608 applies."

4. The following sections shall be inserted after section 590—

"590A. Section 590: supplementary provisions

(1) For the purposes of section 590(3)(*e*) and (*f*) two or more employments are relevant associated employments if they are employments in the case of which—

(*a*) there is a period during which the employee has held both or all of them,
(*b*) the period counts under the scheme in the case of both or all of them as a period in respect of which benefits are payable, and
(*c*) the period is one during which both or all of the employers in question are associated.

(2) For the purposes of section 590(3)(*g*) and (*h*) the scheme is connected with another scheme in relation to an employee if—

(*a*) there is a period during which he has been the employee of two persons who are associated employers,
(*b*) the period counts under both schemes as a period in respect of which benefits are payable, and
(*c*) the period counts under one scheme by virtue of service with one employer and under the other scheme by virtue of service with the other employer.

(3) For the purposes of subsections (1) and (2) above, employers are associated if (directly or indirectly) one is controlled by the other or if both are controlled by a third person.

(4) In subsection (3) above the reference to control, in relation to a body corporate, shall be construed—

(*a*) where the body corporate is a close company, in accordance with section 416, and
(*b*) where it is not, in accordance with section 840.

590B. Section 590: further supplementary provisions

(1) For the purposes of section 590(3)(*e*) the relevant amount, in relation to an employee, shall be found by applying the following formula—

$$\frac{A \times C}{60}$$

(2) For the purposes of section 590(3)(*f*) the relevant amount, in relation to an employee, shall be found by applying the following formula—

$$\frac{3 \times A \times C}{80}$$

(3) For the purposes of section 590(3)(*g*) the relevant amount, in relation to an employee, shall be found by applying the following formula—

$$\frac{B \times C}{60}$$

(4) For the purposes of section 590(3)(*h*) the relevant amount, in relation to an employee, shall be found by applying the following formula—

$$\frac{3 \times B \times C}{80}$$

(5) For the purposes of this section A is the aggregate number of years service (expressing parts of a year as a fraction), subject to a maximum of 40, which, in the case of the employee, count for the purposes of the scheme at the time the benefits in respect of service in the employment become payable.

(6) But where the same year (or part of a year) counts for the purposes of the scheme by virtue of more than one of the relevant associated employments it shall be counted only once in calculating the aggregate number of years service for the purposes of subsection (5) above.

(7) For the purposes of this section B is the aggregate number of years service (expressing parts of a year as a fraction), subject to a maximum of 40, which, in the case of the employee, count for the purposes of any of the following—

(*a*) the scheme, and
(*b*) the other scheme or schemes with which the scheme is connected in relation to him

at the time the benefits become payable.

(8) But where the same year (or part of a year) counts for the purposes of more than one scheme it shall be counted only once in calculating the aggregate number of years service for the purpose of subsection (7) above.

(9) For the purposes of this section C is the permitted maximum in relation to the year of assessment in which the benefits in question become payable, that is, the figure found for that year by virtue of subsections (10) and (11) below.

(10) For the years 1988–89 and 1989–90 the figure is £60,000.

(11) For any subsequent year of assessment the figure is the figure found for that year, for the purposes of section 590C, by virtue of section 590C(4) and (5).

590C. Earnings cap

(1) In arriving at an employee's final remuneration for the purposes of section 590(3)(*a*) or (*d*), any excess of what would be his final remuneration (apart from this section) over the permitted maximum for the year of assessment in which his participation in the scheme ceases shall be disregarded.

(2) In subsection (1) above "the permitted maximum", in relation to a year of assessment, means the figure found for that year by virtue of subsections (3) and (4) below.

(3) For the years 1988–89 and 1989–90 the figure is £60,000.

(4) For any subsequent year of assessment the figure is also £60,000, subject to subection (5) below.

(5) If the retail prices index for the month of December preceding a year of assessment falling within subsection (4) above is higher than it was for the previous December, the figure for that year shall be an amount arrived at by—

(*a*) increasing the figure for the previous year of assessment by the same percentage as the percentage increase in the retail prices index, and
(*b*) if the result is not a multiple of £600, rounding it up to the nearest amount which is such a multiple.

(6) The Treasury shall in the year of assessment 1989–90, and in each subsequent year of assessment, make an order specifying the figure which is by virtue of this section the figure for the following year of assessment."

5.—(1) Section 592 (exempt approved schemes) shall be amended as follows.

(2) In subsection (8) there shall be inserted at the beginning the words "Subject to subsection (8A) below,".

(3) After subsection (8) there shall be inserted—

"(8A) Where an employee's remuneration for a year of assessment includes remuneration in respect of more than one employment, the amount allowed to be deducted by virtue of subsection (7) above in respect of contributions paid by the employee in that year by virtue of any employment (whether under a single scheme or under two or more schemes) shall not exceed 15 per cent, or such higher percentage as the Board may in a particular case prescribe, of his remuneration for the year in respect of that employment."

(4) After subsection (8A) there shall be inserted—

"(8B) In arriving at an employee's remuneration for a year of assessment for the purposes of subsection (8) or (8A) above, any excess of what would be his remuneration (apart from this subsection) over the permitted maximum for that year shall be disregarded.

(8C) In subsection (8B) above "permitted maximum", in relation to a year of assessment, means the figure found for that year by virtue of subsections (8D) and (8E) below.

(8D) For the year 1989–90 the figure is £60,000.

(8E) For any subsequent year of assessment the figure is the figure found for that year, for the purposes of section 590C, by virtue of section 590C(4) and (5)."

6.—(1) Section 594 (exempt statutory schemes) shall be amended as follows.

(2) In subsection (1) the word "relevant" shall be inserted before the words "statutory scheme".

(3) In subsection (2) there shall be inserted at the beginning the words "Subject to subsection (3) below,".

(4) After subsection (2) there shall be inserted—

"(3) Where a person's remuneration for a year of assessment includes remuneration in respect of more than one office or employment, the amount allowed to be deducted by virtue of subsection (1) above in respect of contributions paid by the person in that year by virtue of any office or employment (whether under a single scheme or under two or more schemes) shall not exceed 15 per cent, or such higher percentage as the Board may in a particular case prescribe, of his remuneration for the year in respect of that office or employment."

(5) After subsection (3) there shall be inserted—

"(4) In arriving at a person's remuneration for a year of assessment for the purposes of subsection (2) or (3) above, any excess of what would be his remuneration (apart from this subsection) over the permitted maximum for that year shall be disregarded.

(5) In subsection (4) above "permitted maximum", in relation to a year of assessment, means the figure found for that year by virtue of subsections (6) and (7) below.

(6) For the year 1989–90 the figure is £60,000.

(7) For any subsequent year of assessment the figure is the figure found for that year, for the purposes of section 590C, by virtue of section 590C(4) and (5)."

7. Section 595(2) and (3) (charge to tax in certain cases) shall be omitted.

8.—(1) Section 596 (exceptions from section 595) shall be amended as follows.

(2) In subsection (1)—

  (*a*) for the words "Neither subsection (1) nor subsection (2) of section 595 shall" there shall be substituted the words "Section 595(1) shall not"; and
  (*b*) in paragraph (*b*) the word "relevant" shall be inserted before the words "statutory scheme".

(3) In subsection (2) for the words "Neither subsection (1) nor subsection (2) of section 595 shall" there shall be substituted the words "Section 595(1) shall not".

(4) In subsection (3)(*a*) the words "either" and "or subsection (2)" shall be omitted.

9. The following section shall be inserted after section 596—

"**596A. Charge to tax: benefits under non-approved schemes**

(1) Where in any year of assessment a person receives a benefit provided under a retirement benefits scheme which is not of a description mentioned in section 596(1)(*a*), (*b*) or (*c*), tax shall be charged in accordance with the provisions of this section.

(2) Where the benefit is received by an individual, he shall be charged to tax under Schedule E for that year.

(3) Where the benefit is received by a person other than an individual, the administrator of the scheme shall be charged to tax under Case VI of Schedule D for that year.

(4) The amount to be charged to tax is—

  (*a*) in the case of a cash benefit, the amount received, and
  (*b*) in the case of a benefit in kind, an amount equal to whatever is the cash equivalent of the benefit.

(5) In the case of the charge under Case VI of Schedule D, the rate of tax is 40 per cent. or such other rate (whether higher or lower) as may for the time being be specified by the Treasury by order.

(6) Tax shall not be charged under this section in the case of a benefit which is chargeable to tax under Schedule E by virtue of section 19(1)1.

(7) But where the amount chargeable to tax by virtue of section 19(1)1 is less than the amount which would be chargeable to tax under this section—

  (*a*) subsection (6) above shall not apply, and

(b) the amount chargeable to tax under this section shall be reduced by the amount chargeable to tax by virtue of section 19(1)1.

(8) Tax shall not be charged under this section to the extent that the benefit received is attributable to the payment of a sum—

(a) which is deemed to be the income of a person by virtue of section 595(1), and
(b) in respect of which that person has been assessed to tax.

(9) For the purpose of subsection (8) above the provision of a benefit shall be presumed not to be attributable to the payment of such a sum as is mentioned in that subsection unless the contrary is shown.

596B. Section 596A: supplementary provisions

(1) For the purposes of section 596A the cash equivalent of a benefit in kind is—

(a) in the case of a benefit other than living accommodation, the amount which would be the cash equivalent of the benefit under Chapter II of Part V if it were chargeable under the appropriate provision of that Chapter (treating any sum made good by the recipient as made good by the employee), and
(b) in the case of living accommodation, an amount equal to the value of the accommodation to the recipient determined in accordance with the following provisions of this section less so much of any sum made good by him to those at whose cost the accommodation is provided as is properly attributable to the provision of the accommodation.

(2) Where the cost of providing the accommodation does not exceed £75,000, the value of the accommodation to the recipient in any period is the rent which would have been payable for the period if the premises had been let to him at an annual rent equal to their annual value as ascertained under section 837.

(3) But for a period in which those at whose cost the accommodation is provided pay rent at an annual rate greater than the annual value as so ascertained, the value of the accommodation to the recipient is an amount equal to the rent payable by them for the period.

(4) Where the cost of providing the accommodation does exceed £75,000, the value of the accommodation to the recipient shall be taken to be the aggregate of the value of the accommodation to him determined in accordance with subsections (2) and (3) above and the additional value of the accommodation to him determined in accordance with subsections (5) and (6) below.

(5) The additional value of the accommodation to the recipient in any period is the rent which would have been payable for that period if the premises had been let to him at an annual rent equal to the appropriate percentage of the amount by which the cost of providing the accommodation exceeds £75,000.

(6) Where throughout the period of six years ending with the date when the recipient first occupied the property any estate or interest in the property was held by a relevant person (whether or not it was the same estate, interest or person throughout), the additional value shall be calculated as if in subsection (7) below—

(a) the amount referred to in paragraph (a) were the market value of that property as at that date, and
(b) the amount referred to in paragraph (b) did not include expenditure on improvements made before that date.

(7) For the purposes of this section, the cost of providing any living accommodation shall be taken to be the aggregate of—

(a) the amount of any expenditure incurred in acquiring the estate or interest in the property held by a relevant person, and
(b) the amount of any expenditure incurred by a relevant person before the year of assessment in question on improvements to the property.

(8) The aggregate amount mentioned in subsection (7) above shall be reduced by the amount of any payment made by the recipient to a relevant person, so far as that amount represents a reimbursement of any such expenditure as is mentioned in paragraph (a) or (b) of that subsection or represents consideration for the grant to the recipient of a tenancy of the property.

(9) For the purposes of this section, any of the following persons is a relevant person—

(a) the person providing the accommodation;

    (*b*) any person, other than the recipient, who is connected with a person falling within paragraph (*a*) above,

(10) In this section—

"the appropriate percentage" means the rate applicable for the purposes of section 160 as at the beginning of the year of assessment in question;
"market value", in relation to any property, means the price which that property might reasonably be expected to fetch on a sale in the open market with vacant possession, no reduction being made, in estimating the market value, on account of any option in respect of the property held by the recipient, or a person connected with him, or by any of the persons mentioned in subsection (9) above;
"property", in relation to any living accommodation, means the property consisting of that living accommodation;
"tenancy" includes a sub-tenancy;

and section 839 shall apply for the purposes of this section."

10. In section 598(1)(*b*) (charge to tax: repayment of employee's contributions) the word "relevant" shall be inserted before the words "statutory scheme".

11.—(1) Section 599 (charge to tax: commutation of entire pension in special circumstances) shall be amended as follows.

(2) In subsection (2)(*b*) the word "relevant" shall be inserted before the words "statutory scheme".

(3) After subsection (9) there shall be inserted—

"(10) In subsection (1)(*a*) above "the permitted maximum" means, as regards a charge to tax arising under this section in a particular year of assessment, the figure found for that year by virtue of subsections (11) and (12) below.

(11) For the years 1988–89 and 1989–90 the figure is £60,000.

(12) For any subsequent year of assessment the figure is the figure found for that year, for the purposes of section 590C, by virtue of section 590C(4) and (5)."

12.—(1) The following section shall be inserted after section 599—

"**599A. Charge to tax: payments out of surplus funds**

(1) This subsection applies to any payment which is made to or for the benefit of an employee or to his personal representatives out of funds which are or have been held for the purposes of—

   (*a*) a scheme which is or has at any time been an exempt approved scheme, or
   (*b*) a relevant statutory scheme established under a public general Act,

and which is made in pursuance of duty to return surplus funds.

(2) On the making of a payment to which subsection (1) above applies, the administrator of the scheme shall be charged to income tax under Case VI of Schedule D at the relevant rate on such amount as, after deduction of tax at that rate, would equal the amount of the payment.

(3) Subject to subsection (4) below, the relevant rate shall be 35 per cent.

(4) The Treasury may by order from time to time increase or decrease the relevant rate.

(5) Where a payment made to or for the benefit of an employee is one to which subsection (1) applies, it shall be treated in computing the total income of the employee for the year in which it is made as income for that year which is—

   (*a*) received by him after deduction of income tax at the basic rate from a corresponding gross amount, and
   (*b*) chargeable to income tax under Case VI of Schedule D.

(6) But, subject to subsection (7) below, no assessment to income tax shall be made on, and no repayment of income tax shall be made to, the employee.

(7) Subsection (6) above shall not prevent an assessment in respect of income tax at a rate other than the basic rate.

(8) Subsection (5) above applies whether or not the employee is the recipient of the payment.

(9) Any payment chargeable to tax under this section shall not be chargeable to tax under section 598, 599 or 600 or under the Regulations mentioned in paragraph 8 of Schedule 3 to the Finance Act 1971.

(10) In this section—

"employee", in relation to a relevant statutory scheme, includes any officer;
references to any payment include references to any transfer of assets or other transfer of money's worth."

13.—(1) Section 600 (charge to tax: unauthorised payments to or for employees) shall be amended as follows.

(2) In subsection (1) the words "or have been" and "or has at any time been" shall be omitted.

(3) In subsection (2) for paragraphs (*a*) and (*b*) there shall be substituted the words "is not expressly authorised by the rules of the scheme or by virtue of paragraph 33 of Schedule 6 to the Finance Act 1989."

14. In section 605 (information) the word "relevant" shall be inserted before the words "statutory scheme" in subsections (2), (3)(*a*) and (*b*)(i) and (4).

15. The following section shall be inserted after section 611—

"611A. Definition of relevant statutory scheme

(1) In this Chapter any reference to a relevant statutory scheme is a reference to a statutory scheme—

(*a*) established before 14th March 1989, or
(*b*) established on or after that date and entered in the register maintained by the Board for the purposes of this section.

(2) The Board shall maintain a register for the purposes of this section and shall enter in it the relevant particulars of any statutory scheme established on or after 14th March 1989 which is reported to the Board by the authority responsible for establishing it as a scheme the provisions of which correspond with those of an approved scheme.

(3) The reference in subsection (2) above to the relevant particulars, in relation to a scheme, is a reference to—

(*a*) the identity of the scheme,
(*b*) the date on which it was established,
(*c*) the authority responsible for establishing it, and
(*d*) the date on which that authority reported the scheme to the Board.

(4) Where the Board enter the relevant particulars of a scheme in the register maintained by them for the purposes of this section, they shall inform the authority responsible for establishing the scheme of the date of the entry."

16. In section 828(4) (orders) after "377(8)" there shall be inserted "590C(6)".

17. Paragraph 8 of Schedule 23 (benefits under scheme for additional voluntary contributions causing benefits under main scheme to abate if aggregate benefits exceed limits) shall be omitted.

Effect of amendments

18.—(1) Paragraphs 2, 6(2), 8(2)(*b*), 10, 11(2), 14 and 15 above shall be deemed to have come into force on 14th March 1989.

(2) Paragraphs 3(2) and (3) and 4 above shall have effect in relation to a scheme not approved by the Board before the day on which this Act is passed; but if the scheme came into existence before 14th March 1989 those provisions shall not have effect as regards an employee who became a member of the scheme before 1st June 1989.

(3) Paragraph 3(4) above shall have effect where a determination is made on or after the day on which this Act is passed.

(4) Paragraphs 5 and 6(3), (4) and (5) above shall have effect for the year 1989–90 and subsequent years of assessment, but paragraphs 5(4) and 6(5) above shall not have effect as regards a person's remuneration in respect of an office or employment in such circumstances as the Board may by regulations prescribe for the purposes of this sub-paragraph.

(5) Paragraphs 7 and 8(2)(*a*) and (3) above shall have effect for the year 1988–89 and subsequent years of assessment.

(6) Paragraph 8(4) above shall not have effect where a sum has been deemed to be income of a person by virtue of section 595(2) before 6th April 1988.

(7) Paragraph 9 above shall have effect in relation to payments made and benefits provided on or after the day on which this Act is passed.

(8) Paragraph 11(3) above shall have effect where the charge to tax under section 599 arises on or after 14th March 1989, but not where the scheme came into existence before that date and the employee became a member of it before 1st June 1989.

(9) Paragraphs 12 and 13 above shall have effect in relation to payments made on or after the day on which this Act is passed.

(10) Paragraph 17 above shall have effect in relation to benefits provided on or after the day on which this Act is passed.

PART II

APPROVED SCHEMES: GENERAL

Preliminary

19.—(1) This Part of this Schedule shall be deemed to have come into force on 14th March 1989 and, subject to sub-paragraphs (2) to (4) below, applies in relation to any retirement benefits scheme (within the meaning of Chapter I of Part XIV of the Taxes Act 1988) approved by the Board before the day on which this Act is passed.

(2) The Board may by regulations provide that, in circumstances prescribed in the regulations, this Part of this Schedule or any provision of it shall not apply or shall apply with such modifications as may be so prescribed.

(3) Regulations under sub-paragraph (2) above—

(*a*) may include provision authorising the Board to direct that this Part of this Schedule or any provision of it shall not apply in any particular case where in the opinion of the Board the facts are such that its application would not be appropriate;

(*b*) may take effect (and may authorise any direction given under them to take effect) as from 14th March 1989 or any later date;

(*c*) may make such supplementary provision as appears to the Board to be necessary or expedient.

(4) This Part of this Schedule shall not apply to a scheme if, before the end of 1989, the administrator of the scheme gives written notice to the Board that it is not to apply.

(5) Where a notice is given to the Board under sub-paragraph (4) above, the scheme shall cease to be approved—

(*a*) if it came into existence before 14th March 1989, with effect from 1st June 1989 or (if later) the date with effect from which it was approved;

(*b*) if it came into existence on or after 14th March 1989, with effect from the date with effect from which it was approved.

Remuneration

20.—(1) This paragraph applies—

(*a*) where the scheme came into existence before 14th March 1989, as regards an employee who became a member of the scheme on or after 1st June 1989;

(*b*) where the scheme came into existence on or after 14th March 1989, as regards any employee who is a member of the scheme (whenever he became a member).

(2) The rules of the scheme shall have effect (notwithstanding anything in them to the contrary and notwithstanding the effect of anything in Schedule 23 to the Taxes Act 1988) as if, in arriving at the employee's relevant annual remuneration for the purposes of calculating benefits, any excess of what would be his relevant annual remuneration (apart from this paragraph) over the permitted maximum for the year of assessment in which his participation in the scheme ceases shall be disregarded.

(3) The rules of the scheme shall have effect (notwithstanding anything in them to the contrary) as if, in arriving at the employee's remuneration for the year 1988–89 or any subsequent year of assessment for the purposes of any restriction on the aggregate amount of contributions payable under the scheme by the employee and the employer, there were disregarded any excess of what would be his remuneration for the year (apart from this paragraph) over the permitted maximum for the year.

(4) In this paragraph "the permitted maximum", in relation to a year of assessment, means the figure found for that year by virtue of sub-paragraphs (5) and (6) below.

(5) For the years 1988–89 and 1989–90 the figure is £60,000.

(6) For any subsequent year of assessment the figure is the figure found for that year, for the purposes of section 590C of the Taxes Act 1988, by virtue of section 590C(4) and (5).

21.—(1) The rules of the scheme shall have effect (notwithstanding anything in them to the contrary) as if the amount of contributions payable under the scheme by an employee in the year 1989–90 or any subsequent year of assessment were limited to 15 per cent. of his remuneration for the year in respect of the employment.

(2) Where in relation to any year of assessment a percentage higher than 15 per cent. applies for the purposes of section 592(8) or (8A) of the Taxes Act 1988 (relief in respect of contributions) as regards any employee, sub-paragraph (1) above, as regards him, shall have effect in relation to that year with the substitution for 15 per cent. of that higher percentage.

22.—(1) This paragraph applies—

(*a*) where the scheme came into existence before 14th March 1989, as regards an employee who became a member of the scheme on or after 1st June 1989;
(*b*) where the scheme came into existence on or after 14th March 1989, as regards any employee who is a member of the scheme (whenever he became a member).

(2) For the purposes of paragraph 21(1) above, in arriving at the employee's remuneration for the year any excess of what would be his remuneration for the year (apart from this sub-paragraph) over the permitted maximum for the year shall be disregarded.

(3) In sub-paragraph (2) above "the permitted maximum", in relation to a year of assessment, means the figure found for that year by virtue of sub-paragraphs (4) and (5) below.

(4) For the year 1989–90 the figure is £60,000.

(5) For any subsequent year of assessment the figure is the figure found for that year, for the purposes of section 590C of the Taxes Act 1988, by virtue of section 590C(4) and (5).

Accelerated accrual

23.—(1) This paragraph applies where the scheme allows a member to commute his pension or part of it for a lump sum or sums and—

(*a*) where the scheme came into existence before 14th March 1989, applies as regards an employee who became a member of the scheme on or after 1st June 1989, and
(*b*) where the scheme came into existence on or after 14th March 1989, applies as regards any employee who is a member of the scheme (whenever he became a member).

(2) The rules of the scheme shall have effect (notwithstanding anything in them to the contrary and notwithstanding the effect of paragraph 3 of Schedule 23 to the Taxes Act 1988) as if they did not allow the employee to obtain by way of commutation a lump sum or sums exceeding in all the greater of the following sums—

(*a*) a sum of three-eightieths of his relevant annual remuneration for each year of service up to a maximum of 40;
(*b*) a sum of the pension payable under the scheme to the employee for the first year in which it is payable multiplied by 2.25.

(3) The following rules shall apply in calculating, for the purposes of sub-paragraph (2) above, the pension payable under the scheme to the employee for the first year in which it is payable—

(*a*) if the pension payable for the year changes, the initial pension payable shall be taken;
(*b*) it shall be assumed that the employee will survive for the year;
(*c*) the effect of commutation, and of any allocation of pension to provide benefits for survivors, shall be ignored.

24.—(1) This paragraph applies where the scheme provides a lump sum or sums for a member otherwise than by commutation of his pension or part of it and—

(*a*) where the scheme came into existence before 14th March 1989, applies as regards an employee who became a member of the scheme on or after 1st June 1989, and
(*b*) where the scheme came into existence on or after 14th March 1989, applies as regards any employee who is a member of the scheme (whenever he became a member).

(2) The rules of the scheme shall have effect (notwithstanding anything in them to the contrary and notwithstanding the effect of paragraph 4 of Schedule 23 to the Taxes Act 1988) as if they did not allow the payment to the employee, otherwise than by way of commutation, of a lump sum or sums exceeding in all the greater of the following sums—

(*a*) a sum of three-eightieths of his relevant annual remuneration for each year of service up to a maximum of 40;
(*b*) a sum of the relevant number of eightieths of his relevant annual remuneration.

(3) For the purposes of sub-paragraph (2) above the relevant number shall be found by

taking the number of eightieths (of relevant annual remuneration) by reference to which the pension payable under the scheme to the employee is calculated, multiplying that number by three, and treating the resulting number as 120 if it would otherwise exceed 120.

Associated employments

25.—(1) This paragraph applies—

(*a*) where the scheme came into existence before 14th March 1989, as regards an employee who became a member of the scheme on or after 1st June 1989;

(*b*) where the scheme came into existence on or after 14th March 1989, as regards any employee who is a member of the scheme (whenever he became a member).

(2) Where the employee is a member of the scheme by virtue of two or more relevant associated employments, the rules of the scheme shall have effect as mentioned in sub-paragraph (3) below.

(3) The rules of the scheme shall have effect (notwithstanding anything in them to the contrary) as if they prohibited the amount payable by way of pension in respect of service in any of the relevant associated employments, when aggregated with any amount payable by way of pension in respect of service in the other such employment or employments, from exceeding the relevant amount.

(4) For the purposes of sub-paragraph (3) above the relevant amount, in relation to the employee, shall be found by applying the following formula—

$$\frac{A \times C}{30}$$

(5) For the purposes of this paragraph—

(*a*) section 590B(5) and (6) of the Taxes Act 1988 shall apply for the purpose of defining A, and

(*b*) section 590B(9) to (11) of that Act shall apply for the purpose of defining C,

as they apply for the purposes of section 590B of that Act, except that for the purposes of this paragraph A shall not exceed 20.

(6) The reference to two or more relevant associated employments shall be construed in accordance with section 590A of the Taxes Act 1988.

Connected schemes

26.—(1) This paragraph applies—

(*a*) where the scheme came into existence before 14th March 1989, as regards an employee who became a member of the scheme on or after 1st June 1989;

(*b*) where the scheme came into existence on or after 14th March 1989, as regards any employee who is a member of the scheme (whenever he became a member).

(2) Where in relation to the employee the scheme is connected with another scheme which is (or other schemes each of which is) an approved scheme, the rules of the scheme shall have effect as mentioned in sub-paragraph (3) below.

(3) The rules of the scheme shall have effect (notwithstanding anything in them to the contrary) as if they prohibited the amount payable by way of pension under the scheme, when aggregated with any amount payable by way of pension under the other scheme or schemes, from exceeding the relevant amount.

(4) For the purposes of sub-paragraph (3) above the relevant amount, in relation to the employee, shall be found by applying the following formula—

$$\frac{B \times C}{30}$$

(5) For the purposes of this paragraph—

(*a*) section 590B(7) and (8) of the Taxes Act 1988 shall apply for the purpose of defining B, and

(*b*) section 590B(9) to (11) of that Act shall apply for the purpose of defining C,

as they apply for the purposes of section 590B of that Act, except that for the purposes of this paragraph B shall not exceed 20.

(6) References in this paragraph to the scheme being connected with another scheme in relation to the employee shall be construed in accordance with section 590A of the Taxes Act 1988.

Augmentation

27.—(1) This paragraph applies—

(*a*) where the scheme came into existence before 14th March 1989, as regards an employee who became a member of the scheme on or after 1st June 1989;
(*b*) where the scheme came into existence on or after 14th March 1989, as regards any employee who is a member of the scheme (whenever he became a member).

(2) Where in addition to being a member of the scheme (the main scheme) the employee is also a member of an approved scheme (the voluntary scheme) which provides additional benefits to supplement those provided by the main scheme and to which no contributions are made by any employer of his, sub-paragraph (3) below shall apply in relation to any augmentation of the benefits provided for him by the main scheme after he has ceased to participate in it.

(3) Any rules of the main scheme imposing a limit on the amount of a benefit provided for the employee shall have effect (notwithstanding anything in them to the contrary) as if they provided for the limit to be reduced by the amount of any like benefit provided for the employee by the voluntary scheme.

Centralised schemes

28.—(1) Where the scheme is a centralised scheme, sub-paragraph (1)(*a*) and (*b*) of each of paragraphs 20 and 22 to 27 above shall have effect with the substitution for the reference to the coming into existence of the scheme of a reference to the commencement of the employer's participation in the scheme.

(2) For the purposes of this paragraph a centralised scheme is a retirement benefits scheme (within the meaning of Chapter I of Part XIV of the Taxes Act 1988) established for the purpose of enabling any employer, other than an employer associated with the person by whom the scheme is established, to participate in it as regards his employees.

(3) For the purposes of sub-paragraph (2) above one person is associated with another if (directly or indirectly) one is controlled by the other or if both are controlled by a third person.

(4) In sub-paragraph (3) above the reference to control, in relation to a body corporate, shall be construed—

(*a*) where the body corporate is a close company, in accordance with section 416 of the Taxes Act 1988, and
(*b*) where it is not, in accordance with section 840 of that Act.

Election

29.—(1) In a case where—

(*a*) an employee became a member of the scheme on or after 17th March 1987 and before 1st June 1989, and
(*b*) he gives written notice to the administrator of the scheme that this Part of this Schedule is to apply in his case,

he shall be deemed for the purposes of this Part of this Schedule to have become a member of the scheme on 1st June 1989.

(2) A notice under this paragraph shall be given in such form as the Board may prescribe.

Supplementary

30. In this Part of this Schedule "relevant annual remuneration" means final remuneration or, if the scheme provides for benefits to be calculated by reference to some other annual remuneration, that other annual remuneration.

PART III

APPROVED SCHEMES: ADDITIONAL VOLUNTARY CONTRIBUTIONS

Preliminary

31.—(1) Subject to sub-paragraphs (2) to (4) below, this Part of this Schedule applies in relation to any retirement benefits scheme which was approved by the Board before the day on which this Act is passed and which makes provision for the payment by an employee of voluntary contributions.

(2) Paragraph 32 below only applies where—

(*a*) the provision for the payment of voluntary contributions is freestanding, and
(*b*) the scheme is not one to which contributions are made by any employer of the employee.

(3) The Board may by regulations provide that, in circumstances prescribed in the regulations, this Part of this Schedule or any provision of it shall not apply or shall apply with such modifications as may be so prescribed.

(4) Regulations under sub-paragraph (3) above—

(*a*) may include provision authorising the Board to direct that this Part of this Schedule or any provision of it shall not apply in any particular case where in the opinion of the Board the facts are such that its application would not be appropriate;
(*b*) may make such supplementary provision as appears to the Board to be necessary or expedient.

Abatement of benefits

32.—(1) The scheme shall have effect (notwithstanding anything in it to the contrary) as if its rules included a rule imposing, in the case of each benefit provided for the employee, such a limit on the amount of the benefit as is mentioned in sub-paragraph (2) below.

(2) The limit referred to above is a limit of such an amount as is found by—

(*a*) taking the amount of the limit imposed by the main scheme on the provision of any like benefit for the employee by that scheme, and
(*b*) subtracting from that amount an amount equal to the relevant amount.

(3) For the purposes of sub-paragraph (2) above the relevant amount is—

(*a*) where the employee is not a member of any other relevant scheme, the amount of any like benefit provided for the employee by the main scheme, and
(*b*) where the employee is a member of another relevant scheme or schemes, an amount equal to the aggregate of the amount mentioned in paragraph (*a*) above and the amount of any like benefit provided for the employee by the other relevant scheme or schemes.

(4) In sub-paragraph (3) above, references to the employee being a member of another relevant scheme are references to his being a member of any approved scheme, other than the scheme, which provides additional benefits for him to supplement those provided by the main scheme.

(5) This paragraph shall have effect in relation to benefits provided on or after the day on which this Act is passed.

Return of surplus funds

33.—(1) The scheme shall have effect (notwithstanding anything in it to the contrary) as if its rules included a rule requiring the administrator, in the circumstances mentioned in sub-paragraph (2) or (3) below, as the case may be, to make to the employee or his personal representatives a payment of an amount equal to the prescribed amount out of funds which are or have been held for the purposes of the scheme.

(2) Where the provision for the payment of voluntary contributions is freestanding, the circumstances referred to above are that the amount of any benefit provided for the employee by the scheme would have been greater had the amount of any like benefit provided for him by the main scheme, or any other relevant scheme of which he is a member, been less.

(3) Where the provision for the payment of voluntary contributions is not freestanding, the circumstances referred to above are that the amount of any benefit provided for the employee by virtue of the voluntary contributions would have been greater had the amount of any like benefit provided for him by the principal provisions of the scheme, or any other relevant scheme of which he is a member, been less.

(4) In sub-paragraph (1) above, the reference to the prescribed amount is to an amount calculated in accordance with the method for the time being specified in regulations made for the purposes of section 591 of the Taxes Act 1988 as the method to be used for calculating the amount of any surplus funds.

(5) In sub-paragraph (2) above, the reference to the employee being a member of another relevant scheme is a reference to his being a member of any approved scheme, other than the scheme, which provides additional benefits for him to supplement those provided by the main scheme.

(6) In sub-paragraph (3) above, the reference to the employee being a member of another relevant scheme is a reference to his being a member of any approved scheme, other than the scheme, which provides additional benefits for him to supplement those provided by the principal provisions of the scheme.

Cross references.—See TA 1988, s. 600(2) (unauthorised payments from pension schemes etc.

34. The scheme shall have effect (notwithstanding anything in it to the contrary) as if its rules included a rule enabling the administrator, before making any payment by virtue of paragraph 33 above, to deduct the amount of any tax to which he is charged by section 599A of the Taxes Act 1988 by virtue of making the payment.

Supplementary

35. In this Part of this Schedule—

(*a*) "administrator", "approved scheme", "employee" and "retirement benefits scheme" have the same meanings as in Chapter I of Part XIV of the Taxes Act 1988,
(*b*) "freestanding", in relation to provision for the payment of voluntary contributions, means provision which is contained in a retirement benefits scheme other than the one which provides the benefits which the voluntary contributions are intended to supplement,
(*c*) "the main scheme", in relation to provision for the payment of voluntary contributions which is freestanding, means the retirement benefits scheme which provides the benefits which the voluntary contributions are intended to supplement,
(*d*) "principal provisions", in relation to a retirement benefits scheme which makes provision for the payment of voluntary contributions which is not freestanding, means the provisions of the scheme concerning the provision of the benefits which the voluntary contributions are intended to supplement,
(*e*) references to the provision of a benefit for an employee shall, in relation to a deceased employee, be construed as references to the provision of a benefit in respect of him, and
(*f*) references to an employee being (or not being) a member of a scheme shall, in relation to a deceased employee, be construed as references to his having been (or not having been) a member of a scheme immediately before the time of his death.

SCHEDULE 7

Section 77

PERSONAL PENSION SCHEMES

PART I
AMENDMENTS OF TAXES ACT

1. Chapter IV of Part XIV of the Taxes Act 1988 (personal pension schemes) shall be amended as mentioned in the following provisions of this Part of this Schedule.

2.—(1) Section 635 (lump sum to member) shall be amended as follows.

(2) The following subsection shall be substituted for subsection (3) (lump sum not to exceed one quarter of value of benefits for member)—

"(3) The lump sum must not exceed one quarter of the difference between—

(*a*) the total value, at the time when the lump sum is paid, of the benefits provided for by the arrangements made by the member in accordance with the scheme, and
(*b*) the value, at that time, of such of the member's rights under the scheme as are protected rights for the purposes of the Social Security Act 1986 or the Social Security (Northern Ireland) Order 1986."

(3) Subsection (4) (lump sum not to exceed £150,000 or sum specified by Treasury by order) shall cease to have effect.

(4) This paragraph shall have effect in relation to the approval of a scheme on or after the day on which this Act is passed; but if the scheme came into existence before that day sub-paragraph (2) above shall not have effect as regards arrangements made by a member in accordance with the scheme before that day.

3.—(1) In section 640 (maximum amount of deductions) the following table shall be substituted for the table in subsection (2) (maximum amount by reference to age)—

36 to 45	20 per cent.
46 to 50	25 per cent.
51 to 55	30 per cent.
56 to 60	35 per cent.
61 or more	40 per cent.

(2) This paragraph shall have effect for the year 1989–90 and subsequent years of assessment.

4.—(1) The following section shall be inserted after section 640—

"640A. Earnings cap

(1) In arriving at an individual's net relevant earnings for a year of assessment for the purposes of section 640 above, any excess of what would be his net relevant earnings for the year (apart from this subsection) over the allowable maximum for the year shall be disregarded.

(2) In subsection (1) above "the allowable maximum" means, as regards a particular year of assessment, the figure found for that year by virtue of subsections (3) and (4) below.

(3) For the year of assessment 1989–90 the figure is £60,000.

(4) For the year of assessment 1990–91 and any subsequent year of assessment the figure is the figure found for that year, for the purposes of section 590C, by virtue of section 590C(4) and (5)."

(2) This paragraph shall have effect for the year 1989–90 and subsequent years of assessment.

5.—(1) Section 644 (meaning of relevant earnings) shall be amended as follows.

(2) In subsection (2) for "(5)" there shall be substituted "(6F)".

(3) The following subsections shall be inserted after subsection (6)—

"(6A) Emoluments of an individual as an employee of a company are not income within subsection (2) above if—

(*a*) he is a controlling director of the company at any time in the year of assessment in question or has been a controlling director of the company at any time in the ten years immediately preceding that year of assessment, and

(b) any of subsections (6B) to (6E) below applies in his case.

(6B) This subsection applies in the case of the individual if—

(a) at any time in the year of assessment in question he is in receipt of benefits under a relevant superannuation scheme, and
(b) the benefits are payable in respect of past service with the company.

(6C) This subsection applies in the case of the individual if—

(a) at any time in the year of assessment in question he is in receipt of benefits under a personal pension scheme,
(b) the scheme has received a transfer payment relating to him from a relevant superannuation scheme, and
(c) the transfer payment is in respect of past service with the company.

(6D) This subsection applies in the case of the individual if—

(a) at any time in the year of assessment in question he is in receipt of benefits under a relevant superannuation scheme,
(b) the benefits are payable in respect of past service with another company,
(c) the emoluments are for a period during which the company mentioned in subsection (6A) above has carried on a trade or business previously carried on by the other company, and
(d) the other company carried on the trade or business at any time during the period of service in respect of which the benefits are payable.

(6E) This subsection applies in the case of the individual if—

(a) at any time in the year of assessment in question he is in receipt of benefits under a personal pension scheme,
(b) the scheme has received a transfer payment relating to him from a relevant superannuation scheme,
(c) the transfer payment is in respect of past service with another company,
(d) the emoluments are for a period during which the company mentioned in subection (6A) above has carried on a trade or business previously carried on by the other company, and
(e) the other company carried on the trade or business at any time during the period of service in respect of which the transfer payment was made.

(6F) For the purposes of subsections (6A) to (6E) above—

(a) a person is a controlling director of a company if he is a director (as defined by section 612(1)), and he is within paragraph (b) of section 417(5), in relation to the company;
(b) "relevant superannuation scheme" has the same meaning as in section 645(1);
(c) references to benefits payable in respect of past service with a company include references to benefits payable partly in respect of past service with the company; and
(d) references to a transfer payment in respect of past service with a company include references to a transfer payment partly in respect of past service with the company."

(4) This paragraph shall be deemed to have come into force on 6th April 1989.

6.—(1) Section 645 (earnings from pensionable employment) shall be amended as follows.

(2) In subsection (1)(c) for the words "neither subsection (4) nor subsection (5) below applies" there shall be substituted the words "subsection (4) below does not apply".

(3) In subsection (3) the word "and" following paragraph (a) shall be omitted and after paragraph (b) there shall be inserted "and

(c) which is of a description mentioned in section 596(1)(a), (b) or (c)."

(4) After subsection (4) there shall be inserted—

"(4A) Where the emoluments from an office or employment held by an individual are foreign emoluments within the meaning of section 192, this section shall have effect with the substitution of the following for paragraph (c) of subsection (3) above—

"(c) which corresponds to a scheme of a description mentioned in section 596(1)(a), (b) or (c).""

(5) Subsection (5) shall cease to have effect.

(6) This paragraph shall be deemed to have come into force on 6th April 1989.

7.—(1) In section 646 ("net relevant earnings") in subsection (1) after the words "(7) below" there shall be inserted the words "and section 646A".

(2) This paragraph shall have effect for the year 1989–90 and subsequent years of assessment.

8.—(1) The following section shall be inserted after section 646—

"646A. Earnings from associated employments

(1) This section applies where in the year of assessment in question—

(*a*) an individual holds two or more offices or employments which are associated in that year,
(*b*) one or more of them is an office or employment to which section 645 applies ("pensionable job"), and
(*c*) one or more of them is an office or employment to which that section does not apply ("non-pensionable job").

(2) Where the emoluments for that year from the pensionable job (or jobs) are equal to or exceed the allowable maximum for that year, section 646(1) shall have effect in the case of the individual as if the references to relevant earnings were references to relevant earnings not attributable to the non-pensionable jobs (or jobs).

(3) Where the allowable maximum for that year exceeds the emoluments for that year from the pensionable job (or jobs), the individual's net relevant earnings, so far as attributable to the non-pensionable job (or jobs), shall not be greater than the amount of the excess.

(4) For the purposes of this section two or more offices or employments held by an individual in a year of assessment are associated in that year if the employers in question are associated at any time during it.

(5) For the purposes of subsection (4) above, employers are associated if (directly or indirectly) one is controlled by the other or if both are controlled by a third person.

(6) In subsection (5) above the reference to control, in relation to a body corporate, shall be construed—

(*a*) where the body corporate is a close company, in accordance with section 416, and
(*b*) where it is not, in accordance with section 840.

(7) In this section "the allowable maximum" has the same meaning as in section 640A(1)."

(2) This paragraph shall have effect for the year 1989–90 and subsequent years of assessment.

9. In section 655(5) (provisional approval in the case of applications made before 1st February 1990) the words "in cases where the applications are made before 1st February 1990" shall be omitted.

PART II

SCHEMES APPROVED BEFORE PASSING OF THIS ACT

Interpretation

10. In this Part of this Schedule—

(*a*) "personal pension scheme" has the same meaning as in Chapter IV of Part XIV of the Taxes Act 1988, and
(*b*) references to approval of such a scheme do not include references to provisional approval under regulations made under section 655(5) of that Act.

Lump sum to member

11.—(1) This paragraph applies as regards arrangements made by a member of a personal pension scheme approved by the Board before the day on which this Act is passed, if the arrangements are made by the member in accordance with the scheme on or after that day.

(2) The rules of the scheme shall have effect (notwithstanding anything in them to the contrary) as if any limitation imposed on the maximum amount payable to the member by way of lump sum, and imposed by reference to a fraction of the total value of the benefits for him provided for by the arrangements, were imposed by reference to the same fraction of the difference between—

(*a*) the total value, at the time when the lump sum is paid, of the benefits provided for by the arrangements, and
(*b*) the value, at that time, of such of his rights under the scheme as are protected rights for the purposes of the Social Security Act 1986 or the Social Security (Northern Ireland) Order 1986.

12.—(1) This paragraph applies where on or after the day on which this Act is passed a lump sum becomes payable under a personal pension scheme approved by the Board before that day.

(2) The rules of the scheme shall have effect (notwithstanding anything in them to the contrary) as if any limitation imposed on the maximum amount payable to a member by way of lump sum, and imposed by reference to a figure, did not apply.

(3) The reference in sub-paragraph (2) above to a limitation imposed on the maximum amount payable to a member by way of lump sum does not include a reference to a limitation imposed on the maximum amount so payable out of a transfer payment.

SCHEDULE 8

Section 84

AMENDMENTS OF CHAPTER I OF PART XII OF TAXES ACT 1988 (INSURANCE COMPANIES)

1. In section 431 (interpretative provisions relating to insurance companies), at the end of subsection (2) there shall be added—

""policy holders' fraction" and "shareholders' fraction" shall be construed in accordance with section 89 of the Finance Act 1989."

2. Section 433 (profits reserved for policy holders or annuitants) shall cease to have effect.

3.—(1) In section 434 (franked investment income etc.), for subsection (3) there shall be substituted the following subsections—

"(3) Subject to sections 437 and 438, the policy holders' fraction of the franked investment income from investments held in connection with a company's life assurance business shall not be used under Chapter V of Part VI to frank distributions made by the company and, accordingly, for the purposes of that Chapter (other than the application of franked investment income under section 241), in relation to any unrelieved income of a company falling within subsection (1) above, the surplus of franked investment income for any accounting period means the aggregate of—

(*a*) the policy holders' fraction of that franked investment income; and
(*b*) the amount determined under section 241(3) on the basis that the reference therein to franked investment income is a reference only to the shareholders' fraction of that income."

(3A) The policy holders' fraction of the franked investment income from investments held in connection with a company's life assurance business shall be left out of account in determining, under subsection (7) of section 13, the franked investment income forming part of the company's profits for the purposes of that section."

(2) Subsections (4) and (5) of that section shall be omitted.

(3) In subsection (6) of that section for the words from "such fraction" onwards there shall be substituted "the policy holders' fraction thereof".

(4) In subsection (7) of that section for "(4)" there shall be substituted "(3)" and after the words "against which" there shall be inserted "disregarding relief under section 242".

4. After section 434 there shall be inserted the following section—

"434A. Limitations on loss relief and group relief

(1) In the case of a company carrying on life assurance business, no relief shall be allowable under Chapter II (loss relief) or Chapter IV (group relief) of Part X against the policy holders' fraction of the relevant profits for any accounting period.

(2) For the purposes of subection (1) above, the relevant profits of a company for an accounting period are the total profits of its life assurance business, less any deduction due under section 76, but before allowing any relief under Chapter II or Chapter IV of Part X."

5. Section 435 (taxation of gains reserved for policy holders and annuitants) shall cease to have effect.

6. In section 436 (annuity and pension business: separate charge on profits) in subsection (3)(*a*) for the words "section 433" there shall be substituted "sections 82 and 83 of the Finance Act 1989".

7. In section 441 (foreign life assurance funds) in subsection (5)(*b*) after "which" there shall be inserted "in respect of its general annuity business only".

SCHEDULE 9
Section 90
LIFE POLICIES ETC. HELD BY COMPANIES

1. Chapter II of Part XIII of the Taxes Act 1988 shall be amended as follows.

2. At the end of section 539 there shall be added—

"(9) A policy of life insurance issued in respect of an insurance made before 14th March 1989 shall be treated for the purposes of sections 540(5A), 547(8) and 548(3A) as issued in respect of one made on or after that date if it is varied on or after that date so as to increase the benefits secured or to extend the term of the insurance; and any exercise of rights conferred by the policy shall be regarded for this purpose as a variation."

3.—(1) Section 540 shall be amended as follows.

(2) In subsection (4), for the words "this section" there shall be substituted the words "subsections (1) and (3) above".

(3) After subsection (5) there shall be inserted—

"(5A) Sub-paragraphs (i) and (ii) of subsection (1)(*b*) above shall not apply in relation to a policy issued in respect of an insurance made on or after 14th March 1989 if, immediately before the happening of the event, the rights conferred by the policy were in the beneficial ownership of a company, or were held on trusts created, or as security for a debt owed, by a company."

4.—(1) Section 541 shall be amended as follows.

(2) After subsection (4) there shall be inserted—

"(4A) Where, immediately before the happening of the chargeable event, the rights conferred by a qualifying endowment policy are held as security for a debt owed by a company, then, if—

(*a*) the conditions in subsection (4B) below are satisfied,
(*b*) the amount of the debt exceeds the total amount previously paid under the policy by way of premiums, and
(*c*) the company makes a claim for the purpose within two years after the end of the accounting period in which the chargeable event happens,

this section shall have effect as if the references in subsection (1)(*a*) and (*b*) to that total amount were references to the amount of the debt.

(4B) The conditions referred to in subsection (4A) above are—

(*a*) that, throughout the period beginning with the making of the insurance and ending immediately before the happening of the chargeable event, the rights conferred by the policy have been held as security for a debt owed by the company;
(*b*) that the capital sum payable under the policy in the event of death during the term of the policy is not less than the amount of the debt when the insurance was made;
(*c*) that any sum payable under the policy by reason of the chargeable event is applied in repayment of the debt (except to the extent that its amount exceeds the amount of the debt);
(*d*) that the debt was incurred to defray money applied—

(i) in purchasing an estate or interest in land to be occupied by the company for the purposes of a trade carried on by it, or
(ii) for the purpose of the construction, extension or improvement (but not the repair or maintenance) of buildings which are or are to be so occupied.

(4C) If the amount of the debt is higher immediately before the happening of the chargeable event than it was at some earlier time during the period mentioned in subsection (4B)(*a*) above, the amount to be taken into account for the purposes of subsection (1) above shall be the lowest amount at which it stood during that period.

(4D) If during the period mentioned in subsection (4B)(*a*) above the company incurs a debt by borrowing in order to repay another debt, subsections (4B) and (4C) above shall have effect as if, where appropriate, references to either debt included references to the other."

(3) In subsection (5), after paragraph (*b*) there shall be inserted "and

(c) "qualifying endowment policy" means a policy which is a qualifying policy by virtue of paragraph 2 of Schedule 15;".

5.—(1) Section 547 shall be amended as follows.

(2) In subsection (1), for paragraph (b) there shall be substituted—

"(b) if, immediately before the happening of that event, those rights were in the beneficial ownership of a company, or were held on trusts created, or as security for a debt owed, by a company, the amount of the gain shall be deemed to form part of the company's income (chargeable under Case VI of Schedule D) for the accounting period in which the event happened;".

(3) After subsection (7) there shall be inserted—

"(8) Subsection (1)(b) above shall not have effect as respects—

(a) a policy of life insurance issued in respect of an insurance made before 14th March 1989,
(b) a contract for a life annuity made before that date, or
(c) a capital redemption policy issued in respect of an insurance made before that date, or issued by a company resident in the United Kingdom in respect of an insurance made on or after that date,

6.—(1) Section 548 shall be amended as follows.

(2) In subsection (1)—

(a) in paragraph (a), after the words "an individual's total income" there shall be inserted the words "or the income of a company";
(b) in paragraph (c), after the words "that individual" there shall be inserted the words "or company";
(c) for the words "subsection (3)" there shall be substituted the words "subsections (3) and (3A)".

(3) After subsection (3) there shall be inserted—

"(3A) Subsections (1) and (2) do not apply where the rights conferred by the policy or contract are in the beneficial ownership of a company, or are held on trusts created, or as security for a debt owed, by a company, if the policy was issued in respect of an insurance made before 14th March 1989 or the contract was made before that date."

7. In section 552, in subsection (2), after paragraph (b) there shall be inserted "or

(c) the event is a chargeable event only because of section 540(5A)."

8. Paragraph 5 above shall have effect in relation to chargeable events happening in any accounting period of the company concerned which begins after 31st March 1989; but subject to that this Schedule shall have effect as from 14th March 1989.

SCHEDULE 10

Section 93

DEEP DISCOUNT SECURITIES: AMENDMENTS

1. Schedule 4 to the Taxes Act 1988 (deep discount securities) shall be amended as mentioned in the following provisions of this Schedule.

2.—(1) Paragraph 1 shall be amended as follows.

(2) The following paragraph shall be inserted after sub-paragraph (1)(*d*)—

"(*dd*) "a deep discount security" also means any redeemable security which has been issued by a public body (at whatever time) at a deep discount, other than—

(i) a security such as is mentioned in paragraph (*d*)(ii) above;
(ii) a security falling within sub-paragraph (5), (6) or (7) below;".

(3) In sub-paragraph (1)(*g*) after the words "the company" there shall be inserted the words "or the public body".

(4) The following shall be inserted at the end of sub-paragraph (2)—

"This sub-paragraph applies only in the case of securities issued by a company."

(5) The following sub-paragraphs shall be inserted after sub-paragraph (3)—

"(4) For the purposes of this Schedule a public body is any of the following which is not a company—

(*a*) a government, whether of the United Kingdom or elsewhere;
(*b*) a public or local authority, whether in the United Kingdom or elsewhere.

(5) A security falls within this sub-paragraph if it is a gilt-edged security and—

(*a*) it was issued before 14th March 1989, or
(*b*) it was issued on or after that date but was issued under the same prospectus as any gilt-edged security issued before that date.

(6) A security falls within this sub-paragraph if it is a gilt-edged security and—

(*a*) it was issued under a prospectus under which no securities were issued before 14th March 1989,
(*b*) it was issued otherwise than on the occasion of the original issue under the prospectus, and
(*c*) all the securities issued on the occasion of the original issue under the prospectus are gilt-edged securities which are not deep discount securities.

(7) A security falls within this sub-paragraph if it is not a gilt-edged security and was issued (at whatever time) under the same prospectus as any other security which was issued before the security in question and which is not a deep discount security.

(8) For the purposes of this Schedule "gilt-edged security" has the same meaning as it has for the purposes of the 1979 Act."

3. The following sub-paragraph shall be inserted after paragraph 4(7)—

"(8) In the case of a deep discount security issued by a public body, this paragraph applies where a disposal is made on or after 14th March 1989 (whatever the date of acquisition)."

4. In paragraph 11(1) after the words "deep discount security" there shall be inserted the words "issued by a company".

5. The following paragraph shall be inserted after paragraph 11—

"**11A.** Where any deep discount security issued by a public body is redeemed before the redemption date by the body which issued it, paragraph 4 above shall have effect subject to paragraph 11(2) above (ignoring the words following paragraph (*b*))."

6. The following sub-paragraph shall be inserted after paragraph 13(2)—

"(3) Every public body which issues deep discount securities on or after 1st August 1989 shall cause to be shown on the certificate of each such security the income element for each income period between the date of issue of the security and the redemption date."

7. The following shall be inserted after paragraph 14—

"Retirement benefit schemes

15.—(1) In a case where—

(*a*) paragraph 4 above would apply (apart from this paragraph) to a disposal of a security, and
(*b*) immediately before the disposal was made the security was held for the purposes of an exempt approved scheme (within the meaning of Chapter I of Part XIV),

that paragraph shall not apply to the disposal.

(2) Sub-paragraph (1) above shall not apply unless the disposal is made on or after 14th March 1989.

Stock lending

16.—(1) In a case where—

(*a*) a security is the subject of a transfer which falls within section 129(3), and
(*b*) the transfer constitutes a disposal to which (apart from this paragraph) paragraph 4 above would apply,

that paragraph shall not apply to the disposal.

(2) Sub-paragraph (1) above shall not apply unless the disposal is made on or after 14th March 1989.

Trustees

17.—(1) Where on the disposal by trustees of a deep discount security an amount is treated as income chargeable to tax by virtue of paragraph 4(1) above, the rate at which it is chargeable shall be a rate equal to the sum of the basic rate and the additional rate for the year of assessment in which the disposal is made.

(2) Where the trustees are trustees of a scheme to which section 469 applies, sub-paragraph (1) above shall not apply if or to the extent that the amount is treated as income in the accounts of the scheme.

(3) Sub-paragraph (1) above shall not apply unless the disposal is made on or after 14th March 1989.

Underwriters

18.—(1) An underwriting member of Lloyd's shall be treated for the purposes of this Schedule as absolutely entitled as against the trustees to the securities forming part of his premiums trust fund, his special reserve fund (if any) and any other trust fund required or authorised by the rules of Lloyd's, or required by the underwriting agent through whom his business or any part of it is carried on, to be kept in connection with the business.

(2) Sub-paragraph (1) above applies where a disposal is made on or after 14th March 1989 (whatever the date of acquisition).

(3) Where a security forms part of a premiums trust fund at the end of 31st December of any relevant year, for the purposes of this Schedule the trustees of the fund shall be deemed to dispose of the security at that time; and for this purpose relevant years are 1989 and subsequent years.

(4) Where a security forms part of a premiums trust fund at the beginning of 1st January of any relevant year, for the purposes of this Schedule the trustees of the fund shall be deemed to acquire the security at that time; and for this purpose relevant years are 1990 and subsequent years.

(5) Sub-paragraph (6) below applies where the following state of affairs exists at the beginning of 1st January of any year or the end of 31st December of any year—

(*a*) securities have been transferred by the trustees of a premiums trust fund in pursuance of an arrangement mentioned in section 129(1) or (2),
(*b*) the transfer was made to enable another person to fulfil a contract or to make a transfer,
(*c*) securities have not been transferred in return, and
(*d*) section 129(3) applies to the transfer made by the trustees.

(6) The securities transferred by the trustees shall be treated for the purposes of sub-paragraphs (3) and (4) above as if they formed part of the premiums trust fund at the beginning of 1st January concerned or the end of 31st December concerned (as the case may be).

(7) Paragraph 7 above shall have effect subject to sub-paragraph (3) above.

(8) Paragraph 7(2) above shall not apply where—

(a) the deceased was an underwriting member of Lloyd's who died on or after 14th March 1989, and
(b) immediately before his death the security concerned formed part of a premiums trust fund, a special reserve fund or any other trust fund required or authorised by the rules of Lloyd's, or required by the underwriting agent through whom the deceased's business or any part of it was carried on, to be kept in connection with the business.

(9) In a case where an amount treated as income chargeable to tax by virtue of paragraph 4(1) above constitutes profits or gains mentioned in section 450(1)—

(a) section 450(1)(b) shall apply; and
(b) paragraph 4(1)(b) above shall not apply.

(10) For the purpose of computing income tax for the year 1987–88 sub-paragraph (9) above shall have effect as if—

(a) the reference to section 450(1) were to paragraph 2 of Schedule 16 to the Finance Act 1973, and
(b) the reference to section 450(1)(b) were to paragraph 2(b) of that Schedule.

(11) In this paragraph "business" and "premiums trust fund" have the meanings given by section 457.

Gilts: special rules

19.—(1) In a case where—

(a) securities have been issued by a public body under a prospectus under which no securities were issued before 14th March 1989,
(b) some of the securities issued under the prospectus are gilt-edged securities which are would-be deep discount securities,
(c) some of the securities issued under the prospectus are gilt-edged securities which are not would-be deep discount securities, and
(d) there is a time when the aggregate nominal value of the securities falling within paragraph (b) above (at that time) exceeds the aggregate nominal value of the securities falling within paragraph (c) above (at that time),

sub-paragraph (2) below shall apply in relation to any gilt-edged security which has been or is issued under the prospectus at any time (whether before, at or after the time mentioned in paragraph (d) above).

(2) As regards any event occurring in relation to the security after the time mentioned in sub-paragraph (1)(d) above, paragraphs 4, 7, 8, 11A, 12 and 14 to 18 above shall have effect as if—

(a) the security were a deep discount security,
(b) it had been issued as such (whatever the time it was issued), and
(c) it had been acquired as such (whatever the time it was acquired).

(3) For the purposes of sub-paragraph (1) above a would-be deep discount security is a security which would be a deep discount security apart from paragraph 1(6) above.

(4) For the purposes of sub-paragraph (2) above events, in relation to a security, include anything constituting a disposal for the purposes of the 1979 Act, the death of a person competent to dispose of the security, a disposal mentioned in paragraph 18(3) above, and an acquisition mentioned in paragraph 18(4) above.

Non-gilts: special rules

20.—(1) In a case where—

(a) all the securities issued by a public body on the occasion of the original issue under a particular prospectus (whatever the time of the issue) are neither gilt-edged securities nor deep discount securities,
(b) some of the securities issued under the prospectus are not gilt-edged securities but are new would-be deep discount securities, and
(c) there is a time when the aggregate nominal value of the securities falling within paragraph (b) above (at that time) exceeds the aggregate nominal value of the securities which (looking at the state of affairs at that time) have been issued under the prospectus and are neither gilt-edged securities nor new would-be deep discount securities,

sub-paragraph (2) below shall apply in relation to any security which is not a gilt-edged security but which has been or is issued under the prospectus at any time (whether before, at or after the time mentioned in paragraph (c) above).

(2) As regards any event occurring in relation to the security after the time mentioned in sub-paragraph (1)(c) above, paragraphs 4, 7, 8, 11A, 12 and 14 to 18 above shall have effect as if—

(a) the security were a deep discount security,
(b) it had been issued as such (whatever the time it was issued), and
(c) it had been acquired as such (whatever the time it was acquired).

(3) For the purposes of sub-paragraph (1) above a new would-be deep discount security is a security which—

(a) would be a deep discount security apart from paragraph 1(7) above, and
(b) was issued on or after 14th March 1989.

(4) For the purposes of sub-paragraph (2) above events, in relation to a security, include anything constituting a disposal for the purposes of the 1979 Act, the death of a person competent to dispose of the security, a disposal mentioned in paragraph 18(3) above, and an acquisition mentioned in paragraph 18(4) above."

SCHEDULE 11

Section 94

DEEP GAIN SECURITIES

Cross references.—See FA 1984, s. 64(3A) (CGT exemption for deep gain securities); TA 1988, s. 126(2)(*c*), (3) (Treasury securities issued at a discount).

Deep gain securities

1.—(1) For the purposes of this Schedule a deep gain security is a redeemable security (whenever issued) which fulfils the first and second conditions.

(2) The first condition is that, taking the security at the time it is issued and assuming redemption, the amount payable on redemption might constitute a deep gain; and if the security is capable of redemption on one of a number of occasions, this condition is fulfilled if it is fulfilled as regards any one of them.

(3) For the purposes of sub-paragraph (2) above "redemption" does not include any redemption which may be made before maturity only at the option of the person who issued the security (and no other person).

(4) The second condition is that the security—

(*a*) is not a deep discount security (either because the amount payable on redemption is not known at issue or for some other reason),
(*b*) is not a share in a company,
(*c*) is not a qualifying indexed security,
(*d*) is not a convertible security, and
(*e*) does not fall within sub-paragraph (5), (6) or (7) below.

(5) A security falls within this sub-paragraph if it is a gilt-edged security and—

(*a*) it was issued before 14th March 1989, or
(*b*) it was issued on or after that date but was issued under the same prospectus as any gilt-edged security issued before that date.

(6) A security falls within this sub-paragraph if it is a gilt-edged security and—

(*a*) it was issued under a prospectus under which no securities were issued before 14th March 1989,
(*b*) it was issued otherwise than on the occasion of the original issue under the prospectus, and
(*c*) all the securities issued on the occasion of the original issue under the prospectus are gilt-edged securities which are not deep gain securities.

(7) A security falls within this sub-paragraph if it is not a gilt-edged security and was issued (at whatever time) under the same prospectus as any other security which was issued before the security in question and which is not a deep gain security.

(8) For the purposes of this paragraph—

(*a*) a deep discount security is a security which is a deep discount security for the purposes of Schedule 4 to the Taxes Act 1988,
(*b*) "qualifying indexed security" has the meaning given by paragraph 2 below, and
(*c*) a gilt-edged security is a security which is a gilt-edged security for the purposes of the Capital Gains Tax Act 1979.

(9) For the purposes of this paragraph the amount payable on redemption of a security constitutes a deep gain if the issue price is less than the amount so payable, and the amount by which it is less represents more than—

(*a*) 15 per cent. of the amount so payable, or
(*b*) half Y per cent. of the amount so payable, where Y is the number of complete years between the date of issue and the redemption date.

(10) For the purposes of this paragraph the amount payable on redemption does not include any amount payable by way of interest.

Qualifying indexed securities

2.—(1) For the purposes of paragraph 1 above a qualifying indexed security is a security which fulfils each of the conditions set out below.

(2) The first condition is that—

(*a*) the security is denominated in sterling and under the terms of issue the amount payable on redemption is determined by reference to the movement of the retail prices index,
(*b*) the security is denominated in a currency other than sterling and under the terms of issue the amount payable on redemption is determined by reference to any similar general index of prices which is published by the government, or by an agent of the government, of the territory in whose currency the security is denominated, or
(*c*) the security was issued before 9th June 1989 and was quoted in the official list of a recognised stock exchange on 8th June 1989, and under the terms of issue the amount payable on redemption is determined by reference to the movement of a published index of prices of shares quoted in the official list of a recognised stock exchange.

(3) The second condition is that the terms of issue make no provision for conversion into, or redemption in, a currency other than that in which the security is denominated on issue.

(4) The third condition is that under the terms of issue—

(*a*) interest is payable on the security,
(*b*) not more than one year can elapse between the day of issue and the first day on which interest becomes payable, or between any day on which interest becomes payable and the next day on which it becomes payable,
(*c*) the interest payable is determined by reference to a rate which is not less than a reasonable commercial rate (judged by reference to the date of issue and by reference to securities of a similar nature to the one in question), and
(*d*) the interest payable is also determined by reference to the movement of the index by reference to which the amount payable on redemption is determined.

(5) The fourth condition is that where that index is applied to determine the amount payable on redemption or to determine interest it must, under the terms of issue, be applied precisely and without restriction.

(6) The fifth condition is that—

(*a*) the security is expressed to be issued for a definite period stated on the face of the security, and
(*b*) the period so stated commences with the day of issue and is five years or more.

(7) The sixth condition is that the terms of issue contain no provision enabling the person who holds the security for the time being to require any of the following before the expiry of a period which commences with the day of issue and which is five years or more—

(*a*) the security to be repurchased by the person who issued it;
(*b*) the security to be purchased by a person other than the person who issued it;
(*c*) the security to be converted into another kind of security;
(*d*) the security to be redeemed in circumstances other than any of the qualifying circumstances (set out in sub-paragraph (13) below).

(8) The seventh condition is that, where the issue is handled by an agent for the person making the issue or by an underwriter, the terms on which the agent or underwriter offers the security—

(*a*) contain no provision for the security to be repurchased by the person who issued it, converted into another kind of security, or redeemed, before the expiry of a period which commences with the day of issue and which is five years or more, and
(*b*) contain no provision enabling the person who holds the security for the time being to require the security to be purchased, by a person other than the person who issued it, before the expiry of a period which commences with the day of issue and which is five years or more.

(9) For the purposes of sub-paragraph (5) above "redemption" does not include any redemption which may be made before maturity only at the option of the person who issued the security (and no other person).

(10) In a case where the amount payable on redemption, or the amount of interest, is under the terms of issue determined by reference to the movement of the index for a period (a notional period) in place of a later actual period (a process commonly known as lagging) the fourth condition shall be treated as fulfilled if the following rules are fulfilled—

(a) under the terms of issue the notional period must start not more than eight months before the actual period starts and must end not more than eight months before the actual period ends, and

(b) where the index is applied for the notional period it must, under the terms of issue, be applied precisely and without restriction.

(11) In a case where the terms of issue contain provision for the amount payable on redemption to be not less than an amount stated in the terms, the provision shall not prevent the fourth condition being fulfilled if—

(a) the security was issued before 9th June 1989, and

(b) the amount stated does not constitute a deep gain (within the meaning given by paragraph 1(9) above).

(12) In a case where—

(a) the terms of issue contain provision for the amount payable on redemption in any of the qualifying circumstances (set out in sub-paragraph (13) below) to be not less than an amount stated in the terms, and

(b) the security was issued before 9th June 1989,

the provision shall not prevent the fourth condition being fulfilled.

(13) For the purposes of sub-paragraphs (7) and (12) above the following are qualifying circumstances—

(a) there is a fundamental change in the rules governing the index and the change would be detrimental to the interests of the person who holds the security for the time being;

(b) the index ceases to be published without being replaced by a comparable index;

(c) the person who issued the security fails to comply with the duties imposed on him by the terms of issue;

(d) the security was issued by a company before 9th June 1989 and a person gains control of the company in pursuance of the acceptance of an offer made by that person to acquire shares in the company.

(14) In a case where an issue is handled by an agent for the person making the issue, or by an underwriter, for the purposes of sub-paragraphs (2) to (5) and (10) above the terms of issue shall be taken to include any terms on which the agent or underwriter offers the security.

(15) For the purposes of this paragraph the amount payable on redemption does not include any amount payable by way of interest.

(16) For the purposes of this paragraph "control" (in relation to a company) shall be construed in accordance with section 840 of the Taxes Act 1988.

Convertible securities

3.—(1) For the purposes of paragraph 1 above a security is a convertible security if—

(a) it was issued by a company before 9th June 1989,

(b) under the terms of issue it can be converted into or exchanged for share capital in a company (whether or not the company is the one which issued the security), and

(c) the condition set out in sub-paragraph (2) below is fulfilled.

(2) The condition is that—

(a) at some time in the qualifying period the security was quoted in the official list of a recognised stock exchange,

(b) at some time in that period relevant share capital was so quoted, or

(c) each of paragraphs (a) and (b) above is satisfied (though not necessarily as regards the same time).

(3) For the purposes of sub-paragraph (2) above the qualifying period is the period of one month beginning with the day on which the security was issued.

(4) For the purposes of sub-paragraph (2) above relevant share capital is share capital in the company into whose share capital the security can be converted or for whose share capital the security can be exchanged; and relevant share capital need not be share capital into or for which the security can be converted or exchanged.

(5) References in this paragraph to share capital are to share capital by whatever name called.

Meaning of transfer etc.

4.—(1) This paragraph has effect for the purposes of this Schedule.

(2) "Transfer", in relation to a security, means transfer by way of sale, exchange, gift or otherwise.

(3) Where an agreement for the transfer of a security is made, it is transferred, and the person to whom it is agreed to be transferred becomes entitled to it, when the agreement is made and not on a later transfer made pursuant to the agreement; and "entitled", "transfer" and cognate expressions shall be construed accordingly.

(4) A person holds a security at a particular time if he is entitled to it at the time.

(5) A person acquires a security when he becomes entitled to it; and "acquisition" shall be construed accordingly.

(6) If an agreement is conditional (whether on the exercise of an option or otherwise) for the purposes of sub-paragraph (3) above it is made when the condition is exercised.

Cross references.—See TA 1988, s. 687(3)(*i*) (payments under discretionary trusts).

Charge to tax on transfer

5.—(1) This paragraph applies if—

(*a*) there is a transfer of a deep gain security on or after 14th March 1989 (irrespective of when the person making the transfer acquired it), and
(*b*) the amount obtained on transfer exceeds the amount paid on acquisition.

(2) In such a case—

(*a*) an amount equal to the difference between those two amounts, less the amount of any costs, shall be treated as income of the person making the transfer,
(*b*) the income shall be chargeable to tax under Case III or Case IV (as the case may be) of Schedule D,
(*c*) the income shall be treated as arising in the year of assessment in which the transfer takes place, and
(*d*) notwithstanding anything in sections 64 to 67 of the Taxes Act 1988, the tax shall be computed on the income arising in the year of assessment for which the computation is made.

(3) For the purposes of this paragraph—

(*a*) the amount obtained on transfer is the amount obtained, in respect of the transfer, by the person making it,
(*b*) the amount paid on acquisition is the amount paid by that person in respect of his acquisition of the security (or his last acquisition of it before the transfer), and
(*c*) costs are the costs incurred by that person in connection with the transfer and with his acquisition of the security (or his last acquisition of it before the transfer).

(4) For the purposes of sub-paragraph (3)(*a*) above the person making the transfer shall be treated as obtaining in respect of it—

(*a*) any amount he actually obtains in respect of it, and
(*b*) any amount he is entitled to obtain, but does not obtain, in respect of it.

(5) Sub-paragraph (4) above shall not apply where paragraph 7, 8 or 9 below applies.

Cross references.—See TA 1988, s. 452(8) (Lloyd's underwriters special reserve funds).

Redemption

6.—(1) Paragraph 5 above applies where there is a redemption of a deep gain security as well as where there is a transfer.

(2) In its application by virtue of sub-paragraph (1) above, paragraph 5 above shall have effect as if—

(*a*) references to the person making the transfer were to the person who was entitled to the security immediately before redemption, and
(*b*) other references to transfer were to redemption.

Death

7.—(1) Where an individual who is entitled to a security dies, for the purposes of this Schedule—

(a) he shall be treated as transferring it to his personal representatives immediately before his death, and

(b) he shall be treated as obtaining in respect of the transfer an amount equal to the market value of the security at the time of the transfer.

(2) Where a security is transferred by personal representatives to a legatee, for the purposes of paragraph 5 above they shall be treated as obtaining in respect of the transfer an amount equal to the market value of the security at the time of the transfer.

(3) In sub-paragraph (2) above "legatee" includes any person taking (whether beneficially or as trustee) under a testamentary disposition or on an intestacy or partial intestacy, including any person taking by virtue of an appropriation by the personal representatives in or towards satisfaction of a legacy or other interest or share in the deceased's property.

Connected persons

8.—(1) This paragraph applies where a security is transferred from one person to another (whether or not on or after 14th March 1989) and they are connected with each other.

(2) For the purposes of paragraph 5 above—

(a) the person making the transfer shall be treated as obtaining in respect of it an amount equal to the market value of the security at the time of the transfer, and

(b) the person to whom the transfer is made shall be treated as paying in respect of his acquisition of the security an amount equal to that market value.

(3) Section 839 of the Taxes Act 1988 (connected persons) shall apply for the purposes of this paragraph.

Market value

9.—(1) This paragraph applies where a security is transferred from one person to another (whether or not on or after 14th March 1989) and—

(a) the transfer is made for a consideration which consists of or includes consideration not in money or money's worth, or

(b) the transfer is made otherwise than by way of a bargain made at arm's length.

(2) For the purposes of paragraph 5 above—

(a) the person making the transfer shall be treated as obtaining in respect of it an amount equal to the market value of the security at the time of the transfer, and

(b) the person to whom the transfer is made shall be treated as paying in respect of his acquisition of the security an amount equal to that market value.

Underwriters

10.—(1) An underwriting member of Lloyd's shall be treated for the purposes of this Schedule as absolutely entitled as against the trustees to the securities forming part of his premiums trust fund, his special reserve fund (if any) and any other trust fund required or authorised by the rules of Lloyd's, or required by the underwriting agent through whom his business or any part of it is carried on, to be kept in connection with the business.

(2) Where a security forms part of a premiums trust fund at the end of 31st December of any relevant year, for the purposes of this Schedule—

(a) the trustees of the fund shall be treated as transferring it on that day, and

(b) they shall be treated as obtaining in respect of the transfer an amount equal to the market value of the security at the time of the transfer;

and for this purpose relevant years are 1989 and subsequent years.

(3) Where a security forms part of a premiums trust fund at the beginning of 1st January of any relevant year, for the purposes of this Schedule—

(a) the trustees of the fund shall be treated as acquiring it on that day, and

(b) they shall be treated as paying in respect of the acquisition an amount equal to the market value of the security at the time of the acquisition;

and for this purpose relevant years are 1990 and subsequent years.

(4) Sub-paragraph (5) below applies where the following state of affairs exists at the beginning of 1st January of any year or the end of 31st December of any year—

(a) securities have been transferred by the trustees of a premiums trust fund in pursuance of an arrangement mentioned in section 129(1) or (2) of the Taxes Act 1988,

(*b*) the transfer was made to enable another person to fulfil a contract or to make a transfer,
(*c*) securities have not been transferred in return, and
(*d*) section 129(3) of that Act applies to the transfer made by the trustees.

(5) The securities transferred by the trustees shall be treated for the purposes of sub-paragraphs (2) and (3) above as if they formed part of the premiums trust fund at the beginning of 1st January concerned or the end of 31st December concerned (as the case may be).

(6) Paragraph 7(1) above shall not apply where the individual concerned is an underwriting member of Lloyd's and the security concerned forms part of a premiums trust fund, a special reserve fund or any other trust fund required or authorised by the rules of Lloyd's, or required by the underwriting agent through whom the individual's business or any part of it is carried on, to be kept in connection with the business.

(7) In a case where an amount treated as income chargeable to tax by virtue of paragraph 5(2) above constitutes profits or gains mentioned in section 450(1) of the Taxes Act 1988—

(*a*) section 450(1)(*b*) shall apply, and
(*b*) paragraph 5(2)(*c*) above shall not apply.

(8) For the purpose of computing income tax for the year 1987–88 sub-paragraph (7) above shall have effect as if—

(*a*) the reference to section 450(1) of the Taxes Act 1988 were to paragraph 2 of Schedule 16 to the Finance Act 1973, and
(*b*) the reference to section 450(1)(*b*) were to paragraph 2(*b*) of that Schedule.

(9) In this paragraph "business" and "premiums trust fund" have the meanings given by section 457 of the Taxes Act 1988.

Cross references.—See TA 1988, s. 687(3)(*i*) (payments under discretionary trusts).

Trustees

11.—(1) Where on a transfer or redemption of a security by trustees an amount is treated as income chargeable to tax by virtue of paragraph 5 above, the rate at which it is chargeable shall be a rate equal to the sum of the basic rate and the additional rate for the year of assessment in which the transfer is made.

(2) Where the trustees are trustees of a scheme to which section 469 of the Taxes Act 1988 applies, sub-paragraph (1) above shall not apply if or to the extent that the amount is treated as income in the accounts of the scheme.

Foreign currency

12.—(1) Where, for the purposes of paragraph 5 above and apart from this paragraph, the amount obtained on transfer would be an amount expressed in a currency other than sterling, it shall be treated for those purposes as the sterling equivalent on the day of the transfer of the amount so expressed.

(2) Where, for the purposes of paragraph 5 above and apart from this paragraph, the amount paid on acquisition would be an amount expressed in a currency other than sterling, it shall be treated for those purposes as the sterling equivalent on the day of the acquisition of the amount so expressed.

(3) Where, for the purposes of paragraph 5 above and apart from this paragraph, the amount of the costs incurred by a person in connection with a transfer would be an amount expressed in a currency other than sterling, it shall be treated for those purposes as the sterling equivalent on the day of the transfer of the amount so expressed.

(4) Where, for the purposes of paragraph 5 above and apart from this paragraph, the amount of the costs incurred by a person in connection with an acquisition would be an amount expressed in a currency other than sterling, it shall be treated for those purposes as the sterling equivalent on the day of the acquisition of the amount so expressed.

(5) In sub-paragraphs (1) and (3) above "transfer" includes "redemption".

(6) For the purposes of this paragraph the sterling equivalent of an amount on a particular day is the sterling equivalent calculated by reference to the London closing rate of exchange for that day.

Receipts in United Kingdom

13.—(1) Sub-paragraph (2) below applies where—

(a) by virtue of paragraph 5(2) above an amount is treated as income of a person and as chargeable to tax under Case IV of Schedule D, and
(b) the person satisfies the Board, on a claim in that behalf, that he is not domiciled in the United Kingdom, or that (being a Commonwealth citizen or a citizen of the Republic of Ireland) he is not ordinarily resident in the United Kingdom.

(2) In such a case—

(a) any amounts received in the United Kingdom in respect of the amount treated as income shall be treated as income arising in the year of assessment in which they are so received, and
(b) paragraph 5(2) above shall have effect with the substitution of paragraph (a) above for paragraph 5(2)(c).

(3) For the purposes of sub-paragraph (2) above—

(a) there shall be treated as received in the United Kingdom all amounts paid, used or enjoyed in, or in any manner or form transmitted or brought to, the United Kingdom, and
(b) subsections (6) to (9) of section 65 of the Taxes Act 1988 shall apply as they apply for the purposes of subsection (5) of that section.

Retirement benefit schemes

14. In a case where—

(a) paragraph 5 above would apply (apart from this paragraph) to a transfer or redemption of a security, and
(b) immediately before the transfer or redemption was made the security was held for the purposes of an exempt approved scheme (within the meaning of Chapter I of Part XIV of the Taxes Act 1988),

that paragraph shall not apply to the transfer or redemption.

Charities

15.—(1) In a case where—

(a) paragraph 5 above would apply (apart from this paragraph) to a transfer or redemption of a security,
(b) immediately before the transfer or redemption was made the security was held by a charity, and
(c) the amount which would (apart from this paragraph) be treated as income by virtue of paragraph 5 above is applicable and applied for charitable purposes,

that paragraph shall not apply to the transfer or redemption.

(2) In this paragraph "charity" has the same meaning as in section 506 of the Taxes Act 1988.

Stock lending

16. In a case where—

(a) a security is the subject of a transfer which falls within section 129(3) of the Taxes Act 1988, and
(b) paragraph 5 above would apply to the transfer (apart from this paragraph),

that paragraph shall not apply to the transfer.

Accrued income scheme

17. In a case where—

(a) a security is the subject of a transfer to which paragraph 5 above applies, and
(b) apart from this paragraph, the transfer would be a transfer for the purposes of sections 710 to 728 of the Taxes Act 1988,

the transfer shall not be a transfer for those purposes.

Other provisions excluded

18. In a case where paragraph 5 above applies to the redemption of a security, sections 123 and 348 to 350 of the Taxes Act 1988 shall not apply to any proceeds of the redemption.

Identification of securities

19. Section 88 of the Finance Act 1982 shall apply to the identification, for the purposes of this Schedule, of deep gain securities transferred or redeemed as it applies to the identification, for the purposes of capital gains tax, of deep discount securities disposed of.

Gilts: special rules

20.—(1) In a case where—

(*a*) securities have been issued under a prospectus under which no securities were issued before 14th March 1989,
(*b*) some of the securities issued under the prospectus are gilt-edged securities which are would-be deep gain securities,
(*c*) some of the securities issued under the prospectus are gilt-edged securities which are not would-be deep gain securities, and
(*d*) there is a time when the aggregate nominal value of the securities falling within paragraph (*b*) above (at that time) exceeds the aggregate nominal value of the securities falling within paragraph (*c*) above (at that time),

sub-paragraph (2) below shall apply in relation to any gilt-edged security which has been or is issued under the prospectus at any time (whether before, at or after the time mentioned in paragraph (*d*) above).

(2) As regards any event occurring in relation to the security after the time mentioned in sub-paragraph (1)(*d*) above, paragraphs 5 to 19 above shall have effect as if—

(*a*) the security were a deep gain security, and
(*b*) it had been acquired as such (whatever the time it was acquired).

(3) For the purposes of sub-paragraph (1) above a would-be deep gain security is a security which would be a deep gain security apart from paragraph 1(6) above.

(4) In sub-paragraph (1) above "gilt-edged security" has the same meaning as in paragraph 1 above.

(5) For the purposes of sub-paragraph (2) above events, in relation to a security, include anything constituting a transfer or acquisition for the purposes of this Schedule.

Non-gilts: special rules

21.—(1) In a case where—

(*a*) all the securities issued on the occasion of the original issue under a particular prospectus (whatever the time of the issue) are neither gilt-edged securities nor deep gain securities,
(*b*) some of the securities issued under the prospectus are not gilt-edged securities but are new would-be deep gain securities, and
(*c*) there is a time when the aggregate nominal value of the securities falling within paragraph (*b*) above (at that time) exceeds the aggregate nominal value of the securities which (looking at the state of affairs at that time) have been issued under the prospectus and are neither gilt-edged securities nor new would-be deep gain securities,

sub-paragraph (2) below shall apply in relation to any security which is not a gilt-edged security but which has been or is issued under the prospectus at any time (whether before, at or after the time mentioned in paragraph (*c*) above).

(2) As regards any event occurring in relation to the security after the time mentioned in sub-paragraph (1)(*c*) above, paragraphs 5 to 19 above shall have effect as if—

(*a*) the security were a deep gain security, and
(*b*) it had been acquired as such (whatever the time it was acquired).

(3) For the purposes of sub-paragraph (1) above a new would-be deep gain security is a security which—

(*a*) would be a deep gain security apart from paragraph 1(7) above, and
(*b*) was issued on or after 14th March 1989.

(4) In sub-paragraph (1) above "gilt-edged security" has the same meaning as in paragraph 1 above.

(5) For the purposes of sub-paragraph (2) above events, in relation to a security, include anything constituting a transfer or acquisition for the purposes of this Schedule.

Cross references.—See FA 1984, s. 64(3B), (5B) (CGT exemption for deep gain securities treated as such by virtue of sub-para. (2) above).

Indexed securities: special rules

22.—(1) Sub-paragraph (2) below applies where—

(*a*) a qualifying indexed security has been issued,
(*b*) the person by whom it was issued and the person for the time being holding it make an agreement, on or after 14th March 1989, varying the terms under which it is held, and
(*c*) the terms as varied are such that, had the security been issued on those terms, it would be a deep gain security.

(2) As regards any event occurring in relation to the security after the agreement is made, paragraphs 5 to 19 above shall have effect as if—

(*a*) the security were a deep gain security, and
(*b*) it had been acquired as such (whatever the time it was acquired).

(3) For the purposes of sub-paragraph (2) above events, in relation to a security, include anything constituting a transfer or acquisition for the purposes of this Schedule.

(4) In this paragraph "qualifying indexed security" has the meaning given by paragraph 2 above.

Cross references.—See FA 1984, s. 64(3C), (5C) (CGT exemption for deep gain securities treated as such by virtue of sub-para. (2) above).

Power to modify

23.—(1) The Treasury may make regulations amending paragraph 2 above so as to do one or more of the following—

(*a*) vary any condition for the time being set out in that paragraph;
(*b*) omit any condition for the time being so set out;
(*c*) add a new condition to any for the time being so set out;
(*d*) substitute a condition or conditions for any condition or conditions for the time being so set out.

(2) Regulations under sub-paragraph (1) above—

(*a*) shall be made by statutory instrument subject to annulment in pursuance of a resolution of the House of Commons,
(*b*) shall apply where there is a transfer within the meaning of this Schedule, or a redemption, on or after such day as may be specified in the regulations, and
(*c*) may include such supplementary, incidental, consequential or transitional provisions as appear to the Treasury to be necessary or expedient.

SCHEDULE 12

Section 107

CLOSE COMPANIES

PART I
ADMINISTRATIVE PROVISIONS

Interpretation

1. In this Part of this Schedule "the relevant provisions" means—

(*a*) sections 13A, 231 and 419 to 422 of the Taxes Act 1988, and
(*b*) Chapter III of Part XI of that Act (as it has effect in relation to accounting periods beginning before 1st April 1989).

Provision of information by company

2. The inspector may, by notice, require any company which is, or appears to him to be, a close company to furnish him within such time (not being less than 30 days) as may be specified in the notice with such particulars as he thinks necessary for the purposes of the relevant provisions.

Provision of information by shareholders

3.—(1) If for the purposes of the relevant provisions any person in whose name any shares are registered is so required by notice by the inspector, he shall state whether or not he is the beneficial owner of the shares and, if not the beneficial owner of the shares, shall furnish the name and address of the person or persons on whose behalf the shares are registered in his name.

(2) This paragraph shall apply in relation to loan capital as it applies in relation to shares.

Information about bearer securities

4.—(1) The inspector may, for the purposes of the relevant provisions, by notice require—

(*a*) any company which appears to him to be a close company to furnish him with particulars of any bearer securities issued by the company, and the names and addresses of the persons to whom the securities were issued and the respective amounts issued to each person, and
(*b*) any person to whom bearer securities were issued by the company, or to or through whom such securities were subsequently sold or transferred, to furnish him with such further information as he may require with a view to enabling him to ascertain the names and addresses of the persons beneficially interested in the securities.

(2) In this paragraph—

"loan creditor" has the same meaning as in Part XI of the Taxes Act 1988, and
"securities" includes shares, stocks, bonds, debentures and debenture stock and also any promissory note or other instrument evidencing indebtedness to a loan creditor of the company.

PART II
AMENDMENTS CONNECTED WITH REPEAL OF CHAPTER III OF PART XI OF TAXES ACT 1988

The Taxes Management Act 1970 (c. 9)

5. In the first column of the Table in section 98 of the Taxes Management Act 1970 (penalty for failure to give particulars etc) there shall be added at the end—

"Paragraphs 2 to 4 of Schedule 12 to the Finance Act 1989.".

The Capital Gains Tax Act 1979 (c. 14)

6.—(1) In section 136 of the Capital Gains Tax Act 1979 (relief in respect of loans to traders) in subsection (10)(*b*) for the words "paragraph 7 of Schedule 19 to the Taxes Act 1988" there shall be substituted the words "paragraph 1 of Schedule 20 to the Finance Act 1985".

(2) This paragraph shall have effect where the claim under section 136 is made after 31st March 1989.

The Income and Corporation Taxes Act 1988 (c. 1)

7. In section 13 of the Taxes Act 1988 (small companies' rate) in subsection (9) for the words "paragraph 17 of Schedule 19" there shall be substituted the words "paragraphs 2 to 4 of Schedule 12 to the Finance Act 1989".

8.—(1) In section 168(11) of the Taxes Act 1988 (cases in which a person has a material interest in a company for the purposes of Chapter II of Part V of that Act) for the words from "in a company" to the end of paragraph (*b*) there shall be substituted—

"in a company if he, either on his own or with one or more associates, or if any associate of his with or without such other associates,—

(*a*) is the beneficial owner of, or able, directly or through the medium of other companies, or by any other indirect means to control, more than 5 per cent. of the ordinary share capital of the company, or

(*b*) in the case of a close company, possesses, or is entitled to acquire, such rights as would, in the event of the winding-up of the company or in any other circumstances, give an entitlement to receive more than 5 per cent. of the assets which would then be available for distribution among the participators.";

and at the end there shall be added the words ", and "participator" has the meaning given by section 417(1)".

(2) This paragraph shall have effect in relation to accounting periods beginning after 31st March 1989.

9.—(1) In section 187(3) of the Taxes Act 1988 (cases in which a person has a material interest in a company for the purposes of sections 185 to 187 of, and Schedules 9 and 10 to, that Act) for the words from "in a company" to the end of paragraph (b) there shall be substituted—

"in a company if he, either on his own or with one or more associates, or if any associate of his with or without such other associates,—

(*a*) is the beneficial owner of, or able, directly or through the medium of other companies, or by any other indirect means to control, more than 25 per cent. or, in the case of a share option scheme which is not a savings-related share option scheme, more than 10 per cent., of the ordinary share capital of the company, or

(*b*) where the company is a close company, possesses, or is entitled to acquire, such rights as would, in the event of the winding-up of the company or in any other circumstances, give an entitlement to receive more than 25 per cent., or in the case of a share option scheme which is not a savings-related share option scheme more than 10 per cent., of the assets which would then be available for distribution among the participators.";

and at the end there shall be added the words "and "participator" has the meaning given by section 417(1)".

(2) This paragraph shall have effect in relation to accounting periods beginning after 31st March 1989.

10.—(1) In section 214 of the Taxes Act 1988 (chargeable payments connected with exempt distributions) in subsection (1)(*c*) for the words from "338(2)(*a*)" to "Schedule 19" there shall be substituted the words "and 338(2)(*a*)".

(2) This paragraph shall have effect in relation to accounting periods beginning after 31st March 1989, except in any case where section 427(4) of the Taxes Act 1988 has effect by virtue of section 103(2) of this Act.

11. In section 234 of the Taxes Act 1988 (information relating to distributions) in subsection (9) for the words from "paragraph 17" to "that Schedule" there shall be substituted the words "paragraphs 2 to 4 of Schedule 12 to the Finance Act 1989 for the purposes of the relevant provisions (as defined in paragraph 1 of that Schedule)".

12.—(1) Section 360 of the Taxes Act 1988 (loan to buy interest in a close company) shall be amended in accordance with this paragraph.

(2) In subsection (1)(*a*) for the words from "satisfying" to "424(4)" there shall be substituted the words "complying with section 13A(2)".

(3) In subsections (2)(*a*) and (3)(*a*) for the words "satisfy any of the conditions of section 424(4)" there shall be substituted the words "comply with section 13A(2)".

(4) This paragraph shall have effect in relation to interest paid on or after the day on which this Act is passed (and, accordingly, the conditions of section 424(4) of the Taxes Act 1988 shall continue to have effect for the purposes of section 360 of that Act in relation to interest paid before that day).

13.—(1) Section 360A of the Taxes Act 1988 (cases in which a person has a material interest in a company for the purposes of section 360(2)(*a*)) shall be amended in accordance with this paragraph.

(2) In subsection (1) for the words from "in a company" onwards there shall be substituted—

"in a company if he, either on his own or with one or more associates, or if any associate of his with or without such other associates,—

(*a*) is the beneficial owner of, or able, directly or through the medium of other companies, or by any other indirect means to control, more than 5 per cent. of the ordinary share capital of the company, or
(*b*) possesses, or is entitled to acquire, such rights as would, in the event of the winding-up of the company or in any other circumstances, give an entitlement to receive more than 5 per cent. of the assets which would then be available for distribution among the participators."

(3) In subsection (10) after the word "section" there shall be inserted the words ""participator" has the meaning given by section 417(1) and".

(4) This paragraph shall have effect in relation to accounting periods beginning after 31st March 1989.

14.—(1) In section 576 of the Taxes Act 1988 (which relates to relief for losses on certain unquoted shares) in subsection (5), for paragraph (*a*) of the definition of "trading company" there shall be substituted—

"(*a*) a company whose business consists wholly or mainly of the carrying on of a trade or trades".

(2) This paragraph shall have effect in relation to disposals made after 31st March 1989.

15.—(1) In section 623 of the Taxes Act 1988 (meaning of "relevant earnings" for the purposes of Chapter III of Part XIV of that Act) in subsection (2) for the words "(construed in accordance with paragraph 7 of Schedule 19)" there shall be substituted the words "(that is to say, income which, if the company were an individual, would not be earned income)".

(2) This paragraph shall have effect in relation to accounting periods beginning after 31st March 1989.

16.—(1) In section 644 of the Taxes Act 1988 (meaning of "relevant earnings" for the purposes of Chapter IV of Part XIV of that Act) in subsection (6) for the definition of "investment income" there shall be substituted—

""investment income" means income which, if the company were an individual, would not be earned income."

(2) This paragraph shall have effect in relation to accounting periods beginning after 31st March 1989.

17. In section 745 of the Taxes Act 1988 (power to obtain information for the purposes of Chapter III of Part XVII of that Act) in subsection (4) for the words from "trading" onwards there shall be substituted the words "companies whose business consists wholly or mainly of the carrying on of a trade or trades.".

18.—(1) Paragraph 7 of Schedule 8 to the Taxes Act 1988 (cases in which a person has a material interest in a company for the purposes of a profit-related pay scheme) shall be amended in accordance with this paragraph.

(2) In sub-paragraph (2) for the words from "in a company" onwards there shall be substituted—

"in a company if he, either on his own or with one or more associates, or if any associate of his with or without such other associates,—

(*a*) is the beneficial owner of, or able, directly or through the medium of other companies, or by any other indirect means to control, more than 25 per cent. of the ordinary share capital of the company, or
(*b*) in the case of a close company, possesses, or is entitled to acquire, such rights as would, in the event of the winding-up of the company or in any other circumstances, give an entitlement to receive more than 25 per cent. of the assets which would then be available for distribution among the participators".

(3) In sub-paragraph (3) the second "and" shall be omitted and after the definition of "control" there shall be inserted "and

"participator" has the meaning given by section 417(1)".

(4) This paragraph shall have effect in relation to accounting periods beginning after 31st March 1989.

SCHEDULE 13

Section 121

CAPITAL ALLOWANCES: MISCELLANEOUS AMENDMENTS

Buildings etc. bought after use

1.—(1) In the Capital Allowances Act 1968 ("the 1968 Act") after section 5 (buildings and structures bought unused) there shall be inserted—

"5A. Buildings and structures bought after use

(1) This section applies where—

  (a) expenditure is incurred on the construction of a building or structure by a person carrying on a trade which consists, in whole or part, in the construction of buildings or structures with a view to their sale, and
  (b) after the building or structure has been used, he sells the relevant interest in it in the course of that trade or, as the case may be, of that part of that trade.

(2) Where this section applies, this Chapter shall have effect in relation to the person who buys the interest as if—

  (a) the original expenditure had been capital expenditure,
  (b) all appropriate writing-down allowances had been made to the person incurring it, and
  (c) all appropriate balancing allowances or charges had been made on the occasion of the sale."

(2) This paragraph shall have effect in any case where the purchase price payable on any sale becomes payable on or after the day on which this Act is passed.

Roads on industrial estates

2.—(1) In section 7 of the 1968 Act (definition of "industrial building or structure"), after subsection (3A) there shall be inserted—

"(3B) A road on an industrial estate shall be treated as used for the purposes of a trade which falls within subsection (1) above if the buildings and structures on the estate are used wholly or mainly for such purposes."

(2) This paragraph shall have effect in relation to any chargeable period or its basis period ending on or after the day on which this Act is passed.

Contributions to expenditure

3.—(1) Section 84 of the 1968 Act (under which certain contributions etc. reduce allowable expenditure) shall be amended as follows.

(2) At the end of paragraph (b) of subsection (2) there shall be added the words "and not being expenditure which is allowed to be deducted in computing the profits or gains of a trade, profession or vocation carried on by that person".

(3) After subsection (2) there shall be inserted—

"(2A) In determining for the purposes of subsection (2)(b) above whether an allowance could be made under the provisions of section 85 below, it shall be assumed that the person by whom expenditure has been or is to be met is within the charge to tax, whether or not that is in fact the case."

(4) This paragraph shall have effect in relation to expenditure incurred on or after the day on which this Act is passed except in so far as a contribution to the expenditure was made before that day.

4.—(1) In section 85 of the 1968 Act (which gives allowances in respect of certain contributions), after subsection (3) there shall be inserted—

"(3A) References in this section, and in Schedule 9 to this Act, to a trade shall be construed as including references to a profession or vocation."

(2) This paragraph shall have effect in relation to contributions made on or after the day on which this Act is passed.

5.—(1) This paragraph applies where allowances are made in respect of a contribution to capital expenditure by virtue of section 85 of the 1968 Act as applied by paragraph 15(6) of Schedule 8 to the Finance Act 1971.

(2) Where this paragraph applies in relation to a contribution made for the purposes of a trade carried on or to be carried on by the contributor, it shall be assumed for the purposes of section 44 of the Finance Act 1971—

> (*a*) that the contribution was made for the purposes of a trade carried on by the contributor separately from any trade actually carried on by him, and
> (*b*) that the separate trade is discontinued or transferred (in whole or in part) when the trade actually carried on is discontinued or transferred (in whole or in part);

and any allowance or charge which would on those assumptions fall to be made for any chargeable period in the case of the separate trade shall be made for that period in the case of the trade for the purposes of which the contribution was actually made.

(3) References in sub-paragraph (2) above to a trade shall be construed as including references to a profession or vocation.

(4) This paragraph shall have effect in relation to contributions made on or after the day on which this Act is passed.

6.—(1) In its application in relation to allowances under Schedule 15 to the Finance Act 1986 (agricultural land and buildings), Schedule 9 to the 1968 Act shall have effect—

> (*a*) with the omission of paragraph 4, and
> (*b*) as if, in paragraph 3, the references to section 11 of the 1968 Act and to expenditure incurred on the construction of a building or structure were references to paragraph 3 of Schedule 15 to the Finance Act 1986 and to expenditure falling within paragraph 1(1) of that Schedule.

(2) This paragraph shall have effect in relation to contributions made on or after the day on which this Act is passed.

Scientific research

7.—(1) In section 91 of the 1968 Act (allowances for expenditure on scientific research), after subsection (1B) there shall be inserted—

> "(1C) Subject to subsections (1A) and (1B) above, where a person incurs capital expenditure which is partly within subsection (1) above and partly not, such apportionment of the expenditure shall be made for the purposes of this Part of this Act as may be just."

(2) This paragraph shall have effect in relation to expenditure incurred on or after the day on which this Act is passed.

8. The amendments made in section 92 of the 1968 Act (assets ceasing to be used for scientific research) by section 63 of the Finance Act 1985 shall have effect in relation to any case where the relevant event (within the meaning given in section 92(1)) occurs on or after 1st April 1989 (as well as in the cases provided for by section 63(7) where it occurs before that date).

9.—(1) In section 94 of the 1968 Act (interpretation of Part II), after subsection (4) there shall be added—

> "(4A) Any reference in this Part of this Act to the time when an asset ceases to belong to a person shall, in the case of a sale, be construed as a reference to the time of completion or the time when possession is given, whichever is the earlier."

(2) This paragraph shall have effect in any case where the sale is effected, or the contract for sale entered into, on or after the day on which this Act is passed.

Hire-purchase, leases etc.

10.—(1) In section 45(1) of the Finance Act 1971 (machinery or plant held by a person under a hire-purchase or similar agreement to be treated as belonging to him), in paragraph (*a*), after the words "to him" there shall be inserted the words "(and not to any other person)".

(2) This paragraph shall have effect in relation to capital expenditure incurred under contracts entered into on or after the day on which this Act is passed.

11. In section 46 of the Finance Act 1971 (machinery and plant on lease) after subsection (2) there shall be inserted—

> "(2A) In this section "lease" includes an agreement for a lease where the term to be covered by the lease has begun, and any tenancy, but does not include a mortgage, and "lessee" and other cognate expressions shall be construed accordingly."

12.—(1) In section 48 of the Finance Act 1971, after subsection (4) (which provides for the manner of making capital allowances and imposes restrictions in certain cases where the machinery or plant is on lease), there shall be inserted—

"(4A) Section 403(3) of the Taxes Act (group relief) shall not apply to an allowance if or to the extent that, by virtue of the proviso to subsection (4) above, subsection (3) of the said section 74 does not apply to it."

(2) This paragraph shall have effect in any case where the accounting period of the surrendering company (within the meaning of Chapter IV of Part X of the Taxes Act 1988) ends on or after the day on which this Act is passed.

Gifts of machinery or plant

13.—(1) Paragraph 7 of Schedule 8 to the Finance Act 1971 (effect of use after user not attracting capital allowances, or after receipt by way of gift) shall be amended as follows.

(2) In sub-paragraph (1) the words "Subject to sub-paragraph (2) below" and the words from "by reason of" to the end of paragraph (*b*) shall cease to have effect.

(3) After sub-paragraph (1A) there shall be inserted—

"(1B) Where a person is treated as having incurred capital expenditure on the provision of machinery or plant by virtue of sub-paragraph (1)(*b*) above, he shall for the purposes of paragraph 3 above be treated as having done so by way of purchase from the donor."

(4) This paragraph shall have effect in cases where machinery or plant is brought into use on or after the day on which this Act is passed.

Allowances for ships

14.—(1) In paragraph 8A of Schedule 8 to the Finance Act 1971 (which enables shipowners to elect to defer allowances in certain cases), in sub-paragraph (1)(*b*), for the words from "the expenditure" to "falling" there shall be substituted the words "the ship is not provided for leasing or letting on charter otherwise than by way of lease, or is so provided but it appears that the ship will be used in the requisite period (within the meaning of section 64 of the Finance Act 1980) for a qualifying purpose (within the meaning of that section) and will not at any time in that period be used for any other purpose, and the expenditure does not fall".

(2) This paragraph shall have effect in relation to expenditure incurred on or after the day on which this Act is passed.

15.—(1) In section 58 of the Finance Act 1985 (extension of first-year allowances to ships which are not new), after subsection (2) there shall be added—

"(3) In consequence of subsection (1) above—

(*a*) no disclaimer or claim under section 41(3) of the Finance Act 1971 may be made in respect of any ship,
(*b*) section 66(7) of the Finance Act 1980 and paragraph 3 of Schedule 11 to the Finance Act 1982 shall have effect with the omission of the word "new" in each place where it occurs, and
(*c*) section 59(4)(*c*) and (6)(*c*) of the Finance Act 1984 shall have effect with the omission of the word "new"."

(2) Paragraph (*a*) of section 58(3) of the Finance Act 1985 shall have effect in relation to disclaimers and claims made on or after the day on which this Act is passed, paragraph (*b*) of that subsection shall have effect in any case where the requisite period begins on or after that day and paragraph (*c*) of that subsection shall come into force on that day.

Sales etc. and succession to trades between connected persons

16.—(1) In paragraph 13 of Schedule 8 to the Finance Act 1971 (successions to trades between connected persons), after sub-paragraph (3) there shall be inserted—

"(3A) Section 48(1) of the Capital Allowances Act 1968 and section 65(5) of the Finance Act 1980 shall not apply in any case where an election is made under this paragraph."

(2) This paragraph shall have effect in relation to successions occurring on or after the day on which this Act is passed.

17. In section 68(4) of the Finance Act 1972 (which modifies the restrictions on allowances imposed by paragraph 3 of Schedule 8 to the Finance Act 1971 in the case of sales etc. between connected persons) for paragraphs (*b*) and (*c*) there shall be substituted—

"(b) where capital expenditure was incurred by the seller on the provision of the machinery or plant, the amount of that expediture;
(c) where capital expenditure was incurred by any person connected with the seller on the provision of the machinery or plant, the amount of the expenditure incurred by that person."

Leased assets

18. In section 73(5) of the Finance Act 1980 (application of sections 64 to 72 to activities other than trades), for the words "first-year" there shall be substituted the words "writing-down".

19. In Schedule 11 to the Finance Act 1982, in paragraph 4(3), for the reference to section 243(2) of the Taxes Act 1988 there shall be substituted a reference to section 343(2).

Dwelling-houses

20.—(1) In paragraph 4(5)(c) of Schedule 12 to the Finance Act 1982 (application of section 78 of and Schedule 7 to the 1968 Act to certain sales of dwelling-houses), for the words "are at the time of the sale" there shall be substituted the words "at the time of the sale are or at any earlier time were".

(2) This paragraph shall have effect in any case where the time of the sale referred to in paragraph 4(5)(c) is after 14th January 1989.

Short-life assets

21.—(1) In section 57(6) of the Finance Act 1985 (election for certain machinery or plant to be treated as short-life assets)—

(a) for the words "the short-life asset" there shall be substituted the words "a short-life asset provided for leasing", and
(b) in paragraph (b)—

(i) after the word "expenditure", where it first appears, there shall be inserted the words "in respect of the notional trade",
(ii) for the words following "1980)" there shall be substituted the words "be, or be added to, the trader's qualifying expenditure for that chargeable period."

(2) The amendment made by sub-paragraph (1)(b)(i) above is to section 57(6) of the Finance Act 1985 as it has effect as amended by section 57(6) of the Finance Act 1986 and as it has effect by virtue of section 57(7) of that Act and the amendment made by sub-paragraph (1)(b)(ii) above is to section 57(6) of the Finance Act 1985 as it has effect by virtue of section 57(7) of the Finance Act 1986.

(3) This paragraph shall have effect in relation to any chargeable period or its basis period ending on or after the day on which this Act is passed.

22.—(1) In Schedule 15 to the Finance Act 1985 (machinery and plant excluded from treatment as short-life assets), for paragraph 8 (leased assets) there shall be substituted—

"**8.** Machinery or plant provided for leasing, except—

(a) machinery or plant which it appears will be used in the requisite period (within the meaning of section 64 of the Finance Act 1980) for a qualifying purpose (within the meaning of that section) and will not at any time in that period be used for any other purpose,
(b) vehicles of the kind mentioned in subsection (12) of that section."

(2) In paragraph 9 of that Schedule (leased assets) for the words from "1980" to the end there shall be substituted the word "applies".

(3) This paragraph shall have effect in relation to expenditure incurred on or after the day on which this Act is passed.

Machinery and plant which are fixtures

23.—(1) In Schedule 17 to the Finance Act 1985, in paragraph 9 (disposal value of fixtures) in sub-paragraph (10), for the words "another person" onwards there shall be substituted the words "—

(a) another person incurs expenditure on the provision of the fixture, and
(b) the former owner brings a disposal value into account in accordance with section 44 of the Finance Act 1971,

there shall be disregarded for material purposes so much (if any) of that expenditure as exceeds that disposal value".

(2) This paragraph shall have effect in relation to expenditure incurred on or after the day on which this Act is passed.

Mineral extraction

24.—(1) In Schedule 13 to the Finance Act 1986 (new code for minerals), in paragraph 16(5) (unrelieved value for the purposes of qualifying expenditure), for the reference to section 55 of that Act there shall be substituted a reference to Schedule 15.

(2) This paragraph shall have effect in cases where buildings or structures cease, on or after the day on which this Act is passed, permanently to be used for any purpose.

Agricultural land and buildings

25. At the end of section 56(3) of the Finance Act 1986 (interpretation of new provisions relating to agriculture), there shall be added the words "and section 4(11) of and Chapter VI of Part I of the Capital Allowances Act 1968 shall apply in relation to Schedule 15 as they apply in relation to section 68 of that Act".

26. In paragraph 7(3) of Schedule 15 to the Finance Act 1986 (amount of writing-down allowances after a balancing event) the words "subject to paragraph 9 below" shall be omitted.

Patent rights

27.—(1) Section 521 of the Taxes Act 1988 shall be amended as follows.

(2) In subsection (5) (which limits allowable expenditure in the case of certain sales entered into between connected persons or for the purpose of obtaining an allowance)—

(*a*) the words "within the terms of section 839" shall be omitted, and
(*b*) for the words "the disposal value" onwards there shall be substituted the words "the relevant amount determined in accordance with subsection (6) below".

(3) After subsection (5) there shall be added—

"(6) The relevant amount referred to in subsection (5) above is—

(*a*) in a case in which, by virtue of subsections (2) to (4) above, a disposal value falls to be brought into account by reason of the sale, an amount equal to that disposal value,
(*b*) in a case in which no disposal value falls to be brought into account as mentioned in paragraph (*a*) above, but the seller receives on the sale a capital sum in respect of which he is chargeable to tax in accordance with section 524, an amount equal to that sum,
(*c*) in any other case, an amount equal to whichever of the following is the smallest—

(i) the price which the rights would have fetched if sold in the open market,
(ii) where capital expenditure was incurred by the seller on acquiring the rights, the amount of that expenditure,
(iii) where capital expenditure was incurred by any person connected with the seller on acquiring the rights, the amount of the expenditure incurred by that person.

(7) Section 839 (connected persons) shall apply for the purposes of this section."

(4) This paragraph shall have effect in relation to expenditure incurred on or after the day on which this Act is passed.

Exclusion of double allwances

28.—(1) Where an allowance is made to any person in respect of capital expenditure under one of the provisions specified in sub-paragraph (4) below—

(*a*) no allowance shall be made to him under any other of those provisions—

(i) in respect of that expenditure, or
(ii) in relation to the construction, provision or acquisition of any asset to the construction, provision or acquisition of which the first-mentioned allowance relates, and

(*b*) that expenditure and any expenditure relating to the provision of any asset to the provision of which the first-mentioned allowance relates shall not be taken into account in determining his qualifying expenditure for the purpose of any allowance or charge under section 44 of the Finance Act 1971.

(2) Where in the case of any person an allowance or charge under that section is made by reference to an amount of qualifying expenditure which took account of a particular amount of capital expenditure, no allowance shall be made to him under any of the provisions specified in sub-paragraph (4) below—

(*a*) in respect of that capital expenditure, or
(*b*) in relation to the provision of any asset if that capital expenditure related to the provision of that asset.

(3) In this paragraph—

"asset" means asset of any kind, including a building or structure, and
"capital expenditure" includes any contribution to capital expenditure,

and references to the provision of an asset include references to its construction or acquisition.

(4) The provisions referred to in sub-paragraphs (1) and (2) above are—

(*a*) Chapter I of Part I of the 1968 Act (industrial buildings and structures),
(*b*) Chapter IV of Part I of that Act (dredging),
(*c*) Chapter V of Part I of that Act (agricultural land and buildings),
(*d*) Part II of that Act (scientific research),
(*e*) Schedule 12 to the Finance Act 1982 (certain let dwelling-houses),
(*f*) Schedule 13 to the Finance Act 1986 (mineral extraction),
(*g*) Schedule 15 to the Finance Act 1986 (agricultural land and buildings).

(5) The following provisions (which are superseded by sub-paragraphs (1) to (4) above) shall cease to have effect—

(*a*) sections 9(*b*),14, 50(2), 67(11) and 93(1) and (2) of the 1968 Act,
(*b*) paragraph 2 of Schedule 8 to the Finance Act 1971,
(*c*) paragraph 8 of Schedule 6 to the Finance Act 1978,
(*d*) in sections 74(6) and 75(6) of the Finance Act 1980, the words from the beginning to "and",
(*e*) paragraph 11 of Schedule 12 to the Finance Act 1982, and
(*f*) section 56(5) of the Finance Act 1986,

and in section 92(5) of the 1968 Act the words "allowed or" and "balancing allowance or" shall cease to have effect.

(6) This paragraph shall have effect in relation to any chargeable period or its basis period ending on or after the day on which this Act is passed.

Time when expenditure incurred

29.—(1) In section 56 of the Finance Act 1985 (time when capital expenditure is incurred) at the end of subsection (1) there shall be added "and

(*g*) sections 117 and 118 of the Finance Act 1989."

(2) This paragraph shall have effect in relation to expenditure incurred on or after 6th April 1989.

30.—(1) In section 56(8) of the Finance Act 1985 (preservation of certain provisions under which expenditure is taken to have been incurred later than section 56 provides), for the words "or the Finance Act 1971" there shall be substituted the words "the Finance Act 1971, Schedule 12 to the Finance Act 1982 or Schedules 13 and 15 to the Finance Act 1986".

(2) This paragraph shall have effect in relation to any chargeable period or its basis period ending on or after the day on which this Act is passed.

SCHEDULE 14

Section 124

CAPITAL GAINS TAX: GIFTS ETC.

Gifts of business assets

1.—(1) Section 126 of the Capital Gains Tax Act 1979 shall be amended as follows.

(2) For subsection (1) there shall be substituted—

"(1) If—

(*a*) an individual (in this section referred to as "the transferor") makes a disposal otherwise than under a bargain at arm's length of an asset within subsection (1A) below, and

(*b*) a claim for relief under this section is made by the transferor and the person who acquires the asset (in this section referred to as "the transferee") or, where the trustees of a settlement are the transferee, by the transferor alone,

then, subject to subsection (2) and sections 126A and 126B below, subsection (3) below shall apply in relation to the disposal.

(1A) An asset is within this subsection if—

(*a*) it is, or is an interest in, an asset used for the purposes of a trade, profession or vocation carried on by—

(i) the transferor, or
(ii) his family company, or
(iii) a member of a trading group of which the holding company is his family company, or

(*b*) it consists of shares or securities of a trading company, or of the holding company of a trading group, where—

(i) the shares or securities are neither quoted on a recognised stock exchange nor dealt in on the Unlisted Securities Market, or
(ii) the trading company or holding company is the transferor's family company."

(3) At the end of subsection (2) there shall be added the words "or

(*c*) in the case of a disposal of qualifying corporate bonds within the meaning of section 64 of the Finance Act 1984, a gain is deemed to accrue by virtue of paragraph 10(1)(*b*) of Schedule 13 to that Act, or

(*d*) subsection (3) of section 147A below applies in relation to the disposal (or would apply if a claim for relief were duly made under that section)."

(4) In subsection (7)—

(*a*) in paragraph (*a*), for the words "has the meaning" there shall be substituted the words ", "holding company", "trading company" and "trading group" have the meanings", and
(*b*) paragraph (*b*) shall be omitted.

(5) After subsection (8) there shall be added—

"(9) Where a disposal in respect of which a claim is made under this section is (or proves to be) a chargeable transfer for inheritance tax purposes, there shall be allowed as a deduction in computing (for capital gains tax purposes) the chargeable gain accruing to the transferee on the disposal of the asset in question an amount equal to whichever is the lesser of—

(*a*) the inheritance tax attributable to the value of the asset, and
(*b*) the amount of the chargeable gain as computed apart from this subsection,

and, in the case of a disposal which, being a potentially exempt transfer, proves to be a chargeable transfer, all necessary adjustments shall be made, whether by the discharge or repayment of capital gains tax or otherwise.

(10) Where an amount of inheritance tax—

(*a*) falls to be redetermined in consequence of the transferor's death within seven years of making the chargeable transfer in question, or
(*b*) is otherwise varied,

after it has been taken into account under subsection (9) above, all necessary adjustments shall be made, whether by the making of an assessment to capital gains tax or by the discharge or repayment of such tax."

2. After section 126 there shall be inserted—

"**126A. Section 126 relief: gifts to non-residents**

(1) Section 126(3) above shall not apply where the transferee is neither resident nor ordinarily resident in the United Kingdom.

(2) Section 126(3) above shall not apply where the transferee is an individual or a company if that individual or company—

(*a*) though resident or ordinarily resident in the United Kingdom, is regarded for the purposes of any double taxation arrangements having effect by virtue of section 788 of the Taxes Act 1988 as resident in a territory outside the United Kingdom, and
(*b*) by virtue of the arrangements would not be liable in the United Kingdom to tax on a gain arising on a disposal of the asset occurring immediately after its acquisition.

126B. Section 126 relief: gifts to foreign-controlled companies

(1) Section 126(3) above shall not apply where the transferee is a company which is within subsection (2) below.

(2) A company is within this subsection if it is controlled by a person who, or by persons each of whom,—

(*a*) is neither resident nor ordinarily resident in the United Kingdom, and
(*b*) is connected with the person making the disposal.

(3) For the purposes of subsection (2) above, a person who (either alone or with others) controls a company by virtue of holding assets relating to that or any other company and who is resident or ordinarily resident in the United Kingdom shall be regarded as neither resident nor ordinarily resident there if—

(*a*) he is regarded for the purposes of any double taxation arrangements having effect by virtue of section 788 of the Taxes Act 1988 as resident in a territory outside the United Kingdom, and
(*b*) by virtue of the arrangements he would not be liable in the United Kingdom to tax on a gain arising on a disposal of the assets.

126C. Section 126 relief: emigration of controlling trustees

(1) Subsection (2) below applies where—

(*a*) relief under section 126 above is given in respect of a disposal of an asset to a company which is controlled by the trustees of a settlement ("the relevant disposal"),
(*b*) at the time of the relevant disposal the person making it is connected with the trustees, and
(*c*) at a time when the company has not disposed of the asset and the trustees have not ceased to control the company, they become neither resident nor ordinarily resident in the United Kingdom.

(2) Where this subsection applies then, subject to the following provisions of this section, a chargeable gain shall be deemed to have accrued to the trustees immediately before the time mentioned in subsection (1)(*c*) above, and its amount shall be equal to the held-over gain (within the meaning of section 126 above) on the relevant disposal.

(3) For the purposes of paragraph (*c*) of subsection (1) above, the company shall be taken to have disposed of an asset before the time referred to in that paragraph only if it has made a disposal or disposals in connection with which the whole of the held-over gain on the relevant disposal was represented by reductions made in accordance with section 126(3)(*b*) above; and where the company has made a disposal in connection with which part of that gain was so represented, the amount of chargeable gain deemed by virtue of this section to accrue to the trustees shall be correspondingly reduced.

(4) The disposals by the company that are to be taken into account under subsection (3) above shall not include any disposal to which section 273 of the Taxes Act 1970 (transfers within a group) applies; but where the company disposes of an asset by a disposal to which that section applies, the first subsequent disposal of the asset by another member of the group which is a disposal to which that section does not apply shall be taken into account under subsection (3) above as if it had been made by the company.

(5) Where an amount of tax assessed on trustees by virtue of this section is not paid within the period of twelve months beginning with the date when the tax becomes payable

then, subject to subsection (6) below, the transferor may be assessed and charged (in the name of the trustees) to all or any part of that tax.

(6) No assessment shall be made under subsection (5) above more than six years after the end of the year in which the relevant disposal was made.

(7) Where the transferor pays an amount of tax in pursuance of subsection (5) above, he shall be entitled to recover a corresponding sum from the trustees.

(8) Gains on disposals made after a chargeable gain has under this section been deemed to accrue by reference to a held-over gain shall be computed without any reduction under section 126(3)(*b*) above in respect of that held-over gain.

(9) Section 126B(3) above shall apply for the purposes of subsection (1)(*c*) above as it applies for the purposes of section 126B(2)."

3.—(1) Schedule 4 to the Capital Gains Tax Act 1979 shall be amended as follows.

(2) In paragraph 1—

(*a*) in sub-paragraph (1)(*b*), for the words "section 126(1)(*a*)" there shall be substituted the words "section 126(1)" and for the words "that paragraph" there shall be substituted the words "section 126(1A)(*a*)"; and

(*b*) in sub-paragraph (2), the words "at the rate of 50 per cent." shall be omitted, and at the end of paragraph (*b*) there shall be added the words ", or

(*c*) would be so made but for section 124A of that Act (assuming, where there is no chargeable transfer on that occasion, that there were)."

(3) For paragraph 2 there shall be substituted—

"**2.**—(1) If—

(*a*) the trustees of a settlement make a disposal otherwise than under a bargain at arm's length of an asset within sub-paragraph (2) below, and

(*b*) a claim for relief under section 126 of this Act is made by the trustees and the person who acquires the asset (in this Schedule referred to as "the transferee") or, where the trustees of a settlement are also the transferee, by the trustees making the disposal alone,

then, subject to subsection (2) of section 126 and to sections 126A and 126B, subsection (3) of section 126 shall apply in relation to the disposal.

(2) An asset is within this sub-paragraph if—

(*a*) it is, or is an interest in, an asset used for the purposes of a trade, profession or vocation carried on by—

(i) the trustees making the disposal, or
(ii) a beneficiary who had an interest in possession in the settled property immediately before the disposal, or

(*b*) it consists of shares or securities of a trading company, or of the holding company of a trading group, where—

(i) the shares or securities are neither quoted on a recognised stock exchange nor dealt in on the Unlisted Securities Market, or
(ii) not less than 25 per cent. of the voting rights exercisable by shareholders of the company in general meeting are exercisable by the trustees at the time of the disposal.

(3) Where section 126(3) applies by virtue of this paragraph, references to the trustees shall be substituted for the references in sections 126(3)(*a*) and 126C to the transferor; and where it applies in relation to a disposal which is deemed to occur by virtue of section 54(1) or 55(1) of this Act, section 126(6) shall not apply."

(4) In paragraph 3—

(*a*) in sub-paragraph (1)—

(i) the words from "by virtue" to "(settled property)" shall be omitted,
(ii) for the words "(*a*) of paragraph 2(1)" there shall be substituted "2(1)(*a*)", and
(iii) for the words "the said paragraph (*a*)" there shall be substituted the words "paragraph 2(2)(*a*) above", and

(*b*) in sub-paragraph (2), the words "at the rate of 50 per cent." shall be omitted, and at the end of paragraph (*b*) there shall be added the words ", or

(*c*) would be so made but for section 124A of that Act (assuming, where there is no chargeable transfer on that occasion, that there were)."

(5) In paragraph 4—

(a) in sub-paragraph (2)(a), for the words "section 126(1)" there shall be substituted the words "section 126(1A)", and for the words "sub-paragraph (1)" there shall be substituted the words "sub-paragraph (2)";
(b) for sub-paragraph (2)(c) there shall be substituted—

"(c) "the transferor" has the same meaning as in section 126 of this Act except that, in a case where paragraph 2 above applies, it refers to the trustees mentioned in that paragraph,"; and

(c) for sub-paragraph (3) there shall be substituted—

"(3) In this Part of this Schedule—

(a) any reference to a disposal of an asset is a reference to a disposal which falls within subsection (1) of section 126 of this Act by virtue of subsection (1A)(a) of that section or, as the case may be, falls within sub-paragraph (1) of paragraph 2 above by virtue of sub-paragraph (2)(a) of that paragraph, and
(b) any reference to a disposal of shares is a reference to a disposal which falls within subsection (1) of section 126 of this Act by virtue of subsection (1A)(b) of that section or, as the case may be, falls within sub-paragraph (1) of paragraph 2 above by virtue of sub-paragraph (2)(b) of that paragraph."; and

(d) in sub-paragraph (4), for the words "as the case may be" there shall be substituted the words "where it applies", and the words "(taking account" onwards shall be omitted.

(6) At the end of each of paragraph 5 and paragraph 6 there shall be added—

"(2) This paragraph shall not apply where the circumstances are such that a reduction in respect of the asset—

(a) is made under Chapter II of Part V of the Inheritance Tax Act 1984 in relation to a chargeable transfer taking place on the occasion of the disposal, or
(b) would be so made if there were a chargeable transfer on that occasion, or
(c) would be so made but for section 124A of that Act (assuming, where there is no chargeable transfer on that occasion, that there were)."

(7) For paragraph 7 there shall be substituted—

"**7.**—(1) If in the case of a disposal of shares assets which are not business assets are included in the chargeable assets of the company whose shares are disposed of, or, where that company is the holding company of a trading group, in the group's chargeable assets, and either—

(a) at any time within the period of twelve months before the disposal not less than 25 per cent. of the voting rights exercisable by shareholders of the company in general meeting are exercisable by the transferor, or
(b) the transferor is an individual and, at any time within that period, the company is his family company,

the amount of the held-over gain shall be reduced by multiplying it by the fraction defined in sub-paragraph (2) below.

(2) The fraction referred to in sub-paragraph (1) above is that of which—

(a) the denominator is the market value on the date of the disposal of all the chargeable assets of the company, or as the case may be of the group, and
(b) the numerator is the market value on that date of those chargeable assets of the company or of the group which are business assets.

(3) For the purposes of this paragraph—

(a) an asset is a business asset in relation to a company or a group if it is or is an interest in an asset used for the purposes of a trade, profession or vocation carried on by the company, or as the case may be by a member of the group; and
(b) an asset is a chargeable asset in relation to a company or a group at any time if, on a disposal at that time, a gain accruing to the company, or as the case may be to a member of the group would be a chargeable gain.

(4) Where the shares disposed of are shares of the holding company of a trading group, then for the purposes of this paragraph—

(a) the holding by one member of the group of the ordinary share capital of another member shall not count as a chargeable asset, and
(b) if the whole of the ordinary share capital of a 51 per cent. subsidiary of the holding company is not owned directly or indirectly by that company, the value of the chargeable assets of the subsidiary shall be taken to be reduced by multiplying it by the fraction of

which the denominator is the whole of the ordinary share capital of the subsidiary and the numerator is the amount of that share capital owned directly or indirectly by the holding company.

(5) Expressions used in sub-paragraph (4) above have the same meanings as in section 838 of the Taxes Act 1988."

Gifts on which inheritance tax is chargeable etc.

4. The following sections shall be inserted after section 147 of the Capital Gains Tax Act 1979—

"147A. Gifts on which inheritance tax is chargeable etc.

(1) If—

(*a*) an individual or the trustees of a settlement (in this section referred to as "the transferor") make a disposal within subsection (2) below of an asset,
(*b*) the asset is acquired by an individual or the trustees of a settlement (in this section referred to as "the transferee"), and
(*c*) a claim for relief under this section is made by the transferor and the transferee or, where the trustees of a settlement are the transferee, by the transferor alone,

then, subject to subsection (6) and section 147B below, subsection (3) below shall apply in relation to the disposal.

(2) A disposal is within this subsection if it is made otherwise than under a bargain at arm's length and—

(*a*) is a chargeable transfer within the meaning of the Inheritance Tax Act 1984 (or would be but for section 19 of that Act) and is not a potentially exempt transfer (within the meaning of that Act),
(*b*) is an exempt transfer by virtue of—

(i) section 24 of that Act (transfers to political parties),
(ii) section 26 of that Act (transfers for public benefit),
(iii) section 27 of that Act (transfers to maintenance funds for historic buildings etc.), or
(iv) section 30 of that Act (transfers of designated property),

(*c*) is a disposition to which section 57A of that Act applies and by which the property disposed of becomes held on trusts of the kind referred to in subsection (1)(*b*) of that section (maintenance funds for historic buildings etc.),
(*d*) by virtue of subsection (4) of section 71 of that Act (accumulation and maintenance trusts) does not constitute an occasion on which inheritance tax is chargeable under that section,
(*e*) by virtue of section 78(1) of that Act (transfers of works of art etc.) does not constitute an occasion on which tax is chargeable under Chapter III of Part III of that Act, or
(*f*) is a disposal of an asset comprised in a settlement where, as a result of the asset or part of it becoming comprised in another settlement, there is no charge, or a reduced charge, to inheritance tax by virtue of paragraph 9, 16 or 17 of Schedule 4 to that Act (transfers to maintenance funds for historic buildings etc.).

(3) Where this subsection applies in relation to a disposal—

(*a*) the amount of any chargeable gain which, apart from this section, would accrue to the transferor on the disposal, and
(*b*) the amount of the consideration for which, apart from this section, the transferee would be regarded for the purposes of capital gains tax as having acquired the asset in question,

shall each be reduced by an amount equal to the held-over gain on the disposal.

(4) Subject to subsection (5) below, the reference in subsection (3) above to the held-over gain on a disposal is a reference to the chargeable gain which would have accrued on that disposal apart from this section.

(5) In any case where—

(*a*) there is actual consideration (as opposed to the consideration equal to the market value which is deemed to be given by virtue of any provision of this Act) for a disposal in respect of which a claim for relief is made under this section, and
(*b*) that actual consideration exceeds the sums allowable as a deduction under section 32 above,

the held-over gain on the disposal shall be reduced by the excess referred to in paragraph (*b*) above or, if part of the gain on the disposal is relieved under Schedule 20 to the Finance Act 1985 (retirement relief), by so much, if any, of that excess as exceeds the part so relieved.

(6) Subsection (3) above does not apply in relation to a disposal of assets within section 67(1) above on which a gain is deemed to accrue by virtue of paragraph 10(1)(*b*) of Schedule 13 to the Finance Act 1984.

(7) In the case of a disposal within subsection (2)(*a*) above there shall be allowed as a deduction in computing the chargeable gain accruing to the transferee on the disposal of the asset in question an amount equal to whichever is the lesser of—

(*a*) the inheritance tax attributable to the value of the asset, and
(*b*) the amount of the chargeable gain as computed apart from this subsection.

(8) Where an amount of inheritance tax is varied after it has been taken into account under subsection (7) above, all necessary adjustments shall be made, whether by the making of an assessment to capital gains tax or by the discharge or repayment of such tax.

(9) Where subsection (3) above applies in relation to a disposal which is deemed to occur by virtue of section 54(1) or 55(1) above, subsection (5) above shall not apply.

(10) Where a disposal is partly within subsection (2) above, or is a disposal within paragraph (*e*) of that subsection on which there is a reduced charge such as is mentioned in that paragraph, the preceding provisions of this section shall have effect in relation to an appropriate part of the disposal.

147B. Section 147A relief: gifts to non-residents

(1) Section 147A(3) above shall not apply where the transferee is neither resident nor ordinarily resident in the United Kingdom.

(2) Section 147A(3) above shall not apply where the transferee is an individual who—

(*a*) though resident or ordinarily resident in the United Kingdom, is regarded for the purposes of any double taxation arrangements having effect by virtue of section 788 of the Taxes Act 1988 as resident in a territory outside the United Kingdom, and
(*b*) by virtue of the arrangements would not be liable in the United Kingdom to tax on a gain arising on a disposal of the asset occurring immediately after its acquisition."

Payment of tax by instalments

5. The following section shall be inserted after section 7 of the Capital Gains Tax Act 1979—

"7A. Payment by instalments of tax on gifts

(1) Subsection (2) below applies where—

(*a*) the whole or any part of any assets to which this section applies is disposed of by way of gift or is deemed to be disposed of under section 54(1) or 55(1) below, and
(*b*) the disposal is one—

(i) to which neither section 126(3) nor section 147A(3) below applies (or would apply if a claim were duly made), or
(ii) to which either of those sections does apply but on which the held-over gain (within the meaning of the section applying) is less than the chargeable gain which would have accrued on that disposal apart from that section.

(2) Where this subsection applies, the capital gains tax chargeable on a gain accruing on the disposal may, if the person paying it by notice in writing to the inspector so elects, be paid by ten equal yearly instalments.

(3) The assets to which this section applies are—

(*a*) land or an estate or interest in land,
(*b*) any shares or securities of a company which, immediately before the disposal, gave control of the company to the person by whom the disposal was made or deemed to be made, and
(*c*) any shares or securities of a company not falling under paragraph (*b*) above and not quoted on a recognised stock exchange nor dealt in on the Unlisted Securities Market.

(4) Where tax is payable by instalments by virtue of this section, the first instalment shall be due on the day on which the tax would be payable apart from this section.

(5) Subject to the following provisions of this section—

(a) tax payable by instalments by virtue of this section shall carry interest in accordance with Part IX (except section 88) of the Taxes Management Act 1970, and
(b) the interest on the unpaid portion of the tax shall be added to each instalment and paid accordingly.

(6) Tax payable by instalments by virtue of this section which is for the time being unpaid, with interest to the date of payment, may be paid at any time.

(7) Tax which apart from this subsection would be payable by instalments by virtue of this section and which is for the time being unpaid, with interest to the date of payment, shall become due and payable immediately if—

(a) the disposal was by way of gift to a person connected with the donor or was deemed to be made under section 54(1) or 55(1) below, and
(b) the assets are disposed of for valuable consideration under a subsequent disposal (whether or not the subsequent disposal is made by the person who acquired them under the first disposal)."

Minor and consequential amendments

6.—(1) In section 56A of the Capital Gains Tax Act 1979 (gifts relief in cases within section 55 or 56)—

(a) in subsection (1), for the words "79 of the Finance Act 1980" there shall be substituted the words "126 or 147A below", and
(b) in subsection (4), for the words "79(1) of the Finance Act 1980" there shall be substituted the words "126 or, as the case may be, 147A below".

(2) In section 155(1) of that Act, the following definition shall be inserted after the definition of "quoted"—

"recognised stock exchange" has the meaning given by section 841 of the Taxes Act 1988,".

(3) In section 79 of the Finance Act 1981 (emigration of donee)—

(a) in subsection (1), for paragraph (a) there shall be substituted—

"(a) relief is given under section 126 of the Capital Gains Tax Act 1979 in respect of a disposal to an individual or the trustees of a settlement or under section 147A of that Act in respect of any disposal ("the relevant disposal");",

and for the words "the said section 79" there shall be substituted the words "section 126 or 147A", and
(b) for the words "subsection (1)(b) of the said section 79" in subsection (2) and for the words "section 79(1)(b) of the Finance Act 1980" in subsections (6) and (10) there shall be substituted the words "section 126(3)(b) or 147A(3)(b) of the Capital Gains Tax Act 1979".

(4) In section 64(5)(b) of the Finance Act 1984 (qualifying corporate bonds), for the words "of that Act or section 79 of the Finance Act 1980" there shall be substituted the words "or 147A of that Act".

(5) In section 58 of the Finance Act 1986 (gifts into dual resident trusts)—

(a) in subsection (1), for the words "79 of the Finance Act 1980 (general relief" there shall be substituted the words "126 or 147A of the Capital Gains Tax Act 1979 (relief", and for the words "subsection (1)" there shall be substituted the words "subsection (3)",
(b) subsection (2)(b) shall be omitted, and
(c) in subsections (3) and (5), for the words "the 1980 provision" in each place where they occur there shall be substituted the words "section 126 or 147A of the Capital Gains Tax Act 1979".

(6) In paragraph 3(3) of Schedule 28 to the Taxes Act 1988 (offshore income gains), for the words "79 of the Finance Act 1980 (relief for gifts), that section" there shall be substituted the words "126 or 147A of the Capital Gains Tax Act 1979 (relief for gifts), the claim".

SCHEDULE 15

Section 141

CAPITAL GAINS: RE-BASING TO 1982 ETC.

Postponed charges etc.: pre-1st April 1982 events

1.—(1) None of the enactments specified in sub-paragraph (2) below shall apply in consequence of an event occurring on or after 6th April 1988 if its application would be directly attributable to the disposal of an asset on or before 31st March 1982.

(2) The enactments referred to in sub-paragraph (1) above are—

(*a*) section 268A(4) of the Taxes Act 1970 (postponement of charge where securities acquired in exchange for business acquired by non-resident company);
(*b*) section 84 of the Capital Gains Tax Act 1979 (postponement of charge or loss where gilts acquired on compulsory acquisition of shares);
(*c*) section 111B(3) of that Act (postponement of charge where depreciating asset acquired on compulsory acquisition of land); and
(*d*) section 117(2) of that Act (postponement of charge where depreciating asset acquired as replacement for business asset).

2. Paragraph 3(1) of Schedule 9 to the Finance Act 1988 (halving of charges deferred from before 6th April 1988) shall have effect, and shall be deemed always to have had effect, with the insertion of the words "and to paragraph 1 of Schedule 15 to the Finance Act 1989" after the words "sub-paragraph (3) below".

Reduction of 1982 value in certain cases

3.—(1) Sub-paragraph (2) below applies where—

(*a*) subsection (2) of section 96 of the Finance Act 1988 applies in relation to the disposal of an asset,
(*b*) if that subsection did not apply, any of the enactments specified in sub-paragraph (3) below would operate to disallow expenditure as a deduction in computing a gain accruing on the disposal, and
(*c*) the disallowance would be attributable to the reduction of the amount of the consideration for a disposal made after 31st March 1982 but before 6th April 1988.

(2) Where this sub-paragraph applies the amount allowable as a deduction on the disposal shall be reduced by the amount which would be disallowed if section 96(2) did not apply.

(3) The enactments referred to in sub-paragraph (1) above are—

(*a*) section 21(2) of the Capital Gains Tax Act 1979 (disallowance of allowable expenditure where allowance already given against receipts of compensation or insurance money);
(*b*) section 72(4) of that Act (disallowance where allowance already given against capital distribution);
(*c*) section 83(4) of that Act (disallowance where allowance already given against premium on conversion of securities); and
(*d*) section 109 of that Act (disallowance where allowance already given against gain from small part disposal).

(4) This paragraph shall apply to disposals on or after 6th April 1989.

No gain/no loss disposals

4.—(1) Section 68(7A) of the Finance Act 1985 shall have effect, and shall be deemed always to have had effect—

(*a*) as if in paragraph (*a*) for "146(3)" there were substituted "146(2) or (3), 146A(2)", and
(*b*) as if after paragraph (*e*) there were inserted—

"(*ee*) section 130(3) of the Transport Act 1985;".

(2) Paragraph 1(3) of Schedule 8 to the Finance Act 1988 shall have effect, and shall be deemed always to have had effect, as if after paragraph (*e*) there were inserted—

"(*ee*) section 130(3) of the Transport Act 1985;".

Elections

5. Paragraph 13(5) of Schedule 8 to the Finance Act 1988 shall have effect, and shall be deemed always to have had effect, as if for the words "subsection (5)" there were substituted the words "subsection (6)".

SCHEDULE 17

Section 187

REPEALS

PART IV
INCOME AND CORPORATION TAX: GENERAL

Chapter	Short title	Extent of repeal
1970 c. 9.	The Taxes Management Act 1970.	In section 15(11), paragraph (*b*) and the word "and" preceding it.
1988 c. 1.	The Income and Corporation Taxes Act 1988.	In section 131(2), the words "for the same or another chargeable period".
		In section 149(1), the words "for that period" and the words "for that or any other period".
		Section 170.
		Section 175(3).
		In section 176(1), the words "(but not more than six months)".
		In section 178(2), paragraph (*b*) and the word "or" preceding it.
		Section 203(4).
		In section 231, in subsection (4) the words "and where" onwards, and subsection (5).
		Section 433.
		Section 434(4) and (5).
		Section 435.
		Section 436(3)(*b*).
		Section 507(2).
		In section 590(3)(*d*), the words "(disregarding any excess of that remuneration over the permitted maximum)".
		Section 595(2) and (3).
		In section 596(3)(*a*), the word "either" and the words "or subsection (2)".
		In section 600(1), the words "or have been" and the words "or has at any time been".
		Section 635(4).
		In section 645, in subsection (3), the word "and" following paragraph (*a*) and sub-section (5).
		In section 655(5), the words "in cases where the applications are made before 1st February 1990".
		Section 769(7)(*b*) and (*c*).
		In section 824(10), the definition of "United Kingdom estate".
		In Schedule 8, in paragraph 7(1), the words ", or is an associate of a person who has,"; in paragraph 13, in sub-paragraph (1) the word "fixed" and sub-paragraphs (2) and (3); and, in paragraph 14, sub-paragraph (2), in sub-paragraph (5) the words "specified in, or" and sub-paragraph (7).
		In Schedule 9, in paragraph 10, paragraph (ii) of sub-paragraph (*c*) and the word "and" preceding it.
		In Schedule 23, paragraph 8.
1988 c. 39.	The Finance Act 1988.	In section 68(1), the words from "at the fixed price" to "tendered".

1. The repeals in sections 131 and 149 and of section 170 of the Income and Corporation Taxes Act 1988 have effect in accordance with section 42 of this Act.

2. The repeals in sections 231 and 824 of the Income and Corporation Taxes Act 1988 have effect in accordance with sections 110 and 111 of this Act.

3. The repeals in sections 433 to 435 of the Income and Corporation Taxes Act 1988 have effect in accordance with section 84(5) of this Act and the repeal of section 436(3)(*b*) of that Act has effect in accordance with section 87(5) of this Act.

4. The repeals in sections 590, 595, 596 and 600 of, and in Schedule 23 to, the Income and Corporation Taxes Act 1988 have effect in accordance with Schedule 6 to this Act.

5. The repeals in sections 635, 645 and 655 of the Income and Corporation Taxes Act 1988 have effect in accordance with Schedule 7 to this Act.

6. The repeal of section 769(7)(*b*) and (*c*) of the Income and Corporation Taxes Act 1988 has effect in accordance with section 100 of this Act.

7. The repeal in the Finance Act 1988 has effect in relation to offers made on or after 11th October 1988.

PART V
CLOSE COMPANIES

Chapter	Short title	Extent of repeal
1970 c. 9.	The Taxes Management Act 1970.	Section 29(2). In section 31(3)(*b*), the words "426,". In the Table in section 98, in the first column, the reference to paragraph 17 of Schedule 19 to the principal Act. In Schedule 3, in rule 8, the words from "or relating" to "Schedule 19 to the principal Act".
1972 c. 41.	The Finance Act 1972.	In Schedule 24, paragraph 6.
1979 c. 14.	The Capital Gains Tax Act 1979.	In section 89(1), paragraph (*b*) and the word "or" preceding it.
1988 c. 1.	The Income and Corporation Taxes Act 1988.	In section 127(3), paragraph (*b*) and the word "or" preceding it. In section 230, the word "either", the words from "or to" to "Schedule 19" and the words "in either case". In section 239(7), the words "subsections (5) to (7) of section 430 and". In section 249(3), the words "and paragraph 12(1) to (3) of Schedule 19". In section 250(7), the words "and paragraph 12 of Schedule 19". Section 414(3). In section 416(1), the words from "except" to "Schedule 19". Sections 423 to 430. In section 539(1), the words "including tax under section 426". In section 681, in subsection (1), paragraph (*b*) and the word "and" preceding it and subsections (2) and (3). Section 686(3) and (4). Section 687(3)(*b*) and (*c*). In section 701(8), the words "426(3)". Section 742(9)(*d*) and (10). In section 825(1)(*a*), the words from "and any" to "430(7)(*a*)". In Schedule 4, paragraph 10(3). In Schedule 8, in paragraph 7(3), the second "and". Schedule 19. In Schedule 29, in the Table in paragraph 32, the entries relating to section 29(2) of the Taxes Management Act 1970 and sections 89(1)(*b*) and 136(10)(*b*) of the Capital Gains Tax Act 1979.
1988 c. 39.	The Finance Act 1988.	Section 102(2)(*a*).

1. The repeal in section 98 of the Taxes Management Act 1970 and the repeal of paragraph 17 of Schedule 19 to the Income and Corporation Taxes Act 1988 have effect on and after the day on which this Act is passed.

2. The repeal in section 89 of the Capital Gains Tax Act 1979 (and the corresponding repeal in Schedule 29 to the Income and Corporation Taxes Act 1988) have effect where the due date of issue of

the share capital issued to a close company falls in an accounting period of the company beginning after 31st March 1989.

3. The repeal of section 414(3) of the Income and Corporation Taxes Act 1988 has effect from 1st April 1989.

4. The repeal of sections 423 to 430 of, and Schedule 19 to, the Income and Corporation Taxes Act 1988 has effect in accordance with section 103 of this Act.

5. The repeals in section 681 of the Income and Corporation Taxes Act 1988 have effect in relation to the income of bodies corporate for accounting periods beginning after 31st March 1989.

6. The remaining repeals have effect in relation to accounting periods beginning after 31st March 1989.

PART VI
CAPITAL ALLOWANCES

Chapter	Short title	Extent of repeal
1968 c. 3.	The Capital Allowances Act 1968.	Section 9(*b*). Section 14. Section 50. Section 67(11). In section 68, in subsections (1) and (3), the words "or forestry", in each place where they occur, and in subsection (2), the words "and forestry income". Section 80. In section 87(4), the words "or forestry", in both places where they occur. In section 92(5), the words "allowed or" and the words "balancing allowance or". Section 93(1) and (2). Schedule 8.
1971 c. 68.	The Finance Act 1971.	In Schedule 8, paragraph 2 and, in paragraph 7, in sub-paragraph (1) the words "Subject to sub-paragraph (2) below" and the words from "by reason of" to the end of paragraph (*b*) and sub-paragraph (2).
1978 c. 42.	The Finance Act 1978.	In Schedule 6, paragraph 8.
1980 c. 48.	The Finance Act 1980.	In section 74(6), the words from the beginning to "and". In section 75(6), the words from the beginning to "and".
1982 c. 39.	The Finance Act 1982.	In Schedule 12, paragraph 11.
1986 c. 41.	The Finance Act 1986.	Section 56(5). In Schedule 15, in paragraphs 1 to 3, the words "or forestry", in each place where they occur, in paragraph 7(3), the words "subject to paragraph 9 below", and in paragraph 11, the words "and forestry income" and the words "or forestry income".
1988 c. 1.	The Income and Corporation Taxes Act 1988.	In section 521(5), the words "within the terms of section 839".

1. The repeal in paragraph 7(1)(*b*) of Schedule 8 to the Finance Act 1971 has effect in cases where machinery or plant is brought into use on or after the day on which this Act is passed.

2. The repeals in sections 68 and 87(4) of the Capital Allowances Act 1968 and in paragraphs 1 to 3 and 11 of Schedule 15 to the Finance Act 1986 have effect in relation to chargeable periods beginning on or after 6th April 1993.

3. The repeal in section 521(5) of the Income and Corporation Taxes Act 1988 has effect in accordance with paragraph 27 of Schedule 13 to this Act.

4. The repeals of the provisions listed in sub-paragraph (5) of paragraph 28 of Schedule 13 to this Act have effect in accordance with that paragraph.

PART VII
CAPITAL GAINS

Chapter	Short title	Extent of repeal
1973 c. 51.	The Finance Act 1973.	In section 38(3B)(*a*), the words "within the period of two years ending at the date of the disposal".

Chapter	Short title	Extent of repeal
1979 c. 14.	The Capital Gains Tax Act 1979.	Section 126(7)(*b*). Section 142A(5)(*c*). In Schedule 4, in paragraph 1(2) the words "at the rate of 50 per cent.,", in paragraph 3(1), the words from "by virtue" to "(settled property)", in paragraph 3(2) the words "at the rate of 50 per cent.," and in paragraph 4(4), the words "(taking account" onwards.
1980 c. 48.	The Finance Act 1980.	Section 79.
1981 c. 35.	The Finance Act 1981.	Section 78. Section 96(3)(*e*) and (4).
1982 c. 39.	The Finance Act 1982.	Sections 81 and 82.
1984 c. 43.	The Finance Act 1984.	Section 64(2)(*a*).
1984 c. 51.	The Inheritance Tax Act 1984.	In section 97(2), the words from "and in this section" to the end.
1985 c. 54.	The Finance Act 1985.	In section 70(10), paragraph (*a*) and the word "and" following it.
1986 c. 41.	The Finance Act 1986.	In section 58(2), paragraph (*b*) and the word "and" preceding it. Section 101(2).
1987 c. 51.	The Finance (No. 2) Act 1987.	Section 78.
1988 c. 1.	The Income and Corporation Taxes Act 1988.	In Schedule 29, in the Table in paragraph 32, the entry relating to section 126(7) of the Capital Gains Tax Act 1979.

1. The repeal in the Finance Act 1973 has effect in accordance with section 130 of this Act.

2. The repeal in section 142A of the Capital Gains Tax Act 1979 has effect in accordance with section 92 of this Act.

3. The repeal of section 81 of the Finance Act 1982 has effect in relation to disposals on or after 6th April 1989 or, in the case of section 81(1)(*b*), assets acquired on or after that date.

4. The repeal of section 64(2)(*a*) of the Finance Act 1984 has effect in accordance with section 139(1) of this Act.

5. The repeal in section 97(2) of the Inheritance Tax Act 1984 has effect in accordance with section 138(7) of this Act.

6. The repeal in the Finance (No. 2) Act 1987 has effect in accordance with section 140 of this Act.

7. The remaining repeals have effect in relation to disposals on or after 14th March 1989 (except that they shall not have effect in relation to such a disposal in a case where the enactment in question operates in consequence of relief having been given under section 79 of the Finance Act 1980 in respect of a disposal made before that date).

PART VIII
MANAGEMENT

Chapter	Short title	Extent of repeal
1970 c. 9.	The Taxes Management Act 1970.	Section 16(6). In section 20, subsections (4) and (5) and, in subsection (6), the words "and in relation" onwards. In section 20B(7), the words from "to a person" to "daughter". Sections 37 to 39. In section 40(2), the words "Subject to section 41 below,". Section 41. In section 53(1), the words "and the reference" onwards. In section 61(5), the words "within the said five days" and the words from "The costs" to "the collector, and". Section 62(3), so far as unrepealed. Section 64(3), so far as unrepealed. Section 70(5). Section 86(6). Section 87(4) and (5).

Chapter	Short title	Extent of repeal
1970 c. 9— cont.	The Taxes Management Act 1970— cont.	In section 98, in the Table, in column 1, in the entry relating to Part III of the Taxes Management Act 1970, the words ", except sections 16 and 24(2)" and the entry relating to section 481(5)(k) of the Income and Corporation Taxes Act 1988. In section 118(1), the definition of "neglect".
1973 c. 51.	The Finance Act 1973.	In Schedule 16A, paragraph 10.
1975 c. 45.	The Finance (No. 2) Act 1975.	In section 47(1), the words "of not less than £25".
1976 c. 24.	The Development Land Tax Act 1976.	In Schedule 8, paragraphs 17 and 18, so far as unrepealed.
1980 c. 48.	The Finance Act 1980.	Section 62.
1982 c. 39.	The Finance Act 1982.	Section 69.
1987 c. 51.	The Finance (No. 2) Act 1987.	In section 84, subsections (1) to (3) and (5) to (8).
1988 c. 1.	The Income and Corporation Taxes Act 1988.	In section 824, in subsections (1)(a) and (b), the words "of not less than £25" and, in subsection (5), the words "of not less than £25" and paragraph (b) and the word "and" preceding it. In section 825(2), the words "of not less than £100". In Schedule 19A, paragraph 10.
1988 c. 39.	The Finance Act 1988.	In section 126, subsection (1) and, in subsection (4)(b), the words "and (9)". In Schedule 3, paragraph 29.
1989 c.26	The Finance Act 1989.	Section 165(2).

1. The repeals in sections 16, 53 and 98 of the Taxes Management Act 1970 have effect in accordance with section 164 of this Act.

2. The repeals in sections 20 and 20B of the Taxes Management Act 1970 and section 126 of the Finance Act 1988 have effect with respect to notices given, or warrants issued, on or after the day on which this Act is passed.

3. The repeals of sections 37 to 39, in section 40, of section 41 and in section 118 of the Taxes Management Act 1970 and in Schedule 3 to the Finance Act 1988 have effect in accordance with section 149 of this Act.

4. The repeals in section 61 of the Taxes Management Act 1970 come into force on the day appointed under section 152(7) of this Act.

5. The repeals in sections 86 and 87 of the Taxes Management Act 1970, the Finance (No. 2) Act 1975, the Finance Act 1980 and sections 824 and 825 of the Income and Corporation Taxes Act 1988 have effect in accordance with section 158 of this Act.

6. The repeal in the Finance Act 1982 has effect in accordance with section 156(2) of this Act.

7. The repeal of subsection (2) of section 165 of this Act has effect in relation to failures beginning on or after the day appointed under that subsection.

PART X

RATES OF INTEREST

Chapter	Short title	Extent of repeal
1970 c. 9.	The Taxes Management Act 1970.	Section 89.
1970 c. 24.	The Finance Act 1970.	Section 30.
1970 c. 21 (N.I.).	The Finance Act (Northern Ireland) 1970.	Section 1(1) and (2).
1973 c. 51.	The Finance Act 1973.	In Schedule 16A, in paragraph 3(4), paragraph (a) and the word "and" following it and the words "they apply".
1975 c. 22.	The Oil Taxation Act 1975.	In Schedule 2, in the Table in paragraph 1, the entry relating to section 89 of the Taxes Management Act 1970.
1975 c. 45.	The Finance (No. 2) Act 1975.	Section 47(2).
1980 c. 1.	The Petroleum Revenue Tax Act 1980.	Section 2(3).
1984 c. 51.	The Inheritance Tax Act 1984.	Section 233(2) and (4).
1986 c. 41.	The Finance Act 1986.	Section 92(4) and (5). In Schedule 19, paragraph 32.

Chapter	Short title	Extent of repeal
1987 c. 51.	The Finance (No. 2) Act 1987.	Section 89.
1988 c. 1.	The Income and Corporation Taxes Act 1988.	In section 824, subsection (1A), in subsection (2) the words "and (1A)" and in subsection (6) the words "Without prejudice to subsection (1A) above". In section 825, subsection (2A) and in subsection (5) the words "Without prejudice to subsection (2A) above". In Schedule 19A, in paragraph 3(4), paragraph (*a*) and the word "and" following it and the words "they apply".
1988 c. 39.	The Finance Act 1988.	In Schedule 13, paragraphs 7(*b*) and (*f*) and 8.

These repeals have effect in accordance with section 178(7) of this Act.

PART XIV
TITHE REDEMPTION

Chapter	Short title	Extent of repeal
1979 c. 14.	The Capital Gains Tax Act 1979.	In Schedule 2, in Part II, the entry relating to securities issued under Part II of the Tithe Act 1936.

These repeals have effect from the day appointed under section 187(2) of this Act.

Note.—Other repeals in this Part have been omitted as being irrelevant to this work.

INDEX

Definitions are included in a separate index **WORDS AND PHRASES** *post.*

ABROAD
    assets leased. *See under* MACHINERY AND PLANT
    partnership controlled..TA 1980 s 112
    residence. *See* RESIDENCE
    trade carried on..TA 1988 s 391
    trade partly. *See under* WORK DONE ABROAD
    work done. *See* WORK DONE ABROAD

ACCOMMODATION
    charge to tax..TA 1988 s 154
    employee, provided for—
        charge to tax..TA 1988 s 145, 146
        directors..TA 1988 s 145(5)
        exceptions..TA 1988 s 145(4)
        expenses..TA 1988 s 163
        expensive houses..TA 1988 s 46
        family or household..TA 1988 s 145(6)
        value..TA 1988 s 146(3)
    holiday. *See* FURNISHED HOLIDAY LETTING
    job-related..TA 1988 s 354
    MP's allowance..TA 1988 s 198, 200
    representative occupation, expenses connected with..TA 1988 s 163
    work done abroad..TA 1988 s 193(4)

ACCOUNT
    incorrect—
        assisting..TMA 1970 s 99
        delay in correcting..TMA 1970 s 97
        penalties..TMA 1970 s 95 96
    power to obtain..TMA 1970 s 20–20D
    public revenue dividends..TA 1988 Sch 3

ACCOUNTING DATE
    meaning..TA 1988 s 834

ACCOUNTING PERIOD
    controlled foreign company..TA 1988 s 751
    corporation tax..TA 1988 s 8, 12
    profit-related pay..TA 1988 Sch 8 para 10
    qualifying distribution made outside..TA 1988 Sch 13 para 9

ACCUMULATION SETTLEMENT
    meaning..FA 1988 s 100(2)
    capital gains tax..FA 1988 s 100(1)
    child..TA 1988 s 664

ACT
    meaning..TA 1988 s 832(1)

ADDITIONAL RATE
    meaning..TA 1988 s 832(1)
    discretionary trusts..TA 1988 s 686(1)

ADMINISTRATION OF ESTATE
    absolute interest—
        meaning..TA 1988 s 701(2)
        benefits received, meaning..TA 1988 s 697(3)
        CTT relief..TA 1988 s 699
        foreign estate..TA 1988 s 696(3)(6)
        payments taxable..TA 1988 s 696
        successive..TA 1988 s 698(2)
    accrued income, relief..TA 1988 s 699

ADMINISTRATION OF ESTATE—*continued*
adjustments..TA 1988 s 700
administration period, meaning..TA 1988 s 695(1)
aggregate income, meaning..TA 1988 s 701(8)
capital gains tax..CGTA 1979 s 47
charges on residue, meaning..TA 1988 s 701(6)
differing residuary dispositions..TA 1988 s 701(11)
discretionary payments..TA 1988 s 689(3)
foreign estate—
  meaning..TA 1988 s 701(10)
  absolute interest..TA 1988 s 696(3)(6)
  limited interest..TA 1988 s 695(4)
information..TA 1988 s 700(4)
inheritance tax relief..TA 1988 s 699
limited interest—
  meaning..TA 1988 s 701(3)
  deemed payments..TA 1988 s 695(5)
  foreign estate..TA 1988 s 695(4)
  payments taxable..TA 1988 s 695(6)
personal representative's rights as to another estate..TA 1988 s 698(1)
residuary income—
  meaning..TA 1988 s 696(2)
  ascertainment..TA 1988 s 697(1)
  charge to tax..TA 1988 s 696
  company..TA 1988 s 696(8)
Scotland..TA 1988 s 702
specific disposition, meaning..TA 1988 s 701(5)
successive absolute interests..TA 1988 s 698(2)
sum paid or payable, meaning..TA 1988 s 701(12)
time for assessment etc..TA 1988 s 700(3)
UK estate, meaning..TA 1988 s 701(9)

ADVANCE CORPORATION TAX
assessment..TA 1988 Sch 13 para 10
carry back, surrender of limited right to..TA 1988 s 498, 499
change in company ownership..TA 1988 s 245
close company apportionment..TA 1988 s 430(2)
company purchase of own shares..TA 1988 s 240(9)
corporation tax provisions distinguished..TA 1988 s 14(4)
demergers. *See under* DEMERGER
distribution made outside accounting period..TA 1988 Sch 13 para 9
double taxation relief and..TA 1988 s 797(4)
franked payment, meaning..TA 1988 s 238(1)
gross amount of dividend, on..TA 1988 s 255
group income..TA 1988 s 247(6)(7)
income tax..TA 1988 s 233
interest on overdue..TMA 1970 s 87
liability, qualifying distributions..TA 1988 s 14(2)
notional distribution date, meaning..TA 1988 s 499(2)
oil extraction activities..OTA 1975 s 16 TA 1988 s 497, 499
payment of—
  franked investment income received after..TA 1988 Sch 13 para 4
  time for..TA 1988 Sch 13 para 3
payments not qualifying distributions..TA 1988 Sch 13 para 7
principal accounting period, meaning..TA 1988 s 498(2)
public corporation, transfer of assets..TA 1988 s 410
qualifying distribution—
  meaning..TA 1988 s 14(2)
  liability..TA 1988 s 14(1)
rate—
  changes..TA 1988 s 246
  1988..TA 1988 s 14
redeemable preference shares, on..TA 1988 s 497(3)(4)
regulations, power to make..TA 1988 s 253
repayment..TA 1988 Sch 13 para 10
repayment supplement..TA 1988 s 825
return—
  contents..TA 1988 Sch 13 para 1
  duty to make..TA 1988 Sch 13 para 1
  errors..TA 1988 Sch 13 para 8
set-off—
  asset transferred after change of ownership, where..TA 1988 s 245B
  change of ownership, on..TA 1988 s 245A, 245B
  claim for..TA 1988 s 239(3)

ADVANCE CORPORATION TAX—*continued*
set-off—*continued*
  corporation tax on profits, against. . TA 1988 s 239
  excessive. . TA 1988 s 252(1)
  restriction. . FA 1984 s 52(3) TA 1988 s 245A 245B
  subsidiary's liability, against. . TA 1988 s 240
surplus—
  meaning. . TA 1988 s 238(1)
  set-off. *See* set-off *supra*
  treatment. . TA 1988 s 240
surrendered, meaning. . TA 1988 s 498(2) 499(2)
surrendering company, meaning. . TA 1988 s 240(1)
tax credit. . TA 1988 s 231
transactions in securities—
  appeals. . TA 1988 s 705
  Board's notice. . TA 1988 s 703
uncertain payments. . TA 1988 Sch 13 para 7

ADVANCE PETROLEUM REVENUE TAX
deduction for corporation tax. . TA 1988 s 500

AFRICA
Central African Pension Fund. . TA 1988 s 615

AGE ALLOWANCE
entitlement. . TA 1988 s 257(2)
restriction. . TA 1988 s 257(5)

AGENCY
meaning. . TMA 1970 s 118(1) CGTA 1979 s 12(3) TA 1988 s 834(1)
non-resident's profits—
  capital gains tax. . TMA 1970 s 84
  corporation tax. . TMA 1970 s 85
  income tax. . TMA 1970 s 79
  profession or vocation through. . CGTA 1979 s 12(2A), FA 1989 s 126

AGENCY WORKER
excluded services. . TA 1988 s 134(5)
remuneration, meaning. . TA 1988 s 134(7) Sch 29 para 6
return of employees. . TA 1988 Sch 29 para 7
Sch E. . TA 1988 s 134(1)(6)

AGENT
copyright royalties. . TA 1988 s 536(3)
non-resident, of, investment transactions. . TMA 1970 s 78(2)
Sch A collected from. . TA 1988 s 23(7)(8)
unauthorised. . TMA 1970 s 82

AGGREGATION
retirement relief—
  gains. . FA 1985 Sch 20 para 6–8 12
  spouse's interest. . FA 1985 Sch 20 para 16
wife's income. *See under* HUSBAND AND WIFE

AGREEMENT
appeal settled by. . TMA 1970 s 54
capital allowances, as to. . FA 1982 s 79
payment without deduction of tax. . TMA 1970 s 106(2)
postponed tax. . TMA 1970 s 55(7)(8)
stock relief, as to. . FA 1982 s 79

AGRICULTURAL BUILDING
allowances and charges—
  balancing. . FA 1986 Sch 15 para 6
  forestry land, on, abolition. . FA 1989 s 120
  manner of making. . FA 1986 Sch 15 para 11
  restrictions on. . FA 1986 Sch 15 para 10
balancing events. . FA 1986 Sch 15 para 7
bought unused. . FA 1986 Sch 15 para 5
capital allowances. . FA 1986 s 56
expenditure qualifying for allowances. . FA 1986 Sch 15 para 2
land values, exclusion of. . FA 1986 Sch 15 para 8

AGRICULTURAL BUILDING—*continued*
  relevant interest—
    meaning..FA 1986 Sch 15 para 3
    transfers of..FA 1986 Sch 15 para 4
  sales..FA 1986 Sch 15 para 9
  writing-down allowance..CAA 1968 s 75 FA 1986 Sch 15 para 1

AGRICULTURAL INCOME
  meaning..CAA 1968 s 69

AGRICULTURAL LAND
  meaning..CAA 1968 s 69 TA 1988 s 33(3)
  allowances and charges—
    balancing..FA 1986 Sch 15 para 6
    manner of making..FA 1986 Sch 15 para 11
  balancing events..FA 1986 Sch 15 para 7
  capital allowances..FA 1986 s 56
  expenditure qualifying for allowances..FA 1986 Sch 15 para 2
  land values, exclusion of..FA 1986 Sch 15 para 8
  relevant interest—
    meaning..FA 1986 Sch 15 para 3
    transfers of..FA 1986 Sch 15 para 4
  sales..FA 1986 Sch 15 para 9
  Sch A, allowance..TA 1988 s 33
  writing-down allowance..CAA 1968 s 75 FA 1986 Sch 15 para 1

AGRICULTURAL PROPERTY
  gift of business assets..CGTA 1979 Sch 4 para 1

AGRICULTURAL SOCIETY
  meaning..TA 1988 s 510(2)
  exemption..TA 1988 s 510(1)

AIRCRAFT
  leasing..FA 1982 s 70(1) FA 1986 s 57(4)
  rollover relief..CGTA 1979 s 118
  short-term leasing..FA 1980 s 64(6) 73(3)
  work done abroad..TA 1988 Sch 12 para 5

ALLOWANCE
  balancing. *See* BALANCING ALLOWANCE
  bereavement..TA 1988 s 262
  capital. *See* CAPITAL ALLOWANCE
  indexation. *See* INDEXATION ALLOWANCE
  initial. *See* INITIAL ALLOWANCE
  investment. *See* INVESTMENT ALLOWANCE
  mobility..TA 1988 s 617(1)
  personal. *See* PERSONAL ALLOWANCE
  supplementary. *See* SUPPLEMENTARY ALLOWANCE
  writing-down. *See* WRITING-DOWN ALLOWANCE

ANIMAL
  exhibition, for..TA 1988 Sch 5 para 9(5)
  farm. *See* FARM ANIMALS; HERD BASIS
  racing..TA 1988 Sch 5 para 9(5)
  trades other than farming..TA 1988 Sch 5 para 9

ANNUAL PAYMENT
  capital gains..CGTA 1979 s 144
  charge on income, not being..TA 1988 s 51A
  charity, to..TA 1988 s 338, 339, 347A(2)(*b*)
  close company apportionment..TA 1988 s 423(3)
  deduction of income tax—
    certificate of..TA 1988 s 352
    payments not out of profits..TA 1988 s 349, 350
    payments out of profits..TA 1988 s 348
  existing obligations..FA 1988 s 356(4)(5)
  general rule..TA 1988 s 347A
  loss relief..TA 1988 s 387, 388
  non-allowable deductions..TA 1988 s 817(1)
  non-resident, paid to..TA 1988 s 82, 340
  non-taxable consideration, for..TA 1988 s 125
  not out of profits or gains brought into charge, meaning..TA 1988 s 350(2)
  personal representative, made by..TA 1988 s 347A(3)

ANNUAL PAYMENT—*continued*
  relief..TA 1988 s 353
  Sch A..TA 1988 s 15(1)
  Sch D Case III..TA 1988 s 18(3)
  share acquisition schemes..TA 1988 s 688
  spouses between..FA 1988 Sch 3 para 32
  under deduction..TA 1988 s 821(2)

ANNUITY. *See also* ANNUAL PAYMENT
  annuity business, meaning..TA 1988 s 431(1)
  annuity fund, meaning..TA 1988 s 431(1)
  capital gains..CGTA 1979 s 144
  foreign, deduction..TA 1988 s 65(1), 196
  general annuity business, meaning..TA 1988 s 431(1)
  life annuity, meaning..TA 1988 s 539(3)
  life annuity contract. *See* LIFE ANNUITY CONTRACT
  non-allowable deductions..TA 1988 s 817(1)
  payments for non-taxable consideration..TA 1988 s 125
  payments securing..TA 1988 s 273, FA 1988 Sch 3 para 10
  personal pension scheme, paid under..TA 1988 s 633, 634, 636
  public, Sch E..TA 1988 s 19(1)
  purchased life. *See* PURCHASED LIFE ANNUITY
  retirement. *See* RETIREMENT ANNUITY
  Sch D Case III..TA 1988 s 18(3)
  Sch E..TA 1988 s 19(1)
  under deduction..TA 1988 s 821(2)
  victims of Nazi persecution, paid to..TA 1988 s 30

ANTI-AVOIDANCE. *See* TAX AVOIDANCE

APPEAL
  meaning..TMA 1970 s 48(1)
  agreement, settled by..TMA 1970 s 54
  assessment, against—
    double assessment..TMA 1970 s 32(2)
    error or mistake..TMA 1970 s 33(4)
    income tax..TMA 1970 s 29(4)
    right of..TMA 1970 s 31
    time for..TMA 1970 s 31(1)
  capital gains tax regulations..TMA 1970 s 57
  case stated. *See* CASE STATED
  chargeable gains..TMA 1970 s 57
  claim, as to..TMA 1970 s 42(3)(4)(9)
  close company apportionment..TA 1988 Sch 19 paras 13, 18
  company payments not distributions..TA 1988 Sch 16 para 10(3)(4)
  controlled foreign company, as to..TA 1988 s 753, 754(3)(4)
  corporation tax return, penalty, against..F(No 2)A 1987 s 84(6)
  Court of Appeal, to..TMA 1970 s 56(8)
  determination of penalty, against..TMA 1970 s 100B, 100C(4)
  double assessment, against..TMA 1970 s 32(2)
  evidence..TMA 1970 s 52
  General Commissioners, to..TMA 1970 s 31(4)(6)
  High Court, from..TMA 1970 s 56(8)
  House of Lords, to..TMA 1970 s 56(10)
  increase of assessment on..TMA 1970 s 50(7)(8)
  jurisdiction—
    Board, from..TMA 1970 Sch 2 para 3
    inspector, from..TMA 1970 Sch 2 para 1 2
  Lands Tribunal, to..TMA 1970 s 47(1)(2)
  lease at undervalue..TA 1988 s 42
  Northern Ireland..TMA 1970 s 59
  notice of..TMA 1970 s 31
  notice of hearing..TMA 1970 s 50(1)(2)
  offshore fund, as to..TA 1988 Sch 27 para 16
  out of time..TMA 1970 s 49
  payment of tax pending..TMA 1970 s 56(9)
  personal pension scheme, as to..TA 1988 s 651
  postponement..TMA 1970 s 50(4)
  profit-related pay, as to..TA 1988 s 182
  profit sharing scheme, as to..TA 1988 Sch 9 para 5
  purchased life annuity..TA 1988 s 658(1)
  recovery of tax not postponed..TMA 1970 s 55
  reduction of assessment on..TMA 1970 s 50(6)(8)
  rehearing..TMA 1970 s 57B(1)(*c*)

APPEAL—*continued*
   repayment to wife, as to. . TA 1988 s 281(3)(4)
   representation. . TMA 1970 s 50(5)
   Scotland. . TMA 1970 s 56(10)
   share option scheme approval, as to. . TA 1988 Sch 9 para 5
   Special Commissioners, to. *See under* SPECIAL COMMISSIONERS
   sub-contractor's certificate, as to. . TA 1988 s 561(9)
   summary penalty, against. . TMA 1970 s 53(2)
   surrender of life policy, as to. . TA 1988 s 272(5)
   time limit—
     assessments. . TMA 1970 s 31(1)
     claims. . TMA 1970 s 42(3)
   transactions in securities—
     advance corporation tax. . TA 1988 s 705(6)
     generally. . TA 1988 s 705(1)
     tribunal. . TA 1988 s 706
   transfer to Special Commissioners. . TMA 1970 s 44(3)(3A)
   tribunal. . TA 1988 s 706
   underwriting agent, by. . FA 1988 Sch 5 para 5
   unremittable overseas income. . TA 1988 s 584(9)
   venue—
     capital gains tax. . TMA 1970 Sch 3 para 1–6
     corporation tax. . TMA 1970 Sch 3 para 7 8
     income tax. . TMA 1970 Sch 3 para 1–6
   withdrawal. . TMA 1970 s 54(3)(4)
   witnesses. . TMA 1970 s 52(2)(3) 53

APPLICATION
   determination of amount, for. . TMA 1970 s 55(4)(5)
   postponement of tax. . TMA 1970 s 55(3)(3A)

APPORTIONMENT
   additional personal allowance. . TA 1988 s 260
   capital allowances—
     procedure. . CAA 1968 s 81
     sale etc of property. . CAA 1968 s 77
   child, relief for. . TA 1988 s 260
   close company. *See* CLOSE COMPANY APPORTIONMENT
   company reconstructions. . TA 1988 s 343(9)(10)
   controlled foreign company, as to. *See under* CONTROLLED FOREIGN COMPANY
   corporation tax. . TA 1988 s 72
   first-year allowance. . FA 1971 Sch 8 para 15(4)
   furnished holiday lettings. . TA 1988 s 503(6)
   gain etc over period of ownership. . CGTA 1979 Sch 5 para 11
   group relief. . TA 1988 s 409(2)
   hire-purchase payments, cars. . CAA 1968 Sch 2 para 10
   loan interest relief. . TA 1988 s 367(4)
   sale etc of industrial building, on. . CAA 1968 s 17(3)
   Sch D Cases I, II and VI. . TA 1988 s 72
   tied premises. . TA 1988 s 98(3)
   time basis. . TA 1988 s 834(4)

ARMED FORCES
   abroad, life assurance relief. . TA 1988 s 266(9)
   allowances, bounties and gratuities. . TA 1988 s 316
   awards pensions. . TA 1988 s 317
   leave travel facilities. . TA 1988 s 197
   wounds and disability pensions. . TA 1988 s 315

ARTIST
   relief. . TA 1988 s 538

ASSESSMENT
   advance corporation tax. . TA 1988 Sch 13 para 10
   allowances, transfer of. . TMA 1970 s 37A
   annual, income tax. . TA 1988 s 2(2)
   appeal against. *See under* APPEAL
   basis of—
     corporation tax. . TA 1988 s 70
     non-resident company. . TA 1988 s 70(3)
   Board, by. . TMA 1970 s 29(2)(3)(7)
   business expansion scheme. . TA 1988 s 307
   capital allowances agreements. . FA 1982 s 79
   claim, election, application or notice, making of. . TMA 1970 s 43A 43B

ASSESSMENT—*continued*
  claim, following..TMA 1970 s 42(10)
  company payments not distributions..TA 1988 Sch 16 para 10
  controlled foreign company..TA 1988 s 754
  current year basis..TA 1988 s 69
  deposit-taker, deduction of tax by..TA 1988 s 479(2)(4)
  determination of tax assessed..TMA 1970 s 88 88A 118(4)
  double..TMA 1970 s 32
  error or mistake..TMA 1970 s 33
  fraud..TMA 1970 s 36 37, FA 1988 Sch 3 para 29
  furnished holiday lettings..TA 1988 s 503
  further..TMA 1970 s 43A
  increase on appeal..TMA 1970 s 50(7)(8)
  inspector, by..TMA 1970 s 29(1)–(3)
  loss etc..TMA 1970 s 112
  neglect—
    capital gains tax..TMA 1970 s 36 37, FA 1988 Sch 3 para 29
    corporation tax..TMA 1970 s 39
    deceased persons..TMA 1970 s 40(2)
    income tax..TMA 1970 s 36 37, FA 1988, Sch 3 para 29
    leave..TMA 1970 s 41
    partnerships..TMA 1970 s 38
  notice of..TMA 1970 s 29(5)(6)
  partnership—
    method..TA 1988 s 111
    neglect..TMA 1970 s 38
    Scotland..TMA 1970 s 118(3)
  PAYE..TA 1988 s 203
  personal pension schemes..TA 1988 s 647(3)
  personal representatives..TMA 1970 s 40, FA 1989 s 151
  preceding year basis—
    Sch D Cases I and II..TA 1988 s 60
    Sch D Case III..TA 1988 s 64, 73
    Sch D Cases IV and V..TA 1988 s 65, 73
  procedure..TMA 1970 s 29
  profit-related pay..TA 1988 s 170
  profits prior to year of assessment..TA 1988 s 71
  recovery of overpayments..TMA 1970 s 30
  reduction on appeal..TMA 1970 s 50(6)(8)
  Sch A..TA 1988 s 22
  Sch E. *See under* SCHEDULE E
  separate. *See under* HUSBAND AND WIFE
  separate taxation of wife's earnings..TA 1988 s 287
  single assessment of Cases III, IV and V..TA 1988 s 73
  stock relief agreements..FA 1982 s 79
  subsequent income..TMA 1970 s 35
  time for—
    claim, following..TMA 1970 s 42(10)
    generally..TMA 1970 s 34(1)
    personal representatives..TMA 1970 s 40(1)(2)
  trustees, of..FA 1989 s 151
  validity..TMA 1970 s 114
  wilful default..TMA s 36 37, FA 1988 Sch 3 para 29
  year of. *See* YEAR OF ASSESSMENT

ASSET
  meaning (CGT)..CGTA 1979 s 19(1)
  anticipated normal working life..TA 1988 s 782(6)
  apportionment of gain or loss over period of ownership..CGTA 1979 Sch 5 para 11
  available for distribution, meaning..TA 1988 s 704(E)(3)
  business. *See under* CAPITAL GAINS TAX; RETIREMENT RELIEF; ROLLOVER RELIEF; TRANSFER OF ASSETS
  chargeable business asset, meaning..FA 1985 Sch 20 para 12(2)
  classes, CGT..CGTA 1979 s 118
  disposal, meaning..CGTA 1979 s 19(2)
  distribution—
    group relief..TA 1988 Sch 18
    mutual business..TA 1988 s 491
  gift. *See under* CAPITAL GAINS TAX
  held-over gain..CGTA 1979 Sch 4 para 5 6
  leasing. *See under* LEASING; MACHINERY AND PLANT
  location, CGT..CGTA 1979 s 18(4)
  replacement. *See* ROLLOVER RELIEF
  short-term leasing. *See under* MACHINERY AND PLANT
  traders etc, leased to..TA 1988 s 781

ASSET—continued
transfer abroad. *See under* TRANSFER OF ASSETS
transfer between resident companies..TA 1988 s 209(6)
valuation, inspection powers..TMA 1970 s 111
wasting asset—
  meaning..CGTA 1979 s 37(1)
  CGT. *See under* CAPITAL GAINS TAX
  lease..CGTA 1979 Sch 3 para 1

ASSOCIATED OPERATION
meaning..TA 1988 s 742(1)
transfer of assets abroad..TA 1988 s 739

ASSOCIATED PERSONS. *See* CLOSE COMPANY: CONNECTED COMPANIES: CONNECTED PERSONS

ASSURED TENANCY
application of CAA 1968..FA 1982 Sch 12 para 14
approved body, meaning..FA 1982 Sch 12 para 15(1)
balancing allowances and charges..FA 1982 Sch 12 para 4–6 9
buildings bought unused..FA 1982 Sch 12 para 8
common parts, meaning..FA 1982 Sch 12 para 1(5)
construction costs..FA 1982 Sch 12 para 8 15(2)(3)
date of expenditure..FA 1985 s 56
deemed sales..FA 1982 Sch 12 para 6(1)
double allowance exclusion..FA 1982 Sch 12 para 11
excluded houses..FA 1982 Sch 12 para 3(3)
expenditure limit..FA 1982 Sch 12 para 1(4)
expenditure on building..FA 1988 s 95
holding over..FA 1982 Sch 12 para 12
initial allowance..FA 1982 Sch 12 para 1 FA 1984 s 58(1)(c) Sch 12 para 3
  claim for, extension of time limit..F(No 2)A 1987 s 72(2)
manner of relief etc..FA 1982 Sch 12 para 9
purchase price of building bought unused..FA 1984 Sch 12 para 3(3)
qualifying houses..FA 1982 Sch 12 para 3
reduction of proceeds of sale etc..FA 1982 Sch 12 para 15(4)
relevant interest, meaning..FA 1982 Sch 12 para 13
repairs..FA 1982 Sch 12 para 10
residue of expenditure..FA 1982 Sch 12 para 7
spreading of expenditure under certain contracts..FA 1984 Sch 12 para 7–9
temporary disuse..FA 1982 Sch 12 para 6(2)
writing-down allowance..FA 1982 Sch 12 para 2
written off expenditure..FA 1982 Sch 12 para 7

ATOMIC ENERGY AUTHORITY
exemption..TA 1988 s 512

ATTORNEY GENERAL
recovery of penalties..TMA 1970 s 100(2)

AUCTIONEER
chargeable gains, information as to..TMA 1970 s 25(7)

AUTHOR
meaning..TA 1988 s 534(7) 535(11)
copyright payments. *See* COPYRIGHT

BALANCING ALLOWANCE
assets leased abroad..FA 1982 s 70(2)(4)
assured tenancies..FA 1982 Sch 12 para 4–6
car—
  part-time use..CAA 1968 Sch 2 para 5
  restriction..CAA 1968 Sch 2 para 4
enterprise zones..FA 1981 s 75(4)(5)
hotels..FA 1978 Sch 6 para 4 FA 1981 s 75(4)(5)
industrial buildings..CAA 1968 s 3 FA 1972 s 69
know-how..TA 1988 s 530(2)
machinery and plant—
  entitlement..CAA 1968 s 33
  notional sales—
    certain cases..CAA 1968 s 34
    effect on other party..CAA 1968 s 35
  previous user..CAA 1968 s 39

BALANCING ALLOWANCE—*continued*
mines, oil wells etc..CAA 1968 s 58
mining structures, carry back..CAA 1968 s 15
patent rights..TA 1988 s 520(4)–(6)
scientific research..CAA 1968 s 3(4)–(6)
short-term leasing..FA 1980 s 65
transfers under Oil and Gas (Enterprise) Act 1982..FA 1984 s 60

BALANCING CHARGE
assets leased abroad..FA 1982 s 70(2)
assured tenancy..FA 1982 Sch 12 para 4–6 9
enterprise zones..FA 1981 s 75(4)(5)
hotels..FA 1978 Sch 6 para 4 FA 1981 s 75(4)(5)
industrial building..CAA 1968 s 3
know-how..TA 1988 s 530(2)
loss relief..TA 1988 s 383(2)
machinery and plant—
  charge..CAA 1968 s 33
  notional sales—
    certain cases..CAA 1968 s 34
    effect on other party..CAA 1968 s 35
  previous user..CAA 1968 s 39
  replacement, option on..CAA 1968 s 40
mines, oil wells etc..CAA 1968 s 58
patent rights..TA 1988 s 520(4)–(6)
scientific research..CAA 1968 s 3(4)–(6)
short-term leasing..FA 1980 s 65
transfers under Oil and Gas (Enterprise) Act 1982..FA 1984 s 60

BANK. *See also* DEPOSIT-TAKER
composite rate, determination of..TA 1988 s 483
conversion of circulating capital..TA 1988 s 473
deduction of tax on interest. *See under* DEPOSIT-TAKER
double taxation relief..TA 1988 s 794, 808
foreign currency accounts..CGTA 1979 s 18(4)(*j*)
information from—
  deposits..TA 1988 s 483(5)
  transfer of assets abroad..TA 1988 s 765(4)
interest on borrowed money..TA 1988 s 475
non-resident central banks..TA 1988 s 516
non-resident, double taxation relief..TA 1988 s 794
overdraft..TA 1988 s 353(3)
personal pension scheme established by..TA 1988 s 632
Reserve Bank of India..TA 1988 s 517
State Bank of Pakistan..TA 1988 s 517
tax-free income..TA 1988 s 474
tax-free Treasury securities..TA 1988 s 475

BANK OF ENGLAND
public revenue dividends..TA 1988 s 17, Sch 13 Pt I

BANK OF IRELAND
public revenue dividends..TA 1988 s 17, Sch 13 Pt I

BARRISTER
appeal hearing..TMA 1970 s 50(5)

BASIS PERIOD
meaning (capital allowances)..CAA 1968 s 72

BASIS YEAR
meaning (scientific research)..CAA 1968 s 91(3)

BENEFICIAL LOAN
cash equivalent—
  meaning..TA 1988 Sch 7 para 3
  alternative calculation..TA 1988 Sch 7 para 5
  generally..TA 1988 Sch 7 para 3
  interest relief..TA 1988 Sch 7 Pt III
  normal calculation..TA 1988 Sch 7 para 4
charge to tax..TA 1988 s 160
death of employee..TA 1988 s 161(6)
determination of eligibility..TA 1988 Sch 7 Pt III
election as to calculation..TA 1988 Sch 7 para 5(3)

BENEFICIAL LOAN—*continued*
  exception from charge..TA 1988 s 161
  fixed term and interest..TA 1988 s 161
  husband and wife..TA 1988 Sch 7 para 10–12
  interest relief..TA 1988 Sch 7 Pt III
  loan, meaning..TA 1988 s 160(6)
  obtained by reason of employment, meaning..TA 1988 Sch 7 Pt I
  termination of employment..TA 1988 s 160(3)

BENEFICIARY
  becoming entitled against trustee..CGTA 1979 s 54
  capital payment, meaning..FA 1981 s 83(1)(2)
  chargeable gains attributed to..FA 1981 s 80–82
  controlled foreign company..TA 1988 s 752(7)
  foreign dividends..TA 1988 s 123(5)
  migrant settlements..FA 1981 s 81 82
  non-resident trust, postponement of tax. *See under* POSTPONEMENT OF TAX
  recovery of higher rate tax from..TA 1970 s 689
  retirement relief, qualifying. *See* RETIREMENT RELIEF

BENEFITS IN KIND
  accommodation. *See* ACCOMMODATION
  annual value of use of asset..TA 1988 s 156(6)
  asset used partly for security..FA 1989 s 51
  beneficial loan. *See* BENEFICIAL LOAN
  benefits chargeable as emoluments..TA 1988 s 154(2)
  calculation of emoluments..TA 1988 s 167(2)
  car. *See* CAR
  car fuel..TA 1988 s 158
  car parking space, provision of..TA 1988 s 155(1A)
  cash equivalents..TA 1988 s 156
  charge to tax..TA 1988 s 154
  cost of, meaning..TA 1988 s 156(2)
  credit-tokens..TA 1988 s 142
  director, meaning..TA 1988 s 168(8)
  director's or higher-paid employment, meaning..TA 1988 s 167(1)
  directorships excluded..TA 1988 s 167(5)
  employee shareholdings..TA 1988 s 162
  exceptions..TA 1988 s 155
  expenses, charge to tax..TA 1988 s 153
  market value of asset..TA 1988 s 168(7)
  non-cash vouchers..TA 1988 s 141
  notice of nil liability..TA 1988 s 166
  notional loan..TA 1988 s 162
  scholarships. *See* SCHOLARSHIP
  security asset or service..FA 1989 s 50–52
  tax paid by employer..TA 1988 s 164
  transfer of assets..TA 1988 s 156(3)(4)
  transport vouchers..TA 1988 s 141(6)
  two or more employments with same employer..TA 1988 s 167(3)
  vouchers. *See* VOUCHER

BEREAVEMENT ALLOWANCE
  entitlement..TA 1988 s 262

BETTERMENT LEVY
  CGT allowance..CGTA 1979 Sch 6 para 21

BETTING
  gains not chargeable..CGTA 1979 s 19(4)

BILL OF EXCHANGE
  discounted. *See* DISCOUNTED BILL

BLIND PERSON
  relief..TA 1988 s 265, FA 1988 Sch 3 para 8

BOARD OF INLAND REVENUE
  administration by..TMA 1970 s 1
  appeal from, jurisdiction..TMA 1970 Sch 2 para 3
  assessment by..TMA 1970 s 29(2)(3)(7)
  Commissioners' hearings..TMA 1970 s 50(3)
  declaration on taking office..TMA 1970 s 6(3)(5) Sch 1 Pt II
  entry powers..TMA 1970 s 20C

BOARD OF INLAND REVENUE—*continued*
  information. *See under* INFORMATION
  notice of appeal meeting..TMA 1970 s 50(2)
  officer attending appeal..TMA 1970 s 50(3)
  payroll deduction scheme. *See* CHARITY
  stock exchange, designation..TA 1988 s 841(2)

BOARD OF REFEREES
  dissolution..FA 1982 s 156

BODY OF PERSONS
  meaning..TMA 1970 s 118(1)
  chargeability—
    capital gains tax..TMA 1970 s 77
    income tax..TMA 1970 s 71

BOND WASHING
  anti-avoidance..TA 1988 s 729–737
  dealers in securities..TA 1988 s 732
  Eurobonds..TA 1988 s 732(5)
  manufactured dividends..TA 1988 s 737
  securities, transferred or accrued interest. *See* SECURITIES

BONUS ISSUE
  close company apportionment..TA 1988 Sch 19 para 3
  disallowance of reliefs..TA 1988 s 237
  repayment of share capital, with or after..TA 1988 s 210
  value..TA 1988 s 209(8)

BOUNTY
  armed forces..TA 1988 s 316

BRANCH
  meaning..TMA 1970 s 118(1) CGTA 1979 s 12(3) TA 1988 s 834(1)
  non-resident banks, double taxation relief..TA 1988 s 794(2)
  non-resident carrying on profession or vocation through..CGTA 1979 s 12(2A) FA 1989 s 126

BRANCH PROFITS
  branch, meaning..TMA 1970 s 118(1)
  non-resident—
    capital gains tax..TMA 1970 s 84
    corporation tax..TMA 1970 s 85
    income tax..TMA 1970 s 79

BRIDGE
  Sch D Case I..TA 1988 s 55

BRITISH AIRWAYS BOARD
  company reconstructions..TA 1988 s 513
  transfer of assets..TA 1988 s 513

BRITISH NATIONAL OIL CORPORATION
  transfer of assets..FA 1982 s 146

BRITISH STEEL
  successor company, corporation tax..BSA 1988, s 11

BROKER. *See also* STOCKBROKER
  meaning..TMA 1970 s 21(7) TA 1988 s 737(6)
  manufactured dividends..TA 1988 s 737
  money broker as deposit-taker..TA 1988 s 481(5)
  unauthorised..TMA 1970 s 82

BUDGET RESOLUTION
  income tax..PCTA 1968 s 1
  payments and deductions made on account..PCTA 1968 s 2
  provisional effect..PCTA 1968 s 5

BUILDER
  sub-contractor. *See* SUB-CONTRACTOR

BUILDING
  enterprise zone. *See* ENTERPRISE ZONE
  first letting or occupation. *See* FIRST LETTING CHARGE

BUI   *Index*   [12]

BUILDING—*continued*
    industrial. *See* INDUSTRIAL BUILDING
    lost or destroyed, CGT..CGTA 1979 s 22(3)

BUILDING ALTERATIONS
    machinery and plant, for..CAA 1968 s 45 FA 1971 Sch 8 para 15(2)

BUILDING SOCIETY
    meaning..TA 1988 s 832(1)
    amalgamation etc..TA 1988 Sch 29 para 29
    computation of profits..TA 1988 s 476(3)
    contractual savings schemes..TA 1988 s 326
    corporation tax—
        payment dates..TA 1988 Sch 30 para 1
        reduced rate, determination of..TA 1988 s 483
        time for payment..TA 1988 s 478
        treatment..TA 1988 s 476(3)
    dividend, meaning..TA 1988 s 476(11)
    income tax..TA 1988 s 476
    information, Board's power to require..TA 1988 s 483(5)
    investment..TA 1988 s 477
    mortgage interest. *See* MORTGAGE INTEREST RELIEF
    pension funds investing in..TA 1988 s 476(7)
    reduced rate, determination of..TA 1988 s 483
    shares, indexation allowance not applying to..FA 1988 s 113(1)
    transfer of business—
        capital allowances..FA 1988 Sch 12 para 3
        capital gains..FA 1988 Sch 12 para 4, 5
        contractual savings schemes..FA 1988 Sch 12 para 7
        distributions..FA 1988 Sch 12 para 6
        financial trading stock..FA 1988 Sch 12 para 2
        gilt-edged securities..FA 1988 Sch 12 para 2
        stamp duty..FA 1988 Sch 12 para 8

BUSINESS ASSETS
    gift. *See under* CAPITAL GAINS TAX
    replacement. *See* ROLLOVER RELIEF
    retirement relief. *See* RETIREMENT RELIEF
    transfer. *See* TRANSFER OF ASSETS

BUSINESS ENTERTAINMENT
    meaning..TA 1988 s 577(5)
    charge to tax..TA 1988 s 577(3)
    gifts..TA 1988 s 577(8)
    non-deductible..TA 1988 s 577(1), FA 1988 s 72

BUSINESS EXPANSION SCHEME
    anti-avoidance provisions..TA 1988 s 289(11)
    certificate..TA 1988 s 306
    CGT..TA 1988 Sch 29 para 29
    claim..TA 1988 s 289(8)–(10), 306
    companies qualifying..TA 1988 s 293
    disposals..TA 1988 s 299
    eligible shares..TA 1988 s 289(4)
    entitlement..TA 1988 s 289(1)
    false statements..TA 1988 s 306(6)
    husband and wife..TA 1988 s 304, FA 1988 Sch 3 para 12
    individuals qualifying..TA 1988 s 291
    information..TA 1988 s 310
    interest on overdue tax..TA 1988 s 306(9)
    investment funds..TA 1988 s 311
    land, interests in ..TA 1988 s 294–296
    limits..TA 1988 s 290
    method..TA 1988 s 289(5)
    nominees..TA 1988 s 311
    permitted maximum, amounts exceeding..TA 1988 s 290A
    private rented housing—
        already let, house being..FA 1988 Sch 4 para 15
        already qualifying for relief..FA 1988 Sch 4 para 16
        capital allowances, house qualifying for..FA 1988 Sch 4 para 17
        dwelling houses, for provision of..FA 1988 s 50(3)
        expensive dwelling houses..FA 1988 Sch 4 para 13
        modification of provisions..FA 1988 Sch 4 Pt I
        qualifying activities..FA 1988 s 50

BUSINESS EXPANSION SCHEME—*continued*
  private rented housing—*continued*
    sub-standard dwelling-houses..FA 1988 Sch 4 para 14
    unfit dwelling houses..FA 1988 Sch 4 para 14
  relevant period..TA 1988 s 289(12)
  replacement capital..TA 1988 s 302
  research and development companies..TA 1988 s 289(1)
  returns..TA 1988 s 310
  ships, letting..TA 1988 s 290A(7)
  statement..TA 1988 s 306(3)(5)(6)
  subsidiary—
    conditions..TA 1988 s 308(1)–(4)
    provisions as to..TA 1988 s 309
    qualifying, meaning..TA 1988 s 308(5)
  value received..TA 1988 s 300, 303
  winding-up etc..TA 1988 s 289(13), 293(5)
  withdrawal of relief..TA 1988 s 307

CANAL
  Sch D Case I..TA 1988 s 55

CAPITAL
  interest charged to..TA 1988 s 388

CAPITAL ALLOWANCE. *See also* BALANCING ALLOWANCE; BALANCING CHARGE; FIRST-YEAR ALLOWANCE; INITIAL ALLOWANCE; WRITING-DOWN ALLOWANCE
  meaning..TA 1988 s 832(1)
  agreement as to, assessment..FA 1982 s 79
  agricultural land and buildings..FA 1986 s 56
  apportionment procedure..CAA 1968 s 81
  assured tenancies. *See* ASSURED TENANCY
  basis period, meaning..CAA 1968 s 72
  building society, transfer of business by..FA 1988 Sch 12 para 3
  business entertainment..CAA 1968 s 82(2)
  car. *See* CAR
  carry forward..CAA 1968 s 70(4)–(5) 74
  cemeteries etc..TA 1988 s 91
  CGT, assets held 1965..CGTA 1979 Sch 5 para 15
  chargeable period—
    meaning..CAA 1968 s 87(1)
    scientific research..CAA 1968 s 91(2)(3)
  coal industry nationalisation..CAA 1968 Sch 8 Pt I
  commencement of legislation..CAA 1968 s 96(1)
  company reconstruction..TA 1988 s 343(2)
  connected persons—
    contributions by..CAA 1968 s 85(1A)
    long lease..FA 1978 s 37(6)
    machinery and plant..CAA 1968 s 78 Sch 7 para 3
    sales between..CAA 1968 s 78 Sch 7
    sales without change of control..CAA 1968 Sch 7 para 4
  contributions to expenditure..CAA 1968 s 85 Sch 9
  controlled foreign company, assumptions as to..TA 1988 Sch 24 para 10, 11
  corporation tax allowances etc—
    other than trade..CAA 1968 s 74
    trade..CAA 1968 s 73
  Crown, references to..CAA 1968 s 4(13)
  date of expenditure—
    post-December 1984..FA 1985 s 56(6)
    pre-December 1984..CAA 1968 s 82(3)
  development area, transitional relief..FA 1984 Sch 12 para 4
  double, exclusion of..FA 1989 Sch 13 para 28
  dredging..CAA 1968 s 67, 75 FA 1985 s 61
  exceptional depreciation allowance..CAA 1968 s 89
  excluded expenditure..CAA 1968 s 82(1)(2)
  fire safety expenditure..FA 1974 s 17 FA 1975 s 15
  first-year allowance. *See* FIRST-YEAR ALLOWANCE
  franked investment income surplus..TA 1988 s 242(2)
  group relief..TA 1988 s 407(2)
  hotels..FA 1978 s 38 FA 1985 s 66(2)
  income tax allowances etc—
    other than trade..CAA 1968 s 71 FA 1985 Sch 12 para 2
    trade..CAA 1968 s 70

CAPITAL ALLOWANCE—*continued*
industrial building or structure. *See* INDUSTRIAL BUILDING
initial allowance. *See* INITIAL ALLOWANCE
investment grants..CAA 1968 s 83 FA 1971 Sch 8 para 1
know-how..TA 1988 s 532(4), 533(7)
leasehold interest—
  meaning (Scotland)..CAA 1968 s 88
  apportionment..CAA 1968 s 77(3)
long lease—
  meaning..FA 1978 s 37(4)
  connected persons..FA 1978 s 37(6)
  election..FA 1978 s 37(1)–(3)
loss relief..TA 1988 s 383, 385
machinery and plant. *See* MACHINERY AND PLANT
manner of making—
  industrial buildings..CAA 1968 s 6
  machinery and plant..CAA 1968 s 46 FA 1971 s 48
  mines, oil wells etc..CAA 1968 s 66
mills, factories etc..CAA 1968 s 89
mines etc. *See* MINES, OIL WELLS ETC
motor vehicles—
  cars. *See* CAR
non-resident companies..CAA 1968 s 76
oil extraction activities..TA 1988 s 492(5)–(7)
oil wells. *See* MINES, OIL WELLS ETC
patent rights..TA 1988 s 520–523, 532(3), 533
postponement for double taxation relief..TA 1988 s 810
redundancy schemes..TA 1988 Sch 21 para 6
regional projects, transitional relief..FA 1984 Sch 12 para 4
sale, insurance, salvage or compensation moneys, meaning..CAA 1968 s 86
sale of property—
  apportionment..CAA 1968 s 77
  connected persons..CAA 1968 s 78
sales for obtaining..CAA 1968 s 78 Sch 7
scientific research. *See* SCIENTIFIC RESEARCH
Scotland, application to..CAA 1968 s 88
security asset, for..FA 1989 s 117 118
set-off..CAA 1968 s 71
sports grounds..F(No 2)A 1975 s 49 FA 1978 s 40 FA 1989 s 119
sports pavilions..CAA 1968 s 10
subsidies etc..CAA 1968 s 84
succession to trades etc..CAA 1968 s 79
terminal losses..TA 1988 s 389(6)(7)
thermal insulation..FA 1975 s 14
transport industry nationalisation..CAA 1968 Sch 8 Pt II
Trustee Savings Bank..TSBA 1985 Sch 2 para 1
wasting assets, CGT..CGTA 1979 s 39
withdrawal of..FA 1984 s 58 Sch 12
woman, made to..FA 1988 Sch 3 para 23, 24

CAPITAL GAINS TAX. *See also* CHARGEABLE GAINS
accumulation settlement, gains accruing to..FA 1988 s 100
administration by Board..TMA 1970 s 1(1)
administration expenses..CGTA 1979 s 47
agricultural land..CGTA 1979 s 112
agricultural property..CGTA 1979 Sch 4 para 1
aircraft shares, compulsory acquisition..FA 1976 s 54
annual payments..CGTA 1979 s 144
annuities—
  deferred..CGTA 1979 s 143
  generally..CGTA 1979 s 144
April 1965—
  capital allowances..CGTA 1979 Sch 5 para 15
  close companies, transfers to..CGTA 1979 Sch 5 para 16
  compensation and insurance money..CGTA 1979 Sch 5 para 18
  husband and wife..CGTA 1979 Sch 5 para 17
  land..CGTA 1979 Sch 5 Pt II
  other assets..CGTA 1979 Sch 5 Pt III
  quoted securities..CGTA 1979 Sch 5 Pt I
appeal—
  jurisdiction..TMA 1970 s 47
  regulations..TMA 1970 s 57

CAPITAL GAINS TAX—*continued*
  apportionment over period of ownership..CGTA 1979 Sch 5 para 11
  asset—
    meaning..CGTA 1979 s 19(1)
    acquired before April 1979..CGTA 1979 Sch 6 para 10
    capital sum from..CGTA 1979 s 20
    disposal..CGTA 1979 s 19(2)
    held April 1965. *See* April 1965 *supra*
    insolvent's..CGTA 1979 s 61
    lost or destroyed etc..CGTA 1979 s 22
    other assets, derived from..CGTA 1979 s 36
  authorised unit trust..FA 1980 s 81
  bare trustees..CGTA 1979 s 46
  beneficiary under non-resident trust..FA 1984 Sch 14 para 6(5)
  BNOC..FA 1982 s 146
  building society, transfer of business by..FA 1988 Sch 12 para 4, 5
  buildings..CGTA 1979 s 22(3)
  capital allowances, assets held since 1965..CGTA 1979 Sch 5 para 15
  capital distribution—
    meaning..CGTA 1979 s 72(5)(*b*)
    disposal of right to acquire shares..CGTA 1979 s 73
    distribution not new holding..CGTA 1979 s 72
  capital sum—
    meaning..CGTA 1979 s 20(3)
    assets, from..CGTA 1979 s 20
    compensation..CGTA 1979 s 21
    insurance money..CGTA 1979 s 21
  charge to—
    Continental Shelf..FA 1973 s 38
    exploration etc, disposals by non-residents..FA 1973 s 38(3A)–(3C)
    generally..CGTA 1979 s 1
  chargeable persons..TMA 1970 s 77
  charges..CGTA s 23
  charities—
    chargeable gains..CGTA 1979 s 145
    gifts to..CGTA 1979 s 146
  chattels..CGTA 1979 s 128
  Chevening Estate..TA 1988 s 147
  close company. *See under* CLOSE COMPANY
  collective investment schemes..FA 1989 s 140
  commencement..CGTA 1979 s 156
  commodities—
    held April 1965..CGTA 1979 Sch 5 para 13
    identification..CGTA 1979 s 132
  commodity futures..FA 1985 s 72 Sch 21
  company migration, on—
    branch or agency, trade carried on through..FA 1988 s 105(4)
    deemed disposal of assets on..FA 1988 s 105
    postponement of charge..FA 1988 s 107
    roll-over relief..FA 1988 s 105(3) 106(3)
    75 per cent subsidiary of resident company, by..FA 1988 s 107
  company reconstruction etc. *See* COMPANY RECONSTRUCTION
  company's chargeable gains..TA 1988 s 345
  compensation—
    chargeable..CGTA 1979 s 21
    compulsory acquisition..CGTA 1979 s 110
    not chargeable..CGTA 1979 s 19(5)
    pre-April 1965..CGTA 1979 Sch 5 para 18
  computation—
    apportionment..CGTA 1979 s 43(4)
    assets derived from other assets..CGTA 1979 s 36
    consideration—
      chargeable to income tax..CGTA 1979 s 31 TA 1988 Sch 29 para 20
      due after disposal..CGTA 1979 s 40
    contingent liabilities..CGTA 1979 s 41
    double deduction restriction..CGTA 1979 s 43(1)
    expenditure—
      deductible..CGTA 1979 s 32
      excluded..CGTA 1979 s 33 TA 1988 Sch 29 para 21
    income or profits, meaning..CGTA 1979 s 43(2)(3)
    losses...*See* losses *infra*
    market value..CGTA 1979 s 29A
    part disposals..CGTA 1979 s 35

CAPITAL GAINS TAX—continued
computation—continued
- public money..CGTA 1979 s 42
- wasting assets. See wasting assets infra

connected persons—
- meaning..CGTA 1979 s 63
- series of transactions between..FA 1985 s 71
- transactions between..CGTA 1979 s 62

construction..CGTA 1979 s 159
contract, disposal under..CGTA 1979 s 27
conversion of securities—
- meaning..CGTA 1979 s 82(3)(a)
- accrued interest, transfer with..TA 1988 s 711
- assets held April 1965..CGTA 1979 Sch 5 para 14
- circulating capital..TA 1988 s 473
- compensation stock..CGTA 1979 s 84
- converted securities and new holding..CGTA 1979 s 82
- pre-April 1979..CGTA 1979 Sch 6 para 20
- premiums..CGTA 1979 s 83
- securities, meaning..CGTA 1979 s 82(3)(b)

corporate bond. See CORPORATE BOND
death—
- annuitant..CGTA 1979 s 57
- general provisions..CGTA 1979 s 49
- life tenant's..CGTA 1979 s 56
- Scotland..CGTA 1979 s 50

debts..CGTA 1979 s 134
deep discount securities. See DEEP DISCOUNT SECURITIES
deferred annuity..CGTA 1979 s 143
demergers..FA 1980 Sch 18 para 9 10 15
discretionary settlement, gains accruing to..FA 1988 s 100
disposal—
- meaning—
  - assets..CGTA 1979 s 19(2)
  - offshore fund..TA 1988 s 757(2)
- acquisition, before..CGTA 1979 Sch 6 para 25
- asset derived from other assets..FA 1988 Sch 8 para 5
- assets..CGTA 1979 s 19
- capital allowance on re-acquisition..FA 1988 Sch 8 para 3
- chargeable under Sch D Case VII..CGTA 1979 Sch 6 para 12
- excluded persons..CGTA 1979 s 29A(3)–(5)
- market value..CGTA 1979 s 29A
- no gain/no loss..FA 1988 Sch 8 para 1, 2
- non-resident, by..CGTA 1979 s 32(5) (6)
- part..CGTA 1979 s 35, FA 1988 Sch 8 para 4
- right to acquire shares..CGTA 1979 s 73
- time of, under contract..CGTA 1979 s 27
- 31st March 1982, deemed to be on..FA 1988 s 96 Sch 8

dispositions pre-1974..CGTA 1979 Sch 6 para 14
double taxation relief..CGTA 1979 s 10
dual resident company, deemed disposal by..FA 1989 s 132(2)–(4)
emigration of donee..FA 1981 s 79
employee trusts..CGTA 1979 s 149
excess liability, charge in respect of..FA 1988 s 102(1)(2)
excluded gains..CGTA 1979 s 19(4)(5)
excluded persons..CGTA 1979 s 29A(3)–(5)
exemption—
- annual, individuals..CGTA 1979 s 5
- corporate bonds..FA 1984 s 64(1)
- indexation..CGTA 1979 s 5(1B)(1C)

exploration and exploitation assets..FA 1973 s 38(3A)–(3C) FA 1989 s 131
financial futures..FA 1985 s 72 Sch 21
financial option..CGTA 1979 s 137(4)(aa)(9)(c) 138(1)(aa)
foreign assets—
- delayed remittance..CGTA 1979 s 13, FA 1988 s 104(3)
- domicile abroad..CGTA 1979 s 14 TA 1988 s 761(5)

foreign currency accounts..CGTA 1979 s 18(4)(j)
foreign currency for personal use..CGTA 1979 s 133
foreign currency loan..CGTA 1979 Sch 6 para 17
foreign securities..CGTA 1979 Sch 6 para 17 18
foreign tax, allowance..CGTA 1979 s 11
fund in court..CGTA 1979 s 99 FA 1980 s 81
furnished holiday lettings..FA 1984 Sch 11 para 4 5

CAPITAL GAINS TAX—*continued*
gains—
  meaning..CGTA 1979 s 1(1)
  chargeable..CGTA 1979 s 4
  excluded..CGTA 1979 s 19(4)(5)
  pre-31st March 1982, deferred charge on..FA 1988 Sch 9
gift—
  business assets. *See* gift of business assets *infra*
  CTT on death, pre-1974 disposition..CGTA 1979 Sch 6 para 15
  housing association, to..CGTA 1979 s 146A
  inheritance tax chargeable on..CGTA 1979 s 147A
  non-resident, to..CGTA 1979 s 147B
  payment of tax by instalments..CGTA 1979 s 7A
  recovery from donee..CGTA 1979 s 59
  settlement, into..CGTA 1979 s 53
  small..CGTA 1979 s 6
gift of business assets—
  agricultural property..CGTA 1979 Sch 4 para 1
  controlling trustees, emigration of..CGTA 1979 s 126C
  foreign-controlled company, to..CGTA 1979 s 126B
  held-over gain. *See* held-over gain *infra*
  non-resident, to..CGTA 1979 s 126A
  relief..CGTA 1979 s 126
  settled property..CGTA 1979 Sch 4 para 2 3
gilt-edged securities. *See* GILT-EDGED SECURITIES
held-over gain—
  assets..CGTA 1979 Sch 4 para 5 6
  disposal, meaning..CGTA 1979 Sch 4 para 4(3)
  retirement relief..CGTA 1979 Sch 4 para 8
  shares..CGTA 1979 Sch 4 para 7
hire-purchase..CGTA 1979 s 24
Historic Buildings and Monuments Commission..TA 1988 Sch 29 para 29
Hops Marketing Board..FA 1982 s 148
husband and wife—
  assets held 1965..CGTA 1979 Sch 5 para 17
  capital gains and losses..CGTA 1979 s 4(2), FA 1988 s 104(1)(*a*)
  disposals between..CGTA 1979 s 44 FA 1985 s 71(2)
  exempt amount..CGTA 1979 Sch 1 para 2 3, FA 1988 s 104(1)(*c*)
  gilt-edged securities..CGTA 1979 s 69
  losses, deduction of..CGTA 1979 s 4(2), FA 1988 s 104(1)(*a*)
  married woman's gains..CGTA 1979 s 45 FA 1988 s 104(1)(*b*)
  rate for..FA 1988 s 99
identification rules—
  acquisition post-April 1985..FA 1985 Sch 19 para 17(2)
  disposal before acquisition..CGTA 1979 s 66 FA 1985 Sch 19 para 16–19
  general provisions..CGTA 1979 s 65
  indexation allowance. *See under* INDEXATION ALLOWANCE
  post-April 1985 disposals..FA 1985 Sch 19 para 16–19
  priority..FA 1985 Sch 19 para 19
indexation allowance. *See* INDEXATION ALLOWANCE
insolvents' assets..CGTA 1979 s 61
insurance money..CGTA 1979 s 21 Sch 5 para 18
insurance policies..CGTA 1979 s 140, TA 1988 s 547(1)(*a*), FA 1988 s 102(3)
insurance premiums..CGTA 1979 s 141
International Maritime Satellite Organisation..TA 1988 Sch 29 para 29
investment trusts..FA 1980 s 81
land—
  agricultural..CGTA 1979 s 112
  betterment levy..CGTA 1979 Sch 5 para 10
  betterment levy allowance..CGTA 1979 Sch 6 para 21
  compulsory acquisition..CGTA 1979 s 110 111
  part disposal—
    allowable expenditure..CGTA 1979 s 109
    compulsory acquisition..CGTA 1979 s 108
    small..CGTA 1979 s 107
  rollover relief..CGTA 1979 s 111A 111B
  valuation at April 1965..CGTA 1979 Sch 5 para 9
lease—
  meaning..CGTA 1979 Sch 3 para 10(1)
  allowable expenditure restriction..CGTA 1979 Sch 3 para 1
  duration..CGTA 1979 Sch 3 para 8
  other than land..CGTA 1979 Sch 3 para 9
  premiums..CGTA 1979 Sch 3 para 2 3 5

CAPITAL GAINS TAX—*continued*
lease—*continued*
   Sch A, premiums taxed under..CGTA 1979 Sch 3 para 5
   sub-lease out of short lease..CGTA 1979 Sch 3 para 4
   wasting asset..CGTA 1979 Sch 3 para 1
letters patent..TA 1988 Sch 29 para 31
life assurance..CGTA 1979 s 143
life interest terminated where CTT chargeable..CGTA 1979 Sch 6 para 16
loans to traders..CGTA 1979 s 136
location of assets..CGTA 1979 s 18(4)
losses—
   basis of computation..CGTA 1979 s 29
   capital allowances etc..CGTA 1979 s 34
   renewals allowances..CGTA 1979 s 34
market value—
   meaning—
      assets generally..CGTA 1979 s 150(1) Sch 6 para 2(1)
      unit holders' rights..CGTA 1979 Sch 6 para 2(4)
   determination..CGTA 1979 s 150
   linked transactions, disposals under..FA 1985 Sch 21
   offshore fund..TA 1988 s 759(9)
married woman's gains..CGTA 1979 s 45
migrant settlement—
   disregard of capital payments..FA 1981 s 81(1)
   information..FA 1981 s 84
   resident period..FA 1981 s 81
   transfers between..FA 1981 s 82
mineral royalties..TA 1988 s 122(1)(*b*)
mortgages..CGTA 1979 s 23
movable property—
   chattel exemption..CGTA 1979 s 128
   lease..CGTA 1979 Sch 3 para 9
   passenger vehicles..CGTA 1979 s 130
   valour award..CGTA 1979 s 131
   wasting assets..CGTA 1979 s 127
National Heritage Memorial Fund..TA 1988 Sch 29 para 29
nominees..CGTA 1979 s 46
non-marketable securities..CGTA 1979 s 71
non-resident—
   chargeability..TMA 1970 s 84
   company..CGTA 1979 s 15
   deemed disposals..FA 1989 s 127
   disposals by, special rules..CGTA 1979 s 32(5) (6)
   group of companies..CGTA 1979 s 16
   post-cessation disposals..CGTA 1979 s 12(1A)
   profession or vocation, carrying on..CGTA 1979 s 12(2A) FA 1989 s 126
   roll-over relief..FA 1989 s 129
   UK branch or agency..CGTA 1979 s 12
non-resident trust—
   gains post-April 1981..FA 1981 s 80
   information..FA 1981 s 84
   postponement of tax due from beneficiary. *See under* POSTPONEMENT OF TAX
   pre-April 1981..CGTA 1979 s 17
   transfers between..FA 1981 s 82
notice of liability..TMA 1970 s 11A 12
offshore fund. *See* OFFSHORE FUND
option—
   disposal, as..CGTA 1979 s 137
   wasting assets..CGTA 1979 s 138
partner, charge to tax..CGTA 1979 s 60
partnerships, residence..CGTA 1979 s 60
passenger vehicles..CGTA 1979 s 130
personal equity plans..TA 1988 Sch 29 para 29
personal representatives..CGTA 1979 s 48 Sch 1 para 4
persons chargeable..CGTA 1979 s 2
pooling. *See* POOLING
private residence—
   absence from..CGTA 1979 s 102
   dependent relative..CGTA 1979 s 105
   let as accommodation..FA 1980 s 80
   main residence, determination..CGTA 1979 s 101
   relief..CGTA 1979 s 102
   restrictions..CGTA 1979 s 103
   settled property..CGTA 1979 s 104

CAPITAL GAINS TAX—*continued*
  quoted options..CGTA 1979 s 91 137(9)(*a*) 139
  quoted securities held April 1965. *See under* QUOTED SECURITIES
  rates..FA 1988 s 98 102
  re-basing—
    assets derived from other assets..FA 1988 Sch 8 para 5
    assets held on 31st March 1982..FA 1988 s 96
    business assets, replacement of..FA 1988 Sch 8 para 9
    capital allowances..FA 1988 Sch 8 para 3
    close companies..FA 1988 Sch 8 para 7
    election—
      excluded disposals..FA 1988 Sch 8 para 12
      group of companies..FA 1988 Sch 8 para 13 14
    group transactions..FA 1988 Sch 8 para 6
    indexation allowance..FA 1988 Sch 8 para 11
    part disposal..FA 1988 Sch 8 para 4
    postponed charges..FA 1989 Sch 15 para 1
    pre-1965 gains and losses, apportionment of..FA 1988 Sch 8 para 10
    previous no gain/no loss disposals..FA 1988 Sch 8 para 1 2
    private residence relief..FA 1988 Sch 8 para 8
    reduction of 1982 value..FA 1989 Sch 15 para 3
  recovery of tax not postponed..TMA 1970 s 55
  remittance basis, resident with foreign domicile..CGTA 1979 s 14
  repayment supplement..F(No 2)A 1987 s 47
  replacement of business assets. *See* ROLLOVER RELIEF
  residence..CGTA 1979 s 18
  retirement relief. *See* RETIREMENT RELIEF
  rollover relief. *See* ROLLOVER RELIEF
  savings certificates etc..CGTA 1979 s 71
  securities—
    meaning..CGTA 1979 s 65(7)
    conversion. *See* conversion of securities *supra*
    gilt-edged. *See* GILT-EDGED SECURITIES
    identification. *See* identification rules *supra*
  settled property—
    meaning..CGTA 1979 s 51
    death of annuitant..CGTA 1979 s 57
    death of life tenant..CGTA 1979 s 56
    disposals..CGTA 1979 s 58
    gains arising from..FA 1988 Sch 10
    gifts..CGTA 1979 s 53
    gifts of business assets..CGTA 1979 Sch 4 para 2 3
    held-over gain..CGTA 1979 s 56A
    persons becoming absolutely entitled..CGTA 1979 s 54
    private residence..CGTA 1979 s 104
    termination of life interest..CGTA 1979 s 55
    trustees..CGTA 1979 s 52
    works of art..CGTA 1979 s 147(3)(4)
  share capital, reorganisation or reduction. *See under* SHARE CAPITAL
  share option schemes..CGTA 1979 s 76
  shipbuilding shares, compulsory acquisition..FA 1976 s 54
  sterling devaluation..CGTA 1979 Sch 6 para 17 18
  stock dividends..CGTA 1979 s 89 90
  stock in trade..CGTA 1979 s 122
  subordinate legislation, validity..CGTA 1979 Sch 6 para 28
  superannuation funds..CGTA 1979 s 144
  termination of life interest..CGTA 1979 s 55
  time for payment..CGTA 1979 s 7
  traded option..CGTA 1979 s 137(4)(*aa*)(9)(*b*) 138(1)(*aa*) FA 1985 s 72 Sch 21
  trust expenses..CGTA 1979 s 47
  trustee—
    charge to tax..CGTA 1979 s 48
    exempt amount..CGTA 1979 Sch 1 para 6
    liability..CGTA 1979 Sch 1 para 5
  underwriters..CGTA 1979 s 142
  unit trust—
    exempt unit holders..CGTA 1979 s 96 98
    treatment..CGTA 1979 s 93
  unquoted shares held at April 1965..CGTA 1979 Sch 5 para 13
  unrelieved Case VII losses..CGTA 1979 Sch 6 para 13
  valour awards..CGTA 1979 s 131
  valuation—
    April 1965, election for..CGTA 1979 Sch 5 para 12
    CTT/inheritance tax..CGTA 1979 s 153

CAPITAL GAINS TAX—continued
valuation—continued
  estate duty valuation..CGTA 1979 Sch 6 para 9
  inheritance tax..CGTA 1979 s 153
  market value. *See* market value *supra*
  original rules..CGTA 1979 Sch 6 para 2
  quoted securities at April 1965..CGTA 1979 Sch 6 para 3
  series of transactions..CGTA 1979 s 151 FA 1985 s 71 Sch 21
  Stock Exchange, meaning..CGTA 1979 Sch 6 para 4
  unquoted shares—
    acquisition on death..CGTA 1979 Sch 6 para 7
    determination..CGTA 1979 s 152
    prior part disposal..CGTA 1979 Sch 6 para 7
value-shifting—
  acquisition after disposal..CGTA 1979 s 26(8)
  charge to tax..CGTA 1979 s 25 26
  disposal of another company's assets..CGTA 1979 s 26(7)
  disposal within group followed by disposal of shares..CGTA 1979 s 26B
  distributions followed by disposal of shares..CGTA 1979 s 26A
  excluded disposals..CGTA 1979 s 26(3)(6)
  pre-March 1977..CGTA 1979 Sch 6 para 11
  reorganisation of share capital, transactions treated as..CGTA 1979 526D
  schemes for..CGTA 1979 s 26
  subsequent disposal of asset..CGTA 1979 s 26C
wasting assets—
  meaning..CGTA 1979 s 37(1)
  capital allowances..CGTA 1979 s 39
  leases..CGTA 1979 Sch 3 para 1
  movable property..CGTA 1979 s 127
  options..CGTA 1979 s 138
  residual or scrap value..CGTA 1979 s 37(2)
  restriction of allowable expenditure..CGTA 1979 s 38
woodlands..CGTA 1979 s 113
works of art etc..CGTA 1979 s 147

CAPITAL REDEMPTION BUSINESS. *See also under* INSURANCE COMPANY
meaning..TA 1988 s 458(3)

CAPITAL REDEMPTION POLICY
meaning..TA 1988 s 539(3)
allowable aggregate amount..TA 1988 s 546(3)
bonus, treatment..TA 1988 s 539(4)
certificate by insurers..TA 1988 s 552
charge to tax..TA 1988 s 539(1)
chargeable event..TA 1988 s 545(1), 553
computation of gains..TA 1988 s 547
loans..TA 1988 s 548
method of charge..TA 1988 s 547
new offshore—
  chargeable events..TA 1988 s 553
  notification to inspector..TA 1988 s 552
post-March 1968..TA 1988 s 539(5)
reckonable aggregate value..TA 1988 s 546(2)
recovery of tax from trustees..TA 1988 s 551(1)
relief where gain charged directly..TA 1988 s 550
top-slicing relief..TA 1988 s 550

CAPITAL TRANSFER TAX. *See* INHERITANCE TAX
accrued income, relief..TA 1988 s 699
loan for payment of..TA 1988 s 364
market value, CGT..CGTA 1979 s 153

CAR
meaning..TA 1988 s 168(5)(*a*)
age..TA 1988 s 168(5)(*b*)
balancing allowances restriction..CAA 1968 Sch 2 para 4
business travel, meaning..TA 1988 s 168(5)(*c*)
capital allowances..FA 1971 Sch 8 para 10–12A
cash equivalent—
  additional cars..TA 1988 Sch 6 para 5(3)
  application of Tables..TA 1988 Sch 6 para 1(1)
  car unavailable for use..TA 1988 Sch 6 para 2

CAR—*continued*
  cash equivalent—*continued*
    employee paying for use..TA 1988 Sch 6 para 4
    insubstantial business use..TA 1988 Sch 6 para 5
    mainly business use..TA 1988 Sch 6 para 3
    Tables..TA 1988 s 158(2) Sch 6 Pt I
  charge to tax..TA 1988 s 158(1)
  connected persons..FA 1971 Sch 8 para 10(4)
  contributions towards..CAA 1968 Sch 2 para 6
  date of first registration..TA 1988 s 168(5)(*d*)
  disabled person's grant..TA 1988 s 327
  excluded expenditure..TA 1988 s 157(3)
  first-year allowance..FA 1971 s 43
  fuel..TA 1988 s 158
  hire—
    capital allowance..FA 1971 Sch 8 para 12
    deductions limit..CAA 1968 Sch 2 para 9
  hire-purchase, apportionment..CAA 1968 Sch 2 para 10
  inclusive price, meaning..TA 1988 s 168(5)(*f*)
  initial allowance..CAA 1968 Sch 2 para 2
  lease-back..FA 1971 Sch 8 para 10(4)
  motor car, meaning..FA 1971 Sch 8 para 9
  original market value..TA 1988 s 168(5)(*e*)
  part-time use..CAA 1968 Sch 2 para 5
  part trade use..FA 1971 Sch 8 para 10(5)
  pooled..TA 1988 s 159
  previous user..CAA 1968 Sch 2 para 3
  private use, meaning..TA 1988 s 168(5)(*f*)
  removal of double charge..TA 1988 s 157(5)
  renewals allowances limit..CAA 1968 Sch 2 para 8
  replacement of machinery or plant..CAA 1968 Sch 2 para 7
  short-life asset, whether..FA 1985 Sch 15 para 7
  short-term leasing..FA 1980 s 69
  subsidies..CAA 1968 Sch 2 para 6
  time for claims..CAA 1968 Sch 2 para 11(3)
  wear and tear subsidy..FA 1971 Sch 8 para 10(5)
  writing-down allowance—
    amount..CAA 1968 s 32(1)(2)
    previous user..CAA 1968 Sch 2 para 3
    qualifying cars..CAA 1968 s 32(4)–(7)
    special rules..FA 1971 Sch 8 para 10(3) 11

CAR PARKING
  benefit in kind, as..TA 1988 s 155(1A)
  credit-token for..TA 1988 s 142(3A)
  expenses of..TA 1988 s 197A
  voucher for..TA 1988 s 141(6A)

CARAVAN
  meaning..TA 1988 s 367(1)
  large, meaning..TA 1988 s 367(1)
  loan interest..TA 1988 s 354(1)(3)
  restriction on interest relief..TA 1988 s 355, 357, FA 1988 s 44

CARRY-BACK
  interest..TA 1988 s 390
  surplus ACT..TA 1988 s 239(3)
  terminal losses..TA 1988 s 380, 381

CARRY FORWARD
  capital allowances..CAA 1968 s 70(4)–(5) 74
  interest..TA 1988 s 390
  loss relief. *See under* LOSS RELIEF
  retirement annuity relief..TA 1988 s 625
  stock relief—
    corporation tax..TA 1988 Sch 30 para 19
    income tax..TA 1988 Sch 30 para 19
  surplus ACT..TA 1988 s 239(4)(5)

CASE STATED
  Court of Appeal..TMA 1970 s 56A
  High Court..TMA 1970 s 56
  Northern Ireland..TMA 1970 s 59(4)(5)
  notice requiring..TMA 1970 s 56(2)(3)

CEMETERY
capital expenditure, meaning..TA 1988 s 91(2)(8)
change in trader..TA 1988 s 91(5)
deductible expenditure..TA 1988 s 91(1)
residue of expenditure..TA 1988 s 91(4)

CENTRAL BANK
non-resident, government securities..TA 1988 s 516

CERTIFICATE
deduction of tax at source..TA 1988 s 352
unpaid tax..TMA 1970 s 70

CERTIFICATE OF DEPOSIT. *See also* DEPOSIT-TAKER
meaning..TA 1988 s 56(5)
qualifying, meaning..TA 1988 s 482(6)
transactions in..TA 1988 s 56, 398

CERTIFICATE OF TAX DEPOSIT
interest period..FA 1982 s 145

CHANNEL ISLANDS
Trustee Savings Bank..TSBA 1985 Sch 2 para 3

CHARGE ON INCOME
corporation tax. *See under* CORPORATION TAX
general annuity business..TA 1988 s 437(1)
general rule..TA 1988 s 347A
income tax relief, effect..TA 1988 s 276
interest charged to capital..TA 1988 s 388
oil extraction activities..TA 1988 s 494

CHARGEABLE GAINS. *See also* CAPITAL GAINS TAX
meaning..TA 1988 s 832(1)
appeal—
　regulations..TMA 1970 s 57
artificial transactions in land..TA 1988 s 776 777
capital gains tax, relationship..TA 1988 s 345(2)–(4)
charities..TA 1988 s 505(5)
company reconstruction etc..TA 1970 s 267
computation..TA 1988 s 345
controlled foreign company..TA 1988 Sch 26
co-operative housing associations..TA 1988 s 488(5)
corporate bond. *See* CORPORATE BOND
double taxation relief..TA 1988 s 797
foreign life assurance fund..TA 1988 s 441(7)
gilt-edged securities..TA 1970 s 270
groups of companies. *See* GROUP (COMPANIES)
harbour reorganisation schemes..TA 1988 Sch 29 para 25
interest charged to capital..TA 1970 s 269
life policies etc. *See* CAPITAL REDEMPTION POLICY; LIFE ANNUITY CONTRACT; LIFE POLICY
liquidator, assets vested in..TA 1988 s 345(5)
local constituency associations, relief..F(No 2)A 1983 s 7(4)–(7)
nominees..TMA 1970 s 26
non-resident company—
　charge..TA 1988 s 11
　information..TMA 1970 s 28
non-resident trust, information..TMA 1970 s 28
notice requiring information..TMA 1970 s 25
postponement of charge..TA 1970 s 268A
recovery of tax from shareholder..TA 1988 s 346
regulations, power to make..TMA 1970 s 57
returns..TMA 1970 s 12
Sch C exempt stock and dividends..TA 1988 Sch 29 para 29
self-build societies..TA 1988 s 489(3)
settled property, information as to..TMA 1970 s 27
share incentive scheme..TA 1988 s 138, Sch 29 para 29
shares disposed of within prescribed period of acquisition..F(No 2)A 1975 s 58
transfer of assets—
　company reconstruction etc..TA 1970 s 267
　non-resident company, to..TA 1970 s 268A
underwriters, premiums trust fund..TA 1988 s 450

CHARGEABLE PERIOD
meaning..TMA 1970 s 118(1) 526(5) TA 1988 s 832(1)

CHARGEABLE PERSON
bodies of persons..TMA 1970 s 71
capital gains tax..TMA 1970 s 77
coupons..TA 1988 Sch 3 para 6
foreign dividends..TA 1988 Sch 3 para 6
guardian..TMA 1970 s 72 73
incapacited person..TMA 1970 s 72
infants..TMA 1970 s 73
non-residents..TMA 1970 s 78 83
personal representative..TMA 1970 s 74
public revenue dividends..TA 1988 Sch 3 para 6
receiver appointed by court..TMA 1970 s 75
Schedule A..TA 1988 s 21
trustee—
    incapacited persons..TMA 1970 s 72
    protection in certain cases..TMA 1970 s 76
tutor..TMA 1970 s 72 73

CHARITABLE TRUST
disposals, CGT..CGTA 1979 s 145

CHARITY
meaning..TA 1988 s 506(1)
avoidance of tax by..TA 1988 s 505(7)
chargeable gains..CGTA 1979 s 145
covenant. *See* COVENANTED PAYMENT TO CHARITY
deep discount securities, exemption..TA 1988 Sch 4 para 14
deep gain security, holding..FA 1989 Sch 11 para 15
donations to—
    companies, by..TA 1988 s 339
    traders, by..TA 1988 s 715(1)
employee seconded to..TA 1988 s 86
exemption..TA 1988 s 505, 761(6)
gifts to..CGTA 1979 s 146
ministers' houses..TA 1988 s 332
non-qualifying expenditure..TA 1988 s 506, Sch 20 Pt III
offshore income gain, exemption..TA 1988 s 761(6)
payments charged as annual payments..TA 1988 s 505(2)
payroll deduction scheme—
    approval by Board..TA 1988 s 202(3)(8)
    maximum sum..TA 1988 s 202(7)
    participating employer or agent..TA1988 s 202(9)(10)
    prescribed information..TA 1988 s 202(9)
    relief for donations under..TA 1988 s 202
public revenue dividends..TA 1988 Sch 3 para 4
qualifying expenditure..TA 1988 s 506
qualifying investments..TA 1988 Sch 20 Pt I
qualifying loans..TA 1988 Sch 20 Pt II
restriction of tax exemptions..TA 1988 s 505
transfer of securities: accrued interest..TA 1988 s 715(1)(3)

CHATTEL
chargeable gains..CGTA 1979 s 128

CHEVENING ESTATE
exemption..TA 1988 s 147

CHILD
meaning (settlement)..TA 1988 s 670
additional relief for widows etc—
    apportionment..TA 1988 s 260
    entitlement..TA 1988 s 259, FA 1988 Sch 3 para 5
double claim..TA 1988 s 259(4A)
employee not domiciled in UK, of..TA 1988 s 195(6)
settlement. *See* CHILDREN'S SETTLEMENTS

CHILDREN'S SETTLEMENTS
accumulation settlements..TA 1988 s 664
adjustments between disponor and trustees..TA 1988 s 667
income arising under, meaning..TA 1988 s 666(4)
income of settlor..TA 1988 s 663(1)

CHILDREN'S SETTLEMENTS—*continued*
information..TA 1988 s 669
interest paid by trustees..TA 1988 s 666
irrevocable, meaning..TA 1988 s 665
more than one settlor..TA 1988 s 668
offshore income gain..TA 1988 s 663(2)
pre-1936 irrevocable dispositions..TA 1988 Sch 30 para 10

CLAIM
affidavit supporting..TMA 1970 s 42(5)
appeal as to..TMA 1970 s 42(3)(4)(9)
assessment following..TMA 1970 s 42(10)
business expansion scheme..TA 1988 s 289, 306
company payments not distributions, set-off..TA 1988 Sch 16 para 5, 6
company reconstructions..TA 1988 s 343
co-operative housing association, by..TA 1988 s 488
error or mistake..TMA 1970 s 42(8)
fluctuating profits relief..TA 1988 s 96(8)
form of..TMA 1970 s 42(5)
franked investment income surplus..TA 1988 s 242, 243
group relief..TA 1988 s 412
inspector, to..TMA s 42(2)
loss relief..TA 1988 s 380(1), 381(1), 382(1)
non-resident, by..TA 1988 s 278(5)
person under disability..TMA 1970 s 42(6)
personal pension scheme, relief under..TA 1988 s 639
postponement of tax due from beneficiary..FA 1984 Sch 14 para 2
satisfaction of..TMA 1970 s 42(7)
self-build society, by..TA 1988 s 489
set-off of franked investment income..TA 1988 Sch 16 para 5, 6
supplementary..TMA 1970 s 42(8)
time limits..TMA 1970 s 43
variation of decision..TMA 1970 s 42(9)

CLEARING HOUSE
information as to chargeable gains..TMA 1970 s 25(6)

CLERK TO GENERAL COMMISSIONERS
appointment and remuneration..TMA 1970 s 3
compensation for loss of office etc..FA 1972 s 130
declaration on taking office..TMA 1970 s 6(2)(5) Sch 1
retiring age..TMA 1970 s 3(5)

CLOSE COMPANY
meaning..TA 1988 s 414, 415
accommodation etc expenses..TA 1988 s 418(2)–(4)
apportionment. *See* CLOSE COMPANY APPORTIONMENT
approved share option scheme..TA 1988 Sch 9 para 8
assets transferred to, pre-April 1965..CGTA 1979 Sch 5 para 16
associate—
    meaning..TA 1988 s 417(3)
associated company, meaning..TA 1988 s 416(1)
beneficial ownership of rights under life policies etc..TA 1988 s 547(1)
capital gains tax—
    assets transferred at undervalue..CGTA 1979 s 75
    relief, shortfall in distributions..CGTA 1979 s 74
companies with quoted shares..TA 1988 s 415
control, meaning..TA 1988 s 416(2)(3)
controlled foreign company..TA 1988 s 756(3)
deep discount securities..TA 1988 Sch 4 para 10
director, meaning..TA 1988 s 417(5)
distribution, meaning..TA 1988 s 418(1)
employee trust..CGTA 1979 s 149
exempt approved scheme, shares held on trust..TA 1988 s 414(7)
information, provision of..FA 1989 Sch 12 para 2–4
investment holding—
    meaning..TA 1988 s 13A
    small companies' rate, application of..TA 1988 s 13
loan creditor, meaning..TA 1988 s 417(7)–(9)
loan for acquisition of interest in..TA 1988 s 360
loans to participators—
    controlled companies..TA 1988 s 422
    corporation tax..TMA 1970 s 109
    release of debt..TA 1988 s 421

CLOSE COMPANY—*continued*
  loans to participators—*continued*
    taxing provisions..TA 1988 s 419, 420, FA 1988 Sch 3 para 16
  material interest in..TA 1988 s 187(3)
  participator—
    meaning..TA 1988 s 417(1)
    associate. *See* associate *supra*
    loans to. *See* loans to participators *supra*
    payments etc to..TA 1988 s 418(7)
  settlement, connected with..TA 1988 s 681(5)
  transactions in securities..TA 1988 s 704(D)

CLOSE COMPANY APPORTIONMENT
  business requirements of..TA 1988 Sch 19 para 8, 9
  cessations..TA 1988 Sch 19 para 10
  distributable income..TA 1988 Sch 19 para 4, 6
  distributions—
    determining..TA 1988 Sch 19 para 3
    legal restrictions on..TA 1988 Sch 19 para 11
  estate of trading income..TA 1988 Sch 19 para 5, 6
  liquidations..TA 1988 Sch 19 para 10
  relevant income—
    meaning..TA 1988 Sch 19 para 1
    maximum amount of..TA 1988 Sch 19 para 2
  stock dividends..TA 1988 Sch 19 para 12
  trading company, meaning..TA 1988 Sch 19 para 7
  trading group, member of..TA 1988 Sch 19 para 7

COLLECTIVE INVESTMENT SCHEME
  exchange of rights..FA 1989 s 140

COLLECTION OF TAX
  budget resolution. *See* BUDGET RESOLUTION
  company payments not distributions—
    appeal..TA 1988 Sch 16 para 10(3)(4)
    assessment..TA 1988 Sch 16 para 10
    claim for set-off..TA 1988 Sch 16 para 5, 6
    deposit-taker, interest..TA 1988 s 479(5)–(7)
    due date..TA 1988 Sch 16 para 10(2)
    errors..TA 1988 Sch 16 para 8
    payment of tax..TA 1988 Sch 16 para 4
    payments outside accounting period..TA 1988 Sch 16 para 9
    recovery of tax..TA 1988 Sch 16 para 11
    relevant payment, meaning..TA 1988 Sch 16 para 1
    repayments..TA 1988 Sch 16 para 10(4)
    returns..TA 1988 Sch 16 para 2, 3
    set-off..TA 1988 Sch 16 para 5, 7
  Continental Shelf..FA 1973 Sch 15 para 4–8
  demand note..TMA 1970 s 60(1)
  deposit-takers, from ..TA 1988 s 479(5)–(7)
  distress..TMA 1970 s 61
  priority of tax..TMA 1970 s 62
  receipt..TMA 1970 s 60(2)
  recovery. *See* RECOVERY OF TAX
  Sch A, lessees and agents..TA 1988 s 23
  surrender of life policy, on..TA 1988 s 272
  wife, from..TA 1938 s 285

COLLECTOR OF TAXES
  appointment..TMA 1970 s 1(2)
  certificate—
    interest on unpaid tax..TMA 1970 s 70(2)
    unpaid tax..TMA 1970 s 70(1)
  collection by. *See* COLLECTION OF TAX
  continuation of proceedings..TMA 1970 s 1(3)
  declaration on taking office..TMA 1970 s 6(4)(5) Sch 1 Pt III
  recovery of tax. *See* RECOVERY OF TAX

COLONIAL PENSION
  exemption..TA 1988 s 615
  Sch E..TA 1988 s 19(4)

COLONIAL PENSION FUND
  tax credit..TA 1988 s 232(2)

COMMERCIAL BUILDING
meaning..FA 1980 s 74(4)
balancing adjustments on non-qualifying use..FA 1981 s 75(4)(5)
enterprise zone. *See* ENTERPRISE ZONE
sales post-March 1981..FA 1981 s 76

COMMISSION
returns..TMA 1970 s 16

COMMISSIONERS
meaning..TMA 1970 s 48(1)
disclosure of information between..FA 1972 s 127
   imports, as to..FA 1988 s 8
General. *See* GENERAL COMMISSIONERS
national heritage: transfer of functions to..FA 1985 s 95
Special. *See* SPECIAL COMMISSIONERS
venue on appeal. *See under* APPEAL

COMMODITY
futures—
  meaning..TA 1988 s 128
  dealings, capital gains tax..FA 1985 s 72(1)–(4)
  loss relief..TA 1988 s 399
held at April 1965...CGTA 1979 Sch 5 para 13
identification..CGTA 1979 s 132
offshore fund..TA 1988 Sch 27 para 4, 11

COMMONWEALTH AGENT
Agent-General, meaning..TA 1988 s 320(4)
High Commissioner, meaning..TA 1988 s 320(4)
immunity..TA 1988 s 320
mission, meaning..TA 1988 s 320(4)
self-governing colony..TA 1988 s 320(4)

COMPANY
meaning..TA 1988 s 832
ACT. *See* ADVANCE CORPORATION TAX
amalgamation. *See* COMPANY RECONSTRUCTION
associated—
  meaning..TA 1988 s 416(1), 774(4)(*d*)
  deep discount securities..TA 1988 Sch 4 para 9
  sales at under- or overvalue..TA 1988 s 770, 772, 773
  transactions with dealing company..TA 1988 s 774
business transferred to, rollover relief..CGTA 1979 s 123 Sch 6 para 23
capital gains. *See* CHARGEABLE GAINS
change in ownership—
  ACT..TA 1988 s 245
  ascertainment..TA 1988 s 469
  disallowance of trading losses..TA 1988 s 468
chargeable gains. *See* CHARGEABLE GAINS
claim for repayment of tax deducted from receipts..TA 1988 s 7(5)
close. *See* CLOSE COMPANY; CLOSE COMPANY APPORTIONMENT
connected. *See* CONNECTED COMPANIES
consortium, meaning..TA 1988 s 247(9), 413(6)
control, meaning..CAA 1968 s 87(1) TA 1988 s 168(12), 416(2), 840
corporation tax. *See* CORPORATION TAX
Crown, controlled by..TA 1988 s 414(4)
dealing company—
  meaning..TA 1988 s 774(4)(*b*)
  reduction in value of holding..TA 1988 s 736
  transactions with associated company..TA 1988 s 774
demerger. *See* DEMERGER
distributions. *See* COMPANY DISTRIBUTION
donation to charity..TA 1988 s 339
dual resident—
  meaning..FA 1989 s 132(1) 133(4)
  deemed disposals by..FA 1989 s 132(2)–(4)
  roll-over relief..FA 1989 s 133
employee seconded to charity..TA 1988 s 86
employee-controlled, investment in—
  conditions..TA 1988 s 361(2)(4)
  recovery of relief..TA 1988 s 363
  relief..TA 1988 s 361, FA 1988 Sch 3 para 15
  subsequent loans..TA 1988 s 363(4)

COMPANY—*continued*
  Export Credits Guarantee Dept payments..TA 1988 s 88, 441(9), 584(5)
  family. *See* FAMILY COMPANY
  first-year allowance..FA 1971 s 41(3)
  franked investment income..*See* FRANKED INVESTMENT INCOME
  government investment written-off..TA 1988 s 400
  group. *See* GROUP (COMPANIES); GROUP INCOME; GROUP RELIEF
  holding company, meaning..TA 1988 s 229(1), 413(3)
  income tax—
    collection, payment not distributions. *See under* COLLECTION OF TAX
    interest on overdue..TMA 1970 s 87
    regulations..TA 1988 s 350(6)(7)
  insurance. *See* INSURANCE COMPANY
  investment. *See* INVESTMENT COMPANY
  investment in corporate trades. *See* BUSINESS EXPANSION SCHEME; BUSINESS START-UP SCHEME
  limited liability, meaning..TA 1988 s 518(10)
  losses. *See under* LOSS RELIEF
  material interest in, meaning..TA 1988 s 168(11) 360A
  merger, meaning..TA 1970 s 278A(2)
  migration..TA 1988 s 765
    capital gains tax. *See* CAPITAL GAINS TAX
    failure to pay tax..FA 1988 s 131 132
    outstanding tax, securing payment of..FA 1988 s 130
    requirements preceding..FA 1988 s 130
    Treasury Consent, meaning..FA 1988 s 105(5) 130(6)
  mutual business..TA 1988 s 490
  non-resident. *See* NON-RESIDENT COMPANY; OVERSEAS LIFE INSURANCE COMPANY
  officer's responsibility..TMA 1970 s 108
  partnership. *See under* PARTNERSHIP
  payments between related companies..TA 1988 s 341
  proper officer, meaning..TMA 1970 s 108(3)
  purchase of own shares—
    ACT..TA 1988 s 240(9)
    dealer, from..TA 1988 s 95
    fixed-rate preference shares, meaning..TA 1988 s 95(5)
    unquoted trading company. *See* UNQUOTED TRADING COMPANY
  reconstruction. *See* COMPANY RECONSTRUCTION
  repayment supplement..TA 1988 s 825
  residence..FA 1988 s 66 Sch 7
  residuary income..TA 1988 s 696(8)
  service on..TMA 1970 s 108(1)
  small, mitigation of liability..TA 1988 s 13
  sub-contractor's certificate..TA 1988 s 565
  subsidiary. *See* SUBSIDIARY
  terminal losses..TA 1988 s 394
  trading company, meaning..TA 1988 s 247(a)(*b*) 756
  trading income, meaning..TA 1988 s 393(8)
  trading or holding company, meaning..TA 1988 s 247(9)(*a*)
  trading with members..TA 1988 s 486(10)(11)
  transfer of assets. *See* TRANSFER OF ASSETS
  trustee savings bank as..FA 1984 s 44
  UK, incorporated in..FA 1988 s 66(1)
  unquoted—
    meaning..TA 1988 s 229(1)
    purchase of own shares. *See* UNQUOTED TRADING COMPANY
  winding-up. *See* WINDING-UP

COMPANY DISTRIBUTION
  meaning..TA 1988 s 209, 418
  ACT. *See* ADVANCE CORPORATION TAX
  assets, out of..TA 1988 s 254(9)
  bonus issue. *See* BONUS ISSUE
  building society, transfer of business by..FA 1988 Sch 12 para 6
  capital distributions..CGTA 1979 s 72
  close company apportionment. *See* CLOSE COMPANY APPORTIONMENT
  corporation tax exemption..TA 1988 s 209
  dealers in securities..TA 1988 s 736
  deep discount securities..TA 1988 Sch 4 para 5(5)
  exempt funds etc, to..TA 1988 s 235, 236
  friendly societies..TA 1988 s 461(3)
  gross rate or amount..TA 1988 s 255
  groups of companies..TA 1988 s 254(1)–(4)
  income tax..TA 1988 s 20
  issue at less than amount repayable..TA 1988 s 254(11)

COMPANY DISTRIBUTION—continued
mutual business..TA 1988 s 490
new consideration, meaning..TA 1988 s 210(4) 254(1)
ordinary shares, meaning..TA 1988 s 210(4)
preference share, meaning..TA 1988 s 210(4)
profit distribution..TA 1988 Sch 18 para 2
profits etc available for, group relief..TA 1988 Sch 18
qualifying, meaning..TA 1988 s 14(2)
reciprocal arrangements..TA 1988 s 254(8)
redeemable share capital..TA 1988 s 209(8)
regulations, powers..TA 1988 s 253
repayment of share capital..TA 1988 s 211
returns..TA 1988 s 234(5)–(9)
Sch F..TA 1988 s 20
securities, meaning..TA 1988 s 254(1)
share, meaning..TA 1988 s 254(1)
statement of..TA 1988 s 234(1)(2)
stock dividends..TA 1988 s 230
transfer of assets etc..TA 1988 s 209(6)

COMPANY RECONSTRUCTION
advance clearance..CGTA 1979 s 88
apportionment..TA 1988 s 343(9)(10)
BOAC, BEA, and British Airways Board..TA 1988 s 513
capital allowances..TA 1988 s 343(2)
cessation by successor..TA 1988 s 343(5)(6)
change of ownership, without..TA 1988 s 343
claim for relief..TA 1988 s 343(11)
connected persons..CGTA 1979 s 87(3)
controlled foreign company, assumption as to..TA 1988 Sch 24 para 8
corporate bonds..FA 1984 s 64(7) Sch 13 Pt II
deep discount securities..TA 1988 Sch 4
exchange of securities..CGTA 1979 s 85 TA 1988 s 757(5)
exemption for certain mergers..TA 1970 s 278A
indexation allowance..FA 1982 Sch 13 para 5
issue of securities..CGTA 1979 s 86
losses, leasing contracts..TA 1988 s 395
merger, meaning..TA 1970 s 278A(2)
recovery of tax..CGTA 1979 s 87(4)
relative, meaning..TA 1988 s 344(5)
restrictions on relief..TA 1988 Sch 10 para 5
scheme of, meaning..CGTA 1979 s 86(2)
securities as trading stock..TA 1988 s 343(5)
share of trade..TA 1988 s 344(1)(2)
small holdings..CGTA 1979 s 87(2)
subsidiary, meaning..TA 1988 s 344(3)(*b*)
tax avoidance..CGTA 1979 s 87(1)
terminal losses..TA 1988 s 343(3)
transfer of assets, chargeable gains..TA 1988 s 347(1)

COMPENSATION. *See also* DAMAGES
capital gains tax—
    chargeable..CGTA 1979 s 21
    compulsory acquisition..CGTA 1979 s 110
    not chargeable..CGTA 1979 s 19(5)
    pre-April 1965..CGTA 1979 Sch 5 para 18
clerks to General Commissioners..FA 1972 s 130
loss of office. *See* TERMINATION PAYMENT
Nazi persecution..TA 1988 s 330

COMPENSATION STOCK
conversion of securities..CGTA 1979 s 84

COMPULSORY ACQUISITION
aircraft and shipbuilding shares..FA 1976 s 54
authority exercising or having compulsory powers, meaning..CGTA 1979 s 108(5)
CGT—
    compensation..CGTA 1979 s 110
    part disposal..CGTA 1979 s 108
compensation stock..CGTA 1979 s 84
dealers in securities..TA 1988 s 472

CONNECTED COMPANIES
meaning..TA 1988 s 839(5)–(7)
deep discount securities..TA 1988 Sch 4 para 9
oil extraction activities..TA 1988 s 502(3)(4)
purchase of own shares..TA 1988 s 223(1), 228
relevant income, close company apportionment..TA 1988 Sch 19 para 9
unilateral relief..TA 1988 s 790(6)

CONNECTED PERSONS
meaning—
   CGT..CGTA 1979 s 63
   generally..TA 1988 s 839(1)–(4), (7)
   leased assets..TA 1988 s 783
capital allowances. *See under* CAPITAL ALLOWANCES
capital gains tax..CGTA 1979 s 62 FA 1985 s 71
cars..FA 1971 Sch 8 para 10(4)
companies. *See* CONNECTED COMPANIES
company reconstruction etc..CGTA 1979 s 87(3)
controlled foreign company..TA 1988 s 755(5)
determination..TA 1988 s 839(1)
interest in shares, acquiting..FA 1988 s 83
know-how sales..TA 1988 s 531(7)
land purchase etc loans..TA 1988 s 355(5)
local enterprise agencies..TA 1988 s 79(9)
long lease..FA 1978 s 37(6)
machinery and plant..CAA 1968 Sch 7 para 3 FA 1971 s 44(7) Sch 8 para 3
partnership..TA 1988 s 839(4)
patent rights, sale..TA 1988 s 521(4)(5)
sales at under- or overvalue..TA 1988 s 770
series of transactions between..FA 1985 s 71
share acquisition rights..TA 1988 s 136(2)
short-life asset, disposal to..FA 1985 s 57(6)–(8)
short-term leasing..FA 1980 s 73(6)
succession to trade..FA 1971 Sch 8 para 13
transactions between..CGTA 1979 s 62
transactions between dealing company and associated company..TA 1988 s 774
trustees..TA 1988 s 839(3)

CONSTRUCTION INDUSTRY
sub-contractor. *See* SUB-CONTRACTOR

CONSUL
meaning..TA 1988 s 321(3)
exemption..TA 1988 s 321(1)(2)
official agents..TA 1988 s 321

CONSULAR OFFICER
employees..TA 1988 s 322(2)
exemption..TA 1988 s 322

CONTINENTAL SHELF
charge to tax..TA 1988 s 830
collection of tax..FA 1973 Sch 15 para 4–8
divers etc..TA 1988 s 314
information..FA 1973 Sch 15 para 2
UK, part of..TA 1988 s 830(1)

CONTRACTUAL SAVINGS SCHEME
meaning..TA 1988 s 326(2)(3)
building society—
   meaning..TA 1988 s 832(1)
   transfer of business..FA 1988 Sch 12 para 7
exemption..TA 1988 s 326(1)

CONTROL
meaning (company)..CAA 1968 s 87(1) TA 1988 s 168(12) 416(2) 840

CONTROLLED FOREIGN COMPANY
meaning..TA 1988 s 747(1)(2)
acceptable distribution policy..TA 1988 Sch 25 Pt I
accounting period—
   appropriate, meaning..TA 1988 Sch 26 para 1(2)(*a*)
   dates for..TA 1988 s 751
   less than 12 months..TA 1988 Sch 25 para 3(2)

CONTROLLED FOREIGN COMPANY—*continued*
  ACT..TA 1988 Sch 24 para 7, Sch 26 para 2
  advances by, meaning..TA 1988 Sch 25 para 11(5)(*b*)
  amendment of direction..TA 1988 s 753(3)
  appeal..TA 1988 s 753(4)–(7), 754(4)
  apportionment—
    beneficiaries..TA 1988 s 752(7)
    corporation tax..TA 1988 s 747(4)(5)
    interest holders, among..TA 1988 s 752(1)
    interests, determination of..TA 1988 s 752(2)
    method..TA 1988 s 752(4)–(8)
    powers..TA 1988 s 747(3)
    same interest held directly and indirectly..TA 1988 s 752(6), 754(6)–(8)
  assessment..TA 1988 s 754(1)–(4)
  associated persons..TA 1988 s 756(2)(*b*)
  assumptions—
    capital allowances..TA 1988 Sch 24 para 10, 11
    company reconstruction..TA 1988 Sch 24 para 8
    earlier losses..TA 1988 Sch 24 para 9
    general..TA 1988 Sch 24 para 1–4
    group relief..TA 1988 Sch 24 para 5–7
    unremittable foreign income..TA 1988 Sch 24 para 12
  available profits, computation..TA 1988 Sch 25 para 3
  banking, interest payments..TA 1988 Sch 25 para 11(3)
  banking business..TA 1988 Sch 25 para 9(3)
  branch or agency, services provided through..TA 1988 Sch 25 para 8(4)
  business establishment, meaning..TA 1988 Sch 25 para 7(1)
  capital interest..TA 1988 Sch 25 para 11(4)(*a*)
  capital losses, meaning..TA 1988 Sch 25 para 3(4)
  capital profits, meaning..TA 1988 Sch 25 para 3(4)
  charge to tax..TA 1988 s 747(1)
  chargeable profits, meaning..TA 1988 s 747(6)
  close company..TA 1988 s 756(3)
  connected persons..TA 1988 s 756(2)(*a*)
  corporation tax—
    apportionment of profits..TA 1988 s 747(4)(5)
    determination of amount..TA 1988 s 750(3)(4)
  creditable tax, meaning..TA 1988 s 751(6)
  diversion of profits, for..TA 1988 Sch 25 para 19
  dividend—
    meaning..TA 1988 Sch 25 para 2(3)
    related company, derived from..TA 1988 Sch 25 para 4
    relief..TA 1988 Sch 26 para 4–6
    specified profits, out of..TA 1988 Sch 25 para 3(5)
  double taxation relief..TA 1988 Sch 26 para 4–6
  elections, assumption as to..TA 1988 Sch 24 para 4(1)(2)
  exclusions—
    acceptable distribution policy..TA 1988 Sch 25 Pt I
    exempt activities..TA 1988 Sch 25 Pt II
    public quotation condition..TA 1988 Sch 25 Pt III
    reduction in UK tax and diversion of profits..TA 1988 Sch 25 Pt IV
  exempt activities—
    conditions..TA 1988 Sch 25 para 6
    number of employees, ..TA 1988 Sch 25 para 8
    residence..TA 1988 Sch 25 para 5(2)
    services, conditions as to..TA 1988 Sch 25 para 8
  foreign subsidiary—
    meaning..TA 1988 s 755(1)
    controlling company, meaning..TA 1988 s 755(2)
    information..TA 1988 s 755
  gains on disposal of shares..TA 1988 Sch 26 para 3
  gift to..CGTA 1979 s 126B
  goods delivered into territory of residence..TA 1988 Sch 25 para 10
  gross trading receipts, insurance business..TA 1988 Sch 25 para 11(7)–(9)
  group relief..TA 1988 Sch 24 para 5–7, Sch 26 para 1(4)
  guarantor's liability, value of capital interest..TA 1988 Sch 25 para 11(4)(*b*)(*c*)
  holding company—
    meaning..TA 1988 Sch 25 para 12(1)
    conditions..TA 1988 Sch 25 para 6(3)(4)
    connected companies..TA 1988 Sch 25 para 12(5)
    determination whether..TA 1988 Sch 25 para 12(2)
    local holding company..TA 1988 Sch 25 para 6(3)
  inspection of books etc..TA 1988 s 755(3)–(7)
  insurance business..TA 1988 Sch 25 para 11(6)–(8)

CONTROLLED FOREIGN COMPANY—*continued*
  interest in, persons having..TA 1988 s 749(5)–(7)
  investment business, meaning..TA 1988 Sch 25 para 9(1)
  loan creditor..TA 1988 s 749(7) 752(3)
  local reinsurance contract, meaning..TA 1988 Sch 25 para 11(8)
  losses..TA 1988 Sch 24 para 9, Sch 26 para 1
  lower level of taxation, determination of..TA 1988 s 750
  majority interest, meaning..TA 1988 Sch 24 para 4(3)
  non-trading income, meaning..TA 1988 Sch 25 para 12(6)
  non-voting fixed-rate preference shares, meaning..TA 1988 Sch 25 para 2(7)
  notice of declaration..TA 1988 s 753(5)
  notice of direction..TA 1988 s 753(1)–(4)
  notice of liability..TA 1988 s 754(6)–(8)
  outstanding capital, meaning..TA 1988 Sch 25 para 11(4)(*e*)
  premises, meaning..TA 1988 Sch 25 para 7(2)
  principal member of..TA 1988 Sch 25 para 15(2)
  proceeds of sale of property etc..TA 1988 Sch 25 para 11(2)
  public quotation condition..TA 1988 Sch 25 Pt III
  recovery of tax..TMA 1970 s 55(1)(*g*)
  reduction in UK tax—
    limitation on direction-making..TA 1988 s 748(3)
    main purpose, meaning..TA 1988 Sch 25 para 18
    transaction, meaning..TA 1988 Sch 25 para 16(2)
    transactions achieving..TA 1988 Sch 25 para 17
  related company—
    meaning..TA 1988 Sch 25 para 4(2) 19(2)
    dividend derived from..TA 1988 Sch 25 para 4(1)
  relief—
    ACT..TA 1988 Sch 26 para 2
    dividends..TA 1988 Sch 26 para 4, 5
    entitlement..TA 1988 s 754(5)
    group relief..TA 1988 Sch 24 para 5–7, Sch 26 para 1(4)
    relevant allowance, meaning..TA 1988 Sch 26 para 1(3)
    relevant maximum, meaning..TA 1988 Sch 26 para 2(3)
    set-off against liability..TA 1988 Sch 26 para 1(5)
    share disposals..TA 1988 Sch 26 para 3, 6
    time for claim..TA 1988 Sch 26 para 1(6)
    trading losses..TA 1988 Sch 26 para 1
  residence—
    determination of..TA 1988 s 749(1)–(4)
    exempt activities..TA 1988 Sch 25 para 5(2)
  restriction on liability..TA 1988 s 748
  revised amount..TA 1988 s 751(6)
  shares issued—
    indirect interests..TA 1988 Sch 25 para 2(8)
    single class..TA 1988 Sch 25 para 2(4)
    two classes..TA 1988 Sch 25 para 2(5)–(7)
  trade investments, meaning..TA 1988 Sch 25 para (1)(5)(*a*)
  trading company, meaning..TA 1988 s 756(1)
  value of fixed assets..TA 1988 Sch 25 para 11(4)(*d*)
  voting and non-voting shares..TA 1988 Sch 25 para 2(5)–(7)
  voting power..TA 1988 Sch 25 Pt III
  wholesale, distributive etc business—
    meaning..TA 1988 Sch 25 para 11(1)
    conditions..TA 1988 Sch 25 para 6(2)

CO-OPERATIVE
  loan for acquisition of interest in..TA 1988 s 361

CO-OPERATIVE ASSOCIATION
  meaning..TA 1988 s 486(12)
  agriculture and fisheries..TA 1988 s 486(9)
  distributions by..TA 1988 s 486

CO-OPERATIVE HOUSING ASSOCIATION
  adjustment of member's liability..TA 1988 s 488(4)
  approval..TA 1988 s 488(6)(7)
  chargeable gains..TA 1988 s 488(5)
  claim..TA 1988 s 488(9)
  conditions for relief..TA 1988 s 488(6)(10)
  special treatment..TA 1988 s 488
  time for claim..TA 1988 s 488(9)

COPYRIGHT
  agent's commission..TA 1988 s 536(3)
  assignment—
    before 10 years after publication..TA 1988 s 534
    less than 6 years, for..TA 1988 s 535(3)
    more than 6 years, for..TA 1988 s 535(2)
    ten years after publication..TA 1988 s 535
  cessation of profession..TA 1988 s 535(6)
  death of author..TA 1988 s 535(4)
  double relief exclusion..TA 1988 s 534(6), 535(9)
  first publication, meaning..TA 1988 s 534(7)
  husband and wife..TA 1988 s 535(5)
  loss relief exclusion..TA 1988 s 387(3)(e)
  lump sum payment, meaning..TA 1988 s 535(11)
  non-resident owner..TA 1988 s 536
  notice of election..TA 1988 s 535(7)
  owner, meaning..TA 1988 s 536(2)
  personal representatives, election by..TA 1988 s 535(5)
  public lending right..TA 1988 s 537
  relief—
    generally..TA 1988 s 534
    loss relief..TA 1988 s 387(3)(e)
    ten years, sale after..TA 1988 s 535
  under deduction..TA 1988 s 821(3)(a)

CORPORATE BOND
  meaning..FA 1984 s 64(2)
  company reconstruction etc—
    relevant transaction, meaning..FA 1984 Sch 13 para 7(1)
    relief..FA 1984 s 64(7) Sch 13 Pt II
  exemption..FA 1984 s 64(1)
  group of companies..FA 1984 s 64(6)
  issue, time of..FA 1984 s 64(8)
  new asset, meaning..FA 1984 Sch 13 para 7(2)(3)
  old asset, meaning..FA 1984 Sch 13 para 7(2)(3)
  qualifying—
    meaning..FA 1984 s 64(4)(a)
    becoming..FA 1984 s 64(4)(b)
    identification: capital gains tax..FA 1982 s 88(9) 89
    indexation allowance..FA 1985 s 68(2)(a)
  relevant transaction, meaning..FA 1984 Sch 13 para 7(1)
  United Kingdom—
    meaning..TA 1988 Sch 4 para 2(8)
    deep discount securities..TA 1988 Sch 4 para 2(2)

CORPORATION TAX
  accounting period—
    basis of assessment..TA 1988 s 12(1)
    beginning..TA 1988 s 12(2)
    end..TA 1988 s 12(3)
    group relief..TA 1988 s 408
    uncertain..TA 1988 s 12(8)
    winding-up..TA 1988 s 12(7)
  administration by Board..TMA 1970 s 1(1)
  advance. *See* ADVANCE CORPORATION TAX
  advance petroleum revenue tax, deduction..TA 1988 s 500
  application of provisions to..TA 1988 s 832(3)(4)
  apportionment between financial years..TA 1988 s 8(3)
  assessment, payable without..TA 1988 s 10(2)–(4)
  basis of assessment..TA 1988 s 70
  British steel, successor company..BSA 1988 s 11
  building societies..TA 1988 s 476(3)
  capital allowances—
    other than trade..CAA 1968 s 74
    trade..CAA 1968 s 73
  certified unit trust, on..TA 1988 s 468B
  charge on income—
    meaning..TA 1988 s 338(2)
    allowance..TA 1988 s 118(1), 338
    charity donations..TA 1988 s 339
    franked investment income..TA 1988 s 242(2)
    interest payable to—
      non-resident..TA 1988 s 340
      related company..TA 1988 s 341

CORPORATION TAX—*continued*
  charge to—
    commencement..TA 1988 s 12(4)
    Continental Shelf..TA 1988 s 830(5)
    general provisions..TA 1988 s 6 8
  close company. *See* CLOSE COMPANY
  close investment-holding company..TA 1988 s 13
  company in liquidation..TA 1988 s 342
  company reconstruction where no change of ownership..TA 1988 s 343
  computation—
    income tax principles..TA 1988 s 9
    special rules..TA 1988 s 337
  controlled foreign company..TA 1988 s 747 750
  credit union..TA 1988 s 487
  deep discount securities. *See* DEEP DISCOUNT SECURITIES
  discounted bills..TA 1988 s 78
  distribution—
    meaning..TA 1988 s 209, 418(1)
    received by UK company..TA 1988 s 7(2)
  double taxation relief by credit..TA 1988 s 797
  Electricity Council and Boards..TA 1988 s 511
  franked investment income. *See* FRANKED INVESTMENT INCOME
  friendly societies..TA 1988 s 461 463
  gain or loss outside accounting period..TA 1988 s 12(6)
  Gas Council and Boards..TA 1988 s 511(7)
  general scheme of..TA 1988 s 8
  gilt-edged securities..TA 1970 s 270
  group income. *See* GROUP INCOME; GROUP RELIEF
  group of companies. *See* GROUP (COMPANIES)
  harbour reorganisation scheme..TA 1988 s 518
  industrial and provident societies..TA 1988 s 486
  insurance company. *See* INSURANCE COMPANY; OVERSEAS LIFE INSURANCE COMPANY
  interest claims, effect on..FA 1989 s 157
  International Maritime Satellite Organisation..TA 1988 s 515
  investment company. *See* INVESTMENT COMPANY
  life assurance gains..TA 1988 s 435(2)
  loans to participators..TMA 1970 s 109
  local authority bonds etc held by non-resident..TA 1988 s 581(1)
  local constituency associations, relief..F(No 2)A 1983 s 7(4)
  loss relief. *See under* LOSS RELIEF
  mineral rights, deductions..TA 1988 s 121
  mineral royalties..TA 1988 s 122
  mitigation of liability—
    small companies..TA 1988 s 13
  non-resident, chargeability..TMA 1970 s 85 246
  Northern Ireland Electricity Service..TA 1988 s 511(4)(5)
  notice of liability..TMA 1970 s 10
  offshore fund. *See* OFFSHORE FUND
  oil extraction activities..TA 1988 s 492 500
  overdue, interest on..TMA 1970 s 87A
  overpaid—
    interest on..TA 1988 s 826
    recovery of..TMA 1970 s 30
  overseas life insurance company, set-off..TA 1988 s 447(4)
  payment dates—
    building societies..TA 1988 s 478
    companies..TA 1988 s 510, Sch 30 para 1
  petroleum revenue tax, deduction..TA 1988 s 500
  preceding years..TA 1988 s 8(4)
  pre-trading expenditure..TA 1988 s 401
  profits, meaning..TA 1988 s 6(4)(*a*)
  rate—
    change of..TA 1988 s 8(5)
    small companies..TA 1988 s 26(1)
    1989..FA 1989 s 34
  recovery—
    proper officer, from....TMA 1970 s 108(2)
    tax not postponed..TMA 1970 s 55
  repayment supplement..TA 1988 s 825
  residuary income..TA 1988 s 696(8)
  return of profits..TMA 1970 s 11
    delivery of..TMA 1970 s 11(4)
    failure to make..TMA 1970 s 94
      penalty arising from..F(No 2)A 1987 s 84

CORPORATION TAX—*continued*
  return of profits—*continued*
    information required..TMA 1970 s 11(6)–(8)
    specified period, relating to..TMA 1970 s 11(2)
  sale and repurchase of securities..TA 1988 s 729(2)
  set-off of income tax against, overseas life insurance companies..TA 1988 s 447(4)
  several accounting dates..TA 1988 s 12(5)
  small companies..TA 1988 s 13 FA 1989 s 35
  stock relief. *See* STOCK RELIEF
  time basis, apportionment..TA 1988 s 834(4)
  time for payment—
    building societies..TA 1988 s 478
    generally..TA 1988 s 10
  trade union provident benefits..TA 1988 s 467(2)
  transfer of income from securities..TA 1988 s 730(6)
  Trustee Savings Bank, exemption..TSBA 1985 Sch 2 para 6
  UK company distributions..TA 1988 s 208

CORPORATION TAX ACTS
  meaning..TA 1988 s 831(1)(*a*)

CO-TENANT
  income tax relief..TA 1988 s 277

COUNTY COURT
  recovery of tax..TMA 1970 s 66

COUPON
  meaning..TA 1988 s 45
  chargeable persons..TA 1988 Sch 3 para 6
  foreign dividends..TA 1988 s 123(3)
  overseas public revenue dividends..TA 1988 s 17

COURT OF APPEAL
  appeal to..TMA 1970 s 56(8)
  case stated..TMA 1970 s 56A

COVENANT
  charitable. *See* CHARITABLE COVENANT
  restrictive. *See* RESTRICTIVE COVENANT

COVENANTED PAYMENT TO CHARITY
  meaning..TA 1988 s 339(8) 660(3) FA 1989 s 59
  British Museum..TA 1988 s 339(9)
  charge on income, as..TA 1988 s 51A(2)(*b*), 347A(2)(*b*)
  corporation tax..TA 1988 s 339
  exemption limit..TA 1988 s 683(3)
  Historic Buildings and Monuments Commission..TA 1988 s 339(9)
  National Heritage Memorial Fund..TA 1988 s 339(9)
  revocable settlements..TA 1988 s 671(2)
  time limit..TA 1988 s 660(2) 671(2)

CREDIT CARD. *See* CREDIT-TOKEN

CREDIT TOKEN
  meaning..TA 1988 s 142(4)
  benefits in kind..TA 1988 s 142
  car parking space, for..TA 1988 s 142(3A)
  entertainment, for..TA 1988 s 142(3B)

CREDIT TRANSACTION
  anti-avoidance provisions..TA 1988 s 786

CREDIT UNION
  meaning..TA 1988 s 487(5)
  exemption..TA 1988 s 487(1)–(3)
  share interest payments..TA 1988 s 487(3)
  surplus funds, meaning..TA 1988 s 487(5)

CREMATORIUM. *See* CEMETERY

CRIMINAL PROCEEDINGS
  saving for..TMA 1970 s 104
  Scotland..TMA 1970 s 107

CROPS
meaning..CAA 1968 s 7(5)

CROWN
company controlled by..TA 1988 s 414(4)
Income Tax Acts..TA 1988 s 829
industrial buildings..CAA 1968 s 4(12) 13(1)
Sch C exemption..TA 1988 s 49(2)

CROWN SERVANT
foreign service allowance..TA 1988 s 319

CUSTOMS AND EXCISE
disclosure of information..FA 1972 s 127

DAMAGES
gain not chargeable..CGTA 1979 s 19(5)
interest on, personal injuries..TA 1988 s 329

DEALER IN SECURITIES
companies..TA 1988 s 736
compulsory acquisition..TA 1988 s 472(1)
conversion of circulating capital..TA 1988 s 473
double taxation relief..TA 1988 s 808
Eurobonds..TA 1988 s 732(5)
exchange of securities..TA 1988 s 471
interest on borrowed money..TA 1988 s 475
overseas securities..TA 1988 s 732(4)
purchase and sale provisions..TA 1988 s 732
sale and repurchase etc..TA 1988 s 729(4)(5)
securities, meaning..TA 1988 s 471(4)
tax-free income..TA 1988 s 474
tax-free Treasury securities..TA 1988 s 475
winding-up..TA 1988 s 427

DEALING COMPANY
offshore fund with interests in..TA 1988 Sch 27 para 12

DEATH
administration on. *See* ADMINISTRATION OF ESTATE
author..TA 1988 s 535(4)
beneficiary under non-resident trust..FA 1984 Sch 14 para 6(3)
CGT. *See under* CAPITAL GAINS TAX
deep discount securities..TA 1988 Sch 4 para 7(2)
offshore fund, disposal of material interest..TA 1988 s 757(3)
patent rights..TA 1988 s 525(2)
personal pension scheme payments on..TA 1988 s 633(1)(*d*), 636, 637
transfer of securities: accrued interest..TA 1988 s 721
underwriter..TA 1988 s 455
unquoted shares acquired on..CGTA 1979 Sch 6 para 7

DEBT
bad debts, discontinued trade..TA 1988 s 89
chargeable gains..CGTA 1979 s 134
interest on, funding bonds..TA 1988 s 582
interest relief restriction..TA 1988 s 353(3)
post-cessation receipts..TA 1988 s 103(4)(5)
set-off and released..TA 1988 s 94
transactions in..TA 1988 s 56

DECEASED PERSON
administration of estate. *See* ADMINISTRATION OF ESTATE

DECLARATION
jointly held property, as to..TA 1988 s 282B
taking office, on..TMA 1970 s 6 Sch 1

DEDUCTION AT SOURCE
annual interest..TA 1988 s 349
annual payments—
    certificate..TA 1988 s 352
    not out of profits..TA 1988 s 349 350

DEDUCTION AT SOURCE—*continued*
  annual payments—*continued*
    profits or gains..TA 1988 s 348
  basic rate..TA 1988 s 4(1)
  certificate..TA 1988 s 352
  deposit-taker, by. *See under* DEPOSIT-TAKER
  loan interest..TA 1988 s 354
  mortgage interest. *See* MORTGAGE INTEREST RELIEF
  over-deduction before annual Act..TA 1988 s 822
  relevant year of assessment..TA 1988 s 4(2)
  under-deduction before annual Act..TA 1988 s 521

DEEP DISCOUNT SECURITIES
  meaning..TA 1988 Sch 4 para 1
  accrued income, meaning..TA 1988 Sch 4 para 4(2)
  adjusted issue price, meaning..TA 1988 Sch 4 para 1
  amount payable on redemption, meaning..TA 1988 Sch 4 para 1
  anti-avoidance provision..TA 1988 Sch 4 para 5(6)
  associated companies..TA 1988 Sch 4 para 9
  charge to tax..TA 1988 Sch 4 para 2–4
  charities, exemption..TA 1988 Sch 4 para 14
  close companies..TA 1988 Sch 4 para 10
  company distributions..TA 1988 Sch 4 para 5(5)
  contract, time of disposal under..TA 1988 Sch 4 para 8
  converted securities..TA 1988 Sch 4 para 7(3)
  costs of obtaining loan finance..TA 1988 s 577
  deemed issue..TA 1988 Sch 4 para 1(3)
  discount—
    meaning..TA 1988 Sch 4 para 1
    deep discount, meaning..TA 1988 Sch 4 para 1
  disposal—
    meaning..TA 1988 Sch 4 para 7
    time of, disposal under contract..TA 1988 Sch 4 para 8
  early redemption..TA 1988 Sch 4 para 11
  exchanged securities..TA 1988 Sch 4 para 1(2), 7(3)
  gilts..TA 1988 Sch 4 para 19
  group of companies..TA 1988 Sch 4 para 9
  identification of securities..TA 1988 Sch 4 para 12
  income element—
    certificate, shown on..TA 1988 Sch 4 para 13(1)
    charge on income..TA 1988 Sch 4 para 5
    computation..TA 1988 Sch 4 para 4(3)(4)
    deduction from company profits..TA 1988 Sch 4 para 5
    linked, meaning..TA 1988 Sch 4 para 9(2)
  income period, meaning..TA 1988 Sch 4 para 1
  information..TA 1988 Sch 4 para 13
  no gain/no loss disposals..TA 1988 Sch 29 para 27
  non-gilts..TA 1988 Sch 4 para 20
  non-residents..TA 1988 Sch 4 para 4(5)(6)
  oil extraction activities..TA 1988 Sch 4 para 6
  pooling, exclusion..FA 1983 Sch 6 para 1(2)(*aa*)
  premiums trust fund, part of..TA 1988 Sch 4 para 18
  public body, issued by..TA 1988 Sch 4 para 1, 11A, 13(3)
  redemption date, meaning..TA 1988 Sch 4 para 1
  retirement benefit scheme, held by..TA 1988 Sch 4 para 15
  Sch D Cases III and IV..TA 1988 Sch 4 para 4(7)
  stock lending..TA 1988 Sch 4 para 16
  trustees, disposal by..TA 1988 Sch 4 para 17
  United Kingdom corporate bonds..TA 1988 Sch 4 para 2(2)
  yield to maturity, meaning..TA 1988 Sch 4 para 1

DEEP GAIN SECURITY
  meaning..FA 1989 Sch 11 para 1
  accrued income scheme, and..FA 1989 Sch 11 para 17
  acquisition of..FA 1989 Sch 11 para 4
  charity, held by..FA 1989 Sch 11 para 15
  convertible..FA 1989 Sch 11 para 3
  death of person entitled to..FA 1989 Sch 11 para 7
  gilts..FA 1989 Sch 11 para 20
  holding..FA 1989 Sch 11 para 4
  identification of..FA 1989 Sch 11 para 19
  indexed..FA 1989 Sch 11 para 22
  modification of provisions..FA 1989 Sch 11 para 23
  non-gilts..FA 1989 Sch 11 para 21

DEEP GAIN SECURITY—*continued*
premiums trust fund, part of..FA 1989 Sch 11 para 10
qualifying indexed securities..FA 1989 Sch 11 para 2
redemption of—
  charge to tax..FA 1989 Sch 11 para 6
  provisions not applying to..FA 1989 Sch 11 para 18
  trustees, by..FA 1989 Sch 11 para 11
retirement benefit scheme, held for..FA 1989 Sch 11 para 14
stock lending..FA 1989 Sch 11 para 16
transfer of—
  meaning..FA 1989 Sch 11 para 4
  charge to tax..FA 1989 Sch 11 para 5
  connected persons, between..FA 1989 Sch 11 para 8
  foreign currency, in..FA 1989 Sch 11 para 12
  market value, at..FA 1989 Sch 11 para 9
  trustees, by..FA 1989 Sch 11 para 11
trustees, transfer or redemption by..FA 1989 Sch 11 para 11
UK, receipts in..FA 1989 Sch 11 para 13

DEFERRED ANNUITY
capital gains..CGTA 1979 s 143
excess relief restriction..TA 1988 Sch 14 para 4
industrial assurance companies..TA 1988 Sch 14 para 3

DEFINITIONS. *See separate index* WORDS AND PHRASES *post*

DEMAND
payment of tax, for..TMA 1970 s 60(1)

DEMERGER
ACT relief—
  conditions..TA 1988 s 213
  exempt distributions..TA 1988 s 213(2)
CGT relief..FA 1980 Sch 18 para 9 10 15
chargeable payments—
  meaning..TA 1988 s 214(2)
  capital gains..FA 1980 Sch 18 para 15
  returns..TA 1988 s 216
  tax on..TA 1988 s 214(1)
clearance..TA 1988 s 215
income tax. *See* ACT relief *supra*
information..TA 1988 s 217(1)
returns..TA 1988 s 216
subsidiary, determination..TA 1988 s 218(3)

DEMOLITION
industrial buildings..CAA 1968 s 4(11)
machinery and plant..CAA 1968 s 36 FA 1971 Sch 8 para 14
mines, oil wells etc..CAA 1968 s 55
scientific research, as to..CAA 1968 s 92(4) 93(3)

DEPOSIT
meaning..TA 1988 s 481(3)
transactions in..TA 1988 s 56, 398

DEPOSIT-TAKER
meaning..TA 1988 s 481(2)
assessment to income tax etc..TA 1988 s 479(2)–(4)
certificate of deposit issued pre-13 March 1984..TA 1988 s 482(8)
composite rate, determination of..TA 1988 s 483
deduction of tax on interest..TA 1988 s 479(1)
deposit—
  meaning..TA 1988 s 481(3)
  appropriate person, meaning..TA 1988 s 482(6)
  branch, held at..TA 1988 s 482(7)
  composite rate deposit..TA 1988 s 480
  general client account deposit, meaning..TA 1988 s 482(6)
  pre-13 March 1984..TA 1988 s 482(8)
  pre-6 July 1984..TA 1988 s 482(9)
  qualifying time deposit, meaning..TA 1988 s 482(6)
  regulations, powers..TA 1988 s 482(11)(12)
  relevant deposit, meaning..TA 1988 s 481(4)(5)
  treatment as relevant deposit..TA 1988 s 482(5)
inspection of declarations..TA 1988 s 482(3)(4)

DEPOSIT-TAKER—continued
non-residents..TA 1988 s 481(5)(j)
prescribed classes..TA 1988 s 482(10)
qualifying certificate of deposit, meaning..TA 1988 s 482(6)

DESIGN
fees etc, deductibility..TA 1988 s 83
owner abroad, taxation in event of..TA 1988, s 537B
payment in respect of, relief for..TA 1988, s. 537A

DEVELOPMENT AREA
meaning..FA 1970 s 15(3)
capital allowances, transitional relief..FA 1984 Sch 12 para 4

DEVELOPMENT GAINS
tax on, abolition..FA 1985 s 93

DEVELOPMENT LAND TAX
abolition..FA 1985 s 93

DIRECTOR
meaning—
  benefits..TA 1988 s 168(8)
  close company..TA 1988 s 417(5)
  receipts basis assessment..TA 1988 s 202B(5)(6)
benefits. *See* BENEFITS IN KIND
director's or higher-paid employment, meaning..TA 1988 s 167(1)
full-time, meaning..TA 1988 s 139(11)
full-time working, meaning..TA 1988 s 168(10)
living accommodation provided for..TA 1988 s 145(5)
priority share allocation..FA 1988 s 68
return as to..TMA 1970 s 15(3)–(11)
share acquisition. *See* SHARE ACQUISITION SCHEME
tax paid by employer..TA 1988 s 164

DISABILITY PENSION
exemption..TA 1988 s 315

DISABLED PERSON
trust—
  meaning..TA 1988 s 715(8)
  transfer of securities: accrued interest..TA 1988 s 715(1)(e)
vehicle maintenance grant..TA 1988 s 327

DISABLEMENT PENSION
exemption..TA 1988 s 315

DISCLAIMER
writing-down and first-year allowances, machinery and plant..FA 1971 s 44(2A)

DISCOUNT
discounted bill. *See* DISCOUNTED BILL
Sch D Case III..TA 1988 s 18(3)

DISCOUNT HOUSE
meaning..TA 1988 s 78(6)
bills of exchange..TA 1988 s 78

DISCOUNTED BILL
bank, meaning..TA 1988 s 78(6)
conditions for relief..TA 1988 s 78(1)
discount house, meaning..TA 1988 s 78(6)
incidental costs..TA 1988 s 78(4)(5)
relief..TA 1988 s 78(2)
restriction on relief..TA 1988 s 78(3)

DISCRETIONARY SETTLEMENT
meaning..FA 1988 s 100(2)
capital gains tax..FA 1988 s 100(1)

DISCRETIONARY TRUST
additional rate..TA 1988 s 686
overseas tax, relief..TA 1988 s 809

DISCRETIONARY TRUST—*continued*
  payments under..TA 1988 s 687
  recovery of higher rate from beneficiary..TA 1988 s 689

DISPOSITION
  meaning..TA 1988 s 660(3)

DISTRESS
  tax, for..TMA 1970 s 61

DISTRIBUTION. *See* COMPANY DISTRIBUTION

DIVER
  Sch D Case I..TA 1988 s 314

DIVIDEND. *See also* STOCK DIVIDEND
  meaning..TA 1988 s 45
  abnormal, meaning..TA 1988 s 709(4)
  date of payment..TA 1988 s 834(3)
  dividend stripping..TA 1970 s 281
  foreign. *See* FOREIGN DIVIDEND
  manufactured..TA 1988 s 737
  preference—
    meaning..TA 1988 s 832(1)
    over-deduction..TA 1988 s 822
  public revenue. *See* PUBLIC REVENUE DIVIDEND

DIVIDEND WARRANT
  statement of tax deductions..TA 1988 s 234

DOCK
  meaning..CAA 1968 s 7(5)
  Sch D Case I..TA 1988 s 55

DOCUMENT
  meaning..TMA 1970 s 20D(3)
  copies..TMA 1970 s 20B(4)
  delivery of..TMA 1970 s 115
  entry powers..TMA 1970 s 20C
  falsification etc of..TMA 1970 s 20BB
  loss etc..TMA 1970 s 112
  power to require. *See under* INFORMATION
  removal, procedure for..TMA 1970 s 20CC
  service of..TMA 1970 s 115

DOMESTIC SERVICES
  charge to tax..TA 1988 s 154(2)

DOMICILE
  abroad, CGT..CGTA 1979 s 14
  Sch E, determination..TA 1988 s 207

DOUBLE TAXATION RELIEF
  ACT, and..TA 1988 s 797(4)(5)
  agreement, by—
    effect..TA 1988 s 788
    power to make regulations..TA 1988 s 791
    UK partners of non-resident partnership..TA 1988 s 112(4)
  arrangements specified in Orders in Council..TA 1988 s 788(1)
  branches of non-resident banks..TA 1988 s 794(2)
  business carried on by non-resident..TA 1988 s 808
  capital gains tax..CGTA 1979 s 10
  chargeable gains..TA 1988 s 797
  commencement years—
    meaning..TA 1988 s 804(8)
    relief..TA 1988 s 804
  controlled foreign company..TA 1988 Sch 26 para 4–6
  credit, by—
    computation..TA 1988 s 795
    corporation tax..TA 1988 s 797
    election against..TA 1988 s 805
    income tax..TA 1988 s 796
    reduction of UK taxes by credit due..TA 1988 s 793
    residence..TA 1988 s 794

DOUBLE TAXATION RELIEF—continued
  credit, by—*continued*
    time limit..TA 1988 s 806
    transfer of securities: accrued income..TA 1988 s 807
  deduction for foreign tax..TA 1988 s 811
  disclosure of information..TA 1988 s 816
  discretionary trusts..TA 1988 s 809
  foreign loan interest..TA 1988 s 798
  foreign tax—
    meaning..TA 1988 s 792(1)
    deduction where no credit..TA 1988 s 811
  income eligible for, meaning..TA 1988 s 278(7)
  insurance companies..TA 1988 s 802
  interest on overseas loans..TA 1988 s 798
  offshore fund..TA 1988 Sch 27 para 5(4)
  overseas life insurance companies..TA 1988 s 449
  overseas tax, meaning..TA 1988 s 804(8)
  postponement of capital allowances, post-1970 expenditure..TA 1988 s 810
  qualifying reliefs..TA 1988 s 788
  related companies—
    dividends not covered by arrangements..TA 1988 s 800
    UK and third country taxes..TA 1988 s 801
  spared tax, meaning..TA 1988 s 798(4)
  subsidiary, meaning..TA 1988 s 792(2)
  tax credits..FA 1989 s 115
  transfer of securities: accrued income..TA 1988 s 807
  UK taxes, meaning..TA 1988 s 792(1)
  underlying tax—
    meaning..TA 1988 s 792(1)
    computation..TA 1988 s 799
    insurance companies trading overseas..TA 1988 s 802
    interest on loans..TA 1988 s 803
    less than 10% voting power..TA 1988 s 790(6)–(10)
    related companies..TA 1988 s 800
    UK and third country taxes..TA 1988 s 801
  unilateral—
    meaning..TA 1988 s 790(2)
    Channel Islands..TA 1988 s 790(5)
    connected companies..TA 1988 s 790(6)
    credit, by..TA 1988 s 790(1)
    Isle of Man..TA 1988 s 790(5)
    Sch D Case VI..TA 1988 s 790(11)
  USA..TA 1988 Sch 30 para 14

DREDGING
  capital allowances..CAA 1968 s 67
  initial allowance, withdrawal..FA 1985 s 61
  writing-down allowance..CAA 1968 s 75

DWELLING
  scientific research: provision of..CAA 1968 s 91(1B)

DWELLING-HOUSE
  assured tenancy, capital allowances. *See* ASSURED TENANCY
  business expansion scheme. *See* BUSINESS EXPANSION SCHEME
  qualifying, meaning (assured tenancy)..FA 1982 Sch 12 para 3(1), FA 1988 s 50(3)

EASEMENT
  meaning..TA 1988 s 119(3)
  electric lines etc..TA 1988 s 120
  mines, quarries etc..TA 1988 s 119
  Schedule A..TA 1988 s 15(3)

EDUCATION
  technical, deductible expense..TA 1988 s 84

EDUCATIONAL BODY
  employees seconded to..TA 1988 s 86

ELECTION
  appeal to Special Commissioners..TMA 1970 s 31(3)–(6) Sch 2 para 1(1)–(1E)
  beneficial loan, as to..TA 1988 Sch 7 para 5

ELECTION—*continued*
   capital allowances, long lease..FA 1978 s 37(1)–(3)
   carry-back, post-cessation receipts..TA 1988 s 108
   copyright payments, as to..TA 1988 s 535(5)–(7)
   double taxation relief by credit..TA 1988 s 805
   eligible expenditure, writing-down allowances..FA 1976 s 39(5)
   group income..TA 1988 s 248
   herd basis..TA 1988 Sch 5 para 2, 12
   maintenance fund for historic building..TA 1988 s 27, 691(2)–(4)
   payment by instalments, share options..TA 1988 s 137
   pooling, for. *See* POOLING
   replacement of machinery or plant, on..CAA 1968 s 40
   retirement relief—
      reorganisation, equation of shares..FA 1985 Sch 20 para 2
      spouse's interest, aggregation..FA 1985 Sch 20 para 16(2)
   separate assessment..TA 1988 s 283
   separate taxation..TA 1988 s 287, 288
   stock relief—
      succession, on..TA 1988 Sch 30 para 19
   terminal loss relief, minerals..FA 1970 Sch 6 para 5
   valuation at April 1965..CGTA 1979 Sch 5 para 12
   woodlands, Sch D..TA 1988 s 54

ELECTRIC LINE
   wayleave rents..TA 1988 s 120

ELECTRICITY BOARD
   meaning..TA 1988 s 511(6)
   corporation tax..TA 1988 s 511

ELECTRICITY COUNCIL
   corporation tax..TA 1988 s 511

EMOLUMENT
   employees', return of..TMA 1970 s 15
   evidence as to..TMA 1970 s 70(4)
   foreign. *See* FOREIGN EMOLUMENT
   Sch E..TA 1988 s 19
   termination payments..TA 1988 Sch 11 para 8
   UK, received in..TA 1988 s 132(5)
   year of assessment, received after..TMA 1970 s 35

EMPLOYEE
   meaning..TMA 1970 s 15(11)(*a*) TA 1988 s 612(1)
   accommodation provided for. *See under* ACCOMMODATION
   benefits. *See* BENEFITS IN KIND
   charity, seconded to..TA 1988 s 86
   educational body, seconded to..TA 1988 s 86
   full-time, meaning..TA 1988 s 361(8)
   investment in employee-controlled companies..TA 1988 s 361(3)(4)
   non-resident, employed by..FA 1974 s 24
   overseas, pension funds..TA 1988 s 614
   priority share allocations..FA 1988 s 68
   retirement relief, disposal..FA 1985 s 70(1)(2) Sch 20 para 4(1)(*b*)
   return of emoluments..TMA 1970 s 15
   securities, new holding, pooling..FA 1985 Sch 19 para 8(2)
   share acquisition. *See* SHARE ACQUISITION SCHEME
   share schemes..TA 1988 s 185–187, Sch 9
   training, costs of, relief for..TA 1988 s 588
   work done abroad. *See* WORK DONE ABROAD

EMPLOYEE SHARE OWNERSHIP TRUST
   acquisition, rules about..FA 1989 Sch 5 para 11
   beneficiaries..FA 1989 Sch 5 para 4
   borrowing..FA 1989 s 71
   chargeable amounts..FA 1989 s 70 72
   chargeable events..FA 1989 s 69 72
   charges to tax..FA 1989 s 68 71
   continuation of..FA 1989 Sch 5 para 12 13
   establishment of..FA 1989 Sch 5 para 2
   features not to be included in..FA 1989 Sch 5 para 10
   information, inspector requiring..FA 1989 s 73
   material interest, person having..FA 1989 Sch 5 para 16
   payments to, tax relief..FA 1989 s 67

EMPLOYEE SHARE OWNERSHIP TRUST—*continued*
    qualifying company..FA 1989 s 68(6)
    qualifying purposes..FA 1989 s 67(4), 69(5)
    qualifying trusts..FA 1989 Sch 5 para 1
    retention of securities..FA 1989 Sch 5 para 11
    securities held by..FA 1989 Sch 5 para 7–9 14
    transfer of securities..FA 1989 Sch 5 para 11
    trustees—
        functions of..FA 1989 Sch 5 para 5
        rules for..FA 1989 Sch 5 para 3
        sums received, use of..FA 1989 Sch 5 para 6

EMPLOYEE TRUST
    capital gains..CGTA 1979 s 149

EMPLOYERS' ASSOCIATION
    exemptions..TA 1988 s 467, FA 1988 Sch 3 para 17
    registration..TA 1988 s 467(4)(*b*)

EMPLOYMENT
    meaning..TA 1988 s 168(2)
    benefits. *See* BENEFITS IN KIND
    income from. *See* SCHEDULE E
    payment on removal from. *See* TERMINATION PAYMENT

ENTERPRISE ALLOWANCE
    charge to tax under Schedule D Case VI..TA 1988 s 127

ENTERPRISE ZONE
    meaning..FA 1980 s 74(2)
    balancing adjustments on non-qualifying use..FA 1981 s 75(4)(5)
    commercial building, meaning..FA 1980 s 74(4)
    initial allowance..FA 1980 Sch 13 para 1 2
    qualifying hotels..FA 1980 s 74(3)
    relief..FA 1980 s 74(1)
    sales post-March 1981..FA 1981 s 76
    short-term leasing..FA 1980 s 74(6)
    thermal insulation..FA 1980 s 74(6)
    use as qualifying building or structure..FA 1980 Sch 13 para 4
    writing-down allowance..FA 1980 Sch 13 para 3

ENTERTAINER
    activity treated as part of trade..TA 1988 s 556
    charge on profits or gains..TA 1988 s 557
    income attributed to..TA 1988 s 556(2)–(4)
    payment of tax..TA 1988 s 555
    valuation..TA 1988 s 558

ENTERTAINMENT
    business. *See* BUSINESS ENTERTAINMENT
    capital allowances..CAA 1968 s 82(2)
    charge to tax..TA 1988 s 154(2)
    credit token for..TA 1988 s 142(3B)
    director and higher-paid employees, of..TA 1988 s 155(7)
    voucher used for..TA 1988 s 141(6B)

ENTRY POWERS
    valuation of land..TMA 1970 s 110
    warrant, with..TMA 1970 s 20C

ERROR. *See* MISTAKE

ESTATE
    administration. *See* ADMINISTRATION OF ESTATE
    foreign. *See* FOREIGN ESTATE
    United Kingdom estate, meaning..TA 1988 s 701(9)

ESTATE DUTY
    valuation..CGTA 1979 Sch 6 para 9 26
    works of art..CGTA 1979 Sch 6 para 24

EUROBOND
    meaning..TA 1988 s 732(5)
    interest on quoted..TA 1988 s 124

EUROBOND—*continued*
  quoted, meaning..TA 1988 s 124(6)
  recognised clearing system, meaning..TA 1988 s 124(6)
  returns..TA 1988 s 124(3)

EUROPEAN ASSEMBLY
  terminal grants to representatives..TA 1988 s 190

EUROPEAN ECONOMIC COMMUNITY
  disclosure of information..FA 1978 s 77

EVIDENCE
  appeals..TMA 1970 s 52
  emoluments, of..TMA 1970 s 70(4)
  fraud etc, where..TMA 1970 s 105
  profits, of..TMA 1970 s 101
  recovery of tax..TMA 1970 s 70

EXCHANGE CONTROL
  interest on overdue tax..TMA 1970 s 92

EXEMPT FUND
  distributions of..TA 1988 s 235 236

EXPENSES
  business entertaining. *See* BUSINESS ENTERTAINMENT
  defrayed from emoluments..TA 1988 s 199
  directors' and higher-paid employees'..TA 1988 s 153
  living accommodation provided for employee..TA 1988 s 145
  relief under Sch E..TA 1988 s 198
  Special Commissioners'..TMA 1970 s 4(6)
  work done abroad. *See* WORK DONE ABROAD

EXPORT CREDITS
  payments under investment insurance scheme..TA 1988 s 88 441(9) 584(5)

EXTENSION OF TIME
  general provision..TMA 1970 s 118(2)

FAIR
  chargeable person..TA 1988 s 59(3)
  Sch D Case I..TA 1988 s 55

FAMILY
  company.. *See* FAMILY COMPANY
  credit..TA 1988 s 617(2)

FAMILY COMPANY
  meaning..CGTA 1979 s 124(8) FA 1985 Sch 20 para 1(2)
  chargeable business asset..FA 1985 Sch 20 para 12(2)
  dealing by individual..CGTA 1979 s 120
  gifts of business assets..CGTA 1979 s 126
  retirement relief—
    capital distribution..CGTA 1979 s 125 FA 1985 s 69(2)(*c*)
    post-April 1985 disposal..FA 1985 s 69 Sch 20
    transfer pre-April 1985..CGTA 1979 s 124

FAMILY INCOME POLICY
  relief..TA 1988 Sch 15 para 9

FARM ANIMALS
  death or destruction..TA 1988 Sch 5 para 3(12)
  herd basis. *See* HERD BASIS
  immature..TA 1988 Sch 5 para 8(2)–(4)
  maturity, time of..TA 1988 Sch 5 para 8(3)
  replacements..TA 1988 Sch 5 para 3(5)
  Sch D Case I..TA 1988 s 97
  stock relief..TA 1988 Sch 30 para 19
  trading stock—
    general provisions..TA 1988 Sch 5 para 1
  working animals..TA 1988 Sch 5 para 7

FARM LAND
meaning..TA 1988 s 832(1)

FARMING
animals. *See* FARM ANIMALS; HERD BASIS
fluctuating profits..TA 1988 s 96
loss relief..TA 1988 s 397
machinery and plant..FA 1971 Sch 8 para 2(2)
Sch D Case I..TA 1988 s 53

FEE
professional bodies etc..TA 1988 s 201
returns..TMA 1970 s 16

FERRY
Sch D Case I..TA 1988 s 55

FEU DUTY
Schedule A..TA 1988 s 15(1)

FILM
meaning..FA 1982 s 72(2)
accounting periods..FA 1982 s 72(3)
allocation of expenditure..FA 1982 s 72(3)(4)
British..Films Act 1972 Sch 1 para 4
certification..FA 1982 s 72(8)
expenditure of a revenue nature, meaning..FA 1982 s 72(9)
labour costs..Films Act 1972 Sch 1 para 6–8
post-March 1982..FA 1982 s 72
pre-March 1984..FA 1982 s 72(7)
qualifying, certification of..Films Act 1972 Sch 1
trading receipts..FA 1982 s 72(6)
trading stock, as..FA 1982 s 72(5)

FINANCIAL FUTURES
meaning..TA 1988 s 128
dealings by pension funds etc..TA 1988 s 659
dealings, capital gains tax..FA 1985 s 72(1)–(4)

FIRE PRECAUTIONS
capital allowances..FA 1974 s 17 FA 1975 s 15

FIRST-YEAR ALLOWANCE
assets leased abroad..FA 1982 s 70(4)
exclusion..FA 1971 Sch 8 para 1
machinery and plant. *See under* MACHINERY AND PLANT
restriction of set-off..FA 1976 s 41
ships..FA 1971 Sch 8 para 8
short-term leasing..FA 1980 s 64
television sets etc..FA 1980 Sch 12 Pt II
withdrawal..FA 1976 s 41(3) FA 1984 s 58 Sch 12

FISHINGS
chargeable person..TA 1988 s 59(3)
Sch D Case I..TA 1988 s 55

FIXTURES
meaning..FA 1985 s 59(1)
machinery and plant, allowances..FA 1985 s 56 Sch 17

FOREIGN COMPANY. *See* CONTROLLED FOREIGN COMPANY; NON-RESIDENT COMPANY; OVERSEAS LIFE INSURANCE COMPANY

FOREIGN CONCESSION
meaning..CAA 1968 s 87(1) FA 1971 Sch 8 para 7(2)

FOREIGN CURRENCY
assets acquired with borrowed..CGTA 1979 Sch 6 para 17
bank accounts..CGTA 1979 s 18(4)(*j*)
deposit with deposit-taker..FA 1984 Sch 8 para 6(1)
interest payments..TA 1988 s 82(2) 340(1)
local authority borrowing..TA 1988 s 581
personal use, CGT..CGTA 1979 s 133

FOREIGN CURRENCY—*continued*
  statutory corporation borrowing..TA 1988 s 581
  transfer of securities: accrued interest..TA 1988 s 710(12) 713(8)

FOREIGN DIVIDEND
  meaning..TA 1988 s 123(1)
  anti-avoidance provisions..TA 1988 s 123(6)
  beneficiary..TA 1988 s 123(5)
  charge to tax..TA 1988 s 123(2)
  chargeable persons..TA 1988 Sch 3 para 6
  collected abroad..TA 1988 s 123(3)
  non-residents..TA 1988 s 123(4)
  paying agents..TA 1988 s 123(2)
  public revenue..TA 1988 s 48(4)
  recognised clearing system, in, TA 1988 s 48(4)

FOREIGN EMOLUMENT. *See also* FOREIGN INCOME
  meaning..TA 1988 s 192(1)
  amount..TA 1988 s 192(5)
  deduction allowable..TA 1988 s 192(3)(4)
  excepted..TA 1988 s 192(2)
  Sch E..TA 1988 s 19(1)
  seafarers, of..TA 1988 Sch 12 para 3(2A) FA 1988 s 67
  work done abroad..TA 1988 Sch 12 para 3

FOREIGN ESTATE
  meaning..TA 1988 s 701(10)
  absolute interest..TA 1988 s 696(3)(6)
  limited interest..TA 1988 s 695(4)

FOREIGN INCOME
  delayed remittance..TA 1988 s 585
  Export Credits Guarantee Dept..TA 1988 s 584(5)
  unremittable—
    meaning..TA 1988 s 584(1)
    appeal..TA 1988 s 584(9)
    controlled foreign company..TA 1988 Sch 24 para 12
    deceased persons..TA 1988 s 484(7)
    determination..TA 1988 s 484(8)
    relief..TA 1988 s 484(2)

FOREIGN PENSION
  deduction..TA 1988 s 196
  Sch D Case V..TA 1988 s 58

FOREIGN POSSESSIONS
  Sch D Case V..TA 1988 s 18(3)

FOREIGN SECURITIES. *See* OVERSEAS SECURITIES

FOREIGN SERVICE
  termination payments..TA 1988 Sch 11 para 10

FOREIGN STATE
  tax credit..TA 1988 s 232

FOREIGN TAX
  meaning..TA 1988 s 792(1)

FOREIGN TRADE
  stock relief..TA 1988 Sch 30 para 19

FOREIGN TRAVEL. *See also* WORK DONE ABROAD
  expenses connected with..TA 1988 s 80 81 193–195

FORESTRY INCOME
  meaning..CAA 1968 s 69

FORESTRY LAND. *See also* WOODLAND
  meaning..CAA 1968 s 69
  agricultural buildings allowance, abolition..FA 1989 s 120

FRANKED INVESTMENT INCOME
meaning..TA 1988 s 238 832(1)
ACT calculation..TA 1988 s 241
capital allowances..TA 1988 s 242(2)(*d*)
capital redemption business..TA 1988 s 458(2)
claim for set-off..TA 1988 Sch 13 para 5, 6
errors..TA 1988 Sch 13 para 4
general annuity business..TA 1988 s 437(4)(5)
insurance companies..TA 1988 s 434
life insurance business..TA 1988 s 434
pension business..TA 1988 s 438(3)–(6)
receipt after payment of ACT..TA 1988 Sch 13 para 4
returns..TA 1988 Sch 13 para 1, 2
set-off brought forward..TA 1988 s 243
surplus—
  meaning..TA 1988 s 238
  set-off against..TA 1988 s 242
terminal losses..TA 1988 s 243(5)
time for claims..TA 1988 s 242(8) 243(6)

FRANKED PAYMENT
meaning..TA 1988 s 238 832(1)
errors..TA 1988 Sch 13 para 8
returns..TA 1988 Sch 13 para 1 2

FRAUD
assessment where..TMA 1970 s 36 37
evidence..TMA 1970 s 105
interest on overdue tax..TMA 1970 s 88
penalties. *See* PENALTY

FRIENDLY SOCIETY
amalgamation..TA 1988 s 460(9)(10) 466(3)(4)
appeal..TA 1970 s 335(4A)
deduction from premium..TA 1988 Sch 14 para 3
exemption limits..TA 1988 s 460(2)–(7) 464
incorporation..TA 1988 s 460(11) 461(4)
insurances between June 1984 and March 1985..TA 1988 s 462(3)
life assurance business, meaning..TA 1988 s 466(2)
life assurance relief..TA 1988 Sch 13 para 3, 4, 6
life or endowment business, meaning..TA 1988 s 466(2)
part payments to, relief..TA 1988 s 266(6)
policy, meaning..TA 1988 s 466(2)
qualifying distributions..TA 1988 s 461(3)
registered—
  amalgamation..TA 1988 s 466(3)(4)
  contracts made pre-1966..TA 1988 s 462(2)
  corporation tax..TA 1988 s 463
  exemption..TA 1988 s 460
  life or endowment business..TA 1988 s 463, 466(1)
  new societies, meaning..TA 1988 s 466(2)
  old societies—
    meaning..TA 1988 s 465(1)
    life or endowment business..TA 1988 s 460(2)
    post-March 1985 control..TA 1988 s 465
tax exempt business—
  conditions for..TA 1988 s 462
tax exempt life or endowment business, meaning..TA 1988 s 466(2)
tax exempt limits..TA 1988 s 460(2)–(7) 464
tax liability..TA 1988 s 461
transfer of engagements..TA 1988 s 460(9)(10)
unregistered, exemption..TA 1988 s 459

FUND IN COURT
accrued income scheme..TA 1988 s 328(2)–(4)
meaning..CGTA 1979 s 99(3)
capital gains..CGTA 1979 s 99 FA 1980 s 81
claim..TA 1988 s 328(1)
designation agreement..TA 1988 s 328(7)
exemption..TA 1988 s 328(1)
fresh income..TA 1988 s 328(5)
information, duty to provide..TA 1988 s 328(6)
Northern Ireland..TA 1988 s 328(8)

FUNDING BOND
meaning..TA 1988 s 582(4)
interest on debt..TA 1988 s 582

FURNISHED HOLIDAY LETTING
adjustment of tax charged..TA 1988 s 503(7)
apportionment..TA 1988 s 503(6)
capital gains tax..FA 1984 Sch 11 para 4 5
claims..TA 1988 s 504(6)(7)
commercial letting, meaning..TA 1988 s 504(2)
deductible expenditure..TA 1988 s 503(5)
holiday accommodation—
   meaning..TA 1988 s 504(2)
   determination whether..TA 1988 s 504(4)(5)
let, meaning..TA 1988 s 504(9)
losses..TA 1988 s 503(3)(4)
part holiday accommodation..TA 1988 s 503(6)
pre-trading expenditure..TA 1988 s 503(2)–(4)
private residence relief..FA 1984 Sch 11 para 5
Sch D Case VI..TA 1988 s 503(1)
trade, treatment as..TA 1988 s 503

GAS BOARD
corporation tax..TA 1988 s 511(7)

GAS COUNCIL
corporation tax..TA 1988 s 511(7)

GENERAL COMMISSIONERS
appeal from..TMA 1970 s 56
appeal to—
   out of time..TMA 1970 s 49(2)
   right of..TMA 1970 s 31(4)(6)
appointment..TMA 1970 s 2
Board member's attendance..TMA 1970 s 50(3)
case stated. *See* CASE STATED
certificate, interest on unpaid tax..TMA 1970 s 70(3)
clerk. *See* CLERK TO GENERAL COMMISSIONERS
declaration on taking office..TMA 1970 s 6(1)(5) Sch 1 Pt I
divisions..FA 1973 s 41
finality of decision..TMA 1970 s 46(2)
jurisdiction..TMA 1970 s 44
personal interest..TMA 1970 s 5(1)
power to obtain information..TMA 1970 s 51 53
quorum..TMA 1970 s 44(5)
Scotland..TMA 1970 s 2(3)(4)
service on..TMA 1970 s 115(4)
summary penalties..TMA 1970 s 53
term of office..TMA 1970 s 2(7)
transfer of appeal..TMA 1970 s 44(3) (3A)
validity of proceedings..TMA 1970 s 2(8)

GIFT
business assets. *See under* CAPITAL GAINS TAX
business entertainment..TA 1988 s 577(8)
charity, to..CGTA 1979 s 146
emigration of donee..FA 1981 s 79
foreign-controlled company, to..CGTA 1979 s 126B
housing association, to..CGTA 1979s 146A
inheritance tax chargeable on..CGTA 1979 s 147A
instalments, payment of tax by..CGTA 1979 s 7A
non-resident, to..CGTA 1979 s 5A 147B
offshore income gain..TA 1988 Sch 28 para 3(3)
recovery from donee..CGTA 1979 s 59
settlement, into..CGTA 1979 s 53 FA 1986 s 58

GILT-EDGED SECURITIES
meaning..CGTA 1979 Sch 2 para 1
authorised unit trusts..TA 1988 s 468
building society, transfer of business by..FA 1988 Sch 12 para 2
company disposals..TA 1970 s 270
compensation stock..CGTA 1979 s 84

GILT-EDGED SECURITIES—*continued*
indexation allowance..FA 1985 s 68(2)(*a*)
index-linked..TA 1988 s 439(6)–(8)
list..CGTA 1979 Sch 2 Pt II
long-term gains, exemption..CGTA 1979 s 67
publication..CGTA 1979 Sch 2 para 2
redemption date pre-1979..CGTA 1979 Sch 6 para 19(1)

GOODWILL
know-how sales..TA 1988 s 531(2)
rollover relief..CGTA 1979 s 118

GOVERNMENT INVESTMENT
written-off..TA 1988 s 400

GOVERNMENT SECURITIES. *See also* GILT-EDGED SECURITIES
converted..TA 1988 s 52
interest paid without deduction—
  Northern Ireland securities..TA 1988 s 51
  UK..TA 1988 s 50
non-resident, held by—
  foreign..TA 1988 s 48
  UK..TA 1988 s 47
non-resident central banks, held by..TA 1988 s 516
restricted—
  meaning..TA 1988 s 439(5)
  gains etc, treatment..TA 1988 s 439(1)–(4)

GRANT
disabled person's vehicle..TA 1988 s 327
investment. *See* INVESTMENT GRANT

GRATUITY
armed forces..TA 1988 s 316

GRAVEL PIT
Sch D Case I..TA 1988 s 55(2)

GROUND RENT
Schedule A..TA 1988 s 15(1)

GROUP (COMPANIES)
meaning..TA 1970 s 272(1)(*b*)
approved share option scheme..TA 1988 Sch 9 para 1(3)(4)
cessation of membership—
  charge to tax..TA 1970 s 278
  mergers..TA 1970 s 278A
  shares in subsidiary..TA 1970 s 279
company leaving, deemed disposal by..TA 1970 s 278
company, meaning..TA 1970 s 272(2)
controlled foreign company, assumptions..TA 1988 Sch 24 para 5–7
corporate bonds..FA 1984 s 64(6)
demerger. *See* DEMERGER
depreciatory transaction, meaning..TA 1970 s 280(1)
disposal or acquisition outside..TA 1970 s 275
distributions..TA 1988 s 254
dividend stripping..TA 1970 s 281
factors determining..TA 1970 s 272(1A)–(1D)
group income. *See* GROUP INCOME
group relief. *See* GROUP RELIEF
identification of securities..FA 1982 s 89(2)
London Transport Executive..TA 1970 s 272(6)
loss-making transactions..TA 1970 s 280
mergers, exemption..TA 1970 s 278A
non-resident, CGT..CGTA 1979 s 16
pooling, election for..CGTA 1979 Sch 5 para 5
principal company, meaning..TA 1970 s 272(1)(*c*)
profit-related pay, scheme employers..TA 1988 s 173(2)(3)
purchase of own shares..TA 1988 s 222
recovery of tax..TA 1988 s 347
replacement of business assets..TA 1970 s 276
share option schemes..TA 1988 Sch 9 para 1(3)
tax refund, surrender of..FA 1989 s 102
trading group, meaning..TA 1988 s 576(5)

GROUP (COMPANIES)—*continued*
transfers within—
 disposals..TA 1970 s 273 FA 1985 s 71(6)(7) Sch 21 para 4
 trading stock..TA 1970 s 274
transport boards..TA 1970 s 272(5)
value-shifting. *See* CAPITAL GAINS TAX

GROUP INCOME
ACT..TA 1988 s 247(6)(7)
consortia..TA 1988 s 247(9)(*c*)
controlled foreign company, assumptions..TA 1988 Sch 24 para 5–7
election for..FA 1972 s 91(4) TA 1988 s 248
exclusions..TA 1988 s 247(5)
income tax..TA 1988 s 247(6)(7)
qualifying income..TA 1988 s 247(1)–(4)
regulations..TA 1988 s 248(1)
subsidiary, determination..TA 1988 s 247(8)

GROUP RELIEF
accounting periods..TA 1988 s 408
adjustments..TA 1988 s 412(4)
apportionment..TA 1988 s 409
capital allowances..TA 1988 s 407(2)
change in group membership..TA 1988 s 409
claim..TA 1988 s 402(1) 412
consortia..TA 1988 s 405 413(6)
controlled foreign company..TA 1988 Sch 24 para 5–7 Sch 26 para 1(4)
convertible shares or securities, treatment of..TA 1988 Sch 18 para 1
double allowance exclusion..TA 1988 s 411
dual resident companies—
 accounting periods covering 1 April 1987..TA 1988 Sch 17 para 1–3
 appeals..TA 1988 Sch 17 para 7
 charges on income, early payment of..TA 1988 Sch 17 para 6
 companies joining or leaving group..TA 1988 Sch 17 para 8
 interest, early payment of..TA 1988 Sch 17 para 5
 limitation of relief..TA 1988 s 404
entitlement—
 conditions..TA 1988 s 402
limited partners..TA 1988 s 118
normal commercial loan, meaning..TA 1988 Sch 18 para 1(5)
notional winding-up..TA 1988 Sch 18 para 3
oil extraction activities..TA 1988 s 492(8)
partnerships involving companies..TA 1988 s 116
payment for—
 meaning..TA 1988 s 402(6)
 treatment..TA 1988 s 402
profit distribution..TA 1988 Sch 18 para 2
profits or assets available for distribution..TA 1988 Sch 18
public corporation, transfer of assets..TA 1988 s 410(7)
qualifying companies..TA 1988 s 413(3)
relation to other relief..TA 1988 s 407
subsidiary, determination..TA 1988 s 413(5)
transfer of company to another group..TA 1988 s 410
types..TA 1988 s 403

GUARANTEE
qualifying loan, repayment of..CGTA 1979 s 136(4)

GUARDIAN
chargeability—
 capital gains tax..TMA 1970 s 77
 income tax..TMA 1970 s 72 73
 protection..TMA 1970 s 76

HARBOUR AUTHORITY
meaning..TA 1988 s 518(10)
transfer of trade to..TA 1988 s 518(1)

HARBOUR REORGANISATION SCHEME
meaning..TA 1988 s 518(10)
chargeable gains..TA 1988 s 518(7)
corporation tax..TA 1988 s 518

HERD BASIS
additions to herd..TA 1988 Sch 5 para 3, 8(3)
adjustments..TA 1988 Sch 5 para 11
computation..TA 1988 Sch 5 para 3
election..TA 1988 Sch 5 para 2, 12
herd, meaning..TA 1988 Sch 5 para 8
information..TA 1988 Sch 5 para 10
production herd—
  meaning..TA 1988 Sch 5 para 8(5)
  cessation..TA 1988 Sch 5 para 4
  class..TA 1988 Sch 5 para 8(6)
  slaughter..TA 1988 Sch 5 para 6
  transfer..TA 1988 Sch 5 para 5
repayments..TA 1988 Sch 5 para 11
sale of herd..TA 1988 Sch 5 para 3(8)–(11)
stock relief..TA 1988 Sch 30 para 19

HIGH COURT
appeal from..TMA 1970 s 56(8)
appeal to..TMA 1970 s 56
recovery of tax..TMA 1970 s 68

HIRE
vehicles—
  capital allowance..FA 1971 Sch 8 para 12
  deductions limit..CAA 1968 Sch 2 para 9
  first-year allowance..FA 1971 s 43(2)

HIRE-PURCHASE
capital gains tax..CGTA 1979 s 24
cars..CAA 1968 Sch 2 para 10
hire-purchase agreement, meaning..TA 1988 s 784(6)
leased assets..TA 1988 s 784
machinery and plant..CAA 1968 Sch 3 FA 1971 s 45

HISTORIC BUILDING
maintenance fund. *See under* MAINTENANCE FUND

HISTORIC BUILDINGS AND MONUMENTS COMMISSION
exemption..TA 1988 s 507(1)

HOLDING COMPANY
meaning..TA 1988 s 413(3)

HOLIDAY LETTING. *See* FURNISHED HOLIDAY LETTING

HOME IMPROVEMENT
housing association, loan to..FA 1988 s 43(3)
loan interest..TA 1988 s 355(2A)–(2C) 356(1A) 372

HOPS MARKETING BOARD
transfer of assets..FA 1982 s 148

HOTEL
balancing adjustments on non-qualifying use..FA 1981 s 75(4)(5)
balancing allowances and charges..FA 1978 Sch 6 para 4
capital allowances..FA 1978 s 38 FA 1985 s 66(2)
enterprise zone. *See* ENTERPRISE ZONE
initial allowances..FA 1978 Sch 6 para 1 FA 1985 s 66
household accommodation..FA 1978 s 38(6)(*b*)
letting bedroom, meaning..FA 1978 s 38(3)
qualifying, meaning..FA 1978 s 38(2)
sales post-March 1981..FA 1981 s 76
season, meaning..FA 1978 s 38(3)
temporary disuse..FA 1978 Sch 6 para 7
workers' accommodation..FA 1978 s 38(6)(*a*)

HOUSE. *See* ASSURED TENANCY; DWELLING-HOUSE

HOUSE OF LORDS
appeal to..TMA 1970 s 56(10)

HOUSEBOAT
restriction on interest relief..TA 1988 s 354–357, FA 1988 s 44

HOUSING ASSOCIATION
meaning..FA 1988 s 43(3)(*a*)
co-operative. *See* CO-OPERATIVE HOUSING ASSOCIATION
disposals of land..TA 1970 s 342A(1) 342B
gift of land to..CGTA 1979 s 146A
home improvement loan, interest on..FA 1988 s 43(3)
Northern Ireland..TA 1970 s 341A(12)
registered, meaning..TA 1970 s 342A(2)
relevant loan interest..FA 1988 s 44(6)
self-build. *See* SELF-BUILD SOCIETY

HOUSING BENEFIT
exemption from income tax..TA 1988 s 617(2)

HOUSING CORPORATION
disposal of land—
    housing associations..TA 1970 s 342A(1)
    housing societies..TA 1970 s 342
    related assets, meaning..TA 1970 s 342

HOUSING GRANT
exemption..TA 1988 s 578

HOUSING SOCIETY
meaning..TA 1970 s 342
Housing Corporation and, disposal of land between..TA 1970 s 342
Northern Ireland..TA 1970 s 341A(12)

HOVERCRAFT
meaning..CGTA 1979 s 118
rollover relief..CGTA 1979 s 118

HUSBAND AND WIFE
aggregation of income—
    abolition..FA 1988 s 32
    collection from wife..TA 1988 s 285
    deceased wife's income..TA 1988 s 286
    general rule..TA 1988 s 279
beneficial loans, determination of eligibility..TA 1988 Sch 7 para 10–12
business expansion scheme..TA 1988 s 304
    disposals..TA 1988 s 304, FA 1988 Sch 3 para 12
capital gains. *See under* CAPITAL GAINS TAX
collection of tax from wife..TA 1988 s 285
commencement of trade, charge to tax on..TA 1988 s 62(2A)
copyright payments..TA 1988 s 535(5)
deceased wife's income..TA 1988 s 286
deduction or set-off against income of other spouse..TA 1988 s 280
deductions transferable..TA 1988 s 280
identification of securities..FA 1982 s 89(1)
interest relief..TA 1988 s 280
jointly held property—
    declarations..TA 1988 s 282B
    income arising from..TA 1988 s 282A
living together, meaning..TA 1988 s 282, FA 1988 Sch 3 para 11
loss relief—
    farming etc..TA 1988 s 397(10)
    set-off..TA 1988 s 382(2)(3)
marriage in year of assessment..TA 1988 s 257(8)
National Savings Bank interest..TA 1988 s 325
personal relief..TA 1988 s 257 257A
    indexation..TA 1988 s 257C
    transfer of..TA 1988 s 257B
    transitional..TA 1988 s 257D–257F
repayments to wife..TA 1988 s 281
retirement annuity..TA 1988 s 623(1)
retirement relief, aggregation of spouse's interest..FA 1985 Sch 20 para 16
rights under the life policies etc..TA 1988 s 547(1)
separate assessment—
    effect on reliefs..TA 1988 s 284
    option for..TA 1988 s 283
    withdrawal..TA 1988 s 283(4)(5)
separate taxation of wife's earnings. *See* SEPARATE TAXATION
trade, discontinuance of..TA 1988 s 63
trade losses in early years..TA 1988 s 381(5)

HUS   *Index*   [52]

HUSBAND AND WIFE—*continued*
   transactions in securities..TA 1988 s 703(7)
   transfer of assets abroad..TA 1988 s 742(9)
   underpayment of PAYE, recovery of..TA 1988 s 203(3A)
   wife's earned income relief..TA 1988 s 257(6)(7)
   year of marriage, claim in..TA 1988 s 261 FA 1988 Sch 3 para 6

INCAPACITATED PERSON
   meaning..TMA 1970 s 118(1)
   chargeable persons..TMA 1970 s 72 77
   claim on behalf..TMA 1970 s 42(6)

INCOME
   meaning—
      capital allowances..CAA 1968 s 87(1)
      settlor..TA 1988 s 670
   charge on. *See* CHARGE ON INCOME
   distributable, meaning..TA 1988 Sch 19 para 4(1)
   distributable investment income, meaning..TA 1988 Sch 19 para 4(2)
   earned income, meaning..TA 1988 s 833(4)(5), FA 1988 Sch 3 para 21
   eligible for double taxation relief, meaning..TA 1988 s 278(7)
   estate or trading, meaning..TA 1988 Sch 19 para 5
   highest part..TA 1988 s 833(3)
   other person's, return of..TMA 1970 s 13
   received after year of assessment..TMA 1970 s 35
   relevant, close company. *See under* CLOSE COMPANY
   support—
      amount accruing, tax on..FA 1989 s 41
      amount taxable, notification of..TA 1988 s 152
      income, not being..TA 1988 s 617(2)
      income tax, charge to..TA 1988 s 151
   trade unions, of, relief in respect of..TA 1988 s 467
   total income..TA 1988 s 835, 836, FA 1988, Sch 3 para 22
   unrelieved income, meaning..TA 1988 s 434(7)

INCOME TAX
   additional rate—
      meaning..TA 1988 s 832(1)
      discretionary trust..TA 1988 s 686
   administration by Board..TMA 1970 s 1(1)
   adjustment of reliefs..TA 1988 s 823
   agreement for payment without deduction..TMA 1970 s 106(2)
   bands..TA 1988 s 1(2)(*b*)
   basic rate, charge to..TA 1988 s 1(2)(*a*), FA 1988 s 23 FA 1989 s 30(1)
   benefits in kind. *See* BENEFITS IN KIND
   budget resolution..PCTA 1968 s 1
   building societies..TA 1988 s 476
   capital allowances—
      other than trade..CAA 1968 s 71
      trade, as to..CAA 1968 s 70
   charge to—
      Continental Shelf..TA 1988 s 830(5)
      generally..TA 1988 s 1
   chargeable persons. *See* CHARGEABLE PERSON
   claim for repayment of tax deducted from receipts..TA 1988 s 7(5)
   close company apportionment..TA 1988 s 426 427 429
   company distributions..TA 1988 s 20
   composite rate for banks..TA 1988 s 483
   continuation of legislation..TA 1988 s 820
   Crown..TA 1988 s 829
   dates for payment..TA 1988 s 5
   deduction at source. *See* DEDUCTION AT SOURCE
   deductions, effect..TA 1988 s 835(3)–(5)
   deep discount securities. *See* DEEP DISCOUNT SECURITIES
   demergers. *See under* DEMERGER
   distributions etc received by UK company..TA 1988 s 7
   double taxation relief by credit..TA 1988 s 796
   enterprise allowance..TA 1988 s 127
   fractions of a pound..TA 1988 s 2(1)
   friendly societies..TA 1988 s 461
   group income..TA 1988 s 247(4)(5)
   higher rate band..FA 1988 s 24(1), FA 1989 s 30(2)

INCOME TAX—*continued*
  higher rate band—*continued*
    recovery from beneficiary..TA 1988 s 689
  income received after year of assessment..TMA 1970 s 35
  indexation..TA 1988 s 1(4) FA 1988 s 24(2)
  International Maritime Satellite Organisation..TA 1988 s 515
  investment income. *See* INVESTMENT INCOME
  letters patent..TA 1988 s 829(4)
  maintenance fund, historic buildings. *See under* MAINTENANCE FUND
  method of charging..TA 1988 s 1
  mineral royalties..TA 1988 s 122(1)
  mobility allowance..TA 1988 s 617(1)
  non-resident, chargeability..TMA 1970 s 78
  notice of liability..TMA 1970 s 7
  offshore fund. *See* OFFSHORE FUND
  oil extraction activities..OTA 1975 s 13
  over-deductions from interest..TA 1988 s 822
  overseas life insurance company, set-off..TA 1988 s 447(4)
  PAYE. *See* PAYE
  partnership return..TMA 1970 s 9
  patent rights..TA 1988 s 524
  payroll deduction scheme. *See* CHARITY
  personal equity plans..TA 1988 s 333
  personal reliefs. *See* PERSONAL RELIEFS
  public departments..TA 1988 s 829(3)
  recovery where not postponed..TMA 1970 s 55
  reduced rate for building societies..TA 1988 s 483
  refusal to allow deduction of..TMA 1970 s 106(1)
  repayment supplement—
    companies..TA 1988 s 825
    other..TA 1988 s 824
  returns..TMA 1970 s 8
  Schedules A–F. *See appropriate Schedule*
  statement on dividend warrants etc..TA 1988 s 234(3)(4)
  statute, no exemption by..TA 1988 s 829(4)
  stock relief. *See* STOCK RELIEF
  supplementary allowance. *See* SUPPLEMENTARY ALLOWANCE
  under deduction, payments made before annual Act..TA 1988 s 821
  underwriters' special reserve fund..TA 1988 s 454
  yearly assessment..TA 1988 s 2(2)

INCOME TAX ACTS
  meaning..TA 1988 s 831(1)(*b*)
  continuation..TA 1988 s 820
  public departments..TA 1988 s 829(1)–(3)

INDEXATION
  income tax allowances etc..TA 1988 s 1(4)
  underwriter's premiums trust funds..FA 1985 Sch 19 para 22 23

INDEXATION ALLOWANCE
  meaning..FA 1982 s 86(4) FA 1983 Sch 6 para 5(2)(*b*), FA 1988 Sch 11 para 6(3)
  assets held March 1982—
    assets derived from other assets..FA 1985 s 68(6)
    post-April 1985 disposal..FA 1985 s 68(4)(5)
  building society shares..FA 1988 s 113(1)
  calculation..FA 1982 s 87 Sch 13 para 10 FA 1985 Sch 19 para 11
  calls on shares..FA 1982 Sch 13 para 6
  capital gains..CGTA 1979 s 5(1B)
  disposal of linked company debt, on..FA 1988 Sch 11 para 1, 2
  disposal of linked company shares, on..FA 1988 Sch 11 para 3, 5
  disposals after no gain/no loss..FA 1985 s 68(7)(8)
  disposals post-February 1986..FA 1985 s 68(2)(*b*)
  disposals post-March 1982..FA 1982 s 86
  gilt-edged securities..FA 1985 s 68(2)(*a*)
  gross gain, meaning..FA 1982 s 86(2)(*a*)
  identification of securities—
    generally..FA 1982 s 88
    groups..FA 1982 s 89(2)
    husband and wife..FA 1982 s 89(1)
    pools at April 1982..FA 1982 Sch 13 para 9
    post-April 1985 disposals..FA 1985 Sch 19 para 16–19
    third party, disposals to..FA 1982 s 89(3)
  indexed securities, meaning..FA 1982 s 89(5)

INDEXATION ALLOWANCE—*continued*
    industrial and provident society shares..FA 1988 s 113(1)
    linked company, meaning..FA 1988 Sch 11 para 4
    local constituency associations..F(No 2)A 1983 s 7(5)
    losses..FA 1982 s 86
    no gain/no loss disposals..FA 1982 Sch 13 para 2
    offshore income gain..TA 1988 Sch 28 para 3(1), 4(3)
    options..FA 1982 Sch 13 para 7 FA 1983 Sch 6 para 10
    part disposals..FA 1982 Sch 13 para 1
    pooling. *See* POOLING
    qualifying corporate bonds..FA 1985 s 68(2)(*a*)
    receipts affecting allowable expenditure..FA 1982 Sch 13 para 4
    relevant allowable expenditure..FA 1982 s 86(2)(*b*)
    relevant securities, meaning..FA 1982 s 88(9)
    reorganisation etc..FA 1982 Sch 13 para 5
    unindexed gains or loss, meaning..FA 1982 s 86(2)(*a*)

INDIA
    family pension funds..TA 1988 s 614(2)
    Reserve Bank..TA 1988 s 517

INDUSTRIAL AND PROVIDENT SOCIETY
    amalgamation..TA 1988 s 486(8)
    co-operative association—
        meaning..TA 1988 s 486(12)
        agriculture and fisheries..TA 1988 s 486(9)
    group relief..TA 1988 s 413(4)
    interest payments by..TA 1988 s 486(1)–(6)
    loan interest, meaning..TA 1988 s 486(12)
    registered, meaning..TA 1988 s 486(12)
    returns..TA 1988 s 486(6)
    share interest, meaning..TA 1988 s 486(12)
    shares, indexation allowance not applying to..FA 1988 s 113(1)
    trading with members..TA 1988 s 486(10)(11)

INDUSTRIAL ASSURANCE
    qualifying policies..TA 1988 Sch 15 para 7, 8
    relief..TA 1988 Sch 14 para 2, 3

INDUSTRIAL BUILDING
    meaning..CAA 1968 s 7
    appointed day..CAA 1968 s 16
    apportionment on sale etc..CAA 1968 s 17 (3)
    balancing allowance—
        entitlement..CAA 1968 s 3
        non-qualifying use..FA 1981 s 75(4)(5)
        restriction..FA 1972 s 69
    balancing charge—
        imposition..CAA 1968 s 3
        non-qualifying use..FA 1981 s 75(4)(5)
    bought after use..CAA 1968 s 5A
    coal industry nationalisation..CAA 1968 Sch 8 para 5 6
    commercial rent, meaning..FA 1972 s 69(4)
    Crown..CAA 1968 s 4(12) 13(1)
    demolition..CAA 1968 s 4(11)
    enterprise zone. *See* ENTERPRISE ZONE
    exceptional depreciation allowance..CAA 1968 s 89
    excluded expenditure..CAA 1968 s 17(1)
    expenditure post-March 1983..FA 1983 s 30(2)
    extension of relief..FA 1983 s 30(2)
    holding over of leased land..CAA 1968 s 13(2)
    hotels..FA 1978 s 38
    initial allowance—
        chargeable period..CAA 1968 s 1(4)
        development areas..FA 1970 s 15 FA 1971 s 51
        entitlement..CAA 1968 s 1
        intermediate areas..FA 1970 s 15 FA 1971 s 51
        manner of making..CAA 1968 s 6(2)
        Northern Ireland..FA 1971 s 51
        rate..CAA 1968 s 1(2)
        restriction..CAA 1968 s 1(5)
        withdrawal of..FA 1984 s 58(1)(*a*) Sch 12 para 1
    licensees..FA 1982 s 74(2)
    maintenance trades..CAA 1968 s 7(2A)

INDUSTRIAL BUILDING—*continued*
  method of making allowances and charges..CAA 1968 s 6
  mining structures, balancing allowances carried back..CAA 1968 s 15
  non-qualifying use..FA 1981 s 75(4)(5)
  outside UK..CAA 1968 s 7(9)
  part trade use..CAA 1968 s 7(2)(4)
  premium, meaning..FA 1972 s 69(4)
  relevant interest, meaning..CAA 1968 s 11
  rent, meaning..FA 1972 s 69(4)
  repair..CAA 1968 s 8
  requisitioned land..CAA 1968 s 13(1)
  residue of expenditure, meaning..CAA 1968 s 4
  sale after end of qualifying use..FA 1981 s 74(5)(6)
  sales post-March 1981..FA 1981 s 76
  scientific research..CAA 1968 s 3(4)–(6)
  sites for machinery and plant..CAA 1968 s 9
  small workshop. *See* SMALL WORKSHOP
  sports pavilions..CAA 1968 s 10
  spreading of expenditure on contracts between 13 March 1984 and 31 March 1986..FA 1984 Sch 12 para 5 8–10
  subordinate interest, meaning..FA 1972 s 69(4)
  temporary disuse..CAA 1968 s 12
  tenancies..FA 1980 s 76
  thermal insulation..FA 1975 s 14
  unused buildings..CAA 1968 s 5
  very small workshops..FA 1982 s 73 FA 1983 s 31
  writing-down allowances..CAA 1968 s 2
  writing off expenditure..CAA 1968 s 4

INDUSTRIAL GRANT
  capital allowances restriction..CAA 1968 s 84(1) 95(6)
  Northern Ireland..TA 1988 s 93(2)
  trading receipt..TA 1988 s 93

INDUSTRY
  rationalisation. *See* RATIONALISATION OF INDUSTRY

INFANT. *See also* CHILD
  chargeable persons..TMA 1970 s 73

INFORMATION
  close company, as to..FA 1989 Sch 12 para 2–4
  disclosure—
    certification of offshore fund..TA 1988 Sch 27 para 18
    deep discount securities..TA 1988 Sch 4 para 13
    double taxation relief..TA 1988 s 816
    EEC states, to..FA 1978 s 77
    revenue departments, between..FA 1972 s 127
    unlawful..FA 1989 s 174
  document, meaning..FA 1988 s 127
  power to require—
    administration of estates..TA 1988 s 700(4)
    approved share option scheme..TA 1988 Sch 4 para 9
    artificial transactions in land..TA 1988 s 778
    bank, from..TA 1988 s 483(5)
    building society, from..TA 1988 s 483(5)
    business expansion scheme..TA 1988 s 310
    chargeable gains..TMA 1970 s 25
    children's settlements..TA 1988 s 669
    collection of tax from wife..TA 1988 s 285(6)
    Commissioners..TMA 1970 s 51 53
    company purchase of own shares..TA 1988 s 226(3)(4)
    computer records..FA 1988 s 127(2)–(6)
    controlled foreign company..TA 1988 s 755
    demergers..TA 1988 s 217(1)
    deposit-taker, from..TA 1988 s 483(5)
    entry..TMA 1970 s 20C
    herd basis..TA 1988 Sch 5 para 10
    income from securities..TMA 1970 s 24
    judicial authority..TMA 1970 s 20D(1)
    migrant settlements..FA 1981 s 84
    nominees..TMA 1970 s 26
    non-resident companies..TMA 1970 s 28
    non-resident trusts..TMA 1970 s 28 FA 1981 s 84

INFORMATION—continued
power to require—continued
payments out of public funds..TMA 1970 s 18A
petroleum production..FA 1973 Sch 15 para 2
postponement of tax due from beneficiary of non-resident trust..FA 1984 Sch 14 para 15(1)(2)
profit-related pay..TA 1988 s 180 181
profit sharing schemes..TA 1988 Sch 9 para 6
register of securities..TMA 1970 s 23
restrictions..TMA 1970 s 20B
revocable settlements..TA 1988 s 680
sale and repurchase of securities..TA 1988 s 729(11)
sale of income..TA 1988 s 778
savings-related share option scheme..TA 1988 Sch 9 para 6
settled property..TMA 1970 s 27
share incentive scheme, authorised unit trust..TA 1988 s 139(6)
surrender of life policy..TA 1988 s 272(7)
tax accountant, from..TMA 1970 s 20A
taxpayer, from..TMA 1970 s 20
transactions in securities..TA 1988 s 708
transfer of assets abroad..TA 1988 s 745
transfer of income from securities..TA 1988 s 730(8)
transfer of securities: accrued interest..TA 1988 s 728

INHERITANCE TAX
accrued income, relief..TA 1988 s 699
gift, where chargeable on..CGTA 1979 s 147A
loan for payment of..TA 1988 s 364
market value, CGT..CGTA 1979 s 153

INITIAL ALLOWANCE
assured tenancies..FA 1984 s 58(1)(c) Sch 12 para 3
cars..CAA 1968 Sch 2 para 2
completion date, meaning..FA 1984 Sch 12 para 5(2) 6(2) 7(2)
contract date, meaning..FA 1984 Sch 12 para 5(2) 6(2) 7(2)
contract price, meaning..FA 1984 Sch 12 para 5(2) 6(2) 7(2)
contributions to expenditure..CAA 1968 s 85
development area, meaning..FA 1970 s 15(3)
enterprise zone..FA 1980 Sch 13 para 1 2
hotels..FA 1978 Sch 6 para 1 FA 1985 s 66
industrial buildings. *See under* INDUSTRIAL BUILDING
intermediate area, meaning..:FA 1970 s 15(3)
investment allowance. *See* INVESTMENT ALLOWANCE
investment grants..CAA 1968 s 83
machinery and plant..CAA 1968 s 18
maximum allowable expenditure..FA 1984 Sch 12 para 9
mines, oil wells etc—
    entitlement..CAA 1968 s 56
small workshops..FA 1980 Sch 13 para 1 2
spreading of expenditure under certain contracts..FA 1984 Sch 12 para 5–10
tenancies..FA 1980 s 76
withdrawal of..FA 1984 s 58 Sch 12

INJURY PENSION
exemption..TA 1988 s 315(2)(e)

INLAND REVENUE
meaning..TMA 1970 s 1(1)
Board of. *See* BOARD OF INLAND REVENUE

INMATE
returns..TMA 1970 s 14

INSPECTION
books etc, controlled foreign company..TA 1988 s 755
public revenue dividends etc..TA 1988 Sch 3 para 13
valuation of assets..TMA 1970 s 111

INSPECTOR OF TAXES
appeal from..TMA 1970 Sch 2 para 1 2
appointment..TMA 1970 s 1(2)
assessment by..TMA 1970 s 29
certificate of tax due..TMA 1970 s 70(1)
claims to..TMA 1970 s 42(2)
continuation of proceedings..TMA 1970 s 1(3)

INSPECTOR OF TAXES—*continued*
  declaration on taking office..TMA 1970 s 6(4)(5) Sch 1 Pt III
  notice of appeal meeting..TMA 1970 s 50(2)
  power to require information. *See under* INFORMATION

INSTALMENTS
  Sch D..TA 1988 s 5(2)
  share options..TA 1988 s 137

INSURANCE
  capital gains..CGTA 1979 s 140 141
  investment insurance scheme, export credits payments..TA 1988 s 88
  life policy. *See* LIFE ASSURANCE RELIEF; LIFE POLICY
  medical, relief for—
    certification of contracts..FA 1989 s 56
    eligible contracts..FA 1989 s 55
    regulations, power to make..FA 1989 s 57
    requirements..FA 1989 s 54
  re-insurance, underwriters..TA 1988 s 450(4)

INSURANCE COMPANY
  meaning..TA 1988 s 431(1) 767(5)
  annuity business, meaning..TA 1988 s 431(1)
  annuity fund, meaning..TA 1988 s 431(1)
  base date, meaning..TA 1988 s 440(10)
  capital redemption business—
    meaning..TA 1988 s 458(3)
    losses..TA 1988 s 458(2)
    pre-1938 contracts..TA 1988 s 458(4)
    separate business, as..TA 1988 s 458(1)
  classes of business..TA 1988 s 432
  controlled foreign company..TA 1988 Sch 25 para 11
  conversion of circulating capital..TA 1988 s 473
  distributions taken into account..TA 1988 s 436(3)(*e*)
  double taxation relief..TA 1988 s 808
  foreign life assurance fund—
    meaning..TA 1988 s 441(6)
    charge to tax..TA 1988 s 441(1) 724(3)(4)
    exempt securities..TA 1988 s 441(2)(4) 724(3)(4)
    income from abroad..TA 1988 s 441(3)
  franked investment income..TA 1988 s 434 437(4)(5) 438(3)(6)
  general annuity business—
    meaning..TA 1988 s 431(1)
    charges on income..TA 1988 s 437(1)
    computation of profits..TA 1988 s 437(2)
    franked investment income..TA 1988 s 437(4)(5)
    non-resident company..TA 1988 s 437(6)
    offshore income gains..TA 1988 Sch 28 para 3(4)
    separate charge..TA 1988 s 436
  indexed-linked stock..TA 1988 s 439(6)(7)
  interest on borrowed money..TA 1988 s 475
  life assurance business. *See* LIFE ASSURANCE BUSINESS
  life policies with non-money rights..TA 1988 s 443
  long term assets—
    meaning..TA 1988 s 440(11)
    identification or exchange..TA 1988 s 440
  long term business, meaning..TA 1988 s 439(5) 440(11)
  long term business levy, relief..TA 1988 s 76(7)
  machinery and plant..TA 1970 s 306
  management expenses..TA 1988 s 76 724(1)
  migration of companies..TA 1988 s 765(3)
  mutual business..TA 1988 s 490
  non-resident. *See* OVERSEAS LIFE INSURANCE COMPANY
  offshore income gain..TA 1988 s 431(1) 441(8) Sch 28 para 3(4)
  overseas business..TA 1988 s 442
  overseas life. *See* OVERSEAS LIFE INSURANCE COMPANY
  pension business—
    computation of profits..TA 1988 s 436(3)(*d*)
    exemption..TA 1988 s 438(1)(2)
    franked investment income..TA 1988 s 438(3)(4)
    offshore income gains..TA 1988 s 431(1) 441(8) Sch 28 para 3(4)
    premiums..TA 1988 s 431(4)(6)
    restricted government securities..TA 1988 s 439(1)–(5)
    separate charge..TA 1988 s 436

INSURANCE COMPANY—*continued*
  pension business—*continued*
    tax credit..TA 1988 s 438
    periodical return, meaning..TA 1988 s 431(1)
    pre-1965 life polices..TA 1988 s 444
    relief for levies on..TA 1988 s 76(7)
    restricted government securities..TA 1988 s 439
    taxed income, meaning..TA 1988 s 437(3)
    tax-free income..TA 1988 s 474
    tax-free Treasury securities..TA 1988 s 475
    trading overseas, underlying tax..TA 1988 s 802
    unrelieved income, meaning..TA 1988 s 434(7)

INSURANCE MONEY
  capital gains tax..CGTA 1979 s 21 Sch 5 para 18

INTER-AMERICAN DEVELOPMENT BANK
  exemption..TA 1988 s 583

INTEREST. *See also* INTEREST RELIEF; MORTGAGE INTEREST RELIEF
  meaning..TA 1988 s 711(9) 832(1)
  accrued: transfer of securities. *See* SECURITIES
  annual, deduction at source..TA 1988 s 349(2)
  bank, deduction of tax by. *See under* DEPOSIT-TAKER
  bank overdraft..TA 1988 s 353(3)(*a*)
  capital, charged to..TA 1988 s 338
  close company apportionment..TA 1988 s 423 424
  companies, related, payments between..TA 1988 s 341
  debt, on, funding bonds..TA 1988 s 582
  fixed net amount..TA 1988 s 818
  government securities. *See* GOVERNMENT SECURITIES
  industrial and provident society payments..TA 1988 s 486(1)–(5)
  loss relief..TA 1988 s 390
  National Savings Bank..TA 1988 s 325
  Netherlands Antilles subsidiary, paid to..FA 1989 s 116
  non-resident, payable to—
    charge on income..TA 1988 s 340
    deductibility..TA 1988 s 82
  over-deduction..TA 1988 s 822
  overdue tax, on—
    ACT..TMA 1970 s 87
    certificates as to..TMA 1970 s 70(2)(3)
    civil service industrial action..FA 1981 s 51
    company payments..TMA 1970 s 87
    corporation tax..TMA 1970 s 87A
    date applicable..TMA 1970 s 86(4)
    disallowance of relief..TMA 1970 s 90
    effect of reliefs..TMA 1970 s 91
    fraud etc..TMA 1970 s 88
    liability..TMA 1970 s 86(1)(2)
    non-business days..TMA 1970 s 86(5)
    reckonable date, meaning..TMA 1970 s 86(3)
    recovery..TMA 1970 s 69
    remission—
      exchange restrictions..TMA 1970 s 92
      generally..TMA 1970 s 86(6)
  overpaid tax, on..TA 1988 s 826
  overseas loans..TA 1988 s 798
  payment "less tax"..TA 1988 s 818
  personal injuries damages..TA 1988 s 329
  PRT overpaid, on..TA 1988 s 501
  rates of..FA 1989 s 178
  related companies, payments between..TA 1988 s 341
  relief. *See* INTEREST RELIEF; MORTGAGE INTEREST RELIEF
  repayments, on. *See* REPAYMENT SUPPLEMENT
  returns as to..TMA 1970 s 17 18
  Sch D Case III..TA 1988 s 18(3)
  share acquisition schemes..TA 1988 s 688
  tax reserve certficates, exemption..TA 1988 s 46(2)
  under deduction..TA 1988 s 821(2)

INTEREST RELIEF. *See also* MORTGAGE INTEREST RELIEF
  apportionment..TA 1988 s 367(4)
  beneficial loans..TA 1988 Sch 7 Pt III

INTEREST RELIEF—*continued*
  bridging loans..TA 1988 s 354(5)
  capital transfer tax, loan for..TA 1988 s 364
  close company, acquisition of interest in..TA 1988 s 360
  co-operative, acquisition of interest in..TA 1988 s 361
  credit for money due..TA 1988 s 367(3)
  debts..TA 1988 s 353
  deduction for capital recovered..TA 1988 s 363(1)(2)
  double relief exclusion..TA 1988 s 368
  entitlement..TA 1988 s 353
  husband and wife..TA 1988 s 280
  information..TA 1988 s 366(1)
  inheritance tax, loan for..TA 1988 s 364
  investment in employee-controlled company—
    both spouses full-time employees..TA 1988 s 361(7)
    conditions..TA 1988 s 361(4)
    recovery of relief..TA 1988 s 363(1)(2)
    relief..TA 1988 s 361(3)
  job-related accommodation..TA 1988 s 356
  land purchase etc..TA 1988 s 354
  life annuity, loan for..TA 1988 s 365
  limited loans..TA 1988 s 357
  limited partners..TA 1988 s 117(1)
  limits..TA 1988 s 357(1) 365(3)
  loan replacing another loan..TA 1988 s 360(1)(*c*)
  machinery or plant..TA 1988 s 359
  mortgage interest. *See* MORTGAGE INTEREST RELIEF
  partnership, acquisition of interest in..TA 1988 s 362
  personal representatives..TA 1988 s 358
  qualifying maximum..TA 1988 s 367(5)
  residence basis—
    married couples..TA 1988 s 356B, FA 1988 Sch 3 para 14
    more than one loan, on..TA 1988 s 356D(6)(7)
    period of interest..TA 1988 s 356D(3)
    proportion eligible for relief..TA 1988 s 356D(5)
    qualifying interest, meaning..TA 1988 s 356D(1)
    residence, meaning..TA 1988 s 356D(2)
    sharer's limit, meaning..TA 1988 s 356A(3)
    shortfall, meaning..TA 1988 s 356A(8)
    two persons, payable by..TA 1988 s 356A 356D(8)
    1st August 1988, payments after..TA 1988 s 356C
  restriction—
    debts..TA 1988 s 353(3)
    land purchase etc..TA 1988 s 354
    loans to reduce tax liability..TA 1988 s 787
  street works..TA 1988 s 354(2)
  Trustee Savings Bank..TSBA 1985 Sch 2 para 7

INTERNATIONAL MARITIME SATELLITE ORGANISATION
  exemption..TA 1988 s 515

INTERNATIONAL ORGANISATION
  designation for tax exemption..TA 1988 s 324

INVENTOR
  know-how..TA 1988 s 530(5)
  patent rights..TA 1988 s 529

INVESTMENT ALLOWANCE
  machinery and plant..CAA 1968 Sch 1 para 2
  pre-April 1959 expenditure..CAA 1968 Sch 1 para 5
  ships..CAA 1968 Sch 1 para 3
  transitory provisions..CAA 1968 Sch 1 para 1

INVESTMENT COMPANY
  meaning..TA 1988 s 130
  costs of obtaining loans..TA 1988 s 77
  Export Credits..TA 1988 s 88
  group relief..TA 1988 s 403(4)(5)
  local enterprise agency contributions..TA 1988 s 79(2)
  machinery and plant..TA 1970 s 306 FA 1971 s 47(2)
  management expenses..TA 1988 s 75
  profits..FA 1988 s 75(1)

INVESTMENT COMPANY—*continued*
  receipts basis, computation of profits on..FA 1989 s 41
  regional development grant, exemption..TA 1988 s 92(2)

INVESTMENT FUND
  business expansion scheme..TA 1988 s 311(3)–(6)

INVESTMENT GRANT
  meaning..CAA 1968 s 83(4)
  first-year allowance..FA 1971 Sch 8 para 1
  initial allowance..CAA 1968 s 83

INVESTMENT INCOME
  distributable, meaning..TA 1988 Sch 19 para 4(2)
  policy holders, reserved for..TA 1988 s 434(4)
  underwriter's payments from special reserve fund..TA 1988 s 456(1)(2)

INVESTMENT TRANSACTIONS
  meaning..TMA 1970 s 78(3)
  non-resident, by agent of..TMA 1970 s 78(2)

INVESTMENT TRUST
  meaning..TA 1988 s 842(1)
  CGT exemption..FA 1980 s 81
  holding—
    meaning..TA 1988 s 842(3)(*a*)
    acquired pre-1965..TA 1988 s 842(2)(*a*)

IRELAND, REPUBLIC OF
  double taxation relief. *See under* DOUBLE TAXATION RELIEF
  interest relief..TA 1988 s 353(1)(*b*)
  premiums on leases..TA 1988 s 746
  public revenue dividends..TA 1988 s 17, Sch 3 Pt IV

ISSUING HOUSE
  chargeable gains, returns..TMA 1970 s 25(2)

JOB-RELATED ACCOMMODATION
  meaning..TA 1988 s 356(3)
  interest relief..TA 1988 s 356

JOB RELEASE SCHEME
  allowances chargeable..TA 1988 s 150(*a*)
  exemption..FA 1988 s 191

JOBBER. *See also* STOCKJOBBER
  meaning..TMA 1970 s 21(7)

JURISDICTION
  appeal—
    Board, from..TMA 1970 Sch 2 para 3
    chargeable gains..TMA 1970 s 47
    inspector, from..TMA 1970 Sch 2 para 1 2
  determination as to..TMA 1970 s 44(3)(4)
  General Commissioners..TMA 1970 s 44

KNOW-HOW
  meaning..TA 1988 s 533(7)
  balancing allowance..TA 1988 s 530(2)
  balancing charge..TA 1988 s 530(3)
  charge to tax..TA 1988 s 531(2)(3)
  connected persons..TA 1988 s 531(7)
  date of expenditure..FA 1985 s 56(8)
  disposal value, accountability..TA 1988 s 530(5) 531(4)
  goodwill..TA 1988 s 531(2)
  inventor's income..TA 1988 s 531(6)
  restrictive undertakings..TA 1988 s 531(8)
  trading receipts..TA 1988 s 531(1)
  writing-down allowance..TA 1988 s 530(2) 531(6)(7)

LAND
abroad, mines, oil wells etc..CAA 1968 s 54 Sch 5 para 4 5
annual value—
  meaning..TA 1988 s 837(1)(2)
  business expense..TA 1988 Sch 30 para 5
  determination..TA 1988 s 837(3)
artificial transactions..TA 1988 s 776 777
capital gains. *See under* CAPITAL GAINS TAX
current use value. *See under* DEVELOPMENT GAINS
development, loan interest..TA 1988 s 354
development value, with—
  betterment levy..CGTA 1979 Sch 5 para 10
  valuation at April 1965..CGTA 1979 Sch 5 para 9
farm land, meaning..TA 1988 s 832(1)
interest in—
  Sch A..TA 1988 s 15(1)
loan for purchase etc, interest relief..TA 1988 s 354
machinery and plant..CAA 1968 s 47
occupation..TA 1988 s 53(3)(4)
purchase, interest relief..TA 1988 s 354
restriction on interest relief..TA 1988 s 357, FA 1988 s 44
rollover relief..CGTA 1979 s 119
sale and lease back—
  limit on relief..TA 1988 s 779
  tax on consideration..TA 1988 s 780
sales at under- or overvalue..TA 1988 s 777
scientific research, acquisition for..CAA 1968 s 91(1A)
valuation—
  adjustment of..TA 1988 s 294(5A)
  entry powers..TMA 1970 s 110

LANDS TRIBUNAL
jurisdiction..TMA 1970 s 47(1)(2)

LEASE
meaning—
  capital allowances..CAA 1968 s 87(1)
  Sch A..TA 1988 s 24(1)
  tied premises..TA 1988 s 98(8)
capital gains. *See under* CAPITAL GAINS TAX
duration—
  application of provisions..TA 1988 Sch 30 para 2
  ascertainment..TA 1988 Sch 30 para 4
  determination..CGTA 1979 Sch 3 para 8
  rules..TA 1988 s 38
full rent, at, meaning..TA 1988 s 24(7)
industrial building, capital allowances..CAA 1968 s 13(2)–(5)
long, capital allowances..FA 1978 s 37
pre-1963, Sch A..TA 1988 s 39
sale and leaseback. *See* LEASEBACK
tenant's repairing lease, meaning..TA 1988 s 24(6)
undervalue, at—
  appeals..TA 1988 s 42
  assignment, Sch D..TA 1988 s 35
  information..TA 1988 s 42(7)

LEASEBACK
cars..FA 1971 Sch 8 para 10(4)
land—
  consideration, tax on..TA 1988 s 780
  limit on relief..TA 1988 s 779
machinery and plant..FA 1971 Sch 8 para 3

LEASEHOLD INTEREST
meaning (Scotland)..CAA 1968 s 88
capital allowances, apportionment..CAA 1968 s 77(3)

LEASING
abroad. *See under* MACHINERY AND PLANT
aircraft..FA 1982 s 70(1) FA 1986 s 57(4)
apportionment..TA 1988 s 783(9)
associated persons, meaning..TA 1988 s 783(10)
chargeable sums..TA 1988 s 783
hire-purchase agreements..TA 1988 s 784

LEASING—*continued*
  losses, company reconstruction..TA 1988 s 395
  new expenditure on..FA 1986 s 57
  partnerships involving companies..TA 1988 s 116
  machinery and plant, capital allowances..FA 1971 s 46
  ships..FA 1986 s 57(4)
  short-term. *See under* MACHINERY AND PLANT
  special cases..TA 1988 s 782
  traders etc, to..TA 1988 s 781
  transport containers..FA 1986 s 57(4)

LESSEE
  holding over, assured tenancy..FA 1982 Sch 12 para 12
  industrial buildings..CAA 1968 s 1(1A)(3)
  machinery and plant..CAA 1968 s 43
  Sch A collected from..TA 1988 s 23

LESSOR
  machinery and plant..CAA 1968 s 43

LETTERS PATENT
  exemption by..TA 1988 s 829(4)

LICENCE
  oil..FA 1986 Sch 13 para 22

LICENSEE
  capital allowances..FA 1982 s 74(2)
  industrial building, meaning..CAA 1968 s 7(3A)

LIFE ANNUITY CONTRACT. *See also* PURCHASED LIFE ANNUITY
  allowable aggregate amount..TA 1988 s 546(3)
  assigned contract—
    meaning..TA 1988 s 544(2)
    chargeable person..TA 1988 s 544(6)
    loan for home-purchase etc..TA 1988 s 544(7)(*b*)
    reassignment etc..TA 1988 s 544(3)
  bonus, treatment..TA 1988 s 539(4)
  certificate by insurers..TA 1988 s 552
  charge to tax..TA 1988 s 539(1)
  chargeable event..TA 1988 s 542
  computation of gain..TA 1988 s 543
  excess liability..TA 1988 s 549
  life annuity, meaning..TA 1988 s 539(3)
  loans on..TA 1988 s 548
  method of charge..TA 1988 s 547
  notification to inspector..TA 1988 s 552
  post-March 1968..TA 1988 s 539(5)
  reckonable aggregate value..FA 1988 s 546(2)
  recovery of tax from trustees..TA 1988 s 551
  relevant capital payments, meaning..TA 1988 s 543(3)
  relief where gain charged at higher rate..TA 1988 s 559
  top-slicing relief..TA 1988 s 550(7)

LIFE ASSURANCE BUSINESS
  meaning..TA 1988 s 76(8) 431(1)
  basic—
    meaning..FA 1989 s 84(1)
    acquisition expenses, spreading of relief for..FA 1989 s 86
    management expenses..FA 1989 s 86(5)
    receipts, charge of..FA 1989 s 85
  franked investment income..TA 1988 s 434(3)
  group relief, limitations on..TA 1988 s 434A
  loss relief, limitations on..TA 1988 s 434A
  machinery and plant..FA 1971 s 47(2)
  mutual business..TA 1988 s 490
  profits—
    calculation of..FA 1989 s 82
    policy holders' fraction..FA 1989 s 89
      corporation tax rate..FA 1989 s 88
      distributions, not used to frank..TA 1988 s 434(3)
    receipts basis, calculation on..FA 1989 s 44
    receipts brought into account..FA 1989 s 83
    shareholders' fraction..FA 1989 s 89

LIFE ASSURANCE BUSINESS—*continued*
  separate business, as..TA 1988 s 432
  straddling period..FA 1989 s 82(5) 83(3) 84(2) (3)

LIFE ASSURANCE RELIEF
  armed forces abroad..TA 1988 s 266(9)
  certification..TA 1988 Sch 15 para 22
  connected policies..TA 1988 Sch 15 para 13, 14
  deduction from premiums, by..TA 1988 s 266(5)
  endowment assurance..TA 1988 Sch 15 para 2
  exceptional mortality risk..TA 1988 Sch 15 para 12
  family income policies..TA 1988 Sch 15 para 9
  fraud or negligence..TA 1988 Sch 14 para 7(3)
  friendly society policies..TA 1988 Sch 15 para 3–6
  industrial assurance policies..TA 1988 Sch 14 para 2, 3 Sch 15 para 7
  mortgage protection policies..TA 1988 Sch 15 para 9
  part payments—
    friendly societies..TA 1988 s 266(6)
    trade unions..TA 1988 s 266(7)
  post-1916 policies—
    entitlement..TA 1988 s 266(1)
    limit..TA 1988 s 274(1)
    qualifying premiums..TA 1988 s 266(2)
    restrictions..TA 1988 s 266(3)
  post-13 March 1984..TA 1988 s 266(3) 268(7)(*a*) 269 Sch 14 para 8
  premiums paid from sums due under previous policies..TA 1988 Sch 15 para 15
  regulations..TA 1988 Sch 14 para 7(1)(2)
  substitution of policy..TA 1988 Sch 15 para 8(17), 17
  surrender..TA 1988 s 269
  term assurance..TA 1988 Sch 15 para 1
  time of payment of premiums..TA 1988 s 266(4)
  variation in life assured..TA 1988 Sch 14 para 8(6)
  variation of policy..TA 1988 Sch 14 para 8, Sch 15 para 18
  whole life..TA 1988 Sch 15 para 1

LIFE INTEREST
  pre-1974 dispositions terminated on death..CGTA 1979 Sch 6 para 16

LIFE POLICY
  allowable aggregate amount..TA 1988 s 546(3)
  assigned policy—
    meaning..TA 1988 s 544(1)
    chargeable person..TA 1988 s 544(6)
    reassignment etc..TA 1988 s 544(3)
  bonus, treatment..TA 1988 s 539(4)
  borrowing against..TA 1988 s 554
  capital gains..CGTA 1979 s 143
  certification—
    new non-resident policies..TA 1988 Sch 15 para 24
    pre-April 1976 policies..TA 1988 Sch 15 para 22(2)
    qualifying policies..TA 1988 Sch 15 para 21
    requirements..TA 1988 Sch 552(3)–(5), Sch 15 para 22
  charge to tax..TA 1988 s 539
  chargeable events..TA 1988 s 540, 553
  computation of gain..TA 1988 s 541
  connected policies—
    meaning..TA 1988 Sch 15 para 14(2)
    disqualification..TA 1988 Sch 15 para 14
    post-22 August 1983..TA 1988 Sch 15 para 14(9)
    relief..TA 1988 Sch 15 para 13
  early surrender etc—
    amounts payable..TA 1988 s 268(2)–(5)
    charge to tax..TA 1988 s 268(1)
    collection of tax..TA 1988 s 272
    policies affected..TA 1988 s 268(2)
    premium increased, where..TA 1988 s 268(6)
    relief, reduction for..TA 1988 s 270
  excess liability..TA 1988 s 549
  excess relief restriction..TA 1988 Sch 14 para 4
  friendly society..TA 1988 Sch 14 para 3
  husband and wife..TA 1988 Sch 14 para 1
  industrial assurance—
    premiums under..TA 1988 Sch 14 para 3
    relief..TA 1988 Sch 14 para 2

LIFE POLICY—*continued*
  loans..TA 1988 s 548
  method of charge..TA 1988 s 547
  new non-resident policy—
    meaning..TA 1988 Sch 15 para 24(1)
    amendment of qualifying conditions..TA 1988 Sch 15 para 25
    capital redemption policy..TA 1988 s 553
    certification..TA 1988 Sch 15 para 24
    issuing company, meaning..TA 1988 Sch 15 para 24(1)
    substitutions..TA 1988 Sch 15 para 26
    variation..TA 1988 Sch 15 para 24
  notification to inspector..TA 1988 s 552
  post-March 1968..TA 1988 s 539(5)
  pre-March 1968..TA 1988 s 539(6)
  pre-1965, chargeable gains..TA 1988 s 444
  qualifying—
    amendment of conditions..TA 1988 Sch 15 para 19
    certification..TA 1988 Sch 15 para 21
    determination as to..TA 1988 Sch 15 para 19
    friendly society policy, exclusion..TA 1988 Sch 15 para 21(4)
    industrial assurance..TA 1988 Sch 15 para 8
    loan against assigned policy..TA 1988 s 544(3)(*c*)
    non-resident policy. *See* new non-resident policy *supra*
    reckonable aggregate value..TA 1988 s 546(2)
    recovery of tax—
      assessment..TA 1988 Sch 14 para 6
      trustees, from..TA 1988 s 551
    refusal to certify..TA 1988 Sch 15 para 21(3)
  relevant capital payments, meaning..TA 1988 s 541(5)
  relief—
    gain charged directly..TA 1988 s 550
    manner of making..TA 1988 s 266(5)–(8)
    premiums, on. *See* LIFE ASSURANCE RELIEF
    variation, on..TA 1988 Sch 14 para 8, Sch 15 para 18
  repayment of tax..TA 1988 Sch 14 para 6
  rights not in money..TA 1988 s 443
  short-term assurances..TA 1988 Sch 15 para 10
  spouse, meaning..TA 1988 Sch 14 para 1
  substitution, relief..TA 1988 Sch 14 para 8, Sch 15 para 17
  surrender—
    capital sum, determination..TA 1988 Sch 15 para 1(6)
    charge to tax..TA 1988 s 269(1)
    collection of tax..TA 1988 s 272
    computation..TA 1988 s 269(2)
    early. *See* early surrender *supra*
    industrial assurance..TA 1988 Sch 15 para 8
    information..TA 1988 s 272(7)
    policies affected..TA 1988 s 269(5)
    qualifying policies. *See* qualifying *supra*
    relevant premiums..TA 1988 s 270(2)
    relief, reduction for..TA 1988 s 270
    returns..TA 1988 s 272(1)
    successive..TA 1988 s 269(3)
  variation in life assured..TA 1988 Sch 14 para 8(6), Sch 15 para 20

LIQUIDATION. *See* WINDING-UP

LOAN
  anti-avoidance provisions..TA 1988 s 786
  beneficial. *See* BENEFICIAL LOAN
  bridging loan..TA 1988 s 354(5) 357(4)
  capital payment to beneficiary by..FA 1981 s 83(4)
  capital transfer tax, for..TA 1988 s 364
  close company participator, to..TA 1988 s 419
  controlled company, by..TA 1988 s 422
  costs of obtaining..TA 1988 s 77
  foreign loan interest, double taxation relief..TA 1988 s 798
  home improvement. *See* HOME IMPROVEMENT.
  inheritance tax, for..TA 1988 s 364
  interest relief. *See* INTEREST RELIEF; MORTGAGE INTEREST RELIEF
  life policies etc, on..TA 1988 s 548 554
  normal commercial, meaning..TA 1988 Sch 18 para 1(5)
  notional, employee shareholdings..TA 1988 s 162
  qualifying, CGT..CGTA 1979 s 136(1)

LOAN—*continued*
  reduction of tax liability, for..TA 1988 s 787
  related, meaning..TA 1988 s 139(8)
  trader, to..CGTA 1979 s 136
  underlying tax reflecting interest on..TA 1988 s 803

LOAN CAPITAL
  over-deduction from interest..TA 1988 s 822

LOAN CREDITOR
  meaning (close company)..TA 1988 s 417(7)–(9)
  close company apportionment..TA 1988 s 425(3)
  controlled foreign company..TA 1988 s 749(7) 752(3)

LOAN INTEREST. *See* INTEREST RELIEF; MORTGAGE INTEREST RELIEF

LOCAL AUTHORITY
  meaning..TA 1988 s 519(4)
  exemption..TA 1988 s 519
  foreign currency borrowing..TA 1988 s 581

LOCAL AUTHORITY ASSOCIATION
  meaning..TA 1988 s 519(3)
  exemption..TA 1988 s 519

LOCAL CONSTITUENCY ASSOCIATION
  meaning..F(No 2)A 1983 s 7(2)
  disposals of land, relief..F(No 2)A 1983 s 7(4)–(7)
  political party, meaning..F(No 2)A 1983 s 7(8)
  relevant date..F(No 2)A 1983 s 7(1)(9)
  successor, meaning..F(No 2)A 1983 s 7(3)

LOCAL EDUCATIONAL AUTHORITY
  employee seconded to..TA 1988 s 86(3)

LOCAL ENTERPRISE AGENCY
  approval..TA 1988 s 79(5)(6)
  approved, meaning..TA 1988 s 79(4)
  benefit received from..TA 1988 s 79(3)(9)
  connected persons..TA 1988 s 79(3)
  contributions deductible..TA 1988 s 79(1)(2)

LODGER
  return of..TMA 1970 s 14

LONDON TRANSPORT EXECUTIVE
  group provisions..TA 1970 s 272(6)

LORD ADVOCATE
  recovery of penalties..TMA 1970 s 100(2)
  Special Commissioners—
    appointment of..TMA 1970 s 4(1)
    procedural rules..TMA 1970 s 57B

LOSS
  allowable, meaning..TA 1988 s 834(1)
  capital gains tax. *See under* CAPITAL GAINS TAX
  capital redemption business..TA 1988 s 458(2)
  compensation, trade etc..TA 1988 s 382(4)
  controlled foreign company, assumptions as to..TA 1988 Sch 24 para 9, Sch 26 para 1
  furnished holiday lettings..TA 1988 s 503(3)(4)
  government investment written-off..TA 1988 s 400
  indexation allowance..FA 1982 s 86
  leasing contracts and company reconstructions..TA 1988 s 395
  oil extraction activities..TA 1988 s 492(2)–(4)
  pre-trading expenditure..TA 1988 s 114(1)(*b*) 401
  relief. *See* LOSS RELIEF; TERMINAL LOSS
  Sch D Case VI—
    corporation tax..TA 1988 s 396
    income tax..TA 1988 s 392
  terminal. *See* TERMINAL LOSS
  trade, profession or vocation. *See* LOSS RELIEF
  underwriter's..TA 1988 s 450(3)(4) 453(1)–(4)
  unquoted shares in trading companies..TA 1988 s 573 574

LOSS OF OFFICE. *See also* TERMINATION PAYMENT
  clerks to General Commissioners..FA 1972 s 130

LOSS RELIEF
  business transferred to company..TA 1988 s 386
  capital payments..TA 1988 s 387(2)
  carry-back—
    interest..TA 1988 s 390
    terminal losses..TA 1988 s 388
  carry-forward—
    business transferred to company..TA 1988 s 386
    entitlement..TA 1988 s 380(2)
    interest..TA 1988 s 390
    subsequent profits, against..TA 1988 s 385
  cessation of trade..TA 1988 s 380(3)
  claim for..TA 1988 s 380(1)
  commodity futures..TA 1988 s 399(2)–(4)
  computation of loss..TA 1988 s 382(4)
  corporation tax—
    losses other than terminal..TA 1988 s 118 393
    terminal losses..TA 1988 s 394
  early years..TA 1988 s 381
  exclusions..TA 1988 s 387(2)(3)
  farming..TA 1988 s 397
  husband and wife—
    farming etc..TA 1988 s 397(10)
    set-off..TA 1988 s 382(1)(2)
  income of corresponding class, meaning..TA 1988 s 382(2)
  limited partners..TA 1988 s 117
  market gardening..TA 1988 s 397
  Sch D Case VI losses—
    corporation tax..TA 1988 s 396
    income tax..TA 1988 s 392
  set-off—
    capital allowances..TA 1988 s 383
    husband and wife..TA 1988 s 382(1)(2)
    income, against..TA 1988 s 382
    restrictions..TA 1988 s 384
  terminal loss. *See* TERMINAL LOSS
  transitional provisions..TA 1988 Sch 30 para 6, 7
  woodlands..TA 1988 s 382(4)

LOTTERY
  gains not chargeable..CGTA 1979 s 19(4)

LUMP SUM PAYMENT
  meaning (copyright)..TA 1988 s 535(11)
  personal pension scheme, under..TA 1988 s 633(1)(*b*) 635 637
  retirement..TA 1988 s 189

MACHINERY AND PLANT
  appointed day..CAA 1968 s 49(1)
  balancing allowances and charges—
    amount..FA 1971 s 44(2)(*b*)(3)
    entitlement..CAA 1968 s 33
    non-trade use..CAA 1968 s 37
    notional sales—
      certain cases..CAA 1968 s 34
      effect on other party..CAA 1968 s 35
    previous user..CAA 1968 s 39
    Sch A..TA 1988 s 32
    short-life assets..FA 1985 s 57(3)–(9)
    wear and tear subsidies..CAA 1968 s 38
  basis period, meaning..FA 1971 s 50(2)
  building alterations..CAA 1968 s 45
  capital expenditure, meaning..FA 1971 s 50(1)
  cars..CAA 1968 s 32 Sch 2 para 7
  chargeable period, meaning..FA 1971 s 50(1)
  coal industry nationalisation..CAA 1968 Sch 8 para 7
  date of expenditure post-December 1984..FA 1985 s 56
  demolition..CAA 1968 s 36
  disclaimer of writing-down and first-year allowances..FA 1971 s 44(2A)

MACHINERY AND PLANT—*continued*
  disposal before use..FA 1971 Sch 8 para 4
  estate management..FA 1971 s 47(2) TA 1988 s 32
  exceptional depreciation allowance..CAA 1968 s 89
  expenditure unallowed, meaning..CAA 1968 s 41
  films etc..FA 1982 s 72
  fire safety expenditure..FA 1974 s 17 FA 1975 s 15
  first-year allowance—
    meaning..FA 1971 s 41(1)
    apportionment..FA 1971 Sch 8 para 15(4)
    building alterations..FA 1971 Sch 8 para 15(2)
    companies..FA 1971 s 41(3)
    connected persons..FA 1971 Sch 8 para 3
    contributions to expenditure..FA 1971 Sch 8 para 15(6)
    demolition..FA 1971 Sch 8 para 14
    disclaimer..FA 1971 s 44(2A)
    double allowance exclusion..FA 1971 s 40(1)
    entitlement..FA 1971 s 41(1)
    fixtures..FA 1985 Sch 17 para 1(4)(*a*)
    investment grant..FA 1971 Sch 8 para 1
    lease-back..FA 1971 Sch 8 para 8
    leased abroad..FA 1982 s 70(4)
    new ships..FA 1971 Sch 8 para 8
    partnership..FA 1971 Sch 8 para 15(1)
    qualifying date..FA 1971 s 40(1)
    rate..FA 1971 s 42(1)
    road vehicles..FA 1971 s 43
    second-hand..FA 1971 s 40(2) FA 1972 s 68(1)
    short-life assets and..FA 1985 s 57(10) Sch 15(8) (9)
    subsidies..FA 1971 Sch 8 para 15(5)
    succession between connected persons..FA 1971 Sch 8 para 13
    succession to trade..FA 1971 Sch 8 para 15(3)
    withdrawal of..FA 1984 s 58(1)(*b*) Sch 12 para 2
  fixtures, expenditure on—
    assignment by equipment lessor..FA 1985 Sch 17 para 8
    chargeable period..FA 1985 Sch 17 para 1(4)
    consideration, included in..FA 1985 Sch 17 para 4
    disposal value..FA 1985 Sch 17 para 9
    equipment lease..FA 1985 Sch 17 para 3(4) 4(2)
    equipment lessor, by..FA 1985 Sch 17 para 3 8
    holder of interest in land, by..FA 1985 Sch 17 para 2
    incoming lessee, by..FA 1985 Sch 17 para 5 6
    leased..FA 1971 s 46(2)(*b*)
    post-July 1984..FA 1985 s 59
    qualifying interest, ceasing to have..FA 1985 Sch 17 para 7
    sale by equipment lessor..FA 1985 Sch 17 para 8
    security, land as..FA 1985 Sch 17 para 1(3)
  gifts..FA 1971 Sch 8 para 7
  hire-purchase..CAA 1968 Sch 3 FA 1971 s 45
  initial allowances..CAA 1968 s 18
  insurance company..TA 1970 s 306
  investment allowance..CAA 1968 Sch 1 para 2
  investment company..TA 1970 s 306 FA 1971 s 47(2)
  joint lessees..FA 1980 s 68 FA 1982 Sch 11 para 6
  land, profits from..CAA 1968 s 47
  leased—
    fixtures..FA 1971 s 46(2)(*b*)
    lessee's entitlement..FA 1971 s 46
    losses, company reconstructions..TA 1988 s 395(1)
    new expenditure on..FA 1986 s 57
    outside UK. *See* leased abroad *infra*
    short-term. *See* short-term leasing *infra*
  leased abroad—
    balancing adjustments..FA 1982 s 70(2)(4)
    conditions..FA 1982 s 70(1)
    first-year allowance..FA 1982 s 70(4)
    joint lessees..FA 1986 Sch 16 para 9
    period of use..FA 1982 s 70(3)
    pooling of writing-down allowances..FA 1982 Sch 11 para 2
    post-March 1982..FA 1982 s 70(10)–(12)
    recovery of excess relief..FA 1982 s 70(5) Sch 11 para 3 4 FA 1986 Sch 16 para 8
    writing-down allowance..FA 1982 s 70(2)(4) Sch 11 para 2
  lessees..CAA 1968 s 43
  lessors..CAA 1968 s 42

MACHINERY AND PLANT—*continued*
  life assurance company..FA 1971 s 47(2)
  limit of recharge, meaning..CAA 1968 Sch 7 para 3(4)
  loan interest..TA 1988 s 359
  machinery or plant allowance, meaning..CAA 1968 s 52(2)
  manner of making allowances etc..CAA 1968 s 46 FA 1971 s 48
  mineral exploration..CAA 1968 s 52 Sch 5 para 1 FA 1971 Sch 8 para 2(2)
  mining..CAA 1968 Sch 5 para 2
  new, meaning..FA 1971 s 50(1)
  new machinery or plant, meaning..CAA 1968 s 19(4)
  new ship..CAA 1968 s 31
  notional sales—
    certain cases..CAA 1968 s 34
    effect on other party..CAA 1968 s 35
  open market price, meaning..CAA 1968 s 33(2)(*a*) 34(4)
  open market value, meaning..FA 1972 s 68(10)
  part trade use..FA 1971 Sch 8 para 5
  partnership using partner's property..CAA 1968 s 44
  postponement of allowance for double taxation relief..TA 1988 s 810
  predictable life..CGTA 1979 s 37(1)(*c*)
  professions, vocations etc..CAA 1968 s 47 FA 1971 s 47(1)
  replacement option—
    cars..CAA 1968 Sch 2 para 7
    entitlement..CAA 1968 s 40
  restriction of allowance..FA 1972 s 68
  rollover relief..CGTA 1979 s 118
  sales between connected persons etc..CAA 1968 Sch 7 para 3
  second-hand—
    first-year allowance..FA 1971 s 40(2)
    restriction..FA 1972 s 68(1)
  short-life asset—
    meaning..FA 1985 s 57(1)
    connected person, disposal to..FA 1985 s 57(7)–(9)
    excluded from treatment as..FA 1985 s 57(1)(*b*) Sch 15
    treatment as, election..FA 1985 s 57
  short-term leasing—
    meaning..FA 1980 s 64(3)
    aircraft..FA 1980 s 64(6)
    cars..FA 1980 s 69
    connected persons..FA 1980 s 73(6)
    containers..FA 1980 s 64(7)
    enterprise zones..FA 1980 s 74(6)
    first-year allowance..FA 1980 s 64
    individuals, by..TA 1988 s 384(6)
    joint lessees..FA 1980 s 68
    leasing, meaning..FA 1980 s 73(3)
    pre-1980 contracts..FA 1980 s 72
    qualifying purposes..FA 1980 s 64(2)
    recovery of excess relief..FA 1980 s 66
    ships..FA 1980 s 64(5)(6A)
    television sets etc..FA 1980 Sch 12 Pt II
    writing-down allowance..FA 1980 s 65
  sites for, expenditure on..CAA 1968 s 9
  sports grounds..F(No 2)A 1975 s 49
  spreading of expenditure under certain contracts..FA 1984 Sch 12 para 6 8–10
  succession to trades..CAA 1968 s 48
  thermal insulation..FA 1975 s 14
  use after user not attracting allowances..FA 1971 Sch 8 para 7
  wear and tear subsidies..FA 1971 Sch 8 para 6
  woodlands..FA 1971 s 47(1)
  writing-down allowance—
    meaning..CAA 1968 s 49(2)(3)
    adjustments..CAA 1968 s 24
    calculation—
      alternative method..CAA 1968 s 21
      change from normal to alternative..CAA 1968 s 22
      mines etc..CAA 1968 s 23
      normal method..CAA 1968 s 20
      post-October 1970..FA 1971 s 44(2)
    connected persons..FA 1971 s 44(7)
    disclaimer..FA 1971 s 44(2A) FA 1984 s 59(4)–(8)
    disposal value..FA 1971 s 44(5)(6)
    entitlement..CAA 1968 s 19(1) FA 1971 s 44(1)
    fixtures..FA 1985 Sch 14 para 1(4)(*b*)

MACHINERY AND PLANT—*continued*
writing-down allowance—*continued*
fractions and percentages..CAA 1968 s 19(3)
limit..CAA 1968 s 27
mines, oil wells etc..CAA 1968 s 23
non-trade use..CAA 1968 s 28
part year..CAA 1968 s 25
percentages, determination of..CAA 1968 s 26
post-November 1962..CAA 1968 Sch 4 para 2 3
post 1968–69..CAA 1968 Sch 4 para 1
post-1970..FA 1971 s 44
previous user..CAA 1968 s 30
qualifying expenditure..FA 1971 s 44(4)
relevant capital amount..CAA 1968 Sch 4 para 3(3)
short-life asset..FA 1985 s 57(3)–(9)
short-term leasing..FA 1980 s 65
wear and tear subsidies..CAA 1968 s 29

MAGISTRATES' COURT
recovery of tax..TMA 1970 s 65

MAINTENANCE FUND
historic buildings—
election by trustees..TA 1988 s 691
income tax—
charge to..TA 1988 s 694(1)(4)(5)
exemption..TA 1988 s 694(3)
rate..TA 1988 s 694(2)(2A)
resettlement..TA 1988 s 694(6)
tax-free transfers..TA 1988 s 694(7)
reimbursement of settlor..TA 1988 s 692
one-estate election..TA 1988 s 27
part settled property..TA 1988 s 693

MAINTENANCE PAYMENT
meaning..TA 1988 s 347A(4)
child of the family, meaning..TA 1988 s 51B(7) 347B(7) FA 1988 s 40(1)
existing obligations, under—
new rules, election for..FA 1988 s 39
1988–89..FA 1988 s 37
1989–90 onwards..FA 1988 s 38
outside UK, arising..TA 1988 s 51A(4) 347A(4)
qualifying—
meaning..TA 1988 s 51B(1) 347B(1)
deductions in respect of..TA 1988 s 51B(2)–(7) 347B(2)–(7)
recipient..FA 1988 s 40(2)

MANAGEMENT COMPANY
offshore fund with interests in..FA 1984 Sch 19 para 12

MANAGEMENT EXPENSES
costs as to loan finance..TA 1988 s 77
insurance company..TA 1988 s 76
investment company..TA 1988 s 75
local enterprise agency contributions..TA 1988 s 79(2)
long term business levy..TA 1988 s 76(7)
mineral rights..TA 1988 s 121
mineral royalties..TA 1988 s 122(2)
overseas life insurance company..TA 1988 s 76(6)
redundancy payments..TA 1988 s 579(3)(4)
unit trusts..TA 1988 s 468(4)
war injuries payments..TA 1988 s 587(2)
war risk premiums..TA 1988 s 586(2)

MARKET
chargeable person..TA 1988 s 59(3)
Sch D Case I..TA 1988 s 55

MARKET GARDEN
fluctuating profits..TA 1988 s 96
land, meaning..TA 1988 s 832(1)
loss relief..TA 1988 s 397
Sch D Case I..TA 1988 s 53

MARKET MAKER
meaning..TA 1988 s 737(6)
liability to tax..TA 1988 s 737(3)

MARKETING BOARD
reserve fund..TA 1988 s 509

MARRIAGE
election to disregard..TA 1988 s 261
year of assessment, in..TA 1988 s 257(8)

MARRIED COUPLE
meaning..TA 1988 s 151(2)
living together, meaning..TA 1988 s 282(1) FA 1988 s 40(3)

MARRIED WOMAN. *See also* HUSBAND AND WIFE
living with husband, meaning..TA 1988 s 282
separate taxation. *See* SEPARATE TAXATION

MATERNITY PAY
Sch E..TA 1988 s 150

MEMBER OF PARLIAMENT
accommodation allowance..TA 1988 s 200
pension—
 contributions..TA 1988 s 613(1)
 payments..TA 1988 s 613(3)
pensionable salary, meaning..TA 1988 s 629(2) 654(3)
personal pension scheme..TA 1988 s 654
retirement annuity premiums..TA 1988 s 629
terminal grants..FA 1988 s 190

MEMORIAL GARDEN
capital expenditure..TA 1988 s 91(7)

MERGER
meaning..TA 1970 s 278A(2)
chargeable gains..TA 1970 s 278A

MINERAL
meaning..TA 1988 s 122(6)
Continental Shelf..FA 1973 s 38

MINERAL DEPLETION
writing-down allowances..CAA 1968 s 60

MINERAL DEPOSITS
meaning..CAA 1968 s 87(1) FA 1971 Sch 8 para 7

MINERAL RIGHTS
corporation tax, deductions..TA 1988 s 121(3)
management expenses..TA 1988 s 121
overseas, capital allowances..CAA 1968 s 53 Sch 5 para 3 5

MINERAL ROYALTIES
meaning..TA 1988 s 122(5)
charge to tax..TA 1988 s 122
management expenses..TA 1988 s 122(2)
mineral, meaning..TA 1988 s 122(6)
mineral lease or agreement, meaning..TA 1988 s 122(6)
Northern Ireland..TA 1988 s 122(7)
statutory instrument..FA 1970 s 29(8)
terminal loss relief—
 allowable loss..FA 1970 Sch 6 para 6
 CGT..FA 1970 Sch 6 para 9
 claim..FA 1970 Sch 6 para 4
 deduction, by..FA 1970 Sch 6 para 7
 election..FA 1970 Sch 6 para 5
 relevant event..FA 1970 Sch 6 para 3(2)
 terminal loss, meaning..FA 1970 Sch 6 para 4(3)
 time limit..FA 1970 Sch 6 para 8(1)
under deduction..TA 1970 s 521(3)(*d*)

MINES, OIL WELLS ETC
appointed day..CAA 1968 s 65(1)
appointed day expenditure—
  meaning..CAA 1968 Sch 6 para 2
  assets purchased from predecessor..CAA 1968 Sch 6 Pt III
  computation..CAA 1968 Sch 6 Pt II
assets—
  meaning..CAA 1968 s 65(2) FA 1986 Sch 13 para 1
  limitation on expenditure..FA 1986 Sch 13 para 20
  non-trader, formerly owned by..FA 1986 Sch 13 para 24
  part of expenditure..FA 1986 Sch 13 para 21
  traders, formerly owned by..FA 1986 Sch 13 para 19
balancing allowances and charges..CAA 1968 s 58 FA 1986 Sch 13
capital allowances..FA 1986 s 55 Sch 13 para 2
carry-back..CAA 1968 s 15
commencement of trade, expenditure before..CAA 1968 s 64
demolition..CAA 1968 s 55 FA 1986 Sch 13 para 14
disposal receipts..FA 1986 Sch 13 paras 10 18
exploration—
  abortive..CAA 1968 s 62
  machinery and plant..CAA 1968 Sch 5 para 1 FA 1971 Sch 8 para 2(2)
initial allowance—
  amount..CAA 1968 s 56
land acquired outside UK..CAA 1968 s 54 Sch 5 para 4 5
machinery and plant for exploration..CAA 1968 s 52
mine, charge under Sch D Case I..TA 1988 s 55
mineral deposits, meaning..CAA 1968, s 87(1)
old expenditure..FA 1986 Sch 14 paras 1–8
overseas mineral rights..CAA 1968 s 53 Sch 5 para 3 5
persons not in trade of mining..CAA 1968 s 59
pre-trading exploration expenditure..FA 1986 Sch 13 para 6
public services etc outside UK..CAA 1968 s 61 75 FA 1986 Sch 13 para 7
qualifying expenditure..CAA 1968 s 51 FA 1986 Sch 13
regulations, power to make..CAA 1968 s 63
restoration expenditure..FA 1986 Sch 13 para 8
terminal losses..TA 1988 s 389(2)
time when expenditure incurred..FA 1986 Sch 13 para 3
writing-down allowance—
  calculation..CAA 1968 s 23
  entitlement and computation..CAA 1968 s 57 FA 1986 Sch 13 para 9
  mineral depletion..CAA 1968 s 60

MINING RENT
meaning..TA 1988 s 119(3)
charge to tax..TA 1988 s 119

MINISTER OF RELIGION
houses and expenditure..TA 1988 s 332

MISTAKE
appeal as to..TMA 1970 s 33(4)
assessment, in..TMA 1970 s 33
claim, in..TMA 1970 s 42(8)

MOBILITY ALLOWANCE
exemption..TA 1988 s 617

MORTGAGE
capital gains tax..CGTA 1979 s 23
interest. *See* MORTGAGE INTEREST RELIEF
protection policy, relief..TA 1988 Sch 15 para 9

MORTGAGE INTEREST RELIEF
combined payment, meaning..TA 1988 s 377(10)
conditions..TA 1988 s 370
deduction of tax..TA 1988 s 369
determination whether relevant interest..TA 1988 s 370
home improvement..TA 1988 s 355(2A)–(2C) 372
joint borrowers..TA 1988 s 343(6)
limit..TA 1988 s 357(1)
limited loans..TA 1988 s 373
loan agreement, meaning..TA 1988 s 377(10)
non-deductible..TA 1988 s 574(*o*)
qualifying borrowers..TA 1988 s 376(1)–(3)

MORTGAGE INTEREST RELIEF—*continued*
qualifying lenders..TA 1988 s 376(4)–(6)
regulations, power to make..TA 1988 s 378
relevant loan interest, meaning..TA 1988 s 370(1)
repayment of tax to lender..TA 1988 s 7(3) 11(4) 369(6)
set-off against taxable income..TA 1988 s 369(4)
variation of repayment terms..TA 1988 s 377

MOTOR VEHICLE
car. *See* CAR
first-year allowance..FA 1971 s 43
passenger vehicle..CGTA 1979 s 130
short-life asset, whether..FA 1985 Sch 15

MUTUAL BUSINESS
meaning..TA 1988 s 491(9)
distributions..TA 1988 s 490 491

NATIONAL DEBT
funds for reducing..TA 1988 s 514

NATIONAL DEBT COMMISSIONERS
public revenue dividends..TA 1988 Sch 3 Pt I
Sch C exemption..TA 1988 s 49(1)

NATIONAL FREIGHT CORPORATION
transfer of assets..TA 1988 s 513(2)

NATIONAL HERITAGE
transfer of Treasury functions to Board..FA 1985 s 95

NATIONAL HERITAGE MEMORIAL FUND
covenanted donations..TA 1988 s 339(9)
exemption..TA 1988 s 507(1)

NATIONAL INSURANCE
Class 4 contributions, relief..TA 1988 s 617(5)
personal pension schemes..TA 1988 s 649
profit-related pay..TA 1988 s 172(2)(3)

NATIONAL RADIOLOGICAL PROTECTION BOARD
exemption..TA 1988 s 512

NATIONAL SAVINGS
bank interest..TA 1988 s 325

NATIONAL-SOCIALIST PERSECUTION
compensation for..TA 1988 s 330

NATIONALISATION
aircraft and shipbuilding shares..FA 1976 s 54
capital allowances..CAA 1968 s 80
dealers in securities..TA 1988 s 471 472

NEGLECT
assessment where—
    capital gains tax..TMA 1970 s 36 37
    income tax..TMA 1970 s 36 37
    personal representatives..TMA 1970 s 40(2)
interest on overdue tax..TMA 1970 s 88

NOMINEE
business expansion scheme..TA 1988 s 311(1)–(3)
capital gains tax..CGTA 1979 s 46
funds in court..CGTA 1979 s 99(1)
information as to chargeable gains..TMA 1970 s 26
transfer of securities: accrued interest..TA 1988 s 720(1)(2)

NON-RESIDENT
agency profits..TMA 1970 s 79
branch profits..TMA 1970 s 79

NON-RESIDENT—*continued*
  CGT. *See under* CAPITAL GAINS TAX
  charge on percentage of turnover..TMA 1970 s 80
  chargeability—
    capital gains tax..TMA 1970 s 84
    corporation tax..TMA 1970 s 85
    income tax..TMA 1970 s 78
  copyright royalties..TA 1988 s 536
  deep discount securities..TA 1988 Sch 4 para 4(5)(6)
  deposit with deposit-taker..TA 1988 s 481(5)(*h*)(*j*)
  double taxation relief..TA 1988 s 808
  dual resident, meaning..FA 1989 s 129(7)
  entertainer..TA 1988 s 555
  foreign dividends..TA 1988 s 123
  foreign government securities held by..TA 1988 s 48
  gift to..CGTA 1979 s 147B
  indemnity..TMA 1970 s 83(2)
  Inter-American Development Bank..FA 1976 s 131
  interest paid to—
    charge on income..TA 1988 s 340
    deductibility..TA 1988 s 82
  Irish resident..TA 1988 s 746
  life policy. *See under* LIFE POLICY
  local authority bonds held by..TA 1988 s 581(1)
  merchanting profits..TMA 1970 s 81
  personal reliefs..TA 1988 s 278
  premiums taxable under Sch A and Sch D..TA 1988 Sch 2
  recovery of tax assessed on, petroleum production..FA 1973 Sch 15 para 4A
  responsibilities of chargeable persons..TMA 1970 s 83(1)
  Sch A..TA 1988 s 43
  Sch D Case VI..TA 1988 s 43
  sportsman..TA 1988 s 555
  tax credit..TA 1988 s 232 813
  transfer of securities: accrued interest..TA 1988 s 715(1)(5)
  UK government securities held by..TA 1988 s 47
  unauthorised agent or broker..TMA 1970 s 82

NON-RESIDENT COMPANY
  basis of assessment..TA 1988 s 70(3)
  capital allowances..CAA 1968 s 76
  capital gains tax..CGTA 1979 s 15
  chargeable gains..TA 1988 s 11(2)
  controlled. *See* CONTROLLED FOREIGN COMPANY
  corporation tax..TA 1988 s 11
  information as to chargeable gains..TMA 1970 s 28
  life insurance. *See* OVERSEAS LIFE INSURANCE COMPANY
  non-payment of tax by..FA 1989 s 134
  offshore fund, material interest..TA 1988 s 759
  offshore income gains..TA 1988 s 762
  set-off of income tax deducted..TA 1988 s 11(3)
  tax credits, withdrawal..TA 1988 s 813
  transfer of assets to..TA 1970 s 268A
  trustees, gains..FA 1981 s 85

NON-RESIDENT TRUST
  capital gains—
    information..TMA 1970 s 28
    postponement of tax due from beneficiary. *See under* POSTPONEMENT OF TAX
    post-April 1981..FA 1981 s 80
    pre-April 1981..CGTA 1979 s 17
  disposals..FA 1981 s 88
  information..TMA 1970 s 28 FA 1981 s 84
  losses deductible from chargeable gains..FA 1981 s 83(6)
  offshore income gain..TA 1988 s 762(2)–(4)

NORTHERN IRELAND
  appeals in..FA 1988 s 134
  capital allowances, transitional relief..FA 1984 Sch 12 para 4
  case stated..TMA 1970 s 58 59(4)(5)
  company returns..TMA 1970 s 11(9)
  credit unions..TA 1988 s 487
  educational body, employee seconded to..TA 1988 s 86(3)(*c*)(*d*)
  ejectment..TMA 1970 s 117

NORTHERN IRELAND—continued
family credit..TA 1988 s 617
friendly societies..TA 1988 Sch 15 para 3
funds in court..TA 1988 s 328(8)
government securities, interest paid without deduction..TA 1988 s 51
grants for industry..TA 1988 s 93(2)(3)
housing associations and societies..TA 1988 s 488(6)(8) 489(12)
housing benefit..TA 1988 s 617
income support..TA 1988 s 151(9) 617
initial allowance, industrial buildings..FA 1971 s 51
mineral royalties..TA 1988 s 122(7)
Northern Ireland Electricity Service..TA 1988 s 511(4)(5)
proceedings—
   meaning..TMA 1970 s 58(3)(*a*)
   county court..TMA 1970 s 59
   tax cases..TMA 1970 s 58
recoverable as civil debt, meaning..TMA 1970 s 65(4)
recovery of penalties..TMA 1970 s 100

NOTICE
appeal, of..TMA 1970 s 31
assessment. *See* NOTICE OF ASSESSMENT
close company apportionment..TA 1988 Sch 19 para 13, 14
controlled foreign company, as to..TA 1988 s 753 754(6)–(8)
determination of amount, for..TMA 1970 s 55(4)(5)
election for hearing by Special Commissioners..TMA 1970 s 46(1)
employees' emoluments, as to..TMA 1970 s 15
information, requiring. *See under* INFORMATION
lease at undervalue, as to..TA 1988 s 42(1)
liability to tax—
   capital gains..TMA 1970 s 11A 12
   corporation tax..TMA 1970 s 10
   income tax..TMA 1970 s 7
nil liability, benefits in kind..TA 1988 s 166
offshore fund, as to—
   application for certification, inviting..TA 1988 Sch 27 para 15 18
payment out of public funds, information as to..TMA 1970 s 18A
postponement of tax, as to..TMA 1970 s 55(3)(3A)
profit-related pay, as to..TA 1988 s 181
service of. *See* SERVICE OF DOCUMENTS
statement of case, as to..TMA 1970 s 56(2)(3)(5)
stockjobber, to..TMA 1970 s 21
underwriting agent, to..FA 1988 Sch 5 para 2
withdrawal of appeal..TMA 1970 s 54(3)(4)

NOTICE OF ASSESSMENT
date of..F(No 2)A 1975 s 67(1)
form..TMA 1970 s 113(3)
general provisions..TMA 1970 s 29(5)(6)
service of..TMA 1970 s 29(5)

OCCUPATIONAL PENSION SCHEME *See also* RETIREMENT BENEFITS SCHEME
approved before 23rd July 1987..TA 1988 Sch 23
refund of contributions..FA 1971 Sch 3 para 8

OFFICE
payment on removal from. *See* TERMINATION PAYMENT

OFFSHORE FUND
meaning..TA 1988 s 759(1)
ability to realise interests..TA 1988 s 759(4)
account period..TA 1988 s 760(8)–(10)
appeals..TA 1988 Sch 27 para 16
assessment, effect of non-certification..TA 1988 Sch 27 para 17, 18
capital gain, deduction of offshore income gain..TA 1988 s 763
certification—
   appeal..TA 1988 Sch 27 para 16
   application for..TA 1988 Sch 27 para 15
   breach of conditions, power to disregard..TA 1988 Sch 27 para 14
   dealing company, interests in..TA 1988 Sch 27 para 12
   determination as to..TA 1988 Sch 27 para 15, 18(4)–(6)
   disclosure of decisions etc..TA 1988 Sch 27 para 20

OFFSHORE FUND—*continued*
  certification—*continued*
    fund investing in trading company..TA 1988 Sch 27 para 10
    information, notice requiring..TA 1988 Sch 27 para 15(4)
    investments, disregard of certain..TA 1988 Sch 27 para 13
    investments, exclusion..TA 1988 Sch 27 para 6–9
    invitation to apply for..TA 1988 Sch 27 para 18(2)
    management company, interests in..TA 1988 Sch 27 para 12
    modification of conditions..TA 1988 Sch 27 Pt II
    notice of refusal..TA 1988 Sch 27 para 15(3)
    postponement of tax pending..TA 1988 Sch 27 para 19
    subsidiaries dealing in commodities..TA 1988 Sch 27 para 11
    time for application..TA 1988 Sch 27 para 15(2)
  charge to tax..TA 1988 s 761
  charities, exemption..TA 1988 s 761(6)
  children's settlements..TA 1988 s 663(2)
  commodities—
    income..TA 1988 Sch 27 para 4
    subsidiaries dealing in..TA 1988 Sch 27 para 11
  corporation tax, charge to..TA 1988 s 761(2)
  death, disposal on..TA 1988 s 757(3)(4)
  deduction of offshore income gain to determine capital gain..TA 1988 s 763
  disposal—
    meaning..TA 1988 s 757(2)
    material time..TA 1988 s 757(7)
    post-31 December 1984..TA 1988 s 757(1)(*b*)
    1979 Act disposal, meaning..TA 1988 s 763(1)
  distributing fund—
    certification. *See* certification *supra*
    conditions..TA 1988 Sch 27 para 1
    investments, exclusion..TA 1988 Sch 27 para 6–9
  equalisation arrangements..TA 1988 Sch 27 para 2
  exchange of securities..TA 1988 s 757(5)(6)
  failure to prepare accounts..TA 1988 Sch 27 para 1(3)
  foreign tax, deduction for..TA 1988 Sch 27 para 5(4)
  full distribution policy, requirements..TA 1988 Sch 27 para 1
  gifts, unindexed gain..TA 1988 Sch 28 para 3(3)
  income tax—
    charge to..TA 1988 s 761(1)
    charities, exemption..TA 1988 s 761(6)
  indexation allowance..TA 1988 Sch 28 para 3(1) 4(3)(4)
  insurance company..TA 1988 s 441(8), Sch 28 para 3(4)
  losses, unindexed gain..TA 1988 Sch 28 para 3(5)
  market value, determination..TA 1988 s 759(9)
  material interest—
    meaning..TA 1988 s 759
    more than one class..TA 1988 s 760(7)
  more than 10 per cent of assets as interest in single company..TA 1988 s 760(3)–(5)
  non-resident company, gain accruing to..TA 1988 s 762(1)(5)(6)
  non-qualifying—
    meaning..TA 1988 s 760(1)
    identification: capital gains tax..FA 1982 s 88(9)
  non-resident settlements..TA 1988 s 762(2)–(4)
  offshore income gain, meaning..TA 1988 Sch 28 para 5
  overseas company, shares in..TA 1988 s 759(1)(*a*)(8)
  part disposal..TA 1988 s 763(4)
  post-1983 gains..TA 1988 Sch 28 para 4
  primary fund, meaning..TA 1988 Sch 27 para 6(1)(*a*)
  qualifying, meaning..TA 1988 Sch 27 para 6(2)
  remittance basis, resident not domiciled in UK..TA 1988 s 761(5)
  restriction on distributions under foreign law..TA 1988 Sch 27 para 1(6)
  rollover relief, effect..TA 1988 s 763(5) Sch 28 para 3(2)
  Sch D Case IV or V, charge under..TA 1988 Sch 27 para 3
  scope of legislation..TA 1988 s 757(1)
  settled property..TA 1988 s 761(7)
  trustees, charge to tax..TA 1988 s 764
  UK equivalent profits..TA 1988 Sch 27 para 5
  unindexed gain, calculation..TA 1988 Sch 28 para 2,3

OIL EXTRACTION ACTIVITIES
  meaning..TA 1988 s 502(1)
  ACT, restriction on set-off..TA 1988 s 497
  associated companies, meaning..TA 1988 s 502(3)
  capital allowances..TA 1988 s 492(5)–(7)

OIL *Index* [76]

OIL EXTRACTION ACTIVITIES—*continued*
capital gains tax, charge to..FA 1973 s 38(3A)–(3C)
charges on income..TA 1988 s 494
company owned by consortium..TA 1988 s 499
corporation tax treatment..TA 1988 s 492(1)
deep discount securities..TA 1988 Sch 4 para 6
disregard of grant-aided expenditure..TA 1988 s 495
group relief..TA 1988 s 492(8)
income tax treatment..TA 1988 s 492(1)
licence. *See* OIL LICENCE
losses..TA 1988 s 492(2)–(4)
non-resident, disposal of assets by..FA 1973 s 38(3A)–(3C)
oil, meaning..TA 1988 s 502(1)
oil rights, meaning..TA 1988 s 502(1)
petroleum revenue tax. *See* PETROLEUM REVENUE TAX
recovery of tax assessed on non-resident..FA 1973 Sch 15 para 4A
ring fence income, meaning..TA 1988 s 492(2)
transfer of assets within group..FA 1986 Sch 13 para 23
valuation of oil..TA 1988 s 493

OIL LICENCE
appraisal work, meaning..FA 1988 s 64(6)(*b*)
corresponding expenditure..FA 1986 Sch 13 para 22(3)
disposal of—
  balancing charges..FA 1988 s 63(5)
  material, meaning..FA 1988 s 62(2)
  relevant qualifying expenditure..FA 1988 s 63
  scientific research, expenditure on..FA 1988 s 61(3)
  undeveloped areas, relating to..FA 1988 s 62
exploration work, meaning..FA 1988 s 64(6)(*a*)
original licensee..FA 1986 Sch 13 para 22(2)
qualifying expenditure..FA 1986 Sch 13 para 22(1)
undeveloped area, relating to..FA 1988 s 64(1)

OIL WELL
capital allowances. *See* MINES, OIL WELLS ETC

OLD AGE PENSIONER
increased personal relief for..TA 1988 s 257(2)

OPTION
disposal of asset..CGTA 1979 s 137
indexation allowance..FA 1982 Sch 13 para 7 FA 1983 Sch 6 para 10 FA 1985 Sch 19 para 15
material interest test..TA 1988 Sch 9 para 38
quoted, disposal, as..CGTA 1979 s 137(4)
traded option..CGTA 1979 s 137(4)(*aa*)(9) 138(1)(*aa*)
wasting assets..CGTA 1979 s 138

OVERDRAFT
interest relief restriction..TA 1988 s 353(3)(*a*)

OVERDUE TAX
interest on. *See under* INTEREST
recovery of. *See* RECOVERY OF TAX

OVERSEAS INCOME. *See* FOREIGN INCOME

OVERSEAS LIFE INSURANCE COMPANY
meaning..TA 1988 s 431(1)
annuity business..TA 1988 s 446
double taxation agreements..TA 1988 s 449
general annuity business..TA 1988 s 437(6)
investment income..TA 1988 s 445 724(5)
management expenses..TA 1988 s 76(6)
set-off against corporation tax..TA 1988 s 447
tax credit..TA 1988 s 447(4) 448

OVERSEAS PENSION
exemption..TA 1988 s 614(5) 615 616

OVERSEAS SECURITIES
meaning..TA 1988 s 732(4)
anti-avoidance provisions..TA 1988 s 732(4)

OVERSEAS SERVICE
employees' pension funds..TA 1988 s 614(5)
pension..TA 1988 s 615
pension fund..TA 1988 s 614(4) 615(2)

OVERSEAS TERRITORY
meaning..TA 1988 s 615(7)

PAINTER
relief..TA 1988 s 538

PAKISTAN
pension..TA 1988 s 615(2)
State Bank..TA 1988 s 517

PARLIAMENTARY CONSTITUENCY
former, meaning..F(No 2)A 1983 s 7(1)(*a*)
new, meaning..F(No 2)A 1983 s 7(1)(*b*)
relief on reorganisation..F(No 2)A 1983 s 7

PARTICIPATOR. *See under* CLOSE COMPANY

PARTNER
limited—
   meaning..TA 1988 s 117(2)
   reliefs, restrictions of..TA 1988 s 117
machinery and plant, partnership using..CAA 1968 s 44
personal relief..TA 1988 s 277
retirement annuity payments..TA 1988 s 628
sub-contractor's certificate..TA 1988 s 563

PARTNERSHIP
assessment..TMA 1970 s 118(3)
basis period, meaning..TA 1988 s 115(6)
change in ownership..TA 1988 s 113
company, involving—
   rules..TA 1988 s 114
   transfer of relief..TA 1988 s 116
connected persons..TA 1988 s 839(4)
control, meaning..TA 1988 s 168(12) 840
controlled abroad..TA 1988 s 112
loan for acquisition of interest in..TA 1988 s 362
losses—
   capital allowances..TA 1988 s 383(8)(11)
   Sch D Case VI..TA 1988 s 392
machinery and plant—
   first-year allowance..FA 1971 Sch 8 para 15(1)
   loan interest..TA 1988 s 359
   partner's..CAA 1968 s 44
method of assessment..TA 1988 s 111
partner's machinery and plant, using..CAA 1968 s 44
patent rights..TA 1988 s 525(3)(4)
profit-related pay scheme employer, as..TA 1988 s 183
retirement annuity payments..TA 1988 s 628 683 FA 1988 Sch 3 para 19
return—
   chargeable gains..TMA 1970 s 12
   income..TMA 1970 s 9
stock relief..TA 1988 Sch 30 para 19
sub-contractor's certificate..TA 1988 s 564
terminal losses..TA 1988 s 388(5) 389(5)

PASSENGER VEHICLE
chargeable gains..CGTA 1979 s 130

PATENT FEES
deductibility..TA 1988 s 83

PATENT RIGHTS
meaning..TA 1988 s 533(1)
balancing allowance..TA 1988 s 520(4)
balancing charge..TA 1988 s 520(6)
capital allowances..TA 1988 s 520–522 532

PATENT RIGHTS—*continued*
  capital sums—
    death, winding-up etc..TA 1988 s 525
    income, as..TA 1988 s 524
  commencement of patent, meaning..TA 1988 s 533(1)
  connected persons, transactions between..TA 1988 s 521(4)(5)
  Crown use..TA 1988 s 533(4)
  date of expenditure..FA 1985 s 56(8)
  death..TA 1988 s 525
  expenses, relief..TA 1988 s 526
  future patents..TA 1988 s 533(5)(6)
  income from patents, meaning..TA 1988 s 533(1)
  inventor's income..TA 1988 s 529
  licences..TA 1988 s 533(2)(3)
  manner of making allowances etc..TA 1988 s 529
  partnership changes..TA 1988 s 525(3)(4)
  royalties, spread over several years..TA 1988 s 527
  sales..TA 1988 s 523
  UK patent, meaning..TA 1988 s 533(1)
  under deduction..TA 1988 s 821(3)(*b*)
  winding-up..TA 1988 s 525(1)
  writing-down allowance—
    entitlement..TA 1988 s 520(4) 521(1)(*b*) 522
    manner of making..TA 1988 s 528

PAYE
  agency workers..TA 1988 Sch 29 para 6
  assessment..TA 1988 s 203
  cash vouchers..TA 1988 s 143
  director's tax paid by employer..TA 1988 s 164
  payment, meaning..TA 1988 s 203A
  profit sharing schemes..TA 1988 Sch 10 para 7
  repayments, restriction..TA 1988 s 204
  tax tables..TA 1988 s 203(6)

PAYROLL DEDUCTION SCHEME. *See* CHARITY

PAYMENT OF TAX
  ACT..TA 1988 Sch 13 para 3 10(2)
  appeal, pending..TMA 1970 s 56(9)
  beneficiary under non-resident trust..FA 1984 Sch 14 para 11
  capital gains tax..CGTA 1979 s 7
  company payments not distributions..TA 1988 Sch 16 para 4
  corporation tax—
    generally..TA 1988 s 10
    payment dates..TA 1988 Sch 30 para 1
  date for, income tax..TA 1988 s 5
  postponed tax..TMA 1970 s 55(9)
  share options..TA 1988 s 137

PENALTY
  agent's default, Sch A..TA 1988 s 23(7)(8)
  assessment of amounts..F(No 2)A 1987 s 84
  criminal liability, Scotland..TMA 1970 s 107
  determination of—
    appeal..TMA 1970 s 100B
    death of person incurring..TMA 1970 s 100A
    officer of Board, by..TMA 1970 s 100
  dividend warrants etc..TA 1988 s 234(4)
  evidence—
    fraud etc..TMA 1970 s 104
    profits..TMA 1970 s 101
  failure to give notice of liability..TMA 1970 s 7(3) 10 (2)
  failure to make return—
    capital gains tax..TMA 1970 s 93 FA 1988 Sch 3 para 27, 28
    corporation tax..TMA 1970 s 94
    income tax..TMA 1970 s 93 FA 1988 Sch 3 para 27, 28
    special return..TMA 1970 s 98
  false statement—
    purchased life annuity..TA 1988 s 658(5)
    retirement annuity..TA 1988 s 619(7)
  incorrect return or accounts—
    assisting..TMA 1970 s 99
    capital gains tax..TMA 1970 s 95 FA 1988 Sch 3 para 27, 28

PENALTY—*continued*
  incorrect return or accounts—*continued*
    corporation tax..TMA 1970 s 96
    delay in correcting..TMA 1970 s 97
    income tax..TMA 1970 s 95 FA 1988 Sch 3 para 27, 28
  migration of companies..TA 1988 s 766(3) FA 1988 s 131 132
  mitigation..TMA 1970 s 102
  proceedings—
    Commissioners, before..TMA 1970 s 100C
    court, before..TMA 1970 s 100D
  recovery of..TMA 1970 s 100 103
  refusal to allow deduction of income tax..TMA 1970 s 106(1)
  savings for criminal proceedings..TMA 1970 s 103
  special..TMA 1970 s 98A
  special return etc, as to..TMA 1970 s 98
  sub-contractor's certificate, as to..TA 1988 s 561(10)–(12)
  summary—
    appeal against..TMA 1970 s 53(2)
    Commissioners, awarded by..TMA 1970 s 53
  time limits..TMA1970 s 103
  two or more in respect of same tax..TMA 1970 s 97B
  underwriting agent, on..FA 1988 Sch 5 para 10
  witness, default..TMA 1970 s 52(3) 53

PENSION. *See also* PENSION FUND *and* PERSONAL PENSION SCHEMES
  amount accruing, tax on..FA 1989 s 41
  colonial. *See* COLONIAL PENSION
  foreign. *See* FOREIGN PENSION
  Indian, Pakistan and colonial..TA 1988 s 615
  investment in building societies..TA 1988 s 476(7)
  overseas service..TA 1988 s 614(4) 615
  public..TA 1988 s 19(2)
  Sch E..TA 1988 s 19(2)–(4)
  social security. *See under* SOCIAL SECURITY
  Special Commissioners..TMA 1970 s 4(6)
  victims of Nazi persecution..TA 1988 s 330
  Victoria Cross etc..TA 1988 s 317
  war service, exemption..TA 1988 s 318
  wounds pension..TA 1988 s 315

PENSION FUND. *See also* PERSONAL PENSION SCHEMES
  Central African..TA 1988 s 615(2)
  exempt, meaning..TA 1988 s 476(7)
  financial futures, dealings in..TA 1988 s 659
  Indian family..TA 1988 s 614(2)
  Indian, Pakistan and colonial..TA 1988 s 615
  occupational schemes. *See* OCCUPATIONAL PENSION SCHEME
  overseas employees..TA 1988 s 614(5)
  Overseas Service..TA 1988 s 614(4) 615(2)
  Parliamentary..TA 1988 s 613
  sponsored superannuation scheme, meaning..TA 1988 s 624(1)
  supplementary schemes..TA 1988 s 614
  traded options, dealings in..TA 1988 s 659

PENSION SCHEME
  occupational. *See* OCCUPATIONAL PENSION SCHEME
  personal. *See* PERSONAL PENSION SCHEMES

PERSON UNDER DISABILITY. *See* INCAPACITATED PERSON

PERSONAL ALLOWANCE
  entitlement..TA 1988 s 257
  indexation..TA 1988 s 1(4)

PERSONAL INJURY
  meaning..TA 1988 s 329(4)
  interest on damages..TA 1988 s 329

PERSONAL PENSION SCHEMES
  meaning..TA 1988 s 630
  amendment of without approval..TA 1988 s 631(4)
  annuity, payment of—
    death of member, after..TA 1988 s 634(5) 636
    earned income, treated as..TA 1988 s 643(3)

PERSONAL PENSION SCHEMES—*continued*
  annuity, payment of—*continued*
    member, to..TA 1988 s 633(1)(*a*) 634
  appeal to Special Commissioners..TA 1988 s 651
  approval—
    application for..TA 1988 s 631
    cessation of..TA 1988 s 631(4)
    grant of..TA 1988 s 631(2)
    refusal of..TA 1988 s 631(2)
      appeal..TA 1988 s 631(3)
      grounds for, disclosure of..TA 1988 s 631(3)
      written notice of..TA 1988 s 631(3)
    restrictions on—
      benefits..TA 1988 s 633
      contributors..TA 1988 s 638(6)(7)
      excess contributions..TA 1988 s 638(3)–(5)
      persons establishing scheme..TA 1988 s 632
      scheme administrator..TA 1988 s 638(1)
      transfer payments..TA 1988 s 647
    transitional provisions..TA 1988 s 655
    withdrawal of..TA 1988 s 650
  assessment of—
    contributions under unapproved arrangements..TA 1988 s 648
    unauthorised payments..TA 1988 s 647
  associated employments, earnings from..TA 1988 s 646A
  authorised insurance company, *meaning*..TA 1988 s 630
  bank, scheme established by..TA 1988 s 632
  benefits, allowable..TA 1988 s 633
  building society, schemes established by..TA 1988 s 632
  carry-back of contributions..TA 1988 s 641
  carry-forward of relief..TA 1988 s 642
  claim for relief..TA 1988 s 639(1)
  contributions—
    carry-back..TA 1988 s 641
    excess, restriction of..TA 1988 s 638(3)–(5)
    information about..TA 1988 s 652
    relevant earnings, deduction from..TA 1988 s 639(1)
    relief by deduction from..TA 1988 s 639(2)–(4)
    repayment on death of member..TA 1988 s 637(2)
    unapproved arrangements, under..TA 1988 s 618
  contributors, permitted..TA 1988 s 638(6)(7)
  death of member—
    annuity paid after..TA 1988 s 634(5) 636
    contributions, return of..TA 1988 s 637(2)
    lump sum paid on..TA 1988 s 633(1)(*c*) 637
  earnings cap..TA 1988 s 640A
  excess contributions, restriction of..TA 1988 s 638(3)–(5)
  information..TA 1988 s 652
    penalties..TMA 1970 s 98 TA 1988 s 653
  lump sum payment—
    death of member..TA 1988 s 633(1)(*c*) 637
    member, to..TA 1988 s 633(1)(*b*) FA 1989 Sch 7 para 11 12
  member, *meaning*..TA 1988 s 630
  Member of Parliament..TA 1988 s 654
  national insurance..TA 1988 s 649
  net relevant earnings, calculation of..TA 1988 s 646
  penalties..TA 1988 s 653
  personal pension arrangements..TA 1988 s 630
  regulations, power to make..TA 1988 s 632(4) 828
  relevant earnings—
    calculation of..TA 1988 s 644
    pensionable employment, exclusion of earnings from..TA 1988 s 644(3) 645
  scheme administrator, *meaning*..TA 1988 s 630
  Special Commissioners, appeal to..TA 1988 s 651
  tax relief—
    adjustment of..TA 1988 s 639(1)
    annuities..TA 1988 s 643(3)
    carry-back of contributions..TA 1988 s 641
    carry-forward of relief..TA 1988 s 642
    claims for..TA 1988 s 639(1)
    deduction from contributions..TA 1988 s 639(2)–(4)
    deduction from relevant earnings..TA 1988 s 639(1)
    double, exclusion of..TA 1988 s 639(7)
    employer's contributions..TA 1988 s 643(2)

PERSONAL PENSION SCHEMES—*continued*
  tax relief—*continued*
    net relevant earnings, calculation of.. TA 1988 s 646
    relevant earnings, calculation of.. TA 1988 s 644 645
    scheme investments, exemption of.. TA 1988 s 643(2)
  transfer payments, provision for.. TA 1988 s 638(2)
  transitional provisions.. TA 1988 s 655
  unauthorised payments.. TA 1988 s 647
  unapproved arrangements, contributions paid under.. TA 1988 s 618

PERSONAL RELIEFS
  additional for child.. TA 1988 s 259
  age allowance.. TA 1988 257(2)(3)
  bereavement allowance.. TA 1988 s 262
  blind persons.. TA 1988 s 265 FA 1988 Sch 3 para 8
  charges on income.. TA 1988 s 276
  children, apportionment.. TA 1988 s 260
  disregard of marriage.. TA 1988 s 261
  entitlement.. TA 1988 s 256
  indexation.. FA 1988 s 257(9)
  joint interests.. TA 1988 s 277
  life assurance premiums.. TA 1988 s 266 FA 1988 Sch 3 para 9
  life policies, limit on.. TA 1988 s 274
  married couple—
    elderly, relief for.. TA 1988 s 257E
    entitlement.. TA 1988 s 257A
    indexation.. TA 1988 s 257C
    separated.. TA 1988 s 257F
    transfer of.. TA 1988 s 257B
    transitional relief.. TA 1988 s 257D–257E
  national insurance Class 4 contributions.. TA 1988 s 617(5)
  non-residents.. TA 1988 s 278
  partners.. TA 1988 s 277
  personal allowance.. TA 1988 s 257
  separate assessment.. TA 1988 s 284
  separate taxation.. TA 1988 s 287
  those aged 80 and over.. TA 1988 s 257(3)
  wife's earned income.. TA 1988 s 267(6)(7)

PERSONAL REPRESENTATIVE
  meaning.. TA 1988 s 701(4)
  administration. *See* ADMINISTRATION OF ESTATE
  annual payment made by.. TA 1988 s 347A(3)
  assessment on.. TMA 1970 s 40 FA 1989 s 151
  capital gains tax.. CGTA 1979 s 48 Sch 1 para 4
  chargeability.. TMA 1970 s 74
  copyright payments.. TA 1988 s 535(5)
  interest relief.. TA 1988 s 358
  profit sharing schemes.. TA 1988 Sch 10 para 1(2)
  residence of.. FA 1989 s 111
  rights under life policies etc.. TA 1988 s 547(1)(*c*)
  stock dividends.. TA 1988 s 249(5)
  transactions in securities.. TA 1988 s 703(11)
  transfer of securities: accrued interest.. TA 1988 s 715(1)(*c*)
  underwriter's.. TA 1988 s 455(4)

PETROL
  benefit in kind.. TA 1988 s 158

PETROLEUM COMPANY
  meaning.. TA 1988 s 771(1)
  oil extraction activities. *See* OIL EXTRACTION ACTIVITIES
  petroleum revenue tax. *See* PETROLEUM REVENUE TAX
  sales at under- or overvalue—
    arm's length price.. TA 1988 s 771(6)
    associated companies.. TA 1988 s 771(5)
    determination of questions.. TA 1988 s 772(8)
    resident buyer or seller, as.. TA 1988 s 771(4)

PETROLEUM REVENUE TAX
  deduction for corporation tax.. TA 1988 s 500
  interest on overpaid.. TA 1988 s 501

PILOT'S BENEFIT FUND
  meaning..TA 1988 s 607(4)
  approval..TA 1988 s 607

PLANT. *See* MACHINERY AND PLANT

POINDING
  recovery of tax..TMA 1970 s 63

POLICE PROVIDENT BENEFITS
  exemption..TA 1988 s 467

POOLING
  adjustments..FA 1983 Sch 6 para 11
  deep discount securities..FA 1983 Sch 6 para 1(2)(*aa*)
  effect..FA 1983 Sch 6 para 3
  election for..CGTA Sch 5 para 4 5 FA 1983 Sch 6 para 2 FA 1985 s 68(3)(*d*) Sch 19 para 20
  entitlement..FA 1983 s 34(1)
  exchanges etc..CGTA 1979 Sch 5 para 6
  exclusion..CGTA 1979 Sch 5 para 3
  identification rules—
    generally..CGTA 1979 s 65
    indexation allowance. *See under* INDEXATION ALLOWANCE
    post-April 1985 disposals..FA 1985 Sch 19 para 17
  indexation allowance..FA 1983 Sch 6 para 5–8
  indexed pool..FA 1983 Sch 6 para 7
  indexed rise in indexed pool..FA 1983 Sch 6 para 8
  new holding—
    meaning..FA 1985 Sch 19 para 9(3)
    computation of allowances..FA 1985 Sch 19 para 11
    employee, securities held by..FA 1985 Sch 19 para 8(2)
    identification rules post-April 1985..FA 1985 Sch 19 para 17 19
    indexed pool of expenditure..FA 1985 Sch 19 para 13 14
    operative event, meaning..FA 1985 Sch 19 para 13(4)
    option consideration..FA 1985 Sch 19 para 15
    part disposal..FA 1985 Sch 19 para 10 11(1) 12
    post-April 1982 holding..FA 1985 Sch 19 para 9(1)
    post-April 1985 holding..FA 1985 Sch 19 para 9(2)
    qualifying expenditure..FA 1985 Sch 19 para 12
  1982 holding—
    meaning..FA 1985 Sch 19 para 6
    identification..FA 1985 Sch 19 para 19
    relevant allowable expenditure..FA 1985 Sch 19 para 7(2)
    single asset, regarded as..FA 1985 Sch 19 para 7
  no gain/no loss transfers..FA 1983 Sch 6 para 9
  operative event, meaning..FA 1983 Sch 6 para 7(3)
  options..FA 1983 Sch 6 para 10
  parallel..FA 1983 Sch 6 para 9 FA 1985 Sch 19 para 20
  post-March 1982—
    computation of allowance..FA 1982 Sch 13 para 10
    effect..FA 1982 Sch 13 para 8
    identification rules..FA 1982 Sch 13 para 9(4)
    operative date..FA 1982 Sch 13 para 8(4)
    relevant allowable expenditure..FA 1982 Sch 13 para 9
  qualifying securities..FA 1983 Sch 6 para 1(2)
  relevant allowable expenditure..FA 1982 s 86(2)(*b*)(3) FA 1985 Sch 19 para 8(1)(*c*)
  underwriters..CGTA 1979 Sch 5 para 7
  unindexed pool..FA 1983 Sch 6 para 6

POST-CESSATION RECEIPTS
  Sch D. *See under* SCHEDULE D

POSTPONEMENT OF TAX
  appeal, pending, amount..TMA 1970 s 55(6)(7)
  application for..TMA 1970 s 55(3)(3A)
  beneficiary, non-resident trust—
    meaning..FA 1984 Sch 14 para 1(1)
    attributed gain—
      meaning..FA 1984 Sch 14 para 1(1)
      claim, specified in..FA 1984 Sch 14 para 2(5)(6)
      personal representatives..FA 1984 Sch 14 para 2(7)
      tax referable to..FA 1984 Sch 14 para 3
    balance of capital payments..FA 1984 Sch 14 para 12
    basic rules..FA 1984 Sch 14 para 6

POSTPONEMENT OF TAX—*continued*
beneficiary, non-resident trust—*continued*
calculation period, meaning..FA 1984 Sch 14 para 5(1)
capital gains tax..FA 1984 Sch 19 para 6(5)
capital transfer tax, consequential relief..FA 1984 Sch 14 para 16
claims..FA 1984 Sch 14 para 2
close relative—
meaning..FA 1984 Sch 14 para 1(1)
payments received by..FA 1984 Sch 14 para 9
conditions for..FA 1984 s 70(1)
death of beneficiary..FA 1984 Sch 14 para 6(3)
ineligible gain, meaning..FA 1984 Sch 14 para 1(1)
information..FA 1984 Sch 14 para 15
initial calculations..FA 1984 Sch 14 para 4
notification of disposals..FA 1984 Sch 14 para 15(3)
payment of postponed tax..FA 1984 Sch 14 para 11
personal representatives, claim by..FA 1984 Sch 14 para 2(7)(8)
previous postponement..FA 1984 Sch 14 para 2(3)
related benefits—
capital payments..FA 1984 Sch 14 para 10(2)–(5)
determination..FA 1984 Sch 14 para 10
offshore income gains..FA 1984 Sch 14 para 10(2)
payments received by close relatives..FA 1984 Sch 14 para 9
related settlement—
meaning..FA 1984 Sch 14 para 5(6)
relevant benefits..FA 1984 Sch 14 para 5(2)–(5)
relevant benefits..FA 1984 Sch 14 para 5
relevant year of assessment, meaning..FA 1984 Sch 14 para 1(1)
second or later claims..FA 1984 Sch 14 para 14
subsequent capital payments received..FA 1984 Sch 14 para 7 8
tax already paid, meaning..FA 1984 Sch 14 para 4(5)
unpaid tax, meaning..FA 1984 Sch 14 para 6(4)
Commissioners..TMA 1970 s 55(11)
payment on determination..TMA 1970 s 55(9)
recovery of tax not postponed..TMA 1970 s 55
transfer of assets to non-resident company..TA 1970 s 268A
transfer of proceedings..TMA 1970 s 55(11)

POULTRY
herd basis..TA 1988 Sch 5 para 9

PREFERENCE DIVIDEND
meaning..TA 1988 s 832(1)

PREMISES
meaning..TA 1988 s 24(1)

PREMIUM
meaning—
industrial buildings..FA 1972 s 69(4)
insurance..TA 1988 s 431(4)
lease..TA 1988 s 24(1)(3)
capital gains..CGTA 1979 Sch 3 para 2 3
conversion of securities..CGTA 1979 s 83
deduction—
premiums and rents received, from..TA 1988 s 37
Sch D Cases I and II..TA 1988 s 87
deemed..TA 1988 s 24(2)
life assurance relief. *See* LIFE ASSURANCE RELIEF
reinsurance, Lloyd's..TA 1988 s 450(5)
relief where taxable under Sch A and D..TA 1988 Sch 2
rent or Sch D profits, as..TA 1988 s 34
retirement annuity. *See* RETIREMENT ANNUITY
Sch A, taxed under, CGT..CGTA 1979 Sch 3 para 5
taxable, dealers in land..TA 1988 s 99

PREMIUMS TRUST FUND
underwriters..TA 1988 s 450

PRIORITY OF TAX
England and Wales..TMA 1970 s 62
Scotland..TMA 1970 s 64

PRIVATE RESIDENCE
  CGT—
   acquisition to realise gain..CGTA 1979 s 103(3)
   adjustment..CGTA 1979 s 103(2)
   business use..CGTA 1979 s 103(1)
   exemption..CGTA 1979 s 101
   let as residential accommodation..FA 1980 s 80
   periods of absence..CGTA 1979 s 102
  dependent relative..CGTA 1979 s 105
  furnished holiday lettings..FA 1984 Sch 11 para 5
  mortgage interest. *See* MORTGAGE INTEREST RELIEF
  rollover relief exclusion..CGTA 1979 s 111B(1)
  settled property..CGTA 1979 s 104

PRIZES
  gains not chargeable..CGTA 1979 s 19(4)

PROFESSION. *See also* TRADE
  computation of tax. *See* SCHEDULE D Cases I and II
  employee seconded to charity..TA 1988 s 86
  losses. *See* LOSS RELIEF
  machinery and plant allowances..CAA 1968 s 47
  Sch D Case II..TA 1988 s 18(3)
  stock relief..TA 1988 Sch 30 para 19

PROFESSIONAL BODY
  fees and subscriptions..TA 1988 s 201

PROFIT
  meaning—
   CGT..TMA 1970 s 29(8)(*b*)
   corporation tax..TMA 1970 s 29(8)(*c*) TA 1988 s 6(4)(*a*)
   income tax..TMA 1970 s 29 (8)(*a*)
  annual, Sch D Case VI..TA 1988 s 18(3)
  conventional basis, meaning..TA 1988 s 110(4)
  distributable, meaning..TA 1988 Sch 19 para 4(1)
  distribution, available for, group relief..TA 1988 Sch 18
  earnings basis, meaning..TA 1988 s 110(3)
  evidence of..TMA 1970 s 101
  fluctuating, farming etc..TA 1988 s 96
  investment company..TA 1988 s 75
  non-allowable deductions..TA 1988 s 817
  Sch D..TA 1988 s 18
  trade, profession or vocation. *See* SCHEDULE D Cases I and II

PROFIT-RELATED PAY
  meaning..TA 1988 s 169(1)
  accounting periods, identification of..TA 1988 Sch 8 para 9, 10
  accountant, report by..TA 1988 s 175(2) 180(1)(*b*)
  administration..TA 1988 s 179–182
  alteration of terms..TA 1988 s 177B
  annual returns..TA 1988 s 180
   time limit..TA 1988 s 180(2)(3)
  appeal to Special Commissioners..TA 1988 s 182
  Crown employment, exclusion of..TA 1988 s 174(1)(2)
  disposal of property..TA 1988 s 417(6)
  distributable pool—
   meaning..TA 1988 Sch 8 para 11
   calculation of..TA 1988 Sch 8 para 11–15
   payments from..TA 1988 Sch 8 para 16–18
  employee benefit trust, and..TA 1988 s 417(4)–(12)
  employees—
   excluded..TA 1988 Sch 8 para 7, 8
   meaning..TA 1988 s 169(2)
   minimum percentage in scheme..TA 1988 Sch 8 para 6
  employer, *see* scheme employer
  employment—
   meaning..TA 1988 s 169(1)
   excluded..TA 1988 s 174
   dual..TA 1988 s 172(1)
   unit..TA 1988 s 169(1)
  group of companies, application for registration by..TA 1988 s 173(2)(3)

PROFIT-RELATED PAY—*continued*
  independent accountant—
    meaning..TA 1988 s 184
    reports by..TA 1988 s 175(2) 180(1)(*b*)
  information required by Board..TA 1988 s 175(1)(*e*) 181
    penalties..TMA 1970 s 98
  local authority employment, exclusion of..TA 1988 s 174
  losses—
    meaning..TA 1988 s 169(1)
    ascertainment of..TA 1988 Sch 8 para 19, 20
  material interest held by employee..TA 1988 Sch 8 para 7
  minimum wage legislation, compliance with..TA 1988 s 175(1)(*c*)(4)
  national insurance exemption, effect of..TA 1988 s 172(2)(3)
  partnerships..TA 1988 s 183
  parts of undertakings..TA 1988 Sch 8 para 21 22
  pay, *meaning*..TA 1988 s 169(1)
  penalties..TMA 1970 s 98
  percentage of employees within scheme..TA 1988 Sch 8 para 6–8
  profit and loss account, preparation of..TA 1988 Sch 8 para 19, 20
  profit-period—
    meaning..TA 1988 s 169(1)
    identification of..TA 1988 Sch 8 para 9
    length of..TA 1988 Sch 8 para 10
  profits—
    meaning..TA 1988 s 169(1)
    ascertainment of..TA 1988 Sch 8 para 19, 20
  recovery of tax..TA 1988 s 179
  registration of scheme—
    accountant, report by..TA 1988 s 175(2) 180(1)(*b*)
    amendment of, change of employer..TA 1988 s 177
    application for..TA 1988 s 173–177
      amendment of..TA 1988 s 177
      form of..TA 1988 s 175(1)
      refusal of..TA 1988 s 176(2)(*a*)(4)(5)
      time limit..TA 1988 s 176
    Board of Inland Revenue, by..TA 1988 s 176(1)(*c*)(2)
    cancellation of..TA 1988 s 178
      appeal against..TA 1988 s 182
      notice of..TA 1988 s 178(6)
    conditions—
      distributable pool, calculation of..TA 1988 Sch 8 para 11–14
      employees, excluded..TA 1988 Sch 8 para 7, 8
      employees, included..TA 1988 Sch 8, para 5, 6
      employer, identification of..TA 1988 Sch 8 para 2
      employment unit, identification of..TA 1988 Sch 8 para 4
      minimum percentage of employees in scheme..TA 1988 Sch 8 para 6
      payments to employees..TA 1988 Sch 8 para 6–8
      profit and loss account, preparation of..TA 1988 Sch 8 para 19, 20
      writing, terms of scheme in..TA 1988 Sch 8 para 1
    Crown employment..TA 1988 s 174(1)(2)
    employer—
      application by..TA 1988 s 173
      change of..TA 1988 s 177
    excluded employments..TA 1988 s 174
    form of application..TA 1988 s 175(1)
    group of companies, application by..TA 1988 s 173(2)(3)
    information..TA 1988 s 175(1)(*e*)
    local authority employment..TA 1988 s 174
    notification of..TA 1988 s 176(7)
    person eligible to apply for..TA 1988 s 173
    refusal to register..TA 1988 s 176(2)(*a*)(4)(5)
      appeal against..TA 1988 s 182(1)(*a*)
      notification of..TA 1988 s 176(8)
    time limit for..TA 1988 s 176(1)
  relief from tax—
    calculation of..TA 1988 s 171
    dual employment..TA 1988 s 172(1)
    exceptions from..TA 1988 s 172
    national insurance exemption, effect of..TA 1988 s 172(2)(3)
  return, submission of..TA 1988 s 180
  scheme employer—
    application for registration by..TA 1988 s 173
    change of, amendment of registration..TA 1988 s 177
    death of..TA 1988 s 177A

PROFIT-RELATED PAY—*continued*
scheme employer—*continued*
group of companies as..TA 1988 s 173(2)(3)
identification of..TA 1988 Sch 8 para 2
partnership as..TA 1988 s 183
recovery of tax from..TA 1988 s 179
Special Commissioners, appeal to..TA 1988 s 182
taxation of—
recovery of tax from scheme employer..TA 1988 s 179
relief from..TA 1988 s 171

PROFIT-SHARING SCHEME
appropriate allowance..TA 1988 s 186(12)
appropriate percentage..TA 1988 Sch 10 para 3
appropriated shares..TA 1988 s 186
approval—
alteration to scheme..TA 1988 Sch 9 para 4, 30(2)
appeals..FA 1988 Sch 9 para 5
application for..TA 1988 Sch 9 para 1(1)(2)
conditions for..TA 1988 Sch 9 para 1
withdrawal of..TA 1988 Sch 9 para 3
capital gains tax..TA 1988 Sch 29 para 28
capital receipts..TA 1988 s 186(3)(12) Sch 10 para 4
company reconstruction etc..TA 1988 Sch 10 para 5
consortium..TA 1988 s 187(7)
disposals..TA 1988 s 186(4)–(10) 187(8)
excess shares..TA 1988 Sch 10 para 6
group scheme..TA 1988 Sch 9 para 1(3)(4)
income, not treated as..TA 1988 s 186(2)
information..TA 1988 Sch 9 para 6
initial market value..TA 1988 Sch 9 para 30(4)
limit on appropriations..TA 1988 Sch 9 para 30(5)
locked-in value, meaning..TA 1988 s 186(5)
market value, meaning..TA 1988 s 187(2)
material interest test..TA 1988 Sch 9 para 37–39
obligations under..TA 1988 Sch 10 para 1
participant, meaning..TA 1988 s 186(2)
participant's salary, meaning..TA 1988 s 187(5)
PAYE..TA 1988 Sch 10 para 7
period of retention..TA 1988 Sch 10 para 2
permitted transactions..TA 1988 Sch 10 para 1(1)
personal representatives..TA 1988 Sch 10 para 1(2)
release date, meaning..TA 1988 s 187(2)
relevant amount, meaning..TA 1988 s 187(2)
Sch D deduction..TA 1988 s 85
shares—
meaning..TA 1988 s 187(2)
conditions..TA 1988 Sch 9 Pt II
trustees..TA 1988 Sch 9 para 30(1)
unauthorised shares..TA 1988 Sch 10 para 6

PUBLIC CORPORATION
transfer of assets—
ACT and group relief..TA 1988 s 410(7)
successor companies..TA 1988 s 513

PUBLIC DEPARTMENT
Income Tax Acts..TA 1988 s 829(3)
public revenue dividends..TA 1988 Sch 3 para 5

PUBLIC LENDING RIGHT
tax treatment..TA 1988 s 537

PUBLIC REVENUE DIVIDEND
meaning..TA 1988 s 45
accounts..TA 1988 Sch 3 para 1, 6
Bank of England, payable to..TA 1988 s 17 Sch 3 Pt I
Bank of Ireland, payable to..TA 1988 s 17 Sch 3 Pt I
chargeable persons..TA 1988 Sch 3 para 6
charities..TA 1988 Sch 3 para 4
foreign..TA 1988 s 48(4)
inspection powers..TA 1988 Sch 3 para 13
Ireland, double taxation relief..TA 1988 Sch 3 para 15
National Debt Commissioners..TA 1988 s 17 Sch 13 Pt I

PUBLIC REVENUE DIVIDEND—*continued*
overseas, meaning..TA 1988 s 45
public offices and departments..TA 1988 Sch 3 para 5
public revenue, meaning..TA 1988 s 45
Sch C..TA 1988 s 17
Sch D..TA 1988 s 17(5) 18(3)

PUBLIC SERVICES
mining, contributions outside UK..CAA 1968 s 61 FA 1986 Sch 13 para 7

PUBLIC TRUSTEE
funds in court..TA 1988 s 328

PURCHASED LIFE ANNUITY
meaning..TA 1988 s 657(1)
appeals..TA 1988 s 658(1)
capital element..TA 1988 s 656
determination of capital element..TA 1988 s 656(2)(3)
elderly, by..TA 1988 s 271(2)(*b*), 365
exclusions..TA 1988 s 657(2)
false statements..TA 1988 s 658(5)
inspector, determination by..TA 1988 s 658(1)
interest relief..TA 1988 s 365
life annuity, meaning..TA 1988 s 657(1)
notices..TA 1988 s 656(5)(6)
regulations, powers..TA 1988 s 656(2)(3)
tax deduction..TA 1988 s 656(5)(6)

QUARRY
rents..TA 1988 s 119
Sch D Case I..TA 1988 s 55

QUOTED SECURITIES
meaning..CGTA 1979 Sch 5 para 1(1)
held April 1965—
  actual cost, reference to..CGTA 1979 Sch 5 para 2
  deemed acquisition value..CGTA 1979 Sch 5 para 1
  pooling—
    election for..CGTA 1979 Sch 5 para 4 5
    exclusion..CGTA 1979 Sch 5 para 3
    subsequent disposals..CGTA 1979 Sch 5 para 6
    underwriters..CGTA 1979 Sch 5 para 7
value at April 1965..CGTA 1979 Sch 6 para 3

RADIO RELAY SERVICE
easements and wayleaves..TA 1988 s 120

RAILWAY
Sch D Case I..TA 1988 s 55

RATE OF TAX. *See under relevant tax*

RATIONALISATION OF INDUSTRY
cancellation of certification..TA 1988 s 571
certification..TA 1988 s 568(2)
contributions—
  meaning..TA 1988 s 568(5)
  deductible..TA 1988 s 568
  repayment..TA 1988 s 569
damage payments..TA 1988 s 570(2)
payments as trading receipts..TA 1988 s 570
post-cessation payments..TA 1988 s 570(3)
redundancy schemes..TA 1988 s 572

RECEIPT
tax paid..TMA 1970 s 60(2)

RECEIVER
chargeability..TMA 1970 s 75

RECOGNISED INVESTMENT EXCHANGES
regulations extending enactments to include..F(No 2)A 1987 s 73

RECONSTRUCTION. See COMPANY RECONSTRUCTION

RECOVERY OF PENALTIES. See PENALTY

RECOVERY OF TAX
business expansion scheme..TA 1988 s 307
certificate that tax due..TMA 1970 s 70
civil debt, as..TMA 1970 s 65
company, from..TMA 1970 s 108(2)
company payments not distributions..TA 1988 Sch 16 para 11
company reconstructions etc..CGTA 1979 s 87(4)
Continental Shelf..FA 1973 Sch 15 para 4–8
corporation tax..TMA 1970 s 108(2)
county court..TMA 1970 s 66
distress..TMA 1970 s 61
evidence..TMA 1970 s 70
group of companies..TA 1988 s 347
High Court..TMA 1970 s 68
higher rate tax from beneficiary..TA 1988 s 689
inferior courts in Scotland..TMA 1970 s 67
interest on tax..TMA 1970 s 69
life assurance relief..TA 1988 Sch 14 para 6 Sch 15 para 16
magistrates' court..TMA 1970 s 65
non-resident, petroleum production..FA 1973 Sch 15 para 4A
Scotland..TMA 1970 s 63 67
shareholder, from..TA 1988 s 346
tax not postponed..TMA 1970 s 55

REDUNDANCY PAYMENT. See also TERMINATION PAYMENT
meaning..TA 1988 s 580(1)
additional payments..TA 1988 s 90
deductible..TA 1988 s 579(2)
employer's payment, meaning..TA 1988 s 580(1)
income tax exemption..TA 1988 s 579 580(3)
management expenses..TA 1988 s 579(3)(4)

REDUNDANCY REBATE
meaning..TA 1988 s 580(1)
trading receipt..TA 1988 s 579(2)

REDUNDANCY SCHEME
capital allowances..TA 1988 Sch 21 para 6(2)
contribution—
  meaning..TA 1988 Sch 21 para 1(1)
  deductible, meaning..TA 1988 Sch 21 para 1(1)
  paid after relief given..TA 1988 Sch 21 Pt III
  repayment of..TA 1988 Sch 21 para 1(2)
  statutory schemes..TA 1988 s 572
damage—
  meaning..TA 1988 Sch 21 para 1(1)
  qualifying..TA 1988 Sch 21 para 6
payment, meaning..TA 1988 Sch 21 para 1(1)
person chargeable, meaning..TA 1988 Sch 21 para 1(1)
relief—
  computation..TA 1988 Sch 21 para 5
  conditions..TA 1988 Sch 21 para 3, 4
  entitlement..TA 1988 Sch 21 para 2
  exclusion..TA 1988 Sch 21 Pt III
scheme, meaning..TA 1988 Sch 21 para 1(1)
statutory, meaning..TA 1988 s 572(3)

REGIONAL DEVELOPMENT GRANT
meaning..TA 1988 s 592(3)
exemption..TA 1988 s 92
oil extraction activities..TA 1988 s 495

REGISTERED FRIENDLY SOCIETY. See FRIENDLY SOCIETY

REGULATIONS
CGT—
  appeals..TMA 1970 s 57B
  exemption..CGTA 1979 s 5(1C)
deposit taker: relevant deposits..TA 1988 s 481(6) 482(11)(12)
life assurance relief..TA 1988 Sch 14 para 7

REGULATIONS—*continued*
mines, oil wells etc..CAA 1968 s 63
mortgage interest..TA 1988 s 378
purchased life annuity..TA 1988 s 658(2)(3)
repayments to wife..TA 1988 s 281(5)
sub-contractors in construction industry..TA 1988 s 566

RELATIVE
meaning..TA 1988 s 275
connected person..TA 1988 s 839(2)

RELIEF
adjustment..TA 1988 s 823
artists' receipts..TA 1988 s 538
business expansion scheme. *See* BUSINESS EXPANSION SCHEME
copyright. *See* COPYRIGHT
double taxation. *See* DOUBLE TAXATION RELIEF
group. *See* GROUP RELIEF
interest on overdue tax—
    disallowance..TMA 1970 s 90
    effect..TMA 1970 s 91
losses. *See* LOSS RELIEF
overseas tax. *See* DOUBLE TAXATION RELIEF
payroll deduction scheme. *See* CHARITY
personal. *See* PERSONAL RELIEFS
premiums taxable under Sch A and D..TA 1988 Sch 2
profit-related pay. *See* PROFIT-RELATED PAY
replacement of business assets. *See* ROLLOVER RELIEF
retirement. *See* RETIREMENT RELIEF
termination payments..TA 1988 s 188
transfer of securities: accrued interest..TA 1988 s 713 714
work done abroad. *See* WORK DONE ABROAD

REMISSION OF TAX
interest on overdue tax—
    exchange restrictions..TMA 1970 s 92
    generally..TMA 1970 s 86(6)

RENT
meaning—
    mines etc..TA 1988 s 119(3)
    Sch A..TA 1988 s 24(6)
    self-build society..TA 1988 s 489(11)
commercial rent, meaning..FA 1972 s 69(4)
deductions from, Sch A—
    general rules..TA 1988 s 25
    land managed as one estate..TA 1988 s 26
electric line wayleaves..TA 1988 s 120
mines, quarries etc..TA 1988 s 119
non-payment, Sch A relief..TA 1988 s 41
restriction on Sch A deductions..TA 1988 Sch 1
Schedule A..TA 1988 s 15(1)
tied premises..TA 1988 s 98
under deduction..TA 1988 s 821(2)

RENTCHARGE
land sold and leased back..TA 1988 s 780(2)
Schedule A..TA 1988 s 15(1)

REPAIR
industrial buildings..CAA 1968 s 8

REPAYMENT OF TAX
assessment as to..TMA 1970 s 30
claim, on..TMA 1970 s 42(7)
error or mistake, for..TMA 1970 s 33(2)
false statements, Scotland..TMA 1970 s 107
furnished holiday lettings..TA 1988 s 503(7)
life policies, relief..TA 1988 Sch 14 para 7(2)
supplement. *See* REPAYMENT SUPPLEMENT
wife, to..TA 1988 s 281

REPAYMENT SUPPLEMENT
companies..TA 1988 s 825
persons other than companies..F(No 2)A 1975 s 47 TA 1988 s 824

REPLACEMENT OF BUSINESS ASSETS. *See* ROLLOVER RELIEF

REPUBLIC OF IRELAND. *See* IRELAND, REPUBLIC OF

RESEARCH AND DEVELOPMENT
meaning..TA 1988 s 312(1)
business expansion scheme..TA 1988 s 289(1)(*b*)(*c*)

RESEARCH ASSOCIATION
payments to..CAA 1968 s 90

RESETTLEMENT GRANT
European Assembly representatives..TA 1988 s 190

RESIDENCE
capital gains tax..CGTA 1979 s 18
Commonwealth citizen temporarily abroad..TA 1988 s 334
company..FA 1988 s 66 Sch 7
company purchase of own shares..TA 1988 s 220
controlled foreign company..TA 1988 s 749(1)–(4) Sch 25 para 5(2)
double taxation relief by credit..TA 1988 s 794
person working abroad..TA 1988 s 335
personal representatives, of..FA 1989 s 111
Sch E, determination..TA 1988 s 207
temporary, in UK..TA 1988 s 336
trustees, of..FA 1989 s 110

RESTRICTIVE COVENANT
know-how sales..TA 1988 s 531(8)
taxation of..TA 1988 s 313 FA 1988 s 73

RETIREMENT ANNUITY
approval—
  conditions..TA 1988 s 618 620(2)(4)
  dependants, contracts for..TA 1988 s 621
carry-forward of relief..TA 1988 s 625
dependants, contracts for..TA 1988 s 621
false statements..TA 1988 s 619(7)
financial futures, dealings in..TA 1988 s 659
fund, exemption..TA 1988 s 620(6)
life insurance, contracts for..TA 1988 s 621
Lloyd's underwriters..TA 1988 s 627
Ministers and others..TA 1988 s 629
net relevant earnings, meaning..TA 1988 s 623(6)
older contributors..TA 1988 s 626
partnership—
  earned income..TA 1988 s 628
  relevant earnings..TA 1988 s 623(9)
pensionable office, meaning..TA 1988 s 623(3)
pilots' benefit fund..TA 1988 s 607
qualifying conditions..TA 1988 s 623(2)–(4)
qualifying premium..TA 1988 s 620(1)
relevant earnings—
  individual..TA 1988 s 623(2)(5)
  partner..TA 1988 s 623(9)
relief—
  entitlement..TA 1988 s 619(1)
  nature and amount..TA 1988 s 619
  sponsored superannuation scheme, meaning..TA 1988 s 624(1)
trust schemes..TA 1988 s 620(5)
wife's earnings..TA 1988 s 623(1)
withdrawal of approval..TA 1988 s 620(7)

RETIREMENT BENEFITS SCHEME
meaning..TA 1988 s 611(1)
administrator—
  meaning..TA 1988 s 612(1)
  responsibility of..TA 1988 s 606
alteration and approval..TA 1988 s 590(6)

RETIREMENT BENEFITS SCHEME—*continued*

approval—
  alteration of scheme..TA 1988 s 590(6)
  application for..TA 1988 s 604
  conditions..TA 1988 s 590(2) (3) FA 1988 Sch 3 para 18
  discretionary..TA 1988 s 591
  mandatory..TA 1988 s 590(3)
  method..TA 1988 s 590(7)
  withdrawal..TA 1988 s 590(5)
approved—
  meaning..TA 1988 s 612(1)
  accelerated accrual..FA 1989 Sch 6 para 23 24
  additional voluntary contributions..FA 1989 Sch 6 para 31–35
  application of provisions..FA 1989 Sch 6 para 19
  associated employments..FA 1989 Sch 6 para 25
  augmentation..FA 1989 Sch 6 para 27
  centralised..FA 1989 Sch 6 para 28
  connected schemes..FA 1989 Sch 6 para 26
  election for application of provisions..FA 1989 Sch 6 para 29
  exemption and reliefs..TA 1988 s 592
  relevant annual remuneration..FA 1989 Sch 6 para 30
  remuneration..FA 1989 Sch 6 para 20 22
associated employers..TA 1988 s 590A(3) (4) 590B
charge to tax—
  commutation..TA 1988 s 599
  conditions..TA 1988 s 595
  employer, repayments to..TA 1988 s 601(5)
  exceptions..TA 1988 s 596
  repayment of contributions..TA 1988 s 598
  Sch E..TA 1988 s 597
commutation—
  charge to tax..FA 1971 Sch 3 para 8
  entire pension..TA 1988 s 599
connected..TA 1988 s 590A(2)
deep discount security, holding..TA 1988 Sch 4 para 14
deep gain security held for..FA 1989 Sch 11 para 14
differing classes of employees..TA 1988 s 611(3) (4)
employer, sums paid by..TA 1988 s 595
financial futures, dealing in..TA 1988 s 659
information..TA 1988 s 605
lump sum, exemption..TA 1988 s 189
non-approved, benefits under..TA 1988 s 596A
non-deductible expenses..FA 1989 s 76
permitted maximum, final remuneration over..TA 1988 s 590C
pilots' benefit fund..TA 1988 s 607
prescribed conditions..TA 1988 s 590(2)–(4)
regulations..TA 1988 s 612(3)
relevant associated employments..TA 1988 s 590A(1)
relevant benefits, meaning..TA 1988 s 612(1)
scheme, meaning..TA 1988 s 611(2)
statutory—
  meaning..TA 1988 s 612(1)
  exemptions..TA 1988 s 594
  relevant, meaning..TA 1988 s 611A
surplus funds, payments out of..TA 1988 s 599A
surpluses, reduction of..TA 1988 Sch 22
unauthorised payments..TA 1988 s 600

RETIREMENT PAYMENT
relief. *See* TERMINATION PAYMENT

RETIREMENT RELIEF
aggregation of gains..FA 1985 Sch 20 para 6–8
amount available..FA 1985 Sch 20 para 4(3) 13
associated disposals—
  meaning..FA 1985 s 70(7)
  generally..FA 1985 Sch 20 para 4(1)(*d*)
  part of gain accruing..FA 1985 Sch 20 para 10
business assets, disposal of—
  generally..FA 1985 s 69(2)
  material, *meaning*..FA 1985 s 69(3)–(5) 70(8) Sch 20 para 4(1)(*a*)

RETIREMENT RELIEF—continued
chargeable business assets—
  meaning..FA 1985 Sch 20 para 12(2)
  capital distribution..FA 1985 Sch 20 para 11 12(5)
  disposal, aggregation of gains on..FA 1985 Sch 20 para 6–8
date of claim..FA 1985 Sch 20 para 5(2)
disposals eligible for..FA 1985 Sch 20 para 5 FA 1987 s 47
earlier business periods, aggregation..FA 1985 Sch 20 para 14
earlier disposal, relief given on..FA 1985 Sch 20 para 15
employee's disposal—
  meaning..FA 1985 Sch 20 para 4(1)(*b*)
  relevant..FA 1985 s 70(1)(2)
furnished holiday lettings..FA 1985 Sch 14 para 1(2)(*g*)
gains qualifying for..FA 1985 Sch 20 para 6–12
ill-health grounds, retirement on..FA 1985 s 69(1)(*b*) 70(1)(*b*) Sch 20 para 3
individual qualifications..FA 1985 s 69
operation of..FA 1985 Sch 20 para 5–16
post-April 1985 disposal..FA 1985 s 69 Sch 20 para 5(1)
pre-April 1985—
  capital distribution..CGTA 1979 s 125
  generally..CGTA 1979 s 124 Sch 4 para 8
qualifying beneficiary—
  meaning..FA 1985 s 70(3)(*b*)
  conditions as to..FA 1985 s 70(3)–(5)
  disposal by, amount of relief..FA 1985 Sch 20 para 13(2)(3)
  interest in part of settled property..FA 1985 Sch 20 para 9
qualifying disposal—
  meaning..FA 1985 Sch 20 para 4(1)
  holding company..FA 1985 Sch 20 para 8
qualifying period—
  earlier periods, aggregation..FA 1985 Sch 20 para 14
  generally..FA 1985 Sch 20 para 4(2)
relevant disposal of assets..FA 1985 s 70
reorganisation of share capital, equation, election as to..FA 1985 Sch 20 para 2
spouse's interest, aggregation..FA 1985 Sch 20 para 16
trustees, disposal by—
  aggregation of gains..FA 1985 Sch 20 para 6–8
  amount of relief..FA 1985 Sch 20 para 13(2)(3)
  capital distribution..FA 1985 Sch 20 para 11
  earlier disposal, relief given on..FA 1985 Sch 20 para 15
  generally..FA 1985 s 70(3)–(5) Sch 20 para 4(1)(*c*) 5(3)
  qualifying and other beneficiaries..FA 1985 Sch 20 para 9

RETURN
meaning..TMA 1970 s 118(1)
advance corporation tax..TA 1988 Sch 13 para 1, 2
annual..TMA 1970 s 113(1)
capital gains tax..TMA 1970 s 12
chargeable gains..TMA 1970 s 12
commission..TMA 1970 s 16
company distributions not qualifying distributions..TA 1988 s 234(5)–(9)
company officer, by..TMA 1970 s 108(1)
company payments not distributions..TA 1988 Sch 16 para 2, 3
company purchase of own shares..TA 1988 s 226(1)(2)
corporation tax..TMA 1970 s 11
delivery of..TMA 1970 s 11(4)
demergers..TA 1988 s 216
director's or higher-paid employment..TMA 1970 s 15(3)–(11)
employees, of—
  agency workers..TA 1988 Sch 29 para 6
  persons treated as employees..FA 1974 s 24
employees' emoluments..TMA 1970 s 15
Eurobonds, as to..TA 1988 s 124(3)
extension of time..TMA 1970 s 118(2)
failure to make—
  capital gains tax..TMA 1970 s 93 FA 1988 Sch 3 para 27, 28
  corporation tax..TMA 1970 s 94
  income tax..TMA 1970 s 93 FA 1988 Sch 3 para 27, 28
  special return..TMA 1970 s 98
false statements, Scotland..TMA 1970 s 107
fees..TMA 1970 s 16
form..TMA 1970 s 113
franked investment income..TA 1988 Sch 13 para 1, 2
franked payments..TA 1988 Sch 13 para 1, 2

RETURN—*continued*
  income—
    income tax..TMA 1970 s 8 FA 1988 Sch 3 para 26
    partnership..TMA 1970 s 9
    total..TA 1988 s 863
  incorrect—
    assisting..TMA 1970 s 99
    capital gains tax..TMA 1970 s 95 FA 1988 Sch 3 para 27, 28
    corporation tax..TMA 1970 s 96
    income tax..TMA 1970 s 95 FA 1988 Sch 3 para 27, 28
    remedy of error..TMA 1970 s 97
    information required..TMA 1970 s 11(6)–(8)
    specified period, relating to..TMA 1970 s 11(2)
  interest—
    loan..FA 1972 Sch 10 para 7
    paid without tax deducted..TMA 1970 s 18
    received without tax deducted..TMA 1970 s 17
  life policy premiums..FA 1976 Sch 4 para 17
  lodgers and inmates..TMA 1970 s 14
  loss etc..TMA 1970 s 112
  notice requiring..TMA 1970 s 8(1)–(4)
  partnership—
    chargeable gains..TMA 1970 s 12
    income..TMA 1970 s 9
  penalties as to. *See* PENALTY
  profit-related pay..TA 1988 s 180
  profits, corporation tax..TMA 1970 s 11
  Schedule A..TMA 1970 s 19 s 69(2)
  separate taxation of wife's earnings..TA 1988 s 287(10)
  services, payments for..TMA 1970 s 16
  share acquisitions..TA 1988 s 139(5)
  special, failure to deliver..TMA 1970 s 98
  special penalties..TMA 1970 s 98A
  stock dividends..TA 1988 s 250
  stockjobbers'..TMA 1970 s 21
  surrender of life policy..TA 1988 s 272
  surtax..TMA 1970 s 22
  tax credit..TMA 1970 s 8(9)
  taxable income of others..TMA 1970 s 13
  total income..TA 1988 s 863
  underwriting agent, by..FA 1988 Sch 5 para 2
  validity..TMA 1970 s 114

REVOCABLE SETTLEMENT
  associated payment, meaning..TA 1988 s 678(3)
  capital sum—
    meaning..TA 1988 s 677(9)
    associated body, by..TA 1988 s 678
  close company connected with..TA 1988 s 681(5)
  discretionary benefit of settlor..TA 1988 s 674
  excess repayments..TA 1988 s 675(4)
  income arising under, meaning..TA 1988 s 681(1)
  information..TA 1988 s 680
  more than one settlor..TA 1988 s 679
  non-deductible payments..TA 1988 s 677
  recovery of tax paid..TA 1988 s 675(3)
  release of obligation, allowing..TA 1988 s 671
  reversion, allowing..TA 1988 s 672
  Sch D Case VI..TA 1988 s 675(1)
  settlement, meaning..TA 1988 s 681(4)
  settlor retaining an interest..TA 1988 s 673
  sums paid to settlor other than income..TA 1988 s 677
  undistributed income—
    ascertainment..TA 1988 s 682(1)
    interest paid by trustees..TA 1988 s 682(2)–(6)

ROLLOVER RELIEF
  activities other than trades..CGTA 1979 s 121
  business transferred to company..CGTA 1979 s 123 Sch 6 para 23
  capital allowances option..CAA 1968 s 40
  Class 1 assets..CGTA 1979 s 119
  classes of assets..CGTA 1979 s 118
  compulsory acquisition, on..CGTA 1979 s 111A 111B
  depreciating asset, meaning..CGTA 1979 s 117(6)

ROLLOVER RELIEF—*continued*
  dual resident company..FA 1989 s 133
  entitlement..CGTA 1979 s 115
  family company—
    dealing by individual..CGTA 1979 s 120
    gifts of business assets..CGTA 1979 s 126 FA 1984 Sch 11 para 1(2)(*h*)
  furnished holiday lettings..FA 1984 Sch 11 para 1(2)(*f*)
  groups of companies..TA 1970 s 276
  held over gain, meaning..CGTA 1979 s 117(1)(*a*)
  land..CGTA 1979 s 119
  local constituency associations..F(No 2)A 1983 s 7(6)
  new assets depreciating assets..CGTA 1979 s 117
  non-residents..FA 1989 s 129
  offshore income gain and..TA 1988 s 763(5) Sch 28 para 3(2)
  oil licences, exclusion of..F(No 2)A 1987 s 80
  part replacement..CGTA 1979 s 116
  pre-July 1970 acquisitions..CGTA 1979 Sch 6 para 22
  private residence..CGTA 1979 s 111B(1)
  retirement, on. *See* RETIREMENT RELIEF
  tied premises..CGTA 1979 s 119(4)

ROYALTY PAYMENT. *See also* COPYRIGHT
  minerals. *See* MINERAL ROYALTIES
  public lending right..TA 1988 s 537

SAFETY EXPENDITURE
  sports grounds..F(No 2)A 1975 s 49 FA 1978 s 40 FA 1989 s 119

SALE
  cum dividend. *See* SALE CUM DIVIDEND
  herd basis, where..TA 1988 Sch 5 para 3
  income derived from personal activities..TA 1988 s 775
  land. *See* SALE OF LAND
  leaseback, and. *See* LEASEBACK
  securities—
    purchase, and. *See under* TAX AVOIDANCE
    repurchase, and..TA 1988 s 729
    under- or overvalue, at..TA 1988 s 770

SALE OF LAND
  cemeteries..TA 1988 s 91
  receipts and outgoings, Sch A and D..TA 1988 s 40
  reconveyance right, with..TA 1988 s 36(1)
  sale and lease back..TA 1988 s 779

SAVINGS BANK
  exemption..TA 1988 s 484
  National Savings Bank, relief..TA 1988 s 325

SAVINGS CERTIFICATE
  meaning..CGTA 1979 s 71(2)(*a*)
  capital gains tax..CGTA 1979 s 71
  excess holdings..TA 1988 s 46(3)
  income, exemption..TA 1988 s 46(1)
  Ulster Savings Certificates..TA 1988 s 46(4)(5)

SAVINGS-RELATED SHARE OPTION SCHEME. *See* SHARE OPTION SCHEME

SCHEDULE A
  agricultural land..TA 1988 s 33
  assessment..TA 1988 s 22
  assignment of lease granted at undervalue..TA 1988 s 35
  charge to..TA 1988 s 15(1)
  chargeable persons..TA 1988 s 21
  charities..TA 1988 s 505(1)(*a*)
  collection from lessees etc..TA 1988 s 23
  deductions—
    definitions..TA 1988 s 24
    entitlement..TA 1988 s 25(1)
    exclusions..TA 1988 s 31(5)
    premiums paid..TA 1988 s 37
    receipts other than rent..TA 1988 s 28

SCHEDULE A—*continued*
  deductions—*continued*
    rents, from—
      general rules..TA 1988 s 25
      land managed as one estate..TA 1988 s 26
    sea walls..TA 1988 s 30 Sch 1 para 3
    sporting rights..TA 1988 s 29
  duration of leases, rules..TA 1988 s 38
  easements..TA 1988 s 15(3)
  exceptions..TA 1988 s 15(1)
  individuals, special relief..TA 1988 s 39(3)
  machinery and plant..TA 1988 s 32
  non-receipt of rent etc..TA 1988 s 41
  non-residents..TA 1988 s 43
  notice of election..TA 1988 s 515(2)
  premises, meaning..TA 1988 s 24(1)
  premiums—
    deductions from..TA 1988 s 37
    non-resident relief..TA 1988 Sch 2
    rent or Sch D profits, as..TA 1988 s 34
  pre-1963 leases..TA 1988 s 39(1)(2)
  pre-1964 expenditure..TA 1988 Sch 1
  receipts not rents..TA 1988 Sch 1 para 6
  recovery of tax not postponed..TMA 1970 s 55
  rent..TA 1988 s 15(1) Sch 1 para 1
  restriction on deductions—
    receipts not rents..TA 1988 Sch 1 para 2
    rents..TA 1988 Sch 1 para 1
    sea walls..TA 1988 Sch 1 para 3
  returns..TMA 1970 s 19
  sale of land—
    receipts etc..TA 1988 s 40
    right to reconveyance..TA 1988 s 36
  sea walls..TA 1988 s 30 Sch 1 para 3
  statement of receipts etc..TA 1988 s 22(2)(3)
  tied premises..TA 1988 s 98(4)(5)

SCHEDULE B
  occupation of commercial woodlands, abolition of charge..FA 1988 Sch 6 para 2

SCHEDULE C
  charge to..TA 1988 s 17
  charities..TA 1988 s 505(1)(*c*)(*d*)
  exemptions—
    Crown..TA 1988 s 49(2)
    National Debt Commissioners..TA 1988 s 49(1)
    Treasury..TA 1988 s 49(1)
  government securities. *See* GOVERNMENT SECURITIES
  mode of charge..TA 1988 s 44
  non-resident—
    foreign government securities..TA 1988 s 48
    UK government securities..TA 1988 s 47
  recovery of tax not postponed..TMA 1970 s 55
  tax reserve certificates..TA 1988 s 46(2)

SCHEDULE D
  Case I and II—
    apportionment..TA 1988 s 72
    bridges..TA 1988 s 55
    canals..TA 1988 s 55
    cemeteries etc..TA 1988 s 91
    charge to..TA 1988 s 18(3)
    charitable donations..TA 1988 s 577(9)
    commencement of trade—
      early years following..TA 1988 s 62
      year of assessment, in..TA 1988 s 61
    corporation tax..TA 1988 s 70
    dealers in land..TA 1988 s 99
    deductions—
      bad debts..TA 1988 s 89
      debts set off and released..TA 1988 s 94
      interest paid to non-residents..TA 1988 s 82
      patent fees etc..TA 1988 s 83
      security service or asset..FA 1989 s 112 113

SCHEDULE D—*continued*
Case I and II—*continued*
deductions—*continued*
technical education..TA 1988 s 84
trading stock..TA 1988 s 100
work in progress..TA 1988 s 101
discontinuance..TA 1988 s 63
divers..TA 1988 s 314
entertainer..TA 1988 s 577
Export Credits Dept payments..TA 1988 s 88
farm animals. *See* FARM ANIMALS; HERD BASIS
farming..TA 1988 s 53
ferries..TA 1988 s 55
film production..FA 1982 s 72(1)(9)
fishings..TA 1988 s 55
local enterprise agency, benefits from..TA 1988 s 88(9)
loss relief. *See* LOSS RELIEF
market gardening..TA 1988 s 53
market rights etc..TA 1988 s 55
mines, quarries etc..TA 1988 s 55
non-deductible items..TA 1988 s 74
non-resident entertainer or sportsman..TA 1988 s 557
occupation of land..TA 1988 s 53(3)
preceding year basis..TA 1988 s 60
post-cessation receipts. *See under* Case VI *infra*
railways..TA 1988 s 55
sportsman..TA 1988 s 557
taxable premiums..TA 1988 s 87
tied premises..TA 1988 s 98
trade abroad..TA 1988 s 65(3)
trading stock, valuation..TA 1988 s 100
trustee savings banks..TA 1988 s 130 484
waterworks..TA 1988 s 55
woodlands, purchase and sale..TA 1988 s 99
work in progress..TA 1988 s 101

Case III—
annual payments, rule as to..TA 1988 s 347A
cessation of income..TA 1988 s 67
charge to..TA 1988 s 18(3)
charity, payment to..TA 1988 s 505(2)
companies, payments between..TA 1988 s 341
corporation tax..TA 1988 s 70(1) 73
fresh income..TA 1988 s 66
funds in court..TA 1988 s 328(1)(*b*)
preceding year basis..TA 1988 s 64
public revenue dividends..TA 1988 s 17(5) 18(3)
single assessment with other Cases..TA 1988 s 73
small maintenance payments..TA 1988 s 351(4)

Case IV and V—
cessation of income..TA 1988 s 67
charge to..TA 1988 s 18(3)
corporation tax..TA 1988 s 70 71 73
foreign pension..TA 1988 s 58
fresh income..TA 1988 s 66
offshore funds..TA 1988 Sch 27 para 3
partnership controlled abroad..TA 1988 s 112
preceding year basis..TA 1988 s 105
single assessment with Case III..TA 1988 s 73
tied premises..TA 1988 s 98(6)
transfer of securities: accrued interest..TA 1988 s 715(1)(*j*)

Case VI—
apportionment..TA 1988 s 78
artificial transactions in land..TA 1988 s 776(3)(*a*)
assignment of lease granted at undervalue..TA 1988 s 35(2)
cash option under life annuity contract..TA 1988 s 547(6)
certificates of deposit..TA 1988 s 56(2)
charge to..TA 1988 s 18(3)
corporation tax..TA 1988 s 70(1) 72
current year basis..TA 1988 s 69
duration of leases, rules..TA 1988 s 38
enterprise allowance..TA 1988 s 127
furnished holiday lettings..TA 1988 s 503(1)
know-how..TA 1988 s 531(5)

SCHEDULE D—*continued*
Case VI—*continued*
local enterprise agency, benefits from . . TA 1988 s 88(9)
leased assets . . TA 1988 s 781(1)
losses—
  corporation tax . . TA 1988 s 396
  income tax . . TA 1988 s 392
non-residents . . TA 1988 s 43
post-cessation receipts—
  carry-back . . TA 1988 s 108
  change in basis . . TA 1988 s 103(2) 104
  charge to tax . . TA 1988 s 103(1)
  conventional basis . . TA 1988 s 104
  debts . . TA 1988 s 103(4)(5)
  deductions . . TA 1988 s 105
  deemed discontinuance . . TA 1988 s 110(2)
  earned income, as . . TA 1988 s 107
  earnings basis . . TA 1988 s 103(2)(*a*) 110(3)
  exceptions . . TA 1988 s 103(3)
  persons born pre-1917 . . TA 1988 s 109
  right to payments transferred . . TA 1988 s 106
  work in progress . . TA 1988 s 104(6)
premium under lease . . TA 1988 s 34(5)
pre-1963 leases . . TA 1988 s 39(1)
receipts etc on sale of land . . TA 1988 s 40(5)
revocable settlements . . TA 1988 s 675
sale of income from personal activities . . TA 1988 s 775(2)
sale of land with right to reconveyance . . TA 1988 s 36
transfer of assets abroad . . TA 1988 s 743(1)
transfer of securities: accrued interest . . TA 1988 s 714(2)
under deduction . . TA 1988 s 821(1)
unilateral relief . . TA 1988 s 790(11)
waiver etc of income . . TA 1988 s 786(4)(5)

Case VII—
assets acquired on disposals chargeable under . . CGTA 1979 Sch 6 para 12
unrelieved losses . . CGTA 1979 Sch 6 para 13

charge to—
  Cases, under . . TA 1988 s 18(3)
  general provisions . . TA 1988 s 18(1)
chargeable persons . . TA 1988 s 89
charities . . TA 1988 s 505
corporation tax, assessment etc . . TA 1988 s 70–73
electric line wayleaves . . TA 1988 s 120
foreign dividends . . TA 1988 s 123(2)
mining rents etc . . TA 1988 s 119
premiums, non-residents . . TA 1988 Sch 2
profit sharing schemes . . TA 1988 s 85
profits prior to year of assessment . . TA 1988 s 71
receipts basis, computation on . . FA 1989 s 43
recovery of tax not postponed . . TMA 1970 s 55
temporary residents . . TA 1988 s 336
underwriters . . TA 1988 s 451

SCHEDULE E
agency workers . . TA 1988 s 134(1)
approved share option schemes . . TA 1988 s 185
assessment—
  additional . . TA 1988 s 206
  formal assessment unnecessary . . TA 1988 s 205
  PAYE . . TA 1988 s 203 204
  receipts basis, on . . TA 1988 s 202A
Cases, charge under . . TA 1988 s 19(1)
domicile, determination . . TA 1988 s 207
emoluments—
  calculation of . . TA 1988 s 167
  office or employment not held in year of assessment, from . . TA 1988 s 19(1)
  paid before 6th April 1989 . . FA 1989 s 40
  received in UK . . TA 1988 s 132
  unpaid . . FA 1989 s 38
  unremitted . . FA 1989 s 39
expenses—
  car parking facilities . . TA 1988 s 197A
  defrayed . . TA 1988 s 199
  relief . . TA 1988 s 198

SCHEDULE E—*continued*
Job Release allowances..TA 1980 s 150
living accommodation provided for employee..TA 1988 s 145(1)
maternity pay..TA 1988 s 150
ministers of religion, houses etc..TA 1988 s 332
occupational pension..TA 1988 s 597
offices and employments—
  not held in year of assessment, where..TA 1988 s 19(1)
  place of performance..TA 1988 s 132
  scope of charge..TA 1988 s 131
  UK, performed in..TA 1988 s 132(4)
PAYE. *See* PAYE
pensions. *See* PENSION; PENSION FUND
personal pension scheme, unauthorised payments..TA 1988 s 648
profit-related pay..TA 1988 s 169 170
receipts basis—
  assessment on..TA 1988 s 202A
  receipt, meaning of..TA 1988 s 202B
residence, determination..TA 1988 s 207
retirement payment. *See* TERMINATION PAYMENT
share acquisition rights..TA 1988 s 135–140
sick pay..TA 1988 s 149
statutory sick pay..TA 1988 s 150
subscriptions to professional bodies etc..TA 1988 s 201
temporary residents..TA 1988 s 336(2)
termination payments. *See* TERMINATION PAYMENT
voluntary pensions..TA 1988 s 133

SCHEDULE F
company distributions..TA 1988 s 20
recovery of tax not postponed..TMA 1970 s 55
returns..TMA 1970 s 8(9)

SCHOLARSHIP
meaning..TA 1988 s 165(6) 331(2)
benefits in kind—
  charge to tax..TA 1988 s 165
  payments post-March 1983..TA 1988 s 165(4)
  relevant scholarship, meaning..TA 1988 s 165(6)(*b*)
  trust payments..TA 1988 s 165(3)
exemption..TA 1988 s 331(1)
trust payments..TA 1988 s 165(3)

SCIENTIFIC RESEARCH
meaning..CAA 1968 s 94(1) TA 1988 s 508(3)
asset, meaning..CAA 1968 s 94(1)
balancing allowances and charges..CAA 1968 s 3(4)–(6)
basis year—
  meaning..CAA 1968 s 91(3)
  overlapping..CAA 1968 s 91(4)
capital allowances..CAA 1968 s 91
chargeable period—
  meaning..CAA 1968 s 94(2)
  corporation tax..CAA 1968 s 91(2)
  income tax..CAA 1968 s 91(3)
corporation tax, pre-November 1962..CAA 1968 Sch 10 para 3
demolition of asset..CAA 1968 s 92(4) 93(3)
determination as to..CAA 1968 s 95(8)
disposal value of asset..CAA 1968 s 92
dwelling, expenditure on provision of..CAA 1968 s 91(1B)
expenditure, meaning..CAA 1968 s 94(1)
grants..CAA 1968 s 95(6)
income tax—
  allowable deductions..CAA 1968 s 95(1)
  pre-November 1962..CAA 1968 Sch 10 para 1
land, expenditure on acquisition of..CAA 1968 s 91(1A)
limit on writing-down allowances for machinery etc..CAA 1968 s 27(1)
non-capital expenditure..CAA 1968 s 90
post-April 1946..CAA 1968 Sch 10 para 4
pre-November 1962—
  corporation tax..CAA 1968 Sch 10 para 3
  income tax deductions..CAA 1968 Sch 10 para 1
  termination of user..CAA 1968 Sch 10 para 2 3

SCIENTIFIC RESEARCH—*continued*
research associations etc, payments to..CAA 1968 s 90
scientific research allowance, meaning..CAA 1968 s 87(1)
termination of user—
  assets disposed of etc..CAA 1968 s 92
  post-April 1946..CAA 1968 Sch 10 para 4
  pre-November 1962..CAA 1968 Sch 10 para 2 3
writing off expenditure..CAA 1968 s 4(4)

SCIENTIFIC RESEARCH ASSOCIATION
exemption..TA 1988 s 508
payments to..CAA 1968 s 90
scientific research, meaning..TA 1988 s 508(3)

SCOTLAND
administration of estates..TA 1988 s 702
appeals..TMA 1970 s 56(10)
capital allowances, transitional relief..FA 1984 Sch 12 para 4(1)(3)
CGT on death..CGTA 1979 s 50
educational body, employee seconded to..TA 1988 s 86(3)(*b*)
false statements..TMA 1970 s 107
General Commissioners..TMA 1970 s 2(3)(4)
leasehold interest, meaning..CAA 1968 s 88
poinding..TMA 1970 s 63
priority of tax..TMA 1970 s 64
recovery of penalties..TMA 1970 s 100
recovery of tax—
  inferior courts..TMA 1970 s 67
  poinding..TMA 1970 s 63

SCULPTOR
relief..TA 1988 s 538

SEAFARER
foreign earnings..TA 1988 Sch 12 para 3(2A), FA 1988 s 67

SEA WALL
Sch A..TA 1988 s 30 Sch 1 para 3

SECURITIES. *See also* SHARE
meaning—
  accrued interest or transfers..TA 1988 s 710(2)(3)
  dealers in..TA 1988 s 471(4)
  information..TMA 1970 s 24(4)
accrued interest on transfers—
  capital gains..TA 1988 Sch 29 para 23
  charities..TA 1988 s 715(1)(*d*)(3)
  conversion..TA 1988 s 710(13)
  death, effect..TA 1988 s 721
  foreign currency..TA 1988 s 710(12) 713(7)–(9)
  foreign securities: delayed remittances..TA 1988 s 723
  information..TA 1988 s 728
  insurance companies..TA 1988 s 724
  interest—
    meaning..TA 1988 s 711(9)
    applicable to securities..TA 1988 s 711(7)(8)
    payment day..TA 1988 s 711(2)
    periods..TA 1988 s 711(3)(4)
      unrealised..TA 1988 s 716
  nominal value of securities..TA 1988 s 710(11)
  nominees..TA 1988 s 720(1)(2)
  settlement day..TA 1988 s 712
  settlements..TA 1988 s 713(2)–(6)
  trade profit and losses..TA 1988 s 715(1)
  trading stock: appropriations..TA 1988 s 722
  transfer of assets abroad..TA 1988 s 742(4)–(7)
  transfer with..TA 1988 s 711(5)(6)
  transfer without..TA 1988 s 711(5)
  trustees..TA 1988 s 720
  underwriters..TA 1988 s 710(14) 720(3) 725
  unrealised interest..TA 1988 s 716
bonus issue. *See* BONUS ISSUE
charge under Sch D..TA 1988 s 18(3)
circulating capital, conversion etc..TA 1988 s 473

SECURITIES—*continued*
  conversion. *See under* CAPITAL GAINS TAX
  copies of registers, power to require..TMA 1970 s 23
  corporate bond. *See* CORPORATE BOND
  dealer in. *See* DEALER IN SECURITIES
  deep discount. *See* DEEP DISCOUNT SECURITIES
  disposal within prescribed period of acquisition..F(No 2)A 1975 s 58
  dividend stripping..TA 1970 s 281
  entitlement..TA 1988 s 710(6)–(9)
  exchange..CGTA 1979 s 85 TA 1988 s 757(5)(6)
  foreign. *See* FOREIGN SECURITIES
  FOTRA—
    meaning..TA 1988 s 715(8)
    transfer: accrued interest..TA 1988 s 715(1)(*h*)
  gilt-edged. *See* GILT-EDGED SECURITIES
  government. *See* GOVERNMENT SECURITIES
  holdings, meaning..TA 1988 s 710(7)
  identification, indexation allowance. *See under* INDEXATION ALLOWANCE
  information as to income from..TMA 1970 s 24
  interest on—
    accrued, transfer. *See* ACCRUED INTEREST ON TRANSFER, *supra*
  manufactured dividends..TA 1988 s 735
  new consideration..TA 1988 s 254(1)(6)(7)
  non-marketable, CGT..CGTA 1979 s 71(2)(*b*)
  pooling. *See* POOLING
  prescribed period, meaning..F(No 2)A 1975 s 58(10)
  purchase and sale. *See under* TAX AVOIDANCE
  qualifying (pooling)..FA 1983 Sch 6 para 1(2)
  quoted. *See* QUOTED SECURITIES
  quoted options, CGT..CGTA 1979 s 91 139
  similar, meaning..TA 1988 s 709(4)
  sale and repurchase..TA 1988 s 729
  stock lending..TA 1988 s 129
  tax-free Treasury securities, meaning..TA 1988 s 475(7)
  transfer, meaning..TA 1988 s 710(5)(6)
  transfer of income from..TA 1988 s 730
  transfer with accrued interest—
    meaning..TA 1988 s 711(5)(6)
    capital gains..TA 1988 Sch 29 para 23
    generally..TA 1988 s 713(2)(4)
  transfer without accrued interest—
    meaning..TA 1988 s 711(5)
    capital gains..TA 1985 Sch 29 para 23
    generally..TA 1988 s 713(3)(5)
  transactions in. *See* TRANSACTIONS IN SECURITIES
  United Kingdom securities, meaning..TMA 1970 s 24(4)
  unquoted. *See* UNQUOTED SECURITIES
  value, appeal jurisdiction..TMA 1970 s 47(3)

SECURITY ASSET
  meaning..FA 1989 s 113 118
  benefit in kind, as..FA 1989 s 50–52
  capital allowances..FA 1989 s 117 118
  deduction for..FA 1989 s 112

SECURITY SERVICE
  meaning..FA 1989 s 113
  benefit in kind, as..FA 1989 s 50–52
  deduction for..FA 1989 s 112

SELF-BUILD SOCIETY
  meaning..TA 1988 s 489(11)
  adjustment of liability..TA 1988 s 489(2)
  approval..TA 1988 s 489(4)(5)
  chargeable gains..TA 1988 s 489(3)
  claim..TA 1988 s 489(7)(10)
  conditions for relief..TA 1988 s 489(8)(9)
  disposals of land..TA 1970 s 342A(1)
  exemption..TA 1988 s 489(1)
  rent, meaning..TA 1988 s 489(11)
  unregistered, meaning.....TA 1970 s 342A(2)

SELF-EMPLOYED. *See also* SCHEDULE D; TRADE
job-related accommodation..TA 1988 s 356
work done abroad. *See under* WORK DONE ABROAD

SEPARATE TAXATION
assessment..TA 1988 s 287(9)
charge to tax..TA 1988 s 287(3)
deductions..TA 1988 s 287(7)
effect..TA 1988 s 287(3)
election..TA 1988 s 287 288
personal reliefs..TA 1988 s 287(4)–(6)
returns..TA 1988 s 287(10)
wife's earnings, meaning..TA 1988 s 287(2)

SERVICE OF DOCUMENTS
company, on..TMA 1970 s 108(1)
General Commissioners, on..TMA 1970 s 115(4)
methods..TMA 1970 s 115(2)(4)
notice of assessment..TMA 1970 s 29(5)

SERVICES
return of payments for..TMA 1970 s 16

SET-OFF
capital allowances..CAA 1968 s 71
franked investment income..TA 1988 Sch 13 para 5
overseas life insurance company..TA 1988 s 447(4)
stock relief..TA 1988 Sch 30 para 19

SETTLED PROPERTY
meaning..CGTA 1979 s 51
gains arising from, taxation of..FA 1988 Sch 10
offshore fund..TA 1988 s 761(7)

SETTLEMENT OF PROPERTY. *See also* SETTLOR
meaning..TA 1988 s 670
adjustments between disponer and trustees—
    children's settlements..TA 1988 s 667
    generally..TA 1988 s 661
capital gains. *See under* CAPITAL GAINS TAX
children. *See* CHILDREN'S SETTLEMENTS
discretionary trust. *See* DISCRETIONARY TRUST
disponor—
    adjustment between trustees and..TA 1988 s 661 667
    more than one..TA 1988 s 662
disposition, meaning..TA 1988 s 660(3)
income of settlor..TA 1988 s 660
information as to chargeable gains..TMA 1970 s 27
non-resident. *See* NON-RESIDENT TRUST
post-1965, settlor's liability..TA 1988 s 683
pre-1965 and post-1946..TA 1988 s 685
revocable. *See* REVOCABLE SETTLEMENT
settled property, meaning..CGTA 1979 s 51
transfer of securities: accrued interest..TA 1988 s 420(7)(8)
works of art, CGT..CGTA 1979 s 147(3)(4)
6 years, less than—
    income of disponor..TA 1988 s 660(1)
    more than one disponor..TA 1988 s 662

SETTLOR
meaning—
    children's settlement..TA 1988 s 670
    non-resident trustees..FA 1981 s 83(7)
    revocable settlement..TA 1988 s 681(4)
discretionary power for benefit of..TA 1988 s 674
excess liability—
    meaning..TA 1988 s 683(2)
    post-1965 settlements..TA 1988 s 683
    pre-1965 settlements..TA 1988 s 684
income, meaning..TA 1988 s 670
interest in settled property, retaining..TA 1988 s 673 674A
more than one—
    children's settlements..TA 1988 s 668
    generally..TA 1988 s 662

SETTLOR—*continued*
  more than one—*continued*
    revocable settlements..TA 1988 s 679
    non-deductible payments..TA 1988 s 676
    property originating from..FA 1988 Sch 10 para 6(1)
    recovery of tax by..TA 1988 s 675(3)
    reimbursement, maintenance funds for historic buildings..TA 1988 s 692
    sums other than income..TA 1988 s 677

SEWERAGE AUTHORITY
  meaning..CAA 1968 s 85(3)
  contribution to capital expenditure..CAA 1968 s 85(3)

SHARE. *See also* SECURITIES
  meaning—
    distributions..TA 1988 s 254(1)
    tax avoidance..TA 1988 s 704 E(3)
  acquisition rights. *See* SHARE ACQUISITION SCHEME; SHARE OPTION SCHEME
  aircraft, compulsory acquisition..FA 1976 s 54
  approved profit sharing scheme..TA 1988 Sch 9 para 39
  calls, indexation allowance..FA 1982 Sch 13 para 6
  company purchase of own. *See under* COMPANY; UNQUOTED TRADING COMPANY
  corporate trades. *See* BUSINESS EXPANSION SCHEME; BUSINESS START-UP SCHEME
  disposal within prescribed period of acquisition..F(No 2)A 1975 s 58
  employee, priority allocation for..TA 1988 s 65
  employee share schemes..TA 1988 s 187 Sch 9
  employee shareholdings, benefits..TA 1988 s 162
  held on trust for approved schemes..TA 1988 s 414(7)
  held-over gain..CGTA 1979 Sch 4 para 7
  ordinary, meaning..TA 1988 s 210(4)
  personal equity plans..CGTA 1979 s 149D(2A) TA 1988 s 33
  pooling. *See* POOLING
  preference, meaning..CGTA 1979 Sch 5 para 8(1) TA 1988 s 210(4)
  redeemable preference, ACT on..TA 1988 s 497(2)–(7)
  returns of acquisitions..TA 1988 s 139(5)
  shipbuilding, compulsory acquisition..FA 1976 s 54
  unquoted. *See* UNQUOTED SECURITIES
  value, appeal jurisdiction..TMA 1970 s 47(3)

SHARE ACQUISITION SCHEME
  acquisition of right..TA 1988 s 140(1)
  arrangements..TA 1988 s 138(10)(11)
  assignments..TA 1988 s 136(1)
  associated transactions..TA 1988 s 136(2)(3)
  beneficial interest, person ceasing to have..TA 1988 s 139(13)
  computation of gain..TA 1988 s 136(3)(4)
  conditions..TA 1988 s 138(3)(5)
  connected persons..TA 1988 s 139(3) 140(2)
  director, meaning..TA 1988 s 136(5)
  employee, meaning..TA 1988 s 136(5)
  gains charged under Sch E..TA 1988 s 135(1)
  information as to unit trust scheme..TA 1988 s 139(6)
  interest, exemption..TA 1988 s 688
  notice to inspector..TA 1988 s 136(6)
  original shares..TA 1988 s 138(10)(11)
  other persons, gains by..TA 1988 s 135(6)
  period when charge to tax arises..TA 1988 s 138(9)
  pre-May 1966..TA 1988 s 136(4)
  profit-sharing schemes..TA 1988 s 138(2)–(7)
  receipt of right, tax on..TA 1988 s 135
  reduction of chargeable amount..TA 1988 s 138(8)
  related loans..TA 1988 s 139(8)
  relevant period..TA 1988 s 138(9)
  restrictions..TA 1988 s 138(6)
  returns..TA 1988 s 139(5)
  Sch E charge..TA 1988 s 138(1)
  shares in authorised unit trusts..TA 1988 s 138(3)(*b*)(7)
  shares subject to restrictions..TA 1988 s 139
  unapproved
    application of provisions..FA 1988 s 77
    assignment of rights..FA 1988 s 87(4)
    associated company, meaning..FA 1988 s 87(1)
    capital gains tax..FA 1988 s 84
    changes in interest..FA 1988 s 81

SHARE ACQUISITION SCHEME—*continued*
  unapproved—*continued*
    charge to tax
      dependent subsidiary..FA 1988 s 79, 86
      restrictions removed, where..FA 1988 s 78
      special benefits, on..FA 1988 s 80
    chargeable event, event not being..FA 1988 s 78(4)(5)
    company reorganisation..FA 1988 s 82
    connected persons..FA 1988 s 83
    dependent subsidiary
      meaning..FA 1988 s 86
      shares in..FA 1988 s 79
    director, meaning..FA 1988 s 87(1)
    employee-controlled company..FA 1988 s 87(2)
    employee, meaning..FA 1988 s 87(1)
    group, meaning..FA 1988 s 86(3)
    information..FA 1988 s 85
    intra-group transactions..FA 1988 s 86(3)
    period of account, meaning..FA 1988 s 86(3)
    principal company, meaning..FA 1988 s 86(3)
    shares..FA 1988 s 87(1)
    subsidiary, meaning..FA 1988 s 87(1)
    transitional provisions..FA 1988 s 88
    value, meaning..FA 1988 s 87(1)

SHARE CAPITAL
  fixed-rate preference, meaning..TA 1988 s 312(1)
  new consideration..TA 1988 s 254(6)(7)
  ordinary—
    meaning..TA 1988 s 832(1)
    determination of ownership..TA 1988 s 838(4)–(10)
  redeemable, value..TA 1988 s 209(8)
  reduction—
    meaning..CGTA 1979 s 77(1)(3)
    CGT. *See* reorganisation or reduction *infra*
  reorganisation or reduction—
    meaning..CGTA 1979 s 77
    assets held April 1965..CGTA 1979 Sch 5 para 14
    composite new holdings..CGTA 1979 s 81
    consideration..CGTA 1979 s 79
    original shares and new holding—
      generally..CGTA 1979 s 78
      retirement relief, election as to..FA 1985 Sch 20 para 2
    part disposal of new holding..CGTA 1979 s 80
    pre-April 1979..CGTA 1979 Sch 6 para 20
  repayment—
    bonus issues..TA 1988 s 210
    distribution treated as..TA 1988 s 211(2)(3)
    treatment as..TA 1988 s 211
  stock dividends. *See* STOCK DIVIDEND

SHARE INCENTIVE SCHEME. *See* SHARE ACQUISITION SCHEME

SHARE OPTION SCHEME
  approved—
    alterations to scheme..TA 1988 Sch 9 para 4
    appeal as to approval..TA 1988 Sch 9 para 5
    application for approval..TA 1988 Sch 9 para 1
    associated companies..TA 1988 s 187(1)
    chargeable gains, allowable expenditure..TA 1988 s 185(7)
    close companies..TA 1988 Sch 9 para 8
    consortia..TA 1988 s 187(7)
    eligibility of scheme..TA 1988 Sch 9 para 8, 27
    exemption..TA 1988 s 185(2)(3)
    grantor, meaning..TA 1988 Sch 9 para 1(1)
    group scheme..TA 1988 Sch 9 para 1(3)
    information, power to require..TA 1988 Sch 9 para 6
    limitation of rights..TA 1988 Sch 9 para 28
    notional loans..TA 1988 s 185(8)
    participating company, meaning..TA 1988 Sch 9 para 1(4)
    persons eligible..TA 1988 s 185(1)
    relevant emoluments, meaning..TA 1988 Sch 9 para 28(4)
    Sch E, charge under..TA 1988 s 185(6)
    scheme shares, requirements..TA 1988 Sch 9 para 10–14

SHARE OPTION SCHEME—*continued*
approved—*continued*
share price..TA 1988 Sch 9 para 29
transfer of rights..TA 1988 Sch 9 para 27
valuation of shares, time for..TA 1988 Sch 9 para 28(3)
withdrawal of approval..TA 1988 Sch 9 para 3
capital gains tax..CGTA 1979 s 76
group of companies..TA 1988 Sch 9 para 1(3)(4)
instalments, payment of tax in..TA 1988 s 137
savings-related—
approval..TA 1988 Sch 9 Pt I
bonus date, meaning..TA 1988 Sch 9 para 17
exemption..TA 1988 s 185
general conditions..TA 1988 Sch 9 para 16–26
group scheme..TA 1988 Sch 9 para 1(3)(4)
information..TA 1988 Sch 9 para 6
persons eligible..TA 1988 Sch 9 para 26
scheme shares..TA 1988 Sch 9 para 10–14
value of right..TA 1988 s 135(5)

SHARE POOLING. *See* POOLING

SHAREHOLDER
recovery of tax from..TA 1988 s 346

SHIP
disclaimer of writing-down and first-year allowances..FA 1971 Sch 8 para 8(1)(6)
first-year allowance..FA 1971 Sch 8 para 8
investment allowance..CAA 1968 Sch 1 para 3
investment grant..FA 1971 Sch 8 para 1(4)
leasing..FA 1986 s 57(4)
new, meaning..CAA 1968 s 31(2)
rollover relief..CGTA 1979 s 118
short-life asset, treatment as, excluded..FA 1985 Sch 15 para 1
short-term leasing..FA 1980 s 64(5)(6A) 73(3)
work done abroad..TA 1988 Sch 12 para 5
writing-down allowance—
amount..CAA 1968 s 31
disclaimer..FA 1971 Sch 8 para 8(1)(6)
excluded expenditure..FA 1976 s 39(4)(*a*)
provisions as to..FA 1971 Sch 8 para 8A

SHOP
retail shop, meaning..CAA 1968 s 7(5)

SICK PAY
charge to tax..TA 1988 s 149
statutory..TA 1988 s 150

SMALL WORKSHOP
meaning..FA 1980 s 75(2)
capital allowances..FA 1980 s 75
conversions to very small workshops..FA 1983 s 31
initial allowance..FA 1980 Sch 13 para 1 2
thermal insulation..FA 1980 s 75(6)
very small..FA 1982 s 73
writing-down allowance..FA 1980 Sch 13 para 3

SOCIAL SECURITY
amount accruing, tax on..FA 1989 s 41
benefits chargeable..TA 1988 s 617(1)
contributions—
non-deductible..TA 1988 s 617(3)
stock relief..TA 1988 Sch 30 para 19
family credit..TA 1988 s 617
housing benefit..TA 1988 s 617
income support..TA 1988 s 151 152 617(2)
supplementary pension funds..TA 1988 s 614

SOLICITOR
appeal hearing..TMA 1970 s 50(5)
artificial transactions in land..TA 1988 s 778(3)
power to require information from..TMA 1970 s 20A 20B
transfer of assets abroad..TA 1988 s 745(3)

SPECIAL COMMISSIONERS
  appeal from..TMA 1970 s 56
  appeal to—
    disregard of election..TMA 1970 s 31(5A)–(5E) Sch 2 para 1(1A)–(1E)
    election for..TMA 1970 s 46(1)
    error, as to..TMA 1970 s 33(4)
    out of time..TMA 1970 s 49(2)
    rehearing..TMA 1970 s 57B(1)(*c*)
    right of..TMA 1970 s 31(3)–(6)
    transfer, by..TMA 1970 s 44(3)(3A)
  appointment..TMA 1970 s 4
  authority..TMA 1970 s 4(4)
  Board member's attendance..TMA 1970 s 50(3)
  case stated. *See* CASE STATED
  certificate, interest on unpaid tax..TMA 1970 s 70(3)
  declaration on taking office..TMA 1970 s 6(1)(5) Sch 1 Pt I
  deputy..TMA 1970 s 4A
  finality of decision..TMA 1970 s 46(2)
  personal interest..TMA 1970 s 5(1)
  power to obtain information..TMA 1970 s 51 53
  Presiding..TMA 1970 s 4(1) 45(3)
  procedural rules..TMA 1970 s 57B
  qualifications..TMA 1970 s 4(2)
  quorum..TMA 1970 s 45
  removal..TMA 1970 s 4(3)
  salary and expenses..TMA 1970 s 4(6)
  summary penalties..TMA 1970 s 53
  transfer of appeal to..TMA 1970 s 44(3)(3A)
  value of shares etc..TMA 1970 s 47(3)

SPORTING RIGHTS
  meaning..TA 1988 s 29(5)
  Sch A deduction..TA 1988 s 29

SPORTS GROUND
  safety expenditure..F(No 2)A 1975 s 49 FA 1978 s 40
  stands, expenditure on..FA 1989 s 119

SPORTS PAVILION
  capital allowances..CAA 1968 s 10

SPORTSMAN
  activity treated as part of trade..TA 1988 s 556(1)
  charge on profits or gains..TA 1988 s 557
  income attributed to..TA 1988 s 556(2)
  non-resident..TA 1988 s 555
  payment of tax..TA 1988 s 555 558
  valuation..TA 1988 s 558(3)

SPOUSE. *See* HUSBAND AND WIFE

STATUTE
  exemption by..TA 1988 s 829(4)

STATUTORY CORPORATION
  borrowing in foreign currency..TA 1988 s 581

STATUTORY DECLARATION
  transactions in securities..TA 1988 s 703(9)–(11)

STATUTORY SICK PAY
  charge under Sch E..TA 1988 s 150

STOCK DIVIDEND
  appropriate amount in cash, meaning..TA 1988 s 251(2)
  bonus share capital, meaning..TA 1988 s 251(1)
  capital gains..CGTA 1979 s 90
  close companies..TA 1988 s 430(2), Sch 19 para 12
  consideration for new holding..CGTA 1979 s 89
  distributions..TA 1988 s 230
  income, treated as..TA 1988 s 249(4)
  joint entitlement..TA 1988 s 249(3)
  market value, meaning..TA 1988 s 251(3)
  personal representatives..TA 1988 s 249(5)

STOCK DIVIDEND—*continued*
  relevant cash dividend, meaning..TA 1988 s 251(4)
  returns..TA 1988 s 250
  trustees..TA 1988 s 249(6)

STOCK EXCHANGE
  designation..TA 1988 s 841(2)
  interpretation..CGTA 1979 Sch 6 para 4
  money broker as deposit-taker..TA 1988 s 481(5)
  recognised futures exchange, meaning..CGTA 1979 s 155(3A)
  recognised investment exchanges..F(No 2)A 1987 s 73
  recognised, meaning..TA 1988 s 841(2)

STOCK RELIEF
  agreement as to, assessment..FA 1982 s 79

STOCKBROKER
  broker, meaning..TMA 1970 s 21(7)
  chargeable gains, information as to..TMA 1970 s 25(4)
  stockjobbers' transactions..TMA 1970 s 21

STOCKJOBBER
  jobber, meaning..TMA 1970 s 21(7)
  return of transactions..TMA 1970 s 21

STREET WORKS
  meaning..TA 1988 s 367(1)
  loan interest..TA 1988 s 354(2)

STUDENT
  scholarship income..TA 1988 s 331

SUB-CONTRACTOR
  meaning..TA 1988 s 560(1)
  amount of deduction..TA 1988 s 559(4)
  application of sums deducted..TA 1988 s 559(5)
  construction operations—
    meaning..TA 1988 s 567(1)
    excluded..TA 1988 s 567(3)
    included..TA 1988 s 567(2)
  contractors affected..TA 1988 s 560(2)
  deductions on account of tax..TA 1988 s 559 FA 1989 s 115
  exceptions..TA 1988 s 561
  exemption certificate—
    appeal as to..TA 1988 s 561(9)
    cancellation..TA 1988 s 561(8)
    companies..TA 1988 s 565
    firms..TA 1988 s 564
    individuals..TA 1988 s 562
    partners..TA 1988 s 563
    regulations..TA 1988 s 566
  false statements..TA 1988 s 561(10)
  limited exception..TA 1988 s 561(5)
  regulations, power to make..TA 1988 s 566

SUB-LEASE
  short lease, out of..CGTA 1979 Sch 3 para 4

SUBSCRIPTION
  professional bodies etc..TA 1988 s 201

SUBSIDIARY
  meaning (company distributions)..TA 1988 s 209(4)
  business expansion scheme..TA 1988 s 293(3) 308
  group income. *See* GROUP INCOME; GROUP RELIEF
  non-resident, interest payments to..TA 1988 s 340(3)
  ordinary share capital, ownership..TA 1988 s 838(4)–(10)
  owned directly or indirectly, meaning..TA 1988 s 838(2)
  set-off of ACT..TA 1988 s 240
  51 per cent, meaning..TA 1988 s 838(1)(*a*)
  75 per cent—
    meaning..TA 1988 s 838(1)(*b*)
    determination..TA 1988 s 340(4)
  90 per cent, meaning..TA 1988 s 838(1)(*c*)

SUBSIDY
capital allowances..CAA 1968 s 84
first-year allowance..FA 1971 Sch 8 para 15(5)
wear and tear—
   cars..FA 1971 Sch 8 para 10(5)
   machinery and plant..CAA 1968 s 38 FA 1971 Sch 8 para 6
   writing-down allowances..CAA 1968 s 29

SUPERANNUATION FUND. *See also* OCCUPATIONAL PENSION SCHEME
approved under repealed provisions..TA 1988 s 608
capital gains..CGTA 1979 s 144
close company, shares held on trust..TA 1988 s 414(7)
financial futures, dealings in..TA 1988 s 659

SUPPLEMENTARY ALLOWANCE
benefit officer, meaning..TA 1988 s 152(7)
notification of amount taxable..TA 1988 s 152(1)
objections..TA 1988 s 152(2)–(5)
PAYE repayments..TA 1988 s 204

TAX ACCOUNTANT
meaning..TMA 1970 s 20D(2)
appeal hearing..TMA 1970 s 50(5)
power to require information from..TMA 1970 s 20A 20B

TAX ACTS
meaning..TA 1988 s 831(2)

TAX ADVANTAGE
meaning..TA 1988 s 709(1)
transactions in securities. *See* TRANSACTIONS IN SECURITIES

TAX AVOIDANCE
artificial transactions in land—
   charging provisions..TA 1988 s 776 777
   information..TA 1988 s 778
   prescribed transactions..TA 1988 s 777(3)
associated persons—
   dealing company and associated company..TA 1988 s 774
   sales etc at undervalue..TA 1988 s 770
business expansion scheme..TA 1988 s 289(11)
cancellation of tax advantages from transactions in securities. *See* TRANSACTIONS IN SECURITIES
capital amount, meaning..TA 1988 s 777(13)
company—
   change in ownership—
      ascertainment..TA 1988 s 769
      trading losses..TA 1988 s 768
   dealing in securities..TA 1988 s 736
   migration..TA 1988 s 765
   purchase of own shares..TA 1988 s 223(2)(3) 226(3)(4)
   reconstruction etc..CGTA 1979 s 87(1)
credit transactions..TA 1988 s 786
deep discount securities..TA 1988 Sch 4 para 5(6)(7)
demergers..TA 1988 s 215(2)
distribution reducing value of holding..TA 1988 s 736
leased assets—
   charging provisions..TA 1988 s 781
   special cases..TA 1988 s 782
loans or credit transactions..TA 1988 s 786
manufactured dividends..TA 1988 s 737
non-resident companies, withdrawal of tax credits..TA 1988 s 814
purchase and sale of securities—
   after Stock Exchange reforms..TA 1988 s 738(1)
   application of provisions..TA 1988 s 731
   appropriate amount in respect of interest..TA 1988 s 735
   dealers in securities..TA 1988 s 732
   exemptions, effect..TA 1988 s 733
   persons not dealers..TA 1988 s 734
sale and lease back of land..TA 1988 s 779
sale and repurchase of securities..TA 1988 s 729

TAX AVOIDANCE—*continued*
   sale at under- or overvalue—
     associated companies etc..TA 1988 s 770
     petroleum company. *See* PETROLEUM COMPANY
   sale of income derived from personal activities..TA 1988 s 775 777
   transfer of assets abroad. *See* TRANSFER OF ASSETS ABROAD
   transfer of income from securities..TA 1988 s 730
   value shifting. *See under* CAPITAL GAINS TAX

TAX CREDIT
   meaning..TA 1988 s 832(1)
   advance corporation tax..TA 1988 s 231
   excessive set-off..TA 1988 s 252
   incorrectly paid, recovery..TA 1988 s 813
   insurance companies..TA 1988 s 76(3) 438(4)(5)
   international organisations etc..TA 1988 s 232(3)
   non-residents—
     generally..TA 1988 s 232
     withdrawal of right to..TA 1988 s 813
   overseas life insurance company..TA 1988 s 447(4) 448
   repayment supplement..TA 1988 s 825
   returns..TMA 1970 s 8(9)
   unitary state—
     meaning..TA 1988 s 812(2)
     non-resident company in..TA 1988 s 812

TAX RESERVE CERTIFICATE
   interest on, exemption..TA 1988 s 46(2)

TAX TABLES
   PAYE..TA 1988 s 203(2)(*a*)(6)

TAXES ACT
   meaning..TMA 1970 s 118(1)

TAXPAYER
   power to require information from..TMA 1970 s 20 20B

TECHNICAL EDUCATION
   deductible expense..TA 1988 s 84

TELEVISION SET
   leased, first-year allowance..FA 1980 Sch 12 Pt II
   short-life asset, whether..FA 1985 Sch 15 para 10

TEMPORARY TAX
   meaning..PCTA 1968 s 2(2)
   budget resolution. *See* BUDGET RESOLUTION

TERMINAL LOSS
   meaning..TA 1988 s 388(1)
   capital allowances..TA 1988 s 388(7)
   carry-back..TA 1988 s 388
   company reconstruction..TA 1988 s 343(3)
   computation..TA 1988 s 389(1)
   corporation tax..TA 1988 s 394
   discontinuance, meaning..TA 1988 s 389(4)
   franked investment income surplus..TA 1988 s 243
   mineral royalties. *See under* MINERAL ROYALTIES
   partnership..TA 1988 s 388(5)(6) 389(5)

TERMINATION PAYMENT
   charge under Sch E..TA 1988 s 148
   election as to relief..TA 1988 Sch 11 Pt II
   emoluments..TA 1988 Sch 11 para 8
   exemptions..TA 1988 s 188
   foreign service..TA 1988 Sch 11 para 10
   ill-health..TA 1988 s 188(2)
   relevant date, meaning..TA 1988 Sch 11 para 11
   relief—
     eligible payments..TA 1988 s 188
     payments over £75,000..TA 1988 Sch 11 para 5(2)
     reduction of sums chargeable..TA 1988 Sch 11 para 3
     restriction..TA 1988 Sch 11 para 3

THERMAL INSULATION
enterprise zones..FA 1980 s 74(6)
industrial buildings..FA 1975 s 14
small workshops..FA 1980 s 75(6)

TIED PREMISES
meaning..TA 1988 s 98(2)
apportionment..TA 1988 s 98(3)(5)
lease, meaning..TA 1988 s 98(8)
part only..TA 1988 s 98(3)
rent as trading receipt..TA 1988 s 98(1)
rollover relief..CGTA 1979 s 119(4)
Sch A exemption..TA 1988 s 98(4)
Sch D Case V exemption..TA 1988 s 98(5)
trader equitably entitled..TA 1988 s 98(7)

TOP-SLICING RELIEF
effect..TA 1988 s 833(3)

TRADE
meaning..TMA 1970 s 118(1) TA 1988 s 6(4)(*b*)
abroad—
  carried on..TA 1988 s 391
  partly. *See under* WORK DONE ABROAD
change in ownership..TA 1988 s 113
commencement—
  during year of assessment..TA 1988 s 61
  2 years following..TA 1988 s 62
computation of tax. *See* SCHEDULE D Cases I and II
contribution to..TA 1988 s 117(3)
discontinuance—
  additional redundancy payments..TA 1988 s 90
  bad debts..TA 1988 s 89
  deemed..TA 1988 s 110(2)
  loss relief..TA 1988 s 382(3)
  post-cessation receipts. *See under* SCHEDULE D Case VI
  special basis..TA 1988 s 63
  trading stock..TA 1988 s 100
  work in progress..TA 1988 s 101
foreign, expenses connected with..TA 1988 s 80
local enterprise agency, contributions to..TA 1988 s 79
losses. *See* LOSS RELIEF
major change in nature or conduct, meaning..TA 1988 s 786(4)
non-allowable deductions..TA 1988 s 817
partly abroad. *See under* WORK DONE ABROAD
post-cessation receipts. *See under* SCHEDULE D Case VI
regional development grant, exemption..TA 1988 s 92
Sch D Case I..TA 1988 s 18(3)
succession to—
  capital allowances..CAA 1968 s 79
  machinery and plant..CAA 1968 s 48

TRADE DISPUTE
PAYE repayments..TA 1988 s 204

TRADE EFFLUENT
meaning..CAA 1968 s 85(3)
contributions towards treatment..CAA 1968 s 85(3)

TRADE MARK
fees etc, deductibility..TA 1988 s 83

TRADE UNION
certain income, relief in respect of..TA 1988 s 467, FA 1988 Sch 3 para 17
part payments to, premium relief..TA 1988 s 266(7)
provident benefits—
  meaning..TA 1988 s 467(2)
  exemption..TA 1988 s 467
  police..TA 1988 s 467(4)
registered, meaning..TA 1988 s 467(4)

TRADED OPTION
meaning..CGTA 1979 s 137(9)
dealings, capital gains tax..FA 1985 s 72(1)–(4)

TRADED OPTION—*continued*
  disposal..CGTA 1979 s 137(4)(*aa*)
  wasting asset..CGTA 1979 s 138(1)(*aa*)

TRADER
  donation to charity..TA 1988 s 577(9)
  employee seconded to charity..TA 1988 s 86
  loans to..CGTA 1979 s 136
  tied premises..TA 1988 s 98(7)

TRADING COMPANY
  losses on unquoted shares..TA 1988 s 573–576
  offshore fund investing in..TA 1988 Sch 27 para 10
  unquoted, purchase of own shares. *See* UNQUOTED TRADING COMPANY

TRADING INCOME
  meaning..TA 1988 s 393(8)

TRADING STOCK. *See also* STOCK RELIEF
  meaning..TA 1988 s 100(2)
  capital gains..CGTA 1979 s 122
  deductible expense..TA 1988 s 100(1)
  farm animals..TA 1988 Sch 5 para 1
  film etc..FA 1982 s 72(5)
  land, artificial transactions..TA 1988 s 776 777
  securities, appropriation, accrued interest..TA 1988 s 710
  transfers within a group..TA 1970 s 274
  valuation..TA 1988 s 100

TRAINING
  employees, of, relief for costs of..TA 1988 s 588
  qualifying courses of..TA 1988 s 589

TRANSACTIONS IN SECURITIES
  meaning..TA 1988 s 709(2)
  abnormal dividend—
    meaning..TA 1988s 709(4)
    prescribed circumstances..TA 1988 s 704(A)(C)
  advance corporation tax—
    appeals..TA 1988 s 705(6)
    Board's notice..TA 1988 s 703(5)–(6)
  appeals—
    advance corporation tax..TA 1988 s 705(6)
    generally..TA 1988 s 705
    tribunal..TA 1988 s 706
  assets available for distribution, meaning..TA 1988 s 704(E)(3)
  cancellation of tax advantage..TA 1988 s 703
  clearance..TA 1988 s 707
  close companies..TA 1988 s 704(D)
  company, meaning..TA 1988 s 709(2)
  excepted transactions..TA 1988 s 703(1)
  group relief..TA 1988 s 704(B)(2)
  husband and wife..TA 1988 s 703(7)
  information..TA 1988 s 703
  method of cancelling tax advantage..TA 1988 s 703(3)(4)
  non-taxable, meaning..TA 1988 s 704(E)(3)
  personal representatives..TA 1988 s 703(11)
  prescribed circumstances..TA 1988 s 704
  securities, meaning..TA 1988 s 709(2)
  statutory declaration..TA 1988 s 703(9)–(11)
  time limit..TA 1988 s 703(12)
  trading stock, meaning..TA 1988 s 709(2)
  tribunal..TA 1988 s 706
  winding-up..TA 1988 s 703(2)

TRANSFER OF ASSETS
  abroad. *See* TRANSFER OF ASSETS ABROAD
  benefits in kind..TA 1988 s 156(3)(4)
  BNOC..FA 1982 s 146
  British Airways Board..TA 1988 s 513
  company reconstruction etc..TA 1970 s 267
  resident companies..TA 1988 s 209(4)–(6)

TRANSFER OF ASSETS ABROAD
anti-avoidance provisions..TA 1988 s 739
assets, meaning..TA 1988 s 742(9)
associated operations..TA 1988 s 739(1)–(3)
banks..TA 1988 s 745(5)
computation of liability..TA 1988 s 743(2)
husband and wife..TA 1988 s 742(9)
income tax..TA 1988 s 743(1)
information..TA 1988 s 745
Irish residents, lease premiums..TA 1988 s 746
non-resident company, to..TA 1970 s 268A
non-residents..TA 1988 s 743(3)
non-transferor's liability..FA 1988 s 740
solicitor..TA 1988 s 745(3)
transfer, meaning..TA 1988 s 742(9)

TRANSPORT BOARDS
group provisions..TA 1970 s 272(5)

TRANSPORT CONTAINER
short-term leasing..FA 1980 s 64(7) 73(3) FA 1986 s 57(4)

TRANSPORT VOUCHER
meaning..TA 1988 s 141(7)
exemption..TA 1988 s 141(6)

TRAVELLING EXPENSES
armed forces..TA 1988 s 197
employee not domiciled in UK..TA 1988 s 195
expenses connected with foreign trades etc..TA 1988 s 193 194
work done abroad..TA 1988 s 193

TREASURY
national heritage: transfer of functions to Board..FA 1985 s 95
Sch C exemption..TA 1988 s 49

TREASURY SECURITIES
discounted..TA 1988 s 126

TRIBUNAL
declaration on taking office..TMA 1970 s 6(1)(5) Sch 1
transactions in securities..TA 1988 s 49(1)

TRUST. *See also* SETTLEMENT OF PROPERTY
capital gains. *See under* CAPITAL GAINS TAX
capital payment—
  meaning..FA 1981 s 83(1)(2)
  benefit treated as..FA 1981 s 83(3)
  loans..FA 1981 s 83(4)
  received, meaning..FA 1981 s 83(5)
disabled person's—
  meaning..TA 1988 s 715(8)
  transfer of securities: accrued interest..TA 1988 s 715
discretionary. *See* DISCRETIONARY TRUST
dual resident, gift into..FA 1986 s 58
employee share ownership. *See* EMPLOYEE SHARE OWNERSHIP TRUST
foreign dividends held under..TA 1988 s 123(5)
material interest test..TA 1988 Sch 9 para 37
migrant. *See under* CAPITAL GAINS TAX
non-resident. *See* NON-RESIDENT TRUST
trust gains..FA 1981 s 80(2)
United Kingdom trust, meaning..TA 1988 s 231(5)

TRUSTEE
adjustments between disponor and—
  children's settlements..TA 1988 s 667
  generally..TA 1988 s 661
assessment of income tax on..FA 1979 s 151
CGT—
  administration expenses..CGTA 1979 s 47
  bare trustees..CGTA 1979 s 46
  charge to tax..CGTA 1979 s 48
  chargeability..TMA 1970 s 77
  settled property..CGTA 1979 s 52

TRUSTEE—*continued*
chargeability—
  capital gains tax..TMA 1970 s 77
  income tax..TMA 1970 s 72
  protection in certain cases..TMA 1970 s 76
connected person..TA 1988 s 839(2)
interest paid by, children's settlements..TA 1988 s 666
life policies etc, recovery of tax from..TA 1988 s 551
non-resident, gains from non-resident company..FA 1981 s 85
persons becoming absolutely entitled against..CGTA 1979 s 54
residence of..FA 1989 s 110
retirement relief on disposal by. *See* RETIREMENT RELIEF
share acquisition scheme..TA 1988 s 688
transfer of securities: accrued interest..TA 1988 s 720

TRUSTEE SAVINGS BANK
capital allowances..TSBA 1985 Sch 2 para 1
chargeable gains..TSBA 1985 Sch 2 paras 2–5
corporation tax, exemption from..TSBA 1985 Sch 2 para 6
deemed body corporate..FA 1984 s 44(1)(3)(4)
exemption..TA 1988 s 484
existing subsidiary..TSBA 1985 s 4
existing TSB group..TSBA 1985 s 1
gain or loss accruing to successor..TSBA 1985 Sch 2 para 6
group relief..TSBA 1985 Sch 2 para 6
loan interest, deduction of tax..TSBA 1985 Sch 2 para 7
new TSB group..TSBA 1985 s 1
successor..TSBA 1985 s 1
taxation, generally..TSBA 1985 s 5
trading stock..TSBA 1985 Sch 2 para 6
transfer of assets within group..TA 1970 s 272(2)(*d*)
vesting day..TSBA 1985 s 1

TURNOVER
charge on percentage, non-residents..TMA 1970 s 80

TUTOR
chargeability..TMA 1970 s 72 73

UNDERWRITER
agent—
  meaning..FA 1988 Sch 5 para 1(1)
  appeal against determination..FA 1988 Sch 5 para 5
  liability for..FA 1988 Sch 5 para 9
  payments on account of tax..FA 1988 Sch 5 para 3
  penalties..FA 1988 Sch 5 para 10
  returns by..FA 1988 Sch 5 para 2
business, meaning..TA 1988 s 457(1)
certificate of loss..TA 1988 s 453
closing year, meaning..FA 1988 Sch 5 para 1(1)
interest on tax paid..FA 1988 Sch 5 para 4, 11
Lloyd's—
  reinsurance premium paid by..TA 1988 s 450(5)
  retirement annuity relief..TA 1988 s 627
member, meaning..TA 1988 s 457(1)
pooling..CGTA 1979 Sch 5 para 7
premiums trust fund—
  meaning..TA 1988 s 457(1)
  assessment on agent..TA 1988 s 450(2)
  capital gains tax..CGTA 1979 s 142(2)–(4)
  deep discount security as part of..TA 1988 Sch 4 para 18
  deep gain security as part of..FA 1989 Sch 11 para 9
  disposals..TA 1988 s 450(6)
  indexation..FA 1985 Sch 19 para 22 23
re-insurance..TA 1988 s 450
special reserve fund—
  approval..TA 1988 s 452(1)
  cancellation of approval..TA 1988 s 456(4)
  cessation of trade..TA 1988 s 454(5)
  death..TA 1988 s 455
  income held on trust..TA 1988 s 452(4)
  income tax..TA 1988 s 454

UNDERWRITER—*continued*
  special reserve fund—*continued*
    investment income..TA 1988 s 456(1)(2)
    lower limit..TA 1988 s 455(1)
    payments into..TA 1988 s 452
    payments out of..TA 1988 s 453
    personal representatives..TA 1988 s 455(4)
    provisional payments..TA 1988 s 453(5)(6)
    setting up..TA 1988 s 452(1)–(4)
    variation..TA 1988 s 456(3)
  syndicate—
    meaning..FA 1988 Sch 5 para 1(1)
    profit and loss. *See* syndicate profit or loss, *below*
  syndicate profit or loss—
    meaning..FA 1988 Sch 5 para 1(1)(2)
    apportionment of..FA 1988 Sch 5 para 7
    determination of—
      appeals..FA 1988 Sch 5 para 5
      members, effect on..FA 1988 Sch 5 para 8
      modifications pending appeal..FA 1988 Sch 5 para 6
      power to make..FA 1988 Sch 5 para 4
  transfer of securities: accrued interest..TA 1988 s 710(14) 720(3) 725
  underwriting year, meaning..TA 1988 s 457(1)

UNEMPLOYMENT BENEFIT
  PAYE repayments..TA 1988 s 204

UNMARRIED COUPLE
  meaning..TA 1988 s 151(2)

UNIT TRUST
  authorised—
    meaning..TA 1988 s 468(6) FA 1989 s 80(4)
    CGT exemption..FA 1980 s 81
    income..TA 1988 s 468(1)(2)
  certified—
    meaning..TA 1988 s 468A
    corporation tax..TA 1988 s 468B
    distributions..TA1988 s 468C
  distribution period, meaning..TA 1988 s 468(6)
  distributions, treatment..TA 1988 s 468
  fund of funds—
    meaning..TA 1988 s 468C(6)
    distributions..TA 1988 s 468D
  gilt..FA 1989 s 80
  managers' remuneration..TA 1988 s 468(4)
  other..TA 1988 s 469
  personal pension schemes..TA 1988 s 468(2)
  scheme, meaning..TA 1988 s 468(6) 469
  unit holder, meaning..TA 1988 s 468(6)

UNIT TRUST SCHEME
  meaning..CGTA 1979 s 92 TA 1988 s 468(6) 469

UNITED STATES
  double taxation convention..TA 1988 Sch 30 para 14

UNIVERSITY
  payments to for research..CAA 1968 s 90

UNPAID TAX. *See* OVERDUE TAX

UNQUOTED SECURITIES
  acquisition on death..CGTA 1979 Sch 6 para 7
  held at April 1965..CGTA 1979 Sch 5 para 13
  prior part disposal..CGTA 1979 Sch 6 para 8
  trading companies, in, loss relief..FA 1988 s 573 574
  valuation..CGTA 1979 s 152

UNQUOTED TRADING COMPANY
  purchase of own shares—
    anti-avoidance provisions..TA 1988 s 223(2)(3) 226(3)
    approval..TA 1988 s 225(1)(2)
    associates..TA 1988 s 222 227

UNQUOTED TRADING COMPANY—*continued*
purchase of own shares—*continued*
CGT..TA 1988 s 219(2)
conditions..TA 1988 s 220–223
connected companies..TA 1988 s 223(1) 228(2)
distribution, not treated as..TA 1988 s 219(1)
group membership..TA 1988 s 222
information..TA 1988 s 226
ownership period..TA 1988 s 220(5)
purchase, meaning..TA 1988 s 219(1)
residence..TA 1988 s 220(1)–(4)
restriction..TA 1988 s 219(2)
returns..TA 1988 s 226
vendor, meaning..TA 1988 s 219(1)
relief for investment in. *See* BUSINESS EXPANSION SCHEME
unquoted company, meaning..TA 1988 s 229(1)

UNREMITTABLE FOREIGN INCOME. *See under* FOREIGN INCOME

VALOUR AWARD
annuities..TA 1988 s 317
CGT..CGTA 1979 s 131

VALUATION
assets, inspection powers..TMA 1970 s 111
capital gains, for. *See under* CAPITAL GAINS TAX
estate duty..CGTA 1979 Sch 6 para 26
land, entry powers..TMA 1970 s 110
oil disposed of or appropriated..TA 1988 s 493
securities sold within 12 months of death..FA 1975 Sch 10 Pt II
trading stock..TA 1988 s 100
work in progress..TA 1988 s 101

VALUE-SHIFTING. *See under* CAPITAL GAINS TAX

VENUE
appeals. *See under* APPEAL

VESSEL. *See also* SHIP
work done abroad..TA 1988 Sch 12 para 5

VIEWDATA RECEIVER
leased, first-year allowance..FA 1980 Sch 12 Pt II

VISITING FORCES
exemption..TA 1988 s 323

VOCATION. *See also* TRADE
computation of tax. *See* SCHEDULE D Cases I and II
employee seconded to charity..TA 1988 s 86
losses. *See* LOSS RELIEF

VOUCHER
meaning..TA 1988 s 141(7)
car parking space, for..TA 1988 s 141(6A)
cash—
  meaning..TA 1988 s 143(3)
  PAYE..TA 1988 s 143
cheque voucher, meaning..TA 1988 s 141(7)
entertainment, for..TA 1988 s 141(6B)
other than cash..TA 1988 s 141
transport voucher..TA 1988 s 141(7)

WAR DAMAGE
meaning..TA 1988 s 586(5)
premium—
  deductible..TA 1988 s 586(4)
  management expenses..TA 1988 s 586(2)
  non-deductible..TA 1988 s 586(1)

WAR INJURIES
meaning..TA 1988 s 587(8)
employees, disallowance of payments..TA 1988 s 587

WAR INSURANCE PREMIUM
meaning..TA 1988 s 274(4)
disregard..TA 1988 s 274(4)

WAR RISK
meaning..CAA 1968 s 33(7)
premiums, disallowance of deductions..TA 1988 s 586

WAR SERVICE PENSION
exemption..TA 1988 s 318

WATERWORKS
Sch D Case I..TA 1988 s 55

WIDOW OR WIDOWER
additional relief for child..TA 1988 s 259 260
bereavement allowance..TA 1988 s 262 FA 1988 Sch 3 para 7

WIFE. *See* HUSBAND AND WIFE; MARRIED WOMAN

WILFUL DEFAULT
assessment where..TMA 1970 s 36
evidence..TMA 1970 s 105
interest on overdue tax..TMA 1970 s 88

WINDING-UP
accounting period..TA 1988 s 12(7)
business expansion scheme..TA 1988 s 289(13)
chargeable gains..TA 1988 s 345(5)
close company—
    apportionment..TA 1988 s 423(6)
    relevant income..TA 1988 Sch 19 para 10
corporation tax..TA 1988 s 8(2) 342
dealers in securities..TA 1988 s 472(2)
notional..TA 1988 Sch 18 para 3
patent rights..TA 1988 s 525(1)

WITNESS
appeal, at..TMA 1970 s 52(2)(3) 53
default..TMA 1970 s 52(3) 53

WOODLAND
commercial, meaning..FA 1988 Sch 6 para 1
dealers in land..TA 1988 s 99
forestry purposes, used for..FA 1988 Sch 6 para 4(3)(4)
Schedule B charge to tax, abolition of..FA 1988 Sch 6 para 2
Schedule D election, abolition of..FA 1988 Sch 6 para 3
transitional provisions..FA 1988 Sch 6 para 4

WORDS AND PHRASES. *See separate index post*

WORK DONE ABROAD
absence, meaning..TA 1988 Sch 12 para 4
aircraft..TA 1988 Sch 12 para 5
Continental Shelf..TA 1988 Sch 12 para 5
double relief restriction..TA 1988 s 192(5)
emoluments eligible..TA 1988 Sch 12 para 2
expenses—
    board and lodging..TA 1988 s 193(4)
    foreign trade, connected with..TA 1988 s 80
    home visits..TA 1988 s 194(2)
    relief..TA 1988 s 193(2)
    travel between trades..TA 1988 s 81
    travelling..TA 1988 s 193(3)(6) 195
    two or more offices..TA 1988 s 193(5)
    visits by family..TA 1988 s 194(2)
foreign employment..TA 1988 s 192(4)
incidental duties..TA 1988 Sch 12 para 6
qualifying period..TA 1988 Sch 12 para 3
relief..TA 1988 s 193

WORK DONE ABROAD—*continued*
    residence..TA 1988 s 335
    vessels..TA 1988 Sch 12 para 5

WORK IN PROGRESS
    increase in value. *See* STOCK RELIEF
    post-cessation receipts..TA 1988 s 104(6)
    valuation..TA 1988 s 101

WORK OF ART
    capital gains..CGTA 1979 s 147
    estate duty..CGTA 1979 Sch 6 para 24

WORKER'S CO-OPERATIVE
    meaning..TA 1988 s 187(10)

WOUNDS PENSION
    exemption..TA 1988 s 315

WRITING-DOWN ALLOWANCE
    meaning—
        generally..CAA 1968 s 87(1)
        machinery and plant..CAA 1968 s 49(2)(3)
        scientific research..CAA 1968 s 94(2)
    agricultural land and buildings..CAA 1968 s 75 FA 1986 Sch 15 para 1
    apportionment..CAA 1968 s 75
    assets leased abroad..FA 1982 s 70(2)(4) Sch 11 para 2
    assured tenancies..FA 1982 Sch 12 para 2
    cars. *See under* CAR
    chargeable periods..CAA 1968 s 75
    computation, rate..FA 1976 s 39(2)
    contributions to expenditure..CAA 1968 s 85
    dredging..CAA 1968 s 75
    eligible expenditure—
        meaning..FA 1976 s 39(3)
        election as to..FA 1976 s 39(5)
    first new chargeable period..FA 1976 s 39(1)
    industrial buildings..CAA 1968 s 2 6(3)
    know-how..TA 1988 s 530(2)
    machinery and plant. *See under* MACHINERY AND PLANT
    mineral depletion..CAA 1968 s 60
    mines, oil wells etc..CAA 1968 s 23 57
    new chargeable period, meaning..FA 1976 s 39(6)
    patent rights. *See under* PATENT RIGHTS
    previous user, effect..CAA 1968 s 30
    ships..CAA 1968 s 31 FA 1971 Sch 8 para 8A(2)
    short-term leasing—
        cars..FA 1980 s 69
        determination..FA 1980 s 65
    small workshops..FA 1980 Sch 13 para 3

YEAR
    assessment, of. *See* YEAR OF ASSESSMENT
    financial year, meaning..TA 1988 s 834(1)
    underwriting year..TA 1988 s 487(1)

YEAR OF ASSESSMENT
    meaning..TA 1988 s 832(1)
    profits prior to, where no profits during..TA 1988 s 71
    second, meaning..TA 1988 s 62(1)
    third, meaning..TA 1988 s 62(1)

WORDS AND PH...

Words in brackets indicate the context in which the w...

abnormal dividend..TA 1988 s 709(4)
absence..TA 1988 Sch 12 para 4
absolute interest..TA 1988 s 701(2)
acceptable distribution policy..TA 1988 Sch 25 para 2
accounting date..TA 1988 s 834
accounting period (corporation tax)..TA 1988 s 12(2)(3)
Act..TMA 1970 s 118(1) TA 1988 s 832(1)
additional rate..TA 1988 s 32(1)
adjusted issue price..TA 1988 Sch 4 para 1(1)
adjusted net cost (balancing allowances etc, scientific research)..CAA 1968 s 3(5)
administration period..TA 1988 s 695(1)
administrator (retirement benefits scheme)..TA 1988 s 612(1)
agent (underwriter)..FA 1988 Sch 5 para 1(1)
Agent-General..TA 1988 s 320(4)
aggregate income of estate..TA 1988 s 701(8)
agricultural—
   income..CAA 1968 s 69
   land..CAA 1968 s 69 TA 1988 s 33(3)
   society..TA 1988 s 323(8)
allied headquarters..TA 1988 s 323(8)
allowable—
   expenditure (land)..CGTA 1979 s 109(2)
   loss..TA 1988 s 834(1)
amount payable on redemption (deep discount securities)..TA 1988 Sch 4 para 1
annual value (land)..TA 1988 s 837(1)(2)
annuity business..TA 1988 s 431(1)
annuity fund..TA 1988 s 431(1)
anticipated normal working life (asset)..TA 1988 s 782(6)
appeal..TMA 1970 s 48(1)
appointed day expenditure (mines, oil wells etc)..CAA 1968 Sch 6 para 2
apportioned amount..TA 1988 s 430(1)
appropriate—
   accounting period..TA 1988 Sch 26 para 1(2)
   amount in cash (stock dividend)..TA 1988 s 251(2)
   judicial authority..TMA 1970 s 20D(1)
   person (deposit)..TA 1988 s 482(6)
   rate (controlled foreign company)..TA 1988 s 747(4) Sch 26 para 1(2)
approved—
   body (housing)..FA 1982 Sch 12 para 15(1)
   local enterprise agency..TA 1988 s 79(4)
   (personal pension scheme)..TA 1988 s 630
   scheme..TA 1988 s 612(1)
arrangements (double taxation relief)..TA 1988 s 792(1)
assessable company..TA 1988 s 752(6)
assessable value..TA 1988 s 16(3)(*a*)
asset—
   (CGT)..CGTA 1979 s 19(1)
   (transfers abroad)..TA 1988 s 742(9)
   new (corporate bond)..FA 1984 Sch 13 para 7(2)(3)
   old (corporate bond)..FA 1984 Sch 13 para 7(2)(3)
assigned contract (life annuity)..TA 1988 s 544(2)
assigned policy..TA 1988 s 544(1)
assignment (Scotland)..TA 1988 s 24(5)
associate (close company)..TA 1988 s 417(3)
associated—
   company..TA 1988 s 416(1) 502(3) 774(4)(*d*)
   disposals (retirement relief)..FA 1985 s 70(7)
   operation..TA 1988 s 742(1)
   payment (revocable settlement)..TA 1988 s 678(3)
   person (leasing)..TA 1988 s 783(10)
attributed gain..FA 1984 Sch 14 para 1(1)
author..TA 1988 s 534(7) 535(11)

chargeable period—*continued*
  (discontinuance of trade)..TMA 1970 s 118(1)
  (income and corporation tax)..TA 1988 s 832(1)
  (scientific research)..CAA 1968 s 94(2)
chargeable profits (controlled foreign company)..TA 1988 s 747(6)
chargeable sum..TA 1988 Sch 2 para 2
charity..TA 1988 s 506(1)
cheque voucher..TA 1988 s 141(7)
child (settlement)..TA 1988 s 670
child of the Family..TA 1988 s 51B(7) 347B(7) FA 1988 s 40(1)
claim..FA 1984 Sch 14 para 1(1)
claimant company..TA 1988 Sch 26 para 3(1)(*c*)
close company..TA 1988 s 414 415
close investment-holding
  company..TA 1988 s 13A
close relative..FA 1984 Sch 14 para 1(1)
closing year..FA 1988 Sch 5 para 1(1)
collector..TA 1988 s 832(1)
colliery concern..CAA 1968 Sch 8 para 1
combined payment (mortgage)..TA 1988 s 377(10)
commencement of the patent..TA 1988 s 533(1)
commercial building or structure..FA 1980 s 74(4)
commercial letting..TA 1988 s 504(2)
commercial rent (industrial building)..FA 1972 s 69(4)
commercial woodlands..FA 1988 Sch 6 para 1
Commissioners..TMA 1970 s 48(1)
commodities..TA 1988 Sch 27 para 4(2)(*a*)
commodity futures..TA 1988 s 128
common parts (building)..FA 1982 Sch 12 para 1(5)
company..TA 1988 s 709(2) 832
company distribution..TA 1988 s 209 418
completion date (capital expenditure)..FA 1984 Sch 12 para 5(2) 6(2) 7(2)
connected company..TA 1988 s 839(5)–(7)
connected or associated company..TA 1988 s 755(5)
connected persons—
  (CGT)..CGTA 1979 s 63
  (income and corporation taxes)..TA 1988 s 839(1)–(4), (7)
  (leased assets)..TA 1988 s 783
connected policies..TA 1988 Sch 15 para 14(2)
consortium..TA 1988 s 247(9) 413(6)
construction operations..TA 1988 s 567(1)
consul..TA 1988 s 321(3)
consular employee..TA 1988 s 322(3)
contract date (capital expenditure)..FA 1984 Sch 12 para 5(2) 6(2) 7(2)
contract price (capital expenditure)..FA 1984 Sch 12 para 5(2) 6(2) 7(2)
contractual savings scheme..TA 1988 s 326(2)(3)
contribution—
  (rationalisation of industry)..TA 1988 s 568(5)
  (redundancy)..TA 1988 Sch 21 para 1(1)
  deductible..TA 1988 Sch 21 para 1(1)
control—
  (capital allowances)..CAA 1968 s 87(1)
  (close company)..TA 1988 s 416(2)(3)
  (income and corporation tax)..TA 1988 s 840
  (partnership)..TA 1988 s 168(12) 840
  (profit-related pay)..TA 1988 s 840 Sch 8, para 7(3)
controlled foreign company..TA 1988 s 747(1)(2)
controlling company..TA 1988 s 755(2)
conventional basis..TA 1988 s 110(4)
conversion of securities..CGTA 1979 s 82(3)(*a*) TA 1988 s 710(13)
co-operative association..TA 1988 s 486(12)
corporate bond..FA 1984 s 64(2)
Corporation Tax Acts..TA 1988 s 831(1)(*a*)
cost of (benefits in kind)..TA 1988 s 156(2)
coupon..TA 1988 s 45
court investment fund..CGTA 1979 s 92
covenanted payment to charity..TA 1988 s 339(8) 660(3)
credit token..TA 1988 s 142(4)
credit union..TA 1988 s 487(5)
creditable tax..TA 1988 s 751(6)
crops..CAA 1968 s 7(5)
dealing..TA 1988 Sch 27 para 4(2)(*b*)
dealing company..TA 1988 s 744(4)(*b*)
dealing in commodities..TA 1988 Sch 27 para 4(2)

debentures..TA 1988 s 767(5)
deductible contributions (redundancy)..TA 1988 Sch 21 para 1(1)
deep discount..TA 1988 Sch 4 para 1
deep discount security..TA 1988 Sch 4 para 1
deep gain security..FA 1989 Sch 11 para 1
deposit—
   (deposit-taker)..TA 1988 s 481(3)
   composite rate deposit..TA 1988 s 481(4)
   qualifying time deposit..TA 1988 s 482(6)
   relevant..TA 1988 s 481(4)(5)
deposit-taker..TA 1988 s 481(3)
depreciating asset..CGTA 1979 s 117(6)
depreciatory transaction..TA 1988 s 280(1)
designated area..FA 1973 s 38(2)(*e*)
development area..FA 1970 s 15(3)
development corporation..TA 1988 s 560(5)
direction period (controlled foreign company)..TA 1988 Sch 26 para 3(1)(*a*)
director—
   (benefits)..TA 1988 s 168(8)
   (close company)..TA 1988 s 417(5)
   (receipts basis assessment)..TA 1988 s 202B(5)(6)
   (share acquisition scheme)..TA 1988 s 136(5)
director's or higher-paid employment..TA 1988 s 167(1)
disabled person's trusts..TA 1988 s 715(8)
discontinuance (terminal loss)..TA 1988 s 389(4)
discount..TA 1988 Sch 4 para 1
discount house..TA 1988 s 78(6)
disposal—
   (CGT)..CGTA 1979 s 19(2)
   (deep discount securities)..TA 1988 Sch 4 para 7
   (held-over gain)..CGTA 1979 Sch 4 para 4(3)
   (offshore fund)..TA 1988 s 757(2)
   equalisation element, involving..TA 1988 Sch 28 para 6(3)
disposal value of asset (scientific research)..CAA 1968 s 92(3A)
disposition..TA 1988 s 660(3)
distributable pool..TA 1988 Sch 8 para 1
distribution (corporation tax)..TA 1988 s 209 418(1)
distribution period (unit trust)..TA 1988 s 468(6) 469(6)
dividend—
   (building society)..TA 1988 s 476(11)
   (controlled foreign company)..TA 1988 Sch 25 para 2(3)
   (Sch C)..TA 1988 s 45
dock..CAA 1968 s 7(5)
dock undertaking..CAA 1968 s 7(5)
documents..TMA 1970 s 20D(3)
double taxation relief arrangements..TA 1988 s 616(4)
dual resident..TA 1988 s 468C(4) FA 1989 s 129(7)
dual resident company..FA 1989 s 132(1) 133(4)
earlier claim..FA 1984 Sch 14 para 1(1)(*a*)
earned income..TA 1988 s 833(4)
earnings basis..TA 1988 s 110(3)
easement..TA 1988 s 119(3)
electricity board..TA 1988 s 511(6)
electricity undertaking..CAA 1968 s 7(5)
eligible expenditure..FA 1976 s 39(3)
eligible shares (business expansion)..TA 1988 s 289(4)
employee—
   (company)..TA 1988 s 612(1)
   (profit-related pay)..TA 1988 s 169(2)
   (returns)..TMA 1970 s 15(11)(*a*)
   (share acquisition scheme)..TA 1988 s 136(5)
employee's disposal (retirement relief)..FA 1985 Sch 20 para 4(1)(*b*)
employer's payment..TA 1988 s 580(2)
employment..TA 1988 s 168(2) 169(1)
employment unit..TA 1988 s 169(1)
enactment..TMA 1970 s 118(1)
enterprise zone..FA 1980 s 74(2)
equalisation account..TA 1988 s 758(1)
equipment lease (machinery and plant)..FA 1985 Sch 17 para 3(4)
estate (Schedule A)..TA 1988 s 833(3)
estate or trading income..TA 1988 Sch 19 para 5
Eurobond..TA 1988 s 732(5)
exceptional depreciation allowance..CAA 1968 s 89
excess liability (settlor)..TA 1988 s 683(2)

excluded company..TA 1988 s 576(5)
excluded employer..TA 1988 s 174(2)
excluded persons (CGT)..CGTA 1979 s 29A(5)
exempt—
   approved scheme..TA 1988 s 592(1)
   distribution (demerger)..TA 1988 s 213(2)
   pension fund..TA 1988 s 476(7)
existing association..F(No 2)A 1983 s 7(2)(a)
expenditure (scientific research)..CAA 1968 s 94(1)
expenditure of a revenue nature..FA 1982 s 72(9)
expenditure unallowed (machinery and plant)..CAA 1968 s 41
family company..FA 1985 Sch 20 para 1(2)
farm land..TA 1988 s 832(1)
film..TA 1988 s 298(5)
final remuneration..TA 1988 s 612(1)
financial futures..TA 1988 s 128
financial option..CGTA 1979 s 137(9)(c)
financial year..TA 1988 s 834(1)
first publication..TA 1988 s 534(7)
first-year allowance..FA 1971 s 41(1)
fixed-rate preference share—
   (group relief)..TA 1988 Sch 18 para 1(3)
   (purchase of own shares)..TA 1988 s 95(5)
fixed-rate preference share capital..TA 1988 s 312(1)
fixture (machinery and plant)..FA 1985 s 59(1) Sch 17 para 1(1)
foreign—
   concession..CAA 1968 s 87(1) FA 1971 Sch 8 para 7(2)
   dividends..TA 1988 s 123(1)
   emolument..TA 1988 s 192(1)
   estate..TA 1988 s 701(10)
   life assurance fund..TA 1988 s 441(6)
   period of assessment..TA 1988 s 804(8)
   plantation..CAA 1968 s 7(5)(6)
   securities..CGTA 1979 Sch 6 para 17(4)
   service..TA 1988 Sch 11 para 10
   subsidiary..TA 1988 s 755(1)
   tax..TA 1988 s 792(1)
forestry income..CAA 1968 s 69
forestry land..CAA 1968 s 69
former parliamentary constituency..F(No 2)A 1983 s 7(1)(a)
FOTRA securities..TA 1988 s 715(8)
franked investment income..TA 1988 s 238 832(1)
franked payment..TA 1988 s 238(1) 832(1)
full rent, at (Sch A)..TA 1988 s 24(7)
full-time—
   director or employee..TA 1988 s 139(11)
   employee..TA 1988 s 361(8)
   working director..TA 1988 s 168(10)
fund in court..CGTA 1979 s 99(3)
fund of funds..TA 1988 s 468C(6)
funding bond..TA 1988 s 582(4)
general annuity business..TA 1988 s 431(1)
general client account deposit..TA 1988 s 482(6)
gilt-edged securities..CGTA 1979 Sch 2 para 1
grantor (share option scheme)..TA 1988 Sch 9 para 1(1)
gross attributed tax..TA 1988 Sch 26 para 4(3)
gross gain (indexation allowance)..FA 1982 s 86(2)(a)
group of companies..TA 1970 s 272(1)(b) TA 1988 s 173(3) Sch 9 para 2(4)
group scheme (share option)..TA 1988 Sch 9 para 1(3)
harbour authority..TA 1988 s 518(10)
harbour reorganisation scheme..TA 1988 s 518(10)
harvesting..CAA 1968 s 7(5)
held over gain..CGTA 1979 s 117(1)(a)
herd..TA 1988 Sch 5 para 8(1)
High Commissioner..TA 1988 s 320(4)
hire-purchase agreement..TA 1988 s 784(6)
holders..TA 1988 s 752(5)
holding company—
   (controlled foreign company)..TA 1988 Sch 25 para 12(1)
   (group relief)..TA 1988 s 229(1) 413(3)
   (retirement relief)..FA 1985 Sch 20 para 1(2)
holiday accommodation..TA 1988 s 504(2)
home improvement loan..TA 1988 s 355(2B) 372(3) FA 1988 s 43(3)(b)

housing—
    association..TA 1988 s 560(5) FA 1988 s 43(3)(*a*), 44(6)
    association tenancy..FA 1982 Sch 12 para 3(4)
    society..TA 1970 s 342
hovercraft..CGTA 1979 s 118
hydraulic power undertaking..CAA 1968 s 7(5)
incapacitated person..TMA 1970 s 118(1)
incidental costs (discounted bill)..TA 1988 s 78(5)
inclusive price (car)..TA 1988 s 168(5)(*e*)
income—
    (capital allowances)..CAA 1968 s 87(1)
    (settlor)..TA 1988 s 670
    arising under a settlement..TA 1988 s 681(1)
    corresponding class, of..TA 1988 s 382(2)
    element, linked..TA 1988 Sch 4 para 9(2)
    eligible for double taxation relief..TA 1988 s 278(7)
    patents, from..TA 1988 s 533(1)
    period (deep discount securities)..TA 1988 Sch 4 para 1(1)(*f*)
    relevant earnings..TA 1988 s 644(1)
Income Tax Acts..TA 1988 s 831(1)(*b*)
independent accountant (profit-related pay)..TA 1988 s 184
indexed securities..FA 1982 s 89(5)
indexation allowance..FA 1982 s 86(4) FA 1983 Sch 6 para 5(2)(*b*)
industrial assurance business..TA 1988 s 832(1)
industrial building or structure..CAA 1968 s 7
ineligible gain..FA 1984 Sch 14 para 1(1)
initial dividend..TA 1988 Sch 25 para 4(1)(*a*)
initial storage (oil)..TA 1988 s 502(2)
inland revenue..TMA 1970 s 1(1)
inspector..TA 1988 s 832(1)
insurance company—
    (migration)..TA 1988 s 767(5)
    (tax treatment)..TA 1988 s 431(2)
insurance contract..TA 1988 Sch 25 para 11(7)
interest..TA 1988 s 711(9) 832(1)
interest in land..FA 1985 Sch 17 para 1(2) TA 1988 s 294(5)
interest payment day (securities)..TA 1988 s 711(2)
interest period (securities)..TA 1988 s 711(3)
interim payments (friendly societies)..TA 1988 Sch 15 para 3(11)
intermediate area..FA 1970 s 15(3)
international organisation..TA 1988 s 232(3)
investment—
    business (controlled foreign company)..TA 1988 Sch 25 para 9(1)
    company..TA 1988 s 130
    grant..CAA 1968 s 83(4)
    trust..TA 1988 s 842(1)
    trust holding..TA 1988 s 842(3)
irrevocable (settlement)..TA 1988 s 665
issuing company (non-resident policy)..TA 1988 Sch 15 para 24(1)
jobber..TMA 1970 s 21(7)
job-related living accommodation..TA 1988 s 356(3)
know-how..TA 1988 s 533(7)
large caravan..TA 1988 s 367(1)
later claim..FA 1984 Sch 14 para 14(1)(*b*)
later gain..FA 1984 Sch 14 para 14(1)(*b*)
lease—
    (asset)..TA 1988 s 789
    (capital allowances)..CAA 1968 s 87(1)
    (CGT)..CGTA 1979 Sch 3 para 10(1)
    (Schedule A)..TMA 1970 s 19(3)(*a*) 90(1) TA 1988 s 24(1)
    (tied premises)..TA 1988 s 98(8)
leasehold interest (Scotland)..CAA 1968 s 88
leasing (machinery and plant)..FA 1980 s 73(3)
legatee..CGTA 1979 s 47(2)(3)
lessee (Schedule A)..TMA 1970 s 19(3)(*a*)
lessee/lessor..FA 1984 Sch 12 para 2(3)
let (holiday accommodation)..TA 1988 s 504(9)
letting bedroom..FA 1978 s 38(3)
life—
    annuity..TA 1988 s 539(3) 657(1)
    assurance business..TA 1988 s 76(8) 431(1)
    assurance gains..TA 1988 s 435(1)
life or endowment business..TA 1988 s 466(1)
limit of recharge..CAA 1968 Sch 7 para 3(4)

limited interest..TA 1988 s 701(3)
limited liability company..TA 1988 s 518(10)
limited partner..TA 1988 s 117(2)
linked company..FA 1988 Sch 11 para 4
linked company funded subscription..FA 1988 Sch 11 para 3(4)
linked company loan..FA 1988 Sch 11 para 3(4)
linked company subscription—financing loan..FA 1988 Sch 11 para 3(5)
linked income element..TA 1988 Sch 4 para 9(2)
living together (spouses)..TA 1988 s 282
loan—
  (beneficial)..TA 1988 s 160(6)
  agreement..TA 1988 s 377(10)
  creditor..TA 1988 s 417(7)–(9)
  interest..TA 1988 s 486(12)
local authority..TA 1988 s 519(4)
local authority association..TA 1988 s 519(3)
local constituency association..F(No 2)A 1983 s 7(2)
local holding company..TA 1988 Sch 25 para 6(3)
local reinsurance contract..TA 1988 Sch 25 para 11(8)
locked-in value..TA 1988 s 186(5)
long lease..FA 1978 s 37(4)
long term assets (insurance company)..TA 1988 s 440(11)
long term business (insurance company)..TA 1988 s 440(11)
losses (profit-related pay)..TA 1988 s 169(1)
lump sum payment (copyright)..TA 1988 s 535(11)
machinery or plant allowance..CAA 1968 s 52(2)
main offer..TA 1988 s 139(1)(b)
major change in nature or conduct of trade..TA 1988 s 768(4)
majority interest..TA 1988 Sch 24 para 4(3)
managers..TA 1988 Sch 27 para 2(2)(d)
market garden land..TA 1988 s 832(1)
market value—
  (assets)..CGTA 1979 Sch 6 para 2(1)
  (CGT)..CGTA 1979 s 150(1)
  (profit-sharing scheme)..TA 1988 s 187(2)
  (share capital)..TA 1988 s 251(3)
  (unit holders' rights)..CGTA 1979 Sch 6 para 2(4)
married couple..TA 1988 s 151(2)
married woman living with husband..TA 1988 s 282
material interest—
  (company)..TA 1988 s 168(11) 360A
  (offshore fund)..TA 1988 s 759
  (profit-related pay)..TA 1988 Sch 8 para 7(2)
material year of assessment..FA 1984 Sch 14 para 13(5)
maximum allowable expenditure..FA 1984 Sch 12 para 7(2)
maximum rate commutable pension..TA 1988 Sch 23 para 3(4)
maximum rate lump sum..TA 1988 Sch 23 para 3(4)
maximum rate non-commutable pension..TA 1988 Sch 23 para 4(4)
member (Lloyd's)..TA 1988 s 457(1)
member (personal pension scheme)..TA 1988 s 630
member of a trading group..TA 1988 Sch 19 para 7
Member's pensionable salary..TA 1988 s 629(2) 654(3)
mentally disabled person..CGTA 1979 Sch 1 para 5(2)
merger..TA 1970 s 278A(2)
mineral—
  (royalties)..TA 1988 s 122(6)
  assets..CAA 1968 s 65(2)
  deposits..CAA 1968 s 87(1) FA 1971 Sch 8 para 7
  lease or agreement..TA 1988 s 122(6)
  royalties..TA 1988 s 122(5)
minimum wage legislation..TA 1988 s 175(4)
mining rent..TA 1988 s 119(3)
mission..TA 1988 s 320(4)
motor car..FA 1971 Sch 8 para 9
mutual business..TA 1988 s 491(9)
neglect..TMA 1970 s 118(1)
net relevant earnings (retirement annuity)..TA 1988 s 623(6) 646(7)
new—
  (ship)..CAA 1968 s 31(2)
  association..F(No 2)A 1983 s 7(2)(b)
  chargeable period (writing-down allowance)..FA 1976 s 39(6)
  consideration derived from ordinary shares..TA 1988 s 254(1)
  consideration not derived from ordinary shares..TA 1988 s 210(4)
  holding (pooling)..FA 1985 Sch 19 para 9(3)

new—*continued*
    machinery or plant..CAA 1968 s 19(4) FA 1971 s 50(1)
    non-resident policy..TA 1988 Sch 15 para 24(1)
    parliamentary constituency..F(No 2)A 1983 s 7(1)(*b*)
    society (friendly society)..TA 1988 s 466(2)
non-basis period..TA 1988 s 804(8)
non-cash voucher..TA 1988 s 141(7)
non-marketable securities..CGTA 1979 s 71(2)(*b*)
non-qualifying distribution..TA 1988 s 233(2)
non-qualifying offshore fund..TA 1988 s 760(1)
non-taxable..TA 1988 s 704(E)(3)
non-trading income..TA 1988 Sch 25 para 12(6)
non-voting fixed-rate preference shares..TA 1988 Sch 25 para 2(7)
normal commercial loan..TA 1988 Sch 18 para 1(5)
notional distribution date..TA 1988 s 499(2)
notional winding-up..TA 1988 Sch 18 para 3(2)
obtained by reason of employment (loan)..TA 1988 Sch 7 Pt I
occupier (woodlands)..TA 1988 s 516(5)
official agent (consular)..TA 1988 s 321(3)
offshore fund..TA 1988 s 759(1)
offshore income gain..TA 1988 Sch 28 para 5
oil..TA 1988 s 502(1)
oil extraction activities..TA 1988 s 502(1)
oil rights..TA 1988 s 502(1)
old society (friendly society)..TA 1988 s 465(1)
open market price (machinery and plant)..CAA 1968 s 33(2)(*a*) 34(4)
open market value (machinery and plant)..FA 1972 s 68(10)
operative event (pooling)..FA 1983 Sch 6 para 7(3) FA 1985 Sch 19 para 13(4)
ordinary share..TA 1988 s 210(4)
ordinary share capital..TA 1988 s 832(1)
ordinary trade debt..TA 1988 s 301(5)
outstanding capital..TA 1988 Sch 25 para 11(4)(*e*)
overseas—
    company..TA 1988 s 759(6)
    life insurance company..TA 1988 s 431(1)
    public revenue dividend..TA 1988 s 45
    securities..TA 1988 s 732(4)
    tax..TA 1988 s 804(8)
    territory..TA 1988 s 615(7)
owned directly or indirectly..TA 1988 s 838(2)
owner of copyright..TA 1988 s 536(1)
parent company..TA 1988 s 173(3)
participant (profit sharing scheme)..TA 1988 s 186(2)
participant's salary..TA 1988 s 187(5)
participating company (share option scheme)..TA 1988 Sch 9 para 1(4)
participator..TA 1988 s 417(1)
passenger transport undertaking..TA 1988 s 141(7)
patent rights..TA 1988 s 533(1)
pay (profit-related)..TA 1988 s 169(1)
payment (redundancy scheme)..TA 1988 Sch 21 para 1(1)
payment for group relief..TA 1988 s 402(6)
payment for transferred tax refund..FA 1989 s 97(7)
payment not out of profits or gains brought into charge..TA 1988 s 350(2)
pension..TA 1988 s 615(7)
Pensions (Increase) Acts..TA 1988 s 615(7)
period of absence (dwelling-house)..CGTA 1979 s 102(3)
period of ownership (deep discount securities)..TA 1988 Sch 4 para 4(1)
period of retention (appropriated shares)..TA 1988 Sch 10 para 2
periodical payment..TA 1988 s 51B(7) 347B(7)
periodical return (insurance company)..TA 1988 s 431(1)
person—
    affected (small maintenance order)..TA 1988 s 351(9)
    chargeable (redundancy scheme)..TA 1988 Sch 21 para 1(1)
personal injuries..TA 1988 s 329(4)
personal pension—
    arrangements..TA 1988 s 630
    scheme..TA 1988 s 630
    scheme administrator..TA 1988 s 630
personal representative..TA 1988 s 701(4)
petroleum..TA 1988 s 771(7)
petroleum company..TA 1988 s 771(1)
petroleum products..TA 1988 s 771(7)
pilots' benefit fund..TA 1988 s 607(4)
policy (insurance)..TA 1988 s 466(2) Sch 15 para 14

political party..F(No 2)A 1983 s 7(8)
post-1983 gain..TA 1988 Sch 28 para 4(2)
pre-direction period..TA 1988 Sch 24 para 9(1)
preference dividend..TA 1988 s 832(1)
preference share—
  (bonus issue)..TA 1988 s 210(4)
  (pooling)..CGTA 1979 Sch 5 para 8(1)
premises..TA 1988 s 24(1) Sch 25 para 7(2)
premium—
  (industrial buildings)..FA 1972 s 69(4)
  (insurance)..TA 1988 s 431(4)
  (lease)..TA 1988 s 24(1)(3)
premiums trust fund..TA 1988 s 457(1)
prescribed period (shares etc)..F(No 2)A 1975 s 58(10)
prescribed rate (interest on overdue tax)..TMA 1970 s 89(1)
previous owner..TA 1988 Sch 28 para 4(3)
primary fund..TA 1988 Sch 27 para 6(1)(*a*)
principal accounting period..TA 1988 s 498(2)
principal Act..TMA 1970 s 118(1)
principal company..TA 1970 s 272(1)(*c*)
prior five years (loss)..TA 1988 s 397(5)
prior period of loss..TA 1988 s 397(5)
private use (car)..TA 1988 s 168(5)(*f*)
proceedings in Northern Ireland..TMA 1970 s 58(3)(*a*)
product obtainable from the living animal..TA 1988 Sch 5 para 8(3)
production herd..TA 1988 Sch 5 para 8(5)
profit-related—
  pay..TA 1988 s 169(1)
  pay scheme..TA 1988 s 169(1)
profits—
  (CGT)..TMA 1970 s 29(8)(*b*)
  (corporation tax)..TMA 1970 s 29(8)(*c*) TA 1988 s 6(4)(*a*)
  (income tax)..TMA 1970 s 29(8)(*a*)
  (profit-related pay)..TA 1988 s 169(1)
proper officer (company)..TMA 1970 s 108(3)
provident benefits (trade union)..TA 1988 s 467(2)
public company (profit-related pay)..TA 1988 s 180(4)
public revenue..TA 1988 s 45
public revenue dividend..TA 1988 s 45
purchase (own shares)..TA 1988 s 219(1)
purchased life annuity..TA 1988 s 657(1)
qualifying—
  beneficiary..FA 1985 s 70(3)(*b*)
  certificate of deposit (deposit-taker)..TA 1988 s 482(6)
  corporate bond..FA 1984 s 64(4)(*a*)
  disposal (retirement relief)..FA 1985 Sch 20 para 4(1)
  distribution (ACT)..TA 1988 s 14(2)
  dwelling-house (assured tenancy)..FA 1982 Sch 12 para 3(1)
  expenditure (mines etc)..CAA 1968 s 51
  fund (offshore)..TA 1988 Sch 27 para 6(2)
  hotel..FA 1978 s 38(2)
  interest..TA 1988 s 356D(1)
  loan (CGT relief)..CGTA 1979 s 136(1)
  maintenance payment..TA 1988 s 51B(1) 347B(1)
  maximum (limited loan)..TA 1988 s 357(1)
  office (MP's annuity premium)..TA 1988 s 629(2)
  period (work done abroad)..TA 1988 Sch 12 para 3
  premium (retirement annuity)..TA 1988 s 620(1)
  securities (pooling)..FA 1983 Sch 6 para 1(2)
  subsidiary (business expansion scheme)..TA 1988 s 308(5)
  tenancy..FA 1988 s 49(3)
  time deposit (deposit-taker)..TA 1988 s 482(6)
quoted Eurobond..TA 1988 s 124(6)
quoted option..CGTA 1979 s 137(9)(*a*)
quoted securities..CGTA 1979 Sch 5 para 1(1)
radio relay service..TA 1988 s 120(5)
reckonable aggregate value (life policy)..TA 1988 s 546
reckonable date (interest on overdue tax)..TMA 1970 s 86(3)
recognised clearing system (Eurobonds)..TA 1988 s 124(6)
recognised futures exchange..CGTA 1979 s 155(3A)
recognised stock exchange..TA 1988 s 841(1)
recoverable summarily as a civil debt..TMA 1970 s 65(4)
redeemable preference shares..FA 1988 Sch 11 para 6
redemption date (deep discount securities)..TA 1988 Sch 4 para 1

RED *Words and Phrases* [126]

reduction of share capital..CGTA 1979 s 77(1)(3)
redundancy payment..TA 1988 s 580(1) Sch 21 para 1
redundancy rebate..TA 1988 s 580(1)
regional development grant..FA 1984 s 54(3) Sch 12 para 4(3), TA 1988 s 92(3)
registered—
   housing association..TA 1970 s 342A(2)
   industrial and provident society..TA 1988 s 486(12)
   scheme (profit-related pay)..TA 1988 s 169(1)
   trade union..TA 1988 s 467(4)
regulated tenancy..FA 1982 Sch 12 para 3(4)
related—
   assets..TA 1970 s 342
   company..TA 1988 Sch 25 para 4(2) 19(2)
   loan..TA 1988 s 139(8)
   settlement..FA 1984 Sch 14 para 6(6)
   tax-credit..TA 1988 s 734(3)
relative—
   (child)..TA 1988 s 275
   (company reconstruction)..TA 1988 s 344(5)
   close relative..FA 1984 Sch 14 para 1(1)
release date (appropriated shares)..TA 1988 s 187(2)
relevant—
   allowable expenditure (indexation allowance)..FA 1982 s 86(2)(*b*)
   allowance..TA 1988 Sch 26 para 1(3)
   amount (profit sharing scheme)..TA 1988 s 187(2)
   annual remuneration..TA 1988 Sch 23 para 9 FA 1989 Sch 6 para 30
   assessment to tax..TA 1988 s 642(5)
   beneficiary (friendly society)..TA 1988 Sch 15 para 3(8)
   benefit..FA 1984 Sch 14 para 5 TA 1988 s 612(1)
   capital payments..TA 1988 s 541(5) 543(3)
   cash dividend..TA 1988 s 251(4)
   company..TA 1988 s 138(3)
   date (termination payment)..TA 1988 Sch 11 para 9
   deposit..TA 1988 s 481(4)
   earnings (retirement annuity)..TA 1988 s 623(2)(5) 644
   emoluments (approved share option scheme)..TA 1988 Sch 9 para 28(4)
   expenditure, of lender..TA 1988 s 803(4)
   foreign securities..TA 1988 s 124(6)
   income of company..TA 1988 Sch 19 para 1
   interest..FA 1986 Sch 15 para 3
   loan interest (mortgage interest relief)..TA 1988 s 370(1)
   maximum..TA 1988 Sch 26 para 2(3)
   Netherlands Antilles subsidiary..FA 1989 s 116(3)
   payment (company)..TA 1988 Sch 16 para 1
   percentage..TA 1988 Sch 23 para 3, 4
   period (balancing allowances etc, scientific research)..CAA 1968 s 3(5)
   scholarship..TA 1988 s 165(6)
   securities (indexation allowance)..FA 1982 s 88(9)
   superannuation scheme..TA 1988 s 645(3)
   transaction (corporate bond)..FA 1984 Sch 13 para 7(1)
   voting power..TA 1988 s 790(9)
   year of assessment (attributed gain)..FA 1984 Sch 14 para 1(1)
relevant interest—
   (assured tenancy)..FA 1982 Sch 12 para 13
   (industrial building)..CAA 1968 s 11
remuneration (agency worker)..TA 1988 s 134(7) Sch 29 para 6
renewals allowance..CGTA 1979 s 34(5)
rent—
   (mining)..TA 1988 s 119(3)
   (Schedule A)..TA 1988 s 24(6)
   (self-build society)..TA 1988 s 489(11)
reorganisation of share capital..CGTA 1979 s 77
research and development..TA 1988 s 312(1)
residence..TA 1988 s 356D(2)
residual or scrap value..CGTA 1979 s 37(2)
residuary income..TA 1988 s 696(2)
restricted government securities..TA 1988 s 439(5)
retail shop..CAA 1968 s 7(5)
retirement benefits scheme..TA 1988 s 611(1)
return..TMA 1970 s 118(1)
return period (company distribution)..TMA 1970 s 87(6)
reversion (Scotland)..TA 1988 s 24(5)
ring fence income..TA 1988 s 492(2)
salary (profit sharing scheme)..TA 1988 s 187(5)

sale, insurance, salvage or compensation moneys..CAA 1968 s 86
savings certificates..CGTA 1979 s 71(2)(*a*)
scheme—
    administrator (personal pension schemes)..TA 1988 s 630
    employer (profit-related pay)..TA 1988 s 169(1)
    (occupational pensions)..TA 1988 s 611(2)
    profit-related pay..TA 1988 s 169(1)
    (redundancy)..TA 1988 Sch 21 para 1(1)
    reconstruction or amalgamation, of..CGTA 1979 s 86(2)
    shares..TA 1988 Sch 9 para 9(1)
scholarship—
    (benefit in kind)..TA 1988 s 165(6)
    (income)..TA 1988 s 331(2)
scientific research..CAA 1968 s 94(1) TA 1988 s 508(3)
scientific research allowance..CAA 1968 s 87(1)
scientific research expenditure..CAA 1968 s 94(1)
season (hotel)..FA 1978 s 38(3)
second year of assessment..TA 1988 s 62(1)
securities—
    (conversion)..CGTA 1979 s 82(3)(*b*)
    (dealers in)..TA 1988 s 471(4)
    (distribution)..TA 1988 s 254(1)
    (information)..TMA 1970 s 23(3) 24(4)
    (pooling)..CGTA 1979 s 65(7) FA 1985 s 68(7)
    (stockjobber)..TMA 1970 s 21(7)
    (transactions in)..TA 1988 s 709(2)
    (transfers: accrued interest)..TA 1988 s 711 (5)(6)
security asset..FA 1989 s 113 118
security service..FA 1989 s 113
self-build society..TA 1988 s 489(11)
self-governing colony..TA 1988 s 320(4)
settled property..CGTA 1979 s 51 FA 1981 s 83(7)
settlement..TA 1988 s 670 720(8)
settlor—
    (children's settlement)..TA 1988 s 671(3)
    (non-resident trustees)..FA 1981 s 83(7)
    (revocable settlement)..TA 1988 s 681(4)
sewerage authority..CAA 1968 s 85(3)
share—
    (distributions)..TA 1988 s 254(1)
    (profit-sharing scheme)..TA 1988 s 187(2)
    (tax advantage)..TA 1988 s 704(E)(3)
    interest..TA 1988 s 486(12)
sharer's limit..TA 1988 s 356A(3)
short-life asset..FA 1985 s 57(1)(*c*)
short-term leasing..FA 1980 s 64(3)
similar securities..TA 1988 s 709(4)
small workshop..FA 1980 s 75(2)
sound recording (film)..TA 1988 s 298(5)
spared tax (foreign loan interest)..TA 1988 s 798(4)
specific disposition..TA 1988 s 701(5)
sponsored superannuation scheme..TA 1988 s 624(1)
sporting rights..TA 1988 s 29(5)
spouse (life policy)..TA 1988 Sch 14 para 1
statutory—
    increases (pension)..TA 1988 s 616(4)
    provision..CAA 1968 s 80(1)(5)
    redundancy scheme..TA 1988 s 572(3)
    scheme..TA 1988 s 612(1)
Stock Exchange..CGTA 1979 Sch 6 para 4
street works..TA 1988 s 367(1)
sub-contractor (construction industry)..TA 1988 s 560(1)
subsidiary—
    (company distribution)..TA 1988 s 209(4)
    (company reconstruction)..TA 1988 s 344(3)(*b*)
    (double taxation relief)..TA 1988 s 792(2)
    51 per cent..TA 1988 s 838(1)(*a*)
    75 per cent..TA 1988 s 838(1)(*b*)
    90 per cent..TA 1988 s 838(1)(*c*)
successor (local constituency association)..F(No 2)A 1983 s 7(3)
sums payable or paid..TA 1988 s 701(12)
surplus—
    advance corporation tax..TA 1988 s 283(1)

surplus—*continued*
  franked investment income..TA 1988 s 238
  funds (credit union)..TA 1988 s 487(5)
surrendered ACT..TA 1988 s 498(2) 499(2)
surrendering company..TA 1988 s 498(2)
syndicate..FA 1988 Sch 5 para 1(1)
syndicate profit or loss..FA 1988 Sch 5 para 1(1)
tax..TMA 1970 s 118(1) TA 1988 s 832(3)
tax accountant..TMA 1970 s 20D(2)
Tax Acts..TA 1988 s 831(2)
tax advantage..TA 1988 s 709(1)
tax already paid..FA 1984 Sch 14 para 4(5)
tax credit..TA 1988 s 832(1)
tax exempt life or endowment business..TA 1988 s 466(2)
taxed income (insurance company)..TA 1988 s 437(3)
Taxes Acts..TMA 1970 s 118(1)
tax-free transfer (historic building)..TA 1988 s 694(7)
tax-free Treasury securities..TA 1988 s 475(7)
tax refund relating to an accounting period..FA 1989 s 97(3)
tax unpaid..TMA 1970 s 94(7)
temporary tax..PCTA 1968 s 2(2)
tenant (holiday accommodation)..TA 1988 s 504(9)
tenant's repairing lease..TA 1988 s 24(6)
terminal loss..FA 1970 Sch 6 para 4(3) TA 1988 s 388(1)
third year of assessment..TA 1988 s 62(1)
tied premises..TA 1988 s 98(2)
total income..TA 1988 s 835
trade (generally)..TMA 1970 s 118(1) TA 1988 s 6(4)(*b*) 832(1)
trade effluent..CAA 1968 s 85(3)
trade investments..TA 1988 Sch 25 para 11(5)(*a*)
traded option..CGTA 1979 s 137(9)(*b*) TA 1988 s 659
trading—
  company..TA 1988 Sch 19 para 7
  group..TA 1988 s 576(5)
  income..TA 1988 s 393(8)
  stock..TA 1988 s 100(2) 709(2)
trading or holding company..TA 1988 s 247(9)(*a*)
transactions in securities..TA 1988 s 709(2)
transfer—
  (assets abroad)..TA 1988 s 742(9)
  (securities)..TA 1988 s 711(5)(6)
transport voucher..TA 1988 s 141(7)
Treasury Consent..FA 1988 s 105(5) 130(6)
trust gains..FA 1981 s 80(2)
UCITS directive..TA 1988 s 468A(2)
Ulster Savings Certificates..TA 1988 s 832(1)
underlying tax..TA 1988 s 792(1)
undertaking..CAA 1968 s 7(5)
underwriting year..TA 1988 s 487(1)
unilateral relief..TA 1988 s 790(2)
unindexed gain or loss (indexation allowance)..FA 1982 s 86(2)(*a*)
unindexed securities..FA 1982 s 89(5)
unit holder..TA 1988 s 468(6)
unit trust scheme..CGTA 1979 s 92 TA 1988 s 468(6) 469
unitary state..TA 1988 s 812(2)
United Kingdom—
  corporate bond..TA 1988 Sch 4 para 2(8)
  estate..TA 1988 s 701(9)
  patent..TA 1988 s 533(1)
  period of assessment..TA 1988 s 804(8)
  securities..TMA 1970 s 24(4)
  taxes..TA 1988 s 792(1)
  trust territory..TA 1988 s 615(7)
unmarried couple..TA 1988 s 151(2)
unpaid tax..FA 1984 Sch 14 para 4(4)
unquoted company..TA 1988 s 229(1)
unregistered self-build society..TA 1970 s 342A(2)
unrelieved income..TA 1988 s 434(7)
unremittable overseas income..TA 1988 s 584(1)
vendor (shares)..TA 1988 s 219(1)
voucher..TA 1988 s 141(7)
war—
  damage..TA 1988 s 586(5)
  injuries..TA 1988 s 587(8)

war—*continued*
   insurance premiums..TA 1988 s 274(4)
   risk..CAA 1968 s 33(7)
wasted relief..TA 1988 Sch 26 para 4(4)
wasting asset..CGTA 1979 s 37(1)
water undertaking..CAA 1968 s 7(5)
wholesale distribution..TA 1988 s 297(3)
wholesale, distributive or financial business..TA 1988 Sch 25 para 11(1)
wife's earnings..TA 1988 s 287(2)
workers' co-operative..TA 1988 s 187(10)
writing-down allowance..CAA 1968 s 49(2)(3) 87(1) 94(2)
year of assessment..TA 1988 s 832(1)
year of commencement..TA 1988 s 804(8)
yearly equivalent..TA 1988 Sch 2 para 2
yield to maturity (deep discount securities)..TA 1988 Sch 4 para 1
1979 Act disposal..TA 1988 s 763(1)

TYPESET, PRINTED AND BOUND IN GREAT BRITAIN BY
WILLIAM CLOWES LIMITED, BECCLES AND LONDON